BIOLOGICAL
SCIENCE 1 & 2

BIOLOGICAL SCIENCE 1 & 2

N.P.O. GREEN B.Sc., C.Biol., M.I.Biol.
Headmaster
St George's College, Buenos Aires, Argentina

G.W. STOUT B.Sc., M.A., M.Ed., C.Biol., F.I.Biol.
Headmaster
International School of Bophuthatswana, Mafikeng/Mmabatho,
Republic of Bophuthatswana, Southern Africa

D.J. TAYLOR B.Sc., Ph.D., C.Biol., F.I.Biol.
Head of Biology
Strode's Sixth Form College, Egham

Editor
R. SOPER B.Sc., C.Biol., F.I.Biol.
Formerly Vice-Principal and Head of Science
Collyers Sixth Form College, Horsham

CAMBRIDGE
UNIVERSITY PRESS

Published by the Press Syndicate of the University of Cambridge
The Pitt Building, Trumpington Street, Cambridge CB2 1RP
40 West 20th Street, New York, NY 10011-4211, USA
10 Stamford Road, Oakleigh, Victoria 3166, Australia

First published as Books 1 & 2 1984
Ninth printing 1989
First published in this edition 1990
Third printing 1992

Printed in Great Britain by Ebenezer Baylis & Son Ltd
The Trinity Press, Worcester and London

British Library cataloguing in publication data

Green, N. P. O. (Nigel P. O.) – Combined ed.
Biological science.
1. Biology
I. Title   II. Stout, C. W. (C. Wilf)   III. Taylor, D. J.
(Dennis James) *1947*–   IV. Soper, R. (Roland) *1921*–
574

ISBN 0 521 38380 3

Contents

Preface   xi
Acknowledgements   xiii

Chapter One   Introduction to the subject   1

**Chapter Two   Variety of life – prokaryotes,
viruses and fungi**   3
2.1   Prokaryotes compared with eukaryotes   3
      Kingdom Prokaryotae   4
2.2   Bacteria   4
2.3   Viruses   13
      Kingdom Fungi   17
2.4   Fungi   17
2.5   Benefits and uses of micro-organisms   24
2.6   Harmful organisms   30
2.7   Practical work   33

**Chapter Three   Variety of life – protoctists
and plants**   39
      Kingdom Protoctista   40
3.1   Characteristics and classification of
      protoctists   40
3.2   Algae   40
3.3   Phylum Euglenoidea   49
3.4   Phylum Oomycota   49
3.5   Phyla Rhizopoda, Zoomastigina,
      Apicomplexa, Ciliophora   51
      Kingdom Plantae   59
3.6   Phylum Bryophyta   59
3.7   Phyla Lycopodophyta (clubmosses),
      Sphenophyta (horsetails) and Filicinophyta
      (ferns)   64
3.8   Seed-bearing plants   73
3.9   Comparative survey of land plants   81

Chapter Four   Variety of life – animals   85
4.1   Kingdom Animalia   85
4.2   Origins and trends   85
4.3   Phylum Cnidaria (Coelenterata)   88
4.4   Phylum Platyhelminthes   92
4.5   Body cavities   98
4.6   Phylum Nematoda   100
4.7   Phylum Annelida   100
4.8   Phylum Mollusca   106
4.9   Phylum Arthropoda   106
4.10 Phylum Echinodermata   119
4.11 Phylum Chordata   119

Chapter Five   Chemicals of life   125
5.1   Introduction to biochemistry   125
5.2   Carbohydrates (saccharides)   130
5.3   Lipids   138
5.4   Amino acids   143
5.5   Proteins   146
5.6   Nucleic acids   154
5.7   Other biochemically important molecules   160
5.8   Identification of biochemicals   160

Chapter Six   Enzymes   167
6.1   Catalysis and energy of activation   167
6.2   Enzyme cofactors   169
6.3   The rate of enzyme reactions   172
6.4   Factors affecting the rate of enzyme
      reactions   172
6.5   Enzyme inhibition   176
6.6   Allosteric enzymes   178
6.7   Control of metabolism   179
6.8   Enzyme classification   180
6.9   Enzyme technology   180

Chapter Seven   Cells   185
7.1   Typical animal and plant cells   192
7.2   Structures common to animal and plant cells   192
7.3   Structures characteristic of plant cells   211

Chapter Eight   Histology   215
8.1   Simple plant tissues – tissues consisting
      of one type of cell   215
8.2   Plant tissues consisting of more than one
      type of cell   225
8.3   Animal epithelial tissue   230
8.4   Animal connective tissue   234
8.5   Muscle tissue   243
8.6   Nervous tissue   244

Chapter Nine   Autotrophic nutrition   249
9.1   Grouping of organisms according to their
      principal sources of energy and carbon   249
9.2   Photosynthesis   250
9.3   The structure of the leaf   251
9.4   Biochemistry of photosynthesis   259
9.5   Factors affecting photosynthesis   268
9.6   Measuring rates of photosynthesis   272
9.7   Compensation points   274

9.8 Photorespiration and C_4 photosynthesis 275
9.9 Photosynthetic bacteria 280
9.10 Chemosynthesis 281
9.11 Mineral cycles (biogeochemical cycles) 281
9.12 Mineral nutrition of plants and animals 284

Chapter Ten   Heterotrophic nutrition 289
10.1 Modes of heterotrophic nutrition 289
10.2 Feeding mechanisms in a range of animals 292
10.3 Nutrition in mammals 300
10.4 The alimentary canal in humans 304
10.5 The control of digestive secretions 318
10.6 The fate of absorbed food materials 319
10.7 Regulation of food intake in humans 319
10.8 Variations in the mammalian alimentary canal 320

Chapter Eleven   Energy utilisation 323
11.1 Role of respiration 324
11.2 ATP (adenosine triphosphate) 324
11.3 Biological oxidation 325
11.4 Shuttle systems 332
11.5 Mitochondria 334
11.6 Gaseous exchange 340
11.7 Gaseous exchange in a mammal 349
11.8 Unusual conditions in ventilation 356
11.9 Flowering plants 357

Chapter Twelve   Organisms and their environment *with Rosalind Taylor and Stephen Tomkins* **359**
12.1 Approaches to ecology 360
12.2 The ecosystem 363
12.3 Energy and nutrient relationships 364
12.4 Biogeochemical cycles – the cycling of matter 377
12.5 The abiotic component of ecosystems: the physical habitat factors 387
12.6 Community ecology and ecological succession 398
12.7 Population ecology 404
12.8 Agriculture and horticulture 419
12.9 The Green Revolution 425
12.10 Conservation 427

Chapter Thirteen   Quantitative ecology 439
13.1 Methods of measuring environmental factors 439
13.2 Biotic analysis 444
13.3 Ecological research projects and investigations 452
13.4 A synecological investigation 453
13.5 An autecological investigation 456

Answers and discussion for chapters 2–13 461
Chapter 2 461
Chapter 3 462
Chapter 5 462

Chapter 6 463
Chapter 7 464
Chapter 9 464
Chapter 10 467
Chapter 11 467
Chapter 12 468
Chapter 13 471

Chapter Fourteen   Transport 473
Transport in plants 473
14.1 Plant water relations 474
14.2 Movement of water through the flowering plant 481
14.3 Transpiration and movement of water through the leaf 482
14.4 Ascent of water in the xylem 492
14.5 Uptake of water by roots 493
14.6 Uptake of mineral salts and their transport across roots 495
14.7 Translocation of mineral salts through plants 497
14.8 Translocation of organic solutes in phloem 497
Transport in animals 506
14.9 General characteristics of a circulatory system 506
14.10 The development of transport systems in animals 507
14.11 Composition of mammalian blood 511
14.12 The mammalian circulatory system 514
14.13 Functions of mammalian blood 526
14.14 The immune system 533

Chapter Fifteen   Coordination and control in plants 543
15.1 Plant movements 543
15.2 Plant growth substances 544
15.3 Synergism and antagonism 559
15.4 Phytochrome and effects of light on plant development 562
15.5 Vernalisation and flowering 565

Chapter Sixteen   Coordination and control in animals 567
16.1 The nervous system 567
16.2 The vertebrate nervous system 576
16.3 The phylogenetic development of the nervous system 587
16.4 Sensory receptors 588
16.5 Structure and function of receptors 592
16.6 Effectors – the endocrine system 603
16.7 The study of behaviour (ethology) 613
16.8 Innate behaviour 613
16.9 Learned behaviour 624

Chapter Seventeen   Movement and support 627
17.1 Skeletal systems 627

17.2	Skeletal tissue	629
17.3	Anatomy of the skeleton of a mammal (the rabbit)	631
17.4	The muscle system	637
17.5	Innervation of skeletal muscle	644
17.6	Locomotion in selected non-vertebrates	648
17.7	Locomotion in vertebrates	655
17.8	Support in plants	666

Chapter Eighteen   Homeostasis   667

18.1	Control systems in biology	667
18.2	Temperature regulation	673
18.3	Ectothermic animals	676
18.4	Endothermic animals	677
18.5	The mammalian liver	686

Chapter Nineteen   Excretion and osmoregulation   695

19.1	The significance of excretion and osmo-regulation	695
19.2	Nitrogenous excretory products	697
19.3	Nitrogenous excretion and osmoregulation	698
19.4	A phylogenetic review of organs and processes of nitrogenous excretion and osmoregulation	701
19.5	The mammalian kidney	712
19.6	Anti-diuretic hormone (ADH) and the formation of a concentrated or dilute urine	721
19.7	Control of blood sodium level	722
19.8	Control of blood pH	723

Chapter Twenty   Reproduction   725

20.1	Asexual and sexual reproduction	725
20.2	Sexual reproduction in plants	735
20.3	Human sexual reproduction	752
20.4	Phylogenetic review of sexual reproduction in vertebrates	769

Chapter Twenty-one   Growth and development   771

21.1	Measurement of growth	771
21.2	Patterns of growth	774
21.3	Control of growth and development	776
21.4	Development	776
21.5	Morphogenesis	777
21.6	Growth and development in the flowering plant	778
21.7	Metamorphosis	788
21.8	Development in vertebrates	792
21.9	Repair and regeneration	794
21.10	Dormancy	794

Chapter Twenty-two   Continuity of life   797

22.1	The cell cycle	797
22.2	Mitosis	798
22.3	Meiosis	802
22.4	The structure of chromosomes	811
22.5	The nature of genes	816
22.6	Protein synthesis	821
22.7	Genetic control	824
22.8	The genetic control of development	828

Chapter Twenty-three   Variation and genetics   833

23.1	Mendel's work	833
23.2	The chromosomal basis of inheritance	838
23.3	Linkage	840
23.4	Gene mapping	843
23.5	Linkage groups and chromosomes	844
23.6	Sex discrimination	845
23.7	Gene interactions	848
23.8	Variation	853
23.9	Mutation	854

Chapter Twenty-four   Evolution – history of life   859

24.1	Theories of the origin of life	859
24.2	The nature of the earliest organisms	863
24.3	Summary of the 'theories' of the origin of life	864
24.4	The theory of evolution	864
24.5	Natural selection	866
24.6	Modern views on evolution	868
24.7	Evidence for the theory of evolution	868
24.8	Human evolution *by Stephen Tomkins*	886

Chapter Twenty-five   Mechanisms of speciation   891

25.1	Population genetics	891
25.2	Factors producing changes in populations	894
25.3	Selection	896
25.4	Artificial selection	899
25.5	Natural selection	902
25.6	The concept of species	906
25.7	Speciation	906
25.8	Intraspecific speciation	906
25.9	Interspecific hybridisation	909

Answers and discussion for chapters 14–25   911

Chapter	14	911
Chapter	15	913
Chapter	16	916
Chapter	17	916
Chapter	18	917
Chapter	20	917
Chapter	21	918
Chapter	22	919
Chapter	23	920
Chapter	24	923
Chapter	25	924

Appendix 1	Biological chemistry	925
Appendix 2	Biological techniques	936
Appendix 3	Classification	950
Appendix 4	Nomenclature and units	952
Appendix 5	The geological time scale	954

Index   957

Biological Science
Software

Brian Kahn
General editor, Computer software for *Biological Science*

Cambridge University Press has developed some programs which link to *Biological Science* for use by students following advanced level Biology courses. Each program is accompanied by full documentation, containing user instructions, worksheets and teacher's notes.
The software runs on Acorn BBC machines. The titles are:
Crossover   Nervous system   Hardy-Weinberg

For further details of *Biological Science software*, please write to: The Schoolbooks Marketing Department, Cambridge University Press, The Edinburgh Building, Shaftesbury Road, Cambridge CB2 2RU

Other software of interest and available from Cambridge University Press:

Balance Your Diet   Netherhall Educational Software
Population Growth   Netherhall Educational Software
Menstruation and Pregnancy   Netherhall Educational Software
Water Balance in Plants   Netherhall Educational Software

To order an evaluation copy, please contact the Schoolbooks Marketing Department at the above address.

Preface

The fundamental aim underlying the writing of *Biological Science* was the desire to emphasise the unifying scientific nature of biological systems despite the amazing diversity in structure and function seen at all levels of biological organisation.

This combined edition consists of the second edition of Books 1 and 2 (which are also printed as separate volumes). It comprises a complete text for the A-level student, following all syllabuses in Biological Sciences and incorporating all the topic areas recommended by the GCE Interboard Working Party on the A-level common core in Biology (published 1983). The text will also be relevant to all first-year University and Further Education College students studying the Biological Sciences.

Each chapter is designed to provide comprehensive, up-to-date information on all topics in Biological Sciences, and the accuracy and relevance of this information has been checked by leading authorities in the appropriate fields and by practising teachers and examiners. The text includes:
- clearly written factual material,
- a carefully selected series of thoroughly pretested practical investigations relevant to the A-level course,
- a variety of types of question designed to stimulate an enquiring approach and answers to them.

The second edition of *Biological Science* has incorporated information which is relevant to recent curriculum innovations. These include:
- the introduction of Advanced Supplementary (AS) Level syllabuses and examinations,
- revised Advanced Level syllabuses which emphasise the social, environmental and technological relevance of biological science,
- the introduction of the Sixth Form Entrance Papers for the purposes of university entrance,
- the requirements associated with the development of the Advanced Level modular curriculum.

Rather than dramatically increase the extent of the text, which is already comprehensive, some of the original text and illustrations have been removed as they are no longer considered necessary for students studying at these levels. New information has been introduced which both updates existing material and enables the book to justify its claim as the most comprehensive text in the biological sciences at these levels.

Greater attention is paid to the effects of humans on the environment in chapter 12. Organisms and their environment, with many new case studies, are also included in this chapter. For example pollution is linked with disruption of biogeochemical cycles, and issues such as the 'greenhouse effect', eutrophication, the ozone layer and acid rain are discussed in detail. More applications of population ecology are included, for example fisheries management, and there are new sections on agricultural and horticultural practices and pesticides where the environment and conservation are considered.

Recent advances in our knowledge of the appearance of HIV and its associated disease, AIDS, have resulted in the incorporation of additional information. Theories of phloem translocation have been substantially revised; similarities in the energetics of mitochondria and chloroplasts have been stressed; the usefulness of ecological pyramids is reassessed; the original meaning of the term 'symbiosis' has been adopted in line with current trends; and classification of relationships between organisms is discussed, including research on the importance of mycorrhizas. These are just a few examples of the many changes, some major, some minor, which have been made.

Another important influence in preparing this second edition was the *Report of Recommendations on Biological Nomenclature* published by the Institute of Biology and the Association for Science Education in 1989. One of the Report's most significant recommendations concerns classification and this has resulted in a major revision of chapters 2, 3 and 4. Recommendations on the terms, units and symbols used in describing water relations have been adopted throughout.

The appendices, which provide information and techniques vital to the study of Biological Sciences at this level, recognise that many students do not study Physics and Chemistry to the same level. Mathematical, physical and chemical concepts related to Biological Sciences are emphasised throughout the text, as appropriate.

Acknowledgements

The authors and publisher wish to acknowledge the many friends, colleagues, students and advisers who have helped in the production of *Biological Science*.

In particular, we wish to thank:
Dr R. Batt, Dr Claudia Berek, Professor R.J. Berry, Dr. A.C. Blake, Dr John C. Bowman, Mr R. Brown, Dr Fred Burke, Mr Richard Carter, Dr Norman R. Cohen, Dr K.J.R. Edwards, Mr Malcolm Emery, Mr Nick Fagents, Dr James T. Fitzsimons, Dr John Gay, Dr Brij L. Gupta, Vivienne Hambleton, Dr David E. Hanke, the late Dr R.N. Hardy, the late Reverend J.R. Hargreaves, Dr S.A. Henderson, Mr Michael J. Hook, Mr Colin S. Hutchinson, Dr Alick Jones, Mrs Susan Kearsey, Dr Simon P. Maddrell FRS, Professor Aubrey Manning, Dr Chris L. Mason, Mrs Ruth Miller, Dr David C. Moore, A.G. Morgan, Dr Rodney Mulvey, Dr R.E. Riley, Dr David Secher, Dr John M. Squire, the late Professor James F. Sutcliffe, Miss Anne C. Tallantire, Dr R.M. Taylor, Dr Eric R. Turner, the late Dr Paul Wheater, Dr Brian E.J. Wheeler, Dr Michael Wheeler, Mr L. Williams.

The authors are particularly indebted to Mrs Adrienne Oxley, who patiently and skilfully organised the pretesting of all the practical exercises. Her perseverance has produced exercises that teachers, pupils and laboratory technicians can depend upon.

In preparing the second edition we are indebted to Dr Rosalind Taylor of the School of Geography, Kingston Polytechnic, Kingston-upon-Thames, Surrey and to Mr Stephen Tomkins of Hills Road Sixth Form College, Cambridge. Dr Taylor undertook a thorough review of the Ecology chapter, Chapter 12, and is responsible for much of the new material included, especially the influence of humans on the environment. Stephen Tomkins made a significant contribution to the content and organisation of material in the Conservation section. One of the authors, Dr Dennis Taylor, spent a valuable term at Jesus College, Cambridge as a Teacher Fellow Commoner during the preparation of the second edition, and would like to thank all those at the College who gave such friendly encouragement, assistance and hospitality during that time.

However, the authors accept full responsibility for the final content of these books.

Finally, the authors wish to express their thanks to their wives and families for the constant support and encouragement shown throughout the preparation and publication of these books.

We also wish to thank the following for permission to use their illustrations, tables and questions.
Figures: 2.4, 2.5, 2.19a, 2.23c, 3.5c, 3.16b, 3.29c, 3.29d, 7.6, 7.10, 7.15, 7.19b, 7.21, 7.22, 8.2e, 8.2f, 8.3a, 8.3b, 8.4d, 8.5e, 8.6, 8.8c, 8.8d, 8.9b, 8.11b, 8.11c, 8.11e, 8.12b, 8.12d, 9.3, 9.6, 10.30c, Biophoto Associates; 2.9, Professor L. Caro/Science Photo Library; 2.13b, Dr H.G. Pereira (1965) *Journal of Molecular Biology*, **13**; 2.13c, R.W. Horne, I. Pasquali-Ronchetti & Judith M. Hobart (1975) *J. Ultrastruct. Res.*, **51**, 233; 2.14, from *The structure of viruses*, R.W. Horne, copyright © 1963 by Scientific American Inc., all rights reserved; 2.15a, R.W. Horne (1974) *Virus structure*, Academic Press, London; 2.15b, Dr Lee D. Simon/Science Photo Library; 2.17, Dr Thomas F. Anderson & Dr Lee D. Simon/Science Photo Library; 2.26a, 2.26b, National Institute for Research in Dairying, Reading; 3.5a, 8.1b, 8.4c, 8.5d, 8.11f, 9.13, 13.1, 13.2, 13.6, 13.10, Centre for Cell and Tissue Research, York; 3.28b, Roy Edwards; 3.28c, 3.29e, 3.39a, 3.39b, 10.3. Heather Angel; 3.19a, 3.19b, Dr Lawrence Bannister; 4.1, Jane Burton/Bruce Coleman Ltd; 4.26, R. Buchsbaum (1948) *Animals without backbones*, vol.2, University of Chicago Press; 4.29, 4.30, H.G.Q. Rowett (1962) *Dissection guides*, John Murray, London; 4.31b, 4.31c, 4.33b, 4.33c, C. James Webb; 4.31d, Barnabys Picture Library; 4.32b, 4.32c, 4.34d, Stephen Dalton/Natural History Photographic Agency; 4.33d, E.J. Hudson/Frank W. Lane; 4.34b, 4.34c, Shell International Petroleum Co; 4.41, Oxford Local Examinations, A62-P, special sheet 2, summer 1978; 5.10c, Nigel Luckworth; 5.33, D-G. Smyth, W.H. Stein & S. Moore (1963) *J. Biol. Chem.*, **238**, 227; 5.36, 5.39, R.E. Dickerson & I. Geis (1969) *The structure and action of proteins*, W.A. Benjamin, California; 5.38b, 5.38d, Sir John Kendrew; 5.38c, R.E. Dickerson (1964) *The proteins*, ed. H. Neurath, 2nd ed., vol.2, Academic Press Inc., New York; 5.45, Dr J.M. Squire, Biopolymer Group, Imperial College; 5.49, Professor M.H.F. Wilkins, Biophysics Department, King's College, London; 6.3, reprinted by permission from *Nature*, vol. 213, p. 864, copyright © 1967 Macmillan Journals Limited; 6.5, C.F. Stoneman & J.C. Marsden (1974) *Enzymes and equilibria*, Scholarship Series in Biology, Heinemann Educational Books, London; 7.5, Dr Glenn L. Decker, School of Medicine, John Hopkins University; 7.11b, Cancer Research Campaign and Paul Chantrey; 7.14, from *Biochemistry*, 2nd ed. by L. Stryer, W.H. Freeman and Company, copyright © 1981; 7.19a, M.A. Tribe, M.R. Erant & R.K. Snook (1975) *Electron microscopy and cell structure*, Cambridge University Press;; 7.20a, 8.13b, 8.14b, 8.15c, 8.16b, 8.17c, 8.18b, 8.19, 8.21, 8.22, 8.23, 8.24, 8.25, 8.26, 8.27, 8.28a, 8.29, 8.32a, 8.32b, 8.33, 8.34, 8.37, 8.39, 8.40, 8.41, 10.22b, 10.23, 10.25, 10.26 10.28a, 10.28b, 10.30, 11.15d, 11.31, Dr Paul Wheater; 7.25, Dr Klaus Weber; 7.26, Dr Elias Lazarides, California Institute of Technology; 7.27, E. Frei & R.D. Preston FRS; 8.2d, Rothamsted Experimental Station; 8.17d, 10.30b, Mr P. Crosby, Department of Biology, University of York; 8.20, W.H. Freeman & B. Bracegirdle (1967) *An atlas of histology*, 2nd ed., Heinemann Educational Books, London; 8.31, John Currey (1970) *Animal skeletons*, Studies in Biology no. 22, Edward Arnold, London; 9.4, Gene Cox; 9.8, 9.16, 9.29b, Dr A.D. Greenwood; 9.18, D.O. Hall & K.K. Rao (1972) *Photosynthesis*, 1st ed., Studies in Biology no. 37, Edward Arnold, London; 9.28, Dr Alex B. Novikoff, Albert Einstein School of Medicine, & Saunders College Publishing; 9.29a, C.C. Black (1971) *Plant Physiology*, **47**, 15–23, with permission of the publisher; 10.6, J.P. Harding; 10.7a, Kim Taylor/Bruce Coleman Ltd.; 10.7b, Dr Brad Amos/Science Photo Library; 10.8, Topham; 10.9b, Dr Tony Brain/Science Photo Library; 10.12, Griffin & George; 10.13, Nuffield Biology Text III, *The maintenance of life* (1970), Longman; 10.17a, Charles Day; 10.17b, King's College School of

Medicine and Dentistry, London; 10.21*a*, 10.21*b*, 10.21*c*, 10.21*d*, Dr C.A. Saxton, Unilever Research; 10.22*a*, Dr L.M. Beidler/ Science Photo Library; 10.32, Nuffield Text *Maintenance of the organism* (1970) Nuffield Foundation, Longman; 10.33, from *An introduction to human physiology*, 4th ed., by J.H. Green, published by Oxford University Press 1976; 11.14*a*, 11.14*b*, 11.15*e*, Dr Brij L. Gupta, Zoology Department, Cambridge University; 11.16, M.A. Tribe & P. Whittaker (1972) *Chloroplasts and mitochondria*, 1st ed., Studies in Biology no. 31, Edward Arnold, London; 11.17, Dr Ernst F.J. van Bruggen, State University of Groningen; 11.31, reproduced with permission from G.M. Hughes, *The vertebrate lung* (2nd edn) 1979, Carolina Biology Reader Series, copyright Carolina Biological Supply Company, Burlington, North Carolina, USA; 11.32, Philip Harris Biological Ltd; 11.33, B. Siegwart, P. Gehr, J. Gil & E.R. Weibel (1971) *Respir. Physiol.*, **13**, 141–59; 12.2, from *Ecology*, 2nd ed. by Eugene P. Odum, copyright © 1975 by Holt, Rinehart & Winston, reprinted by permission of Holt, Rinehart & Winston, CBS Publishing; 12.6*b*, Dr E.J. Popham; 12.7*a*, 12.7*e*, S. Cousins (1985) *New Scientist*, 4/7/85, p.51; 12.8, 12.9, 12.11, 12.19, from *Fundamentals of ecology*, 3rd ed. by Eugene P. Odum, copyright © 1971 by W.B. Saunders Company, reprinted by permission of Holt, Rinehart & Winston, CBS Publishing; 12.10, 12.13, 12.33, M.A. Tribe, M.R. Erant & R.K. Snook (1974) *Ecological principles*, Basic Biology Course 4, Cambridge University Press; 12.15, from *The biosphere*, G. Evelyn Hutchinson, copyright © 1970 by Scientific American Inc.; 12.16, R.J. Chorley & P. Haggett (eds.) (1967) *Physical and information models in geography*, Methuen, London; 12.17, A. Crane & P. Liss (1985) *New Scientist*, 21/11/85; 12.18, M. McElroy (1988) The challenge of global change, *New Scientist*, **119**, 1623, 34–6; 12.20, C.F. Mason (1981) *Biology of freshwater pollution*, Longman; 12.29, W.D. Billings (1972) *Plants, man and the ecosystem*, 2nd ed., Macmillan, London; 12.31, A.G. Tansley (1968) *Britain's green mantle*, 2nd ed., George Allen & Unwin, London; 12.35, B.D. Collier, G.W. Cox, A.W. Johnson & P.C. Miller, *Dynamic ecology* © 1973, p. 321, reprinted by permission of Prentice-Hall Inc., New Jersey; 12.37, A.S. Boughey (1971) *Fundamental ecology*, International Textbook Co.; 12.38, T.R.E. Southwood (1974) *Am. Nature* **108**, 791–804; 12.39, W.G. Abrahamson & M. Gadgil (1973) *Am. Nat.* **107**, 651–61; 12.40, 12.42, 12.43, Open University Foundation Course (S100) unit 20, copyright © 1971 The Open University Press; 12.41, D. Lack (1966) *Population studies of birds*, Clarendon Press, Oxford; 12.44, C.B. Huffaker (1958) *Experimental studies on predation: dispersion factors and predator–prey oscillations*; 12.47, 12.48, M. Graham (1956) *Sea fisheries – their investigation*, Arnold; 12.49, R.V. Tait (1981) *Elements of marine ecology*, 3rd ed., Butterworths; 12.50, Richard North, *The Independent*, February 1988; 12.51, J.P. Dempster (1968) The control of *Pieris rapae* with DDT. II Survival of the young stages of *Pieris* after spraying, *J. Appl. Ecol.* **5**, 451–62; 12.52, 12.53, N.W. Moore (1987) *A synopsis of the pesticide problem* in J.B. Cragg (ed.) *Advances in ecological research*, Blackwell; 12.54, after M. Markkula, K. Tiittanen & M. Nieminen (1972) *Ann. Agr. Fenn.* **11**, 74–8; 12.55, C. Rose (1985) Acid rain falls on British woodlands, *New Scientist*, **108**, 1482, 52–7; 12.56, J. H. Ottaway (1980) *The biochemistry of pollution*, Studies in Biology 123, Arnold; 12.57, F. Pearce (1986) Unravelling a century of acid pollution, *New Scientist*, **111**, 1527, 23; 13.5, John Edward Leigh; 13.22, D.A.S. Smith (1970) *School Science Review*, Association for Science Education; 14.10, 14.13, 14.15*c*, 14.15*d*, 20.1, 20.26, 21.17, Centre for Cell and Tissue Research, York; 14.11*a*, 20.2, 24.8*b*, Heather Angel; 14.11*b*, A–Z Collection; 14.12, data from L.J. Briggs & H.L. Shantz (1916) *J. Agr. Res*, **5**, 583–649; 14.16*c*, 14.16*d*, 14.40, 18.11, 19.4, 20.39, 20.41*a*, 21.26*a*, 21.26*b*, 22.18, 23.15, 23.31, Biophoto Associates; 14.19, data from R.N. Robertson & J.S. Turner (1945) *Austral. J. Exp. Biol. Med. Sci.*, **23**, 63; 14.21*a*, 14.21*b*, 14.21*c*, Dr Chris Marshall; 14.22, Anderson & Cronshaw (1970) *Planta*, **91**, 173–80, Springer-Verlag; 14.25*a*, 14.25*b*, Dr Martin Zimmerman, Harvard University; 14.27, Professor B.E.S. Gunning (1977) *Science Progress*, **64**, 539–68, Blackwell Scientific Publications Ltd.; 14.28, 14.45, E.G. Springthorpe (1973) *An introduction to functional systems in animals*, Longman by permission of the Longman Group Limited; 14.29, A.E. Vines & N. Rees (1972) *Plant and animal biology* (4th ed.) vol. 1, by permission of Pitman Publishing Ltd., London; 14.30, 19.7, J.A. Ramsay (1968) *A physiological approach to lower animals* (2nd ed.) Cambridge University Press; 14.36*a*, 14.36*b*, 14.37*a*, 14.37*b*, 14.46, 14.47, 16.8, 19.21*a*, 19.21*b*, 20.32, Dr Paul Wheater; 14.38, 14.57, A.G. Clegg & P.C. Clegg (1963) *Biology of the mammal* (2nd ed.) Heinemann Medical Books; 14.44, 14.54, 16.27, 17.46, K. Schmidt-Nielsen (1979) *Animal physiology* (2nd ed.) Cambridge University Press; 14.52, 14.53, J.H. Green (1968) *An introduction to human physiology*, Oxford University Press; 14.61, E. Florey (1967) *An introduction to general and comparative animal physiology*, W.B. Saunders & Co.; 14.62, G. Chapman (1967) *The body fluids and their functions*, Studies in Biology no. 8, Edward Arnold; 14.68, Emil Bernstein & Eila Kairinen, Gillette Research Institute *Science*, **173**, cover 27 August 1971, copyright © 1971 by the American Association for the Advancement of Science; 14.70, from *The development of the immune system*, Max Cooper & Alex Lawton, copyright © 1974 by Scientific American Inc., all rights reserved; 14.76, Macfarlane Burnet (1971) *Genes, dreams and realities*, MTP Press Ltd.; 14.78, David Hockley, National Institute for Biological Standards and Control; 15.2*a*, 15.2*b*, 17.49*a*, 17.49*b*, 17.49*c*, Roy Edwards; 15.3, W.O. James (1963) *An introduction to plant physiology* (6th ed.) Oxford University Press; 15.16, Dr B.E. Juniper; 15.17, P.E. Pilet (1975) *Planta*, **122**, 299–302; 15.18, T Swarbrick *Harnessing the hormone*, Grower Publications Ltd.; 15.20, 20.28, Long Ashton Research Station; 15.24, Centre Nationale de la Recherche Scientifique *Regulateurs naturels de la croissance vegetale* (1964); 15.27, Dr Peter Evans, Southampton University; 15.33, Professor Anton Lang (1957) *Proc. Natl. Acad. Sci. USA*, **43**, 709–17; 16.25*a*, E.D. Adrian & Y. Zotterman (1926) *J. Physiol.*, **61**, 151–71; 16.25*b*, B. Katz (1950) *J. Physiol.*, **111**, 261–82; 16.31, R. Schmidt (ed.) (1978) *Fundamentals of sensory physiology*, Springer-Verlag; 16.43*a*, 16.43*b*, Dr I. Hunter-Duvar, The Hospital for Sick Children, Toronto; 16.46, P.J. Bentley (1976) *Comparative vertebrate endocrinology*, Cambridge University Press; 16.65, 16.66, Caroline E.G. Tutin; 16.57*a*, N. Tinbergen (1953) *The herring gull's world*, Collins; 16.57*b*, N. Tinbergen & A. Purdeck (1950) *Behaviour*, **3**, 1–38; 16.58, J. Brady (1979) *Biological clocks*, Studies in Biology no. 104, Edward Arnold; 16.59, Niall Rankin/Eric and David Hosking; 16.60, A. Watson (1970) *J. Reprod. Fert.*, Suppl. **11**, 3–14; 16.61, J.S. Huxley (1914) *Proc. Zool. Soc. Lond.*, **1914(2)**, 491–562; 16.63, R.A. Hinde (1970) *Animal behaviour* (2nd ed.) McGraw-Hill Book Company, reproduced with permission; 16.64, 16.65, N. Tinbergen (1951) *A study of instinct*, Oxford University Press; 16.68, J.B. Messenger (1977) *Symp. Zool. Soc. Lond.*, **38**, 347–76 by permission of the Zoological Society of London; 17.15, Lee D. Peachey (1965) *Journal of Cell Biology*, **25**, 209–31; 17.17, P.M.G. Munro, Biopolymer Group, Imperial College; 17.18, A. Freundlich, Biopolymer Group, Imperial College; 17.19, Dr J. Squire, Biopolymer Group, Imperial College; 17.25*b*, David Harrison (1971) *Advanced biology notes*, by permission of Macmillan, London and Basingstoke; 17.26, D. Lamb, *Physiology of exercise*, Macmillan Inc.; 17.32, 17.36*a*, from *Cells and organelles*, 2nd edition by Alex B. Novikoff & Eric Holtzman, copyright © 1970, 1976 by Holt, Rinehart and Winston, reprinted by permission of Holt, Rinehart and Winston, CBS College Publishing; 17.33, M.A. Sleigh (1974) *Cilia and flagella*, Academic Press Inc.; 17.50, E.J. Sains, *The Racing Pigeon*, London; 17.58, Topham; 18.9 C.J.

Martin (1930) *Lancet*, (2) **108**, 561; 18.14, R.N. Hardy (1979) *Temperature and animal life*, Studies in Biology no. 35 (2nd ed.) Edward Arnold; 18.21, Royal Veterinary College, Histology Department; 19.2, J. Zanefeld (1937) *J. Ecology*, **25**, 431–68; 19.3, E.H. Mercer (1959) *Proc. Roy. Soc. Lond.* B, **150**, 216–36, plate 16; 19.8, J.W.L. Beament (1958) J. Exp. Biol., **35**, 494–519; 19.11, G. Parry (1960) in *The physiology of crustacea* vol. 1, ed. T.H. Waterman, 341–66, Academic Press Inc.; 19.14, A.P.M. Lockwood (1963) *Animal body fluids and their regulation*, Heinemann Educational; 19.19, Professor A. Clifford Barger, Harvard Medical School; 20.11*a*, 20.11*b*, Gurdon (1977) *Proc. Roy. Soc. Lond.* B, **198**, 211–47; 20.23; Hermann Eisenbeiss; 20.25, Howard Jones; 20.31, *Research in reproduction* (1976) **8**, no.4, by permission of the International Planned Parenthood Federation; 20.41*b*, Dr Everett Anderson/Science Photo Library; 20.48, *Research in reproduction* (1972) **4**, no. 5, by permission of the International Planned Parenthood Federation; 20.49*a*, 20.49*b*, 20.49*c*, 20.49*d*, Marion J. Boorman; 21.3, data from L.R. Wallace (1948) *J. Agric. Sci.*, **38**, 93, and H. Palsson & B. Vergés (1952) *J. Agric. Sci.*, **42**, 93; 21.7, A.L. Batt (1980) *Influences on animal growth and development*, Studies in Biology no. 116, Edward Arnold; 21.8, J. Hammond (ed.) (1955) *Progress in the physiology of farm animals*, **2**, 341, Butterworths; 21.12, R. Soper & S.T. Smith (1979) *Modern biology*, by permission of Macmillan, London and Basingstoke; 21.13, J.L. Durrer & J.P. Hannon (1962) *Am. J. Physiol.*, **202**, 375; 21.15, data from R. Desveaux & M. Kogane-Charles (1952) *Annls. Inst. Nat. Rech. Agron. Paris*, **3**, 385–416, © INRA-PARIS 1952; 21.29, Gene Cox; 21.34, The Natural History Photographic Agency; 22.2, 22.7*a*, 22.7*b*, 22.8,, 22.9, Dr S.A. Henderson, Department of Genetics, University of Cambridge; 22.3*a*, 23.26, ARC Poultry Research Centre; 22.11*b*, 22.11*c*, H. G. Callan (1963) *Int. Rev. Cytol.*, **15**, 1; 22.11 Professor H.G. Callan, University of St Andrews; 22.14, 22.24 E.J. Ambrose & D.M. Easty (1977) *Cell biology* (2nd ed.), Nelson, by permission of Van Nostrand Reinhold (UK); 22.20, from *The genetic code I*, F.H.C. Crick, copyright © 1962 by Scientific American Inc., all rights reserved; 22.25*a*, O.L. Miller Jr & B.A. Hamkalo, Visualization of bacterial genes in action, *Science*, **169**, 392–5, 24 July 1970, copyright © 1970 by the American Association for the Advancement of Science; 24.3, RIDA Photo Library; 24.6, G. Matthews (1939) *Climate of evolution* (2nd ed.) vol. 1, New York Academy of Sciences; 24.7, Eric Hosking; 24.8, D. Lack (1947) *Darwin's finches*, Cambridge University Press; 24.9*a*, Bruce Coleman Ltd.; 24.9*b*, Pig farming magazine, Ipswich; 24.14, T.H. Hamilton (1967) *Process and pattern in evolution*, Macmillan, London and Basingstoke; 24.18, The Zoological Society of London; 24.19, V.M. Ingram (1963) *Haemoglobins in genetics and evolution*, © 1963, Columbia University Press, reprinted by permission; 24.20, 24.21, S. Tomkins (1984) *The origins of mankind*, Cambridge University Press; 25.3; M.N. Karn & L.S. Penrose (1951) *Ann. Eugenics, London*, **16**, 147–64; 25.4, D.S. Falconer (1953) *J. Genetics*, 51, 470–501; 25.5*a* 25.5*b*, Photo A.G.P.M.; 25.6 Semences Nickerson, France; 25.8, D.F. Jones, Connecticut Agricultural Experiment Station 25.9, John Haywood; 25.10*a*, 25.10*b*, Dr H.B.D. Kettlewell; 25.11, H.B.D. Kettlewell (1958) *Heredity*, **12**, 51–72, by permission of Longman 25.12, M.A. Tribe, I. Tallan and M.R. Eraut (1978) *Case Studies in Genetics*, Cambridge University Press; 25.13, John Haywood.

Tables: 2.1, A2.4, E.A. Martin(ed.) (1976) *a dictionary of life sciences*, Pan Books, London; 5.1, based on A.L. Lehninger (1970) *Biochemistry*, Worth, New York with permission of Plenum Publishing Corporation, copyright Plenum Publishing Corporation; 6.3, A. Wiseman & B.J. Gould (1971) *Enzymes, their nature and role*, Century Hutchinson Limited, London; 10.4, 10.5, *Manual of nutrition* (1976), reproduced by permission of the Controller of Her Majesty's Stationery Office; 11.3, John E. Smith (1988) *Biotechnology*, 2nd ed. New Studies in Biology, Edward Arnold; 12.1, 12.2, from *Fundamentals of ecology*, 3rd ed. by Eugene P. Odum, copyright © (1971) by W.B. Saunders Company, reprinted by permission of Holt, Rinehart & Winston, CBS Publishing; 12.3, A.N. Duckham & G.B. Masefield (1970) *Farming systems of the world*, Chatto & Windus, London; 12.4, 12.5, 12.7, C.F. Mason (1981) *Biology of freshwater pollution*, Longman; 12.6, B. Moss (1980) *Ecology of fresh waters*, Blackwell Scientific; 12.8, 12.9, by permission of Griffin & George; 12.10, by permission from The Open University Press; 12.15, 12.16, *1981 World population data sheet*, Population Reference Bureau Inc., Washington D.C.; 12.19, Open University Science Foundation Course (S100) unit 20, copyright © 1971 The Open University Press; 14.7, T.E. Weier, C.R. Stocking & M.G. Barbour (1970) *Botany: an introduction to plant biology* (4th ed.), John Wiley & Sons Inc.; 16.1, A.L. Hodgkin (1958) *Proc. Roy. Soc. Lond.*, **148**, 1–37; 16.18, W.H. Thorpe (1963) *Learning and instinct in animals*, Methuen; 19.2, K. Schmidt-Nielsen (1979) *Animal physiology* (2nd ed.), Cambridge University Press; 24.6, M.O. Dayhoff & R.V. Eck (1967–8) *Atlas of protein sequence and structure*, National Biomedical Research Foundation, Silver Spring, Md.

Questions: 2.3, University of Oxford Delegacy of Local Examinations (OLE); 12.11, modified from M.A. Tribe, M.R. Erant & R.K. Snook (1974) *Ecological principles*, Basic Biology Course 4, Cambridge University Press; 12.19, 12.21, Open University Science Foundation Course (S100) Unit 20, copyright © (1971) The Open University Press.

Cover: The cover photograph shows a Leopard frog leaping (*Rana pipiens*), Stephen Dalton/Oxford Scientific Films.

Chapter One

Introduction to the subject

Biology (*bios*, life; *logos*, knowledge) is a science devoted to the study of living organisms. Science has progressed by breaking down complex subjects of study into their component parts so that today there are numerous branches of biology devoted to specialised study of the structure and function of select organisms, as shown in fig. 1.1. This principle is often called the 'reductionist' principle and, carried to its logical conclusions, it has focussed attention on the most elementary forms of matter in living and non-living systems. This approach to study seeks fundamental understanding by looking at the parts rather than the whole. An opposing approach, based upon the 'vitalist' principle, considers that 'life' is something special and unique, and maintains that life cannot be explained solely in terms of the laws of physics and chemistry, having properties which are special to the system as a whole. The aim of biology must ultimately be to explain the living world in terms of scientific principles, although appreciating that organisms behave in ways which often seem beyond the capabilities of their component parts. Certainly the consciousness of living organisms cannot be described in terms of chemistry and physics even though the neuro-physiologist can describe the working of the single neurone in physico-chemical terms. Consciousness may be the collective working of millions of neurones and their electrochemical states, but as yet we have no real concept of the chemical nature of thought and ideas. Nor do we understand completely how living organisms originated and evolved. There have been many attempts to answer this question from theological to biological and chapters 22–25, in book 2, attempt to put the different viewpoints but with the emphasis on the possible biological explanations.

Thus we are reduced to the position that we cannot define precisely what life is or whence it came. All that we can do is to describe the observable phenomena that distinguish living matter from non-living matter. These are as follows.

Nutrition (chapters 9 and 10)

All living organisms need food, which is assimilated and used as a source of energy, and materials for living processes such as growth. The distinction between the majority of plants and animals is based upon their methods of obtaining food. Most plants photosynthesise, incorporating the energy of light, to make their food. This is a form of autotrophic nutrition. Animals and fungi, on the other hand, obtain their food from other organisms, breaking down their organic compounds by enzymes and absorbing the products. This is known as heterotrophic nutrition. Most bacteria are also heterotrophic but some are autotrophic.

Respiration (chapter 11)

All life processes require energy and much of the food obtained by autotrophic and heterotrophic nutrition is used as a source of this energy. The energy is released during the breakdown of certain energy-rich compounds by the process of respiration. The energy released is stored in molecules of adenosine triphosphate (ATP) and this compound has been found to occur in all living cells.

Irritability (chapters 15 and 16)

Living organisms have the ability to respond to changes in both the internal and external environments and thus ensure that they maximise their chances of survival. For example the dermal blood vessels in the skin of a mammal dilate in response to a rise in body temperature, and the consequent heat loss brings about a restoration of the optimum temperature of the body. A green plant on a window sill in a room grows towards one-sided light coming through the window thus ensuring maximum exposure to light for photosynthesis.

Movement (chapter 17)

Animals are distinguished from plants by their ability to move from place to place, that is they locomote. This is necessary in order for them to obtain their food, unlike plants which can manufacture their own food from raw materials obtained in one place. Nevertheless, movement occurs in plants, both within their cells and indeed within

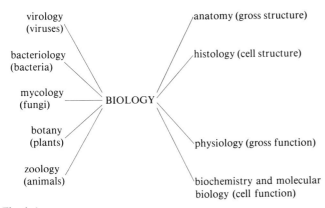

Fig 1.1

whole structures, although at a much slower rate than animals. Some bacteria and unicellular plants are also capable of locomotion.

Excretion (chapter 19)

Excretion is the removal from the body of waste products of metabolism. For example the process of respiration produces toxic waste products which must be eliminated. Animals take in an excess of protein during nutrition and, since this material cannot be stored, it must be broken down and excreted. Animal excretion is, therefore, largely nitrogenous excretion. In addition, the removal of certain unusable materials absorbed by the organism, such as lead, radioactive dust and alcohol can be regarded as excretion.

Reproduction (chapter 20)

The life span of organisms is limited, but they all have the ability to perpetuate 'life', thereby ensuring the survival of the species. The resulting offspring have the same general characteristics as the parents, whether such individuals are produced by asexual or sexual reproduction. The 'reductionist' search for the explanation of this inheritance has now revealed the existence of molecules known as nucleic acids (deoxyribosenucleic acid, DNA, and ribosenucleic acid, RNA) which appear to contain the coded information passed between organisms of succeeding generations.

Growth (chapter 21)

Non-living objects, such as a crystal or a stalagmite, grow by the addition of new material to their outside surface. Living organisms, however, grow from within, using food that they obtain by autotrophic or heterotrophic nutrition. The molecules are formed into new living material during the process of assimilation.

These seven characteristics can be observed to a greater or lesser extent in all living organisms and are our only means of indicating whether life exists or not. However, they are only the *observable* characteristics of the all-important properties of living material, that is, extracting, converting and using energy from the environment. In addition, living material is able to maintain and even increase its own energy content. In contrast to this, dead organic matter tends to disintegrate as a result of the chemical and physical forces of the environment. In order to maintain themselves and prevent this disintegration, organisms have an inbuilt self-regulating system to ensure that there is no net energy loss. This control is referred to as homeostasis and operates at all levels of biological organisation, from the molecular level to the community level.

The characteristics of life outlined above are dealt with in detail in the chapters indicated. Inevitably, many of these chapters extend the explanations in terms of physical and chemical concepts, for it is in these fields that the major research and additions to our knowledge have come in recent years. The study of protein synthesis, DNA, ATP, enzymes, hormones, viruses, antigen–antibody reactions and many other examples, all provide some explanation of what is happening in the cells and bodies of organisms.

In the appendix, in book 2, you will find some basic information required by a biologist, including biochemistry, scientific method, the experimental approach, a glossary of terms and so on. The appendix is designed to supply information to those students who may be lacking in one or more of these areas. With this knowledge the student must strive to develop powers of critical observation and description which are part of the thinking processes underlying scientific enquiry.

Chapter Two

Variety of life – prokaryotes, viruses and fungi

Chapter 2 is concerned with three groups of organisms: bacteria (prokaryotes), viruses and fungi. Although, as will become clear, they are placed in three very different groups taxonomically, they are often studied together in the branch of biology known as **microbiology**. This is because the techniques used in their study are similar in many respects, involving particularly microscopy and sterile (aseptic) procedures. They are of tremendous ecological and economic importance, and are intimately associated with the developing areas of biotechnology and genetic engineering.

2.1 Prokaryotes compared with eukaryotes

All cellular organisms so far studied fall naturally into one of two major groups, the prokaryotes and eukaryotes. **Prokaryotes** appeared about 3 500 million years ago and comprise a variety of organisms collectively known as bacteria. **Eukaryotes** include protoctists, fungi, green plants and animals. Eukaryotes appeared first in the late Pre-Cambrian period, about 2 000 million years ago, and probably evolved from prokaryotes.

The cells of prokaryotes (*pro*, before; *karyon*, nucleus) lack true nuclei. In other words, their genetic material (DNA) is not enclosed by nuclear membranes, and lies free in the cytoplasm. The cells of eukaryotes (*eu*, true) are

Table 2.1 Major differences between prokaryotes and eukaryotes.

Feature	*Prokaryote*	*Eukaryote*
Cell size	Average diameter 0.5–5µm.	Up to 40 µm diameter common; commonly 1 000–10 000 times volume of prokaryotic cells.
Form	Unicellular or filamentous.	Unicellular, filamentous or truly multicellular.
Genetic material	Circular DNA lying naked in the cytoplasm. No true nucleus or chromosomes. No nucleolus.	Linear DNA associated with proteins and RNA to form chromosomes within a nucleus. Nucleolus in nucleus.
Protein synthesis	70S ribosomes (smaller). No endoplasmic reticulum involved. (Many other details of protein synthesis differ, including susceptibility to antibiotics, e.g. prokaryotes inhibited by streptomycin.)	80S ribosomes (larger). Ribosomes may be attached to endoplasmic reticulum.
Organelles	Few organelles. None are surrounded by an envelope (2 membranes). Internal membranes scarce; if present usually associated with respiration or photosynthesis.	Many organelles. Envelope-bound organelles present, e.g. nucleus, mitochondria, chloroplasts. Great diversity of organelles bounded by single membranes, e.g. Golgi apparatus, lysosomes, vacuoles, microbodies, endoplasmic reticulum.
Cell walls	Rigid and contain polysaccharides with amino acids. Murein is main strengthening compound.	Cell walls of green plants and fungi rigid and contain polysaccharides. Cellulose is main strengthening compound of plant walls, chitin of fungal walls.
Flagella	Simple, lacking microtubules. Extracellular (not enclosed by cell surface membrane). 20 nm diameter.	Complex, with '9+2' arrangement of microtubules. Intracellular (surrounded by cell surface membrane). 200 nm diameter.
Respiration	Mesosomes in bacteria, except cytoplasmic membranes in blue-green bacteria.	Mitochondria for aerobic respiration.
Photosynthesis	No chloroplasts. Takes place on membranes which show no stacking.	Chloroplasts containing membranes which are usually stacked into lamellae or grana.
Nitrogen fixation	Some have the ability.	None have the ability.

Based on *A Dictionary of Life Sciences*, E. A. Martin (ed.), (1976), Pan Books.

much more complex and are characterised by a true nucleus, that is genetic material enclosed by membranes (the **nuclear envelope**) to form a definite, easily recognisable structure.

Many other fundamental differences exist between prokaryotes and eukaryotes, the more important of which are summarised in table 2.1. Some of the cell structures mentioned are discussed in more detail in chapter 7. Figs 2.3, 7.3 and 7.4 illustrate typical prokaryote and eukaryote cells.

Fig 2.1 summarises the classification of living organisms used in this book. Five kingdoms are used (see introduction to chapter 3).

Kingdom Prokaryotae

2.2   Bacteria

Bacteria are the smallest organisms having a cellular structure, their average diameter being about 1 μm, enough room for 200 average-sized globular protein molecules (of 5 nm diameter) to fit across the cell. Such a molecule in solution can diffuse about 60 μm per second; thus no special transport mechanisms are needed for these organisms. Bacteria range in length from about 0.1 to 10 μm. They are unicellular, and hence can only be seen individually with the aid of a microscope, that is they are **micro-organisms**. The study of bacteria, or **bacteriology**, is one branch of **microbiology**, the latter also including the study of viruses (**virology**), fungi (**mycology**) and other micro-organisms. Many of the techniques used to handle these organisms are similar.

Bacteria occupy many environments, such as soil, dust, water, air, in and on animals and plants and they can even be found in hot springs at temperatures of 60 °C or higher. Their numbers are enormous; one gram of fertile soil is estimated to contain 100 million and 1 cm³ of fresh milk

may contain more than 3 000 million. Together with fungi their activities are vital to all other organisms because they cause the decay of organic material and the subsequent recycling of nutrients. In addition, they are of increasing importance to humans, not only because some cause disease, but because they can be utilised in many economically important processes. Their importance is discussed further in sections 2.5 and 2.6.

2.2.1   Classification

There are a number of distinct groups of organisms at this level of organisation, the smallest and simplest of which are little more complex than viruses. The only group of concern here is the 'true bacteria' or Eubacteria. Fig 2.2 illustrates the range of organisms that are generally classified as bacteria.

2.2.2   Structure

Fig 2.3 shows the structure of a generalised bacterium. Fig 2.4 is an electron micrograph of a section through a rod-shaped bacterium and reveals how little structure is visible compared with a eukaryotic cell (for instance figs 7.5 and 7.6).

Capsules and slime layers

Capsules and slime layers are slimy or gummy secretions of certain bacteria which show up clearly after negative staining (when the background, rather than the specimen, is stained). A **capsule** is relatively thick and compact, whereas a **slime layer** is diffuse. In some cases these layers unite bacteria into colonies. Both offer useful additional protection to bacteria, for example capsulate strains of pneumococci grow in their human hosts causing pneumonia, whereas non-capsulate strains are easily attacked and destroyed by phagocytes, and are therefore harmless.

Cell wall

The cell wall confers rigidity and shape and can be clearly seen in a section (fig 2.4). As with plant cells, it prevents the cell from swelling and bursting as a result of osmosis when, as often occurs, it is in a medium of higher water potential (section 14.1.3). Water, various ions and small molecules can pass freely through tiny pores in the wall, but larger molecules like proteins and nucleic acids are excluded. The wall also has antigenic properties, caused by both proteins and polysaccharides.

Bacteria fall into two natural groups according to their cell wall structure. Some are stained with Gram's stain and are termed **Gram positive**, others do not retain the stain

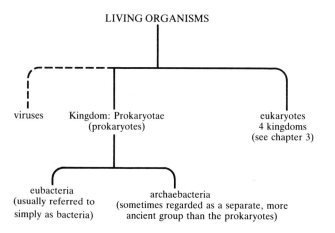

Fig 2.1   *Summary classification of living organisms*

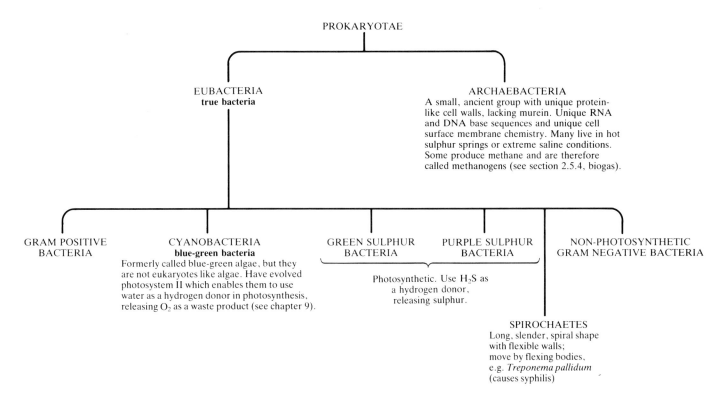

PROKARYOTAE

EUBACTERIA
true bacteria

ARCHAEBACTERIA
A small, ancient group with unique protein-like cell walls, lacking murein. Unique RNA and DNA base sequences and unique cell surface membrane chemistry. Many live in hot sulphur springs or extreme saline conditions. Some produce methane and are therefore called methanogens (see section 2.5.4, biogas).

GRAM POSITIVE BACTERIA

CYANOBACTERIA
blue-green bacteria
Formerly called blue-green algae, but they are not eukaryotes like algae. Have evolved photosystem II which enables them to use water as a hydrogen donor in photosynthesis, releasing O_2 as a waste product (see chapter 9).

GREEN SULPHUR BACTERIA

PURPLE SULPHUR BACTERIA

Photosynthetic. Use H_2S as a hydrogen donor, releasing sulphur.

NON-PHOTOSYNTHETIC GRAM NEGATIVE BACTERIA

SPIROCHAETES
Long, slender, spiral shape with flexible walls; move by flexing bodies, e.g. *Treponema pallidum* (causes syphilis)

Other organisms resembling bacteria, but of doubtful affinity, include **mycobacteria** (slime bacteria) which move by gliding; **mycoplasmas** or **pleuropneumonia-like organisms** (**PPLO**s), extremely small parasites lacking cell walls; **rickettsias**, organisms similar to large viruses which cause typhus.

Fig 2.2 *Classification of prokaryotes*

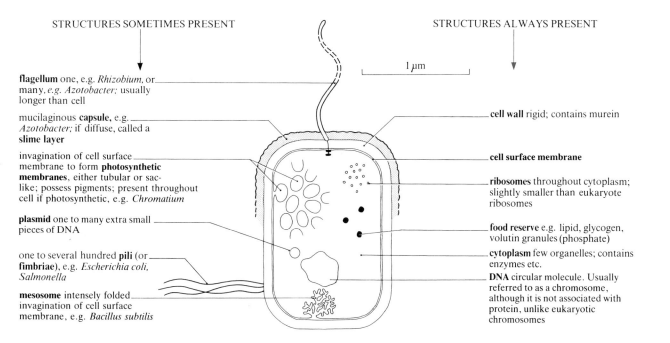

STRUCTURES SOMETIMES PRESENT

STRUCTURES ALWAYS PRESENT

1 μm

flagellum one, e.g. *Rhizobium,* or many, *e.g. Azotobacter;* usually longer than cell

mucilaginous **capsule**, e.g. *Azotobacter;* if diffuse, called a **slime layer**

invagination of cell surface membrane to form **photosynthetic membranes**, either tubular or sac-like; possess pigments; present throughout cell if photosynthetic, e.g. *Chromatium*

plasmid one to many extra small pieces of DNA

one to several hundred **pili** (or **fimbriae**), e.g. *Escherichia coli, Salmonella*

mesosome intensely folded invagination of cell surface membrane, e.g. *Bacillus subtilis*

cell wall rigid; contains murein

cell surface membrane

ribosomes throughout cytoplasm; slightly smaller than eukaryote ribosomes

food reserve e.g. lipid, glycogen, volutin granules (phosphate)

cytoplasm few organelles; contains enzymes etc.

DNA circular molecule. Usually referred to as a chromosome, although it is not associated with protein, unlike eukaryotic chromosomes

Fig 2.3 *A generalised rod-shaped bacterium*

during the decolourising procedure (section 2.7) and are termed **Gram negative**. Both types of wall have a rigid, unique framework of **murein**, a molecule consisting of parallel polysaccharide chains cross-linked in a regular fashion by short peptide chains. Each cell is thus effectively surrounded by a net-like sac which is really one molecule. (The polysaccharide portion is described in table 5.7.)

In Gram positive bacteria, such as *Lactobacillus*, the murein net is infilled with other components, mainly polysaccharides and proteins, to form a relatively thick, rigid box. The walls of Gram negative bacteria, such as *Escherichia coli* and *Azotobacter*, are thinner but more complex. Their murein layer is coated on the outside with a smooth, soft, lipid-rich layer. This protects them from **lysozyme**, an antibacterial enzyme found in tears, saliva and other body fluids and egg white. Lysozyme breaks the polysaccharide backbone of murein by catalysing hydrolysis of certain sugar linkages. The wall is thus punctured and lysis (osmotic swelling and bursting) of the cell occurs if the organism is in a solution of higher water potential. The same lipid-rich layer also confers resistance to penicillin, which attacks Gram positive bacteria by interfering with the cross-linking in growing cells, thus making the walls less rigid and more susceptible to osmotic shock.

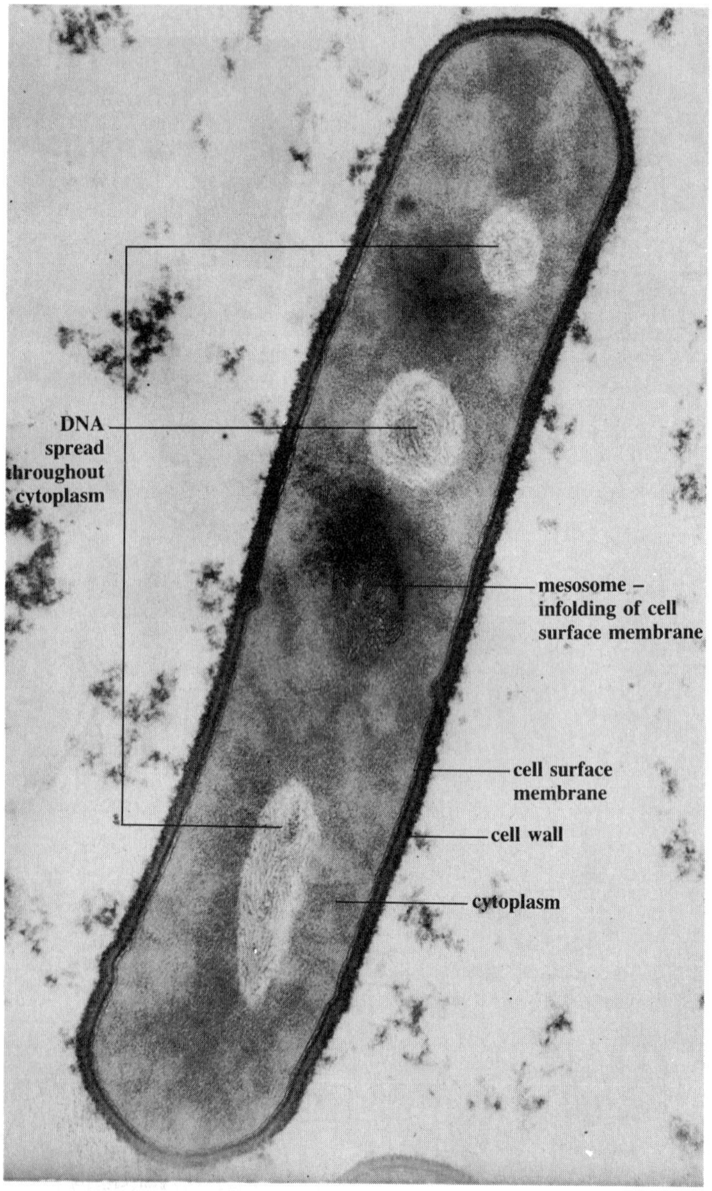

Flagella

Many bacteria are motile due to the presence of one or more flagella.

Bacterial flagella are much simpler in structure than those of eukaryotes (section 17.6.2, table 2.1) resembling just one of the microtubules of eukaryotic flagella. They are made of identical spherical subunits of a protein called **flagellin**, similar to the actin of muscle and arranged in eleven helical spirals to form a hollow cylinder, about 10–20 nm in diameter. The flagellum is rigid, though shaped into a wave, and has a unique mechanism of action. The base apparently rotates on ring-shaped bearings so that the flagellum does not beat but performs a corkscrew motion to propel the cell along. This is apparently the only structure in nature where the principle of the wheel is used. Another interesting feature is that a solution of flagellin subunits will associate spontaneously into helical threads. Spontaneous self-assembly is an important feature of many complex biological structures and in this case is due entirely to the particular sequence of amino acids (primary structure) of the protein.

Motile bacteria can move in response to certain stimuli, that is show tactic movements. For example, aerobic bacteria will swim towards oxygen (positive aerotaxis) and motile photosynthetic bacteria are positively phototactic (that is swim towards light).

Flagella are most easily seen with the electron microscope if the technique of metal shadowing, described in section A2.5, is used (see fig 2.5).

Pili (sing. pilus) or fimbriae (sing. fimbria)

Projecting from the walls of some Gram negative bacteria are protein rods called **pili** or **fimbriae** (fig 2.5). They are shorter and thinner than flagella and are concerned with cell to cell, or cell to surface, attachments, conferring a specific 'stickiness' on those strains that possess them. Various types occur, but of particular interest is the F pilus, coded for by a plasmid (section 2.2.4) and involved in sexual reproduction.

Fig 2.4 *Electron micrograph of a section of a typical rod-shaped bacterium,* Bacillus subtilis *(× 50 000). The light areas contain DNA*

Cell surface membrane, mesosomes and photosynthetic membranes

Like all cells, the living material of bacterial cells is surrounded by a partially permeable membrane. The structure and functions of the cell surface membrane are similar to those in eukaryotic cells (section 7.2.1). It is also the site of some respiratory enzymes. In addition, in some bacteria it forms mesosomes and/or photosynthetic membranes.

Mesosomes are infoldings of the cell surface membrane (figs 2.3 and 2.4) which may be artefacts created by the techniques used in specimen preparation for electron microscopy. They appear to be associated with DNA during cell division, facilitating the separation of the two daughter molecules of DNA after replication and aiding in the formation of new cross-walls between the daughter cells.

Among photosynthetic bacteria, sac-like, tubular or sheet-like infoldings of the cell surface membrane contain the photosynthetic pigments, always including bacterio-chlorophyll. Similar membranes are associated with nitrogen fixation.

Genetic material (bacterial 'chromosome')

Bacterial DNA is a single circular molecule of about 5×10^6 base pairs and of length 1 mm. The total DNA (the **genome**), and hence the amount of information encoded, is much less than that of a eukaryotic cell: typically it contains

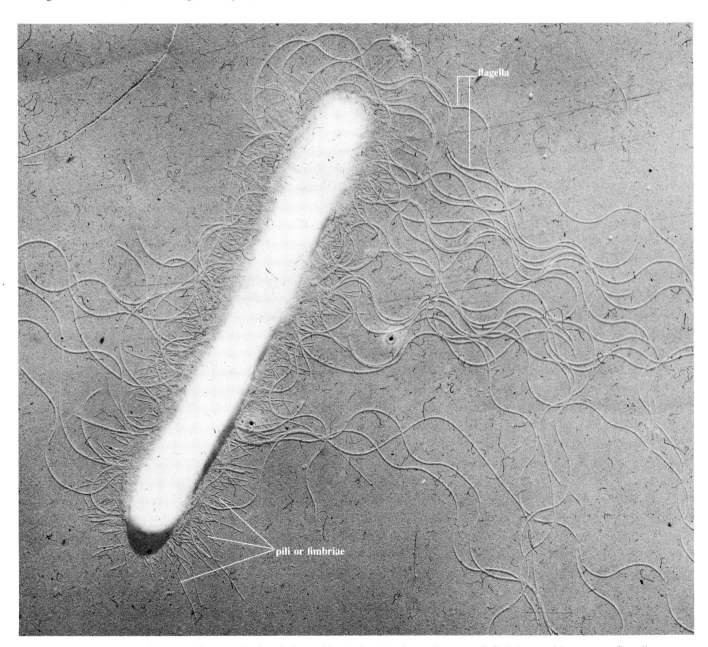

Fig 2.5 *Transmission electron micrograph of rod-shaped bacterium to show shape, wall, fimbriae and long wavy flagella* (× 28 000)

7

several thousand genes, about 500 times fewer than a human cell. (See also table 2.1 and fig 2.3.)

Ribosomes

See table 2.1 (protein synthesis) and fig 2.3.

Spores

Some bacteria, mainly of the genera *Clostridium* and *Bacillus*, form endospores (spores produced inside cells). They are thick-walled, long-lived and extremely resistant, particularly to heat and short-wave radiations. Their position in the cell is variable and is of importance in recognition and classification (see fig 2.6). If a whole cell forms a dormant, resistant structure it is called a cyst, as in some *Azotobacter* species.

2.2.3   Form

Bacterial shape is an important aid to classification. The four main shapes found are illustrated in fig 2.6. Examples of both useful and harmful bacteria are given.

2.2.4   Growth and reproduction

Growth of individuals and asexual reproduction

Bacteria have a large surface area to volume ratio and can therefore gain food sufficiently rapidly from their environment by diffusion and active transport mechanisms. Therefore, providing conditions are suitable, they can grow very rapidly. Important environmental factors affecting growth are temperature, nutrient availability, pH and ionic concentrations. Oxygen must also be present for obligate aerobes and absent for obligate anaerobes.

On reaching a certain size, dictated by the nucleus to cytoplasm ratio, bacteria reproduce asexually by binary fission, that is by division into two identical daughter cells. Cell division is preceded by replication of the DNA and while this is being copied it may be held in position by a mesosome (figs 2.3 and 2.4). The mesosome may also be attached to the new cross-walls that are laid down between the daughter cells, and plays some role in the synthesis of cell wall material. In the fastest growing bacteria such divisions may occur as often as every 20 min; this is known as the **generation time**.

---

(1) COCCI (sing. coccus) spherical

Cocci

Streptococci (chains)

e.g. many *Streptococcus* spp.; some infect upper respiratory tract and cause disease, e.g. *S. pyogenes* causes scarlet fever and sore throats; *S. thermophilus* gives yoghurt its creamy flavour; *S. lactis*, see section 2.3.4

Staphylococci (like a bunch of grapes)

e.g. *Staphylococcus aureus*, lives in nasal passages; different strains cause boils, pneumonia, food poisoning and other diseases

Diplococci (pairs)

the pneumococci *(Diplococcus pneumoniae)* are the only members; cause pneumonia

(2) BACILLI (sing. bacillus) rod-shaped

single rods   **rods in chains**

e.g. *Escherichia coli*, common gut-living symbiont; *Lactobacillus*, see section 2.3.4; *Salmonella typhi* causes typhoid fever

e.g. *Azotobacter*, a nitrogen-fixer; *Bacillus anthracis* causes anthrax

Bacilli with endospores showing various positions, shapes and sizes of spores

oval spore

central not swollen e.g. *Bacillus anthracis*, causes anthrax

spherical spore

terminal swollen e.g. *Clostridium tetani*, causes tetanus

subterminal swollen e.g. *Clostridium botulinum* (spores may also be central), causes botulism

(4) VIBRIOS comma-shaped

e.g. *Vibrio cholerae*, causes cholera single flagellum

(3) SPIRILLA (sing. spirillum) spiral-shaped

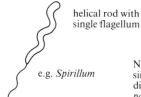

helical rod with single flagellum

e.g. *Spirillum*

NB body of spirochaetes is similar in form but locomotion differs, e.g. *Treponema pallidum* causes syphilis

Fig 2.6   *Forms of bacteria, illustrated by some common useful and harmful types*

Population growth

2.1 Consider the situation where a single bacterium is placed in a nutrient medium under optimal growth conditions. Assuming it, and its descendants, divide every 20 min, copy table 2.2 and complete it.

Using the data from the table, draw graphs of number of bacteria (graph A) and $\log_{10}$ number of bacteria (graph B) on the vertical axes against time (horizontal axis). What do you notice about the shapes of the graphs?

Table 2.2 Growth of a model population of bacteria.

Time (in units of 20 min)	0	1	2	3	4	5	6	7	8	9	10
A Number of bacteria											
B $\log_{10}$ number of bacteria (to one decimal place)											
C Number of bacteria expressed as power of 2											

The kind of growth shown in table 2.2 is known as logarithmic, exponential or geometric. The numbers form an exponential series. This can be explained by reference to line C in table 2.2 where the number of bacteria is expressed as a power of 2. The power can be called the logarithm or exponent of 2. The logarithms or exponents form a linearly increasing series 0, 1, 2, 3, etc., corresponding with the number of generations.

Returning to table 2.2, the numbers in line A could be converted to logarithms to the base 2 as follows:

A Number of bacteria	1	2	4	8	16	32	64	128	256	512	1024
D $\log_2$ number of bacteria	0	1	2	3	4	5	6	7	8	9	10

Compare line C with line D. However, it is conventional to use logarithms to the base 10, as in line B. Thus 1 is 10^0, 2 is $10^{0.3}$, 4 is $10^{0.6}$, etc.

The curve in graph A is known as a **logarithmic** or **exponential curve**. Such growth curves can be converted to straight lines by plotting the logarithms of growth against time. Under ideal conditions, then, bacterial growth is theoretically exponential. This mathematical model of bacterial growth can be compared with the growth of a real population. Fig 2.7 shows such growth. The growth curve shows four distinct phases. During the **lag phase** the bacteria are adapting to their new environment and growth has not yet achieved its maximum rate. The bacteria may,

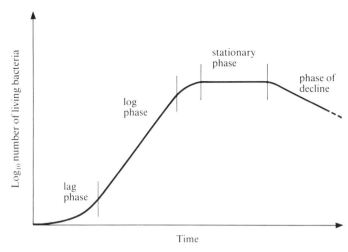

Fig 2.7 *Typical growth curve of a bacterial population*

for example, be synthesising new enzymes to digest the particular spectrum of nutrients available in the new medium.

The **log phase** is the phase when growth is proceeding at its maximum rate, closely approaching a logarithmic increase in numbers when the growth curve would be a straight line. Eventually growth of the colony begins to slow down and it starts to enter the **stationary phase** where growth rate is zero, and there is much greater competition for resources. Rate of production of new cells is slower and may cease altogether. Any increase in the number of cells is offset by the death of other cells, so that the number of living cells remains constant. This phase is a result of several factors, including exhaustion of essential nutrients, accumulation of toxic waste products of metabolism and possibly, if the bacteria are aerobic, depletion of oxygen.

During the final phase, the **phase of decline**, the death rate increases and cells stop multiplying. Methods of counting bacteria are described in the practical work at the end of this chapter.

Table 2.3 Culture of bacteria at 30°C.

Time/h	Number of cells in millions	
	living	living and dead
0	9	10
1	10	11
2	11	12
5	18	20
10	400	450
12	550	620
15	550	700
20	550	850
30	550	950
35	225	950
45	30	950

Sexual reproduction or genetic recombination

Bacteria exhibit a primitive form of sexual reproduction which differs from eukaryote sexual reproduction in that there are no gametes and cell fusion does not occur. However, the essential feature of sexual reproduction, namely exchange of genetic material, does take place and is called **genetic recombination**. Part (rarely all) of the DNA from the donor cell is transferred to the recipient cell whose DNA is genetically different. Parts of the donor DNA can replace parts of the recipient DNA, the process involving breakage and reunion of DNA strands by certain enzymes. The DNA formed contains genes from both parent cells and is called **recombinant DNA**. The offspring, or **recombinants**, will show variation as a result of the mixing of genes. This is the basic advantage of sexual reproduction because variation contributes to the process of evolution.

Three methods are known by which recombination can be achieved. In order of their discovery they are transformation, conjugation and transduction.

In **transformation** the donor and recipient do not come into contact. The process was discovered by Griffith in 1928. He was working with a pneumococcus, a bacterium causing pneumonia. The colonies were of two types, rough(R) and smooth(S) in appearance. The former were non-pathogenic and had no capsules; the latter were pathogenic and had large capsules (see section 2.2.2). Griffith discovered that if a mouse was injected with living R cells and dead (heat-killed) S cells it would die within a few days, and from its blood living S cells could be isolated. He concluded that the dead S cells had released a factor which enabled R cells to develop capsules and thus resist destruction by the host. This 'transformation' proved to be heritable, and since the molecule of inheritance was at that time unknown, though suspected to be protein, great efforts were made to identify the transforming factor.

In 1944, Avery, MacLeod & McCarty succeeded in isolating and identifying the factor and were surprised to find that it was DNA, not protein. This was the first direct evidence that the genetic material is DNA.

It is now known that during transformation a short piece of DNA is released by the donor and actively taken up by the recipient, in which it replaces a similar, though not necessarily identical, piece of DNA. It only occurs in a few genera, including some pneumococci, in so-called 'competent' strains where DNA can penetrate the recipient. A possible mechanism for transformation is shown in fig 2.8.

Conjugation involves DNA transfer between cells in direct contact. In contrast to transformation and transduction, large fractions of the donor DNA may be exchanged. It was discovered in 1946 in *Escherichia coli* in the following experiment. Normally *E. coli* can make all of its own amino acids, given a supply of glucose and mineral salts. Random

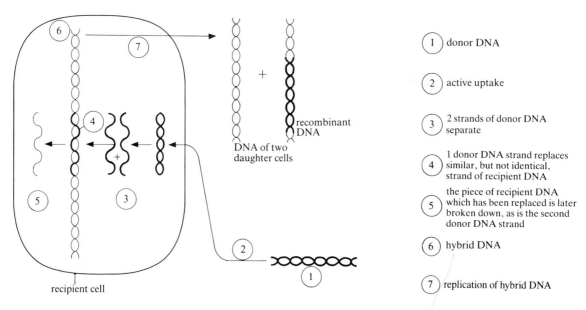

DNA of two daughter cells

recombinant DNA

recipient cell

1. donor DNA
2. active uptake
3. 2 strands of donor DNA separate
4. 1 donor DNA strand replaces similar, but not identical, strand of recipient DNA
5. the piece of recipient DNA which has been replaced is later broken down, as is the second donor DNA strand
6. hybrid DNA
7. replication of hybrid DNA

Fig 2.8 *A possible method for transformation. The precise method for active uptake of donor DNA is not known*

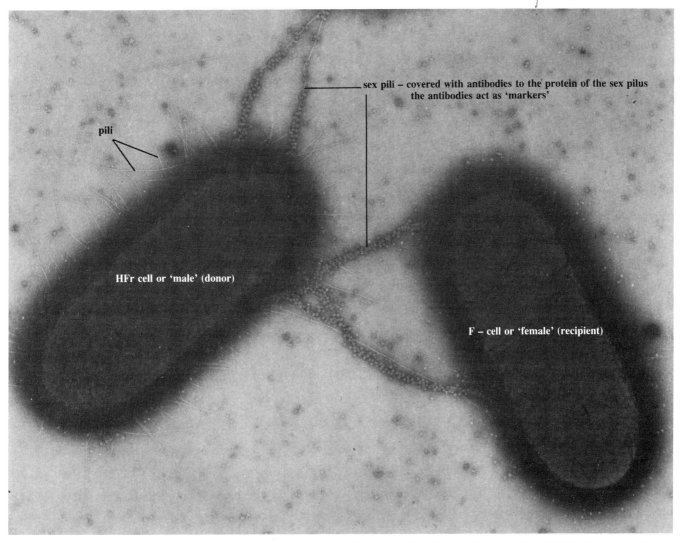

pili

**sex pili – covered with antibodies to the protein of the sex pilus
the antibodies act as 'markers'**

HFr cell or 'male' (donor)

F – cell or 'female' (recipient)

Fig 2.9 *Transmission electron micrograph of conjugating bacteria, one 'male' with two 'females' (× 19 475). The second 'female' cell is beyond the top of the photograph*

mutations were induced by exposure to radiation and two particular mutants selected. One could not make biotin (a vitamin) or the amino acid methionine. Another could not make the amino acids threonine and leucine. About 10^8 cells of each mutant were mixed and cultured on media lacking all four growth factors. Theoretically, none of the cells should have grown, but a few hundred colonies developed, each from one original bacterium, and these were shown to possess genes for making all four growth factors. Exchange of genetic information had therefore occurred, but no chemical responsible could be isolated. Eventually it was shown with the electron microscope that direct cell to cell contact, that is conjugation, can occur in *E. coli* (fig 2.9).

The ability to serve as a donor is determined by genes in a small circular piece of DNA called the sex factor, or **F factor** (F for fertility), a type of plasmid (see below) which codes for the protein of a special type of pilus, the F pilus or sex pilus. The sex pilus enables cell to cell contact to be established. DNA is a double-stranded molecule and

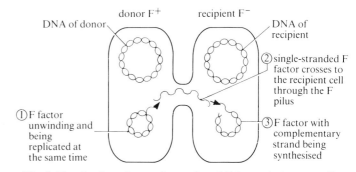

donor F$^+$ recipient F$^-$

DNA of donor

DNA of recipient

① F factor unwinding and being replicated at the same time

② single-stranded F factor crosses to the recipient cell through the F pilus

③ F factor with complementary strand being synthesised

Fig 2.10 *Conjugation and transfer of F factor between cells. 1, 2 and 3 represent successive stages in transfer*

during conjugation one of the two strands of F factor DNA passes through the sex pilus from the donor (F$^+$) to the recipient (F$^-$). The process is summarised in fig 2.10 which shows that the donor retains the F factor while the recipient also receives a copy. 'F$^+$ness' can therefore be spread throughout a population. Donor cells may become F$^-$ cells by spontaneously losing the F factors.

11

The F factor is particularly important because in a few cases, about 1 in 100 000, it becomes integrated with the rest of the DNA in the host cell. In such cases, the process of conjugation involves transfer of not only the F factor, but also the rest of the DNA. This takes about 90 min and separation may occur before exchange is complete. Such strains consistently donate all or large portions of their DNA and are called Hfr strains (H = high, f = frequency, r = recombination), because the donor DNA can recombine with the recipient DNA.

During **transduction** a small, double-stranded piece of DNA is transferred from donor to recipient by a bacteriophage (a virus, see section 2.3). The probable mechanism is shown in fig 2.11.

Some viruses have the ability to integrate their DNA with bacterial DNA; it is replicated at the same time as their host's DNA and passed from one bacterial generation to the next. Occasionally it becomes active and codes for the production of new viruses. The host (bacterial) DNA breaks down and odd pieces may get included inside new virus coats, sometimes to the exclusion of the viral DNA. The new 'viruses', or **transducing particles**, then carry the DNA to other bacteria.

Plasmids and episomes

Plasmids and episomes are small pieces of DNA separate from the bulk of the DNA. They often, though not always, replicate in step with the host DNA and are not essential for the survival of the host.

Originally a distinction was drawn between plasmids, which could not integrate with the host DNA, and episomes, which could do so. Episomes include F factors and temperate phages (section 2.3.4). In recent years the general term plasmid has been adopted for both. Plasmids are now known to be extremely common and can be regarded as subcellular parasites or symbionts even simpler than viruses. The question of whether viruses are living is discussed in section 2.3.2; with plasmids, which are only

DNA molecules, the question is even more difficult to answer.

Plasmids confer various abilities on their hosts. Some are 'resistance factors' (R plasmids or R factors), that is factors that confer resistance to antibiotics. An example is the penicillinase plasmid of staphylococci which can be transduced by bacteriophages. This contains a gene for the enzyme penicillinase which breaks down penicillin, thus conferring resistance to penicillin. Spread of such factors by sexual reproduction among bacteria has important implications for medicine. Other plasmid genes confer resistance to disinfectants; cause disease, such as staphylococcal impetigo; are responsible for the fermentation of milk to cheese by lactic acid bacteria; and confer ability to utilise complex substances as food, such as hydrocarbons, with potential applications in cleaning oil spills and producing protein from petroleum.

To conclude, it should be said that all forms of sexual reproduction in bacteria are rare, but significant because of the vast numbers of cells occurring in bacterial colonies. Sexual reproduction is much less organised than in eukaryotes and the complete genome (total DNA) can only be exchanged during conjugation of bacteria and then it is a rare event. It has particular significance in spreading resistance to antibiotics and disinfectants.

2.2.5 Nutrition

At the beginning of chapter 9, and summarised in table 9.1, organisms are placed into four nutritional categories. There are examples of bacteria in all four categories, as shown in table 2.4. The most important group is the chemoheterotrophic bacteria. In their feeding strategies these bacteria resemble fungi. As with fungi there are three groups, namely saprotrophs, mutualists and parasites (see sections 2.4.1 and 10.1).

A **saprotroph** is an organism that obtains its food from dead and decaying matter. The saprotroph secretes

Fig 2.11 *Mechanism of transduction*

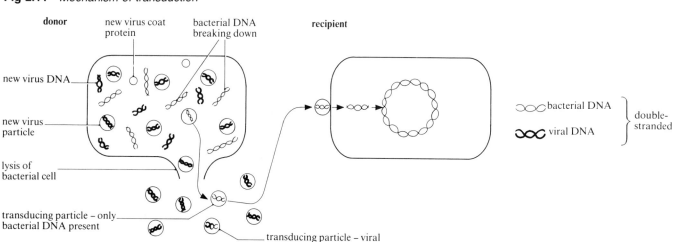

Table 2.4 The four nutritional categories of bacteria and some of their characteristics.

	Autotrophic (carbon source is carbon dioxide (inorganic))		Heterotrophic (carbon source is organic compounds made by other organisms)	
	Photoautotrophic*	Chemoautotrophic (chemosynthetic)	Photoheterotrophic*	Chemoheterotrophic
Energy source	Light	Chemical – from oxidation of inorganic substances during respiration	Light	Chemical – from oxidation of organic substances during respiration
Types	Only green and blue-green bacteria, purple sulphur bacteria and some purple non-sulphur bacteria	Nitrifying bacteria, sulphur bacteria and others	Only purple non-sulphur bacteria, extremely few in number	Most bacteria – important as saprotrophs, parasites and mutualists, utilising enormous range of chemical substances as food
Further information	section 9.9	section 9.10	—	section 2.2.5

* photoautotrophic + photoheterotrophic types comprise the *photosynthetic* bacteria.

enzymes onto the organic matter, so that digestion is outside the organism. Soluble products of digestion are absorbed and assimilated within the body of the saprotroph.

Saprotrophic bacteria and fungi constitute the **decomposers** and are essential in bringing about decay and recycling of nutrients. They produce humus from animal and plant remains, but also cause decay of materials useful to humans, especially food. Their importance in the biosphere is stressed in section 2.5, and also in chapter 12.

Mutualism is the name given to any form of close relationship between two living organisms in which both partners benefit. Examples of bacterial mutualists are *Rhizobium*, a nitrogen-fixer living in the root nodules of legumes, such as pea and clover, and *Escherichia coli*, which inhabits the gut of humans, and probably contributes vitamins of the B and K groups.

A **parasite** is an organism that lives in or on another organism, the **host**, from which it obtains its food and, usually, shelter. The host is usually of a different species and suffers harm from the parasite. Parasites which cause disease are called **pathogens**. Some examples are given in section 2.6. Some parasites can only survive and grow in living cells and are called **obligate parasites**. Others can infect a host, bring about its death and then live saprotrophically on the remains; these are called **facultative parasites**. It is a characteristic of parasites that they are very exacting in their nutritional requirements, needing 'accessory growth factors' that they cannot manufacture for themselves but can only find in other living cells.

2.2.6 Useful and harmful bacteria/Practical work

See sections 2.5 and 2.6, and 2.7 respectively.

2.3 Viruses

2.3.1 Discovery

In 1852, the Russian botanist D. J. Ivanovsky prepared an infectious extract from tobacco plants that were suffering from mosaic disease. When the extract was passed through a filter able to prevent the passage of bacteria, the filtered fluid was still infectious. In 1898 the Dutchman Beijerink coined the name 'virus' (Latin for poison) to describe the infectious nature of certain filtered plant fluids. Although progress was made in isolating highly purified samples of viruses and in identifying them chemically as nucleoproteins (nucleic acids combined with proteins), the particles still proved elusive and mysterious because they were too small to be seen with the light microscope. As a result, they were among the first biological structures to be studied when the electron microscope was developed in the 1930s.

2.3.2 Characteristics

Size

Viruses are the **smallest living organisms**, ranging in size from about 20 nm to 300 nm; on average they are about 50 times smaller than bacteria. As stated above they cannot be seen with the light microscope (since they are usually smaller than half a wavelength of light) and they pass through filters which retain bacteria.

The question is often posed, 'Are viruses living?'. If, to be defined as living, a structure must possess genetic material (DNA or RNA), and be capable of reproducing itself, then the answer must be that viruses are living. If to be living demands a cellular structure then the answer is that they are not. It should also be noted that viruses are not capable of reproducing outside the host cell. They are on the borderline between living and non-living and remind us that there is a continuous spectrum of increasing complexity from simple molecules to the elaborate enclosed systems of cells.

Habit

Since viruses can only reproduce themselves inside living cells, they are all obligate parasites. They usually cause obvious signs of disease. Once inside the host cell, they 'switch off' (inactivate) the host's DNA and, using their own DNA or RNA, instruct the cell to make new copies of the virus (section 2.3.3). Viruses are transmitted from cell to cell as inert particles.

Structure

Viruses have a very simple structure consisting of a length of genetic material, either DNA or RNA, forming a **core** surrounded and protected by a coat of protein called a **capsid**. The fully assembled, infective particle is called a **virion**. A few viruses, such as herpes and influenza viruses, have an additional lipoprotein **envelope** derived from the surface membrane of the host cell. Unlike all other organisms viruses are non-cellular.

Virus coats are often built up of identical repeating subunits called **capsomeres**. These form highly symmetrical structures that can be crystallised, enabling information about their structure to be obtained by X-ray crystallography as well as electron microscopy. Once the subunits of a virus have been made by the host, they show the property of self-assembly into a virus. Self-assembly is characteristic of many other biological structures and is of fundamental importance in biology. Fig 2.12 shows a simplified, generalised structure of a virus.

Icosahedron and dodecahedron (such as adenovirus, polyoma/papilloma virus, polio virus). An icosahedron has 20 triangular faces with 12 corners and 30 edges. Fig 2.13a shows a regular icosahedron. Using the technique of negative staining the detailed structure of viruses can be observed because the stain can penetrate between, and show up, all the surface features. For example figs 2.13b and c reveal that, in the case of the

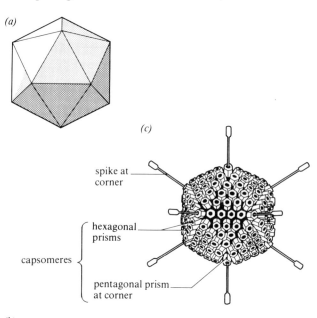

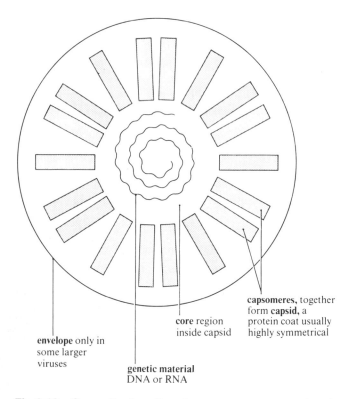

Fig 2.12 *Generalised section of a capsomere-possessing virus*

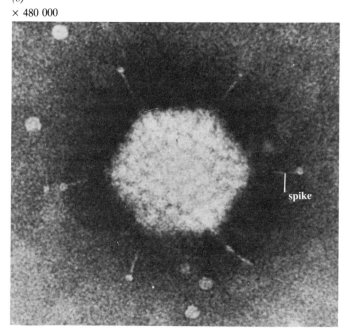

Fig 2.13 *(a) Solid model of an icosahedron. (b) Adenovirus particle, an icosahedral virus showing spikes at the corners. Electron micrograph of a negatively stained preparation. (c) Drawing from a three-dimensional model of an adenovirus. The capsid is made of 252 capsomeres, 12 at corners, 240 on faces and edges. Adenoviruses are DNA viruses which have been isolated from a variety of mammals and birds. They infect lymphoid tissue in humans and cause respiratory disease*

14

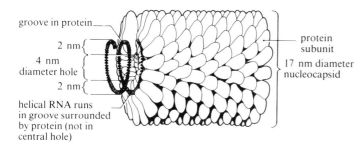

groove in protein

2 nm

4 nm diameter hole

2 nm

helical RNA runs in groove surrounded by protein (not in central hole)

protein subunit

17 nm diameter nucleocapsid

Fig 2.14 *Structure of tobacco mosaic virus. Drawing of part of the rod-shaped virus based on X-ray diffraction, biochemical and electron microscope data*

Helical symmetry. This is best illustrated by the tobacco mosaic virus (TMV), an RNA virus (fig 2.14). The 2 130 identical protein subunits, together with the RNA, form an integrated structure called a **nucleocapsid**. In some viruses the nucleocapsid is enclosed in an envelope, for instance the mumps and influenza viruses.

Bacteriophage type. Viruses that attack bacteria form a group called bacteriophages. Some of these have a distinct icosahedral head, with a tail showing helical symmetry (fig 2.15).

Complex types. Some viruses have a complex structure, such as rhabdoviruses and pox viruses.

adenovirus, each of the 20 faces is made up of a number of capsomeres. The overall number of capsomeres is 252 (240 hexagonal, 12 pentagonal at the corners). This number varies between viruses, for instance herpes has 162, polyoma 42, $\Phi \times 174$ bacteriophage 12. All have 12 pentagonal capsomeres, the latter having no hexagonal capsomeres and forming a shape called a **dodecahedron**.

2.3.3 Life cycle of a bacteriophage

The life cycle of a typical bacteriophage is shown in fig 2.16; fig 2.17 shows the scale of the phage in relation to the bacterium. *E. coli* is a typical host and it can be attacked by at least seven strains of phage, known as T_1 to T_7. A T-even phage (for instance T_2) is illustrated in figs 2.15 and 2.16.

(a)

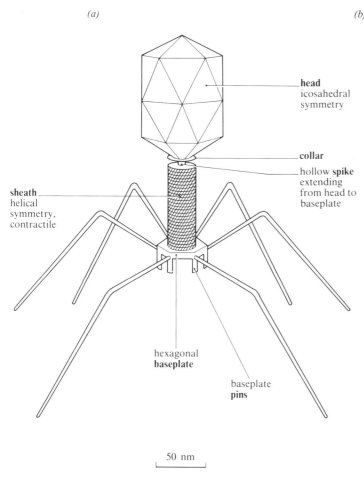

head
icosahedral symmetry

collar

hollow **spike** extending from head to baseplate

sheath helical symmetry, contractile

hexagonal **baseplate**

baseplate **pins**

50 nm

(b)

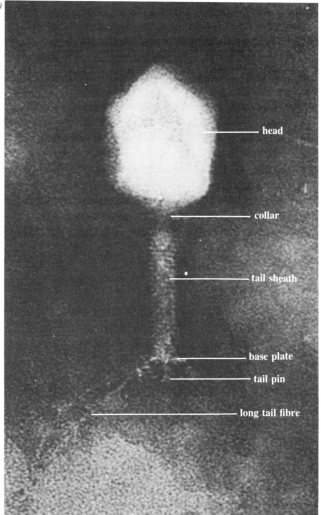

head

collar

tail sheath

base plate

tail pin

long tail fibre

Fig 2.15 *(a) Structure of a bacteriophage. (b) Electron micrograph of negatively stained bacteriophage*

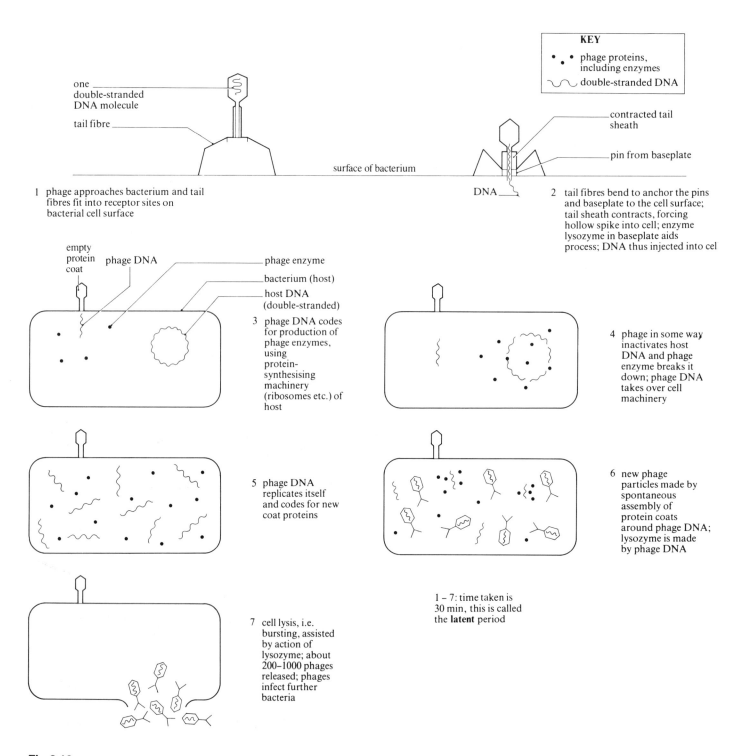

one double-stranded DNA molecule

tail fibre

KEY

• • • phage proteins, including enzymes

‿‿ double-stranded DNA

contracted tail sheath

pin from baseplate

surface of bacterium

1 phage approaches bacterium and tail fibres fit into receptor sites on bacterial cell surface

DNA

2 tail fibres bend to anchor the pins and baseplate to the cell surface; tail sheath contracts, forcing hollow spike into cell; enzyme lysozyme in baseplate aids process; DNA thus injected into cel

empty protein coat

phage DNA

phage enzyme

bacterium (host)

host DNA (double-stranded)

3 phage DNA codes for production of phage enzymes, using protein-synthesising machinery (ribosomes etc.) of host

4 phage in some way inactivates host DNA and phage enzyme breaks it down; phage DNA takes over cell machinery

5 phage DNA replicates itself and codes for new coat proteins

6 new phage particles made by spontaneous assembly of protein coats around phage DNA; lysozyme is made by phage DNA

1 – 7: time taken is 30 min, this is called the **latent** period

7 cell lysis, i.e. bursting, assisted by action of lysozyme; about 200–1000 phages released; phages infect further bacteria

Fig 2.16 *Life cycle of a bacteriophage*

2.3.4 Life cycles of other viruses

A similar life cycle probably occurs in most viruses. The penetration process differs in bacterial, plant and animal viruses because bacterial and plant viruses have to penetrate cell walls. This does not always involve the injection process described in fig 2.16 and protein coats are not always left outside the cell.

Some phages do not replicate once inside the host cell but instead their nucleic acid becomes incorporated into the DNA of the host cell. They may then remain without influence through several generations, being replicated

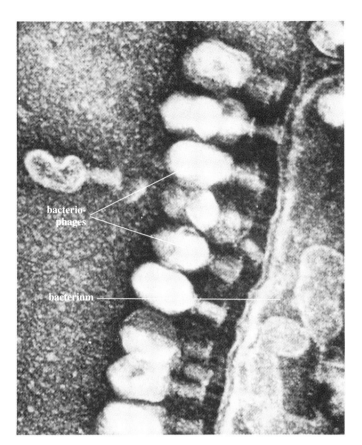

Fig 2.17 *Electron micrograph of bacteriophages heavily infesting a bacterium* Escherichia coli

only as the host replicates its own DNA. Such phages are known as **temperate phages** and the bacteria that harbour them **lysogenic**, meaning that they have the potential for lysis, but that this is not shown until the phage resumes activity. The inactive phage is called a **prophage** or **provirus**.

2.3.5 Evolutionary origin of viruses

The most plausible hypothesis for the origin of viruses is that they represent escaped nucleic acid, that is nucleic acid that has become capable of replicating itself independently of the cell from which it originated, even though it means using (parasitising) the machinery of that, or other, cells. Viruses would thus be derived from cellular organisms and should not be regarded as primitive forerunners of cellular organisms.

How common such 'escapes' have been cannot be easily judged, but it is likely that our increasing knowledge of genetics will reveal more variations on the theme of parasitic nucleic acids.

2.3.6 Viruses as agents of disease

See section 2.6.2.

Kingdom Fungi

2.4 Fungi

The fungi are a large and successful group of organisms of about 80 000 named species. They range in size from the unicellular yeasts to the large toadstools, puffballs and stinkhorns, and occupy a very wide range of habitats, both aquatic and terrestrial. They are also of major importance for the essential role that they play in the biosphere, and for the way in which they have been exploited by humans for economic and medical purposes.

Fungi include the numerous moulds growing on damp organic matter (such as bread, leather, decaying vegetation and dead fish), the unicellular yeasts which are abundant on the sugary surfaces of ripe fruits and many parasites of plants. The latter cause some economically important diseases of crops, such as mildews, smuts and rusts. A few fungi are parasites of animals, but are less significant in this respect than bacteria.

The study of fungi is called **mycology** (*mykes*, mushroom). It constitutes a branch of microbiology because many of the handling techniques used, such as sterilising and culturing procedures, are the same as those used with bacteria.

2.4.1 Characteristics and classification of Fungi

Fungi are eukaryotes that lack chlorophyll, and are therefore heterotrophic, like animals. However, they have rigid cell walls and are non-motile, like plants. Traditionally, they have been regarded as plants*, but more modern classifications, such as that shown in fig. 3.1, place them in a separate kingdom. Their characteristics and classification are summarised in fig 2.18 and table 2.5. The two largest and most advanced groups are the Ascomycota and the Basidiomycota.

> **2.5** Using those features of the kingdom Fungi given in table 2.5, prepare a table of differences between fungi and chlorophyll-containing plant cells.

Structure

The body structure of the fungi is unique. It consists of a mass of fine, tubular branching threads called **hyphae** (singular, hypha), the whole mass being called a **mycelium**. Each hypha has a thin, rigid wall whose chief component is chitin, a nitrogen-containing polysaccharide also found as a

---

* At one time fungi were given the status of a class, and together with the class Algae formed the division Thallophyta of the plant kingdom. The **Thallophyta** were those plants whose bodies could be described as a thallus. A **thallus** is a body, often flat, which is not differentiated into true roots, stems and leaves and lacks a true vascular system.

structural component in the exoskeletons of arthropods (section 5.2.4). The hyphae are not divided into true cells. Instead, the protoplasm is either continuous or interrupted at intervals by cross-walls called **septa** which divide the hyphae into compartments similar to cells. Unlike normal cell walls their formation is not a consequence of nuclear division, and a pore normally remains at their centre allowing protoplasm to flow between compartments. Each compartment may contain one, two or more nuclei, which are distributed at more or less regular intervals along the hyphae. Hyphae lacking cross-walls are called **non-septate (aseptate)** or **coenocytic**, the latter term applying to any mass of protoplasm containing many nuclei and not split into cells. Hyphae having cross-walls are called **septate**. Within the cytoplasm the usual eukaryote organelles are found, such as mitochondria, Golgi apparatus, endoplasmic reticulum, ribosomes and vacuoles. In the older parts, vacuoles are large and cytoplasm is confined to a thin peripheral layer. Sometimes hyphae aggregate to form more solid structures such as the fruiting bodies of the Basidomycota.

Nutrition

Fungi are heterotrophic, that is require an organic source of carbon. In addition, they require a source of nitrogen, usually organic such as amino acids; inorganic ions such as K^+ and Mg^{2+}; trace elements such as Fe, Zn and Cu; and organic growth factors such as vitamins. The exact range of nutrients required, and hence substrates on which they are found, is variable. Some fungi, particularly obligate parasites, require a wide range of ready-made components; others can synthesise their own requirements given only a source of carbohydrate and mineral salts. Some may synthesise most of their requirements but need one or more particular amino acids or vitamins. The nutrition of fungi can be described as **absorptive** because they absorb nutrients directly from outside their bodies. This is in contrast to animals, which normally **ingest** food, and then **digest** it *within their bodies* before **absorption** takes place.

With fungi, digestion, if necessary, is external using extracellular enzymes.

Fungi obtain their nutrients as saprotrophs, parasites or mutualists. In this respect they are like most bacteria and the three terms have already been defined in section 2.2.5. (See also section 10.1.)

Saprotrophs. Fungal saprotrophs produce a variety of digestive enzymes. If they secrete the three main classes of digestive enzymes, namely carbohydrases, lipases and proteases, they can utilise a wide range of substrates, for example the *Penicillium* species which form green and blue moulds on substrates such as soil, damp leather, bread and decaying fruit.

The hyphae of saprotrophic fungi are usually chemotropic, that is they grow towards certain substrates in response to chemicals diffusing from these substrates (section 15.1.1).

Fungal saprotrophs usually produce large numbers of light, resistant spores. This allows efficient dispersal to other food sources. Examples are *Mucor*, *Penicillium* and *Agaricus*.

Saprotrophic fungi and bacteria together form the **decomposers** which are essential in the recycling of nutrients. Especially important are the few that secrete the enzyme cellulase, which breaks down cellulose. Cellulose is an important structural component of plant cell walls, and the rotting of wood and other plant remains is achieved partly by decomposers secreting cellulase.

Some fungal saprotrophs are of economic importance, such as *Saccharomyces* (yeast) and *Penicillium* (section 2.4.3).

Parasites. Fungal parasites may be facultative or obligate (section 2.2.5), and more commonly attack plants than animals. Obligate parasites do not normally kill their hosts, whereas facultative parasites frequently do, and live saprotrophically off the dead remains. Obligate parasites include the powdery mildews, downy mildews,

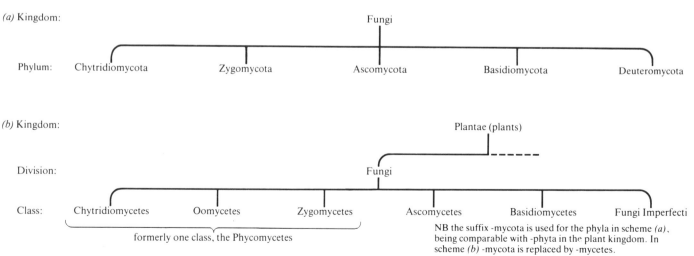

Fig 2.18 *Classification of fungi: (a) a modern scheme, (b) a traditional scheme*

Table 2.5 Classification and characteristics of fungi.

Kingdom Fungi

General characteristics
Heterotrophic nutrition because they lack chlorophyll and therefore non-photosynthetic. They can be parasites, saprotrophs or mutualists
Rigid cell walls containing chitin as the fibrillar material
Body is usually a mycelium, a network of fine tubular filaments called hyphae
If carbohydrate is stored, it is usually as glycogen, not starch
Reproduce by means of spores
Non-motile

Phylum Zygomycota	*Phylum Ascomycota*	*Phylum Basidiomycota*
Sexual reproduction by conjugation, involving fusion of two gametangia to produce a zygospore	Sexual reproduction involves production of spores (ascospores) inside a special structure called an ascus	Sexual reproduction involves production of basidia which bear spores (basidiospores) externally
Asexual reproduction by conidia or sporangia containing spores. No zoospores	Asexual reproduction by conidia. No sporangia	Asexual reproduction by formation of spores. Not common
Non-septate hyphae and large well-developed branching mycelium	Septate hyphae	Septate hyphae
e.g. *Rhizopus stolonifer*, common bread mould, a saprotroph. *Mucor*, common moulds, saprotroph	e.g. *Penicillium* and *Aspergillus*, saprotrophic moulds. *Saccharomyces* (yeast), unicellular saprotrophs. *Erysiphe*, obligate parasites causing powdery mildews, e.g. of barley. *Ceratocystis ulmi*, parasite causing Dutch elm disease	e.g. *Agaricus campestris*, field mushroom, saprotroph

---

Phylum Chytridiomycota
A small group of microscopic, often unicellular, fungi, e.g. *Synchytrium endobioticum*, a parasite causing wart disease of potatoes.
Phylum Deuteromycota (Fungi Imperfecti)
Fungi in which sexual reproduction has never been observed, and whose classification is uncertain, e.g. *Trichophyton* which causes athlete's foot and ring-worm.

NB: Phyla end in '-mycota'

rusts and smuts, and are usually restricted to a narrow range of hosts from which they require a specific range of nutrients. Facultative parasites are usually less specialised and may grow on a variety of hosts or substrates.

If the host is a plant, hyphae penetrate through stomata, directly through the cuticle and epidermis, or through wounds. Once inside the plant, hyphae normally ramify between cells, sometimes producing pectinases which digest a path through the middle lamellae. The fungus may be systemic, that is spread throughout the host, or it may be confined to a small part of the host.

Facultative parasites commonly produce sufficient pectinases to cause 'soft rot' of the tissue, reducing it to a mush. Subsequently cells may be invaded and killed with the aid of cellulase which digests the cell walls. Cell constituents may be absorbed directly or digested by secretion of further fungal enzymes. Obligate parasites possess specialised penetration and absorption devices called **haustoria**. Each haustorium is a modified hyphal outgrowth with a large surface area which pushes into living cells without breaking

their cell surface membranes, and without killing them. The success of the parasite depends on the continued life of the host. Haustoria are rarely produced by facultative parasites.

The life cycles of parasitic fungi are sometimes complex. This is particularly true of obligate parasites, such as rust fungi, whose life cycles involve several stages and more than one host. Obligate parasites usually produce resistant spores by sexual reproduction to coincide with the deaths of their hosts. In this way they may overwinter.

Mutualism. Two important types of mutualistic union are made by fungi, namely lichens and mycorrhizae. **Lichens** are mutualistic associations between fungi and algae. The fungus is an ascomycote or a basidiomycote, while the alga is a green alga (or blue-green bacterium). Lichens are commonly encrusted on exposed rocks and trunks of trees; they also hang from trees in wet forests. It is believed that the alga contributes organic food from photosynthesis, while the fungus is

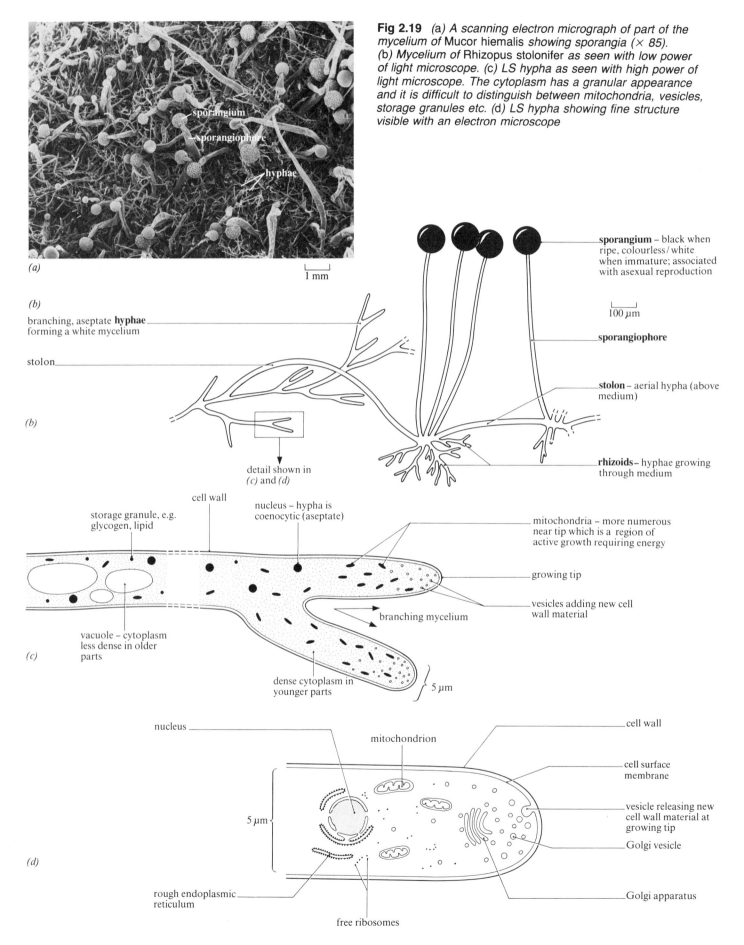

Fig 2.19 (a) *A scanning electron micrograph of part of the mycelium of* Mucor hiemalis *showing sporangia (× 85).* (b) *Mycelium of* Rhizopus stolonifer *as seen with low power of light microscope.* (c) *LS hypha as seen with high power of light microscope. The cytoplasm has a granular appearance and it is difficult to distinguish between mitochondria, vesicles, storage granules etc.* (d) *LS hypha showing fine structure visible with an electron microscope*

(a)

1 mm

(b)

branching, aseptate **hyphae** forming a white mycelium

stolon

(b)

detail shown in
(c) and (d)

sporangium – black when ripe, colourless/white when immature; associated with asexual reproduction

100 μm

sporangiophore

stolon – aerial hypha (above medium)

rhizoids – hyphae growing through medium

cell wall

storage granule, e.g. glycogen, lipid

nucleus – hypha is coenocytic (aseptate)

mitochondria – more numerous near tip which is a region of active growth requiring energy

growing tip

branching mycelium

vesicles adding new cell wall material

vacuole – cytoplasm less dense in older parts

(c)

dense cytoplasm in younger parts

5 μm

nucleus

mitochondrion

cell wall

cell surface membrane

vesicle releasing new cell wall material at growing tip

Golgi vesicle

5 μm

(d)

rough endoplasmic reticulum

Golgi apparatus

free ribosomes

protected from high light intensity and able to absorb water and mineral salts. The fungus can also conserve water, enabling some lichens to grow in dry conditions where no other plants exist.

2.4.2   Phylum Zygomycota

Characteristics of the Zygomycota are given in table 2.5. They are a small group of fungi which are regarded as ancestral to the two main divisions, Ascomycota and Basidiomycota.

An example, *Rhizopus*, is a very common saprotroph, similar in structure and appearance to *Mucor*, but more widespread. Both *Rhizopus* and *Mucor* are called pin moulds for the reason given below (in asexual reproduction). *Rhizopus stolonifer* is a common species and is the common bread mould. It may also grow on apples and other fruit in storage, causing soft rot.

Structure

The structure of the mycelium and individual hyphae is shown in fig 2.19. The mycelium is profusely branching and aseptate. Unlike *Mucor*, the mycelium develops aerial stolons which arch above the medium and produce hyphae called **rhizoids** where they touch down. From these points sporangiophores develop.

Life cycle

The life cycle of *Rhizopus stolonifer* is summarised diagrammatically in fig 2.20.

Asexual reproduction

After two or three days in culture, *Rhizopus* begins to produce vertically growing hyphae called **sporangiophores** (*-phore*, stalk). These are negatively geotropic. Each sporangiophore tip swells into a **sporangium** which becomes separated from the sporangiophore by a domed cross-wall called the **columella** as shown in fig 2.21. Inside the sporangium the protoplasm splits up into portions, each

of which acquires a wall and becomes a spore containing several nuclei. The appearance of the sporangiophores and sporangia resembles a collection of pins; hence *Rhizopus* and the other closely related fungi such as *Mucor* are called **pin moulds**. As the sporangium matures it becomes black and dries, the wall eventually cracking unevenly to expose a dry, powdery mass of spores. The columella collapses, as shown in fig 2.21, providing a wide platform from which spores are easily blown away and dispersed. Under wet conditions, the sporangia would not dry and crack, thus preventing release of spores when conditions are unfavourable for dispersal. The haploid spores germinate if they land on a suitable substrate and produce a new mycelium.

> **2.6   What is the purpose of the sporangiophores?**

Sexual reproduction

Many fungi exist in two different mating strains. Sexual reproduction can only occur between different strains, even if both produce male and female sex organs. Such self-sterile fungi are called **heterothallic** and the two strains are usually designated plus and minus (*not* male and female). They are structurally identical but physiologically slightly different. Fungi in which there is only one strain, and which are therefore self-fertile, are called **homothallic**. The advantage of heterothallism is that cross-fertilisation occurs and greater variation is ensured.

Rhizopus stolonifer is heterothallic. The events of sexual reproduction are summarised in fig 2.22. The initial events

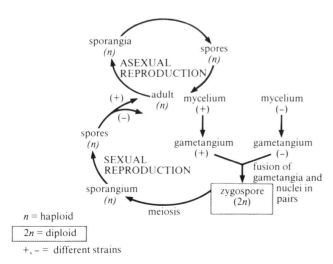

Fig 2.20 *Diagrammatic life cycle of* Rhizopus stolonifer

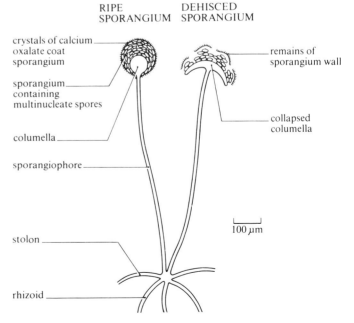

Fig 2.21 *Asexual reproduction in* Rhizopus stolonifer, *showing LS ripe and dehisced sporangia*

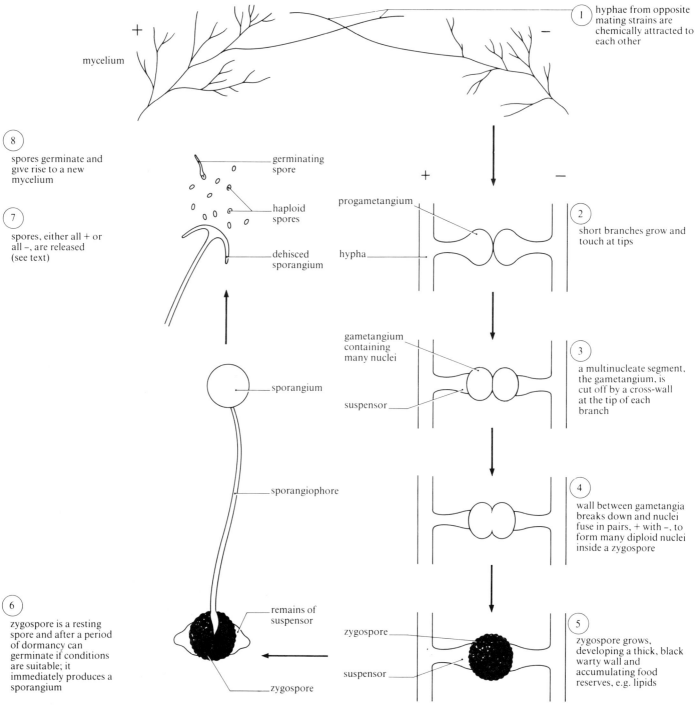

Fig 2.22 *Sexual reproduction in* Rhizopus stolonifer, *+ and − represent opposite mating strains, (1) to (8) sequence of events*

① hyphae from opposite mating strains are chemically attracted to each other

② short branches grow and touch at tips

③ a multinucleate segment, the gametangium, is cut off by a cross-wall at the tip of each branch

④ wall between gametangia breaks down and nuclei fuse in pairs, + with −, to form many diploid nuclei inside a zygospore

⑤ zygospore grows, developing a thick, black warty wall and accumulating food reserves, e.g. lipids

⑥ zygospore is a resting spore and after a period of dormancy can germinate if conditions are suitable; it immediately produces a sporangium

⑦ spores, either all + or all −, are released (see text)

⑧ spores germinate and give rise to a new mycelium

mycelium

germinating spore

haploid spores

dehisced sporangium

sporangium

sporangiophore

remains of suspensor

zygospore

progametangium

hypha

gametangium containing many nuclei

suspensor

zygospore

suspensor

are caused by diffusion of hormones between the strains. The hormones stimulate growth of long hyphae between the colonies. These probably release volatile chemical signals which attract the opposite strain, a form of chemotropism.

There are no typical gametes and fertilisation is a process of nuclei fusing in pairs as described in fig 2.22. Since the gametangia are of equal size, the process of sexual reproduction is described as **isogamy**.

The product of nuclear fusion is a zygospore containing many diploid nuclei. It is thought that all of these degenerate except for one. This divides by meiosis to form four haploid nuclei only one of which survives. It is a matter of chance whether this is of a plus or minus strain.

The zygospore, unlike the asexually produced spores, is not specialised for dispersal but rather for a period of dormancy, since it has food reserves and a thick protective wall. Dispersal is achieved immediately after germination, when asexual reproduction occurs by production of a sporangium as shown in fig 2.22. Within the germinating

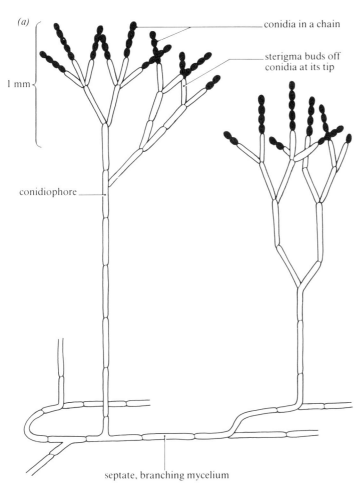

(a)

1 mm

conidia in a chain

sterigma buds off
conidia at its tip

conidiophore

septate, branching mycelium

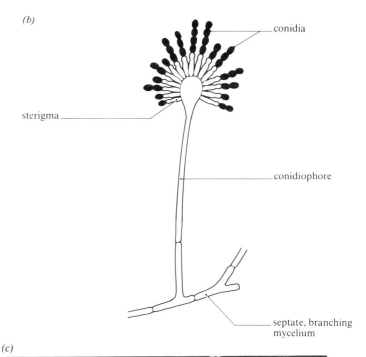

(b)

conidia

sterigma

conidiophore

septate, branching
mycelium

(c)

conidia

sterigma

conidiophore

Fig 2.23 *Two common members of the Ascomycota showing asexual reproduction. (a)* Penicillium, *with a brush-like arrangement of conidia. (b)* Aspergillus, *with a spherical mass of conidia. (c) Scanning electron micrograph (SEM) of conidiophore of* Aspergillus niger *(× 1 372)*

structure, the remaining haploid nucleus divides by mitosis and repeated divisions form many haploid nuclei, each of which can form the nucleus of a spore in the sporangium. Thus all the spores are of the same strain. Fig 2.20 gives a non-pictorial summary of sexual reproduction.

2.4.3 Phylum Ascomycota

Characteristics of the Ascomycota are given in table 2.5. They are the largest group of fungi and are relatively advanced, showing more complexity than the Zygomycota, especially in their sexual structures. They

include the yeasts, some common moulds, powdery mildews, cup fungi, morels and truffles.

Penicillium is a widespread saprotroph, forming blue, green and sometimes yellow moulds on a variety of substrates. It reproduces asexually by means of **conidia**. Conidia are spores formed at the tips of special hyphae called **conidiophores**. They are not enclosed in a sporangium, but are naked and free to be dispersed as soon as they mature. The structure of *Penicillium* is shown in fig 2.23a. Its mycelium forms a circular colony of small diameter and its spores give colour to the colony so that the young outer edge of the mycelium is usually white, whereas the more mature central portion, where spores have developed, appears coloured. The economic importance of *Penicillium* species is discussed in section 2.5.4.

Aspergillus generally grows on the same substrates as *Penicillium* and resembles it closely. It forms black, brown, yellow and green moulds. Fig 2.23*b* shows an asexually reproducing mycelium for comparison with *Penicillium*.

2.4.4 Phylum Basidiomycota

Characteristics of the Basidiomycota are given in table 2.5. They are almost as large a group as the Ascomycota, together with which they form the 'higher' fungi, that is the most advanced fungi. Their large 'fruiting bodies' make them some of the most conspicuous fungi, including those commonly known as mushrooms or toadstools,* puffballs, stinkhorns and bracket fungi. The group also contains important obligate parasites, namely the smuts and rusts.

Agaricus (*Psalliota*) belongs to the group of gill-bearing toadstools. The toadstool, or mushroom, is a short-lived 'fruiting body'. The mycelium grows saprotrophically on organic matter in the soil and may live for a number of years. It forms thick strands called **rhizomorphs** in which the hyphae are compacted to form tissues. Rhizomorphs can resist adverse conditions, becoming dormant until favourable conditions return. They grow from the tips and are responsible for vegetative spread of the fungus. The external features of *Agaricus* are shown in fig 2.24, together with the structure of the gills.

The 'fruiting body', or **sporophore**, appears above ground in the autumn in temperate regions and is made entirely from hyphae which compact to form tissues. The edges of the gills are made of **basidia**, which produce spores (**basidiospores**). The gills exhibit positive geotropism so hang down vertically. The spores, which are produced in large numbers (about half a million per minute from a large mushroom), are forcibly ejected from the basidia and drop down between the gills to be carried away by air currents.

2.4.5 Useful and harmful fungi

See sections 2.5 and 2.6.

2.5 Benefits and uses of micro-organisms

Micro-organisms are important for their natural roles in the biosphere, the fact that they can be deliberately exploited by humans in a number of ways, and because they are sometimes harmful, particularly as disease-causing agents (pathogens). Examples of these

* Mushrooms and toadstools are really synonymous terms, although edible species are sometimes called mushrooms and poisonous species toadstools.

three main areas of importance are discussed below in sections 2.5.1 to 2.5.4 and in section 2.6, with reference to bacteria, viruses and fungi. Protozoans and some algae are also micro-organisms; the latter are dealt with in section 3.2.

2.5.1 Micro-organisms and soil fertility

Micro-organisms play an important part in soil fertility. Below is a summary of information discussed in more detail elsewhere.

Decay and formation of humus. The formation of humus from the litter and fermentation layers above it is discussed in chapter 12. Humus is a layer of decayed organic matter which, besides containing nutrients, has important physical and chemical properties, such as water-retaining ability. The action of saprotrophic bacteria and fungi (together known as decomposers) in decaying organic matter is also discussed in 9.11.1. Inorganic products which can be recycled as a result include carbon dioxide, ammonia, mineral salts (for instance phosphates and sulphates) and water.

Nutrient or biogeochemical cycles. The nitrogen, sulphur and phosphorus cycles are discussed in section 9.11. The nitrogen cycle involves:
(*a*) nitrogen-fixing bacteria, including free-living saprotrophs, such as *Azotobacter*, mutualists, such as *Rhizobium*, and the free-living photosynthetic blue-green bacteria.
(*b*) nitrifying bacteria which can convert organically combined nitrogen (for instance protein) to nitrate, such as *Nitrosomonas* and *Nitrobacter*.
(*c*) denitrifying bacteria which can convert nitrate to nitrogen gas, such as *Thiobacillus*.

Further information concerning bacteria and fungi in the nitrogen cycle is given in section 9.11.1.

2.5.2 Sewage disposal

The activities of decomposers in sewage works closely resemble those of decomposers in the soil because they break down organic matter to harmless, soluble, inorganic materials. The sewage, separated into liquid and sludge in settling tanks, is often digested in several stages by a combination of aerobic and anaerobic bacteria. Methane gas produced by anaerobic bacteria is sometimes utilised as fuel to run the machinery at the works. The products of a sewage farm are a liquid, which is normally recycled by emptying into rivers, and a sludge that contains harmless organic and inorganic materials and micro-organisms (mainly bacteria and protozoans) and can be dried and used as fertiliser unless contaminated with heavy metals. Saprotrophic fungi and bacteria, together with protozoans, are part of the jelly-like film of living organisms covering the stones of 'filterbeds' at sewage works.

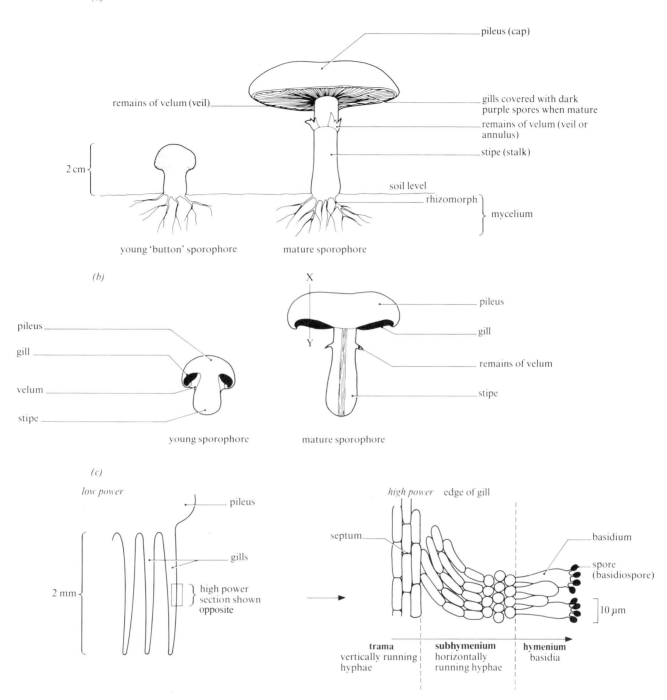

Fig 2.24 *Structure of* Agaricus campestris, *the field mushroom.* Agaricus bisporus, *the cultivated mushroom, is very similar but the basidia bear two, not four, spores.*
(a) Entire sporophores with mycelium. (b) VS sporophores.
(c) Part of VS pileus from X to Y

2.5.3   Mutualistic micro-organisms

Mammals and other animals cannot digest cellulose since they lack the enzyme cellulase. For herbivores, cellulose constitutes a large proportion of the diet, and they have cellulose-digesting bacteria and protozoa living mutualistically in the gut. In rabbits, the bacteria occupy the caecum and the appendix; in cows and sheep, they are present in the rumen. This is of indirect significance to humans who use these animals as a source of food.

Of more direct use is the 'flora' of human intestines. Many bacteria inhabit the intestines and some, such as *E. coli*, synthesise vitamins of the B group and vitamin K.

Some skin micro-organisms of humans offer protection against invasion by pathogenic organisms.

Some important further examples of mutualism involving micro-organisms are given in table 10.1.

2.5.4 Biotechnology and genetic engineering

Biotechnology may be defined as the application of organisms, biological systems or processes to the manufacturing and service industries (The Royal Society, 1981). Where whole organisms are involved, these are generally micro-organisms, such as bacteria, viruses, fungi and algae. The estimated market for biotechnology is about £40 billion per annum by the end of the century. Some of the products will be produced in bulk at relatively low cost, others will be 'fine' products, produced in small quantities for relatively high prices.

At the heart of biotechnology are the 'fermentation' processes. Originally the term 'fermentation' was reserved for anaerobic activity, but it is now applied more loosely to any process in which microbes are cultured in containers (**fermenters** or **bioreactors**). The use and design of fermenters is described in section 11.3.10. The traditional fermentation industries include brewing, baking, cheese and butter manufacture, but there is now an enormous range of products, as indicated in table 11.3.

Brewing

The oldest fermentation industry is that of brewing. Beer is brewed from barley which has been partially germinated to convert its starch store to the sugar maltose. Gibberellins (section 15.2.6) are used to speed up this process and to control it precisely. The subsequent fermentation is carried out in a large vat and is brought about by the unicellular fungus yeast *Saccharomyces* (for instance *S. cerevisiae*, *S. carlsbergensis*). During this process sugar is converted to carbon dioxide and alcohol which reaches a final concentration of 4–8%. Hops are added at an earlier stage for their flavour and antimicrobial properties.

Wine manufacture depends on the fermentation of grape juice by wild yeasts present on the skin of grapes. The final concentration of alcohol is 8–15%, high enough to kill the yeasts, and the wine is often left to mature over a number of years. Some unconverted sugar may remain.

Other common drinks prepared by fermentation are cider from apple juice and the Japanese saké made from rice.

Industrial alcohol can be prepared from carbohydrate-containing waste substances such as molasses.

Cheese manufacture

Cheese manufacture usually depends on the combined activities of bacteria and fungi. During the process the milk sugar lactose is fermented to lactic acid which causes the milk protein, casein, to curdle. The solid curds, containing protein and fat, are separated from the liquid whey and acted on by bacteria and/or fungi. Inoculation with different microbes produces different varieties of cheese, such as cheddar from *Lactobacillus* species. Some famous cheeses are ripened with *Penicillium* species, such as roquefort (*P. roqueforti*), camembert (*P. camemberti*), Danish blue and Italian gorgonzola.

The souring of cream during butter manufacture and the flavour of butter are caused by lactic acid streptococci. *Lactobacillus* species are also used in the production of sauerkraut (from cabbages), silage and pickles. A useful article on cheese manufacture was published in *Scientific American* of May 1985, pp. 66–73.

Baking

Another important fermentation industry which utilises yeast is baking. Strains of *S. cerevisiae* selected for their high production of carbon dioxide, the raising agent, are used by bakeries. The alcohol produced at the same time is driven off as a vapour by the heat of baking.

Antibiotics

Since the 1930s a great deal of research has been devoted to isolating from bacteria and fungi natural chemicals that have antibiotic properties, that is which inhibit the growth of, or kill, other micro-organisms. They have found application in medicine, veterinary science, agriculture, industry and pure research. Soil-dwelling organisms are a particularly rich source of antibiotics since in the micro-ecosystems in which they exist there is much competition, and antibiotics form part of the natural 'armoury' for establishing ecological niches. Soil samples from all over the world are continually being screened for potentially useful new antibiotics.

The first antibiotic to be exploited was **penicillin**, which is produced by several species of the fungus *Penicillium*, notably *P. notatum* and *P. chrysogenum*, the latter being the current commercial source. The impact of its introduction during the 1940s was enormous because it was active against all staphylococcal infections, a wide range of Gram positive bacteria and yet virtually non-toxic to the patient. It is still the most important antibiotic, and new synthetic derivatives of it are continually being introduced to improve its effectiveness, the starting material still being penicillin prepared from large-scale culture (fermentation) of the fungus.

Griseofulvin is another antibiotic obtained from *Penicillium* species (particularly *P. griseofulvum*). It has antifungal properties and is especially effective against athlete's foot and ringworm when taken orally. **Fumagillin** is a particular type of antibiotic obtained from *Aspergillus fumigatus*. It is frequently used against amoebic dysentery.

One of the most productive sources of antibiotics has been the genus *Streptomyces*, a bacterium resembling a miniature fungus, of which there are many species and from which over 500 antibiotics have been identified. More than 50 of these have found practical applications, including **streptomycin**, **chloramphenicol** and the **tetracyclines**.

Streptomycin was discovered soon after penicillin. It proved almost as dramatically successful, increasing the range of pathogens that could be treated. For example, unlike penicillin, it is active against the tuberculosis bacillus. *Bacillus* species have also proved fruitful, such as *Bacillus brevis* which produces **gramicidin**.

Single cell protein (SCP) and new food sources

A new food source of recent years is 'single cell protein' (SCP), a term which refers to protein derived from the large-scale growth of micro-organisms such as bacteria, yeasts and other fungi, and algae. The protein may be used for human consumption or animal feed. It may also be a useful source of minerals and vitamins (as well as containing fat and carbohydrate). There are several advantages in using micro-organisms as a food source: they occupy less room than conventional crops and animals, grow much more rapidly and can grow on a wide variety of cheap or waste products of agriculture or industry. Examples of these are petroleum products, methane, methanol, ethanol, sugars, molasses, cheese whey and waste from pulp and paper mills.

One of the major products is **Pruteen**, whose production is described in section 11.3.10. Early hopes for SCP have been dampened for various reasons.

(a) Agricultural surpluses, particularly of the high protein products like grain and dairy products, are now common in developed countries such as the USA and Europe.

(b) Developing countries where protein is scarce cannot afford the investment in equipment, and lack relevant expertise.

(c) There has been an increase in production, and reduction in price, of competitive animal feed additives like soyabean, fishmeal and gluten from maize (the latter being a by-product of biotechnological fuel programmes).

(d) There was a rise in oil prices in the late 1970s; SCP production is energy-intensive.

ICI and Rank, Hovis, McDougall now produce a mycoprotein from the fungus *Fusarium*. This protein is unusual in being used for human consumption, and ICI may produce it on a larger scale using the expertise gained from Pruteen manufacture.

New energy sources: biogas and gasohol

Many methods are being explored for exploiting living organisms and biological processes for energy supplies. Artificial photosynthesis generating hydrogen gas (a fuel) from water, is a long-term possibility. Another basic strategy is to exploit the energy trapped in biomass. This usually means upgrading the raw material (biomass) to a higher fuel value by fermentation. Although this may result in a *net loss* of energy from the original biomass, the product has a higher energy content per unit mass and is therefore more easily stored and transported. Among the raw materials currently being investigated are waste materials such as animal manures, sewage sludge, domestic wastes, food wastes, paper wastes, spoilt crops, sugar cane tops and molasses. Various crops (such as maize, sugarcane, sugarbeet) and water plants (such as kelps and water hyacinth) might also be used. Two processes currently dominate, namely production of **biogas** (methane) by anaerobic digestion and of ethanol by yeast fermentation.

Biogas
Overall equation:

$$C_6H_{12}O_6 \longrightarrow 3CH_4 + 3CO_2$$

glucose   methane   carbon dioxide

energy value: 16 kJ per g   56 kJ per g

Biogas is about 54–70% methane. Most of the rest is carbon dioxide, with traces of nitrogen, hydrogen and other gases. (Natural gas is about 80% methane.) A mixture of micro-organisms is used in the fermentation, including a group of bacteria called **methanogens** which can produce methane from carbon dioxide and hydrogen. These are **archaebacteria** (see fig 2.2). A wide range of waste materials or plant products can be used for fermenting (see above). In the USA the water hyacinth, a vigorous plant which can block canals and water ways, has been used. Most operations are small-scale and for local fuel use, as is common in India and China.

The manure from one cow in one year can be converted to methane equivalent of over 227 litres of petrol; 0.5 kg of cow manure could generate enough gas to cook a family's meals for a day.

In China, over 18 million family-scale digesters have been built. The gas is typically used for cooking, lighting, tractor or car fuel and for running electricity generators.

On a larger scale, the gas can be a by-product of landfill, sewage or factory waste (such as sugar factories, distilleries). It can be used to drive electricity generators in sewage works and waste treatment plants. In Britain, rubbish could be a major source of methane (up to 20 litres of gas per kilogram of refuse). At the moment the gas is collected from landfill sites by sinking pipes into the compacted rubbish and sucking out the gas.

Ethanol
Overall equation:

$$C_6H_{12}O_6 \longrightarrow 2C_2H_5OH + 2CO_2$$

glucose   ethanol

energy value: 16 kJ per g   30 kJ per g

Ethanol, or 'power alcohol', has been produced successfully in Brazil in the '**Proalcool**' programme. Sugarcane juice (with some molasses) is the starting material. Ethanol is distilled from the fermented product. Over 11 000 million litres were produced in 1985 and cars in Brazil are adapted to run on ethanol (its main use). In the USA the product is known as **Gasohol** and the initial biomass is starch from maize. Over 2280 million litres per year were being produced in the mid-1980s. As a motor fuel it can be used either pure or blended with petrol.

Toxic chemicals and xenobiotics

A xenobiotic is a chemical compound synthesised by humans which is not naturally found in living organisms and cannot normally be metabolised (broken down) by them. It is not surprising, therefore, that many toxic chemicals are xenobiotics. About 300 million tonnes of hazardous waste are produced per year in the USA and, in 1979, 2 million tonnes of pesticide were used in the western hemisphere. One approach to the cleaning up of all of the toxic waste is to 'design' or discover micro-organisms with the relevant enzymes to break down the chemicals. Such organisms can be cultured in fermenters with the waste. Some plasmids (see section 2.2.4) carry genes coding for suitable enzymes. These may be brought together in bacteria for the purposes of degrading specific chemicals. For example, a strain of the bacterium *Pseudomonas putida* has been created which breaks down octane, xylene and camphor. Genetic engineering may be used more extensively in the future.

Waste disposal

See above for sewage disposal (technically a type of biotechnology), new energy sources, toxic chemicals and xenobiotics, and SCP (new foods). Treatment of waste water from domestic and industrial sources uses biological processes similar to those in sewage works.

Extraction of metals from minerals and solutions

Bacteria can be used to chemically extract ('leach') copper and other metals from rocks containing low concentrations of metals. These are often the waste from mines. Micro-organisms may similarly be used to remove toxic heavy metal pollution from waste waters of mining operations and other industrial processes. Thus both economic and environmental benefits are possible. Bacterial leaching is currently used on a commercial scale for copper and uranium extraction. One possible important future use of environmental significance is the leaching out of inorganic sulphur from coal. If other bacteria could be used to remove organic sulphur, the burning of desulphurised coal would not release sulphur dioxide, thought to be one of the main contributors to acid rain.

Enzyme technology and biosensors

Using the versatility of the enzymes of micro-organisms, new methods of making many industrially important chemicals are being introduced. In section 6.9 a detailed account of the procedures involved and the use of enzymes is given, together with an account of the related technology of biosensors and biochips.

Genetic engineering

Genetic engineering is the manipulation of genes. The process is variously referred to as **genetic manipulation**, **gene cloning** (since a clone of genetically identical organisms can be grown from the original altered cell), or **recombinant DNA technology**. In genetic engineering, pieces of DNA (genes) are introduced into a host by means of a carrier (vector) system. The foreign DNA becomes a permanent feature of the host, being replicated and passed on to daughter cells along with the rest of its DNA. The donated DNA could come from another organism or might be an artificially synthesised gene.

In fig 2.25 an outline of the normal procedure is given, but it should be noted that some knowledge of DNA and genetics will be necessary to understand this (see chapters 22 and 23). In fig 2.25 the vector is a plasmid (see section 2.2.4), but bacteriophages or other viruses are sometimes used, the latter mainly for animal cells. **Restriction endonucleases** are enzymes which cut (cleave) DNA. There are many different types, each of which cuts at a different specific base sequence. Some leave overlapping ends of DNA called '**sticky ends**' because their base sequences are complementary.

Only a very small proportion of treated bacterial cells will be successfully transformed, and in order to recognise these cells the vector used usually contains a '**marker gene**'. This is often a gene for resistance to a particular antibiotic, for example tetracycline resistance. At the end of the process, any transformed bacterial cells can therefore be identified by growing the bacteria on a medium containing tetracycline. Two early examples of the commercial application of this technique are the production of human insulin and human growth hormone.

Insulin production. Ever since the cause of diabetes mellitus was established as a shortage of the hormone insulin, sufferers have been provided with insulin derived from the pancreases of slaughtered sheep and cattle. Due to minor differences in the chemical composition of insulin from different species, some patients showed damaging side-effects as a result of the injections. Insulin is a protein, and it was argued that if the genes for this protein could be inserted into a bacterium, then it might be possible to culture the bacterium on a commercial scale. One of the potential problems in transferring genes between eukaryotes and prokaryotes is that different regulatory mechanisms exist, even if the genes themselves can be transferred. But successful transfer of human insulin genes into bacteria has now been achieved and the bacteria are grown by the fermentation methods described in section 11.3.10. The process developed by Eli Lilly is described here; their product is known as **Humulin**.

The procedure is complicated by the fact that insulin has two polypeptide chains (fig 5.32), the A chain and the B chain. The amino acid sequences of these chains are known and the first procedure developed involves synthesising two

NB A double-stranded DNA molecule, ∞∞∞∞∞ is represented as:

complementary strands of DNA

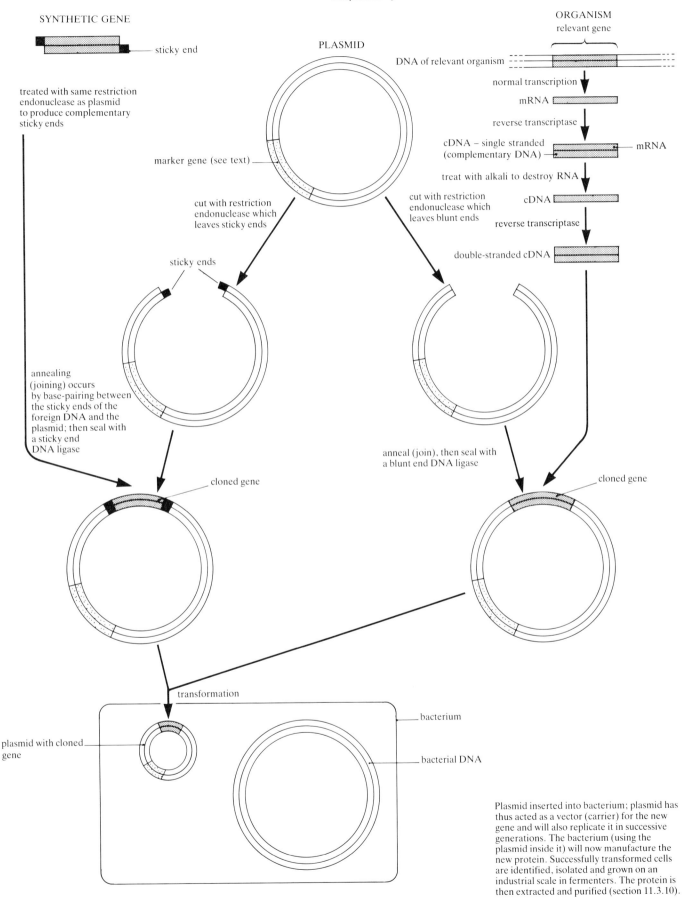

SYNTHETIC GENE

sticky end

treated with same restriction
endonuclease as plasmid
to produce complementary
sticky ends

PLASMID

ORGANISM
relevant gene

DNA of relevant organism

normal transcription

mRNA

reverse transcriptase

cDNA – single stranded
(complementary DNA)

mRNA

treat with alkali to destroy RNA

cDNA

reverse transcriptase

double-stranded cDNA

marker gene (see text)

cut with restriction
endonuclease which
leaves sticky ends

cut with restriction
endonuclease which
leaves blunt ends

sticky ends

annealing
(joining) occurs
by base-pairing between
the sticky ends of the
foreign DNA and the
plasmid; then seal with
a sticky end
DNA ligase

anneal (join), then seal with
a blunt end DNA ligase

cloned gene

cloned gene

transformation

bacterium

plasmid with cloned
gene

bacterial DNA

Plasmid inserted into bacterium; plasmid has
thus acted as a vector (carrier) for the new
gene and will also replicate it in successive
generations. The bacterium (using the
plasmid inside it) will now manufacture the
new protein. Successfully transformed cells
are identified, isolated and grown on an
industrial scale in fermenters. The protein is
then extracted and purified (section 11.3.10).

Fig 2.25 *Outline of two procedures for genetic engineering. A virus may be used as a vector instead of a plasmid, in which case the final stage is 'transduction', not 'transformation'*

29

artificial DNA molecules (genes) which code for the two appropriate amino acid chains. The synthesised DNA molecules are then introduced into separate bacteria by the process for synthetic genes shown in fig 2.25. After growing large quantities of the bacteria in fermenters, the bacteria are lysed (split open) and the chains purified. The two chains are then chemically combined in an oxidation reaction, and have been shown to function exactly as natural human insulin. More recently, an alternative procedure, using one synthetic gene which mimics the normal human gene and codes for a molecule called **proinsulin**, has been developed. Once purified, proinsulin is converted into insulin by digesting away part of the molecule.

Insulin was the first genetically engineered protein to be used in humans and it is now used in routine clinical practice throughout the world.

Growth hormone (somatotrophin). The role and importance of growth hormone (GH) is discussed in section 21.8.1. Unlike insulin, GH from animals other than humans is not effective in humans. In roughly one child in 5 000 too little GH is secreted during childhood, and in extreme cases the child suffers from pituitary dwarfism (IQ is unaffected). Injections of GH can overcome this problem, but the hormone is in short supply and is very expensive because it can only be obtained from pituitary glands of human cadavers. Trials of GH produced by genetic engineering began first in the USA and then followed in Britain in the late 1980s. Although very expensive, hopefully all requirements will eventually be met at reasonable cost.

Other proteins. Some success has been achieved with a group of anti-viral proteins called **interferons** which can be used to help fight viral diseases. The genes have been cloned in *E. coli*, yeasts and animal cells, with the best yields coming from yeast cells. One advantage of using yeast in genetic engineering is that it is a eukaryote and therefore gene expression is easier to achieve if the foreign genes are also from eukaryotes. Another important application of genetic engineering is in the development of vaccines. Vaccines contain antigens, which are normally proteins. Genetically engineered vaccines are now available for hepatitis B and foot-and-mouth disease, both viral diseases. There is currently intensive research to find vaccines for AIDS and malaria, where one of the main problems is the isolation of a suitable antigen.

2.6 Harmful micro-organisms

2.6.1 Deterioration of food and materials

Saprotrophic bacteria and fungi attack and decompose organic materials and can therefore present many problems to humans, despite their vital role as decomposers in the biosphere. Foods such as grain and fruit which are stored in large quantities must be protected, and food spoilage generally is a constant problem. There are many different and economically costly ways of preserving food. Natural fabrics, leather and other consumer goods manufactured from raw materials are also subject to attack, particularly by fungi. Fungi which live on cellulose cause rots in damp timber and fabrics. Much money is spent on preservation of all these materials.

2.6.2 Bacteria, viruses and fungi as agents of disease

Organisms which cause disease are called **pathogens**. They are parasitic on their hosts. All viruses are parasitic and therefore usually cause symptoms of disease in their hosts. Some bacteria and fungi are also pathogenic. Pathogenic bacteria more commonly affect animals than plants, whereas the reverse is true of fungi. Viruses are more indiscriminate. Human disease and disease of our domestic animals and crops is the inevitable consequence.

Bacterial and viral diseases

Some important animal diseases that are caused by viruses are foot-and-mouth disease of cattle, swine fever, fowl pest and myxomatosis of rabbits. Virus infections of plants commonly cause a yellow mottling of leaves called **leaf mosaic**, and crinkly or dwarfed leaves. They also cause stunting of growth with consequent reductions in yields. Some important crop diseases are turnip yellow mosaic virus (TYMV), tobacco mosaic virus (TMV), tomato bushy stunt and tomato spotted wilt virus. The striped appearance of some tulip varieties is caused by a virus and these tulips are sold as a specific variety by horticulturists. Plant viruses are apparently always RNA viruses.

Important bacterial diseases of animals include *Salmonella* food poisoning of pigs and poultry. Bacterial diseases of plants include crown gall of fruit trees and fire blight of apples and pears (*Agrobacterium tumefaciens* and *Erwinia amylovorum* respectively).

Table 2.6 describes some common viral diseases of humans and can be compared with table 2.7 which gives similar information for bacterial diseases. Further information is contained in fig 2.6.

Methods of transmission

It is convenient to discuss the transmission of viral and bacterial diseases together since the principal methods are the same. Examples of all the methods described below are given in tables 2.6 and 2.7.

Droplet infection

Respiratory infections in particular are usually spread by droplet infection. Sneezing and coughing result in a violent expulsion of millions of tiny droplets of liquid (mucus and saliva) which can carry living microbes and be inhaled by other people, particularly in crowded and poorly ventilated places. Standard hygiene should include appropriate use of handkerchiefs or tissues and ventilation of rooms.

Some microbes, like the smallpox virus and the tuberculosis bacterium, are quite resistant to drying out, so may be carried in dust containing the dried remains of droplets. Even talking can result in microscopic droplets of saliva being released, so such infections are difficult to prevent if the microbe is virulent.

Contagion (direct physical contact)

Relatively few diseases are spread by direct physical contact with an infected person or animal. They include the **venereal**, that is sexually transmitted, diseases such as gonorrhoea and syphilis. A disease closely related to syphilis, namely yaws, is common in tropical countries and requires direct skin contact. Contagious viral diseases include trachoma, a common eye disease of tropical countries, the common wart and herpes simplex which causes 'cold sores'. Leprosy and tuberculosis are caused by *Mycobacterium* species and are contagious bacterial diseases.

Vectors

A **vector** is an organism that transmits a pathogen. It picks up the infection from an organism called the **reservoir**. For example the flea is the vector of the two bacterial diseases endemic typhus and plague (bubonic plague or Black Death) and the reservoir is the rat. In the case of rabies, a viral disease, the vector and reservoir are the same, for example dog or bat.

2.7 What are (a) the vectors and (b) the reservoirs for (i) epidemic typhus and (ii) yellow fever? (See tables 2.6 and 2.7.)

Table 2.6 Some common viral diseases of humans.

Name of disease	Caused by	Parts of body affected	Method of spread	Type of vaccination*
Influenza	A myxovirus (DNA virus) three types, A, B, and C, of varying severity	Respiratory passages: epithelial lining of trachea and bronchi	Droplet infection	Killed virus: must be of right strain
Common cold	Large variety of viruses, most commonly rhino-virus (RNA virus)	Respiratory passages: usually upper passages only	Droplet infection	Living or inactivated virus given as intramuscular injection; not very effective because so many different strains of rhinovirus
Smallpox**	Variola virus (DNA virus) a pox virus	Respiratory passages, then skin	Droplet infection (contagion possible via wounds in skin)	Living attenuated virus applied by scratching skin; no longer carried out
Mumps	A paramyxovirus (RNA virus)	Respiratory passages, then generalised infection throughout body via blood, particularly salivary glands; also testes in adult males	Droplet infection (or contagion via infected saliva to mouth)	Living attenuated virus
Measles	A paramyxovirus (RNA virus)	Respiratory passages (mouth to bronchi) spreading to skin and intestines	Droplet infection	Living attenuated virus
German measles (Rubella)	Rubella virus	Respiratory passages, lymph nodes in neck, eyes and skin	Droplet infection	Living attenuated virus; more essential for girls because disease causes complication in pregnancy
Poliomyelitis ('polio')	Poliovirus (a picornavirus) (RNA virus), three strains exist	Pharynx and intestines, then blood; occasionally motor neurones in spinal cord, when paralysis may occur	Droplet infection or via human faeces (see cholera, table 2.8)	Living attenuated virus given orally, usually on sugar lump
Yellow fever	An arbovirus, that is arthropod-borne virus (RNA virus)	Lining of blood vessels and liver	Vector – arthropods, e.g. ticks, mosquitoes	Living attenuated virus (control of vectors also important)
AIDS (see section 14.14.3)	Retrovirus (RNA virus)	Skin cancer (Kaposi's sarcoma), blood (septicaemia), brain (dementia)	Sexual intercourse – homo- and heterosexuals	Not available

* types of vaccination – see table 2.8
** last recorded natural case in Somalia, October 1977; disease extinct, though virus kept in a few laboratories

Table 2.7 Some common bacterial diseases of humans.

Name of disease	Caused by	Parts of body affected	Method of spread	Type of vaccination* or antibiotic
Diphtheria	*Corynebacterium diphtheriae* (rod-shaped, Gram +)	Upper respiratory tract, mainly throat. Harmful toxin spread by blood to all parts of body. Toxin affects heart.	Droplet infection	Toxoid
Tuberculosis (TB)	*Mycobacterium tuberculosis* (rod-shaped, member of Actinomycetes)	Mainly lungs	Droplet infection. Drinking milk from infected cattle.	BCG living attenuated bacteria. Must test first to see if already immune. Antibiotics, e.g. streptomycin.
Whooping cough	*Bordetella pertussis* (rod-shaped, Gram −)	Upper respiratory tract, inducing violent coughing	Droplet infection	Killed bacteria
Gonorrhoea	*Neisseria gonorrhoeae* (coccus, Gram −)	Reproductive organs: mainly mucous membranes of urino-genital tract. Newborn infants may acquire serious eye infections if they pass through infected birth canal.	Contagion by sexual contact	Antibiotics, e.g. penicillin, streptomycin
Syphilis	*Treponema pallidum* (a spirochaete)	Reproductive organs, then eyes, bones, joints, central nervous system, heart and skin	Contagion by sexual contact	Antibiotics, e.g. penicillin
Typhus	*Rickettsia*	'Epidemic typhus' more serious than 'endemic typhus'. Similar to typhoid. Linings of blood vessels causing clots. Skin rash.	Epidemic typhus: vector – louse. Endemic typhus: vector – rat flea. From rat to rat by flea and lice.	Killed bacteria or living non-virulent strain. Antibiotics, e.g. tetracyclines, chloramphenicol (control of vectors also important).
Tetanus	*Clostridium tetani* (rod-shaped, Gram +)	Blood. Toxin produced which affects motor nerves of spinal cord and hence muscles, causing lockjaw and spreading to the muscles. Often fatal.	Wound infection	Toxoid
Cholera	*Vibrio cholerae* (comma-shaped, Gram −)	Alimentary canal: mainly small intestine. Toxin affects lining of intestine.	Faecal contamina-tion: (*a*) food- or water-borne of material contaminated with faeces from infected person; (*b*) handling of con-taminated objects; (*c*) vector, e.g. flies moving from human faeces to food.	Killed bacteria: short-lived protection and not always effective. Antibiotics, e.g. tetracyclines, chloramphenicol.
Typhoid fever	*Salmonella typhi* (= *S. typhosa*) (rod-shaped, Gram −)	Alimentary canal, then spreading to lymph and blood, lungs, bone marrow, spleen	As cholera	Killed bacteria (TAB vaccine)
Bacterial dysentery (bacillary dysentery)	*Shigella dysenteriae* (rod-shaped, Gram −)	Alimentary canal, mainly ileum and colon	As cholera	No vaccine. Antibiotic, e.g. tetracyclines.
Bacterial food poisoning (gastro-enteritis or salmonellosis)	*Salmonella* spp. (rod-shaped, Gram −)	Alimentary canal	Mainly foodborne-meat from infected animals, mainly poultry and pigs. Also via faecal con-tamination as cholera.	No vaccine. Antibiotics, e.g. tetracyclines; usually not necessary and not very effective.

* types of vaccination – see table 2.8

Table 2.8 Types of vaccine.

(1) **Attenuated living micro-organism**

An **attenuated** micro-organism is one whose virulence has been greatly reduced by some laboratory procedure, e.g. growing it in a high temperature. It may be a mutant variety with the same antigens, but lacking virulence.

(2) **Killed micro-organism**

Killed by some laboratory procedure, e.g. exposure to 75% alcohol (TAB vaccine). Antigens still present.

(3) **Toxoids**

A toxoid is an inactivated toxin that retains its antigenic properties. It is inactivated by laboratory treatment, e.g. treatment with formaldehyde.

(4) **Mild strain of virus**

Closely related but non-pathogenic strain, e.g. formerly smallpox/cowpox.

In the cases mentioned the vector acts as a second host in which the pathogen can multiply. Insects can also carry pathogens on the outsides of their bodies. For example, houseflies walking and feeding on faeces from a person infected with a gut disease, such as cholera, typhoid or dysentery, might transmit the pathogen to food likely to be consumed by humans.

Faecal contamination

With diseases that affect the alimentary canal the pathogens leave the body in the faeces. Three common means of transmitting disease arise from this.

Waterborne. The classic waterborne diseases are cholera, typhoid (both caused by flagellated bacteria) and dysentery. If insanitary conditions prevail, faeces of infected individuals are often deposited in or near water which may be used for drinking. In this way disease spreads rapidly through a population.

Foodborne. Food may be contaminated by traces of faecal matter by washing it in contaminated water, touching it with unwashed hands or when a vector such as a housefly touches it.

Contamination of objects. Various objects may become contaminated with faecal matter either directly or via handling. Subsequent handling by another person may lead to hand-to-mouth passage of the disease.

'True' foodborne

Salmonella food poisoning is commonly spread in the meat of infected animals if it is undercooked. *Clostridium botulinum* (fig 2.6) is a bacterium which causes **botulism**, an often fatal form of food poisoning because the toxin it produces is one of the most toxic substances known (the lethal dose for mice is $5 \times 10^{-5}\,\mu\mathrm{g}$). It can grow in protein-rich foods, particularly tinned meats.

Contamination of wounds

Ignoring the bites of animal vectors, there are certain diseases associated with contamination of wounds. Gas gangrene and tetanus are both infections of deep wounds caused by *Clostridium* species, usually picked up from the soil. More superficial wounds and burns are easily infected with staphylococci and streptococci.

Fungal diseases

Some important and familiar diseases are shown in table 2.9. The best-known obligate parasites, namely mildews, rusts and smuts, are included in the table. Although obligate parasites do not kill their hosts, they cause yield losses and make them more vulnerable to other diseases and adverse conditions. They are of great economic importance when they attack crop plants. For example, powdery mildews can cause total yield losses of up to 10% in cereals such as barley. A large industry has grown up to produce fungicides which can be used to protect crops.

Parts of plants infected include underground organs, as in wart disease of potatoes; leaves by rusts, powdery mildews, downy mildews and black spot; flowers, by smuts and ergot; ripe fruit, by soft rots and moulds.

2.7 Practical work

The following practical work is designed to cover some of the basic microbiological techniques associated with bacteriology, using milk as a relatively safe source of bacteria. Milk is a useful food source for bacteria as well as mammals, and certain bacteria are characteristically associated with it.

2.7.1 Bacterial content of milk

Bacteria inevitably enter milk during milking and handling, even under the most hygienic conditions. Milking is normally followed immediately by cooling to retard bacterial growth. The untreated (raw) milk is pasteurised, a heat process intended to kill pathogenic bacteria, though many non-pathogenic bacteria survive. Bacteria present are:

15–30°C *Streptococcus lactis* (Gram +) dominates, together with many other streptococci (Gram +) and coryneform bacteria (for example *Microbacterium*, *Brevibacterium*) which resemble

Table 2.9 Some common fungal diseases. Also included is the phylum Oomycota, now classified in the kingdom Protoctista, not Fungi.

Phylum	Disease	Host	Fungus	Notes
Oomycota	Potato blight	Potato	*Phytophthora infestans*	Caused Irish potato famine of 1845, with many people emigrating to America as a result.
	Downy mildews	Vine	*Plasmopara viticola*	One of the most destructive diseases of vineyards. Accidentally introduced into Europe from America in nineteenth century.
		Onion, tobacco, cabbage, wallflower	*Peronospora* spp.	Not normally serious diseases.
	(Water-)mould	Fish and fish eggs	*Saprolegnia* spp.	Many do significant damage in fish hatcheries.
Zygomycota	Soft rot	Apples and other fruit in storage	*Rhizopus stolonifer*	Not normally a serious disease. Other fungi cause more serious soft rots.
Ascomycota	Powdery mildews	Hop, cereals, apple, rose and others	*Erysiphe* and other genera *E. graminis* attacks cereals	Serious obligate parasites. Economically important, particularly with cereals.
	Dutch elm disease	Elm	*Ceratocystis ulmi*	Has devastated elms in many parts of the world, including America, Britain and the rest of Europe.
	Brown rot	Stone fruits, e.g. peach, plum	*Monilinia fructigena*	Serious disease worldwide.
	Apple scab	Apple	*Venturia inaequalis*	One of the most important parasites of apples. Infects leaves, twigs, young fruit, weakening host and reducing fruit quality.
	Ergot	Rye	*Claviceps purpurea*	Produces sclerotia* known as ergots in place of host ovaries. Ergots contain alkaloids related to the hallucinogen LSD which can be fatal if eaten.
	Black spot	Rose	*Diplocarpon rosae*	Common infection of roses.
	Aspergillosis (farmer's lung)	Humans, birds	*Aspergillus fumigatus*	Disease of lungs similar to tuberculosis. Rare in humans. Sometimes associated with mouldy hay.
Basidiomycota	Rusts	Many, e.g. bean, cereals, coffee, carnation	Numerous, e.g. *Puccinia graminis* (black stem rust of wheat) *Albugo* (white blister rusts)	Economically important. Patches of spores formed at surface, often rust-coloured.
	Smuts	Many, e.g. onion, cereals	Numerous, e.g. *Ustilago avenae* (loose smut of oats)	Produce black, sooty masses of spores. Economically important, mainly in cereals. Grain itself may be infected, making it useless.
Fungi Imperfecti	Ringworm, Athlete's foot	Humans	*Trichophyton* spp. and others	Ringworm more common in children, athlete's foot in adults. Skin infections.
	Vascular wilt	Potato, flax, tomato, banana, palm	*Fusarium* spp.	Infects vascular (conducting) tissue, causing wilting.

* sclerotia (sing. sclerotium) – hard-walled, resistant, resting body produced by some fungi, often as a means of overwintering.

Lactobacilli but may have swollen ends to the rods (coryneform means club-shaped).

Streptococcus lactis grows well at 10 °C but growth ceases at > 40 °C.

30–40 °C *Lactobacillus* (Gram +) and coliform (gut-living) bacilli (Gram −) dominate, such as *E. coli*.

Streptococcus lactis and *Lactobacillus* are lactic acid bacteria. They produce lactic acid during fermentation (anaerobic respiration) of lactose (milk sugar) and the accumulating acid causes souring of milk. Colonies of *S. lactis* and *Lactobacillus* are relatively small (maximum diameter of a few millimetres on a culture) and never pigmented, appearing chalky white. *S. lactis* forms smooth-textured colonies with entire edges. If finely divided calcium carbonate is included in the nutrient agar, streptococci show clear zones around each colony where lactic acid dissolves the calcium carbonate. Streptococci are responsible for the normal souring of milk. They have the usual appearance under the microscope (fig 2.26). Lactobacilli are rods which tend to stick together in long chains (fig 2.26). Colonies may have a rough surface texture with irregular edges.

A number of other bacteria may be found in milk, including the gut-living rod *Alcaligenes* (Gram −) found singly or in chains. It may be recognised on MacConkey's agar by a yellowish (alkaline) zone around each colony.

2.7.2 Bacteriology experiments

The following three experiments are exercises in the use of microbiological techniques. The second and third experiments are extensions of the first. The first experiment is to culture milk bacteria. The second is to stain bacteria for examination with a light microscope. The third involves the counting of bacterial colonies using the technique of serial dilution.

Experiment 2.1: To investigate the bacterial content of fresh and stale milk

The aims of the experiment are to determine the effect of leaving milk unrefrigerated for 24 h and why milk becomes stale. Milk is almost a complete food for humans and the experiments show that it is also a good culture medium for certain bacteria.

Materials

4 sterile nutrient agar plates	fresh pasteurised milk
inoculating loop	stale milk (milk left at room temperature for 24 h)
Bunsen burner	incubator set at 35 °C
indelible marker or wax pencil	

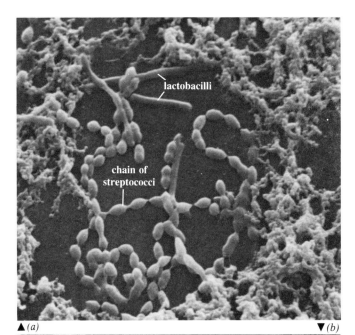
▲ *(a)*

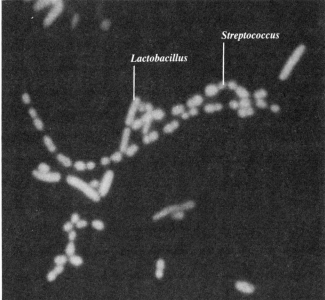
▼ *(b)*

Fig 2.26 *(a) Scanning electron micrograph of bacteria recovered from milk. (b) Bacteria recovered from milk by membrane filtration. Chains of streptococci and rods are clearly visible*

Method

(1) Place the inoculating loop in the Bunsen burner flame until the loop is red-hot (fig 2.27a).

(2) Allow the loop to cool and then dip it into a sample of fresh, well-shaken milk.

(3) Lift the lid of a sterile agar plate slightly with the other hand and lightly spread the contents of the inoculating loop over the surface of the agar as described in fig 2.27b.

(4) Close the lid of the plate and return the loop to the Bunsen burner flame until red-hot.

(5) Label the base of the plate with an indelible marker (or wax pencil).

(6) Repeat with a second plate and another sample of fresh milk.

(7) Flame the loop again and having allowed it to cool, dip it into a sample of stale milk.

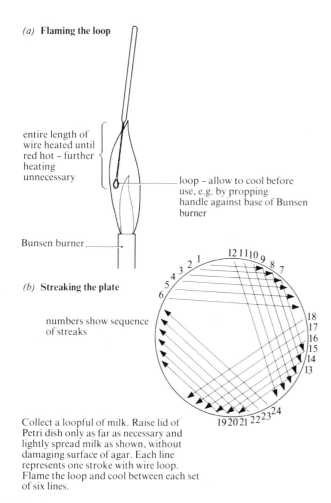

(a) Flaming the loop

entire length of wire heated until red hot – further heating unnecessary

loop – allow to cool before use, e.g. by propping handle against base of Bunsen burner

Bunsen burner

(b) Streaking the plate

numbers show sequence of streaks

Collect a loopful of milk. Raise lid of Petri dish only as far as necessary and lightly spread milk as shown, without damaging surface of agar. Each line represents one stroke with wire loop. Flame the loop and cool between each set of six lines.

Fig 2.27 *Flaming a wire loop and inoculating nutrient agar with milk bacteria using the streaking technique*

(8) Spread the contents of the loop over the surface of a third plate and then close the lid.

(9) Label the base of the plate with an indelible marker.

(10) Repeat with a fourth plate and a second sample of stale milk.

(11) Place the four plates in an incubator at 35 °C for about three days. They should be placed upside down to prevent condensation falling onto the cultures. After incubation, the two halves of each plate should be taped together for safety reasons.

(12) Record the appearance of the colonies and compare with the description in section 2.7.1.

Notes

(1) Students may pour their own plates, if McCartney tubes of sterile, molten, nutrient agar are supplied.

(2) The particular streaking technique used progressively reduces the number of bacteria in each streak. It is suitable in situations where large numbers of bacteria are present, as in milk, and is normally used to isolate pure colonies of bacteria from mixed cultures.

(3) The plates can be placed in a refrigerator after incubation until required. This prevents further bacterial growth.

(4) When the plates are no longer required they should be placed in a disposable autoclave bag and autoclaved for 15 min before final disposal.

(5) Other experiments using milk could be performed. The experiment above is the simplest. The effect of refrigeration could be studied. Also if samples of raw (unpasteurised) milk could be obtained (for instance direct from a dairy farm) the effect of the process of pasteurisation on the bacterial content of milk could be studied. Pasteurisation of milk can be accomplished by placing raw milk in a sterile test-tube plugged with cotton wool and heating at 63 °C for 35 min in a water bath. A third variation would be to incubate some plates at 10 °C instead of 35 °C. This lower temperature favours growth of *Streptococcus lactis* compared with *Lactobacillus*.

Experiment 2.2: To stain bacteria for examination with a light microscope

Although direct microscopic examination of living bacteria is possible using a phase contrast microscope, it is more common to kill and stain bacteria before examination.

One stain which is important in the identification of bacteria is the Gram stain. It was first developed by a Danish physician, Christian Gram, in 1884. Before staining, all bacteria are colourless. Afterwards **Gram positive** bacteria are stained **violet** and **Gram negative** bacteria stained **red**. The difference between the two types of bacteria is described in section 2.2.2 (cell walls).

Materials

basic stain = crystal violet (0.5% aqueous)
mordant = Lugol's iodine
decolouriser = acetone–alcohol (50:50 acetone: absolute alcohol)
counterstain = safranin (1% aqueous)
wire loop
Bunsen burner
glass slides scrupulously clean (wipe with alcohol)
forceps
staining rack set up over sink or dish
distilled water in a wash bottle
blotting paper
immersion oil and microscope with oil immersion lens

Method

(Stages 1 to 6 should take about 5 min.) (Based on *Bacteriology*, Humphries, J., John Murray, 1974.)

(1) **Prepare a smear** of bacteria on the slide as follows. Flame a wire loop and cool. Place a loopful or two of tap water on the centre of a clean slide. Touch the wire loop lightly on a selected bacterial colony from the experiment above, opening the lid of the plate a minimal amount for safety reasons. Transfer the bacteria to the slide and gently mix with the water. Spread the bacteria over the slide, using the loop, to cover an area about 3×1 cm. Flame the loop again. It is important to achieve the correct thickness of the smear. It should appear only faintly opalescent and is more usually too thick than too thin. It should also be of even thickness. Allow the smear to become perfectly dry in air (a few minutes).

(2) **Fix the smear.** Holding the slide with forceps, pass it horizontally just over a yellow bunsen flame three times. It is important that it is not overheated and should feel comfortable against the skin after each passage over the flame. Fixing kills the bacteria by coagulating the cytoplasm and also makes them stick to the slide.

(3) Staining is likely to soil the bench so should be done on a rack over a sink or dish. A rack can be made by arranging two glass or metal rods across the sink or dish 5 cm apart and absolutely horizontal. If supported on plasticine they are easily adjusted. Flood the slide with crystal violet stain. Leave for 30 s.

(4) Wash off with Lugol's iodine; flood with Lugol's iodine and leave for 30 s. Wash off the iodine with distilled water from a wash bottle.

(5) Flood the slide with acetone–alcohol until no more colour is seen to come off (about 3 s); *immediately* wash with water to prevent excessive decolourisation. Repeat if necessary (only experience will show how much washing is needed).

(6) Flood the slide with safranin and leave for 1 min. Wash off the stain with water. Gently dry the slide between sheets of clean blotting paper and allow to dry finally in air.

(7) Apply a drop of immersion oil and examine under the oil immersion lens (section A2.3.2).

Results

Are your observations in agreement with the description given in section 2.7.1 of the bacterial content of milk?

Experiment 2.3: To compare the numbers of bacteria present in fresh and stale milk

If a single bacterium is placed on nutrient agar it will grow to form a colony which is easily seen with the naked eye, unlike the original bacterium. This can be made use of when counting bacteria.

After sterilising the apparatus, the first part of the experiment involves the technique of serial dilution. The numbers of bacteria in milk are vast, so counting can be made more manageable by diluting by a known factor and taking a small sample of known volume. A series of dilutions is prepared. In the second part of the experiment samples of each dilution are cultured and the one giving the most suitable number of colonies (a reasonably large number but with no overlap of colonies) when grown on agar is used to calculate the number of bacteria in a given volume of milk.

Materials

6 sterile nutrient agar plates	indelible marker
8 $1 cm^3$ graduated pipettes	Bunsen burner
1 $10 cm^3$ graduated pipette	$100 cm^3$ distilled water
6 test-tubes and test-tube rack	fresh milk
cotton wool	stale milk
	70% alcohol
	aluminium foil
	glass spreader

Sterilisation of apparatus

(1) Place cotton wool plugs in each of six test-tubes and cover the plugs loosely with aluminium foil.

(2) Place a small piece of cotton wool in the top of each of eight $1 cm^3$ graduated pipettes and one $10 cm^3$ graduated pipette and wrap each pipette separately in aluminium foil.

(3) Place the test-tubes and pipettes in a hot air oven at $160 °C$ for 60 min (bottles of media and water should not be sterilised in an oven).

(4) Allow all the apparatus to cool before use.

Serial dilution of milk and inoculation of agar plates

(1) Label the six sterile plugged test-tubes F1, F2, F3, S1, S2 and S3, and remove the aluminium foil covers from the plugs.

(2) Label the base of each of six sterile nutrient agar plates F1, F2, F3, and S1, S2, S3.

(3) Transfer $9.9 cm^3$ of sterile distilled water to each of the six test-tubes using the following technique.

   (*a*) Remove the cotton wool plug from the flask containing sterile distilled water using the little finger and fourth finger of one hand.

   (*b*) Whilst holding the plug, draw up $9.9 cm^3$ of water using the sterile $10 cm^3$ graduated pipette held in the other hand.

   (*c*) Replace the plug.

   (*d*) Remove the plug from the first test-tube using the same method as in (*a*).

   (*e*) Transfer $9.9 cm^3$ of water to the test-tube.

   (*f*) Replace the plug.

   (*g*) Repeat for the five remaining test-tubes.

(4) Shake the sample of fresh milk and transfer 0.1 cm^3 of this milk using a sterile 1 cm^3 pipette to tube F1, removing and replacing the plug as before. This gives a ×100 dilution.

(5) Shake the tube gently to ensure thorough mixing.

(6) Using a fresh pipette, transfer 0.1 cm^3 from tube F1 to the sterile plate labelled F1, lifting the lid by a minimal amount.

(7) Dip a glass spreader in 70% alcohol, allow excess alcohol to drip off and then hold the spreader vertically in a Bunsen burner flame.

(8) Cool the spreader and spread the sample of milk over the surface of the plate.

(9) Re-sterilise the spreader.

(10) Using the same pipette as in point (6), transfer 0.1 cm^3 from tube F1 to tube F2, removing and replacing the bungs as before.

(11) Shake the tube F2 to ensure thorough mixing. This gives a ×10 000 dilution.

(12) Repeat the procedure from (6)–(9), substituting F2 for F1.

(13) Repeat from (10)–(11), using F3 for F2. This gives a × 1 000 000 dilution. Repeat (6)–(9) using F3 for F1.

(14) Repeat the serial dilution technique using the sample of stale milk and prepare plates S1, S2 and S3.

(15) Incubate the six plates upside down at 35 °C for about three days.

(16) The lids of the plates should then be taped down to avoid the risk of pathogens being spread.

(17) Examine the plates for bacterial growth. Count the numbers of individual colonies where practical. Record results in the form of a table and use them to calculate the number of bacteria in 1 cm^3 of undiluted milk.

Notes

See notes (3) and (4) at the end of experiment 2.1.

2.7.3   Practical work with fungi

The methods for handling fungi are in many cases the same as those for bacteria, being standard microbiological techniques. Many saprotrophic fungi, like bacteria, can be cultured on nutrient agar and, if pure cultures are required, the sterile techniques described in section 2.7.2 should be used. Common fungi suitable for culture in this way are *Mucor*, *Rhizopus*, *Penicillium* and *Aspergillus*, and a suitable culture medium is a 2% malt agar prepared in petri dishes. Selected fungi can be isolated from mixed cultures grown by chance contamination of substrates such as bread, fruit, and other moist foods. Spores can be transferred and added to the culture medium by a sterile mounted needle. Cultures can be conveniently examined with low power stereoscopic microscopes.

Chapter Three

Variety of life – protoctists and plants

In chapter 2 it was stated that all cellular organisms seem to fall into two natural groups, prokaryotes and eukaryotes. The eukaryotes have certain important features in common, summarised in table 2.1; one of these is the presence of nuclei in their cells.

There is evidence that a key event in the evolution of eukaryotes was the invasion of a primitive ancestor by aerobic prokaryotes that developed into mitochondria (the **endosymbiont theory** – see section 9.3.1). Another important event is thought to have been a subsequent invasion by photosynthetic prokaryotes (blue-green bacteria) that developed into chloroplasts. Cells from this line of evolution are believed to have given rise to the ancestors of plants. A plant is a **photosynthetic eukaryote** or an **autotrophic eukaryote**, autotrophic meaning that it uses carbon dioxide as a source of carbon. Eukaryotes that lack chloroplasts are non-photosynthetic and described as **heterotrophic** (using an organic source of carbon). Among the early eukaryotes are thought to have been the algae, fungi, slime moulds and protozoa. The basic stock of

eukaryotes from which these groups arose were probably simple unicellular organisms which moved by beating flagella. Many of these organisms exhibited both animal- and plant-like characteristics. Evolutionary relationships among these primitive groups are still not clear, and it is therefore difficult to divide the groups into kingdoms. Margulis and Schwartz* proposed a system in 1982 which, like any other system, cannot be regarded as perfect, but which has been widely adopted and is currently recommended by the Institute of Biology. Five kingdoms are proposed, one prokaryote kingdom, the Prokaryotae and four eukaryote kingdoms (see fig 3.1).

The most controversial group is the **Protoctista (protoctists)** because it is probably an unnatural group. It contains eukaryotes that are generally regarded as identical or similar to the ancestors of modern plants, animals and fungi. The Protoctista includes two groups, the algae and the protozoans, which formerly had taxonomic status, and

* Margulis, L. & Schwartz, K.V. (1982), *Five kingdoms: an illustrated guide to the phyla of life on Earth*, W.H. Freeman & Co.

Table 3.1 Differences between plants and animals.

	Typical animal	*Typical plant*
Nutrition	Heterotrophic (see chapter 10)	Autotrophic (see chapter 9)
Locomotion	Motile – essential for finding food	Non-motile
Sensitivity	Controlled by hormones and nervous system – latter allows rapid reactions and is essential for movement and locomotion	Controlled by hormones only – no nervous system. Responds slowly to stimuli, usually by growth.
Excretion	Special excretory structures in most multi-cellular animals, particularly for nitrogenous excretion	Few excretory products and no special excretory organs
Osmoregulation	Special structures to carry out osmoregulation	Active osmoregulation not required owing to presence of cell walls
Growth	Occurs throughout body	Restricted to certain regions called meristems (in multicellular plants)
Surface area to volume ratio	Compact body for ease of movement	Large surface area to volume ratio for efficient trapping of light and exchange of materials. Branching often occurs
Cell structure	No rigid cell wall	Rigid cell wall containing cellulose
	Vacuoles small and temporary	Large permanent vacuole containing cell sap
	No chloroplasts or other plastids	Chloroplasts (containing chlorophyll) or other plastids present
	Stores carbohydrate as glycogen	Stores carbohydrate as starch
	Centrioles present	Centrioles absent

which are now regarded as containing organisms too widely different to be placed in one phylum. In addition, it includes one group of organisms which were previously placed in the fungi, the Oomycota or oomycetes, but which are now regarded as ancestral to fungi. The slime moulds, a group of organisms which are motile but which produce spores in sporangia, are also included in the Protoctista.

Further discussion on classification is given later in this chapter (see algae) and at the beginning of chapter 4. Plants are distingished from animals according to the features shown in table 3.1.

Kingdom Protoctista

(Gk. *protos*, very first; *ktistos*, to establish)

3.1 Characteristics and classification of protoctists

Protoctists include all eukaryotic organisms which are no longer classified as animals, plants or fungi. Many are unicellular organisms or collections of similar cells, and the kingdom includes all algae, protozoa, slime moulds and the Oomycota. Algae and protozoa are adapted for aquatic habitats. The classification and characteristics of the Protoctista are summarised in fig 3.1 and given in more detail later in fig 3.2 (algae), table 3.4 (Oomycota) and table 3.5 (protozoa).

3.2 Algae

3.2.1 Characteristics and classification of algae

The algae form a large group of protoctistans of great biological importance and significance to humans (section 3.2.7). Their bodies lack true stems, roots and leaves. Originally therefore, they were classified with fungi in the division Thallophyta (see footnote page 17). However, as more has been discovered about the group it has become obvious that there is great variety among the algae. They are best thought of as oxygen-producing photosynthetic eukaryotes that evolved in, and have exploited, an aquatic environment. It is true that some have escaped on to the land, but the worldwide productivity of

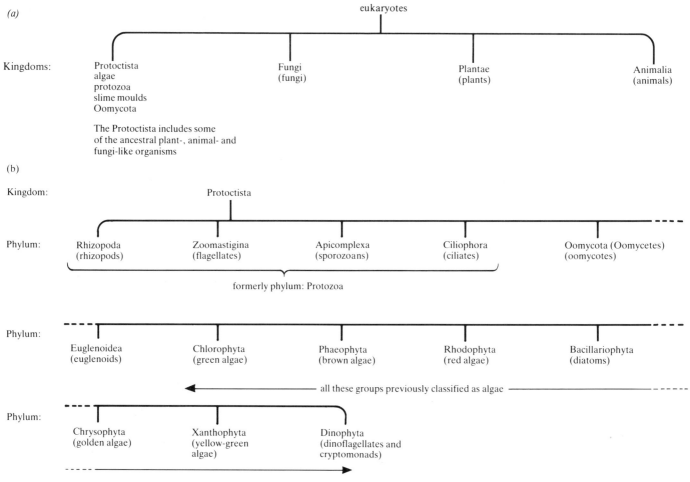

Fig 3.1 (a) *Eukaryotic kingdoms,* (b) *classification of Protoctista*

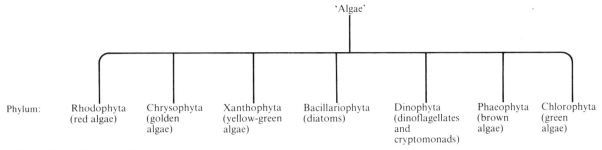

Fig 3.2 *The phyla of eukaryotic algae*

these coastal and land forms is insignificant compared with those in the oceans and fresh water.

If algae are thought of in this way, the blue-green bacteria (cyanobacteria), formerly known as the blue-green algae, have to be excluded from the group, since they are prokaryotes. There remains the important point, however, that blue-green bacteria produce oxygen in photosynthesis, whilst other photosynthetic prokaryotes do not. This requires the presence of chlorophyll *a* and photosystem II (section 9.4.2) so that water can be split into hydrogen and oxygen, an important advance over other photosynthetic bacteria. Little is known about how this advance was achieved, though some types intermediate between blue-green bacteria and other bacteria are being discovered. Our understanding of the link between blue-green bacteria, algae and plants is improved by the evidence of the endosymbiont theory which suggests that chloroplasts originated as blue-green bacteria (section 9.3.1).

Fortunately, the eukaryotic algae seem to fall naturally into distinct groups, chiefly on the basis of their photosynthetic pigments. These groups are given the status of phyla in modern classifications. The relationship between the phyla is still the subject of research which is fundamental to our knowledge of the origins of plants and the link between prokaryotes and eukaryotes.

The phyla are shown in fig 3.2 and a current view of their relationships in fig 3.3. Characteristics of the algae and of some of the main phyla are shown in table 3.2.

3.2.2 Asexual reproduction in the algae

Algae show both asexual and sexual reproduction. Below is a summary of the asexual types found, which range from simple to complex.

Vegetative reproduction. In some colonial forms, the colonies fragment to produce separate, smaller colonies. In the larger, thalloid algae, such as *Fucus*, new thalli may develop from the main thallus and break off.

Fragmentation. This occurs in filamentous algae, such as *Spirogyra*. The filament breaks in a controlled manner somewhere along its length to form two filaments and could be regarded as a form of vegetative reproduction.

Table 3.2 Classification and characteristics of two of the main groups of algae.

Algae	
General characteristics Body is a photosynthetic thallus Almost all are specialised for an aquatic existence Great range of size and form	
Phylum Chlorophyta ('green algae')	*Phylum Phaeophyta* ('brown algae')
Dominant photosynthetic pigment is chlorophyll; therefore green in appearance. Chlorophylls *a* and *b* present (as in plants)	*Dominant photosynthetic pigment is brown and called fucoxanthin. Chlorophylls *a* and *c* present
Store carbohydrate as starch (insoluble)	*Store carbohydrate as soluble laminarin and mannitol. Also store fat
Mostly freshwater	Nearly all marine (three freshwater genera only).
Large range of types, e.g. unicellular, filamentous, colonial, thalloid	Filamentous or thalloid, often large

e.g. *Chlamydomonas*, a unicellular, motile alga
   Spirogyra, a filamentous alga
   Ulva, a thalloid, marine alga
	e.g. *Fucus*, a thalloid, marine alga
	   Laminaria, large thalloid, marine alga; one of the kelps

* a diagnostic feature.

41

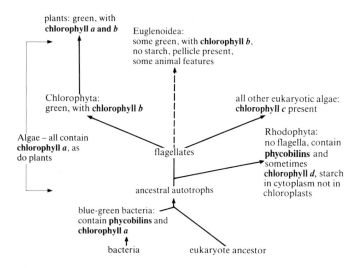

Fig 3.3 *Possible relationships between different groups of algae, bacteria, euglenoids and plants. For further discussion, see B. S. Rushton,* School Science Review, *62, no. 221, 648–54, June 1981*

Binary fission. In this process a unicellular organism divides into two equal halves, the nucleus dividing by mitosis.

Zoospores. These are motile, flagellate spores produced by many algae, for example *Chlamydomonas.*

Aplanospores. These are non-motile spores produced, for example, by some brown algae.

3.2.3 Sexual reproduction in the algae

Sexual reproduction involves the combination of genetic material from two individuals of the same species. The commonest method in the algae is by fusion of two morphologically (structurally) identical gametes. The process is called **isogamy**, and the gametes **isogametes**. *Spirogyra* and some species of *Chlamydomonas* are isogamous.

Sometimes, one of the gametes is less motile, or larger, and the process is then called **anisogamy**. In *Spirogyra* the gametes are structurally identical, but one moves while the other is stationary. This could be regarded as physiological anisogamy. A third variation occurs when one gamete is large and stationary while the other is small and motile. The gametes are known as female and male respectively and the process is called **oogamy**. *Fucus* and some species of *Chlamydomonas* are oogamous. The female gamete is larger because it contains food reserves for the developing zygote after fertilisation.

The three types of sexual reproduction are associated with an increase in complexity of body structure because, although some simple algae such as *Chlamydomonas* show

oogamy, it is more widespread in the complex algae, such as the Phaeophyta. Oogamy is the only type occurring in plants.

Unfortunately, a confusing variety of terms is associated with gametes and organs of sexual reproduction in the algae and plants, especially algae. The main terms are explained below.

The gametes of the fungi, algae, mosses and ferns are produced in structures called **gametangia**. The male gametangium is called an antheridium and the female gametangium an oogonium or archegonium.

An **oogonium*** is a simple female gametangium found in many algae and fungi, and the female gamete or gametes it contains are called **oospheres**. A fertilised oosphere is called an **oospore** and this typically develops into a thick-walled resting spore capable of surviving adverse conditions. A general term for a female gamete is an **ovum** or **egg-cell**, although the term oosphere is sometimes used more loosely to mean ovum.

An **archegonium** is a more complex female gametangium, characteristic of bryophytes, ferns and many conifers, and is described later in the chapter.

An **antheridium** produces male gametes called **antherozoids** or **spermatozoids**. They are motile because they possess one or many flagella. They are characteristic of the

---

* The term oogonium also refers to a cell of an animal that divides to produce oocytes in the ovary (see chapter 20).

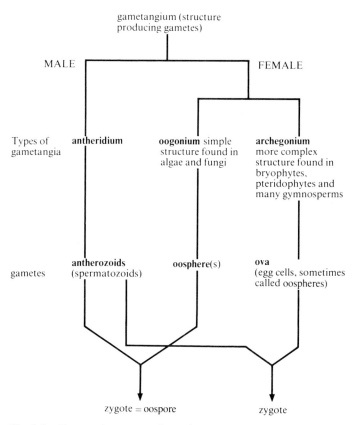

Fig 3.4 *Types of gametangia and gametes*

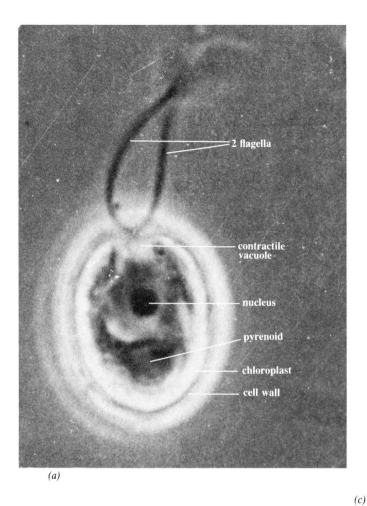

(a)

2 flagella

contractile
vacuole

nucleus

pyrenoid

chloroplast

cell wall

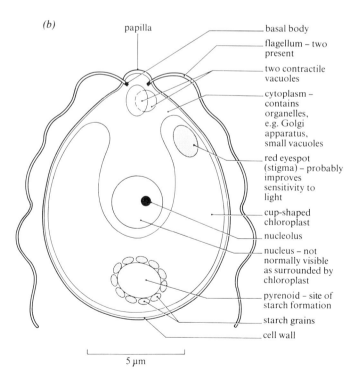

(b)

papilla

basal body

flagellum – two
present

two contractile
vacuoles

cytoplasm –
contains
organelles,
e.g. Golgi
apparatus,
small vacuoles

red eyespot
(stigma) – probably
improves
sensitivity to
light

cup-shaped
chloroplast

nucleolus

nucleus – not
normally visible
as surrounded by
chloroplast

pyrenoid – site of
starch formation

starch grains

cell wall

5 μm

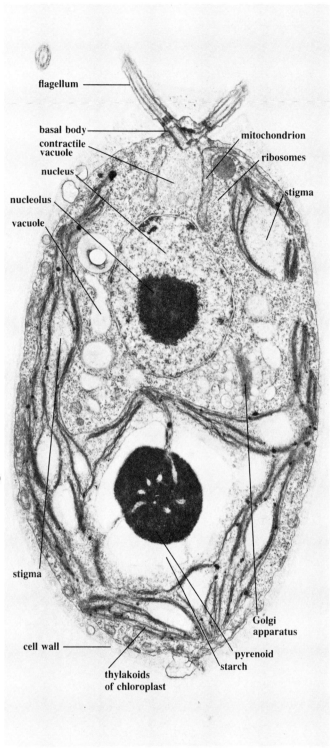

(c)

flagellum

basal body

contractile
vacuole

nucleus

nucleolus

vacuole

mitochondrion

ribosomes

stigma

stigma

cell wall

thylakoids
of chloroplast

starch

pyrenoid

Golgi
apparatus

Fig 3.5 (a) Chlamydomonas *as seen with the light microscope (× 600)*. (b) *Diagram of structure of* Chlamydomonas. *(c) Electron micrograph of* Chlamydomonas reinhardtii *(× 1400)*

43

fungi, algae, mosses, ferns and some conifers. Male gametes produced by animals are called **spermatozoa** (**sperm** or **sperms**). These terms are summarised in fig 3.4.

For the purposes of this chapter there is little point in preserving the distinction between the different names for gametes of the same sex, so all male gametes will be referred to as sperm and all female gametes as ova.

Like fungi, some algae show heterothallism (section 2.4.2).

3.2.4 Phylum Chlorophyta

Characteristics of the Chlorophyta are summarised in table 3.2.

Chlamydomonas is a unicellular motile alga living mainly in stagnant water, such as in ponds and ditches, particularly where it is rich in soluble nitrogenous compounds, as in farmyards. The cells often occur in numbers large enough to impart a green colour to the water. A few species are marine, or live in brackish coastal waters.

Structure

Chlamydomonas is motile and possesses contractile vacuoles. Its structure is illustrated in fig 3.5. The electron micrograph reveals the presence of eukaryote organelles in

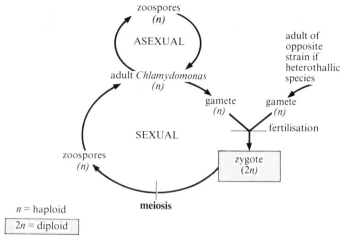

n = haploid

$2n$ = diploid

Fig 3.6 *Diagrammatic life cycle of* Chlamydomonas

the cytoplasm, such as Golgi apparatus, mitochondria, ribosomes and small vacuoles. The **pyrenoid** is a structure found in the chloroplasts of most algae. It is a protein body and probably consists mainly of the carbon-dioxide-fixing enzyme ribulose bisphosphate carboxylase. It is associated with the storage of carbohydrates such as starch. The **red eye spot** detects changes in light intensity and the cell responds by moving towards, or staying in, light of

Fig 3.7 *Reproduction in* Chlamydomonas. (a) *Asexual reproduction.* (b) *Sexual reproduction in an isogamous species*

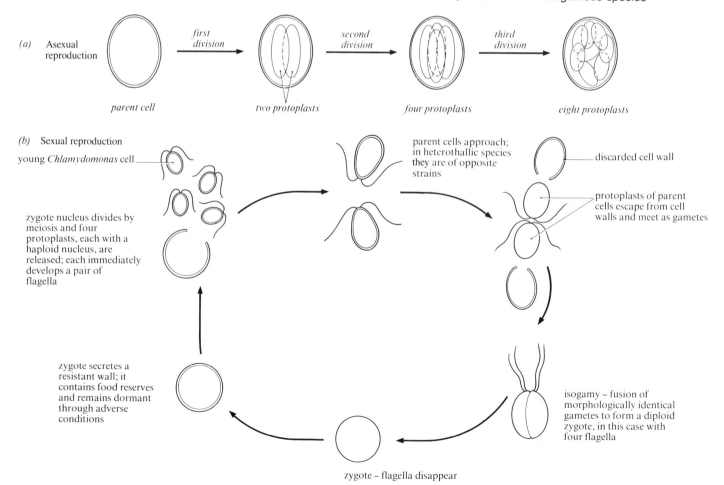

optimum intensity for photosynthesis. Such a response to light is called **phototaxis** (section 15.1.2). The cell moves by beating its two flagella and has a corkscrew motion because it rotates as it moves forward.

Life cycle

The life cycle of *Chlamydomonas* is summarised in fig 3.6. The adult is haploid.

Asexual reproduction

Asexual reproduction is by **zoospores**. The parent cell withdraws its flagella and the protoplast inside the cell wall divides into 2–16 daughter protoplasts (usually four). During this process the nuclear division is by mitosis and the chloroplast also divides. The daughter protoplasts develop new cell walls, eye spots and flagella. Centrioles (basal bodies) are involved in the formation of new flagella. The daughter cells, now called zoospores, are liberated by gelatinisation of the parent cell wall. Each grows to a full-sized *Chlamydomonas* cell. The process is illustrated in fig 3.7a.

Sexual reproduction

Some *Chlamydomonas* species are homothallic and some are heterothallic, and different species may be isogamous, anisogamous or oogamous. Reproduction of an isogamous species is illustrated in fig 3.7b. At germination, the first division of the zygote nucleus is by meiosis, resulting in a return to the haploid condition of the adult. The young *Chlamydomonas* cells released may be called zoospores until they reach maturity.

Spirogyra is a non-branching filamentous alga, living in ponds and other bodies of still, fresh water. The majority of species are floating and they are characteristically slimy.

Structure

The cylindrical walls are joined end to end to form a filament as shown in fig 3.8. Each cell is identical, so there is no division of labour. It has a narrow peripheral layer of cytoplasm and a large vacuole across which run strands of cytoplasm. The nucleus is suspended by these strands in a central position. The peripheral cytoplasm contains one or more chloroplasts that are spiral in form.

Growth and reproduction

Growth of the filament is intercalary, that is can occur by division and subsequent growth of any cell along the length of the filament (contrast most plants where primary growth is confined to apical regions). The nucleus of a given cell divides by mitosis, which is followed by division of the whole cell as a new cell wall grows from the edges of the filament inwards. The two daughter cells thus formed grow to normal size, causing the filament to grow in length.

Asexual reproduction is by fragmentation, as mentioned earlier (section 3.2.2).

Sexual reproduction is by a method confined to the filamentous algae in which two filaments line up alongside each other and adjacent cells become connected by short tubular outgrowths of the cells. The whole cell contents behave like gametes and the process can be regarded as *anisogamous* because, although the gametes are morphologically identical, one is motile and crosses through the connecting tube to the other. The process is called **conjugation**.

3.2.5   Phylum Phaeophyta

Characteristics of the Phaeophyta are summarised in table 3.2.

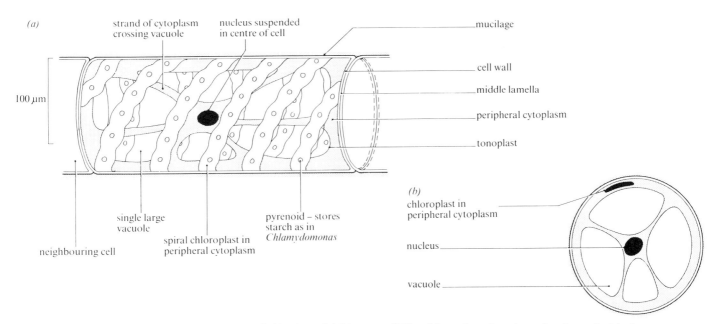

Fig 3.8 *Structure of* Spirogyra. *(a) Diagram of side view. (b) Diagram of TS cell in region of nucleus showing cylindrical nature of cells*

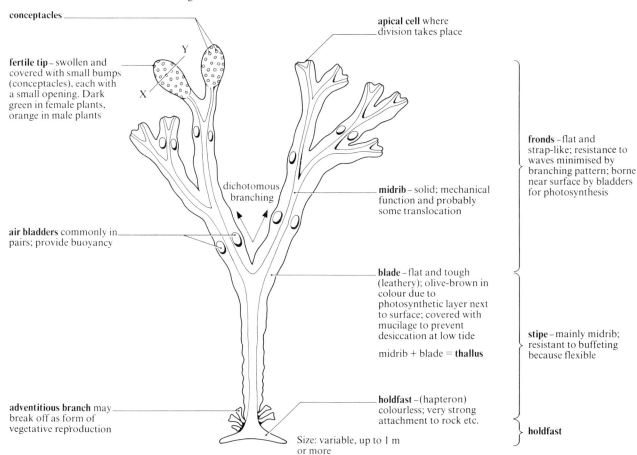

X–Y see fig 3.10

conceptacles

fertile tip – swollen and covered with small bumps (conceptacles), each with a small opening. Dark green in female plants, orange in male plants

apical cell where division takes place

dichotomous branching

midrib – solid; mechanical function and probably some translocation

fronds – flat and strap-like; resistance to waves minimised by branching pattern; borne near surface by bladders for photosynthesis

air bladders commonly in pairs; provide buoyancy

blade – flat and tough (leathery); olive-brown in colour due to photosynthetic layer next to surface; covered with mucilage to prevent desiccation at low tide

midrib + blade = **thallus**

stipe – mainly midrib; resistant to buffeting because flexible

adventitious branch may break off as form of vegetative reproduction

holdfast – (hapteron) colourless; very strong attachment to rock etc.

holdfast

Size: variable, up to 1 m or more

Fig 3.9 *External features of* Fucus vesiculosus, *with notes on structure, particularly adaptations to environment*

Species of the genus *Fucus* are common on rocky shores off the British coast. They are well adapted to the relatively harsh conditions of the littoral zone, the zone alternately exposed and covered by the tides.

There are three common species and these are often found at three different levels, or zones, on the shore, a phenomenon called **zonation**. They are principally zoned according to their ability to withstand exposure to air. Their chief recognition features and positions on the shore are noted below.

F. spiralis (flat wrack) – towards high tide mark. If suspended, the thallus adopts a slight spiral twist.

F. serratus (common, serrated or saw wrack) – middle zone. Edge of the thallus is serrated.

F. vesiculosus (bladder wrack) – towards low tide mark. Possesses air bladders for buoyancy.

The external features of *F. vesiculosus* are shown in fig 3.9 and some of the main features of internal structure in fig 3.10.

The body, or thallus, shows some division of labour between different tissues. This trend is carried further in the Phaeophyta than in any other algal group. Adaptations to environment are discussed below.

Reproductive structures

Sexual reproduction is oogamous. *F. vesiculosus* and *F. serratus* are dioecious, that is they have separate male

and female organisms. *F. spiralis* is hermaphrodite, having male and female organs on the same organism and in the same conceptacles. The sex organs develop inside conceptacles on the 'fertile' tips of some fronds. Each conceptacle has a pore (**ostiole**) for later release of the sex organs. Their structures are shown in fig 3.10.

The adult is diploid and the gametes are produced by meiosis.

Adaptations to environment

Before discussing the adaptations of *Fucus* to its environment, some mention must be made of the nature of this environment, which is relatively hostile. Being intertidal, the different species are subjected to varying degrees of exposure to air when the tide recedes. Therefore they must be protected against drying out. Temperatures may change rapidly, as when a cold sea advances into a hot rock pool. Salinity is another factor to which the organism has adapted, and this may increase in an evaporating rock pool, or decrease during rain. The surge and tug of the tide, and the pounding of waves, are additional factors which demand mechanical strength if they are to be withstood. Large waves can pick up stones and cause great damage as they crash down.

Morphological adaptations (overall structure)

The thallus is firmly anchored by a **holdfast** (fig 3.9). This forms an intimate association with its substrate, usually rock, and is extremely difficult to dislodge. In fact, the rock often breaks before the holdfast.

The thallus is dissected owing to its dichotomous branching in one plane, and this minimises resistance to water. It is also tough but non-rigid. The midrib of the thallus is strong and flexible.

F. vesiculosus possesses air bladders for buoyancy, thus holding its fronds up near the surface for maximum interception of light for photosynthesis.

Chloroplasts are mainly located in the surface layers for maximum exposure to light for photosynthesis.

Physiological adaptations

The dominant photosynthetic pigment is the brown pigment **fucoxanthin**. This is an adaptation to photosynthesising under water because fucoxanthin strongly absorbs blue light, which penetrates water much further than longer wavelengths such as red light.

The thallus secretes large quantities of mucilage which fills spaces within the body and exudes on to its surface. This helps to prevent desiccation by retaining water.

The solute potential of the cells is lower than that of sea water, so water is not lost by osmosis.

Reproductive adaptations

Release of gametes is synchronised with the tides. At low tide the thallus dries and squeezes the sex organs, which are protected by mucilage, out of the conceptacles. As the tide advances, the walls of the sex organs dissolve and release the gametes.

The male gametes are motile and chemotactic, attracted by a chemical secretion of the female gametes.

The zygote develops immediately after fertilisation, minimising the risk of being swept out to sea.

3.2.6 Trends in the algae

Even among the few examples described, it can be seen that there is a wide range of algal types, ranging from unicellular organisms such as *Chlamydomonas* to relatively large seaweeds, such as *Fucus*, with differentiated bodies showing some division of labour. Some large brown algae even possess conducting tissues, although none possess true vascular tissue (xylem and phloem).

Within the algae there is also a trend in sexual reproduction from simple isogamy and anisogamy to oogamy. Caution has to be exercised in trying to use these trends to establish evolutionary relationships between algal groups. The relationships are still not clear and the group from which land plants are thought to have evolved, the Chlorophyta (green algae), contains simple unicellular types as well as complex types, together with a range of sexual reproduction from isogamy to oogamy.

3.2.7 Importance of the algae

The role of algae in the biosphere

Modern estimates are that at least half the world's productivity, that is carbon fixation, comes from the oceans. This is contributed by the algae, the only vegetation in the sea. Considering their large surface area, the oceans might be expected to contribute a larger fraction, but photosynthesis is confined to the surface layers where light is available and here nutrient availabil-

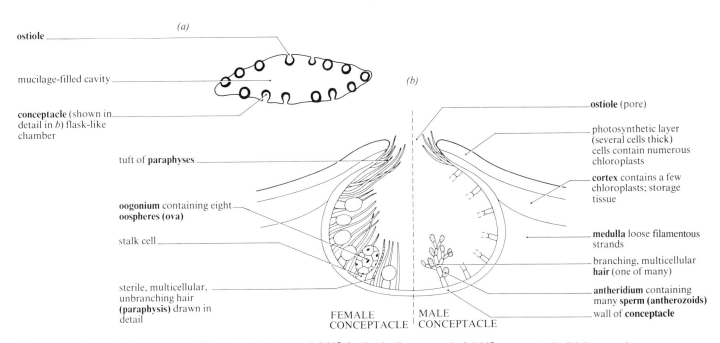

Fig 3.10 *Reproductive organs of* Fucus vesiculosus. *(a) VS fertile tip (low power). (b) VS conceptacle (high power)*

ity, particularly nitrogen and phosphorus, is a limiting factor.

Algae are vital as primary producers (chapter 12), being at the start of most aquatic food chains, including freshwater as well as virtually all ocean food chains. These chains lead through zooplankton*, crustaceans, and so on to fish. Many of the algae are microscopic unicells and these are the chief components of phytoplankton.*

Carbon fixation is not the only consequence of photosynthesis (section 9.2). The oxygen in the atmosphere is maintained by photosynthesis and at least half of this must therefore come from the algae, more than is contributed by forests on land.

Alginic acid, agar and carrageenin

A number of useful substances, including alginic acid, agar and carrageenin, are extracted from algae. **Alginic acid** and its derivatives (alginates) are polysaccharides extracted from the middle lamellae and cell walls of brown algae, such as *Laminaria*, *Ascophyllum* and *Macrocystis*. The fronds of the algae (seaweeds) are harvested in large quantities from shallow coastal waters, such as *Macrocystis* off the coast of California. The purified alginates are non-toxic and readily form gels. They are used as thickeners and gelling agents in a wide variety of industrial products; for example hand creams in cosmetics, emulsifiers in ice cream, polishes, medicines and paints, gelling agents in confectionery and glazes in ceramics.

Agar is a polysaccharide extracted from red algae. Like alginates, it forms gels and is probably most familiar as a convenient medium on which to culture bacteria and fungi. Here it is prepared as a dilute solution, mixed with nutrients and allowed to set as a jelly. It is also used for much the same purposes as alginates.

Carrageenin (**carragheen**) is another cell wall polysaccharide and is extracted mainly from the red alga *Chondrus crispus*. It is chemically very similar to agar and is used for the same purposes.

Diatomite (kieselguhr)

Algae of the phylum Bacillariophyta are mainly unicellular and are called **diatoms**. They have a characteristic cell wall structure containing silica. When they die they sediment, so that on the sea bed or lake bottom extensive deposits can be built up over long periods of time. The resulting 'diatomaceous earth' has a high proportion of silica (up to 90%) and when purified can be used as an inert filtering material, as in sugar refining and brewing, as a filler in paints and paper, and can be used in insulation materials that have to withstand extremes of temperature.

Fertiliser

A traditional but small-scale use of the larger seaweeds (red and brown algae) has been as a fertiliser on coastal

farms. They are richer in potassium, but poorer in nitrogen and phosphorus, than farm manure, and are of limited success.

Food

Some algae are used directly for human consumption, particularly in the Far East. *Porphyra*, a delicate red seaweed, and *Laminaria*, a large brown seaweed, are commonly used either raw or prepared in some way. *Porphyra* is made into laver bread in South Wales, a traditional dish in which the boiled alga is mixed with oatmeal and cooked in butter. In the search for new foods, much attention has been paid to mass culture of algae. Few have provided greater success in this field. However, the blue-green bacterium *Spirulina* shows promise as a food source.

Sewage disposal

Algae contribute to some extent to the microbial life of sewage works, the sewage providing nutrients for microscopic green algae as well as for bacteria, fungi and protozoa. Algae are particularly useful to humans in open 'oxidation ponds', which are used especially in tropical and subtropical countries. Ponds between 1 m and 1.5 m deep receive raw sewage, and oxygen provided by algal photosynthesis is vital for the other aerobic microorganisms that utilise the sewage. The algae can also be harvested occasionally and processed for animal fodder.

Research

Unicellular algae show characteristics typical of plants and often make ideal research material since they can be grown in large numbers under precisely controlled conditions without occupying a great deal of space. For example, the use of *Chlorella* in research on photosynthesis has been rewarding, as described in section 9.4.3. Algae are also used in ion uptake experiments and were important in early work on the structure of cell walls and flagella.

Harmful effects

Under certain conditions algae produce 'blooms'; that is dense masses of material. This is particularly true in relatively warm conditions when there is high nutrient availability. The latter may be artificially induced by human activity, as when sewage is added to water, or inorganic fertilisers run off from agricultural land into rivers and lakes. As a result, an explosive growth of primary producers (algae) occurs and far more than usual therefore die before being eaten. The subsequent process of decomposition is carried out by aerobic bacteria which, in turn, multiply and deplete the water of oxygen. This sequence may be rapid and the lack of oxygen may lead to the death of fish and other animals and plants. The increase of nutrients which starts the process is called **eutrophication**, and if rapid constitutes a form of pollution.

Toxins produced by algal blooms (and by blue-green bacteria) can also increase mortality. They can be a

---

* Plankton are minute algae (phytoplankton) and animals (zooplankton) floating in the surfaces of the oceans and lakes. They are of great economic and ecological importance.

serious problem in lakes, including those of fish farms, especially where intensive addition of fertilisers to farmlands adds to the eutrophication problems. Similar problems may occur as a result of algal blooms in the oceans. In addition, toxins may be stored by shellfish feeding on the algae and be passed on to humans causing, for example, paralytic shellfish poisoning.

Algae also cause problems in water storage reservoirs, where their products may taint the water and where they can grow on and block the beds of sand used as filters.

> **3.1** The problems just mentioned are greater in lowland reservoirs. Why should this be so?
>
> **3.2** Algae are not associated with disease, unlike many fungi and bacteria. What is the reason for this?

3.3 Phylum Euglenoidea (euglenoids)

Characteristics of the Euglenoidea are summarised below. The phylum shows a mixture of features that makes these organisms difficult to classify. In the past it has been included in both the plant and animal kingdoms.

Euglena is a common unicellular organism of freshwater ponds, ditches and any other water that is rich in soluble organic matter. Like *Chlamydomonas* it may be present in numbers sufficient to impart a green colour to the water, chlorophyll being the dominant pigment. Its structure is shown in fig 3.11, together with notes on some of its features.

Euglena lacks a cell wall. The outer layer of the cell is the cell surface membrane, immediately below which is the proteinaceous **pellicle**. This is flexible and permits the organism to assume various shapes. As the pellicle surrounds the cytoplasm, it can be regarded as a form of **exoskeleton**. It consists of a number of thickened longitudinal strips and microfibrils articulating with each other. When minute fibrils within the cytoplasm, called **myo-**

Table 3.3 Characteristics of Euglenoidea.

Phylum Euglenoidea ('euglenoids')
Dominant photosynthetic pigment is chlorophyll; therefore green in appearance.
Chlorophylls *a* and *b* present
Store carbohydrate as paramylum (similar to starch)
Mostly freshwater
Unicellular and motile
*Pellicle present instead of cellulose cell wall
Eye spot and contractile vacuoles present
e.g. *Euglena*

* a diagnostic feature.

nemes, contract, they cause the strips of the pellicle to slide over one another and effect a change in body shape. This is called **euglenoid movement**. Details of its more usual method of locomotion by means of its long flagellum are included in fig 3.11 (see eye spot, photoreceptor and long flagellum) and in section 17.6.3.

Asexual reproduction is by longitudinal binary fission. No sexual reproduction occurs.

Nutrition

Green species of *Euglena* are autotrophic, synthesising their own food from carbon dioxide, water and mineral salts. However, they are dependent on an external supply of vitamins B_1 and B_{12} which, like animals, they cannot synthesise for themselves. Although *Euglena* resembles animals in this respect, a large number of protoctists in other groups also share this inability.

A few *Euglena* species lack chloroplasts and are therefore colourless and non-photosynthetic (heterotrophic). They have a saprotrophic mode of nutrition, carrying out extracellular digestion, and grow most abundantly where putrefaction is taking place since decaying material is rich in organic compounds. Other colourless forms may be capable of ingesting small food particles at the base of the gullet, where the pellicle is absent, and carrying out intracellular digestion (holozoic nutrition, section 10.1.1). Food may be driven into the gullet by the action of the flagella. These species resemble the protozoan *Peranema* (section 3.5.2).

If green species of *Euglena* are kept in darkness for a prolonged period they lose their chloroplasts and become colourless. If the medium contains organic nutrients, they survive saprotrophically. Chloroplasts return when the organisms are returned to light.

3.4 Phylum Oomycota (oomycetes)

Characteristics of the Oomycota are given in table 3.4. In the phylum are a number of pathogenic organisms, including the downy mildews (see table 2.10). One of these, *Phytophthora infestans*, will be studied as an example of a parasite.

Phytophthora infestans is a pathogen of economic importance because it parasitises potato crops, causing a potentially devastating disease known as potato blight. It is similar in its structure and mode of attack to another member of the Oomycota, *Peronospora*, which is a common, but less serious, disease of wall-flower, cabbage and other members of the plant family Cruciferae.

Blight is usually first noticed in the leaves in August, though infection normally starts in the spring when the organism grows up to the leaves from the tubers in which the mycelium has over-wintered.

A mycelium of branched, aseptate hyphae ramifies through the intercellular spaces of the leaves, giving off **branched haustoria** which push into the mesophyll cells and

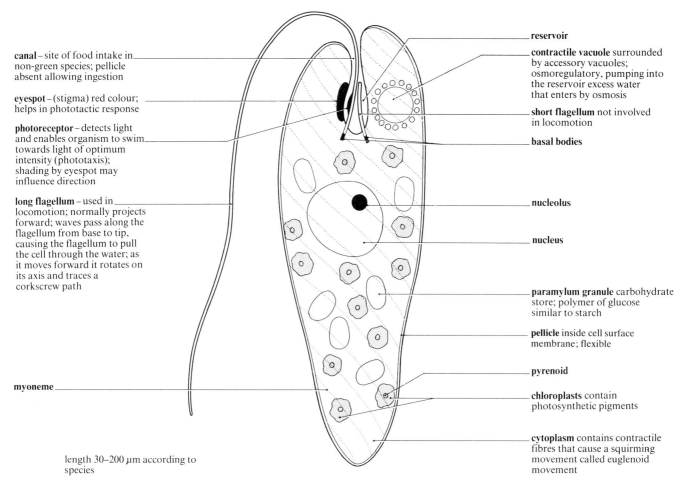

canal – site of food intake in non-green species; pellicle absent allowing ingestion

eyespot – (stigma) red colour; helps in phototactic response

photoreceptor – detects light and enables organism to swim towards light of optimum intensity (phototaxis); shading by eyespot may influence direction

long flagellum – used in locomotion; normally projects forward; waves pass along the flagellum from base to tip, causing the flagellum to pull the cell through the water; as it moves forward it rotates on its axis and traces a corkscrew path

myoneme

reservoir

contractile vacuole surrounded by accessory vacuoles; osmoregulatory, pumping into the reservoir excess water that enters by osmosis

short flagellum not involved in locomotion

basal bodies

nucleolus

nucleus

paramylum granule carbohydrate store; polymer of glucose similar to starch

pellicle inside cell surface membrane; flexible

pyrenoid

chloroplasts contain photosynthetic pigments

cytoplasm contains contractile fibres that cause a squirming movement called euglenoid movement

length 30–200 μm according to species

Fig 3.11 *Structure of* Euglena gracilis

absorb nutrients from them (fig 3.12). In warm, humid conditions the mycelium produces long, slender structures called **sporangiophores** which emerge from the lower surface of the leaf through stomata or wounds. These branch and give rise to **sporangia** (fig 3.12). In warm conditions sporangia may behave as spores, being blown or splashed by raindrops on to other plants, where further infection takes place. A hypha emerges from the sporangium and penetrates the plant via a stoma, lenticel or wound. In cool conditions, the sporangium contents may divide to form motile zoospores (a primitive feature) which, when released, swim in surface films of moisture.

Table 3.4 Characteristics of Oomycota.

Phylum Oomycota

Sexual reproduction by oogamy, involving fusion of an oosphere (female gamete) with a male gamete to produce an oospore

Asexual reproduction by means of biflagellate zoospores produced in sporangia

Non-septate hyphae

Cell walls contain cellulose

e.g. *Phytophthora infestans*, facultative parasite causing potato blight
Pythium, many important facultative parasites, some cause damping-off of seedlings
Peronospora, obligate parasites, causing downy mildews of crucifers, e.g. cabbages

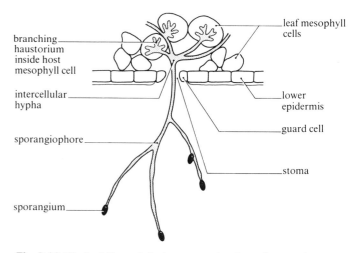

branching haustorium inside host mesophyll cell

intercellular hypha

sporangiophore

sporangium

leaf mesophyll cells

lower epidermis

guard cell

stoma

Fig 3.12 Phytophthora infestans *growing in a diseased potato leaf, with sporangiophores emerging from the underside of the leaf*

50

They may encyst until conditions are suitable once more for hyphal growth, then produce new infections.

Diseased plants show individual leaflets with small, brown, dead, 'blighted' areas. Inspection of the lower surface of an infected leaflet reveals a fringe of white sporangiophores around the dead area. In warm, humid conditions, the dead area spreads rapidly through the whole leaf and into the stem. Some sporangia may fall to the ground and infect potato tubers where infection spreads very rapidly causing a form of dry rot in which the tissues are discoloured a rusty brown in an irregular manner from the skin to the centre of the tuber.

First the base and then the rest of the plant becomes a putrid mass as the dead areas become secondarily infected with decomposing bacteria (saprotrophs). *Phytophthora* thus kills the whole plant, unlike its close relative *Peronospora* which is an obligate parasite. In this respect, *Phytophthora* is not a typical obligate parasite and it is sometimes described as facultative, though the distinction is perhaps not worth stressing here.

The organism normally overwinters as a dormant mycelium within lightly infected potato tubers. Except where the potato is native (Mexico, Central and South America) it is thought that the organism rarely reproduces sexually, unlike *Peronospora*, but under laboratory conditions it can be induced to do so. Like *Peronospora*, it produces a resistant resting spore. It is the result of fusion between an antheridium and an oogonium, and a thick-walled oospore is produced. This can remain dormant in the soil over winter and cause infection in the following year.

In the past, *Phytophthora* epidemics have had serious consequences. The disease is thought to have been accidentally introduced into Europe from America in the late 1830s and caused a series of epidemics that totally destroyed the potato crop in Ireland in 1845 and in subsequent years. Widespread famine resulted and many starved to death, victims as much of complex economic and political influences as of the disease. Many Irish families emigrated to North America as a result.

The disease is also of interest because in 1845 Berkeley provided the first clear demonstration that micro-organisms cause disease by showing that the organism associated with potato blight *caused* the disease, rather than being a by-product of decay.

Knowledge of the life cycle of potato blight has since led to methods of controlling the disease. These are summarised below.

(1) Care must be taken to ensure that no infected tubers are planted.

(2) New plantings must not be made in soil known to have carried the disease a year previously, since the organism can survive up to one year in the soil. Crop rotation may therefore help.

(3) All diseased parts of infected plants should be destroyed before lifting tubers, for example by burning or spraying with a corrosive solution such as sulphuric acid. This is because tubers can be infected from decaying haulms (stems) and aerial parts.

(4) Since the organism can overwinter in unlifted tubers, care must be taken to ensure that all tubers are lifted in an infected field.

(5) The organism can be attacked with copper-containing fungicides, such as Bordeaux mixture. Spraying must be carried out at the correct time to prevent an attack, since infected plants cannot be saved. It is usual to spray at fortnightly intervals, from the time that the plants are a few centimetres high until they are well matured. Tubers intended as seed potatoes can be sterilised externally by immersion in a dilute mercury(II) chloride solution.

(6) Accurate monitoring of meteorological conditions, coupled with an early warning system for farmers, can help to decide when spraying should be carried out.

(7) Breeding for resistance to the blight has been carried out for some years. The wild potato, *Solanum demissum*, is known to show high resistance and has been used in breeding experiments. One great obstruction to producing the required immunity lies in the fact that the organism exists in many strains and no potato has been found to be resistant to all of them. New strains of the organism may appear as new strains of potato are introduced. This is a familiar problem in plant pathology and emphasises the need for conservation of the wild ancestors of our modern crop plants as sources of genes for disease resistance.

3.5 Phyla Rhizopoda, Zoomastigina, Apicomplexa, Ciliophora

At the beginning of chapter 3 it was stated that the fungi, algae, slime moulds and protozoans might have evolved from an earlier group of eukaryote ancestors which moved by means of flagella (see fig 3.14). These flagellate organisms, represented by present-day forms belonging to the Kingdom Protoctista, probably displayed both plant- and animal-like characteristics. Some may have possessed chlorophyll and carried out photosynthesis only; some may have lost their chlorophyll, probably by mutation and fed heterotrophically exclusively; whilst some may have photo-synthesised and fed heterotrophically. This suggests that there were few real differences between plant and animal cells at an early stage in evolution.

The earliest 'animal-like' unicellular organisms were probably similar in their basic features to present-day protozoans, as represented by organisms belonging to the phyla Rhizopoda, Zoomastigina, Apicomplexa and Ciliophora.

The earliest 'plant-like' organisms were probably similar in their basic features to present-day euglenoids (phylum Euglenophyta, section 3.3), which display a mixture of plant and animal features.

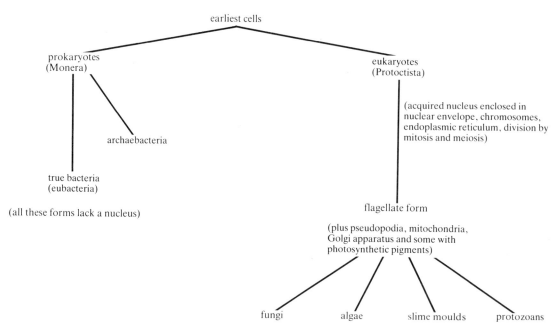

Fig 3.13 *Possible early cell evolution*

3.5.1 Protozoans

The protozoa (*protos*, first; *zoon*, animal) are a diverse group of organisms. There are over 50 000 known species, and they are found in all environments where water is present. Each protozoan functions as an independent unit and is able to perform effectively all the activities necessary for life (table 3.5).

Within the protozoans there exists a range of different levels of **cellular organisation**. In the simplest forms (such as *Amoeba proteus)* the cell is relatively undifferentiated and there are few organelles which can be related to any specific activity. In the more differentiated protozoa (for example *Paramecium caudatum*) organisation has become highly complex. Here, elaboration of the living material into numerous highly efficient **organelles** has enabled these organisms to perform particular activities much more effectively.

It is a matter of debate whether a protozoan should be regarded as **unicellular** or **non-cellular** (acellular). The term unicellular will be used in this book. Non-cellular implies an equivalence between the whole body of the protozoan, which exhibits all the attributes of life, and the whole body of a multicellular animal. If protozoans are to be called unicellular, then comparison must be made between the whole protozoan body and a single cell of the body of a multicellular animal.

When the body of a multicellular animal is compared with that of a protozoan, it is obvious that structurally the protozoan is much simpler. However, if individual cells from multicellular animals are compared with protozoans the story is quite the opposite. Because the protozoan has to accomplish all of life's processes it is not surprising that it exhibits a much more complex organisation than that of multicellular animal cells. Cells of these animals are usually designed to perform only one specific function. Consequently these cells exhibit a diminished level of structural complexity but an increased efficiency in performing their specific functions.

3.5.2 Phylum Zoomastigina

Peranema (fig 3.14) is an example of a flagellate, and its resemblance to some species of *Euglena* is mentioned in section 3.3.

Peranema is predatory and feeds on organisms such as *Euglena*. A '**rod organelle**' located near the cytostome touches the prey, protrudes and becomes attached to its surface. The anterior end then dilates and envelops the victim, the rods helping to push it through the cytostome.

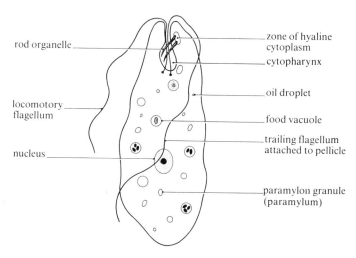

Fig 3.14 Peranema trichophorum *showing the main structures visible under the light microscope*

Table 3.5 Classification of the protozoa.

Characteristic features
Unicellular
No tissues
Specialised parts of living material form organelles
Exhibit all forms of heterotrophism
Reproduction by fission; gametic fission when whole animal breaks up into gametes

NB Compound protozoans – these have more elaborate organelles and their structure foreshadows the multicellular animal phyla
(*a*) every cell is capable of reproduction
(*b*) all cells are structurally and physiologically similar and not organised into primary germ layers

Phylum Zoomastigina	*Phylum Rhizopoda*	*Phylum Ciliophora*	*Phylum Apicomplexa*
Some possess chromatophores, others do not	No chromatophores	No chromatophores	No chromatophores
Semi-rigid cell Covering is a pellicle	Some secrete tests, shells or skeleton, others possess no specific outer covering	Pellicle	Pellicle
Definite shape Adult movement by one or several flagella	Variable shape Adult movement by pseudopodia	Definite shape Adult movement by numerous cilia arranged in tracts	Definite shape Most exhibit no external structures for locomotion, any movement is limited
One nucleus	One nucleus	Macronucleus and micronucleus	One nucleus
Asexual reproduction by longitudinal binary fission	Asexual reproduction by binary fission	Asexual reproduction by transverse binary fission	Asexual reproduction by spores and schizogony (growth and reproduction)
		Sexual reproduction by conjugation	Sexual reproduction occurs in the life history
Multiple fission in cyst	May sporulate	Rarely sporulate	Large numbers of resistant spores after syngamy
e.g. *Euglena* *Peranema* *Trypanosoma*	e.g. *Amoeba* *Arcella* *Polystomella*	e.g. *Paramecium* *Vorticella* *Stentor*	e.g. *Monocystis* *Plasmodium*

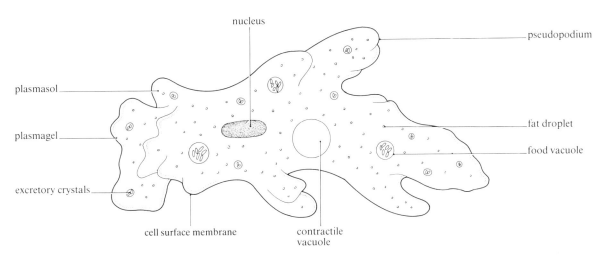

Fig 3.15 Amoeba proteus – *structures visible under the light microscope*

They may also shred the prey to some extent, so exposing its inner parts to enzyme action. Swallowing takes about eight minutes to complete, and the prey is then digested within food vacuoles.

3.5.3 Phylum Rhizopoda

Amoeba (fig 3.15) is a well-known example of the Rhizopoda. When compared with ciliates or flagellates

Amoeba shows little real differentiation either in its surface layer or within the cell. This may, in part, be due to the nature of its locomotory process which requires considerable cytoplasmic mobility. Nevertheless, its apparent simple construction is deceptive and it should be remembered that this animal is sufficiently well organised to carry out effectively all of the processes for life within its own minute mass of living material.

Amoeba is a free-living microscopic animal found living on the mud at the bottom of shallow freshwater ponds and streams where there is some movement of water. It is **omnivorous** feeding on a varied diet of algae, ciliates and flagellates. It measures approximately 0.1 mm in diameter and is subdivided into a nucleus and cytoplasm surrounded by a delicate cell surface membrane. The nucleus is embedded in the cytoplasm but occupies no fixed position. It is concerned with the organisation and integration of the animal's metabolic and reproductive processes.

The cytoplasm is differentiated into an outer layer of clear **plasmagel** called **ectoplasm**, and an inner mass of granular **plasmasol**, or **endoplasm**. The endoplasm contains fat droplets and a variety of vacuoles containing food matter in various stages of digestion, indigestible remains of food and crystals of excretory materials. It possesses a variable number of transient contractile vacuoles, which regularly become filled with water from the cytoplasm and then ultimately expel it into the surrounding pond water. The vacuoles perform an osmoregulatory function for the animal.

The animal constantly changes shape. This is brought about by temporary outpushings of the cytoplasm, called **pseudopodia**, which are regularly formed at any part of the animal's surface. These lobose pseudopodia are used for locomotion and feeding.

Amoeba does not possess any specific sensory organelles, however it is able to respond to a variety of stimuli. For example, it can discriminate between different types of food, it moves away from bright light, strong chemical solutions and persistent mechanical irritation. Violent disturbances cause it to withdraw all pseudopodia and remain stationary for some time.

Asexual reproduction takes place by binary fission. This form of mitotic cell division is triggered off in response to limits imposed either by the surface area to volume ratio, and/or the ratio between cytoplasmic volume and nuclear volume. The nucleus, which contains between 500–600 very small chromosomes, divides first. This is followed by a constriction and elongation of the cytoplasm which forces the daughter chromosomes apart and towards their respective poles. Ultimately two daughter amoebae of roughly equal proportions separate from each other. Under ideal conditions the whole process can be completed within 30 min. Each daughter *Amoeba* then proceeds to feed and grow to maximum size.

This particular form of reproduction is thought to be the only one that occurs in *Amoeba proteus*. Earlier reports of sporulation and cyst formation are now disregarded.

However both of these activities do take place in other species of *Amoeba*.

3.5.4 Phylum Ciliophora

Paramecium (fig 3.16) is a well-known ciliate. It demonstrates a very high degree of **cellular differentiation**, exhibiting many complex organelles which have been designed to perform specific functions for the organism. Not only does its structure show specialisation, but its reproductive activity is also complex.

Paramecium lives in stagnant water, or slow-flowing fresh water containing decaying organic matter. It possesses a constant elongate body shape with a blunt anterior end and a tapered posterior. Its whole body is covered by a thin, flexible **pellicle**. The pellicle has a uniform appearance, being composed of a lattice of hexagonally shaped pits each perforated by a pair of **cilia**. The whole body of the organism is covered with cilia, which are generally arranged in longitudinal rows, diagonally aligned along its length (fig 3.17). Perforating the ridges of each pit are holes which provide the exits for flask-shaped structures called **trichocysts**. When stimulated, fine, sharply tipped threads are discharged from them. They serve as a means of anchorage during feeding activity (fig 3.18).

Beneath the pellicle is a clear layer of firm plasmagel, the ectoplasm, which exhibits considerable complexity. **Kinetosomes**, the structures from which cilia are formed, are found here. A single fibril (kinetodesmal fibril) arises from each kinetosome and extends forwards and obliquely to its right. It joins other fibrils from adjacent kinetosomes to form a longitudinal bundle of striated fibrils, called a **kinetodesma**. The kinetosomes and fibrils of a particular row are collectively known as a **kinety**. There is also a dense network of fibrils situated in the endoplasm near the cytostome. This is the **motorium**. It has branches which interconnect with the fibrils of the ectoplasm, and the whole fibrillar system is thought to be the controlling centre for ciliary activity.

At the boundary between the ectoplasm and the more granular endoplasm are large bundles of microfilaments called **M fibres** (myonemes). These are contractile in their activity and promote a change of shape in *Paramecium* to enable it to squeeze through narrow spaces.

Near the anterior end of the animal, and on its ventral surface, is a permanent ciliated shallow depression called the **oral groove**. It extends backwards, and tapers into a much narrower tube-like gullet at the end of which is a portion of naked endoplasm, the **cytostome** (mouth). Within the gullet are rows of closely packed cilia arranged into sheets (undulating membranes). When feeding, the cilia of the oral groove suck a current of water, containing bacteria and other suspended particles, into the gullet. The gullet cilia drive the food into the cytostome. Here the food particles, together with a drop of water are enclosed in a food vacuole and ingested into the endoplasm. These vacuoles move away from the cytostome and begin to follow a distinct pathway through the endoplasm as a result of cyclosis (the circulation of organelles within the cell cytoplasm). Any indigestible material is egested at a fixed point, the **cytoproct**, by active vacuolar activity (exocytosis).

Two fixed contractile vacuoles are present in the endoplasm. Both are dorsally situated, one at the anterior end, the other at the posterior end. Around each contractile vacuole are a number of radial canals which fill with fluid before emptying into the main vacuole. The posterior contractile vacuole empties and fills at a faster rate than the anterior one, because of greater endosmosis (intake of water) in the region of the gullet.

Dorsal to the gullet, and towards the centre of the body, lie the **two nuclei**. The larger, bean-shaped **macronucleus** is polyploid; it controls metabolism and differentiation within the animal. The **micronucleus** is diploid; it controls reproductive activity and gives rise to new macronuclei. It is always active when nuclear reorganisation takes place during the life history of the animal.

Paramecium swims by the rhythmic beating of its cilia. Each cilium beats a little in advance of the one immediately behind so that waves of ciliary activity pass over the animal (metachronal rhythm). The direction of each wave is slightly oblique, causing the animal to swim in a spiral manner and at the same time to rotate about its longitudinal axis.

Detection of external stimuli probably takes place through the cilia, especially the stiff, non-locomotory ones at the posterior end. *Paramecium* is sensitive to touch, different concentrations of chemicals, oxygen and carbon dioxide levels, and changes in light intensity. If it encounters unfavourable conditions, or meets an obstruction, *Paramecium* is able to stop its cilia beating, reverse

(a)

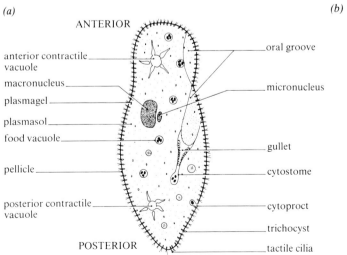

(b)

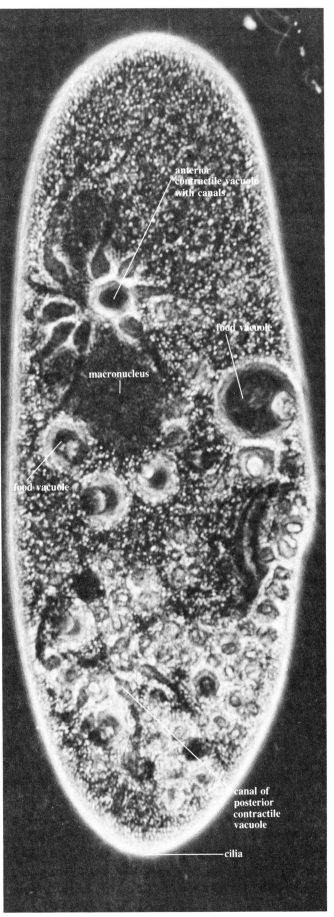

Fig 3.16 *(a)* Paramecium caudatum – *structures visible under the light microscope.* (b) *Micrograph of* Paramecium caudatum *showing structural details* (× 832)

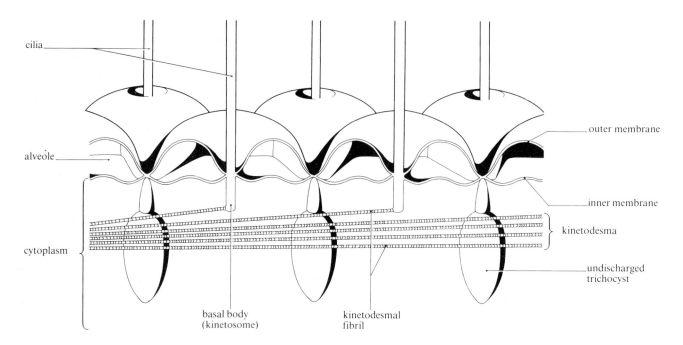

cilia

alveole

cytoplasm

outer membrane

inner membrane

kinetodesma

undischarged trichocyst

basal body (kinetosome)

kinetodesmal fibril

Fig 3.17 *Pellicle and infraciliature of* Paramecium caudatum, *taken from electron micrographs and based upon the work of Grell, Ehret and Powers*

their beat, and then swim forward at an angle to its original path. This is continued until a clear route, or favourable conditions, are restored. It is an example of trial and error behaviour and tends to keep the animal in an optimum environment. The position of the motorium near the mouth, and its connections with the kinetodesmata make it ideally placed to receive and respond in advance of conditions ahead of the animal (fig 3.19).

Most species of *Paramecium* divide asexually by means of transverse binary fission. Both nuclei increase in size elongate and pull themselves apart. The macronucleus divides amitotically, randomly distributing its chromosomes between the two newly formed macronuclei. The micronucleus undergoes mitosis. A spindle forms within its nuclear envelope and very small chromosomes are shared between the two daughter micronuclei in the normal manner. A cytoplasmic constriction forms around the middle of the animal which finally ruptures, producing two daughter paramecia. By the time separation is complete, both daughters have a full complement of organelles.

At times of food shortage, a form of sexual reproduction called **conjugation** occurs (fig 3.20). It only takes place between compatible mating types of the same species. Meiosis and nuclear exchange take place resulting in the production of offspring with a wide variety of genotypes. The process is as shown in fig 3.20.

(1) Two different compatible mating types (**conjugants**) adhere to each other at their oral grooves.

(2) The pellicle breaks down and a **cytoplasmic bridge** is established between them. Attachment can last several hours. Respective macronuclei disintegrate. Each micronucleus divides meiotically to form four daughter micronuclei.

(3) Three micronuclei disintegrate and disappear. Which shall disappear and which survive depends on their relative positions in the cytoplasm.

(4) The remaining nucleus in each conjugant divides once mitotically to form two identical gametic nuclei. One gamete remains stationary ('female' nucleus), whilst the other ('male' nucleus) migrates via the cytoplasmic bridge into the opposite conjugant.

(5) The male and female nuclei fuse to form a **zygotic nucleus** (synkaryon). Exchange of genetic material is now complete.

(6) Conjugants separate and are called ex-conjugants. The zygotic nucleus of each divides mitotically to form eight daughter nuclei.

(7) Four become macronuclei and four micronuclei; then three micronuclei degenerate.

(8) Binary fission of each ex-conjugant takes place. Two macronuclei enter each new cell and each micronucleus undergoes mitosis.

(9) Further binary fission results in separation of macronuclei and another mitotic division of the micronucleus. The end result is four daughter paramecia formed from each ex-conjugant.

Continued amitotic division of the macronucleus during binary fission leads to unequal distribution of its chromosomes. This upsets the normal coordinated activity of *Paramecium* and leads to 'depression'. The situation can be rectified by a process called **autogamy**, a modified form of sexual reproduction which occurs every 3–4 weeks (fig 3.21). It leads to the production of new macronuclei containing the 'normal' number of chromosomes, and is a

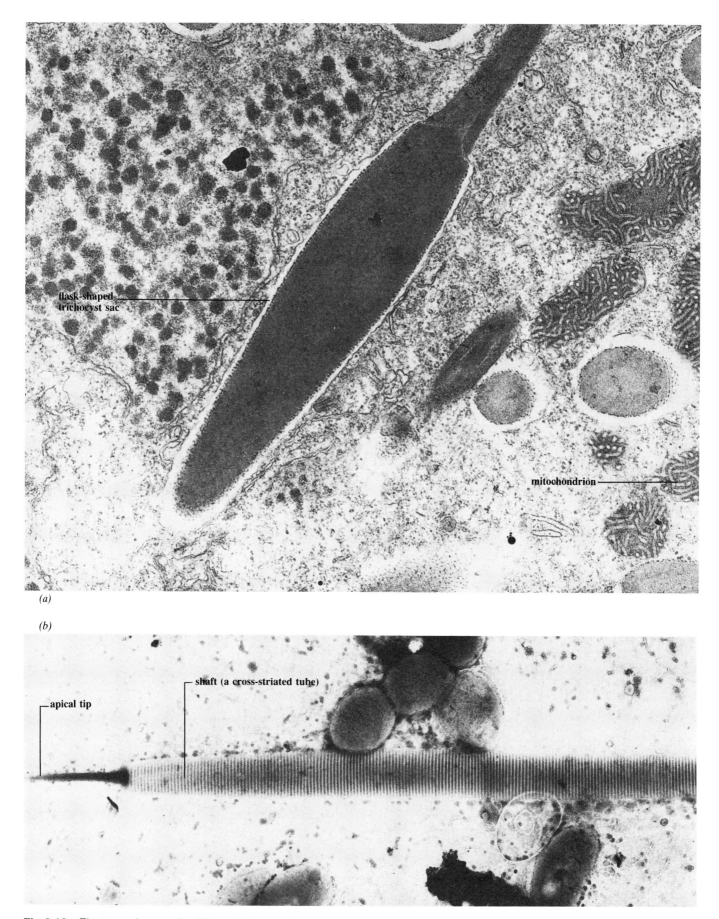

(a)

(b)

Fig 3.18 *Electron micrograph of (a) undischarged and (b) discharged trichocyst of* P. caudatum *(× 50 000)*

type of self-fertilisation occurring within a single individual. It occurs as shown in fig 3.21.

(1) The micronucleus divides into eight haploid nuclei. Six of the nuclei break down. The macronucleus degenerates.
(2) The two remaining nuclei fuse to form a zygotic nucleus.

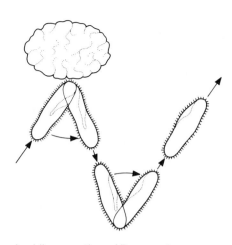

Fig 3.19 *Avoiding reaction of* Paramecium

(3) The zygotic nucleus divides twice to form four nuclei, two of which become macronuclei and two micronuclei.
(4) Binary fission occurs to produce two daughter paramecia. Normal nuclear condition of the macronucleus has thus been restored.

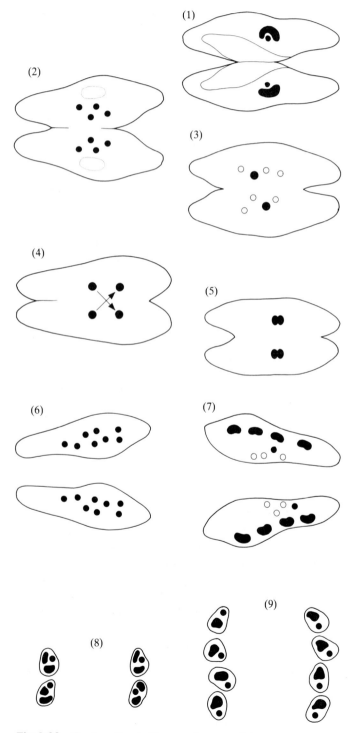

Fig 3.20 *Conjugation in* Paramecium caudatum

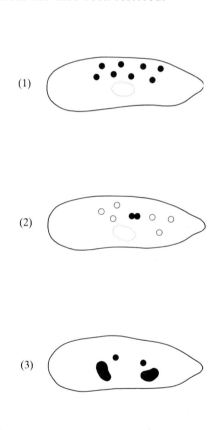

Fig 3.21 *Autogamy in* Paramecium caudatum

Kingdom Plantae

Plants are described as **autotrophic eukaryotes** at the beginning of this chapter. This definition excludes fungi since fungi are heterotrophic. For the purposes of this book, fungi have been classified as a separate kingdom. The only other autotrophic eukaryotes, apart from plants, are algae.

The *International Code of Botanical Nomenclature* recommends that each major group of the plant kingdom should be called a division, rather than a phylum as in the animal kingdom. Strictly speaking the terms phylum and division are not equivalent, but for the sake of simplicity phylum is used rather than division in this book.

3.6 Phylum Bryophyta – liverworts and mosses

There are fossil records of blue-green bacteria living 3 000 million years ago and eukaryotic organisms have existed for more than 1 000 million years. However, the first organisms to colonise the land, primitive plants, did not do so until about 420 million years ago. Probably the greatest single problem to overcome in making the transition from water to land is that of desiccation. Any plant not protected in some way, for example by a waxy cuticle, will tend to dry out and die very rapidly. Even if this difficulty is overcome, there remain other problems, notably that of successfully achieving sexual reproduction. In the algae this usually involves a male gamete which must swim in water to reach the female gamete.

The first plants to colonise the land are generally thought to have evolved from the green algae (fig 3.3), a few advanced members of which evolved reproductive organs, namely archegonia (female) and antheridia (male), that enclosed and thus protected the gametes within. This, and certain other factors that helped to prevent desiccation, enabled some of them to invade the land.

One of the main themes that will be stressed when considering the different groups of land plants will be their gradually increasing independence from water.

The main problems associated with the transition from an aquatic to a terrestrial environment are summarised below.

Desiccation. Air is a drying medium and water is essential for life for many reasons (section 5.1.2). Means of obtaining water and conserving it are required.

Reproduction. Delicate sex cells must be protected and motile male gametes (sperm) require water if they are to reach the female gametes.

Support. Air, unlike water, offers no support to the plant body.

Nutrition. Plants require light and carbon dioxide for photosynthesis, so at least part of the body must be above ground. Minerals and water, however, are at ground level or below ground, and to make efficient use of these, part of the plant must grow below ground in darkness.

Gaseous exchange. For photosynthesis and respiration, carbon dioxide and oxygen must be exchanged with the atmosphere rather than a surrounding solution.

Environmental variables. Water, particularly large bodies of water like lakes and oceans, provides a very constant environment. A terrestrial environment, however, is much more subject to changes in important factors such as temperature, light intensity, ionic concentration and pH.

It will be seen in the remainder of this chapter that plants have successfully exploited the land by gradual changes in structure and function. It is the main changes that the student should try to understand rather than the detailed differences between plants.

3.6.1 Classification and characteristics of Bryophyta

The simplest group of land plants is the phylum Bryophyta, which includes two main classes, the Hepaticae (liverworts) and the Musci (mosses). The classification and characteristics of the Bryophyta are summarised in table 3.6.

The bryophytes are relatively poorly adapted to life on land, so are mainly confined to damp, shady places. They are small simple plants, with strengthening and conducting tissues absent or poorly developed. There is no true vascular tissue (xylem or phloem). They lack true roots, being anchored by thin filamentous outgrowths of the stem called **rhizoids**. Water and mineral salts can be absorbed by the whole surface of the plant, including the rhizoids, so that the latter are mainly for anchorage, unlike true roots. (*True* roots also possess vascular tissue, as do *true* stems and leaves.) Thus the stems and leaves of bryophytes are not homologous with stems and leaves of vascular plants, where they are part of a diploid sporophyte not a haploid gametophyte. The plant surface lacks a cuticle, or has only a delicate one, and so has no barrier against loss (or entry) of water. Nevertheless, most bryophytes have adapted to survive periods of dryness using mechanisms that are not fully understood. For example, it has been shown that the well-known xerophytic moss *Grimmia pulvinata* can survive total dryness for longer than a year at 20 °C. Recovery is rapid as soon as water becomes available.

Alternation of generations

In common with all land plants[*] and some advanced algae, such as *Laminaria*, bryophytes exhibit **alternation of**

---

[*] All plant groups are terrestrial, although a few species have returned to water as a secondary adaptation, such as aquatic ferns and the flowering plant *Zostera*. 'Land plants' will refer to all plants. (Note that algae are no longer classified as plants.)

Table 3.6 Classification and characteristics of the Bryophyta.

Phylum Bryophyta

General characteristics
Alternation of generations in which the gametophyte generation is dominant
No vascular tissue, that is no xylem or phloem
Body is a thallus, or differentiated into simple 'leaves' and 'stems'
No true roots, stems or leaves: the gametophyte is anchored by filamentous rhizoids
Sporophyte is attached to, and is dependent upon, the gametophyte for its nutrition
Spores are produced by the sporophyte in a spore capsule on the end of a slender stalk above the gametophyte
Live mainly in damp, shady places

Class Hepaticae (or *Hepaticopsida*) (liverworts)	*Class Musci* (or *Bryopsida*) (mosses)
Gametophyte is a flattened structure that varies from being a thallus(rare) to 'leafy' with a stem(majority), with intermediate lobed types	Gametophyte 'leafy' with a stem and generally more differentiated than liverworts
'Leaves' (of leafy types) in three ranks along the stem	'Leaves' spirally arranged
Rhizoids unicellular	Rhizoids multicellular
Capsule of sporophyte splits into four valves for spore dispersal: elaters aid dispersal	Capsule of sporophyte has an elaborate mechanism of spore dispersal, dependent on dry conditions and involving teeth or pores; elaters absent

e.g. *Pellia*, a thallose liverwort
    Marchantia, a thallose liverwort, with antheridia and archegonia on stalked structures above the thallus
    Lophocolea, a leafy liverwort, common on rotting wood
	e.g. *Funaria*
	    Mnium, a common woodland moss similar in appearance to *Funaria*
	    Sphagnum, bog-moss: forms peat in wet acid habitats (bogs)

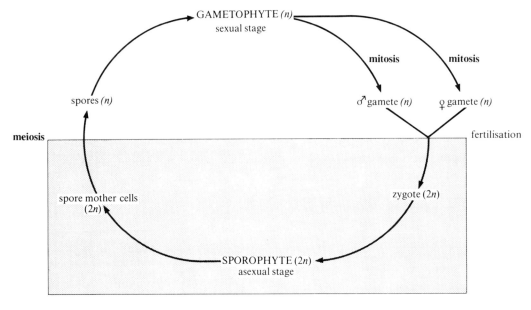

Fig 3.22 *Generalised life cycle of a plant showing alternation of generations. Note the haploid stages (n) and diploid stages (2n). The gametophyte is always haploid and always produces gametes by mitosis. The sporophyte is always diploid and always produces spores by meiosis*

generations. Two types of organism, a **haploid gametophyte** generation and a **diploid sporophyte** generation, alternate in the life cycle (the cycle from the zygote of one generation to the zygote of the next generation). The cycle is sum-marised in fig 3.22. The haploid generation is called the gametophyte (*gameto*, gamete; *phyton*, plant) because it undergoes sexual reproduction to produce gametes. Pro-duction of gametes involves mitosis, so the gametes are also haploid. The gametes fuse to form a diploid zygote which grows into the next generation, the diploid sporophyte generation. It is called the sporophyte because it undergoes asexual reproduction to produce spores. Production of spores involves meiosis, so that there is a return to the haploid condition. The haploid spores give rise to the gametophyte generation.

One of the two generations is always more conspicuous and occupies a greater proportion of the life cycle; this is said to be the **dominant generation**. In the bryophytes, the gametophyte generation is dominant. In all other land plants the sporophyte generation is dominant. It is customary to place the dominant generation in the top half of the life cycle diagram.

Fig 3.22 should be studied carefully because it summarises the life cycle of all land plants, including the flowering plants, which are the most advanced. One point that must be remembered is that gamete production involves mitosis, not meiosis as in animals; meiosis occurs in the production of spores.

3.6.2 Class Hepaticae – liverworts

Characteristics of the Hepaticae are summarised in table 3.6. They are more simple in structure than mosses and, on the whole, more confined to damp and shady habitats. They are found on the banks of streams, on damp rocks and in wet vegetation. Most liverworts show regular lobes or definite 'stems' with small, simple 'leaves'. The simplest of all though are the thalloid liverworts where the body is a flat thallus with no stem or leaves. One of these, *Pellia*, is used as an example.

Pellia is a liverwort common throughout Britain. The plant is a dull green with flat branches about 1 cm wide. Its external features are shown in fig 3.23.

3.6.3 Class Musci – mosses

Characteristics of the mosses are summarised in table 3.6. They have a more differentiated structure than liverworts but, like liverworts, are small and found mainly in damp habitats. They often form dense cushions.

Funaria is a common moss of fields, open woodland and disturbed ground, being one of the early colonisers of such ground. It is especially associated with freshly burned areas, for example after heath fires. It is also a common weed in greenhouses and gardens. Its external features are illustrated in fig 3.26.

Life cycle

The sex organs, male antheridia and female archegonia, are found at the tips of separate shoots on the gametophyte generation (see fig 3.25). Within them male and female gametes are produced from gamete mother cells whose nuclei divide by mitosis. A diagrammatic summary of the life cycle is shown in fig 3.24. Note that the sex organs protect the developing gametes from desiccation. The

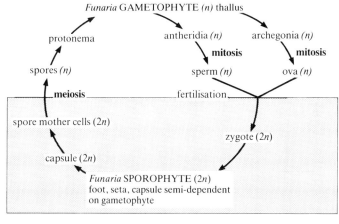

n = haploid

$2n$ = diploid

Fig 3.24 *Diagrammatic life cycle of* Funaria

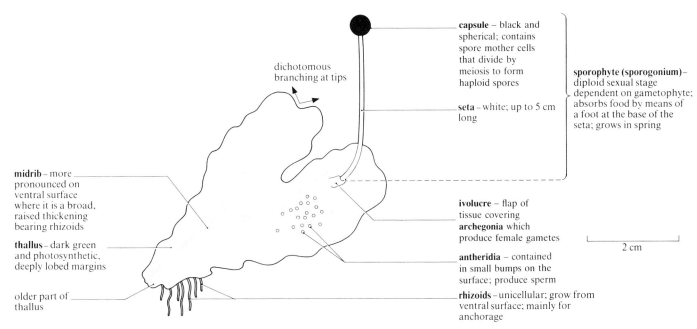

Fig 3.23 *External features of* Pellia. *The gametophyte is shown with the dependent sporophyte generation attached*

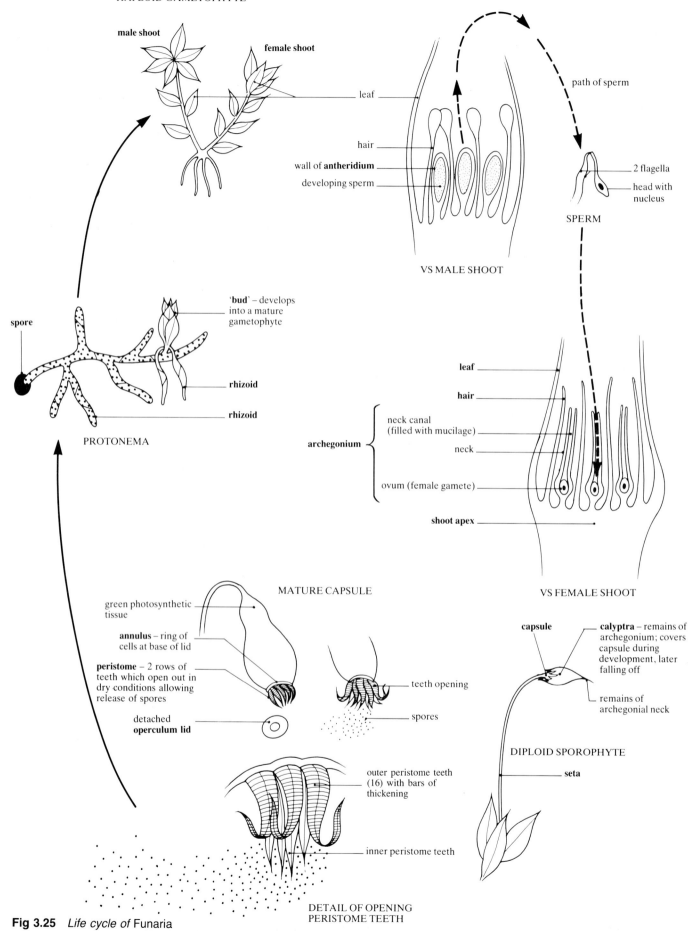

HAPLOID GAMETOPHYTE

male shoot

female shoot

leaf

hair

wall of **antheridium**

developing sperm

VS MALE SHOOT

path of sperm

2 flagella

head with nucleus

SPERM

spore

'**bud**' – develops into a mature gametophyte

rhizoid

rhizoid

PROTONEMA

leaf

hair

neck canal (filled with mucilage)

archegonium

neck

ovum (female gamete)

shoot apex

VS FEMALE SHOOT

MATURE CAPSULE

green photosynthetic tissue

annulus – ring of cells at base of lid

peristome – 2 rows of teeth which open out in dry conditions allowing release of spores

detached **operculum** lid

teeth opening

spores

outer peristome teeth (16) with bars of thickening

inner peristome teeth

DETAIL OF OPENING PERISTOME TEETH

capsule

calyptra – remains of archegonium; covers capsule during development, later falling off

remains of archegonial neck

DIPLOID SPOROPHYTE

seta

Fig 3.25 *Life cycle of* Funaria

ovum is also protected by mucilage found in the neck canal of the archegonium.

Fertilisation. Water is essential for fertilisation. When the surface of the plant is wet, mature antheridia absorb water and burst, releasing the male gametes (antherozoids or sperms) on to the surface. The sperms are biflagellate (have two flagella) and are produced in such large numbers that the fluid covering the plant has a milky appearance. They swim towards the archegonia, attracted by sucrose secreted by the archegonial necks. Such movement is an example of chemotaxis (section 15.1.2). Sperms swim down the neck of each archegonium to the venter at its base, which contains the female gamete or ovum. Fertilisation, that is fusion of the sperm nucleus with the ovum nucleus, takes place in the venter and the product is a diploid zygote.

Development of the zygote. Usually only one zygote develops. The zygote grows into a sporophyte, consisting of a foot, seta (stalk), and capsule. The foot grows back into the gametophyte and acts as an absorptive organ through which it obtains nutrients (fig 3.26). The developing sporophyte contains chloroplasts and therefore appears green and is capable of producing some of its own food requirements by photosynthesis. It is therefore, only semi-dependent on the gametophyte. As the sporophyte grows, the archegonium enlarges at first to contain it and is called the **calyptra**. Later, the sporophyte seta elongates and the calyptra ruptures and remains like a cap on the capsule until the latter is almost mature (fig 3.25).

Asexual reproduction. The sporophyte capsule contains spore mother cells that divide by meiosis to produce haploid spores. When mature the thin-walled cells of the annulus swell with water and force the lid off the capsule, exposing an inner and an outer ring of teeth (inner and outer peristome). Each ring contains 16 teeth. The outer teeth have specially thickened (lignified) walls which result in the teeth curling inwards and closing over the end of the capsule in damp conditions. In dry conditions they curl back and the inner teeth part, so allowing escape of spores (fig 3.25). Dry conditions favour dispersal (rain would quickly carry spores to the ground). The fact that the capsule is borne about 3 cm above the gametophyte by the seta also increases the chances of wind currents catching and dispersing the very light spores.

Germination. The spore germinates on finding a suitable damp habitat and grows to form a filamentous structure called a **protonema**, resembling a filamentous green alga. It produces several 'buds', each of which develops into a moss gametophyte. The life cycle of *Funaria* is summarised in fig 3.25.

Success of adaptation to land

Mosses are well adapted to a terrestrial environment in their mode of spore dispersal, which depends on the drying out of the capsule and the dispersal of small, light spores by wind. However, they still show a great reliance on water for the following reasons.

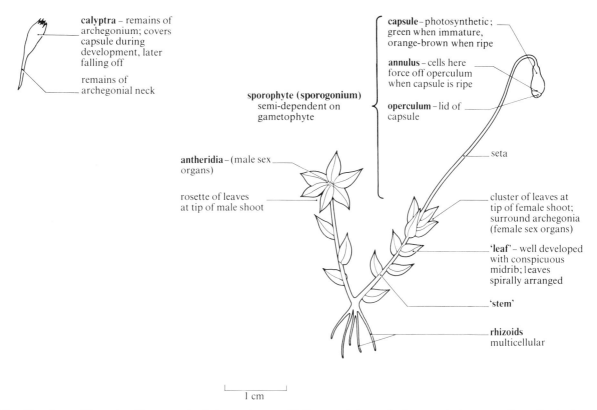

1 cm

Fig 3.26 *Structure of* Funaria. *The gametophyte is shown with the semi-dependent sporophyte generation attached*

(1) They are still dependent on water for reproduction because sperms must swim to the archegonia. They are adapted to release their sperms when water is available since only then do the antheridia burst. They are partly adapted to land because the gametes develop in protective structures, the antheridia and archegonia.

(2) There are no special supportive structures, so the plants are restricted in upward growth.

(3) They are dependent on availability of water and mineral salts close to or at the surface of the soil, because they have no roots to penetrate the substrate. However, rhizoids are present for anchorage, an adaptation to a solid substratum.

3.3 Liverworts and mosses have sometimes been described as the amphibians of the plant world. Briefly explain why this should be so.

3.7   Phyla Lycopodophyta (clubmosses), Sphenophyta (horsetails) and Filicinophyta (ferns)

The oldest known of these plants are fossils from the end of the Silurian period, 380 million years old. Whether these plants evolved from bryophytes or independently from algae is not known, but they are the earliest known vascular plants. **Vascular plants** are those containing **vascular tissue**, that is the conducting tissues of xylem and phloem. In order to emphasise what a major advance vascular tissue represents compared with the simple conducting cells of some bryophytes and algae, all vascular plants were formerly included in one division, the **Tracheophyta**, with clubmosses, horsetails and ferns and the more advanced group, the seed-bearing plants, being classified as subdivisions.

Vascular tissue is a feature of the sporophyte generation, that generation which in the bryophytes is small and dependent on the gametophyte. Its occurrence in the sporophyte and not the gametophyte generation is one reason why the sporophyte generation becomes conspicuous in all vascular plants.

Vascular tissue has two important properties of relevance here. Firstly, it forms a **transport system**, conducting food and water around the multicellular body, thus allowing development of large, complex bodies. Secondly, these bodies can be **supported** because xylem, apart from being a conducting tissue, contains lignified cells of great strength and rigidity. In some extinct ferns, xylem developed extensively as a result of secondary growth to form wood, which is the major supporting tissue of trees and shrubs. Another lignified tissue, sclerenchyma, also develops in vascular plants and supplements the mechani-

cal role of xylem (section 8.2.1). The vascular tissue of ferns shows certain basic features compared with flowering plants. The xylem contains tracheids rather than vessels and the phloem contains sieve cells rather than sieve tubes (section 8.2.2).

The earliest known vascular plants, the Psilopsida, a group which is now almost extinct, lacked roots, but these appeared later. Roots penetrate the soil with the result that water can be obtained more easily, the xylem conducting it to other parts of the plant. From the early groups of rooted plants the clubmosses, horsetails and ferns have survived to the present.

Once plant bodies could achieve support above the ground, there must have been competition for light and a tendency for taller forms to evolve. The period following the Silurian, the Devonian, is marked by the appearance of 'trees' up to 3 m tall and sometimes with woody trunks 2 m thick. By the next period, the Carboniferous, great swampy forests of giant clubmosses and horsetails were widespread, eventually giving rise to the coal seams of today. In these forests insects and amphibians first became abundant. Elsewhere, ferns and tree-ferns (not supported by any wood) also occurred, and these were the dominant vegetation for about 70 million years, from the Devonian to the Permian, when conifers and later flowering plants largely replaced them (see the geological time scale in appendix 5).

Despite these advances in adapting to a land environment, which are associated with the sporophyte generation, there remains the major problem of the gametophyte. This is even smaller and more susceptible to desiccation than the bryophyte gametophyte and is called a **prothallus**, dying as soon as it has reproduced to form the sporophyte. It produces sperms which must swim to reach the female gametes.

Heterospory

In some clubmosses and ferns, the gametophyte is protected by remaining in the spores of the previous sporophyte generation. In such cases there are two types of spore and the plants are therefore described as **heterosporous**. Plants producing one type of spore, like the bryophytes, are described as **homosporous**.

Heterosporous plants produce large spores called **megaspores** and small spores called **microspores**. Certain technical terms are applied to the structures associated with spore production and for convenience these are summarised in table 3.7 and fig 3.27.

Megaspores give rise to female gametophytes (prothalli) that bear archegonia, and microspores give rise to male gametophytes (prothalli) that bear antheridia. Sperms produced by the antheridia then travel to a female prothallus. Both male and female prothalli remain protected inside their respective spores. The microspore is small, can be produced in large numbers, and is dispersed by wind from the parent sporophyte; the male prothallus that the microspore contains is therefore dispersed with it.

Table 3.7 Glossary of terms associated with spore production.

strobilus or cone – a collection of sporophylls
sporophyll – a leaf which produces sporangia (*phyllon*, leaf)
megasporophyll – a leaf which produces a megasporangium
microsporophyll – a leaf which produces a microsporangium
sporangium – a structure in which spores are produced by plants; it is associated with asexual reproduction
megasporangium – a sporangium which produces megaspores
microsporangium – a sporangium which produces microspores
megaspore – a relatively large spore which grows to produce a female gametophyte
microspore – a relatively small spore which grows to produce a male gametophyte
homosporous – producing only one type of spore, e.g. *Pellia, Funaria, Dryopteris*
heterosporous – producing two types of spore, megaspores and microspores, e.g. *Selaginella* and all spermatophytes

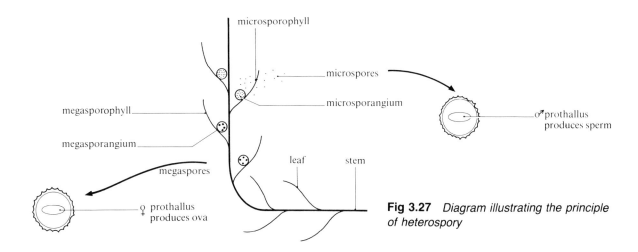

Fig 3.27 *Diagram illustrating the principle of heterospory*

Table 3.8 Classification and characteristics of the ferns, clubmosses and horsetails.

General characteristics
Alternation of generations in which the sporophyte generation is dominant
Gametophyte is reduced to a small, simple prothallus
Sporophyte has true roots, stems and leaves with vascular tissues

Phylum Lycopodophyta (clubmosses)	*Phylum Sphenophyta* (horsetails)	*Phylum Filicinophyta* (ferns)
Leaves relatively small (microphyllous*) and spirally arranged around the stem	Leaves relatively small (microphyllous*) and arranged in whorls around the stem	Leaves relatively large (macrophyllous*) and called fronds; spirally arranged around the stem
Homosporous and heterosporous forms	Homosporous	Homosporous (mostly)
Sporangia usually in strobili (cones)	Sporangia in strobili (cones) on distinctive sporangiophores	Sporangia usually in clusters (sori)
e.g. *Selaginella*, a heterosporous clubmoss *Lycopodium*, a homosporous clubmoss	e.g. *Equisetum* (only surviving genus)	e.g. *Dryopteris filix-mas* (male fern) *Pteridium* (bracken)

* microphyllous – having a single mid-vein. Usually small.   macrophyllous – having branching veins. Large.

The evolution of heterospory is an important step in the evolution of seed-bearing plants, as will be shown later.

3.7.1 Phylum Filicinophyta – ferns

Characteristics of the Filicinophyta are summarised in table 3.8. They are usually restricted to damp, shady habitats. Few ferns are capable of growing in full sunlight, although bracken (*Pteridium*) is a common exception. Ferns are common in tropical rain forests, where temperature, light and humidity are favourable.

The male fern (*Dryopteris filix-mas*) is probably the most common British fern and is found in damp woods, hedgerows and other shady places throughout the country.

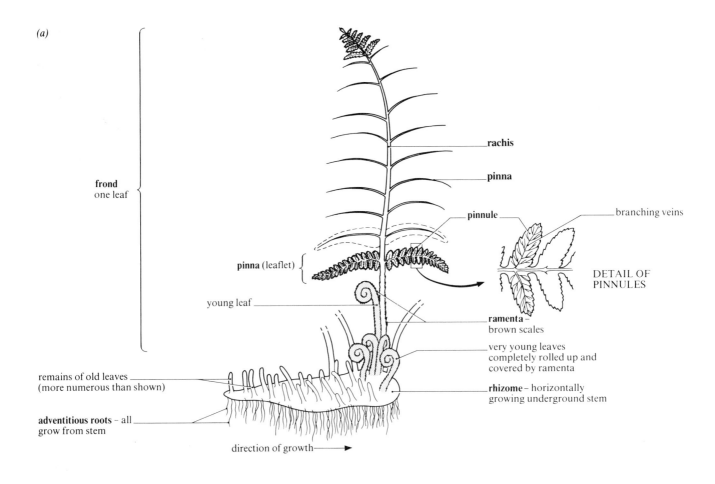

(a)

frond
one leaf

rachis

pinna

pinnule

branching veins

pinna (leaflet)

DETAIL OF
PINNULES

young leaf

ramenta –
brown scales

very young leaves
completely rolled up and
covered by ramenta

remains of old leaves
(more numerous than shown)

rhizome – horizontally
growing underground stem

adventitious roots – all
grow from stem

direction of growth →

(b)

(c)

rachis

pinna

pinnule

placenta
sorus

indusium

Fig 3.28 *External features of the sporophyte generation of Dryopteris filix-mas, the male fern. (a) Diagram with details of one pair of pinnae; others have the same structure. (b) The fronds. (c) Underside of frond showing sori (some covered with indusium)*

The **fronds** (leaves) of the sporophyte may reach a metre or more in height and grow from a thick horizontal stem, or **rhizome**. This bears **adventitious roots**. Branches from the main stem may eventually break away and give rise to separate plants, a form of vegetative reproduction. The bases of the fronds are covered with dry brown scales called **ramenta** that protect the young leaves from frost or drought. The young leaves show a characteristic tightly rolled structure. The ramenta gradually become smaller and less dense up the main axis of the frond. This axis is called the **rachis**, and the leaflets either side the **pinnae**. The small rounded subdivisions of the pinnae are called **pinnules**. The external features of the sporophyte of *Dryopteris filix-mas* are shown in fig 3.28.

Life cycle

A diagrammatic summary of the life cycle of *Dryopteris* is shown in fig 3.29.

Asexual reproduction. Spores are produced during late summer in structures called **sporangia**. Sporangia develop in clusters called **sori** on the undersides of pinnules (fig 3.29a). Each sorus has a protective covering called an **indusium**. Inside each sporangium diploid spore mother cells divide by meiosis to produce haploid spores. All the spores are identical, so *Dryopteris* is homosporous. When mature, the indusium shrivels and drops off, and the exposed sporangium walls begin to dry out. In each wall is a conspicuous strip of cells, the **annulus**, with thickenings on their inner and radial walls (fig 3.29b). The annulus extends only part of the way around the sporangium, and completing the circuit are thin-walled cells forming a region called the **stomium**. As the cells of the annulus dry, their thin outer walls are pulled inwards by the shrinking cytoplasm. The tension thus caused across the whole strip makes the cells of the adjacent stomium suddenly rupture and the annulus curl back. At the moment of rupture spores are catapulted from the sporangium. Eventually the cytoplasm pulls away from the annulus walls altogether, suddenly releasing the tension across the annulus so that it returns violently to its original position, throwing out the remaining spores.

Germination. The spores can remain dormant for a short period and when suitable moist conditions are present germinate to form the gametophyte generation. The gametophyte is a thin heart-shaped plate of cells about 1 cm in diameter (fig 3.29a). It is green and photosynthetic and is anchored by unicellular rhizoids to the soil. This delicate prothallus lacks a cuticle and is prone to drying out, so can only survive in damp conditions.

Sexual reproduction. The gametophyte (prothallus) produces simple antheridia and archegonia on its lower surface (fig 3.29a). These sex organs protect the gametes within them. Gametes are produced by mitosis of gamete mother cells, the antheridia producing sperm and

each archegonium an ovum, as in the bryophytes. Each sperm has a tuft of flagella. When ripe, and conditions are wet, each antheridium releases its sperm, which swim through a film of water towards the archegonia. This is a chemotactic response to malic acid (2-hydroxybutanedioic acid) secreted by the necks of the archegonia. Cross-fertilisation usually occurs because the antheridia mature before the archegonia. The product of fertilisation is a diploid zygote. Note that fertilisation is still dependent on water as in the bryophytes.

Development of the zygote. The zygote grows into the sporophyte generation. The young embryo develops a foot with which to absorb nutrients from the gametophyte until its own roots and leaves can take over the role of nutrition. The gametophyte soon withers and dies.

The life cycle is summarised non-pictorially in fig 3.30.

3.4 How are ferns better adapted to life on land than liverworts or mosses?

3.5 Which of the following are nutritionally self-supporting?
(a) Mature liverwort and moss gametophytes
(b) Mature liverwort and moss sporophytes
(c) Mature fern gametophytes
(d) Mature fern sporophytes

3.6 In what main respects are mosses, liverworts and ferns poorly adapted to life on land?

3.7 How can ferns spread?

3.8 How is the zygote of liverworts (or mosses) and ferns (a) protected, (b) supplied with food?

3.7.2   Phylum Lycopodophyta – clubmosses

Characteristics of the Lycopodophyta are summarised in table 3.8. Note that, despite their superficial resemblance to mosses, these plants are structurally more advanced than true mosses which are bryophytes. The Lycopodophyta were once far more extensive than they are today, with many tree species as mentioned on page 64. They are intermediate between ferns and seed plants in their adaptation to land.

Selaginella is a mainly tropical genus, with one British species, *S. selaginoides*. It is quite common in mountainous areas of north-west Britain, favouring moist conditions on wet rocks and pastures and being common near streams. It has a creeping stem, that is one that usually lies flat on the ground, with short erect branches. The external features of a common greenhouse species of *Selaginella, S. kraussiana*, are shown in fig 3.31. It has small leaves produced in four rows and arranged in opposite pairs, each pair having one larger (lower) and one smaller (upper) leaf. Each leaf has a **ligule**, a small, membranous outgrowth near its base.

Fig 3.29 *(a) Life cycle of* Dryopteris filix-mas

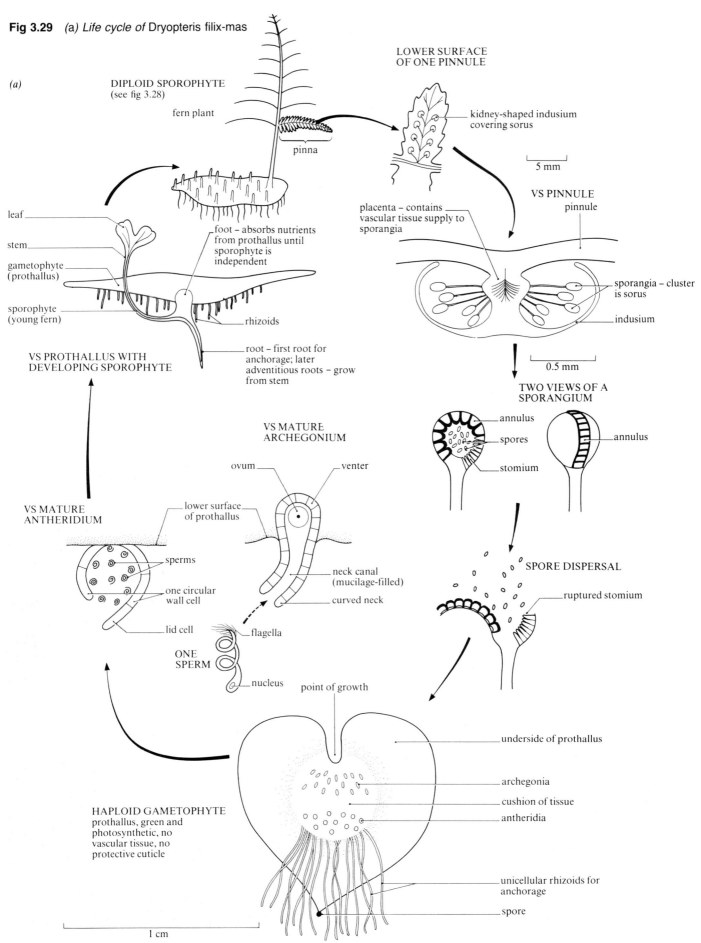

(a)

DIPLOID SPOROPHYTE
(see fig 3.28)

fern plant

pinna

LOWER SURFACE
OF ONE PINNULE

kidney-shaped indusium
covering sorus

5 mm

VS PINNULE
pinnule

placenta – contains
vascular tissue supply to
sporangia

sporangia – cluster
is sorus

indusium

0.5 mm

leaf

stem

gametophyte
(prothallus)

sporophyte
(young fern)

foot – absorbs nutrients
from prothallus until
sporophyte is
independent

rhizoids

root – first root for
anchorage; later
adventitious roots – grow
from stem

VS PROTHALLUS WITH
DEVELOPING SPOROPHYTE

TWO VIEWS OF A
SPORANGIUM

annulus

spores

stomium

annulus

VS MATURE
ARCHEGONIUM

ovum

venter

lower surface
of prothallus

neck canal
(mucilage-filled)

curved neck

VS MATURE
ANTHERIDIUM

sperms

one circular
wall cell

lid cell

flagella

ONE
SPERM

nucleus

SPORE DISPERSAL

ruptured stomium

point of growth

underside of prothallus

archegonia

cushion of tissue

antheridia

unicellular rhizoids for
anchorage

spore

HAPLOID GAMETOPHYTE
prothallus, green and
photosynthetic, no
vascular tissue, no
protective cuticle

1 cm

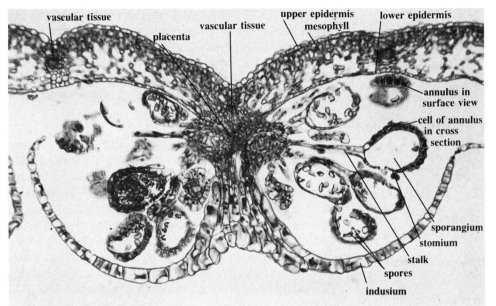

vascular tissue

placenta

vascular tissue

upper epidermis
mesophyll

lower epidermis

annulus in
surface view

cell of annulus
in cross
section

sporangium

stomium

stalk

spores

indusium

(b)

Fig 3.29 (cont.) *(b)–(e) photomicrographs. (b) LS of a sorus. (c) LS antheridia. (d) LS archegonium. (e) prothallus with first frond emerging.*

(c)

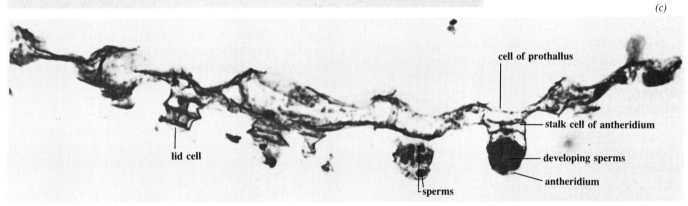

cell of prothallus

stalk cell of antheridium

developing sperms

antheridium

sperms

lid cell

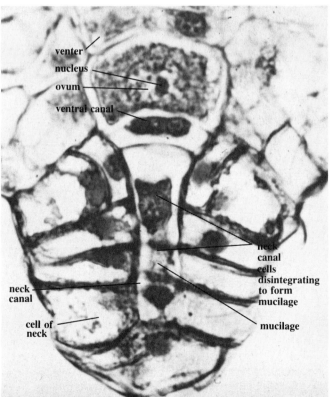

venter

nucleus

ovum

ventral canal

neck
canal
cells
disintegrating
to form
mucilage

mucilage

neck
canal

cell of
neck

(d)

1mm

first
sporophyte leaf

sporophyte stem

gametophyte
prothallus

apical notch
of prothallus

(e)

69

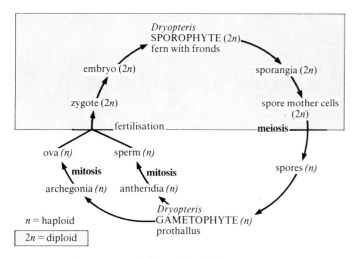

Fig 3.30 *Diagrammatic life cycle of* Dryopteris filix-mas

Root-like structures called **rhizophores** grow down from the stem and branch into adventitious roots at their free ends.

Reproduction involves the production of vertical branches called **strobili**, or **cones**, differing in structure from the rest of the plant. They consist of four vertical rows of leaves of equal size that produce sporangia on their dorsal surfaces, and are therefore **sporophylls**.

Life cycle

A diagrammatic summary of the life cycle of *Selaginella* is shown in fig 3.32. For the meanings of some of the terms used below, consult table 3.7.

Asexual reproduction. *Selaginella* produces strobili or cones as described above. The lower leaves are megasporophylls producing megasporangia, while the upper leaves are microsporophylls producing microsporangia (fig 3.33). Each megasporangium produces four megaspores and each microsporangium produces many microspores; in both cases the spore mother cells undergo meiosis. Since there are two types of spore, *Selaginella* is described as heterosporous.

Spore development and sexual reproduction. The microspores develop into male gametophytes. During development the microspores are released and they may be dispersed or sift down the strobilus to the megasporophylls. The contents of each microspore become a male prothallus, consisting of one vegetative cell and a single antheridium, inside which flagellate sperm are produced by mitosis. The prothallus, a reduced gametophyte generation, is non-photosynthetic and entirely dependent on food stored within the microspore. This food can therefore be traced back to the sporophyte generation.

The megaspores develop into female gametophytes. Again development begins before the spores are shed and the contents of each megaspore become a female prothallus, a reduced gametophyte generation. The top of the prothallus is revealed by the spore splitting. It develops rhizoids and becomes partially green and photosynthetic. However, most of its food, like that of the male gametophyte, comes from a food store in the spore and is derived from the previous sporophyte generation. The female prothallus produces archegonia at its surface, inside each of which an ovum is produced by mitosis.

Note that the mature gametophytes are *not* independent plants, unlike all the previous examples of land plants studied in this chapter. This is an important evolutionary

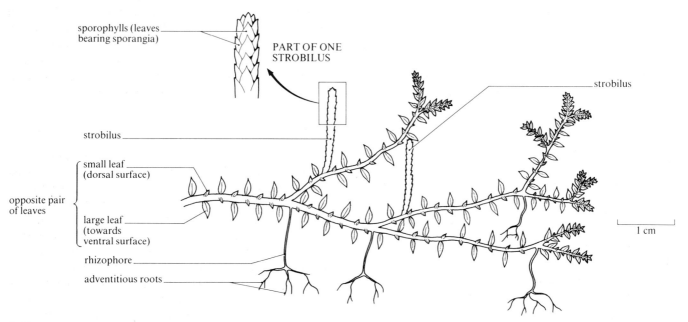

3.31 *External features of the sporophyte generation of* Selaginella kraussiana, *a common greenhouse species. In* Selaginella selaginoides, *the only naturally occurring British species, all leaves are the same size. Also, it lacks rhizophores, having adventitious roots only*

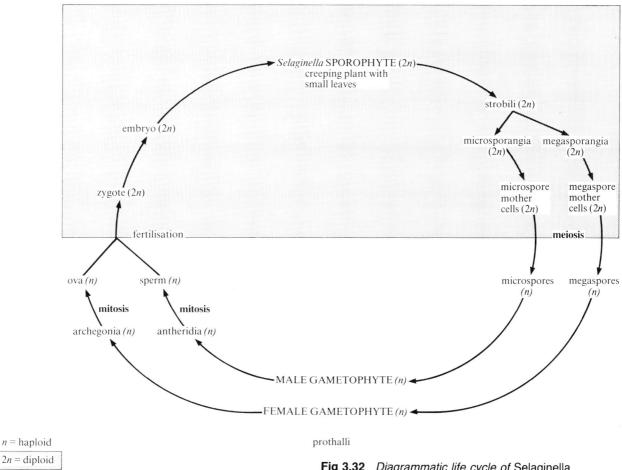

n = haploid

2*n* = diploid

prothalli

Fig 3.32 *Diagrammatic life cycle of* Selaginella

advance, an adaptation to life on land that results in the gametophyte generation, previously vulnerable to desiccation, now being partly protected by the spore. No longer free-living, it is supplied with food stored in the spore by the preceding sporophyte generation.

This advantage is accompanied by the disadvantage that sperm have to travel from the male prothallus, inside the microspore, to the female prothallus inside the megaspore. Self-fertilisation of the gametophyte is no longer possible, and the spores (and hence gametophytes) may be widely separated if dispersed.

Fertilisation. The walls of the microspores rupture and the sperm escape. Moist conditions are still needed for this to occur, and sperm swim to the archegonia of the female prothallus. The latter is still in the megaspore, and this may still be on the parent sporophyte or may have been released. Sperm swim down the neck of the archegonium and one will fuse with the ovum to produce a diploid zygote.

Development of the zygote. The zygote develops into an embryo sporophyte. The upper part of the embryo becomes an elongated structure, the **suspensor**, that pushes the embryo down into the food store of the gametophyte and megaspore. The embryo develops a root,

stem and leaves, obtaining food through an absorptive foot until it is an independent, photosynthetic plant.

Note that the larger size of the megaspore compared with the microspore is due to the food it contains, enabling both the female gametophyte and the embryo of the succeeding sporophyte generation to grow. Thus food made by one sporophyte generation is used in the early development of the next sporophyte generation. The life cycle of *Selaginella* is summarised pictorially in fig 3.33.

3.7.3 Phylum Sphenophyta – horsetails

Characteristics of the Sphenophyta are summarised in table 3.8. *Equisetum* is the only surviving genus and has about 25 species distributed throughout the world (except in Australia). Many are associated with damp or wet habitats, such as ponds and marshes. However, *Equisetum arvense*, the common or field horsetail, is common throughout Britain in drier places such as fields and roadsides, wasteground and gardens.

The sporophytes have horizontal underground stems (rhizomes) and aerial shoots usually less than a metre in height. The shoots have characteristic whorls of small pointed scale leaves at each node. They may be 'sterile' vegetative shoots or 'fertile' shoots bearing strobili (cones).

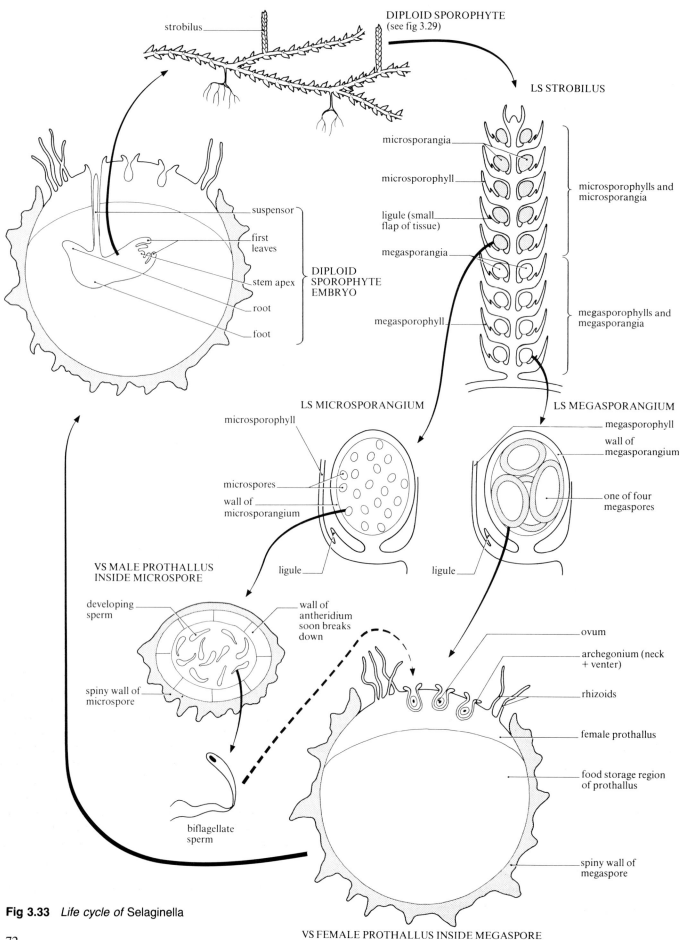

strobilus

DIPLOID SPOROPHYTE
(see fig 3.29)

LS STROBILUS

microsporangia

microsporophyll

ligule (small
flap of tissue)

megasporangia

megasporophyll

microsporophylls and
microsporangia

megasporophylls and
megasporangia

suspensor

first
leaves

stem apex

root

foot

DIPLOID
SPOROPHYTE
EMBRYO

LS MICROSPORANGIUM

microsporophyll

microspores

wall of
microsporangium

ligule

LS MEGASPORANGIUM

megasporophyll
wall of
megasporangium

one of four
megaspores

ligule

VS MALE PROTHALLUS
INSIDE MICROSPORE

developing
sperm

spiny wall of
microspore

wall of
antheridium
soon breaks
down

ovum

archegonium (neck
+ venter)

rhizoids

female prothallus

food storage region
of prothallus

spiny wall of
megaspore

biflagellate
sperm

VS FEMALE PROTHALLUS INSIDE MEGASPORE

Fig 3.33 *Life cycle of* Selaginella

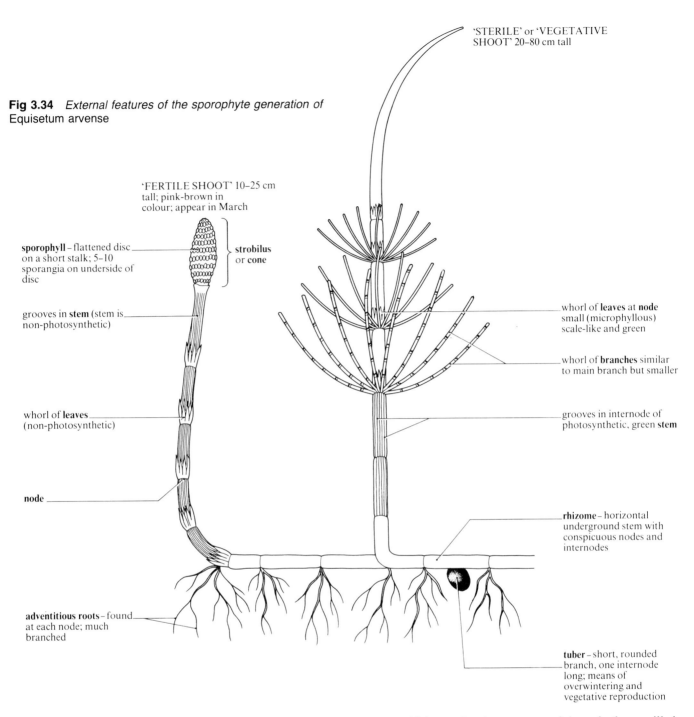

Fig 3.34 *External features of the sporophyte generation of* Equisetum arvense

'STERILE' or 'VEGETATIVE SHOOT' 20–80 cm tall

'FERTILE SHOOT' 10–25 cm tall; pink-brown in colour; appear in March

sporophyll – flattened disc on a short stalk; 5–10 sporangia on underside of disc

strobilus or **cone**

grooves in **stem** (stem is non-photosynthetic)

whorl of **leaves** (non-photosynthetic)

node

adventitious roots – found at each node; much branched

whorl of **leaves** at **node** small (microphyllous) scale-like and green

whorl of **branches** similar to main branch but smaller

grooves in internode of photosynthetic, green **stem**

rhizome – horizontal underground stem with conspicuous nodes and internodes

tuber – short, rounded branch, one internode long; means of overwintering and vegetative reproduction

Sterile shoots are green and have a whorl of narrow branches, as well as scale leaves, at each node. Fertile shoots of most species are pale brown to colourless, unbranched, and with a single strobilus at the apex; in some species they are green and branching. Internodes (the regions between nodes) of all parts have a number of longitudinally running grooves and the main branches are hollow. The external features of *E. arvense* are illustrated in fig 3.34.

3.8 Seed-bearing plants

The most successful group of land plants have seeds. In this section stress will be placed on the adapta-tions which made them successful and they will be compared with the less advanced groups already studied.

The seed-bearing plants probably have their origin among extinct seed-producing members of the clubmosses, horsetails and ferns. If the clubmoss *Selaginella* has been studied it will be noted that its life cycle is essentially the same as that of seed plants, except that in *Selaginella* the megaspore is released whereas in seed plants it is retained. However, it will be assumed in the following discussion that *Selaginella* has not been studied and the life cycle of seed plants will be compared with that of homosporous plants like the ferns.

One of the main problems for plants living on land is the vulnerability of the gametophyte generation. For example, in ferns the gametophyte is a delicate prothallus and it produces male gametes, or sperm, dependent on water for swimming. In seed plants, however, the gametophyte generation is protected and very much reduced. It is only by comparing the life cycle of seed plants with those of more primitive plants that it becomes obvious that alternation of generations still occurs in seed plants. Three important advances have been made by seed plants, first the development of heterospory, secondly the development of seeds, and thirdly the development of non-swimming male gametes.

Heterospory

An important advance towards the seed-plant life cycle came with the evolution of plants that produced two types of spore, microspores and megaspores. Such plants are termed **heterosporous** and are discussed in the introduction (section 3.7). Table 3.7 contains a glossary of terms relating to spore production in the life cycle of heterosporous types (see also fig 3.27). All seed plants are heterosporous.

The contents of a microspore become a male gametophyte, and those of a megaspore become a female gametophyte. In both cases the mature gametophyte is very reduced and is not released from the spore, unlike the free-living independent gametophytes of homosporous plants such as *Dryopteris*. By being retained within the spores, the gametophytes are protected from desiccation, an important adaptation to life on land. They are non-photosynthetic and dependent on food stored in the spores by the preceding sporophyte generation. The most extreme reduction of gametophytes takes place in the flowering plants, as will be discussed later.

Megaspores are produced in megasporangia on megasporophylls and microspores in microsporangia on microsporophylls. The equivalent structure to a megasporangium in a seed plant is called an **ovule**. Within an ovule only

one megaspore or female gametophyte develops, and this is called an **embryo sac**. The equivalent structure to a microsporangium is called a **pollen sac**. Within the pollen sac many microspores develop which are called **pollen grains**.

Evolution of seeds

In seed plants, the megaspores are not released from the sporophyte, unlike the situation in more ancestral heterosporous plants. Instead they are retained in the ovules (megasporangia) still attached to the sporophyte. Inside each megaspore, the female gametophyte (embryo sac) develops and produces one or more female gametes, or ova. Once the female gamete is fertilised, the ovule is called a **seed**. Thus a seed is a fertilised ovule. The ovule, later the seed, has the following main advantages associated with it.

(1) The female gametophyte is protected by the ovule. It is totally dependent upon the parent sporophyte and is not susceptible to desiccation as would be a free-living gametophyte.

(2) After fertilisation it develops a food store, supplied by the parent sporophyte plant to which it is still attached. The food will be used by the developing zygote (the next sporophyte generation) at germination.

(3) The seed is specialised to resist adverse conditions and can remain dormant until conditions are suitable for germination.

(4) The seed may be modified to facilitate dispersal from the parent gametophyte.

The seed is a complex structure because it contains cells from three generations, a parent sporophyte, a female gametophyte and the embryo of the next sporophyte

Fig 3.35 *Relationships between the gametophyte and sporophyte generations in different groups of plants*

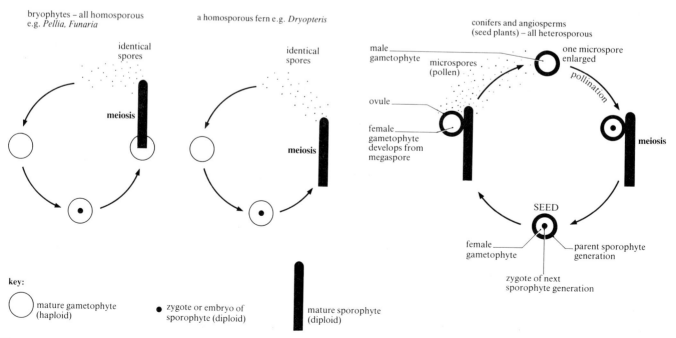

key:

mature gametophyte (haploid)

zygote or embryo of sporophyte (diploid)

mature sporophyte (diploid)

74

generation. This is summarised in fig 3.35. All the essentials for life are supplied by the parent sporophyte and it is not until the seed is mature, containing a food store and an embryo sporophyte, that it is dispersed from the parent sporophyte.

Evolution of non-swimming male gametes, and fertilisation independent of water

In the groups previously studied, sexual reproduction has been achieved by sperm swimming in surface moisture to the ova. With seed plants certain problems arise. Male gametes must reach the female gametes for fertilisation to be achieved and it has already been noted that male and female gametophytes develop separately, the latter being retained in the ovules of the sporophyte. Male gametes are produced by the male gametophytes inside the microspores, or pollen grains. Instead of developing as swimming sperm, the male gametes remain non-motile and are carried by pollen grains from the pollen sacs (microsporangia) to the vicinity of the ovules. This transfer is called **pollination**. The final stage of transfer involves growth of a **pollen tube** towards the ovule, down which the non-motile male gametes can pass to achieve fertilisation. At no stage then is water necessary for sperm. Only in a few primitive seed plants, such as the cycads, are sperm released from the pollen tubes, an indication of a link with non-seed-bearing plants. Fig 3.35 compares the life cycle of seed plants with representative non-seed-bearing plants in a way that emphasises the nature of seeds and the relationships between sporophyte and gametophyte generations.

The requirement for pollination is a possible disadvantage since the process is likely to be haphazard and difficult to achieve, and the production of large amounts of pollen is biologically expensive. Originally pollination is thought to have been achieved by wind. However, early in the evolution of seed plants flying insects appeared (in the Carboniferous era about 300 million years ago) bringing the possibility of more efficient pollination by insects. One group of seed plants, the flowering plants, have exploited this method to a high degree.

> **3.9** The chances of survival and development of wind-blown pollen grains (microspores) are much less than those of spores of *Dryopteris*. Why?
>
> **3.10** Account for the fact that megaspores are large and microspores are small.

3.8.1 Classification and characteristics of seed-bearing plants

Classification and characteristics of the seed-bearing plants are summarised in table 3.9.

Table 3.9 shows the two groups of seed-bearing plants, the **conifers** and **angiosperms**. The latter are commonly known as the flowering plants. In conifers ovules, later seeds, are located on the surfaces of specialised leaves called megasporophylls or **ovuliferous scales**. These are arranged in cones. In angiosperms seeds are enclosed, affording even more protection to the gametophyte and subsequent zygote. The structures enclosing the seeds are **carpels** and are thought to be equivalent to megasporophylls (leaves) which are folded up to enclose the ovules (megasporangia). One or more carpels may be present.

The hollow base of a carpel, or group of fused carpels, is

Table 3.9 Classification and characteristics of the seed-bearing plants.

Seed-bearing plants
General characteristics
Heterosporous, i.e. two types of spore: microspores and megaspores; microspore = pollen grain, megaspore = embryo sac
The embryo sac (megaspore) remains completely enclosed in the ovule (megasporangium); a fertilised ovule is a seed.
Sporophyte is the dominant generation; gametophyte generation is severely reduced
Water is not needed for sexual reproduction because male gametes do not swim (except in a few primitive members); they are conveyed to the ovum by a pollen tube to effect fertilisation
Complex vascular tissues in roots, stems and leaves

Phylum Coniferophyta (mainly conifers; yews, cycads, ginkgos and others belong to different phyla (see below))	*Phylum Angiospermophyta* (flowering plants)
'Naked' seeds: this means that the seeds are exposed, i.e. not enclosed in an ovary	Seeds are enclosed in an ovary
Usually cones on which sporangia and spores develop	Produce flowers in which sporangia and spores develop
No fruit because no ovary	After fertilisation, the ovary develops into a fruit
No vessels in xylem, only tracheids; no companion cells in phloem, only albuminous cells (similar in function to companion cells, but different in origin)	Xylem contains vessels; phloem contains companion cells
Phylum Cycadophyta – cycads *Phylum* Ginkgophyta – ginkgos	*Classes* Dicotyledoneae and Monocotyledoneae (see table 3.9)

called an **ovary**. The ovary encloses the ovules. After fertilisation the ovary is called a **fruit** and the ovules are called **seeds**. Either the fruit or the seed (sometimes both) is modified to assist in dispersal.

Fig 3.36 compares, by means of simple diagrams, the different spore-bearing structures of vascular plants and enables a comparison to be made of some of the terms which have been used.

3.8.2 Phylum Coniferophyta

Characteristics of the Coniferophyta are summarised in table 3.9.

Conifers are a successful group of plants of worldwide distribution, accounting for about one-third of the world's forests. They are trees or shrubs, mostly evergreen, with needle-like leaves. Most of the species are found at higher altitudes and further north than any other trees. Conifers are commercially important as 'softwoods', being used not only for timber but for resins, turpentine and wood pulp. They include pines, larches (which are deciduous), firs, spruces and cedars. A typical conifer *Pinus sylvestris*, the Scots pine, is described below.

Pinus sylvestris is found throughout central and northern Europe, Russia and North America. It is native to Scotland, though it has been introduced elsewhere in Britain. It is planted for ornament and timber, being a stately, attractive tree up to 36 m in height with a characteristic pink to orange-brown flaking bark. It grows most commonly on sandy or poor mountain soils and consequently the root system is often shallow and spreading. Its external features are illustrated in fig 3.37.

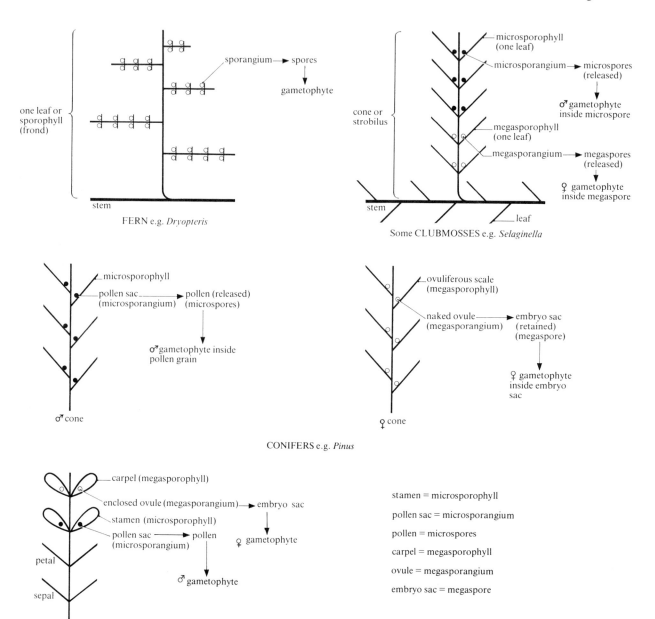

Fig 3.36 *Diagrammatic comparison of spore-bearing structures in vascular plants*

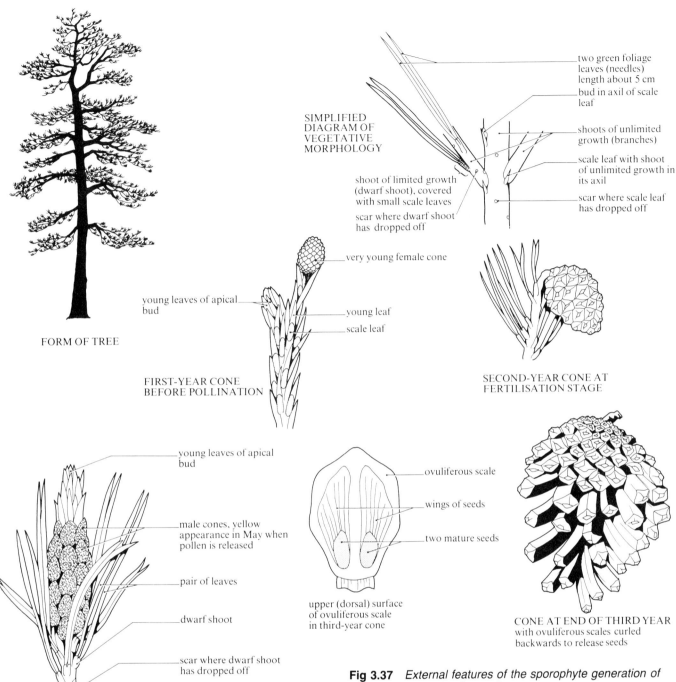

FORM OF TREE

SIMPLIFIED
DIAGRAM OF
VEGETATIVE
MORPHOLOGY

two green foliage
leaves (needles)
length about 5 cm

bud in axil of scale
leaf

shoots of unlimited
growth (branches)

scale leaf with shoot
of unlimited growth in
its axil

scar where scale leaf
has dropped off

shoot of limited growth
(dwarf shoot), covered
with small scale leaves

scar where dwarf shoot
has dropped off

young leaves of apical
bud

very young female cone

young leaf

scale leaf

FIRST-YEAR CONE
BEFORE POLLINATION

SECOND-YEAR CONE AT
FERTILISATION STAGE

young leaves of apical
bud

male cones, yellow
appearance in May when
pollen is released

pair of leaves

dwarf shoot

scar where dwarf shoot
has dropped off

ovuliferous scale

wings of seeds

two mature seeds

upper (dorsal) surface
of ovuliferous scale
in third-year cone

CONE AT END OF THIRD YEAR
with ovuliferous scales curled
backwards to release seeds

GROUP OF MALE CONES

Fig 3.37 *External features of the sporophyte generation of* Pinus sylvestris, *the Scots pine*

Each year a whorl of lateral buds around the stem grows out into a whorl of branches. The roughly conical appearance of *Pinus* and other conifers is due to the transition from whorls of shorter (younger) branches at the tops to longer (older) branches lower down. The latter usually die and drop off as the tree grows, leaving the mature trees bare for some distance up their trunks (fig 3.37).

The main branches and trunk continue growth from year to year by the activity of an apical bud. They are said to show **unlimited growth**. They have spirally arranged scale leaves, in the axils of which are buds that develop into very short branches (2–3 mm) called **dwarf shoots**. These are shoots of **limited growth** and at their tips grow two leaves. Once the shoot has grown, the scale leaf at its base drops off leaving a scar. The leaves are needle-like, reducing the surface area available for the loss of water. They are also covered with a thick, waxy cuticle and have sunken stomata, further adaptations for conserving water. These xeromorphic features ensure that the tree does not lose too much water from its evergreen leaves during cold seasons, when water may be frozen or difficult to absorb from the soil. After two to three years the dwarf shoots and leaves drop off together, leaving a further scar.

The tree is the sporophyte generation and is heterosporous. In spring, male and female cones are produced on the same tree. The male cones are about 0.5 cm in diameter, rounded and found in clusters behind the apical buds at the bases of new shoots. They develop in the axils of scale leaves in the place of dwarf shoots. Female cones arise in the axils of scale leaves at the tips of new strong shoots, at some distance from the male cones and in a more scattered arrangement. Since they take three years to complete growth and development, they are of various sizes, ranging from about 0.5–6 cm on a given tree. They are green when young, becoming brown or reddish-brown in their second year. Both male and female cones consist of spirally arranged, closely packed sporophylls around a central axis (fig 3.37).

Each sporophyll of a male cone has two microsporangia or pollen sacs on its lower surface. Inside each pollen sac, pollen mother cells divide by meiosis to form pollen grains or microspores. Each grain has two large air sacs to aid in wind dispersal. During May the cones become yellow in appearance as they release clouds of pollen. At the end of the summer they wither and drop off.

Each sporophyll of a female cone consists of a lower bract scale and a larger upper ovuliferous scale. On its upper surface are two ovules side by side, inside of which one megaspore mother cell divides by meiosis to produce four megaspores. Only one of these develops. Pollination takes place during the first year of the cone's development, but fertilisation does not take place until the pollen tubes grow during the following spring. The fertilised ovules become winged seeds. They continue to mature during the second year and are dispersed during the third year. By this time the cone is relatively large and woody and the scales bend outwards to expose the seeds prior to wind dispersal.

3.8.3 Phylum Angiospermophyta – flowering plants

Characteristics of the Angiospermophyta are summarised in table 3.9.

Angiosperms are better adapted to life on land than any other plants. After their appearance during the Cretaceous period, 135 million years ago, they rapidly took over from conifers as the dominant land vegetation on a world scale, and proliferated as different habitats were successfully exploited. Some angiosperms even returned to fresh water, and a few to salt water.

One of the most characteristic features of angiosperms, apart from the enclosed seeds already mentioned, is the presence of flowers instead of cones. This has enabled many of them to utilise insects, and occasionally birds or even bats, as agents of pollination. In order to attract these animals, flowers are usually brightly coloured, scented and offer pollen or nectar as food. In some cases the flowers have become indispensable to the insects. The result is that, in some cases, the evolution of insects and flowering plants has become closely linked and there are many highly specialised, mutually dependent, relationships. The flower generally becomes adapted to maximise the chances of pollen transfer by the insect and the process is therefore more reliable than wind pollination. Insect-pollinated plants need not, therefore, produce as much pollen as wind-pollinated plants. Nevertheless, many flowers are specialised for wind pollination.

Life cycle

The life cycle of a typical flowering plant is summarised in fig 3.38.

The purpose of fig 3.38 is to emphasise the links with the life cycles of more primitive plants, a detailed description of the life cycle being reserved for section 20.2. It is still the same, in essence, as that shown in fig 3.22. Note particularly the stages at which meiosis and mitosis occur. Gametes are still produced by mitosis, and spores by meiosis, as in other plants with alternation of generations. Strictly speaking, the flower is an organ of both asexual and sexual reproduction since it produces spores (asexual reproduction) within which gametes are produced (sexual reproduction). Note that a pollen grain is a spore, not a male gamete, as it *contains* male gametes. As noted before, the pollen grain carries the male gametes to the female parts, thus avoiding the need for swimming sperm.

The process of endosperm development is also shown in fig 3.38. The endosperm develops into a food store and the manner of its formation is unique to angiosperms.

Dicotyledons and monocotyledons

The angiosperms are divided into two major groups that are given the status of classes. The most commonly used names for the two groups are the monocotyledons and dicotyledons, usually abbreviated to **monocots** and **dicots**. A summary of the ways in which they differ is given in table 3.10. Few of the differences are diagnostic if used alone, since exceptions may exist, but a combination of several characters would lead to positive identification. The modern view is that monocots probably evolved from ancestral dicots.

Angiosperms may be **herbaceous** (non-woody) or **woody**. Woody plants become shrubs or trees. They grow large amounts of secondary xylem (wood) that offers support, as well as being a conducting tissue, and is produced as a result of the activity of the vascular cambium. Herbaceous plants, or herbs, rely on turgidity and smaller quantities of mechanical tissues such as collenchyma, sclerenchyma and xylem for support, and they are consequently smaller plants. They either lack a vascular cambium or, if present, it shows restricted activity. Many herbaceous plants are **annuals**, completing their life

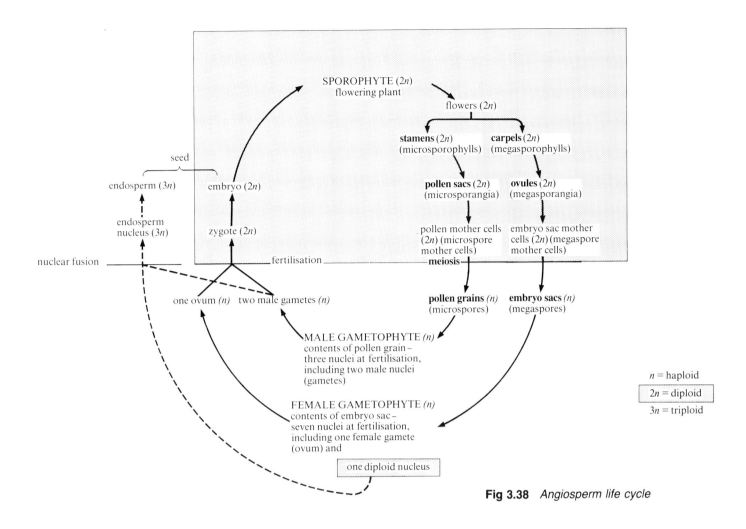

Fig 3.38 *Angiosperm life cycle*

Table 3.10 Major differences between dicotyledons and monocotyledons.

	Class Dicotyledoneae	*Class Monocotyledoneae*
Leaf morphology	Reticulate venation (net-like pattern of veins)	Parallel venation (veins are parallel)
	Lamina (blade) and petiole (leaf stalk)	Lanceolate (elongate)
	Dorso-ventral (dorsal and ventral surfaces differ)	Identical dorsal and ventral surfaces
Stem anatomy	Ring of vascular bundles	Vascular bundles scattered
	Vascular cambium usually present, giving rise to secondary growth	Vascular cambium usually absent, so no secondary growth (exceptions occur, e.g. palms)
Root morphology	Primary root persists as a tap root that develops lateral roots (secondary roots)	Adventitious roots from the base of the stem take over from the primary root, giving rise to a fibrous root system
Root anatomy	Few groups of xylem (2–8) (see section 14.5)	Many groups of xylem (commonly up to 30)
	Vascular cambium often present, giving rise to secondary growth	Vascular cambium usually absent, so no secondary growth
Seed morphology	Embryo has two cotyledons (seed leaves)	Embryo has one cotyledon
Flowers	Parts mainly in fours and fives	Parts usually in threes
	Perianth segments usually differ forming a calyx and corolla.	Perianth segments identical, with no distinct calyx and corolla
	Often insect pollinated	Often wind pollinated
Examples	Pea, rose, buttercup, dandelion	Grasses, iris, orchids, lilies

cycles from germination to seed production in one year. Some produce organs of perennation such as bulbs, corms and tubers by means of which they overwinter or survive periods of adverse conditions such as drought (section 20.1.1). They may then be **biennial** or **perennial**, that is they produce their seeds and die in their second year or they survive from year to year. Shrubs and trees are perennial, and may be **evergreen**, producing and shedding leaves all year round so that leaves are always present, or **deciduous**, shedding leaves in seasons of cold or drought.

The morphology (structure) of representative angiosperms will be described in figs 3.40–43 to illustrate their diversity.

(a)

(b)

Fig 3.39 *Structure of a (a) monocot and (b) a dicot leaf*

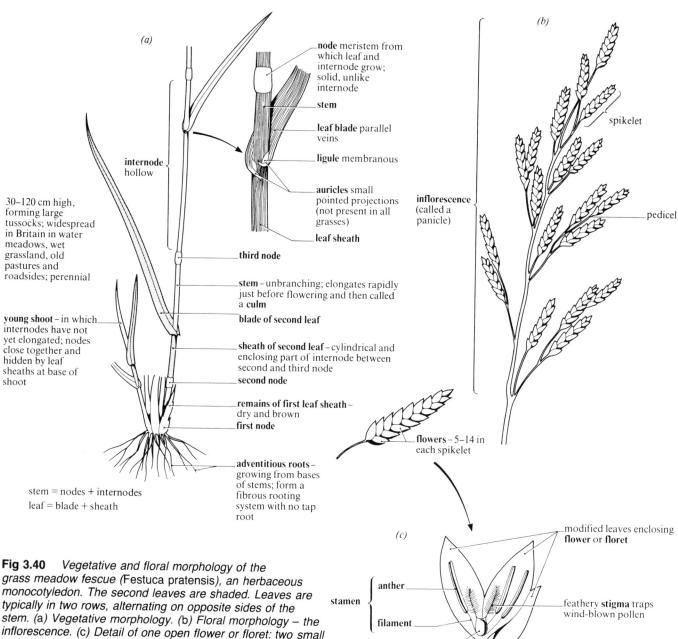

(a)

(b)

node meristem from which leaf and internode grow; solid, unlike internode

stem

leaf blade parallel veins

ligule membranous

auricles small pointed projections (not present in all grasses)

leaf sheath

third node

stem – unbranching; elongates rapidly just before flowering and then called a **culm**

blade of second leaf

sheath of second leaf – cylindrical and enclosing part of internode between second and third node

second node

remains of first leaf sheath – dry and brown

first node

adventitious roots – growing from bases of stems; form a fibrous rooting system with no tap root

internode hollow

30–120 cm high, forming large tussocks; widespread in Britain in water meadows, wet grassland, old pastures and roadsides; perennial

young shoot – in which internodes have not yet elongated; nodes close together and hidden by leaf sheaths at base of shoot

stem = nodes + internodes
leaf = blade + sheath

inflorescence (called a **panicle**)

spikelet

pedicel

flowers – 5–14 in each spikelet

(c)

modified leaves enclosing **flower** or **floret**

stamen { **anther** **filament** }

feathery **stigma** traps wind-blown pollen

ovary

Fig 3.40 *Vegetative and floral morphology of the grass meadow fescue* (Festuca pratensis), *an herbaceous monocotyledon. The second leaves are shaded. Leaves are typically in two rows, alternating on opposite sides of the stem. (a) Vegetative morphology. (b) Floral morphology – the inflorescence. (c) Detail of one open flower or floret: two small petal-like structures (lodicules) which enclose the ovary have been omitted*

80

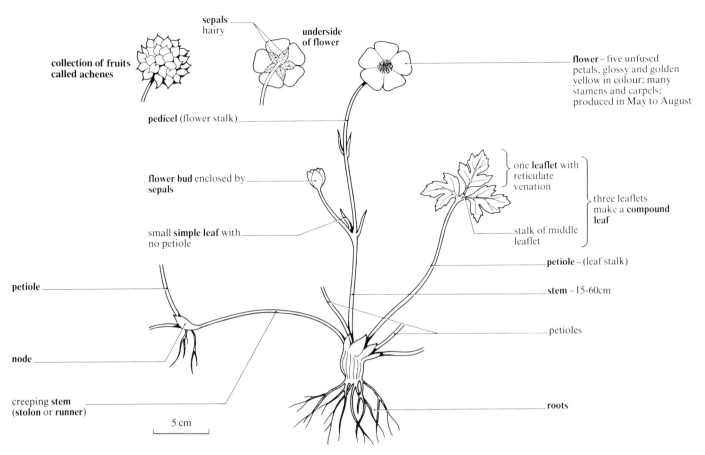

collection of fruits called achenes

sepals hairy

underside of flower

flower – five unfused petals, glossy and golden yellow in colour; many stamens and carpels; produced in May to August

pedicel (flower stalk)

one **leaflet** with reticulate venation

three leaflets make a **compound leaf**

stalk of middle leaflet

flower bud enclosed by **sepals**

small **simple leaf** with no petiole

petiole – (leaf stalk)

stem – 15-60cm

petioles

petiole

node

creeping stem (**stolon** or **runner**)

5 cm

roots

3.8.4 Summary of adaptations of conifers and angiosperms to life on land

In section 3.6 the problems associated with the transition from an aquatic to a terrestrial environment were discussed and summarised. Having studied representatives of the major groups of land plants we can return to consider why the conifers and angiosperms are so well adapted to life on land. Their major advantage over other plants is related to their reproduction. Here they are better adapted in three important ways.

(1) The gametophyte generation is very reduced. It is always protected inside sporophyte tissue, on which it is totally dependent. In mosses and liverworts, where the gametophyte is conspicuous, and in ferns where it is a free-living prothallus, the gametophyte is susceptible to drying out.

(2) Fertilisation is not dependent on water as it is in other plant groups, where sperm swim to the ova. The male gametes of seed plants are non-motile and are carried within pollen grains that are suited for dispersal by wind or insect. Final transfer of the male gametes after pollination is by means of pollen tubes, the ova being enclosed within ovules.

(3) Conifers and flowering plants produce seeds. Development of seeds is made possible by the retention of ovules and their contents on the parent sporophyte.

Other ways in which spermatophytes are adapted to life on land are summarised below and discussed in more detail elsewhere in the book.

(a) Xylem and sclerenchyma are lignified tissues provid-

Fig 3.41 *Vegetative and floral morphology of the creeping buttercup* (Ranunculus repens), *an herbaceous dicotyledon. It is a common perennial plant throughout Britain, found in wet fields, woods, gardens and on waste ground*

ing support in all vascular plants. Many of these show secondary growth with deposition of large amounts of wood (secondary xylem). Such plants become trees or shrubs.

(b) True roots, also associated with vascular plants, enable water in the soil to be exploited efficiently.

(c) The plant is protected from desiccation by an epidermis with a waterproof cuticle, or by cork after secondary thickening has taken place.

(d) The epidermis of aerial parts, particularly leaves, is perforated by stomata, allowing gaseous exchange between plant and atmosphere.

(e) Plants show other adaptations to hot dry environments (xeromorphic adaptations) as described in sections 18.2.3 and 19.3.2.

3.9 Comparative summary of land plants

Fig 3.44 provides a summary of some of the key features of the land plants discussed in this chapter, with particular emphasis on life cycles.

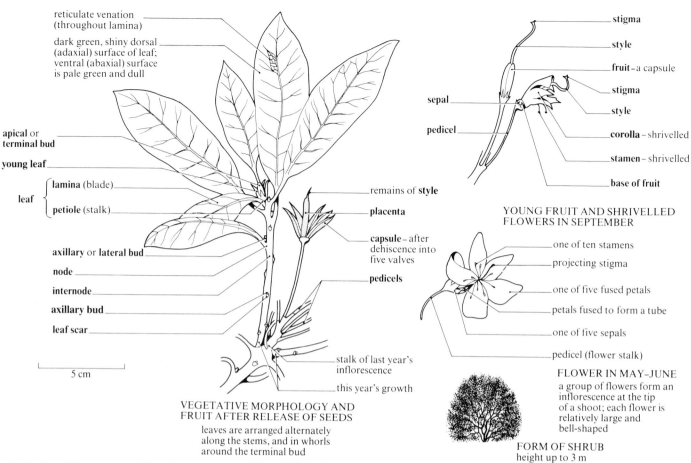

reticulate venation (throughout lamina)

dark green, shiny dorsal (adaxial) surface of leaf; ventral (abaxial) surface is pale green and dull

apical or **terminal bud**

young leaf

leaf { **lamina** (blade) / **petiole** (stalk) }

axillary or **lateral bud**

node

internode

axillary bud

leaf scar

5 cm

remains of **style**

placenta

capsule – after dehiscence into five valves

pedicels

stalk of last year's inflorescence

this year's growth

VEGETATIVE MORPHOLOGY AND FRUIT AFTER RELEASE OF SEEDS
leaves are arranged alternately along the stems, and in whorls around the terminal bud

stigma

style

fruit – a capsule

stigma

style

corolla – shrivelled

stamen – shrivelled

base of fruit

sepal

pedicel

YOUNG FRUIT AND SHRIVELLED FLOWERS IN SEPTEMBER

one of ten stamens

projecting stigma

one of five fused petals

petals fused to form a tube

one of five sepals

pedicel (flower stalk)

FLOWER IN MAY–JUNE
a group of flowers form an inflorescence at the tip of a shoot; each flower is relatively large and bell-shaped

FORM OF SHRUB
height up to 3 m

Fig 3.42 *Vegetative and floral morphology of the wild* Rhododendron, R. ponticum, *an evergreen dicotyledonous shrub. It is commonly planted in woods and gardens. Originally introduced, it has become naturalised, favouring acid soils (sandy or peaty) on heaths and in woods*

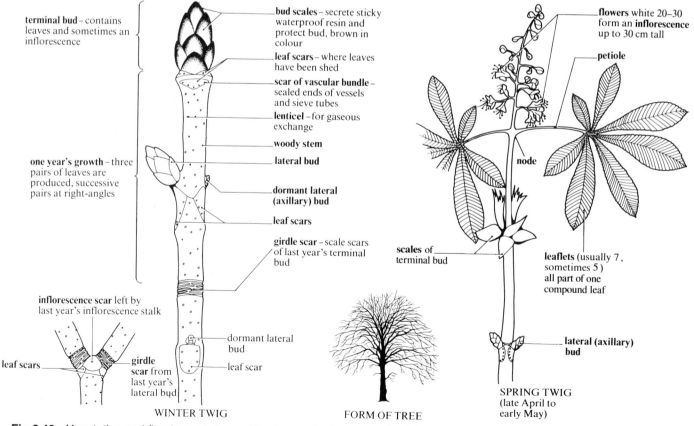

terminal bud – contains leaves and sometimes an inflorescence

one year's growth – three pairs of leaves are produced, successive pairs at right-angles

inflorescence scar left by last year's inflorescence stalk

leaf scars

girdle scar from last year's lateral bud

bud scales – secrete sticky waterproof resin and protect bud, brown in colour

leaf scars – where leaves have been shed

scar of vascular bundle – sealed ends of vessels and sieve tubes

lenticel – for gaseous exchange

woody stem

lateral bud

dormant lateral (axillary) bud

leaf scars

girdle scar – scale scars of last year's terminal bud

dormant lateral bud

leaf scar

WINTER TWIG

FORM OF TREE

flowers white 20–30 form an **inflorescence** up to 30 cm tall

petiole

node

scales of terminal bud

leaflets (usually 7, sometimes 5) all part of one compound leaf

lateral (axillary) bud

SPRING TWIG
(late April to early May)

Fig 3.43 *Vegetative and floral morphology of the horse chestnut* (Aesculus hippocastanum), *a deciduous dicotyledonous tree. The tree may reach 30 m or more in height*

	Phylum BRYOPHYTA (liverworts and mosses) *Pellia*, a liverwort *Funaria*, a moss	Phyla LYCOPODOPHYTA, SPHENOPHYTA and FILICINOPHYTA (clubmosses, horsetails, ferns and others)		Phyla CONIFEROPHYTA and ANGIOSPERMOPHYTA (seed plants) Angiospermophyta (flowering plants)
		Dryopteris, a fern	*Selaginella*, a clubmoss	
Presence or absence of vascular tissue (xylem and phloem)	non-vascular	vascular	vascular	vascular
Relative importance of sporophyte and gametophyte generations in life cycle	gametophyte (n); gametophyte conspicuous; sporophyte (2n)	sporophyte conspicuous	sporophyte conspicuous	sporophyte conspicuous
Mature gametophyte	thallus; lobed or with simple 'leaves', free-living and photosynthetic	prothallus; free-living and photosynthetic	♀ prothallus retained in megaspore; semi-dependent on sporophyte food; megaspore released from sporophyte ♂ prothallus retained in microspore; dependent on sporophyte food; microspore released from sporophyte	♀ only eight nuclei; retained in megaspore (embryo sac); dependent on sporophyte food; megaspore released from sporophyte ♂ only three nuclei; retained in microspore (pollen grain); dependent on sporophyte food; microspore released from sporophyte
Male gametes	free-swimming sperm; therefore water needed	free-swimming sperm; therefore water needed	free-swimming sperm; therefore water needed	non-motile nuclei inside pollen; pollination followed by growth of pollen tube towards ♀ gamete ensures fertilisation; water not needed
Mature sporophyte	dependent *(Pellia)* or semi-dependent *(Funaria)* on gametophyte; no stem, leaves or roots; only capsule, seta and foot	fern plant with true leaves (fronds), stem and roots	clubmoss with true leaves, stem and roots	flowering plant with true leaves, stem and roots
Homosporous or heterosporous	homosporous	homosporous	heterosporous	heterosporous
Habitat	moist, shady places	often moist and shady	moist	wide range, including very dry habitats (dependent on species)
Life cycle	spores produced in a capsule	spores produced on unmodified leaves	spores produced in cones (strobili)	spores (pollen and embryo sac) produced in flowers; no antheridia or archegonia

Fig 3.44 *Comparison of the major groups within the kingdom Plantae*

Chapter Four

Variety of life – animals

4.1 Kingdom Animalia

As discussed at the beginning of chapter 2, it is believed that at some point in time two distinct lines evolved from the very earliest cell forms. They were a group without a nuclear envelope enclosing the nuclear material, the prokaryotes, and a group with a nuclear envelope enclosing a true nucleus, the eukaryotes.

4.2 Origins and trends

All animal phyla are composed of multicellular, heterotrophic organisms. One group, the sponges (phylum Porifera), do not form true tissues (table 4.1), but in all other animals within the multicellular body similar cells operate collectively and become specialised functionally to form **tissues**. Many different tissues can be formed, each performing different functions. This is called differentiation or **division of labour** within the organism and it may be extensive. The advantage of this is that tissues generally perform specific tasks more effectively than individual cells.

Cellular activity in a tissue is coordinated so that the cells collectively function as a unit. A number of tissues may work together as an **organ**, and a group of organs working together forms an **organ system**. Just as cells are unable to act independently within a tissue, so organs and organ systems are subordinate to some means of coordination by the body. The net effect is an overall cooperation between the various systems which enables the organism to live as an effective, unique individual entity. The development of specific tissues, organs and organ systems is a feature of multicellular organisation and will be discussed in greater detail throughout the course of this chapter.

4.2.1 Phylogenetic origins of the kingdom Animalia

It is most probable that multicellular animals originated from the Protoctista, but it is much less certain which of the protoctistan groups, or how many of them, might have been ancestral. Two main hypotheses have been discussed in recent years. The first was put forward by

Table 4.1 Classification of phylum Porifera.

Phylum Porifera (pore-bearing) – sponges

Characteristic features
Some cellular differentiation, but no tissue organisation
Two layers of cells – outer pinacoderm and inner choanoderm (of collared flagellate cells)
Adults sessile
All marine
Body frequently lacks symmetry
Single body cavity
Numerous pores in body wall
Usually a skeleton of calcareous or siliceous spicules, or horny fibres
No differentiated nervous system
Asexual reproduction by budding
All are hermaphrodite, most protandrous
Embryonic development includes blastula and larval stages
Great regenerative power
'Dead-end' phylum – it has not given rise to any other group of organisms

Class Calcarea (calcareous spicules) e.g. *Leucosolenia*, *Sycon*

Class Hexactinellida (siliceous six-rayed spicules) e.g. *Euplectella* Venus flower basket) (fig 4.1)

Class Demospongiae (siliceous spicules, not six-rayed; or spongin fibres; or without skeletal elements), bath sponges e.g. *Halichondria*

Haeckel in 1866. He suggested that certain protoctistans, probably protozoans, divided repeatedly into daughter cells which failed to separate. Some anatomical and functional differences arose between the collection of cells, leading to specialisation. This produced a multicellular organism showing limited division of labour: in effect a forerunner of the cnidarians. It is probably true that the Porifera arose in this way. Some poriferan cells are almost identical to a family of flagellates called choanoflagellates, and it is likely that the sponges evolved from a colonial form of them (**colonial theory**).

The second hypothesis was put forward by Hadzi in 1944, who suggested that the nucleus of a protozoan divided repeatedly to give a multinucleate protozoan. This condition is seen today in the ciliated opalinids and in the Cnidosporidia. Subsequent internal division produced a multicellular condition (**syncitial theory**). This hypothesis has been widely accepted as a means of explaining how all multicellular animals other than the sponges have originated. What is more, Hadzi proposed that the turbellarian platyhelminths were more primitive than the Cnidaria. He suggested that the platyhelminths evolved as a result of internal division of multinucleate protozoa, and that the Cnidaria arose from the Turbellaria after some of them had adopted a sessile mode of life. To support his line of argument Hadzi pointed out that bilateral symmetry already existed in many of the protoctistans and that the cnidarians may not be strictly diploblastic (two-layered), as cells are often found in the mesogloea (fig 4.5). The covering of cilia over the turbellarian body also suggests possible relationships with ciliates.

Nevertheless, because the cnidarian type studied in this book possesses a construction that is simpler than in the platyhelminths mentioned, it has been decided to place it before the platyhelminths in the study of the various animal phyla. However, this must not be judged to be an indication of its actual point of origin. This is still a point of great debate amongst zoologists.

4.2.2 Trends in the kingdom Animalia

The onset of multicellularity and the increasing size of the organisms produced many physiological and anatomical problems which it was necessary for the animals to solve if they were to be successful. Some of the more important ones, and the ways they have been overcome, are summarised as follows.

(1) Large animals with many cells require much more food than the unicellular protozoa.

(2) Animals have become entirely heterotrophic, and in most cases holozoic (section 10.1.1).

(3) Development of an **alimentary canal** has enabled the animals to ingest large food particles, digest them and absorb the soluble products. This is followed by the egestion of insoluble food remains.

(4) A variety of feeding habits has been developed, incorporating carnivorous, herbivorous and omnivorous modes of life. Some are parasitic.

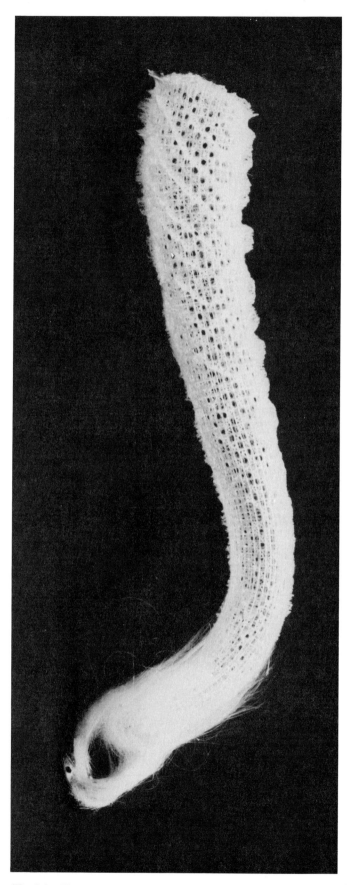

Fig 4.1 *The siliceous 'skeleton' of Venus flower basket* (Euplectella). *This is a deep sea member of the subkingdom Parazoa – the sponges*

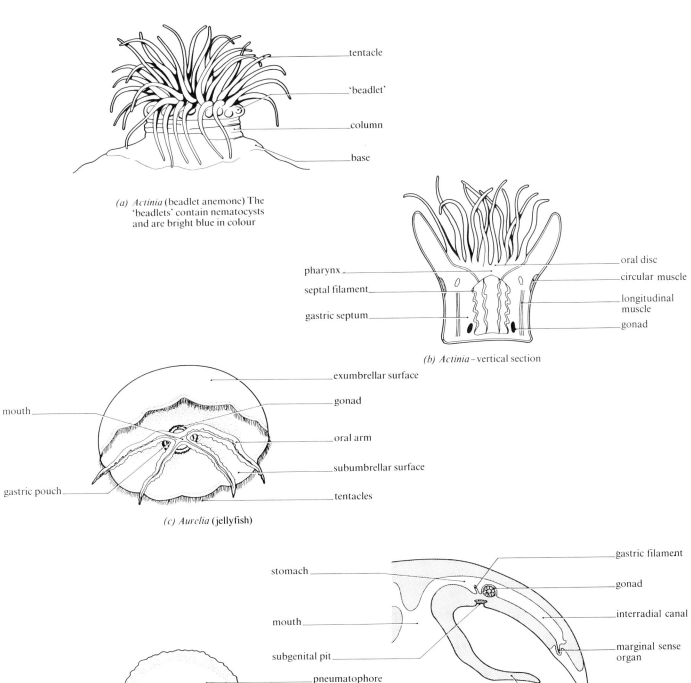

(a) *Actinia* (beadlet anemone) The 'beadlets' contain nematocysts and are bright blue in colour

- tentacle
- 'beadlet'
- column
- base

(b) *Actinia* – vertical section

- pharynx
- septal filament
- gastric septum
- oral disc
- circular muscle
- longitudinal muscle
- gonad

(c) *Aurelia* (jellyfish)

- exumbrellar surface
- gonad
- oral arm
- subumbrellar surface
- tentacles
- mouth
- gastric pouch

(d) *Aurelia* – radial section through an adradial canal and marginal sense organ

- stomach
- mouth
- subgenital pit
- gastric filament
- gonad
- interradial canal
- marginal sense organ
- oral arm

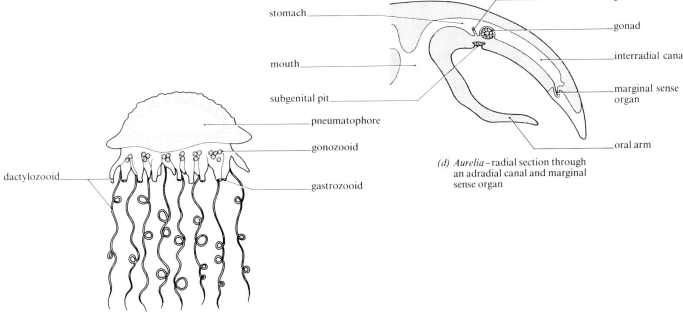

(e) *Physalia* diagrammatic

- pneumatophore
- gonozooid
- gastrozooid
- dactylozooid

Fig 4.2 *A variety of cnidarians*

87

(5) To meet increased demands for food, and to enable organisms to search for it, an efficient means of locomotion has been devised.

(6) **Muscle** and **skeletal systems** (exo- or endoskeletons) have been developed to (a) aid maintenance of general body shape, (b) protect and provide support for inner structures, and (c) provide propulsive forces that will enable the organism to move.

(7) Most animals have adopted a **bilaterally symmetrical shape**. This gives a compact, generally elongated form which offers least resistance to movement. It also confers anterior, posterior, dorsal, ventral, right and left aspects to the animals. These areas may undergo further specialisation in different organisms. (NB Cnidaria and echinoderms are notable exceptions. They are sessile or slow moving. The former exhibit radial symmetry whilst the latter exhibit pentamerous symmetry. This enables them to encounter environmental changes from all directions.)

(8) Development of a central nervous system has occurred to coordinate all body activities. Sense organs receive stimuli, the central nervous system processes the information, and effectors produce an appropriate response.

(9) The major sense organs and nerve centres become situated at the anterior end of the body. Here they are ideally placed to be the first structures to encounter any environmental changes ahead. This process is called **cephalisation** and results in the formation of a definite head region.

(10) The nervous system is complemented by the parallel development of another coordinating system, the **endocrine system** (section 16.6). Together they serve to maintain the animal's steady state.

(11) Increase in size causes the spatial problem of the separation of central tissue from the body wall and the environment. Hence there has been the development of a **transport system**. This consists of a fluid tissue, usually **blood**, pumped around the body in vessels by a muscular heart or contractile vessels.

(12) The transport system provides a means by which oxygen, carbon dioxide, soluble food and excretory materials are transported throughout the body. At various points they may be taken up and utilised by the tissues, or expelled from the body.

(13) The relatively impermeable outer covering of an animal means that there are few areas which can be used for exchange of materials between the body and its surrounding environment. This adds to the need for an efficient transport system.

(14) The development of a multicellular animal from a single-celled zygote is often a long, complex process. It is therefore necessary for a period of **embryonic development** to take place, quite often followed by a larval phase and **metamorphosis** before the adult form is achieved.

4.3 Phylum Cnidaria (Coelenterata)

4.3.1 Class Hydrozoa

The majority of animals in this class are marine, but the genus *Hydra* is found in fresh water.

Obelia (fig 4.3) is a marine form and lives in shallow coastal waters attached to rocks, shells, seaweeds or wooden piles. It exists in two distinctly different forms during its life history. There is a sessile form, comprising of branching colonies of numerous minute **hydroid polyps**. Growing in the angles of the lower branches are **blastostyles** which give rise, by budding, to small swimming **medusae**. The medusa is the active free-living form of the animal. It provides a means of dispersal, and is the only form that is able to reproduce sexually. There are no special osmoregulatory mechanisms in either form as their cell contents are isosmotic with sea water. Gaseous exchange is by diffusion over the whole surface.

The colonial form

The colony consists of many hydroid individuals, each interconnected by a thin hollow tube, the **coenosarc**. Characteristically the coenosarc consists of a continuous cavity, the **enteron**, running throughout the colony, surrounded by a wall composed of outer **ectodermis**, **mesogloea** and inner **endodermis**. At the end of each branch the coenosarc continues into a cup-shaped structure, the **hydranth** (hydroid polyp). The coenosarc secretes outside itself a thin protective exoskeleton of chitin, the **perisarc**. This expands around the hydranth to form a **hydrotheca**. All hydranths are feeding structures and their collective activity supplies the whole colony with an adequate means of nourishment. Much of the structural organisation of the hydranths can be directly related to their function. Each hydranth is sac-like in shape and possesses an oral aperture at its apex. Surrounding the oral aperture is a circle of approximately 24 **tentacles** which are used to capture food which is generally small crustacea. Each tentacle consists of an internal layer of endodermal cells surrounded by an external covering of ectodermal cells. Being sessile, *Obelia* has to rely for its food source on water currents carrying prey, or prey swimming towards it. The radial symmetry of the hydranths and the branched nature of the whole colony enable the tentacles to sweep through large quantities of water and to encounter food from all directions. Each tentacle possesses batteries of **nematoblasts**, cells which each contain a **nematocyst**. There are three main types of nematocysts: penetrants, volvants and glutinants; they operate as the food-collecting structures of *Obelia*. When the projecting **cnidocils** are touched the nematocyst contents are automatically discharged, usually in large numbers (fig 4.4). They penetrate, hold and generally kill the prey, depending on the type of nematocyst. The highly developed longitudinal muscle tails of the tentacles holding the prey contract and succeed in carrying the prey to the mouth where it is ingested and passed into the enteron.

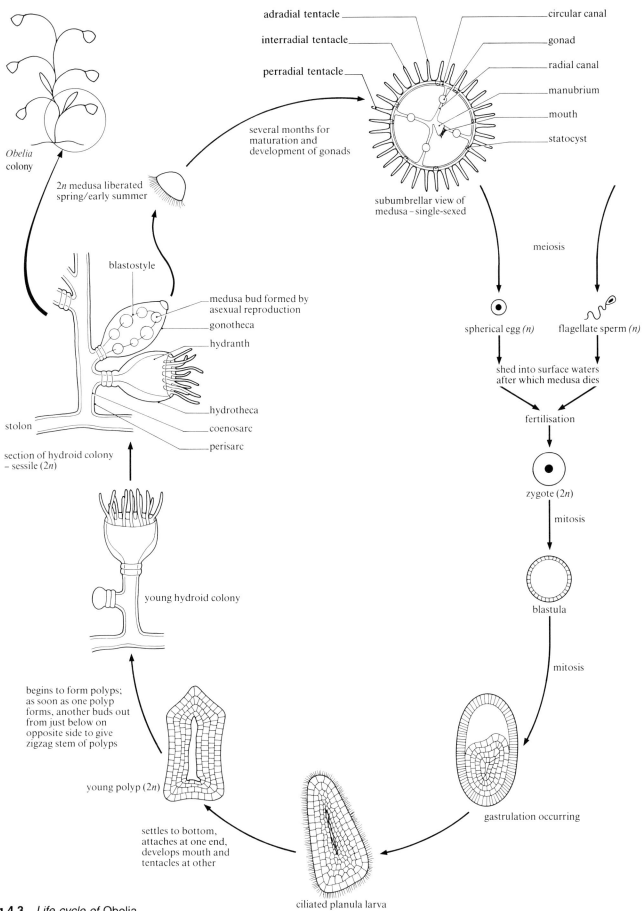

adradial tentacle
interradial tentacle
perradial tentacle

circular canal
gonad
radial canal
manubrium
mouth
statocyst

subumbrellar view of
medusa – single-sexed

several months for
maturation and
development of gonads

2n medusa liberated
spring/early summer

Obelia
colony

blastostyle

medusa bud formed by
asexual reproduction
gonotheca
hydranth

hydrotheca
coenosarc
perisarc

stolon

section of hydroid colony
– sessile (2n)

young hydroid colony

begins to form polyps;
as soon as one polyp
forms, another buds out
from just below on
opposite side to give
zigzag stem of polyps

young polyp (2n)

settles to bottom,
attaches at one end,
develops mouth and
tentacles at other

ciliated planula larva

meiosis

spherical egg (n)   flagellate sperm (n)

shed into surface waters
after which medusa dies

fertilisation

zygote (2n)

mitosis

blastula

mitosis

gastrulation occurring

Fig 4.3 *Life cycle of* Obelia

Table 4.2 Classification of phylum Cnidaria.

Phylum Cnidaria (Coelenterata)

Characteristic features
Diploblastic animals: body wall composed of two layers of cells, an outer ectoderm and an inner endoderm; these layers are separated by a structureless, gelatinous layer of mesogloea which may contain cells that have migrated from the other layers
Tissue level of organisation achieved
Single cavity, corresponds to the coelenteron; primarily inhalent, secondarily exhalent
Single opening for ingestion and egestion
Radial symmetry exhibited
Sedentary polyp forms which may be solitary or colonial; medusoid forms, free swimming and solitary
Nervous system is a collection of cells forming an irregular net or plexus
Asexual reproduction by budding or strobilation
Sexual reproduction produces characteristic planula larva
Polymorphism exhibited, but most individuals reducible either to hydroid or medusoid type

Class Hydrozoa	*Class Scyphozoa*	*Class Anthozoa*
Polyp dominant	Polyp present	Polyp only
Medusa simple	Large medusa dominant	No medusa
No mesenteries	Mesenteries present only in young polyp	Large mesenteries normally present
No gullet	No gullet	Gullet lined by ectoderm
Gonads ectodermal	Gonads endodermal	Gonads endodermal
Polyps solitary or colonial	Polyp is the hydratuba	Polyps solitary or colonial (in corals)
Nematocysts	Nematocysts	Nematocysts
e.g. *Hydra*	e.g. *Aurelia* (jellyfish)	e.g. *Actinia* (anemone)
Obelia		*Madrepora* (coral)

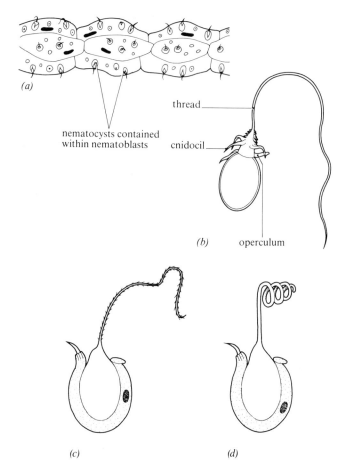

(a)

thread

nematocysts contained
within nematoblasts

cnidocil

(b)   operculum

(c)   (d)

Fig 4.4   (a) *Portion of tentacle of hydranth showing batteries of nematoblasts. (b) Discharged penetrant nematocyst. (c) Volvant nematocyst. (d) Glutinant nematocyst*

Glandular cells (fig 4.5) in the endodermis secrete proteolytic enzymes into the enteron which begin extracellular digestion of the food. **Flagellate cells**, also of the endodermis, assist in the circulation of food particles and fluid in the enteron, whilst **pseudopodial cells** ingest food particles by phagocytic activity. Intracellular digestion within the food vacuoles completes the digestive process.

Many of the endodermal cells possess muscle tails containing contractile proteinaceous fibres embedded in the mesogloea. The muscle tails of the endodermis are arranged horizontally to the long axis of the body. Contraction of these enables the hydranth to become longer and thinner. The ectodermis of the hydranth also possesses **musculo-epithelial** cells, but their muscle tails are arranged parallel to the long axis of the body and allow the hydranth to become shorter and fatter and to retract more or less completely into its protective hydrotheca if it is irritated in any way. **Sensory cells** and undifferentiated **interstitial** cells are also present in the ectodermis.

Flagellate cells found in the endodermis circulate food particles throughout the coenosarc to all parts of the colony. At any point endodermal cells can engulf food for their own needs. After digestion has been completed in the endodermis, soluble food diffuses to the ectodermis through the mesogloea (fig 4.5). Any unwanted food remains are egested via the oral aperture.

On either side of the mesogloea is a **nerve net** composed of numerous **multipolar nerve cells**. The network is denser in the region of the oral disc and the tentacles, and is in contact with the sensory cells of the ectodermis and endodermis.

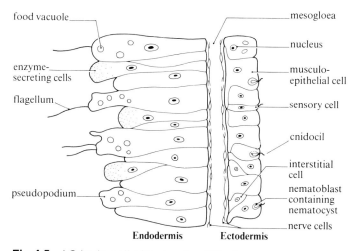

food vacuole

mesogloea

nucleus

enzyme-secreting cells

musculo-epithelial cell

flagellum

sensory cell

cnidocil

interstitial cell

nematoblast containing nematocyst

pseudopodium

nerve cells

Endodermis **Ectodermis**

Fig 4.5 *LS body wall of hydranth of* Obelia

Each blastostyle is a hollow extension of the coenosarc. It has no mouth or tentacles and is surrounded by a portion of the perisarc called the **gonotheca** which is open at its free end. Medusae are budded off and eventually expelled via the gonothecal opening into the sea.

The medusa

This is the **pelagic** sexual stage in the life history of *Obelia*. It is a bell-shaped, inverted polyp and possesses a convex exumbrellar and a concave subumbrellar surface. Hanging down from the centre of the subumbrellar surface is the **manubrium** at the end of which is a four-lobed oral aperture.

The whole of the outer surface is covered by ectodermal cells. The oral aperture provides the opening for the gullet which leads into the enteron. From here, four radial canals pass outwards to the edge of the bell and link up with a circular canal. The gullet, enteron and canals are lined with endodermis possessing numerous flagellate cells.

Initially about 24 tentacles hang vertically downwards from the edge of the bell, but more are added as the medusa matures. Their structure is essentially the same as in the hydranth, but in addition they each possess a swelling at their base where interstitial cells have accumulated. The interstitial cells are used to replace lost or damaged tentacular nematoblasts. Ingestion is aided by the tentacles, which bend over towards the mouth by infolding of the medusa margin. Digestion and distribution of food is accomplished in a similar way to that of the hydranth.

Halfway along each radial canal, and protruding from the subumbrellar surface, are the **gonads**. They consist of an outer layer of ectodermal cells and a core of endodermal cells derived from the radial canal itself. Germ cells originate in the ectoderm of the manubrium and migrate to the gonads. It is here that meiosis occurs. Each medusa is unisexual and will produce either **flagellate sperms** or **spherical eggs**. Liberation of the gametes occurs when the sacs burst. After this the medusa dies.

At the base of each adradial tentacle is a fluid-filled sac

lined with ectodermal cells called a **statocyst**. Each sac possesses a **statolith** of calcium carbonate (fig 4.6). Alongside, and attached to, the statolith is a series of sensory protoplasmic processes. The whole apparatus enables the medusa to detect changes in its orientation during swimming.

The medusa swims actively by contracting the margin of its body inwards towards the manubrium. This forces a jet of water out and backwards from the subumbrellar surface and propels the animal forward. The whole process is effected by contraction of musculo-epithelial cells of the ectodermis, in particular a ring of well-developed, striated circular muscle fibres at the edge of the bell on the subumbrellar side. There are also muscle tails arranged radially on the subumbrellar surface. The normal shape of the medusa is regained by the elasticity of the thick layer of mesogloea that is present between the exumbrellar and subumbrellar surfaces of the animal.

In order to coordinate the overall activity of the medusa the nervous system has necessarily to be more complex than that of the polyp. As well as the characteristic nerve net, nerve cells have been concentrated into two rings, one external and one internal to the circular canal. Primarily the inner ring controls the subumbrellar muscle fibres whilst the outer ring receives impulses from the statocysts. However, they also interconnect with each other, the sensory cells and with processes innervating the tentacles.

The medusa normally swims through the water with the margins of its bell horizontally aligned, however if the bell is tilted, angular displacement of the statoliths will cause impulses to be produced by the sensory processes which are passed to the outer nerve ring. They are then relayed to the inner ring and the subumbrellar musculature will be stimulated to take the appropriate **reflex corrective action** to restore equilibrium.

In *Obelia* it can be seen that the organisation of cells into tissues has permitted different regions of the animal to specialise in performing particular tasks well. This is called

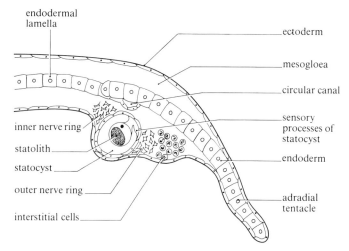

endodermal lamella

ectoderm

mesogloea

circular canal

sensory processes of statocyst

inner nerve ring

statolith

statocyst

endoderm

outer nerve ring

adradial tentacle

interstitial cells

Fig 4.6 *VS statocyst of* Obelia *medusa at base of an adradial tentacle*

differentiation and may lead to **division of labour**. However, there has to be cooperation between different areas of the colony. In a differentiated organism each cell is no longer able to perform all those processes necessary to keep itself alive and must depend to some extent on the activities of neighbouring tissues. For example, the tentacles, equipped with nematocysts, adequate musculature and innervation, capture prey and pass it to the enteron. Here the endodermis is specialised to digest the food. The soluble food materials are then passed back to the tentacles, among other areas, to provide them with the energy and raw materials they need to capture the next meal, and so on. This mutual cooperation between cells and tissues, as seen in *Obelia*, has become an established characteristic of all multicellular animals.

4.3.2 Polymorphism

The occurrence of structurally and functionally different types of individual within the same organism during its life history is called polymorphism. In *Obelia* there are feeding individuals (**gastrozooids**), individuals only capable of asexual reproductive activity (**gonozooids**), and free-living sexually reproductive zooids (medusae).

4.3.3 Alternation of generations and metagenesis

Whilst it is clear that *Obelia* undergoes an alternation of asexual and sexual phases during its life history, this should not be confused with alternation of generations in plants. In the majority of plants there is a regular alternation between a haploid gametophyte and a diploid sporophyte (section 3.6.1), whereas in *Obelia* both asexual and sexual phases are diploid. The only haploid cells in the life cycle of *Obelia* are the gametes. Since the colonial form does not produce gametes it may be regarded as the juvenile stage and the term **metagenesis** would be more appropriate to describe the life cycle of *Obelia*. Metagenesis implies deferment of the sexually reproductive phases rather than alternating phases of mitosis and meiosis.

4.4 Phylum Platyhelminthes

4.4.1 The triploblastic condition

This is the embryological situation where a third layer, the **mesoderm**, has developed which separates the ectoderm from the endoderm. The presence of mesoderm in the body is significant in several respects. It allows triploblastic organisms to increase in size and this results in considerable separation of the alimentary canal from the body wall. This poses problems of transport of materials between the endodermal and ectodermal layers. In animals where the mesoderm completely fills the space between the endoderm and ectoderm (**acoelomate condi-**

tion), transport problems are overcome by a dorso-ventral flattening of the body and maintenance of a large surface area in relation to volume. Thus diffusion of materials between environment and tissues is adequate to satisfy metabolic requirements. In animals where a space (the **coelom**) develops within the mesoderm (**coelomate condition**) transport systems are developed which carry materials from one part of the body to another. The presence of the mesoderm layer has been utilised to form a variety of organs, which may combine together and contribute towards an organ system level of organisation. Examples of such systems include the central nervous system and digestive, excretory and reproductive systems. The muscular activity of triploblastic organisms is also much improved. This is necessary as their increased size renders the ciliary mode of locomotion inadequate.

The platyhelminths are designed on the triploblastic body plan and are the most ancestral group of organisms to utilise mesoderm. They are the earliest animals to have developed organs and organ systems from the mesoderm. Much of the mesoderm, though, remains undifferentiated and forms a packing tissue, the **mesenchyme** or parenchyma, which supports and protects the organs of the body.

The phylum is divided into three classes; two of these are completely parasitic, whereas the other class, the most typical, contains free-living forms. The platyhelminths possess a clearly differentiated 'head' situated anteriorly, and a distinct posterior end. There are clearly defined dorsal and ventral surfaces. Many structures (such as eyes) are symmetrically arranged on the right- and left-hand sides of the body. Such organisation, where the right side is approximately the mirror image of the left and where there is a distinct anterior end, is said to constitute **bilateral symmetry**.

No transport system has developed, hence in the basic body structure all parts are in close proximity to food and oxygen supplies. All platyhelminths are thin and flat to provide a large surface area to volume ratio for gaseous exchange, and many forms possess a much-branched gut ramifying throughout the body to facilitate digestion and absorption of food materials. In addition, excretory material is collected from all parts by a branched system of excretory tubes ending in **flame cells** (see chapter 19).

4.4.2 Class Turbellaria

Planaria is a free-living, carnivorous flatworm found in freshwater streams and ponds. It remains under stones during the day, emerging only at night to feed. It is black in colour and can measure up to 15 mm in length. It has an elongated, extremely flattened body, with a relatively broad anterior 'head' possessing a pair of dorsal eyes, and a posterior end that is clearly tapered. *Planaria* is bilaterally symmetrical, a body design associated with an active mode of life (fig 4.7).

There is a single gut opening, the mouth, which is located on its ventral surface towards the posterior end of the body.

Table 4.3 Classification of phylum Platyhelminthes.

Phylum Platyhelminthes

Characteristic features
Triploblastic
Bilaterally symmetrical
Unsegmented
Acoelomate
Central nervous system anteriorly placed; very simple network; ganglia
Excretory system of branching tubes ending in flame cells
Flattened dorsoventrally
Mouth but no anus
Complex hermaphroditic reproductive system
Larval form usually present

Class Turbellaria	*Class Trematoda*	*Class Cestoda*
Free living; aquatic	Endoparasitic	Endoparasitic
Delicate, soft, leaf-like body	Leaf-like	Elongated body divided into proglottides which are able to break off
Suckers rarely present	Usually ventral sucker in addition to sucker on proscolex	Suckers and hooks on proscolex
Ciliated cellular outer covering; cuticle absent	Thick cuticle; no cilia in adult	Thick cuticle; no cilia in adult
Enteron present	Enteron	No enteron
Sense organs in adult	Sense organs only in free-living stages	Sense organs only in free-living stages
Simple life history	Complex life history	Complex life history
e.g. *Planaria*	e.g. *Fasciola* (liver fluke)	e.g. *Taenia* (tapeworm)

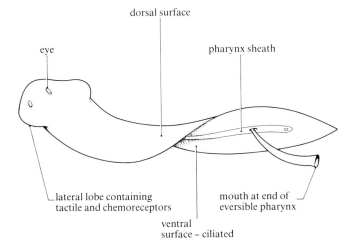

dorsal surface

eye

pharynx sheath

lateral lobe containing
tactile and chemoreceptors

mouth at end of
eversible pharynx

ventral
surface – ciliated

Fig 4.7 Planaria lugubris *showing external features*

Planaria has a complex body wall which contributes towards the mechanisms of locomotion, protection and capture of prey (fig 4.8). The epidermis consists of columnar cells which are ciliated at the sides and on the ventral surface of the organism. Interspersed between the ventral ciliated cells are tracts of glandular cells which secrete slime. The epidermal cells also possess **rhabdites**. These are secreted during food capture and help entangle the prey.

Below the epidermis are several layers of muscle cells. There is an outer circular, a middle diagonal and an inner longitudinal layer. There are also dorso-ventral muscle

tracts. Each layer consists of collections of individual muscle fibres, not just muscle tails of epithelial cells as in the cnidarians. The complex pattern of musculature enables the animal to perform all kinds of agile movements in the water, and therefore contributes to its complex behavioural activities.

Planaria feeds on small worms, crustacea and on the dead bodies of larger organisms. Anteriorly the body wall possesses sense cells which enable the animal to detect prey from some distance away. *Planaria* takes up a position on top of the prey and pins it down by means of muscular contractions of its body. Rhabdites and slime are exuded from the worm's ventral surface and the sticky fluid helps entangle the prey. An **eversible pharynx** protrudes and engulfs the prey. If the prey is large, enzymes are secreted on to it to begin extracellular digestion, and pumping activity of the pharynx breaks the food into smaller particles. These are then ingested into the intestine. Endodermal cells line the three main branches of the intestine, one branch leading to the front and two to the rear of the animal (fig 4.9). Numerous blind-ending lateral caecae arise from each of these branches. The intestine thus possesses a large surface area for digestion and absorption. The large size of the intestine penetrates most parts of the body and facilitates diffusion of materials to and from the body cells. Additional enzymes are secreted by the gland cells of the intestine and continue the process of extracellular digestion. Small particles of food are finally engulfed by phagocytic cells. Digestion is completed intracellularly. From here the soluble food passes to the

93

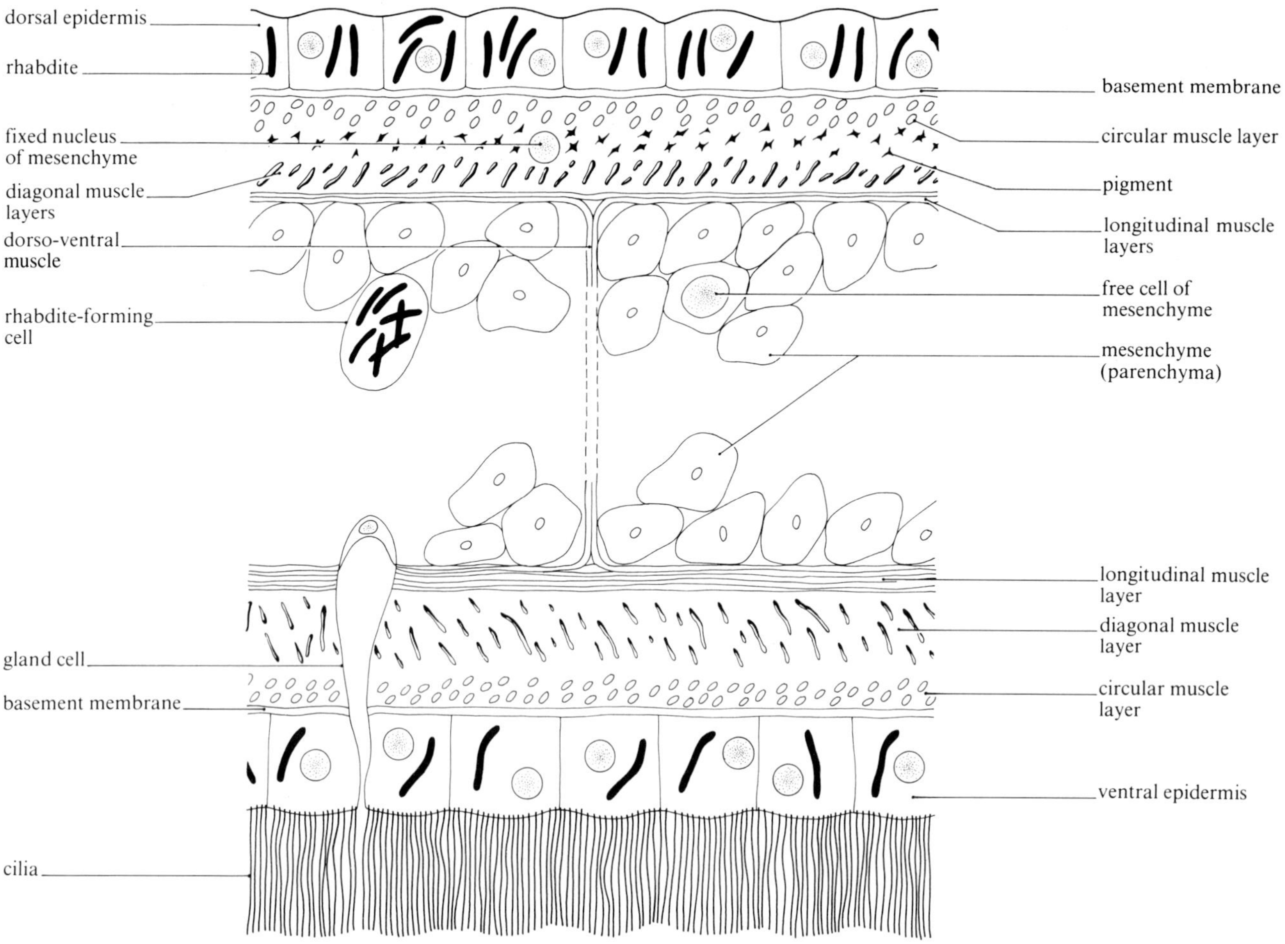
dorsal epidermis
rhabdite
basement membrane
fixed nucleus of mesenchyme
circular muscle layer
pigment
diagonal muscle layers
dorso-ventral muscle
longitudinal muscle layers
free cell of mesenchyme
rhabdite-forming cell
mesenchyme (parenchyma)
longitudinal muscle layer
diagonal muscle layer
gland cell
basement membrane
circular muscle layer
ventral epidermis
cilia

Fig 4.8 *LS through* Planaria lugubris *showing both dorsal and ventral body walls*

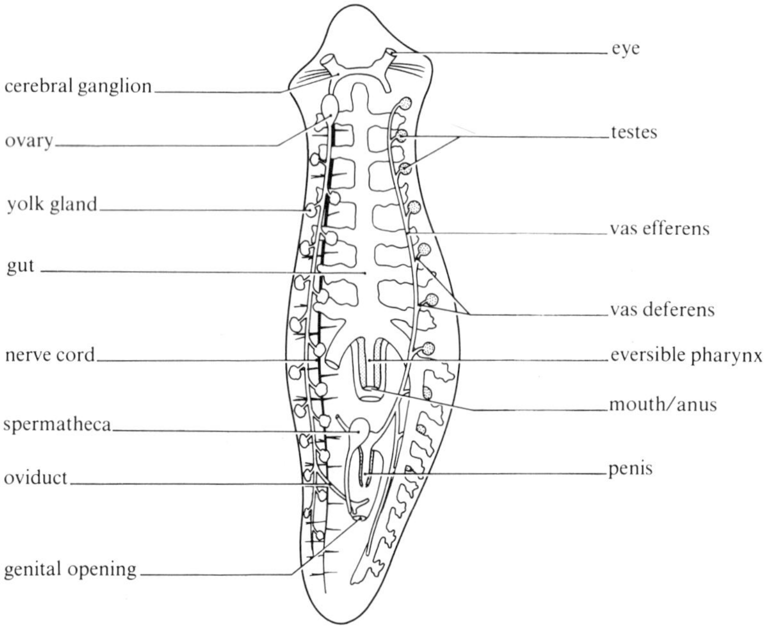
eye
cerebral ganglion
ovary
testes
yolk gland
vas efferens
gut
vas deferens
nerve cord
eversible pharynx
mouth/anus
spermatheca
penis
oviduct
genital opening

Fig 4.9 *Anatomy of* Planaria lugubris

rest of the body by diffusion via the mesenchyme and by amoeboid cells. Undigested food remains are egested through the mouth.

A distinct excretory system has differentiated within the mesodermal layer. It consists of two longitudinal excretory canals which open on to the dorsal surface via a number of pores. Each canal has many branches which end in flame cells (section 19.4.3). Excretory substances are actively secreted into the flame cells and ultimately passed out of the body via ducts. The flame cell system also provides an efficient osmoregulatory mechanism for the planarian.

Asexual reproduction occurs by **transverse fission**. The posterior end of the flatworm adheres to the substrate by the secretion of slime, while the anterior half pulls away from it until the worm splits in two. The split takes place just behind the pharynx. Both portions then proceed to regenerate all missing parts.

Planarians are hermaphrodite and possess a complex reproductive system. The arrangement is shown in fig 4.9. Sperm are produced by the germinal epithelium of numerous **testes** and pass into **vasa efferentia**, which in turn empty their contents into two longitudinally arranged **vasa deferentia**. Mature sperm are stored in **seminal vesicles** until required. Each seminal vesicle leads to a muscular, protrusible **penis** contained in the **genital atrium**.

Ova are produced by the paired **ovaries** which are situated laterally within the mesenchyme. Each ovary is connected, via a short portion of the **oviduct**, to a **receptaculum seminis**. This is where fertilisation will take place. Each oviduct passes to the rear of the body. Along its length it receives lateral ducts from **yolk** and **shell glands**. Both oviducts finally join together in the **genital atrium**. Another structure, the **copulatory sac** (or spermatheca) also opens into the genital atrium.

Copulation takes place prior to fertilisation. Two worms adhere to each other by their ventral surfaces. Sperms from one worm are transferred to the copulatory sac of the other when its penis is inserted into the genital atrium of its partner. After this, the worms separate. Within each organism the sperm swim from the copulatory sac, up the oviducts to each receptaculum seminis where fertilisation occurs. The fertilised eggs then pass down the oviducts and become coated with yolk cells and shell substances. **Cocoons** containing several eggs and many yolk cells are formed in the genital atrium and eventually expelled from the body. Within a few weeks the eggs hatch and small worms emerge.

4.4.3 Class Trematoda

Fasciola hepatica (figs 4.10 and 4.11) belongs to the class Trematoda, which is one of the major groups of parasites in the animal kingdom. It is endoparasitic, living in the bile ducts of sheep, its most important, or **primary**, **host**. Other primary hosts are cattle and, occasionally, humans. Many differences exist between *Fasciola* and the free-living *Planaria lugubris*. These differences can be attributed to the adaptations that *Fasciola* has evolved in order to survive as an endoparasite. Associated with its parasitic mode of life is a complex life history, involving three larval stages (the miracidium, redia and cercaria), and opportunities for increasing their numbers during the life cycle. Within some of the larval forms are germinal cells, as distinct from somatic cells, which undergo normal mitotic division to produce even more individuals. Such a process is called **polyembryony**, the cells of each new individual being products of divisions of the original zygotic cell. The large numbers of offspring produced in this way help to offset the high mortality rate that inevitably occurs during infection of new hosts. For a part of its life history *Fasciola* infests a **secondary host**, the freshwater snail *Limnea truncatula*, in which some of its larval stages are able to live and multiply.

Each stage in the life history of *Fasciola* exhibits structural, physiological and reproductive adaptations suited to its mode of life. Some of these are listed below.

Adult fluke. The body is thin and flat and pressed against the side of the bile duct so that it does not interrupt the bile flow. It is attached to the wall of the bile duct by oral and ventral suckers which enable it to maintain its position in the duct, and spines on the body wall, which point backwards, prevent it from being flushed down the duct in the bile flow. The body wall protects the worm against the host's enzymes. The gland cells situated here secrete material which protects the parasite against the host's antitoxins (fig 4.11). The body wall is also the area of nitrogenous excretion (primarily ammonia) and the site of gaseous exchange for the parasite. Respiration is thought to be largely anaerobic (but oxygen is utilised if present). However, no relationship has been established between oxygen uptake and carbon dioxide output. The muscular pharynx has a pumping action which enables the ingestion of viscous materials such as blood, other tissues and mucus.

A complex, hermaphrodite reproductive system ensures that fertilisation (either self- or cross-fertilisation) can occur.

Miracidium. This is the first of the larval stages of *Fasciola* (fig 4.12). It has a ciliated epidermis which provides means for swimming in water or in moisture on vegetation. The miracidium is attracted to its molluscan secondary host by chemotaxis. An apical papilla attaches it to the snail's foot and an apical gland secretes proteolytic enzymes on to the surface of the snail to assist in the penetration of the host's tissues. Penetration is further aided by circular and longitudinal muscle cells which help the larva to wriggle through the tissues of the host. In this way it migrates to the digestive glands of the secondary host via the lymph channels. There are germ cells present which give rise to subsequent larval forms.

Sporocyst. This is an immobile, closed germinal sac containing germinal cells. The cells proliferate by

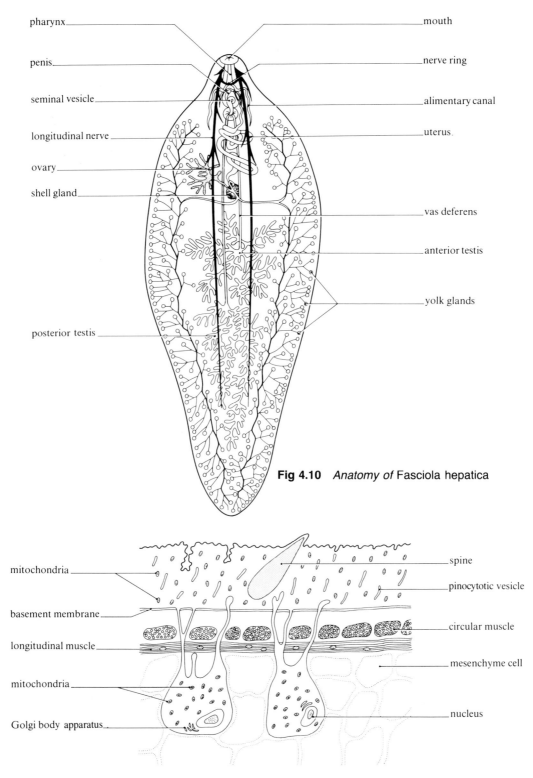

pharynx

mouth

penis

nerve ring

seminal vesicle

alimentary canal

longitudinal nerve

uterus

ovary

shell gland

vas deferens

anterior testis

yolk glands

posterior testis

Fig 4.10 *Anatomy of* Fasciola hepatica

mitochondria

spine

pinocytotic vesicle

basement membrane

circular muscle

longitudinal muscle

mesenchyme cell

mitochondria

Golgi body apparatus

nucleus

Fig 4.11 *Section through body wall of* Fasciola hepatica *showing ultrastructure*

polyembryony into many rediae. This is therefore a multiplicative phase in the life history of *Fasciola*.

Redia. This stage has a muscular pharynx to suck in fluids and tissues from its host. Circular and longitudinal muscle cells aid locomotion of the larva; two posterior lateral flaps provide purchase at the posterior end, whilst an anterior collar provides 'grip' at the other end.

Germinal cells proliferate into more rediae, or into cercariae, by polyembryony; so this is also a multiplicative phase. There is a birth pore for the escape of the second generation of rediae or the cercariae.

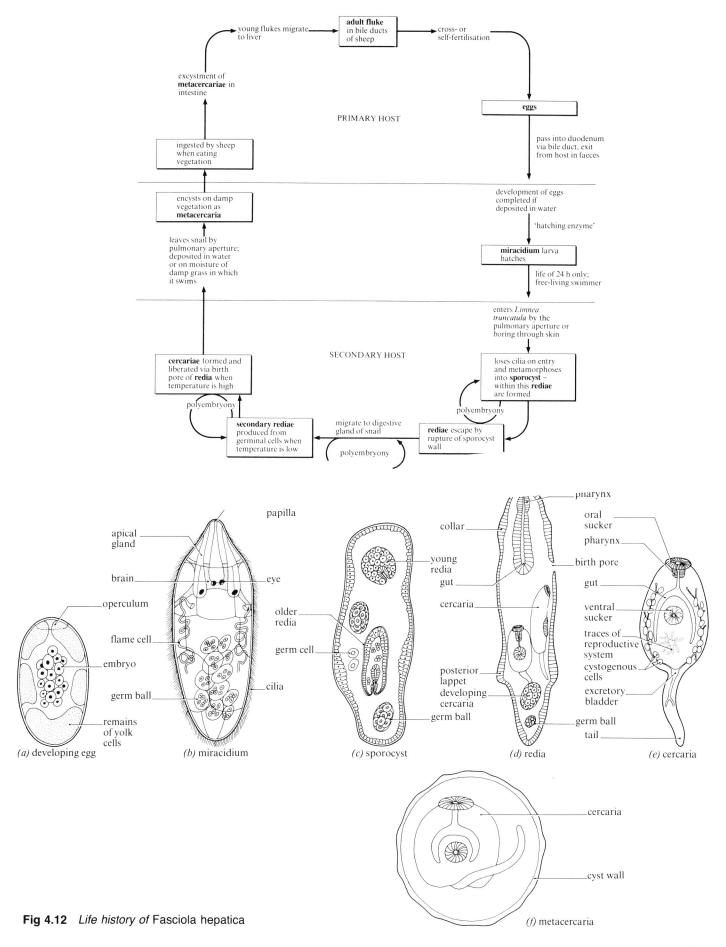

PRIMARY HOST

adult fluke
in bile ducts
of sheep

young flukes migrate
to liver

cross- or
self-fertilisation

excystment of
metacercariae in
intestine

eggs

pass into duodenum
via bile duct, exit
from host in faeces

ingested by sheep
when eating
vegetation

development of eggs
completed if
deposited in water

encysts on damp
vegetation as
metacercaria

'hatching enzyme'

leaves snail by
pulmonary aperture;
deposited in water
or on moisture of
damp grass in which
it swims

miracidium larva
hatches

life of 24 h only;
free-living swimmer

SECONDARY HOST

enters *Limnea
truncatula* by the
pulmonary aperture or
boring through skin

cercariae formed and
liberated via birth
pore of **redia** when
temperature is high

loses cilia on entry
and metamorphoses
into **sporocyst** –
within this **rediae**
are formed

polyembryony

polyembryony

secondary rediae
produced from
germinal cells when
temperature is low

migrate to digestive
gland of snail

rediae escape by
rupture of sporocyst
wall

polyembryony

papilla

apical
gland

brain

eye

operculum

flame cell

embryo

germ ball

remains
of yolk
cells

cilia

(a) developing egg

(b) miracidium

young
redia

older
redia

germ cell

(c) sporocyst

collar

pharynx

gut

cercaria

posterior
lappet
developing
cercaria

germ ball

(d) redia

pharynx

oral
sucker

pharynx

birth pore

gut

ventral
sucker

traces of
reproductive
system

cystogenous
cells

excretory
bladder

germ ball

tail

(e) cercaria

cercaria

cyst wall

(f) metacercaria

Fig 4.12 *Life history of* Fasciola hepatica

Cercaria. This bears many features in common with the adult fluke, which include oral and ventral suckers for anchorage to suitable substrates, such as grass. There is also a tail to assist in locomotion through water or moisture on vegetation. Cystogenous glands are present which secrete a cyst wall to form a metacercaria.

Metacercaria. No further development of this stage occurs until it is swallowed by sheep. It has considerable powers of resistance to low temperatures, but is susceptible to desiccation (fig 4.12).

Limnea truncatula is an amphibious snail inhabiting ponds, muddy tracks and damp vegetation. It is able to withstand adverse conditions. Therefore the sporocyst and redia stages of *Fasciola's* life history, which develop within the snail, are themselves directly protected from such unfavourable conditions. Indeed, in conditions of low temperature, rediae produce daughter rediae instead of cercariae. The rediae remain within the snail and can overwinter within the host, only producing cercariae when warmer weather returns in the spring. *Limnea* is also a very rapid breeder. It has been estimated that one snail may produce up to 160 000 offspring in 12 weeks. If all of these offspring contain developmental stages of *Fasciola*, then the chances of cercariae escaping from the snails and entering new, uninfected primary hosts will be considerably increased. The amphibious mode of life of *Limnea* ensures that when the cercariae escape there is water available in which to disperse.

The release of young adult flukes from the metacercaria (excystment) takes place in the gut of the sheep or cow. The process is initiated in the stomach by high carbon dioxide levels and a temperature of around 39 °C. Under these conditions the parasite releases proteolytic enzymes which digest a hole in the cyst wall at one point. Emergence of young flukes is triggered off by the presence of bile in the digestive juices of the small intestine.

The young flukes burrow through the intestinal wall and migrate to the liver via the coelom. For a time they feed on liver tissue, but about six weeks after infection they become permanently attached in the bile ducts.

Fasciola can have several effects on its host. A heavy infection can cause death. Liver metabolism of the host is interfered with when cercariae migrate through it. Cells are destroyed and bile ducts may be blocked; large-scale erosion of the liver (liver rot) will cause dropsy. Little, or absence of, bile in the gut can affect digestion, and the excretory wastes of *Fasciola* can have a toxic effect on the host.

The following measures can be taken against *Fasciola*. Drainage of the pasture land and introduction of snail-eating geese and ducks to the pastures (a method of biological control) will help to remove the secondary host *Limnea*. The filling in of ponds and use of elevated drinking troughs will also help to achieve this. Use of lime on the land will help to prevent the hatching of the eggs of the parasite, as they will not hatch in water with a pH of more than 7.5. For sheep which are already infected, the administration of carbon tetrachloride kills some of the fluke stages in the liver.

4.5   Body cavities

It has been seen in the platyhelminths that the mesoderm completely fills the space between the ectodermal and endodermal layers and forms a solid middle layer. The only cavity present is the **archenteron**. Since its lumen is, in reality, in contact with the exterior environment, the archenteron cannot be regarded as a true internal body cavity (coelom). Such a condition, without a coelom, as illustrated by the platyhelminths is said to be **acoelomate** (fig 4.13*a*).

In most recent groups, an extensive internal space or body cavity is developed, called a **coelom**, which separates

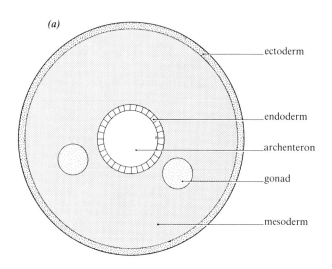
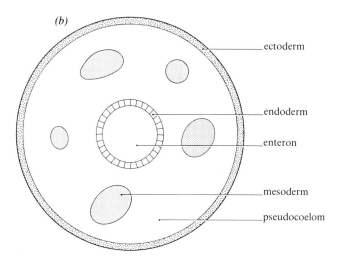

Fig 4.13 *The (a) acoelomate and (b) pseudocoelomate condition*

the body wall from the alimentary tract. The space is generally filled with fluid and may perform the following functions:

(1) may act as a hydrostatic skeleton;
(2) enable activities of the body wall and alimentary canal to operate independently of each other;
(3) permit animals to become much larger;
(4) the fluid of the cavity may act as a circulatory medium for the transport of food, waste materials and gases;
(5) waste materials and excess fluids may be temporarily stored here;
(6) provides space for the enlargement of internal organs;
(7) may play a part in the osmoregulatory activity of organisms.

4.5.1 Types of body cavity

The **pseudocoelom**, which is found in nematodes and rotifers (fig 4.13*b*), is derived from the hollow space situated in the blastula at an early stage in embryological development. It is bounded on the outside by ectoderm and on the inside by the endodermal wall of the alimentary canal. The internal organs remain free within the pseudocoelom, and the spaces between them are filled with large, vacuolated mesodermal cells. Thus the organs are separated and can operate independently of each other, and the mesodermal cells, which are easily deformed, enable the organism to change its body shape readily. The pseudocoelom appears to be the forerunner of another type of body cavity, the coelom.

The **coelom** is preceded by the blastocoel during embryological development, hence the coelom should be regarded as the **secondary body cavity**. When it develops it reduces the blastocoel to a series of blood-filled spaces bound by mesodermally derived walls. The coelom arises when a split occurs within the embryonic mesoderm. The cavity of the coelom is thus bounded by a lining of mesodermal cells called the **peritoneum**. Vertical portions of the peritoneum are called **mesenteries** and they help in the suspension of the alimentary canal from the body wall. The coelomic cavity is filled with **coelomic fluid**.

Examination of the embryological development of the coelom in various organisms indicates that it may arise in more than one way. Opinion is divided as to which method is the most ancestral. Three methods of coelom formation are shown in fig 4.14.

The result of coelom formation is that a layer of mesoderm (**somatic**) is applied to the ectoderm and

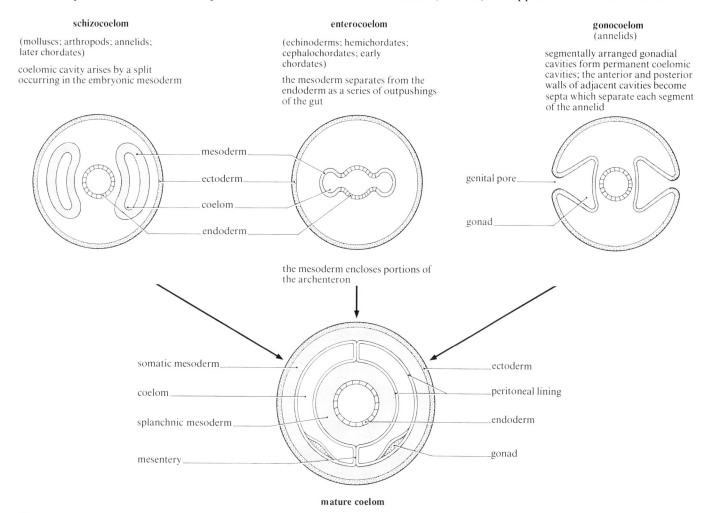

schizocoelom

(molluscs; arthropods; annelids; later chordates)

coelomic cavity arises by a split occurring in the embryonic mesoderm

enterocoelom

(echinoderms; hemichordates; cephalochordates; early chordates)

the mesoderm separates from the endoderm as a series of outpushings of the gut

gonocoelom
(annelids)

segmentally arranged gonadial cavities form permanent coelomic cavities; the anterior and posterior walls of adjacent cavities become septa which separate each segment of the annelid

mesoderm
ectoderm
coelom
endoderm

genital pore
gonad

the mesoderm encloses portions of the archenteron

somatic mesoderm
coelom
splanchnic mesoderm
mesentery

ectoderm
peritoneal lining
endoderm
gonad

mature coelom

Fig 4.14 *Methods of coelom formation*

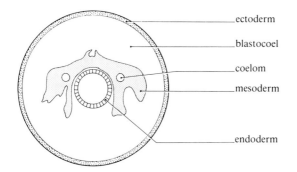

ectoderm

blastocoel

coelom

mesoderm

endoderm

Fig 4.15 *The haemocoel condition*

becomes part of the body wall, and a layer of mesoderm (**splanchnic**) associates with the endoderm of the alimentary tract to form the musculature of the gut. The relatively stationary coelomic fluid separates the body wall from the alimentary canal, and any organs which protrude into the cavity are bounded by peritoneum.

In the case of the **haemocoel**, which is found in arthropods and molluscs, the coelom has been almost completely obliterated by a greatly enlarged blastocoel (fig 4.15). The blastocoel consists of sinuses filled with blood. The blood is generally circulated in the haemocoel. Gonads are never differentiated from the haemocoel wall, and the coelom is confined to cavities of excretory organs and the gonoducts.

4.6 Phylum Nematoda

Ascaris lumbricoides is a common nematode which parasitises humans and pigs. The worms possess slender, elongated bodies, tapering at each end. The male is smaller than the female and is more curved at its posterior end. Covering the body of each worm is a cuticle made of three layers of diagonally arranged collagen fibres. This allows the body some degree of contraction and extension. Beneath the cuticle the epidermis is thickened into four longitudinal internal ridges, one dorsal, one ventral and two lateral. The epidermis forms a **syncitium**, since it is a mass of cytoplasm containing many nuclei and is bounded by a cell surface membrane. Below the epidermis

Table 4.4 Characteristics of phylum Nematoda.

Phylum Nematoda

Characteristic features
Triploblastic, pseudocoelomate
Bilaterally symmetrical
Unsegmented
Elongated, round 'worms' with pointed ends
Alimentary canal with mouth and anus
Sexes separate (dioecious)
Some free living, many important plant and animal parasites
Anterior end shows a degree of cephalisation

is a single layer of longitudinal, obliquely striated muscle fibres. The layer is divided into four bands, each band occupying the space between two ridges of epidermis. Each muscle cell has its contractile elements located peripherally. Its other end is bulbous and possesses a slender cytoplasmic extension which connects with a longitudinal nerve cord. (This contrasts with other organisms where nerve fibres pass to the muscles.)

The mouth is surrounded by three 'lips' which possess sensory papillae. It leads into a muscular pharynx lined by cuticle and epidermis. The pharynx pumps some of its host's food into the straight intestine of the worm. The gut is provided with valves at both ends which prevent regurgitation of the food. Microvilli are present in the intestine which is secretory and absorptive in its anterior and posterior regions respectively. Unwanted material is egested via the anus.

The pseudocoel which separates the alimentary canal from the body wall consists of a small number of vacuolated cells filled with a protein-rich fluid. The so-called excretory system (it may be entirely osmoregulatory in function) consists of two longitudinally orientated lateral canals which unite anteriorly to form a single canal leading to the exterior by a ventral excretory pore. There is a nerve ring around the pharynx which is associated with a number of ganglia. From it, distinct dorsal, ventral and lateral cords run the length of the worm. Anteriorly, six nerves pass from the ring to the head sense organs.

Locomotion is achieved by undulating waves of contraction and relaxation of the muscle bands acting against the turgidity of the pseudocoel. Absence of circular muscle permits bending in only the dorso-ventral plane.

The female has two ovaries which pass their contents via oviducts to the uteri where the eggs are gathered. The uteri lead to a vagina which opens on the ventral surface by the female genital pore. The single testis of the male is a long tube which enlarges into a sperm duct and opens to the surface near the posterior end. A seminal vesicle is present which joins the rectum just before the cloaca. During copulation the male inserts its copulatory spicules into the genital atrium of the female and distends the vagina. The amoeboid sperm are ejected into the vagina and pass to the uteri where fertilisation occurs. Details of the life cycle of *A. lumbricoides* can be seen in fig 4.16.

4.7 Phylum Annelida

4.7.1 The coelomate body plan and metameric segmentation

Whereas the nematodes possess a pseudocoel, later groups, from the annelids onwards, have developed a fluid-filled coelom. Coelomic fluid separates the body wall from the alimentary tract. The majority of the mesoderm which lines the coelom develops into muscle; that of the body wall aids locomotion of the whole animal, whilst that of the gut causes **peristalsis** of food. Transport of

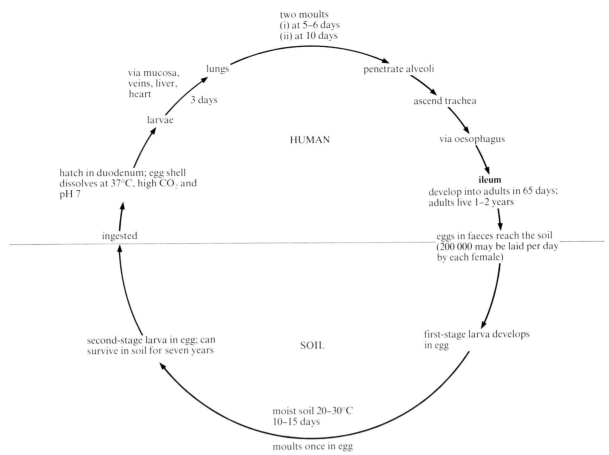

two moults
(i) at 5–6 days
(ii) at 10 days

lungs   penetrate alveoli

via mucosa,   ascend trachea
veins, liver,
heart   3 days   via oesophagus

larvae   HUMAN

hatch in duodenum; egg shell   **ileum**
dissolves at 37°C, high CO_2 and   develop into adults in 65 days;
pH 7   adults live 1–2 years

ingested   eggs in faeces reach the soil
          (200 000 may be laid per day
          by each female)

second-stage larva in egg; can   first-stage larva develops
survive in soil for seven years   SOIL   in egg

moist soil 20–30°C
10–15 days

moults once in egg

Fig 4.16 *Life cycle of* Ascaris lumbricoides

Table 4.5 Classification of phylum Annelida.

Phylum Annelida

Characteristic features
Triploblastic, coelomate
Bilaterally symmetrical
Metamerically segmented
Perivisceral coelom
Pre-oral prostomium
Central nervous system of paired supra-oesophageal ganglia connected to ventral nerve cord by commissures
Solid, ventral nerve cord, usually double with segmented nerves
Excretory organs are segmental, ectodermal in origin, ciliated, and called nephridia
Definite cuticle secreted by ectoderm
Chaetae of chitin arranged segmentally (except leeches)
Larva typically a trochophore

Class Polychaeta	*Class Oligochaeta*	*Class Hirudinea*
Marine	Inhabit freshwater or damp earth	Ectoparasitic with suckers anterior and posterior
Distinct head	No distinct head	No distinct head
Chaetae numerous on parapodia	Few chaetae – in pairs or single, no parapodia	Small fixed number of segments, no chaetae or parapodia
Dioecious	Hermaphrodite	Hermaphrodite
Gonads not localised but extending throughout whole body	Gonads localised in few segments	Gonads localised in small number of segments
Fertilisation is external	Copulation and cross-fertilisation	Cross-fertilisation
No cocoon	Clitellum with eggs laid in cocoon	Eggs laid in cocoon
Free-swimming trochophore larva	No larval stage, development direct	No larval stage
e.g. *Nereis* (ragworm) *Arenicola* (lugworm)	e.g. *Lumbricus* (earthworm)	e.g. *Hirudo* (leech)

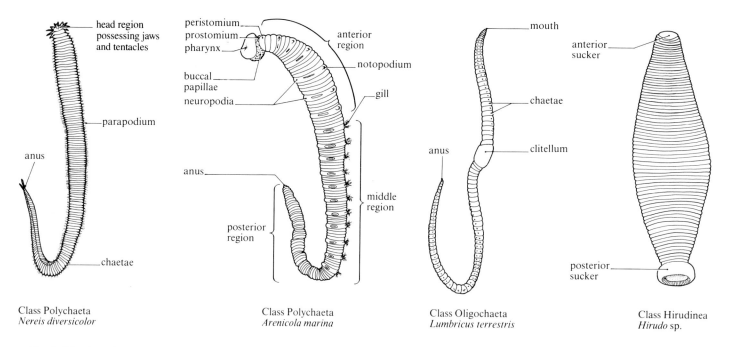

Class Polychaeta
Nereis diversicolor

Class Polychaeta
Arenicola marina

Class Oligochaeta
Lumbricus terrestris

Class Hirudinea
Hirudo sp.

Fig 4.17 *A variety of annelids*

materials between the gut wall and the body wall (and vice versa) is achieved by a well-developed **blood vascular system**.

Another evolutionary advance which took place amongst the coelomates was that of **metameric segmentation**. It is a phenomenon which originates in the mesoderm but usually affects both mesodermal and ectodermal regions of the body. As a result the body becomes divided transversely into a number of similar parts or segments. In the annelids, where it is clearly seen, the subdivisions may be indicated externally by constrictions of the body surface. Internally the segments are separated from each other by septa extending across the coelom. However the segments are not entirely independent, as a number of organ systems run the length of the body, penetrating each individual segment in turn.

Once segmentation has been established, individual or small groups of segments may become further modified and specialised in many ways to perform a variety of different functions. Such differences may occur by elaboration of organs within a segment, by fusion or even loss of segments.

It is thought that the coelom arose in the immediate ancestors of the annelids and was exploited as an adaptation for the burrowing habit. Burrowing would have given the annelids a two-fold advantage over their competitors: protection against predators, and exploitation of new ecological niches. The coelom of the annelid provided a form of **hydrostatic skeleton** against which its muscles could act during locomotion and burrowing. Contraction of the circular muscles produces a pressure in the coelomic fluid that forces the body to elongate. Similarly contraction of the longitudinal muscles would produce a pressure in the coelomic fluid that would cause

the body to widen. It would be a further advantage if the action of the circular and longitudinal muscles could be localised to certain regions as this would facilitate burrowing. Metameric segmentation, resulting in a subdivision of the muscle layers, provided this mechanism. Segmentation of the nervous system to coordinate muscle activity, and of the blood and excretory systems to accommodate the needs of the muscles is then thought to have followed.

4.7.2 Class Polychaeta

Nereis is an elongated, cylindrical bristle-worm. It lives in estuaries under stones or in mud burrows. The segmented nature of its body is clearly visible externally. All segments, apart from those most anterior and posterior, are very similar to each other. On either side of each segment is a lateral projection, the **parapodium**. It is **biremous** and consists of an upper **notopodium** and a lower **neuropodium** (fig 4.18). Rods called **acicula** support both these processes, and two tufts of **chaetae** emanate from each structure forming fan-like bodies. Two additional outgrowths of the parapodia are noticeable: a dorsal and a ventral **cirrus**.

The body wall of the worm consists of a thin cuticle secreted by a single layer of columnar epithelium. There is a thin outer layer of circular muscle below which is a thicker layer of longitudinal muscle. The longitudinal muscle is split into two dorso-lateral and two ventro-lateral bundles which run lengthways in the body. Oblique muscles extend from the midline to mid-lateral regions and join with circular muscles. All are obliquely striated.

Septa, composed of a double layer of peritoneum, separate the coelom into individual segments. Coelomic fluid is present which contains amoeboid cells and a variety of dissolved materials. It bathes all organs and aids both excretory and reproductive processes.

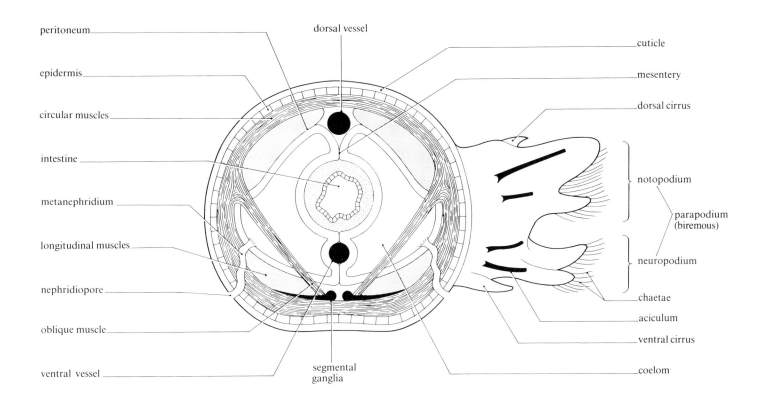

peritoneum

epidermis

circular muscles

intestine

metanephridium

longitudinal muscles

nephridiopore

oblique muscle

ventral vessel

dorsal vessel

segmental ganglia

cuticle

mesentery

dorsal cirrus

notopodium

parapodium (biremous)

neuropodium

chaetae

aciculum

ventral cirrus

coelom

Fig 4.18 *Cross-section of trunk segment of* Nereis diversicolor

The alimentary canal runs from mouth to anus and is more complex anteriorly. Prey is captured by two horny jaws at the end of an eversible pharynx. It is swallowed when the pharynx is retracted.

Nereis possesses a clearly differentiated head which displays a considerable degree of **cephalisation** (fig 4.19). The head consists of an anterior **prostomium** and a **posterior peristomium**. On the prostomium is a pair of dorsal sensory **tentacles** and two pairs of eyes, whilst a pair of fleshy palps extend from its ventro-lateral regions. The mouth is situated between the two head parts, and on the peristomium are four pairs of long, flexible tactile **cirri**.

Internally, there is an increase of nerve cells and nerve tissue at the anterior end compared with the platyhelminths and nematodes. This concentration of nerve tissue is composed of a pair of relatively large fused **cerebral ganglia** which supply the prostomium via the prostomial nerves. The cerebral ganglia are connected to a **double ventral nerve cord** by a pair of circumoesophageal commissures.

The double ventral nerve cord runs throughout the length of the worm. In each segment the ventral cord bears a pair of ganglia from which lateral nerves extend. These nerves are mixed, containing sensory and motor nerve components.

The excretory organs are **nephridia**. A pair is found in all but the first and the last segments. Nitrogenous waste is principally ammonia. The blood and tissue fluids of the animal can remain isotonic with the marine environment over a wide range of salinities. Thus there are few problems of osmoregulation.

There is an efficient blood vascular system with blood confined to closed vessels. Blood flows forwards in a dorsal longitudinal vessel and passes into a ventral vessel in each segment via two pairs of lateral segmental vessels. These run into the parapodia where they branch into capillaries and rejoin before joining the ventral vessel. Circulation is maintained by contractile activity of the major vessels and by waves of muscular contraction running along the body wall which squeeze the blood vessels, forcing blood along.

The parapodia are extensively vascularised and function as the animal's gaseous exchange surface. Haemoglobin, dissolved in the plasma, increases the blood's oxygen carrying capacity.

Nereis crawls by using its parapodia in an oar-like manner, and swims by the coordinated activity of the parapodia and lateral flexing of the body brought about by contraction and relaxation of the body wall musculature.

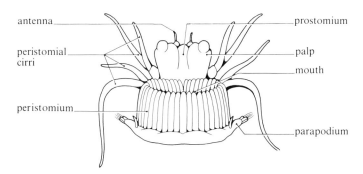

antenna

peristomial cirri

peristomium

prostomium

palp

mouth

parapodium

Fig 4.19 *Ventral view of head of* Nereis diversicolor

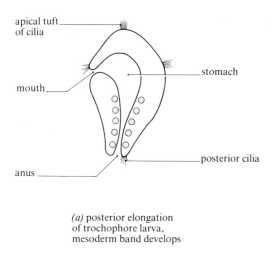

(a) posterior elongation of trochophore larva, mesoderm band develops

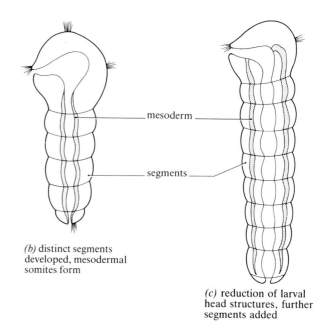

(b) distinct segments developed, mesodermal somites form

(c) reduction of larval head structures, further segments added

Fig 4.20 *Development of segmentation in polychaetes during metamorphosis of the trochophore larva*

The sexes are separate in nereids. Gametes are formed in most segments from germinal cells in the peritoneum. Prior to fertilisation, worms leave their burrows and swim near the surface of the water. Spawning occurs at a definite time of the year, generally in early spring. Males shed their sperm into the water, and segments of the female burst to release eggs, millions of gametes being present in the sea at the same time. After discharge of the gametes the adult worms die.

Fertilisation is external. The zygote develops into a ciliated **trochophore larva** (fig 4.20). This later metamorphoses; its lower region elongates and develops several segments. Its ciliated bands disappear, and the trochophore settles on the sea bed where it develops into the adult form.

4.7.3 Class Oligochaeta

Lumbricus, an earthworm, is an elongated, cylindrical organism, approximately 12–18 cm in length. The anterior end of the body is tapered, whilst the posterior end is dorso-ventrally flattened. Despite being a terrestrial animal, it has not fully overcome all the problems associated with life on land. In order to protect itself from desiccation it lives underground in burrows in damp soil, and emerges only at night to feed and reproduce. The differences in body form exhibited by *Lumbricus* as compared with *Nereis* are the result of its adaptation to a subterranean life.

The body is streamlined with no projecting structures which might impede its passage through the soil. The prostomium is a small, rounded structure without sensory appendages overlying the mouth. Each segment, except

the first and last, possesses four pairs of chaetae, two positioned ventrally and two ventro-laterally. The chaetae protrude from chaetigerous sacs located in the body wall and are able to be protracted or retracted by the action of specialised muscle blocks (fig 4.21). They are used during locomotory activity. Longer chaetae are present on segments 10–15, 26 and 32–37, and are used during copulation. Another reproductive structure, the **clitellum**, is situated on segments 32–37 (fig 4.22). Here the epidermis is dorsally and laterally swollen with gland cells that form a very noticeable saddle. The clitellum aids in the processes of copulation and cocoon formation.

The structure of the body wall is similar to that of *Nereis* and is shown in fig 4.21. There is a terminal mouth and anus. Food is ingested by the muscular action of a non-eversible pharynx. The gut is straight, and its digestive and absorptive surface is increased by the presence of a **typhlosole** (a dorsal longitudinal fold on the intestine which protrudes into the gut lumen). *Lumbricus* is a detritus

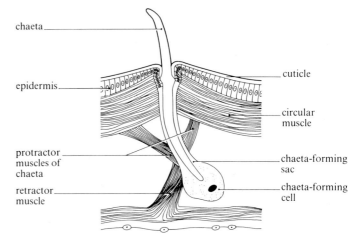

Fig 4.21 *VS body wall of* Lumbricus terrestris *through chaeta*

104

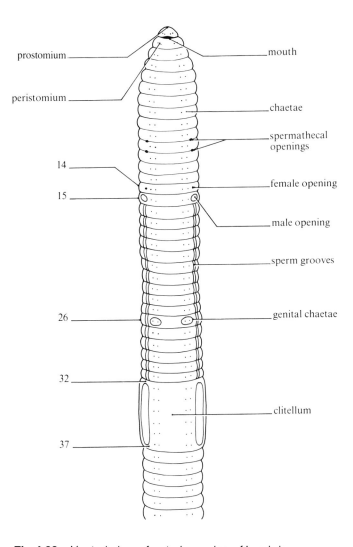

Fig 4.22 *Ventral view of anterior region of* Lumbricus terrestris

feeder, digesting organic materials from the soil it swallows. Food is absorbed into blood capillaries lining the intestinal wall. The majority of the soil passes straight through the worm, much of it eventually being deposited as castings onto the surface of the ground.

Secretions of coelomic fluid via dorsal pores, and mucus from epidermal mucous glands, keep the worm's thin cuticle moist. It is here that gaseous exchange occurs by diffusion, a process that is helped by the presence of networks of looped blood capillaries in the epidermal layer.

There is a pair of excretory and osmoregulatory nephridia in every segment except the first three and the last one. They open on to the surface of the worm in front of the ventro-lateral chaetae via nephridiopores. **Chloragogenous cells** found around the gut also aid in excretion.

Blood, collected from the segments, flows forwards in the dorsal contractile vessel. It is passed to the median ventral vessel by five pairs of muscular, lateral **pseudohearts** in segments 7–11. Valves present in the hearts and the dorsal vessel prevent backflow. The ventral

vessel distributes blood to all segments via lateral branches.

Though there is no noticeable aggregation of sensory structures at its anterior end, *Lumbricus* possesses sensory cells which respond to touch, chemicals and light. These are distributed throughout the epidermis. The central nervous system is similar to that of *Nereis*. Giant fibres present in the ventral cord enable the worm to contract its whole body in response to particularly irritating stimuli, whilst the general design of the nervous system permits the coordinated activity of the muscle layers necessary for the normal burrowing and locomotory activity of the worm.

The reproductive system and behaviour of earthworms is very complex. This can be associated with their terrestrial mode of life and the necessity to avoid desiccation of gametes and fertilised eggs. *Lumbricus* is hermaphrodite (fig 4.23). This is an adaptation to a relatively sedentary existence. Contact between worms is infrequent, but when it does occur, because they are hermaphrodite, any two worms of the same species will be able to copulate. This involves reciprocal transfer of male gametes and leads to mutual fertilisation.

The sex organs are grouped at the anterior end of each worm. The exact location of the reproductive organs in specific segments is shown in fig 4.23. Mating and subsequent laying of fertilised eggs in **cocoons** is a complicated process which can be summarised as follows.

During the spring and summer months, on warm, moist nights, worms protrude from their burrows, rarely leaving them completely, and pair with one of their neighbours. The ventral surfaces of two worms press against each other, the head of one worm pointing to the tail of the other. Such a position ensures that segments 9–11 of one worm are opposite the clitellum of the other and vice versa.

The long chaetae of the clitellar region and segments 10–15 and 26 are thrust into the body of each mating partner to maintain close contact during copulation.

The epidermis of each worm secretes a **mucus sheath** around itself from segments 11–31; this keeps the sperms of each partner separate during copulation and provides a closed channel for their passage.

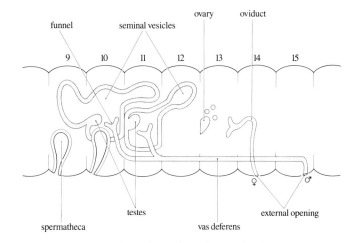

Fig 4.23 *Lateral view of position of reproductive organs*

In the clitellar regions a tube common to both partners is secreted which binds them tightly together.

Sperms from the seminal vesicles leave each worm via the openings of the vasa deferentia on segment 15 and are propelled backwards along the ventral seminal grooves of each worm. Their movement is facilitated by contraction of arch-shaped muscles found among the longitudinal muscle layer of segments 15–32. When the sperms reach segments 9 and 10 of their partner they pass into its **spermathecae**.

Once sperm have been exchanged (the process takes 3–4 h), the worms separate. Two days later **cocoon** formation begins.

The glandular epithelium secretes a tough chitinous tube around itself. This becomes the sheath of the cocoon. **Albumen** is secreted into the cocoon by the clitellum. This later nourishes the embryo. Expansion of the segments behind the cocoon force it towards the anterior of the worm. As this is happening 10–12 eggs are passed into it from the oviducal openings of segment 14. When the cocoon passes the spermathecal openings on segments 9 and 10, sperm are deposited in it and the eggs are fertilised. The cocoon is eventually forced clear of the worm. Its ends seal quickly, thus preventing desiccation. Initially the cocoon is yellow, but later dries and darkens in colour.

Cocoons are formed every 3–4 days until all sperms have been used. This can continue for a whole year without further pairing being necessary.

Development is direct, there being no free-swimming larval stage. Usually only one embryo develops per cocoon, and a young worm hatches 2–12 weeks after laying, depending on environmental conditions.

Agricultural importance of earthworms

Burrowing activity permits greater penetration of air into the soil, and improves the drainage capacity of the soil. It also enables roots to grow downwards through the soil more easily. Mixing and churning of the soil is brought about when earth which contains inorganic particles is brought up to the surface from lower regions.

Worms do not swallow particles greater than 2 mm in diameter. Thus when soil is deposited on the surface as casts, it is stone-free and provides a good medium for seed germination. Earthworm activity at the soil surface may cover seeds and promote more effective germination.

Leaves may be pulled underground by worms and partially digested. The remainder of the leaves will add to the organic content of the soil, as will the excretory wastes and secretions of worms and the bodies of dead worms.

The pH of worm casts is approximately 7. This has the advantage of preventing soils becoming excessively acid or alkaline.

4.8 Phylum Mollusca

The phylum Mollusca consists of a diverse group of organisms which include slow-moving snails and slugs, relatively sedentary bivalves, such as clams, and highly active cephalopods (fig 4.24). With over 80 000 living species and 35 000 fossil species it is second only in size to the Arthropoda. One of the molluscs, the giant squid, is the largest non-vertebrate animal, weighing several tonnes and measuring 16 m in length.

The formation of a protective shell, possession of external or internal fertilisation mechanisms, and use of gills or lungs for gaseous exchange has enabled molluscs to colonise aquatic and terrestrial environments and thus occupy a wide range of ecological niches. However a shell can be a handicap to locomotion, and some of the more active molluscs show a reduction or loss of the shell.

There is strong evidence that molluscs may have evolved from an ancestral annelid-like ancestor. For instance, molluscs and annelid polychaetes exhibit spiral cleavage during embryological development, and form almost identical trochophore larvae. Also the discovery of a molluscan 'living fossil' *Neopilina*, which possesses segmentally arranged gills, gonads, excretory organs and shell muscle, suggests that the early molluscs were built on a segmental plan, as are the annelids.

However, there is equally as much evidence to suggest that the Mollusca may have had an ancestor among the early platyhelminth turbellarians. The ancestry of the molluscs, therefore, is still far from clear.

4.9 Phylum Arthropoda

The phylum Arthropoda contains more species than any other phylum. Arthropods have exploited every type of habitat on land and in water and exist at all latitudes. Within each class there is tremendous **adaptive radiation** (section 24.7.6). The arthropod body design can be regarded as an elaboration of the segmented body plan of annelids. Ancestral arthropods possessed a series of similar simple appendages along the length of their bodies, which probably served a variety of purposes such as gaseous exchange, food gathering, locomotion and detection of stimuli. The success of the arthropods is said to be

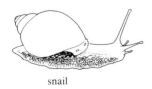
snail

clam

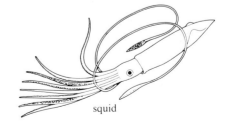
squid

Fig 4.24 *A variety of molluscs*

Table 4.6 Classification of phylum Mollusca.

Phylum Mollusca

Characteristic features
Unsegmented, triploblastic coelomates
Usually bilaterally symmetrical
Body divided into a head, ventral muscular foot and dorsal visceral hump
Skin soft, and over the hump it forms a mantle which secretes a calcareous shell
Heart and open haemocoelic system
Respiratory pigment usually haemocyanin
Nervous system consisting of circumoesophageal ring with cerebral and pleural ganglia, pedal cords and visceral loops
Basically oviparous with a trochophore larva

There are six classes of molluscs but only the three major classes are described here.

Class Gastropoda	Class Pelycopoda (Bivalvia)	Class Cephalopoda
Terrestrial, marine and freshwater	Aquatic	Aquatic
Asymmetrical	Bilateral symmetry	Bilateral symmetry, long axis of body dorso-ventral
At some stage in their development they show torsion of the visceral mass	No torsion of visceral mass	No torsion of visceral mass
Anus is anterior		
Shell of one piece, usually coiled	Body laterally compressed and is enclosed by two valves (hence the term 'bivalve')	Chambered shell often reduced and internal or wholly absent
Head, eyes and sensory tentacles	Head greatly reduced in size, tentacles absent	Head highly developed. Tentacles and well-developed eyes
Land forms lost gills and converted mantle cavity into a lung	Large plate-like gills	Gills
Radula	Filter feeder	Radula and horny beak
Internal fertilisation	External fertilisation	Internal fertilisation
e.g. *Helix aspersa* (land snail) *Patella* (limpet) *Buccinum* (whelk) *Limax* (slug)	e.g. *Mytilus edulis* (marine mussel) *Ostrea* (oyster)	e.g. *Sepia officinalis* (cuttlefish) *Loligo* (squid) *Octopus vulgaris* (octopus)

the result of a process called '**arthropodisation**', which is the exploitation of potentialities latent within the annelid body plan. Many factors have contributed to this success and some of the major ones are listed below.

(1) The evolution of a firm **exoskeleton** (cuticle) which is resistant to changes of shape. This has been used to form a sytem of levers. **Joints** have developed between many of them leading to the formation of serially arranged, **jointed appendages**. Each segment is attached to its neighbour by means of a modified portion of cuticle which is thin and flexible. This allows each segment or lever to be moved independently of its adjacent component (fig 4.25). Constituents of the insect exoskeleton are as follows.

The **epicuticle** is composed of an outer cement layer of lipoprotein, two waterproof wax layers and a cuticulum layer associated with polyphenols. It is 3–6 μm thick and is the main waterproofing layer. It is almost impermeable and affords protection against entry of micro-organisms.

The **procuticle** is composed of chitin, arthropodin and resilin. Chitin is an amino polysaccharide which gives the cuticle a degree of flexibility. Arthropodin is a protein which complexes with the chitin. Its degree of hardness is increased if it is tanned, that is the arthropodin/chitin complex reacts with phenols, and during this reaction its molecular structure becomes much firmer due to the formation of many additional cross linkages.

$$\text{Arthropodin} \xrightarrow[\text{process}]{\text{tanning}} \text{Sclerotonin}$$
$$\text{(soft)} \qquad\qquad\qquad \text{(hard)}$$

Resilin is an elastic protein. It is a natural rubber made up of amino acid chains running in all directions and randomly joined together.

(2) Portions of the exoskeleton, including many appendages, have been modified to form a variety of structures serving many different purposes. In addition, groups of adjacent appendages may carry out similar functions. This further increases the efficiency and complexity of the activity (fig 4.26).

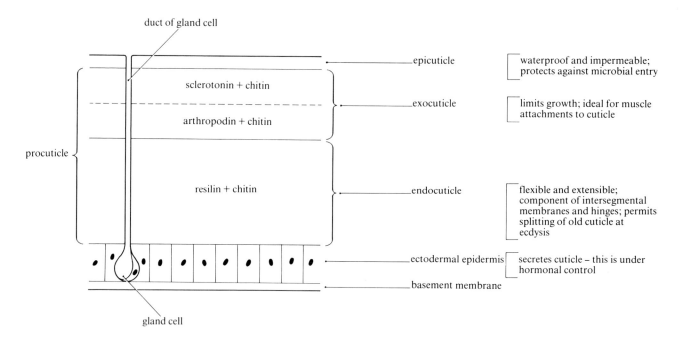

Fig 4.25 *VS body wall of insect to show layers of exoskeleton*

(3) The division of labour which occurs in the arthropods has contributed to the development of distinct regions of the body, namely the **head**, and in many cases a **thorax** and an **abdomen**. The head incorporates sensory receptors (such as eyes, antennae and statocysts) and feeding appendages. The brain is much larger than in annelids, and **cephalisation** is more pronounced.

(4) The cuticle is waterproof, enabling some arthropod species, notably the insects, to exploit terrestrial habitats.

(5) A firm surface for muscle attachment is provided by the inner surface of the exoskeleton. The continuous muscle layers of the annelids are no longer apparent in arthropods. Instead, **antagonistic** pairs of muscles are present which facilitate the separate movement of individual appendages or segments (fig 4.27).

(6) Arthropod muscle has become **striated**. This increases the speed of muscle contraction and hence the animal's speed of response.

(7) A hard exoskeleton has imposed a size limitation on the arthropods, by virtue of its weight. Growth is difficult and can only take place if the exoskeleton is periodically shed; hence **ecdysis (moulting)** has evolved. However the arthropod is vulnerable to attack by predators during this period, and generally seeks the protection of shelter before undergoing the process.

(8) A coelom is not present as the main body cavity. Instead a **haemocoel** has developed. This is used to distend the body during moulting so that the old cuticle can be split open and cast off.

4.9.1 General adult insect morphology

External anatomy

The body of an adult insect is usually divided into three distinct regions, the head, thorax and abdomen (fig 4.29). The head bears one pair of jointed **antennae** whose form may vary considerably, eyes which may be of two types (**compound** and **simple**), and movable mouthparts. The mouthparts of insects are very diverse in form and function. Indeed insects may be classified into two groups on the basis of the construction of their mouthparts: chewing insects or mandibulate, and sucking insects or haustellate.

Whilst the two types of mouthparts differ considerably in appearance, their components are homologous (parts of different species that have the same evolutionary origin but serve different purposes because the organisms possessing them have undergone adaptive radiation). The mandibulate type is the more ancestral. Three pairs of appendages make up the mouthparts of an adult insect. They are the **mandibles, maxillae** and **segmental palps,** and the second maxillae which are usually divided into an upper lip (**labrum**) and a lower lip (**labium**).

The thorax is subdivided into three regions, the **pro-, meso-,** and **metathoracic segments**. A pair of **spiracles** is present on the meso- and metathoracic segments. The thorax also bears three pairs of **legs**. Again there is tremendous variation in the construction of the legs and the functions they perform. The legs may be modified for walking, running, leaping, swimming, grasping or even the production of sound. Most insects possess wings, but some orders such as Thysanura and Collembola, are entirely wingless. Usually there are two pairs of **wings**, one pair on

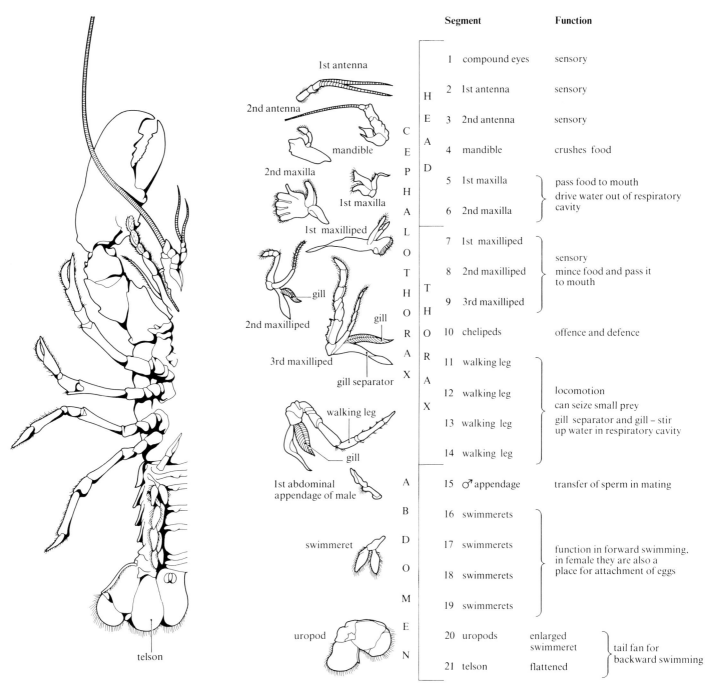

Segment		Function
H E A D	1 compound eyes	sensory
	2 1st antenna	sensory
	3 2nd antenna	sensory
	4 mandible	crushes food
	5 1st maxilla	pass food to mouth
	6 2nd maxilla	drive water out of respiratory cavity
T H O R A X	7 1st maxilliped	sensory
	8 2nd maxilliped	mince food and pass it to mouth
	9 3rd maxilliped	
	10 chelipeds	offence and defence
	11 walking leg	locomotion
	12 walking leg	can seize small prey
	13 walking leg	gill separator and gill – stir up water in respiratory cavity
	14 walking leg	
A B D O M E N	15 ♂ appendage	transfer of sperm in mating
	16 swimmerets	function in forward swimming, in female they are also a place for attachment of eggs
	17 swimmerets	
	18 swimmerets	
	19 swimmerets	
	20 uropods	enlarged swimmeret · tail fan for backward swimming
	21 telson	flattened

Fig 4.26 *Appendages of lobster (after Buchsbaum) to illustrate their variety in structure and function*

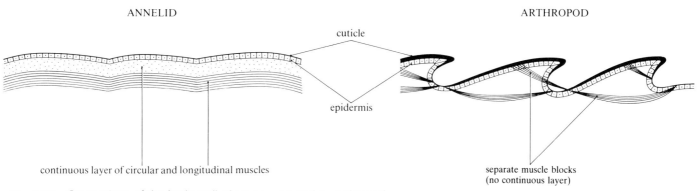

Fig 4.27 *Comparison of the body wall of an annelid and an arthropod*

109

Table 4.7 Classfication of phylum Arthropoda.

Phylum Arthropoda

Characteristic features
Triploblastic, coelomate
Segmented, bilaterally symmetrical
Coelom much reduced, perivisceral cavity a haemocoel
Central nervous system of paired pre-oral ganglia connected by commissures to a ventral nerve cord; the ventral nerve cord is double, solid with segmental ganglia and nerves
No nephridia
Secreted exoskeleton of chitin and sometimes calcareous matter
Each segment typically bears a pair of jointed appendages used for locomotion or feeding or sensory purposes
Cilia completely lacking externally
Dorsal heart with open vascular system
Many larval forms found within the phylum

*Superclass Crustacea**	*Class Chilopoda*	*Class Insecta*	*Class Arachnida*
Mainly aquatic	Mainly terrestrial	Mainly terrestrial	Terrestrial
Ill-defined cephalothorax	Clearly defined head	Well-defined head, thorax, abdomen	Divisions into prosoma and opisthosoma
Head of six segments 2 pairs of antennae	Head of six segments 1 pair of antennae	Head of six segments 1 pair of antennae	Prosoma of six segments not in any way homologous with the head of other arthropods – no antennae
Pair of compound eyes raised on stalks	Eyes simple, compound or absent	Pair of compound eyes and simple eyes	Simple eyes
At least three pairs of mouthparts (gnathites)	One pair of gnathites	Usually three pairs of gnathites	No true gnathites
	Numerous segments each bearing one pair of similar appendages	Three thoracic segments each with a pair of legs. Second and third thoracic segments usually have one pair of wings each	Segments 4–7 each possess a pair of walking legs
Abdomen typically 11 segments	Body segments all similar	Abdomen typically 11 segments	Abdomen typically 13 segments not all externally visible in some cases
Genital apertures in thoracic segments	Median genital opening	Genital apertures near anus on abdomen	Genital apertures on second abdominal segment
Straight gut	Straight gut	Gut may be coiled	Highly specialised gut to deal with liquid food
Hepatic caecae open into mesenteron	No hepatic caecae	No hepatic caecae	Hepatic caecae open into mesenteron
Typically nauplius or other larval form. May be direct development	No larval form	Commonly a complicated metamorphosis. Development may be direct with a nymphal stage or indirect with larval stages	No larval form
Typically gaseous exchange by gills – outgrowths of the body wall or limbs	Gaseous exchange by tracheae	No gills in adult. Gaseous exchange by tracheae	Gaseous exchange by internal air spaces 'lungs' or 'gill' books or tracheae
e.g. *Daphnia* (water-flea) *Astacus* (crayfish)	e.g. *Lithobius* (centipede) *Iulus* (millipede)	e.g. *Periplaneta* (cockroach) *Apis* (bee) *Pieris* (white butterfly)	e.g. *Scorpio* (scorpion) *Epeira* (web-spinning spider)

*This superclass contains many classes e.g. Malacostraca

the mesothorax and the other pair on the metathorax. The most primitive forms of wing are the membranous wings as seen in the Hymenoptera and Diptera. Other forms evolving from these include the hairy wings of the Trichoptera, scaly wings of the Lepidoptera, the leathery covers (tegmina) of the Orthoptera, and the horny wing covers (elytra) of the Coleoptera. In the Diptera the second pair of wings has been replaced by a pair of balancing organs, the **halteres**.

The number of abdominal segments varies from between 3–11. Most segments are without any appendages, but segments 8 and 9 may possess reproductive appendages. In

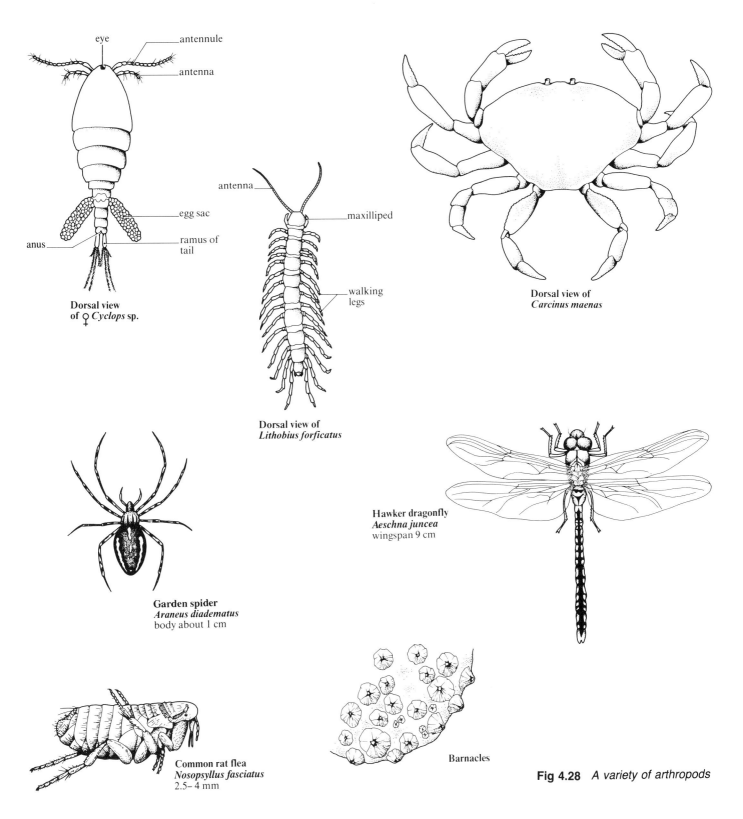

eye

antennule

antenna

egg sac

ramus of tail

anus

Dorsal view of ♀ *Cyclops* sp.

antenna

maxilliped

walking legs

Dorsal view of *Lithobius forficatus*

Dorsal view of *Carcinus maenas*

Garden spider *Araneus diadematus* body about 1 cm

Hawker dragonfly *Aeschna juncea* wingspan 9 cm

Common rat flea *Nosopsyllus fasciatus* 2.5–4 mm

Barnacles

Fig 4.28 *A variety of arthropods*

some species the 11th segment bears **cerci**. Spiracles are usually present on abdominal segments 1–8.

Internal anatomy

The alimentary canal generally consists of a mouth, pharynx, oesophagus, crop, gizzard and intestine (fig 4.30).

The size of the organs varies according to the nature of the diet of the insect.

The blood of an insect does not circulate through its body in arteries and veins; instead it flows through a haemocoel. The dorsal heart is a tube closed posteriorly and open at its anterior. It is perforated at points along its length by pairs of lateral holes called **ostia**. Contractions of the heart,

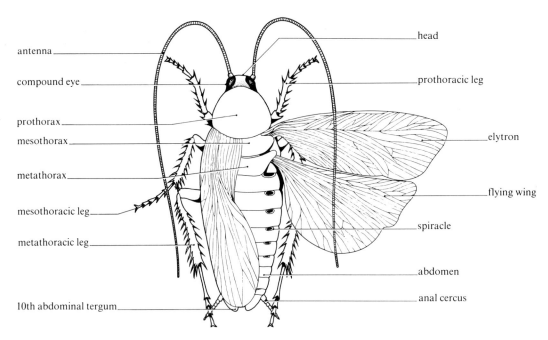

antenna

compound eye

prothorax

mesothorax

metathorax

mesothoracic leg

metathoracic leg

10th abdominal tergum

head

prothoracic leg

elytron

flying wing

spiracle

abdomen

anal cercus

Fig 4.29 *Dorsal view of a cockroach (male)*

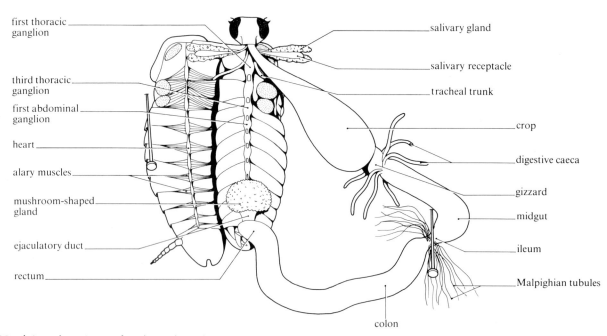

first thoracic ganglion

third thoracic ganglion

first abdominal ganglion

heart

alary muscles

mushroom-shaped gland

ejaculatory duct

rectum

salivary gland

salivary receptacle

tracheal trunk

crop

digestive caeca

gizzard

midgut

ileum

Malpighian tubules

colon

Fig 4.30 *Internal anatomy of male cockroach*

beginning posteriorly and moving forwards, force the blood towards the anterior end of the insect. The blood is pumped out into the haemocoel where it bathes all tissues. It later percolates back into the heart.

Commissures connect the dorsal cerebral ganglion to a ventral suboesophageal ganglion. The ventral nerve cord consists of segmentally arranged ganglia joined by connectives. It runs the length of the insect body. Cephalisation is considerable, this being correlated with the highly developed antennae and eyes.

Gaseous exhange is effected by a **tracheal system** consisting of a number of air tubes which pass to all parts of the body. The tubes open out onto the surface of the insect via apertures called **spiracles** (fig 4.29). The spiracles may be opened and closed, the mechanism being closely related to the levels of oxygen and carbon dioxide in the blood.

Malpighian tubules are the chief organs of nitrogenous excretion in most insects. They excrete **uric acid**. The uric acid is mixed with faeces in the hindgut and eventually expelled via the rectum. If necessary, water can be reabsorbed by the rectum.

The sexes are separate in insects. Typically the female reproductive system consists of two ovaries and two lateral oviducts which unite to form a common oviduct. This leads to the vagina. Accessory glands and a spermatheca are also present. The male possesses a pair of testes and a pair of lateral sperm ducts (vasa deferentia). The lower part of each duct is enlarged to form a seminal vesicle in which sperm are stored. The sperm ducts unite to form a common ejaculatory duct which leads into an extensible or eversible penis. Accessory glands which secrete seminal fluid are also present (fig 4.30).

4.9.2 Insect life histories

Life histories of insects are very variable and often highly complex. In many, a process called **metamorphosis** (*meta*, change; *morphe*, form) occurs. This is an abrupt change of form or structure of the animal during the course of its life cycle.

In the more primitive insect groups the larval stages often resemble the adult (**imago**) during development. Each successive larval form (called a **nymph** or **instar**) usually looks more and more like the adult. This form of development is termed **hemimetabolous** metamorphosis. It may be further subdivided into **gradual** metamorphosis, where the nymph lives in the same habitat as the adult and eats the same food, or **incomplete** metamorphosis, where the nymph possesses adaptive features which enable it to live in a different habitat and eat different food from that of the adult. This avoids competition for food between juvenile and adult.

In later groups, the larval stages are morphologically quite distinct from the adult. The final **larval** moult produces a sedentary **pupa**, inside which the drastic metamorphosis produces the adult tissues, using components from the degenerating larval tissues. This is called **holometabolous** or **complete** metamorphosis. Metamorphosis is under hormonal control, and is discussed more fully in section 21.7.

4.9.3 Classification of insects based on types of metamorphosis used in the life history

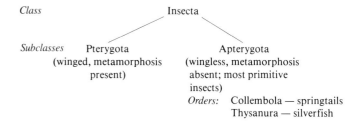

Hemimetabolous metamorphosis	Holometabolous metamorphosis
Direct development	Indirect development
Wings develop externally	Wings develop internally
Miniature stages – nymphs resemble adults	Immature stages – larvae differ in structure and function from adults
	Last pre-adult stage a pupa
Orders:	*Orders:*
Ephemeroptera – mayflies	Diptera – blowflies, mosquitoes
Dictyoptera – cockroaches	Lepidoptera – butterflies, moths
Orthoptera – locusts	

4.9.4 Implications of metamorphosis

Metamorphosis enables the juvenile and adult forms to live in different habitats and exploit different sources of food, that is to occupy different ecological niches. This reduces competition between juveniles and adults. For instance, dragonfly nymphs (naiads) prey upon aquatic insects and exchange gases via gills, whereas the adults attack terrestrial insects, live in air and exchange gases via tracheae. Also, lepidopteran larvae generally feed on foliage and possess chewing mouthparts, whereas the adults drink nectar and have sucking mouthparts.

Since adults seldom grow after the last moult, metamorphosis also allows the immature stages to provide the feeding and growing periods of the insect's life history.

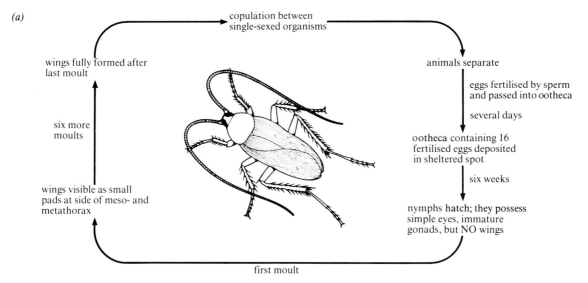

(a)

copulation between
single-sexed organisms

wings fully formed after
last moult

animals separate

eggs fertilised by sperm
and passed into ootheca

six more
moults

several days

ootheca containing 16
fertilised eggs deposited
in sheltered spot

wings visible as small
pads at side of meso- and
metathorax

six weeks

nymphs hatch; they possess
simple eyes, immature
gonads, but NO wings

first moult

NB nymph lives in the same habitat as the adult
and eats the same food – gradual metamorphosis

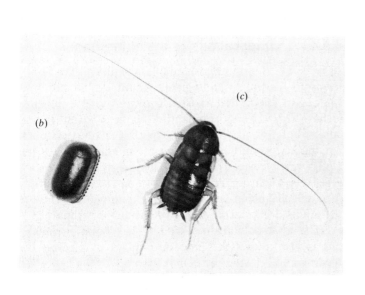

(b)

(c)

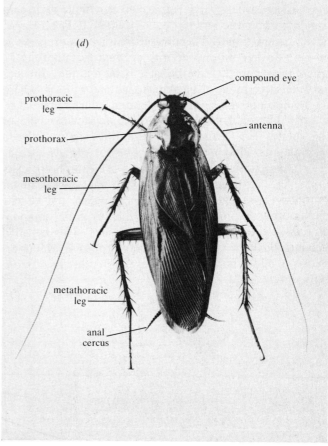

(d)

compound eye

prothoracic
leg

antenna

prothorax

mesothoracic
leg

metathoracic
leg

anal
cercus

Fig 4.31 *Dictyoptera*, Periplaneta americana *(cockroach): (a) life cycle* (b) *ootheca, (c) nymph, (d) imago*

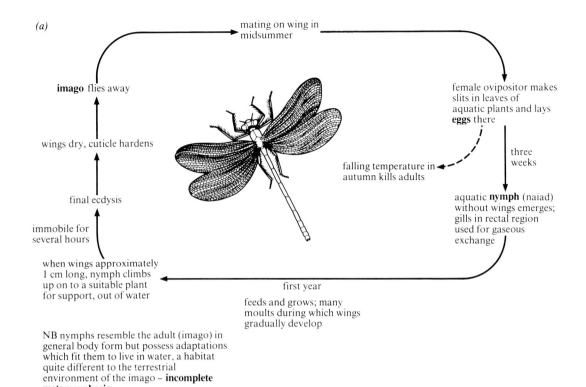

(a)

mating on wing in midsummer

imago flies away

wings dry, cuticle hardens

final ecdysis

immobile for several hours

when wings approximately 1 cm long, nymph climbs up on to a suitable plant for support, out of water

female ovipositor makes slits in leaves of aquatic plants and lays **eggs** there

falling temperature in autumn kills adults

three weeks

aquatic **nymph** (naiad) without wings emerges; gills in rectal region used for gaseous exchange

first year

feeds and grows; many moults during which wings gradually develop

NB nymphs resemble the adult (imago) in general body form but possess adaptations which fit them to live in water, a habitat quite different to the terrestrial environment of the imago – **incomplete metamorphosis**

(b)

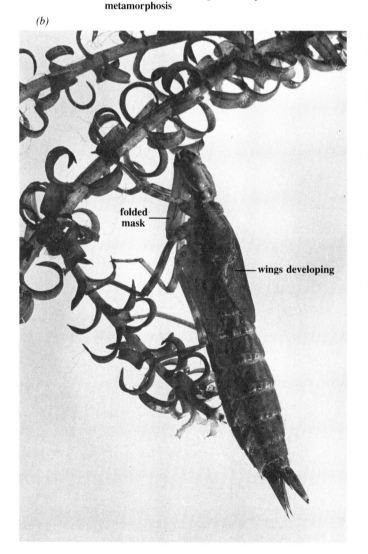

folded mask

wings developing

(c)

Fig 4.32 *Odonata,* Aeschna juncea *(dragonfly): (a) life cycle, (b) aquatic nymph, (c) imago*

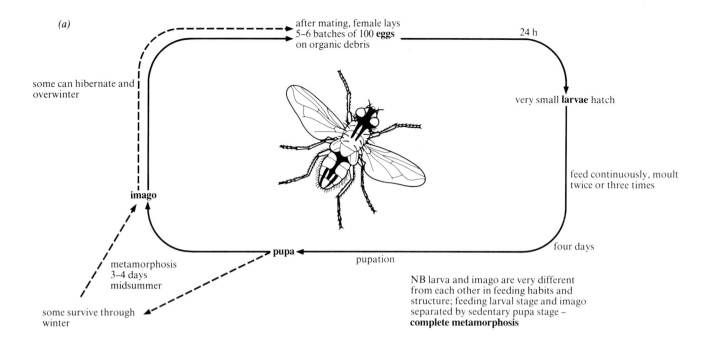

(a)

after mating, female lays
5–6 batches of 100 **eggs**
on organic debris

24 h

some can hibernate and
overwinter

very small **larvae** hatch

feed continuously, moult
twice or three times

imago

pupa

pupation

four days

metamorphosis
3–4 days
midsummer

some survive through
winter

NB larva and imago are very different
from each other in feeding habits and
structure; feeding larval stage and imago
separated by sedentary pupa stage –
complete metamorphosis

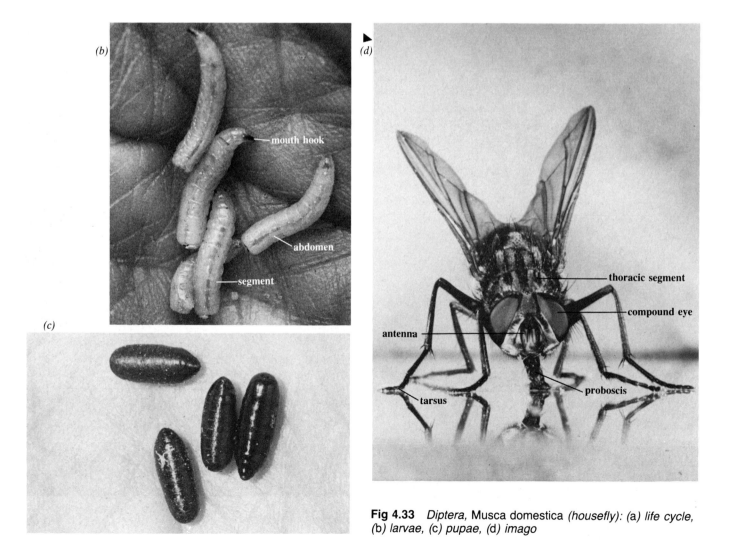

(b)

mouth hook

abdomen

segment

(c)

(d)

thoracic segment

compound eye

antenna

proboscis

tarsus

Fig 4.33 *Diptera*, Musca domestica *(housefly): (a) life cycle,*
(b) larvae, (c) pupae, (d) imago

116

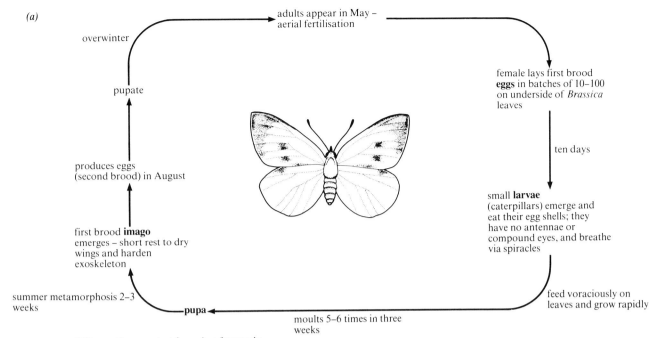

(a)

overwinter → adults appear in May – aerial fertilisation

pupate

produces eggs (second brood) in August

first brood **imago** emerges – short rest to dry wings and harden exoskeleton

summer metamorphosis 2–3 weeks

pupa

NB pupation may last for only a few weeks in summer; if insect overwinters, then the pupa is the state maintained – **complete metamorphosis**

female lays first brood **eggs** in batches of 10–100 on underside of *Brassica* leaves

ten days

small **larvae** (caterpillars) emerge and eat their egg shells; they have no antennae or compound eyes, and breathe via spiracles

feed voraciously on leaves and grow rapidly

moults 5–6 times in three weeks

(b)

(c)

thorax

head

wing pad

abdomen

(d)

Fig 4.34 *Lepidoptera*, Pieris brassicae *(cabbage white butterfly): (a) life cycle, (b) larvae, (c) pupa, (d) imago (female feeding from a garden buddleia bush)*

Table 4.8 Classification of phylum Echinodermata.

Phylum Echinodermata

Characteristic features
Triploblastic, coelomate
All marine
Water vascular system is part of the coelom
Tube feet
Calcareous exoskeleton
No special excretory organs present
Sexes are separate
Basic larval stage called dipleurula, possesses ciliated band and is the main dispersive phase – pelagic
Larva bilaterally symmetrical, adult shows pentamerous symmetry

Class Stelleroidea	*Class Echinoidea*	*Class Crinoidea*	*Class Holothuroidea*	*Subclass Ophiuroidea*
Free-living	Free-living	Attached during part or all of its life by aboral stalk	Free-living	Free-living
Star-shaped, flattened	Globular	Star-shaped	Cucumber-shaped	Star-shaped
Arms not sharply demarcated from disc	Does not possess arms	Arms	Body not drawn into arms	Very long arms sharply demarcated from central disc
Few calcareous plates in body wall; movable spines	Numerous plates in body wall	No spines	No external spines	Spines and calcareous plates
e.g. *Asterias* (starfish)	e.g. *Echinocardium* (sea urchin)	e.g. *Antedon* (feather star)	e.g. *Holothuria* (sea cucumber)	e.g. *Ophiothrix* (brittle star)

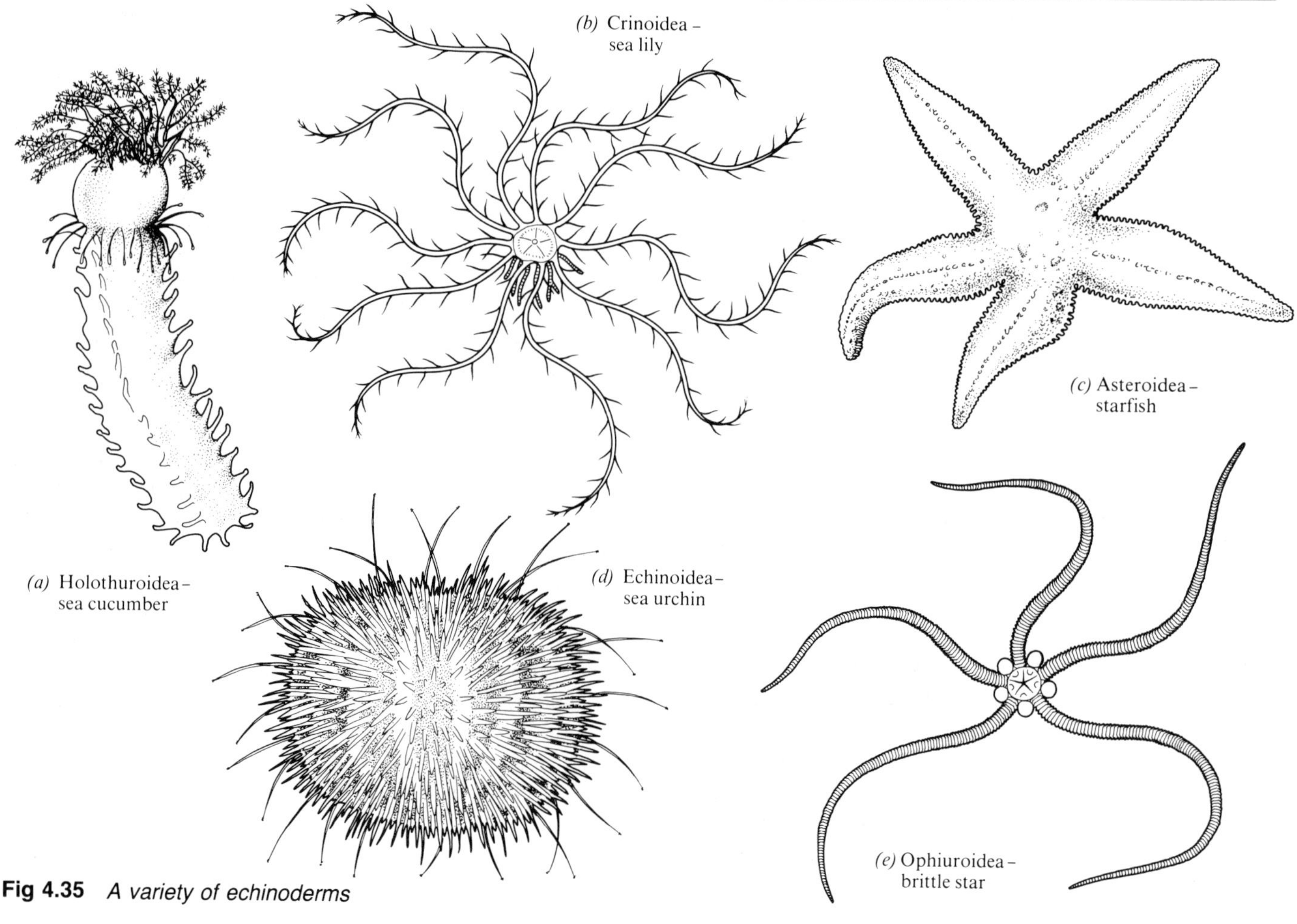

(a) Holothuroidea – sea cucumber

(b) Crinoidea – sea lily

(c) Asteroidea – starfish

(d) Echinoidea – sea urchin

(e) Ophiuroidea – brittle star

Fig 4.35 *A variety of echinoderms*

4.10　Phylum Echinodermata

There are over 5 000 known species of echinoderms. They are all marine and are largely bottom-dwellers inhabiting shorelines and shallow seas. The adult forms exhibit **pentamerous symmetry** (a modified form of radial symmetry), this being secondarily developed from a bilateral ancestor (fig 4.35). Their most unique characteristic is the possession of a **water vascular system**, a complex of tubes surrounding the mouth and passing into the arms and tube feet.

There are a number of striking resemblances between the echinoderms and chordates that lend support to the suggested affinities between them. For example, **radial cleavage** occurs during the development of echinoderm and chordate embryos. This contrasts with the **spiral cleavage** of annelids, molluscs and arthropods (fig 4.36). The **blastopore** (the opening of the blastocoel) forms the anus in echinoderms and chordates whereas it becomes the mouth in the annelids, molluscs and arthropods. On the basis of the fate of the blastopore, the former organisms are classed as **deuterostomes**, whilst the latter are termed **protostomes**.

4.11　Phylum Chordata

Table 4.9 Characteristic features of chordates.

Phylum Chordata

Characteristic features
Notochord present at some stage in the life history. This is a flexible rod of tightly packed, vacuolated cells held together within a firm sheath
Triploblastic, coelomate
Bilateral symmetry
Pharyngeal (visceral) clefts present
Dorsal, hollow nerve cord
Segmental muscle blocks (myotomes) on either side of the body
Post-anal tail
Closed blood system
Blood flows forwards ventrally, backwards dorsally
Ventral vessel connected to dorsal vessel by blood vessels located in the visceral arches
Limbs formed from more than one body segment

4.11.1　Non-vertebrate chordates

A brief review of the major features of the three non-vertebrate classes Hemichordata, Urochordata and Cephalochordata shows a gradual trend towards possession of all chordate features throughout the entire life cycle. It establishes links between the protostome (non-vertebrate) phyla, the echinoderms and the vertebrates and suggests a course for chordate evolution.

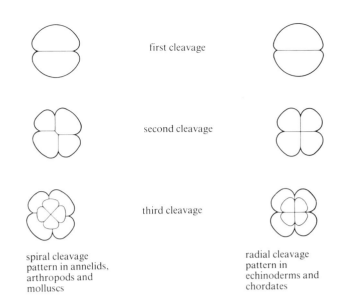

first cleavage

second cleavage

third cleavage

spiral cleavage pattern in annelids, arthropods and molluscs

radial cleavage pattern in echinoderms and chordates

Fig 4.36 *Comparison of methods of cleavage in animals*

4.11.2　Chordate phylogeny

It has been proposed that the urochordate **ascidian tadpole** evolved into a pelagic fish-like chordate by **neoteny**, a process whereby the organism becomes sexually mature and reproduces whilst retaining the body form of the larval stage (fig 4.38).

It is thought that the ascidian larva shared a common ancestor with the echinoderm larva (fig 4.39). The ciliated circumoral band of the echinoderm larva, in moving to a dorsal position and rolling inwards with its associated nervous tissue, gave rise to the **dorsal hollow nerve cord**. The tail muscle and notochord evolved and increased the locomotory power and internal support of the larva, hence increasing the organism's size and activity.

During the late Devonian and lower Carboniferous periods land generally rose whilst the sea level was lowered. Consequently there was a redistribution of the aquatic medium. Professor Romer has suggested that it was this increasing lack of water and drying up of large areas that forced the crossopterygians (lobe-finned fish) onto land to seek new aquatic habitats (fig 4.40). As a result they began to spend more time on land. In order to exploit the terrestrial environment vertebrates had to overcome the following major problems.

(1) Breathing gaseous oxygen – crossopterygians possessed well-developed lungs and were therefore well equipped at the outset. Even so, they still possessed gills which were their main respiratory organs, with the lungs as a secondary means.

(2) Desiccation – there is evidence that early amphibia retained their fish ancestor's scales and they are thought never to have ventured far from water. It was during the Permian that they evolved resilient body coverings.

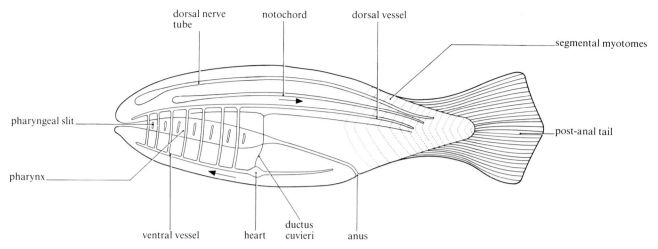

Fig 4.37 *Diagram showing basic chordate features*

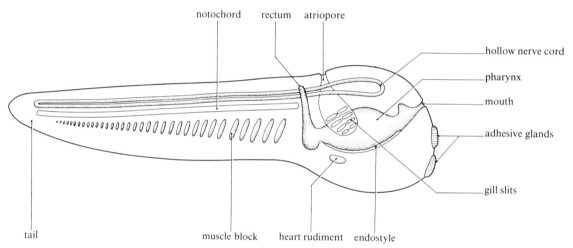

Fig 4.38 *Ascidian tadpole*

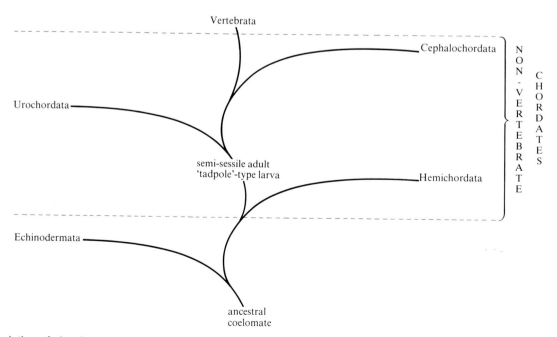

Fig 4.39 *Evolution of chordates*

Table 4.10 Classification of non-vertebrate chordates.

	Class Hemichordata	*Class Urochordata*	*Class Cephalochordata*
Non-chordate features	Terminal anus Blood flows forward in dorsal blood vessel Pelagic larva similar to holothurian echinoderm larva	No trace of notochord in adult No nerve cord in adult Adult a sessile filter feeder, structurally nothing like a chordate	
Chordate features	Tripartite body plan of preoral proboscis, collar and trunk Pharyngeal slits, may have arisen initially to dispose of excess water created by feeding mechanism. Latterly developed into food-collecting device	Gill slits in adult multiplied to form large filter-feeding pharynx Larva an ascidian tadpole, possesses the following features: notochord, pharyngeal slits, dorsal tubular nerve cord, segmental myotomes, post-anal tail	Fish-like animals showing all recognisable chordate features Notochord extends length of body in larval and adult stages Large pharynx with clefts forms feeding mechanism Ciliated gill bars Pharyngeal slits open into atrium Segmental myotomes No head or limbs
	e.g. *Saccoglossus*	e.g. *Ciona intestinalis*	e.g. *Amphioxus lanceolatus*

Table 4.11 Classification of subphylum Vertebrata.

Subphylum Vertebrata

Characteristic features
Well-developed central nervous system including brain
Internal skeleton
Pharyngeal clefts few in number
Kidneys for nitrogenous excretion and osmoregulation
Muscular ventral heart
Two pairs of limbs

Class Agnatha (Cyclostomata)	*Class Chondrichthyes*	*Class Osteichthyes*	*Class Amphibia*	*Class Reptilia*	*Class Aves*	*Class Mammalia*
Slimy skin	Skin with placoid scales	Skin with cycloid scales	Soft skin	Skin dry with horny scales and bony plates	Skin bears feathers, legs have scales	Skin bears hair with two types of glands, sebaceous or sudoriparous
	Cartilaginous skeleton	Bony skeleton				
Paired limbs present	Paired, fleshy pectoral and pelvic fins	Paired pectoral and pelvic fins supported by rays	Paired pentadactyl limbs	Paired pentadactyl limbs usually present	Paired pentadactyl limbs, front pair form wings	Paired pentadactyl limbs
	Visceral clefts present as separate gill openings	Visceral clefts present as separate gill openings, but covered by a bony flap (operculum)	Visceral clefts present in tadpole only, lungs in adult	Visceral clefts never develop gills	Visceral clefts never develop gills	Visceral clefts never develop gills
	Lateral line system well developed	Lateral line system well developed	Lateral line system in tadpole only	No lateral line	No lateral line	No lateral line
	Inner ear, no middle or external ear	Inner ear, no middle or external ear	Inner and middle ear, no external ear	Inner and middle ear, no external ear	Inner and middle ear, no external ear	External, middle and inner ear, middle ear develops 3 ear ossicles
	No larval stage	Larval stage	Larval stage	No larval stage	No larval stage	No larval stage
	Eggs produced, internal fertilisation	Eggs produced, external fertilisation	Eggs produced, external fertilisation	Oviparous eggs laid, or eggs retained until hatching (ovoviviparous), internal fertilisation	Yolky eggs in calcareous shells, oviparous, internal fertilisation	Eggs develop within mother (except two genera), viviparous, internal fertilisation
						Muscular diaphragm between thorax and abdomen
e.g. *Myxine* (hag fish) *Lampetra* (lamprey)	e.g. *Scyliorhinus* (dogfish)	e.g. *Clupea* (herring)	e.g. *Rana* (frog) *Bufo* (toad)	e.g. *Natrix* (grass snake) *Crocodylus* (crocodile)	e.g. *Columba* (pigeon) *Aquila* (eagle)	e.g. *Homo* (human) *Canis* (dog)

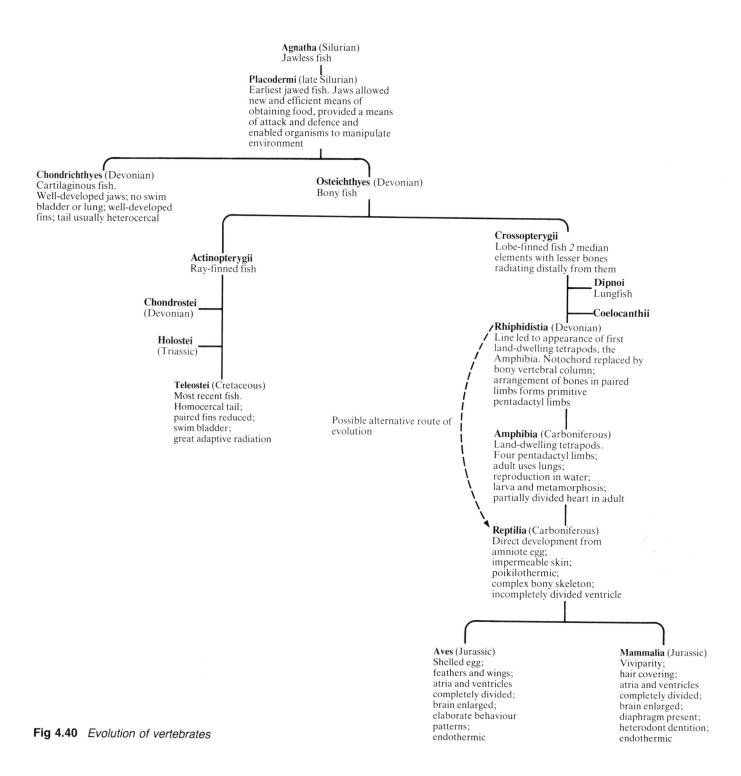

Agnatha (Silurian)
Jawless fish

Placodermi (late Silurian)
Earliest jawed fish. Jaws allowed
new and efficient means of
obtaining food, provided a means
of attack and defence and
enabled organisms to manipulate
environment

Chondrichthyes (Devonian)
Cartilaginous fish.
Well-developed jaws; no swim
bladder or lung; well-developed
fins; tail usually heterocercal

Osteichthyes (Devonian)
Bony fish

Crossopterygii
Lobe-finned fish 2 median
elements with lesser bones
radiating distally from them

Actinopterygii
Ray-finned fish

Dipnoi
Lungfish

Coelocanthii

Chondrostei
(Devonian)

Rhiphidistia (Devonian)
Line led to appearance of first
land-dwelling tetrapods, the
Amphibia. Notochord replaced by
bony vertebral column;
arrangement of bones in paired
limbs forms primitive
pentadactyl limbs

Holostei
(Triassic)

Teleostei (Cretaceous)
Most recent fish.
Homocercal tail;
paired fins reduced;
swim bladder;
great adaptive radiation

Possible alternative route of
evolution

Amphibia (Carboniferous)
Land-dwelling tetrapods.
Four pentadactyl limbs;
adult uses lungs;
reproduction in water;
larva and metamorphosis;
partially divided heart in adult

Reptilia (Carboniferous)
Direct development from
amniote egg;
impermeable skin;
poikilothermic;
complex bony skeleton;
incompletely divided ventricle

Aves (Jurassic)
Shelled egg;
feathers and wings;
atria and ventricles
completely divided;
brain enlarged;
elaborate behaviour
patterns;
endothermic

Mammalia (Jurassic)
Viviparity;
hair covering;
atria and ventricles
completely divided;
brain enlarged;
diaphragm present;
heterodont dentition;
endothermic

Fig 4.40 *Evolution of vertebrates*

(3) Increased effect of gravity – the apparent increase in body weight in air meant new stresses on the vertebral column. It changed from being a compression strut to being a girder. Limbs and girdles were developed.

(4) Change in locomotion – paired appendages became the main locomotory structures with the tail used for balance. In fish, locomotion is effected by the body and tail with the paired fins being used for balance.

(5) Reproduction – tetrapods must either develop methods for protecting eggs from desiccation or return to water to reproduce. Amphibia have not solved this problem and adopt the latter alternative.

(6) Irritability – changes in the sensory receptors had to be made to cope with the new stimuli present in the terrestrial environment.

4.1 Using the key provided in fig 4.41 attempt to classify as far as you can the range of animals provided by your teacher.

Fig 4.41 *Key for the classification of some non-vertebrate animals found in moist terrestrial or freshwater habitats*

1. Organism unicellular, or colony of similar cells .... PROTOCTISTA
   Organism multicellular, some or all cells specialised for different functions 2

2. Animal forming whitish or greenish encrusting growth on stones or branches etc.; pierced by small holes; texture spongy .... PORIFERA (Spongillidae)
   Animals not forming an encrusting growth 3

3. Animal attached, with tubular body surmounted by tentacles; flexible and retracting on disturbance .... CNIDARIA (Hydrozoa)
   Animal microscopic, usually under 2 mm with conspicuous crown of cilia. The body usually with a capsule or cuticle often of definite plates; often a 'foot' ending in two terminal small processes .... ROTIFERA
   Animal not as above 4

4. Animal under 2 mm, elongate, body forked posteriorly; cuticle usually bearing spines and scales. Cilia at front and on parts of surface .... GASTROTRICHA
   Animal very small, with one or two suckers; with or without forked tail (cercaria stage) .... TREMATODA
   Animal unlike either of above 5

5. Animal colonial, with a number of tentaculate heads, the tentacles bearing cilia. Usually attached but capable in few cases of slow creeping .... POLYZOA
   Animal not colonial 6

6. Animals with a hard inflexible shell (MOLLUSCA), from which a soft, unsegmented, body projects 7
   Animals without a hard inflexible shell 8

7. Snails, with single coiled shell, or limpet-like .... GASTROPODA
   Bivalves, with two valves or shells joined by a hinge ..... PELYCOPODA

8. Segmented or unsegmented worm-like animals, never with jointed limbs, where segmented with more than 14 segments 9
   Segmented animals with a hard jointed integument and usually with jointed limbs (ARTHROPODA)   18

9. Unsegmented animals without bristles or suckers 10
   Segmented animals either with bristles on the segments or a sucker at front and hind ends 12

10. Round-sectioned, elongate, with body enclosed in cuticle; no cilia, ends of body usually pointed .... NEMATODA
    Animal variable shape, often flat, not very elongate. No cuticle; body capable of contraction. Ciliated 11

11. Reddish-yellow worm about 1 cm long with protrusible proboscis above the mouth (usually protruded when animal dropped into spirit)   NEMERTINA
    Flat, often with proboscis bearing the mouth; movement characteristically gliding over substratum or surface of water. Colour usually black, yellowish, brown, or whitish .... PLATYHELMINTHES: TURBELLARIA

12. Animals bearing a sucker at both ends; segmentation well marked; never bearing bristles (leeches) .... HIRUDINEA
    Animals never with sucker at both ends, (and only in one small group of parasites, on crayfish with any suckers). Usually with bristles grouped into bundles, one on each side ventrally and one or more on each side dorsally per segment (OLIGOCHAETA) 13

13. Lacking bristles, sucker posteriorly .... BRANCHIOBDELLIDAE
    Bristles present, free-living, no suckers 14

14. Rather small, transparent worms with long chaetae .. NAIDIDAE
    Larger worms, or if small, without prominent chaetae   15

15. Usually more than two chaetae per bundle 16
    Never more than two chaetae per bundle 17

16. Small (to 36 mm) whitish, reddish, or yellowish worms with straight or S-shaped, pointed bristles ... ENCHYTRAEIDAE
    Small to large (to 200 mm) worms, some of the bristles forked at the tip .... TUBIFICIDAE

17. The families Lumbriculidae, Phreoryctidae, Criodrilidae and Lumbricidae are

123

all here and are best separated on characters of the reproductive system

18. Arthropods: small animals with globular or pear shaped, usually transparent bodies; three or four pairs of limbs, usually with hairs or bristles and often branched .... IMMATURE CRUSTACEA

Arthropods also with globular but usually opaque bodies, often bright red and mostly lacking visible segments; four pairs of limbs when adult; three when immature .... ARACHNIDA
19

Arthropods with elongate bodies, bearing 3 pairs of legs or lacking legs; head bearing antennae (1 pair) and mouth parts, thorax bearing legs, abdomen usually legless except for cerci or gills .... INSECTA

Arthropods with more than six legs, segmentation well marked, head bearing antennae (2 pairs), usually with abdominal appendages .... CRUSTACEA
21

19. Animal a typical spider, hairy body, unwetted by water and building air-filled 'bell' chamber .... *Argyronecta aquatica*

Animal smaller, without attached air bubble
20

20. Animals small (1 mm), elongate, with short, stumpy legs, living usually among wet moss, etc .... TARDIGRADA

Animals with rounded body, elongate legs, palps with 4 or 5 joints, often brightly coloured (red) or patterned brown. Usually above 1 mm, adults often free swimming, sometimes crawling .... ACARINA (mites)

21. Small crustacea, less than 3 mm, variable number of legs, usually transparent and free swimming in surface waters (zooplankton); often with carapace and with branched appendages bearing bristles .... MICROCRUSTACEA

Large crustacea, more than 3 mm, bottom living or swimming above the bottom 22

22. More than 5 pairs legs 23
5 pairs legs only 24

23. Animal flattened laterally from side to side, swimming on side, abdominal appendages of two kinds, the longest at the back ...... AMPHIPODA (Gammaridae)

Animal dorso-ventrally flattened, all limbs of equal size, resembling woodlouse .... ISOPODA (Asellotidae)

24. Body crab-like .... *Eriocheir sinensis* (mitten crab)

Body longer, lobster-like ..... *Astacus pallipes* (crayfish)

Chapter Five

Chemicals of life

5.1   Introduction to biochemistry

The study of the chemicals of living organisms, or biochemistry, has been closely associated with the great expansion in biological knowledge that has taken place during this century. Originally a supporting subject, particularly for medicine, biochemistry has grown into a discipline in its own right, studied to degree level in most centres of higher education. Its importance lies in the fundamental understanding it gives us of physiology, that is the way in which biological systems work. This in turn finds application in fields like agriculture (development of pesticides, herbicides and so on); medicine (including the whole pharmaceutical industry); fermentation industries with their vast range of useful products, including alcoholic drinks; food and nutrition, including dietetics, food production and preservation; and some more recent applications like enzyme technology and production of new types of food and fuel.

Biochemistry is also one of the great unifying themes in biology. At this level, what is often striking about living organisms is not so much their differences as their similarities.

5.1.1   Elements found in living organisms

The Earth's crust contains approximately 100 chemical elements and yet only 16 of these are essential for life. These 16 are listed in table 5.1. The four most common elements in living organisms are, in order, hydrogen, carbon, oxygen and nitrogen. These account for more than 99% of the mass and numbers of atoms found in all living organisms. The four most common elements in the Earth's crust, however, are oxygen, silicon, aluminium, and

sodium. The biological importance of hydrogen, oxygen, nitrogen and carbon is largely due to their having valencies of 1, 2, 3 and 4 respectively and their ability to form more stable covalent bonds than any other elements with these valencies (see appendix A1.1.3).

The importance of carbon

Carbon exhibits many unique features in its chemistry that are fundamental to life. A whole branch of chemistry, organic chemistry, is devoted to the study of carbon and its compounds. What are these unique features? Carbon has an atomic number of six because it has six electrons orbiting a nucleus containing six protons (fig A1.1). The nucleus also contains six neutrons, the protons and neutrons combining to give it a mass number of 12. In its chemistry it acquires a full (stable) outer shell of eight electrons by sharing four electrons. Thus, it is covalent (shares electrons) and has a valency of four (it shares four electrons).

A simple example of this sharing is shown in fig A1.2d, for the compound methane, whose **molecular formula** is CH_4 and whose **structural formula** is also shown in fig A1.2d.

> **5.1**   From what you have read, what is the difference between molecular and structural formulae?

When carbon is joined to four atoms or groups, the four bonds are arranged symmetrically in a tetrahedron (fig 5.1). If the three-dimensional arrangement of atoms is important, the convention shown in fig 5.1b can be used. Another convention commonly used is to omit carbon

Table 5.1 The elements found in living organisms.

Chief elements of organic molecules		Ions		Trace elements			
H	hydrogen	Na$^+$	sodium	Mn	manganese	B	boron
C	carbon	Mg^{2+}	magnesium	Fe	iron	Al	aluminium
N	nitrogen	Cl$^-$	chlorine	Co	cobalt	Si	silicon
O	oxygen	K$^+$	potassium	Cu	copper	V	vanadium
P	phosphorus	Ca^{2+}	calcium	Zn	zinc	Mo	molybdenum
S	sulphur					I	iodine

Elements in each column are arranged in order of atomic mass, not abundance. Those in the first three columns are found in all organisms.
(Based on A. L. Lehninger, *Biochemistry*, Worth. N.Y. 1970)

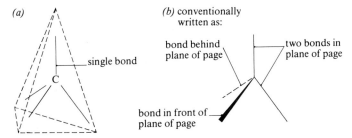

(a) single bond

(b) conventionally written as:

bond behind plane of page — two bonds in plane of page

bond in front of plane of page

Fig 5.1 *Tetrahedral arrangement of carbon bonds*

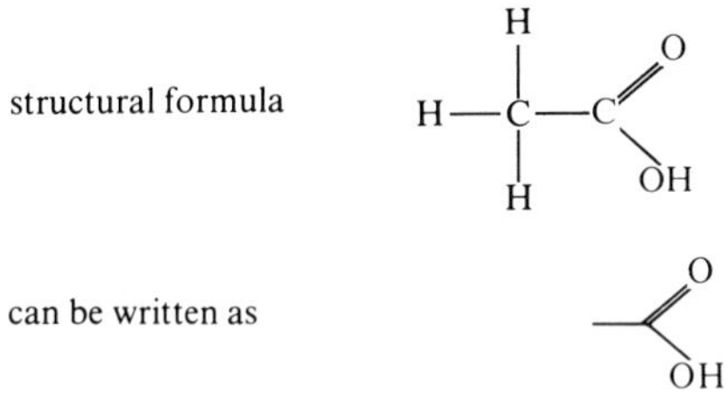

structural formula

$$H - \overset{\displaystyle H}{\underset{\displaystyle H}{C}} - C \overset{\displaystyle O}{\underset{\displaystyle OH}{}}$$

can be written as

$$\overset{O}{\underset{OH}{}}$$

Fig 5.2 *Two ways of representing the structural formula of ethanoic acid (acetic acid), CH_3COOH*

atoms, and any hydrogen atoms joined to carbon atoms, from the structural formula. A simple example is ethanoic acid (acetic acid), shown in fig 5.2. You will see also from this figure why its molecular formula can be represented as $CH_3.COOH$.

Knowing that the valency of carbon is 4, it is possible to deduce the location of missing hydrogen atoms. The advantage of this convention is two-fold: it simplifies diagrams of structural formulae and allows stress to be placed on the more important chemical groups.

The importance of carbon, then, lies in the way it forms strong, stable covalent bonds. This it can do with other carbon atoms, and with other types of atoms.

Carbon can form covalent bonds with other carbon atoms to form stable chains or rings, a property not shown to such an extent by any other element (fig 5.3). This ability is largely responsible for the vast variety of organic compounds; C—C bonds can be regarded as the skeletons of organic molecules.

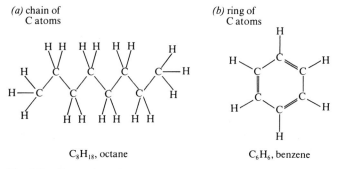

(a) chain of C atoms

C_8H_{18}, octane

(b) ring of C atoms

C_6H_6, benzene

Fig 5.3 *Examples of chain and ring structures formed by C–C bonds*

5.2 Draw the structural formulae of *(a)* octane and *(b)* benzene, using the convention described in fig 5.2.

Carbon atoms commonly form covalent bonds with H, N, O, P, and S. Combination with these and other elements contributes to the large variety of organic compounds.

Multiple bonds. A further important property of carbon is its ability to form strong multiple bonds, a property shared with oxygen and nitrogen. The multiple bonds are:

double bonds: $>C=C<$ $>C=O$ $>C=N-$

triple bonds: $-C\equiv C-$ $-C\equiv N$
(rare in nature)

Compounds containing double = or triple ≡ carbon–carbon bonds are called unsaturated. In a saturated carbon compound, all carbon–carbon bonds are single.

5.3 Draw the structural formula for the unsaturated organic compound ethene (ethylene), C_2H_4.

Summary. The important chemical properties of carbon are
(1) it is a relatively small atom with a low mass,
(2) it has the ability to form four strong, stable covalent bonds,
(3) it has the ability to form carbon–carbon bonds, thus building up large carbon skeletons with ring and/or chain structures,
(4) it has the ability to form multiple covalent bonds with other carbon atoms, oxygen and nitrogen.

This unique combination of features is responsible for the enormous variety of organic molecules. Variation occurs in three major ways: **size**, determined by the carbon skeleton, **chemistry**, determined by the associated elements and chemical groups and how saturated the carbon skeleton is, and **shape**, determined by geometry, that is angles of the bonds.

5.1.2   Simple biological molecules

Having seen which elements are found in organisms, it is necessary to examine which compounds they form. Again, there is a fundamental similarity between all living organisms. Water is the most abundant compound, typically constituting between 60–95% of the fresh mass of an organism. Certain simple organic molecules are also universally found; these act as building blocks for larger molecules and are listed in table 5.2. They are discussed more fully later.

Thus relatively few types of molecule give rise to the larger molecules and structures of living cells. They are the kinds of molecules which biologists speculate could have

Table 5.2 Chemical 'building blocks' of organic compounds.

Small molecules ('building blocks')	Constituent of
amino acids	proteins
sugars (monosaccharides)	polysaccharides and nucleic acids
fatty acids, glycerol and choline	lipids
aromatic bases	nucleic acids

been synthesised in the 'primeval soup' of chemicals which is thought to have existed in the early history of the planet, before life itself appeared (section 24.1). These simple molecules are made in turn from even simpler, inorganic molecules, notably carbon dioxide, nitrogen and water.

Importance of water

Without water, life could not exist on this planet. It is doubly important to living organisms because it is both a vital chemical constituent of living cells and, for many, a habitat. It is worth while, then, looking at some of its chemical and physical properties.

These are rather unusual and due mostly to its small size,

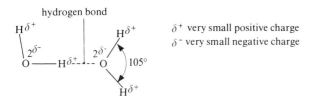

Fig 5.4 *Two water molecules, showing polarity of the molecules and formation of a hydrogen bond between them*

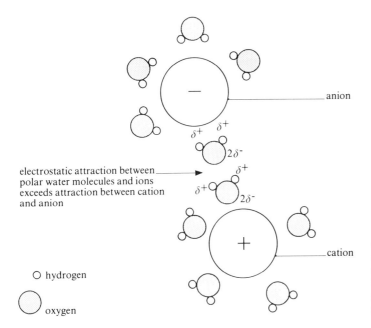

electrostatic attraction between polar water molecules and ions exceeds attraction between cation and anion

○ hydrogen

◯ oxygen

its polarity and to hydrogen-bonding between its molecules. Polarity is an uneven charge distribution over a molecule. In water, one end of the molecule is slightly positive and the other slightly negative. This is known as a **dipole**. The more electronegative oxygen atom tends to attract the single electrons of the hydrogen atoms. Water molecules therefore have an electrostatic attraction for each other, opposite charges coming together and causing them to behave as if they were 'sticky' (fig 5.4). These attractions are not as strong as normal ionic bonds and are called **hydrogen bonds**. With these features in mind, some of the biologically significant properties of water can be examined.

Biological significance of water

Solvent properties. Water is an excellent solvent for polar substances. These include ionic substances like salts, whose charged particles (ions) dissociate (separate) in water when the substance dissolves as described in fig 5.5, and some non-ionic substances like sugars and simple alcohols which contain charged (polar) groups within the molecules, such as the hydroxyl (—OH) groups of sugars and alcohols.

Once a substance is in solution its molecules or ions can move about freely, thus making it more chemically reactive than if it were solid. Thus the majority of the cell's chemical reactions take place in aqueous solutions. Non-polar substances, such as lipids, are immiscible with water and can serve to separate aqueous solutions into compartments, as with membranes. Non-polar parts of molecules are repelled by water and usually group together in its presence, as when oil droplets coalesce in water to form larger oil droplets, that is non-polar molecules are **hydrophobic** (water-hating). Such hydrophobic interactions are important in maintaining the stability of membranes, many protein molecules, nucleic acids and other subcellular structures.

Water's solvent properties also mean that it acts as a transport medium, as in the blood, lymphatic and excretory systems, the alimentary canal and in xylem and phloem.

High heat capacity. The specific heat capacity of water is the amount of heat, measured in joules, required to raise the temperature of 1 kg of water by 1 °C. Water has a high heat capacity. This means that a large increase in heat energy results in a relatively small rise in temperature. This is because much of the energy is used in breaking the hydrogen bonds (overcoming the 'stickiness') which restrict the mobility of the molecules.

Fig 5.5 (left) *Distribution of water molecules around an anion (−) and a cation (+). Note that the more negatively charged oxygen atom of water faces inwards to the cation but outwards from the anion. This occurs when ionic substances dissolve in water. Due to their polarity, water molecules weaken the attraction between ions of opposite charge and then surround the ions, keeping them apart. The ions are said to be hydrated*

Temperature changes within water are minimised as a result of its high heat capacity. Biochemical processes therefore operate over a smaller temperature range, proceeding at more constant rates and are less likely to be inhibited by extremes of temperature. Water also provides a very constant external environment for many cells and organisms.

High heat of vaporisation. Latent heat of vaporisation (or relative latent heat of vaporisation) is a measure of the heat energy required to vaporise a liquid, that is to overcome the attractive forces between its molecules so that they can escape as a gas. A relatively large amount of energy is needed to vaporise water. This is due to the hydrogen bonding. As a result, water has an unusually high boiling point for such a small molecule.

The energy imparted to water molecules to vaporise them thus results in loss of energy from their surroundings, that is a cooling effect occurs. This is made use of in sweating and panting of mammals, the opening of the mouth of some reptiles in sunshine, such as crocodiles, and may be important in cooling transpiring leaves. The high heat of vaporisation means that a large amount of heat can be lost with minimal loss of water from the body.

High heat of fusion. Latent heat of fusion (or relative latent heat of fusion) is a measure of the heat energy required to melt a solid, in this case ice. With its high heat capacity, water requires relatively large amounts of heat energy to thaw it. Conversely, liquid water must lose a relatively large amount of heat energy to freeze. Contents of cells and their environments are therefore less likely to freeze. Ice crystals are particularly damaging if they develop inside cells.

Density and freezing properties. The density of water decreases below 4 °C and ice therefore tends to float. It is the only substance whose solid form is less dense than its liquid form.

Since ice floats, it forms at the surface first and the bottom last. If ponds froze from the bottom upwards, freshwater life could not exist in temperate or arctic climates. Ice insulates the water below it, thus increasing the chances of survival of organisms in the water. This is important in cold climates and cold seasons, and must have been particularly so in the past, such as during Ice Ages. Also, the ice thaws more rapidly by being at the surface. The fact that water below 4 °C tends to rise also helps to maintain circulation in large bodies of water. This may result in nutrient cycling and colonisation of water to greater depths.

High surface tension and cohesion. Cohesion is the force whereby individual molecules stick together. At the surface of a liquid, a force called surface tension exists between the molecules as a result of inwardly acting cohesive forces between the molecules. These cause the surface of the liquid to occupy the least possible surface area (ideally a sphere). Water has a higher surface tension than any other liquid. The high cohesion of water molecules is important in cells and in translocation of water through xylem in plants (section 14.4). At a less fundamental level, many small organisms rely on surface tension to settle on water or to skate over its surface.

Water as a reagent. Water is biologically significant as an essential metabolite, that is it participates in the chemical reactions of metabolism. In particular, it is used as a source of hydrogen in photosynthesis (section 9.4.2) and is used in hydrolysis reactions.

Water and evolutionary change. The importance of water to living organisms is reflected in the fact that its shortage appears to have been a major selection pressure in the development of species. This is a recurrent theme in chapters 3 and 4 where, for example, the restrictions placed on certain plants by their motile gametes are discussed. All terrestrial organisms are adapted to obtain and conserve water, and the extreme adaptations of xerophytes, desert animals and so on, provide some fascinating examples of biological design.

Some of the biologically important functions of water are summarised in table 5.3.

Table 5.3 Some biologically important functions of water.

All organisms
Structure – high water content of protoplasm
Solvent and medium for diffusion
Reagent in hydrolysis
Support for aquatic organisms
Fertilisation by swimming gametes
Dispersal of seeds, gametes and larval stages of aquatic organisms, and seeds of some terrestrial species e.g. coconut

Plants
Osmosis and *turgidity* (important in many ways, such as growth (cell enlargement), support, guard cell mechanism)
Reagent in photosynthesis
Transpiration and *translocation* of inorganic ions and organic compounds
Germination of seeds – swelling and breaking open of the testa and further development

Animals
Transport
Osmoregulation
Cooling by evaporation, such as sweating, panting
Lubrication, as in joints
Support – hydrostatic skeleton
Protection, for example lachrymal fluid, mucus
Migration in ocean currents

5.1.3 Macromolecules

The simpler organic molecules associate to form larger molecules. A **macromolecule** is a giant molecule made from many repeating units; it is therefore a **polymer** and the unit molecules are called **monomers**. There are three types of macromolecule, namely polysaccharides, proteins and nucleic acids and their constituent monomers are monosaccharides, amino acids and nucleotides respectively.

Macromolecules account for over 90% of the dry mass of cells. Table 5.4 summarises the important properties of macromolecules.

Differences between macromolecules are discussed in detail later, but one key point is that nucleic acids and proteins can be regarded as 'informational' molecules, whereas polysaccharides are 'non-informational'. This means that the *sequence* of subunits is important in proteins and nucleic acids and is much more variable than in polysaccharides, where only one or two different subunits are normally used. The reasons for this will become clear later. In the rest of this chapter, we shall be studying the three classes of macromolecules and their subunits in detail. In addition, lipids, although generally much smaller molecules (average M_r 750–2 500) will be included since they generally associate with each other into much larger groups of molecules.

Table 5.4 Characteristics of macromolecules.

Property	Polysaccharides	Proteins	Nucleic acids
M_r (relative formula mass or molecular mass)	10^4–10^6 (typical)	10^4–10^6 (typical)	10^4–10^{10} (typical)
Subunits	**monosaccharides** (Many types, though few commonly used. Usually only 1 type per molecule. Sometimes 2 types alternate.)	**amino acids** (20 common types. All may be used in 1 molecule.)	**nucleotides** (5 types, 4 used in DNA, 4 in RNA.)
Branching or non-branching	May be branched	No branching	No branching
Type of bond joining subunits	Glycosidic bond – 2 types	Peptide bond	Phosphodiester bond (Sugar–phosphate bond)

Other properties common to all three types of macromolecule:
(i) bonds between subunits are formed by elimination of water (**condensation**),
(ii) formation of bonds requires energy,
(iii) bonds between subunits are broken by addition of water (**hydrolysis**).

Table 5.5 Some common chemical groups found in organic molecules.

Aldehyde group	$-C\begin{smallmatrix}H\\\\O\end{smallmatrix}$ or —CHO $\xrightarrow[\text{oxidation}]{O}$ —COOH carboxylic acid $\xrightarrow[\text{reduction}]{2H}$ —CH$_2$OH primary alcohol	
Keto group (compound containing this group is called a ketone)	C=O $\xrightarrow[\text{reduction}]{2H}$ —CHOH secondary alcohol	
Hydroxyl group	—OH	
Primary alcohol group	—CH$_2$OH or $-C\begin{smallmatrix}H\\-H\\OH\end{smallmatrix}$	
Secondary alcohol group	CHOH or $>C\begin{smallmatrix}H\\OH\end{smallmatrix}$	
Carboxyl group	>COOH or $-C\begin{smallmatrix}O\\OH\end{smallmatrix}$	
Carbonyl group	>C=O note that this group is present in aldehydes, ketones and carboxylic acids	

5.2   Carbohydrates (saccharides)

Carbohydrates are substances with the general formula $C_x(H_2O)_y$, where x and y are variable numbers; their name (hydrate of carbon) is derived from the fact that hydrogen and oxygen are present in the same proportions as in water. All carbohydrates are aldehydes or ketones and all contain several hydroxyl groups. Their chemistry is determined by these groups. For example, aldehydes are very easily oxidised and hence are powerful reducing agents. The structures of these and some related groups are shown in table 5.5, together with some typical chemical reactions of aldehydes and ketones.

Carbohydrates are divided into three main classes, mono-, di- and polysaccharides, as shown in fig 5.6.

5.2.1   Monosaccharides

Monosaccharides are single sugar units. Their general formula and some of their properties are shown in fig 5.6. They are classified according to the number of carbon atoms as trioses (3C), tetroses (4C), pentoses (5C), hexoses (6C) and heptoses (7C). Of these, pentoses and hexoses are the most common.

5.4 What would be the molecular formula of each of these types of sugar?

The chief functions of monosaccharides are summarised in table 5.6.

It will be seen from table 5.6 that monosaccharides are important as energy sources and as building blocks for the synthesis of larger molecules. They are suitable for the latter role because they are chemically reactive molecules and show a wide variety of structures, including the variation in number of carbon atoms already mentioned. Some other important features which contribute to their variety are discussed below.

Aldoses and ketoses

In monosaccharides, all the carbon atoms except one have a hydroxyl group attached. The remaining carbon atom is either part of an aldehyde group, in which case the monosaccharide is called an **aldose** or **aldo sugar**, or is part of a keto group, when it is called a **ketose** or **keto sugar**. Thus all monosaccharides are aldoses or ketoses. The two simplest monosaccharides are the trioses glyceraldehyde and dihydroxyacetone. Glyceraldehyde has an aldehyde

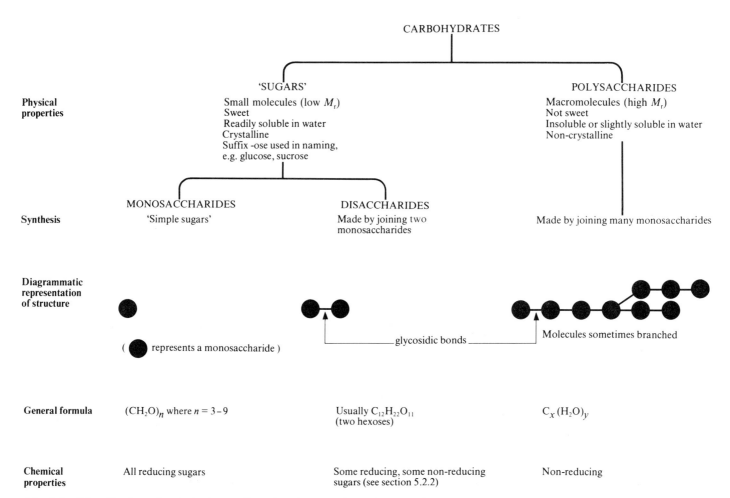

Fig 5.6 *Classification of carbohydrates. Note that the term 'sugar' is superfluous but convenient because mono- and disaccharides share certain properties, such as sweetness of taste*

Table 5.6 Chief functions of monosaccharides.

Trioses $C_3H_6O_3$ e.g. glyceraldehyde, dihydroxyacetone
Intermediates in respiration (see glycolysis), photosynthesis (see dark reactions) and other branches of carbohydrate metabolism
Glyceraldehyde→glycerol→triglyceride(lipid)

Tetroses $C_4H_8O_4$
Rare in nature, occurring mainly in bacteria (not discussed further in this chapter)

Pentoses $C_5H_{10}O_5$ e.g. ribose, ribulose
Synthesis of nucleic acids; ribose is a constituent of RNA, deoxyribose of DNA
Synthesis of some coenzymes, e.g. NAD, NADP, coenzyme A, FAD, FMN
Synthesis of AMP, ADP, and ATP
Synthesis of the polysaccharides called pentosans (see polysaccharides)
Ribulose bisphosphate is the CO_2 acceptor in photosynthesis

Hexoses $C_6H_{12}O_6$ e.g. glucose, fructose, galactose, mannose
Source of energy when oxidised in respiration; glucose is the most common respiratory substrate and the most common monosaccharide
Synthesis of disaccharides; monosaccharide units can link together to form larger molecules; combinations of 2–10 monosaccharides
are termed oligosaccharides, the most commonly occurring oligosaccharides are the disaccharides, made up of two monosaccharides
Synthesis of the polysaccharides called hexosans (see polysaccharides), glucose is particularly important in this role

Derivatives of Monosaccharides
Some important derivatives of monosaccharides are sugar alcohols, sugar acids, deoxy sugars and amino sugars

(i) Sugar $\xrightarrow[\text{reduction}]{2H}$ **sugar alcohol,** e.g. glycerol, used in lipid synthesis. Sugar alcohols sometimes act as storage carbohydrates, e.g. mannitol in *Fucus* and some fruits.

—CHO (aldose) $\xrightarrow{2H}$ —CH_2OH
>C=O (ketose) $\xrightarrow{2H}$ >CHOH

(ii) Sugar $\xrightarrow[\text{oxidation}]{O}$ **sugar acid** Sugar acids are important intermediates in carbohydrate metabolism. Some, e.g. glucuronic acid, are constituents of the polysaccharides used in gums, mucilages and cell walls. Vitamin C (ascorbic acid) is a sugar acid derived from a hexose.

—CHO (aldose) $\xrightarrow{O}$ —COOH
—CH_2OH (aldose $\xrightarrow{-2H}$ CHO $\xrightarrow{O}$ —COOH
or ketose)

(iii) Sugar $\xrightarrow[\text{lost by}]{\text{oxygen atom}}$ **deoxy sugar** Most important is deoxyribose, formed by deoxygenation of ribose, and used in DNA synthesis.
replacing —OH group
with—H

(iv) Sugar $\xrightarrow[\text{(amino group)}]{\text{add —NH}_2}$ **amino sugar** e.g. glucosamine, used in synthesis of chitin and formed in many polysaccharides of vertebrates. Galactosamine used in synthesis of cartilage.
—OH of carbon 2→ —NH_2

group and dihydroxyacetone a keto group, and they can be regarded as the parent compounds of the aldoses and ketoses respectively (fig 5.7).

5.5 If you have little experience of chemistry, it might be useful to answer the following with reference to fig 5.7.
(a) What is the valency of each element?
(b) What is the total number of each type of atom? Does it conform with the molecular formula?
(c) How many hydroxyl groups does each molecule contain? Could this have been predicted knowing they were trioses?
(d) Can you recognise any other chemical groups not labelled in this diagram?

Fig 5.8 shows some other common aldoses and ketoses. In general, aldoses, such as ribose and glucose, are more common than ketoses, such as ribulose and fructose.

5.6 Which sugars in fig 5.8 are pentoses and which are hexoses?

Optical isomerism

Another important structural characteristic of monosaccharides is the occurrence of isomerism. If two different compounds have the same molecular formula, they are said to be isomers of each other. Two types of isomerism occur, structural and stereoisomerism. **Structural isomerism** is due to different linkings of the atoms or groups within the molecules. Thus all hexoses are structural isomers of each other (fig 5.8 – compare glucose, mannose, galactose and fructose, all with the same molecular formula, $C_6H_{12}O_6$).

Stereoisomerism occurs when the same atoms or groups are joined together but are arranged differently in space. Two kinds of stereoisomerism occur, geometric and optical isomerism. We are not concerned with geometric isomerism, which involves certain compounds containing double bonds. Optical isomerism, however, is an important, biologically significant feature of monosaccharides and amino acids.

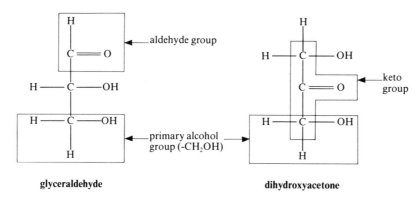

Fig 5.7 *Structures of glyceraldehyde and dihydroxyacetone. Note carefully the positions of the aldehyde and keto groups. Aldehyde groups are always at the end of the chain of C atoms*

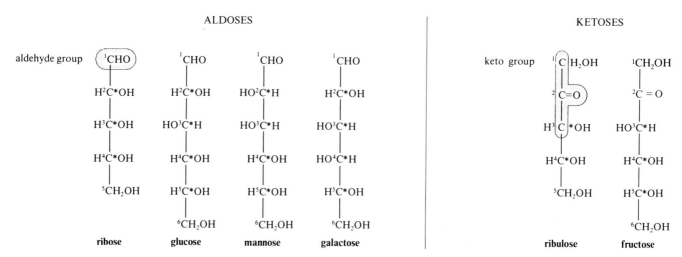

Fig 5.8 *Some common aldoses and ketoses. C atoms are numbered according to convention. * asymmetric C atoms – see optical isomerism*

Certain solid compounds when dissolved to form a solution (and certain liquid compounds) possess the power to rotate the plane of vibration of plane-polarised light, and are said to be **optically active**. Plane-polarised light is light vibrating in one plane only, whereas light normally vibrates in all planes perpendicular to its direction of transmission. It is easier to understand this by studying fig 5.9, which shows normal light being artificially converted to plane-polarised light by a **polariser**, and then having its plane of polarisation changed by an optically active substance.

If the substance rotates the plane of polarisation to the right, it is said to be **dextro-rotatory** and if to the left **laevo-rotatory**. The degree of rotation can be measured by an instrument called a polarimeter.

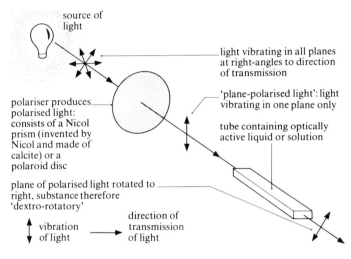

Fig 5.9 *Principles of optical isomerism*

Optical isomerism is a property of any compound which can exist in two forms whose structures are mirror images. Like right- and left-handed gloves, such structures cannot be superimposed on each other. In organic compounds this occurs when a carbon atom has four different atoms or groups attached to it. Such a carbon atom is called an **asymmetric carbon atom**. The principle is illustrated in fig 5.10*a* where it can be seen that the tetrahedral arrangement of bonds about the central, asymmetric carbon atom means that there are two possible arrangements of the groups in space, forming two mirror images. Glyceraldehyde provides a simple example of a monosaccharide showing optical isomerism. It possesses one asymmetric carbon atom and exists in two forms as shown in fig 5.10*b*.

Dextro-rotatory compounds are given the prefix 'd'- or more recently (+) and laevo-rotatory compounds 'l'- or more recently (−). The two isomers of glyceraldehyde are called the D-isomer (dextro-rotatory) and the L-isomer (laevo-rotatory). (Note the use of *small* capitals.) All optical isomers of monosaccharides can be structurally related to one of these two forms of glyceraldehyde. By convention, if the asymmetric carbon atom furthest from the aldehyde or ketone group has its hydroxyl group in the same position as in D-glyceraldehyde, the isomer is called the D-isomer, and if in the same position as in L-glyceraldehyde, it is called the L-isomer. **This is irrespective of the direction in which they rotate plane-polarised light**. All the isomers shown in fig 5.8 are D-isomers, as are virtually all naturally occurring monosaccharides. However, the direction in which they rotate plane-polarised light varies. D-glucose for example rotates it to the right, whereas D-fructose rotates it to the left. The D- and L-isomers of glucose are shown in fig 5.11 and it will be seen that they are mirror images.

Although D- and L-isomers of the same substance have the same chemical and physical properties, and are therefore given the same chemical name, such as D- and L-glyceraldehyde, their three-dimensional differences have biological significance in one important respect, namely that enzymes, which depend on recognition by shape, can distinguish between the mirror images. It is possible that early in evolution an arbitrary bias to accept the D-isomers of sugars was established since their L-isomers are rare in nature. Naturally occurring amino acids, however, are all L-isomers.

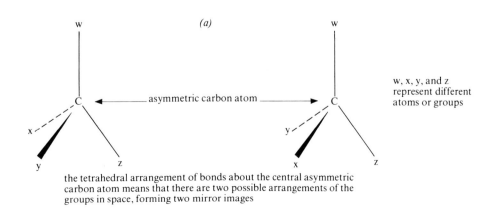

the tetrahedral arrangement of bonds about the central asymmetric carbon atom means that there are two possible arrangements of the groups in space, forming two mirror images

Fig 5.10 *Optical isomerism (a) Diagram illustrating the principle of asymmetry of carbon atoms.*

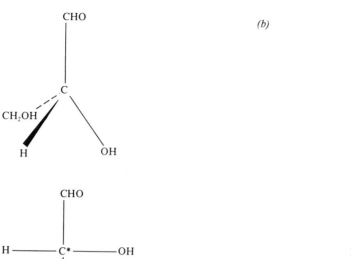

(b)

D(+)-glyceraldehyde

L(−)-glyceraldehyde

* asymmetric carbon atom

(c)

Fig 5.10 (cont.) *(b) Two ways of representing optical isomers (mirror images) of glyceraldeyde and (c) molecular models of the two isomers*

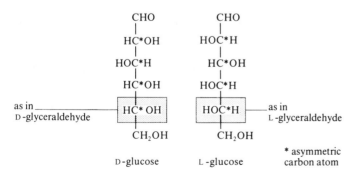

as in D-glyceraldehyde

as in L-glyceraldehyde

D-glucose   L-glucose

* asymmetric carbon atom

Fig 5.11 *D- and L-isomers of glucose. Note that they are mirror images*

Ring structures

Fig 5.8 shows pentoses and hexoses represented as straight chain molecules. Because of the bond angles between carbon atoms, however, it is possible for sugars with five and six carbon atoms to form stable ring structures. In pentoses, the first carbon atom joins with the oxygen atom on the fourth carbon atom to give a five-membered ring called a **furanose ring**, as shown in fig 5.12. In hexoses which are aldoses, for example glucose, the first carbon atom combines with the oxygen atom on carbon five to give a six-membered ring, as shown in fig 5.13. This structure is known as a **pyranose ring**. In hexoses which are ketoses, such as fructose, the *second* carbon atom combines with the oxygen atom on carbon five to give a furanose ring.

The ring structures of pentoses and hexoses are the usual forms, with only a small proportion of the molecules existing in the 'open chain' form at any one time. The ring structure is the form incorporated into disaccharides and polysaccharides.

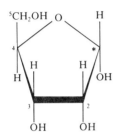

H
|
$^1C = O$
|
$H —^2C —OH$
|
$H —^3C —OH$
|
$H —^4C —OH$
|
$^5CH_2OH$

D-ribose

carbon 1 shown to right of ring by convention

$^5CH_2OH$ O   H
   ^4C ^1C
H   H   H   OH
      $_3C$——$_2C$
      | |
      OH   OH

D-ribose with 5-membered furanose ring

conventionally written as:

$^5CH_2OH$ O   H
   4   *
      H   H
   H   OH
      3   2
      OH   OH

* see α - and β - isomers

The ring is at right-angles to the plane of the paper. The front portion is represented by thicker lines. The side-groups are located above and below the ring.

Fig 5.12 *Three conventional ways of representing the structure of ribose*

H
|
$^1C = O$
|
$H —^2C——OH$
|
$HO—^3C——H$
|
$H —^4C——OH$
|
$H —^5C——OH$
|
$^6CH_2OH$

D-glucose

$^6CH_2OH$
         5   O
H   H
      H   OH   H   *
   4   1
   OH   OH
            3   2
         H   OH

D-glucose with 6-membered pyranose ring
* see α - and β - isomers

Fig 5.13 *Two conventional ways of representing the structure of glucose*

α- and β-isomers

The ring structures have biological significance because their formation results in another carbon atom becoming asymmetric. This carbon atom is asterisked in figs 5.12 and 5.13 and you will notice that each has a hydroxyl group (–OH) attached to it. This may be below the plane of the ring, as shown in figs 5.12 and 5.13, or above the plane of the ring. The former is the α-isomer, the latter the β-isomer. The existence of α- and β-isomers leads to greater chemical variety and is of importance in, for example, the formation of starch and cellulose (see polysaccharides).

> **5.7** (*a*) Draw side by side, for comparison, the α- and β-isomers of D-ribose and D-glucose. (*b*) What type of isomerism is this?

5.2.2 Disaccharides

Fig 5.6 summarises some of the properties of disaccharides. They are formed by condensation reactions between two monosaccharides, usually hexoses, as shown in fig 5.14.

The bond formed between two monosaccharides is called a **glycosidic bond** and it normally forms between carbon atoms 1 and 4 of neighbouring units (a 1,4 bond). The process can be repeated indefinitely to build up the giant molecules of polysaccharides (fig 5.14). The monosaccharide units are called **residues** once they have been linked. Thus a maltose molecule contains two glucose residues.

The most common disaccharides are maltose, lactose and sucrose:

glucose + glucose   = maltose,
glucose + galactose = lactose,
glucose + fructose = sucrose.

Maltose is formed by the action of amylases (enzymes) on starch during digestion, for example in animals or germinating seeds. It is converted to glucose by the action of a maltase. Lactose, or milk sugar, is found exclusively in milk. Sucrose, or cane sugar, is most abundant in plants, where it is translocated in large quantities through phloem tissue. It is sometimes stored because it is relatively inert metabolically. It is obtained commercially from sugar cane and sugar beet and is the 'sugar' we normally buy in shops.

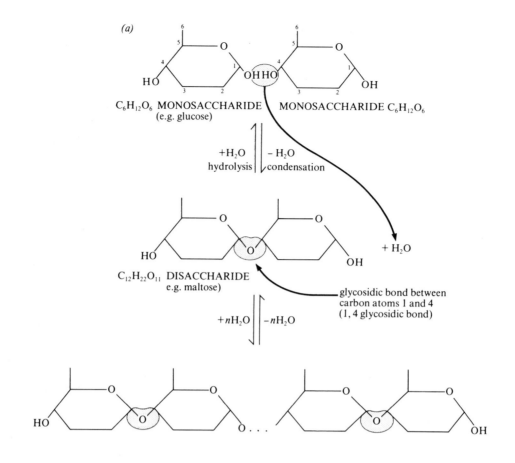

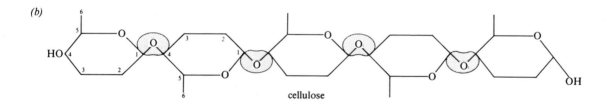

(b)

cellulose

Fig 5.14 *(a) Formation of a disaccharide and a polysaccharide. NB Only the relevant parts of the molecules are shown. A complete glucose molecule is shown in fig 5.13. (b) Structure of cellulose. In some polysaccharides, units may be spun through 180° at each successive condensation, as in cellulose*

Reducing sugars

All monosaccharides and some disaccharides, including maltose and lactose, are reducing sugars. Sucrose is a non-reducing sugar. The chemistry of reduction is related to the activity of the aldehyde group of aldo sugars and the combined ketone and primary alcohol groups of keto sugars. In non-reducing sugars, these groups are not available to participate in a reaction since they are linked together in the glycosidic bond. Two common tests for reducing sugars, Benedict's test and Fehling's test (section 5.8) make use of the ability of these sugars to reduce copper from a valency of 2 to a valency of 1. Both tests involve use of an alkaline solution of copper(II) sulphate ($CuSO_4$) which is reduced to insoluble copper(I) oxide (Cu_2O).

Ionic equation: $Cu^{2+} + e^- \longrightarrow Cu^+$
blue solution   brick-red precipitate

5.2.3 Polysaccharides

Fig 5.6 summarises some of the properties of polysaccharides. They function chiefly as food and energy stores (for example starch and glycogen) and as structural materials (for example cellulose). They are convenient storage molecules for several reasons: their large size makes them more or less insoluble in water, so they exert no osmotic or chemical influence in the cell; they fold into compact shapes (see below) and they are easily converted to sugars by hydrolysis when required.

As we have already seen, polysaccharides are polymers of monosaccharides; polymers of pentoses are called **pentosans** and polymers of hexoses are called **hexosans**. Polymers of glucose are **glucosans**.

Starch

Starch is a polymer of glucose. It is a major fuel store in plants, but is absent from animals where the equivalent is glycogen (see below). Starch has two components, amylose and amylopectin. Amylose has a straight chain structure consisting of several thousand glucose residues, though the chain coils helically into a more compact shape. Amylopectin is also compact as it has many branches, formed by 1,6 glycosidic bonds (fig 5.15). It has up to twice as many glucose residues as amylose.

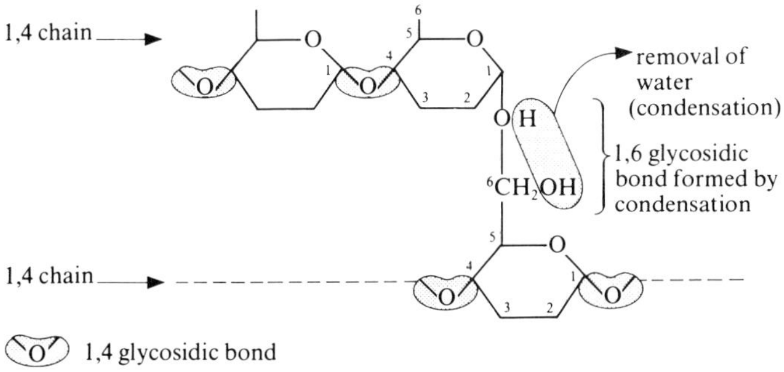

Fig 5.15 *Structure of amylopectin showing formation of one branch*

A suspension of amylose in water gives a blue-black colour with iodine–potassium iodide solution, whereas a suspension of amylopectin gives a red-violet colour. This forms the basis of the test for starch (section 5.8). Starch molecules accumulate to form starch grains. These are visible in many plant cells, notably in the chloroplasts of leaves (fig 9.6), in storage organs such as the potato tuber, and in seeds of cereals and legumes. The grains appear to be made of layers of starch and are usually of a characteristic size and shape for a given plant species.

> **5.8** With reference to your answer to question 5.7, which isomer, α- or β-glucose, is used in making starch?

Glycogen

Glycogen is the animal equivalent of starch, being a storage polysaccharide made from glucose; many fungi also store it. In vertebrates, glycogen is stored chiefly in the liver and muscles, both centres of high metabolic activity where it provides a useful source of glucose for use in respiration. It is very similar in structure in amylopectin, but shows more branching. It forms tiny granules inside cells which are usually associated with smooth endoplasmic reticulum (fig 7.5). The metabolism of glycogen is described in chapter 11.

Cellulose

Cellulose is another polymer of glucose.

> **5.9** Study the structure of cellulose in fig 5.14*b*. Is it made of α- or β- glucose residues? (This should reveal why successive glucose residues are rotated at 180° in the cellulose molecule.)

About 50% of the carbon found in plants is in cellulose and it is the most abundant organic molecule on Earth. It is virtually confined to plants, although it is found in some non-vertebrates and ancestral fungi. Its abundance is a result of its being a structural component of all plant cell walls, constituting about 20–40% of the wall on average. The structure of the molecule reveals its suitability for this role. It consists of long chains of glucose residues with about 10 000 residues per chain (fig 5.14*b*). Hydroxyl groups (—OH) project outwards from each chain in all directions and form hydrogen bonds with neighbouring chains, thus establishing a rigid cross-linking between chains. The chains associate in groups to form microfibrils, which are arranged in larger bundles to form macrofibrils. These have tremendous tensile strength (some idea of this strength can be obtained by testing cotton, which is almost pure cellulose) and their arrangement in layers in a cementing matrix of other polysaccharides is described in section 7.3.1. Despite their combined strength, the layers are fully permeable to water and solutes, an important property in the functioning of plant cells. Apart from being a structural compound, cellulose is an important food source for some animals, bacteria and fungi. The enzyme cellulase, which catalyses the digestion of cellulose to glucose, is relatively rare in nature and most animals, including humans, cannot utilise cellulose despite its being an abundant and potentially valuable source of glucose. Ruminant mammals like the cow, however, have bacteria living symbiotically in their guts which digest cellulose. The abundance of cellulose and its relatively slow rate of breakdown in nature have ecological implications because it means that substantial quantities of carbon are 'locked up' in this substance, and carbon is one of the chief materials required by living organisms. Commercially, cellulose is extremely important. It is used, for example, to make cotton goods and is a constituent of paper.

Callose

Callose is an amorphous polymer of glucose found in a wide variety of locations in plants and often formed in response to wounding or stress. It is particularly important in phloem sieve tubes (chapter 14). It has 1,3 glycosidic linkages.

Inulin

Inulin is an unusual polysaccharide, being a polymer of fructose. It is used as a food store, particularly in roots and tubers of the family Compositae, for example *Dahlia* tubers.

5.2.4 Compounds closely related to polysaccharides

Brief mention has already been made of amino sugars and sugar acids in table 5.6. These molecules often participate in the same ways as simple sugars in the formation of polysaccharides, and their products are generally called mucopolysaccharides. They are of great biological significance.

Chitin

Chitin is closely related to cellulose in structure and function, being a structural polysaccharide. It occurs in some fungi, where its fibrous nature contributes to cell wall structure, and in some animal groups, particularly the arthropods where it forms an essential part of the exoskeleton. Structurally it is identical to cellulose except that the hydroxyl (—OH) group at carbon atom 2 is replaced by —NH.CO.CH$_3$. This is a result of the amino sugar glucosamine combining with an acetyl group (CH$_3$.CO—). Chitin is therefore a polymer of acetylglucosamine (fig 5.16). It forms bundles of long parallel chains like cellulose.

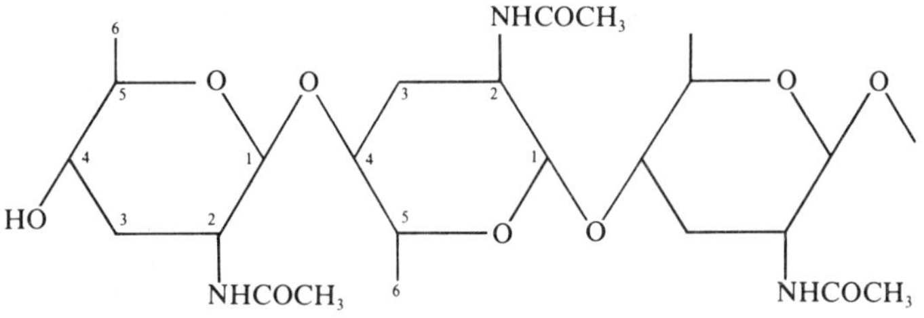

Fig 5.16 *Structure of chitin*

Glycoproteins and glycolipids

Glycoproteins and glycolipids are important molecules containing a polysaccharide unit, and the structure and biological functions of glycolipids are described further in section 5.3.8. Table 5.7 gives further examples of the many roles played by polysaccharides and closely related compounds. The chief point to note is the existence of a great variety of molecules with different structures which, in turn, leads to a wide range of functions.

> **5.10** Summarise the structures and functions of starch, glycogen, cellulose and chitin in a table similar to table 5.7.
>
> **5.11** What structural features of carbohydrates account for the wide variety of polysaccharides?

5.3 Lipids

Lipids are sometimes classified loosely as those water-insoluble organic substances which can be extracted from cells by organic solvents such as ether, chloroform and benzene. They cannot be defined precisely because their chemistry is so variable, but we could say that true lipids are esters of fatty acids and an alcohol.

Esters are organic compounds formed by a reaction between an acid and an alcohol:

$$
\begin{array}{l}
\text{acid} \quad + \text{alcohol} \xrightarrow{\text{'esterification'}} \text{ester} \quad\quad + \text{water} \\
\text{e.g. CH}_3\text{.COOH} + \text{C}_2\text{H}_5\text{OH} \quad\quad \text{CH}_3\text{COOC}_2\text{H}_5 + \text{H}_2\text{O} \\
\text{ethanoic} \quad\quad \text{ethanol} \quad\quad\quad \text{ethyl ethanoate} \quad \text{water} \\
\text{acid} \quad\quad\quad \text{(ethyl alcohol)} \\
\text{(acetic acid)}
\end{array}
$$

—COO— is an ester linkage. Note that an ester linkage is formed by a condensation reaction.

> **5.12** What is a condensation process?

5.3.1 Constituents of lipids

Fatty acids

Fatty acids contain the acidic group —COOH (the carboxyl group) and are so named because some of the larger molecules in the series occur in fats. They have the general formula R.COOH where R is hydrogen or an alkyl group such as —CH$_3$, —C$_2$H$_5$, and so on (increasing by —CH$_2$ for each subsequent member of the series). R usually has many carbon atoms in lipids. Most fatty acids have an even number of carbon atoms between 14 and 22 (most commonly 16 or 18). The most common fatty acids are shown in fig 5.17. Note the characteristically long chain of carbon and hydrogen atoms forming a hydrocarbon tail. Many of the properties of lipids are determined by these tails, including their insolubility in water. The tails are hydrophobic (*hydro*, water; *phobos*, fear).

Fatty acids sometimes contain one or more double bonds (C=C), such as oleic acid (fig 5.17). In this case they are said to be **unsaturated**, as are lipids containing them. Fatty acids and lipids lacking double bonds are said to be **saturated**. Unsaturated fatty acids melt at much lower temperatures than saturated fatty acids. Oleic acid, for example, is the chief constituent of olive oil and is liquid at normal temperatures (M.pt. 13.4 °C), whereas palmitic and stearic acids (M.pts. 63.1 °C and 69.6 °C respectively) are solid at temperatures to which living organisms are normally exposed.

Table 5.7 Further examples of polysaccharides and closely related compounds.

	Structure	Name of 'polysaccharide'	Units (residues)	Function
Structural	Cell wall matrix in plants	Pectins	Galactose (a hexose) and galacturonic acid (the acid sugar of galactose). Pectic acid is polygalacturonic acid.	Often form gels (commercial jellying agents).
		Hemicelluloses	Very mixed. Sugar residues (mainly pentoses) and sugar acids.	Further information on cell wall matrix in chapter 7.
	Bacterial cell walls	Murein	A polysaccharide cross-linked with amino acids. Polysaccharide is alternating units of 2 amino sugars (acetyglucosamine and another similar nitrogen-containing monosaccharide – compare chitin).	A structural component equivalent to cellulose of plant cell walls. Unique to prokaryotes.
		Other polysaccharides		Some are *antigens* in Gram positive bacteria.
	Outer coats of animal cells	Glycoprotein, glycolipids and other polysaccharides, e.g. hyaluronic acids		Important in ability of cells to 'recognise' each other and in antigenic properties. Intercellular lubrication.
	Connective tissue	Hyaluronic acid	Alternating sugar acid and amino sugar residues.	Part of ground substance of vertebrate connective tissue. Important lubricant – found in synovial fluid in joints and vitreous humour of eye. Forms very viscous solution. Major component of cartilage, bone and other connective tissues. Also cornea.
	'mucopolysaccharides' – repeating pairs of units, one of which is always an amino sugar, e.g. glucosamine	Chondroitin sulphate	Similar to hyaluronic acid.	
Protective		Heparin	Related to chondroitin.	Anticoagulant in mammalian blood and connective tissue. Secreted by most cells.
		Gums and mucilages	Sugars (arabinose, galactose, xylose and rhamnose), and sugar acids (glucuronic and galacturonic acids).	Swell in water; gums form gels or sticky solutions, mucilages form looser gels or a slimy mass. Large, open, flexible molecules, often complex and highly branched. Formed as a result of injury as hard, glossy exudates, e.g. gum arabic from *Acacia*. May also retain water for drought resistance.
Food storage		Mannan, arabinan	Mannose, arabinose.	In some plants.
		Hemicelluloses	See above.	Some seeds, e.g. dates.

NB The suffix -an is used for polymers, e.g. glucose→glucans (e.g. starch); mannose→mannans etc.

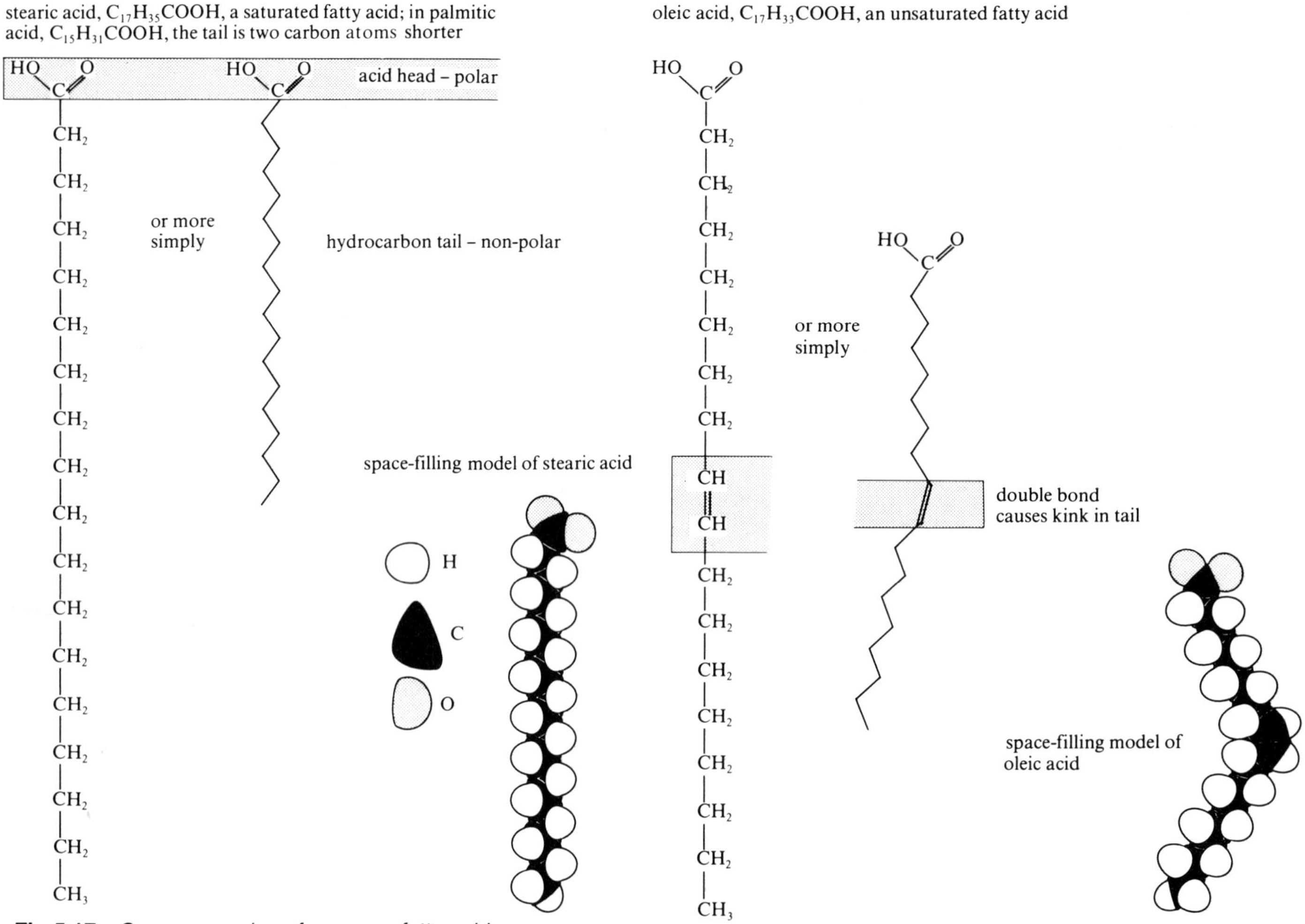

stearic acid, $C_{17}H_{35}COOH$, a saturated fatty acid; in palmitic acid, $C_{15}H_{31}COOH$, the tail is two carbon atoms shorter

oleic acid, $C_{17}H_{33}COOH$, an unsaturated fatty acid

acid head – polar

or more simply

hydrocarbon tail – non-polar

space-filling model of stearic acid

H

C

O

or more simply

double bond causes kink in tail

space-filling model of oleic acid

Fig 5.17 *Some examples of common fatty acids*

5.13 Cells of poikilothermic ('cold-blooded') animals usually have a higher proportion of unsaturated fatty acids than homeothermic ('warm-blooded') animals. Can you account for this?

Alcohols

Most lipids are esters of the alcohol **glycerol** (fig 5.18), and are therefore called **glycerides**.

5.3.2 Formation of a lipid

Glycerol has three hydroxyl (—OH) groups, all of which can condense with a fatty acid to form an ester. Usually all three undergo condensation reactions as shown in fig 5.18, and the lipid formed is therefore called a **triglyceride**.

5.3.3 Properties and functions of triglycerides

Triglycerides are the commonest lipids in nature and are further classified as fats or oils, according to whether they are solid (fats) or liquid (oils) at 20 °C. The higher the proportion of unsaturated fatty acids, the lower their melting points.

5.14 Tristearin and triolein are both lipids. Which is more likely to be an oil?

Triglycerides are non-polar and therefore relatively insoluble in water. They are less dense than water and therefore float.

A major function of lipids is to act as energy stores. They have a higher calorific value than carbohydrates, that is a given mass of lipid will yield more energy on oxidation than an equal mass of carbohydrate (see also chapter 11). This is because lipids have a higher proportion of hydrogen and an almost insignificant proportion of oxygen compared with carbohydrates.

Animals store extra fat when hibernating, and fat is also found below the dermis of the skin of vertebrates where it serves as an insulator. Here it is extensive in mammals living in cold climates, particularly in the form of blubber in aquatic mammals such as whales, where it also contributes to buoyancy. Plants usually store oils rather than fats. Seeds, fruits and chloroplasts are often rich in oils and some seeds are commercial sources of oils, for example the coconut, castor bean, soyabean and sunflower seed. When fats are oxidised, water is a product. This metabolic water can be very useful to some desert animals, such as the kangaroo rat, which stores fat for this purpose (section 19.3.4).

5.15 A camel stores fat in the hump primarily as a water source rather than as an energy source. (*a*) By what metabolic process would water be made available from fat? (*b*) Carbohydrate could also be used as a water source in the same process. What advantage does fat have over carbohydrate?

5.3.4 Waxes

Waxes are esters of fatty acids with long-chain alcohols. Their functions are summarised in table 5.8.

5.3.5 Phospholipids

Phospholipids are lipids containing a phosphate group. The commonest type, phosphoglycerides, are formed when one of the primary alcohol groups (—CH$_2$OH) of glycerol forms an ester with phosphoric acid (H$_3$PO$_4$) instead of a fatty acid (fig 5.19).

The molecule consists of a phosphate head (circled in fig 5.19) with two hydrocarbon tails (the fatty acids).

5.3.6 Steroids and terpenes

Steroids and terpenes can be classified as lipids from the substances involved in their synthesis, although they do not contain fatty acids. They are derived from 5-carbon hydrocarbon building blocks called isoprene units, C$_5$H$_8$. Steroids all contain a nucleus composed of 17 carbon atoms, methyl groups (—CH$_3$) are usually attached at positions 18 and 19 as shown in fig 5.20 and a side-chain generally occupies position 17.

In humans, the steroid present in largest amounts is cholesterol (fig 5.20), a key intermediate in the synthesis of related steroids, as well as being an important constituent of membranes. It is a steroid alcohol, or sterol and is made in the liver.

Steroids are abundant in plants and animals and have many important biochemical and physiological roles, as table 5.8 reveals. It is interesting to note that some plant steroids can be converted into animal hormones in the presence of relevant enzymes.

Terpenes also have a wide range of physiological roles, particularly in plants (see table 5.8).

5.3.7 Lipoproteins

Lipoproteins are associations of lipids with proteins. Their functions are summarised in table 5.8.

5.3.8 Glycolipids

Glycolipids are associations of lipids with carbohydrates. The carbohydrate forms a polar head to the molecule, and glycolipids, like phospholipids, are found in membranes (table 5.8).

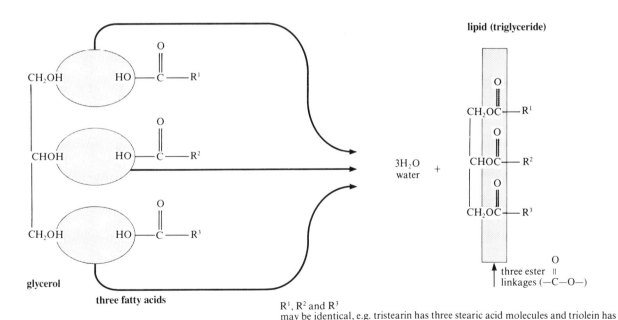

R^1, R^2 and R^3 may be identical, e.g. tristearin has three stearic acid molecules and triolein has three oleic acid molecules; however R^1, R^2 and R^3 are more usually different

Fig 5.18 *Formation of a lipid from fatty acids and glycerol by condensation reactions*

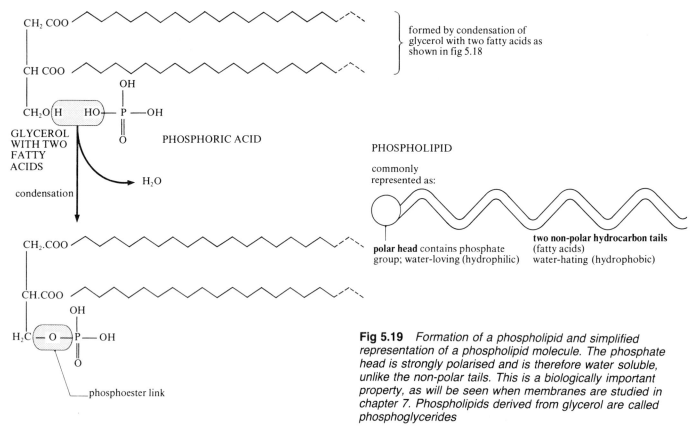

CH₂ COO⎯

CH COO⎯

CH₂O[H   HO]⎯P⎯OH
                |
                OH
                ‖
                O

GLYCEROL WITH TWO FATTY ACIDS   PHOSPHORIC ACID

condensation

→ H₂O

CH₂.COO⎯

CH.COO⎯
                    OH
                    |
H₂C[⎯O⎯]P⎯OH
                    ‖
                    O

phosphoester link

formed by condensation of glycerol with two fatty acids as shown in fig 5.18

PHOSPHOLIPID

commonly represented as:

polar head contains phosphate group; water-loving (hydrophilic)

two non-polar hydrocarbon tails (fatty acids) water-hating (hydrophobic)

Fig 5.19 *Formation of a phospholipid and simplified representation of a phospholipid molecule. The phosphate head is strongly polarised and is therefore water soluble, unlike the non-polar tails. This is a biologically important property, as will be seen when membranes are studied in chapter 7. Phospholipids derived from glycerol are called phosphoglycerides*

Table 5.8 Functions of lipids other than fats and oils.

Waxes
Mainly used as waterproofing material by plants and animals as in:
additional protective layer on cuticle of epidermis of some plant organs, e.g. leaves, fruits, seeds (particularly xerophytes), skin, fur and feathers of animals,
exoskeleton of insects (see chitin).
Beeswax is a constituent of the honeycomb of bees.

Phospholipids
Constituents of membranes.

Steroids
Bile acids, e.g. cholic acid. Constituents of bile, forming part of bile salts which emulsify and solubilise lipids during digestion (chapter 10).
Sex hormones, e.g. oestrogen, progesterone, testosterone (chapter 20).
Cholesterol (absent from plants (see text)).
Vitamin D – rickets occurs if deficient.
Cardiac poisons e.g. digitalis, used for heart therapy.
Adrenocortical hormones (corticosteroids) e.g. aldosterone, corticosterone, cortisone (chapter 16).

Terpenes
Scents and flavours in 'essential oils' of plants e.g. menthol in mint, camphor (2, 3, or 4 isoprene units).
Gibberellins – plant growth substances with 4 isoprene units (see chapter 15).
Phytol – component of chlorophyll (chapter 9) and vitamins A, E, and K, has 4 isoprene units.
Cholesterol – derived from terpenes with 6 isoprene units.
Carotenoids – photosynthetic pigments with 8 isoprene units (chapter 9).
Natural rubber – thousands of isoprene units in regular linear arrangements.

Lipoproteins
Membranes are lipoprotein structures.
Form in which lipids are transported in blood plasma and lymph.

Glycolipids
Components of cell membranes, particularly in myelin of nerve cells and on outer surfaces of nerve cells; chloroplast membranes.

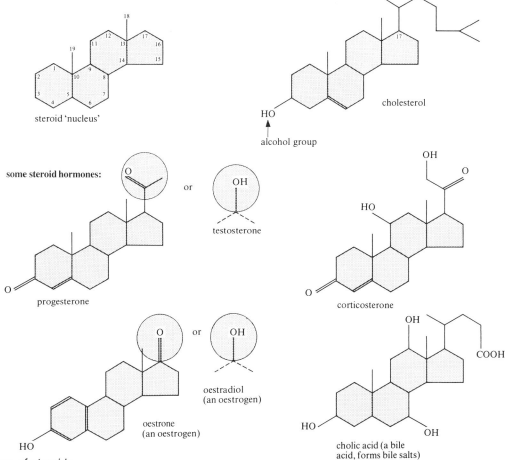

Fig 5.20 *Structures of steroids*

5.4   Amino acids

Over 170 amino acids are currently known to occur in cells and tissues. Of these, 26 are constituents of proteins, 20 occurring commonly in protein structure (table 5.9).

Plants are able to make all the amino acids they require from simpler substances. However, animals are unable to synthesise all that they need, and therefore must obtain some 'ready-made' amino acids directly from their diet. These are termed **essential amino acids**. It must be emphasised, however, that when considered as components of proteins within the animal body, the essential amino acids are no more important than those that the animals synthesise themselves. They are simply 'essential' because they cannot be synthesised by them.

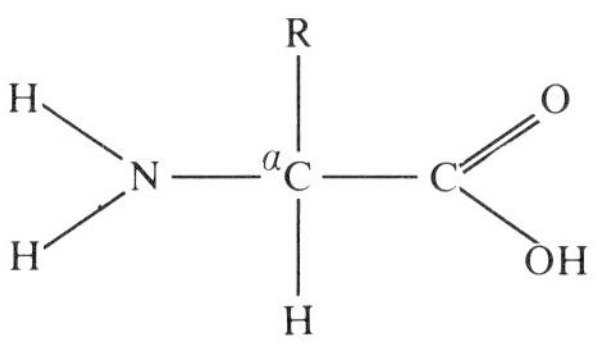

Fig 5.21 *General formula of an amino acid*

5.4.1   Structure and range of amino acids

With the exceptions of proline and hydroxy-proline which are imino acids (table 5.9), all amino acids are α amino acids, that is the amino (—NH₂) group is attached to the α carbon of the related carboxylic (—COOH) group. The general formula of an amino acid can be seen in fig 5.21.

The majority of amino acids possess one acidic carboxylic group and one basic amino group and are termed 'neutral' amino acids. However, in some cases there may be more than one amino group present, giving rise to **basic amino acids**, or more than one carboxylic group giving rise to **acidic amino acids**. The R group represents the residual part of the molecule. Its composition varies considerably in different amino acids and is responsible for the unique properties they display.

The simplest amino acid, glycine (fig 5.22), is formed when R is substituted by H. When the R group is anything but H, the groups attached to the α carbon will all be different. The carbon is therefore asymmetric. This means that the amino acid will possess two optically active forms. In fact, all amino acids but glycine are optically active and may exist in either the D or L forms. In nature amino acids are generally found in their L form. Optical isomerism is discussed earlier in this chapter.

Table 5.9 Common amino acids in proteins.

Amino acid	Abbreviation	R group	Notes
Alanine	Ala	$-CH_3$	
Arginine	Arg	$-[CH_2]_3-NH-C{\overset{\nearrow NH}{\searrow NH_2}}$	Basic amino acid, essential for children
Asparagine	Asn	$-CH_2-CO-NH_2$	R contains amide group
Aspartic acid	Asp	$-CH_2-COOH$	Acidic amino acid
Cysteine	Cys	$-CH_2-SH$	R contains sulphur
Glutamine	Gln	$-[CH_2]_2-CO-NH_2$	R contains amide group
Glutamic acid	Glu	$-[CH_2]_2-COOH$	Acidic amino acid
Glycine	Gly	$-H$	
Histidine	His	$-CH_2$ (imidazole ring with N, NH)	Basic amino acid, essential for children
Isoleucine	Ile	$-C{\overset{H}{\underset{CH_3}{}}}----C_2H_5$	Essential amino acid
Leucine	Leu	$-CH_2-CH{\overset{\nearrow CH_3}{\searrow CH_3}}$	Essential amino acid
Lysine	Lys	$-[CH_2]_4-NH_2$	Basic amino acid, essential
Methionine	Met	$-[CH_2]_2-S-CH_3$	Essential amino acid, R contains sulphur
Phenylalanine	Phe	$-CH_2-$ (benzene ring)	Essential amino acid, R contains aromatic ring
Proline	Pro	CH_2*-CH_2 / CH_2 / NH — H COOH (structure of whole molecule)	$=NH$ instead of $-NH_2$, called an **imino** acid. *$H{\searrow}{\nearrow}OH$ over $C-$ in hydroxyproline.
Serine	Ser	$-CH_2-OH$	
Threonine	Thr	$-C{\overset{\nearrow OH}{\underset{H}{}}}----CH_3$	Essential amino acid
Tryptophan	Trp	$-CH_2$ (indole ring with NH)	R contains aromatic ring, essential amino acid
Tyrosine	Tyr	$-CH_2-$ (benzene ring) $-OH$	R contains aromatic ring
Valine	Val	$-CH{\overset{\nearrow CH_3}{\searrow CH_2}}$	Essential amino acid

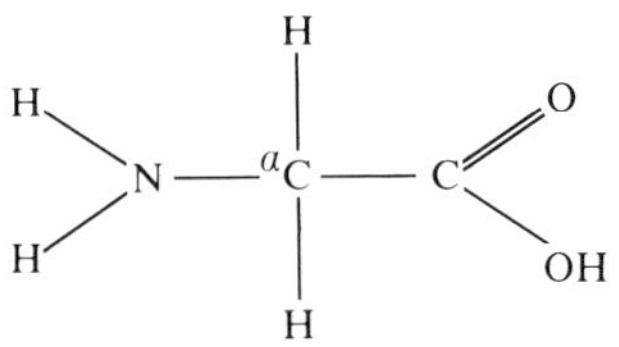

Fig 5.22 *Glycine*

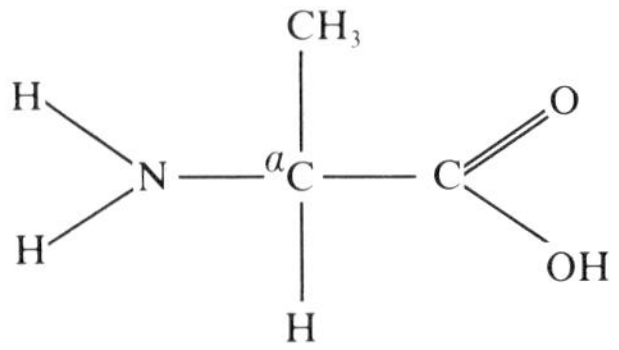

Fig 5.23 *Alanine*

When R is substituted by —CH$_3$, the amino acid alanine is formed (fig 5.23).

Table 5.9 shows the names, three-letter abbreviations and R groups of the commonly occurring amino acids.

Rare amino acids

A small number of rare amino acids occur in organisms. They are derivatives of some of the common amino acids. For example, hydroxyproline is a derivative of proline, and is found in collagen; hydroxylysine is a derivative of lysine, and is also found in collagen.

There is no DNA triplet code for the rare amino acids, and they are derived by the modification of their parent amino acids after they have been incorporated into a polypeptide chain.

Non-protein amino acids

Over 150 of these are known to occur, either free or in a combined form in cells, but never in proteins. For example, ornithine and citrulline are important metabolic intermediates in the synthesis of arginine. Also GABA (γ-amino butyric acid) is virtually unique to the nervous system. It is an inhibitory neurotransmitter, important in the brain.

5.4.2 Properties of amino acids

Amino acids are colourless, crystalline solids. They are generally soluble in water, but insoluble in organic solvents. In neutral aqueous solutions they exist as dipolar ions (**zwitterions**) and are **amphoteric**, possessing both basic and acidic properties.

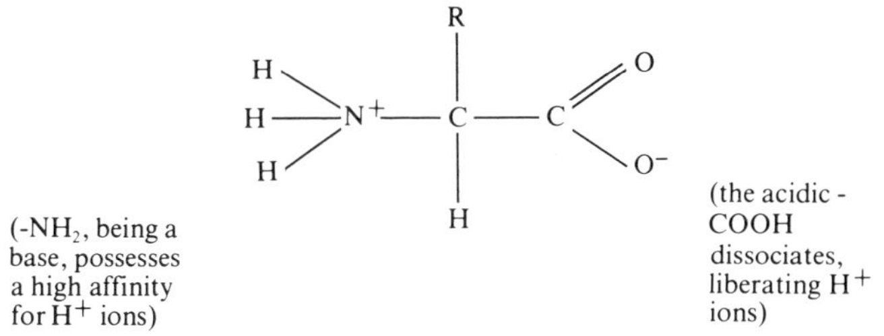

(-NH$_2$, being a base, possesses a high affinity for H$^+$ ions)

(the acidic -COOH dissociates, liberating H$^+$ ions)

Fig 5.24 *Neutral zwitterion form of an amino acid*

Each amino acid has its own specific pH at which it will exist in its neutral zwitterion form and will be strongly dipolar (fig 5.24). If it is placed in an electric field at this pH, the amino acid will migrate neither to the cathode nor to the anode. The pH causing this electrical neutrality is called the **isoelectric point** of the amino acid. Thus each amino acid possesses its own specific isoelectric point.

The amphoteric nature of amino acids is useful biologically as it means that they can act as buffers in solutions, resisting changes in pH. They do this by donating H$^+$ ions as pH increases and accepting H$^+$ ions as pH decreases. Fig 5.25 demonstrates what happens when an amino acid at the pH of its isoelectric point (*a*) has an acid added to it, and (*b*) has a base added to it.

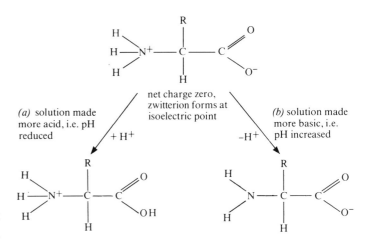

net charge zero, zwitterion forms at isoelectric point

(*a*) solution made more acid, i.e. pH reduced   + H$^+$

(*b*) solution made more basic, i.e. pH increased   −H$^+$

H$^+$ions accepted. The amino acid becomes positively charged and will migrate to the negative electrode (cathode) if placed in an electric field. Net charge +

H$^+$ions donated. The amino acid becomes negatively charged and will migrate to the positive electrode (anode) if placed in an electric field. Net charge −

Fig 5.25 *Effect of (a) acid and (b) alkali on the isoelectric point of an amino acid*

5.4.3 Linkages

Amino acids are able to form a variety of chemical bonds with other reactive groups. These will later be shown to be of great significance in protein structure and function.

Peptide bond

This is formed when a water molecule is eliminated during interaction between the amino group of one amino acid and the carboxylic group of another. Elimination of water is known as **condensation** and the linkage formed is a covalent carbon–nitrogen bond, called a **peptide bond** (fig 5.26). The compound formed is a **dipeptide**. It possesses a free amino group at one end, and a free carboxylic group at the other. This enables further combination between the dipeptide and other amino acids. If many amino acids are joined together in this way, a **polypeptide** is formed (fig 5.27).

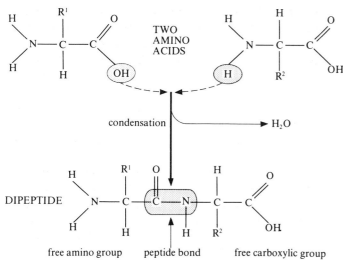

Fig 5.26 *Formation of a dipeptide by condensation of two amino acids*

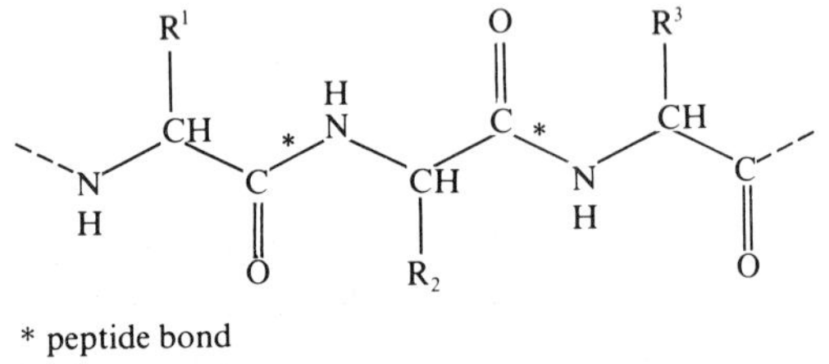

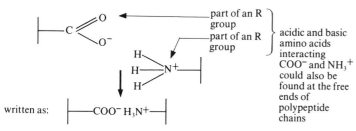

* peptide bond

Fig 5.27 *Part of a polypeptide showing the joining of three amino acids*

5.16 Write down the structural formula of the tripeptide formed by alanine, glycine and serine joined together in that order.

Ionic bond

At a suitable pH an interaction may occur between ionised amino and carboxylic groups. The result is the formation of an ionic bond (fig 5.28). In an aqueous environment this bond is much weaker than a covalent bond and can be broken by changing the pH of the medium.

part of an R group
part of an R group
acidic and basic amino acids interacting COO^- and NH_3^+ could also be found at the free ends of polypeptide chains

written as: $-COO^- \, H_3N^+-$

Fig 5.28 *Ionic bond formation*

Disulphide bond

When two molecules of cysteine combine, neighbouring cysteine sulphydryl (—SH) groups are oxidised and subsequently form a disulphide bond (fig 5.29). Interchain or intrachain disulphide bonds may be formed. This is significant in protein structure (figs 5.32 and 5.33).

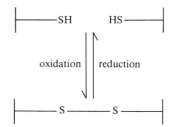

Fig 5.29 *Formation of a disulphide bond*

Hydrogen bond

Electropositive hydrogen atoms attached to oxygen or nitrogen in —OH or —NH groups have a tendency to share the electrons of a neighbouring electronegative oxygen atom such as the O of a =CO group (fig 5.30). The hydrogen bond is weak, but as its occurrence is frequent, the total effect makes a considerable contribution towards molecular stability, as in the structure of silk (fig 5.35a).

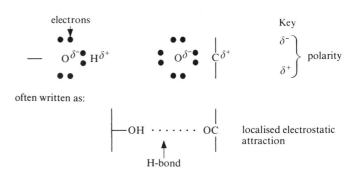

Fig 5.30 *Formation of a hydrogen bond*

5.5   Proteins

Proteins are complex organic compounds always containing the elements carbon, hydrogen, oxygen and nitrogen, and in some cases sulphur. Some proteins form complexes with other molecules containing phosphorus, iron, zinc and copper. Proteins are macromolecules of high M_r (relative formula mass or molecular mass), between several thousands and several millions, consisting of chains of amino acids. Twenty different amino acids are commonly found in naturally occurring proteins. The potential variety of proteins is unlimited because the sequence of amino acids in each protein is specific for that protein (section 22.6) and is genetically controlled by the DNA of the cell in which it is manufactured. Proteins are the most abundant organic molecules to be found in cells and comprise over 50% of their total dry mass. They are an essential component of the diet of animals and may be converted to both fat and carbohydrate by the cells. Their structural diversity enables them to display a great range of structural and metabolic activities within the organism.

5.5.1 Size of protein molecules

Simple peptides containing two, three or four amino acid residues are called di-, tri- and tetrapeptides respectively. Polypeptides are chains of many amino acid residues (up to several thousand – table 5.10). A protein may possess one or more polypeptide chains.

5.5.2 Classification of proteins

Because of the complexity of protein molecules and their diversity of function, it is very difficult to classify them in a single, well-defined fashion. Three alternative methods are given in tables 5.11, 5.12 and 5.13.

5.5.3 Structure of proteins

Each protein possesses a characteristic three-dimensional shape, its **conformation**. In describing the three-dimensional structure of proteins it is usual to refer to four separate levels of organisation as follows.

Primary structure

The primary structure is the number and sequence of amino acids held together by peptide bonds in a polypeptide chain (fig 5.31). It was the double Nobel prizewinner F. Sanger, working in Cambridge, who pioneered work on elucidating the amino acid sequence of proteins. He worked specifically with insulin (fig 5.32), a hormone, and this was the first protein to have its amino acid sequence determined. It took him ten years (1944–54) to discover the sequence. Insulin is a compound of 51 amino acids, with a M_r of 5 733. The protein is composed of two polypeptide chains held together by disulphide bridges.

Today, much of the amino acid sequencing is accomplished by machine and an estimated 8 000 protein primary structures are known. Another example, lysozyme is shown in fig 5.33.

There are over 10 000 proteins in the human body, all composed of different arrangements of the 20 fundamental amino acids. The sequence of amino acids of a protein dictates its biological function. In turn, this sequence is strictly controlled by the sequence of bases in DNA (section 22.6). Substitution of just a single amino acid can cause a major alteration in a protein's function, as in the condition of sickle cell anaemia (section 23.9). Analysis of amino acid sequences of homologous proteins from different species is of interest, because it offers evidence about the possible taxonomic relationships between different species. This is dealt with in chapter 24.

5.17 (*a*) Let the letters A and B represent two different amino acids. Write down the sequences of all the possible tripeptides that could be made with just these two amino acids.
(*b*) From your answer to (*a*), what is the formula for calculating the number of different tripeptides that can be formed from two different amino acids?
(*c*) How many polypeptides, 100 amino acids in length, could be formed from two different amino acids?
(*d*) How many polypeptides, 100 amino acids in length (a modest length for a protein), could be made using all 20 common amino acids?
(*e*) How many peptides/polypeptides could be made (any length) from all 20 common amino acids?

Table 5.10 Sizes of some proteins.

Protein	M_r (molecular mass)	Number of amino acid residues	Number of polypeptide chains
Ribonuclease	12 640	124	1
Lysozyme	13 930	129	1
Myoglobin	16 890	153	1
Haemoglobin	64 500	574	4
α amylase	97 600	Not known	2
TMV (Tobacco mosaic virus)	≈ 40 000 000	≈ 336 500	2 130

The largest protein complexes are found in viruses where M_rs of over 40 000 000 are commonly found.

Table 5.11 Classification of proteins according to structure.

Type	Nature	Function
Fibrous 	Secondary structure most important (little or no tertiary structure) Insoluble in water Physically tough Long parallel polypeptide chains cross-linked at intervals forming long fibres or sheets	Perform structural functions in cells and organisms, e.g. components of connective tissue, collagen (tendons, bone matrix), myosin (in muscle sarcomere), silk (spiders' webs), keratin (hair, horn, nails, feathers)
Globular 	Tertiary structure most important Polypeptide chains tightly folded to form spherical shape Easily soluble to form a colloidal suspension	Globulins of blood serum – important in immunology Form enzymes, antibodies and some hormones, e.g. insulin Important in protoplasm as they hold water and other substances and serve to maintain molecular organisation
Intermediate	Fibrous but soluble	e.g. fibrinogen – forms insoluble fibrin when blood clots

Table 5.12 Classification of proteins according to composition.

Proteins

(i) *Simple*
Only amino acids form their structure

(ii) *Conjugated*
Complex compounds consisting of globular proteins and non-proteinaceous material; the non-proteinaceous material is called a **prosthetic** group

(i) *Simple proteins*

Name	Properties	Location
Albumins	Neutral Soluble in water Soluble in dilute salt solution	Egg albumen Serum albumin of blood
Globulins	Neutral Insoluble in water Soluble in dilute salt solution	Antibodies in blood Blood fibrinogen
Histones	Basic Soluble in water Insoluble in dilute ammonia solution	Associated with nucleic acids, in nucleo-proteins of cell
Scleroproteins (only in animal kingdom)	Insoluble in water and most other solvents	Keratin of hair, skin, feathers; collagen of bone matrix and tendon; elastin of ligament

(ii) *Conjugated proteins*

Name	Prosthetic group	Location
Phosphoprotein	Phosphoric acid	Casein of milk Vitellin of egg yolk
Glycoprotein	Carbohydrate	Blood plasma Mucin (component of saliva)
Nucleoprotein	Nucleic acid	Component of viruses Chromosomes Ribosome structure
Chromoprotein	Pigment	Haemoglobin – haem (iron-containing pigment) Phytochrome (plant pigment) Cytochrome (respiratory pigment)
Lipoprotein	Lipid	Membrane structure Lipid transported in blood as lipoprotein
Flavoprotein	FAD (flavin adenine dinucleotide, see section 11.3.6)	Important in electron transport chain in respiration
Metal proteins	Metal	E.g. nitrate reductase, the enzyme in plants which converts nitrate to nitrite

Table 5.13 Protein classification according to function. Proteins are also important in membranes where they function as enzymes, receptor sites and transport sites.

Type	Examples	Occurrence/function
Structural	Collagen	Component of connective tissue, bone, tendons, cartilage
	Sclerotin	Exoskeleton of insects
	α-keratin	Skin, feathers, nails, hair, horn
	Elastin	Elastic connective tissue (ligaments)
	Mucoproteins	Synovial fluid, mucous secretions
	Viral coat proteins	'Wraps up' nucleic acid of virus
Enzymes	Trypsin	Catalyses hydrolysis of protein
	Ribulose bisphosphate carboxylase	Catalyses carboxylation (addition of CO_2) of ribulose bisphosphate in photosynthesis
	Glutamine synthetase	Catalyses synthesis of the amino acid glutamine from glutamic acid + ammonia
Hormones	Insulin } Glucagon }	Help to regulate glucose metabolism
	ACTH	Stimulates growth and activity of the adrenal cortex
Transport	Haemoglobin	Transports O_2 in vertebrate blood
	Haemocyanin	Transports O_2 in some non-vertebrate blood
	Myoglobin	Transports O_2 in muscles
	Serum albumin	Transport in blood, e.g. fatty acids, lipids
Protective	Antibodies	Form complexes with foreign proteins
	Fibrinogen	Precursor of fibrin in blood clotting
	Thrombin	Involved in clotting mechanism
Contractile	Myosin	Moving filaments in myofibril of sarcomere
	Actin	Stationary filaments in myofibril of sarcomere
Storage	Ovalbumin	Egg white protein
	Casein	Milk protein
Toxins	Snake venom	Enzymes
	Diphtheria toxin	Toxin made by diphtheria bacteria

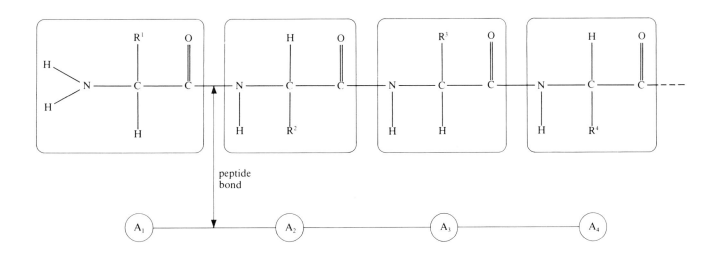

Fig 5.31 *Portion of a polypeptide chain to show primary structure. A_1, A_2, A_3 and A_4 represent different amino acids*

Fig 5.32 *(below) Primary structure (sequence of amino acids) of insulin. The molecule consists of two polypeptide chains held together by two disulphide bridges*

Fig 5.33 *(right) The primary structure of lysozyme. Lysozyme is an enzyme that is found in many tissues and secretions of the human body, in plants, and in the whites of eggs. Its function is to catalyse the breakdown of the cell walls of bacteria. The molecule consists of a single polypeptide chain of 129 amino acid residues. There are four intrachain disulphide bridges*

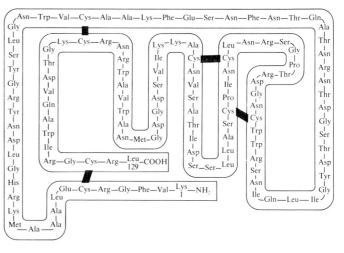

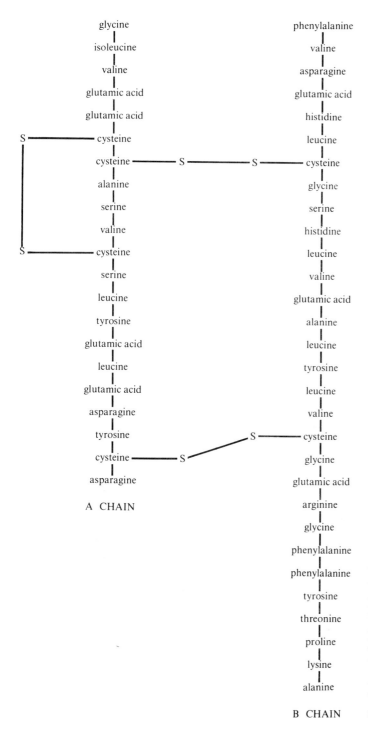

A CHAIN

B CHAIN

Secondary structure

In addition to the primary structure there is a specific secondary structure. It usually takes the form of an extended spiral spring, the α-helix, whose structure is maintained by many hydrogen bonds which are formed between adjacent CO and NH groups. The H atom of the NH group of one amino acid is bonded to the O atom of the CO group three amino acids away (fig 5.34). X-ray diffraction analysis data indicate that the α-helix makes one complete turn for every 3.6 amino acids.

A protein which is entirely α-helical, and hence fibrous, is keratin. It is the structural protein of hair, wool, nails, claws, beaks, feathers and horn, as well as being found in vertebrate skin. Its hardness and stretchability vary with the degree of cross-linking by disulphide bridges between neighbouring chains.

Theoretically, all CO and NH groups can participate in hydrogen bonding as described, so the α-helix is a very stable, and hence a common, structure. In spite of this, most proteins are globular molecules in which there are also regions of β-sheet (see below) and irregular structure. This is due mainly to interference in hydrogen bonding by certain R groups, the occurrence of disulphide bridges between different parts of the same chain and the inability of the amino acid proline to make hydrogen bonds.

Another type of secondary structure is the β-pleated sheet. Silk fibroin, the protein used by silkworms when spinning their cocoon threads, is entirely in this form. This protein comprises a number of adjacent chains which are more extended than the α-helices. They are arranged in a parallel fashion but running in opposite directions to each other. They are joined together by hydrogen bonds formed between the C=O and NH groups of one chain and the NH and C=O groups of adjacent chains. Again, all NH and C=O groups are involved in hydrogen bonding, so the structure is very stable. This is called the β-**configuration**, and the whole structure is known as a β-**pleated sheet** (fig 5.35). The sheet of fibroin has a high tensile strength and cannot be stretched, but the arrangement of the polypeptides makes the silk very supple. In globular proteins a single polypeptide chain may fold back on itself and form regions of β-pleated sheet.

Yet another arrangement is seen in the fibrous protein collagen. Here three polypeptide chains are wound around each other to form a triple helix. There are about 1 000 amino acid residues in each chain, and the complete triple helix compound is called **tropocollagen** (fig 5.36). Again the protein cannot be stretched and this is an essential part of its functioning, for example in tendons, bone and other connective tissue. Proteins which exist entirely in the form of helical coils, such as keratin and collagen, are exceptional.

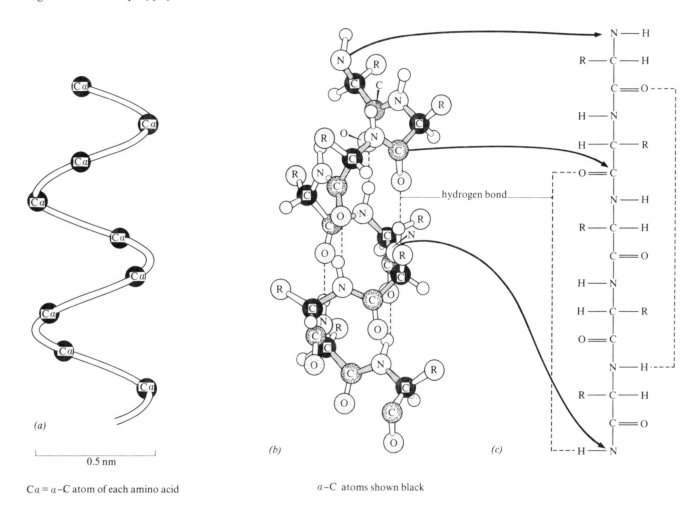

(a)

0.5 nm

$Ca = a$–C atom of each amino acid

(b)

a–C atoms shown black

hydrogen bond

(c)

Fig 5.34 *Structure of the α-helix. (a) The α-C atoms are shown. A line joining them describes an α-helix. (b) the entire α-helix. (c) Part of the α-helix straightened out. Hydrogen bonds hold the helix in place*

Fig 5.35 *(below) Beta-pleated sheet. The chains are held parallel to each other by the hydrogen bonds that form between the NH and CO groups. The side-groups (R) are above and below the plane of the sheet. (a) Two antiparallel polypeptide chains. (b) Drawing of three parallel chains to show pleating of structure between R groups*

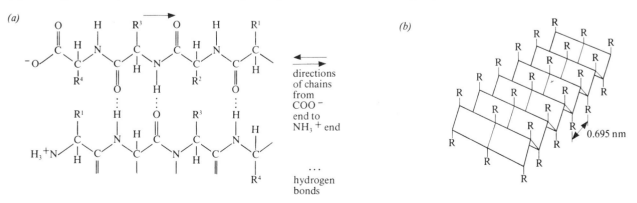

(a)

directions of chains from COO⁻ end to NH₃⁺ end

... hydrogen bonds

(b)

0.695 nm

Fig 5.36 *Collagen triple-helix structure*

Tertiary structure

Usually the polypeptide chain bends and folds extensively, forming a precise, compact 'globular' shape. This is the protein's tertiary conformation and it is maintained by the interaction of the three types of bond already discussed, namely ionic, hydrogen and disulphide bonds as well as hydrophobic interactions (fig 5.37). The latter are quantitatively the most important and occur when the protein folds so as to shield hydrophobic side-groups from the aqueous surroundings, at the same time exposing hydrophilic side-chains.

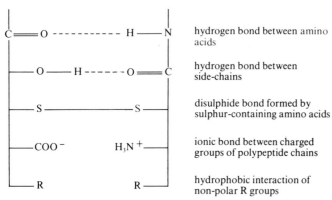

hydrogen bond between amino acids

hydrogen bond between side-chains

disulphide bond formed by sulphur-containing amino acids

ionic bond between charged groups of polypeptide chains

hydrophobic interaction of non-polar R groups

Fig 5.37 (above) *Summary of types of bond stabilising secondary and tertiary structures of proteins. Hydrophobic interactions (associations of non-polar molecules or parts of molecules) to exclude water molecules in the aqueous environment of the cell are particularly important in maintaining structure, as in membranes*

The tertiary structure of a protein can be determined by X-ray crystallography. By early 1963, and after many years work, Kendrew and Perutz had elucidated the secondary and tertiary structures of myoglobin using this technique (fig 5.38):

primary structure – single polypeptide chain of 153 amino acids, the sequence was elucidated in the early 1960s;

secondary structure – about 75% of the chain is α-helical (eight helical sections);

tertiary structure – non-uniform folding of the α-helical chain into a compact shape;

prosthetic group – haem group (contains iron).

Further information about the functions of myoglobin can be found in chapter 14. The elucidation of tertiary structure is still very time-consuming and there are still only about 300 proteins whose tertiary structure is known. Use of computers and other techniques to predict tertiary structure, based on knowledge of primary and secondary structures, is a fast-growing area of molecular biology. There would follow the possibility of designing proteins with particular shapes for particular functions, with important applications in industry and medicine.

Quaternary structure

Many highly complex proteins consist of an aggregation of polypeptide chains held together by hydrophobic interactions and hydrogen and ionic bonds. Their precise arrangement is the quaternary structure. Haemoglobin exhibits such a structure. It consists of four separate polypeptide chains of two types, namely two α-chains and two β-chains. The two α-chains each contain 141 amino acids, while the two β-chains each contain 146 amino acids.

H_2N— Val — Leu — Ser — Glu — Gly — Glu — Trp — Gln — Leu — Val(10) — Leu — His — Val — Tyr — Ala — Lys — Val —

Glu(20) — Ala — Asp — Val — Ala — Gly — His — Gly — Gln — Asp — Ile — Leu — Ile(30) — Arg — Leu — Phe — Lys —

Ser — His — Pro — Glu(40) — Thr — Leu — Glu — Lys — Phe — Asp — Arg — Phe — Lys — His — Leu — Lys(50) — Thr —

Glu — Ala — Glu — Met — Lys — Ala — Ser — Glu — Asp(60) — Leu — Lys — Gly — His — His — Glu — Ala — Glu —

Leu — Thr(70) — Ala — Leu — Gly — Ala — Ile — Leu — Lys — Lys — Gly(80) — His — His — Glu — Ala — Glu —

Leu — Lys — Pro — Leu(90) — Ala — Gln — Ser — His — Ala — Thr — Lys — His — Lys — Ile(100) — Pro — Ile — Lys —

Tyr — Leu — Glu — Phe — Ile — Ser — Glu — Ala(110) — Ile — Ile — His — Val — Leu — His — Ser — Arg — His —

Pro(120) — Gly — Asn — Phe — Gly — Ala — Asp — Ala — Gln — Gly — Ala(130) — Met — Asn — Lys — Ala — Leu — Glu —

Leu — Phe — Arg — Lys(140) — Asp — Ile — Ala — Ala — Lys — Tyr — Lys — Glu(150) — Leu — Gly — Tyr — Gln — Gly —COOH

Fig 5.38 (above and opposite) *(a) Primary structure of myoglobin. (b) X-ray diffraction pattern of myoglobin (sperm whale). The regular array of spots is a result of scattered (diffracted) beams of X-rays striking the photographic film. The photograph is a two-dimensional section through a three dimensional array of spots. The pattern and intensity of the spots are used to determine the arrangement of atoms in the molecule. From J. C. Kendrew,* Scientific American, *December 1961. (c) Conformation of myoglobin deduced from high resolution X-ray data. (d) Structure of myoglobin*

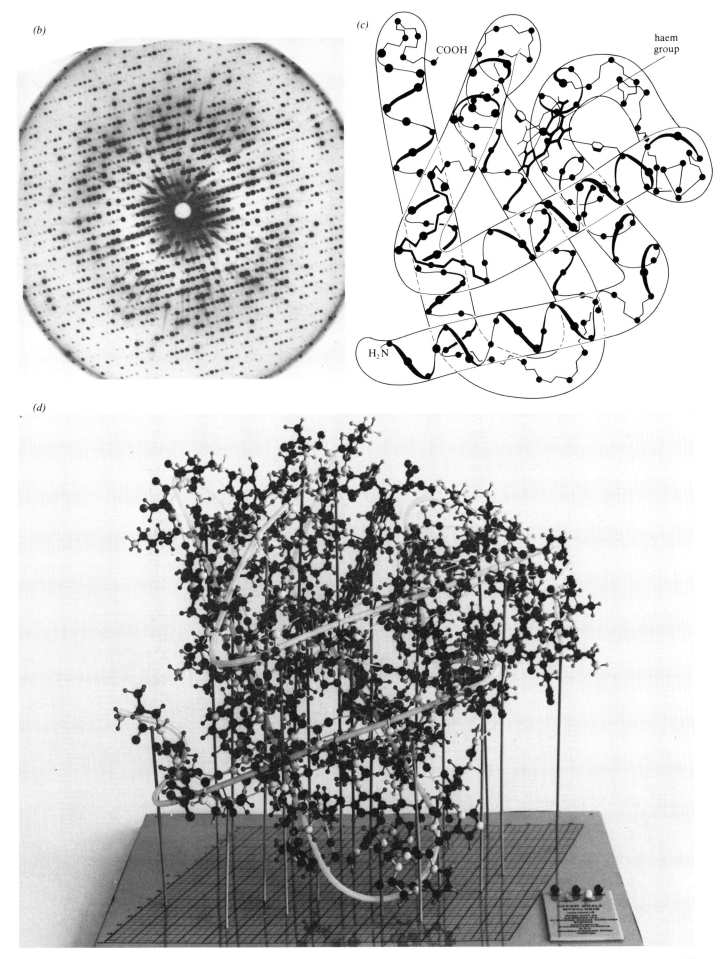

(b)

(c)

COOH

haem group

H₂N

(d)

153

Fig 5.39 *Structure of haemoglobin. The molecule consists of four chains: two alpha chains and two beta chains. Each chain carries a haem to which one molecule of oxygen binds. The assembly of a protein from separate subunits is an example of quaternary structure*

The complete structure of haemoglobin was worked out by Kendrew and Perutz and is illustrated in fig 5.39.

The protein coats of some viruses, such as the tobacco mosaic virus, are composed of many polypeptide chains arranged in a highly ordered fashion (fig 2.14).

5.5.4 Electrical properties of proteins

A considerable number of positive and negative electrical charges are carried by protein molecules. Accordingly, proteins demonstrate amphoteric properties similar to those of amino acids, and also possess their own specific isoelectric points. At its isoelectric point a protein has no net charge. At pHs below its isoelectric point the protein is positively charged, and above its isoelectric point it is negatively charged. In either case the net charge which the protein bears is the same (either all positive or all negative) for all its molecules. The net electrostatic effect that this causes is repulsion between adjacent protein molecules, thus preventing their aggregation. At its isoelectric point the protein is at its least soluble due to the absence of electrostatic repulsion which would otherwise keep the molecules apart. The process of souring of milk illustrates this well. Casein is a soluble protein component of fresh milk. The pH of fresh milk is well above the isoelectric point of casein. However, when milk is soured by the production of lactic acid by bacteria, its pH is lowered to that of the isoelectric point of casein (pH 4.7). At this point casein is precipitated in the form of white curds. Most cytoplasmic proteins possess an isoelectric point at about pH 6. However since the cytoplasmic pH is approximately 7, the proteins are in an environment more alkaline than their isoelectric points, and hence carry negative charges.

5.5.5 Denaturation and renaturation of proteins

Denaturation is the loss of the specific three-dimensional conformation of a protein molecule. The change may be temporary or permanent, but the amino acid sequence of the protein remains unaffected. If denaturation occurs, the molecule unfolds and can no longer perform its normal biological function. A number of agents may cause denaturation as follows.

Heat or radiation. e.g. infra-red or ultra-violet light. Kinetic energy is supplied to the protein causing its atoms to vibrate violently, so disrupting the weak hydrogen and ionic bonds. Coagulation of the protein then occurs.

Strong acids and alkalis and high concentrations of salts. Ionic bonds are disrupted and the protein is coagulated. Breakage of peptide bonds may occur if the protein is allowed to remain mixed with the reagent for a long period of time.

Heavy metals. Cations form strong bonds with carboxylate anions and often disrupt ionic bonds. They also reduce the protein's electrical polarity and thus increase its insolubility. This causes the protein to precipitate out of solution.

Organic solvents and detergents. These reagents disrupt hydrophobic interactions and form bonds with hydrophobic (non-polar) groups. This in turn causes the disruption of intramolecular hydrogen bonding. When alcohol is used as a disinfectant it functions to denature the protein of any bacteria present.

Renaturation

Sometimes a protein will spontaneously refold into its original structure after denaturation, providing conditions are suitable. This is called **renaturation**, and is good evidence that tertiary structure can be determined purely by primary structure and that biological structures can spontaneously assemble according to a few general principles.

5.5.6 Mammalian protein metabolism

Fig 5.40 provides a summary of mammalian protein metabolism.

5.6 Nucleic acids

Nucleic acids, like proteins, are essential for life. They constitute the genetic material of all living organisms, including the simplest virus.

The elucidation of the structure of DNA, one of the two types of nucleic acid, represents one of the outstanding milestones in biology because it finally solved the problem of how living cells, and therefore organisms, accurately replicate themselves and encode the information needed to control their activities. Table 5.4 shows that nucleic acids are made up of units called **nucleotides**. These are arranged to form extremely long molecules known as **polynucleotides**. Thus, to understand their structure, it is necessary first to study the structure of the nucleotide.

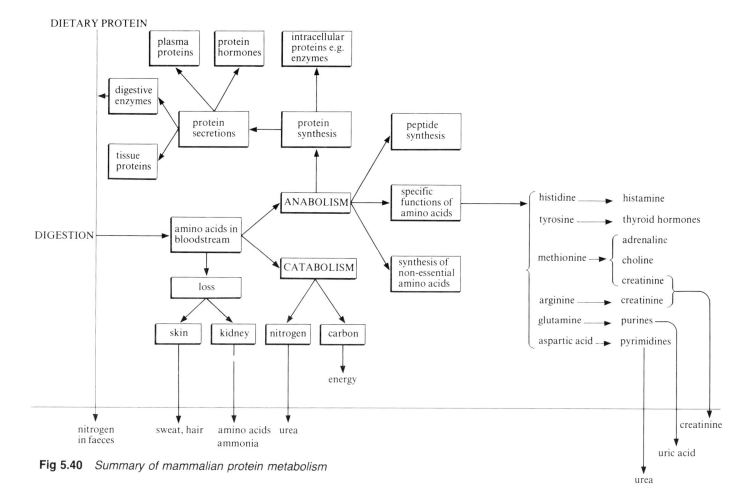

Fig 5.40 *Summary of mammalian protein metabolism*

5.6.1 Structure of nucleotides

A nucleotide has three components, a 5-carbon sugar, a nitrogenous base and phosphoric acid.

Sugar. The sugar has five carbon atoms, therefore it is a pentose. There are two types of nucleic acids, depending on the pentose they contain. Those containing ribose are called ribonucleic acids (RNA) and those containing deoxyribose (ribose with an oxygen atom removed from carbon atom 2) deoxyribonucleic acids (DNA) (fig 5.41).

Bases. Each nucleic acid contains four different bases, two derived from purine and two from pyrimidine. The nitrogen in the rings gives the molecules their basic nature. The bases are the purines, adenine (A) and guanine (G), and the pyrimidines, thymine (T) in DNA or uracil (U) in RNA and cytosine (C). Purines have two rings and pyrimidines one ring in their structure. Note that RNA contains uracil in place of thymine in DNA. Thymine is chemically very similar to uracil (it is 5-methyl uracil, that is uracil with a methyl group on carbon atom 5). The bases are commonly represented by their initial letters A, G, T, U and C.

Phosphoric acid (fig 5.41). This gives nucleic acids their acid character. Fig 5.42 shows how the sugar, base and phosphoric acid combine to form a nucleotide.

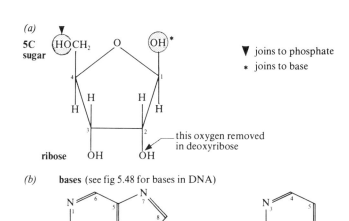

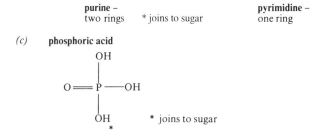

Fig 5.41 *Components of nucleotides*

155

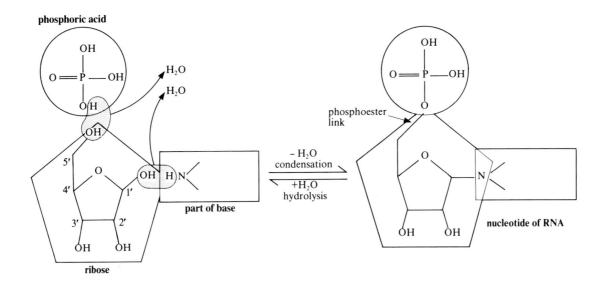

diagrammatically:

◯ phosphate

⬠ sugar (pentose)

▭ base

+ 2H₂O

nucleotide

Fig 5.42 *Formation of a nucleotide. Carbon atoms of ribose are, by convention, numbered 1' to 5' to avoid confusion with C atoms 1 to 9 of bases*

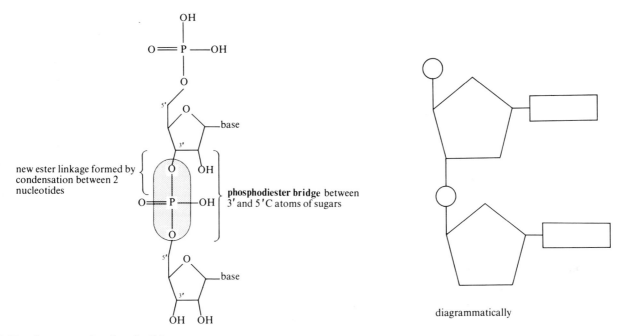

new ester linkage formed by condensation between 2 nucleotides

phosphodiester bridge between 3' and 5'C atoms of sugars

diagrammatically

Fig 5.43 *Structure of a dinucleotide*

The combination of a sugar with a base forms a compound called a **nucleoside**. This occurs with the elimination of water and therefore is a condensation reaction. A nucleotide is formed by further condensation between the nucleoside and phosphoric acid forming a phosphoester link.

Different nucleotides are formed according to the sugars and bases used. Nucleotides are not only used as building blocks for nucleic acids, but they and their derivatives form several important coenzymes, including adenosine monophosphate (AMP), diphosphate (ADP) and triphosphate (ATP), cyclic AMP, coenzyme A, nicotinamide adenine dinucleotide (NAD) and its phosphate NADP, and flavin adenine dinucleotide (FAD) (chapter 6).

5.6.2 Structure of dinucleotides and polynucleotides

Two nucleotides join to form a **dinucleotide** by condensation between the phosphate group of one with the sugar of the other to form a phosphodiester bridge, as shown in fig 5.43. The process is repeated up to several million times to make a **polynucleotide**. An unbranched sugar–phosphate backbone is formed by phosphodiester bridges between the 3′ and 5′ carbon atoms of the sugars as shown in fig 5.44.

Phosphodiester linkages are formed from strong covalent bonds and this confers strength and stability on the polynucleotide chain. This is an important point in preventing breakage of the 'chain' during DNA replication (chapter 22).

5.6.3 Structure of DNA

Like proteins, polynucleotides can be regarded as having a primary structure, which is the sequence of nucleotides, and a three-dimensional structure. Interest in the structure of DNA intensified when it was realised in the early part of this century that it might be the genetic material. Evidence for this is presented in section 22.4.

By the early 1950s the Nobel prize-winning chemist Linus Pauling of the USA had worked out the α-helical structure which is common to many fibrous proteins, and was applying himself to the problem of the structure of DNA, which evidence suggested was also a fibrous molecule. At the same time Maurice Wilkins and Rosalind Franklin of King's College, London were tackling the same problem using the technique of X-ray crystallography. This involved the difficult and time-consuming process of preparing pure fibres of the salt of DNA from which they managed to get complex X-ray diffraction patterns. These reveal the gross structure of the molecule but are not as detailed as those from pure crystals of proteins (fig 5.45). Meanwhile, James Watson and Francis Crick of the Cavendish Laboratory in Cambridge had chosen what was to prove the successful approach. Using all the chemical and physical information they could gather, they began

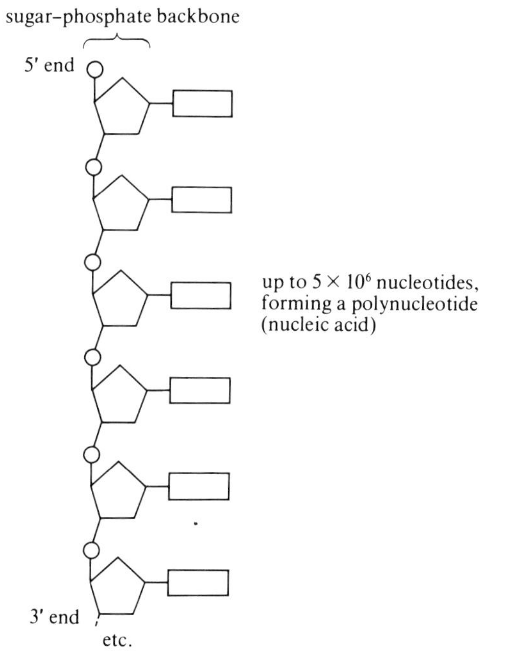

Fig 5.44 *Formation of a polynucleotide*

building scale models of polynucleotides in the hope that a convincing structure would emerge. Watson's book *The Double Helix* provides a fascinating insight into their work.

Two lines of evidence proved crucial. Firstly, they were in regular communication with Wilkins and had access to the X-ray diffraction data, against which they were able to test their models. These data strongly suggested a helical structure (fig 5.45) with regularity at a spacing of 0.34 nm along its axis. Secondly, they realised the significance of some evidence published by Erwin Chargaff in 1951 concerning the ratio of the different bases found in DNA. Although important, this evidence had generally been overlooked. Table 5.14 shows some of Chargaff's data, and supporting data obtained since.

5.18 Examine the table. What does it reveal about the ratios of the different bases?

Watson and Crick had been exploring the idea that there may be two helical chains of polynucleotides in DNA, held together by pairing of bases between neighbouring chains. The bases would be held together by hydrogen bonds.

5.19 If this model were correct, can you predict from Chargaff's data which base combines with which in each pair?

Fig 5.46 shows how the base pairs are joined by hydrogen bonds. Adenine pairs with thymine, and guanine with cytosine; the adenine–thymine pair has two hydrogen bonds and the guanine–cytosine pair has three hydrogen bonds. Watson tried pairing the bases in this way, and recalls 'my morale skyrocketed, for I suspected that we

Table 5.14 Relative amounts of bases in DNA from various organisms.

Source of DNA	Adenine	Guanine	Thymine	Cytosine
Man	30.9	19.9	29.4	19.8
Sheep	29.3	21.4	28.3	21.0
Hen	28.8	20.5	29.2	21.5
Turtle	29.7	22.0	27.9	21.3
Salmon	29.7	20.8	29.1	20.4
Sea urchin	32.8	17.7	32.1	17.3
Locust	29.3	20.5	29.3	20.7
Wheat	27.3	22.7	27.1	22.8
Yeast	31.3	18.7	32.9	17.1
Escherichia coli (a bacterium)	24.7	26.0	23.6	25.7
ΦX174 bacteriophage (a virus)	24.6	24.1	32.7	18.5

Amounts are in molar proportions on a percentage basis.

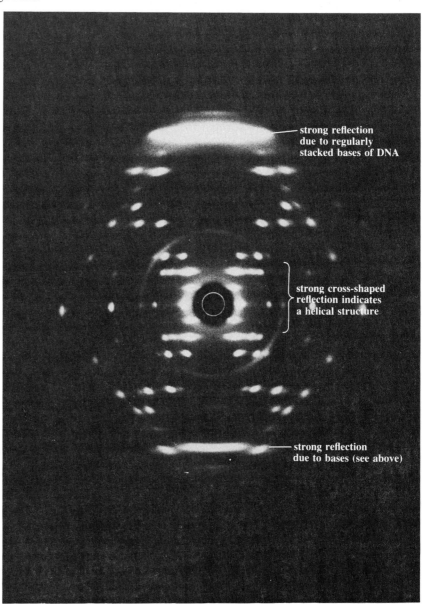

strong reflection due to regularly stacked bases of DNA

strong cross-shaped reflection indicates a helical structure

strong reflection due to bases (see above)

Fig 5.45 *X-ray diffraction photograph of a fibre of DNA. This is the kind of pattern from which the double helical structure was originally deduced (photograph by courtesy of Dr J. M. Squire)*

now had the answer to the riddle of why the number of purine residues exactly equalled the number of pyrimidine residues'.* He noticed the neat way in which the bases fit and that the overall size and shape of the base pairs was identical, both being three rings wide (fig 5.46). Hydrogen bonding between other combinations of bases, while possible, is much weaker. The way was finally open to building the correct model of DNA, whose structure is summarised in figs 5.47–49.

Features of the DNA molecule

Watson and Crick showed that DNA consists of two polynucleotide chains. Each chain forms a right-handed helical spiral and the two chains coil around each other to form a double helix (fig 5.47). The chains run in opposite directions, that is are **antiparallel**, the so-called 3' end of one being opposite the 5' end of the other (remember the 3',5' phosphodiester linkages). Each chain has a sugar–phosphate backbone with bases which project at right-angles and hydrogen bond with the bases of the opposite chain across the double helix (fig 5.48). The sugar–phosphate backbones are clearly seen in a space-filling model of DNA (fig 5.49). The width between the two backbones is constant and equal to the width of a base pair, that is the width of a purine plus a pyrimidine. Two purines would be too large, and two pyrimidines too small, to span the gap between the two chains. Along the axis of the molecule the base pairs are 0.34 nm apart, accounting for the regularity indicated by X-ray diffraction. A complete turn of the double helix comprises 3.4 nm, or ten base pairs. There is no restriction on the sequence of bases in one chain, but because of the rules of base pairing, the sequence in one chain determines that in the other. The two chains are thus said to be **complementary**.

* From *The Double Helix*, James D. Watson, Weidenfeld & Nicolson, 1968.

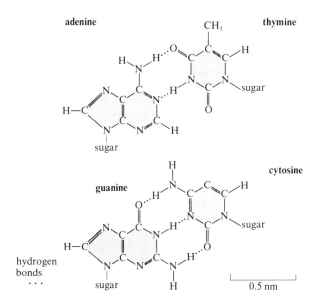

Fig 5.46 *Adenine–thymine and guanine–cytosine base pairs*

Watson and Crick published their model in 1953 in the journal *Nature*, and together with Maurice Wilkins were awarded the Nobel Prize for their work in 1962, the same year that Kendrew and Perutz received Nobel prizes for their work on the three-dimensional structure of proteins, also based on X-ray crystallography.

To act as genetic material, the structure had to be capable of carrying coded information and of accurate replication. Its suitability for this was not overlooked by Watson and Crick who, with masterly understatement near the end of their paper said 'It has not escaped our notice that the specific pairing we have postulated immediately suggests a possible copying mechanism for the genetic material.'* In a second paper that year they discussed the

* Watson, J. D. & Crick, F.H.C. (1953) *Nature* **171**, 737.

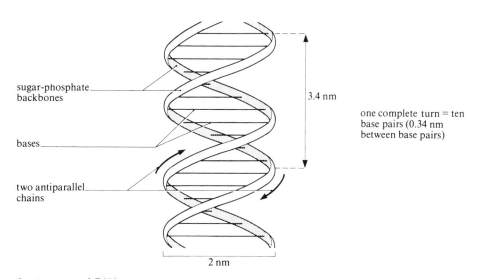

Fig 5.47 *Diagrammatic structure of DNA*

159

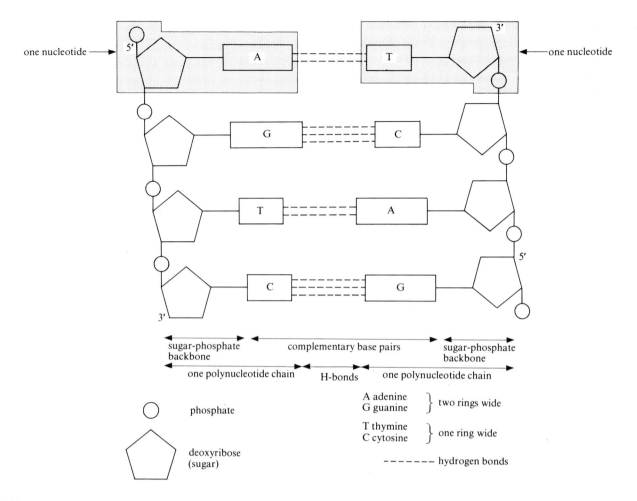

one nucleotide ⟶

one nucleotide ⟵

sugar-phosphate backbone   complementary base pairs   sugar-phosphate backbone

one polynucleotide chain   H-bonds   one polynucleotide chain

◯ phosphate

⬠ deoxyribose (sugar)

A adenine
G guanine } two rings wide

T thymine
C cytosine } one ring wide

- - - - - - - hydrogen bonds

Fig 5.48 *DNA – diagrammatic structure of straightened chains*

genetic implications of the structure, and these are dealt with in chapter 22. This discovery, in which structure was shown to be so clearly related to function even at the molecular level, gave great impetus to the science of molecular biology.

5.6.4 Structure of RNA

RNA is normally single stranded, unlike DNA. Certain forms of RNA do assume complex structures, notably transfer RNA (tRNA) and ribosomal RNA (rRNA). Another form is messenger RNA (mRNA). These are involved in protein synthesis and are discussed in chapter 22.

5.7 Other biochemically important molecules

Apart from the well-defined classes of organic molecule already discussed, many other complex organic compounds occur in living cells. Of particular note are the vitamins and a group of substances which assist enzymes in their functioning, the cofactors or coenzymes. They contain miscellaneous chemical structures, some being nucleotides or their derivatives. Vitamins are discussed in section 10.3.10 and cofactors in section 6.2.

Inorganic ions and molecules of biochemical importance are discussed in section 9.12 with mineral nutrition.

5.8 Identification of biochemicals

It is recommended that you first familiarise yourself with the following tests by using pure samples of the chemicals being tested. Once the techniques have been mastered and familiarity with the colour changes obtained, various tissues can be studied.

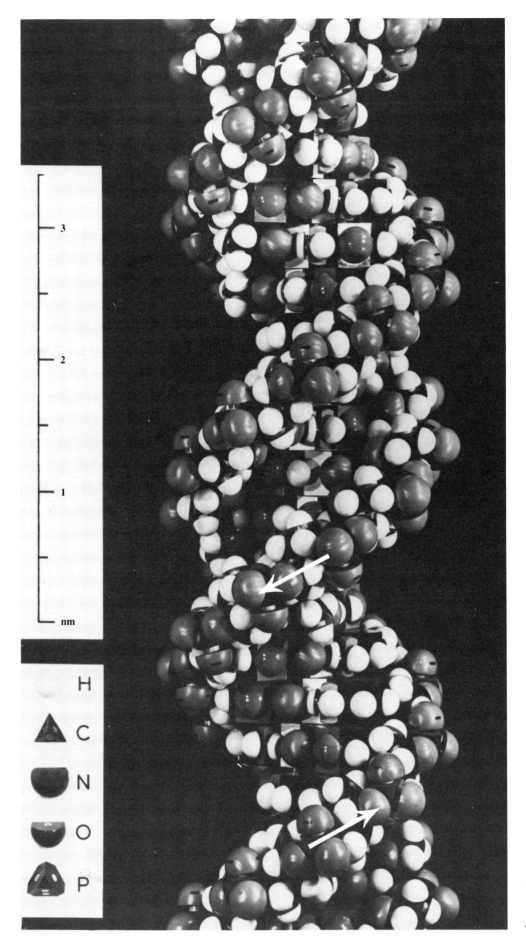

Fig 5.49 *Space-filling model of DNA. Arrows indicate the directions of the two antiparallel sugar–phosphate backbones*

Experiment 5.1: Identification of biochemicals in pure form

N.B. Any heating that has to be done in the following tests should be carried out in a water bath at the boiling point of water. Direct heating of test-tubes should not take place.

Materials

pH paper
test-tubes
test-tube rack
Bunsen burner
teat pipettes
spatula
1 cm³ syringe
iodine/potassium iodide solution
Benedict's reagent

dilute sulphuric acid
sodium hydrogencarbonate
Sudan III
Millon's reagent
5% potassium hydroxide solution
1% copper sulphate solution
DCPIP (dichlorophenolindophenol) solution
1% starch solution (cornflour is a recommended source)
1% glucose solution
1% sucrose solution (Analar sucrose must be used to avoid contamination with a reducing sugar)
olive oil or corn oil
absolute ethanol
egg albumen
1% lactose solution
1% fructose solution

Carbohydrates

Reducing sugars. The reducing sugars include all monosaccharides, such as glucose and fructose, and some disaccharides, such as maltose. Use 0.1–1% sugar solutions.

Test	Observation	Basis of test
Benedict's test		
Add 2 cm³ of a solution of the reducing sugar to a test-tube. Add an equal volume of Benedict's solution. Shake and bring gently to the boil, shaking continuously to minimise spitting.	The initial blue colouration of the mixture turns green, then yellowish and may finally form a brick-red precipitate.	Benedict's solution contains copper sulphate. Reducing sugars reduce soluble blue copper sulphate, containing copper(II) ions (Cu²⁺) to insoluble red-brown copper oxide containing copper(I). The latter is seen as a precipitate.

Additional information

The mixture is likely to bump violently during heating and extra care should therefore be taken. The test is **semi-quantitative**, that is a rough estimation of the amount of reducing sugar present will be possible. The final precipitate will appear green to yellow to orange to red-brown with increasing amounts of reducing sugar. (The initial yellow colour blends with the blue of the copper sulphate solution to give the green colouration.)

Test	Observation	Basis of test
Fehling's test		
Add 2 cm³ of a solution of the reducing sugar to a test-tube. Add 1 cm³ of Fehling's solution A and 1 cm³ of Fehling's solution B. Shake and bring to the boil.	The initial blue colouration of the mixture turns green to yellow and finally a brick-red precipitate is formed.	As Benedict's test.

Additional information

Not as convenient as Benedict's test because Fehling's solutions A and B have to be kept separate until the test. Also it is not as sensitive.

Non-reducing sugars. The most common non-reducing sugar is sucrose, a disaccharide. If reducing sugars have been shown to be absent (negative result in above test) a brick-red precipitate in the test below indicates the presence of a non-reducing sugar. If reducing sugars have been shown to be present, a heavier precipitate will be observed in the following test than with the reducing test if non-reducing sugar is also present.

Test	Observation	Basis of test
Add 2 cm³ of sucrose solution to a test-tube. Add 1 cm³ dilute hydrochloric acid. Boil for one minute. Carefully neutralise with sodium hydrogencarbonate (check with pH paper) – care is required because effervescence occurs. Carry out Benedict's test.	As Benedict's test.	A disaccharide can be hydrolysed to its monosaccharide constitutents by boiling with dilute hydrochloric acid. Sucrose is hydrolysed to glucose and fructose, both of which are reducing sugars and give the reducing sugar result with the Benedict's test.

Starch. This is only slightly soluble in water, in which it forms a colloidal suspension. It can be tested in suspension or as a solid.

Test	Observation	Basis of test
Iodine/potassium iodide test		
Add 2 cm³ 1% starch solution to a test-tube. Add a few drops of I₂/KI solution. Alternatively add the latter to the solid form of starch.	A blue-black colouration.	A polyiodide complex is formed with starch.

Cellulose and lignin. See appendix A2.4.2 (staining).

Lipids

Lipids include oils (such as corn oil and olive oil), fats and waxes.

Test	Observation	Basis of test
Sudan III		
Sudan III is a red dye. Add 2 cm³ oil to 2 cm³ of water in a test-tube. Add a few drops of Sudan III and shake.	A red-stained oil layer separates on the surface of the water, which remains uncoloured.	Fat globules are stained red and are less dense than water.
Emulsion test		
Add 2 cm³ fat or oil to a test-tube containing 2 cm³ of absolute ethanol. Dissolve the lipid by shaking vigorously. Add an equal volume of cold water.	A cloudy white suspension	Lipids are immiscible with water. Adding water to a solution of the lipid in alcohol results in an emulsion of tiny lipid droplets in the water which reflect light and give a white, opalescent appearance.

Proteins

A suitable protein for these tests is egg albumen.

Test	Observation	Basis of test
Millon's Test Add 2 cm³ protein solution or suspension to a test-tube. Add 1 cm³ Millon's reagent and boil. *NB* Millon's reagent is poisonous: take care!	A white precipitate forms which coagulates on heating and turns red or salmon pink.	Millon's reagent contains mercury acidified with nitric acid, giving mercury(II) nitrate and nitrite. The amino acid tyrosine contains a phenol group which reacts to give a red mercury(II) complex. This is a reaction given by all phenolics and is not specific for proteins. Protein usually coagulates on boiling, thus appearing solid. The only common protein lacking tyrosine likely to be used is gelatin.
Biuret Test Add 2 cm³ protein solution to a test-tube. Add an equal volume of 5% potassium hydroxide solution and mix. Add 2 drops of 1% copper sulphate solution and mix. No heating is required.	A mauve or purple colour develops slowly.	A test for peptide bonds. In the presence of dilute copper sulphate in alkaline solution, nitrogen atoms in the peptide chain form a purple complex with copper(II) ions (Cu^{2+}). Biuret is a compound derived from urea which also contains the —CONH— group and gives a positive result.

Vitamin C (ascorbic acid)

This test can be conducted on a quantitative basis if required, in which case the volumes given below must be measured accurately. A suitable source of vitamin C is a 50/50 mix of fresh orange or lemon juice with distilled water. Vitamin C tablets may also be purchased.

Test	Observation	Basis of test
Using 0.1% ascorbic acid solution as a standard. Add 1 cm³ of DCPIP solution to a test-tube. Fill a 1 cm³ syringe with 0.1% ascorbic acid: Add the acid to the DCPIP drop by drop, stirring gently with the syringe needle. Do not shake.* Add until the blue colour of the dye just disappears. Note the volume of ascorbic acid solution used.	Blue colour of dye disappears to leave a colourless solution.	DCPIP is a blue dye which is reduced to a colourless compound by ascorbic acid, a strong reducing agent.

* Shaking the solution would result in oxidation of the ascorbic acid by oxygen in the air. The effects of shaking and of boiling could be investigated.

5.20 How could you determine the concentration of ascorbic acid in an unknown sample?

5.21 You are provided with three sugar solutions. One contains glucose, one a mixture of glucose and sucrose, and one sucrose.
(a) How could you identify each solution?
(b) Supposing that the apparatus were available, and time permitted, briefly discuss any further experiments you could perform to confirm your results.

5.22 How would you make 100 cm³ of a 10% glucose solution?

5.23 Starting with stock solutions of 10% glucose and 2% sucrose how would you make 100 cm³ of a mixture of final concentration 1% sucrose and 1% glucose?

Experiment 5.2: Identification of biochemicals in tissues

A biochemist is often faced with the problem of wanting to identify chemicals (qualitative analysis) or to measure their amounts (quantitative analysis) in living tissue. Sometimes the chemical can be tested for directly, but often some kind of extraction and purification process must first be embarked upon.

A convenient exercise is to take a range of common foods and plant material and to test for the range of biochemicals listed in experiment 5.1 above. An extraction procedure is designed where possible to give a clear, colourless solution for testing, and you should note the rationale behind the procedures so that you could design your own if necessary.

Materials

As for experiment 5.1 up to DCPIP solution
pestle and mortar
microscope
slides and cover-slips
razor blade
watch glass
Schultz's solution
phloroglucinol + conc. hydrochloric acid
potato tuber
apple
cotton wool
woody stem
seeds/nuts
soaked peas
beans

Microscopic examination of thin sections of tissue

Suitable for: Visible storage products, particularly starch grains, such as potato tuber.

As above with appropriate staining or other chemical testing

Suitable for: Reducing sugars – Mount in a few drops of Benedict's reagent, heat gently to boiling; add water if necessary to prevent drying.

Starch – Mount section in dilute iodine/potassium iodide solution.

Protein – Mount in a few drops of Millon's reagent, heat gently to boiling; add water if necessary to prevent drying.

Oil and fat – Stain material, such as seed, with Sudan III and wash with water and/or 70% ethanol. Then section and mount.

Cellulose, lignin, etc. – see appendix A2.4.2 for staining.

Testing a clear, aqueous solution

Decolourise tissue if necessary: Pigments may interfere with colour tests but can usually be removed with an organic solvent such as 80% ethanol or 80% propanone. *Care must be taken to avoid naked flames.* However, remember these solvents may also remove lipids and soluble sugars.
Suitable for: Removing chlorophyll from leaves.

Homogenise (grind) material: Sugars and proteins – Small pieces of solid material can be ground with a small quantity of water using a pestle and mortar or a food mixer. The ground material should be squeezed through several layers of pre-moistened fine muslin or nylon and/or filtered or centrifuged to remove solid material. This may be unnecessary if a fairly colourless, fine suspension is obtained. The clear solution can be tested as usual, with further dilution if necessary. The solid residue may also be tested if appropriate.

Lipids – Grind material, transfer to a test-tube and boil. Lipids will escape as oil droplets. Perform the Sudan III test. Alternatively take thin shavings of nuts or other foods, including coloured foods, and do the emulsion test.
Suitable for:

Fruit, such as apple, orange	(vitamin C, sugars)
Nuts	(oils)
Castor oil seed	(oil)
Pea seed	(protein)
Pine kernels	(protein and oil)
Potato	(starch, vitamin C)
Egg	(protein)

Subdivision of the above materials, such as into seeds, flesh, skin and juice, may be possible.

Chapter Six

Enzymes

Enzymes are protein molecules produced by living cells. Each cell contains several hundred enzymes. They are used to promote a vast number of rapid chemical reactions between temperature limits suitable for the particular organism, that is approximately 5–40 °C. In order to achieve the same speeds of reaction outside the organism, high temperatures would be necessary, as well as marked changes in other conditions. These would be lethal to a living cell, which operates in such a way as to prevent any marked change in its normal working conditions. Thus enzymes can be defined as biological **catalysts**, that is they speed up reactions. They are vitally important because in their absence reactions in the cell would be too slow to sustain life.

Enzyme reactions may be either **anabolic** (involved in synthesis) or **catabolic** (involved in breakdown). The sum total of all these reactions in a living cell or organism constitutes its metabolism. Therefore metabolism consists of anabolism and catabolism. An example of an enzyme involved in anabolism is glutamine synthetase:

$$\text{glutamic acid} + \text{ammonia} + \text{ATP} \xrightarrow[\text{synthetase}]{\text{glutamine}} \text{glutamine} + \text{water} + \text{ADP} + \text{P}_\text{i}$$

(ATP is adenosine triphosphate, ADP is adenosine diphosphate and P_i is inorganic phosphate.) An example of an enzyme involved in catabolism is maltase:

$$\text{starch} + \text{water} \xrightarrow{\text{amylase}} \text{maltose}$$

Commonly, a number of enzymes are used in sequence to convert one substance into one or several products via a series of intermediate compounds. The chain of reactions is referred to as a **metabolic pathway**. Many such pathways can proceed simultaneously in the cell. The reactions proceed in an integrated and controlled manner and this can be attributed to the **specific** nature of enzymes. A single enzyme generally will catalyse only a single reaction. Thus enzymes serve to control the chemical reactions that occur within cells and ensure that they proceed at an efficient rate.

6.1 Catalysis and energy of activation

Biological catalysts (that is enzymes) possess the following major properties: all are globular proteins; they increase the rate of a reaction without themselves

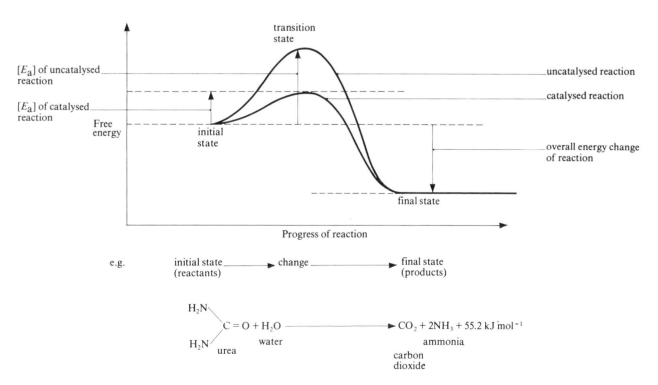

Fig 6.1 *Energy diagram showing a catalysed and uncatalysed chemical reaction (see also appendix 1)*

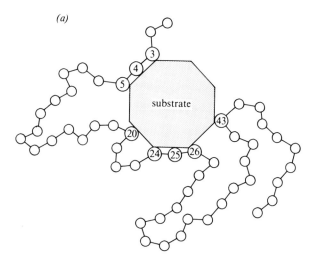

(a)

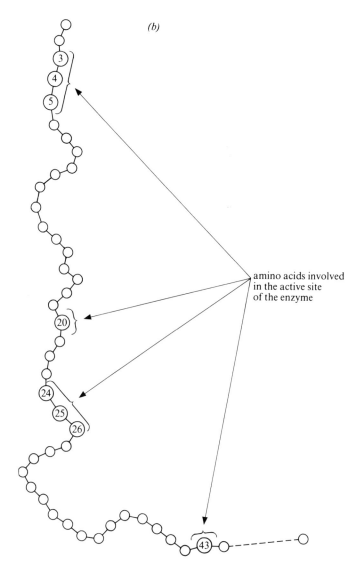

(b)

amino acids involved
in the active site
of the enzyme

Fig 6.2 *(a) Diagrammatic representation of substrate complexing with an enzyme active site. (b) Position of the amino acids of the active site shown on the primary structure of the enzyme*

being used up; their presence does not alter the nature or properties of the end product(s) of the reaction; a very small amount of catalyst effects the change of a large amount of substrate; their activity varies with pH, temperature, pressure and substrate and enzyme concentrations; the catalysed reaction is reversible; they are specific, that is an enzyme will generally catalyse only a single reaction.

Consider a mixture of petrol and oxygen maintained at room temperature. Although a reaction between the two substances is thermodynamically possible, it does not occur unless energy is applied to it, such as a simple spark. The energy required to make substrates react is called **activation energy** [E_a]. The greater the amount of activation energy required, the slower will be the rate of reaction at a given temperature. Enzymes, by functioning as catalysts, serve to reduce the activation energy required for a chemical reaction to take place (fig 6.1). They speed up the overall rate without altering, to any great extent, the temperature at which it occurs.

An **enzyme** combines with its **substrate** to form a short-lived enzyme/substrate complex (fig 6.2). Within this complex the chances of reactions occurring are greatly enhanced. Once a reaction has occurred, the complex breaks up into **products** and enzyme. The enzyme remains unchanged at the end of the reaction and is free to interact again with more substrate.

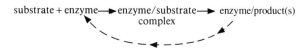

substrate + enzyme ⟶ enzyme/substrate ⟶ enzyme/product(s)
complex

6.1.1 Mechanism of enzyme action

Detailed study has revealed that most enzymes are far larger molecules than the substrates they act on and that only a very small portion of the enzyme, between 3–12 amino acids, comes into direct contact with the substrate in the enzyme/substrate complex. This region is called the **active site** of the enzyme. It is here that binding of the substrate or substrates occurs (fig 6.2). The remaining amino acids, which comprise the bulk of the enzyme, function to maintain the correct globular shape of the molecule which, as will be explained below, is important if the active site is to function at the maximum rate (fig 6.3).

Enzymes are very specific and it was suggested by Fischer in 1890 that this was because the enzyme had a particular shape into which the substrate or substrates fit exactly. This is often referred to as the '**lock and key**' hypothesis, where the substrate is the **key** whose shape is complementary to the enzyme or **lock** (fig 6.4).

When an enzyme/substrate complex is formed it is 'activated' into forming the products of the reaction. Once formed, the products no longer fit into the active site and escape into the surrounding medium, leaving the active site free to receive further substrate molecules.

In 1959 Koshland suggested a modification to the 'lock and key' analogy. Working from evidence that suggested that enzymes and their active sites were physically rather

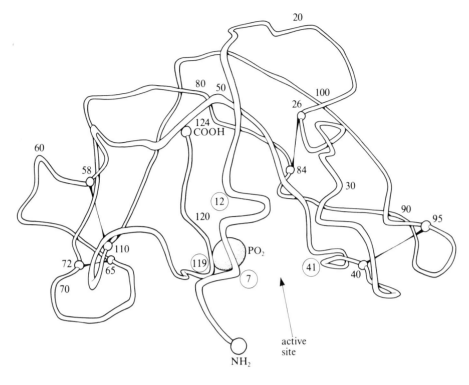

Fig 6.3 *Tertiary structure of ribonuclease. The amino acids involved at the active site are numbers 12 and 119 (histidines) and 7 and 41 (lysines). Ribonuclease hydrolyses ribonucleic acids to nucleotides (From Kartha, Bello & Harker (1967) Nature, 213, 864.)*

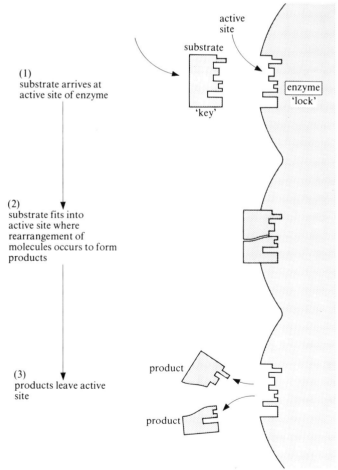

(1) substrate arrives at active site of enzyme

(2) substrate fits into active site where rearrangement of molecules occurs to form products

(3) products leave active site

Fig 6.4 *Fischer's 'lock and key' hypothesis (1890). Sequence of events when the union of a substrate with its enzyme occurs*

more flexible structures than hitherto described, he envisaged a dynamic interaction occurring between enzyme and substrate. He argued that when a substrate combines with an enzyme, it induces changes in the enzyme structure. The amino acids which constitute the active site are moulded into a precise formation which enables the enzyme to perform its catalytic function most effectively (fig 6.5). This is called the '**induced-fit**' hypothesis. A suitable analogy would be that of a hand changing the shape of a glove as the glove is put on. Further refinements to the hypothesis have been made as details of individual reactions became known. In some cases, for example, the substrate molecule changes shape slightly before binding.

6.2 Enzyme cofactors

Many enzymes require non-protein components called **cofactors** for their efficient activity. They were discovered as substances that had to be present for enzyme activity, even though, unlike enzymes, they were stable at relatively high temperatures. Cofactors may vary from simple inorganic ions to complex organic molecules, and may either remain unchanged at the end of a reaction or be regenerated by a later process. The **enzyme/cofactor** complex is called a **holoenzyme**, whilst the enzyme portion, without its cofactor, is called an **apoenzyme**. There are three recognised types of cofactor: inorganic ions, prosthe-

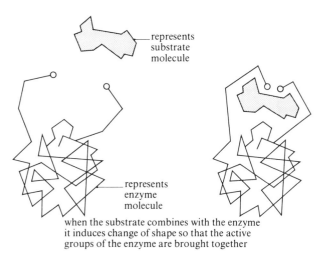

represents substrate molecule

represents enzyme molecule

when the substrate combines with the enzyme it induces change of shape so that the active groups of the enzyme are brought together

larger and smaller compounds are unsuitable for reacting with the enzyme

Fig 6.5 *Diagram to show Koshland's 'induced-fit' hypothesis. (From J. C. Marsden & C. F. Stoneman (1977) Enzymes and equilibria, Heinemann Educational Books)*

tic groups and coenzymes. Many organic molecules, some related to vitamins, act as cofactors. The molecule may be tightly bound to the enzyme (as in prosthetic groups) or only loosely associated with it (as in coenzymes). In both cases the molecules act as carriers of groups of atoms, single atoms or electrons that are being transferred from one place to another in an overall metabolic pathway.

6.2.1 Inorganic ions (alternatively known as enzyme activators)

These are thought to mould either the enzyme or the substrate into a shape such that an enzyme/substrate complex can be formed, hence increasing the chances of a reaction occurring between them and therefore increasing the rate of reaction catalysed by that particular enzyme. For example, salivary amylase activity is increased in the presence of chloride ions.

6.2.2 Prosthetic groups (for example FAD, FMN, biotin, haem)

The organic molecule is integrated in such a way that it effectively assists the catalytic function of its enzyme, as in flavin adenine dinucleotide (FAD). This contains riboflavin (vitamin B_2) which is the hydrogen-accepting part of FAD (fig 6.6). It is concerned with cell oxidation pathways such as part of the respiratory chain in respiration (chapter 11).

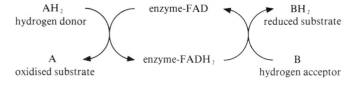

AH$_2$
hydrogen donor

enzyme-FAD

BH$_2$
reduced substrate

A
oxidised substrate

enzyme-FADH$_2$

B
hydrogen acceptor

Net effect: 2H transferred from A to B. One holoenzyme acts as a link between A and B.

Haem

Haem is an iron-containing prosthetic group. It has the shape of a flat ring (a '**porphyrin ring**' as is found in

chlorophyll) with an iron atom at its centre. It has a number of biologically important functions.

Electron carrier. Haem is the prosthetic group of cytochromes (see respiratory chain, chapter 11), where it acts as an electron carrier. In accepting electrons the iron is reduced to Fe(II); in handing on electrons it is oxidised to Fe(III). In other words it takes part in oxidation/reduction reactions by reversible changes in the valency of the iron.

Oxygen carrier. Haemoglobin and myoglobin are oxygen-carrying proteins that contain haem groups. Here the iron remains in the reduced, Fe(II) form (see section 14.13,1).

Other enzymes. Haem is found in catalases and peroxidases, which catalyse the decomposition of hydrogen peroxide into water and oxygen. It is also found in a number of other enzymes.

6.2.3 Coenzymes (for example NAD, NADP, coenzyme A, ATP)

Nicotinamide adenine dinucleotide (NAD) (fig 6.7)

This is derived from the vitamin nicotinic acid and can exist in both a reduced and an oxidised form. In the oxidised state it functions in catalysis as a hydrogen acceptor

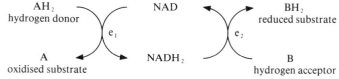

AH$_2$
hydrogen donor

NAD

e_1

BH$_2$
reduced substrate

e_2

A
oxidised substrate

NADH$_2$

B
hydrogen acceptor

where e_1 and e_2 are two different dehydrogenase enzymes.

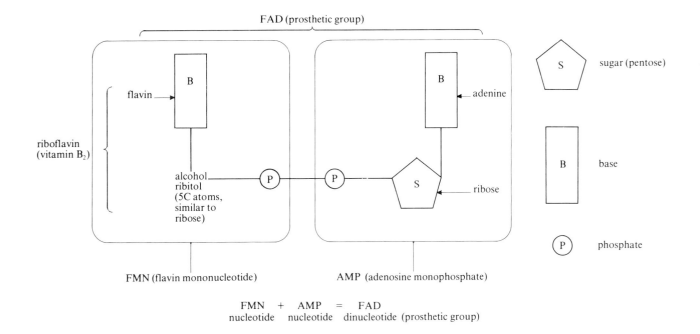

Fig 6.6 *Vitamin and prosthetic group interrelationship. The structure of FAD (flavin adenine dinucleotide) is shown*

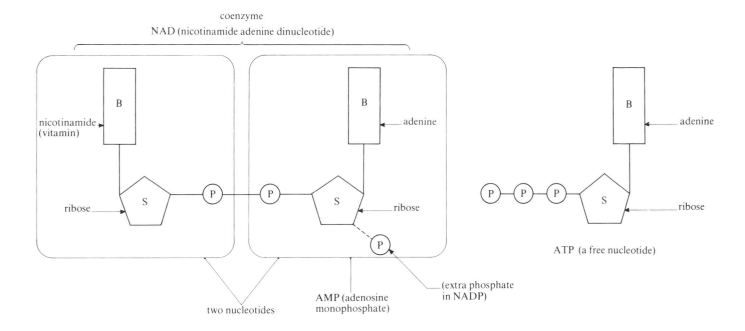

Fig 6.7 *Vitamin and coenzyme interrelationship. The structures of NAD, NADP and ATP are shown*

Net effect: 2H transferred from A to B. Here the coenzyme acts as a link between two different enzyme systems e_1 and e_2.

6.3 The rate of enzyme reactions

The rate of an enzyme reaction is measured by the amount of substrate changed or amount of product formed, during a period of time.

The rate is determined by measuring the slope of the tangent to the curve in the initial stage of the reaction (shown as (a) in fig 6.8). The steeper the slope, the greater is the rate. If activity is measured over a period of time, the rate of reaction usually falls, most commonly as a result of a fall in substrate concentration (see next section).

6.4 Factors affecting the rate of enzyme reactions

When investigating the effect of a given factor on the rate of an enzyme-controlled reaction, all other factors should be kept **constant** and at **optimum levels** wherever possible. Initial rates only should be measured, as explained above.

Computer program. ENZYME: The program simulates enzyme-controlled reactions. The user can generate four types of graph: free energy vs. reaction coordinate; kinetic energy vs. temperature; amount of product or reaction rate vs. time, substrate concentration, enzyme concentration, pH or temperature.

6.4.1 Enzyme concentration

Provided that the substrate concentration is maintained at a high level, and other conditions such as pH and temperature are kept constant, the rate of reaction is proportional to the enzyme concentration (fig 6.9). Invariably reactions are catalysed by enzyme concentrations which are much lower than substrate concentrations. Thus as the enzyme concentration is increased, so will be the rate of the enzymatic reaction.

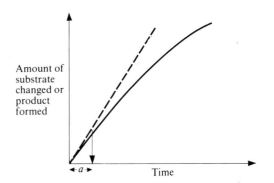

Fig 6.8 *The rate of an enzyme-controlled reaction*

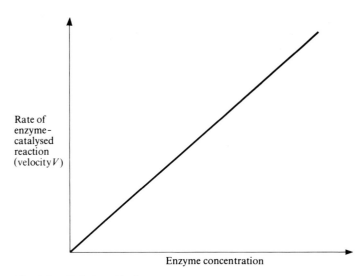

Fig 6.9 *Relationship between enzyme concentration and the rate of an enzyme-controlled reaction*

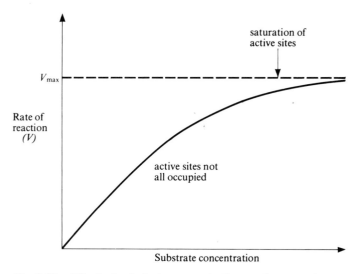

Fig 6.10 *Effect of substrate concentration on the rate of an enzyme-controlled reaction*

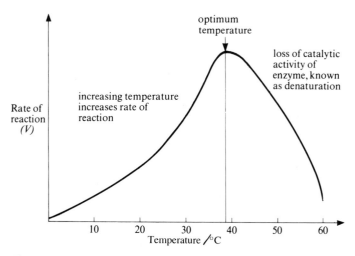

Fig 6.11 *The effect of temperature on the activity of an enzyme such as salivary amylase*

172

Experiment 6.1: To determine the effect of enzyme concentration on the hydrolysis of sucrose by sucrase (invertase)

Materials

2% sucrose solution
1%, 0.75%, 0.5% sucrase (invertase) solutions
Benedict's reagent
12 test-tubes and rack
water baths at 38 °C and 100 °C
glass rods
stopclock
distilled water
labels
Bunsen burner

Method

(1) Add 2 cm³ of clear blue Benedict's reagent to 2 cm³ of clear colourless 1% sucrase solution. Heat the mixture in the water bath maintained at 100 °C for 5 min (Benedict's test).
(2) Repeat (1) using 2 cm³ of clear colourless 2% sucrose solution and then 2 cm³ of distilled water.
(3) Boil 5 cm³ 1% sucrase solution.
(4) Take 8 clean, dry test-tubes, label 1–8, and add 1 cm³ Benedict's reagent to each.
(5) Add 5 cm³ of 2% sucrose solution to a test-tube labelled S and place in the water bath maintained at 38 °C throughout the experiment.
(6) Add 5 cm³ of 1% sucrase solution to a test-tube labelled E and place in the water bath at 38 °C.
(7) Leave both test-tubes and contents in the water bath for 5 min to allow them to equilibrate with their surroundings.
(8) Add the enzyme solution to the sucrose solution, invert the test-tube to thoroughly mix the two solutions.
(9) Immediately start the stopclock and replace the tube containing the reaction mixture in the water bath.
(10) Throughout the experiment agitate the mixture continuously to ensure thorough mixing.
(11) After 30 s of incubation remove 1 cm³ of mixture and place in test-tube 1.
(12) Repeat this procedure every 30 s placing the samples in tubes 2–8 in turn.
(13) Heat tubes 1–8 in the water bath at 100 °C for 5 min. Note the time when the first positive reducing sugar test is obtained indicated by a brick-red precipitate.
(14) Repeat the experiment using the boiled enzyme from (3).
(15) Repeat the entire sequence/experiment twice using the 0.75% and 0.5% sucrase solutions.
(16) Record your observations and comment on your results.

6.4.2 Substrate concentration

For a given enzyme concentration, the rate of an enzymatic reaction increases with increasing substrate concentration (fig 6.10). The theoretical maximum rate (V_{max}) is never quite obtained, but there comes a point when any further increase in substrate concentration produces no significant change in reaction rate. This is because at high substrate concentrations the active sites of the enzyme molecules at any given moment are virtually saturated with substrate. Thus any extra substrate has to wait until the enzyme/substrate complex has dissociated into products and free enzyme before it may itself complex with the enzyme. Therefore at high substrate levels, both enzyme concentration, and the time it takes for dissociation of the enzyme/substrate molecule, limit the rate of the reaction.

6.4.3 Temperature

The effect of temperature on the rate of a reaction can be expressed as the temperature coefficient, Q_{10}.

$$Q_{10} = \frac{\text{rate of reaction at } (x + 10)°\text{C}}{\text{rate of reaction at } x °\text{C}}$$

Over a range of 0–40 °C, Q_{10} for an enzyme-controlled reaction is 2. In other words, the rate of an enzyme-controlled reaction is doubled for every rise of 10 °C. Heat increases molecular motion, thus the reactants move more quickly and chances of their bumping into each other are increased. As a result there is a greater probability of a reaction being caused. The temperature that promotes maximum activity is referred to as the optimum temperature. If the temperature is increased above this level, then a decrease in the rate of the reaction occurs despite the increasing frequency of collisions. This is because the secondary and tertiary structures of the enzyme have been disrupted, and the enzyme is said to be **denatured** (fig 6.11).

> **6.1** Explain how denaturing an enzyme may affect its efficiency as a catalyst.

If temperature is reduced to near or below freezing point, enzymes are **inactivated**, not denatured. They will regain their catalytic influence when higher temperatures are restored.

Today techniques of quick-freezing food are in widespread use as a means of preserving food for extensive periods. This not only prevents growth and multiplication of micro-organisms, but also deactivates their digestive enzymes thus making it impossible for them to decompose food. The natural enzymes in the food itself are also inactivated. However, once frozen, it is necessary to keep the food at subzero temperatures until it is to be prepared for consumption.

Experiment 6.2: To investigate the distribution of catalase in a soaked pea, and to determine the effect of different temperatures on its activity

Catalase is an enzyme which catalyses the decomposition of hydrogen peroxide, liberating oxygen gas as shown by effervescence:

$$2H_2O_2 \xrightarrow{\text{catalase}} 2H_2O + O_2$$

Hydrogen peroxide is a toxic by-product of metabolism in certain plant and animal cells, and is efficiently removed by catalase, which is one of the fastest acting enzymes known (at 0 °C one molecule of catalase can decompose 40 000 molecules of hydrogen peroxide per second). Catalase is found in microbodies (see chapter 7) and peroxisomes (see chapters 7 and 9).

Materials

a supply of soaked peas
hydrogen peroxide solution
test-tubes and rack
water baths at 40 °C, 60 °C, 70 °C, 80 °C and 100 °C
clock
thermometer
scalpels, scissors and forceps
test-tube holder
glass rod
white tile

Method

(1) Test for the presence of catalase by crushing a soaked pea and adding a few drops of hydrogen peroxide solution.
(2) Remove the seed coats from three soaked peas and test separately for catalase activity in both the seed coats and the cotyledons.
(3) Place two test-tubes containing distilled water in a water bath at 40 °C.
(4) Boil three whole peas in a test-tube and then place the boiled peas in one of the tubes in the water-bath.
(5) Place three whole unboiled peas in the other test-tube in the water bath.
(6) Allow enough time for the peas to reach the temperature of the water bath (at least 10 min).
(7) Test each pea for catalase activity.
(8) Repeat the experiment at 50, 60, 70, 80 and 100 °C.
(9) Record your observations and comment on your results.

> **6.2** Study fig 6.12 carefully and comment on the shapes of the curves given for the enzymatic reaction at different temperatures.

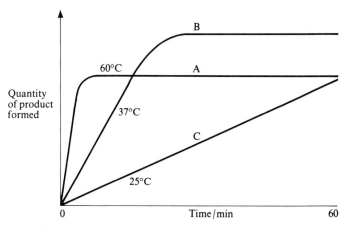

Fig 6.12 *Time course of an enzyme reaction at various temperatures*

6.4.4 pH

Under conditions of constant temperature, every enzyme functions most efficiently over a narrow pH range. The optimum pH is that at which the maximum rate of reaction occurs (fig 6.13 and table 6.1). When the pH is altered above or below this value, the rate of enzyme activity diminishes. Changes in pH alter the ionic charge of the acidic and basic groups that help to maintain the specific shape of the enzyme (section 5.5.4). The pH change leads to an alteration in enzyme shape, particularly at its active site. If extremes of pH are encountered by an enzyme, then it will be denatured. The optimum pH of an enzyme is not always the same as the pH of its immediate intracellular environment. This suggests that the enzyme's surroundings may be exerting some form of control over its activity.

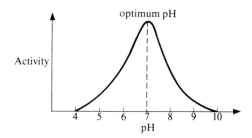

Fig 6.13 *Activity/pH curve for an enzyme*

Table 6.1 Optimum pH values for some enzymes.

Enzyme	Optimum pH
Pepsin	2.00
Sucrase	4.50
Enterokinase	5.50
Salivary amylase	6.80
Catalase	7.60
Chymotrypsin	7.00–8.00
Pancreatic lipase	9.00
Arginase	9.70

Experiment 6.3: To investigate the effect of different pH values on enzyme activity

Materials

Benedict's reagent
buffer solutions at pH 3,5,7,9,11
1% starch solution
water bath at 38 °C
Bunsen burner
asbestos mat
test-tube holder, test-tubes and rack
5 cm³ graduated pipettes
thermometer
stopclock
distilled water
stock solution of salivary
amylase (such as contained in saliva)

Method

(1) Rinse out the mouth with 5 cm³ of distilled water and spit this out.
(2) Swill 10 cm³ of distilled water round the mouth for 1 min and then collect this liquid.
(3) Make up the volume of salivary amylase to 40 cm³ with distilled water.
(4) Test the salivary amylase, starch and buffer solutions for the presence of reducing sugar using Benedict's reagent.
(5) Label a test-tube pH3 and add 2 cm³ of starch solution.
(6) Add 2 cm³ of buffer solution pH3 to the same test-tube and mix the two solutions thoroughly.
(7) Boil at least 4 cm³ of enzyme solution and place 4 cm³ in a labelled test-tube.
(8) Add 4 cm³ of unboiled enzyme solution to another labelled test-tube and place all three test-tubes in the water bath and allow the solutions to reach 38 °C (approximately 1 min).
(9) Place a small quantity of Benedict's reagent in each of 11 test-tubes and label them 1–11.

The following three stages must be carried out very quickly:

(10) When the solutions in the water bath have equilibrated, add the buffered starch solution to the unboiled enzyme solution.
(11) Mix the two solutions thoroughly by inverting the test-tube and replace the tube in the water bath.
(12) Start the stopclock and immediately remove a small quantity of reaction mixture (approximately the same volume as the Benedict's reagent) and place it in the test-tube labelled 1.
(13) Throughout the experiment the mixture must be shaken vigorously.
(14) After one minute of incubation remove a second, approximately equal volume, of the mixture and place it in test-tube 2.
(15) Repeat the removal of similar-sized samples of mixture at minute intervals for a further 9 min and place in test-tubes 3–11.
(16) Perform Benedict's tests on test-tubes 1–11 and note the time of incubation at which a positive result (a brick-red precipitate) is first achieved.
(17) Repeat the experiment using the boiled enzyme solution from (7).
(18) Repeat the entire experiment using each of the other buffer solutions.
(19) Plot a graph of time taken for hydrolysis to occur against pH and comment on your results.

6.3 (a) In fig 6.14, what is the optimum pH for the activity of enzyme B?
(b) Give an example of an enzyme which could be represented by (i) activity curve A, (ii) activity curve B.
(c) Why does the enzyme activity of C decrease at pH values between 8 and 9?
(d) Why is pH control important *in vivo*?
(e) 1 cm³ of a catalase solution was added to hydrogen peroxide solution at different pH values and the time taken to collect 10 cm³ of oxygen was measured. The results are given below.

pH of solution	Time (min) to collect gas
4.00	20.00
5.00	12.50
6.00	10.00
7.00	13.60
8.00	17.40

Draw a graph of these results and comment on them.

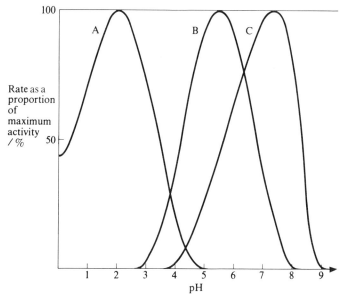

Fig 6.14 *The effect of pH on the activity of three enzymes, A, B and C*

6.5 Enzyme inhibition

A variety of small molecules exist which can reduce the rate of an enzyme-controlled reaction. They are called **enzyme inhibitors**. Inhibition may be reversible or irreversible.

6.5.1 Reversible inhibition

The inhibitor may be easily removed from the enzyme under certain conditions.

Competitive reversible inhibition

Here a compound, structurally similar to that of the usual substrate, associates with the enzyme's active site, but is unable to react with it. While it remains there it prevents access of any molecules of true substrate. As the genuine substrate and inhibitor **compete** for position in the active site, this form of inhibition is called competitive inhibition. It is able to be reversed, for if the substrate concentration is increased, the rate of reaction will be increased.

6.4 Why should the rate of reaction increase under these conditions?

An example of competitive inhibition is illustrated in fig 6.15.

The knowledge of competitive inhibition has been utilised in **chemotherapy**. This is the use of chemicals to destroy infectious micro-organisms without damaging host tissues. During the Second World War, **sulphonamides**, chemical derivatives of sulphanilamide, were used extensively to prevent the spread of microbial infection. The sulphonamides are similar in structure to para-aminobenzoate (PAB), a substance essential to the growth of many pathogenic bacteria. The bacteria require PAB for the production of folic acid, an important enzyme cofactor. Sulphonamides act by interfering with the synthesis of folic acid from PAB.

Animal cells are insensitive to sulphonamides even though they require folic acid for some reactions. This is because they use pre-formed folic acid and do not possess the necessary metabolic pathway for making it.

(a)

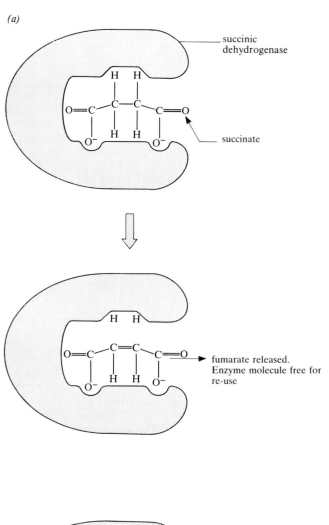

(b)

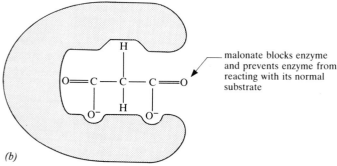

Fig 6.15 *An example of competitive inhibition. (a) The action of the enzyme succinic dehydrogenase on succinate. (b) Competitive inhibition of the enzyme by malonate*

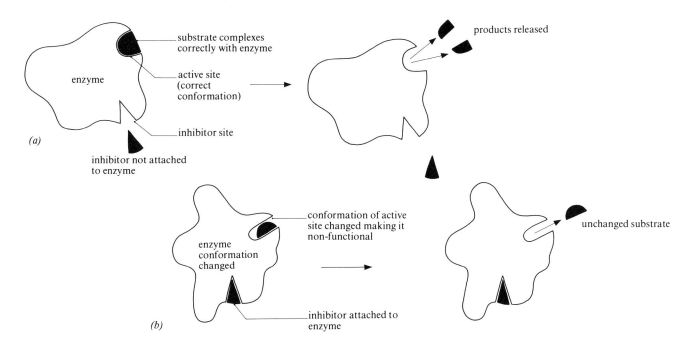

Fig 6.16 *The principle of non-competitive inhibition. (a) Normal reaction. (b) Non-competitive inhibition*

Non-competitive reversible inhibition

This type of inhibitor has no real structural similarity to the substrate and forms an enzyme/inhibitor complex at a point on the enzyme other than its active site (fig 6.16). It has the effect of altering the globular structure of the enzyme, so that even though the genuine substrate may be able to bind with the enzyme, catalysis is unable to take place. For example, cyanide combines with metallic ions (acting as prosthetic groups) of some enzymes (such as copper ions of cytochrome oxidase) and inhibits their activity. The rate of reaction will continue to decrease with increasing inhibitor concentration. When inhibitor saturation is reached, the rate of the reaction will be almost nil.

6.5.2   Irreversible inhibition (fig 6.17)

Very small concentrations of chemical reagents such as the heavy metal ions mercury (Hg^{2+}), silver (Ag^+) and arsenic (As^+), or iodoacetic acid, completely inhibit some enzymes. They combine permanently with sulphydryl ($-SH$) groups and cause the protein of the enzyme molecule to precipitate. If these are components of the active site then the enzyme is inhibited.

> **6.5** What would be the effect on the rate of reaction between an inhibitor of this kind and the substrate if substrate concentration is increased?

Diisopropylfluorophosphate (DFP), a nerve gas used in warfare, forms an enzyme/inhibitor complex with the amino acid serine at the active site of the enzyme acetylcholinesterase. This enzyme deactivates the chemical transmitter substance acetylcholine. One of the functions of acetylcholine is to aid the passage of a nerve impulse from one neurone to another across a synaptic gap (section 16.1). When the impulse has been transmitted acetylcholinesterase functions to deactivate acetylcholine almost immediately by hydrolysing it into choline and ethanoate. Once this has been completed the neurone is free to pass on another impulse. If acetylcholinesterase is inhibited, acetylcholine accumulates and nerve impulses are constantly propagated, causing prolonged muscle contraction. Paralysis or death is the end result. Some insecticides currently in use (such as parathion) have a similar effect on insects.

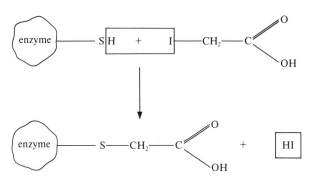

Fig 6.17 *Irreversible inhibition of an enzyme by iodoacetic acid*

6.6   Allosteric enzymes

The activity of these enzymes is regulated by compounds which are not their substrates and which bind to the enzyme at specific sites well away from the active site. They modify enzyme activity by causing a reversible change in the structure of the enzyme's active site. Compounds of this nature are called **allosteric effectors** and they may speed up (**allosteric activators**) or slow down (**allosteric inhibitors**) the reaction rate of an allosteric enzyme by increasing or decreasing the affinity of the enzyme for its substrate. An example of this is provided by the enzyme phosphofructokinase which catalyses the phosphorylation of fructose-6-phosphate to fructose-1-6-diphosphate. This reaction occurs during the glycolysis section of the respiratory pathway. When ATP is at a high concentration, it inhibits the enzyme phosphofructokinase allosterically. However, when cell metabolism increases and more ATP is used up, the overall concentration of ATP decreases and the pathway once again comes into operation (figs 6.18 and 6.19).

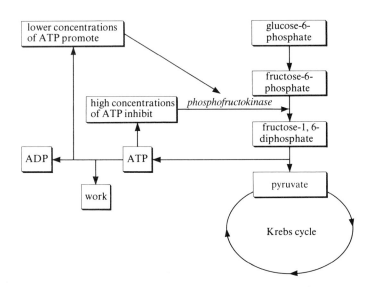

Fig 6.18 *Possible mechanism of the allosteric effect of ATP on phosphofructokinase. (After D. Harrison (1975)* Patterns in Biology, *Arnold)*

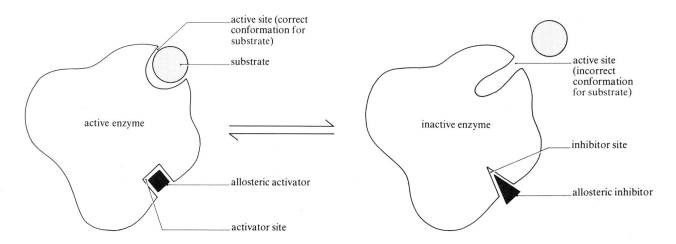

Fig 6.19 *Schematic representation of allosteric enzyme activity*

6.6.1 End-product inhibition (negative feedback inhibition)

When the end product of a metabolic pathway begins to accumulate, it may act as an allosteric inhibitor on the enzyme controlling the first step of the pathway. The affinity of the enzyme for its substrate would therefore be lowered, and further production of the end product decreased or prevented. This is called end-product inhibition and is an example of a negative feedback mechanism (section 18.1) serving to control an aspect of metabolic activity (fig 6.20).

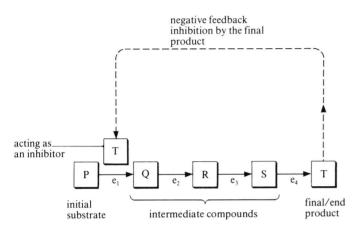

Fig 6.20 *Final/end-product inhibition. $e_1 - e_4$ are specific enzymes of a metabolic pathway*

6.7 Control of metabolism

There are over 500 enzymes present in a typical cell. Their activity and concentration will fluctuate continuously. How then, is control and integration of metabolism achieved? The answer lies in the specificity of action of enzymes, their spatial organisation and their functional interaction with other cellular components. Two distinct types of metabolic pathway exist in a cell which clearly demonstrate these features; these are the linear and branched metabolic pathways.

6.7.1 The linear metabolic pathway

A number of enzymes are arranged together in an organised fashion as a **multi-enzyme complex**. They are usually membrane-bound (fig 6.21a). The linear order of enzymes permits **self-regulation** by negative feedback inhibition, the rate of the pathway being controlled by the concentration of the end product. Such close-knit organisation also serves to reduce to a minimum interference from other reactions. Each enzyme is interdependent with the ones adjacent to it, and molecules are passed as products from one enzyme, to become the substrate of the next enzyme in the chain until the specific end product is formed.

6.7.2 The branched metabolic pathway.

In this pathway, a number of different end products may be formed. Which one would depend on the conditions prevailing in the cell at the time (fig 6.21b). Control of end-product formation would be influenced by feedback inhibition. Here again, a multi-enzyme system is in operation, but the enzymes are in solution and in no way closely associated with each other.

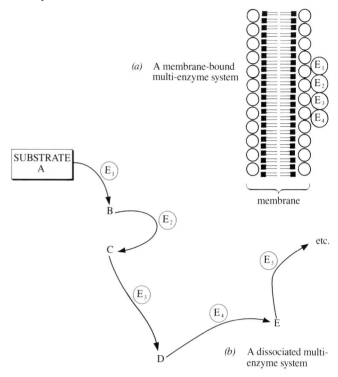

Fig 6.21 *Multi-enzyme systems. (a) A membrane-bound multi-enzyme system. (b) A dissociated multi-enzyme system, where B, C, D and E could be products depending upon the conditions in the cell*

6.6 Consider the multi-enzyme system shown below:

(a) If e_1 is specific for A, and the end-product X inhibits e_1, what does this tell you about the binding sites of A and X on the enzyme?
(b) How might an excess of X regulate the metabolic pathway?
(c) What is the name given to the type of control system operating here?
(d) Why are several enzymes needed in any metabolic pathway?

6.7 Summarise the characteristic properties of enzymes.

Table 6.2 Enzyme classification.

Group	Reaction catalysed	Examples
Oxidoreductase	Transfer of H or O atoms, or electrons, from one molecule to another	Two types, dehydrogenases and oxidases $$AH_2 + B \xrightleftharpoons[\hphantom{dehydrogenase}]{dehydrogenase} A + BH_2 \qquad \text{transfer of } H_2$$ e.g. $CH_3CHO + NADH_2 \xrightleftharpoons[\text{dehydrogenase}]{\text{alcohol}} CH_3CH_2OH + NAD$ (p. 330) ethanal, alcohol (ethanol) $$AH_2 + O \xrightleftharpoons[\hphantom{oxidase}]{oxidase} A + H_2O$$ e.g. reduced cytochrome $+ \tfrac{1}{2}O_2 \xrightleftharpoons[\text{oxidase}]{\text{cytochrome}}$ cytochrome $+ H_2O$ (p. 328)
Transferase	Transfer of a specific group from one molecule to another. The group may be methyl-, acyl-, amino- or phosphate	$AB + C \rightleftharpoons A + BC$ e.g. transaminases (transfer amino groups) (pp. 268 & 340) phosphorylases (add inorganic phosphate) glycogen $+ P_i \xrightleftharpoons[\text{phosphorylase}]{\text{glycogen}}$ glucose-1-phosphate in respiration
Hydrolase	Formation of two products from a substrate by hydrolysis (splitting molecule with water)	$AB + H_2O \rightleftharpoons AOH + BH$ e.g. lipase, amylase, peptidases, other digestive enzymes (section 10.4.9)
Lyase	Non-hydrolytic addition or removal of groups from substrates. C–C, C–N, C–O or C–S bonds may be split	e.g. decarboxylases (remove CO_2) $CH_3COCOOH \xrightleftharpoons[\text{decarboxylase}]{\text{pyruvate}} CH_3CHO + CO_2$ (p. 330) pyruvic acid, ethanal e.g. carboxylases (add CO_2) $RuBP + H_2O + CO_2 \xrightleftharpoons[\hphantom{RuBP carboxylase}]{RuBP\ carboxylase} 2GP$ (p. 265)
Isomerase	Intramolecular rearrangement – one isomer converted into another	$AB \rightleftharpoons BA$ e.g. glucose-1-phosphate $\xrightleftharpoons[\hphantom{phosphoglucomutase}]{phosphoglucomutase}$ glucose-6-phosphate in respiration glucose-6-phosphate $\xrightleftharpoons[\text{isomerase}]{\text{phosphoglucomutase}}$ fructose-6-phosphate (p. 327)
Ligase	Join together two molecules by synthesis of new C–C, C–N, C–O or C–S bonds using energy from ATP	$X + Y + ATP \rightleftharpoons XY + ADP + P_i$ e.g. synthetases e.g. aminoacyl tRNA synthetases (p. 822)

NB This classification is often not followed in the common names of enzymes, e.g. DNA **polymerase** (p. 814).

6.8 Enzyme classification

In 1961 a systematic nomenclature for enzymes was recommended by a commission of the International Union of Biochemistry. The enzymes were placed into six groups according to the general type of reaction which they catalyse. Each enzyme was given a systematic name, accurately describing the reaction it catalyses. However, since many of these names were very long and complicated, each enzyme was allocated a 'trivial' name for everyday use. This consists of (i) the name of the substrate acted upon by the enzyme, (ii) the type of reaction catalysed, and (iii) the suffix -ase. For example, ribulose bisphosphate carboxylase; substrate: ribulose bisphosphate $(+CO_2)$; type of reaction: carboxylation (addition of CO_2). The enzymes are classified as in table 6.2.

6.9 Enzyme technology

Use of enzymes in industry is growing and, with the versatility of micro-organisms in producing

Table 6.3 Summary of some common industrial uses of enzymes.

Application	Enzymes used	Uses	Problems
Biological detergents	Primarily proteases, produced in an extracellular form from bacteria	Used for pre-soak conditions and direct liquid applications	Allergic response of process workers; now overcome by encapsulation techniques
	Amylase enzymes	Detergents for machine dishwashing to remove resistant starch residues	
Baking industry	Fungal alpha-amylase enzymes; normally inactivated about 50 °C, destroyed during baking process	Catalyse breakdown of starch in the flour to sugar. Yeast action on sugar produces carbon dioxide. Used in production of white bread, buns, rolls	
	Protease enzymes	Biscuit manufacture to lower the protein level of the flour	
Baby foods	Trypsin	To pre-digest baby foods	
Brewing industry	Enzymes produced from barley during mashing stage of beer production	Degrade starch and proteins to produce simple sugars, amino acids and peptides used by the yeasts to enhance alcohol production	
	Industrially produced enzymes: amylases, glucanases, proteases betaglucanase amyloglucosidase proteases	Now widely used in the brewing process: split polysaccharides and proteins in the malt improve filtration characteristics low-calorie beer remove cloudiness during storage of beers	
Fruit juices	Cellulases, pectinases	Clarify fruit juices	
Dairy industry	Rennin, derived from the stomachs of young ruminant animals (calves, lambs, kids)	Manufacture of cheese, used to split protein	Older animals cannot be used as with increasing age rennin production decreases and is replaced by another protease, pepsin, which is not suitable for cheese production. In recent years the great increase in cheese consumption together with increased beef production has resulted in increasing shortage of rennin and escalating prices
	Microbially produced enzyme	Now finding increasing use in the dairy industry	
	Lipases	Enhance ripening of blue-mould cheeses (Danish blue, Roquefort)	
	Lactases	Break down lactose to glucose and galactose	
Starch industry	Amylases, amyloglucosidases and glucoamylases	Converts starch into glucose and various syrups	
	Glucose isomerase	Converts glucose into fructose (high-fructose syrups derived from starchy materials have enhanced sweetening properties and lower calorific values)	
	Immobilised enzymes	Production of high fructose syrups	Widely used in USA and Japan but EEC restrictive practices to protect sugar beet farmers prohibits use
Rubber industry	Catalase	To generate oxygen from peroxide to convert latex to foam rubber	
Paper industry	Amylases	Degrade starch to lower viscosity product needed for sizing and coating paper	
Photographic industry	Protease (ficin)	Dissolve gelatin off scrap film allowing recovery of silver present	

Based on Table 5.2, *Biotechnology*, 2nd ed., John E. Smith, New Studies In Biology (1988), Edward Arnold and *Enzymes, their nature and role*, Wiseman & Gould, Hutchinson Educational.

enzymes, new methods of making many industrially important chemicals are possible. High cost, purified enzymes are also being increasingly used in medicine, notably for diagnostic purposes in blood and urine tests. Enzymes can accomplish reactions at normal temperatures and pressures which would otherwise require expensive, energy-demanding high temperatures and/or pressures, or might not be possible at all.

Enzymes may be extracted from cells and purified before use, used within whole cells or, in the near future, it is anticipated that 'designer enzymes' will be 'tailor made' for specific tasks (**protein engineering**). The latter depends on being able to predict the three-dimensional shape into which a given primary structure will fold. Once a protein has been designed with the desired shape, an artificial gene could be made which would code for the protein and the gene could be inserted, say, into the bacterium *E. coli* for mass production. Table 6.3 summarises some of the current uses of enzymes in industry.

6.9.1 Immobilisation of enzymes

Apart from the problem of obtaining the enzyme in a suitable form in the first place (usually from a micro-organism), other major problems in enzyme technology include how to keep the organism functioning for a long period of time (**stabilisation**) and, in particular, how to immobilise the enzyme. **Immobilisation** is the process of attaching the enzyme to, or trapping it in, an inert solid support or carrier. This enables the reactants to be passed over the enzyme in a **continuous** process, or for the enzyme to be used in a **batch reactor** (a reactor that deals with one batch at a time), the important point being that in both cases the enzyme can be recovered at the end of the reaction for re-use. The alternative of mixing the enzyme in solution with the reactants is technically simpler, but once

the reaction is over this will involve either wasteful loss of the enzyme or potentially expensive recovery techniques. Therefore, where possible, it is used only for cheaper enzymes such as amylases and proteases.

Insoluble polymers, in the form of membranes or particles, are typically used as supports for the enzyme. Immobilised whole microbial cells are also sometimes used, for example inside polyacrylanide beads. Glucose isomerase (see starch industry, table 6.3) is currently the enzyme most commonly used in immobilised form, and can operate continuously for 1 000 hours at 60 °C. Class experiments using alginate beads to immobilise enzymes, for example urease, can provide a demonstration of this principle (consult, for example, the London Centre for Biotechnology, or NCSB Reading).

6.9.2 Biosensors

In industry, medicine, agriculture and environmental science, it is sometimes useful to be able to monitor the presence of specific chemicals both accurately and rapidly. For example, continuous monitoring of an industrial fermentation process would allow conditions such as pH, temperature, and substrate concentration to be maintained precisely at optimum levels; or in medicine, rapid diagnosis might be possible, based on detection of chemicals such as sodium, potassium or glucose in blood or urine samples. Biosensors are a relatively new and important innovation in this field. Our taste buds and olfactory (smell) areas may be regarded as biosensors. A **biosensor** uses an **immobilised** biological molecule (usually an enzyme or an antibody) or a whole microbial cell to detect or 'sense' a particular substance. The biosensor does this by reacting specifically with the substance to be detected (hence the use of enzymes or antibodies) to give a product which is used to generate an electrical signal by means of a

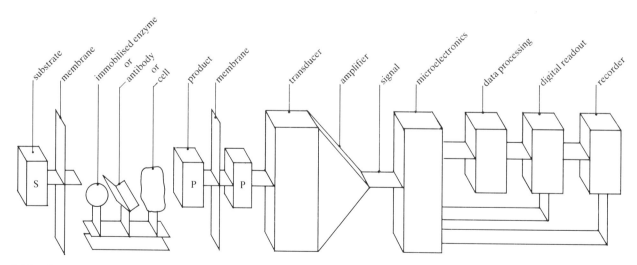

Fig 6.22 *Schematic outline of a biosensor. The substance to be measured (substrate) passes through a thin membrane and then encounters the biological sensing agent – usually an enzyme, an antibody or a whole microbial cell. The substrate and sensor interact to give a product which may be an electrical current, heat, a gas, or a soluble chemical. The product then passes through another membrane to the transducer which detects and measures the product, producing an electrical signal which is amplified and used to give an immediate read-out*

device called a **transducer**. The product of the reaction could be heat, a gas, a soluble chemical or an electric current generated by electron or proton flow during the reaction. The nature of the transducer varies with the nature of the product it has to detect, but it always produces an electrical signal in response to the product. This electrical signal is amplified and processed to give an instant read-out (fig 6.22).

Details of an experiment to detect urea using the enzyme urease are available from the London Centre for Biotechnology.

A number of sensing devices have already been introduced, such as glucose monitors for medical purposes and nerve gas sensors for military use. Enzymes are being used increasingly in medicine for routine automatic analysis of body fluids, for example for metabolites, drugs and hormones. A glucose oxidase 'electrode' or biosensor is one of the most developed products. This can measure the amount of glucose in a blood sample. It is hoped that in the relatively near future it will be possible to implant such devices in blood vessels in the skin of diabetics, allowing them to monitor more accurately their insulin requirements. Ultimately, it may be possible to link the biosensor to a minipump, so that insulin is automatically released when needed, thus in effect providing the diabetic with an automatic pancreas. This fine control would reduce the common secondary effects of diabetes, such as eye and kidney damage, suffered by some diabetics as a result of relatively crude treatment by occasional injections.

One of the major future developments in biosensor research will be towards making more-sensitive miniature sensors. This could be the result of developing 'biochips'. Just as large computers have been reduced in size by the introduction of silicon microchips containing the complex circuits required, so further size reduction may be possible by using **semiconducting organic molecules**, such as proteins in place of silicon. Electrical signals will then pass along these molecules; electrical circuits could be just one molecule wide. Biochips would be small enough to implant in the human body. Interfaced with the relevant devices, numerous medical applications become possible, such as artificial sense organs or artificial regulation of heartbeat.

Another important development in biosensor research will be multifunctional biosensors, each of which it is anticipated will be sensitive to at least ten different stimuli.

183

Chapter Seven

Cells

The basic unit of structure and function in living organisms is the **cell**. This concept, known as the **cell theory**, evolved gradually during the nineteenth century as a result of microscopy. The study of cells by microscopy came to be known as **cytology**. Later in the nineteenth century, and during this century, much more experimentation was brought into the study of cells, and there is now a large branch of biology called **cell biology** in which many techniques are combined to gain an understanding of living organisms at the cellular level. Like biochemists, cell biologists often deal with fundamental processes which are common to most or all cells, so that cell biology, like biochemistry, is a unifying theme in biology. Table 7.1 summarises some of the historically important events in the development of cell biology.

There is good reason why life should have a cellular basis. The cell, in essence, is a self-perpetuating chemical system. In order to maintain the concentration of chemicals required the system has to be physically separate from its environment, yet capable of exchange with its environment so that chemicals which are raw materials can be acquired and those which are waste products can be removed. In this way, by doing work, the system can maintain stability (homeostasis, chapter 18). In all cases the barrier between the chemical system and its environment is the cell surface membrane; this helps to control exchanges between the two and so forms the boundary of the cell.

Cells always contain cytoplasm, as well as genetic material in the form of DNA. The DNA controls the activities of the cell and can replicate itself so that new cells are formed. The concept that new cells only come from pre-existing cells also dates from the nineteenth century (table 7.1) and is an essential part of the cell theory.

Table 7.1 Some historically important events in cell biology.

1590	Jansen invented the **compound microscope**, which combines two lenses for greater magnification.
1665	Robert Hooke, using an improved compound microscope, examined cork and used the term 'cell' to describe its basic units. He thought the cells were empty and the walls were the living material.
1650–1700	Antony van Leeuwenhoeck, using a good quality simple lens (mag. ×200), observed nuclei and unicellular organisms, including bacteria. In 1676, bacteria were described for the first time as '**animalcules**'.
1700–1800	Further descriptions and drawings published, mainly of plant tissues, although the microscope was generally used as a toy.
1827	Dolland dramatically improved the quality of lenses. This was followed by a rapid spread of interest in microscopy.
1831–3*	Robert Brown described the nucleus as a characteristic spherical body in plant cells.
1838–9*	Schleiden (a botanist) and Schwann (a zoologist) produced the '**cell theory**' which unified the ideas of the time by stating that **the basic unit of structure and function in living organisms is the cell.**
1840*	Purkinje gave the name **protoplasm** to the contents of cells, realising that the latter were the living material, not the cells walls. Later the term **cytoplasm** was introduced (cytoplasm + nucleus = protoplasm).
1855*	Virchow showed that all cells arise from pre-existing cells by cell division.
1866	Haeckel established that the nucleus was responsible for storing and transmitting hereditary characters.
1866–88	Cell division studied in detail and chromosomes described.
1880–3	Plastids, e.g. chloroplasts, discovered.
1890	Mitochondria discovered.
1898	Golgi apparatus discovered.
1887–1900	Improvements in microscopes, fixatives, stains and sectioning. Cytology† started to become experimental. Embryology was studied to establish how cells interact during growth of a multicellular organism. Cytogenetics‡, with its emphasis on the functioning of the nucleus in heredity, became a branch of cytology.
1900	Mendel's work, forgotten since 1865, was rediscovered giving an impetus to cytogenetics. Light microscopy had almost reached the theoretical limits of resolution, thus slowing down the rate of progress.
1930s	Electron microscope developed, enabling much improved resolution.
1946 to present	Electron microscope became widely used in biology, revealing much more detailed structure in cells. This 'fine' structure is called **ultrastructure**.

* significant events in the origin and development of the cell concept.
† **cytology** – the study of cells, especially by microscopy.
‡ **cytogenetics** – the linking of cytology with genetics, mainly relating structure and behaviour of chromosomes during cell division to results from breeding experiments.

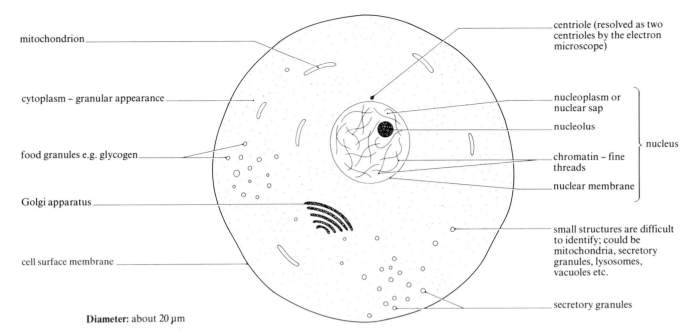

Fig 7.1 (above) *Typical animal cell such as an epithelial cell from lining of cheek as seen with a light microscope*

mitochondrion

cytoplasm – granular appearance

food granules e.g. glycogen

Golgi apparatus

cell surface membrane

Diameter: about 20 µm

centriole (resolved as two centrioles by the electron microscope)

nucleoplasm or nuclear sap

nucleolus

chromatin – fine threads

nuclear membrane

nucleus

small structures are difficult to identify; could be mitochondria, secretory granules, lysosomes, vacuoles etc.

secretory granules

Fig 7.2 (below) *Ultrastructure of a generalised animal cell as seen with the electron microscope. NB for simplicity, only some of the rough endoplasmic reticulum is shown covered with ribosomes. Similarly only some of the free ribosomes are shown*

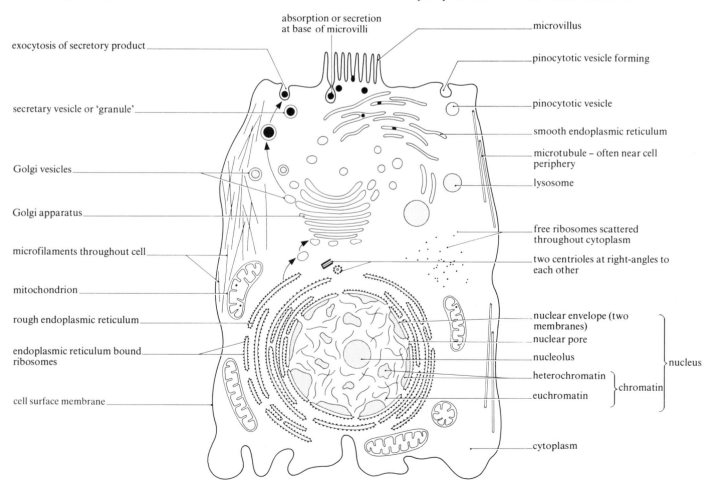

exocytosis of secretory product

secretary vesicle or 'granule'

Golgi vesicles

Golgi apparatus

microfilaments throughout cell

mitochondrion

rough endoplasmic reticulum

endoplasmic reticulum bound ribosomes

cell surface membrane

absorption or secretion at base of microvilli

microvillus

pinocytotic vesicle forming

pinocytotic vesicle

smooth endoplasmic reticulum

microtubule – often near cell periphery

lysosome

free ribosomes scattered throughout cytoplasm

two centrioles at right-angles to each other

nuclear envelope (two membranes)

nuclear pore

nucleolus

heterochromatin

euchromatin

nucleus

chromatin

cytoplasm

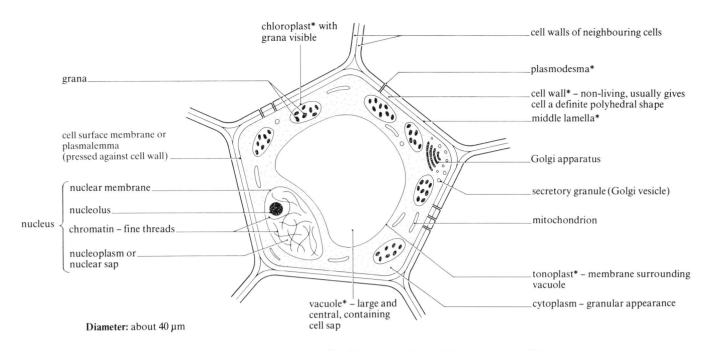

chloroplast* with grana visible

cell walls of neighbouring cells

grana

plasmodesma*

cell wall* – non-living, usually gives cell a definite polyhedral shape

middle lamella*

cell surface membrane or plasmalemma (pressed against cell wall)

Golgi apparatus

secretory granule (Golgi vesicle)

nucleus {
nuclear membrane
nucleolus
chromatin – fine threads
nucleoplasm or nuclear sap
}

mitochondrion

tonoplast* – membrane surrounding vacuole

cytoplasm – granular appearance

vacuole* – large and central, containing cell sap

Diameter: about 40 µm

Fig 7.3 (above) *Typical plant cell such as a leaf mesophyll cell as seen with a light microscope. *Features characteristic of plant cells but not animal cells*

Fig 7.4 (below) *Ultrastructure of a generalised plant cell as seen with the electron microscope*

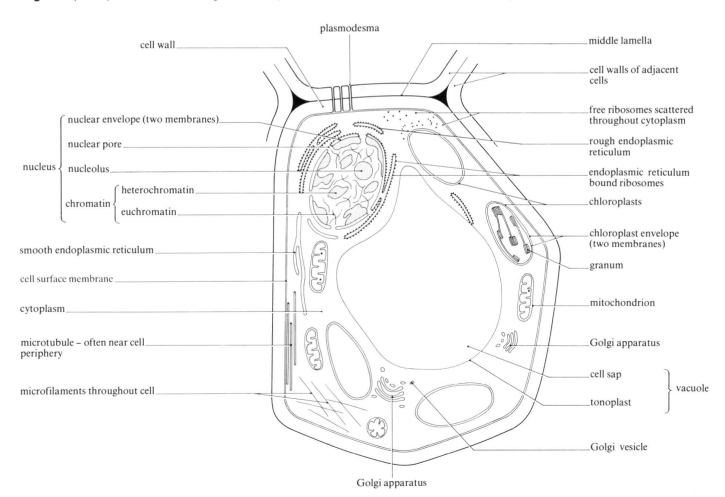

cell wall

plasmodesma

middle lamella

cell walls of adjacent cells

nucleus {
nuclear envelope (two membranes)
nuclear pore
nucleolus
chromatin {
heterochromatin
euchromatin
}
}

free ribosomes scattered throughout cytoplasm

rough endoplasmic reticulum

endoplasmic reticulum bound ribosomes

chloroplasts

chloroplast envelope (two membranes)

granum

smooth endoplasmic reticulum

cell surface membrane

cytoplasm

microtubule – often near cell periphery

microfilaments throughout cell

mitochondrion

Golgi apparatus

cell sap

tonoplast

vacuole

Golgi vesicle

Golgi apparatus

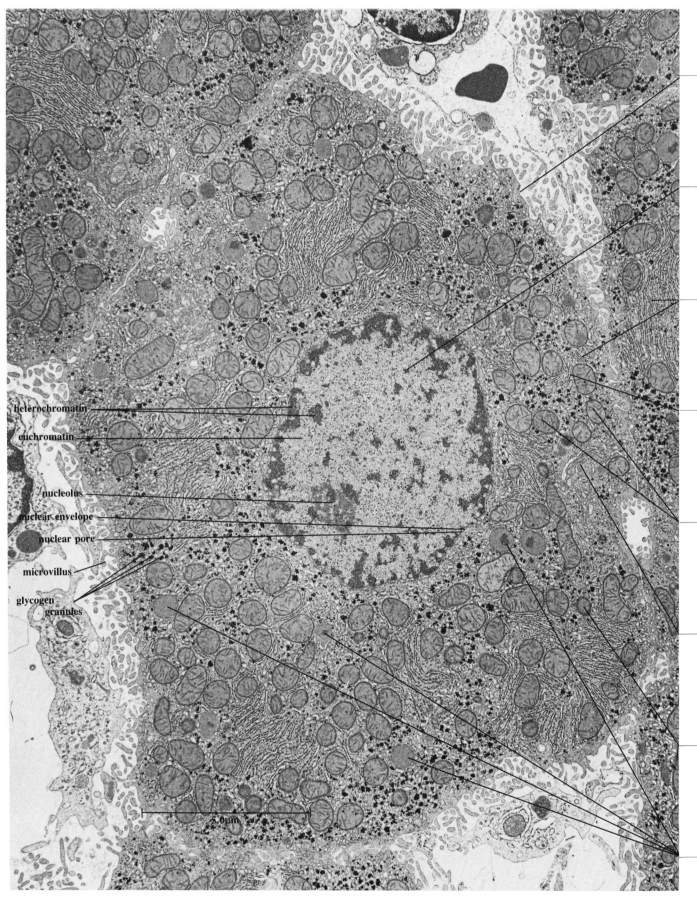

heterochromatin

euchromatin

nucleolus

nuclear envelope

nuclear pore

microvillus

glycogen
granules

5.0μm

Fig 7.5 *Electron micrograph of a thin section of a representative animal cell, a rat liver cell (hepatocyte × 9 600)*

	Diagram	Structure	Functions
cell surface membrane	**Cell surface membrane (plasmalemma)** — protein, lipid bilayer, protein	Two layers of lipid (bilayer) sandwiched between two protein layers	A partially permeable barrier controlling exchange between the cell and its environment
nucleus	**Nucleus** — nuclear envelope (two membranes), nuclear pore, heterochromatin, euchromatin (chromatin), nucleolus, nucleoplasm	Largest cell organelle, enclosed by an **envelope** of two membranes that is perforated by **nuclear pores**. It contains **chromatin** which is the extended form taken by chromosomes during interphase. It also contains a **nucleolus**.	Chromosomes contain DNA, the molecule of inheritance. DNA is organised into genes which control all the activities of the cell. Nuclear division is the basis of cell replication, and hence reproduction. The nucleolus manufactures ribosomes.
endoplasmic reticulum	**Endoplasmic reticulum (ER)** — ribosomes, cisterna	A system of flattened, membrane-bounded sacs called **cisternae**, forming tubes and sheets. It is continuous with the outer membrane of the nuclear envelope.	If ribosomes are found on its surface it is called **rough ER**, and transports proteins made by the ribosomes through the cisternae. **Smooth ER,** (no ribosomes) is a site of lipid and steroid synthesis.
ribosomes	**Ribosomes** — large subunit, small subunit	Very small organelles consisting of a large and a small subunit. They are made of roughly equal parts of protein and RNA. Slightly smaller ribosomes are found in mitochondria (and chloroplasts in plants).	Sites of protein synthesis, holding in place the various interacting molecules involved. They are either bound to the ER or lie free in the cytoplasm. They may form **polysomes** (polyribosomes), collections of ribosomes strung along messenger RNA.
mitochondria	**Mitochondria (sing. mitochondrion)** — phosphate granule, ribosome, matrix, crista, envelope (two membranes), circular DNA	Surrounded by an envelope of two membranes, the inner being folded to form **cristae**. Contains a **matrix** with a few ribosomes, a circular DNA molecule and phosphate granules.	In aerobic respiration cristae are the sites of oxidative phosphorylation and electron transport, and the matrix is the site of Krebs cycle enzymes and fatty acid oxidation.
Golgi apparatus	**Golgi apparatus** — Golgi vesicles, dictyosome or Golgi body	A stack of flattened, membrane-bounded sacs, called **cisternae**, continuously being formed at one end of the stack and budded off as vesicles at the other. Stacks may form discrete dictyosomes as in plant cells, or an extensive network as in many animal cells.	Processing in cisternae and transport in vesicles of many cell materials, such as enzymes from the ER. Often involved in secretion and lysosome formation.
lysosome	**Lysosomes**	A simple spherical sac bounded by a single membrane and containing digestive (hydrolytic) enzymes. Contents appear homogeneous.	Many functions, all concerned with breakdown of structures or molecules. See text for role in autophagy, autolysis, endocytosis and exocytosis.
microbodies	**Microbodies**	A roughly spherical organelle bounded by a single membrane. Its contents appear finely granular except for occasional striking crystalloid or filamentous deposits.	All contain catalase, an enzyme that breaks down hydrogen peroxide. All are associated with oxidation reactions. In plants, are the site of the glyoxylate cycle.

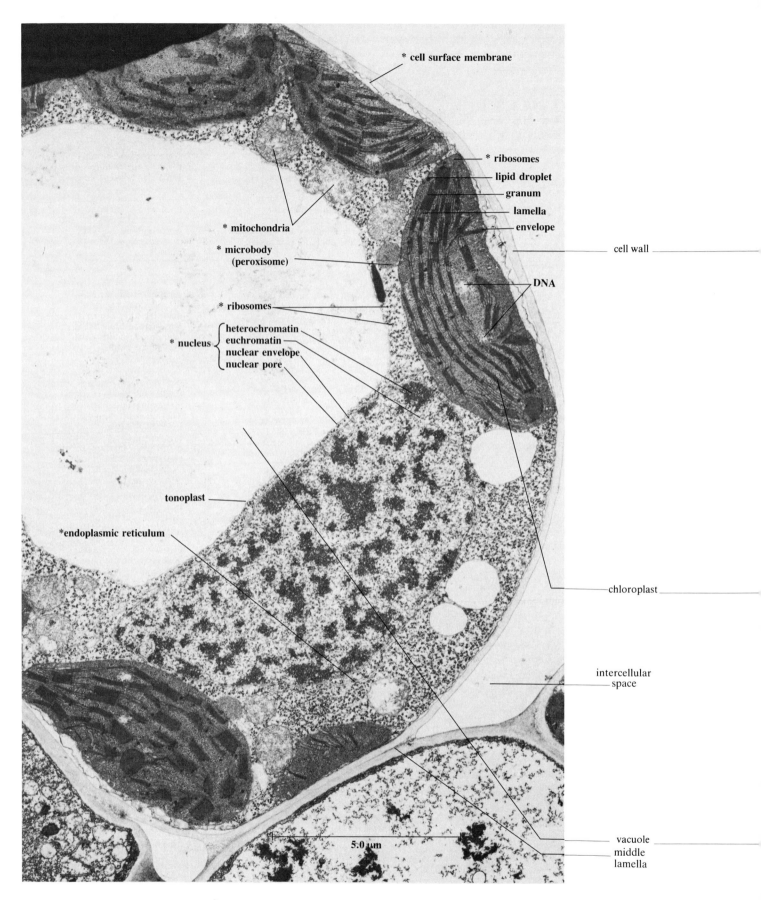

* cell surface membrane

* ribosomes

lipid droplet

granum

lamella

envelope

cell wall

* mitochondria

* microbody
(peroxisome)

DNA

* ribosomes

heterochromatin
euchromatin
nuclear envelope
nuclear pore

* nucleus

tonoplast

*endoplasmic reticulum

chloroplast

intercellular
space

5.0 µm

vacuole

middle
lamella

Fig 7.6   *Electron micrograph of a thin section of a representative plant cell, a leaf mesophyll cell (× 15 000)*
Notes provided on fig 7.5

Diagram	Structure	Functions
Cell wall, middle lamella, plasmodesmata (sing. **plasmodesma**) cell wall intercellular air space cell surface membrane middle lamella plasmodesma Detail of plasmodesma ER tubular core	A rigid cell wall surrounding the cell, consisting of cellulose microfibrils running through a matrix of other complex polysaccharides, namely hemicelluloses and pectic substances. May be secondarily thickened in some cells.	Provides mechanical support and protection. It allows a pressure potential to be developed which aids in support. It prevents osmotic bursting of the cell. It is a pathway for movement of water and mineral salts. Various modifications, such as lignification, for specialised functions.
	Thin layer of pectic substances (calcium and magnesium pectates).	Cements neighbouring cells together.
	A fine cytoplasmic thread linking the cytoplasm of two neighbouring cells through a fine pore in the cell walls. The pore is lined with the cell surface membrane and has a central tubular core, often associated at each end with ER.	Enables a continuous system of cytoplasm, the **symplast**, to be formed between neighbouring cells for transport of substances between cells.
Chloroplast photosynthetic membranes with chlorophyll lamella granum stroma envelope (two membranes) circular DNA lipid droplet ribosomes starch grain	Large plastid containing chlorophyll and carrying out photosynthesis. It is surrounded by an envelope of two membranes and contains a gel-like **stroma** through which runs a system of membranes that are stacked in places to form **grana**. It may store starch. The stroma also contains ribosomes, a circular DNA molecule and lipid droplets.	It is the organelle in which photosynthesis takes place, producing sugars and other substances from carbon dioxide and water using light energy trapped by chlorophyll. Light energy is converted to chemical energy.
Large central vacuole (Smaller vacuoles may occur in plant and animal cells such as food vacuoles, contractile vacuoles.)	A sac bounded by a single membrane called the **tonoplast**. It contains **cell sap**, a concentrated solution of various substances, such as mineral salts, sugars, pigments, organic acids and enzymes. Typically large in mature cells.	Storage of various substances including waste products. It makes an important contribution to the osmotic properties of the cell. Sometimes it functions as a lysosome.

Protoplasm is the nineteenth-century term given to the living contents of cells, which were observed at the time as little more than a fluid in which the processes of life took place. It is now known, particularly as a result of electron microscopy, that division of labour takes place in the protoplasm, with minute structures having particular functions. These definite structures are called organelles, that is 'small organs'. All eukaryotic cells are built on the same basic plan with a limited number of organelles carrying out the different biochemical activities in separate compartments. **This 'compartmentation' is the key to understanding cell organisation**.

The first organelle to be discovered was the nucleus, described by Robert Brown in 1831 (table 7.1). The smallest organelles are ribosomes, and these are found in all cells. Some organelles are found only in specialised cells, such as chloroplasts which are found in photosynthetic cells.

In section A2.3 details of the use of a light microscope are given and differences between light microscopes and electron microscopes are described, together with some of the techniques used with microscopy which will be referred to in this chapter. In this chapter the structure of the eukaryote cell will be described. Chapter 2 should be referred to for a comparison with the prokaryotic cell. Eukaryotes comprise protoctists, fungi, plants and animals.

7.1 Typical animal and plant cells

Figs 7.1 and 7.2 show the appearance of typical animal and plant cells as seen with the light microscope at the maximum resolution of × 1 500. Figs 7.3 and 7.4 show the increased detail that can be seen with the aid of the electron microscope.

> **7.1** With reference to figs 7.1–7.4, what additional structures are revealed by the electron microscope compared with the light microscope?
>
> **7.2** With reference to figs 7.1–7.4, what structures are found (*a*) in plant cells but not in animal cells, and
> (*b*) in animal cells but not in plant cells?

Figs 7.5 and 7.6 show actual electron micrographs of representative animal and plant cells, together with summaries of the structures and functions of the different parts seen.

7.2 Structures common to animal and plant cells

7.2.1 Cell membranes

Cell membranes are important for a number of reasons. They separate the contents of cells from their external environments, controlling exchange between the two, and they enable separate compartments to be formed inside cells in which specialised metabolic pathways can take place. Chemical reactions, such as the light reactions of photosynthesis in chloroplasts and oxidative phosphorylation of respiration in mitochondria, sometimes take place on the membranes themselves. They also act as receptor sites for recognising external stimuli such as hormones and other chemicals, either from the external environment or from other parts of the organism. An understanding of their properties is essential to an understanding of cell function.

It has been known since the turn of the century that cell membranes do not behave simply like semi-permeable membranes that allow only the passage of water and other small molecules such as gases. Instead they are better described as **partially permeable**, since other substances such as glucose, amino acids, fatty acids, glycerol and ions can diffuse slowly through them, and they also exert a measure of active control over what substances they allow through.

Early work showed that organic solvents, such as alcohol, ether and chloroform, penetrate membranes even more rapidly than water. This suggested that membranes have non-polar portions; in other words that they contain lipids. This was later confirmed by chemical analysis which showed that membranes are comprised almost entirely of proteins and lipids. The proteins are discussed later. The lipids are mainly phospholipids, glycolipids and sterols.

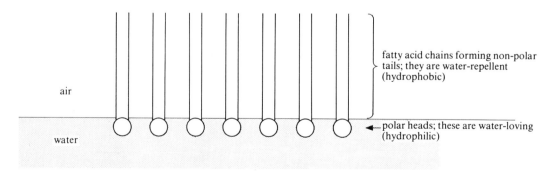

Fig 7.7 *Monolayer of polar lipid molecules, such as phospholipids, at the surface of water*

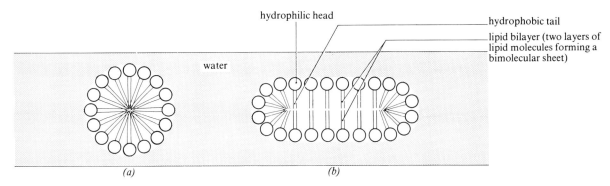

hydrophilic head

hydrophobic tail

lipid bilayer (two layers of lipid molecules forming a bimolecular sheet)

water

(a)   (b)

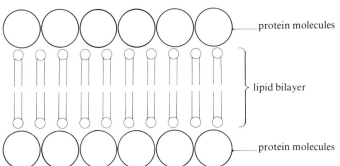

protein molecules

lipid bilayer

protein molecules

Fig 7.8 (above) *Sections through (a) a spherical micelle and (b) a rod-shaped micelle formed by polar lipids in water*

Fig 7.9 (left) *Davson–Danielli model of membrane structure*

Fig. 7.10 (below) *Electron micrograph showing the surface membrane of a red blood cell (× 250 000). The arrows indicate the three-layered structure of the membrane (dense-light-dense). The stain used contained osmium which is taken up by the hydrophilic regions of proteins and lipids*

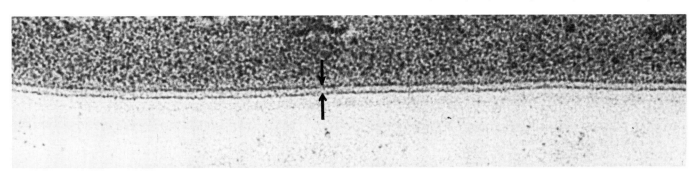

Phospholipids (containing a phosphate group) have a polar* head and two non-polar tails (fig 5.19). **Glycolipids** are lipids combined with carbohydrate. Like phospholipids, glycolipids have polar heads and non-polar tails. **Sterols** are steroid alcohols. The most abundant sterol is cholesterol (fig 5.20). Unlike phospholipids and glycolipids, cholesterol is completely non-polar.

If a thin layer of polar lipids, such as phospholipids, is spread over the surface of water, the molecules orientate themselves into a single monomolecular layer, a **monolayer**, as shown in fig 7.7. The non-polar hydrophobic tails project out of the water, whilst the polar hydrophilic heads lie in the surface of the water.

If the polar lipid is present in large enough amounts to more than cover the surface of the water, or if it is shaken up with the water, particles known as **micelles** are formed, in which hydrophobic tails project inwards away from the water as shown in fig 7.8.

Fig 7.8 shows a type of micelle in which two layers of lipid molecules occur, known as a **lipid bilayer**. Phospholipid bilayers like this have many of the properties of living cell

membranes. Davson and Danielli proposed, in 1935, that such a structure, coated with protein molecules on both surfaces, might occur in cell membranes. Their membrane model is summarised in fig 7.9. With the introduction of the electron microscope membranes could be clearly seen for the first time, and surface membranes of both animal and plant cells showed a characteristic three-layered (**trilaminar**) appearance. An example of this is shown in fig 7.10.

In 1959 Robertson combined the available evidence and put forward the '**unit membrane**' hypothesis which proposed that all biological membranes shared the same basic structure:

(*a*) they are about 7.5 nm wide;

(*b*) they have a characteristic trilaminar appearance when viewed with the electron microscope;

(*c*) the three layers are a result of the same arrangement of proteins and polar lipids as proposed by Davson and Danielli (fig 7.9) and represent two protein layers surrounding a central lipid layer.

The unit membrane hypothesis has since been modified in the light of evidence from a variety of sources, notably freeze fracturing, a technique described in section A2.5 that is very important in the investigation of membrane structure. The technique allows membranes to be split and

* Remember that polar groups or molecules are charged and have an affinity for water (hydrophilic); non-polar groups or molecules do not mix with water (hydrophobic) (section 5.1.2).

193

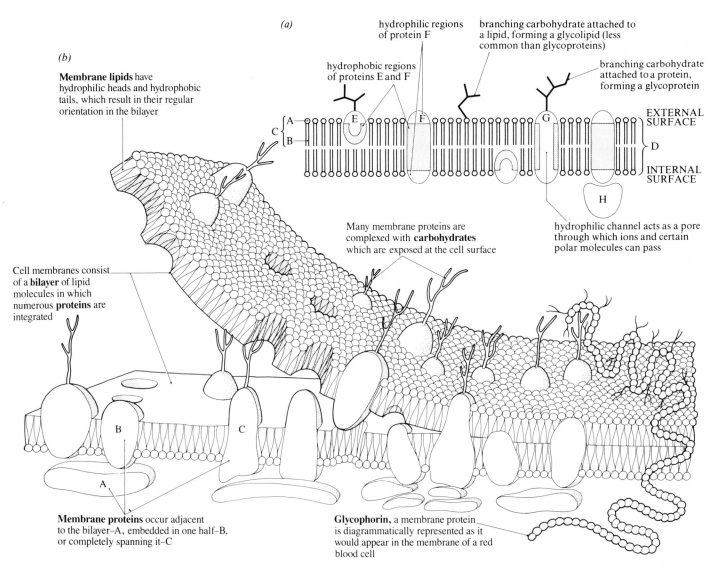

(a)

(b)

Membrane lipids have hydrophilic heads and hydrophobic tails, which result in their regular orientation in the bilayer

hydrophilic regions of protein F

hydrophobic regions of proteins E and F

branching carbohydrate attached to a lipid, forming a glycolipid (less common than glycoproteins)

branching carbohydrate attached to a protein, forming a glycoprotein

EXTERNAL SURFACE

INTERNAL SURFACE

Many membrane proteins are complexed with **carbohydrates** which are exposed at the cell surface

hydrophilic channel acts as a pore through which ions and certain polar molecules can pass

Cell membranes consist of a **bilayer** of lipid molecules in which numerous **proteins** are integrated

Membrane proteins occur adjacent to the bilayer–A, embedded in one half–B, or completely spanning it–C

Glycophorin, a membrane protein is diagrammatically represented as it would appear in the membrane of a red blood cell

Fig 7.11 *(a) Modern fluid mosaic model of membrane structure. Glycoproteins and glycolipids are associated only with the external surfaces of membranes. (b) Three-dimensional model of membrane structure*

7.3 (*a*) What are the structures represented by the labels A, B, C and D in fig 7.11 (*a*)? (*b*) What common component of structure D has been omitted?

the surfaces inside to be examined. It has the advantage that the membranes are preserved in a life-like state by instant freezing, rather than being subjected to chemical fixation which might alter the arrangement of the components. Freeze fracturing reveals the presence of particles (mainly proteins) which penetrate into, and sometimes right through, the lipid bilayer. In general, the more metabolically active the membrane, the more protein particles that are found; chloroplast membranes (75% protein) have many particles (fig 9.13), whereas the metabolically inert myelin sheath (18% protein) has none. The inner and outer faces of membranes also differ in their particle distribution.

In 1972, Singer and Nicolson put forward the '**fluid mosaic' model** of membrane structure in which a mosaic of protein molecules floats in a fluid lipid layer. This model is shown in its modern form in fig 7.11.

In this model the lipid bilayer remains unchallenged as the unit membrane, but it is regarded as a dynamic structure in which proteins can float in the lipid like islands, some moving about freely while others are fixed in position, sometimes by microfilaments running into the cytoplasm. Lipids also move about.

Proteins

Some proteins penetrate only part of the way into the membrane while others penetrate all the way through. Usually they have hydrophobic portions which interact with the lipids, with hydrophilic portions facing the aqueous contents of the cell at the membrane surface. In all there are thousands of different proteins which can occur in cell membranes. They may be purely structural or have some additional function. Some, for example, act as **carrier** molecules, transporting specific substances through the membrane. The carrier may be part of an active pump mechanism (discussed later). It is believed that hydrophilic **channels** or **pores** sometimes occur within a protein, or between adjacent protein molecules. The pore spans the membrane, allowing the passage through the membrane of polar molecules that would otherwise be excluded by the lipid region. Such a protein-lined pore is shown in fig 7.11a.

Other membrane proteins may act as enzymes, specific receptor molecules, electron carriers and energy transducers in photosynthesis and respiration, and so on. Also present in membranes are glycoproteins. These have branching carbohydrate portions resembling antennae on their free surfaces, as shown in fig 7.11. The 'antennae' are made up of a number of sugar residues and may be of many different, but precisely defined, patterns owing to the diversity of linkages between sugars and the existence of α- and β-isomers as described in chapter 5. They are important as recognition features in a number of ways. For example, sugar-recognition sites of two neighbouring cells may bind to each other causing cell-to-cell adhesion. This may enable cells to orientate themselves and to form tissues, such as during cell differentiation. Recognition is also the basis of various control systems and of the immune response, where glycoproteins act as antigens. Certain molecules in solution may bear recognition sites which enable them to be taken up specifically by cells with complementary recognition sites. The addition of sugar residues (glycosylation) to proteins by the Golgi apparatus for this purpose is discussed later (section 7.2.7). Sugars can therefore function as informational molecules and in this sense are comparable with proteins and nucleic acids.

Lipids

Variations in lipid composition affect such properties as fluidity and permeability, the usual consistency of the lipids being similar to that of olive oil. Unsaturated lipids have kinks in their fatty acid tails (section 5.3.1 and fig 5.17). These prevent close packing of the molecules and make the membrane structure more open and fluid. Fluidity also increases with decreasing length of fatty acid tails and the lipid cholesterol is important in regulating fluidity within certain limits. Fluidity affects membrane activity, such as the ease with which membranes fuse with each other, and the activity of membrane-bound enzymes and transport proteins.

Glycolipids contribute to recognition sites in the same way as glycoproteins.

Summary of cell membranes

A summary of the features of biological membranes is given below.

(1) Different types of membranes differ in thickness but most fall within the range 5–10 nm, for example cell surface membranes are 7.5 nm wide.
(2) Membranes are lipoprotein structures (lipid + protein), with carbohydrate (sugar) portions attached to the *external* surfaces of some lipid and protein molecules. Typically, 2–10% of the membrane is carbohydrate.

(3) The lipids spontaneously form a bilayer owing to their polar heads and non-polar tails.
(4) The proteins are variable in function.
(5) The sugars are involved in recognition mechanisms.
(6) The two sides of a membrane may differ in composition and properties.
(7) Both lipids and proteins show rapid lateral diffusion in the plane of the membrane unless anchored or restricted in some way.

7.2.2 Transport across the cell surface membrane

In chapter 14 the problems of long-distance transport within the bodies of multicellular plants and animals are discussed. Living organisms are also faced with the problem of short-distance transport across cell membranes which, although only 5–10 nm wide, present barriers to the movement of ions and molecules, particularly polar molecules such as glucose and amino acids that are repelled by the non-polar lipids of membranes. Transport across membranes is vital for a number of reasons, for example to maintain a suitable pH and ionic concentration within the cell for enzyme activity, to obtain certain food supplies for energy and raw materials, to excrete toxic substances or secrete useful substances and to generate the ionic gradients essential for nervous and muscular activity. In the following account, movement across the cell surface membrane will be discussed, although similar movements occur across the membranes of cell organelles within cells. There are four basic methods of entry into, or exit from, cells, namely diffusion, osmosis, active transport and endocytosis or exocytosis. The first two processes are passive, that is they do not require the expenditure of energy by the cell; the latter two are active, energy-consuming processes.

Diffusion and facilitated diffusion

Gases, like the respiratory gases oxygen and carbon dioxide, diffuse rapidly in solution through membranes, moving from regions of high concentration to regions of low concentration down diffusion gradients. Ions and small polar molecules such as glucose, amino acids, fatty acids and glycerol normally diffuse slowly through membranes. Uncharged and fat soluble (lipophilic) molecules pass through membranes much more readily, as already noted.

A modified form of diffusion known as **facilitated diffusion** exists in which the substance is allowed through the membrane by a specific molecule. This molecule may possess a specific channel that admits only one type of substance. An example is the movement of glucose into red blood cells, which is not inhibited by respiratory inhibitors and is therefore not an active process.

Osmosis

Water diffuses through membranes, a process called osmosis (see section A1.5).

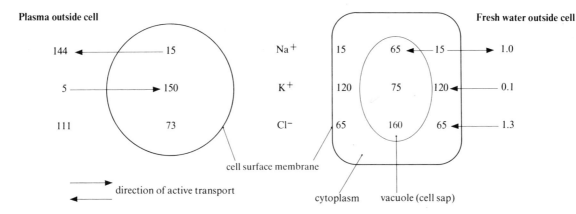

Fig 7.12 *Concentrations (mM) of Na$^+$, K$^+$ and Cl$^-$ ions in two types of cell and their environments*

Active transport

Active transport is the energy-consuming transport of molecules or ions across a membrane against a concentration gradient. Energy is required because the substance must be moved against its natural tendency to diffuse in the opposite direction. Movement is usually unidirectional, unlike diffusion which is reversible.

When movement of ions is considered, two factors will influence the direction in which they diffuse. One is concentration, the other is electrical charge. An ion will usually diffuse from a region of its high concentration to a region of its low concentration. It will also generally be attracted towards a region of opposite charge, and move away from a region of similar charge. Thus ions are said to move down **electrochemical gradients**, which are the combined effects of both electrical and concentration gradients. Strictly speaking then, active transport of ions is their movement against an electrochemical gradient. It has been shown that cells maintain a potential difference, that is a charge, across their cell surface membranes and that, for almost all cells studied, the inside of the cell is negative with respect to the outside medium. Thus cations (positively charged ions) are usually electrically attracted into the cells and anions repulsed. However, their relative concentrations inside and outside of the cell also helps to determine in which direction they actually diffuse.

The major ions of extracellular and intracellular fluids are sodium (Na$^+$), potassium (K$^+$) and chloride (Cl$^-$) ions. Study fig 7.12 which shows the concentrations of certain ions in the cytoplasm and cell sap of a plant cell, and the cytoplasm of an animal cell.

The data show that both of these types of cell have ionic compositions very different from their external solutions. For example, like most cells, they have a much higher potassium content inside than outside. Another typical feature is the higher concentration of potassium inside relative to sodium.

If respiration of the red blood cells is specifically inhibited, for example with cyanide, the ionic composition of the cells gradually changes until it comes into equilibrium with the plasma. This suggests that the ions can diffuse passively through the cell surface membrane of the red blood cells, but that normally respiration supplies the energy for active transport to maintain the concentrations shown in fig 7.12. In the case of both types of cell shown in fig 7.12, sodium is actively pumped out of the cell and potassium is actively pumped in. It is possible to calculate that there is no net tendency for chloride ions to enter red blood cells from the plasma, despite the higher concentration of chloride ions in the plasma. This is due to the strictly negative charge of the cell contents relative to the outside, which tends to repulse chloride ions; in other words it is the **electrochemical gradient** that determines the movement of the ions, as already explained, and this is true of all cells. A careful study of the figures provided for *Nitella* in fig 7.12 will show similar examples of how movement of ions is not solely determined by concentration. The potential difference across the cell surface membrane of red blood cells is −10 mV, and of *Nitella* is −140 mV.

In recent years it has been shown that the cell surface membranes of most cells possess **sodium pumps** that actively pump sodium ions out of the cell. Usually, though not always, the sodium pump is coupled with a potassium pump which actively accumulates potassium ions from the external medium and passes them into the cell. The combined pump is called the **sodium–potassium pump** (Na$^+$–K$^+$ pump).

Since this pump is a common feature of cells and has a number of important functions, it provides a good example of active transport.

It has been studied in animal cells and has been shown to be driven by ATP. Its physiological importance is revealed by the observation that more than a third of the ATP consumed by a resting animal is used to pump sodium and potassium. This is essential in controlling cell volume (osmoregulation), in maintaining electrical activity in nerve and muscle cells and in driving active transport of some other substances such as sugars and amino acids. Also, high cell concentrations of potassium are needed for protein synthesis, glycolysis, photosynthesis and other vital processes.

The pump is essentially a protein which spans the membrane from one side to the other. On the inside it accepts sodium and ATP, while on the outside it accepts potassium. The transfer of sodium and potassium across the membrane is thought to be brought about by conformational changes in the protein. The protein also acts as an ATPase, catalysing the hydrolysis of ATP with release of energy to drive the pump. A possible sequence of events is summarised in fig 7.13. Note that for every $2K^+$ taken into the cell, $3Na^+$ are removed. Thus a negative potential is built up inside the cell and a potential difference across the membrane.

As sodium is pumped out, it generally diffuses back in passively. However, the membrane is relatively impermeable to sodium so that back diffusion is very slow. Membranes are usually about 100 times more permeable to potassium ions than to sodium, so potassium diffuses in much more rapidly.

7.4 Try to explain the following observations.
(a) When K^+ ions are removed from the medium surrounding red blood cells, sodium influx into the cells and potassium efflux (outflux) increase dramatically.
(b) If ATP is introduced into cells, Na^+ efflux is stimulated.

Active transport is carried out by all cells but it assumes particular significance in certain physiological processes. The process is particularly associated with epithelial cells as in the gut lining and kidney tubules, because these are active in secretion and absorption.

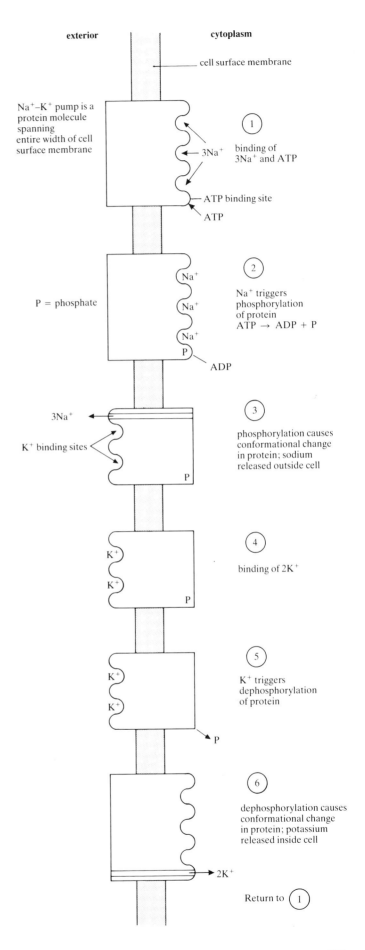

Fig 7.13 *Outline of a possible scheme for the operation of a sodium–potassium pump in red blood cells. Each event in the cycle is a consequence of the previous event. Given a supply of sodium, potassium and ATP the pump will continue to run. Changes in the conformation of the protein are caused by addition or removal of phosphate (phosphorylation or dephosphorylation respectively)*

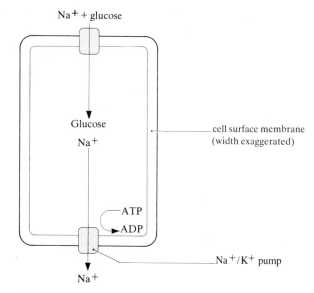

Na+ + glucose

Glucose
Na+

cell surface membrane
(width exaggerated)

ATP
ADP

Na+/K+ pump

Na+

Fig 7.14 *Active transport of glucose through the cell surface membrane of an intestinal cell or kidney cell. (Based on Fig 36–12, L. Stryer (1981) Biochemistry, 2nd ed., Freeman)*

Active transport in the intestine. When the products of digestion are absorbed in the small intestine they must pass through the epithelial cells lining the gut wall. Glucose, amino acids and salts then pass through the cells of the blood capillary walls, into the blood and thence to the liver. Soon after feeding, relatively high concentrations of digested foods are found in the gut and absorption is partly a result of diffusion. However, this is very slow and must be supplemented by active transport. Such active transport is coupled to a sodium–potassium pump as shown in fig 7.14.

As sodium is pumped out by the sodium–potassium pump, so it tends to diffuse back in. Situated in the membrane is a protein which requires both sodium and glucose to function. These are transported together **passively** into the cell. Sodium thus 'pulls' the glucose into the cell. A similar sodium–amino-acid carrier protein operates in the active transport of amino acids into cells, the active part of the process being the pumping back of sodium ions. In the absence of a sodium gradient the carriers may still act, providing that the external concentration of glucose or amino acids is greater than the internal concentration, that is facilitated diffusion can occur.

Active transport in nerve cells and muscle cells. In nerve cells and muscle cells a sodium–potassium pump is responsible for the development of a potential difference, called the **resting potential**, across the cell surface membrane (see conduction of nervous impulses, section 16.1, and muscle contraction, section 17.4). A pump similar to the Na+–K+ pump occurs in the membranes of the sarcoplasmic reticulum in muscle cells, where calcium is actively pumped into the sarcoplasmic reticulum at the expense of ATP (chapter 17).

Active transport in the kidney. Active transport of glucose and sodium occurs from the proximal convoluted tubules of the kidney (fig 19.27) and the kidney cortex actively transports sodium. These processes are described more fully in chapter 19.

Endocytosis and exocytosis

Endocytosis and exocytosis are active processes involving the bulk transport of materials through membranes, either into cells (endocytosis) or out of cells (exocytosis).

Endocytosis occurs by an infolding or extension of the cell surface membrane to form a vesicle* or vacuole*. It is of two types.

(1) Phagocytosis ('cell eating') – material taken up is in solid form. Cells specialising in the process are called **phagocytes** and are said to be **phagocytic**; for example some white blood cells. The sac formed during uptake is called a **phagocytic vacuole**. (See section 7.2.8.)

(2) Pinocytosis ('cell drinking') – material taken up is in liquid form (a solution, colloid or fine suspension). Vesicles formed are often extremely small, in which case the process is known as **micropinocytosis** and the vesicles as **micropinocytotic**.

Pinocytosis is particularly associated with amoeboid protozoans and many other, often amoeboid, cells, such as leucocytes, embryo cells, liver cells, and certain kidney cells involved in fluid exchange. It can also occur in plant cells.

Exocytosis is the reverse process of endocytosis by which materials are removed from cells, such as solid, undigested remains from food vacuoles or reverse pinocytosis in secretion (see section 7.2.7).

7.2.3   The nucleus

Nuclei are found in all eukaryotic cells, the only common exceptions being mature phloem sieve tube elements and mature red blood cells of mammals. In some protozoa, such as *Paramecium*, two nuclei exist, a micronucleus and a meganucleus. Normally, however, cells contain only one nucleus. Nuclei are conspicuous because they are the largest of cell organelles, and they were the first to be described by light microscopists. They are typically spherical to ovoid in shape and about 10 μm in diameter by 20 μm in length.

The nucleus is vitally important because it controls the cell's activities. This is because it contains the genetic (hereditary) information in the form of DNA. Not only this, but the DNA is capable of replication and this can be followed by nuclear division thus ensuring that the daughter nuclei also contain DNA. Nuclear division precedes cell division, and all daughter cells possess nuclei. The nucleus is surrounded by a nuclear envelope and contains chromatin, one or more nucleoli and nucleoplasm.

The single membrane (**nuclear membrane**) surrounding

---

* Vacuole – fluid-filled, membrane-bound sac. Vesicle – small vacuole.

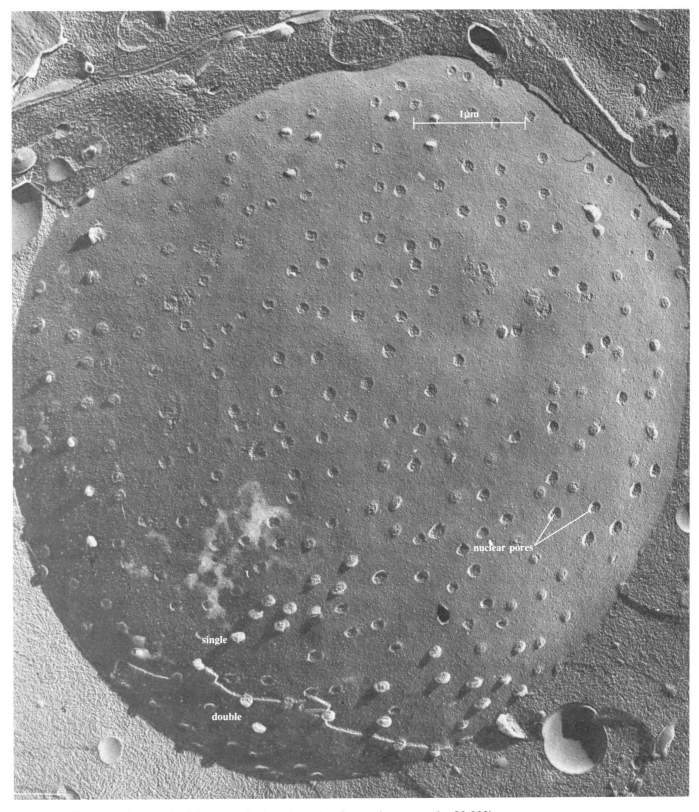

Fig 7.15 *Electron micrograph of freeze-etched nucleus showing nuclear pores (× 30 000)*

the nucleus, as shown by the light microscope, is actually a **nuclear envelope** composed of two membranes. The outer membrane is continuous with the endoplasmic reticulum (ER) as shown in figs 7.3 and 7.4, and like the ER may be covered with ribosomes engaged in protein synthesis. The nuclear envelope is perforated by **nuclear pores** (fig 7.5) and these are particularly well revealed by freeze etching as shown in fig 7.15. Nuclear pores allow exchange of substances between the nucleus and the cytoplasm, for example the exit of messenger RNA (mRNA) and of ribosomal subunits and the entry of ribosomal proteins, nucleotides and molecules that regulate the activity of DNA. The pore has a definite structure formed by fusion of the outer and inner membranes of the envelope. This controls the passage of molecules through the pore.

Within the nucleus is a gel-like matrix called **nucleoplasm** (or nuclear sap) which contains chromatin and one or more nucleoli. Nucleoplasm contains a variety of chemical substances such as ions, proteins (including enzymes) and nucleotides, either in true or colloidal solution.

Chromatin is composed mainly of coils of DNA bound to basic proteins called **histones**. The organisation of histones and DNA into bead-like structures called nucleosomes, and the packing of the nucleosomes in the chromatin, are described in section 22.4.

The term chromatin means 'coloured material' and refers to the fact that this material is easily stained for viewing with the microscope. During nuclear division chromatin stains more intensely and hence becomes more conspicuous because it condenses into more tightly coiled threads called **chromosomes**. During interphase (the period between nuclear divisions) it becomes more dispersed. However, some remains tightly coiled and continues to stain intensely. This is called **heterochromatin** and is seen as characteristic dark patches usually occurring near the nuclear envelope (figs 7.3–6). The remaining, loosely coiled chromatin is located towards the centre of the nucleus and is called **euchromatin**. These individual fibres are too dispersed to be visible under the light microscope and they are thought to contain the DNA which is genetically active during interphase. Thus cells in which a wide variety of genes are being expressed, as in liver cells, will show more euchromatin and less heterochromatin than cells in which few genes are being expressed, such as mucus-producing cells.

Until recently, it was imagined that interphase chromosomes lie randomly, like spaghetti, inside the nucleus. Recent work, using serial sectioning through nuclei, suggests that chromosomes are held in precise domains. The relative positions of chromosomes and their genes may influence such events as chromosome mutation and gene expression, and may change during development.

The **nucleolus** is a conspicuous rounded structure within the nucleus, whose function is the manufacture of ribosomal RNA (fig 7.5). One or more nucleoli may be present. It stains intensely because of the large amounts of DNA and RNA it contains. It has a dense fibrillar region of DNA of one or several different chromosomes, called the **nucleolar organiser**. This contains many copies of the genes that code for ribosomal RNA. The nucleoli disperse and are no longer visible during prophase (the early stage of cell division) and the organisers re-organise the nucleoli during telophase (at the end of nuclear division).

Around the central region of the nucleolus is a less dense, peripheral region containing granules where ribosomal RNA is beginning to be folded and assembled with proteins into ribosomes. The partly assembled ribosomes move out through the nuclear pores into the cytoplasm, where assembly is completed.

7.2.4 Cytoplasm

In the introduction to this chapter it was pointed out that the living contents of eukaryote cells are divided into nucleus and cytoplasm, the two together forming the protoplasm. Cytoplasm consists of an aqueous ground substance containing a variety of cell organelles and other inclusions such as insoluble waste or storage products.

The cytosol or ground substance

The **cytosol** is the soluble part of the cytoplasm. It forms the ground substance or 'background material' of the cytoplasm and is located between the cell organelles. It contains a system of microfilaments (see section 7.2.10) but otherwise appears transparent and structureless in the electron microscope. It is about 90% water and forms a solution which contains all the fundamental biochemicals of life. Some of these are ions and small molecules forming true solutions, such as salts, sugars, amino acids, fatty acids, nucleotides, vitamins and dissolved gases. Others are large molecules which form colloidal solutions (section A1.4), notably proteins and to a lesser extent RNA. A colloidal solution may be a sol (non-viscous) or a gel (viscous); often the outer regions of cytoplasm are more gel-like, as with the ectoplasm of *Amoeba* (section 17.6).

Apart from acting as a store of vital chemicals, the ground substance is the site of certain metabolic pathways, an important example being glycolysis. Synthesis of fatty acids, nucleotides and some amino acids also takes place.

The most common view of cytoplasm is the static one of cells that have been killed and prepared for microscopy. However, when *living* cytoplasm is examined, great activity is usually seen as cell organelles move about and occasional '**cytoplasmic streaming**' occurs. This is an active mass movement of cytoplasm which may be particularly prominent in certain cells such as young sieve tube elements.

7.2.5 Endoplasmic reticulum (ER)

One of the most important discoveries to be made when the electron microscope was introduced was the occurrence of a complex system of membranes running through the cytoplasm of all eukaryotic cells. This network, or reticulum, of membranes was named the **endoplasmic reticulum** and although it is often extensive, it is below the limits of resolution of the light microscope. The membranes were seen to be covered with small particles which later became known as ribosomes. At about the same time a cell fraction was isolated by differential centrifugation

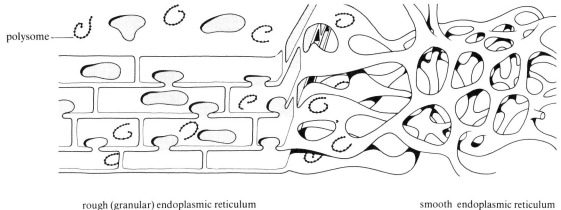

polysome

rough (granular) endoplasmic reticulum   smooth endoplasmic reticulum

Fig 7.16   *Three-dimensional model of endoplasmic reticulum*

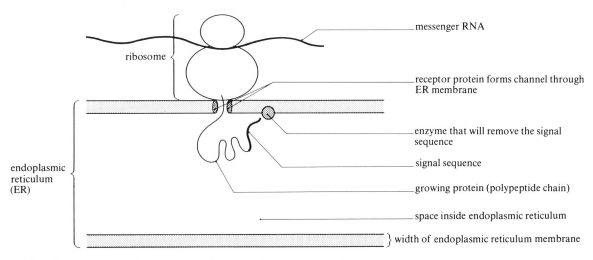

messenger RNA

ribosome

receptor protein forms channel through ER membrane

enzyme that will remove the signal sequence

endoplasmic reticulum (ER)

signal sequence

growing protein (polypeptide chain)

space inside endoplasmic reticulum

} width of endoplasmic reticulum membrane

Fig 7.17   *Entry of newly synthesised protein into the endoplasmic reticulum*

which was shown to be capable of protein synthesis. Examination of this fraction in the electron microscope revealed many small membrane-bound sacs (vesicles), each covered externally with ribosomes. These sacs were called **microsomes**. The **microsomal fraction** is now known to be formed during the homogenisation procedure. When the ER is broken up into small pieces it reseals into vesicles. Thus microsomes do not exist as such in intact cells.

Typically, the ER appears in thin sections as pairs of parallel lines (membranes) running through the cytoplasm, as shown in figs 7.3–6. Occasionally though, a section will glance through the surface of these membranes and show that, in three dimensions, the ER is usually sheet-like rather than tubular. A possible three-dimensional structure is shown in fig 7.16. The ER consists of flattened, membrane-bound sacs called **cisternae**. These may be covered with ribosomes, forming **rough ER**, or ribosomes may be absent, forming **smooth ER**, which is usually more tubular. Both types are concerned with the synthesis and transport of substances.

Rough ER is concerned with the transport of proteins which are made by ribosomes on its surface. Details of protein synthesis are given in chapter 22. For the present it is sufficient to know that the growing protein, which consists of a chain of amino acids called a polypeptide chain, is bound to the ribosome until its synthesis is complete. At the beginning of protein synthesis, the first part of the growing chain may consist of a 'signal sequence' which fits a specific receptor in the ER membrane, thus binding the ribosome to the ER. The receptor forms a channel through which the protein can pass into the ER cisternae (fig 7.17). Once inside, the signal sequence is removed and the protein folds up into its tertiary structure, thus trapping it inside the ER.

7.5 A high proportion of amino acid residues in signal sequences are non-polar. Suggest a reason for this.

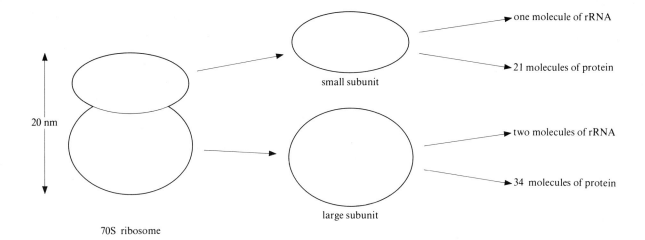

The protein is now transported through the cisternae, usually being extensively modified en route. For example, it may be phosphorylated or converted into a glycoprotein. A common route for the protein is via smooth ER to the Golgi apparatus from whence it can be secreted from the cell or passed on to other organelles in the same cell, such as storage bodies or lysosomes.

If a protein is made which does not possess a signal sequence, the ribosome making it remains free in the cytoplasm and the protein is released into the cytosol for use in the cell.

One of the chief functions of smooth ER is lipid synthesis. For example, in the epithelium of the intestine the smooth ER makes lipids from fatty acids and glycerol absorbed from the gut and passes them on to the Golgi apparatus for export. Steroids are a type of lipid and smooth ER is extensive in cells which secrete steroid hormones, such as the adrenal cortex and the interstitial cells of the testis. In the liver both rough and smooth ER are involved in detoxication. In muscle cells a specialised form of smooth ER, called sarcoplasmic reticulum, is present (section 17.4).

7.2.6   Ribosomes

Ribosomes are minute organelles, about 20 nm in diameter, found in large numbers throughout the cytoplasm of living cells, both prokaryotic and eukaryotic. A typical bacterial cell contains about 10 000 ribosomes, while eukaryotic cells possess many times more than this number. They are the sites of protein synthesis.

Each ribosome consists of two subunits, one large and one small as shown in fig 7.18. Being so small they are the last organelles to be sedimented in a centrifuge, requiring a force of 100 000× gravity for 1–2 h. Sedimentation has revealed two basic types of ribosome, called 70S* and 80S ribosomes. The 70S ribosomes are found in prokaryotes

* S=Svedberg unit. This is related to the rate of sedimentation in a centrifuge, the greater the S number, the greater the rate of sedimentation.

Fig 7.18 *Structure of a 70S ribosome. (The subunits of 80S ribosomes possess more proteins and the large subunit possesses three rRNA molecules)*

and the slightly larger 80S ribosomes occur in the cytoplasm of eukaryotes. It is interesting to note that chloroplasts and mitochondria contain 70S ribosomes, suggesting that these eukaryotic organelles are related in some way to prokaryotes (section 9.3.1).

Ribosomes are made of roughly equal amounts by mass of RNA and protein (hence they are ribonucleoprotein particles). The RNA is termed **ribosomal RNA (rRNA)** and is made in nucleoli. The distribution of rRNA molecules and protein molecules is given in fig 7.18. Together these molecules form a complex three-dimensional structure which is capable of spontaneous self-assembly.

During protein synthesis at ribosomes, amino acids are joined together one by one to form polypeptide chains. The process is described in detail in chapter 22. The ribosome acts as a binding site where the molecules involved can be precisely positioned relative to each other. These molecules include messenger RNA (mRNA), which carries the genetic instructions from the nucleus, transfer RNA (tRNA), which brings the required amino acids to the ribosome, and the growing polypeptide chain. In addition there are chain initiation, elongation and termination factors to be accommodated. The process is so complex that it could not occur efficiently, if at all, without the ribosome.

Two populations of ribosomes can be seen in eukaryotic cells, namely free and ER-bound ribosomes (figs 7.3, 7.5 and 7.16). All of the ribosomes have an identical structure but some are bound to the ER by the proteins that they are making, as explained in the previous section. Such proteins are usually secreted. An example of a protein made by free ribosomes is haemoglobin in young red blood cells.

During protein synthesis, the ribosome moves along the thread-like mRNA molecule. Rather than one ribosome at a time passing along the RNA, the process is carried out more efficiently by a number of ribosomes moving simultaneously along the mRNA, like beads on a string. The resulting chains of ribosomes are called **polyribosomes** or **polysomes**. They form characteristic whorled patterns on the ER as shown in fig 7.16 and they can be isolated intact by centrifugation.

7.2.7 Golgi apparatus

The Golgi apparatus was discovered by Camillo Golgi in 1898, using special staining techniques. However, its structure was only revealed by electron microscopy. It is found in virtually all eukaryotic cells and consists of a stack of flattened, membrane-bound sacs called **cisternae**, together with a system of associated vesicles called **Golgi vesicles**. In plant cells a number of separate stacks called **dictyosomes** are found (fig 7.6). In animal cells a single larger stack is thought to be more usual. It is difficult to build up a three-dimensional picture of the Golgi apparatus from thin sections but it is believed from such evidence as negative staining that a complex system of interconnected tubules is formed around the central stack, as shown in fig 7.19.

At one end of the stack new cisternae are constantly being formed by fusion of vesicles which are probably derived from buds of the smooth ER. This 'outer' or 'forming' face is convex, whilst the other end is the concave 'inner' or 'maturing' face where the cisternae break up into vesicles once more. The whole stack consists of a number of cisternae thought to be moving from the outer to the inner face.

The function of the Golgi apparatus is to transport and chemically modify the materials contained within it. It is

(a)

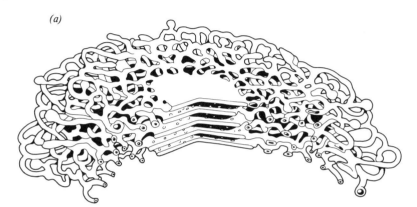

Fig 7.19 *(a) The three-dimensional structure of the Golgi apparatus. (b) Transmission electron micrograph showing two Golgi apparatuses. The left-hand one shows a dictyosome in vertical section. The right-hand one shows the topmost cisternum viewed from above (× 50 000)*

(b)

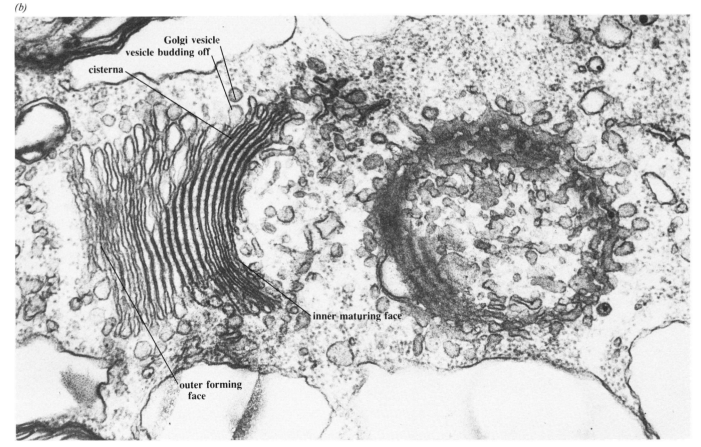

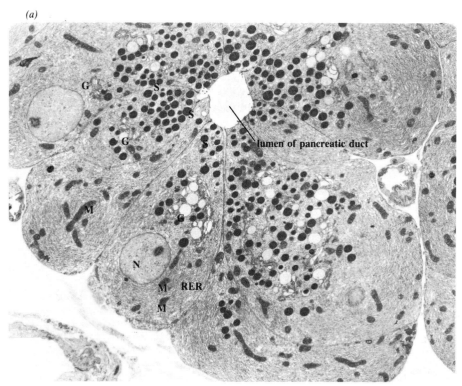

(a)

Fig 7.20 (left) *(a) Electron micrograph of an acinus, a group of pancreatic acinar cells (× 10 400) N, nucleus; M, mitochondrion; G, Golgi apparatus; S, secretory granules; RER, rough endoplasmic reticulum. (below) (b) Diagrammatic representation of the synthesis and secretion of a protein (an enzyme) in a pancreatic acinar cell*

lumen of pancreatic duct

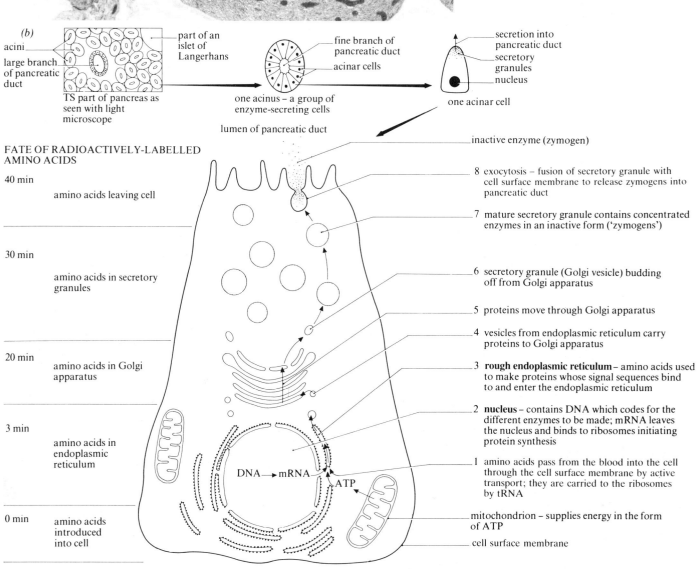

(b)

acini
large branch of pancreatic duct
part of an islet of Langerhans
TS part of pancreas as seen with light microscope

fine branch of pancreatic duct
acinar cells
one acinus – a group of enzyme-secreting cells

secretion into pancreatic duct
secretory granules
nucleus
one acinar cell

lumen of pancreatic duct

FATE OF RADIOACTIVELY-LABELLED AMINO ACIDS

40 min — amino acids leaving cell

30 min — amino acids in secretory granules

20 min — amino acids in Golgi apparatus

3 min — amino acids in endoplasmic reticulum

0 min — amino acids introduced into cell

inactive enzyme (zymogen)

8 exocytosis – fusion of secretory granule with cell surface membrane to release zymogens into pancreatic duct

7 mature secretory granule contains concentrated enzymes in an inactive form ('zymogens')

6 secretory granule (Golgi vesicle) budding off from Golgi apparatus

5 proteins move through Golgi apparatus

4 vesicles from endoplasmic reticulum carry proteins to Golgi apparatus

3 **rough endoplasmic reticulum** – amino acids used to make proteins whose signal sequences bind to and enter the endoplasmic reticulum

2 **nucleus** – contains DNA which codes for the different enzymes to be made; mRNA leaves the nucleus and binds to ribosomes initiating protein synthesis

1 amino acids pass from the blood into the cell through the cell surface membrane by active transport; they are carried to the ribosomes by tRNA

mitochondrion – supplies energy in the form of ATP

cell surface membrane

DNA → mRNA
ATP

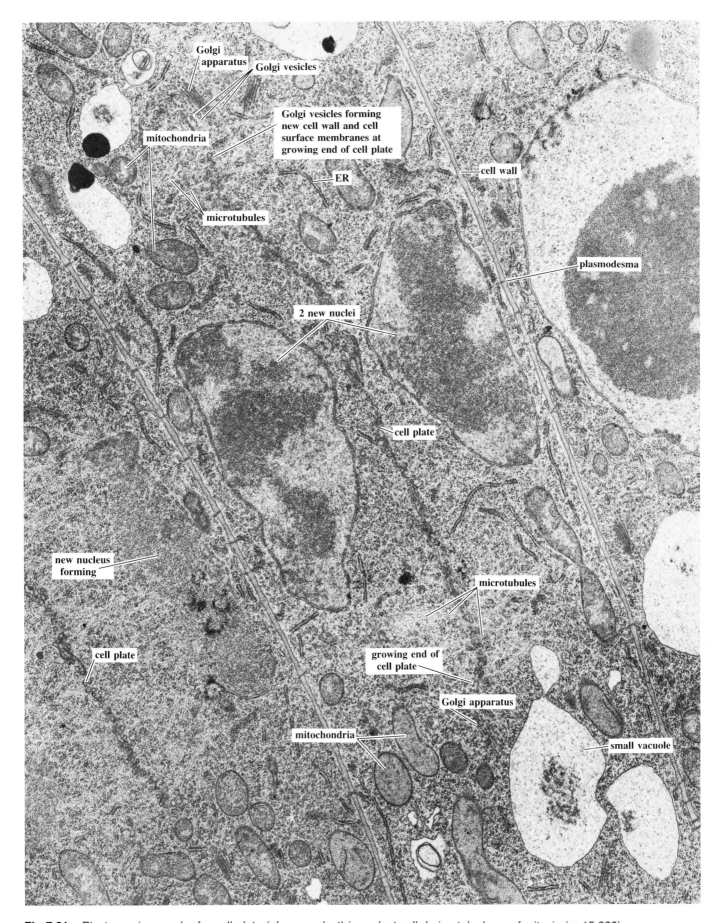

Fig 7.21 *Electron micrograph of a cell plate (phragmoplast) in a plant cell during telophase of mitosis (× 15 000)*

particularly important and prominent in secretory cells, a good example being provided by the acinar cells of the pancreas. These cells secrete the digestive enzymes of the pancreatic juice into the pancreatic duct, along which they pass to the duodenum. Fig 7.20a is an electron micrograph of such a cell, and fig 7.20b a diagrammatic representation of the secretion pathway.

Details of the pathway have been confirmed by using radioactively labelled amino acids and following their incorporation into protein and subsequent passage through different cell organelles. This can be done by homogenising samples of tissue at different times after supplying the amino acids, separating the cell organelles by centrifugation and finding which organelles contain the highest proportion of the amino acids. After concentration in the Golgi apparatus, the protein is carried in Golgi vesicles to the cell surface membrane. The final stage in the pathway is secretion of the inactive enzyme by reverse pinocytosis. The digestive enzymes secreted by the pancreas are synthesised in an inactive form so that they do not attack and destroy the cells that make them. An inactive enzyme is called a **proenzyme** or **zymogen**. An example is trypsinogen which is converted to active trypsin in the duodenum.

In general, proteins received by the Golgi apparatus from the ER have had short carbohydrate chains added to become glycoproteins (like the membrane proteins shown in fig 7.11). These carbohydrate 'antennae' can be remodelled in the Golgi apparatus, possibly to become markers that direct the proteins to their correct destinations. However, the exact details of how the Golgi apparatus sorts and directs molecules are unknown. The process of combining carbohydrates with proteins to form glycoproteins is called **glycosylation** and occurs during the production of many proteins.

The Golgi apparatus is also sometimes involved in the secretion of carbohydrates, an example being provided by the synthesis of new cell walls by plants. Fig 7.21 shows the intense activity which goes on at the 'cell plate', the region between two newly formed daughter nuclei where the new cell wall is laid down after nuclear division (mitosis or meiosis).

Golgi vesicles are steered into position at the cell plate by microtubules (described later) and fuse. Their membranes become the new cell surface membranes of the daughter cells, while their contents contribute to the middle lamella and new cell walls. Radioactively labelled glucose fed to dividing plant cells has been shown by autoradiography to appear in the Golgi apparatus and subsequently to be incorporated into cell wall polysaccharides within Golgi vesicles. These are polysaccharides of the cell wall matrix rather than cellulose, whose synthesis does not occur in Golgi vesicles.

Secretion by the pancreatic acinar cell and the formation of new plant cell walls are examples of the way in which many cell organelles can combine to perform one function.

An important glycoprotein secreted by the Golgi apparatus is **mucin**, which forms **mucus** in solution. It is secreted by goblet cells of the respiratory and intestinal epithelia. The root cap cells of plants contain Golgi apparatus which secretes a mucous polysaccharide, helping to lubricate the tip of the root as it penetrates the soil. The Golgi apparatus in leaf glands of the insectivorous plants *Drosera* (sundews) and *Pinguicula* (butterworts) secretes a sticky slime and enzymes which trap and digest insects. The slime, wax, gum and mucilage secretions of many cells are released by Golgi apparatus.

The Golgi apparatus is also sometimes involved in lipid transport. When digested, lipids are absorbed as fatty acids and glycerol in the small intestine. They are resynthesised to lipids in the smooth ER, coated in protein and then transported through the Golgi apparatus to the plasma membrane where they leave the cell, mainly to enter the lymphatic system.

A second important function of the Golgi apparatus, in addition to the secretion of proteins, glycoproteins, carbohydrates and lipids, is the formation of lysosomes, described below.

7.2.8 Lysosomes

Lysosomes (*lysis*, splitting; *soma*, body) are found in most eukaryotic cells, but are particularly abundant in animal cells exhibiting phagocytic activity. They are bounded by a single membrane and are simply sacs that contain hydrolytic (digestive) enzymes, such as proteases, nucleases, lipases and acid phosphatases. The contents of the lysosome are acidic and the enzymes have a low optimum pH. The enzymes have to be kept apart from the rest of the cell or they would destroy it. In animal cells, lysosomes are usually spherical and 0.2–0.5 μm in diameter. They have a characteristically homogeneous appearance in electron micrographs (fig 7.22).

In plant cells the large central vacuoles may act as lysosomes, although bodies similar to the lysosomes of animal cells are sometimes seen in the cytoplasm, particularly in dying cells. Most of the work on lysosomes has been done with animal cells.

The enzymes contained within lysosomes are synthesised on rough ER and transported to the Golgi apparatus. Golgi vesicles containing the processed enzymes later bud off and are called **primary lysosomes**. These have a number of functions, mostly involving digestive processes within the cell, but sometimes involving secretion of digestive enzymes. Their functions are summarised below and in fig 7.23.

Digestion of material taken in by endocytosis

The process of endocytosis is explained in section 7.2.2. Primary lysosomes may fuse with the vesicles or vacuoles formed by endocytosis to form **secondary lysosomes** in

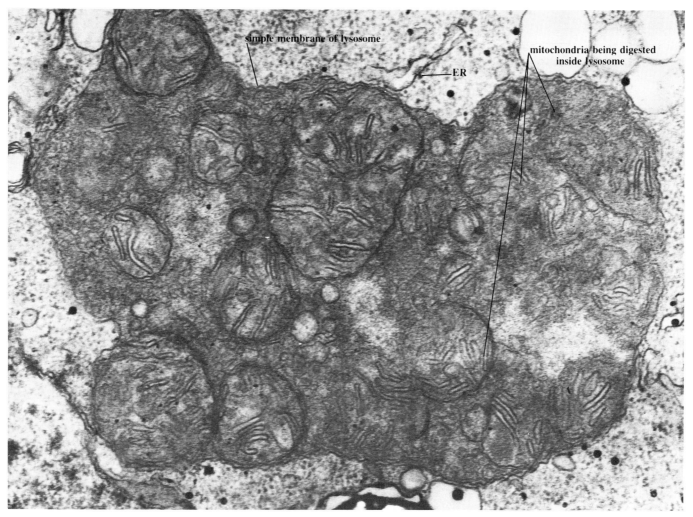

Fig 7.22 *Electron micrograph of a secondary lysosome (× 90 750)*

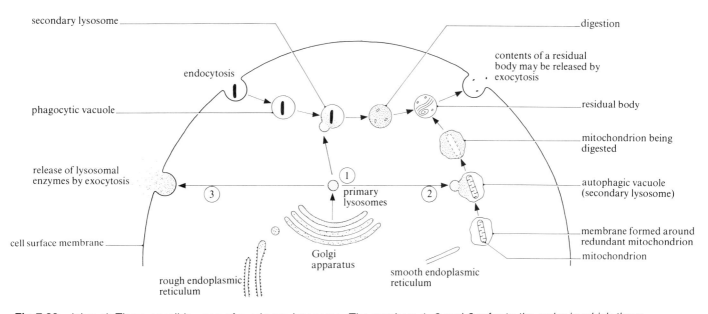

Fig 7.23 (above) *Three possible uses of a primary lysosome. The numbers 1, 2 and 3 refer to the order in which these pathways are discussed in the text*

which the material taken in by endocytosis is digested. This material might be taken in for food, as in some protozoans such as *Amoeba*, or for defensive purposes, as is the case when phagocytic white blood cells and macrophages ingest bacteria. The secondary lysosome may also be called a **food vacuole**. The products of digestion are absorbed and assimilated by the cytoplasm of the cell leaving undigested remains. The secondary lysosome is now termed a **residual body**. These usually migrate to the cell surface membrane and egest their contents (exocytosis). In certain cells, such as heart muscle and liver cells (hepatocytes), the residual bodies are stored.

An interesting example of the role of lysosomes occurs in the thyroid gland, where cells are stimulated by thyroid-stimulating hormone (TSH) to take up thyroglobulin by pinocytosis. The pinocytic vesicles so formed fuse with primary lysosomes and the thyroglobulin is partially hydrolysed to produce the active hormone thyroxine before the lysosome fuses with the cell surface membrane, thus secreting the hormone into the blood.

Autophagy

Autophagy is the process by which unwanted structures within the cell are removed. They are first enclosed by a single membrane, usually derived from smooth ER, and this structure then fuses with a primary lysosome to form a secondary lysosome, the **autophagic vacuole**, in which the unwanted material is digested. This is part of the normal turnover of cytoplasmic organelles, old ones being replaced by new ones. It becomes more frequent in cells undergoing reorganisation during differentiation.

Release of enzymes outside the cell (exocytosis)

Sometimes the enzymes of primary lysosomes are released from the cell. This occurs during the replacement of cartilage by bone during development. Similarly the matrix of bone may be broken down during the remodelling of bone that can occur in response to injury, new stresses and so on. In this case the enzymes are secreted from the lysosomes of cells known as **osteoclasts**.

Autolysis

Autolysis is the self-destruction of a cell by release of the contents of lysosomes within the cell. In such circumstances lysosomes have sometimes been aptly named 'suicide bags'. Autolysis is a normal event in some differentiation processes and may occur throughout a tissue, as when a tadpole tail is resorbed during metamorphosis. It also occurs after cells die. Sometimes it occurs as a result of certain lysosomal diseases or after cell damage.

7.2.9   Peroxisomes or microbodies

Peroxisomes or microbodies are common organelles of eukaryotic cells (fig 7.5). They are spherical, 0.3–1.5 μm in diameter (slightly smaller on average than mitochondria) and bounded by a single membrane. Their contents are finely granular, sometimes with a distinctive crystalline core which is a crystallised protein (enzyme) and they are derived from the ER, with which they often remain in close association.

Their most distinctive feature is the presence of the enzyme **catalase**, which catalyses the decomposition of hydrogen peroxide to water and oxygen (hence the name peroxisome). Hydrogen peroxide is a by-product of certain cell oxidations and is also very toxic, so must be eliminated immediately. Catalase is the fastest-acting enzyme known and its activity can be demonstrated by dropping a piece of fresh, preferably ground, liver into hydrogen peroxide, when rapid evolution of oxygen is observed. The cells of liver contain large numbers of peroxisomes (fig 7.5). Animal peroxisomes participate in a number of metabolic processes involving oxidation, but more details are known about plant peroxisomes. They can be divided into three types. **Glyoxysomes**, so called because they metabolise a compound called glyoxylate, are concerned with conversion of lipids to sucrose in lipid-rich seeds, such as in the endosperm of castor oil seeds (see question 21.7 and glyoxylate cycle, section 11.5). **Leaf peroxisomes** are important in the process of photorespiration in which they are intimately associated with chloroplasts and mitochondria, the three organelles often being found in close proximity as shown in fig 9.28. Hydrogen peroxide is produced during the photorespiratory pathway as shown in fig 9.28. A third group of **non-specialised peroxisomes** is found in other tissues.

7.2.10   The cytoskeleton

With the advent of electron microscopy it quickly became obvious that the cytoplasm of cells had a great deal more organisation than had previously been realised, and that extensive division of labour occurred between membrane-bound cell organelles and small organelles like ribosomes and centrioles. More recently structure has been revealed at an even finer level in the apparently structureless 'background' or ground substance of the cytoplasm. Complex networks of fibrous protein structures have been shown to exist in all eukaryotic cells. Collectively known as the **cytoskeleton**, these fibres are of at least three types: **microtubules**, **microfilaments** and **intermediate filaments**. They are concerned with movement, either by or within cells, and with the ability of cells to maintain their shapes.

Microtubules

Nearly all eukaryotic cells contain unbranched, hollow cylindrical organelles called **microtubules**. They are very fine tubes, having an external diameter of about 24 nm and with walls about 5 nm thick made up of helically arranged globular subunits of a protein called **tubulin**, as shown in fig 7.24. Their typical appearance in electron micrographs is shown in fig 7.21. They may extend for several micrometres in length. At intervals, cross-bridges (arms) sometimes project from their walls and these are probably involved in

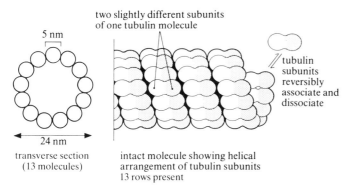

two slightly different subunits
of one tubulin molecule

5 nm

24 nm

transverse section
(13 molecules)

tubulin
subunits
reversibly
associate and
dissociate

intact molecule showing helical
arrangement of tubulin subunits
13 rows present

Fig 7.24 (above) *Probable arrangement of tubulin subunits in a microtubule*

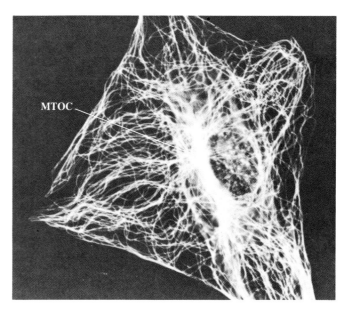

MTOC

Fig 7.25 *Immunofluorescence micrograph showing the distribution of microtubules in a cell (fibroblast) by reaction with a fluorescent antibody. The microtubules radiate from the microtubule-organising centre (MTOC) lying just outside the nucleus. The MTOC contains the centriole at its centre*

linking with adjacent microtubules, as occurs in cilia and flagella. Growth of microtubules occurs at one end by addition of tubulin subunits. It is inhibited by a number of chemicals, such as **colchicine**, which have been used to investigate the functions of microtubules. Growth apparently requires a template to start and certain very small ring-like structures that have been isolated from cells, and which consist of tubulin subunits, appear to serve this function. In intact animal cells, centrioles probably also serve this function and are therefore sometimes known as microtubule-organising centres, or MTOCs. Centrioles contain short microtubules as shown in fig 22.3.

The network of microtubules in cells has been strikingly revealed by a technique known as **immunofluorescence microscopy** in which fluorescent markers are tagged to antibody molecules that bind specifically to the protein whose distribution is being investigated. If an antibody to tubulin is used, a distribution like that shown in fig 7.25 is revealed by the light microscope. The microtubules radiate from the centrosphere around the centrioles. Satellite proteins around the centrioles act as MTOCs.

Microtubules are involved in a number of cell processes, some of which are listed below.

Centrioles, basal bodies, cilia and flagella. Centrioles are small hollow cylinders (about 0.3–0.5 μm long and about 0.2 μm in diameter) that occur in pairs in most animal and lower plant cells in a distinctly staining region of the cytoplasm known as the **centrosome** or **centrosphere**. Each contains nine triplets of microtubules as shown in fig 22.3. At the beginning of nuclear division the centrioles replicate themselves and the two new pairs migrate to opposite poles of the spindle, the structure on which the chromosomes become aligned (section 22.2). The spindle itself is made of microtubules ('spindle fibres') presumably synthesised using centrioles as MTOCs. The microtubules control separation of chromatids or chromosomes as described in chapter 22. Cells of higher plants lack centrioles, although they do produce spindles during nuclear division. The cells are thought to contain smaller MTOCs that are not easily visible even with the electron microscope. Another possible function of

centrioles as MTOCs is discussed in intracellular transport below.

Identical in structure to centrioles are **basal bodies**, formerly known as **kinetosomes** or **blepharoplasts**. They are always found at the base of cilia and flagella and probably originate from replication of centrioles. They also seem to act as MTOCs because cilia and flagella contain a characteristic '9 + 2' arrangement of microtubules (section 17.6 and figure 17.31).

In spindles, as well as in cilia and flagella, microtubules undergo sliding motions which in the former case move chromosomes or chromatids and in the latter are responsible for beating movements. Further details of these activities are given in chapters 17 and 22.

Intracellular transport. Microtubules have also been implicated in the movements of other cell organelles such as Golgi vesicles, an example being the guiding of Golgi vesicles to the cell plate shown in fig 7.21. There is a constant traffic in cells of Golgi vesicles and of vesicles from the ER to the Golgi apparatus, and time-lapse photography reveals regular movements of larger organelles, such as lysosomes and mitochondria, in many cells. Such movements may be both random and non-random and are believed to be typical of most cell organelles. They are suspended if the microtubule system is disrupted.

Cytoskeleton. Microtubules also have a passive architectural role in cells, their long, fairly rigid, tube-like structure acting in a skeletal fashion to form a '**cytoskeleton**'. They help to determine the shape of cells during development and to maintain the shape of differentiated cells, often being found in a zone just beneath the

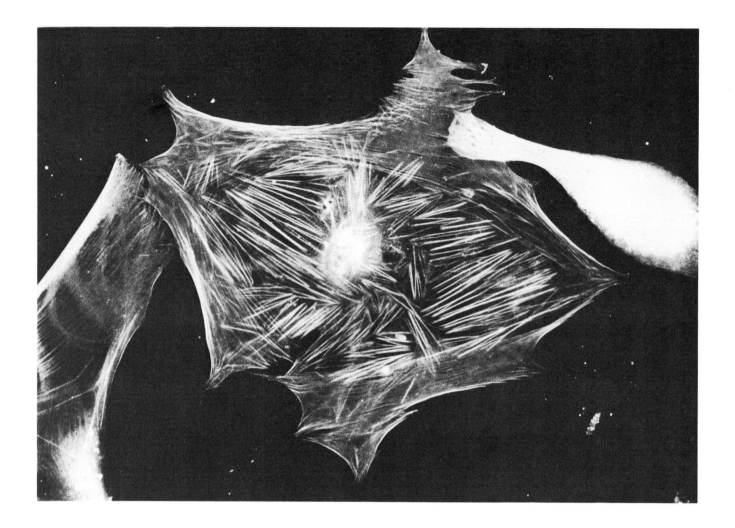

cell surface membrane. The axons of nerve cells, for example, contain longitudinally running bundles of microtubules (possibly involved in transport along the axons). Animal cells in which microtubules are disrupted revert to a spherical shape. In plant cells the alignment of microtubules exactly corresponds with the alignment of cellulose fibres during deposition of the cell wall, thus indirectly establishing cell shape.

Microfilaments

Microfilaments are very fine protein filaments about 7 nm in diameter. Recently it has been shown that they are abundant in all eukaryotic cells and consist of the protein **actin** which is found in muscle. In fact, 10–15% of the total protein of all cells so far examined has proved to be actin and immunofluorescence microscopy shows a cytoskeleton of actin similar to that of microtubules (fig 7.26).

Microfilaments often occur in sheets or bundles (stress fibres) just below the cell surface membrane and at the interface between stationary and moving cytoplasm where cytoplasmic streaming is taking place. They are probably involved in endocytosis and exocytosis. A much smaller proportion of myosin filaments is also found in cells, myosin being the other major protein of muscle. Interac-

Fig 7.26 *Immunoflorescence micrograph showing the distribution of actin microfilaments in a cell (fibroblast) by reaction with a fluorescent antibody. Long stress fibres are revealed. Fluorescence staining of tropomyosin indicates that actin and tropomysin are found in the same fibre bundles.*

tions between actin and myosin are the cause of muscle contraction, as described in section 17.4. This and other evidence suggests that microfilaments are involved in cell motility (whether of the whole cell or within the cell), although this is not controlled in exactly the same way as in muscle. Actin filaments may operate alone in some cases, and with myosin in others. A good example of the latter is in microvilli (section 7.2.11). Microfilaments are constantly being assembled and disassembled in cells that show motility (see, for example, amoeboid movement, section 17.6). A final example of the use of microfilaments is during cleavage of animal cells which is brought about by constriction of a ring of microfilaments after nuclear division.

Intermediate filaments

A third distinct type of filament of intermediate size (8–10 nm in diameter) also has certain cytoskeletal and motility roles.

7.2.11 Microvilli

One of the best understood cytoskeletal systems is that of microvilli. Microvilli are finger-like extensions of the cell surface membrane of some animal cells. They increase the surface area by as much as 25 times and are particularly numerous on cells specialised for absorption, such as on intestinal epithelium and kidney tubule epithelium. The fringe of the microvilli can just be seen with a light microscope and is called a **brush border**. More irregular and transitory extensions of the cell surface membrane also occur, as shown in figs 7.3 and 7.5, and these play roles in exocytosis and endocytosis.

Each microvillus contains bundles of about 40 cross-linked actin filaments which are associated with myosin filaments at the base of the microvillus in a region called the **terminal web**. The terminal web contains actin and intermediate filaments and extends across the whole cell just below the microvilli. The system as a whole ensures that the microvilli remain upright and retain their shape, while still probably allowing backward and forward movement through the interactions of actin and myosin (compare muscle contraction). The increase in surface area provided by the microvilli not only improves the efficiency of absorption, but also, in the gut, of digestion because certain digestive enzymes are associated with their surface (see section 10.4.9).

Plant cells lack microvilli because their rigid cell walls impose restrictions on extensions of the cell surface membrane. However, it is interesting to note the comparable increases in membrane surface area achieved by transfer cells for purposes of transport (fig 14.27 and section 14.8.4).

7.2.12 Mitochondria

Mitochondria are found in all aerobic eukaryotic cells and their structure and function are briefly summarised in figs 7.3–6. Their chief function is aerobic respiration and they are described in detail in section 11.5.

7.3 Structures characteristic of plant cells

As noted already, the cells of higher plants contain all the organelles found in animal cells with the exception of centrioles. They also possess extra structures which are the theme of this section.

7.3.1 Cell walls

Plant cells, like those of prokaryotes and fungi, are surrounded by a relatively rigid wall which is secreted by the living cell (the protoplast) within. Plant cell walls differ in chemical composition from those of the prokaryotes and the fungi, as reference to table 2.1 will show. However, they share some of the same functions, such as protection and support, and impose the same physical restraints on cell movement. The wall laid down during cell division of plants is called the **primary wall**. This may later be thickened to become a **secondary wall**. Formation of the primary wall is described in this section and a micrograph of an early stage in wall formation is shown in fig 7.21.

Structure of the cell wall

The primary wall consists of cellulose microfibrils running through a **matrix** of complex polysaccharides. Cellulose is a polysaccharide whose chemical structure is described in section 5.2.3. Of particular relevance to its role in cell walls is its fibrous nature and high tensile strength, which approaches that of steel. Individual molecules of cellulose are long chains cross-linked by hydrogen bonds to other molecules to form strong bundles called **microfibrils**. Microfibrils form the framework of the cell wall within the cell wall matrix. The matrix consists of polysaccharides which are usually divided for convenience into **pectins** and **hemicelluloses** according to their solubility in a number of solvents used in extraction procedures. **Pectins**, or **pectic substances**, are usually extracted first, having relatively high solubility. They are a mixed group of acidic polysaccharides (built up from the sugars arabinose and galactose, the sugar acid galacturonic acid, and methanol). They form long branching or straight molecules. The **middle lamella** that holds neighbouring cell walls together is composed of sticky, gel-like magnesium and calcium pectates. In the walls of ripening fruit certain insoluble pectic substances are converted back to soluble pectins. These form gels when sugar is added and are therefore used as commercial gelling agents.

Hemicelluloses are a mixed group of alkali-soluble polysaccharides (including polymers of the sugars xylose, galactose, mannose, glucose and glucomannose). Like cellulose they form chain-like molecules, but the chains are less organised, shorter and more branched. Cell walls are hydrated and 60–70% of their mass is usually water. Water can move freely through free space in the cell wall and also contributes to the chemical and physical properties of the cell wall polysaccharides.

Mechanically strong materials, like cell walls, in which more than one component is present are known as **composite materials** and they are generally stronger than any of their components in isolation. Fibre–matrix systems are used widely in engineering and a study of their properties is an important branch of both modern engineering and biology. The matrix transfers stress to the fibres, which have a high tensile strength. The matrix also improves resistance to compression and shear, spreads out the fibres and protects them from abrasion and possible chemical attack. An example of a matrix traditionally used

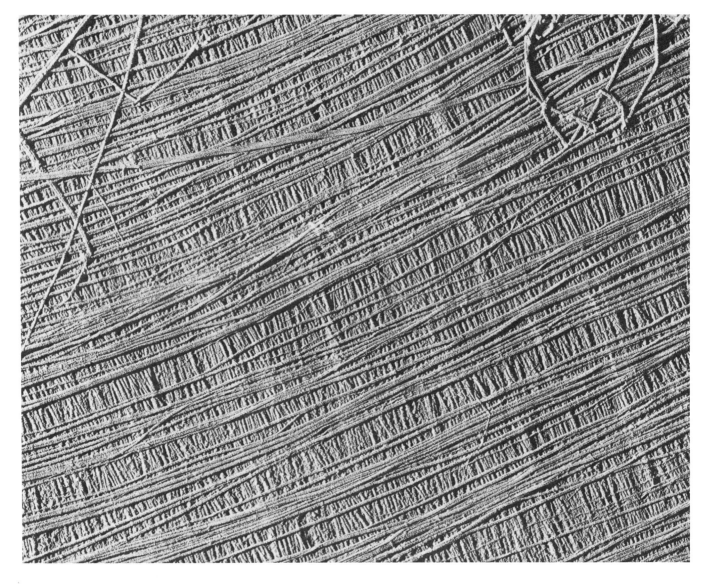

Fig 7.27 *Electron micrograph of layers from the wall of the green seaweed* Chaetomorpha melagonium *showing cellulose microfibrils some 20 nm wide; the contrast is due to shadowing with a platinum/gold alloy*

in engineering is concrete which may be reinforced in various ways, such as by steel rods. A more modern and lighter structural material is a glass or carbon fibre reinforced plastic in which the plastic acts as the matrix. Wood is a composite whose strength is due to its cell walls. Other rigid biological composites include bone, cartilage and arthropod cuticles. Pliant composites also exist such as connective tissue and skin.

In some cells, such as leaf mesophyll cells, the primary wall remains the only wall. In most, however, extra layers of cellulose are laid down on the inside surface of the primary wall (the outside surface of the cell surface membrane), thus building up a secondary wall. This usually occurs after the cell has reached a maximum size; but a few cells, such as those of collenchyma, continue to grow during this phase. Secondary thickening of plant cell walls should not be confused with secondary thickening (secondary growth) of the whole plant, which is an increase in girth resulting from the addition of new cells.

The cellulose fibres of a given layer of secondary thickening are usually orientated at the same angle, but different layers are orientated at different angles, forming an even stronger cross-ply structure. This is shown in fig 7.27.

Some cells such as xylem vessel elements and sclerenchyma undergo extensive **lignification** whereby lignin, a complex polymer (not a polysaccharide), is deposited in all the cellulose layers (often a primary layer and three secondary layers). In some cells, such as protoxylem, the lignin is laid down in annular, spiral or reticulate patterns as shown in fig 8.11. In others it is complete, apart from pits which represent areas of the primary wall originally occupied by groups of plasmodesmata and known as pit fields (section 8.1.3 and fig 8.7). Lignin cements and anchors cellulose fibres together. It acts as a very hard and rigid matrix giving the cell wall extra tensile and particularly compressional strength (prevents buckling). It further protects the cells from physical and chemical damage. Together with the cellulose, which remains in the wall, it is responsible for the unique characteristics of wood as a construction material.

Functions of the cell wall

The main functions of plant cell walls are summarised below.

(1) Mechanical strength and skeletal support is provided for individual cells and for the plant as a whole. Extensive lignification increases strength in some walls (small amounts are present in most walls).

(2) Cell walls are fairly rigid and resistant to expansion and therefore allow development of turgidity when water enters the cell by osmosis. This contributes to the support of all plants and is the main source of support in herbaceous plants and organs such as leaves which do not undergo secondary growth. The cell wall prevents the cell from bursting when exposed to a dilute solution.

(3) Orientation of cellulose microfibrils limits and helps to control cell growth and shape because the cell's ability to stretch is determined by their arrangement. If, for example, cellulose microfibrils form hoops in a transverse direction around the cell, the cell will stretch, as it fills with water by osmosis, in a longitudinal direction.

(4) The system of interconnected cell walls (the **apoplast**) is a major pathway of movement for water and dissolved mineral salts. The walls are held together by middle lamellae. The cell walls also possess minute pores through which structures called **plasmodesmata** can pass, forming living connections between cells, and allowing all the protoplasts to be linked in a system called the **symplast**.

(5) Cell walls develop a coating of waxy cutin, the cuticle, on exposed epidermal surfaces reducing water loss and risk of infection. Cork cell walls undergo impregnation with suberin which serves a similar function after secondary growth.

(6) The walls of xylem vessels, tracheids and sieve tubes (with their sieve plates) are adapted for long-distance translocation of materials through the cells, as explained in chapters 8 and 14.

(7) The cell walls of root endodermal cells are impregnated with suberin forming a barrier to water movement (section 14.1.7).

(8) Some cell walls are modified as food reserves, as in storage of hemicelluloses in some seeds.

(9) The cell walls of transfer cells develop an increased surface area and the consequent increase in surface area of the cell surface membrane increases the efficiency of transfer by active transport (section 14.8.4).

7.3.2 Plasmodesmata

Plasmodesmata are living connections that pass between neighbouring plant cells through very fine pores in adjacent walls. Fig 7.6 summarises what little is known about their structure and function. They are sometimes found in groups known as primary pit fields as described in section 8.1.3. Sieve plate pores of phloem sieve tubes are derived from plasmodesmata.

7.3.3 Vacuoles

A vacuole is a fluid-filled sac bounded by a single membrane. Animal cells contain relatively small vacuoles, such as phagocytic vacuoles, food vacuoles, autophagic vacuoles and contractile vacuoles. However, plant cells, notably mature parenchyma and collenchyma cells, have a large central vacuole surrounded by a membrane called the **tonoplast** (fig 7.4). The fluid they contain is called **cell sap**. It is a concentrated solution of mineral salts, sugars, organic acids, oxygen, carbon dioxide, pigments and some waste and 'secondary' products of metabolism. The functions of vacuoles are summarised below.

(1) Water generally enters the concentrated cell sap by osmosis through the differentially permeable tonoplast. As a result a pressure potential builds up within the cell and the cytoplasm is pushed against the cell wall. Osmotic uptake of water is important in cell expansion during cell growth, as well as in the normal water relations of plants.

(2) The vacuole sometimes contains pigments in solution called **anthocyans**. These include **anthocyanins**, which are red, blue and purple, and other related compounds which are shades of yellow and ivory. They are largely responsible for the colours in flowers (for example in roses, violets and *Dahlia*), fruits, buds and leaves. In the latter case they contribute to autumn shades, together with the photosynthetic pigments of chloroplasts. They are important in attracting insects, birds and other animals for pollination and seed dispersal.

(3) Plant vacuoles sometimes contain hydrolytic enzymes and act as lysosomes during life. After cell death the tonoplast, like all membranes, loses its partial permeability and the enzymes escape causing autolysis.

(4) Waste products and certain secondary products of plant metabolism may accumulate in vacuoles. For example, crystals of waste calcium oxalate are sometimes observed. The role of secondary products is not always clear, as in the case of alkaloids which may be stored in vacuoles. They, like tannins (which are astringent to the taste), may offer protection from consumption by herbivores. Tannins are particularly common in vacuoles (as well as in the cytoplasm and cell walls) of leaves, wood, bark, unripe fruits and seed coats. Latex may accumulate in vacuoles, usually in a milky emulsion, as in dandelion stems. Certain cells, known as **laticifers**, are specialised for this function. The latex of the rubber tree *Helvea brasiliensis* contains the enzymes and intermediates needed for rubber synthesis, and the latex of the opium poppy contains alkaloids.

(5) Some of the dissolved substances act as food reserves, which can be utilised by the cytoplasm when necessary, for example sucrose, mineral salts and inulin.

7.3.4 Plastids

Plastids are organelles found only in plant cells and in higher plants develop from small bodies called **proplastids** found in meristematic regions. They are surrounded by two membranes (the envelope). Proplastids can develop into several types of plastid depending on where they are found in the plant. There are various ways of classifying the different types and a simple scheme is given below.

Chloroplasts. These are plastids that contain chlorophyll and carotenoid pigments and carry out photosynthesis. They are found mainly in leaves and are described in section 9.3.1 in the context of photosynthesis.

Chromoplasts. These are non-photosynthetic coloured plastids containing mainly red, orange or yellow pigments (carotenoids). They are particularly associated with fruits (such as the tomato and red pepper) and flowers in which their bright colours serve to attract insects, birds and other animals for pollination and seed dispersal. The orange pigment of carrot roots is also contained in chromoplasts.

Leucoplasts. These are colourless plastids lacking pigments. They are usually modified for food storage, and are particularly abundant in storage organs such as roots, seeds and young leaves. They are further classified according to food stored; for example **amyloplasts** store starch (see fig 15.16), **lipidoplasts** (elaioplasts or oleoplasts) store lipids either as oil or fat, as in oily nuts and sunflower seeds, and **proteoplasts** store protein, as in some seeds.

Chapter Eight

Histology

All multicellular organisms possess groups of cells of similar structure and function assembled together to form tissues. The study of tissues is called **histology**. A **tissue** can be defined as a group of physically linked cells and associated intercellular substances that is specialised for a particular function or functions. This specialisation, whilst leading to an increased efficiency of action by the organism as a whole, means that the collective activity of different tissues must be coordinated and integrated if the organism is to be viable.

Different tissues are often grouped together into larger functional units called **organs**. Internal organs are more obvious in animals than in plants, where they do not exist as such except perhaps for the vascular bundles. In animals, organs form the parts of the even larger functional units known as **systems**, for example the digestive system (pancreas, liver, stomach, duodenum and so on) and the vascular system (heart and blood vessels).

The cells of a tissue may be all of one type, for example parenchyma, collenchyma and cork in plants and squamous epithelium in animals. Alternatively, the tissues may contain a mixture of different cell types, as in xylem and phloem in plants and areolar connective tissue in animals. Generally the cells of a tissue share a common embryological origin.

The study of tissue structure and function relies heavily on light microscopy and the associated techniques of preserving, staining and sectioning material. These techniques are described in section A2.4.

In this chapter the histology of flowering plants is studied at the level of detail which can be seen with the light microscope. In some cases, though, reference is made to structure as revealed by the scanning electron microscope in order to provide greater clarification. In relating structure to function in tissues it is important to bear in mind the three-dimensional structures of the cells and their relationship to one another. This kind of information is usually 'pieced together' by examining material in thin section, most commonly in transverse section (TS) and longitudinal section (LS). Neither type of section alone can give all the information required, but a combination of the two can often reveal the necessary information. Some cells,

such as xylem vessels and tracheids in plants, can easily be examined whole by macerating the tissues. This involves the breakdown of soft tissues leaving behind the harder, lignified xylem vessels, tracheids and fibres.*

Plant tissues can be divided into two groups, either consisting of one type of cell or of more than one type. Animal tissues are divided into four groups: epithelial, connective, muscle and nervous tissue. Table 8.1 shows the characteristic features, functions and distribution of plant tissues.

8.1 Simple plant tissues – tissues consisting of one type of cell

8.1.1 Parenchyma

Structure

The structure of parenchyma is shown in fig 8.1. The cells are usually roughly spherical (isodiametric) though they may be elongated.

Functions and distribution

The cells are unspecialised and act as **packing tissue** between more specialised tissues, as in the pith, cortex and medullary rays. They form a large part of the bulk of various organs, such as the stem and root, and they also occur among the xylem vessels (xylem parenchyma) and phloem cells (phloem parenchyma).

The osmotic properties of parenchyma cells are important because when turgid they become tightly packed and provide support for the organs in which they are found. This is particularly important in the stems of herbaceous plants, where they form the main means of support. During periods of water shortage the cells of such plants lose water and this results in the plants wilting.

Although structurally unspecialised, the cells are **metabolically active** and are the sites of many of the vital activities of the plant body.

A system of air spaces runs between the cells through which gaseous exchange can take place between living cells and the external environment through stomata or lenticels. Oxygen for respiration and carbon dioxide for photosynthesis can thus diffuse through the spaces, such as in the spongy mesophyll layer of the leaf.

---

* The structure of some plant tissues is dealt with elsewhere in this book. More detailed structure of phloem is given in chapter 14 where its structure is related to its function in translocation. Development of plant tissues from meristematic cells is discussed in chapter 21, together with secondary growth and the structure of wood (secondary xylem) and cork.

Table 8.1 Characteristic features, functions and distribution of plant tissues.*

Tissue	Living or dead	Wall material	Cell shape	Main functions	Distribution
Parenchyma	Living	Cellulose, pectins and hemicelluloses	Usually isodiametric, sometimes elongated	Packing tissue. Support in herbaceous plants. Metabolically active. Intercellular air spaces allow gaseous exchange. Food storage. Transport of materials through cells or cell walls.	Cortex, pith, medullary rays and packing tissue in xylem and phloem
Modified parenchyma *(a)* epidermis	Living	Cellulose, pectins and hemicelluloses, and covering of cutin	Elongated and flattened	Protection from desiccation and infection. Hairs and glands may have additional functions.	Single layer of cells covering entire primary plant body
(b) mesophyll	Living	Cellulose, pectins and hemicelluloses	Isodiametric, irregular or column-shaped depending on location	Photosynthesis (contains chloroplasts). Storage of starch.	Between the upper and lower epidermis of leaves
(c) endodermis	Living	Cellulose, pectins and hemicelluloses, and deposits of suberin	As epidermis	Selective barrier to movement of water and mineral salts (between cortex and xylem) in roots. Starch sheath with possible role in geotropic response in stems.	Around vascular tissue (innermost layer of cortex)
(d) pericycle	Living	Cellulose, pectins and hemicelluloses	As parenchyma	In roots it retains meristematic activity producing lateral roots and contributing to secondary growth if this occurs.	In roots between central vascular tissue and endodermis

NB The pericycle in the stem is made of sclerenchyma and has a different origin.

Tissue	Living or dead	Wall material	Cell shape	Main functions	Distribution
Collenchyma	Living	Cellulose, pectins and hemicelluloses	Elongated and polygonal with tapering ends	Support (a mechanical function)	Outer regions of cortex, e.g. angles of stems, midrib of leaves
Sclerenchyma *(a)* fibres	Dead	Mainly lignin. Cellulose, pectins and hemicelluloses also present.	Elongated and polygonal with tapering interlocking ends	Support (purely mechanical)	Outer regions of cortex, pericycle of stems, xylem and phloem
(b) sclereids	Dead	As fibres	Roughly isodiametric, though variations occur	Support or mechanical protection	Cortex, pith, phloem, shells and stones of fruits, seed coats

Xylem	Mixture of living and dead cells. Xylem also contains fibres and parenchyma which are as previously described.				
tracheids and vessels	Dead	Mainly lignin. Cellulose, pectins and hemicelluloses also present.	Elongated and tubular	Translocation of water and mineral salts. Support.	Vascular system

Phloem	Mixture of living and dead cells. Phloem also contains fibres and sclereids which are as previously described.				
(a) sieve tubes	Living	Cellulose, pectins and hemicelluloses	Elongated and tubular	Translocation of organic solutes (food)	Vascular system
(b) companion cells	Living	Cellulose, pectins and hemicelluloses	Elongated and narrow	Work in association with sieve tubes	Vascular system

* Tissues associated with secondary growth, such as wood and cork, are described in chapter 21.

(a)

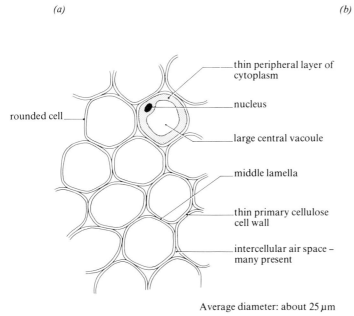

thin peripheral layer of cytoplasm

nucleus

large central vacoule

middle lamella

rounded cell

thin primary cellulose cell wall

intercellular air space – many present

Average diameter: about 25 μm

Fig 8.1 *Structure of parenchyma cells. (a) TS, cells are usually roughly isodiametric (spherical), though may be elongated. (b) TS* Helianthus *stem pith*

(b)

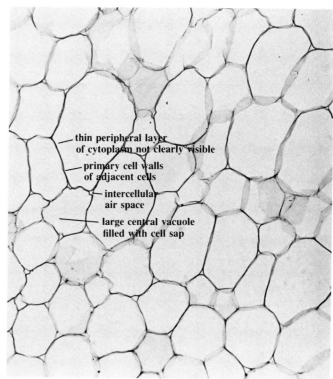

thin peripheral layer of cytoplasm not clearly visible

primary cell walls of adjacent cells

intercellular air space

large central vacuole filled with cell sap

Parenchyma cells are often sites for food storage, most notably in storage organs, such as potato tubers where the parenchyma cortex stores starch in **amyloplasts**. Food is also stored in medullary rays. Rare examples occur of parenchyma cells storing food in thickened cell walls, for example the hemicelluloses of date seed endosperm.

The walls of parenchyma cells are important pathways of water and mineral salt transport through the plant (part of the 'apoplast pathway' described in chapter 14). Substances may also move through cytoplasmic routes between neighbouring cells.

Parenchyma cells may become modified and more specialised in certain parts of the plant. Some examples of tissues that can be regarded as modified parenchyma are discussed below.

Epidermis. This is the layer, one cell thick, that covers the whole of the primary plant body. Its basic function is to protect the plant from desiccation and infection. During secondary growth it may be ruptured and replaced by a cork layer as described in section 21.6.6. The structure of typical epidermal cells is shown in fig 8.2.

The epidermal cells secrete a waxy substance called **cutin** which forms a layer of variable thickness called the **cuticle** within and on the outer surface of the cell walls. This helps to reduce water loss by evaporation from the plant surface as well as helping to prevent the entry of pathogens.

If the surfaces of leaves are examined in a light microscope it can be seen that the epidermal cells of dicotyledonous leaves are irregularly arranged and often have wavy margins, while those of monocotyledons tend to be more regular and rectangular in shape. At intervals,

specialised epidermal cells called **guard cells** occur in pairs side by side, with a pore between them called a **stoma**. These features are shown in figs 8.2b and c. Guard cells have a distinctive shape and are the only epidermal cells that contain chloroplasts, the rest being colourless. The size of the stoma is adjusted by the turgidity of the guard cells as described in chapter 14. The stomata allow gaseous exchange to occur during photosynthesis and respiration and are most numerous in the leaf epidermis, though they are also found in the stem. Water vapour also escapes through the stomata, and this is part of the process called transpiration.

Sometimes epidermal cells grow hair-like extensions which may be unicellular or multicellular and serve a wide variety of functions. In roots, unicellular hairs grow from a region just behind the root tip and increase the surface area for absorption of water and mineral salts (fig 14.16). In climbing plants, such as goosegrass (*Galium aparine*), hooked hairs often occur and function to prevent the stems from slipping from their supports.

More often epidermal hairs are an additional protective feature. They may assist the cuticle in reducing water loss by trapping a layer of moist air next to the plant, as well as reflecting radiation. Some hairs are water absorbing, notably on xerophytic plants. Others may have a mechanical protective function as with short, stiff bristles. The hairs of the stinging nettle (*Urtica dioica*) are hard with a bulbous tip and as they knock against an animal's body their fragile tip breaks off and the jagged end pierces the skin. The cell contents at their bases enter the wound, acting as an irritant poison. Hairs may form barriers around the nectaries of flowers preventing access to crawling

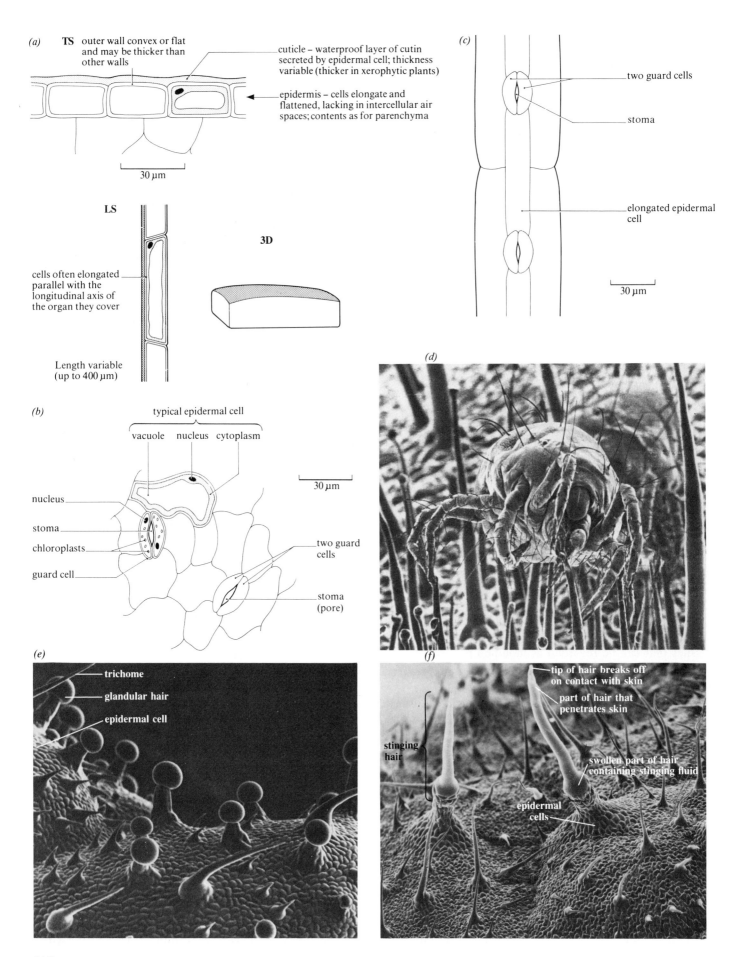

(a) **TS** outer wall convex or flat and may be thicker than other walls

cuticle – waterproof layer of cutin secreted by epidermal cell; thickness variable (thicker in xerophytic plants)

epidermis – cells elongate and flattened, lacking in intercellular air spaces; contents as for parenchyma

30 μm

LS

3D

cells often elongated parallel with the longitudinal axis of the organ they cover

Length variable (up to 400 μm)

(c) two guard cells

stoma

elongated epidermal cell

30 μm

(b) typical epidermal cell

vacuole   nucleus   cytoplasm

30 μm

nucleus

stoma

chloroplasts

guard cell

two guard cells

stoma (pore)

(d)

(e) trichome

glandular hair

epidermal cell

(f) tip of hair breaks off on contact with skin

part of hair that penetrates skin

stinging hair

swollen part of hair containing stinging fluid

epidermal cells

218

Fig. 8.2 (opposite) *Structure of epidermal cells. (a) Epidermal cells seen in TS, LS and three-dimensions. (b) Surface view of dicotyledon leaf epidermis (for TS stoma see fig 14.16). (c) Surface view of monocotyledon leaf epidermis. (d) Spider mite trapped and killed by the hair glands of a potato leaf. An enzyme capable of digesting animal matter has been found in one type of glandular hair in the potato, so the potato could be regarded as a carnivorous plant. Many other plants not normally thought of as carnivorous may have similar abilities. (e) Young leaf of* Cannabis sativa *with adaxial glands and trichomes. (f) Leaf surface of* Urtica dioica *(stinging nettle)*

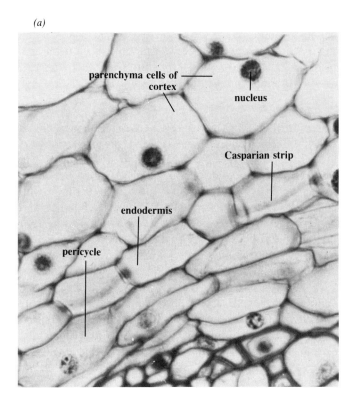

(a)

(b)

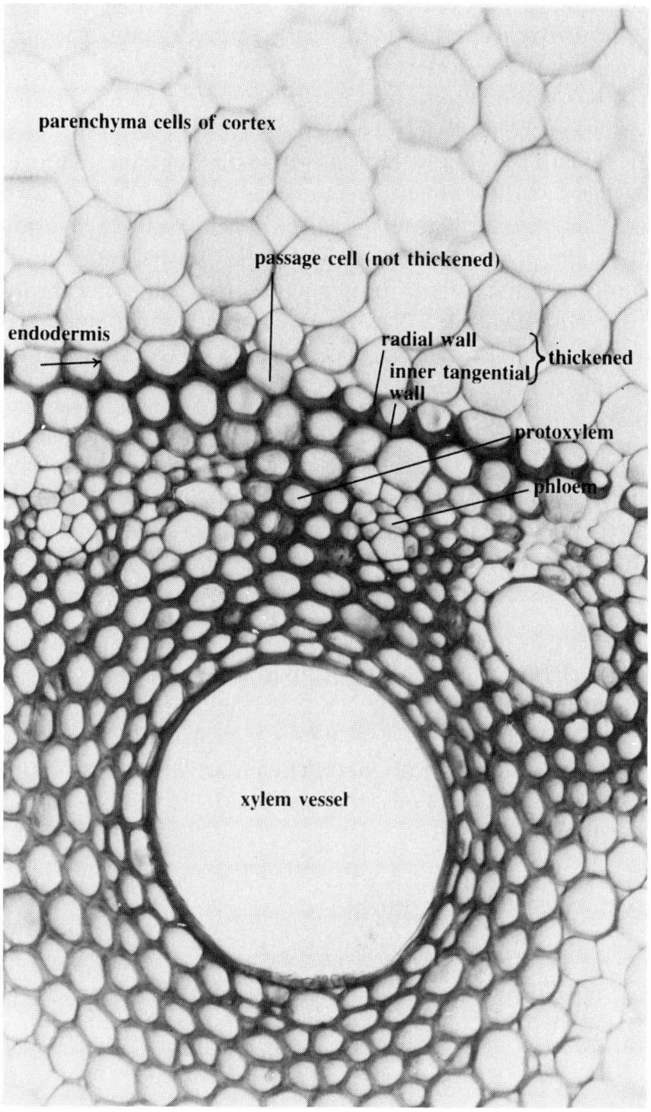

Fig 8.3 *Structure of root endodermis. (left) (a) TS young endodermis with Casparian band (HP). (above) (b) TS old dicotyledonous root showing endodermis*

insects and helping to promote cross-pollination by larger flying insects (see white dead-nettle, fig 20.17).

Glandular cells are also a common feature of the epidermis and these may be hair-like. They may secrete a sticky substance that traps and kills insects, either for protection or, if the exudate contains enzymes, for digestion and subsequent absorption of food. Such plants may be regarded as carnivorous (fig 8.2*d*). Glandular hairs are sometimes responsible for the scents given off by plants, such as on the leaves of lavender (*Lavendula*).

Mesophyll (see also figs 9.3 and 9.4). This is the packing tissue found between the two epidermal layers of leaves and consists of parenchyma modified to carry out photosynthesis. Photosynthetic parenchyma is sometimes called **chlorenchyma**. The cytoplasm of such cells contains numerous chloroplasts where the reactions of photosynthesis occur. In dicotyledons there are two distinct layers of

mesophyll, an upper layer consisting of column-shaped cells forming the **palisade mesophyll**, and a lower layer of more irregularly shaped cells, containing fewer chloroplasts, called **spongy mesophyll**. Most photosynthesis is carried out in the palisade mesophyll, while large intercellular air spaces between spongy mesophyll cells allow efficient gaseous exchange.

Endodermis (see also fig 14.17). This is the layer of cells surrounding the vascular tissue of plants and can be regarded as the innermost layer of the cortex. The cortex is usually parenchymatous, but the endodermis may be modified in various ways, both physiologically and structurally. It is more conspicuous in roots, where it is one cell thick, than in stems because in roots each cell develops a **Casparian strip**, a band of **suberin** (a fatty substance) that runs round the cell (fig 8.3). At a later stage further thickenings of the wall may take place. The structure and function of root endodermis are shown in fig 14.17.

In the stems of dicotyledons the vascular bundles form a ring and the endodermis is the layer, one to several cells thick, immediately outside of this ring (fig 14.15). In this situation the endodermis often appears no different from the rest of the cortex, but may store starch grains and form a **starch sheath** which becomes visible when stained with iodine solution. These starch grains may sediment inside the cells in response to gravity, making the endodermis important in the geotropic response in the same way as root cap cells (section 15.2.2). In monocotyledonous stems the vascular bundles are scattered and no endodermis can be distinguished around them.

Pericycle. Roots possess a layer of parenchyma, one to several cells thick, called the **pericycle**, between the central vascular tissue and the endodermis (fig 14.17). It retains its meristematic capacity and produces lateral roots. It also contributes to secondary growth if this occurs. In stems there is usually no equivalent layer.

Companion cells. These are specialised parenchyma cells found adjacent to sieve tubes and vital for the functioning of the latter. They are very active metabolically and have a denser cytoplasm with smaller vacuoles than normal parenchyma cells. Their origin, structure and function are described later in this chapter (section 8.2.2).

8.1.2 Collenchyma

Collenchyma consists, like parenchyma, of living cells but is modified to give support and mechanical strength.

Structure

The structure of collenchyma is shown in fig 8.4. It shows many of the features of parenchyma but is characterised by the deposition of extra cellulose at the corners of the cells. The deposition occurs after the formation of the primary cell wall. The cells also elongate parallel to the longitudinal axis of the organ in which they are found.

Function and distribution

Collenchyma is a mechanical tissue, providing support for those organs in which it is found. It is particularly important in young plants, herbaceous plants and in organs such as leaves where secondary growth does not occur. In these situations it is an important strengthening tissue supplementing the effects of turgid parenchyma. It is the first of the strengthening tissues to develop in the primary plant body and, because it is living, can grow and stretch without imposing limitations on the growth of other cells around it.

In stems and petioles its value in support is increased by

its location towards the periphery of the organ. It is often found just below the epidermis in the outer region of the cortex and gradually merges into parenchyma towards the inside, thus forming a hollow cylinder in three dimensions. Alternatively strengthening ridges may be formed, as along the fleshy petioles of celery (*Apium graveolus*) and the angular stems of plants such as dead-nettle (*Lamium*). In dicotyledonous leaves it appears as solid masses running the length of the midrib, providing support for the vascular bundles.

8.1.3 Sclerenchyma

The sole function of **sclerenchyma** is to assist in providing support and mechanical strength for the plant. Its distribution within the plant is related to the stresses to which different organs are subjected. Unlike collenchyma, the mature cells are dead and incapable of elongation so they do not mature until elongation of the living cells around them is complete.

Structure

There are two types of sclerenchyma cell, namely **fibres**, which are elongated cells, and **sclereids** or **stone cells**, which are usually roughly spherical, although both may vary considerably in size and shape. Their structures are shown in figs 8.5 and 8.6 respectively. In both cases the primary cell wall is heavily thickened with deposits of **lignin**, a hard substance with great tensile and compressional strength. A high tensile strength means that it does not break easily on stretching, and a high compressional strength means that it does not buckle easily.

Deposition of lignin takes place in and on the primary cellulose cell wall, and as the walls thicken, the living contents of the cells are lost with the result that the mature cells are dead. In both fibres and sclereids structures called **simple pits** appear in the walls as they thicken. These represent areas where lignin is not deposited on the primary wall owing to the presence of groups of **plasmodesmata** (strands of cytoplasm that connect neighbouring cells through minute pores in the adjacent cell walls). Each group of plasmodesmata forms one pit. The pits are described as simple because they are tubes of constant width. Their development is best explained diagrammatically as shown in fig 8.7.

Function and distribution of fibres

Individual sclerenchyma fibres are strong owing to their lignified walls. Collectively their strength is enhanced by their arrangement into strands or sheets of tissue that extend for considerable distances in a longitudinal direction. In addition, the ends of the cells interlock with one another, increasing their combined strength.

Fibres are found in the pericycle of stems, forming a solid

Fig 8.4 *Structure of collenchyma cells. (a) TS, cells are polygonal in outline. (b) LS, cells are elongated (up to 1 mm in length). (c) TS collenchyma from* Helianthus *stem. (d) LS collenchyma from* Helianthus *stem*

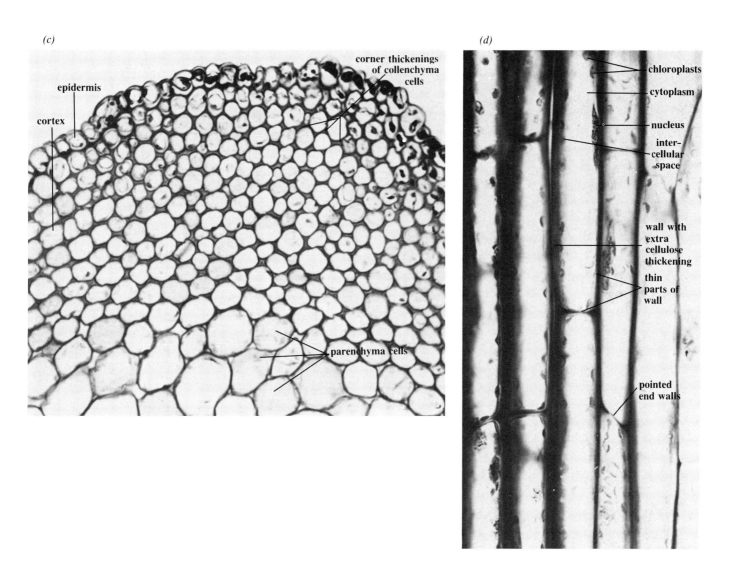

(a) **TS** Cells are polygonal in outline

vacuole
nucleus

normal living cell contents

cytoplasm

intercellular air spaces extremely small or non-existent

middle lamella

20 μm

thinner side walls

thickenings of extra cellulose at each corner

(b) **LS** Cells are elongated (up to 1 mm in length)

end walls often pointed

thick part of wall – thickenings run length of cell

thin part of wall

(c)

epidermis

cortex

corner thickenings of collenchyma cells

parenchyma cells

(d)

chloroplasts

cytoplasm

nucleus

inter-cellular space

wall with extra cellulose thickening

thin parts of wall

pointed end walls

221

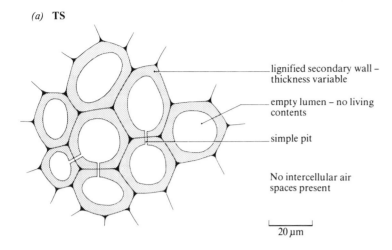

(a) **TS**

lignified secondary wall – thickness variable

empty lumen – no living contents

simple pit

No intercellular air spaces present

20 μm

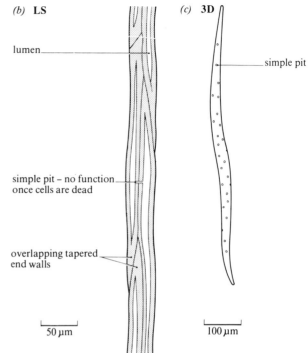

(b) **LS**

lumen

simple pit – no function once cells are dead

overlapping tapered end walls

50 μm

(c) **3D**

simple pit

100 μm

Fig 8.5 *Structure of sclerenchyma cells. (a) TS, cells are polygonal in outline. (b) LS, cells are elongated (length very variable, commonly > 1 mm, up to 250 mm reported). (c) Three-dimensional appearance. (d) TS sclerenchyma from* Helianthus *stem. (e) LS sclerenchyma from* Helianthus *stem*

(d)

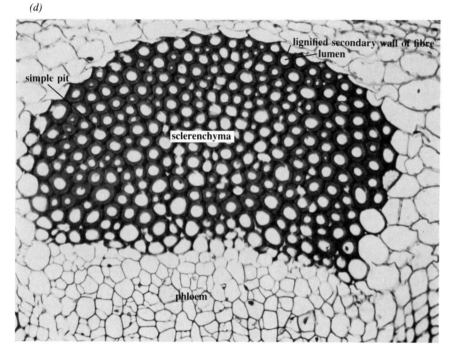

lignified secondary wall of fibre
lumen

simple pit

sclerenchyma

phloem

(e)

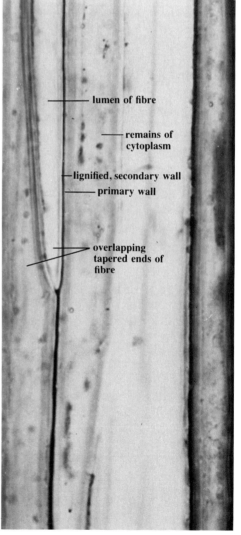

lumen of fibre

remains of cytoplasm

lignified, secondary wall
primary wall

overlapping tapered ends of fibre

(a)

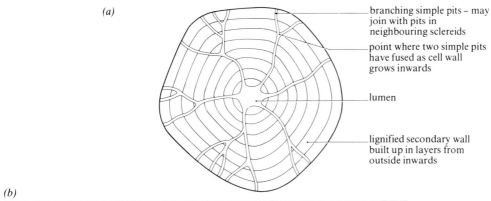

branching simple pits – may join with pits in neighbouring sclereids

point where two simple pits have fused as cell wall grows inwards

lumen

lignified secondary wall built up in layers from outside inwards

(b)

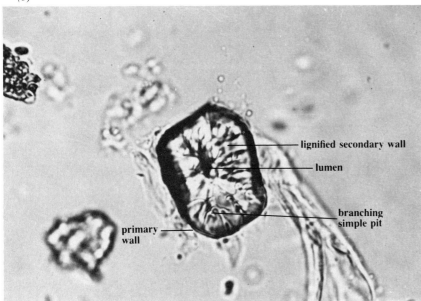

lignified secondary wall

lumen

branching simple pit

primary wall

Fig 8.6 *Structure of sclerenchyma sclereids. (a) TS or LS, cells are isodiametric. (b) Entire sclereid from macerated flesh of pear fruit (× 400)*

Fig 8.7 (below)   *Development of simple pits in sclerenchyma fibres and sclereids*

TS before lignification

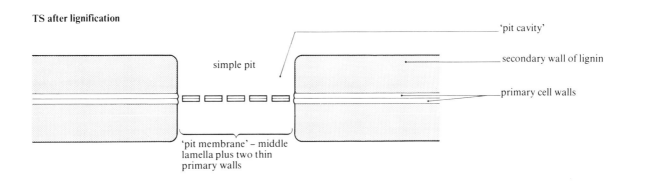

close group of plasmodesmata ('primary pit field') – primary cell walls are thinner in this area as a result of slower growth

adjacent primary cell walls of two cells

middle lamella

plasmodesma

TS after lignification

'pit cavity'

simple pit

secondary wall of lignin

primary cell walls

'pit membrane' – middle lamella plus two thin primary walls

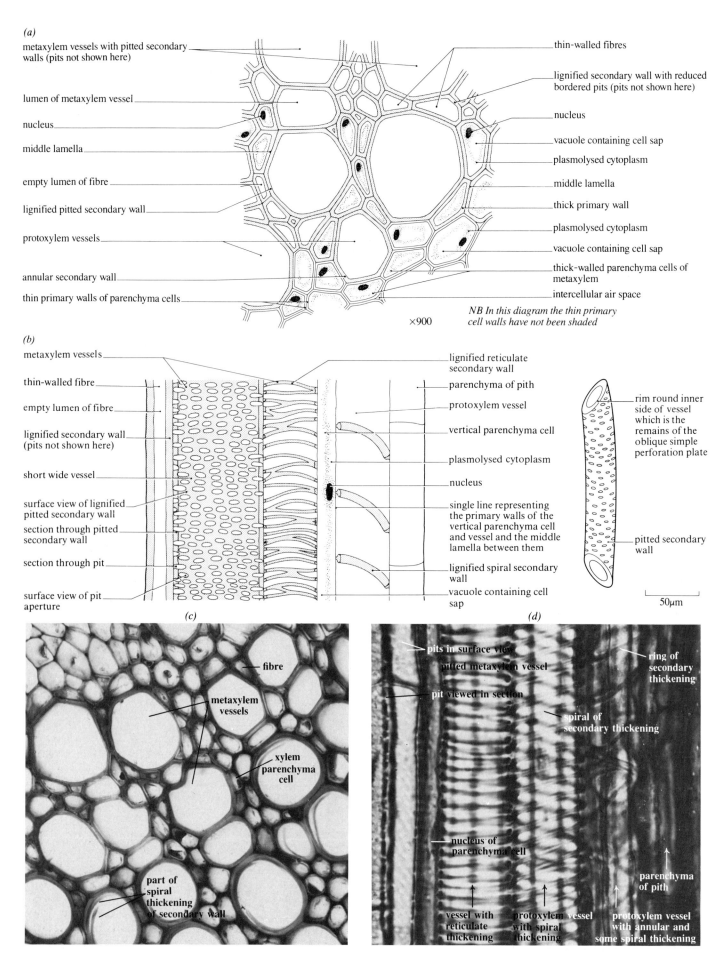

(a)

metaxylem vessels with pitted secondary walls (pits not shown here)

lumen of metaxylem vessel

nucleus

middle lamella

empty lumen of fibre

lignified pitted secondary wall

protoxylem vessels

annular secondary wall

thin primary walls of parenchyma cells

thin-walled fibres

lignified secondary wall with reduced bordered pits (pits not shown here)

nucleus

vacuole containing cell sap

plasmolysed cytoplasm

middle lamella

thick primary wall

plasmolysed cytoplasm

vacuole containing cell sap

thick-walled parenchyma cells of metaxylem

intercellular air space

×900

NB In this diagram the thin primary cell walls have not been shaded

(b)

metaxylem vessels

thin-walled fibre

empty lumen of fibre

lignified secondary wall (pits not shown here)

short wide vessel

surface view of lignified pitted secondary wall

section through pitted secondary wall

section through pit

surface view of pit aperture

lignified reticulate secondary wall

parenchyma of pith

protoxylem vessel

vertical parenchyma cell

plasmolysed cytoplasm

nucleus

single line representing the primary walls of the vertical parenchyma cell and vessel and the middle lamella between them

lignified spiral secondary wall

vacuole containing cell sap

rim round inner side of vessel which is the remains of the oblique simple perforation plate

pitted secondary wall

50μm

(c)

fibre

metaxylem vessels

xylem parenchyma cell

part of spiral thickening of secondary wall

(d)

pits in surface view

pitted metaxylem vessel

pit viewed in section

ring of secondary thickening

spiral of secondary thickening

nucleus of parenchyma cell

parenchyma of pith

vessel with reticulate thickening

protoxylem vessel with spiral thickening

protoxylem vessel with annular and some spiral thickening

224

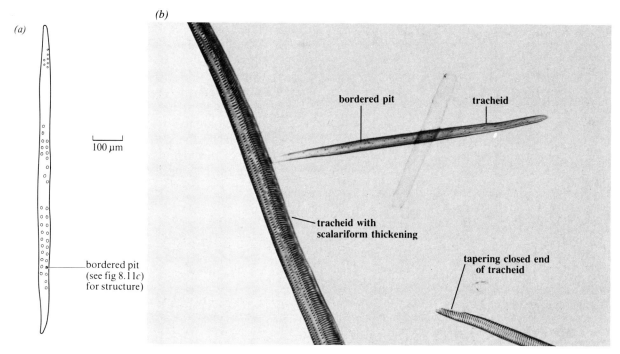

(a)

(b)

100 μm

bordered pit
(see fig 8.11c)
for structure)

bordered pit

tracheid

tracheid with
scalariform thickening

tapering closed end
of tracheid

Fig 8.8 (opposite) *Structure of primary xylem. (a) TS.
(b) LS. (c) TS primary xylem from Helianthus stem.
(d) LS primary xylem from Helianthus stem*

Fig 8.9 (above) *Structure of tracheids. (a) Tracheid with
bordered pits (tracheids may also have annular, spiral,
scalariform and reticulate thickening, like vessels, see fig
8.11g). (b) Tracheids from macerated wood of* Pinus *(× 120)*

rod of tissue 'capping' the vascular bundles of dicotyledons, and a hollow cylinder around the vascular bundles of monocotyledons (see fig 14.15). They often form a layer in the cortex below the epidermis of stems or roots, in the same way as collenchyma, forming a hollow cylinder that contains the rest of the cortex and vascular tissue. Fibres also occur in both xylem and phloem, either individually or in groups, as described in section 8.2.

Function and distribution of sclereids

Sclereids are generally scattered singly or in groups almost anywhere in the plant body, but are most common in the cortex, pith, phloem and in fruits and seeds.

Depending on numbers and position, they confer firmness or rigidity on those structures in which they are found. In the flesh of pear fruits they occur in small groups and are responsible for the 'grittiness' of these fruits when eaten. In some cases they form very resilient, solid layers, as in the shells of nuts, and the stones (endocarp) of stone fruits. In seeds they commonly toughen the testa (seed coat).

8.2 Plant tissues consisting of more than one type of cell

There are two types of conducting tissue in plants, namely **xylem** and **phloem**, both of which contain more than one type of cell. Together they constitute the **vascular tissue** whose function in translocation is described in chapter 14. Xylem conducts mainly water and mineral salts from the roots up to other parts of the plant, while phloem conducts mainly organic food from the leaves both up and down the plant. Both tissues may be increased in amount as a result of secondary growth as described in chapter 21. Secondary xylem may become extensive, when it is known as **wood**. The structure of wood is shown in figs 21.25 and 21.26.

8.2.1 Xylem

Xylem has two major functions, the conduction of water and mineral salts, and support. Thus it has both a physiological and a structural role in the plant. It consists of four cell types, namely tracheids, vessel elements, parenchyma and fibres. These are illustrated in TS and LS in fig 8.8.

Tracheids

Tracheids are single cells that are elongated and lignified. They have tapering end walls that overlap with adjacent tracheids in the same way as sclerenchyma fibres. Thus they have mechanical strength and give support to the plant. They are dead with empty lumens when mature. Tracheids represent the original, primitive water-conducting cells of vascular plants and are the only cells found in the xylem of the more ancestral vascular plants. They have given rise, in

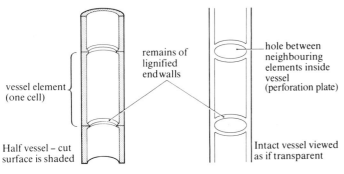

vessel element (one cell)

remains of lignified endwalls

Half vessel – cut surface is shaded

hole between neighbouring elements inside vessel (perforation plate)

Intact vessel viewed as if transparent

Fig 8.10 (above) *Fusion of vessel elements to form a vessel*

Fig 8.11 (below) *Structure of protoxylem and metaxylem vessels. (a) Protoxylem vessels. (b) Micrograph of annular and spiral protoxylem vessels. (c) Micrograph of metaxylem reticulate vessels from macerated wood.*

other plants, to xylem fibres and vessels which are described later. Despite their ancestral nature, they obviously function efficiently because conifers, most of which are trees, rely exclusively on tracheids to conduct water from the roots to the aerial parts. Water can pass through the empty lumens without being obstructed by living contents. It passes from tracheid to tracheid through the pits via the 'pit membranes', formed as described in fig 8.7, or through unlignified portions of the cell walls. The pattern of lignification of the walls resembles that of vessels which are described below. Fig 8.9 illustrates the structure of tracheids. Angiosperms have relatively fewer tracheids than vessels, and vessels are thought to be more effective transporting structures, possibly necessary owing to the larger leaves and higher transpiration rates of this group.

Vessels

Vessels are the characteristic conducting units of angiosperm xylem. They are very long, tubular structures formed by the fusion of several cells end to end in a row.

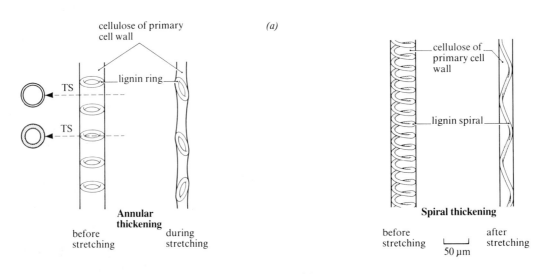

(a)

cellulose of primary cell wall

lignin ring

TS

TS

Annular thickening

before stretching

during stretching

cellulose of primary cell wall

lignin spiral

Spiral thickening

before stretching

after stretching

50 µm

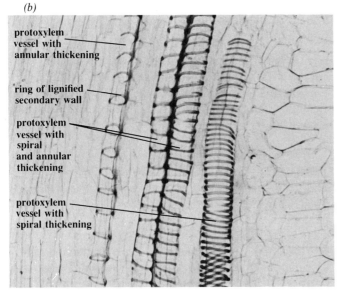

(b)

protoxylem vessel with annular thickening

ring of lignified secondary wall

protoxylem vessel with spiral and annular thickening

protoxylem vessel with spiral thickening

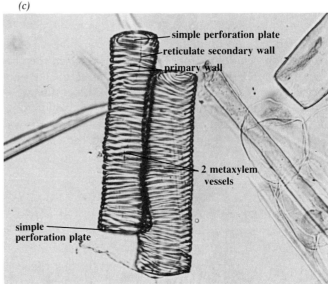

(c)

simple perforation plate

reticulate secondary wall

primary wall

2 metaxylem vessels

simple perforation plate

Fig 8.11 (cont.)   *(d) Pitted and reticulate metaxylem vessels.*
(e) Micrograph of metaxylem pitted vessel from macerated
wood. (f) Scanning electron micrograph of metaxylem vessels
(× 18 000). Appearance of these vessels in TS will vary
according to which part of the vessel is sectioned as indicated
in the diagram of extreme left vessel in part (a). (g) TS
bordered pit to show structure

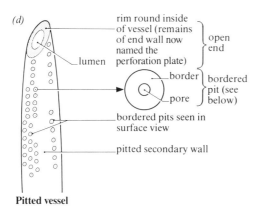

(d)

rim round inside
of vessel (remains
of end wall now
named the
perforation plate) — open end

lumen

border ⎤
pore ⎦ bordered pit (see below)

bordered pits seen in surface view

pitted secondary wall

Pitted vessel

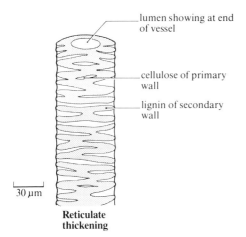

lumen showing at end of vessel

cellulose of primary wall

lignin of secondary wall

30 μm

Reticulate thickening

Size is very variable; the longest are several
metres in length, though commonly several
centimetres long.

Scalariform thickening is similar to reticulate but with fewer
interconnections between the bars of thickening. It is less
commonly seen. It usually grades into reticulate thickening by
progressive lignification

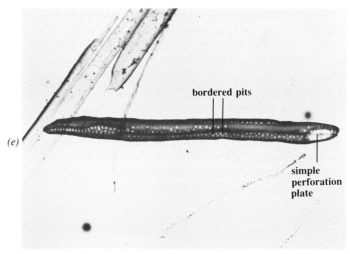

(e)

bordered pits

simple
perforation
plate

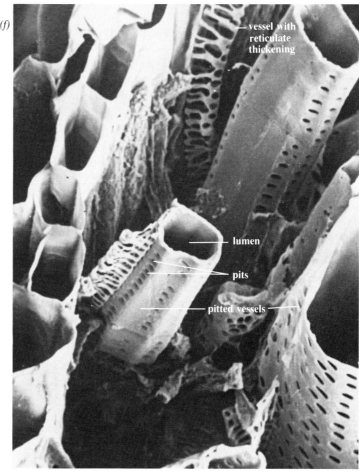

(f)

vessel with
reticulate
thickening

lumen

pits

pitted vessels

(g)

TS bordered pit to show structure

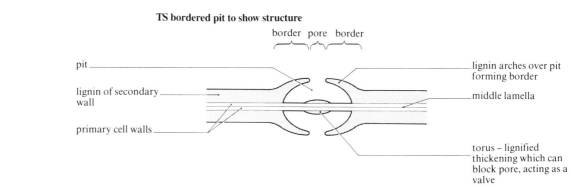

border pore border

pit

lignin of secondary wall

primary cell walls

lignin arches over pit forming border

middle lamella

torus – lignified
thickening which can
block pore, acting as a
valve

227

Each of the cells forming a xylem vessel is equivalent to a tracheid and is called a **vessel element**. However, vessel elements are shorter and wider than tracheids. The first xylem to appear in the growing plant is called **primary xylem** and develops in the root and shoot apices. Differentiated xylem vessel elements appear in rows at the edges of the procambial strands (shown in figs 21.18 and 21.20). A vessel is formed when the neighbouring vessel elements of a given row fuse as a result of their end walls breaking down. A series of rims is left around the inner side of the vessel marking the remains of the end walls. The fusion of elements is shown in fig 8.10.

Protoxylem and metaxylem

The first vessels form the **protoxylem**, located in the part of the apex, just behind the apical meristem, where elongation of surrounding cells is still occurring. Mature protoxylem vessels can be stretched as surrounding cells elongate because lignin is not deposited over the entire cellulose wall, but only in rings or in spirals as shown in fig 8.11. These act as reinforcement for the tubes during elongation of the stem or root. As growth proceeds more xylem vessels develop and these undergo more extensive lignification completing their development in the mature regions of the organ and forming **metaxylem**. Meanwhile, the earliest protoxylem vessels have stretched and collapsed. Mature metaxylem vessels cannot stretch or grow because they are dead, rigid, fully lignified tubes and were they to develop before the living cells around them had finished elongating they would impose severe restraints on elongation.

Metaxylem vessels show three basic patterns of lignification, namely scalariform, reticulate and pitted, as shown in fig 8.11.

The long, empty tubes of xylem provide an ideal system for translocating large quantities of water over long distances with minimal obstruction to flow. As with tracheids, water can pass from vessel to vessel through pits or through unlignified portions of the cell wall. The walls also have high tensile strength, being lignified, another important feature because it prevents tubes collapsing when conducting water under tension (section 14.4).

The second main function of xylem, namely support, is also fulfilled by the collection of lignified tubes. In the primary plant body the distribution of xylem in the roots is central, helping to withstand the tugging strains of the aerial parts as they bend or lean over. In the stems the vascular bundles are arranged either peripherally in a ring, as in dicotyledons, or scattered, as in monocotyledons, so that in both cases separate rods of xylem run through the stem and provide some support. The supporting function becomes much more important if secondary growth takes place. During this process extensive growth of secondary xylem occurs which supports the large structure of trees and shrubs, taking over from collenchyma and sclerenchyma as the chief mechanical tissue. The nature and extent of the thickness is modified to some extent by the stresses received by the growing plant, so that reinforcement growth can occur and give maximum support.

Xylem parenchyma

Xylem parenchyma occurs in both primary and secondary xylem but it is more extensive and assumes greater importance in the latter. It has thin cellulose cell walls and living contents, as is typical of parenchyma.

Two systems of parenchyma exist in secondary xylem, derived from meristematic cells called ray initials and fusiform initials, as described in section 21.6.6 and fig 21.21. The ray parenchyma is the more extensive (fig 21.24). It forms radial sheets of tissue called medullary rays which maintain a living link through the wood between the pith and cortex. Its functions include food storage, deposition of tannins, crystals and so on, radial transport of food and water, and gaseous exchange through the intercellular spaces.

Fusiform initials normally give rise to xylem vessels or phloem sieve tubes and companion cells but occasionally they give rise to parenchyma cells. These form vertical rows of parenchyma in the secondary xylem.

Xylem fibres

Xylem fibres, like xylem vessels, are thought to have originated from tracheids. They are shorter and narrower than tracheids and have much thicker walls, but they have pits similar to those in tracheids and are often difficult to distinguish from them in section because intermediate cell types occur. Xylem fibres closely resemble the sclerenchyma fibres already described, having overlapping end walls. Since they do not conduct water they can have much thicker walls and narrower lumens than xylem vessels and are therefore stronger and confer additional mechanical strength to the xylem.

8.2.2 Phloem

Phloem resembles xylem in possessing tubular structures modified for translocation. However, the tubes are composed of living cells with cytoplasm and have no mechanical function. There are five cell types in the phloem, namely sieve tube elements, companion cells, parenchyma, fibres and sclereids.

Sieve tubes and companion cells

Sieve tubes are the long tube-like structures that translocate solutions of organic solutes like sucrose throughout the plant. They are formed by the end-to-end fusion of cells called **sieve tube elements** or **sieve elements**. Rows of these cells can be seen developing from the procambial strands of apical meristems where primary phloem develops, together with primary xylem, in vascular bundles.

The first phloem formed is called **protophloem** and, like protoxylem, it is produced in the zone of elongation of the growing root or stem (figs 21.18 and 21.20). As the tissues around it grow and elongate it becomes stretched and much of it eventually collapses and becomes non-functional.

Fig 8.12 *Structure of phloem. (a) Diagram of TS. (b) Micrograph of TS of primary phloem of* Helianthus *stem (× 450). (c) Diagram of LS. (d) Micrograph of LS of primary phloem of* Cucurbita *stem (× 432)*

(b)

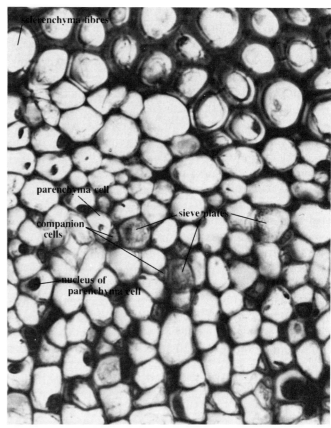

sclerenchyma fibres

parenchyma cell

companion cells

sieve plates

nucleus of parenchyma cell

(a) **TS**

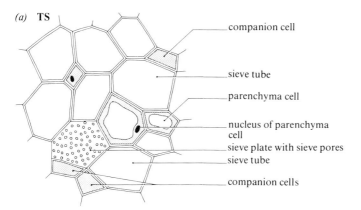

companion cell

sieve tube

parenchyma cell

nucleus of parenchyma cell

sieve plate with sieve pores

sieve tube

companion cells

(c) **LS**

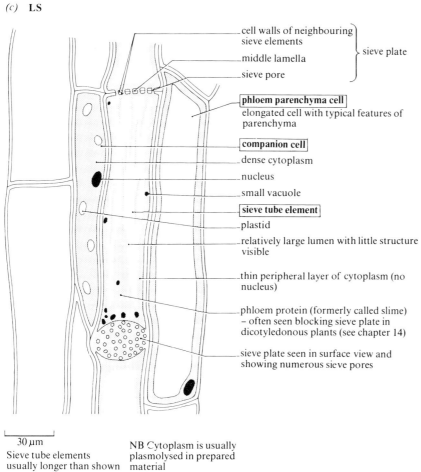

cell walls of neighbouring sieve elements

middle lamella

sieve pore

} sieve plate

phloem parenchyma cell
elongated cell with typical features of parenchyma

companion cell

dense cytoplasm

nucleus

small vacuole

sieve tube element

plastid

relatively large lumen with little structure visible

thin peripheral layer of cytoplasm (no nucleus)

phloem protein (formerly called slime) – often seen blocking sieve plate in dicotyledonous plants (see chapter 14)

sieve plate seen in surface view and showing numerous sieve pores

30 μm

Sieve tube elements usually longer than shown

NB Cytoplasm is usually plasmolysed in prepared material

(d)

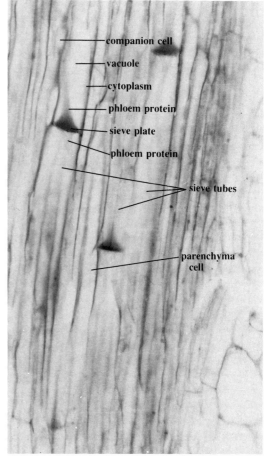

companion cell

vacuole

cytoplasm

phloem protein

sieve plate

phloem protein

sieve tubes

parenchyma cell

229

Meanwhile, however, more phloem continues to be produced and the phloem that matures after elongation has ceased is called **metaphloem**.

Sieve tube elements have a very distinctive structure. Their walls are made of cellulose and pectic substances, like parenchyma cells, but their nuclei degenerate and are lost as they mature and the cytoplasm becomes confined to a thin layer around the periphery of the cell. Although they lack nuclei, the sieve elements remain living but are dependent on the adjacent companion cells which develop from the same original meristematic cell. The two cells together form a functional unit, the companion cell having dense, very active cytoplasm. The detailed structure of the cells is revealed by the electron microscope and is described in chapter 14 (see figs 14.22 and 14.23 and section 14.2.2).

A conspicuous and characteristic feature of sieve tubes that is visible in the light microscope is the **sieve plate**. This is derived from the two adjoining end walls of neighbouring sieve elements. Originally plasmodesmata run through the walls but the canals enlarge to form pores, making the walls look like a sieve and allowing a flow of solution from one element to the next. Thus sieve tubes are spanned at intervals by sieve plates that mark successive sieve elements. The structure of sieve tubes, companion cells and phloem parenchyma as seen with the electron microscope is shown in fig 8.12.

Secondary phloem, which develops from the vascular cambium like secondary xylem, appears similar in structure to primary phloem except that it is crossed by bands of lignified fibres and medullary rays of parenchyma as shown in figs 21.25 and 21.26. It is much less extensive than secondary xylem and is constantly being replaced as described in section 21.6.

Phloem parenchyma, fibres and sclereids

Phloem parenchyma and fibres are found in dicotyledons but not in monocotyledons. Phloem parenchyma has the same structure as parenchyma elsewhere, though the cells

are generally elongated. In secondary phloem, parenchyma occurs in medullary rays and vertical strands as already described for xylem parenchyma. Phloem parenchyma and xylem parenchyma have the same functions.

Phloem fibres are exactly similar to the sclerenchyma fibres already described. They occur occasionally in the primary phloem, but more frequently in the secondary phloem of dicotyledons. In secondary phloem they form vertically running bands of cells. Since the secondary phloem is subject to stretching as growth continues, the sclerenchyma probably helps to resist this pressure.

Sclereids occur frequently in phloem, especially in older phloem.

8.3   Animal epithelial tissue

Epithelial tissue is arranged in single or multilayered sheets and covers the internal and external surfaces of the body of an organism. True epithelial tissue arises embryonically from either the ectoderm, which provides epithelium for the skin, nervous system and parts of the fore- and hindgut, or the endoderm, which provides epithelium for the remainder of the alimentary canal, the liver and pancreas. It should be mentioned here that the inner lining of blood vessels, called endothelium, is not true

Table 8.2 Classification of epithelial tissues.

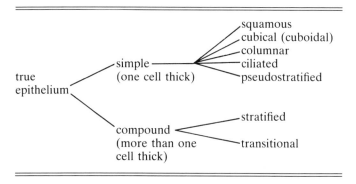

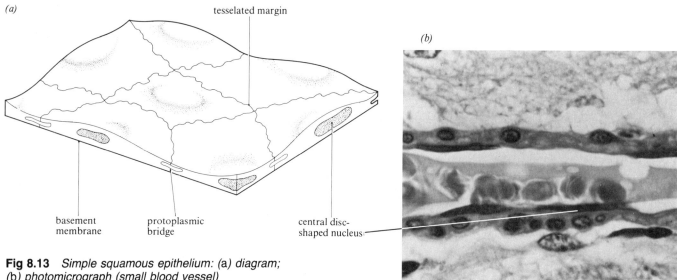

Fig 8.13 *Simple squamous epithelium: (a) diagram; (b) photomicrograph (small blood vessel)*

epithelium as it is derived from embryonic mesoderm.

Epithelial cells are held together by small amounts of cementing substance containing a carbohydrate derivative called hyaluronic acid. The bottom layer of cells rests on a **basement membrane** composed of a network of collagenous fibres usually secreted by underlying tissues. As epithelial cells are not supplied with blood vessels, they rely on diffusion of oxygen and nutrients from lymph vessels which ramify adjacent intercellular spaces. Nerve endings may penetrate the epithelium.

Epithelial tissue functions to protect underlying structures from injury through abrasion or pressure, and from infection. Stress is combated by the tissue becoming thickened and keratinised, and where cells are sloughed off due to constant friction the epithelium shows a very rapid rate of cell division so that lost cells are speedily replaced. The free surface of the epithelium is often highly differentiated and may be absorptive, secretory or excretory in function, or bear sensory cells and nerve endings specialised for stimulus reception.

Epithelial tissues are classified into the following types indicated in table 8.2 according to the number of cell layers and the shape of the individual cells. In many areas of the body the different cell types intermix and the epithelia cannot be classified into distinct types.

(a)

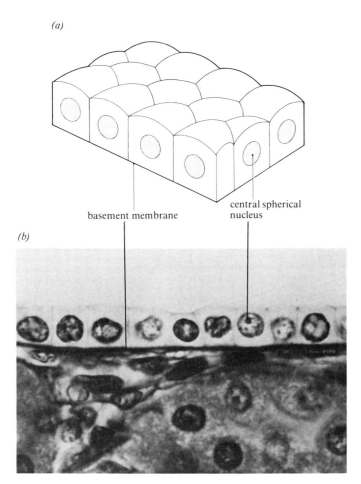

basement membrane

central spherical nucleus

(b)

Fig 8.14 *Cubical (cuboidal) epithelium: (a) diagram; (b) photomicrograph (kidney)*

8.3.1 Simple epithelia

Squamous epithelium

The cells are thin, flattened and contain little cytoplasm enclosing a centrally placed disc-shaped nucleus (fig 8.13). The margins of squamous cells are tesselated (irregular) and provide a mosaic outline in surface view. There are often protoplasmic connections between adjacent cells which help to bind them firmly together. Squamous epithelium occurs in areas such as the Bowman's capsules of the kidney, the alveolar lining of the lungs and the blood capillary walls where its thinness permits diffusion of materials through it. It also provides smooth linings to hollow structures such as blood vessels and the chambers of the heart where it allows the relatively friction-free passage of fluids through them.

Cubical epithelium

This is the least specialised of all epithelia and, as the name implies, the cells are cube-shaped and possess a central spherical nucleus (fig 8.14). When viewed from the surface the cells are either pentagonal or hexagonal in outline. They form the lining of many ducts such as the salivary, pancreatic and collecting ducts of the kidney where they are non-secretory. Cubical epithelium in other parts of the body is secretory and is found in many glands such as the salivary, mucus, sweat and thyroid glands.

Columnar epithelium

These cells are tall and quite narrow, thus providing more cytoplasm per unit area of epithelium (fig 8.15). Each cell possesses a nucleus situated at its basal end. Secretory goblet cells are often interspersed among the epithelial cells and the epithelium may be secretory and/or absorptive in function. There is frequently a conspicuous striated border of **microvilli** at the free surface end of each cell which increases the surface area of the cell for absorption and secretion. Columnar epithelium lines the stomach, where mucus secreted by goblet cells protects the stomach lining from the acidic contents of the stomach and from digestion by enzymes. It also lines the intestine where mucus again protects it from self-digestion and at the same time lubricates the passage of food. In the small intestine digested food is actually absorbed through the epithelium into the bloodstream. Columnar epithelium lines and protects many kidney ducts, and is a component of the thyroid gland and gall bladder.

Ciliated epithelium

Cells of this tissue are usually columnar in shape but bear numerous cilia at their free surfaces (fig 8.16). They are always associated with mucus-secreting goblet cells producing fluids in which the cilia set up currents. Ciliated epithelium lines the oviducts, ventricles of the brain, the spinal canal and the respiratory passages, where it serves to move materials from one location to another.

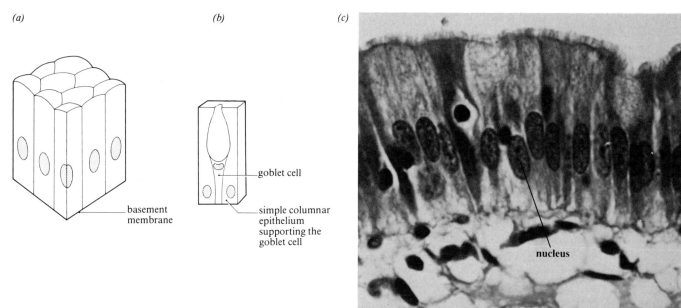

(a)   *(b)*   *(c)*

goblet cell

simple columnar
epithelium
supporting the
goblet cell

basement
membrane

nucleus

Fig 8.15 *(a) Columnar epithelium, (b) showing goblet cell,
(c) photomicrograph of columnar epithelium (trachea)*

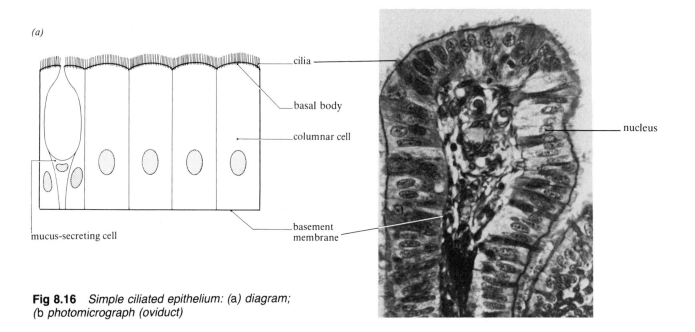

(a)

cilia

basal body

columnar cell

nucleus

mucus-secreting cell

basement
membrane

Fig 8.16 *Simple ciliated epithelium: (a) diagram;
(b photomicrograph (oviduct)*

Pseudostratified epithelium

When viewed in section the nuclei of this type of epithelium
appear to be at several different levels because all the cells
do not reach the free surface (fig 8.17). Nevertheless the
epithelium is still only one layer of cells thick with each cell
attached to the basement membrane. This epithelium is
found lining the urinary tract, the trachea (as pseudostratified columnar), other respiratory passages as (pseudostratified columnar ciliated) and as a component of the
olfactory mucosa.

8.3.2   Compound epithelia

Stratified epithelium

This tissue comprises a number of layers of cells, is
correspondingly thicker than simple epithelium and forms
a relatively tough, impervious barrier. The cells are formed
by mitotic division of the germinal layer which rests on the
basement membrane (fig 8.18). The first-formed cells are
cuboid in shape, but as they are pushed outwards towards
the free surface of the tissue they become flattened. In this
condition the cells are called **squames**. They may remain
uncornified, as in the oesophagus, where the epithelium
protects the underlying tissues against mechanical damage

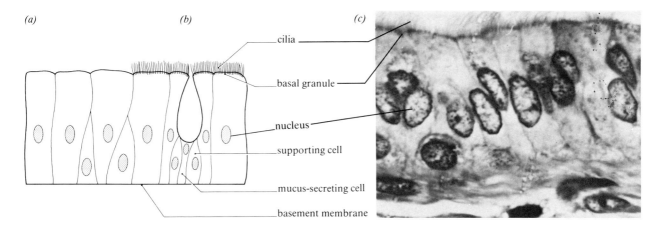

cilia

basal granule

nucleus

supporting cell

mucus-secreting cell

basement membrane

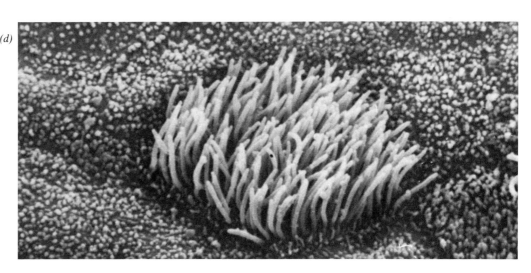

Fig 8.17 *Pseudostratified epithelium: (a) columnar; (b) ciliated; (c) photomicrograph of respiratory, ciliated epithelium; (d) scanning electron micrograph of cilia*

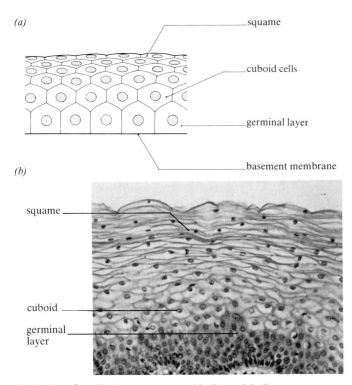

(a)

squame

cuboid cells

germinal layer

basement membrane

(b)

squame

cuboid

germinal layer

Fig 8.18 *Stratified squamous epithelium: (a) diagram; (b) photomicrograph (vagina)*

by friction with food just swallowed. In other areas of the body the squames may be transformed into a dead horny layer of **keratin** which ultimately flakes away. In this condition the epithelium is said to be **cornified**, and is found in particular abundance on external skin surfaces, lining the buccal cavity and the vagina, where it affords protection against abrasion.

According to the shape of the cells which make up the stratified epithelium, it may be termed stratified squamous (located in parts of the oesophagus), stratified cuboidal (in the sweat gland ducts), stratified columnar (in the mammary gland ducts), and stratified transitional (in the bladder).

Transitional epithelium

This is often regarded as a modified type of stratified epithelium. It consists of 3–4 layers of cells all of similar size and shape except at the free surface where they are more flattened (fig 8.19). The superficial cells do not slough off, and all cells are able to modify their shape when placed under differing conditions. This property is important in locations where structures are subjected to considerable distention such as the urinary bladder, ureter and the pelvic region of the kidney. The thickness of the tissue also prevents urine escaping into the surrounding tissues.

233

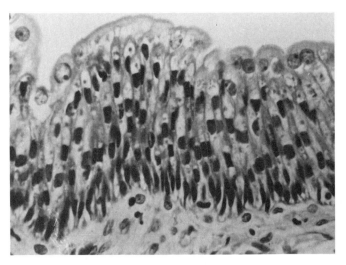

Fig 8.19 *Transitional epithelium (bladder)*

surface via ducts (table 8.3). **Endocrine** are glands where the secretion is passed directly into the bloodstream. Endocrine glands possess no ducts and are alternatively termed **ductless glands** (section 16.6 and fig 8.20).

The secretions produced by glandular cells are released in three different ways. In **merocrine glands** the secretion, produced within the cells, is simply passed through the cell membrane at the cell's free surface. No cytoplasm is lost. This occurs in simple goblet cells, the sweat glands and the exocrine regions of the vertebrate pancreas. In **apocrine glands** a portion of the cell's distal cytoplasm is lost as the secretion is released, as in the secretions of the mammary glands. In **holocrine glands** the whole cell breaks down to release its secretory product and is extruded from the epithelial layer. Sebaceous glands show this mode of secretion.

Sometimes a cell may secrete different materials each by

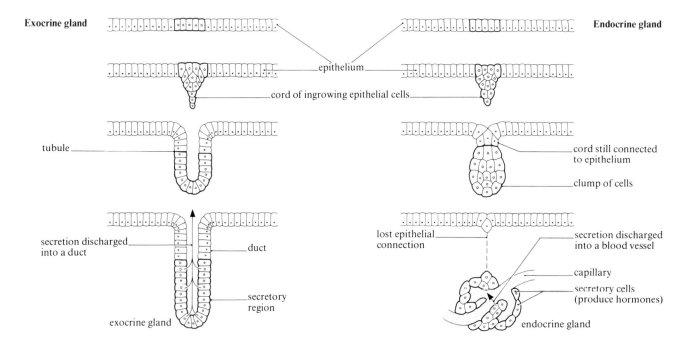

Fig 8.20 *The development of exocrine and endocrine glands (From Freeman & Bracegirdle (1975)* An atlas of histology, *Heinemann Education Books Ltd., London.)*

8.3.3 Glandular epithelia

Amongst the epithelial cells there may be individual glandular cells, such as the **goblet cells**, or aggregates of glandular cells forming a **multicellular gland**. An epithelium containing many goblet cells is called a mucous membrane.

Two types of glandular cell exist, called exocrine and endocrine. **Exocrine** are those where the secretion is delivered to the free surface of the epithelium (fig 8.20). Multicellular exocrine glands pass their products to the

a different method. Such an example can be found in the mammary gland where a lipid product is secreted by the apocrine mechanism and a protein secretion is released in a merocrine fashion.

If the glandular cells secrete a viscous mucous product they are called **mucous cells** or **mucocytes**, whereas if the secretion is clear, watery in consistency and contains enzymes they are termed **serous cells** or **serocytes**. If both kinds of secretion are produced within the same gland then the gland is called a **mixed gland**.

Multicellular exocrine glands exist in a number of forms of variable complexity as shown in table 8.3.

8.4 Animal connective tissue

Connective tissue is the major supporting tissue of the body. It includes the skeletal tissue, bone and

Type of gland	Structure	Location	Type of gland	Structure	Location
Simple tubular	secretory portion tubular in design	Crypts of Lieberkühn in the ileum of higher vertebrates Fundic region of stomach	Simple alveolar	secretory portion sac-like in construction	Mucus glands in skin of frog
Simple coiled tubular		Sweat glands in Man	Simple branched alveolar		Sebaceous glands in mammalian skin
Simple branched tubular		Fundic region of stomach Brunner's glands in mammalian small intestine	Compound alveolar		Exocrine parts of pancreas Mammary gland
Compound tubular		Brunner's glands in mammal Salivary glands	Compound tubular-alveolar	many branched ducts possessing a mixture of tubular and alveolar secretory portions	Submaxillary glands Mammary glands Salivary glands

Table 8.3 Different forms of multicellular exocrine glands.

Table 8.4 Types of connective tissue.

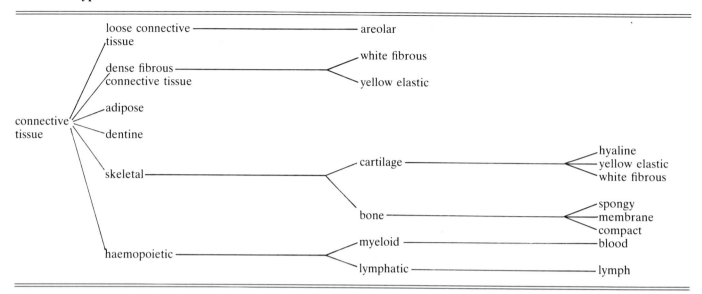

cartilage, and in addition it binds other tissues together, for example the skin with underlying structures, or the epithelia of mesenteries. This tissue also forms sheaths around the organs of the body, separating them so that they do not interfere with each other's activities, as well as embedding and protecting blood vessels and nerves where they enter or leave organs. Connective tissue is a composite structure made up of a variety of cells developed from mesenchyme originating in the embryonic mesoderm, several types of fibre which are non-living products of the cells, and a fluid or semi-fluid intercellular matrix consisting of hyaluronic acid, chondroitin, chondroitin sulphate and keratin sulphate.

The cells are usually widely separated from each other and their metabolic needs relatively small. An extensive vascular network is often present in various parts of the body (as in the dermis of the skin) but this is primarily concerned with supplying other structures, such as the epithelium, with oxygen and nutrients rather than the connective tissue itself. Connective tissue may be subdivided into a number of types as indicated in table 8.4.

This tissue fulfils many functions other than packing and binding other structures together, such as providing protection against wounding or bacterial invasion (areolar), insulation of the body against heat loss (adipose), providing a supportive framework for the body (cartilage and bone) and producing blood (haemopoietic tissue).

8.4.1 Loose connective tissue

This tissue contains cells widely dispersed in intercellular material and has fibres loosely woven in a random manner.

Areolar

Areolar tissue possesses a transparent semi-fluid matrix which contains a mixture of mucin, hyaluronic acid and chondroitin sulphate. Scattered throughout are numerous

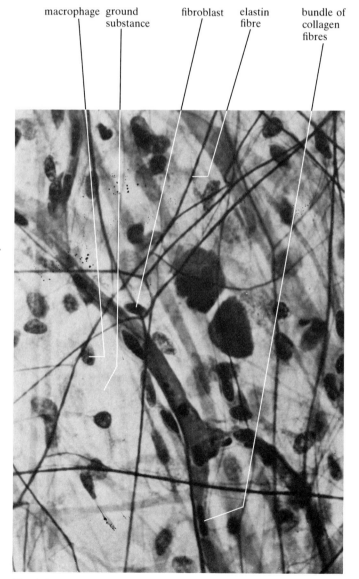

Fig 8.21 *Loose areolar tissue*

wavy bundles of **collagen fibres** and a loose anastomosing network of thin straight fibres of **elastin** (fig 8.21). Collagen fibres are flexible but inelastic whilst elastin fibres are flexible and elastic. Together the fibres endow the tissue with considerable tensile strength and resilience. Very fine and thread-like **reticular fibres** are present, located around blood vessels and nerves, and form the connective tissue covering around muscle fibres. It is thought that reticular fibres may be immature collagen fibres. Interspersed in the matrix are a variety of different cell types. They include fibroblasts, macrophages, mast cells, plasma cells, chromatophores, fat and mesenchyme cells. **Fibroblasts** are the cells which produce the fibres. They are flattened and spindle-shaped and contain an oval nucleus. Generally they lie closely applied to the fibres they synthesise, but can migrate towards wounded tissue and secrete more fibres in this region to effectively seal off the injured area. **Macrophages (histiocytes)** are polymorphic cells capable of amoeboid locomotion, which engulf bacteria or other foreign particles. Generally they are immobile, but at times cells wander to areas of bacterial invasion and therefore provide a means of defence for the body. Together with the reticular cells of the lymphatic system they comprise the **reticulo-endothelial system** of the body (section 14.11.2). **Mast cells** are oval-shaped, small and contain granular cytoplasm. They secrete the matrix as well as heparin and histamine, and are found in abundance close to blood vessels. **Heparin** is an anticoagulant present in all mammalian tissues. It neutralises the action of thrombin, preventing the conversion of prothrombin to thrombin. **Histamine** is released from tissues when they are injured or disrupted in any way. It causes vasodilation, contraction of smooth muscle and stimulates gastric secretion. **Plasma**

cells are rare and are the products of mitotic cell division by migratory lymphocytes. When present they produce antibodies which are important components of the body's immune system (section 14.14). **Chromatophores** are present in specialised areas, such as the skin and the eye. The cells are much branched and densely packed with melanin granules. Each **fat cell** contains a large lipid droplet which fills the bulk of the cell. The cytoplasm and nucleus are confined to the margins. **Mesenchyme cells** act as a reserve of undifferentiated cells for the tissue. They can be stimulated to transform into one of the above cell types as the need arises.

Areolar tissue is found around all the organs of the body, it connects the skin to the structures below, and binds sheets of epithelia to form mesenteries. It also ensheathes blood vessels and nerves where they enter or leave organs.

8.4.2 Dense (compact) fibrous connective tissue

This tissue has more fibres situated in the matrix than cells. The fibres may be irregularly arranged, or orientated such that the individual fibres lie more or less parallel to each other.

White fibrous

This is a tough, shiny tissue composed of numerous highly organised bundles of collagen fibres closely packed together and running parallel to each other (fig 8.22). Rows of fibroblasts are interspersed among the collagen and run alongside the bundles. Each bundle is bound to its neighbours by areolar tissue. The tissue is strong, flexible, yet inextensible and its tensile strength is achieved by the presence of collagen. Each strand of collagen possesses

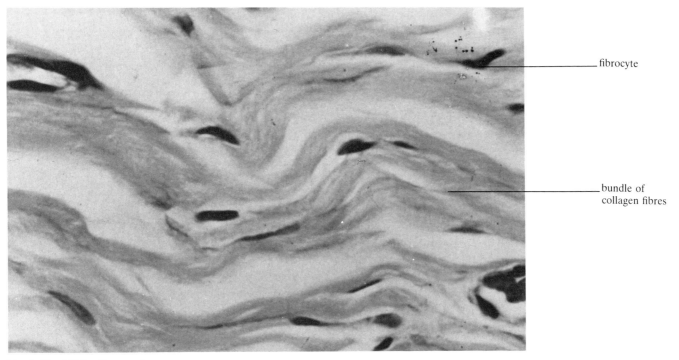

fibrocyte

bundle of collagen fibres

Fig 8.22 *White fibrous tissue*

237

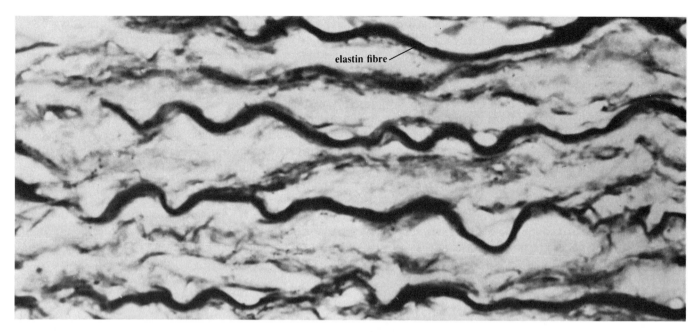

elastin fibre

three chains of tropocollagen plaited together as in a rope (section 5.5.3). The fibres are precisely organised so that they run parallel to the lines of stress which are encountered as a result of the functions carried out by the structures containing collagen.

White fibrous tissue is abundant in tendons, some ligaments, the sclerotic and cornea of the eye, the kidney capsule, and the perichondrium and periosteum of cartilage and bone respectively.

Yellow elastic

In contrast to white fibrous tissue, this possesses a loose network of irregularly arranged branched yellow elastic fibres (fig 8.23). The fibroblasts are randomly scattered throughout the matrix and some fine collagen fibres are also present. The elastic fibres endow the tissue with elasticity and flexibility and the collagen gives it strength. The tissue is located in ligaments, the walls of arteries, as a component of the lung and associated air passages, and in the great cords of the neck.

8.4.3 Adipose tissue

This tissue has no specific matrix of its own and is really areolar tissue containing large numbers of fat cells arranged into lobules. Each cell is filled almost entirely by a central fat droplet which squeezes the cytoplasm and nucleus to the periphery (fig 8.24).

In mammals, adipose tissue is found in the dermis of the skin, the mesenteries, and around the kidneys and heart. It provides a considerable energy reserve, acts as a shock absorber, and insulates against heat loss.

8.4.4 Skeletal tissues

Cartilage

Cartilage is a connective tissue consisting of cells embedded in a resilient matrix of chondrin. The matrix is

Fig 8.23 (above) *Yellow elastic tissue*
Fig 8.24 (below) *Adipose tissue*

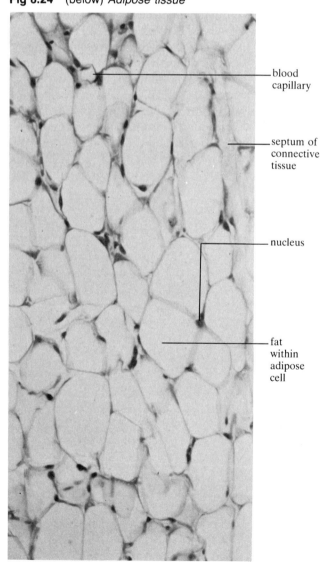

blood capillary

septum of connective tissue

nucleus

fat within adipose cell

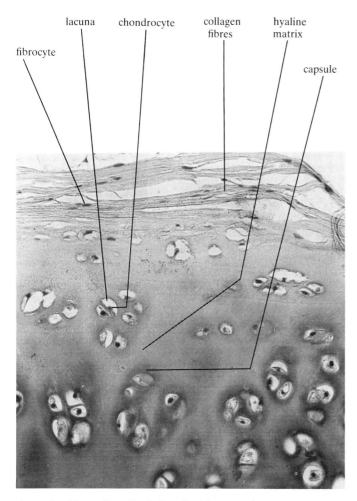

fibrocyte — lacuna — chondrocyte — collagen fibres — hyaline matrix — capsule

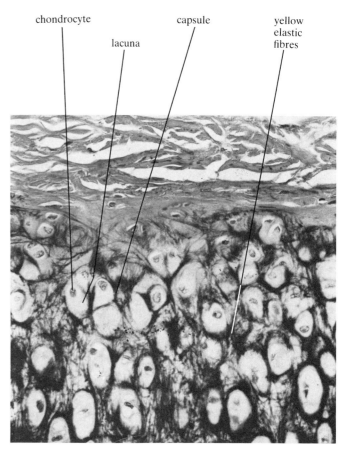

chondrocyte — lacuna — capsule — yellow elastic fibres

Fig 8.25 (left) *Hyaline cartilage*

Fig 8.26 (above) *Elastic cartilage*

deposited by cells called **chondroblasts** and possesses many fine fibrils mostly made up of collagen. Eventually the chondroblasts become enclosed in spaces called **lacunae**. In this condition they are termed **chondrocytes**. The margin of a piece of cartilage is enclosed by a dense layer of cells and fibrils called the **perichondrium**. From here new chondroblasts are produced, which are constantly added to the internal matrix of the cartilage.

Cartilage is a hard but flexible tissue. It is highly adapted to resist any strains that are placed upon it. The matrix is compressible and elastic and is able to absorb mechanical shocks such as frequently occur between the articular surfaces of bones. The collagen fibrils resist any tension which may be imposed on the tissue.

Three types of cartilage are recognisable. For each type the organic components of the matrix are quite distinct.

Hyaline cartilage (fig 8.25). The matrix is a semi-transparent material consisting of chondroitin sulphate and frequently fine collagen fibrils. The peripheral chondrocytes are flattened in shape whereas those situated internally are angular. Each chondrocyte is contained in a lacuna, and each lacuna may enclose one, two, four or eight chondrocytes.

Unlike bone, no processes extend from the lacunae into the matrix, neither are there blood vessels in this area. All exchange of materials between the chondrocytes and the

matrix occurs by diffusion.

Hyaline cartilage is an elastic, compressible tissue located at the ends of bones, in the nose and air passages of the respiratory system and in parts of the ear. It is the only type of skeletal material found in elasmobranchs and forms the embryonic skeleton in bony vertebrates.

Yellow elastic cartilage (fig 8.26). The matrix is semi-opaque and contains a network of yellow elastic fibres. They confer greater elasticity and flexibility than is found in hyaline cartilage and permit the tissue to quickly recover its shape after distortion. It is located in the external ear, eustachian tube, the epiglottis and cartilages of the pharynx.

White fibrous cartilage (fig 8.27). This consists of large numbers of bundles of densely packed white collagen fibres embedded in the matrix. This provides greater tensile strength than hyaline cartilage, as well as a small degree of flexibility. White fibrous cartilage is located as discs between adjacent vertebrae (intervertebral discs) where it provides a cushioning effect. It is also found in the symphysis pubis (the region between the two pubic bones of the pelvis) and the ligamentous capsules of joints.

Bone

Bone is the most abundant of all animal skeletal materials

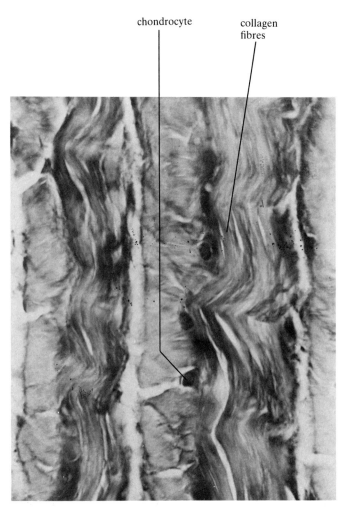

chondrocyte   collagen fibres

Fig 8.27 *White fibrous cartilage*

providing supportive, metabolic and protective functions for those possessing it. It is a calcified connective tissue made up of cells embedded in a firm matrix. About 30% of the matrix is composed of organic material consisting chiefly of collagen fibrils, whilst 70% is inorganic bone salts. The chief inorganic constituent of bone is hydroxyapatite, $Ca_{10}(PO_4)_6(OH)_2$, but sodium, magnesium, potassium, chloride, fluoride, hydrogencarbonate and citrate ions are also present in variable amounts.

Bone cells, called **osteoblasts**, are contained in lacunae which are present throughout the matrix. They lay down the inorganic components of bone. Fine canals containing cytoplasm connect the lacunae to each other and blood vessels passing through them provide the means by which osteoblasts exchange materials.

The structure of bone is specially designed to withstand the compression strains falling upon it and to resist tension. When the bone fibrils are laid down they are impregnated by apatite crystals. This arrangement provides maximum strength for the bone.

Bone resorption and reconstruction processes enable a particular bone to adapt its structure to meet any change in the mechanical requirements of the animal during its development. Calcium and phosphate may be released into the blood as needed, under the control of two hormones, **parathormone** and **calcitonin** (sections 16.6.4 and 16.6.5).

Compact or dense bone (fig 8.28). A transverse section of compact bone shows it to consist of numerous cylinders of concentric bony **lamellae** each surrounding a central **Haversian canal**. One such cylinder plus its canal is termed an **Haversian system** or **osteon**.

Interspersed between the lamellae are numerous lacunae containing living bone cells called **osteoblasts**. Each cell is capable of bone deposition. Its cytoplasm possesses a well-defined rough endoplasmic reticulum and Golgi apparatus and is rich in RNA. When osteoblasts are not active they are termed **osteocytes**. In this condition they contain reduced quantities of cell organelles and often store glycogen. If structural changes in the bone are required they are activated and quickly differentiate into osteoblasts.

Radiating from each lacuna are many fine channels called **canaliculi** containing cytoplasm which may link up with the central Haversian canal, with other lacunae or pass from one lamella to another.

An artery and a vein run through each Haversian canal, and capillaries branch from here and pass via the canaliculi to the lacunae of that particular Haversian system. They facilitate the passage of nutrients, metabolic waste and respiratory gases towards and away from the cells. A Haversian canal also contains a lymph vessel and nerve fibres tightly packed with areolar tissue. Transverse Haversian canals communicate with the marrow cavity and also interconnect with the longitudinal Haversian canals. These contain larger blood vessels and are not encircled by concentric lamellae.

At the outer and inner surfaces of the bone the lamellae are not in the form of concentric cylinders but are orientated circumferentially over it. The **canals of Volkman** ramify these areas. The canals contain blood vessels which pass through them to link with those in the Haversian canals.

The matrix of compact bone is composed of bone collagen, manufactured by the osteoblasts, and hydroxyapatite together with quantities of magnesium, sodium, carbonates and nitrates. The combination of organic with inorganic material produces a structure of great strength. The lamellae are laid down in a manner that is suited to the forces acting upon the bone, and the load that has to be carried.

Covering the bone is a layer of dense connective tissue called the **periosteum**. Bundles of collagen fibres called **Sharpey–Schafer** fibres from the periosteum pierce the bone and provide an intimate connection between the underlying bone and periosteum and act as a firm base for tendon insertions. The inner region of the periosteum is vascular and forms a layer which contains undifferentiated potential osteoblasts.

Spongy or trabecular bone (fig 8.29). Spongy bone consists of a meshwork of thin, interconnect-

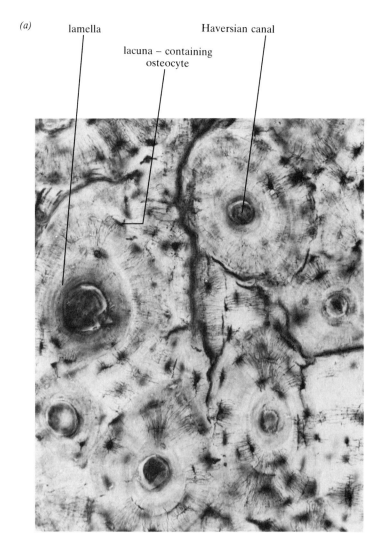

(a) lamella   Haversian canal

lacuna – containing osteocyte

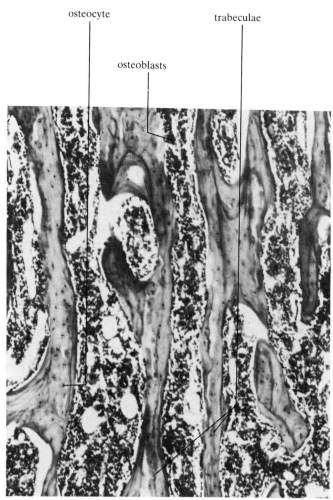

osteocyte   trabeculae

osteoblasts

Fig 8.29 *Spongy bone*

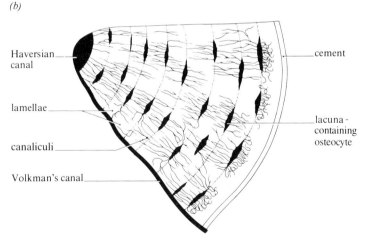

(b)

Haversian canal

lamellae

canaliculi

Volkman's canal

cement

lacuna - containing osteocyte

Fig 8.28 *(a) Part of a transverse section of a long bone. (b) TS Haversian system. The presence of large numbers of lamellae provides the bone with great strength despite its light weight*

ing bony struts called **trabeculae**. Its matrix contains less inorganic material (60–65%) than compact bone. The organic material is primarily composed of collagen fibres. The spaces between the trabeculae are filled with soft marrow tissue. If the marrow is red, as at the epiphyses of long bones such as the femur, the cells are predominantly red blood cells, whereas if it is yellow, as in the diaphyses of long bones, the cells are primarily fat cells. Three different types of cell appear to be present in spongy bone, which may be three different functional stages of the same cell type. These are **osteoblasts** which synthesise the spongy bone, **osteocytes** which are resting osteoblasts, and **osteoclasts** which can resorb the calcified matrix.

The trabeculae are orientated in the direction in which the bone is stressed. This enables the bone to withstand tension and compression forces effectively whilst at the same time keeping the weight of the bone to a minimum.

Spongy bone occurs in the embryo, growing organisms, and the epiphyses of long bones.

Membrane or dermal bone (fig 8.30). Such bones have no cartilage forerunner but are formed directly by intramembranous ossification in the dermis of the skin. Aggregations of osteoblasts appear in this region and form

241

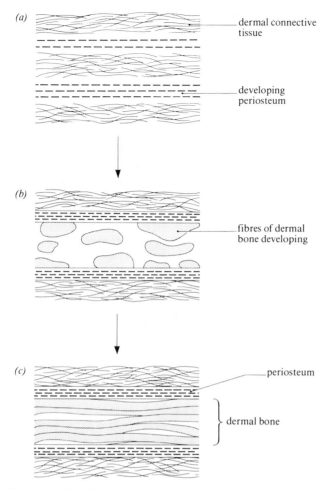

(a) — dermal connective tissue

— developing periosteum

(b) — fibres of dermal bone developing

(c) — periosteum

} dermal bone

Fig 8.30 *Development of dermal bone*

rows of cells which manufacture bone trabeculae. In this way, flat bony plates are produced very close to the surface of the body. They increase in size when more bone is deposited on their inner and outer surfaces, and then may sink further into the body to become part of the skeleton. Membrane bones form components of the skull, jaws and pectoral girdle.

8.4.5 Dentine

The composition of dentine (commonly called ivory) is very much like that of bone. However it contains a higher inorganic content (75%) and is consequently harder. Dentine contains no lacunae or osteons, and the arrangement of osteoblasts is quite different from that in bone (fig 8.31). In dentine they are confined to the dentinal inner margins and perforate the matrix with many odontoblastic processes which contain **microtubules**, and frequently blood vessels and nerve endings sensitive to touch and low temperatures. Collagen fibres, manufactured and laid down at the apices of the processes ultimately become calcified by impregnation with apatite crystals to form new dentine. Dentine is located between the enamel and pulp cavity in teeth, above and below gum level.

8.4.6 Haemopoietic tissue

Haemopoietic tissue forms red and white blood cells and is located in the red bone marrow and lymphoid tissue of adult mammals. Bone marrow or myeloid tissue produces red blood cells and granulocytes,

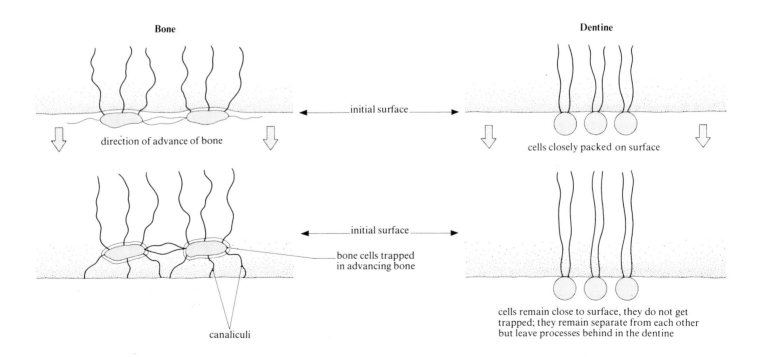

Bone

Dentine

← initial surface →

direction of advance of bone

cells closely packed on surface

← initial surface →

bone cells trapped in advancing bone

cells remain close to surface, they do not get trapped; they remain separate from each other but leave processes behind in the dentine

canaliculi

Fig 8.31 *Comparison of growth in bone and dentine (Modified after John Currey (1970) Animal Skeletons, Arnold.)*

whilst lymphocytes and monocytes are differentiated in lymphoid tissue. Haemopoietic tissue consists of free cells enmeshed in a stroma of loose scleroprotein fibres, often termed reticular connective tissue.

Bone marrow/myeloid tissue

The stroma here consists of very loose, reticular connective tissue permeated by wide intercellular spaces. It is traversed by numerous thin-walled, wide blood sinuses through which mature blood cells escape into the bloodstream. Lining the sinuses are phagocytic cells which form part of the body's reticulo-endothelial system.

It is thought that all blood cells are derived from primitive cells called **haemocytoblasts** which in turn differentiate into **erythroblasts**, the precursors of erythrocytes, **myelocytes**, the precursors of granulocytes, **lymphoblasts**, the precursors of lymphocytes, **monoblasts**, the precursors of monocytes, and **megakaryocytes** which produce platelets.

Further details of the structure and functions of these cells can be found in section 14.11.

Lymphoid tissue

This is responsible for the differentiation of lymphocytes. Three types of the tissue exist: **loose lymphoid tissue**, where the stroma of reticular connective tissue predominates over the free cells, **dense lymphoid tissue**, where there are many more free cells embedded in the stroma, and **nodular lymphoid tissue**, which possesses dense aggregates of free cells.

The free cells are composed primarily of lymphocytes of various sizes and functions. There are also plasma cells present which have developed from lymphocytes, and occasionally monocytes and eosinophils are evident. Some of the cells are phagocytic. Further details of the lymphatic system are given in section 14.12.1.

8.5 Muscle tissue

Muscle tissue makes up 40% of a mammal's body weight. It is derived from embryonic mesoderm and consists of highly specialised contractile cells or fibres held

Table 8.5 The similarities and differences between voluntary, involuntary and cardiac muscle.

Features	Voluntary	Involuntary	Cardiac
Other names	Striated, striped, skeletal	Unstriated, unstriped, smooth	Heart
Specialisation	Most highly specialised	Least specialised	More specialised than involuntary
Structure	Very long cells, usually called fibres, subdivided into units called sarcomeres. Fibres bound together by vascular connective tissue.	Consists of individual, spindle-shaped cells, associated in bundles or sheets	Cells terminally branched and connected to each other by special interdigitating surface processes, the **intercalated discs**. Arrangement of fibres is three-dimensional.
Nucleus	Several in variable positions near periphery of fibre	Single, elongated in shape and centrally placed	Several centrally placed
Cytoplasmic contents	Mitochondria in rows in periphery and between fibres, prominent SER forming network of tubules, T-system well developed, glycogen granules and some lipid droplets	Prominent mitochondria, individual tubules of the SER, glycogen granules	Numerous large mitochondria in columns between cells, poorly developed SER consisting of network of tubules, T-system well developed
Sarcolemma	Present	Absent	Present
Myofilaments/myofibrils	Very conspicuous, length 1–40 mm, diameter 10–60 µm	Inconspicuous, length 0.02–0.5 mm, diameter 5–10 µm	Conspicuous, length 0.08 mm or less, diameter 12–15 µm
Innervation	Under control of the voluntary nervous system via motor nerves from the brain and spinal cord (neurogenic)	Under control of autonomic nervous system (neurogenic)	Myogenic, but rate of contraction can be influenced by the autonomic nervous system
Cross striations	Present	Absent	Present
Intercalated discs	Absent	Absent	Present
Activity	Powerful, rapid contractions, short refractory period, therefore fatigues quickly	Shows sustained rhythmical contraction and relaxation, as in peristalsis	Rapid rhythmical contraction and relaxation, long refractory period, therefore does not fatigue; contraction not sustained
Location	Attached to the skeleton in the trunk, limbs and head	In walls of intestinal, genital, urinary and respiratory tracts, and the walls of blood vessels	Found only in the walls of the heart chambers

SER – Smooth endoplasmic reticulum.

together by connective tissue. Three types of muscle are present in the body, classified according to their method of innervation and they are **voluntary** (striated), **involuntary** (unstriated) and **cardiac**. Table 8.5 shows the main points of similarity and difference between them. Further details can be found elsewhere in sections 14.12 and 17.4. (Also see figs 8.32–4.)

8.6 Nervous tissue

Nervous tissue is derived from embryonic mesoderm. It is composed of densely packed interconnected nerve cells called **neurones** (as many as 10^{10} in the human brain), specialised for conduction of nerve impulses, and accessory neuroglial cells. There is little intercellular space between them. Nervous tissue also contains receptor cells, and is frequently ensheathed by vascularised connective tissue.

8.6.1 Neurones

These are the functional units of the nervous system. Neurones are excitable cells, that is they are capable of transmitting electrical impulses, and this provides the means of communication between **receptors** (cells or organs which receive stimuli, such as the sensory cells in the skin) and **effectors** (tissues or organs which react to stimuli, such as muscles or glands). Neurones which conduct impulses towards the central nervous system (the brain and spinal cord) are called **afferent** or **sensory neurones**, whilst **efferent** or **motor neurones** conduct impulses away from the central nervous system. **Internuncial**, intermediate, relay or association neurones frequently interconnect afferent neurones with efferents. The structure of these neurones is shown in fig 8.35.

Each neurone possesses a cell body (perikaryon) 3–100 μm in diameter (fig 8.35), which contains a nucleus, the majority of the cell's other organelles embedded in a mass of cytoplasm, and a variable number of cytoplasmic processes extending from it. The arrangement of these processes forms the basis of one means of classifying neurones (fig 8.36), there being uni-, pseudouni-, bi-, and multipolar neurones. Processes which conduct impulses towards the cell body are called **dendrons**. They are small, relatively wide, and break up into fine terminal branches. Processes conducting impulses away from the cell body are termed **axons** or nerve fibres and may be several metres long. They are thinner than dendrons.

The terminal region of an axon is neurosecretory and breaks up into many fine branches with swollen endings. It communicates with adjacent neurones at sites called **synapses** which may be excitatory or inhibitory (section 16.1.2). The bulbous endings possess small vesicles containing transmitter substance (acetylcholine or noradrenaline) and many mitochondria, for these regions are extremely active metabolically. Nissl's granules, which are

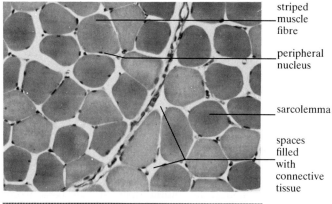

(a)

- striped muscle fibre
- peripheral nucleus
- sarcolemma
- spaces filled with connective tissue

(b)

- striations
- nucleus
- striped muscle fibril

Fig 8.32 *(a) TS and (b) LS of voluntary (striped) muscle*

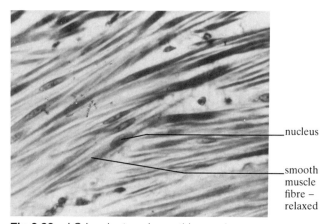

- nucleus
- smooth muscle fibre – relaxed

Fig 8.33 *LS involuntary (smooth) muscle*

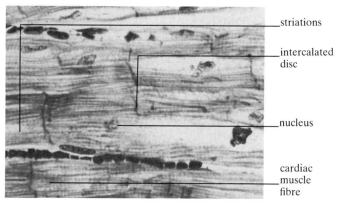

- striations
- intercalated disc
- nucleus
- cardiac muscle fibre

Fig 8.34 *Section of cardiac muscle*

groups of ribosomes associated with protein synthesis, and Golgi apparatus are present in the cell body (fig 8.37). Microtubules, neurofibrils, rough endoplasmic reticulum and mitochondria are present throughout the axoplasm of the neurone.

Nerve fibres may be **myelinated** (as, for example, in cranial and spinal nerves) or **non-myelinated** (as in autonomic nerves). In the former case, the fibres are completely surrounded by a fatty **myelin sheath** formed by many **Schwann cells**. The sheath is constricted at intervals along its length by **nodes of Ranvier** (fig 8.35). One Schwann cell nucleus is visible in the sheath between a pair of nodes. Surrounding the sheath is a tough inelastic membrane, the **neurilemma**.

Non-myelinated fibres do not possess nodes of Ranvier, and are incompletely enclosed by a Schwann cell (fig 8.38). Indeed there may be up to nine fibres partially shrouded by a single Schwann cell.

8.6.2 Nerves

These consist of bundles of nerve fibres ensheathed in connective tissue called the **epineurium**. Inward extensions of the epineurium, called the **perineurium**, divide the fibres into smaller bundles, whilst each fibre is itself surrounded by connective tissue called the **endoneurium** (fig 8.39). Nerves are classified according

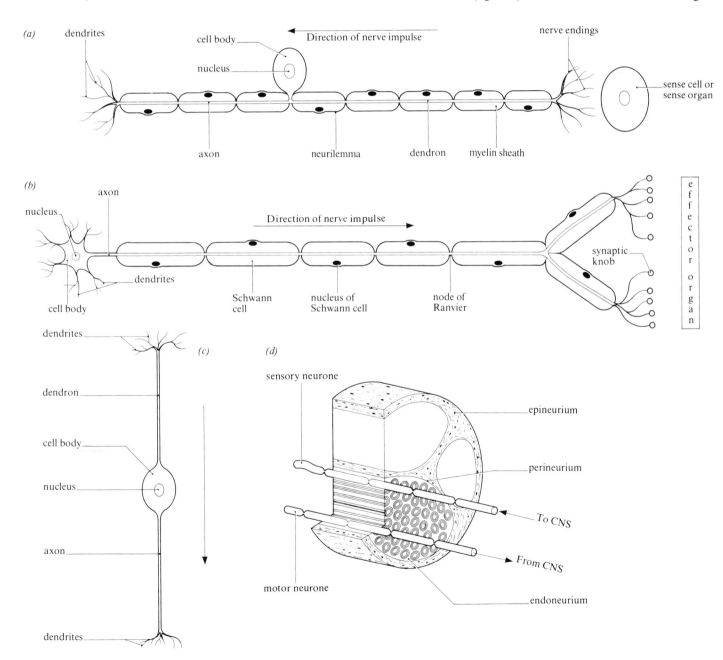

Fig 8.35 *Schematic representation of (a) sensory neurone, (b) motor neurone, (c) internuncial neurone, (d) section of myelinated nerve*

245

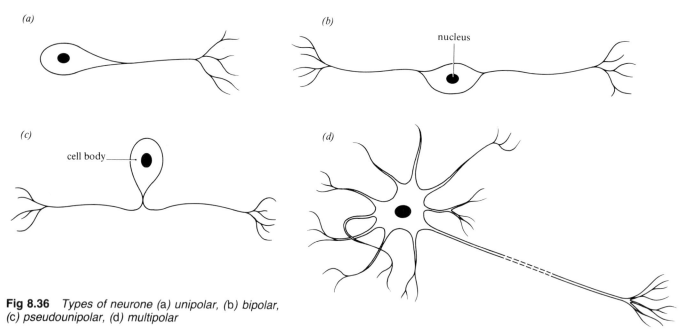

Fig 8.36 *Types of neurone (a) unipolar, (b) bipolar, (c) pseudounipolar, (d) multipolar*

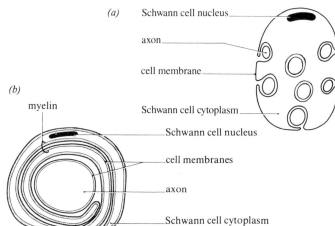

Fig 8.38 (a) *Non-myelinated nerve fibre. (b) Myelinated nerve fibre*

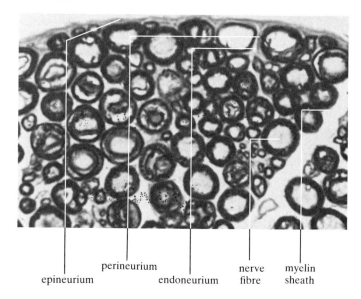

Fig 8.37 *Neurone with synapses*

Fig 8.39 *TS myelinated nerve*

to the direction in which they convey impulses. Sensory or afferent nerves convey impulses into the central nervous system (such as the olfactory, optic and auditory nerves), whilst efferent or motor nerves conduct impulses away from the central nervous system (as in the oculomotor, pathetic and abducens). Mixed nerves convey impulses in both directions (for example the trigeminal, facial, glossopharyngeal, vagus and all spinal nerves).

8.6.3 Neuroglia

These cells are ten times more numerous than neurones and are found packed around the neurones throughout the central nervous system, thus supporting them mechanically by filling up the majority of inter-neurone space. It is thought that their metabolic activity is closely allied to that of the neurones they surround and that they might be involved in the memory processes by storing

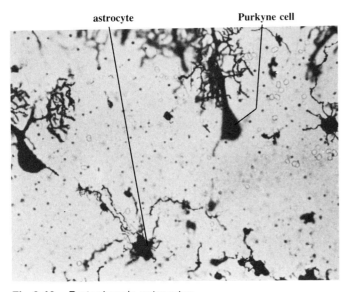

Fig 8.40 *Protoplasmic astrocytes*

information in the form of an RNA code. They may also nourish the cytoplasmic extensions of neurones. Satellite neuroglia, called **Schwann cells**, synthesise the myelin sheath of myelinated nerve fibres whilst others are phagocytic in function. The different kinds of neuroglial cells are classified as follows. **Ependymal cells** line the brain cavities and spinal canal and form an epithelial layer in the choroid plexus. They serve to connect the cavities with underlying tissues (section 16.2.4). **Macroglia** are divided into two categories, astrocytes and oligodendrocytes. **Protoplasmic astrocytes** are located in the grey matter (fig 8.40). Numerously branched, short thick processes radiate from the cell body which contains an ovoid nucleus and much glycogen. **Fibrous astrocytes** are located in the white matter. Fewer branched, long processes radiate from the cell body which itself possesses an ovoid nucleus and much glycogen. Some of the branches actually abut upon the walls of blood vessels. These cells convey nutrients from the bloodstream to the neurones. Both types of astrocytes are interconnected forming an extensive three-dimensional meshwork in which the neurones are embedded. They also divide frequently to form scar tissue if the central nervous system is injured.

Oligodendrocytes are located in grey and white matter. They are smaller than astrocytes and the single nucleus is spherical. Fewer, finer branches radiate from the cell body, which itself contains cytoplasm rich in ribosomes. Schwann cells are specialised oligodendrocytes which synthesise the myelin sheath of myelinated fibres.

Microglia are located in grey and white matter but are more numerous in the grey. A thick process arises from each end of the small, elongated cell body which itself contains lysosomes and a well-developed Golgi apparatus. All branches possess further lateral branches. When the brain is damaged these cells are stimulated to become phagocytic and move around in amoeboid fashion to combat invasion of foreign particles.

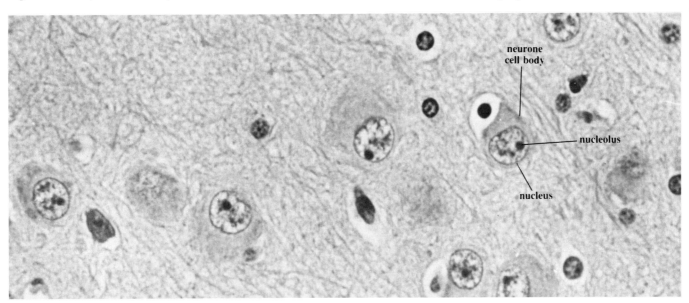

Fig 8.41 *Neurones and glial cells in human cortex*

Chapter Nine

Autotrophic nutrition

In chapters 9–11 we shall be concerned with living organisms as consumers of food, that is energy and materials. The process of *acquiring* energy and materials is called **nutrition** and this is the theme of chapters 9 and 10. In chapter 11 **respiration** is considered, the process whereby organisms *release* energy from the energy-rich compounds acquired by nutrition.

Energy can neither be created nor destroyed (**the law of conservation of energy**). It may occur in various forms, such as light, chemical, heat, electrical, mechanical and sound, and these can be converted from one form to another, that is they are **interconvertible**. A simple example would be striking a match, where, in the matchhead, chemical energy is converted to heat, light and sound energy.

Energy may be defined as the capacity to do work. All living organisms may be regarded as working machines which require a continuous supply of energy in order to keep working, and so to stay alive. This energy is required in order to carry out a variety of vital processes. The forms of work include:

chemical synthesis of substances for growth and repair;

active transport of substances into and out of cells;

electrical transmission of nerve impulses;

mechanical contraction of muscles (movement);

maintenance of a constant body temperature in birds and mammals;

bioluminescence (that is the production of light by living organisms, such as fireflies, glow-worms and some deep sea animals);

electrical discharge, as in the electric eel.

9.1 Grouping of organisms according to their principal sources of energy and carbon

Living organisms can be grouped on the basis of their source of energy or source of carbon. Carbon is the most fundamental material required by living organisms (section 5.1.1)

Energy source

Despite energy existing in several forms, only two are suitable as energy sources for living organisms, namely light and chemical energy. Organisms utilising light energy to synthesise their organic requirements are called **phototrophs** or **phototrophic** (*photos*, light; *trophos*, nourishment), while those utilising chemical energy are called **chemotrophs** or **chemotrophic**. Phototrophs are character-

ised by the presence of pigments, including some form of chlorophyll, which absorb light energy and convert it to chemical energy. An alternative term for the process of phototrophism is **photosynthesis**.

Carbon source

In this alternative grouping organisms which have an inorganic source of carbon, namely carbon dioxide, are called **autotrophs** or **autotrophic** (*autos*, self) and those having an organic source of carbon are called **heterotrophs** or **heterotrophic** (*heteros*, other). Unlike heterotrophs, autotrophs synthesise their own organic requirements from simple inorganic materials.

Table 9.1 summarises the groupings and shows how they interact. An important principle to emerge is that chemotrophic organisms are totally dependent on phototrophic organisms for their energy, and heterotrophic organisms are totally dependent on autotrophic organisms for their carbon.

By far the most important groups are the photoautotrophic organisms, including all green plants, and the chemoheterotrophic organisms, including all animals and fungi. Ignoring a few bacteria the position is simplified by saying that heterotrophic organisms are ultimately dependent on green plants for their energy and carbon. Photoautotrophic organisms are sometimes described as **holophytic** (*holos*, whole; *phyton*, plant).

> **9.1** Define photoautotrophism and chemoheterotrophism.

In ignoring the two minor groups, it should be stressed that the activities of the chemosynthetic organisms are of great importance, as will be shown in sections 9.10 and 9.11.

A few organisms do not fit neatly into these groups. *Euglena*, for example, is normally autotrophic, but some species can survive heterotrophically in darkness if an organic carbon source is present. Fig 9.1 illustrates further the relationship between the two main nutritional categories. It also illustrates how energy flows and carbon is cycled through living organisms and the environment, themes which are important in ecology (chapter 12).

In the carbon cycle, the carbon is released as carbon dioxide by respiration and converted to organic compounds by photosynthesis. Further details of the carbon cycle, including the role of chemosynthetic organisms, are shown in fig 9.2.

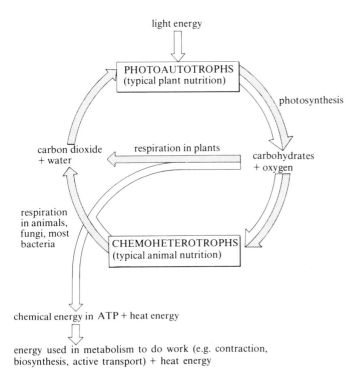

Fig 9.1 (above) *Flow of energy (open arrows) and cycling of carbon (solid arrows) through photoautotrophs and chemoheterotrophs, and balance between photosynthesis and respiration. Light energy is converted to chemical energy in photosynthesis and used in the synthesis of organic materials from inorganic materials. Organic materials form the energy and carbon source for chemoheterotrophs and are released again in the process of respiration (also carried out by plants). Every energy conversion is accompanied by some loss of energy as heat*

9.2 Examine fig 9.2. Which nutritional categories are indicated by (*a*) the darker background shading and (*b*) the white background?

9.3 What is the total natural annual productivity (turnover) of carbon in the carbon cycle?

9.2 Photosynthesis

Table 9.1 shows that there are two types of photosynthetic organisms, photoautotrophs and photo-heterotrophs. The majority of these organisms are photo-autotrophs and it is these that will be studied in detail in this chapter.

9.2.1 Importance of photosynthesis

All life on Earth depends on photosynthesis, either directly or, as in the case of animals, indirectly. Photosynthesis makes both carbon and energy available to living organisms and produces the oxygen in the atmosphere which is vital for all aerobic forms of life. Humans also depend on photosynthesis for the energy-containing fossil fuels which have developed over millions of years. One recent estimate of the annual fixation of carbon (not carbon dioxide) by photosynthesis is 75×10^{12} kg year^{-1} (fig 9.2). About 40% of this is contributed by phytoplankton living in the oceans. Of the total amount of solar radiation intercepted by our planet, about half reaches its surface after absorption, reflection and scattering in the atmosphere. Of this, only about 50% is of the right wavelength to stimulate photosynthesis and, although estimates vary, it is

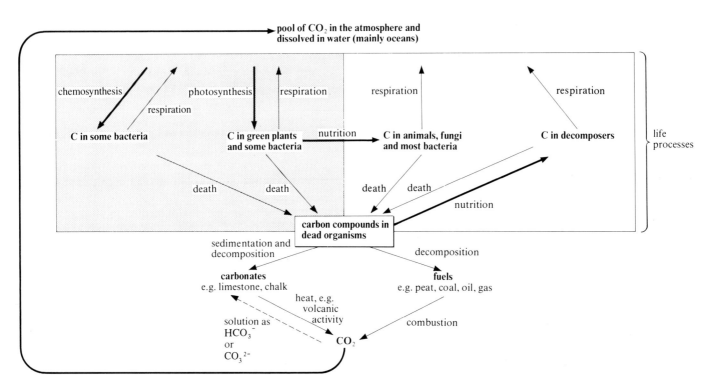

Table 9.1 Grouping of living organisms according to principal sources of carbon and energy.

		CARBON SOURCE	
		AUTOTROPHIC use carbon dioxide (inorganic)	HETEROTROPHIC use organic source of carbon
ENERGY SOURCE	PHOTOTROPHIC (PHOTOSYNTHETIC) use light energy	PHOTOAUTOTROPHIC all green plants, blue-green bacteria and green and purple sulphur bacteria	PHOTOHETEROTROPHIC few organisms, e.g. some purple non-sulphur bacteria
	CHEMOTROPHIC use chemical energy	CHEMOAUTOTROPHIC (CHEMOSYNTHETIC) a few bacteria, e.g. *Nitrosomonas* and some other nitrogen cycle bacteria	CHEMOHETEROTROPHIC all animals and fungi, most bacteria, some parasitic flowering plants, e.g. dodder (*Cuscuta*)

NB Majority of living organisms occur in photoautotrophic and chemoheterotrophic categories.

likely that only about 0.2% of this is used in net plant production (about 0.5% of the energy actually reaching plants). From this small fraction of the available energy virtually all life is sustained.

One potentially important use of photosynthesis is as an alternative source of energy to our depleting natural reserves of oil and gas. Attempts are currently being made to mimic the early stages of the photosynthetic process in plants whereby water is split into hydrogen and oxygen using light (solar) energy. Hydrogen could be burned as a fuel, and the waste material would be water. This system would therefore provide an attractive alternative or supplement to nuclear and other forms of energy.

Research into photosynthesis is also of great importance in agriculture because, as the figures above suggest, there is great scope for improving the efficiency of agriculture. New sources of food are being produced from micro-organisms such as algae and photosynthetic bacteria which are often more efficient as 'crops'. If grown on sewage or industrial waste, these substances could be purified or made use of at the same time as food is produced.

Fig 9.2 (left) *The carbon cycle. Heavy arrows indicate the dominant of the two pathways. Some rough estimates of actual quantities involved:*
Oceans (mainly phytoplankton): 40×10^{12} kg carbon per year fixed as carbon dioxide by photosynthesis. Most of this is released in respiration
Land: 35×10^{12} kg carbon per year fixed as carbon dioxide by photosynthesis
10×10^{12} kg carbon per year released as carbon dioxide by respiration of plants and animals
25×10^{12} kg carbon per year released as carbon dioxide by respiration of decomposers
5×10^{12} kg carbon per year released as carbon dioxide by burning of fossil fuels, enough to be causing a gradual increase in carbon dioxide concentration in atmosphere and oceans NB 10^3 kg = 1 tonne

> **9.4** What advantages would production of hydrogen fuel by the action of light on water have over nuclear power?

9.3 The structure of the leaf

In higher plants the major photosynthetic organ is the leaf. As with all living organs, structure and function are closely linked. From the equation for photosynthesis

$$CO_2 + H_2O \xrightarrow[\text{chlorophyll}]{\text{sunlight}} (CH_2O)_n + O_2$$
carbon   water   carbohydrate oxygen
dioxide

it can be deduced that first the leaf requires a source of carbon dioxide and water, secondly it must contain chlorophyll and be adapted to receive sunlight, thirdly oxygen will escape as a waste product and finally the useful product, carbohydrate, will have to be exported to other parts of the plant or stored. In its structure the leaf is highly adapted to satisfy these requirements. Figs 9.3 and 9.4 show labelled photomicrographs of leaf sections which will aid you in interpreting sections of monocotyledonous and dicotyledonous leaves. Fig 9.5 is a simplified drawing of a vertical section through a dicotyledonous leaf. The epidermis of different leaf types are shown in fig 8.2 and details of stomatal structure and function are dealt with in chapter 14.

The structure and function of different tissues in a dicotyledonous leaf are summarised in table 9.2.

> **9.5** Make a list of the ways in which the structure of the leaf contributes to its successful functioning.

251

Table 9.2 Structure and function of tissues in a dicotyledonous leaf.

Tissue	Structure	Function
Upper and lower epidermis	One cell thick. Colourless flattened cells. External walls covered with a cuticle of cutin (waxy substance). Contains stomata (pores) which are normally confined to, or more numerous in, the lower epidermis. Each stoma is surrounded by a pair of guard cells.	Protective. Cutin is waterproof and protects from desiccation and infection. Stomata are sites of gaseous exchange with the environment. Their size is regulated by guard cells, special epidermal cells containing chloroplasts.
Palisade mesophyll	Column-shaped ('palisade') cells with numerous chloroplasts in a thin layer of cytoplasm.	Main photosynthetic tissue. Chloroplasts may move towards light.
Spongy mesophyll	Irregularly shaped cells fitting together loosely to leave large air spaces.	Photosynthetic, but fewer chloroplasts than palisade cells. Gaseous exchange can occur through the large air spaces via stomata. Stores starch.
Vascular tissue	Extensive finely branching network through the leaf.	Conducts water and mineral salts to the leaf in xylem. Removes products of photosynthesis (mainly sucrose) in phloem. Provides a supporting skeleton to the lamina, aided by collenchyma of the midrib, turgidity of the mesophyll cells, and sometimes sclerenchyma.

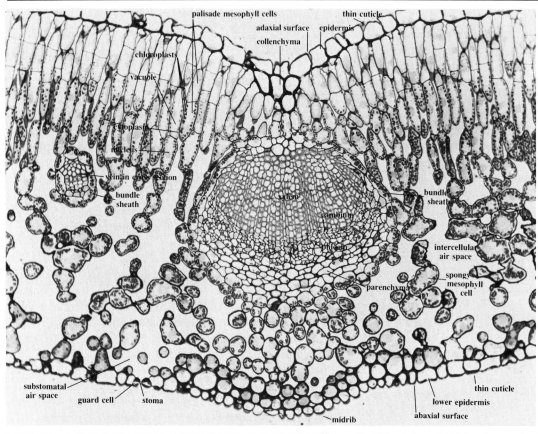

Fig 9.3 (above) *TS lamina and midrib of a privet leaf* (Ligustrum), *a typical dicotyledon*

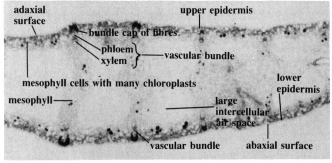

Fig 9.4 (left) *TS lamina of an* Iris *leaf, a typical monocotyledon*

252

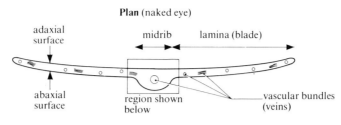

Plan (naked eye)

adaxial surface

midrib

lamina (blade)

abaxial surface

region shown below

vascular bundles (veins)

NB All mesophyll cells contain chloroplasts

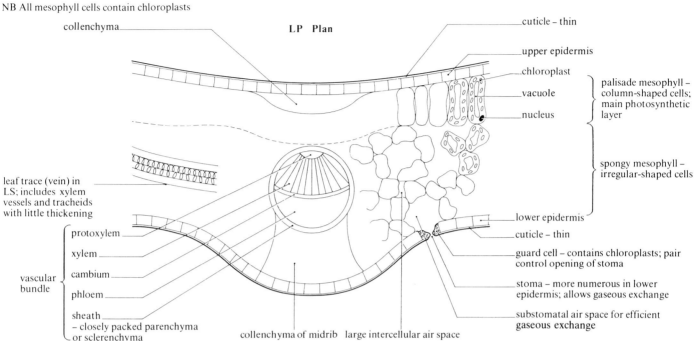

LP Plan

collenchyma

cuticle – thin

upper epidermis

chloroplast

vacuole

palisade mesophyll – column-shaped cells; main photosynthetic layer

nucleus

spongy mesophyll – irregular-shaped cells

leaf trace (vein) in LS; includes xylem vessels and tracheids with little thickening

lower epidermis

cuticle – thin

protoxylem

xylem

cambium

phloem

sheath – closely packed parenchyma or sclerenchyma

vascular bundle

guard cell – contains chloroplasts; pair control opening of stoma

stoma – more numerous in lower epidermis; allows gaseous exchange

substomatal air space for efficient gaseous exchange

collenchyma of midrib   large intercellular air space

A final point to note is the arrangement of the leaves for minimal overlapping. Such leaf mosaics are particularly noticeable in some plants, such as ivy. Etiolation (rapid extension growth in the dark) and phototropism (growth towards light) are further phenomena which ensure that leaves reach the light.

9.3.1 Chloroplasts

In eukaryotes, photosynthesis takes place in organelles called chloroplasts, distributed in the cytoplasm in numbers varying from one (as in *Chlamydomonas* and *Chlorella*) to about 100 (palisade mesophyll cells). In higher plants chloroplasts are usually biconvex in section and circular in surface view. They are about 3–10 μm (average 5 μm) in diameter, and so are visible with a light microscope. They are more variable in form in the algae, for example they are spiral in *Spirogyra* and cup-shaped in *Chlamydomonas*, and usually possess pyrenoids, as in *Spirogyra* (section 3.2.4).

Chloroplasts arise from small, undifferentiated bodies called **proplastids** found in the growing regions of plants (meristems) and are surrounded by two membranes, which form the **chloroplast envelope**. They always contain chlorophyll and other photosynthetic pigments located on a system of membranes running through a ground substance, or stroma. Their detailed structure is revealed

Fig 9.5 *Diagrammatic transverse section of a typical dicotyledon leaf*

by electron microscopy. Fig 7.6 shows the typical appearance of chloroplasts in a leaf mesophyll cell as seen at low power in the electron microscope. Figs 9.6 and 9.8 show electron micrographs and fig 9.7 a diagram of a chloroplast, illustrating the membrane system. The membrane system is the site of the **light reactions** in photosynthesis (section 9.4.2). The membranes are covered with chlorophyll and other pigments, enzymes and electron carriers. The system consists of many flattened, fluid-filled sacs called **thylakoids** which form stacks called **grana** at intervals, with lamellae (layers) between the grana. Each granum resembles a pile of coins and the lamellae are often sheet-like (fig 9.8). Grana are just visible under the light microscope as grains.

The stroma is the site of the **dark reactions** of photosynthesis (section 9.4.3). The structure is gel-like, containing soluble enzymes, notably those of the Calvin cycle, and other chemicals such as sugars and organic acids. Excess carbohydrate from photosynthesis is also stored as grains of starch mainly in the light. Spherical lipid droplets are often associated with the membranes. They become more conspicuous as membranes break down during senescence, presumably accumulating lipids from the membranes. In chromoplasts they are often very large and accumulate carotenoid pigments.

253

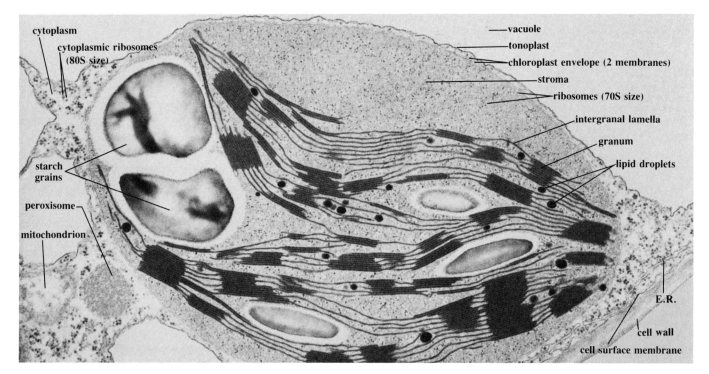

Fig 9.6 *Electron micrograph of a chloroplast (× 15 800)*

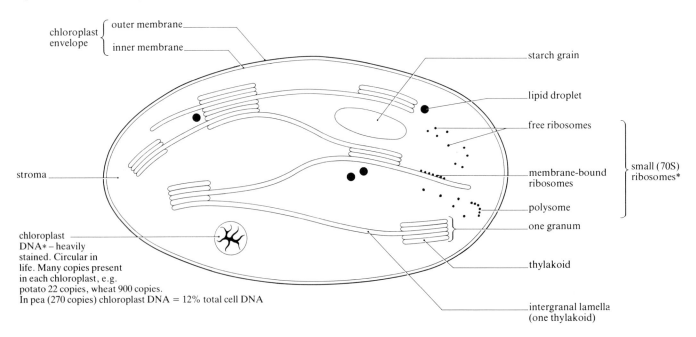

Fig 9.7 *Chloroplast structure. The membrane system has been reduced for convenience (*prokaryote-like protein synthesising machinery)*

Protein-synthesising machinery and the endosymbiont theory

An interesting feature of chloroplasts, apart from photo-synthesis, is their protein-synthesising machinery. During the 1960s it was shown that both chloroplasts and mitochondria contain DNA and ribosomes. This led to speculation that these organelles may be partially or completely independent of the control of the nucleus in the cells containing them. It was further suggested that they might represent prokaryotic organisms which invaded eukaryotic cells at an early stage in the history of life. Thus the organelles represent an extreme form of symbiosis, a

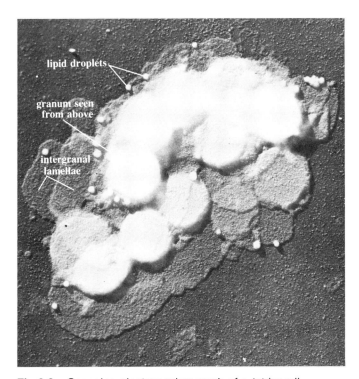

Fig 9.8 *Scanning electron micrograph of a 'stripped' chloroplast (a chloroplast whose outer envelope has been removed) looking down from above on the lamellae and grana which can be seen in three dimensions. Note that the lamellae are sheet-like and interconnect the grana. The preparation is a shadowed replica (see appendix 2)*

lipid droplets

granum seen from above

intergranal lamellae

theory known as the **endosymbiont theory**. Some of the evidence for this is presented in table 9.3.

Photosynthetic prokaryotes (blue-green bacteria and other photosynthetic bacteria) do not contain chloroplasts. Instead their photosynthetic pigments are located in membranes distributed throughout the cytoplasm. Thus the whole cell is similar to one chloroplast, and is approximately the same size. It is now believed that chloroplasts are the descendants of blue-green bacteria.

It has been shown that, while chloroplasts and mitochondria do code for and make some of their own proteins, they no longer contain enough DNA to code for all of them, and the task is shared with nuclear DNA.

9.3.2 Photosynthetic pigments

The photosynthetic pigments of higher plants fall into two classes, the chlorophylls and carotenoids. The role of the pigments is to absorb light energy, thereby converting it to chemical energy. They are located on the chloroplast membranes and the chloroplasts are usually arranged within the cells so that the membranes are at right-angles to the light source for maximum absorption. Table 9.4 shows the range of pigments found within each of the main groups of plants.

Chlorophylls

Chlorophylls absorb mainly red and blue-violet light, reflecting green light and therefore giving plants their characteristic green colour, unless masked by other pigments. Fig 9.9 shows the absorption spectra of chlorophylls *a* and *b* compared with carotenoids.

Chlorophylls are characterised by a porphyrin ring (fig 9.10) which is a structure found in several important biological compounds, such as the haem of haemoglobin, myoglobin and cytochromes. The porphyrin ring is a flat, square structure containing four smaller rings (I–IV), each possessing a nitrogen atom which can bond with a metal atom, such as magnesium in the chlorophylls and iron in haem. The 'head' is joined to a long hydrocarbon tail by an ester linkage formed between an alcohol group (−OH) at the end of phytol and a carboxyl group (−COOH) on the head. Different chlorophylls have different side-chains on the head and this modifies their absorption spectra.

Table 9.3 Comparison of prokaryotes, chloroplasts and mitochondria with eukaryotes.

	Prokaryotes, chloroplasts and mitochondria	*Eukaryotes*
DNA	Circular Not contained in chromosomes Not contained in nucleus	Linear Contained in chromosomes Contained in a nucleus
Ribosomes	Smaller (70S)	Larger (80S)
Sensitivity to antibiotics	Protein synthesis inhibited by chloramphenicol, not cycloheximide	Protein synthesis inhibited by cycloheximide, not chloramphenicol
Average diameter	Prokaryote cell: 0.5–3 μm Chloroplast: 3–5 μm Mitochondrion: 1 μm	Eukaryote cell: 20 μm

Table 9.4 The main photosynthetic pigments, their colours and distribution.

Class of pigment with examples	Colour	Distribution
Chlorophylls		
chlorophyll *a*	yellow-green	All photosynthetic organisms except some photosynthetic bacteria
chlorophyll *b*	blue-green	Higher plants and green algae
chlorophyll *c*	green	Brown algae, a few unicellular algae including diatoms
chlorophyll *d*	green	Some red algae
bacteriochlorophylls *a–d*	pale blue	Photosynthetic bacteria
Carotenoids (carotenes and xanthophylls)		
Carotenes		
β-carotene	orange	All photosynthetic organisms except photosynthetic bacteria
Xanthophylls (carotenols)		
Great variety	all yellow	Fucoxanthin helps give brown algae their colour. It has a very broad absorption spectrum

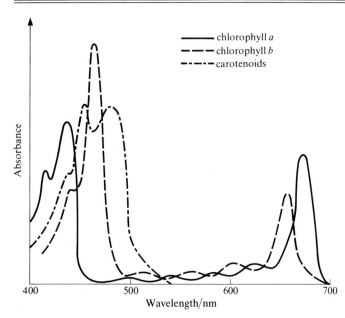

Fig 9.9 (above) *Absorption spectra of chlorophylls* a *and* b, *and carotenoids*

Fig 9.10 (right) *Structure of chlorophylls*

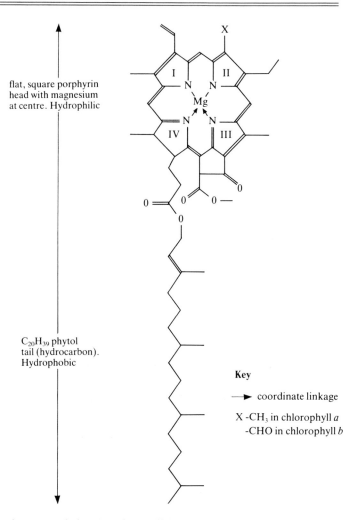

The structure is related to function in the following ways:
(*a*) the long tail is lipid soluble (hydrophobic) and so is anchored in the thylakoid membrane;
(*b*) the head is hydrophilic (water loving) and so generally lies in the surface of the membrane next to the aqueous solution of the stroma;
(*c*) the flat head is parallel to the membrane surface for light absorption;
(*d*) modifications of side-groups on the head cause changes in the absorption spectrum so that different energies of light are absorbed;
(*e*) absorption of light energy by the head causes changes in the energy levels of electrons within the head.

Chlorophyll *a* is the most abundant photosynthetic pigment and is the only one found in all photosynthetic plants due to its central role as a primary pigment. It exists in several forms, depending on its arrangement in the membrane. Each form differs slightly in its red absorption peak; for example, the peak may be at 670 nm, 680 nm, 690 nm or 700 nm.

> **9.6** How does the absorption spectrum of chlorophyll *a* differ from that of chlorophyll *b*?

256

Carotenoids

Carotenoids are yellow, orange, red or brown pigments that absorb strongly in the blue-violet range. They are usually masked by the green chlorophylls but can be seen in leaves prior to leaf-fall since chlorophylls break down first. They are also found in the chromoplasts of some flowers and fruits where the bright colours serve to attract insects, birds and other animals for pollination or dispersal; for example the red skin of the tomato is due to lycopene, a carotene.

Carotenoids have three absorption peaks in the blue-violet range of the spectrum (fig 9.9) and apart from acting as accessory pigments, they may also protect chlorophylls from excess light and from oxidation by oxygen produced in photosynthesis.

Carotenoids are of two types, carotenes and xanthophylls. **Carotenes** are hydrocarbons, the majority being

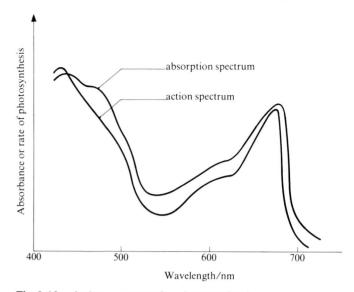

Fig 9.12 *Action spectrum for photosynthesis compared with absorption spectrum of photosynthetic pigments*

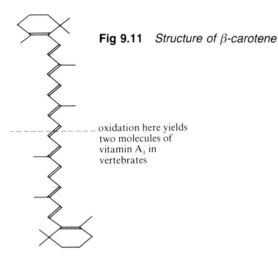

oxidation here yields two molecules of vitamin A_1 in vertebrates

Fig 9.11 *Structure of β-carotene*

C_{40} compounds (tetraterpenes). The most widespread and important is β-carotene (fig 9.11), which is familiar as the orange pigment of carrots. Vertebrates are able to break the molecule into two during digestion to form two molecules of vitamin A. **Xanthophylls** are chemically very similar to carotenes but contain oxygen.

Absorption and action spectra

When investigating a process such as photosynthesis that is activated by light, it is important to establish the action spectrum for the process and to use this to try to identify the pigments involved. An **action spectrum** is a graph showing the effectiveness of different wavelengths of light in stimulating the process being investigated, in this case photosynthesis, where the response could be measured for example in terms of oxygen production at different wavelengths. An **absorption spectrum** is a graph of the relative absorbance of different wavelengths of light by a pigment. An action spectrum for photosynthesis is shown in fig 9.12, together with an absorption spectrum for the

combined photosynthetic pigments. Note the close similarity, which indicates that the pigments, chlorophylls in particular, are those responsible for absorption of light in photosynthesis.

Excitation of pigments by light

Pigments are chemicals that absorb visible light and this causes the excitation of certain electrons to '**excited states**', that is the electrons absorb energy. The shorter the wavelength of light, the greater its energy and the greater its potential to promote electrons to these excited states. The excited state is usually unstable and the molecule returns to its '**ground state**' (original low energy state), losing its energy of excitation as it does so. This energy can be lost in several ways, including reversal of absorption either by **fluorescence** or **phosphorescence**. Here some of the energy is lost as heat and some as light. The emitted light has a longer wavelength (less energy) than the absorbed light. This can be observed when solutions of chlorophyll are irradiated and then observed in darkness.

In the light reactions of photosynthesis, the excited primary pigments lose electrons, leaving positive 'holes' in their molecules; for example

$$\text{chlorophyll} \xrightarrow{\text{light energy}} \text{chlorophyll}^+ + e^-$$
(reduced form)　　　　　　(oxidised form)　　electron

Each electron lost is accepted by another molecule, the so-called **electron acceptor**, so this is an oxidation–reduction process (see section A1.2). The chlorophyll is oxidised and the electron acceptor is reduced. Chlorophyll is described as an **electron donor**.

257

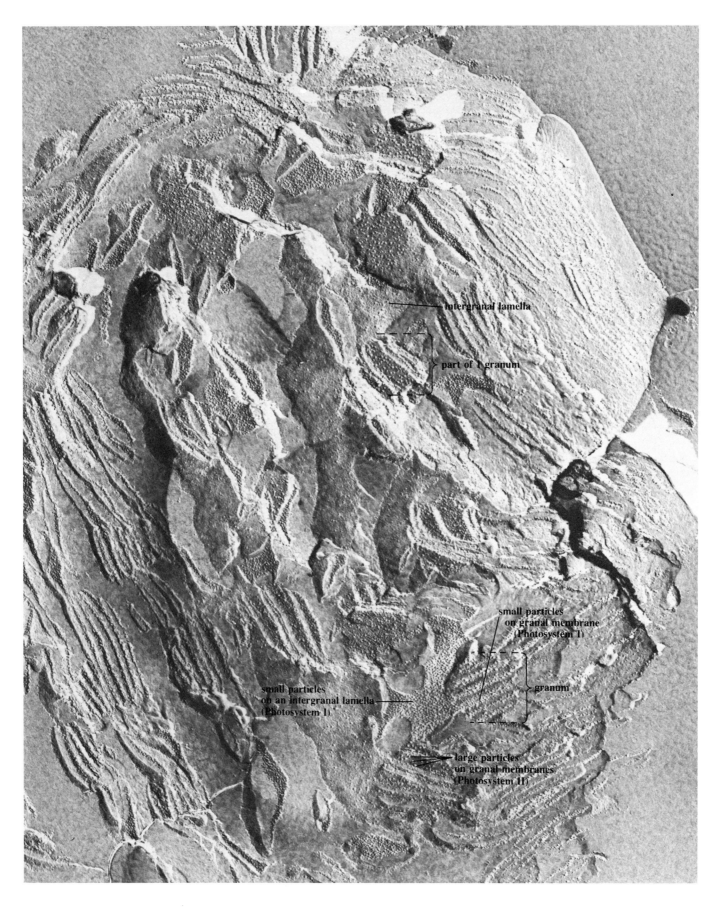

Fig 9.13 *Freeze-fractured isolated thylakoids of a chloroplast. The surfaces of fractured granal and intergranal membranes are visible. Note the aggregates of particles on the membranes*

Primary and accessory pigments

The photosynthetic pigments are of two types, **primary pigments** and **accessory pigments**. The latter pass the energy they emit to primary pigments. The electrons emitted by primary pigments are those that drive the reactions of photosynthesis.

There are two primary pigments, both forms of chlorophyll *a*; they are called P680 and P700 (see below). P stands for pigment. The accessory pigments are the other chlorophylls (including other forms of chlorophyll *a*) and the carotenoids.

> **9.7** Movement of energy from one pigment molecule to another must involve some loss of energy as heat, since energy cannot be transferred with 100% efficiency. Chlorophyll *b* passes energy to chlorophyll *a*. Can you predict whether chlorophyll *a* or chlorophyll *b* has the lower energy of excitation?

Photosystems and reaction centres

Over the last twenty years a great deal has been learned about the precise structural arrangement of the pigments and associated molecules in the thylakoid membranes. It is currently believed that there are two types of **photosystem**, called **photosystems I** and **II** (**PSI** and **PSII**) (photosystem I probably being the first to evolve). Evidence for this comes from both biochemical and electron microscopic observations. The latter come from the technique of freeze fracturing described in section A2.5, and are a good example of how this technique has contributed to biological research. Fig 9.13 shows the regular arrangement of two sizes of particle in the thylakoid membranes. It is thought that the small and large particles represent photosystems I and II respectively. Each has its own characteristic set of chlorophyll molecules, summarised in fig 9.14. PSII particles seem to be mostly associated with grana, and PSI particles with intergranal lamellae.

Each photosystem contains a collection of molecules involved in the light reactions of photosynthesis. Each contains about 300 chlorophyll molecules which act as a light-harvesting 'antenna'. A quantum of light energy absorbed by any of these molecules will pass downhill in energy terms to a **reaction centre** which consists of one specialised chlorophyll *a* molecule called **P680** or **P700**, depending on its absorption peak in nanometres. P680 and P700 are energy traps; they are the molecules which absorb light of the longest wavelength and hence the lowest energy. Other specialised forms of chlorophyll *a*, such as chlorophyll *a* 670, may be regarded as accessory pigments, like chlorophyll *b* 650. (Energy of excitation is transferred from one pigment molecule to another by resonance. The mechanism is known as **sensitised fluorescence** and is most efficient when the molecules are close together; hence their

arrangement in photosystems.) At the reaction centre energy from light causes electrons to leave P680 or P700, so driving a chemical reaction (see section 9.4.2). Thus it is here that light energy is converted to chemical energy and this is the energy conversion central to photosynthesis. The concept of a photosynthetic unit is sometimes used to include both photosystems and the electron transport chain that links them (section 9.4.2).

Computer program. LIGHT HARVEST, PHOTOSYNTHESIS: A double package. LIGHT HARVEST simulates the random walk of photons during light harvesting and demonstrates the concept of chlorophyll fluorescence. PHOTOSYNTHESIS is a simulation of the light phase of photosynthesis. The user controls the emission and wavelength of photons and can introduce blocking and uncoupling agents to explore some of the crucial experiments on which the light reaction is based.

9.4 Biochemistry of photosynthesis

A commonly used equation for photosynthesis is

$$6CO_2 + 6H_2O \xrightarrow[\text{chlorophyll}]{\text{light energy}} C_6H_{12}O_6 + 6O_2$$

carbon dioxide ___ water _____ sugar ___ oxygen
_____ e.g. glucose

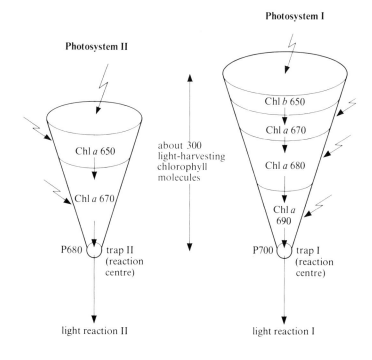

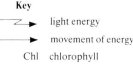

Key

→ light energy
→ movement of energy
Chl chlorophyll
Chl *a* 670 chlorophyll *a* with absorption peak at 670 nm
P pigment, i.e. primary pigment molecule of chlorophyll *a*

Fig 9.14 *Diagrammatic representation of energy traps in photosystems I and II*

This is useful for showing the formation of one molecule of sugar, but it should be realised that it is an overall summary of events. A better summary is

$$CO_2 + H_2O \xrightarrow[\text{chlorophyll}]{\text{light energy}} [CH_2O] + O_2$$

CH_2O does not exist as such, but represents a carbohydrate.

9.4.1 Source of oxygen

Looking at the equation a chemist would speculate about what type of reaction is involved, and a key question is whether the oxygen produced comes from carbon dioxide or water. The most obvious answer would seem to be carbon dioxide, so that the remaining carbon would be added to water to make carbohydrate. With the use of isotopes (section A1.3) in biology during the 1940s it became possible to answer the question directly.

The common isotope of oxygen has a mass number of 16 and is therefore represented as ^{16}O (8 protons, 8 neutrons). A rare isotope has a mass number of 18 (^{18}O). This is stable, but can be detected by virtue of its greater mass with a mass spectrometer, an important analytical instrument which distinguishes between different atoms and molecules according to their masses. In 1941 an experiment was carried out which produced results summarised in the following equation

$$CO_2 + H_2^{18}O \xrightarrow{\hspace{2cm}} [CH_2O] + {}^{18}O_2$$

The source of oxygen was thus shown to be water. The equation shows two atoms of oxygen coming from one molecule of water. So the balanced equation should be

$$CO_2 + 2H_2O \xrightarrow[\text{chlorophyll}]{\text{light energy}} [CH_2O] + O_2 + H_2O$$

This is the most accurate summary of photosynthesis and provides the extra information that water is produced, as well as used, in photosynthesis. This experiment confirmed indirect evidence put forward at about the same time by van Niel, who showed that bacteria do not produce oxygen during photosynthesis, although they use carbon dioxide. He concluded that all photosynthesising organisms need a source of hydrogen; for plants this is water, with oxygen being released; for sulphur bacteria, for example, it is hydrogen sulphide, sulphur being released instead of oxygen:

$$CO_2 + 2H_2S \xrightarrow[\text{chlorophyll}]{\text{light energy}} [CH_2O] + 2S + H_2O$$

This equation for sulphur bacteria is analogous to the plant equation.

These experiments provided a profound insight into the nature of photosynthesis because they showed that it takes place in two stages, the first of which involves acquiring hydrogen; in plants hydrogen is obtained by splitting water into hydrogen and oxygen. This requires energy which must be provided by light (hence the process used to be called **photolysis**: *photos*, light; *lysis*, splitting). Oxygen is released as a waste product. In the second stage, hydrogen combines with carbon dioxide to produce carbohydrate. Addition of hydrogen is an example of a type of chemical reaction called **reduction** (section A1.2).

The fact that photosynthesis is a two-stage process was first established in the 1920s and 1930s. The first stage was characterised by reactions requiring light and was called the **light reaction**. The second stage did not require light, and was called the **dark reaction**, although it takes place in light. It is now known that these are two sets of reactions which are also separated in space, the light reactions occurring on the chloroplast membranes and the dark reactions in the chloroplast stroma.

Having established that photosynthesis proceeds by light reactions followed by dark reactions, it remained in the 1950s to elucidate the nature of these reactions.

9.4.2 Light reactions

See reference to the computer program PHOTOSYNTHESIS, p. 259.

In 1958, Arnon and his co-workers showed that isolated chloroplasts, when exposed to light, could synthesis ATP from ADP and phosphate (**phophorlaytion**), reduce NADP to NADPH$_2$. and evolve oxygen.

He also showed that carbon dioxide could be *reduced* to carbohydrate *in the dark* if ATP and NADPH$_2$ (section 6.2.3) were provided. It therefore seemed that the role of the light reactions was to provide ATP and NADPH$_2$. Arnon noted the resemblance to respiration, where phosphorylation also occurs. This requires energy. In respiration it comes from oxidation of a food, usually glucose, and it is therefore called oxidative phosphorylation. In photosynthesis the energy comes from light and the process is therefore called photophosphorylation. Hence **oxidative phosphorylation** is the conversion of $ADP + P_i$ to ATP using chemical energy obtained from food by respiration, and **photophosphorylation** is the conversion of $ADP + P_i$ to ATP using light energy in photosynthesis. (P_i = inorganic phosphate.)

Arnon accurately predicted that photophosphorylation, like oxidative phosphorylation, would be coupled to the transfer of electrons in membranes. Electron transfer is fundamental to an understanding of both photosynthesis and respiration.

Cyclic and non-cyclic photophosphorylation

The role of the light reactions is to synthesise ATP and NADPH$_2$ using light energy. The process depends on a flow of electrons from primary pigments, and light provides the energy that causes this flow.

$$\text{chlorophyll } a \xrightarrow{\text{light energy}} \text{chlorophyll } a^+ + e^-$$
(reduced chlorophyll)   (oxidised chlorophyll)   excited electron

The fate of the electrons is summarised in fig 9.15. The pathway shown is sometimes known as the 'Z-scheme' from its shape. Remember that losing an electron is oxidation, gaining an electron is reduction (see section A1.2). In the Z-scheme two electrons are shown for convenience, though in practice they enter the scheme one at a time.

Fate of electrons. First, an electron from photosystem I or II is boosted to a higher energy level, that is it acquires excitation energy. Instead of falling back into the photosystem and losing its energy as, for example, fluorescence, it is captured by an electron acceptor (X or Y in fig 9.15). This represents the important conversion of light energy to chemical energy. The electron acceptor is thus reduced and a positively charged (oxidised) pigment is left in the photosystem. The electron then travels downhill, in energy terms, from one electron acceptor to another in a series of oxidation–reduction (redox) reactions. This electron flow is '**coupled**' to the formation of ATP in both cyclic and non-cyclic pathways; in addition, NADP is reduced in the non-cyclic pathway.

Non-cyclic photophosphorylation

Non-cyclic photophosphorylation is initiated by light shining on photosystems I and II. Excited electrons from P680 (PSII) and P700 (PSI) reduce electron acceptors X and Y respectively. P680 and P700 are now positively charged (oxidised). P680 is neutralised by electrons from water: electrons flow downhill from the latter to P680 via two electron carriers and oxygen is produced as a waste product of photosynthesis.

P700 is neutralised by electrons moving downhill from X via a chain of electron carriers, the energy from this flow being coupled to ATP production. Up to two ATP molecules may be made per pair of electrons, but this number is probably variable (two are shown in fig 9.15). Finally, electrons pass downhill from Y to NADP and combine with hydrogen ions to form $NADPH_2$. Note that the excess hydrogen ions are available from the 'splitting' of water.

Cyclic photophosphorylation

In cyclic photophosphorylation, electrons from Y are recycled back to P700 via the chain of electron carriers.

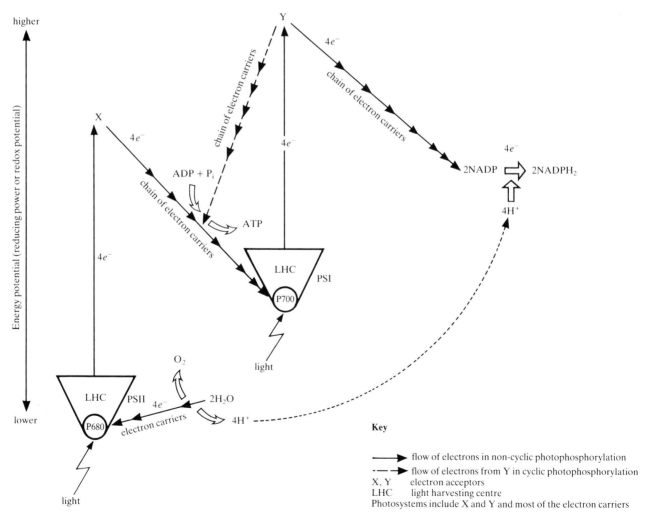

Fig 9.15 *'Z'-scheme of electron flow in cyclic and non-cyclic photophosphorylation*

Table 9.5 Comparison of cyclic and non-cyclic photophosphorylation.

	Non-cyclic	Cyclic
Pathway of electrons	Non-cyclic	Cyclic
First electron donor (source of electrons)	Water	Photosystem I (P700)
Last electron acceptor (destination of electrons)	NADP	Photosystem I (P700)
Products	Useful: ATP, NADPH$_2$ Waste: O$_2$	Useful: ATP only
Photosystems involved	I and II	I only

Their excitation energy is coupled to ATP production just as in non-cyclic photophosphorylation.

Table 9.5 shows the differences between cyclic and non-cyclic photophosphorylation.

The overall equation for non-cyclic photophosphorylation is

$$H_2O + NADP + 2ADP + 2P_i \xrightarrow[\text{chlorophyll}]{\text{light energy}} \tfrac{1}{2}O_2$$
$$+ NADPH_2 + 2ATP$$
$$\text{(maximum of 2ATP --}$$
$$\text{may be less than 2)}$$

Extra ATP can be made via cyclic photophosphorylation. The efficiency of energy conversion in the light reactions is high and estimated at about 39%.

The Hill reaction

In 1939 Robert Hill, working in Cambridge, discovered that isolated chloroplasts were capable of liberating oxygen in the presence of an oxidising agent (electron acceptor). This has since been called the Hill reaction. A number of so-called **Hill oxidants** substitute for the naturally occurring electron acceptor NADP, one of which is the blue dye DCPIP (2,6 dichlorophenolindophenol) that turns colourless when reduced:

$$\text{oxidised DCPIP} \xrightarrow{\text{light + chloroplasts}} \text{reduced DCPIP}$$

(blue) H_2O $\tfrac{1}{2}O_2$ (colourless)

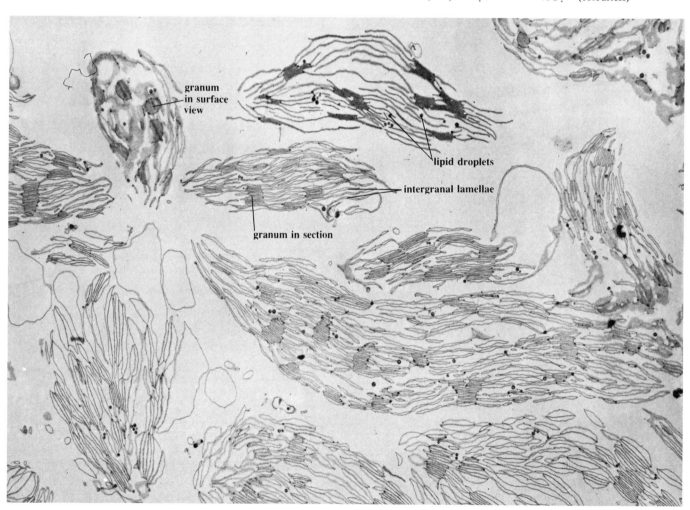

Fig 9.16 *Electron micrograph of chloroplasts after isolation in a dilute medium (× 13 485). Envelopes and stroma are lost*

Experiment 9.1: Investigating the Hill reaction

Isolation of chloroplasts

Materials

spinach, lettuce or cabbage leaves
scissors
cold pestle and mortar (or blender or food mixer)
muslin or nylon
filter funnel
centifuge and centrifuge tubes
ice–water–salt bath
glass rod

Solutions (see notes)

0.05 M phosphate buffer solution, pH 7.0
isolation medium
DCPIP solution (reaction medium)

Method

Chloroplasts can be isolated by grinding spinach, lettuce or cabbage leaves in a cold medium of suitable osmotic and ionic strength and pH, such as 0.4 M sucrose, 0.01 M KCl and 0.05 M phosphate buffer, pH 7.0. Solutions and apparatus must be kept cold during the isolation procedure if biochemical activity is to be preserved. The operation should also be performed as rapidly as possible, so study the method carefully and assemble the apparatus first.

Sufficient chloroplasts can be isolated using this method to supply several groups of students, if it is not practicable for all groups to prepare their own.

(1) Cut three small spinach, lettuce or cabbage leaves into small pieces with scissors, avoiding midribs and petioles. Place in a cold mortar or blender containing 20 cm³ of cold isolation medium (scale up quantities for blender if necessary).
(2) Grind vigorously and rapidly (or blend for about 10 s).
(3) Place four layers of muslin or nylon in a funnel and wet with cold isolation medium.
(4) Filter the homogenate through the funnel and collect in pre-cooled centrifuge tubes supported in an ice–water–salt bath. Gather the edges of the muslin and wring thoroughly into the tubes.
(5) Ensure that each centrifuge tube contains about the same volume of filtrate.
(6) If your bench centrifuge has a fixed speed, spin the filtrate for 2–5 min (a small pellet is required, but the time taken should be minimal).

If a bench centrifuge with variable speed is available, spin the filtrate at 100–200 times gravity for 1–2 min. Respin the supernatant (the liquid above the sediment) at 1 000–2 000 times gravity for up to 5 min (sufficient time to get a small chloroplast pellet).
(7) Pour away the supernatant. Resuspend the pellet of one centrifuge tube in about 2 cm³ of isolation medium using a glass rod. Transfer the suspension from this tube to the second centrifuge tube and resuspend the

pellet in that tube. (Alternatively, if more than one student group is to be supplied, use 2 cm³ in each tube and use one tube per group.)
(8) Store this chloroplast suspension in an ice–water–salt bath and use as soon as possible.

The Hill reaction

The chloroplast suspension can now be used to study the Hill reaction. The DCPIP solution should be used at room temperature.
Prepare the following tubes:
(1) 0.5 cm³ chloroplast suspension + 5 cm³ DCPIP solution. Leave in a bright light.
(2) 0.5 cm³ isolation medium + 5 cm³ DCPIP solution. Leave in a bright light.
(3) 0.5 cm³ chloroplast suspension + 5 cm³ DCPIP solution. Place immediately in darkness.
(4) It is useful to add 0.5 cm³ chloroplast suspension to 5 cm³ distilled water as a colour standard, showing what the final colour will be if the DCPIP is reduced.
Record your observations after 15–20 min.

If a colorimeter is available, the progress of the reaction can be followed by measuring the decrease in absorbance of the dye as it changes from the blue oxidised to the colourless reduced state. Prepare the mixtures given above for tubes (2) to (4) in colorimeter sample tubes. Insert a red (or yellow) filter and set the colorimeter at zero absorbance using tube (4) as a blank. Then set up tube (1) and immediately take a reading from this tube and return it to the light. Take further readings at 30 s intervals. Plot the rate of the reaction graphically. Once reduction is complete, take a reading from tube (3). Tube (2) can be checked for reduction of dye by first setting the colorimeter at zero with a blank of isolation medium. Ideally the time for complete reduction is about 10 min.

Notes

Prepare the solutions as follows.
0.05 M phosphate buffer solution, pH 7.0
$Na_2HPO_4.12H_2O$ 4.48 g (0.025 M)
KH_2PO_4 1.70 g (0.025 M)
Make up to 500 cm³ with distilled water and store in a refrigerator at 0–4 °C.
Isolation medium
sucrose   34.23 g (0.4 M)
KCl   0.19 g (0.01 M)
Dissolve in phosphate buffer solution at room temperature and make up to 250 cm³ with the buffer solution. Store in a refrigerator at 0–4 °C.
DCPIP solution (reaction medium)
DCPIP   0.007–0.01 g (10^{-4} M approx.)
KCl   0.93 g (0.05 M)
Dissolve in phosphate buffer solution at room temperature and make up to 250 cm³. Store in a refrigerator at 0–4 °C. Use at room temperature.
(NB Potassium chloride is a cofactor for the Hill reaction.)

9.8 What change, if any, did you observe in tube (1)?

9.9 What was the purpose of tubes (2) and (3)?

9.10 What other organelles apart from chloroplasts might you expect in the chloroplast suspension?

9.11 What evidence have you that these were not involved in the reduction of the dye?

9.12 Why was the isolation medium kept cold?

9.13 Why was the isolation medium buffered?

9.14 What was (*a*) the electron donor, and (*b*) the electron acceptor, in the Hill reaction?

9.15 During the Hill reaction, DCPIP acts between X and PSI in the Z-scheme (fig 9.15) and oxygen is evolved. Does the Hill reaction involve cyclic or non-cyclic photophosphorylation, or both? Give your reasons.

9.16 Fig 9.16 shows the appearance of the chloroplasts after being used in the experiment. The photograph demonstrates the consequences of transferring chloroplasts from the hypertonic isolation medium containing sucrose to the hypotonic reaction medium.

(*a*) How do the chloroplasts in fig 9.16 differ in appearance from normal chloroplasts?
(*b*) Can you explain why transferring the chloroplasts to a medium lacking sucrose should bring about this change?
(*c*) Why was this change desirable before carrying out the Hill reaction?

9.17 What significance do you think the discovery of the Hill reaction might have had on the understanding of the photosynthetic process?

9.4.3 Dark reactions

The dark reactions which take place in the stroma do not require light and use the energy (ATP) and reducing power ($NADPH_2$) produced by the light reactions to reduce carbon dioxide. The reactions are controlled by enzymes and their sequence was determined by Calvin, Benson and Bassham of the USA during the period 1946–53, work for which Calvin was awarded the Nobel prize in 1961.

Calvin's experiments

Calvin's work was based on use of the radioactive isotope of carbon, ^{14}C (half-life 5 570 years, see section A1.3) which only became available in 1945. He also used paper chromatography, which was a relatively new but neglected technique. Cultures of the unicellular green alga *Chlorella* were grown in the now famous 'lollipop' apparatus (fig

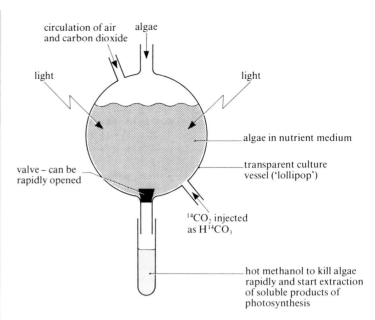

Fig 9.17 *Diagram illustrating the principle of Calvin's 'lollipop' apparatus. This comprises a thin, transparent vessel in which unicellular algae are cultured. Carbon dioxide containing radioactive carbon is bubbled through the algal suspension in experiments to determine the path taken by carbon in photosynthesis*

9.17). The *Chlorella* culture was exposed to $^{14}CO_2$ for varying lengths of time, rapidly killed by dropping into hot methanol, and the soluble products of photosynthesis extracted, concentrated and separated by **two-dimensional paper chromatography** (fig 9.18 and section A1.8.2). The aim was to follow the route taken by the labelled carbon through intermediate compounds into the final product of photosynthesis. Compounds were located on the chromatograms by **autoradiography**, whereby photographic film sensitive to radiation from ^{14}C was placed over the chromatograms and became darkened where radioactive compounds were located (fig 9.18). After only one minute of exposure to $^{14}CO_2$ many sugars and organic acids, including amino acids, had been made. However, using 5 s exposures or less, Calvin was able to identify the first product of photosynthesis as a 3C acid (an acid containing three carbon atoms), **glycerate-3-phosphate** (GP). He went on to establish the sequence of compounds through which the fixed carbon passed and the various stages involved are summarised below. They have since become known as the **Calvin cycle** (or Calvin–Benson–Bassham cycle).

9.18 What is the advantage of using a radioactive isotope with a long half-life in biological experiments?

9.19 What advantage might be gained by using *Chlorella* rather than a higher plant?

9.20 Why was the 'lollipop' vessel thin in section rather than spherical?

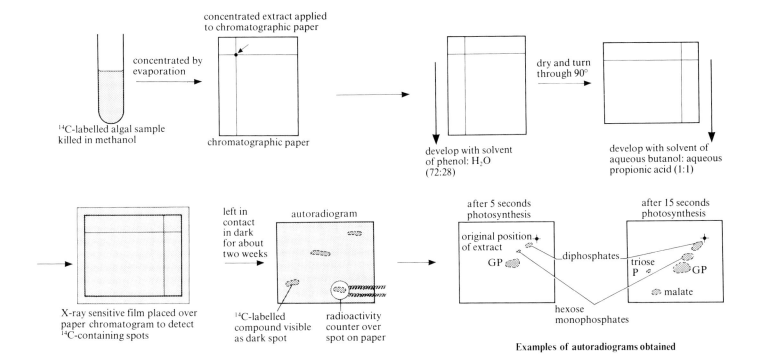

Fig 9.18 (a) Detection of the products of $^{14}CO_2$ fixation in algae after brief periods of illumination by the use of paper chromatography and autoradiography. (b) Autoradiographs of the photosynthetic products from $^{14}CO_2$ added to algae illuminated for short periods of time

Stages in carbon pathway

Acceptance of carbon dioxide (carbon dioxide fixation).

$$\underset{\substack{\text{(ribulose}\\\text{bisphosphate)}\\\text{5C sugar}}}{\text{RuBP}} + CO_2 + H_2O \xrightarrow{\text{RuBP carboxylase}} \underset{\substack{\text{(glycerate-3-phosphate)}\\\text{3C acid}\\\textbf{first product of}\\\textbf{photosynthesis}}}{2\text{GP}}$$

The carbon dioxide acceptor is a 5C sugar (a pentose), **ribulose bisphosphate** (ribulose with two phosphate groups, formerly known as ribulose diphosphate, RuDP). Addition of carbon dioxide to a compound is called **carboxylation**; the enzyme involved is a **carboxylase**. The 6C product is unstable and breaks down immediately to two molecules of **glycerate-3-phosphate** (GP). The latter is the first product of photosynthesis. The enzyme ribulose bisphosphate carboxylase is present in large amounts in the chloroplast stroma, and is in fact the world's most common protein.

Reduction phase

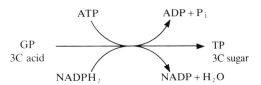

GP is glycerate-3-phosphate, a 3C **acid**. It contains the acidic carboxyl group (–COOH). TP is triose phosphate or glyceraldehyde-3-phosphate, a 3C **sugar**. It contains an aldehyde group (–CHO).

The reducing power of $NADPH_2$ and energy of ATP are used to remove oxygen from GP (reduction). The reaction takes place in two stages, the first using some of the ATP produced in the light reactions and the second using all the $NADPH_2$ produced in the light reactions. The overall effect is to reduce a carboxylic acid group (–COOH) to an aldehyde group (–CHO). The product is a 3C sugar phosphate (a triose phosphate), that is a sugar with a phosphate group attached. This contains more chemical energy than GP, and is the first carbohydrate made in photosynthesis.

Regeneration of the carbon dioxide acceptor, RuBP. Some of the triose phosphate (TP) has to be used to regenerate the ribulose bisphosphate consumed in the first reaction. This process involves a complex cycle, containing 3, 4, 5, 6 and 7C sugar phosphates. It is here that the remaining ATP is used. Fig 9.19 provides a summary of the dark reactions. In it the Calvin cycle is represented as a 'black box' into which carbon dioxide and water are fed and TP emerges. The diagram shows that the remaining ATP is used to phosphorylate ribulose phosphate to ribulose

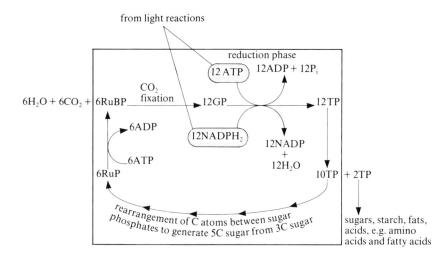

from light reactions

Fig 9.19 (left) *Summary of the dark reactions of photosynthesis (Calvin cycle). RuBP, ribulose bisphosphate; RuP, ribulose phosphate; GP, glycerate-3-phosphate; TP, triose phosphate*

Fig 9.20 (opposite) *Metabolism of GP and TP showing the relationship between photosynthesis and synthesis of food in plants. Main pathways only are shown. Some intermediate steps are omitted*

bisphosphate, but details of the complex series of reactions are not shown.

The overall equation which can be derived from fig 9.19 is

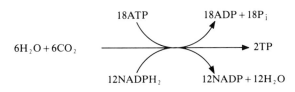

The important point to note is that six molecules of carbon dioxide have been used to make two molecules of a 3C sugar, triose phosphate. The equation can be simplified by dividing by six:

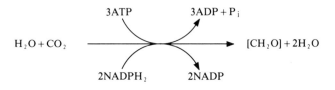

9.21 Redraw fig 9.19 showing only the numbers of C atoms involved; for example 6RuBP = 6 × 5C.
A summary of photosynthesis is given in table 9.6.

9.4.4 Metabolism of glycerate-3-phosphate and triose phosphate

Although triose phosphate (phosphoglyceraldehyde) is the end product of the Calvin cycle, it does not accumulate in large quantities since it is immediately converted to other products. The most familiar of these are glucose, sucrose and starch, but fats and organic acids (such as fatty acids and amino acids) are also rapidly made. Photosynthesis can strictly be regarded as complete once triose phosphate is made, because subsequent reactions can also occur in non-photosynthetic organisms, like animals and fungi. However, it is important to show here how glycerate-3-phosphate and triose phosphate can be used in the synthesis of all the basic food requirements of plants. Fig 9.20 summarises some of the main pathways involved and shows what a central position the reactions of glycolysis and Krebs cycle have in metabolism. The latter two pathways are discussed in chapter 11. Both glycerate-3-phosphate and triose phosphate are intermediates in glycolysis.

Synthesis of carbohydrates

Carbohydrates are synthesised in a process which is, in effect, a reversal of glycolysis. The two most common carbohydrate products are sucrose and starch. Sucrose is the form in which carbohydrate is exported from the leaf in the phloem (section 14.8). Starch is a storage product and is the most easily detected product of photosynthesis.

Synthesis of lipids

Glycerate-3-phosphate enters the glycolytic pathway and is converted to an acetyl group which is added to coenzyme A to form acetyl coenzyme A. This is converted to fatty acids in both cytoplasm and chloroplasts (not in mitochondria, where *breakdown* of fatty acids occurs). Glycerol on the other hand is made from triose phosphate.

Synthesis of proteins

Glycerate-3-phosphate and triose phosphate contain the

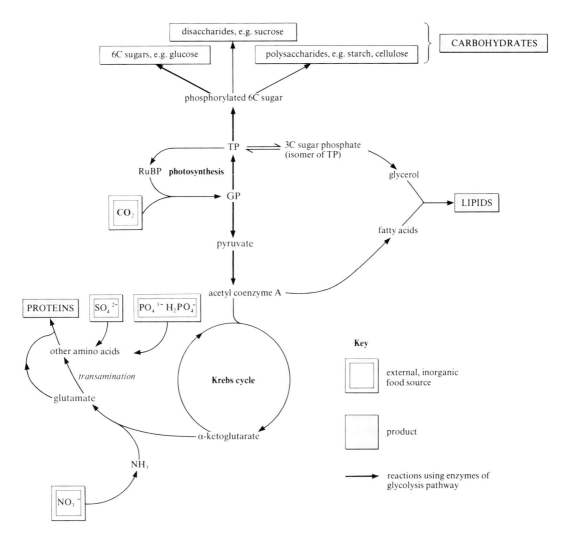

Table 9.6 Summary of photosynthesis.

	Light reactions	*Dark reactions*
Location in chloroplasts	Thylakoids	Stroma
Reactions	Photochemical, i.e. require light. Light energy causes the flow of electrons from electron 'donors' to electron 'acceptors', along a non-cyclic or a cyclic pathway. Two photosystems, I and II, are involved. These contain chlorophylls which emit electrons when they absorb light energy. Water acts as an electron donor to the non-cyclic pathway. Electron flow results in production of ATP (photophosphorylation) and NADPH$_2$. (See also table 9.5.)	Do not require light. Carbon dioxide is fixed when it is accepted by a 5C-compound ribulose bisphosphate (RuBP), to form two molecules of a 3C-compound glycerate-3-phosphate (GP), the first product of photosynthesis. A series of reactions occurs called the Calvin cycle in which the carbon dioxide acceptor RuBP is regenerated and GP is reduced to a sugar. (See also fig 9.19.)
Overall equation	$2H_2O + 2NADP \xrightarrow[\text{chlorophyll}]{\text{light}} O_2 + 2NADPH_2$ also $ADP + P_i \longrightarrow ATP$ (variable amount)	$CO_2 + H_2O \;\; \underset{\underset{2NADPH_2 \qquad 2NADP}{}}{\overset{\overset{3ATP \qquad 3ADP + 3P_i}{}}{\rightleftarrows}} \;\; [CH_2O] + 2H_2O$
Results	Light energy is converted to chemical energy in ATP and NADPH$_2$. Water is split into hydrogen and oxygen. Hydrogen is carried to NADPH$_2$ and oxygen is a waste product.	Carbon dioxide is reduced to carbon compounds such as carbohydrates, using the chemical energy in ATP and hydrogen in NADPH$_2$.
Combined equations		

$$\text{light} + \text{chlorophyll} \underset{O_2 \quad 4H^+ + 4e^-}{\overset{2H_2O}{\rightleftarrows}} \qquad \underset{CO_2 + H_2O}{\overset{[CH_2O]}{\rightleftarrows}}$$

$$\text{Net equation: } CO_2 + H_2O \xrightarrow[\text{chlorophyll}]{\text{light}} [CH_2O] + O_2$$

elements carbon, hydrogen and oxygen. Nitrogen, sulphur and occasionally phosphorus are also needed if amino acids and hence proteins are to be made. Plants obtain these elements from the soil water (or surrounding water in aquatic plants) as inorganic salts (nitrates, sulphates and phosphates respectively).

Many plants are able to synthesise all their amino acids using ammonia or nitrate as the nitrogen source, and given a supply of glycerate-3-phosphate from photosynthesis. Mammals are unable to synthesise some of the common amino acids (the essential amino acids, see section 5.4) and have to rely on plants as the source. Glycerate-3-phosphate is first converted to one of the acids of the Krebs cycle via acetyl coenzyme A (fig 9.20). Subsequent synthesis of the amino acid is summarised below.

(1)

$$NO_3^- \xrightarrow[\text{nitrate reductase}]{\text{reduction}} NO_2^- \xrightarrow[\text{nitrite reductase}]{\text{reduction}} NH_3$$
(nitrate)   (nitrite)
from roots

(2)

$$NH_3 + \text{Krebs cycle acid} \xrightarrow[\text{+ reduction}]{\text{amination}} \text{amino acid}$$
(ammonia)

For example,

$$NH_3 + \alpha\text{-ketoglutarate} + NADPH_2 \underset{\text{transaminase}}{\rightleftharpoons} \text{glutamate} + NADP$$

Reaction (2) is the major route of entry of ammonia into amino acids. By a process called **transamination** other amino acids can be made by transferring the amino group ($-NH_2$) from one acid to another. For example,

$$\text{glutamate} + \text{oxaloacetate} \underset{\text{transaminase}}{\rightleftharpoons} \alpha\text{-ketoglutarate} + \text{aspartate}$$
(amino acid) (a Krebs cycle acid)   (a Krebs cycle acid)   (amino acid)

Other synthetic pathways for amino acids also occur. Some amino acids are made in the chloroplasts. About one-third of the carbon fixed and about two-thirds of the nitrogen taken up by plants are commonly used directly to make amino acids.

9.5   Factors affecting photosynthesis

The rate of photosynthesis is an important factor in crop production since it affects yields. An understanding of those factors affecting the rate is therefore likely to lead to an improvement in crop management.

Computer program. PHOTOPLOT generates graphs of oxygen production against a selected variable under different conditions for both C_3 and C_4 plants.

9.22 From the equation for photosynthesis what factors are likely to affect its rate?

9.5.1   The concept of limiting factors

The rate of a biochemical process which, like photosynthesis, involves a series of reactions, will theoretically be limited by the slowest reaction in the series. For example, in photosynthesis the dark reactions are dependent on the light reactions for $NADPH_2$ and ATP. At low light intensities the rate at which these are produced is too slow to allow the dark reactions to proceed at maximum rate, so light is a limiting factor. The principle of limiting factors can be stated thus:

when a chemical process is affected by more than one factor its rate is limited by that factor which is nearest its minimum value: it is that factor which directly affects a process if its quantity is changed.

The principle was first established by Blackman in 1905. Since then it has been shown that different factors, such as carbon dioxide concentration and light intensity, interact and can be limiting at the same time, although one is often the major factor. Consider one of these factors, light intensity, by studying fig 9.21 and trying to answer the following questions.

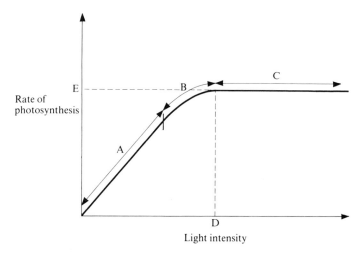

Fig 9.21   *Effect of light intensity on rate of photosynthesis*

9.23 In fig 9.21 (*a*) what is the limiting factor in region A?
(*b*) what is represented by the curve at B and C?
(*c*) what does point D represent on the curve?
(*d*) what does point E represent on the curve?

Fig 9.22 shows the results from four experiments in which the same experiment is repeated at different temperatures and carbon dioxide concentrations.

9.24 In fig 9.22 what do the points X, Y and Z represent on the three curves?

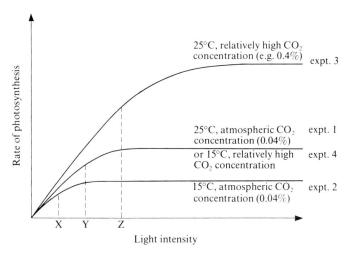

Fig 9.22 *Effect of various factors on rate of photosynthesis*

In fig 9.22, experiments 1–4 show that once light intensity is no longer limiting, both temperature and carbon dioxide concentration can become limiting. Enzyme-controlled reactions like the dark reactions of photosynthesis are sensitive to temperature; thus an increase in temperature from 15 °C to 25 °C results in an increased rate of photosynthesis (compare experiments 2 and 1, or 4 and 3) providing light is not a limiting factor. Carbon dioxide concentration can also be a limiting factor in the dark reactions (compare experiments 2 and 4, or 1 and 3). Thus in experiment 2, for example, both temperature and carbon dioxide concentration are limiting, and an increase in either results in increased photosynthetic rate.

9.5.2   Reaction rate graphs

The chief external factors affecting rate of photosynthesis are light intensity, carbon dioxide concentration and temperature. Graphs representing their effects all have the form of fig 9.21, with external factors plotted on the horizontal axis. All show an initial linear increase in photosynthetic rate where the factor being investigated is limiting, followed by a decrease in the rate of increase and stabilising of rate as another factor, or factors, becomes limiting.

In the following it is assumed that factors other than the one under discussion are optimal.

Light

When considering the effect of light on a process it is important to distinguish between the effects of light intensity, light quality and duration of exposure to light.

Light intensity. In low light intensities the rate of photosynthesis increases linearly with increasing light intensity (fig 9.21). Gradually the rate of increase falls off as the other factors become limiting. Illumination on a clear summer's day is about 100 000 lux (10 000 ft candles), whereas light saturation for photosynthesis is reached at about 10 000 lux. Therefore, except for shaded

plants, light is not normally a major limiting factor. Very high light intensities may bleach chlorophyll and retard photosynthesis, but plants naturally exposed to such conditions are usually protected by devices such as thick cuticles and hairy leaves.

Light duration (photoperiod). Photosynthesis only occurs during periods of light, but is otherwise unaffected by light duration.

Light quality (wavelength of colours). The effect of light quality is revealed by the action spectrum for photosynthesis (see fig 9.12).

Carbon dioxide concentration

Carbon dioxide is needed in the dark reactions where it is fixed into organic compounds. Under normal field conditions, carbon dioxide is the major limiting factor in photosynthesis. Its concentration in the atmosphere varies between 0.03% and 0.04%, but increases in photosynthetic rate can be achieved by increasing the percentage (see experiment 3, fig 9.22). The short-term optimum is about 0.5%, but this can be damaging over long periods; then the optimum is about 0.1%. This has led to some greenhouse crops, such as tomatoes, being grown in carbon-dioxide-enriched atmospheres. At the moment there is much interest in a group of plants which are capable of removing the available carbon dioxide from the atmosphere more efficiently, hence achieving greater yields. These 'C_4' plants are discussed in section 9.8.2, where the effects of high carbon dioxide concentrations on inhibiting photorespiration, thus stimulating photosynthesis, are also discussed.

Temperature

The dark reactions and, to a certain extent, the light reactions are enzyme-controlled and therefore temperature-sensitive. For temperate plants the optimum temperature is usually about 25 °C. The rate doubles for every 10 °C rise up to about 35 °C, although other factors mean that the plant grows better at 25°C.

9.25 Why should the rate decrease at higher temperatures?

Water

Water is a reactant (raw material) in photosynthesis but so many cell processes are affected by lack of water that it is impossible to measure the direct effect of water on photosynthesis. Nevertheless, by studying the yields (amounts of organic matter synthesised) of water-deficient plants, it can be shown that periods of temporary wilting can lead to severe yield losses. Even slight water deficiency, with no visible effects, might significantly reduce crop yields. The reasons are complex and not fully understood. One obvious factor is that plants usually close their stomata in response to wilting and this would prevent access of carbon dioxide for photosynthesis. Abscisic acid, a growth inhibitor, has also been shown to accumulate in water-deficient leaves of some species.

Chlorophyll concentration

Chlorophyll concentration is not normally a limiting factor, but reduction in chlorophyll levels can be induced by several factors, including disease (such as mildews, rusts and virus diseases), mineral deficiency (section 9.12) and normal ageing processes (**senescence**). If the leaf becomes yellow it is said to be **chlorotic**, the yellowing process being called **chlorosis**. Chlorotic spots are thus often a symptom of disease or mineral deficiency. Iron, magnesium and nitrogen are required during chlorophyll synthesis (the latter two elements being part of its structure) and are therefore particularly important minerals. Potassium is also important. Lack of light can also cause chlorosis since light is needed for the final stage of chlorophyll synthesis.

Oxygen

Relatively high concentrations of oxygen, such as the 21% in the atmosphere to which plants are normally exposed, generally inhibit photosynthesis. In recent years it has been shown that oxygen competes with carbon dioxide for the active site in the carbon-dioxide-fixing enzyme RuBP carboxylase, thus reducing the overall rate of photosynthesis. In the subsequent reactions carbon dioxide is produced, again reducing net photosynthesis. These reactions comprise 'photorespiration' and are discussed in section 9.8.

Specific inhibitors

An obvious way of killing a plant is to inhibit photosynthesis, and various herbicides have been introduced with this intention. A notable example is DCMU (dichlorophenyl dimethyl urea) which short-circuits non-cyclic electron flow in chloroplasts and thus inhibits the light reactions. DCMU has been useful in research on the light reactions.

Pollution

Low levels of certain gases of industrial origin, notably ozone and sulphur dioxide, are very damaging to the leaves of some plants, although the exact reasons are still being investigated. It is estimated, for example, that cereal crop losses as high as 15% may occur in badly polluted areas, particularly when compounded with dry conditions as in the British summer of 1976. Lichens are very sensitive to sulphur dioxide. Soot can block stomata and reduce the transparency of the leaf epidermis.

> **9.26** Suggest some habitats or natural circumstances in which (*a*) light intensity, (*b*) oxygen concentration or (*c*) temperature might be limiting factors in photosynthesis.

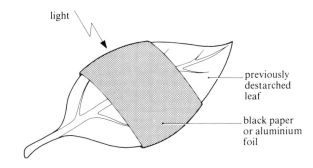

During experiment

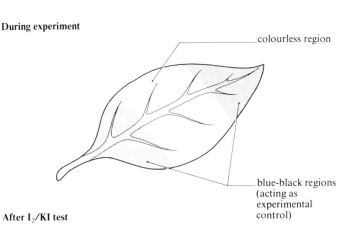

After I₂/KI test

Fig 9.23 *Investigating the need for light in photosynthesis*

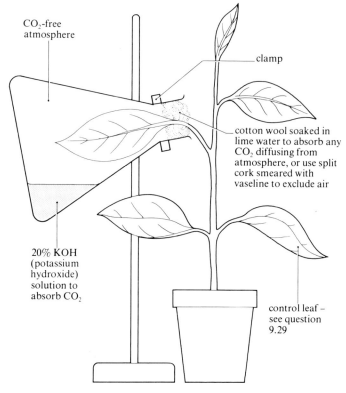

Fig 9.24 *Investigating the need for carbon dioxide in photosynthesis*

Experiments: To investigate conditions required for, and products of photosynthesis

As an indication that photosynthesis has occurred some product of the process can be identified. The first product is phosphoglyceric acid which is rapidly converted to a number of compounds, including sugars and thence starch. The latter can be tested for very easily and can be taken as an indication that photosynthesis has occurred, providing that the precaution is taken of starting the experiment with a destarched leaf or plant.

Destarching a plant

A plant can be destarched by leaving it in the dark for 24–48 h. It is advisable to check that destarching is complete before attempting the following experiment.

9.27   Why does this result in destarching?

Experiment 9.2: To test a leaf for starch

Materials

leaf to be tested	hot water bath
test tube	90% ethanol
forceps	iodine/potassium
white tile	iodide solution

Method

Starch can be detected using iodine/potassium iodide solution (I_2/KI) but the leaf must first be decolourised because the green colour of the chlorophyll masks the colour change. This is achieved by placing the leaf in a test-tube of boiling 90% ethanol in a water bath for as long as necessary (naked flames must be avoided because ethanol is highly inflammable).

The decolourised leaf is rinsed in hot water to remove ethanol and soften the tissues, spread on a white tile, and iodine solution poured on its surface. The red-brown solution stains any starch-containing parts of the leaf blue-black.

Experiment 9.3: To investigate the need for light

Materials

destarched leafy plant	black paper or metal foil
light source such as	starch test materials
a bench lamp	

Method

Although the destarching process itself demonstrates the need for light, the requirement can be investigated further by placing strips of black paper or metal foil over destarched leaves and exposing them to light for several hours. Procedure and expected results are shown in fig 9.23.

9.28   How would you criticise the experimental design and modify the experiment to take into account your criticisms?

Experiment 9.4: To investigate the need for carbon dioxide

Materials

destarched leafy plant such as potted geranium (*Pelargonium*)	starch test materials
	250 cm³ conical flask
	clamp and clamp stand
	limewater
light source such as a bench lamp	
cotton wool	
20% potassium hydroxide solution	

Method

Fig 9.24 illustrates a suitable procedure for investigating the need for carbon dioxide. The plant should be left for several hours in the light before testing the relevant leaves for starch.

9.29   Describe the conditions to which you would subject the control leaf.

A more satisfactory experiment showing the use of carbon dioxide is one involving the uptake of $^{14}CO_2$ (radioactively labelled carbon dioxide) into sugars and other compounds.

Experiment 9.5: To investigate the need for chlorophyll

Materials

plant with variegated leaves such as *Chlorophyton*, variegated ivy, geranium, maple or privet
starch test materials

Method

A number of plants have variegated leaves, that is leaves with green and non-green areas, the latter having no chlorophyll. Examples are given above. If the starch test is carried out on such a leaf, after careful mapping of the green and white (non-green) areas, it will be seen that only the green, chlorophyll-containing areas contain starch.

Experiment 9.6: To investigate the evolution of oxygen

Materials

Canadian pondweed
   (*Elodea*)
test-tube
glass funnel
light source such as a
   bench lamp

sodium hydrogen-
   carbonate
400 cm³ beaker
wooden splint
plasticine

Method

The simplest method to demonstrate that oxygen is a product of photosynthesis is to use a well-illuminated aquatic plant, such as *Elodea*, from which oxygen gas can be collected over water as shown in fig 9.25. A quantitative method is discussed in the next section.

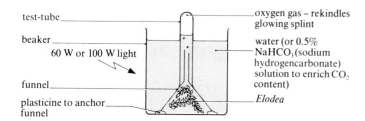

Fig 9.25 *Investigating the evolution of oxygen during photosynthesis*

9.6   Measuring rates of photosynthesis

> **9.30** From the equation for photosynthesis, what changes in the substances taken up and produced might be used to measure the rate of photosynthesis?

In section 9.5 certain external factors (such as light intensity, carbon dioxide concentration and temperature) were shown to affect the rate of photosynthesis. When a particular factor is being investigated, it is essential that other factors are kept constant and, if possible, at optimum levels so that no other factor is limiting.

9.6.1   The rate of oxygen evolution

Measuring the rate of oxygen evolution from a water plant is the simplest way to measure the rate of photosynthesis.

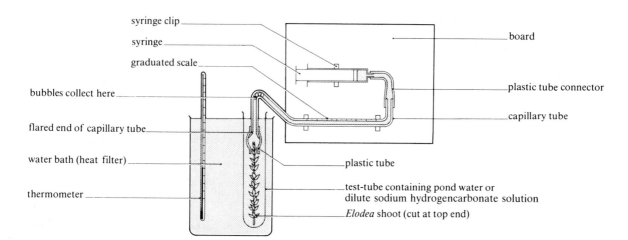

Fig 9.26 *Apparatus for measuring the rate of oxygen evolution by a water plant during photosynthesis*

Experiment 9.7: To investigate the effect of light intensity on the rate of photosynthesis

Materials

apparatus for collecting gas as shown in fig 9.26
test-tube
400 cm³ beaker
thermometer
mercury vapour lamp or projector lamp
sodium hydrogen-carbonate
metre rule
stopclock
light source such as bench lamp
Canadian pondweed (*Elodea*), previously well illuminated for several hours
detergent (washing-up liquid)

Method

It is advisable to use *Elodea* that has been well illuminated and is known to be photosynthesising actively. The addition of 2–10 g of sodium hydrogencarbonate to each litre of pond water may stimulate photosynthesis if there are no obvious signs of bubbles being produced (this increases carbon dioxide availability). The water could also be aerated for an hour before the experiment.

(1) Cut the stem of a bubbling piece of *Elodea* to about 5 cm long with a sharp scalpel and place it, cut surface upwards, in a test-tube containing the same water that it has been kept in.

(2) Stand the test-tube in a beaker of water at room temperature. Record the temperature of the water, which acts as a heat shield, and check it at intervals throughout the experiment. It should remain constant and the water be renewed if necessary.

(3) Fill the apparatus with tap water, ensuring that no air bubbles are trapped in it and push the plunger well in to the end of the syringe (fig 9.26).

(4) Darken the laboratory. Place a bright light source 5 cm from the plant.

(5) Allow the plant to adjust to the light intensity (equilibrate) for 2–3 min. Ensure that the rate of bubbling is adequate (such as more than 10 bubbles per minute). A trace of detergent is sometimes sufficient to lower the surface tension to allow freer escape of bubbles.

(6) Position the *Elodea* so that its bubbles are collected in the capillary tube of the apparatus. Start timing.

(7) Collect a suitable volume of gas in a known period (for example 5–10 min). Measure the length of the bubble by drawing it slowly along the capillary tube by means of a syringe. The bubble can thus be positioned along the scale.

(8) Draw the bubble into the plastic tube connector where it will not interfere with subsequent measurements and repeat the procedure at increasing distances between the light source and *Elodea*, such as 10, 15, 20, 30, 40 and 80 cm. In each case allow time for the plant to equilibrate. The following three measurements are required under each condition: (*a*) the distance between plant and light source, (*b*) the time taken to collect the gas, and (*c*) the length of the gas bubbles collected (this measurement is directly proportional to volume and is used as a measurement of volume).

Results

The intensity of light falling on a given object is inversely proportional to the square of the distance from the source. In other words, doubling the distance between the weed and the lamp does not halve the light intensity received by the weed, but quarters it.

$$LI \propto \frac{1}{d^2}$$

where *LI* is the light intensity and *d* is the distance between object and light source. Plot a graph with rate of photosynthesis on the vertical axis (as length of gas bubble per unit time) and *LI* on the horizontal axis (as $1/d^2$ or, more conveniently, $1\,000/d^2$).

> **9.31** (*a*) State the relationship between gas production and light intensity demonstrated by your results.
> (*b*) Why was the laboratory darkened and the temperature kept constant?
> **9.32** What are the main sources of inaccuracy in this experiment?
> **9.33** If the gas is collected and analysed it is found *not* to be pure oxygen. Can you account for this?
> **9.34** Why is it advisable to aerate the water before beginning the experiment?

If a simpler, quicker, though slightly less accurate method is required, the rate of oxygen evolution can be determined by counting the number of bubbles evolved from the cut end of a stem of *Elodea* in a given time period. This can be just as satisfactory, but errors may occur through variations in bubble size. This problem is less likely to arise if a trace of detergent is added to lower the surface tension (see (5) above). The *Elodea* can be anchored to the bottom of the tube with plasticine if necessary.

9.7   Compensation points

Photosynthesis results in uptake of carbon dioxide and evolution of oxygen. At the same time respiration uses oxygen and produces carbon dioxide. If light intensity is gradually increased from zero, the rate of photosynthesis gradually increases accordingly (fig 9.22). There will come a point, therefore, when photosynthesis and respiration exactly balance each other, with no net exchange of oxygen and carbon dioxide. This is called the **compensation point**, or more precisely the **light compensation point**, that is the light intensity at which net gaseous exchange is zero.

Since carbon dioxide concentration affects the rate of photosynthesis there also exists a **carbon dioxide compensation point**. This is the carbon dioxide concentration at which net gaseous exchange is zero for a given light intensity. The higher the carbon dioxide concentration, up to about 0.1% (1 000 ppm, parts per million), the faster the rate of photosynthesis. For most temperate plants the carbon dioxide compensation point, beyond which photosynthesis exceeds respiration, is 50–100 ppm, assuming light is not a limiting factor. Atmospheric carbon dioxide concentrations are normally in the range 300–400 ppm, and therefore under normal circumstances of light and atmospheric conditions this point is always exceeded.

Experiment 9.8: To investigate gaseous exchange in leaves

Materials

four test-tubes	unbleached cotton wool
thoroughly cleaned	no. 12 cork borer
and fitted with rubber	water bath with
bungs	test-tube clamps
forceps	bench lamp
test-tube rack	freshly picked leaves
2 cm³ syringe	hydrogencarbonate
aluminium foil	indicator

The hydrogencarbonate indicator (bicarbonate indicator) solution should be freshly equilibrated with the atmosphere by bubbling fresh air through it until cherry red. Hydrogencarbonate indicator is supplied as a concentrated solution and must be diluted by a factor of ten for experimental use. To equilibrate with atmospheric carbon dioxide, air from *outside* the laboratory should be pumped through the solution. A suitable method is to place the solution in a clear glass wash-bottle to which a tube is attached whose free end is hung from a window. A filter pump is then used to bubble air through the solution until there is no further colour change. The colour of the indicator at this stage is a deep red but will appear orange-red in the test-tubes. Time must be allowed for this procedure before the start of the experiment (100 cm³ of indicator will need to be aerated for at least 20 min).

Method

(1) Label four test-tubes A, B, C and D.
(2) Rinse the four tubes and a 2 cm³ syringe with a little of the indicator solution.
(3) Add 2 cm³ of the indicator solution to each tube by means of the syringe. Avoid putting fingers over the ends of the tubes since the acid in sweat will affect the indicator. Also avoid breathing over the open ends of the tubes.
(4) Cover the outside of the tubes A and C with aluminium foil.
(5) Set up the tubes as shown in fig 9.27, using two leaf discs per tube, cut from a fresh leaf with a number 12 cork borer.
(6) Arrange the tubes in such a way that they are equally illuminated by a bench lamp.
(7) Place a heat filter in the form of a glass tank of water between the tubes and the light source to prevent a rise in temperature during the experiment. Alternatively, the tubes can be clamped in a water bath.
(8) Note the colour of the indicator in each tube.
(9) At intervals shake the tubes gently and leave for at least 2 h, preferably overnight. Record the final colour of the indicator in each tube as seen against a white background.

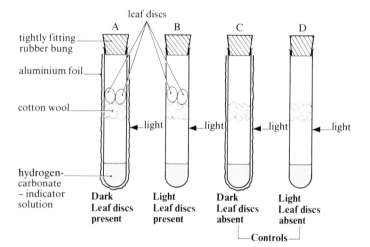

Fig 9.27 *Experiment to investigate gaseous exchange in leaf discs*

Results

Results can be interpreted using the following guide to colour changes.

yellow   orange   red   purple

◄— net carbon dioxide production —| |— net carbon dioxide uptake —►

◄————————— increasing acidity —————————

————————— increasing alkalinity —————————►

If conditions become more acidic, this can be assumed to be the result of carbon dioxide being produced and dissolving in the indicator solution. If conditions become less acidic, this indicates a lowering of carbon dioxide concentration.

Modifications of this experiment

(1) **Comparing rates of photosynthesis.** By using leaf discs as described, rather than whole leaves, comparative studies may be carried out using different light intensities, or, for example, old and young leaves on the same plant, yellow and green areas of variegated leaves, leaves of different species (such as a C_3 and a C_4 plant – see C_4 photosynthesis). To compare rates of photosynthesis, colours of the indicator solutions can be compared during or at the end of the experiment as appropriate. If light intensity is investigated, a mercury vapour lamp should be used. An interesting comparison can be made between shade-loving plants, such as enchanter's nightshade (*Circaea lutetiana*), and other species to determine whether the former are capable of photosynthesising at lower light intensities (that is they have lower light compensation points).

(2) **Using water plants instead of leaf discs.** Water plants such as *Elodea* may be used, providing they are washed well in distilled water to remove traces of dirt and pond water in order to minimise any contribution from micro-organisms. The plants should be placed directly in sufficient indicator solution to cover them. The solution has little effect on the plants during the course of the experiment.

9.8 Photorespiration and C_4 photosynthesis

9.8.1 Photorespiration

Photosynthesis is believed to have evolved in an atmosphere much richer in carbon dioxide than it is today, but one containing relatively little oxygen, probably about 0.02% oxygen compared with 21% today. Since 1920 it has been known that oxygen generally inhibits photosynthesis and the reason for this was discovered in 1971. It was shown that the carbon-dioxide-fixing enzyme, ribulose bisphosphate carboxylase (RuBP carboxylase) will accept not only carbon dioxide but also oxygen as a substrate. The two gases compete, in fact, for the same active site.

If oxygen is accepted the following reaction is catalysed:

$$(1) \quad O_2 + RuBP \xrightarrow{\text{RuBP oxygenase}} \text{phosphoglycolate} + GP$$
$$ 5C \phantom{\xrightarrow{\text{RuBP oxygenase}} \text{phosphoglycolate} +} 2C 3C$$

Compare with the usual carbon dioxide-fixing process:

$$(2) \quad CO_2 + RuBP \xrightarrow{\text{RuBP carboxylase}} 2GP$$
$$ 5C \phantom{\xrightarrow{\text{RuBP carboxylase}} } 2\times3C$$

Reaction (1) is called an **oxygenation**; the same enzyme is therefore called **RuBP oxygenase** in this reaction and RuBP carboxylase in reaction (2). The enzyme is therefore often called ribulose bisphosphate carboxylase-oxygenase, or RUBISCO. In reaction (1), one molecule each of glycerate-3-phosphate and phosphoglycolate are formed instead of the two GP molecules in reaction (2). Phosphoglycolate (phosphoglycolic acid) is converted immediately to glycolate (glycolic acid) by removal of the phosphate group.

Oxygen is therefore a **competitive inhibitor** (section 6.5) of carbon dioxide fixation and any increase in oxygen concentration will favour the uptake of oxygen rather than carbon dioxide, and so inhibit photosynthesis. Conversely an increase in carbon dioxide concentration will favour the carboxylation reaction.

The plant now has the problem of what to do with the glycolate and the pathway which deals with it is called **photorespiration**. Photorespiration is defined as a light-dependent uptake of oxygen and output of carbon dioxide. It is in no way related to normal respiration (now sometimes called **dark respiration** to avoid confusion) and only resembles it in that oxygen is used and carbon dioxide produced. It is light-dependent because a supply of RuBP is only available when photosynthesis is operating, RuBP being a product of the Calvin cycle. The function of photorespiration is to recover some of the carbon from the excess glycolate. The pathway involved is illustrated in fig 9.28. Details of the pathway can be ignored but the following four main points emerge.

(1) **Oxygen is used** (*a*) when glycolate is oxidised to glyoxylate in the peroxisome, and (*b*) when glycine is oxidised to serine in the mitochondrion.

(2) There is a **wasteful loss of carbon as carbon dioxide** when glycine is oxidised to serine.

(3) There is a **wasteful loss of energy** as $NADPH_2$ and ATP are used. Although ATP is produced when glycine is oxidised to serine, the overall process is energy-consuming.

(4) **Three different organelles are involved**, that is chloroplasts, peroxisomes and mitochondria. Peroxisomes are briefly described in chapter 7 (fig 7.6).

Overall, one molecule of PGA containing 3C atoms is produced from two molecules of glycolate ($2 \times 2C$ atoms), that is three carbon atoms out of four are recovered from the waste glycolate. Since intermediates such as glycine can be made more efficiently by other pathways, there seems to be no other function for the pathway.

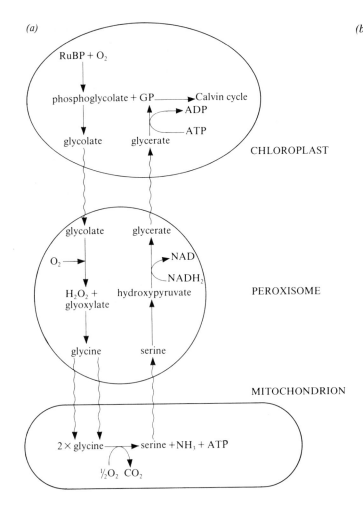

(a)

RuBP + O$_2$

phosphoglycolate + GP ——→ Calvin cycle

→ ADP

— ATP

glycolate   glycerate

CHLOROPLAST

glycolate   glycerate

O$_2$ →

→ NAD

— NADH$_2$

H$_2$O$_2$ +   hydroxypyruvate

glyoxylate

PEROXISOME

glycine   serine

MITOCHONDRION

2 × glycine ——→ serine + NH$_3$ + ATP

½O$_2$ CO$_2$

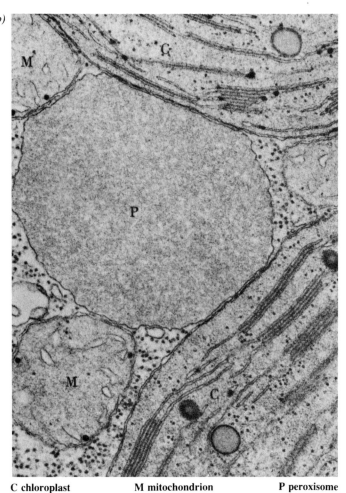

(b)

C chloroplast   M mitochondrion   P peroxisome

Fig 9.28 *(a) Pathway of photorespiration. Note oxygen is used and carbon dioxide produced. Also RuBP is used and this can only be produced by photosynthesis in the light. (b) Electron micrograph showing the intimate relationship between chloroplasts, peroxisomes and mitochondria typical of leaf mesophyll cells (× 38 700)*

The carbon lost represents carbon that had previously been fixed at the cost of energy. Also, the ammonia released when glycine is oxidised to serine must be reincorporated into amino acids at the expense of ATP.

9.37 How does a knowledge of photorespiration help to explain the known effects of carbon dioxide and oxygen concentration on rates of photosynthesis?

9.38 What environmental conditions favour photorespiration?

Summary of photorespiration

(1) It is a light-dependent uptake of oxygen and output of carbon dioxide.

(2) It bears no relation to normal respiration ('dark respiration').

(3) It occurs as a result of RuBP carboxylase accepting oxygen as well as carbon dioxide; unwanted glycolate is produced as a result. The remaining reactions are a means of recovering some of the carbon from glycolate.

(4) Two molecules of glycolate (total four carbon atoms) are converted to one molecule of PGA (three carbon atoms) at the expense of energy. Oxygen is used and wasteful loss of the fourth carbon atom as carbon dioxide occurs.

(5) It reduces the potential yield of C$_3$ plants by 30–40%.

9.8.2   C$_4$ photosynthesis

In 1965 it was shown that the first products of photosynthesis in sugarcane, a tropical plant, appeared to be acids containing four carbon atoms (malic, oxaloacetic and aspartic) rather than the 3C-acid PGA of *Chlorella* and most temperate plants. Many plants, mostly tropical and some of great economic importance, have since been identified in which the same is true and these are called **C$_4$ plants**. Examples are the monocotyledons maize (*Zea*),

Sorghum, sugarcane (*Saccharum*) and millet (*Eleusine*); the dicotyledons include *Amaranthus* and some *Euphorbia* species. Plants in which the first product of photosynthesis is the C_3-acid GP are called C_3 plants. It is the biochemistry of the latter plants which has been described so far in this chapter.

In 1966, two Australian workers, Hatch and Slack showed that C_4 plants were far more efficient at taking up carbon dioxide than C_3 plants: they could remove carbon dioxide from an experimental atmosphere down to 0.1 ppm compared with the 50–100 ppm of temperate plants, that is they had **low carbon dioxide compensation points**. Such plants show no apparent photorespiration.

The new carbon pathway in C_4 plants is called the **Hatch–Slack pathway**. Subtle variations exist but the process in a typical C_4 plant, maize, will be described. C_4 plants possess a characteristic leaf anatomy in which two rings of cells are found around each of the vascular bundles. The inner ring, or **bundle sheath cells**, contains chloroplasts which differ in form from those in the **mesophyll cells** in the outer ring. The chloroplasts in the plants are therefore described as **dimorphic**. Figs 9.29 (*a*) and (*b*) illustrate this so-called '**Kranz**' anatomy (Kranz means crown or halo, referring to the two distinct rings of cells). The biochemical pathway that takes place in these cells is summarised below and in fig 9.30.

Hatch–Slack pathway

The Hatch–Slack pathway is a pathway for transporting carbon dioxide and hydrogen from mesophyll cells to bundle sheath cells. Here carbon dioxide is fixed as in C_3 plants, as shown in fig 9.30, and reduced using the hydrogen.

Acceptance of carbon dioxide (carbon dioxide fixation) in mesophyll cells. Carbon dioxide is fixed in the **cytoplasm** of the mesophyll cells as shown below:

$$\underset{\substack{\text{(phosphoenolpyruvate)} \\ \text{3C}}}{\text{PEP}} + CO_2 \xrightarrow{\text{PEP carboxylase}} \underset{\text{4C}}{\text{oxaloacetate}}$$

The carbon-dioxide-acceptor is phosphoenolpyruvate (PEP) instead of RuBP and the enzyme is PEP carboxylase instead of RuBP carboxylase. PEP carboxylase has two enormous advantages over RuBP carboxylase. First, it has a much higher affinity for carbon dioxide, and secondly it does not accept oxygen and hence does not contribute to photorespiration. Oxaloacetate is converted to malate or aspartate, both 4C-acids. They possess two carboxyl (—COOH) groups, that is they are **dicarboxylic acids**.

Malate shunt. Malate is shunted through plasmodesmata in the cell walls to the chloroplasts of the bundle sheath cells, where it is used to produce carbon dioxide (decarboxylation), hydrogen (oxidation) and pyruvate. The hydrogen reduces NADP to $NADPH_2$.

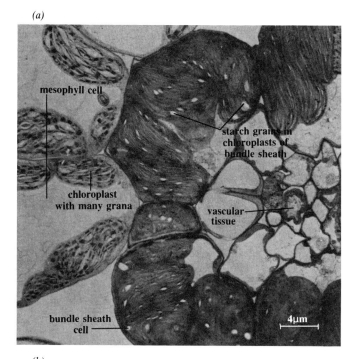

(*a*)

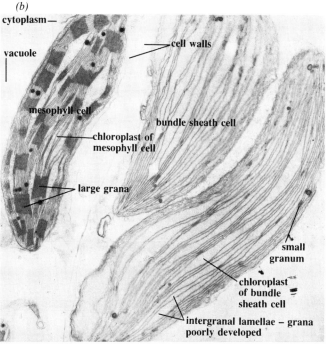

(*b*)

Fig 9.29 (a) 'Kranz' anatomy, characteristic of C_4 plants. Micrograph of a crabgrass (Digitaria sargurnalis) leaf cross section to show the dimorphism between bundle sheath Chloroplasts and mesophyll chloroplasts. Grana in the bundle sheath are only rudimentary, whereas they are prominent in the mesophyll. Starch grains are present in both. (Magnification × 4 000). (b) Electron micrograph of maize leaf showing two types of chloroplasts found in bundle sheath cells and mesophyll cells (× 9 900)

277

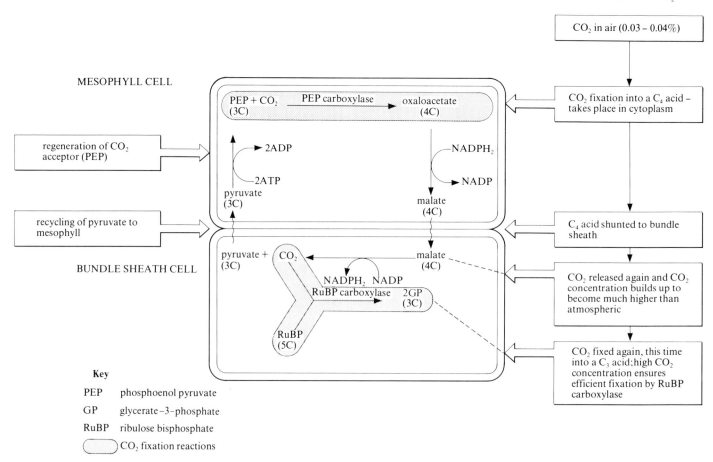

Fig 9.30 *Simplified outline of C₄ pathway coupled with C₃ fixation of carbon dioxide. Transport of carbon dioxide from air to bundle sheath is shown, together with final fixation of carbon dioxide into the C₃ acid PGA*

Regeneration of the carbon dioxide acceptor. Pyruvate is returned to the mesophyll cells and is used to regenerate PEP by addition of phosphate from ATP. This requires the energy from two high-energy phosphate bonds.

Net result of C₄ pathway

The net result of the C₄ pathway is the use of two high energy phosphate bonds to transport carbon dioxide and hydrogen from the mesophyll cells to the chloroplasts of the bundle sheath cells.

Refixation of carbon dioxide in the bundle sheath cells

Carbon dioxide and NADPH₂ are produced, as well as pyruvate, in the bundle sheath chloroplasts (see malate shunt above). The carbon dioxide is refixed by RuBP carboxylase in the conventional C₃ pathway, and the latter also uses the NADPH₂

Since every carbon dioxide molecule has had to be fixed twice, the energy requirement is roughly double in C₄ photosynthesis compared with C₃ photosynthesis. At first sight then, the transport of carbon dioxide by the C₄ pathway seems pointless. However, fixation using PEP carboxylase in the mesophyll is so efficient that a high concentration of carbon dioxide accumulates in the bundle sheath. This means that the RuBP carboxylase works at an

advantage compared with the same enzyme in C₃ plants, where carbon dioxide is at atmospheric concentration. There are two reasons for this: firstly, like any enzyme it works much more efficiently at high substrate concentrations; and secondly, photorespiration is inhibited, because oxygen is competitively excluded from the enzyme by carbon dioxide.

The main advantage of C₄ photosynthesis therefore is that it improves the efficiency of carbon dioxide fixation and prevents wasteful loss of carbon by photorespiration. It is an addition rather than an alternative to the C₃ pathway. As a result, C₄ plants are photosynthetically more efficient because the rate of carbon dioxide fixation is normally the limiting factor in photosynthesis. C₄ plants consume more energy by using the C₄ pathway, but energy is not normally the limiting factor in photosynthesis, and C₄ plants grow in regions of high light intensity as well as having modified chloroplasts for making more efficient use of available energy (see below).

Table 9.7 Differences between mesophyll and bundle sheath chloroplasts in C₄ plants.

Mesophyll chloroplasts	Bundle sheath chloroplasts
Large grana	No grana (or very few and small)
Therefore photosystem II activity high, so plenty of ATP, $NADPH_2$ and O_2 generated.	Therefore photosystem II activity low, so little $NADPH_2$ or O_2 generated (some ATP from photosystem I)
Virtually no RuBP carboxylase so no CO_2 fixation (CO_2 fixation occurs in cytoplasm by PEP carboxylase)	High concentration of RuBP carboxylase so CO_2 fixation occurs
Little starch	Abundant starch grains

Mesophyll and bundle sheath chloroplasts

Table 9.7 summarises the important differences between mesophyll and bundle sheath chloroplasts, some of which are visible in fig 9.29.

9.39 Which type of chloroplast is specialised for light reactions and which for dark reactions?

9.40 Why is it an advantage that bundle sheath chloroplasts lack grana?

9.41 The malate shunt is, in effect, a carbon dioxide and hydrogen pump. What is the advantage of this?

9.42 What would be the effect of lowering oxygen concentrations on (a) C₃ photosynthesis, (b) C₄ photosynthesis? Explain your answers.

In addition to C₃ and C₄ plants, there is a small group of plants, mainly succulents, in which carbon dioxide is incorporated into organic compounds, such as citrate and malate, *during the hours of darkness*. In the light, these compounds undergo decarboxylation, releasing carbon dioxide within the leaf which is then taken up by the chloroplasts and built up into sugars via the C₃ pathway. These are referred to as **CAM** plants (**C**rassulacean, the family of plants into which many of the succulents are classified; **A**cid **M**etabolism which need not concern us further except to note that by having, in effect, an internal store of carbon dioxide, the stomata need to open for less time in the light, thereby reducing water loss).

Compared with C₃ plants, C₄ plants can cope with higher light intensities before light saturation occurs. They also have a higher affinity for carbon dioxide because the initial carboxylating enzyme is more efficient in C₄ plants. The overall optimum temperature for photosynthesis is higher for C₄ plants. As a result of the increased physiological efficiency, the stomata need to open for shorter periods and hence in C₄ plants there is a higher rate of production of dry mass per unit of water taken up by the plants.

Table 9.8 Summary of the physiological differences between C₃ and C₄ plants.

	C_3	C_4
Representative species	Most crop plants cereals, tobacco, beans	Maize, sugar species
Rate of photo-respiration	High	Low
Light intensity for maximum rate of photosynthesis	10 000–30 000 foot candles	Not saturated at 10^5 lux
Effect of temperature on net rate (25 °C v. 35 °C)	No change or less at the warmer temperature	50% greater at the warmer temperature
'First product' produced in light	Glycerate-3-phosphate	Malate and oxaloacetate
Compensation point	40–60 ppm CO_2	Around zero
Water loss per g dry mass producer	450–950	250–350

Photorespiration is also reduced in C₄ plants and since

net assimilation rate = total amount of photosynthetic products produced − respiration losses

it follows that if photorespiration could be reduced in C₃ plants, higher yields would be produced overall. Attempts have been made, by the use of potential inhibitors sprayed on the leaf, to inhibit photorespiration. However, whilst these inhibitors have been shown to block certain enzyme steps in the photorespiration pathway, they have as yet been unsuccessful under field conditions; an example are the hydroxysulphonates which inhibit glycolic acid oxidase.

Attempts are being made to extend the environmental range of a number of crop and foliage plants having the C₄ type of metabolism by breeding new varieties and by selection within a species. For example, certain varieties of maize and soya bean have been shown to give consistently higher rates of photosynthesis than other varieties in different environmental conditions. C₄ plants do not appear to perform too well under temperate conditions.

9.8.3 Significance of photorespiration and the C₄ pathway

Photorespiration can be regarded as an unfortunate consequence of the increase in the oxygen concentration of the Earth's atmosphere (itself a result of photosynthesis) and of the ability of RuBP carboxylase to accept oxygen as well as carbon dioxide. It is wasteful of both carbon and energy and it has been estimated that it reduces the net rate of photosynthesis, and hence the potential yield, of C₃ plants by as much as 30–50%. Hence

Table 9.9 Comparison of C$_3$ and C$_4$ plants.

	C$_3$ plants	C$_4$ plants	
Carbon dioxide fixation	Occurs once	Occurs twice, first in mesophyll cells, then in bundle sheath cells	
Carbon dioxide acceptor	RuBP, a 5C-compound	**Mesophyll cells** PEP, a 3C-compound	**Bundle sheath cells** RuBP
Carbon dioxide – fixing enzyme	RuBP carboxylase, which is inefficient	PEP carboxylase which is very efficient	RuBP carboxylase, working efficiently because carbon dioxide concentration is high
First product of photosynthesis	A C$_3$ acid, GP	A C$_4$ acid, e.g. oxaloacetate	
Leaf anatomy	Only one type of chloroplast	'Kranz' anatomy, i.e. two types of cell, each with its own type of chloroplast	
Photorespiration	Occurs; therefore oxygen is an inhibitor of photo-synthesis	Is inhibited by high carbon dioxide concentration. Therefore atmospheric oxygen is not an inhibitor of photosynthesis.	
Efficiency	Less efficient photo-synthesis than C$_4$ plants. Yields usually much lower.	More efficient photosynthesis than C$_3$ plants. Yields usually much higher.	

it is of great economic significance, notably in crop plants. Various ways of inhibiting the process are being sought. One method would be to grow crops in atmospheres with artificially reduced oxygen concentrations, but this is difficult. Another is to artificially increase carbon dioxide concentrations to 0.1–1.5%, a five-fold increase over atmospheric, though this is commercially viable only for high-cash crops grown in greenhouses, such as tomatoes and flowers. Breeding C$_4$ genes into C$_3$ plants may prove possible and the techniques of genetic engineering may eventually prove useful.

The C$_4$ pathway is thought to be more recently evolved than the C$_3$ pathway and involves both a superior carbon-dioxide-fixing mechanism and a means of inhibiting photorespiration. Thus C$_4$ plants increase in dry mass more rapidly than C$_3$ plants and are more efficient crop plants.

They have evolved chiefly in the drier regions of the tropics, for which they are adapted in two major ways. First, their maximum rate of carbon dioxide fixation is greater; therefore the higher light intensities and tempera-tures of the tropics are more efficiently exploited. Second-ly, C$_4$ plants are more tolerant of dry conditions. Plants usually reduce their stomatal apertures in order to reduce water loss by transpiration, and this also reduces the area for carbon dioxide entry. Carbon dioxide is fixed so rapidly in C$_4$ plants that a steep carbon dioxide diffusion gradient can still be maintained between external and internal atmospheres, thus allowing faster growth than C$_3$ plants. C$_4$ plants lose only about half the water that C$_3$ plants lose for each molecule of carbon dioxide fixed.

However, in cooler, moister, temperate regions with fewer hours of high light intensity, the extra energy (about 15% more) required by C$_4$ plants to fix carbon dioxide is more likely to be a limiting factor and C$_3$ plants may even have a competitive advantage in such situations.

9.9 Photosynthetic bacteria

Since photosynthesis probably first appeared in prokaryotes, details of the process in these organisms are of interest. In table 9.10 some of the more important comparisons between pro- and eukaryotes are made.

Four groups of photosynthetic bacteria occur as follows.

Green sulphur bacteria (for example *Chlorobium*). Anaerobic bacteria using hydrogen sul-phide (H$_2$S) or other reduced sulphur compounds as hydrogen (electron) donors.
For example,

$$2H_2S + CO_2 \xrightarrow[\text{bacteriochlorophyll}]{\text{light}} [CH_2O] + 2S + H_2O$$

Sulphur is deposited.

Purple sulphur bacteria (for example *Chromatium*). Red and brown pigments (carotenoids) dominate bacteriochlorophyll making the cells appear purple. They are mostly anaerobic and details of photo-synthesis are as above.

Purple non-sulphur bacteria (for example *Rhodospirillum*). Bacteria using organic compounds as a source of hydrogen to reduce either carbon dioxide (photoautotrophic) or an organic carbon source (photo-heterotrophic).

Blue-green bacteria (see table 9.10). Re-semble many plants in using water as a hydrogen donor.

Table 9.10 Comparison of photosynthesis in prokaryotes and eukaryotes.

	Prokaryotes	Eukaryotic plants
Bacteria	Blue-green bacteria	
No chloroplasts	No chloroplasts	Chloroplasts (each equivalent to a prokaryotic cell?)
Membranes present as extensions of the plasma membrane; called chromatophores	Membranes present throughout cytoplasm	Membranes in chloroplasts
Membranes not stacked	Membranes not stacked	Membranes usually stacked, forming grana in higher plants
Photosystem II absent; therefore no oxygen produced	Photosystem II present; therefore oxygen produced from water	Photosystem II present; therefore oxygen produced from water
Hydrogen donor variable e.g. H_2S, H_2, organic compounds, not water	Water acts as hydrogen donor	Water acts as hydrogen donor
Primary pigment is bacteriochlorophyll	Primary pigment is chlorophyll	Primary pigment is chlorophyll
No phycobilins	Also contain phycobilins (a third class of photosynthetic pigment)	Phycobilins only in red algae (a primitive feature)

9.10 Chemosynthesis

Chemosynthetic organisms (chemoautotrophs) are bacteria using carbon dioxide as a carbon source but obtaining their energy from chemical reactions rather than light. The energy is obtained by oxidising inorganic materials such as hydrogen, hydrogen sulphide, sulphur, iron(II), ammonia and nitrite.

Iron bacteria (for example *Leptothrix*).

$$Fe^{2+} \xrightarrow{\text{oxygen}} Fe^{3+} + \text{energy}$$

Full equation:

$$4FeCO_3 + O_2 + 6H_2O \longrightarrow 4Fe(OH)_3 + 4CO_2 + \text{energy}$$

Colourless sulphur bacteria (for example *Thiobacillus*).

$$S \xrightarrow[\text{nitrate}]{\text{oxygen or}} SO_4^{2-}$$
$$\text{sulphur} \qquad\qquad \text{sulphate} + \text{energy}$$

Full equation: $2S + 3O_2 + 2H_2O \longrightarrow 2H_2SO_4 + \text{energy}$

Under anaerobic conditions some species use nitrate as a

hydrogen acceptor, thus carrying out denitrification (see section 9.11.1).

Nitrifying bacteria (see section 9.11.1).

$$NH_4^+ \xrightarrow{\text{oxygen}} NO_2^- + \text{energy} \text{ (for example}$$
$$\text{ammonium} \qquad \text{nitrite} \qquad\qquad\quad \textit{Nitrosomonas)}$$

Full equation: $2NH_3 + 3O_2 \longrightarrow 2HNO_2 + 2H_2O + \text{energy}$

$$NO_2^- \xrightarrow{\text{oxygen}} NO_3^- + \text{energy} \text{ (for example } \textit{Nitrobacter)}$$

Full equation: $2HNO_2 + O_2 \longrightarrow 2HNO_3 + \text{energy}$

In the above examples oxygen is an electron (hydrogen) acceptor and the bacteria are aerobic.

Chemosynthetic bacteria play important roles in the biosphere, principally in maintaining soil fertility through their activities in the nitrogen cycle.

9.11 Mineral cycles (biogeochemical cycles)

9.11.1 The nitrogen cycle

The atmosphere contains 79% by volume of nitrogen, yet nitrogen is relatively scarce in combined (fixed) form because it is rather inert chemically. Nitrogen is an essential constituent of amino acids, and hence proteins, and it limits the supply of food available in ecosystems more than any other plant nutrient. The only way in which it can be made available to living organisms is via **nitrogen fixation**, an ability confined to certain prokaryotes, although the techniques of genetic engineering may eventually lead to introduction of the relevant genes into green plants. The nitrogen cycle is summarised in fig 9.31.

Nitrogen fixation

Nitrogen fixation is energy-consuming because the two nitrogen atoms of the nitrogen molecule must first be separated. Nitrogen-fixers achieve this by an enzyme, nitrogenase, using energy from ATP. Non-enzymic separation requires the much greater energy of industrial processes or of ionising events in the atmosphere, such as lightning and cosmic radiation.

Nitrogen is so important for soil fertility, and the demand for food production so great, that colossal amounts of ammonia are produced industrially each year to be used mainly for nitrogenous fertilisers such as ammonium nitrate (NH_4NO_3) and urea ($CO(NH_2)_2$). The amounts of nitrogen fixed commercially are now roughly equal to the amounts fixed naturally. We are still relatively ignorant as to the effects which the gradual accumulation of fixed nitrogen, which is now occurring, will have in the biosphere. We have learned through experience of some of the problems, such as run-off of nitrate fertilisers into lakes

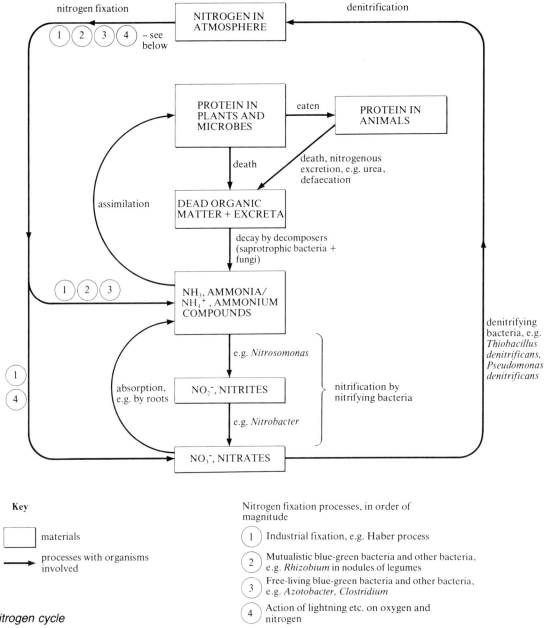

Fig 9.31 *Nitrogen cycle*

Key

☐ materials

→ processes with organisms involved

Nitrogen fixation processes, in order of magnitude

① Industrial fixation, e.g. Haber process

② Mutualistic blue-green bacteria and other bacteria, e.g. *Rhizobium* in nodules of legumes

③ Free-living blue-green bacteria and other bacteria, e.g. *Azotobacter, Clostridium*

④ Action of lightning etc. on oxygen and nitrogen

and rivers causing an imbalance of salts. This can result in the complete loss of life from the water.

A relatively small amount of fixed nitrogen (5–10%) is formed by ionising events in the atmosphere. The resulting nitrogen oxides dissolve in rain, forming nitrates.

The legumes, such as clover, soyabean, lucerne and pea, are probably the greatest natural source of fixed nitrogen. Their roots possess characteristic swellings called **nodules** which are caused by colonies of nitrogen-fixing bacilli (genus *Rhizobium*) living within the cells. The relationship is mutualistic because the plant gains fixed nitrogen in the form of ammonia from the bacteria and, in return, the bacteria gain energy and certain nutrients, such as carbohydrates, from the plants. In a given area legumes can contribute as much as 100 times more fixed nitrogen than free-living bacteria. It is not surprising, therefore, that they

are frequently used to add nitrogen to the soil, especially since they have the added benefit of making good fodder crops.

> **9.43** Farmers often say that legumes are 'hard on the soil', meaning that they place a large demand on soil minerals. Why should this be so?

All nitrogen-fixers incorporate nitrogen into ammonia, but this is immediately used to make organic compounds, mainly proteins (fig 9.31).

Decay and nitrification

Most plants depend on a supply of nitrate from the soil for their nitrate source. Animals in turn depend directly or indirectly on plants for their nitrogen supply. Fig 9.31 shows how nitrates are recycled from proteins in dead organisms by saprotrophic bacteria and fungi. The sequence from proteins to nitrate is a series of oxidations, requiring oxygen and involving aerobic bacteria. Proteins are decomposed via amino acids to ammonia when an organism dies. Animal wastes and excreta are similarly decomposed. Chemosynthetic bacteria (section 9.10) then oxidise ammonia to nitrate, a process call **nitrification**.

9.44 In which of the nutritional categories would you place bacteria and fungi which are decomposers?

Denitrification

Nitrification can be reversed by denitrifying bacteria (**denitrification**) whose activities can therefore reduce soil fertility. They only do this under anaerobic conditions, when nitrate is used instead of oxygen as an oxidising agent (electron acceptor) for the oxidation of organic compounds. Nitrate itself is reduced. The bacteria are therefore **facultative aerobes**. It should not be assumed that their activities on a global scale are detrimental to the biosphere because it has been estimated that most of the atmospheric nitrogen might now be in the oceans or locked up in sediments were it not for denitrification.

9.45 What natural areas or situations might favour denitrification?

9.46 Why should good drainage and ploughing increase soil fertility?

9.11.2 The sulphur cycle

Fig 9.32 shows the sulphur cycle. Sulphur is abundant in the Earth's crust and is available to plants principally as sulphate. It is an essential constituent of virtually all proteins.

As with nitrogen, animals depend ultimately on plants for their sulphur requirements. In addition to the natural sulphur cycle shown in fig 9.32, oxides of sulphur, such as sulphur dioxide (SO_2), are increasingly being added to the atmosphere as a result of burning fossil fuels and the smelting of sulphur ores. These are pollutants and when dissolved in rain make it acidic. A growing body of

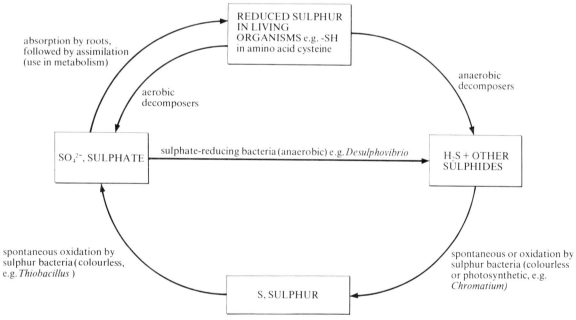

Fig 9.32 (above) *Sulphur cycle*

Fig 9.33 (below) *Phosphorus cycle*

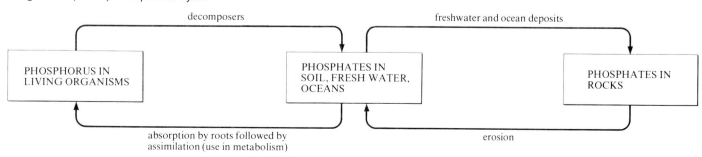

evidence is suggesting that acid rainfall can have widespread ecological repercussions.

9.11.3 The phosphorus cycle

Phosphorus is an essential constituent of nucleic acids, proteins, ATP and some other vital organic compounds. It is a relatively uncommon element and, like nitrogen and potassium, is often a limiting factor in the productivity of ecosystems. The cycle, shown in fig 9.33, is simple because phosphorus forms no natural gaseous compounds. Much of the phosphorus that finds its way to the oceans becomes locked up in sedimentary deposits.

9.11.4 The carbon and oxygen cycles

The carbon cycle is discussed in section 9.1 and shown in fig 9.2. The oxygen cycle is closely related.

9.11.5 Summary

The cycling of materials in the biosphere has been shown to involve complex nutritional relationships between living organisms. These form part of the study of ecology and certain aspects of them are discussed in more detail in chapter 12. Bacteria are an integral part of each cycle and their activities can therefore be seen to be essential in maintaining all life. The different modes of nutrition involve autotrophic, heterotrophic, photosynthetic and chemosynthetic activity. An understanding of these cycles is essential to humans if we are to make the best use of available materials and to understand the consequences of interference with them.

9.12 Mineral nutrition of plants and animals

Autotrophic nutrition involves not only the synthesis of carbohydrates from carbon dioxide and a hydrogen donor, such as water, but the subsequent use of minerals like nitrates, sulphates and phosphates to make other organic requirements, such as proteins, nucleic acids and so on. Heterotrophic organisms also require certain minerals to supplement their organic food. In many cases the same nutrients are required, and for the same reasons, so it is convenient to consider the whole area of mineral nutrition as a bridge between autotrophic nutrition (chapter 9) and heterotrophic nutrition (chapter 10).

A nutritional element essential for the successful growth and reproduction of an organism is called an **essential element**. The major essential elements for life are carbon, hydrogen, oxygen, nitrogen, sulphur, phosphorus, potassium, sodium, magnesium, calcium and chlorine. In addition, certain elements, the **trace elements**, are essential in trace amounts (a few parts per million). Of these, all organisms require manganese, iron, cobalt, copper and

zinc; some also require combinations of molybdenum, vanadium, chromium and other heavy metals, as well as boron, silicon, fluorine and iodine (see table 5.1). All except carbon, hydrogen and oxygen are taken up as minerals from soil or water by green plants. The mechanism of uptake is discussed in chapter 14.

For heterotrophic organisms (animals and fungi) the trace elements (inorganic) are sometimes grouped with vitamins (organic) as **micronutrients**, since both are required in trace amounts and have similar fundamental roles in cell metabolism, often as enzyme cofactors. Vitamins are considered in chapter 10. Autotrophic organisms synthesise their own vitamins. The other essential elements are called **macronutrients**. Deficiency of any of the nutrients mentioned can lead to **deficiency diseases**.

Some examples of the functions of the major minerals are given in table 9.11. A study of the table will reveal that mineral elements are taken up by plants as separate ions, either anions (negatively charged) or cations (positively charged). This is also true of trace elements, though their ions are not shown in the table.

Cations fall into two broad categories, namely light metals, whose roles in cell metabolism are usually associated with their high mobility, and the heavy metals, such as iron and copper, which are generally fixed in the membranes of mitochondria and chloroplasts. Animals do not obtain all their essential elements in the form of minerals. Much of their nitrogen, for example, is ingested in the form of proteins.

The geographical distribution of the minerals, particularly trace elements, can vary enormously and is one of the factors in the environment determining the distribution of different plants, and hence, animal species. A balance of trace elements is essential for soil fertility. Extreme cases are known of plants thriving in areas of high metal contamination, such as on spoilage tips from mines or over natural mineral deposits, and such plants can prove toxic to grazing animals. Conversely, these plants can be useful to humans if they help to cover formerly unsightly areas.

9.12.1 Mineral element deficiencies

It is not always easy, or possible, to isolate the effects of individual minerals. In plants, for example, chlorosis (lack of chlorophyll) can be caused by lack of magnesium or iron, both having different roles in chlorophyll synthesis (table 9.11). A common deficiency disease of sheep and cattle called scour, which causes diarrhoea, is due to copper deficiency induced by high levels of molybdenum in the pastures. Different effects may occur in different organisms; lack of manganese, for example, causes grey speck in oats, marsh spot in beans and poor flavour in oats.

The close interaction and varied effects of mineral elements are due to their fundamental effects on cell metabolism. However, it is possible by various means, such

Table 9.11 Some essential mineral elements and examples of their uses in living organisms.

MACRONUTRIENTS

Element and symbol	Taken up by plants as	General importance	Common deficiency diseases or symptoms — Plants	Humans	Common food source for humans
Nitrogen, N	Nitrate, NO_3^- Ammonium, NH_4^+	Synthesis of proteins, nucleic acids and many other organic compounds, e.g. coenzymes and chlorophyll.	Stunted growth and strong chlorosis, particularly of older leaves	Kwashiorkor due to lack of protein	Protein, e.g. lean meat, fish and milk. Milk is rich in phosphorus
Phosphorus, P	Phosphate, PO_4^{3-} Orthophosphate, $H_2PO_4^-$	Synthesis of nucleic acids, ATP and some proteins. Also, phosphate is a constituent of bone and enamel. Phospholipids in membranes.	Stunted growth, particularly of roots		
Potassium, K	K^+	Mainly associated with membrane function, e.g. conduction of nervous impulses, maintaining electrical potentials across membranes Na^+/K^+ pump in active transport across membranes, anion/cation and osmotic balance. Cofactor in photosynthesis and respiration (glycolysis). Common in cell sap of plant vacuoles.	Yellow and brown leaf margins and premature death	Rarely deficient	Vegetables, e.g. brussels sprouts (= buds), and meat.
Sulphur, S	Sulphate, SO_4^{2-}	Synthesis of proteins (e.g. keratin) and many other organic compounds, e.g. coenzyme A.	Chlorosis, e.g. 'tea-yellow' of tea		Protein, e.g. lean meat, fish and milk.
Sodium, Na	Na^+	Similar to potassium, but usually present in lower concentrations. Often exchanged for potassium.		Muscular cramps	Table salt (sodium chloride) and bacon.
Chlorine, Cl	Chloride, Cl^-	Similar to Na^+ and K^+, e.g. anion/cation and osmotic balance. Involved in 'chloride shift' during carbon dioxide transport in blood. Constituent of hydrochloric acid in gastric juice.		Muscular cramps	Table salt and bacon.
Magnesium, Mg	Mg^{2+}	Part of structure of chlorophyll. Bone and tooth structure. Cofactor for many enzymes, e.g. phosphatases (e.g. ATPase).	Chlorosis		Vegetables and most other foods.
Calcium, Ca	Ca^{2+}	Formation of middle lamella (calcium pectate) between plant cell walls and normal cell wall development. Constituent of bone, enamel and shells. Activates ATPase during muscular contraction. Blood clotting.	Stunted growth	Poor skeletal growth, possibly leading to rickets	Milk, hard water.

TRACE ELEMENTS – all cations except boron, fluorine and iodine

Element and symbol	Substance containing	Examples of functions	Common deficiency diseases or symptoms — Plants	Humans	Common food source for humans
Manganese, Mn	Phosphatases (transfer PO_4 groups)	Bone development (a 'growth factor')	Leaf-flecking, e.g. 'grey-speck' in oats	Poor bone development	Vegetables and most other foods.
	Decarboxylases Dehydrogenases	Oxidation of fatty acids, respiration, photosynthesis.			
Iron, Fe	Haem group in: haemoglobin and myoglobin	Oxygen carriers.		Anaemia	Liver and red meat. Some vegetables, e.g. spinach.
	Cytochromes	Electron carriers, e.g. respiration, photosynthesis.			

Element and symbol	Substance containing	Examples of functions	Common deficiency diseases or symptoms		Common food source for humans
			Plants	Humans	
Iron, Fe *cont.*	Catalase and peroxidases	Break down H_2O_2.	Strong chlorosis, particularly in young leaves		
	Other porphyrins	Chlorophyll synthesis.			
Cobalt, Co	Vitamin B_{12}	Red blood cell development.		Pernicious anaemia	Liver and red meat (as vitamin B_{12}).
Copper, Cu	Cytochrome oxidase	Terminal electron carrier in respiratory chain – oxygen converted to water.	Dieback of shoots		
	Haemocyanin	Oxygen carrier in certain invertebrates.			
	Plastocyanin	Electron carrier in photosynthesis.			
	Tyrosinase	Melanin production.		Albinism	
Zinc, Zn	Alcohol dehydrogenase	Anaerobic respiration in plants (alcohol fermentation).	'Mottle leaf' of *Citrus*		Most foods.
	Carbonic anhydrase	Carbon dioxide transport in vertebrate blood.	Malformed leaves, e.g. 'sickle leaf' of cocoa		
	Carboxypeptidase	Hydrolysis of peptide bonds in protein digestion.			
Molybdenum, Mo	Nitrate reductase	Reduction of nitrate to nitrite during amino acid synthesis in plants.	Slight retardation of growth; 'scald' disease of beans		
	Nitrogenase	Nitrogen fixation (prokaryotes).			
Boron, B	—	Plants only. Normal cell division in meristems. Mobilisation of nutrients?	Abnormal growth and death of shoot tips, 'heart-rot' of beet; 'stem-crack' of celery	Not needed	
Fluorine, F	Associated with calcium as calcium fluoride in animals	Component of tooth enamel and bone.		Dental decay more rapid	Milk, drinking water in some areas.
Iodine, I	Thyroxine (Probably not required by higher plants)	Hormone controlling basal metabolic rate.		Goitre; cretinism in children	Seafoods, salt.

as experimentally manipulating mineral uptake, to show that specific sets of symptoms are associated with deficiencies of certain elements.

Such knowledge is of importance in both medicine and agriculture because deficiency diseases are common worldwide, both in humans and in their crops and animals.

Experiments on plants were done in the late nineteenth and early twentieth century, particularly by German botanists, using the now classic water culture or sand culture techniques. In these experiments, plants are grown in prepared culture solutions of known composition. Many economically important plant deficiency diseases are now catalogued with the aid of colour photography, enabling rapid diagnosis. Although many of the essential roles of the mineral elements are established, further physiological and biochemical research remains to be done.

9.12.2 Special methods for obtaining essential elements

Insectivorous plants

Insectivorous or carnivorous plants are green plants which are specially adapted for trapping and digesting small animals, particularly insects. In this way they supplement their normal autotrophic nutrition (photosynthesis) with a form of heterotrophic nutrition. Such plants typically live in nitrogen-poor habitats, and use the animals principally as a source of nitrogen. Having lured the insect with colour, scent or sweet secretions, the plant traps it in some way and then secretes enzymes and carries out extracellular digestion. The products, notably amino acids, are absorbed and assimilated.

Some of the plants are interesting for the elaborate nature of their trap mechanisms, notably the Venus fly trap (*Dionaea muscipula*), pitcher plants (*Nepenthes*) and sundews (*Drosera*). *Drosera* is one of the few British examples, most being tropical or subtropical. It is found on the wetter heaths and moors which are typically acid, mineral-deficient habitats. The details of the various mechanisms are outside the scope of this book.

Mycorrhizas

A mycorrhiza is a mutualistic association between a fungus and a plant root. It is likely that the great majority of land plants enter into this kind of relation with soil fungi. They are of great significance because they are probably the major route of entry of mineral nutrients into roots. The fungus receives organic nutrients, mainly carbohydrates and vitamins, from the plant and in return absorbs mineral salts (particularly phosphate, ammonium, potassium and nitrate) and water, which can pass to the plant root. Generally only young roots are infected. Root hair production either ceases or is greatly reduced on infection. A network of hyphae spreads through the surrounding soil, covering a much larger surface area than the root could, even with root hairs. It has been suggested that plants of the same species, or even different species may have common interconnections with mycorrhizas, a concept which could radically alter our view of natural ecosystems.

Two groups of mycorrhizas occur, the ectotrophic and endotrophic mycorrhizas. **Ectotrophic mycorrhizas** form a sheath around the root and penetrate the air spaces between the cells in the cortex, but do not enter cells. An extensive intercellular net is formed. They are found mainly in forest trees such as conifers, beech, oak and many others, and involve fungi of the Basidiomycota. Their 'fruiting bodies' (mushrooms) are commonly seen near the trees.

Endotrophic mycorrhizas occur in virtually all other plants. Like ectotrophic mycorrhizas, they also form an intercellular network and extend into the soil, but they appear to penetrate cells (although in fact they do not break through the cell surface membranes of the root cells).

As we learn more about mycorrhizas, it is likely that the knowledge will be applied with advantage to agriculture, forestry and land reclamation.

Root nodules

Nitrogen fixation in root nodules of leguminous plants has already been discussed in section 9.11.1 of this chapter. The bacteria which inhabit the nodules stimulate growth and division of the root parenchyma cells resulting in the swelling or nodule.

Chapter Ten

Heterotrophic nutrition

Heterotrophs are organisms that feed on complex ready-made organic food (their carbon source is organic, p. 249). They use it as a source of (i) energy for their vital activities, (ii) building materials, that is specific atoms and molecules for cell maintenance and repair and growth, and (iii) vitamins (coenzymes) that cannot be synthesised in the organism but which are vital for specific cellular processes.

The survival of heterotrophs is dependent either directly or indirectly on the synthetic activities of autotrophs. All animals and fungi and the majority of bacteria are heterotrophic. A few bacteria, such as purple non-sulphur bacteria, possess **bacteriochlorophyll** and are able to utilise energy to synthesise their organic requirements from other organic raw materials, and are called **photoheterotrophs** (table 9.1).

The manner in which heterotrophs procure and take in their food varies considerably; nevertheless the way in which it is processed into a utilisable form within the body is very similar in most of them. It involves two distinct processes: first a method of reducing large complex food molecules into simpler soluble ones (**digestion**), and secondly a means of **absorbing** the soluble molecules from the region of digestion into the tissues of the organism.

For convenience, the main forms of heterotrophic nutrition may be classified as holozoic, saprotrophic (or saprophytic), mutualistic and parasitic, although some overlap between groups may occur.

10.1 Modes of heterotrophic nutrition

10.1.1 Holozoic nutrition

All organisms feeding in this way take food into the body where it is then digested into smaller soluble molecules which can be absorbed and assimilated. The term holozoic is applied to mainly free-living animals which have a specialised digestive tract (alimentary canal) in which these processes occur. Most animals and insectivorous plants are holozoic.

The characteristic processes involved in holozoic nutrition are defined as follows.

Ingestion is the taking in of complex organic food.

Digestion is the breakdown of large complex insoluble organic molecules into small, simple soluble diffusible molecules. This is achieved by mechanical breakdown and enzymatic hydrolysis. Digestion may be either extra- or intracellular.

Absorption is the uptake of the soluble molecules from the

digestive region, across a membrane and into the body tissue proper. The food may pass directly into cells or initially pass into the bloodstream to be transported to appropriate regions within the body of the organism.

Assimilation is the utilisation of the absorbed molecules by the body to provide either energy or materials to be incorporated into the body.

Egestion is the elimination from the body of undigested waste food materials.

The stages involved in holozoic nutrition are summarised in fig 10.1.

Animals which feed on plants are called **herbivores**, those that feed on other animals **carnivores**, and those that eat a mixed diet of animal and vegetable matter are termed **omnivores**. If they take in food in the form of small particles the animals are **microphagous** feeders, for example

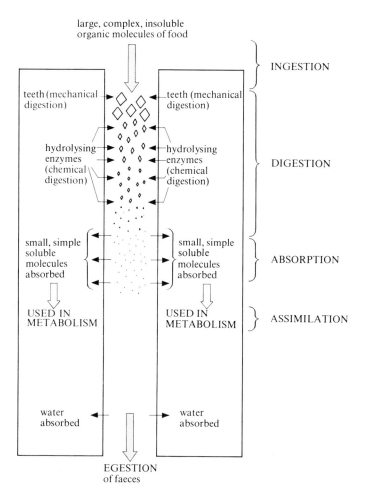

Fig 10.1 *Stages in the holozoic nutrition of a mammal*

289

earthworms, whereas if the food is ingested in liquid form they are classed as **fluid feeders**, such as aphids and mosquitoes. Animals which take in food in the form of large pieces are termed **macrophagous**. A summary of holozoic feeding methods is given below.

(1) Microphagous
    (*a*) pseudopodial
    (*b*) ciliary
    (*c*) filter-feeding – setose (setae are hair-like structures)
                – ciliary
(2) Macrophagous
    (*a*) tentacular
    (*b*) scraping/boring
    (*c*) seizing prey
    (*d*) detritus/deposit-feeding
(3) Fluid-feeding
    (*a*) sucking
    (*b*) piercing and sucking

10.1.2 Saprophytic or saprotrophic nutrition
(*sapros*, rotten; *phyton* plant; *trophos*, feeder)

Organisms which feed on dead or decaying organic matter are called **saprophytes** or **saprotrophs**. Many fungi and bacteria are saprophytes, for example the fungus *Mucor hiemalis*. They were once regarded as plants, hence the use of 'phyte' in saprophyte. A more recent term, saprotroph, avoids this problem. Saprotrophs secrete enzymes onto potential food where it is digested. The soluble end-products of this extracellular chemical decomposition are then absorbed and assimilated by the saprotroph. Saprotrophs feed on the dead organic remains of plants and animals and contribute to the removal of such organic refuse by decomposing it. Many of the simple substances formed are not used by the saprotrophs themselves but are absorbed by plants. In this way the activity of the saprotrophs provides important links in nutrient cycles serving to return vital chemical elements from the dead bodies of organisms to living ones.

The saprotrophic nutrition of Mucor hiemalis

Nutritive fungal hyphae penetrate the substrate on which *Mucor* is growing and secrete hydrolysing enzymes from their tips which results in extracellular digestion as shown in fig 10.2. Carbohydrase and protease enzymes carry out the extracellular digestion of starch to glucose and protein to amino acids respectively. The thin, much-branched nature of the mycelium of *Mucor* ensures that there is a large surface area for absorption. Glucose is used during respiration to provide energy for the organism's metabolic activities whilst glucose and amino acids are used for growth and repair. Surplus glucose is converted to glycogen and fat, and excess amino acids to protein granules. These products are stored in the hyphal cytoplasm.

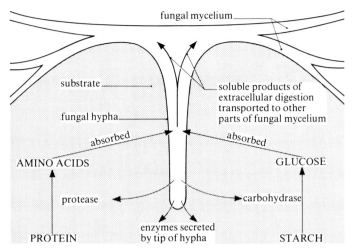

Fig 10.2 *Extracellular digestion and absorption in* Mucor hiemalis

10.1 Briefly describe the ways in which *Mucor* is economically important to humans.

10.1.3 Symbiosis: mutualism, parasitism and commensalism

The term symbiosis means literally 'living together' (*syn*, with; *bios*, life). It was introduced by the German scientist de Bary in 1879 and broadly defined as 'the living together of dissimilarly named organisms'; in other words, as an association between two or more organisms of different species. Since de Bary's time the term symbiosis has been restricted by many biologists to meaning a **close** relationship between two or more organisms of different species **in which all partners benefit**.

Since the 1970s symbiosis has assumed more importance as a topic in biology. For example, the endosymbiont theory of 1967 (section 9.3.1) launched the field of intracellular symbiosis; the ecological importance of symbiosis has received greater attention with the realisation that the great majority of plants obtain their minerals with the assistance of mycorrhizas, and that much nitrogen fixation is carried out by symbiotic bacteria; and rumen fermentation, involving symbiotic organisms, is of potential importance in increasing cattle productivity. At the same time biologists have become increasingly aware that degree of closeness and degree of benefit (or harm) of an association are two variables about which it is difficult to be precise and that there is a continuous spectrum of degrees of closeness and benefit or harm. Most modern biologists therefore prefer to use something like de Bary's original definition of symbiosis, a move approved by the Society for Experimental Biology in 1975*.

The following definitions will therefore be adopted in

---

* *References*: SEB Symposia XXIX, *Symbiosis*, CUP (1975) D.H. Jennings & D.L. Lee (eds.); G.H. Harper, (1985) 'Teaching symbiosis', *J.Biol.Ed.* **19** (3), 219–23; D.C. Smith & A.E. Douglas (1987) *The Biology of Symbiosis*, Arnold.

this book. For convenience (and to preserve existing terms) emphasis is placed on whether the relationship is beneficial or not to both partners, but **closeness** of association could equally well be a criterion for classification (see G.H. Harper*, footnote p. 290).

Symbiosis – the living together in close association of two (or more) organisms of different species. (Note: many associations involve three or more partners. Interactions commonly, but not necessarily, involve nutrition. 'Close' is difficult to define.)

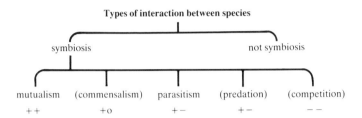

Key:
+, a partner benefits;
–, a partner receives harm;
o, a partner is unaffected;
( ) additional terms included by some biologists under symbiosis
Parasitism is regarded as a form of predation by some biologists.

Ectosymbiont – a symbiont external to its partner, e.g. leech, dodder (ectoparasites).
Endosymbiont – a symbiont within its partner –
  intracellular, e.g. chloroplasts, mitochondria
  extracellular, e.g. tapeworm (endoparasite).
Obligate symbiont – a symbiont which cannot survive without its partner.
Facultative symbiont – a symbiont which can survive without its partner.

Mutualism

Mutualism is a close association between two living organisms of different species which is beneficial to both partners. The larger organism may be referred to as the **host**. (This is the narrow definition of symbiosis, no longer recommended.) (Note, 'benefit' has been defined as increasing fitness for survival. Some biologists include brief interactions, such as pollination of flowers by insects, which is of benefit to flower and insect.) The association may be between two organisms of the same or different kingdoms. For example, the sea anemone *Calliactis parasitica* attaches itself to a shell used by the hermit crab *Eupagurus* (fig 10.3). The anemone obtains nourishment from the scraps of food left by the crab, and is transported from place to place when the crab moves. The crab is camouflaged by the anemone and may also be protected by nematocysts. It seems that the anemone is unable to survive unless attached

Fig 10.3 *Sea anemones,* Calliactis parasitica, *attached to a whelk shell inhabited by the hermit crab* Eupagurus bernhardus

to the crab's shell, and, if the anemone is removed, the crab will seek another anemone and actually place it on the shell it is inhabiting.

Herbivorous ruminants harbour a vast fauna of cellulose-digesting ciliates, such as *Entodinium* (see section 10.8.3). These can only survive in anaerobic conditions such as are found in a ruminant's alimentary canal. Here the ciliates feed on the cellulose contained in the host's diet, converting it into simple compounds which the ruminant is then able to further digest, absorb and assimilate itself. Some other examples of mutualism involving micro-organisms are given in table 10.1. See also mycorrhizas (section 9.12.2) and endosymbiosis (section 9.3.1).

Commensalism (com-, together; mensa, table)

Commensalism is a close association between two living organisms of different species which is beneficial to one (the **commensal**) and does not affect the other (the **host**). Commensalism means literally 'eating at the same table' and is used to describe symbiotic relationships which do not fit conveniently into the mutualism and parasitism categories. For example, the colonial hydrozoan *Hydractinia echinata* attaches itself to whelk shells inhabited by hermit crabs. It obtains nourishment from the scraps of food left by the crab after it has eaten. In this particular case the crab is totally unaffected by the association. An orchid or lichen (the commensal) growing on a tree (the host) would be another example.

Parasitism (para, beside; sitos, food)

Parasitism is a close association between two living organisms of different species which is beneficial to one (the **parasite**) and harmful to the other (the **host**). The parasite obtains food from the host and generally shelter. A successful parasite is able to live with the host without

Table 10.1 Some examples of mutualism involving micro-organisms (based on D.C. Smith & A.E. Douglas (1987) *The Biology of Symbiosis*, Arnold).

Host (larger partner)	Symbiont (smaller partner)	Benefit for host	Benefit for symbiont
Blue-green bacteria (cyanobacteria)	Aerobic bacteria	Nitrogen fixation enhanced (takes place in anaerobic conditions)	Oxygen from photosynthesis
Hydra	*Chlorella* (intracellular)	Maltose	All nutrients available
Legumes	*Rhizobium* spp. (intracellular)	Ammonia (fixed nitrogen)	Products of photosynthesis
Plants	Blue-green bacteria in soil	Ammonia (fixed nitrogen)	Products of photosynthesis
Plants	Blue-green bacteria in cells (= chloroplasts)	Photosynthesis	All nutrients available for protein formation
Plants ⎫ Mycorrhiza formed	Fungi ⎭	Mineral nutrients taken up, particularly N, PO_4 and K; roots protected against pathogens; drought resistance enhanced	Products of photosynthesis
Lichen fungi ⎫ Lichen formed	Blue-green bacteria ⎭	Glucose, ammonia (fixed nitrogen)	Shielded from high light intensity and water loss is reduced; some joint synthesis of metabolites
Lichen fungi ⎫ Lichen formed	Algae ⎭	Polyhydric alcohols (closely related to carbohydrates)	
Vertebrates with a rumen (ruminants)	Various prokaryotes, protozoans and fungi living in rumen	Formation of food, e.g. cellulose converted to fatty acids; protection from some gut parasites	Food ingested by host
Some teleost fish, squids and tunicates	Luminescent bacteria	Luminous light organs, e.g. angler fish (tip of projection from head acts as bait)	Nutrients and oxygen

causing it any great harm. The degree of benefit or harm may be difficult to establish (see G.H. Harper*, footnote p. 290).

Parasites which live on the outer surface of a host are termed **ectoparasites** (for example ticks, fleas and leeches). Such organisms do not always live a fully parasitic existence. Those that live within a host are **endoparasites** (such as *Plasmodium* and *Taenia*). If the organism has to live parasitically at all times it is said to be an **obligate** parasite. **Facultative** parasites are fungi that feed parasitically initially, but having eventually killed their host continue to feed saprotrophically on the dead body. Some green plants are partial parasites; they photosynthesise but nevertheless obtain micronutrients from their host. Mistletoe is such an example; its haustoria penetrate the xylem of the host from where they absorb mineral salts and water.

The very nature of the parasitic niche means that parasites are highly specialised, possessing numerous adaptations, many of which are associated with their host and its mode of life. Table 10.2 shows some of the structural, physiological and reproductive modifications used by various parasites in order to cope with the rigours of their existence. Micro-organisms which cause disease may be regarded as parasites (tables 2.6, 2.7 and 3.4).

> **10.2** List the structural, physiological and reproductive features that make *Fasciola* (liver fluke) a successful parasite.

10.2 Feeding mechanisms in a range of animals

10.2.1 Microphagous feeders

Pseudopodial

Amoeba consumes rotifers, diatoms, desmids, bacteria, flagellates, ciliates and minute particles of debris. It ingests its food by means of phagocytosis. **Pseudopodia** envelop the material and enclose it, together with a variable amount of water, in a **food vacuole** (fig 10.4). The vacuole then becomes surrounded by many tiny lysosomes which ultimately fuse with its membrane and discharge their enzymatic contents into it. Hence digestion is intracellular. At this stage the vacuole becomes known as a **digestive vacuole**. Initially it decreases in size as water is withdrawn,

Table 10.2 Some structural, physiological and reproductive specialisations of parasites.

	Type of modification	Examples
Structural	Absence or degeneration of feeding and locomotory organs – characteristic of gut parasites.	*Fasciola* (liver fluke), *Taenia* (tapeworm)
	Highly specialised mouthparts as in fluid feeders.	*Pulex* (flea), *Aphis* (aphid)
	Development of haustoria in some parasitic green plants.	*Cuscuta* (dodder)
	Boring devices to effect entry into a host.	nematodes, fungi
	Attachment organs such as hooks or suckers.	*Taenia, Hirudo* (leech), *Fasciola*
	Resistant outer covering.	*Taenia, Fasciola*
	Degeneracy of sense organs associated with the constancy of the parasite's environment.	*Taenia*
Physiological	Exoenzyme production to digest host tissue external to parasite.	fungi, *Plasmodium* (a protozoan (Apicomplexa) which infects mammals and birds, and in the case of humans causes malaria)
	Anticoagulant production in blood feeders.	*Pulex, Hirudo*
	Chemosensitivity in order to reach the optimum location in the host's body.	*Plasmodium, Monocystis* (a protozoan (Apicomplexa) parasitic in the seminal vesicles of earthworms)
	Production of cytolytic substances to aid penetration into host.	*Cuscuta* (a flowering plant belonging to the family Convolvulaceae, which does not possess chlorophyll and parasitises a variety of green plants)
	Production of anti-enzymes.	gut parasites
	Ability to respire adequately in anaerobic conditions.	gut parasites
Reproductive	Hermaphrodite condition thus aiding possible self-fertilisation.	*Taenia, Fasciola*
	Enormous numbers of reproductive bodies, i.e. eggs, cysts and spores.	*Taenia, Fasciola*
	Resistance of reproductive bodies when external to the host.	*Monocystis, Phytophthora* (e.g. potato blight)
	Employment of specialised reproductive phases in life cycle.	*Fasciola*
	Use of secondary hosts as vectors.	*Taenia, Fasciola, Plasmodium*

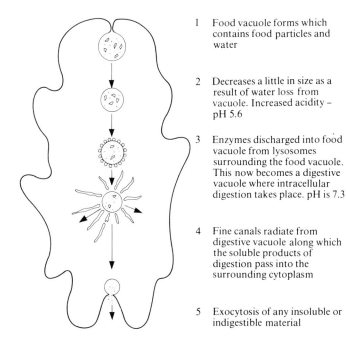

1 Food vacuole forms which contains food particles and water

2 Decreases a little in size as a result of water loss from vacuole. Increased acidity – pH 5.6

3 Enzymes discharged into food vacuole from lysosomes surrounding the food vacuole. This now becomes a digestive vacuole where intracellular digestion takes place. pH is 7.3

4 Fine canals radiate from digestive vacuole along which the soluble products of digestion pass into the surrounding cytoplasm

5 Exocytosis of any insoluble or indigestible material

Fig 10.4 *Ingestion, digestion and absorption in* Amoeba

and its contents become first acid (approximately pH 5.6) and then alkaline (about pH 7.3).

The enzymes poured into the digestive vacuole include carbohydrases, amino-, exo- and endopeptidases, esterase, collagenase and nuclease. They are secreted at different times so that their digestive effects are separated by time rather than spatially as in higher organisms. When digestion is complete the digestive vacuole membrane is drawn out into numerous fine canals. The soluble products of digestion are passed into the canals and finally into the surrounding cytoplasm of the animal by micropinocytosis. Undigested material is voided from the organism by **exocytosis** at any point on its surface.

Ciliary

The main diet of *Paramecium* consists of bacteria. Specialised tracts of cilia along the oral groove sweep the microorganisms in feeding currents towards the cytopharynx (fig 10.5). Any bacteria present are conveyed along the cytopharynx towards the cytostome or 'mouth' by the cilia of the undulating membrane. At the 'mouth' are a number of specialised cilia arranged in a criss-cross fashion which act as a filter to prevent large particles being taken in.

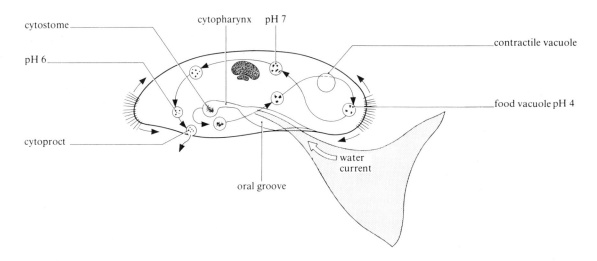

Fig 10.5 *Feeding currents and the pathway of food and digestive vacuoles in* Paramecium

Small particles together with a quantity of water pass into the plasmasol of the organism. Every so often the plasmasol actively segregates the collected food particles into a food vacuole which then follows a consistent pathway through the endoplasm. Once again the vacuole contents become acid initially (pH 2–4) and then alkaline (pH 7–8). The acid phase usually kills the prey, whilst most digestive activity takes place as the vacuole contents become less acid. For example, proteolytic enzymes work best at a pH of 5.7–5.8.

The soluble end-products of this intracellular digestion are finally absorbed into the cytoplasm of the organism and any undigested material is eliminated at the cytoproct by the process of **exocytosis**.

Experiment 10.1: To investigate ingestion of yeast cells and the formation of food vacuoles in *Paramecium*

Materials

Paramecium culture
cavity slides and cover-slips
dissecting needles
10% methyl cellulose
cotton wool
yeast culture stained in Congo red
monocular microscopes

Method

(1) Mount a drop of culture solution containing *Paramecium* on a cavity slide.
(2) Add one or two drops of 10% methyl cellulose and mix. This slows down the movements of *Paramecium*.
(3) Add a few cotton wool fibres. This supports the cover-slip when it is applied and also creates partitions which confine the movements of the animal and make it easier to observe.

(4) Add a drop of yeast suspension stained with Congo red dye. Congo red is an indicator in the pH range 3–5:

red/orange	pH 5.1
purple	pH 3–5
blue/violet	pH 3

(5) Cover the slide with a cover-slip and examine under the high power objective of the microscope.
(6) Observe the fate of the yeast cells as they enter the oral groove and are ingested at the cystosome. Food vacuoles containing yeast cells should be seen forming.
(7) Note if any colour changes take place in the food vacuoles. Comment on any changes that occur.

10.2.2 Filter feeding

Setose

Daphnia pulex, the common water flea, possesses a number of broad limbs with numerous stiff bristles (setae), all enclosed under a **carapace** (fig 10.6). When the limbs collectively move forward they draw water, containing suspended food particles, towards themselves. The bristles filter off the food from this feeding current and when the limbs move in a backward direction the food is propelled towards the mouth along a food groove by setae located at the base of each limb. At the mouth entrance the food particles become enmeshed by sticky mucus secretions prior to being swallowed.

Ciliary

Mytilus edulis, the common mussel, is found attached to rocks and stones in shallow coastal waters. It is a sedentary bivalve mollusc and possesses two 'gills', or ctenidia, covered with cilia on each side of its body. The movement of the cilia causes a current of water to enter the animal via an inhalant siphon and leave via an exhalant siphon. The

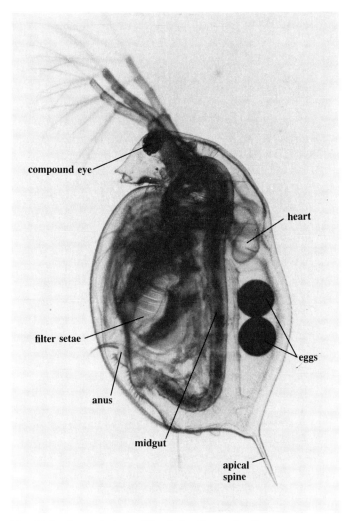

compound eye

heart

filter setae

anus

eggs

midgut

apical
spine

Fig 10.6 *Lateral view of* Daphnia, *the water flea*

water which enters contains the food of the mussel such as microscopic protozoa and algae. Numerous secretory cells scattered among the cilia produce streams of sticky mucus which entangle the food particles. The trapped food is then swept by tracts of cilia towards the mouth which is located in a dorsal position near the anterior end of the 'gill'. Ciliated labial palps encircling the mouth sort out the food particles to some extent before they enter the mouth. The alimentary canal of the mussel consists of a stomach and short intestine which terminates via an anus located close to the exhalant siphon.

Experiment 10.2: To investigate feeding in *Daphnia pulex* (water flea)

Materials

Daphnia culture
cotton wool
cavity slides and cover-slips
dissecting needles
yeast culture coloured with neutral red
binocular and monocular microscopes

Method

(1) Place a culture of *Daphnia* on a cavity slide.
(2) Add cotton wool fibres to slow down the animal's movement.
(3) Add a drop of yeast solution coloured with neutral red. Neutral red is an indicator for the pH range 6–8:

red	pH 6.8
rose-red	pH 7.7
orange/yellow	pH 8.0

(4) Add a cover-slip and view a *Daphnia* in the lateral position under a microscope (fig 10.6).
(5) Note the nature and beating of the thoracic appendages and their setae under the carapace.
(6) Observe the movement of the yeast as it is swept towards the filtering region before ingestion.
(7) Note any colour change in the ingested yeast as it passes along the gut and comment on your observations.

10.2.3 Macrophagous feeders

Tentacular

The cnidarian *Hydra* feeds primarily on *Daphnia* and *Cyclops* and digestion is partly extracellular and partly intracellular. When these organisms brush against the projecting cnidocils of nematoblasts located on the tentacles of *Hydra* the nematocyst contents are automatically discharged. Penetrant nematocysts paralyse the prey whilst volvants and glutinants hold it tightly against the tentacle. The tentacle then bends over towards the 'mouth' which in turn opens widely enabling the prey to enter the enteron (fig 10.7).

Glandular **zymogen cells** in the endodermis secrete powerful proteolytic enzymes which initiate extracellular digestion. Endodermal flagellate cells and contractions of the body assist in the circulation of food and enzymes, and in breaking it up into fine particles. Extracellular digestion is completed in 4 h after which time the food particles are engulfed by the phagocytic action of endodermal amoeboid cells where digestion is completed intracellularly as in *Amoeba*.

The soluble products of digestion ultimately diffuse from the endodermis via the mesogloea to the ectodermis. Undigested material is egested via the single oral aperture.

Sepia officinalis, the cuttlefish, is a carnivore. The activity of pigment cells in its skin enables it to camouflage itself well. Suitably coloured, it lies in wait for its prey, which may be shrimps or crabs.

The cuttlefish has efficient eyesight and when it spots suitable prey it quickly extends two long prehensile tentacles which adhere tightly to the prey by means of their terminal suckers. The tentacles are then rapidly retracted towards the mouth carrying the prey with them. Sometimes a small quantity of toxic venom is injected into the prey from posterior salivary glands to assist in paralysing and killing it.

The other eight short tentacles of *Sepia* hold the prey against the mouth where a pair of beak-shaped horny jaws break up and bite off pieces of the prey (fig 10.8). Within the mouth is a radula which rasps the food into small pieces which are then swallowed. This mechanical breakdown of the food is assisted by proteases secreted from the salivary glands.

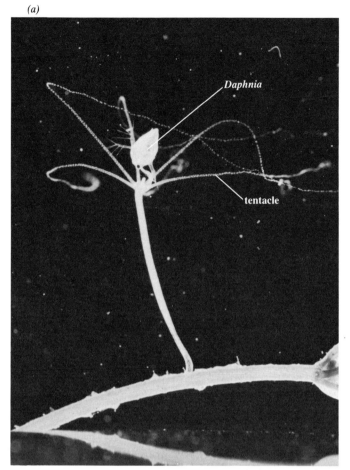

(a)

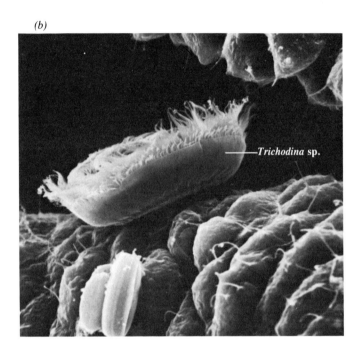

(b)

Fig 10.7 (above) *(a)* Hydra vulgaris *capturing a* Daphnia *(left)* *(b)* Scanning electron micrograph of Trichodina *lodged on the tentacles of a brown hydra*

Fig 10.8 *(below)* Sepia officinalis *(squid) showing tentacles covering mouth*

Scraping and boring

Helix aspersa, the common garden snail, feeds by using a rasping organ, the **radula**, in conjunction with a horny jaw plate (fig 10.9). The radula consists of about 150 rows of backwardly pointing 'teeth' with just over 100 teeth per row.

Leaves are held by the lips of the snail. The radula moves back and forth over the leaves with its teeth tearing the food whilst at the same time pressing it against the jaw plate. In this way minute fragments of vegetation are obtained which are gradually pushed backwards towards the pharynx. This type of activity wears down the front 'teeth' of the radula which become loose and eventually fall out to be swallowed with the food. They are rapidly and continuously replaced by new teeth. The rasping action of the radula ensures that the tough cellulose walls of the vegetation acted upon are broken down so that the cell contents are exposed to the hydrolytic action of enzymes, especially proteases, further along the digestive tract.

Biting and chewing mouthparts

Exoskeletal appendages in segments four, five and six form the feeding apparatus which surrounds a ventrally situated mouth in the grasshopper *Chorthippus*. The mouth is bordered anteriorly by the plate-like **labrum** or upper lip (fig 10.10). Beneath this lies a pair of stout, strong **mandibles** or jaws. Each mandible possesses an anterior ridged cutting surface and a posterior grinding surface which works against that of its partner and serves to cut, tear and crush food. A pair of **maxillae** is situated behind the mandibles. Each maxilla bears an **olfactory palp**. Hanging down behind the maxillae is an exoskeletal flap called the **labium** or lower lip. This assists in manoeuvring the food and also has a sensory function. The grasshopper is herbivorous and feeds mainly on leafy vegetation. It grips the leaf between its lips whilst the mandibles bite fragments from it. Activity of the maxillae and labium propels the food towards the mouth where it is swallowed. In the hypopharynx it is moistened with saliva secreted from

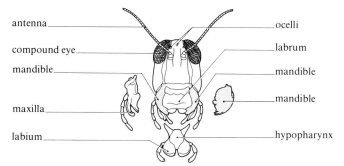

Fig 10.10 *Mouthparts of the common grasshopper* Chorthippus

salivary glands. The saliva contains amylase and sucrase, and so carbohydrate digestion begins immediately.

Seizing and swallowing

Scyliorhinus caniculus, the spotted dogfish, is a predatory carnivore and feeds on crustacea, shellfish, annelid worms, small fish and fragments of dead or dying animals. Its wide mouth is ventrally situated and enables the dogfish to swallow some animals whole. The buccal cavity is wide and flattened dorsoventrally. It possesses large, backwardly pointing **dermal denticles** which act as teeth and prevent prey from escaping once it has been seized in the mouth.

The buccal cavity leads into a wide pharynx which contains a tough muscular pad, the tongue. This assists in swallowing the food by moving it in an upward and backward direction into the oesophagus. The lining of the oesophagus is considerably folded. These folds extend around the food when it is swallowed and at the same time prevent much water from entering the gut. The shape of the stomach is asymmetrical, consisting of a dilated cardiac limb where the acid phase of digestion occurs, and a smaller, narrower pyloric limb. The alkaline phase of digestion takes place in the duodenum, which is relatively short and follows the stomach. The bile and pancreatic ducts open separately into the duodenum.

The duodenum leads into the ileum which contains the

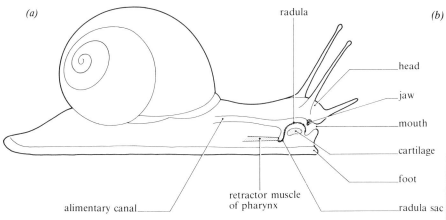

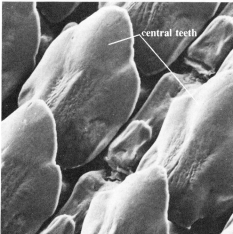

Fig 10.9 *(a)* Helix aspersa *radula location. (b) Scanning electron micrograph of the radula of the giant land snail*

spiral valve. This structure possesses many infoldings of the intestinal lining which slow down the passage of food and increase the surface area for its absorption. All absorbed food passes directly to the extremely large liver.

Throughout the length of the alimentary canal are numerous mucous glands whose secretions assist the smooth passage of the food. Undigested material is collected in the rectum and defaecated via the anus.

Detritus feeder

Lumbricus terrestris, the common earthworm, consumes fragments of fresh or decaying organic matter, especially vegetation, either at the soil surface, or after the food has been pulled into its burrow. Pieces of food are torn off by the mouth, moistened by alkaline secretions of the pharynx and drawn into the buccal cavity by the pumping action of the muscular pharynx. The food is then swallowed into the pharynx by **peristalsis**. Earthworms can also feed on organic material contained in the substrate which they swallow during burrowing activity.

The alimentary canal is straight and runs from mouth to anus. It is specialised at various points along its length for digestion and absorption of the ingested food. Table 10.3 indicates the sections of the alimentary canal involved in these activities, the segments which they occupy and their

structure and specific functions. Any undigested material is propelled to the posterior of the alimentary canal by peristaltic activity and voided via the anus as 'worm casts'.

Fluid feeding

Sucking. The housefly, *Musca domestica*, possesses a **proboscis tube** constructed from a highly modified labium. There are no mandibles, and the maxillae are reduced to a pair of palps. At the proximal end of the proboscis is a centrally placed mouth whilst at the distal end are two lobes called **labella**. Each of these contains numerous fine food channels termed **pseudotracheae** which ultimately converge into a central proboscis canal.

Generally the proboscis is held pressed against the underside of the insect's body, but when the insect feeds, it is extended by blood pressure so that the labella are placed on the food. If the food is solid, saliva from salivary glands is secreted onto it via an opening above the mouth. The saliva contains a number of enzymes which make the food soluble. When the food has been made soluble, or if the food is liquid in the first place, it passes into the pseudotracheae by capillary action. From here it is sucked up into the body by the activity of the muscles of the pharynx (fig 10.11*b*).

The feeding device of a butterfly such as *Pieris brassicae*

Table 10.3 Structure and functions of various regions of the earthworm gut.

Region of alimentary canal	Segments	Structure	Function
Mouth	–	–	Tears off pieces of food. Grips food as it is drawn into the worm's burrow.
Buccal cavity	1–3	Wide, thin-walled	Food moistened and softened by secretions of pharyngeal glands. Secretions include mucus and a proteolytic enzyme. Food eventually swallowed by peristalsis.
Pharynx	4–5	Dilatable, muscular and thick-walled	Possesses patches of glandular material, exudations of which help to soften the food.
Oesophagus	6–13	Narrow, tubular and thin-walled	Oesophageal pouches open into it from segment 10. Openings of two pairs of calciferous glands from segments 11 and 12; these glands secrete a fluid containing calcium carbonate particles. They are excretory in function rather than digestive and represent the manner in which excess calcium is removed from the body.
Crop	14–16	Wide and thin-walled	Acts as a storage chamber for the food. Some preliminary digestion occurs here.
Gizzard	17–19	Spherical, thick-walled, hard and muscular	Contains sharp fragments of stone. Mastication of food occurs here. Pieces of food are reduced in size by abrasion against the stones and the cuticularised lining of the gizzard.
Intestine	20	Surrounded by longitudinal and circular muscles. Its surface area is increased by the presence of a typhlosole.	A large surface area is presented for secretion of enzymes and absorption of digested food. Digestion is extracellular and food is absorbed into a network of capillaries lining the intestine. Three types of cell are present in the intestine: (1) glandular cells secrete proteolytic, amylolytic and lipolytic enzymes; (NB cellulase is secreted.) (2) ciliated cells help mix food with enzymes; (3) mucus cells lubricate food and protect gut lining from the digestive action of enzymes.
Anus	–	–	Faeces voided as worm casts.

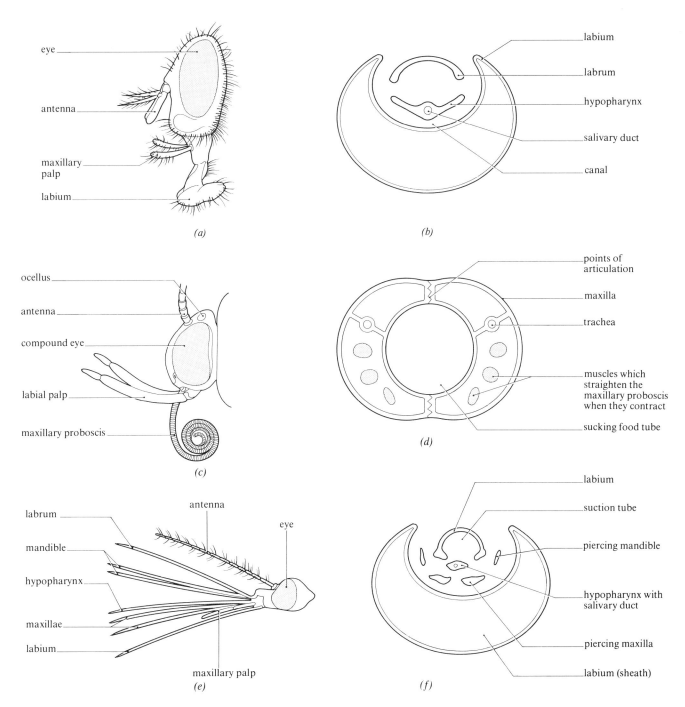

eye

antenna

maxillary palp

labium

(a)

labium

labrum

hypopharynx

salivary duct

canal

(b)

ocellus

antenna

compound eye

labial palp

maxillary proboscis

(c)

points of articulation

maxilla

trachea

muscles which straighten the maxillary proboscis when they contract

sucking food tube

(d)

labrum

antenna

eye

mandible

hypopharynx

maxillae

labium

maxillary palp

(e)

labium

suction tube

piercing mandible

hypopharynx with salivary duct

piercing maxilla

labium (sheath)

(f)

Fig 10.11 *(a) Mouthparts of the housefly* Musca domestica. *(b) TS mouthparts of* M. domestica. *(c) Mouthparts of the large white butterfly* Pieris brassicae. *(d) TS mouthparts of* P. brassicae. *(e) Mouthparts of the female mosquito* Anopheles *sp. (f) TS mouthparts of* Anopheles *sp.*

is its proboscis. In contrast to that of the housefly the proboscis is formed from the two maxillae. The part of each maxilla which together form the long tube through which the food is sucked (**galea**) is greatly elongated and grooved on its inner surface. These two structures fit together to form the proboscis tube. Mandibles are absent and the maxillary palps are either absent or poorly developed.

At rest, the proboscis is in the form of a coiled tube held under the head. When *Pieris* feeds, reflex contraction of the oblique galea muscles uncoils the proboscis. The proboscis is extended into the corolla of a flower and its tip placed directly on the food which is nectar, a dilute solution of sugar. It is frequently the case that the depth of the corolla tube corresponds to the length of the butterfly's proboscis. Muscles in the pharynx then begin to contract causing the nectar to be sucked into the mouth of the insect (fig 10.11*d*).

Piercing and sucking mouthparts. The **female mosquito** such as *Anopheles* sp., feeds on the blood of mammals. In order to obtain its meal it has to pierce the mammal's skin. This it does by using its mandibles or maxillae which have been highly modified into four sharp **stylets**. The stylets are contained in a grooved sheath, the proboscis sheath, formed by a greatly elongated labium.

Also present in the proboscis are the deeply grooved labrum and the hypopharynx. When the hypopharynx presses against the labrum it forms a food channel along which the fluid food is pumped. The hypopharynx also contains a salivary duct. During feeding, saliva containing an **anticoagulant** is secreted into the blood to prevent it clotting as it is sucked up into the pharynx via the narrow food channel (fig 10.11*f*).

10.3 Nutrition in mammals

10.3.1 Dietary requirements

Every mammal requires a daily supply of energy-providing foods (carbohydrates and fats), growth-promoting foods (proteins) and sufficient amounts of mineral salts, water, roughage and vitamins. For a diet to be adequate and balanced, these foodstuffs must be ingested in the correct proportions. Such a diet does not necessarily prevent illness but it certainly reduces the chances of the individual contracting a nutritionally based disease. The optimum nutritional value of any particular meal intake will vary markedly in different individuals depending on their sex, age, activity, body size and the temperature of their external environment (less food is eaten per individual in warm climates).

The Netherhall Education Software program *Balance your Diet* enables the user to enter their own diet and to compare it with a standard recommended diet. Protein, carbohydrate, fat and certain mineral and vitamin contents of diet can be examined separately.

> **10.3** Why does a mouse require a larger number of joules per unit weight than a man?

10.3.2 Measurement of the energy value of foodstuffs

An adequate diet must contain sufficient energy for the body's daily metabolic needs. This energy is measured as heat energy and expressed as joules. The energy value of a foodstuff can be calculated by burning a known mass of it in oxygen in a **bomb calorimeter**. The heat generated by this oxidation is transmitted to a known mass of water whose corresponding temperature rise is measured. Using the knowledge that 4.18 J of heat energy raises the temperature of 1 g of water by 1 °C, the number of joules generated by the burning of the food can be calculated (fig 10.12).

Table 10.4 indicates the recommended daily intake of energy and nutrients for humans in the UK for a variety of ages and activities and for both sexes. Table 10.5 shows the composition of a selection of foods per 100 g edible portion and is based on values published in the *Manual of Nutrition*, HMSO, 1976.

> **10.4** How many kilojoules are produced if 1 g of sugar burned in oxygen raises the temperature of 500 g of water by 7.5 °C?

10.3.3 Measurement of energy expenditure by humans

In order to calculate energy expenditure in humans a method of 'indirect calorimetry' is used. Accurate measurements of oxygen consumption, carbon dioxide excretion, and sometimes nitrogen excretion in the urine are used in the calculation of energy expenditure. The theory behind this method is that the same quantity of heat is released, oxygen consumed, and carbon dioxide and water produced when one gram of foodstuff is burned in the air as when it is burned in the body. However, this is only an approximate value since complete oxidation of food materials does not occur in the body.

> **10.5** It has been calculated that 1 g glucose combines with 774 cm^3 oxygen releasing 15.8 kJ heat, and 1 g long-chain fatty acid combines with 2012 cm^3 oxygen releasing 39.4 kJ heat. Why does 1 g of fatty acid give rise to more than twice as much heat as 1 g glucose?
>
> **10.6** Why is it that protein and fats subjected to combustion in a bomb calorimeter liberate more heat than when exactly the same weight of each foodstuff is burned in the body?

10.3.4 Malnutrition

This situation arises when an organism is deficient in (**undernutrition**) or receives excess (**overnutrition**) of one or more nutrients or energy-providing foods over a long period of time. In many underdeveloped parts of the world undernutrition is the most common form of malnutrition, whereas in the industrialised West obesity, coronary heart disease and reduced life expectancy are all symptoms of overnutrition.

10.3.5 Carbohydrates, proteins and fats

Detailed information concerning the structure and functions of these foodstuffs is provided in chapter 5. However, a note about the quality of dietary protein is necessary here. The nutritional value of a protein depends upon the composition of its amino acids and whether or not it can be digested by the animal concerned. Vegetable

Table 10.4 Recommended daily intakes of energy and nutrients for humans in the UK (Department of Health and Social Security (1969)) for a variety of ages and activities, and for both sexes.

Age range and occupational category	Body wt kg	Energy kcal	MJ	Protein[1] g	Thiamin mg	Riboflavin mg	Nicotinic acid mg equivalents	Ascorbic acid mg	Vitamins A µg retinol equivalents[2]	Vitamins D µg cholecalciferol	Calcium mg	Iron mg
BOYS and GIRLS												
0 up to 1 year	7.3	800	3.3	20	0.3	0.4	5	15	450	10	600	6
2 up to 4 years	13.5	1400	5.9	35	0.6	0.7	8	20	300	10	500	7
4 up to 7 years	20.5	1800	7.5	45	0.7	0.9	10	20	300	2.5	500	8
BOYS												
9 up to 12 years	31.9	2500	10.5	63	1.0	1.2	14	25	575	2.5	700	13
12 up to 15 years	45.5	2800	11.7	70	1.1	1.4	16	25	725	2.5	700	14
15 up to 18 years	61.0	3000	12.6	75	1.1	1.7	19	30	750	2.5	600	15
GIRLS												
9 up to 12 years	33.0	2300	9.6	58	0.9	1.2	13	25	575	2.5	700	13
12 up to 15 years	48.6	2300	9.6	58	0.9	1.4	16	25	725	2.5	700	14
15 up to 18 years	56.1	2300	9.6	58	0.9	1.4	16	30	750	2.5	600	15
MEN												
18 up to 35 years												
sedentary	65	2700	11.3	68	1.1	1.7	18	30	750	2.5	500	10
moderately active		3000	12.6	75	1.2	1.7	18	30	750	2.5	500	10
very active		3600	15.1	90	1.4	1.7	18	30	750	2.5	500	10
35 up to 65 years												
sedentary	65	2600	10.9	65	1.0	1.7	18	30	750	2.5	500	10
moderately active		2900	12.1	73	1.2	1.7	18	30	750	2.5	500	10
very active		3600	15.1	90	1.4	1.7	18	30	750	2.5	500	10
65 up to 75 years ⎱ assuming a	63	2350	9.8	59	0.9	1.7	18	30	750	2.5	500	10
75 and over ⎰ sedentary life	63	2100	8.8	53	0.8	1.7	18	30	750	2.5	500	10
WOMEN												
18 up to 55 years												
most occupations	55	2200	9.2	55	0.9	1.3	15	30	750	2.5	500	12
very active		2500	10.5	63	1.0	1.3	15	30	750	2.5	500	12
55 up to 75 years ⎱ assuming a	53	2050	8.6	51	0.8	1.3	15	30	750	2.5	500	10
75 and over ⎰ sedentary life	53	1900	8.0	48	0.7	1.3	15	30	750	2.5	500	10
pregnancy, 2nd and 3rd trimester		2400	10.0	60	1.0	1.6	18	60	750	10	1200	15
lactation		2700	11.3	68	1.1	1.8	21	60	1200	10	1200	15

[1] Recommended intakes calculated as providing 10% of energy.
[2] 1 retinol equivalent = 1 µg retinol or 6 µg β-carotene or 12 µg other biologically active carotenoids.

foods generally contain small quantities of protein and the amino acids present are rarely in the proportions required by animal tissues. Therefore there is a danger of malnutrition if only one vegetable food forms the major component of the diet. However, a good vegetarian diet can be worked out which provides the complete range of protein requirements by using a wide variety of protein-containing vegetable foods. These include cereals, legumes, nuts, fruit and other vegetables. An exception to the low protein content of many vegetable foods is soya bean protein which is as good as most animal proteins. Many, though not all animal proteins contain a high proportion of essential amino acids in balanced amounts and are termed 'first-class' proteins.

10.3.6 Mineral salts

A wide variety of inorganic elements is present in the body, all of which must be obtained from food or drink consumed by the mammal concerned. They are required for many metabolic activities and in the structure of a number of tissues. The different functions of the elements are considered in table 9.11.

10.3.7 Water

Water is essential to mammals as all bodily metabolic reactions take place in solution. Since water makes up 65–70% of the total body weight, and this weight remains relatively constant each day, it follows that the 2–3 dm³ of water lost daily from the body must be replaced by fluids or food consumed by the mammal each day. The importance of water to life becomes clear when one

Table 10.5 Composition of selected foods per 100g edible portion, based on values published in *Manual of Nutrition* **(1976).**

	Energy kcal	kJ	Protein g	Fat g	Carbo-hydrate g	Minerals Ca mg	Fe mg	Vitamins A µg	D µg	B_1 mg	B_2 mg	Nicotinic acid equivalents mg	C mg
Almonds	580	2397	20.5	53.5	4.3	247	4.2	0	0	0.32	0.25	4.9	0
Apples	46	197	0.3	0	12.0	4	0.3	5	0	0.04	0.02	0.1	5
Apricots, canned	106	452	0.5	0	27.7	12	0.7	166	0	0.02	0.01	0.3	5
Bacon, rashers, cooked	447	1852	24.5	38.8	0	12	1.4	0	0	0.40	0.19	9.2	0
Bananas	76	326	1.1	0	19.2	7	0.4	33	0	0.04	0.07	0.8	10
Beans, canned in tomato sauce	63	266	5.1	0.4	10.3	45	1.4	50	0	0.07	0.05	1.4	3
Beans, runner	23	100	2.2	0	3.9	27	0.8	50	0	0.05	0.10	1.4	20
Beef, average	226	940	18.1	17.1	0	7	1.9	0	0	0.06	0.19	8.1	0
Beef, corned	216	905	26.9	12.1	0	14	2.9	0	0	0.01	0.23	9.0	0
Beer, bitter, draught	30	127	0	0	2.3	11	0	0	0	0	0.05	0.7	0
Beetroot, boiled	44	189	1.8	0	9.9	30	0.7	0	0	0.02	0.04	0.4	5
Biscuits, plain, semi-sweet	431	1819	7.4	13.2	75.3	126	1.8	0	0	0.17	0.06	2.0	0
Bread, brown	230	981	9.2	1.4	48.3	88	2.5	0	0	0.28	0.07	2.7	0
Bread, white	251	1068	8.0	1.7	54.3	100	1.7	0	0	0.18	0.03	2.6	0
Bread, wholemeal	241	1025	9.6	3.1	46.7	28	3.0	0	0	0.24	0.09	1.9	0
Brussels sprouts, boiled	17	75	2.8	0	1.7	25	0.5	67	0	0.06	0.10	1.0	41
Butter	731	3006	0.5	81.0	0	15	0.2	995	1.25	0	0	0.1	0
Cabbage, boiled	15	66	1.7	0	2.3	38	0.4	50	0	0.03	0.03	0.5	23
Carrots	23	98	0.7	0	5.4	48	0.6	2000	0	0.06	0.05	0.7	6
Cauliflower	13	56	1.9	0	1.5	21	0.5	5	0	0.10	0.10	1.0	64
Cheese, Cheddar	412	1708	25.4	34.5	0	810	0.6	420	0.35	0.04	0.05	5.2	0
Chicken, roast	148	621	24.8	5.4	0	9	0.8	0	0	0.08	0.19	12.8	0
Chocolate, milk	578	2411	8.7	37.6	54.5	246	1.7	6.6	0	0.03	0.35	2.5	0
Coconut, desiccated	608	2509	6.6	62.0	6.4	22	3.6	0	0	0.06	0.04	1.8	0
Cod, fried in batter	199	834	19.6	10.3	7.5	80	0.5	0	0	0.04	0.10	6.7	0
Cod, haddock, white fish	76	321	17.4	0.7	0	16	0.3	0	0	0.08	0.07	4.8	0
Coffee, instant	155	662	4.0	0.7	35.5	140	4.0	0	0	0	0.10	45.7	0
Cornflakes	354	1507	7.4	0.4	85.4	5	0.3	0	0	1.13[a] 0.04[b]	1.41[a] 0.10[b]	10.6[a] 0.8[b]	0
Cream, double	449	1848	1.8	48.0	2.6	65	0	420	0.28	0.02	0.08	0.4	0
Cream, single	189	781	2.8	18.0	4.2	100	0.1	155	0.10	0.03	0.13	0.8	0
Eggs	147	612	12.3	10.9	0	54	2.1	140	1.50	0.09	0.47	3.7	0
Fish fingers	178	749	12.6	7.5	16.1	43	0.7	0	0	0.09	0.06	3.1	0
Flour, white	348	1483	10.0	0.9	80.0	138	2.1	0	0	0.30	0.03	2.7	0
Fruit cake, rich	368	1546	4.6	15.9	55.0	71	1.6	57	0.80	0.07	0.07	1.2	0
Ham, cooked	269	1119	24.7	18.9	0	9	1.3	0	0	0.44	0.15	8.0	0
Honey	288	1229	0.4	0	76.4	5	0.4	0	0	0	0.05	0.2	0
Ice-cream, vanilla	192	805	4.1	11.3	19.8	137	0.3	1	0	0.05	0.20	1.1	1
Jam	262	1116	0.5	0	69.2	18	1.2	2	0	0	0	0	10
Kipper	184	770	19.8	11.7	0	60	1.2	45	22.20	0.02	0.30	6.9	0
Lamb, roast	291	1209	23.0	22.1	0	9	2.1	0	0	0.10	0.25	9.2	0
Lettuce	8	36	1.0	0	1.2	23	0.9	167	0	0.07	0.08	0.4	15
Liver, fried	244	1020	24.9	13.7	5.6	14	8.8	6000	0.75	0.27	4.30	20.7	20
Luncheon meat	313	1298	12.6	26.9	5.5	15	1.0	0	0	0.07	0.12	4.5	0
Margarine	734	3019	0.2	81.5	0	4	0.3	900[c]	8.00	0	0	0.1	0
Marmalade	261	1114	0.1	0	69.5	35	0.6	8	0	0	0	0	10
Milk, liquid, whole	65	274	3.3	3.8	4.8	120	0.1	44[d] 37[e]	0.05[d] 0.01[e]	0.04	0.15	0.9	1
Oils, cooking and salad	899	3696	0	99.9	0	0	0	0	0	0	0	0	0
Onions	23	98	0.9	0	5.2	31	0.3	0	0	0.03	0.05	0.4	10
Oranges	35	150	0.8	0	8.5	41	0.3	8	0	0.10	0.03	0.3	50
Parsnips	49	210	1.7	0	11.3	55	0.6	0	0	0.10	0.09	1.3	15
Peaches, canned	88	373	0.4	0	22.9	4	1.9	41	0	0.01	0.02	0.6	4
Peanuts, roasted	586	2428	28.1	49.0	8.6	61	2.0	0	0	0.23	0.10	20.8	0
Pears, fresh	41	175	0.3	0	10.6	8	0.2	2	0	0.03	0.03	0.3	3
Peas, fresh or quick frozen, boiled	49	208	5.0	0	7.7	13	1.2	50	0	0.25	0.11	2.3	15
Pineapple, canned	76	325	0.3	0	20.0	13	1.7	7	0	0.05	0.02	0.3	8
Plain cake, Madeira	426	1785	6.0	24.0	49.7	67	1.4	82	1.20	0.08	0.11	1.7	0
Plums	32	137	0.6	0	7.9	12	0.3	37	0	0.05	0.03	0.6	3
Pork, average	330	1364	15.8	29.6	0	8	0.8	0	0	0.58	0.16	6.9	0
Potatoes, boiled	80	339	1.4	0	19.7	4	0.5	0	0	0.08	0.03	1.2	4–15[f]
Potato chips, fried	236	1028	3.8	9.0	37.3	14	1.4	0	0	0.10	0.04	2.2	6–20[f]

302

Table 10.5 (*cont.*)

	Energy kcal	kJ	Protein g	Fat g	Carbo-hydrate g	Minerals Ca mg	Fe mg	Vitamins A µg	D µg	B$_1$ mg	B$_2$ mg	Nicotinic acid equivalents mg	C mg
Potatoes, roast	111	474	2.8	1.0	27.3	10	1.0	0	0	0.10	0.04	2.0	6–23(f)
Prunes	161	686	2.4	0	40.3	38	2.9	160	0	0.10	0.20	1.7	0
Raspberries	25	105	0.9	0	5.6	41	1.2	13	0	0.02	0.03	0.5	25
Rhubarb	6	26	0.6	0	1.0	103	0.4	10	0	0.01	0.07	0.3	10
Rice	359	1531	6.2	1.0	86.8	4	0.4	0	0	0.08	0.03	1.5	0
Rice pudding	142	594	3.6	7.6	15.7	116	0.1	96	0.08	0.05	0.14	1.0	1
Sausage, pork	367	1520	10.6	32.1	9.5	41	1.1	0	0	0.04	0.12	5.7	0
Soup, tomato, canned	55	230	0.8	3.3	5.9	17	0.4	35	0	0.03	0.02	0.2	6
Spaghetti	364	1549	9.9	1.0	84.0	23	1.2	0	0	0.09	0.06	1.8	0
Spinach	21	91	2.7	0	2.8	70	3.2	1000	0	0.12	0.20	1.3	60
Spirits, 70% proof	221	914	0	0	0	0	0	0	0	0	0	0	0
Steak and kidney pie, cooked	304	1266	13.3	21.1	14.6	37	5.1	126	0.55	0.11	0.47	6.0	0
Strawberries	26	109	0.6	0	6.2	22	0.7	5	0	0.02	0.03	0.5	60
Sugar, white	394	1680	0	0	105.0	1	0	0	0	0	0	0	0
Sweet corn, canned	79	336	2.9	0.8	16.1	3	0.1	35	0	0.05	0.08	0.3	4
Syrup	298	1269	0.3	0	79.0	26	1.4	0	0	0	0	0	0
Tomatoes, fresh	12	52	0.8	0	2.4	13	0.4	117	0	0.06	0.04	0.7	21
Watercress	14	60	2.9	0	0.7	222	1.6	500	0	0.10	0.16	2.0	60
Wine, red	67	277	0	0	0.3	6	0.8	0	0	0.01	0.02	0.2	0
Yoghurt, fruit	96	410	4.8	1.0	18.2	160	0.2	10	0.02	0.05	0.23	1.2	1
Yoghurt, natural	53	224	5.0	1.0	6.4	180	0.1	10	0.02	0.05	0.26	1.3	0

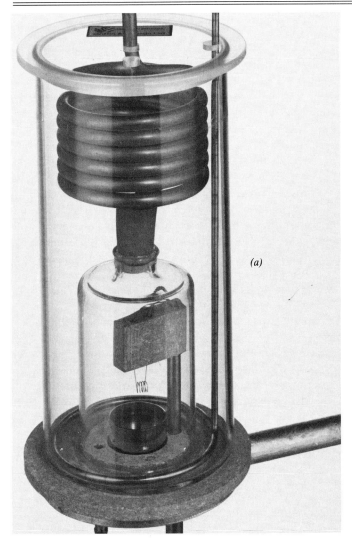

(a)

Notes:

Carbohydrates are given as monosaccharides.

Vitamin A is given in the form of µg retinol equivalents, i.e. values include estimated contributions from carotene precursors. 1 µg retinol is equivalent to 3.33 i.u. (international units).

Vitamin D is given as µg: 1 µg vitamin D is equivalent to 40 i.u.

Vitamin B$_1$ is *thiamin*.

Vitamin B$_2$ is *riboflavin*.

Nicotinic acid is given in two forms; *total* being the nicotinic acid present as the vitamin itself. Nicotinic acid *equivalents* include the contribution estimated to be supplied by tryptophan, assuming 60 mg tryptophan gives rise to 1 mg nicotinic acid.

(a) fortified; (b) unfortified; (c) some margarines contain carotene; (d) summer value; (e) winter value; (f) high in new potatoes falling during storage.

(b)

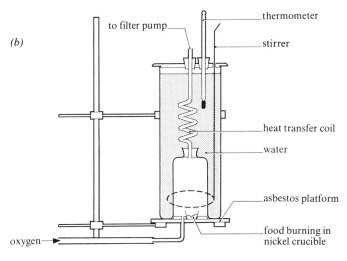

Fig 10.12 *(a) Calorimeter designed to investigate the energy content of food materials. The small electric heating coil is used to ignite the food. (b) Diagram to show the labelled parts*

considers that a man deprived of food may live for more than 60 days, but for only a few days if deprived of water. A full account of the functions of water in both animals and plants can be found in chapters 5 and 14.

10.3.8 Roughage

In humans, roughage or dietary fibre consists of indigestible cellulose of the cell walls of plants. It has a water-holding capacity and provides bulk to the intestinal contents, especially in the large intestine. Here, stretching of the colon wall stimulates reflex peristaltic activity and hence aids movement of the colon contents towards the rectum, and promotes defaecation. Absence of dietary fibre can lead to constipation and other disorders of the large intestine.

10.3.9 Milk

The only dietary item that most mammals receive during the first weeks of their lives is milk. It provides an almost complete diet during this stage of their development, containing carbohydrate, protein, fat, minerals (especially calcium, magnesium, phosphorus and potassium) and a variety of vitamins. The one major element that milk lacks is iron, a constituent of haemoglobin in blood. However, this problem is overcome by the embryo accumulating iron from its mother and storing a sufficient quantity of it in its body prior to birth. This sustains embryonic development, and development after birth until the offspring begins to ingest solid food.

> **10.7** Early this century, Frederick Gowland Hopkins in Cambridge performed a famous experiment where he took two sets of eight young rats and fed both on a diet of pure casein, starch, sucrose, lard, inorganic salts and water. The first set received additionally 3 cm³ of milk per day for the first 18 days. On day 18, the extra milk was denied the first set, but given to the second set of rats instead. The result of the experiment is shown in fig 10.13.
> (a) What hypothesis can you deduce from the graph?
> (b) Support your answer with comments.
> (c) Why is a diet of milk inadequate for an adult?

10.3.10 Vitamins

Vitamins are complex organic compounds present in very small quantities in natural food and absorbed into the body from the small intestine. They possess no energy value but are essential for the good health of the body and in maintaining its normal metabolic activities. If the diet is deficient in a particular vitamin, metabolic activity is impaired. This produces a disorder symptomatic with that particular vitamin deficiency, which is termed a **deficiency disease**. When the dietary intake of a

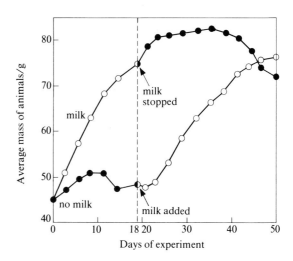

Fig 10.13 *Gowland Hopkins's experiment on feeding milk to rats*

particular vitamin is inadequate, the deficiency disease it might cause can be avoided by supplementing the diet with the necessary vitamin. Table 10.6 indicates some of the sources and functions of the principal vitamins required in the human diet and the deficiency diseases caused by a lack of them.

10.4 The alimentary canal in humans

Digestion and absorption occurs in the alimentary canal, digestive or gastrointestinal tract, or more plainly the gut, which runs from the mouth to the anus. As the gut wall is continuous with the outside surface of the body, the food it contains is considered to be external to the body in a positional and physiological sense. Food can only be absorbed into the body when its highly complex molecules are broken down physically by the teeth and muscles of the gut wall, and chemically by its enzymes into molecules of a suitably small size to be absorbed into the blood capillaries surrounding the small intestine. From here they are delivered to the cells of the body tissues where they undergo assimilation. The pattern of enzymatic digestion can be seen in fig 10.14.

The gut is a locally differentiated structure, that is it is specialised at various points along its length, with each region designed to carry out a different role in the overall processes of digestion and absorption. It begins with the mouth and buccal cavity which are followed by the pharynx, oesophagus, stomach, the small intestine comprising the duodenum and ileum, the large intestine consisting of the caecum, bearing the appendix, colon and rectum and terminating at the anus (fig 10.15 and table 10.7).

Whilst each different portion of the digestive tract possesses its own special characteristics, all conform to a basic common structure as shown in fig 10.16. This consists

Table 10.6 Sources and functions of principal vitamins required in the human diet.

Name of vitamin and its designated letter	Principal sources	Function	Deficiency diseases and symptoms
Fat-soluble vitamins			
A Retinol	Halibut and cod-liver oil; ox liver; milk and derivatives; carrots; spinach; watercress	Controls normal epithelial structure and growth. The aldehyde form of vitamin A, retinal, is essential for the formation of the visual pigment rhodopsin, which aids 'night vision'.	Skin becomes dry, cornea becomes dry and mucous membranes degenerate. Poor 'night vision'. Serious deficiency results in complete night blindness. **Xerophthalmia** – permanent blindness may occur if the vitamin is not added to the diet.
D Calciferol	Halibut and cod-liver oil; egg yolk; margarine; made by the action of sunlight on lipids in the skin; milk	Controls calcium absorption from the digestive tract, and concerned with calcium metabolism. Important in bone and tooth formation. Aids absorption of phosphorus.	**Rickets** – this is the failure of growing bones to calcify. Bow legs are a common feature in young children and knock knees in older ones. Deformation of the pelvic bones in adolescent girls can occur which may lead to complications when those girls give birth. **Osteomalacia** – an adult condition where the bones are painful and spontaneous fractures may occur.
E Tocopherol	Wheat germ; brown flour; liver; green vegetables	In rats, it affects muscles and the reproductive system and prevents haemolysis of red blood corpuscles. Function in humans is unknown.	Can cause sterility in rats. Muscular dystrophy. **Anaemia** – increased haemolysis of red blood corpuscles.
K Phylloquinone	Spinach; cabbage; brussels sprouts; synthesised by bacteria in the intestine	Essential for final stage of prothrombin synthesis in the liver. Therefore it is a necessary factor for the blood-clotting mechanism.	Mild deficiency leads to a prolonged blood-clotting time. Serious deficiency means blood fails to clot at all.
Water-soluble vitamins			
B_1 Thiamin	Wheat or rice germ; yeast extract; wholemeal flour; liver; kidney; heart	Acts as a coenzyme for decarboxylation. Aids chemical changes in respiration, especially in Krebs cycle.	**Beriberi** – nervous system affected. Muscles become weak and painful. Paralysis can occur. Heart failure. Oedema. Children's growth is impaired. Keto acids, e.g. pyruvic acid, accumulate in the blood.
B_2 Riboflavin	Yeast extract; liver; eggs; milk; cheese	Forms part of the prosthetic group of flavoproteins which are used in electron transport.	Tongue sore. Sores at the corners of the mouth.
B_6 Pyridoxine	Eggs; liver; kidney; whole grains; vegetables; fish	Phosphorylated pyridoxine acts as a coenzyme for amino acid and fatty acid metabolism.	Depression and irritability. Anaemia. Diarrhoea. Dermatitis.
B_5 Pantothenic acid	In most foods	Forms part of coenzyme A molecule which is involved in activation of carboxylic acids in cellular metabolism.	Poor neuromotor coordination. Fatigue. Muscle cramp.
B_3(pp) Nicotinic acid (niacin)	Meat; wholemeal bread; yeast extract; liver	Essential component of the coenzymes NAD, NADP which operate as hydrogen acceptors for a range of dehydrogenases. Also a part of coenzyme A.	**Pellagra** – skin lesions, rashes. Diarrhoea.
M or Bc Folic acid	Liver; white fish; green vegetables	Formation of red blood corpuscles. Synthesis of nucleoproteins.	**Anaemia** – particularly in women during pregnancy.
B_{12} Cyanocobalamin	Meat; milk; eggs; fish; cheese	RNA nucleoprotein synthesis. Prevents pernicious anaemia.	Pernicious anaemia.
H Biotin	Yeast; liver; kidney; egg white; synthesis by intestinal bacteria	Used as a coenzyme for a number of carboxylation reactions. Involved in protein synthesis and transamination.	Dermatitis. Muscle pains.
C Ascorbic acid	Citrus fruits; green vegetables; potatoes; tomatoes	Concerned with the metabolism of connective tissue and the production of strong skin. Essential for collagen fibre synthesis.	**Scurvy** – skin of gums becomes weak and bleeds. Wounds fail to heal. Connective tissue fibres fail to form. Anaemia. Heart failure.

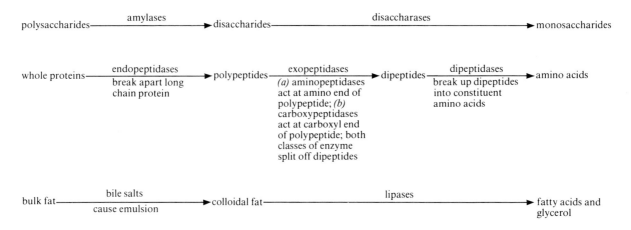

Fig 10.14   *General pattern of enzyme digestion in the human alimentary canal*

Table 10.7 Summary of the functions of the different parts of the human digestive system.

Specialised part	Function
Buccal cavity	Ingestion, mastication
Pharynx	Swallowing
Oesophagus	Links pharynx to stomach
Stomach	Food storage and digestion of protein
Duodenum	Digestion and absorption
liver (bile)	Emulsification of fats
pancreas	
(pancreatic juice)	Digestion of starch, protein and fat
Ileum	Completion of digestion and absorption of food
Colon	Absorption of water
Rectum	Formation and storage of faeces
Anus	Egestion

of four distinct layers: the mucosa, submucosa, muscularis externa and serosa.

Mucosa.   This is the innermost layer of the gut and is composed of glandular epithelium which secretes copious quantities of mucus and possess enzymes embedded in the brush border. The mucus lubricates the food and facilitates its easy passage along the digestive tract. It also prevents digestion of the gut wall by its own enzymes. The epithelial cells rest on a basement membrane beneath which is the **lamina propria**, containing connective tissue, blood and lymph vessels. Outside this is a thin layer of smooth muscle, the **muscularis mucosa**.

Submucosa.   This is a layer of connective tissue containing nerves, blood and lymph vessels, collagen and elastic fibres. It may contain some mucus-secreting glands which deposit their contents onto the surface via ducts, such as Brunner's glands in the duodenum.

Muscularis externa.   This layer is composed of an inner circular and an outer longitudinal layer of

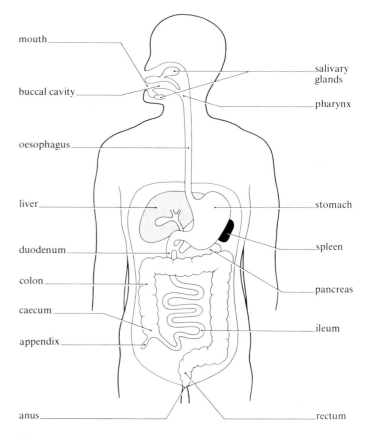

Fig 10.15   *General layout of human alimentary canal*

smooth muscle. Coordinated movements of the two layers provide the wave-like peristaltic activity of the gut wall which propels food along. At a number of points along the gut the circular muscle thickens into structures called **sphincters**. When these relax or contract they control the movement of food from one part of the alimentary canal to another. They are found at the junctions of the oesophagus and stomach (cardiac sphincter), stomach and duodenum (pyloric sphincter), ileum and caecum, and at the anus.

Between the circular and longitudinal muscle layers is

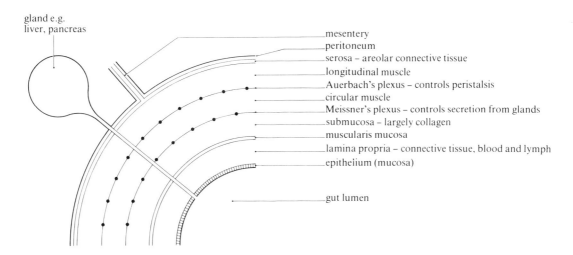

Fig 10.16 *General plan of gut structure as seen in transverse section*

Auerbach's plexus. This consists of nerves from the autonomic nervous system which control peristalsis. Impulses travelling along sympathetic nerves cause the gut muscles to relax and the sphincters to close, whilst impulses travelling via the parasympathetic nerves stimulate the gut wall to contract and the sphincters to open (section 16.2). Between the circular muscle and submucosa is another nerve plexus, **Meissner's plexus**. This controls secretion from glands in the gut wall.

Serosa. This is the outermost coat of the gut wall. It is composed of loose fibrous connective tissue.

The whole of the outer surface of the gut is covered by **peritoneum**. This tissue also lines the abdominal cavity, where most of the gut is located, and constitutes the **mesenteries** which suspend and support the stomach and intestines from the dorsal body wall. Mesenteries consist of double layers of peritoneum containing nerves, blood vessels and lymph vessels that pass to and from the gut. The peritoneum cells are moist and help to reduce friction when the gut wall slides over other portions of itself or other organs.

10.4.1 Human dentition

In humans there are two jaws, the fixed upper jaw and the movable lower jaw, with the tongue between each half of the lower jaw. Both jaws bear teeth which are used to chew or **masticate** food into smaller pieces. This is mechanical digestion and increases the surface area of food for efficient enzyme attack. The teeth are very hard structures and ideally suited to their task. Humans have two successive sets of teeth, a condition called **diphyodont**. The **deciduous** or milk teeth appear first, only to be progressively replaced by the **permanent** teeth. Human teeth have different shapes and sizes and possess uneven

biting surfaces, which is known as **heterodont**. This is in contrast to the **homodont** condition of fish and reptiles where all teeth are similar and usually cone-shaped. Humans possess 32 permanent teeth consisting of eight incisors, four canines, eight premolars and twelve molars. These replace the eight incisors, four canines and eight premolars of the deciduous dentition. The arrangement of the teeth can be conveniently expressed in the form of a **dental formula**. Human permanent dentition is:

$$2 \left[\text{i} \, \frac{2}{2} \quad \text{c} \, \frac{1}{1} \quad \text{pm} \, \frac{2}{2} \quad \text{m} \, \frac{3}{3} \right]$$

where the letters indicate the type of tooth, the numerator represents the number of each type of tooth in the upper jaw on one side of the head and the denominator represents the teeth in the lower part of the jaw on the same side (fig 10.17).

The number, size and shape of the teeth differ within the buccal cavity of humans and also between different mammals. This can be correlated with their different functions and different diets respectively. The basic structure and function of each type of tooth is as follows. **Incisors** are situated at the front of the buccal cavity. They have flat, sharp edges which are used for cutting and biting food (fig 10.18a). **Canines** are prominently pointed teeth (fig 10.18b). They are poorly developed in humans, but highly developed in carnivores where they are designed for piercing and killing prey, and tearing flesh. **Premolars** possess one or two roots and two cusps (projections on the surface of a tooth) (fig 10.18c). They are specialised for crushing and grinding food, although in humans they may also be used to tear food. **Molars** have more than one root; upper molars have three roots, lower molars two (fig 10.18d). Each has four or five cusps. They are used to crush and grind food. They are not present in the deciduous dentition of humans.

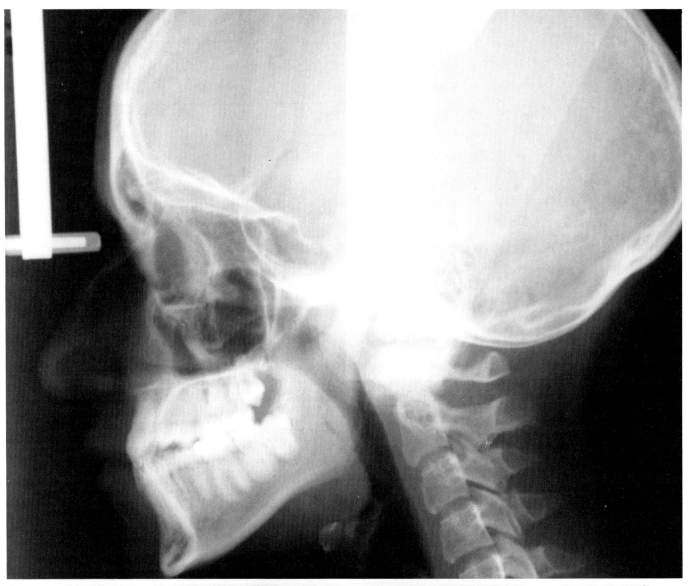

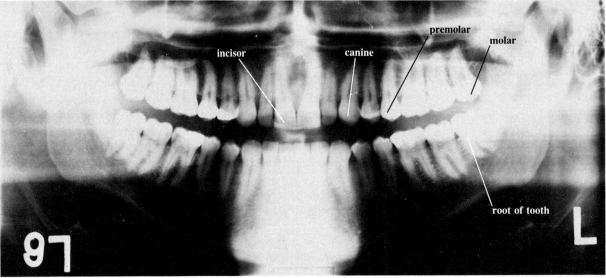

Fig 10.17 (a) *X-ray of side of human head to show permanent dentition on one side.*

(b) *X-ray from the front to show a complete permanent dentition. Dental formula* $2\left[\text{i}\,\dfrac{2}{2}\quad \text{c}\,\dfrac{1}{1}\quad \text{pm}\,\dfrac{2}{2}\quad \text{m}\,\dfrac{3}{3}\right]$

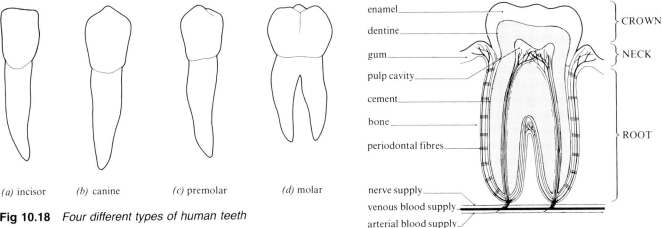

(a) incisor   (b) canine   (c) premolar   (d) molar

Fig 10.18 *Four different types of human teeth*

Fig 10.19 *Vertical section of a premolar tooth*

10.4.2 Generalised structure of a tooth

The visible part of the tooth, termed the **crown**, is covered with enamel (fig 10.19), the hardest substance in the body. It is relatively resistant to decay. The neck of the tooth is surrounded by the **gum** whilst the root is embedded in the jawbone. Beneath the enamel is **dentine** which forms the bulk of the tooth. Though tough, it is not as hard as enamel or as resistant to decay. It is ramified by numerous canaliculi containing cytoplasmic extensions of **odontoblasts** (section 8.4.5), the dentine-producing cells. The **pulp cavity** contains odontoblasts, sensory endings of nerves and blood vessels which deliver nutrients to the living tissues of the tooth and remove their waste products.

The root of the tooth is covered with **cement**, a substance similar to bone. Numerous **periodontal fibres**, connected to the cement at one end and the jawbone at the other, anchor the tooth firmly in place. However it is still able to move slightly and this reduces the chances of it being sheared off during chewing.

10.4.3 The development of teeth in humans

Teeth begin to form in the embryo after about the sixth week of its development. Cells in the buccal epithelium divide to form tooth buds. Each bud extends into the mesoderm and is termed an **enamel organ**. Gradually this organ becomes concave and develops the characteristic shape of a tooth. The enamel organ differentiates into outer and inner epithelia. The inner cells enclose a mesodermal core, the **dental papilla**, from which the dentine-producing cells and pulp develop. When dentine begins to form, the inner enamel layer differentiates into **ameloblasts** which produce enamel. Finally the jawbone becomes fashioned into a tooth socket to house the growing tooth. Fig 10.20 shows the stages in tooth development. The first tooth appears through the gum of a baby at about six months after birth.

Deciduous dentition is usually complete by the age of

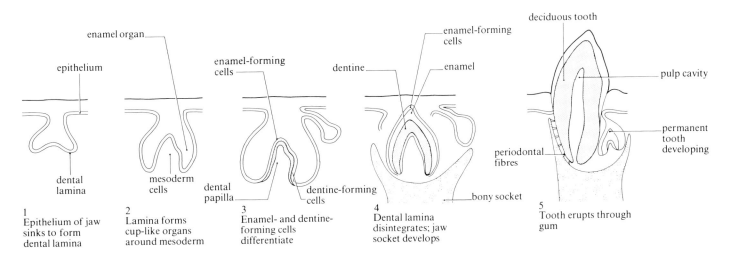

1 Epithelium of jaw sinks to form dental lamina

2 Lamina forms cup-like organs around mesoderm

3 Enamel- and dentine-forming cells differentiate

4 Dental lamina disintegrates; jaw socket develops

5 Tooth erupts through gum

Fig 10.20 *Stages in the development of a tooth*

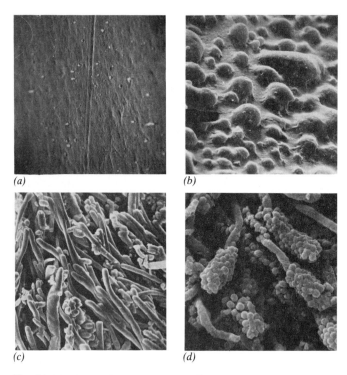

three years but the jaws continue growing and these teeth soon become too small. At the age of six years the deciduous teeth begin to loosen and are replaced by the first of the larger permanent teeth. By the age of 13, 28 of the permanent teeth should have appeared. The four

(a)

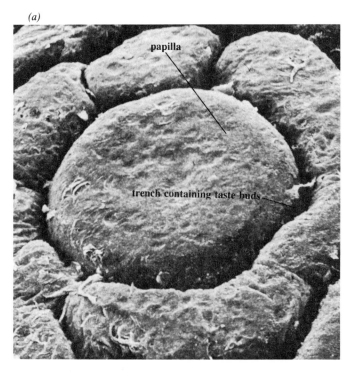

Fig 10.21 (above) *Development of dental plaque. (a) Coccal bacteria deposit as pioneer species and then multiply to form a film. (b) Organisms embedded in a matrix of extracellular polymers of bacterial and salivary origin. (c) The complexity of the community increases and rod- and filament-shaped populations appear. (d) In the climax community many unusual associations between different populations can be seen, including 'corn cob' arrangements*

Fig 10.22 (above) *(a) Scanning electron micrograph of circumvallate papilla of a three-week-old puppy. The taste buds are in the trenches surrounding the surface papillae (below) (b) VS taste buds in the tongue*

(b)

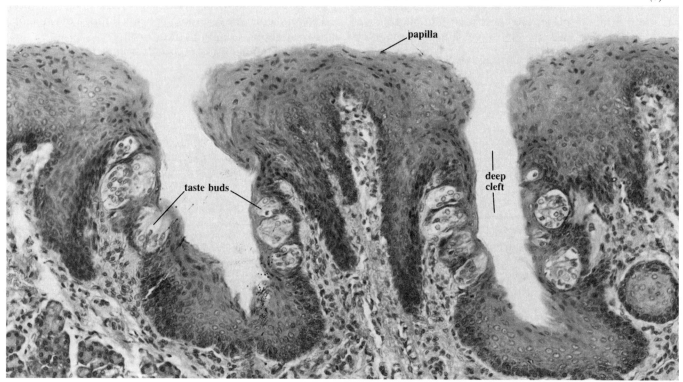

remaining molars, or wisdom teeth, usually appear after the age of 17.

In humans and carnivores the hole at the base of the pulp cavity closes when each tooth reaches a particular size and prevents it from growing any further. However, in herbivores, this does not occur to the same extent and nutrients continue to pass to the tooth which grows continuously.

10.4.4 Dental disease

Two major dental diseases exist, periodontal disease and dental caries. Both are caused by **plaque** which is a mixture of bacteria and salivary materials. If allowed to accumulate, the bacteria cause inflammation of the gums (**periodontal disease**). Plaque also combines with certain chemicals in the saliva which make it harden and calcify to form deposits of **calculus** which cannot be removed by brushing. Some of the bacteria in plaque convert sugar into acid which initiates the process of **dental caries** (fig 10.21).

Periodontal disease

This is a disease of the gums caused by micro-organisms that are normally present in the mouth in dental plaque, especially in the areas between the gums and the teeth. Neglect of oral hygiene creates favourable conditions for the spread of this disease. Initially periodontal disease causes inflammation of the gums. If this condition, which is generally painless, is allowed to continue, the inflammation may spread to the root of the tooth and destroy the periodontal fibres which anchor it in place. Eventually the tooth becomes loose and may have to be extracted.

Dental caries

The micro-organisms in dental plaque convert sugar in the buccal cavity to acid. Initially the enamel is slowly and painlessly dissolved by the acid. However when the dentine and pulp of the tooth are attacked this is accompanied by severe pain or 'toothache', and the possible loss of teeth.

Several factors contribute to the spread of dental caries. They include prolonged exposure to sugary foodstuffs, disturbance of saliva composition, lack of oral hygiene and low levels of fluoride in drinking water. Prevention of dental caries may be aided by adding fluoride to drinking water, fluoridation of some foods such as milk, children taking fluoride tablets, brushing teeth with fluoridated toothpaste, good oral hygiene and regular visits to the dentist and oral hygienist and care with the composition of the diet.

10.4.5 Buccal cavity

The buccal cavity is the region enclosing the jaws and tongue, and is lined by stratified squamous epithelium. During mastication the muscular tongue moves food around the mouth and mixes and moistens it with saliva. The tongue possesses **taste buds** (fig 10.22) that are sensitive to sweet, salty, sour and bitter substances and this aids in food discrimination. In humans the tongue is also important in speech.

About 1.5 dm³ of saliva are produced by humans each day by three pairs of **salivary glands** (fig 10.23) and numerous **buccal glands** in the mucosa of the buccal cavity. Saliva is a watery secretion containing the enzymes **salivary amylase** and **lysozyme**, sodium chloride and sodium hydrogencarbonate, phosphates, carbonates, Ca^{2+}, K^+, Mg^{2+}, sulphocyanide and mucus. The mucus moistens and lubricates the food and makes it easier to swallow. Salivary amylase begins the digestion of starch first to dextrins, shorter polysaccharides, and then to the disaccharide maltose. Carnivorous mammals which rapidly gulp large chunks of food into their stomachs possess no digestive enzymes in their saliva. Lysozyme helps in keeping the buccal cavity clear of pathogenic micro-organisms by catalysing the breakdown of their cell walls. Ultimately the semi-solid, partially digested food particles are stuck together by **mucin** and moulded into a **bolus** (or pellet) by the tongue, which then pushes it towards the pharynx. From here as a result of a reflex action it is swallowed into the oesophagus via the pharynx.

10.4.6 Swallowing

This is initially a voluntary action, but once begun it continues involuntarily to its completion. Fig 10.24 shows the stages involved in swallowing in humans.

10.4.7 Oesophagus

This is a narrow muscular tube lined by stratified squamous epithelium containing mucus glands. In humans it is about 25 cm long and quickly conveys food and fluids by peristalsis from the pharynx to the stomach.

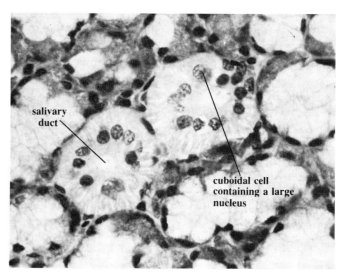

Fig 10.23 *Salivary gland tissue*

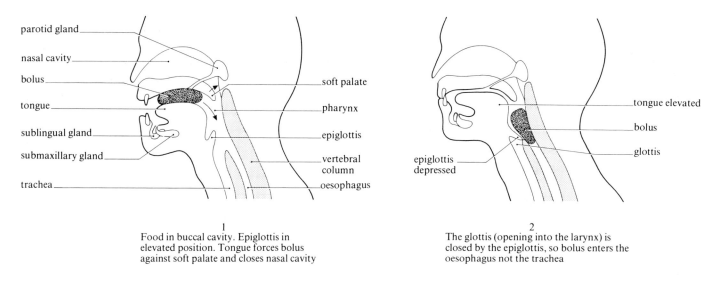

1
Food in buccal cavity. Epiglottis in elevated position. Tongue forces bolus against soft palate and closes nasal cavity

2
The glottis (opening into the larynx) is closed by the epiglottis, so bolus enters the oesophagus not the trachea

Fig 10.24 *Actions involved in the swallowing of food in humans*

The upper part of the oesophagus contains striated muscle, the middle section a mixture of striated and smooth muscle and the lower region purely smooth muscle. Carnivores which gulp their food in large pieces possess striated muscle along the whole length of the oesophagus.

10.4.8 Stomach

The stomach in humans is situated below the diaphragm and on the left side of the abdominal cavity. It is a distensible muscular bag whose function is to store and partially digest food. Unlike the other regions of the gut it consists of three smooth muscle layers, the outer longitudinal, middle circular and inner oblique layers which serve to churn and mix the food with the gastric secretions. When undistended the stomach lies in folds, but when fully distended it can hold nearly $5\,dm^3$ of food. The thick mucosa is liberally supplied with mucus-secreting epithelial cells and possesses numerous gastric pits (figs 10.26 and 10.27). These possess zymogen cells, oxyntic cells and enzymes and hydrochloric acid. Collectively the secretions of the stomach are called **gastric juice**. The mucus provides a barrier between the stomach mucosa and gastric juice and prevents the stomach self-digesting. The cardiac sphincter, at the junction between the oesophagus and upper cardiac region of the stomach, and pyloric sphincter, at the junction of the stomach and the duodenum, prevent the uncontrolled exit of food from the stomach. Both act as valves and serve to retain food in the stomach for periods of up to 4 h. Periodic relaxation of the pyloric sphincter releases small quantities of the food into the duodenum. The mucosa of the cardiac region of the stomach contains only mucus glands, whilst the main body of the stomach, the fundus, contains many long, tubular **zymogen** or **chief glands** (fig 10.27). These possess zymogen cells, oxyntic cells and argentaffine cells.

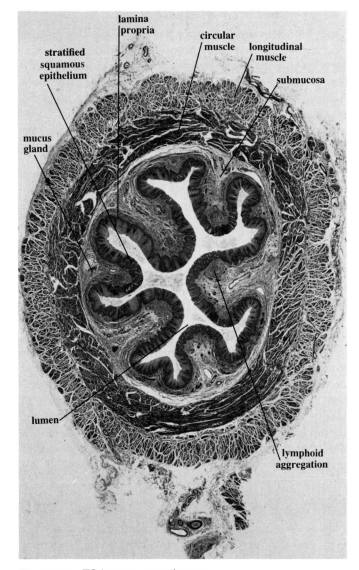

Fig 10.25 *TS human oesophagus*

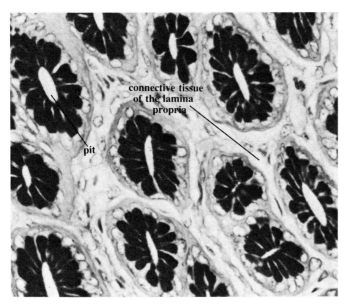

Fig 10.26 *TS gastric pits of a mammal*

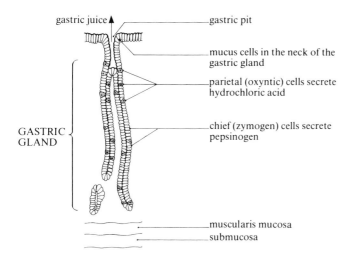

Fig 10.27 *VS stomach wall showing gastric gland*

Zymogen or chief cells. These secrete the inactive enzymes pepsinogen and prorennin.

> **10.8** Why is it necessary for pepsin to be secreted in an inactive state?

Oxyntic or parietal cells. These secrete a 0.04–0.05% solution of hydrochloric acid which makes the pH of the stomach contents 1–2.5, ideal for the optimum activity of the stomach enzymes. The acid kills many bacteria, loosens fibrous and cellular components of tissue and promotes the conversion of pepsinogen to its active form pepsin. Pepsin hydrolyses protein into smaller polypeptides and converts more molecules of pepsinogen to pepsin, a process known as **autocatalysis**. Hydrochloric acid converts prorennin to rennin which, in turn, coagulates caseinogen, the soluble protein of milk, into the

insoluble calcium salt of casein, in the presence of calcium ions. This calcium salt is then digested by pepsin. Hydrochloric acid renders calcium and iron salts suitable for absorption in the intestine, begins hydrolysis of sucrose to glucose and fructose and splits nucleoproteins into nucleic acid and protein.

Argentaffine cells. These produce the **intrinsic gastric factor** which aids absorption of molecules of the vitamin B_{12} complex.

The muscles of the stomach wall thoroughly mix up the food with gastric juice and eventually convert it into a semi-liquid mass called **chyme**. Gradually the stomach empties the chyme into the duodenum via the relaxed pyloric sphincter.

10.4.9 Small intestine

This consists in humans of an upper tube, 20 cm long, called the **duodenum**, into which open the pancreatic and bile ducts. The duodenum leads on to the **ileum** which is about 5 m long (fig 10.28*a* and *b*). The submucosa of the small intestine is thrown into many folds. The mucosa possesses numerous finger-like projections called **villi** whose walls are richly supplied with blood capillaries and lymph vessels and contain smooth muscle (fig 10.30). They are able to constantly contract and relax, thus bringing themselves into close contact with the food in the small intestine. The individual cells on the surface of the villi possess tiny microvilli on their free surfaces (fig 10.30 and section 7.2.11).

> **10.9** (*a*) List the features of the small intestine which increase its surface area.
> (*b*) Why is this an advantage to the animal concerned?

Throughout the small intestine, certain mucosal cells secrete mucus. Submucosal Brunner's glands also secrete mucus and alkaline fluid in the first part of the duodenum, so protecting the intestinal mucosa against the acid pH of the stomach and providing an optimum pH of 7–8 at which the intestinal enzymes are active.

> **10.10** What would happen to the activity of the intestinal enzymes if the pH in the duodenum remained at 2?

Until the mid-1960s it was believed that digestion of foodstuffs was completed by a group of enzymes collectively called the succus entericus secreted into the lumen of the small intestine by the epithelial cells lining this region. However, this is now known not to be the case.

The disaccharase and peptidase enzymes involved in the final digestive process are, in fact, bound to membranes of the microvilli of the epithelial mucosa (fig 10.30*b*). Other peptidases are located within these cells. It is at these sites

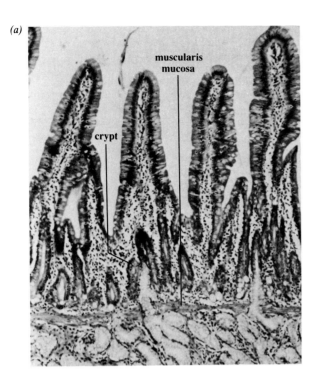

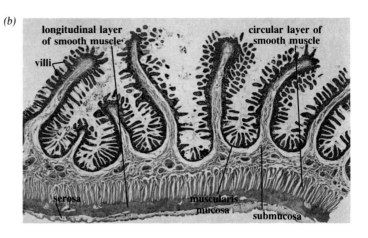

Fig 10.28 *(a) VS duodenum. (b) VS ileum*

Table 10.8 Summary of digestive secretions and their action.

Secretion	Enzymes	Site of action	Optimum pH	Substrate	Products
Saliva (from salivary glands)	Salivary amylase	Buccal cavity	6.5–7.5	Amylose in starch	Maltose
Gastric juice (from stomach mucosa)	(Pro)rennin (in young)	Stomach	2.00	Caseinogen in milk	Casein
	Pepsin(ogen)	Stomach	2.00	Proteins	Peptides
	Hydrochloric acid (not an enzyme)	Stomach	—	Pepsinogen	Pepsin
				Nucleoproteins	Nucleic acid and protein
Membrane-bound enzymes in small intestine	Amylase	Microvilli of	8.5	Amylose	Maltose
	Maltase	brush border	8.5	Maltose	Glucose
	Lactase	of	8.5	Lactose	Glucose + galactose
	Sucrase	epithelial	8.5	Sucrose	Glucose + fructose
(exopeptidases)	{Aminopeptidase	mucosa of	8.5	Peptides and	Amino acids
	{Dipeptidase	small intestine	8.5	dipeptides	Amino acids
Intestinal juice	Nucleotidase	Small intestine	8.5	Nucleotides	Nucleosides
	Enterokinase	Small intestine	8.5	Trypsinogen	Trypsin
Pancreatic juice (from pancreas)	Amylase	Small intestine	7.00	Amylose	Maltose
	Trypsin(ogen)	Small intestine	7.00	{Proteins	Peptides
				{Chymotrypsinogen	Chymotrypsin
(endopeptidases)*	{Elastase	Small intestine	7.00	Proteins	Peptides
	{Chymotrypsin(ogen)	Small intestine	7.00	Proteins	Amino acids
(exopeptidase)*	Carboxypeptidase	Small intestine	7.00	Peptides	Amino acids
	Lipase	Small intestine	7.00	Fats	Fatty acids + glycerol
	Nuclease	Small intestine	7.00	Nucleic acid	Nucleotides
	Bile salts (not enzymes)	Small intestine	7.00	Fats	Fat droplets

* Exopeptidases split off terminal amino acids from proteins (polypeptides)
Endopeptidases break bonds between amino acids within proteins thus producing smaller peptides

Collectively these enzymes break up polypeptides into their constituent amino acids so that they can be absorbed by the villi of the ileum

that the final hydrolysis of disaccharides, dipeptides and some tripeptides occurs (fig 10.29). The end-products are monosaccharides and amino acids respectively, which are liberated into the lumen of the small intestine. A full list of the enzymes involved can be found in table 10.8.

Also present in the small intestine is nucleotidase, which converts nucleotides to nucleosides, and enterokinase, a non-digestive enzyme which converts inactive trypsinogen of the pancreatic juice into active trypsin. In addition to its own set of enzymes the small intestine receives alkaline pancreatic juice and bile from the pancreas and liver respectively. Bile, produced by liver cells (section 18.4), is stored in the gall bladder and contains a mixture of salts, notably sodium glycocholate and taurocholate, which reduce the surface tension of fat globules and emulsify them into droplets, so increasing their total surface area. In this form they are acted upon more effectively by lipase. Further information about the composition of bile is given in section 18.4.

The pancreas is a large gland whose exocrine tissue resembles that of salivary glands (fig 10.31). This tissue is composed of groups of cells called **acini** (singular acinus) which produce a variety of digestive enzymes that are poured into the duodenum via the pancreatic duct. They include amylase to convert amylose to maltose, **lipase** to convert fats to fatty acids and glycerol, **trypsinogen**, which when converted to trypsin by enterokinase digests proteins into smaller polypeptides and more trypsinogen into trypsin, **chymotrypsinogen** which is converted to chymotrypsin to digest proteins to amino acids, **carboxypeptidases** to convert peptides to amino acids and **nucleases** to convert nucleic acids to nucleotides.

A summary of the enzymes secreted by the human gut and their action is given in table 10.8. Table 10.9 indicates the differences in structure between the major regions of the alimentary canal in humans.

10.4.10 Absorption of food in the small intestine

Absorption of the end-products of digestion occurs through the microvilli (section 7.2.11) of the epithelial cells of villi lining the ileum. The structure of the villus is ideally suited for this function as can be seen in fig 10.30. Monosaccharides, dipeptides and amino acids are absorbed either by diffusion or active transport into the blood capillaries (section 7.2.2).

> **10.11** Why is it important that active transport is employed in the absorption of the foodstuffs monosaccharides, dipeptides and amino acids?

From the villi the blood capillaries converge to form the hepatic portal vein which delivers the absorbed food to the liver. Fatty acids and glycerol enter the columnar epithelial cells of the villi. Here they are reconverted into fats. These fats then enter the lacteals. Proteins present in these lymph vessels coat the fat molecules to form lipoprotein droplets called **chylomicrons**. These pass into the bloodstream via the thoracic lymphatic duct. The lipoproteins are subsequently hydrolysed by a blood plasma enzyme and enter cells as fatty acids and glycerol where they may be used in respiration or stored as fat in the liver, muscles, mesenteries or subcutaneous tissue.

Inorganic salts, vitamins and water are also absorbed in the small intestine.

10.4.11 Peristalsis in the alimentary canal of humans

Whilst the food is in the alimentary canal it is subjected to a number of peristaltic movements. Alternate rhythmic contractions and relaxation of its wall produce **segmenting movements** which constrict parts of the small intestine and bring chyme and the absorptive mucosal lining close together. **Pendular movements** are produced when loops of the intestine suddenly shorten vigorously,

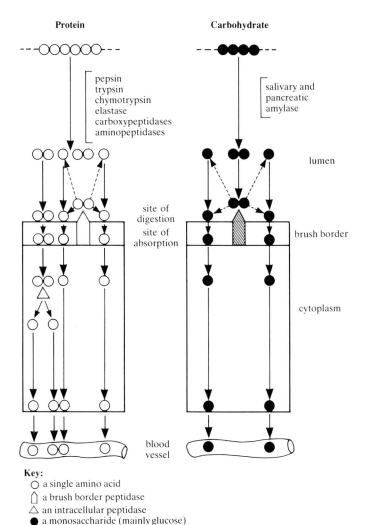

Key:
○ a single amino acid
⌂ a brush border peptidase
△ an intracellular peptidase
● a monosaccharide (mainly glucose)
▨ sucrase, maltase or lactase

Fig 10.29 *Schematic diagram of two epithelial cells, the one on the left bringing about the final phase of protein digestion, with the subsequent absorption of amino acids; and the one on the right the corresponding processes for carbohydrates*

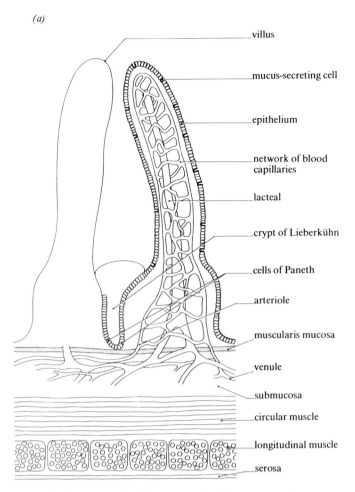

(a)

villus

mucus-secreting cell

epithelium

network of blood capillaries

lacteal

crypt of Lieberkühn

cells of Paneth

arteriole

muscularis mucosa

venule

submucosa

circular muscle

longitudinal muscle

serosa

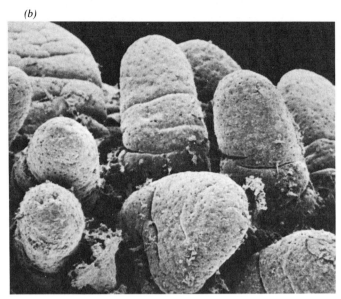

(b)

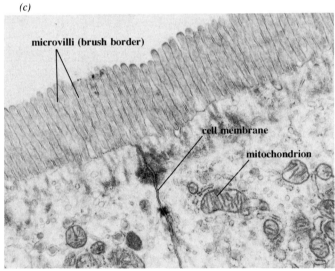

(c)

microvilli (brush border)

cell membrane

mitochondrion

Fig 10.30 *(a) TS wall of human small intestine showing a villus. (b) Scanning electron micrograph showing villi on surface of small intestine. (c) Electron micrograph of mucosal cell showing microvilli*

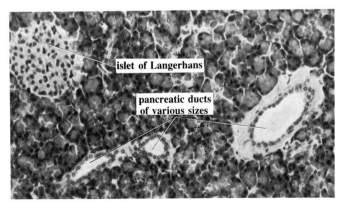

islet of Langerhans

pancreatic ducts of various sizes

Fig 10.31 *TS pancreas tissue showing pancreatic ducts and one islet of Langerhans*

throwing food from one end to the other thus thoroughly mixing it. As well as this, normal peristaltic activity occurs which propels the intestinal contents further along the alimentary canal. The ileocaecal sphincter opens and closes from time to time, to allow small amounts of residue from the ileum to enter the large intestine.

10.4.12 Large intestine

In the human large intestine the bulk of the water and any remaining inorganic nutrients are absorbed, whilst some metabolic waste and inorganic substances, notably calcium and iron, in excess in the body are excreted as salts. Mucosal epithelial cells secrete mucus which

Table 10.9 Comparison of structures of the major regions of the alimentary canal in humans.

Layer	Oesophagus	Stomach	Small intestine	Large intestine
Mucosa (a) epithelium lining lumen	Stratified, squamous	Simple columnar	Simple columnar, absorptive and mucus cells	Simple columnar, absorptive and mucus cells
	Specialisation – a few mucus glands located in the lamina propria and sub-mucosa	Specialisation – gastric glands located in lamina propria, four cell types: (i) mucus (ii) parietal (iii) peptic (iv) endocrine	Specialisation – (i) intestinal glands in crypts of Lieberkühn (ii) Paneth cells (iii) endocrine cells (iv) duodenal mucus glands	Specialisation – intestinal glands in lamina propria
(b) lamina propria	Some mucus glands	Many gastric glands	Intestinal glands and prominent lacteals	Tubular glands
(c) muscularis mucosa	Present	Present	Present	Present
Submucosa	Some deep mucus glands	Present	Duodenal glands	Intestinal glands
Muscularis inner circular, outer longitudinal	Transitional from striated muscle in upper region to smooth muscle in lower region in Man	With additional inner-most layer of oblique muscle. Circular muscle forms cardiac and pyloric sphincters	Present	Present
Serosa	Present	Present	Present	Incomplete serosa

lubricates the solidifying food residue or faeces. Many symbiotic bacteria present in the large intestine synthesise amino acids and some vitamins, especially vitamin K, which are absorbed into the bloodstream.

In humans the appendix is a blindly ending pouch leading from the caecum and possesses no known function. It is, however, of great significance in herbivores (section 10.8.3). The bulk of the faeces consists of dead bacteria, cellulose and other plant fibres, dead mucosal cells, mucus, cholesterol, bile pigment derivatives and water. Faeces can remain in the colon for 36 h before being passed on to the rectum where it is stored briefly before egestion via the anus. Two sphincters surround the anus, an internal one of smooth muscle and under the control of the autonomic nervous system, and an outer one of striated muscle controlled by the voluntary nervous system.

In a young baby reflex defaecation occurs when distension of the rectum causes relaxation of the internal sphincter. Gradually the child learns to bring this reflex under control of its higher nervous centres and defaecation usually only occurs when the external sphincter is relaxed.

Experiment 10.3: To investigate the anatomy of the stomach, small and large intestines and to analyse the amino acid content of each region

Materials

freshly killed adult rat	dissection kit
mammal Ringer's solution	distilled water
specimen tubes	thin-layer chromatogram plate
binocular microscope	wire loop
chromatogram jar and lid	fume cupboard
n-butanol	ninhydrin spray
glacial ethanoic acid	oven at 100 °C

Method

(1) Dissect the freshly killed rat under Ringer's solution. Ligature and remove separately the stomach, small intestine and large intestine, open them and wash out the contents of each region with mammal Ringer's solution into separate labelled specimen tubes.

(2) Cut small sections of the wall of each region and examine under a binocular microscope. Observe and make notes on the nature of their internal surfaces.

(3) Add a small quantity of distilled water to the contents of the specimen tubes, shake well and allow to settle for 15 min.

(4) Take a drop of the clear liquid above the sediment from each specimen tube and place it on separate, prepared thin-layer chromatogram plates and dry. Repeat the procedure to increase the amount of specimen present. When the spots are dry, place them in a chromatogram jar containing a solvent composed of 40 parts n-butanol, 10 parts glacial acetic acid and 15 parts distilled water to about 1 cm depth. Place a lid on the chromatogram jar (fig 10.32).

(5) Allow to run for 90 min, then dry the plates in a fume cupboard and spray with ninhydrin.

(6) Heat the plates to 100 °C in an oven.

(7) Examine each plate for purple and other coloured spots. The spots indicate the presence of amino acids in the solutions being examined.

(NB This practical is based on Nuffield A-level Biology, *Maintenance of the organism*.)

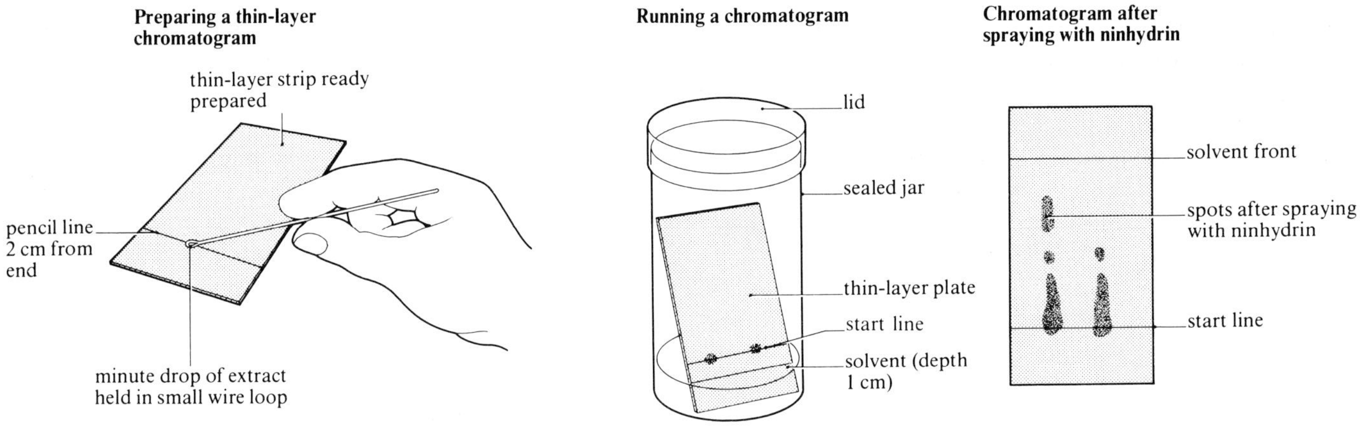

Running a chromatogram

Chromatogram after
spraying with ninhydrin

Fig 10.32 *Preparing a thin-layer chromatogram*

Experiment 10.4: To investigate digestion and absorption using a model gut

Materials

freshly killed adult rat
watchglasses
1% starch solution
three 15 cm lengths of
visking tubing
cotton
boiling tubes
paper clips
water bath at 30 °C
stopclock

iodine/potassium iodide
solution
Benedict's solution
bunsen burner
asbestos mat
test-tubes and rack
teat pipette

Method

(1) Dissect a freshly killed rat and ligature and extract the stomach, small intestine and large intestine separately.

(2) Put each in a watchglass and cover with 1% starch suspension. Mix and break up the tissue whilst in the watchglass.

(3) Take three 15 cm lengths of visking tubing (1 cm diameter) and tie a knot at one end.

(4) Pour the macerated tissue of each region into the three lengths of visking tubing, one for each region, and top up with more starch solution until the total volume is about 10 cm³. Mix each solution thoroughly.

(5) Lower the three tubes into separate boiling tubes containing 10 cm³ of distilled water and prevent each open end falling into the water by attaching it to the side of the boiling tube with a paper clip.

(6) Set up a control with the visking tubing containing 10 cm³ of 1% starch solution only.

(7) Incubate all tubes in a water bath at 30 °C for 30 min.

(8) After 30 min perform the following tests on each tube and its contents:
 (*a*) take a drop of solution from each of the visking tubing contents and test each separately for the presence of starch with iodine/potassium iodide solution;
 (*b*) take a further drop of solution from each of the visking tubing contents and test for reducing sugar using Benedict's solution. Record your results;
 (*c*) perform separate starch and reducing sugar tests on the water surrounding the visking tubing in each tube.

(9) Construct a table of your results.

(10) Is there any evidence that gut tissue changes starch to reducing sugar? If so which region produces most reducing sugar?

(11) What do your observations indicate about the nature of visking tubing?

10.5 The control of digestive secretions

Secretion of digestive enzymes is an energy-consuming process, and it would be extremely wasteful if the body was constantly producing them, especially in the absence of food. Instead the bulk of digestive juice is produced only when there is digestive work to be done. In this way the overall control of digestive activity is coordinated and regulated as an orderly sequence during the digestion of food.

In the buccal cavity salivary secretion is released by two reflex reactions. First an unconditional cranial reflex occurs when food is present in the buccal cavity. Contact with the taste buds of the tongue elicits impulses which travel to the brain and from there to the salivary glands which are stimulated to secrete saliva. Secondly, there are the conditioned reflexes of seeing, smelling or thinking of food.

Secretion of gastric juice occurs in three phases. The first is the **nervous** (or vagus) phase. The presence of food in the buccal cavity and its swallowing initiate impulses which pass via the vagus nerve to the stomach whose mucosa is stimulated to secrete gastric juice. This takes place before the food has reached the stomach and therefore prepares it to receive food. The nervous phase of gastric secretion lasts for approximately 1 h. The second phase is the distension phase in which distension of the stomach by the food it contains also stimulates the flow of gastric juice. Thirdly, there is the gastric (or humoral) phase, in which the presence of food in the stomach stimulates the pyloric mucosa to produce a hormone, gastrin, which reaches the rest of the stomach mucosa via the bloodstream and stimulates it to produce gastric juice rich in hydrochloric acid for about 4 h.

The phases of gastric secretion can be seen in fig 10.33.

Enterogastrone is another hormone that is released by the stomach mucosa in response to the presence of fatty acids in the food. This generally inhibits hydrochloric acid secretion, slows down stomach peristalsis and delays its emptying. The intrinsic gastric factor which aids absorption of vitamin B_{12} is also released by the gastric mucosa.

When acidified chyme enters and makes contact with the walls of the duodenum it triggers the duodenal mucosa to secrete intestinal juice and also to produce two hormones **cholecystokinin–pancreozymin** and secretin. The pancreozymin component of the former hormone is conveyed by the bloodstream to the pancreas as is secretin which also reaches the liver along with cholecystokinin. Pancreozymin induces the formation of pancreatic juice rich in enzymes. Secretin stimulates the flow of pancreatic juice rich in hydrogencarbonate, and bile synthesis by the liver. Cholecystokinin causes contraction of the gall bladder and subsequent release of bile into the duodenum.

Table 10.10 summarises the endocrine control of the various secretions of the alimentary canal and its associated organs.

10.6 The fate of the absorbed food materials

Carbohydrates and amino acids are both absorbed into the bloodstream surrounding the small intestine and passed to the liver via the hepatic portal vein. Most of the glucose is stored here or in muscle as glycogen and fats, though some leaves via the hepatic vein to be distributed round the body where it is oxidised during respiration. Between meals, if the body requires more energy, glycogen can be reconverted to glucose and transported by the blood to those tissues in need.

Amino acids are used for the synthesis of new protoplasm, the repair of damaged parts of the body and the formation of enzymes and hormones. Surplus amino acids cannot be stored and are deaminated in the liver. Their amino (NH_2) groups are removed and converted to urea which is delivered via the bloodstream to the kidneys and excreted in the urine. The remainder of the amino acid molecule is converted to glycogen and stored.

Absorbed fats bypass the liver and enter the venous bloodstream via the thoracic lymphatic duct. Fats represent the major energy store of the body. Normally, however, glucose is in adequate supply and the fats are not required for energy production. In this case they are stored in subcutaneous adipose tissue, around the heart and kidneys and in the mesenteries. Some fat is incorporated into cell and nuclear membranes.

10.7 Regulation of food intake in humans

The regulation of food intake in humans is under the general control of two centres in the **hypothalamus** of the brain, the **hunger** and **satiety** centres. Stimulation of the hunger centre causes the individual to seek and eat food, whilst stimulation of the satiety centre inhibits food intake. The most important factor influencing both these centres is the level of glucose in the blood. This is monitored by the hypothalamus and gives a good indication of the nutritional condition of the body.

Shortly after a meal, blood glucose level is high and this stimulates the satiety centre to inhibit the body from eating any further food. A long time after a meal the blood glucose level will be low, and this condition triggers the hunger centre into action (fig 10.34).

This seemingly quite simple explanation is not by any means the complete story. Whether or not food is

Table 10.10 Summary of endocrine control of the secretions of the alimentary canal and its associated organs in humans.

Hormone	Site of production	Stimulus for secretion	Target organ	Response
Gastrin	Stomach mucosa	Distension of stomach by food	Stomach	Increased secretion of HCl
Enterogastrone	Stomach mucosa and small intestine	Fatty acids in food	Stomach	Inhibits HCl secretion, slows peristaltic activity, delays emptying
Pancreozymin	Duodenal mucosa	Food in the duodenum	Pancreas	Increased secretion of pancreatic enzymes
Cholecystokinin	Duodenal mucosa	Fatty food in the duodenum	Gall bladder	Contraction of gall bladder to release bile
Secretin	Duodenal mucosa	Acid and food in the duodenum	Pancreas	Increased flow of hydrogencarbonate in pancreatic juice
			Liver	Synthesis of bile

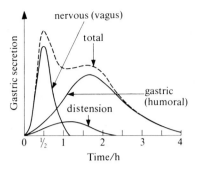

Fig 10.33 (left) *Phases of gastric secretion (From J. H.Green (1968) An introduction to human physiology, Oxford Medical Publications.)*

Fig 10.34 (below) *Hypothalamic control of food intake*

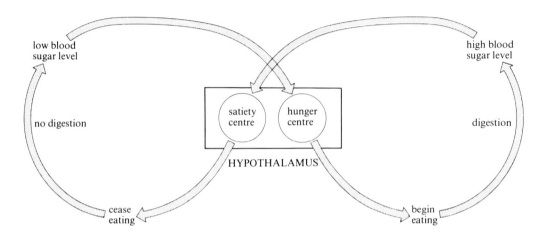

consumed is also affected by other subsidiary factors which include stretch reflexes in the alimentary canal, the psychological state of the individual, conscious habits and damage to or impairment of the brain. Any of these may upset the activity of the hypothalamic centres and cause abnormal responses towards food intake.

10.8 Variations in the mammalian alimentary canal

10.8.1 A carnivore – the cat

The cat is a carnivore and has teeth adapted for catching and breaking down animal food. The dental formula is:

$$2 \left[i\frac{3}{3} \quad c\frac{1}{1} \quad pm\frac{3}{2} \quad m\frac{1}{1} \right]$$

The closely fitting incisors are small and chisel-shaped and used to tear away flesh near the bone surface. The enlarged canines are curved and fang-like and used to seize and kill prey, and tear off flesh. Two cheek teeth on each side of the jaws are considerably enlarged – with prominent ridges running parallel with the line of the jaw. These are the **carnassial** teeth (third upper pm and first lower m). They act rather like the two blades of a pair of scissors with the

inner surfaces of the teeth of the upper jaw moving closely against the outer surfaces of the teeth in the lower jaw as they shear flesh from the prey. The other cheek teeth are flattened and possess sharp edges used for cutting flesh and cracking bones.

The jaw joint operates as a closely fitting hinge and permits only up-and-down movement. The cheek teeth, which require the greater force for their operation, are placed nearest the joint.

Contraction of the **temporal** muscle closes the lower jaw. It is attached to a prominent bony extension from the lower jaw which projects upwards towards the ears. This particular arrangement provides efficient leverage on the food as it is being sheared by the teeth, or when the cat's mouth is snapping shut whilst killing its prey. Another muscle, the **masseter**, pulls the base of the lower jaw upwards and reduces the strain on the jaw joint (fig 10.35).

10.8.2 A herbivore – the sheep

A sheep eats grass and its dentition is closely correlated with its feeding habits and diet. Its dental formula is:

$$2 \left[i\frac{0}{3} \quad c\frac{0}{1} \quad pm\frac{3}{2} \quad m\frac{3}{3} \right]$$

Upper incisors and canines are absent. In their place is a horny pad against which the chisel-shaped lower incisors

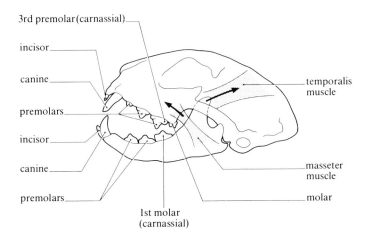

Fig 10.35 *Jaws, dentition and musculature of the cat*

and canines bite when the sheep is cropping grass. Between the front and cheek teeth is a large gap, the **diastema**, which provides space for the tongue to manipulate the cropped grass in such a way that grass being chewed is kept apart from that freshly gathered.

The cheek teeth possess broad grinding surfaces whose area is further increased by the surfaces of the upper teeth being folded into a W-shape and those of the lower teeth being folded into an M-shape. The ridges of the teeth are composed of hard enamel whilst the troughs are of dentine.

The jaw joint is very loose and allows forward, backward and sideways movement. During chewing the lower jaw moves from side to side, with the W-shaped ridges of the upper cheek teeth fitting closely into the grooves of the M-shaped lower teeth as they grind the grass. The masseter muscle is large, and the temporal small, the reverse arrangement of that of the cat (fig 10.36).

10.8.3 Cellulose digestion in ruminants (such as sheep and cattle)

Ruminants possess highly complex alimentary canals. A number of compartments precede the true stomach, the first of which is the **rumen**. This acts as a fermentation chamber where food, mixed with saliva,

undergoes fermentation by mutualistic micro-organisms. Many of these produce cellulases which digest cellulose. Their presence is absolutely essential to the ruminant as it is unable to manufacture cellulase itself. The end-products of fermentation are ethanoic, propanoic and butanoic acids, carbon dioxide and methane. The acids are absorbed by the host, who uses them as a major source of energy during oxidative metabolism. In return the micro-organisms obtain their energy requirements through the chemical reactions of fermentation and an ideal temperature in which to live.

A ruminant is able to regurgitate and rechew partially digested material from the rumen. This is called rumination or 'chewing the cud'. The food is then reswallowed and undergoes further fermentation. Eventually the partially digested food is passed through the initial compartments of the alimentary canal until it reaches the **abomasum** which corresponds to the stomach in humans. From here onwards food undergoes digestion by the usual mammalian digestive enzymes (fig 10.37).

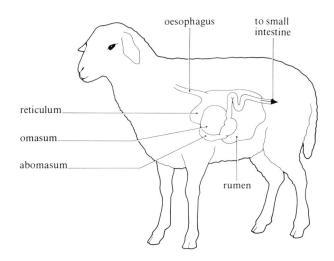

Fig 10.37 *Complex arrangement of compartments preceding the small intestine in a ruminant*

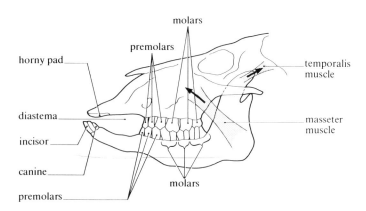

Fig 10.36 *Jaws, dentition and musculature of the sheep*

Chapter Eleven

Energy utilisation

Each living cell is a complex entity characterised by a high degree of order within its system. Experiments have revealed that the cell interior as a whole is continuously active, with materials constantly entering and leaving it. All reactions proceeding in the cell can be grouped into two categories. **Anabolic** reactions are the synthesis of large molecules from smaller, simpler molecules. Energy is used in this process (that is the process is **endergonic**).

$$A + B \rightarrow AB \quad [+\Delta G]$$

(Where ΔG = free energy change of a reaction.)

Catabolic reactions are the breakdown of large molecules to smaller, simpler molecules usually accompanied by release of energy (so the process is **exergonic**). Sometimes the simpler molecules can be used for biosynthesis again.

$$AB \rightarrow A + B \quad [-\Delta G]$$

[NB It is important to note that not every catabolic reaction liberates energy. Some degradations that the cell performs in order to eliminate unwanted substances are actually endergonic.]

The sum total of catabolic and anabolic reactions occurring at any time in a cell represents its **metabolism**:

catabolism + anabolism = metabolism

Organic compounds that enter a cell provide it with two essentials. These are small 'building' molecules, which are used for biosynthesis of new cellular components or the replacement of components past their useful life, and chemical energy. Generally when nutrients are degraded within a cell, energy is liberated. Much of it is utilised by the cell to maintain its own life processes. It is transferred to various sites in the cell and converted into different forms. Each form of energy may then be used for a particular job of work within the cell. This may be biosynthesis, mechanical work, cell division, active transport, osmotic activity, and, in some specialised cells, muscular contraction, bioluminescence or electrical discharge (fig 11.1). Chemical energy is most appropriate for use by living cells as it can be transferred within and between cells quickly, and released in economically regulated amounts as, and when, required. All energy is derived from the sun. Energy is readily convertible into its different forms by organisms, but to enter the food chains solar energy must be absorbed by green plants (**autotrophs**), and converted by their chlorophyll-containing cells into chemical energy (contained in the simple sugar glucose or polysaccharide starch) by the process of photosynthesis. A portion of this energy is liberated and used by plants for their own requirements. Animals have to

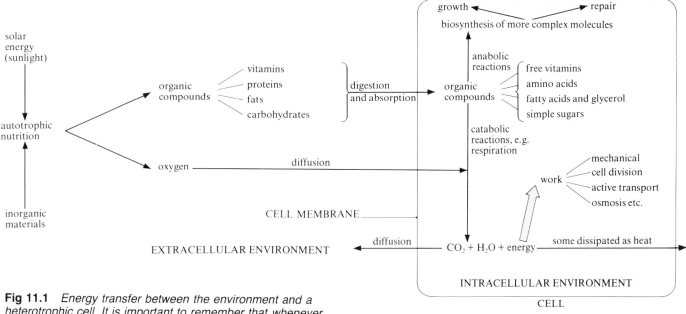

Fig 11.1 *Energy transfer between the environment and a heterotrophic cell. It is important to remember that whenever one form of energy is converted into another, a certain proportion of it is dissipated as heat*

find a ready-made source of energy (that is foodstuffs). Some of them obtain this by feeding on plants (**herbivores**), whilst others (**carnivores**) devour the tissues of herbivores for their energy supply (see chapter 12).

11.1 Role of respiration

Respiration may be defined as generally any process that liberates chemical energy when organic molecules are oxidised. Where the process occurs within cells it is called **internal**, **tissue** or **cell respiration**. If it requires oxygen, it is **aerobic** respiration; whereas if the reaction takes place in the absence of oxygen, it is **anaerobic** respiration.

Organic molecules (usually carbohydrate or fat) are broken down bond by bond, by a series of enzyme-controlled reactions. Each releases a small amount of energy, much of which is channelled into molecules of a chemical nucleotide called **adenosine triphosphate** (ATP).

Tissue respiration must not be confused with the processes of acquiring and extracting oxygen from, and discharging carbon dioxide into, the environment. These are collectively termed **external respiration**, or preferably **gas exchange**. They may involve organs or structures with specialised surfaces for the efficient exchange of gases, over which air or water is pumped by various respiratory movements (section 11.6).

11.2 ATP (adenosine triphosphate)

ATP is composed of the purine adenine linked to the 5C sugar ribose and three phosphate groups (fig 11.2). When the bonds of the two end phosphate groups of ATP are hydrolysed, the free energy yield for each is of the order of 30.6 kJ, whereas if the third phosphate group is hydrolysed the energy yield is only 13.8 kJ (table 11.1). It is because of this that ATP and ADP (adenosine diphosphate) are popularly, though erroneously, believed to possess 'energy-rich' bonds (often signified ($\sim$)). The reason why ATP releases more energy on hydrolysis than many other compounds is not clear. However it is thought to involve the distribution of charges within the molecule.

Table 11.1 Free energy of hydrolysis of phosphate compounds.

Compound	ΔG (free energy change) (kJ mol^{-1})
Phosphoenolpyruvate	−62.1
1,3 diphosphoglycerate	−49.5
Creatine phosphate	−43.3
ATP (to ADP and phosphate)	−30.6
ADP (to AMP and phosphate)	−30.6
AMP (to adenosine and phosphate)	−13.8
Glucose-6-phosphate	−13.8

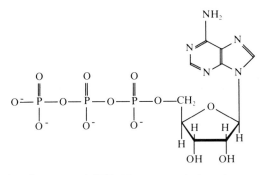

Fig 11.2 *Structure of ATP. The two end phosphate groups are attached by pyrophosphate bonds, which when hydrolysed yield a large quantity of free energy*

More chemical energy is said to be required to maintain its integrity. This is not contained in any one bond, but is a property of the whole molecule.

> **11.1** Table 11.1 shows that ATP is not by any means the most 'energy-rich' compound in cells. What is the significance of ATP lying in an intermediate position in the table?

11.2.1 Importance of ATP

ATP is the standard unit in which the energy released during respiration is stored. To make one ATP molecule from ADP and phosphate 30.6 kJ of energy are required. Therefore it can only be formed from reactions that yield more than 30.6 kJ mol^{-1}. Any energy liberated in excess of 30.6 kJ mol^{-1}, and all that from reactions that yield less than 30.6 kJ mol^{-1}, cannot be stored in ATP and is lost as heat.

Because all the chemical energy is in one form (ATP), the energy-consuming processes need only one system that can accept chemical energy from ATP. Thus a great economy of mechanism is achieved.

ATP is an instant source of energy within the cell. It is mobile and transports chemical energy to energy-consuming processes anywhere within the cell. When the cell requires energy, hydrolysis of ATP is all that has to occur for the energy to be made available. ATP is found in all living cells, and hence is often known as the **universal energy carrier**.

ADP may be rephosphorylated to ATP by respiratory activity (fig 11.3), or by another 'high-energy' compound, such as creatine phosphate which is present in muscle cells. If all available ADP of a muscle cell has been converted to ATP, phosphate is transferred from ATP to creatine to form creatine phosphate. This releases a quantity of ADP which can combine with more phosphate to make extra ATP. The reverse occurs when ATP levels decrease: phosphate is transferred from creatine phosphate to ADP thus restoring ATP stocks (fig 11.4).

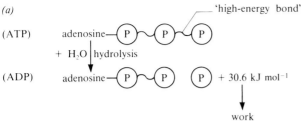

(a)

(b) respiratory activity

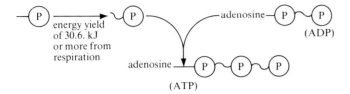

Fig 11.3 (left) (a) *Hydrolysis, and (b) rephosphorylation, of ATP by respiratory activity*

Fig 11.4 (below) *Energy-phosphate transfer between ATP and creatine*

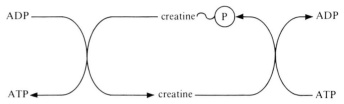

A third way to rephosphorylate ADP is by photophosphorylation by chlorophyll-containing cells of green plants (section 9.4).

The metabolic role of ATP is significant in that it lies at the centre of cellular activity, acting as a common intermediate between respiration and energy-requiring processes, with phosphate being consistently removed and replaced.

11.2 'The role of ATP can be compared with that of a battery.' Explain this statement.

11.3 Biological oxidation

In general, cell oxidations are of three types:

(1) $$A + O_2 \rightarrow AO_2$$

direct oxidation by molecular oxygen;

(2) $$AH_2 + B \rightarrow A + BH_2$$

where A is oxidised at the expense of B;

11.3 What is this type of oxidation called?

11.4 What are enzymes which carry out this type of oxidation called?

(3) $$Fe^{2+} \rightarrow Fe^{3+} + e^-$$

where an electron transfer occurs, such as the oxidation of one ionic form of iron (Fe^{2+}) to another (Fe^{3+}).

Each type of oxidation is to be found in the series of reactions which are collectively termed **aerobic respiration**.

11.3.1 Cell respiration in outline

Cell respiration involves oxidation of a substrate to yield chemical energy (ATP). Organic compounds which are used as substrates in respiration are carbohydrates, fats and proteins.

Carbohydrates. These are usually the first choice of most cells. In fact brain cells of mammals cannot use anything but glucose.

Polysaccharides are hydrolysed to monosaccharides before they enter the respiratory pathway:

Fats. They form the 'first reserve' and are mainly used when carbohydrate reserves have been exhausted. However in skeletal muscle cells, if glucose and fatty acids are available, these cells respire the acids in preference to glucose.

Proteins. Since proteins have other essential functions, they are only used when all carbohydrate and fat reserves have been used up, as during prolonged starvation.

When glucose is the substrate, its oxidation can be divided into three distinct phases: glycolysis (the Embden–Meyerhof pathway); oxidative decarboxylation (Krebs, or citric acid cycle or TCA, tricarboxylic acid cycle); oxidative phosphorylation (respiratory chain incorporating hydrogen and electron transfer). Glycolysis is common to anaerobic and aerobic respiration, but the other two phases only occur when aerobic conditions prevail. Details of each of the processes are to be found later in this chapter, but an outline is given below.

11.3.2 Glycolysis and the Krebs cycle

During aerobic respiration glucose is oxidised by a series of dehydrogenations. At each dehydrogenation, hydrogen is removed and used to reduce a coenzyme:

AH_2	+	B	$\xrightarrow{\text{dehydrogenase}}$	A	+	BH_2
reduced respiratory substrate		coenzyme (hydrogen acceptor)		oxidised respiratory substrate		reduced coenzyme

Most of these oxidations occur in the mitochondrion, where the usual coenzyme hydrogen acceptor is NAD (nicotinamide adenine dinucleotide):

$$NAD + 2H \rightarrow NADH_2$$

or, more accurately,

$$NAD^+ + 2H \rightarrow NADH + H^+$$

$NADH_2$ then enters the respiratory chain to be reoxidised.

11.3.3 The respiratory chain and oxidative phosphorylation

$NADH_2$ is oxidised back to NAD and the hydrogen released is passed along a chain of at least five carrier substances to the end of the chain where the hydrogen combines with molecular oxygen to form water. The passage of hydrogen along this 'respiratory chain' of carriers involves a series of redox reactions. The energy released from some of these is sufficient to make ATP, a process called **oxidative phosphorylation**. The net yield per molecule of glucose completely oxidised to water and carbon dioxide is 38 molecules of ATP, synthesised from ADP and inorganic phosphate. Glycolysis yields two ATP, Krebs cycle two ATP and the respiratory chain 34 ATP (fig 11.5).

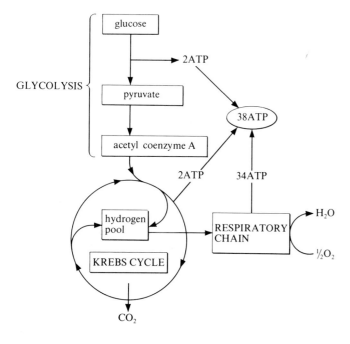

Fig 11.5 *Aerobic respiration in outline*

11.3.4 Glycolysis in detail

Glycolysis represents a series of reactions in which a glucose molecule is broken down into two molecules of pyruvate (fig 11.6). It occurs in the cytoplasm of cells, not in the mitochondria, and does not require the presence of oxygen. The process may be sub-divided into

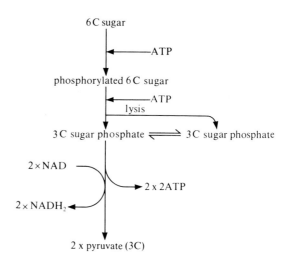

Fig 11.6 *Glycolysis in outline*

two steps, first the conversion of glucose into fructose 1,6-diphosphate, and secondly the splitting of fructose-1,6-diphosphate into 3C sugars which are later converted into pyruvate. Two ATP molecules are used up for phosphorylation reactions in the first step, whilst four ATP molecules are produced in the second step. Therefore there is a net gain of two ATP molecules. Four hydrogen atoms are also released. Their fate will be discussed later. The equation of the overall reaction is:

$$C_6H_{12}O_6 \rightarrow 2C_3H_4O_3 + 4H + 2ATP$$
glucose   pyruvic acid   (net gain)

The input and output of materials during glycolysis is shown in table 11.2.

Table 11.2 Input and output of materials during glycolysis.

Total input	Total output
1 molecule of glucose (6C)	2 molecules of pyruvate (2×3C)
2 ATP	4 ATP
4 ADP	2 ADP
2×NAD	2×NADH_2
2×P_i	2×H_2O

The ultimate fate of pyruvate depends on the availability of oxygen in the cell. If it is present, pyruvate will enter a mitochondrion and be completely oxidised into carbon dioxide and water (**aerobic respiration**). If oxygen is unavailable, pyruvate will be converted into ethanol or lactate (**anaerobic respiration**).

11.5 Study fig 11.7 carefully and answer the following questions:
(a) What is the process occurring at B and D?
(b) What class of enzyme controls reaction C?
(c) Name the processes occurring at E.
(d) Which vitamin contributes to the molecule of NAD?

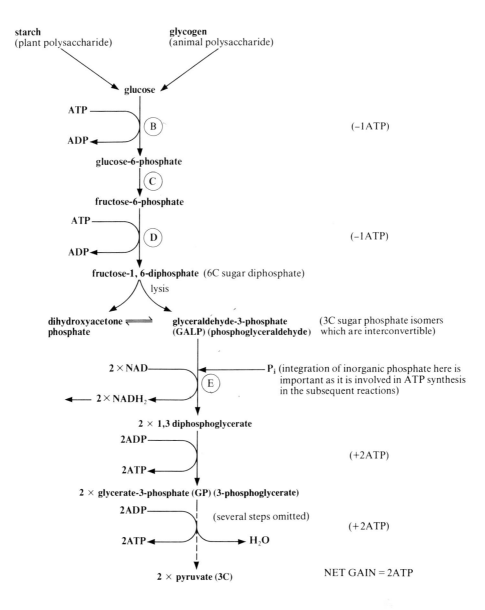

starch
(plant polysaccharide)

glycogen
(animal polysaccharide)

glucose

ATP

ADP

(B)

(–1ATP)

glucose-6-phosphate

(C)

fructose-6-phosphate

ATP

ADP

(D)

(–1ATP)

fructose-1, 6-diphosphate (6C sugar diphosphate)

lysis

dihydroxyacetone ⇌ glyceraldehyde-3-phosphate
phosphate   (GALP) (phosphoglyceraldehyde)

(3C sugar phosphate isomers which are interconvertible)

$2 \times NAD$

$2 \times NADH_2$

(E)

P_i (integration of inorganic phosphate here is important as it is involved in ATP synthesis in the subsequent reactions)

$2 \times 1,3$ diphosphoglycerate

2ADP

2ATP

(+2ATP)

$2 \times$ glycerate-3-phosphate (GP) (3-phosphoglycerate)

2ADP

2ATP

(several steps omitted)

H_2O

(+2ATP)

$2 \times$ pyruvate (3C)

NET GAIN = 2ATP

11.3.5 Aerobic respiration

There are two phases involved in aerobic respiration. First, if sufficient oxygen is available, each pyruvate molecule enters a mitochondrion where its oxidation is completed by aerobic means. This involves oxidative decarboxylation of pyruvate, that is the removal of carbon dioxide together with oxidation by dehydrogenation. During these reactions pyruvate combines with a substance called coenzyme A (often written CoAS—H) to form acetyl coenzyme A. Sufficient energy is released to form an 'energy-rich' bond in the acetyl CoA molecule. In reality the complete reaction is much more complex than this description suggests and involves five different coenzymes and three different enzymes.
The overall reaction is:

$$CH_3COCOOH + CoAS—H + NAD \rightarrow$$
$$CH_3CO\sim S—CoA + CO_2 + NADH_2$$
acetyl CoA

Fig 11.7 *Glycolysis in detail. General biochemistry of glycolysis. It is important to note that because two 3C compounds are formed when fructose-1,6-diphosphate is cleaved, four ATP are produced during subsequent reactions, two for each 3C compound converted to pyruvate*

The $NADH_2$ formed as a result of acetyl CoA formation is collected and channelled into the respiratory chain in the mitochondrion.

The second phase is the Krebs cycle (named after its discoverer, Sir Hans Krebs). The acetyl component of acetyl CoA possesses two carbons and is passed into the Krebs cycle when acetyl CoA is hydrolysed. The acetyl component combines with oxaloacetate, a 4C compound, to form citrate (6C). This reaction requires energy which is provided at the expense of the energy-rich bond of acetyl CoA. A cycle of reactions follows during which the acetyl groups fed in by acetyl CoA are dehydrogenated to release

327

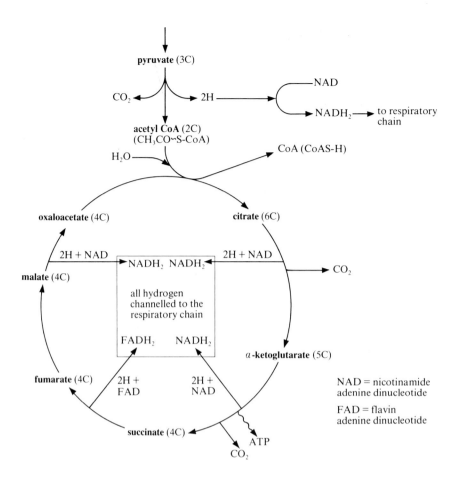

pyruvate (3C)

CO_2 ← | → 2H → NAD → NADH$_2$ → to respiratory chain

acetyl CoA (2C)
(CH$_3$CO~S-CoA)

H_2O → CoA (CoAS-H)

oxaloacetate (4C) | **citrate (6C)**

2H + NAD | 2H + NAD

malate (4C)

NADH$_2$ NADH$_2$

all hydrogen channelled to the respiratory chain

FADH$_2$ NADH$_2$

→ CO_2

α-**ketoglutarate (5C)**

fumarate (4C)

2H + FAD | 2H + NAD

NAD = nicotinamide adenine dinucleotide

FAD = flavin adenine dinucleotide

succinate (4C)

CO_2 ATP

Fig 11.8 *Simplified diagram of the Krebs cycle*

four pairs of hydrogen atoms and decarboxylated to form two molecules of carbon dioxide. During the latter process oxygen is taken from two molecules of water and used to oxidise two carbon atoms to carbon dioxide. This is termed **oxidative decarboxylation**. At the end of the cycle oxaloacetate is regenerated and able to link up once again with another molecule of acetyl CoA, and so the cycle continues. One molecule of ATP, four pairs of hydrogen atoms and two molecules of carbon dioxide are released per molecule of acetyl CoA oxidised. The hydrogen atoms are accepted by NAD or FAD (section 6.2.3) and are eventually passed into the respiratory chain. As two molecules of acetyl CoA are formed from one oxidised glucose molecule, Krebs cycle must rotate twice for each molecule respired. Therefore the net result is two ATP synthesised, four carbon dioxide liberated and eight pairs of hydrogen atoms released for entry into the respiratory chain (fig 11.8).

The overall reaction for glycolysis, acetyl CoA formation and Krebs cycle is:

$$C_6H_{12}O_6 + 6H_2O \rightarrow 6CO_2 + 4ATP + 12 \square H_2$$

where $\square$ = hydrogen acceptor.

11.3.6 Oxidative phosphorylation and the respiratory chain

The pairs of hydrogen atoms removed from respiratory intermediates by dehydrogenation reactions during glycolysis and the Krebs cycle are ultimately oxidised to water by molecular oxygen with accompanying phosphorylation of ADP to form ATP molecules. This is accomplished when hydrogen, released from NADH$_2$ or FADH$_2$, is passed along a chain of at least five intermediate substances, which include flavoprotein, coenzyme Q and a number of different cytochromes, until at the end the hydrogen combines with molecular oxygen to form water. As a result of the passage of hydrogen the intermediate carriers undergo a series of **redox** reactions, and they are arranged in such a way that at three points in the chain, each time the hydrogen atoms are passed from one intermediate to another, a small amount of energy is liberated and incorporated into a molecule of ATP. Fig 11.9 represents the respiratory chain (or electron transport chain). In fact the initial part of the chain effects mainly hydrogen transfer whilst the latter portion operates purely electron transfer. Carriers X, Y and Z are **cytochromes**. X and Y contain a protein pigment with an iron-containing prosthetic group called **haem**, as occurs also in haemoglobin. During each redox reaction the iron ion is alternately in its oxidised (Fe^{3+}) and reduced (Fe^{2+}) forms. Finally, at the terminal stage, carrier Z, which contains copper and is commonly called **cytochrome oxidase** (cytochrome a/a_3), promotes the reduction of molecular oxygen to water. This

328

stage of cell oxidation can be inhibited by potassium cyanide or carbon monoxide.

11.3.7 Hydrogen and electron carriers

NAD and NADP (nicotinamide adenine dinucleotide (phosphate))

These are closely related coenzymes, both derived from nicotinic acid (vitamin B complex). Each molecule is electropositive (lacks one electron) and can carry an electron as well as a hydrogen atom. When a hydrogen pair is accepted, one hydrogen atom dissociates with its electron and proton:

$$H \longrightarrow H^+ + e^-$$

hydrogen atom → proton electron
or
hydrogen ion

The other hydrogen atom remains whole and becomes attached to NAD(P).

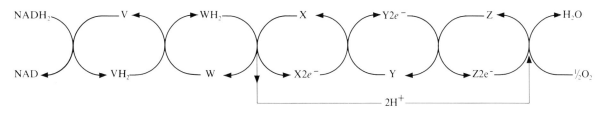

Fig 11.9 (above) *Diagrammatic representation of the respiratory chain which effects hydrogen-electron transfer. Points at which enough energy is liberated to form ATP are not shown. Not all carriers are shown*

Fig 11.10 (below) *Respiratory chain. Each cytochrome can only carry one electron, and it is thought that there are two ranks of cytochromes in each respiratory pathway. Only one is shown in the figure, but values have been doubled in order to obtain the correct end-product of the reaction. The electrons flow downhill in energy terms*

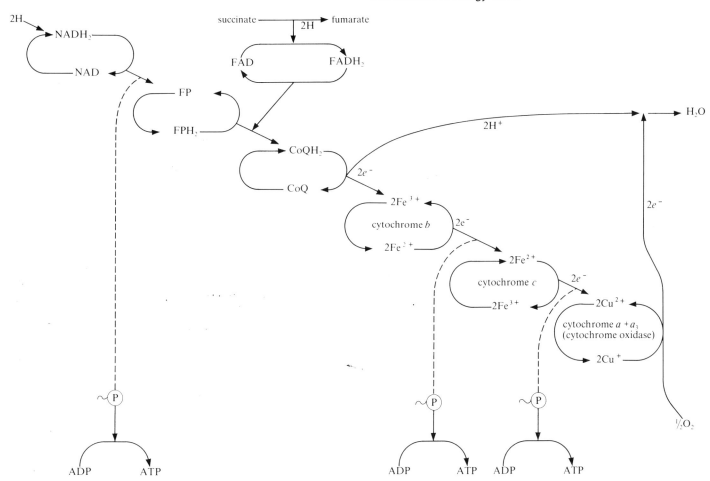

The overall reaction is:

$$NAD(P)^+ + H \quad [H^+ + e^-] \longrightarrow NAD(P)H + \quad H^+$$

whole   dissociated   reduced   free proton
atom   hydrogen atom   coenzyme   in medium

or, more simply,

$$NAD(P) + H_2 \longrightarrow NAD(P)H_2$$

The free proton is used later to reoxidise the coenzyme when the hydrogen is released.

Flavoproteins

These are coenzymes derived from vitamin B_2. FAD (flavin adenine dinucleotide) is the prosthetic group, whilst the protein part of the molecule acts as an enzyme. In the respiratory chain the protein part acts as **NAD dehydrogenase** and catalyses the oxidation of reduced NAD. The hydrogen is carried by the flavoprotein in the form of whole atoms.

In the Krebs cycle the protein part of FAD acts as **succinic dehydrogenase**. It catalyses the oxidation of succinate to fumarate. Reduced FAD enters the respiratory chain at a point after the first ATP synthesis site. Therefore only two ATP will be formed from its reoxidation (fig 11.10).

Coenzyme Q

This has a 6C ring structure. It accepts hydrogen from flavoprotein and passes it on to cytochrome b.

Cytochromes

All are proteins of relatively low molecular mass. They possess tightly bound haems as prosthetic groups, and carry electrons rather than hydrogen atoms. The electron-carrying component of cytochromes is the iron of the haem group. It normally exists in its oxidised state (Fe^{3+}), but when it accepts an electron it is reduced to its ferrous state (Fe^{2+}). What happens is that each hydrogen atom passing from coenzyme Q dissociates into a hydrogen ion and an electron:

$$H \rightarrow H^+ + e^-$$

The electron is then accepted by an ion of iron:

$$Fe^{3+} + e^- \rightleftharpoons Fe^{2+}$$
oxidised   reduced

The hydrogen ions are temporarily deposited in the surrounding medium until they are required at the end of the respiratory chain.

The electron is passed from cytochrome b to c and finally to cytochrome $a + a_3$, a tight-knit complex of two cytochromes commonly known as cytochrome oxidase. This complex contains copper as well as iron, and undergoes a redox reaction when cytochrome a_3 finally passes on electrons to oxygen (fig 11.10). Only one electron at a time can be carried by a cytochrome and it is thought

that there are two ranks of cytochromes in each respiratory chain handling pairs of electrons:

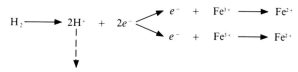

With this information about hydrogen and electron carriers you should now be able to appreciate a much more detailed study of the respiratory chain which is given in fig 11.10.

Final analysis of aerobic respiration

(1) $C_6H_{12}O_6 + 6H_2O \xrightarrow[\text{Krebs cycle}]{\text{glycolysis}} 6CO_2 + 12H_2 + 4ATP$

(2) $12H_2 + 6O_2 \xrightarrow[\text{chain}]{\text{respiratory}} 12H_2O + 34ATP$

Add (1) and (2):

$$C_6H_{12}O_6 + 6O_2 \longrightarrow 6CO_2 + 6H_2O + 38ATP$$

11.3.8   Anaerobic respiration

A variety of microorganisms (anaerobes) employ anaerobic respiration as their major ATP-yielding process. Indeed, some bacteria are actually killed by substantial amounts of oxygen and of necessity have to live where there is no oxygen. They are termed **obligate anaerobes** (for example *Clostridium botulinum* and *C. tetani*).

Other organisms such as yeasts and alimentary canal parasites (such as tapeworms), can exist whether oxygen is available or not. These are called **facultative anaerobes**. Also some cells that are temporarily deprived of oxygen (such as muscle cells) are able to respire anaerobically. (See reference to computer program in section 16.4)

With no oxygen available to accept the hydrogen atoms released during glycolysis, an alternative acceptor must be used instead of $NADH_2$. Pyruvate becomes that acceptor, and depending on the metabolic pathways within the organisms or cells themselves the end-products of anaerobic respiration will either be ethanol and carbon dioxide (as in yeasts, for example):

$$CH_3COCOOH \longrightarrow CH_3CHO + CO_2$$
pyruvic acid   ethanal

$$CH_3CHO + NADH_2 \longrightarrow CH_3CH_2OH + NAD$$
ethanal   ethanol

(this process is termed **alcoholic fermentation**) or lactate, as in animals when cells are temporarily deprived of oxygen and in some bacteria, for example **lactate fermentation** in muscle cells:

$$CH_3COCOOH + NADH_2 \longrightarrow CH_3CHOHCOOH + NAD$$
pyruvic acid   lactic acid

A summary of the pathways of anaerobic respiration is given in fig 11.11.

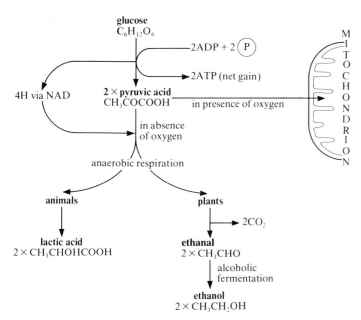

Fig 11.11 *Summary of pathways of anaerobic respiration*

No further ATP is produced by either process and so the energy yield per glucose molecule respired in this way is two ATP. In fact a considerable amount of energy remains trapped in ethanol and lactate. Hence when later compared with aerobic respiration (section 11.3.9) it must be regarded as an inefficient process (fig 11.11). The lactate has to be removed from muscle cells by the blood to prevent fatigue. It is reconverted to glucose and then to glycogen in the liver aerobically. Further details of this process are discussed in section 16.4.

11.3.9 Energy conversion efficiency of aerobic and anaerobic respiratory processes

Aerobic respiration

$$C_6H_{12}O_6 + 6O_2 \rightarrow 6CO_2 + 6H_2O + 38ATP \quad \Delta G = -2880 \text{ kJ mol}^{-1}$$

$$\text{Therefore efficiency} = \frac{38 \times -30.6}{-2880} = 40.37\%$$

(where -30.6 kJ represents the free energy liberated on hydrolysis of ATP to ADP).

Anaerobic respiration

(1) Yeast (alcoholic) fermentation

$$C_6H_{12}O_6 \rightarrow 2C_2H_5OH + 2CO_2 + 2ATP \quad \Delta G = -210 \text{ kJ mol}^{-1}$$

$$\text{Therefore efficiency} = \frac{2 \times -30.6}{-210} = 29.14\%$$

(2) Muscle glycolysis (lactate fermentation)

$$C_6H_{12}O_6 \rightarrow 2CH_3CHOHCOOH + 2ATP \quad \Delta G = -150 \text{ kJ mol}^{-1}$$
$$\text{lactic acid}$$

$$\text{Therefore efficiency} = \frac{2 \times -30.6}{-150} = 40.80\%$$

Study of the above figures indicates that the efficiency of each system is relatively high when compared with petrol engines (25–30%) and steam engines (8–12%). The amount of energy captured as ATP during aerobic respiration is 19 times as much as for anaerobic respiration. This is because a great deal of energy remains locked within lactate and ethanol. The energy in ethanol is permanently unavailable to yeast, which clearly indicates that alcoholic fermentation is an inefficient energy-producing process. However, much of the energy locked in lactate may be liberated at a later stage if oxygen is made available. In the presence of oxygen, lactate is converted to pyruvate in the liver. Pyruvate then enters Krebs cycle and is fully oxidised to carbon dioxide and water, releasing many more ATP molecules in the process (section 17.4.8).

11.3.10 Fermentation in industry

Fermentation processes are commercial or experimental processes in which micro-organisms are cultured in containers, called **fermenters** or **bioreactors**, in a liquid or solid medium. The term was originally applied only to anaerobic cultures, as in brewing, but it is important to realise that it is now more loosely applied to both anaerobic and aerobic processes, such as the growth of *Penicillium* in the penicillin industry, involving the culture of micro-organisms in artificial vessels.

Fig 11.12 shows a typical fermenter (one that is sealed from the atmosphere during operation) and gives some information on its use. The contents of most fermenters are stirred during operation, but this is not always the case, as with the production of the single cell protein 'Pruteen' by ICI, where air introduced at high velocity at the bottom of the vessel is used to achieve mixing. The **product** is either the cells themselves (biomass) or some useful cell product. *All* operations must be carried out under *sterile conditions* to avoid contamination of the culture. In addition, all inlets and outlets of the fermenter must be capable of being kept sterile. The fermenter and the medium used are sterilised before use, either together or separately. Stock cultures of the organism to be used in the fermentation are kept in an inactive form (for example stored frozen). A sample is re-activated, grown up to sufficient bulk using aseptic techniques (**scale-up**), and then added to the fermenter, a process known as **inoculation**. Once inside the fermenter, the organism grows and multiplies, using the nutrient medium.

Two basic types of fermentation are possible, **batch fermentation** (or **closed system**) and **continuous culture** (or **open system**). In the more common batch fermentation the process is stopped once sufficient product has been formed. The contents of the fermenter are removed, the product isolated, the micro-organism discarded and the fermenter is then cleaned and set up for a fresh batch. Continuous culture involves continuous long-term operation over many weeks, during which nutrient medium is added as fast as it is used, and the overflow is harvested. Continuous

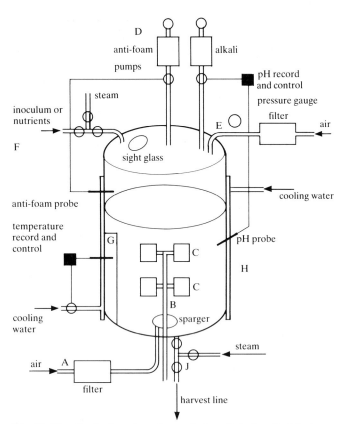

Fig 11.12 *Typical enclosed, aerated, agitated, cylindrical fermentation vessel (bioreactor) (adapted from S.B. Primrose (1987)* Modern Biochemistry, *Blackwell.)*

Size of the vessel is very variable, ranging from 1 dm³ (experimental) to 500 000 dm³ for commercial production. Shape and material used in construction are also variable, although cylindrical, stainless steel vessels are common

Key:

A *Air main – most fermentations are aerobic, requiring large volumes of sterile air. The 'sparger' is a specially designed part that releases air. Air bubbles may help the mixing process, provide oxygen for aerobic respiration and aid release of volatile waste products.*

B *Stirrer shaft – present in most fermenters. Agitation needed to*

  (i) increase rate at which O₂ dissolves;
  (ii) maintain diffusion gradients of O₂ and nutrients into cells and products out of cells;
  (iii) prevent clumping of cells or mycelia of fungi;
  (iv) promote heat exchange between medium and cooling surfaces.
  Shaft bearings must be strong and sterile.

C *Stirrer paddles – usually flat and vertical.*

D *Alkali and anti-foam inlets – alkali added if, as is usual, acidity increases during fermentation (to maintain a constant pH). Aeration and agitation generate foam, particularly from proteins, and prevent escape of contents through the exhaust, so anti-foaming agents are added.*

E *Exhaust – contents of fermenter are under pressure; therefore pressure gauge and safety valve attached.*

F *Top of fermenter has a part for addition of medium, inoculum (micro-organism), access for cleaning etc.*

G *Baffle – vertical fin on inside wall; helps to prevent vortex formation as culture is rotated.*

H *Cooling jacket – reduces temperature; needed because culture generates heat.*

J *Harvest – samples may be taken during fermentation in order to monitor process.*

culture has found only limited application, but is used for the production of single cell protein where a large biomass of cells is required. ICI, for example, produce a single cell protein (SCP), that is a microbial protein, called 'Pruteen' from the bacterium *Methylophilus methylotrophus* (see also section 2.5.4). The cell is provided with methanol, oxygen (in air), nitrogen in the form of ammonia and inorganic nutrients such as calcium and phosphorus. The plant at Billingham has the largest continuous culture fermenter in the world, with a 1½ million litre capacity. The temperature must be carefully monitored within the range 30–40 °C and the pH kept at 6.7. The final product, Pruteen, is 72% protein and also has a high vitamin content. It is ideal for use in animal feeds. The fermenter has been run continuously for as long as 100 days and can produce 150 tonnes per day. Unfortunately, it is not economic to produce SCP for animal feeds, other sources of protein being cheaper at present in developed countries. Developing countries cannot afford to run such large-scale technology, and do not have the necessary expertise.

Downstream processing

Downstream processing is the name given to the phase following fermentation when the desired product is recovered and purified. Many techniques are used, including precipitation, chromatography (for example with streptomycin and interferon), electrophoresis, centrifugation, distillation (as with propanone, ethanoic acid, and spirits such as whisky), concentration, drying, solvent extraction (as with penicillin) and filtration (as with beer and soft drinks). As an indication of the importance of downstream processing, it involves over 90% of the 200 staff employed by Eli Lilly in their human insulin producing plant.

An enormous range of products is now produced by fermentation processes, some of which are shown in table 11.3. Living cells have the advantage over traditional chemical technology in that they can operate at lower temperatures, neutral pH, produce higher yields, show greater specificity, include production of particular isomers, and very often produce chemicals such as antibiotics and hormones that cannot be produced easily (if at all) by any other means. However, there are specialist techniques, such as aseptic techniques and complex methods of separation, which can make the process more technically demanding.

11.4 Shuttle systems

Although the sequence of events for aerobic respiration shown in this text indicates that 38 ATP are produced for each glucose molecule oxidised, it must be stated that the total number of ATP molecules produced in aerobic respiration can vary according to the tissue involved. Two NADH₂ complexes are produced during glycolysis in the cytoplasm. Cytoplasmic NADH₂ cannot pass through the mitochondrial membrane and therefore

Table 11.3 Fermentation products according to industrial sectors. Adapted from table 3.1, John E. Smith (1988), *Biotechnology*, New Studies in Biology, 2nd ed. Arnold.

Sector	Activities
Chemicals	
Organic (bulk)	Ethanol, acetone, butanol
Organic (fine)	Enzymes
	Perfumeries
	Polymers (mainly polysaccharides)
Inorganic	Metal beneficiation, bioaccumulation and leaching (Cu, U)
Pharmaceuticals	Diagnostic agents (enzymes, monoclonal antibodies)
	Enzyme inhibitors
	Steroids
	Vaccines
	Antibiotics, e.g. penicillin, streptomycin
Energy	Ethanol (gasohol)
	Methane (biogas)
Food	Dairy products (cheeses, yoghurts, fish and meat products)
	Beverages (alcoholic, tea and coffee)
	Baker's yeast
	Food additives (antioxidants, colours, flavours, stabilisers)
	Novel foods (soy sauce, tempeh, miso)
	Mushroom products
	Amino acids, vitamins
	Starch products
	Glucose and high-fructose syrups
	Functional modifications of proteins, pectins
Agriculture	Animal feedstuffs (SCP)
	Veterinary vaccines
	Composting processes: silage for cattle fodder
	Microbial pesticides
	Rhizobium and other N-fixing bacterial inoculants
	Mycorrhizal inoculants
	Plant cell and tissue culture (vegetative propagation, embryo production, genetic improvement)

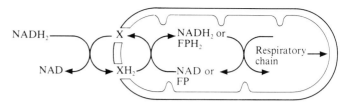

Fig 11.13 *Model of shuttle system (see text for full explanation). NAD, nicotinamide adenine dinucleotide; FP, flavoprotein*

Experiment 11.1: To investigate the oxidation of a Krebs cycle intermediate

The most efficient way of releasing energy from a substrate and storing this for future use is by a series of smaller reactions, each one reversible and enzyme-mediated. One of the intermediate reactions involved is the oxidation, by removal of hydrogen, of succinic acid to fumarate.

There are substances which accept such hydrogen atoms and, in doing so, change colour. One example is 2:6 dichlorophenolindophenol (DCPIP). It is blue in its oxidised form but loses its colour when reduced.

If the coloured form of DCPIP is decolorised by a tissue extract, one explanation could be that it has accepted hydrogen atoms from succinic acid. If the rate of decolorisation increased when succinic acid was added this would tend to confirm the hypothesis that DCPIP was a hydrogen acceptor of atoms from succinic acid.

As most living processes are governed by enzymes, these must be present before the oxidation will occur. The enzyme succinic dehydrogenase reduces succinic acid and further experiments could reveal the presence of the enzyme. In this experiment mitochondria are isolated from germinating mung bean seedlings and a suspension of these used as a source of enzyme. It is essential to carry out the extraction as quickly as possible. Once cells are disrupted, further metabolism is short-lived.

The experiment is divided into two parts. The first part consists of the extraction of the enzyme required and the second uses the extracted enzyme to oxidise succinic acid. DCPIP is used to indicate that a reaction has or has not occurred.

Ideally all the apparatus concerned with the first part of this experiment (the preparation of the enzyme extract) should be placed in a refrigerator for at least one hour before it is required for the experiment.

Materials

4 centrifuge tubes (capacity 15 cm³)
2 glass rods
2 × 10 cm³ graduated pipettes
2 × 1000 cm³ beakers (polythene preferably)
ice
salt
mung beans

the electrons derived from glycolysis have to enter via indirect routes or **shuttles**. According to which shuttle operates, the number of ATP molecules produced from cytoplasmic NADH₂ can be four or six, thus making the total either 36 or 38 ATP. The principle of this shuttle is illustrated in fig 11.13. X acts as a carrier molecule, carrying hydrogen from the cytoplasm into the mitochondrion. It can pass through the mitochondrial membranes, whereas NADH₂ cannot.

NAD → NADH₂ in heart and liver cells, giving three ATP on reoxidation.
FP → FPH₂ in muscle and nerve cells, giving two ATP on reoxidation.
Therefore 38 ATP are formed in heart and liver cells, whilst 36 ATP are formed in muscle and nerve cells.

The shuttles constantly transfer electrons from the cytoplasm to mitochondria and at the same time reoxidise cytoplasmic NADH₂. This effectively prevents a build-up of hydrogen atoms in the cytoplasm and explains why no lactate accumulates during aerobic respiration.

test-tubes and rack
1 × 1 cm³ graduated pipette
stopclock

Solutions (see notes)
buffer/sucrose solution
buffer/sucrose + succinic acid solution (succinate solution)
0.1% DCPIP (solution made up in buffer/sucrose solution)
distilled water

Method

(1) Germinate some mung beans by placing the dry beans on damp cotton wool in the dark for 3–4 days (24 beans are needed for the whole experiment per student or group).
(2) Prepare an ice bath by placing ice in a 1000 cm³ polythene beaker and adding a little salt to lower the temperature further.
(3) Place the flask containing buffer/sucrose solution and two centrifuge tubes in the ice bucket.
(4) Take 12 mung beans and remove their testas and radicles.
(5) Place six beans in each centrifuge tube.
(6) Add 1 cm³ of buffer/sucrose solution which does not contain succinic acid to each tube.
(7) Crush the beans thoroughly using a cold glass rod, keeping the tubes in the ice bucket.
(8) Add a further 10 cm³ of buffer/sucrose solution to each centrifuge tube.
(9) Place the centrifuge tubes on opposite sides of the centrifuge head and spin the tubes at maximum speed for 3 min.
(10) Place the centrifuge tubes back in the ice bucket.
(11) Pipette 15 cm³ of distilled water into a test-tube and mark the position of the meniscus.
(12) Pour off the distilled water and carefully fill the tube to the mark with supernatant from the centrifuge tubes.
(13) The next step must be carried out very quickly: add 0.5 cm³ of DCPIP solution to the reaction tube and mix the contents by placing a thumb over the end of the tube and inverting the tube.
(14) Start the stopclock as the solutions are mixing.
(15) Note the colour of the solution after 20 min.
(16) Repeat the entire experiment using the buffer/sucrose solution containing succinic acid.

The experiment can be monitored colorimetrically. This is done as follows.

(1) Using a red filter, switch on the colorimeter and allow it to warm up for 5 min.
(2) Add 0.5 cm³ of DCPIP solution to 15 cm³ of supernatant as before.
(3) Mix the solutions and start the stopclock.
(4) Place the tube in the colorimeter and adjust the needle to 0% transmission.
(5) Take readings after 1, 2, 5, 10 and 20 min.

(6) Repeat the experiment using buffer/sucrose containing succinic acid.
(7) Plot a graph of percentage transmission (vertical axis) against time.
(8) Draw your own conclusions from the results that you obtain.

Notes on how to make solutions

Buffer/sucrose solution (100 cm³)

disodium hydrogen phosphate (Na_2HPO_4)	0.76 g
potassium dihydrogen phosphate (KH_2PO_4)	0.18 g
sucrose	13.60 g
magnesium sulphate	0.10 g

Buffer/sucrose + succinic acid (100 cm³)

As for buffer/sucrose, plus

succinic acid	1.36 g
sodium hydrogencarbonate	1.68 g

The best method for making up these solutions is to make up enough buffer/sucrose solution for both halves of the experiment (solutions are made up in distilled water). Divide the solution into two and add succinic acid and sodium hydrogencarbonate (in the correct concentration) to one half.

There will be effervescence when succinic acid and sodium hydrogencarbonate are added to the buffer/sucrose solution. The solution should be shaken well to get rid of as much carbon dioxide as possible as this could affect the experiment.

DCPIP solution

Use 0.1 g of dichlorophenolindophenol in 10 cm³ of buffer/sucrose solution (without succinic acid for both experiments). The solid does not dissolve very well and so after thorough mixing the suspension should be filtered.

11.5 Mitochondria

Mitochondria are present in all eukaryotic cells and are the major sites of aerobic respiratory activity within cells. They were first seen as granules in muscle cells by Kolliker in 1850. Later, in 1898, Michaelis demonstrated that they played a significant role in respiration by showing experimentally that they produced a colour in redox dyes.

The number of mitochondria per cell varies considerably and depends on the type of organism and nature of the cell. Cells with high energy requirements possess large numbers of mitochondria (for example, liver cells contain upwards of 1 000 mitochondria) whilst less active cells possess far fewer. Mitochondrial shape and size are also tremendously variable. They may be spiral, spherical, elongate, cup-shaped and even branched, and are usually larger in active cells than in less active ones. Their length ranges from 1.5–10 μm, and width 0.25–1.00 μm, but their diameter does not exceed 1 μm.

11.6 Why should the diameter of mitochondria remain fairly constant when the length is so variable?

Mitochondria are able to change shape, and some are able to move to areas in the cell where a lot of activity is taking place. This is facilitated by **cytoplasmic streaming** and provides the cell with a large concentration of mitochondria in areas where ATP need is greater. Other mitochondria assume a more fixed position (as in insect flight muscle, fig 11.14).

11.5.1 Structure of mitochondria

Mitochondria can be extracted from cells in pure fractions by cell homogenisation and ultracentrifugation techniques. Once isolated they may be examined with an electron microscope using various techniques such as sectioning or negative staining. Each mitochondrion is bounded by two membranes (an envelope), the outer one being separated from the inner by a space some 6–10 nm wide. A semi-rigid matrix is enclosed by the inner membrane which itself is folded inwards into a number of shelf-like **cristae** (fig 11.15). Techniques using ultrasonic vibration and detergent action can be used to separate the two membranes, making it easier to study their individual structure and activity. Even so, knowledge of the outer membrane is still scarce. It is said to be permeable to substances with molecular weights below 21 000, and that such molecules are able to diffuse across it. The cristae of the inner membrane effectively increase its surface area, serving to provide abundant space for **multi-enzyme systems**, and greater access to enzymes present in the matrix. The inner membrane exhibits selectivity over what materials are allowed through it, and it is known that active transport mechanisms involving **translocase** enzymes are responsible for the movement of ADP and ATP across it. Negative staining techniques which stain the space around structures rather than the structures themselves (fig 11.15b) indicate the presence of **elementary particles** on the matrix side of the inner membrane. Each particle consists of a head piece, stalk and base. Whilst the photograph (fig 11.15e) suggests that the particles stick out from the membrane into the matrix, it is generally recognised that this is an artefact produced by the method of preparation, and that probably the particles are tucked into the membrane. The head piece is associated with ATP synthesis and is a coupling enzyme, ATPase (formerly termed F_1), which acts to link the phosphorylation of ADP to the respiratory chain. At the base of the particle, and extending through the inner membrane, are the components of the respiratory chain itself. They are arranged in precise positions relative to each other. The mitochondrial matrix contains most of the enzymes controlling the Krebs cycle and fatty acid oxidation. In addition, mitochondrial

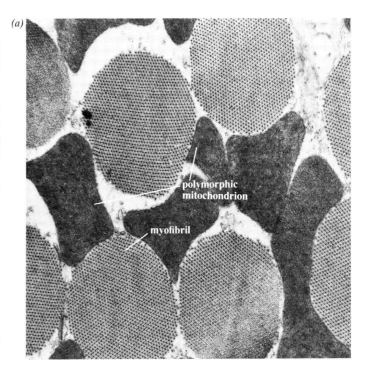

(a)

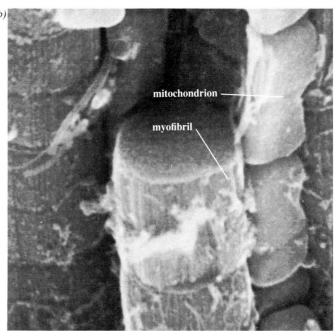

(b)

Fig 11.14 *(a) Transmission electron micrograph, and (b) scanning electron micrograph of the flight muscle from the house fly* Musca *to show that each myofibril is surrounded by polymorphic mitochondria.*

DNA, RNA and ribosomes are present as well as a variety of small proteins (section 7.2.12).

11.7 What chemical substances would be exchanged between the cytoplasm and the mitochondria? Indicate whether they are entering or leaving the mitochondria.

335

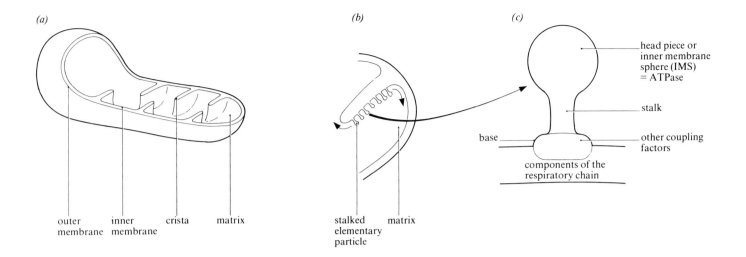

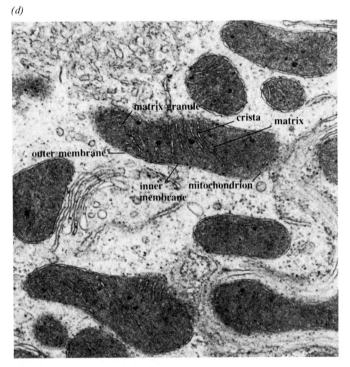

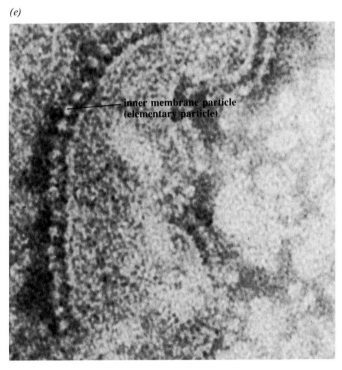

Fig 11.15 *Structure of mitochondrion: (a) Diagram of mitochondrion. (b) Diagram of crista showing inner membrane particles. (c) Structure of inner membrane particle. (d) Low power electron micrograph of mitochondrion.*

(e) Transmission electron micrograph of inner membrane particles (F_1-F_0 ATPase) from osmotically disrupted mitochondria of the house-fly (Musca)

11.5.2   Mitochondrial assembly

Whilst mitochondrial DNA carries enough information for the synthesis of about 30 proteins, this is not enough for it to be able to build all the proteins that are required to make a new mitochondrion. Therefore reproduction of a mitochondrion must rely to some extent on nuclear DNA, cytoplasmic enzymes and other molecules supplied by cells. Fig 11.16 summarises current information concerning the interaction between the mitochondrion and the rest of the cell during mitochondrial assembly.

11.5.3   Evolution of mitochondria – the endosymbiont theory

It is suggested that mitochondria were originally independent prokaryotic, bacteria-like organisms which gained access, by accident, to a host cell and entered into a succesful mutualistic (**symbiotic**) union with it. Presumably conditions in the host cell were favourable for the prokaryote, whilst in return the prokaryote provided a greatly increased capacity to manufacture ATP, and conferred upon the host an ability to respire aerobically. A number of observations support this theory. First,

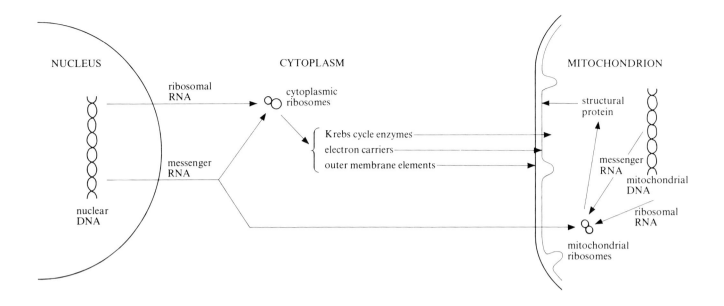

Fig 11.16 *Control of mitochondrial assembly (From Tribe & Whittaker,* Chloroplasts and mitochondria, *Series in Biology, No. 31, Arnold.)*

mitochondrial DNA is generally circular (fig 11.17). This is very much like that found in present-day bacteria. Secondly, mitochondrial ribosomes are smaller than those of the cytoplasm but equivalent in size to bacterial ribosomes. Thirdly, mitochondrial and bacterial synthesis mechanisms are sensitive to different antibiotics when compared with the cytoplasmic mechanism, for example chloramphenicol and streptomycin inhibit mitochondrial and bacterial protein synthesis, whereas cycloheximide inhibits cytoplasmic protein synthesis (see section 9.3.1 for endosymbiotic theory and chloroplasts).

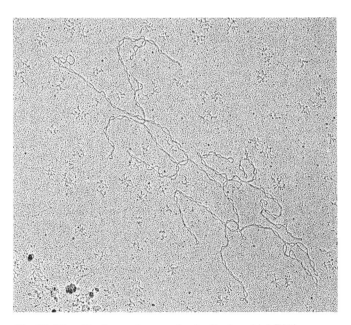

Fig 11.17 *Electron micrograph of mitochondrial DNA from the brewer's yeast* Saccharomyces carlsbergensis. *The molecule is a 'supercoiled' circle of double-strand DNA with a circumference of 26 micrometres. It is made up of some 75 000 nucleotides*

11.5.4 ATP synthesis

The mechanism for the coupling of ATP synthesis to electron transport has been the subject of intensive research for over 30 years. Experimental evidence is now overwhelmingly in favour of the **chemiosmotic** hypothesis (now given the status of a theory) which was unpopular when first postulated by the British biochemist Mitchell in 1961. Mitchell was awarded the Nobel Prize for his work in 1978. The theory applies to both mitochondria and chloroplasts (and to ATP generation in bacteria). Mitchell argued that ATP synthesis was intricately associated with the ways in which electrons and protons are passed along the respiratory chain. Certain conditions are necessary if the theory is correct. They are summarised as follows.

(1) The inner mitochondrial membrane must be intact and impermeable to movement of protons (hydrogen ions) from the outside to the inside.

(2) Respiratory chain activity results in protons being drawn into the electron transport chain from the internal matrix and then removed to the space between the inner and outer membranes of the mitochondrion. (From here protons pass to the outside of the mitochondrion since the outer membrane is freely permeable to small molecules.)

(3) Movement of the protons to the outside of the mitochondrion causes an accumulation of hydrogen ions and creates a pH gradient across the mitochondrial inner membrane. It is thought that this occurs because the electron carriers involved are located in the inner

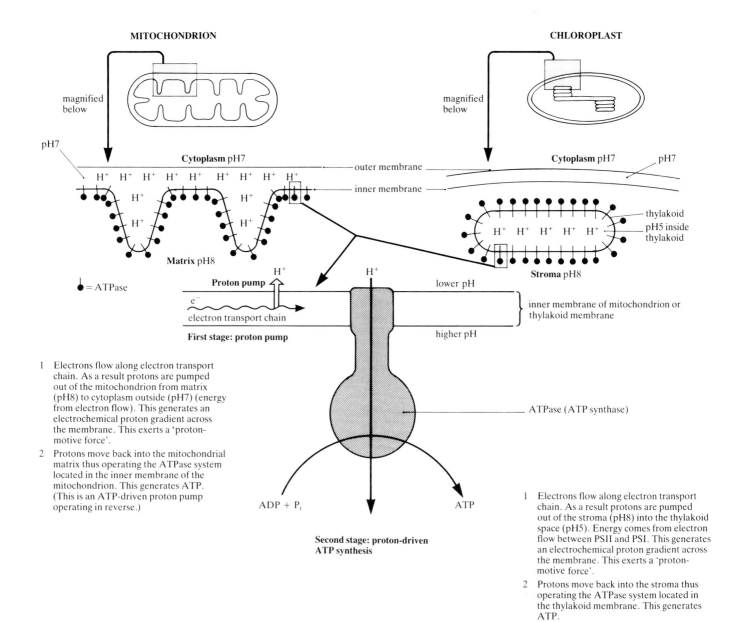

MITOCHONDRION

CHLOROPLAST

magnified below

magnified below

pH7

Cytoplasm pH7 ——— outer membrane ——— inner membrane

Cytoplasm pH7 — pH7

H⁺ H⁺ H⁺ H⁺ H⁺ H⁺ H⁺ H⁺ H⁺
H⁺
H⁺
H⁺
H⁺
H⁺

Matrix pH8

⊥• = ATPase

thylakoid
pH5 inside thylakoid

H⁺ H⁺ H⁺ H⁺ H⁺

Stroma pH8

H⁺
Proton pump
e⁻
electron transport chain

First stage: proton pump

lower pH

inner membrane of mitochondrion or thylakoid membrane

higher pH

H⁺

ATPase (ATP synthase)

ADP + Pᵢ

ATP

Second stage: proton-driven ATP synthesis

1 Electrons flow along electron transport chain. As a result protons are pumped out of the mitochondrion from matrix (pH8) to cytoplasm outside (pH7) (energy from electron flow). This generates an electrochemical proton gradient across the membrane. This exerts a 'proton-motive force'.

2 Protons move back into the mitochondrial matrix thus operating the ATPase system located in the inner membrane of the mitochondrion. This generates ATP. (This is an ATP-driven proton pump operating in reverse.)

1 Electrons flow along electron transport chain. As a result protons are pumped out of the stroma (pH8) into the thylakoid space (pH5). Energy comes from electron flow between PSII and PSI. This generates an electrochemical proton gradient across the membrane. This exerts a 'proton-motive force'.

2 Protons move back into the stroma thus operating the ATPase system located in the thylakoid membrane. This generates ATP.

Fig 11.18 *ATP generation by chemiosmosis in mitochondria and chloroplasts (Mitchell's hypothesis)*

membrane in such a position as to allow only uptake from the inside and loss to the outside.

(4) Normally a pH gradient could not be maintained, as hydrogen ions would pass back into the mitochondrion by diffusion. Therefore the maintenance of this gradient is energy-requiring. The energy obtained from the transfer of electrons down the electron (respiratory) transport chain is thought to provide the energy needed.

(5) The combined pH gradient and electrical potential across the membrane is referred to as the **electrochemical proton gradient**. This gradient can be used to do work; this is usually referred to as **proton-motive force (PMF)**. In respiration (and photosynthesis)

protons move back across the membrane, down their concentration gradients, through specific sites where the enzyme ATPase, otherwise known as ATP synthase, is located (see section 11.5.1). The energy released by the protons is used to drive ATP synthesis (see fig 11.18).

Proton-motive force can power certain processes other than ATP synthesis, for example transport of small molecules across the mitochondrial inner membrane and rotation of bacterial flagella.

Mitchell's hypothesis explains why the membrane must be intact (because the proteins required are located in the membrane and alteration of the structure of the membrane would also alter the protein positions and structure). It also explains why the membrane needs to be impermeable to hydrogen ions (from outside to inside), because if the membrane was completely permeable a pH gradient would not form, and a pH gradient is vital to this theory.

11.5.5 Other respiratory pathways

Pentose phosphate shunt (hexose monophosphate shunt)

This particular pathway requires oxygen and is a major source of 5C sugars which are components of important nucleotides (ATP, NAD, FAD) and nucleic acids. The shunt may operate simultaneously alongside the normal glycolytic pathway and in different cells can contribute between 10 and 90% of energy supplied by carbohydrate respiration.

In essence, six molecules of glucose-6-phosphate are initially dehydrogenated and then decarboxylated. NADP acts as the hydrogen acceptor molecule. Six molecules of ribulose-5-phosphate (5C sugar phosphate) are the result of these processes, and six carbon dioxide molecules are formed as by-products. The ribulose-5-phosphate molecules then undergo an intricate series of reactions which finally result in the resynthesis of five molecules of glucose-6-phosphate. Glyceraldehyde-3-phosphate is also formed and may be redirected into the glycolytic pathway, converted into pyruvate and finally passed into the Krebs cycle. The net result of the shunt is a yield of 36 ATP. This compares favourably with the 38 ATP formed by the glycolytic and Krebs pathway. Fewer reactions are involved in the shunt and consequently fewer enzymes required. The overall reaction is:

$$6 \times \text{glucose-6-P} + 12\text{NADP}^+ + 6\text{H}_2\text{O}$$
$$\downarrow$$
$$5 \times \text{glucose-6-P} + 12(\text{NADPH} + \text{H}^+) + 6\text{CO}_2 + \text{P}$$
$$6\text{O}_2 \longrightarrow \downarrow$$
$$12\text{NADP}^+ + 12\text{H}_2\text{O}$$

The shunt also functions to generate NADPH_2 which serves as a hydrogen and electron donor (a reducing agent) in the synthesis of a number of biochemicals. For instance, in adipose tissue the shunt operates to generate large amounts of NADPH_2 which are in turn consumed in the reduction of acetyl CoA to fatty acids during lipid synthesis.

Glyoxylate cycle

This occurs in seeds that possess tissues rich in fat, and enables stored fat to be converted into carbohydrate. The enzymes responsible for the cycle are mostly contained in organelles called **glyoxysomes** (a type of peroxisome because they contain catalase), which are active when seeds are germinating, although the cycle does occur in other organelles. However, once all the fat reserves have been consumed, the cycle ceases to operate.

During germination fats are hydrolysed to fatty acids and glycerol. Subsequently fatty acids are broken down by the process of β-oxidation (section 11.5.6) producing substantial amounts of acetyl CoA. Acetyl CoA enters the Krebs cycle as usual, but the glyoxylate cycle is added to the reactions of the Krebs cycle. For each turn of the glyoxylate cycle the overall reaction shown below occurs:

$$\text{2 acetyl CoA} \longrightarrow \text{succinate} + 2\text{H} + 2\text{CoA}$$
$$2 \times 2\text{C} \qquad\qquad 4\text{C}$$

The pair of hydrogen atoms released passes to oxygen in the respiratory chain causing production of ATP. Succinate may be used to supply the carbon skeleton in the manufacture of a range of compounds. Thus the glyoxylate cycle uses a 2C compound in the form of acetyl CoA as a fuel and provides energy and 4C intermediates for biological synthesis.

11.5.6 Fat as a respiratory substrate

Some animal tissues such as liver, and seeds possessing large deposits of fat, are able to use fat as a respiratory substrate without first converting it to carbohydrate. Initially fat is hydrolysed by enzymes called lipases into fatty acids and glycerol.

Glycerol

Glycerol is first phosphorylated by ATP into glycerol phosphate and then dehydrogenated by NAD to the sugar dihydroxyacetone phosphate. This is next converted into its isomer glyceraldehyde-3-phosphate (fig 11.19). As can be seen the process consumes one ATP, but yields three ATP when hydrogen is transferred to oxygen along the respiratory chain. Glyceraldehyde-3-phosphate is subsequently incorporated into the glycolysis pathway and Krebs cycle, liberating a further 17 ATP. Therefore the yield per one molecule of glycerol aerobically respired is $20 - 1 = 19$ ATP.

Fatty acid

Each fatty acid molecule is oxidised by a process called β-**oxidation** which, in essence, involves 2C fragments of acetyl coA being split off from the acid so that the long fatty acid molecule is shortened 2C atoms at a time. Each acetyl CoA formed can enter Krebs cycle as usual to be oxidised to carbon dioxide and water (fig 11.22). The process takes place in the matrix of the mitochondrion. A great deal of energy is released from each fatty acid molecule thus oxidised, for instance 147 ATP per molecule of stearate. Not surprisingly, therefore, fatty acids are important energy sources, contributing, for example, at least half the normal energy requirements of heart muscle, resting skeletal muscle, liver and kidneys.

11.5.7 Protein as a respiratory substrate

Very occasionally, when carbohydrate and fat reserves have been exhausted, proteins are utilised as respiratory material. They are first hydrolysed into their constituent amino acids and then deaminated (their amino groups are removed). This may occur in two ways, oxidative deamination or transamination.

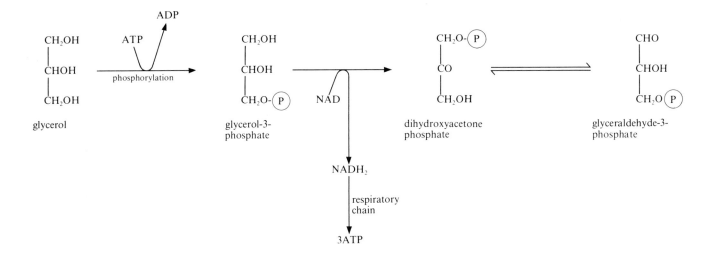

Fig 11.19 *Conversion of glycerol into glyceraldehyde-3-phosphate*

Oxidative deamination

This takes place in vertebrate liver cells. An ammonia molecule is removed from the amino acid by dehydrogenation and hydrolysis. Later it is excreted as ammonia, uric acid or urea depending on the animal concerned (section 18.5). The deaminated amino acid is an α-keto acid. According to the nature of its R group, it may be respired like a carbohydrate (**glucogenic**) or via the fatty acid pathway (**ketogenic**) (fig 11.20).

Transamination

This occurs in all cells and is controlled by **transaminase** enzymes. It is the transfer of an amino group from an amino acid to a keto acid. In this way one amino acid can be converted into another. The process also produces **α-keto acids** which are able to enter the normal respiratory pathways. Some examples are shown in fig 11.21. A summary of the major metabolic pathways in respiration is shown in fig 11.22.

11.6 Gaseous exchange

Whether aerobic or anaerobic respiration is occurring, the constant passage of gases between organisms and their environments has to be maintained. Aerobes require oxygen for oxidation of foodstuffs and energy release, whilst aerobes and most anaerobes must expel carbon dioxide, a waste product of respiration. Exchange of carbon dioxide and oxygen between environment and organism is termed **gaseous exchange**, and the area where gaseous exchange actually takes place is called the **respiratory surface**. Gaseous exchange takes place in all organisms by the physical process of **diffusion**. In order for this to occur effectively the respiratory surface must satisfy the following criteria:

it must be **permeable**, so that gases can pass through;

it must be **thin**, because diffusion is only efficient over distances of 1 mm or less;

it should possess a **large surface area** so that sufficient amounts of gases are able to be exchanged according to the organism's need.

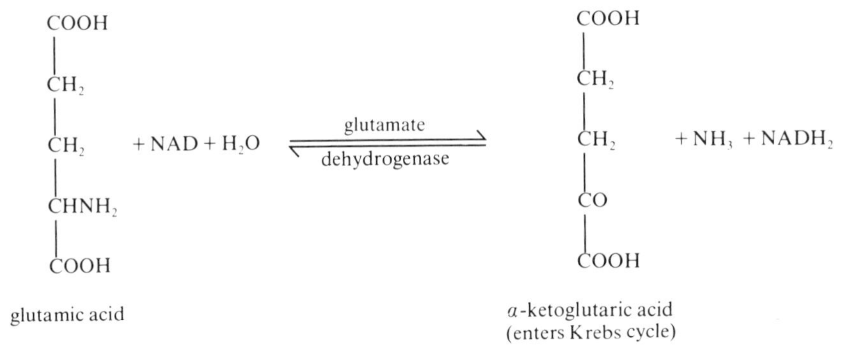

Fig 11.20 *Oxidative deamination of glutamic acid*

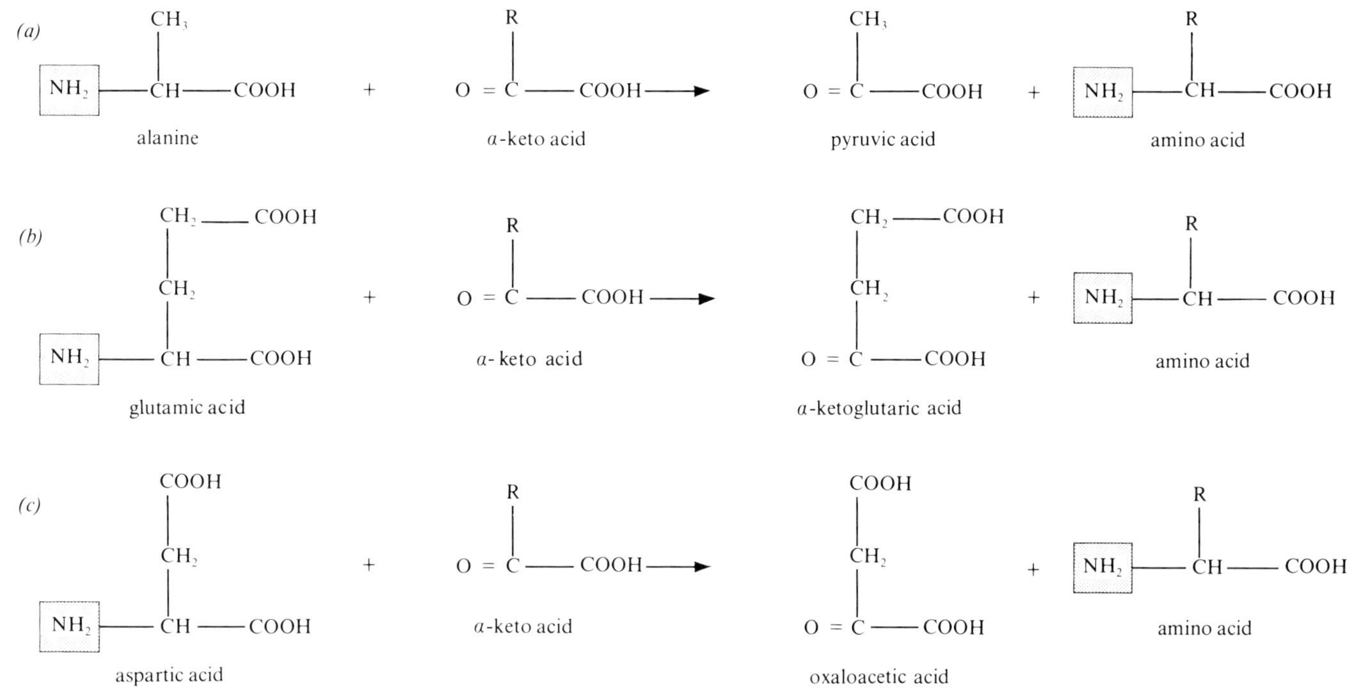

(a)

$$\underset{\text{alanine}}{\boxed{NH_2}\text{—}\underset{\overset{|}{CH_3}}{CH}\text{—COOH}} \;+\; \underset{\alpha\text{-keto acid}}{O=\underset{\overset{|}{R}}{C}\text{—COOH}} \longrightarrow \underset{\text{pyruvic acid}}{O=\underset{\overset{|}{CH_3}}{C}\text{—COOH}} \;+\; \underset{\text{amino acid}}{\boxed{NH_2}\text{—}\underset{\overset{|}{R}}{CH}\text{—COOH}}$$

(b)

$$\underset{\text{glutamic acid}}{\boxed{NH_2}\text{—}\underset{\overset{|}{\underset{\overset{|}{CH_2}}{CH_2\text{—COOH}}}}{CH}\text{—COOH}} \;+\; \underset{\alpha\text{-keto acid}}{O=\underset{\overset{|}{R}}{C}\text{—COOH}} \longrightarrow \underset{\alpha\text{-ketoglutaric acid}}{O=\underset{\overset{|}{\underset{\overset{|}{CH_2}}{CH_2\text{—COOH}}}}{C}\text{—COOH}} \;+\; \underset{\text{amino acid}}{\boxed{NH_2}\text{—}\underset{\overset{|}{R}}{CH}\text{—COOH}}$$

(c)

$$\underset{\text{aspartic acid}}{\boxed{NH_2}\text{—}\underset{\overset{|}{\underset{\overset{|}{CH_2}}{COOH}}}{CH}\text{—COOH}} \;+\; \underset{\alpha\text{-keto acid}}{O=\underset{\overset{|}{R}}{C}\text{—COOH}} \longrightarrow \underset{\text{oxaloacetic acid}}{O=\underset{\overset{|}{\underset{\overset{|}{CH_2}}{COOH}}}{C}\text{—COOH}} \;+\; \underset{\text{amino acid}}{\boxed{NH_2}\text{—}\underset{\overset{|}{R}}{CH}\text{—COOH}}$$

Fig 11.21 *Examples of transaminations*

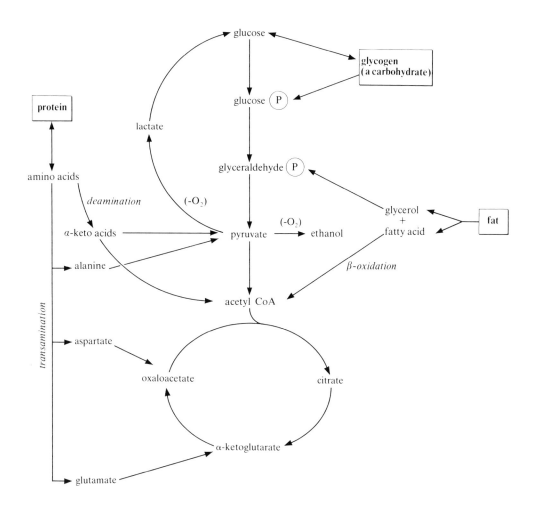

Fig 11.22 *Summary of major metabolic pathways in respiration*

Organisms acquire their oxygen either direct from the atmosphere or from oxygen dissolved in water. There are marked differences in the oxygen content of air and water. A unit volume of air contains far more oxygen in it than an equal volume of water. Therefore it follows that an aquatic organism such as a fish must pass a correspondingly much greater volume of water over its gaseous exchange surface than a terrestrial vertebrate passes air in order to obtain sufficient oxygen for its metabolic needs.

11.6.1 Protoctista

The rhizopod *Amoeba proteus* measures less than 1 mm in diameter and possesses a large surface area to volume ratio. Diffusion of gases occurs over the whole surface of the animal via the cell membrane, and is enough to satisfy its metabolic needs.

11.6.2 Cnidaria

In the multicellular, diploblastic *Hydra* and *Obelia*, all cells are in contact with the surrounding aquatic medium, and each is able to exchange gases sufficient for its own needs through the cell membrane adjacent to the surrounding water.

11.6.3 Platyhelminthes

A free-living platyhelminth, such as *Planaria*, acquires the oxygen it needs by means of diffusion over its body surface. This is facilitated by the worm's extremely flattened body (no more than 0.06 cm thick) which increases the surface area to volume ratio, and by the fact that it generally lives in well-aerated streams or ponds.

Many platyhelminths such as the tapeworm *Taenia* are internal parasites, surviving in regions where there is little available oxygen. In this case they operate as **anaerobes**. Their size or shape is not limited by any need for oxygen diffusion, although they still retain a large surface area to volume ratio.

> **11.8** What other advantage does a large surface area to volume ratio confer on the platyhelminths?

11.6.4 The need for special respiratory structures and pigments

As animals increase in size, so their surface area to volume ratio decreases, rendering simple diffusion over the body surface inadequate to supply oxygen to cells of the organism not in direct contact with the surrounding medium. Also the increased metabolic activity of many of these larger animals increases their rate of oxygen consumption.

In order to cope with the increased demand, certain regions of the body have developed into specialised respiratory surfaces. Different organisms possess different types of gaseous exchange surface. Each is designed to work efficiently in a specific environment. They can be classified as shown in fig 11.23. Generally their surface area is greatly increased and often associated with a transport system, such as a blood vascular system. The possession of a transport system puts the respiratory surface in contact with all other tissues of the organism and enables oxygen and carbon dioxide to be continuously exchanged between the respiratory surface and cells. The presence of a respiratory pigment in the blood further increases the efficiency of the blood's oxygen-carrying capacity. In addition there may be special ventilation movements which assist in ensuring a rapid exchange of gases between the animal and the surrounding environment by maintaining steep diffusion gradients.

Respiratory pigments

Blood that contains any form of respiratory pigment is a more efficient oxygen carrier than blood without one. This is because the pigment permits far greater amounts of oxygen to be taken up and transported. The pigment may be in the blood plasma or enclosed in specific cells. It is interesting to note that the relative molecular masses of pigments confined to cells are relatively low when compared with those of pigments in plasma. In fact, the plasma-based pigments are aggregates of many small molecules behaving as one large molecule. This arrangement permits an increase in the amount of pigment in the blood without increasing the number of dissolved molecules in solution.

> **11.9** Why is this important?
>
> **11.10** What is the advantage of confining the pigment to cells?

All known respiratory pigments are linked to protein molecules. They are able to bind reversibly to oxygen. At high oxygen concentrations, the pigment unites easily with oxygen, whereas at low oxygen concentrations the oxygen is quickly released. A more detailed account of the transport of oxygen by haemoglobin can be found in chapter 14. The common respiratory pigments of animals are shown in table 11.4.

11.6.5 Annelida

There are no organ systems especially designed for gaseous exchange, and consequently respiratory exchange takes place by diffusion over the whole body surface. Any such systems would appear to be unnecessary, as the general cylindrical shape of the worms maintains a high surface area to volume ratio, and their relative inactivity necessitates only a small oxygen consumption rate per unit body mass.

Table 11.4 Table of common respiratory pigments.

Pigment	Metal	Colour $+O_2 \rightleftharpoons -O_2$	Animal groups	Location in blood	cm³ of O_2 carried per 100 ml of blood
Haemocyanin	copper	blue $\rightleftharpoons$ colourless	some snails	plasma	2
			crustacea	plasma	3
			cephalopods	plasma	8
Haemerythrin	iron	red $\rightleftharpoons$ colourless	some annelids	always in cells	2
Chlorocruorin	iron	red $\rightleftharpoons$ green	some annelids	plasma	9
Haemoglobin	iron	orange $\rightleftharpoons$ purple red red	some molluscs	plasma	2
			some annelids	plasma or cells	7
			fishes	cells	9
			amphibia	cells	11
			reptiles	cells	10
			birds	cells	18
			mammals	cells	25

NB Compare the above figures with the fact that the amount of physically dissolved oxygen is 0.2 cm³ of O_2 per 100 ml of blood.

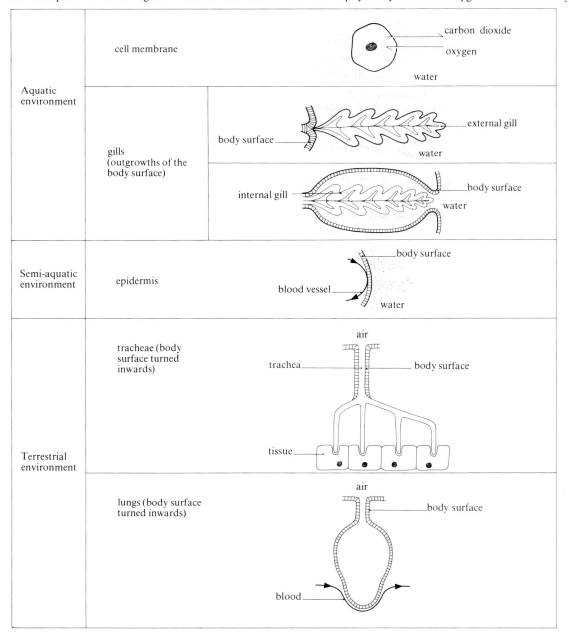

Fig 11.23 *Types of respiratory surface*

The worms do possess a blood vascular system which contains the respiratory pigment **haemoglobin** in solution. Contractile pumping activity by the blood vessels facilitates the passage of blood and dissolved gases round the body and maintains steep diffusion gradients.

Terrestrial oligochaetes (such as *Lumbricus*) keep their thin cuticles moist by glandular secretions from the epidermis and fluid exuded from the dorsal pores. **Looped blood capillaries** are present in the epidermis immediately below the cuticle. The distance between body surface and blood vessels is small enough to enable rapid diffusion of oxygen into the blood. Earthworms have little protection against desiccation and consequently their behavioural responses are designed to confine them to moist conditions.

Aquatic polychaetes (such as *Nereis* sp.) possess pairs of segmental **parapodia** along the lengths of their bodies (fig 4.19). They are mobile extensions of the body wall which are heavily vascularised, and serve to increase the respiratory surface of the animal. Once again, the blood in the parapodia is close enough to the body surface for rapid diffusion of gases to occur.

11.6.6 Arthropoda

A basic form of the arthropodan gaseous exchange system can be seen in the insects. Here gaseous exchange occurs via a system of pipes called the **tracheal system**. This allows gaseous oxygen to diffuse from the outside air directly to the tissues without the need for transportation by blood. This is much faster than diffusion of dissolved oxygen through the tissues and permits high metabolic rates.

Pairs of holes called **spiracles**, found on the second and third thoracic, and first eight abdominal, segments lead into air-filled cavities. Extending from these are branched tubes called **tracheae** (fig 11.24). Each trachea is bounded by squamous epithelium which secretes a thin layer of

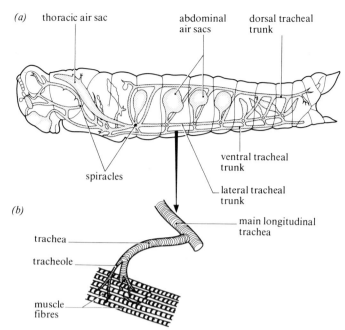

Fig 11.24 *(a) VLS tracheal system of grasshopper. (b) Structure of insect trachea*

chitinous material over itself. This is usually further strengthened by spiral or annular patterns of thickening which function to maintain an open pipeline even when the lumen of the trachea is subjected to reduced pressure (compare the cartilage hoops in trachea and bronchi of humans). In each segment the tracheae branch into numerous smaller tubes called **tracheoles** which ramify among the insect tissues, and in the more active ones, such as flight muscle, end blindly within cells. Tracheoles lack a chitinous lining; moreover the degree of branching may be adjusted according to the metabolic needs of individual tissues.

At rest the tracheoles are filled with watery fluid (fig 11.25) and diffusion of oxygen through them, and carbon

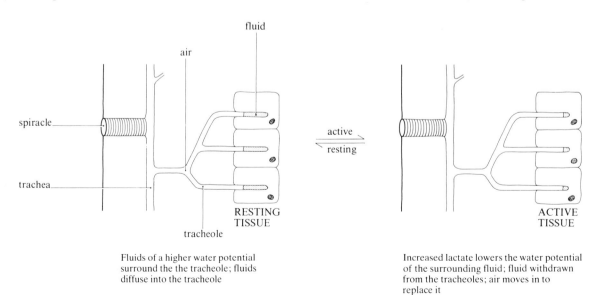

Fig 11.25 *Conditions in resting and active insect tissues – the functioning of tracheoles*

dioxide in the reverse direction, satisfies the insect's requirements. However, during exercise, increased metabolic activity by the muscles leads to accumulation of metabolites, especially lactate, so increasing the tissue's solute potential. When this occurs the fluid in the tracheoles is drawn osmotically into the tissues, causing more air and therefore more oxygen to enter the tracheoles and come into close contact with the tissues just at the time when it is required.

The overall flow of air in and out of the insect is regulated by a spiracular closing mechanism. Each spiracular opening is controlled by a system of valves operated by tiny muscles. It also has hairs around its edges which prevent foreign bodies entering and undue loss of water vapour. The size of the aperture is adjusted according to the level of carbon dioxide in the body.

Increased activity leads to increased carbon dioxide production. This is detected by chemoreceptors and the spiracles are opened accordingly. Ventilation movements by the body may also be initiated by the same stimulus, notably in larger insects. Dorso-ventral muscles contract and flatten the insect body, decreasing the volume of the tracheal system, thus forcing air out (expiration). Inspiration (intake of air) is achieved passively, when the elastic nature of the body segments returns them to their original shape.

There is evidence to suggest that the thoracic and abdominal spiracles open and close alternately, and that this, in conjunction with ventilation movements, provides a unidirectional flow of air through the animal, with air entering in through the thorax and out via the abdomen.

However, even though the tracheal system is a highly effective means of gaseous exchange it must be realised that it relies solely on diffusion of gaseous oxygen through the body. Since this can only occur efficiently across small distances, it imposes severe limitations on the size that insects can attain. Diffusion is only effective over distances of up to 1 cm; therefore, even though some insects may be up to 16 cm in length, they cannot be more than 2 cm broad!

11.6.7 Chondrichthyes

Cartilaginous fish (for example, the dogfish)

Situated on either side of the pharynx of the dogfish are five pairs of gill pouches, each of which contains a gill. Typically each gill is supported by a vertical rod of cartilage called the **branchial arch**. The septum overlying the arch is extended into a series of horizontal folds called **lamellae**. Each lamella in turn possesses further vertical folds on its upper and lower surface; these are termed secondary lamellae or **gill plates** (fig 11.26). The free edge of each gill septum is considerably elongated and forms an effective flap valve. It is used to close periodically the gill slit immediately posterior to it during ventilation activity. The spaces between the flap valves and gill lamellae represent the parabranchial cavities.

Deoxygenated blood from the ventral aorta is passed into each gill via an afferent branchial artery. In the gill plate region the artery branches repeatedly into many fine capillaries. It is here that gas exchange takes place. The capillaries finally reunite into efferent branchial arteries and leave the gill at its base.

Ventilation movements, taking the form of a buccal pressure pump operating in front of the gills and a suction pump behind them, serve to draw an almost continuous stream of water across the gills. Water enters the fish through the mouth and spiracles when the floor of the buccal cavity and pharynx is lowered. This is because the increased volume of the pharyngeal region reduces its pressure and consequently water rushes in (fig 11.27a). At the same time, the reduced pressure developed in the pharynx pulls the flap valves of the gills securely over the gill slits so preventing entry of water from this quarter. Whilst this is happening the suction pump mechanism is also working. Lateral movement of the flap valves causes the parabranchial cavities to expand and develop a lower hydrostatic pressure than that in the pharynx. Hence because of this differential pressure gradient, water not

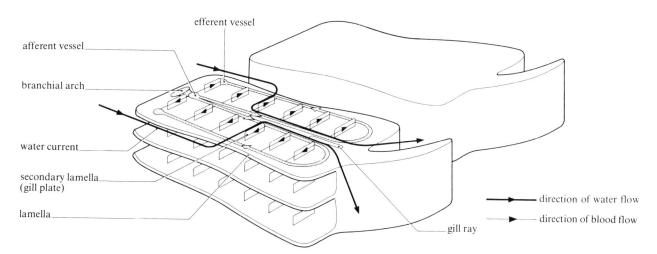

Fig 11.26 *Water flow over the lamellae in the dogfish*

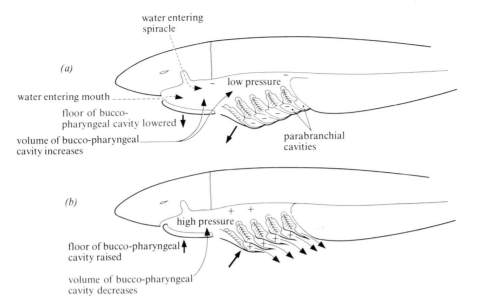

Fig 11.27 (above) *Side view of dogfish to show path of respiratory current. Pressures in the cavities are indicated with respect to zero pressure outside the fish. (a) Intake of water into bucco-pharyngeal cavity. (b) Expulsion of water via gills*

only moves into the pharynx but also simultaneously moves between the gill filaments, creating an almost continuous flow through the fish.

When the pharyngeal cavity is full of water, the mouth and spiracles close, the flap valves open, and the floor of the buccal cavity and pharynx is raised. This action forces water through the gill pouches over the respiratory epithelium of the lamellae and finally out of the fish through the gill slits (fig 11.27b). Whilst the water is being passed through the pharyngeal region and oesophageal sphincter muscle contracts, closing the oesophagus, thus preventing water from passing into the alimentary canal. Even though oxygen is absorbed by haemoglobin found in red blood cells, less than 50% of it is actually extracted by the dogfish, whereas 80% is absorbed by bony fish. This is because dogfish have relatively small gill surfaces when compared with bony fish and also because much of the water that flows over the gills travels in a direction parallel to the blood flow.

11.11 Why should blood flowing in the same direction as the water current be a relatively inefficient mechanism for exchange of gases?

11.6.8 Osteichthyes

Bony fish (for example, the herring)

A bony fish possesses four branchial arches on either side of the pharynx separating five pairs of gill clefts (or gill slits). Each gill on the arches is composed of two rows of fragile gill filaments arranged in the shape of a V (fig 11.28). The

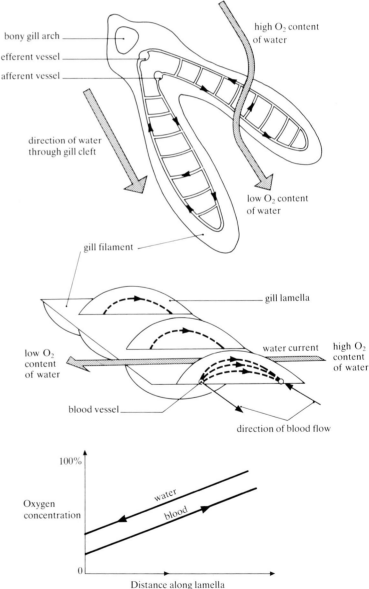

Fig 11.28 *Gill filaments of a bony fish*

filaments possess lamellae of a design similar to those found in the dogfish, and have a rich supply of blood capillaries. A movable gill cover, the operculum, which is reinforced with thin layers of bone, encloses and protects the gills in an opercular cavity. It also plays a part in the fish's ventilation mechanism.

During inspiration the buccal cavity expands, and this decreases the pressure within, causing water to be drawn in. Simultaneously the outside water pressure presses the valve at the posterior end of the operculum shut preventing entry of water from this region. However, also active at this time are opercular muscles which contract causing the opercular cavity to be enlarged. The pressure in the opercular cavity is less than that in the buccal cavity and hence water is drawn from the buccal cavity over the gills into the opercular cavity. Therefore gaseous exchange is able to continue even when the fish is engaged in taking in a fresh volume of water.

When expiration takes place the mouth closes, as does the oesophageal entrance, and the floor of the buccal cavity is raised. This forces water over the gills, through the gill slits and ultimately to the outside via the now open posterior end of the operculum. The coordinated activity of the buccal cavity and the opercular muscles ensures that a continuous flow of water passes over the gills for the majority of the time.

Adjacent gill filaments overlap at their tips, providing resistance to water flow. This slows down the passage of water over the gill lamellae thus increasing the time available for gaseous exchange to take place. The blood in the lamellae flows in the opposite direction to that of the water. Such a countercurrent system ensures that blood will constantly meet water with a relatively higher concentration of dissolved oxygen in it, and that a concentration gradient wll be maintained between blood and water throughout the entire length of the filament and across each lamella. In this way bony fish are able to extract 80% of the oxygen in water.

11.6.9 Amphibia

A frog is able to exchange gases in three different ways: through its skin by **cutaneous respiration**, via the epithelium of the buccal cavity in **buccal respiration**, and in a lung in **pulmonary respiration**.

Cutaneous respiration   The skin of the frog is richly supplied with blood capillaries and maintained in a moist condition by secretions of mucus from mucus glands. Thus atmospheric oxygen is able to dissolve in the mucus and subsequently diffuse into the blood. This is called cutaneous respiration. Oxygen uptake through the skin is almost constant throughout the year, due to the constant oxygen concentration in the atmosphere maintaining a constant diffusion gradient. In winter it supplies almost all the oxygen required by the animal, whereas in the spring when the frogs are most active it may represent only a

quarter of the frog's needs. The extra oxygen required is taken in via the buccal cavity and lungs.

Buccal respiration   Visible bucco-pharyngeal movements of the throat maintain a constant exchange of gases between the buccal cavity and the atmosphere. This is called buccal respiration. For inhalation to occur the mouth and glottis must be closed, the nostrils open, and the floor of the buccal cavity lowered, this being achieved by contraction of **sternohyoid muscles** attached to the hyoid cartilage (fig 11.29a). The buccal cavity is lined with moist, heavily vascularised epithelium, and it is here that gaseous exchange occurs. Exhalation follows when **petrohyoid muscles**, also attached to the hyoid cartilage, contract, raising the floor of the buccal cavity.

Pulmonary respiration.   The lungs are a pair of hollow sacs which hang down in the abdominal cavity. Their surface is extremely folded, but even so they present a relatively small surface area when compared with the lungs of a mammal. The epithelial lining of the lungs is moistened with mucus and profusely supplied with blood. Leading from each lung is a short tube, the **bronchus**. The two bronchi join forming the **trachea**. This is connected to a

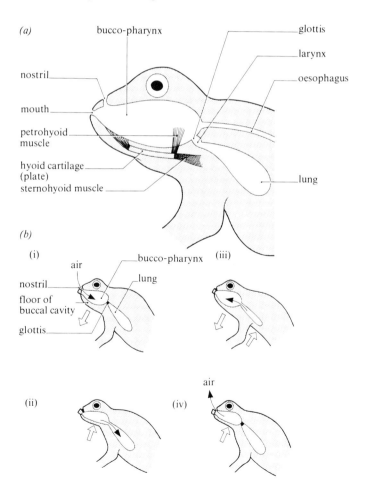

Fig 11.29 (a) VS through head of frog to show hyoid cartilage (plate) and associated musculature. (b) Ventilation of the lungs in a frog

small chamber, the **larynx**, which runs into the buccal cavity via a structure called the **glottis** (fig 11.29*a*).

At infrequent intervals violent swallowing movements are observed to occur in the frog. This is pulmonary ventilation working. The sequence of events is as follows:

(1) (fig 11.29*b* (i)) With the mouth closed, the nostrils open, the glottis closed, the floor of the buccal cavity is lowered. Air enters the buccopharynx.

(2) (fig 11.29*b* (ii)) The nostrils close, the glottis opens. Air from the lungs is forced into the buccopharynx by muscle action and elastic recoil of the lungs, thus mixing it with freshly inhaled air.

(3) (fig 11.29*b* (iii)) The floor of the buccal cavity is raised, and accompanied by vigorous gulping movements. This forces the mixed air into the lungs. When the lungs are full of air, the glottis closes and air is trapped there for some time. It is here that gas exchange between the blood capillaries in the epithelium of the lungs and the inspired air occurs.

(4) After a short interval, exhalation occurs. The nostrils close, the glottis opens and the floor of the buccal cavity is once again lowered. Air is sucked into the buccal cavity from the lungs (fig 11.29*b* (iv)). The nostrils open, the glottis closes and the floor of the buccal cavity is raised. This forces air out of the body via the nostrils.

11.6.10   Reptilia

Reptiles possess a horny body covering which is generally impermeable to gases and therefore not able to be used in a respiratory capacity. Gaseous exchange occurs exclusively via the lungs. These are sac-like in construction and exhibit much more complex folding than the amphibian lungs. Reptiles possess ribs, but no true diaphragm separates the thorax from the abdomen. Ventilation occurs when the ribs are moved by intercostal muscle contractions. The mechanism is very similar to that found in mammals.

11.6.11   Aves

Birds are homeothermic organisms and require a high rate of metabolism in order to maintain their body temperature. An efficient respiratory mechanism has been developed in order to make this possible.

Bird lungs are small, compact structures composed of numerous branching air tubes called **bronchi**. The smallest of these, the **parabronchi**, are heavily vascularised and it is here that gaseous exchange occurs. Extending from the lungs are large, thin-walled **air sacs**. These are poorly vascularised and do not take part in gaseous exchange. Functionally the air sacs can be divided into an anterior group and a posterior group, and they serve to move air in and out of the respiratory system.

Ventilation movements are complex, but basically they occur in the following sequence:

first inhalation – air flows directly to the posterior sacs (fig 11.30);

first exhalation – air in the posterior sac is passed to the lungs;

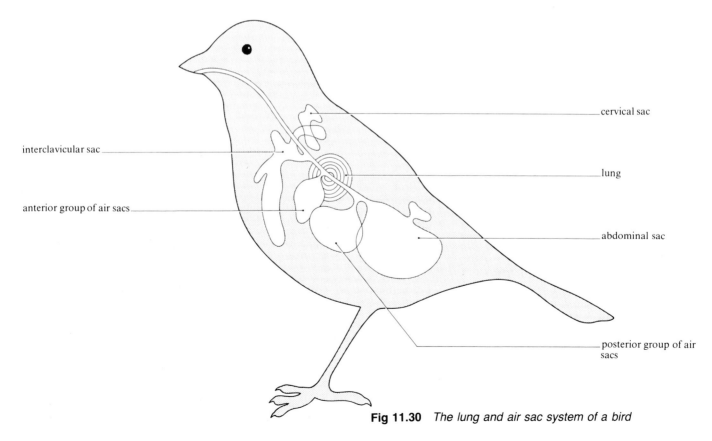

interclavicular sac

anterior group of air sacs

cervical sac

lung

abdominal sac

posterior group of air sacs

Fig 11.30 *The lung and air sac system of a bird*

348

second inhalation – air passes from the lungs to the anterior sacs;

second exhalation – air from the anterior sacs is forced to the outside.

This method of ventilation ensures that there is a unidirectional flow of air from the posterior sacs, through the lungs to the anterior sacs, before it leaves the bird's body.

Quiet respiratory movements are carried out in a similar manner to mammals, with intercostal and abdominal muscles producing inspiratory and expiratory movements respectively. When a bird is in flight, ventilation of the lungs is augmented by vigorous contraction of the pectoral muscles acting on a large keeled sternum. In these circumstances greater volumes of air are exchanged between bird and atmosphere in order to satisfy its metabolic needs.

11.7   Gaseous exchange in a mammal

The respiratory system of a mammal consists of a series of air tubes connecting a pair of lungs, which are situated in the thoracic cavity, to the atmosphere. Air is passed into the lungs through these tubes in the following sequence: nasal passages, pharynx, larynx, trachea, bronchi, bronchioles, alveoli of lungs. Twelve pairs of bony ribs surround and protect the lungs and heart in the thoracic cavity. Dorsally, each rib articulates with a thoracic vertebra and is able to be moved up or down. The anterior ten pairs of the ribs join to a bony plate, the **sternum**. The remaining pairs of ribs are called free or floating ribs. **Intercostal muscles** are attached to the ribs, and a large **diaphragm**, which effectively separates the thorax from the abdomen, are also vital parts of the system.

Air enters the body through two external nostrils, each of which possesses a border of large hairs which trap particles in the air and filter them out of the system. The walls of the passage are lined with **ciliated epithelial** and **mucus**-secreting goblet cells. Mucus serves two functions. First it traps any particles that have managed to pass through the hairs of the external nostrils. Epithelial cilia then beat in such a fashion as to carry the trapped particles to the back of the buccal cavity where its expulsion from the respiratory tract is completed by swallowing. Secondly, it moistens the incoming air, which incidentally is also warmed by the temperature of the superficial blood vessels in the nasal channels of the organism. In the roof of the posterior part of the nasal cavity is a mass of olfactory epithelium consisting of neurosensory and supporting cells, richly supplied with blood. Here odours in the air are detected. At the end of the nasal passages the air enters the pharynx via two internal openings. By the time this occurs the air has been generally freed from particles, warmed, moistened and its odour detected.

Next the air must traverse the pharynx in order to enter the larynx. As both food and air pass through the **pharynx**, the slit-like opening to the larynx, the **glottis**, has to be protected against the entry of food which could block the air breathing channels. This is achieved by a triangular flap of cartilaginous tissue, the **epiglottis**.

The **larynx** consists of a collection of nine cartilages forming a box-like structure at the entrance of the trachea. Muscles attached to the cartilages move them relative to each other. Within the box are two sets of horizontally aligned fibro-elastic ligaments, the **vocal cords**. When air is expelled over the vocal cords and through the glottis, sound waves are formed. By varying the tension of the cords, the pitch of the sound can be changed.

Air from the larynx enters the **trachea**. This is a tube which lies directly in front of the oesophagus and extends into the thoracic cavity. The wall of the tube is strengthened and held open by horizontally arranged C-shaped cartilages. The open section of the C is applied against the oesophagus. The cartilage prevents collapse of the tube during inspiration (fig 11.31). Lining the trachea is a carpet of pseudostratified, ciliated columnar epithelium. Mucus from goblet cells interspersed in the epithelium traps dust and germs, and the rhythmic beating of the cilia in a direction towards the back of the buccal cavity removes unwanted materials from the trachea.

At its lower end the trachea splits into two **bronchi**. The right bronchus further divides into three bronchi. They extend separately into the three lobes of the right lung. The left bronchus divides into two bronchi, and similarly these penetrate the two lobes of the left lung (fig 11.32). Within the lungs each bronchus subdivides many times into much smaller tubes called **bronchioles**. The C-shaped cartilages of the bronchi are initially replaced in the smaller tubes by irregularly shaped plates of cartilage, but when the internal diameter of the bronchioles is less than 1 mm, cartilaginous support ceases altogether. At this point, the thin bronchiole wall consists merely of smooth muscle, connective tissue possessing elastic fibres which promotes inflation and recoil of the bronchiole, and an inner lining of ciliated epithelium interspersed by mucus-secreting cells. The smallest tubes, called **respiratory bronchioles**, are about 0.5 mm in diameter. They, in turn, divide repeatedly into many **alveolar tubes** lined with cuboidal epithelium, which terminate in hollow, lobed air sacs called **alveoli** (figs 11.33 and 11.34). Collectively the alveoli form the gaseous exchange surface of the mammal.

There are over 700 million alveoli present in the lungs of a mammal, representing a total surface area of 80–90 m². The wall of each alveolus is only 0.0001 mm thick. On its outside is a dense network of blood capillaries, all of which have originated from the pulmonary artery and will ultimately rejoin to form the pulmonary vein. Lining each alveolus is moist squamous epithelium. Collagen and elastic fibres are also present and they provide flexibility for the alveoli, enabling them to expand and recoil easily during breathing.

Giant alveolar cells in the alveolus wall provide a secretion that is released inside the alveolus and lines its

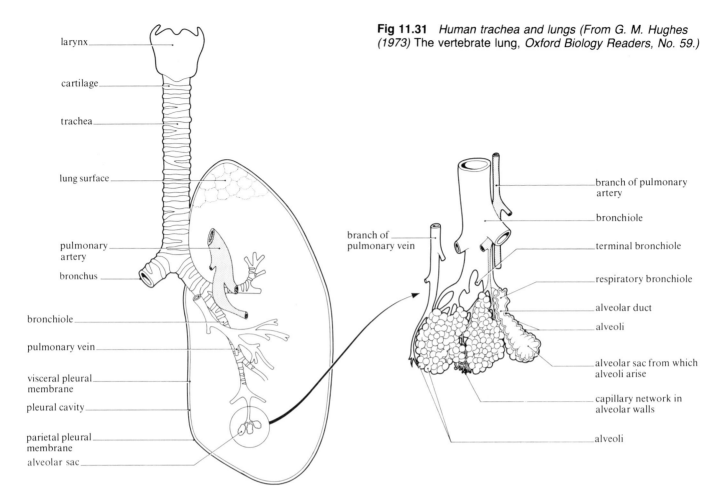

larynx

cartilage

trachea

lung surface

pulmonary artery

bronchus

bronchiole

pulmonary vein

visceral pleural membrane

pleural cavity

parietal pleural membrane

alveolar sac

Fig 11.31 *Human trachea and lungs (From G. M. Hughes (1973) The vertebrate lung, Oxford Biology Readers, No. 59.)*

branch of pulmonary vein

branch of pulmonary artery

bronchiole

terminal bronchiole

respiratory bronchiole

alveolar duct

alveoli

alveolar sac from which alveoli arise

capillary network in alveolar walls

alveoli

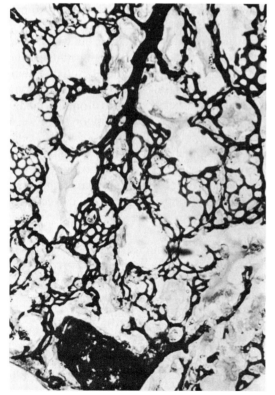

Fig 11.32 *Human lung injected to show airways and pulmonary circulation*

walls. This secretion contains a detergent-like lipoprotein called a **surfactant**. It lowers the surface tension of the alveoli, and hence the amount of effort needed to breathe in and inflate the lungs.

Surfactant also speeds up the transport of oxygen and carbon dioxide between the air and liquid phases and has a bactericidal effect, helping to remove any potentially harmful bacteria which reach the alveoli. Surfactant is constantly being secreted and reabsorbed in a healthy lung.

Surfactant is lacking in premature babies, resulting in the condition known as **respiratory distress syndrome**, in which breathing is very difficult and which may result in death.

The oxygen diffuses across the thin membranous barrier represented by the alveolar epithelium and capillary endothelium, and passes initially into the blood plasma. It then combines with haemoglobin in the red blood corpuscles to form oxyhaemoglobin. Carbon dioxide diffuses in the reverse direction from the blood to the alveolar cavity.

The diameter of the alveolar capillaries is smaller than the diameter of the red blood corpuscles passing through them. This means that the corpuscles have to be squeezed through the capillaries by blood pressure. During this process more of their surface area is exposed to the gaseous exchange surface of the alveolus permitting greater uptake of oxygen. Progress of the corpuscles is also relatively slow, thus increasing the time available for gaseous exchange to take place. When blood leaves the alveolus it possesses the

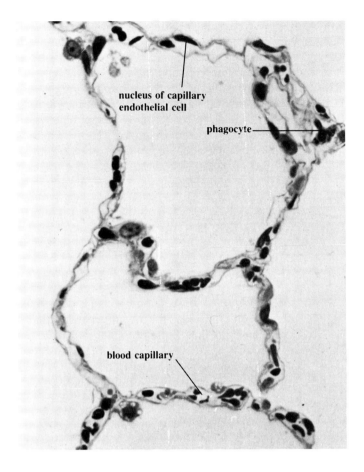

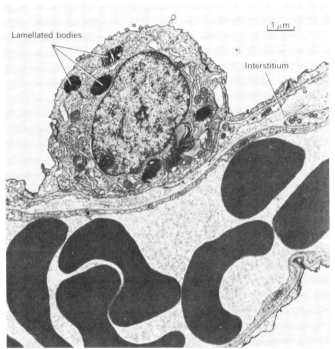

Fig 11.34 (above) *Electron micrograph of a longitudinal section through an alveolar capillary in dog lung (From G. M. Hughes (1973) The vertebrate lung, Oxford Biology Readers, No. 59).*

Fig 11.33 (left) *Histology of lung alveolus*

same partial pressure of oxygen and carbon dioxide as alveolar air.

11.7.1 Structure of the thorax

Each lung is surrounded by a **pleural cavity**. This is a space lined by two flexible, transparent pleural membranes (**pleura**). The inner visceral membrane is in contact with the lungs, whilst the outer parietal membrane lines the walls of the thorax and diaphragm. The pleural cavity contains a fluid, secreted by the membranes. This lubricates the pleura, thus reducing friction as the membranes rub against each other during breathing movements. The cavity is air-tight and its pressure stays at 3–4 mmHg lower than that in the lungs. This is important for it causes the lungs almost to fill the thorax. The negative pressure of the pleural cavity is maintained during inspiration and this allows the alveoli to inflate and fill any extra available space provided by the expanding thorax.

11.7.2 The mechanism of ventilation

Air is passed in and out of the lungs by movements of the intercostal and diaphragm muscles which alter the volume of the thoracic cavity. There are two types of intercostal muscle between each rib. The **external intercostals** slant forwards and downwards, whilst the **internal intercostals** slant backwards and downwards

(fig 11.35). The diaphragm consists of circular and radial muscle fibres arranged around the edge of a circular inelastic sheet of white fibres.

Inspiration is an active process. The external intercostal muscles contract and the internal intercostals relax. This produces a forward and outward movement of the rib cage away from the vertebral column. Simultaneously, the diaphragm contracts and flattens. Both actions increase the volume of the thorax. As a result the pressure in the thorax,

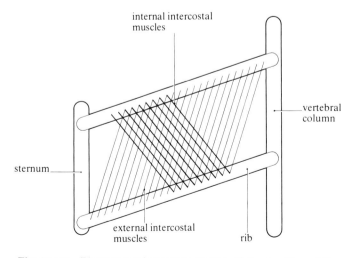

Fig 11.35 *Diagrammatic representation of the position of the intercostal muscles*

351

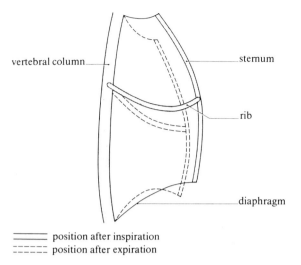

vertebral column

sternum

rib

diaphragm

——— position after inspiration
------- position after expiration

Fig 11.36 *Side view of thorax to show movements during breathing (only one rib shown)*

and hence the lungs, is reduced to less than atmospheric pressure, so permitting air to rush in and inflate the alveoli, until the air pressure in the lungs is equal to that of the atmosphere (fig 11.36).

Expiration is largely a passive process under resting conditions and is brought about by the elastic recoil of the lung tissue and respiratory muscles. The external intercostal and diaphragm muscles relax and return to their former size and position, whilst the internal intercostals contract. This reduces the volume of the thorax and raises its pressure above that of the atmosphere. Consequently air is forced out of the lungs and expiration completed. Under conditions of exercise, forced breathing occurs. When this happens additional muscles are brought into action and expiration becomes a much more active, energy-consuming process. The internal intercostals contract more strongly and move the ribs vigorously downwards. The abdominal muscles also contract strongly, causing more active upward movement of the diaphragm.

11.7.3 Control of ventilation

Involuntary control of breathing is carried out by a **breathing centre** located in the medulla of the brain (fig 11.37). The ventral portion of the breathing centre acts to increase inspiratory rate and is called the **inspiratory centre**, whilst its dorsal and lateral portions cut off inspiratory activity and promote expiration. These regions are collectively termed the **expiratory centre**. The brea-

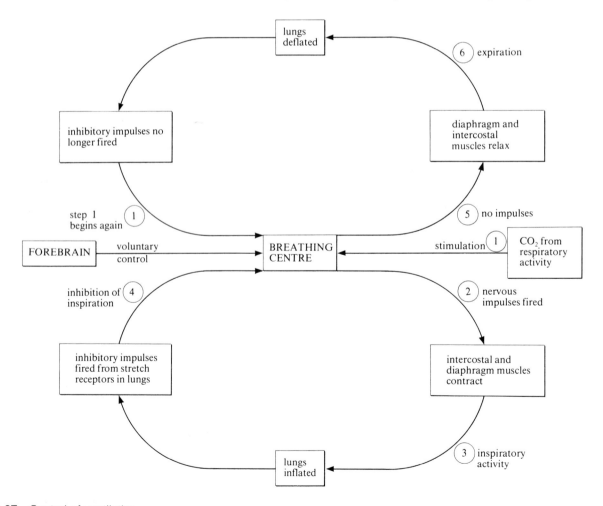

Fig 11.37 *Control of ventilation*

352

thing centre communicates with the diaphragm via phrenic and thoracic nerves. The bronchial tubes and alveoli are innervated by branches of a cranial nerve, the vagus.

The main stimulus that controls the breathing rate is the concentration of carbon dioxide in the blood. When carbon dioxide levels increase, **chemoreceptors** in the carotid and aortic bodies of the blood system are stimulated to discharge nerve impulses which pass to the inspiratory centre. The inspiratory centre then sends out impulses via the phrenic and thoracic nerves to the diaphragm and intercostal muscles causing them to increase the rate at which they contract. This automatically increases the rate at which inspiration takes place. Inspiratory activity inflates the alveoli, and stretch receptors located here and in the bronchial tree are stimulated to discharge impulses to the expiratory centre which automatically cuts off inspiratory activity. The respiratory muscles therefore relax and expiration takes place. After this has occurred, the alveoli are no longer stretched and the stretch receptors no longer stimulated. Therefore the expiratory centre becomes inactive and inspiration can begin again. The whole cycle is repeated rhythmically throughout the life of the organism.

Within limits, the rate and depth of breathing are under voluntary control. When such control is being exerted, impulses originating in the cerebrum pass to the breathing centre which then carries out the appropriate action. Oxygen concentration also has an effect on the breathing rate (section 11.8). However, under normal circumstances there is an abundance of oxygen available, and its influence is relatively minor.

11.7.4 Lung volumes and capacities

The average man has a lung capacity of approximately 5 dm³ (fig 11.38). During quiet breathing he will breathe in and out about 450 cm³ of air. This is called the **tidal volume**. If after a normal tidal inspiration he continues to inhale, he can take in a further 1 500 cm³ of air. This is called his **inspiratory reserve volume**. If after a tidal expiration the man continues to exhale he can force out a further 1 500 cm³ of air. This is termed his **expiratory**

reserve volume. The amount of air exchanged after a forced inspiration followed immediately by a forced expiration is termed the **vital capacity**. Even after forced expiration 1 500 cm³ of air remain in the lungs. This cannot be expelled and is called **residual air**.

During inspiration about 300 cm³ of the tidal volume reaches the lungs, whilst the remaining 150 cm³ remains in the respiratory tubes, where gaseous exchange does not occur. When expiration follows, this air is expelled from the body as unchanged room air and is termed **dead space air**. The air that reaches the lungs mixes with the 1 500 cm³ of air already present in the alveoli. Its volume is small compared to that of the alveolar air and complete renewal of air in the lungs is therefore a necessarily slow process. The intermittent slow exchange between fresh air and alveolar air affects the composition of gases in the alveoli to such a small extent that they remain relatively constant at 13.8% oxygen, 5.5% carbon dioxide and 80.7% nitrogen. Comparison of the composition of gases of inspired, expired and alveolar air is interesting (table 11.5). It is clear that one-fifth of the oxygen inspired has been retained for use by the body, and 100 times the amount of carbon dioxide expelled. The air that comes into close contact with the blood is alveolar air. It contains less oxygen than inspired air, but more carbon dioxide.

Table 11.5 Percentage composition by volume of gases in inspired, alveolar and expired air.

Gas	Inspired air	Alveolar air	Expired air
Oxygen	20.95	13.8	16.4
Carbon dioxide	0.04	5.5	4.0
Nitrogen	79.01	80.7	79.6

11.7.5 Measurement of respiratory activity

An instrument commonly used in schools, laboratories and hospitals for measuring the volume of air which enters and leaves the lungs is the spirometer. Essentially it consists of an air-filled box with a capacity of

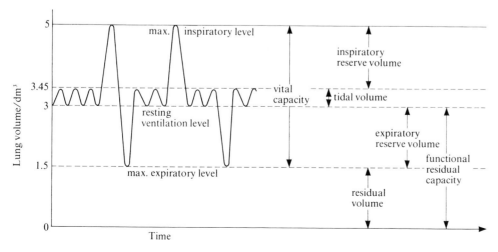

Fig 11.38 *Lung volumes and capacities*

six or more litres, suspended freely over water. The air in the box is connected by a series of pipes to the subject so that the air in the subject's lungs and the air in the box is a sealed system.

The box is counterbalanced so that when gas is passed in or out, the box rises or falls accordingly. When the subject breathes out, the box is raised; when he breathes in, the box is lowered. A pen attached to the box writes on a slowly rotating drum (kymograph) recording all the movements of the box.

Detailed instructions for the operation of the spirometer are supplied by the manufacturer and will not be dealt with here. However, it is important to be able to analyse the tracings recorded by the spirometer, and to understand what information can be derived from them.

From spirometer tracings the metabolic rate, respiratory quotient, tidal volume, rate of breathing and consumption of oxygen can be measured.

The **respiratory rate** is calculated as the number of breaths taken per minute. **Pulmonary ventilation (PV)** is expressed in terms of the respiratory rate multiplied by the tidal volume:

$$PV = \text{respiratory rate} \times \text{tidal volume}$$

For example, if respiratory rate is 15 breaths per minute and tidal volume is 400 cm³, then PV = 15 × 400 cm³ = 6 000 cm³ per minute (that is 6 000 cm³ of air will be exchanged between subject and outside environment each minute).

Alveolar ventilation (AV) is the volume of air that actually reaches the lungs. It is less than that of the pulmonary ventilation.

$$AV = \text{respiratory rate} \times (\text{tidal volume} - \text{dead space air})$$

For example if TV = 400 cm³, dead space air = 150 cm³ and respiratory rate = 15 breaths per minute,

$$
\begin{aligned}
\text{then } AV &= 15 \times (400 - 150) \text{ cm}^3 \\
&= 15 \times 250 \text{ cm}^3 \\
&= 3\,750 \text{ cm}^3 \text{ per minute (that is 3 750 cm}^3 \text{ of air}
\end{aligned}
$$
will be exchanged between the lungs of the subject and outside environment each minute).

> **11.12** Why is the volume of alveolar air less than that of the pulmonary ventilation?

Measuring the metabolic rate of an organism

As respiration is directly involved with most metabolic activities within the body, its measurement gives a relatively accurate indication of metabolic activity. The metabolic rate can be calculated by measuring the rate of oxygen consumption.

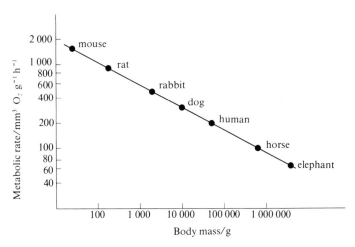

Fig 11.39 *Metabolic rate of animals, calculated per gram body mass, plotted on logarithmic coordinates*

> **11.13** Consider fig 11.39. It can be seen that the smaller the mammal the higher its metabolic rate. Why is this so?
>
> **11.14** How can you compare the metabolic rates of mammas of different size?

11.7.6 The basal metabolic rate (BMR)

The BMR of an organism is the minimum rate of energy conversion required just to stay alive during complete rest or sleep. Before the BMR of human subjects is measured they undergo a standardised rest period of 12–18 h physical and mental relaxation. No meal is eaten during this time. This ensures that the alimentary canal is empty before measurements are taken. The BMR varies with age, sex, size and state of health of the individual and is clearly correlated with body surface area to volume ratio.

11.7.7 Respiratory quotient (RQ)

Consider the equation:

$$C_6H_{12}O_6 + 6O_2 \longrightarrow 6CO_2 + 6H_2O + \text{energy}$$

From this it is quite clear that in a given time the volume of carbon dioxide produced during respiration of carbohydrate is equal to the volume of oxygen consumed (remember, one mole of any gas occupies the same volume under the same conditions of temperature and pressure). The ratio of $CO_2:O_2$ is called the respiratory quotient, and for metabolism of carbohydrate its value is 1,

$$
\text{that is RQ} = \frac{\text{volume of } CO_2 \text{ evolved}}{\text{volume of } O_2 \text{ absorbed}}
$$
(from direct observations)

$$
\text{Or} \quad \frac{\text{moles or molecules of } CO_2 \text{ evolved}}{\text{moles or molecules of } O_2 \text{ evolved}}
$$
(from equations)

Therefore, from the above equation, $RQ = \dfrac{CO_2}{O_2} = \dfrac{6}{6} = 1$

11.15 The equation for respiration of the fat tripalmitin is:

$$2C_{51}H_{98}O_6 + 145O_2 \longrightarrow 102CO_2 + 98H_2O$$

What is the RQ for tripalmitin?

11.16 What is the RQ when glucose is respired anaerobically to ethanol and carbon dioxide?

Analysis of respiratory quotients can yield valuable information about the nature of the substrate being used for respiration and the type of metabolism that is taking place (table 11.6).

11.17 Why is the usual RQ for humans between 0.7 and 1.0?

11.18 From the spirometer trace given in fig 11.40 calculate
(a) respiratory rate;
(b) tidal volume;
(c) pulmonary ventilation;
(d) oxygen consumption.

Table 11.6 Respiratory quotients of a variety of substrates.

RQ	Substrate	
>1.0	Carbohydrate plus some anaerobic respiration	
1.0	Carbohydrates	
0.9	Protein	
0.7	Fat, such as tripalmitin	
0.5	Fat associated with carbohydrate synthesis	The carbon dioxide released during respiration is being put to other uses and therefore not released from the body
0.3	Carbohydrate with associated organic acid synthesis	

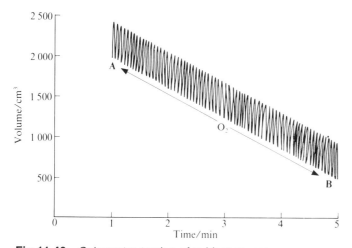

Fig 11.40 *Spirometer tracing of subject at rest*

Experiment 11.2: To measure the oxygen uptake in small terrestrial non-vertebrates such as woodlice

The oxygen uptake by the non-vertebrates in this experiment is measured using a manometer. Fig 11.41 shows the apparatus which is used.

In respiration, oxygen is taken up and carbon dioxide is given off, and so to ensure that the manometer is recording oxygen consumption alone, soda-lime is incorporated in the apparatus in order to absorb the carbon dioxide evolved.

The apparatus is used to investigate the effect of temperature on oxygen uptake. A water bath is used in order to keep the temperature of the atmosphere surrounding the organisms constant whilst readings are being taken.

Materials

manometer	clamps and stands
manometer fluid	water bath
1 cm³ syringe	thermometer
2 boiling tubes	stopclock
2 pieces of zinc gauze (to fit the diameter of a boiling tube)	graph paper
	small non-vertebrates such as woodlice or blow-fly larvae
glass beads (or any equivalent non-absorbent material of equal volume to the invertebrates)	soda-lime

Method

(1) Half fill a manometer with fluid and connect a 1 cm³ syringe to the three-way tap attached to one arm of the manometer.
(2) Place equal volumes of soda-lime in the bottom of each of two boiling tubes and then place a zinc-gauze platform 1 cm above the soda-lime.
(3) Place some invertebrates in one boiling tube (experimental) and an equal volume of glass beads in the other tube (control). The animals must not come into contact with the soda-lime and so the platform must be an absolute barrier between the animals and the soda-lime.
(4) Connect the manometer to the two boiling tubes as shown in fig 11.41, and adjust the three-way tap and screw-clip so that the apparatus is open to the atmosphere.
(5) Clamp the apparatus so that the boiling tubes are in a water bath at 20 °C and leave the apparatus at this temperature with the taps open for at least 15 min.
(6) Close the tap and screw-clip, note the position of the manometer fluid and start the stopclock.
(7) At regular intervals, read off the position of the manometer fluid against the scale.
(8) At the end of the experiment open the tap and screw-clip again.

Fig 11.41 *Apparatus used in the investigation of oxygen uptake in small terrestrial non-vertebrates*

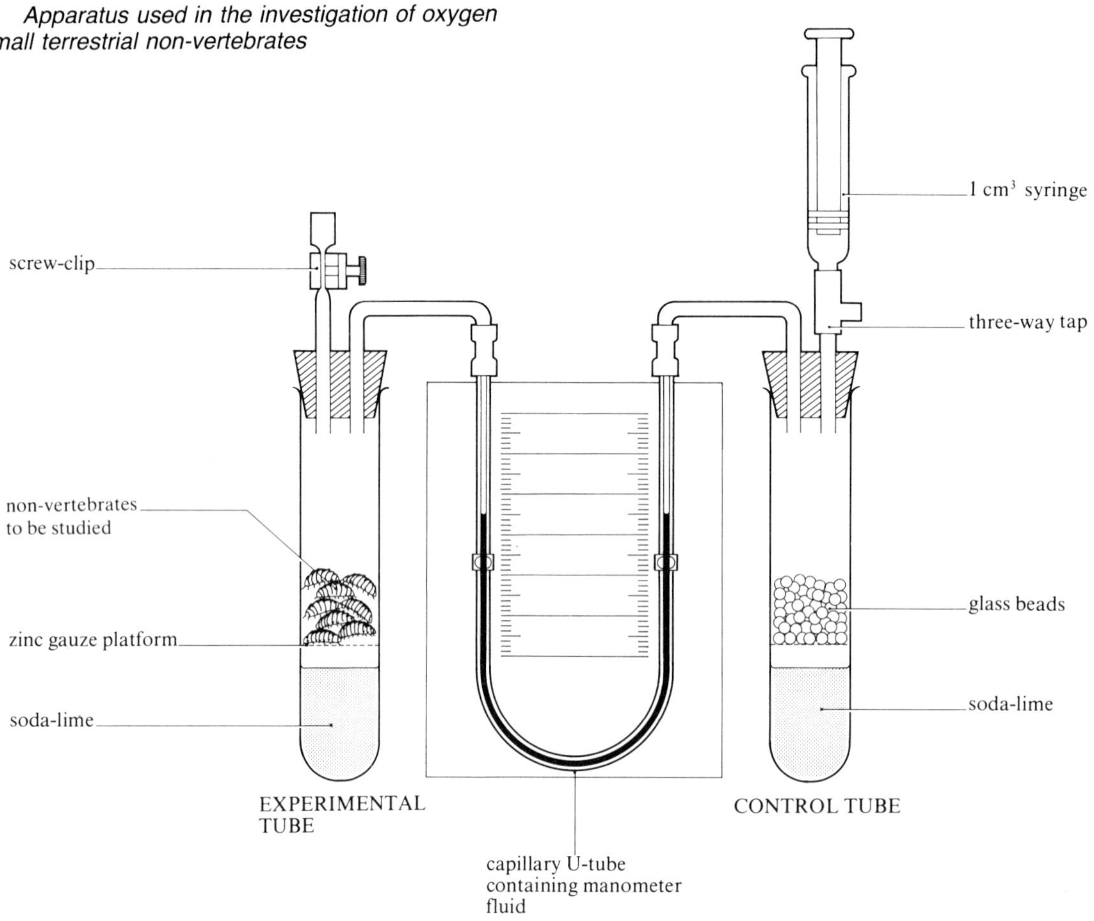

screw-clip

non-vertebrates to be studied

zinc gauze platform

soda-lime

EXPERIMENTAL TUBE

capillary U-tube containing manometer fluid

1 cm³ syringe

three-way tap

glass beads

soda-lime

CONTROL TUBE

(9) Plot a graph of the change in fluid level against time.
(10) Calculate the rate of oxygen uptake.
(11) Repeat the experiment several times over a range of temperatures, such as 20, 25, 30, 35 and 40 °C.
(12) Plot a graph of rate of oxygen consumption against temperature.

Notes

(1) The fluid that is used in the manometer can be dyed water, oil or mercury. The less dense the fluid, the greater the displacement in the manometer.

(2) In order to measure the change in the manometer fluid levels, a scale must be attached to the manometer. This can be done by attaching the manometer U-tube to a piece of hardboard on which a scale or graph paper has been glued. Alternatively an adhesive metric scale can be attached to the arm of the manometer itself. The tape is available from Philip Harris Ltd.

(3) Before any readings are taken in the experiment, the apparatus must be checked to ensure that it is air-tight. This can be done by pushing air into the apparatus using the syringe, causing the manometer fluid to be displaced. The tap should then be used to close off the apparatus to the atmosphere and if the apparatus is air-tight, the difference in levels of fluid should not decrease.

11.8 Unusual conditions in ventilation

11.8.1 The effects of altitude and acclimatisation

As mountaineers ascend high mountains they suffer from inadequate oxygenation of the blood. This condition is known as **anoxia** or hypoxia. It occurs because the partial pressure of oxygen, along with the other gases of the atmosphere falls with increasing altitude, for example at 5 450 m the barometric pressure of the atmosphere is 0.5 bar which is exactly half that at sea level. Although the percentage of oxygen by volume is the same at this altitude when compared with the other gases of the atmosphere, the actual amount is half that found at sea level.

Respiratory activity is stimulated by chemoreceptors, and at high altitudes, in the quest for more oxygen, the increased ventilation expels large quantities of carbon dioxide from the lungs causing the acidity of the blood to decrease. The increase in alkalinity (greater pH) causes a condition known as **alkalaemia**. This greater pH inhibits the activity of the chemoreceptors. Consequently pulmonary ventilation is hampered and becomes relatively inadequate, causing great discomfort and fatigue.

Given time, the respiratory and circulatory systems are able to adjust somewhat to the lower partial pressure of oxygen at altitude. After several days alkaline urine is expelled from the body thus reducing the alkalaemia. With the chemoreceptors no longer inhibited, pulmonary ventilation will increase, and carbon dioxide concentration will once again become the main chemical stimulus in the regulation of breathing. At the same time the bone marrow is stimulated to produce more red blood cells (erythrocytes). This raises the oxygen-carrying capacity of the blood, offsetting to some extent the incomplete oxygen saturation of the blood caused by the low partial pressure of oxygen. When these adjustments are complete the body is said to be **acclimatised** to its new conditions.

11.8.2 Diving mammals

Seals frequently remain submerged in the water for periods of up to 15 min. Their blood has a much higher oxygen-carrying capacity than human blood, being able to carry between 30 and 40 cm^3 of oxygen per 100 cm^3 of blood.

During the dive, considerable modifications to the circulatory and respiratory system occur which ensure the effective distribution of oxygen within the animal and its efficient use. Generally this is what happens. At the onset of a dive, a nervous reflex decreases the rate at which the heart contracts, thus slowing blood flow. Blood pressure in the arteries is maintained because the blood vessels constrict. Certain blood vessels constrict completely and bring about a redistribution of the blood supply so that only the vital organs, such as the heart, brain and other parts of the nervous system, receive blood. Such modification means that oxygen in the blood will be used up slowly but is always available to those organs which are very sensitive to anoxia. With little oxygen available to them, the muscles of the seal respire anaerobically, accumulating lactate. Because there is little blood passing from the muscles to the general circulation, no great quantity of lactate will be distributed around the body and the body will not suffer any harmful effects. On returning to the surface, the first breath taken is the signal for the heartbeat to increase, and blood circulation to return to normal. When this happens lactate is passed into circulation and metabolised in the liver. The air in the lungs is rapidly replaced as each breath can exchange as much as 80% of the air in the lungs.

11.9 Flowering plants

Plants require less energy per unit mass than animals as they possess lower metabolic rates. Whereas some small plants can carry out gaseous exchange by diffusion over their whole surfaces, large flowering plants exchange gases through stomata in their leaves and on their green stems (herbaceous stems), or if the stems are woody. through cracks in the bark or via lenticels (section 21.6.6).

Once inside the plant, movement of oxygen is determined by the diffusion gradients that exist in the intercellular air spaces. In this way oxygen travels towards the cells and dissolves in the surface moisture of their walls. From here it passes by diffusion into the cells themselves. Carbon dioxide leaves the plant by the same pathway but in the reverse direction.

The whole situation becomes more complex in chlorophyll-containing cells if the plant is also photosynthesising at the same time. Here oxygen produced by the chloroplasts may be immediately used up by mitochondria contained in the same cell, and carbon dioxide issuing from the mitochondria consumed by the chloroplasts.

Further information concerning gaseous exchange in flowering plants can be found in chapter 9.

> **11.19** (a) Construct a table showing the major differences between photosynthesis and aerobic respiration. (b) Make a list of similarities (including biochemical similarities), between photosynthesis and aerobic respiration.

Chapter Twelve

Organisms and their environment

Ecology is the study of the relationships of living organisms to each other and their surroundings. As stated by Cousins (*New Scientist*, 4 July 1985), 'Ecology is a science, from which much is expected. It provides the foundations of our understanding of agriculture, forestry and fisheries and is called upon to predict the effects of everything from pollutants to the construction of dams.'

The term 'ecology' was first used by the German biologist Ernst Haeckel in 1869 and is derived from the Greek roots *oikos* meaning a 'house' or 'living-place' and *logos* meaning the 'study' or 'science' of. Thus, literally, ecology means the study of the Earth's households. It adopts a **holistic** approach, that is one in which a whole picture is built up which is more important than the parts. Although the various parts often have to be analysed separately, as described in chapter 13, it is the synthesis of all the available information into an overall picture of the living systems and their surroundings that is important.

Ecology has its roots in natural history and has ranked alongside physiology, genetics and other disciplines as a branch of biology from about 1900. Since the mid-1950s the scope and importance of ecology have increased greatly, and modern ecology is best viewed as an important interdisciplinary science linking physical, biological and social sciences. Its relationship with other branches of biology is summarised in fig 12.1, which shows that living organisms can be studied at different levels of organisation. Ecology spans the right-hand portion of the diagram, which includes organisms, populations and communities. Ecologists regard these as the living part (**biotic component**) of a system called the **ecosystem**. This also includes a non-living

part (the **abiotic component**) which contains matter and energy. Populations, communities and ecosystems are terms which have precise meanings in ecology, and they are defined in fig 12.1. The different ecosystems are united to form the **biosphere**, or **ecosphere**, which includes all the living organisms and the physical environment with which they interact. Thus, the oceans, land surface and lower parts of the atmosphere all form part of the ecosphere.

Within ecology, studies have traditionally been of two types, namely autecology and synecology. **Autecology** focusses on the relationships between an organism or population and the environment, whereas **synecology** looks at communities and the environment. Thus, while in an autecological study one might examine the ecology of a single oak tree, or the species *Quercus robur* (pedunculate oak), or the genus *Quercus* (oak), in a synecological study it is the whole oakwood community which is examined (sections 13.4 and 13.5).

As Southwood noted in 1981* in a useful review summarising the changing nature of ecology, the first ecological article in the journal *New Scientist* (in 1956) dealt with the reintroduction of reindeer into Scotland in an essentially autecological study. More recently, emphasis in ecological work has shifted to ecosystem (that is community and environment) and even ecosphere (whole planet) studies. It is at these levels of organisation that the important contribution to ecology of sciences other than biology, notably chemistry, physics, pedology (the study of soils) and hydrology (the study of water), as well as the various social sciences, can most clearly be understood.

* Southwood, T. R. E. *New Scientist*, **92**, 512–4 (19 Nov 1981).

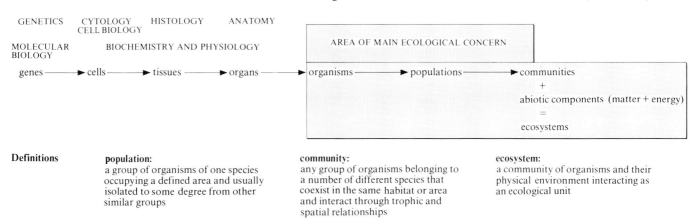

Fig 12.1 *Levels of organisation from genes to ecosystems*

The growing public awareness of ecology, particularly of the interaction between human societies and the environment, is seen in many ways. In the USA developers are required by law to prepare Environmental Impact Statements (EIS) before any new project may begin. In Britain, though this is not yet a legal requirement, major industries and environmental groups who may oppose developments prepare similar assessments of new proposals. No company can afford to alienate public opinion, and planning officials are unlikely to allow development without a proper environmental appraisal. An example is BP's extensive environmental appraisal of the Wytch Farm on-shore oil development in Dorset. Many local planning authorities now employ ecologists or seek advice from County Naturalists Trusts and ecologists have increasingly found a place in government committees dealing with the environment, such as the permanent Royal Commission on Environmental Pollution (RCEP).

Ecology has also formed the basis for a new political perspective, called 'environmentalism'. In Europe, this is encapsulated by the various national Green parties. Under the West German electoral system *die Grünen* (the Greens) have achieved formal political representation. In Britain, the Green party has adopted a lobbyist approach and seeks, with other major environmental organisations such as Greenpeace and Friends of the Earth, to inform and persuade politicians and industrialists of the importance of environmental concerns. Recent well-publicised industrial accidents as at Seveso (Italy), Bhophal (India) and Chernobyl (USSR) have heightened public and political awareness of the relevance of ecology to industry. The current controversy in Britain over nuclear waste disposal, the growing international concern over toxic chemical wastes (as highlighted by the case of *Karin B*, summer 1988), and the failure, in European eyes, of the British government to act effectively on acid rain or respond wholeheartedly to initiatives on North Sea pollution, further emphasise the political relevance and international dimension of ecology.

One positive response has been the emergence over the last two decades of environmental consultancies and agencies supplying advice to industry and other interested parties. Designing in an environmentally benign manner and thus avoiding the need for subsequent costly modification may make the difference between profit and loss, success and failure, in an ever more environmentally aware market. The success of enterprises such as Environmental Data Services, established in 1978, which has trebled the circulation of its journal during the 1980s testifies to this process.

E.P. Odum's assertion in 1971 that 'ecology is the branch of science most relevant to the everyday life of all people' thus seems vindicated by events of the last 20 years.

Student action

1 Look at the job advertisements in *New Scientist* or the quality daily newspapers on 'Public appoint-

ments' day (for example *Guardian*, *Times*, *Independent*). How many jobs require ecological knowledge?

2 Watch the main evening television news programme every day for one week and list the environmentally related issues reported.

12.1   Approaches to ecology

The holistic approach (see introduction above) is the distinctive characteristic of ecological science. A proper understanding of ecology requires simultaneous consideration of all factors interacting in a particular place. The sheer scope of this task presents problems, and in practice most ecologists adopt one of several main approaches when undertaking a new investigation. These approaches may be summarised as the ecosystem approach, community approach (synecology), population approach (autecology), habitat approach and the evolutionary–historical approach.

These five approaches to ecology interact and overlap to some extent. However, they provide a useful framework for study. In this text it is not possible to consider all in equal depth. Instead, attention will be focussed on the ecosystem, community and population approaches which between them include the essence of the subject. A brief summary of the chief characteristics and contributions to ecological thought, and the problem-solving possibilities of the five main approaches is given below.

Ecosystem approach

The ecosystem was first defined by Tansley in 1935 as the living world and its habitat (see also definitions in fig 12.1 and section 12.2.1). The ecosystem approach focusses on the **flow of energy** and **cycling of matter** between living and non-living components of the ecosphere. A systems ecologist, therefore, is usually concerned with the functional relationships (such as feeding) between organisms and between them and their environment, rather than with species composition of communities and identification of rarities or special variations. The ecosystem approach also highlights the similarity in organisation of all living systems irrespective of differing taxonomy or habitat. A simple comparison of aquatic and terrestrial ecosystems, as shown in fig 12.2, serves to stress this point. Note the similarities in structure and functional units between the two systems despite the widely differing habitats and species contained within them.

At the same time, the ecosystem approach introduces the concept of **homeostasis** (self-regulation) in living systems, shows how this operates by means of feedback mechanisms (see section 12.4, biogeochemical cycles), and makes clear that breakdown of the regulatory mechanisms, for example by pollution, may lead to biological imbalance, such as excess of an organism as with a plankton bloom. The ecosystem approach is also relevant to the future development of scientifically sound agricultural practices.

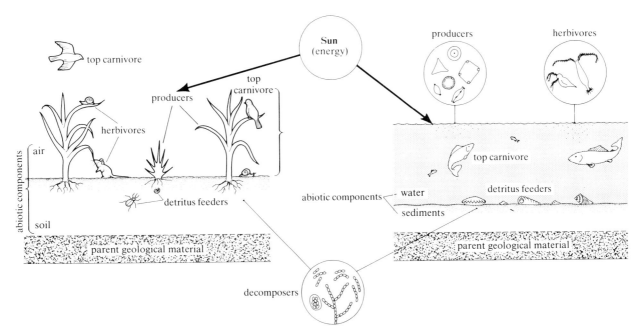

Fig 12.2 *A simple comparison of the gross structure of an aquatic (freshwater or marine) and a terrestrial ecosystem. Necessary units for function are: abiotic components (basic inorganic and organic compounds); producers (vegetation on land, phytoplankton in water); animals – direct or 'grazing herbivores' (grasshoppers, meadow mice etc. on land,* *zooplankton etc. in water); indirect or detritus-feeding consumers (soil non-vertebrates on land, bottom non-vertebrates in water); 'top' carnivores (hawks and large fish); decomposers (bacteria and fungi of decay). Animals and decomposers comprise the consumers. (Modified from E.P. Odum (1975)* Ecology, *2nd ed., Holt, Rinehart & Wilson.)*

Community approach

The term community is defined in fig 12.1.

Community ecology focusses in particular on the biotic components of ecosystems. It is synonymous with a synecological approach (sections 12.6 and 13.4). Thus in community studies one examines the plants, animals and microbiology of a recognisable biotic unit such as a woodland, grassland or heathland. Limiting factors may be identified, but functional aspects of the physical environment, such as weathering, are not usually studied in any detail. Emphasis is placed instead on the identification and description of the species present, as well as an examination of factors which control their presence, such as dispersal, competition and resource partitioning.

One important aspect of community studies is the concept of **succession** and **climax communities** (section 12.6) which is an important consideration for rational conservation management.

Population approach

The term population is defined in fig 12.1.

Population ecology covers the area studied in autecology (sections 12.7 and 13.5). Modern population studies are concerned with the characteristic mathematical forms of the growth, maintenance and decline of species populations. They embrace a number of important concepts, such as natality (birth rate), survivorship and mortality. Population ecology provides the theoretical basis for understand-

ing the 'outbreaks' of pests in agriculture and medicine, the possibilities for biological control methods (the control of pest organisms by biological means, such as the introduction of their predators or parasites), and the critical numbers of individuals needed for continued survival of a species. This latter point is important for the design and management of nature reserves and game parks, and also links strongly with evolutionary and historical ecology.

Recent application of ecological ideas to palaeontology has given new insights into how species interacted in fossil communities. Population ecology provides an important theoretical basis for examining species expansion and extinction since the very beginnings of life on this planet.

Habitat approach

Habitat is a spatial concept. It describes the typical environment of a particular organism, population, community or ecosystem. On the grand scale, Earth has four major habitats, that is marine, estuarine, freshwater and terrestrial. Each is characterised by physical conditions or limiting factors, such as salinity or temperature, that influence the presence and survival of organisms in that habitat and their distribution within it. The organism is adapted to the physical conditions of the habitat. On the local scale, habitat studies give unity to, and a readily understood basis for, field studies. Local habitats could include a hedgerow, freshwater pond, oakwood or rocky shore. Details of the application of the habitat approach to ecological investigation are given in chapter 13. Some communities are so intimately linked with particular habitats that they cannot meaningfully be studied in any other context, such as sand dune or saltmarsh communities. However, an adequate study of, for example, sand dune ecology will incorporate the four main approaches. Particular locations within the same overall habitat may have their own special conditions and are sometimes referred to as **microhabitats**, such as the bark of a rotting log in an oakwood.

An organism's habitat is not solely a matter of *physical conditions*. Its environment may be modified, or even primarily determined, by *other living organisms*. A related, useful and important concept is the **ecological niche** which combines the ideas of spatial habitat with the functional relationships of an organism, especially its feeding activities and other interactions with other species. An organism's niche thus describes both its location and function ('address' and 'profession') within a particular community or ecosystem. To understand more completely why an organism not only exists but flourishes in a particular place one must study its absolute physical and biotic constraints, which will determine its **potential niche**, and its preferences and behaviour, which will determine the more restricted range of its **realised niche** (actual niche). (See reference to computer program ECOSPACE, p. 373.)

If two species occupy the same niche they will generally compete with one another until one is displaced. Similar habitats have similar ecological niches and in different parts of the world may contain morphologically similar, but taxonomically different, animal and plant species. Open grassland and scrub, for example, will typically provide a niche for fast running herbivores, but these may be horses, antelope, bison, kangaroos, and so on.

The habitat approach is also convenient for studying those characteristics of the physical environment which are intimately linked with plants and animals such as soils, moisture and light. Here, links with the ecosystem and community approaches are particularly strong. The continued development of related sciences such as hydrology, pedology, meteorology, climatology and oceanography has opened important new interdisciplinary areas of study. Unfortunately it also makes the challenge too wide for reasonable study by any one individual, so teamwork is important and individual ecologists generally focus on one aspect of plant or animal and environment interactions, such as forest hydrology, crop climatology and derelict land reclamation. Again it is expected that functional approaches (ecosystem, community and population approaches) will be incorporated into the studies.

Evolutionary and historical approach

By studying how ecosystems, communities and populations have changed over time we gain important insights into why changes occurred and a good basis for predicting the likely nature of future changes. **Evolutionary ecology** views the changes over time since life evolved. Most importantly it

gives us an understanding of the nature of the ecosphere before humans became a major environmental influence. It may be studied using, for example, fossil evidence or sedimentary sequences. Typical studies include attempts to reconstruct the ecosystems of the past, comparisons of ancient and modern distributions of taxa, and analysis of the interplay of genetic and environmental change. Evolutionary ecology thus has strong links with geological science. The application of ecosystem ideas to the past is a relatively new development in traditional palaeontology. Evolutionary ecology in general is an expanding and fruitful field of study.

Historical ecology is concerned with change since the developing technology and culture of the human species made human activity a major influence on ecological systems. In Britain and the rest of Europe the major technological and cultural advance that led to the beginning of widespread forest clearance dates from the New Stone Age or Neolithic times, which began about 5000 BP (before present). Pollen analysis and archaeological artefacts form the main evidence for pre-documentary times (in cultural terms 'pre-historic'). Written records, early maps and tree-ring analysis are important additional tools for more recent historical times.

The long-term perspective is a valuable aid to ecological understanding. Trends and strategies may be identified which contemporary studies alone cannot reveal, for example the periodicity of drought in the Sahel and the possibility of cyclical phases of abundance and decline in North Sea herring stocks.

Another example is provided by the checkerspot butterfly (*Euphydryas ethida*). In parts of its range it lays eggs on just one plant, a species of Indian paint brush *Castilleja linariifolia*. Other plants around, and used elsewhere in its range, are ignored. The area concerned experiences occasional drought phases which return periodically between 50–100 years. Chance opportunity to observe a drought phase showed that unlike the alternative host species, *C. linariifolia* was drought-resistant. The survival benefits of the checkerspot's highly selective egg-laying strategy in this part of its range thus became clear.

Historical ecology is a vital aspect of effective conservation management of plagioclimax communities, such as the lowland heaths of Britain and the rest of Europe (see section 12.6.1). These heaths are a result of forest clearance followed by centuries of grazing and burning management. Their present species and landscape value cannot be conserved without maintaining or simulating traditional land-use practice. Without this, succession to some form of scrub or woodland is inevitable.

Evolutionary studies of species dispersal, adaptive radiation and extinction, like historical studies, form the basis of models of nature reserve design and species conservation. The study of past communities and populations has traditionally been part of palaeontology, but the application of ecosystem ideas to the past is relatively recent.

12.2 The ecosystem

12.2.1 Definitions and key concepts

Ecosystems are made up of living and non-living components, known as **biotic** and **abiotic** components respectively. The organisms which comprise the biotic component are collectively known as the **community**. The term 'ecosystem' was first used by Tansley in 1935 to describe 'the whole complex of living organisms living together as a sociological unit and its habitat,' or, to put it more simply, 'the living world and its habitat'. The terms 'microcosm' in North America and 'biogeocenose' in Soviet and Central European literature embrace similar ideas. Numerous restatements of the concept have tried to improve or elaborate on Tansley's original definition. Two useful examples are given below.

Lindeman (1942): 'a system composed of physical–chemical–biological processes active within a space–time unit of any magnitude'.

Odum (1963): 'the basic functional unit of nature including both organisms and their non-living environment, each interacting with the other and influencing each other's properties and both necessary for the maintenance and development of the system'.

Several key points about ecosystems emerge from these definitions.

(a) Living (biotic) and non-living (abiotic) components are equally important and therefore demand equivalent study and understanding.

(b) The close association of living and non-living components; both affect each other.

(c) Ecosystems can be studied at any scale. This makes individual systems difficult to define since boundaries are not clear-cut. The 'fuzzy' boundaries, however, make us constantly aware of the potential importance of factors beyond the immediate focus of interest. For example, damming the River Nile 700 miles upstream at Aswan reduced freshwater discharge and sediment load downstream and led to increased salinity and decreased nutrient status in the eastern Mediterranean. An associated decline in the eastern Mediterranean fisheries and rapid recession of the delta coastline was seen.

(d) All organisms and all features of the physical environment are necessary for the maintenance and flourishing of the system. Any change will bring a reaction (homeostasis). This may not necessarily be detrimental, but human manipulation of ecosystems has often brought unwished-for 'side-effects', such as pests in simplified agricultural ecosystems. Changes may not be immediately obvious. Some scientists consider that we are only now beginning to see the consequences of continuing human ignorance of this point, for example

global warming due to increased atmospheric carbon dioxide from accelerating use of fossil fuels, chlorofluorocarbons (CFCs) and the ozone hole, pollutants and acid rain. These three examples in particular reflect failure to understand the importance of the abiotic environment for the well-being of living systems. These issues will be discussed more fully in sections 12.4 and 12.10.

12.2.2 Overall structure of ecosystems

Ecosystems are complex, but a convenient starting point is fig 12.2 which shows in a simplified way the overall structures of a terrestrial and an aquatic ecosystem.

The biotic component can usefully be subdivided into autotrophic and heterotrophic organisms. All living organisms fit into one of these two categories, as has been described in table 9.1. Autotrophic organisms synthesise their own organic requirements from simple inorganic molecules and, with the exception of chemosynthetic bacteria, do this by photosynthesis, using light as an energy source. Heterotrophic organisms require a source of organic food and, with the exception of a few bacteria, rely on a chemical source of energy derived usually from the organic food they consume. It will be shown that heterotrophs are dependent on autotrophs for their existence, and that an understanding of their relationships is essential to an understanding of ecosystems. It is also fundamental to human manipulation of ecosystems as, for example, in agriculture.

The non-living or abiotic component of an ecosystem is principally divided into soil or water, and climate. Soil and water contain a mixture of inorganic and organic nutrients. The underlying bedrock from which soil is partly derived and on which it is based contributes to the properties of the soil. Climate includes such environmental variables as light, temperature and water, which are important in determining the types of living organisms that can flourish in the ecosystem. In aquatic ecosystems salinity is another major variable.

The essence of ecosystem studies, however, lies in understanding how connections between the different organisms and their abiotic environment work. Two important ways in which these connections are seen are energy flow and nutrient cycling. These aspects are discussed more fully in the following sections.

With the ecosystem approach, the ultimate aim is a synthesis of our knowledge to give an understanding of a complex system. This should always be kept in mind as different parts of the system are analysed separately.

12.3 Energy and nutrient relationships

12.3.1 Energy flow and nutrient cycling

The organisms of an ecosystem are linked by their energy and nutrient relationships and the distinction between energy and nutrients must be fully appreciated. Chapters 9–11 have already dealt with living organisms as consumers of energy and nutrients and it is strongly recommended that the opening sections of chapter 9 are read so that this is fully understood.

In section 9.1 energy is defined as the capacity to do work and living organisms are likened to machines in that they require energy to keep working, that is to stay alive. The ecologist can regard the whole ecosystem as one machine which is kept working by an input of energy and nutrients (materials or matter). Nutrients are derived originally from the abiotic components of the ecosystem, to which they eventually return by way of the decomposition of waste products or dead bodies or organisms. Thus a constant recycling of nutrients occurs within an ecosystem. Both living and non-living components are involved, so the cycles are called **biogeochemical cycles**. They are described further in section 12.4.

The energy to drive these cycles is supplied ultimately by the Sun. In the biotic component, photosynthetic organisms utilise the Sun's energy directly and pass it on to other organisms. The net result is a flow of energy and a cycling of nutrients through the ecosystem as illustrated in fig 12.3. It should also be pointed out that in the abiotic component climatic factors such as temperature, movement of the atmosphere, evaporation and rainfall are also regulated by the input of solar energy.

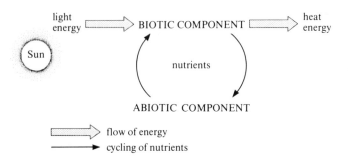

Fig 12.3 *Flow of energy and cycling of nutrients through an ecosystem*

To understand why energy flows through the ecosystem in a linear fashion, rather than being recycled and re-used like the nutrients, a brief consideration of thermodynamics is necessary.

Energy can be thought of as existing in various forms, such as mechanical, chemical, heat and electrical energy, all of which are interconvertible. The change of energy from one form to another, known as the **transformation of energy**, is governed by the laws of thermodynamics. The first law, **the law of conservation of energy**, states that

energy may be transformed from one form into another, but can be neither created nor destroyed. The second law states that, in performing work, no energy conversion can be 100% efficient and that some energy must escape as heat. Heat is the result of the random movement of molecules, whereas work always involves a non-random (ordered) use of energy.* The concept of 'work' can be applied to any energy-consuming process carried out by living organisms, from processes at the cellular level, such as the maintenance of electrical gradients across membranes and protein synthesis, to processes at the level of the whole organism, such as growth, development, repair and reproduction.

Thus living organisms are energy transformers and each time an energy transformation is carried out some energy is lost as heat. Ultimately *all* the energy that enters the biotic component of the ecosystem is lost as heat. It may be imagined that since heat can be used to do work, as in a steam locomotive, there is no reason why heat should not be recycled. However, the process that generates the heat requires more energy than can be reclaimed by recycling the heat, so that an overall rundown of useable energy would still occur. In practice, living organisms do not use heat as a source of energy to do work, but use light or chemical energy.

The study of energy flow through ecosystems is called **energetics** and since this, together with nutrient cycling, is a dominant theme in the study of ecosystems it is important to become familiar with the energy units used.

12.3.2 Energy units

The SI unit of energy is the joule, though the traditional unit of the calorie is still in common use. Both units are defined in table 12.1, which also includes references to the energy content of representative foods and organisms, and to daily food requirements of representative organisms.

> **12.1** Why are the figures for energy content in table 12.1 quoted for dry mass rather than fresh (wet) mass?
>
> **12.2** Account for the large difference in daily energy requirements of humans and small birds or mammals on a weight for weight basis.

12.3.3 The Sun as a source of energy

The ultimate source of energy in ecosystems is the Sun. The Sun is a star which releases vast amounts of solar energy into space. The energy travels through space as electromagnetic waves and a small fraction of it, about 1/2000 millionth, amounting to $10.8 \times 10^6 \, kJ \, m^{-2} \, yr^{-1}$,

---

* The increase in disorder that is involved in energy transformations is measured as a term called **entropy**. In the universe as a whole entropy is continuously increasing.

Table 12.1 Units of energy and energy content of some living organisms and biological molecules.

Energy units

calorie (cal) or gram calorie	– the amount of heat (or energy) needed to raise the temperature of one gram of water through 1 °C (14.5 °C to 15.5 °C)
kilocalorie (kcal or Cal)	– 1 000 cal
joule (J)	– 10^7 ergs: 1 erg is the amount of work done when 1 newton moves through 1 metre (1 newton (N) is a unit of force) Alternatively 981 ergs is the work done in raising a gram weight against the force of gravity to a height of 1 cm
kilojoule (kJ)	– 1 000 J

$$1 \text{ J} = 0.239 \text{ cal} \qquad 1 \text{ cal} = 4.186 \text{ J}$$

Energy content (averages or approximations)

	joules per gram dry mass (energy value)
carbohydrate	16.7
protein	20.9
lipid	38.5
terrestrial plants	18.8
algae	20.5
non-vertebrates (excl. insects)	12.6
	22.6
vertebrates	23.4

(differences between these groups of organisms are due partly to different mineral contents)

Daily food requirements	kJ per kg live body mass
humans	167 (about 12 500 kJ day^{-1} for a 70 kg adult)
small bird or mammal	4 186
insect	2 093

Based on data from table 3.1, Odum, E. P. (1971) *Fundamentals of Ecology*, 3rd ed. Saunders.

is intercepted by the Earth. Of this, about 40% is reflected immediately from the clouds, dust in the atmosphere and the Earth's surface without having any heating effect. This is termed the planetary **albedo**. A further 15% is absorbed and converted to heat energy in the atmosphere, particularly by ozone in the stratosphere, and by water vapour. The ozone layer absorbs almost all short-wave ultraviolet radiation which is important because such radiation is lethal to exposed living material. The remaining 45% of incoming energy penetrates to the Earth's surface. This represents an average of about $5 \times 10^6 \text{ kJ m}^{-2} \text{ yr}^{-1}$, though the actual amount for a given locality varies with latitude and local features such as aspect. Just under half the radiation striking the Earth's surface is in the photosynthetically active range (PAR), the visible wavelengths. However, under optimum conditions only a very small proportion, about 5% of incoming radiation (or 10% PAR) is converted in photosynthesis into gross primary produc-

tivity (GPP). A more typical figure for good conditions is 1% of total radiation (2% PAR) while the biosphere average is about 0.2% of total incident radiation. Net primary productivity (NPP) (the net gain of organic material in photosynthesis after allowing for losses due to respiration) varies between 50% and 80% of gross primary productivity (see section 12.3.7).

As a global average the energy fix by Earth's green plants is only 0.1% of total sunlight. Terrestrial systems, which cover one-third of the planetary surface, fix half the total sunlight captured. Cultivated crops achieve higher rates of GPP and NPP during their short cultivation periods, but so far it has proved impossible to achieve higher rates of photosynthetic fixation on a sustained basis under normal field conditions.

12.3.4 Energy transfers: food chains and trophic levels

Within the ecosystem, the energy-containing organic molecules produced by autotrophic organisms are the source of food (materials and energy) for heterotrophic organisms; a typical example is a plant being eaten by an animal. This animal may in turn be eaten by another animal, and in this way energy is transferred through a series of organisms, each feeding on the preceding organism and providing raw materials and energy for the next organism. Such a sequence is called a **food chain**. Each stage of the food chain is known as a **trophic level** (*trophos*, feeding), the first trophic level being occupied by the autotrophic organisms, the so-called **primary producers**. The organisms of the second trophic level are usually called **primary consumers**, those of the third level are **secondary consumers**, and so on. There are usually four or five trophic levels, and seldom more than six for reasons stated in section 12.3.7 and obvious from fig 12.12. Further characteristics of each link in the chain are as follows, and the sequence is summarised in fig 12.4.

Primary producers

The primary producers are autotrophic organisms, and are mainly green plants and algae. Some prokaryotic organisms, namely a few bacteria (including blue-green bacteria), are also photosynthetic but their contribution is relatively small. Photosynthetic organisms transform solar energy (light energy) to chemical energy which is contained within the organic molecules that make up their tissues. A small contribution is also made by chemosynthetic bacteria which obtain their energy from inorganic compounds.

The major primary producers of aquatic ecosystems are algae, often minute unicellular algae that make up the phytoplankton of the surface layers of oceans and lakes. On land the major primary producers are the larger plants, namely angiosperms and conifers, which form forests and grasslands.

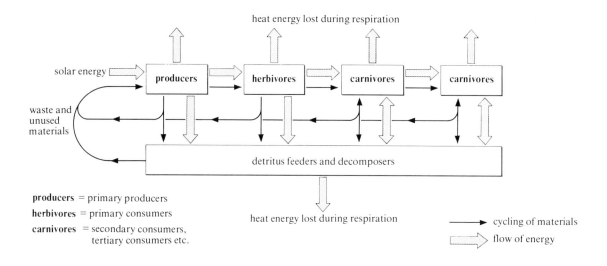

Fig 12.4 *Flow of energy and cycling of materials through a typical food chain. Note that a two-way exchange is possible between carnivores and detritus feeders/decomposers. The latter feed on dead carnivores; carnivores may eat living detritus feeders/decomposers*

Primary consumers

Primary consumers feed on primary producers and are therefore **herbivores**. On land, typical herbivores include insects as well as reptiles, birds and mammals. Two important groups of herbivorous mammals are rodents and ungulates. The latter are hoofed grazing animals such as horses, cattle and sheep that are adapted for running on the tips of their digits.

In aquatic ecosystems (freshwater and marine) the herbivores are typically small crustaceans and molluscs. Most of these organisms, such as water fleas, copepods, crab larvae, barnacles and bivalves (for example mussels and clams) are filter-feeders and extract the minute primary producers from the water as described in section 10.2.2. Together with protozoa, they make a large contribution to the zooplankton which feed on the phytoplankton. Life in the oceans and lakes is almost totally dependent on plankton since it is found at the beginning of virtually all food chains.

Primary consumers also include parasites (fungi, plants or animals) of plants.

Secondary and tertiary consumers

Secondary consumers feed on herbivores and are therefore carnivores. Tertiary consumers feed on secondary consumers and are also carnivores.

Secondary and tertiary consumers may be **predators**, which hunt, capture and kill their prey; **carrion feeders**, which feed on corpses; or **parasites**, in which case they are smaller than their hosts. Parasite food chains are excep-

tional and are included with pyramids of numbers in section 12.3.6 (see questions 12.4 and 12.5).

In a typical predator food chain the carnivores get larger at successive trophic levels:

plant (such as nectar)→fly→**spider**→**shrew**→**owl**

rosebush sap→aphid→**ladybird**→**spider**→**insectivorous bird**→**hawk**

In a typical parasite food chain the parasites get smaller at successive levels (questions 12.4 and 12.5). Some further examples of food chains are given below.

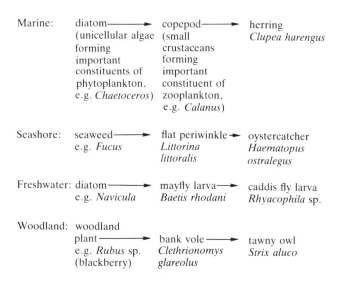

Decomposers and detritivores (detritus food chains)

Two basic types of food chain exist, namely grazing food chains and detritus food chains. The examples quoted so far are of **grazing food chains**, in which the first trophic level is occupied by a green plant (or alga), the second by a 'grazing' animal (herbivore) (the term grazing being used in a broad sense to include the eating of a plant by any animal), and subsequent levels by carnivores. When plants and animals die their bodies still contain energy and raw materials, as do the waste products such as urine and faeces which they deposit during lives. These organic materials are decomposed by micro-organisms, namely fungi and bacteria, which live saprotrophically on the remains. They are called **decomposers** and secrete digestive enzymes onto the dead or waste material, subsequently absorbing the products of digestion. The rate of decomposition varies with substrate and climate. The organic matter of animal urine, faeces and corpses is consumed within a matter of weeks, whereas fallen trees and branches may take many years to decompose. Essential to the breakdown of wood (and other plant material) is the action of fungi which produce cellulase, softening the wood and allowing small animals to penetrate and ingest material.

Decomposition is rapid in warm and moist environments, such as tropical rain forest, but takes place slowly in cool and/or dry conditions. The virtual absence of litter from the rain forest floor and the low content of humus in rain forest soils by comparison with the conspicuous litter layer and significant humus content of soils in temperate oakwoods or beechwoods illustrates this point. This has important implications for human use of these systems.

Fragments of decomposing material are called **detritus**, and many small animals feed on these, contributing to the process of breakdown. They are called **detritivores**. Because the combined activities of the true decomposers (fungi and bacteria) and detritivores (animals) lead to breakdown (decomposition) of materials, they are sometimes all referred to collectively as decomposers, although strictly the term decomposer relates to saprotrophic organisms.

Detritivores may in turn be fed upon by larger organisms, building up another type of food chain which can be regarded as starting with detritus. Thus:

detritus→detritivore→carnivore.

Some detritivores of woodland and seashore communities are shown in fig 12.5.

Two typical detritus food chains of woodlands are:

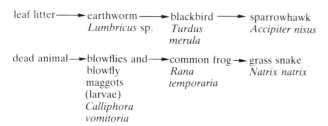

Fig 12.5 *Some woodland and seashore detritivores*

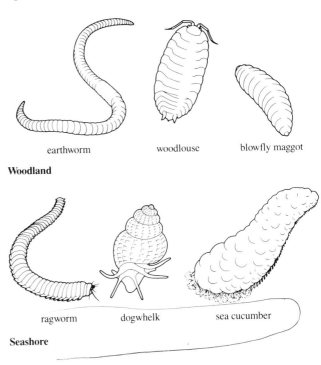

Some typical terrestrial detritivores are earthworms, woodlice, millipedes and the smaller (<0.5 mm) animals such as mites, springtails, nematode worms and enchytraeid worms. Methods for isolating and examining these are given in section 13.2.

12.3.5 Food webs

In food chains each organism is depicted as feeding on only one other type of organism. However, the feeding relationships within an ecosystem are more complex than this because each animal may feed on more than one organism in the same food chain, or may feed in different food chains. This is particularly true of carnivores at the higher trophic levels. Some animals, most notably humans, feed on plants, animals and fungi and are called **omnivores**. In reality then, the food chains interconnect in such a way as to produce a **food web**. Fig 12.6 illustrates woodland and freshwater food webs. Only some of the many possible interrelationships can be shown on such diagrams and it is usual to include only one or two carnivores at the highest level. Such diagrams illustrate the feeding relationships among organisms in an ecosystem and provide a basis for more quantitative studies of energy flow and exchange of material through the biotic component of ecosystems. This is discussed more fully in the next two sections.

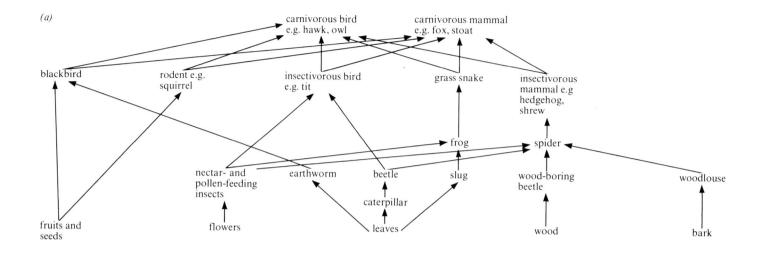

(a)

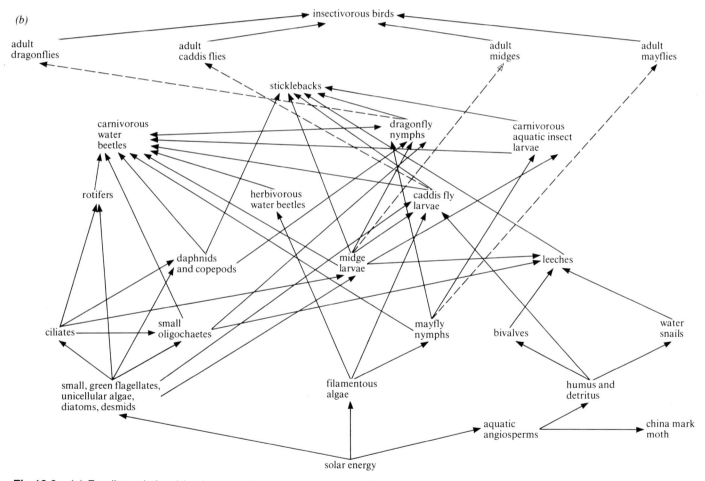

(b)

Fig 12.6 (a) Feeding relationships in a woodland, forming a food web. (b) Food web of a freshwater habitat (Based on Popham (1955) Some aspects of life in fresh water, Heinemann.)

12.3.6 Ecological pyramids

Feeding relationships and energy transfer through the biotic component of ecosystems may be quantified and shown diagrammatically as ecological pyramids. These give an apparently simple and fundamental basis for comparing different ecosystems, or even seasonal variation of pollution-induced change within a single system. However, ecologists working on the International Biological Programme (IBP), which aimed to gather data for quantitative comparison of all major world ecosystems during the decade 1964–74, have questioned the usefulness of pyramids as summaries of energy flow. One difficulty lies with deciding the trophic level of an organism. This and other problems will be considered later (see 'Criticism of ecological pyramids').

Pyramid of numbers

In a given area of ecosystem, small organisms usually outnumber large organisms. A pyramid of numbers of animals in different size classes can readily be constructed (fig 12.7a) (autotrophic organisms are omitted). This is the original basis of the pyramid of numbers as first proposed by Charles Elton in the 1920s. Elton also noted that typically predators are larger than their prey, and his original model based on *size* classes was therefore adapted by Lindeman to a trophic model, that is one based on the *feeding* levels of the organisms concerned irrespective of their size (figs 12.7b, c, d). Though theoretically this may seem a reasonable extension of Elton's ideas, in practice it is much more difficult to collect data for trophic levels than for size classes (see 'Criticism of ecological pyramids' later). Fig 12.7e shows how Elton's size-based and Lindeman's trophic models are related.

In a trophic-level based pyramid of numbers the organisms of a given area are first counted and then grouped into their trophic levels (as best one can). When this is done it is usually found that there is a progressive decrease in the number of animals at each successive level. Plants in the first trophic level also often outnumber animals at the second trophic level, though this will depend on the relative sizes of organisms, such as a tree compared with phytoplankton. A *pyramid* of numbers typically results.

For diagrammatic purposes the number of organisms in a given trophic level can be represented as a rectangle whose length (or area) is proportional to the number of organisms in a given area (or volume if aquatic). Figs 12.7b, c and d illustrate three types of naturally occurring pyramids of numbers. The carnivores in the highest trophic level are known as the **top carnivores**.

12.3 In pyramid (b) (fig 12.7) the primary producers (plants) are small in size and outnumber the herbivores. Describe and explain the difference in pyramid (c) compared with (b).

12.4 *Leptomonas* is a parasitic flagellate protozoan, thousands of which may be found in a single flea. Construct a pyramid of numbers based on the following food chain:

grass→herbivorous mammal→flea→*Leptomonas*

12.5 Give a possible explanation of the difference between pyramids (b) and (d) in fig 12.7.

Although the data needed to construct pyramids of numbers may be relatively easy to collect by straightforward sampling techniques, there are a number of complications associated with their use. Three important problems are as follows.
(1) Deciding to which trophic level an organism belongs.
(2) The producers vary greatly in size, but a single grass plant or alga, for example, is given the same status as a single tree. This explains why a true pyramid shape is often not obtained. Also parasitic food chains may give inverted pyramids (see questions 12.3–12.5).
(3) The range of numbers is so great that it is often difficult to draw the pyramids to scale, although logarithmic scales may be used.

Pyramid of biomass

The disadvantages of using pyramids of numbers can be overcome by using a **pyramid of biomass** in which the total mass of the organisms (**biomass**) is estimated for each trophic level. Such estimates involve weighing representative individuals, as well as recording numbers, and so are more laborious and expensive in terms of time and equipment. Ideally, dry masses should be compared. These can either be estimated from wet masses or can be determined by destructive methods (experiment 13.1). The rectangles used in constructing the pyramid then represent the masses of organisms at each trophic level per unit area or volume. Fig 12.8a shows a typical pyramid of biomass in which biomass decreases at each trophic level.

The biomass at the time of sampling, in other words at a given moment in time, is known as the **standing biomass** or **standing crop biomass**. It is important to realise that this figure gives no indication of the *rate* of production (**productivity**) or consumption of biomass. This can be misleading in two ways.
(1) If the rate of consumption (loss through being used as food) more or less equals the rate of production, the standing crop does not necessarily give any indication of productivity, that is the amounts of material and energy passing from one trophic level to the next in a given time period such as one year. For example, a fertile, intensively grazed pasture may have a smaller standing crop of grass, but a higher productivity, than a less fertile and ungrazed pasture.

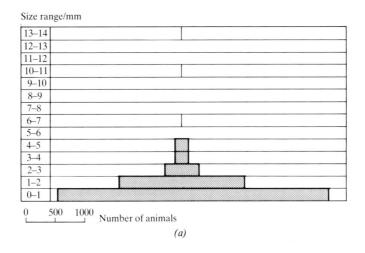

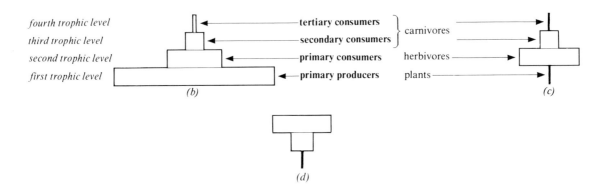

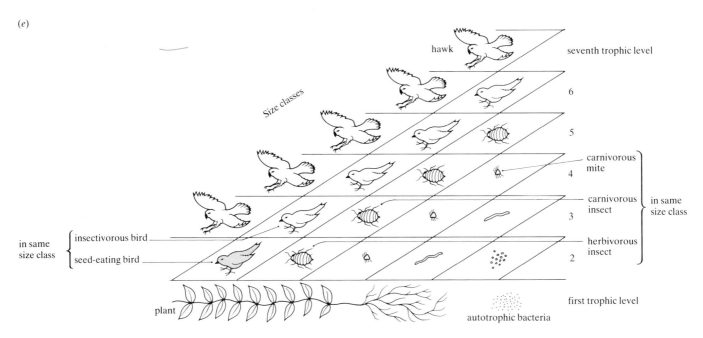

Fig 12.7 (a) *An Eltonian pyramid of numbers based on size class, in this case for animals on the floor of a forest in Panama. (From S. Cousins,* New Scientist, *4.7.85, p. 51). Elton noted that predators are typically larger than their prey, but the size difference is never so great that prey are too small to see and handle easily or too big to catch and eat without difficulty. In short, the size of prey is 'about right' for the predator. Two common types of pyramids of number, (b) and (c), and an inverted pyramid (d). These are explained in the text. (e) The Lindeman and Elton models, rearranged so that they relate to one another: a hawk feeds at five trophic levels. Organisms in the same trophic level are in the same horizontal row. Size classes are arranged diagonally and omit autotrophic organisms. Note that trophic levels usually contain organisms of a variety of sizes, and that the hawk, for example, should be divided between trophic levels 3 to 7.*

(a) old field, Georgia USA

(b) English Channel

Fig 12.8 (above) *Pyramids of biomass. Type (a) is the more common. Type (b) is an inverted pyramid (see text). Figures represent g dry mass m⁻². (From E. P. Odum (1971)* Fundamentals of ecology, *3rd ed., W. B. Saunders.)*

Fig 12.9 (above) *Seasonal changes in pyramids of biomass for an Italian lake. Figures represent mg dry mass m⁻³. (From E. P. Odum (1971)* Fundamentals of ecology, *3rd ed., W. B. Saunders.)*

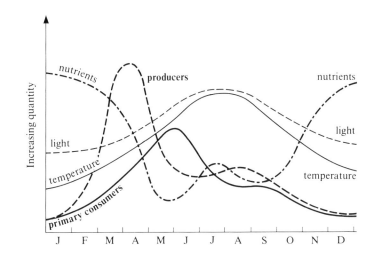

Fig 12.10 (right) *Changes in standing crop biomass of producers and primary consumers and in certain environmental variables in a lake during one year. (From M. A. Tribe, M. R. Erant & R. K. Snook (1974)* Ecological principles, Basic Biology Course 4, *Cambridge University Press.)*

(2) If the producers are small, such as algae, they have a high turnover rate, that is a high rate of growth and reproduction balanced by a high rate of consumption or death. Thus, although the standing crop may be small compared with large producers such as trees, the productivity may be the same, trees accumulating their biomass over a long time period. Put another way, an amount of phytoplankton with the same productivity as a tree would have a much smaller biomass than a tree, even though it could support the same amount of animal life. In general, the larger, longer-lived plants and animals have lower 'turnover rates' than the smaller, shorter-lived plants or algae and animals, and accumulate materials and energy over a longer time period. One possible consequence of this is shown in fig 12.8*b*, where an inverted pyramid of biomass is illustrated for an English Channel community. The zooplankton is shown to have a higher biomass than the phytoplankton on which it feeds. This is characteristic of ocean and lake planktonic communities at certain times of year;

phytoplankton biomass exceeds zooplankton biomass during the spring 'bloom', but at other times the reverse might be true. Such apparent anomalies are avoided by using pyramids of energy as described below.

Equally, these differences may highlight useful information. For example, persistence of an algal bloom and a broad-based biomass pyramid in an aquatic ecosystem may indicate the onset of eutrophication (a form of water pollution discussed more fully in section 12.4.1). Similarly, the frequent inversion of marine pyramids suggests that for these systems harvesting plant or algal rather than animal biomass is not the sensible strategy it appears to be for many terrestrial ecosystems.

12.6 Consider the two pyramids of biomass shown in fig 12.9. They represent plankton in an Italian lake at two different times of year, spring and winter. Account for the inversion of the pyramid during the year.

Pyramid of energy

The most fundamental and ideal way of representing relationships between organisms in different trophic levels is by means of a pyramid of energy. This has a number of advantages.

(1) It takes into account the *rate* of production, in contrast to pyramids of numbers and biomass which depict the standing states of organisms at a particular moment in time. Each bar of a pyramid of energy represents the amount of energy per unit area or volume that flows through that trophic level in a given time period. Fig 12.11 shows a pyramid of energy for an aquatic ecosystem. Note that the units used are for energy flow.

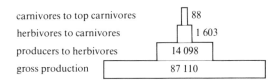

carnivores to top carnivores	88
herbivores to carnivores	1 603
producers to herbivores	14 098
gross production	87 110

Fig 12.11 *Pyramid of energy for Silver Springs, Florida. Figures represent energy flow in kJ m⁻² yr⁻¹. (From E. P. Odum (1971) Fundamentals of ecology, 3rd ed., W. B. Saunders.)*

(2) Weight for weight, two species do not necessarily have the same energy content, as table 12.1 indicates. Comparisons based on biomass may therefore be misleading.

(3) Apart from allowing different ecosystems to be compared, the relative importance of populations within one ecosystem can be compared and inverted pyramids are not obtained. This is illustrated by table 12.2, where energy flow (energy output) through primary consumers of different biomass is compared. Note, for example, that the great importance of soil bacteria in terms of energy flow is not obvious from their small biomass.

(4) Input of solar energy can be added as an extra rectangle at the base of a pyramid of energy.

Although pyramids of energy are sometimes considered the most useful of the three types of ecological pyramid, they are the most difficult to obtain data for because they require even more measurements than pyramids of

Table 12.2 Density, biomass and energy flow of five primary consumer populations.

	Approximate density (no. m⁻²)	Biomass (g m⁻²)	Energy flow (kJ m⁻² day⁻¹)
Soil bacteria	10^{12}	0.001	4.2
Marine copepods (*Acartia*)	10^5	2.0	10.5
Intertidal snails (*Littorina*)	200	10.0	4.2
Salt marsh grasshoppers (*Orchelimum*)	10	1.0	1.7
Meadow mice (*Microtus*)	10^{-2}	0.6	2.9
Deer (*Odocoileus*)	10^{-5}	1.1	2.1

From Odum, E. P. (1971).

biomass. One extra piece of information needed is the energy values for given masses of organisms. This requires combustion of representative samples. In practice, pyramids of biomass can sometimes be converted to pyramids of energy with reasonable accuracy, based on previous experiments.

Criticisms of ecological pyramids

The pyramids of numbers, biomass and energy described depend on assigning living organisms to trophic levels. While the correct level is obvious for plants and obligate herbivores, many carnivores and omnivores eat a varied diet and thus their trophic level varies according to the food selected, which may in turn be an animal with a range of possible trophic levels. This point is clear from the discussion of food webs and from figs 12.6*a* and *b*.

From question 12.9 the problem of assigning a hawk to a particular trophic level is self-evident. Even if its typical diet was studied, one would still need to know the feeding histories of the prey organisms. Thus, even for the hawk alone, a great deal of fieldwork would be needed; on an ecosystem basis one can only resort to very approximate generalisations.

Another major problem is where to place dead and waste material. Such material is ecologically important as a food source. For example, it is estimated that up to 80% of the energy fixed by terrestrial plants enters decay pathways rather than being passed on to herbivores, yet it is hard to fit dead material (detritus) and its consumers into conventional pyramids. One solution is to regard dead material as a new trophic level 1, and to split the ecosystem into a herbivore pathway and a detritus pathway.

These and other problems mean that our ideas about ecological pyramids are currently subject to radical reappraisal, and this should be borne in mind when studying pyramids of numbers, biomass and energy.

Computer program. PYRAMID and ECO-SPACE: A double package. PYRAMID allows population numbers, biomass or energy to be plotted for different trophic levels in the traditional bar format, but the bars expand and contract as the user steps through the changing seasons for selected ecosystems. ECOSPACE allows the concept of the ecological niche to be visualised.

12.3.7 Efficiency of energy transfer: production ecology

The study of productivity is known as production ecology, and involves the study of energy flow through ecosystems.

Energy enters the biotic component of the ecosystem through the primary producers, and the rate at which this energy is stored by them in the form of organic substances which can be used as food materials is known as **primary productivity**. This is an important parameter to measure as it determines the total energy flow through the biotic component of the ecosystem, and hence the amount (biomass) of life which the ecosystem can support.

12.10 In considering the primary productivity of an ecosystem, which groups of organisms other than plants make a contribution?

As mentioned in section 12.3.3, the amount of the Sun's radiation intercepted by Earth's surface varies with latitude and with details of location such as aspect and altitude. The amount intercepted by plants also varies with light quality and the organisation and amount of vegetation cover. In Britain, incident radiation on plants averages about 1×10^6 kJ m^{-2} yr^{-1}. Of this, as much as 95–99% is immediately lost from the plant by reflection, radiation or heat of evaporation. The remaining 1–5% of incoming radiation is absorbed by the chlorophyll and used in the production of organic molecules. The rate at which this chemical energy is stored by plants is known as **gross primary productivity** (**GPP**). Between 20–50% of the GPP is used by the plant in simultaneous respiration and photorespiration, leaving a net gain known as the **net primary productivity** (**NPP**) which is stored in the plant. It is this energy which is potentially available to the next trophic level.

In the example given in fig 12.12 NPP is given as 8 000 kJ m^{-2} yr^{-1}, or 0.8% of received radiation (1% of absorbed radiation and 80% of the GPP). All these figures are on an annual basis, productivity being higher in the summer and lower during winter.

When herbivores and carnivores consume other organisms, food (materials and energy) is thereby transferred from one trophic level to the next. Some of the food remains undigested and is lost immediately in the process of egestion. For animals with alimentary canals this is usually in the form of faeces. Collectively, egested substances are known as **egesta**. They contain energy, as do

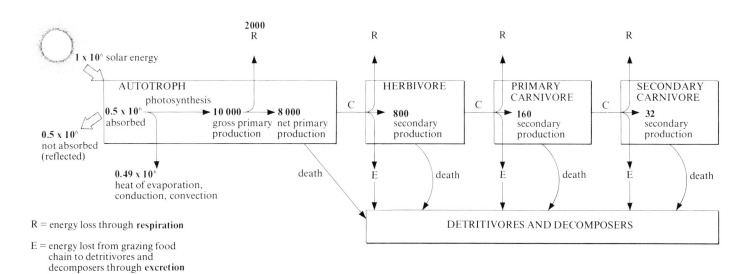

R = energy loss through **respiration**

E = energy lost from grazing food chain to detritivores and decomposers through **excretion** (e.g. urine) and **egestion** (e.g. faeces)

C = **consumption** by organisms at the higher trophic level

all energy values given in kilojoules (kJ)

Fig 12.12 *Energy flow through a grazing food chain, such as a grazed pasture. Figures represent kJ m^{-2} yr^{-1}*

373

organic excretory products (**excreta**) such as urea. Excreta are products of the animal's own metabolism, unlike egesta. Animals, like plants, also lose energy as a result of respiration. The energy remaining in heterotrophs after losses through egestion, excretion and respiration is available for production, that is growth, repair and reproduction.

Production by heterotrophs is called **secondary production** (whatever the trophic level). The following word equation summarises the fate of energy consumed by an animal:

food consumed = growth + respiration + egesta + excreta

Some of these terms can be measured easily in domestic animals or in laboratory studies of wild animals. Growth is measured as increase in biomass, or better as increase in energy value of the body, with time. Faeces and excreta can be collected, weighed and subtracted from the mass of food consumed to determine food retained and used for growth and respiration.

Measurement of productivity

As a result of photosynthesis, there is an increase in dry mass. The **relative growth rate** (R) is defined as the gain in mass per unit of plant mass in unit time.

$$R = \frac{\text{increase in dry mass in unit time}}{\text{dry mass of plant}}$$

The increase in dry mass in unit time is equal to

$$\frac{W_t - W_0}{t}$$

where W_t is the dry mass after time t and W_0 is the dry mass at the start of the time period.

The **net assimilation rate** (NAR, also called unit leaf rate) relates increase in dry mass to leaf area.

$$\text{NAR} = \frac{\text{increase in dry mass in unit time}}{\text{leaf area}}$$

Note that the increase in dry mass is equal to the difference between the real rate of photosynthesis minus the losses in dry mass due to respiration.

Measured rate (or apparent = true rate − respiratory losses rate of photosynthesis)

Biomass is the total dry mass of all organisms in an ecosystem.

Total biomass	=	biomass of primary producers	+	biomass of consumers	+	biomass of decomposers	+	biomass of dead organisms

Even though it is difficult to measure biomass accurately, biomass provides a useful comparison between different land areas or ecosystems.

Not all the organic material produced by a crop is suitable for commercial sale. For example, in cereals the aim is to produce maximum yield of grain and the remainder of the plant is not of general economic importance (although some straw will be used for the bedding of animals). The **harvestable dry matter**, as the name suggests, is the dry mass of the crop useful for commercial exploitation. It may therefore be advantageous to alter the distribution of the newly synthesised carbohydrate in the plant, more being directed to storage organs. The **harvest index** represents the economic yield compared with total yields. Indolyl acetic acid (IAA) has been shown to increase the movement of synthesised materials into storage tissue. Further, a reduced oxygen level retards reproductive growth and deflects carbohydrates into storage regions, that is economically important regions.

Solar radiation is intercepted by the leaves. In a tropical rain forest the tree canopy will be very dense, but in other situations the available leaf area for absorption of light may be quite small and most light falls on the base soil.

The **leaf area index** is a measure of the leaf area per unit of ground area, that is plants with a large index will absorb most of the light. The index for clover plants has been cited as around 33%, that for *Holium regidum* (a grass) around 16%.

Fig 12.12 shows clearly that energy is lost at every stage in the food chain and the length of the food chain is obviously limited by the extent of these losses. The proportion of energy lost in the first transfer of energy from solar energy received to net primary production is high. Subsequent transfers are at least ten times more efficient than this initial transfer. The average efficiency of transfer from plants to herbivores is about 10% and from animal to animal is about 20%. In general, herbivores make less efficient use of their food than do carnivores because plants contain a high proportion of cellulose and sometimes wood (which contains cellulose and lignin) which are relatively indigestible and therefore unavailable as energy sources for most herbivores.

Energy lost in respiration cannot be transferred to other living organisms. However, the energy lost from a food chain in the form of excreta and egesta is not lost to the ecosystem because it is transferred to detritivores and decomposers. Similarly, any dead organisms, fallen leaves, twigs and branches and so on will start detritus and decomposer food chains. The proportion of net primary production flowing directly into detritus and decomposer food chains varies from one system to another. In a forest ecosystem most of the primary production enters the detrital rather than the grazing pathway with the result that the litter and humus on the forest floor is the centre of much of the consumer activity, even though the organisms involved are mostly inconspicuous. However, in an ocean ecosystem or an intensively grazed pasture more than half the net primary production may enter the grazing food chain.

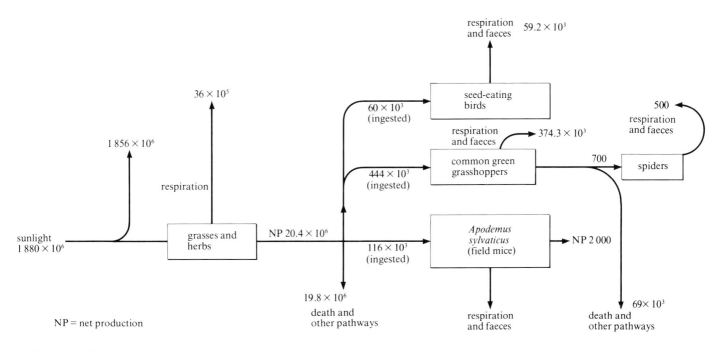

Fig 12.13 *Movement of energy through a small portion of grassland ecosystem. Figures are given in kJ m^{-2} yr^{-1}. (From M. R. Tribe* et al. *(1974)* Ecological principles, *Basic Biology Course 4, Cambridge University Press.)*

12.11 Fig. 12.13 shows the energy flow through a small portion of a grassland ecosystem. The figures are given in kJm^{-2} yr^{-1}.
(a) What is the gross primary production of grasses and herbs?
(b) What is the photosynthetic efficiency (that is the efficiency of conversion of incident solar energy to gross primary production)?
(c) What is the net production of the seed-eating birds, spiders and common green grasshoppers respectively?
(d) How much energy is lost via respiration and faeces by field mice?
(e) Which of the organisms are producers, primary consumers and secondary consumers?
(f) Which of the organisms are heterotrophic?
(g) What are the 'other pathways' likely to be? (Name three.)
(Modified from Tribe, M. A. *et al.* (1975) *Ecological Principles*, CUP).

Detrital pathways are often complex and are less well understood than the conventionally described grazing pathways. Nevertheless they are just as important and, in terms of energy flow, frequently more important than grazing pathways. Globally, 80% of the NPP enters the detrital pathway. Most intensive agricultural systems ignore the potential value of detritus-based food production.

The figures quoted in this section have been on an annual basis. If the ecosystem is stable and not increasing overall in biomass, the total biomass at the end of the year will be the same as at the beginning. All the energy that went into primary production will then have passed through the various trophic levels and none retained as net production. Normally, however, a system will be in a process of change. A young forest, for example, would retain some of the energy input in the form of increased biomass at the end of the year. A year is a useful period over which to express productivity because it takes into account seasonal variations where these exist. For example, primary productivity is usually greater in the part of the year when new plant or algal growth commences and secondary production increases later.

One of the reasons for studying energy flow through ecosystems is that it has important implications for the way in which humans obtain their own food and energy requirements. It opens the way to analysing traditional systems of agriculture for their efficiency, and suggests where improvements can be made. Since energy is lost at each trophic level, it is clear that, for omnivores like humans, eating plants is a more efficient way of extracting energy from a system (table 12.3). However, in suggesting improved methods for providing food, other factors must be considered. For example, animal protein is generally a better source of the essential amino acids, though some pulse crops, such as soya bean, are richer sources than most plants. Also animal protein is more easily digested, since the tough plant cell walls must first be broken down before

Table 12.3 Outputs of agricultural food chains in UK.

Food chain		Example	Energy yield of food to humans (kJ × 10³ ha⁻¹)	Protein yield of food to humans (kg ha⁻¹ yr⁻¹)
(a) Cultivated plant crop→humans		Monocultures of wheat and barley	7 800–11 000	42
(b) Cultivated plant crop→ livestock→humans		Barley-fed beef and bacon pigs	745–1 423	10–15
(c) Intensive grassland→ livestock→humans		Intensive beef herd on carefully managed pasture		
	Meat		339	4
	Milk		3 813	46
(d) Grassland and crops→ livestock→humans		Mixed dairy farm		
	Milk		1 356	17

Data from Duckham, A. N. & Mansfield, G. B. (1970) *Farming Systems of The World*, Chatto and Windus.

the plant protein is released. Finally, there are many ecosystems where animals can concentrate food from large areas where it would be difficult to grow or harvest plant crops. Examples are grazing on poor quality pasture land, such as by sheep in Britain, reindeer in Scotland and Scandinavia and eland in East Africa, or taking fish from aquatic ecosystems.

Rational cropping of ecosystems

Cropping is the removal of any organism from an ecosystem for food, whether plant or animal. Rational cropping is using the ecosystem to produce food in the most efficient way. This may mean increasing the productivity of the crop and decreasing the effects of disease and predation by other animals, or by using a crop which is better adapted to conditions in the ecosystem.

Increasing productivity of plant crops may be achieved by adding fertilisers to the soil, and by adding water to the soil by irrigation or removing excess water by drainage, as necessary. Disadvantages of carrying out these processes are that, over a long period of time, the use of man-made fertilisers can lead to deterioration of the soil structure (section 12.5.1), which will eventually lead to a decrease in productivity, and addition of fertilisers or water is often energy-expensive.

Decreasing the effects of predation, generally insects and birds in the case of plant crops, and disease is usually carried out by the selection of resistant genetic strains of the crop or the use of chemicals to kill the pest or disease-producing organisms. Using such chemicals must be done with care; persistent chemicals, those not rapidly broken down in the ecosystem, may have disastrous effects on other trophic levels (sections 12.3.8 and 12.8.9), and effective pesticides used too frequently may bring about outbreaks of resistant strains of the pest which are more difficult to control, as in the attempts to control aphids on chrysanthemums and early season pests on cotton.

The use of C_4 plants, such as sugarcane and maize, rather than C_3 plants in conditions of relatively high light intensity and temperature is an example of using crops better suited to the environment. In these conditions C_4 plants photosynthesise more efficiently, and therefore have a higher productivity, than C_3 plants (section 9.8.2). A further example is the possible use of wild ungulates rather than domestic livestock as the 'crop' in East Africa. The wild ungulates, such as eland, have a greater year-long biomass ($82.2–117.5 \times 10^5$ kg ha⁻¹ compared with $13.2–37.6 \times 10^5$ kg ha⁻¹ for domestic livestock and cattle) as they are more efficient at digesting and assimilating nutrients from poor quality herbage, which is particularly important during the dry season in the savanna, and possibly also because they have a higher resistance to diseases which occur in the area.

An important concept in the management of animal 'crops' which take several years to reach sexual maturity is that of **maximum sustainable yield**. This is discussed more fully in section 12.7.7.

12.3.8 Concentration effects in food chains

Since the Second World War there has been a dramatic increase in the number of man-made chemicals released into the environment. These include herbicides and pesticides designed to kill those organisms, particularly weeds and insects, that are harmful to crops, livestock and humans themselves. Among the first of the successful pesticides was a group of chlorinated hydrocarbons (organochlorines) which included DDT (dichlorodiphenyltrichloroethane), dieldrin and aldrin. These chemicals are toxic to a broad spectrum of animal species, including humans, although birds, fish and non-vertebrates are worst affected. To the surprise of many scientists, it was reported in the mid-1960s that DDT had been detected in the livers of penguins in the Antarctic, a habitat very remote from areas where DDT might have been used.

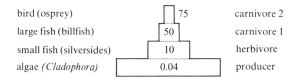

bird (osprey)	75	carnivore 2
large fish (billfish)	50	carnivore 1
small fish (silversides)	10	herbivore
algae (*Cladophora*)	0.04	producer

Fig 12.14 *Biomass and amounts of DDT at different trophic levels in a food chain. Figures represent amounts of DDT in parts per million (ppm)*

12.12 Fig 12.14 shows the amount of DDT at different levels in a food chain, the data for which were collected in the USA.

(a) If the concentration of DDT in the water surrounding the algae was 0.02 ppm, what was the final concentration factor for DDT in passing **from water** into (i) primary producers, (ii) small fish, (iii) large fish, (iv) the top carnivore.

(b) What conclusions can you draw from your answer to (a)?

(c) At which trophic level (i) is DDT likely to have the most marked effect, (ii) would DDT be most easily detected, (iii) are insect pests of crops found (a typical target of DDT)?

(d) Suggest ways in which the penguins might have come to contain DDT.

(e) Clear Lake, California, is a large lake used for recreational activities such as fishing. Disturbance of the natural ecosystem by eutrophication (nutrient enrichment, see sections 3.2.7 and 12.4) led to increased populations of midges during the 1940s and these were treated by spraying with DDD, a close relative of DDT, in 1949, 1954 and 1957. The first and second applications killed about 99% of the midges but they recovered quickly and the third application had little effect on the population.

Analysis of small fish from the lake showed levels of 1–200 ppm of DDD in the flesh eaten by humans, and 40–2 500 ppm in fatty tissues. A population of 1 000 western grebes that bred at the lake died out and levels of 1 600 ppm of DDD were found in their fatty tissues.

(i) Suggest a reason why the DDD did not succeed in eradicating the midges and why they recovered so quickly after the third application.

(ii) It has been observed that many animals die from DDT poisoning in times of food shortage. Suggest a reason for this based on the data given so far.

(f) In Great Britain, the winters of 1946–7 and 1962–3 were particularly severe. The death toll of birds was high in both winters, but much higher in 1962–3. Suggest a possible reason for this in the light of the data given about DDT.

Pesticide poisoning has had devastating effects on some top carnivores, most notably birds. The peregrine falcon, for example, has disappeared completely from the eastern USA as a result of DDT poisoning. Birds are especially vulnerable because DDT induces hormonal changes that effect calcium metabolism and result in the production of thinner egg shells with a consequently high loss of eggs through breakage. Levels of DDT in human body fat are 12–16 ppm in the USA, where the upper legal limit of DDT content for sale of food is 7 ppm.

In more recent years, some powerful but non-persistent pesticides have been developed, such as organophosphates (for example malathion), and the use of DDT has been severely reduced. However, DDT is relatively cheap to produce and continues to be more suitable for certain tasks, such as malaria control. When considering whether to use pesticides it is often a case of choosing the lesser of two evils. DDT has completely eradicated malaria in many parts of the world. In Mauritius, for example, although the birth rate has not changed significantly since 1900, a population explosion has occurred because far fewer babies are dying from malaria. Infant mortality fell from 150 per 1 000 to 50 per 1 000 in 10 years as a result of post-war spraying with DDT.

12.13 In trying to develop a new pesticide what properties would you ideally want it to have?

12.4 Biogeochemical cycles – the cycling of matter

Biogeochemical cycling is the second major function of ecosystems (along with energy flow). Each cycle summarises the movement of chemical elements through the living component of the ecosystem, namely the build-up in food chains of complex organic molecules incorporating the element and the breakdown in decomposition to simpler organic and subsequently inorganic forms which can be used again to make the living material of living organisms. As well as this actively cycling pool of an element, all cycles have a larger reservoir pool. Exchanges between the reservoir and active cycling pools are typically limited and often slow processes, for example the chemical weathering of phosphate rock, and fixation by lightning of nitrogen into nitrates during thunderstorms.

Cycles can be recognised for all chemical elements that occur in living systems. The biogeochemical cycles for carbon (C), nitrogen (N), sulphur (S) and phosphorus (P), four important macronutrients, were summarised diagrammatically in figs 9.2 and 9.31–33. These cycle diagrams, section 9.11 and table 9.10, which deal with mineral nutrition, should be referred to when reading this section (see also fig 12.15).

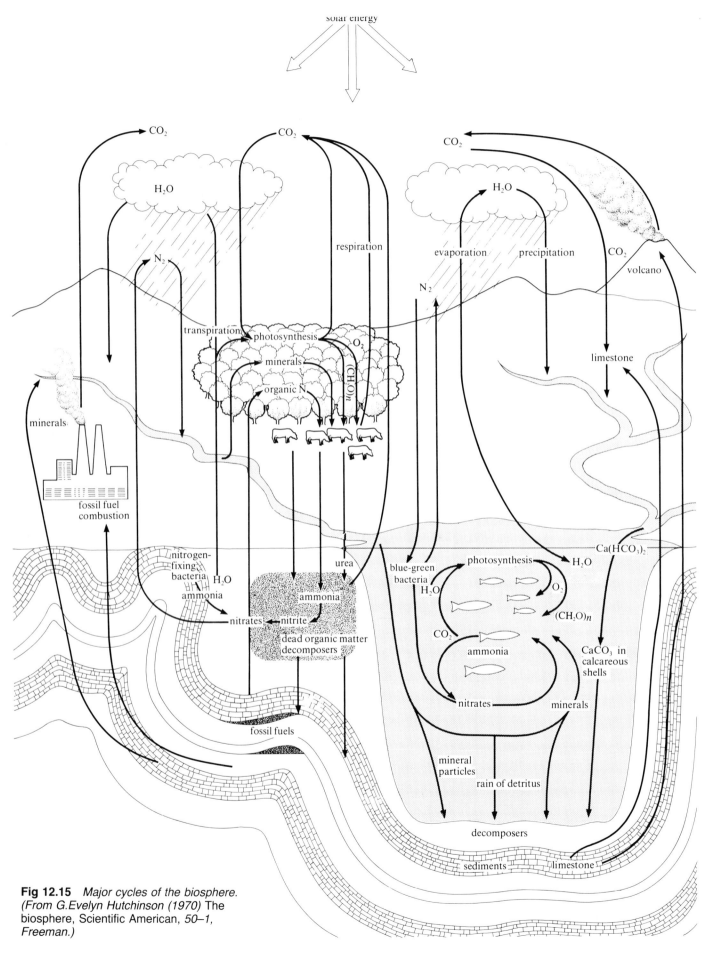

Fig 12.15 *Major cycles of the biosphere. (From G.Evelyn Hutchinson (1970) The biosphere, Scientific American, 50–1, Freeman.)*

Humans require as many as 40 different elements for their biological well-being. Furthermore, the highly technological culture of modern human societies makes demands on virtually all other elements and many new synthetic substances. Some of these have become incorporated into living organisms and their potential for, and rate of, breakdown and recycling is an important contemporary concern. An understanding of biogeochemical cycling and maintenance of effective cycling is thus important for human society. Human activity generally speeds movement of material through the cycles and may fundamentally upset the balance of cycles. This may lead to build-up of material at one point in the cycle, in other words, **pollution**. Typically build-up occurs when more of an element (or new synthetic substance) is injected into one stage of a cycle than can be removed by the natural counterbalancing removal mechanisms. An obvious and topical example is the build-up of carbon as carbon dioxide in the atmosphere. This is discussed more fully in section 12.4.1.

As pointed out, all biogeochemical cycles have an active or cycling pool and a reservoir pool of an element. Reservoirs may be broadly divided into **sedimentary reservoirs**, as for phosphorus, and **fluid reservoirs**, the latter including both the oceans and the atmosphere, which displays some of the properties of fluids. Examples of elements with fluid reservoirs are nitrogen (atmosphere), and carbon with both atmospheric and oceanic reservoirs. Hydrogen, an important macronutrient not previously discussed, cycles in the water cycle (**hydrological cycle**) (fig 12.16). This cycle interacts in an important and complex way with the global energy budget because it plays a role in weather systems and is a gas which is important in the greenhouse effect (section 12.4.1).

Transfers in cycles are termed **fluxes**. These are measured as the quantity of nutrient exchanged per unit time per unit area or volume. On a global scale such measurement is difficult and our knowledge of the quantities of nutrients in different parts of cycles is, at best, only very approximate. Some of the more reliable estimates come from designed and accidental experiments using radioactive tracers (for example from nuclear weapons testing and from leaks and accidents at nuclear power plants such as Sellafield, Three Mile Island and Chernobyl). A useful and related idea is **turnover rate**. Turnover rate measures the flux to and from a particular pool in relation to the quantity of nutrient held in that pool. For example, if fixation of carbon as a result of photosynthesis took place in a field at the rate of 2 g of carbon m^{-2} day^{-1}, this would be termed the flux of carbon. If there were 200 g of carbon m^{-2} of field, the turnover rate of carbon would be $2/200 = 0.01$ (the **turnover time** would be 100 days).

Human-induced turnover rate measures the additional rate of movement to or from a major reservoir due to human activity. In some cases human-induced turnover exceeds the natural turnover rate. The human-induced turnover rates for copper, zinc, lead and phosphorus are all more than ten times the natural rate. The chief concern with high human-induced turnover rates lies with the biologically active elements, such as lead, which is readily ingested and stored in the body and which is thought to affect behaviour and learning as well as being directly toxic in larger quantities. In the case of phosphorus the rate of loss of this important macronutrient from the exchange pool to the deep sea sedimentary reservoir (from which there is no practicable prospect of recovery on a human time scale) exceeds gains from natural weathering and new

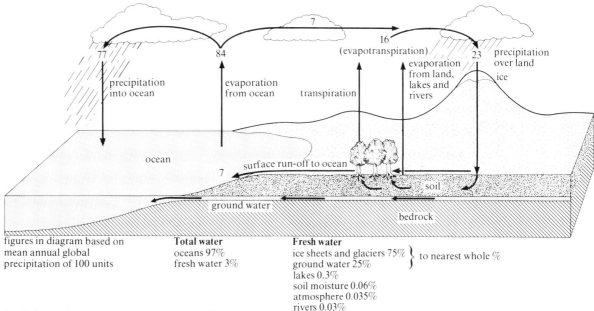

figures in diagram based on mean annual global precipitation of 100 units

Total water
oceans 97%
fresh water 3%

Fresh water
ice sheets and glaciers 75%
ground water 25% } to nearest whole %
lakes 0.3%
soil moisture 0.06%
atmosphere 0.035%
rivers 0.03%

Fig 12.16 *The hydrological cycle and water storage. (Based on R.J. Chorley & P. Haggett (eds.) (1967) Physical and information models in geography, Methuen.)*

deposition in guano deposits. Furthermore, rock phosphate in a form readily recoverable in current technological and economic frameworks is limited. Future supplies depend substantially on recovery and recycling from dead material and sewage. This would simultaneously help to prevent phosphate enrichment of waters, which is a major cause of accelerated eutrophication in aquatic ecosystems (see section 12.4.1) and reduce permanent losses to deep sediments.

In general, cycles such as the nitrogen and carbon cycles with large numbers of negative feedback mechanisms, that is actions which tend to favour maintenance of the status quo, are considered more stable than those with fewer negative feedback mechanisms such as the phosphorus cycle. Unfortunately, it is often easier to understand the simpler cycles and to predict the likely effects of human activity. The cycles of the individual elements are not isolated but tend to interact, another factor that makes accurate prediction very difficult. In a classic experiment at Hubbard Brook,* the effects of land-use change on biogeochemical cycling in small water-shed ecosystems were monitored. After several years measuring the undisturbed systems the woodland cover of one small catchment was felled and the area treated with herbicide to prevent 'weed' growth before planting with commercial timber species. Since renewed plant growth was suppressed, exchange of soil nitrogen in the ammonium form with new plants (refer to fig 9.31) was prevented and breakdown to nitrite and nitrates took place more rapidly than in the undisturbed system. The process released hydrogen ions to the soil (H^+) which in turn displaced important cations (positively charged ions) from the soil. High levels of sodium, potassium and subsequently calcium and magnesium occurred in waters draining from the disturbed catchment, resulting in less fertile soil. This important study highlights the value of a continued vegetation cover, even 'weeds', in maintaining soil fertility.

12.4.1 Disrupted cycles and pollution

The carbon cycle – carbon dioxide and the planetary greenhouse effect

The main exchange pathways in the carbon cycle were summarised in fig 9.2. The additional human-induced turnover is estimated at 5×10^{12} kg yr^{-1} released by human use of fossil fuels. Some scientists think that forest clearance is an equally important source of additional atmospheric carbon dioxide and that the total annual rate of human-induced release to the atmosphere may be nearer 10×10^{12} kg yr^{-1}.

*F.H. Bormann & G.E. Likens (1967) 'Nutrient cycling', *Science*, **155**, 424–9.

12.14 How does deforestation increase atmospheric carbon dioxide?

Carbon dioxide is normally present in the lower atmosphere, the troposphere, in very small amounts, about 300 ppm or 0.03% by volume (see fig 12.17). Its importance lies in its contribution to the planetary greenhouse effect. Carbon dioxide is transparent to incoming short-wave radiation from the Sun, but absorbs strongly the long-wave radiation which the Earth typically re-radiates into Space. It therefore 'traps' outgoing radiation, warming the lower atmosphere which in turn radiates energy back to the surface (as well as losing some in upward and lateral radiation). Ultimately, of course, any given 'package' of incoming energy will eventually be dissipated and lost to Space, but the atmosphere–surface exchanges induced by

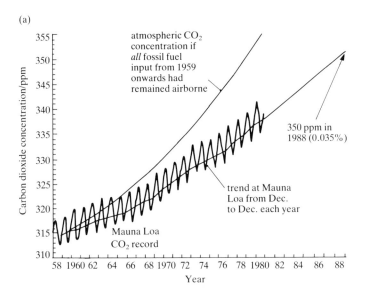

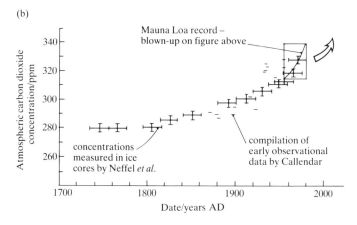

Fig 12.17 *Changes in atmospheric carbon dioxide concentrations since the year 1700: (a) 1958 to 1982 with projection to known level of 1988; (b) 1700 to 2000 (prediction). (From A. Crane & P. Liss (1985) New Scientist 21.11.85.)*

the presence of carbon dioxide (and other near-surface greenhouse gases) are sufficient to raise planetary surface temperatures about 40 °C above those that would otherwise occur. It is important to realise that without this basic greenhouse effect, which has varied little for millions of years, living systems as we know them would not exist. The contemporary concern lies with the clear evidence that carbon dioxide levels (and those of other greenhouse gases, notably carbon monoxide, methane and chlorofluorocarbons (CFCs)), are rising at a rate unprecedented in recent Earth history and their increased presence will logically favour an increasingly warmer surface environment (see fig 12.18). This may in turn lead to increased evaporation and a greater atmospheric water vapour content. Since water vapour also acts as a powerful long-wave absorber, this may further increase surface temperatures. The resulting rise in surface temperatures will cause changes in the distribution pattern and intensity of the major planetary weather systems which may profoundly affect human activities.

Some meteorologists and governments have discounted the greenhouse warming threat, suggesting that increased dustiness of the atmosphere (linked with accelerating soil erosion associated with forest clearance, agricultural intensification, hedgerow removal, overgrazing and so on) will have a compensating cooling effect*, giving negligible change overall. However, unusual and socially catastrophic weather effects on a planetary scale during the summer of 1988, such as severe drought in the mid-western USA, floods in China and Sudan, more rain-bearing depressions than usual over Britain (the track is usually further north in summer), together with the now undisputed effects of CFCs on the ozone layer, have led to wider recognition of the possibility of pollution-induced global climatic changes and concern for the potential severity of its consequences. Whether or not these current events are directly caused by greenhouse warming, government action to control pollutant greenhouse gases is a welcome trend since the natural removal mechanisms for these gases are either too slow to alleviate the problem, as in the case of carbon dioxide, or induce further problems, as with the destruction of ozone in the stratosphere by CFCs (see section 12.10.2).

Carbon dioxide is removed from the atmosphere by photosynthesis, by exchange with the oceans, and by deposition as carbonates. The chief process is exchange with the oceans. The surface 75 m of the oceans is a well-mixed layer, heated by the Sun and agitated by wind. These properties combined with its carbonate chemistry make it a relatively rapid absorber of carbon dioxide. Ultimately the rate of carbon dioxide uptake is determined by exchange between this layer and the deep ocean waters renewing the capacity of the surface waters to absorb further carbon dioxide. Exchange with the deep waters is in most areas a slow process. The vast cold (<5 °C) oceanic deeps are isolated from the surface mixed waters by a

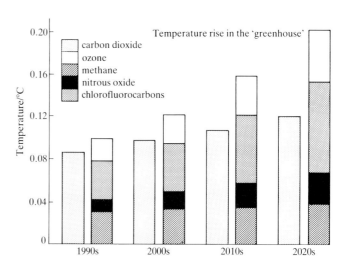

Fig 12.18 *Contributions of different greenhouse gases to predicted rise in global temperatures between now and the 2020s. (From M. McElroy (1988) The challenge of global change,* New Scientist, **119**, *1623, 34–6.)*

stagnant zone of decreasing temperature and increasing density, the **oceanic thermocline** (see fig 12.19), which extends to about 1000 m from the surface. It is estimated that over hundreds of years surface waters see only about 10% of total ocean water. Thus, although the oceans have the potential for absorbing all the human-induced excess atmospheric carbon dioxide, in practice the slow transfer between surface and deep waters prevents realisation of its full potential as a carbon dioxide sink, at least within a human time-scale. It is also possible that as the surface oceanic waters become saturated with carbon dioxide, the proportion of atmospheric carbon dioxide that the oceans can absorb may be reduced, making the carbon dioxide problem even worse.

Predictions of future levels of atmospheric carbon dioxide are difficult. This is partly because of our poor understanding of the detailed chemistry of oceanic absorption (more seems to be absorbed than the chemical models predict) and also because increasing environmental awareness may both curtail deforestation and accelerate development of alternative energy sources, reducing rates of increase in fossil fuel consumption. Nevertheless it is widely assumed that atmospheric carbon dioxide will rise to 600 ppm by the mid-twenty-first century, more than double the level for the late nineteenth century (see fig 12.17). Climatic consequences are also hard to predict due to the large number of possible feedback effects. Most models predict an overall global warming by the mid-twenty-first century of 3±1.5 °C. In high latitudes the problem may be made worse due to positive feedback mechanisms. As snow and ice melt, surface albedo (reflectivity) decreases, leading to increased absorption of radiation, a consequent increase in evaporation and finally increased water vapour in the atmosphere. Since water vapour is itself a greenhouse gas, this will mean that the temperature rise in high

---

* Dusts in the atmosphere reduce incoming short-wave radiation more than outgoing long-wave.

latitudes for a doubling of atmospheric carbon dioxide concentration should be two or three times greater than that at the tropics. Possible environmental consequences range from extensive flooding of coastal lowlands (serious, for example, for S.E. England, the Netherlands, Bangladesh and tropical islands on coral atolls such as the Maldives) to major shifts in world climatic zones. This could have profound implications for food production and the balance of trade and political power. Some small compensation may be gained from increased terrestrial photosynthesis (carbon dioxide is usually a limiting factor in photosynthesis).

Marine phytoplankton production may increase, especially in coastal waters where pollutants generate additional nitrates and phosphates, the key limiting factors for phytoplankton productivity. While this may aid carbon dioxide removal from the atmosphere, its desirability is questionable. Such increased productivity favours rapid growing species, reducing phytoplankton variety, and new dominant species may be less palatable to consumers. This does not favour secondary production in the grazing pathway and resulting excess decomposition may lead to oxygen depletion and death among consumer organisms.

A review of the greenhouse effect is presented in *New Scientist* of 22nd October 1988.

Eutrophication

Eutrophication means nutrient enrichment. Over a long time period, typically several thousand years, lake ecosystems classically show a natural progression from an **oligotrophic** (few nutrients) to a **eutrophic** or even **dystrophic** (rich in nutrients) state (see table 12.4). In the twentieth century, however, rapid eutrophication has occurred in many lakes, such as Lake Erie (N. America), Lake Zurich (Switzerland) and Lough Neagh (Northern Ireland); in semi-enclosed seas such as the Baltic and Black Seas; and in river systems worldwide. This is due to human activity. The main factors are heavy use of nitrogen fertilisers on agricultural land and the increased discharge of phosphates from sewage works. The phosphate problem reflects not only a larger human population but also the modern tendency for greater concentration of settlement into urban areas and the development of mains sewage systems. Thus, not only has the absolute amount of phosphate-containing waste increased but also its distribution has been locally concentrated with direct and more immediate discharge to rivers, lakes and seas compared with traditional systems (such as septic tanks). Sewage discharge into lake ecosystems generates particularly acute problems as, for example, seen in Lake Washington, USA. Here dense phytoplankton blooms occurred in the mid-1950s, accompanied by severe oxygen depletion in deep waters (hypolimnion – see fig 12.19). These changes were directly attributed to an increased sewage discharge from the developing city of Seattle. The situation was remedied by diverting all sewage to the Pacific via Puget Sound and at the same time improving the quality of the discharge to

Table 12.4 The general characteristics of oligotrophic and eutrophic lakes.

	Oligotrophic	*Eutrophic*
Depth	Deeper	Shallower
Summer oxygen in hypolimnion	Present	Absent
Algae and blue-green bacteria	High species diversity, with low density and productivity, often dominated by green algae	Low species diversity with high density and productivity, often dominated by blue-green bacteria
Blooms	Rare	Frequent
Plant nutrient flux	Low	High
Animal production	Low	High
Fish	Salmonids (e.g. trout, char) and coregonids (whitefish) often dominant	Coarse fish (e.g. perch, roach, carp) often dominant

(Source: C.F. Mason (1981) *Biology of freshwater pollution*, Longman.)

Note

In the classic mode of natural lake eutrophication a newly formed deep lake (a classic situation would be following retreat of an ice sheet) contains few nutrients since there has been no opportunity for weathering and sediment removal from the surrounding catchment. Primary and secondary productivity are hence low, the waters are clear, and oxygen status is good throughout.

With time, as weathering proceeds, nutrient status increases, primary and secondary productivity rise, organic and inorganic sediments accumulate and the lake becomes shallower. The more productive waters are less clear and the hypolimnion (see fig 12.19) may become seasonally oxygen-depleted.

A **dystrophic** lake is one which receives large quantities of organic matter from terrestrial plants giving the water a brown colouration. Such lakes typically have peat-filled margins and may develop into peat bogs.

prevent acute pollution in Puget Sound itself. Problems of eutrophication have been reported for lake systems throughout the world. Wherever possible, sewage discharge to lakes or virtually enclosed waters, such as coastal bays, should be avoided.

This human-induced accelerated eutrophication process is properly termed 'cultural eutrophication' (though it is commonly referred to as eutrophication). It reflects disruption of the normal nitrogen and phosphorus cycles. Human activity has increased the active or cycling part of these cycles beyond the self-regulatory (homeostatic) capacity of the systems, at least in the immediate time-scale. Cultural eutrophication generates acute economic as well as ecological problems. Good quality water resources are important for many industrial processes, vital for human and livestock drinking water supplies, essential for commercial and recreational fisheries and necessary for the maintenance of recreational amenities and navigation routes on major waterways (see table 12.5).

Nitrates and phosphates are the nutrients most commonly limiting primary productivity in aquatic ecosystems. Additional nitrate and phosphate, therefore, favours an increase in the more rapidly growing competitive planktonic species, such as *Oscillatoria rubescens*, and an overall

Table 12.5 The main effects of eutrophication on the receiving ecosystem and the problems for human societies associated with these effects.

Effects
(1) Species diversity decreases and the dominant biota change
(2) Plant, algal and animal biomass increases
(3) Turbidity increases
(4) Rate of sedimentation increases, shortening the life span of the lake
(5) Anoxic conditions may develop

Problems
(1) Treatment of drinking water may be difficult and the supply may have an unacceptable taste or odour
(2) The water may be injurious to health
(3) The amenity value of the water may decrease
(4) Increased vegetation may impede water flow and navigation
(5) Commercially important species (such as salmonids and coregonids) may disappear

(Source: C.F. Mason (1981) *Biology of freshwater pollution*, Longman.)

reduction in phytoplankton diversity. Such changes often also result in a disproportionate increase in less palatable species (species less suitable as food for consumers). This factor and the typically longer life histories and hence larger response times to environmental change of secondary producers or consumer organisms means that not all the increased primary production is eaten by the consumer organisms. Instead the excess material enters the decomposition pathway. Breakdown to simple inorganic nutrients is an oxygen-demanding process. Dissolved oxygen levels may be reduced below those necessary for successful growth and reproduction of sensitive species such as salmon and trout (*Salmo* spp.). In extreme cases fish death and the subsequent decomposition in turn impose a further oxygen demand making the situation increasingly worse (positive feedback). This may not just be a problem for the immediately affected area. Zones of oxygen depletion on an otherwise unaffected river system may be sufficient to disrupt breeding in migratory species such as salmon and eels.

The problem of eutrophic oxygen depletion may be made worse by seasonal thermally induced water stratification in deep lakes. In mid-latitudes thermal stratification typically establishes in early summer (fig 12.19). This prevents diffusion of new oxygen supplies to the deep waters of the hypolimnion until the stratification pattern breaks down with seasonal cooling and higher wind speeds in autumn. The waters of streams and rivers entering the lake, since they are relatively shallow, are warm and therefore the dissolved nutrients and oxygen they contain mix only with the waters of the epilimnion (fig 12.19). Fauna requiring stable temperatures are mainly found in the hypolimnion. Excess phytoplankton production, encouraged by the warmth and increased nutrient status of the epilimnion, on death falls to the hypolimnion where its decomposition makes an additional oxygen demand on a restricted oxygen resource. Providing sufficient oxygen is present to meet this extra demand, and the needs of existing fauna, no major problem arises. However, if the situation is not carefully monitored, sudden and catastrophic fish kills may result in late summer when oxygen supplies approach exhaustion.

Case study

In the Norfolk Broads nitrate, and especially phosphate, levels have risen dramatically since the nineteenth century, especially during the last 40 years (table 12.6). At the same time clear waters with low phytoplankton productivity and many bottom-growing plants, such as stonewort (*Chara* spp.), have changed to phytoplankton-rich, turbid (cloudy) waters with few plants. At Barton Broad, transparency as measured by a Secchi disc*, was only 11 cm in 1973. Although most of the pre-1800 fauna of broadland,

* Disc with four segments, alternately black and white. The disc is lowered on a graduated string until the contrasting segments can no longer be distinguished. This gives an index of water turbidity.

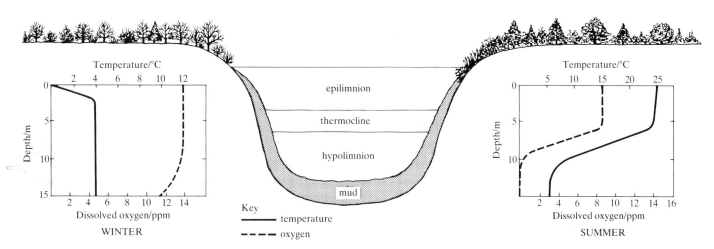

Fig 12.19 *Thermal stratification in a mid-latitude lake (data from Linsley ponds, Conn.). In summer a warm oxygen-rich circulating layer of water, the epilimnion, is separated from cold oxygen-poor hypolimnion waters by a broad zone of rapid temperature change called the thermocline. A similar gradient of oxygen status is also evident – see text for explanation. (Modified from E.P. Odum (1971)* Fundamentals of ecology, *Saunders p. 310.)*

Table 12.6 Phosphate levels in lakes and the Norfolk Broads since 1800.

General data	$\mu g\,dm^{-3}$ phosphate
Clear water upland lake	5
Naturally fertile lowland lake	10–30
Norfolk Broads pre-1800	10–20
Norfolk Broads 19th century following land enclosure	up to 80
Norfolk Broads 20th century following conversion to modern sewage disposal methods and population increase	max. 2 000 typically 150–300

(Source: B. Moss (1979) *Alarm call for the Broads*, Geographical Magazine.)

Changing phosphate levels at Barton Broad, Norfolk and the principal sources of phosphate

Date	$\mu g\,dm^{-3}$ phosphate	Sewage	Land drainage
1800	13.3	zero	13.3
1900	52.0	(separate data not available)	
1920	72.0	(separate data not available)	
1940	119.0	72	47
1975	361.0	287	74

(Source: B. Moss, 1980, *Ecology of fresh waters*, Blackwell Scientific Publications.)

including game fish (such as trout), have been lost, by the mid-twentieth century the area was a world-renowned centre for coarse fish and angling. However, the continued steep rise in nutrients, especially phosphorus, together with other complexly interacting factors have meant that these coarse fisheries are now also threatened. Additional threats include periodic marine flooding, now made worse by river bank erosion, and the physical disturbance of sediments and destruction of fringing reed banks. The latter protect river banks and are important fish spawning sites. Their destruction is due to the expanding and changing holiday and boating industry, where yachting is being replaced by activities with diesel-powered launches.

Recent experiments suggest that eutrophication can be reversed. Access points to two small broads, Alderfen and Cockshoot, were dammed, blocking new supplies of nutrient-rich river water*. At Alderfen no further action was taken. Initial improvement and return to a clear-water system was lost when a complex interaction occurred between existing sediments and new organic decomposition associated with a new spring phytoplankton bloom. This triggered renewed phosphate release from the nutrient-rich sediments. At first algal growth was restricted by nitrate availability but eventually nitrogen-fixing planktonic species became established and by summer 1985, six years after the experimental closure, the waters were again turbid. At Cockshoot damming was accompanied by dredging and removal of the phosphate-rich sediment. Aquatic plants are steadily recolonising this broad and fish stocks are increasing. Dredging Cockshoot, in 1982, cost

* The Broads are former peat-cuttings abandoned due to flooding during the late thirteenth and fourteenth centuries. Many typically have narrow and shallow connections to the main river system, hence damming is a practicable proposition.

£75 000. A more typical-sized broad would cost £250 000. However, in many cases navigation rights would preclude damming and isolation of a broad, especially on a permanent basis.

General effects and remedies

Physical isolation of water bodies will often be impracticable, but the experiments described above show that recovery is possible, if complex. They also increase our scientific understanding of the eutrophication process. Phosphate removal at sewage works is now widely used on sewage outfalls entering broadland rivers and at many other seriously affected locations. This involves chemical precipitation and removal of phosphorus using lime or iron salts. This can greatly aid recovery of a receiving waterway, especially when accompanied by initial dredging. Sediment removed may be beneficially used as fertiliser, at least partly offsetting costs. Dredging also benefits the system by deepening lakes and river channels. This favours increased flow which should improve oxygenation. In lake systems it may lead to increased water volume, thus having a further diluting effect on nutrients. In deeper stratified lakes an associated increase in hypolimnion volume and hence potential oxygen supply may result. Deepening may even induce stratification and thus limit nutrient supply to the epilimnion, in turn reducing phytoplankton productivity. Nutrient levels may also be reduced by bottom sealing using polythene sheeting, or by chemical removal by precipitation, such as with aluminium sulphate.

Algal blooms may be directly controlled chemically using algicides but this poses problems of unwanted harmful effects on non-target species which may be difficult to predict.

Eutrophication in water reservoirs is a serious economic problem. Algae may block filters at purification plants. This seriously reduces the throughput of water and cleaning may necessitate temporary shut-down of a plant. Small algae may persist into consumer supplies where subsequent decomposition in feeder pipes can impart an unpleasant (though harmless) taste and smell to drinking water supplies.

Most efforts in eutrophication control are concentrated on phosphate reduction. This is mainly because phosphates are typically added at clearly identifiable 'point-sources' whereas the main sources of additional nitrate are overland flow linked with agricultural practice. Nitrate entry to water systems is thus more diffuse, and control or remedy, aside from a radical change in farming practice, is less practicable. Nitrate levels in drinking water supplies are, however, a cause for concern. The European health standards set thresholds of 50 mg dm^{-3} nitrate for drinking water supplies with levels up to 100 mg dm^{-3} acceptable. In lowland England, river water intakes frequently exceed 100 mg dm^{-3} nitrate and must be mixed with waters with low nitrate values before entering public supply.

Monitoring eutrophication

Changes associated with eutrophication can be monitored biologically and chemically. This gives the opportunity for remedial action before catastrophic ecosystem damage occurs. Changes in phytoplankton species present may be indicative of eutrophication. Blue-green bacterial blooms are common, for example *Oscillatoria rubescens* at Lake Washington and *Anabaena flos-aquae* at Lough Neagh. Table 12.7 summarises characteristic plankton groups for oligotrophic and eutrophic lakes. Eutrophic waters characteristically show high abundance and low species diversity of phytoplankton. Reference slides to aid basic plankton identification are available from Philip Harris Ltd. Another approach monitors chlorophyll *a* abundance as an index of algal biomass. Mean summer values for oligotrophic lakes lie between 0.3–2.5 mg m^{-3}, whereas for eutrophic lakes values range from 5–140 mg m^{-3}.

Field records of large non-vertebrate fauna are useful indicators of river water quality. A simple five-point scheme is shown in table 12.8. Care must be taken to standardise sample procedure and ensure adequate replication for representative samples of each location. In Britain the two schemes most widely used in the water industry and by other professionals are the Trent Biotic Index (TBI) (table 12.9) and the Chandler Biotic Score (CBS). The simpler five-part scheme is based on these. The TBI monitors the presence or absence of key species together with species richness but does not include abundance estimates for different species. This makes calculation rapid but has the disadvantage that a single individual of a sensitive species may have a disproportionate influence on the index. In estimating the Chandler score, the value for each individual species is weighted according to five levels of abundance. A criticism of the method is, however, that assignment of

Table 12.7 Characteristic algal associations of oligotrophic and eutrophic lakes.

	Algal group	Examples
Oligotrophic lakes	Desmid plankton	*Staurodesmus*, *Staurastrum*
	Chrysophycean plankton	*Dinobryon*
	Diatom plankton	*Cyclotella*, *Tabellaria*
	Dinoflagellate plankton	*Peridinium*, *Ceratium*
	Chlorococcal plankton	*Oocystis*
Eutrophic lakes	Diatom plankton	*Asterionella*, *Fragillaria crotonensis*, *Stephanodiscus astraea*, *Melosira granulata*
	Dinoflagellate plankton	*Peridinium bipes*, *Ceratium*, *Glenodinium*
	Chlorococcal plankton	*Pediastrum*, *Scenedesmus*
	Myxophycean plankton	*Anacystis*, *Aphanizomenon*, *Anabaena*

(Source: Mason, C. F. (1981) *Biology of freshwater pollution*, Longman.)

Table 12.8 Five-point scale for water pollution studies using presence and absence indicator species.

Level of pollution	Oxygen concentration	Indicator organisms
(A) Clean water or very low pollution levels	High	stonefly nymph
		mayfly nymph
(B) Low pollution levels		caddis fly larva
		freshwater shrimp
(C) High pollution levels		water louse
		bloodworm
(D) Very high pollution levels	Low	sludgeworm
		rat tailed maggot
(E) Extreme pollution levels	No oxygen	No apparent life

This point scheme is used in the Philip Harris and Griffin water pollution study packs. The Philip Harris scheme includes colour photographs of key indicator species. The Griffin package has an excellent series of black and white drawings of a wider range of indicator organisms as well as procedures for calculating the Trent Biotic Index and other simple pollution indicator tests. The drawings are reproduced from *The biology of polluted waters* by H. B. N. Hynes, Liverpool Press 1971.

abundance scores is somewhat arbitrary. Further, since taxa must be counted as well as identified the Chandler Score takes much longer to determine than the Trent Biotic Index. (Appropriate microcomputer packages can be used for this work.) Full details of these methods, including worked examples, are given in C.F. Mason (1981) *Biology of Freshwater Pollution*, Longman.

A useful chemical indicator of eutrophication is the **biochemical oxygen demand (BOD)**. The BOD measures the rate of oxygen depletion by organisms. It is assumed this primarily reflects micro-organism activity in decomposing organic matter present in waters. (As discussed, organic matter typically increases as waters become nutrient-enriched.) Oxygen consumption by algal respiration will inevitably also be included in the test. In practice this is normally not important, but in some cases it may account for up to 50% of the total BOD. BOD is thus an approximate rather than precise guide to water quality. It is

Table 12.9 The Trent Biotic Index.

Summary table

	Indicator species		Total number of groups present				
			0–1	2–5	6–10	11–15	16+
			Trent	*Biotic*	*Index*		
Clean	Plecoptera nymph present	More than one species	−	7	8	9	10
		One species only	−	6	7	8	9
	Ephemeroptera nymph present	More than one species*	−	6	7	8	9
		One species only*	−	5	6	7	8
	Trichoptera larvae present	More than one species†	−	5	6	7	8
		One species only†	4	4	5	6	7
	Gammarus present	All above species absent	3	4	5	6	7
	Asellus present	All above species absent	2	3	4	5	6
	Tubificid worms and/or red chironomid larvae present	All above species absent	1	2	3	4	−
	All above types absent	Some organisms such as *Eristalis tenax* not requiring dissolved oxygen may be present	0	1	2	−	−

Organisms in order of tendency to disappear as degree of pollution increases

Heavily polluted

Groups list
The term 'group' here denotes the limit of identification which can be reached without restoring to lengthy techniques.
Thus the groups are as follows:
Each known species of Platyhelminthes (flatworms).
Annelida (worms) excluding genus *Nais*.
Genus *Nais* (worms).
Each known species of Hirudinae (leeches).
Each known species of Mollusca (snails).
Each known species of Crustacea (*Asellus*, shrimps).
Each known species of Plecoptera (stone-fly).
Each known genus of Ephemeroptera (may-fly) excluding *Baetis rhodani*.
Baetis rhodani (may-fly).
Each family of Trichoptera (caddis-fly).
Each species of Neuroptera (alder-fly).
Family Chironomidae (midge larvae) except *Chironomus thummi*.
Chironomus thummi (blood worms).
Family Simulidae (black-fly larvae).
Each known species of other fly larvae.
Each known species of Coleoptera (beetles and beetle larvae).
Each known species of Hydracarina (water-mites).

* *Baetis rhodani* excluded
† *Baetis rhodani* (Ephemeroptera) is counted in this section for the purpose of classification.
The maximum value is 10. Biotic indices are effectively marks out of ten with zero representing virtually lifeless heavily polluted waters.

Procedure
(1) Sort each sample, separating the animals according to group (see above groups list). Count the total number of groups present.
(2) Note which indicator species are present, starting from the top of the list.
(3) To find the Trent Biotic Index, take the highest indicator species, e.g. caddis fly, *Trichoptera*, and work along the line. Note from the top the group number and read off the Trent Biotic Index.

e.g.	Highest indicator animal	Trichoptera
	Number of indicator species	more than one
	Total numbers of groups	7
	Trent Biotic Index	6

Source: The Griffin Pollution test kit: handbook for users

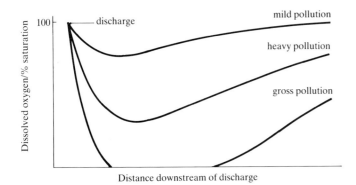

Fig 12.20 *The effect of an organic discharge on the oxygen content of river water. (From C.S. Mason (1981) Biology of fresh water pollution, Longman.)*

most useful when used in conjunction with other water quality indicators. The standard measure of BOD is the weight of oxygen in milligrams consumed from a decimetre cubed of sample when stored in darkness for five days at $20°C$. Clean river water normally has a BOD of 3 mg dm^{-3} compared with 10 mg dm^{-3} for a badly polluted stream. Typical BOD values for domestic sewage are between 250–350 mg dm^{-3} (see table 12.10).

Deoxygenation of a river caused by organic wastes is a slow process so that the point of maximum deoxygenation may occur considerably downstream of a discharge (see fig 12.20).

12.15 List the factors that will determine the degree of deoxygenation.

In the River Thames in 1967, at low flow in autumn, minimum oxygen conditions prevailed for 40 km downstream of London Bridge, whereas in spring with high flow only 12 km had minimum oxygen. Furthermore, depletion was immediately associated with this major conurbation at low flow but did not occur until 22 km downstream at high flow.

Table 12.10 (*a*) **A guide to water quality as measured by BOD.** (*b*) **Comparative BOD strengths of some typical industrial liquid wastes.**

(*a*)

Rivers		Sewage	
BOD (mg dm^{-3})	Quality	BOD (mg dm^{-3})	Quality
1	very good	600	strong sewage
2	good	350	moderate sewage
3	fairly good	200	weak sewage
5	doubtful	20	maximum Royal Commission
10	poor		standard effluent assuming ×
20	very poor		10 dilution in receiving stream

(*b*)

Waste type	5 day BOD (mg dm^{-3})
cotton	200–1 000
tannery	1 000–2 000
laundry	1 600
brewery	850
distillery	7 000
dairy	600–1 000
cannery: peas	570
fruit (citrus)	2000
farm waste	1 000–2 000
silage	50 000
paper board	100–450
coke oven	780
oil refinery	100–500

(Adapted from Open University, *Clean and dirty water*.)

12.5 The abiotic component of ecosystems: the physical habitat factors

The abiotic, or non-living, component of an ecosystem may be conveniently divided into edaphic factors (concerning soil), climatic factors, topographic factors and other physical factors that might be operating, such as wave action, ocean currents and fire.

As we have seen in the discussion of biogeochemical cycling, the abiotic components are often intimately linked with the living components of an ecosystem. On the grand scale the physical factors of the environment determine the extent of the biosphere (that part of the planet which is suitable for life). At a regional and local level they influence the distribution of species and, in close association with biotic controls such as competition and predation, influence the structure of communities and the nature of ecosystems. Biotic factors are more fully discussed in the sections on communities and population ecology.

12.5.1 Edaphic factors

The scientific study of soil is called **pedology**. Early work on soils stressed their importance as sources of nutrients for plants, or examined them from a geological viewpoint. Work was therefore concentrated on the physics and chemistry of soils and they were seen as inert inorganic substances. The first scientist to describe soil as a dynamic rather than an inert medium was the Russian Dokuchaev in his classic work on Russian soils dating from 1870. He saw soil as a constantly changing and developing material, a dynamic zone in which physical, chemical and biological activities occur. He recognised five major soil-forming factors, namely climate, parent material (geology), topography (relief), organisms and time.

Although soil is included here with abiotic factors, it is better to regard it as a vital link between the biotic and abiotic components of terrestrial ecosystems. The term 'soil' is applied to the layer of material overlying the rocks of the Earth's crust. A suitable nutrient content and structure are essential for successful crop production. Though modern technology can, with some success, overcome poor soil conditions, a proper scientific understanding is vital to avoid unwanted environmental side-effects. Examples of these are the depletion of soil nutrient reserves so often associated with forest clearance, especially in the tropics, and the constant over-enrichment of the soil by fertilisers in many intensively farmed areas which leads to nutrient rich run-off and associated eutrophication of waters, such as in the East Anglian broadlands and fenlands.

Soil has four important structural components, namely the mineral skeleton (typically 50–60% of the total soil composition), organic matter (up to 10%), air (15–25%) and water (25–35%). Methods of analysing these components are given in section 13.1.1. In addition, there is a biotic component which has been considered in the previous section, and is also dealt with further in chapter 13.

Mineral skeleton (inorganic content)

The mineral skeleton of soil is the inorganic component and is derived from the parent rock by weathering.

Soil texture. The mineral fragments comprising the soil skeletal material vary in size from boulders and stones down to sand grains and minute clay particles. The skeletal material is usually divided arbitrarily into **fine earth** (particles <2 mm) and larger fragments. Particles <1 µm in diameter are termed **colloidal**. The mechanical and chemical properties of soil are largely determined by the fine earth material. The distribution of soil particle sizes within the fine earth is examined by mechanical analysis in the laboratory (section 13.1.1) or, with experience, by 'feel' methods in the field. Fig 12.21 summarises two of the most widely used thresholds for sand, silt and clay. In all cases clay consists of particles <0.002 mm (2 µm) in diameter.

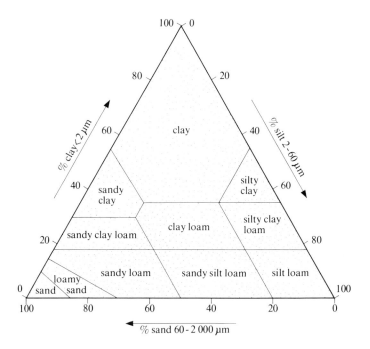

Fig 12.22 *Triangular diagram of soil textural classes as used by the Soil Survey of England and Wales, 1974*

International Society of Soil Science

clay	silt	fine sand	coarse sand	gravel

0.002　　　　　0.02　　　　　0.2　　　　　2.0

British Standards System (used by the Soil Survey of England and Wales)

clay	silt	fine sand	medium sand	coarse sand	stones

0.002　　　　　0.06　　0.2　　0.6　　2.0

Diameter of soil particle/mm
(log scale)

Fig 12.21 *Particle-size classes of soil*

The relative proportions of sand, silt and clay determine the soil texture. Fig 12.22 shows a standard soil texture triangle and indicates the limits of 11 major soil textural classes in routine use by the Soil Survey of England and Wales.

Soil texture is important agriculturally. Medium- and fine-textured soils such as clays, clay loams and silt loams are generally more suitable for plant growth because they have the most satisfactory nutrient and water retention. Sandy soils are faster draining and lose nutrients through leaching, but may be advantageous in obtaining early crops as the surface dries more rapidly than that of a clay soil in early spring, resulting in a warmer soil. Stone content of the soil (particles >2 mm) may also have importance agriculturally since it will affect wear and tear on agricultural implements, and will modify the drainage characteristics of fine earth. Generally, as the stone content of a soil increases, its water holding capacity decreases.

The implications of soil texture can be partly understood by comparing the properties of pure sand and clay, as shown in table 12.11. An ideal soil would contain roughly equal quantities of clay and sand, combined with a range of intermediate particle sizes. In these circumstances a porous crumb structure is formed and such soils are called **loams**. They usually combine the advantages and eliminate the disadvantages of the extreme soil types. Thus mechanical analysis of a given soil, which is easily carried out, is a useful guide to the soil's properties.

Agriculturally, soils are sometimes referred to as heavy (clays) or light (sands) reflecting the power needed to work the soil with agricultural implements. Heavy soils are poorly drained and are usually wet and sticky. Clodding and compacting make it difficult to obtain a fine tilth. Light soils are well drained and a fine tilth is readily obtained as the particles separate easily.

Chemistry of the mineral skeleton. Soil chemistry is partly determined by the mineral skeleton and partly by the organic matter, which is described later. A high proportion of the minerals in soil are present as crystalline structures, left as the resistant products of weathering of the original parent rock. Sand and silt consist mainly of the mineral quartz, SiO_2, which is extremely inert and is otherwise known as silica. Silica is also the basis of silicate ions, SiO_4^{4-}, which typically combine with cations, particularly aluminium (Al^{3+}) and iron (Fe^{3+}, Fe^{2+}), to form electrically neutral crystals. Silicates are the predominant soil minerals.

Table 12.11 Comparison of the properties of sand and clay.

Property	Sand	Clay
Texture	Coarse, particle size >0.06 mm	Fine, particle size <0.002 mm
Structure	Structureless	Forms large sticky masses (clods) when wet, becomes hard and cracks on drying
Porosity	Pore spaces relatively large, good aeration, rapid drainage	Pore spaces relatively small, poor aeration, slow drainage
Water-holding capacity	Poor water retention, little water held by capillarity (surface tension) or adsorption, does not become waterlogged	Good water retention, relatively large amounts of water held by capillarity (surface tension) and adsorption, easily waterlogged
Temperature	Warm due to low moisture content*	Cold due to high moisture content*
Nutrient retention	Low, rapidly leached (sandy soils tend to become acidic as bases are leached out and humic acids accumulate)	High, not leached, clay particles attract cations and some anions

* Water has a high specific heat capacity and a high latent heat of evaporation.

One particularly abundant and important group of minerals affecting nutrient and water retention are the clay minerals. Most of these occur as minute flat crystals, often hexagonal in shape, which form a colloidal suspension in water. Each crystal contains layers of silicate sheets combined with sheets of aluminium hydroxide, with spaces between the layers. The combined surface area of the layers with their spaces is very large compared with the volume of the crystals (5–800 m^2 g^{-1} clay). The important feature of these minerals is that they have a permanent negative charge which is neutralised by cations adsorbed from the soil solution. The cations are thereby prevented from being leached out of the soil and remain available for exchange with other cations in the soil solution and in plants. The extent to which cations are freely exchangeable is referred to as the **cation exchange capacity** and is an important indicator of soil fertility. Water is also attracted into the spaces, causing hydration and swelling of the clay.

Organic matter

The organic content of the soil is derived from the decay of dead organisms, parts of organisms (such as shed leaves), excreta and egesta. The dead organic matter is utilised as food by a combination of detritivores, which ingest and help to break down the material, and decomposers (fungi and bacteria) which complete the process of decomposition. Undecomposed material is called **litter** and the final, fully decomposed amorphous material in which the original material is no longer recognisable is called **humus**. Humus is a dark brown to black colour and chemically very complex and variable in composition, consisting of many types of organic molecule. These consist mainly of phenolic acids, carboxylic acids and esters of fatty acids. Humus, like clay, is in a colloidal state. Some of it adheres strongly to the clay to form a **clay–humus complex**. Like the clay,

the humus has a large surface area and high cation exchange capacity, the anions in humus being carboxyl and phenolic groups. This capacity is particularly important in soils with a low clay content. Humus is very important for soil structure, generally improving aeration and water and nutrient retention through its chemical and physical properties.

At the same time as **humification** (formation of humus) occurs, essential elements pass from organic compounds into inorganic compounds, such as nitrogen into ammonium ions (NH_4^+), phosphorus into orthophosphate ions ($H_2PO_4^-$) and sulphur into sulphate ions (SO_4^{2-}). This process is called **mineralisation**. Carbon is released as carbon dioxide as a result of respiration (see carbon cycle, fig 9.2).

In order for any type of humus to develop the soil must be reasonably well drained, because decay is extremely slow under waterlogged conditions where lack of oxygen restricts growth of aerobic decomposers. Under such conditions the structure of the animal and plant remains is thus preserved for long periods of time and they gradually become compressed to form peat which may accumulate to great depths. The method of determining the humus content of a soil sample is described in experiment 13.2.

Air content

The soil atmosphere, together with the soil water, occupies the pores between soil particles. Porosity (pore space) varies with different soils, increasing in the series from clays through loams to sands. There is free exchange of gases between the soil and external atmosphere with the result that the air in both has a similar composition. Generally, the soil air has a slightly lower level of oxygen and a higher level of carbon dioxide than outside owing to respiration by soil organisms. Oxygen is required by the roots of plants, by soil animals and by decomposers. Some of the soil gases are in solution and it is in this form that they are exchanged with living organisms. If the soil becomes waterlogged, the air spaces fill with water and the soil becomes anaerobic. Minerals like those of iron, sulphur and nitrogen will tend to exist in their reduced states (Fe^{2+}, sulphide, sulphite, nitrite) and may trap any oxygen that becomes available by becoming oxidised. The soil will become acidic because anaerobic organisms continue to produce carbon dioxide. Humus turnover is reduced, so humic acids also accumulate. Unless the soil is rich in bases it may become extremely acidic and this, like the oxygen depletion, adversely affects the soil micro-organisms. Changes in the oxidation state of iron affect the colour of the soil. The oxidised form of iron, Fe^{3+}, imparts yellow, red and brown colours while the reduced form, Fe^{2+}, gives the grey colour characterstic of waterlogging. A prolonged period of anaerobic conditions will result in plant death. The method of determining the air content of a soil sample is described in experiment 13.3.

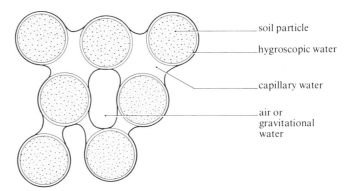

Fig 12.23 *Three types of soil water*

Water content

Some water is retained around the soil particles, while the remaining water, sometimes called **gravitational water** (fig 12.23), is free to drain downwards through the soil. The latter is important in causing the phenomenon known as **leaching**, which is the washing-out of minerals, including nutrients. The level to which gravitational water drains is called the **water table** and this may fluctuate in depth depending on rainfall.

Water may be retained as a thin, tightly bound film around individual colloidal particles. This is sometimes called **hygroscopic water** (fig 12.23). It is adsorbed by hydrogen bonding, for example, to the surfaces of silica and clay minerals or to the cations that are associated with clay minerals and humus. It is the water least available to plant roots and is the last water to remain in very dry soils. The amount present depends on the colloidal content of the soil and is therefore much greater in clay soils (about 15% by weight) than in sandy soils (about 0.5% by weight).

As water layers build up around soil particles, water begins to fill the finer pores between soil particles and spreads to larger and larger pores. The hygroscopic water grades into **capillary water** which is the water held round soil particles by surface tension (fig 12.23). This is the water that can move upwards through fine pores and channels from the water table by capillarity, a phenomenon caused by the high surface tension of water. Capillary water is easily utilised by plants and is their most important regular supply of water. It is easily lost by evaporation, unlike hygroscopic water. Fine-textured soils like clays hold more capillary water than coarse-textured soils like sands.

The total amount of water that can be retained by a soil (determined by adding water until it drains out and then stops dripping) is called the **field capacity** (section 13.1.1).

Water is required by all living organisms in the soil, and enters living cells by osmosis (section 14.1). It is also important as a solvent for nutrients and respiratory gases which are taken up from an aqueous solution by plant roots. It contributes to the weathering process of parent rocks in ways described in the next section.

12.5.2 Formation of soil

Soil is formed as a result of the interaction of many variables, the five most important of which are climate, parent material (geology), topography (relief or surface morphology), organisms, and time. These are considered separately below.

Climate and weathering

Weathering is the action of climate and, to a lesser extent, living organisms in bringing about the physical and chemical breakdown of the parent rock or material. The two most important factors in weathering are water and temperature and so it is most conveniently dealt with in the context of climate. The more general influence of climate on soil formation will be described after weathering.

Physical weathering can be caused by temperature changes, as when rocks alternately expand and contract in response to diurnal (daily) changes in temperature. This process causes rocks to shatter. If water is present in the cracks and alternate freeze and thaw cycles occur, the expansion of ice can cause tremendous pressures to build up, also shattering the rock. Other causes of physical weathering are particles of various sizes like sand, which, when carried by wind, water or glaciers, scour exposed surfaces.

Chemical weathering may be influenced by biological and climatic factors. It is generally accelerated by higher temperatures. Water acts as a solvent and also as a reagent in the hydrolysis of certain rock minerals. Rocks which are slightly water soluble, such as the calcium carbonate of chalk and limestone, are particularly liable to erosion by solution. The effectiveness of water may be increased when carbon dioxide from the atmosphere, or from the respiration of soil organisms, dissolves to form the dilute acid carbonic acid. Lichens are among the few living organisms that can grow on bare rock surfaces, and they contribute to chemical erosion by extracting certain nutrients from weathering rocks.

As with weathering, temperature and precipitation (such as rainfall and snowfall) are the two key climatic factors operating. The amount of precipitation is particularly important. If it exceeds evaporation, the soil may be subject to leaching, or if drainage is poor to waterlogging. If evaporation exceeds precipitation, capillarity will occur from the water table and movement of soluble materials will be in a predominantly upward direction, again affecting the nature of the soil that develops. A dry climate will result in sparse vegetation cover which, in turn, reduces humus production. Soils may be less acidic as a result. Lack of water also inhibits chemical weathering and leaching.

Some of the effects of climate are shown in the summary diagram of fig 12.24.

Parent material

All rocks can be traced back in origin to the solidification of molten magma which was released from below the Earth's crust. The rocks formed directly by the cooling of this magma are called **igneous rocks**, and may be acidic, such as granite, or basic, such as basalt, according to their mineral composition. When acid rocks weather, a high proportion of silicon remains as SiO_2, or quartz, which is seen as sand grains. When basic rocks weather, however, much of the silicon is present in a rich variety of silicates which pass through various sequences of weathering, giving rise to the different minerals of silt and clay.

Sedimentary rocks are formed by the deposition of material derived from the weathering of other rocks, or from the remains of living organisms. The material accumulates and becomes compacted, possibly over millions of years. Typical sedimentary rocks are sandstones, chalk and limestone and their effect on soil development is described in section 12.5.3.

Metamorphic rocks are rocks which have been changed after their formation by periods of heating and recrystallisation, such as slate and marble. They are generally more resistant to weathering than other rocks.

Finally, some soils develop on transported materials such as wind-blown sand, alluvial deposits and glacial moraines. The influence of parental material here is obviously related to the original parent rock from which these materials were derived.

Topography

Topography, or relief, exerts its influence chiefly through altitude, steepness of slope and aspect. These affect local climate and drainage. Drainage is generally better on slopes, getting progressively poorer towards lowland and valley bottoms where peats may develop if soils are permanently waterlogged. On slopes, a certain proportion of water will be lost as run-off and this causes losses of weathered rock and soil. Soils on slopes tend to be thinner as a result. Soil is also lost as it creeps slowly downhill in response to gravity. This process is called **solifluction** and

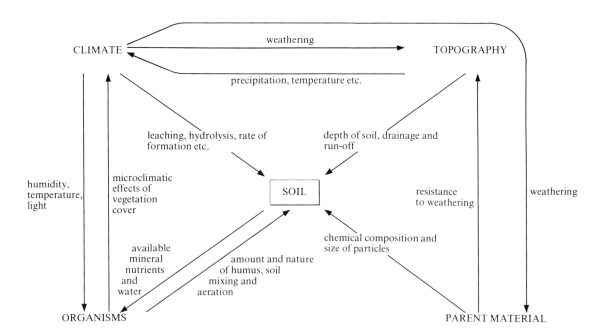

Fig 12.24 *Interactions of the four direct agents of soil formation. Note the major influence of climate. Time is a fifth, indirect factor which is not included*

leads to the accumulation of soil on lower slopes. Vegetation cover may limit these processes.

Climatic factors such as precipitation and temperature are affected by topography, which thereby indirectly influences the soil-forming process. Aspect can be an important factor as well as altitude in influencing the climate. Temperatures are higher on the sunnier aspects, resulting in faster soil development, drier soils and often influencing the vegetation. Windward slopes are generally wetter than leeward slopes.

Organisms

Organisms contribute the organic part of the soil (litter and humus), the physical and chemical properties of which have been described already.

Vegetation may influence the development of soils as well as climate and parent material. There is some evidence, for example, that podzols (section 12.5.3) are more likely to form under heath and coniferous forest communities than under deciduous forest communities. This is probably related to the nature of the chemicals leached from the plant litter and their inhibiting effects on decomposition by soil micro-organisms. Also, the acid litter of heaths and pine forests is unfavourable for earthworms, unlike that of deciduous forests.

The activity of soil detritivores, particularly earthworms in temperate regions, is important in a number of ways, and these in turn are influenced by vegetation. In general, detritivores speed up the process of decomposition by breaking up and increasing the surface area of litter. In addition, their faeces and excretory products contribute to the volume of processed organic and inorganic material. Soil, in passing through the gut of an earthworm, is made finer in texture and the mineral and organic components are mixed in a way that improves the structure of the soil. Earthworm burrows improve aeration and provide passages for root growth. Similarly, burrowing vertebrates such as moles and rabbits improve soil mixing and aeration.

Human influence. The delicate and dynamic balance of a mature soil is potentially at risk when humans use soil for agricultural purposes, and in many cases destruction of soil structure, depletion of nutrients and soil erosion have been the consequences.

Soil structure is particularly at risk when heavy agricultural machinery is used for working the land, soil compaction having a number of consequences such as reducing pore size and hence reducing aeration and drainage. Soil compaction may also be caused by large numbers of livestock. Repeated use of the soil, particularly for the same crops, may reduce the levels of important nutrients. Ploughing soil may increase its erosion by wind and water, particularly on slopes. Similarly, removal of a protective layer of vegetation through overgrazing by livestock, or by forest clearance, can expose soil to greater erosion. Clearance of tropical rain forest can have very serious consequences on the thin soils typical of such regions. On bare soil there is increased surface run-off which may not only increase soil erosion but also wash out soil nutrients. The consequences for humans are a decreased soil fertility and, in some extreme cases, a change towards barren conditions is triggered resulting in a large drop in productivity of the ecosystem. For example, in some areas of Malaya and parts of the Brazilian Amazon there has been massive erosion accompanied by silting of rivers. Soil management is therefore one of the key areas of interest to agriculturalists and soil scientists.

Time

Time has an indirect but important influence on soil formation. The rate of formation is very variable, from a few decades on volcanic ash to several thousand years starting from a bare rock surface in a temperate climate. Over geological periods of time, climatic and topographic changes occur which in turn influence soil development.

To summarise, it should be stressed again that the soil-forming factors mentioned do not act in isolation. Each, apart from time, has a direct effect on soil formation, but may also act indirectly by influencing the other factors. Fig 12.24 summarises the interactions of these factors.

12.5.3 Types of soil

Soils have been shown to be the products of the interaction between the biotic and abiotic components of the ecosystem. As a result they show great complexity and variety, and they are very difficult to classify. Of the many soil types that have been recognised and described, three very different types which are found in moist temperate zones like Britain are chosen here as examples, namely podzols, brown earths and rendzinas. Soils can be examined by digging soil pits or using a soil auger as described in section 13.1.1. There is a standard nomenclature for the characteristic layers or **horizons** seen when a soil is viewed in profile. The nomenclature for freely drained soils, such as the three examples chosen, is shown and explained in fig 12.25.

Podzols

The name originates from the Russian words *pod*, meaning under, and *zola*, meaning ash, and a typical profile is shown in fig 12.26.

Podzols are characteristic of sandstone, gravel deposits (from glacial drift) and alluvial deposits, and are associated mainly with heathland and coniferous forests in cool, humid climates. The litter layer is deep as it contains materials with a high concentration of phenols, such as conifer 'needles', which are resistant to microbial decay.

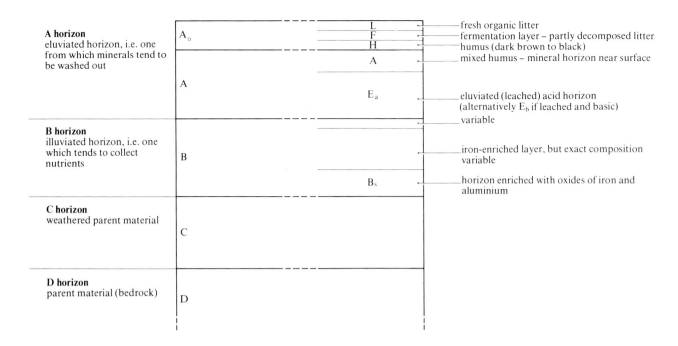

Fig 12.25 (above) *Generalised profile for a typical, freely drained soil showing the nomenclature used for soil horizons*

Fig 12.26 (below) *Profile of a podzol*

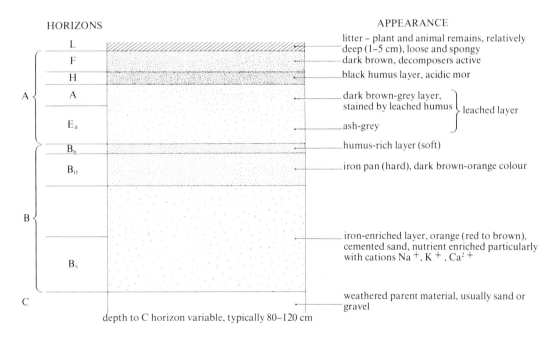

The calcium content of the soil is low so conditions are too acidic (pH 3–6.5) to support significant numbers of earthworms and other animals which ingest soil. Hence decay of the litter is mainly carried out by fungi, which is a relatively slow process, and results in a deep acidic humus layer, known as **mor**, which remains quite separate from the lower layers.

The E_a horizon is characteristically ash grey in colour and stands out clearly from the layers above and below. It consists mainly of separate grains of sand and is heavily leached, and hence nutrient deficient, as a result of either (or both) very high precipitation and very pervious bedrock. Organic acids from the humus contribute to the leaching process by carrying cations down through the soil.

Beneath the leached layer collect the iron, humus and other materials that have been washed down through the soil. Humus and iron oxide may cement into a '**hard pan**' or '**iron pan**' which may be so hard and thick that it prevents the penetration of roots to the layers below. Between the pan and the parent rock is a nutrient-rich layer where the leached materials accumulate.

The leached layer, in which most of the plant roots grow, is acidic (pH 3–4) and low in nitrates and other plant nutrients. Podzols are therefore relatively infertile soils. Much of the nutrient in a coniferous forest is present in the biomass of trees and litter rather than in the soil. Cycling of nutrients and decomposition are slow. Such soils tend to be a dominant factor in determining the vegetation of an area because they favour acid-loving plants (**calcifuges**). There are relatively few calcifuge species and these include many typical heathland species such as the heathers (*Calluna vulgaris, Erica tetralix, Erica cinerea*), heath bedstraw (*Galium saxatile*), sheep's sorrel (*Rumex acetosella*) and *Rhododendron*.

Brown earths (brown forest soils)

Brown earths have a relatively simple appearance in profile, consisting of uniform brown or dark brown A and B horizons which grade in conspicuously into each other (fig 12.27). They are associated with temperate deciduous forests, often in warmer areas of lower altitude than the coniferous forests and podzols. Decomposition rates are greater than on podzols owing to the higher temperature and lower resistance of deciduous leaves to decomposition, so there is a faster turnover of litter. This layer is usually shallow as the soil is rich enough in calcium (giving a pH of 4.5–8) to support large numbers of organisms, such as earthworms, which mix the top layers of soil. The humus formed is of the type known as **mull**. Nutrient richness increases towards the B horizon (as in podzols). The absence of a pan means that plant roots have unrestricted

access to the deeper, more nutrient-rich layers and the soils are generally relatively fertile. They weather to a loamy texture.

The mineral nutrient content of deciduous forest biomass and of the soil is higher than in coniferous forest and there is a more rapid cycling of nutrients.

Rendzinas

The name originates from the Polish word *rzedzic*, to tremble, as the soil is shallow and implements used in farming strike the rock below.

Rendzinas are very shallow soils consisting of a thin dark brown or black calcium-rich layer covering a calcareous bedrock (fig 12.28). They are characteristic of limestone and chalk.

Climate has little influence on their development and they are therefore found in a wide range of climatic conditions. Chalk and limestone generally form hills (such as the Downs and Cotswolds) since, being very permeable, water tends to penetrate the rock rapidly rather than form streams and cause erosion.

Rendzinas generally form steep slopes where the soil remains, in effect, permanently underdeveloped due mainly to soil creep. The rapid water penetration of the soil means that over a period of time the calcareous material, which is slightly soluble, is leached out, leaving behind any siliceous material in the surface layer of the soil. There is no B horizon and no definite layers can be distinguished. The important features of the soil from a biological viewpoint are its high calcium carbonate content (up to 80%), which gives it a basic character with a pH value greater than 8.0, and its rapid drainage which causes drying out. Plants growing on rendzinas are, therefore, usually specialised for

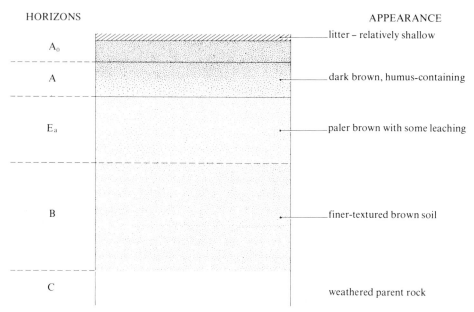

Fig 12.27 *Profile of a brown earth*

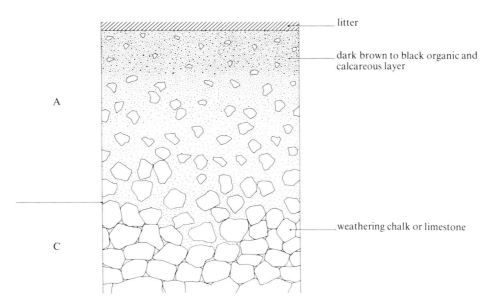

litter

dark brown to black organic and
calcareous layer

A

weathering chalk or limestone

C

Fig 12.28 *Profile of a rendzina*

reducing water loss and for making maximum use of
available water, often possessing laterally extensive roots
or deep roots which penetrate the bedrock. Some plants
thrive particularly well in conditions of high pH and are
called **calcicoles**. Examples are *Clematis* (traveller's joy or
old man's beard), milkwort (*Polygala calcarea*), wild
marjoram (*Origanum vulgare*) and basil-thyme (*Acinos
arvensis*). Rendzinas generally have a relatively rich flora.
Like podzols, they are an example of a soil which has a
particularly strong influence on the biotic component of the
ecosystem.

12.5.4   Climatic factors

The chief climatic variables in an ecosystem
are light, temperature, water availability and wind. Their
effects on soil formation have already been described in
section 12.5.2 and their direct effects on the biotic
component of the ecosystem are described below.

Light

As the source of energy for photosynthesis light is essential
for life, but it influences living organisms in many other
ways. In considering its effects it is useful to remember that
the intensity, quality (wavelength or colour), and duration
(photoperiod) of light can all have different effects.

Light intensity is affected by the angle of incidence of the
Sun's rays to the surface of the Earth. This varies with
latitude, season, time of day and aspect of slope.

Photoperiod or daylength is a more or less constant 12 h
at the equator but at higher latitudes it varies seasonally.
Plants and animals of higher latitudes typically show

photoperiodic responses that synchronise their activities
with the seasons, such as flowering and germination of
plants (section 15.4), migration, hibernation and reproduction of animals (section 16.8.5).

The need for light by plants has an important effect on
the structure of communities. Aquatic plants are confined
to surface layers of water and in terrestrial ecosystems
competition for light favours certain strategies such as
gaining height through growing tall or climbing, and
increasing leaf surface area. In woodland this results in
stratification as explained in section 12.6.1.

Some of the major processes in which light is involved,
and which are discussed in other chapters, are summarised
in table 12.12.

Temperature

The main source of heat is the Sun's radiation, with
geothermal sources being important only in a minority of
habitats, such as the growth of bacteria and blue-green
algae in hot springs.

A given organism will survive only within a certain
temperature range for which it is metabolically and
structurally adapted. If the temperature of a living cell falls
below freezing, the cell is usually physically damaged and
killed by the formation of ice crystals. At the other
extreme, if temperatures are too high, enzymes become
denatured. Between the extremes enzyme-controlled reactions, and hence metabolic activity, double in rate with
every 10°C rise. Most organisms are able to exert some
degree of control over their temperatures by a variety of
responses and adaptations so that extremes and sudden
changes of environmental temperature can be 'smoothed

Table 12.12 Major processes of plants and animals in which light is involved.

Photosynthesis (see chapter 9 and section 12.3.4)
  On average 1–5% of the radiation incident on plants is used in photosynthesis
  Source of energy for rest of food chain
  Light is also needed for chlorophyll synthesis

Transpiration (see section 14.3)
  About 75% of the radiation incident on plants is wasted in causing water to evaporate thereby causing transpiration
  Important implications for water conservation

Photoperiodism (see sections 15.4 and 16.8.5)
  Important for synchrony of plant and animal behaviour (particularly reproduction) with seasons

Movement (see section 15.1 and chapter 17)
  Phototropism and photonasty in plants; important for reaching light
  Phototactic movements of animals and unicellular plants; important for locating suitable habitat

Vision in animals (see section 16.5)
  One of the major senses

Other roles
  Synthesis of vitamin D in humans
  Prolonged exposure to ultra-violet damaging, particularly to animals, therefore pigmentation, avoidance behaviour, etc.

out' (sections 18.3 and 18.4). Aquatic environments undergo less extreme temperature changes, and therefore provide more stable habitats, than terrestrial environments owing to the high heat capacity of water.

As with light intensity, temperature is broadly dependent on latitude, season, time of day and aspect of slope. However, local variations are common, particularly in microhabitats, which have their own microclimates. Vegetation usually has some microclimatic effect on temperature, as in forests (section 12.6.3) or on a smaller scale within individual clumps of plants or the shelter of leaves and buds of individual plants.

Moisture and salinity

Water is essential for life and is a major limiting factor in terrestrial ecosystems. It is precipitated from the atmosphere as rain, snow, sleet, hail or dew. There is a continuous cycling of water, the **hydrological cycle** (section 12.4), which basically governs water availability over land surfaces. For terrestrial plants water is absorbed mainly from the soil. Rapid drainage, low rainfall and high evaporation, or a combination of these factors, can result in dry soils, whereas the opposite extremes can lead to permanent waterlogging. The amount of water in the soil therefore depends on the water-retaining capacity of the soil itself, and the balance between precipitation and the combined effects of evaporation and transpiration (evapotranspiration), evaporation taking place from the surface of wet vegetation as well as from the soil surface.

Plants can be classified according to their ability to tolerate water shortage as xerophytes (high tolerance), mesophytes (medium tolerance) and hydrophytes (low tolerance/water-adapted). Some of the xeromorphic adaptations will be discussed in section 14.3.7 with transpiration and in section 19.3.2, and are also summarised in table 12.13. Similarly, terrestrial animals show adaptations for gaining and conserving water, particularly in dry habitats (see section 19.3.4 and table 12.13).

Aquatic organisms also have problems of water regulation (section 19.4.6). Salinity of water is relevant, as a comparison between freshwater and marine species will reveal. Relatively few plants and animals can withstand large fluctuations in salinity. Those that can are usually associated with estuaries or salt marshes, such as the snail *Hydrobia ulvae* which can survive a range of salinities from 50–1 600 mmol dm^{-3} of sodium chloride. Salinity may also be relevant in terrestrial habitats; if evaporation exceeds precipitation soils may become saline and this is a problem in some irrigated areas.

Atmosphere

The atmosphere is a major part of the ecosphere, to which it is linked by a number of biogeochemical cycles which have gaseous components, principally the carbon, nitrogen, oxygen and hydrological cycles. Its physical properties are also of importance, for its low resistance to movement and lack of physical support for terrestrial organisms has had a direct influence on their structure and, in addition, several animal groups have exploited flight as a means of locomotion. The atmosphere, like the oceans, is constantly circulating. This is a mass flow phenomenon, the energy for which comes from the Sun.

On a large scale, atmospheric circulation is particularly relevant to the distribution of water vapour because this can be picked up locally (by evaporation), carried by mass flow in moving air masses and deposited locally (by precipitation). If the release of other gases into the atmosphere is local, for example pollutant gases such as sulphur dioxide from industrial areas, then the pattern of atmospheric circulation will affect their distribution and eventual precipitation as solutions in rainfall.

Wind can interact with other environmental variables to affect growth of vegetation, particularly trees in exposed places, where they may become stunted and distorted on their windward sides. Wind is also important in increasing evapotranspiration under conditions of low humidity.

Dispersal of spores, seeds, and so on through the atmosphere, aided by wind, increases the spread of non-motile organisms like plants, fungi and some bacteria. Winds may also influence the dispersal or migration of flying animals.

Another atmospheric variable is atmospheric pressure, which decreases with altitude. This reduces oxygen availability and affects animals as described in section 11.8.1, and increases transpiration from plants, the latter resulting in adaptations to conserve water, as, for example, those shown by many alpine plants.

Table 12.13 Adaptations of plants and animals to dry conditions.

	Examples
Reducing water loss	
Leaves reduced to needles or spines	Cactaceae, Euphorbiaceae (spurges), conifers
Sunken stomata	*Pinus, Ammophila*
Leaf rolls into cylinder	*Ammophila*
Thick waxy cuticle	Leaves of most xerophytes; insects
Swollen stem with large volume to surface area ratio	Cactaceae and Euphorbiaceae ('succulents')
Hairy leaves	Many alpine plants
Leaf-shedding in drought	*Fouquieria splendens* (ocotillo or candle plant)
Stomata open at night, close during day	Crassulaceae (stonecrops)
Efficient carbon dioxide fixation at night with partial opening of stomata	C_4 plants, e.g. *Zea mais*
Uric acid as nitrogenous waste	Insects, birds and some reptiles
Long loop of Henlé in kidneys	Desert mammals, e.g. camel, desert rat
Tissues tolerant of high temperatures, reducing sweating or transpiration	Many desert plants, camel
Burrowing behaviour	Many small desert mammals, e.g. desert rat
Spiracles covered with flaps	Many insects
Increasing water uptake	
Extensive shallow root system and deep roots	Some Cactaceae, e.g. *Opuntia*, and Euphorbiaceae
Long roots	Many alpine plants, e.g. *Leontopodium alpinum* (edelweiss)
Burrow for water	Termites
Water storage	
In mucilaginous cells and cell walls	Cactaceae and Euphorbiaceae
In specialised bladder	Desert frog
As fat (water is a product of oxidation)	Desert rat
Physiological tolerance of water loss	
Apparent dehydration can occur without death	Some epiphytic ferns and clubmosses, many bryophytes and lichens, *Carex physiodes* (sedge)
Loss of high proportion of body mass with rapid recovery when water is available	*Lumbricus terrestris* (70% loss of body mass), camel (30% loss)
Evasion	
Pass unfavourable season as seed	Californian poppy
Pass unfavourable season as bulbs or tubers	Some lilies
Seed dispersal, with some reaching more favourable conditions	
Escape behaviour	Soil organisms, e.g., mites, earthworm
Aestivation in mucus-containing sheath	Earthworm, lungfish

Microclimates

The particular climatic conditions associated with a habitat or microhabitat may be different from those of surrounding areas and are known as **microclimates**. An understanding of microclimates and microhabitats is important to an understanding of the complexity of ecosystems. One example will serve to illustrate the general principle. A group of crustaceans known as isopods (woodlice and related forms) contains species such as *Porcellio* which are confined to the moist air of leaf litter and other species such as *Armadillidium* which are able to withstand drier conditions and wander more freely.

12.5.5 Topography

The influence of topography is intimately connected with the other abiotic factors since it can strongly influence local climate and soil development, as already discussed.

The main topographic factor is altitude. Higher altitudes are associated with lower average temperatures and a greater diurnal temperature range, higher precipitation (including snow), increased wind speeds, more intense radiation, lower atmospheric pressures and reduced gas concentrations, all factors which have an influence on plant and animal life. As a result, vertical zonations are common, as shown in fig 12.29.

Mountain chains can act as climatic barriers. As air rises over mountains it cools and precipitation tends to occur. Thus a rain 'shadow' occurs on the leeward side of the mountains where air is drier and precipitation is less. This affects the ecosystems. Mountains also act as barriers to dispersal and migration and may play important roles as isolating mechanisms in the process of speciation as described in section 25.7.

Another important topographic factor is aspect. In the northern hemisphere south-facing slopes receive more sunlight, and therefore higher light intensities and temperatures, than valley bottoms and north-facing slopes (the reverse being true in the southern hemisphere). This has

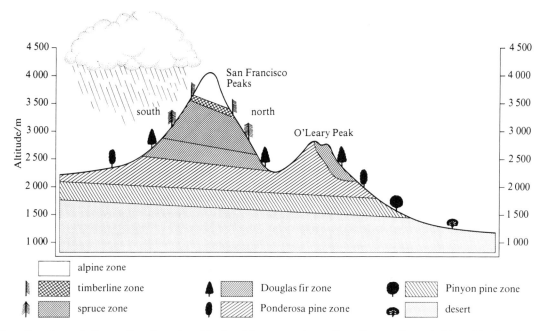

Fig 12.29 *Zonation of vegetation on San Francisco Peaks, Arizona, as viewed from the south-east. (From Merriam (1890). Redrawn and modified from W. D. Billings (1972)* Plants, man and the ecosystem, *2nd ed., Macmillan: London and Basingstoke.)*

striking effects on the natural vegetation and on land use by humans.

Steepness of slope (**inclination**) is a third topographic factor. Steep slopes generally suffer from faster drainage and run-off and the soils are therefore thinner and drier, with more xeromorphic vegetation. At slope angles in excess of 35° soil and vegetation are typically unable to develop, and screes of loose material form.

12.6 Community ecology and ecological succession

A **community** is a group of interacting populations living in a given area, and represents the living part of an ecosystem. It functions as a dynamic unit with trophic levels, a flow of energy and a cycling of nutrients through it as described in section 12.4.

Some of the interactions have also been mentioned in section 12.3, such as predator–prey relationships (including grazing) and parasitism. Others may exist, such as mutualism (section 2.5.3) and competition (section 12.7.6).

The structure of a community is always built up over a period of time. An example which can be used as a model for the development of a community is the invasion and colonisation of bare rock, as on a recently created volcanic island. Trees and shrubs cannot grow on bare rock since there is insufficient soil. Algae and lichens, however, can invade and colonise such areas, coming in by various methods of dispersal and forming the **pioneer community**. The accumulation of dead and decomposing organisms, and the erosion of rock by weathering, leads to the accumulation of sufficient soil for invasion and colonisation by larger plant species such as mosses or ferns. Ultimately these plants will be succeeded by even larger and more nutrient-demanding plants such as seed-bearing plants, including grasses, shrubs and trees. Fig 12.30 shows a typical succession.

Such replacement of some species by others through time is called an **ecological succession**. The final stable and self-perpetuating community, which is in equilibrium with its environment, is called the **climax community** and is the most productive that environment **can sustain** (see also section 12.6.2). The animals of such a community will also have shown a succession, to a large extent dictated by the plant succession, but also being influenced by what animals are available to migrate from surrounding communities.

The type of succession described above, in which there is an initial colonisation of bare rock or other surface lacking organic soil, such as sand dunes or glaciated surfaces, is called **primary succession. Secondary succession** is said to occur when the surface is completely or largely denuded of vegetation but has already been influenced by living organisms and has an organic component, for example a cleared forest or a previously burned or farmed area. Seeds and spores and organs of vegetative reproduction, such as rhizomes, may be present in the ground and thus influence the succession. In both primary and secondary succession the flora and fauna of surrounding areas are major factors influencing the types of plants and animals entering the successions through chance dispersal and migration.

> **12.16** What factors are likely to affect the number and diversity of species reaching an area?

The complete succession is sometimes called a **sere**, the sere being made up of a series of **seral communities (seral stages)**. Seres of particular environments tend to follow similar successions and may therefore be classified according to environment; for example a **hydrosere** develops in an aquatic environment as a result of the colonisation of open water and a **halosere** develops in a saltmarsh.

398

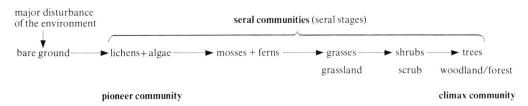

major disturbance of the environment → bare ground ——→ lichens+algae ——→ mosses + ferns ——→ grasses ——→ shrubs ——→ trees

seral communities (seral stages)

grassland · scrub · woodland/forest

pioneer community · climax community

Fig 12.30 *A typical terrestrial succession*

The climax community is often described as having one **dominant** or several **co-dominant** species. The term dominance is rather subjective but normally refers to those species with the greatest collective biomass or productivity, although physical size of individuals is also usually considered important. In practice, however, the concept of dominance is often of little value, as will become apparent in section 12.6.2.

The idea of succession was first discussed in detail in 1916 by Clements, who studied communities in North America and came to the conclusion that climate is the dominant factor in determining the composition of the climax community. His view, known as the **monoclimax hypothesis**, was that only one climax community was ultimately possible for a given climate, and this was called the **climatic climax community**. Any interruption in the progression towards this climax caused by local conditions of topography, microclimate, land use, and so on might still lead to a stable community, but this could not be regarded as a climax because, in the long term, climatically determined factors should lead to the theoretical climax. Mountains and hills, for example, would gradually be eroded away with consequent changes in community structure. The more modern concept is that of the **polyclimax**, which is a climax influenced by all physical factors, one or several of which may be dominant, such as drainage, soil, topography or incidence of fire. The community is regarded as a true climax community if it is 'stable' with respect to time. Any change occurring is relatively slow compared with the time taken to establish the climax through succession.

Zonation

Within a community at any one time species may be spatially distributed according to variations of the physical environment. This is called **zonation**. A good example is the zonation of seaweeds and marine animals that occurs on rocky shores from low-tide to high-tide level and into the splash zone. Physical conditions vary through these zones, notably length of exposure to air between successive tides, and each zone is occupied by species adapted for its particular conditions. Zonation on a seashore is described and illustrated in section 13.4. Another good example of zonation is the vertical zonation that occurs on mountains with increasing altitude (fig 12.29). Superficially zonations may resemble succession, but it is important to recognise the basic difference, namely that with zonation the species vary in space (spatially), whereas with succession the species vary in time (temporally).

12.6.1 Examples of natural and human-made climax communities in Britain

As a result of pollen analysis it has been possible to build up a picture of vegetational changes in Britain since the end of the last Ice Age about 10 000 years ago. At the beginning of the Neolithic period, about 5 000 years ago, much of lowland Britain was covered with a climax community that was forest, predominantly oak. Neolithic Man introduced agriculture and large-scale clearing of forest for the first time. He cultivated mainly the drier upland areas, such as the chalk of the South Downs and the limestone of the Cotswolds. The areas were reduced to grassland for grazing and were sometimes tilled for crops. By the Iron Age there appears to have been fairly extensive cultivation and grazing of these areas. A typical climax community of, for example, Roman times (when Britain was in the late Iron Age) would have been a lowland forest with oak as the dominant species, or a mixed oak–beech climax, and herbivores such as deer, omnivores such as bears and carnivores such as wolves and lynxes. The Weald (the area between the North and South Downs) and Midland Plain are examples of areas that were covered with such forests. Pine and birchwoods would have occupied poorer, sandier soils and higher altitudes. Ash was common on limestone and chalk hills, alder and willow at wetter sites.

The modern distribution of beech shows a link with chalk and limestone areas. This reflects past human use of beech and oak and the greater climatic sensitivity of beech in Britain. Beech can grow on a wide variety of soils and will dominate oak on well-drained loams. Its patchy modern distribution on loamy soils in part reflects human preference for oak throughout history. Oak timber, for structural purposes, and bark, for tanning, were highly valued. Adequate supplies of beech, used in furniture making, could be obtained from beechwoods in areas where oak could not compete (the shallow soils of calcareous areas – see below). Furthermore, oak produces acorns every three or four years whereas heavy beech 'mast' (seed) years are less frequent in Britain. Frost susceptibility and cool summers are key factors affecting seed production, germination and establishment of beech in Britain. Oak regeneration thus occurred more regularly, reinforcing the human-induced tendency for more widespread and abundant oakwoods.

Cultivation spread from the hills to the more fertile and easily worked lowland soils. There has been a progressive clearing of natural forest and increasing interference in natural communities until the present day, when there are only a few 'relic' woodlands left that can be regarded as near natural. As a result, some of the apparently natural vegetation that occurs today is not a natural climax vegetation but a man-made climax or a 'sub-climax' (sometimes called a **plagioclimax**). Two good examples are chalk grassland and lowland heaths.

Much of the vegetation of chalk hills, such as the North and South Downs, is described as grassland and is notable for the rich variety of its flowers, many of which, like certain orchids, are relatively rare. The vegetation could be regarded as a **biotic climax** because the dominant influence in maintaining its stability has been the biological effects of grazing. Sheep and cattle were the dominant herbivores and, since its introduction by the Normans, the rabbit. Rabbits became a serious pest on parts of the chalk downs by cropping the grass too short for use by other herbivores, but in 1953 the viral disease myxomatosis was 'accidentally' introduced into England. The disease spread so rapidly through the rabbit populations of Britain that by the end of 1955 the rabbit population had decreased by 90%. The disease still recurs at intervals and the rabbit population is still much smaller than formerly. As a result of the reduction of both rabbit and domestic grazing, young saplings of shrubs and trees survived. This, and possibly other factors, mean that **regeneration** of woodland is now a

'problem' in some areas where conservationists are trying to preserve the chalk grassland. The typical regeneration sequence (really a secondary succession) is through scrub in which shrubs dominate (such as bramble, hawthorn, dogwood, juniper and blackthorn) to a climax consisting of beech woodland. Beech is able to dominate oak in the drier chalk soils and is particularly characteristic of the steeper slopes. It is a good competitor partly because it shades out other species. Furthermore, on the drier shallow chalk soils the characteristically dense surface root mat of beech successfully absorbs water and nutrients and gives stability, whereas oak with its deep tap-root system cannot survive. On gentler slopes with deeper, moister soils, ash may precede beech in the succession and on heavier, wetter clay soils, oak is a better competitor than beech and becomes dominant. Here, then, the edaphic factor is important in the succession. Fig 12.31a summarises a succession from chalk grassland to woodland in south-east England.

Fig. 12.31b shows a succession from heath to woodland. Lowland heaths also tend to be associated with a particular soil type, being typical of acid, sandy soils. Like chalk grassland, they are also a man-made climax. In the past they were used for grazing by horses, cattle, pigs and rabbits, the dominant plants being heathers, particularly ling (*Calluna vulgaris*). The heath was managed by burning off older heaths to allow regeneration of young succulent shoots from underground parts that survive the fire. Fire is

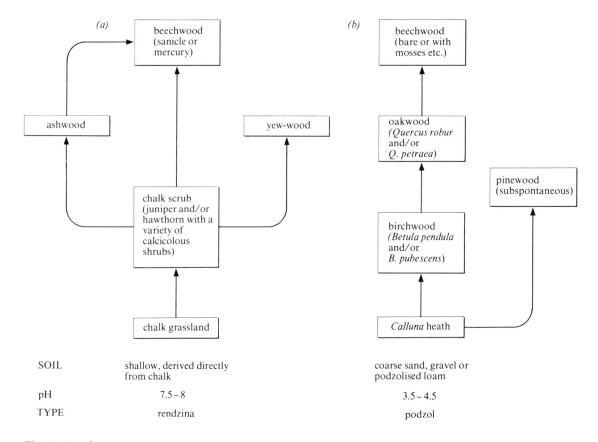

Fig 12.31 *Successions in south-east England.* (a) *Chalk grassland to woodland.* (b) *Heath to woodland (From A. G. Tansley (1968)* Britain's green mantle, *2nd ed., Allen & Unwin.)*

thus an important abiotic factor in development of this community. If unmanaged, the heath gradually reverts to woodland, passing through a scrub stage in which gorse, broom, hawthorn and other species may dominate. Birch is often the first tree to become established, followed by oak, the whole succession taking about 200 years. Pine, and less commonly beech, may also compete with oak. If lowland heaths are to be maintained, then active measures to remove shrubs and trees are necessary. Such management is desirable in the context of conservation because they contribute to the diversity of habitats found in Britain and certain rare species, such as the natterjack toad and the Dartford warbler (in Dorset), are found on heaths or heath scrubs.

A climax woodland

A typical terrestrial climax community is a deciduous woodland. Such communities are very rich in species. In a wood near Oxford, which has been the subject of a long and detailed study, about 4 000 animal species have been found. Part of the reason for species richness is the complex structure of the woodland which contains many niches and microhabitats.

The food web of an oak woodland has already been shown in fig 12.6a. Fig 12.32 illustrates the structure of a typical deciduous woodland. An important feature is the layering, or **stratification**, that is present. Most of the primary production occurs in the tree canopy and most of the decomposition at ground level, with animals occupying niches in all layers.

12.6.2   Underlying features of succession

A number of attempts have been made to explain succession in terms of some underlying principle which determines the progress towards the climax.

Ecological dominance

The observations of ecological dominance suggest that successions might always progress towards a climax in which one species is dominant, such as oak woodland, or a few species are codominant, such as beech–oak woodland. These impose restrictions, such as shading, on the species that can grow in association with them. However, the concept of dominance is difficult to apply in some situations, as in planktonic communities, among animals, and in the tropical rain forests where several hundred tree species may be found in roughly equal numbers.

Productivity and biomass

Lindeman in 1942 proposed that succession involved increasing productivity until a climax community was reached in which the maximum efficiency of energy conversion occurred. This is a logical and attractive hypothesis because the amount of energy flowing through an ecosystem is a major limiting factor in determining the number and biomass of the organisms it can support.

Evidence shows that the later stages of successions do become more productive, but that there is usually a decline in gross productivity associated with the climax community. Thus older forests have lower productivities than younger forests, which in turn may have lower productivities than the more species-rich herb layers that precede them. A similar decline has been observed in some aquatic systems. Maximum productivity is now believed to be attained very quickly in many successions, although data are still few. The reasons for the decrease in productivity can only be speculated upon, but using a forest as an example, older trees might be expected to be less productive than younger trees for several reasons. One is that the accumulation of nutrients in the increasing standing crop biomass may lead to a reduction in nutrient recycling. However, a simple reduction in vigour as the average age of the individuals in the community increases to a constant point would presumably cause a reduction in productivity.

Although it does not seem possible to argue that successions lead to maximum efficiency of energy conversion (maximum gross productivity) it *is* possible to argue that they lead to maximum accumulation of biomass. This is most obvious in the case of forest communities, where the plants become larger and larger during the succession, but the accumulated biomass of other climax communities is also normally greater than in the successional stages. Changes in gross productivity, respiration and biomass during a typical succession are summarised in fig 12.33. This shows that in the climax community these terms become more or less constant. It also shows that an upper limit of biomass is reached when total respiratory losses (R) from the system almost equal gross primary productivity (P), that is the P/R ratio is almost equal to 1. These and other trends that can be expected to occur in successions are summarised in table 12.14.

During a succession more and more of the available nutrients become locked up in the biomass of the community with a consequent decrease in nutrients in the abiotic component of the ecosystem (such as soil and water). The amount of detritus produced also increases and detritus feeders take over from grazers as the main primary consumers. Appropriate changes in food webs occur and detritus becomes the main source of nutrients.

12.6.3   Interactions between organisms and their abiotic environment

Early in a succession the most important interactions are those between living organisms and the abiotic environment. The latter is changed as a result of the activity of the organisms. A striking example of this is the formation of sand dunes as a result of the accumulation of wind-blown sand around shoots of *Ammophila* (marram grass or *Psamma*). This is described in fig 12.34. The stabilisation of sand dunes takes place over a period of a

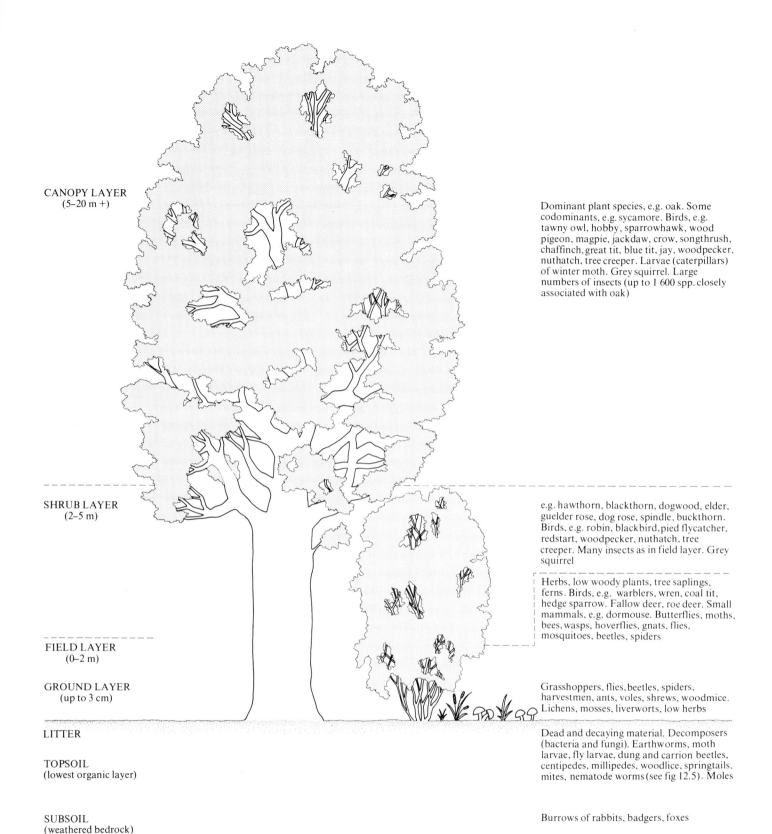

CANOPY LAYER
(5–20 m +)

Dominant plant species, e.g. oak. Some codominants, e.g. sycamore. Birds, e.g. tawny owl, hobby, sparrowhawk, wood pigeon, magpie, jackdaw, crow, songthrush, chaffinch, great tit, blue tit, jay, woodpecker, nuthatch, tree creeper. Larvae (caterpillars) of winter moth. Grey squirrel. Large numbers of insects (up to 1 600 spp. closely associated with oak)

SHRUB LAYER
(2–5 m)

e.g. hawthorn, blackthorn, dogwood, elder, guelder rose, dog rose, spindle, buckthorn. Birds, e.g. robin, blackbird, pied flycatcher, redstart, woodpecker, nuthatch, tree creeper. Many insects as in field layer. Grey squirrel

Herbs, low woody plants, tree saplings, ferns. Birds, e.g. warblers, wren, coal tit, hedge sparrow. Fallow deer, roe deer. Small mammals, e.g. dormouse. Butterflies, moths, bees, wasps, hoverflies, gnats, flies, mosquitoes, beetles, spiders

FIELD LAYER
(0–2 m)

GROUND LAYER
(up to 3 cm)

Grasshoppers, flies, beetles, spiders, harvestmen, ants, voles, shrews, woodmice. Lichens, mosses, liverworts, low herbs

LITTER

Dead and decaying material. Decomposers (bacteria and fungi). Earthworms, moth larvae, fly larvae, dung and carrion beetles, centipedes, millipedes, woodlice, springtails, mites, nematode worms (see fig 12.5). Moles

TOPSOIL
(lowest organic layer)

SUBSOIL
(weathered bedrock)

Burrows of rabbits, badgers, foxes

BEDROCK

Fig 12.32 *Layered structure of a typical deciduous woodland community. NB Some animals move between layers. For example grey squirrels forage on ground and sleep, breed and move among trees; birds may rest in one layer and feed in another, such as the tawny owl which takes mammals from the field and ground layers and nests in the canopy*

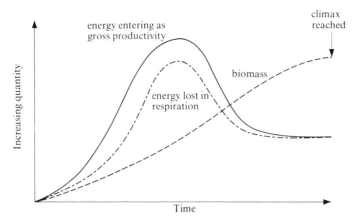

Fig 12.33 *Changes in gross productivity, respiration and biomass during a typical succession (Modified from M. R. Tribe et al. (1974) Ecological principles, Basic Biology Course 4, Cambridge University Press).*

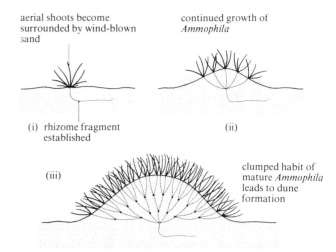

Fig 12.34 *Dune formation by gradual deposition of wind-blown sand around aerial shoots of* Ammophila

few years. A sand dune succession around Lake Michigan in North America has been well documented and here dune stabilisation allows the growth of larger plants with low nutritional requirements such as cottonwood (a tree) and pine trees. Over a long period of time a soil develops, typically accumulating organic carbon from the litter layer. Also an increase in nitrogen-fixing organisms leads to an increase in nitrogen in the soil. In parts this has allowed growth of oak which has become the dominant species. Once oak has become fully established soil conditions apparently remain constant over an indefinite period with nutrient demand being balanced by nutrient input from recycling of leaf litter and the like. Here edaphic factors have been a dominant influence in the succession and have themselves been modified during the succession. It may take a thousand years, however, for the soil to reach a stable chemical composition and for the succession to be regarded as complete.

The relatively short period for early stages of succession compared with later stages is an important general principle illustrated by this example. Further development of a climax community will obviously occur in response to changes in environmental conditions, either sudden or long term. The succession of Ice Ages over the last 1.8 million years is a good example of climatic change that profoundly changed the communities of affected areas.

There are other ways in which the biotic community can influence the physical environment, and hence the succession. Local modifications of climate may be induced, forming microclimates within the ecosystem.

> **12.17** In what ways might a group of trees influence the environment under the canopy in terms of (*a*) light, (*b*) temperature, (*c*) wind and (*d*) moisture?

Table 12.14 Summary of changes in an ecosystem during a typical secondary succession.

Characteristic	Stage of ecosystem development	
	Immature (early)	Mature (late)
Gross production/community respiration (P/R ratio)	high (>1)	approaches 1
Net community production	high	low
Food chains	linear, mainly grazing	web-like, mainly detritus-feeding
Total organic matter (or biomass)	small	large
Species diversity	low	high*
Structure of community	simple	complex (stratification, many microhabitats)
Niche specialisation	broad	narrow
Size of organism	small	large
Strategies adopted by species (section 12.7.4)	'r-strategy'	'K-strategy'

* Most plant and some animal examples of succession show a peak of species diversity before climax.

Similarly, microhabitats may be generated, such as dead wood (which in a given area may support about 200 species of animals), dung (inhabited by more than 300 animal species, chiefly beetles and flies) and carrion (also colonised by beetles and flies).

12.6.4 Interactions between organisms within the community

In the latter stages of succession, biotic interactions become more important in forming the detailed community structure. The variety of living organisms tends to increase, so inevitably their interactions become more complex. The tropical rain forest communities, which are among the longest established climax communities, are renowned for their species richness and the extreme complexity of their biotic interactions. What we are concerned with in community ecology are the dynamic interactions between species rather than between members of the same species. A number of different kinds of interaction occur. Predator–prey interactions, including grazing, have already been mentioned with food chains and food webs in section 12.3, where the dependence of some organisms on others was made clear. Parasitic, symbiotic and other mutualistic relationships are also important. Studies of these interactions are bound to overlap with population ecology as some of the examples given in section 12.7.6 show.

What gradually occurs is the filling of the available ecological niches and there may be competition for a given niche (section 12.1). The chances of an animal becoming established will depend on many factors, including the likelihood of its chance migration into the area, the availability of suitable food, its ability to find a suitable niche and if necessary the ability to compete effectively for this niche. The more specialised it becomes for a particular niche, the less chance there is of direct competition.

A useful concept related to that of the ecological niche is **resource partitioning**, which is the sharing of the available resources among the different species of the community. Specialisation by different species to make use of different resources leads to less competition and a more stable community structure. Resource partitioning may take several forms, for example:

(1) specialisation of morphology and behaviour for different foods, such as the beaks of birds which may be modified for picking up insects, drilling holes, cracking nuts, tearing flesh, and so on;

(2) vertical separation, such as canopy dwellers and forest floor dwellers;

(3) horizontal separation, such as the occupation of different microhabitats.

One or a combination of these three factors would serve to separate the organisms into groups of species with reduced competition between the groups because each occupies its own niche. For example, ecological groupings have been devised for birds based on feeding location (air,

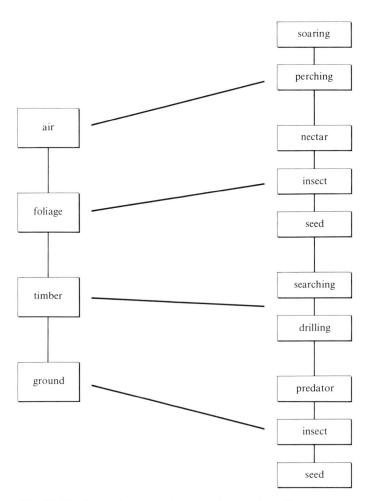

Fig 12.35 *Ecological groupings used to analyse three California bird communities. (From B. D. Collier* et al. *(1974) Dynamic ecology, Prentice Hall.)*

foliage, timber or ground) and subdivided according to major food type as shown in fig 12.35.

When plants are considered, each species will have its own set of optimum conditions of moisture, altitude, soil pH, and so on, in which it will be favoured, once again restricting direct competition.

Despite a tendency for each species to evolve its own particular niche, some direct competition between species for available resources is inevitable. This is discussed in section 12.7.6.

12.7 Population ecology

In the introduction to this chapter, a **population** was defined as a group of organisms of one species occupying a defined area and usually isolated to some degree from other similar groups by geographical or topographical boundaries, or even arbitrarily delimited by an investigator. Thus one might study, for example, the roe deer of a particular woodland, the frogs of a particular valley or trout of a particular lake. Many biogeographers widen this definition and use similar principles to study major plant and animal taxa, rather than single species, on a global or regional scale. In studying populations we are concerned not just with the numbers of a given species living in a given area at a given moment in time, but rather with an understanding of how populations grow, are maintained and decline in response to their environments. This aspect of population ecology is called **population dynamics**. It focusses on properties of a group rather than the individuals within the group. Thus one examines characteristics such as density, natality, mortality, survivorship, age structure, biotic potential, dispersion and growth form. Populations also have properties related to their ecology such as adaptiveness and reproductive fitness. Population interactions such as competition, predation and parasitism not only regulate growth of a given population but influence the structure of communities. Successions (section 12.6) may also be examined from the viewpoint of population interactions. Knowledge of how numbers of individuals of different species change through time can also be used in biomass and energy flow studies and therefore in building up knowledge of ecosystems. As discussed in section 12.1, the study of populations has many important applications, as in the control of pests and in species conservation.

Apart from some long-term studies on phytoplankton, most work on population dynamics has been done on animals and micro-organisms. With plants, especially crop plants, it is more useful, and easier in some cases, to collect data on biomass rather than numbers. The dynamics of plant populations exert a strong influence on those of animal populations so, for example, the study of human populations (**demography**) is usually studied in geography alongside the availability of food resources based on plants.

Some information on how to sample animal and plant populations with the aims of collecting data on numbers and distribution is given in section 13.2.

12.7.1 Birth rate (natality) and death rate (mortality)

Population size may increase as a result of **immigration** from neighbouring populations, or by reproduction of individuals within the population. One measure of reproduction is known as **fecundity** and concerns the numbers of offspring produced by individual females of the species. Fecundity is expressed in different ways, depending on convenience and the species involved. It could be defined, for example, as the average number of fertilised eggs produced in an average breeding cycle or in a lifetime. For mammals, fecundity is expressed as **birth rate** or **natality**, the number of young produced per female per unit time (usually per year). In the case of humans, birth rate is usually expressed as the number of births per thousand head of population per year (table 12.15) and generally less-developed countries, where birth control is not practised extensively, have birth rates about twice those of

Table 12.15 Birth rate statistics from selected countries and regions. Figures are the number of live births per year per thousand head of population.

Countries		Regions	
Kenya	53	Africa	46
Congo	45	Latin America	32
Iran	44	Asia	29
Egypt	41	North America	16
India	36	Australia	16
South Africa	36	Europe	14
Mexico	33		
Malaysia	31		
Jamaica	27		
Israel	25		
Chile	22		
China	18		
United States	16		
Cuba	15		
Japan	14		
East Germany	14		
United Kingdom	13		
Italy	12		
Sweden	12		
West Germany	10		

Data from the 1981 World Population data sheet.

Table 12.16 Death rate statistics from selected countries and regions. Figures are the number of deaths per year per thousand head of population.

Countries		Regions	
Ethiopia	25	Africa	17
Congo	19	Asia	11
India	15	Europe	10
East Germany	14	Latin America	9
Iran	14	North America	9
Kenya	14	Australia	7
South Africa	12		
United Kingdom	12		
West Germany	12		
Egypt	11		
Sweden	11		
Italy	9		
United States	9		
Mexico	8		
Malaysia	8		
Chile	7		
Israel	7		
China	6		
Cuba	6		
Jamaica	6		
Japan	6		
Costa Rica	4		

Data from the 1981 World Population data sheet.

better developed countries. Sociologists refer to the cultural change by a society from the higher to the lower rate as the **demographic transition**.

Population size may decrease as a result of **emigration** or death (**mortality**). In population biology, mortality strictly means *rate* of death and may be expressed in terms of per cent, or numbers per thousand, dying per year. Table 12.16 shows that generally speaking the well-developed countries have a lower mortality rate than the less-developed countries, owing to their better medical care and nutrition. Where medical and food aid programmes have been introduced, as in India since the Second World War, the statistics reveal a decreasing mortality rate. The very low mortality rates of places like Japan and Costa Rica are due to a relatively high proportion of young people.

12.7.2 Survivorship curves

The percentage of individuals that die before reaching reproductive age (**pre-reproductive mortality**) is one of the chief factors affecting population size, and for a given species is much more variable than fecundity. If population size is to remain constant, on average only two offspring from each male–female pair must survive to reproductive age.

If we start with a population of newborn individuals and the decrease in numbers of survivors is plotted against time, a **survivorship curve** is obtained. On the vertical axis, actual numbers of survivors may be plotted, or percentage survival:

$$\frac{\text{number of survivors}}{\text{number in original population}} \times 100\%$$

Different species have characteristic survivorship curves, depending partly on their pre-reproductive mortality. Some representative examples are shown in fig 12.36.

Most animals and plants exhibit a phenomenon called senescence or ageing, manifested as a declining vigour with increasing age beyond maturity. Once senescence begins, there is increasing likelihood of death occurring within a given time period. The immediate cause of death can vary, but the underlying cause is a reduced resistance to external factors such as disease. Curve (a) in fig 12.36 shows an almost ideal curve for a population in which senescence is the major factor affecting mortality. An example would be a human population in a modern industrialised country in which high standards of medicine and nutrition are maintained. Most people live to old age, but little can yet be done to prolong life expectancy beyond about 75 years. The main deviation of curve (a) from the ideal is due to infant mortality, shown by the dip at the start of the curve. Although infant mortality is much lower in industrialised countries, there are still above-average risks to life in early infancy. Another factor which will combine with senescence to affect the curve to some extent is accidental death, the cause of which may vary with age. In England, for example, deaths through car accidents reach a peak among people in their early twenties. A curve like (a) would also be obtained for an annual crop plant such as wheat, where all the plants in a given field senesce simultaneously.

Curve (b) is for a population with a high mortality rate early in life, such as might occur for mountain sheep or for humans in a country in which starvation and disease are prevalent. Curve (c) shows the kind of smooth curve that would be obtained if there was a constant mortality rate throughout life (50% per unit time). Such a curve is obtained if chance is the major factor influencing mortality and the organisms die out before senescence becomes evident. A curve similar to this was once obtained for a population of glass tumblers in a cafeteria. Some animal populations show survivorship curves which approximate closely to this model curve, for example *Hydra*, where there is no special risk attached to being young. Most non-vertebrates and plants show a curve similar to (c) but with high juvenile mortality superimposed so that the initial part of the curve descends even more steeply.

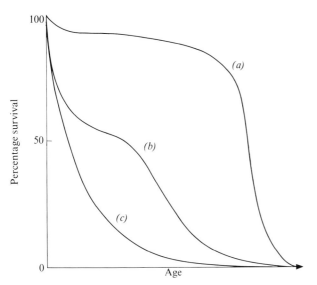

Fig 12.36 *Three types of survivorship curve. Letters (a), (b) and (c) are explained in the text*

Minor variations in survivorship curves may occur within species for various reasons, a common one being sexual differences. In humans, for example, female life expectancy is slightly greater than for males, although the precise reasons for this are unknown.

By plotting survivorship curves of species it is possible to determine the mortality rates of individuals of different ages and hence to determine at which ages they are most vulnerable. By identifying the factors causing death at these ages, an understanding can be gained of how population size is regulated.

12.21 The following figures apply to sockeye salmon in a Canadian river system. Each female salmon lays 3 200 eggs in a gravelly shallow in the river in autumn. 640 fry (young fish derived from these eggs) enter a lake near the shallow in the following spring. 64 smolts (older fish survivors from the fry) leave the lake one year later and migrate to the sea. Two adult fish (survivors of these smolts) return to the spawning grounds $2\frac{1}{2}$ years later; they spawn and then die. Calculate the percentage mortalities for sockeye salmon for each of the following periods:

(a) from laying eggs to movement of fry into the lake six months later;

(b) from entering the lake as fry to leaving the lake as smolts 12 months later;

(c) from leaving the lake as smolts to returning to the spawning grounds as adult salmon 30 months later;

Draw a survivorship curve for the sockeye salmon in this river system (plot percentage survival against age). What is the pre-reproductive mortality for these salmon?

Source of question: Open University, S100, Unit 20, *Species and Populations*, p. 71.

12.7.3 Population growth and growth curves

Populations grow and decline in characteristic ways. The size of population increase will be determined by the reproductive potential of the organisms concerned and by environmental resistance. The maximum reproductive potential is the rate of reproduction given unlimited environmental resources. This is termed the intrinsic rate of natural increase or the **biotic potential** (and is symbolised r in the growth curve equation). Biotic potential will vary according to the age structure of a population and obviously may also be influenced by male:female ratios. Thus, theoretically, one can identify the population structure that maximises biotic potential (r-max). This point is put to practical use in fisheries management. By regulating catches the population age structure can be manipulated to human advantage to maximise recruitment and growth rates.

In practice the full biotic potential of an organism is not realised. The difference between the actual occurring rate of increase and the biotic potential reflects environmental resistance. **Environmental resistance** means the sum total of limiting factors, both biotic and abiotic, which act together to prevent the biotic potential from being realised. It encompasses external factors such as predation, food supply, heat, light and space, and internal regulatory mechanisms such as intraspecific competition and behavioural adaptations. Strong feedback links exist between all these factors, for example intraspecific competition arises in response to some resource (such as space) which is in limiting supply.

Growth curves

Two basic forms of growth curve can be identified, the **J-shaped** growth curve and the **S-shaped** or sigmoidal growth curve. These contrasting forms may be combined or modified in various ways according to the particular circumstances of an organism's environment and life history. Human intervention may deliberately, or by chance, modify a population's growth form. An example is that of the Kaibab deer, more fully discussed in 12.7.6. In this case the population growth form changed from an S-shaped curve (density-dependent – see later) to a J-shaped form (density-independent – see later) primarily due to the deliberate removal by humans of predatory control. Eventually a new equilibrium was established marking a return to density-dependent control. Similarly many 'pest' problems arise as a result of human removal of a predator or competitor species, triggering a shift from sigmoidal to J-shaped population growth.

The S-shaped or sigmoidal growth curve describes a situation in which, in a new environment, the population density of an organism increases slowly initially, as it adapts to new conditions and establishes itself, then increases rapidly, approaching an exponential growth rate. It then shows a declining rate of increase until a zero population growth rate is achieved where rate of reproduction (natality) equals rate of death (mortality) (fig 12.37*a*). The declining rate of increase reflects increasing environmental resistance, which becomes proportionately more important at higher population densities. In other words, as numbers increase so competition for essential resources, such as food or nesting materials, increases until eventually feedback in terms of increased mortality and reproduction failures (fewer matings, stress-induced abortion) reduces population growth to zero with natality and mortality in approximate equilibrium.

This type of population growth is said to be **density-dependent** or density-conditioned since, for a given set of resources, growth rate depends on the numbers present in the population. The point of stabilisation or zero growth rate is the maximum **carrying capacity** of the given environment for the organism concerned. It represents the point where the sigmoidal curve levels off (the upper **asymptote**) and is symbolised K in population growth equations (see fig 12.37*a* and table 12.17 equation (*a*)).

The growth of a great variety of populations representing micro-organisms, plants and animals, under both laboratory and field conditions has been shown broadly to follow this basic sigmoidal pattern. A useful example is the model used in chapter 2 to describe bacterial population growth, in which a fresh culture medium is inoculated with bacteria (fig 2.7; see also section 21.1.2 and fig 21.1*d* for yeast). Phytoplankton in lakes and oceans may show sigmoidal growth in spring as could insects such as flour beetles or mites introduced into a new habitat with abundant food and no predators. In plants and animals which have complicated life histories and long periods of development there are often delays in build-up of numbers and limiting factors, and hence delayed density-conditioning. Such time lags may, for example, derive from the time of approximately one generation which elapses before the depression of birth rates at high densities shows up as a decrease in the adult population. An approximate way of incorporating such time delays into the equation for S-shaped growth is shown in table 12.17, equation (*b*). If the time-delay factor is long compared with the natural response time there will be a tendency for the population to overshoot carrying capacity and then overcompensate, giving an oscillatory rather than smooth return to the equilibrium point K, the carrying capacity.

The J-shaped growth curve describes a situation in which, after the initial establishment phase (lag phase), population growth continues in an exponential form until stopped *abruptly*, as environmental resistance becomes *suddenly* effective (fig 12.37*b*, table 12.17, equation (*c*)). Growth is said to be **density-independent** since regulation of growth rate is not tied to the population density until the final crash. The crash may be triggered by factors such as seasonality or the end of a breeding phase, either of the organism itself or of an important prey species. It may be associated with a particular stage in the life cycle, such as seed production, or it may be induced by human intervention as when an insecticide is used to control an insect pest

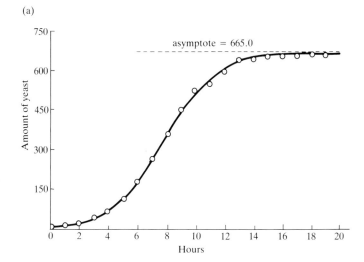

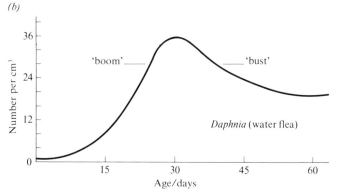

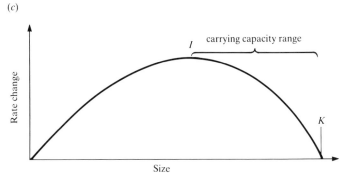

Fig 12.37 *Types of population growth curve. (a) The sigmoidal growth curve (S-shaped curve). The growth of yeast in a culture. A simple case of the sigmoid growth form in which environmental resistance (in this case detrimental factors produced by the organisms themselves) is linearly proportional to the density. (From E.P. Odum (1983) Basic ecology, Holt-Saunders International.) (b) 'Boom-and-bust' (J-shaped) curve of water fleas grown in culture. (Based on A.S. Boughey (1971) Fundamental ecology, International Textbook Co.) (c) S-shaped curve redrawn to show changing rate of increase in relation to changing population size. I, the inflexion point, represents the maximum level (highest growth rate) and is thus the theoretical point for maximum sustainable yield for a game or fish population. The range between I and K represents a secure or desirable density. It maximises returns but minimises risk of sudden environmental change triggering either underproduction or overshooting carrying capacity and damaging the environment as might occur for an organism with a long generation time and hence delayed response to environmental change. (Source as in a.)*

Table 12.17 Equations for the sigmoid (S-shaped) and J-shaped ('boom-and-bust') growth curves.

Symbols:
r is the intrinsic rate of increase or biotic potential
N is the number of individuals in the populations
t represents time
d is the conventional mathematical symbol for instantaneous change
K represents carrying capacity
T represents the lag effect as in generation time (explained in text)

(a) Sigmoid growth curve $\dfrac{dN}{dt} = rN\dfrac{(K-N)}{K}$ or $rN(1-N/K)$

(b) Time-delayed regulation of sigmoidal growth $\dfrac{dN}{dt} = rN\,[1-N(t-T)/K]$

(c) J-shaped growth curve $\dfrac{dN}{dt} = rN$ with a definite limit on N

Note the clear relationship between the J-shaped and S-shaped curves.

The expressions $\dfrac{(K-N)}{K}$ or $(1-N/K)$ are alternative ways of indicating environmental resistance created by the growing population itself, which brings about an increasing reduction in the potential reproduction rate as the populations size approaches carrying capacity (K). In word form, equation (a) above may be summarised as:

| rate of population increase | equals | maximum possible rate of increase times the numbers present in the population | times | degree of realisation of maximum rate of increase |

population. Following the crash, such populations typically show a fluctuating recovery pattern giving the 'boom-and-bust' cycles characteristic of some insect species and

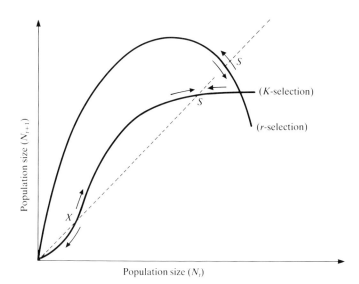

Fig 12.38 *The population growth curves of r- and K-strategists showing stable (S) equilibrium points and an unstable point, the extinction point (x) for K-strategists. Note that though an equilibrium point exists for r-selected species it is not monotonic as for K-species but subject to continuous marked oscillations (the boom-and-bust cycles). (Taken from T.R.E. Southwood (1976) Bionomic strategies and population parameters in Theoretical ecology, principles and applications, ed. R.M. May, Blackwell.)*

associated with algal blooms. In very general terms the J-shaped growth form may be considered an incomplete sigmoid curve where a sudden limiting effect comes in to play before the self-limiting effects within the population assume importance. Studies of thrips on roses illustrate this point. A J-shaped growth form is evident in favourable years when seasonality triggers a halt in population increase. In climatically less favourable years population growth is more sigmoidal in form as limiting effects within the population, such as competition for food resources, become operative before seasonality intervenes.

As discussed, the maximum population of an organism that a particular environment can sustain is termed the carrying capacity. This is identified theoretically as the K value (or upper asymptote) of the sigmoidal growth curve. Populations showing J-shaped growth do not achieve stability in this way, instead showing characteristic boom-and-bust cycles (see also fig 12.38, section 12.7.4). In practical terms carrying capacity implies continuing yield at maximum population densities without environmental damage. However, as fig 12.37c shows, greater productivity, or rates of population increase, will be achieved at lower densities than carrying capacity. Thus in fisheries or livestock management, where a regular annual crop of good size and quality is sought, maximum sustained yield will be achieved at population densities below carrying capacity. A good strategy aims to maintain the population between I (maximum population growth) and K (carrying capacity). If carrying capacity is exceeded then environmental resources will be depleted. Carrying capacity, at least temporarily, is reduced. The resulting lower population density then allows recovery of environmental resources. If human intervention or some other agencies cause carrying capacity to be greatly exceeded, then a permanent environmental change may result leading to an environment which is no longer suitable for that organism or which is capable of permanently sustaining only a much smaller population. Grazing-induced or grazing-exacerbated desertification of large areas of tropical rangelands reflects this process.

12.7.4 Population strategies

In the last section the terms r and K were used in equations for population growth. Species that reproduce rapidly and have a high value of r are termed r-species or r-strategists. They are generally opportunist species and represent the typical pioneer species of new and disturbed habitats. Migration and dispersal are an important part of their strategy. Selection pressure in such species favours high reproduction rate and short generation time. Since they may even be the sole colonisers of an area, competitive ability has little importance and r-strategists are typically small in size. Mortality rates are high. Although extinction is regularly the fate of individual populations (as habitats are modified and K-strategists arrive and out-compete), the species as a whole is very resilient. Mobility and low generation time ensure species survive as individuals, seeds or propagules, move on to new situations, such as newly dug ground, and rapidly colonise.

K strategists reproduce relatively slowly, for example trees and humans. The dominant thrusts of their survival strategy are mortality avoidance and competitive ability. Thus they are characteristic of stable, relatively undisturbed habitats where competitive ability rather than reproductive speed is a major survival attribute. They tend to be more typical of the later stages of succession. Such species are not very adapted to recover from population densities significantly below their equilibrium level (the K value or carrying capacity). If population numbers are greatly depressed these species tend towards extinction (fig 12.38). In contemporary times, when human activity often triggers rapid habitat change, such as deforestation, extreme K-strategists require active conservation measures rather more often than predominant r-strategists.

These two strategies, r and K, represent two different solutions to the same problem, which is long-term survival. Both are effective and the precise strategy of any species, or species population, will reflect the interplay of factors such as habitat variability in space and time and the longevity, size and fecundity of the organism concerned. In consequence a broad continuum of strategies from small, opportunist extreme r-selected species to large, dominant extreme K-selected species occurs (sometimes termed the **r-K continuum**). Some of the characteristics typical of extreme r- and K- strategists are summarised in table 12.18.

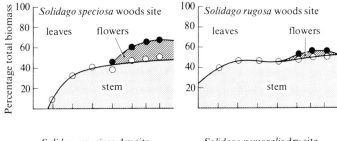
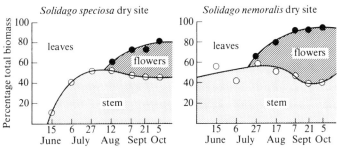

Fig 12.39 *Percentage biomass allocated to production of leaves, stems and flowers in four goldenrod populations (From R. M. May (ed.) (1976) Theoretical ecology, Blackwell.)*

12.22 Study fig 12.39 which shows the allocation of standing crop biomass to reproduction (flowers) in three species of goldenrod (*Solidago*) in the eastern USA. They grow either on woodland sites or on open, dry, disturbed sites of earlier successional stages, as indicated in the figure.
(a) Which species devotes most biomass to reproduction?
(b) Which species is most heavily r-selected?
(c) Which species is most heavily K-selected?
(d) What general conclusion can be made by comparing the reproductive behaviour of *S. speciosa* on woodland and dry sites?

Computer program. POPULATION MODELLER: A program concerning population dynamics. Population size vs. time for one species (e.g. r-strategy species, K-strategy species), or two species (e.g. competitors, predator–prey).

Table 12.18 Characteristics of r- and K-species.

r-species (opportunist species)	K-species (equilibrium species)
Reproduce rapidly (high fecundity, short generation time); therefore high value of r (the intrinsic rate of increase)	Reproduce slowly (low fecundity, long generation time); therefore low value of r
Reproduction rate not sensitive to population density	Reproduction rate sensitive to population density, rising rapidly if density falls
Investment of energy and materials spread over many offspring	Investment of energy and materials concentrated on a few offspring, with parental care in animals
Population size fluctuates greatly showing marked oscillations about a theoretical balance point which is not maintained over a long period (fig 12.38)	Population size stays close to equilibrium level determined by K
Species not very persistent in a given area	Species persistent in a given area
Disperse widely and in large numbers; with animals, migration may occur every generation	Disperse slowly
Reproduction is relatively expensive in terms of energy and materials	Reproduction is relatively inexpensive in terms of energy and materials; more energy and materials devoted to non-reproductive (vegetative) growth
Small size	Large size; woody stems and large roots if plants
Individuals short-lived	Individuals long-lived
Can occupy open ground	Not well adapted to growing in open sites
Habitats short-lived (e.g. ripe fruit for *Drosophila* larva)	Habitats stable and long-lived (e.g. forest for monkeys)
Poor competitors (competitive ability not required)	Good competitors
Relatively lacking in defensive strategies	Good defence mechanisms
Do not become dominant	May become dominant
More adaptable to changes in environment (less specialised)	Less resistant to changes in environmental conditions (highly specialised for stable habitat)
Examples bacteria *Paramecium* aphids flour-beetles annual plants	*Examples* large tropical butterflies condor (large bird of prey) albatross humans trees

12.7.5 Factors affecting population size

In section 12.7.3 population growth was examined. Once a population has finished its initial growth phase there usually continues to be fluctuations in population size from generation to generation. An example is shown in fig 12.40 for caterpillars of the winter moth (*Operophthera brumata*) in an oakwood near Oxford.

Important influences are likely to be variations in climatic conditions (such as temperature), food supply and predation. Sometimes fluctuations are regular and may be called **cycles**. Their study is laborious and time-consuming since data for field organisms often must be collected over several years. In some cases data have been obtained by using laboratory organisms with short life cycles, such as fruit flies, rats and mites. These are used as model populations where conditions can be controlled more rigorously than in the field.

Basically, population size may change as a result of changes in fecundity or mortality, or possibly both. When

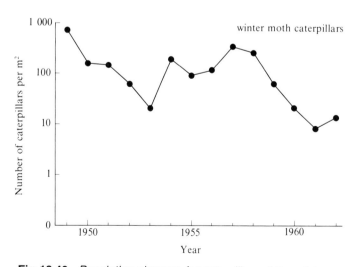

Fig 12.40 *Population changes for caterpillars of the winter moth (*Operophthera brumata*) in Wytham Wood near Oxford. Note that the numbers are plotted on a logarithmic scale. (From Open University Science Foundation Course (S100) Unit 20 (1971) Open University Press.)*

studying change it is usual to search for the 'key factor', that is the factor responsible for the greatest proportion of the observed change from one generation to the next. In most cases studied this is a factor affecting mortality.

Whereas fluctuations in population size might be expected to be purely random, in practice some factors operate to regulate population size within certain limits. These are factors which reduce numbers by increasing mortality or reducing fecundity, and which become more effective as population density increases. Hence they may be described as **density-dependent factors**. Food shortage and increased predation are two factors which sometimes operate in this way. They have direct effects on mortality for obvious reasons. Two regulatory mechanisms which have been well studied and which affect fecundity are territorial behaviour and the physical effects of overcrowding.

Territorial behaviour

Territorial behaviour or **territoriality** occurs in a wide range of animals, including certain fish, reptiles, birds, mammals and social insects. It has been particularly well studied in bird populations. Either the male bird, or both the male and the female, of a pair may establish a breeding territory which they will defend against intruders of the same species. The song of the bird and sometimes a visual display, such as that of the robin's red breast, are means of asserting territorial claims, and intruders usually retreat, sometimes after a brief 'ritual fight' in which neither competitor is seriously damaged (section 16.8.6). This has obvious advantages over a series of 'real' fights. There is little or no overlap between neighbouring territories of the same species and, in areas where the territory includes the food of the species, it will contain sufficient food to support the birds and their young. As population sizes grow, territories usually become smaller and able to support fewer new birds. In extreme cases, some birds may be unable to establish territories and therefore fail to breed. Regulation is therefore due to spatial interactions.

Overcrowding

Another form of regulation in which space is an important factor is that due to overcrowding. Laboratory experiments with rats show that when a certain high population density is reached, fecundity is greatly reduced even if there is no food shortage. Various hormonal changes occur which affect reproductive behaviour in a number of ways; for example, failure to copulate, infertility, number of abortions and eating of young by the parents all increase, and parental care decreases. The young abandon the nest at an earlier age, with consequent reduction in chances of survival. There is also an increase in aggressive behaviour. Changes like these have been demonstrated for a number of mammals and could operate under natural circumstances outside the laboratory. Natural populations of voles, for example, show a similar kind of regulation.

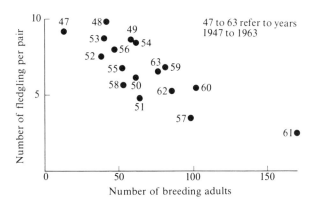

Fig 12.41 *Breeding success of the great tit in Marley Wood, near Oxford, in relation to the number of breeding pairs present from 1947–63. (From M. E. Solomon (1976) Population dynamics, 2nd ed., Studies in Biology No. 18, Arnold.)*

There are many examples where breeding success and population density have been shown to be related. Cyclic variations in population size and density-dependent breeding success was shown during an investigation of great tits in Marley Wood near Oxford, as shown in fig 12.41.

In the laboratory it has been shown that the number of eggs laid per day by fruit flies (*Drosophila melanogaster*) decreases as the population density of flies increases. With plants, the number of seeds produced by each plant may similarly be reduced at higher plant densities. In these examples it is not always obvious what the regulatory factors are, but food availability, competition for territory, mutual physical disturbance with possible hormonal changes are all factors which may be involved.

The regulatory factors help to smooth out and compensate for other factors which might have a random, non-regulatory effect on population size, such as climate. For example, the particularly low number of breeding great tits in Marley Wood in the year 1947 (fig 12.41) might have been due to high mortality during the very cold winter of 1946–7. This may have been compensated for by the relatively high breeding successes of 1947 and 1948, but the reasons for these successes are probably complex.

It was noted above that the key factor affecting population size is often one that affects mortality. This is clearly shown in the case of the winter moth, whose life cycle is illustrated in fig 12.42. Its numbers have been studied over many years in an oakwood near Oxford. Table 12.19 shows the average number of individuals killed by each of six factors affecting mortality.

The table shows that on average each pair of adults replaces itself each year with two surviving offspring, but fig 12.43 shows that in reality the population varies from year to year. Assuming that fecundity is constant, at least one of the six mortality factors must fluctuate and be density-dependent since the average size of the population remains constant. Fig 12.43 shows how the mortality factors fluctuated between 1950 and 1961. The key factor

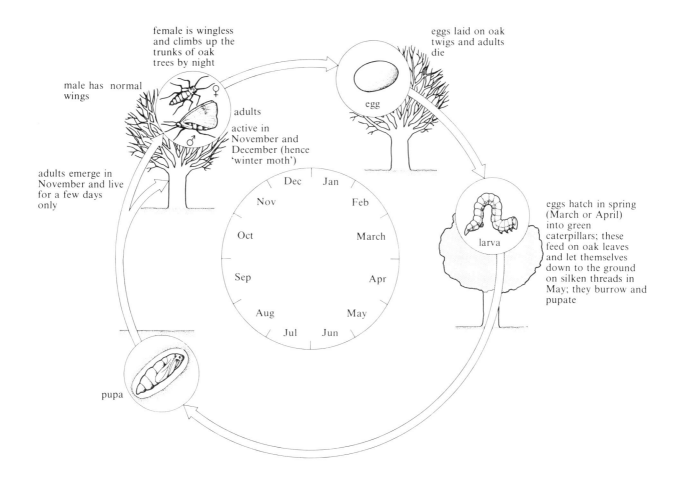

Fig 12.42 *Annual life cycle of the winter moth. (Based upon Open University Science Foundation Course Unit 20 (1971) Open University Press.)*

Table 12.19 Average number of individuals of the winter moth killed by six mortality factors acting in succession.

Number of eggs laid by the female moth	200

Mortality factor	Number killed
Winter disappearance (death of a few eggs and very high mortality of newly hatched caterpillars)	184
Parasitic fly living on caterpillars	1
Other parasites living on caterpillars	1.5
Disease of caterpillars	2.5
Predators killing pupae in soil (beetles, shrews)	8.5
Parasitic wasp living on pupae	0.5
Total	198

Therefore number of adults surviving to breed:	2

Based on Open University S100 Unit 20 (see fig 12.42).

affecting total mortality (pre-reproductive mortality) is winter disappearance because this accounts for the greatest proportion of deaths and is most closely correlated with total mortality. The high mortality at this stage is explained by the fact that the hatching of the young caterpillars is closely, but not always exactly, synchronised with bud burst and young leaf growth of the oak trees. If the caterpillars hatch slightly early many starve, and if too late many will not have completed development before the leaves become too tough and full of tannin to be eaten. If, however, exact synchrony is achieved, the population of caterpillars may reach pest proportions and trees may be completely defoliated.

Although winter disappearance is the key factor affecting mortality, some other factor appears to be acting to regulate population size because fluctuations in mortality are less dramatic than those for winter disappearance in most years (the years 1960 and 1961 being exceptions). The regulating factor therefore causes relatively more deaths in years when, as a result of reduced winter disappearance, the population becomes larger. In other words, the regulatory factor is density-dependent. Both pupal predation and pupal parasitism show a relationship with total mortality which suggests that they could be regulatory

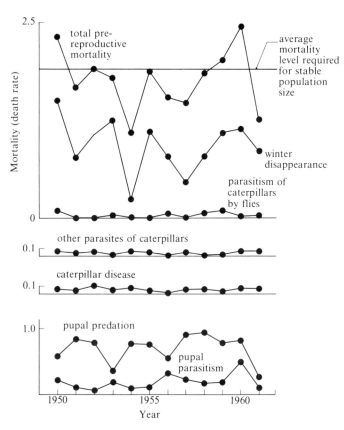

Fig 12.43 *Total pre-reproductive mortality and contributions to total mortality made by six different factors for winter moth in Wytham Wood between 1950 and 1961. (From Open University Science Foundation Course Unit 20 (1971) Open University Press.)*

factors. Pupal predation is highest in years when numbers of pupae are high (low winter disappearance). The relationship with parasitism is more complex because parasite density tends to be out of phase with host density. The parasite of winter moth pupae is a wasp whose larvae feed on the caterpillars. Parasite–host relationships are complex, but briefly a year of high host density will result in successful parasite breeding followed a year later by higher parasite density and hence higher pupal parasitism.

Very accurate models are now available for predicting winter moth numbers. Such models have practical application when the species is a pest, as is the winter moth in eastern Canada. The models suggest ways in which the pest might be controlled and, in the case of winter moth, enabled the consequences of introducing parasites as a means of biological control to be predicted with success.

Another density-dependent factor that may affect the population size of a species is migration (or dispersal). For example, at high aphid densities not only does the rate of reproduction of the aphids decrease but a higher proportion develop wings and leave the plant on which they are feeding.

Some factors regulating population sizes such as climate have been regarded as density-independent, but it is inevitable that they interact with other factors that are density-dependent. Thus, although the terms are useful, it is better to avoid stressing the difference between density-dependent and density-independent factors and to study each case on its merits with the awareness that complex interactions may occur. The study of population fluctuations and regulation is a complex area of ecology and the examples quoted are chosen merely to illustrate some of the more obvious ways in which these factors operate.

12.7.6 Factors affecting population size: interspecific factors

It is seldom possible to confine studies of population dynamics to single species. It has already been shown, for example, that an understanding of the fluctuations in winter moth populations depends on a knowledge of parasites of the moth. A number of well-recognised types of interaction may occur between populations of different species (interspecific interactions). At a given trophic level there may be **interspecific competition**, that is competition between members of different species, for available resources such as food and space. It is here that the study of niches is important in community ecology. Populations from different trophic levels may also interact, as, for example, in the cases of predator–prey relationships and host–parasite relationships. Other relationships exist, some of which are subtle and complex, including some symbiotic relationships where both partners benefit.

Interactions between members of the same species (**intraspecific interactions**) also occur, such as territoriality and other forms of agonistic behaviour (section 16.8.8).

Predator–prey relationships

(See reference to computer program, p. 410.)

In trying to understand interspecific interactions, simple and well-controlled situations can be set up in the laboratory. It is hoped that they represent 'models' of real situations.

A commonly used and simple model of predator–prey relationships is one that has been well illustrated by laboratory experiments with two mites, one predatory (*Typhlodromus*) and one herbivorous (*Eotetranychus*). Fig 12.44 shows the cyclic fluctuations that occur in their numbers, the cycles for the two species being slightly out of phase with each other.

The explanation for these cycles is that an increase in numbers of the prey supports a subsequent increase in numbers of the predator. The predators then cause a crash in numbers of the prey, followed by an inevitable decline in numbers of predators. The cycles are completed when the decline in predators allows an increase in numbers of the prey. Each cycle occurs over a number of generations. These laboratory models must be applied with caution to

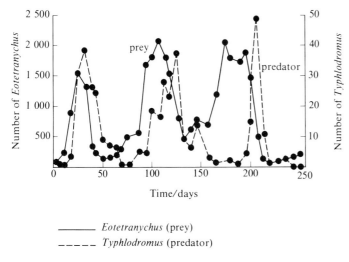

Fig 12.44 *Oscillations in the populations of the predatory mite* Typhlodromus *and its prey, the plant mite* Eotetranychus, *in a laboratory habitat.* (From M. K. Sands (1978) Problems in ecology, Mills & Boon Ltd).

Legend:
——— *Eotetranychus* (prey)
– – – – *Typhlodromus* (predator)

natural predator–prey relationships, which will be subject to other influences. Some herbivorous mammals show regular cycles of numbers in the populations, an example being the lemmings of North America and Scandinavia, which have a four-year cycle. Their predators, the arctic fox and the snowy owl, consequently show a similar cycle, but the factor causing the lemming cycle could be overgrazing rather than predation. Occasionally, when populations of Scandinavian lemmings reach exceptionally high densities, they emigrate *en masse*, many plunging to their deaths in fjords or drowning in rivers. Other cyclic changes in herbivores may also be influenced more by availability of food plants than by predators. Death through disease is another factor which could operate in a density-dependent manner since epidemics are more likely to spread through populations of high density. There is some evidence that this might contribute to the population cycles of the snowshoe hare of northern Canada. Here again one of its main predators, the Canadian lynx, follows a similar, but out-of-phase, cycle. Hares form 80–90% of the diet of the lynx.

Although it may not be the only factor, there is no doubt that predation plays an important part in regulating natural populations. Some indication of the importance of predator–prey relationships in this respect, and the long-term advantage it has for the prey, can be gained from the fate of a population of deer on the Kaibab Plateau in Arizona. In 1906 the area was declared a wild-life refuge, and in order to protect the deer their predators, such as pumas, wolves and coyotes, were systematically exterminated over the next 30 years. Up to 1906 the deer population had remained stable at about 4000, but subsequently a 'population explosion' occurred, as shown in fig 12.45 with the result that the carrying capacity of the environment, estimated to be about 30 000 deer, was exceeded. The

population reached an estimated 100 000 by 1924, following a 'boom-and-bust' curve, but the overgrazing resulted in starvation and, together with disease, a subsequent population crash. In addition, the vegetation had been seriously damaged and did not recover to its 1906 level, with the result that the carrying capacity of the environment dropped to 10 000 deer.

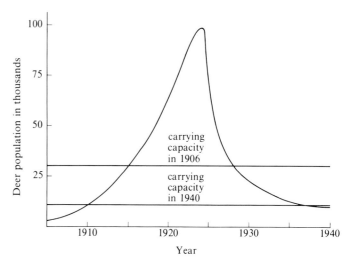

Fig 12.45 *Deer population on the Kaibab Plateau following eradication of predators*

Host–parasite relationships

In some of the cases studied host and parasite populations show similar out-of-phase cycles to those described above, notably when insects parasitise other insects (see also the case of the winter moth, section 12.7.5).

Interspecific competition

(See reference to computer program, p. 410.)

Competition may occur between populations within an ecosystem for any of the available resources, such as food, space, light or shelter. If two species occur at the same trophic level then they are likely to compete with each other for food. Adaptive radiation by one or both species may then occur over a period of time with the result that they come to occupy separate niches within the trophic level, thus minimising the extent of competition. Alternatively, if the competitors occupy the same niche, or strongly overlapping niches, an equilibrium situation may be reached in which neither succeeds as well as it would in the absence of the competitor, or one of the competitors declines in numbers to the point of extinction. The latter phenomenon is known as **competitive exclusion**. It is difficult to study in wild populations but some classic work on laboratory populations has been done, originally by the Russian biologist Gause in 1934 who worked on competition between several species of *Paramecium*. Some of his results are shown in fig 12.46.

415

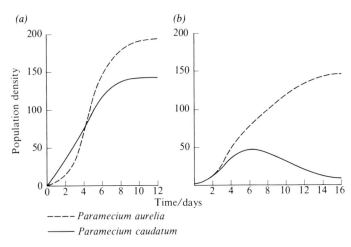

(a)   (b)

Population density (y-axis, both graphs: 0, 50, 100, 150, 200)

Time/days

- - - - Paramecium aurelia
———— Paramecium caudatum

Fig 12.46 *Population growth of two species of* Paramecium.
(a) Cultured separately. (b) Cultured together

12.23 With reference to fig 12.46,
(a) what type of population growth curve is shown by the two species when grown in isolation?
(b) what resources might the two species be competing for in the mixed culture?
(c) what factors give *P. aurelia* a competitive advantage over *P. caudatum*?

When the two species are cultured together *P. aurelia* has a competitive advantage over *P. caudatum* for gaining food and after five days the numbers of *P. caudatum* start to decrease until, after about 20 days, the species has become 'extinct', that is it has been competitively excluded. *P. aurelia* takes longer to reach the stationary phase of growth than when grown in isolation, so is also affected adversely by the competition, even though it is more successful than its competitor. This helps to explain the selection pressure for competitors to adapt to separate niches. Under natural circumstances, the less successful competitor rarely becomes extinct, but merely becomes rare and may even increase in numbers again before achieving an equilibrium position.

The **competitive exclusion principle** (or **Gausian exclusion principle**) has since been confirmed in further animal experiments carried out by other workers. Competitive exclusions have been shown to occur in plant populations; in mixed cultures of duckweed (*Lemna*) species; *L. gibba* was capable of excluding *L. polyrrhiza*.

The study of natural populations is made more complex by the larger number of interacting populations and by the fact that the environmental variables such as temperature, moisture and food supply cannot be controlled.

Among plant populations one form of competition which has attracted a lot of interest is allelopathy. It is part of the more general phenomenon of allelochemistry whereby plants and micro-organisms produce as secondary products of metabolism a variety of complex organic molecules which affect the growth of other living organisms. They include antibiotics and growth inhibitors, such as penicillin which is produced by the fungus *Penicillium* and has antibiotic properties against Gram positive bacteria (section 2.2.2). Chemical competition among micro-organisms is very intense and the relationships between them very complex. When chemicals affect other populations at the same trophic level the interspecific competitive effect that results is termed **allelopathy**. The odours of aromatic plants are volatile secondary products which are sometimes involved in interactions of this kind. For example, Muller in 1966 showed that the volatile terpenes released from aromatic plants of the Californian chaparral (a type of scrubland) are adsorbed on to surrounding soil particles and inhibit the germination or growth of surrounding plants. Phenolic compounds that are leached into the soil from the litter of some plants have a similar effect. Many plants of chalk grassland are aromatic and this may be an additional factor to grazing in maintaining the rich variety of herbaceous plants present. Recent studies of allelochemical interactions suggest that they are probably widespread in occurrence, both within and between trophic levels. Among the important plant chemicals involved are phenolics, terpenoids and alkaloids. They are extremely interesting because they are often physiologically active in animals. One example of allelopathy involving animals is provided by the monarch butterfly (*Danaus plexippus*). Its caterpillar stage feeds on the milkweed plant which produces chemicals that act as strong cardiac (heart) poisons in vertebrates. This, or its unpleasant taste, presumably discourages grazing herbivores from eating the plant. However, the caterpillars can tolerate the poison, and can store it and carry it into the adult butterfly stage. The butterfly, in turn, gains protection from predatory birds. The bright colouration and striking markings of the butterfly therefore serve as a warning to potential predators and act as a protective device. An incidental consequence of this is that some butterflies mimic the markings of the monarch, thus also gaining protection. This case study serves to show just how complex species interactions can become. Generally speaking, many plants subjected to grazing contain toxic chemicals to which only a few herbivore species are tolerant.

Two other important processes, in which interaction occurs between flowering plants and animals, are discussed in section 20.2, namely seed dispersal and pollination. The latter, in particular, is a good example of another general principle, namely that of **co-evolution**, where species become adjusted to each other's presence and develop over a period of time varying degrees of mutual dependence and benefit. In the case of toxic plants, the most beneficial and stable arrangement would be for the toxin-tolerant herbivores to provide a service to the plant, such as the pollination by butterflies whose caterpillars feed on the plant.

12.7.7 Applications: fisheries management

The practical relevance of population ecology has already been mentioned, as in species extinction, pest control, conservation and game and fisheries management. A further discussion of fisheries management, with particular reference to North Sea fisheries, is given below. The use of population models in pest control is discussed in section 12.8.

Fisheries, especially marine fisheries, are an important source of human food. Unlike most other food species, fish have not been domesticated nor are they owned by individuals. Modern fishing still depends on hunter-gathering techniques and fishermen compete for stock. Biological, economic, social and political factors complexly interact in the story of modern fishing and quota systems.

Over the last century technological advances have greatly improved human hunting ability. Furthermore, developments in refrigeration and freezing methods have meant that vessels can fish to capacity without the pressure to return quickly to port to ensure landings arrive in good condition. A summary of the main changes in fishing practice is given in table 12.20. Fifty years ago it was already evident that problems existed in the North Sea haddock fisheries. The proportion of small fish in the catch was rising markedly (fig 12.47). Furthermore, twentieth-century records for haddock catches show a downward trend in peacetime with peaks immediately following the two World Wars during which fishing activities had largely ceased (fig 12.48). The trend for world landings of sea fish since the Second World War is similar, the graph flattening out in the late 1970s despite increasing fishing effort (fig 12.49).

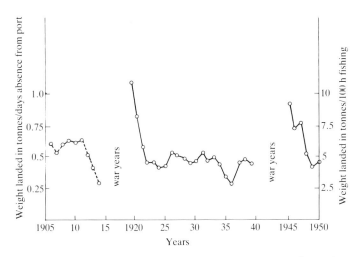

Fig 12.47 *Haddock catch per unit of fishing effort by Scottish trawlers in the North Sea. Dashed line, landings/days absence; full line, landings/100h. (From M. Graham (1956) Sea fisheries – their investigation in the UK, Arnold.)*

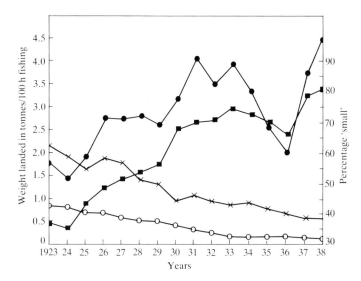

Fig 12.48 *Catch, per unit of fishing effort of North Sea haddock, and percentage of the 'small' category, 1923–38. Open circles, large; crosses, medium; full circles, small; open squares, percentage 'small'. (From M. Graham (1956) Sea fisheries – their investigation in the UK, Arnold.)*

Table 12.20 The main changes in fishing practice since the late-nineteenth century.

Major innovation	Consequent benefits
(1) Steam ships replace sailing ships	(a) Larger nets can be used (b) Greater independence of wind and tide results
(2) Diesel replaces steam	(a) Even faster, more powerful ships can search larger areas (b) Even less weather-dependent
(3) Development of plastic nets which are stronger, lighter and longer-lasting	(a) The use of even larger nets is possible (b) By using different densities of synthetic fibres in different parts of the net, improved control and manipulation is possible
(4) Development of radar and sonic detection techniques	(a) Improved hunting and detection of fish shoals (b) Better net handling
(5) Development of large-scale on-board refrigeration and freezing facilities	(a) Fishing boats can travel further from port and continue fishing without deterioration of the catch

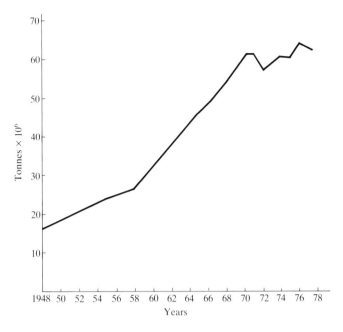

Fig 12.49 *World landings of sea fish 1948–77. (From R.V. Tait (1981)* Elements of marine ecology, *3rd ed., Butterworths, p. 305)*

In the 1940s Russell* proposed a model for fisheries management based on the ideas of population dynamics. His summary equation is:

$$S_2 = S_1 + (A + G) - (C + M)$$

S_1 = weight of stock at the beginning of a year,
S_2 = weight of stock at the end of that year,
A = annual increment by recruitment of young fish to the stock,
G = annual increment due to growth of all fish in the stock,
C = total weight of fish removed during the year by fishing, 'the catch',
M = weight of fish lost during the year by death from all the other causes, that is the natural mortality.

The amount by which stock weight increases if there is no fishing is the natural yield, $A + G - M$ in Russell's formula. If the stock remains unchanged then annual recruitment and growth $(A + G)$ must be balanced by mortality and catch $(M + C)$. In short, catch must equal natural yield. Relatively simple data on fish landings and fishing techniques can enable reasonable prediction (plus or minus 20%) of the balanced catch. Quotas, permissible mesh sizes and other key criteria can be adjusted accordingly. Furthermore, equilibrium between catch and natural yield can be established for any population size. The maximum possible

* E.S. Russell (1942) *The Overfishing Problem*, CUP.

sustained yield will be achieved when fishing effort is adjusted so that the population is maintained at or just above inflexion point, I, the maximum growth rate described for S-shaped population growth in section 12.7.3 (see fig 12.37c). In other words the fishery must be neither overfished nor underfished if a maximum yield is to be achieved and sustained.

Underfishing

Under conditions of light fishing a fish population grows to the limits of food supply, the carrying capacity (K) in the absence of significant human predation. Competition for food restricts the numbers surviving and the size to which individuals grow. Slow-growing older fish compete successfully with new recruits for food. Fish catches show a predominance of older fish but, due to age, persistent undernourishment and associated disease vulnerability, they are typically of poor quality. Such a fishery is underfished and landings may command a poor price. The population could sustain a larger more profitable fishery of better quality fish if more fish were caught (that is, if the balance were shifted back from K towards I in fig 12.37c). Reduction in population size by removing the excess older fish would achieve a better growth rate through the remaining stock and improve the condition of the fish.

Overfishing

Heavy fishing, by contrast, generates a population of mainly young small specimens, since fish are caught as soon as they reach a catchable size. Again such fish may fetch poor prices since they have little edible flesh in relation to bone. (Scarcity value may to some extent offset this tendency for price reduction.) The stock is overfished. These young fish would make rapid growth if left longer in the sea and would soon reach a more valuable size, giving heavier landings of better quality fish per unit fishing effort, giving an improved profit margin. Productivity and prices would thus improve if fishing were reduced. However, individual fishermen are tempted to achieve weight quotas and improve immediate income by catching more rather than fewer fish. This triggers positive feedback favouring further reductions in fish stock and size, requiring more effort (cost) to achieve reasonable landings. If this reaches the point where fish are caught before spawning so that the reproductive capacity of the stock is seriously impaired then a catastrophic reduction in numbers occurs and local extinction may result. Overfishing which involves fish being caught before reproductive age is called **recruitment overfishing**; overfishing of fish before optimum age is called **growth overfishing**, and typically occurs before recruitment overfishing.

These basic fish management models may be further refined by studying the fate of particular age cohorts rather than the population overall. This requires more detailed measurement of fish landings but gives valuable insights into population structure and a more-sensitive basis for prediction. Current events in the North Sea cod fisheries illustrate this point. Catches during 1987 were good, prompting fishermen to ask for increased quotas. On the other hand, scientists advising the Council of European Fisheries Ministers decided that cod catches should be reduced by about one-third. According to the scientists, during the past 15 years fishermen have been taking an increasingly higher proportion of cod stocks from the North Sea. Up to 60% of the cod aged over 18 months were being caught each year and this has lead to a reduction in spawning stock to its lowest post-war level (figs 12.50 *a* and *b*). How far the spawning stock can decline before the

reproduction rate crashes is unknown for North Sea cod (that is the point of no return or *X* on fig 12.38). This worrying picture is complicated by extreme variability in the rate at which 18-month-old fish enter the fisheries, the recruitment rate (fig 12.50*c*). Scientists suspect that these vast natural variations are masking a general downward trend. Hence advice on quotas tends to be cautious. Low recruitment in 1986 and 1987 suggests future problems unless quotas are reduced. Paradoxically, this advice has coincided with a temporary, it is assumed, abundance of cod in the North Sea reflecting good recruitment in 1985. Age cohort data are clearly fundamental to prediction in this instance.

If the biological basis of fisheries management seems complex, the intricacies of fisheries economics and social factors equally cannot be ignored. A biologically optimum fishing rate may glut the market, reducing prices; high catches per unit fishing effort leave expensive equipment and skilled personnel idle once quotas have been attained. The issues of fishing rights and quotas are matters of international politics. Scientific studies can usefully supply the basis for good decision-making; however, a viable policy must be workable in social and economic terms as well as scientifically ensuring the maintenance of valuable food resources.

(a)

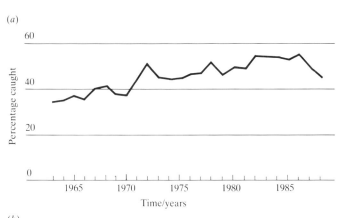

(b)

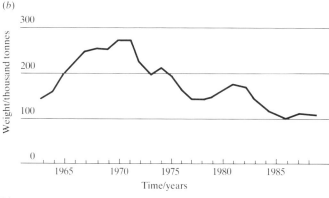

(c)

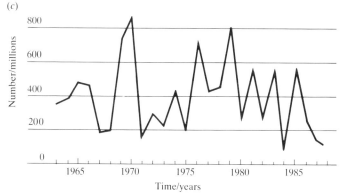

Fig 12.50 (a) *Percentage of North Sea cod stock caught annually.* (b) *Spawning stock of cod in the North Sea.* (c) *Recruitment of cod to North Sea stock as monitored by the number of one-year-old fish. (From Richard North, The Independent, Feb. 1988)*

12.8   Agriculture and horticulture

Tremendous advances in crop production have taken place throughout the world in the last 20 years as a result of the widespread implementation of the results of technological and scientific research. A number of examples are given below.

12.8.1   Ploughing

Used for the breaking down of the soil to produce seed beds, and converting grassland to arable crops by turning over or burying the grass sward. In the UK this is carried out in the autumn, the winter frosts breaking down the soil clods.

Curved steel blades are pulled by a tractor through the soil. Modern hydraulic devices on the tractor automatically control the working depth of the ploughing. Disc ploughs are then used to break up the hard soil to produce a good tilth and final preparation of the seed bed may involve the use of steel-framed or disc harrows.

12.8.2   Direct drilling

After a cereal harvest, the stubble is treated with a herbicide, such as Paraquat, to destroy any weeds. Using a seed drill which is able to break through the undisturbed soil, the seeds are sown directly thus avoiding the cost of ploughing (thereby reducing fuel costs).

12.8.3 Crop rotation

Historically, cultivation in the UK was based on a three-year cycle; winter wheat was followed by spring wheat and then the field left unplanted for one year to preserve and restore soil fertility. With the development of root crops and the recognition of the importance of legumes (nitrogen fixation and a source of green manure), a four-course rotation was developed of roots, wheat, grassland or legumes, and barley; this rotation was modified as a wider variety of crops was introduced, such as kale and sugar beet. The rotation not only maintained soil fertility but also prevented the build-up of harmful pests. With the development of pesticides however, monoculture has become possible. Here only one type of crop is grown successfully on the same land from one year to another; an intensive system of agriculture.

In developing countries, or in opening-up new areas for cultivation, a system described as **slash-and-burn** may be carried out. The existing vegetation is cut down and then burnt, a method returning important mineral nutrients to the soil. The clearing formed may be cultivated continuously for several years until soil fertility falls, and then the site is abandoned for a number of years and other areas brought into cultivation. Cropping is usually mixed, several different kinds of crop being grown on the same plot.

12.8.4 Harvesting

This depends on the type of crop and ranges from the modern use of combine harvesters to the hand-picking of fruits. The crop is harvested when, by experience, it is judged to be at a suitable stage of development (percentage moisture content for grain crops; ripeness in fruit, allowing for further changes during transit to the markets). However, in modern intensive cultivation the grain may be dried artificially to the correct level. The crop may be delivered directly to the commercial market or factories (such as sugar beet) or undergo a period of storage.

12.8.5 Storage

The main aims are to prevent or reduce deterioration of the quality of the crop whilst awaiting favourable market conditions. Losses are due mainly to insect and fungal attack. Details of storage again depends on the crop, such as cereals in silos and grain stores, potatoes and root crops in clamps, fruit in special fruit stores.

It was found that the storage life of fruits is inversely related to their rate of respiration. This rate can be reduced by refrigeration and in some instances by circulating an air stream enriched with 10% carbon dioxide. However, ethene (which is produced by ripening fruits) hastens the onset of ripening and reduces storage life. Various volatile substances can be added to the air stream circulating through potato stores to prevent premature sprouting, and similarly fungicides may be used in fruit stores.

12.8.6 Weed control

A weed may be defined as a plant growing in the 'wrong' place. Weeds are characterised by rapid seed germination and growth and the production of a large number of fertile seeds. The seeds may remain dormant for several years. The adult plant, by virtue of tap roots or rhizomes and rapid regeneration of injured tissue, may withstand hoeing, grazing and contact herbicides thereby making eradication difficult.

Weeds, by virtue of these characteristics, compete with planted crops, particularly in the seedling stage, for water, nutrients and light so successfully that crop yields may be reduced. At the later stage of harvesting, the weed seeds may contaminate the harvest of cereal crops, for example false oat plants in cereal crops.

12.8.7 Herbicides

One of the earliest goals of agricultural research was to increase the yield of cereal crops using plant hormones. Application of auxins led to the discovery of herbicide action and to the use of the phenoxyacetic acids such as MCPA. Many different herbicides have now been developed, superceding the old 'contact' herbicides such as sodium chlorate. These more recent compounds are called systemic herbicides (systemic because they are translocated about the plant) and act as selective weedkillers. For example, paraquat and diquat interfere with the photosynthetic processes and can be used to kill weeds amongst well-established woody species of plants. Atrazine and simazine remain in the soil and prevent seed germination.

12.8.8 Insecticides

Insecticides, like other pesticides, are effective by inhibiting some metabolic process. They differ widely in composition, effectiveness, mode and speed of action and the dosage required. Ideally they should have a very limited range of action so that other organisms are not directly affected (table 12.21).

12.8.9 Pesticides and environment

Pesticides are chemical substances used by humans to control pests, those living organisms thought to be harmful to human interests. The term pesticide is an all-embracing word for **herbicides** (kill plants), **insecticides** (kill insects), **fungicides** (act on fungi), and so on. Most pesticides are poisons and aim to kill the target species, but the term also includes chemosterilants (chemicals causing sterility) and growth inhibitors. In Britain pesticide use is mainly associated with agriculture and horticulture, though pesticides are also widely used in food storage and to protect wood, wool and other natural products. In many countries pesticides are used in forestry and they are also used extensively to control human and animal disease

Table 12.21 Examples of the three main insecticides and their major uses.

Type	Example	Comments
(1) *Contact* – penetrate through the cuticle of the insects	(*a*) *Natural* nicotine (developed from tobacco) pyrethrum (extracted from the flowers of *Chrysanthemum* sp.) rotenone (from the roots of *Derris*)	Useful for destroying insects such as aphids which pierce the epidermal layers to suck out the plant juices
	(*b*) *Synthetic* compounds are now widely developed and are constantly being modified as resistant strains are built up as a result of selection, e.g. DDT, gammexane, parathion, malathion	Earlier examples used were chlorinated hydrocarbons (DDT) but these were persistent in soil and very toxic. Use is banned in some countries and replaced by organophosphates (e.g. parathion)
(2) *Systemic* – absorbed through the alimentary canal. Often stomach poisons. Newer insecticides interfere with the transmission of nervous impulses	Some of the contact poisons have been used as systemic insecticides, e.g. parathion, DDT	Used against insects with biting mouthparts. May be used in foliage against leaf-eating insects or as poison-bait ingredients against locusts
(3) *Fumigants* – compounds which, when volatilised, destroy insects	Formaldehyde, ethene oxide	Used in greenhouses

vectors (see section 12.3.8, malaria). Pesticides are used worldwide and in a wide variety of habitats. The more persistent disperse into all environments including those which are never sprayed, for example the open oceans and subpolar regions. Most life on Earth is thus in contact with pesticides. Natural organic pesticides, such as pyrethrum, and inorganic substances, such as $CuSO_4$ in Bordeaux mixture (as applied to vines), have been used for centuries, but widespread use of new synthetic organic substances (about 90% of all present pesticide applications) is a development of the post-Second World War era. The world's species have no previous evolutionary experience of these substances. Pesticides are thus a new environmental factor. The ecological effects of pesticides can be hard to predict, making pesticide ecology a fascinating and important new area of study. Our understanding of unwanted 'side-effects', such as loss of non-target species, pest resurgence and chronic effects on human populations, is still rudimentary.

The important ecological characteristics of pesticides are toxicity, persistence and their non-specific and density-independent mode of action. Toxicity and persistence are linked in that a lethal but non-persistent chemical may in the long run do less damage than a sublethal persistent chemical. This is because the latter has more opportunity for incorporation into food chains where it may be metabolised to a more toxic form or more typically accumulate to toxic concentrations in predators at the top of the chain (see section 12.3.8). Pesticide applications as dusts and sprays lead to their wide dispersal in air and water and incorporation into food chains in non-target areas. The organochlorines (for example DDT) which are both persistent and fat-soluble are probably the most widely distributed pesticides. Organochlorine residues have been found in all British bird species and, more noteworthy perhaps, are present in the bodies of Antarctic penguins.

Though persistence is generally an undesirable quality, particularly on food crops, in some instances, for example in the control of animal parasites and soil-borne diseases, some degree of persistence is an important practical and economic requirement. Toxicity for a particular species is commonly defined by the **lethal dose 50** (LD_{50}). This is the single dose administered orally which kills half an experimental laboratory population. In the field when the organism is subjected to additional environmental stresses a higher proportion may die. Nevertheless, by definition, some survive. (In short the aim in agriculture is to reduce crop injury to an acceptable level, the balance being largely a question of economics.) Unfortunately the survivors form the basis of a resistant pest population and, in organisms such as insects with a rapid life cycle, resistance and pest resurgence are common problems. The typical response is to develop an alternative pesticide, but this is both expensive and, many ecologists would argue, inevitably destined for a similar fate.

12.24 Why are pesticide resistance and pest resurgence associated with the use of pesticides?

Most pesticides are discovered empirically, that is by trial and error or chance observation. It is not always known how they cause death in the target species. Toxicity may vary greatly between taxa and even between closely related species, for example in mammals the LD_{50} for DDT is four times greater per unit body weight for sheep than for rats. In some organisms a sexual difference is seen. The LD_{50} for male mice for DDT is 500 mg kg^{-1} compared with 550 mg kg^{-1} for females. These differential responses and especially those between different taxa and major organism groups can be put to practical advantage so that, for example, dicotyledonous weeds in cereal crops can be selectively eliminated without apparently harming the crop plant or its human consumers. Fleas and similar animal parasites may be controlled without harming their animal host. However, there is need for caution with these assumptions. Recent reports of illness among farm workers regularly exposed over many years to organophosphates* as, for example, used in sheep dips, suggest a need for a radical reappraisal of safety standards. Long-term consequences of pesticide exposure, even at low doses, and possible synergistic links with other contaminants or disease vectors are little known due to the relative newness of most pesticides. There is mounting concern that the 'harmless' traces of pesticide metabolites left as residues on food, though not directly toxic and certainly not lethal, may, nevertheless, lower disease resistance or be biologically accumulated to significant levels. Pesticide residues in the North Sea are thought by many scientists to be linked with the rapid spread of viral

* Organophosphates – nerve poisons now widely used in place of the more persistent organochlorines.

disease in the common seal population during summer 1988.

Agriculturally, when non-target organisms affected by pesticides are also predators of target species serious economic problems may result due to pest resurgence. A good example of this was seen in a study of the use of DDT to control cabbage white butterfly, *Pieris rapae*, on brussels sprouts. Initial pesticide application gave good control but subsequently numbers of butterfly larvae *exceeded* those in an unsprayed control area. This effect was even more pronounced following repeat applications of DDT to 'control' the new infestation. Examination of the crop ecosystem showed that pesticide concentrations on the leaves were rapidly reduced due to subsequent growth of existing and new leaves. However, levels in the soil remained high, especially if crop residues were ploughed in. Thus eggs deposited by adults from surrounding areas after spraying were little affected by the pesticide, but the main larval predators, the soil-dwelling ground beetle *Harpalus rufipes* and harvestman *Phalangium opilio*, showed reduced numbers and survivors fed less frequently. Larval predation was thus significantly reduced and larval numbers exceeded pre-spraying levels. Further applications of DDT merely made this situation worse (fig 12.51).

Predatory species are generally most disadvantaged by pesticide use. This is because they occur in lower numbers than their prey and therefore the population is more vulnerable and recovers more slowly. This is made worse when the predator also feeds on resistant prey with residues in the body fat. In addition, poisoned, dead, dying or ailing and behaviourally conspicuous prey are more readily

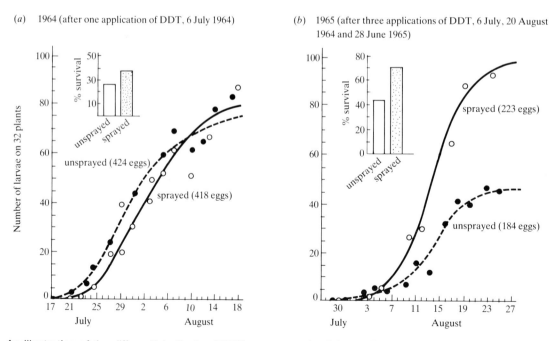

(a) 1964 (after one application of DDT, 6 July 1964)

(b) 1965 (after three applications of DDT, 6 July, 20 August 1964 and 28 June 1965)

Fig 12.51 *An illustration of the differential effects of DDT on crop and soil fauna.* Pieris *lives on crops; spraying with DDT to control it is effective for only a very short period in the first year (a). Because the soil-living predators of* Pieris *are affected by residuals in the soil,* Pieris *in fact increases markedly after repeated spraying (b). (From J.P. Dempster (1968) The control of* Pieris rapae *with DDT: II Survival of the young stages of* Pieris *after spraying. J. Appl. Ecol., 5, 451–62.)*

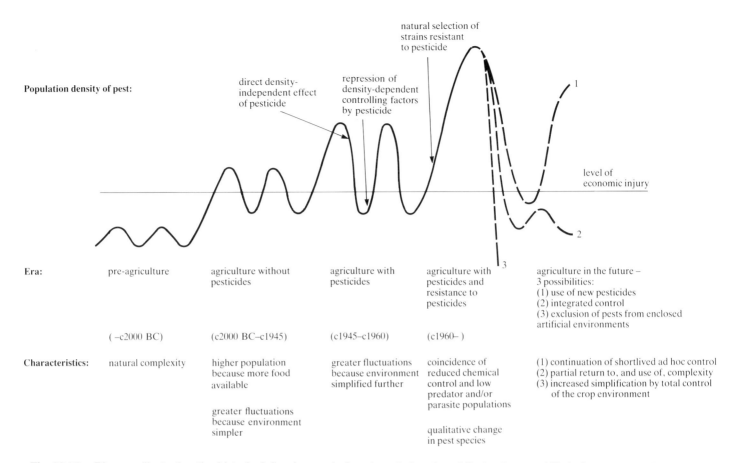

Population density of pest:

natural selection of
strains resistant
to pesticide

direct density-
independent effect
of pesticide

repression of
density-dependent
controlling factors
by pesticide

level of
economic injury

1

2

3

Era:	pre-agriculture	agriculture without pesticides	agriculture with pesticides	agriculture with pesticides and resistance to pesticides	agriculture in the future – 3 possibilities: (1) use of new pesticides (2) integrated control (3) exclusion of pests from enclosed artificial environments
	(–c2000 BC)	(c2000 BC–c1945)	(c1945–c1960)	(c1960–)	
Characteristics:	natural complexity	higher population because more food available greater fluctuations because environment simpler	greater fluctuations because environment simplified further	coincidence of reduced chemical control and low predator and/or parasite populations qualitative change in pest species	(1) continuation of shortlived ad hoc control (2) partial return to, and use of, complexity (3) increased simplification by total control of the crop environment

Fig 12.52 *Diagram illustrating the historical development of pest control and pest fluctuations and likely future trends depending on the control methods. (From N.W. Moore (1987) A synopsis of the pesticide problem, Advances in Ecological Research, Blackwell.)*

caught than healthy unaffected organisms. The general effect of pesticide use is to reduce species diversity. It also tends to increase productivity at lower levels of ecosystems and lessen productivity at higher levels. The effects on decomposer organisms are poorly understood and the implications of all these for nutrient cycling and soil fertility need further study. Fig 12.53 summarises the main ways in which pesticides affect ecosystems. You should consider the implications of these changes (see also fig 12.52).

Problems such as those outlined, especially resistance, resurgence and health risk to the human population, have led to more extensive consideration of alternative control techniques. The main alternatives, **biological control** and **integrated control** (more carefully targeted use of pesticides linked with biological control), are briefly considered below. Two useful sources of further information are the Studies in Biology booklets numbers 50 and 132.*

*H.F. van Emden (1974) *Pest control and its ecology*, Studies in Biology 50, Edward Arnold.
M.J. Samways (1981) *Biological control of pests and weeds*, Studies in Biology 132, Edward Arnold.

Biological control

Biological control of pests has traditionally meant regulation by natural enemies: predators, parasites and pathogens. As such it represents a form of population management preventing unchecked exponential growth of pest species (see section 12.7.3, growth curves). Some scientists take a wider view and include other techniques, such as genetic manipulation, within the scope of biological control. **Cultural control** methods such as crop rotation, tillage, mixed cropping, removal of crop residues and adjustment of harvest or sowing times to favour crop or natural enemies rather than pest may also be considered biological control. Classic biological control has been most successfully applied to introduced species which may lack natural controls, either biological or physical, as in the form of seasonal checks, in a new environment. The control of cottony cushion scale, *Icerya purchasi*, on newly established citrus plantations in California in the late-nineteenth century is the first truly successful example of scientifically planned biological control. This pest was introduced with nursery stock from its native Australia. Field searches in Australia identified two natural enemies, a parasitic fly *Cryptochetum iceryae* and a predatory lady beetle *Rodolia cardinalis*, commonly known as Vedalia. These were taken

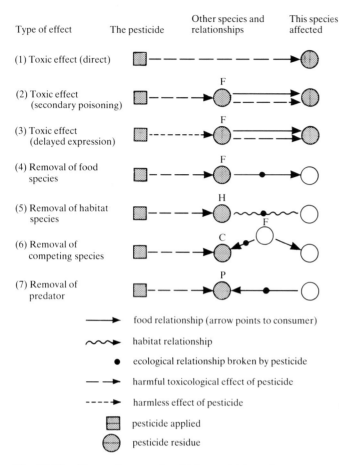

Type of effect	The pesticide	Other species and relationships	This species affected

(1) Toxic effect (direct)

(2) Toxic effect (secondary poisoning)

(3) Toxic effect (delayed expression)

(4) Removal of food species

(5) Removal of habitat species

(6) Removal of competing species

(7) Removal of predator

⟶ food relationship (arrow points to consumer)

〜〜➤ habitat relationship

● ecological relationship broken by pesticide

— ➤ harmful toxicological effect of pesticide

---➤ harmless effect of pesticide

▦ pesticide applied

◉ pesticide residue

Fig 12.53 *The main ways in which pesticides affect ecosystems. Note C, competing species; F, food species; H, habitat species; P, predator species. (From N.W. Moore (1967) A synopsis of the pesticide problem, Advances in Ecological Research. J.B. Cragg (ed.), pp. 75–126, Blackwell.)*

caterpillar-moth *Cactoblastis cactorum*. This New World cactus became a serious pest of warm grazing lands in the Old World and Australia. Entomologists searching for a suitable natural enemy found 150 possible species. Of these 51 were introduced into quarantine in Australia, 19 were released and 12 became established, but long-term control was achieved by just one species, *C. cactorum*. With plant-feeding insects, a high degree of specificity is needed and it is preferable if the insect feeds on only one type of plant. Once released into a new environment the predator cannot be re-called. Exhaustive testing and monitoring in the native environment is necessary to ensure that there is no chance that the introduced predator will develop an affinity for a plant of economic value.

Biological control is also widely used in commercial glasshouses. Tomatoes and cucumbers are grown in this way in most temperate countries. Two major glasshouse pests are the two-spotted spider mite, *Tetranychus urticae*, and the glasshouse white fly, *Trialeurodes vaporariorum*. Soil sterilisation in winter kills all beneficial predatory controls. New plants introduced the following spring typically bring in some white fly, and new spider mites emerge from hibernation in the glasshouse structure. With no natural enemies present, populations grow rapidly unless pesticides are used or natural enemy control is re-established. Fig 12.54 compares the resultant population fluctuations of spider mite using these two alternatives. Growers opting for biological control must act rapidly for the method to be effective. The natural white fly enemy, the parasite *Encarsia formosia*, and the spider mite

to California and, after careful study and successful controlled release in canvas tents, were released into the wild. Both parasite and predator spread rapidly and effective and persistent control was achieved within months.

Success is not always so immediate. Careful matching of climatic conditions and monitoring of interactions with native species is essential. In attempts to control the walnut aphid, *Chromaphis juglandicola*, in California a parasitic wasp, *Trioxys pallidus*, was introduced from Cannes in France. It was moderately successful in coastal areas but in the hot interior, the main walnut-growing area, the wasp died out after one season. Ten years later after extensive searching in similar hot and dry environments a new strain of *Trioxys* was introduced from Iran. It successfully overwintered and within a year over 50 000 square miles were cleared of the pest and parasitisation exceeded 90%.

Biological control can be particularly effective against exotic (foreign) weeds that threaten to smother indigenous vegetation or pastureland. A classic example is the control of prickly pear, *Opuntia*, in Australia by the introduced

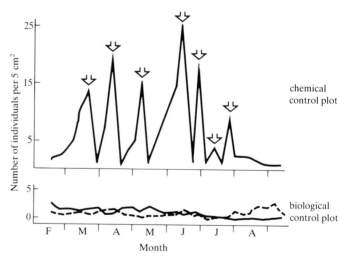

Fig 12.54 *Control of the two-spotted spider mite, Tetranychus urticae (full line), on glasshouse cucumbers in Finland by chemical control using dicofol (arrowed) and biological control employing the predatory mite Phytoseiulus persimilis (dashed line). With chemical control the spider mite population fluctuates wildly, whereas with biocontrol the pest population is maintained at a fairly low and steady level. (After M. Markkula, K. Tiittanen, & M. Nieminen, (1972) Ann. Agr. Fenn., 11, 74–8.)*

predator *Phytoseiulus persimilis* are bred commercially to ensure abundant supplies. In the 'pest-in-first' method of control, the white fly and spider mite pests are first deliberately introduced followed, after about seven days, by the parasite and predator once sufficient food (that is pest) has established for their survival. There is some understandable grower resistance to this 'unnecessary' introduction of pest species. An alternative approach is to make repeated releases of the natural enemy at about 10-day intervals around the time that infestation is typically expected. For successful control it is vital to have natural enemies present in the first stages of infestation. If that critical period is missed natural enemies never seem to catch up and overtake the pests.

Integrated control

Integrated control is pest population management which combines and integrates biological and chemical controls in a sensitive way. Pesticides are used as necessary in a manner least disruptive to complementary biological control. Integrated control programmes have the twin objectives of economic and ecologically acceptable management of pest populations.

They aim to keep pest populations below the level of economic injury, or even prevent their development, while causing minimum harm and disruption to a crop (agroecosystem) or 'natural' ecosystems and especially the beneficial natural enemies of the crop or host species. Most programmes seek to limit the use of expensive and environmentally damaging chemicals and target their use more carefully. One way of achieving this is to design more-selective chemicals. For example, the development of the aphicide pirimor, a carbamate insecticide which is highly selective for aphids but causes minimal harm to their natural enemies, has enabled development of an integrated control programme for peach–potato aphid, *Myzus persicae*, and red spider mite, *Tetranychus*, on glasshouse chrysanthemums in Britain. Both were formerly controlled by organophosphate insecticides, which are relatively unselective and to which the aphid was developing resistance. The spider mite is now controlled biologically with the predatory mite *Phytoseiulus*, and the aphid controlled by pirimor.

However, for economic reasons (research and development costs versus the smaller market for selective chemicals) a more practicable universal approach is better targeted use of broad-spectrum chemicals. Targeting may be improved spatially and by better timing of pesticide applications. The development of pheromones* has greatly aided spatial targeting. Sex attractants can be used to lure insects to some other control measure, a pesticide or chemosterilant. Alternatively, a pheromone might be used to aggregate a population in an area to be treated with a

pesticide. In this way much less pesticide is used with minimal effects on non-target species and the wider environment. Another promising use of pheromones alone is to inhibit behavioural responses such as mating by saturating the atmosphere with the appropriate pheromone (very low concentrations will do this). Insects become habituated to the constant stimulus and the appropriate reaction is suppressed. Frequency of pesticide application can be reduced by careful timing to cause maximum damage to the pest (such as at mating) while minimising effects on associated species. This requires close study of the life histories of all the species concerned and a clear understanding of the ecosystems involved.

Successful integrated control schemes have been used on many crop ecosystems where previous blanket spraying of broad-spectrum chemicals has destroyed the natural balance of pest and natural enemy controls. For example the combined use of pheromones and pesticide has enabled recovery of the natural enemies of the cabbage white butterfly and development of new control measures for this pest on *Brassica* crops.

Integrated control measures are now widely used in commercial cotton growing where on a world-wide scale the use of broad-spectrum chemicals to control early season pests such as boll weevil, *Anthonomus grandis*, led to depletion of natural enemies and emergence of new pests, often pesticide-resistant. Economic costs were high. In the Canete valley, Peru, spraying of cotton monocultures resulted in the collapse of associated faunal control giving economic and ecological disaster. Legislative controls in the mid-1950s restricted use of broad-spectrum chemicals and instigated control based on cultural practices including mixed cultivations, reintroduction of beneficial insects and return to older, more-sensitive insecticides. By the late 1950s cotton yields rose dramatically. Similar schemes have been used in other badly affected cotton-growing areas. Worldwide integrated control measures have been developed for many crops of major economic and social importance such as alfalfa, apple, citrus, oil palm, rubber and cocoa, and furthermore such techniques are used extensively on glasshouse crops.

12.9   The Green Revolution

Originally this term was applied to the successful introduction of high-yielding rice and wheat varieties as a means of increasing production in developing countries.

In the late 1940s short-stem varieties of wheat from Japan were crossed with semi-dwarf American varieties. With dwarf varieties the problem of lodging (plants collapsing with a heavy ear) is greatly reduced so that increased application of nitrogenous fertilisers (to boost crop yield) and improved irrigation methods could be exploited. This resulted in yields increasing by a factor of 2.

* Synthetic production of chemical substances used by insects to signal behavioural activity such as mating and aggregation.

The success of the wheat programme led to the setting up of the International Rice Research Institute in the Philippines. Successful breeding of tall, vigorous varieties from Indonesia with dwarf varieties from Taiwan produced the very successful strain 1R8. This responded to high nitrogen fertiliser application by early maturing and enabled two crops to be taken in one growing season.

However, in some respects these innovations proved disappointing since success depended on a high input of expensive fertilisers. They were therefore of no particular advantage to the peasant farmers. Furthermore, due to unfamiliar taste and texture, the rice produced by the new varieties was often unpopular with the indigenous population.

The choice of food crop may be greatly influenced by factors unconnected with primary food production. The commonly grown cereal crops may be deficient in certain of the essential amino acids, for example maize is low in the amino acids lysine and tryptophan. Affluent societies prefer to obtain their amino acids from animal meat proteins rather than plant proteins (such as beans and cereals). The grain is fed to animals which adds an extra consumer to the food chain and is therefore a relatively inefficient system of converting plant protein into high class animal proteins.

A solution to these problems is being sought by:

(1) intensive breeding programmes to select mutants and to develop varieties better adapted to climatic conditions or able to withstand temporary conditions such as drought;
(2) genetic engineering by which favourable genes can be transferred to the host plants, for example to confer disease resistance. Attempts are being made to transfer the NIF genes (the nitrogen-fixation genes) involved in the legume/*Rhizobium* interaction to non-leguminous crops. If successful, this will reduce the requirement for expensive nitrogenous fertilisers.

Plants which have considerable salt tolerance are being developed for semi-arid regions; for example some species have genes which allow, as a detoxication mechanism, the accumulation of ions in the vacuole. Other plants appear to tolerate higher levels of sodium ions in the leaf without their adversely affecting plant growth as in other plants.

Toleration of desiccation in some plants may be related to inherent properties of the cellular contents, such as cytoplasmic factors which are in some way able to limit the damage caused by desiccation and so can be rapidly reactivated on rehydration. However, other investigators have claimed that successful tolerance depends on the mechanical structural properties of the cell wall, or on the size and shape of the cells and on the size of the vacuole.

The term 'Green Revolution' is now used more broadly for the successful application of scientific agricultural principles to tropical crop plants.

Agricultural techniques resulting in increased production of organic materials have been responsible for sustaining large increases in world population. Neverthe-less in Europe, the potential for food production by conventional and alternative agricultural methods is undergoing extensive review (EEC Agricultural Policy) and reorganisation as a consequence of over-production resulting in the 'food mountains'. However, worldwide there remains the question of underproduction with a marked dependence of final crop yield on climatic factors, particularly rainfall.

Claims have been made that the world can be divided into three main groups according to their increase in population.

Group 1: Where the population growth is less than 1.5% per year, for example North America, Western Europe and the USSR, which overall represents about 26% of the total world population.
Group 2: Where the growth rate lies between 1.5 and 2.5% per year, such as China, Japan, South Africa, representing about 28% of the total world population.
Group 3: Where the growth rate is greater than 2.5% per year, for example India, Pakistan, Indonesia and most of Africa, representing about 46% of the world population. It has been estimated that India requires an increase of about 3 million tonnes of grain per annum merely to cope with the increase in population. In addition, it is these areas which are most subject to sudden climatic disasters (such as flooding, lack of rain) and therefore where famine conditions are most likely to occur.

Agricultural systems attempt to improve the efficiency of the photosynthetic system in order to increase production of dry matter for human purposes (the harvest index). This efficiency is based on the conversion of solar radiation into production. The choice of crop species, however, is heavily influenced by factors unconnected with this production, such as food preferences, ease of cultivation, religious and social pressures and secondary constraints such as climate, particularly temperature ranges, and prevalence of pests. As a result of the need to provide food to satisfy population increases, particularly in the developing countries, there is a pressure to push the growth of desirable crops towards the geographical limits of their climatic adaptations, that is to exploit new growing regions, and to develop crops capable of growing successfully in these marginal regions.

Western agriculture depends on a high energy input (mechanisation) and on high rates of application of nitrogenous fertilisers. The production of these fertilisers, involving the reduction of atmospheric nitrogen, also requires a high energy input. Intensive cultivation is therefore possible only in a small percentage of agricultural lands. Worldwide, therefore, there is an emphasis on breeding new varieties of plants capable of producing more food of higher quality, but requiring lower energy input and less dependence on the use of nitrogenous fertilisers. This emphasis is coupled with the need to exploit new habitats for the growth of crops, and to encourage diversification by sowing a wider range of crops, for example in the UK, rape seed is now a common crop and the possibility of growing sunflowers (for oil) is being promoted.

Intensive agricultural programmes based upon artificially optimising environmental conditions have enabled high crop yields to be obtained. The use of greenhouses and hydroponics highlight many of the principles associated with such intensive programmes.

12.9.1 Greenhouses

In addition to the physiological and genetic factors already mentioned, the rate of photosynthesis under field conditions has been shown to be influenced by:

(1) mineral nutrition of the plant;
(2) water management, such as availability;
(3) presence of plant pathogens;
(4) heat stress;
(5) wind;
(6) age of the plant and leaves: factors which delay senescence lead to higher rates. For example, cytokinins delay the onset of senescence in leaves. Leaves sprayed with cytokinins (benzyl adenine and kinetin) have higher rates of photosynthesis compared with control plants.

To obtain higher crop yields, it is important that these factors should be maximised and controlled. By growing crops under glass or inexpensive plastics, such as polyethylene films, greater control of the conditions becomes possible, enabling crops to be grown out of season and thereby exploiting lucrative markets. Greenhouses are also useful for the propagation of seedlings.

The management of greenhouse crops is influenced by the type of plants being grown but general principles include the following.

(1) *Temperature control*. Most plants have an optimum temperature range. Control can be achieved by additional heating in winter, shading in summer and by controlled ventilation. In large commercial greenhouses, temperature is carefully controlled by automatically opening and closing ventilators.
(2) *Ventilation*. This ensures an adequate supply of fresh air, replenishing carbon dioxide levels, and also controls atmospheric moisture levels.
(3) *Water levels and humidity*. Plants vary considerably in their response to moisture; for example cacti thrive best in dry air conditions, foliage plants require higher humidities. Control of humidity is also needed to control the spread of fungal diseases. Humidity levels can be monitored and increased by sprays and mist propagators. Many of these operations are now con-

trolled by computers. Attempts have been made to increase artificially the levels of carbon dioxide in closed greenhouses. This has led to increased yields but the technique has been expensive to operate.

Sheets or cones of plastic film, often called hot caps, are sometimes placed over the tops of plants growing in the field and this has been used especially in Israel for winter vegetable production using plastic tunnels, the higher temperature in the tunnel favouring early crop production.

12.9.2 Hydroponics

This technique was based on earlier experiments investigating the mineral nutrition of plants by growing plants in a range of nutrient solutions. The plants are now usually grown in greenhouses with a continuous liquid culture which is circulated around the plants by pumps. These also give adequate aeration to the nutrient solutions. The nutrient content can be monitored and continuously adjusted (by computers) to maintain optimum growth conditions. The root system is supported in a sand and gravel base. Hydroponics is useful in areas where (*a*) the agriculture soil is poor, (*b*) water is limited, (*c*) there is a demand for off-season speciality crops of high market value.

Table 12.22 Reported increases in crops grown hydroponically.

	Usual agriculture methods	By hydroponics
tomatoes kg/plant	5.4	7.3–10.2
potatoes tonnes/hectare	12.1	26.3
rice kg/hectare	551.0	1 652

12.10 Conservation

Conservation may be defined as the human management of Earth's physical and biological resources in such a way as to give all forms of life, including humans, the best chances in a shared future. Conservation implies both taking action and expressing concern to protect the environment and keep it healthy. It is grounded in the belief, developed through the study of ecology, that well-managed resources of water, land and wildlife will continue to support human requirements for food, shelter, industrial products, recreation, knowledge and health well into the future.

The term conservation is often used to mean preservation of such things as historic buildings and other artefacts (human-made structures). However, conservation in its biological and environmental sense is a more dynamic and interactive process that implies a concern for the natural world which is itself always changing. We need to understand what is happening in our environment to be able to know how to look after it. This knowledge comes from ecology and the other environmental sciences.

Implicit in conservation practice and thinking is an attitude to the world we live in. This is called the **conservation ethic**. Here are just three ways in which it has been expressed.

'We have not so much inherited the world from our parents as borrowed it from our children' (a 'Green' slogan)
'Cheat the Earth and the Earth will cheat you' (an old Chinese proverb)
'Extinction is forever!' (a 'T' Shirt to 'Save the Whale')

Conservation, therefore, often has a moral and political dimension.

Effective conservation management requires integration of scientific and social objectives. In the long term the well-being of human societies and the health of the biosphere are inseparable. In the immediate time scale, however, the objectives of conservation can often seem in conflict with human aims for development and techno-logical progress. Conservation issues are thus often highly contentious; they are also very wide-ranging. Some examples of what conservation may mean in practice are given below.

Conservation of genetic variety. This is one argument for tropical rain forest conservation since these forests have high species diversity. It is also important for maintaining domesticated plants and animals. Worldwide establish-ment of seed and sperm banks ensures survival of potential material from which to develop new varieties of food crops and domestic livestock in the event of major physical or biotic environment change, such as changing patterns of global climate associated with 'greenhouse' warming, or emergence of a new pest or disease due to natural or human-induced mutation.

Restoration of land, such as mine-waste or gravel pits for wildlife, recreation, agriculture and landscape enhance-ment, or even new building land thus relieving pressure on high-quality, relatively undisturbed countryside.

Waste recycling to avoid excessive use of resources. Recycling paper, often needlessly burned or thrown away, reduces timber needs for the paper industry. Domestic refuse can be used to generate power, particularly for local district heating schemes, though care must be taken when incinerating wastes to avoid air pollution problems.

Maintenance of forest cover on watersheds thus pre-venting erosion and rapid run-off and flooding and at the same time maintaining timber stocks for future human use.

Avoidance of overcropping both in the seas (see section 12.7.7) and on the land.

12.10.1 Spaceship Earth

For thousands of years humans were in equilibrium with their environment. Whenever a resource ran out locally the human population moved on. Another clearing could be made in the forest or a new search could bring ample supplies of fresh food. This balance between environmental requirements and human needs was found in hunter–gatherer societies; most recently it has been seen amongst the Kalahari bushmen, Australian aboriginies, or Inuit Indians (eskimos).

A series of revolutions in human history have broken down this balance between humans and nature. The origins of agriculture and of animal husbandry 10 000 years ago caused a huge expansion of farming people which led eventually to the first large settlements. Since then further revolutions in food production, disease control and indus-trialisation have changed a tiny global human population into a huge expanding and technological society that places ever greater demands on Earth's resources. In the 1960s, when humans first ventured off the planet, Earth was seen from space for the first time. This had a profound effect on people emphasising the finite limits to population growth and the exploitation of resources.

Ecologists have come to view Earth as a 'spaceship' that is completely equipped for long-term travel, but without any support other than its own original resources and the radiant energy of its nearest star, the Sun. Life has been sustained on this planet for an estimated 3 500 million years; there is no reason to suppose that it will not go on for at least as long into the future, if we look after it.

As discussed in section 12.3, the energy for life comes principally from the Sun, as light, feeding useful energy into food chains by photosynthesis of green plants and driving the biogeochemical cycles. Solar energy also powers the planetary weather systems and ocean currents that more immediately generate environments amenable to life.

In 1980 three worldwide bodies (UNEP, IUCN and WWF) drew up a **World Conservation Strategy** in which they presented an ecological analysis of how to run the spaceship, Earth. This document identified the conserva-tion of Earth's physical environments and plant communi-ties as the first essential of the life support system. The atmosphere, oceans and soils sustain plant life and plants sustain all animals. Furthermore on the terrestrial (land) surface it is largely plant cover that in turn conserves the soil from erosion.

Secondly the World Conservation Strategy recognised the need to conserve the Earth's genetic diversity. Evolu-tion has produced a vast variety of life forms, both naturally and artificially selected. The extinction of species repre-sents a permanent loss of biological resources and future opportunities. The World Conservation Strategy set out, for the first time, a programme for the sustained use of Earth's ecosystems. It argued that it must be possible to give every human being a satisfactory quality of life, whilst not abusing the life support system or threatening the other inhabitants of the spaceship with extinction. Many of the wild plants and animals of Earth may well prove more useful in the future than we suspect at present.

12.10.2 Abuse of the life support system – pollution

Until very recent Earth history, living systems evolved in rough balance with the atmosphere, hydrosphere and lithosphere, unaffected by human activity. Since the development of agriculture and technology, an increasing human impact on environment has occurred. In the last two centuries especially, widespread industrialisation has led to potentially damaging environmental pollution.

Pollution may be defined as the release into the environment of substances or energy in such quantities and for such duration that they cause harm to people or their environment. Pollution can affect all aspects of environment, human-made and natural, physical and biotic, and is readily transferred between components of the life support system. For example, pollutant gases in the atmosphere generate 'acid rain' (hydrosphere) which may in turn lead to soil acidification (lithosphere) and which also has profound effects on forests and aquatic ecosystems (biosphere), as well as damaging buildings and other artefacts (human-made structures).

Atmospheric pollution

Until the 1960s air pollutants were generally considered a local problem associated with urban and industrial centres. Subsequently it has become apparent that pollutants may be transported long distances in the air, causing adverse effects in environments far removed from the source of emission. Air pollution and its control is thus a global issue demanding international cooperation. Important atmospheric pollutants include gases such as chlorofluorocarbons (CFCs), sulphur dioxide (SO_2), hydrocarbons (HCs) and the oxides of nitrogen (NO_x). Gases occurring naturally in the atmosphere may be seriously depleted by pollution, such as ozone (O_3) in the stratosphere. Paradoxically in some locations ozone is occurring with increasing frequency as a ground-level air pollutant with mean monthly concentrations up to 200 ppm compared with normal monthly values peaking at 0.04 ppm. At these higher levels ozone damages many crop plants, for example tomatoes in California (total crop losses due to O_3 damage in California amount to about $1 billion per annum). In association with other hydrocarbons and NO_x pollutants, ozone may generate a direct human health hazard and is an important constituent of photochemical smog. Dusts, noise, waste heat, radioactivity and electromagnetic pulses may also pollute the atmosphere. Detailed consideration of the full range of pollutants, their effects and controls, is beyond the scope of this text*. The rising levels of atmospheric carbon dioxide and its role, with other gases, in the planetary 'greenhouse' effect was discussed in section 12.4.1. Two further topical global issues, ozone depletion and 'acid rain' are considered now.

Ozone depletion. The atmosphere provides a thermal blanket and radiation shield to the Earth. In the upper atmosphere, 15–50 km above the Earth, oxygen and ozone absorb much of the incoming short-wave radiation. These are ultraviolet (UV), X- and gamma-rays which are in the main very harmful to living organisms, damaging their genetic material. In the USA it has been estimated that a 5% reduction in stratospheric ozone would lead to a 7.5–15% increase in ground-level UV radiation† which might increase the incidence of skin cancer by tens or hundreds of thousands of cases a year. Furthermore radiation absorption by stratospheric ozone warms the stratosphere creating a deep temperature inversion layer (temperature usually *decreases* with height in the troposphere, the lower atmosphere). This effectively limits convective motion in the atmosphere. Any change or weakening of this temperature inversion layer, by extending the depth through which convection may operate, would profoundly alter global weather patterns and hence Earth surface climates.

High in the atmosphere oxygen molecules (O_2) are dissociated by radiation into oxygen atoms (O) which combine with oxygen molecules to make ozone (O_3). The reaction is reversible by sunlight ($O_3 + O \rightleftharpoons 2O_2$). Ozone exists at an equilibrium level in the 'ozone layer' at a concentration of 1 ppm.

Chlorofluorocarbons are a group of chemicals including carbon tetrachloride and chloroform. These are commonly used as solvents, aerosol propellants and refrigerator coolants. They are not readily broken down in the troposphere where they may contribute to increased 'greenhouse' warming as discussed in section 12.4.1. They rise eventually into the stratosphere. Above 25 km CFCs are broken down by sunlight, releasing chlorine and fluorine. These react with ozone, one atom of chlorine or fluorine destroying 10^5 molecules of ozone, and break it down into oxygen faster than it can be reformed from oxygen into ozone.

CFC pollution shifts the oxygen–ozone equilibrium. At the present levels of CFC pollution a 10% depletion of ozone may occur over the next 20 years, and it has been suggested that as much as two-thirds of the ozone could be destroyed in half a century. In 1987 a seasonal but complete depletion of the ozone layer occurred above Antarctica for the first time.

Acid rain. Acid rain is neither a simple nor a single phenomenon. The acid gases sulphur dioxide (SO_2) and oxides of nitrogen (NO_x) are produced by burning

---

* See D. Elsom. (1987) *Atmospheric Pollution*, Blackwell, for a fuller discussion of climatic and health effects.
† UV radiation of certain wavelengths also has an important *beneficial* effect converting skin steroids to vitamin D.

fossil fuels. Incomplete combustion of these fuels releases hydrocarbons. These may have effects as dry gases or they may be washed out of the atmosphere to produce acid precipitation in rain and snow (see figure 12.55). The most industrialised areas of the world, such as the eastern USA, western Europe, north-east China and Japan, have all experienced rainfall with a pH well below 4.0. (pH 5 is the conventionally accepted lower limit for natural rainfall acidity*.)

Acid rainfall (pH<5) is often accompanied by major changes in ecosystems and damage to buildings. This often happens in countries bordering those which are major sources of pollutants. Norway and Sweden, for example, receive acid rain as a result of air pollutants emitted in the UK and industrial centres of Europe which are transported by prevailing high-level winds (see figure 12.56). Acid rainfall in central Sweden and southern Norway has affected salmon and trout fisheries (see figure 12.57) and damaged forests. Tree injury associated with acid pollution is now widespread in Europe and evidence for damage to beech and yew has been recorded in Britain.

It is commonly found that where the soil on which precipitation falls does not neutralise the acid (being derived from carbonate-poor bedrock such as granite) the fauna of lakes and rivers suffers. Young fish fry and spawn are particularly susceptible. In Scandinavia, winter accumulation of acid pollutants in snow cover which is released as an acid 'pulse' in spring melt water, coinciding with the appearance of spawn and fry, makes this problem worse. Magnesium and calcium are leached from soils and from

damaged leaves, eventually aluminium, manganese and heavy metals come into solution and may reach toxic concentrations, causing damage to tree roots and the breakdown of mycorrhizas. This decreases the capacity of the tree to take up water and nutrients. Disease induced by mineral deficiencies becomes common, a situation made worse by dry conditions. 'Acid rain' also includes the phenomenon of ozone-acid mists, thought to be an important cause of die-back in the Black Forest in Germany, and dry deposition of acid pollutants. Ozone is generated as a ground-level pollutant as hydrocarbons react with nitrogen oxides in sunny conditions. Even at levels where they are individually harmless, ozone, sulphur dioxide, nitrogen oxides, heavy metals and other photo-oxidants may together produce severe and damaging reductions of plant growth. Combined with climatic stress, especially drought, such pollution 'cocktails' can lead to tree death.

The expression 'acid rain' therefore describes more than one phenomenon. Cures, such as adding lime to lakes (Sweden) and forests (W. Germany) can only be viewed as temporary stop-gaps. The remedy lies in reducing the release of pollutant gases. Attention has been focussed on reducing sulphur dioxide emissions since these have significant and clearly identifiable industrial sources, most notably coal-fired electricity generators. Furthermore the desulphurisation technology is available and effective, though costly*. In the long term, however, it may be equally important to reduce hydrocarbon and nitrogen oxide emissions.

* Carbon dioxide naturally present in the atmosphere can reduce rainfall pH to 5.6. Sea- or volcanic-derived sulphur may further reduce natural rainfall pH to as low as pH 4.7.

* High cost particularly applies when desulphurisation units are fitted retrospectively rather than included in initial plant design.

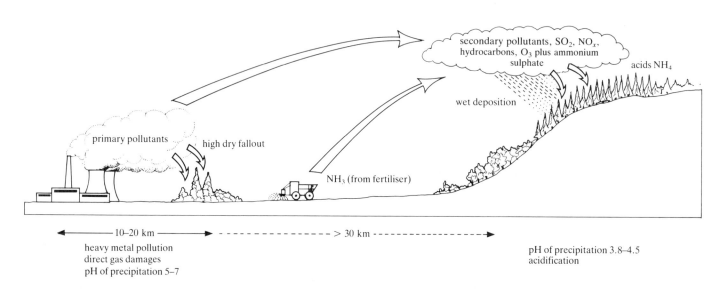

Fig 12.55 *The complexity of 'acid rain', a schematic representation of how air pollutants interact in complex ways to produce different effects in different areas. (From C. Rose (1985) Acid rain falls on British woodland, New Scientist, 108, 1482, 52–7.)*

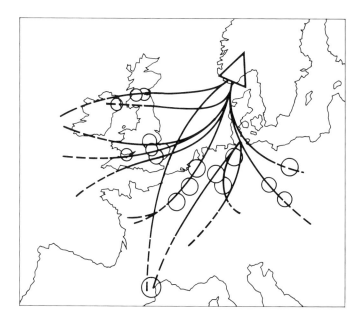

Fig 12.56 *Accumulation of acid pollutants over southern Norway. The arrows show the prevailing winds on 12 successive days of January 1974. The open circles represent centres of population or industry in western Europe. (From J.H. Ottaway (1980) The biochemistry of pollution, Studies in Biology, 123, Edward Arnold.)*

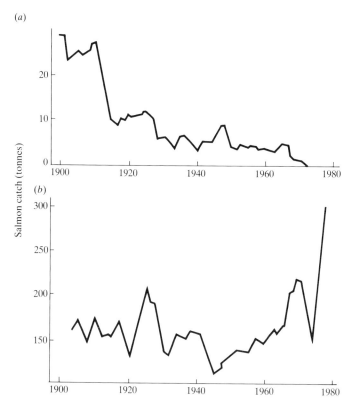

Fig 12.57 *Trends in the salmon catch from Norwegian rivers. (a) Southern rivers, the area most affected by acid pollution. (b) 68 other rivers of Norways. (From F. Pearce (1986) Unravelling a century of acid pollution, New Scientist, 11, 1527, p. 23.)*

Water pollution

Until recently water pollution has been a relatively local problem of the developed world. The problem of eutrophication associated with excessive use of fertilisers in intensive agriculture and phosphate-rich sewage effluents was discussed in section 12.4.1. Such problems are increasingly occurring on a world-wide basis and affect marine as well as freshwater ecosystems. For example an algal bloom, many miles in extent, covered parts of the North Sea approaches to the Baltic in the summer of 1988. Sewage from coastal settlements discharges, sometimes untreated, into coastal waters where it generates a direct health hazard for recreational bathers as well as marine organisms. Land drainage from urban areas, industrial and waste disposal sites is often contaminated with heavy metals or hydrocarbons. Biological concentration by heavy metals in marine food chains may give lethal doses as occurred following the industrial discharge of mercury into coastal waters at Minimata in Japan. Concentrations in fish led to deaths of many humans and other animal predators. At sub-lethal levels heavy metals and contaminants such as pesticide and oil derivatives may weaken disease resistance. In the North Sea polychlorinated biphenyls (PCBs), which are also carcinogens, are present at concentrations of 0.000002 ppm. Dolphins at the end of the marine food chain have levels of 16 ppm. Measures to control and eventually stop toxic waste dumping and incineration at sea have recently been introduced by countries bordering the North Sea. Legislative controls of oil pollution associated with oil terminals and the discharge of ballast water from oil tankers were introduced much earlier after the problems were highlighted by major oil spills from oil tankers such as the Torrey Canyon (1967). Studies have shown that the less spectacular, small but persistent spills and leakages have a more damaging influence on marine ecosystems than the well-published major incidents. Use of detergents to disperse oil slicks is often more damaging to the environment than the oil itself. Further research and better marine pollution monitoring is urgently needed. Legislation to control marine pollution is difficult to police, particularly in open oceans. Easy profits can be made from criminal dumping, especially since waste disposal has become a major problem for human societies. Noxious chemicals and radioactive wastes are of course eventually dispersed by ocean currents and wave action, but if discharged into the shallow seas of the continental shelf, and especially the intertidal zone, they may damage ecosystems before effective dispersal can occur. Small seas are particularly vulnerable. The Irish Sea is a more radioactive marine environment than other coastal waters due to leaks from the Sellafield nuclear power station.

Another major problem relates to soil erosion on the continental surfaces. This increases the silt load of rivers and coastal waters. The silt may beneficially enrich fisheries, though even this is debatable (see section 12.4.1). Silt deposition is certainly leading to coral reef destruction. For example the Australian Great Barrier reef is adversely influenced by deforestation on the continental mainland.

Global deforestation

Forests are the natural climax vegetation of many parts of the world covering, until recent years, a third of the land surface. Although temperate forests are not significantly decreasing, tropical forests are declining at a rate that will decrease their 1950 extent (15% of global land surface) to 300 million hectares (7% of global land surface) by the year 2000 AD. Twelve million hectares of forest, an area the size of England, are disappearing annually and a further ten million hectares are being degraded by removal of good timber species, inappropriate management and inattention to conservation needs. Tropical forests are in urgent need of conservation. The responsibility for their care is international for their destruction is linked with our global economic system and the problem of Third World poverty.

Traditional practices of forest clearance for farming, by 'slash and burn,' did no long-term damage to forests at low human population densities. It is important to realise that, given time, the period of 'bush fallow' between clearances provided a natural rotation system that allowed the forest and its soils time to recover and did not threaten the forest's wildlife or endanger its soil in the long term. Human population expansion and competing land uses, such as plantation agriculture and hydroelectric power development, have forced a reduction in this fallow period and, because there is not enough land for people to farm, this is leading to the decline of forests. Not only are forests under much pressure from peasant farming systems but also importantly from fuel-wood gathering, from commercial logging for tropical hardwoods (such as teak and mahogany) and from wholesale burning and clearance for cattle ranching. The Third World countries alone are not to blame for this situation; global deforestation is a product of both population expansion (which increases the demands of poor farmers for more land and fuel) and the exploitative demands of rich countries for the very best timber and beef at cheap prices.

Loss of forests is serious for many reasons.

(a) There is a loss of traditionally harvested products such as timber, poles, twine, fuel-wood, honey, fruit, game animals and herbs, that at one time supplied local people with their needs.
(b) The demand for softwood timber (for building), pulp wood (for making paper) and tropical hardwood (for furniture) is rising globally. Long-term supplies are very much threatened.
(c) Forests are often on uplands and on watersheds, catching large amounts of rain and releasing the water slowly into streams and rivers. Deforestation of uplands is a major cause of floods in the plains below. India spends more than $1 000 million on flood damage repairs each year. In Bangladesh, in the summer of 1988, flooding occurred on an unprecedented scale affecting most of the country, largely due to the

deforestation in the mountains to the north in India and Nepal. International aid and cooperation is essential for an effective remedy.
(d) Deforestation results in soil erosion which causes economic losses and hunger. Clean water supplies may be fouled with resulting disease, as occurred in Bangladesh. The silting of reservoirs reduces their useful life, whilst harbours and estuaries must be continually dredged to keep them open.
(e) Deforestation increases global carbon dioxide (see section 12.4.1) and increases Earth surface albedo. Both of these changes may have long-term effects on the global climate.
(f) Removal of forest may alter the amount and frequency of rainfall and as a result sustained spring water supplies to communities may be lost.
(g) Forests have the most species-rich and diverse wildlife communities. Their destruction will lead to innumerable extinctions of little-known forms of life with the consequent loss of genetic variety and potential resources.

Soil erosion and the loss of agricultural land

Deforestation is not the only cause of soil erosion. Mismanagement of farmland and grassland may lead to a rapid loss of soil. Soil formation is a slow process (see section 12.5) and, globally, soil destruction currently far outreaches new soil formation. High rainfall, hilly areas with steep slopes and regularly cultivated soils are especially susceptible to soil erosion. Parts of south-east Asia have long-established systems of terracing that have proved very effective in holding soil. These are in areas where forests have been cleared. Principal soil conservation measures are terrace cultivation, contour ploughing and tying ridges to stop run-off of rain. Examples of such good conservation practices are found in Bali, whereas in neighbouring Java rapid population expansion and poor farming practice have led to considerable devastation. Annually, five million hectares of farmed land are coming out of crop production, worldwide, because of erosion losses.

Grasslands that are overgrazed by livestock frequently lose the plant cover that holds the topsoil. Plants are eaten to their roots and die, with the result that water running freely across the land surface causes sheet erosion, carrying off the topsoil. Channelled rainwater forms gullies which cut deep into the land surface. About seven million hectares of grazing land are lost this way each year and much of this will become desert.

Deserts may form naturally, but their creation may be accelerated by human activity in a process called **desertification**. One third of the global land surface is arid or semi-arid, and in these regions some 700 million people live a precarious and marginal existence. Much soil erosion is due to the activities of relatively poor people living on marginal land because they have few other choices. The Sahel, a semi-arid belt across the continent of Africa south of the Sahara, has increased in extent as a result of overpopulation by people and overgrazing by their cattle. Desertification may be checked and deserts made 'green' again by conservation measures: excluding people and their cattle, and planting trees. However, this is administratively, socially, economically and politically difficult. If deserts are 'made green' again they may generate higher and more regular rainfall through changed albedo effects on climate.

Thought question

1(a) For any one of the topics discussed in this section or section 12.4.1 (the greenhouse effect or eutrophication), prepare a summary table showing who pays for the pollution and who benefits.

(b) When polluters are forced to pay for pollution control the costs previously borne by society (as pollution) are included in the production process as pollution control. This is termed the **polluter pays principle**. What are the main likely benefits and difficulties associated with this idea?

12.10.3   Conservation of genetic diversity
Rare and endangered species

Throughout evolution species have been extinguished in the struggle for existence. Extinction is forever: the dodo and the dinosaurs cannot be brought back. Today there is an accelerating rate of extinction largely due to the fast rate of habitat destruction, the powerful forces exploiting wild populations and the shrinking of available spaces for wildlife in the face of human expansion. It is estimated that a species a day is lost at the present time. Many, most notably tropical rain forest species, are being lost before they can be described and named by taxonomists. Most losses are of insects. For every ten described species of higher plant or animal there is one in imminent danger of extinction. The plight of endangered species is well illustrated by the giant panda.

The giant panda, *Ailuropoda melanoleuca*, symbol of the Worldwide Fund for Nature (WWF), is found in eastern Tibet and southwest China. Its doleful face and cuddly-looking nature have endeared it to millions of sympathetic humans! At one time it was very much endangered since its habitat, of bamboo forest, was being encroached upon increasingly by the human population. Since interest in its survival has developed and forest reserves for it have been made, the panda population has increased to nearly a thousand members. The giant panda feeds almost exclusively on arrow bamboo, a plant that goes through cycles of abundance and scarcity. In Sichuan province in 1983 large areas of forest suddenly died back and at least 59 pandas died of starvation. Without human help this endangered species might at such a time have become extinct altogether. It has only been in the last few years that sufficient studies have been made of this species to begin to understand its physiology and ecology in the wild. It is now easy to see how ill-equipped giant pandas are to compete with people in the modern world. Pandas live solitary lives and only come together for breeding. Adults spend 95% of their waking hours feeding on bamboo, which is a poor diet, and will rarely eat anything else in preference. Although breeding captive pandas in zoos in this country has been a failure, the Chinese have been more successful at the 'Panda Farm' at Wolong in Sichuan province. Use has been made of the latest techniques in reproduction technology, such as artificial fertilisation and sperm banking, and several young have been born in captivity. It is now more possible to predict the female oestrus and ensure mating at the right moment. With environmental protection and a little human help the giant panda will survive.

There are many well-documented examples of endangered species and many programmes have been developed to save them. Some species, like the Californian condor, became endangered because of pesticide poisoning; others, such as the Philippines monkey-eating eagle, are declining because their habitat is disappearing. Each of these eagles requires more than 50 km^2 of forest and there are less than 300 of them left in the whole of southeast Asia. For some species decline is due to incompatibility with humans. The tiger in India, traditionally the enemy of humans, was close to extinction until several large tiger reserves were created. Poaching for ivory and rhinoceros horn have reduced elephant and rhino numbers to very low levels, a trend increased by the availability of automatic weapons. Other rare animals, such as mountain gorillas, are particularly sensitive to human disturbance. All endangered species of both plants and animals are documented in the 'Red Data Books' produced by the International Union for the Conservation of Nature and Natural Resources (IUCN). Successful species conservation requires public education, publicity, ecological research and financial support for game parks, nature reserves, zoos and botanic gardens.

Genetic resources for human use

Recently it has been realised that there is a considerable extinction of valuable alleles if an existing species' gene pool becomes too reduced. This is certainly happening with crop plants and domesticated animals. Of the estimated 80 000 plants that are edible, only 20 species have been cultivated on a large scale for human food. It is very common in developed countries for a very few varieties of these species to be grown. Selected, attested high-yielding varieties are often all that is available in bulk for sowing (half of all the wheat on the Canadian wheatlands is of one variety, 'Neepawa'). Plant breeders have for some time been aware of the genetic erosion that crop monoculture produces. They are therefore collecting many old crop varieties and conserving them, either in cultivation or in seed banks. The largest plant breeders 'gene bank' is at the International Rice Research Institute in the Philippines where thousands of traditional rice varieties are being kept (see section 12.9). Many of these are unproductive and do not respond well to fertilisers, but on the credit side they possess alleles for pest and disease resistance.

In Britain the Rare Breeds Survival Trust maintains a considerable variety of native forms of farm animal in approved collections. The rare Cornish chicken was recently used to provide an input of fast growth genes to modern poultry varieties. The Tamworth pig has proved highly successful as a free-range pig in Australia.

Undomesticated species are also a potential resource for humankind, and their conservation is only prudent. The rosy periwinkle, for example, came originally from the forests of Madagascar and produces a drug used in cancer therapy. Recently a variant of this plant was found in the West Indies that had the capacity to produce ten times more of the valuable cancer drug.

It has become increasingly clear that the best guarantee for the survival of wild species of plants and animals lies in conserving the environments in which the species are found. This requires an ecosystem approach. Each nation is at present seeking to set aside representative environments and will give them a high conservation status so that the genetic diversity of the world's plants and animals may be the better looked after (see section 12.10.6).

> **Thought question**
> 2 How could sperm banks be used to enlarge the gene pool of a species like the African rhinoceros, populations of which must become increasingly isolated and unable to meet each other?

12.10.4 Thinking 'Green'

Ecological knowledge and the perception of the Earth's life support systems and its evolved genetic diversity has forced many people to look critically at our management of the Earth's resources. We need to 'think green' if we are to make sustained use of plant and animal communities and maintain environmental quality.

Sustainable use of plant and animal resources

Rational cropping of ecosystems was discussed in section 12.3.7. The relevance of population dynamics to sustained and profitable use of fish resources was considered in section 12.7. In the long-term economic prosperity and ecological well-being are inseparable.

Forest management illustrates the need to take a long-term view, for the timber needed by one generation has to be planted at least a generation in advance. Furthermore where land use is changed to accommodate human needs, as when forest is cleared for new agricultural land, it is important that the new system should be sustainable in the long term. In parts of Amazonia agricultural success following rain forest clearance has been very transient. Even schemes with substantial external

financial support and agricultural expertise have been abandoned after 10 or 15 years. Weed invasion, pest and disease problems, and, above all, declining soil fertility make projects no longer economically viable. For a variety of reasons mature rain forest rarely re-establishes at such sites. In the intervening period soil nutrients are lost and structure is impaired; no forest seed store remains and, even when dispersal brings seeds of mature rain forest species, germination is poor in the exposed conditions. (Rain forest species require the high humidity found beneath a mature canopy for successful germination.) At best a secondary forest of lower productivity than the original rain forest is established in which only very low intensity shifting cultivation can be practised. Intensive agriculture is clearly not a sustainable use of these areas. It wastes resources since the replacing forest is less productive than the original. At the same time many mature forest species are permanently lost. Sustainable use of tropical moist forests which also allows economic and social development of the region concerned is a major contemporary challenge for the world community.

Recycling of materials

An important aspect of conservation is the need to imitate the cycling processes of nature. Materials are used over and over again in nature; why not with human materials? If commodities are uncommon, like rare metals, this may be done, but generally ours is a 'throw-away society'. During the Second World War Britain recycled a great deal of paper effectively. Poor Third World countries do the same today. Since we are rich enough to pay the world price for wood pulp relatively little is recycled in Britain and many other developed countries. Paper recycling technology is improving to such an extent that the wasteful use of paper could at least be halved.

Sewage processing is a technological use of the decay micro-organisms, normally present in the soil and fresh water, to break down human wastes. Sewage works employ this natural process and produce, as a by-product, nutrient-rich dried sludge. Providing it has not become contaminated with heavy metals (such as by lead from petroleum wastes) this may be returned to the land as fertiliser. Sewage sludge is also often used in reclamation schemes since it improves 'soil' structure as well as providing vital missing nutrients. Energy from the organic sewage may be used to generate methane (biogas) to provide the energy to run the sewage processing works.

New sources of energy

An awareness of the rate of depletion of fossil fuels and an unease about nuclear power has prompted many people to think creatively about alternative sources of energy.

The Sun may be considered to be a nuclear fusion reactor. It has the advantage of being 150 million kilometres away. The heat of the Sun indirectly causes the wind and waves of the sea. It also runs the hydrological cycle and provides all the energy for photosynthesis in the biosphere. Harnessing wind and wave power, hydroelectric power and direct solar power are all options open to us for the future. Even the use of plant materials to provide energy for fuel is feasible. Brazil has large industrial plants for converting sugar, from cane, into ethanol (gasohol) to run its cars. Such uses of 'biomass' to produce energy are potentially cleaner and less exploitive of the fossil fuel reserves of the planet. These should not be burned for they may be very valuable to us in the long-term and should be regarded as finite resources. They cannot last forever.

Reclamation from industrial and urban dereliction

Conservation may imply acting to restore the use of some exploited part of the environment for some useful biological production or human amenity or industrial use. Abandoned mining wastes and industrial sites often pose a considerable hazard, as demonstrated by the land-slip disaster at Aberfan, S. Wales in 1963. Establishing a vegetation cover on such areas will ameliorate the extreme drainage, flood, water quality and slope stability problems they pose.

The main problems for revegetating abandoned industrial and urban sites lie with establishing a suitable stable 'soil' medium for germination and sustained growth. Temperature and moisture extremes commonly impair germination. Deficiencies of nitrogen and phosphorus are major problems for plant growth. Mine spoil and industrial wastes may also be contaminated with heavy metals. Returning these wastes to agricultural or forestry use is difficult due to the risk of bioaccumulation of metal toxicity in food chains. Extremes of pH and recurring extreme acidity, as found in colliery spoil containing iron pyrites, also require amendment before a successful and sustained vegetation sward can be established. However, these areas can be reclaimed for new industrial sites, thus relieving pressure on remaining countryside resources.

Spoil heaps from mines in the Midlands and north of England have been landscaped and sown with mineral-tolerant grasses. To many people they now look like ordinary hills. Old gravel pits are very commonly landscaped and managed for wildlife, or for fishing, boating or waterskiing. In Northamptonshire 5 700 hectares of open cast mining have been reclaimed by landscaping, by clearing the boulders and by planting grass and clover mixtures. After 20 years the build-up of soil has been sufficient to return the land to arable farming once again, providing wild areas of countryside in the mean time.

12.10.5 United Kingdom conservation concerns

Britain has almost no 'natural' communities. Since Neolithic times people have been an important influence shaping the countryside (see section 12.6.1). The upland moors and lowland heaths (considered in 12.6.1) have been formed by centuries of deforestation and subsequent grazing and burning management. The structure and species composition of British woodlands has been modified by grazing and silvicultural practice. Thus, concern for maintaining the 'natural landscape' is in fact a demand for the retention of a pattern of rural appearances only a few hundred years old. Within this framework there are many seminatural communities that are worthy of conservation which will die out if they are not managed well. These are described below.

Broad-leaved woodland

As discussed in section 12.6.1, oak was the dominant species in the primeval forests of Britain. Beech was also important in the south and like ash sometimes dominated on limestone and chalk hills. Lime was particularly important during the warmest phase since the last Ice Age. Birch and, in the north, pine were characteristic on nutrient-poor sandy soils. Alder, another warmth-loving species, favoured wetter fertile sites with willow more prevalent on wet nutrient-poor sites.

A very few contemporary woodlands are primary forest remnants and even these have been modified by human activities. Most broad-leaved woodlands are secondary, having developed from formerly cleared sites. 'Ancient woodlands' are those that date from before 1600 AD; those with a later origin are termed 'recent'. Ancient woodlands have the highest conservation value. Although they may not be original primary forest, they often contain great species diversity, particularly of slow-growing long-lived plants such as lichens, and they bear the marks of human management back to very early times. Most woodlands were managed in one of two traditional systems as wood pastures or coppice. **Wood pastures** were common on poorer soils and livestock grazing as well as timber produce was important in these woodlands. Grazing pressure restricted regeneration, a problem overcome by **pollarding** (cutting the main stem above the browse line (c. 2 m) to encourage new growth of lateral branches which could be periodically harvested). The Ancient and Oriental woodlands of the New Forest, Hampshire are good examples of wood pastures. These woodlands are typically less species-rich than former coppice woodlands. Over centuries the more palatable species have been lost and browse-tolerant species such as holly and hawthorn have become dominant in the understorey. The future of many of these woodlands depends on regeneration success now largely dependent on the control of grazing pressure.

On richer soils the **coppice system** predominated. Understorey species such as ash and hazel were cut close to ground level on a 5–20 year cycle depending on the rate of regrowth and the products required. The larger coppice poles were used to provide materials for house building, furniture and fencing; lighter materials were used for basket weaving, sheep hurdles or wattle (to hold wall plaster) or were used in thatching. Woods provided much fuel and of all the products very little was wasted. Occasional standard trees were allowed to grow to near full maturity. These were felled on a longer time scale and sawn into planks or fashioned into beams. This management pattern, of **coppice with standards**, resulted in periodic expanses of flowers on the woodland floor. Such woods have a species-rich ground flora, with many rare and historically interesting plants. In the late nineteenth and early twentieth centuries economic and social changes led to the decline of coppice management and many woods were untouched for over 50 years. The re-establishment of coppice cycles, mainly by voluntary conservation groups, has restored the interest and beauty of many of these woodlands. Conserving ancient woodland helps to retain the rich plant and animal communities of the primary forests, many members of which are rare. Such places provide an experimental 'control' or baseline from which to judge other environmental change as well as being a living museum more ancient than our built historical monuments.

Hedgerows

Hedgerows may have high value to wildlife conservation. Hedges were used by the Saxons to divide and demarcate land plots and to contain livestock. Hedgerows are traditionally managed by periodic laying, in which upright stems are selected in the line of the hedge, half cut through and layed down, weaving them between stakes. The resulting structure, a layed hedge, is both alive and stockproof. Over the centuries such hedgerows have increased their species richness. One new species of woody shrub is added to every 27 m length of hedgerow, on average, every hundred years. Ancient hedgerows have therefore the greatest diversity of wildlife and some are even the only places in an arable area where plants typical of ancient woodland are found. Many thousands of kilometres of hedgerow were lost in lowland Britain between 1950 and 1980; between 1957 and 1969 the rate of removal was fastest. The enlarged field sizes released many hectares of land to arable farming, freed farmers from having to maintain them by trimming or proper laying, facilitated ploughing and harvesting by large machines, and removed from the countryside what farmers perceived as a reservoir of weeds, pests and diseases. Hedgerows, however, undoubtedly conserved many species of animals which act as predators of many plant pests. They reduce windspeeds providing important areas of livestock shelter in their lee and helping to reduce soil erosion. Hedgerows also provide a refuge and home for song birds, game birds and other woodland species.

Grasslands and meadows

Today most of the grazing used by farmers are sown leys of productive species, typically rye grass (*Lolium*) mixtures. Ancient grassland is much richer in plant species, and hence retains many more species of other wildlife. The richest of these ancient grass communities are the chalk grasslands (see also section 12.6.1) found on calcareous soils, and the ill-drained lush grass pastures of the lowland wetlands. Traditionally grass may be grazed (pasture) or mown for hay (meadow) or left for winter grazing (foggage). Management systems vary, but to conserve the diversity of grassland a traditional system should be maintained, avoiding the use of herbicides and nutrient enrichment with fertilisers. The addition of nitrogen will quickly deplete pastures of orchids, for example. Where a ley may have barely ten species of plant in it, an ancient meadow may have over a hundred. Many old meadows and pastures, characterised by such plants as cowslips, ox-eye daisies and ladies bedstraw, have disappeared under the plough. Wetlands have been drained and turned to profitable arable farming. The Halvergate marshes in East Anglia, Somerset levels and the flood meadows of the Test and Avon valleys (Hampshire), some of the best remaining wet grazing lands, have all been threatened. Once lost, such plant and animal communities are almost impossible to regain.

Upland moors (see section 12.6.1 for lowland heaths)

The northern uplands of Britain are characterised by a virtually treeless region of short vegetation, some of which is dominated by heather (*Calluna vulgaris*). It covers over a million hectares of Scotland and northern England on acid free-draining (podzolic) soils; it is rare on the continent of Europe where similar communities have been afforested. A distinction is sometimes made between upland heaths and moors based on the damper thicker peat of the latter. However, there is little difference in vegetation apart from an increased frequency of rare liverworts and lichens on the wetter moors. Moorland is partly man-made, being a product of the deforestation of primary upland forest followed by intensive sheep grazing and occasional burning. Moorlands have been conserved for their scenic beauty, recreational value to walkers and because game shooting (grouse and red deer) are still major recreations for the minority. Moorlands are rich in non-vertebrate species and many nationally rare birds, such as the curlew, the golden eagle and the merlin falcon, favour such open habitats. A trend in recent years has been towards planting forests on these uplands. There has also been much drainage of water-logged bogs that formerly defied any alternative land use. This has been seen in the Flow country of Scotland. The planting of coniferous monocultures of lodgepole pine (*Pinus contorta*) and sitka spruce (*Picea sitchensis*) is welcomed by those who see them as a means of meeting national timber needs, but opposed by those who see the plantations as an eyesore to the landscape, of doubtful real economic benefit, and an impoverishment of native wildlife. Satisfying a diversity of recreational needs together with economic and wildlife conservation imperatives requires careful long-term planning. The voice of conservation dictates that the existing diversity should be maintained without loss of species.

12.10.6 Conservation agencies

There are many individuals, groups and organisations concerned with conservation from local level up to international level. The groups to which individuals belong are diverse and specialised in their particular interest. All contribute in different ways to changing the way we think about and act towards the environment.

Local and national non-governmental bodies

Every county and major urban area in Britain has a Trust for Nature Conservation which owns and manages small nature reserves. Trusts, at the local level, provide a considerable protection for species-rich sites and involve many of their members in wildlife recording and fund raising. All such Trusts, which collectively have about 1 400 nature reserves, are affiliated to the Royal Society for Nature Conservation. Their junior club is called 'WATCH'.

The Royal Society for the Protection of Birds, has a larger membership, reflecting the popularity of birds in Britain. They too own a small number (126) of generally larger 'bird reserves'. These not only provide great publicity for the conservation movement, but importantly also conserve a wide variety of other wildlife as well. The RSBP junior membership is in the Young Ornithologist Club.

The British Trust for Conservation Volunteers unites a large number of groups of predominantly young adults working at physical conservation tasks as unpaid volunteers. This Trust provides training in woodland management practices (such as coppicing), hedge-laying, dry-stone walling and the use of power tools, and so on.

Other conservation charities, such as the National Trust (NT), are not solely concerned with wildlife and landscape conservation, although the NT has 340 properties of SSSI status (see below). Others, such as the Wildfowl Trust (ducks, geese and swans), the Rare Breeds Trust (conserving domesticated animal varieties) and the Woodland Trust, are more specific in their concerns. Groups such as Friends of the Earth and Greenpeace (which is also an important international agency) are concerned with political lobbying and direct action at a wider level.

Statutory conservation bodies

Although the voluntary movement is powerful in Britain there are also many statutory (government and state-funded) bodies concerned with conservation and the environment. The Nature Conservancy Council has powers to safeguard Sites of Special Scientific Interest (SSSIs) through notification procedures to local authorities and is responsible for running National Nature Reserves (NNRs) which tend to be larger and of higher conservation status than most wildlife sanctuaries. Many are on private land and have limited public access. There is just one Marine Nature Reserve (MNR) established around Lundy in 1986. The Countryside Commission (CC) is responsible for the wider countryside. It is an advisory and promotional body but does not own land or facilities. Formed in 1968, it replaced the National Parks Commission and still maintains an important advisory role for management and countryside issues within the National Parks. The Countryside Commission's chief function today is the designation of Areas of Outstanding Natural Beauty (AONBs), the definition of heritage coasts and the establishment of long distance footpaths (see table 12.23). It advises local and regional planning authorities on countryside matters, taking a particular interest in urban fringe areas. It has encouraged the setting up of Country Parks whose recreational and educational emphasis has relieved pressure on the more-sensitive and scientifically important sites managed by the NCC.

Each National Park is administered by a National Park Authority (NPA) with funding (about 75%) from the Department of the Environment. Since 1987 government funds (from MAFF, Ministry of Agriculture, Fisheries and Food) have also been available for Environmentally Sensitive Areas (ESAs) giving support to farmers to maintain traditional agricultural practices in countryside that might otherwise be spoilt by modern farming methods. The government research body most concerned with wildlife conservation is the Natural Environment Research Council. This body does outstanding work on all aspects of nature conversation and environmental protection, and coordinates with those also doing research in universities and polytechnics. The Forestry Commission is a statutory body whose responsibilities relate to timber production. It is required to take account of conservation interests on its estates and cooperates with the NCC and Country Trusts for Nature Conservation.

International conservation concerns

Within Britain there are voluntary organisations that concern themselves with conservation issues internationally. The Fauna and Flora Preservation Society funds much specific species conservation research and protection, whilst the Worldwide Fund for Nature (formerly the World Wildlife Fund, WWF) raises very large sums of money for both research into and purchases of endangered environments. The International Union for the Conservation of

Table 12.23 Protected landscapes in England and Wales

A. *National Parks* (see footnote (iii) re. Scotland)

Park	Area designated (km²)	Date of confirmation
Peak District	1 404	1951
Lake District	2 243	1951
Snowdonia	2 171	1951
Dartmoor	945	1951
Pembrokeshire Coast	583	1952
North York Moors	1 432	1952
Yorkshire Dales	1 761	1954
Exmoor	686	1954
Northumberland (including Roman Wall)	1 031	1956
Brecon Beacons	1 344	1957
Total	13 600	

(i) Since 1.1.88 the East Anglian Broads have been granted equivalent status to the National Parks. The area is administered by the Broads Authority which operates similarly to the individual National Parks authorities.

(ii) The Countryside Commission, Nature Conservancy Council and Forestry Commission all regard the New Forest, Hampshire as an area of equivalent status to a National Park and top grade NNR.

(iii) Scotland has no National Parks. There are however 40 designated (1980) National Scenic Areas. These were identified by the Countryside Commission for Scotland (CCS) on a subjective assessment of their beauty. They give some limited protection from development but many ecological and recreational agencies think a better defined and more rigorous system is needed. For a fuller discussion see MacEwen, A. & MacEwen, M. (1983). *National Parks: conservation or cosmetics?*, George Allen & Unwin.

B. *Other Countryside Commission designated areas in England and Wales* (1988)

38	AONBs
39	heritage coasts
13	long distance footpaths
227	country parks
251	picnic sites

About 22% of the land surface lies within a National Park or AONB.

Nature and Natural Resources (IUCN) is a wider network and forum for those concerned with conservation, allowing them to coordinate action and monitor the survival of endangered species all over the world. The latter are described in the 'Red Data Books', which list in detail animals and plants on the verge of extinction. At intergovernmental level the United Nations Environment Programme (UNEP) has done much, particularly for the marine environment, that is not within any one country's national sovereignty. UNEP, IUCN and WWF published an important charter in 1980 called *The World Conservation Strategy* in which many conservation ideas, of importance to the world's future, were discussed.

Chapter Thirteen

Quantitative ecology

The principles of ecology, as outlined in the previous chapter, are based on qualitative and quantitative data obtained from studies carried out on animals, plants, micro-organisms and the abiotic environment. This chapter deals with both qualitative and quantitative aspects of ecological investigation and presents a general introduction to some of the methods and techniques of obtaining, presenting and analysing data relating to the abiotic and biotic environments.

Before attempting any ecological investigation it is essential to identify the exact aims and objectives of the study and the degree of accuracy required. These, in turn will clarify the methods and techniques to be employed and will ensure that the data collected is relevant to the study and is adequate to form a basis for valid conclusions. In many cases, it simplifies the methods and techniques and reduces the time, money, resources and effort needed for the study. However it must be stressed that investigations frequently have to be modified in the light of problems encountered during the investigation.

13.1 Methods of measuring environmental factors

The main environmental factors which must be studied in order to complement biotic analyses, are edaphic, topographic and climatic factors such as water, humidity, temperature, light and wind. Many of the methods used to measure environmental factors are included below in experiments. Other methods of quantitative study are described in outline only.

13.1.1 Edaphic factors

Soils vary considerably in structure and chemical composition as described in section 12.4. In order to obtain a basic idea of the structure or profile of the soil, a pit is dug so that a clean-cut vertical section of the soil can be seen. The various thicknesses of clearly differentiated bands (horizons), shown in terms of colour and texture, can be measured directly, and samples removed from these horizons and used for the various analyses described below.

Alternatively a soil auger, which is an elongated cork-screw implement, is screwed into the ground to the desired depth and then removed. Soil trapped in the threads of the screw at various levels is removed into separate polythene bags for subsequent analysis. When using this method of obtaining a soil sample, it is important to keep a record of the level each part of the sample occupied in the ground. This information should be recorded on the relevant bag.

Experiment 13.1: To investigate the water content of a soil sample

Materials

about 80 g soil
aluminium foil pie dish
balance accurate to 0.1 g
thermostatically controlled oven
thermometer reading up to 150 °C
desiccator
tongs

Method

(1) Weigh aluminium foil pie dish while still empty. Record the mass (a).
(2) Add a broken-up soil sample to the pie dish and weigh. Record the mass (b).
(3) Place the pie dish containing the soil sample in the oven at 110 °C for 24 h.
(4) Remove the sample from the oven and cool in a desiccator.
(5) Weigh the sample when cool, and record the mass.
(6) Return the sample to the oven at 110 °C for a further 24 h.
(7) Repeat stages (4) and (5) until consistent weighings are recorded (constant mass). Record the mass (c).
(8) Calculate the percentage water content as follows:

$$\frac{b - c}{b - a} \times 100$$

(9) Retain the soil sample in the desiccator for experiment 13.2.

Notes

The value obtained in the experiment is the percentage total water present. This amount will depend upon recent rainfall. Alternative estimates of water content include field capacity and available water. The **field capacity** is the amount of water retained in the soil after excess water has drained off under the influence of gravity. To obtain this value the soil in the field should be flooded until surface water persists for several minutes, 48 h before the sample is removed for investigation. The **available water** is the water which is available to be taken up by plants and may be estimated by drying the weighed sample to constant mass at room temperature. The difference between wet mass and dry mass is the amount of available water present.

Experiment 13.2: To investigate the organic (humus) content of a soil sample

Materials

dried soil sample from experiment 13.1 in desiccator
crucible and lid
tripod, Bunsen burner, asbestos mat, fireclay triangle
desiccator
tongs

Method

(1) Heat the crucible and lid strongly in the Bunsen flame to remove all traces of moisture. Place in the desiccator to cool. Weigh and record the mass (a).
(2) Add the dried soil sample (kept from the previous experiment) from the desiccator and weigh. Record the mass (b).
(3) Heat the soil sample in the crucible, covered with the lid, to red-heat for 1 h to burn off all the organic matter. Allow to cool for 10 min and remove to the desiccator.
(4) Weigh the crucible and sample when cool.
(5) Repeat (3) and (4) until constant mass is recorded.
(6) Calculate the percentage organic content as follows:

$$\frac{b - c}{b - a} \times 100$$

(7) Repeat the experiment on soil samples taken from different areas to demonstrate variations in organic content.

Note

The percentage organic content obtained in this experiment is relative to dried soil and not to fresh (wet) soil. The organic content of a soil may be quoted as a percentage of fresh (wet) soil using the data obtained in experiment 13.1.

13.1 60 g of a fresh sample of soil produced the following data on analysis. After repeatedly heating at 110 °C and cooling in a desiccator, the consistent readings of dry mass of 45 g were obtained. The dry soil was heated repeatedly to red-heat in a crucible, cooled in a desiccator and weighed. The mass was now found to be 30 g. Calculate the water content and organic content of the fresh soil sample.

Experiment 13.3: To investigate the air content of a soil sample

Materials

tin can of volume about 200 cm³
500 cm³ beaker
water
chinagraph pencil
metal seeker

Method

(1) Place the empty can open end uppermost into the 500 cm³ beaker and fill the beaker with water above the level of the can. Mark the water level in the beaker.
(2) Carefully remove the can containing the water and measure this volume of water in a measuring cylinder. Record the volume (a). The water level in the beaker will fall by an amount corresponding to the volume of water in the can.
(3) Perforate the base of the can using a drill, making about eight small holes.
(4) Push the open end of the can into soil from which the surface vegetation has been removed until soil begins to come through the perforations. Gently dig out the can, turn it over and remove soil from the surface until it is level with the top of can.
(5) Place the can of soil, with open end uppermost, gently back into the beaker of water and loosen soil in the can with seeker to allow air to escape.
(6) The water level in the beaker will be lower than the original level because water will be used to replace the air which was present in the soil.
(7) Add water to the beaker from a full 100 cm³ measuring cylinder until the original level is restored. Record volume of water added (b).
(8) The percentage air content of the soil sample can be determined as follows:

$$\frac{b}{a} \times 100$$

(9) Repeat the experiment on soil samples from different areas.

Experiment 13.4: To investigate the approximate relative proportions of solid particles (soil texture) in a soil sample

Materials

500 cm³ measuring cylinder
100 cm³ soil sample
300 cm³ water

Method

(1) Add the soil sample to the measuring cylinder and cover with water.
(2) Shake the contents vigorously.
(3) Allow the mixture to settle out, according to density and surface area of particles, for 48 h.
(4) Measure the volume of the various fractions of soil sample.

Results

A gradation of soil components is seen. Organic matter floats at the surface of the water, some clay particles remain in suspension, larger clay particles settle out as a layer on top of sand and stones which are layered according to their sizes.

Experiment 13.5: To investigate the pH of a soil sample

Materials

long test-tube (145 mm) and bung
test-tube rack
barium sulphate
BDH universal indicator solution and colour chart
soil sample
spatula
distilled water
10 cm³ pipette

Method

(1) Add about 1 cm of soil to the test-tube and 1 cm of barium sulphate, which ensures flocculation of colloidal clay.
(2) Add 10 cm³ of distilled water and 5 cm³ of BDH universal indicator solution. Seal the test-tube with the bung. Shake vigorously and allow contents to settle for 5 min.
(3) Compare the colour of liquid in the test-tube with the colours on the BDH reference colour chart and read off the corresponding pH.
(4) Repeat the experiment on soil samples from different areas.

Note

pH is one of the most useful measurements which can be made on a soil. Although a simple measurement, it is a product of many interacting factors and is likely to be a good guide to nutrient status and to types of plants (and therefore animals) that flourish. Acid soils tend to be less nutrient rich (poorer cation-holding capacity).

13.1.2 Climatic factors

Water, air and light are the most important climatic parameters to measure and this section outlines some of the basic practical methods used in their measurement.

Experiment 13.6: To investigate the pH of a water sample

Materials

universal indicator test paper or pH meter
water sample

Method

(1) Dip a piece of universal indicator test paper into the water sample and compare the colour produced with the colour chart. Read off the pH value.

OR

(2) Rinse the probe of the pH meter with distilled water, dip it into the water sample and read off the pH value. (This method is more accurate, but the meter must be accurately calibrated using prepared solutions of known pH before the experiment begins.) Rinse the probe with distilled water before returning it to buffer solution for storage.
(3) Repeat the experiment on water samples from different sources.

Experiment 13.7: To investigate the chloride content of a water sample (giving a rough estimate of salinity)

Materials

water sample
10 cm³ pipette
burette
distilled water in a wash bottle
3 conical flasks
white tile
potassium chromate indicator
50 cm³ silver nitrate solution (2.73 g 100 cm⁻³)

Method

(1) Place 10 cm³ of the water sample into a conical flask and add two drops of potassium chromate indicator solution.
(2) Titrate silver nitrate solution from the burette, shaking the conical flask constantly.
(3) The end-point of the titration is given by a reddening of the silver chloride precipitate.

(4) Repeat the titration on a further two 10 cm³ water samples. Calculate the mean volume of silver nitrate used.

(5) The volume of silver nitrate solutions used is approximately equal to the chloride content of the water sample (in g dm⁻³).

Experiment 13.8: To investigate the oxygen content of a water sample

Dissolved oxygen

The technique described here is the Winkler method which gives an accurate measure of oxygen content but requires many reagents. A simpler but less accurate method is described in Nuffield Advanced Science, Biological Science.

Materials

10 cm³ of alkaline iodide solution (3.3 g NaOH, 2.0 g KI in 10 cm³ distilled water) (CARE)
10 cm³ of manganese chloride solution (4.0 g $MnCl_2$ in 10 cm³ distilled water)
5 cm³ of concentrated hydrochloric acid (CARE)
starch solution (as indicator)
distilled water in a wash bottle
0.01 M sodium thiosulphate solution (see point (8) in method)
3 × 5 cm³ graduated pipettes
burette
white tile
3 conical flasks
250 cm³ water sample in glass bottle with ground glass stopper

Method

(1) Collect the water sample carefully without splashing and stopper the sample bottle under water to prevent entry of air bubbles.

(2) Add 2 cm³ of manganese chloride solution and 2 cm³ of alkaline iodide solution to the sample using pipettes whose tips are placed at the bottom of sample bottle. The heavier salt solutions will displace an equal volume of water from the top of the sample bottle.

(3) Add 2 cm³ of concentrated hydrochloric acid and stopper the bottle so that no air bubbles are trapped. Shake the bottle thoroughly to dissolve the precipitate. This leaves a solution of iodine in an excess of potassium iodide. The dissolved oxygen is now fixed and exposure to air will not affect the result.

(4) Remove a 50 cm³ sample of this solution and place it in a conical flask. Titrate with 0.01 M sodium thiosulphate solution from the burette as follows:

(a) add thiosulphate solution whilst shaking conical flask until the yellow colour becomes pale:

(b) add three drops of starch solution and continue to titrate and shake until the blue-black colouration of the starch disappears.

Record the volume of thiosulphate used.

(5) Repeat stage (4) with two further 50 cm³ samples of water and obtain the mean volume used ($\bar{x}$).

(6) Using these solutions, 1 cm³ of 0.01 M thiosulphate solution corresponds to 0.056 cm³ of oxygen at STP (standard temperature and pressure).

(7) Calculate the concentration of oxygen per litre of water using the following formula:

$$\text{oxygen in cm}^3\,\text{dm}^{-3} = \frac{0.056 \times \bar{x} \times 1000}{50} \text{ at STP}$$

Where $\bar{x}$ = volume of thiosulphate solution required for the titration of 50 cm³ of samples.

(8) In comparative studies for water pollution work and estimating BOD, dissolved oxygen levels are commonly expressed in mg dm⁻³. Calculation of the final result is simpler if a working solution of 0.0125 M sodium thiosulphate is used. Then 1 cm³ sodium thiosulphate solution is equivalent to 0.1 mg oxygen.

(a) Prepare a stock solution of 0.1 M sodium thiosulphate. To do this dissolve 24.82 g $Na_2S_2O_3.5H_2O$ in distilled water. Add a pellet of NaOH and dilute to 1 dm³ (litre). Store in a brown bottle. This solution may be kept for two or three weeks.

(b) Prepare, as needed, a working solution of 0.0125 M sodium thiosulphate. To do this take 125 cm³ of stock solution and dilute to 1 dm³ (×8 dilution).

(c) Carry out the method following the procedure outlined above but using 0.0125 M sodium thiosulphate in step (4).

$$\text{mg O}_2 \text{ in dm}^3 \text{ (1 litre) sample} = \frac{\bar{x} \times 0.1 \times 1000}{50}$$

$$\text{or } \bar{x} \times 2$$

$\bar{x}$ = mean volume of 0.0125 M thiosulphate solution required for the titration of 50 cm³ of sample.

NB It is quite common to use 25 cm³ water samples, thus saving on reagent with appropriate adjustment of the final calculation (mg O_2 dm⁻³ = $\bar{x}$ × 4).

Biochemical oxygen demand (BOD)

Materials

Either

(1) Reagents and glassware as described for the Winkler method in experiment above (dissolved oxygen),

or

an appropriately calibrated oxygen electrode.

(2) 500 cm³–1 dm³ water sample.

Method

A. Pre-checks

(1) If necessary adjust the sample pH to the range of 6.5–8.5 (to optimise micro-organism activity).

(2) If the oxygen content of the sample is known to be very low (e.g. already measured dissolved oxygen) the sample should be oxygenated for 5–10 min. This is important since the test measures the rate of oxygen consumption and organism activity. The results will be misleading if there is an insufficient initial oxygen supply.

(3) If high organic contamination is suspected, prepare sample dilutions* (see footnote at end of method) before incubating. Remember to check that the BOD of the dilution water itself is negligible. To do this incubate dilution water in the same way as samples. If necessary (that is if there is a significant decrease in dissolved oxygen) adjust results for oxygen loss in dilution water controls as well as for dilution factor itself.

Test procedure

(1) Place portions of the sample (dilute if necessary) into three glass stoppered bottles of 125 cm^3 or 250 cm^3 capacity. Pour carefully to avoid trapping air bubbles. Ensure bottles are completely full.

(2) Immediately determine the oxygen content of one bottle (express as $mg\,dm^{-3}$).

(3) Incubate the remaining two bottles *in the dark* (no photosynthesis) at a standard temperature (20 °C) or the temperature of the original sample for 1–5 days. The standard procedure is to incubate in darkness at 20 °C for five days.

(4) Determine the oxygen content of the incubated bottles ($mg\,dm^{-3}$).

(5) Subtract the mean value for the incubated samples from the original sample. This gives the sample BOD in $mg\,dm^{-3}$ unless the sample was diluted before incubation. In this case use the following formula:

$$BOD = (x-y)(a+1)\,mg\,dm^{-3}$$

where x is the initial dissolved oxygen in $mg\,dm^{-3}$.
y is the mean final dissolved oxygen in $mg\,dm^{-3}$.
a is the volume(s) of dilution water to 1 volume of sample.

Water current

The simplest method of measuring water current is to record the time taken for a floating object to cover a known distance. In order to eliminate the effects of wind it is preferable to use an object which is mainly submerged. Alternatively an L-shaped tube 50 cm high, 10 cm long and 2 cm in diameter can be placed in a stream with the short end facing upstream. By measuring the height to which water rises in the long limb the velocity of the current can be measured using the formula:

$$v = \sqrt{(2hg)}$$

where v is the speed of the current ($cm\,s^{-1}$), g is the acceleration due to gravity ($981\,cm\,s^{-2}$) and h is the height of the column (cm).

Humidity

The relative humidity of air is a measure of the moisture content of air relative to air fully saturated with water vapour. Relative humidity varies with temperature, since air expands on heating and can hold more water vapour. This is measured by a **whirling hygrometer** consisting of a wet and a dry thermometer mounted on a wooden frame resembling a football rattle (fig 13.1). It is whirled around until both thermometers give constant temperature readings. These temperatures are then examined in hygrometer tables and the corresponding relative humidity read off.

Temperature

Air, water and soil temperatures can be measured using a mercury thermometer, but measurements of temperature at a point in time provide little real information of ecological significance. It is the range of temperatures over a period of time which have more significance in ecological studies. Hence sophisticated time-based recordings of temperature are normally used or the maximum and minimum temperatures recorded using a maximum–minimum thermometer. Temperatures in microhabitats and inaccessible habitats, such as the centre of a tree, are measured using a **thermistor** (fig 13.2). This is an electrical device which can be miniaturised to fit into the tip of a ballpoint pen and whose resistance varies with temperature. By measuring the resistance of the thermistor and comparing this with previous temperature-calibrated resis-

---

* River water does not usually require dilution. A badly polluted stream or pond might require up to four parts dilution water to one part sample. Such contaminated water is a health risk and requires great care in handling and is best avoided for student class work. Tapwater was formerly commonly used for dilution but high chlorination now often makes this unsuitable. Synthetic dilution water is preferable (distilled or deionised water with appropriate chemicals added). Advice on the preparation of synthetic dilution waters is given in H.L. Golterman, R.S. Clymo & M.A.M. Ohnstad (1978) *Methods for physical and chemical analysis of fresh waters*, IBP Handbook No. 8, Blackwell Scientific Publications 2nd edition.

Any samples absorbing more than 6 $mg\,dm^{-3}$ oxygen or having a final dissolved oxygen content less than 40% saturation should be diluted.

In some cases a considerable part of the BOD may be due to oxidation of ammonia. If wished this nitrification can be inhibited by adding 1 cm of 0.5 $g\,dm^{-3}$ solution of allylthiourea to each sample. For a fuller discussion see Golterman *et al.* as cited above.

443

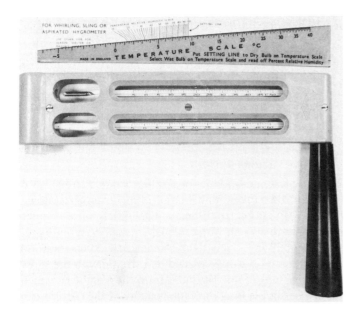

Fig 13.1 *Whirling hygrometer*

Fig 13.2 *A thermistor in use*

Light

Light varies in intensity, duration and quality (wavelength). Measurements of all three aspects are required to provide the information relevant to ecological study and specialised techniques are required to record them. For practical purposes some indication of intensity related to particular areas is generally required, so that the incident light in different areas can be compared. For this purpose an ordinary photographic exposure meter is adequate. Light intensities over a given period of time are recorded using Ozalid papers which have a cumulative sensitivity to light.

Wind speed and direction

The wind speed in a habitat at a given point in time is not as ecologically significant as the degree of exposure to wind experienced by the habitat. In this respect wind frequency, intensity and direction are all important. However, for most practical purposes a simple wind-gauge indicating the direction of the wind and a simple anemometer (fig 13.3) indicating wind speed are adequate for comparing features of wind in different habitats.

13.2 Biotic analysis

In analysing the organisms living in a given habitat (the biotic component of the ecosystem) the community structure must be determined in terms of species present in the habitat and numbers within each population. It is obviously impractical to attempt to find and count all the members of a given species, and so sampling techniques have to be devised which will give

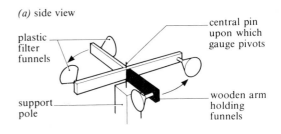

(a) side view

plastic filter funnels

support pole

central pin upon which gauge pivots

wooden arm holding funnels

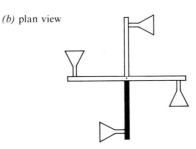

(b) plan view

Fig 13.3 *Simple anemometer which may be used to determine wind speed in terms of the rate of turning of the wooden arm painted black*

tances the environmental temperature can be obtained. The temperature extremes of microhabitats (microclimates) are also useful in ecological studies since they can often explain the disappearance of a particular species from an area, such as frost-sensitive plants.

indications of species present and their numbers. Generally speaking, the more accurate the results required the more time-consuming the method, so it is necessary to be clear about objectives. Also, if possible, non-destructive techniques should be used.

In all cases reliable methods of sampling (recording and/or collecting) organisms are required and it is safe to say that 'no stone should be left unturned' (providing it is replaced!) since organisms will occupy almost all available microhabitats. For example, at first sight a square metre of grass, soil, sand, rocky shore or stream bed may not appear to support many species, but closer examination, involving hand-sorting the soil, grass and weeds, turning over stones and examining roots, stems, flowers and fruits of plants and holdfasts of seaweeds, will reveal many more species.

In recording data, as many species as possible (plant and animal) should be identified in the field, using keys if necessary. Only if the species are obviously common locally and not known to be rarities should they be collected. Over-collection can have serious effects on local communities. In the case of collected animals, attempts should be made to keep them alive and to release them in a similar microhabitat to that in which they were collected. It is necessary to identify the organisms as accurately as possible, that is to the level of species. This cannot always be done but it should be possible to identify them at least as far as class, order or family. Identification of specimens depends upon familiarity with keys. The principles of classification, key construction and details of how to use a key are described in appendix 3.

A list of all the species in the habitat gives some indication of the diversity of structure of the community, the **species richness** or **diversity**.

(There are various numerical ways of expressing species richness using mathematical formulae. The numerical value is called the **diversity index** but details of this will not be considered here.)

These data provide information enabling possible food chains and food webs to be constructed, but are inadequate in providing information related to quantitative aspects of the community. The extent of the diversity is only fully revealed when the numbers of organisms within each species, that is the population sizes, are determined. This information enables a more detailed picture of the community to be constructed, such as a pyramid of numbers (section 12.3.6).

Obtaining the qualitative and quantitative data of a habitat depends on specific methods of collecting, sampling and estimating organisms within the habitat, and the method chosen is related to the mode of life, behaviour and size of the organism.

13.2.1 Methods of collecting organisms

There are several points to consider when collecting organisms and these are summarised below.
(1) Observe the Countryside Code at all times.

(2) Always obtain permission from the landowner before beginning an ecological study in an area.
(3) Consult the local Natural History Society, university, college or the Nature Conservancy about where and what you are to collect.
(4) Never remove organisms from their habitat or destroy them unnecessarily.
(5) Leave the habitat as undisturbed as possible, for example replace stones, turf, logs and so on to their original positions.
(6) Where it is necessary to remove organisms from the habitat for identification, take as few as possible and, if practicable, return them to the habitat.
(7) Keep specimens separate when removing them to the laboratory for identification to prevent contamination or being eaten by predators, for example do not put ragworm and crabs in the same collecting vessel. Useful collecting equipment includes jam jars, Kilner jars, polythene bottles, specimen tubes and polythene bags.
(8) Always record as much information as possible concerning the topography of the habitat and climate at the time of collection as the information may have a bearing on what is collected:
  (a) nature of rock or substratum (grass, mud, soil etc.);
  (b) nature of aspect (for example flat, south-facing, angle of slope etc.);
  (c) drainage;
  (d) soil, mud or sand profile;
  (e) temperature of substrate, water and air;

Table 13.1 Field booking sheet for recording edaphic, physiographic and climatic features.

Area .... Grid reference .... Date ....

(1) **Underlying rock**
(2) **Substratum/soil**
  (a) surface feature ....
  (b) depth of horizon A ....
  (c) ,, ,, ,, B ....
  (d) ,, ,, ,, C ....
  (e) pH ....
  (f) temperature ....
(3) **Topography**
  (a) aspect, direction .... angle ....
  (b) height above sea level ....
  (c) relief ....
  (d) drainage ....
  (e) land use ....
  (f) high or low water, time .... height ....
(4) **Climate**
  (a) air temperature, range ....
  (b) rainfall ....
  (c) cloud cover/sunlight ....
  (d) relative humidity ....
  (e) wind direction ....
  (f) wind speed ....
  (g) light intensity (horizontal), N ..., S ..., E ..., W ....
  (h) time of day ....

Table 13.2 A summary of various methods used to collect organisms.

Collecting method	Structure and function	Organisms collected
beating tray	A fabric sheet of known area is attached to a collapsible frame and held under a branch which is beaten with a stick or shaken. Organisms fall onto the sheet and are removed using a pooter (see later notes).	non-flying insects, larval stages, spiders
kite net	A muslin net is attached to a handle and swept through the air. Organisms become trapped in the net. All netting techniques must be standardised to ensure uniformity of sampling, e.g. eight, figure-of-eight sweeps per examination of the net.	flying insects
sweep net	A nylon net is attached to a steel handle and swept through grass, bushes, ponds or streams.	insects, crustaceans
plankton net	A bolting silk net is attached to a metal hoop and rope harness and towed through the water. A small jar is attached to the rear of the net to collect specimens.	plankton
sticky trap	Black treacle and sugar are boiled together and smeared onto a sheet of thick polythene which is then attached to a piece of chipboard with drawing pins. This can be hung in various situations and at various heights. Jam and beer can be added to the sticky substances to act as attractants.	flying insects
pitfall trap	A jam jar or tin is buried in the soil with the rim level with ground level. This is best placed where the ground falls away from rim level to prevent water entering the jar. A piece of slate supported on three stones acts as a lid preventing rainwater from entering. The trap can be baited with either sweet foods such as jam or decaying meat. Traps should be regularly cleared (fig 13.4).	walking/crawling insects, myriapods, spiders, crustacea
light trap	A mercury vapour light trap attracts flying organisms which hit baffles and fall down into the base and become trapped in cardboard egg boxes or crumpled-up paper. Cotton wool soaked in chloroform is added before examining the contents to anaesthetise or kill the organisms (fig 13.5).	night-flying insects, particularly moths and caddis flies
mammal trap	A Longworth mammal trap (fig 13.6) is left in a runway and filled with bedding material. Bait, e.g. grain or dried fruit, can be left outside and inside the trap. The trap can be left unset for some time until organisms become accustomed to it and then set. Animals are captured alive so the trap must be visited regularly. Some animals may remain 'trap shy' and never enter it, whereas others become 'trap happy' and visit it regularly. These two patterns can present problems when using the technique to estimate population sizes.	shrews, voles and mice
kick sampling	This is used for collecting in running fresh water. An open sweep or plankton net is held vertically downstream of the area being sampled by turning over stones and scraping off organisms which are then swept into the net. Alternatively the area being sampled is agitated by kicking and stamping so that organisms are displaced vertically and swept into the net by the current.	aquatic insects and crustaceans
pooter	This is used to collect small insects from beating trees or directly off vegetation for closer examination and/or counting (fig 13.10).	aphids, small insects and spiders
hand-sorting	Samples of soil or vegetation, e.g. grass, leaf litter, pond and seaweed, are placed at one end of a tray and small amounts of material are systematically examined between the fingers, specimens are removed to a collecting jar and sorted material passed to the other end of the tray. The sample is then examined as it is moved back to the original end of the tray.	mites, enchytraeid worms, insect larvae and small insects
extractions	5 cm^3 of 4% formaldehyde are added to 50 cm^3 of water and used to water a square metre of lawn or grassland. Earthworms are driven out from their burrows and collected and immediately washed in water to remove the formaldehyde.	earthworms
flotation	Add a known mass of soil to a beaker of saturated salt solution, stir vigorously for several minutes and allow soil to settle. Organisms float to surface in dense salt solution. Pour off surface layer of fluid into a Petri dish and examine under binocular microscope. Remove all specimens into another Petri dish containing 70% alcohol to kill and fix the specimens. Mount each specimen separately in glycerine on a microscope slide, cover with a cover-slip and identify under binocular microscope or low power of compound microscope.	mites, insects, eggs, cocoon, larval and pupal stages
Tullgren funnel (dry extraction)	Many soil and leaf litter-dwelling organisms move away from a source of heat and towards moister conditions. A soil or leaf litter sample is placed in the sieve about 25 cm below a 100 W bulb in a metal reflector (fig 13.7). Every two hours the bulb is moved 5 cm nearer to the sample until the bulb is 5 cm from the soil sample. The apparatus is left for a total of 24 h. All small arthropods move downwards and drop through the metal gauze into the alcohol beneath.	small arthropods e.g. millipedes, centipedes, mites, springtails and collembola
Baermann funnel (wet extraction)	A soil sample is placed in a muslin bag, submerged in a funnel containing water and suspended 25 cm from a 100 W in a metal reflector (fig 13.8). The apparatus is left for 24 h. The water and the gentle heating encourage organisms to leave the sample, move out into the water and sink to the base of the funnel. They are removed at intervals by opening the clip in the apparatus and allowing them to fall into the alcohol.	small arthropods, enchytraeid worms and nematodes

(*f*) substrate or water pH;

(*g*) cloud cover and rainfall;

(*h*) relative humidity of air;

(*i*) light intensity (such as shaded or open, possibly a meter reading);

(*j*) wind speed and direction (such as still, gentle breeze, gale, south-west);

(*k*) time of day and date.

An example of how some of these features may be recorded is shown in table 13.1.

There are a variety of methods of collecting specimens. A summary of methods and their applications is shown in table 13.2 and in figs 13.4–9.

Specimens should be collected from traps at regular intervals, identified, counted and, where possible, released. In the case of pitfall traps it should be realised that if natural predators and prey are collected it is probable that the prey will not be present when the trap is emptied. Where this is believed to be happening, 70% alcohol should be placed in the trap to kill the organisms as they fall in. Imagination and ingenuity are required in collecting specimens.

Generally, sites where specimens are collected are not randomly chosen and consequently the results obtained from the collections must be interpreted in the light of biased selection of collecting site. Whilst this may not affect the species of organism collected, so that community structure will be accurately represented, it is likely to give biased indications of numbers present. For example, the use of baits and lures to attract organisms to sticky traps, pitfall traps and mammal traps will influence the results, and conclusions based on quantitative data will reflect this

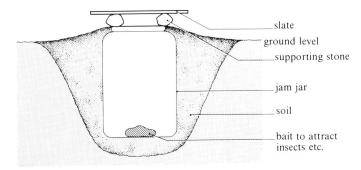

Fig 13.4 *Simple pitfall trap made by sinking a jam jar into the soil*

Fig 13.5 (below) *Mercury vapour lamp in use attracting insects*

Fig 13.6 (at bottom of page) *Longworth mammal trap*

447

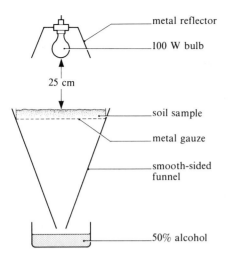

metal reflector

100 W bulb

25 cm

soil sample

metal gauze

smooth-sided funnel

50% alcohol

Fig 13.7 *Tullgren funnel*

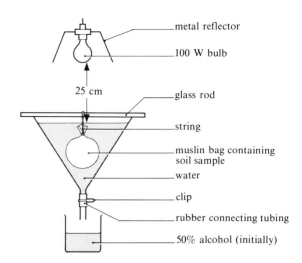

metal reflector

100 W bulb

25 cm

glass rod

string

muslin bag containing soil sample

water

clip

rubber connecting tubing

50% alcohol (initially)

Fig 13.8 *Baermann funnel*

Fig 13.9 *The position of a line transect across a rocky shore*

bias. Therefore in discussion of results it is necessary to state clearly that bias exists.

13.2.2 Methods of sampling an area

In order to standardise the sites where abiotic and biotic aspects of ecosystems are investigated, transects and/or quadrats are commonly used and collecting and sampling is confined to the area of the transect or quadrat.

Line transect. This may be used to sample a uniform area but is particularly useful where it is suspected that there is a transition in habitats and populations through an area (fig. 13.9). For example, a tape or string running along the ground in a straight line between two poles indicates the position of the transect and sampling is rigorously confined to species actually touching the line.

Belt transect. A belt transect is simply a strip of chosen width through the habitat, made by setting up two line transects, say 0.5 m or 1 m apart, between which species are recorded. An easier method of obtaining both

qualitative and quantitative data from a belt transect is to use a quadrat frame in conjuction with a line transect.

Height variations recorded along line or belt transects produce a profile of the transect, sometimes known as a **profile transect**, and this is used when presenting data (fig 13.19).

A decision over which type of transect to use depends on the qualitative and quantitative nature of the investigation, the degree of accuracy required, the nature of the organisms present, the size of the area to be investigated and the time available. Over a short distance a line transect might be used and a continuous record kept of each plant species lying immediately beneath it. Alternatively, over a longer distance the species present every metre, or other suitable distance along the transect, may be recorded.

Quadrat. A quadrat frame is a metal or wooden frame, preferably collapsible to facilitate carrying, which forms a square of known area, such as 0.25 m² or 1 m² (fig 13.11). It is placed to one side of a line transect and sampling carried out. It is then moved along the line transect to different positions. Both the species present within the frame and the numbers or abundance (section 13.2.3) of these may be recorded depending upon the nature of the investigation. In all cases the method of recording the species must be consistent, for example all species partially or completely visible within the quadrat are listed. The structure of the quadrat frame can be modified according to the demands of the investigation. For example, it can be divided by string or wire into convenient sections to assist in counting or estimating numbers or abundance of the species (fig 13.11). This is particularly useful when studying a habitat supporting several species of plants.

A quadrat may be used without a transect when studying an apparently uniform habitat. In this case the quadrat is used randomly. One fairly random sampling technique is to

Fig 13.10 *Pooter in use collecting small non-vertebrates*

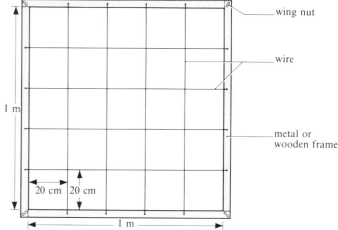

Fig 13.11 *Quadrat frame (1 m²) with wire sub-quadrats (each 400 cm²) forming a graduated quadrat*

449

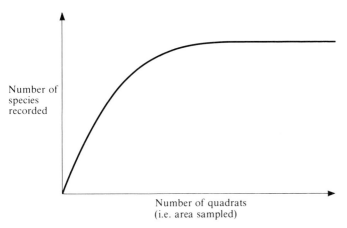

Fig 13.12 *Graph showing the relationship between the number of species recorded in an area and the number of quadrats studied. (In quantitative studies there is no point in sampling more quadrats beyond a certain point as it is unrewarding and uneconomical on time.)*

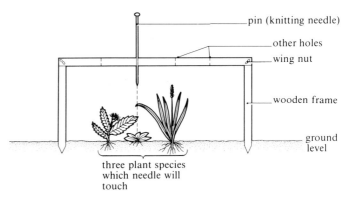

Fig 13.13 *Pin frame or point quadrat*

fling a robust quadrat over the shoulder and record the species within it wherever it falls. This is repeated several times so that a representative sample of the area is covered. Alternatively a sampling point may be chosen by using a table of random numbers, also generated by some calculators, to select a random coordinate on an imaginary grid laid over the area. The sides of the grid may be marked by measuring tapes. Investigations have shown that in a uniform habitat there comes a point beyond which analysing the species within a quadrat becomes unnecessary as it does not increase the number of different species recorded. This relationship is shown in fig 13.12. As a rule of thumb, once five quadrats have failed to show any new species it may be assumed that no further species will be found. However, when an assumption such as this is made it must be stated in the ecological report as it may affect the reliability of the results.

Pin frame (point quadrat). This is a frame bearing a number of holes through which a 'pin', such as a knitting needle can be passed (fig 13.13). It is particularly useful with transect studies of overgrown habitats where several plant species may overlap. All species touched by the pin as it descends to the ground are recorded for each of the holes.

Permanent quadrat. In long-term ecological investigations involving the study of community change (succession) or seasonal changes, a permanent quadrat or transect is used. Metal pegs and nylon rope are used to mark out an area of ground. Periodic samples of abiotic and biotic factors can be taken and the results presented in such a way as to reveal trends and changes and possible factors accounting for, or associated with, these changes.

Computer program. SAMPLE: Two programs on ecological sampling: quadrat and capture–recapture.

13.2.3 Methods of estimating population size

In all studies in quantitative ecology it is essential to be able to estimate, with a degree of accuracy, the number of organisms within a given area of ground or volume of water or air. In most cases this is equivalent to estimating the population size, and methods employed are determined by the size and mode of life of organisms involved and the size of the area under investigation. The numbers of plants and sessile or slow-moving animals in a small area may be counted directly, or their percentage cover or abundance estimated, whereas indirect methods may be required for fast-moving organisms in large open areas. In habitats where organisms are difficult to observe, because of their behaviour and mode of life, it is necessary to estimate numbers of organisms using either the **removal** method or the **capture–recapture** method. Methods of estimating populations may be either objective or subjective.

Objective methods

The use of quadrats, direct observation and photography are known as direct counting methods, whereas the removal and capture–recapture techniques are indirect counting methods.

Quadrat. If the number of organisms within a number of quadrats, representing a known fraction of the total area, are determined, an estimate of the total numbers in the whole area can be obtained by simple multiplication. This method provides a means of calculating three aspects of species distribution.

(1) **Species density.** This is the number of individuals of a given species in a given area, such as 10 m^{-2}. It is obtained by counting the number of organisms in randomly thrown quadrats. The method has the advantages of being accurate, enabling different areas and different species to be compared and providing an absolute measure of abundance. The disadvantages are that it is time-consuming and requires individuals to be defined, for example is a grass tussock counted as one plant or does each plant of the tussock need to be counted?

(2) **Species frequency.** This is a measure of the probability (chance) of finding a given species with any one throw of a quadrat in a given area. For example, if the species occurs once in every ten quadrats it has a frequency of 10%. This measure is obtained by recording the presence or absence of the species in a randomly thrown quadrat. (The number present is irrelevant.) In this method the size of the quadrat must be stated since it will influence the results, and also whether the frequency refers to 'shoot' or 'rooted' frequency. (For 'shoot' frequency the species is only recorded as present if foliage overlaps into the quadrat from outside. For 'rooted' frequency the species is only recorded as present if it is actually rooted in the quadrat.) This method has the advantage of being quick and easy and useful in certain large-scale ecosystems such as woodland. The disadvantages are that quadrat size, plant size and spatial distribution (that is random, uniform or clumped) (section A2.8) all affect the species frequency.

13.2 What is the species frequency of the species recorded in 86 quadrats out of 200 thrown?

(3) **Species cover.** This is a measure of the proportion of ground occupied by the species and gives an estimate of the area covered by the species as a percentage of the total area. It is obtained either by observing the species covering the ground at a number of random points, by the subjective estimate of percentage of quadrat coverage or by the use of a pin frame (fig 13.13). This is a useful method for estimating plant species, especially grasses, where individuals are hard to count and are not as important as cover. However it has the disadvantages of being slow and tedious.

13.3 If a pin frame containing ten pins was used ten times and 36 units were recorded for plant X, what is the percentage cover of X?

Direct observation. Direct counting is not only applicable to sessile or slow-moving animals but also to many larger mobile organisms such as deer, wild ponies and lions, and wood pigeons and bats as they leave their roost.

Photography. It is possible to obtain population sizes of larger mammals and sea birds which congregate in open spaces by direct counting from aerial photographs.

Removal method. The removal method is very suitable for estimating numbers of small organisms, particularly insects, within a known area of grassland or volume of water. Using a net in some form of standard sweep, the number of animals captured is recorded and the animals kept. This procedure is repeated a further three

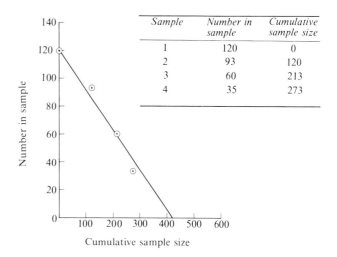

Sample	Number in sample	Cumulative sample size
1	120	0
2	93	120
3	60	213
4	35	273

Fig 13.14 *Graph of number in sample against cumulative sample size. Extrapolation of the line to the point when sample size equals zero gives an estimate of the number in the population*

times and the gradually reducing numbers recorded. A graph is plotted of number of animals captured per sample against the previous cumulative number of animals captured. By extrapolating the line of the graph to the point at which no further animals would be captured (that is number in sample = 0) the total population may be estimated, as shown in fig 13.14.

Capture–recapture method. (See reference to computer program, p. 450.) This method involves capturing the organism, marking it in some way, without causing it any damage, and replacing it so that it can resume a normal role in the population. For example, fish are netted and their operculum tagged with aluminium discs, birds are netted and rings attached to their legs, small mammals may be tagged by dyes, or by clipping the ear or removing a toe, and arthropods are marked with paint. In all cases some form of coding may be adopted so that individual organisms are identified. Having trapped, counted and marked a representative sample of the population the individuals are released in the same area. At a later stage the population is retrapped and counted and the population size estimated using the expression below:

$$\text{Estimated total population} = \frac{\begin{array}{c}\text{number of organisms} \times \text{number of organisms}\\ \text{in initial sample} \quad\quad \text{in second sample}\end{array}}{\text{number of marked organisms recaptured}}$$

This estimate of population size is called the **Lincoln index**. It relies on a number of assumptions which are summarised below.

(1) Organisms mix randomly within the population. (This does not always apply since some organisms live in colonies, troops or shoals.)
(2) Sufficient time must elapse between capture and

recapture to allow random mixing. The less mobile the species the longer the time lapse must be.

(3) It is only applicable to populations whose movement is restricted geographically.
(4) Organisms disperse evenly within the geographical area of the population.
(5) Changes in population size as a result of immigration, emigration, births and deaths are negligible.
(6) Marking does not hinder the movement of the organisms or make them conspicuous to predators.

Where plants and small animals, such as barnacles, are concerned, direct counting becomes very tedious and, depending upon the degree of accuracy required from the study, may be replaced by estimating percentage cover or abundance within a quadrat frame. In the early stages of estimation it is advisable to use a graduated quadrat frame (fig 13.11) to increase the accuracy of estimation. Various schemes may be adopted for representing percentage cover or abundance, some being totally subjective, others partially, or completely, objective.

> **13.4** In an attempt to estimate the number of trout in a small lake, 625 trout were netted, marked and released. One week later 873 trout were netted and of these 129 had been marked. What was the estimated size of the population?

Subjective methods

These involve some form of frequency assessment, frequency scale or estimate of abundance in terms of cover. For example, an arbitrary scale devised by Crisp and Southward for limpets on a rocky shore uses the following letters, frequencies and percentages.

A abundant > 50%
C common 10–50%
F frequent 1–10%
O occasional < 1%
R rare   present – only a few found in 30 min searching

These assessments and scales are arbitrary and the frequencies can be adjusted to varying percentage values, for example in a particular study, abundant may represent > 90%. The value of using the five categories above is that they can be applied to methods of presenting data, such as in constructing kite diagrams, as described in section A2.7.3. The major disadvantage of this method is that it is subjective and tends to rate small species with poor cover lower than conspicuous species, flowering species and species occurring in clumps.

13.3 Ecological research projects and investigations

Ecological projects are broadly concerned with studying either the organisms in an area (**synecology**) or a single species (**autecology**). In both cases it is necessary to spend time reading about and discussing the project so as to clarify the aims, nature and extent of the project. All investigations should include problems which have to be solved or hypotheses to be tested.

The aims of the project should be stated clearly and should include both general and specific aims. For example:

(1) to develop and encourage an attitude of curiosity and enquiry;
(2) to develop the ability to plan an investigation, construct hypotheses and design experiments;
(3) to develop the ability to formulate questions and collect relevant qualitative and quantitative data to answer these;
(4) to develop practical and observational skills including the use of apparatus and biological keys;
(5) to develop the ability to record data accurately;
(6) to develop the ability to apply existing knowledge to the interpretation of data;
(7) to develop a critical attitude to data, assessment of their validity and conclusions based on them;
(8) to develop the ability to communicate biological information by means of tables, graphs and the spoken and written word;
(9) to develop an appreciation of organisms and the importance of conservation;
(10) to develop an understanding of the interrelationships between organisms, between organisms and their environment, and the dynamic aspects of ecology. This can be extended to further aims which are specific to the study as described in section 13.5.

13.3.1 Writing up the project or investigations

Irrespective of the quality of both the investigation and the data obtained, the project or investigation is of little use to other scientists until it is presented as a report and this should take the following form.

(1) **Introduction**: including the idea, the problems, hypotheses and aims (that is what you set out to do and why).
(2) **Method**: the strategy of the project (that is what you did (was done), where and how it was done including all practical details of apparatus and techniques employed both in the field and in the laboratory).
(3) **Results and observations**: tabulated data, graphs, histograms, profiles, presence–absence graphs, kite diagrams and any other relevant and realistic way of representing data and relationships clearly and concisely.
(4) **Discussion of results**: this involves an analysis of the results, preferably quantitative if possible, tentative conclusions based on data presented and references to already published material.

(5) **Discussion of significance of conclusions**: criticisms of the techniques employed, sources of error and suggestions for further study.

(6) **List of references consulted**.

13.4 A synecological investigation

A synecological investigation involves studying the abiotic and biotic elements associated with a natural community (biotic element of ecosystem) found in a particular defined geographical area (or ecosystem) such as an oak woodland or a rocky shore, which may contain several plant and animal species and possibly several habitats. In such an investigation it is necessary to carry out the following exercises:

(1) map the area and habitat(s) in plan view and, if necessary, in profile;

(2) identify the species and estimate the number of each species present;

(3) measure (possibly collect and analyse) the abiotic factors within the habitat(s).

The overall aim of such an investigation is to determine the qualitative and quantitative relationships between the plant and animal populations within the area being studied and the possible interactions between these and edaphic, topographic and climatic factors. Given this information, it is possible to explain the nature and extent of the factors governing the number and distribution of organisms in terms of a food web and, depending upon the sophistication of the investigation, pyramids of numbers, standing-crop biomass and energy.

13.4.1 Mapping an area

Plan view

The following simple method is designed primarily for mapping a small area, such as a grassland 10 m × 10 m or a small pond, but can be used on a larger scale, for example to map the whole rocky shore of a bay.

(1) Select the approximate area to study and stretch a measuring tape along one side of the area. This marks the base-line AY (fig 13.15).

(2) From the base-line measure the perpendicular distance to certain natural landmarks within the area or marker poles showing the limit of the study area. Record these measurements.

(3) Transfer the measurement of AY and the various perpendicular distances to a sheet of squared paper using a suitable scale.

(4) Using the base-line and measured distances to perpendicular landmarks drawn in (3) above as a guide, complete the map freehand.

(5) If the area is relatively small divide the actual base-line AY into an equal number of sections and from these lay out perpendicular string line transects. Repeat the

procedure using the extreme left transect AF as a new base-line to produce a string-grid, as shown in fig 13.16. Draw these grid lines on the map and label them using A, B, C etc. along one edge and 1, 2, 3 etc. along the other edge.

(6) Mark the positions of obvious structural and vegetational zones.

(7) Using a quadrat frame, pin frame or sweep net, depending on the area, systematically sample the area from, say, left to right and record the species present and their numbers or abundance.

(8) If the area is extremely large and a qualitative and quantitative study is required, belt transects spaced out at set intervals across the area, and set at right-angles to any suspected zonation, can be used in conjunction with quadrats to sample the area at particular points called **stations**. Direct measurements of the abiotic features of the environment should be made as frequently as possible or samples removed for subsequent analysis.

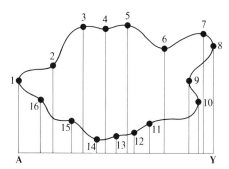

Fig 13.15 *A suggested method of mapping the significant aspects of an area, such as a small, irregularly shaped pond*

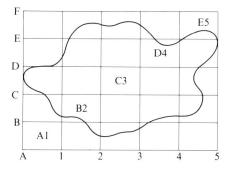

Fig 13.16 *Map of the area under investigation showing the various subsections, for example A1-E5, obtained by the use of a string grid. These provide reference areas for subsequent study*

453

Plotting a height profile

In some areas, distribution of organisms may be influenced by a factor related to height, such as on a rocky shore. Here the length of time each part of the shore is exposed due to the vertical motion of tides is height dependent. In such cases it is necessary to produce a height profile showing how the height along the transect varies, as from high to low water marks in the rocky shore example used below. At each point (station) along the transect where the community is sampled the height should be obtained accurately by the use of a surveying theodolite and measuring points. Over short distances a simple home-made levelling device attached to a reference pole, and a graduated pole can achieve relatively accurate results as described below (fig 13.17).

(1) Attach the levelling device at a convenient height (h_1), such as 1.5 m, on the measuring pole.
(2) Set out a line transect from high water mark to the water's edge.
(3) Set up the reference pole at a specific point, such as high water mark, on the transect and the marker pole at a known distance (x) further down the shore. Mark these positions on the transect and label them A and B. Keep to one side of the transect line whilst taking readings to avoid trampling on the specimens to be studied.
(4) When the wooden sighting bar is horizontal, look along the sighting tube with a point on the marker pole. The exact position of this point is then located by the person holding the marker pole and the height (h_2) recorded. The height difference between the stations is equal to $h_2 - h_1$.

Table 13.3 Horizontal and vertical distances recorded at stations A–K on a rocky shore. Northumberland 1968.

Station	Horizontal distance/m (x, x_1 etc.)	Height between stations/m ((h_2-h_1) etc.)	Height above low water/m ((h_2-h_1) etc.)
A	0		9.6
B	20	1.5	8.1
C	40	1.7	6.4
D	60	1.8	4.6
E	80	0.8	3.8
F	100	0.6	3.2
G	120	0.7	2.5
H	140	0.9	1.6
I	160	0.8	0.8
J	180	0.4	0.4
K	200	0.4	0

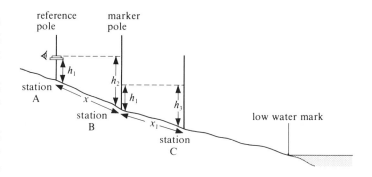

Fig 13.18 *Methods of obtaining heights and horizontal distances of stations above low water mark*

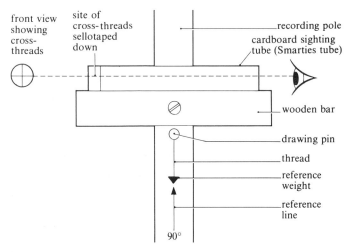

Fig 13.17 *A simple home-made levelling device attached to a reference pole. The position of the pole is adjusted until the sighting bar is shown to be horizontal by the thread indicating 90° on the reference point on the pole. Holding the pole steady, the observer looks along the sighting tube and indicates to the person holding the graduated pole the corresponding level position on his pole, as shown by the cross-wire sites. This height is recorded*

(5) Move the reference pole to station B and the marker pole a known distance (x_1) to station C. Repeat stages (3) and (4) and record the new height (h_3) (fig 13.18).
(6) Continue to obtain readings h_4, h_5 and so on, distances x_3, x_4 and so on and stations D, E and so on to the water's edge at low water. Record all distances as shown in table 13.3, and calculate the heights and horizontal distances of the stations above the low water mark.
(7) Transfer these data to a scale representation of the shore profile and mark on the positions of the stations (fig 13.19).

13.4.2 Identifying and estimating the number of each species present

Line and belt transects, frame quadrats and pin frames are used to sample systematically the area as described in section 13.2.2. Specimens are identified using a key and the number of organisms are either counted directly or estimated as described in section 13.2.3.

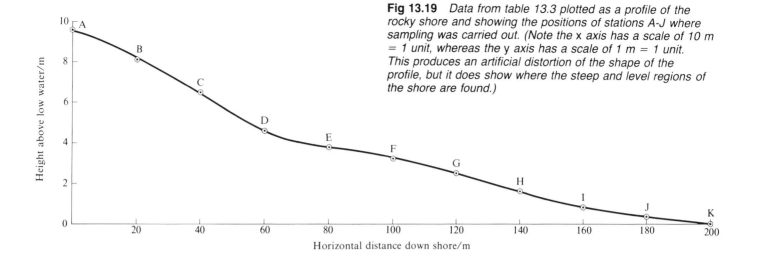

Fig 13.19 *Data from table 13.3 plotted as a profile of the rocky shore and showing the positions of stations A-J where sampling was carried out. (Note the x axis has a scale of 10 m = 1 unit, whereas the y axis has a scale of 1 m = 1 unit. This produces an artificial distortion of the shape of the profile, but it does show where the steep and level regions of the shore are found.)*

13.4.3 Recording and representing data

Data should be recorded directly they are obtained using some form of field booking sheet. In the case of synecological investigations of marine habitats the information shown on the booking sheets illustrated in tables 13.4 and 13.5 has proved successful. These sheets are best attached to a clip-board, completed in pencil and kept in a large polythene bag to protect them from rain. Once all the data have been collected they must be represented in some suitably efficient diagrammatic form that will highlight relationships between organisms and/or the nature of the environment. Methods of representing data are given in section A2.7 and include presence–absence graphs, kite diagrams, and histograms. Trophic pyramids are described in section 12.3.6. Some examples of the use of all four methods of representation are included in figs 13.20–13.22.

Table 13.4 Suggested format of field booking sheet.

Field Booking Sheet – Marine Ecology
(1) Name of site and grid reference ....
(2) Nature of profile (rocky, sandy, muddy, dune) ....
(3) Sketch map of area showing area(s) of study/position(s) of transects.

(4) Special features (exposure, aspect, etc.) ....
(5) Date ....
(6) Weather, conditions ....
(7) Tide data:
    predicted high water ....
    ,,   low water ....
    observed high water ....
    ,,   low water ....
    predicted tidal range ....
(8) Notes and key to recorded data (abundance scales – % cover, reference height of level, e.g. h_1 etc.)

Table 13.5 Data required on a booking sheet for investigating the synecology of marine habitats.

Station name	Horizontal distance from origin/m	Level reading (h_2)/m etc.	Change in height ($h_2 - h_1$ etc.)/m	Height above low water/m	Time exposed	Time covered	ANIMALS (species and abundance)	PLANTS (species and abundance)	NOTES

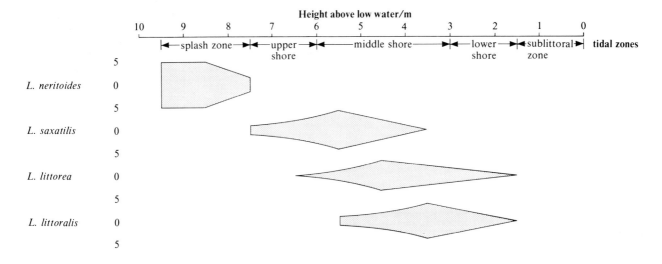

Fig 13.20 *Kite-diagrams showing the frequency and distribution of four common species of periwinkle,* Littorina, *on a rocky shore on the Dale peninsula, Pembrokeshire, April 1976. See table 13.6 for data*

13.4.4 Collecting and analysing abiotic factors

The amount of time spent on this stage of a synecological investigation will depend upon the nature of the area being studied. It is more applicable to areas where edaphic factors predominate, such as woodland, grassland and salt marsh, than to a rocky shore. The abiotic factors to be studied and the methods of study are described in section 13.1.

13.5 An autecological investigation

An autecological investigation involves studying all the ecological factors related to a single plant or animal species throughout its life cycle. The aim of the investigation is to describe as precisely as possible the ecological niche of the species. The species selected for study should be one which is both common and locally available. Initially the investigation should concern itself with undertaking extensive background reading on the species selected. During the reading, notes should be made on all aspects of the biology of the species and also on opportunities for practical work. This may involve either repeating investigations carried out by others or developing new investigations to be undertaken as part of the current study.

A straightforward approach to an autecological study is to prepare a comprehensive list of the questions which must be answered in order to reveal all there is to know about the species under investigation. The study should be undertaken as rigorously as possible and treated as a research project. Therefore it must involve some measure of original investigation including observation, measurement and experimentation. It must not simply be a report based on knowledge gleaned from reading books, journals and magazines. The species under investigation should be studied over a period of at least one full year.

A guide to the sorts of questions to be asked in the investigations of an **animal** is given below.

(1) **Classification.** What is the name of the species? What other groups of organisms does it resemble most closely? What are the similarities and differences between related species? What is its full taxonomic description?

(2) **Habitat.** Where is it found? What are the characteristic abiotic features of the area? How do these factors change over the course of a year?

(3) **Structure.** What is its adult structure? What are its characteristic external features? What are its dimensions and mass?

(4) **Movement.** How does it move from place to place? Which parts of the organism are involved in the movement and what are the functions of these parts? How are these parts adapted to the environment?

(5) **Nutrition.** What are the food sources of the organism? When does the organism feed? How much food is eaten? How is the food captured and ingested? What special features assist ingestion? Are there any unusual features of digestion and absorption?

(6) **Respiration.** Where is the gaseous exchange surface? How does gaseous exchange occur? How much oxygen is required by the organism?

(7) **Excretion.** What are the waste products of metabolism? How are these removed from the organism? What special organs of excretion are present?

(8) **Reproduction.** Are the sexes separate? What visible external differences are there between the sexes? Does any form of courtship occur? Does the organism defend a territory? How does mating occur? When does mating occur? How often does mating occur? How many gametes are produced? Where does fertilisation occur?

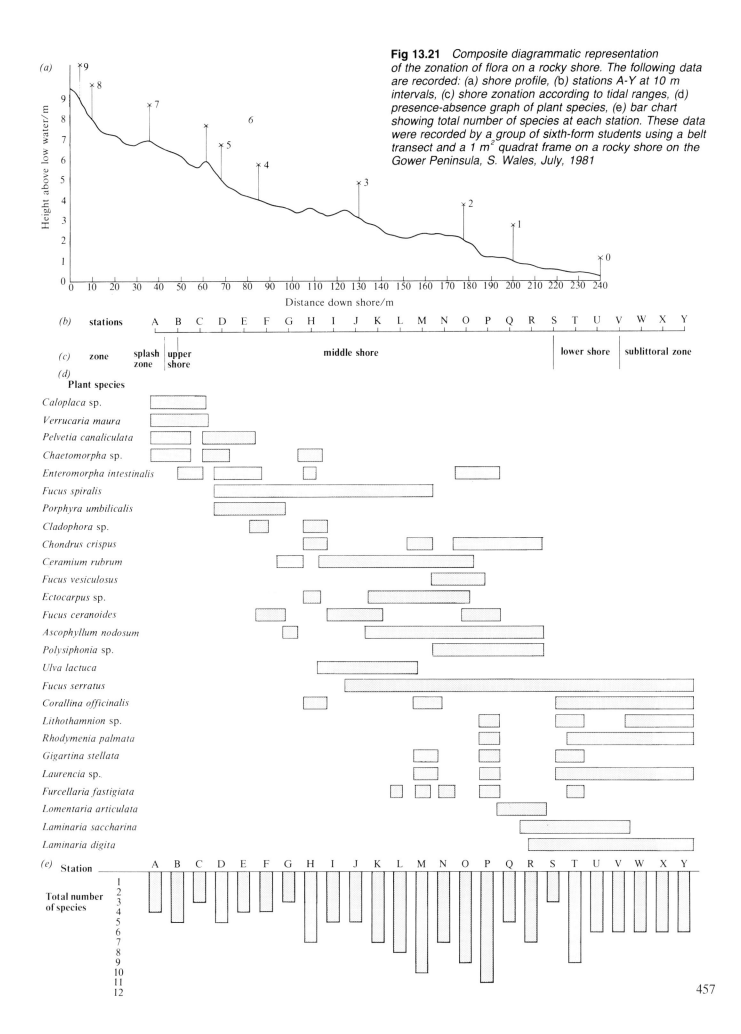

Fig 13.21 *Composite diagrammatic representation of the zonation of flora on a rocky shore. The following data are recorded: (a) shore profile, (b) stations A-Y at 10 m intervals, (c) shore zonation according to tidal ranges, (d) presence-absence graph of plant species, (e) bar chart showing total number of species at each station. These data were recorded by a group of sixth-form students using a belt transect and a 1 m^2 quadrat frame on a rocky shore on the Gower Peninsula, S. Wales, July, 1981*

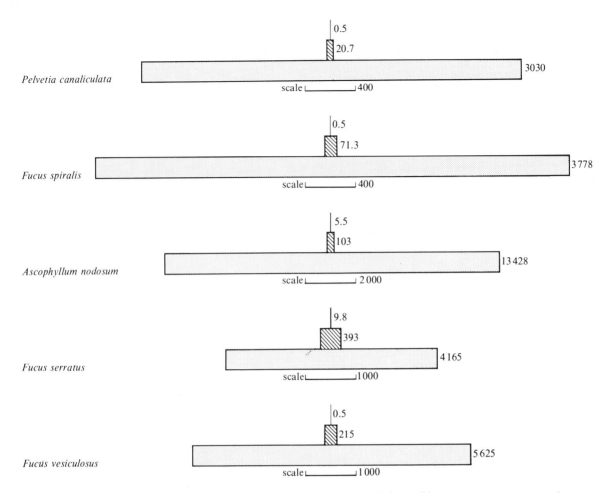

Fig 13.22 *Trophic pyramids of standing crop biomass for five rocky shore communities based on particular algal primary producers. The numerical values represent estimates of standing crop biomass in g m⁻². The stippled areas represent primary producers, the cross-hatched areas represent primary consumers (herbivores and detritus feeders) and the solid areas represent secondary consumers (carnivores). It must not be assumed however, that each trophic level is supported entirely by the level beneath. Northumberland coast, March 1969. (After D. A. S. Smith (1970) School Science Review, ASE).*

Table 13.6 The distribution of four common species of the periwinkle, *Littorina* on a rocky shore on the Dale peninsula, Pembrokeshire. April 1976. These data are represented graphically by the kite-diagrams shown in fig 13.20.

Height above low water/m	L. neritoides		L. saxatalis		L. littorea		L. littoralis	
	number	scale	number	scale	number	scale	number	scale
9–10	63	10	–	–	–	–	–	–
8–9	54	10	–	–	–	–	–	–
7–8	7	4	3	2	–	–	–	–
6–7	–	–	8	4	1	1	–	–
5–6	–	–	17	8	3	2	2	2
4–5	–	–	6	4	13	6	9	4
3–4	–	–	1	1	6	4	16	8
2–3	–	–	–	–	2	2	5	4
1–2	–	–	–	–	1	1	1	1
0–1	–	–	–	–	–	–	–	–

Abundance scale: ⩾20 = 10; 19–15 = 8; 14–10 = 6; 9–5 = 4; 4–2 = 2; 1 = 1.

(9) **Life cycle.** How long does development take? What degree of parental care is shown? Are there larval stages? When do adults become sexually mature? What is the typical life span of an individual of the species?

(10) **Behaviour.** How does the organism receive stimuli? To which stimuli does the organism mainly respond? How are the major sense organs adapted to the mode of life of the organism? To what extent does learning occur? How does the organism react to other members of the same species? How does the species react to unfavourable weather conditions? How does the organism communicate?

(11) **Ecology.** How many organisms occur in the population? What other organisms live in the same habitat? How are the various species distributed within the habitat? How is the species related to other species in the same habitat in terms of position in food chains and food webs? Is the organism a host, parasite or symbiont? What is the ecological niche of the species?

Similarly the sorts of questions to be asked in the investigation of a **flowering plant** are given below.

(1) **Classification.** What is the name of the species? What subspecies, varieties and ecotypes of the species exist? What are the similarities and differences between closely related species? What is its full taxonomic description?

(2) **Habitat**
(*a*) *Edaphic factors* – What is the parent rock type? What type of soil profile is shown? How thick are the various horizons? What is the percentage water content (field capacity) of the soil? What is the percentage organic content of the soil? What is the mineral composition of the soil? What is the pH of the soil? What is the height and seasonal variation of the water table in relation to the life history and distribution of the species?

(*b*) *Climatic factors* – What are the extremes and mean temperatures in the habitats? What is the annual rainfall in the habitats? What is the mean relative humidity of the air in the habitats? What is the direction of the prevailing wind? How much light is received by the plant?

(*c*) *Topographical factors* – To which direction is the species normally exposed? Does the species appear to prefer exposed or sheltered sites? Does the species appear to prefer sloping or flat

habitats? Does altitude appear to affect the distribution of the species?

(3) **Structure.** How extensive is the root system? What form does the root system take? How does the stem branch? How many leaves are carried on each branch? What shapes are the leaves? What variations in length and breadth exist between the leaves? How tall does the plant grow?

(4) **Physiology.** What pigments are present in the leaves and petals? Which surface of the leaf has the highest transpiration rate? What effect has darkness on transpiration rate? Do diurnal changes in water content of leaves occur?

(5) **Reproduction.**
(*a*) *Flower* – How many flowers are produced per plant? How many and of what shape and size are the sepals, petals, anthers, carpels or pistil? What variation in petal colour exists? What pigments are present in the leaves? When does flowering begin? How long is the flowering period? How does pollination occur? What adaptations to insect or wind pollination are shown?

(*b*) *Fruit and seeds* – How are the fruits formed? What is the structure of the fruit? How many seeds are produced per flower? How are fruits and seeds dispersed? How far are fruits and seeds dispersed?

(*c*) *Perennation* – How does vegetative propagation occur? What are the organs of perennation? At what rate does the species colonise an area?

(6) **Life cycle.** What type of seed is produced? What conditions are required for germination? When do the seeds germinate? What percentage of seeds germinate? Which form of germination occurs? At what rate does the shoot system develop? What is the extent of growth in terms of space and time? (Why do some of the seedlings not become mature?)

(7) **Ecology.** Does the species grow as solitary plants or in patches? What size are the patches? Which species grow in the same habitat? What degree of competition exists between the species being studied and other species? Is the species a parasite, host or symbiont? How is the species related to animals in terms of position in the food web? Does the species offer protection or shelter to animals? If so, which animals and how is this provided? What is the ecological niche of the species?

Fungi, algae, mosses, liverworts or conifers may be used in autecological studies and the questions above may be modified as appropriate to the species under investigation.

Answers and discussion

Chapter 2

2.1

Time (in units of 20 min)	0	1	2	3	4	5	6	7	8	9	10
A Number of bacteria	1	2	4	8	16	32	64	128	256	512	1024
B Log₁₀ number of bacteria	0.0	0.3	0.6	0.9	1.2	1.5	1.8	2.1	2.4	2.7	3.0
C Number of bacteria expressed as power of 2	2^0	2^1	2^2	2^3	2^4	2^5	2^6	2^7	2^8	2^9	2^{10}

Graph A (an arithmetic plot) increases in steepness as time progresses. Graph B (a logarithmic plot) is a straight line (increases linearly with time). See fig 2.1(ans).

2.2 The graph would be as fig 2.7.

2.3 See fig 2.3(ans).

Factors responsible for the changes are discussed in section 2.2.4. The difference in the growth curve of living bacteria compared with living and dead bacteria is due to the following:

(a) a few cells die during lag and log phases;

(b) during the stationary phase the combined total of living plus dead cells continues to increase slowly for some time since some cells are still reproducing.

(c) during the phase of decline the combined total of living plus dead cells remains constant, though many are dying.

2.4 Generation time is the time taken for numbers to double during the log phase. This is about 2.5 h.

2.5 (i)(a) louse (b) human

(ii)(a) mosquito or tick (b) human (also monkeys)

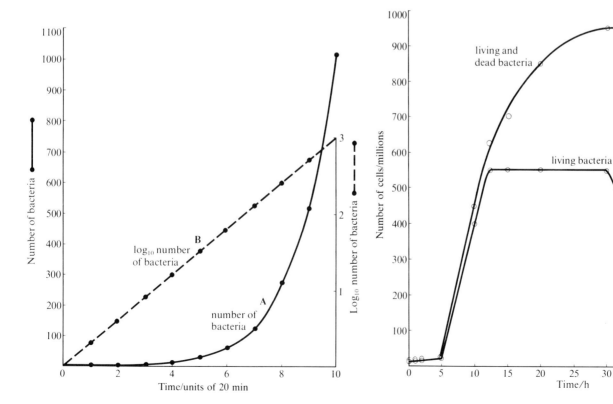

Fig 2.1(ans) *Growth of a model population of bacteria as plotted on arithmetic and logarithmic scales*

Fig 2.3(ans) *Growth of a bacterial population*

Chapter 3

2.6 Consult tables 2.6 and 2.7, chapter 2.

2.7 The sporangiophores bear the sporangia above the main mycelium so that the spores are more likely to catch air currents and be dispersed.

Chapter 3

3.1 There is greater nutrient availability in lowland reservoirs because the rivers flowing into them have had longer to accumulate nutrients, particularly from cultivated areas where fertilisers may be used.

3.2 Algae have autotrophic nutrition. Pathogens are parasites or saprotrophs, obtaining food from their hosts.

3.3 Amphibians, like liverworts and mosses, are only partially adapted to life on land, having bodies which easily lose water, and they still rely on water for sexual reproduction. Both groups of organisms are also believed to represent intermediate stages in the evolution towards more advanced forms which are better adapted to life on land.

3.4 The sporophyte has become adapted for life on land although the gametophyte is still dependent on water for swimming gametes. The sporophyte generation has true vascular tissue and true roots, stem and leaves with which to exploit the land environment more successfully.

The sporophyte is the dominant generation, the life of the gametophyte being short.

The mature sporophyte is no longer dependent on the gametophyte.

3.5 (*a*), (*c*) and (*d*)

3.6 Sexual reproduction is dependent on water since it involves free-swimming sperm.

The gametophyte thallus is susceptible to desiccation.

The plants are often relatively intolerant of high light intensities.

3.7 By asexual reproduction, either vegetative (see text) or by dissemination of spores. (Sexual reproduction does not result in spread because the zygote grows from the previous gametophyte generation – contrast seed-bearing plants.)

3.8 (*a*) The zygote is located in the venter of an archegonium of the previous gametophyte generation. Thus it is protected by the archegonium and the surrounding tissues of the gametophyte.

(*b*) The gametophyte generation from which the zygote develops is photosynthetic and provides the zygote with food.

3.9 The *Dryopteris* spore can develop wherever it falls, providing conditions are moist and fertile. Pollen grains must reach the female parts of the sporophyte.

3.10 The megaspore is large because it must contain sufficient food reserves to support the female gametophyte and subsequent development of the embryo sporophyte until the latter becomes self-supporting. Microspores, by being small, can be produced economically in large numbers and are light enough to be carried by air currents, thus increasing the chances of the male gametes that they contain reaching the female parts of the plants.

Chapter 5

5.1 The molecular formula shows the number of each type of atom. The structural formula shows the arrangement of the atoms relative to each other. Note that angles of bonds can also be shown; see figs 5.3 and 5.4, for example.

5.2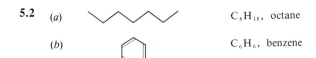

(*a*) C_8H_{18}, octane

(*b*) C_6H_6, benzene

5.3

H$\diagdown$C$=$C$\diagup$H (with H's at corners)

5.4 triose $C_3H_6O_3$ hexose $C_6H_{12}O_6$
tetrose $C_4H_8O_4$ heptose $C_7H_{14}O_7$
pentose $C_5H_{10}O_5$

5.5 (*a*) Valency of C = 4, O = 2, H = 1.

(*b*) Molecular formula is $C_3H_6O_3$ in both cases; the compounds are therefore trioses.

(*c*) Each contains two hydroxyl groups. This could have been predicted, since it has already been explained that in monosaccharides all the carbon atoms except one have a hydroxyl group attached.

(*d*) Glyceraldehyde contains a secondary alcohol group,

$$>CHOH$$

Dihydroxyacetone contains a primary alcohol group —CH_2OH at both ends of the molecule.

(Hydroxyl and carbonyl groups are parts of these larger groups.)

5.6 Pentoses: ribose, ribulose

Hexoses: glucose, mannose, galactose, fructose

5.7 (*a*) See fig 5.7(ans).

(*b*) This is optical isomerism.

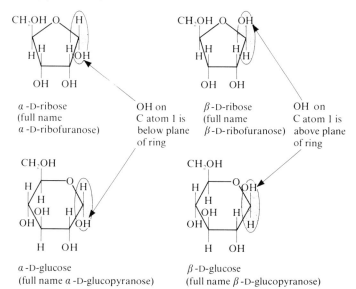

a-D-ribose (full name *a*-D-ribofuranose)   OH on C atom 1 is below plane of ring

β-D-ribose (full name *β*-D-ribofuranose)   OH on C atom 1 is above plane of ring

a-D-glucose (full name *a*-D-glucopyranose)

β-D-glucose (full name *β*-D-glucopyranose)

Fig 5.7(ans) *The α and β isomers of D-glucose and D-ribose*

5.8 α-glucose

5.9 Cellulose is made of β-glucose residues. The —OH group on C atom 1 is at 180° to the —OH group on C atom 4. Since these groups must come alongside each other in adjacent residues to form a glycosidic link, adjacent residues have to be at 180° to each other.

5.10 Relevant information is provided in sections 5.2.3 and 5.2.4.

5.11 The principal sources of variation are as follows.

(*a*) Use of both pentoses and hexoses. Although normally

only one monosaccharide is used, sometimes two are used in alternating sequence (such as in murein) and in a few complex polysaccharides more may be used.

(b) Two types of linkage, 1,4 and 1,6, are common between residues. Thus branching can occur. (Other linkages, such as 1,2 and 1,3, are possible because every hydroxyl group in a monosaccharide can participate in a condensation.)

(c) Lengths of chains and branches, and extent of branching can vary enormously.

(d) Different optical isomers exist. Most naturally occurring isomers are D- rather than L-isomers so little extra variation comes from this. However α- and β-forms are important. (Compare starch and cellulose.)

(e) Sugars may be ketoses or aldoses. Ketohexoses form five-membered, and aldohexoses six-membered rings.

(f) The high chemical reactivity of sugars (aldehyde, ketone and hydroxyl groups) means that they combine readily with other substances to form related compounds, such as amino sugars and acid sugars. These can participate in building polysaccharides.

5.12 One that occurs when two compounds are joined by the elimination of a water molecule.

5.13 Body temperatures of poikilothermic animals become lower in cold environments. Lipids rich in unsaturated fatty acids (which have low melting points) generally remain liquid at temperatures lower (usually 5 °C or lower) than those rich in saturated fatty acids. This may be necessary if the lipid is to maintain its function, such as a constituent of membranes.

5.14 Triolein because it contains three *unsaturated* oleic acid molecules. Tristearin is a fat, triolein an oil.

5.15 (a) Cell respiration (internal or tissue respiration). Fat undergoes oxidation.

(b) Only the hydrogen part of carbohydrate and fat molecules yields water on oxidation ($2H_2 + O_2 \rightarrow 2H_2O$) and fats contain relatively more hydrogen than carbohydrates on a weight basis (nearly twice as much).

5.16

*peptide bond.

5.17 (a) AAA AAB ABA ABB
BAA BAB BBA BBB

(b) $2^3 = 8$

(c) $2^{100} = 1.27 \times 10^{30}$

(d) $20^{100} = 1.27 \times 10^{130}$ This is much larger than the number of atoms in the Universe (estimated at about 10^{100})! Thus, there is an effectively infinite potential for variation among protein structures.

(e) 20^n where n is the number of amino acids in the molecule.

5.18 The outstanding feature is that the ratio of adenine to thymine is always about 1.0, and so is the ratio of guanine to cytosine. In other words, the number of adenine molecules equals the number of thymine molecules and guanine = cytosine. Note also that the number of purine residues (adenine + guanine) therefore equals the number of pyrimidine residues (thymine + cytosine). Also revealed is the fact that the DNAs of different organisms have different base compositions, in other words the ratio of A:G or T:C is variable.

5.19 Adenine must pair with thymine and guanine with cytosine to account for the observed base ratios.

5.20 Compare the volume of the unknown sample needed to reduce the dye with the volume of 0.1% ascorbic acid solution needed in the standard described.

Percentage ascorbic acid in unknown sample =

$$\frac{\text{volume 0.1\% ascorbic acid used in standard}}{\text{volume of unknown sample used}} \times \frac{0.1}{100}$$

5.21 (a) Carry out Benedict's test on all three solutions. The sucrose solution would not give a brick-red precipitate on boiling. The glucose and glucose/sucrose solutions could be distinguished by pre-treating both as for hydrolysis (see non-reducing sugar test) and repeating Benedict's test. The glucose/sucrose mix will now show a greater amount of reducing sugar. (In practice, different dilutions of the solutions may have to be tried for convincing results. 0.05% glucose solution, 0.5% sucrose solution and a mixture of equal volumes of 0.1% glucose solution and 1.0% sucrose solution are suitable.)

(i) Paper chromatography or thin-layer chromatography.

(ii) Effect on plane-polarised light using a polarimeter (both sucrose and glucose are dextro-rotatory, but sucrose produces a greater degree of rotation than glucose).

(iii) Sucrose is converted to reducing sugars (glucose + fructose) by the enzyme sucrase (invertase). The reaction may either be followed using a polarimeter or by Benedict's test.

5.22 Dissolve 10 g glucose in distilled water and make up to 100 cm³. (Do not add 10 g glucose to 100 cm³ distilled water because the final volume would be greater than 100 cm³.)

5.23 Add 10 cm³ of 10% glucose to 50 cm³ of 2% sucrose solution and make up to 100 cm³ with distilled water.

Chapter 6

6.1 Excess heat irreversibly changes the secondary and tertiary structure of the enzyme. This means that its specific shape will be changed and that the amino acids normally located close to each other in the functional active site will no longer be in such a position. Therefore the active site will be non-functional. Normally enzyme conformation is easily disrupted by high temperatures.

6.2 (a) Initially the reactions A and B are fast and a lot of product is formed. Later, product formation levels off and there is no further increase. This may be because (i) all substrate has been converted to product, (ii) the enzyme has become inactivated, or (iii) the equilibrium point of a reversible reaction has been reached, and substrate and product are present in balanced concentrations.

(b) When the temperature is raised, (i) initial reaction rate is increased, and (ii) the enzyme becomes less stable and is inactivated more rapidly.

(c) Sensitivity to heat is an indication of the protein nature of the enzymes.

(d) At lower temperatures (as in curve C) rate of formation of product remains constant over 1 h.

6.3 (a) 5.50

(b) (i) pepsin, (ii) salivary amylase

(c) The active site of the enzyme is being destroyed. The ionisable groups of the enzyme, especially those of the active site, are being modified. Hence the substrate no longer fits easily into the active site and catalytic activity is diminished.

(d) A change in pH results in a change in the activity of most enzymes. Each enzyme would have its rate of reaction modified to a different extent as each possesses its own particular pH activity curve. All cells rely on a delicate

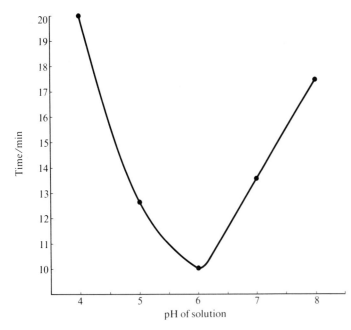

Fig 6.3(ans) *Activity of catalase on hydrogen peroxide at varying pH*

balance between their enzyme systems, and so any changes in enzyme activity could cause the death of the cell or multicellular organism.

(*e*) See fig 6.3(ans).

Optimum pH for enzyme activity is 6.00.

From pH 4–6, ionisable groups of the active site are modified such that the active site becomes more efficient at receiving and complexing with its substrate. The reverse is true when the pH changes from 6–8.

6.4 Increasing the substrate concentration increases the probability of substrate molecules fitting into the active sites rather than inhibitor molecules.

6.5 Increased substrate concentration has no effect on the overall rate as there is no competition for the active site. Inhibition is therefore irreversible.

6.6 (*a*) The two sites are located on different parts of the enzyme, an active site for complexing with A, and another site specific for binding with X.

(*b*) (i) X could inhibit e_1 and therefore only permit production of S along the A–S pathway. This situation could remain until the surplus of X had been used up.

(ii) X could accelerate the catalytic activity of e_5, again enhancing the production of S at the expense of X.

(*c*) Feedback inhibition.

(*d*) Because of enzyme specificity, each step requires specific enzymes and this allows for fine control of the pathway.

6.7 (1) All are proteins and synthesised within living organisms.

(2) They catalyse chemical reactions by lowering the activation energy required to start the reaction.

(3) Only small amounts of enzyme are needed to catalyse reactions.

(4) At the end of a reaction the enzymes are unchanged.

(5) Each enzyme is specific and possesses an active site where enzyme and substrate combine temporarily to form an enzyme/substrate complex before products are released.

(6) Enzymes work best at an optimum pH and optimum temperature.

(7) Being proteins enzymes are denatured by extremes of pH and temperature.

(8) The Q_{10} of enzymes over a temperature range of 0–40 °C is approximately 2.

(9) Some enzymes work in conjunction with cofactors.

(10) Certain chemical reagents inhibit enzyme activity, as can end-products of metabolic pathways.

Chapter 7

7.1 Endoplasmic reticulum, ribosomes, microtubules, microfilaments, microvilli (visible as a 'brush border' in the light microscope).

In addition, small structures that are difficult to identify with certainty using a light microscope can be easily identified with the electron microscope, such as lysosomes and mitochondria.

7.2 (*a*) cell wall with middle lamella and plasmodesmata, chloroplasts (plastids in general), large central vacuole (animal cells do possess small vacuoles, such as food vacuoles, contractile vacuoles)

(*b*) centrioles, microvilli, pinocytotic vesicles are more commonly seen in animal cells.

7.3 (*a*) A: polar head of phospholipid (hydrophilic)

B: non-polar hydrocarbon tails of phospholipid (hydrophobic)

C: phospholipid

D: lipid layer

(*b*) cholesterol (the most common sterol)

7.4 (*a*) A Na^+/K^+ pump operates whereby efflux of Na^+ is linked to influx of K^+. Without K^+, no Na^+ efflux can occur, so Na^+ accumulates within the cells by diffusion and K^+ leaves the cells by diffusion. (*b*) ATP is a source of energy for active transport of Na^+ ions.

7.5 Non-polar amino acids are hydrophobic (repelled by water). Therefore the signal sequence tends to be repelled by the aqueous cytosol around the ribosome until it finds the receptor protein in the ER.

Chapter 9

9.1 Photoautotrophism is the process by which light energy from the Sun is used as an energy source for synthesising organic compounds from inorganic materials, with carbon dioxide as a source of carbon. Chemoheterotrophism is the process by which organic compounds are synthesised from pre-existing organic sources of carbon, using energy from chemical reactions.

9.2 (*a*) autotrophic organisms (*b*) heterotrophic organisms

9.3 75×10^{12} kg carbon per year [$(40 \times 10^{12}) + (35 \times 10^{12})$]

9.4 Solar energy is free; the raw material, water, is abundant; the product of combustion is also water, which is non-toxic and would not pollute the environment (nuclear power involves safety and pollution hazards).

9.5 **Overall form and position**

Large surface area to volume ratio for maximum interception of light and efficient gaseous exchange.

Blade often held at right-angles to incident light, particularly in dicotyledons.

Stomata

Pores in the leaf allow gaseous exchange. Carbon dioxide needed for photosynthesis, with oxygen a waste product.

In dicotyledons, stomata are located mainly in the shady lower epidermis, thus minimising loss of water vapour in transpiration.

Guard cells
Regulate opening of stomata (ensure stomata open only in light when photosynthesis occurs).

Mesophyll
Contains special organelles for photosynthesis, the chloroplasts, containing chlorophyll.

In dicotyledons, palisade mesophylls cells, with more chloroplasts, are located near the upper surface of the leaf for maximum interception of light. Length of the cells increases the chance for light absorption.

Chloroplasts are located near the periphery of the cell for easier gas exchange with intercellular spaces.

Chloroplasts may be phototactic (that is move within the cell towards light).

In dicotyledons, spongy mesophyll has large intercellular spaces for efficient gaseous exchange (monocotyledons also have extensive intercellular spaces).

Vascular system
Supplies water, a reagent in photosynthesis; also mineral salts. Removes the products of photosynthesis.

Supporting skeleton provided together with collenchyma and sclerenchyma.

9.6 Chlorophyll *a* absorption in red light is about twice that of chlorophyll *b* and the absorption peak is at a slightly longer wavelength (lower energy). Absorption in the blue is lower and shifted to a slightly shorter wavelength (higher energy). Note that only very slight differences in chemical structure cause these differences.

9.7 Chlorophyll *a* has the lower energy of excitation. It is possible therefore for chlorophyll *b* to transfer energy to chlorophyll *a* whilst still losing some energy as heat during the transfer.

9.8 The dark blue colour of the dye should disappear as it is reduced, leaving the green of the chloroplasts.

9.9 The DCPIP should have remained blue in tubes (2) and (3), which were controls. Tube (2) shows that light alone cannot induce the colour change, and that chloroplasts must be present for the Hill reaction to occur. Tube (3) shows that light must be present as well as chloroplasts for the Hill reaction to occur.

9.10 The two organelles closest in size to the chloroplasts are nuclei (slightly larger) and mitochondria (slightly smaller). More rigorous differential centrifugation or density gradient centrifugation would be necessary to isolate pure chloroplasts.

9.11 Indirect evidence suggests that nuclei and mitochondria were not involved in reducing DCPIP because light was needed, and these organelles lack chlorophyll or any other conspicuous pigment.

9.12 To reduce enzyme activity. During homogenisation destructive enzymes may be released from other parts of the cell, such as from lysosomes or vacuoles.

9.13 Cell reactions operate efficiently only at certain pHs; any significant change in pH, caused for example by release of acids from other parts of the cell, might have affected chloroplast activity.

9.14 (*a*) water (*b*) DCPIP

9.15 Non-cyclic photophosphorylation only: (i) oxygen was evolved (ii) electrons were accepted by DCPIP, therefore they could not recycle into PSI.

9.16 (*a*) The chloroplasts lack chloroplast envelopes (bounding membranes) and stroma. Only the internal membrane system remains.

(*b*) The medium lacking sucrose was hypotonic to the chloroplasts. Without the protection of the cell walls, broken during homogenisation, chloroplasts absorb water by osmosis, swell and burst. The stroma dissolves, leaving only membranes.

(*c*) The change was desirable because bursting the chloroplasts allows more efficient access of DCPIP to the membranes where the Hill reaction is located.

9.17 The discovery of the Hill reaction was a landmark for several reasons:

(1) it showed that oxygen evolution could occur without reduction of carbon dioxide, providing evidence for separate light and dark reactions and the splitting of water;

(2) it showed that chloroplasts could carry out a light-driven reduction of an electron acceptor;

(3) it gave biochemical evidence that the light reaction of photosynthesis was entirely located in the chloroplast.

9.18 If an isotope has a shorter half-life (for example ^{11}C, 20.5 min) it rapidly decays to the point at which it is undetectable, thus severely restricting its usefulness in biological experiments, which often take hours or days to complete.

9.19 Photosynthesis in *Chlorella* and higher plants is biochemically similar so that *Chlorella* was used for the following reasons:

(1) *Chlorella* culture is virtually a chloroplast culture since a large volume of every cell is occupied by a single chloroplast;

(2) greater uniformity of growth can be achieved;

(3) the cells are very rapidly exposed to radioactive carbon dioxide and also quickly killed, so handling techniques are easier.

9.20 For maximum illumination of algae.

9.21

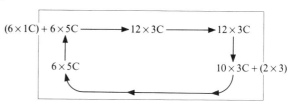

This emphasises the cyclic flow of carbon; the complexity of Calvin's cycle is due mainly to the difficulty of converting $10 \times 3C$ into $6 \times 5C$.

9.22 Availability of carbon dioxide, water, light and chlorophyll.

9.23 (*a*) In region A light intensity is the limiting factor.

(*b*) B: some factor other than light intensity is becoming the limiting factor. In region B, both light intensity and the other factor(s) are limiting. C: light intensity is no longer a limiting factor.

(*c*) D: the 'saturation point' for light intensity under these conditions, that is the point beyond which an increase in light intensity will cause no further increase in the rate of photosynthesis.

(*d*) E: the maximum rate of photosynthesis attainable under the conditions of the experiment.

9.24 X, Y and Z are the points at which light ceases to be the major limiting factor in the four experiments. Up to these points there is a linear relationship between light intensity and rate of photosynthesis.

9.25 Enzymes would start to become denatured.

9.26 Some likely situations would be (*a*) in a shaded community such as a wood; dawn and twilight in a warm climate; (*b*) carbon dioxide is normally limiting, but it would be particularly so in a crowded stand of plants, such as a crop under sunny, warm conditions; (*c*) a bright winter's day.

465

9.27 The plant continues to use sugars in the dark, for example for respiration. Photosynthesis ceases in the dark, so as sugars are depleted starch reserves are converted to sugars, including sucrose which travels from the leaves to other parts of the plant.

9.28 It could be argued that paper or foil prevents photosynthesis by restricting diffusion of carbon dioxide to the covered parts. This can be disproved by arranging an air gap between paper and leaf as shown below in fig 9.28(ans).

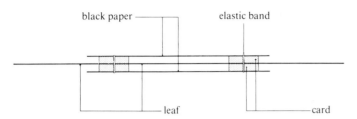

Fig 9.28(ans) *Section through leaf wrapped in black paper*

9.29 It should be placed in an identical flask but with water replacing potassium hydroxide solution. Unsoaked cotton wool should secure the leaf stalk. (The stalk itself could be surface-treated with lime water to check whether possible injury here could affect photosynthesis.)

9.30 Rates of carbon dioxide uptake, oxygen production and carbohydrate production could be used. Rate of increase in the dry mass of leaves may also be measured. This is particularly suitable for crop plants over a growing season when relatively large samples may be taken. An experiment for measuring carbon dioxide uptake is described in section 9.7.

9.31 (a) The rate of gas production is directly proportional to LI up to a LI of x units. At this point light saturation began to occur and this was complete at y units (x and y values depend on experimental conditions). Thereafter some factor other than light was limiting the rate of gas production.

(b) The laboratory was darkened to avoid extra light which could have stimulated extra photosynthesis. Temperature was kept constant because this also affects the rate of photosynthesis.

9.32 (a) Temperature may vary as the lamp heats the water (this should be avoided by the water bath).

(b) The carbon dioxide concentration of the water may vary during the experiment, especially if potassium hydrogen-carbonate was added earlier.

(c) Any stray light which is admitted to the laboratory will affect photosynthesis.

9.33 As the bubble of oxygen rises through the water, some of the dissolved nitrogen will come out of solution and enter the bubble, and some of the oxygen will dissolve. This exchange is due to the different partial pressures (concentrations) of oxygen and nitrogen in the bubble and the water, there being a tendency for them to come to equilibrium with time. Traces of water vapour and carbon dioxide will also be present in the collected gas. Once the gas has been collected, it will tend to come into equilibrium with atmospheric air by diffusion of gases through the water.

9.34 The amount of oxygen produced by photosynthesis in the experiment must all be collected. If the water is not saturated with air, some of the oxygen released in photosynthesis will dissolve in the water and reduce the amount recorded.

9.35 Specimen results are given in the following table.

Time/h	Colour of indicator			
	tube A	tube B	tube C	tube D
0	red	red	red	red
18	yellow	purple	red	red

The control tubes, C and D, were necessary to prove that any changes that took place in tubes A and B were due to the presence of leaves. In tube A conditions became more acidic as a result of carbon dioxide being produced during respiration. Photosynthesis did not take place in the absence of light. In tube B conditions became less acidic, indicating a net uptake of carbon dioxide. The carbon dioxide produced by respiration was used in photosynthesis, together with that already in the air inside the leaf and dissolved in the indicator solution. The rate of photosynthesis was greater than the rate of respiration.

9.36 The carbon dioxide compensation point. At this point rate of photosynthesis equals rate of respiration.

9.37 The higher the concentration of carbon dioxide, up to 0.1%, the greater the rate of photosynthesis. As carbon dioxide concentration increases, it competes more effectively with oxygen for the active site in RuBP carboxylase, thereby increasing the rate of carbon dioxide fixation, that is photosynthesis. Increase in oxygen concentration inhibits photosynthesis for the opposite reason, oxygen tending to exclude carbon dioxide and to stimulate photorespiration, which releases carbon dioxide.

9.38 High oxygen concentration and low carbon dioxide concentration (maximum rate achieved at 100% oxygen). High light intensities are also needed for high rates since the process is light-dependent.

9.39 Mesophyll chloroplasts for light reactions, bundle sheath chloroplasts for dark reactions.

9.40 Oxygen production is associated with grana (major location of PSII) and oxygen would compete with carbon dioxide for RuBP carboxylase and stimulate photorespiration. Also grana occupy a large volume of the chloroplast and in their absence there is more stroma, and hence more RuBP carboxylase and storage space for starch.

9.41 Carbon dioxide pump. By acting as a carbon dioxide pump, the malate shunt increases carbon dioxide concentration in the bundle sheath cells, thus increasing the efficiency with which RuBP carboxylase works.

Hydrogen pump. Malate carries hydrogen from $NADPH_2$ in the mesophyll to NADP in the bundle sheath cells, where $NADPH_2$ is regenerated. The advantage is that $NADPH_2$ is generated by the efficient light reaction in the mesophyll chloroplasts (PSII present) and can be used as reducing power in the Calvin cycle of bundle sheath chloroplasts, whose own synthesis of $NADPH_2$ is limited.

9.42 (a) Lowering oxygen concentrations stimulates C_3 photosynthesis because it reduces photorespiration.

(b) Lowering oxygen concentration does not affect C_4 photosynthesis because photorespiration is already inhibited.

9.43 Mutualistic bacteria in the root nodules of legumes fix nitrogen which leads to increased growth and thus to increased demand for other minerals, notably potassium and phosphorus. (However, ploughing-in of legumes is sometimes done, thus keeping the minerals in the soil.)

9.44 Chemoheterotrophic. They can be classified further as saprotrophic.

9.45 Anywhere there is insufficient oxygen for decomposition of all accumulating organic matter, such as bogs, aquatic sediments like mud deposits, arctic tundra, deeper zones of soil and waterlogged soils.

9.46 Both increase aeration and hence oxygen content of soil. This stimulates decomposition and nitrification. It also inhibits denitrification, oxygen being used instead of nitrate.

Chapter 10

10.1 (1) Decomposes organic matter and therefore helps recycling of elements from dead to living organisms.
(2) Removes organic refuse.
(3) Renders food unfit for human consumption (such as makes bread mouldy).
(4) In the Far East *Mucor* has been used to produce alcohol. A mixture of *Mucor* and yeast was added to rice. *Mucor* converted the rice to sugars which the yeast then converted to alcohol.

10.2 See section 4.5.3.

10.3 Because of the continual heat loss from the relatively larger body surface of the mouse.

10.4 4.18 J raise the temperature of 1 g water through 1 °C,
7.5×4.18 J raise the temperature of 1 g water through 7.5 °C,
$7.5 \times 4.18 \times 500$ J raise the temperature of 500 g water through 7.5 °C,
therefore 15.675 kJ are produced when 1 g of sugar is burned in oxygen.

10.5 Fats are much richer in hydrogen than carbohydrates. As most of the energy that is released in the body arises by the oxidation of hydrogen to water, so fats liberate more heat than carbohydrates.

10.6 Less energy is released in the body because both of these substances are not completely oxidised; for example the nitrogen in protein is excreted as urea in urine rather than being oxidised to nitrogen dioxide, therefore excretion of urea from the body actually expels some energy.

10.7 (*a*) Certain 'factors' (now known as vitamins) are needed in small amounts in the diet, which are essential for healthy growth and development.
(*b*) The growth 'factors' must be contained in the 3 cm³ rations of milk provided for the rats, which confirms that only minute amounts are required. When the milk was stopped, growth was quickly curtailed. Rats without milk did grow initially, therefore they must have had a small store of vitamins in their body initially.
(*c*) It is deficient in iron, vitamin B and roughage.

10.8 Active pepsin would digest cells that produce it, there being no mucus barrier within the zymogen glands.

10.9 (*a*) The small intestine wall is thrown into folds, the presence of villi and the presence of microvilli.
(*b*) It increases tremendously the secretory and absorptive surface of the small intestine and makes it very efficient at these processes.

10.10 Enzyme activity would be impaired as the enzymes would be denatured by the low pH.

10.11 It ensures that even if the soluble food molecules are in concentrations lower than those already in the blood, they will still pass into the blood.

Chapter 11

11.1 Those substances which yield more energy than ATP when hydrolysed are able to transfer their phosphate groups to ADP to form ATP. Those that liberate less energy than ATP when hydrolysed will receive phosphate groups from ATP.

11.2 ATP can be compared with a battery in the sense that its manufacture requires energy and that it is a convenient short-term carrier of energy. It is manufactured during respiration and can move to any part of the cell requiring energy, be 'run down' (converted to ADP), then 'recharged' (converted back to ATP) by respiration.

11.3 dehydrogenation

11.4 dehydrogenases (see table 6.3)

11.5 (*a*) phosphorylation
(*b*) isomerases
(*c*) (i) dehydrogenation/oxidation
    (ii) phosphorylation
(*d*) a vitamin of the B complex

11.6 For rapid diffusion of intermediates between cytoplasm and mitochondrion.

11.7

Entering	Leaving
pyruvate	
oxygen	carbon dioxide
reduced hydrogen carrier	oxidised hydrogen carrier
ADP	ATP
phosphate	water

11.8 Provides an increased surface area for absorption of digested food materials.

11.9 Large concentrations of dissolved molecules would increase the solute potential of the plasma, which in turn could affect many other physiological processes.

11.10 (1) Within the cell, the pigment is separated from the more variable chemical environment of the plasma.
(2) Enclosing the pigment will decrease the viscosity of the blood and reduce the work the heart has to do to pump the blood around the body.

11.11 Initially when blood and water first meet, the concentration gradient of oxygen between them would be great. However, as blood and water flow along together the gradient will decrease until blood shows a percentage saturation for oxygen equal to that of the water. This would be well below the blood's maximum saturation point and therefore inefficient (fig 11.11(ans)).

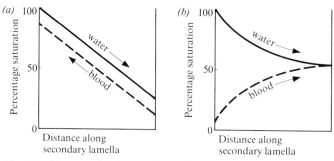

Fig 11.11(ans) (*a*) *Counterflow of water and blood.*
(*b*) *Parallel flow of water and blood*

11.12 Because the dead space air forms part of the pulmonary ventilation volume.

11.13 Smaller mammals have a large surface area to volume ratio from which heat can be lost and therefore must use up more oxygen in order to maintain a constant body temperature.

11.14 By relating oxygen consumption to body mass and

calculating the volume of oxygen consumed per gram of body weight in unit time.

11.15 $RQ = \dfrac{CO_2}{O_2} = \dfrac{102}{145} = 0.70$

11.16 $RQ = \dfrac{CO_2}{O_2} = \dfrac{2}{0} = \infty$

11.17 Because Man generally respires carbohydrate and fat substrates.

11.18 (a) Respiratory rate is about 17 breaths min^{-1}.
(b) Tidal volume is 450 cm^3 (average).
(c) Pulmonary ventilation is $17 \times 450\ cm^3 = 7.65\ dm^3\ min^{-1}$.
(d) Oxygen uptake is given by the slope of the line AB. Therefore oxygen consumption is 1500 cm^3 in 4 min = 375 $cm^3\ min^{-1}$.

11.19 (a)

Aerobic respiration	Photosynthesis
This is a catabolic process and results in the breakdown of carbohydrate molecules into simple inorganic compounds	An anabolic process which results in the synthesis of carbohydrate molecules from simple inorganic compounds.
Energy is incorporated into ATP for immediate use.	Energy is accumulated and stored in carbohydrate. Some ATP is formed.
Oxygen is used up.	Oxygen is released.
Carbon dioxide and water are released.	Carbon dioxide and water are used up.
The process results in a decrease in dry mass.	Results in an increase in dry mass.
In eukaryotes the process occurs in mitochondria.	In eukaryotes the process occurs in chloroplasts.
Takes place continuously throughout the lifetime of all cells, and is independent of chlorophyll and light.	Occurs only in cells possessing chlorophyll and only in the presence of light.

(b) *List of similarities between photosynthesis and aerobic respiration*
Both are energy-converting processes.
Both require mechanisms for exchange of carbon dioxide and oxygen.
Both require special organelles in eukaryotes, that is mitochondria for respiration and chloroplasts for photosynthesis; mitochondria and chloroplasts resemble prokaryotic organisms in possessing circular DNA and a prokaryote-type protein-synthesising system.
The light reactions of photosynthesis resemble cell respiration in the following ways:
(i) phosphorylation occurs (that is synthesis of ATP from ADP and P_i);
(ii) this is coupled to flow of electrons along a chain of electron carriers;
(iii) the electron carriers must be organised on membranes for coupling to take place; these are cristae in mitochondria and thylakoids in chloroplasts.
Both also involve cyclic pathways that take place in solution in the matrix around the membranes (Krebs cycle in respiration, Calvin cycle in photosynthesis).
Part of the glycolytic sequence of enzymes is common to both processes.

Chapter 12

12.1 Dry mass is used because the water content of food samples or organisms may vary and water contributes no energy.

12.2 Small birds or mammals have a much higher surface area to volume ratio than humans and therefore lose body heat relatively more rapidly. Since small mammals and birds are endothermic ('warm-blooded') like humans they must consume relatively more energy to maintain body heat. (Birds also have a higher metabolic rate and body temperature than mammals.)

12.3 In pyramid (c) the primary producers are large, such as trees, and therefore fewer in numbers than the herbivores they support. A situation like this would be obtained, for example, with aphids feeding on a rose bush, or caterpillars on a tree.

12.4

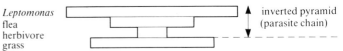

Leptomonas / flea / herbivore / grass — inverted pyramid (parasite chain)

12.5 Pyramid (d) is based on a parasite food chain, where a parasite is itself parasitised. The pyramid of numbers that results is unusual in being inverted since the organisms become progressively smaller and more numerous along the food chain. The first trophic level shown could be a tree or shrub, although parasite food chains are sometimes represented as starting with the host, whether it be plant or animal.

12.6 As conditions become suitable in the spring there is rapid growth and reproduction of the algae that form the phytoplankton (an algal bloom) and their mass exceeds that of their grazers. This is presumably followed by an increase in numbers and biomass of the primary consumers, and then by an increase in secondary consumers as materials and energy flow from one trophic level to the next. The biomass of phytoplankton decreases as the grazers increase and as the unfavourable conditions of winter return. At some point the biomass of the longer-lived consumers exceeds that of the producers. Such seasonal fluctuations in pyramids of biomass are typical of lake and ocean ecosystems based on phytoplankton.

12.7 (a) May, June and July
(b) (i) Increase in light intensity and duration, and increase in temperature coupled with the availability of nutrients. Photosynthesis and growth are therefore favoured.
(ii) Grazing by primary consumers, such as zooplankton, and decrease in production due to depletion of nutrients. (The latter is due to the dead remains of producers sinking through the lake to colder, non-circulating water.)
(iii) Decline in numbers of zooplankton. Increase in nutrients (circulation of nutrients improves in the autumn as the surface layers of water cool and mix more freely with the colder, deeper layers). Temperature and light are still favourable.
(iv) Light and temperature unfavourable for photosynthesis and growth.

12.8 Transfer of energy between trophic levels cannot be 100% efficient, so successive levels have less energy and can support, on average, fewer animals.

12.9 seed – blackbird – hawk; trophic level 3, T3
leaf litter – earthworm – blackbird – hawk, T4
leaf – caterpillar – beetle – insectivorous bird – hawk, T5
rose bush (sap) – aphid – ladybird – spider – insectivorous bird – hawk, T6

12.10 Blue-green bacteria and some other bacteria are also photosynthetic (they are prokaryotes, not plants). Chemosynthetic bacteria are also autotrophic (table 9.1) and therefore make a contribution to primary productivity. The total contribution of all these organisms is small compared with autotrophic eukaryotes (photosynthetic protoctista and plants).

12.11 (a) 24×10^6 kJ m^{-2} yr^{-1}

(b) 1.3%

(c) 800, 200 and 69 700 kJ m^{-2} yr^{-1} respectively

(d) 114×10^3 kJ m^{-2} yr^{-1}

(e) Grasses and herbs (producers), seed-eating birds, common green grasshoppers and field mice (primary consumers), spiders (secondary consumers)

(f) All except grasses and herbs

(g) Other primary or secondary consumers, decomposers, detritivores (also possibly emigration)

12.12 (a) (i) ×2 (ii) ×500 (iii) ×2 500 (iv) ×3 750

(b) DDT is subject to progressive concentration as it passes along the food chain. This suggests that it is a persistent chemical, not easily broken down, and that it is stored rather than metabolised in living organisms. (In fact, it remains active for 10–15 years in soil.)

(c) (i) and (ii) 4th trophic level (top carnivore) (iii) 2nd trophic level (herbivore)

(d) DDT has spread all over the world as a result of two factors. First, it is carried at very low concentrations in water. If it is washed off agricultural land and into rivers some of it reaches the sea and becomes concentrated in marine food chains. Penguins feed on fish and are part of these food chains. Secondly, DDT can be carried in the atmosphere, both because it is volatile and because it is sprayed as a dust which can be carried by wind systems over large distances.

(e) (i) A small proportion of the original midges were resistant to DDD and these were not killed by the spraying procedure. Between sprays their numbers increased and after successive sprays they continued to breed and eventually constituted the greater part of the population. In other words the population had undergone intensive selection pressure (see chapter 25).

(ii) The data given suggest that DDD (and therefore DDT) is stored predominantly in fatty tissues. (This is because DDD and DDT are soluble in fat rather than water.) During times of food shortage, fat is mobilised and used so that the DDD or DDT accumulated over a long period is released into the bloodstream in relatively high concentrations.

(f) It has been suggested that the high death toll of birds in the winter of 1962–3 compared with 1946–7 was due to the additional effects of DDT mobilisation from fatty tissues. In 1946–7 the use of DDT was limited; in the late 1950s and early 1960s its use was widespread.

12.13 (1) Maximum possible specificity so that it has minimal effects on species other than pests. The greater the specificity, however, the smaller the potential market and the more expensive it will be!

(2) Inexpensive to manufacture.

(3) Relatively non-persistent, if toxic to non-pest species.

12.14 (a) Deforestation reduces the total world volume of photosynthetic material and thus reduces consumption of atmospheric carbon dioxide in photosynthesis.

(b) Removal of the tree canopy exposes the forest floor to sunlight and warmer temperatures. In forests or woodlands with significant litter and soil humus contents this exposure will favour accelerated rates of decomposition and carbon dioxide release.

12.15 BOD of discharge
BOD of receiving water

Nature of organic material
Total organic load of the river
Temperature
Extent of aeration from atmosphere (varies with wind etc.)
Dissolved oxygen in stream
Numbers and type of bacteria in effluent and stream
Ammonia content of effluent

12.16 Geographical barriers, such as oceans; ecological barriers, such as unfavourable habitats separating areas of favourable habitats; distance over which dispersal must operate; air and water currents; size and nature of invasion areas

12.17 Various environmental factors may be altered.

(a) *Light* – Light intensity at the forest floor may be only 1–6% of that striking the canopy.

– Light quality may also change: light passing through leaves is enriched in far-red light (shorter wavelengths of red being filtered out). This has physiological implications for the phytochrome system (see chapter 15).

(b) *Temperature* – Daily and seasonal fluctuations of temperature are less within a forest than outside it. Lower maximum and higher minimum temperatures are usual. The mean temperature is relatively lower in summer and higher in winter compared with the air temperature outside the canopy.

(c) *Wind* – Plants below the canopy are protected from wind, and wind speeds on average are only 40–80% of those outside.

(d) *Moisture* – Interception of rainfall and subsequent evaporation from the canopy will reduce the amount of water reaching the vegetation below. Relative humidity is usually greater in the woodland than outside, partly as a result of lower temperatures during the day.

12.18 Birth rate $= \dfrac{10\,000}{500\,000} \times 1\,000 = 20$ per thousand head per year.

12.19 (a) Two eggs from each female must, on average, survive.

(b)

	Number of fertilised eggs that must die for stable population	Pre-reproductive mortality
oyster	$(100 \times 10^6) - 2$	>99.9%
codfish	$(9 \times 10^6) - 2$	>99.9%
plaice	$(35 \times 10^4) - 2$	>99.9%
salmon	$(10 \times 10^4) - 2$	>99.9%
stickleback	498	498/500 = 99.6%
winter moth	198	99.0%
mouse	48	96.0%
dogfish	18	90.0%
penguin	6	75.0%
elephant	3	60.0%
Victorian Englishwoman	8	80.0%

(c) The stickleback and dogfish give birth to live young, that is they are viviparous. Therefore fewer eggs need to be produced owing to the greater degree of parental involvement in the development of offspring. Also, the female parent could not physically support any greater numbers of offspring.

12.20 Population (b), since a high percentage of individuals would die before reproductive age is reached. Population (a) would have to combine its high survival rate with low reproductive rate to maintain a stable population size.

12.21 (*a*) Out of 3 200 eggs, 640 survive, so 2 560 die – a mortality of 80%.

(*b*) Out of 640 fry, 64 survive, so 576 die – a mortality of 90%.

(*c*) Out of 64 smolts, 2 survive, so 62 die – a mortality of about 97%.

The total pre-reproductive mortality for salmon is 3 198 out of 3 200 = 99.97% (see fig 12.21(ans)).

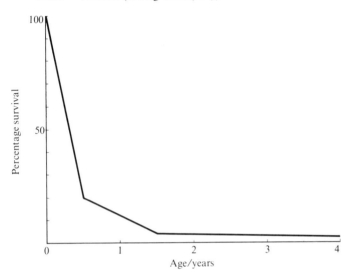

Fig 12.21 (ans) *Graph showing pre-reproductive mortality for salmon*

12.22 (*a*) *S. nemoralis* (*b*) *S. nemoralis* (*c*) *S. rugosa* (*d*) The results for *S. speciosa* show that it has flexibility of response to its environment. When colonising a woodland site, which is a stable K-selecting habitat, it behaves more like a K-strategist in devoting less biomass to reproduction than when it grows in the disturbed habitat of an earlier successional stage.

A general conclusion that might be drawn is that some species may have variable levels of '*r*' depending on environmental conditions. This in fact appears to be true for some plant and animal populations. If either strategy is selected for over a period of time, speciation might occur as has happened with *S. rugosa* and *S. nemoralis*.

12.23 (*a*) A sigmoid (S-shaped) growth curve.

(*b*) Food and space. Food is more likely in this case.

(*c*) Faster reproductive rate. More efficient feeding. Greater resistance to toxic waste products, either of *Paramecium* or of bacteria growing in the same culture (*P. aurelia* has been shown to be more resistant than *P. caudatum*). Production of a poison or growth inhibitor (allelopathy). Predation.

12.24 (*a*) Natural variation in the target population leaves some resistant survivors.

(*b*) LD$_{50}$ toxicity definition means that not all of the target population will be eliminated, just sufficient of the damaging surplus.

(*a*) and (*b*) together ensure a viable pool of resistant organisms from which the population can recover to be a pest once more.

Thought questions

1 (*a*) E.g. acid rain

Costs	*Benefits*
(i) Local and/or long distance air pollution hazard may be caused.	(i) Cheaper electricity generation gives more profits to generating board.
(ii) Use of high-level dis-	(ii) Cheaper supplies for

persal in the atmosphere distributes pollution over large distances. Countries far removed from the catchment of the generator may experience serious pollution requiring expensive remedial action.

(iii) Crop damage

(iv) Human and animal health hazard

domestic industrial consumers in the catchment of that generator.

(*b*) The answer to (*b*) should promote a lively discussion. The main benefit is a cleaner environment and reduction of the hidden costs of industrial activity. Environmental costs are often not fully accounted in conventional cost:benefit analyses.

The chief snag is that the polluter may pass on the extra costs of pollution control to the consumer. The system will only work if the consumer supports the clean manufacturer by buying the more expensive product, even if cheaper alternatives produced by the manufacturers not using pollution control are available.

An obvious related example currently seen in many British supermarkets is the relative price of organically produced food compared with fruit and vegetables grown under conventional farming systems using chemical fertilisers and pest control. Other difficulties lie with enforcing pollution legislation. A possible benefit is revenue from the manufacture and export of pollution control technology, for example, W. Germany exports desulphurisation technology.

2 A population with a common gene pool (deme) will slowly evolve over time. If the population is very small its members may become inbred and lose vigour. In the recent past the black rhino has been hunted, for its horn, to near extinction. Each local population is now a tiny fraction of the original population and physically isolated. Such animals will be increasingly inbred. Outbreeding strengthens genetic diversity and where populations are very small this may be important for the health of the animals. Semen may be collected from anaesthetised wild or captive males and used to inseminate anaesthetised captive females at oestrus (the time of ovulation). Such artificial insemination technology makes it less necessary to move the animals themselves yet allows the spread of genes. It also makes possible the storage of genetic material (by cryopreservation – deep-frozen semen) in the event of a lack of males, in a local population, where females are still found.

Student action/role-playing game (p. 437)

The main points 'for' and 'against' are summarised below.

For

(*a*) A larger proportion of national timber needs could be supplied. Home-grown timber currently supplies 10% of Britain's timber needs.

(*b*) Job creation in areas of rural unemployment.

(*c*) Increased landscape and habitat (creates woods) diversity.

(*d*) Source of local revenue.

(*e*) Long-term investment for land-owner and nation.

Against

(*a*) Exotic conifer monocultures are vulnerable to disease and support little wildlife at the closed canopy stage. (In the early scrub stages they can be good habitats, but unless managed on a well-planned rotation basis this is short-lived.)

(*b*) Deep ploughing destroys peatlands leading to permanent species loss and alien landscape change (an eyesore to some).

(c) Serious detrimental changes in land drainage and water quality may result.

(d) The promised local jobs may not materialise. Forestry is not very labour-intensive and requires prior expertise.

(e) Conifer forests are poor recreation areas which may deter tourism.

In a role-playing exercise students could argue these, and other points, as representatives of major interested parties. These could include

(a) Nature Conservancy Council
(b) Countryside Commission for Scotland
(c) Council for the Protection of Rural Scotland
(d) Friends of the Earth
(e) Royal Society for the Protection of Birds
(f) Forestry Commission
(g) Estate owner(s)
(h) Scottish Tourist Board
(i) Water Authority
(j) Local and strategic regional planning authorities
(k) Local residents
(l) The local Member of Parliament

An eminent chairperson and supporting experts/dignitaries (two or three) will also be needed. Their role is to report to national government advising an appropriate course of action in the light of evidence presented.

Chapter 13

13.1

Fresh mass of soil $= 60 \text{ g}$

dry mass of soil $= 45 \text{ g}$

therefore mass of water $= 60 \text{ g} - 45 \text{ g} = 15 \text{ g}$

therefore percentage water content of fresh soil $= \frac{15}{60} \times 100 = 25\%$

Dry mass of soil $= 45 \text{ g}$

dry mass of soil after combustion $= 30 \text{ g}$

therefore mass of organic material $= 15 \text{ g}$

therefore percentage organic content of fresh soil $= \frac{15}{60} \times 100 = 25\%$

13.2 43%

13.3 36%

13.4 4 230

Chapter Fourteen

Transport

The exchange of substances between individual cells and their environments takes place by the physical process of diffusion (which includes osmosis) and the active processes of active transport and endocytosis or exocytosis. Within cells, substances generally move by diffusion, but active processes, such as cytoplasmic streaming, can also occur. Over short distances these means of transport are rapid and efficient and in unicellular organisms, and multicellular organisms which possess a large surface area to volume ratio, they operate efficiently enough for specific transport systems to be unnecessary. For example, respiratory gases are exchanged by diffusion between the body surface and the environment in small organisms such as the earthworm.

In larger and more complex organisms, cells may be too widely separated from each other and from their external environments for these processes to be adequate. Specialised long-distance transport systems which can move substances more rapidly become necessary. Materials are generally moved by a mass flow system, **mass flow** being the bulk transport of materials from one point to another as a result of a pressure difference between the two points. It is a characteristic of mass flow that all the materials, whether they be in solution or suspension, are swept along at similar speeds as in a river, unlike diffusion, where molecules move independently of each other according to their diffusion gradients. Some of the mass flow systems of plants and animals are summarised in table 14.1.

Transport in plants

Table 14.2 page 474 summarises the major groups of substances that move through plants and gives details of the major routes and mechanisms for uptake, transport and elimination.

The movement of substances through the conducting, or vascular, tissues of plants is termed **translocation**. In vascular plants the vascular tissues are highly specialised and are called **xylem** and **phloem**. Xylem translocates mainly water, mineral salts, some organic nitrogen and hormones from the roots to the aerial parts of the plant. Phloem translocates a variety of organic and inorganic solutes, mainly from the expanded leaves to other parts of the plant.

The study of translocation has important economic applications. For example, it is useful to know how herbicides, fungicides, growth regulators and nutrients enter plants, and the routes that they take through plants, in order to know how best to apply them, and to judge possible effects that they might have. Also, plant pathogens such as fungi, bacteria and viruses are sometimes translocated and such knowledge could influence treatment or preventive measures. In the 1960s, for example, a new group of fungicides was introduced which were described as **systemic** because they were translocated throughout plants. They provide longer-term, and more thorough, protection from important diseases like mildews.

Table 14.1 Some mass flow systems of animals and plants.

Mass flow system	Material(s) moved	Driving force	Location
Plants			
vascular system:			
xylem (chapter 14)	mainly water and mineral salts	transpiration and root pressure	vascular plants
phloem (chapter 14)	mainly organic food, e.g. sucrose	mechanism not fully understood	
Animals			
alimentary system (chapter 10)	food and water	muscles of alimentary canal	Annelida, Mollusca, Arthropoda, Chordata
respiratory system (chapter 11)	air or water	respiratory muscles	Mollusca, Chordata
blood vascular system (chapter 14)	blood	heart or contractile blood vessels	Annelida, Mollusca, Arthropoda, Chordata
lymphatic system (chapter 14)	lymph	general muscular activity in the body	Mammalia

Table 14.2 Movement of substances through plants.

	Uptake	Transport	Elimination
Water			
route	root hairs	xylem	stomata (small loss from cuticle and lenticels)
mechanism	osmosis	mass flow	diffusion of water vapour
Solutes			
route	root hairs	xylem (mainly inorganic solutes) phloem (mainly organic solutes)	shedding of leaves, bark, fruits and seeds; otherwise retained until death or passed to next generation in embryo of seed
mechanism	diffusion or active transport	mass flow	controlled by plant growth substances
Gases*			
route	stomata, lenticels, root epidermis	intercellular spaces and through cells	stomata, lenticels, root epidermis
mechanism	diffusion	diffusion	diffusion

* Movement of gases is considered in further detail in chapter 11.

14.1 Plant water relations

14.1.1 Osmosis

An understanding of plant water relations depends upon an understanding of the physical processes of osmosis and diffusion, which are explained in section A1.5. There it is pointed out that osmosis can be regarded as a special kind of diffusion in which water molecules are the only molecules diffusing owing to the presence of a partially permeable membrane which does not allow the passage of solute particles. Water molecules move from a region of their high concentration (a dilute solution) to a region of their low concentration (a more concentrated solution) through a partially permeable membrane. It is thought that this process may occur more rapidly than can be accounted for by straightforward diffusion, and that mass flow is involved because the membrane is also permeable to some solute molecules. It can, however, be largely explained in terms of diffusion.

14.1.2 Terms used

In 1988 the Institute of Biology recommended the standardisation of the terms used in describing water movement through membranes. Use of the term **water potential**, which had come to be accepted by plant physiologists as the most fundamental and useful concept for understanding water movement, was recommended, and is therefore used here. The two main factors determining the water potential of plant cells are solute concentration and the pressure generated when water enters and inflates plant cells. These are expressed in the terms **solute potential** and **pressure potential** respectively. All of these terms are explained below.

A useful aid in the understanding of these terms is the computer program *Water balance in plants* produced by Netherhall Educational Software (CUP) for use in schools. The Teacher's Handbook provides background information which, in addition to considering the terms used in describing water movement, provides some useful tables showing typical values of water potential in different environments (such as atmosphere, soils, salt-marshes) and plant tissues (for example mesophytes, desert plants, water plants). Further reference to this program is made in section 14.1.9.

14.1.3 Water potential (symbol ψ, the Greek letter psi)*

Water potential is a fundamental term derived from thermodynamics (see section A1.6). Water molecules possess kinetic energy, which means that in liquid or gaseous form they move about rapidly and randomly from one location to another. The greater the concentration of water molecules in a system, the greater the total kinetic energy of water molecules in that system and the higher its so-called water potential. Pure water therefore has the highest water potential. If two systems containing water are in contact (such as soil and atmosphere, or cell and solution) the random movements of water molecules will result in the net movement of water molecules from the system with the higher energy to the system with the lower energy until the concentration of water molecules in both systems is equal. This process is called **diffusion** (see section A1.5.1). In thermodynamic terms, water molecules (like other molecules) move according to the laws of entropy from a region of higher to lower 'free energy'. This movement down gradients of free energy is diffusion.

Water potential can be measured in energy units (for example joules per m^3), but is more commonly expressed in pressure units by biologists (such as pascals; 1 pascal = 1 newton per m^2).** Since pure water has the highest water potential, this is used as a reference. By convention, the water potential of pure water at atmospheric pressure (at a defined temperature) is zero.

---

* Technically, ψ means potential and water potential should be represented as ψ_w. Since in living systems the solvent we are concerned with is always water, it is simpler to use ψ and assume the w.

The following main points emerge:

(a) pure water has the maximum water potential, which by definition is zero;

(b) water **always** moves from a region of higher ψ to one of lower ψ;

(c) all solutions have lower water potentials than pure water and therefore have negative values of ψ (at atmospheric pressure and a defined temperature);

(d) **osmosis** can be defined as the movement of water molecules from a region of higher water potential to a region of lower water potential through a partially permeable membrane:

(e) the **water potential** of a system may be defined as the difference between the free energy of water in that system and the free energy of pure water at atmospheric pressure and a defined temperature.

Advantage of using water potential

Water potential can be regarded as the tendency of water to leave a system. A higher (less negative) water potential implies a greater tendency to leave. If two systems are in contact, water will move from the system with the higher water potential to the one with the lower water potential. The two systems do not necessarily have to be separated by a membrane.

Using the term water potential, the tendency for water to move between any two systems can therefore be measured, not just from cell to cell in a plant, but also, for example, from soil to root, from leaf to air or from soil to air. Water can be said to move through a plant down a continuous gradient of water potential from soil to air. The steeper the potential gradient, the faster the flow of water along it.

14.1.4 Solute potential, ψ_s

The term solute potential (symbol ψ_s) is recommended by the Institute of Biology, although osmotic potential is also commonly used and has the same meaning. (The disadvantage of using osmotic potential is that it is often confused with osmotic pressure. As explained in A1.5.2, osmotic pressure increases as osmotic potential decreases).

The effect of dissolving solute molecules in pure water is to reduce the concentration of water molecules and hence to lower the water potential. All solutions therefore have lower water potentials than pure water. The magnitude of this lowering is known as the **solute potential**. In other words, solute potential is a measure of the change in water potential of a system due to the presence of solute molecules. ψ_s is always negative. The more solute molecules present, the lower (more negative) is ψ_s (see also

** Pressure was formerly measured in atmospheres (atm), but now pascals are used (Pa) (see section A4.3).

1 Pa	$= 1\,Nm^{-2}$ (N = newton)
1 bar	$= 0.987\,atm = 10^5\,Pa = 100\,kPa$
1 atm	$= 1.0132\,bar = 1.0132 \times 10^5\,Pa$
1 000 kPa	$= 1\,MPa$

section A1.5.2). For a solution at atmospheric pressure, $\psi = \psi_s$.

14.1.5 Pressure potential, ψ_p

If a pressure greater than atmospheric pressure is applied to pure water or a solution, its water potential increases. It is equivalent to pumping water from one place to another. Such a situation may arise in living systems. For example, water potential of blood plasma is raised to a positive value by the high blood pressure in the glomerulus of the kidney. Also, when water enters plant cells by osmosis, pressure may build up inside the cell making the cell turgid and increasing the pressure potential (section 14.1.8). Pressure potential is usually positive, but in certain circumstances, as in xylem when water is under tension (negative pressure) it may be negative.

Summary

Water potential is affected by both solute potential and pressure potential, and the following equation summarises the relationship between the two terms.

$$\underset{\text{water potential}}{\psi} = \underset{\substack{\text{solute}\\\text{potential}}}{\psi_s} + \underset{\substack{\text{pressure}\\\text{potential}}}{\psi_p}$$

14.1.6 Movement of water between solutions by osmosis

The terms mentioned above can only be used with confidence if they are properly understood. Question 14.1 on page 476, together with questions 14.5–14.8, can be a useful test of this understanding.

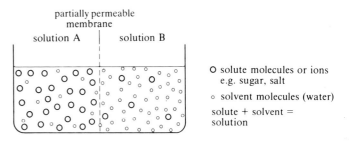

Fig 14.1 *Two solutions separated by a partially permeable membrane*

14.1.7 Osmosis and plant cells

The partially permeable membranes of particular relevance in the water relations of plant cells are shown in fig 14.2. The cell wall is usually freely permeable to substances in solution, so is not an osmotic barrier. The cell contains a large central vacuole whose contents, the cell sap or vacuolar sap, contribute to the solute potential of the cell. The two important membranes are the cell surface membrane and the tonoplast. In plant water relations, the cell surface membrane, cytoplasm and tonoplast can be regarded as acting together as one partially permeable membrane.

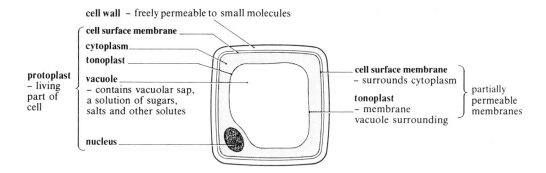

Fig 14.2 *Partially permeable membranes of a typical vacuolated plant cell. Note that the cell surface membrane would normally be pressed tightly up against the cell wall*

cell wall – freely permeable to small molecules

cell surface membrane

cytoplasm

tonoplast

protoplast – living part of cell

vacuole – contains vacuolar sap, a solution of sugars, salts and other solutes

nucleus

cell surface membrane – surrounds cytoplasm

tonoplast – membrane vacuole surrounding

partially permeable membranes

14.1 Study fig 14.1 in which two solutions are separated by a partially permeable membrane.
(a) Which solution has the higher concentration of water molecules?
(b) Which solution is more concentrated, that is has the higher concentration of solute?
(c) In which direction will osmosis occur?
(d) Which of the following two values of ψ is higher: (i) $-2\,000\,kPa$, (ii) $-1\,000\,kPa$?
(e) Which solution has the higher water potential (ψ)?
(f) Which solution has the higher solute potential?
(g) What is the relationship between ψ_s and ψ of a solution at atmospheric pressure?

Experiment 14.1: To investigate osmosis in living plant cells

Materials

onion bulb or young rhubarb epidermis	distilled water
microscope	1 M sucrose solution
2 slides and cover-slips	2 teat pipettes
scalpel and forceps	filter paper

Method

Remove a strip of epidermis from the inner surface of one of the fleshy storage leaves of the onion bulb, or from the young rhubarb petiole. Rhubarb has the advantage of having coloured cell sap, but onion epidermis is easier to peel off. The epidermis can be removed by first slitting it with a scalpel, then lifting and tearing back the single layer of cells with fingers or forceps. Quickly transfer the epidermal strip to a slide and add two or three drops of distilled water. Carefully add a cover-slip and examine the cells with a microscope. Identify and draw a few epidermal cells. Repeat using another strip of epidermis and 1 M sucrose solution instead of distilled water. Observe the strip over a period of 15 min and draw any changes observed in one or more representative cells at high power. The possibility of reversing the process observed can be investigated by irrigating with distilled water under the cover-slip to wash away the sucrose solution. Use filter paper to absorb any excess liquid.

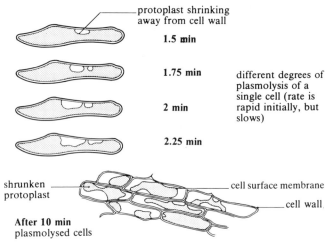

protoplast shrinking away from cell wall

1.5 min

1.75 min

2 min

different degrees of plasmolysis of a single cell (rate is rapid initially, but slows)

2.25 min

shrunken protoplast

cell surface membrane

cell wall

After 10 min plasmolysed cells

Fig 14.3 *Appearance of onion epidermal cells during plasmolysis. Strips of epidermal cells were left in 1 M sucrose solution for varying lengths of time*

Results

Fig 14.3 shows the appearance of onion epidermal cells left in 1 M sucrose solution for varying lengths of time.

14.1.8 Plasmolysis and pressure potential

If a cell is in contact with a solution of lower water potential than its own contents, then water leaves the cell by osmosis through the cell surface membrane. Water is lost first from the cytoplasm and then from the vacuole through the tonoplast. The protoplast, that is the living contents of the cell within the cell wall, shrinks and eventually pulls away from the cell wall. This process is called **plasmolysis**, and the cell is said to be **plasmolysed**. The point at which **plasmolysis** is just about to happen is called **incipient plasmolysis**. At incipient plasmolysis the protoplast has just ceased to exert any pressure against the cell wall, so the cell is **flaccid**. Water will continue to leave the protoplast until its contents are of the same water potential as the external solution. No further shrinkage then occurs.

14.2 What occupies the space between the cell wall and the shrunken protoplast in plasmolysed cells?

The process of plasmolysis is usually reversible without

permanent damage to the cell. If a plasmolysed cell is placed in pure water or a solution of higher water potential than the contents of the cell, water enters the cell by osmosis. As the volume of the protoplast increases it begins to exert pressure against the cell wall and stretches it. The wall is relatively rigid, so the pressure inside the cell rises rapidly. The pressure exerted by the protoplast against the cell wall is called the **pressure potential** (ψ_p). As the pressure potential of the cell gradually increases, due to water entering by osmosis, the cell becomes **turgid**. Full turgidity, that is maximum ψ_p, is achieved when a cell is placed in pure water. When the tendency for water to enter a cell is exactly balanced by pressure potential, the amount of water leaving the cell equals that entering the cell. There is no further net uptake of water and the cell is now in equilibrium with the surrounding solution. The contents of the cell are still likely to be of lower solute potential than the external solution because only a small amount of water is needed to raise the pressure potential to the equilibrium point, and this is not sufficient to dilute the cell contents significantly. Pressure potential therefore accounts for the fact that at equilibrium the solute potential of a plant cell can still be lower than that of the external solution.

Pressure potential is a real pressure rather than a potential one, and can only develop to any extent if a cell wall is present. Animal cells have no cell wall and the cell surface membrane is too delicate to prevent the cell expanding and bursting in a solution of higher water potential. Animal cells must therefore be protected by osmoregulation (chapter 19).

> **14.3** What is the ψ_p of a flaccid cell?
> **14.4** Which organisms, apart from plants, possess cell walls?

14.1.9 Movement of water between solutions and cells by osmosis

When considering the tendency for water to move by osmosis between a plant cell and an external solution, the water potential of the cell must be compared with the water potential of the solution, since water always moves from higher to lower water potential. The water potential of the cell must equal the water potential of the external solution at equilibrium.

As previously stated, at atmospheric pressure the water potential of a solution is determined by its solute potential:

$$\psi^{solution} = \psi_s^{solution}$$

The water potential of a cell is determined by two factors, its solute potential and its pressure potential. As with the external solution, the lower the solute potential of the solution inside the cell, the lower its water potential. However, an increase in pressure potential inside a cell increases the tendency for water to leave the cell (or resists

water entry), that is an increase in pressure potential increases the water potential of the cell. This can be summarised in the equation below:

$$\psi^{cell} = \psi_s^{cell} + \psi_p^{cell}$$

At equilibrium, $\psi^{cell} = \psi^{solution}$ or $\psi^{int} = \psi^{ext}$

where 'int' means internal solution, and 'ext' means external solution.

The problems below are useful in testing understanding of the terms used so far. It will be necessary to remember the following points:
(1) water always moves from higher water potential to lower water potential;
(2) for two systems to be in equilibrium, they must have equal water potential;
(3) in most cases the quantities of water entering and leaving plant cells are not sufficient to significantly change their solute potentials (solute potential is therefore assumed to remain constant in the following calculations) though pressure potentials do change significantly.

> **14.5** Describe what happens if a cell at incipient plasmolysis, with a ψ_s of $-2\,000\,kPa$, is placed in a solution of $\psi = -1\,200\,kPa$. What are the ψ and ψ_s of the cell at equilibrium?
> **14.6** If the ψ of the vacuolar sap of a cell in equilibrium with pure water at atmospheric pressure is $-1\,100\,kPa$. What is its ψ_p?
> **14.7** If a cell is equilibrated with pure water and then transferred to a sucrose solution with a water potential of $-800\,kPa$,
> (a) what is the difference in ψ between the cell contents and the external solution at the time of transfer?
> (b) would water enter or leave the cell?
> (c) would the ψ_p of the cell increase or decrease?

Further appreciation of the dynamic nature of events can be gained by using the computer program *Water balance in plants*, already mentioned in section 14.1.2. This demonstrates by graphics the effects of different concentrations of external solutions on the whole plant (degree of wilting), blocks of tissues such as potato chips, layers of cells such as epidermal strips (fig 14.4a) and single cells. It also includes a more-detailed molecular model (see fig 14.4b).

14.1.10 Movement of water between cells by osmosis

Consider the situation in fig 14.4, in which two vacuolated cells possessing different water potentials are in contact.

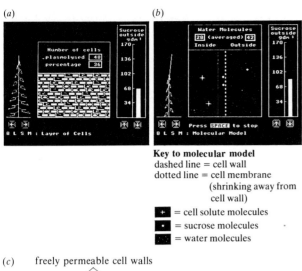

Key to molecular model
dashed line = cell wall
dotted line = cell membrane
(shrinking away from cell wall)
[+] = cell solute molecules
[•] = sucrose molecules
[▓] = water molecules

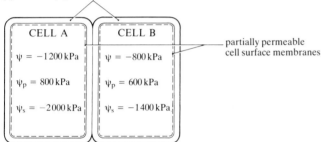

freely permeable cell walls

CELL A	CELL B
$\psi = -1200\,kPa$	$\psi = -800\,kPa$
$\psi_p = 800\,kPa$	$\psi_p = 600\,kPa$
$\psi_s = -2000\,kPa$	$\psi_s = -1400\,kPa$

partially permeable cell surface membranes

Fig 14.4 (a) *Epidermal strip* (b) *molecular model* (c) *two adjacent vacuolated cells*

14.8 (a) Which cell has the higher water potential?
(b) In which direction will water move by osmosis?
(c) What will be the water potential of the cells at equilibrium?
(d) What will be the solute potentials and pressure potentials of the cells at equilibrium?

Experiment 14.2: To determine the mean solute potential of the cell sap in a sample of plant cells using the method of incipient plasmolysis

There are several methods available for determining the solute potential of plant cells, but the most convenient is that of incipient plasmolysis. It makes use of the following relationships:

(1) ψ of a cell = $\psi_s + \psi_p$; ψ of a solution = ψ_s.
(2) $\psi^{cell} = \psi^{solution}$ when the two are in equilibrium.

Samples of the tissue being investigated are allowed to come to equilibrium in a range of solutions of different concentrations (water potentials) and the aim is to find which solution causes incipient plasmolysis, that is shrinkage of the protoplasts to the point where they just begin to pull away from the cell walls. At this point pressure potential is zero since no pressure is exerted by the protoplasts against the cell walls, so $\psi^{cell} = \psi_s^{cell} = \psi^{solution} = \psi_s^{solution}$ (from (1) and (2) above). In other words,

the solution causing incipient plasmolysis has the same solute potential as the cell sap.

In practice, solute potential varies between cells in the same tissue and so some plasmolyse in more dilute solutions than others. Incipient plasmolysis is said to have been reached when 50% of the cells have plasmolysed. At this point 50% of the cells are unplasmolysed and the average cell can be said to be at incipient plasmolysis. The solute potential obtained is a mean value for the tissue.

Materials

onion bulb or rhubarb petiole
6 petri dishes
6 test-tubes
test-tube rack
labels or wax pencil
2 ×10 cm³ or 25 cm³ graduated pipettes
2 × 100 cm³ beakers
brush (fine paintbrush)
distilled water
1 M sucrose solution
fine forceps
Pasteur pipettes
slides and cover-slips
microscope
graph paper
razor blade or sharp scalpel

Method

(An alternative method using beetroot is described after this first method.)

(1) Label six petri dishes and six test-tubes appropriately for each of the following sucrose solutions: 0.3 M, 0.35 M, 0.4 M, 0.45 M, 0.5 M and 0.6 M.
(2) Using a 10 cm³ or 25 cm³ graduated pipette, a beaker of distilled water and a beaker of 1M sucrose solution, make up 20 cm³ of sucrose solution of the required concentration in each test-tube. Table 14.3 shows the amounts used.
(3) Make sure that the solutions are mixed thoroughly by shaking. This is very important. Add the solutions to the appropriate petri dishes.
(4) **Onion.** Remove one of the fleshy storage leaves of an onion. While it is still attached to the leaf, cut the inner epidermis into six squares of approximately 5 mm side using a razor blade or scalpel. Remove each of

Table 14.3 Sucrose dilution table for experiment 14.2.

Concentration of sucrose solution	Volume of distilled water/cm³	Volume of 1M sucrose solution/cm³
0.30 M	14	6
0.35 M	13	7
0.40 M	12	8
0.45 M	11	9
0.50 M	10	10
0.60 M	8	12

the six squares using fine forceps and immediately place one square of tissue into each petri dish. Agitate each dish gently to ensure that the tissue is completely immersed and washed with the sucrose solution. Leave for about 20 min.

Rhubarb. Score the outer epidermis into six squares of approximately 5 mm side and remove the epidermis as described for the onion.

(5) Remove the tissue from the 0.60 M solution and, using a brush, mount it on a slide in sucrose solution of the same concentration. Add a cover-slip and examine with a microscope.

(6) Select a suitable area of cells using low power. Switch to a medium or high power objective and move the slide through the selected area, recording the state (plasmolysed or unplasmolysed) of the first 100 cells viewed. Cells in which there is any sign of the protoplast pulling away from the cell wall should be counted as plasmolysed.

(7) Repeat for all other squares of tissue, mounting them in their respective solutions.

(8) From the total number of cells counted and number plasmolysed determine the percentage of plasmolysed cells for each solution. Plot a graph of percentage of plasmolysed cells (vertical axis) against molarity of sucrose solution (horizontal axis).

(9) Read off from the graph the molarity of the sucrose solution which causes 50% of the cells to plasmolyse.

(10) Plot a graph of solute potential (vertical axis) against molarity of sucrose solution (horizontal axis) using the data provided in table 14.4.

Table 14.4 Solute potentials of given sucrose solutions at 20 °C.

Concentration of sucrose solution (molarity)	Solute potential/kPa	Solute potential/atm
0.05	−130	−1.3
0.10	−260	−2.6
0.15	−410	−4.0
0.20	−540	−5.3
0.25	−680	−6.7
0.30	−820	−8.1
0.35	−970	−9.6
0.40	−1 120	−11.1
0.45	−1 280	−12.6
0.50	−1 450	−14.3
0.55	−1 620	−16.0
0.60	−1 800	−17.8
0.65	−1 980	−19.5
0.70	−2 180	−21.5
0.75	−2 370	−23.3
0.80	−2 580	−25.5
0.85	−2 790	−27.5
0.90	−3 010	−29.7
0.95	−3 250	−32.1
1.00	−3 510	−34.6
1.50	−6 670	−65.8
2.00	−11 810	−116.6

(11) From this graph determine the solute potential of the solution which caused 50% plasmolysis. This is equal to the mean solute potential of the cell sap.

Results

A typical graph for onion epidermis is shown in fig 14.5. Similar results are obtained using rhubarb epidermis.

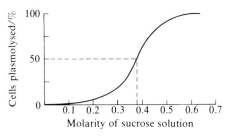

Fig 14.5 *Percentage of onion epidermal cells plasmolysed in different concentrations of sucrose solution*

14.9 What is the solute potential of onion epidermal cells if 50% of the cells were plasmolysed in 0.38 M sucrose solution?

Use of beetroot tissue

Beetroot is a less convenient material to use, but a combination of this experiment with experiment 14.3 would enable an estimation of the pressure potential of beetroot cells to be made, although it should be pointed out that different beetroots may have different water potentials and solute potentials. Beetroots normally have a lower solute potential than onion or rhubarb because they have more sugar and inorganic salts in their vacuoles.

Modifications to the method are as follows.

(1)–(3) As for onion and rhubarb experiment above, except use solutions of the following concentrations: 0.4 M, 0.45 M, 0.5 M, 0.55 M, 0.6 M and 0.7 M.

(4) Cut a rectangular 'chip' of beetroot with square ends of approximately 5 × 5 mm. Thin sections (maximum 0.5 mm thick) should be cut from the end of this chip using a razor blade. The thinner the sections, the easier it is to count plasmolysed cells. The coloured sap enables easy detection of plasmolysis. The sections could be cut immediately before the practical class and kept in distilled water. Add several sections of beetroot tissue to each sucrose solution, and leave for about 30 min. Meanwhile examine similar sections, mounted in distilled water, with a microscope to become familiar with the appearance of the unplasmolysed cells. The margins of the sections are likely to be thinner and easier to examine. Some damaged cells may be colourless, and some small cells near vascular tissue may be seen. These can be ignored in subsequent counts.

(5)–(11) As before, starting with tissue from 0.7 M solution.

Results

A set of results obtained for beetroot is given in table 14.5.

Table 14.5 Percentage of beetroot cells plasmolysed in different concentrations of sucrose solution.

Molarity of sucrose solution	Percentage of plasmolysed cells*
0.30	2.5
0.40	3.5
0.45	13.5
0.50	74.0
0.55	100.0
0.60	100.0

* Sample size 200 cells.

14.10 What is the mean solute potential of the beetroot cells used in this experiment? (You will need to draw a graph to determine this.)

Experiment 14.3: To determine the water potential of a plant tissue

Water potential is a measure of the tendency of water molecules to pass from one place to another. The principle in this experiment is to discover a solution, of known water potential, in which the tissue being examined neither gains nor loses water. Samples of the tissue are allowed to come to equilibrium in a range of solutions of different concentrations and the solution which induces neither an increase nor a decrease in mass or volume of the tissue has the same water potential as the tissue. The method described below relies on volume rather than mass changes.

Materials

fresh potato tuber or fresh beetroot
6 petri dishes
5 test-tubes
test-tube rack
labels or wax pencil
2×10 cm^3 or 25 cm^3 graduated pipettes
tile
distilled water
1 M sucrose solution
scalpel or knife
2×100 cm^3 beakers
graph paper

Method

(1) Label six petri dishes appropriately, one for each of the following: distilled water, 0.1 M, 0.25 M, 0.5 M, 0.75 M and 1.0 M sucrose solutions. Label five test-tubes appropriately, one for each of the sucrose solutions.

(2) Using a graduated pipette, a beaker of distilled water and a beaker of 1 M sucrose solution, make up 20 cm^3 of sucrose solution of the required concentration in each test-tube. A dilution table is useful as described in experiment 14.2 (table 14.3).

(3) Shake the tubes to mix the solutions thoroughly.

(4) Pour the solutions into the appropriate petri dishes. Add 20 cm^3 of distilled water to the sixth petri dish.

(5) Place the petri dishes on graph paper, making sure their lower surfaces are dry.

(6) Using the knife or scalpel, cut 12 rectangular strips of tissue approximately 2 mm thick, 5 mm wide and as long as possible (about 5 cm) from a slice of tissue (2 mm thick) taken from the middle of a large beetroot or potato. It is important to work quickly to avoid loss of water through evaporation as this would lower the water potential of the tissue.

(7) Completely immerse two strips in each petri dish and immediately measure their lengths against the graph paper seen through the bottoms of the dishes. Agitate the contents of each dish to wash the strips.

(8) Leave in covered petri dishes for at least 1 h, preferably 24 h.

(9) Measure the lengths again, and calculate the mean percentage change in length. Plot a graph of the mean percentage change in length (vertical axis) against the molarity of the sucrose solution (horizontal axis). Changes in length are proportional to changes in volume.

(10) Read off from the graph the molarity of the sucrose solution which causes no change in length.

(11) Plot a graph of solute potential (vertical axis) against molarity of sucrose solution (horizontal axis) using the data provided in table 14.4.

(12) From this graph, determine the solute potential of the solution which caused no change in length. The water potential of the tissue is determined according to the following:

$$\psi^{cell} = \psi^{external\ solution} = \psi_s$$

(13) If beetroot has been used and its solute potential determined from experiment 14.2, calculate the pressure potential from:

$$\psi = \psi_s + \psi_p$$

Results

More accurate results are likely to be obtained by pooling class results. See table 14.6 for specimen results.

14.1.11 Effect of heat and alcohols on membranes

The partial permeability of cell membranes can be destroyed by certain chemicals and treatments, such as ethanol and high temperatures. The membranes are still present but behave as if holes had been punched through them and they no longer provide a barrier to the passage of large molecules such as sucrose. High temperature and alcohols denature membrane proteins and increase fluidity of membrane lipids; alcohols at high concentrations can also dissolve lipids.

14.11 What is the mean water potential of beetroot cells from the data in table 14.6? (You will need to determine mean percentage changes in length and draw graphs.)

14.12 Why are at least two strips of tissue added to each dish?

14.13 Why are the petri dishes covered when left?

14.14 If the solute potential of beetroot cells is −1400 kPa and their water potential is −950 kPa, what is their mean pressure potential?

14.15 Consider the experiment illustrated in fig 14.6 in which the hollow inflorescence stalk (scape) of a dandelion (*Taraxacum officinale*) is first cut longitudinally into four strips 3 cm long, and the pieces then immersed in distilled water or sucrose solutions of different concentrations.

(a) Why did cutting the scape longitudinally result in immediate curling back of the cut strips?

(b) Why did scape B bend further outwards in distilled water?

(c) Why did scape C bend inwards in concentrated sucrose solution?

(d) Why did scape A retain the same curvature in dilute sucrose solution?

(e) Which of the following could be determined for scape cells using this method: solute potential, water potential or pressure potential? Design an experiment to determine the relevant value, giving full experimental details.

Table 14.6 Lengths of beetroot strips left in distilled water or different concentrations of sucrose solution for 24 h.

Molarity of sucrose solution	Length of beetroot strip at start/cm			Length of beetroot strip after 24 h/cm		
	1	2	3	1	2	3
0.00 (distilled water)	4.8	5.0	5.3	5.0	5.3	5.6
0.10	5.1	4.8	4.9	5.3	4.9	5.1
0.20	5.1	4.9	4.9	5.2	4.9	5.0
0.25	5.2	4.8	5.0	5.2	4.9	5.0
0.30	4.9	4.9	5.0	4.9	5.0	5.1
0.40	4.9	5.0	4.8	4.9	5.0	4.8
0.50	5.0	4.8	5.1	4.8	4.7	5.0
0.60	4.8	5.0	5.0	4.6	4.9	4.9
0.75	4.9	4.9	5.0	4.6	4.7	4.8
0.90	4.9	5.0	4.9	4.5	4.7	4.7
1.00	4.8	4.9	4.9	4.7	4.6	4.4
1.50	4.9	4.9	4.9	4.5	4.1	4.5

14.16 The red colour of beetroot is contained in the cell vacuoles. Using this information, design experiments to investigate the effects of heat and ethanol on the differential permeability of beetroot cell membranes.

14.2 Movement of water through the flowering plant

Water in the plant is in direct contact with water in the soil and with water vapour in the air around the

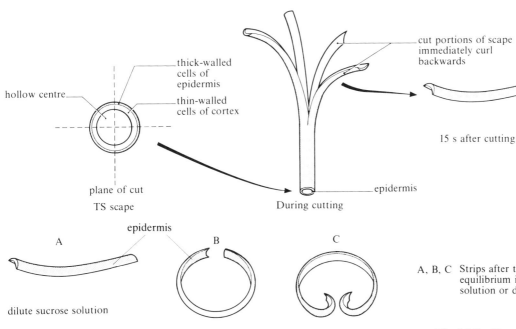

thick-walled cells of epidermis

thin-walled cells of cortex

hollow centre

plane of cut

TS scape

During cutting

epidermis

cut portions of scape immediately curl backwards

15 s after cutting

A

epidermis

dilute sucrose solution

B

distilled water

C

concentrated sucrose solution (1 M) or drying in air

A, B, C Strips after they have been allowed to come to equilibrium in different concentrations of sucrose solution or distilled water (about 30 min)

Fig 14.6 *Experiment on dandelion scapes. Investigation of the effects of distilled water and sucrose solutions on the curvature of strips of dandelion scape*

481

plant. It has already been stated that water moves from higher to lower water potentials. Plant physiologists therefore think of water as moving through plants from a region of higher water potential in the soil to a region of lower water potential in the atmosphere, down a gradient of water potentials. The water potential of moderately dry air is several tens of thousands of kilopascals below that of the plant; hence there is a great tendency for water to leave the plant.

Most of the water entering the plant does so via the root hairs. It travels across the root cortex to the xylem, ascends in the xylem to the leaves and is lost by evaporation from the surface of the mesophyll cells before diffusing out through the stomata. This latter process is called **transpiration**, and the flow of water from the roots to the transpiring surfaces forms the **transpiration stream**. It is estimated that less than 1% of the water absorbed is used by the average plant. Uses of water are given in section 5.1.2.

14.3 Transpiration and movement of water through the leaf

Water normally leaves the plant as a vapour. The change from a liquid state to a vapour state requires the addition of energy, called the **latent heat of evaporation**. This energy is provided by the Sun (solar energy) and according to the most widely accepted theory of transpiration, the **cohesion–tension theory**, it is this energy that maintains the flow of water through the entire plant. Transpiration is the loss of water vapour from the surface of a plant, and may occur from the following three sites (relative losses when stomata are open are indicated in brackets).

(1) **Stomata:** by evaporation of water from cells and diffusion of the water vapour through stomata, the pores found in the epidermis of leaves and green stems (about 90%).
(2) **Cuticle:** by evaporation of water from the outer walls of epidermal cells through the waxy cuticle covering the epidermis of leaves and stems (about 10%, varying with thickness of cuticle).
(3) **Lenticels:** by evaporation of water through lenticels (minute proportions, although this is the main source of water loss from deciduous trees after leaf fall).

The quantities of water lost by transpiration can be very large. A herbaceous plant, such as cotton or sunflower, can lose between 1–2 dm^3 of water per day, and a large oak tree more than 600 dm^3 per day.

Water is brought to the leaf in the xylem of vascular bundles which spread to form a fine branching network throughout the leaf. The branches end in one or a few xylem vessels or tracheids possessing little lignification. Water can therefore escape easily through their cellulose walls to the mesophyll cells they supply. Fig 14.7 shows the three pathways which water can subsequently follow, namely the apoplast pathway (cell walls), the symplast

pathway (cytoplasm and plasmodesmata) and the vacuolar pathway (from vacuole to vacuole).

14.17 Why does transpiration occur mainly through leaves?

14.3.1 The apoplast (apoplasm) pathway

The **apoplast** is the system of adjacent cell walls which is continuous throughout the plant (except for the Casparian strip in roots, section 14.5.2). Up to 50% of a cellulose cell wall may be 'free space' which can be occupied by water. As water evaporates from the mesophyll cell walls into the intercellular air spaces, tension develops in the continuous stream of water in the apoplast, and water is drawn through the walls in a mass flow by the cohesion of water molecules (section 14.4). Water in the apoplast is supplied from the xylem.

14.3.2 The symplast (symplasm) pathway

The **symplast** is the system of interconnected protoplasts in the plant. The cytoplasm of neighbouring protoplasts is linked by the plasmodesmata, the cytoplasmic strands which extend through pores in adjacent cell walls (fig 14.7b). The exact structure of plasmodesmata is not yet fully explained, so to what extent they form channels for the movement of materials is not known. However, it seems likely that once water, and any solutes it contains, is taken into the cytoplasm of one cell it can move through the symplast without having to cross further membranes. Water would move down a water potential gradient, as in the vacuolar pathway (section 14.3.3). Movement might be aided by cytoplasmic streaming. The symplast is a more important pathway of water movement than the vacuolar pathway.

14.3.3 The vacuolar pathway

In the vacuolar pathway water moves from vacuole to vacuole through neighbouring cells, crossing the symplast and apoplast in the process and moving through membranes and tonoplasts by osmosis (fig 14.7b). It moves down a water potential gradient, set up as follows.

Water evaporates from the wet walls of the mesophyll cells into the intercellular air spaces, particularly into the larger substomatal air spaces. Taking cell A in fig 14.7a as an example, loss of water from the cell would result in a decrease in its pressure potential and its water potential. Cell B would then have a higher water potential than cell A (at equilibrium they would be equal). Water will therefore move from cell B to cell A, thus lowering the water potential of cell B relative to cell C. In this way a gradient of water potential is set up across the leaf from a higher potential in the xylem to a lower potential in the mesophyll cells. Water enters the mesophyll cells from the xylem by osmosis. Although it is convenient to describe the move-

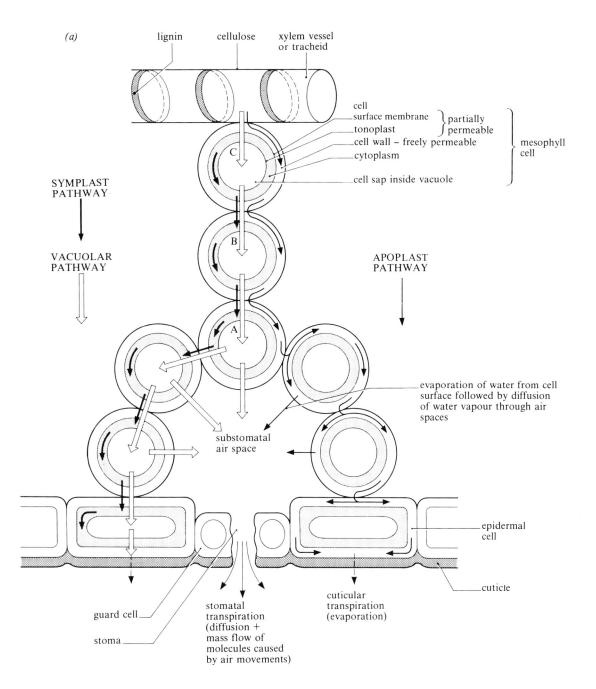

lignin   cellulose   xylem vessel or tracheid

cell
surface membrane } partially permeable
tonoplast
cell wall – freely permeable
cytoplasm
cell sap inside vacuole
} mesophyll cell

SYMPLAST PATHWAY

VACUOLAR PATHWAY

APOPLAST PATHWAY

C

B

A

evaporation of water from cell surface followed by diffusion of water vapour through air spaces

substomatal air space

epidermal cell

cuticle

guard cell

stoma

stomatal transpiration (diffusion + mass flow of molecules caused by air movements)

cuticular transpiration (evaporation)

Fig 14.7 *(a) Diagrammatic representation of water movement through a leaf. There are three possible pathways: the symplast and vacuolar pathways are shown to the left, the apoplast pathway to the right. Cells A, B and C are referred to in the text. Thickness of cell walls has been exaggerated. (b) (right) Diagrammatic representation of a group of cells summarising possible pathways of water (and solute) movement. More than one pathway may be used simultaneously. Such pathways may be used across the leaf and across the root cortex. Movement of ions by the vacuolar pathway would involve active transport. The apoplast pathway is the most important, and the vacuolar pathway the least important (negligible)*

(b)

cell wall   plasmodesma   cytoplasm   cell surface membrane   tonoplast   vacuole

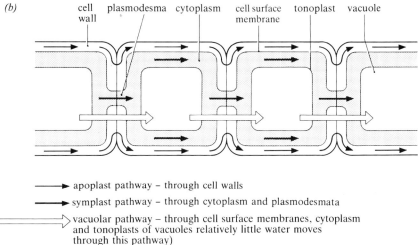

→ apoplast pathway – through cell walls

➤ symplast pathway – through cytoplasm and plasmodesmata

⇨ vacuolar pathway – through cell surface membranes, cytoplasm and tonoplasts of vacuoles relatively little water moves through this pathway)

ment of water in a step-by-step fashion, it should be stressed that the water potential gradient that develops across the leaf is a continuous one, and water moves smoothly down the gradient as a liquid would in moving along a wick.

It is sometimes imagined that water moves across the leaf in response to a gradient of solute potentials. However, although a water potential gradient exists, there is no evidence to suggest that solute potentials of the relevant cells differ significantly from one another. Differences in water potential are due mainly to differences in pressure potential (remember that loss of a small amount of water from a cell has a much greater effect on pressure potential than on solute potential). The same applies to the root (section 14.5) where gradients of pressure potential and water potential, but not necessarily of solute potential, exist.

14.3.4   Exit of water through stomata

The three pathways described above end with water evaporating into air spaces. From here water vapour diffuses through the stomata, following the path of least resistance in moving from a high water potential inside the leaf to a much lower one outside the leaf. In dicotyledons, stomata are usually confined to, or are more numerous in, the lower epidermis. Control of stomatal opening is discussed in section 14.3.9. Immediately next to the leaf is a layer of stationary air whose thickness depends on the dimensions and surface features of the leaf, such as hairiness, and also on wind speed. Water vapour must diffuse through this layer before being swept away by moving air (mass flow). The thinner the stationary layer, the faster is the rate of transpiration. There is a diffusion gradient from the stationary layer back to the mesophyll cells. Theoretically each stoma has a diffusion gradient, or 'diffusion shell' around it, as shown in fig 14.8. In practice the diffusion shells of neighbouring stomata overlap in still air to form one overall diffusion shell.

14.3.5   Measuring the rate of transpiration

Transpiration can easily be demonstrated by placing a bell jar over a potted plant with the pot enclosed in a plastic bag to prevent water loss from the soil. As transpiration occurs, a fluid collects on the inside of the bell jar which is shown to contain water when tested with cobalt(II) chloride paper (blue to pink in water) or anhydrous copper(II) sulphate crystals (white to blue in water).

Measuring absolute rates of transpiration can be difficult, but satisfactory results, at least for the purposes of comparison, can be obtained by means of the two simple experiments described below.

Experiment 14.4: To investigate and measure factors affecting rate of transpiration using a potometer

A **potometer** is a piece of apparatus designed to measure the rate of water uptake by a cut shoot or young seedling. It does not measure transpiration directly, but since most of the water taken up is lost by transpiration, the two processes are closely related. Potometers are available commercially, but a simple version may be set up as shown in fig 14.9.

Materials

potometer (fig 14.9: conical filter flask, short rubber tubing, rubber bung with a single hole, hypodermic syringe and needle, graduated capillary tube)

large black polythene bag	stop clock
large transparent polythene bag	thermometer
	vaseline (petroleum jelly)
small electric fan	leafy shoot, such as lilac
retort stand and clamp	bucket

Method

(1) Select a suitable leafy plant, cut off the shoot and immerse the cut end immediately in a bucket of water

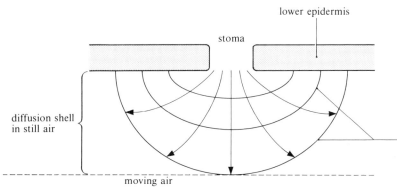

lower epidermis

stoma

diffusion shell in still air

moving air

Arrows represent curved paths of diffusion of water molecules

Fig 14.8 *Diffusion of water molecules from a stoma. Note that the diffusion gradient is steeper at the edges of the pore*

Lines represent contours of equal concentration of water molecules (equal water potential); the steeper the water potential gradient, the closer together the contours and the faster the rate of diffusion. The fastest rates are therefore from the edges of the pores. This 'edge effect' means that water loss and gaseous exchange are more rapid through a large number of small holes than through a smaller number of large holes with the same total area

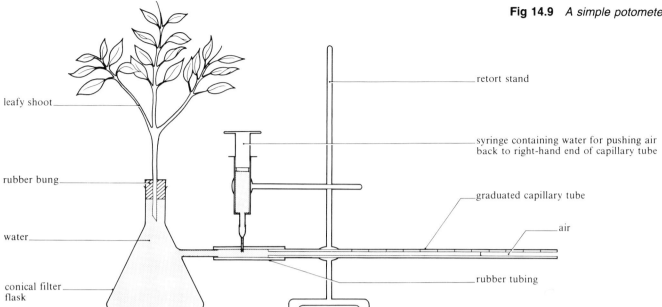

Fig 14.9 *A simple potometer*

leafy shoot

rubber bung

water

conical filter flask

retort stand

syringe containing water for pushing air back to right-hand end of capillary tube

graduated capillary tube

air

rubber tubing

to minimise the risk of air being drawn into the xylem. Immediately cut the shoot again under water, with a slanting cut, a few centimetres above the original cut. The stem must be thick enough to fit tightly into the bung of the potometer.

(2) Submerge a conical filter flask in a sink of water to fill it with water. Transfer the leafy shoot from bucket to sink and again immediately make a slanting cut a few centimetres above the last cut. Fit the shoot into the bung of the flask under water and push the bung in to make a tight fit.

(3) Submerge the graduated capillary tube, with rubber tubing attached, in the sink, fill it with water and attach it to the side arm of the filter flask.

(4) Remove the apparatus from the sink and set up the syringe with the needle pushed into the rubber tubing as shown in fig 14.9. The syringe can be clamped in a vertical position. The joint between shoot and bung should be smeared with vaseline to make certain it is airtight.

(5) As the shoot takes up water the end of the water column in the capillary tube can be seen to move. It may be returned to the open end of the tube by pushing in water from the syringe. Allow the shoot to equilibrate for 5 min whilst regularly replacing the water taken up.

(6) Measure the time taken for the water column to move a given distance along the capillary tube and express the rate of water uptake in convenient units, such as cm min^{-1}. A number of readings should be taken to ensure that the rate is fairly constant, and the mean result calculated. The temperature of the air around the plant should be noted.

(7) Each time the air bubble reaches the end of the graduated section of the tube return it to its original position with the syringe.

(8) The effects of some of the following factors on rate of uptake of water could be investigated:
   (a) wind – use a small electric fan (do not strongly buffet the leaves or the stomata will close);
   (b) humidity – enclose the shoot in a transparent plastic bag;
   (c) darkness – enclose the shoot in a black polythene bag;
   (d) removal of half the leaves – is the transpiration rate halved?
   (e) vaselining upper and/or lower epidermises of the leaves to prevent water loss.

In each case sufficient time should be allowed to ensure that the new rate has been attained. It is not always possible to change only one condition at a time; for example, enclosing the plant in a transparent bag will also lead to some reduction in light intensity.

Absolute rate of water uptake

Results can be converted to actual volume of water taken up per unit time, such as cm^3 h^{-1}, if the volume of the graduated scale corresponding to each division is determined.

Most of the water taken up is lost through the leaves. An estimate of rate of water loss per unit leaf area can be obtained by measuring the volume of water lost as described above and then removing all the leaves and determining their surface area. The latter can be obtained by drawing the outlines of the leaves on graph paper and counting the enclosed squares. Using these data results can be expressed as cm^3 h^{-1} m^{-2} leaf area.

Results

The effects of wind, temperature, humidity and darkness are discussed in section 14.3.6.

14.3.6 Effects of environmental factors on transpiration

Plants exhibit many morphological and anatomical features which enable them to reduce transpiration losses if dry conditions are encountered. Such features are described as **xeromorphic** and are considered below. Plants growing in dry habitats and thus subjected to drought are called **xerophytes** and possess many xeromorphic features which are described in more detail in section 19.3.2. Plants growing under conditions in which there is normally an adequate water supply are called **mesophytes**, but nevertheless can show xeromorphic features.

Light

Light affects transpiration because stomata usually open in the light and close in darkness. At night, therefore, only small amounts of water are lost by cuticular, and possibly lenticular transpiration. As stomata open in the morning, transpiration rates increase.

One group of succulent plants, the Crassulaceae, open their stomata at night and close them during the day as a means of reducing water losses. Carbon dioxide enters the stomata at night, is fixed into an organic acid, and then released again inside the leaf for photosynthesis during the day.

Temperature

Given the presence of light, the external factor which has the greatest effect on transpiration is temperature. The higher the temperature, the greater the rate of evaporation of water from mesophyll cells and the greater the saturation of the leaf atmosphere with water vapour. At the same time, a rise in temperature lowers the relative humidity of the air outside the leaf. Both events result in a steeper concentration gradient of water molecules from leaf atmosphere to external atmosphere. The steeper this gradient, the faster is the rate of diffusion. Alternatively, it can be said that water potential increases inside the leaf while decreasing outside the leaf.

The temperature of the leaf is raised by solar radiation. Pale-coloured leaves reflect more of this radiation than normal leaves and therefore do not heat up as rapidly. The pale colour is usually due to a thick coat of epidermal hairs, waxy deposits or scales, and is a xeromorphic feature.

Humidity and vapour pressure

Low humidity (low water vapour pressure) outside the leaf favours transpiration because it makes the diffusion gradient of water vapour (or water potential gradient) from the moist leaf atmosphere to the external atmosphere steeper. As the concentration of water vapour in the external atmosphere, that is the humidity, rises, the diffusion gradient becomes less steep. Water vapour pressure of the atmosphere also decreases with altitude as atmospheric pressure decreases. High altitude plants therefore often show xeromorphic adaptations to reduce transpiration rates.

A xeromorphic feature of some leaves is the presence of sunken stomata, that is stomata in grooves or infoldings of the epidermis, around which a high humidity can build up and reduce transpiration losses. In some cases the whole leaf may roll up enclosing a humid atmosphere, such as in *Ammophila* (marram grass) (fig 14.10). A coat of epidermal hairs or scales will tend to trap a layer of still moist air next to the leaf, thus reducing transpiration.

Wind

In still air a shell of highly saturated air builds up around the leaf, thus reducing the steepness of the diffusion gradient between leaf atmosphere and external atmosphere. Any disturbance, that is mass flow of the air, will generally sweep away this shell. Thus windy conditions result in increased transpiration rates, the increase being most pronounced at low wind speeds. High winds may result in stomatal closure and cessation of stomatal transpiration.

Hairs and scales trap still air as described above, tending to reduce transpiration rates.

Availability of soil water

As soil dries out, water usually binds more tightly to soil particles. Also, though of less importance, the soil solution becomes more concentrated, that is its water potential decreases. There is therefore less tendency for water to enter by osmosis. Reduced water uptake is followed shortly by a reduction in transpiration rate as there is greater resistance to movement of water through the plant, and a less steep water potential gradient from the soil through the plant to the atmosphere.

14.3.7 Effect of plant or internal factors on the rate of transpiration

The effects of some xeromorphic adaptations on transpiration rates have been considered above. Further examples of the ways in which such 'internal' as opposed to 'external' (environmental) factors can operate are given below.

Leaf surface area and surface area to volume ratio

Transpiration of a plant increases with its total leaf surface area, and with leaf surface area to volume ratio. Reduction of leaf surface is achieved when leaves are reduced to needles, such as in *Pinus* and other conifers, or to spines, as in cacti. There may also simply be a reduction in size in dry conditions. The shedding of leaves in dry or cold seasons by deciduous plants is a xeromorphic adaptation. In cold seasons water may be unavailable through being frozen and the rate of water movement through the plant is also lower at low temperatures.

Surface area to volume ratio can be reduced by using the stem as the main photosynthetic organ, as in cacti. Fig 14.11 shows the characteristic reduction in leaf surface area of succulents like cacti.

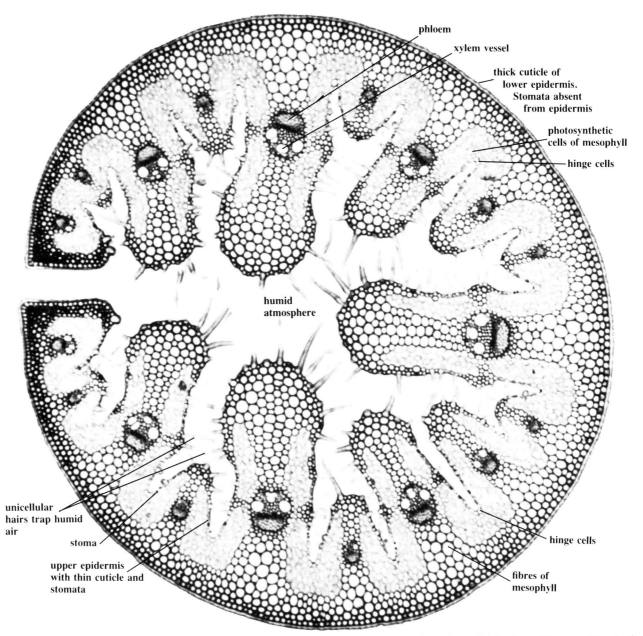

phloem

xylem vessel

thick cuticle of
lower epidermis.
Stomata absent
from epidermis

photosynthetic
cells of mesophyll

hinge cells

humid
atmosphere

hinge cells

unicellular
hairs trap humid
air

stoma

upper epidermis
with thin cuticle and
stomata

fibres of
mesophyll

Fig 14.10 *A transverse section of the xeromorphic leaf of* Ammophila *(marram grass) to show distribution of tissues. The leaf is shown in the rolled condition*

Fig. 14.11 *Succulent plants. (left) Silver Cholla (*Opuntia echinocarpa*) (right) Kalanchoe verticilitta*

Cuticle

In general, the thinner the cuticle the greater the rate of cuticular transpiration, although the composition of the cuticle is also important. Where it is thin, as in ferns, 30–45% of the transpiration losses can be through the cuticle. It may assume particular importance if stomatal transpiration is minimal and water is scarce.

The upper surfaces of dicotyledonous leaves, which are exposed to direct solar radiation and are less protected from air currents than the lower surfaces, often possess thicker cuticles than their lower surfaces. Increased wax deposits on leaves can virtually eliminate cuticular transpiration. Also, waxy leaves are usually shiny and so reflect more solar radiation.

Stomata

In general, the greater the number of stomata per unit area, the greater is the rate of stomatal transpiration; however, their distribution is also important. For example, the lower surfaces of dicotyledonous leaves usually have more stomata than their upper surfaces (table 14.7), whereas monocotyledonous leaves, which are generally held vertically rather than horizontally, have similar upper and lower surfaces with similar stomatal distributions (see maize and oat, table 14.7). On average, fewer stomata occur in plants adapted to dry conditions. The number may vary within the same species as a result.

Table 14.7 Stomatal densities in the leaves of some common plants

| Plant | Number of stomata/cm^{-2} | |
	upper epidermis	lower epidermis
Monocotyledons		
maize (*Zea mais*)	5 200	6 800
oat (*Avena sativa*)	2 500	2 300
Dicotyledons		
apple (*Malus* spp.)	0	29 400
bean (*Phaseolus vulgaris*)	4 000	28 100
cabbage (*Brassica* spp.)	14 100	22 600
lucerne (*Medicago sativa*)	16 900	13 800
Nasturtium	0	13 000
oak (*Quercus* spp.)	0	45 000
potato (*Solanum tuberosum*)	5 100	16 100
tomato (*Lycopersicon esculentum*)	1 200	13 000

Based on Weier, T. E., Stocking, C. R. and Barbour, M. G. (1970) *Botany, an Introduction to Plant Biology*, 4th ed., John Wiley & Sons, p. 192.

Experiment 14.5: To investigate stomatal distribution

Materials

    clear nail varnish
    slides and cover-slips
    fine forceps
    fresh fully expanded leaves
    microscope

Method

A convenient means of examining stomatal distribution is to make a replica of the leaf surface using clear nail varnish. Spread a thin layer of the nail varnish over the leaf using the brush in the bottle. Allow it to dry, then peel off the thin replica with fine forceps, lay it on a slide and add a cover-slip. It may be mounted in water for convenience. Examine with a microscope. Count the number of stomata in a given field of view and repeat several times in different areas. Obtain a mean value. Determine the area of the field

of view of the microscope by measuring the diameter with a calibrated slide or transparent ruler and using the formula πr^2 for the area, where r is the radius and $\pi = 3.142$. The number of stomata per square centimetre can then be calculated.

Compare the densities of stomata in upper and lower epidermises of the same leaf, and in different species. Is there any correlation between stomatal densities and the habitats of plants?

14.18 Examine fig 14.12. Describe and explain the relationships between the three variables shown.

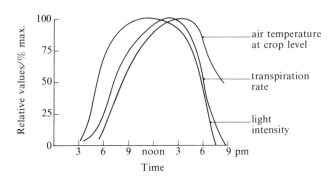

Fig 14.12 *Relationship between light intensity, air temperature and transpiration rate from lucerne leaves. (From data by L. J. Briggs & H. L. Shantz (1916) J. Agr. Res., 5, 583–649; cited by A. C. Leopold (1964) Plant growth and development, p. 396. McGraw-Hill)*

14.3.8 Functions of transpiration

Transpiration has been described as a 'necessary evil' because it is an inevitable, but potentially harmful, consequence of the existence of wet cell walls from which evaporation occurs. Water vapour escapes along the route used for gaseous exchange between the plant and its environment, which is essential for the processes of photosynthesis and respiration. The route is mainly through stomata, as already discussed. If there was no cuticle, stomata would be unnecessary and gaseous exchange would be even more efficient. However, loss of water could not then be controlled. The cuticle reduces water loss and further control is exercised by the stomata, which in most plants are highly sensitive to water stress and close, for example, under conditions of drought. They also usually close during the night when photosynthesis ceases. Loss of water can lead to wilting, serious desiccation, and often death of a plant if conditions of drought are experienced. There is good evidence that even mild water stress results in reduced growth rate and, in crops, to economic losses through reductions in yield.

Despite its apparent inevitability, it is worth questioning whether there might be some advantages associated with transpiration. Two possibilities are as follows.

(1) It has been suggested that the transpiration stream is necessary to distribute mineral salts throughout the plant, since these move with the water. Whilst this may be true, it seems probable that very low transpiration rates would suffice. For example, mineral salt supply to leaves is just as great at night, when transpiration is low, as during the day because the xylem sap is more concentrated at night. Uptake of mineral salts is largely independent of the transpiration stream, but high rates of water uptake may serve to draw water and dissolved substances from more remote regions of the soil.

(2) The evaporation of water from mesophyll cells that accompanies transpiration requires energy and therefore results in cooling of the leaves in the same way that sweating cools the skin of mammals. This is sometimes important under conditions of direct sunlight when leaves absorb large amounts of radiant energy and experience rises in temperature which, under extreme conditions, can inhibit photosynthesis. However, it is unlikely that the cooling effect is of significance under normal conditions. Plants that live in hot climates usually have other means of counteracting heat stress.

14.3.9 Stomata – structure and mechanism of opening and closing

Stomata are pores in the epidermis through which gaseous exchange occurs. They are found mainly in leaves, but also in stems. Each stoma is bounded by two guard cells which, unlike the other epidermal cells, possess chloroplasts. The guard cells control the size of the stoma by changes in their turgidity. The appearance of guard cells

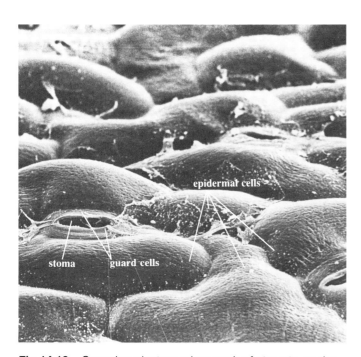

Fig 14.13 *Scanning electron micrograph of stomata on the lower surface of a leaf*

and stomata is well revealed by the scanning electron microscope, as shown in fig 14.13.

The appearance of epidermal cells, guard cells and stomata in surface view, as seen with the light microscope, is dealt with in section 8.1. Fig 14.14 is a diagram of a section through a typical stoma, and shows that the guard cell walls are unevenly thickened, the wall furthest from the pore (termed the dorsal wall) being thinner than that next to the pore (the ventral wall). Also, the cellulose microfibrils that make up the walls are arranged so that the ventral wall is less elastic than the dorsal wall, and some

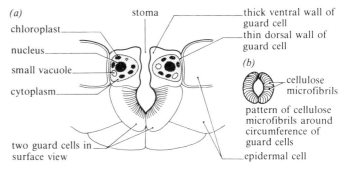

Fig 14.14 *(a) Vertical section through a stoma, showing also part of the lower surface of the leaf. (b) Pattern of cellulose microfibrils in guard cell walls*

form hoops around the sausage-shaped guard cells as shown in fig 14.14b. As the cells inflate with water, that is become turgid, the hoops tend to restrict the cells to an increase in length only. Because the ends of the guard cells are joined, and also because the thin dorsal walls stretch more easily than the thick ventral walls, each cell assumes a semicircular shape (fig 14.14). Thus a hole, the stoma, appears between the guard cells. The same effect can be obtained by inflating a sausage-shaped balloon which has had a piece of adhesive tape stuck along one side to mimic the non-elastic ventral wall of the guard cell.

Conversely, when the guard cells lose water and turgidity, the pore closes. The question remains as to how the turgidity changes are brought about.

A traditional hypothesis, the 'starch–sugar hypothesis', suggested that an increase in sugar concentration in guard cells during the day lead to a decrease in their solute potential (solute potential more negative) and entry of water by osmosis. However, sugar has never been shown to accumulate in guard cells to the extent necessary to cause the observed changes in solute potential. It has now been shown that an accumulation of potassium ions and associated anions occurs in guard cells during the day in response to light and is sufficient to account for the observed changes. In darkness, potassium ions (K^+) move out of the guard cells into surrounding epidermal cells. There is still doubt about which anions balance the potassium. In some, but not all, species studied large quantities of organic acid anions, such as malate, accumulate. At the same time the starch grains that appear in guard cell chloroplasts in

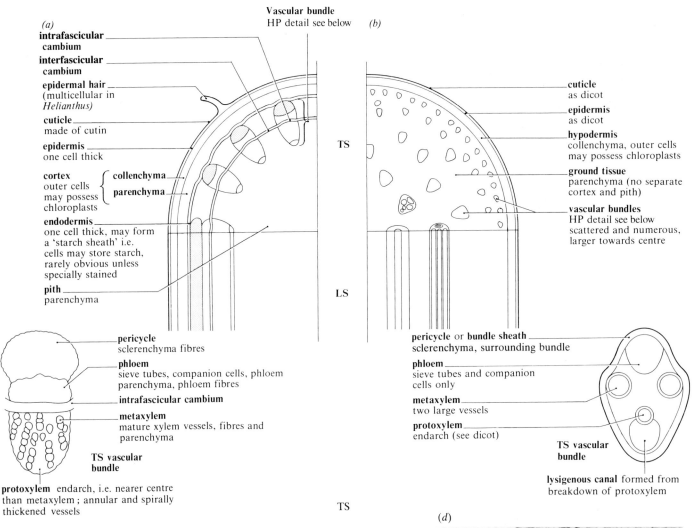

(a)

intrafascicular cambium

interfascicular cambium

epidermal hair (multicellular in *Helianthus*)

cuticle made of cutin

epidermis one cell thick

cortex outer cells may possess chloroplasts { **collenchyma** **parenchyma** }

endodermis one cell thick, may form a 'starch sheath' i.e. cells may store starch, rarely obvious unless specially stained

pith parenchyma

Vascular bundle HP detail see below

TS

LS

pericycle sclerenchyma fibres

phloem sieve tubes, companion cells, phloem parenchyma, phloem fibres

intrafascicular cambium

metaxylem mature xylem vessels, fibres and parenchyma

TS vascular bundle

protoxylem endarch, i.e. nearer centre than metaxylem; annular and spirally thickened vessels

(b)

cuticle as dicot

epidermis as dicot

hypodermis collenchyma, outer cells may possess chloroplasts

ground tissue parenchyma (no separate cortex and pith)

vascular bundles HP detail see below scattered and numerous, larger towards centre

pericycle or bundle sheath sclerenchyma, surrounding bundle

phloem sieve tubes and companion cells only

metaxylem two large vessels

protoxylem endarch (see dicot)

TS vascular bundle

lysigenous canal formed from breakdown of protoxylem

TS

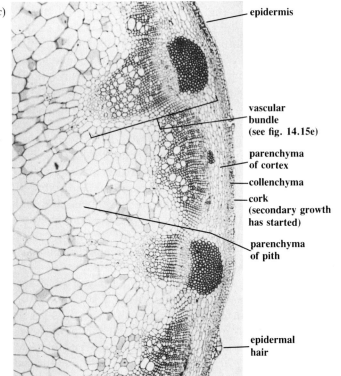

(c)

epidermis

vascular bundle (see fig. 14.15e)

parenchyma of cortex

collenchyma

cork (secondary growth has started)

parenchyma of pith

epidermal hair

(d)

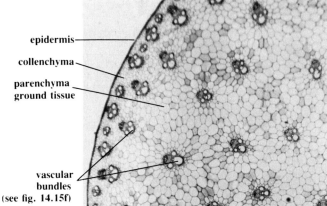

epidermis

collenchyma

parenchyma ground tissue

vascular bundles (see fig. 14.15f)

Fig 14.15 *(a) (top left) Primary anatomy of the stem of a typical dicotyledon,* Helianthus annuus *(sunflower). (b) (top right) Anatomy of the stem of a typical monocotyledon,* Zea mais *(maize). (c) (above left) Low power micrograph of part of a TS of the stem of* Helianthus. *(d) (above right) Low power micrograph of part of a TS of the stem of* Zea. *(e) (facing page, top left) High power micrograph of a TS of a vascular bundle from a stem of* Helianthus. *(f) (facing page, top right) High power micrograph of a TS of a vascular bundle from a stem of* Zea *(g) (facing page, centre) Micrograph of an LS of the stem of* Helianthus *(h) (facing page, bottom) Micrograph of an LS of the stem of* Zea

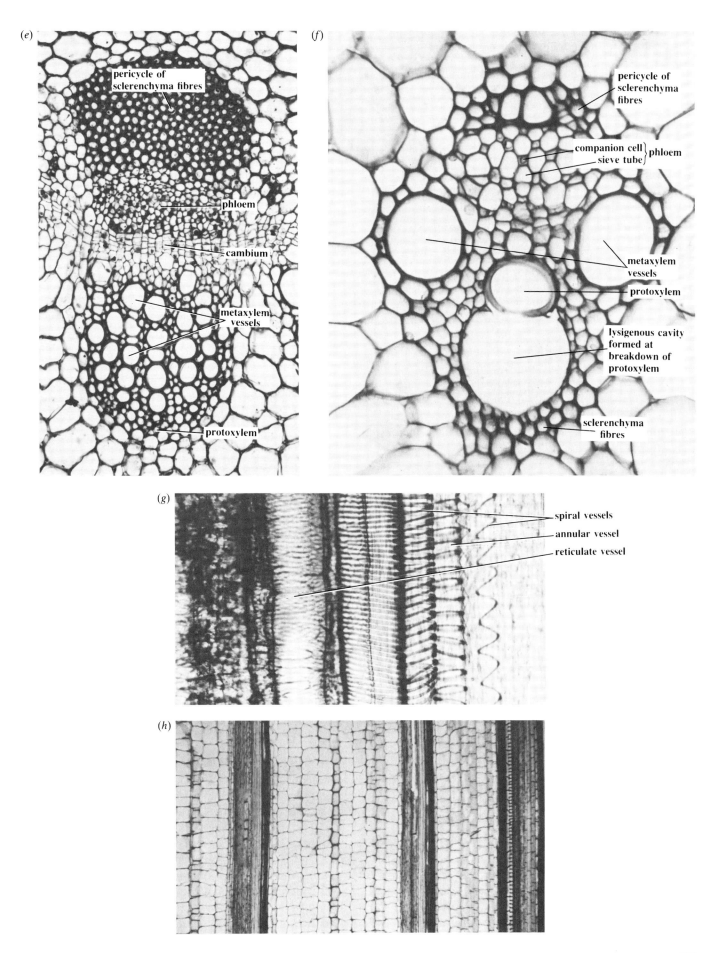

(e) pericycle of
sclerenchyma fibres

phloem

cambium

metaxylem
vessels

protoxylem

(f) pericycle of
sclerenchyma
fibres

companion cell
sieve tube } phloem

metaxylem
vessels

protoxylem

lysigenous cavity
formed at
breakdown of
protoxylem

sclerenchyma
fibres

(g) spiral vessels

annular vessel

reticulate vessel

(h)

491

darkness decrease in size, suggesting that starch is converted to malate in light. A possible route is:

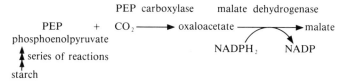

(Compare C_4 photosynthesis, section 9.8.2.)

Some species, such as *Allium cepa* (onion), have no starch in their guard cells. Here malate does not accumulate during stomatal opening and inorganic anions, such as chloride (Cl^-), may be taken up with the cations.

Certain questions remain to be answered. For example, why is light necessary for stomatal opening, and what function is served by the chloroplasts apart from starch storage? Is malate converted back to starch in darkness? In 1979 it was shown that the enzymes of the Calvin cycle are absent from the chloroplasts of guard cells of *Vicia faba* (broad bean), and the thylakoid system is poorly developed, although chlorophyll is present. Normal C_3 photosynthesis therefore cannot occur and starch cannot be made by this route. This might help to explain why starch is made at night rather than during the day as in normal photosynthetic cells. Another interesting fact is that guard cells lack plasmodesmata and are therefore relatively isolated from other epidermal cells.

14.4 Ascent of water in the xylem

Xylem in flowering plants contains two types of water-transporting cell, the tracheid and the vessel, whose structures as seen in the light microscope are discussed in section 8.2.1, together with the appearance of vessels as seen with the scanning electron microscope (fig 8.11). The structure of the secondary xylem (wood) is dealt with in section 21.6.6.

Xylem, together with phloem, forms the vascular or conducting tissue of higher plants. Vascular tissue consists of bundles of tubes called **vascular bundles** whose structure and arrangement in the primary stems of dicotyledonous plants (dicots) and monocotyledonous plants (monocots) are shown in fig 14.15.

> **14.19** Summarise in table form the major differences in primary structure between dicot and monocot stems.
>
> **14.20** What is the overall shape of the following tissues in three dimensions: (*a*) epidermis, (*b*) xylem, (*c*) pericycle of dicots and (*d*) pith?

The fact that water can move up the xylem may be demonstrated by immersing the cut end of a shoot in a dilute solution of a dye, such as eosin. The dye rises in the xylem and spreads through the network of veins in the leaves. Sectioning and examination with a light microscope reveals the stain to be in the xylem.

Better evidence that xylem conducts water is given by 'ringing' experiments. These were among earlier experiments done before radioactive isotopes made the tracing of substances through living organisms much easier. In one type of ringing experiment an outer ring of bark, including phloem, is removed and, in the short term, this does not affect the upward movement of water. However, lifting a flap of bark, removing a section of xylem, and replacing the flap of bark leads to rapid wilting.

Any theory for water movement up the xylem has to account for the following observations.

(1) Xylem vessels are dead tubes with narrow lumens ranging in diameter from 0.01 mm in 'summer wood' to about 0.2 mm in 'spring wood'.
(2) Large quantities of water are carried at relatively high speeds, up to 8 m h^{-1} being recorded in tall trees and commonly in other plants at 1 m h^{-1}.
(3) To move water through such tubes to the height of a tall tree requires pressures of around 4 000 kPa. The tallest trees, the giant sequoias or redwoods of California (conifers and therefore possessing only tracheids, not vessels) and *Eucalyptus* trees or blue gums of Australia, can reach heights greater than 100 m. Water will rise in fine capillary tubes due to its high surface tension, a phenomenon called **capillarity**, but could rise only about 3 m in even the finest xylem vessels by this method.

The **cohesion–tension theory** (or cohesion theory) of water movement adequately accounts for these observations. According to this theory, evaporation of water from the cells of a leaf is responsible for raising water from the roots. Evaporation results in a reduced water potential in the cells next to the xylem as described in section 14.3. Water therefore enters these cells from the xylem sap which has a higher water potential, passing through the moist cellulose cell walls of the xylem vessels at the ends of the veins, as shown in fig 14.7.

The xylem vessels are full of water and as water leaves them a tension is set up in the columns of water. This is transmitted back down the stem all the way to the root by **cohesion** of water molecules. Water molecules have high cohesion, that is tend to 'stick' to each other, because, being polar, they are electrically attracted to each other and are held together by hydrogen bonding (section 5.1.2). They also tend to stick to the vessel walls, a force called **adhesion**. The high cohesion of water molecules means that a relatively large tension is required to break a column of water, that is a water column has a high tensile strength. The tension in the xylem vessels builds up to a force capable of pulling the whole column of water upwards by means of mass flow, and water enters the base of the columns in the roots from neighbouring root cells. It is essential that the xylem walls should also have high tensile strength if they are not to buckle inwards, as happens when sucking up a soggy straw. Lignin and cellulose both provide this strength. Evidence that the contents of xylem vessels are under high tension comes from measuring diurnal changes in the diameters of tree trunks using an instrument called a dendrogram. The minimum diameters are recorded during daylight hours when transpiration rates are highest. The minute shrinkage of each xylem vessel under tension combines to give a measurable shrinkage in diameter of the whole trunk.

Estimates of the tensile strength of a column of xylem sap vary from about 3 000–30 000 kPa, the lower estimates being the more recent. Water potentials of the order required to generate enough tension to raise water, about −4 000 kPa, have been recorded in leaves, and it seems likely that xylem sap has the required tensile strength to withstand this tension, though there may be a tendency for the columns to break, particularly in vessels of relatively large diameter.

Critics of the theory point to the fact that any break in a column of sap should stop its flow, the vessel tending to fill with air and water vapour, a process known as **cavitation**. Shaking, bending and shortage of water can all induce cavitation. It is well known that the water content of tree trunks gradually decreases during summer as the wood becomes filled with air. This is made use of in the lumber industry because such wood floats more easily. However, breaks in water columns do not greatly affect water flow rates. The explanation may be that water flows from one vessel to another, or by-passes air-locks by moving through neighbouring parenchyma cells and their walls. Also, it is calculated that only a small proportion of the vessels need be functional at any one time to account for the observed flow rates. In some trees and shrubs water moves only through the younger outer wood, which is therefore called **sapwood**. In oak and ash, for example, water moves mainly through the vessels of the current year, the rest of the sapwood acting as a water reserve. New vessels are added throughout the growing season, mostly early in the season when flow rates are higher.

A second force involved in water movement up the xylem is **root pressure**. This can be observed and measured when a freshly cut root stump continues to exude sap from its xylem vessels. The process is inhibited by respiratory inhibitors such as cyanide, lack of oxygen and low temperatures. The mechanism probably depends on active secretion of salts or other solutes into the xylem sap, thus lowering its water potential. Water then moves into the xylem by osmosis from neighbouring root cells.

The positive hydrostatic pressure of around 100–200 kPa (exceptionally 800 kPa) that is generated by root pressure is usually not sufficient alone to account for water movement up the xylem but it is no doubt a contributing factor in many plants. It can be sufficient, however, in slowly transpiring herbaceous plants, when it can cause guttation. **Guttation** is the loss of water as drops of liquid from the surface of a plant (as opposed to vapour in transpiration). It is favoured by the same conditions that favour low transpiration rates, including dim light and high humidity. It is common in many rain forest species and is frequently seen at the tips of the leaves of young grass seedlings.

14.21 Summarise the properties of xylem which make it suitable for the long-distance transport of water and solutes.

14.5 Uptake of water by roots

The primary structures of typical dicot and monocot roots are shown in fig 14.16.

14.22 Summarise in table form the major differences in primary structure between typical dicot and monocot roots.

Water is absorbed mainly, but not exclusively, by the younger parts of roots in the regions of the root hairs. As a root grows through the soil, new root hairs develop a short distance behind the zone of elongation and older hairs die. These hairs are tubular extensions of epidermal cells (fig 14.16) and greatly increase the available surface area for uptake of water and mineral salts. They form a very intimate relationship with soil particles.

Fig 14.17a is a diagrammatic representation of the pathway taken by water across a root. A water potential gradient exists across the root from higher potential in the piliferous layer to lower potential in the cells adjacent to the xylem. This gradient is maintained in two ways:

(1) by water moving up the xylem, as described, setting up tension in the xylem and thus lowering the water potential of its sap;

(2) the xylem sap has a lower (more negative) solute potential than the dilute soil solution.

Water moves across the root by pathways similar to those in the leaf, namely apoplast, symplast and vacuolar pathways.

14.5.1 Symplast and vacuolar pathways

As water moves up the xylem in the root, it is replaced by water from neighbouring parenchyma cells, such as cell A in fig 14.17a. As water leaves cell A, the water potential of cell A decreases and water enters it from cell B by osmosis or through the symplast in exactly the same way as described for cells A and B in the leaf (section 14.3.2). Similarly the water potential of cell B then decreases and water enters it from cell C and so on across the root to the piliferous layer.

The soil solution has a higher water potential than cells of the piliferous layer, which include the root hair. Water therefore enters the root from the soil by osmosis.

14.23 Arrange the following in order of ψ: soil solution, xylem sap, cell A, cell B, cell C, root hair cell. (Use the symbol > (greater than).)

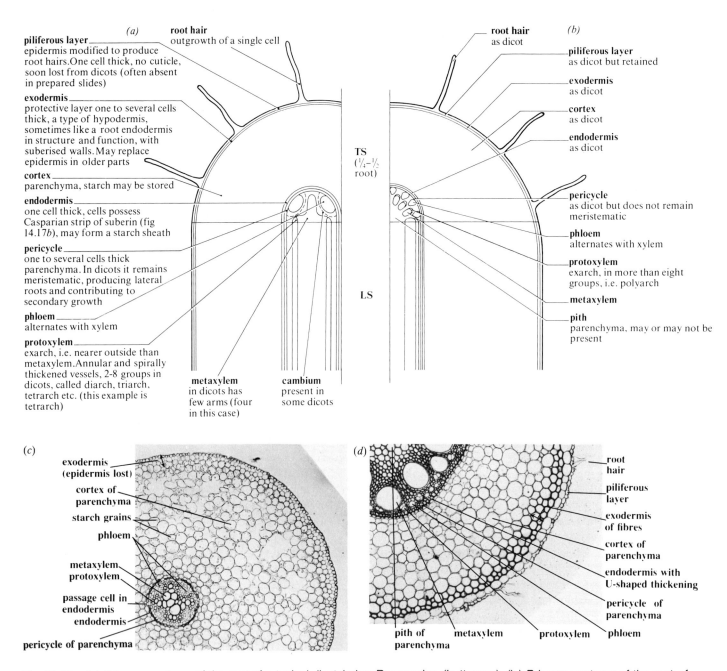

Fig 14.16 *(a) Primary anatomy of the root of a typical dicotyledon,* Ranunculus *(buttercup). (b) Primary anatomy of the root of a typical monocotyledon,* Zea mais *(maize). (c) Low power micrograph of a TS of the root of* Ranunculus *(d) Low power micrograph of a TS of the root of* Zea

14.5.2 Apoplast pathway

The apoplast pathway operates in much the same way as in the leaf (section 14.3.1). However, there is one important difference. When water moving through spaces in the cell walls reaches the endodermis its progress is barred by the waterproof substance called **suberin** which is deposited in the cell walls in the form of bands called **Casparian strips**. These strips prevent apoplastic movement of water (fig 14.17b) and therefore water and salts must pass through the cell surface membrane under the cytoplasmic control of the endodermal cell. In this way, it is believed, control by living cells is exercised over the movement of water and of mineral salts from soil to xylem. Such control is necessary to regulate salt movement and may be a protective measure against entry of toxic substances, fungal pathogens and so on. It is interesting to note that when endodermal cells are plasmolysed, their cytoplasm remains attached to the Casparian strip even when shrinking away from the rest of the cell wall. As roots get older suberisation in the endodermis often gets more extensive as shown in fig 14.17b. This blocks the normal exit of water and mineral salts through the inner tangential wall. However, plasmodesmata may stay as pores in these

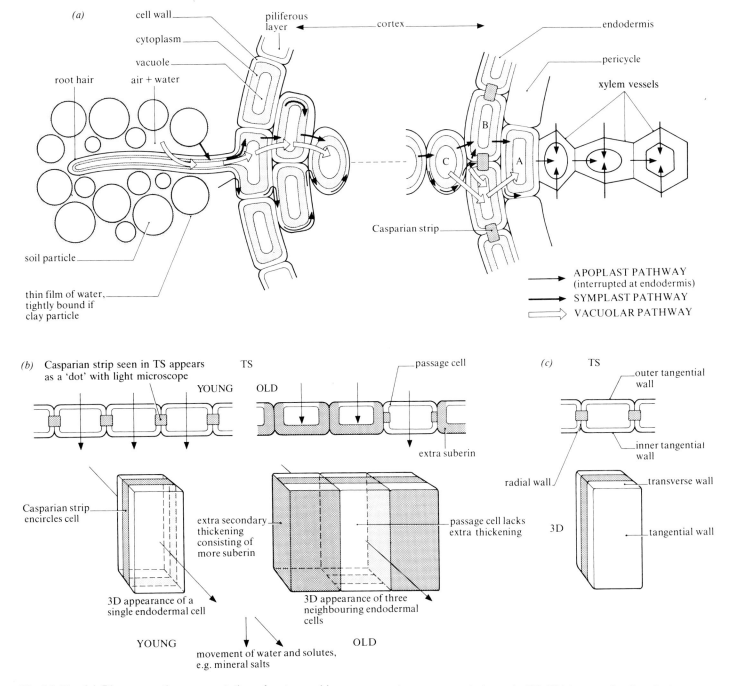

Fig 14.17 (a) Diagrammatic representation of water and ion movement across a root shown in TS. Thickness of cell walls is exaggerated for clarity. Cells A, B, C are referred to in the text. The apoplast pathway is of greatest importance for both water and solutes. The symplast pathway is less important, except for salts in the region of the endodermis. Movement along the vacuolar pathway is negligible. (b) Structure and function of root endodermis showing Casparian strip in young endodermal cells and deposition of extra suberin in older endodermal cells, with exception of 'passage cells'. (c) Naming of walls. The transverse and radial walls are anticlinal (at right-angles to the surface of the root) and the tangential wall is periclinal (parallel).

walls, and 'passage cells' in which no extra thickening occurs also remain to allow water and solute movement.

The relative importance of apoplast, symplast and vacuolar pathways is not known.

14.6 Uptake of mineral salts and their transport across roots

As part of their nutrition, plants require certain mineral elements in addition to the carbohydrates made in photosynthesis. The uses of these elements are described in table 9.11. In green plants minerals are taken up from the soil or surrounding water by roots. Uptake is greatest in the region of the root hairs. The possibly important involvement of mycorrhizas is discussed in section 9.12.2.

Mineral elements exist in the form of ions in salts, and in solution the ions dissociate and move about freely. In attempting to explain the uptake and movement of mineral ions, the following facts must be taken into account.

(1) Cell membranes, including the cell surface membrane and tonoplast, are not truly semi-permeable but differentially permeable, allowing to varying extents the passage of substances other than water, such as ions.

(2) Active transport can occur across cell membranes. This requires energy in the form of ATP, made during respiration, and can lead to an accumulation of ions against a concentration gradient (section 7.2.2).

(3) There is a continuous system of cell walls, the apoplast, extending inwards from the piliferous layer of the root. Water, and any solutes it contains, enters the system from the soil by mass flow and to a lesser extent by diffusion.

(4) Water moves through the apoplast as part of the transpiration stream.

Fig 14.18 shows the uptake of potassium ions by young cereal roots which had previously been thoroughly washed in pure water. After 90 min the respiratory inhibitor potassium cyanide was added to the solutions.

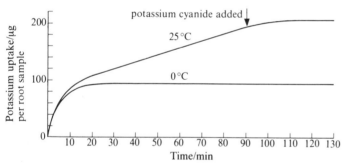

Fig 14.18 Absorption of potassium ions by young cereal plants in aerated solution

14.24 (a) Describe the uptake of potassium ions at 0 °C and 25 °C.
(b) Explain the differences described, and the effect of potassium cyanide (KCN).

Similar results to those in fig 14.18 can be obtained with isolated tissues, those of storage organs, such as carrot, being commonly used. The data shown in fig 14.19 confirm the inhibition of respiration by potassium cyanide.

To summarise so far, the uptake of ions by roots is a combination of **passive uptake**, whereby ions move by mass flow and diffusion through the apoplast, and **active uptake**, or **active transport**, whereby ions can be taken up

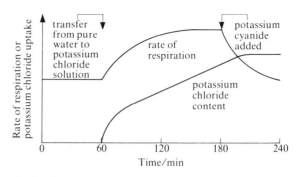

Fig 14.19 Rate of respiration and uptake of potassium chloride by carrot discs. (Based on data by Robertson & Turner (1945))

14.25 Fig 14.19 shows that the rate of respiration of carrot discs increases when they are transferred from pure water to potassium chloride solution. From the results shown, account for this increase.

14.26 Why does the rise in potassium chloride content stop when KCN is added?

14.27 In an experiment similar to that described in fig 14.18, but involving phosphate uptake, 16% of the phosphate taken up by barley roots over a short period could be washed out after transferring to pure water again. Explain.

14.28 Could ions reach the xylem entirely by means of the apoplast pathway?

into cells against a concentration gradient using energy from respiration.

Active transport is selective and dependent on respiration, whereas diffusion is non-selective and not dependent on respiration. Each cell of the root cortex is bathed in a solution similar in composition to that of the soil solution as a result of passive uptake. Thus there is a large surface area for ion uptake.

Ions moving in the apoplast can only reach the endodermis, where the Casparian strip prevents further progress as described in section 14.5.2. To cross the endodermis, ions must pass by diffusion or active transport through the cell surface membranes of endodermal cells, entering their cytoplasm and possibly their vacuoles. Thus the plant monitors and controls which types of ions eventually reach the xylem.

14.29 How could you demonstrate, using a radioactive ion and autoradiography, that the endodermis is a barrier to the movement of ions through cell walls?

Ions can also move through the symplast pathway. Once they are taken into the cytoplasm of one cell, they can move through the symplast without having to cross further membranes. The symplast extends from the piliferous layer right through to the xylem. Fig 14.17a summarises the possible ways in which ions can cross the root.

The final stage in the movement of mineral salts across the root is the release of ions into the xylem. To achieve this, ions must leave living cells at some stage, crossing back through a cell surface membrane. This could be by diffusion or active transport.

14.7 Translocation of mineral salts through plants

The pathway of mineral salts across the root to the xylem, described above, is the first stage in their translocation. Once in the xylem, they are distributed throughout the plant by the transpiration stream, in which they move by mass flow. Movement of the mineral elements in the xylem can be demonstrated by ringing experiments like those already described, in which removal of tissues external to the xylem, such as phloem, has no effect on upward movement of ions. Analysis of the xylem sap also reveals that although some of the nitrogen travels as inorganic nitrate or ammonium ions, much of it is carried in the organic form of amino acids and related compounds. Some conversion of these ions to amino acids must therefore take place in the roots. Similarly small amounts of phosphorus and sulphur are carried as organic compounds.

Thus, although xylem and phloem are traditionally regarded as conducting inorganic and organic materials respectively, the distinction is not clear-cut. In addition, a small amount of exchange between xylem and phloem is common and phloem carries significant quantities of mineral elements away from organs other than the root, as discussed below.

The chief **sinks**, that is sites of utilisation, for mineral elements are the growing regions of the plant, such as the apical and lateral meristems, young leaves, developing fruits and flowers, and storage organs. Unloading of solutes from xylem occurs at the fine vein endings and entry of solutes into cells can take place by diffusion and active uptake. Transfer cells (section 14.8.6) may sometimes be involved.

14.7.1 Recirculation and remobilisation

Very often the path from roots to sinks via xylem or phloem is not the end of translocation of mineral elements. Generally speaking, xylem makes the initial delivery of a given element to an organ, and then phloem carries away the element for continued translocation up or down the plant if it is not required by that organ. This **recirculation** can be investigated with radioactive isotopes and is shown to be a common phenomenon. In one experiment, the roots of a maize plant were separated into two beakers of nutrient solution, one containing radio-

active phosphorus. Within 6 h the phosphorus had travelled up the stem in the xylem, back down in the phloem and had been detected in the second beaker. This is part of the evidence which suggests that phosphorus circulates continuously and rapidly within the xylem and phloem of plants. Other elements are less mobile. Sulphur, for example, is mainly removed during its first circulation, and calcium is notoriously immobile, being virtually trapped in any organ where it is deposited because it has poor mobility within the phloem.

Often an element will stay in an organ for some time and then be **remobilised**, that is leave the organ for some other part of the plant after having served some useful function. This occurs during sequential senescence (ageing) of leaves, when older dying leaves export much of their mineral content to younger leaves. Similarly, prior to abscission of leaves by deciduous trees and shrubs useful minerals can be conserved by remobilising them for storage elsewhere. Development of flowers, fruits and seeds, and storage organs also involves remobilisation. Directional control of the movement of nutrients is under the influence of plant growth substances, particularly cytokinins (section 15.2.7). The elements most readily mobilised are phosphorus, sulphur, nitrogen and potassium.

14.8 Translocation of organic solutes in phloem

In those multicellular plants where certain parts of the plant, such as roots, are some distance from the sites of photosynthesis, there is a need for a transport system to circulate the products of photosynthesis. In vascular plants phloem is the tissue which carries these organic products away from the leaves, the main organs of photosynthesis, to other parts. Phloem consists of sieve elements, companion cells, parenchyma, fibres and sclereids. Its structure, as revealed by the light microscope, is described in section 8.2.2. The sieve elements are arranged end to end to form sieve tubes, each element being separated from the next by a sieve plate. Fig 14.20 summarises the relationship between autotrophic cells producing organic food and those receiving the food. Note from fig 14.20 that movement of organic solutes must be up

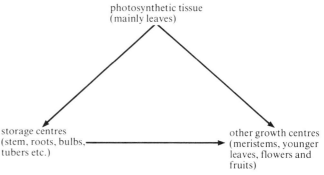

Fig 14.20 *Movement of organic solutes in a green plant*

and down in the same plant, that is bidirectional. This contrasts with movement in the xylem, which is only upwards. Note also that storage organs act either as sources (losing food) or as sinks (gaining food) at different times.

Typically, about 90% of the total solute carried in the phloem is the carbohydrate sucrose, a disaccharide. This is a relatively inert and highly soluble sugar, playing little direct role in metabolism and so making an ideal transport sugar, being unlikely to be used in transit. Once at its destination it can be converted back to the more active monosaccharides. It can be present in very high concentrations, up to 25% mass to volume in the phloem of plants such as sugarcane.

It should be noted that phloem also carries certain mineral elements in various forms, particularly nitrogen and sulphur in the form of amino acids, phosphorus in the form of inorganic phosphate ions and sugar phosphates, and potassium ions. Small amounts of vitamins, growth substances such as auxins and gibberellins, artificially applied chemicals, viruses and other components may also be present. The importance of phloem in recirculation and remobilisation of mineral elements is in section 14.7.1.

Evidence for the circulation of carbon within the plant can be obtained by supplying leaves with carbon dioxide containing the radioactive isotope ^{14}C. Radioactive carbon

(b)

(a)

(c)

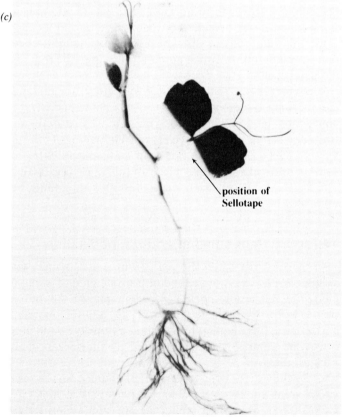

position of Sellotape

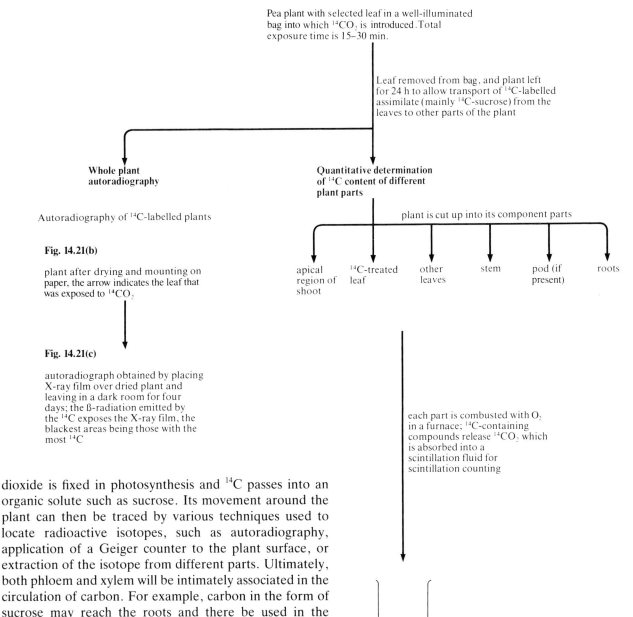

dioxide is fixed in photosynthesis and ^{14}C passes into an organic solute such as sucrose. Its movement around the plant can then be traced by various techniques used to locate radioactive isotopes, such as autoradiography, application of a Geiger counter to the plant surface, or extraction of the isotope from different parts. Ultimately, both phloem and xylem will be intimately associated in the circulation of carbon. For example, carbon in the form of sucrose may reach the roots and there be used in the conversion of nitrates to amino acids. The latter, containing the carbon, can then travel up the shoots in the xylem.

Experiment 14.6: To investigate the pattern of distribution of the products of photosynthesis in a pea plant

The experiment and data below are based on the Independent Television schools' programme *An investigation of photosynthesis and assimilate transport.* Providing the terms of licence granted by the Independent Television Companies to local authorities are complied with, this programme could be usefully recorded on a videocassette recorder.

In the experiment below, carbon dioxide containing the radioactive isotope of carbon, ^{14}C, is supplied to photosynthesising pea plants (*Pisum sativum*). ^{14}C is a useful

Fig 14.21 (opposite and above) *Stages in an experiment to investigate the pattern of distribution of ^{14}C-labelled assimilates in a pea plant*

isotope because it has a long half-life (5 570 years) and therefore retains its radioactivity throughout the experiment. (Compare ^{11}C which has a half-life of 20.5 min.) It is also relatively safe to handle because it emits only weak radiation (low energy β particles).

499

$^{14}CO_2$ is used by the plant in photosynthesis in exactly the same way as the usual carbon dioxide ($^{12}CO_2$) and is incorporated into the products of photosynthesis (assimilates). The movement of these assimilates can be followed in the experiment because they contain ^{14}C; they are said to be ^{14}C-labelled.

Method

Fig 14.21 outlines the stages of an experiment in which $^{14}CO_2$ is fed either to a lower leaf or an upper leaf of separate pea plants with one pod. After feeding and allowing 24 h for transport of ^{14}C-labelled assimilates from the leaves to other parts of the plant, the pattern of distribution of activity is revealed either by autoradiography (fig 14.21) or by measuring the amount of ^{14}C in each plant part. If autoradiography is done first, the plants can subsequently be cut up and used for the second determination which involves combustion.

Results

Fig 14.21 shows the results of autoradiography. Table 14.8 shows the results of counting the ^{14}C in each plant part.

Table 14.8 Radioactivity of different parts of a pea plant 24 h after feeding with $^{14}CO_2$.

Plant part	Upper leaf treated/counts min^{-1}*	Lower leaf treated/counts min^{-1}*
apical region of shoot	1 123	759
^{14}C-treated leaf	11 325	11 372
other leaves	234	168
stem	819	1 160
pod	9 055	4 937
roots	842	2 700

* Corrected for background radiation which is always present as a result of cosmic radiation.

> **14.30** (a) From table 14.8 calculate the percentage distribution of radioactivity in each plant and thereby compare directly the patterns of ^{14}C-assimilate distribution in the two plants. What are the main similarities and differences in the pattern of ^{14}C export from the upper and lower leaves?
> (b) Consider the significance of these similarities and differences in relation to the growth of the plant and its parts. (It may help you if you draw a simple diagram of a pea plant with about eight leaves, with a pod positioned by the third leaf from the top, then indicate the direction and degree of assimilate movement from both an upper and lower leaf to the pod and to the root system.)

14.8.1 Features of phloem translocation

Although an adequate hypothesis for xylem translocation has been established, there is still controversy about the mechanism of phloem translocation. Before considering possible mechanisms for phloem translocation it is useful to list some outstanding facts which any hypothesis has to account for, and which make the problem such a difficult one to solve.

(1) **The quantity of material moved can be very large.** It is estimated, for example, that as much as 250 kg of sugar can be conducted down the trunk of a large tree during a growing season.

(2) **The rate of flow is high, commonly 20–100 cm h^{-1}.** Maximum rates in excess of 600 cm h^{-1} have been recorded.

> **14.31** If sucrose were moving at 100 cm h^{-1} through sieve tubes where sieve elements were 200 µm long, how long would it take a given molecule of sucrose to pass through one sieve element?

Translocation values of 10–25 g dry mass h^{-1} cm^{-2} of sieve tube cross-sectional area are commonly obtained for dicotyledonous stems.

(3) **The distances travelled can be very large.** The tallest trees, such as *Eucalyptus*, may be over 100 m tall. The leaves of *Eucalyptus* trees are located mainly near the top of the trunk, so assimilates must travel the length of the stem and often a considerable distance through the roots.

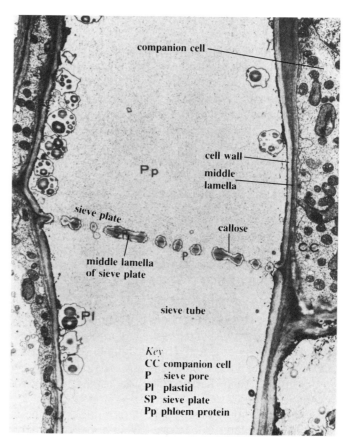

Fig 14.22 *Electron micrograph of a mature sieve element*

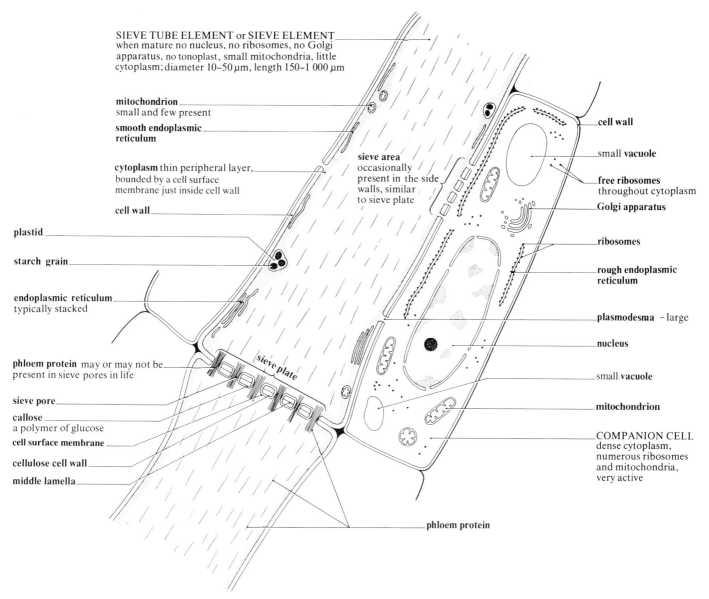

SIEVE TUBE ELEMENT or SIEVE ELEMENT
when mature no nucleus, no ribosomes, no Golgi
apparatus, no tonoplast, small mitochondria, little
cytoplasm; diameter 10–50 μm, length 150–1 000 μm

mitochondrion
small and few present

smooth endoplasmic
reticulum

cytoplasm thin peripheral layer,
bounded by a cell surface
membrane just inside cell wall

cell wall

plastid

starch grain

endoplasmic reticulum
typically stacked

phloem protein may or may not be
present in sieve pores in life

sieve pore

callose
a polymer of glucose

cell surface membrane

cellulose cell wall

middle lamella

sieve plate

sieve area
occasionally
present in the side
walls, similar
to sieve plate

cell wall

small vacuole

free ribosomes
throughout cytoplasm

Golgi apparatus

ribosomes

rough endoplasmic
reticulum

plasmodesma – large

nucleus

small vacuole

mitochondrion

COMPANION CELL
dense cytoplasm,
numerous ribosomes
and mitochondria,
very active

phloem protein

Fig 14.23 *Diagrammatic LS of sieve tube elements and a companion cell as seen with the electron microscope. If the sieve tube is damaged, for example by a grazing animal, more callose is rapidly deposited, blocking the sieve plate and preventing loss of valuable solutes from the sieve tube*

(4) **The amount of phloem is not great.** In a tree trunk, the functional phloem tissue is a layer only about the thickness of a postcard around the circumference. It forms the innermost layer of the bark of woody stems and roots, the older phloem becoming stretched and dying as the plant grows and its circumference increases.

(5) **The sieve tubes are very fine, not more than 30 μm in diameter.** This is comparable with a very fine human hair. At regular intervals the tubes are spanned by sieve plates with pores of even smaller diameter. The smaller the diameter of the tubes and pores, the greater is their resistance to the passage of fluid, and the greater the

force required to move it. Pressure inside sieve tubes is high.

(6) Apart from sieve plates, sieve tubes have other structural features which must be taken into account (see next section).

14.8.2 Ultrastructure of sieve tubes

In contrast with xylem vessels, which are dead empty tubes with few, if any, internal obstructions, phloem sieve tubes are living and do apparently contain obstructions to the flow of solution, namely the sieve plates and, to a lesser extent, the cytoplasm. Since the mechanism of movement is still unclear, it is important in the search for evidence to study the structure of sieve tubes in more detail than can be revealed by the light microscope. Fig 14.22 is an electron micrograph of a mature sieve element, and fig 14.23 is a diagram showing the main features of sieve elements and their neighbouring companion cells.

> **14.32** How many sieve plates per metre would be encountered by a sucrose molecule moving through a sieve tube whose sieve elements were 400 μm long?

During development of a sieve element from a meristematic cell its nucleus degenerates, making it an unusual example of a living cell with no nucleus; in this respect it is like mammalian red blood cells. At the same time many other profound changes take place, the results of which are shown in fig 14.23. The cell walls at each end of the element develop into sieve plates. These are formed when the plasmodesmata of the end walls enlarge greatly to form sieve pores. A surface view of a sieve plate is shown in fig 8.12. The effect of all the changes is to leave a tube-like structure with a wide lumen and a very narrow, indistinct, peripheral layer of living cytoplasm bounded by a cell surface membrane.

Closely associated with each sieve element are one or more companion cells, parenchyma cells which are derived from the same parent cell as the neighbouring sieve element. Companion cells have dense cytoplasm with small vacuoles, and the usual cell organelles. They are metabolically very active, as indicated by their numerous mitochondria and ribosomes (fig 14.23). They show a very close structural and physiological relationship with sieve elements, being essential for their survival because when companion cells die, so do some elements. In leaves, they function as transfer cells, absorbing sugars and transferring them to sieve elements (see section 14.8.6).

In some dicotyledonous and monocotyledonous plants sieve elements develop large quantities of a fibrous protein called **phloem protein** (P-protein). This sometimes forms deposits large enough to be seen with the light microscope. Such deposits were once called 'slime bodies' or 'slime plugs', but the material is not carbohydrate in nature and therefore not a true mucilaginous slime. There is much debate as to whether or not the fibres of protein are normally present in the sieve pores, where they are sometimes, but not always, seen in the electron microscope. One of the great problems of preparing phloem tissue for electron microscopy is that the contents of sieve tubes are under high hydrostatic pressure, possibly as great as 3 000 kPa (about 30 atmospheres). Cutting a specimen for fixation therefore releases this pressure and the sudden surge of sieve tube contents might result in phloem protein and the other contents being swept into and plugging the plates. Any phloem protein seen in the sieve pores might therefore be due to a surge artefact. A number of attempts have been made to get round this problem. For example, wilting a plant before cutting it should eliminate or reduce hydrostatic pressure. Electron microscopy of wilted plants reveals the sieve pores are sometimes plugged, sometimes unplugged and sometimes partially plugged. On balance this and other modern techniques, such as rapid freezing, favour the view that the pores are normally open.

14.8.3 Evidence for movement in phloem

It is important, especially in view of the discussion so far, to be certain that organic solutes really are carried in the phloem sieve tubes. The earliest evidence for movement of sugars and other compounds in phloem came from ringing experiments, in which a ring of tissue containing phloem was removed from the outer region of the stem, leaving the xylem intact. Malpighi obtained evidence in 1675 for ascent of water in wood and descent of food in 'bark'. He removed rings of bark from trees (bark contains the phloem) and found that the leaves did not wilt, but that growth below the ring was greatly reduced.

Mason and Maskell, working with cotton plants in Trinidad during the 1920s and 1930s, did many ringing experiments, one of which is described in fig 14.24. From the results of the experiments shown in fig 14.24, Mason and Maskell concluded that some lateral exchange of sugars can take place between xylem and phloem when they are in contact and the phloem is interrupted (fig 12.24a) but that downward movement occurs in phloem (b and c).

Two simple types of experiment have been done to show the movement of sucrose in phloem. In 1945 a non-radioactive isotope of carbon, ^{13}C, was introduced into a plant as $^{13}CO_2$ and detected by mass spectrometry. A ring of phloem was killed with a fine jet of steam and translocation of ^{13}C-labelled sucrose through this section was shown to be prevented. Movement of mineral elements in the xylem is not affected by such treatment. In the second experiment, microautoradiography of stem sections from plants fed with $^{14}CO_2$ revealed radioactivity in the phloem. The introduction of radioactive tracers in the 1930s and 1940s provided a tremendous boost to work on translocation.

Confirmation that movement is through the sieve tubes comes from a neat type of experiment in which the ability of aphids to feed on translocating sugars is made use of. The aphid penetrates the plant tissues with its specially modified mouthparts; these include extremely fine, tube-like 'stylets' which are pushed slowly through the plant's tissues to the phloem. They can be shown to penetrate individual sieve tubes, as revealed by fig 14.25.

If the aphid is anaesthetised with carbon dioxide and the body removed, leaving the stylets in the plant, the contents of the sieve tube will continue to be forced up the tube of the mouthparts by the hydrostatic pressure in the sieve tube, and the oozing fluid can be collected by microcapillary tubes. This technique has found a number of useful applications, for example in estimating rate of flow through sieve tubes (rate of exudation from tube) and in analysing their contents.

Finally, improvements in the sensitivity of film used in microautoradiography have enabled precise location of the weakly emitting isotope of hydrogen, tritium (^3H), in sieve tubes rather than other phloem cells. The isotope is supplied as part of an amino acid or sucrose.

Experiments have also established that different materials are carried up and down the phloem at the same time, although it is probable that this bidirectional movement is in neighbouring sieve tubes rather than in the same sieve tube.

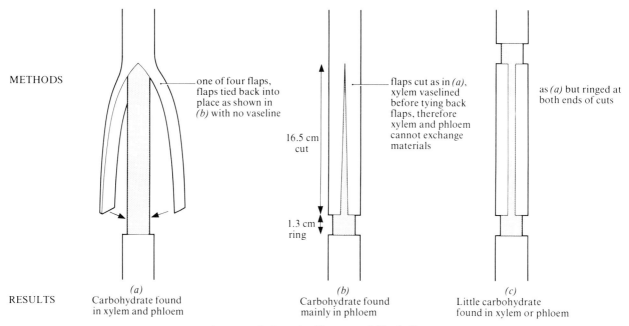

METHODS

one of four flaps, flaps tied back into place as shown in *(b)* with no vaseline

16.5 cm cut

1.3 cm ring

flaps cut as in *(a)*, xylem vaselined before tying back flaps, therefore xylem and phloem cannot exchange materials

as *(a)* but ringed at both ends of cuts

RESULTS

(a)
Carbohydrate found in xylem and phloem

(b)
Carbohydrate found mainly in phloem

(c)
Little carbohydrate found in xylem or phloem

Fig 14.24 *Ringing experiments on cotton plants carried out by Mason and Maskell*

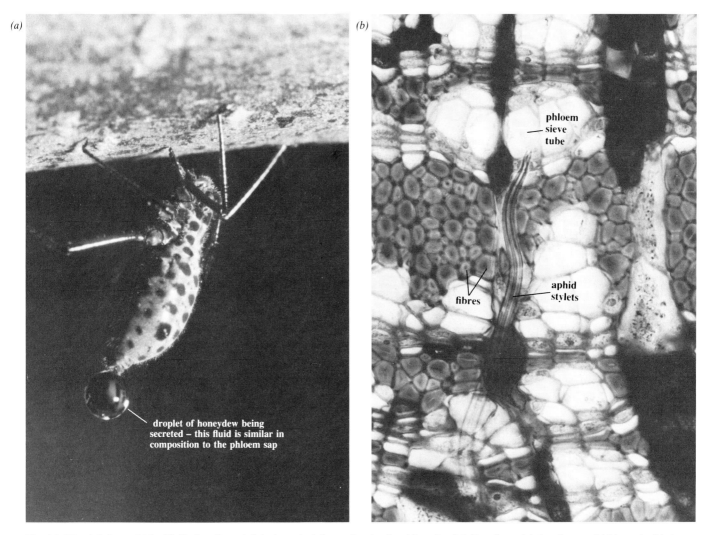

(a)

droplet of honeydew being secreted – this fluid is similar in composition to the phloem sap

(b)

phloem sieve tube

fibres

aphid stylets

Fig 14.25 *(a) An aphid with its feeding stylets inserted through a leaf epidermis. (b) Feeding stylets of an aphid inserted into a sieve tube*

503

14.8.4 Mechanism of translocation in phloem

The facts which any hypothesis must account for are summarised in section 14.8.1. A picture of active phloem has been presented in the previous sections in which large quantities of material move at relatively rapid speeds through very fine sieve tubes. Within the tubes are apparent obstructions, the sieve plates, and other structural features such as phloem protein for which no certain roles have been found. Combine these facts with the further fact that the system is delicate and easily damaged by interference, and it is not surprising that research workers have found it difficult to establish the mechanism of translocation through sieve tubes.

Most workers now believe that a mass flow of solution occurs through sieve tubes, involving the bulk movement of water and solutes in the same direction, unlike diffusion in which molecules and ions move independently of each other. Diffusion itself is too slow to account for the rates observed. The evidence for mass flow through sieve tubes is summarised below.

(1) When phloem is cut, sap can be induced to exude, apparently by mass flow. This is sometimes utilised commercially as a source of sugar. For example the sugar palm exudes 10 dm^3 of sugar-rich sap per day.

(2) The prolonged exudation of sucrose solution from aphid stylets, as described in section 14.8.3, is evidence of hydrostatic pressure in sieve tubes.

(3) Certain viruses are moved in the phloem translocation stream, indicating mass flow rather than diffusion since the virus is incapable of locomotion and not in solution.

The main debate concerns the mechanism by which mass flow is brought about, and the major hypotheses will be discussed.

Münch's hypothesis and the pressure-flow hypothesis

In 1930, Münch put forward a purely physical hypothesis to explain how mass flow might be brought about in sieve tubes. It can be illustrated by the model shown in fig 14.26.

In the model there is an initial tendency for water to pass by osmosis into A and C, but the tendency is greater for A because the solution in A is more concentrated than that in C. As water enters A, a pressure potential (hydrostatic pressure) builds up in the closed system A–B–C, forcing water out of C. Mass flow of solution occurs through B along the hydrostatic pressure gradient so generated. There is also an osmotic gradient from A to C. Eventually the system comes into equilibrium as water dilutes the contents of A and solutes accumulate at C. The model can be applied to living plants. The leaves which make sugar during photosynthesis, thus lowering the ψ_s of the leaf cells, are represented by A. Water, brought to the leaf in xylem (D) enters the leaf cells by osmosis, raising their pressure potential. At the same time, sugars are used in the sinks, such as roots (C), for various purposes including respiration and synthesis of cellulose. This raises the ψ_s of these cells. A hydrostatic pressure gradient exists from leaves to roots, or, in more general terms, from sources to sinks, resulting in mass flow. Equilibrium is not reached because solutes are constantly being used at the sinks (C) and made at the sources (A).

The Münch hypothesis is a purely physical explanation and so does not explain why sieve tubes must be living and metabolically active. It also does not explain the observation that leaf cells are capable of loading sieve tubes against a concentration gradient, that is the fact that the ψ_s of sieve tubes is lower than that of the leaf cells. The hypothesis has

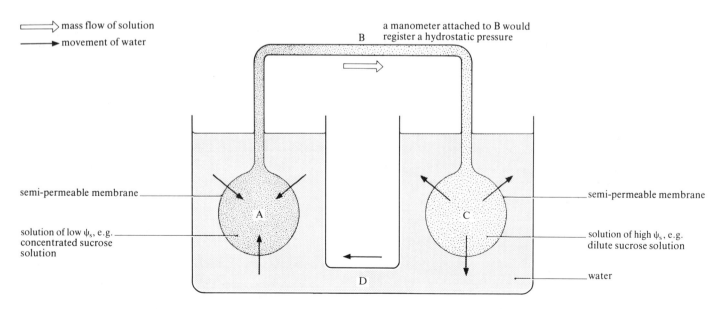

Fig 14.26 *Physical model to illustrate Münch's mass flow hypothesis of phloem translocation*
Equivalents in living plant
A: source, such as leaf; B: phloem; C: sink, such as roots, meristems, fruits; D: xylem, cell walls and intercellular spaces

therefore been modified to include an active loading mechanism of solutes into the sieve tubes. The osmotic and hydrostatic pressure gradient therefore starts in the tubes rather than in the photosynthetic cells. It is also believed that unloading at the sinks is an active process. The modern version of Münch's hypothesis is known as the pressure flow hypothesis.

Loading sieve tubes

It has been shown that the sucrose concentration in sieve tubes in leaves is commonly between 10 and 30% whereas it forms only about a 0.5% solution in the photosynthetic cells where it is produced. As stated above, loading of sieve tubes therefore takes place against a concentration gradient. The mechanism of loading has been the subject of much research in recent years. The problem is to get organic solutes from the chloroplasts to the sieve tubes, a journey of 3 mm at most. Both symplast and apoplast routes are involved.

In 1968 a modified type of companion cell was reported by Gunning and fellow workers. It has numerous internal protuberances of the cell wall, a result of extra thickening. This in turn results in an approximately tenfold increase in surface area of the cell surface membrane lining the wall. It is thought that such cells are thus modified for active uptake of solutes from neighbouring photosynthetic cells and that they actively load their adjacent sieve elements through complex, extensive plasmodesmata. The numerous mitochondria in their cytoplasm provide energy for this. These modified cells are called **transfer cells**, and similar examples of plant cells with wall ingrowths have since been found in many situations where short-distance transport occurs, including xylem parenchyma. Similar cells can easily be seen in a toluidine blue-stained, hand-cut section of a *Tradescantia* node. They are not found in all plants, but are common in the pea family and some other families. Fig 14.27 shows their appearance when viewed with an electron microscope.

Even when transfer cells are absent, similar active transport processes are believed to operate. Active loading of sucrose (and other metabolites such as amino acids, phosphates, potassium and reduced nitrogen) into companion cells is presumably carried out by specific carrier protein molecules in the cell surface membranes of the companion cells.* It results in a very negative solute potential in the companion cells. As a result, water enters by **osmosis** and a mass flow of solution, which includes the sucrose, occurs into the sieve elements via the numerous

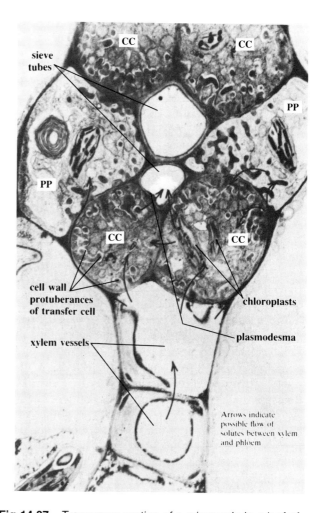

Fig 14.27 *Transverse section of a minor vein in a leaf of* Senecio vulgaris. *The phloem region, in the top half of the picture, shows six cells arranged around two sieve elements. There are two pairs of companion cells (cc) modified as transfer cells. These have dense cytoplasm and lie above and below the sieve elements. There are phloem parenchyma cells (pp) to each side. These have less dense cytoplasm and wall ingrowths only on the sides facing the sieve elements. Plasmodesmata between sieve elements and companion cells are common, but are very rare between sieve elements and phloem parenchyma cells. In the lower half of the picture two xylem elements occupy the centre, while to each side there are parts of two large bundle sheath cells. Arrows indicate some of the possible routes for movement of solutes into sieve elements, including some solutes delivered to the apoplast in the xylem. Magnification ×6 560*

---

* These carrier systems are thought to be similar to those in animal and bacterial cells in which transport of organic molecules is linked with transport of H^+ ions (protons). Protons are pumped out of the cell by a carrier which uses ATP as an energy source (like the Na^+/K^+ pump, see fig 7.13). The proton gradient thus established represents potential energy. The protons diffuse rapidly back into the cell by way of specific carrier proteins that only function if they co-transport sucrose or other specific organic molecules. The active part of this process is therefore the establishment of a proton gradient across the membrane, with a lower pH (higher H^+ concentration) outside of the cell.

plasmodesmata that link the companion cells with the sieve elements. The high pressures and mass flow predicted by the Münch hypothesis are thus generated in the sieve tubes (not in the mesophyll cells as imagined by Münch). Some substances enter phloem by passive diffusion, such as some growth substances.

Little is known of unloading, except that it is probably active and is probably an important means of regulating internal distribution of solutes in plants.

Critical assessment of the pressure-flow hypothesis

(a) The hypothesis predicts that mass flow will occur through sieve tubes and this seems to occur (the evidence has been given).

(b) The hypothesis requires the existence of an osmotic gradient and high pressure potential (hydrostatic pressure) in the phloem. These have been demonstrated in a number of plants.

The hydrostatic pressure gradients required to move solutes at the observed rates are relatively high. Assuming that the sieve pores are completely open, a *gradient* of $100\,kPa\,m^{-1}$ has been theoretically calculated as adequate and until recently it was doubted that such large gradients existed. Several attempts have been made to measure pressure in phloem directly, a very difficult task. An average **gradient** of about $60\,kPa\,m^{-1}$ in the phloem of oak was recorded in 1968. Indirect calculations of pressure potentials based on measured solute potentials and water potentials suggest similar gradients of about $70\,kPa\,m^{-1}$. Actual pressures varying from $1\,000$–$2\,000\,kPa$ have been reliably recorded in recent years. It is therefore likely that the required pressure gradients *are* generated.

(c) Another criticism of the pressure-flow hypothesis has been that it does not explain why sieve tubes should be living as opposed to the dead tubes of xylem. However, only living cells can maintain functional cell surface membranes, and the latter are required to prevent leakage of sucrose from the sieve tubes. Recent studies indicate that little metabolic energy is expended by living sieve tubes, suggesting that movement of solutes through them is passive, as predicted by the pressure-flow hypothesis.

(d) Sieve plates are thought to be necessary, despite the resistance to flow which they create, to support the sieve tubes, preventing them from bulging and splitting or exploding outwards with the high internal pressures.

(e) No role for phloem protein is suggested by the pressure-flow hypothesis (see section 14.8.5).

14.8.5 First-aid mechanisms – a possible role for sieve plates, phloem protein and plastids

One danger faced by all plants is damage from being eaten by animals. If sieve tubes are ruptured, leakage of high energy substances such as sucrose would be costly to the plant. Usually, damaged sieve tubes are sealed within minutes by deposition of callose across the sieve plates, blocking the sieve pores. This represents a possible role for sieve plates. It has been suggested that in dicotyledons that possess large quantities of phloem protein, the latter serve even more of a first-aid function by blocking the sieve pores as soon as the tube is broken. This is due to the pressure surge mentioned in section 14.8.2. This suggestion is partly supported by the fact that the plants with high quantities of phloem protein, such as vines and peas (climbers), tend to have relatively few, but large, sieve tubes (hence their common use in phloem studies) and are therefore more likely to suffer as a result of sieve tube damage.

14.8.6 Other hypotheses

It should be noted that other hypotheses for phloem transport have been put forward, including some form of cytoplasmic streaming, 'activated diffusion' (no known mechanism), and the existence of cytoplasmic strands ('transcellular strands') supported by the sieve plates and extending long distances through the sieve tubes. In the latter case it was suggested that solutions could in some way be pumped along the strands. A mechanism involving a phenomenon known as electro-osmosis, which envisaged a potential difference being actively maintained across sieve plates, had attractions in the 1970s because a role for living sieve tubes, companion cells, sieve plates and even the presence of phloem protein in sieve pores could be argued. All of the alternative theories to pressure-flow are interesting, but are supported by little, if any, experimental evidence.

Transport in animals

In the animal kingdom, the cnidarians and platyhelminths lack a specific system for the transport and distribution of materials. The organisms in these phyla possess a large surface area to volume ratio, and diffusion of gases over the whole body surface is sufficient for their needs. Internally the distance that materials have to travel is again small enough for them to move by diffusion or cytoplasmic streaming (section 7.2.4).

As organisms increase in size and complexity so the quantity of materials moving in and out of the body increases. The distance that materials have to travel within the body also increases, so that diffusion becomes inadequate as a means for their distribution. Some other method of conveying materials from one part of the organism to another is therefore necessary. This generally takes the form of a mass flow system.

14.9 General characteristics of a circulatory system

The purpose of a circulatory system is to provide rapid mass flow of materials from one part of the body to another over distances where diffusion would be too slow. On reaching their destination the materials must be able to pass through the walls of the circulatory system into the organs or tissues. Likewise, materials produced by these structures must also be able to enter the circulatory system.

Every circulatory system possesses three distinct characteristics:
(1) a circulatory fluid, generally called blood;
(2) a contractile, pumping device to propel the fluid around the body, this may either be a modified blood vessel or a heart;
(3) tubes through which the fluid can circulate, called blood vessels.

Two distinct types of circulatory system are found in the non-vertebrates and vertebrates. They are the open and closed vascular systems.

The open vascular system (most arthropods, some cephalopod molluscs, tunicates). Blood is pumped by the heart into an aorta which branches into a number of arteries. These open into a series of blood spaces collectively called the **haemocoel**. Blood under low pressure moves slowly between the tissues, gradually percolating back into the heart via open-ended veins. Distribution of blood to the tissues is poorly controlled.

The closed vascular system (echinoderms, cephalopod molluscs, annelids, vertebrates). Blood is pumped by the heart rapidly around the body under sustained high pressure and back to the heart. It is confined to a series of specific vessels and not permitted to come into contact with the body tissues. Distribution of blood to the tissues is able to be adjusted. The only entry and exit to this system is through the walls of the blood vessels.

Blood vessels are named according to their structure and function. Vessels conveying blood away from the heart are called **arteries**. These branch into smaller arteries called **arterioles**. The arterioles divide many times into microscopic **capillaries** which are located between the cells of nearly all the body tissues. It is here that exchange of materials between blood and tissues takes place.

Within the organ or tissue the capillaries reunite forming **venules** which begin the process of returning blood to the heart. The venules join to form **veins**. It is these blood vessels that actually pass the blood back into the heart. The anatomy of each type of blood vessel is discussed in detail later in section 14.12.

14.10 The development of transport systems in animals

In the protozoans circulation of materials is primarily achieved by cytoplasmic streaming. Cnidarians rely on movements of their body wall to create water currents in the enteron which circulate food, water and dissolved gases. The musculo-epithelial and flagellate cells of the endoderm assist in this activity. Platyhelminths have a very thin, flattened shape, enabling materials to be exchanged within the organism and with its environment by diffusion.

14.10.1 Annelids

Annelids are coelomate animals. The presence of a coelom separates the body wall from the internal organs and confers the advantage of independence of movement of internal structures such as the gut. However, this is countered by the need for some form of connecting system between the two regions which enable food, gases and waste substances to be transported between the environment and the gut or vice versa. It is at the coelomate level that a blood system evolved in order to connect gut and body wall.

The earthworm – a closed blood vascular system

There is a well-developed blood system in which blood circulates around the body through a system of closed blood vessels. The largest blood vessel is the longitudinal, **dorsal vessel** which has muscular walls. It is situated above the alimentary canal. Peristaltic contractions originate at the rear end of the vessel and drive blood forwards towards the anterior end of the animal, backflow being prevented by a series of valves. Each valve is formed from a fold of endothelium within the blood vessel. The dorsal vessel is the main collecting vessel and receives blood from the body wall, gut, nerve cord and nephridia. The names of the main segmental vessels are given in figs 14.28 and 14.29.

The dorsal vessel connects with the smaller, more

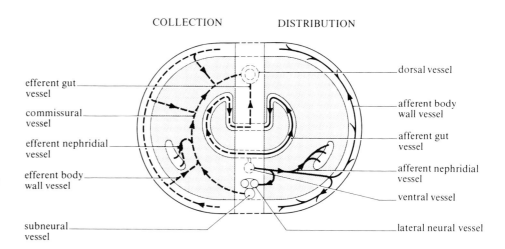

COLLECTION   DISTRIBUTION

dorsal vessel
afferent body wall vessel
afferent gut vessel
afferent nephridial vessel
ventral vessel
lateral neural vessel

efferent gut vessel
commissural vessel
efferent nephridial vessel
efferent body wall vessel
subneural vessel

Fig 14.28 *Segmental distribution of blood in* Lumbricus *in regions behind the clitellum. (From A. E. Vines & N. Rees (4th edition, 1972) Plant and animal biology, Vol. I, Pitman)*

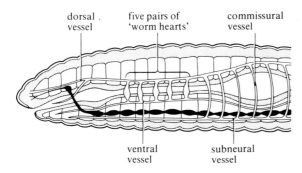

Fig 14.29 (below) *Main blood vessels in the earthworm (Lumbricus terrestris). (From E. G. Springthorpe (1973) An introduction to functional systems in animals, Longman)*

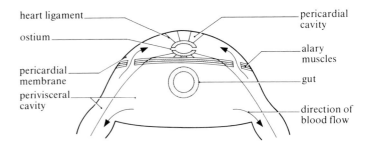

Fig 14.30 *Schematic transverse section to show open blood vascular system of·an insect. (After Ramsay (1968) A physiological approach to lower animals, Cambridge University Press)*

contractile, ventral vessel via five pairs of contractile 'pseudohearts' located in segments 7–11. Each 'pseudoheart' possesses four valves which permit the blood to flow only towards the ventral vessel.

The blood flows posteriorly in the ventral vessel. It is distributed to the nephridia, nerve cord, gut and body wall by a series of segmental blood vessels. In addition the nerve cord is supplied with blood by the longitudinal, subneural vessel which runs below it.

Within the various organs of the worm, capillary networks enable materials to be exchanged between blood and tissues. Eventually the blood passes back to the dorsal vessel, when it can once again begin its journey through the closed blood vascular system of the worm.

The blood itself is red in colour, containing haemoglobin (section 14.13.1) dissolved in the plasma. It transports oxygen, carbon dioxide, soluble excretory materials and foodstuffs around the body. Colourless amoeboid cells which have a defensive function also circulate in the blood.

14.10.2 Arthropods

The coelom is drastically reduced in the arthropods and its place taken by the haemocoel. This is a network of blood-filled spaces called **sinuses** in which the internal organs are suspended. Gaseous exchange in most arthropods is effected by the tracheal system (section 4.9), and the blood vascular system is not used for transporting respiratory gases. Arthropod blood is colourless, containing no haemoglobin, and serves to transport dissolved foodstuffs and excretory materials and to circulate colourless amoeboid leucocytes.

The cockroach – an open blood vascular system

There is only one blood vessel in the cockroach, the dorsal blood vessel, and the posterior part of it is modified into a distinct heart, whilst the anterior end is called the **aorta**. The heart lies in a large sinus which is a modified part of the haemocoel called the **pericardium** (fig 14.30). There are 13 dilations or chambers in the heart, three are located in the thoracic segments and ten in the abdomen. Every chamber except the most posterior possesses a pair of lateral

openings called **ostia**. Each ostium is fitted with a valve which permits blood to enter but not leave the chamber. Between adjacent chambers are more valves which prevent backward flow of the blood. Intersegmental alary muscles are attached to the ventral wall of the heart, and when these muscles contract they increase the volume of the heart and create a negative pressure. This draws in blood from the pericardium through the ostia. When the alary muscles relax and the heart contracts, blood is propelled forwards into the aorta. This divides into several arteries which are open-ended. Consequently blood pours out of them into blood sinuses where it bathes the organs of the insect directly. Eventually the blood percolates back into the pericardium and ultimately into the heart.

14.10.3 Vertebrate circulatory systems

All vertebrate circulatory systems possess a well-defined muscular heart, lying in a ventral position in the region of the pectoral girdle. The heart is responsible for conveying blood rapidly to all parts of the animal's body. Arteries convey blood away from the heart, whilst veins pass blood from the body to the heart. Another system, the lymphatic system, is also present and supplements the activities of the circulatory system.

Comparative embryological studies indicate that, in all vertebrate embryos, six lateral arterial arches emanate from the ventral aorta and unite to form a pair of lateral dorsal aortae which eventually merge into a single median dorsal aorta (fig 14.31). Fish are the only vertebrates to exhibit this arrangement in anything like its original form in the adult condition. In all other vertebrates the embryonic pattern has been extensively modified.

The dogfish

The dogfish heart (fig 14.32*b*), which is confined within a pericardial cavity, is S-shaped and consists of two main chambers, an **atrium** and a **ventricle**. Blood from the general body circulation enters a thin-walled chamber, the **sinus venosus**, which precedes the heart. From here it passes into the weakly muscular atrium by a negative pressure developed in the surrounding pericardium. It is passed on to the thicker, more muscular ventricle. When

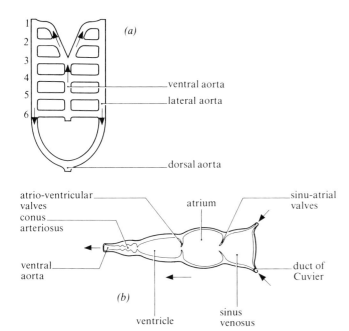

Fig 14.31 (a) *Vertebrate embryo condition of the blood vascular system. Six arterial arches branch from the ventral aorta, eventually rejoining to form lateral aortae.* (b) *Embryonic heart*

this contracts, blood is pumped via the **conus arteriosus** into a ventral aorta. Valves between the atrium and ventricle and the ventricle and conus arteriosus prevent backflow of blood. The conus arteriosus is highly elastic and easily stretched by the pressure of the blood leaving the ventricle. In turn, its elastic walls act on the blood and force it forwards at a more uniform speed, thus enhancing a continuous flow of blood in the ventral aorta.

In the dogfish five pairs of afferent branchial arteries branch from the ventral aorta and carry deoxygenated blood to the gills (fig 14.32a). Within the gills the arteries divide many times into numerous fine capillaries. Eventually they rejoin to form efferent branchial arteries. These carry oxygenated blood and form a series of four loops which encircle the perimeter of each of the first four internal branchial clefts. A single blood vessel from the anterior part of the fifth branchial cleft opens into the fourth loop. Four epibranchial vessels from either side of the body convey the blood from the loops backwards and towards the midline where they join to form the dorsal aorta. Anteriorly the dorsal aorta divides and joins the internal carotid arteries, and supplies oxygenated blood to the head. Posteriorly the dorsal aorta branches many times

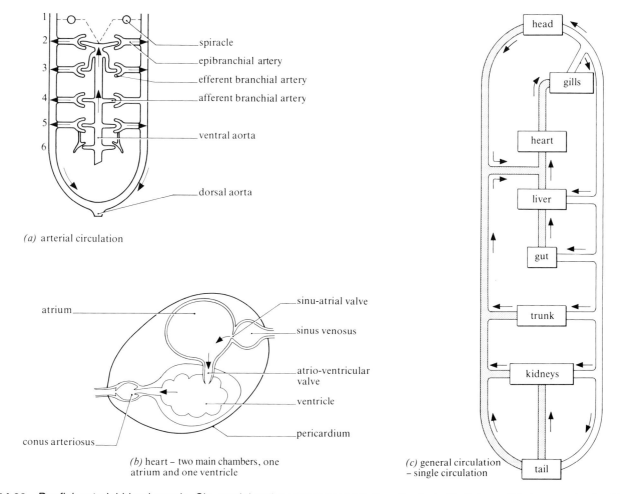

(a) arterial circulation

(b) heart – two main chambers, one atrium and one ventricle

(c) general circulation – single circulation

Fig 14.32 *Dogfish arterial blood supply. Six arterial arches are reduced to five, the first gill slit is modified as a spiracle. Direct branchial vessels have split up to form afferent, efferent and epibranchial arteries. This gives a greater surface area of the blood system in the gill region for gaseous exchange*

into arteries which supply the rest of the body with oxygenated blood.

As blood flows through the heart only once during each circuit of the body, the dogfish is said to possess a single circulation (fig 14.32c). The blood pressure falls as it passes through the gill capillaries and is low in the dorsal aorta. The blood pressure falls even further after it has passed through the capillaries of the body organs. This is because of the resistance to its flow exerted by the various capillary networks of the body. Consequently, return of blood to the heart is very slow. To offset this apparent disadvantage, large blood spaces called **sinuses**, which provide little resistance to blood flow, are present. Raised anterior and posterior cardinal sinuses, together with laterally placed veins, return blood to the region of the heart where it passes to the sinus via a pair of Cuvierian veins. Backflow of blood in the veins is prevented by valves, and forward flow enhanced by the body muscles squeezing these vessels.

In the posterior region of the fish there are blood vessels called **portal veins**. These are blood vessels with capillary beds at both ends. Blood from the small intestine passes to the liver via the hepatic portal vein, and blood from the tail to the kidney via renal portal veins. Thus the blood of the dogfish having already passed through the capillaries of the gills passes through two sets of capillaries of the portal systems – three sets of capillaries in all.

Dogfish blood contains oval-shaped, nucleated red blood cells and amoeboid leucocytes suspended in plasma. The lymphatic system is comprised of lymphatic vessels emptying into two dorsal longitudinal collecting ducts which finally return their contents (that is lymph) to the blood via the cardinal sinuses.

Amphibia – the frog

In the adult frog the heart and aortic circulation show modifications which can be correlated with its semi-terrestrial mode of life. Lungs have developed and replaced gills as respiratory organs, and a new circulation, the pulmonary circulation between the lungs and heart, has been established. There is no longer a need to retain all the aortic arches to supply branchial arches, and some have been put to new uses whilst others have been lost. The third arch has become the carotid artery and transports blood anteriorly to the head (fig 14.33a). The fourth is the systemic, conveying oxygenated blood to the rest of the body via the dorsal aorta, whilst the sixth arch transports

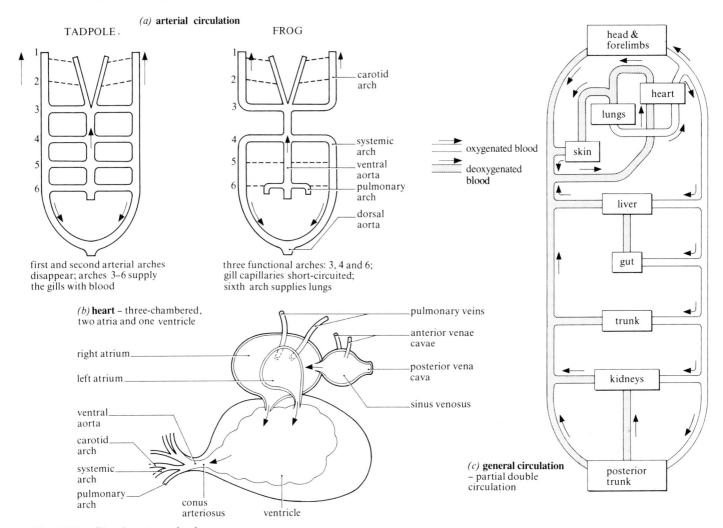

Fig 14.33 *Blood system of a frog*

deoxygenated blood from the heart to the lungs via the pulmonary artery. The first, second and fifth arches have disappeared.

The heart consists of three main chambers, two atria and one ventricle (fig 14.33b). Blood which has been oxygenated at the lungs is returned to the left atrium via the pulmonary vein, whilst deoxygenated blood from the body is passed to the right atrium via the sinus venosus by the anterior and posterior venae cavae. At no time does the blood in the atria mix. However, both atria contract at the same time and deliver their blood to the single ventricle. The inner surface of the dorsal and ventral walls of the ventricle is built up into ridges which prevent mixing of the blood to some extent. When the blood passes from the ventricle to the conus arteriosus, mixing is further prevented by a spiral valve which incompletely divides the conus into two distinct corridors. The dorsal passage, called the **cavum pulmocutaneous**, leads to the pulmonary arch which, besides running to the lungs, also sends branches to the skin, whilst the ventral **cavum aorticum** takes blood to the carotid and systemic arches.

It is clear that there are two distinct circuits which the blood can take, one to the lungs and one to the body. This may be regarded as a partial double circulation, where blood, after passing from the heart to the lungs, is returned again to the heart before passing to the body (fig 14.33c). The separation of oxygenated and deoxygenated blood in this system is not entirely complete.

The blood vascular system of a frog is a very special system suitable for an amphibious animal. When the frog is relatively inactive, oxygen diffuses into the capillaries under the skin and is transported to the right atrium of the heart via the subclavian vein. The lungs are not used except under conditions of strenuous action. Thus normally the left atrium receives little oxygenated blood.

Veins replace sinuses in the venous system of the frog. Blood is returned to the sinus venosus by anterior and posterior venae cavae which receive blood from veins leaving the major organs of the body. Renal and hepatic portal veins are also present.

Intercellular channels containing lymph (section 14.12.1) drain into lymphatic vessels. Eventually the lymph is pumped into the venous system at two points, one anterior and one posterior. A pair of small contractile lymph hearts in each region drive the lymph into the veins.

Frog's blood consists of nucleated erythrocytes containing haemoglobin, and a variety of white cells suspended in the plasma. They include macrophages, lymphocytes, granulocytes and monocytes (section 14.11.2).

Reptilia – the crocodile

Here the heart consists of four chambers, two atria and two ventricles, the right side being more or less completely separated from the left side (fig 14.34). Therefore the crocodile possesses a double circulatory system with almost complete separation of oxygenated blood in the left side from deoxygenated blood on the right side. The conus

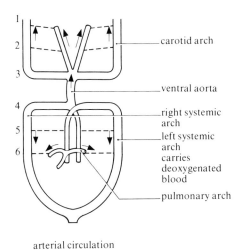

arterial circulation

Fig 14.34 *Reptile arterial blood supply – the crocodile*

arteriosus has been replaced by three distinct arteries which form arches directly from the ventricle. They are the right systemic arch, which gives rise to the carotid arteries, the left systemic arch, and the pulmonary arch.

Aves and Mammalia – general

The heart is four-chambered in birds and mammals. The right atrium and ventricle are completely separated from the left atrium and ventricle (fig 14.35b(ii)). This means that oxygenated and deoxygenated blood are kept completely separate. In order for blood in the right side of the heart to get to the left side, it must first pass through the lungs (fig 14.35b(iii)). For blood from the left side to get to the right side it has first to pass round the body. This double circulation ensures that oxygenated blood flowing to the tissues is under high pressure and not, as is the case of fish, under low pressure. As the blood passes through the lungs before it passes to the body, this ensures that it is well oxygenated before it reaches the actively respiring organs.

14.33 Why is it an advantage in birds and mammals for oxygenated blood to flow to the tissues under high pressure?

The arterial system is further reduced in birds and mammals. Birds retain only the right half of the systemic arch, whilst mammals retain the left half (fig 14.35b(i)). The third arch persists as the carotid arch and the sixth as the pulmonary arch. Within the venous system the posterior vena cava replaces the renal portal system. Therefore blood from the posterior parts of the body is returned directly to the heart, thus increasing the speed at which blood can be supplied back to the tissues.

14.11 Composition of mammalian blood

Blood is composed of cells bathed in a fluid matrix called **plasma**. The cells constitute about 45% by

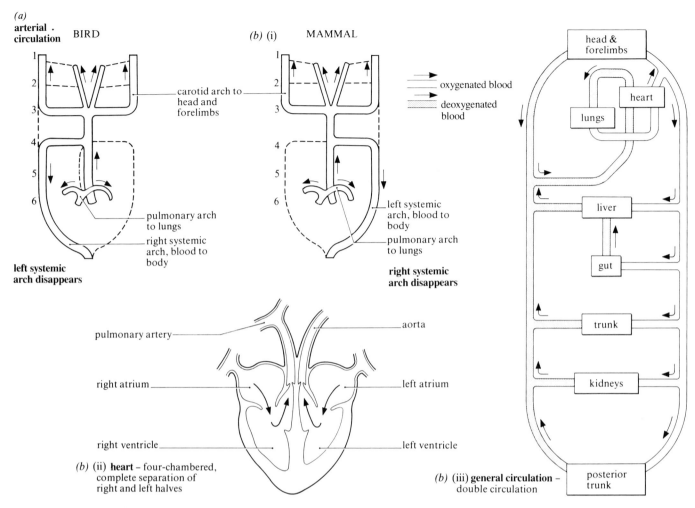

(a) **arterial circulation** BIRD

1
2 — carotid arch to head and forelimbs
3
4
5
6 — pulmonary arch to lungs — right systemic arch, blood to body

left systemic arch disappears

(b) (i) MAMMAL

1
2
3
4
5
6 — left systemic arch, blood to body — pulmonary arch to lungs

right systemic arch disappears

→ oxygenated blood
→ deoxygenated blood

pulmonary artery — aorta

right atrium — left atrium

right ventricle — left ventricle

(b) (ii) **heart** – four-chambered, complete separation of right and left halves

head & forelimbs
heart
lungs
liver
gut
trunk
kidneys
posterior trunk

(b) (iii) **general circulation** – double circulation

Fig 14.35 *(a) Bird and (b) mammal arterial blood systems*

volume of the blood, whilst the other 55% is represented by the plasma.

14.11.1 Plasma

Plasma is a pale yellow liquid. It consists of 90% water and 10% of a variety of substances in solution and suspension, some of which are normally maintained at constant concentrations, whilst the concentrations of others may fluctuate within narrow limits according to their rates of removal or supply from particular organs. The major components of blood plasma together with their functions are shown in table 14.9.

14.11.2 Blood cells

Erythrocytes

These are the red blood cells. Characteristically in humans they are small, enucleated and appear as circular, biconcave discs. Their average diameter is 7–8 μm, which is approximately the same as the internal diameter of blood capillaries. Their particular shape permits a larger surface area to volume ratio than that of a sphere and therefore increases the area which can be used for gaseous exchange. Each cell is very thin, thus permitting efficient diffusion of gases from its surface inwards. Its membrane is pliable and this property allows the erythrocyte to squeeze through capillaries whose internal diameters are smaller than its own.

The mechanism of production of erythrocytes is known as **haemopoiesis** and the tissue which gives rise to them is called **haemopoietic tissue**. In an infant, all bones contain haemopoietic tissue, whilst in adults the principal regions of erythrocyte production are the bones of the pelvis, ribs, sternum, vertebrae, clavicles, scapulae and skull. There are approximately five million erythrocytes per cubic millimetre of blood. However this figure varies according to the age, sex and state of health of each individual.

An important characteristic of erythrocytes is the presence of haemoglobin which combines reversibly with oxygen to form oxyhaemoglobin in areas of high oxygen concentration, and releases the oxygen in regions of low oxygen concentration. They also contain the enzyme carbonic anhydrase which plays a role in carbon dioxide transport (section 14.13.4).

In the adult, each erythrocyte has a life span of about

Table 14.9 Components of blood plasma and their functions.

Constituent	Function
Constituents maintained at a constant concentration	
Water	Major constituent of lymph. Provides tissue cells with water. Conveys many dissolved materials round the body. Aids maintenance of blood pressure and blood volume
Plasma proteins	
Serum albumin	Very abundant. Binds plasma calcium
Serum globulins:	
α-globulin	Binds thyroxine and bilirubin
β-globulin	Binds iron, cholesterol and the vitamins A, D and K
γ-globulin	Binds antigens and is important in the body's immunological reactions. Generally called antibody. Also binds histamine
Prothrombin	A catalytic agent which takes part in the blood-clotting process
Fibrinogen	Takes part in blood-clotting process
Enzymes	Participate in metabolic activities
Mineral ions	
These include: Na^+, K^+, Ca^{2+}, Mg^{2+}, $H_2PO_4^-$, HPO_4^{2-}, PO_4^{3-}, Cl^-, HCO_3^-, SO_4^{2-}	All help collectively to regulate osmotic pressure and pH levels of the blood. They also exert a variety of other effects on the cells of the body; e.g. Ca^{2+} may act as a clotting factor, regulate muscle and nerve cell sensitivity, influence the sol–gel condition within cells
Constituents that occur in varying concentrations	
Dissolved products of digestion	
Dissolved excretory products	All are being constantly transported to and from cells within the body
Vitamins	
Hormones	

three months after which time it is destroyed in the spleen or liver. The protein portion of the erythrocyte is broken down into its constituent amino acids; the iron of the haem portion is extracted and stored in the liver as ferritin (an iron-containing protein). It may be re-used later in the production of further erythrocytes or as a component of cytochrome. The remainder of the haem molecule is broken down into two bile pigments, bilirubin and biliverdin. Both are ultimately excreted by way of the bile into the gut.

Between 2–10 million erythrocytes are destroyed and replaced each second in the human body. The rate of destruction and replacement is determined by the amount of oxygen in the atmosphere which is available for carriage by the blood. If the quantity carried is low, then the marrow is stimulated to produce more erythrocytes than the liver destroys. This is one of the ways in which mammals acclimatise to the reduced oxygen content at high altitudes. When the oxygen content is high, the situation is reversed.

White blood cells – leucocytes

These cells are larger than erythrocytes, and present in much smaller numbers, there being about 7 000 per cubic millimetre of blood. All are nucleated. They play an important role in the body's defence mechanisms against disease. Although they are nucleated their life span in the bloodstream is normally only a few days. There are two main groups of white blood cell, the granulocytes and the agranulocytes.

Granulocytes (polymorphonuclear leucocytes). These originate in the bone marrow but are produced by cells different from those that make erythrocytes. Each cell contains a lobed nucleus and granular cytoplasm (table 14.10). All are capable of amoeboid movement. Granulocytes can be further subdivided into neutrophils, eosinophils and basophils.

Neutrophils (phagocytes). These constitute 70% of the total number of white cells. They are able to squeeze between the cells of the capillary walls and enter the intercellular spaces. This process is called **diapedesis**. From here they move to infected areas of the body. They are actively phagocytic and engulf and digest disease-causing bacteria (section 14.13.5).

Eosinophils. They possess cytoplasmic granules which stain red when the dye eosin is applied to them. Generally they represent only 1.5% of the total number of white cells, but their population increases in people with allergic conditions such as asthma or hayfever. It is thought that eosinophils possess anti-histamine properties. The number of eosinophils present in the bloodstream is under the control of hormones produced by the adrenal cortex.

Basophils. They represent 0.5% of the white blood cell population and produce heparin and histamine. The granules in these cells stain blue with basic dyes such as methylene blue.

Agranulocytes (mononuclear leucocytes). These cells possess non-granular cytoplasm and either an oval or bean-shaped nucleus. Two main types exist.

Table 14.10 Cellular components of blood (diagrams not drawn to scale).

Component	Origin	Number of cells/mm^{-3}	Function	Structure
Erythrocytes	bone marrow	5 000 000	transport of oxygen and some carbon dioxide	
Leucocytes	bone marrow			
(a) Granulocytes (72% of total white blood cell count) neutrophils (70%)		4 900	engulf bacteria	
eosinophils (1.5%)	bone marrow	105	anti-histamine properties	
basophils (0.5%)		35	produce histamine and heparin	
(b) Agranulocytes (28%) monocytes (4%)	bone marrow	280	engulf bacteria	
lymphocytes (24%)	bone marrow lymphoid tissue spleen	1 680	production of antibodies	
Platelets	bone marrow	250 000	initiate blood-clotting mechanism	

Monocytes (4%). These are formed in the bone marrow and have a bean-shaped nucleus. They are actively phagocytic and ingest bacteria and other large particles. They are able to migrate from the bloodstream to inflamed areas of the body and act in the same manner as neutrophils.

Lymphocytes (24%). These are produced in the thymus gland and lymphoid tissues from precursor cells which originate from the bone marrow. The cells are rounded and possess only a small quantity of cytoplasm. Amoeboid movement is limited. Their major function is to cause or mediate immune reactions (such as antibody production, graft rejection and tumour cell killing). The life span of these particular cells can vary from a matter of days in rodents up to ten years or more in humans.

14.11.3 Platelets

Platelets are irregularly shaped membrane-bound cell fragments, frequently enucleated and formed from large bone marrow cells called **megakaryocytes**. They

function to initiate the mechanism of blood clotting. There are about 250 000 platelets per cubic millimetre of blood.

14.12 The mammalian circulatory system

As blood circulates continuously round the body it passes through a series of arteries, capillaries and veins. Basically each artery and vein consists of three layers, an inner lining of squamous endothelium, the **tunica intima**, a middle layer of smooth muscle and elastic fibres, the **tunica media**, and an external layer of fibrous connective tissue possessing collagen fibres, the **tunica externa** (table 14.11 and fig 14.37a).

The large arteries in close proximity to the heart (that is the aorta, subclavians and carotids) must be able to contend with the high pressure of blood leaving the ventricles of the heart. The walls of these vessels are thick and the middle layer is mainly composed of elastic fibres. This enables them to dilate but not rupture during

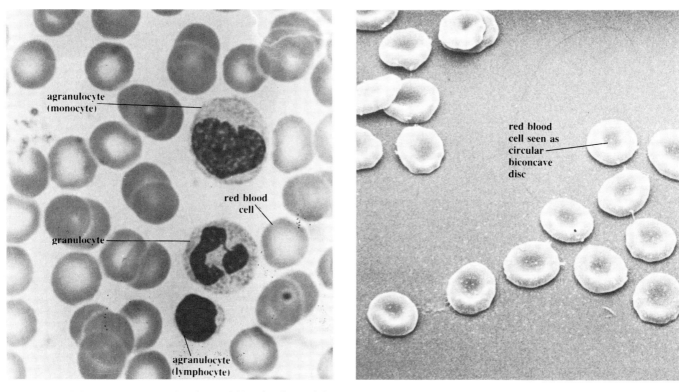

Fig 14.36 *(a) A blood smear showing red blood cells and three types of white cell. (b) A scanning electron micrograph of red blood cells of a mammal*

Table 14.11 Comparison in structure and function of an artery, capillary and vein (diagrams are not drawn to scale).

Artery	Capillary	Vein
Transport blood away from the heart	Link arteries to veins. Site of exchange of materials between blood and tissues	Transport blood towards the heart
Tunica media thick and composed of elastic, muscular tissue	No tunica media. Only tissue present is squamous endothelium. No elastic fibres	Tunica media relatively thin and only slightly muscular. Few elastic fibres
No semi-lunar valves	No semi-lunar valves	Semi-lunar valves at intervals along the length to prevent backflow of blood
Pressure of blood is high and pulsatile	Pressure of blood falling and non-pulsatile	Pressure of blood low and non-pulsatile
Blood flow rapid	Blood flow slowing	Blood flow slow
Low blood volume	High blood volume	Increased blood volume
Blood oxygenated except in pulmonary artery	Mixed oxygenated and deoxygenated blood	Blood deoxygenated except in pulmonary vein

515

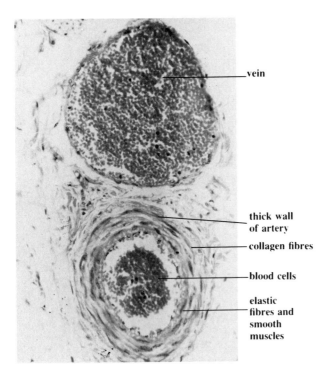

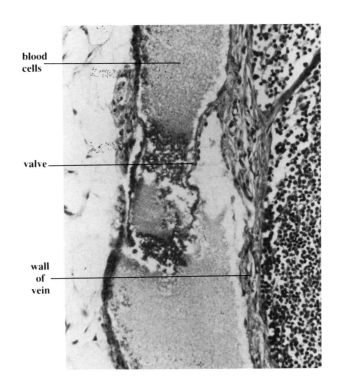

Fig 14.37 *(a) TS of an artery and a vein. (b) LS of a vein showing a valve*

ventricular systole (section 14.12.3). When systole ceases, the arteries contract and promote an even flow of blood along their length (fig 14.38).

The arteries further away from the heart have a similar structure but possess more smooth muscle fibres in the middle layer. They are supplied with neurones from the sympathetic nervous system. Stimulation from this system regulates the diameter of these arteries and this is important in controlling the flow of blood to different parts of the body.

Blood passes from the arteries into smaller vessels called arterioles. In all of these except the pulmonary arterioles, the tunica media consists entirely of smooth muscle fibres supplied with neurones from the sympathetic nervous system (section 16.2). Many arterioles possess precapillary 'sphincters' (figs 14.39 and 14.40) at their capillary ends. When these structures contract, blood is prevented from flowing through the capillary network. Also present in certain regions of the body are arterio-venous cross-connections, which act as short-circuit routes between arterioles and venules and serve to regulate the quantity of blood which flows through the capillary beds according to the needs of the body.

Blood passes from the arterioles into capillaries, the smallest of all blood vessels in the body. They form a vast network of vessels pervading all parts of the body, and are so numerous that no capillary is more than 0.5 mm from any cell. They are 7–10 μm in diameter and their walls, consisting solely of endothelium, are permeable to water and dissolved substances. It is here that exchange of materials between the blood and body cells takes place.

Blood from the capillary beds drains into venules, whose walls consist of a thin layer of collagen fibres. They pass the blood into veins which eventually convey it back to the heart.

A vein possesses less muscle and elastic fibres in its middle layer than an artery and the diameter of its lumen is greater. Semi-lunar valves (fig 14.41) are present, being

(a)

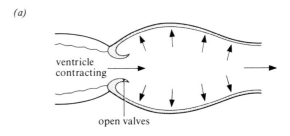

(b)

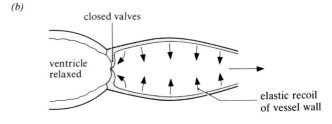

Fig 14.38 *Diagram demonstrating how the arteries near the heart assist in maintaining a continuous flow of blood in spite of a discontinuous flow received from the ventricles. (From Clegg & Clegg (2nd edition, 1963) Biology of the mammal, Heinemann Medical Books)*

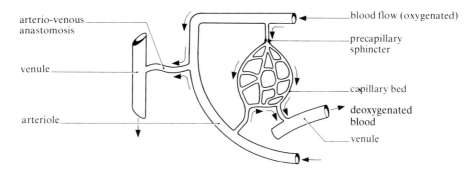

Fig 14.39 *The possible routes that blood may take between arteriole, capillary bed and venule*

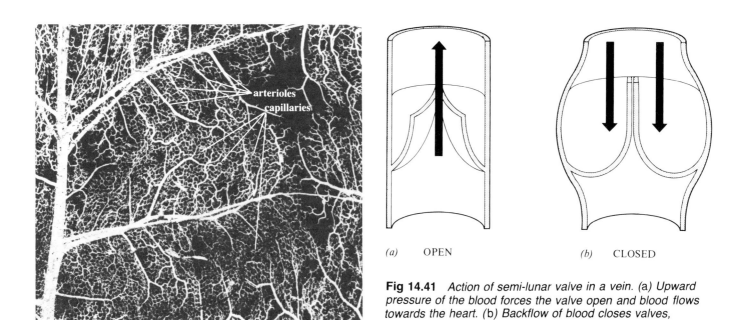

Fig 14.40 *Capillary bed showing arterioles and capillaries*

Fig 14.41 *Action of semi-lunar valve in a vein. (a) Upward pressure of the blood forces the valve open and blood flows towards the heart. (b) Backflow of blood closes valves, blood therefore cannot flow away from the heart*

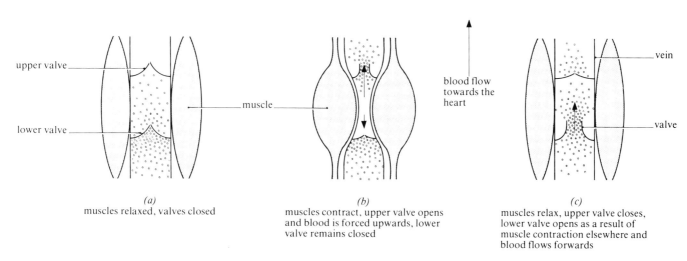

Fig 14.42 *Diagram illustrating how muscle contraction around a vein aids one-way flow of blood towards the heart*

formed from folds of the inner walls of the vein which are permeated by elastic fibres. They function to prevent backflow of blood thereby maintaining a unidirectional blood flow. A number of veins are located between the large muscles of the body (as in the arms and legs). When these muscles contract they exert pressure on the veins and squeeze them flat (fig 14.42). This assists the venous flow to the heart. A general plan of the mammalian double circulation is shown in fig 14.43.

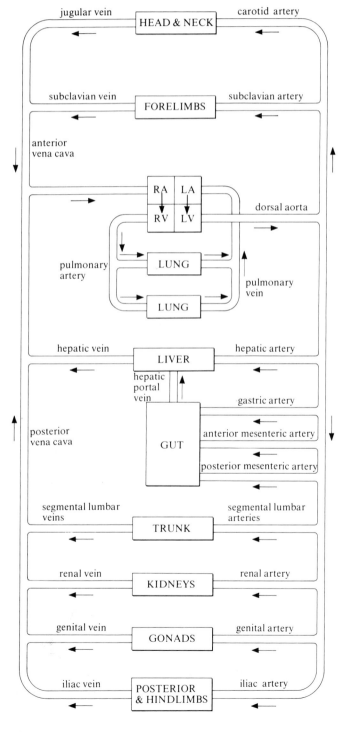

Fig 14.43 *Mammalian double circulatory system. Principal blood vessels are shown but not capillary beds*

14.12.1   Formation of intercellular fluid

Intercellular, or tissue, fluid is formed when blood passes through the capillaries. The capillary walls are permeable to all components of the blood except the erythrocytes and plasma proteins.

The solute potential exerted by the plasma proteins is about 3.3 kPa and this far exceeds the solute potential in the tissue fluid. Under these conditions one would normally expect tissue fluid to flow into the blood plasma. However, the blood pressure at the arterial end of a capillary is about 4.3 kPa. Therefore fluid passes from the capillary into the minute spaces between the cells to form the intercellular fluid. It is through the tissue fluid that exchange of materials between blood and tissues occurs.

The blood cannot afford to constantly lose so much fluid and therefore much of it is returned. This occurs in two ways.

(1) At the venous end of the capillary blood pressure has fallen to 1.6 kPa and therefore below the solute potential exerted by the plasma proteins. Thus there is a net flow of tissue fluid back into the capillary (fig 14.44).

(2) The rest of the intercellular fluid drains into blindly ending lymphatic capillaries, and once inside these the fluid is termed **lymph**. The lymphatic capillaries join to form larger lymphatic vessels. The lymph is moved through the vessels by contraction of the muscles surrounding them, and backflow is prevented by valves present in the major vessels which act in a similar fashion to those found in veins (fig 14.46).

The lymphatic vessels of the legs join to those from the alimentary canal to form the thoracic duct. This empties the lymph into the blood system in the neck region via the left subclavian vein. The right lymphatic duct drains lymph back into the bloodstream via the right subclavian vein (fig 14.45).

Situated at intervals along the lymphatic system are lymph glands or nodes. Lymphocytes, in the course of circulation through the blood and lymph, 'rest' and accumulate in the lymph nodes. They produce antibodies and are an important part of the body's immune system. The nodes (fig 14.47) also filter out bacteria and foreign particles from the lymph, which are ultimately ingested by phagocytes.

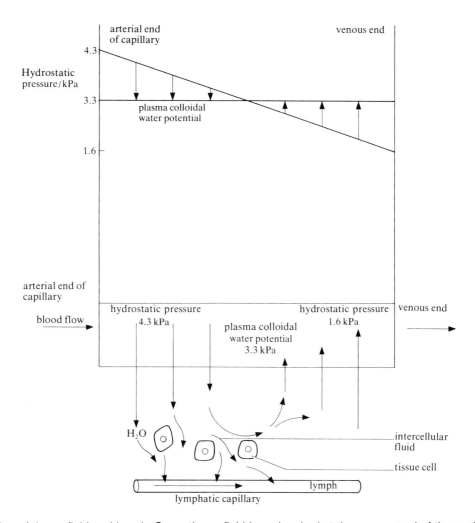

Fig 14.44 *Formation of tissue fluid and lymph. Some tissue fluid is reabsorbed at the venous end of the capillary whereas the remainder is collected in lymphatic capillaries. (After K. Schmidt-Nielsen (1980)* Animal physiology, *2nd ed., Cambridge University Press)*

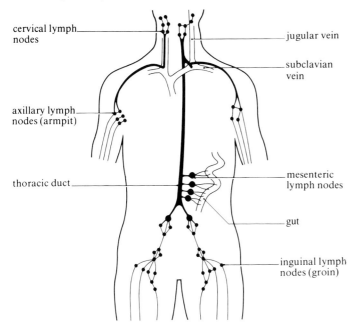

Fig 14.45 *Human lymphatic system. (From E. G. Springthorpe 1973)* An introduction to functional systems in animals, *Longman)*

14.12.2 The mammalian heart

The heart is situated between the two lungs and behind the sternum in the thorax. It is surrounded by a conical-shaped sac, the pericardium, the outer part of which consists of non-distensible white fibrous tissue, whilst the inner part is made up of two membranes. The inner of the two membranes is attached to the heart whilst the outer one is attached to the fibrous tissue. Pericardial fluid is secreted between them which reduces the friction between the heart walls and surrounding tissues when the heart is beating. The general inelastic nature of the pericardium as a whole prevents the heart from being overstretched or overfilled with blood.

There are four chambers in the heart, two upper thin-walled atria and two lower thick-walled ventricles (fig 14.48). The right side of the heart is completely separated from the left. The atria function to collect and retain blood temporarily until it can pass to the ventricles. The distance from atrium to ventricle is very small, hence the power of contraction of the atria does not have to be very great. The right atrium receives deoxygenated blood from the general circulation of the body whilst the left

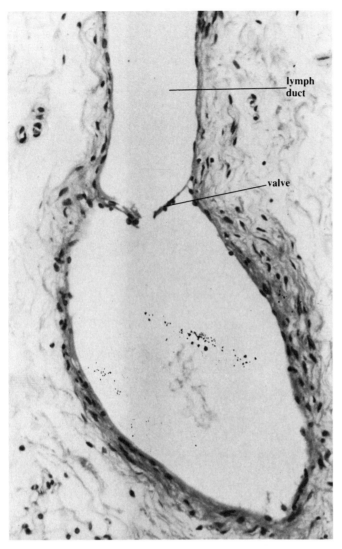

Fig 14.46 *LS through lymph vessel showing an internal valve*

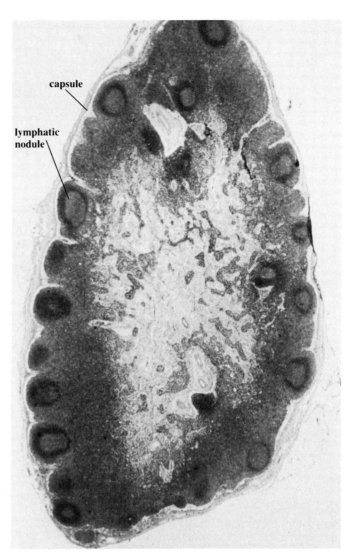

Fig 14.47 *Section through a lymph gland*

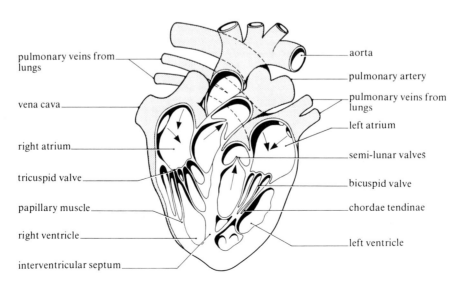

Fig 14.48 *Section through mammalian heart*

520

atrium receives oxygenated blood from the lungs. The muscular wall of the left ventricle is at least three times as thick as that of the right ventricle. This difference can be correlated with the fact that the right ventricle has only to supply the pulmonary circulation whilst the left ventricle pumps blood through the much larger systemic circulation of the body. Correspondingly the blood entering the aorta from the left ventricle is at a much higher blood pressure (approximately 14.0 kPa) than the blood entering the pulmonary artery (2.1 kPa).

14.34 What other advantages are there in supplying the pulmonary circulation with blood at a lower pressure than that of the systemic circulation?

As the atria contract they force blood into the ventricles, and rings of muscle which surround the venae cavae and pulmonary veins at their point of entry into the atria contract and close off the veins. This prevents reflux of blood into the veins. The left atrium is separated from the left ventricle by a bicuspid (two-flapped) valve, whilst a tricuspid valve separates the right atrium from the right ventricle. Attached to the ventricular side of the flaps are fibrous cords which in turn attach to conical-shaped papillary muscles which are extensions of the inner wall of the ventricles. These valves are pushed open when the atria contract, but when the ventricles contract the flaps of each valve press tightly closed so preventing reflux of blood to the atria. At the same time the papillary muscles contract so tightening the fibrous cords. This prevents the valves from being turned inside out. Pulmonary and aortic pocket

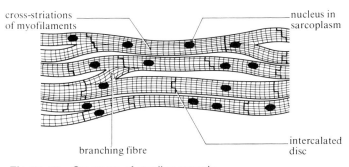

Fig 14.49 *Structure of cardiac muscle*

Fig 14.50 *Photograph of cardiac muscle*

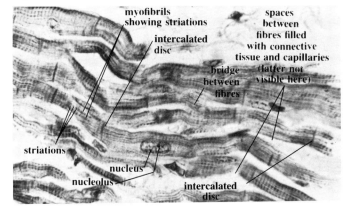

valves guard the point of entry of blood into these vessels and prevent regurgitation of blood back into the ventricles.

Just beyond the aortic valve cusps are the openings of the two coronary arteries. These are the only blood vessels which supply oxygenated blood to the walls of the heart.

The walls of the heart are composed of cardiac muscle fibres, connective tissue and tiny blood vessels. Each muscle fibre possesses one or two nuclei, myofilaments and many large mitochondria. The fibres branch and cross-connect with each other to form a complex net-like arrangement. This permits contraction waves to spread quickly amongst the fibres and enhance the contraction of the chambers as a whole. No neurones are present in the wall of the heart (figs 14.49 and 14.50).

14.12.3 The cardiac cycle

The cardiac cycle refers to the sequence of events which take place during the completion of one heartbeat. It is as follows.

(1) Deoxygenated blood, under low pressure, enters the right atrium and oxygenated blood enters the left atrium. These chambers gradually become distended. Initially the bicuspid and tricuspid valves are closed, but as pressure in the atria rises, as they fill with blood, it eventually exceeds that of the ventricles and the valves are pushed open. Some of the blood flows into the relaxed ventricles. This resting period of the heart chambers is called **diastole** (fig 14.51a).

(2) When diastole ends, the two atria contract simultaneously. This is termed **atrial systole** and results in more blood being conveyed into the ventricles (fig 14.51b). Almost immediately the ventricles contract. This is called **ventricular systole** (fig 14.51c). When this occurs the bicuspid and tricuspid valves are closed. The ventricular pressure rises and soon exceeds the blood pressure in the aorta and pulmonary artery, forcing the aortic and pulmonary valves open. Thus blood is expelled from the heart into these elastic-walled vessels. During ventricular systole blood is forced against the closed atrio-ventricular valve and this produces the first heart sound ('lub').

(3) Ventricular systole ends and is followed by **ventricular diastole** (fig 14.51d). The high pressure developed in the aorta and pulmonary artery tends to force some blood back towards the ventricles and this closes the aortic and pulmonary artery pocket valves. Hence back-flow is prevented. The impact of this backflow against the valves causes the second heart sound ('dub'):

ventricular systole = 'lub'
ventricular diastole = 'dub'

The repeated recoil of the elastic arterial vessels as a result of ventricular systole forces the blood into the pulmonary and systemic circulations as a series of pulses. As blood is propelled further and further away from the heart, the pulses become less and less

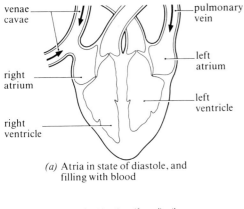

venae cavae — right atrium — right ventricle — pulmonary vein — left atrium — left ventricle

(a) Atria in state of diastole, and filling with blood

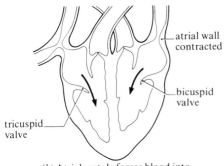

atrial wall contracted — bicuspid valve — tricuspid valve

(b) Atrial systole forces blood into ventricles. Bicuspid and tricuspid valves open. Sphincters of venae cavae and pulmonary veins closed

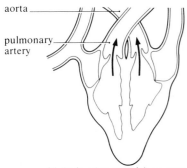

aorta — pulmonary artery

(c) Atria relax, ventricles contract. Blood propelled into aorta and pulmonary artery

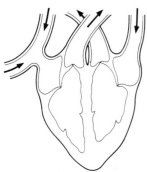

(d) Pocket valves of aorta and pulmonary artery close. Atria begin to refill. Ventricles in state of diastole

Fig 14.51 *Sequence of heart actions involved in one complete heartbeat – the cardiac cycle*

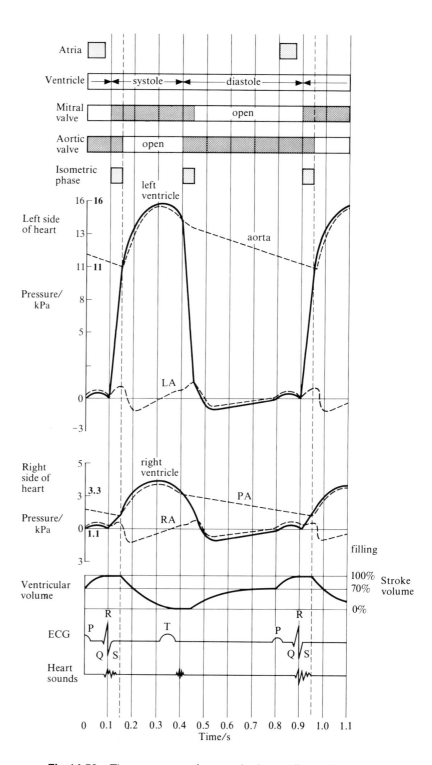

Fig 14.52 *The sequence of events in the cardiac cycle starting with the onset of atrial systole. Part of the subsequent cycle is shown. PA, blood pressure in the pulmonary artery; RA, right atrial pressure; LA, left atrial pressure. (From J. H. Green (1968)* An introduction to human physiology, *Oxford University Press)*

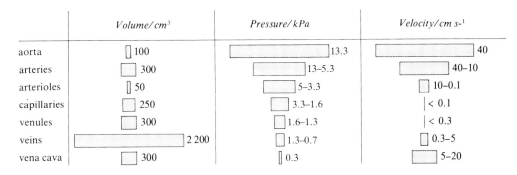

	Volume/cm³	Pressure/kPa	Velocity/cm s⁻¹
aorta	100	13.3	40
arteries	300	13–5.3	40–10
arterioles	50	5–3.3	10–0.1
capillaries	250	3.3–1.6	< 0.1
venules	300	1.6–1.3	< 0.3
veins	2 200	1.3–0.7	0.3–5
vena cava	300	0.3	5–20

Fig 14.53 *Distribution of blood volume, pressure and velocity in the human vascular system. (From K. Schmidt-Nielsen (1980)* Animal physiology, *2nd ed., Cambridge University Press)*

Fig 14.54 *Blood pressure throughout the human circulatory system. (From J. H. Green (1968)* An introduction to human physiology, *Oxford University Press)*

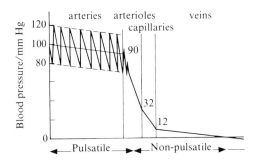

pronounced until, in the capillaries and veins, blood flows evenly (figs 14.53 and 14.54).

One complete heartbeat consists of one systole and one diastole and lasts for about 0.8 s (fig 14.52).

14.12.4 Mechanism of heart excitation and contraction

When a heart is removed from a mammal and placed in well-oxygenated Ringer solution at 37 °C it will continue to beat rhythmically for a considerable time, without stimuli from the nervous or endocrine systems. This demonstrates the myogenic nature of the heart, that is it possesses its own inherent or 'built-in' mechanism for initiating contraction of the cardiac muscle fibres.

Myogenic control of heartbeat rate

The stimulus for contraction of the heart originates in a specific region of the right atrium called the **sino-atrial node** (or S-A node for short) close to the point of entry of the venae cavae. The S-A node is a vestige of the sinus venosus seen in the heart of lower vertebrates. It consists of a small number of diffusely orientated cardiac fibres, possessing few myofibrils, and a few nerve endings from the autonomic nervous system. The S-A node initiates the

heartbeat, but the rate at which it beats can be varied by stimulation from the autonomic nervous system.

The cells of the S-A node maintain a differential ionic concentration across their membranes of −90 mV. These cells have a permanently high sodium conductance, that is to say that sodium ions continually diffuse into the cells. This produces a depolarisation which leads to a propagated action potential (section 16.1.1) being set up in the cells adjacent to the S-A node. As this wave of excitation passes across the muscle fibres of the heart it causes them to contract. The S-A node is known as the pacemaker of the heart because each wave of excitation begins here and acts as the stimulus for the next wave of excitation.

Once contraction has begun it spreads through the walls of the atria via the network of cardiac fibres at the rate of 1 m s⁻¹. Both atria contract more or less simultaneously. The atrial muscle fibres are completely separated from those of the ventricles by the atrio-ventricular septum of connective tissue, except for a region in the right atrium called the **atrio-ventricular node** (A-V node).

The tissues of the A-V node are similar to those of the S-A node and supply a bundle of specialised fibres, the A-V bundle, which provide the only route for the transmission of the wave of excitation from the atria to the ventricles. There is a delay of approximately 0.15 s in conduction from the S-A node to the A-V node, thus permitting atrial systole to be completed before ventricular systole begins.

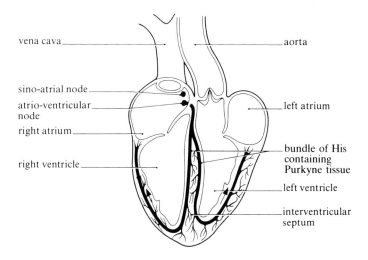

Fig 14.55 *Position of the sino-atrial and atrio-ventricular nodes, and the bundle of His*

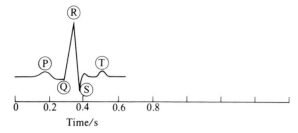

Fig 14.56 *An electrocardiogram (ECG) trace demonstrating the change in electrical potential across the heart during one cardiac cycle. P, atrial depolarisation over the atrial muscle and spread of excitation from the sino-atrial node equivalent to atrial systole; Q, R and S, ventricular systole; T, ventricular diastole begins*

The A-V bundle is connected to the **bundle of His**, a strand of modified cardiac fibres which gives rise to finer branches known as **Purkyne tissue**. Impulses are conducted rapidly along the bundle at 5 m s⁻¹, ultimately proceeding to all parts of the ventricles. Both ventricles are stimulated to contract simultaneously, and the wave of ventricular contraction begins at the apex of the heart and spreads upwards squeezing blood out of the ventricles towards the arteries which pass vertically upwards out of the heart (figs 14.55 and 14.56).

Certain characteristics of cardiac muscle make it suited to its role of pumping blood round the body throughout the life of the mammal. Once cardiac muscle has begun to contract it cannot respond to any other stimulus until it begins to relax. This is known as the **refractory period**. The length of time that the cardiac muscle is in this condition is called its absolute refractive period (fig 14.57). This period is longer than that of other types of muscle, and enables muscle to contract vigorously and rapidly without becoming fatigued. It is thus impossible for the heart to develop a state of sustained contraction called **tetanus**, or to develop an oxygen debt.

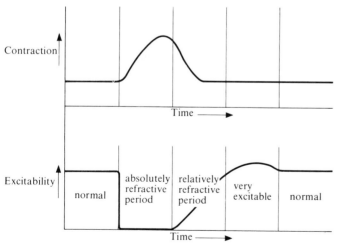

Fig 14.57 *The refractory period of cardiac muscle. The upper figure shows a record of the contraction of the muscle, the lower figure shows the varying excitability of the muscle to stimuli. (From Clegg & Clegg (2nd edition, 1963) Biology of the mammal, Heinemann Medical Books)*

14.12.5 Regulation of heartbeat rate

The intrinsic rate of the heartbeat is controlled by the activity of the S-A nodes as described earlier. Even when removed from the body and placed into an artificial medium the heart will continue to beat rhythmically, albeit more slowly. In situ, however, the body's demands on its circulatory system are constantly changing and the heart rate has to be continuously adjusted accordingly. This is achieved by the dynamic and integrated activity of two types of control system, one nervous and the other chemical. This is a homeostatic response whose overall function is to maintain constant conditions within the bloodstream even though conditions around it are constantly changing.

The amount of blood flowing from the heart over a given period of time is known as the **cardiac output** and depends upon the volume of blood expelled at each beat (the stroke volume) and the heart rate. These three variables are related by the expression

$$\text{cardiac output} = \text{stroke volume} \times \text{heart rate}$$

and it is the cardiac output which is the important variable. One way of controlling cardiac output is by varying the heart rate.

Nervous control of heart rate

Within the medulla oblongata of the hindbrain are several regions concerned with cardiovascular control. In all regions, part of their function is to control the heart rate. Two vagus nerves carrying parasympathetic fibres leave the cardio-inhibitory centre of the medulla oblongata and run, one on either side of the trachea, to the heart. Here nerve fibres lead to the S-A node, A-V node and the bundle of His. Impulses passing along the vagus nerve reduce the heart rate. Other nerves, of the sympathetic system, have their origin in the pressor region of the vasomotor centre of the medulla, run parallel to the spinal cord and emerge from the thoracic region to the S-A node. Stimulation by these nerves results in an increase in the heart rate. It is the integrated activity of the inhibiting and accelerating effects, occurring within the medulla oblongata, that controls the heart rate.

Sensory fibres from stretch receptors within the walls of the aortic arch, the carotid sinuses and the vena cava run to the cardio-inhibitory centre in the medulla. Impulses received from the aorta and carotids decrease the heart rate, whilst those from the vena cava stimulate the pressor centre which increases the heart rate. As the volume of blood passing to any of these vessels increases so does the distension of the vessels, and this increases the number of impulses transmitted to the cardiovascular centres in the medulla.

For example, under conditions of intense activity body muscles contract strongly and this increases the rate at which venous blood returns to the heart. Consequently the vena cava is distended by large quantities of blood and the heart rate is increased. At the same time the increased

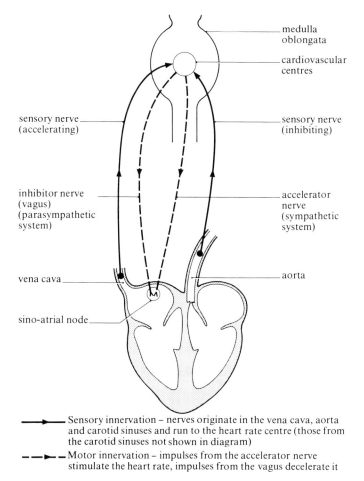

Key:

—————▶ Sensory innervation – nerves originate in the vena cava, aorta and carotid sinuses and run to the heart rate centre (those from the carotid sinuses not shown in diagram)

– – –▶ – Motor innervation – impulses from the accelerator nerve stimulate the heart rate, impulses from the vagus decelerate it

Fig 14.58 *Neurones connecting the heart to the cardiovascular system*

Table 14.12 Non-nervous agencies affecting heart rate.

Non-nervous stimulus	Effect on heart rate
High pH	Decelerates
Low pH (e.g. high CO_2 levels, as is the case during active exercise)	Accelerates
Low temperature	Decelerates
High temperature	Accelerates
Mineral ions Endocrine factors (e.g. thyroxine, insulin, sex hormones, adrenaline, pituitary hormones)	The rate is influenced directly or indirectly

blood flow to the heart places the cardiac muscle of the heart under tension. Cardiac muscle responds to this tension by contracting more strongly during systole and pumping out an increased volume of blood (the stroke volume). This relationship between the volume of blood returned to the heart and cardiac output was named after the English physiologist Starling and is known as **Starling's law**.

The increased stroke volume stretches the aorta and carotids which in turn, via stretch reflexes, signal the cardio-inhibitory centre to slow the heart rate. Therefore there is an automatic fail-safe mechanism which serves to prevent the heart from working too fast, and to enable it to adjust its activity in order to cope effectively with the volume of blood passing through it at any given time (fig 14.58).

Non-nervous control of heart rate

There are a number of non-nervous stimuli which act directly on cardiac muscle or on the S-A node. They are briefly summarised in table 14.12.

Many activities affect the cardiovascular centre in some way or other, for example emotions, such as blushing or turning white with anger, sights and sounds. In such instances sensory impulses are transmitted to the brain where they pass to the cardiovascular centre via intercon-

necting pathways. Under such stimulation the cardiovascular centre responds accordingly (table 14.12).

It should be noted that this centre is influenced at any given moment by a combination of nervous and non-nervous agencies, and never by a single one. The activity of the cardiovascular centre also fluctuates according to the health and age of the individual.

Effects of exercise on heart rate

During bouts of continuous heavy exercise the output of blood from the left ventricle of the heart may increase from its resting condition of 5–$6\,dm^3\,min^{-1}$ to 30–$35\,dm^3\,min^{-1}$. This is brought about by an increased rate of contraction and a more complete emptying of the ventricles (stroke volume).

In anticipation of exercise, and during its early phase, the sympathetic nervous system stimulates an increased heart rate. However during a period of prolonged exercise, the rate is sustained by nervous and hormonal factors. The anticipatory rise may also be assisted by increased hormonal flow from the adrenal glands.

14.12.6 Regulation of blood pressure

Blood pressure depends on several factors: heart rate, strength of heartbeat, blood output (stroke volume) and resistance to blood flow by the blood vessels (peripheral resistance). Heart rate and stroke volume have been discussed in the last section. Resistance to blood flow is altered by contraction (**vasoconstriction**) or relaxation (**vasodilation**) of the smooth muscle in the blood vessel walls, especially those of the arterioles. This peripheral resistance is increased by vasoconstriction but decreased by vasodilation. Increased resistance leads to a rise in blood pressure, whereas a decrease produces a fall in blood pressure. All such activity is controlled by a vasomotor centre in the medulla oblongata.

Nerve fibres run from the vasomotor centre to all arterioles in the body. Changes in the diameter of these blood vessels are produced principally by variation in the activity of constrictor muscles. The dilator muscles play a somewhat less important role.

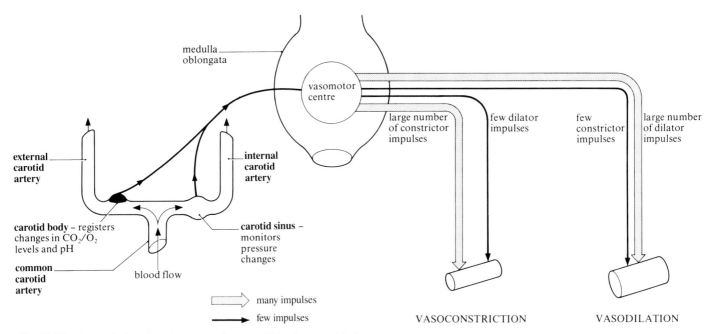

Fig 14.59 *Interrelationships between the carotid body, carotid sinus, vasomotor centre and general circulatory system*

Vasomotor centre activity is regulated by impulses coming from pressure receptors (**baroreceptors**) located in the walls of the aorta and carotid sinuses in the carotid arteries (fig 14.59). Stimulation of parasympathetic fibres in these areas, caused by increased cardiac output, produces vasodilation throughout the body and consequent reduction in blood pressure, as well as a slowing of the heart rate. The converse occurs when blood pressure is low. In this case, a fall in blood pressure increases impulse transmission along sympathetic fibres. This causes body-wide vasoconstriction and a compensatory rise in blood pressure.

Chemical control of the vasomotor centre

Blood arriving at the carotid bodies carrying a high concentration of carbon dioxide stimulates chemoreceptors in these regions to transmit impulses to the vasomotor centre (fig 14.59). Nerve fibres leaving the chemoreceptors synapse with fibres from the carotid sinus prior to passing to the vasomotor centre. When the vasomotor centre is stimulated in this way it sends impulses to the blood vessels to vasoconstrict and therefore raises blood pressure. As increased carbon dioxide concentration in the body is usually brought about by increased activity by body tissues, the blood containing the carbon dioxide will be transported more rapidly to the lungs where expulsion of carbon dioxide in exchange for oxygen can take place more quickly.

Carbon dioxide can also directly affect the behaviour of the smooth muscle of the blood vessel itself. When a tissue suddenly becomes very active, producing a large quantity of carbon dioxide, the carbon dioxide acts directly on the blood vessels in the vicinity and stimulates them to dilate. This increases their own blood supply thus allowing more oxygen and glucose to reach the active cells. It must be

remembered, however, that when the carbon dioxide leaves this localised area it will have the effect of promoting vasoconstriction elsewhere via vasomotor activity. This is a good illustration of how dynamic and adjustable the control of blood pressure and therefore circulation and distribution of blood can be.

Other agencies, such as types of emotional stress (for example excitement, pain and annoyance), increase sympathetic activity and therefore blood pressure. Also when the adrenal medulla is stimulated to produce adrenaline by impulses from higher nervous centres this again increases the rate of heartbeat, promotes bodywide vasoconstriction and therefore raises blood pressure. The significance of the control of heart rate and blood pressure is described further in section 18.1.5.

> **14.35** When an animal is wounded, its overall blood pressure rises, but the area in the vicinity of the wound swells as a result of local vasodilation. Why?
>
> **14.36** Outline the main adjustments that occur to the heart rate and circulatory system just before, during and after a 100 m race.

14.13 Functions of mammalian blood

Mammalian blood performs many major functions. In the following list, the first five functions are carried out solely by the plasma.

(1) Transport of soluble organic compounds from the small intestine to various parts of the body where they are stored or assimilated, and transport from storage areas to places where they are used.

(2) Transport of soluble excretory materials from tissues where they are produced to the organs of excretion.

(3) Transport of metabolic by-products from areas of production to other parts of the body.

(4) Transport of hormones from the glands where they are produced to all parts of the body or certain target organs. This facilitates communication within the body.

(5) Distribution of heat from the deeply seated organs. This serves to dissipate excess heat and to aid the maintenance of a uniform body temperature.

(6) Transport of oxygen from the lungs to all parts of the body, and carriage of carbon dioxide produced by the tissues in the reverse direction.

(7) Defence against disease. This is achieved in three ways:
   (a) clotting of the blood which prevents excessive blood loss and entry of pathogens;
   (b) phagocytosis, performed by the granulocytes which engulf and digest bacteria which find their way into the bloodstream;
   (c) immunity mediated by antibodies and/or lymphocytes.

(8) Maintenance of a constant blood osmotic pressure and pH as a result of plasma protein activity. As the plasma proteins and haemoglobin possess both acidic and basic amino acids they can combine with or release hydrogen ions and serve to minimise pH changes over a wide range of pH values.

14.13.1 Oxygen carriage

It is the haemoglobin molecule, found in the erythrocytes, which is responsible for the transport of oxygen round the body. Haemoglobin is a tetrameric protein with a relative molecular mass of 68 000. It possesses four haem prosthetic groups, responsible for the characteristic red colour of the blood, linked to four globin polypeptide chains. A ferrous iron atom is located within each haem group, and each of these can combine loosely with one molecule of oxygen (fig 14.60).

$$Hb + 4O_2 \rightleftharpoons HbO_8$$

whole haemoglobin molecule   oxyhaemoglobin

(Sometimes the biochemist's standard abbreviation HbO_2 is used to represent oxyhaemoglobin.)

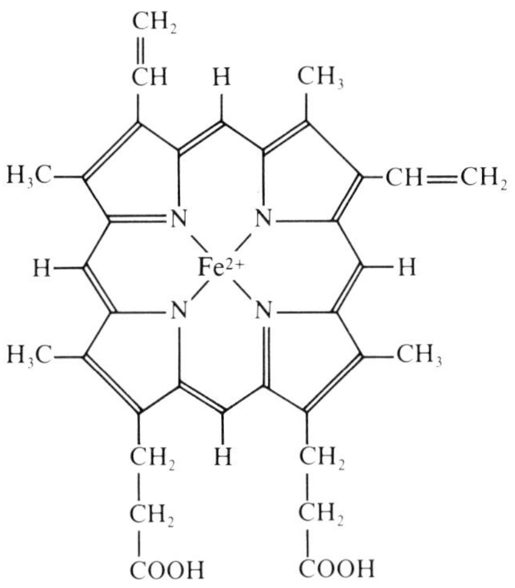

Combination of oxygen with haemoglobin, to form oxyhaemoglobin, occurs under conditions when the partial pressure of oxygen is high, such as in the lung alveolar capillaries. When the partial pressure of oxygen is low, as in the capillaries which supply metabolically active tissues, the bonds holding oxygen to haemoglobin become unstable and oxygen is released. This diffuses in solution into the surrounding cells.

The amount of oxygen that can combine with haemoglobin is determined by the oxygen tension. This is expressed as a partial pressure and is the fraction of oxygen found in

Fig 14.60 *A single haem molecule*

the air. It is still measured in millimetres of mercury. For example, atmospheric pressure at sea level is 760 mm Hg. Approximately one-fifth of the atmosphere is oxygen, therefore the partial pressure of oxygen in the atmosphere at sea level is $\frac{1}{5} \times 760 = 152$ mm Hg. When the percentage oxygen saturation of blood is plotted against the partial pressure of oxygen an S-shaped curve, called the **oxygen dissociation curve**, is obtained (fig 14.61).

Analysis of the curve indicates that for physiological reasons haemoglobin is completely saturated with oxygen at a point known as the **loading tension**. This is taken as the tension when 95% of the pigment is saturated and coincides with a partial pressure of about 73 mm Hg in the example given in fig 14.61. At higher partial pressures of oxygen further uptake of oxygen can occur, but 100% saturation of haemoglobin is rarely achieved. At an oxygen partial pressure of approximately 30 mm Hg only 50% of the

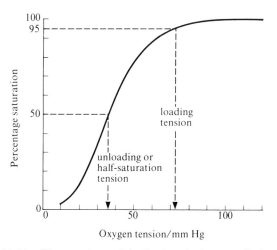

Fig 14.61 *Diagram to explain the terminology applied to oxygen dissociation curves of oxygen-carrying pigments. Loading tension is the tension at which 95% of the pigment is saturated with oxygen; unloading tension is the tension at which 50% of the pigment is saturated with oxygen. (From Florey (1966) An introduction to general and comparative physiology, W.B. Saunders & Co.)*

haemoglobin is present as oxyhaemoglobin, and at a partial pressure of zero no oxygen is attached to the haemoglobin molecule. Over the steep part of the curve, a small decrease in the oxygen partial pressure of the environment will bring about a sizeable fall in the percentage saturation of haemoglobin. The oxygen given up by the pigment is available to the tissues.

But why is the curve S-shaped? The explanation lies in the way that haemoglobin binds to oxygen. It involves the phenomenon of allostery (section 6.6). When an oxygen molecule combines with the ferrous iron atom of a single haem unit it distorts its shape slightly. This distortion is registered by the whole molecule which changes its shape accordingly. Further structural alterations occur when oxygen molecules attach to the second and third haem groups, each one facilitating much faster uptake of oxygen than the preceding one. When the last haem monomer is ready to pick up oxygen it does so several hundred times faster than the first.

The converse reaction occurs when oxyhaemoglobin is exposed to regions where the partial pressure of oxygen is low, as in actively respiring tissues. The first oxygen molecule is released to the tissues very rapidly, but the second, third and fourth molecules are given up much less readily and only at a very reduced partial pressure of oxygen.

In regions with an increased partial pressure of carbon dioxide the oxygen dissocation curve is shifted to the right. This is known as the **Bohr effect** or **shift** (fig 14.62).

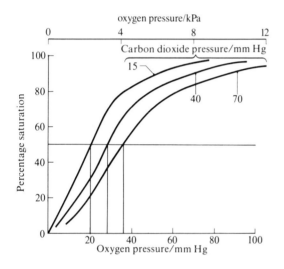

Fig 14.62 (above) Oxygen dissociation curves of haemoglobin illustrating the Bohr effect at different pressures of carbon dioxide. (From Garth Chapman (1967) The body fluids and their functions, Studies in Biology No. 8, Arnold)

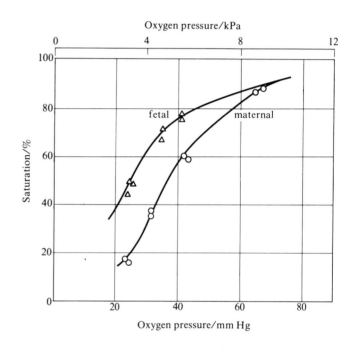

Fig 14.63 (above) Oxygen dissociation curves of fetal and maternal blood of a goat

Fig 14.64 (left) Oxygen dissociation curves of the llama and other mammals

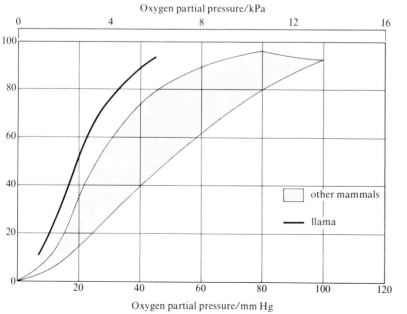

Computer program. DISSOCIATION OF HAEMOGLOBIN (CUP Micro Software) allows the user to examine the dissociation of haemoglobin under a variety of conditions and for different haemoglobins. (Double package with ZWITTERION.)

14.37 What is the physiological significance of the Bohr effect?

14.38 Consider fig 14.63. The oxygen dissociation curve of the fetus is to the left of that of its mother. Why is this so?

14.39 The oxygen dissociation curve of the South American llama, which lives in the High Andes at an altitude of about 5 000 m above sea level, is located to the left of most other mammals (fig 14.64). Why is this so?

14.13.2 Myoglobin

The myoglobin molecule is widely distributed in animals and is particularly common in skeletal muscle tissues of mammals. It displays a great affinity for oxygen and its oxygen dissociation curve is displaced well to the left of haemoglobin (fig 14.65). In fact it only begins to release oxygen when the partial pressure of oxygen is below 20 mm Hg. In this way it acts as a store of oxygen in resting muscle, only releasing it when supplies of oxyhaemoglobin have been exhausted. Myoglobin is very similar to the haemoglobin subunits with respect to both amino acid sequence and three-dimensional structure, but the myoglobin molecules do not associate to form tetramers and so cannot show cooperative oxygen binding. The two proteins have presumably evolved from a common ancestral molecule.

14.13.3 Carbon monoxide and haemoglobin

The affinity of the ferrous ions in haemoglobin for carbon monoxide is several hundred times as great as it is for oxygen. Therefore haemoglobin will combine with any carbon monoxide available in preference to oxygen to form a relatively stable compound called **carboxyhaemo-**

globin. If this occurs oxygen is prevented from combining with haemoglobin, and therefore the transport of oxygen round the body by the blood is no longer possible. In humans collapse follows quickly after exposure to carbon monoxide and unless the victim is removed from the gas, asphyxiation is inevitable. Removal from the gas must be followed by administering a pure oxygen–carbon dioxide mix since the oxygen tension in air is insufficient to replace the carbon monoxide attached to the haemoglobin.

14.13.4 Carriage of carbon dioxide

Carbon dioxide is carried by the blood in three different ways.

In solution (5%). Most of the carbon dioxide carried in this way is transported in physical solution. A very small amount is carried as carbonic acid (H_2CO_3).

Combined with protein (10–20%). Carbon dioxide combines with the amine (NH_2) group of haemoglobin to form a neutral carbamino-haemoglobin compound. The amount of carbon dioxide that is able to combine with haemoglobin depends on the amount of oxygen already being carried by the haemoglobin. The less the amount of oxygen being carried by the haemoglobin molecule, the more carbon dioxide that can be carried in this way:

$$HHbNH_2 + CO_2 \longrightarrow HHbN-C \overset{O}{\underset{OH}{\diagdown}}$$

haemoglobin

carbamino-haemoglobin

As hydrogencarbonate (85%). Carbon dioxide produced by the tissues diffuses passively into the bloodstream and passes into the erythrocytes where it combines with water to form carbonic acid. This process is catalysed by the enzyme carbonic anhydrase found in the erythrocytes and takes less than one second to occur.

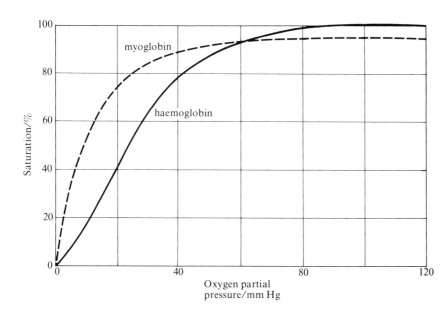

Fig 14.65 *Comparison of haemoglobin and myoglobin oxygen dissociation curves. Myoglobin remains 80% saturated with oxygen until the partial pressure of oxygen falls below 20 mm Hg. This means that myoglobin retains its oxygen in the resting cell but gives it up when vigorous muscle activity uses up the available oxygen supplied by haemoglobin*

529

Carbonic acid then proceeds to dissociate into hydrogen and hydrogencarbonate ions:

$$CO_2 + H_2O \rightleftharpoons H_2CO_3 \rightleftharpoons H^+ + HCO_3^-$$

When the erythrocytes leave the lungs their oxyhaemoglobin (represented as HbO_2) is weakly acidic and associated with potassium ions. This may be represented as $KHbO_2$. In areas of high carbon dioxide concentrations (as at the tissues), oxygen is easily given up by oxyhaemoglobin. When this happens the haemoglobin becomes strongly basic. In this state it dissociates from the potassium ions and readily accepts hydrogen ions from carbonic acid forming haemoglobinic acid (H.Hb). The potassium ions associate with hydrogencarbonate ions to form potassium hydrogencarbonate.

$$KHbO_2 \rightleftharpoons KHb + O_2$$
$$H^+ + HCO_3^- + KHb \rightleftharpoons H.Hb + KHCO_3$$
$$\text{(haemoglobinic acid)}$$

By accepting hydrogen ions, haemoglobin acts as a buffer molecule and so enables large quantities of carbonic acid to be carried to the lungs without any major alteration in blood pH.

The cell surface membrane of an erythrocyte is relatively impermeable to the passage of sodium and potassium ions, however a cation pump operates and expels large numbers of sodium ions into the plasma. The majority of hydrogencarbonate ions formed within the erythrocyte diffuse out into the plasma along a concentration gradient and combine with sodium to form sodium hydrogencarbonate. The loss of hydrogencarbonate ions from the erythrocyte is balanced by chloride ions diffusing into the erythrocyte from the plasma. Thus electrochemical neutrality is maintained. This phenomenon is called the '**chloride shift**'. Potassium hydrogencarbonate, formed in the erythrocyte, is also capable of dissociating, and some of the chloride ions which enter the erythrocyte combine with potassium ions to form potassium chloride, whilst the hydrogencarbonate ions diffuse out. When hydrogencarbonate leaves the

erythrocyte, the excess H^+ ions which remain decrease the pH within the erythrocyte causing the dissociation of potassium oxyhaemoglobin ($KHbO_2$) into oxygen and potassium haemoglobin (fig 14.66).

When the erythrocytes reach the lungs the reverse process occurs.

14.40 Summarise how carbon dioxide in the blood is expelled as gaseous carbon dioxide by the lungs.

14.13.5 Defensive functions of the blood

Every mammal is equipped with a complex system of defensive mechanisms which are designed to enable it to withstand attacks by pathogens, and to remove foreign materials from its system. Three defensive mechanisms are discussed here:
(1) clotting of blood ⎫ both contributing to
(2) phagocytosis ⎬ wound healing
(3) immune response to infection.

Clotting

When a tissue is wounded blood flows from it, and coagulates to form a blood clot. This prevents further blood loss and entry of pathogenic micro-organisms and is of clear survival value to the animal concerned. It is just as important that blood in undamaged vessels does not clot. The highly complex series of reactions that take place in order for coagulation to be achieved serves at the same time to prevent it from occurring unnecessarily. The whole clotting process depends on at least 12 clotting factors working in harmony with each other. Only the main factors are described in this account.

Blood escaping from a superficial wound is exposed to the air, and mixes with substances oozing from the damaged cells and ruptured platelets. Thromboplastin, a lipoprotein released from injured tissues, together with clotting factors VII and X (plasma enzymes) and calcium ions, catalyses the conversion of inactive plasma protein

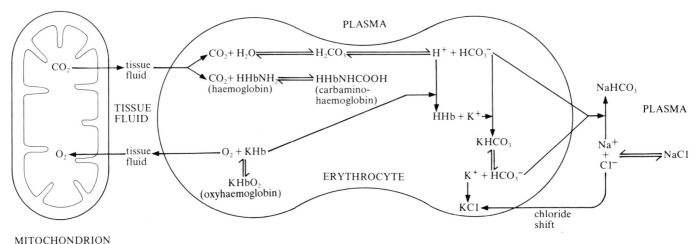

Fig 14.66 *Carbon dioxide carriage by the plasma and erythrocyte and its role in the release of oxygen at the tissues*

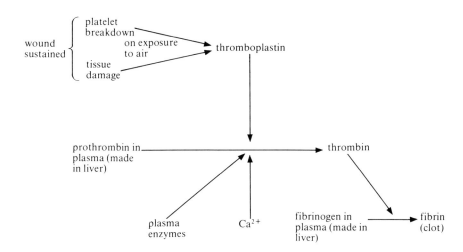

Fig 14.67 *Major features involved in the clotting process*

prothrombin to thrombin. Thrombin is a proteolytic enzyme that hydrolyses the large soluble globular plasma protein molecule, fibrinogen, into smaller units which then associate to form a meshwork of long tangled needle-like fibres of insoluble fibrillar fibrin (fig 14.67). When fibrinogen has been removed from the plasma, the fluid which remains is called **serum**. Blood cells become trapped in the meshwork (fig 14.68) and a blood clot is formed. It dries to form a scab which acts to prevent further blood loss, and as a mechanical barrier to the entry of pathogens.

Because the clotting process is so elaborate, it means that the absence or low concentration of any of the essential clotting factors could produce excessive bleeding. Such a condition is known as **haemophilia**. For example, if an essential factor necessary for the action of thromboplastin is absent or only present in minute amounts, the individual will bleed profusely from any minor cut. Haemophilia is due to an inheritable gene mutation and is transmitted on an X chromosome. The condition is usually seen only in males, with females being carriers, since the abnormal allele is carried on the X chromosome and is recessive to the normal allele on the other X chromosome (section 23.6.1).

Clotting does not occur in undamaged blood vessels because the lining of the vessels is very smooth and does not promote platelet or cell rupture. Also present are substances which actively prevent clotting. One of these is heparin, present in low concentrations in the plasma and produced by most cells found in the connective tissues and the liver. It serves to prevent the conversion of prothrombin into thrombin, and fibrinogen to fibrin and is widely used clinically as an anticoagulant.

If a clot does form within the blood circulation it is called a **thrombus** and leads to a medical condition known as **thrombosis**. This may happen if the endothelium of a blood vessel is damaged and the roughness of the damaged area promotes platelet breakdown and sets in motion the clotting process. Coronary thrombosis, a thrombus developing in the coronary artery of the heart, is particularly dangerous and can lead to a swift death.

Phagocytosis

This function is generally carried out by neutrophils. These are amoeboid cells which are attracted to areas where cell and tissue damage has occurred. The stimulus for this migration appears to be some of the chemicals liberated by the ruptured blood cells and tissues. The neutrophils are able to recognise any invading bacteria. This capability is enhanced by plasma proteins called **opsonins**, which become attached to the surfaces of the bacteria and in some way make them more recognisable. Then the bacteria are engulfed in an amoeboid fashion and a phagosome is formed (fig 14.69). Small lysosomes fuse with the phagosome, forming a phagolysosome. Lysozyme and other hydrolytic enzymes, together with acid, are poured into the phagolysosome from the lysosomes and the bacteria are digested. Ultimately the soluble products of bacterial digestion are absorbed into the surrounding cytoplasm of the neutrophil.

Neutrophils are able to squeeze through the walls of blood capillaries, a process called **diapedesis**, and move about in the tissue spaces. In organs such as the liver, spleen and lymph nodes, large resident phagocytes, usually termed **macrophages**, are present. Their role is to engulf toxic foreign particles as well as microbes, and to retain them for long periods of time, often permanently. In this way infection can often be localised. The macrophages together with the neutrophils form the body's reticulo-endothelial system.

Inflammation

When an area of the body is wounded, the localised reaction of the tissue surrounding the wound is to become swollen and painful. This is called inflammation and is due to the escape of chemicals, including histamine and 5-hydroxytryptamine, from the damaged tissues. Collectively they cause local vasodilation of capillaries. This increases the amount of blood in the area and raises the temperature locally. Permeability of the capillaries is also increased, permitting escape of plasma into the surrounding tissues and a consequent swelling of the area, a

531

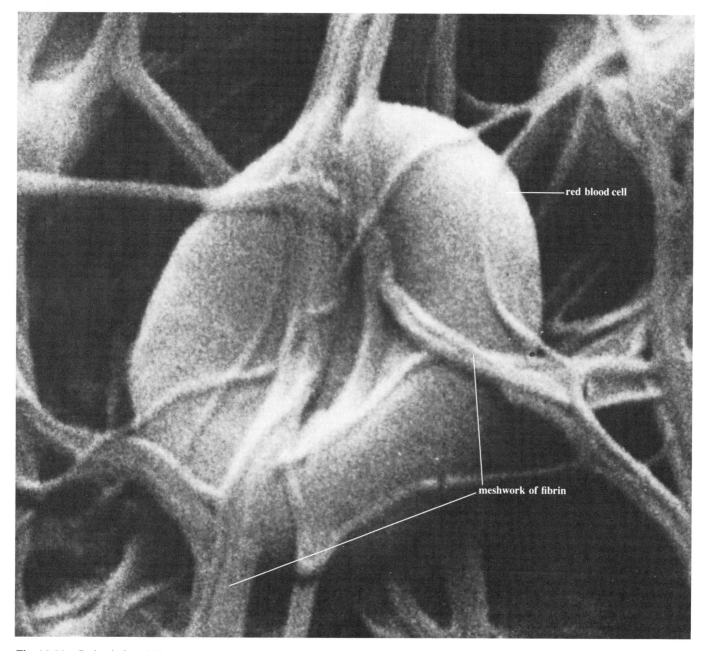

Fig 14.68 (below) *A red blood cell enmeshed in fibrin in a blood clot*

condition known as **oedema**. This plasma contains bacteriocidal factors, antibodies and neutrophils, all of which help to combat spread of infection. Fibrinogen is also present to assist blood clotting if necessary, and the excess tissue fluid tends to dilute and negate any potential toxic irritants.

Wound healing

Towards the end of the inflammatory phase, cells called fibroblasts appear and secrete collagen. This is a fibrous protein and becomes linked to polysaccharide to form a meshwork of randomly arranged fibrous scar tissue. Vitamin C is important for collagen formation; without it hydroxyl groups cannot be attached to the collagen

molecule and so it remains incomplete. After about 14 days the disorganised mass of fibres is reorganised into bundles arranged along the lines of stress of the wound. Numerous small blood vessels begin to ramify through the wound. They function to provide oxygen and nutrients for the cells involved in repairing and healing the wound.

Whilst these processes are going on within the wound, the epidermis around it is also engaged in repair and replacement activity. Some epidermal cells migrate into the wound and ingest much of the debris and fibrin of the blood clot which has formed over the wound. When the epidermal cells meet, they unite to form a continuous layer under the scar. When this is complete the scab sloughs off thus exposing the epidermis to the surrounding atmosphere.

Summary of events

(1) Wound occurs, blood flows.
(2) Clotting process occurs.
(3) Inflammation occurs.
(4) White cells migrate into wound. They absorb foreign matter and bacteria, and remove cell debris.

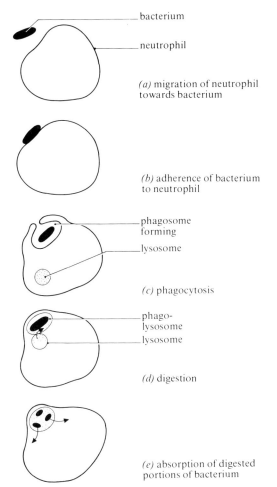

bacterium

neutrophil

(a) migration of neutrophil towards bacterium

(b) adherence of bacterium to neutrophil

phagosome forming

lysosome

(c) phagocytosis

phago-lysosome

lysosome

(d) digestion

(e) absorption of digested portions of bacterium

Fig 14.69 *Phagocytosis of a bacterium by a neutrophil* (above)

(5) Fibroblasts enter the wound and synthesise collagen which is built up into scar tissue.
(6) Epidermal cells remove any final debris in the wound, and also begin to dismantle the scar.
(7) Epidermis creates a new skin surface in the area of the wound.
(8) Scab sloughs off.

If the wound is small, phagocytosis is usually sufficient to cope with any pathogenic invasion. However, if there is considerable damage, the immune response of the body is put into action.

14.14 The immune system

Immunity has been defined by Sir Macfarlane Burnet as

'the capacity to recognise the intrusion of material foreign to the body and to mobilise cells and cell products to help remove that particular sort of foreign material with greater speed and effectiveness'.

Basic definitions

An **antibody** is a molecule synthesised by an animal in response to the presence of foreign substances for which it has a high affinity. Each antibody is a protein molecule called an **immunoglobulin** (formerly globulin). Its structure consists of two heavy H-chains of 50 000–60 000 relative molecular mass, and two light L-chains of 23 000 relative molecular mass. Functionally the antibody has a constant and variable part, the variable part acting something like a key which specifically fits into a lock (fig 14.70). Each organism can produce thousands of antibodies with different specificities, recognising all kinds of foreign substances.

The name **antigen** or **immunogen** is given to the foreign material that elicits antibody formation. Antigen usually

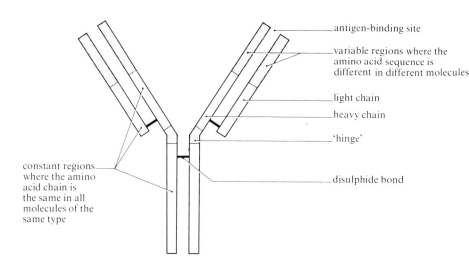

antigen-binding site

variable regions where the amino acid sequence is different in different molecules

light chain

heavy chain

'hinge'

constant regions where the amino acid chain is the same in all molecules of the same type

disulphide bond

Fig 14.70 *Immunoglobulin antibody molecule. Antigens are bound between the light and heavy chains of the variable regions. (From M. Cooper & A. Lawton (1972) The development of the immune system, Scientific American)*

takes the form of a protein or polysaccharide structure on the surface of microbial organisms or as a free molecule. Two systems of immunity have been developed by mammals, a cell-mediated immune response and a humoral response.

The division of labour in the immune system is caused by the development of two types of lymphocytes, the T and B cells. Both types arise from precursor cells in the bone marrow. The influence of the thymus gland is essential in making the T cells immunologically competent, and it is thought that the placenta, fetal liver and bone marrow exert a similar influence over the development of the B cells. Within each type there is an enormous capacity for recognising each of the millions of antigens that exist. When an antibody–antigen reaction occurs it serves to fix and nullify the action of the antigen, thereby preventing it from acting upon the body in a harmful way.

Cell-mediated response. T cells possessing membrane receptors which recognise antigen are stimulated to proliferate and produce a clone of T cells. These cells then either combat micro-organisms and/or effect the rejection of foreign tissues.

Humoral immune response. B cells recognise antigen in a similar way to T cells. However their response is different. They are stimulated to proliferate and form a plasma cell clone. The plasma cells synthesise and liberate antibodies into the blood plasma and tissue fluid. Here the antibodies adhere to the surfaces of bacteria and speed up their phagocytosis, or combine with and neutralise toxins produced by micro-organisms.

14.14.1 The thymus gland and the development of T cells

The thymus gland is situated in the thorax under the sternum and close to the ventral side of the heart. It begins to function during the embryonic period of the individual and is at its most active at the time of, and just after, birth. After the period of weaning it decreases in size and soon ceases to function.

Evidence that the thymus gland is important in the development of the immune response can be demonstrated by the following experiments.
(1) Removal of the gland from a newborn mouse results in death from a chronic deficiency of lymphocytes in its tissue fluid and blood.
(2) Tissue from another mouse grafted onto an experimental newborn mouse with the gland removed is unable to recognise and react with antigens.
(3) If the thymus gland is removed from a much older mouse, this mouse suffers no adverse effects.

The stem cells of the bone marrow, which give rise to T lymphocytes, must pass through the tissue of the thymus gland before they can become fully functional. The mechanism employed for the maturation of T lymphocytes has yet to be clearly understood, but it is known that the

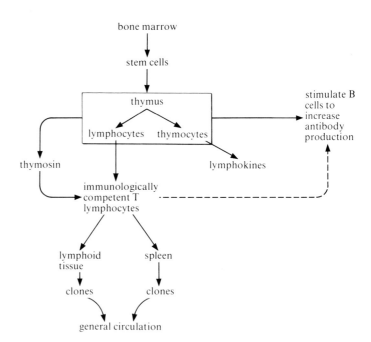

Fig 14.71 *T-cell differentiation and activity*

thymus secretes a hormone called **thymosin** which may promote T lymphocyte maturation. However, the role of the thymus as an endocrine organ has yet to be clearly established. The spleen and other lymph glands possess small numbers of lymphocytes at birth.

The cortex of the thymus gland is packed with lymphocytes, and those resident in the gland are called **thymocytes**, in order to distinguish them from the T lymphocytes circulating in the blood and body fluids (fig 14.71). Most thymocytes are immature, but a few are capable of reacting with antigen. When they do, they proliferate and manufacture complex molecules called **lymphokines** which aid in the attack and elimination of foreign particles. Mature, antigen-specific T lymphocytes are also required to help B lymphocytes mature and produce their antibody.

T cells constantly leave the thymus and pass to the lymph nodes and spleen. Here, if an antigen is recognised by a T cell, the T cell divides to form a clone of cells, all of which can identify and react with the antigen (fig 14.72). An individual T lymphocyte combats foreign cells by producing a receptor for antigen which is built into its surface membrane. When this sensitised lymphocyte recognises a complementary antigen, it attaches itself to it, rather like a key fitting into a lock, and destroys it. T cells regularly leave the lymphoid tissues to circulate in the blood and tissue fluid. Their constant circulation increases their chances of meeting and combating antigens.

14.14.2 B cell production

Stem cells that will eventually become B lymphocytes must undergo further differentiation outside the bone marrow. This may be in the liver, spleen or lymph nodes.

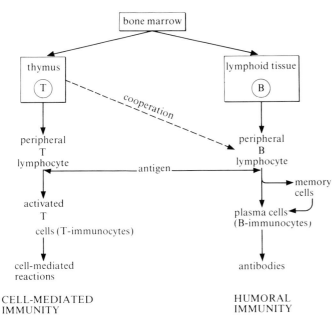

Fig 14.72 *Comparison of cell-mediated and humoral immunity*

When surface receptors (immunoglobulins) on the B lymphocytes detect complementary antigens, the B lymphocytes are stimulated to divide repeatedly and differentiate into plasma cell clones and memory cells (fig 14.72). The plasma cells, being genetically identical with each other, proceed to synthesise large quantities of antibody of the same kind.

These antibody-producing cells live for only a few days, but during that time they are able to synthesise and secrete nearly 2 000 identical antibody molecules per second.

The lymphatic memory cells are important in activating the body's response to a second infection of the antigen. Very little is known about memory cells, only that they exist and that in some way they enable an individual who has been exposed to an antigen once to respond more promptly and vigorously in a second encounter. This is called the **secondary response** and it results in a massive outpouring of antibody which quickly neutralises the harmful effect of the antigen (fig 14.74). Thus immunity is achieved. However it must be remembered that immunity

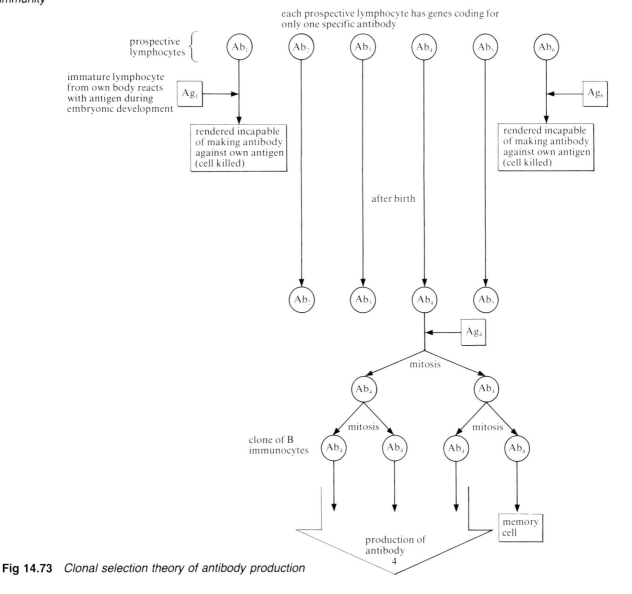

Fig 14.73 *Clonal selection theory of antibody production*

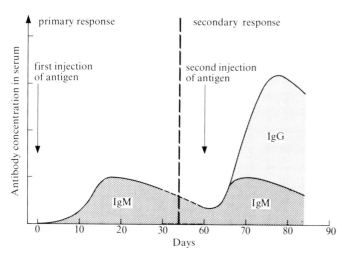

primary response | secondary response

first injection of antigen

second injection of antigen

IgG

IgM | IgM

Antibody concentration in serum

Days

Fig 14.74 *Primary and secondary response to an initial and later dose of antigen. The secondary response is more rapid and intense than the first*

to one antigen does not protect the individual against any other antigens. Each time a new antigen gains entry into the body, the appropriate complementary antibody must be produced if disease is to be prevented.

14.14.3 AIDS – Acquired Immune Deficiency Syndrome

AIDS is a disorder which impairs the body's T4 lymphocyte cell immune system in humans, in that the virus replicates within the T4 or 'helper' cells (see section 14.14.1). Thus these cells can no longer 'help' or induce other T cells, called killers, to fight invaders. The body's immune system breaks down, leaving the patient exposed to a variety of diseases (see section on *Signs, symptoms and nature of the disease* p. 537). It is important to realise, however, that infection with the virus (HIV) does not necessarily result in AIDS. As with other diseases, some people remain symptomless and are therefore termed 'carriers'.

Origin of AIDS

AIDS is thought to have originated somewhere in Central Africa, possibly sharing an ancestor with a virus found in several species of African monkey. The virus then appears to have migrated to Haiti and thence to the USA, and has subsequently been identified in 71 other countries throughout the world. It has already infected an estimated 10 million people.

Causative agent

The syndrome that we now know as AIDS was first recognised in the USA in 1981. Doctors reported a number of deaths which were associated with a breakdown of the body's immune system. In 1983 the French physician Dr Luc Montagnier identified the virus in the lymph nodes of a male homosexual. He termed the virus 'Lymphadenopathy Virus' or LAV. In Britain Abraham Karpas, working at Cambridge University, also isolated the virus (C-LAV)

from an AIDS patient. Shortly afterwards Dr Robert Gallo of the National Cancer Research Institute of America isolated an almost identical virus which he called 'Human T cell Lymphotropic Virus' or HTLV-III. These viruses are all essentially the same, and now the virus is internationally known as the 'Human Immunodeficiency Virus', its symbol being HIV. It is an RNA virus.

Transmission

The HIV virus can only survive in body fluids and is transmitted by blood or semen. In 90% of cases the transmission is achieved by sexual contact. People can contract the disease as follows.

(1) *Intimate sexual contact.* The disease was first associated with homosexual communities, notably in American cities such as San Francisco, Los Angeles and Miami where there were high levels of promiscuity amongst homosexuals. Since then it has become clear that transmission can also take place between heterosexuals. It passes from the infected partner to his/her unaffected partner through vaginal or anal intercourse, or oral sex. The risk becomes proportionately greater amongst those who are promiscuous. In America and Europe the disease is still largely confined to homosexuals, but in Africa it is also present in the heterosexual community. There the most rapid spread is amongst prostitutes and this pattern may be occurring in the Western World.

In October 1988 it was estimated that 50 000 people in the United Kingdom had the HIV in their blood and most of them were homosexuals (85%) who would develop the fatal disease in the next 10–15 years. Up to then 1 794 people had developed AIDS of whom 965 had died; 9 512 were known through blood tests to carry the HIV and of that only 400 were believed to had been infected through heterosexual intercourse. Probably 3 000 men and women had been infected heterosexually.

(2) *Infected blood entering the bloodstream.*

(*a*) AIDS can also be contracted by intravenous drug users practising self-injection by means of unsterilised needles and syringes. HIV has spread rapidly amongst intravenous drug users. Of the quarter of a million heroin addicts in New York, it is officially estimated that 60% have already been infected by the virus. Once in the bloodstream of the drug addict it can be further passed on through sexual activity, not only to other drug users but also to the general public.

(*b*) Some haemophiliacs have unfortunately contracted the disease after being given blood or blood products already infected with HIV. As a result of extensive screening programmes and other measures which include heat treatment of blood products to inactivate the virus, the treatment of haemophilia has been prevented from being a means of HIV transmission in countries with adequate medical facilities.

(c) Close contact between infected and non-infected people through cuts and open wounds has also been known to pass on the virus.

(d) Other ways:

An infected pregnant woman can pass on the virus to her baby through the placenta, at birth or through breast milk during suckling. The chances of the infection being transmitted from the mother to her baby are currently estimated to be 25–50%.

Mode of replication of HIV

The virus binds to receptors present in the surface of the T4 lymphocytes. From here it enters the lymphocyte by endocytosis or fusing with the cell surface membrane and injecting its viral RNA directly into the cell (see fig 2.16). The viral RNA is then copied into DNA by the activity of a unique enzyme called reverse transcriptase. The DNA enters the lymphocyte nucleus and becomes incorporated into the cell's own DNA. Thus it becomes a permanent part of the cells of an infected individual. Every time the human cell divides, so does the viral DNA, and thus spread of the viral genes is rapid.

The viral DNA may remain dormant for at least six years. However, suddenly, for some reason unknown, the lymphocyte begins to make copies of the viral genes in the form of messenger RNA. These then migrate from the nucleus into the lymphocyte cytoplasm and organise the synthesis of viral proteins and RNA. These assemble to form new AIDS viruses which leave the lymphocyte by budding out from underneath the cell surface membrane. The viruses spread and infect many other lymphocytes and brain cells. Eventually the cells in which the virus has multiplied are killed.

Signs and symptoms and nature of the disease

Current information suggests that 1–2% of HIV infected persons will develop AIDS each year, and that 5–10% of HIV infected persons will develop AIDS-related symptoms each year. First signs and symptoms are a short flu-like illness, followed by no further effects for months or years. AIDS involves a defect in the cell-mediated immune response, hence the term 'immune deficiency'. Opportunistic infections then ensue, that is micro-organisms that we normally live with, and which we can easily destroy, may cause killer diseases. Cause of death is commonly a rare type of pneumonia. Many patients suffer a rare and disfiguring form of skin cancer known as Kaposi's sarcoma. Other common signs and symptoms of AIDS include weight loss, fever, dementia, diarrhoea, septicaemia (blood poisoning) and other forms of cancer. Severity of immune deficiency varies and bouts of illness may persist for years.

As well as affecting lymphocytes, HIV may directly infect brain cells in more than 50% of cases, causing irreversible dementia and eventual death. The brain shrinks, with a loss of memory and mental agility, and behavioural changes occur. Long-term brain damage may emerge in the future as a common feature of the disease. It has been estimated that perhaps 50% of those infected with the virus may eventually show long-term brain disease, even if these patients do not develop AIDS.

Test for the disease

A blood test is used to tell whether or not a person has been infected by the AIDS virus. Under normal circumstances the immune system reacts to infection by producing antibodies, such as when the HIV enters the body, anti-HIV antibodies are produced. The blood of the person being tested is added to HIV proteins which have been commercially prepared. If there are anti-HIV antibodies in the blood sample they will bind to the viral proteins. This union of antibody to HIV protein indicates that the blood is from an infected person who is then designated HIV+.

However if the test proves negative that person may still be infected. This is because up to three months or longer must elapse between infection and production of HIV antibodies.

Control – treatment and prevention

An enormous international effort is being made to devise methods of treating and preventing the disease. There are two lines of research, one into developing drugs which can be used to cure the disease, and one into developing a vaccine. Both approaches are at an early stage and require heavy financial investment.

In the short-term the aim is to develop drugs to inactivate the virus, the method being to block a vital part of the pathogen's metabolism. An obvious target is the enzyme reverse transcriptase which is essential for replication of the virus.

The best-known drug in use by 1987 was azidothymidine or zidovudine (formerly known as AZT) which slows progression of the disease and can attack the virus even in the brain (a major reservoir of infection). Other drugs are being examined such as Ribavarin, a drug used to treat other viral infections which has been found to suppress the AIDS virus under laboratory conditions. Sumarin, an antiparasitic drug, has shown promise by acting to inhibit reverse transcriptase.

The only other treatment at the moment is relief of symptoms where possible, and attempts to restrict complications such as pneumonia.

Prevention

There are some obvious precautions which can be followed in trying to prevent the disease.

(1) The use of a barrier during intercourse can prevent the virus from infecting sex organs through blood or semen. Thus the use of the sheath or condom is advocated. This practice has been encouraged through many advertis-

ing campaigns throughout the world. There is evidence that this advice is beginning to be understood and used.

(2) The use of one sexual partner and the absence of promiscuity will clearly reduce the risk of infection.

(3) The reduction in the spread of HIV could be brought about by the use of clean needles and sterile syringes by drug addicts. Some health authorities in European countries, such as Holland, provide free sterile needles and syringes for drug users, but this has been questioned in this country. It is suggested that this will lead to increased drug addiction. Until December 1986, the Health Minister was still refusing to set up a free needle scheme, but at last a trial scheme to distribute free needles and syringes was announced in that month.

(4) Since October 1985 all blood donated in Britain has been tested for the presence of antibodies to HIV which indicates whether or not the donor is infected. Blood containing these antibodies is not used.

(5) Education about the disease has an important part to play, particularly in reassuring the public about the real risks. There is no evidence that infection can occur by droplet infection through the nose or mouth, or by casual contact such as shaking hands (see section 2.3.6). Healthcare staff who tend AIDS patients have never contracted the disease in this way.

14.14.4 Classes of immunoglobulins and their biological activities

There are five classes of immunoglobulin antibodies. Each class is determined by the type of heavy chain in its molecule, and demonstrates different activities. The light chains in the immunoglobulins are specified as either **kappa** or **lambda**. Their structural details need not be discussed here. Table 14.13 indicates some of the activities of the immunoglobulins.

Table 14.13 Classes of immunoglobulins and their biological activities.

Immuno-globulin	Heavy chain		Activity
IgM	mu		First class of antibody to appear in the serum after injection of antigen. It initiates the body's primary response
IgG	gamma	1	Principal antibody in serum. Initiates the
	,,	2	body's secondary response
	,,	3	
	,,	4	
IgA	alpha	1	Major class of antibody in external secre-
	,,	2	tions such as saliva, tears, bronchial and intestinal mucus. Operates as body's first line of defence against bacterial and viral antigens
IgD	delta		Little secreted. It is membrane-bound, but its function is as yet unknown
IgE	epsilon		Possibly involved in reactions to allergens. Functions otherwise unknown

14.14.5 The clonal selection theory of antibody formation

This theory was developed by Jerne, Burnet, Talmage and Lederberg in the 1950s and is generally accepted as a working model for antibody production (fig 14.73). Its essential points are as follows.

(1) There exists in every individual a very wide range of lymphocytes, each of which is capable of recognising only one specific antigen.

(2) The specificity of an antibody (which is a protein) is determined by its amino acid sequence, which in turn is determined by the lymphocyte's own unique DNA base sequence. Therefore the ability to synthesise a specific antibody is predetermined before the cell ever meets the antigen.

(3) Small amounts of antibody are produced by each cell as it matures and some of it becomes interlocked into its cell surface membrane where it acts as a receptor site for its complementary antigen.

(4) It is thought that if an immature lymphocyte meets with an antigen corresponding to its antibody during embryonic life, then the lymphocyte is killed. Therefore an animal will not synthesise antibody against its own macromolecules and becomes self-tolerant.

(5) When antigen locks into the receptor site of a mature lymphocyte, somehow the genetic apparatus of the lymphocyte is stimulated to produce antibody. Contact with the antigen is necessary for the lymphocyte to differentiate and divide into a clone of plasma cells synthesising antibody, and into memory cells.

(6) As all plasma cells are genetically identical, they all make the same antibody.

(7) The memory cells persist after the disappearance of the antigen, and in some way retain the capacity to be stimulated by antigen if it reappears. This is called **immunological memory** (fig 14.74), and is responsible for the body's secondary response which generally confers immunity on an animal against the specific antigen.

14.14.6 Types of immunity

Natural passive immunity

Preformed antibodies from one individual are passed into another individual of the same species. This only affords temporary protection against infection, for as the antibodies do their job, or are broken down by the body's natural processes, their number diminishes and protection is slowly lost. For example, antibodies from a mother can cross the placenta and enter her fetus. In this way they provide protection for the baby until its own immune system is fully functional. Passive immunity may also be conferred by colostrum, the initial secretion of the mammary glands, from which antibodies are absorbed from the intestines of the baby.

Acquired passive immunity

Here antibodies which have been preformed in one individual are extracted and then injected into the blood of another individual which may or may not be of the same species. For example, specific antibodies used for combating tetanus and diphtheria are cultured in horses and later injected into humans. They act prophylactically to prevent tetanus and diphtheria respectively. This type of immunity is again short-lived.

Natural active immunity

The body manufactures its own antibodies when exposed to an infectious agent. Because memory cells, produced on exposure to the first infection, are able to stimulate the production of massive quantities of antibody when exposed to the same antigen again, this type of immunity is most effective and generally persists for a long time, sometimes even for life (fig 14.74).

Acquired active immunity

This is achieved by injecting (or less commonly administering orally) small amounts of antigen, called the **vaccine**, into the body of an individual. The whole process is called **vaccination** or **immunisation**. If the whole organism is administered it should be safe because the organism is either killed or attenuated. This ensures that the individual does not contract the disease itself, but is stimulated to manufacture antibodies against the antigen. Often a second, booster injection is given and this stimulates a much quicker production of antibody which is long lasting and which protects the individual from the disease for a considerable time. Several types of vaccine are currently in use.

(1) **Toxoids.** Exotoxins produced by tetanus and diphtheria bacilli are detoxified with formaldehyde, yet their antigen properties remain unimpaired. Therefore vaccination with the toxoid will stimulate antibody production without producing symptoms of the disease.

(2) **Killed organisms.** Some dead viruses and bacteria are able to provoke a normal antigen–antibody response and are used for immunisation purposes.

(3) **Attenuated organisms.** Modified but living organisms are injected into the body. They are able to multiply without producing disease. Attenuation may be achieved by culturing the organisms at higher temperatures than normal or by adding specific chemicals to the culture medium for long periods of time. Attenuated vaccines for tuberculosis, measles, rubella and poliomyelitis are now in general use.

14.14.7   Blood groups

When a patient receives a blood transfusion it is imperative that he receives blood that is compatible with his own. If it is incompatible, a type of immune response occurs. This is because the donor's red cell membranes possess mucopolysaccharides known as **agglutinogens** which act as antigens and react with antibodies (agglutinins) in the recipient's plasma. The result is that the donor's cells are agglutinated (the cells link or attach to each other when the antigens on the surface of their cells interact with the antibodies). Two agglutinogens exist and they are named A and B respectively. The complementary plasma agglutinins are named a and b, and are present in the plasma all of the time. They are not produced in response to the donor's agglutinogen as is the case in the immune reactions already studied. A person with a specific agglutinogen in the red cells does not possess the corresponding agglutinin in the plasma. For example, anyone with agglutinogen A in the red cell membranes has no agglutinin a in the plasma and is classified under blood group A. If only B agglutinogens are present the blood group is B. Should both agglutinogens be present the blood group will be AB, whilst if no agglutinogens are present the blood group is designated O (table 14.14).

When transfusion occurs it is important to know what will happen to the cells of the donor. If there is a likelihood of them being agglutinated by the recipient's plasma antibodies then transfusion should not take place.

Fig 14.75 indicates the consequences of mixing different

Table 14.14 Blood groups.

Blood group	O	A	B	AB
Percentage of population	46%	42%	9%	3%
Agglutinogen	–	A	B	A + B
Agglutinin	a + b	b	a	–

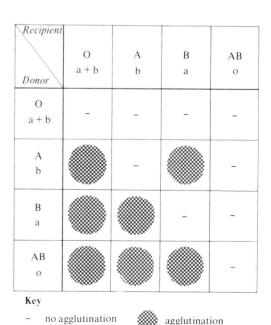

Key

–   no agglutination   agglutination

Fig 14.75 *Interactions between human blood groups. Cell agglutinogens are denoted by capital letters, agglutinins by small letters*

539

blood groups together. Individuals with blood group O are termed **universal donors** because their blood can be given to anyone. It possesses cells which will not be agglutinated by the recipient's plasma agglutinins. Although group O possesses a and b agglutinins there will be very little agglutination of the recipient's cells because the donated plasma is diluted so much by the recipient's blood that it is ineffective in its agglutination activity. Individuals with group AB can receive blood from anyone and are called **universal recipients**. However, they can only donate to blood group AB.

14.14.8 The rhesus factor

Of the total population, 85% possess red cells containing an agglutinogen called the rhesus factor and are termed **rhesus positive**. The remainder of the population lack the rhesus agglutinogen and are therefore regarded as **rhesus negative**. Rhesus negative blood does not usually contain rhesus agglutinins in its plasma. However, if rhesus positive blood enters a rhesus negative individual the recipient responds by manufacturing rhesus agglutinins.

The practical importance of this observation is made obvious when a rhesus negative mother bears a rhesus positive child. During the later stages of the pregnancy, fragments of the rhesus positive cells of the fetus may enter the mother's circulation and cause the mother to produce rhesus agglutinins. These can infiltrate to the fetus and destroy fetal red cells. Normally the agglutinins are not formed in large enough quantities to unduly affect the first-born child. However, subsequent rhesus positive children can suffer chronic destruction of their red cells. A rhesus baby is usually premature, anaemic and jaundiced, and its blood needs to be completely replaced by a transfusion of healthy blood. This treatment may now be undertaken whilst the baby is still in the womb.

Protection against the rhesus positive–negative reaction

(1) Consider a rhesus negative mother of blood group O, carrying a rhesus positive child of any blood group other than O. Should fetal cells enter the maternal circulation, the mother's a and b agglutinins will destroy them before the mother has time to manufacture anti-rhesus agglutinins.

(2) If an intravenous injection of anti-rhesus agglutinins, called **anti-D**, is given to a rhesus negative mother within 72 h of her giving birth, sensitisation of the rhesus negative mother by rhesus positive fetal cells is prevented. Apparently the anti-D attaches itself to the fetal cells which are in the mother's circulation and affects them in such a way that they are not recognised by the mother's antibody forming cells and hence the antibody process in the mother is not set in motion (fig 14.76).

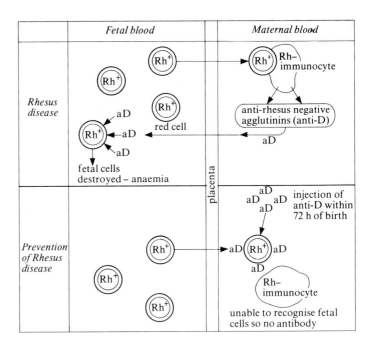

Fig 14.76 *The basis of Rhesus disease and its prevention. (From Burnet (1978)* Genes, dreams and realities, *Pelican)*

14.14.9 Transplantation

Replacement of diseased tissues or organs by healthy ones is called transplantation and is a technique used increasingly in surgery today. However, when foreign tissue is inserted into or onto another individual it is rejected by the recipient because it acts as an antigen, so stimulating the immune response in the recipient. The following terms are used for the different kinds of transplantation.

Autograft – tissue grafted from one area to another on the same individual.

Isograft – a graft between two genetically identical individuals such as identical twins.

Allograft – a tissue grafted from one individual to another individual of the same species but of different genetic constitution.

Xenograft – a graft between individuals of different species such as from pig to human.

Only allografting will be discussed here.

As blood is a fluid tissue, then simple blood transfusion can be regarded as an allograft. Here rejection results in agglutination of the donor's red cells as discussed earlier. When rejection of tissue, such as skin, occurs the following sequence of events takes place.

(1) The skin allograft initially develops blood vessels in the first 2–3 days and generally looks healthy.

(2) During the next six days its vascularisation decreases, and a great number of T lymphocytes and monocytes (sections 14.14.1 and 14.11.2) gather in the vicinity of the graft.

(3) Two days later the graft cells begin to die and the graft is eventually cast off.

Prevention of graft rejection

There are several means of preventing graft rejection currently in use, listed as follows.

(1) Tissue matching – this is an obvious and necessary precaution to take prior to any surgery.

(2) Exposure of bone marrow and lymph tissues to X-irradiation tends to inhibit blood cell production and therefore slows down rejection.

(3) Immunosuppression – here the principle is to use agents which inhibit the entire activity of the immune system. When this occurs graft rejection is delayed, but the main problem with this technique is that the patient becomes susceptible to all other kinds of infections. It has also been shown that immunosuppression may make the patients more prone to develop cancer.

If the disadvantages of non-specific immunosuppression are to be overcome then ways must be found of suppressing only the T cells response to the antigens of the graft. In this way the rest of the patient's immune system would remain unimpaired and continue to function normally. The most promising approach is to treat the patient (or his bone marrow) with antibody that recognises and destroys the T lymphocytes responsible for the graft rejection.

14.14.10 The interferon system

Interferon is a generic term which it is now realised applies to a number of proteins with similar properties. Human interferons have been divided into three groups α, β and γ depending on which type of cell they are produced by. The interferon α group consists of several species. They are all of similar molecular mass (about 20 000).

The most widely studied property of interferon is its ability to 'interfere' with the replication of viruses. It is produced in mammalian and avian cells in response to viral attack and appears to be an effective anti-viral agent on most types of cell against all viruses to a greater or lesser extent.

When a cell is attacked by a virus, a number of things happen. The virus will multiply, but at the same time the host cell is stimulated to produce interferon (fig 14.77). This is released from the cell and when it comes into contact with adjacent cells it renders them resistant to virus attack. To do this interferon triggers a series of events which lead to an inhibition of viral protein synthesis, viral RNA transcription and in some cases assembly and release of virus particles. Thus interferon, itself, is not anti-viral but brings about an 'anti-viral state' which involves cellular changes that then inhibit virus replication. The production of interferon can be stimulated by a whole variety of factors apart from virus attack, such as some inactivated viruses, double-stranded RNA, man-made double-stranded oligo-nucleotides and bacterial endotoxins. It would seem that interferon is produced as a result of an 'abuse' of the cell.

Interferon is biologically extremely active. Mouse interferon has an activity of 2×10^9 units per milligram of protein, where one unit will bring about a 50% reduction in virus production. This means that as little as one molecule per cell may be necessary to render a cell resistant to virus infection.

The interferons have a wide range of other effects including inhibiting cell growth. Recent results show that this effect may mean that they will be useful as anti-cancer agents under certain circumstances. There are also effects on the immune system and marked changes in the properties of cell membranes.

Thus it would seem that the interferon system may play an important role in the protection of the body against viruses.

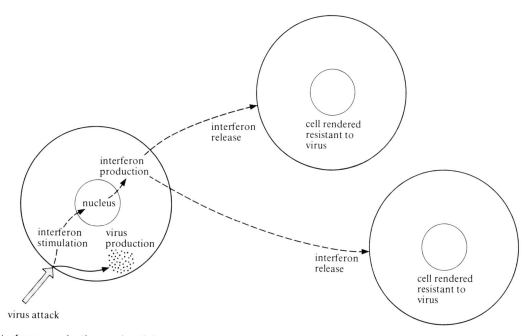

Fig 14.77 *Interferon production and activity*

541

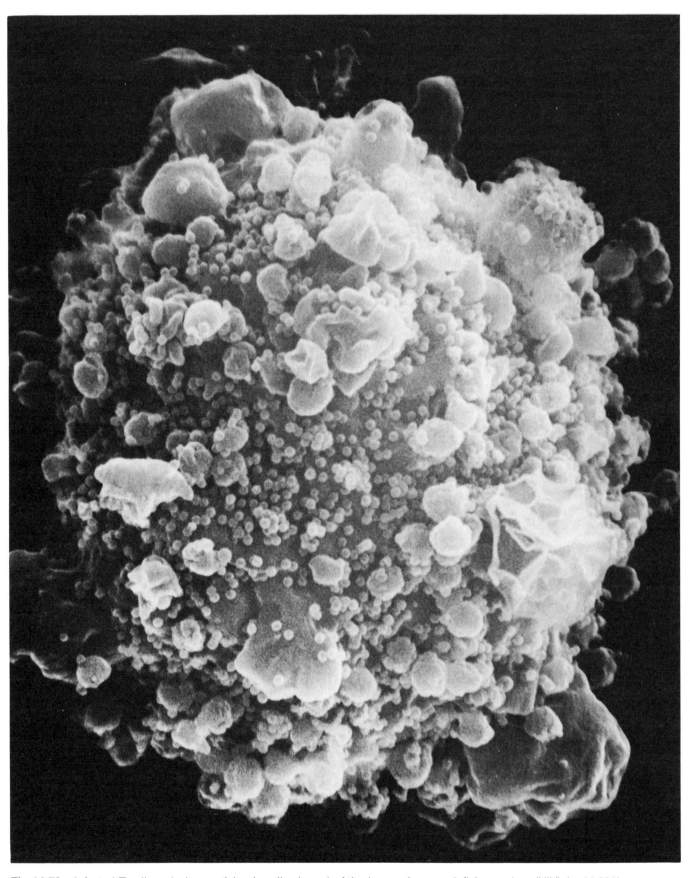

Fig 14.78 *Infected T cell producing particles (small spheres) of the human immunodeficiency virus (HIV) (× 20 000)*

Chapter Fifteen

Coordination and control in plants

Plants, like animals, need some form of internal coordination if their growth and development is to proceed in an orderly fashion, with suitable responses to their environment. Unlike animals, plants do not possess nervous systems and rely entirely on chemical coordination. Their responses are therefore slower and they often involve growth. Growth, in turn, can result in movement of an organ. In this chapter plant movements will be examined before studying the various ways in which plants coordinate their activities.

15.1 Plant movements

It is a characteristic of all but a few unicellular plants that they do not show locomotion (movement of the entire organism). However, movements of individual plant organs are possible and are modified by the sensitivity of the plant to external stimuli. Movements induced by external stimuli fall into three categories: tropisms (tropic movements), nasties (nastic movements) and taxes (tactic movements).

> **15.1** What is the basic reason for the fact that animals show locomotion whereas plants do not?

15.1.1 Tropisms

A **tropism** is a movement of part of a plant in response to, and directed by, an external stimulus. The movement is almost always a growth movement. Tropic responses are described as positive or negative depending on whether growth is towards or away from the stimulus respectively. Some examples of tropisms are shown in table 15.1.

> **15.2** Complete a fourth column to table 15.1 to show for each response how it is advantageous to the plant involved.
>
> **15.3** How could growth be modified to cause a tendril to coil round a solid object?

Phototropism and geotropism will be discussed in more detail later in this chapter (sections 15.2.1 and 15.2.2).

Table 15.1 Examples of tropisms.

Stimulus	Type of tropism	Examples
Light	Phototropism	Shoots and coleoptiles positively phototropic Some roots negatively phototropic, e.g. adventitious roots of climbers like ivy
Gravity	Geotropism	Shoots and coleoptiles negatively geotropic Roots positively geotropic Rhizomes, runners, dicotyledonous leaves **diageotropic*** Lateral roots, stem branches **plagiogeotropic***
Chemical	Chemotropism	Hyphae of some fungi positively chemotropic, e.g. *Mucor* Pollen tubes positively chemotropic in response to chemical produced at micropyle of ovule
Water	Hydrotropism (special kind of chemotropism)	Roots and pollen tubes positively hydrotropic
Solid surface or touch	Haptotropism (thigmotropism)	Tendrils positively haptotropic, e.g. leaves of pea Central tentacles of sundew, an insectivorous plant positively haptotropic (section 9.12.2)
Air (oxygen)	Aerotropism (special kind of chemotropism)	Pollen tubes negatively aerotropic

*diageotropism: growth at 90° to gravity, that is horizontal growth.
plagiogeotropism: growth at some other angle to gravity, that is not horizontal or directly towards or away from gravity.

15.1.2 Taxes

A **taxis** is a movement of an entire cell or organism (that is locomotion) in response to, and directed by, an external stimulus. As with tropisms they can be described as positive or negative, and can be further classified according to the nature of the stimulus. Note that this kind of movement is not confined to plants. Examples are given in table 15.2.

> **15.4** Design an experiment to demonstrate the preferred light intensity of *Euglena* or *Chlamydomonas* in phototaxis.

Table 15.2 Examples of taxes.

Stimulus	Taxis	Examples
Light	Phototaxis	Positive: *Euglena* swims towards light, chloroplasts move towards light Negative: Earthworms, blowfly larvae, woodlice and cockroaches move away from light
Chemical	Chemotaxis	Positive: Sperms of liverworts, mosses and ferns swim towards substances released by the ovum, motile bacteria move towards various food substances Negative: Mosquitoes avoid insect repellent
Air (oxygen)	Aerotaxis (special kind of chemotaxis)	Positive: motile aerobic bacteria move towards oxygen
Gravity	Geotaxis	Positive: Planula larvae of some cnidarians swim towards sea bed Negative: ephyra larvae of some cnidarians swim away from sea bed
Magnetic field	Magnetotaxis	Certain motile bacteria
Resistance	Rheotaxis	Positive: *Planaria* move against water current, moths and butterflies fly into the wind

15.5 Fig 15.1 illustrates the distribution of motile bacteria 10 min after being placed under a cover-slip with a filament of a green alga. (*a*) Name a genus of a suitable alga for the experiment. (*b*) Put forward a hypothesis to account for the final distribution of the bacteria. (*c*) How could you check your hypothesis?

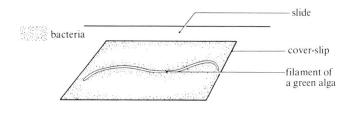

Fig 15.1 *Distribution of motile bacteria on a slide*

15.1.3 Nasties

A **nasty** is a non-directional movement of part of a plant in response to an external stimulus. The direction of movement is determined by the structure of the responding organ. Movement is the result of growth or a turgor change and small movements are typically amplified by the particular positioning of the responding cells.

The 'sleep movements' (**nyctinasty**) of certain flowers and leaves, whereby they open and close in response to light intensity (**photonasty**) or temperature (**thermonasty**), are nastic because they are merely triggered by external stimuli and are directed internally. Some flowers, such as crocus and tulip, close at night by the lower sides of petals growing more rapidly (**hyponasty**). Opening is caused by more rapid growth of the upper sides (**epinasty**). Many leaves or leaflets, particularly of leguminous plants, such as clover and *Mimosa*, have structures called pulvini. A **pulvinus** is a swelling at the base of a petiole or leaflet which possesses large parenchyma cells. Rapid turgor pressure changes in these cells result in the pulvinus acting as a hinge and bringing about movement.

Haptonastic movements, where the stimulus is touch, are among the most fascinating of plant movements, since they include rapid and elaborate responses. The well-known 'sensitive plant' *Mimosa pudica* is sensitive to touch as well as a variety of other stimuli. It exhibits normal sleep movements but responds very rapidly to shock (**seismonasty**) such as a sharp blow, injury, or sudden change in temperature or light intensity. If leaflets at the tip are shocked, they fold upwards in seconds. If the stimulus is strong or sustained, successive pairs of leaflets fold up and the stimulus eventually passes through the whole leaf, resulting in the petiole drooping (fig 15.2). The stimulus will pass in the reverse direction if the stem is stimulated. Fig 15.2 shows the three sites at which pulvini are found. The stimulus is thought to be transmitted by a hormone moving through the xylem; electrical changes are associated with its passage but there is no nervous system.

Insectivorous plants show some of the most elaborate movements in the plant kingdom, some of which are haptonastic.

15.1.4 Kinesis

A type of locomotory response not so far mentioned is **kinesis**. Since this is virtually confined to the animal kingdom it is discussed in chapter 16 with animal behaviour.

15.2 Plant growth substances

Chemical coordination in animals is controlled by **hormones**, chemicals working in minute concentrations at sites some distance from their sites of synthesis. Plants are coordinated by chemicals which do not necessarily move from their sites of synthesis and hence, by definition, should not always be termed hormones. In view of this and because their effects are usually on some aspect of growth, they are called **growth substances**. It is also important to stress that the precise mechanisms of action of the plant growth substances so far discovered are far from clear and that analogies with the better understood animal hormones may be misleading. Plant growth substances are certainly essential for plant development, but to what extent they act

Fig 15.2 *Response of the 'sensitive plant'* (Mimosa pudica) *to shock.* (left) *before* (right) *after*

as 'triggers' for changes in growth or as 'integrating chemicals', modifying processes triggered by other unknown events, is not certain. It should be borne in mind that growth can be divided into the three stages of cell division, cell enlargement and cell differentiation (specialisation) and that these have particular locations in plants (section 21.6). It can be expected, therefore, that the action and distribution of different plant growth substances will reflect this. Five major types of growth substance are recognised: auxins, gibberellins, cytokinins, abscisic acid and ethene (ethylene). Generally speaking, cytokinins are associated with cell division, auxins and gibberellins with cell enlargement and differentiation, abscisic acid with resting states (such as lateral buds) and ethene with senescence (ageing).

In this chapter, each type of growth substance will first be

discussed separately, and then key stages in the life cycle of a plant will be discussed to emphasise the fact that growth substances often work in association with each other to achieve their effects.

15.2.1 Auxins and phototropism

Discovery of auxins

The discovery of auxins was the result of investigations into phototropism that began with the experiments of Charles Darwin and his son Frances. Using oat coleoptiles as convenient material (fig 15.3), they showed that the growth of shoots towards light was the result of some 'influence' being transmitted from the shoot tip to the region of growth behind it. Some of their experiments are summarised in

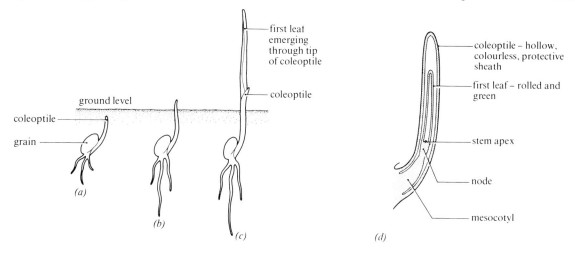

Fig 15.3 *Germination of a typical grass seedling:* (a) (b) and (c) *stages in germination,* (d) *section of coleoptile at stage* (b)

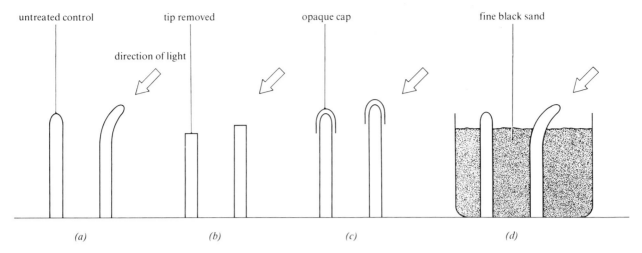

untreated control   tip removed   opaque cap   fine black sand

direction of light

(a)   (b)   (c)   (d)

Fig 15.4 *Darwin's experiments on phototropism using oat coleoptiles. (a), (b), (c) and (d) separate experiments showing treatment* (left) *and result* (right)

fig 15.4, the diagrams representing results obtained from many seedlings.

If the tropic response is analysed in terms of the following: stimulus → receptor → transmission → effector → response, then the largest gap in our knowledge remains the nature of the transmission. In 1913 the Danish plant physiologist Boysen-Jensen added to our knowledge. Fig 15.5 summarises some of his experiments.

In 1928 the Dutch plant physiologist Went finally proved the existence of a chemical transmitter. His aim had been to intercept and collect the chemical as it passed back from the tip and to demonstrate its effectiveness in a variety of tests. He reasoned that a small diffusing molecule should pass freely into a small block of agar jelly, whose structure is such that relatively large spaces exist between its molecules. Fig 15.6 illustrates some of his experiments.

A further experiment of note carried out by Went is illustrated in fig 15.7. In control experiments the tip was exposed to uniform light or darkness before transfer of agar blocks, and the degree of curvature induced by blocks A and B was the same. Unilateral illumination of the tip, however, resulted in unequal distribution of the chemical in blocks A and B (fig 15.7). Not only does this support the

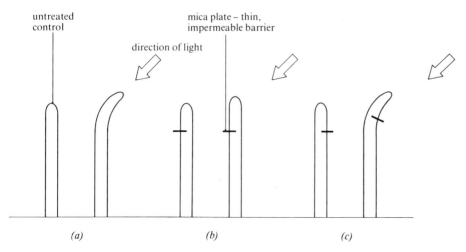

untreated control   mica plate – thin, impermeable barrier

direction of light

(a)   (b)   (c)

Fig 15.5 *Boysen-Jensen's experiments on phototropism using oat coleoptiles, (a), (b) and (c), separate experiments showing treatment* (left) *and result* (right)

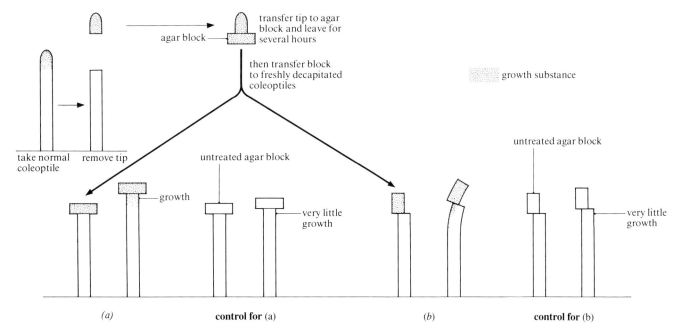

Fig 15.6 *Went's experiments, (a) and (b), separate experiments showing treatment* (left) *and result* (right). *Control experiments are shown alongside. All treatments were carried out in darkness or uniform light*

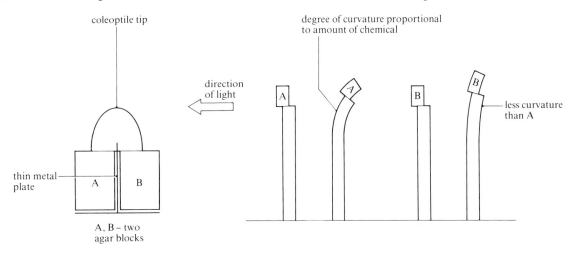

Fig 15.7 *Went's experiment showing effect of unilateral light on distribution of the chemical (auxin)*

conclusions from Boysen-Jensen's experiments about the effect of light on the distribution of the chemical, but it shows how a test for measuring the amount of the chemical present, that is a bioassay, can be set up. A **bioassay** is an experiment in which the amount of a substance is found by measuring its effects in a biological system. Went showed that the degree of curvature of oat coleoptiles was directly proportional to the concentration of the chemical (at normal physiological levels).

The chemical was subsequently named 'auxin' (from the Greek *auxein*, to increase). In 1934 it was identified as indoleacetic acid (IAA). IAA was soon found to be widely distributed in plants and to be intimately concerned with cell enlargement. Fig 15.8 summarises present beliefs concerning the movement of IAA during unilateral illumination of coleoptiles. It should be pointed out, however, that the coleoptile is the simplest system so far

studied and that others appear to be more complex. Also, there is little evidence for the development of auxin gradients in the critical period before the response is measured.

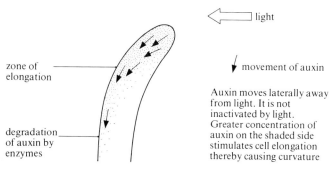

Auxin moves laterally away from light. It is not inactivated by light. Greater concentration of auxin on the shaded side stimulates cell elongation thereby causing curvature

Fig 15.8 *Hypothesis for effect of unilateral illumination on distribution of auxin in a coleoptile*

Structure of IAA

The structure of IAA is shown in fig 15.9.

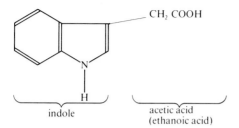

Fig 15.9 *Structure of IAA (indoleacetic acid)*

Other chemicals with similar structures and activity were soon isolated, and some such substances have been synthesised, making a whole class of plant growth substances called auxins. Some of these are discussed below in section 15.2.5.

Synthesis and distribution of auxins

Auxins are made continuously in the shoot apex and young leaves. Movement away from the tip is described as basipetal (from apex to base of the organ) and polar (in one direction only). It moves, apparently by diffusion, from cell to cell and is eventually inactivated and degraded by enzymes. Long-distance transport can also occur via the vascular system (mainly phloem) from shoots to roots. A little auxin is probably made in roots. The effects of different auxin concentrations on shoot growth can be investigated by means of an experiment such as experiment 15.1.

Experiment 15.1: To investigate the effects of indoleacetic acid (IAA) on the growth of oat coleoptiles

The aim of the experiment is to investigate the effect of various concentrations of IAA on growth of oat coleoptiles. Growth is affected by white light and therefore cutting and transferring of coleoptiles during the experiment should be carried out under red light or in the minimum amount of light possible. Sucrose solution is used in the experiment as energy will be required for growth, and sucrose is an energy source. The apical tip (3 mm) of each coleoptile is removed in order to prevent natural auxins produced by the coleoptile from having an effect on growth.

Materials

germinating oat seedlings with coleoptiles at least 1.5 cm long (Soak 100 oat grains in water overnight, place the soaked seeds on damp paper towelling in a dish, cover the dish with aluminium foil and place in the dark to germinate (five days in an incubator at 20 °C). In order to obtain the 60 coleoptiles required for each experiment, at least 100 grains should be soaked to allow for germination failure.)
6 test-tubes in a test-tube rack

6 petri dishes + lids
5 × 5 cm³ graduated pipettes
25 cm³ measuring cylinder or 10 cm³ graduated pipette
coleoptile cutter (fig 15.10)
paint brush
stock IAA solution (1 g dm⁻³) (IAA is not readily soluble in water and is therefore first dissolved in ethanol: dissolve 1 g of IAA in 2 cm³ ethanol and dilute to 900 cm³ with distilled water. Warm the solution to 80 °C and keep at this temperature for 5 min. Make up to 1 dm³ with distilled water. Adjust quantities according to final volume required.)
2% sucrose solution
distilled water

Method

(1) Take six test-tubes and six petri dishes and label them A–F.
(2) Add 18 cm³ of 2% sucrose solution to each test-tube.
(3) Using a clean 5 cm³ pipette, add 2 cm³ of IAA solution to tube A and mix the two solutions thoroughly.
(4) Using a fresh pipette transfer 2 cm³ of solution from tube A to tube B and mix the contents of tube B thoroughly.
(5) Using a fresh pipette each time, transfer 2 cm³ from tube B to tube C, mix, then 2 cm³ from tube C to tube D, mix, then 2 cm³ from tube D to tube E.
(6) Add 2 cm³ distilled water to tube F.
(7) Transfer the solutions from tubes A–F to petri dishes A–F.
(8) Take 60 germinated oat seedlings and cut 10 mm lengths of coleoptile, starting about 2 mm back from the tips. Use a double-bladed cutter with the blades held exactly 10 mm apart by a series of washers, two nuts and two bolts (see fig 15.10). If the tips of the coleoptiles are placed in a line, several lengths can be cut simultaneously.
(9) Using a paint brush, transfer 10 lengths of coleoptile to each dish avoiding cross contamination of the solutions (the greater the number of coleoptiles used, the more statistically valid the results).
(10) Place a lid on each and incubate the dishes at 25 °C for three days in the dark.
(11) Remeasure the lengths of coleoptiles as accurately as possible.

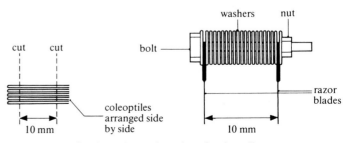

Fig 15.10 *Cutting 10 mm lengths of coleoptiles*

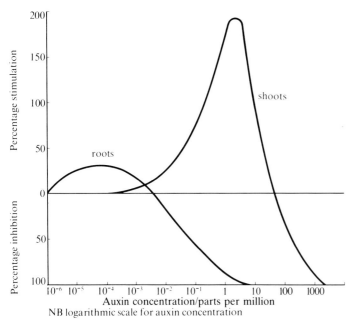

Fig 15.11 *Effect of auxin concentration on growth responses of roots and shoots. Note that concentrations of auxin which stimulate shoot growth inhibit root growth*

(12) Ignoring the largest and smallest figures for each dish, calculate the mean (average) length.

(13) Plot a graph of mean length (vertical axis) against IAA concentration in parts per million (horizontal axis).

> **15.11** What is the concentration in parts per million (ppm) of IAA in each petri dish (1 g dm^{-3} = 1 000 ppm)?

(14) Comment on the results and compare them with fig 15.11. More accurate results can be obtained by combining class results.

15.2.2 Auxins and geotropism

It is a common observation that roots are positively geotropic, that is grow downwards, and shoots are negatively geotropic, that is grow upwards. That gravity is the stimulus responsible can be demonstrated by using a piece of equipment called a **klinostat** (fig 15.12). As the chamber rotates, all parts of the seedling receive, in turn, equal stimulation from gravity. A speed of four revolutions per hour is sufficient to eliminate the one-sided effect of gravity and to cause straight shoot and root growth. A non-rotating control shows the normal response to gravity, with shoot growing up and root growing down. It is important to ensure even illumination during the experiment (or to carry it out in darkness) so that there can be no directional response to light.

The involvement of auxins in geotropism is demonstrated by the experiment shown in fig 15.13, which uses the techniques introduced by Went. Auxin moves out of the horizontally placed coleoptile tip but moves downwards as it does so. The greater auxin concentration on the lower

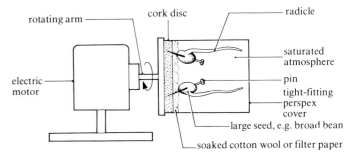

Fig 15.12 *(above) Klinostat showing broad beans after several days growth with rotation*

Fig 15.13 *(below) Effect of gravity on distribution of auxin from a horizontal coleoptile tip*

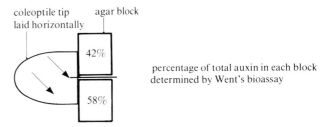

surface of an intact coleoptile would stimulate greater cell elongation here, and hence upward growth.

Decapitation of a root tip removes its sensitivity to gravity, but it is not so easy to demonstrate movement of auxins in roots because very low concentrations are present, and these do not give convincing results in the bioassay described. An interesting result though is obtained from the experiment shown in fig 15.14.

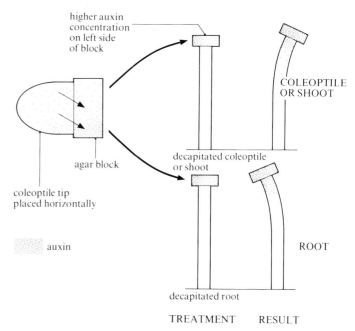

Fig 15.14 *Effect of uneven auxin distribution on growth of decapitated coleoptile and root*

> **15.12** What can you conclude from the experiment shown in fig 15.14?

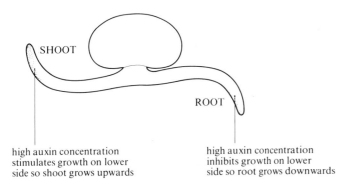

SHOOT

ROOT

high auxin concentration
stimulates growth on lower
side so shoot grows upwards

high auxin concentration
inhibits growth on lower
side so root grows downwards

Fig 15.15 *Hypothesis for redistribution of auxin in a horizontally placed seedling*

Observations of this type led to the hypothesis summarised in fig 15.15, which suggests that the opposite responses of roots and shoots are due to different sensitivities to auxin. Modifications of the hypothesis in the light of recent findings are discussed later in this section.

The different sensitivity of roots to auxin (fig 15.11) could also explain the negative phototropism shown by some; the higher accumulation of auxin on the shaded side would cause inhibition of growth with the result that cells on the light side would elongate faster and the root would grow away from light.

An important aspect of plant growth regulation has thus been revealed. It is not only the nature of the growth substance which is relevant (qualitative control) but the amount of that substance (quantitative control).

The gravity-sensing mechanism

The question now arises as to how the gravity stimulus is detected. Darwin showed that removal of the root cap, the group of large parenchyma cells that protect the root tip as it grows through the soil, abolishes the geotropic response. A section of the root cap reveals the presence of large starch grains contained in amyloplasts within the cells (fig 15.16).

It was suggested as long ago as 1900 that these cells act as **statocytes**, that is gravity receptors, and that the starch grains are **statoliths**, structures which move in response to gravity. The so-called '**starch–statolith hypothesis**' proposes that sedimentation of the starch grains through the cells occurs so that they come to rest on the lower sides of the cells with respect to gravity (fig 15.16). In some unknown way this affects the distribution of growth substances which are known to be produced sometimes in the root apex, sometimes in the root cap and sometimes in both. There is much evidence to support this hypothesis. All plant organs which are sensitive to gravity contain statocytes. They are found, for example, in the vascular bundle sheaths of shoots. Plants from which the starch grains have been removed by certain treatments lose their sensitivity to gravity, but regain it if allowed to make more starch.

15.13 How is this mechanism of gravity detection similar to that in animals?

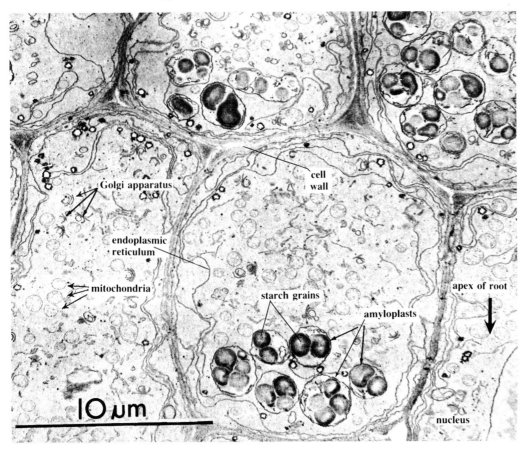

Golgi apparatus

cell wall

endoplasmic reticulum

mitochondria

starch grains

amyloplasts

apex of root

nucleus

10 μm

Fig 15.16 *Electron micrograph of section of root cap showing amyloplasts with starch grains located at the bottoms of the cells*

Modern hypotheses on geotropism

In coleoptiles the gravity response seems to be mediated by auxins as described above, but with most shoots a geotropic response is still obtained if the tip is removed, and there is still doubt as to whether movement of auxin is involved. In roots, auxin redistribution does occur, but probably not dramatically enough to account for the observed changes in growth rates. Transmission of a growth inhibitor from the root cap to the zone of elongation has been shown, but this is not necessarily auxin. Several groups of workers have been unable to find auxin in the root caps of maize seedlings, a common experimental plant. Instead, abscisic acid, a well-known growth inhibitor, has been found. Ethene, another growth inhibitor, could also be involved. Finally, gibberellins (growth promoters) have been found in higher concentrations than normal in the rapidly growing sides of both shoots and roots when they are geotropically stimulated.

> **15.14** What can you conclude from the experiments shown in fig 15.17? Controls, using untreated agar, showed no curvature. When IAA was used instead of abscisic acid no significant curvature was obtained.

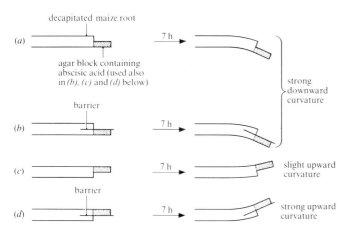

Fig 15.17 *Effect of abscisic acid on geotropic response to decapitated roots. (Based on experiments by Pilet, 1975.)*

15.2.3 Mode of action of auxins

The effect of auxins on cell enlargement is now reasonably well understood. During cell extension the rigid cellulose framework of the cell wall must be loosened. Extension then occurs by a combination of osmotic swelling as water enters the cell and by the laying down of new cell wall material. The orientation of the existing cellulose microfibrils probably helps to determine the direction of extension. 'Wall loosening' is induced by acid conditions, and by auxins. In 1973 four different groups of workers all demonstrated that auxins stimulate hydrogen ion (proton) secretion. This causes a lowering of pH outside the cell (increase in acidity) and hence wall loosening, possibly by an enzyme with a low pH optimum. The ability to maintain a low water potential inside the cell, and availability of water to enter the cell and generate a high pressure potential, are also necessary.

15.2.4 Other effects of auxins

Apart from stimulating cell elongation and hence shoot growth, auxins have a number of other important roles in the plant, summarised in table 15.4. Further details of their roles in differentiation, apical dominance, abscission and fruit growth are given later under the appropriate headings.

15.2.5 Commercial applications of auxins

Discovery of IAA led to the synthesis by chemists of a wide range of active compounds with similar structure.

Synthetic auxins have proved commercially useful in a variety of ways. They are cheaper than IAA to produce, and often more physiologically active because plants generally do not have the necessary enzymes to break them down. Table 15.3 gives some examples with their structures and summaries of their uses. Chlorine substitutions in the structures often increase activity. Fig 15.18 shows the effect of treating tomatoes with a fruit-setting auxin.

Plant growth regulators

It is important to distinguish between naturally occurring **plant growth substances** and synthetic **plant growth regulators** which are often based on the structure of the naturally occurring compounds but are more effective and less easily degraded by the plant and therefore tend to be used commercially, for example:

plant growth substance	auxin (indolyl acetic acid)
plant growth regulators	phenoxyacetic acids (2-4-D)
	indolyl butyric acid
	indolyl propionic acid

15.2.6 Gibberellins

Discovery of gibberellins

During the 1920s a team of Japanese scientists at the University of Tokyo was investigating a particularly damaging worldwide disease of rice seedlings, caused by the fungus *Gibberella* (now called *Fusarium*). Infected seedlings became tall, spindly and pale and eventually died or gave poor yields. By 1926 a fungal extract had been isolated which induced these symptoms in rice plants. An active compound was crystallised by 1935 and a further two

Table 15.3 Commercial applications of auxins.

Type of Auxin	Examples with structures	Uses
Indoles and naphthyls	NAA (naphthalene acetic acid) (structure) —COOH (compare with IAA fig 15.9) Indole propionic acid (structure) —COOH	**Fruiting** – help natural fruit set; sometimes cause fruit setting in absence of pollination (parthenocarpy) **Rooting hormone** – promote rooting of cuttings
Phenoxyacetic acids*	2,4-D (2,4-dichlorophenoxyacetic acid) (structure) O—COOH Cl Cl 2,4,5-T (2,4,5-trichlorophenoxyacetic acid) as above but extra chlorine atom in 5 position of ring MCPA (2-methyl-4-chlorophenoxyacetic acid) as 2,4-D but methyl group (CH_3) in 2 position of ring instead of chlorine	**Selective weedkillers** – kill broad-leaved species (dicotyledons). Used in cereal crops and on lawns. Also in conifer plantations for scrub clearance (conifers unaffected). 2,4-D/2,4,5-T mix used in Vietnam war by US as the defoliant 'Agent Orange' **Potato storage** – inhibit sprouting of potatoes **Fruiting** – prevent premature fruit drop (retard abscission)
Benzoic acids	2,3,6-trichlorobenzoic acid (structure) Cl COOH Cl Cl 2,4,6-trichlorobenzoic acid as above except chlorine atom in 4 position instead of 3 position of ring	Powerful **weedkillers**

*Cause plants to outgrow themselves. Growth distorted. Respiration excessive. 2,4,5-T is being phased out owing to concern about its contaminant, dioxin, which is the most toxic substance known to humans. Dioxin causes, for example, cancer, fetal abnormalities and a particularly severe form of acne called chloracne.

Fig 15.18 (left) *The three large trusses were set by spraying with beta naphthoxy acetic acid. The small one in the bottom left-hand corner was not sprayed – and produced only one normal size tomato*

by 1938. These compounds were called **gibberellins**, after the fungus. Language barriers and then the Second World War delayed the initiation of work in the West, but immediately after the war there was competition between British and American groups to isolate these chemicals. In 1954 a British group isolated an active substance which they called **gibberellic acid**. This was the third, and most active, gibberellin (**GA₃**) isolated by the Japanese. Gibberellins were isolated from higher plants during the 1950s, but the chemical structure of GA₃ was not completely worked out until 1959 (fig 15.19). Now more than 50 naturally occurring gibberellins are known, all differing only slightly from GA₃.

Structure of gibberellins

All are **terpenes**, a complex group of plant chemicals related to lipids; all are weak acids and all contain the '**gibbane**' skeleton (fig 15.19).

gibbane skeleton

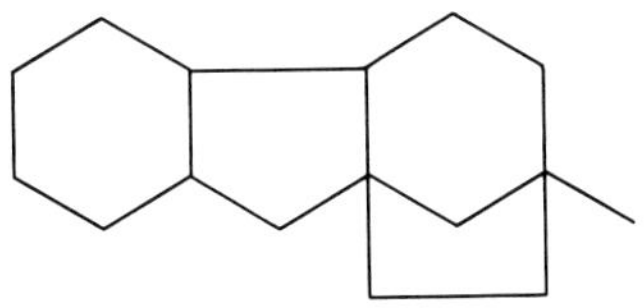

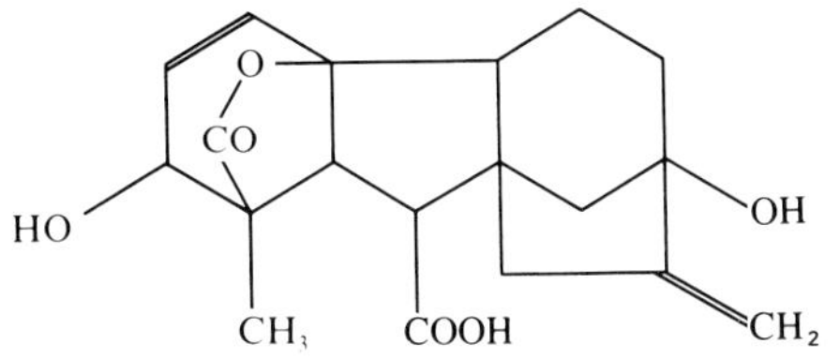

Fig 15.19
Structures of gibbane skeleton and gibberellic acid (GA₃)

gibberellic acid (GA₃)

Synthesis and distribution of gibberellins

Gibberellins are most abundant in young, expanding organs, being synthesised particularly in young apical leaves (possibly in chloroplasts), buds, seeds and root tips. They migrate after synthesis in a non-polar manner, that is up or down the plant from the leaves. They move in phloem and xylem.

Effects of gibberellins

Like the auxins, the principal effect of gibberellins is on stem elongation, mainly by affecting cell elongation. Thus genetically dwarf varieties of peas and maize are restored to normal growth and dwarf beans can be converted into runner beans (fig 15.20). Stem growth of normal plants is promoted. Further information, relating to interaction with auxins, is given in section 15.3.

One of the classic effects of gibberellins, which has been much studied in an attempt to understand their mechanism of action, is the breaking of dormancy of certain seeds, notably of cereals. Germination is triggered by soaking the seed in water. After imbibing water the embryo secretes gibberellin which diffuses to the aleurone layer, stimulating synthesis of several enzymes, including α-amylase (fig 15.21). These catalyse the breakdown of food reserves in the endosperm and the products of digestion diffuse to the embryo, where they are used in growth.

15.15 (*a*) What is the substrate of α-amylase? (*b*) What is the product of the reaction it catalyses? (*c*) What other enzyme is required to complete digestion of its substrate? (*d*) Why is α-amylase so important in cereal seeds?

15.16 Explain the role of storage proteins in the aleurone layer by reference to fig 15.21.

Fig 15.20 *The influence of gibberellic acid (GA) on the growth of variety* Meteor *dwarf pea. The plant on the left received no GA and shows the typical dwarf habit. The remaining plants were treated with GA; the dose per plant in micrograms is shown. With doses up to 5 micrograms there is increased growth of the stems with increase in GA dosage. This is the principle of the dwarf pea assay of gibberellins*

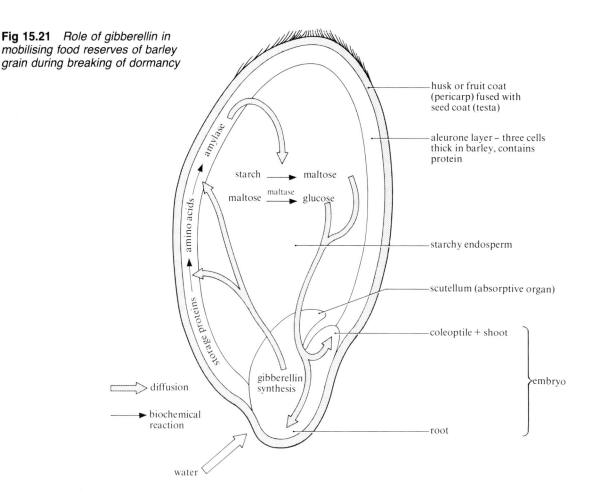

Fig 15.21 *Role of gibberellin in mobilising food reserves of barley grain during breaking of dormancy*

husk or fruit coat (pericarp) fused with seed coat (testa)

aleurone layer – three cells thick in barley, contains protein

amylase

starch ⟶ maltose

maltose ⟶ glucose (maltase)

amino acids

starchy endosperm

scutellum (absorptive organ)

storage proteins

coleoptile + shoot

⟹ diffusion

⟶ biochemical reaction

gibberellin synthesis

embryo

root

water

Experiment 15.2: To test the following two hypotheses, (a) that gibberellin can stimulate breakdown of starch in germinating barley grains and (b) that gibberellin is produced in the embryo

The presence of amylase in barley seeds can be detected by placing a cut seed on the surface of agar containing starch. If the surface is moist, amylase will diffuse from the seed and catalyse digestion of the starch. Addition of iodine to the agar would stain remaining starch blue-black, revealing a clear 'halo' of digestion around the seed. The size of this circular zone gives a rough indication of how much amylase was present. In practice, sterile handling techniques are an important precaution because contaminating bacteria and fungi may also produce amylase.

With careful experimental design, further hypotheses may be tested (see, for example, Coppage, J. & Hill, T. A. (1973) *J. Biol. Ed.* **7**, 11–18).

Materials (per student)

white tile
scalpel
forceps
50 cm³ beaker
labels or chinagraph pencil

iodine/potassium iodide solution
sterile distilled water in sterile flasks (×3)
5% sodium hypochlorite solution or commercial sterilising fluid, e.g. Milton's or 70% alcohol
two starch agar plates (sterile): 1% agar containing 0.5% starch poured to a depth of about 0.25 cm in sterile Petri dishes

two starch–gibberellin agar plates: as above but add gibberellin (GA₃) to the agar before autoclaving at the concentration of 1 cm³ of 0.1% GA₃ solution per 100 cm³ agar (final concentration 10 ppm GA₃) (Gibberellin does not dissolve readily in water and is best dissolved in ethanol; some of the GA₃ is destroyed during autoclaving but the seeds are sensitive to concentrations as low as 10^{-5} ppm GA₃.)

dehusked barley grains: to dehusk barley grains, soak them in 50%(v/v) aqueous sulphuric acid for 3–4 h and then wash thoroughly (about ten times) in distilled water; violent shaking of the grains in a conical flask removes most of the husks; grains should be used immediately, since soaking starts germination. Alternatively, 'embryo' and 'non-embryo' halves can be separated (see below) and stored under dry conditions in a fridge for a maximum of 2–3 days. Wheat grains are naked and do not need dehusking, and may be used as a substitute for barley.

Method

(1) Take two starch agar, and two starch–gibberellin agar plates appropriately labelled +GA or −GA. These have been sterilised. Label one of each type 'embryo' and the other 'non-embryo'.

(2) Cut at least two dry barley grains transversely in half (fig 15.22) on a tile, thus separating into 'embryo' and 'non-embryo' halves.

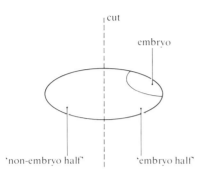

Fig 15.22 *Cutting a barley grain for experiment 15.2*

(3) Sterilise the halves in 5% sodium hypochlorite solution for 5 min. Then wash in three changes of sterile distilled water in sterile flasks.

(4) Using forceps sterilised by rinsing in 70% alcohol, place the halves immediately in the relevant dishes, cut face downwards, with minimal lifting of lids as follows:

−GA	+GA	−GA	+GA
embryo ½	embryo ½	non-embryo ½	non-embryo ½

(5) Incubate for 24–48 h at 20–30 °C.

(6) Test for presence of starch in each dish by flooding surfaces of agar with I₂/KI solution. Draw the final appearance of each dish. Discuss the results.

> **15.17** Using starch agar it is often possible to demonstrate an association of amylase activity with fingerprints. Suggest reasons for this association.
>
> **15.18** What further experiment could you do, given the facilities, to prove that gibberellin causes synthesis of *new* amylase rather than activating pre-existing amylase?
>
> **15.19** How could you prove that amylase synthesis takes place in the aleurone layer?
>
> **15.20** How might the effect of gibberellin on barley seeds be used as a bioassay for gibberellin activity?

Other effects of gibberellins

Further effects of gibberellins on flowering, fruit growth and dormancy and their involvement in photoperiodism and vernalisation are discussed later under the appropriate headings. Their effects are summarised in table 15.4.

Mode of action of gibberellins

The mechanism of action of gibberellins remains unclear. In cereal grains GA_3 has been shown to stimulate synthesis of new protein, particularly α-amylase, and is effective in such low concentrations (as little as 10^{-5} μg cm^{-3}) that it must be operating at a profound level in cell metabolism, such as the 'switching' on or off of genes which takes place during cell differentiation (section 22.7). No conclusive evidence that this is so has yet been obtained, and higher concentrations are required for its other effects. In cell elongation it is dependent on the presence of auxins.

Commercial applications of gibberellins

Gibberellins are produced commercially from fungal cultures. They promote fruit setting and are used for growing seedless grapes (parthenocarpy). GA_3 is used in the brewing industry to stimulate α-amylase production in barley, and hence promote 'malting'. A number of synthetic growth retardants act as 'anti-gibberellins', that is they inhibit the action of gibberellins. Application of these often results in short (dwarf), sturdy plants with deep green leaves and sometimes greater pest and disease resistance. They take up less space and may in the future lead to higher yields per acre; also they are less inclined to blow over.

Uses of plant growth regulators

Most plant growth regulators were discovered as a result of screening for herbicide activity. The rate and timing of the application of the regulator is of critical importance.

Plant regulators increasing yield

Chlormequat chloride	to shorten and stiffen wheat straw to prevent lodging (that is, blowing over) allowing increased use of nitrogenous fertilisers.
Gibberellic acid	to increase fruit set of mandarins, clementines, tangerines and pears.
Gibberellic acid	to overcome losses of apple yield due to frost damage.
Gibberellic acid	to increase berry size in seedless grapes enabling the product to be sold fresh rather than dry as raisins.
Gibberellic acid	to overcome low temperature constraints to sugarcane growth in Hawaii.
Ethephon	to increase latex flow in rubber.
Glysophosine	to ripen sugarcane.

Plant regulators improving quality

Gibberellic acid	coupled with mechanical thinning to increase berry size of seedless grapes in California.

Table 15.4 Roles of plant growth substances in plant growth and development.

Process affected	Auxins	Gibberellins
Stem growth	**Promote cell enlargement in region behind apex.** Promote cell division in cambium.	**Promote cell enlargement in presence of auxin.** Also promote cell division in apical meristem and cambium. **Promote 'bolting' of some rosette plants**
Root growth	**Promote at very low concentrations. Inhibitory at higher concentrations,** e.g. geotropism?	Usually inactive
Root initiation	**Promote growth of roots from cuttings and calluses**	Inhibitory
Bud (shoot) initiation	Promote in some calluses but sometimes antagonistic to cytokinins and inhibitory. Sometimes promote in intact plant if apical dominance broken (see below).	Promote in chrysanthemum callus. Sometimes promote in intact plant if apical dominance broken
Leaf growth*	Inactive	Promote
Fruit growth	**Promote.** Can sometimes induce parthenocarpy.	**Promote.** Can sometimes induce parthenocarpy.
Apical dominance	**Promote, i.e. inhibit lateral bud growth**	Enhance action of auxins
Bud dormancy*	Inactive	**Break**
Seed dormancy*	Inactive	**Break,** e.g. cereals, ash
Flowering*	Usually inactive (promote in pineapple)	**Sometimes substitute for red light.** Therefore promote in long-day plants, inhibit in short-day plants
Leaf senescence	Delay in a few species	Delay in a few species
Fruit ripening	—	—
Abscission	**Inhibit.** Sometimes promote once abscission starts or if applied to plant side of abscission layer	Inactive
Stomatal mechanism	Inactive	Inactive

Process Affected	Cytokinins	Abscisic acid	Ethene
Stem growth	**Promote cell division in apical meristem and cambium** Sometimes inhibit cell expansion	**Inhibitory, notably during physiological stress,** e.g. drought, waterlogging	**Inhibitory, notably during physiological stress**
Root growth	Inactive or inhibit primary root growth	Inhibitory, e.g. geotropism?	Inhibitory, e.g. geotropism?
Root initiation	Inactive or promote lateral root growth	—	—
Bud (shoot) initiation	Promote, e.g. in protonemata of mosses	—	—
Leaf growth*	Promote	—	—
Fruit growth	**Promote.** Can rarely induce parthenocarpy	—	—
Apical dominance	**Antagonistic to auxins, i.e. promote lateral bud growth**	—	—
Bud dormancy*	**Break**	**Promotes,** e.g. sycamore, birch	**Breaks**
Seed dormancy*	**Break**	**Promotes**	—
Flowering*	Usually inactive	Sometimes promote in short-day plants and inhibit in long-day plants (antagonistic to gibberellins)	Promotes in pineapple
Leaf senescence	**Delay**	Sometimes promotes	—
Fruit ripening	—	—	**Promotes**
Abscission	Inactive	**Promotes**	—
Stomatal mechanism	Promotes stomatal opening	**Promotes closing of stomata under conditions of water stress (wilting)**	Inactive?

*Light and temperature are also involved – see photoperiodism and vernalisation.
NB The information presented in this table is generalised. The growth substances do not necessarily always have the effects attributed to them and variation in response between different plants is common. It is best to pay closest attention to the positive effects. Those stressed in bold type are the most important for the A-level student.

Ethene	to de-green citrus fruits.
Gibberellins	to delay ripening and improve storage life of bananas.

Plant regulators increasing the value of crops

Gibberellic acid	to advance or retard maturity of globe artichokes to capture higher prices outside the main production season.
Gibberellic acid	to retard ripening of grapefruit to spread harvest and capture higher-priced market.
Maleic hydrazides	to extend storage life of bulbs and root crops.
Gibberellic acid	to force rhubarb for early production.

Growth retardants

Ethephon	shortening stems of forced daffodils, retarding elongation and stimulating branching in tomatoes, geraniums and roses.
Piproctanyl chloride	dwarfing ornamentals, mainly chrysanthemums.
Dikegulac-sodium	retarding growth of hedges and woody ornamentals.

Other targets for plant growth regulators include:
promotion of root initiation in plant propagation;
breaking or enforcing dormancy in seed buds, storage organs;
controlling development of lateral stems;
increased resistance to pests, adverse weather conditions, such as drought/pollution;
controlling size, shape, colour of crops grown for the processed food market;
suppressing unwanted vegetative growth;
promoting or delaying flowering/controlling fruit set and ripening.

The benefit to cost ratio of using gibberellic acid to increase fruit setting in mandarin oranges has been reported as 9:1, for the production of seedless grapes 40:1, whilst the use of glysophosine has increased sucrose production in sugarcane by 10–15%. However the use of most plant growth regulators is restricted to commercially small and specialist crops with the exception of antilodging compounds. A number of regulators considered potentially useful during laboratory screening tests proved unreliable for commercial usage. Consequently the main thrust in this field centres on the development of herbicides and pesticides. Further manipulation of crops to human need will probably require a balanced mixture of several plant growth regulators.

15.2.7 Cytokinins

Discovery of cytokinins

During the 1940s and 1950s efforts were made to perfect techniques of plant tissue culture. Such techniques provide an opportunity to study development free from the influence of other parts of the organism, and to study effects of added chemicals. While it proved possible to keep cells alive, it was difficult to stimulate growth. During the period 1954–6 Skoog, working in the USA, found that coconut milk contained an ingredient that promoted cell division in tobacco pith cultures. Coconut milk is a liquid endosperm (food reserve) and evidence that it contained growth substances had already been obtained in the 1940s when it had been studied as a likely source of substances to promote embryo growth. In a search for other active substances a stale sample of DNA happened to show similar activity, although a fresh sample did not. However, autoclaving fresh DNA produced the same effect and the active ingredient was shown to be chemically similar to the base adenine, a constituent of DNA (section 5.6). It was called **kinetin**. The term 'kinin' was used by Skoog for substances concerned with the control of cell division. Later the term **cytokinin** was adopted, partly from cytokinesis, meaning cell division, and partly because kinin has an entirely different meaning in zoology (it is a blood polypeptide). The first naturally occurring cytokinin to be chemically identified was from young maize (*Zea mais*) grains in 1963 and hence called **zeatin**. Note again the chemical similarity to adenine (fig 15.23).

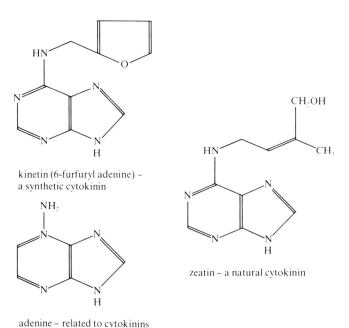

kinetin (6-furfuryl adenine) – a synthetic cytokinin

adenine – related to cytokinins

zeatin – a natural cytokinin

Fig 15.23 *Structures of kinetin, zeatin and adenine*

Synthesis and distribution of cytokinins

Cytokinins are most abundant where rapid cell division is occurring, particularly in fruits and seeds where they are associated with embryo growth. Evidence suggests that in mature plants they are frequently made in the roots and move to the shoots in the transpiration stream (in xylem). Cytokinins may be re-exported from leaves via the phloem.

Effects of cytokinins

Cytokinins, by definition, promote cell division. They do so, however, only in the presence of auxins. Gibberellins may also play a role, as in the cambium. Their interaction with other growth substances is discussed later in section 15.3.2.

One of the intriguing properties of cytokinins is their ability to delay the normal process of ageing in leaves. If a leaf is detached from a plant it will normally senesce very rapidly, as indicated by its yellowing and loss of protein, RNA and DNA. However, addition of a spot of kinetin will result in a green island of active tissue in the midst of yellowing tissue. Nutrients are then observed to move to this green island from surrounding cells (fig 15.24).

> **15.21** Study fig 15.24 and then answer the following.
> (a) What difference is there in the fate of applied amino acid between an old leaf and a young leaf?
> (b) Why should there be this difference?
> (c) What is the effect of kinetin on distribution of radioactive amino acid in old leaves?

Even when kinetin is applied to dying leaves on an intact plant a similar, though less dramatic, effect occurs. It has been shown that levels of natural cytokinins decrease in senescing leaves. A natural programme of senescence may therefore involve movement of cytokinins from older leaves to younger leaves via the phloem.

Cytokinins are also implicated in many stages of plant growth and development (table 15.4 and section 15.3).

Mode of action of cytokinins

The similarity of cytokinins to the base adenine, a component of the nucleic acids RNA and DNA, suggests that they may have a fundamental role in nucleic acid metabolism. Some unusual bases, derived from transfer RNA molecules, have been shown to have cytokinin activity, raising the possibility that cytokinins are involved in transfer RNA synthesis. Whether this is true or not, it does not necessarily account for their role as growth substances, and further evidence is still being sought.

Commercial applications of cytokinins

Cytokinins prolong the life of fresh leaf crops such as cabbage and lettuce (delay of senescence) as well as keeping flowers fresh. They can also be used to break dormancy of some seeds.

15.2.8 Abscisic acid

Discovery of abscisic acid

Plant physiologists have more recently obtained evidence that growth inhibitors, as well as growth promoters like auxins, gibberellins and cytokinins, are important in the normal regulation of growth. It had long been suspected that dormancy was caused by inhibitors when a group at the University of Aberystwyth, led by Wareing, set about trying to find them in the late 1950s. In 1963, an extract from birch leaves was shown to induce dormancy of birch buds. The leaves had been treated with short days to mimic approaching winter. Pure crystals of an active substance

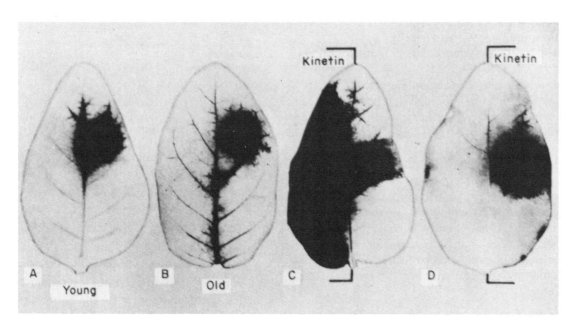

Fig 15.24 *Effect of kinetin upon translocation of an amino acid in tobacco leaves. Radioactive amino acid was supplied as indicated and after a period of translocation the leaves were exposed to photographic film. In the resulting autoradiographs, the areas containing the amino acid appear black*

558

were isolated from sycamore leaves in 1964. The substance was called **dormin**. It turned out to be identical to a compound isolated by another group in 1963 from young cotton fruit. This accelerated abscission and was called **abscisin II** (abscisin I is a similarly acting, but chemically unrelated and less active compound). In 1967 it was agreed to call the substance **abscisic acid (ABA)**. It has been found in all groups of plants from mosses upwards and a substance that plays a similar role, lunularic acid, has been found in algae and liverworts.

Structure of abscisic acid

Like the gibberellins, ABA is a terpenoid and has a complex structure (fig 15.25). It is the only growth substance in its class.

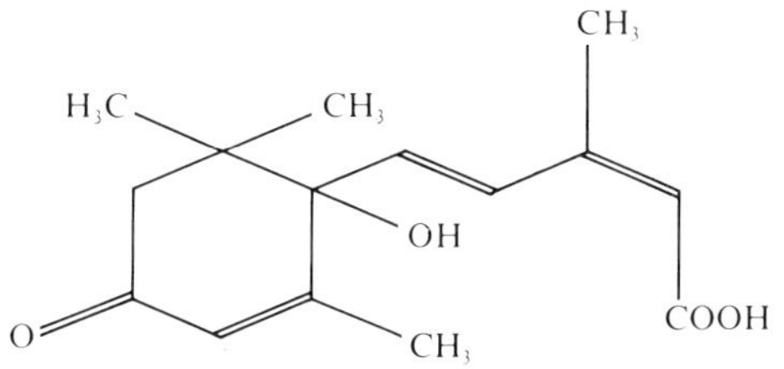

Fig 15.25 *Structure of abscisic acid*

Synthesis and distribution of ABA

ABA is made in leaves, stems, fruits and seeds. The fact that isolated chloroplasts can synthesise it again suggests a link with the carotenoid pigments, which are also made in chloroplasts. Like the other growth substances, ABA moves in the vascular system, mainly in the phloem. It also moves from the root cap by diffusion (see geotropism).

Effects of ABA

Table 15.4 summarises the effects of ABA on growth and development. It is a major inhibitor of growth in plants and is antagonistic to all three classes of growth promoters. Its classical effects are on bud dormancy (including apical dominance), seed dormancy and abscission (see section 15.3.4) but it also has roles in wilting, flowering, leaf senescence and possibly geotropism. It is associated with stress, particularly drought. In wilting tomato leaves, for example, the ABA concentration is 50 times higher than normal and ABA is thought to bring about closure of stomata. High concentrations stop the plant growing altogether.

Mode of action of ABA

This is unknown.

Commercial applications of ABA

ABA can be sprayed on tree crops to regulate fruit drop at the end of the season. This removes the need for picking over a long time-span.

15.2.9   Ethene (Ethylene)

Discovery of ethene as a growth substance

It was known in the early 1930s that ethene gas speeded up ripening of citrus fruits and affected plant growth in various ways. Later it was shown that certain ripe fruits, such as bananas, gave off a gas with similar effects. In 1934 yellowing apples were shown to emit ethene and it was subsequently shown to emanate from a wide variety of ripening fruits and other plant organs, particularly from wounded regions. Trace amounts are normal for any organ.

Structure of ethene

See fig 15.26.

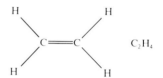

Fig 15.26 *Structure of ethene (ethylene)*

Synthesis and distribution of ethene

As mentioned above, ethene is made by most or all plant organs. Despite being a gas it does not generally move freely through the system of air spaces in the plant because it tends to escape more easily from the plant surface. However, movement of the water-soluble precursor of ethene from waterlogged roots to shoots in the xylem has been demonstrated.

Effects of ethene

Ethene is known chiefly for its effects on fruit ripening and the accompanying rise in rate of respiration (the climacteric) which occurs in some plants (section 15.3.5). Like ABA it acts as a growth inhibitor in some circumstances and can promote abscission of fruits and leaves. Its effects are summarised in table 15.4.

Commercial applications of ethene

Ethene induces flowering in pineapple and stimulates ripening of tomatoes and citrus fruits. Fruits can often be prevented from ripening by storage in an atmosphere lacking oxygen; ripening can subsequently be regulated by application of ethene with oxygen. The commercial compound 'ethephon' breaks down to release ethene in plants and is applied to rubber plants to stimulate the flow of latex.

15.3   Synergism and antagonism

Having studied individual growth substances it has become clear that they generally work by interacting with one another, rather than each controlling its own

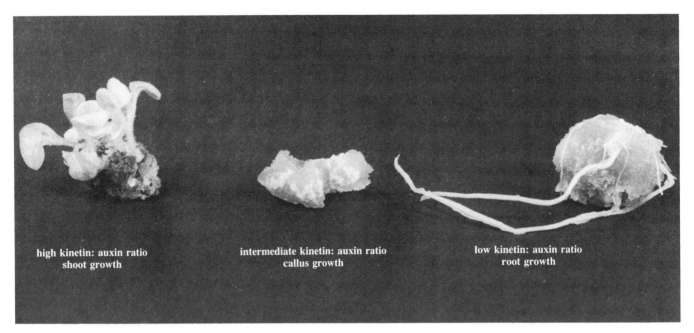

Fig 15.27 *Cultures of tobacco callus. The culture medium in each case contains IAA (2 mg dm⁻³). The culture 0.2 mg dm⁻³ kinetin (centre) continues growth as a callus; with a lower kinetin addition (0.02 mg dm⁻³) it initiates roots and with a higher kinetin addition (0.5 mg dm⁻³) it initiates shoots*

specific aspect of growth. Two kinds of control emerge. In the first, two or more substances supplement each other's activities. It is often found that their combined effect is much greater than the sum of their separate effects. This is called **synergism** and the substances are said to be **synergistic**. The second kind of control occurs when two substances have opposite effects on the same process, one promoting and the other inhibiting. This is called **antagonism** and the substances are said to be **antagonistic**. Here the balance between the substances determines response.

Some of the better understood phases of plant growth and development can now be studied and the importance of synergism and antagonism demonstrated.

15.3.1 Shoot growth

The effect of gibberellins on elongation of stems, petioles, leaves and hypocotyls is dependent on the presence of auxins.

> **15.22** How could you demonstrate this experimentally?

15.3.2 Cell division and differentiation

Cytokinins promote cell division only in the presence of auxins. Gibberellins sometimes also play a role, as in the cambium when auxins and gibberellins come from nearby buds and leaves. The interaction of cytokinins with other growth substances was demonstrated in the classic experiments of Skoog in the 1950s, already mentioned. His team showed the effect of various concentrations of kinetin and auxin on growth of tobacco pith callus. A high auxin to cytokinin ratio promoted root

formation whereas a high kinetin to auxin ratio promoted lateral buds which grew into leafy shoots. Undifferentiated growth would occur if the growth substances were in balance (fig 15.27).

15.3.3 Apical dominance

Apical dominance is the phenomenon whereby the presence of a growing apical bud inhibits growth of lateral buds. It also includes the suppression of lateral root growth by growth of the main root. Removal of a shoot apex results in lateral bud growth, that is branching. This is made use of in pruning when bushy rather than tall plants are required.

> **15.23** (a) What plant growth substance is made in the shoot apex? (b) Design an experiment to show whether it is responsible for apical dominance.

It is interesting to note that auxin levels at the lateral buds are often *not* high enough to cause inhibition of growth. Auxins exert their influence in an unknown way, possibly by somehow 'attracting' nutrients to the apex. In cocklebur it appears that the fall in auxin level in the stem after decapitation permits the lateral buds to inactivate the high levels of ABA that they contain. Gibberellins often enhance the response to IAA. Kinetin application to lateral buds, however, often breaks their dormancy, at least temporarily. Kinetin plus IAA causes complete breaking of dormancy. Cytokinins are usually made in the roots and move in the xylem to the shoots. Perhaps, therefore, they are normally transported to wherever auxin is being made, and they combine to promote bud growth.

Apical dominance is a classic example of one part of a

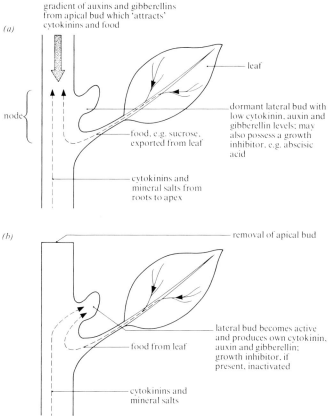

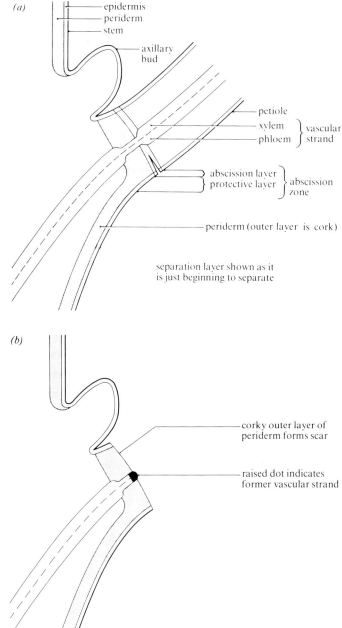

Fig 15.28 *Possible involvement of plant growth substances in apical dominance, (a) in presence of apical bud, (b) after removal of apical bud*

Fig 15.29 *Abscission zone of a leaf, (a) during abscission, (b) after abscission*

plant controlling another via the influence of a growth substance. This is called **correlation** (fig 15.28).

15.3.4 Abscission

Abscission is the organised shedding of part of the plant, usually a leaf, unfertilised flower or fruit. At the base of the organ, in a region called the **abscission zone**, a layer of living cells separates by breakdown of their middle lamellae, and sometimes breakdown of their cell walls. This forms the **abscission layer** (fig 15.29). Final shedding of the organ occurs when the vascular strands are broken mechanically, such as by the action of wind. A protective layer is formed beneath the abscission layer to prevent infection or desiccation of the scar, and the vascular strand is sealed. In woody species the protective layer is corky, being part of the tissue produced by the cork cambium, namely the periderm (section 21.6).

Abscission of leaves from deciduous trees and shrubs is usually associated with the onset of winter, but in the tropics it often occurs with the onset of a dry season. In both cases it affords protection against possible water shortage, leaves being the main organs through which water is lost by transpiration. In winter, for example, soil water may be unavailable through being frozen. In

evergreen species, abscission is spread over the whole year and the leaves are usually modified to prevent water loss.

It has been shown that as a leaf approaches abscission, its output of auxin declines. Fig 15.30 summarises the effect of auxin on abscission. It is worth noting that once abscission has been triggered, auxins seem to accelerate the process.

Abscisic acid (ABA) acts antagonistically to auxin by promoting abscission in some fruits. Unripe seeds produce auxins, but during ripening auxin production declines and ABA production may rise. In developing cotton fruits, for example, two peaks of ABA occur. The first corresponds to

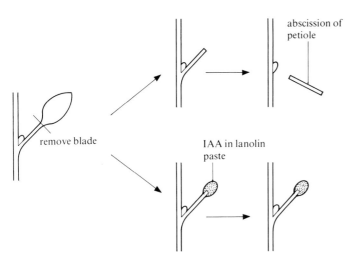

remove blade

IAA in lanolin paste

abscission of petiole

Fig 15.30 *Effect of auxin (IAA) on abscission of a leaf petiole. Removal of leaf blade leads to abscission of the petiole. IAA substitutes for the presence of the leaf blade*

the 'June drop' when self-thinning of the plants occurs: only the aborted immature fruitlets have high ABA levels at this stage. The second corresponds with seed ripening.

There is some doubt as to whether ABA also affects leaf abscission. Applications of high concentrations are effective, but this could be a result of stimulating ethene production. Ethene is produced by senescing leaves and ripening fruits and always stimulates abscission when applied to mature organs. Some deciduous shrubs and trees produce ABA in their leaves just before winter (section 15.5.1) but this may be purely to induce bud dormancy.

Abscission is of immense horticultural significance because of its involvement in fruit drop. Commercial applications of auxins and ABA reflect this and have been discussed earlier in this chapter.

If flowers are not fertilised they are generally abscised (see 'fruit set' below).

15.3.5 Pollen tube growth, fruit set and fruit development

Germinating pollen grains are a rich source of auxins as well as commonly stimulating the tissues of the style and ovary to produce more auxin. This auxin is necessary for 'fruit set', that is retention of the ovary, which becomes the fruit after fertilisation. Without it abscission of the flower normally occurs. After fertilisation, the ovary and the ripe seeds continue to produce auxins which stimulate fruit development.

A few natural examples are known where fruit development proceeds without fertilisation, and therefore without seed development, for example banana, pineapple and some seedless varieties of oranges and grapes. Such development is called **parthenocarpy**. Unusually high auxin levels occur in these ovaries. Parthenocarpy can sometimes be artificially induced by adding auxins, as in tomato, squash and peppers. Seedless pea pods can just as

easily be induced! Gibberellins have the same effect in some plants, such as the tomato, including some that are not affected by auxins, for example cherry, apricot and peach. Developing seeds are not only a rich source of auxins and gibberellins, but also of cytokinins (section 15.2.7). These growth substances are mainly associated with development of the embryo and accumulation of food reserves in the seed, and sometimes in the pericarp (fruit wall) from other parts of the plant.

Fruit ripening is really a process of senescence and is often accompanied by a burst of respiratory activity called the **climacteric**. This is associated with ethene production. The subsequent roles of ethene and ABA in fruit abscission were discussed in section 15.3.4.

15.4 Phytochrome and effects of light on plant development

The importance of environmental stimuli to the growth and orientation of plant organs has already been discussed with plant movements. The stimulus which has the widest influence on plant growth is light. Not only does it provide the energy for photosynthesis and influence plant movements, but it directly affects development. The effect of light upon development is called **photomorphogenesis**.

15.4.1 Etiolation

Perhaps the best way to demonstrate the importance of light is to grow a plant in the dark! Such a plant lacks chlorophyll (is chlorotic) and therefore appears white or pale yellow rather than green. The shoot internodes become elongated and thin and it is described as **etiolated**. In dicotyledonous plants, the epicotyl or hypocotyl (section 21.6.2) elongates in hypogeal or epigeal germination respectively and the plumule tip is hooked. Dicotyledonous leaves remain small and unexpanded. In monocotyledonous plants, the mesocotyl elongates during germination and the leaves may remain rolled up. In all leaves, chloroplasts fail to develop normal membrane systems and are called **etioplasts**. Plants make less supporting tissue and are fragile and collapse easily. Eventually they use up their food reserves and die unless light is reached for photosynthesis. Yet as soon as the plant is exposed to light, normal growth ensues. The significance of etiolation is that it allows maximum growth in length with minimum use of carbon reserves which, in the absence of light, the plant cannot obtain by photosynthesis.

> **15.24** How does the morphology of an etiolated plant suit it for growing through soil?

15.4.2 Discovery of phytochrome

The first stage in any process affected by light must be the absorption of light by a pigment, the so-called **photoreceptor**. The characteristic set of wavelengths of

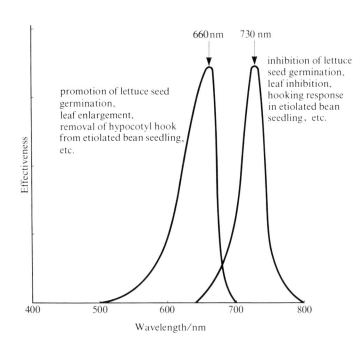

Fig 15.31 *Typical action spectra of a phytochrome-controlled response*

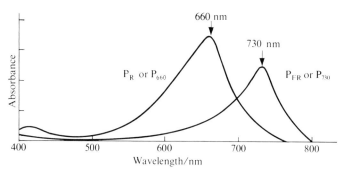

Fig 15.32 *Absorption spectra of the two forms of phytochrome*

light it absorbs form its absorption spectrum (section 9.3.2); remaining wavelengths are reflected and give the substance a characteristic colour (chlorophyll, for example, absorbs red and blue light and reflects green light).

The seeds of many plants germinate only if exposed to light. In 1937 it was shown that, for lettuce seeds, red light promoted germination but far-red light (longer wavelength) inhibited germination. Borthwick and Hendrick, working at the US Department of Agriculture in the 1950s, plotted an **action spectrum** for the germination response (a spectrum of wavelengths showing their relative effectiveness at stimulating the process). Fig 15.31 shows that the wavelength most effective for germination was about 660 nm (red light) and for inhibition of germination about 730 nm (far red light).

They also showed that only brief exposures of light were necessary and that the effects of red light were reversed by far-red light and vice versa. Thus the last treatment in an alternating sequence of red/far-red exposures would always be the effective one. The US team eventually isolated the pigment responsible in 1960 and called it **phytochrome**. Phytochrome, as they predicted, is a blue-green pigment existing in two interconvertible forms. One form, P_{FR} or P_{730} absorbs far-red light and the other, P_R or P_{660}, absorbs red light. Absorption of light by one form converts it rapidly and reversibly to the other form (within seconds or minutes depending on light intensity):

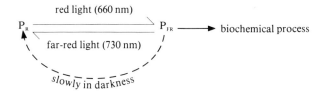

Normal sunlight contains more red than far-red light, so the P_{FR} form predominates during the day. This is the physiologically active form, but reverts slowly to the more stable, but inactive, P_R form at night. Phytochrome was shown to consist of a pigment portion attached to a protein. It is present in minute amounts throughout plants (hence it is not visible, despite its colour (but is particularly concentrated in the growing tips. Its absorption spectrum is shown in fig 15.32.

15.25 What is the difference between an absorption spectrum and an action spectrum?

A number of developmental processes are mediated by low intensities of red light and reversed by far-red light or darkness, showing the involvement of phytochrome (fig 15.31 and table 15.5). The most significant of these is flowering, which is discussed later. The involvement of phytochrome in a process is shown by matching the action spectrum of the response with the absorption spectrum of phytochrome.

15.4.3 Photoperiodism and flowering

One of the important ways in which light exerts its influence on living organisms is through variations in daylength (**photoperiod**). The further from the equator, where days are almost a constant 12 hours, the greater the seasonal variation in daylength. Thus daylength is an important environmental signal in temperate latitudes where it varies between about 9 and 15 hours during the year. The effects of photoperiod on animals are discussed in section 16.8.5. In plants it is a matter of common observation that phenomena such as flowering, fruit and seed production, bud and seed dormancy, leaf fall and germination are closely attuned to seasonal influences like daylength and temperature, and that survival of the plant depends on this.

The process involving the most profound change is flowering, when shoot meristems switch from producing leaves and lateral buds to producing flowers. The importance of photoperiod in flowering was discovered as early as 1910 but was first clearly described by Garner and Allard in 1920. They showed that tobacco plants would flower only

Table 15.5 Some phytochrome-controlled responses in plants.

General process affected	Red light promotes
Germination*	Germination of some seeds, e.g. some lettuce varieties
	Germination of fern spores
Photomorphogenesis (light-controlled development of form and structure)	Leaf expansion in dicotyledons. Leaf unrolling in grasses (monocotyledons). Chloroplast development (etioplasts converted to chloroplasts: see etiolation). Greening (protochlorophyll converted to chlorophyll). Inhibition of internode growth (including epicotyl, hypocotyl, mesocotyl), i.e. preventing of etiolation. Unhooking of plumule in dicotyledons
Photoperiodism	Stimulates flowering in long-day plants. Inhibits flowering in short-day plants. See flowering

*Experiments designed to investigate the effects of light on seed germination are described by J. W. Hannay in *J. Biol. Ed.* (1967) **1**, 65–73. The variety of lettuce suggested, 'Grand Rapids', is no longer available but some modern varieties could be screened for suitability. Such varieties currently available are 'Dandie', 'Kloek' and 'Kweik'. 'Dandie' is probably the most reliable but is fairly expensive because it is a winter-forcing variety. It is available from Suttons in small packets or from E. W. King & Co., Coggeshall, Essex in 10 g packets (enough for about 250 dishes of 50 seeds each). *Phacelia* seeds make an interesting contrast to lettuce.
NB In this experiment a green leaf can be used as a far-red filter.

after exposure to a series of short days. This occurred naturally in autumn, but could be induced by artificially short days of seven hours in a greenhouse in summer. As they examined other plants it became obvious that some required long days for flowering (**long-day plants**) and some would flower whatever the photoperiod once mature (**day-neutral plants**).

Additional complications have since been found. For example, some plants are day-neutral at one temperature, but not at another; some require one daylength followed by another; in some, the appropriate daylength only accelerates flowering and is not an absolute requirement.

An important advance in our understanding came when it was shown that it is really the length of the dark period which is critical. Thus short-day plants are really long-night plants. If they are grown in short days, but the long night is interrupted by a short light period, flowering is prevented. Long-day plants will flower in short days if the long night period is interrupted. Short dark interruptions, however, do not cancel the effect of long days. Table 15.6 summarises the three main categories of plant.

Flowering in chrysanthemums

In the classical work of Garner and Allard, chrysanthemums were described as typical short-day plants. However it was later shown by Schwabe that, in addition, an exposure to cold temperatures (1–7 °C in a refrigerator for

Table 15.6 Classification of plants according to photoperiodic requirements for flowering.

Short-day plants (SDPs)	Long-day plants (LDPs)
e.g. cocklebur (*Xanthium pennsylvanicum*), chrysanthemum, soybean, tobacco, strawberry	e.g. henbane (*Hyoscyamus niger*), snapdragon, cabbage, spring wheat, spring barley
Flowering induced by dark periods longer than a critical length, e.g. cocklebur 8.5 h; tobacco 10–11 h (Under natural conditions equivalent to days shorter than a critical length, e.g. cocklebur 15.5 h; tobacco 13–14 h)	Flowering induced by dark periods shorter than a critical length, e.g. henbane 13 h (Under natural conditions equivalent to days longer than a critical length, e.g. henbane 11 h)

Day-neutral plants

e.g. cucumber, tomato, garden pea, maize, cotton
Flowering independent of photoperiod

NB Tobacco (SDP) and henbane (LDP) both flower in 12–13 h daylength.

around three weeks) hastens flower bud formation in both long- and short-day conditions. In the absence of this cold temperature treatment, the plants may remain vegetative even in short days. For the rapid onset of flowering, short-day photoperiodic treatment and warm temperature are required following exposure to a lower temperature (vernalisation, see section 15.5). Evidence suggests that the vernalisation treatment is more effective if given during the dark period. The growing tip has been shown to be the seat of perception of the vernalisation stimulus. Flowering in chrysanthemums can be inhibited by:
  transfer to long-day treatment;
  transfer to low light intensity during short-day treatment;
  application of auxin paste suggesting that hormone balance may be important in inducing flowering.
It is unusual for short-day plants to require vernalisation. Commercially, chrysanthemum propagation cuttings are taken during January–March when the vernalisation requirement will be met by the prevailing winter temperature.

15.4.4 Quality and quantity of light

The next step is to find the quality (colour) and quantity of light required. Remembering that the cocklebur (SDP) will not flower if its long night is interrupted, experiments revealed that red light was effective in preventing flowering, but that far-red light reversed the effect of red light. Therefore phytochrome is the photoreceptor. These experiments were, in fact, part of the programme which led to the discovery of phytochrome. As would be expected, a LDP held in short days is stimulated to flower by a short exposure to red light during the long night. Again this is reversed by far-red light. The last light treatment always determines response.

In some, though not all, cases low light intensities for a few minutes are effective, again typical of a phytochrome-controlled response. The higher the intensity used, the shorter the exposure time required.

> **15.26** *Xanthium* (cocklebur) is a short-day plant. Flowering is therefore normally induced by long nights. In experiments the effects of red and red/far-red light interruptions of three consecutive 12 h ('long') nights on subsequent flowering were investigated. Flowering intensity was measured by an index of 'floral stage' from 1 to 8, and the results are shown in table 15.7.
>
> Draw graphs of these results, plotting floral stage on the vertical axis and duration of light on the horizontal axis. (The two graphs can be drawn between the same axes.) Comment on the results.

Table 15.7 Effect of red/far-red light interruptions of long nights on flowering of cocklebur (after Downs, R. J. (1956) *Plant Physiol.* **31**, 279–84).

Red light		Two minutes red light followed by FR light	
Floral stage	Duration of red light/s	Floral stage	Duration of FR light/s
6.0	0	0.0	0
5.0	5	4.0	12
4.0	10	4.5	15
2.6	20	5.5	25
0.0	30	6.0	50

Computer program. PHYTOCHROME (CUP Micro Software) demonstrates a model of the photoperiodic control of flowering in the short-day plants and allows the user to simulate the classic Hamner and Bonner flash-of-light-in-the-middle-of-the-night experiment.

15.4.5 Perception and transmission of the stimulus

It was shown in the mid-1930s that the light stimulus is perceived by the leaves and not the apex where the flowers are produced.

> **15.27** How could you demonstrate this with a short-day plant?

In addition to this, a cocklebur plant with just one induced leaf will flower even if the rest of the plant is under non-inductive conditions. This implies that some agent, that is a hormone, must pass from the leaf to the apex to bring about flowering. This concept is supported by the observation that the flowering stimulus can be passed from an induced plant to a non-induced plant by grafting, and that the stimulus is apparently the same for SDP, LDP and day-neutral plants because grafting between these is successful. The hypothetical flowering hormone has been called '**florigen**' but has never been isolated. Indeed, its existence is doubted by some plant physiologists.

15.4.6 Mode of action of phytochrome

How, then, does phytochrome exert its control? At the end of a light period it exists in the active P_{FR} form. At the end of a short night its slow transition back to the inactive P_R form, which takes place in darkness, may not be complete. It can be postulated, therefore, that in LDPs P_{FR} promotes flowering and in SDPs it inhibits flowering. Only long nights remove sufficient P_{FR} from the latter to allow flowering to occur. Unfortunately, short exposures to far-red light, which would have the same effect as a long night, cannot completely substitute for long nights, so the full explanation is more complex. Some time factor is also important.

We do know that gibberellins can mimic the effect of red light in some cases. Gibberellic acid (GA_3) promotes flowering in some LDPs, mainly rosette plants like henbane which bolt before flowering. (Bolting is a rapid increase in stem length.) GA_3 also inhibits flowering in some SDPs. Antigibberellins (growth retardants) nullify these effects.

So, does P_{FR} stimulate gibberellin production, and is this the flowering hormone? There are too many exceptions for this to be the case. Abscisic acid inhibits flowering in some LDPs, such as *Lolium*, but induces it in some SDPs, such as strawberry. In short, our understanding of the flowering process is still incomplete.

15.5 Vernalisation and flowering

Some plants, especially biennials and perennials, are stimulated to flower by exposure to low temperatures. This is called **vernalisation**. Here the stimulus is perceived by the mature stem apex, or by the embryo of the seed, but not by the leaves as in photoperiodism. As with photoperiod, vernalisation may be an absolute requirement (such as in henbane) or may simply hasten flowering (as in winter cereals).

Long-day plants (for example cabbage), short-day plants (such as chrysanthemum) and day-neutral plants (such as ragwort) can all require vernalisation. The length of chilling required varies from four days to three months, temperatures around 4 °C generally being most effective. Like the photoperiodic stimulus, the vernalisation stimulus can be transmitted between plants by grafting. In this case the hypothetical hormone involved was called **vernalin**. It has subsequently been discovered that during vernalisation gibberellin levels increase, and application of gibberellins to unvernalised plants can substitute for vernalisation (fig

Fig 15.33 *Carrot plants (var.* Early french forcing). *left: control; centre: maintained at 17°C but supplied 10 mg of gibberellin daily for 4 weeks; right: plant given vernalizing cold treatment (6 weeks). All photographed 8 weeks after completion of cold treatment*

15.33). It is now believed that 'vernalin' is a gibberellin. It is clear now that photoperiodism and vernalisation serve to synchronise the reproductive behaviour of plants with their environments, ensuring reproduction at favourable times of the year. They also help to ensure that members of the same species flower at the same time and thus encourage cross-pollination and cross-fertilisation, with the attendant advantages of genetic variability.

15.5.1 Photoperiodism and dormancy

The formation of winter buds in temperate trees and shrubs is usually a photoperiodic response to shortening days in the autumn, for example in birch, beech and sycamore. The stimulus is perceived by the leaves and, as mentioned before, abscisic acid (ABA) levels build up. ABA moves to the meristems and inhibits growth. Short days also induce leaf fall from deciduous trees (abscission). Often buds must be chilled before dormancy can be broken ('**bud-break**'). Similarly some seeds require a cold stimulus ('**stratification**') after imbibing water before they will germinate, thus preventing them from germinating prematurely once ripe. This is discussed further in section 21.10. Gibberellins can substitute for the cold stimulus, and natural bud-break is accompanied by a rise in gibberellins as well as, in many cases, a fall in ABA. Breaking of bud dormancy in birch and poplar has been shown to coincide with a rise in cytokinins.

Apart from buds and seeds, storage organs are involved in dormancy and again photoperiod is important. For example, short days induce tuber formation in potatoes, whereas long days induce onion bulb formation.

15.28 Some buds remain dormant throughout the summer. What causes dormancy here?

Chapter Sixteen

Coordination and control in animals

Irritability or **sensitivity** is a characteristic feature of all living organisms and involves their ability to respond to a stimulus. In all organisms some degree of internal coordination and control is necessary in order to ensure that the events of the stimulus and response bear some mutual relationship associated with the maintenance of the steady-state (chapter 18) and survival of the organism.

Animals, unlike plants, have two different but related systems of coordination: the **nervous system** and the **endocrine system**. The former is fast acting, its effects are localised and it involves electrical and chemical transmission, whereas the latter is slower acting, its effects are diffuse and it relies on chemical transmission through the circulatory system. It is thought that the two systems have developed in parallel in the majority of multicellular animals.

16.1   The nervous system

The nervous system is composed of highly differentiated cells whose function is to detect sensory information, code this in the form of electrical impulses and transmit them, often over considerable distances, to other differentiated cells capable of producing a response.

All sensory information (**stimuli**) is detected in multicellular animals by modified nerve cells called **sensory receptors** and the structure and function of these is described in section 16.5. This sensory information is passed on to **effector cells** which produce a response which is associated in some way with the stimulus. The structure and function of effectors is described briefly in section 16.6 and chapter 17.

Interposed between the receptors and effectors are the conductile cells of the nervous system, the **neurones**. These are the basic structural and functional units of the nervous system and ramify throughout the organism forming an elaborate communication network. Types of neurone, and their structures, are shown and described in section 8.6. The structural complexity and organisation of the neurones within the network is related to the phylogenetic position of the organism and ranges from the primitive nerve net of the cnidarians (section 16.3) to the complex central nervous system of mammals (section 16.2). Whereas the former is purely a communication system, the latter provides, in addition, facilities for the storage, retrieval and integration of information.

16.1.1   The nature of the nerve impulse

The transmission of information along neurones as electrical impulses and its effects on muscle contraction and glandular secretion have been known for over 200 years. Details of the mechanisms, however, were established only in the last 50 years following the discovery of certain axons in squid which have a diameter of approximately 1 mm (1 000 µm). These **giant axons** (supplying the muscles of the mantle involved in escape responses) had large enough diameters to permit the earliest electrophysiological investigations to be carried out on them.

The apparatus currently used to investigate electrical activity in neurones is shown in fig 16.1. The **microelectrode**, composed of a small glass tube drawn out to a fine point of 0.5 µm diameter, is filled with a solution capable of conducting an electric current, such as 3 M potassium chloride. This is inserted into an axon and a second electrode, in the form of a small metal plate, is passed into the saline solution bathing the neurone being investigated. Both electrodes are connected by leads to a **preamplifier** to complete the circuit. The preamplifier increases the signal strength in the circuit approximately 1 000 times and provides the input to a **dual-beam cathode ray oscilloscope**. All movements of the microelectrode are controlled by a **micromanipulator**, a device with adjusting knobs similar to those of the microscope, which enables delicate control over the position of the tip of the microelectrode.

When the tip of the microelectrode penetrates the axon cell surface membrane, the beams of the oscilloscope separate. The distance between the beams indicates the potential difference between the two electrodes of the circuit and can be measured. This value is called the **resting potential (RP)** of the axon and is approximately -65 mV in all species investigated. The negative sign for the resting potential indicates that the membrane of the axon is **polarised**, that is the inside of the axon is negative with respect to the outside of the axon. In sensory cells, neurones and muscle cells this value changes with the activity of the cells and hence they are known as **excitable cells**. All other living cells show a similar potential difference across the membrane, known as the **membrane potential**, but in these cells this is constant and so they are known as **non-excitable cells**.

Resting potential

The resting potential of most mammalian neurones is constant as long as the cell remains inactive due to lack of

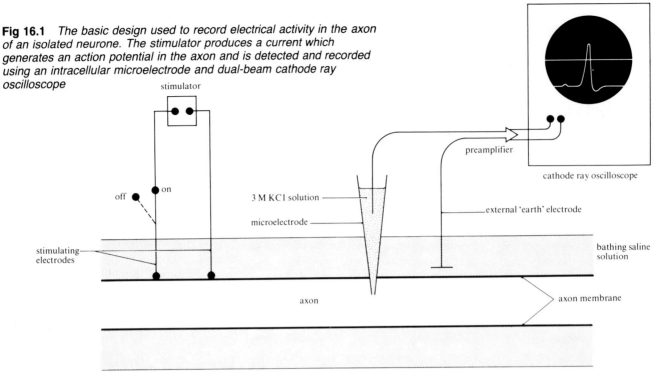

Fig 16.1 *The basic design used to record electrical activity in the axon of an isolated neurone. The stimulator produces a current which generates an action potential in the axon and is detected and recorded using an intracellular microelectrode and dual-beam cathode ray oscilloscope*

stimulation. Curtis and Cole in the USA, and Hodgkin and Huxley in England, in the late 1930s revealed the resting potential to be a physico-chemical phenomenon set up and maintained by the differential concentration of ions across the axon membrane and the selective permeability of the membrane to the ions. Analyses of the intracellular fluid of the axon and the extracellular sea water bathing the axon showed that ionic electrochemical gradients exist as shown in table 16.1.

Table 16.1. Ionic concentrations of extracellular and intracellular fluids in squid axon. (Values given are approximations in mmol kg^{-1} H$_2$O, data from Hodgkin, 1958)

Ion	Extracellular concentration	Intracellular concentration
K$^+$	20	400
Na$^+$	460	50
Cl$^-$	560	100
A$^-$	0	370
(Organic anions)		

The axoplasm inside the axon has a high concentration of potassium (K$^+$) ions and a low concentration of sodium (Na$^+$) ions, in contrast to the fluid outside the axon which has a low concentration of K$^+$ ions and a high concentration of Na$^+$ ions. (The distribution of chloride (Cl$^-$) ions is ignored in the following descriptions since it does not play a vital role in the activities under consideration.)

These electrochemical gradients are maintained by the active transport of ions against their electrochemical gradients by specific regions of the membrane known as **cation** or **sodium pumps**. These constantly active carrier mechanisms are driven by energy supplied by ATP and

couple the removal of Na$^+$ ions from the axon with the uptake of K$^+$ ions as shown in fig 16.2a.

The active movement of these ions is opposed by the **passive** diffusion of the ions which constantly pass down their electrochemical gradients as shown in fig 16.2b at a rate determined by the permeability of the axon membrane to the ion. K$^+$ ions have an ionic mobility and membrane permeability which is 20 times greater than that of Na$^+$ ions, therefore K$^+$ loss from the axon is greater than Na$^+$ gain. This leads to a net loss of K$^+$ ions from the axon, and the production of a **negative** charge within the axon. The value of the resting potential is largely determined by the K$^+$ electrochemical gradient.

Changes in the permeability of the membrane of excitable cells to K$^+$ and Na$^+$ ions lead to changes in the potential difference across the membrane and the formation of action potentials in, and the propagation of nerve impulses along, the axon.

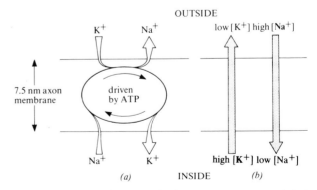

Fig 16.2 *Active and passive ionic movements associated with the production of a negative (−) potential within the axon. (a) The Na$^+$/K$^+$ coupled cation pump actively exchanges ions which pass across the membrane by passive diffusion down their electrochemical gradients as shown in (b)*

Action potential

The experimental stimulation of an axon by an electrical impulse, as shown in fig 16.3, results in a change in the potential across the axon membrane from a negative inside value of about -70 mV to a positive inside value of about $+40$ mV. This polarity change is called an **action potential** or **spike** and appears on the cathode ray oscilloscope as shown in fig 16.3.

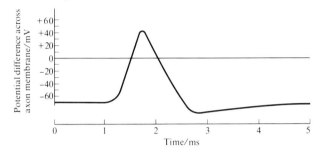

Fig 16.3 *A typical action potential in squid axon*

An action potential is generated by a sudden momentary increase in the permeability of the axon membrane to Na^+ ions which enter the axon. This increase in sodium **conductance** (the electrical equivalent of permeability)

increases the number of positive ions inside the axon and reduces the membrane potential from its resting value of -70 mV. The change in membrane potential is called **depolarisation**. Sodium conductance and depolarisation influence each other by **positive feedback**, that is an increase in one factor reinforces an increase in the other, and this produces the steep rising phase of the action potential. Calculations have revealed that relatively few Na^+ ions (about $10^{-6}\%$ of the internal Na^+ present, depending upon axon diameter) enter the axon and produce the depolarisation of about 110 mV associated with the action potential. At the peak of the action potential, sodium conductance declines (**Na inactivation**) and about 0.5 ms after the initial depolarisation, potassium conductance increases and K^+ ions diffuse out of the axon. As K^+ ions diffuse outwards the internal positive charge is replaced by a negative charge. This **repolarisation** of the membrane is shown by the falling phase of the action potential 'spike' and results in the membrane potential assuming its original level.

From the above account it can be seen that whilst the resting potential is determined largely by K^+ ions, the action potential is determined largely by Na^+ ions (fig 16.4).

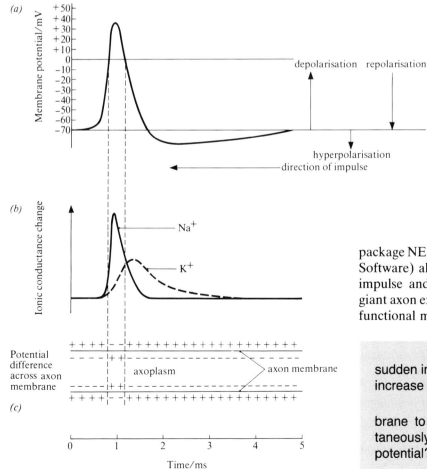

Fig 16.4 *Diagrams to show the relationships between (a) the membrane potential, (b) ionic conductance and (c) the potential distribution across the axon membrane during production of an action potential*

Computer program. The double software package NERVE IMPULSE, BRAIN-SCAN (CUP Micro Software) allows the user to follow the events of a nerve impulse and recreate the original Hodgkin and Huxley giant axon experiments. It also allows the user to develop a functional map of the cerebral cortex.

16.1 Give two reasons why there is a sudden influx of Na^+ ions into the axon following an increase in Na^+ permeability of the axon membrane.

16.2 If the permeability of the axon membrane to Na^+ ions and K^+ ions increased simultaneously what effect would this have on the action potential?

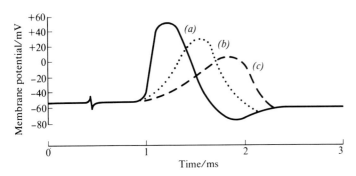

Fig 16.5 *Membrane potentials recorded from squid axons bathed in isosmotic sea water containing different relative concentrations of ions*

16.3 Hodgkin and Katz, in 1949, investigated the effect of Na^+ ions on the production of action potentials in squid axons. Intracellular microelectrodes recorded action potentials from axons bathed in different concentrations of isotonic sea water. The results are shown in fig 16.5. Which action potentials correspond with axons placed in normal sea water, one-half sea water and one-third sea water? Explain the effect of these solutions on the action potentials.

Features of action potentials

Initiation of an action potential. Stimulation of sensory cells leads to depolarisation of their membranes and if this reaches a certain threshold value in the sensory neurone, the **threshold stimulus intensity**, it will set up an action potential. For any given neurone the **amplitude** (fig 16.3) of the action potential is always constant, and increasing the strength or number of stimuli have no effect on this. For this reason action potentials are described as **all-or-nothing** events.

Transmission of nerve impulses. Information is transmitted through the nervous system as a series of nerve impulses, which travel as action potentials. A nerve impulse passes along an axon as a wave of depolarisation accompanied by a wave of negativity along the surface of the axon marking the position, at any instant, of the action potential. Action potentials are **propagated**, that is self-generated, along the axon by the effects of Na^+ ions entering the axon. This creates an area of positive charge and a flow of current is set up in a **local circuit** between this active area and the negatively charged resting region immediately ahead. The current flow in the local circuit reduces the membrane potential in the resting region and this depolarisation produces an increase in sodium permeability and the development of an all-or-nothing action potential in this region. Repeated depolarisations of immediately adjacent regions of the membrane result in the action potential being moved or propagated along the axon. Action potentials are propagated along the axon without change in amplitude and are capable of being transmitted over an infinite distance, that is, they are **non-decremental**. The reason for this is that the production of an action potential at each point along the axon is a self-generating event resulting from a change in the local concentration of ions. So long as the extra- and intracellular environments of the axon have the necessary differential ionic concentrations an action potential at one point will generate another action potential in its adjacent region.

Refractory period. Nerve impulses only pass along the axon in one direction from active region to resting region. This is because the previously active region undergoes a recovery phase during which the axon membrane cannot respond to a depolarisation by a change in sodium conductance, even if the stimulus intensity is increased. The phase is called the **absolute refractory period** and lasts for about 1 ms. Following this is a period lasting for 5–10 ms called the **relative refractory period** during which a high-intensity stimulus may produce a depolarisation. The refractory period is also a limiting factor in the speed of conduction of the nerve impulse.

16.4 Describe the ionic changes occurring across the axon membrane during the refractory period.

Speed of conduction. In non-myelinated axons (section 16.2), typical of those found in nonvertebrates, the velocity of the propagated action potential depends on the longitudinal resistance of the axoplasm. The resistance, in turn, is related to the diameter of the axon such that the smaller the diameter the greater the resistance. In the case of fine axons (<0.1 mm) the high resistance of the axoplasm has an effect on the spread of current and reduces the length of the local circuits so that only the region of the membrane immediately in front of the action potential is involved in the local circuit. These axons conduct impulses at about 0.5 m s^{-1}. Giant axons, typical of many annelids, arthropods and molluscs, have a diameter of approximately 1 mm and conduct impulses at velocities up to 100 m s^{-1}, which are ideal for conducting information vital for survival.

16.5 Explain, in terms of the resistance of the axoplasm and local circuits, why giant axons conduct impulses at greater velocities than fine axons.

In vertebrates, the majority of neurones, particularly those of the spinal and cranial nerves, have an outer covering of myelin derived from the spirally wound Schwann cell (section 8.6.3). Myelin is a fatty material with a high electrical resistance and acts as an electrical insulator in the same way as the rubber and plastic covering of electrical wiring. The combined resistance of the axon membrane and myelin sheath is very high but where breaks in the myelin sheath occur, as at the **nodes of Ranvier**, the resistance to current flow between the axoplasm and the extracellular fluid is lower. It is only at these points that local circuits are set up and current flows across the axon membrane generating the next action potential. This means, in effect, that the action potential 'jumps' from node to node and passes along the myelinated axon faster than the series of smaller local currents in a non-myelinated axon. This type of conduction is called **saltatory** (*saltare*, to jump) and can lead to conduction velocities of up to 120 m s^{-1} (fig 16.6).

Temperature has an effect on the rate of conduction of nerve impulses and as temperature rises to about 40 °C the rate of conduction increases.

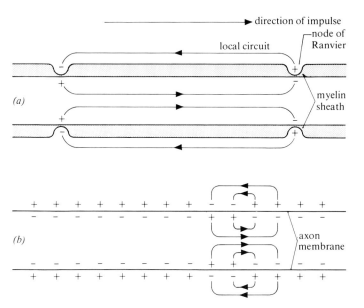

Fig 16.6 *Diagrams showing the difference in lengths of the local circuits produced (a) in a myelinated axon and (b) a non-myelinated axon. In (a) conduction is described as saltatory since the action potential effectively 'jumps' from node to node*

16.6 Why do myelinated axons of frog having a diameter of 3.5 μm conduct impulses at 30 m s^{-1} whereas axons of the same diameter in cat conduct impulses at 90 m s^{-1}?

Coding of nervous information. Nerve impulses pass through the nervous system as propagated, all-or-nothing action potentials with a fixed amplitude for a given species, for example 110 mV in squid axon. Information cannot therefore be passed as an amplitude code and is passed instead as a **frequency code**. This code was first described by Adrian and Zotterman in 1926. They demonstrated that the frequency of nerve impulses is directly related to the intensity of the stimulus giving rise to the impulses.

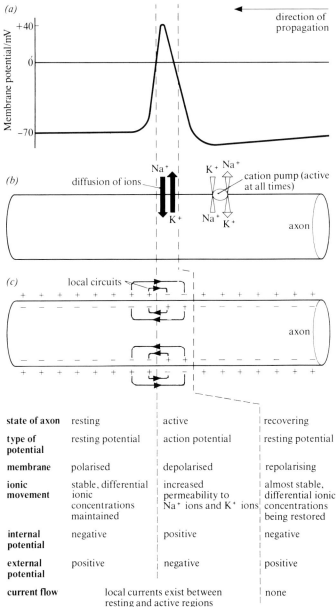

Fig 16.7 *Summary diagrams showing the events accompanying the production of local circuits within the axon and the propagation of an action potential in a non-myelinated axon, (a) action potential and direction of propagation, (b) ionic movements across the axon membrane, (c) current flow in local circuits*

state of axon	resting	active	recovering
type of potential	resting potential	action potential	resting potential
membrane	polarised	depolarised	repolarising
ionic movement	stable, differential ionic concentrations maintained	increased permeability to Na$^+$ ions and K$^+$ ions	almost stable, differential ionic concentrations being restored
internal potential	negative	positive	negative
external potential	positive	negative	positive
current flow	local currents exist between resting and active regions		none

16.1.2 The synapse

A synapse is an area of functional, but not physical, contact between one neurone and another for the purpose of transferring information. Synapses are usually found between the fine terminal branches of the axon of one neurone and the **dendrites** (**axodendritic synapses**) or **cell body** (**axosomatic synapses**) of another neurone. The number of synapses is usually very large, providing a large surface area for the transfer of information. For example, over 1 000 synapses may be found on the dendrites and cell body of a motor neurone in the spinal cord. Some cells in the brain may receive up to 10 000 synapses (fig 16.8).

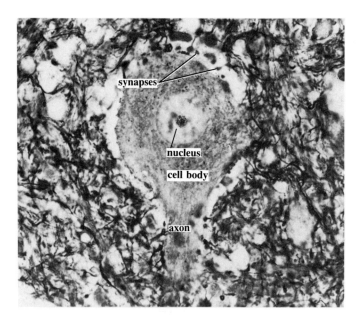

Fig 16.8 *Transmission electron micrograph of a motor neurone at a neuronal synapse*

There are two types of synapses, **electrical** and **chemical**, depending upon the nature of transfer of information across the synapse. A structurally dissimilar, but functionally similar, form of synapse exists between the terminals of a motor neurone and the surface of a muscle fibre and this is called a **neuromuscular junction**. Details of the structure and physiological differences between the synapse and the neuromuscular junction are described later in this section.

Structure of the chemical synapse

Chemical synapses are the commonest type of synapse found in vertebrates and they consist of a bulbous expansion of a nerve terminal called a **synaptic knob** or **bouton terminale** lying in close proximity to the membrane of a dendrite. The cytoplasm of the synaptic knob contains mitochondria, smooth endoplasmic reticulum, microfilaments and numerous **synaptic vesicles**. Each vesicle has a diameter of approximately 50 nm and contains a chemical **neurotransmitter substance** responsible for the transmission of the nerve impulse across the synapse. The membrane of the synaptic knob nearest the synapse is thickened as a result of cytoplasmic condensation and forms the **presynaptic membrane**. The membrane of the dendrite is also thickened and termed the **postsynaptic membrane**. These membranes are separated by a gap, the **synaptic cleft**, of 20 nm. The presynaptic membrane is modified for the attachment of synaptic vesicles and the release of transmitter substance into the synaptic cleft. The postsynaptic membrane contains large protein molecules which act as **receptor sites** for the transmitter substances and numerous **channels** and **pores**, normally closed, for the movement of ions into the postsynaptic neurone (fig 16.10*a*).

Synaptic vesicles contain a transmitter substance which is produced either in the cell body of the neurone and passes down the axon to the synaptic knob by axoplasmic streaming through microtubules, or directly in the synaptic knob. In both cases synthesis of transmitter substances requires enzymes produced by ribosomes in the cell body. In the synaptic knob the transmitter substance is 'packaged' into vesicles and stored pending release. The two main transmitter substances in vertebrate nervous systems are **acetylcholine (ACh)** and **noradrenaline**, although other substances exist and are described at the end of this section. Acetylcholine is an ammonium compound with the formula as shown in fig 16.9. It was the first transmitter substance to be isolated and was obtained by Otto Loewi, in 1920, from the endings of parasympathetic neurones of the vagus nerve (section 16.2) in frog heart. The detailed structure of noradrenaline is described in section 16.6.6. Neurones releasing acetylcholine are described as **cholinergic neurones** and those releasing noradrenaline are described as **adrenergic neurones**.

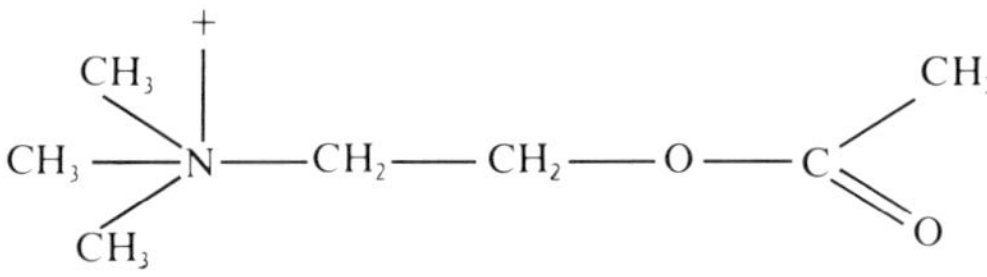

Fig 16.9 *Structural formula of acetylcholine*

Mechanisms of synaptic transmission

The arrival of nerve impulses at the synaptic knob is thought to depolarise the presynaptic membrane and increase the permeability of the membrane to Ca^{2+} ions. As the Ca^{2+} ions enter the synaptic knob they cause the synaptic vesicles to fuse with the presynaptic membrane and rupture (**exocytosis**), discharging their contents into the synaptic cleft. This is known as **excitation–secretion coupling**. The vesicles then return to the cytoplasm where they are refilled with transmitter substance. Each vesicle contains about 3 000 molecules of acetylcholine.

The transmitter substance diffuses across the synaptic cleft, imposing a delay of about 0.5 ms, and attaches to a specific receptor site on the postsynaptic membrane which recognises the molecular structure of the acetylcholine molecule. The arrival of the transmitter substance causes a change in the configuration of the receptor site leading to channels opening up in the postsynaptic membrane and the entry of ions which either **depolarise** or **hyperpolarise** (fig 16.4*a*) the membrane according to the nature of the transmitter substance released and the molecular properties of the postsynaptic receptor sites. Having produced a change in the permeability of the postsynaptic membrane the transmitter substance is immediately lost from the synaptic area by reabsorption by the presynaptic membrane, or diffusion out of the cleft or by hydrolysis by enzymes. In the case of **cholinergic** synapses acetylcholine is hydrolysed to choline by the enzyme **acetylcholinesterase (AChE)**, situated on the postsynaptic membrane, and reabsorbed into the synaptic knob to be recycled into acetylcholine by synthetic pathways in the vesicles (fig 16.10).

At **excitatory** synapses ion-specific channels open up allowing Na$^+$ ions to enter and K$^+$ ions to leave down their respective concentration gradients. This leads to a depolarisation in the postsynaptic membrane. The depolarising response is known as an **excitatory postsynaptic potential (e.p.s.p.)** and the amplitude of this potential is usually small but longer lasting than that of an action potential. The amplitude of e.p.s.p.s fluctuates in steps, suggesting that transmitter substance is released in 'packets' rather than individual molecules. Each 'step' is thought to correspond to the release of transmitter substance from one synaptic vesicle. A single e.p.s.p. is normally unable to produce sufficient depolarisation to reach the threshold required to propagate an action potential in the postsynaptic neurone. The depolarising effect of the e.p.s.p.s is additive, a phenomenon known as **summation**. Two or more e.p.s.p.s arising simultaneously at different regions on the same neurone may produce collectively sufficient depolarisation to initiate an action potential in the postsynaptic neurone. This is **spatial** (related in space) **summation**. The rapid repeated release of transmitter substance from several synaptic vesicles by the same synaptic knob as a result of an intense stimulus produces individual e.p.s.p.s which are so close together that they summate and give rise to an action potential in the postsynaptic neurone. This is **temporal** (related in time) **summation**. Therefore impulses can be set up in a single postsynaptic neurone as a result of either weak stimulation by several of its presynaptic neurones or repeated stimulation by one of its presynaptic neurones.

At **inhibitory** synapses the release of transmitter substance increases the permeability of the postsynaptic membrane by opening up ion-specific channels to Cl$^-$ and K$^+$ ions. As the ions move down their concentration gradients they produce a hyperpolarisation of the membrane known as an **inhibitory postsynaptic potential (i.p.s.p.)**.

Transmitter substances are neither inherently excitatory nor inhibitory. For example, acetylcholine has an excitatory effect at most neuromuscular junctions and synapses, but has an inhibitory effect on neuromuscular junctions in cardiac muscle and visceral muscle. These opposing effects are determined by events occurring at the postsynaptic membrane. The molecular properties of the receptor sites determine which ions enter the postsynaptic cell, which in turn determines the nature of the change in postsynaptic potentials as described above.

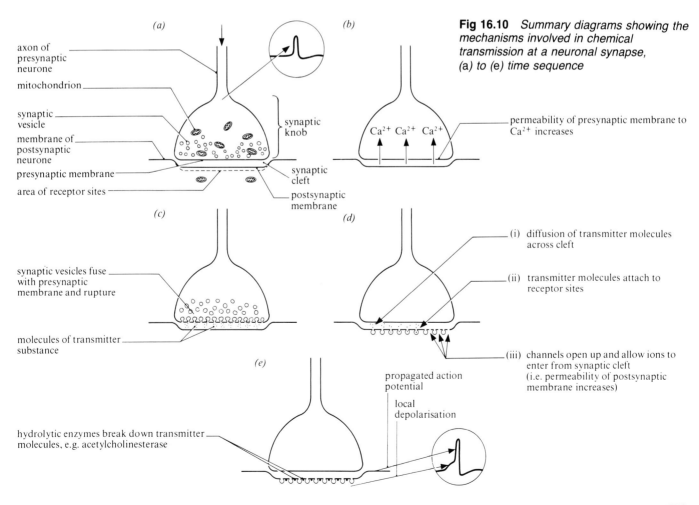

Fig 16.10 *Summary diagrams showing the mechanisms involved in chemical transmission at a neuronal synapse, (a) to (e) time sequence*

(a)

axon of presynaptic neurone

mitochondrion

synaptic vesicle

membrane of postsynaptic neurone

presynaptic membrane

area of receptor sites

synaptic knob

synaptic cleft

postsynaptic membrane

(b)

Ca^{2+} Ca^{2+} Ca^{2+}

permeability of presynaptic membrane to Ca^{2+} increases

(c)

synaptic vesicles fuse with presynaptic membrane and rupture

molecules of transmitter substance

(d)

(i) diffusion of transmitter molecules across cleft

(ii) transmitter molecules attach to receptor sites

(iii) channels open up and allow ions to enter from synaptic cleft (i.e. permeability of postsynaptic membrane increases)

(e)

propagated action potential

local depolarisation

hydrolytic enzymes break down transmitter molecules, e.g. acetylcholinesterase

Electrical synaptic transmission

Transmission across some synapses in many animals, including those of the cnidarian nerve net and vertebrate nervous systems, occurs by the flow of an electrical current between the pre- and postsynaptic membranes. The gap between these membranes is only 2 nm and the combined resistance to the flow of current by membranes and fluid in the cleft is very low. There is no delay in transmission time across the synapses and they are not susceptible to the action of drugs or other chemicals.

Neuromuscular junction

The neuromuscular junction is a specialised form of synapse found between the nerve terminals of a motor neurone and the **endomysium** of muscle fibres (section 17.4.2). Each muscle fibre has a specialised region, the **motor end-plate**, where the axon of the motor neurone divides and forms non-myelinated branches 100 nm wide running in shallow troughs on the membrane cell surface. The muscle cell membrane, the **sarcolemma**, has many deep folds called **junctional folds** as shown in fig 16.11. The cytoplasm of the motor neurone axon terminal has the same contents as the synaptic knob, and on stimulation releases acetylcholine by the same mechanisms as previously described. Changes in the structure of receptor sites on the sarcolemma increase the permeability of the sarcolemma to Na^+ and K^+ ions and a local depolarisation known as **end-plate potential** (**EPP**) is produced which is sufficient to lead to a propagated action potential passing along the sarcolemma and down into the fibre via the **transverse tubule system** (**T-system**) (section 17.4.7). This action potential results in the initiation of muscular contraction.

Functions of synapses and neuro-muscular junctions

The primary function of neuronal synapses and neuro-muscular junctions within the vertebrate nervous system is the transmission of information between receptor and effector. Several other significant functional features arise out of the structure and organisation of these sites of chemical secretion. They are summarised as follows.

(1) **Unidirectionality**. The release of transmitter substance at the presynaptic membrane, and the location of receptor sites on the postsynaptic membrane, ensure that nerve impulses pass in one direction along a given pathway. This gives **precision** to the nervous system.

(2) **Amplification**. Sufficient acetylcholine is released at the neuromuscular junction by each nerve impulse to excite the postsynaptic membrane to produce a propagated response in the muscle fibre. Thus nerve impulses arriving at the neuromuscular junction, however weak, are adequate to produce a response from the effector, thereby increasing the **sensitivity** of the system.

(3) **Adaptation or accommodation**. The amount of transmitter substance released by a synapse steadily falls off in response to constant stimulation until the supply of

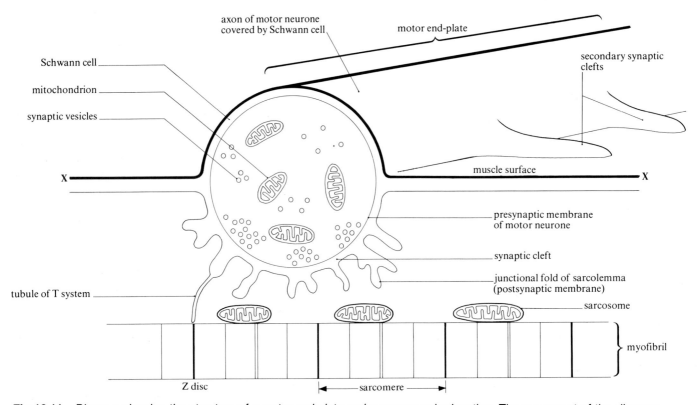

Fig 16.11 *Diagram showing the structure of a motor end plate and neuromuscular junction. The upper part of the diagram above* **X — X** *shows the course of the axon of a motor neurone on the surface of the muscle – the motor end plate. The part of the diagram below* **X — X** *shows the ultrastructure of the neuromuscular junction*

transmitter substance is exhausted and the synapse is described as **fatigued**. Further information passing along this pathway is inhibited and the adaptive significance of fatigue is the prevention of damage to an effector due to overstimulation. Adaptation also occurs at the level of the receptor and this is described in section 16.4.2.

(4) **Integration**. A postsynaptic neurone may receive impulses from a large number of excitatory and inhibitory presynaptic neurones. This is known as **synaptic convergence** and the postsynaptic neurone is able to summate the stimuli from all the presynaptic neurones. This spatial summation enables the synapse to act as one region for the integration of stimuli from a variety of sources and the production of a coordinated response. **Facilitation** occurs at some synapses and this involves each stimulus leaving the synapse more responsive to the next stimulus. In this way subsequent reduced stimuli may evoke a response and this is used to increase the sensitivity of certain synapses. Facilitation is not temporal summation in that it is a chemically mediated response of the postsynaptic membrane and not an electrical summation of postsynaptic membrane potentials.

(5) **Discrimination**. Temporal summation at synapses enables weak background stimuli to be filtered out before it reaches the brain. For example, information from exteroceptors in the skin, the eyes and ears receive constant stimuli from the environment which has little immediate importance for the nervous system. Only *changes* in intensity of stimuli are significant to the nervous system and these increase the frequency of stimuli and pass across the synapse and evoke a response.

(6) **Inhibition**. The transmission of information across synapses and neuromuscular junctions may be prevented postsynaptically by the activity of certain chemical blocking agents, described in the next section, or presynaptically. Presynaptic inhibition occurs at synaptic knobs that are in close contact with synaptic knobs from inhibitory synapses. Stimulation of these inhibitory synapses reduces the number of synaptic vesicles released by the inhibited synaptic knob. This arrangement enables a given nerve terminal to produce a variable response depending upon the activity of its excitatory and inhibitory synapses.

Chemical influences on the synapse and neuromuscular junction

Chemical substances carry out a variety of different functions in the nervous system. The effects of some chemical substances are widespread and well known, such as the excitatory effects of acetylcholine and adrenaline, whereas the effects of other substances are localised and, as yet, require further clarification. Some of these substances and their functions are described in table 16.2.

Several drugs used in the alleviation of psychiatric

Table 16.2. Summary table of chemical substances affecting the synapse and neuromuscular junction in mammals

Substance	Site of action	Function
acetylcholine	vertebrate nervous system	excitation or inhibition
gamma aminobutyric acid(GABA)	mammalian brain	inhibition
dopamine serotonin (5-hydroxytryptamine) noradrenaline	mammalian brain	excitation
lysergic acid diethylamide(LSD) mescaline	mammalian brain	produce hallucinations by mimicking the actions, or acting as antagonists, of other transmitter substances
tetanus toxin	presynaptic membrane	prevents release of inhibiting transmitter substance
botulinum toxin	presynaptic membrane	prevents release of acetylcholine
nicotine	postsynaptic membrane	mimics action of acetylcholine
eserine strychnine organophosphorus weedkillers and insecticides	postsynaptic membrane	inactivates acetylcholinesterase and prevents breakdown of acetylcholine
curare	postsynaptic membrane of neuromuscular junction	blocks action of acetylcholine
atropine	parasympathetic postganglionic endings	blocks action of acetylcholine
muscarine	parasympathetic postganglionic endings	mimics action of acetylcholine

disorders such as anxiety and depression are believed to be effective due to their ability to interact with chemical transmission at synapses. Many tranquillisers and sedatives, such as the tricyclic anti-depressant **imipramine** and **reserpine** and **monoamine oxidase inhibitors**, exert their effects by interacting with transmitter substances or their receptor sites. For example, monoamine oxidase inhibitors prevent the activity of an enzyme involved in the breakdown of adrenaline and noradrenaline and, presumably, are effective in treating depression by prolonging the effects of these transmitter substances. Hallucinogenic drugs, such as **lysergic acid diethylamide (LSD)** and **mescaline**, are believed to produce their effects by either mimicking the actions of naturally occurring brain transmitter substances or having antagonistic effects on other transmitter substances.

Recent research into the activity of the pain-suppressing opiate drugs, **heroin** and **morphine** in the mammalian brain have revealed the presence of naturally occurring (**endogenous**) substances having similar effects. These substances which react with the opiate receptors are collectively called endorphins. Many so far have been identified and the best known are a group of low relative molecular mass peptides known as **enkephalins**, for example **metenkephalin** and β-**endorphin**. They are thought to reduce pain, influence emotion and are involved with certain types of mental illness.

This research has opened up new ideas on brain functioning and offers a biochemical basis for the control of pain and healing by such diverse activities as hypnosis, acupuncture and faith healing. Many more chemical substances of this type have yet to be isolated, identified and have their function determined. As techniques of extracting and analysing substances found in such minute quantities continue to improve, it is only a matter of time before they will help to provide a more complete understanding of brain activity.

16.2 The vertebrate nervous system

The nervous system of vertebrates is characterised by the structural and functional diversity of its neurones and their complex organisation within the body.

There are several systems of classification of the vertebrate nervous system and all have advantages and limitations. The system given in fig 16.12 divides the peripheral nervous system according to the position of innervation in the body. Internuncial neurones, modified nerve cells of the brain and sense organs are not included in this classification.

16.2.1 The peripheral nervous system

Spinal nerves arise from the spinal cord and emerge between adjacent vertebrae along most of the length of the spinal cord. They all carry both sensory and motor neurones and are described as **mixed** nerves. Further details of spinal nerves and the spinal cord are given below. **Cranial nerves** arise from the ventral surface of the brain and, with one exception, supply receptors and effectors of the head. There are 10 pairs of cranial nerves in most vertebrates and 12 in mammals, numbered I–XII in Roman numerals. Not all cranial nerves are mixed (table 16.3).

The tenth cranial nerve, the **vagus**, includes an important motor nerve of the autonomic nervous system supplying the heart, bronchi and alimentary canal.

16.2.2 Reflex action and reflex arcs

The simplest form of irritability associated with the nervous system is **reflex action**. This is a rapid, automatic stereotyped response to a stimulus and because it is not under the conscious control of the brain it is described as an **involuntary action**. The neurones forming the pathway taken by the nerve impulses in reflex action make up a **reflex arc**. The simplest reflex arc found in animals involves a single neurone and the following pathway:

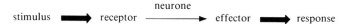

This level of organisation characterises the nervous system of cnidarians. Reflex arcs in all animal groups showing a greater level of structural and functional complexity than cnidarians include at least two neurones, an **afferent** or **sensory neurone** (*a*, towards) carrying impulses from a receptor towards an aggregation of nervous tissue which may be a **ganglion, nerve cord** or the **central nervous system**, and an **efferent** or **motor neurone** (*e*, away from) carrying impulses away from this aggregation to an effector (fig 16.13). There is a wide range of reflexes showing varying structural and functional complexity broadly involving four courses of action.

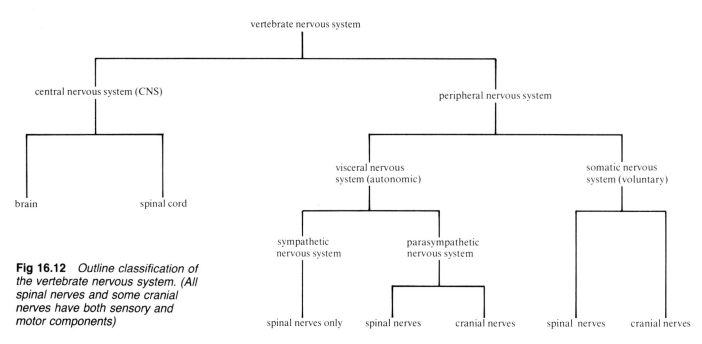

Fig 16.12 *Outline classification of the vertebrate nervous system. (All spinal nerves and some cranial nerves have both sensory and motor components)*

Table 16.3. Summary of mammalian cranial nerves, their innervations and functions

Cranial nerve	Name	Type	Innervation	Function
I	olfactory	sensory	olfactory organ	smell
II	optic	sensory	retina	sight
III	oculomotor	motor	four eye muscles	eye movements
IV	trochlear	motor	one eye muscle	eye movements
V	trigeminal	mixed	jaw muscles, teeth, skin of face	jaw movements, touch and pain receptors
VI	abducens	motor	one eye muscle	eye movements
VII	facial	mixed	cheek, face muscles, tongue	salivation, facial expression, sweet, sour, salt taste
VIII	auditory	sensory	cochlea, semicircular canals	hearing, balance
IX	glossopharyngeal	mixed	tongue, pharyngeal muscle	bitter taste, swallowing
X	vagus	mixed	larynx, pharynx, heart, gut	speech, swallowing, decrease heart rate, stimulus for peristalsis
XI	accessory	motor	head and neck	head movement
XII	hypoglossal	motor	tongue	tongue movement

(1) **Monosyraptic reflex.** This is the simplest reflex arc seen in vertebrates. The sensory neurone synapses directly on to the motor neurone cell body. Only one synapse in the central nervous system is involved in this arc. These reflexes are common in vertebrates and are involved in the control of muscle tone and posture, such as the knee jerk or patellar reflex. In these reflex arcs no neurones pass to the brain and reflex actions are carried out without the involvement of the brain because they are routine and no conscious thought or decision is required for their operation. They are economical on the number of neurones in the central nervous system and do not make trivial demands on the brain which can 'concentrate' on more important matters.

(2) **Polysynaptic spinal reflex.** This has at least two synapses situated within the central nervous system as a result of the inclusion of a third type of neurone in the arc: an **internuncial (intermediate or relay)** neurone. The synapses are found between the sensory neurone and internuncial neurone and between the internuncial neurone and the motor neurone as shown in fig 16.13b. This type of reflex arc provides a simple illustration of localised reflex action within the spinal cord. Fig 16.14 shows a much simplified example of the **spinal reflex** associated with the reflex action following pricking a finger on a pin.

Simple reflex arcs such as (1) and (2) allow the body to make automatic involuntary homeostatic adjustments to changes in the external environment, such as the iris–pupil reflex and balance during locomotion, and also in the internal environment, such as breathing rate and blood pressure, and to prevent damage to the body as in cuts and burns.

(3) **Polysynaptic spinal/brain reflexes.** Here the sensory neurone synapses in the spinal cord with a second

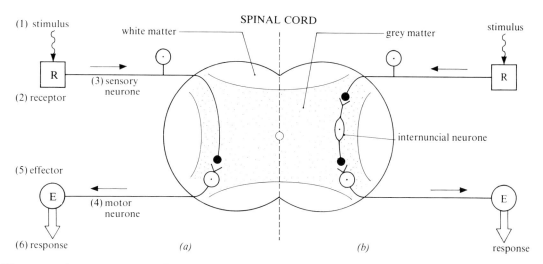

Fig 16.13 *Diagrammatic representation of two simple forms of reflex arc, (a) monosynaptic reflex arc, including the main features of a reflex arc (numbered 1 to 6) (b) simple polysynaptic reflex arc. (**R** represents receptor, **E** represents effector)*

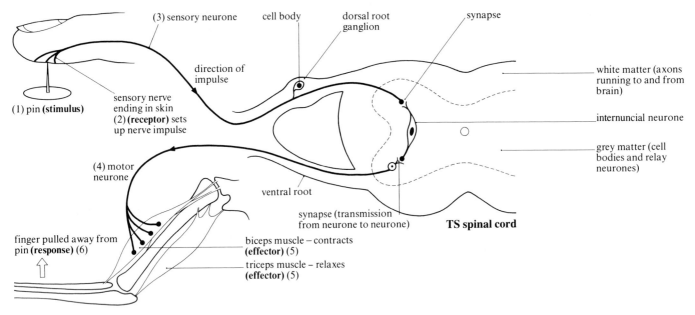

Fig 16.14 *A simplified example of reflex action and a reflex arc. (The numbers in brackets refer to the basic structures in any reflex arc shown in Fig 16.13)*

sensory neurone which passes to the brain. The latter sensory neurones are part of the **ascending nerve fibre tract** and have their origin in the pre-internuncial neurone synapse (fig 16.15*a*). The brain identifies this sensory information and stores it for further use.

Alternatively motor activity may be initiated at any time by the brain and impulses transmitted down motor neurones in **descending nerve fibre tracts** to synapse directly with spinal motor neurones in the post-internuncial synaptic region (fig 16.15*b*).

(4) **Conditioned reflexes**. These are forms of reflex actions where the type of response is modified by past experience. These reflexes are coordinated by the brain. **Learning** forms the basis of all conditioned reflexes, such as in toilet training, salivation on the sight and smell of food and awareness of danger (section 16.9).

Many simple reflex situations arise where there are two immediate responses involving the activity of a given set of muscles which can either contract or relax and produce opposite responses. The normal spinal reflex response in such situations would pass through the reflex arc shown in fig 16.14, but 'conditions' associated with the stimulus may modify the response. In these situations more complex reflex pathways exist involving excitatory and inhibitory neurones.

For example, if an empty metal baking tin is picked up and found to be extremely hot, burning the fingers, it will probably be dropped immediately whereas a boiling hot, cooked casserole in an expensive dish, equally hot and painful, will probably be put down, quickly but gently. The reason for the difference in the response reveals the involvement of conditioning and memory, followed by a conscious decision by the brain.

Fig 16.15 *Simplified diagram of sections through the brain and spinal cord showing (a) the pathway of sensory impulses from receptor, via the spinal cord, to the cerebral cortex, and (b) the pathway of motor impulses, initiated within the cortex to effector, via the spinal cord*

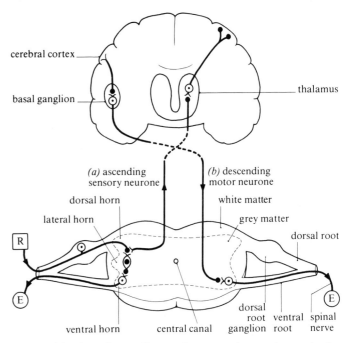

In this situation reflex pathways exist as shown in fig 16.16.

The stimulus in both cases produces impulses passing to the brain in an ascending sensory neurone. When the information reaches the brain it is interpreted and associated with related sensory information coming from other sense organs, for example the eyes, concerning the *cause* of the stimulus. The incoming

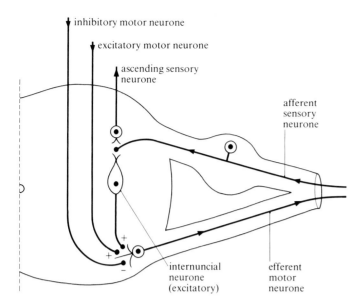

inhibitory motor neurone

excitatory motor neurone

ascending sensory neurone

afferent sensory neurone

internuncial neurone (excitatory)

efferent motor neurone

Fig 16.16 *Simplified diagram showing the relationships within the spinal cord between an internuncial neurone and the modifying effects of excitatory and inhibitory motor neurones from the brain*

information is compared with stored information concerning the nature and cause of the present stimulus and the likely outcome of allowing the spinal reflex to proceed. In the case of the metal tin, the brain computes that no further damage to either the body or the tin will occur if it is dropped and so initiates impulses in an **excitatory** motor neurone. This passes down the spinal cord to the level where the stimulus entered and synapses with the cell body of the motor neurone of the spinal reflex. Such is the speed of conduction through the pathway described above that the impulses from the excitatory motor neurone reach the spinal motor neurone at the same time as impulses from the internuncial neurone. The combined effect of these sends excitatory impulses to the muscle effector along the spinal motor neurone and the tin is dropped.

In the case of the casserole dish, the brain computes that dropping the casserole would probably scald the legs and feet, ruin the meal and break an expensive dish, whereas holding it until it could be put down safely would not cause much more damage to the fingers. If this decision is reached, impulses are initiated which pass down the spinal cord in an **inhibitory** motor neurone. These impulses arrive at the synapse with the spinal motor neurone at the same time as stimulatory impulses from the internuncial neurone and the latter are cancelled out. No impulses pass along the motor neurone to the muscle effector and the dish is held. Simultaneous brain activity would initiate an alternative muscle response which would result in the dish being put down quickly and safely.

The accounts of reflex arcs and reflex activity given above are, of necessity, simplified generalisations. The whole process of the coordination, integration and control

of body functions is much more complex. For example, neurones connect different levels of the spinal cord together, controlling say the arms and legs, so that activity in one can be related to the other whilst at the same time other neurones from the brain achieve overall control.

Whilst combined activity of the brain and endocrine system is important in the coordination of many nervous activities described later in the chapter, another reflex system, based solely on neuronal activity, exists for the control of visceral activities. This is the autonomic nervous system.

16.2.3 The autonomic nervous system

The autonomic nervous system (*autos*, self; *nomos*, governing) is that part of the peripheral nervous system controlling activities of the internal environment that are normally involuntary, such as heart rate, peristalsis and sweating. It consists of motor neurones passing to the smooth muscles of internal organs. Most of the activity of the autonomic nervous system is integrated locally within the spinal cord or brain by **visceral reflexes** and does not involve the conscious control of higher centres of the brain. However, some activities, such as the control of anal and bladder sphincter muscles, are also under the conscious control of the brain and control of these has to be learned. It is thought that many other autonomic activities may be able to be controlled by conscious effort and learning: many forms of meditation and relaxation have their physiological roots in the control of autonomic activities, and considerable success has already been achieved in regulating heart rate and reducing blood pressure by conscious control or 'will power'. The overall control of the autonomic nervous system is maintained, however, by centres in the medulla and hypothalamus (see section 16.2.4). These receive and integrate sensory information and coordinate this with information from other parts of the nervous system to produce the appropriate response.

The autonomic nervous system is composed of two types of neurones, a myelinated **preganglionic** neurone, which leaves the central nervous system in the ventral root of the segmental nerve before synapsing with several unmyelinated **postganglionic** neurones leading to effectors.

There are two divisions of the autonomic nervous system: the **sympathetic** and the **parasympathetic nervous systems**. The two systems differ primarily in the structural organisation of their neurones and these differences are shown in fig 16.17.

In the sympathetic nervous system the synapses and cell bodies of the postganglionic neurones in the trunk region are situated in ganglia close to the spinal cord. Each **sympathetic ganglion** is connected to the spinal cord by a **white ramus communicans** and to the spinal nerve by a **grey ramus communicans** as shown in fig 16.18. Adjacent segmental sympathetic ganglia on each side of the spinal cord are linked together by the sympathetic nerve tract to form a chain of sympathetic ganglia running alongside the

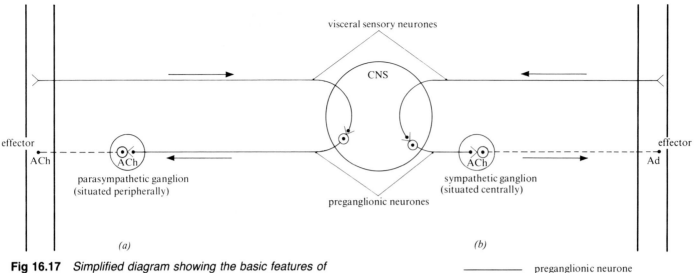

visceral sensory neurones

CNS

effector
ACh

parasympathetic ganglion
(situated peripherally)

preganglionic neurones

sympathetic ganglion
(situated centrally)

effector
Ad

(a)   *(b)*

Fig 16.17 *Simplified diagram showing the basic features of (a) the parasympathetic nervous system and (b) the sympathetic nervous system (visceral sensory neurones are not part of the autonomic nervous system)*

	preganglionic neurone
	postganglionic neurone
ACh	acetylcholine
Ad	noradrenaline

Fig 16.18 *Simplified diagram showing the position of a sympathetic ganglion and its relationship to the spinal cord and spinal nerve*

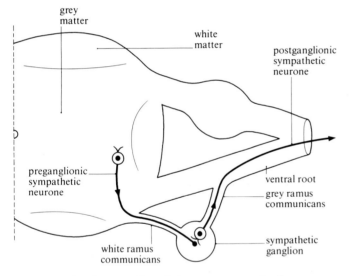

grey matter

white matter

postganglionic sympathetic neurone

preganglionic sympathetic neurone

ventral root

grey ramus communicans

white ramus communicans

sympathetic ganglion

spinal cord. The ganglia of the parasympathetic nervous system are situated close to, or within, the effector organ.

Other differences between the two systems include the nature of the chemical transmitter substance released at the postganglionic effector synapse, their general effects on the body and the conditions under which they are active. These differences are summarised in table 16.4.

The sympathetic and parasympathetic nervous systems generally have opposing effects on organs they supply and this enables the body to make rapid and precise adjustments of visceral activities in order to maintain a steady state. For example, an increase in heart rate due to the release of noradrenaline by sympathetic neurones is compensated for by the release of acetylcholine by parasympathetic neurones. This action prevents heart rate becoming excessive and will eventually restore it to its normal level when secretion from both systems balances out. A summary of the antagonistic effects of these systems is shown in table 16.5.

16.2.4 The central nervous system

The **central nervous system** (**CNS**) develops from an infolding of the ectoderm immediately above the embryonic notochord and forms a dorsal, hollow neural tube running the length of the animal. The neural tube differentiates during development to form an expanded anterior region, the **brain**, and a long cylindrical **spinal cord**.

The central nervous system is covered by three membranes called **meninges** and is completely encased within the protective bones of the skull and vertebral column. The outer membrane forms the tough **dura mater** attached to the periosteum of the skull and vertebrae, and the inner **pia mater** which directly overlies the nervous tissues. Between the two is the **arachnoid** 'membrane', composed of pillars of connective tissue supporting a space beneath it, the **subarachnoid space**, which contains the **cerebrospinal fluid** (**CSF**). Most of this fluid is contained in the central canal of the spinal cord and continues forward to occupy four expanded regions, the **ventricles**, of the brain. The fluid bathes the outside and inside of the brain and blood vessels lie within it for the supply of nutrients and oxygen to the nervous tissues and the removal of wastes (see fig 16.19). The cells of the vascular **anterior** and **posterior choroid plexuses** in the roof of the brain secrete CSF and provide a link between the fluid outside and inside the brain. About 100 cm³ of fluid is present in the CNS and, apart from its nutritive and excretory functions, it supports the nervous tissues and protects them against mechanical shock. A continual circulation of fluid is maintained by ciliated cells lining the ventricles and central canal.

Table 16.4. Summary of the differences between the sympathetic and parasympathetic nervous systems

Feature	Sympathetic	Parasympathetic
Origin of neurones	Emerges from cranial, thoracic and lumbar regions of CNS	Emerges from cranial and sacral regions of CNS
Position of ganglion	Close to spinal cord	Close to effector
Length of fibres	Short preganglionic fibres Long postganglionic fibres	Long preganglionic fibres Short postganglionic fibres
Number of fibres	Numerous postganglionic fibres	Few postganglionic fibres
Distribution of fibres	Preganglionic fibres innervate a wide area	Preganglionic fibres innervate a restricted region
Area of influence	Effect diffuse	Effect localised
Transmitter substance	Noradrenaline released at effector	Acetylcholine released at effector
General effects	Increases metabolite levels Increases metabolic rate Increases rhythmic activities Lowers sensory threshold	Decreases metabolite levels None Decreases rhythmic activities Restores sensory threshold to normal levels
Overall effect	Excitatory homeostatic effect	Inhibitory homeostatic effect
Conditions when active	Dominant during danger, stress and activity; controls reactions to stress	Dominant during rest Controls routine body activities

Table 16.5 Summary of the effects of the sympathetic and parasympathetic nervous systems on the body

Region	Sympathetic	Parasympathetic
Head	Dilates pupils None Inhibits secretion of saliva	Constricts pupils Stimulates secretion of tears Stimulates secretion of saliva
Heart	Increases amplitude and rate of heart beat	Decreases amplitude and rate of heart beat
Lungs	Dilates bronchi and bronchioles Increases ventilation rate	Constricts bronchi and bronchioles Decreases ventilation rate
Gut	Inhibits peristalsis Inhibits secretion of alimentary juices Contracts anal sphincter muscle	Stimulates peristalsis Stimulates secretion of alimentary juices Inhibits contraction of anal sphincter muscle
Blood	Constricts arterioles to gut and smooth muscle Dilates arterioles to brain and skeletal muscle Increases blood pressure Increases blood volume by contraction of spleen	Maintains steady muscle tone in arterioles to gut, smooth muscle, brain and skeletal muscle Reduces blood pressure None
Skin	Contracts erector pili muscles of hair Constricts arterioles in skin of limbs Increases secretion of sweat	None Dilates arterioles in skin of face None
Kidney	Decreases output of urine	None
Bladder	Contracts bladder sphincter muscle	Inhibits contraction of bladder sphincter muscles
Penis	Induces ejaculation	Stimulates erection
Glands	Releases adrenaline from adrenal medulla	None

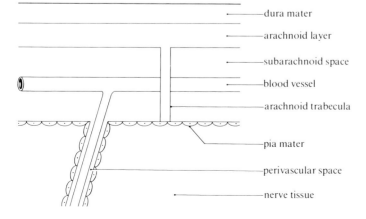

dura mater

arachnoid layer

subarachnoid space

blood vessel

arachnoid trabecula

pia mater

perivascular space

nerve tissue

Fig 16.19 *Diagram showing the structure of the meninges and associated blood vessels. Notice that the channels through the nerve tissue are lined by the pia mater*

The functions of the central nervous system involve the coordination, integration and control of most nervous activities and it works in conjunction with the peripheral nervous system. In vertebrates, advanced forms of nervous activity, such as memory and intelligence, are possible due to the increased size of certain regions of the brain.

The spinal cord

The spinal cord is a dorso-ventrally flattened cylinder of nervous tissue running from the base of the brain to the lumbar region and protected by vertebrae. It consists of an H-shaped central core of **grey matter**, composed of nerve cell bodies, dendrites and synapses surrounding a central canal, and an outer layer, the **white matter**, containing nerve fibres whose fatty myelin sheaths give it its characteristic colour. There are 31 pairs of segmental **spinal nerves** present and these divide close to the spinal cord to form two branches called the **dorsal root** and **ventral root**. Sensory neurones enter the dorsal root and have their cell bodies in a swelling, the **dorsal root ganglion**, close to the spinal cord. The sensory neurones then enter the dorsal horn of the grey matter where they synapse with **internuncial** (intermediate or relay) neurones. These, in turn, synapse with motor neurones in the **ventral horn** and leave the spinal cord via the ventral root (fig 16.15). Since there are many more internuncial neurones than motor neurones, some integration must occur within the grey matter. Some sensory neurones synapse directly with motor neurones in the ventral horn, as in the familiar knee-jerk reflex (fig 16.13a). In the thoracic, upper lumbar and sacral regions a **lateral horn** is present (fig 16.15) containing the cell bodies of the preganglionic autonomic neurones. The white matter is composed of groups of nerve fibres, forming tracts, running between the grey matter and the brain and providing a means of communication between spinal nerves and the brain. **Ascending tracts** carry sensory information to the brain and **descending tracts** relay motor information to the spinal cord.

The functions of the spinal cord include acting as a coordinating centre for simple spinal reflexes, such as the knee-jerk response, and autonomic reflexes, such as contraction of the bladder, and providing a means of communication between spinal nerves and the brain.

The brain

The brain is the swollen anterior end of the vertebrate neural tube and it coordinates and controls the activities of the whole nervous system. The brain is composed entirely of groups of cell bodies, nerve tracts and blood vessels. The **nerve fibre tracts** form the **white matter** of the brain and carry bundles of neurones to and from various regions called '**nuclei**' or **centres** composed of groups of cell bodies and synapses collectively forming the **grey matter** of the brain. The tracts connect the various 'nuclei' together and link the brain and spinal cord. During the phylogenetic development of the vertebrate brain the number of tracts and the complexity of their interconnections have increased. The 'nuclei' vary in size from isolated groups of several hundred cells to large regions such as the cerebral cortex and the cerebellar cortex in humans consisting of several hundred million cells.

The structure of the vertebrate brain. The vertebrate brain differentiates initially into three regions during its embryological development and these are the **forebrain, midbrain** and **hindbrain**. Primitively, these three regions are associated with the coordination of the senses of smell, sight and balance respectively. Subsequent development of the brain varies between and within each vertebrate class, and the original tripartite structure becomes obscured as the forebrain and hindbrain each subdivide. The adult vertebrate brain has five regions, and they assume a particular significance within each class associated with the mode of life and level of structural and functional complexity attained by the class. Some regions of the brain have increased in size reflecting their importance whereas others have diminished. The overall structure of the generalised vertebrate brain is shown in fig 16.20 and a summary showing the development of the regions of the brain in non-mammalian and mammalian vertebrates is given in table 16.6.

Fish are very dependent upon smell in order to find food and have large olfactory lobes to accommodate the sensory input. A large cerebellum coordinates movements, and the large optic lobes act partly in visual responses but mainly as the main coordination centre of the brain. The optic lobes form the dominant feature of the amphibian brain where they have the same functions as in fish. Reptiles show a reduction in the size of the midbrain and an increase in the size of the forebrain. This trend continues in birds with an increase in the sizes of the thalamus and corpora striata where most of the complex, instinctive behavioural activities of birds are coordinated. Finally, mammals are characterised by a large pair of cerebral hemispheres covering a well-developed thalamus. These two structures, containing nuclei and tracts respectively, reflect the dependence placed on the storage of sensory information and the integration of all voluntary activities. The medulla shows little change in relative size throughout the vertebrates and this stresses the importance placed on the reflex control of all essential functions such as heart rate.

Methods of studying brain function

Little knowledge of the functions of the various regions of the brain can be obtained by simply studying their anatomy and histology. Whilst this provides valuable information about structural interrelationships, it does not explain the physiological activities occurring in the brain. Brain activity has been studied using electrophysiological techniques, including the use of **electroencephalograms**. Good electrical contact is made between electrodes and the scalp using electrode jelly and electrical changes produced by the activity of many cells of the cerebral cortex are detected,

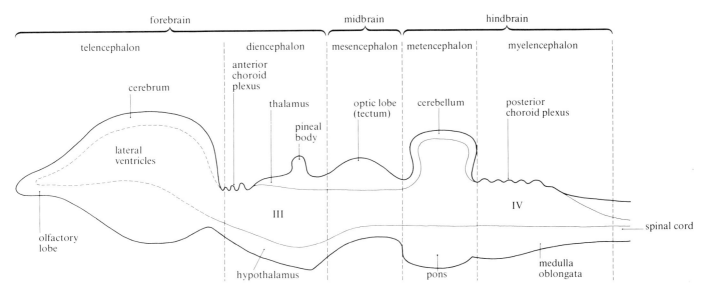

Fig 16.20 *Diagram showing a median section of a generalised vertebrate brain. The numbers refer to the positions of the IIIrd and IVth ventricles*

Table 16.6. The origins and regions of the vertebrate brain

| Embryonic division | Adult region | Structural/functional regions | |
		Non-mammal	Mammal
forebrain	telencephalon	olfactory lobes (fish) / neopallium (reptiles) / corpora striata (birds)	cerebral hemispheres / basal ganglia
	diencephalon	thalamus	thalamus
		hypothalamus	hypothalamus
midbrain	mesencephalon	optic lobes (amphibia)	
		tectum	corpora quadrigemina
hindbrain	metencephalon	cerebellum	cerebellum
		pons	pons
	myelencephalon	medulla oblongata	medulla oblongata

Computer program. BRAIN-SCAN (CUP Micro Software) allows the user to develop a functional map of the cerebral cortex. (Double package with NERVE IMPULSE.)

amplified and recorded on a pen trace. Three major wave frequencies have been detected. α-**waves** are recorded from relaxed subjects with their eyes closed and they usually mask the higher frequency β-**waves** which are present at all times and best seen in patients under anaesthesia. The absence of β-waves or any electrical activity from the brain of a patient indicates 'brain-stem-death' and, along with cessation of heart beat and ventilation is taken as a clinical definition of death. δ-**waves** have the lowest frequency and greatest amplitude and are recorded during sleep. Whilst electroencephalograms yield little immediate information regarding brain function, they are valuable in diagnosing the position of localised brain abnormalities, and, for example, the various forms of epilepsy. Epilepsy is a result of excessive activity of the

CNS and occurs in two forms. The first, *grand mal* produces powerful convulsions lasting from several seconds to minutes whereas the second, *petit mal* produces mild convulsions lasting for much shorter periods of time.

Investigations of brain function are carried out on the brains of patients under local anaesthesia. In one type of investigation patients describe sensations produced whilst various regions of the brain are electrically stimulated. This technique enables motor activities of regions of the cerebral cortex to be mapped (fig 16.23). Likewise recordings of electrical activity obtained using microelectrodes inserted into cell bodies or axons in specific regions during stimulation of sensory cells and organs have enabled maps to be drawn showing regions of brain sensory function.

The structure and functions of the human brain

The following account of the brain is brief and represents a summary of current knowledge of the structures and functions of the human brain. Elaboration of function and evidence for this is omitted except where it is considered necessary for clarification. In this chapter the brain is considered from a structural standpoint and the activities of each region shown in table 16.6 are described in turn. By necessity this approach and account is a gross oversimplification since many brain activities span several regions, and it is useful to bear in mind that functionally there are three main interrelated regions, the cerebrum (cerebral hemispheres), the cerebellum and the brain stem, the latter being composed of the medulla, pons, mesencephalon and thalamus. The brain stem is an extension of the spinal cord and contains complex neuronal pathways controlling cardiovascular function, ventilation, gastrointestinal function, eye movement, equilibrium and most of the stereotyped activities of the body.

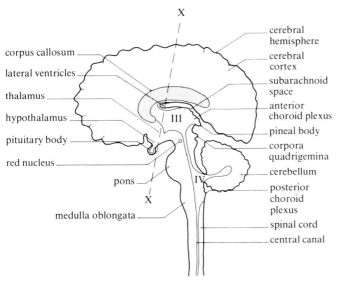

Fig 16.21 (above) *Simplified diagram showing a vertical section through the human brain (the numbers indicate the ventricles of the brain)*

Fig 16.22 (below) *Simplified diagram showing a cross-section of the human brain through X — X on Fig. 16.21*

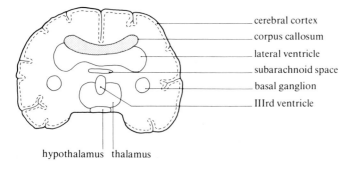

Telencephalon

This is the anterior region of the forebrain and consists of the **cerebrum** and **basal ganglia**. The cerebrum forms the roof and walls of the telencephalon and is greatly enlarged to form the left and right cerebral hemispheres covering most of the brain. The basal ganglia occupy the floor of the telencephalon.

Cerebrum. The cerebral hemispheres are composed of a thin outer layer (3 mm) of densely packed nerve cells (10^9) forming a region of grey matter called the **cerebral cortex**. Beneath this is a central mass of white matter composed of nerve fibre tracts. Left and right cerebral hemispheres are linked by a broad nerve fibre tract called the **corpus callosum** and the surface area of the cortex is increased by numerous infoldings called **convolutions**. Each cerebral hemisphere is divided, for convenience, into four lobes as shown in fig 16.23, and electrophysiological techniques have enabled three discrete areas to be recognised according to the functions their cells perform. These areas are:

(1) **sensory** – receiving impulses indirectly from receptors (input),

(2) **association** – interpreting the input, storing the input and initiating a response in the light of similar past experience, and

(3) **motor** – transmitting impulses to effectors (output).

The interrelationships between the above areas enable the cerebral cortex to dominate and coordinate all voluntary and some involuntary activities of the body, including highly developed functions such as memory, learning, reasoning, conscience and personality. If the cerebral cortex is entirely destroyed it would not cause death but the patient would show no spontaneous activity. The patient would be able to respond to certain stimuli but would be unable to learn or reason and all visible signs of intelligence and personality would disappear. Only those reflexes controlled predominantly by the medulla and cerebellum, such as feeding and sleeping, would remain.

Sensory areas are the input areas of the cortex and receive sensory impulses via ascending tracts from receptors originating from most parts of the body. The sensory areas form localised regions of the cortex associated with certain senses as shown in fig 16.23. The size of the region is related to the number of receptors in the sensory structure.

Association areas are so named for several reasons. First, they associate incoming sensory information with previously perceived information stored in memory units, so that the information is 'recognised'. Secondly, the information is associated with incoming sensory information from other receptors. Thirdly, the information is 'interpreted' and given meaning within its present context and, if necessary, the interpreted information is associated with the 'computed' most appropriate response which the association area initiates and passes to its associated motor area. Association areas, therefore, are involved in memory,

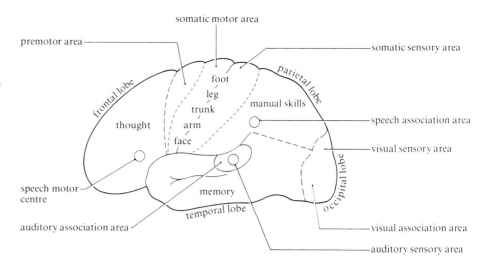

16.23 *Diagram showing the positions of the four main lobes of the brain: frontal, parietal, occipital and temporal. Superimposed on these are the major: sensory, association and motor areas and centres. The positions of certain regions of the brain associated with specific activities and regions of the body are also shown*

learning and reasoning, and the degree of success of the outcome may be loosely termed **intelligence**.

Several major association areas are adjacent to their related sensory area; for example, the **visual association area** is situated immediately anterior to the visual cortex in the **occipital lobe** where, in a visual context, it carries out the association functions described above. Some association areas may have a restricted specialised function and these are linked to other association centres that can further develop the activity. For example, the **auditory association area** only interprets sounds into broad categories which are relayed to more specialised association areas such as the **speech association area** where 'sense' is made of the words. Speech is initiated in the **speech motor centre** which is an example of the third type of functional area found in the cerebrum.

Motor areas are the output areas of the cortex where motor impulses are initiated to pass to voluntary muscles via descending tracts originating in the white matter of the cerebrum.

Many motor impulses pass directly to the spinal cord through two large **pyramidal tracts (corticospinal tracts)** via the brain stem. All other motor impulses pass through **extrapyramidal tracts** which contain motor impulses from other regions of the brain such as the basal ganglia and cerebellum. In the medulla all tracts cross over so that impulses from the left cerebral cortex innervate the right side of the body and vice versa.

Neurones passing through the pyramidal tracts have their cell bodies in the motor cortex and their axons pass directly to synapse with the motor neurones that they activate in the spinal segment at the point where the latter emerge. There are no intervening synapses in the brain, therefore impulses and subsequent responses are neither delayed nor modified en route. Localised regions of the motor cortex have been mapped, and examples of these are shown in fig 16.23. The size of each specific motor area is related to the complexity of the motor activity.

The main extrapyramidal tract is the **reticulospinal tract**

which relays motor neurones from the **reticular formation** situated in the brain stem between the thalamus and medulla. Motor impulses from various regions of the brain controlling muscular activity pass to specific areas of the reticular formation where this activity is modified by impulses from the cortex and becomes either **inhibitory** or **excitatory**. For example, impulses from the cerebellum and **premotor area** of the cortex, a region involved in the control of coordinated movements, pass to an area of the reticular formation in the medulla where the combined effect stimulates **inhibitory motor neurones**. These have a suppressive regulatory effect on muscle activity enabling complex coordinated movements of the body to occur, such as the varied control involved in angling, directing and powering a tennis racquet, cricket ball or violin bow, according to circumstances. Other combinations of motor impulses stimulate **excitatory motor neurones**; in fact, the overall motor output of the reticular formation is excitatory.

Most sensory neurones run to the reticular formation before passing to the cortex via the thalamus. Some of these sensory neurones form the **reticular activating system** and are responsible for activating the cortex and arousing the body from its natural state of sleep. Underactivity or destruction of the reticular activating system induces deep sleep or coma respectively. Many general anaesthetics are thought to act by temporarily blocking synaptic transmission in this system. The reticular activating system is also believed to be responsible for producing and sustaining motivation and concentration hence the inverse relationship between tiredness and concentration.

Finally, the functions of certain regions of the cortex, particularly the large anterior regions, the **prefrontal lobes**, are still uncertain. These regions, along with others in the brain, are called **silent areas** because they fail to produce either sensation or response when stimulated electrically. They are believed to be responsible for our individual characteristics or **personality**. The removal of the lobes or cutting the tracts leading from them to the rest of the brain (**prefrontal lobotomy**) was used to relieve acute anxiety states in patients but it has been discontinued. The side-effects included a reduction in mental awareness, intelligence, judgement and creativity and gave an indication of the functions of the prefrontal lobes.

Basal ganglia. These are regions of the forebrain containing cell bodies receiving motor neurones from parts of the cortex and passing on impulses to the reticular formation. The functions of the basal ganglia are varied, but one ganglion, for example, provides inhibitory stimuli for the antagonistic control of muscle tone during slow movements. Damage to this basal ganglion produces the tremor of the hands associated with Parkinson's disease, a form of muscle paralysis.

Diencephalon

This is the posterior region of the forebrain and its dorsal and lateral regions form the **thalamus** and the ventral region forms the **hypothalamus**. The **pineal body** arises in this region and its function is described in section 16.6.3.

Thalamus. The majority of sensory neurones carrying impulses to the cortex terminate in the thalamus. Here the origin and nature of the impulses are 'analysed' and relayed to the appropriate sensory areas of the cortex by neurones originating in the thalamus. It therefore acts as a processing, integrating and relay centre for all sensory information. In this function it shows similarities to a switchboard in a telephone exchange. Information from certain regions of the cortex is modified by the thalamus, which is also thought to be involved in the perception of pain and pleasure. Part of the reticular formation, whose function was described above for the cerebral motor areas, originates in the thalamus. The dorsal region immediately anterior to the thalamus, the **anterior choroid plexus**, facilitates transfer of substances between the CSF in the third ventricle and the subarachnoid space (fig 16.21).

Hypothalamus. This is the main coordinating and control centre for the autonomic nervous system. It receives sensory neurones from all the visceral receptors and taste and smell receptors. Information is relayed from here to effectors via the medulla and spinal cord, and is used in the regulation and control of heart rate, blood pressure, ventilation rate and peristalsis. Other regions of the hypothalamus contain specific centres for the initiation of feeding, drinking and sleeping, and behavioural activities associated with aggression and reproduction. The hypothalamus is the most vascular region of the brain and monitors the metabolite and hormone levels of the blood as well as blood temperature. Using this information the hypothalamus, in association with the pituitary gland situated immediately beneath it, directs and controls the release of most of the hormones from the body, and maintains the steady-state composition of the blood and tissues. The detailed neuroendocrine role of the hypothalamus is described in section 16.6.2.

Mesencephalon

This connects the anterior two regions of the brain to the posterior two regions and, therefore, all nerve fibre tracts within the brain pass through this region which is part of the brain stem. The roof of the mesencephalon is composed of the **tectum** consisting of the four **corpora quadrigemina** and these function as visual and auditory reflex centres. The superior pair of corpora quadrigemina receive sensory neurones from the eyes and muscles of the head and control visual reflexes. For example, they control the movement of the head and eyes to fix and focus on an object. The inferior pair of corpora quadrigemina receive sensory neurones from the ears and muscles of the head and control auditory reflexes such as the movement of the head to locate and detect the source of a sound.

Situated in the floor of the mesencephalon are many centres or nuclei controlling specific subconscious stereotyped muscular movements, such as bending forwards and backwards and rotation of the head and trunk. For example, stimulation of part of one of these nuclei, the **red nucleus**, causes the head and upper trunk to extend backwards.

Metencephalon

The dorsal region of the metencephalon forms the **cerebellum** and the ventral region forms the **pons**.

Cerebellum. This is made up of the two **cerebellar hemispheres** and, like the cerebrum, has its grey matter on the outside. The grey matter contains characteristically large flask-shaped **Purkyne** cells bearing many dendrites. These cells receive impulses concerning muscular movement from a number of different sources, including sensory receptors in the balance organs (the vestibular apparatus) of the ear concerned with balance, proprioceptors in joints, tendons and muscles and motor centres of the cortex. The cerebellum is thought to integrate this information and produce coordinated muscular activity in all the muscles involved in a given movement including the reflex control of body posture. Damage to the cerebellum results in jerky, poorly controlled movements. The cerebellum is vital to the control of rapid muscular activities such as running, typing and even talking. All the activities of the cerebellum are involuntary but may involve learning in their early stages. During these training periods the cortex directs the control of the cerebellum and concentration is required, such as when learning to walk, swim or ride a bicycle. Once the skill is acquired reflex control by the cerebellum takes over.

Pons. This forms the part of the brain stem in the floor of the metencephalon and, apart from acting as a bridge (*pons*, bridge) carrying ascending and descending tracts, it contains several 'nuclei' relaying impulses to the cerebellum.

Myelencephalon

This is the posterior region of the brain and is continuous

with the spinal cord. It is composed of the dorsally situated **posterior choroid plexus** and the ventro-lateral **medulla oblongata**.

In the medulla the ascending and descending nerve fibre tracts cross over from left to right and vice versa. The eighth to twelfth cranial nerves originate from the medulla and it contains important reflex centres for the regulation of autonomic activities including the control of heart rate (chapters 14 and 18), blood pressure (chapters 14 and 18), ventilation rate (chapters 11 and 18), swallowing, salivation, sneezing, vomiting and coughing.

16.3 The phylogenetic development of the nervous system

A study of animal phylogeny shows a progressive increase in structural and functional complexity from protozoans to mammals. Several trends and patterns in the organisation of organ systems have become established and this is clearly reflected in the development of the nervous system as shown by a study of irritability in protozoans, cnidarians, annelids, arthropods and mammals.

In protozoans the ability to respond to a stimulus resides within a single cell of the organism. There is no spatial separation between the stimulus and response and the cell functions as both receptor and effector. Investigations carried out on irritability in *Amoeba* suggested that the mechanism of transducing a stimulus, for example prodding it with a blunt needle, involves the cell surface membrane and the granular endoplasm. The mechanism probably involves the release of energy by an ATP/ATPase system which provides energy for amoeboid movement (section 17.6.1) thus enabling *Amoeba* to make an avoidance response to the stimulus.

The development of multicellular organisation in the cnidarians has led to an increase in the spatial separation of stimulus and response, receptor and effector. Fortunately, the attainment of the multicellular state was accompanied by tissue differentiation and the appearance of nerve cells linking receptor to effector, thus overcoming difficulties of spatial separation. The nervous system of primitive cnidarians, for example *Hydra*, is a **nerve net** or **plexus** composed of a single layer of short multipolar neurones in synaptic contact throughout the organism. Impulses spread out in all directions from the point of stimulation and at each synapse an impulse is lost. This impulse is used, effectively, to 'charge' the synapse so that subsequent impulses can cross the synapse. This process is called **facilitation** and, since an impulse is lost at each synapse in facilitating (making easier) the passage of the next impulse, the mechanism of conduction is called **decremental conduction**. Nervous conduction in these organism is therefore slow, due to the number of synapses to cross, and spatially restricted because impulses die out as they progress outwards from the stimulus. The system is useful in producing localised

responses, say within a tentacle, but of little value to the whole organism unless the stimulus is **intense** or **prolonged**. In most cnidarians, such as jellyfish and sea anemones, in addition to the nerve net there is a system of elongate bipolar neurones arranged in tracts, called **through conduction tracts**, and able to transmit impulses rapidly over considerable distances and without apparent loss. This system enables the organism to make fairly rapid responses of the whole body to harmful stimuli, such as the withdrawal of tentacles, and this foreshadows the aggregation of neurones into nerves seen in higher organisms.

In the annelids the association of neurones into nerves has resulted in a nervous system consisting of a single longitudinal tract, the **ventral nerve cord**, running the entire length of the organism. This consists of paired segmentally arranged ganglia joined by connecting neurones and supplying segmental nerves to the tissues of each segment as shown in fig 17.38.

As a result of the unidirectional method of locomotion, annelids possess a head. This structure is specialised to assist with feeding and, since it is the first part of the body to come into contact with new environmental situations, it contains all the sensory structures necessary to detect stimuli associated with these situations. The increased input of sensory information from these receptors to the nervous system is dealt with by the enlarged anterior end of the nerve cord. This concentration of feeding apparatus, sense organs and nervous tissue into one region is called **cephalisation**. It should be emphasised though that the term applies to the development of *all* the features associated with the head and not just the nervous tissue. The degree of cephalisation shown by an organism varies according to the level of structural complexity attained by the organism and its mode of life.

The annelid nervous system shows all the basic features found in all other non-vertebrate groups. The enlarged anterior region of the nerve cord forms a pair of **cerebral ganglia** situated above the pharynx and linked to the ventral nerve cord by a pair of **circumpharyngeal connectives**.

In arthropods the basic organisation of the nervous system is almost identical to that of annelids except that the cerebral ganglia overlie the oesophagus and consequently are linked to the ventral nerve cord by **circumoesophageal connectives**. Cerebral ganglia are analogous to the vertebrate brain but do not possess the same degree of autonomy over the entire nervous system as seen in vertebrates. For example, removal of the head of a non-vertebrate has very little effect on movement, whereas in vertebrates the brain initiates and controls all movement of the body. Non-vertebrate cerebral ganglia, in fact, appear to act as relay centres between receptors and effectors and their role in integration and coordination is limited to a few neuroendocrine responses such as the timing of reproductive activities in annelids and the control of ecdysis and moulting in arthropods (section 21.7.3).

16.4 Sensory receptors

The coordinated activity of an organism relies upon a continuous input of information from the internal and external environments. If this information leads to a change in activity or behaviour of the animals, it is a **stimulus**. The specialised region of the body detecting the stimulus is known as a **sensory receptor**.

The simplest and most primitive type of receptor consists of a single unspecialised primary sense cell composed of a single sensory neurone whose terminal end is capable of detecting the stimulus and giving rise to a nerve impulse passing to the central nervous system, for example, skin mechanoreceptors such as the **Pacinian corpuscle** (section 16.5.1). More complex receptors are known as **secondary sense cells**, and they consist of modified epithelial cells able to detect stimuli. These form synaptic connections with their sensory neurones which transmit impulses to the CNS, for example mammalian taste buds (fig 16.31). The most complex receptors are **sensory organs** composed of a large number of sense cells, sensory neurones and associated accessory structures. The mammalian eye and ear show the level of complexity which is attained by sense organs. In the eye there are two types of secondary sense cells, rods and cones, many connecting neurones and many accessory structures such as the lens and iris.

The accessory structures often serve the double function of eliminating the effects of unwanted stimuli and amplifying the effects of desired stimuli.

On the basis of the position of the receptor and the stimulus three types of receptor are identified:

(1) **exteroceptors** – these respond to stimuli originating outside the body, as with the ear and sound;
(2) **interoceptors** – these respond to stimuli originating inside the body, such as blood pressure and carbon dioxide receptors in the carotid arteries;
(3) **proprioceptors** – these respond to stimuli concerned with the relative positions and movements of muscles and the skeleton.

An alternative, and somewhat preferable, system of classification is based on the type of stimulus detected by the receptor, and this is shown in table 16.7.

Table 16.7. Types of receptors and the stimuli detected by them

Type of receptor	Type of stimulus energy	Nature of stimulus
photoreceptor	electromagnetic	light
electroreceptor	electromagnetic	electricity
mechanoreceptor	mechanical	sound, touch, pressure, gravity
thermoreceptor	thermal	temperature change
chemoreceptor	chemical	humidity, smell, taste

Animals only detect stimuli existing in one of the forms of energy shown in table 16.7. Structures transforming stimulus energy into electrical responses in axons are known as **transducers** and, in this respect, receptors act as **biological transducers**.

All receptors transform the energy of the stimulus into a localised non-propagated electrical response which initiates nerve impulses in the neurone leaving the receptor. Thus receptors **encode** a variety of stimuli into nerve impulses which pass into the central nervous system where they are decoded and utilised to produce the required responses as shown in fig 16.13b. The type of response and its extent and duration are all directly related to the nature of the stimulus.

16.4.1 The mechanism of transduction

All sensory cells are excitable cells, and they share with nerve cells and muscle cells the ability to respond to an appropriate stimulus by producing a rapid change in their electrical properties. When not stimulated, sensory cells are able to maintain a resting potential as described in section 16.1.1, but respond to a stimulus by producing a change in membrane potential. Bernard Katz, in 1950, using a specialised stretch receptor known as a muscle spindle was able to demonstrate the presence of a depolarisation in the immediate region of the sensory nerve ending in the muscle spindle. This localised depolarisation is found only in the sensory cell and is known as the **generator** or **receptor potential**. Subsequent investigations involving intracellular recordings, made by penetrating the membranes of receptor cells in muscle spindles and the mechanoreceptors of the skin, the Pacinian corpuscles, have revealed the following information about transduction:

(1) the generator potential results from the stimulus producing a non-selective increase in the permeability of the sensory cell membrane to sodium and potassium ions which flow down their electrochemical gradients;
(2) the magnitude of the generator potential varies with the intensity of the stimulus;
(3) when the generator potential reaches a predetermined threshold it gives rise to a propagated action potential in the sensory axon leading from the sensory cell (fig 16.24);
(4) the frequency of the nerve impulses in the sensory axon is directly related to the intensity of the stimulus.

This latter point was, in fact, established in Cambridge in 1926 by Lord Adrian, who demonstrated that sensory information is carried by all-or-nothing action potentials as a frequency code. We now know that only the generator potential exhibits an amplitude code but, following the attainment of a certain threshold value in the sensory neurone, this gives rise to a propagated all-or-nothing response in the sensory neurone.

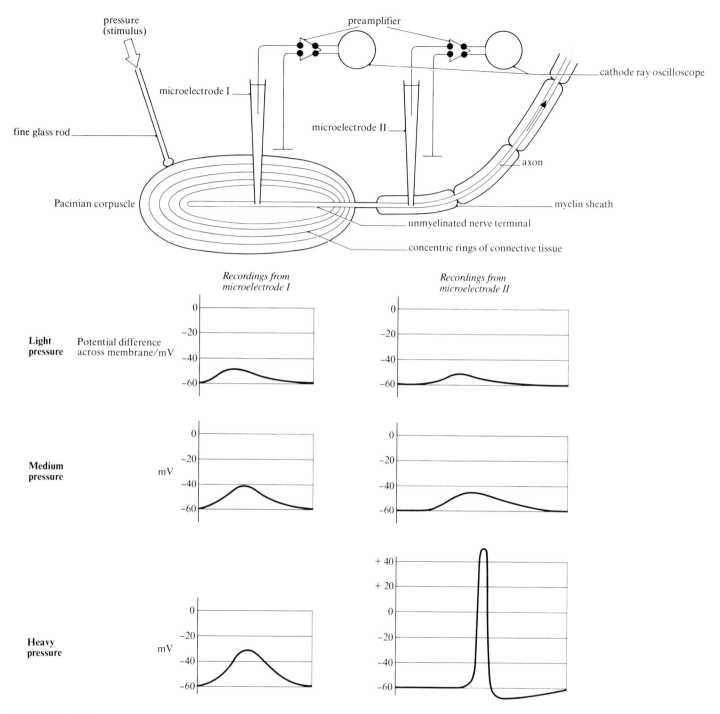

Fig 16.24 *The electrical activity recorded by two microelectrodes (I) and (II) inserted into (I) the axon terminal within a Pacinian corpuscle and (II) the axon of the sensory neurone leaving the corpuscle. As the pressure on the fine glass rod, acting as the stimulus is increased, the amplitude of the localised, non-propagated generator potential increases and at a certain threshold produces a propagated action potential in the sensory neurone*

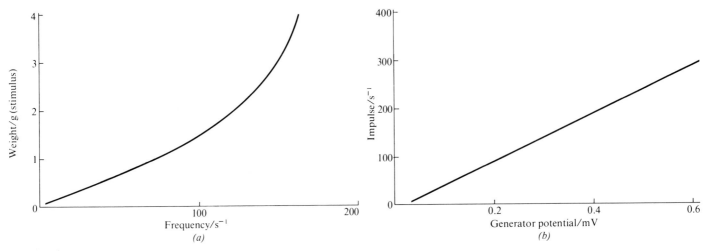

16.25 *Graphs obtained during investigations on frog muscle spindles (a) after Adrian and Zotterman, 1926 and (b) after Katz, 1950*

16.7 Study the graphs shown in fig 16.25, obtained from investigations on frog muscle spindle, and describe the relationship between stimulus, generator potential, and frequency of nerve impulses.

16.4.2 Properties of receptors

The input to the central nervous system from receptors provides the organism with all the essential information to enable it to survive. As a rule a single receptor cell cannot monitor the whole range of a given type of stimulus, however the organism needs to have information concerning the strength or intensity of each stimulus in order to produce the correct response. Receptors have two major properties which increase their effectiveness and efficiency. These are **sensitivity** and **discrimination** and they are obtained by the following structural and functional adaptations.

Parallel sensory cells with various thresholds

Some sense organs, such as stretch receptors in muscle, are composed of many sense cells having a range of thresholds. Those having a low threshold are stimulated by weak stimuli, and as the strength of the stimuli increases they respond by producing an increasing number of impulses in the sensory neurone leaving the sense cell. At a given point saturation occurs and the frequency of impulses in the neurone cannot be increased. A further increase in intensity of stimulus will excite sense cells with higher thresholds, and these too will produce a frequency of responses which is proportional to the intensity of the applied stimulus. In this way the range of receptors is extended (fig 16.26).

Adaptation

Most receptors initially respond to a strong constant stimulus by producing a high frequency of impulses in the sensory neurone. The frequency of these impulses gradually declines and this reduction in response, with time, is called **adaptation**. For example, on entering a room you may immediately notice a clock ticking but after a while become unaware of its presence. The rate and extent of adaptation in a receptor cell is related to its function and there are two types, rapidly and slowly adapting receptors.

Rapidly adapting receptors (phasic receptors) respond to changes in stimulus level by producing a high frequency of impulses at the moments when the stimulus is switched 'on' or 'off'. For example, the Pacinian corpuscle and other receptors concerned with touch and the detection of sudden changes act in this way and register the *dynamic* aspects of a stimulus.

Slowly adapting receptors (tonic receptors) register a constant stimulus with a slowly decreasing frequency of impulses. For example, crayfish stretch receptors register *static* aspects of a stimulus associated with more or less steady conditions.

Adaptation is thought to be related to a decrease in the permeability of the receptor membrane to ions due to sustained stimulation. This progressively reduces the amplitude and duration of the generator potential and when this falls below the threshold level the sensory neurone ceases to fire.

The advantage of adaptation of sense cells is that it provides the animal with precise information about changes in the environment. At other times the cells remain quiescent, thus preventing overloading of the central nervous system with irrelevant and unmanageable information. This contributes to the overall efficiency and economy of the nervous system and enables it to ignore static background information and to concentrate on monitoring aspects of the environment having most survival value.

Convergence and summation

A high degree of sensitivity is achieved in many sense organs by an anatomical arrangement of sense cells and

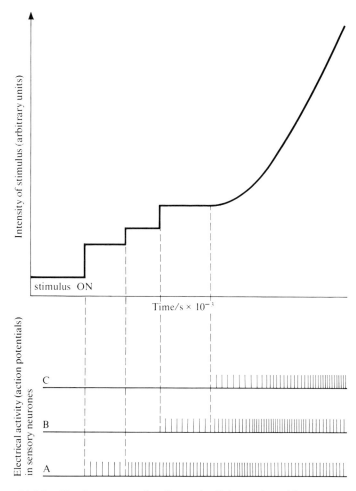

16.26 *The frequency of action potentials produced in sensory neurones leaving three sense cells, **A**, **B** and **C**, each having different threshold levels. In the case of **B** and **C** the point at which the receptors become active coincides with the saturation point of the sense cell with the lower threshold*

sensory neurones known as **convergence**. In such cases, several sense cells are connected to, or converge on, a single sensory neurone. These cells are characteristically small, are found in large numbers and are extremely sensitive to stimuli. Whilst the effect of a stimulus on a single one of these cells would not produce a response in the sensory neurone, the combined effect of the simultaneous stimulation of several cells is cumulative. This cumulative stimulatory effect produced in the sensory neurone is known as **summation** and is similar in function to the summative effect described for synapses in section 16.1.2 and effectors in sections 16.6 and 17.4.5. A good example of convergence and summation is provided by rod cells of the mammalian retina. Some of these cells are capable of detecting a single quantum of light, but the generator potential produced is inadequate to produce a propagated action potential in a neurone of the optic nerve. However, several rods (ranging from two or three to several hundred) are connected to a single optic nerve fibre by a bipolar neurone. Stimulation of at least six rods is required to produce an impulse in an optic nerve fibre. The

increased **visual sensitivity** produced by this arrangement of rods is highly adapted to dim-light vision and is well developed in nocturnal species such as owls, badgers and foxes. This high degree of sensitivity, however, is linked with a decrease in visual precision, as may be observed when attempting to read in poor light. In the human eye and that of many other diurnal species (active during daylight) this problem is counteracted by the presence of cones which, with few exceptions, do not show convergence or summation. What cones lose in sensitivity they gain in **discrimination** as described in section 16.5.4.

Spontaneous activity

Some receptors produce nerve impulses in sensory neurones in the absence of stimulation. This system is not as meaningless as it might appear as it has two important advantages. Firstly it increases the sensitivity of the receptor by enabling it to make an immediate response to a stimulus that would normally be too small to produce a response in the sensory neurone. Any slight change in the intensity of the stimulus will now produce a change in the frequency of impulses along the sensory neurone. Secondly the direction of the change in stimulus can be registered by this system as an increase or decrease in the frequency of the response in the sensory neurone. For example, infra-red receptors in pits in the face of the rattlesnake which act as direction finders in locating prey and predators show spontaneous activity and are sensitive and able to discriminate increases or decreases in temperature of 0.1 °C.

Feedback control of receptors

The threshold of some sense organs can be raised or lowered by efferent impulses from the central nervous system. This 'resets' the sensitivity of the receptor to respond to different ranges of stimulus intensities with equal sensitivity. In many cases the mechanism of control involves feedback from the receptors, which produces changes in accessory structures enabling the receptor cells to function over a new range. This occurs, for example, in the muscle spindle and the iris of the eye.

Lateral inhibition

This phenomenon is important in increasing both sensitivity and discrimination in a receptor. The basic principle involves the mutual inhibition of response from adjacent sense cells when stimulated. Investigations carried out on the individual sense organs (**ommatidia**) of the compound eye of the horseshoe crab, *Limulus*, revealed that adjacent ommatidia produce a lower response if stimulated simultaneously than they do if stimulated independently. This is significant in accentuating the differences between two adjacent areas stimulated by different intensities. Fig 16.27 shows a model system based on visual perception and demonstrates how light falling on two adjacent receptors is enhanced at the bright/dim boundary thereby 'highlighting' the edge. This effect forms the basis of the optical illusion shown in fig 16.28.

Lateral inhibition in the human eye increases the resolving power or **visual acuity** of the eye. The resolving power of a system is its ability to distinguish two or more stimuli of equal intensity as separate stimuli. For example, the distance at which two black lines of equal density can be seen as separate lines and not as a single line is a measure of the eyes' resolving power. The visual acuity of the human eye is very high and in part is due to lateral inhibition but mainly to the anatomical arrangement of cones in the retina. Light from two sources falling on the same or immediately adjacent cones is not resolved as coming from two sources. However, light from two sources falling on cones separated by only one cone can be perceived as separate sources. Approximately 95% of the seven million

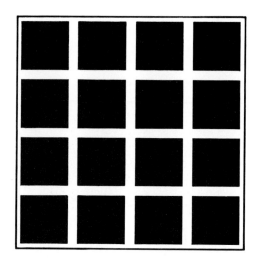

Fig 16.28 *The above diagram illustrates an optical illusion which may be caused by lateral inhibition. The grey spots at the intersections of the white lines are thought to be produced by the image of the white lines inhibiting adjacent receptors which fail to be stimulated. The lack of stimulation from the dark areas and the stimulation from the white lines combine to produce the sensation of grey at the intersections of the white lines*

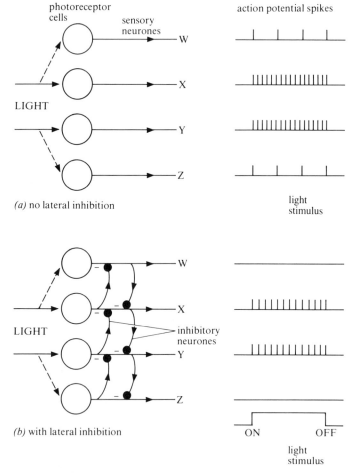

(a) no lateral inhibition

(b) with lateral inhibition

Fig 16.27 *The diagram shows action potentials recorded from four adjacent ommatidia* **W**, **X**, **Y** *and* **Z**. **X** *and* **Y** *are stimulated directly by a narrow beam of light whilst* **W** *and* **Z** *are stimulated weakly by light scattered from the beam stimulating* **X** *and* **Y**. *In (a) with no lateral inhibition* **W** *and* **Z** *are excited and action potentials are recorded in their sensory neurones. In (b) with lateral inhibition direct stimulation excites* **X** *and* **Y** *and inhibitory neurones linking these with* **W** *and* **Z** *prevent any propagated action potentials being set up in the latter. This mechanism sharpens the contrast, as perceived by the cerebral ganglia, as a result of the differential illumination of adjacent photoreceptors. The same principle applies to the rods and cones of the vertebrate eye (after Lamb, Ingram, Johnson and Pitman, 1980)*

cones in the eye are situated within a 1 mm diameter **fovea** in the centre of the retina. Here they each have a bipolar neurone connecting them to their *own* sensory neurone of the optic nerve. It is the absence of convergence and the close packing of cones in the fovea that is responsible for the high visual acuity.

16.5 Structure and function of receptors

The sensations of taste and smell in humans are due to chemical substances exciting specific chemo-receptors and play important roles in feeding, avoiding unfavourable environments and other behavioural activities involving courtship, mating and social organisation.

16.5.1 Mechanoreceptors

Mechanoreceptors are considered the most primitive type of receptors and may respond to a range of mechanical stimuli such as pressure, gravity, displacement and vibration.

Touch and pressure

The distinction between touch and pressure is one of degree, and the detection of these stimuli depends on the position of the receptors within the skin. Touch receptors sensitive to small pressures are found close to the surface of the skin and are composed of many fine, free endings of sensory neurones (primary sense cells). These may be situated in the epidermis or attached to hairs in the hair follicle and respond to deformation of the skin and hairs.

Touch receptors are localised in certain regions of the body and account for the increased sensitivity in these regions. For example, two stimuli may be resolved by the tip of the tongue when 1 mm apart whereas this is only possible at a distance of 60 mm in the middle of the back.

Specialised sense organs known as **Meissner's corpuscles** are situated immediately beneath the epidermis and respond to touch (fig 16.29). They consist of the single convoluted ending of a neurone enclosed within a fluid-filled capsule. **Pacinian corpuscles** are situated in the dermis, joints, tendons, muscles and mesenteries of the gut, and consist of the ending of a single neurone surrounded by connective tissue lamellae. They respond to pressure (fig 16.24).

All touch and pressure receptors are thought to produce a generator potential as a result of deformation of the receptor membrane leading to an increase in the permeability of the receptor cell to ions.

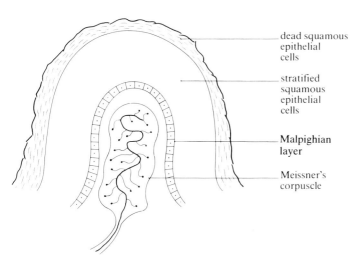

Fig 16.29 *Simplified diagram of a touch receptor, Meissner's corpuscle, showing its relationship to the skin*

dead squamous epithelial cells

stratified squamous epithelial cells

Malpighian layer

Meissner's corpuscle

Muscle spindle

Specialised proprioceptors called muscle spindles have been found in the muscles of mammals, amphibia, crustacea and insects. They respond to changes in tension in the muscles and act as stretch receptors in all activities associated with the control of muscular contraction. The muscle spindle has three main functions, one static and two dynamic:

(1) to provide information to the central nervous system on the state and position of muscles and structures attached to them, a static function;

(2) to initiate reflex contraction of the muscle and return it to its previous length when stimulated by a load, a dynamic function;

(3) to alter the state of tension in the muscle and reset it to maintain a new length, a dynamic function.

The structure and function of the muscle spindle is described in detail in section 17.5.4.

16.5.2 Thermoreceptors

Two types of sense organs found in the dermis are claimed to be responsible for detecting the temperature of the skin. **Organs of Ruffini** are thought to respond to warm temperatures and **bulbs of Krause** are thought to respond to low temperatures. However, it is almost certain that the many free nerve endings in the skin are the major structures detecting temperature (fig 16.30).

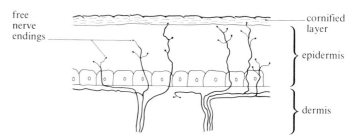

free nerve endings

cornified layer

epidermis

dermis

Fig 16.30 *Free nerve endings in the epidermis and dermis which detect temperature*

16.5.3 Chemoreceptors

The sensations of taste and smell in humans are due to chemical substances exciting specific chemoreceptors and play important roles in feeding, avoiding unfavourable environments and other behavioural activities involving courtship, mating and social organisation.

Taste

Many of the sensations registered as taste are really flavours which are detected both by smell and taste receptors. If a person is blindfolded and pinches his nostrils, thus preventing chemical stimuli from reaching the smell receptors, whilst chewing onion and apple, it is unlikely that the difference between them will be distinguished. This illustrates the lack of sensitivity of taste receptors. Taste or **gustation** is detected by receptor molecules situated in microvilli projecting from sensory cells sunk into goblet-shaped organs known as **taste-buds** found on the top and sides of the tongue (fig 16.31).

There are four 'taste sensations' and the uneven distribution of their receptors may be demonstrated by applying the following stimulating substances to various areas of the tongue: sweet – saccharin; sour – weak acid; salt – sea salt; bitter – quinine. The distribution of these receptor areas is shown in fig 16.31*b*. No correlation has yet been found between the chemical structure of a substance and the taste produced. It is assumed, however, that the production of a generator potential within the receptor cell depends upon substances either penetrating the receptor membrane or attaching to specific receptor sites on the surface of the receptor cell membrane. Taste receptors require higher concentrations of stimulating substances than smell receptors.

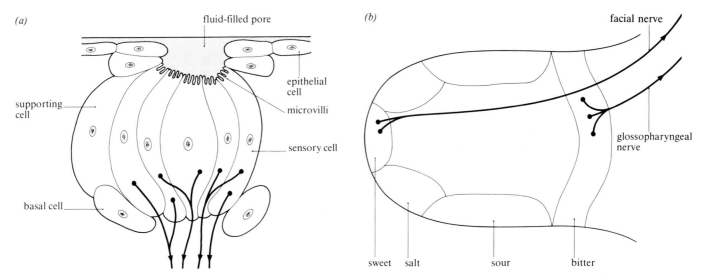

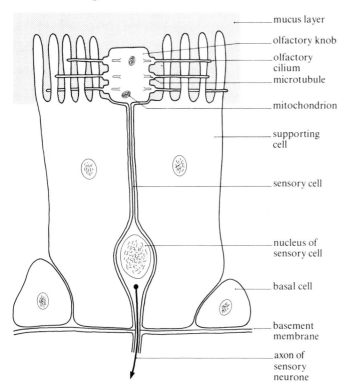

Fig 16.31 *(a) Simplified diagram showing the structure of a tastebud. Substances to be tasted dissolve in the fluid surrounding the microvilli and diffuse to receptor cells embedded in the microvilli. (Redrawn and reproduced with permission, from Schmidt, 1978). (b) Diagram showing the symmetrical distribution of taste receptors of the human tongue and their innervation*

Smell

The sensation of smell is more acute than that of taste and is due to airborne odoriferous substances dissolving in the layer of mucus and stimulating an area of olfactory epithelium situated high up in the nasal passages. Each nostril has an area of 2.5 cm² containing three types of cells as shown in fig 16.32.

Fig. 16.32 *Simplified diagram showing the structure and relationships between sensory cell, supporting cell and basal cell in the olfactory epithelium. Receptor molecules to odoriferous substances are located in the membranes of the olfactory cilia*

Amoore in 1963 proposed a stereochemical theory of olfaction that related the properties of receptor sites on the cilia-like projections of the olfactory cells to the shape and dimension of odour-producing molecules. He proposed that there are seven primary odours such as putrid, pungent, peppery etc. and that they each have specific receptor sites. About 10 000 odours can be differentiated, and this is thought to be due to varying degrees of stimulation of these seven types of receptor sites. Water- and lipid-soluble substances produce the strongest sensations of smell.

Taste and smell in insects

The sense of taste in insects is extremely sensitive and has been studied in detail. Taste organs in insects are known as **taste hairs** and they are situated on the antennae, maxillary and labial palps and feet of insects. They consist of a hollow structure containing endings of sensory neurones and are sensitive to both chemical substances and displacement.

In the blowfly, *Calliphora*, there is a taste reflex which extends the proboscis when the legs are in contact with acceptable food substances. The response threshold in blowfly to sucrose is as low as 0.8×10^{-4} M compared with 0.2×10^{-1} M in humans.

Despite these remarkably low thresholds for taste receptors the sensitivity of insects to smell is even greater. The olfactory receptors are usually situated on the antennae and have been extensively studied in moths. Female silk moths, *Bombyx mori*, are capable of attracting males of the same species at distances of several kilometres as a result of releasing a specific chemical substance. Substances, such as this sex attractant, that act as a form of communication within a species are known as **pheromones**. In one experiment a single silk moth female in a muslin cage attracted 40% of a large population of males released 4 km away. Several species that utilise pheromones over great distances have enlarged antennae carrying, in the case of the male polyphemus moth, *Telea polyphemus*, 15 × 10⁴ sensory cells. Molecules of sex attractant are absorbed on to the antennae as air filters through them.

Contrary to popular belief male moths do not fly up concentration gradients to find female moths. Instead they take off into the wind carrying the pheromone and zig-zag across the aerial trail reversing their direction whenever they lose the scent. Once in the immediate vicinity of the female, her exact location is determined by following the concentration gradient.

16.5.4 Mammalian eye

The mammalian eye is a sense organ composed of many sense cells, the rods and cones of the retina, sensory neurones of the optic nerve and a complex array of accessory structures. This arrangement enables the eye to convert light of various wavelengths reflected from objects at varying distances, the **visual field**, into electrical impulses which nerves transmit to the brain where an image of remarkable precision is perceived.

Light travels as waves of electromagnetic radiation and the wavelengths perceived by the human eye occupy a narrow band, the **visible spectrum**, from 380–760 nm (appendix A 1.7). Light is a form of energy and is emitted and absorbed in discrete packets called **quanta** or **photons**. The wavelengths of the visible spectrum carry sufficient energy in each quantum of radiation to produce a photochemical response in the sense cells of the eye.

The camera and the eye work on the same basic principles and these are:
(1) controlling the amount of light entering the structure;
(2) focusing images of the external world by means of a lens system;
(3) registering the image on a sensitive surface;
(4) processing the 'captured' images to produce a pattern which can be 'seen'.

Structure and function of the human eye

The eyes are held in protective bony sockets of the skull called **orbits** by four **rectus** muscles and two **oblique** muscles which control eye movements. Each human eyeball is about 24 mm in diameter and weighs 6–8 g. Most of the eye is composed of accessory structures concerned with bringing the visual field to the photoreceptor cells situated in the innermost layer of the eye, the **retina**. The eye is composed of three concentric layers: the sclera (sclerotic coat) and cornea; the choroid, ciliary body, lens and iris; and the retina, and is supported by the hydrostatic pressure (3.3 kPa) of the aqueous and vitreous humours.

The gross structure of the human eye is shown in fig 16.33 and brief notes on the function of the various parts are given below.

Sclera – external covering of eye; very tough, containing collagen fibres, protects and maintains shape of eyeball.

Cornea – transparent front part of the sclera; the curved surface acts as a main structure refracting (bending) light towards the retina.

Conjunctiva – thin transparent layer of cells protecting the cornea and continuous with the epithelium of eyelids; the conjunctiva does not cover the cornea overlying the iris.

Eyelid – protects the cornea from mechanical and chemical damage and the retina from bright light by reflex action.

Choroid – rich in blood vessels supplying the retina and covered with pigment cells preventing reflection of light within the eye.

Ciliary body – junction of sclera and cornea; contains tissue, blood vessels and ciliary muscles.

Ciliary muscles – circular sheet of smooth muscle fibres forming bundles of circular and radial muscles which alter the shape of the lens during accommodation.

Suspensory ligament – attaches the ciliary body to the lens.

Lens – transparent, elastic biconvex structure; provides fine adjustment for focusing light on to the retina and separates the aqueous and vitreous humours.

Aqueous humour – clear solution of salts secreted by the ciliary body, finally draining into the blood through the canal of Schlemm.

Iris – circular, muscular diaphragm containing the pigment giving eye its colour; it separates the aqueous humour region into anterior and posterior chambers and controls the amount of light entering eye.

Pupil – opening in iris; all light enters eye through this.

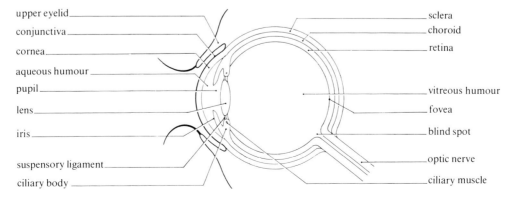

Fig 16.33 *Structure of the mammalian eye*

Vitreous humour – clear semi-solid substance supporting the eyeball.

Retina – contains the photoreceptor cells, rods and cones, and cell bodies and axons of neurones supplying the optic nerve.

Fovea – most sensitive part of retina, contains cones only; most light rays are focused here.

Optic nerve – bundle of nerve fibres carrying impulses from the retina to the brain.

Blind spot – point where the optic nerve leaves eye; there are no rods or cones here, therefore it is not light-sensitive.

> **16.8** List, in order, the structures through which light passes before striking the retina.

Accommodation

Accommodation is the reflex mechanism by which light rays from an object are brought to focus on the retina. It involves two processes and these will be considered separately.

Reflex adjustment of pupil size. In bright light the circular muscle of the iris diaphragm contracts, the radial muscle relaxes, the pupil becomes smaller and less light enters the eye, preventing damage to the retina (fig 16.34). In poor light the opposite muscular contractions and relaxations occur. The added advantage of reducing the pupil size is that it increases the **depth of focus** of the eye so that any displacement of the sense cells in the retina will not impair the focus.

Refraction of light rays. Light rays from distant objects (> 6 m) are parallel when they strike the eye. Light rays from near objects (< 6 m) are diverging when they strike the eye. In both cases the light rays must be **refracted** or bent to focus on the retina and refraction must be greater for light from near objects. The normal eye is able to accommodate light from objects from about 25 cm to infinity. Refraction occurs when light passes from one medium into another with a different refractive index, and this occurs at the air–corneal surface and at the lens. The degree of refraction at the corneal surface cannot be varied and depends on the angle at which light strikes the cornea (which, in turn, depends upon the distance of the object from the cornea). Most refraction occurs here, and consequently the function of the lens is to produce the final refraction that brings light to a sharp focus on the retina; this is regulated by the ciliary muscles. The state of

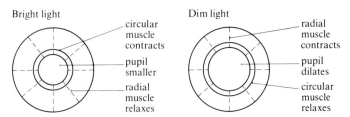

Fig 16.34 *The iris/pupil response to variations in light intensity*

Bright light
- circular muscle contracts
- pupil smaller
- radial muscle relaxes

Dim light
- radial muscle contracts
- pupil dilates
- circular muscle relaxes

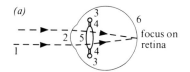 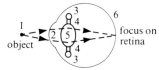

Light from distant object
(a)
focus on retina

1 Parallel light rays reach eye
2 Cornea refracts (bends) light rays
3 Circular ciliary muscle relaxed
4 Suspensory ligament taut
5 Lens pulled out thin
6 Light focused on retina

Light from near object
focus on retina

1 Diverging light rays reach eye
2 Cornea refracts (bends) light rays
3 Circular ciliary muscle contracted
4 Suspensory ligament slack
5 Elastic lens more convex
6 Light focused on retina

(b)

Fig 16.35 *Events occurring during accommodation of light rays from objects at various distances, (a) side views of eye, (b) front views of eye*

Table 16.8. Relationship between structures changing the shape of the lens and the degree of refraction

Ciliary muscle	Tension in suspensory ligament	Radius of curvature	Refraction
contracted	no tension	decreased (lens thick)	increased
relaxed	taut	increased (lens thin)	decreased

contraction of the ciliary muscles changes the tension on the suspensory ligaments. This acts on the natural elasticity of the lens which causes it to change its shape (radius of curvature) and thus the degree of refraction. As the radius of curvature of the lens decreases it becomes thicker and the amount of refraction increases. The complete relationship between these three structures and refraction is shown in table 16.8. Fig 16.35 shows the changes occurring in the eye during accommodation to light from distant and near objects.

The image produced by the eye on the retina is inverted and reversed but the mental image is perceived in the correct position because the brain learns to accept an inverted reversed image as normal.

Structure of the retina

The retina develops as an outgrowth of the forebrain called the **optic vesicle**. During the embryonic formation of the eye the photoreceptor cells of the retina turn inwards (invaginate) and lie against the choroid layer. The cells are covered by the cell bodies and axons linking the photoreceptor cells to the brain as shown in fig 16.36.

The retina is composed of three layers of cells each containing a characteristic type of cell. First there is the **photoreceptor layer** (outermost layer) containing the photosensitive cells, the **rods** and **cones**, partially embedded in the microvilli of pigment epithelium cells of the

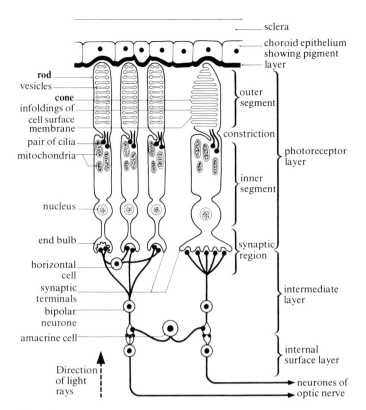

rod
vesicles
cone
infoldings of
cell surface
membrane
pair of cilia
mitochondria

nucleus

end bulb

horizontal
cell
synaptic
terminals
bipolar
neurone
amacrine cell

Direction
of light
rays

sclera
choroid epithelium
showing pigment
layer
outer
segment
constriction
inner
segment
synaptic
region

photoreceptor
layer

intermediate
layer

internal
surface layer

neurones of
optic nerve

Fig 16.36 *Diagrammatic section through the retina of the eye showing the ultrastructure of a rod and a cone. Connections between the sensory cells and the neurones of the optic nerve are shown in the inner segment. Light rays must pass through the ganglion cells and the intermediate layers before reaching the rods and cones*

choroid. Next is the **intermediate layer** containing bipolar neurones with synapses connecting the photoreceptor layer to the cells of the third layer. Horizontal and amacrine cells found in this layer enable lateral inhibition to occur. The third layer is the **internal surface layer** containing ganglion cells with dendrites in contact with bipolar neurones and axons of the optic nerve.

Structure and function of rods and cones

Rods and cones have an essentially similar structure as shown in fig 16.36 and their photosensitive pigments are attached to the outer surfaces of the membranes in the outer segment. They have four similar regions whose structure and function are summarised below.

Outer segment. This is the photosensitive region where light energy is converted into a generator potential. The entire outer segment is composed of flattened membranous vesicles containing the photosensitive pigments. Rods contain 600–1 000 of these vesicles stacked up like a pile of coins and they are enclosed by an outer membrane. Cones have fewer membranous vesicles and they are formed by repeated infoldings of the outer membrane.

Constriction. The outer segment is almost separated from the inner segment by an infolding of the

outer membrane. The two regions remain in contact by cytoplasm and a pair of cilia which pass between the two. These cilia consist of nine peripheral fibres only, the usual central two being absent.

Inner segment. This is an actively metabolic region. It is packed with mitochondria producing energy for visual processes, and polysomes for the synthesis of proteins involved in the production of the membranous vesicles and visual pigment. The nucleus is situated in this region.

Synaptic region. Here the cells form synapses with bipolar cells. **Diffuse bipolar cells** may have synapses with several rods. This is called synaptic convergence, and whilst it lowers visual acuity it increases visual sensitivity. **Monosynaptic bipolar cells** link *one* cone to *one* ganglion cell and this gives the cones greater visual acuity than rods. **Horizontal cells** and **amacrine cells** link certain numbers of rods together and cones together. This allows a certain amount of processing of visual information to occur before it leaves the retina, for instance these cells are involved in lateral inhibition.

Differences between rods and cones

Rods are more numerous than cones, 120×10^6 as opposed to 6×10^6, and have a different distribution. The thin elongate rods ($50 \times 3 \ \mu m$) are distributed uniformly throughout the retina except at the fovea, where the conical elongate cones ($60 \times 1.5 \ \mu m$) have their greatest concentration ($5 \times 10^4 \ mm^{-2}$). Since the cones are tightly packed together at the fovea this gives them higher visual acuity (section 16.4.2). Rods are much more sensitive to light than cones and respond to lower light intensities. Rods only contain one visual pigment, and being unable to discriminate colour are used principally for night vision. Cones contain three visual pigments and these enable the cones to differentiate colours. They are used principally in daylight. The rods have a lower visual acuity because they are less tightly packed together and they undergo synaptic convergence, but this latter point gives them increased collective sensitivity required for night vision.

> **16.9** Explain why synaptic convergence should increase visual sensitivity.
>
> **16.10** Explain why objects are seen more clearly at night by not looking directly at them.

The mechanism of photoreception

Rods contain the photosensitive pigment **rhodopsin** attached to the outer surface of the membranous vesicles. Rhodopsin, or **visual purple**, is a complex molecule formed by the reversible combination of a lipoprotein, **scotopsin**, and a small light-absorbing carotenoid molecule **retinene (retinol)**. The latter is an aldehyde derivative of vitamin A and exists in two isomeric forms according to the light conditions as shown in fig 16.37.

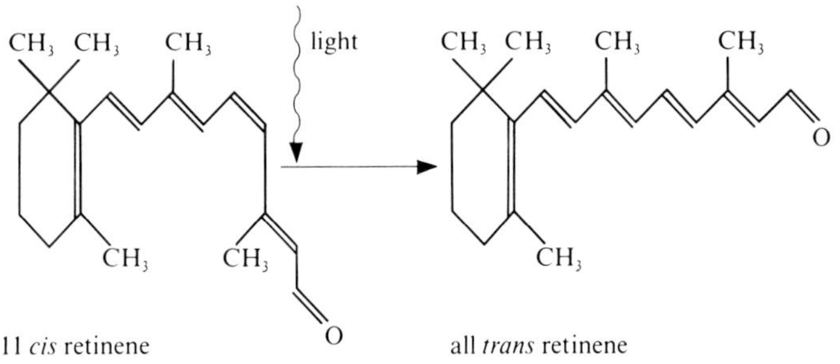

Fig 16.37 *The action of light changes the structure of retinene from the 11* cis *isomer to the all* trans *isomer*

When rhodopsin is exposed to light it is known that one photon of light will produce the above isomeric change. Retinene acts as a prosthetic group and is believed to occupy a certain site on the surface of the scotopsin molecule where it inhibits reactive groups in this molecule involved in initiating electrical activity in the rods. The exact mechanisms of photoreception are not yet known but it is thought that it involves two processes: first the isomeric conversion of 11 *cis* retinene to all *trans* retinene by the action of light, and second the decomposition of rhodopsin via a series of intermediate molecules into retinene and scotopsin, a process known as **bleaching**.

$$\text{rhodopsin} \xrightarrow{\text{bleaching}} \text{retinene} \quad + \quad \text{scotopsin}$$

Rhodopsin is reformed immediately in the absence of further light stimulation. All *trans* retinene is first converted into 11 *cis* retinene in the presence of the enzyme **retinene isomerase**, and is then recombined with scotopsin. This process is called '**dark adaptation**' and in total darkness it takes 30 min for all rods to adapt and the eyes to achieve maximum sensitivity. During the second process, however, the permeability of the outer segment membrane to sodium ions decreases whilst the inner segment continues to pump out sodium ions, thus creating increased negativity within the rod (fig 16.38). This situation gives rise to hyperpolarisation of the rod. This situation is exactly opposite to the effect normally found in sensory receptors where the stimulus produces a depolarisation and not a hyperpolarisation. The hyperpolarisation reduces the rate of release of excitatory transmitter substance from the rod which is released maximally during darkness. The bipolar neurone linked by synapses to the rod cell also responds by producing a hyperpolarisation, but the ganglion cells of the optic nerve supplied by the bipolar neurone respond to this by producing a propagated action potential.

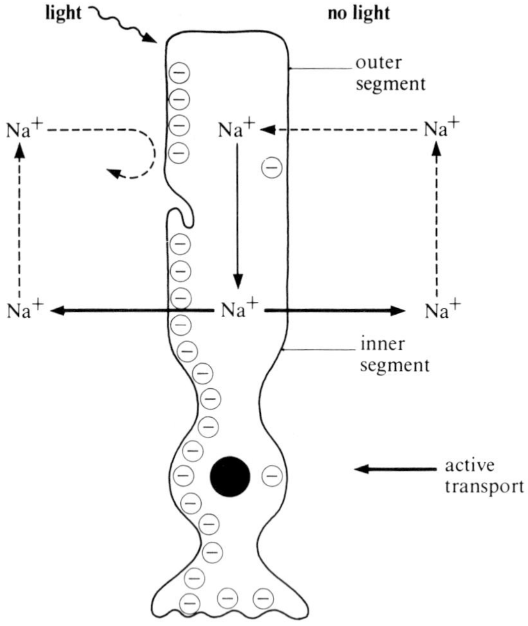

Fig 16.38 *Diagram of a rod showing the proposed changes in sodium permeability of the outer segment produced in the presence of light. The negative charges ⊖ on the right side of the rod indicate the normal resting potential whereas those on the left indicate the hyperpolarisation*

Table 16.9. Colours of the visible spectrum and approximate ranges of their wavelength

Colour	*Wavelength/nm*
red	above 620
orange	590–620
yellow	570–590
green	500–570
blue	440–500
violet	below 440

Colour vision

The human eye absorbs light from all wavelengths of the visible spectrum and perceives these as six colours broadly associated with particular wavelengths as shown in table 16.9. There are three types of cones each possessing a different pigment which electrophysiological investigations have shown absorb light of different wavelengths. There are red, green and blue cones.

Colour vision is explained in terms of the trichromacy theory, which states that different colours and shades are produced by the degree of stimulation of each type of cone produced by the light reflected from an object. For example, equal stimulation of all cones produces the colour sensation of white. The initial discrimination of colour occurs in the retina but the final colour perceived involves the integrative properties of the brain. The mixing effect of pigments forms the basis of colour television, photography and painting.

Colour-blindness. The complete absence of a particular cone or a shortage of one type can lead to various forms of colour-blindness or degrees of 'colour-weakness'. For example, a person lacking red or green cones is 'red–green colour-blind', whereas a person with a reduced number of either cones will have difficulty in distinguishing a range of red–green shades. Colour-blindness, or its extent, is determined using test charts, such as the Ishihara test charts, composed of a series of dots of several colours. Some charts bear a number which a person with normal colour vision can perceive, whilst the colour-blind sufferer sees a different number or no number at all.

Colour-blindness is a sex-linked recessive characteristic resulting in the absence of appropriate colour genes in the X chromosome. About 2% of men are red colour-blind, 6% are green colour-blind, but only 0.4% of women show any sign of colour-blindness.

> **16.11** A person places a green filter over one eye and a red filter over the other eye and looks at an object. Using the data given in table 16.9, describe and explain the apparent colour of the object.

Binocular vision and stereoscopic vision

Binocular vision occurs when the visual fields of both eyes overlap so that the fovea of both eyes are focused on the same object. It has several advantages over monocular vision and these include a larger visual field, damage to one eye being compensated for by the other, for example it cancels the effect of the blind spot, and it provides the basis of stereoscopic vision. Stereoscopic vision depends upon the eyes simultaneously producing slightly different retinal images which the brain resolves as one image. The more frontally the eyes are situated the greater the stereoscopic visual field. For example, humans have a total visual field of 180° and a stereoscopic visual field of 140°. The horse has laterally placed eyes with a limited forward stereoscopic visual field which it uses for viewing distant objects. For nearer objects the horse turns its head and uses monocular vision to examine details. Frontally placed eyes and centrally situated foveas, producing good visual acuity, are essential for good stereoscopic vision which provides an increased appreciation of size and perception of the depth and distance of objects. Stereoscopic vision is found mainly in predatory animals where it is vital when capturing prey by pouncing or swooping, as shown by members of the cat family, hawks and eagles. Animals which are hunted have laterally placed eyes giving wide visual fields but restricted stereoscopic vision, for instance the rabbit has a total binocular visual field of 360° and frontal stereoscopic vision of 26°. The resolution of the two retinal images produced in stereoscopic vision occurs in two areas of the brain called the **visual cortex**.

Visual pathways and the visual cortex

Nerve impulses generated in the retina are carried by the million or so neurones of the optic nerve to the visual cortex, which is situated in the occipital lobe at the rear base of the brain. Here each minute region of the retina,

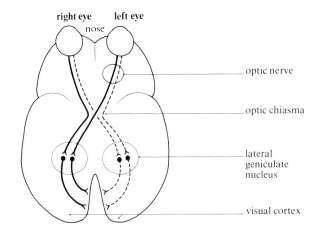

Fig 16.39 *Diagram of the human visual pathway as seen from the underside of the brain*

involving perhaps only a few rods and cones, is represented and it is here that the visual input is interpreted and we 'see'. However, what we see has meaning only after reference to other regions of the cortex and the temporal lobes, where previous visual information is stored and used in the analysis and identification of the present visual input (section 16.2.4). In humans, axons from the left side of the retina of both eyes pass to the left visual cortex and axons from the right side of each retina pass to the right visual cortex. The point where the axons from those regions of the retina closest to the nose cross is called the **optic chiasma** and is included in the visual pathway shown in fig 16.39. About 20% of the optic neurones do not pass to the visual cortex but enter the midbrain, where they are involved in reflex control of pupil size and eye movements.

16.5.5   Arthropod eye

Arthropods have two types of eye: the **simple eye (ocellus)**, which is found in some larval insects, and the more characteristic **compound eye**. The simple eye consists of a single lens covering a few light-sensitive cells and is able to discriminate light and dark but unable to produce images. These eyes are often found in conjunction with the larger, and functionally more important, compound eyes.

Each compound eye is composed of thousands of separate structures called **ommatidia**; for example there are 30 000 in the dragonfly. Each ommatidium is composed of two refractive bodies, a biconvex **lens** formed from cuticle and a **crystalline cone** secreted by **vitrellar cells**. These focus light on to a group of photosensitive **retinulae cells**, whose inner membranes bear microvilli which fuse together to form a structure called a **rhabdome**. The visual pigment is located within the microvilli of the rhabdome where the nerve impulses are set up and pass via the optic nerve to the cerebral ganglia. Each ommatidium is surrounded and isolated from the next by elongate pigment cells (fig 16.40).

Since each ommatidium receives light from a very small area, the image formed by the eye as a whole is made up of a series of separate overlapping points and is known as a

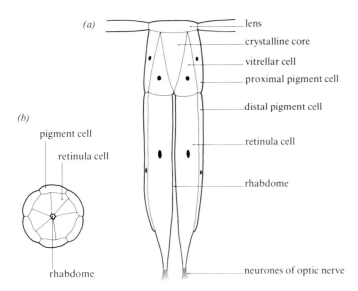

Fig 16.40 *Diagrams of (a) an LS of a single ommatidium and (b) TS of an ommatidium*

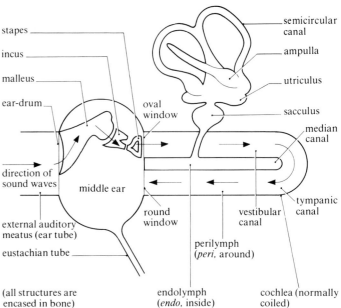

Fig 16.41 *Diagram showing the major structures in the mammalian ear involved in hearing and balance, (not to scale)*

mosaic image. This type of eye lacks the resolution of the mammalian eye but its overlapping images make it very sensitive to movements of objects.

16.5.6 Mammalian ear

The mammalian ear is a sense organ containing mechanoreceptors sensitive to gravity, displacement and sound. Movements and positions of the head relative to gravity are detected by the vestibular apparatus composed of the semicircular canals, the utricle and the saccule. All other structures of the ear are involved in receiving, amplifying and transducing sound energy into electrical impulses and producing the sensation of hearing in the auditory regions of the brain.

Structure and function of the ear

The ear consists of three sections specialising in different functions (fig 16.41). The **outer ear** consists of the **pinna**, strengthened by elastic cartilage, which focuses and collects sound waves into the **ear tube** (external auditory meatus); the sound waves cause the **tympanic membrane** (eardrum) to vibrate. In the **middle ear**, vibrations of the tympanic membrane are transmitted across to the membranous **oval window** by movement of the three ear ossicles, the **malleus, incus** and **stapes** (hammer, anvil and stirrup). A lever system between these three bones and the relative areas of contact of the malleus with the tympanic membrane (60 mm^2) and the stapes with the oval window (3.2 mm^2) amplifies the movement of the tympanic membrane 22 times. Damage to the tympanic membrane, due to atmospheric pressure changes, is prevented by a

connection between the air-filled middle ear and the pharynx, the **eustachian tube**. Finally there is the **inner ear** which consists of a complex system of canals and cavities within the skull bone containing a fluid called **perilymph**. Within these canals are membranous sacs filled with **endolymph** and sensory receptors. Auditory receptors are found in the cochlea and balance receptors are found in the utricle and saccule and the ampullae of the semicircular canals. The perilymph is enclosed by the membranes of the oval window and round window.

The nature of sound

Sound is produced by the vibration of particles within a medium. It travels as waves consisting of alternating regions of high and low pressure and will pass through liquids, solids and gases. The distance between two identical points on adjacent waves is the **wavelength** and this determines the **frequency** of **vibrations** or **pitch** (whether it sounds high or low). The human ear is sensitive to wavelengths between 40 and 20 000 Hz (cycles per second). The audible range of dogs reaches 40 000 Hz, and that of bats 100 000 Hz. Human speech frequencies vary between 500 and 3 000 Hz, and sensitivity to high frequencies decreases with age.

Tone depends upon the number of different frequencies making up the sound. For example, a violin and trumpet playing the same note, say middle C, produce the same fundamental frequency of 256 Hz but sound different. This is due to overtones or harmonics produced by the instrument which give it its distinctive quality or **timbre**. The same principle applies to the human voice and gives it its characteristic sound.

600

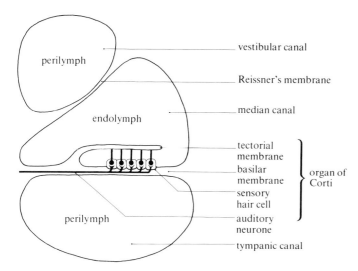

Fig 16.42 *Diagram of a TS cochlea showing the organ of Corti*

The **intensity** (loudness) of a sound depends upon the amplitude of the sound waves produced at the source and is a measure of the energy they contain.

Cochlea and hearing

The cochlea is a spiral canal 35 mm long and subdivided longitudinally by a membranous triangle into three regions as shown in fig 16.42.

Both the vestibular and tympanic canals contain perilymph, and the two canals are connected at the extreme end of the cochlea via a small hole, the **helicotrema**. The median canal contains endolymph. The **basilar membrane** separates the median and tympanic canals and supports sensory hair cells that can be brought into contact with the **tectorial membrane** above. This unit, consisting of basilar membrane, sensory cells and tectorial membrane, is called the **organ of Corti** and is the region where transduction of sound waves into electrical impulses occurs.

Sound waves transmitted from the ear tube to the oval window produce vibrations in the perilymph of the vestibular canal and these are transmitted via **Reissner's membrane** to the endolymph in the median canal. From here they are transferred to the basilar membrane and the perilymph in the tympanic canal, and are finally dissipated into the air of the middle ear as vibration of the round window.

The precise mechanism of transduction of pressure waves into nerve impulses is not known but is believed to involve relative movement of the basilar and tectorial membranes. Vibrations of the basilar membrane, induced by pressure waves, push the sensory hairs against the tectorial membrane and force the two membranes to slide past each other. The distortion produced in the sensory hairs due to the shearing forces causes a depolarisation of the sensory cells, the production of generator potentials and the initiation of action potentials in the axons of the auditory nerve.

Pitch and intensity discrimination

The ability to distinguish the pitch of a sound depends upon the frequency of the vibration producing movement of the basilar membrane and stimulating sensory cells in a specific region of the organ of Corti. These cells supply a particular region of the auditory cortex of the brain where the sensation of pitch is perceived. The basilar membrane becomes broader and more flexible as it passes from the base of the cochlea to its apex and its sensitivity to vibration changes along its length so that only low-frequency sounds can pass to the apex. High-frequency (pitch) sounds stimulate the basilar membrane at the *base* of the cochlea and low frequency sounds stimulate it at the *apical end*. A pure sound, consisting of a single frequency, will only stimulate one small area of the basilar membrane whereas most sounds, containing several frequencies, simultaneously stimulate many regions of the basilar membrane. The auditory cortex integrates the stimuli from these various regions of the basilar membrane and a 'single' blended sound is perceived.

The intensity or loudness of the sound depends upon each region of the basilar membrane containing a range of sensory cells responding to different thresholds of vibration. For example, a quiet sound at a given frequency may only stimulate a few sensory cells, whereas a louder sound at the same frequency would stimulate several other sensory cells having higher thresholds of vibration. This is an example of spatial summation.

Balance

Maintaining balance at rest and during movement of the body relies upon the brain receiving a continual input of sensory information concerning the position of various parts of the body. Information from proprioceptors in joints and muscles indicates the positions and state of the limbs, but vital information related to position and movement of the head is provided by the **vestibular apparatus** of the ear, the **utricle, saccule** and **semicircular canals**.

The basic sensory receptors within these structures consist of cells which have hair-like extensions, **hair cells**, attached to dense structures supported in the **endolymph**. Movement of the head results in deflection of the hairs and the production of a generator potential in the hair cells.

Regions of the walls of the utricle and saccule called **maculae** contain receptor cells which have their hair-like processes embedded in a gelatinous mass containing granules of calcium carbonate called an **otoconium**. Otoconia respond to the pull of gravity acting at right-angles to the Earth's surface and are mainly responsible for detecting the direction of movement of the head with respect to gravity.

The utricle responds to vertical movements of the head and the otoconia produce maximum stimulation when pulling the receptor hairs downwards, such as when the body is upside down.

The saccule responds to lateral (sideways) movement of the head. The hair cells of the saccule are horizontal when

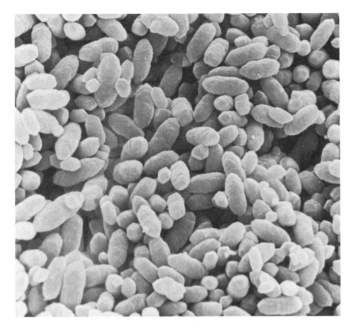 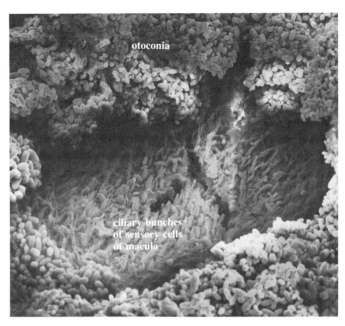

Fig 16.43 *Scanning electron micrographs of the internal structure of the ear. (a) the otoconia and (b) the otoconial layer with a portion removed to show the sensory cells of the macula beneath it*

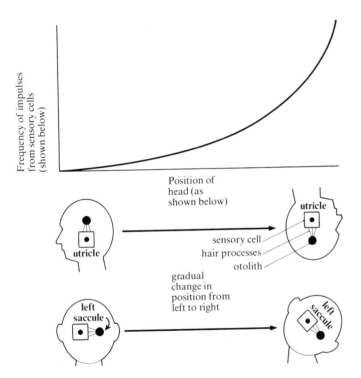

Fig 16.44 *Graph showing the effect of head position on the activity of receptor cells of the utricle and saccule*

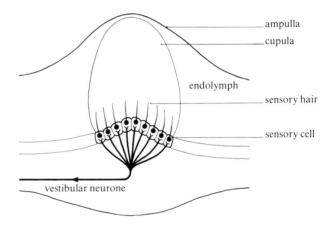

Fig 16.45 *Diagram showing a TS through the ampulla of a semicircular canal*

The three semicircular canals are arranged in three planes at right-angles to each other and detect the direction and rate of change of position of the head. At the base of each canal is a swelling, the **ampulla**, containing a conical gelatinous structure, the **cupula**. This encloses the hair-like projections of the receptor cells. The cupula fully extends across the ampulla (fig 16.45). Rotational movement of the head, semicircular canals and cupula is resisted by the inertia of the endolymph which remains stationary. This produces a relative displacement of the cupula which is bent in the opposite direction to the head movement. The receptor cells respond by producing generator potentials leading to propagated action potentials in the vestibular neurones. The direction and rate of displacement are both detected by the receptor cells. Linear acceleration is detected by both the maculae and cupulae.

the head is upright. Tilting of the head to the left produces a differential response from left and right saccules. The left receives increased stimulation as the otoconia pull downwards on the hairs whereas decreased stimulation occurs on the right. These displacements produce impulses passing to the cerebellum where the orientation of the head is perceived.

16.6   Effectors – the endocrine system

An effector is a differentiated structure, such as a cell, tissue, organ or organ system, performing a specific reaction relative to the environment in response to a stimulus from the nervous system. The most widespread and important effectors are those involved in movement and secretion.

Organisms responding to external stimuli by some form of movement or locomotion may utilise amoeboid, ciliary, flagellate or muscular movements, according to their structure and mode of life, in order to make the response. Details of these mechanisms can be found in chapter 17. In the case of multicellular organisms all types of movement may be involved in response to internal stimuli, and examples include the amoeboid movement of white blood cells through capillary walls to a site of infection in the tissues, the increased movement of cilia in the trachea in response to infection in the lungs, the activation of sperm flagella in response to secretions of the vagina, and reflex contractions of the peristaltic muscles of the oesophagus in response to a food bolus.

Other stimuli, which may be external or internal, bring about a response in the organism involving secretory activity of either an exocrine gland or an endocrine gland (section 8.3.3). For example, exocrine responses may be stimulated by particles of dirt in the eye causing secretion of tears from the tear glands, acidic food in the duodenum causing the release of pancreatic juice and damage to a joint causing an increased production of synovial fluid. Endocrine glands too respond to a variety of stimuli, for example the release of insulin by the cells of the islets of Langerhans in response to rising blood glucose levels, the release of human chorionic gonadotrophin at the beginning of pregnancy by the uterus wall following implantation by a blastocyst and the increased release of thyroxine following prolonged exposure to low temperatures.

16.6.1   The endocrine system

The endocrine and nervous systems function in a coordinated fashion to maintain a homeostatic state within the body. The nervous system transmits nerve impulses whereas the endocrine system utilises the blood as a transport medium. Despite obvious differences in the mechanism of transfer of information, both systems share a common feature in the release of chemical substances as a means of communication between cells. It is believed that these two systems originated and developed side by side as the needs of intercellular communication became more complex due to the increase in the size and complexity of organisms. In both cases the principal role of the systems is the integration, coordination and control of many of the major physiological activities of organisms.

A **gland** is a structure secreting a specific chemical substance, and there are two types of glands in the body; exocrine and endocrine glands. Endocrine glands secrete hormones (*hormon*, to urge on) which are specific chemical substances produced by one part of the body; these then enter the bloodstream and pass to a distant organ, tissue or group of cells where they exert a specific regulatory effect. The major endocrine glands of the body and their hormones and effects are summarised in table 16.10.

Methods of studying glands and hormones

Most of the original information concerning the function of glands and their secretions involved studying the change in body activity associated with overactivity or underactivity of the gland during disease. In some cases the experimental removal of the gland was also used to determine its function. As techniques for the isolation, purification, analysis and synthesis of hormones developed, biologists were able to counteract the symptoms of removing the gland by injecting extracts of the gland or synthetic preparations of the hormone. These techniques clearly established the role of many glands and their secretions but they could not be applied to all glands, for example the liver and kidney. The removal of these glands would produce undesirable conditions other than those connected with their endocrine role.

Radioimmunoassay (RIA) is a technique which is widely used to measure the concentration of hormones, drugs, enzymes, viruses, bacterial and tumour antigens and other organic substances of biological interest in blood, urine or other media. The principle of RIA is simple. The components of the assay consist of a specific anti-serum to the substance (hormone) under investigation, a radioactively labelled form of the substance and the unlabelled substance. The unlabelled substance competes for a limited number of antibody-binding sites with the labelled substance. The amount of inhibition of binding of the labelled substance is proportional to the amount of unlabelled substance present. Measurement of this inhibition is possible by separating (usually precipitating) the antibody-bound material from the unbound, and the technique is made quantitative by comparing the results with a set of tubes containing a *known* concentration of the substance under investigation. This is shown diagrammatically as follows.

$$\text{Ab} + \text{Ag} + \text{Ag}^* \rightleftharpoons \text{Ab.Ag} + \text{Ab.Ag}^*$$

Ab	Ag	Ag*	Ab.Ag	Ab.Ag*
specific antibody	unlabelled antigen	labelled antigen	unlabelled (antibody–antigen complexes)	labelled

Current trends in this field are to replace radioactive labels with enzyme-fluorescent or chemiluminescent labels and thus remove the hazards associated with handling radioactive sources.

Mechanisms of hormone action

All vertebrate hormones belong to one of four chemical groups: derivatives of amines, such as tyrosine; peptides and proteins; steroids; and fatty acids, as summarised in table 16.11. The mechanisms controlling the release of hormones by glands are as follows.

(*a*) The presence of a specific metabolite in the blood. For

Table 16.10. Summary of the major human endocrines, their functions and the control of their secretion

Gland	Hormone	Functions	Secretion control mechanism
Hypothalamus	Releasing and inhibiting hormones and factors, seven identified, possible number unknown (see table 16.2) Posterior pituitary hormones produced here	Control of specific anterior pituitary hormones	Feedback mechanisms involving metabolite and hormone levels
Posterior pituitary gland	No hormones synthesised here, stores and secretes the following: Oxytocin	Ejection of milk from mammary gland, contraction of uterus during birth	Feedback mechanisms involving hormones and nervous system
	Antidiuretic hormone (ADH) (vasopressin)	Reduction of urine secretion by kidney	Blood osmotic potential
Anterior pituitary gland	Follicle stimulating hormone (FSH)	In male, stimulates spermatogenesis In female, growth of ovarian follicles	Plasma oestrogen and testosterone via hypothalamus
	Luteinising hormone (LH)	In male, testosterone secretion	Plasma testosterone via hypothalamus
		In female, secretion of oestrogen and progesterone, ovulation and maintenance of corpus luteum	Plasma oestrogen level via hypothalamus
	Prolactin	Stimulates milk production and secretion	Hypothalamic hormones
	Thyroid stimulating hormone (TSH)	Synthesis and secretion of thyroid hormones, growth of thyroid glands	Plasma T_3 and T_4 levels via hypothalamus
	Adrenocorticotrophic hormone (ACTH or corticotrophin)	Synthesis and secretion of adrenal cortex hormones, growth of gland	Plasma ACTH via hypothalamus
	Growth hormone (GH)	Protein synthesis, growth, especially of bones of limbs	Hypothalamic hormones
Parathyroid gland	Parathormone	Increases blood calcium level Decreases blood phosphate level	Plasma Ca^{2+} level, and plasma PO_4^{3-} level
Thyroid gland	Triiodothyronine (T_3) and thyroxine (T_4)	Regulation of basal metabolic rate, growth and development	TSH
	Calcitonin	Decreases blood calcium level	Plasma Ca^{2+} level
Adrenal cortex	Glucocorticoids (cortisol)	Protein breakdown, glucose/glycogen synthesis, adaptation to stress, anti-inflammatory/allergy effects	ACTH
	Mineralocorticoids (aldosterone)	Na^+ retention in kidney, Na^+ and K^+ ratios in extracellular and intracellular fluids, raises blood pressure	Plasma Na^+ and K^+ levels and low blood pressure
Adrenal medulla	Adrenaline (epinephrine)	Increases rate and force of heartbeat, constriction of skin and visceral capillaries Dilation of arterioles of heart and skeletal muscles, raises blood glucose level	Sympathetic nervous system
	Noradrenaline (norepinephrine)	General constriction of small arteries, elevation of blood pressure	Nervous system
Islets of Langerhans	Insulin (beta cells)	Decreases blood glucose level, increases glucose and amino acid uptake and utilisation by cells	Plasma glucose and amino acid levels
	Glucagon (alpha cells)	Increases blood glucose level, breakdown of glycogen to glucose in liver	Plasma glucose level
Stomach	Gastrin	Secretion of gastric juices	Food in stomach
Duodenum	Secretin	Secretion of pancreatic juice Inhibits gastric secretion	Acidic food in duodenum
	Cholecystokinin (pancreozymin)	Emptying of gall bladder and liberation of pancreatic juice into duodenum	Fatty acids and amino acids in duodenum
Kidney	Renin	Conversion of angiotensinogen into angiotensin	Plasma Na^+ level, decreased blood pressure
Ovarian follicle	Oestrogens (17β-oestradiol)	Female secondary sex characteristics, oestrous cycle	FSH and LH
	Progesterone	Gestation, inhibition of ovulation	LH
Corpus luteum	Progesterone and oestrogen	Uterine growth and development	LH
	Progesterone and oestrogen	Fetal development	Developing fetus
Placenta	Chorionic gonadotrophin	Maintenance of corpus luteum	Developing fetus
	Human placental lactogen	Stimulates mammary growth	Developing fetus
Testis	Testosterone	Male secondary sexual characteristics	LH and FSH

Table 16.11. Summary table showing chemical nature of the major hormones of the body

Chemical group		Hormone	Major source
Amines	catecholamines	Adrenaline	Sympathetic nervous system
		Noradrenaline	Adrenal medulla
	tyrosine	Thyroxine	Thyroid gland
		Triiodothyronine	Thyroid gland
Peptides and proteins		Hypothalamic releasing and inhibiting hormones and factors	Hypothalamus
		Follicle stimulating hormone	
		Luteinising hormone	Anterior pituitary gland
		Prolactin	
		Thyroid stimulating hormone	
		Adrenocorticotrophic hormone	
		Growth hormone	
		Oxytocin	Posterior pituitary gland
		Vasopressin (ADH)	
		Parathormone	Parathyroid gland
		Calcitonin	Thyroid gland
		Insulin	Islets of Langerhans (pancreas)
		Glucagon	
		Gastrin	Stomach mucosa
		Secretin	Duodenal mucosa
Steroids		Testosterone	Testis
		Oestrogens	Ovary and placenta
		Progesterone	
		Corticosteroids	Adrenal cortex
Fatty acids		Prostaglandins	Many tissues

example, excess glucose in the blood causes the release of insulin from the pancreas which lowers the blood glucose level.

(b) The presence of another hormone in the blood. For example, many of the hormones released from the anterior pituitary gland are 'stimulating' hormones which cause the release of other hormones from other glands in the body.

(c) Stimulation by neurones from the autonomic nervous system. For example, adrenaline and noradrenaline are released from the cells of the adrenal medulla by the arrival of nerve impulses in situations of anxiety, stress and danger.

In the first two cases the timing of hormone release and the amount of hormone released are regulated by feedback control. Positive and negative feedback mechanisms both operate in endocrine control but positive feedback, since it tends to increase instability, only operates as part of a larger control system. For example, the release of luteinising hormone under the stimulus of oestrogen is an example of positive feedback but its continued release is prevented by the later release of progesterone.

Hormones which are released by the presence of another circulating hormone are usually under the control of the hypothalamus and pituitary glands and the final metabolic or growth effect may involve the secretion of three separate hormones as shown in fig 16.46. This mechanism, known as the **cascade** effect, is significant because it enables the effect of the release of a small amount of initial hormone to become amplified as it passes along the endocrine pathway.

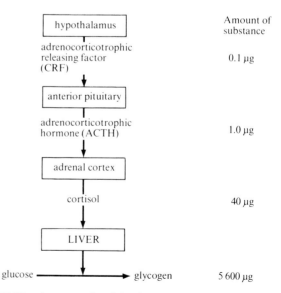

Fig 16.46 *An example of the 'cascade' effect in the control of the conversion of glucose to glycogen as a result of the release of adrenocorticotrophic releasing factor. The total amplification in this example is 56 000 times (data from Bradley, 1976)*

605

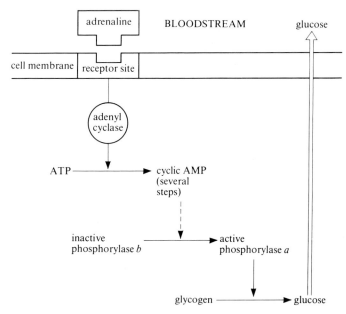

Fig 16.47 *Simplified diagram showing how adrenaline causes the release of glucose from a liver cell. The release of membrane bound adenyl cyclase produces cyclic AMP which activates enzyme systems leading to the breakdown of glycogen to glucose which diffuses out the cells into the blood stream*

Hormones are specific chemical substances and only exert their effects on target cells which possess the specific protein or lipoprotein receptors that interact with the hormone. Non-target cells lack these receptors, therefore there is no response to the circulating hormone. Many hormones have specific regions of their molecular structure for attachment to the receptor, and once attached the hormone may exert its effect at one of the following levels in the cell: (1) the cell membrane, (2) enzymes located in the cell membrane, (3) cellular organelles, and (4) genes. An example of each of these levels follows.

(1) Insulin exerts one of its effects by increasing the uptake of glucose into cells by binding with a receptor site and altering the permeability of the membrane to glucose.

(2) Adrenaline and many peptide hormones bind to receptor sites on the cell membrane and cause the release of a 'second messenger' which initiates a sequence of enzyme mechanisms which produce the appropriate hormonal response. In many cases this 'second messenger' is the nucleotide 3,5–adenosine monophosphate (cyclic AMP) which is formed by the action of the enzyme **adenyl cyclase** on ATP following the enzyme's release from the receptor site. A simplified representation of this mechanism is seen in fig 16.47.

(3) One of the effects of thyroxine is seen at the level of the mitochondrion where it influences the enzymes of the electron carrier system involved with the formation of ATP (section 11.5.4). Much of the energy passing along the electron transport chain in those circumstances is lost as heat.

(4) Steroid hormones, and the insect moulting hormone ecdysone, pass through the cell membrane and bind to a receptor in the cytoplasm. The complex formed passes to the cell nucleus where the hormones exert a direct effect upon the chromosomes by activating genes and stimulating transcription (messenger RNA formation).

In many cases of hormone action hormones appear to exert their effects by influencing enzymes associated with membranes or genetic systems.

16.6.2   The hypothalamus and pituitary gland

Intercellular communication is achieved, as stated earlier, by the activity of nervous and endocrine systems acting independently or together. The major centres in the body for the coordination and integration of the two systems of control are the hypothalamus and pituitary gland. The hypothalamus plays a dominant role in collecting information from other regions of the brain and from blood vessels passing through it. This information passes to the pituitary gland which, by its secretions, directly or indirectly regulates the activity of all other glands.

The hypothalamus

The hypothalamus is situated at the base of the forebrain immediately beneath the thalamus and above the pituitary gland. It is composed of several distinct regions called **nuclei** made up of collections of cell bodies whose axons terminate on blood capillaries in the **median eminence** and **posterior pituitary** as shown in fig 16.48. Many physiological activities such as hunger, thirst, sleep and temperature regulation are regulated by nervous control exercised through nerve impulses passing from the hypothalamus along autonomic neurones. The hypothalamic control of

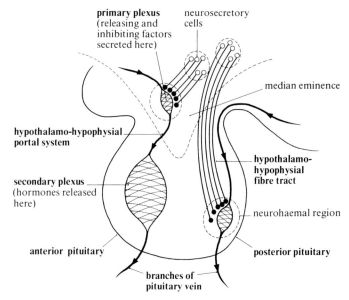

Fig 16.48 *Diagram showing the relationship between neurosecretory cells and blood vessels in the hypothalamus and pituitary gland*

endocrine secretion, however, lies in the ability of the hypothalamus to monitor metabolite and hormone levels in the blood. Information generated this way, together with information from almost all parts of the brain, then passes to the pituitary gland either by the release of 'hormones' into the blood vessels of the median eminence, which supply the pituitary, or by neurones. The information relayed by neurones passes through specialised neurones called **neurosecretory cells**.

All nerve cells release a chemical substance, a transmitter substance, at their terminal synapse, but neurosecretory cells are nerve cells that have developed the secretory capacity to a high level. Chemical substances are produced in the cell bodies of these cells and packaged into granules or droplets before being transported down the axon by axoplasmic streaming. At the terminal end of the neurone these cells synapse on to capillaries into which they release their secretion when stimulated by nerve impulses passing down the axon.

The pituitary gland

The pituitary gland or **hypophysis** (*hypo*, under; *phyein*, to grow) is a small red-grey gland weighing about 0.5 g and connected to the brain by the pituitary stalk (**infundibulum**). It has a dual origin and retains features of those origins in its functions. The two lobes of the pituitary gland are the anterior pituitary and the posterior pituitary.

*Anterior pituitary or adenohypophysis (*aden, gland*).* This is derived from an upgrowth of the glandular roof of the mouth. It is connected to the hypothalamus by blood vessels of the **hypothalamo-hypophysial portal system** which has a capillary bed, the **primary plexus**, in the median eminence of the hypothalamus and a **secondary plexus** in the anterior pituitary.

Nerve terminals from specialised neurosecretory cells release two groups of chemical substances, known as 'releasing factors' and 'inhibiting factors', into the blood capillaries of the primary plexus and these pass to the secondary plexus where they cause the release of six trophic hormones which are produced and stored by the anterior pituitary. These six hormones pass into the blood vessels leaving the pituitary and exert their effects on specific target organs throughout the body, as shown in table 16.12.

The release of the first two hormones is under the dual inhibitory and stimulatory control of the hypothalamus, whereas the release of the other four is regulated by negative feedback of hormones from the target glands acting on receptors in the hypothalamus and anterior pituitary. Pituitary hormones stimulate the release of target gland hormones and as the levels of these rise they inhibit the secretion of hypothalamic and pituitary hormones. When the circulatory level of these target hormones falls below a certain level the hypothalamic and pituitary inhibition ceases allowing the increased secretion from these glands. This control mechanism is described in sections 18.4.4 and 19.6.

*Posterior pituitary or neurohypophysis (*neuro, nerve*).* This is derived from a downgrowth of the floor of the brain. It does not synthesise any hormones but stores and releases two hormones, **antidiuretic hormone (ADH or vasopressin)** and **oxytocin**. Antidiuretic hormone is released in response to a fall in the water content of plasma and leads to an increase in the permeability to water of the distal and collecting tubules of the nephron so that water is retained in the blood plasma. A reduced volume of concentrated urine is excreted (section 19.6). Oxytocin causes contraction of the uterus during birth and the ejection of milk from the nipple (section 20.3.8).

ADH and oxytocin are produced by neurosecretory cell bodies lying in the nuclei of the hypothalamus and pass down the nerve fibres attached to carrier protein molecules called **neurophysins**. These neurosecretory cells are much more specialised than those connected with the secretion of releasing factors and they form structures in the posterior pituitary known as **neurohaemal organs**. These are structures consisting of a swollen synapse attached to a capillary and surrounded by connective tissue (fig 16.49).

Table 16.12. Summary table showing the main hypothalamic hormones, the anterior pituitary hormones influenced by them and their target organs

Hypothalamic hormone	Anterior pituitary hormone and response	Site of action
Growth hormone releasing factor (GHRF) Growth hormone release-inhibiting hormone (GHRIH)* (somatostatin)	Growth hormone (GH) (see section 21.8.1)	Most tissues
Prolactin releasing factor (PRF) Prolactin inhibiting factor (PIF)	Prolactin (luteotrophin) (LTH) Inhibition of prolactin secretion	Ovary and mammary gland
Luteinising hormone releasing hormone (LHRH)*	Follicle stimulating hormone (FSH) Luteinising hormone (LH)	Ovary and testis
Thyrotrophin releasing hormone (TRH)*	Thyroid stimulating hormone (TSH)	Thyroid gland
Adrenocorticotrophin releasing factor (CRF)	Adrenocorticotrophic hormone (ACTH)	Adrenal cortex

*Releasing factors with an established identity are known as 'hormones'. Luteinising hormone releasing hormone is able to stimulate the release of both FSH and LH.

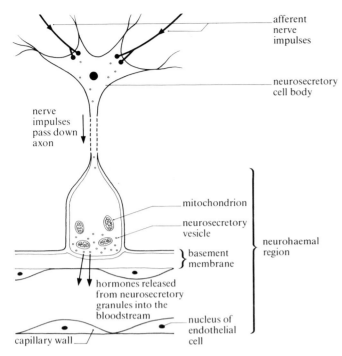

Fig 16.49 *Diagram showing a neurosecretory cell and neurohaemal organ, (not drawn to scale)*

Afferent nerve stimuli are relayed to the cell bodies of these neurosecretory cells from other regions of the brain and transmitted down the axons to the neurohaemal organ where secretions stored in vesicles are released into the bloodstream and carried to target organs. The physiological response produced by such a circuit involving the translation of sensory information into hormonal secretions, and eventually a physiological response, is known as a **neuroendocrine response**. Many neuroendocrine responses result in a type of behavioural pattern known as a **neuroendocrine reflex** and many examples of these are associated with courtship and breeding activity.

16.6.3 Pineal gland or epiphysis, (*epi*, upon: *phyein*, to grow)

The pineal gland is an extremely small gland found in the roof of the forebrain (diencephalon) and covered by the corpus callosum and cerebral hemispheres. It is variable in size and weighs about 150 mg. The Romans believed the pineal gland to be the 'seat of the soul' but it is now recognised as an endocrine gland. It has no direct connection with the central nervous system but is richly vascularised and believed to secrete several hormones, including **melatonin**. It is innervated by sympathetic neurones which are stimulated by centres in the brain controlled by light. Exposure to darkness stimulates melatonin synthesis which acts via the brain and modifies the function of the thyroid and adrenal glands and gonads. There is also evidence to suggest that melatonin acts on the brain and influences several physiological processes which are dependent upon time, such as the onset of puberty, ovulation and sleep. Tumours of the pineal gland in young

boys result in precocious sexual development. The pineal gland, then, appears to function as a 'biological clock' and acts as a **'neuroendocrine transducer'** converting cyclic nervous activity, generated by light, into endocrine secretion. Much more research is required to clarify the many functions of this gland.

16.6.4 Parathyroid glands

In humans there are four small parathyroid glands and they are embedded in the thyroid gland. They produce only one hormone called **parathormone** which is a peptide composed of 84 amino acids. Parathormone and the thyroid hormone **calcitonin** work antagonistically to regulate the plasma calcium and phosphate levels. The release of parathormone increases the plasma calcium level to its normal level of 2.5 mmol dm^{-3} and decreases the plasma phosphate level. The activity of the parathyroid glands is controlled by the simple negative feedback mechanism shown in fig 16.50.

Overactivity of the gland, **hyperparathyroidism**, reduces the level of calcium in the plasma and tissues due to calcium excretion in urine. This can lead to a state of tetany in which muscles remain contracted. Also the rate of excretion of phosphate is reduced and the level of phosphate ions in the plasma rises.

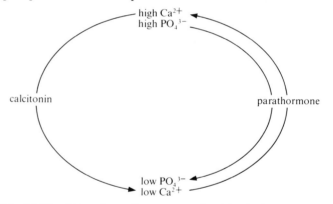

Fig 16.50 *Role of parathormone and calcitonin in the regulation of blood calcium level*

16.6.5 Thyroid gland

The human thyroid gland is a bow-tie shaped structure situated in the neck region with lobes, on each side of the trachea and larynx, connected by a thin band of tissue. The entire gland weighs approximately 25 g and produces three active hormones, **triiodothyronine** (T_3), **thyroxine** (T_4) and **calcitonin**. T_3 and T_4 have a regulatory effect on metabolic rate, growth and development, whilst calcitonin is involved in the regulation of the plasma calcium level.

The structure of the thyroid gland

The thyroid gland is made up of numerous follicles which have a diameter of 0.1 mm and contain a clear colloid composed of the glycoprotein **thyroglobulin**. The wall of each follicle is composed of a single layer of cuboidal cells

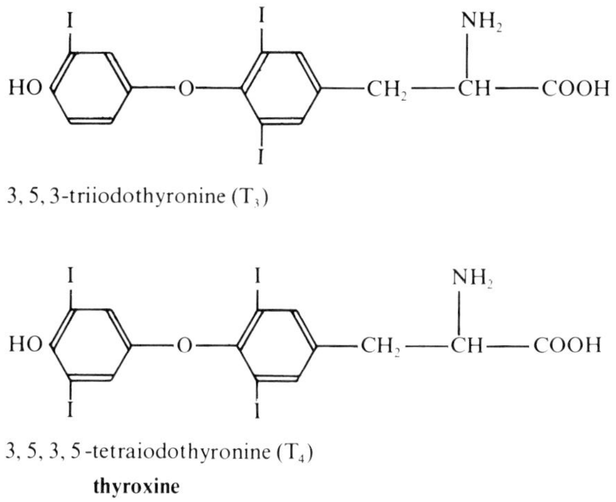

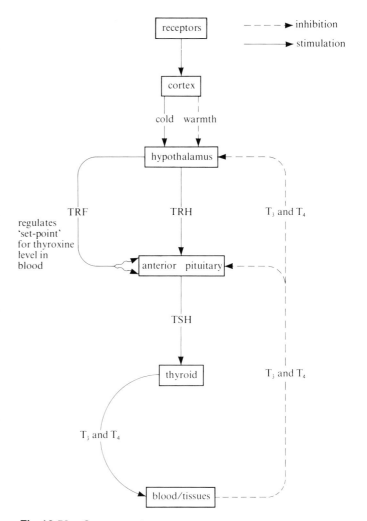

Fig 16.51 *Structural formulae of the main thyroid hormones* T_3 *and* T_4

3, 5, 3-triiodothyronine (T_3)

3, 5, 3, 5-tetraiodothyronine (T_4)

thyroxine

that become columnar and bear microvilli on their inner surface when the gland is activated by **thyroid stimulating hormone (TSH)** from the anterior pituitary gland.

The formation and release of thyroid hormones

Iodine is taken up by active transport from the plasma, in the numerous capillaries surrounding the follicles, as iodine ions (I^-) and secreted into the lumen of the follicle. Here it is bound to a protein molecule and oxidised to iodine by peroxidase enzymes which form part of a cytochrome enzyme system. The iodine formed reacts with the amino acid tyrosine which is bound to thyroglobulin formed by the follicle cells. Further iodination occurs and subsequent interactions give rise to the two main iodinated amino acid hormones shown in fig 16.51.

The function of T_3 and T_4

Whilst T_3 and T_4 have a major influence upon many metabolic processes, including carbohydrate, protein, fat and vitamin metabolism, their main influence is upon the rate of metabolic processes, an effect known as **calorigenesis**, (*calor*, heat, *genesis*, production). The basal metabolic rate (BMR) in humans, $160\,kJ\,m^{-2}$ body surface h^{-1}, is maintained at a steady state by the action of thyroxine which promotes the breakdown of glucose and fats into forms which can readily yield energy (section 18.4.2). Further calorigenic effects include increases in the uptake of oxygen by the body and the rate of enzyme reactions involved in the electron transport chain in the mitochondria. This increases the rate of ATP formation and heat production by the tissues. The exact mechanism of this action is now known.

T_3 and T_4 and the growth hormone, **somatomedin**, have a joint stimulatory effect on protein synthesis leading to an increase in growth rate. This effect is clearly seen in frog metamorphosis (section 21.7.4) and in children suffering from a lack of thyroid hormones.

In many of the metabolic processes with which it is involved thyroxine appears to enhance the effects of other hormones such as insulin, adrenaline and glucocorticoids (section 18.5.2).

Control of T_3 and T_4 release

The effects of T_3 and T_4 are longer lasting than those of most other hormones and hence it is homeostatically vital that fluctuations in their secretion be prevented. This is one of the reasons for the storage of T_3 and T_4 within the gland so that it is readily available for release.

The levels of T_3 and T_4 circulating in the blood control their release from the thyroid gland by negative feedback mechanisms involving the hypothalamus and anterior pituitary.

Thyrotrophic releasing hormone (TRH) and TSH release is inhibited by the amounts of T_3 and T_4 in the blood in excess of those required to maintain the metabolic rate at a steady state. Superimposed on these are environmental factors, such as temperature, which influence higher centres of the brain to stimulate the hypothalamus to secrete TRH. This 'sets' the threshold in the pituitary for the negative feedback mechanisms. These mechanisms of control are shown in fig 16.52.

Fig 16.52 *Summary diagram showing the factors regulating thyroxine secretion and leading to homeostatic control of metabolic rate*

Overactivity of the thyroid gland (hyperthyroidism)

Both over- and underactivity of the thyroid gland can produce a swelling in the neck known as a **goitre**. Overactivity may be due to overproduction of thyroxine from an enlarged thyroid gland. The symptoms are increases in heart rate (tachycardia) (section 18.1.5), ventilation rate and body temperature. The basal metabolic rate may increase by 50% with associated increases in oxygen consumption and heat production. Patients become very nervous and irritable and the hands shake when held out. Extreme hyperthyroidism is termed **thyrotoxicosis** and is associated with increased excitability of cardiac muscle which may lead to heart failure unless treated. This may involve the surgical removal of most of the gland or the destruction of the same amount by administering radioactive iodine.

Underactivity of the thyroid gland (hypothyroidism)

A lack of TSH production by the anterior pituitary, iodine deficiency in the diet or failure of enzyme systems involved in thyroxine production may result in hypothyroidism. If there is a deficiency of thyroxine at birth this will lead to poor growth and mental retardation, a condition known as **cretinism**. If the condition is diagnosed at an early stage thyroxine can be given to restore normal growth and development. Thyroxine deficiency in later life gives rise to a condition known as **myxoedema** and the symptoms are a reduction in metabolic rate accompanied by decreased oxygen consumption, ventilation, heart rate and body temperature. Mental activity and movement become slower and weight increases due to the formation and storage of a semi-fluid material under the skin. This causes the face and eyelids to become puffy, the tongue swells, the skin becomes rough and hair is lost from the scalp and eyebrows. All of these symptoms can be eliminated and the condition treated by taking thyroxine tablets.

Calcitonin

In addition to follicular cells the thyroid gland contains other cells known as **C cells**. These secrete a polypeptide hormone **calcitonin** which works antagonistically towards parathormone and lowers blood calcium levels.

16.6.6 Adrenal glands

There are a pair of adrenal (*ad*, to; *renes*, kidneys) glands weighing approximately 5 g each which are situated anterior to the kidneys. Each gland is composed of cells having two different embryological origins, and these cells function independently. The outer cortex is derived from cells of the neural plate and forms 80% of the gland. It is a firm structure and covered by a fibrous capsule and is essential for life. The inner medulla is derived from cells of the neural crest and has retained its close origin with the nervous system. It is not essential for life.

Table 16.13. Summary table showing the main cytological detail, secretion and functions of the three regions of the adrenal cortex

Region	Cytological detail	Secretion	Function	Notes
Zona glomerulosa	Composed of rounded clusters of small cells containing elongated mitochondria	Mineralocorticoids e.g. aldosterone	Control water and electrolyte metabolism by stimulating cation pumps in membranes to conserve Na^+ and Cl^- and remove K^+. Prevent excessive Na^+ loss in sweat, saliva and urine and maintain osmotic concentration of body fluids at a steady state	Renin released from juxta-glomerular apparatus in kidney produces angiotensin. This stimulates release of aldosterone which increases Na^+ uptake by kidney and leads to release of ADH which increases reabsorption of water by kidney tubules. Release is not stimulated by ACTH
Zona fasciculata	2–3 rows of parallel columns of cells arranged at right-angles to the surface of the gland and containing spherical mitochondria	Glucocorticoids e.g. cortisol	(A) Carbohydrate metabolism (1) promote gluconeogenesis (2) promote liver glycogen formation (3) raise blood glucose level (B) Protein metabolism (1) promote breakdown of plasma protein (2) increase availability of amino acids for enzyme synthesis in the liver (C) Other roles (1) prevent inflammatory and allergic reactions (2) decrease antibody production	Overactivity leads to Cushings' syndrome and patients show abdominal obesity, wasting of muscles, high blood pressure, diabetes and increased hair growth. Overproduction of ACTH by the anterior pituitary is Cushings' disease. Underactivity leads to Addison's disease as shown by muscular weakness, low blood pressure, decreased resistance to infection, fatigue and darkening of the skin
Zona reticularis	Composed of irregularly arranged columns of cells containing elongated mitochondria			

Adrenal cortex

The adrenal cortex has three histologically distinct regions composed of cells grouped around blood capillaries and produces steroid hormones of two types. These regions, their cytological detail, secretions and functions are shown in table 16.13.

All steroids are formed from a common precursor molecule called **cholesterol** which the cortex is able both to synthesise and take up from the circulation following absorption from the diet. The three regions of the cortex then convert it into specific steroid hormones.

Steroids are lipid-soluble substances which diffuse through cell membranes and attach to cytoplasmic receptor proteins. The complexes formed then migrate into the nucleus where they attach to specific areas of the chromosome and de-repress or activate certain genes inducing the formation of messenger RNA.

The size of the adrenal gland is closely linked to the output of ACTH and the ability to withstand stress. During long periods of stress the size of the gland increases. Investigations into the behaviour of organisms under stress have shown that the output of adrenal hormones increases with the rise in number in the population. In organisms where social hierarchies exist, there is a positive correlation between position in the hierarchy and increased size of the adrenal gland.

Control of cortical hormone release

Mineralocorticoid release is stimulated by the activity of **renin** and **angiotensin** as described in table 16.13, whilst glucocorticoids are secreted in response to **adrenocorticotrophic hormone (ACTH)**. The mechanisms of the release of these hormones is shown in fig 16.53.

ACTH is a polypeptide molecule containing 39 amino acids. It attaches to receptors on the surface of the cortical cells and activates adenyl cyclase to convert ATP to cyclic AMP (section 16.6.1). This acts as a cofactor in activating enzymes known as **protein kinases** which stimulate the conversion of cholesterol to pregnenolone. In addition to this ACTH is responsible for the uptake of cholesterol into the cortex, the maintenance of the size of the adrenal cortex and the maintenance of the enzymes involved in steroid production.

Adrenal medulla

The adrenal medulla forms the centre of the adrenal gland. It is a soft tissue composed of strands of cells surrounded by blood capillaries and is richly supplied with nerves. The cells are modified postganglionic sympathetic neurones and when stimulated by preganglionic sympathetic neurones they secrete noradrenaline and adrenaline (section 16.6.1). The adrenal medulla is not essential to life since its function is to augment that of the sympathetic nervous system.

Noradrenaline (norepinephrine) and adrenaline (epinephrine) are formed from the amino acid tyrosine and belong to a group of biologically active molecules called **catecholamines** (fig 16.54). They are both secreted by the cells of the medulla but only noradrenaline is secreted by the postganglionic synapses of the sympathetic nervous system. The effects of both hormones are basically identical as shown in table 16.14, but they differ in their

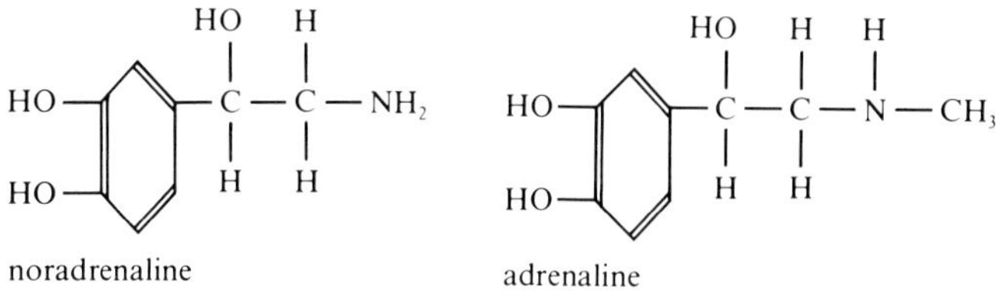

Fig 16.54 *Molecular structure of noradrenaline and adrenaline*

Table 16.14. Physiological effects of noradrenaline and adrenaline

Dilate pupils of eyes
Cause hair to stand on end
Relax bronchioles thus increasing air flow to lungs
Inhibit peristalsis
Inhibit digestion
Prevent bladder contraction
Increase amplitude and rate of heartbeat
Cause almost general vasoconstriction
Increase blood pressure
Stimulate conversion of liver glycogen to glucose
Decrease sensory threshold
Increase mental awareness

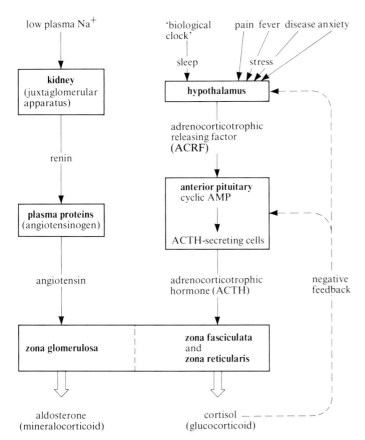

Fig 16.53 *Summary diagram for the control of the main adrenal cortex hormones*

effects on blood vessels. Noradrenaline causes vasoconstriction of all blood vessels whereas adrenaline causes vasoconstriction of blood vessels supplying the skin and gut and vasodilation of blood vessels to muscles and the brain. Both of these hormones activate two types of receptor sites on the target tissues known as α and β **adrenergic receptors**. These release adenyl cyclase (cyclic AMP) into the cell and this leads to the specific tissue response as shown in fig 16.53. Most organs have both α- and β-receptors with α-receptors appearing to be more receptive to noradrenaline than adrenaline and vice versa in the case of β-receptors.

The actions of these hormones are widespread throughout the body and prepare the animal for situations of 'fight or flight' and facilitate the response to sudden demands imposed by stress such as pain, shock, cold, low blood sugar, low blood pressure, anger and passion.

16.6.7 Pancreas

The pancreas has both exocrine and endocrine functions and is associated with the alimentary canal (section 10.4). The bulk of this gland is composed of exocrine acinar cells which form rounded structures enclosing a lumen into which the digestive enzymes of the zymogen granules are secreted (section 10.4.9). Interspersed amongst groups of acinar cells are the **islets of Langerhans** containing a small number of large **alpha (α) cells**, numerous **beta (β) cells** and blood capillaries. Alpha cells secrete glucagon and beta cells **insulin** and these have antagonistic effects on the glucose level.

Insulin

Insulin is a protein composed of 51 amino acids, whose primary structure was determined in 1950 by Sanger in Cambridge. It is released in response to a rise in blood glucose level above $100 \, mg \, 100 \, cm^{-3}$ blood and a rise in glucagon level. It is carried in the plasma bound to β-globulin and has an important anabolic effect on every organ of the body. Receptor sites on cell membranes bind insulin, and this reaction leads to changes both in cell permeability and the activity of enzyme systems within the cell with the following effects:
(1) increase in the rate of conversion of glucose to glycogen (glycogenesis),
(2) increase in the rate of uptake of glucose by muscle and fat by cell membranes,
(3) increase in the rate of protein and fat synthesis,
(4) increase in the formation of ATP, DNA and RNA.

The secretion of insulin is vital to life since it is the only hormone which lowers the blood glucose level. A deficiency in insulin production leads to the metabolic condition known as **diabetes mellitus** in which the blood glucose reaches such a level that it exceeds that which the kidney can reabsorb, the **renal threshold**, and is excreted in the urine. The involvement of the pancreas in diabetes mellitus has been known for almost a hundred years but it was not until 1921 that the Canadian doctors Banting and Best

Table 16.15. Some of the effects of insulin deficiency and excess

Deficiency	Excess
High blood glucose level (hyperglycaemia)	Low blood glucose level (hypoglycaemia)
Breakdown of muscle tissue	Hunger
Loss of weight	Sweating
Tiredness	Irritability
	Double vision

succeeded in treating the condition with insulin extracted from the pancreas of animals. In 1950 Sanger succeeded in determining the primary structure of insulin. The effects of insulin deficiency and excess are summarised in table 16.15. Preparation of human insulin by genetic engineering is described in section 2.5.4. Development of an automatic pancreas is described in section 6.9.2.

Glucagon

Glucagon is a peptide composed of 29 amino acids and is released, along with several other hormones, in response to a fall of blood glucose level induced by an increase in metabolic demand. It stimulates the breakdown of proteins and fats to carbohydrates (gluconeogenesis) (section 18.5.2). Receptor sites in the liver cell membrane bind glucagon which causes the release of adenyl cyclase to form cyclic AMP. The action of glucagon is similar to that of adrenaline and both activate phosphorylase enzymes which stimulate the breakdown of glycogen to glucose-6-phosphate as shown in fig 16.47. Glucagon has no effect on muscle glycogen.

Summary diagrams of the role of insulin and glucagon are shown in figs 18.7 and 18.23.

16.6.8 Differences between nervous and endocrine coordination

The nervous and endocrine systems function separately and together in the coordination of many of the body's activities. This chapter describes both situations but it is useful as a summary to examine the differences between the two systems as this highlights the advantage of each system in the light of their roles (table 16.16).

Table 16.16. Differences between nervous and endocrine coordination

Nervous	Chemical
Information passes as electrical impulses along axons (chemical across synapses)	Information passes as a chemical substance through the bloodstream
Rapid transmission	Slow transmission
Response immediate	Response usually slow, e.g. growth
Response short-lived	Response long-lasting
Response very exact	Response usually widespread

16.7 The study of behaviour (ethology)

Behaviour may be defined as the outwardly expressed course of action produced in organisms in response to stimuli from a given situation. The action modifies, in some way, the relationship between the organism and its environment and its adaptive significance is the perpetuation of the species. All living organisms exhibit a variety of forms of behavioural activity determined by the extent to which they are able to respond to stimuli. This varies from the relatively simple action of the growth of a plant stem towards a light source, to the complex sexual behaviour patterns of territory defence, courtship and mating seen in birds and mammals.

Plant behaviour is restricted to movements produced by growth or turgor changes and is stereotyped and predictable. The two main activities associated with plant behaviour are tropisms and nasties and details of these are described in section 15.1.

Animal behaviour is far more complex and diverse than plant behaviour and therefore it is extremely difficult to investigate and account for with any degree of scientific validity. The three main approaches to behavioural studies are the vitalistic, mechanistic and ethological approaches.

Vitalistic approach. This seeks to account for behavioural activities in terms of what animals are seen to do, and attempts to relate this to changes in the environment. It involves the total rejection of any study of the animal outside its natural environment. The technique has its foundations in natural history and has provided a wealth of valuable data, but it is essentially non-scientific since all the observations relate to past events which cannot be tested experimentally.

Mechanistic approach. This is an experimental approach and involves the study of particular aspects of behaviour under controlled conditions in a laboratory. It may be criticised on the grounds of the artificiality of the experimental situation, the nature of the behavioural activities and the way in which the results are interpreted. This technique is, however, used extensively in psychology and was pioneered by Pavlov.

Ethological approach. This is the contemporary approach to behavioural investigations and attempts to explain responses observed in the field in terms of the stimuli eliciting the behaviour. It involves both of the techniques outlined above and was pioneered by Lorenz, von Frisch and Tinbergen.

In all behavioural studies great care has to be taken in interpreting the results of observations in order to eliminate subjectivity. For example, care must be taken to avoid putting oneself in the place of the animal (**anthropocentrism**), or interpreting what is observed in terms of human experience (**anthropomorphism**) or interpreting the cause of the observation in terms of its outcome (**teleology**).

Recent advances in audio-visual technology have assisted the recording of behavioural activities. Infra-red photography has enabled animals to be filmed at night and time-lapse photography and slow-motion cinematography have enabled respectively slow-moving activities, such as moulting in insects, and fast-moving activities, such as bird flight, to be recorded and subsequently seen at speeds more suited to analysis by behaviouralists. The use of miniature cassette tape recorders for recording sounds and their subsequent analysis using sound spectrographs and computers has helped in the study of auditory communication between organisms. The movement of organisms is now studied either using implanted miniaturised signal generators, emitting signals that can be followed using direction-finding equipment, or by the use of tracking radar. The two techniques are employed successfully in following the migrations of mammals, birds and locusts.

Whatever the approach and techniques used in the investigation of behaviour the fundamental explanation of behavioural activity must begin with a stimulus, end with a response and include all the stages occurring at various levels of organisation within the body linking *cause* and *effect*.

Broadly speaking there are two forms of behaviour, **innate behaviour** and **learned behaviour**, but the distinction between the two is not clear-cut and the majority of behavioural responses in higher organisms undoubtedly contain components of both. However, for simplification in this elementary introduction to behaviour, the various aspects of behaviour are considered under these two headings in the next two sections.

16.8 Innate behaviour

Innate behaviour does not involve a single clear-cut category of behaviour but rather a collection of responses that are predetermined by the inheritance of specific nerve or cytoplasmic pathways in multicellular or acellular organisms. As a result of these 'built-in' pathways a given stimulus will produce, invariably, the same response. These behaviour patterns have developed and been refined over many generations (**selected**) and their primary adaptive significance lies in their survival value to the species. Another valuable feature of innate behaviour is the economy it places on nerve pathways within multicellular organisms, since it does not make enormous demands on the higher centres of the nervous system.

There is a gradation of complexity associated with patterns of innate behaviour which is related to the complexity of nerve pathways involved in their performance. Innate behaviour patterns include orientations (taxes and kineses), simple reflexes and instincts. The latter are extremely complex and include biological rhythms, territorial behaviour, courtship, mating, aggression, altruism, social hierarchies and social organisation. All plant behaviour is innate.

Taxes

A taxis or **taxic response** is a movement of the whole organism in response to an external directional stimulus. Taxic movements may be towards the stimulus (**positive**, $+$), away from the stimulus (**negative**, $-$), or at a particular angle to the stimulus, and are classified according to the nature of the stimulus. Some examples of types of taxes are shown in table 15.2. In some cases organisms are able to move by maintaining a fixed angle relative to the directional stimulus. For example, certain species of ants can follow a path back to their nest by setting a course relative to the Sun's direction. Other organisms orientate themselves so that, for example, their dorsal side is always uppermost. This is called the **dorsal light reaction** and is found in fish such as plaice which maintain their dorsal surface at right-angles to the sky.

Many organisms detect the direction of the stimulus by moving the head, which bears the major sensory receptors, from side to side. This is known as a **klinotaxic response** and enables symmetrically placed receptors on the head, such as photoreceptors, to detect the stimulus. If both receptors are equally stimulated the organism will move forwards in approximately a straight line. This type of response is shown by *Planaria* moving towards a food source and by blowfly larvae moving away from a light source. In all cases of klinotaxis it is thought that successive stimulation of receptors on each side of the body is necessary in order to provide the 'brain' with a continuous supply of information since there is no long-term 'memory'.

Computer program. HYDRA (CUP Micro Software) allows the user to explore a non-teleological model of *Hydra*'s response to light. (Double package with PHYTOCHROME.)

Kineses

A **kinetic response** is a non-directional movement response in which the *rate* of movement is related to the *intensity* of the stimulus and not the *direction* of the stimulus. For example, the direction of movement of the tentacles of *Hydra* in search of food is random and slow, but if saliva, glutathione or water fleas are placed close to the *Hydra* the rate of movement of the tentacles increases.

Both kinetic and taxic responses can be observed through the use of woodlice in a **choice chamber** as described in experiment 16.1.

Experiment 16.1: To investigate orientation behaviour in woodlice by the use of a simple choice chamber.

Materials

old pair of tights	anhydrous calcium
bases of 2 Petri dishes	chloride
Araldite	adhesive tape
hot metal rod	ten woodlice
cotton wool	plasticine

Method

(1) Cut a circle out of an old pair of tights 10 cm in diameter and stretch over the base of an 8.5 cm Petri dish. Attach with Araldite, held in place by an elastic band until it sets.

(2) Burn out a 1.0 cm hole in the bottom of this Petri dish using a hot metal rod.

(3) Divide the base of another Petri dish in half using a plasticine strip 8.5 cm long, 1.4 cm deep and 0.5 cm wide.

(4) Place cotton wool soaked in water in one half of this Petri dish and granules of anhydrous calcium chloride in the other half.

(5) Attach the Petri dish base prepared in (1) above to the Petri dish base prepared in (4) with adhesive tape as shown in fig 16.55.

(6) Introduce ten woodlice into the apparatus through the hole in the upper Petri dish and record the position and number active at 1 min intervals in a table such as table 16.17.

(7) After 20 min plot a graph of numbers present against time for each environment.

(8) Calculate the percentage number of woodlice active in the dry environment for each minute interval and plot on a graph against time.

(9) Explain the nature of the results obtained in terms of kineses and taxes.

Table 16.17. Specimen arrangement of table of results

Time/ min	Humid		Dry		
	Number present	Number active	Number present	Number active	Percentage active dry side
0	4	1	6	4	40%
1	5	2	5	5	50%
2		etc.		etc.	
3					
.					
.					
.					
20					

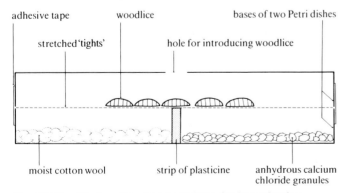

Fig 16.55 *Choice chamber apparatus for investigating orientation behaviour in woodlice.*

adhesive tape   woodlice   bases of two Petri dishes

stretched 'tights'   hole for introducing woodlice

moist cotton wool   strip of plasticine   anhydrous calcium chloride granules

In simple experiments of this type the response of organisms to environments having extremes of a given variable can be investigated. Taxic responses are observed by the preference shown by the organisms for a particular environment. For example, woodlice exposed to areas of high and low humidity in a choice chamber congregate in larger numbers in the area of highest humidity, showing them to be **positively hydrotaxic**. More complex experiments can be devised using combinations of variables in order to determine which is strongest in eliciting a final response.

Kinetic responses are observed by recording the activity of woodlice at, say, 30 s intervals, in relation to their position in the choice chamber. Results of such investigations show that when first introduced into the choice chamber at the junction of two environments some woodlice move around whilst others remain stationary. After a short time all the woodlice begin moving and the speed of movement and rate of turning is always greatest in the drier side of the choice chamber than in the humid side. The increased, apparently random, moving and turning of the woodlice on the dry side is believed to indicate an attempt to find optimal conditions and, when these are found, the moving and turning response diminishes. These responses are examples of **orthokinesis**. The woodlice move more slowly on the humid side and consequently usually congregate there. The preference shown for the humid side of the choice chamber indicates a positive taxic response to humidity.

Not all orientation behaviour patterns are rigid, and the response shown by an organism may vary depending upon other factors such as the degree of hunger, thirst, light, dark, heat, cold and humidity.

16.8.1 Simple reflexes in vertebrates

A simple reflex is an involuntary stereotyped response of part of an organism to a given stimulus. It is determined by the presence of an inherited pattern of neurones forming spinal and cranial reflex arcs, and the structure and function of these is described in section 16.2.

In terms of behaviour, simple spinal reflexes are either **flexion** responses, involving withdrawal of a limb from a painful stimulus, or **stretch** responses, involving the balance and posture of the organism. Both of these responses are primarily involuntary and most require no integration or coordination outside that found in the spinal cord. However both types of response may be modified by the brain according to circumstances and in the light of previous experience. When this happens innate and learned behaviour patterns overlap and the reflex action is now described as 'conditioned' as described in table 16.18. Many simple cranial reflexes too, may be conditioned, for example blinking in response to a sudden movement.

16.8.2 Instincts

Instincts are complex, inborn, stereotyped

behaviour patterns of immediate adaptive survival value to the organism and are produced in response to sudden changes in the environment. They are unique to each species and differ from simple reflexes in their degree of complexity. Konrad Lorenz, a Nobel prize-winning ethologist, defined instincts as 'unlearned species-specific motor patterns'.

Instinctive behaviour is predominant in the lives of nonvertebrate animals where, in insects for example, short life cycles prevent modifications in behaviour occurring as a result of trial-and-error learning. Instinctive behaviour in insects and in vertebrates therefore is a 'neuronal economy measure' and provides the organism with a ready-made set of behavioural responses. These responses are handed down from generation to generation and, having undergone successfully the rigorous test of natural selection, clearly have important survival significance.

However, before concluding that instinctive behaviour patterns are completely inflexible as a result of their genetic origin it must be stressed that this is not so. All aspects of the development of an organism, whether anatomical, biochemical, physiological, ecological or behavioural, are the result of the influence of constantly varying environmental factors acting on a genetic framework. In view of this no behavioural pattern can be purely instinctive (that is genetic) or purely learned (that is environmental), and any subsequently described behavioural activity, whilst being either superficially instinctive or superficially learned, is influenced by both patterns. Some authorities prefer the terms **species-characteristic behaviour**, in preference to instinctive behaviour, and **individual-characteristic behaviour**, in preference to learned behaviour. But despite this terminology the same principle of genetic and environmental interaction applies. This point was demonstrated very clearly by Professor W. H. Thorpe in his investigations of chaffinch song. He found that chaffinches whether reared by parents, reared in isolation, or deaf from the time of hatching, all produce sounds clearly identifiable to the human ear as those of a chaffinch. Sound spectrograms show, however, that these are only rudimentary songs, and that chaffinches reared by parents, listening to the songs of their parents and other chaffinches in the population, develop identical sound patterns to the older birds, characteristic of the local population. It was apparent that bird songs within a species have 'local dialects'. Songs of deaf birds or those in isolation remained rudimentary, thus demonstrating that the environment can significantly modify an instinctive pattern.

16.8.3 Motivation

The extent and nature of any behavioural response is modified by a variety of factors that are collectively known as **motivation**. For example, the *same* stimulus does not always evoke the *same* response in the *same* organism. The difference is always circumstantial and may be controlled by either internal or external factors.

Presenting food to a starved animal will produce a different response from that shown by an animal that has been fed. In between the two extremes responses of varying strengths will be produced depending upon the degree of hunger experienced by the organism. However, if the act of feeding would place a hungry animal in danger of being attacked by a predator the feeding response would be curbed until the danger passed. Many behavioural responses associated with reproduction have a motivational element. For example, many female mammals are only receptive to mating attempts by males at certain times of the year. These times coincide with the period of oestrus and have the adaptive significance of ensuring that mating coincides with the optimum time for fertilisation and therefore the production of offspring at the most favourable time of the year. These behavioural patterns are known as **biological rhythms** and are described in section 16.8.5. In many species the degree of motivation, or 'drive', coincides in males and females, but in other species some system of communication between the sexes is essential to express the degree of motivation. In many primate species the timing of oestrus is signalled by a swelling and change of colour of the genital area of the female and this is displayed to the male. Such behaviour reduces the likelihood of a male attempting to mate at a time when the female is not receptive. The signals used to bring about a change in behaviour are known as **sign stimuli** and, depending upon their origin or function, are classified as motivational, releasing or terminating stimuli.

Motivational stimuli. This type of stimulus may be external, for example increasing day length inducing territorial and courtship behaviour in birds, or internal, for example depleted food stores in the body during hibernation results in awakening and food seeking. Motivational stimuli provide the 'drive' or 'goal' preparing the organism for activity which may be triggered off by the second type of sign stimulus.

Releasing stimuli or 'releasers'. A releaser is either a simple stimulus or a sequence of stimuli produced by a member of a species which evokes a behavioural response in another member of the same species. The term 'releaser' was introduced by Lorenz and its role in behaviour was extensively studied by Tinbergen.

The effect of a releaser was demonstrated during an investigation into feeding in herring gulls. Young herring gulls normally peck at a red spot on the yellow lower mandible of the parent's bill to signal the parent to regurgitate fish which the young then swallow. In a series of controlled experiments, carried out by Tinbergen and Perdeck using cardboard models of adult gulls' heads, they found that the releaser of the begging response was the presence of a contrasting colour on the beak. Such was the strength of the releaser that a pointed stick with alternating coloured bands was able to elicit a greater response than the parent bird, as shown in fig 16.57.

Terminating stimuli. Terminating stimuli, as the name implies, complete the behavioural response and may be external or internal. For example, the external visual stimuli of a successfully completed nest will terminate nest building in birds, whereas the internal satisfaction or 'satiety' accompanying ejaculation in the male will terminate copulation and likewise a full stomach will terminate feeding.

Further examples of sign stimuli for a selection of behavioural mechanisms are discussed in sections 16.8.4–16.8.9.

Fig 16.56 *Female chimpanzee signalling to the male that she is sexually receptive*

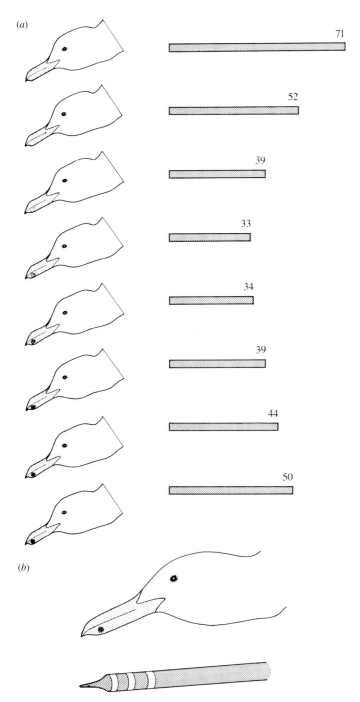

Fig 16.57 *(a) The horizontal bars indicate the number of pecking responses made by herring gull chicks to a series of cardboard models of adult herring gull heads having grey bills and spots of varying shade. (From Hinde, R. A. 1966, after Tinbergen, N., 1951)*
(b) The artificial bill, coloured red with three white bars evoked 20% more pecks than an accurate three-dimensional model of an adult herring gull head and beak, coloured yellow with a red spot. (From Tinbergen and Perdeck, 1950, Behaviour, 3.1)

16.8.4 Innate releasing mechanisms

Lorenz suggested that there must exist a means of filtering out stimuli which are irrelevant from those that are relevant to producing the correct behavioural response. Investigations suggest that this may occur peripherally at the receptors or centrally within the central nervous system. For example, Schneider found that the chemoreceptors on male moth antennae are only sensitive to the sex-attracting chemicals (pheromones) produced by the female of that species and not to those of other species. Modifications of Tinbergen and Perdeck's experiments on the herring gull have been carried out, and the results suggest, as Lorenz postulated, that centrally situated neurosecretory mechanisms control the response to sign stimuli.

16.8.5 Biological rhythms

Many behavioural activities occur at regular intervals and are known as biological rhythms or **biorhythms**. Well-known examples of these include the courtship displays and nesting behaviour of birds in the spring and the migration of certain bird species in autumn. The time interval between activities can vary from minutes to years depending on the nature of the activity and the species. For example, the polychaete lugworm *Arenicola marina* lives in a U-shaped burrow in sand or mud and carries out feeding movements every 6–7 min. This cyclical feeding pattern has no apparent external stimulus nor internal physiological motivational stimulus. It appears that the feeding pattern rhythm is regulated by a biological 'clock' mechanism dependent, in this case, on a 'pacemaker' originating in the pharynx and transmitted through the worm by the ventral nerve cord.

Rhythms involving an internal clock or pacemaker are known as **endogenous rhythms**, as opposed to **exogenous rhythms** which are controlled by external factors. Apart from examples such as the feeding behaviour of *Arenicola*, most biological rhythms are a blend of endogenous and exogenous rhythms.

In many cases the major external factor regulating the rhythmic activity is **photoperiod**, the relative lengths of day and night. This is the only factor which can provide a reliable indicator of time of year and is used to 'set the clock'. The exact nature of the clock is unknown but the clockwork mechanism is undoubtedly physiological and may involve both nervous and endocrine systems. The effect of photoperiod has been studied extensively in relation to behaviour in mammals, birds and insects and, whilst it is evidently important in activities such as preparation for hibernation in mammals, migration in birds and diapause in insects, it is not the only external factor regulating biological rhythms. Lunar rhythms, too, can influence activity in certain species, such as the palolo worm of Samoa. The polychaete worm swarms and mates throughout the whole South Pacific on one day of the year, the first day of the last lunar quarter of the year, on average

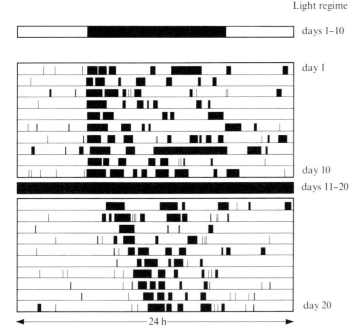

Light regime

days 1-10

day 1

day 10

days 11-20

day 20

← 24 h →

Fig 16.58 *Results of cockroach activity over a 20 day period. During days 1–10 the cockroach received a light regime of 12 hour light: 12 hour dark cycle and between days 11–20 the cockroach was kept in constant darkness as indicated in the figure. The black areas shown for each day represent the time and duration of each 'burst' of activity*

2nd November. The influence of lunar rhythms on tidal variations is well known, and these are two exogenous factors which have been shown to impose a rhythmic behaviour pattern on the midge *Clunio maritimus*. The larvae of *Clunio* feed on red algae growing at the extreme lower tidal limit, a point only uncovered by the tide twice each lunar month. Under natural conditions these larvae hatch, the adults mate and lay eggs in their two-hour-long life during which they are uncovered by the tide. In laboratory conditions of a constant 12 h light – 12 h dark photoperiod the larvae continued to hatch at about 15-day intervals, demonstrating the apparent existence of an endogenous clock programmed to an approximately semi-lunar rhythm coinciding with the 14.8-day tidal cycle.

The behaviour of many completely terrestrial insects appears to be controlled by endogenous rhythms related to periods of light and dark. For example, *Drosophila* emerge from pupae at dawn whereas cockroaches are most active at the onset of darkness and just before dawn. These regularly occurring biological rhythms, showing a periodicity of about 24 h, are known as **circadian** (*circa*, about; *dies*, day) rhythms or **diurnal** rhythms. In an investigation of the activity of a cockroach (*Periplaneta*) under two different light regimes (12 h light and 12 h darkness for 10 days followed by total darkness for 10 days), the cockroach restricted its activity in the later regime to a time approximately related to the period of activity associated with the onset of darkness under the former light regime. The results of this investigation are shown in fig 16.58 and

indicate that in the absence of an exernal time-cue the circadian rhythm persisted even though the onset of activity varied by a small amount each day. These results are consistent with the idea that circadian rhythms are controlled by an endogenous mechanism or 'clock', governed or 'set' by exogenous factors.

Circadian rhythms are believed to have many species-specific adaptive significances and one of these involves orientation. Animals such as fish, turtles, birds and some insects which migrate over long distances are believed to use the Sun and stars as a compass. Other animals, such as honeybees, ants and sandhoppers use the Sun as a compass in locating food and their homes. Compass orientation by Sun or Moon is only accurate if organisms using it possess some means of registering time so that allowances can be made for the daily movement of the Sun and Moon. The increasingly familiar concept of 'jetlag' is an example of a situation where the human internal physiological circadian rhythm is out of step with the day-and-night rhythm of the destination.

16.8.6 Territorial behaviour

A territory is an area held and defended by an organism or group or organisms against organisms of the same, or different, species. Territorial behaviour is common in all vertebrates except amphibia but is rare in non-vertebrates. Research into the nature and function of territoriality has been carried out on birds and groups of primates. In the latter it forms an important part of their social behaviour.

The exact function of territory formation probably varies from species to species, but in all cases it ensures that each mating pair of organisms and their offspring are adequately spaced to receive a share of the available resources, such as food and breeding space. In this way the species achieves optimum utilisation of the habitat. The size of territories occupied by any particular species varies from season to season, according to the availability of environmental resources. Birds of prey and large carnivores have territories several square miles in area in order to provide all their food requirements. Herring gulls and penguins (fig 16.59), however, have territories of only a few square metres, since they move out of their territories to feed and use them for breeding purposes only.

Territories are found, prior to breeding, usually by males. Defence of the area is greatest at the time of breeding and fiercest between males of the same species. There are a variety of behavioural activities associated with territory formation and they involve threat displays between owners of adjacent territories. These threat displays involve certain stimuli which act as releasers. For example, Lack demonstrated that an adult male robin (*Erithacus rubecula*) would attack a stuffed adult male robin displaying a red breast, and a bunch of red breast feathers, but not a stuffed young male robin which did not have a red breast. The level of aggression shown by an

organism increases towards the centre of the territory. The aggressiveness of males is determined partly by the level of testosterone in the body and this can affect territory size. For example, the territory size of a red grouse can be increased by injecting the bird with testosterone. Fig 16.60 shows the changes in territory size of three red grouse treated in this way. The boundary between adjacent territories represents the point where neighbouring animals show equally strong defence behaviour. Despite the apparent conflict and aggression associated with territory formation, actual fighting, which would be detrimental to the species, is rare and is replaced by threats, gestures and postures. Having obtained a territory many species, particularly carnivores, proceed to mark out the boundary by leaving a scent trail. This may be done by urinating or rubbing glandular parts of the body against objects called **scent posts** along the boundary of the territory. Although territorial behaviour involves the sharing of available resources amongst the population there are inevitably some organisms unable to secure and defend a territory. In many bird species, such as grouse, these weaker organisms are relegated to the edges of the habitat where they fail to mate. This appears to be one of the adaptive significances of territoriality as it ensures that only the 'fittest' find a territory, breed and thus pass on their genes to the next generation. Thus a further function of territorial behaviour is associated with **intraspecific competition** and may act as a means of regulating population size.

Fig 16.59 *Aerial photograph showing the territories occupied by penguins*

Fig 16.60 *The solid lines indicate the territories of a group of male red grouse. The dotted lines show changes which occurred after birds **A**, **X** and **Y** had received doses of testosterone. Birds **X** and **Y** had not previously held territories. (After Watson, A (1970). J. Reprod. Fert., Suppl., 11.3.)*

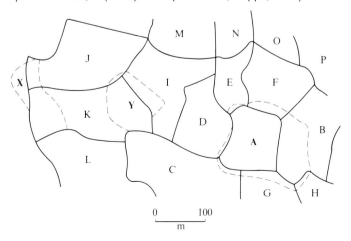

16.8.7 Courtship and mating

There are many elaborate and ritualistic species-specific behaviour patterns associated with courtship and mating. In birds, mammals and some fish these two processes often follow the establishment of a territory by the male. Courtship is a complex behaviour pattern designed to stimulate organisms to sexual activity and is associated with pair formation in those species where both sexes are involved in the rearing of offspring, as in thrushes, or in gregarious mixed-sex groups such as baboons. The majority of these species show rhythmic sexual activity of the type described in section 16.8.5.

Courtship behaviour is controlled primarily by motivational and releasing stimuli and leads to mating which is the culmination of courtship. During mating, the behavioural activities are initiated by releasing stimuli and ended by terminating stimuli associated with the release of gametes by the male.

The motivational stimuli for courtship in most species are external, such as photoperiod, and lead to rising levels of reproductive hormones and the maturation of the gonads. In most species this produces striking changes in the secondary sexual characteristics and other behavioural activities including coloration changes, as in the development of a red belly in male sticklebacks; increase in size of parts of the body, as in the plumage of birds of paradise; mating calls, as in nightingales; postural displays, as in grebes (fig 16.61) and the use of chemical sex attractants, as in butterflies and moths.

Of the variety of signals used in courtship to attract members of the opposite sex, sight, sound and smell play important roles. For example, the male fiddler crab, *Uca*, uses a visual display and attracts females by waving an enlarged chela in a bowing movement similar to that of a violinist. The vigour of the movement increases as a female is attracted to the male.

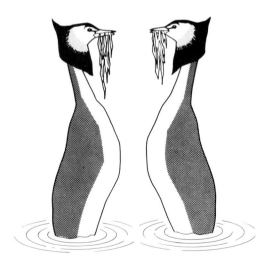

Fig 16.61 *A courtship behavioural activity in great crested grebes. Male and female grebes are shown here presenting nesting material to each other. (After Huxley, J. S. (1914). Proc. Zool. Soc. Lond., 1914 (2), 491–562)*

Many insects, amphibia, birds and mammals use auditory signals in courtship. Some species of female mosquito attract males by the sounds produced by the frequencies of their wing beats whilst grasshoppers, crickets and locusts **stridulate**. This involves either rubbing the hindlegs against each other or the elytron (hardened wing case), or rubbing the elytra together to produce a 'chirping' sound which is species-specific and only produces a response from members of *that* species.

Some species of spiders employ a mechanical means of attracting the opposite sex. Male spiders approach the web of a female sitting at the centre of the web and pluck a thread of the web at a species-specific frequency. The plucking 'serenades' the female and reduces her natural aggressive manner so enabling the male to approach and mate her. Unfortunately, if the male 'woos' a female of the wrong species or 'plays the wrong tune' he is attacked and killed!

The secretion and release by organisms of small amounts of chemical substances, leading to specific physiological or behavioural responses in other members of the same species, is used in courtship and mating and, as described later, the regulation of behaviour within social groups. These substances are called **pheromones** and are usually highly volatile, low relative molecular mass compounds. Many of these compounds function as natural sex attractants and the earliest to be identified were **civetone** from the civet cat and **muscone** from the musk deer. Both of these substances are secretions from the anal glands and are used commercially in the preparation of perfume. Mares, cows and bitches secrete pheromones whilst on 'heat'. This is undetectable by human olfactory epithelium but detectable by the males of the species concerned. **Bombykol**, a pheromone released by eversible glands at the tip of the abdomen of unfertilised adult female silk moths, is capable of attracting males of the same species from considerable distances. The olfactory receptors on the antennae of the male moths detect the presence of the pheromone molecules in great dilutions and the moths make a rheotactic response by flying upwind until they reach the female. Pheromones are used increasingly as a method of **biological control** in insect pest species such as the gypsy moth. In these cases the artificial release of the pheromone, **gyplure**, attracts males to the source of release where they can be captured and killed. This not only immediately reduces the number of male moths in the population but also, in preventing them from breeding, reduces the size of the next generation.

Pheromones are also used to induce mating as in the case of the queen butterfly *Danaus gilippus*. The pheromone is released by the male and brushed on to the female by a pair of brush-like structures, called hairpencils, everted from the tip of the abdomen. The entire courting and mating sequence is shown in fig 16.62.

Courtship in some species is accompanied by conflict behaviour on the part of one or both sexes. In species where individuals normally live a solitary existence,

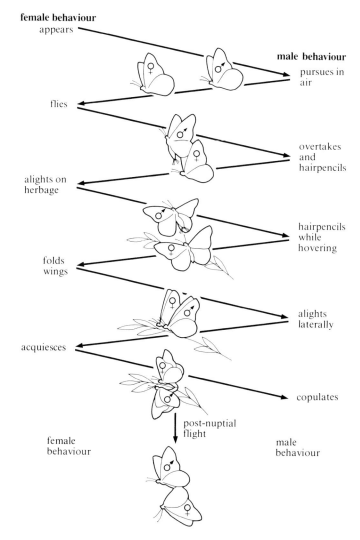

female behaviour
appears

male behaviour
pursues in air

flies

overtakes and hairpencils

alights on herbage

hairpencils while hovering

folds wings

alights laterally

acquiesces

copulates

post-nuptial flight

female behaviour

male behaviour

Fig 16.62 *Courtship and copulation in the queen butterfly. (The arrows indicate the stimuli and responses involved in the behavioural activities). (From Brower, L. P., Brower, J. V. Z. and Cranston, F. P. (1965).* Zoologica, *50, 18)*

courtship conflict may be associated with changing attitudes to other members of the species as a result of increasing hormone levels. Other significances of this behaviour may be the tightening of the pair bond between the mating pair and the synchronisation of gonadial development so that gametes mature at the same time. In certain species of spider, such as wolf spiders, conflict between male and female only diminishes for the act of copulation which culminates in the female killing the male.

16.8.8 Aggression (agonistic behaviour)

Aggression is a group of behavioural activities including threat postures, rituals and occasionally physical attacks on other organisms, other than those associated with predation. They are usually directed towards members of the same sex and species and have various functions including the displacement of other animals from an area, usually a territory or a source of food, the defence of a mate

or offspring and the establishment of rank in a social hierarchy.

The term 'aggression' is emotive and suggests an existence of unnecessary violence within animal groups; the alternative term '**agonistic**' is preferable. Agonistic behaviour has the adaptive significance of reducing intraspecific conflict and avoiding overt fighting which is not in the best interest of the species. Most species channel their 'aggression' into ritual contests of strength and threat postures which are universally recognised by the species. For example, horned animals such as deer, moose, ibex and chamois may resort to butting contests for which 'ground rules' exist. Only the horns are allowed to clash and they are not used on the exposed and vulnerable flank. Siamese fighting fish, *Betta splendens*, resort to threat postures involving increasing their apparent size as shown in fig 16.63.

The threats issued by two organisms in an agonistic conflict situation are settled invariably by one of the organisms, generally the weaker, backing down and withdrawing from the situation by exhibiting a posture of submission or appeasement. In dogs and wolves an appeasement posture may take the form of the animal lying down on its back or baring its throat to the victor.

During actual physical contact animals often refrain from using their most effective weapons on another member of the same species. For example, giraffes will fight each other using the short horns on their heads, but in defence against other animals they use their very powerful feet.

For agonistic behavioural activities to be most effective they must be stereotyped for any species and Tinbergen demonstrated several of these during investigations carried

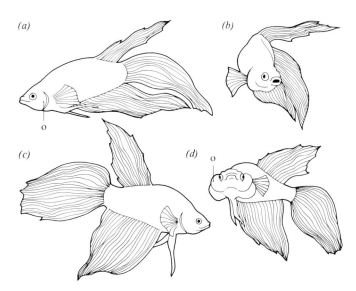

Fig. 16.63 *Stages in threat displays in Siamese fighting fish. (a) and (b) fish not showing threat displays, (c) and (d) operculum, o, and fins erected to increase their apparent size during threat displays. (From Hinde, R. A., 1970, after Simpson, 1968)*

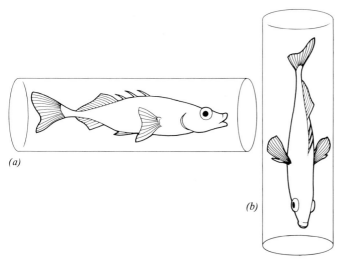

Fig 16.64 (above) (a) Full threat posture in male stickleback (b) Reduced threat posture when contained in a tube held vertically. (After Tinbergen, N., 1951)

Fig 16.65 (below) Models used as releasers of aggressive behaviour in male sticklebacks holding a territory. (a) Accurate model not having a red belly does not elicit aggression from male stickleback. (b)–(c) are models of sticklebacks not having an accurate shape but having a red belly. All these models produced aggressive responses from male sticklebacks. (After Tinbergen, 1951)

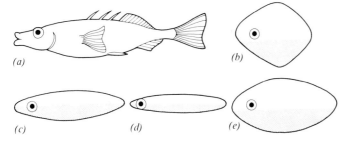

out on sticklebacks. In one series of experiments he demonstrated that the effectiveness of threat posture depended on the stickleback assuming a horizontal position with fins and spines outstretched. When trapped in a specimen tube and kept vertical a male stickleback does not have the same threat potential to ward off other sticklebacks as it has when free-swimming or held horizontally (fig 16.64).

In another series of experiments he demonstrated that agonistic behaviour in male sticklebacks defending a territory is triggered off by 'releasers' which can take the form of almost any object whose underside is coloured red. These objects act as mimics of male sticklebacks whose bellies turn red during the breeding season and who appear to the territory holder as a potential threat (fig 16.65).

At times of stress, for example during conflict situations or during courtship and mating, an organism may perform an action which is trivial and irrelevant to the situation. This is known as **displacement activity** and occurs when motivation is high but two conflicting 'releasers' present themselves. For example, one of a pair of birds involved in a territorial dispute may begin nest-building activities, such as pulling up grass, when presented with a choice between fighting or fleeing. Such displacement activities act as an outlet for pent-up activities. Many human activities may be considered displacement activities in certain circumstances, for example fist clenching, fist banging, nail biting, straightening clothes, finger drumming, etc. A similar form of behaviour is called **vacuum activity** which occurs when motivation is high and no releaser presents itself. In this case the normal response is produced but is not directed towards the normal object or situation, and so provides a means of reducing frustration; for example, showing irritation towards someone who is not the cause of the irritation but acts as a substitute.

16.8.9 Social hierarchies

Many species of insects and most vertebrates show a variety of group behavioural activities associated with numbers of individuals living together temporarily or permanently. This is known as **social behaviour** and the coherence and cooperation achieved has the adaptive significance of increasing the efficiency and effectiveness of the species over that of other species. In a social group of this kind a system of communication is essential, and the efficiency of the organisation is further increased by individuals carrying out particular roles within the society. One aspect of social behaviour arising out of these points is the existence of **social hierarchies** or **pecking orders**.

A pecking order is a **dominance hierarchy**. That is to say that animals within the group are arranged according to status. For example, in a group of hens sharing a hen-house a linear order is found in which hen A will peck any other hen in the group, hen B will peck all hens other than A and so on. Position in the hierarchy is usually decided by some agonistic form of behaviour other than fighting. Similar patterns of dominance have been observed in other species of birds and in mice, rats, cows and baboons. The institutional organisation of all human societies is based on a pattern of dominance hierarchy.

Pecking orders exist only where animals are able to recognise each other as individuals and possess some ability to learn. The position of an animal within a pecking order usually depends on size, strength, fitness and aggressiveness and, within bird hierarchies, remains fairly stable during the lifetime of the individuals. Lower-order male members can be raised up the hierarchy by injections of testosterone which increase their levels of aggressiveness. The experimental removal of lower-order mice from a hierarchy and subsequent provision of unlimited food for them increases their mass, improves their vigour and can raise their position in the hierarchy when reintroduced to the group. Similarly placing lower-order mice into other groups where they are dominant appears to give them a degree of 'self-confidence' (to use an anthropomorphic term) which stays with them when reintroduced to their original groups and results in their rank increasing.

One advantage of pecking order is that it decreases the amount of individual aggression associated with feeding, mate selection and breeding-site selection. Similarly it avoids injury to the stronger animals which might occur if fighting was necessary to establish the hierarchy. Another advantage of pecking order is that it ensures that resources are shared out so that the fittest survive. For example, if a group of 100 hens is provided with sufficient food for only 50 hens it is preferable, in terms of the species, for 50 hens to be adequately fed and the weaker 50 hens die than for them all to live and receive only half rations, as this might prevent successful breeding. In the short term, social hierarchies increase the genetic vigour of the group by ensuring that the strongest and genetically fittest animals have an advantage when it comes to reproducing.

Social organisation

When animals come together to form a cohesive social group individuals often assume specialised roles, which increases the overall efficiency of the group (fig 16.66). These roles include members specialised or designated for food-finding, reproduction, rearing and defence. Cooperation between members of a society sharing division of labour depends upon stereotyped patterns of behaviour and effective means of communication. These patterns of behaviour and methods of communication vary between species and are vastly different for primate and insect societies. Primate societies are flexible, in that roles are interchangeable between members of the group whereas in insect societies differences in body structure and reproductive potential affect their role within the society, a feature called **polymorphism**.

Ants, termites and bees are social insects living in colonies and have an organisation based on a **caste system**. In the honeybee colony there is a single fertile female queen, several thousand sterile female workers and a few hundred fertile male drones. Each type of honeybee has a specific series of roles determined primarily by whether it hatched from a fertilised or an unfertilised egg. Fertilised eggs are diploid and develop into females; unfertilised eggs are haploid and develop into males. Secondly, the type of food provided for female larvae determines whether they will become queens or workers. This food is called **royal jelly** and is one example of the importance of chemical substances in the organisation of the society. Information within the colony is transmitted either by chemical odours and pheromones during the many licking and grooming activities called **trophallaxes**, or by particular forms of visual orientation displays known as **dances**.

Karl von Frisch, a German zoologist and Nobel prize-winner, investigated the nature of these dances using marked worker bees in specially constructed observation hives. Worker bees 'forage' for sources of nectar and communicate the distance and direction of the source to other workers by the nature of a dance generally performed on a vertical comb in the hive. If the distance is less than about 90 m the worker performs a **round dance** as shown in fig 16.67a which intimates that the source is less than 90 m from the hive but gives no indication of direction. The **waggle dance** is performed if the source is greater than 90 m and includes information as to its distance from the hive and its direction relative to the hive and the position of the sun. The dance involves the worker walking in a figure-of-eight and waggling her abdomen during which, according to von Frisch, the speed of the dance is inversely related to the distance of the food from the hive; the angle made

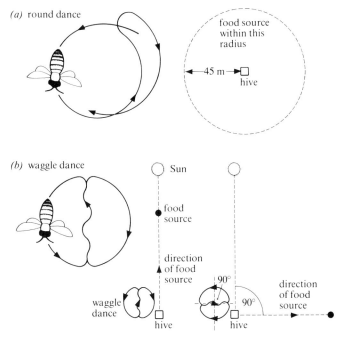

(a) round dance

(b) waggle dance

Fig 16.67 Honeybee dances
(a) Round dance is performed when food is less than 90 metres from hive
(b) Waggle dance shows relation between hive, sun and direction of food source

Fig 16.66 Social grooming in adult chimpanzees provides a means of social cohesion within a group

between the two loops of the figure-of-eight and the vertical equals the angle subtended at the hive by the sun; and the food source and the intensity of the waggles is related to the amount of food at the source (fig 14.67*b*). It is thought that allowances for movement of the sun are made by the use of an inbuilt 'biological clock' and that bees orientate on cloudy days by substituting polarised light from the sun for the position of the sun.

Recent evidence has suggested that bees may use high-frequency sound to communicate sources of food to other workers, but whether this is the main means of communication has yet to be demonstrated clearly. This does not, though, invalidate the data and interpretations of von Frisch and may be an associated communication system which augments the visual dance displays. However, it is known that the returning worker may communicate the type of flower visited by feeding the other workers with some of the nectar collected.

16.8.10 Altruistic behaviour

One area of social behaviour which is not fully understood concerns the way in which certain organisms expend time and energy in caring for other members of the species. This phenomenon is called **altruism** and it refers to a form of social behaviour whereby one organism puts itself either at risk or personal disadvantage for the good of other members of the species.

In the case of activities associated with mating and parental care altruism is not so difficult to comprehend since the action is clearly in the interests of the parents, offspring and species. For example, the female baboon protects and cares for its offspring for almost six years whilst most bird species feed and protect their demanding offspring until they are capable of fending for themselves. What is not so clear is the reason why some organisms give support to organisms which are *not* their offspring, for example, birds and monkeys that call out warnings to others in danger and female monkeys who carry and care for the babies of other monkeys.

One insight into the mechanisms regulating this type of behaviour is seen in the **eusocial** insects such as honeybees, wasps and ants that have a caste system. Here the advantages to the species of division of labour based on a social hierarchy are apparent, but what is slightly obscure is the mechanism by which such behaviour arose.

Here the sterile female workers are prevented, by definition, from producing offspring, yet they spend their lives looking after their brothers and sisters. Investigation of the chromosome composition of the queen, drones and workers show that sisters (queen and workers) are more closely related to each other than mothers are to sons or daughters. This is because the fertile queen is diploid, the sterile worker is diploid and the drone (male) is haploid. Hence by helping their sister (queen) to reproduce they are effectively aiding in the production of queens, workers and drones with a genetic complement closer to their own than if they had offspring of their own. The conferring of a genetic advantage on closely related organisms forms the basis of altruistic behaviour.

Altruistic behaviour is very common amongst primates and varies from the extremes of social protection which exist between members of the same troop (monkeys), through acts of mutual grooming and food sharing (apes) to deliberate acts of self-sacrifice for family, God and country (humans). The extent of the altruistic behaviour appears to be related to close relatives (**kin**) such as offspring and **siblings** (brothers, sisters and cousins) with whom they share certain alleles. Thus the adaptive significance of altruistic behaviour is to increase the frequency of those alleles common both to the donor and recipient(s) of the altruistic behaviour. This behaviour is called **kin selected** and it has led to the establishment of altruism because of the way it confers genetic advantages in kin by promoting survival and reproduction within the species.

In situations where the altruistic behaviour is directed generally towards members of the species rather than to close relatives it is postulated that again the result of the behaviour will enable selection of those alleles responsible for the behaviour to be perpetuated within the benefiting group. This conclusion is backed up by observation which reveals that such general altruistic behaviour is much commoner in species such as the zebra which live in coherent families than in species such as the wildebeest where family groupings are uncommon.

Parallel examples of altruistic behaviour occur in humans too, where once again the intensity of the behaviour is related to kinship and responses are strongest between family members sharing the same alleles.

16.9 Learned behaviour

16.9.1 Memory

Memory is the ability to store and recall the effects of experience and without it learning is not possible. Past experiences, in the form of stimuli and responses, are recorded as a 'memory trace' or **engram**, and since the extent of learning in mammals is proportional to the extent of the cerebral hemispheres it would appear that these are the site of engram formation and storage.

The nature of the engram is not known and it exists only as a hypothetical concept backed up by conflicting data. Of the two broad areas of thought on the nature of the engram one is based on changes in neuronal structure and organisation within the central nervous system and the other based on permanent changes in brain biochemistry.

Histological examination of brain tissue shows the existence of neurones arranged in loops, and this has given rise to the concept of '**reverberating circuits**' as units of the engram. According to this view these circuits are continuously active carrying the memory information. It is doubtful if this activity could last for any length of time and experiments suggest that memory has greater performance and stability than could be achieved by this mechanism alone. For example, cooling the brains of rats down to 0 °C causes all electrical activity in the nervous system to cease, but on restoring the rats to normal temperatures there is no impairment in memory. However, it is thought that such circuits may play a role in **short-term memory**, that is memory lasting at most for minutes such as memorising six-digit telephone numbers in humans and in facilitating particular neural pathways. Events associated with short-term memory take longer to be recalled following concussion or amnesia and gradually disappear in old age. Long-term memory is more stable and suggests that some mechanism for permanent change exists in the brain.

Evidence based on the latter observation suggests that memory is a biochemical event involving the synthesis of substances within the brain. Extracts of the 'brains' of trained flatworms or rats injected into untrained flatworms or rats reduce the time taken by the latter organisms to learn the same task as compared with control groups. The active substance in all the experiments appears to be RNA.

Further evidence exists which suggests that the composition of the RNA of neurones changes during learning and that this may result in the synthesis of specific 'memory proteins' associated with the learned behaviour. Investigations have shown that injections of the protein-inhibiting drug, puromycin, also interfere with memory. For example, injecting puromycin into the brains of mice recently trained to choose one direction in a maze destroyed their ability to retain this learning, whereas a control group, injected with saline, retained the learned behaviour.

In conclusion, it would appear that the nature of memory is far from being clarified but it seems probable that

Table 16.18. Summary of the major types of learned behaviour based on a classification proposed by Thorpe (1963)

Learned behaviour	Features of the learned behaviour
Habituation	Continuous repetition of a stimulus not associated with reward or punishment (reinforcement) extinguishes any response to the stimulus, e.g. birds **learn** to ignore a scarecrow. Important in development of behaviour in young animals in helping to understand neutral elements in the environment, such as movements due to wind, cloud-shadows, wave-action, etc. It is based in the nervous system and is not a form of sensory adaptation since the behaviour is permanent and no response is ever shown to the stimulus after the period of habituation.
Associative learning — Classical conditioning (conditioned reflex)	Based on the research of Pavlov on dogs. It involves the development of a conditioned salivary reflex in which animals **learn** to produce a **conditioned response** (salivation), not only to the natural **unconditioned stimulus** (sight of food) but also to a newly acquired **conditioned stimulus** (ticking of a metronome) which was presented to the dog along with the unconditioned stimulus. Animals learn to **associate** unconditioned stimuli with conditioned stimuli so either produces a response. For example, birds avoid eating black and orange cinnabar moth larvae because of bad taste and avoid all similarly coloured larvae even though they may be nutritious.
Associative learning — Operant conditioning (trial-and-error learning)	Based on the research of Skinner on pigeons. Trial motor activities give rise to responses which are reinforced either by rewarding (positive) or punishment (negative). The **association** of the outcome of a response in terms of reward or punishment increases or decreases respectively future responses. Associative learning efficiency is increased by repetition as shown in investigations carried out on learning in cuttlefish (fig. 16.68).
Latent learning (exploratory learning)	Not all behavioural activities are apparently directed to satisfying a need or obtaining a reward (i.e. appetitive behaviour). Animals explore new surroundings and **learn** information which may be useful at a later stage (hence latent) and mean the difference between life and death. For example in mice, knowledge of the immediate environment of its burrow may help it escape from a predator. At the time of acquiring this knowledge it had no apparent value. This appears to be the method by which chaffinches learn to sing, as described in section 16.8.2.
Insight learning	Probably the 'highest' form of learning. It does not result from immediate trial-and-error learning but may be based on information previously learned by other behavioural activities. Insight learning is based on advanced perceptual abilities such as thought and reasoning. Kohler's work on chimpanzees suggested 'insight learning': when presented with wooden boxes and bananas too high to reach the chimps stacked up the boxes beneath the bananas and climbed up to get them. Observations revealed that this response appeared to follow a period of 'apparent thought' (previous experience of playing with boxes [latent learning] may have increased the likelihood of the response).
Imprinting	A simple and specialised form of learning occurring during receptive periods in an animal's life. The learned behaviour becomes relatively fixed and resistant to change. Imprinting involves young animals becoming associated with, and identifying themselves with, another organism, usually a parent, or some large object. Lorenz found that goslings and ducklings deprived of their parents would follow him and use him as a substitute parent. 'Pet lambs', bottle-fed, show similar behaviour and this may have a profound and not always desirable effect later in life when the animal finds difficulty in forming normal relationships with others of the species. In the natural situation imprinting has obvious adaptive significance in enabling offspring to acquire rapidly skills possessed by the parents, e.g. learning to fly in birds, and features of the environment, e.g. the 'smell' of the stream in which migratory salmon were hatched and to which they return to spawn.

changes in electrical properties of neurones, the permeability of synaptic membranes, enzyme production associated with synapses and synaptic transmission are all concerned with the formation of a 'memory trace'. Certainly it seems that memory is associated closely with events occurring at synapses.

16.9.2 Learning

Learning is an adaptive change in individual behaviour as a result of previous experience (fig 16.68). The degree of permanence of newly acquired learned behaviour patterns depends upon memory storing the information gained from the experience. In humans, acquiring or learning 'facts', for example for examinations, may be short-lived whereas the ability to carry out coordinated motor activities such as toilet training, riding a bicycle or swimming, lasts throughout life. Learning is generally thought of in terms of vertebrates, and mammals in particular, but has been demonstrated in all groups of animals except protozoans, cnidarians and echinoderms where neural organisation is absent or poorly developed. Psychologists have attempted to establish general 'laws of learning' but all attempts so far have failed. It would appear that learning is an individual event and occurs in different ways in different speceis and different contexts. The classification and features of learned behaviour presented

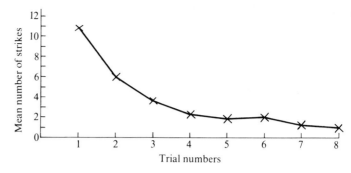

Fig 16.68 *The graph above shows a typical 'learning curve'. The graph shows the results of the number of times a cuttlefish strikes at a prawn kept in a glass tube. The prawn was presented to the cuttlefish on eight successive occasions lasting three minutes each time. As the cuttlefish unsuccessfully attacks the prawn the number of attacks decreases as the cuttlefish 'learns' that it cannot capture the prawn. (The results are based on data obtained from forty cuttlefish, from Messenger, J. B., (1977), Symp. Zoo. Soc. Lond., 38, 347–76)*

in this chapter are artificial and must be recognised as such. They do, however, cover the spectrum on current thinking on types of learning and are backed up by experimental evidence. A summary of the major types of learned behaviour is given in table 16.18 and is designed to provide only an introduction to the topic of learning.

Chapter Seventeen

Movement and support

Movement can occur at the cellular level, for instance cytoplasmic streaming and swimming of gametes, at organ level, such as heartbeat and movement of a limb, or at the level of the organism. Movement of the whole organism from place to place is termed **locomotion**. Plants exhibit cellular and often organ movement, but they do not locomote, that is move from place to place in search of food or water.

Whilst a few animals can survive successfully by remaining attached to one place, the vast majority have complex locomotory systems which presumably evolved to enable them to search for and acquire food. However, even sessile animals exhibit a great degree of mobility of their bodily parts.

Apart from the need for food, some animals use locomotion to avoid capture by predators. It is also used for dispersal purposes and locating new favourable habitats as well as for bringing together individuals for reproductive activity.

Locomotion is the result of the arrangement, interaction and coordination of the nervous, muscular and skeletal systems. Muscles promoting locomotion are attached to the skeleton and are therefore called **skeletal muscles** (section 17.4.1). They act as machines, converting chemical energy into mechanical energy. They have the ability to contract, and when they do they serve to move the systems of levers comprising part of the skeleton. Coordinated movement of the levers enables the animal to move about. The posture of the animal is also maintained by the musculo-skeletal system which is under the overall control of the central nervous system.

Other muscles within the body serve not to move the whole organism but to move materials from place to place within it. Cardiac muscle (section 8.5) of the heart pumps blood round the body, whilst smooth muscle (section 17.5.3) located in the walls of various blood vessels constricts or dilates them and this alters the blood flow. Smooth muscle in the wall of the gut propels food along the intestinal tract by means of peristalsis (section 10.4.11). These are just a few of many such activities constantly occurring within the body.

In this chapter we will be primarily concerned with locomotion, and two systems will be discussed in detail, namely the skeletal and muscle systems. This will be followed by a review of the types of locomotion that occur in a wide variety of organisms.

17.1 Skeletal systems

The vast majority of animals possess some form of supportive structure. It may be from simple rods of strengthening material in the protozoans to the highly complex skeleton of arthropods and vertebrates. Generally speaking, the design of the supporting structure contributes towards the specific shape of the organism. This, in turn, is dictated by the particular requirements of the organism concerned. Structures of different design are needed for aquatic or terrestrial animals, quadripedal or bipedal animals, and for those that move over the ground or through the air.

The general functions of a skeleton are as follows.

(1) **Support**. All skeletons provide a rigid framework for the body and are resistant to compression. They help to maintain the shape of the body. For terrestrial organisms the skeleton supports the weight of the body against gravitational force and in many cases raises it above the ground. This permits more efficient movement over the ground. Within the body, organs are attached to, and suspended, from the skeleton.

(2) **Protection**. The skeleton protects the delicate internal organs in those organisms with an **exoskeleton** (arthropods), and parts of the **endoskeleton** are designed for a similar function. For example, in humans the cranium protects the brain and the sense organs of sight, smell, balance and hearing; the vertebral column protects the spinal cord, and the ribs and sternum protect the heart, lungs and large blood vessels.

(3) **Locomotion**. Skeletons composed of rigid material provide a means of attachment for the muscles of the body. Parts of the skeleton operate as levers on which the muscles can pull. When this occurs, movement takes place. Soft-bodied animals rely on muscles acting against body fluids to produce their form of locomotion.

Three major types of skeleton are generally recognised: hydrostatic, exoskeleton and endoskeleton.

17.1.1 Hydrostatic skeleton

This is characteristic of soft-bodied animals. Here fluid is secreted within the body and enclosed by the body wall muscles. The fluid presses against the muscles which in turn are able to contract against the fluid. The muscles are not attached to any structures and thus they can only pull against each other. The combined effect of muscle contraction and fluid pressure serves to maintain the shape and form of the animal. Generally there are two muscle layers, one longitudinal and the other circular in orientation. When they act antagonistically against each other locomotion is effected. If the body of the organism is unsegmented (as in nematodes), when a particular muscle contracts, the pressure on the fluid will be transmitted to all other parts of the body. If the organism is segmented (such as *Lumbricus terrestris*, the earthworm) then such pressure is localised and only certain segments will move or change shape. A detailed account of the function of the hydrostatic skeleton in locomotion is given for the earthworm in section 17.6.5.

17.1.2   Exoskeleton

This is a particular characteristic of the arthropods. Epidermal cells secrete a non-cellular cuticle, or exoskeleton, composed mainly of **chitin**. It acts as a hard outer covering to the animal and is made up of a series of articulated plates or tubes covering or surrounding organs. It also extends into the anterior (stomodeum) and posterior (proctodeum) ends of the alimentary canal, and into the tracheae. Chitin is very tough, light and flexible; however, it can be strengthened by impregnation with 'tanned' (hardened) proteins, and, particularly in the aquatic crustaceans, by calcium carbonate. Where flexibility is required, as at the joints between plates or tubes, chitin remains unmodified. This combination of a system of plates and tubes joined together by flexible membranes provides both protection and mobility.

Arthropods are the only non-vertebrate group to possess jointed appendages. The joints are hinges, and the levers on either side are operated by flexor and extensor muscles which are attached to inward projections of the exoskeleton (fig 17.1). Chitin is permeable to water and this could lead to desiccation of terrestrial animals like insects. This is prevented by the secretion of a thin waxy epicuticle via ducts from gland cells in the epidermis (fig 4.28). Therefore, the exoskeleton supports and protects the delicate inner parts of the animal and in addition prevents their drying up.

The hollow tubular form of the exoskeleton is very efficient as a supporting and locomotive device for small animals, such as most arthropods, and can support a much greater weight without giving way than a solid cylindrical strut of the same mass. However, it loses this efficiency when organisms become bigger and their weight increases. Here, to do the same job just as efficiently, the exoskeleton would have to increase in weight and thickness. The end product would be very heavy and cumbersome.

Growth takes place by **ecdysis** (moulting) in juvenile stages (larvae and nymphs) in insects and throughout adult life in crustaceans. At various times the exoskeleton is shed (ecdysis), thus exposing a new, soft and extensible exoskeleton. Whilst still soft, growth takes place as the

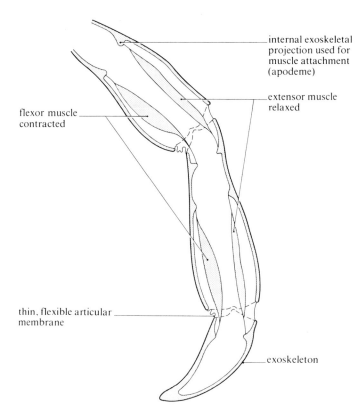

Fig 17.1   *VS of joints and musculature of an arthropod limb*

exoskeleton is extended and moulded into a larger form which often incorporates a change of shape. The new exoskeleton finally hardens. The animal is vulnerable to predators whilst the new exoskeleton is hardening. At this stage the skeleton is unable to support the weight of the animal and movement is virtually impossible. This is less of a problem for aquatic species as their body weight is supported by the water, but aquatic and terrestial organisms usually hide themselves away during this time in an attempt to decrease their chances of being devoured by predators. Moulting is quite expensive in terms of the energy expenditure involved in building the exoskeleton in the first place and material loss when it is shed.

17.1.3   Endoskeleton

This is found in the protoctistan order Radiolaria, where it consists of a skeleton of siliceous spicules, the molluscan class Cephalopoda, where some organisms such as the cuttlefish possess an internal shell, and in vertebrates. Typically the vertebrate skeleton is made either of cartilage or bone, is located within the organism and is internal to the muscles. A further difference between this form of skeleton and the exoskeleton is that the endoskeleton is composed of living tissue and so can grow steadily within the animal thus avoiding the necessity for ecdysis. A number of different types of joint exist and bones that form them are maintained in their correct relative position by elastic ligaments. Skeletal design in quadrupeds and bipeds is essentially the same, but there are slight differences in mobility at the shoulder and the hip. This is correlated with the type of locomotion adopted by the animals concerned and will be discussed in detail later.

17.1.4 The vertebrate skeleton

The vertebrate skeleton is composed either of cartilage or bone. Both tissues provide an internal supporting framework for the body. Only cartilaginous fish (such as dogfish and sharks) possess a whole cartilaginous endoskeleton. All other vertebrates have a bony skeleton in their adult form, but with cartilage also present in certain regions, such as at the joints or between the vertebrae. In the embryo stage the skeleton of bony vertebrates is initially laid down as hyaline cartilage (section 8.4.4). This is of great biological significance, as cartilage is capable of internal enlargement, and so different parts of the skeleton are able to grow in proportion with each other during the development of the organism. Bone is different from cartilage in this respect as it can grow only by addition of material to its outer surface. If this were to occur during development, the articulating surfaces of bones and joints, and their respective points of muscle attachment would be unable to retain their correct spatial relationships.

17.2 Skeletal tissues

17.2.1 Cartilage

Three types of cartilaginous material are recognisable: **hyaline, white fibrous** and **yellow elastic** cartilage. A detailed account of their histology can be found in section 8.4.4. All types consist of a firm matrix penetrated by numerous connective tissue fibres. The matrix is secreted by living cells called chondroblasts. These later become housed in spaces (lacunae) scattered throughout the matrix. In this condition the cells are termed chondrocytes. Hyaline cartilage is the most common type and is found particularly at the ends of bones articulating to form joints. Its matrix of chondroitin sulphate is compressible and elastic, and is well able to withstand heavy weight and absorb sharp mechanical shocks such as might take place at joints. Within the matrix are embedded fine collagen fibres which provide resistance to tension and compression. Dense connective tissue, called the perichondrium, surrounds the outer surface of this cartilage at all places except where it passes into the cavity of a joint.

White fibrous cartilage contains a dense meshwork of collagen fibres and is found as discs between vertebrae and as a component of tendons. It is very strong yet possesses a degree of flexibility. Yellow elastic cartilage possesses many yellow elastic fibres and is located in the external ear, epiglottis and pharyngeal cartilages.

17.2.2 Bone

Bone is a hard, tough connective tissue composed mainly of calcified material. Details of its histology can be found in section 8.4.4. When a vertical longitudinal section of a long bone, such as a femur, is examined microscopically it is seen to be made up of several distinct components. Such a bone consists of a hollow shaft or **diaphysis**, with an expanded head or **epiphysis** at each end. Covering the entire bone is a sheath of tough connective tissue, the periosteum. The diaphysis is composed of compact bone whilst the epiphyses are composed of spongy bone overlain by a thin layer of compact bone. The layout of the bony material is designed to withstand compression forces and to give maximum strength to the bone (fig 17.2).

Fatty yellow marrow occupies the marrow cavity of the diaphysis, whilst red marrow is present amongst the bony struts (**trabeculae**) of the epiphyses. Numerous small openings penetrate the surface of the bone, through which nerves and blood vessels traverse into the bony tissue and marrow.

Apart from the functions listed earlier in the chapter, a bony skeleton also functions to produce red blood corpuscles and white granulocytes. Further it participates in the maintenance of constant calcium and phosphorus levels in the bloodstream (see chapter 16) by providing a store of calcium and phosphate ions which can be mobilised by the action of parathyroid and calcitonin hormones of the parathyroid and thyroid glands respectively.

> **17.1** Indicate for a bone such as the femur, how its structure, articular cartilage, muscle tendons and ligaments are adapted for the functions they perform.

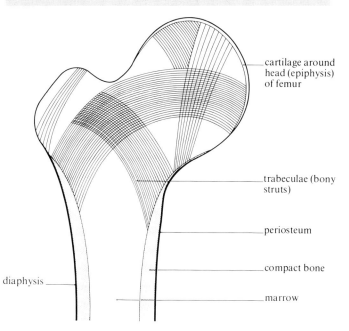

cartilage around head (epiphysis) of femur

trabeculae (bony struts)

periosteum

compact bone

diaphysis

marrow

Fig 17.2 *VS of femur head showing arrangement of trabeculae in spongy bone*

17.2.3 Development of the mammalian bony skeleton

The cartilaginous skeleton of a mammalian embryo is gradually replaced by bone in a growing organism. This involves the removal of existing cartilage, and construction of bone in its place, a process called **ossification**. In a long bone the diaphysis is the first area to be ossified. Here a layer of membrane bone (section 8.4.4) is laid down in the perichondrium forming a complete ring of bone around the diaphysis. When complete, this layer is termed the **periosteum**. Internal to the periosteum, chondrocytes increase in size, the matrix between them becomes calcified and the cells eventually disintegrate. This leads to the appearance of a series of hollow corridors in the cartilage. They are gradually filled by embryonic bone marrow cells and blood vessels arising from the layer of membrane bone in the outlying regions of the diaphysis. Some of the bone marrow cells differentiate into bone forming cells called **osteoblasts**. They position themselves around the remaining bone marrow and secrete layers of bony material. The end product is a strong, hollow tube of bone which surrounds the marrow cavity.

Ossification extends towards the epiphysis, but the cartilage is not completely replaced until the adult structure is attained. Even then, portions of hyaline cartilage remain at the articulating surfaces of the bone. The epiphyses become ossified after the diaphysis. There may be one or several ossification centres present in each epiphysis and they always remain separate from the diaphysis.

Growth in length of the bone occurs at the same time as ossification. It takes place in growth regions towards each end of the bone between the epiphyses and diaphysis. Until the adult form is reached, cartilage continues to be produced and ossified into new bone on either side of these regions. Ultimately growing regions become ossified. When this happens, no further cell division occurs, and growth in length ceases. Increase in girth of the bone is produced by further deposition of bone in the periosteum.

17.2.4 Factors controlling bone deposition

Even after growth is complete, bone absorption, carried out by cells called **osteoclasts**, and bone synthesis and reconstruction still occur. This is important as it permits the shape of the bones to be modified according to the mechanical stresses placed upon them. It is of particular significance in animals that exhibit a marked change in their mode of locomotion during their development into adults. This also generally incorporates a shift in the position of the load that their skeletons have to bear. If continuous pressure is exerted on a specific region of a bone, then that region is absorbed. However, if part of a bone is subjected to periodic stress, bone deposition is stimulated in that region. Such pressures and stresses mould the skeleton into its definitive shape, and in particular, intermittent stresses are responsible for the development of projections and ridges on bones which increase their surface area for muscle attachment. Understressed bone atrophies. This is the subject of much current research because it occurs during prolonged weightlessness in space and presents problems for returning astronauts and cosmonauts. Bone structure may also be weakened by nutritional deficiencies such as lack of vitamins A and D and by lack of growth hormone.

17.2.5 Support in vertebrates

Amphibia evolved from lobe-finned fish and as they migrated from water to land they were faced with the problem of gravity and of holding their bodies off the ground in the absence of any support by the air. As a consequence their vertebrae evolved to become complex structures linked together by interlocking processes. Collectively the vertebrae formed a strong but reasonably flexible girder that supported the weight of the body.

The legs of early amphibians splayed out from the sides of their bodies so that the animals were able to drag themselves over the ground. This type of stance and locomotion is also seen in primitive reptiles (fig 17.3). When in motion most of the muscular energy is used to hold up the trunk from the ground. Such is the effort required to maintain this position that the animals spend the majority of their time whilst on land resting their bellies on the ground.

Later the trend in reptilian evolution was towards bringing the limbs into a position beneath the body and raising the body well clear of the ground (fig 17.3b). This stance provides greater efficiency in locomotion and means that the weight of the body is transmitted through the four relatively straight limbs.

Some reptiles and mammals have evolved a bipedal gait, walking, running or hopping on their hindlimbs. This releases the forelimbs for developing manipulative skills such as feeding, building and cleaning. A special type of locomotion, called **brachiation** characterises some monkeys and apes. These animals swing from tree to tree using

Fig 17.3 *Types of stance in vertebrates:*
(a) a primitive amphibian stance – legs projected laterally from body and then down; (b) modern reptilian stance – intermediate between amphibian and mammals; (c) mammalian stance – legs project straight down from beneath the body

their long arms and elongate hands to grasp the branches. Other animals that climb and move about in trees are too small to brachiate; instead they jump from branch to branch. The most specialised form of aerial locomotion is true flight. This evolved simultaneously during the Jurassic period in the flying reptiles (pterodactyls) and in the first birds (which were descended from reptiles). The forelimbs were modified and adapted into wings. Flying reptiles eventually became extinct, but birds survived and evolved into many highly varied forms.

17.3 Anatomy of the skeleton of a mammal (the rabbit)

All mammalian skeletons possess the same basic divisions. These can be divided into two main groups: the **axial skeleton**, which consists of the skull, vertebral column, ribs and sternum, and the **appendicular skeleton**, which consists of an anterior pectoral and posterior pelvic girdle, attached to each of which is a pair of limbs.

17.3.1 The axial skeleton

The **skull** consists of the cranium to which the upper jaw is fused, and a lower jaw which articulates with the cranium. Muscles connect the lower jaw to the skull and cranium. The **cranium** is composed of a number of flattened bones tightly interlocking forming a series of **immovable joints**. Besides enclosing and protecting the brain, it protects the olfactory organs, middle and inner ear and the eyes. At the posterior end of the cranium are two smooth, rounded protuberances, the **occipital condyles**, that articulate with the atlas vertebra to form a hinge joint which permits the nodding of the head.

The **vertebral column** is the main axis of the body. It consists of a linear series of bones called **vertebrae**, placed end to end, and separated by cartilaginous **intervertebral discs** (fig 17.5). The vertebrae are held together by ligaments which prevent their dislocation, but permit a degree of movement, so that the vertebral column as a whole is flexible. The vertebral column also gives protec-

Table 17.1. Number and types of vertebrae in a range of mammals

Types of vertebra	Region	Number of vertebrae				
		rat	rabbit	cat	cow	human
cervical	neck	7	7	7	7	7
thoracic	chest	13	12–13	13	13	12
lumbar	abdomen	6	6–7	7	6	5
sacral	hip	4	4	3	5	5
caudal	tail	30±	16	18–25	18–20	4

tion to the spinal cord. On the vertebrae are numerous projections for the attachment of muscles. When the muscles are active, they may bend the vertebral column ventrally, dorsally or from side to side.

The total number of vertebrae varies in different mammals. Nevertheless, in all mammals five regions of the vertebral column can be distinguished. The number and types of vertebrae in a variety of mammals are given in table 17.1.

Vertebrae from different regions of the vertebral column all conform to the same basic design. The structure of a typical vertebra is shown in fig 17.4. Note that two facets (articulating surfaces) called **prezygapophyses** are present at the anterior end of the vertebra, whilst two more, the **postzygapophyses** occur at the posterior end. The prezygapophyses of one vertebra fit against the postzygapophyses of the vertebra immediately anterior to it. This arrangement enables the vertebrae to articulate with each other, but it is not a completely rigid arrangement, for the smoothness of the articulating surfaces permits their slight movement over each other. Below each pre- and postzygapophysis is a small notch. When adjacent vertebrae are fixed closely together the anterior notch of one vertebra is placed against the posterior notch of the vertebra immediately in front of it. This arrangement forms a hole through which a spinal nerve can pass. Other structures characteristic of all vertebrae are the **neural spine** and **transverse processes** for muscle attachment. The **centrum** forms a central rigid body to the vertebra over which the **neural arch** encloses the spinal cord.

Whilst there is a great degree of similarity between vertebrae, their design varies in different regions of the vertebral column. This is because of uneven distribution of body weight along the length of the column, and the vertebrae are modified and adapted to perform those specific functions required by each region.

When a rabbit stands up, its vertebral column is supported by the fore- and hindlimbs, with the bulk of the body weight suspended between them. The centra of the vertebrae withstand compression whilst ligaments and muscles which overlay the dorsal parts of the vertebrae withstand tension (fig 17.5)

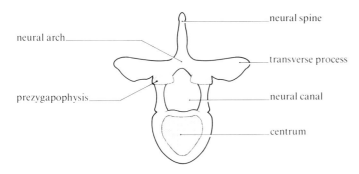

Fig 17.4 *Anterior view of a typical mammalian vertebra*

631

Fig 17.5 *Skeleton of rabbit seen from left side. The centra of the vertebrae serve as compression members whilst the ligaments and muscles which link one vertebra to another form the tension members. The abdominal musculature prevents the weight of the body from forcing the girdles apart*

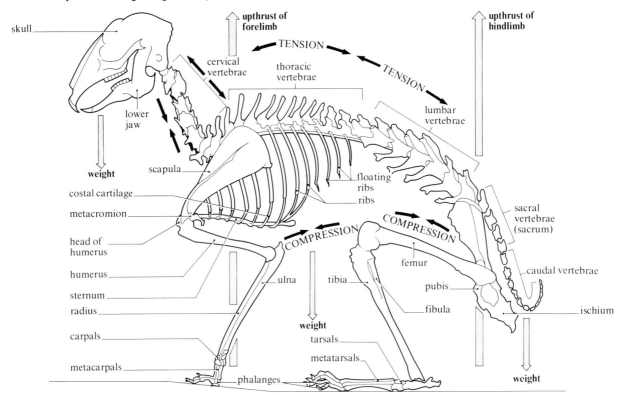

17.3.2 Structure and functions of the vertebrae of a rabbit

Cervical vertebrae

Cervicals 3–7 are very similar in structure (fig 17.6a). They possess a small centrum which is able to withstand compressional forces, and a short neural spine to which the neck muscles are attached. Some of these muscles run from the cervicals to the thoracic vertebrae and are used for holding up the neck, whilst others run to the back of the skull and serve to maintain the head in position. On each side of the centrum is a single hole, the **vertebrarterial canal**, formed by fusion of a cervical rib with the transverse process. As its name implies, it serves as a channel for the vertebral artery to pass through to the brain. Thus this important blood vessel is protected as it traverses the vulnerable region of the neck.

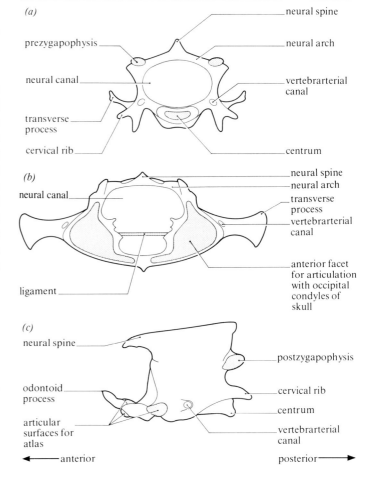

Fig 17.6 (right) (a) Fifth cervical vertebra of a rabbit, anterior view. Note the characteristic vertebrarterial canal; (b) Anterior view of atlas vertebra of a rabbit. Note absence of centrum and anterior facets; (c) Side view (left) of axis vertebra of a rabbit. Note odontoid process and forwardly projecting neural spine

The first two cervical vertebrae possess a quite different design and are modified to support the head and enable it to move in various directions. The first cervical vertebra is the **atlas** (fig 17.6*b*). Zygapophyses and a centrum are absent and the neural spine is reduced to a very small crest. On its anterior surface are two concave depressions, the **articular facets** which articulate with the curved convex occipital condyles of the skull to form a hinge joint. This supports the skull and permits it to be nodded up and down. Wide, flattened transverse processes provide a large surface area for the attachment of those muscles that bring about the nodding action.

The second cervical vertebra is the **axis** (fig 17.6*c*). It possesses a peg-like structure called the **odontoid process** which projects forwards from the centrum. The process is formed by the fusion of the centrum of the atlas to that of the axis, and it fits into the cavity of the atlas below the ligament (fig 17.6*b*) thus being separated from the neural canal. This arrangement gives a pivot joint which enables the head to be rotated from one side to the other (that is to be shaken). Such activity is brought about by muscles on the left and right sides of the neck. They run forwards from the neural spine of the axis to attach to the transverse processes of the atlas (fig 17.7). No prezygapophyses are present.

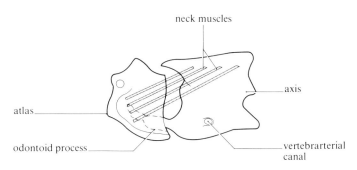

Fig 17.7 *The arrangement of the neck muscles between the atlas and axis vertebrae in a rabbit*

Thoracic vertebrae

These possess long, backwardly pointing neural spines and short transverse processes. Also present on the transverse processes are small, rounded projections called **tubercular facets**. Anterior and posterior half or **demi-facets** are located on the sides of the centrum. Both types of facet are for articulation with the ribs (fig 17.8*a*). The end of the rib which joins to a thoracic vertebra branches into two projections, one being called the **capitulum** and the other the **tuberculum**. The tuberculum articulates with the facet of the transverse process whilst the capitulum articulates with two demi-facets of the centrum. Here the arrangement is quite complex. When two thoracic vertebrae are closely applied to each other, the anterior demi-facet of one vertebra fits closely to the posterior demi-facet of the

Fig 17.8 *(a) Left side view of thoracic vertebra of a rabbit. Note long neural spine and demi-facets. (b) Lumbar vertebra of a rabbit from left side. No hypapophysis is shown. Where it does occur (first and second lumbar vertebrae) it exists as a small projection from the ventral surface of the centrum. (c) Dorsal view of sacrum of a rabbit*

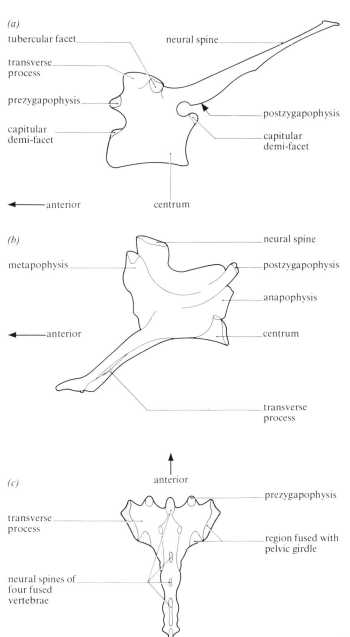

vertebra in front of it to form a common depression. The capitulum of the rib fits into this depression thus effectively articulating with two vertebrae. As a result the thoracic vertebrae serve to support the ribs, but because of the complex arrangement between the vertebrae and ribs, movement between them is strictly limited. Some forward and sideways movement can occur, but in general the thoracic vertebrae are the least flexible of all.

633

Lumbar vertebrae

The vertebrae of this region are subject to the greatest stress in terms of gravity and locomotion. Not only must they provide rigidity for the body, but they must also permit bending, sideways movement and rotation of the trunk. Therefore, not surprisingly this is the region where the large muscles of the back are attached and where there are many adaptive modifications of the vertebrae. The centrum and neural arch are massive, although the centrum is quite short. This arrangement provides greater flexibility between the lumbar vertebrae. The transverse processes are long and wide. They point forwards and downwards. Extra muscle bearing projections called meta-, ana-, and hypapophyses are present on the vertebrae (fig 17.8b). They also interlock with each other and keep the vertebrae in their correct positions relative to each other when this part of the vertebral column is placed under stress.

Sacral vertebrae (sacrum)

The sacral vertebrae are fused together to form a broad structure, the **sacrum** (fig 17.8c). The most anterior sacral vertebrae possess well-developed transverse processes which are fused to the pelvic girdle. It is through the sacrum that the weight of the body of a stationary animal is transmitted to the pelvic girdle and the legs. When an animal moves forwards, the thrust developed by the hindlimbs is transmitted via the pelvic girdle through the sacrum to the rest of the axial skeleton.

Caudal vertebrae

The number of caudal vertebrae varies greatly from one mammal to another (table 17.1) and is related to different lengths of tails in such mammals. In general, as they pass towards the posterior end of the animal, transverse processes, neural arches and zygapophyses all become reduced in size and gradually disappear. This results in the terminal vertebrae only consisting of small centra. Humans possess four caudal vertebrae which are fused to form the **coccyx**. It is not visible externally.

Ribs and sternum

Each rib is a flattened, curved bone. Its dorsal end is forked into the **capitulum** and **tubercle** which provide points of articulation with the thoracic vertebrae. The joints formed permit movement of the ribs by the intercostal muscles during breathing. All of the ribs, thoracic vertebrae and the sternum form a thoracic cage which protects the heart, lungs and major blood vessels (fig 17.9).

In the rabbit the ventral ends of the first seven pairs of ribs are attached to the **sternum**, a flattened, kite-shaped bone, via **costal cartilages**. These are called true ribs. The next two pairs of ribs are also attached ventrally to the cartilage of the seventh rib. The ventral ends of the remaining three or four pairs of ribs are unattached and are called floating ribs (fig 17.5).

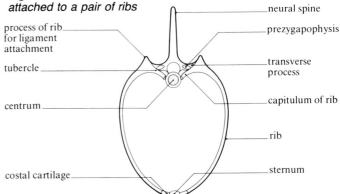

Fig 17.9 *Anterior view of thoracic vertebra of a rabbit attached to a pair of ribs*

17.3.3 The appendicular skeleton

Limb girdles

These provide a connection between the axial skeleton and the limbs. The width of the pectoral girdle separates the forelimbs, and that of the pelvic girdle the hindlimbs, and both contribute to the stability of the animal. A number of areas are modified for muscle attachment and articulation with the limb bones.

Pectoral girdle. This is composed of two distinctly separate halves. Each half consists of the scapula, coracoid process and clavicle. It is not fused to the axial skeleton but flexibly attached to it by ligaments and muscles. This arrangement enables the girdle and its associated limbs to be moved through a great variety of planes of movement and angles. The girdle is strong enough to support the majority of the weight of a quadruped when it is stationary. It also acts as a shock absorber when the animal lands at the end of a jump.

The **scapula** is a flat, triangular-shaped bone which overlies a number of the anterior ribs (fig 17.10a). At its apex is a concave depression, the **glenoid cavity**, which articulates with the head of the humerus to form a ball-and-socket joint. A spine runs along the outer surface of the scapula, and at its free end, close to the glenoid cavity are two projections, the **acromion** and **metacromion** which are both used for muscle attachment. The **coracoid process** is all that remains of a small bone, the coracoid, which has fused with the scapula to form a projection above the glenoid cavity.

The **clavicle** is variable in size and shape in different mammals. In humans it is well developed with one end articulating with the acromion process and the other with the sternum. It is used for muscle attachment and aiding the complex movements of the arms. It is sometimes referred to as the collar bone in humans. Its removal has no serious consequences. In quadrupeds it is much smaller and relatively less important. It forms the 'wishbone' in birds.

17.2 What advantages are there to mammals in possessing a flexible connection between the pectoral girdle and vertebral column?

Fig 17.10 (a) Left scapula of a rabbit. (b) Ventral view of pelvic girdle of a rabbit. Note how sacrum is fused to the ilium

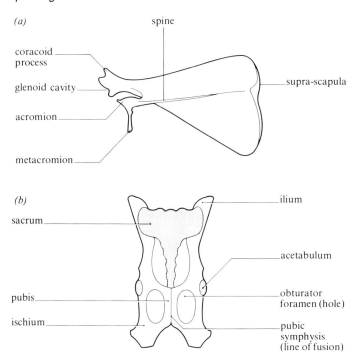

(a)

(b)

Fig 17.11 Vertebrate pentadactyl limb

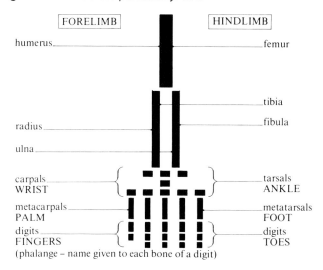

(phalange – name given to each bone of a digit)

Pelvic girdle. Again this consists of two halves, each half comprising three bones, the ilium, ischium and pubis. They are fused to each other forming a single structure, the **innominate** bone. The **ilium** is fused to the sacrum of the vertebral column on each side. On the outer edge of each half is a depression, the **acetabulum**, which articulates with the head of the femur to form the ball-and-socket hip joint (fig 17.10b). The ilium is above the acetabulum. Dorsally it possesses a large crest to which the thigh muscles are attached.

Between the ischium and pubis is a large hole, the **obturator foramen**. Except for a small aperture through which blood vessels and nerves pass to the legs, it is covered by a sheet of tough inflexible connective tissue which provides yet another surface for muscle attachment. Such a design could be an adaptation to reduce the weight of the pelvic girdle and so lighten the load that has to be supported by the hindlegs.

Ventrally a line of fusion can be seen where the two halves of the pelvic girdle meet. This is the **pubic symphysis**. Flexible cartilage in this region permits a widening of the female's girdle at the time of giving birth.

Limbs

The limbs of all mammals are designed on the same basic plan, that of the **pentadactyl limb**, so named because each limb terminates in five digits (fingers or toes) (fig 17.11). There are numerous variations of the general plan, which are adaptations to the different modes of life of different animals. In some cases the number of digits per limb has been reduced during evolution (section 24.7).

Forelimb. The upper part of the forelimb consists of a single bone, the **humerus**. At its upper end is the head which articulates with the glenoid cavity of the scapula to form a ball-and-socket joint at the shoulder allowing universal movement. Near the head are two roughened projections, the greater and lesser **tuberosities**, between which is a groove, the **bicipital groove**. It is along this groove that the tendon of the biceps muscle passes. At its lower end is the **trochlea** which articulates with the forearm to form a hinge joint at the elbow. A hole, the **supra trochlear foramen**, perforates the humerus just above the trochea in the rabbit, but is absent in humans. Also visible is the characteristic **deltoid ridge** running anteriorly along the upper half of the humerus (fig 17.12a). The lower part of the forelimb, the forearm, is composed of two bones, the **ulna** and **radius**. The ulna is the longer of the two. A notch, the **sigmoid notch**, at its upper end articulates with the trochlea of the humerus. Beyond the elbow joint is a projection, the **olecranon process**. This is a most important structure, for when the arm is straightened it prevents any further backward movement of the forearm; hence dislocation does not occur. On the anterior surface of the humerus, above the trochlea, is a hollow, the **supra trochlear fossa**, into which the radius fits when the arm is bent (fig 17.12b).

The radius is a flattened, slightly curved bone which is relatively simple in design. In humans it is not firmly bound to the ulna; muscles are able to rotate the radius about the ulna so that the palm of the hand can be turned downwards or upwards, contributing to human manipulative skills. This freedom of movement is not apparent in the rabbit where both bones are tightly bound and the palm always faces downwards. However, this is not disadvantageous as the limb is in the best position for burrowing and running. Distally the ulna and radius articulate with a number of small **carpal** bones which form the wrist. The carpals articulate with five long **metacarpals** which finally articulate with five **digits**. The first digit on the inside of the limb is composed of two **phalanges** whereas all others contain three.

Fig 17.12 *(a) Left humerus of a rabbit, anterior and posterior views. (b) Ulna and radius of a rabbit, side view*

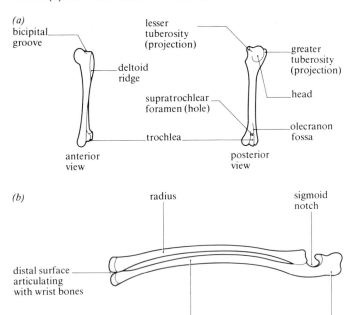

with the tibia to form a hinge joint at the knee. A patella groove separates the two condyles. The patella bone (knee cap) is located here.

The **tibia** and **fibula** bones form the shank of the hindlimb. Two slight depressions at the upper end of the tibia represent the articular surfaces at the knee joint (fig 17.13*b*). The fibula is not a component of this joint. It is a thin bone, and in the rabbit is fused to the tibia at its lower end. At the lower ends of the tibia and fibula are a number of **tarsal** bones. The two longest tarsals, the **astragulus** and **calcaneum** (heel bone), articulate with the tibia and fibula to form the ankle joint. The tarsals articulate distally with long **metatarsal** bones to form the foot, whilst in turn the metatarsals articulate with digits composed of phalanges forming the toes. It is interesting to note that the rabbit hindlimb possesses only four digits.

17.3.4   Joints

In bony vertebrates, where a bone meets another bone, or bones, a joint is formed. Movement of skeletal elements over each other is only possible if there is a joint between them. A variety of different types of joint exist in the mammalian skeleton. They are summarised in table 17.2.

Synovial joints are essentially similar to each other in design. The end surface of each articulating bone is overlain by a smooth covering of hyaline cartilage. Though a living tissue, it contains no blood vessels or nerves. The nutrients and respiratory gases it requires diffuse from the synovial membrane and fluid. The cartilage serves to reduce friction between the bones during movement. Because of its elastic properties, the cartilage also acts as a shock absorber.

The bones of the joint are held in position by a number of ligaments which collectively form a strong fibrous capsule. They run from one side of the joint to the other and are orientated in such a way as to cope effectively with the particular stresses suffered by the joint. The inner surface of the capsule is lined by a thin, cellular synovial membrane which secretes synovial fluid into the synovial cavity (fig 17.14). Synovial fluid, containing mucin, acts as a lubricant

Hindlimb. The upper part of the hindlimb consists of a single bone, the **femur**. At its upper end is a large round head which articulates with the acetabulum of the pelvic girdle to form a ball-and-socket joint at the hip (fig 17.13*a*). Three processes called **trochanters** protrude below the head and provide points of attachment for the thigh muscles. The lower end of the femur possesses two curved convex surfaces, called **condyles**, which articulate

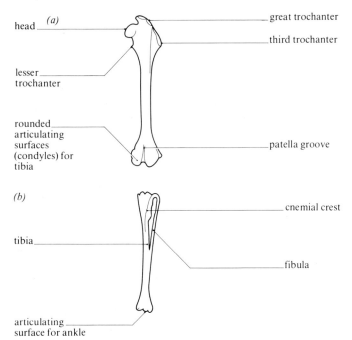

17.13 *(a) Left femur of a rabbit, anterior view. (b) Anterior view of left tibia and fibula of a rabbit*

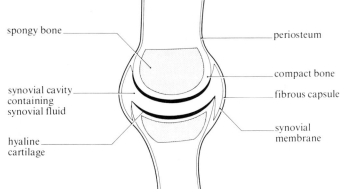

Fig 17.14 *Diarthrodial/synovial joint of a mammal*

Table 17.2. A variety of joints in the endoskeleton of a mammal

Type of joint	General characteristics	Examples	Function
Immovable/suture/ synarthrodial	A thin layer of fibrous connective tissue exists between the bones, holding them firmly in position	Between bones of skull; between sacrum and ilia of pelvic girdle; between bones of pelvic girdle	Provides strength and support for the body, or protection of delicate structures which cannot withstand any kind of deformation
Partially movable/ amphiarthrodial	Bones are separated from each other by cartilaginous pads		
(a) Gliding		Joints between vertebrae; wrist and ankle bones	Bones glide over each other to a limited extent. Collectively they provide a wide range of movement and confer strength on the limb.
(b) Swivel/rotating/ pivot		Joint between atlas and axis vertebrae	Permits shaking of head from side to side
Freely movable/synovial/ diarthrodial (fig 17.14)	Articulating bone surfaces are covered with cartilage and separated from each other by a synovial cavity containing synovial fluid		
(a) Hinge	Relatively few muscles operate this joint	Elbow, knee and finger joints	Permits movement in one plane about one axis. Capable of bearing heavy loads
(b) Ball and socket	Variety of muscles attached to the bones of the joint	Shoulder and hip joints	Permits movement in all planes, and some rotation. Unable to bear very heavy loads

for the joint surfaces and serves to reduce friction between them. The synovial membrane acts as a waterproof seal preventing escape of synovial fluid. Therefore the joint effectively requires no maintenance.

17.4 The muscle system

Muscles are composed of many elongated cells called **muscle fibres** which are all able to contract and relax. During relaxation they are capable of being stretched, but they exhibit the property of elasticity which permits them to regain their original size and form after being stretched. Muscles are well supplied with blood which conveys to them nutrients and oxygen, and takes away metabolic waste products. The amount of blood arriving at a muscle at any one time is able to be adjusted according to its need. Each muscle possesses its own nerve supply. Histologically three distinct types of vertebrate muscle can be identified.

(1) **Skeletal muscle** (section 17.4.1) (also called striated, striped, voluntary). Muscle which is attached to bone. It is concerned with locomotion, contracts quickly and fatigues quickly. It is innervated by the voluntary nervous system.

(2) **Smooth muscle** (section 17.5.3) (also called unstriated, unstriped, plain, involuntary). Muscle which is found in the walls of tubular organs of the body and is concerned with movement of materials through them.

It contracts slowly and fatigues slowly. It is spontaneously active and innervated by the autonomic nervous system.

(3) **Cardiac muscle**. Muscle found only in the heart. It contracts spontaneously and without fatigue. It is innervated by the autonomic nervous system.

17.4.1 Skeletal muscle in detail

A skeletal muscle is attached to bone in at least two places, namely the **origin**, a firm **non-movable** part of the skeleton, and the **insertion**, a freely movable part of the skeleton. Attachment is by means of tough, relatively inextensible tendons made up of connective tissue comprised almost entirely of collagen (section 5.5). At one end a tendon is continuous with the outer covering of the muscle, while the other end combines with the periosteum of the bone to form a very firm attachment.

As muscles can only produce a shortening force (that is contract), it follows that at least two muscles or sets of muscles must be used to move a bone into one position and back again. Pairs of muscles acting in this way are termed **antagonistic** muscles and they may be classified according to the type of movement they bring about (table 17.3).

It is rare that a movement will involve a single pair of antagonistic muscles. Generally, groups of muscles work together to produce a particular individual movement, and such groups are known as **synergists**.

Table 17.3. Types of movement brought about by pairs of antagonistic muscles

Muscle classification	Type of movement brought about
Flexor	Bends a limb by pulling two skeletal elements towards each other
Extensor	Extends a limb by pulling two skeletal elements away from each other
Adductor	Pulls a limb towards the central long axis of the body
Abductor	Pulls a limb away from the central long axis of the body
Protractor	Pulls distal part of a limb forwards
Retractor	Pulls distal part of a limb backwards
Rotator	Rotates whole or part of a limb at one of its joints

17.4.2 Striated muscle

A striated muscle consists of numerous physiological units called muscle fibres or muscle cells. They are cylindrical in shape and arranged parallel to each other. They are between 0.01 and 0.1 mm in diameter, several centimetres long and multinucleate. The nuclei are located near the surface of each fibre. Bundles of muscle fibres are enclosed by collagen fibres and connective tissue. Collagen also occurs between fibres. At the ends of the muscle the collagen and connective tissue forms tendons which attach the muscle to skeletal elements. Each muscle fibre is enclosed by a membrane, the **sarcolemma**. This is very similar in structure to a typical cell surface membrane.

Within the muscle fibres are numerous thin **myofibrils** (*myo*, muscle) which possess characteristic cross-striations. Each myofibril is composed of two types of proteinaceous myofilaments, **actin** and **myosin**. Numerous mitochondria are interposed between the muscle fibres. The cytoplasm of the myofibril is called **sarcoplasm** and contains a network of internal membranes termed the **sarcoplasmic reticulum**. Running transversely across the fibre and between fibrils is a system of tubules known as the **T system**, which is in contact with the surface of the sarcolemma (fig 17.15). At certain points the T tubules pass between the pairs of vesicles which are components of the sarcoplasmic reticulum. A T tubule together with a pair of vesicles is called a **triad**. The tubule and vesicles are held together by membranous cross-bridges. The vesicles are involved in the uptake and release of Ca^{2+} ions. Their activity raises or lowers Ca^{2+} ion concentration in the sarcoplasm, which in turn controls ATPase activity and hence the contractile behaviour of the muscle fibre.

Under a light microscope only the striated nature of the myofibrils can be observed. This is seen as a regular alternation of light and dark bands called the **I and A bands** respectively, traversed by thin, dark lines. Electron microscope studies clearly indicate that the bands are due to the regular arrangement of actin (thin filaments) and myosin (thick filaments). Fig 17.16 shows this clearly.

Traversing the middle of each I band is a dark line called

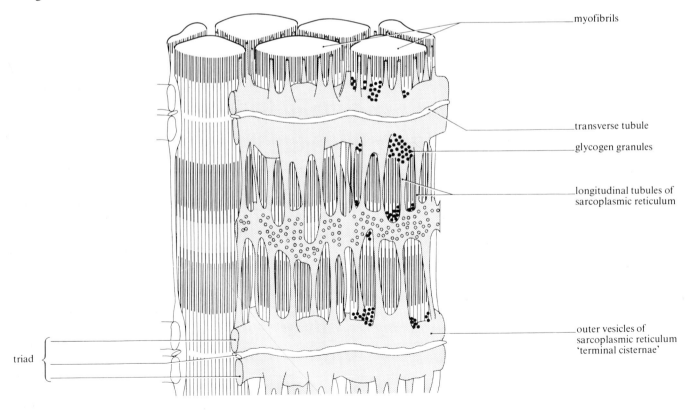

myofibrils

transverse tubule

glycogen granules

longitudinal tubules of sarcoplasmic reticulum

outer vesicles of sarcoplasmic reticulum 'terminal cisternae'

triad

Fig 17.15 *Sarcoplasmic reticulum and T system.*

Fig 17.16 *Fine structure of skeletal muscle*

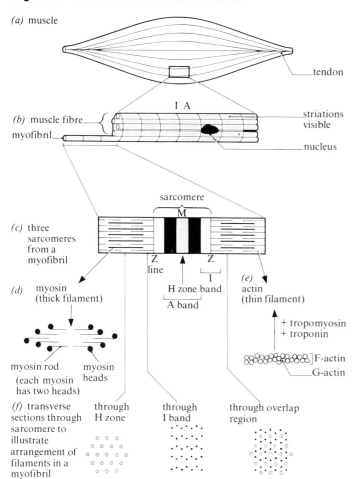

(a) muscle

tendon

(b) muscle fibre

myofibril

I A

striations visible

nucleus

(c) three sarcomeres from a myofibril

sarcomere

M

Z line

H zone band

A band

I

(d) myosin (thick filament)

myosin rod (each myosin has two heads)

myosin heads

(e) actin (thin filament)

+ tropomyosin + troponin

F-actin

G-actin

(f) transverse sections through sarcomere to illustrate arrangement of filaments in a myofibril

through H zone

through I band

through overlap region

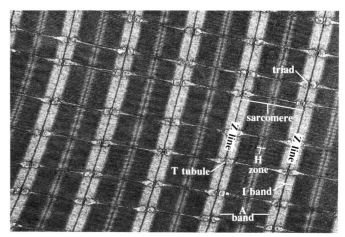

Fig 17.17 *Longitudinal section of fish muscle (roach – Rutilus rutilus). Note the triads and clear myofibrilar structure (× 7 650)*

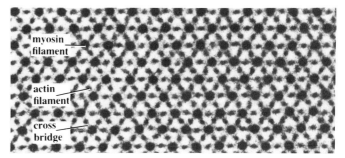

Fig 17.18 *Insect flight muscle (giant water bug). Transverse section of fibril in rigor state (× 137 000)*

the **Z line**. The section of a myofibril between two Z lines is called a **sarcomere**. From the Z line actin filaments extend in both directions, whilst in the centre of the sarcomere are found myosin filaments. These are aligned side by side in a hexagonal lattice (fig 17.17 & 17.18). In certain regions of the sarcomere, actin and myosin filaments overlap. Where they do, transverse sections in these regions indicate that six actin filaments surround each myosin filament. This arrangement of actin and myosin filaments results in a number of other bands being recognisable in the sarcomere. Myosin and actin filaments constitute the A band whilst actin filaments alone constitute the I band. The centre of the A band is lighter than its other regions in a relaxed sarcomere as there is no overlap between actin and myosin in this region. It is called the **H band**. The H band itself may be bisected by a dark line, the **M line**. The M line joins adjacent myosin filaments together at a point halfway along their length.

Myosin (thick filaments)

A molecule of myosin consists of two distinct regions, a long rod-shaped region (myosin rod) on one end of which is a globular region. This globular region consists of two similar globular parts, each called a myosin head. The globular heads are regularly spaced and project from the

sides of the filament except in a short region halfway along its length. This central portion of the filament, which possesses no heads, is termed the bare zone. Where the actin and myosin filaments overlap the myosin heads can attach to neighbouring actin filaments, and while attached they can generate the force which may cause the muscle to shorten. The energy for this force production is derived from ATP hydrolysis since each myosin head is capable of ATPase activity. As described later, the attachment of myosin heads to actin is controlled by the level of Ca^{2+} ions in the sarcoplasm. The myosin ATPase is activated by attachment of myosin to actin. This activity may be inhibited by Mg^{2+} ions. The importance of this will become evident when we deal with the actual contraction mechanism of the sarcomere.

Actin (thin filaments)

Each actin filament is made up of two helical strands of globular actin molecules (G-actin) which twist round each other. The whole assembly of actin molecules is called F-actin (fibrous actin). It is thought that an ATP molecule is attached to each molecule of G-actin. Neither form of actin exhibits any ATPase activity. Actin filaments consist of F-actin together with two accessory proteins, **tropomyosin** and **troponin**. Tropomyosin is a rod-shaped fibrous

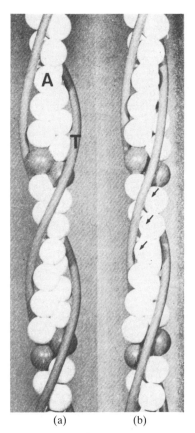

Fig 17.19 *Illustration of changes in actin filament structure (a) 'off' state – low Ca²⁺ level: tropomyosin blocks myosin attachment site. (b) 'on' state – high Ca²⁺ level: tropomyosin moves to expose attachment sites (arrows). A, actin; T, tropomyosin, Troponin, which is not shown, lies nearer to 'grey' actins.*

protein and these rods link end to end to form two helical strands which are wrapped around the F-actin in a longitudinal fashion. Tropomyosin functions to switch on, or off, the contractile mechanism. Troponin is a globular protein with three subunits. Each subunit has a particular function. **Troponin-T** binds troponin to tropomyosin, **troponin-C** is sensitive to, and can reversibly bind to, Ca^{2+} ions, whilst under certain conditions **troponin-I** is able to inhibit any interaction between actin and myosin. Collectively both of these accessory proteins serve to inhibit the actin–myosin interaction in the absence of Ca^{2+} ions (fig 17.19).

17.4.3 The 'all-or-nothing' response

When a skeletal muscle fibre is stimulated by an impulse, the fibre will only contract if the stimulus is at or above a certain threshold level (resting potential). This contraction is maximal for any given set of conditions, and even if the strength of stimulus is considerably increased there will be no increase in the shortening of the muscle or the force that it develops. This phenomenon is referred to as the muscle's 'all-or-nothing' response. A stimulus that is too weak to provoke muscle fibre contraction is referred to as a **subliminal** stimulus.

After response, the muscle endures an **absolute refractory** period when no contraction is possible. This is succeeded by a **relative refractory period**. Only strong stimuli can provoke a response during this time. The refractory period is the time it takes for ionic activity to return the muscle to its resting potential.

17.4.4 Mode of action of vertebrate skeletal muscle

When a muscle is stimulated it exhibits mechanical activity (that is it contracts) and this may either produce a shortening of the muscle, or if the muscle is fixed rigidly at both ends, it may develop tension within the muscle without the muscle changing length. When a muscle shortens against a constant load, this is called **isotonic** contraction, but when there is no change in length, it is **isometric** contraction.

Investigation into the nature of the contractile response of a muscle can be carried out by the use of a **kymograph**. The gastrocnemius muscle of a frog is often used for such investigations. Muscle is excised from a freshly killed frog, placed in a trough on a platform and bathed in a well-oxygenated saline solution. Under these conditions it may perform its contractile activity adequately for several hours. The origin of the muscle is fixed to a rigid station on the platform, whilst its insertion is hooked up to a movable lever. It is then suitably stimulated by an electric current either directly or via a nerve. When the muscle contracts or develops tension it moves the lever, and such movement is recorded as a trace on the revolving drum of the kymograph. The record of events that take place is called a **myogram**. The tension developed by a muscle is a force and is generally measured in terms of grams mass.

17.4.5 Contractile response

Single stimulus. When a single stimulus is applied to a muscle, there is a very short period of about 0.05 s, called the **latent period**, before the muscle responds. Then contraction takes place rapidly and a force is developed. This phase of contraction lasts for about 0.1 s. Following this is a longer period of relaxation where the force declines and the muscle returns to its relaxed state over a period of 0.2 s. A single contraction by a muscle is called a **muscle twitch** (fig 17.20).

Two stimulations. If a long interval of time elapses before a second stimulus is applied, two identical myograms for the muscle are recorded. However, if the time between two stimuli is reduced so that the second stimulus is applied when the muscle is still contracting in response to the first stimulus, a second contraction occurs

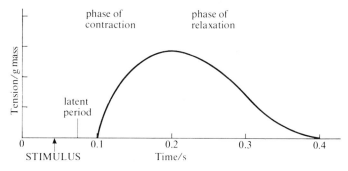

Fig 17.20 *Single muscle twitch of frog gastrocnemius muscle*

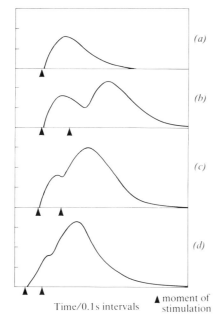

Time/0.1s intervals   ▲ moment of stimulation

Fig 17.21 *Tracings recorded on a kymograph using frog gastrocnemius muscle.*
(a) *Single twitch in response to single stimulus*
(b) ⎧ *Mechanical summation occurring*
(c) ⎨ *when frequency of stimulation*
(d) ⎩ *is increased*

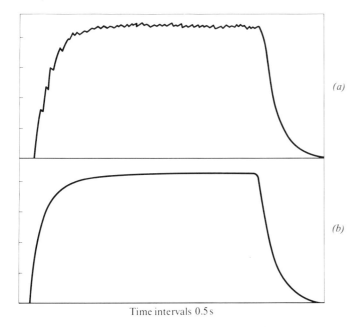

Time intervals 0.5 s

Fig 17.22 *Myogram indicating development of tetany in frog gastrocnemius muscle*
(a) *Unfused tetany, 8 stimulations per 0.5 s*
(b) *Fused tetany, 18 stimulations per 0.5 s*

which is superimposed on the first. This results in a 'bumpy' myogram (fig 17.21). The second contraction also develops a greater force than the first one. This effect is called **mechanical summation**.

Frequent stimulations. If the frequency of stimulation is increased, the bumpiness of the myogram is gradually lost (fig 17.22) and the individual twitches fuse

together (or summate). A smooth trace is drawn which reaches a steady level or plateau and remains there for a relatively long time. When the muscle is in this condition it is said to be in the state of **tetanus**. The plateau of tension developed during tetany is the maximum tension that the muscle can produce. Tetany cannot continue indefinitely as the muscle becomes fatigued.

17.4.6 The sliding filament theory of muscle contraction

In 1954, two independent research groups, namely H. E. Huxley & J. Hanson, and A. F. Huxley & R. Niedergerke, formulated the sliding filament theory of muscle contraction. They discovered independently that the A band of a sarcomere always remained the same length whether the sarcomere was stretched or shortened. This gave rise to the suggestion that there are two interdigitating sets of filaments, actin and myosin, which in some way slide past each other when the sarcomere changes its length. Observations indicated that during contraction the actin filaments move inwards towards the centre of the sarcomere (fig 17.23). The heads of the myosin filaments were thought to operate as 'hooks' attaching to F-actin in a particular way to form cross-bridges, and then changing their relative configuration such that the actin molecules were pulled further into the A band. After the process was completed, the myosin heads detached from the actin and hooked up to another site further along the actin filament. A sarcomere could contract up to 30% of its length, and the cross-bridge attachment/detachment cycles could be repeated many times depending on the speed of shortening. The energy required for this process was provided by the splitting of ATP, one ATP molecule being split for each cross-bridge cycle.

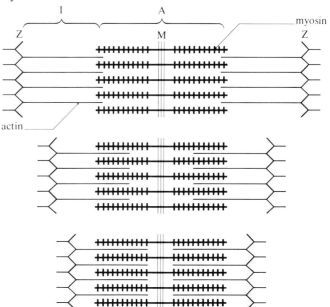

Fig 17.23 *Diagrammatic representation of how a sarcomere contracts by the actin filaments sliding over myosin filaments*

Today the theory is almost universally accepted. However, the actual force-generating process, often called the **excitation–contraction–coupling** mechanism, is still little understood and remains one of the major problems to be resolved by muscle physiologists. Much progress has been made in this field and the following section provides an up-to-date picture of sarcomere contraction.

> **17.3** What happens to the length of the A, H and I bands as the sarcomere contracts?
>
> **17.4** Explain how any change in the A, H and I band lengths are brought about in terms of what happens to the actin and myosin filaments.

17.4.7 Excitation–contraction–coupling

At rest a sarcomere possesses Mg^{2+} ions and ATP in certain concentrations, but Ca^{2+} ions are present only in very low concentrations. Under these conditions the actin filament is in the 'off' position. This is achieved by tropomyosin being positioned on each actin molecule in such a way that it blocks the sites on actin to which myosin will attach. Also the myosin heads are held away from actin in a position close to the long axis of the myosin filament.

When a muscle is stimulated by a nerve impulse, the wave of depolarisation spreads over the muscle and passes from the outside of the muscle fibre membrane into the sarcomere along the T system. As the impulse reaches the triad vesicles it stimulates them to release Ca^{2+} ions into the sarcoplasm, and Ca^{2+} ion concentration consequently rises. Ca^{2+} ions bind to the troponin-C, which in turn interacts with troponin-I and reverses the normally inhibitory effect of the troponin system on actin–myosin interaction. Actin is switched 'on' when the tropomyosin moves to a new position on each actin molecule (fig 17.19) so that the myosin-binding sites are exposed. In some muscle, not vertebrate, the ATPase activity of myosin is also stimulated by the presence of Ca^{2+} ions. It is further enhanced by the presence of actin. In all muscles, when the actin and myosin have been activated, the myosin head moves out from its resting position and links to actin to form an actomyosin cross-bridge. Release of energy by ATP hydrolysis accompanies cross-bridge formation and leads to a change in the angle of the cross-bridge such that the myosin head pulls the actin filament over itself towards the centre of the sarcomere. With all myofilaments acting in this way during sarcomere stimulation the end result is the generation of a force (fig 17.24) which may lead to a shortening of the sarcomere length.

When excitation of the sarcomere ceases, Ca^{2+} ions are actively pumped back into the triad vesicles by an ATP-driven calcium pump. Ca^{2+} ion concentration soon decreases below the threshold for contractile activity and relaxation of the sarcomere begins. The tropomyosin–troponin complex inhibits ATPase activity, cross-bridges are broken, actin and possibly myosin too are switched 'off' and the sarcomere reverts to its normal resting tension.

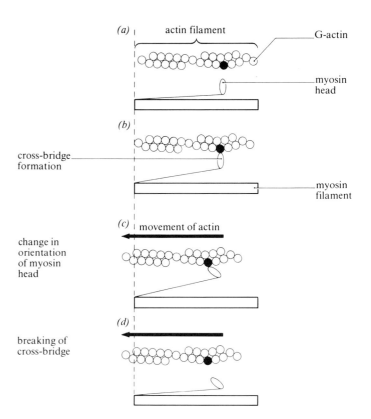

Fig 17.24 *Excitation–contraction coupling. (Tropomyosin and troponin not shown.)*

17.4.8 The energy supply

Within the body the ultimate source of energy for muscle contraction is usually glycogen, but may be fatty acids. When these substrates are metabolised (during respiration), ATP is generated.

Normally the oxygen used in aerobic respiration is supplied by haemoglobin. However muscles also have their own store of oxygen because they contain a protein similar to haemoglobin called **myoglobin** (section 14.13.2), which combines with oxygen and only releases it if the rate of its supply from haemoglobin cannot keep up with demand, as in strenuous exercise.

It is the hydrolysis of ATP that liberates the energy necessary to promote actual muscle contraction:

$$ATP \longrightarrow ADP + P_i + \text{energy for muscle contraction}$$

In resting muscle the level of ATP is low, being sufficient only to power about eight muscle twitches. This condition is maintained by normal aerobic respiration. The ATP is soon used up when a muscle contracts, and has to be quickly restored by other processes.

Restoration of ATP involves a substance located in the muscle called **phosphocreatine** (PCr). The ADP produced during muscle contraction is reconverted to ATP at the expense of phosphocreatine:

$$ADP + PCr \xrightarrow[\text{phosphotransferase}]{\text{creatine}} ATP + Cr$$

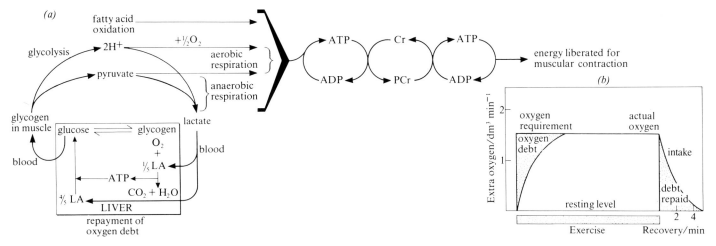

Fig 17.25 (a) Relationship between ATP, phosphocreatine and respiration in the process of muscle contraction. LA, lactate. (b) Oxygen requirements during exercise showing the relationship between oxygen intake and debt

This ensures that there is always a constant supply of ATP in the muscle which it can utilise for immediate contraction. There would only be sufficient phosphocreatine to supply total energy demand for about 5–10 s, and normally about 70% of the store is exhausted after 1 min of heavy exercise. It is therefore useful only for an explosive activity such as a sudden short sprint. At some stage, the phosphocreatine level has to be replenished. This is brought about by oxidation of fatty acids or glycogen. ATP produced here enables phosphocreatine to be resynthesised from creatine:

$$Cr + ATP \longrightarrow PCr + ADP$$

When a muscle becomes very active its oxygen supply rapidly becomes insufficient to maintain adequate oxidative phosphorylation (section 11.3.6) of its respiratory substrates. Under these conditions pyruvate, the end-product of glycolysis, is converted to lactate by addition of H^+ ions. This occurs because there is insufficient oxygen present to attach to the H^+ ions, produced during glycolysis, to form water. Whilst this is happening the muscle is said to be incurring an **oxygen debt**.

$$\underset{\text{pyruvate}}{CH_3COCOOH} + 2H^{\cdot} \longrightarrow \underset{\text{lactate}}{CH_3CHOHCOOH}$$

Lactate formation is relatively inefficient as an energy-liberating process, yielding only about 7% of the energy available from the complete oxidation of glucose. Lactate is toxic and, as it builds up in the muscle, causes muscular tiredness, pain and possibly contributes to muscle cramps. At maximum rate of muscular activity, the system can only meet energy demands for just over one minute, the limit being determined by the body's tolerance to lactate in muscle and body fluid. Therefore sooner or later it has to be removed from the body. This occurs when muscular activity slows down or ceases.

When this happens the oxygen supplies once again become sufficient to oxidise lactate and aid the reconver-

sion of some of it into glycogen. This process generally occurs in the liver where one-fifth of the lactate is fully oxidised to carbon dioxide and water, providing energy which is utilised for the conversion of the remaining lactate into glucose. Some of the glucose is transported back to the muscle where it is finally transformed to glycogen, whilst the remainder is converted to glycogen and stored in the liver. The time taken for lactate to be fully removed from the body represents the time it takes the body to repay the oxygen debt incurred during strenuous muscular activity (fig 17.25).

Training can increase the body's tolerance to lactate and increase the oxygen debt that it can build up.

17.4.9 Effects of exercise on muscles and muscle performance

Basic muscle size is genetically determined, however exercise can increase the size of muscles by up to 60%. This is mainly the result of an increase in the diameter of individual muscle fibres and an increase in their numbers. There is also an increase in the number of myofibrils within each muscle fibre.

Long-term biochemical changes

The number and size of mitochondria increase within the fibres. Processes that take place in mitochondria such as the Krebs cycle, electron transport and oxidation of fatty acids all occur more rapidly.

Stamina training may double the ability of mitochondria to generate ATP. More phosphocreatine, glycogen and fat are stored, and as a result of the presence of more myoglobin, more oxygen is stored. The combined effect of these changes means that the athlete relies less on anaerobic respiration and therefore produces less lactate. There is greater ability to release fatty acids from fat stores for energy liberation. Hence fit people use up more fat during exercise than unfit people.

Long-term increase in muscle strength

Muscle strength is increased only if the muscle is working against a load (resistance) greater than that which it is normally used to. Either intensity or duration of exercise can be increased to achieve this. Muscles working at, or close to, their maximum force of contraction will increase in strength very quickly even if the daily exercise is a matter of minutes.

Regular exercise is necessary to maintain strength of muscle. Without it they revert to their former state and become 'out of condition', losing both speed of contraction and strength.

Muscle tension–length curve

A working muscle is usually at its strongest when its length is slightly longer than its normal resting length. This produces the maximum overlap of the actin and myosin filaments, causing a situation to arise where the maximum number of cross-bridges between these filaments can be established. In this condition the muscle provides its maximum generation of force (fig 17.26). For each square centimetre of cross-sectional area, various muscles can produce about 10–20 newtons of measured force.

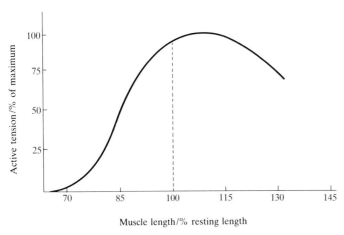

Fig 17.26 *Relationship between muscle length and active tension*

Blood supply to muscles

Regular exercise results in an increase in the number of blood vessels supplying blood to the muscles. This serves to provide a more efficient system for glucose and oxygen transport, and removal of waste products of respiration.

During long-term exercise both circulatory and respiratory systems adapt so that any oxygen debt that builds up at the beginning of the bout of exercise can be adequately repaid during the exercise.

The ability to sustain exercise at a persistently high rate is generally dependent on the rate and efficiency at which oxygen can be taken up and used in relation to body weight.

Coordination

Exercise improves coordination between pairs of antagonistic muscles, thus enabling more complex and skilful movement. Exercise also improves the speed at which muscles relax as well as contract. If a muscle does not relax rapidly enough, it may be torn by the pulling effect of the opposing muscle

Muscles can be overstretched due to over-rigorous training, causing straining or tearing of muscle tissue. The likelihood of this happening can be reduced by the use of warming-up exercises. After strenuous exercise muscles are generally shorter and tighter and more prone to injury. Warming-down exercises, concentrating on flexibility, can help prevent this by gently stretching the muscles.

17.5   Innervation of skeletal muscle

Each muscle is innervated by many motor nerve fibres, all of which branch to supply a group of muscle fibres. This group, together with its motor supply, is called a **motor unit**, and all muscle fibres in it will contract simultaneously when suitably stimulated. The number of muscle fibres in a motor unit is variable and depends on the sophistication of control that the unit is required to exert. For example, there are about ten in eyeball muscle but over 1 000 in a biceps muscle. The fewer the number of muscle fibres in a unit, the greater the nervous control over them.

Where a motor nerve fibre makes contact with a muscle fibre, a neuromuscular junction, or motor end-plate, is formed. Here the axon of the motor nerve fibre loses its myelin sheath, and its terminal dendrites are sunk into grooves which ramify over the end-plate.

The stimulus for muscle contraction to take place is delivered by the central nervous system (fig 17.27). Impulses are propagated along the motor nerve fibre to the motor end-plate. Here, in response to the nervous signal, acetylcholine is released into the synaptic gap which separates the motor fibre and sarcolemma of the muscle

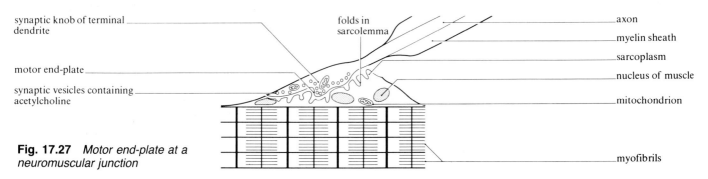

Fig. 17.27 *Motor end-plate at a neuromuscular junction*

Table 17.4. Structure, location and general properties of slow and fast skeletal muscle fibres

	Slow/tonic muscle fibres	*Fast/twitch muscle fibres*
Structure	Many mitochondria Poorly developed sarcoplasmic reticulum Red – due to presence of myoglobin and cytochrome pigments Low in glycogen content Capillaries in close contact with fibres to facilitate fast exchange of materials	Few mitochondria Well-developed sarcoplasmic reticulum White – little or no myoglobin or cytochrome pigments Abundance of glycogen granules
Location	Deeply seated inside the limbs	Relatively superficial
Innervation	Associated with small nerve fibres of 5 μm diameter. A number of end-plates are distributed along the length of the fibre. This is called multi-terminal innervation. Velocity of impulse conductance $2-8$ m s^{-1}	Associated with large nerve fibres of $10-20$ μm diameter. Usually one or possibly two end-plates per fibre $8-40$ m s^{-1}
Excitability	Membrane electrically inexcitable. Each impulse causes release of only small amount of acetylcholine. Therefore amount that membrane is depolarised depends on frequency of stimulation	Membrane electrically excitable. Exhibit 'all-or-none' response when an action potential is elicited.
Response	Slow graded muscular contraction of long duration. Relaxation process slow (up to 100 times slower than twitch fibre)	Fast contraction (3 times faster than slow fibres) Fatigues quite quickly
Physiological activity	Depend on aerobic respiration for ATP production **Many continue to function anaerobically if oxygen is in short supply in which case lactate is formed and an oxygen debt incurred** Carbohydrate or fat store mobilised at same rate as respiratory substrate is oxidised Heat transported away from muscle as soon as it is produced Steady state between muscle activity and its needs is set up	Depend on the anaerobic process of glycolysis for ATP supply Oxygen debt quickly built up Glycogen used extensively as respiratory substrate Heat produced is absorbed by the fibres as the circulatory system does not immediately remove it Muscle contraction occurs during a period when the circulatory system has not had time to increase the oxygen supply to the muscle
Function	Enable sustained muscle contractions to occur. This is used for the maintenance of posture by the organism	Immediate, fast muscle contraction is permitted at a time when the circulatory system is still adjusting to the needs of the new level of muscle activity. Therefore of great importance during locomotion.

The innervation diagram for slow/tonic fibres shows axons branching to multiple end-plates distributed along the length of a single fibre. The diagram for fast/twitch fibres shows a single axon leading to one end-plate on the fibre.

fibre. What happens at the end-plate is remarkably similar to what happens at a neurone–neurone synapse (section 16.1.2). The acetylcholine diffuses towards the sarcolemma and effects a temporary increase in its permeability to ions, especially Na$^+$ and K$^+$. As a result, an end-plate potential is developed and this generates an action potential which passes rapidly along the length of the muscle fibre, also inwards via the T-system, eliciting contraction which is of an all-or-nothing nature.

Acetylcholinesterase, located in large quantities in the region of the sarcolemma, rapidly hydrolyses acetylcholine to choline and ethanoic acid, and thus prevents over-stimulation of the muscle fibre. The motor end-plate rapidly reverts to its resting state once the end-plate potential has passed.

17.5.1 Gradation of response by skeletal muscles

In order for fine control of muscular activity to be exerted, it is important that the degree of tension developed by each muscle should be closely controlled. This is achieved in two ways, either separately or collectively.

(1) The number of muscle fibres that are actually excited at any one time may be varied. It follows that the force generated by a muscle will increase if an increased number of fibres are stimulated, and vice versa. This is what generally happens in vertebrate skeletal muscle.

(2) The frequency of nerve impulses received by muscle fibres may be varied. Repetitive stimulation in this way can increase the force developed by the muscle.

The whole process of muscle contraction within an organism is a smooth, orderly affair. This is achieved by the asynchronous contractions of different groups of muscle fibres in antagonistic muscles.

17.5.2 Types of skeletal muscle fibre

There are two major types of skeletal muscle fibre, each with its own specific physiological properties. They are the slow or **tonic** fibres, and the fast or **twitch** fibres. Table 17.4 indicates their structure, location and general properties. Whilst some muscles may contain purely tonic, or twitch, fibres, some muscles contain proportions of both.

Collectively the two types of fibre endow the organism with the ability to move about and to maintain posture. The twitch fibres enable fast muscle contraction. Predators possess many twitch fibres and use them for fast reactions to capture prey. On the other hand, would-be prey can also react quickly in order to avoid capture by predators. In both cases speed of body movement would influence the probability of survival of the organism concerned. When an animal is still it has to maintain a particular posture. This is achieved by contraction of the tonic muscle fibres. They generate a slower, more sustained contraction, whilst at the same time consuming less fuel than the twitch muscle fibres. The nature of the contraction is usually isometric, and muscles and limbs are held at a constant length, thus resisting the force of gravity.

In humans both types of fibre enter into the composition of all muscles, but one or other usually predominates. The functional significance of this is that the predominantly tonic muscles are suited to long-term slow contractions, and consequently are found in the postural extensor muscles, whilst twitch muscle fibres predominate in the flexor muscles, which are designed to react at speed.

17.5.3 Smooth muscle

Vertebrate smooth muscle is located in the walls of many hollow structures of the body. These include the intestinal tract, bladder, blood vessels, ureter, uterus and vas deferens. The individual cells are uninucleate and spindle-shaped. Connective tissue, consisting largely of collagen, holds them together. They are oriented parallel to each other and form a distinct muscle layer. An example of this is the smooth muscle of the intestine where there is an outer longitudinal, and an inner circular, layer. When the longitudinal muscle contracts, it shortens and dilates the intestinal lumen, whilst contraction of the circular muscle will lengthen and constrict the lumen. Such coordinated activity, called **peristalsis**, aids the movement of the contents of the gut and provides an interesting example of the function of smooth muscle, namely to move along materials within the hollow organs of the body.

Each smooth muscle cell is approximately 50–200 μm long and 2–5 μm in diameter in the extended state. Actin is

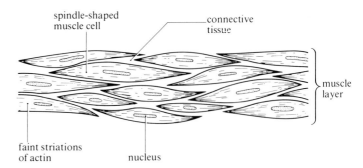

Fig 17.28 *Vertebrate smooth muscle*

arranged in a longitudinal fashion within each cell (fig 17.28). It is now generally accepted that vertebrate smooth muscle has myosin filaments in its normal state, although these may be different from those in striated muscle filaments. Cross-striations are not seen here because the myosin and actin filaments through the cells are not in axial register. It is thought that the contractile mechanism in smooth muscle is essentially similar to that of striated muscle, although regulation of activity may be quite different.

Conduction between cells is relatively slow and this results in prolonged slow contraction of the muscle and an equally slow relaxation period. The muscle is also capable of spontaneous rhythmic contractions and these may vary both in intensity and frequency. Stretching of smooth muscle, caused by the distension of the hollow organ which the muscle surrounds, is generally followed by an immediate contraction of the muscle. This particular property again aids the propulsion of contents within the organ.

The cells are not under voluntary nervous control, but instead are innervated by two sets of nerves from the autonomic nervous system. One set is from the **parasympathetic** and the other from the **sympathetic** system (section 16.2.3). The general opposing effects that they exert on the organs they innervate means that the activity of the organs can be quickly controlled to meet any changing conditions that might occur. Smooth muscle activity may also be modified by adrenaline and other specific hormones.

17.5.4 Muscle spindles and the stretch reflex

Within skeletal muscles are a number of proprioceptors called muscle spindles (fig 17.29). The centre of each muscle spindle is composed of several modified non-contractile muscle fibres called **intrafusal fibres**, enclosed within a connective tissue sheath. These are surrounded by a number of **annulo-spiral nerve endings** which unite to form an afferent nerve which passes to the spinal cord. Surrounding, and in parallel with, the intrafusal fibres are the muscle fibres of the muscle proper (**extrafusal fibres**). The two ends of the spindle consist of contractile muscle fibres innervated by efferent nerves coming from the central nervous system.

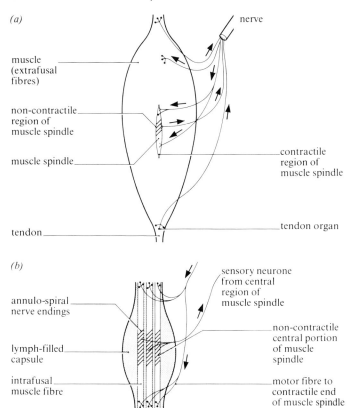

(a)

muscle (extrafusal fibres)

non-contractile region of muscle spindle

muscle spindle

contractile region of muscle spindle

tendon

nerve

tendon organ

(b)

annulo-spiral nerve endings

lymph-filled capsule

intrafusal muscle fibre

sensory neurone from central region of muscle spindle

non-contractile central portion of muscle spindle

motor fibre to contractile end of muscle spindle

When a muscle is stretched, the annulo-spiral nerve endings of the spindle develop a tension and are stimulated to discharge a volley of impulses to the spinal cord via afferent neurones. These synapse directly with efferent neurones which convey impulses to the extrafusal muscle fibres causing a reflex contraction. This is the **stretch reflex**. The greater the degree of stretching incurred by the spindle, the more impulses that are discharged and this leads to a greater degree of muscle contraction. In this way the stretch reflex tries to maintain the constant length of the muscle when the load on it is altered.

Muscle spindles act asynchronously, different ones being active at different times according to the body's needs. There are always some spindles operative at any given time, being stimulated by a constant stream of signals from the central nervous system. This causes a degree of partial muscle contraction within the body called **muscle tone**. Constant use of the muscles, through, for example, physical fitness, is required to maintain good muscle tone.

The two ends of the spindle are important in maintaining muscle tone. When stimulated by impulses from their efferent nerve supply they contract, and this ensures that there is a degree of tension in the muscle before a load is added to it. If the muscle was not maintained in this condition, there would be a danger that it would be overstretched and damaged by the sudden application of such a load.

17.5.5 Inhibitory reflexes

For a limb to be moved to and fro it must be operated by at least two opposing muscles or sets of muscles. When one contracts the other must relax. This is achieved by a simple inhibitory reflex mechanism. It will be recalled that impulses generated by muscle spindles of a muscle arrive at the spinal cord via an afferent neurone and are eventually transmitted to the same muscle causing it to contract. The afferent neurone also synapses with inter-neurones in the grey matter of the spinal cord (fig 17.30). When suitably stimulated, these inhibit the efferent neurones leading to the antagonistic muscle, which is therefore unable to contract and thus remains relaxed.

A good example of this is the mechanism of walking. Initially the limb flexes in order to lift the foot off the ground. During flexion, the antagonistic extensor muscles are stretched but are reflexly inhibited from contracting. After flexion, the limb is straightened and the foot is again brought into contact with the ground. With the flexor muscles no longer contracting, inhibition of the extensor muscles ceases and the stretch reflex now proceeds culminating with the contraction of the extensor muscles. When the limb is straight no stretching in the extensor muscle spindle is detected and the stretch reflex ceases. The whole process is then free to be repeated.

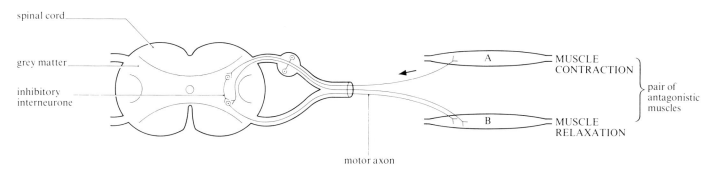

spinal cord

grey matter

inhibitory interneurone

motor axon

A — MUSCLE CONTRACTION

B — MUSCLE RELAXATION

pair of antagonistic muscles

Fig 17.30 *Interneural inhibition. When muscle A contracts, impulses pass to the spinal cord where they meet an inhibitory interneurone. Inhibition of the appropriate motor neurone to muscle B causes it to relax*

17.5.6 Tendon organs

Stretch receptors are also found in tendons. However they only respond when tension becomes severe. Upon stimulation impulses are discharged to the central nervous system where they meet inhibitory interneurones. Stimulation of these causes reflex inhibition of contraction and inhibition of active resistance to stretching. This is significant because it protects the muscle from being damaged when suddenly overloaded, or overcontracting and damaging itself in response to the application of a heavy load.

> **17.5** Examine fig 17.29 and answer the following questions.
> (a) What happens to the muscle spindle when the whole muscle (extrafusal fibres) is stretched?
> (b) What happens next when the extrafusal muscle fibres have contracted?
> (c) What occurs if the muscle is severely stretched, as when a heavy load is suddenly applied to it?
> (d) What occurs when the intrafusal muscle fibres contract?

17.6 Locomotion in selected non-vertebrates

17.6.1 Amoeboid movement

Amoeboid movement is characterised by the formation of temporary projections of the cell called **pseudopodia**. It occurs in protoctistans of the phylum Rhizopoda and in vertebrate white blood cells. During movement the cell produces a definite anterior end which is at the point where new pseudopodia are forming. Analysis of the cytoplasm of an *Amoeba* indicates that there is a peripheral layer of viscous **plasmagel**, the **ectoplasm**, which encloses a more fluid cytoplasm, the **plasmasol** or **endoplasm**. Locomotion is thought to be brought about by alternate changes in the colloidal state of the cytoplasm affected by sol–gel–sol transformations, and the cytoplasmic streaming of plasmasol into the pseudopodia.

Where a pseudopodium is about to form, the plasmagel liquefies into plasmasol. Plasmasol from within the cell now flows towards this point and outwards into the newly forming pseudopodium. Plasmasol in the outer regions of the pseudopodium is rapidly transformed into plasmagel which thus forms a rigid collar around the pseudopodium. At the posterior end of *Amoeba* the plasmagel is rapidly converted to plasmasol which then flows forwards (fig 17.31).

A number of theories exist to explain amoeboid movement. One suggests that the posterior end of the animal contracts and drives plasmasol forwards into the newly formed pseudopodium, slight pressure changes stimulating gel-sol changes and streaming of the cytoplasm from one region of the cell to another. The more-favoured 'fountain-zone' theory suggests that the cell is pulled forwards by contraction of the anterior end of the animal. It is imagined that protein molecules in plasmasol are in an extended state and that their contraction brings about a change in the gel state. Contraction at the anterior end brings about extension at the posterior end.

These theories have been further modified by the discovery of actin and myosin molecules in eukaryotic cells (section 7.2.10). Ectoplasm contains a three-dimensional network of cross-linked actin filaments, whereas endoplasm contains uncross-linked filaments. Proteins which bring about cross-linking may therefore be associated with the gel–sol transition. Such activity is very dependent on calcium ion (Ca^{2+}) concentration and pH, and local control of these variables within the cell may therefore be important.

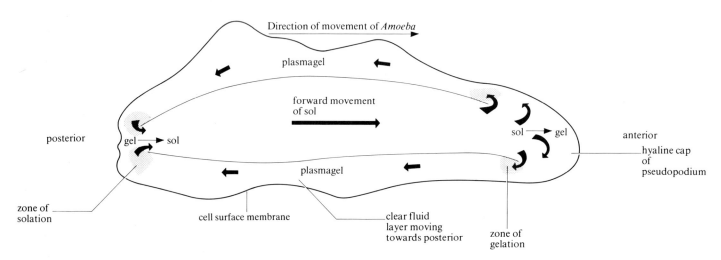

Fig 17.31 *Pseudopodial formation in Amoeba. According to the 'fountain-zone' theory, plasmasol gelates and contracts, thus pulling more plasmasol towards it*

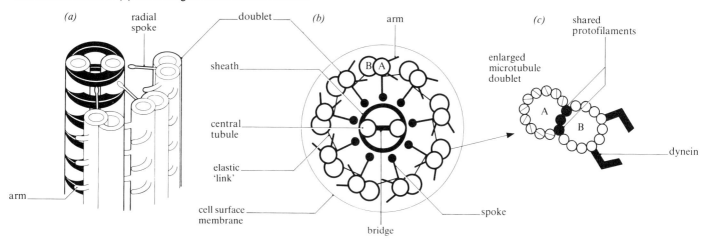

Fig 17.32 *Structure of a cilium or flagellum. (a) An interpretation of the arrangement of tubules and associated material as seen from outside. (b) The structure seen in cross-section. Each doublet consists of an A and a B tubule. Two arms are attached to the A tubule. Note that the A tubule is a complete circle in cross-section, whereas part of the wall of the B tubule is shared with the A. Spokes occur at intervals along the length of each doublet; they connect the doublets to the sheath surrounding the central tubules. (c) An enlarged microtubule doublet.*

17.6.2 Cilia and flagella

Electron micrographs indicate that cilia and flagella possess identical internal structures. Cilia are simply shorter versions of flagella and, unlike flagella, are more commonly found in groups than in isolation. A transverse section of either organelle shows it to consist of a pair of central filaments surrounded by nine peripheral filaments (fig 17.32), the so-called '9+2' array. This bundle of filaments, called an **axoneme**, is surrounded by a membrane that is continuous with the cell surface membrane.

Each peripheral filament is composed of the protein **tubulin** and consists of an A and a B microtubule. Each A microtubule has pairs of 'arms' at regular intervals along its length composed of another protein called **dynein** which is capable of hydrolysing ATP, in other words it is an ATPase. The central filaments are connected to the A microtubule of the peripheral filaments by radial spokes of material.

The end of the cilium or flagellum attached to the cell or organism terminates in a **basal body** which is essentially identical in structure to an axoneme but has a '9 + 0' structure, and is derived from a centriole. It differs from a centriole only in possessing a complex organisation at its basal end known as a **cartwheel structure**. The basal body is thought to act as a template for the assembly of microtubules during development of cilia or flagella. There are often fibres which extend into the cytoplasm from the basal body which act to anchor the basal body in position.

Whilst cilia and flagella possess fundamentally similar internal structures, their mode of action is quite different.

A flagellum possesses a symmetrical beat with several undulations occurring along its length at any given moment (17.33). This wave-like motion may be in one plane, or less commonly such that it beats in a corkscrew (helical) manner which spins the body of the organism about its longitudinal axis as well as propelling it forwards along a helical path (fig 17.34). In some flagellates the flagellum is at the anterior end of the body and beats in such a way as to pull the organism through the water. This sort of flagellum generally possesses minute lateral projections called **mastigonemes** on its surface which aid this type of locomotion. The flagellum itself is sometimes called a '**tinsel**' flagellum. More usually, the flagellum is at the rear of the organism or cell and pushes it through the water, as in the spermatozoan tail. Fig 17.35 shows a summary of the types of movement induced by flagellar activity.

The beat of a cilium is asymmetric (fig 17.33), there being an active, fast, straight downstroke followed by a slower, bent, limp recovery action at the end of which the cilium returns to its original position. With so many cilia occurring together it is essential that some sort of mechanism exists to coordinate their activity. In the ciliate *Paramecium*, a traditional view is that this might involve fibres called **neuronemes** which interconnect the basal bodies. Generally the cilia beat in a synchronised fashion which results in

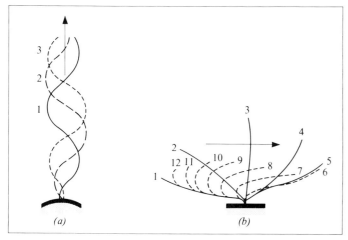

Fig 17.33 *Successive stages in the motion of a flagellum (a) and a cilium (b). The effective stroke of the cilium begins at 1.*

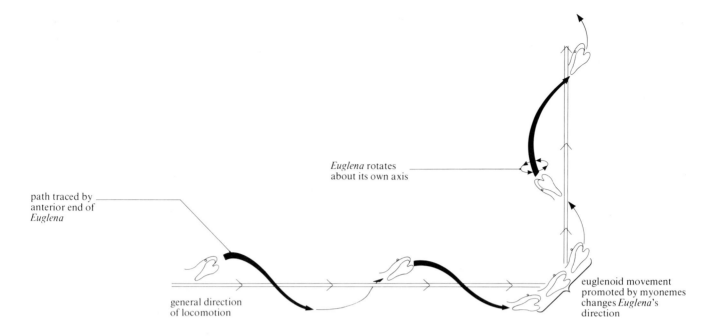

path traced by anterior end of *Euglena*

Euglena rotates about its own axis

general direction of locomotion

euglenoid movement promoted by myonemes changes *Euglena*'s direction

Fig 17.34 *(above)* Euglena*'s path of movement*

Fig 17.35 *(below) Summary of types of movement induced by flagella activity.*

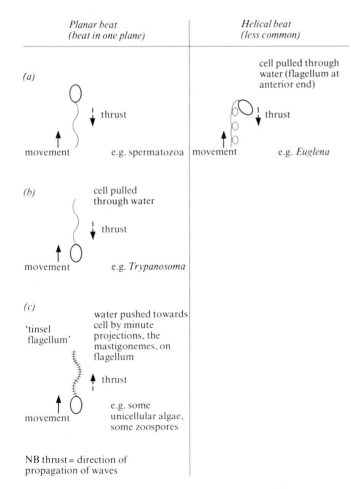

Planar beat (beat in one plane)	Helical beat (less common)
(a)	cell pulled through water (flagellum at anterior end)
movement ↓ thrust e.g. spermatozoa	movement ↓ thrust e.g. *Euglena*
(b) cell pulled through water	
movement ↓ thrust e.g. *Trypanosoma*	
(c) 'tinsel flagellum' water pushed towards cell by minute projections, the mastigonemes, on flagellum	
movement ↑ thrust e.g. some unicellular algae, some zoospores	

NB thrust = direction of propagation of waves

waves of ciliary activity passing along the length of the body in one particular direction. This is called **metachronal rhythm**.

Current evidence concerning the mechanism of beating suggests that a process exists that is essentially similar to that of the sliding filament theory for muscle contraction. A cilium (or flagellum) begins to bend when the two dynein arms of the A microtubule of a doublet forms a cross-bridge with the B microtubule of an adjacent doublet. ATP is hydrolysed to ADP (dynein is an ATPase), the cross-bridge is broken, and another cross-bridge forms further down the B microtubule. The dynein arms thus push the adjacent doublet towards the tip of the cilium.

Successive formation and breakage of cross-bridges causes sliding of the doublets and involves changes in orientation of the dynein arms which have been described as 'walking'. The radial spokes of the cilium tend to resist the sliding process and thus produce local bending (fig 17.36). It is thought that five doublets on one side operate in this manner to produce the initial movement, whilst the remaining four on the other side slide fractionally later, thus inducing the recovery action. It is thought that the central filaments may transmit the signals for sliding from the basal body along the length of the cilium or flagellum. It has also been proved that ciliary activity will only proceed when Mg^{2+} ions are present, and that the direction of the beat of the cilium is dictated by specific levels of intracellular Ca^{2+} ions. Indeed it is interesting to note that the avoiding action of *Paramecium* is controlled in this way. When *Paramecium* encounters an obstacle it reverses the beat of its cilia before moving forward again. Reversal of ciliary beat is stimulated by a sudden influx of Ca^{2+} ions into the cell due to increased permeability of the organism to Ca^{2+} ions.

Both organelles are used extensively by small eukaryotic organisms to propel themselves through water. Locomo-

Fig 17.36 *(a) The sliding of doublets during motion of a cilium in the gills of a mussel. Before bending one of the two tubules of each doublet protrudes further into the tip of the cilium than does the other. Thus, cross-sections at an appropriate constant distance from the tip will show a change in tubule pattern during bending, from all doublets to doublets and single tubules. The entire doublets slide with respect to one another; but the two members of each doublet retain their positions relative to each other. (After P. Satir, from Novikoff & Holtzman.)   (b) Sliding of doublets results in bending*

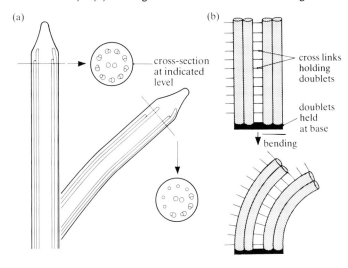

tion brought about in this manner is only effective for small organisms which have a much larger surface area: volume ratio than large animals where the minute forces generated would be quite inadequate. Cilia also frequently occur within the bodies of multicellular organisms where they serve a number of important functions. They may propel fluid through ducts, such as in the nephridia of annelids where metabolic waste is removed. They also propel eggs along mammalian oviducts, and move materials over internal surfaces, such as mucus through the respiratory passages, where this activity helps to keep them free from dust particles and other debris. They can also create feeding currents, as in *Paramecium*, from which food particles can be filtered and removed, often by other cilia.

Some bacteria possess flagella, but these differ markedly from eukaryotic flagella, resembling a single microtubule of a eukaryote flagellum. It is extracellular (not surrounded by a membrane) and rigid. It is rotated (it does not beat) by a 'motor' at its base (see section 2.2.2).

17.6.3   Locomotion in *Euglena*

The locomotory flagellum is at the anterior end of the body and pulls the organism forward. Waves of activity are generated by the flagellum itself, and as they pass in a spiral fashion from its base to its tip they increase in amplitude and velocity. This activity of the flagellum causes the body of *Euglena* to rotate about its axis, at about one complete body turn per second, as well as making it describe a corkscrew pathway through the water. The organism can travel forward at a rate of 0.5 mm s^{-1} which is approximately four times its body length. *Euglena* is able to

change its direction by the action of contractile **myonemes** which lie along the length of its body. When they contract, the shape of the body is changed as well as its direction. This is called **euglenoid motion** (fig 17.34).

17.6.4   Locomotion in *Paramecium*

Surface cilia, arranged in rows, beat diagonally backwards from left to right causing the animal to rotate about its longitudinal axis. At the same time, strongly beating oral groove cilia tend to cause the anterior end of the animal to move in a spiral fashion about its posterior end. The cilia exhibit metachronal rhythm and their coordinated activity may be governed by the **motorium**, a body which is interconnected with the neuronemes and basal bodies. *Paramecium* swims at a speed of about 1 mm s^{-1}, or four times its body length.

17.6.5   Locomotion in the Annelida

An oligochaete, Lumbricus terrestris *(the earthworm)*

The coelom of an earthworm is enclosed by a body wall composed of two antagonistic muscles, an outer circular layer and an inner longitudinal layer. The circular muscle is divided into separate units along the length of the animal by septa between the segments, but the muscle fibres of the longitudinal layer generally extend over several segments. Locomotion is brought about by the coordinated activity of the two muscle layers and those of the **chaetae**.

When an earthworm begins to move forwards, contraction of the circular muscles begins at the anterior end of the body and continues, segment by segment, as a wave along the length of the body. This activity exerts pressure on the coelomic fluid in each segment, stretching the relaxed longitudinal muscle and changing the shape of the segments such that they become longer and thinner. This causes the anterior end of the worm to extend forwards. Chaetae, present in all segments except the first and last, are retracted during the activity of the circular muscles and therefore do not impede the forward movement (fig 17.37).

Whilst the anterior end of the worm is moving forward, longitudinal muscle in more posterior segments contracts, causing this region of the worm to swell and press against the surrounding soil substratum. Chaetae in this region are protruded and help the worm to grip the substratum. This is particularly useful during burrowing for the worm can exert a powerful thrust against the surrounding soil particles during forward locomotion.

Contraction of the circular muscle is quickly followed by contraction of the longitudinal muscles throughout the length of the body, and this means that different parts of the worm may be either moving forward (when the circular muscles contract) or static (when the longitudinal muscles contract) at any given moment. The net effect is a smooth peristaltic wave of activity along the length of the worm as it progresses forwards. The worm is also able to crawl

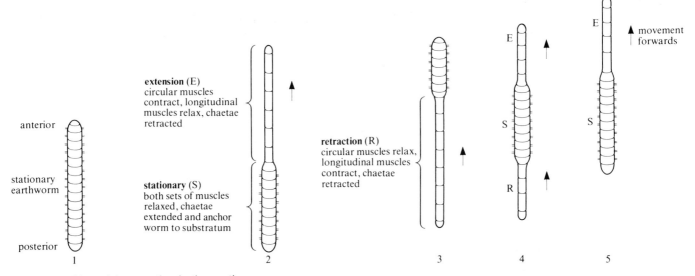

Fig 17.37 (above) *Locomotion in the earthworm*

Fig 17.38 (below) *Segmental innervation of longitudinal muscle in the earthworm (dorsal view). A similar arrangement is present in the circular muscle*

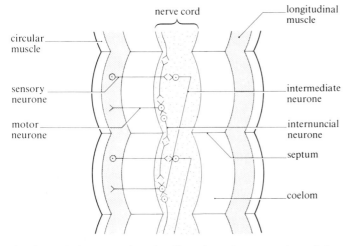

backwards by reversing the direction of contraction of the muscles.

Control of muscle contraction is brought about by a complex network of inter- and intrasegmental neurones. All segments are in contact with the longitudinal nerve cord and also possess their own set of segmental nerves. This means that localised control of each segment is possible, as well as control of overall activity of the animal (fig 17.38).

The ventral nerve cord possesses a **giant axon** which runs centrally along its length and conducts impulses in an anterior-to-posterior direction. Also present in the nerve cord are two longitudinally oriented **lateral fibres** which convey impulses from the tail to the head. When sensory receptors in the head are stimulated, impulses pass along the giant axon stimulating the longitudinal muscles to contract, thus causing the anterior end to be recoiled from the stimulus. If the tail of the worm is similarly stimulated, impulses pass along the lateral fibres from tail to head and cause the tail to be withdrawn. This is the basis of the worm's escape reaction.

A polychaete, Nereis (the ragworm)

In contrast to the earthworm, the longitudinal muscle layer is divided into a pair of dorsal and a pair of ventral muscle blocks (fig 4.18). The circular muscle is relatively weak and segmentally specialised into sets of oblique muscles which run into the **parapodia** and function to move the parapodia and their associated structures. Each parapodium is hollow and ramified by an extension of the coelom which is filled with coelomic fluid. It is subdivided into a dorsal projection, the **notopodium**, and a ventral projection called the **neuropodium**. Both of these structures possess a strengthening rod, the **aciculum**, and a bundle of chaetae.

Interaction between the body wall muscles, parapodia and coelomic fluid brings about several different types of locomotion. Slow creeping movement is achieved by using the parapodia as a system of levers. During its effective stroke a parapodium protrudes its aciculum and chaetae to make contact with the substratum and push against it in a backward direction, thus propelling the animal forwards. Protrusion of these structures is achieved by increased hydrostatic pressure in the coelom of the parapodium. The parapodium moves forward when it lifts from the substratum and its aciculum and chaetae are retracted. Retraction is achieved by contraction of the segmental oblique muscles.

The movements of the right and left parapodia of a segment are coordinated so that whilst one is moving forwards the other is moving backwards. Collectively the parapodia of the worm move as a series of peristaltic waves which pass along the length of the body. In contrast to the earthworm these waves move in a direction from the tail to the head with a group of parapodia on one side all moving generally forwards whilst at the same time their opposite numbers move backwards.

Rapid creeping occurs when the longitudinal muscles on

either side of the body contract alternately throwing the body into a series of lateral undulations. Here the parapodia again come into contact with the substratum. When this occurs, the longitudinal muscles work against these points of contact and effectively pull the animal forwards.

When swimming freely in the water the right and left longitudinal muscles contract alternately to produce waves of lateral movement that pass forward from the tail to the head. The broad, paddle-like parapodia move in a backward direction during their effective stroke. In doing this they push against the water and thrust the animal forwards.

17.6.6 Locomotion in the Arthropoda

Crustacean walking and swimming, Astacus fluviatilis (the crayfish)

The crayfish possesses eight thoracic and six abdominal segments each of which bears appendages of various shapes and sizes which are used for specific functions (fig 4.26). The last four thoracic segments bear walking legs called **pereiopods**, whilst forked paddle-like appendages called **pleopods** are found on abdominal segments 2–5 in the female and 3–5 in the male. The sixth abdominal segment, called the **uropod**, is modified as a flattened tail fin which is most frequently used in swimming.

When walking, the chelipeds of the fourth thoracic segment (section 4.9.1) are raised above the substratum and the abdomen is extended horizontally. Only two legs, one on either side of the body, are out of contact with the ground at any one time, the other six firmly grip the substratum with those of thoracic segments 5–7 pulling the crayfish along while the pair on the eighth thoracic segment push it.

Muscle which promotes movement of the limbs in the crayfish is striated; that in the region of the abdomen is particularly strong. Here thick antagonistic muscles operate to flex and extend the abdomen up and down. When the abdomen is flexed downwards the force exerted on the water by the extended tail is sufficient to cause the crayfish to shoot backwards through the water very quickly. This is the basis of its escape mechanism.

Locomotion in insects

Walking. This is achieved by the coordinated activity of three pairs of legs, one pair being attached to each of the three thoracic segments of the animal. Each leg consists of a series of hollow cylinders whose walls are composed of rigid exoskeletal material. The cylinders are linked together by joints and soft pliable membranes. Where the **coxa** (the basal segment of the insect leg) joins to the body, a form of ball-and-socket joint occurs, but all other joints in the leg are hinge joints. Bending and straightening of the legs is achieved by antagonistic flexor and extensor muscles attached to the inner surface of the exoskeleton on either side of a joint (fig 17.1).

When an insect begins to walk, three legs remain on the ground to support the animal whilst the other three move forward. The first leg on one side pulls the insect, whilst the third leg of the same side pushes. The second leg on the other side serves as a support for this activity. The process is then repeated but with the role of each trio of limbs reversed.

Many insects possess a pair of claws and a sticky pad at the distal ends of their legs. The pad consists of minute hollow tubes which secrete a sticky fluid that helps the insect to adhere to smooth surfaces. Thus, these insects are able to walk up vertical surfaces as well as upside down.

Flight. The wings of insects are flattened extremities of the exoskeleton and are supported by an intricate system of veins. Their movement is controlled by two main groups of muscles, **direct** and **indirect muscles**. In insects with large wings (such as butterflies and dragonflies) the muscles are actually attached to the bases of the wings (fig 17.39); these are the direct muscles. They elevate and depress the wings as well as controlling the angle of the wing stroke during flight. When the angle of one wing is adjusted with respect to the other, turning in the air is accomplished. They are also used to fold up the wings when the insect is stationary.

In insects with smaller wings, the main driving force for flight is developed by two sets of antagonistic, indirect flight muscles; the **dorso-ventrals** are attached to the tergum (roof) and sternum (floor) of the thorax, and the **longitudinals** are attached to the anterior and posterior aspects of the thorax (fig 17.40). There is no direct attachment of the wings to these muscles. However the base of each wing is attached to the tergum and pleura (side) of the thorax. This arrangement acts as a highly efficient lever system, for when either of the indirect muscles shortens fractionally it distorts the shape of the thorax, which in turn produces a large degree of movement by the wings. Because muscle contraction takes place over a very small distance it can be repeated rapidly. This is particularly important for insects that possess very fast wingbeat speeds.

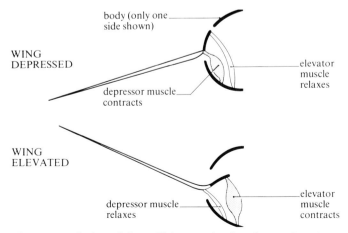

Fig 17.39 *Action of direct flight muscles in a large winged insect, such as a butterfly or dragonfly*

Fig 17.40 *Cross-section of the thorax of an insect from the anterior showing the relationship between wings, pleura, sternum, tergum and muscles during insect flight*

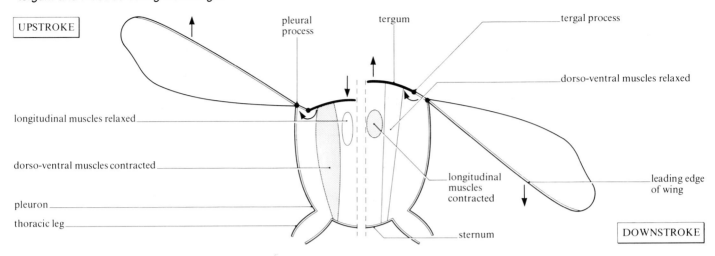

In large, winged insects such as the butterfly and locust the rate of wing beat is between 5–50 beats per second (table 17.5). Here the flight muscles contract each time as a result of a single nerve impulse. Hence impulses are generated at the same rate as the wings beat. Insect flight muscle which responds in this way is called **synchronous muscle**. In the housefly, which has a wing beat frequency of 120–200 beats per second, contraction of the flight muscles is much too fast to be triggered by individual nerve impulses. This muscle is termed **asynchronous** and receives roughly one impulse per 40 wing beats, which is necessary to maintain the muscle in an active state during flight. It can contract further and generate more power than synchronous muscle. Asynchronous muscle can also automatically contract in response to being stretched. This is called the **stretch reflex** and occurs faster than the speed of a nerve impulse.

Table 17.5. Wing speeds of a variety of insects

Wing speeds			
Large butterfly e.g. swallowtail	5 times per second		
Locust	18 ,,	,,	
Hawkmoth	40 ,,	,,	
Housefly	120 ,,	,,	at this speed a humming sound heard
Bee	180 ,,	,,	
Midge	700–1000 ,,	,,	at this speed a high pitched whine heard

In general, the smaller the insect the faster it beats its wings.

NB Some insects have two pairs of wings (such as locusts and dragonflies). In some cases both pairs of wings beat together, as in bees; in others the back pair of wings beats slightly ahead of the front pair, for example locusts. Some insects have one pair of wings, such as flies and beetles. In houseflies the hindwings are reduced and modified to form a pair of club-shaped halteres which are sensory in function. They oscillate rapidly during flight, detect aerodynamic forces and provide information for the maintenance of stability in flight. Some insects (very few) have no wings, for example fleas.

The following account of asynchronous flight is based on detailed observations made by Boettiger on the fly *Sarcophaga bullata*. Whilst flying in a straight line the wings describe a pathway through the air in the form of a figure of eight. The downstroke provides the majority of forward thrust and lift for the insect. During this phase each wing beats forward and downward with its anterior margin inclined at a lower level than its posterior one. On the upstroke the wing moves upward and backward with its anterior margin raised above the posterior one. In this position the wings move through the air with minimum resistance whilst at the same time providing more lift for the body.

In order to raise the wings, the dorso-ventral muscles contract. When this occurs the tergum is lowered and the tergal attachment of each wing is pulled into a position below that of its pleural attachment (fig 17.40). During this process the resistance of the tergum to this distortion increases. However, at a critical point the resistance disappears and the wings click into an elevated position. At the same time that this is happening the longitudinal muscles are stretched, considerably stimulating a stretch reflex which makes them contract instantaneously. The tergum now arches upwards and the tergal attachment of the wing is raised above the pleural one. Once again resistance to such a movement is suddenly overcome and the wings click downwards. This action in turn stretches and stimulates the dorsoventral muscles to contract, and the whole cycle is repeated.

17.6 The sarcoplasmic reticulum of insect flight muscle is modified to increase its surface area by being perforated at intervals. Can you suggest a reason for this?

17.7 Would synchronous or asynchronous muscle be expected to contain more sarcoplasmic reticulum? Give a reason for your answer.

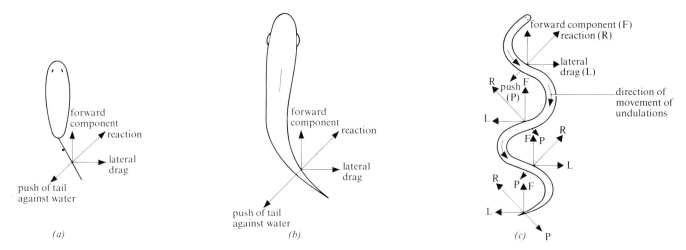

17.7 Locomotion in vertebrates

17.7.1 Swimming in fish

Water, particularly sea water, has a high relative density, many hundreds of times greater than air. As such it represents a comparatively viscous medium to move through. However, its density is made use of by fish as it supports them and also provides a medium against which the fish can thrust during swimming movements.

Any successful organism shows many adaptive features suited to the environment in which it lives and a fish is no exception. The body of most fish is highly streamlined, being tapered at both ends. This means that water flows readily over the body surface and that drag is reduced to a minimum. Apart from the fins no other structures project from a fish, and it seems that the faster the fish, the more perfect is the streamlining. The dermal denticles of cartilaginous fish and the scales of bony fish are moistened by slimy exudation from mucus or oil glands and this also considerably reduces friction between the fish and the water. Other general adaptations possessed by fish for moving efficiently through the water are the fins. Dorsal and ventral, unpaired, median (along the midline of the body) fins help to stabilise the fish, the paired pectoral and pelvic fins are used for steering and balancing the animal, and the caudal or tail fin, in concert with the paired fins, provides the forward movement of the fish through the water. Details of precisely how the fins operate will be discussed later.

17.7.2 Propulsion in fish

Movement is brought about by sets of segmentally arranged antagonistic muscle blocks called **myotomes** located on either side of the vertebral column. Superficially each myotome possesses a zig-zag shape, and internally it traverses the joint formed by two adjacent vertebrae. The vertebral column is a long, flexible rod and, when myotomes on one side of it contract, it bends easily.

The myotomes contract and relax alternately on each side of the vertebral column beginning at the anterior end of the fish and travelling towards its tail. This activity bends the body of the fish into a series of waves, the number increasing the longer and thinner the fish.

Very compact fish such as *Ostracium* (the tunny) show little evidence of this wave-like action with as much as 80% of their forward thrust being achieved purely by the side-to-side lashing of the tail and caudal fin. This locomotion is called **ostraciform**. Longer fish, such as the dogfish and the majority of bony fish, exhibit **carangiform locomotion**; here the posterior half of the fish is thrown into a series of waves. **Anguilliform** locomotion, as demonstrated by eels, is where the body is very long and thrown into many waves so that different parts of the body are moving simultaneously to the left and to the right.

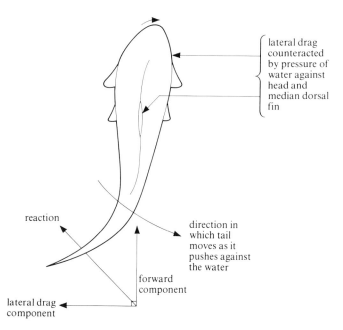

Fig 17.42 *Force components exerted by the caudal fin of a dogfish as it is lashed from side to side*

Fig 17.43 *Action of paired pectoral and pelvic fins and heterocercal tail in the dogfish to provide lift*

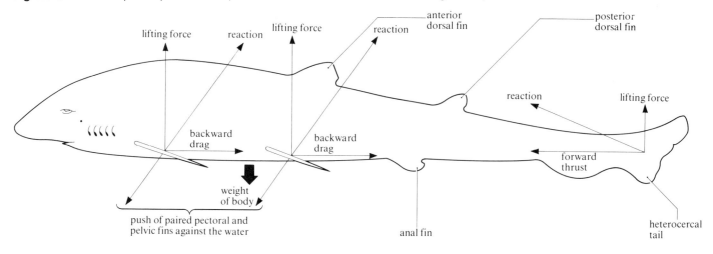

Forward propulsion is generally effected by the side-to-side movement of the tail to which is attached the caudal fin. As the caudal fin is moved in this way it bends slightly and exerts a backward pressure on the relatively viscous water. This force can be resolved into a forward and lateral component. The forward one thrusts the fish through the water whilst the lateral one tends to swing the head of the fish sideways in a direction opposite to that of the tail. This is called **lateral drag** (fig 17.42). Fortunately, it is counteracted by the inertia of the water against the relatively massive anterior end of the body (when compared to the tail) and the large surface area posed by the dorsal median fin. Also it would require a much greater force to move the body laterally through the water than to propel it forwards. The magnitude of the force that the tail and caudal fin apply to the water depends on their speed of action, surface area and the angle at which they are held with respect to the water.

17.7.3 Locomotion in a cartilaginous fish, the dogfish

A dogfish is heavier than sea water and will begin to sink to the bottom if it ceases to swim. To avoid this the paired pectoral and pelvic fins act as **hydrofoils**. They are held at an angle to the long axis of the body, and when the fish wishes to swim up or down in the water their angle is altered accordingly by muscular activity. When held at an angle, the force exerted by the fins can be resolved into an upward component, which forces the head of the fish upwards (positive pitch), and a backward or drag component (fig 17.43). However the drag is considerably less than the forward thrust produced by the tail and is relatively unimportant. The dogfish possesses a **heterocercal** tail, the ventral lobe being proportionately larger than its dorsal counterpart. As the tail thrusts from side to side, once again the force produced by it can be divided into an upwards thrust, termed negative pitch, as well as a lateral component. The positive pitch at the anterior end is balanced by the negative pitch at the rear.

As the fish swims along in a level forward manner it may be subjected to three kinds of displacement or instability. These are **yawing, pitching** and **rolling**. The various fins of the body are generally responsible for maintaining controlled forward locomotion and the way in which they counteract any displacement of the fish can be seen in fig 17.44.

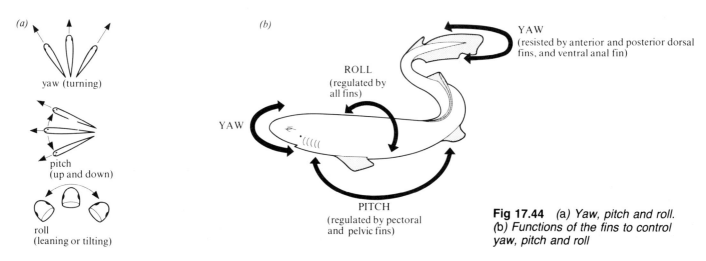

Fig 17.44 *(a) Yaw, pitch and roll.
(b) Functions of the fins to control
yaw, pitch and roll*

Fig 17.45 *Closed swim bladder of a bony fish; (a) location, (b) bladder and circulation*

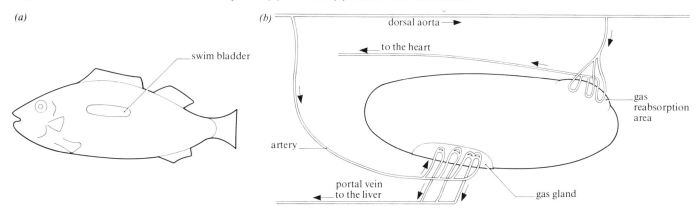

The fins respond almost immediately to any form of instability. This is because of the activity of a set of three semicircular canals located on either side of the head of the fish. Should the body yaw, pitch or roll, then the appropriate semicircular canal is stimulated to fire nerve impulses which pass to the brain. The brain, in turn, immediately sends the appropriate motor impulses to the fin muscles which adjust their position accordingly.

17.7.4 Locomotion in a bony fish, the herring

Bony fish possess a structure called the swim or air bladder. Whilst lobe-finned fish used the swim bladder to perfect the air-breathing habit, bony fish adapted it into a hydrostatic device. The swim bladder is a sac lying between the vertebral column and gut and functions to provide the fish with 'neutral buoyancy'. When this occurs the fish possesses a density equal to that of the surrounding water and therefore does not need to expend energy to keep itself from sinking, so concentrating its efforts on moving through the water.

With the development of such a swim bladder in bony fish, the paired fins were released from their lifting function. Now, they are much smaller than those of the dogfish and are used instead as stabilisers or brakes, in the latter case being spread vertically at 90° to the body. Each pectoral fin may be used independently of its opposite number, and in this way they act as pivots round which the fish can turn rapidly. When the fish is swimming in a straight line the paired fins are pressed firmly against the sides of the body thus improving its streamlined shape. Possession of a swim bladder has also permitted the development of a symmetrical **homocercal** tail which transmits most of the force it develops against the water in a forward direction.

Two types of swim bladder exist.

(1) **Open swim bladder** (as in goldfish, herrings). The bladder is connected to the pharynx by a duct. Air is taken in or expelled from the bladder via the mouth and duct, thus decreasing or increasing the relative density of the fish respectively.

(2) **Closed swim bladder** (as in codfish). The bladder has completely lost its connection with the pharynx. By automatically increasing or decreasing the amount of gas in its bladder, the fish can match the density of the surrounding water and thus preserve 'neutral buoyancy'.

The closed swim bladder is under nervous control. At its anterior end is a structure, the **gas gland**, rich in blood capillaries, which secretes gas rich in oxygen into the bladder. Posteriorly is another heavily vascularized region which can absorb gases from the bladder (fig 17.45). In the gas gland, arterial and venous capillaries are interspersed amongst each other. It is here that a countercurrent system operates in order to facilitate secretion of oxygen into the bladder. The gas gland produces lactate when gas secretion occurs, and as the lactate enters the venous capillaries it reduces the affinity of haemoglobin for oxygen (this is called the root effect). This phenomenon increases the oxygen tension of the blood in the venous capillaries leaving the gas gland, and paradoxically the venous blood

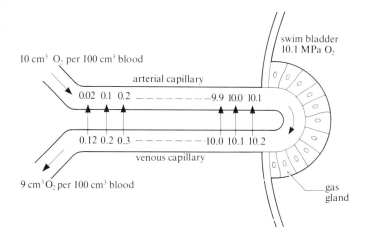

Fig 17.46 *Countercurrent system in the closed swim bladder of a bony fish. The gas gland produces lactate which increases the oxygen tension in the venous capillary. Thus gas diffuses from the venous to arterial capillaries, and remains within the loop. As venous blood leaves the gland it contains less oxygen than the incoming arterial blood. NB For simplification only one venous and one arterial capillary are shown. The gas gland itself contains numerous capillaries*

possesses a higher oxygen tension than that in the arterial capillaries (fig 17.46). Therefore oxygen constantly diffuses from the venous to the arterial capillaries and is secreted into the swim bladder. At the time of gas secretion by the gas gland the blood vessels of the posterior region of the swim bladder are closed off so that no gas can escape from it.

17.8 Summarise the adaptations that fish possess for efficient swimming.

17.7.5 Locomotion in the frog

In the frog the paired limbs are no longer used as fins for stabilising and steering the animal, but are modified to operate as elongated jointed levers, raising the body off the ground whilst at the same time moving the animal over land. The forelimbs are relatively short, with the radius and ulna united. The hindlegs are very long and held underneath the body when the animal is at rest, by being bent at the knee and ankle. The tibia and fibula are fused together and the tarsals greatly elongated. The girdles, which articulate with the limbs, are greatly enlarged when compared with those of fish and support the weight of the animal against the effects of gravity. This is especially true of the pelvic girdle.

When a frog crawls over the substratum its mode of locomotion is effected by diagonally opposite limbs operating in unison with each other. If we begin with a stationary frog with all four limbs on the ground, the following sequence of events takes place when it begins to crawl. The left forelimb retracts at the same time as the right hindlimb extends. Both limbs thrust against the substratum and so propel the animal forwards. This is followed by retraction of the right forelimb and extension of the left hindlimb, the whole process being repeated as long as the animal is crawling. A full explanation is given in fig 17.47.

At take off, during a jump, each joint in the hindlimb is

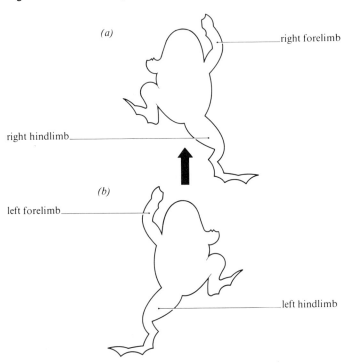

Fig 17.47 *Crawling in a frog viewed dorsally*
(a) Left forelimb retracts, right hindlimb extends, right forelimb extends, left hindlimb placed forwards.
(b) Left forelimb extends, right hindlimb is placed forwards, right forelimb retracts, left hindlimb extends

straightened by rapid contraction of strong extensor muscles. The force exerted against the ground during this activity is transmitted from the limbs to the vertebral column via the pelvic girdle and is at least three times greater than the weight of its body. This is sufficient to propel the animal upwards and forwards into the air against the downward pull of gravity. On landing, the short, compact forelimbs, attached in a flexible manner to the pectoral girdle, dampen down the shock of impact (fig 17.48).

Fig 17.48 *The take-off and jump of a frog*

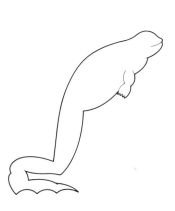
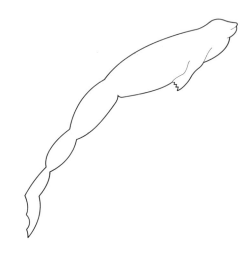

(a)

(b)

(c)

Fig 17.49 *(a) Quill feather, (b) contour feather, (c) down feather*

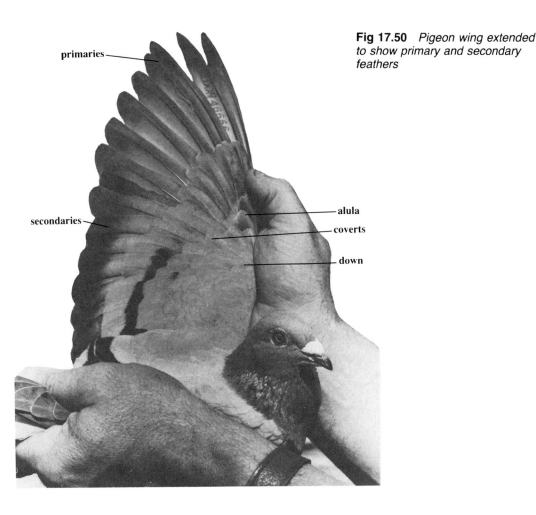

primaries

secondaries

alula

coverts

down

Fig 17.50 *Pigeon wing extended to show primary and secondary feathers*

17.7.6 Bird feathers and flight

The possession of feathers, and considerable modification of their skeleton has enabled most birds to develop structural adaptations which have provided them with the ability to fly, and gain substantial mastery of the air.

Feathers are epidermal structures developed within the skin of birds, evolved from scales of reptiles. Whilst they provide body covering for birds, they are not spread evenly over the body surface. They occur in tracts called **pterylae** (*ptero*, flying) which are separated by featherless areas called **apteria**. Four distinct kinds of feather are recognisable, namely the **quill**, **contour**, **down** and **filoplume**. Details of the structure of each of these can be seen in fig 17.49a–c.

Each bird wing possesses 23 quill feathers called **remiges**. They are positioned in a backward direction over the body and overlap each other. This arrangement provides an upper convex, and lower concave, surface to the wing and therefore enables it to act as an aerofoil, the significance of which will be discussed later. There are 11 remiges attached to the hand (metacarpals and digits), these are called **primaries**, whilst the remaining 12 are attached to the forearm (radius and ulna) and are termed **secondaries** (fig 17.50). The quill feathers of the tail are called **retrices**.

Typically a quill feather is composed of a stiff hollow

lower region, the quill, embedded in the skin, and an upper solid **rachis**. The rachis supports the **vane**, which consists of rows of **barbs** on each side, which themselves bear two rows of **barbules**. The barbules interlock with each other by means of small hooks and grooves (fig 17.51) thus providing a firm, strong and light air-resistant surface to the wing. At the junction between the quill and radius is a smaller tufted structure, the **aftershaft** or afterfeather. It consists of a group of separated barbs.

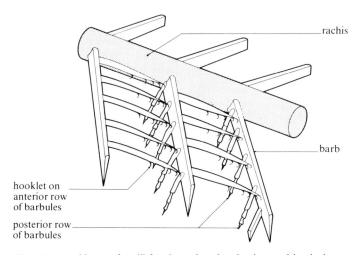

rachis

barb

hooklet on anterior row of barbules

posterior row of barbules

Fig 17.51 *Vane of quill feather showing barbs and barbules*

Contour feathers, though similar in structure, are smaller and more flexible than quill feathers, and their barbs are less firmly attached. They provide the main body covering and wind-proof layer of the bird and establish its body outline.

Down feathers are the only body covering of nestlings. In older birds they are closely applied to the skin in amongst the contour feathers. The barbs of these feathers are long and pliable and their barbules do not possess hooks.

Filoplumes are small hair-like structures. There is no vane as such, just a small tuft of flexible barbs and barbules at the tip of the rachis. These feathers are spread all over the bird and help to retain air close to its body.

Apart from the development of feathers, many other modifications associated with flight have taken place within birds. The major ones are summarised below.

(1) The pectoral girdle is well developed and provides a firm base for the wings. There is a sizeable **keeled sternum** providing a large surface area for the attachment of the powerful pectoral flight muscles (fig 17.52). Flight muscles may approach half the body weight in a strong flying bird such as a racing pigeon.

(2) Considerable fusion and elongation of forelimb bones has provided a large wingspan. Three carpals have fused with three metacarpals to form the **carpometacarpus**, a strong supportive structure for the attachment of the primary flight feathers. Only three digits remain. Loss of the others has helped to lighten the wing. The skeleton is rigid in places; for instance some of the vertebrae are fused, and the vertebral column is fused to the pelvic girdle. This transmits the force of the wings more efficiently and provides better lift. The hindlimbs have been lengthened, which means that the wings do not flap against the ground during take-off.

(3) The body is highly streamlined so that when the bird flies through the air its shape provides little resistance. The skull is compact and generally possesses a streamlined, pointed bill. The arrangement of the feathers provides a smooth surface for the air to flow over. The tail is short. This cuts down drag and increases manoeuvrability. The legs of birds are tucked up to the body during flight.

(4) The possession of a number of hollow spongy bones helps to lighten the body. Many of the cavities are filled by air sacs. These also help to improve ventilation in the bird by being able to supply the lungs with fresh air during inspiration and expiration (section 11.6.11). The insides of the bones of large birds have struts for strength. The beak represents toothless, pointed jaws covered with a horny bill. The absence of teeth precludes the need for heavy jaw muscles for grinding food. This function is carried out by the gizzard which is nearer to the centre of gravity of the bird. It has been estimated that in a pelican weighing 11 kg, and standing 1.5 m tall, its skeleton weighs only 0.65 kg, and that the frigate bird (a sea glider) with a wing span of 2 m possesses a skeleton weighing just 110 g. In fact here the feathers weigh more than the skeleton (1.4–1.8 kg)! The sex organs of birds are very small, only developing fully during the breeding season. This again aids flight economy in terms of keeping the body as light as possible.

(5) Birds have a high body temperature and good insulation which combats the cooling effect of the air as the birds move through it. It also ensures more efficient muscle contraction for flight. The heart of a bird is large and strongly beating thus maintaining high blood pressure.

(6) Birds have excellent visual acuity. A third eyelid, the nictitating membrane, is present which removes particles from the eye during flight. Many birds possess a long flexible neck which enables the head to reach the ground for feeding purposes, and permits it to be rotated, providing good all-round vision.

(7) As would be expected, all birds that fly possess remarkable powers of muscular coordination.

17.7.7 Flight in birds

Consider the horizontal flow of air over an inclined wing surface which has its leading edge raised above its trailing edge. In this context the wing acts as an aerofoil. Air flowing over the upper surface meets less resistance than that flowing over the lower surface (fig 17.53) and therefore develops a greater velocity. The combined effect of these two phenomena is to cause air pressure above the wing to be reduced, and that below to be increased, thus providing the wing with a **lifting force**. The power of this lifting effect depends on the size and shape of the wing, the angle at which it is inclined to the long axis of the body (the angle of attack) and the bird's air speed. There is also a force acting on the bird, exerted by the air, which tends to push the wing backward in the direction of the airstream. This is called **drag**. The

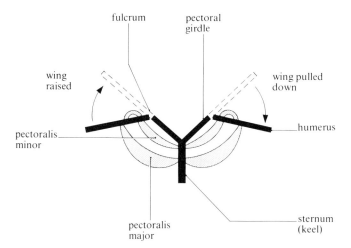

Fig 17.52 *Section of a bird (pigeon) skeleton viewed from the front to show how flight muscles and bones of the wings and pectoral girdle operate together*

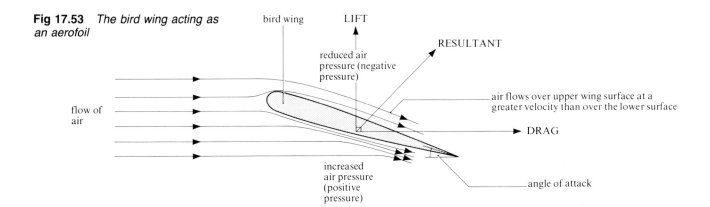

Fig 17.53 *The bird wing acting as an aerofoil*

flow of air

bird wing

LIFT

reduced air pressure (negative pressure)

RESULTANT

air flows over upper wing surface at a greater velocity than over the lower surface

DRAG

angle of attack

increased air pressure (positive pressure)

mechanical efficiency of a wing depends on its ability to develop a big lifting force for a small relative increase in drag.

There are three major types of flight; flapping, gliding and soaring, and hovering.

Flapping flight

In a bird such as the pigeon, which beats its wings two times per second, the main powerstroke is delivered by the downbeat of the wings and is brought about by contraction of the large, powerful **pectoralis major muscles** which are attached at one end to the ventral surface of the humerus and to the keel of the sternum at the other. At take-off the first part of the downstroke is almost vertical with the leading edge of the wing lower than the trailing edge. The primary feathers are bent upwards due to the pressure of the air. They are tightly closed to provide maximum resistance to the air and therefore maximum lift. During the latter part of the downstroke the wing is moved forward

and twists like a propellor so that its front edge is tilted upwards. In this position the wing develops lift for the body. The lifting effect of the air as it moves between the primary feathers tends to separate them and bend them upwards (fig 17.54).

The upstroke starts before the downstroke has been completed. The inner part of the forearm is moved sharply upwards and backwards with its front edge inclined above that of the trailing edge. This action is produced by the **pectoralis minor muscles** attached to the dorsal surface of the humerus and to the sternum. It provides lift for the body. As the wing moves upwards it bends at the wrist and the hand twists round so that the primary feathers are suddenly jerked backwards and upwards until the whole wing becomes more or less straight above the body. On their upward journey the primaries are separated, permitting the air to pass between them thus minimising air resistance. The backward movement of the primaries provides the bulk of the forward propulsive thrust

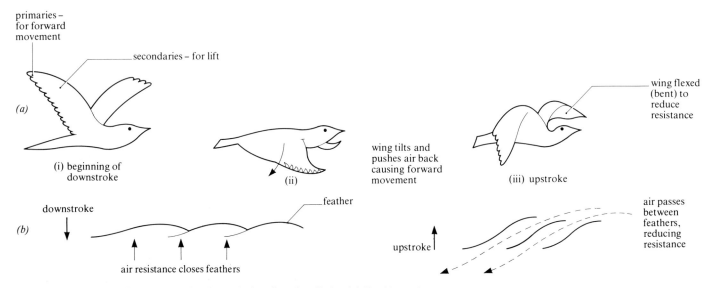

Fig 17.54 *Action of wings and feathers during flapping flight. (a) Position of wings during flapping flight in a pigeon. (b) Position of feathers during downstroke and upstroke of a bird wing during flapping flight*

developed by the animal. Before the primaries have reached their highest point, the pectoralis major muscles begin to contract again, eliciting a new downward beat and the whole process is repeated.

During sustained flapping flight the wing action is considerably modified and requires far less energy than that needed at take-off. Here the wings do not flap so hard, meet each other over the bird's back or move forwards during the latter part of the downstroke. The wings are generally held out straight, and the up and down flapping movements occur mainly at the wrists (junction of lower limb bones and carpals). The active backward lift of the wrist has virtually disappeared and the upstroke is passive, being achieved by air pressure acting against the underside of the wing.

At the end of flight the bird lands by lowering and spreading out its tail. This acts both as a brake and a lifting flap. As lift is achieved, the legs are lowered and the bird comes to rest. The tail is also used to steer the bird in flight, and stability in the air is accomplished by nervous control via the semicircular canals. Impulses are generated here which stimulate accessory muscles to alter the shape and position of the wings and the number of beats of one wing relative to the other.

Different birds fly at different speeds. Such differences are achieved by the shape of the wing, its changing form during flight and the frequency of the wing beat. A comparison of the structure of the wing of a fast flier, the swift, and that of a slow flier, the sparrow, is given in fig 17.55.

Fig 17.55 *Comparison of the structure of the wing of a fast flying bird (such as a swift) and a slow flying bird (such as a sparrow)*

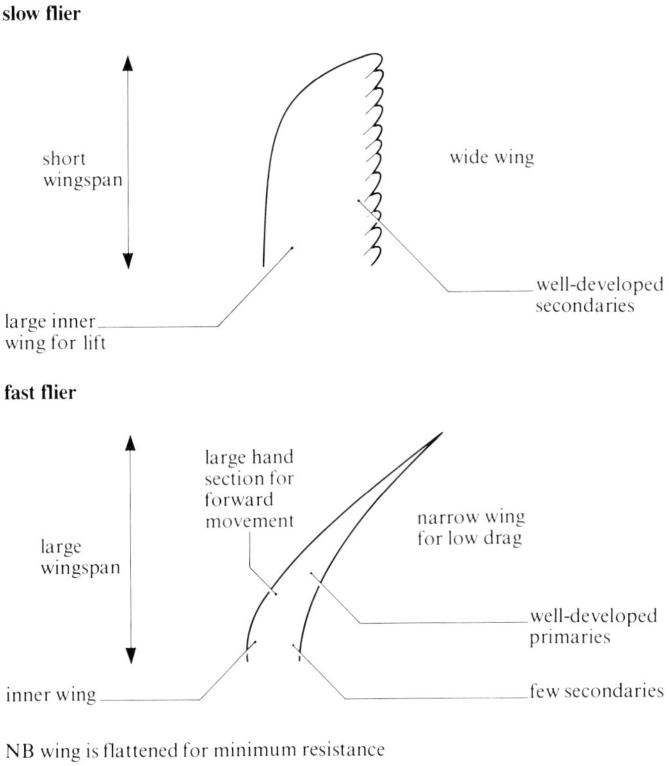

slow flier

short wingspan

wide wing

large inner wing for lift

well-developed secondaries

fast flier

large hand section for forward movement

large wingspan

narrow wing for low drag

inner wing

well-developed primaries

few secondaries

NB wing is flattened for minimum resistance

17.9. List the features which enable the swift to fly so fast.

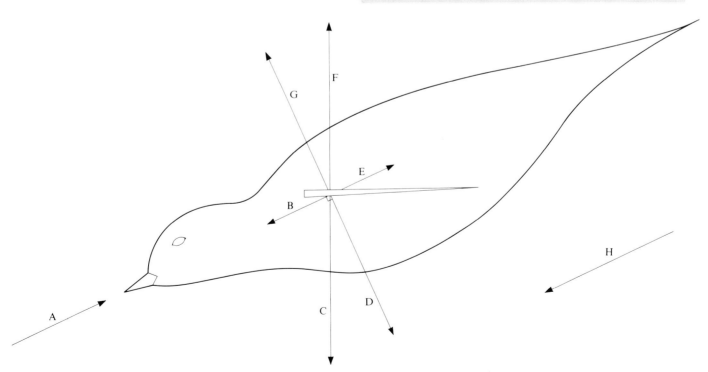

Fig 17.56 *Drawing showing forces exerted against the bird when gliding in still air. A, direction of airflow over bird; B, driving force; C, weight of body; D, sinking force; E, drag; F, resultant aerodyne force; G, lift; H, direction of movement of bird. (Modified after Gray.)*

Gliding and soaring

During gliding the wings are held out at more or less 90° to the body and the bird gradually loses height. As it descends, the force acting on it is called the **driving force** (fig 17.56) and the pull of gravity acting in a downward direction is called the **sinking force**. As the gliding speed increases so the lifting force increases and when lift equals the sinking force, and the driving force equals drag, the bird glides through the air at a constant velocity. The speed and angle of the glide depends on the size, shape and angle of attack of the wings and the weight of the bird.

Land birds make use of thermal upcurrents when gliding. They occur when a horizontal wind is deflected upwards on encountering an obstruction such as a mountain (this is known as slope soaring), or when warm air moves upwards and is replaced by colder air, such as over towns. Birds with light bodies and large wings such as buzzards and eagles are good thermal gliders and they manoeuvre gently upwards in a series of small circles. Rising in the air without flapping is called soaring.

Marine birds, such as the albatross, possess a different shape and glide in a different fashion (fig 17.57). The albatross has a large body, and very long narrow wings, and makes use of gusts of wind that arise above the waves. During its upward glide it ascends to a height of about 7–10 m. Then it turns downwind and descends at great speed with its wings angled in a backward direction. At the bottom of the descent the albatross describes an arc as it turns back into the wind and its wings are placed in a more forward position. The new position of the wings and the forward velocity of the body provide the bird with a lifting force which enables it to gain height in preparation for another rapid descent. Albatrosses are also able to glide for long distances close to, and parallel to, wave ridges, using the small upcurrents of wind from the waves as land birds do in slope soaring.

Hovering

Hovering is flapping the wings while at the same time staying in one place. The wings move backwards and forwards at speeds of up to 50 beats per second, and the upward thrust developed counterbalances the bird's weight. Birds that hover possess enormous flight muscles relative to their size ($\frac{1}{3}$ body weight) and are consequently very strong flappers. Their wings can tilt at almost any angle. The majority of the wing feathers are primaries (only six are secondaries) and are used for developing thrust.

17.7.8 Flight in bats

Bats are the only mammals capable of true flight. Each wing is composed of a thin layer of heavily vascularised skin, stretched between the bat's forearm, all fingers of the hand except the thumb, the sides of its body and the ankle of the hindlimb. The wrist bones are fused and give the wing strength whilst those of the forearm and hand are considerably elongated and function as a supportive framework for the wing. The index and middle

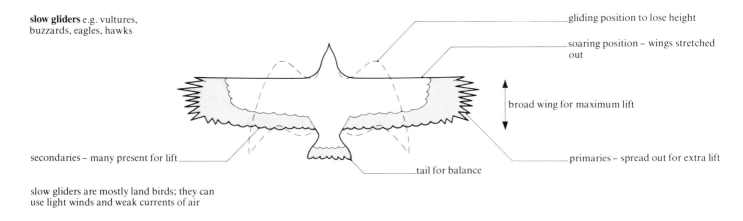

slow gliders e.g. vultures, buzzards, eagles, hawks

gliding position to lose height

soaring position – wings stretched out

broad wing for maximum lift

secondaries – many present for lift

primaries – spread out for extra lift

tail for balance

slow gliders are mostly land birds; they can use light winds and weak currents of air

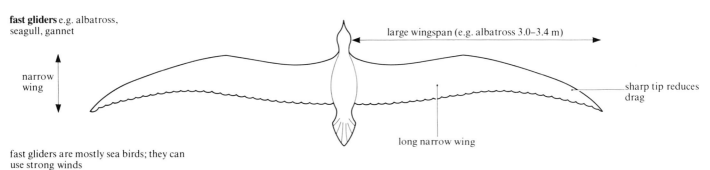

fast gliders e.g. albatross, seagull, gannet

large wingspan (e.g. albatross 3.0–3.4 m)

narrow wing

sharp tip reduces drag

long narrow wing

fast gliders are mostly sea birds; they can use strong winds

Fig 17.57 *A comparison between the body and wing shapes of slow and fast gliders*

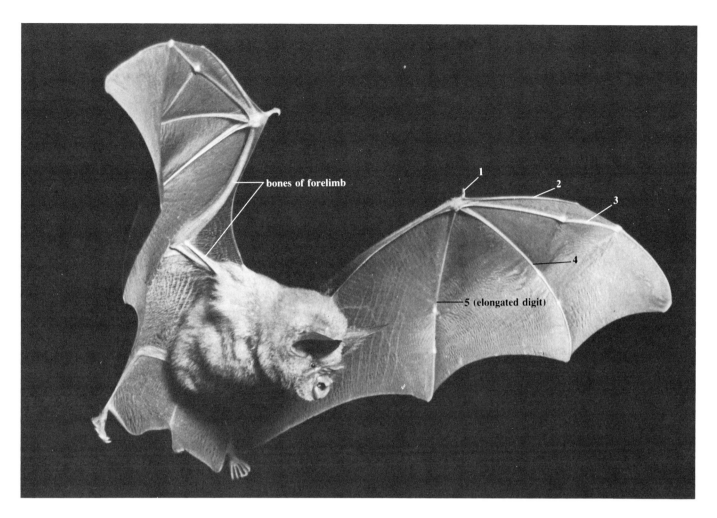

bones of forelimb
1
2
3
4
5 (elongated digit)

fingers of the hand support the leading edge of the wing whilst the other two fingers extend backwards to the trailing edge which eventually links up with the fifth digit of the ankle (fig 17.58). The actual movement of the wings occurs in a similar fashion to the wings of birds, and flight can be powerful and fast.

17.7.9 Locomotion in quadrupeds, the dog

Walking

When a dog walks, its vertebral column remains rigid, and forward movement is achieved by the activity of the hindlimbs. They are moved forwards and backwards by alternate contraction of flexor and extensor muscles respectively.

When its extensor muscle contracts, each hindlimb, acting as a lever, extends and exerts a backward force against the ground, thus thrusting the animal forward and slightly upwards. When the flexor contracts, the limb is lifted clear of the ground and pulled forward. Only one limb is raised at any one time, the other three providing a tripod of support which balances the rest of the body. Beginning with the left forelimb in a stationary dog, the sequence of leg movement is as follows when it walks forward: left forelimb; right hindlimb; right forelimb; left hindlimb; and so on.

Fig 17.58 (above) *Bat wing extended showing attachment of wing to forearm, body and ankle*

Fig 17.59 (below) *Running sequence in a dog (such as a greyhound)*
(a) Backbone fully arched and feet immediately under the body. (b) Backbone fully extended and somewhat concave, limbs fully extended

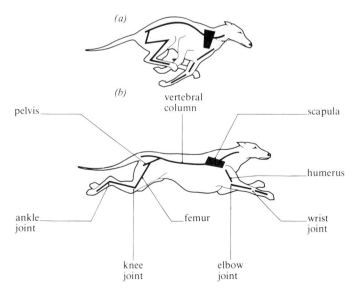

(a)

(b)

pelvis
vertebral column
scapula
humerus
ankle joint
femur
wrist joint
knee joint
elbow joint

Running

As a dog begins to run, it loses its tripod means of suspension and develops a type of movement where the forelimbs move together, followed by the hindlimbs. The feet are in contact with the ground for much less time than in walking, and usually one forelimb touches the ground a split second before the other. This also occurs with the hindlimbs. Therefore the sequence of limbs touching the ground is: left forelimb; right forelimb; right hindlimb; left hindlimb.

As the dog reaches maximum speed, leg movement quickens even further, and as they extend, all four legs may be off the ground at the same time. The strong trunk muscles arch the flexible backbone upwards when all four limbs are underneath it, and downwards when the limbs are fully extended. In this way the thrust of the limbs is increased and the stride of the dog considerably lengthened, both of which enable the dog to increase its speed (fig 17.59).

17.7.10 Bipedal gait, the human

In the standing position the weight of the body is balanced over two legs. When a stride is taken by the right limb the first thing to happen is that the right heel is raised by contraction of the calf muscle. This action serves to push the ball of the right foot against the ground and thus exert a forward thrust. The right limb pushes further against the ground as it is pulled forwards, slightly bent at the knee (fig 17.60). As this occurs, the weight of the body is brought over the left foot which is still in contact with the ground and acting as a prop for the rest of the body. When the right limb extends, the heel is the first part of the foot to touch the ground. The weight of the body is gradually transferred from the left side to a position over the right heel, and then as the body continues to move forwards,

Fig 17.60 *Successive positions of the right leg during a single pace*

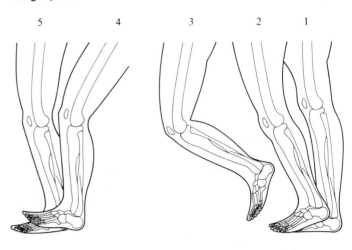

over the right toe, backward pressure against the substratum generally being exerted through the right big toe.

With the weight of the body now over the right leg, the left heel is raised and the whole sequence repeated. This alternating sequence of right and left, heel-and-toe action continues until walking ceases.

> **17.10** Why do sprinters generally run on their toes?

17.8 Support in plants

Four tissues, the parenchyma, collenchyma, sclerenchyma and xylem contribute towards the support of plants. A full account of their supporting role can be found in chapter 8.

Chapter Eighteen

Homeostasis

An organism may be defined as a physico-chemical system existing in a steady state with its external environment. It is this ability to maintain a steady state within a constantly changing environment that contributes towards the success of living systems. In order to maintain this condition organisms, from the morphologically simplest to the most complex, have developed a variety of anatomical, physiological and behavioural mechanisms designed to achieve the same end, that is the preservation of a constant internal environment. The advantage of a constant internal environment in providing optimal conditions in which organisms can live and reproduce most efficiently was first proposed by the French physiologist Claude Bernard in 1857. Throughout his research he had been impressed by the way in which organisms were able to regulate physiological parameters, such as body temperature and water content, and maintain them within fairly narrow ranges. This concept of self-regulation leading to physiological stability was summed up by Bernard in the now classic statement, 'La fixité du milieu interieur est la condition de la vie libre.' (The constancy of the internal environment is the condition of the free life.)

Bernard went on to distinguish between the **external environment** in which organisms live and the **internal environment** in which individual cells live (in mammals, this is tissue, or interstitial, fluid). He realised the importance of conditions in the latter being continuously stable. For example, mammals are capable of maintaining a constant body temperature despite fluctuations in the external temperature. If it is too cold the mammal may move to warmer or more sheltered conditions; if this is not possible, self-regulating mechanisms operate to raise the body temperature and prevent further heat loss. The adaptive significance of this is that the organism as a whole will function more efficiently because its constituent cells are maintained at optimum conditions. In this respect biological systems are seen to operate not only at the level of the organism but also at the level of the cell. An organism is the sum of its constituent cells and the optimum functioning of the whole depends upon the optimum functioning of its parts.

In 1932 the American physiologist Walter Cannon introduced the term **homeostasis** (*homoios*, same; *stasis*, standing) to describe the mechanisms whereby Bernard's 'constancy of the internal environment' is maintained. Homeostatic mechanisms function to maintain the stability of the cellular environment and in so doing provide the

organism with a degree of independence of the environment which is determined by the effectiveness of the mechanisms. Independence of the environment is used as a criterion of the 'success' of an organism and on this basis mammals are seen as 'successful' since they are able to maintain relatively constant levels of activity despite fluctuations in environmental conditions.

In order to achieve a degree of stability the activities of organisms need to be regulated at all levels of biological organisation, from the molecular to the population. This necessitates organisms employing a range of biochemical, physiological and behavioural mechanisms as are most appropriate to their level of complexity and mode of life. In all these respects mammals are seen to be better equipped than protozoans to cope with changes in environmental conditions.

Investigations have shown that the mechanisms of regulation found in organisms show many features in common with mechanisms of regulation in non-living systems, such as machines. The systems of both organisms and machines achieve stability by some form of control, to which Wiener, in 1948, applied the term **cybernetics** (*cybernos*, steersman). Cybernetics is the science of control mechanisms and is commonly referred to as **control theory**. Plant and animal physiologists have used many of the very precise mathematical models of control theory to explain the functioning of biological control systems, hence before studying some of these self-adjusting mechanisms, such as body temperature regulation, gaseous exchange rates, blood metabolite levels and water and ionic balances, it is necessary to have some appreciation of the theoretical considerations underlying control systems.

18.1 Control systems in biology

18.1.1 Introduction to control systems

The rigorous application of control theory to biology has led to a deeper understanding of the functional relationships between the components of many physiological mechanisms and has clarified many concepts which were previously obscure. For example, living systems are now seen to be **open systems**; that is they require a continuous exchange of matter between the environment and themselves. Living systems are, in fact, in steady state with their environment and require a continuous input of

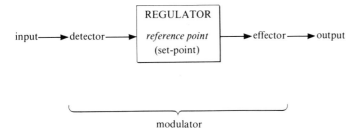

input──▶ detector──▶ | REGULATOR *reference point* (set-point) | ──▶ effector──▶ output

modulator

Fig 18.1 *Basic components of a control system*

energy in order to prevent them coming to equilibrium with the environment. This equilibrium is achieved only upon the death of the organism when it becomes thermodynamically stable with respect to its environment. The basic components of any control system are summarised in fig 18.1.

The efficiency of the control system is measured in terms of how little displacement from the reference point (optimal level) occurs and the speed with which the level is restored. Homeostatic mechanisms must be free to fluctuate, as it is the fluctuations themselves which activate the control systems and return the parameter towards its optimal level. Such control systems rely upon their components being linked together so that the output can be regulated in terms of the input, a concept known as **feedback**.

Feedback requires the action of the system to be referred back to a **reference point** or **set-point**, which is the optimal level of the parameter (or **controlled variable**), so that subsequent action may be modified to restore the set-point. There are two forms of feedback, **negative** and **positive**. The former is most common in the homeostatic mechanisms of organisms.

Negative feedback is associated with increasing stability of systems (fig 18.2). If the system is disturbed, the disturbance or error sets in motion a sequence of events which counteract the disturbance and tend to restore the system to its original state. The principle of negative feedback may be described in terms of the regulation of

oven temperature by the use of a thermostat. In the electric oven the control system includes an **input** (an electric current flowing through an element which acts as a source of heat), an **output** (the oven temperature) and a thermostat which can be set to a desired level, the set-point. The thermostat acts as a modulator. If the thermostat is set to read 150 °C, an electric current will provide a source of heat which will flow until the oven temperature passes the set-point of 150 °C, then the thermostat will cut out and no more heat will be supplied to the oven. When the oven temperature falls below 150 °C the thermostat will cut in and the electric current will increase the temperature and restore the set-point. In this system the thermostat is functioning as an **error detector** where the error is the difference between the output and the set-point, The error is corrected by increasing the input. This is an example of a steady-state closed-loop system which is typical of many of the physiological control mechanisms found in organisms.

Examples of biological negative feedback mechanisms include the control of gas tensions in the blood, heart rate, arterial blood pressure, hormone and metabolite levels, water and ionic balances, the regulation of pH and body temperature. Fig 18.3 illustrates the role of negative feedback in the control of thyroxine release by the thyroid gland. In this example the modulator has three components, a **detector** (the hypothalamus), a **regulator** (the pituitary gland) and an **effector** (the thyroid gland).

Positive feedback is rare in biological systems since it leads to an unstable situation and extreme states. In these situations a disturbance leads to events which increase the disturbance even further (fig 18.2). For example, during the propagation of a nerve impulse, depolarisation of the neuronal membrane produces an increase in its sodium permeability. Sodium ions pass into the axon through the membrane and produce a further depolarisation which leads to the production of an action potential. In this case positive feedback acts as an amplifier of the response whose extent is limited by other mechanisms as described in section 16.1.1.

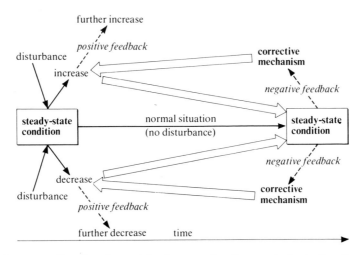

Fig 18.2 *Homeostatic control system. The directions of the lines on the diagram indicate the directions of stimulus and response*

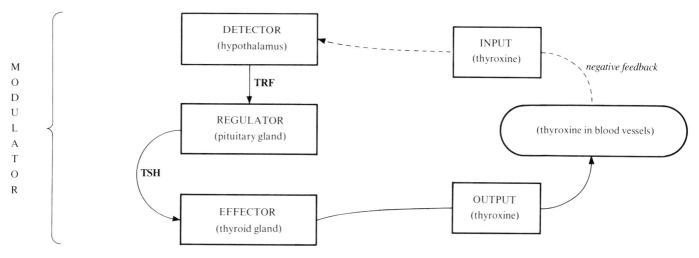

Fig 18.3 *A biological example of a simple control system, the control of thyroxine production. TRF, thyroid releasing factor; TSH, thyroid stimulating hormone; see section 16.6*

There are several control mechanisms in the body which are more complex than those previously described. Broadly they either involve the use of additional detectors (physiological early-warning systems) or effectors ('fail-safe' systems) operating at different levels. For example, temperature detectors situated externally and internally enable homeotherms to maintain an almost constant 'core' body temperature. Temperature receptors in the skin, acting as disturbance detectors of changes in the external environment, send impulses to the hypothalamus which acts as a modulator and initiates corrective measures before any change in blood temperature occurs. Other examples of this system include the control of ventilation during exercise, appetite and thirst. Similarly multiple detectors and effectors provide fail-safe mechanisms for many vital processes, such as regulation of arterial blood pressure where stretch receptors in the carotid sinus and aorta, and baroreceptors in the medulla, respond to blood pressure changes and produce responses in various effectors including the heart, blood vessels and kidneys. Failure of any one of these is compensated for by the others.

18.1.2 The nature and control of the internal environment

The internal environment of an organism and its control may be considered at two levels: the cellular level and the tissue level.

The cell is composed of cytoplasm whose constituents are modulated by the partial permeability of the cell membrane and by enzyme activity under the control of protein synthesis. The cell membrane only permits certain molecules to enter and leave the cell and the rates at which exchange is permitted are strictly controlled by diffusion gradients, osmotic gradients, electrical gradients, active mechanisms involving membrane-bound carrier systems and changes in membrane distribution as shown by pinocytosis (section 7.2.2). Similarly the

nature and amounts of materials synthesised within the cell are controlled by the rates of protein synthesis. Metabolic activities in cells are determined by enzymes produced by the transcription and translation of the base sequence codes of DNA into the primary structure of proteins which act as enzymes. Regions of DNA carrying the code for a specific protein are known as genes and the 'switching on and off' of genes is thought to be controlled by systems of induction and repression which are described in detail in section 22.7. In terms of control systems the maintenance of a steady state within the cell depends upon the rates of supply and utilisation of cellular material, in other words the input and output, and the activity of the modulators (fig 18.4).

Both single-celled organisms and cells of multicellular organisms control their internal environments as described above. In the case of single-celled organisms their immediate environment is the external surroundings over which they have no control. They may, if they possess locomotory mechanisms, move to more favourable surroundings, but for the most part they are at the mercy of the environment. They adapt to, and tolerate, conditions as best they can. The sheer numbers of these minute species reflect their degree of success in surviving in spite of their structural simplicity.

The immediate environment of the cells of multicellular plants and animals is an extracellular fluid. This is called sap in plants, haemolymph in insects, water in echinoderms and tissue fluid in most other animals. The composition of this extracellular fluid can be regulated by the organisms to varying degrees depending upon the efficiency and effectiveness of their homeostatic organs. In mammals the immediate environment of all living cells is tissue fluid. The mechanism of formation of this remarkably stable fluid is described in chapter 14. Since the time of Bernard, the nature of the extracellular fluid and the mechanisms of its control have been widely studied. It is birds and mammals that show most control over the composition of the fluid

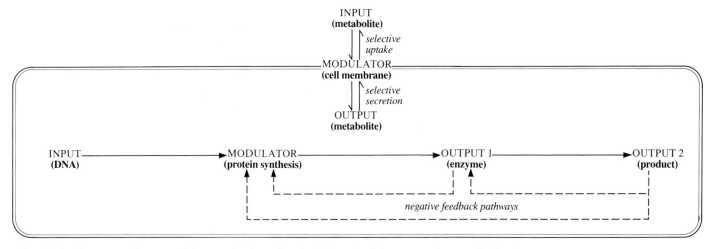

Fig. 18.4 *Summary diagram of the mechanisms involved in maintaining a steady state in the internal environment of a cell*

and its parameters of water, gases, ions, nutrients, hormones, excretory products, pH and temperature. In all cases these parameters have one or several tissues, organs or organ systems to maintain control within narrow limits.

The mechanisms of control in most animals involve responses by endocrine glands, or the nervous system coordinated by control centres in the brain and spinal cord (**regulators**) as shown in fig 18.5.

In conclusion it is worth re-emphasising the adaptive significance of homeostatic mechanisms. All metabolic systems operate most efficiently if maintained within narrow limits either side of optimal conditions. It is the role of homeostatic organs and systems to operate both separately and together to buffer against fluctuations from these optimal conditions caused by variations in the external and internal environments. Some of these mechanisms are discussed in the following sections.

18.1.3 Control of respiratory gases in the blood

The cells of the body require a continuous supply of oxygen from their immediate environment, the tissue fluid, in order to carry out respiration. Carbon dioxide, produced by this process, must not be allowed to accumulate in the cells or in the tissue fluid, as it would upset the equilibria of the reactions involved in respiration

and produce local changes in pH which would affect the rates of enzyme reactions. The body maintains a fine control over the concentration (or tension) of carbon dioxide in the blood despite variations in oxygen availability and metabolic demands which may increase twenty-fold during vigorous activity.

The rate and depth of ventilation (inspiration and expiration) are controlled by **respiratory centres** situated in the pons and the medulla oblongata at the base of the brain (fig 18.6). These centres generate rhythmic impulses to the diaphragm and intercostal muscles which bring about ventilation movements. This rhythm is basically involuntary but can be overridden within limits by higher centres of the brain, as shown by the ability to hold the breath. The rate and depth of ventilation directly governs the composition of the alveolar air which, in turn, determines the oxygen and carbon dioxide tensions in the arterial blood supplied to the body tissues. The mean partial pressures of oxygen and carbon dioxide in alveolar air and the arterial blood are 13.3 kPa and 5.3 kPa respectively in a resting subject at sea level. The maintenance of the above levels is achieved by negative feedback to the respiratory centres in the medulla of impulses from two types of receptors: mechanical stretch receptors (proprioceptors) in the walls of the trachea and lungs, and chemoreceptors in the wall of the aorta, the carotid bodies (situated in the walls of the carotid arteries) and in the medulla itself. Higher centres in

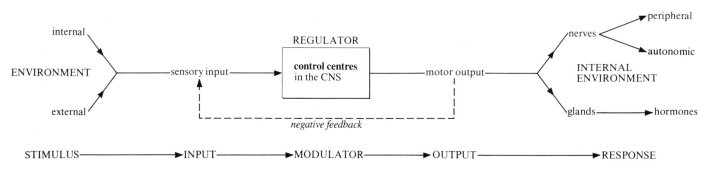

Fig 18.5 *Homeostatic mechanisms for the control of the internal environment*

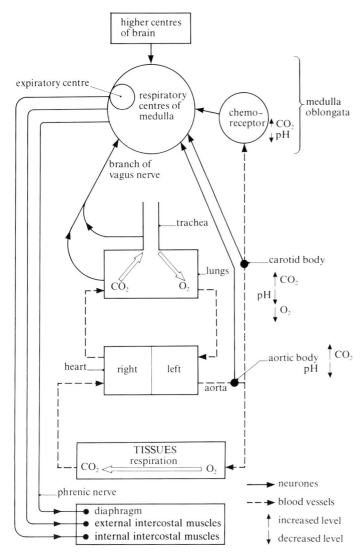

trachea and lungs are no longer stimulated there is no inhibition of the inspiratory respiratory centre and the ventilation cycle repeats. During vigorous activity increased carbon dioxide in the blood stimulates the expiratory centre and impulses pass to the internal intercostal muscles which contract more frequently and this leads to deep or forced breathing.

The rate and depth of ventilation is governed by the activity of chemoreceptors in response to changes in oxygen and carbon dioxide tensions in the blood. Experiments involving subjects breathing air composed of varying concentrations of oxygen and carbon dioxide have shown that the effects of increasing carbon dioxide levels are more important in controlling ventilation than oxygen levels. Reducing the oxygen concentration of air from 20% to 5% produces a doubling of the normal resting ventilation rate, whereas an increase of only 0.2% in carbon dioxide concentration produces the same response.

The influence of carbon dioxide concentrations and reduced blood pH in regulating ventilation rate is mediated almost entirely through chemoreceptors in the aorta, carotid bodies and in the medulla itself. Chemoreceptors in the aorta and carotid bodies are also sensitive to changes in oxygen concentration and are vital when oxygen concentrations are low, because a fall in oxygen concentration depresses activity of the medulla. Increased ventilation facilitates loss of carbon dioxide from the blood by diffusion into the alveolar air which is brought to a new lower equilibrium with atmospheric air. The same effect is achieved by deliberate deep breathing or **hyperventilation**.

18.1 Explain why the ventilation rate decreases and subjects feel dizzy and faint after hyperventilating.

At high altitudes (in excess of 3 000 m) the partial pressures of oxygen and carbon dioxide in the atmosphere are reduced. This results in the oxygen and carbon dioxide concentrations in the alveolar air coming to a new equilibrium with those of the atmosphere. Consequently more carbon dioxide is lost from the blood into the alveolar air due to the lower concentration here. As there is insufficient carbon dioxide in the blood to stimulate the carbon dioxide chemoreceptors the stimulus for ventilation cannot be carbon dioxide. Instead, low oxygen concentrations stimulate chemoreceptors in the carotid body which activates the respiratory centres.

There is a close relationship between the respiratory centres and the cardiovascular centre which are both situated in the medulla. Changes in blood pressure, which are maintained by the cardiovascular centre, affect the ventilation rate, for instance ventilation rate increases as the blood pressure falls and vice versa. Equally, changes in respiratory gas concentrations, as monitored by the respiratory centres, will produce changes in blood pressure (section 14.12.6).

Fig 18.6 *Summary diagram of mechanisms involved in the control of respiratory gases in the blood*

the brain can override this feedback and voluntarily inhibit or increase the activity of the respiratory centres, such as during breath-holding, forced breathing, speech, singing, sneezing and coughing.

The effect of impulses from the stretch receptors is mainly concerned with the mechanics of ventilation movements. Impulses generated by the respiratory centres pass down efferent neurones in the spinal cord; some emerge in the cervical region as the phrenic nerves to the diaphragm, other neurones emerge from the thoracic region of the spinal cord as the external intercostal nerves. Together they produce the inspiratory movements. The lungs inflate, and stretch receptors in the walls of the lungs and trachea activate afferent neurones of the vagus which temporarily inhibit the inspiratory respiratory centre, preventing further inspiratory activity. Elastic properties of the lungs produce recoil as the diaphragm relaxes reducing the volume of the thorax and thus expiration of air from the lungs occurs. As the stretch receptors in the

18.1.4　Control of metabolites in the blood

One of the most important metabolites in the blood whose level must be strictly controlled is glucose. This sugar is the principal respiratory substrate and must be continuously supplied to cells. The brain cells are especially sensitive to glucose and are unable to utilise any other metabolites as an energy source. Lack of glucose results in fainting. The normal level of glucose in the blood is about 90 mg 100 cm^{-3} blood, but may vary from 70 to 150 mg 100 cm^{-3} blood during fasting and following a meal, respectively. The sources of blood glucose and its metabolic interrelationships with other metabolites are described in section 18.5.2.

The control of blood glucose level is an example of a complex, endocrine-regulated homeostatic mechanism involving the integrated secretion of at least six hormones and two negative feedback pathways. A rise in blood glucose level (**hyperglycaemia**) stimulates insulin secretion (section 16.6.7) whereas a fall in blood glucose level (**hypoglycaemia**) inhibits insulin secretion and stimulates the secretion of glucagon (section 16.6.7) and other hormones which raise blood glucose levels (hyperglycaemic factors). The control mechanism is summarised in fig 18.7.

The software program *Insulin* by Brian Kahn provides a simulation of the control of blood sugar level.

18.1.5　Control of heart rate and blood pressure

Variations in heart rate and blood pressure have an indirect effect upon the composition of tissue fluid and enable it to be kept within narrow limits despite fluctuations in the external environment and varying demands imposed on tissues. The mechanisms of control involve the activity of the autonomic system and details of these mechanisms are described in section 14.12.5.

There are two major conditions of abnormal heart rate, tachycardia and bradycardia. **Tachycardia** (*tachys*, swift; *cardia*, heart) is a general term describing an increased heart rate and may be caused by a variety of factors including emotional states, such as anxiety, anger and laughter, and overactivity of the thyroid gland. Severe tachycardia is often the result of changes in the electrical activity of the heart. Regions of the heart, other than the S–A node, can act as foci for the origin of the stimulus producing contraction of the heart muscle and augment the normal heart activity, based on the S–A node, producing tachycardia.

Bradycardia (*bradys*, slow) describes the condition where the heart rate is reduced below the mean level. It is common in athletes who develop an increased stroke volume as a result of training. Therefore, in order to maintain a constant cardiac output at all times their resting heart rate is reduced. Underactivity of the thyroid gland, and changes in the electrical activity of the S–A node and other conductile regions of the cardiac tissue, can also give rise to bradycardia.

The antagonistic regulatory effects of the sympathetic and parasympathetic nervous systems on the S–A node tend to counteract temporary conditions of tachycardia and bradycardia and restore the normal heart rhythm.

Blood pressure is the force developed by the blood pushing against the walls of the blood vessels. It is usually measured in the brachial artery using a **sphygmomano-**

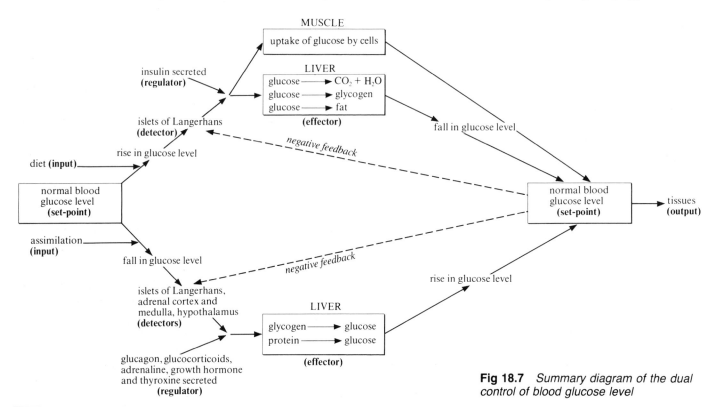

Fig 18.7 *Summary diagram of the dual control of blood glucose level*

meter. The **systolic** pressure is produced by the contraction of the ventricles and the **diastolic** pressure is the pressure in the arteries when the ventricles relax. Blood pressure is affected by age, sex and state of health, and the mean pressures for a healthy young man are 16 kPa (systolic and 10.6 kPa (diastolic). Both pressures are affected by cardiac output and peripheral resistance and indicate the general state of heart and blood vessels. Conditions which lead to narrowing and hardening of the arteries (**atherosclerosis**) or damage to the kidneys may increase the blood pressure, a condition known as **hypertension**, and impose a strain on the heart and blood vessels. This may lead to a weakening of artery walls and their rupture or the clogging of narrowed vessels by blood clots (**thrombosis**). These are very serious if they affect the brain or the heart and lead to cerebral haemorrhage (stroke), cerebral thrombosis or coronary thrombosis.

18.1.6 Control of infection

The many mechanisms of defence against infection are homeostatic in that they attempt to maintain a constant internal environment. The skin is the major defence against infection, but viruses, bacteria, protozoans, roundworms and flatworms can invade the tissues through natural openings, cuts and by boring through the skin. The presence of pathogens and their toxic waste products in the body evokes several defence mechanisms, including the activity of various white blood cells (phagocytes, monocytes and lymphocytes). The mechanisms of blood clotting, wound healing and immunity are described in detail in sections 14.13.5 and 14.14.

18.2 Temperature regulation

Heat is a form of energy with an important influence upon the maintenance of living systems. All living systems require a continuous supply of heat in order to prevent degradation and cessation of those systems.

The major source of heat for all living organisms is the Sun. Solar radiation is converted into an exogenous (outside the body) source of heat energy whenever it strikes and is absorbed by a body. The extent and effect of this solar radiation depends upon geographical location, and is a major factor in affecting the climate of a region. This, in turn, determines the presence and abundance of species. For example, organisms inhabit regions where the normal air temperatures vary from -40 °C, as in the Arctic, to 50 °C in desert regions. In some of the latter regions the surface temperature may rise as high as 80 °C. The majority of living organisms exist within confined limits of temperature, say 10–35 °C, but various organisms show adaptations enabling them to exploit geographical areas at both extremes of temperature (fig 18.8). This is not the only source of heat available to organisms. Solar radiation of wavelengths within those of the visible spectrum are used by photosynthetic autotrophs and this energy becomes

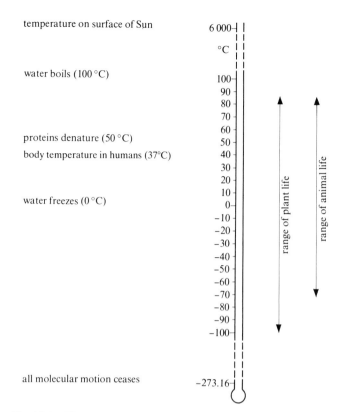

Fig 18.8 *Temperature reference points in living organisms and the ranges of temperature they are able to tolerate*

locked up in the chemical bonds of synthesised organic molecules (chapter 9). This provides an endogenous (within the body) source of heat energy when released by the catabolic reactions of respiration (chapter 11).

Temperature indicates the amount of heat energy in a system and is a major factor determining the rate of chemical reactions in both living and non-living systems. As described in section 6.4.3, heat energy increases the rate at which atoms and molecules move and this increases the probability of reactions occuring between them. The relationship between temperature and the rate of chemical reactions is expressed as the temperature coefficient, or Q_{10}. In living systems temperature has an effect upon enzyme structure which influences the rate of metabolism and exerts the major influence on the distribution and activity of organisms.

18.2.1 The influence of temperature on the growth and distribution of plants

Temperature can act as a limiting factor in the growth and development of plants by influencing the rates of cell division, cell metabolism and photosynthesis. The non-light-requiring reactions of photosynthesis are temperature dependent and control the various metabolic pathways described in chapter 9. The rates of photosynthesis, and the accumulation of sufficient food materials to enable the plant to complete its life cycle, are factors determining the geographical range of plants.

18.2.2 Adaptations to low temperatures in plants

The flora of northern temperate climates and the tundra show many adaptations enabling plants to take maximum advantage of the short, warm summers. For example, the only plant species found are mosses, lichens, a few grasses and fast-growing annuals. Plants living in extreme northerly or southerly latitudes are subjected to long periods of adverse conditions, such as low light intensity, low temperatures and frozen soil. In order to survive in these conditions, plants shown many anatomical, physiological and behavioural adaptations which may be related to stages in the life cycle. For example, most temperate woody perennials are deciduous and lose their leaves, under the influence of the plant growth regulator substance abscisic acid (ABA), in order to prevent water loss by transpiration and evaporation during periods when soil water uptake is limited by low temperatures (section 15.2.8). Wind and snow damage is also avoided by the shedding of leaves during these periods when the rate of photosynthesis would be severely limited by low light intensities, low temperatures and unavailability of water and salts. Throughout these periods the regions of next year's growth, the buds, are protected by scale leaves and their metabolic activity is suppressed by the presence of a growth regulator substance called **dormin**. This is so called because of its effects. Recent investigations, however, have shown this to be abscisic acid. Many coniferous species dominate the vegetation of the more temperate regions, particularly in northern latitudes. These species have needle-like leaves which reduce the amount of snow which can accumulate on them in winter and have a thick cuticle to prevent water loss in summer. Many species of annuals have short growing periods and survive the winter by producing resistant seeds or organs of perennation. Lower plants survive by producing resistant cysts which may remain viable for hundreds of years, as demonstrated by cysts which have germinated following their removal from the permafrost of Siberia.

Low temperatures are required by many plant species in order to break dormancy and initiate vernalisation. For example, lilac buds develop more quickly after being exposed to low temperatures than to high temperatures. Other examples of the effects of low temperature on plant growth are described in chapter 15 and section 21.6.

18.2.3 Adaptations to high temperatures in plants

In many regions of the world high temperatures are associated with water shortage, and many of the adaptations shown by plants in these regions are related to their ability to resist desiccation and their need to lose water in order to cool themselves.

Plants are unable to escape high temperatures by moving to shaded areas and therefore they have to rely on morphological and physiological adaptations to avoid overheating. It is the aerial parts of plants which are exposed to the heating effect of solar radiation, and the largest exposed surface is that of the leaves. Leaves characteristically are thin structures with a large surface area to volume ratio to facilitate gaseous exchange and light absorption. This structure is ideal for preventing damage by excessive heating. A thin leaf has a relatively low heat capacity and therefore will usually assume the temperature of the surroundings, a phenomenon known as **heterothermism**. This effect is offset in hot regions by the development of a shiny cuticle secreted by the epidermis and which reflects much of the incident light, thus preventing heat being absorbed and overheating the plant. The large surface area contains numerous stomatal openings which permit transpiration. As much as $0.5 \text{ kg m}^{-2} \text{ h}^{-1}$ of water may be lost from plants by transpiration in hot, dry weather, which would account for the loss of approximately 350 W m^{-2} in terms of heat energy. This is nearly half the total amount of energy being absorbed. As a result of these mechanisms plants are able to exercise a considerable degree of control over their temperature. This ability is closely coupled to the relative humidity of the air.

> **18.2** Why do plants suffer permanent physiological damage if exposed to temperatures in excess of 30 °C when the humidity is high?

During hot, sunny days many plants in danger of overheating show a phenomenon known as '**photosynthetic slump**'. This is thought to result from a temporary cessation of metabolic activity as a result of changes in enzyme structure, or the closure of stomata as a result of a build-up of respiratory carbon dioxide within the guard cells. It is possible, however, that the reason for closure of the stomata is simply one of transient lack of water in the leaf. Wilting is a common response to high temperatures and reduced water uptake. An imbalance between the rates of transpiration and water uptake results in an overall loss of turgidity by those plant cells lacking a thickened cell wall, such as parenchyma. The adaptive significance of this response is to reduce the leaf surface area which is exposed to direct sunlight, thereby preventing overheating. **Wilting** may be observed in plants growing in greenhouses in response to the very high temperatures which develop in the leaves, even if adequately supplied with water. Once the temperature begins to fall the plants recover very quickly even if the degree of wilting looks severe.

Plants living in dry conditions are called **xerophytes** and show many morphological adaptations which enable them to survive (section 19.3.2). In most cases these adaptations are primarily concerned with regulating water loss, although the characteristic needle-shaped leaves permit maximum heat dissipation. The mechanisms for withstanding high temperatures, on the other hand, are mainly physiological.

18.2.4 The influence of temperature on the growth and distribution of animals

Temperature influences the metabolic activity of animals and plants primarily through its influence on enzymes and the mobility of atoms and molecules. This directly affects the rate of growth of animals (chapter 21). In addition, temperature may also affect the geographical distribution and ecological preferences of animals through its influence on plants as primary producers in the food chains. The ecological range of most animal species, with the exception of some insects, birds and mammals able to migrate, is determined by local availability of particular food materials. Restricted powers of locomotion limit other organisms to feeding on readily available food sources which are determined by the trophic relationships existing in the ecosystem.

The variety of responses shown by animals to temperature depends upon the degree of thermal stability shown by the environment and the degree of control the organism is able to exercise over its own body temperature. Life is believed to have originated in the marine environment, the environment that poses fewest problems to living organisms. Temperature fluctuations in aquatic environments are slight and the biological significance of this is that aquatic organisms occupy a relatively stable environment with regard to temperature. Most of these organisms, including non-vertebrates and fish have a body temperature which varies according to the temperature of the water, though some very active fish such as the tuna are able to maintain body temperature in excess of that of the water. However, aquatic animals rarely need to exhibit the physiological and behavioural responses shown by terrestrial animals because the physical properties of the water buffer them against sudden and extreme fluctuations. Water has a maximum density at $4\,°C$ and consequently only the surface of the water freezes at $0\,°C$ as ice floats. This enables many aquatic animals to continue to be active at times when most terrestrial organisms would be inactive due to sub-zero conditions.

Air has a relatively low specific heat and therefore air temperature can fluctuate widely over a 24 h period. One of the problems associated with the colonisation of land by animals was adapting to, or tolerating, these temperature fluctuations. This has produced many physiological, behavioural and ecological responses, as well as being a major determinant of geographical distribution. The nature of these responses and examples are described in subsequent sections.

18.2.5 Sources of heat for animals

All animals derive heat from two sources, the external environment and from the release of chemical energy within their cells. The extent to which animals are able to generate and conserve this heat depends upon physiological mechanisms associated with their phylogenetic position. All non-vertebrates, fish, amphibia and

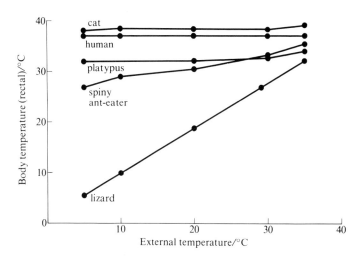

Fig 18.9 *The relationships between external and internal temperatures in vertebrates kept for 2 h at the temperatures indicated*

reptiles are unable to maintain their body temperature within narrow limits. Consequently these animals are described as **poikilothermic** (*poikilos*, various; *therme*, heat). Alternatively, because they rely more on heat derived from the environment than metabolic heat in order to raise their body temperature, they are termed **ectothermic** (*ecto*, outside). These animals used to be described as 'cold-blooded' but this is a misleading and inaccurate term.

Birds and mammals are able to maintain a fairly constant body temperature independently of the environmental temperature. They are described as **homeothermic** (or **homoiothermic** – *homoios*, like) or less correctly as 'warm-blooded'. Homeotherms are relatively independent of external sources of heat and rely on a high metabolic rate to generate heat which must be conserved. Since these animals rely on internal sources of heat they are described as **endothermic** (*endos*, inside). Some poikilotherms may, at times, have temperatures higher than those of homeotherms and in order to prevent ambiguity, the terms ectotherm and endotherm are used throughout the text. Fig 18.9 shows the abilities of several vertebrates to regulate their body temperature in various external temperatures.

18.2.6 Body temperature

Whenever reference is made to body temperature in animal studies it usually refers to the **core temperature**. This is the temperature of the tissues below a level of 2.5 cm beneath the surface of the skin. This temperature is normally determined by taking the rectal temperature. Temperatures in other regions of the body can vary tremendously depending upon position and the external temperatures (fig 18.10).

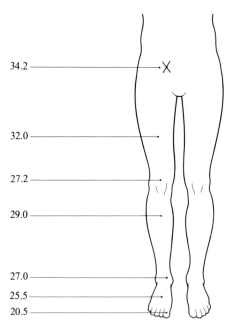
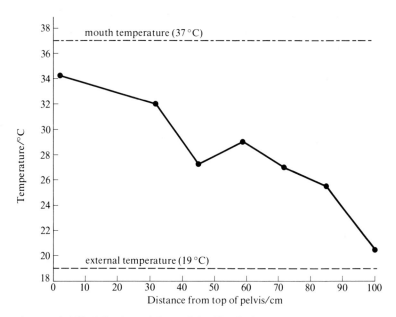

Fig 18.10 *Skin temperatures recorded at various distances from point X at the top of the pelvis. The limb was exposed to an external temperature of 19 °C throughout the period of recording. The low temperature at the knee cap probably reflects the poorer blood supply to this organ*

Whilst the main source of *gaining* heat differs between ectotherms and endotherms, the methods of heat transfer between organism and the environment are the same in both types of organism and these are radiation, convection, conduction and evaporation. Heat can be transferred in either direction by the first three methods depending upon the **thermal gradient** (the direction of the temperature difference from hot to cold) but can only be *lost* from organisms by the latter method.

Radiation. Heat is transferred by electro-magnetic waves which lie in the long-wave, infra-red region of the electromagnetic spectrum, beyond the visible spectrum. Bodies do not radiate heat to air, since it is unable to absorb much radiant heat, but transfer it to other bodies at a rate which is proportional to the temperature difference between the two bodies. Radiation accounts for about 50% of the total heat loss in humans and provides the main route for controlled heat loss in animals.

Convection. Heat is transferred between organism and environment by passage through the air. In the case of endotherms, where the ambient (air) temperature is usually lower than body temperature, the air in contact with the organism rapidly becomes warm, rises, and is replaced by cooler air. The rate of heat transfer by this method is linked to the rate of air movement which continually brings cooler air into contact with the body. It may be reduced by materials covering the skin such as feathers, fur, hair and clothing.

Conduction. Heat is transferred by physical contact between two bodies, for instance the organism and the ground. Heat exchange by this means is relatively insignificant for most terrestrial organisms, but may be considerable for aquatic and soil-dwelling organisms.

Evaporation. Heat is lost from the body surface during the conversion of water to water vapour. The evaporation of 1 cm³ of water (1 g) requires the loss of 2.45 kJ from the body. Water loss by evaporation takes place continuously through the skin and from the lungs, as expired air, and this **insensible** water loss cannot be controlled. It is a limiting factor in the distribution of many plant and animal species. **Regulated** evaporative heat loss is controlled and involves water loss by sweating and panting.

18.3 Ectothermic animals

The majority of animals are ectothermic, and their activity is determined by the prevailing environmental temperature. The metabolic rate of ectotherms is relatively low and they lack mechanisms for conserving heat. Aquatic ectotherms live within a restricted temperature range, or **zone of tolerance**, determined by the size of the body of water in which they live. For example, the temperature of a pond can vary considerably throughout the year, whereas that of an ocean may change by only a few degrees. Despite this wide temperature fluctuation in small bodies of water, many insect species have aquatic larval and pupal, or nymphal, stages, since the aquatic temperatures are more stable and less extreme than terrestrial temperatures during the winter months. Mayflies, dragonflies, caddis-flies, midges and mosquitoes all have an aquatic diapause (section 21.10.1).

Aquatic non-vertebrates are able to tolerate greater temperature fluctuations than aquatic vertebrates due to their relatively simple morphology and physiology. Fish have a higher rate of metabolism than aquatic non-vertebrates but the majority of this endogenous heat is rapidly dissipated around the body and lost to the environment by conduction through the gills and skin. Consequently, fish usually have a body temperature which is at thermal equilibrium with that of the water. Fish cannot maintain a temperature below that of the water but may in some cases, as in the case of tuna fish, retain heat by means of a countercurrent heat exchanger system. This can raise the temperature of the 'red' swimming muscle to about 12 °C above that of the sea water.

Terrestrial ectotherms have to contend with greater temperature fluctuations than those of aquatic ectotherms, but they have the benefit of living at higher environmental temperatures. This allows them to be more active and show a variety of complex behavioural patterns based upon the prevailing temperature conditions. Many species are able to maintain temperatures slightly above or below air temperature and thereby avoid extremes. The relatively poor thermal conductivity of air reduces the rate of heat loss from organisms whilst water loss by evaporation may be used to cool the organism.

18.3.1 Temperature regulation in terrestrial ectotherms

Heat is gained and lost by terrestrial ectotherms by behavioural and physiological activities. The main sources of heat gain are the absorption of solar radiation and conduction from the air and the ground. The amount of heat absorbed depends upon the colour of the organism, its surface area and position relative to the Sun's rays. For example, a species of Australian grasshopper is dark in colour at low temperatures and absorbs solar radiation thus heating up rapidly. As the temperature rises above a set point, further absorption is reduced by the cuticle lightening in colour. This colour change is believed to be a direct response shown in pigment cells to body temperature. These organisms are known as **basking heliotherms** (*helios*, sun).

Changes in orientation of the organism relative to the Sun's rays vary the surface area exposed to heating. This practice is common in many terrestrial ectotherms including insects, arachnids, amphibia and reptiles. It is a form of **behavioural thermoregulation**. For example, the desert locust (*Schistocerca*) is relatively inactive at 17 °C but by aligning itself at right-angles to the Sun's rays it is able to absorb heat energy. As the air temperature rises to approximately 40 °C it re-orientates itself parallel to the Sun's rays to reduce the exposed surface area. Further increase in temperature, which may prove fatal, is prevented by raising the body off the ground or climbing up vegetation. Air temperature falls off rapidly over short distances above ground level and these movements enable the locust to secure a more favourable microclimate (section 12.5.4).

Crocodiles too, regulate their body temperature on land by varying their position relative to the Sun's rays and opening their mouths to increase heat loss by evaporation.

If the temperature becomes too high, they move into the water which is relatively cooler. Conversely, at night they retreat to water in order to avoid the low temperatures which would be experienced on land. Thermoregulation mechanisms have been studied most extensively in lizards.

Many different species of lizard have been studied and show a variety of responses to different temperatures. Lizards are terrestrial reptiles and exhibit many behavioural activities in keeping with other ectotherms; but some species employ a number of physiological mechanisms enabling them to raise and maintain their body temperatures above that of the environment, an example is the Australian monitor (*Varanus*). Other species are able to keep their body temperature within confined limits by varying their activity and taking advantage of shade or exposure. In both these respects lizards foreshadow many of the mechanisms of homeothermy shown by birds and mammals.

Surface temperatures in desert regions can rise to 70–80 °C during the day and fall to 4 °C at dawn. In these circumstances most lizards seek refuge, during these extremes, by living in burrows or beneath stones. This response and certain physiological responses are shown by the horned lizard (*Phrynosoma*) which inhabits the deserts of the south-west of the USA and Mexico. In addition to burrowing, the horned lizard is able to vary its orientation and colour, and as the temperature becomes high it can also reduce its body surface area by pulling back its ribs. Other responses to high temperatures involve panting, which removes heat by the evaporation of water from the mouth, pharynx and lungs, eye bulging and the elimination of urine from the cloaca.

The moist skin of amphibia provides an ideal mechanism to enable heat to be lost by evaporation. This water loss, however, cannot be regulated physiologically as in mammals. Amphibia lose water immediately on exposure to dry conditions and, whilst this aids heat loss, it would lead to dehydration if the amphibia did not find moist shaded conditions where the rate of evaporation would be reduced. The marine iguana (*Amblyrhynchus*), a reptile, normally maintains a temperature of 37 °C as it basks on the rocky shores of the Galapagos Islands, but it needs to spend a considerable time in the sea feeding on seaweed at a temperature of approximately 25 °C. In order to avoid losing heat rapidly when immersed in water the iguana reduces the blood flow between surface and core tissues by slowing its heart rate (bradycardia).

18.4 Endothermic animals

Birds and mammals are endothermic and their activity is largely independent of prevailing environmental temperatures. In order to maintain a constant body temperature, which is normally higher than the ambient (air) temperature, these organisms need to have a high metabolic rate and an efficient means of controlling heat loss from the body surface. The skin is the organ of the body in contact with the environment and therefore monitors the changing temperatures. The actual regulation of temperature by various metabolic processes is controlled by the hypothalamus of the brain.

18.4.1 Skin

The term, skin, applies to the outer covering of vertebrate animals and should not be used to describe the outer covering of annelids, molluscs or arthropods. The skin is the largest organ of the body and is made up of connective tissue, blood vessels, sweat glands and sense cells. These enable it to fulfil a great many different functions. The structure of the skin varies in different vertebrate groups and the major differences will be discussed after the basic structure of human skin has been described.

Human skin structure

The skin is composed of two main layers, the epidermis and dermis, that overly the subcutaneous tissue which contains specialised fat-containing cells known as **adipose tissue**. The thickness of this layer varies according to region of the body and from person to person.

Epidermis. The cells of this region are ectodermal in origin and are separated from the dermis by a basement membrane. The epidermis is composed of many layers of cells forming a stratified epithelium (section 8.3.2). The cells above the basement membrane are cuboid epithelial cells (section 8.3.1) and form an actively dividing region known as the **Malpighian layer**. By repeated division of its cells, this region gives rise to all of the cells of the epidermis. The Malpighian layer forms the lower region of the **stratum granulosum**, which is composed of living cells becoming flatter as they approach the outer region of the epidermis, the **stratum corneum**. Cells in this region become progressively flattened and synthesise **keratin**, which is a fibrous sulphur-containing protein

(a)

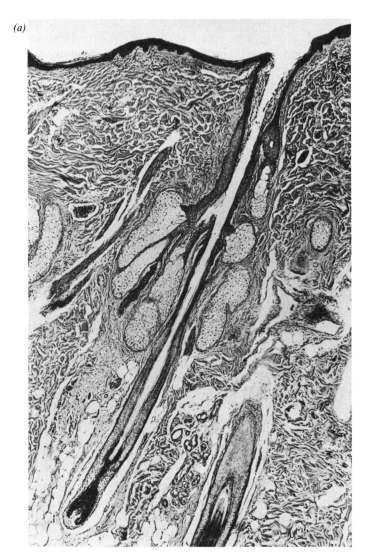

(b)

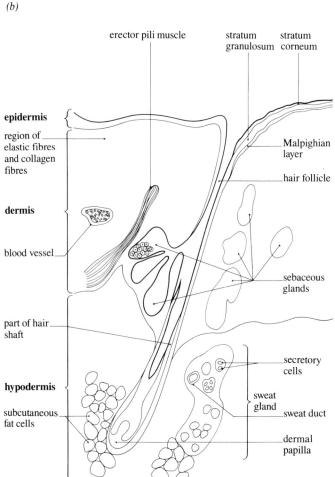

Fig 18.11 (a) VS through human skin. (b) Diagram of skin structure based on (a)

678

which makes the cells waterproof. As the keratin content of the cells increases they become cornified, their nuclei disappear and the cells die. The thickness of the stratum corneum increases in parts of the body where there is considerable friction, such as the ball of the foot and the bases of the fingers. The outer covering of the skin forms a semi-transparent, thin, tough, pliant, waterproof covering pierced by pores, which are the openings of the sweat glands, and by the hair follicles. The outermost squamous epithelial cells are continually being shed as a result of friction.

The stratum corneum has become modified in many vertebrates to produce nails, claws, hooves, horns, antlers, scales, feathers and hair. Keratin is the main component of all these structures.

Dermis. Most of the cells of the dermis are mesodermal in origin. The dermis is a dense matrix composed of connective tissue rich in elastic fibres and containing blood capillaries, lymph vessels, muscle fibres, sensory cells, nerve fibres, chromatophores (pigment cells), sweat glands and hair follicles.

Hair follicles are epidermal invaginations with a root hair, or papilla, at the base from which the hair shaft develops. Hair is composed of cuboid epithelial cells which become cornified by impregnation with keratin. The outer cortex of the hair contains varying amounts of the pigment melanin which determines hair colour. The medulla of the hair may contain air bubbles, and as the number increases with age and melanin production falls off the hair becomes grey. Blood capillaries supply the growing hair with nourishment and remove waste substances. The upper part of the hair projects beyond the epidermis and is kept supple and prevented from becoming wetted by **sebum**, an oily secretion produced by **sebaceous glands** which open into the hair follicle. Sebum contains fatty acids, waxes and steroids, and spreads along the hair and onto the skin where it keeps the follicle free from dust and bacteria, as well as forming a thin waterproof layer over the skin. This not only prevents water loss from the skin but also prevents water entering the skin.

At the base of the follicle is a smooth muscle, the **erector pili muscle** which has its origin on the basement membrane and its insertion on the hair follicle. Contraction of this muscle alters the angle between the hair and the skin which results in variation of the amount of air trapped above the skin. This is used as a means of thermoregulation and also as a behavioural response to danger in some vertebrates. When the hair 'stands on end' it increases the apparent size of the organism which may be sufficient to frighten off would-be attackers. The distribution of hair in humans in much more restricted than in other mammals.

Sweat glands are coiled tubular exocrine glands situated in the dermis and connected to sweat pores by a duct. They are found over the entire human body, but in some mammals are restricted to the pads of the feet. They are absent in birds. Water, salts and urea are brought to the glands by blood capillaries, and the secretory activity of the glands is controlled by the activity of the sympathetic nerve fibres. There are two types of sweat glands, **eccrine** and **apocrine**. The former are most common (approximately 2.5×10^6 in humans), being found in most regions of the body, and the latter are found in the armpits, around the nipples, the pubic region, hands, feet and anus. These release an odourless fluid which may later produce an unpleasant odour due to bacterial activity in the fluid. Certain zinc and aluminium compounds can inhibit the activity of the glands and destroy bacteria. Most antiperspirants and deodorants contain these compounds.

Blood capillaries are numerous in the dermis and supply the various structures already described. Many of the capillaries form loops and have shunts (fig 18.12) which enable the body to vary the amount of blood flowing through the cutaneous capillaries. This is one of the many ways of regulating body temperature, as described in section 18.4.3.

Motor neurones innervate the muscles and glands in the dermis whilst sensory neurones carry nerve impulses from the many sense cells situated in the dermis. These sense cells detect heat, cold, touch, pain and pressure. Some of the sense cells are simple and consist of free nerve endings, whereas others, such as the Pacinian corpuscle, are encapsulated.

Vertebrate skin structure

The skin of other vertebrates differs in various ways from the structure described above. Fish have well-developed scales or dermal plates and mucus-secreting glands. Amphibia have a smooth skin which is made slippery by the secretion of mucus from the many glands in the dermis. This mucus is watery and keeps the skin moist to facilitate gaseous exchange. In some species, such as toads, the secretion is distasteful to predators. The dermis contains numerous pigment cells enabling amphibia to alter their colouration to blend in with the background, and also to absorb or reflect solar radiation. There are many subcutaneous lymph spaces and the skin is only attached to the underlying muscles at intervals which makes the skin extremely loose.

Reptiles have horny scales covering the body and these form an impermeable layer. The skin is always dry, and the numerous chromatophores in the epidermis enable reptiles to alter their colouration. Birds have developed feathers which are outgrowths from the epidermis. There are different types of feathers carrying specific functions (section 17.7.6) but they all contribute to preventing heat loss from the body. Birds maintain relatively high body temperatures, about 40–43 °C, and as they have a large surface area to volume ratio they need an efficient means of preventing heat loss.

All mammals possess sweat glands and hair, and the number and distribution of these two structures reflect the efficiency of control of heat balance.

Functions of mammalian skin

Skin has four main functions. Temperature regulation is described in detail in section 18.4.3. Further functions are as follows.

Protection. The skin protects the internal organs from damage, dehydration and disease. The cornified epidermis prevents damage by friction, particularly in those regions where pressure and chafing develop. The dermis and subcutaneous tissues prevent mechanical damage from bumps and knocks. Melanin, the dark pigment found in chromatophores, protects the body from excessive harmful ultra-violet light. Variations in hair or fur pigment, giving patterns, provide camouflage against the background of the natural habitat. In several species, such as stoat and the arctic hare, the overall colour changes according to the season and thus helps to protect the organism from attack by predators or recognition by its prey. The cornified layer and sebum prevent uncontrolled water loss by evaporation. Sebum also prevents the fur of aquatic mammals, such as the otter, from wetting, which would destroy the insulatory properties of the air trapped in the hair. The entry of pathogens, including bacteria, viruses, fungi, protozoans, roundworms and flatworms into the body is greatly hindered by the structure of the skin. Micro-organisms can nevertheless enter through hair follicles and sweat glands and through the bites of insect vectors. The larval stages of many parasitic worms, such as *Schistosoma*, are capable of boring through the skin.

Vitamin production. Ultra-violet radiations from the Sun convert a group of steroids, known as sterols, to vitamin D. This is only a secondary source of the vitamin since most is obtained in the diet (section 10.3.10).

Energy storage. Fat is deposited as adipose tissue in the lower regions of the dermis and also in a subcutaneous position. The secondary effect of this is to provide thermal insulation as described in section 18.4.3. Many mammals build up a store of fat under the skin in preparation for adverse climatic conditions.

18.4.2 Sources of heat

The major source of heat in endotherms is produced from the exothermic biochemical reactions which occur in living cells. This heat is released by the breakdown of molecules derived from the diet, principally carbohydrates and fats. The amount of heat released in a resting fasting organism is known as the **basal metabolic rate** (BMR) and provides a 'base-line' for comparing the energy demands during various activities, and in different organism (see section 11.7.6). The energy content of food required to meet the demands of the basal metabolic rate for an average-sized male human over a 24 h period is approximately 8 000 kJ. The exact amount per individual depends upon size, age and sex, being slightly higher in males.

Most of the metabolic energy which appears as heat energy comes from active tissues such as the liver and voluntary (skeletal) muscle. The rate of energy release is regulated by other factors such as environmental temperature and hormones. Thyroxine, released from the thyroid gland, increases the metabolic rate and therefore heat production. The effects of this hormone are long term, whereas the effects of adrenaline are mostly short-lived. Other sources of metabolic heat energy are initiated by nerve impulses. Repeated stimulation of voluntary muscle by somatic motor neurones produces the shivering response which can increase heat production by up to five times the basal level. During shivering various groups of muscle fibres within a muscle contract and relax out of phase, so that the overall response is an uncoordinated movement. This response may be reinforced by other muscular activity such as rubbing the hands together, stamping the feet and limited forms of exercise. In many mammals there are areas near the thoracic blood vessels which are rich in brown fat cells; stimulation of these by sympathetic neurones causes the rapid metabolism of the numerous fat droplets in the cells. The subsequent release of energy by enzymes in the mitochondria in these cells is particularly important for hibernating animals since it is instrumental in rapidly raising the core temperature during arousal from hibernation (section 21.10.3). The hypothalamus is the centre initiating heat production for most of the mechanisms described above.

18.4.3 Loss of heat

Heat is lost from endotherms by the four mechanisms described in section 18.2.6, that is conduction, convection, radiation and evaporation. In all cases, the rate of loss depends upon the temperature differences between the body core and the skin, and the skin and the environment. The rate can be increased or decreased depending upon the rate of heat production and the environmental temperature.

There are three factors limiting heat loss, as given below.

The rate of blood flow between the body core and skin. The rate of heat loss from the skin by radiation, convection and conduction depends upon the amount of blood flowing through it. If the blood flow is low the skin temperature approaches that of the environment, whereas if the flow is increased the skin temperature then approaches core temperature. The skin of endotherms is richly vascularised and blood can flow through it by any of three routes: through capillary networks in the dermis, through shunt pathways deep in the dermis linking arterioles and venules, and through subcutaneous, small connecting veins linking cutaneous arterioles and veins.

Arterioles have relatively thick muscular walls which can contract or relax altering the diameter of the vessels and the rate of blood flow through them. The degree of contraction is controlled by sympathetic vasomotor nerves from the vasomotor centre in the brain which receives impulses from the thermoregulatory centre in the hypothalamus. The rate

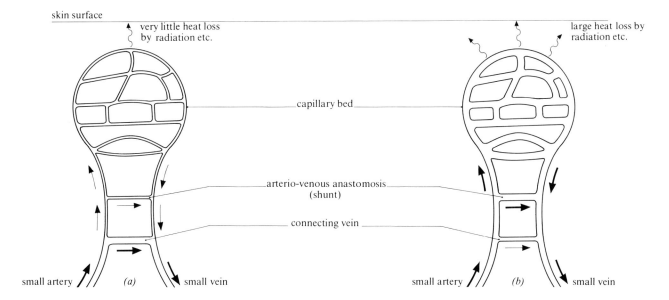

skin surface

very little heat loss by radiation etc.

capillary bed

arterio-venous anastomosis (shunt)

connecting vein

small artery   *(a)*   small vein

large heat loss by radiation etc.

small artery   *(b)*   small vein

of blood flow through the skin in humans can vary from less than $1\,cm^3\,min^{-1}\,100\,g^{-1}$ in cold conditions to $100\,cm^3\,min^{-1}\,100\,g^{-1}$ in hot conditions, and this can account for an increase in heat loss by a factor of five or six. The 'shunt pathways' are known as **arterio-venous anastomoses** and lie beneath the level of the skin capillary beds. Constriction of these vessels forces blood through the low resistance 'connecting veins' from arteries to veins and the bulk of the blood by-passes the capillaries and shunts (fig 18.12). This is a typical response preventing heat loss. Dilation of the shunt vessels encourages blood flow through the capillary beds and shunts and not through the connecting veins. This increases blood flow through the skin and therefore heat is lost more rapidly.

The rate of sweat production and evaporation from the skin. Sweat is a watery fluid containing between 0.1 and 0.4% of sodium chloride, sodium lactate and urea. It is less concentrated than blood plasma and is secreted from tissue fluid by the activity of sweat glands under the control of **sudomotor neurones**. These neurones are part of the sympathetic nervous system and they relay impulses from the hypothalamus. Sweating begins whenever the body temperature rises above its mean value of 36.7 °C. Approximately $900\,cm^3$ of sweat are lost per day in a temperate climate, but the figure can rise as high as $12\,dm^3$ per day in very hot dry conditions, providing that there is adequate replacement of water and salts.

> **18.3** The latent heat of evaporation of sweat is $2.45\,kJ\,cm^{-3}$. Calculate the percentage of energy lost by sweating from a coalminer who loses $4\,dm^3$ per day of sweat and has a daily energy uptake of 50 000 kJ.

When sweat evaporates from the skin surface, energy as latent heat of evaporation is lost from the body and this reduces body temperature. The rate of evaporation is

Fig 18.12 *Mechanism of regulation of blood flow through the skin. (a) Blood flow through the skin preventing heat loss. Constriction of the arteriole reduces blood flow through capillaries and shunt. Only sufficient blood passes into the skin to keep the tissues alive. Most of the blood flowing from the body by-passes the skin through the connecting vein and reduces heat loss. (b) Blood flow through the skin increasing heat loss. Dilation of the arteriole increases blood flow through the capillaries and shunt. The capillaries dilate due to the rise in blood pressure within them. Heat is lost from the blood by radiation, convection and conduction and blood flow is increased to the sweat glands*

reduced by low environmental temperatures, high humidity and lack of wind.

Many mammals have so much hair on their bodies that sweating is restricted to bare areas, for instance pads of the feet of dogs and cats, and the ears of rats. These mammals increase heat loss by licking their bodies and allowing moisture to evaporate, and by panting and losing heat from the moist nasal and buccal cavity. Humans, horses and pigs are able to sweat freely over the entire body surface.

Experiments have now confirmed that sweating only occurs as a result of a rise in core temperature. Experiments on humans and other animals have shown that lowering the core temperature, by swallowing ice water or cooling the carotid blood vessels with an ice pack around the neck, while at the same time exposing the skin to heat, result in a decrease in the rate of sweating. Opposite effects have been recorded by reversing the environmental conditions. Blood from the carotid vessels flows to the hypothalamus and these experiments have indicated its role in thermoregulation. Inserting a thermistor against the eardrum gives an acceptable measure of hypothalamic temperature. The relation between changes in temperature in this region and the skin and rate of evaporation of sweat are shown in fig 18.13. Examine this figure and answer the following questions.

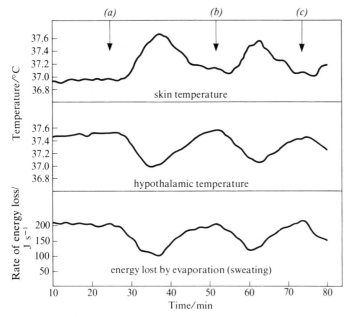

Fig 18.13 *Graphs showing the relation between skin temperature, hypothalamic temperature and rate of evaporation for a human in a warm chamber (45°C). Iced water was swallowed at the points labelled (a), (b) and (c)*

18.4 Account for temperature and evaporation rate remaining relatively constant during the first 20 min.

18.5 Describe the relationship between hypothalamic temperature and rate of sweating.

18.6 Suggest why the skin temperature rises shortly after the ingestion of iced water.

The amount of insulation between the core and the environment. Insulation for the body is provided by air trapped outside the skin and by dermal and subcutaneous fat. Feathers, fur and clothes trap a layer of air, known as stagnant air, between the skin and the environment, and because it is a poor conductor of heat it reduces heat loss. The amount of insulation provided by this means depends upon the thickness of the trapped air. Reflex contractions of the erector pili muscles in response to decreasing temperatures increases the angle between the feathers or fur and the skin and thus there is more air trapped. The response is still present in humans but due to the minimal amount of body hair it only produces the effect known as 'goose-flesh' or 'goose-pimples'. Humans compensate for the lack of body hair by taking advantage of the insulating effects of clothing. The seasonal accumulation of a thick subcutaneous fat is common in mammals, particularly in those species which do not hibernate and manage to withstand cold temperatures. Aquatic mammals, particularly those inhabiting cold waters, such as whale, sea-lion, walrus and seal, have a thick layer of fat known as blubber, which effectively insulates them against the cold.

18.4.4 Heat balance and the role of the hypothalamus

The temperature of any body is determined by the following equation:

heat gained by body = heat lost by body

Endothermic animals are able to generate sufficient heat energy and regulate the amount lost so that the two expressions above are always in equilibrium and equal a

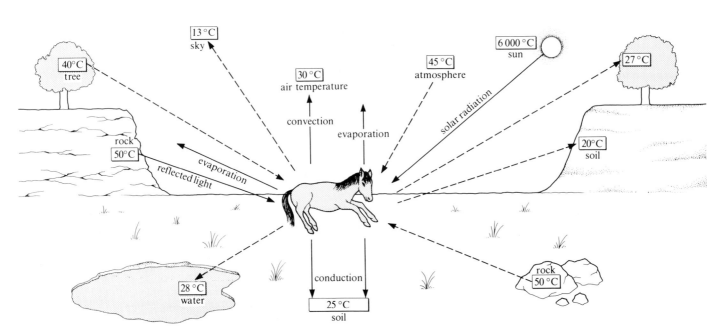

Fig 18.14 *Diagram showing the energy exchanges between a horse, with a body temperature of 38 °C, and the environment on a hot sunny day with an air temperature of 30 °C. The dotted lines represent thermal radiation*

constant (fig 18.14). This is known as **homeothermy**. Any mechanism which has an input and an output and is capable of maintaining a constant value must be regulated by a control system as described earlier in this chapter.

Birds and mammals have a well-developed control system involving receptors and effectors and an extremely sensitive control centre, the hypothalamus. This organ monitors the temperature of the blood, which is in equilibrium with the core temperature, flowing through it. If the hypothalamus is to control a constant core temperature, as is the case with endotherms, it is vital that information regarding changes in the external temperature is also transmitted to the hypothalamus. Without such information the body would gain or lose a great deal of heat before changes in core temperature would activate the hypothalamus to take corrective measures. This problem is overcome by having peripheral thermoreceptors, situated in the skin, which detect changes in the environmental temperature and initiate impulses to the hypothalamus in advance of changes in the core temperature. There are two types of thermoreceptors, hot and cold, which generate impulses in afferent neurones leading from them when suitably stimulated. Some pass to the hypothalamus and others to the sensory areas of the cortex, where the sensations associated with temperature are registered according to the intensity of stimulation, the duration and the numbers of receptors stimulated. There are estimated to be 150 000 cold receptors and 16 000 heat receptors in humans. This enables the body to make rapid and precise adjustments to maintain a constant core temperature. In the context of control systems, the skin receptors act as disturbance detectors anticipating changes in body temperature. Factors bringing about changes in internal temperature such as metabolic rate or disease will immediately affect the core temperature and in these situations be

Table 18.1 Functions of the heat loss and heat gain centres of the hypothalamus. These are situated in the anterior and posterior hypothalamus respectively and have antagonistic effects

Anterior hypothalamus (heat loss centre)	Posterior hypothalamus (heat gain centre)
Activated by increase in the hypothalamic temperature	Activated by impulses from peripheral cold receptors or temperature of the hypothalamus
Increases vasodilation	Increases vasoconstriction
Increases heat loss by radiation, convection and conduction	Decreases heat loss by radiation convection and conduction
Increases sweating and panting	Inhibits sweating and panting
Decreases metabolic activity	Increases metabolic activity through shivering and release of thyroxine and adrenaline
Decreases thickness of air layer by flattening hair or feathers	Increases thickness of air layer by action of hair muscles

detected by thermoreceptors in the hypothalamus. In most cases the activity of both peripheral and hypothalamic receptors is instrumental in controlling body temperature.

Investigations into the thermostatic activity of the hypothalamus have shown that there are two distinct areas concerned with this type of regulation and the functions of these areas are summarised in table 18.1. The interrelationships between the cerebral cortex, the hypothalamic thermoregulatory centres, core temperature, skin temperature and environmental temperatures are shown in fig 18.15 and fig 18.16.

Fig 18.15 *Summary diagram showing the reflex control of body temperature in a mammal involving the environment, hypothalamus and blood temperature*

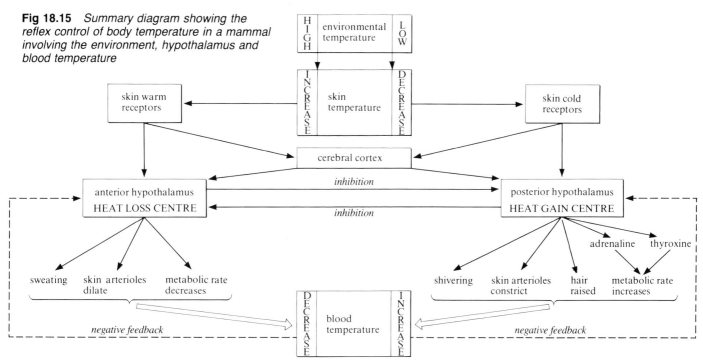

Certain diseases produce an increase in core temperature as a result of the 'thermostat' being set at a higher temperature. It is believed that certain substances known as **pyrogens**, which may be toxins produced by pathogenic organisms or substances released by white blood corpuscles known as neutrophils, directly affect the hypothalamus and increase the set-point. The raised body temperature stimulates the defence responses of the body and aids the destruction of pathogens. Antipyretic drugs such as aspirin lower the set-point and provide relief from the unpleasant symptoms of fever, but probably retard the normal defence mechanisms. In cases of extremely high temperature these drugs are valuable in preventing irreversible damage to the brain.

> **18.7** The onset of fever is often accompanied by shivering and a feeling of cold known as chill. Explain these symptoms in terms of mechanism of control of body temperature.

18.4.5 Adaptations to extreme climates

The size of organs and physiological and behavioural adaptations of organisms vary over their geographical range. The total heat production of endotherms depends upon the volume of metabolically active tissues whilst the rate of heat loss depends upon surface area. The two parameters, surface area and volume, are inversely proportional to each other. For this reason animals living in cold regions tend to be large, for example polar bears and whales, whilst animals living in hot climates are generally smaller, for instance insectivorous mammals. This phenomenon is known as **Bergman's rule** and is observed in many species, including the tiger, which

decreases in size with distance from the Poles. There are exceptions to this rule, but the organisms concerned have adaptations favouring survival in these regions. For example, small mammals in temperate or arctic regions have a large appetite enabling them to maintain a high metabolic rate. They have small extremities to reduce heat loss and are forced to hibernate in winter. Large mammals living in hot regions, such as the elephant and hippopotamus, have the opposite problems. The elephant has extremely large ears which are well supplied with blood, and flapping of these ears encourages heat loss by radiation and convection. The hippopotamus lacks sweat glands and adopts a similar behavioural response to temperature as the crocodile in that it moves between land and water in an attempt to minimise the effects on its body of changes in temperature. The size of the external organs also varies according to environmental temperature such that species living in colder climates have smaller extremities than related species in warmer climates. This is known as **Allen's rule** and may be seen in closely related species of, for instance, the fox (fig 18.17).

18.4.6 Adaptations to life at low temperatures

All ectotherms and many endotherms are unable to maintain a body temperature which permits normal activity during cold seasons, and they respond by showing some form of dormancy, as described in section 21.10. Some of these responses are quite startling; for example, the larva of an insect parasite *Bracon*, which invades the Canadian wheat sawfly, is able to survive exposure to temperatures lower than −40.0 °C. This larva accumulates glycerol in its haemolymph. The glycerol acts as an 'antifreeze' and is able to prevent the formation of ice crystals by a process known as 'super-cooling'.

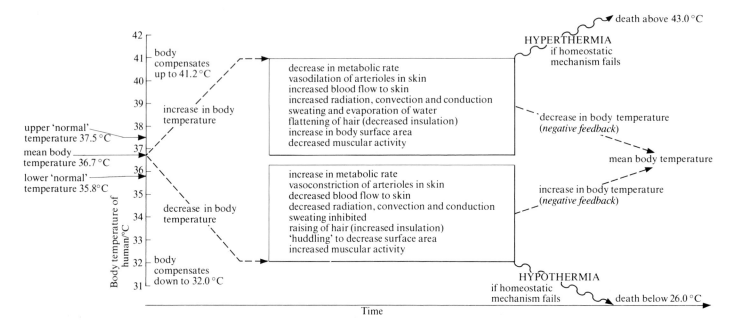

Fig 18.16 *Homeostatic control of body temperature*

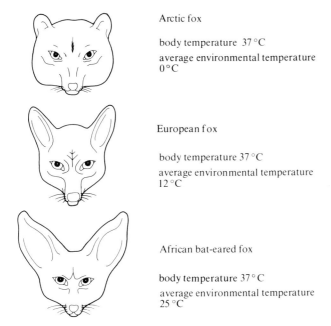

Arctic fox

body temperature 37 °C

average environmental temperature 0 °C

European fox

body temperature 37 °C

average environmental temperature 12 °C

African bat-eared fox

body temperature 37 °C

average environmental temperature 25 °C

Fig 18.17 *Variation in ear length shown by three species of fox (*Lycaon*) which each occupies a different geographical region. This is an example of Allen's rule*

Excessive heat loss to the environment from appendages is prevented in many organisms by the arrangement of blood vessels within the appendages. The arteries carrying blood towards the appendage are surrounded by veins carrying blood back to the body. The warm arterial blood from the body is cooled by the cold venous blood flowing towards the body. Similarly the cold venous blood from the appendage is warmed by the warm arterial blood flowing towards the appendage. Because the blood reaching the appendage is already cooled the amount of heat lost is considerably reduced. This arrangement is known as a **countercurrent heat exchanger** and is found in the flippers and flukes of seals and whales, in the limbs of birds and mammals and in the blood supply to the testes in mammals (fig 18.18).

The countercurrent exchange principle is used for the transfer of materials other than heat, such as respiratory gases and ions (sections 11.7 and 19.5.7).

The induction of a state of hypothermia is being used increasingly in heart surgery since it allows the surgeon to carry out repairs to the heart without the risk of brain damage to the patient. By reducing the body temperature to 15 °C, the metabolic demands of the brain cells are so reduced that blood flow to the brain can be stopped, without any adverse effects, for up to one hour. For operations requiring a longer time than this a heart–lung machine is used, in addition to hypothermia, to maintain blood circulation in the tissues.

18.4.7 Adaptations to life at high temperatures

Animals living in conditions where the air temperatures exceed skin temperature gain heat, and the only means of reducing body temperature is by evaporation of water from the body surface. For climatic reasons hot regions may be, in addition, either dry or humid, and this poses an additional problem. In hot dry regions heat can be lost by the free evaporation of water, but animals in these regions have the problem of finding adequate supplies of water to satisfy the demands of evaporative cooling. In hot humid regions water is freely available to organisms but the humidity gradient between organisms and the environment often prevents evaporation. In the latter case physiological mechanisms of temperature control are often supplemented and there may be behavioural activities which take advantage of the shade and breezes associated with humid forest and jungle habitats.

The **heat load** of an organism is the amount of heat gained by metabolic activities and from the environment, and the latter is approximately proportional to the body

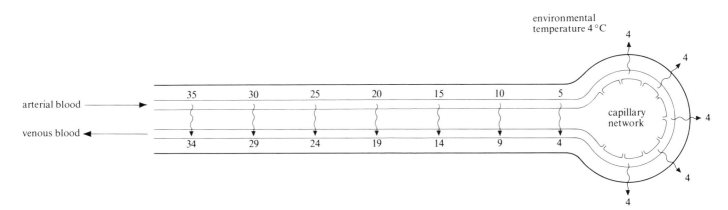

Fig 18.18 *Diagram showing the blood supply between the body of an endotherm with a stable temperature of 35 °C and an appendage in an environment at 4 °C. Heat flows from a warm body to a cool body and the rate of heat loss between the two bodies is proportional to the temperature difference between them. The countercurrent flow shown delivers blood to the capillary network at 5 °C and collects blood from it at 4 °C. The amount of heat lost to the environment is therefore proportional to the temperature difference of 1 °C. Likewise blood returning to the core of the body is only 1 °C cooler than the blood leaving the core. This mechanism prevents the excessive loss of metabolic energy and helps maintain the core temperature at 35 °C*

surface area. The majority of animals living in deserts, therefore, are small, such as the kangaroo rat (*Dipodomys*), and have fewer problems than larger animals, such as camels. In addition they are able to live in burrows in sand and soil where the microclimate poses fewer problems to life.

A camel in hot dry conditions, with free access to water, is able to regulate its body temperature between about 36 and 38 °C. It is able to do this by losing heat through the evaporation of water from the body surface. If the camel is deprived of water, as say during a journey across the desert lasting several days, the difference in the body temperatures at morning and evening steadily increase according to the degree of dehydration. This diurnal fluctuation can be from 34 °C in the early morning to 41 °C in the late afternoon. By effectively storing up heat during the day the camel does not need to lose this heat by the evaporation of water. It functions in fact, like a storage radiator. In a series of investigations carried out by Schmidt-Nielsen it was found that a 500 kg camel tolerating a 7 °C temperature rise stored approximately 12 000 kJ of heat energy. If this amount of heat were lost by evaporative cooling, in order to maintain a constant body temperature, it would require the loss of 5 dm³ of water. Instead this heat is lost by radiation, conduction and convection during the night. A second advantage of becoming 'partially ectothermic' during the day is that this reduces the temperature difference between the hot desert air and the camel, and therefore reduces the rate of heat gain. The fur of the camel acts as an efficient insulating barrier by reducing heat gain and water loss. In an experiment, in which a camel was shorn, the water loss increased by 50% over that of a control camel. The final significant advantage shown by the camel is its ability to tolerate dehydration. Most mammals cannot tolerate dehydration beyond a loss of body mass of 10–14%, but the camel can survive losses up to 30%, because it is able to maintain its plasma volume even when dehydrated. Heat death as a result of dehydration is due to the inability of the circulatory system to transfer heat from the body core to the surface quickly enough to prevent overheating as a result of a fall in volume of the plasma. Contrary to popular belief, the camel is unable to store water in advance of conditions of water shortage, and there is doubt whether it can obtain water from the metabolism of fat stored in the hump. The camel is, however, able to drink a vast volume of water in a short space of time to rehydrate the body tissues after a period of severe dehydration. For example, a 325 kg camel is known to have drunk 30 dm³ of water in less than ten minutes. This is roughly equivalent to a human of average build and weight drinking about 7 dm³ (12 pints) of water!

18.5 The mammalian liver

The liver is the largest visceral organ of homeostasis and controls many metabolic activities essential for the maintenance of the composition of blood at a steady state. The liver is derived from an endodermal outpushing of the alimentary canal and many of its functions are associated with the preparation, production and control of substances derived from absorbed food materials. There is a unique dual blood supply to the liver and because of its rich vascularisation it regulates many activities associated with blood and the circulatory system (fig 18.19). Paradoxically, despite the enormous variety of metabolic activities carried out by the liver its histological structure is relatively uniform and simple.

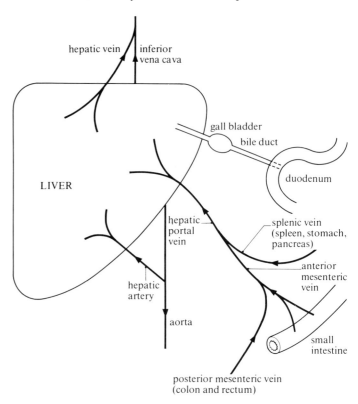

Fig 18.19 *Diagram showing the blood supply to and from the liver and the relative position of the bile duct*

18.5.1 The position and structure of the liver

The human liver is a large organ making up 3–5% of the body weight and lies immediately beneath the diaphragm to which it is attached by the **falciform ligament**. It is made up of several lobes and has a variable shape depending upon the amount of blood present within it. The liver is surrounded by a capsule made up of two layers, the outer layer being a smooth, moist peritoneum and the inner a fibrous covering known as **Glisson's capsule** which surrounds all structures entering and leaving the liver. The fibres of Glisson's capsule form an 'internal skeleton' which supports the rest of the liver.

The cells of the liver are called **hepatocytes** and show no structural or functional differentiation. The only other cells found in the liver are nerve cells and cells associated with blood and lymph vessels. Hepatocytes have prominent nuclei and Golgi apparatus, many mitochondria and

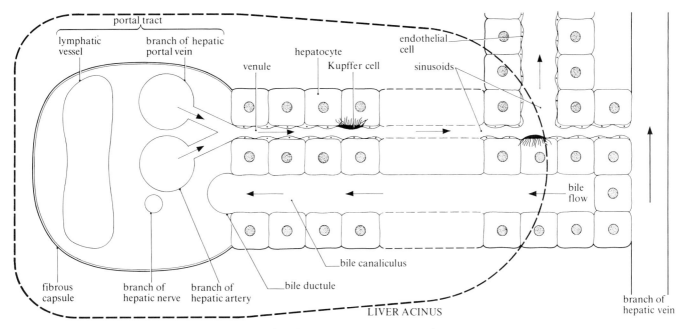

Fig 18.20 *A simplified diagram of a liver acinus showing a transverse section of a portal tract and a longitudinal section through a branch of the hepatic vein*

lysosomes, and are rich in glycogen granules and fat droplets. They are tightly packed together, and where their surface is in contact with blood vessels there are microvilli which are used for the exchange of materials between the two.

The whole internal structure of the liver is complex and not fully understood. It is based upon an arrangement of hepatocytes and two systems of blood vessels which interdigitate with channels called **bile canaliculi**. The hepatic portal vein forms many branches inside the liver and they carry alongside them branches of the hepatic artery, bile duct, nerves, lymphatic vessels and fibrous tissue of Glisson's capsule. This arrangement forms a structure known as a **portal tract**(canal) (fig 18.20). Blood vessels from both the hepatic portal vein, carrying absorbed materials from the alimentary canal, and the hepatic artery, carrying oxygenated blood, join together to form 'venules' which carry blood to the hepatocytes. This arrangement of 'venules' and hepatocytes is believed to form the functional unit of the liver and is known as an **acinus**. Smaller blood vessels called **sinusoids** arise from the 'venules' and form a vast network of capillaries before uniting to carry blood to branches of the hepatic vein. Adjacent sinusoids are separated from each other by 'plates' of hepatocytes which are often only one cell thick. As blood flows along the sinusoids, materials are exchanged between the blood and the hepatocytes. The presence of pores, having a diameter up to 10 nm, in the endothelial lining of the sinusoids, and the microvilli on the hepatocytes where they touch the sinusoids, facilitates the exchange of materials. Bile produced in the hepatocytes does not enter the sinusoids but is secreted into minute bile canaliculi which replace the sinusoids at various points and run between adjacent plates of hepatocytes. These canali-

culi are lined with microvilli and take up bile from the hepatocytes by some form of active transport. The canaliculi form a branching network which unites to form **bile ductules**. These join together in the portal tract to form **bile ducts** and these eventually fuse before leaving the liver as the **common hepatic duct**.

The structure of the liver, as described above, shows it to be a vast network of hepatocytes, blood, blood spaces and bile canaliculi. This produces a structure with an immense surface area where each cell is in direct contact with blood thus facilitating maximum exchange between cell and blood and control of substances in the blood.

The structure of the liver in the pig is much simpler than the human liver but is atypical of other mammals. It is described because its simplicity highlights many of the structural and functional relationships which may not be readily evident from the account of the typical mammalian situation described above. The pig's liver is composed of a large number of discrete units, called **lobules** which are polygonal in transverse section and have a diameter of approximately 1 mm. They form thimble-shaped units about 2–3 mm long and are enclosed in a connective tissue sheath continuous with Glisson's capsule. Between the lobules are the **interlobular blood vessels** consisting of an arteriole of the hepatic artery and a branch of the hepatic portal vein and a bile ductule (as found in the portal tract of other mammals). An **intralobular vein** is situated in the centre of the lobule and receives blood which flows along the sinusoids from the portal vein and artery. Blood from the intralobular veins passes into the hepatic vein. The bulk of the lobule is composed of strands of liver cells running from the periphery of the lobule and converging on the intralobular vein. Exchange of materials between hepatocytes and blood occurs as described previously. The

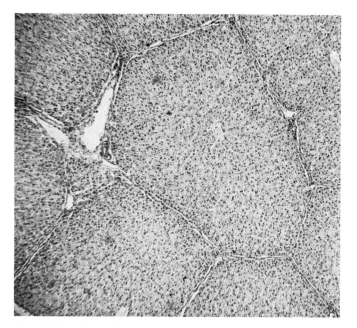

Fig 18.21 *TS pig liver showing lobules*

sinusoids alternate with bile canaliculi which carry bile to the interlobular bile ductule. This relatively simple and regular pattern is shown in figs 18.21 and 18.22.

The functional unit of pig liver is the lobule and its regular structure arises because the intralobular and interlobular blood vessels run parallel to each other. This situation is not generally found in other mammals where lobulation is absent or less definite.

The lymph found in the lymphatic vessels of the portal tract is surprisingly rich in protein and is produced from plasma which escapes from the endothelial pores in the 'venules' and sinusoids.

One other type of cell is found in the liver and it forms part of a more extensive system known as the **reticulo-endothelial system** (see section 14.14). The cells are called **Kupffer cells** and are found attached to the walls of the sinusoids by cytoplasmic projections. They are phagocytic and are involved in the breakdown of old(effete) erythrocytes and the ingestion of pathogenic organisms.

18.5.2 Functions of the liver

It has been estimated that the liver carries out several hundred separate functions involving thousands of different chemical reactions. These functions are related to the position of the liver in the circulatory system and the vast amount of blood which flows through it at any given time (approximately 20% of the total blood volume). The liver and the kidney between them are the major organs responsible for regulating the steady state of blood metabolites and the composition of the blood tissues. All food materials absorbed from the alimentary canal pass directly to the liver where they are stored or converted into some other form as required by the body at that time.

The functions of the liver therefore fall into two main categories: the storage of food materials and synthesis of their derivatives, and the breakdown of substances not required by the body prior to their excretion. Finally, as a result of the number of metabolic activities occurring within the liver, it may be a source of heat production for animals living in cold climates.

Carbohydrate metabolism

Hexose sugars enter the liver from the gut by the hepatic portal vein, which is the only blood vessel in the body having an extremely variable sugar content. This gives a clue to the role of the liver in carbohydrate metabolism as

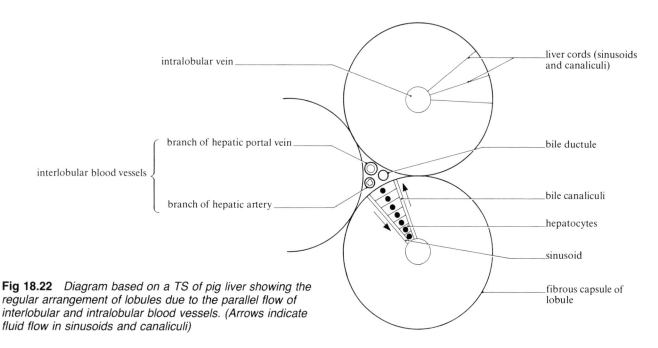

Fig 18.22 *Diagram based on a TS of pig liver showing the regular arrangement of lobules due to the parallel flow of interlobular and intralobular blood vessels. (Arrows indicate fluid flow in sinusoids and canaliculi)*

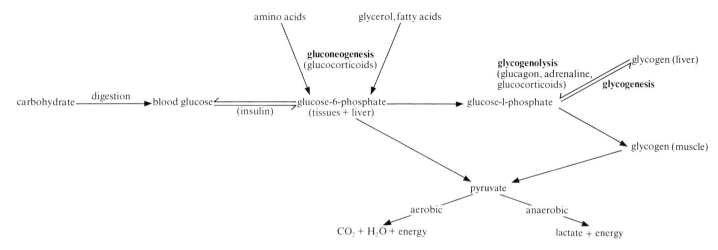

Fig 18.23 *Summary diagram of carbohydrate metabolism*

the organ which maintains the blood glucose level at approximately 90 mg glucose 100 cm^{-3} blood. The liver prevents blood glucose levels from fluctuating according to feeding patterns thus preventing damage to tissues which cannot store glucose, such as the brain. All hexose sugars, including galactose and fructose, are converted to glucose by the liver and stored as the insoluble polysaccharide, glycogen. Up to 100 g of glycogen are stored here but more is stored in muscle. The conversion of glucose to glycogen is known as **glycogenesis** and is stimulated by the presence of insulin:

$$\text{glucose} \underset{\text{(phosphorylation)}}{\overset{\text{insulin}}{\rightleftharpoons}} \text{glucose-6-phosphate} \rightleftharpoons \text{glucose-1-phosphate} \underset{\text{(condensation)}}{\rightleftharpoons} \text{glycogen}$$

Glycogen is broken down to glucose to prevent the blood glucose level falling below 60 mg 100 cm^{-3} blood. This process is called **glycogenolysis** and involves the activation of a phosphorylase enzyme by the pancreatic hormone, glucagon. In times of danger, stress or cold this activity is also stimulated by adrenaline, released by the adrenal medulla, and noradrenaline released by the endings of the sympathetic neurones (section 16.2.3).

$$\text{glycogen} \underset{\text{(store)}}{\overset{\text{phosphorylase}}{\rightleftharpoons}} \text{glucose-1-phosphate} \overset{\text{phosphoglucomutase}}{\rightleftharpoons} \text{glucose-6-phosphate} \underset{\text{(free)}}{\overset{\text{glucose-6-phosphatase}}{\rightleftharpoons}} \text{glucose}$$

Muscle lacks the enzyme glucose-6-phosphatase and cannot convert glycogen directly to glucose via glucose-6-phosphate as shown above. Instead, glucose-6-phosphate is converted into pyruvate which is used to produce ATP during aerobic or anaerobic respiration. Lactate produced by anaerobic respiration in skeletal muscle can be converted later into glucose and hence glycogen in the liver by a biochemical pathway known as the **Cori cycle**.

$$\text{lactate} \rightarrow \text{pyruvate} \rightarrow \text{glucose} \rightarrow \text{glycogen}$$

When the demand for glucose has exhausted the glycogen store in the liver, glucose can be synthesised from non-carbohydrate sources. This is called **gluconeogenesis**. Low blood glucose levels (hypoglycaemia) stimulate the sympathetic nervous system to release adrenaline which helps satisfy immediate demand as described above. Low blood glucose levels also stimulate the hypothalamus to release CRF (section 16.6.2) which in turn releases adrenocorticotrophic hormone (ACTH) from the anterior pituitary gland. This leads to the synthesis and release of increasing amounts of the glucocorticoid hormones, cortisone and hydrocortisone. These stimulate the release of amino acids, glycerol and fatty acids, present in the tissues, into the blood and increase the rate of synthesis of enzymes in the liver which convert amino acids and glycerol into glucose. (Fatty acids are converted into acetyl coenzyme A and used directly in the Krebs cycle.) Carbohydrate in the body which cannot be utilised or stored as glycogen is converted into fats and stored. A summary of carbohydrate metabolism involving the liver, muscles and tissues is shown in fig 18.23.

Protein metabolism

The liver plays an important role in protein metabolism which may be considered under the headings of deamination, urea formation, transamination and plasma protein synthesis.

Deamination. The body is unable to store absorbed amino acids, and those not immediately required for protein synthesis or gluconeogenesis are deaminated in the liver. This involves the enzymic removal of the amino group (–NH$_2$) from the amino acid with the simultaneous oxidation of the remainer of the molecule to form a carbohydrate which is utilised in respiration. The amino group is removed along with a hydrogen atom so that the nitrogenous product of deamination is ammonia (NH$_3$).

For example,

$$2NH_2 \!-\! \underset{\underset{H}{|}}{\overset{\overset{R}{|}}{C}} \!-\! COOH \;+\; O_2 \longrightarrow 2\, \underset{\underset{O}{\|}}{\overset{\overset{R}{|}}{C}} \!-\! COOH \;+\; 2NH_3$$

amino acid oxygen keto acid ammonia

or specifically,

$$2NH_2 \!-\! \underset{\underset{H}{|}}{\overset{\overset{CH_3}{|}}{C}} \!-\! COOH \;+\; O_2 \longrightarrow 2\, \underset{\underset{O}{\|}}{\overset{\overset{CH_3}{|}}{C}} \!-\! COOH \;+\; 2NH_3$$

alanine oxygen pyruvic acid ammonia

This ammonia may be used for the synthesis of certain amino acids or nitrogenous bases, such as adenine and guanine (section 5.6), or excreted.

Urea formation. Ammonia produced by deamination is converted in the liver into the soluble excretory product urea:

$$2NH_3 \;+\; CO_2 \longrightarrow \overset{NH_2}{\underset{NH_2}{>}}C\!=\!O \;+\; H_2O$$

ammonia carbon urea water
    dioxide

This occurs by a cyclic reaction known as the **ornithine cycle** which is summarised in fig 18.24.

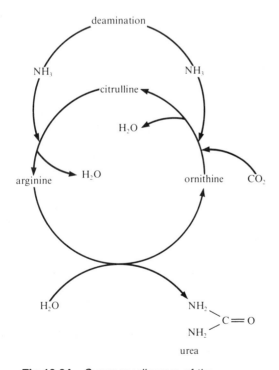

Fig 18.24 *Summary diagram of the ornithine cycle in mammalian liver (ornithine and citrulline are amino acids but are not obtained from the diet)*

Transamination. This is the synthesis of amino acids by the enzymic transfer of the amino group from an amino acid to a carbohydrate in the form of a keto acid (chapter 5). For example the amino acid, glutamic acid, could be synthesised by the following reactions:

$$NH_2 \!-\! \underset{\underset{H}{|}}{\overset{\overset{CH_3}{|}}{C}} \!-\! COOH \;+\; O\!=\!\underset{\overset{|}{CH_2}}{\overset{\overset{CH_2COOH}{|}}{C}}\!-\!COOH \longrightarrow$$

alanine   α-oxoglutaric acid

$$NH_2 \!-\! \underset{\underset{H}{|}}{\overset{\overset{\substack{CH_2COOH \\ | \\ CH_2}}{|}}{C}} \!-\! COOH \;+\; O\!=\!\overset{\overset{CH_3}{|}}{C}\!-\!COOH$$

glutamic acid   pyruvic acid

The general principle underlying these reactions is the mutual exchange of characteristic radicals between the amino acid and the keto acid:

$$NH_2 \!-\! \underset{\underset{H}{|}}{\overset{\overset{\text{Ⓐ}}{|}}{C}} \!-\! COOH \;+\; O\!=\!\overset{\overset{\text{Ⓑ}}{|}}{C}\!-\!COOH \longrightarrow$$

amino acid A   keto acid B

$$NH_2 \!-\! \underset{\underset{H}{|}}{\overset{\overset{\text{Ⓑ}}{|}}{C}} \!-\! COOH \;+\; O\!=\!\overset{\overset{\text{Ⓐ}}{|}}{C}\!-\!COOH$$

amino acid B   keto acid A

Transamination is the means of producing amino acids which are deficient from the diet, and this is yet another of the liver's homeostatic mechanisms. The 'essential' amino acids, described in section 10.3, cannot be synthesised by transamination in the liver and must be obtained from the diet.

Plasma protein production. Plasma proteins are vital components of plasma and the majority of them are synthesised from amino acids in the liver. Plasma albumin is the commonest protein and about 4 g 100cm^{-3} is normally present in the blood. It plays an important part in exerting a colloid osmotic potential which opposes the hydrostatic pressure developed in blood vessels. The antagonistic effects of these two factors maintains the balance of fluids inside and outside of blood vessels (section 14.12.1). Albumins also act as transport molecules within the circulatory system, carrying substances such as calcium, tryptophan, bilirubin, bile salts, aspirin and some steroid hormones. Plasma globulins are very large molecules and blood carries about 34 g dm^{-3}. α- and β-globulins transport hormones, including thyroxine and insulin, cholesterol, lipids, iron and the vitamins B$_{12}$, A, D and K. γ-globulins are produced by lymphocytes and the other cells of the reticulo-endothelial tissues, and are involved in the immune response (section 14.14.3). The other main plasma proteins are the blood-clotting factors, prothrombin and fibrinogen, and their functions are described in section 14.13.5.

Fat metabolism

The liver is involved in the processing and transport of fats rather than their storage. Liver cells carry out the following functions: converting excess carbohydrates to fat; removing cholesterol and phospholipids from the blood and breaking them down or, when necessary, synthesising them and producing globulins to transport lipids.

Vitamin storage

The liver stores some of the water-soluble vitamins B and C, especially those of the B group such as nicotinic acid, vitamin B$_{12}$ and folic acid. Vitamin B$_{12}$ (cyanocobalamin) and folic acid are required by the bone marrow for the formation of erythrocytes and deficiency of these vitamins leads to various degrees of anaemia. The main vitamins stored in the liver, however, are the fat-soluble vitamins A, D, E and K. The liver of certain fish contains high concentrations of vitamins A and D, for example cod and halibut. Vitamin K is a vital factor in blood clotting.

Mineral storage

Those elements required in small amounts such as copper, zinc, cobalt and molybdenum (trace elements) are stored in the liver along with iron and potassium. Iron is stored primarily as a compound called **ferritin** which is a complex of iron and β-globulin. Approximately 1 mg g^{-1} dry mass of liver tissue in humans is iron. Most of this iron in the liver is temporary and comes from the breakdown of old erythrocytes and is stored here for later use in the manufacture of new erythrocytes in the bone marrow.

Storage of blood

The blood vessels leaving the spleen and gut join to form the hepatic portal vein and, together with the blood vessels of the liver, contain a large volume of blood which acts as a reservoir, though this is not a static store. Sympathetic neurones and adrenaline from the adrenal medulla can constrict many of these hepatic vessels and make more blood available to the general circulation. Likewise, if the blood volume increases, as for example during a blood transfusion, the hepatic veins along with other veins can dilate to accommodate the excess volume.

Formation of erythrocytes

The liver of the fetus is responsible for erythrocyte production (**erythropoiesis**) but this function is gradually taken over by cells of the bone marrow (section 14.11.2).

Once this process is established the liver takes an opposite role and assists in breaking down erythrocytes and haemoglobin.

Breakdown of haemoglobin

Erythrocytes have a life-span of about 120 days. By this stage they are effete and are broken down by the activity of phagocytic macrophage cells of the reticulo-endothelial system of the liver, spleen and bone marrow. Haemoglobin is broken down into **haem** and **globin**. The globin is reduced to its constituent amino acids and enters the liver's amino acid pool to be used according to demand. The iron is removed from haem and the remaining **pyrrole rings** form a green pigment **biliverdin**. This is converted to **bilirubin**, which is yellow and a component of bile. The accumulation of bilirubin in the blood is symptomatic of liver disease and produces a yellowing of the skin, a condition known as **jaundice**.

Bile production

Bile is a viscous, greenish yellow fluid secreted by hepatocytes. Between 500–1 000 cm^3 of bile are produced each day and it is composed of 98% water, 0.8% bile salts, 0.2% bile pigments, 0.7% inorganic salts and 0.6% cholesterol. It is involved in digestion, the absorption of fats and is a means of excretion of bile pigments.

Bile salts are derivatives of the steroid **cholesterol** which is synthesised in hepatocytes. The commonest bile salts are sodium glycocholate and sodium taurocholate. They are secreted with cholesterol and phospholipids as large particles called **micelles**. The cholesterol and phospholipids hold the polar bile salt molecules together so that all the hydrophobic ends of the molecules are orientated the same way. The hydrophobic ends attach to lipid droplets whilst the other ends are attached to water. This decreases the surface tension of the droplets and enables the lipids to separate, forming an emulsion. These smaller droplets have an increased surface area for attack by pancreatic lipase which converts the lipids into glycerol and fatty acids so that they can then be absorbed from the gut. Bile salts also activate the enzyme lipase, but their action, in all cases, is purely physical. Too little bile salt in bile increases the concentration of cholesterol which may precipitate out in the gall bladder or bile duct as cholesterol gall stones. These can block the bile duct and cause severe discomfort.

Bile pigments have no function and their presence is purely excretory.

Cholesterol is produced by the liver and is the precursor molecule in the synthesis of other steroid molecules. The major source of cholesterol is the diet, and many dairy products are rich in cholesterol or fatty acids from which cholesterol can be synthesised. Thyroxine both stimulates cholesterol formation in the liver and increases its rate of excretion in the bile. Excessive amounts of cholesterol in the blood can lead to its deposition in the walls of arteries leading to **atherosclerosis** (narrowing of the arteries) and the increased risk of the formation of a blood clot which may block blood vessels, a condition known as **arterial thrombosis**. This is often fatal if it occurs in the heart or brain. Cholesterol is often cited as a major cause of cardiovascular disease but, as yet, much of the evidence is contradictory.

Bile is stored and concentrated in the gall bladder by absorption of sodium ions (and water) into surrounding blood capillaries. The stimulus for the release of bile into the duodenum is the presence of the hormone cholecysto-kinin-pancreozymin (CCK-PZ) as described in section 10.5.

Hormone production and breakdown

Whilst the liver is not generally considered as an endocrine gland, it synthesises and releases growth-promoting factors called **somatomedins** under the influence of the hormone **somatotrophin**, released from the pituitary gland. This control of growth is described in more detail in section 21.8.1. The liver destroys almost all hormones to various extents. Testosterone and aldosterone are rapidly destroyed, whereas insulin, glucagon and gut hormones, female sex hormones, adrenal hormones, ADH and thyroxine are destroyed less rapidly. In this way the liver has a homeostatic effect on the activities of these hormones.

Detoxification

This term covers a range of homeostatic activities carried out by the liver so as to maintain the composition of blood at a steady state. Bacteria and other pathogens are removed from the blood in the sinusoids by Kupffer cells but the toxins they produce are dealt with by biochemical reactions in the hepatocytes. Toxins are rendered harmless by one or more of the following reactions: oxidation, reduction, methylation (the addition of a $-CH_3$ group) or combination with another organic or inorganic molecule. Following detoxification these substances, now harmless, are excreted by the kidney. The major toxic substance in the blood though is ammonia, whose fate is described above in this chapter. The detoxification process also includes harmful substances taken in to the body such as alcohol and nicotine. Alcohol taken in excess (in gradually increasing dosage) can result in liver breakdown, such as cirrhosis of the liver in alcoholics.

Some of the metabolic activities of the liver may be potentially harmful and evidence is growing that certain food additives may be converted into poisonous or carcinogenic substances by liver activity. Even the pain killer paracetamol, if taken in excess, is changed into a substance which affects enzyme systems and can cause liver, and other tissue, damage.

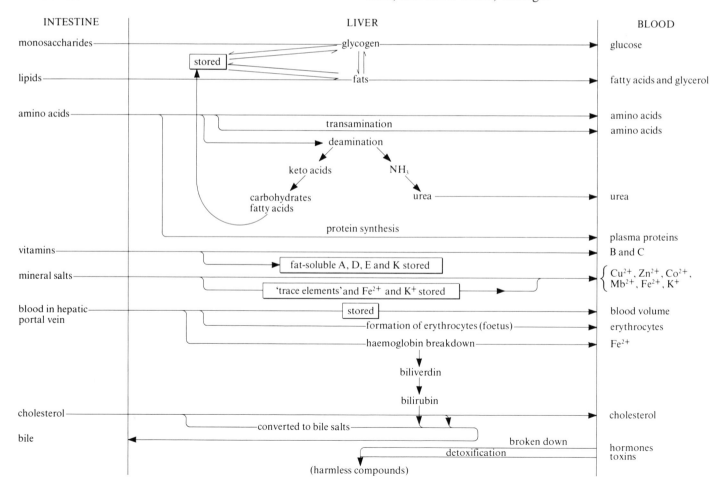

Fig 18.25 *Summary diagram of the functions of the liver*

Heat production

Evidence is accumulating to show that the widespread belief that the metabolic activity of the liver results in it being a major source of heat production in the body of mammals may be false. Many of the liver's metabolic activities are endothermic and therefore require heat energy rather than release it. Under conditions of extreme cold the hypothalamus will increase the ectothermic activity of the liver by its influence on the release of adrenaline by the sympathetic nervous system and the release of thyroxine. In 'normal' temperatures, however, the liver has been shown to be 'thermally neutral' but is usually 1–2 °C hotter than the rest of the body core.

The liver provides yet another example of the intimate relationship which exists in biological systems between structure and function. What is remarkable about the liver is the diversity of function achieved by a highly complex morphological structure which has such a simple, undifferentiated histological structure.

Chapter Nineteen

Excretion and osmoregulation

Excretion and osmoregulation are two important homeostatic processes occurring in living organisms. Each process enables organisms to maintain, to varying degrees, the internal environment at a steady state despite changes in the external environment.

Excretion is the elimination from the body of waste metabolic substances which if permitted to accumulate would prevent the maintenance of a steady state. Many substances which are not metabolic, that is those which have not been synthesised by the organism, are eliminated. To distinguish excretion from these latter functions it is necessary to define them. **Secretion** is the passive or active removal of molecules from cells into the extracellular environment, such as the bloodstream, gastro-intestinal tract or external environment. These molecules have been synthesised *in vivo* (in life), for example hormones and enzymes, and are therefore considered to have been metabolised, but are not regarded as waste substances. Secretion may form part of the process of excretion as is described later in the chapter. **Egestion** is the elimination of waste substances, mainly undigested food, which have never been involved in the metabolic activities of cells.

19.1 The significance of excretion and osmoregulation

Excretion and osmoregulation have a number of functions which may be listed and summarised as follows.

(1) The removal of metabolic waste substances which are often by-products of major metabolic pathways. This is necessary in order to prevent unbalancing the chemical equilibria of reactions. Many metabolic reactions are reversible and the direction of the reaction is determined solely by the relative concentrations of reactants and products in accordance with the law of mass action. For example, in the enzyme-catalysed reaction:

$$A + B \rightleftharpoons C + D$$
$$\text{(reactants)} \qquad \text{(products)}$$

the continued production of C, a vital requirement of metabolism, is ensured by the removal of D, a waste product. This will ensure that the *equilibrium* of the reaction favours the reaction to proceed from reactants to products.

(2) The removal of metabolic waste substances which, if they accumulated, would affect the metabolic activity of the organism. Many of these substances are toxic acting as inhibitors of enzymes involved in metabolic pathways.

(3) The regulation of the ionic content of body fluids. Salts behave as electrolytes and undergo dissociation in the aqueous media of living organisms. For example, sodium chloride, taken in as part of the diet, exists in body fluids as sodium ions (Na^+) and chloride ions (Cl^-). If the balance of these and other ions is not carefully regulated within narrow limits, the efficiency of many physiological and biochemical activities is impaired; for instance a reduction in Na^+ concentration leads to a decrease in nervous coordination. Other important ions whose concentrations must be carefully regulated are K^+, Mg^{2+}, Ca^{2+}, Fe^{2+}, H^+, Cl^-, I^-, PO_4^{3-} and HCO_3^-, as they are vital for many metabolic activities including enzyme activity, protein synthesis, production of hormones and respiratory pigments, membrane permeability, electrical activity and muscle contraction. Their effects on water content, solute potential and pH of body fluids are described below.

(4) The regulation of water content of body fluids. The amount of water within the body fluids and its regulation is one of the major physiological problems faced by organisms in the colonisation of many of the available ecological niches on this planet. The solutions to this problem have produced some of the most important structural and functional adaptations shown by organisms. The mechanisms of obtaining water, preventing water loss and eliminating water are diverse, but they are of great importance in maintaining the osmotic pressure and volume of body fluids at a steady state, as described later in this chapter. Before describing these it is important to emphasise that the solute potential of body fluids depends upon the relative *amounts* of solute and solvent, that is water, present. The mechanisms of regulation of solutes and water are known as **osmoregulation**.

(5) The regulation of hydrogen ion concentration (pH) of body fluids. The nature of pH and methods of its measurement are described in appendix A1.1.5 but the mechanisms of excreting those ions which have a major influence on pH, such as H^+ and HCO_3^-, are considered in this chapter. For example, the pH of urine may vary between 4.5 and 8 in order to maintain the pH of the body fluids at a fairly constant level.

Table 19.1 Summary of the products, sources, functions and fates of the major excretory products

Product	Source	Function/Fate
Oxygen	Photosynthesis in autotrophic organisms	Reactant in aerobic respiration
Carbon dioxide	Aerobic respiration in all organisms Breakdown of urea	Reactant in photosynthesis Decreases pH of body fluids
Water	Aerobic respiration in all organisms Condensation reactions	Solvent in all metabolic activities Reactant in photosynthesis, etc.
Ions (salts)	Nutrient metabolism	Maintenance of solute potentials Recycled through ecosystem
Bile salts	Lipid metabolism in liver	Emulsification of fats
Bile pigments	Breakdown of haem in liver	None
Tannins and other organic acids	Nitrogen and carbohydrate metabolism in certain plant species	Bitter substances deter ingestion by animals
Nitrogenous substances	Protein and nucleic acid metabolism	Decompose and recycled through ecosystem

19.1.1 Excretory products

The major excretory products of animals and plants and their sources are summarised in table 19.1. Not all excretory products are waste in the sense of serving no further useful purpose to the body. Indeed, many serve useful purposes prior to their elimination and afterwards, for reasons described in table 19.1.

19.1.2 Excretion in plants

Plants do not have as many problems regarding excretion as do animals. This is because of fundamental differences in the physiology and mode of life between animals and plants. Plants are producers and they synthesise all their organic requirements according to the demand for them. For example, plants manufacture only the amount of protein necessary to satisfy immediate demand. There is never an excess of protein and therefore very little excretion of nitrogenous waste substances, produced by the catabolism (breakdown) of proteins, occurs. If proteins are broken down into amino acids, the latter can be recycled into new proteins. Three of the waste substances produced by certain metabolic activities in plants, that is oxygen, carbon dioxide and water, are raw materials (reactants) for other reactions, and excesses of carbon dioxide and water are used up in this way. The only major gaseous excretory product of plants is oxygen. During light periods the rate of production of oxygen is far greater than the plant's demand

for oxygen in respiration and this escapes from plants into the environment by diffusion.

Many organic waste products of plants are stored within dead permanent tissues such as the 'heart-wood' or within leaves or bark which are periodically removed. The bulk of most perennial plants is composed of dead tissues into which excretory materials are passed. In this state they have no adverse effects upon the activities of the living tissues. Similarly, many mineral salts, taken up as ions, may accumulate due to the differential use of cations and anions. Organic acids, which might prove harmful to plants, often combine with excess cations and precipitate out as insoluble crystals which can be safely stored in plant cells. For example, calcium ions and sulphate ions are taken up together, but sulphate is used up immediately in amino acid synthesis leaving an excess of calcium ions. These combine freely with oxalic and pectic acids to form harmless insoluble products such as calcium oxalate and calcium pectate. Other ions, such as iron and manganese, and organic acids, such as tannic and nicotinic acids, pass into leaves where they accumulate and contribute to the characteristic autumn tints of leaves prior to their loss during leaf abscission. Substances are not only eliminated through leaf loss but also through petals, fruits and seeds, although this excretory function is not the primary function of their dispersal. Aquatic plants lose most of their metabolic wastes by diffusion directly into the water surrounding them.

19.1.3 Excretion in animals

Any permeable surface which directly connects a region containing excretory products to the external environment is a potential area of excretion. These include the cell membrane of unicellular organisms, the outer covering of annelids, trachea of arthropods, gills and skin of fish and amphibia and the lungs and skin of vertebrates. The cells of organisms having a relatively simple structure are usually in direct contact with the environment and their excretory products are immediately removed by diffusion. As organisms increase in structural complexity, excretory organs develop to convey excretory products from the body directly or indirectly to the external environment through ducts and pores. In the case of the vertebrates specialised excretory structures are present to augment the activity of the vascular system which removes metabolic wastes from cells and transfers them to the excretory organs. The most important excretory organs in these organisms are the skin, lungs, liver and kidney. The roles of the first three only will be described at this stage.

Skin. Water, urea and salts are actively secreted from capillaries in the skin by the tubules of the sweat glands. Sweat is secreted onto the skin where the water evaporates using latent heat of evaporation. In this way heat is lost from the body and this helps to regulate the body temperature.

Lungs. Carbon dioxide and water vapour diffuse from the moist alveolar surfaces of the lungs, which in mammals are the sole excretory organs for carbon dioxide. Some of the water released at the lung surface is metabolic, that is, produced as a waste product of respiration and therefore excretory, but its exact origin is not really important in view of the large volume of water contained within the body.

Liver. Considering the many homeostatic roles of the liver described in section 18.5.2 it is not surprising that these include excretion. Bile pigments are excretory products from the breakdown of the haemoglobin of effete (old) red blood cells. They pass to the duodenum as a constituent of bile for removal from the body along with the faeces, to which they impart a characteristic colour. The most important excretory role of the liver is the formation of nitrogenous waste products by the deamination of excess amino acids (section 18.5.2).

19.2 Nitrogenous excretory products

Nitrogenous waste products are produced by the catabolism of proteins and nucleic acids. The immediate nitrogenous waste product of the deamination of proteins is ammonia, and the basis of this reaction is described in section 18.5.2. Ammonia may be excreted immediately or converted into the major nitrogenous compounds, urea and uric acid, which differ in their solubility and toxicity (fig 19.1). The exact nature of the

Table 19.2. Summary of the relationships between excretory products and stages in the life cycle of various animal groups

Animal	Excretory product	Embryonic environment	Adult habitat
protozoan	ammonia	aquatic	aquatic
poriferan	ammonia	aquatic	aquatic
cnidarian	ammonia	aquatic	aquatic
platyhelminth	ammonia	aquatic	aquatic
aquatic crustacean	ammonia	aquatic	aquatic
terrestrial insect	uric acid	cleidoic egg	terrestrial
gastropod mollusc	uric acid	cleidoic egg	terrestrial
echinoderm	ammonia	aquatic	aquatic
cartilaginous fish	urea	aquatic	aquatic
freshwater bony fish	ammonia	aquatic	aquatic
marine bony fish	urea, trimethyl-amine oxide	aquatic	aquatic
larval amphibian	ammonia	aquatic	aquatic
adult amphibian	urea	—	semi-terrestrial
reptile	uric acid	cleidoic egg	terrestrial
bird	uric acid	cleidoic egg	terrestrial
mammal	urea	aquatic	terrestrial

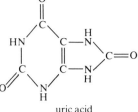

Fig 19.1 *Molecular structure of the three main nitrogenous excretory products*

ammonia   urea   uric acid

excretory product is determined by the metabolic capability of the organism (that is, which enzymes are present), the availability of water to the organism (that is, its habitat), and the extent to which water loss is controlled by the organism.

Animals may be classified according to the nature of their major nitrogenous excretory product and, as shown in table 19.2, there is a degree of correlation between excretory product, embryonic environment and adult habitat. The classification of organisms and the correlation with habitats for the majority of organisms may be summarised thus:

ammonia	**ammoniotelic**	aquatic
urea	**ureotelic**	aquatic/terrestrial
uric acid	**uricotelic**	terrestrial

19.2.1 Ammonia

Ammonia is an extremely soluble molecule with a low relative molecular mass (17) and diffuses rapidly through water. It is toxic to animals and cannot be stored in the body. Mammals are very sensitive to ammonia and cannot tolerate concentrations in excess of 0.02 mg 100 cm^{-3} blood. The high solubility of ammonia aids its rapid excretion as ammonium ions (NH_4^+) in most aquatic organisms from protozoa to amphibia before it reaches concentrations which are toxic to the organisms.

19.2.2 Urea

Urea is formed in the liver of vertebrates by the interaction of ammonia, produced by deamination, and carbon dioxide, produced by respiration, in a cyclical reaction known as the **ornithine cycle**. It is less soluble and less toxic than ammonia and is the main nitrogenous excretory substance in cartilaginous fish, certain bony fish, adult amphibia and mammals. The normal level of urea in mammalian blood is 2.5–6.0 mmol dm^{-3} blood. The metamorphosis of the tadpole stage to the adult form in the frog is marked by the change from ammonia excretion to urea excretion.

19.2.3 Uric acid

Uric acid and its salts are ideal excretory products for terrestrial organisms and a pre-requisite for organisms producing a cleidoic egg (shelled egg) (section 19.4.8) since they combine a high nitrogen content with low toxicity and low solubility. They can be stored in cells, tissues and organs without producing any toxic or adverse osmoregulatory effects, and they require a minimal

697

amount of water for their excretion. As the concentration of uric acid in the tissue rises it settles out as a solid precipitate. The biochemical details of uric acid formation and excretion are described in section 19.4.5. Uric acid and ammonium urate are the forms in which nitrogenous excretion occurs in insects, lizards, snakes and birds. Humans, apes and, because of a kidney defect, the Dalmation dog excrete small quantities of uric acid but this is produced from the breakdown of nucleic acids and not from the breakdown of proteins. The normal level of uric acid in human blood is 3 mg 100 cm^{-3} blood and approximately 1 g of uric acid is excreted in urine per day.

19.2.4 Other nitrogenous excretory compounds

In addition to the excretory products previously described, excess dietary protein is converted in some marine fishes into another excretory substance, trimethylamine oxide.

$$CH_3 \atop CH_3 \!\!\!> \!\! N = O \atop CH_3$$

trimethylamine oxide

This is produced by the addition of methyl groups to ammonia, formed by deamination, and the subsequent oxidation of intermediate molecules. Trimethylamine oxide gives fish its characteristic smell.

The only other source of nitrogenous waste substances is nucleic acid. Foods such as yeast, liver and kidney are rich in small cells and have abundant nuclei. The breakdown of these foodstuffs releases significant amounts of the nucleic acid bases, purines and pyrimidines. Spiders and some mammals excrete the purines adenine and guanine directly, but in other organisms these are broken down into uric acid as described later.

Adenine and guanine have a similar structure to uric acid whereas the pyrimidine bases cytosine, thymine and uracil have a structure which enables them to be broken down into a molecule of ammonia and a molecule of amino acid. The amino acid then undergoes deamination and the nitrogenous waste is excreted in the form which is typical of that organism.

Insects, terrestrial reptiles, birds, humans, apes and the Dalmation dog excrete purines as uric acid. The majority of mammals, however, possess the enzyme uricase in the liver, which converts uric acid directly to the excretory product **allantoin**. Dipteran insects also excrete allantoin. Some bony fish produce allantoin which oxidises to the excretory product **allantoic acid**.

Creatine and its derivative **creatinine** are other nitrogenous waste products. Creatine is formed in the liver of vertebrates from the amino acids, arginine, methionine and glycine. Approximately 2% of the total amount of creatine in the body is lost each day as creatinine. Some creatine is phosphorylated in the muscles to form creatinine phosphate (phosphagen) where it acts as an energy store for the regeneration of muscle ADP to ATP (section 17.4.8).

A final group of nitrogenous waste compounds results from detoxification processes occurring in the liver. The commonest product is hippuric acid (*hippos*, horse) which was discovered in horse urine and is formed by the conjugation of benzoic acid (from plant foods) and the amino acid glycine. Many other phenolic compounds such as benzoic acid are rendered harmless by similar detoxification reactions.

19.3 Nitrogenous excretion and osmoregulation

The major source of waste nitrogenous substances is the deamination of excess amino acids. This produces ammonia which is extremely toxic and must be eliminated. Being soluble, ammonia can be eliminated from the body rapidly and safely if diluted in a sufficient volume of water. This presents no real problems to organisms which have ready access to water but this applies only to those organisms living in the freshwater environment. Marine and terrestrial organisms have an acute problem of gaining or conserving water respectively, therefore very little is available for the elimination of nitrogenous waste. Table 19.2 reveals that organisms living in these environments have developed alternative means of nitrogen excretion. These involve the development of many anatomical, biochemical, physiological and behavioural mechanisms involving the elimination of nitrogenous waste whilst maintaining the composition of the body fluids at a steady state. Since these may involve excretion and osmoregulation the two processes will be considered together.

Osmoregulation is a homeostatic process by which animals and plants maintain the concentration of their body fluids at a steady state. Body fluids are found within cells (**intracellular**) and outside cells (**extracellular**). For example, the fluid within plant cell vacuoles (cell sap) is intracellular whereas the fluid surrounding the cells of the cortex of a plant stem or root is extracellular. In multicellular animals intracellular fluid is dispersed fairly evenly throughout the cell whereas extracellular fluid exists as plasma and interstitial fluid. The latter is further subdivided in vertebrates into tissue fluid and lymph. It is vital that the composition of these fluids should remain at a steady state in order for the metabolic activities of the cells to work efficiently. The nature of the intra- and extracellular fluids and their regulation in plants is described in section 19.3.2.

Osmoregulation is not a term used simply to describe the control of water balance within an organism. It refers to the control of the composition of body fluids, which in all cases are solutions of varying complexity. Details of the physical and chemical properties of solutions are described in appendix A1.4.

In animals, even if the solute potentials of two solutions are the same, solutes will move if their relative concentrations are different. The movement of water molecules between two solutions by osmosis, occurs in response to the relative solute potentials of the two solutions. Solute molecules move across partially permeable membranes in a direction determined by their relative concentrations on either side of the membrane and their size in relation to the pores of the membrane. This movement may be **passive** and molecules move down a concentration gradient from a region of their high concentration by **diffusion**, or they may move against the concentration gradient as a result of **active transport** by carrier mechanisms located in the membrane. Membranes, including the cell surface membrane, cytoplasmic tissue layers, body surfaces and gills, can all act as partially permeable membranes through which water and solutes can pass.

The osmotic concentration of solutions is described in this chapter in terms of solute potential and expressed either in milliosmoles per litre ($mOsm\,dm^{-3}$) or milliosmoles per kilogram of water ($mOsm\,kg^{-1}$).

For biological purposes involving osmoregulation the concentration of a solution may also be described in terms of the **freezing point depression** of the solution. Pure water freezes at $0\,°C$, but as solutes are added the freezing point falls below $0\,°C$ and the new freezing point indicates the concentration of solutes in the solution. For example, sea water has a solute potential of $-1000\,mOsm\,dm^{-3}$ and a freezing point depression (Δ) of $-1.7\,°C$.

19.3.1 Osmoregulatory mechanisms

The body fluids of freshwater organisms are usually more concentrated than their aquatic environment whilst those of many marine organisms, particularly vertebrates, are less concentrated than sea water. Many marine non-vertebrates, on the other hand, are **isosmotic** (have the same concentration) with the marine environment.

If the concentration of solutes in an aquatic environment increases, or the volume of water decreases, animals respond in either of two ways. An **osmoconformer** would alter the concentrations of its body fluids to equal those of the new surroundings, whilst an **osmoregulator** would maintain its osmotic concentration despite changes in the external environment. In homeostatic terms, osmoconformers are described increasingly as **poikilosmotic** and osmoregulators as **homeosmotic**, in line with the prefixes used in temperature regulation.

19.3.2 Osmoregulation in plants

Plant tissue contains a higher proportion of water than animal tissue, and the effective and efficient functioning of the plant cell and the whole plant depends upon maintaining the water content at a steady state. Plants do not have the same problems of osmoregulation as animals and they can be considered simply in relation to their environment. On this basis plants are classified as outlined below.

Hydrophytes

Freshwater aquatic plants such as Canadian pondweed (*Elodea canadensis*), water milfoil (*Myriophyllum*) and the water lily (*Nymphaea*) are classed as hydrophytes and have fewer osmoregulatory problems than any of the other plant types. Plant cells in fresh water are surrounded by a solution of higher water potential and water enters the vacuolar sap by osmosis. The water passes through the freely permeable cell wall and the partially permeable cell surface and tonoplast membranes. As the volume of the vacuole increases due to water uptake, it generates a **turgor pressure** (pressure potential). The cell becomes turgid and a point is reached when the water potential has increased to equal that of the surrounding water (about zero) and no further water enters (see section 14.1.7). This is termed **mechanical osmoregulation**. *Nitella clavata* is a freshwater alga with an extremely concentrated sap, whose osmoregulatory problems only concern the maintenance of the ionic contents of the sap. This is carried out by active uptake from the surrounding water.

Halophytes

The only plants able to live immersed in sea water are algae and they form the major source of vegetation on the seashore. The distribution of algal species down the shore is determined by many factors, including tolerance to wave action, desiccation when exposed by tides and the nature of their photosynthetic pigments. In all cases these species can tolerate increases in salinity and their main osmoregulatory problem is the prevention of water loss by evaporation. Channel wrack (*Pelvetia canaliculata*) occupies the highest

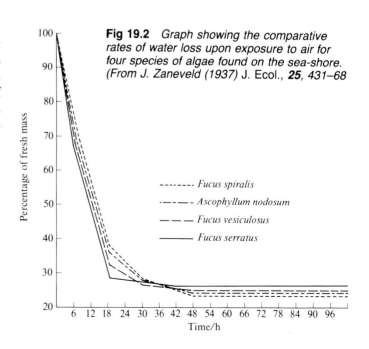

Fig 19.2 *Graph showing the comparative rates of water loss upon exposure to air for four species of algae found on the sea-shore. (From J. Zaneveld (1937) J. Ecol.,* **25**, *431–68*

-------- *Fucus spiralis*

·——· *Ascophyllum nodosum*

— — — *Fucus vesiculosus*

———— *Fucus serratus*

algal zone on sheltered rocky shores surrounding the British Isles, and its habitat tolerance is aided by thick cell walls, a thick covering of mucilage and a stipe shaped as a channel. Fig 19.2 shows the rate of water loss and degree of tolerance of four common British species of seaweed which are zoned according to their ability to retain water when exposed to air.

Halophytes, however, are defined as plants inhabiting areas of high salinity such as those encountered in estuaries and salt marshes where salinity is constantly changing and may exceed that of sea water. Whilst the shoot system is not regularly exposed to high salinities, the root system must tolerate the increased salinities of the sand and mud which accompany hot windy periods when the tide is out. It was thought that these plants must tolerate periods of 'physiological drought' when water is unavailable to the tissues due to the low water potential of the environment of the roots. However, this does not seem to be the case and high transpiration rates and low water potential in root cells enable water to be taken up. Cord grass (*Spartina*) is a common halophyte found low down on estuaries and salt marshes; it has an extensive system of rhizomes for propagation, bearing adventitious roots for anchorage and purposes of water and ion uptake. Other halophytes of estuaries and salt marshes include smaller plants which store water when it is freely available. Common examples of these species are glasswort (*Salicornia*), seablite (*Suaeda maritima*) and sea purslane (*Halimione*). Some species, such as sea milkwort (*Glaux*) and *Spartina*, are able to regulate their salt content by excreting salt from glands at the margins of the leaves.

Mesophytes

The majority of angiosperm plant species are mesophytes, and they occupy habitats with adequate water supplies. They are faced with the problem of water loss by evaporation from all aerial parts. Features which help to reduce water loss are both structural (xeromorphic) and physiological, and include the presence of a cuticle, protected stomata whose diameters can be regulated, a variable leaf shape, abscission and an ecological distribution based upon tolerance to dehydration. Further details and examples of these mechanisms are found in section 14.3.

Xerophytes

Plants adapted to life in dry regions and able to survive long periods of drought are called xerophytes. These form the typical flora of desert and semi-desert regions and are common along the strand line of the seashore and in sand dunes. Some plants respond to extreme conditions by surviving in the seed or spore stage. These are known as **drought evaders** and can germinate following rainfall and grow, flower and complete seed formation in four weeks, for example the Californian poppy (*Escholtzia*). The seeds produced lie dormant until the next rainy spell.

Drought endurers, on the other hand, show many

structural (xeromorphic) and physiological adaptations enabling them to survive in extremely dry conditions. Most of the xerophytic species of the British Isles are associated with the strand line and sand dunes, such as saltwort (*Salsola*) and sea sandwort (*Honkenya*) found growing in small mounds of sand on the shore. Sand couch grass (*Agropyron*) and marram grass (*Ammophila*) are dominant species of embryo dunes and have extensive rhizome systems with adventitious roots for obtaining water from well below sand level. *Agropyron* is able to tolerate salt concentrations in the sand up to 20 times that of sea water. Both *Ammophila* and *Agropyron* are important pioneer plants in the development of sand-dune systems.

Xerophytic plant species of desert regions show several adaptations to reducing water loss and obtaining and storing water. Some of these are summarised in table 19.3.

Table 19.3. Summary of methods of conserving water shown by various plant species (see chapters 14 and 16)

Mechanism of water conservation	Adaptation	Example
reduction in transpiration rate	waxy cuticle } few stomata } sunken stomata stomata open at night and closed by day surface covered with fine hairs	prickly pear (*Opuntia*), pine (*Pinus*), ice plant (*Mesembryanthemum*)
	curled leaves	marram grass (*Ammophila*)
storage of water	fleshy succulent leaves fleshy succulent stems	*Bryophyllum* candle plant (*Kleinia*)
	fleshy underground tuber	*Raphionacme*
water uptake	deep root system below water table shallow root system absorbing surface moisture	acacia oleander cactus

19.3.3 Processes associated with excretion and osmoregulation

Ultrafiltration is the process by which solvent and solute molecules separate from a solution according to their differential abilities to pass through the pores in a filter. The filter in most animals is the layer separating the circulatory system and the osmoregulatory or excretory organ. The force required to produce filtration is a hydrostatic pressure and comes from the blood pressure. The filtered solution is known as **filtrate**. Most of the contents of blood are removed by ultrafiltration, the exceptions being really large molecules, such as proteins, and cells, such as red blood cells.

Selective reabsorption involves the selective uptake of solute molecules and water in amounts which are useful to the body. Those substances which are metabolic wastes are not reabsorbed, nor are solute and water molecules if their reabsorption would result in their exceeding the normal steady-state composition of the body fluids. Reabsorption occurs initially by passive diffusion until the diffusion gradient levels out, after which further reabsorption occurs by active transport. As solutes are reabsorbed, the filtrate becomes progressively less concentrated compared with the body fluids so that water molecules follow the movement of ions by osmosis to produce a filtrate which is isosmotic with the body fluids. A dilute filtrate is produced by the further uptake of ions from the filtrate in a region of the osmoregulatory/excretory organ which is impermeable to water.

Secretion occurs by active transport and removes solutes from the body fluids to the filtrate or directly to the environment. It therefore operates in the opposite direction to reabsorption. This mechanism further decreases the solute potential of the filtrate and increases the solute potential of the body fluids.

The net effect of these three mechanisms of ultrafiltration, selective reabsorption and secretion is homeostatic, in that it maintains the composition of the body fluids at a steady state.

There is a range of osmoregulatory or excretory organs and organelles which show variety in morphological structure and anatomical location, yet they all rely for their function on one or more of the mechanisms described above. Some of the structures are relatively non-specialised and share common characteristics within a range of organisms, for example contractile vacuoles, nephridia and kidneys, whereas others are relatively specialised, such as gills, rectal glands and salt glands.

19.3.4 The effect of environment on excretion and osmoregulation

The nature of the environment produces certain osmoregulatory problems in different groups of organisms. Many aquatic organisms living in an environment of lower water potential (more concentrated) *lose* water by osmosis and *gain* solutes by diffusion. The water loss is replaced in various ways, including drinking and eating, but this increases the solute concentrations of the body fluids and necessitates the removal of excess solute molecules by active transport. Organisms living in an environment of higher water potential (less concentrated) *gain* water by osmosis and *lose* solutes by diffusion. In order to minimise these exchanges the organisms often have an impermeable outer covering and take up ions from the environment by active transport.

All terrestrial organisms face the problem of water and solute loss from their body fluids to the environment. The intracellular body fluid of these organisms is maintained at a steady state by the regulation of the extracellular body fluid by specialised osmoregulatory/excretory organs, such as Malpighian tubules and kidneys. A balance must be achieved between the amount of water and ions lost and gained. The problems of water balance are described in detail in section 19.4.

Adaptations to severe drought

The kangaroo rat (*Dipodomys*) is quite remarkable among mammals in being able to tolerate drought conditions in the deserts of North America. It flourishes in these conditions by possessing a unique combination of structural, physiological and behavioural adaptations. Water loss by evaporation from the lungs is reduced by exhaling air at a temperature below core temperature. As air is inhaled it gains heat from the nasal passages which assume a lower temperature. During exhalation water vapour in the warm air condenses on the nasal passages and is conserved. The kangaroo rat feeds on dry seeds and other dry plant material and does not drink. Water produced by the chemical reactions of respiration, and that present in minute amounts in its food, are its only sources of water. The classic investigations by Knut Schmidt-Nielsen (summarised in table 19.4) revealed the overall water metabolism balance for a kangaroo rat weighing 35 g metabolising 100 g of barley in experimental surroundings at 25 °C and a relative humidity of 20%. Throughout this period the only source of water was the barley grain.

Table 19.4 Water metabolism for a kangaroo rat under experimental conditions. The absorbed water was the water present in the food

Water gains	cm^3	Water losses	cm^3
oxidation water	54.0	urine	13.5
absorbed water	6.0	faeces	2.6
		evaporation	43.9
Total water gain	60.0	Total water loss	60.0

Finally the kangaroo rat avoids excessive evaporative water losses in the wild by spending much of its time in the relatively humid atmosphere of its underground burrow.

The other spectacular example of water conservation is the camel, whose physiological adaptations are described in section 18.4.7.

19.4 A phylogenetic review of organs and processes of nitrogenous excretion and osmoregulation

Throughout this review the following points should be considered:
(1) the environment influences the nature of the excretory product and the process of osmoregulation,
(2) some groups of organisms have species adapted to life in more than one environment,
(3) some organisms are able to withstand considerable changes in the environment.

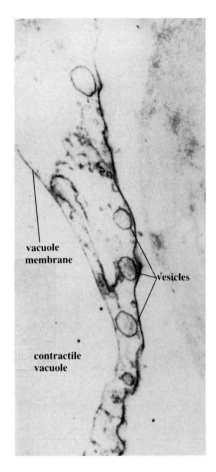

vacuole membrane

vesicles

contractile vacuole

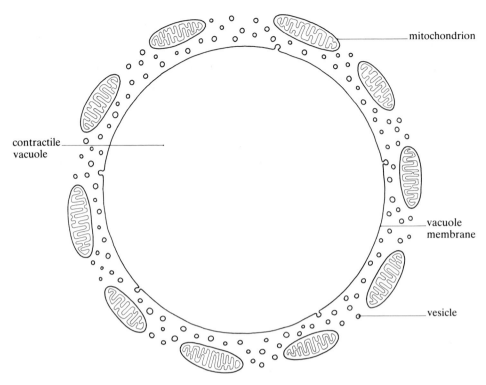

mitochondrion

contractile vacuole

vacuole membrane

vesicle

Fig 19.3 *Electron micrograph of contractile vacuole of* Amoeba. *Water is secreted into tiny vesicles which fuse with the membrane of the contractile vacuole discharging water into the vacuole*

19.4.1 Protozoans

Protozoans are found in freshwater and marine habitats and the body fluids of other organisms. The intracellular fluid of a protozoan is separated from the external environment only by a partially permeable cell surface membrane. Excretion of carbon dioxide and ammonia occurs by diffusion over the entire surface of the cell. This has a relatively large surface area to volume ratio which assists the removal of waste substances.

All freshwater species of protozoans have a lower solute potential than their surroundings and have osmoregulatory organelles known as **contractile vacuoles**. These are necessary to remove water which enters the cell by osmosis from the dilute medium through the cell surface membrane, and to regulate the volume of the cell and prevent it increasing in size. The exact location and structure of the contractile vacuole is extremely variable. In *Amoeba proteus* a contractile vacuole can form anywhere within the cell and release its fluid into the external environment at any point on its outer surface (fig 19.3). In *Paramecium aurelia* there are two contractile vacuoles with fixed positions (fig 19.4). The method of functioning, however, appears to be similar in all species and involves the movement of water from the cytoplasm into small vesicles which fuse with, and empty their water into, the contractile vacuole. Mitochondria collect around contractile vacuoles, and presumably supply the energy for the 'osmotic' work of filling them.

Investigations carried out into the function of the contractile vacuole in the giant amoeba (*Chaos chaos*) show that the calculated osmotic influx of water based on the solute potential of the intracellular fluid agrees with observed estimates of the volume eliminated by the contractile vacuole. The contents of the contractile vacuole have a higher water potential than the intracellular fluid yet have a lower water potential than the external medium. Several hypotheses have been put foward to account for formation of vacuolar fluid. A probable explanation is shown in fig 19.5.

Many of the marine rhizopod protozoans do not have functional contractile vacuoles because their intracellular fluid composition is isosmotic with sea water. This evidence suggests that the primary role of the vacuole is osmoregulation.

19.4.2 Cnidarians

Cnidarians do not appear to possess any excretory or osmoregulatory organs or organelles and the mechanism of osmoregulation is unknown. Carbon dioxide and ammonia are the principal toxic metabolic waste substances and they are removed by diffusion from the cells directly into the water of the extracellular environment.

19.4.3 Platyhelminths

Most of the metabolic waste products of platyhelminths pass into the much-branched gut and are

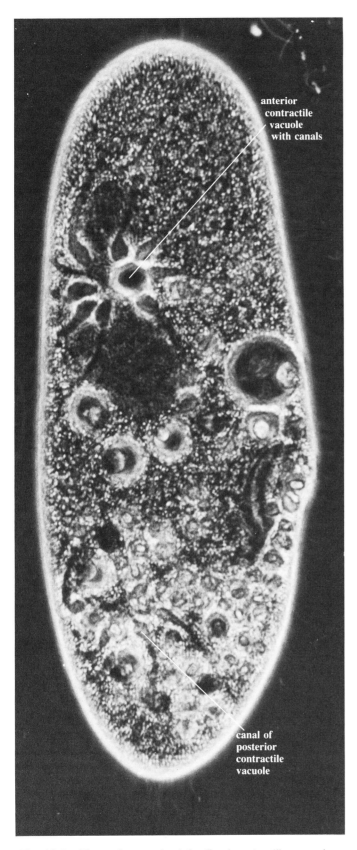

anterior
contractile
vacuole
with canals

canal of
posterior
contractile
vacuole

Fig. 19.4 *Photomicrograph of the fixed contractile vacuoles of* Paramecium

eliminated via the mouth. Some, however, pass into a series of tubules which form a joint excretory and osmoregulatory system. This is a primitive type of nephridium, known as a **protonephridium**, whose principal function is osmoregulation. Protonephridia are found mainly in animals that lack a true body cavity (coelom) such as the platyhelminths and rotiferans. *Planaria* has a pair of protonephridia which run the entire length of the body and open to the exterior via numerous excretory pores (fig 19.6a). Each protonephridium is made up of many tubules which branch and end in enlarged hollow cells from which cilia project into the tubule. If only one cilium is present the cell is known as a **solenocyte** and if several are present it is known as a **flame cell** (fig 19.6b). The cilia of the flame cells undulate, and this movement resembles the flickering of a flame, hence the name. This 'flickering' appears to agitate the fluid in the tubule and propel it along the nephridial ducts towards the excretory pores. The fluid in the flame cell is composed of water and waste substances produced by the tissues. It is thought that some of these wastes are secreted into the tubule by active transport and some by ultrafiltration through the cytoplasm of the flame cell. Water enters the lumen of the flame cell by osmosis. Flame cells are found in some annelids and solenocytes are found principally in the cephalochordate, *Amphioxus*.

19.4.4 Annelids

Annelids have a combined excretory and osmoregulatory organ known as a **metanephridium**, or simply a **nephridium**, which regulates the chemical composition of the body fluids. The exact structure and distribution of nephridia varies in each of the three orders, the Polychaeta, Oligochaeta and Hirudinea, but the basic structure and function is similar in all. Nephridia are unbranched tubules which link the coelom to the exterior. In some species, such as the lugworm (*Arenicola*), the nephridium is formed by the fusion of an ectodermal tubule which opens to the exterior by a pore and a mesodermal tubule or coelomoduct which opens into the coelom. The earthworm (*Lumbricus*) has a pair of nephridia in each segment apart from the first three and the last, but polychaetes and leeches have fewer.

A nephridium consists of a ciliated funnel, the **nephrostome**, which leads via a long ciliated and muscular tubule to a bladder where fluid is stored prior to its release through an external opening, the **nephridiopore**. The waste fluid is called **urine** and is formed by the processes of ultrafiltration, selective reabsorption and active secretion.

Coelomic fluid containing useful and waste substances passes into the nephrostome by pressure created by the beating of cilia (fig 19.7). Fluid passes along the long narrow tube by the action of cilia and muscles but no reabsorption of useful substances occurs here. The cells lining the short middle tube and the longer wide tube reabsorb useful substances into the blood capillaries in their walls, whilst further waste is actively secreted into the

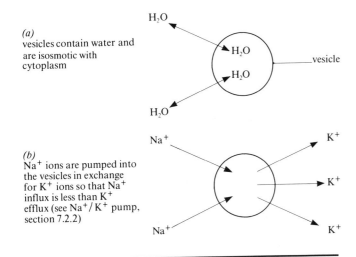

(a)
vesicles contain water and are isosmotic with cytoplasm

H_2O

H_2O
H_2O

vesicle

H_2O

(b)
Na^+ ions are pumped into the vesicles in exchange for K^+ ions so that Na^+ influx is less than K^+ efflux (see Na^+/K^+ pump, section 7.2.2)

Na^+ K^+

K^+

Na^+ K^+

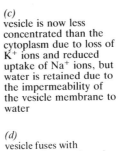

(c)
vesicle is now less concentrated than the cytoplasm due to loss of K^+ ions and reduced uptake of Na^+ ions, but water is retained due to the impermeability of the vesicle membrane to water

Na^+

H_2O

(d)
vesicle fuses with contractile vacuole and the contents are discharged. Na^+ ions lost from the cell in the vacuolar fluid are replaced by active transport from the external medium

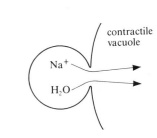

contractile vacuole

Na^+

H_2O

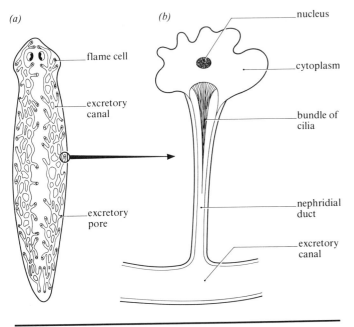

(a)
flame cell

excretory canal

excretory pore

(b)
nucleus

cytoplasm

bundle of cilia

nephridial duct

excretory canal

Fig 19.5 *(above) Diagrammatic explanation of a possible mechanism of water uptake by a contractile vacuole*

Fig 19.6 *(left) Features of the protonephridial excretory system of platyhelminths. (a) Gross structure of the system in Planaria, (b) single flame-cell*

Fig 19.7 *(below) Stages in the formation of urine in the earthworm. Heavy arrows show regions of active secretion of substances. Protein is known to be present in the nephrostome but not in the urine excreted by the nephridiopore. At some stage it is removed from the nephridium but as yet no mechanism is known to account for this uptake. (Graph after Ramsay.)*

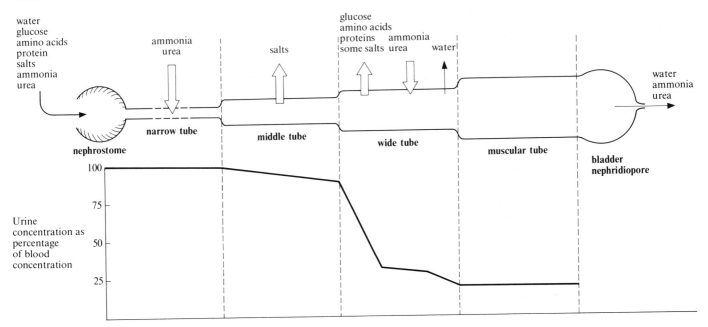

tubule from the capillaries. As substances are reabsorbed the concentration of waste solutes in the urine rises and the urine becomes more dilute. This urine, which is more dilute than coelomic fluid, is excreted through the nephridiopore. The ability to produce dilute urine suggests that the nephridium has an osmoregulatory function. Investigations have revealed that *Lumbricus* behaves as a freshwater osmoregulator since, when placed in salt solutions of various concentrations, it remains more concentrated than its environment yet produces a dilute urine. Although the natural habitat of the earthworm appears terrestrial, it actually lives in direct contact with the water films that surround the soil particles of the walls of its burrow. Hence it may be considered a freshwater organism. The osmoregulatory activities of typically marine polychaete species such as *Nereis diversicolor* are described in section 19.4.6.

19.4.5   Arthropods

Arthropods are adapted to conditions in a vast range of habitats from marine to fully terrestrial. It is not surprising, therefore, that as a phylum they display a range of excretory and osmoregulatory mechanisms. Adaptations shown by insects to terrestrial life and crustaceans to marine, estuarine and freshwater life have been selected as representative of the range of features shown by arthropods and are described in this section.

One of the major problems of life on land is the prevention of water loss. Insects have an almost impermeable cuticle to reduce water loss from the body surface and spiracles to reduce water loss from the gaseous exchange system of tracheae and tracheoles.

The strong cuticle is composed of a chitinous exo- and endocuticle covered by a thin waterproof layer, the epicuticle (0.3 μm thick) as described in section 4.9.1. Water loss by evaporation is prevented by the impermeable properties of the epicuticle produced by a highly organised monolayer of lipid molecules covered by several layers of irregularly orientated lipid molecules. If these wax or grease lipid layers are abraded by sharp particles, such as sand or alumina, the evaporation rate increases and the insect risks dehydration. Interestingly, as the air temperature surrounding an insect is increased steadily there is a gradual increase in the rate of evaporation until a particular temperature is exceeded after which the evaporation rate increases rapidly. This point is known as the **transition temperature**. If the water loss from the insect is plotted against the insect's surface temperature this transition point can be seen more clearly and marks the temperature at which the ordered orientation of the wax monolayer breaks down, as shown in fig 19.8.

Some insects living on dry food in very dry habitats are able to take up water from the air providing that the relative humidity of the air is above a certain value, such as 90% for the mealworm (*Tenebrio*) and 70% for the house mite (*Dermatophagoides*).

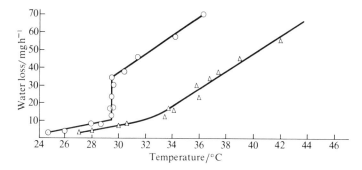

Fig 19.8 (above) Graph showing the water loss from the cuticle of a cockroach at various air temperatures (triangles). The circles indicate water loss plotted against the surface temperature of the cuticle. This shows the dramatic increase in water loss at about 29.5 °C, the **transition temperature**

Fig 19.9 (below) Diagram showing the position of Malpighian tubules in relation to the alimentary canal of Rhodnius prolixus

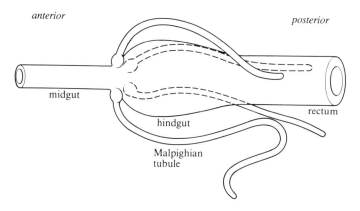

The problem of preventing water loss by excretion is overcome by specialised excretory organs called **Malpighian tubules** which produce and excrete the almost insoluble waste substance **uric acid**.

Malpighian tubules are blind-ending tubules which lie in the intercellular space of the abdomen and are bathed in haemolymph. The number of tubules is variable in insects, some have a pair and others may have several hundred. *Rhodnius*, a blood-sucking hemipteran, has four tubules; in all cases they open into the hindgut at its junction with the midgut and may be long and slender or short and compact (fig 19.9).

Wigglesworth investigated the function of the tubules in uric acid formation in *Rhodnius* and the mechanism appears to be as follows.

The tubule has two histologically distinct regions, an **upper segment** (distal to the gut), composed of a single layer of cells and containing a clear solution, and a **lower segment**. The cells of the lower segment have microvilli on their inner surface and it is here that crystals of uric acid precipitate out of solution (fig 19.10). The contents of the tubule pass into the hindgut or rectum where they mix with waste materials from digestive processes. Rectal glands in the wall of the rectum absorb water from the faeces and uric acid suspension until the waste is dry enough for it to be eliminated from the body as pellets.

Fully terrestrial organisms do not have the same osmoregulatory problems as aquatic or semi-terrestrial organisms. Insects, however, do have to regulate the ionic contents of their haemolymph and this is achieved by maintaining a balance between ions taken up in the diet and those lost through synthesis, egestion and excretion. It is aquatic arthropods such as the freshwater crustacean *Astacus*, the crayfish, and the marine crustacean *Carcinus maenas*, the shore crab, that show most adaptations of their excretory and osmoregulatory organs to their habitats and modes of life.

Astacus lives in freshwater streams which provide a dilute environment. Some waste nitrogenous substances and carbon dioxide are deposited in the cuticle of the nymphal stages and shed during moulting, but in the adult nitrogenous waste is removed as ammonia through specialised excretory/osmoregulatory organs known as **antennal** or **green glands**.

The antennal glands are blind-ending mesodermal structures which lie in the haemocoel just in front of the mouth region and open to the exterior by a pore situated underneath the base of the antennae. Each antennal gland is composed of four regions, a blind-ending sac, a green tube known as the labyrinth, a long white nephridial canal and a thin-walled bladder which opens to the exterior (fig 19.11).

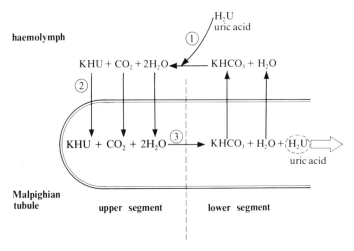

Fig 19.10 *Summary of the suggested mechanism of uric acid excretion by the Malpighian tubule. (1) Uric acid (H_2U) produced by the cells of the body is secreted into the haemolymph where it combines with sodium and potassium hydrogencarbonates and water to form sodium and potassium urates (NaHU and KHU), carbon dioxide and water (only potassium is shown in the diagram). (2) These salts are actively secreted into the lumen of the tubule and water follows by osmosis. (3) As these soluble substances pass down the tubule hydrogencarbonates form and these are actively reabsorbed into the haemolymph. Water follows the hydrogencarbonates by osmosis and as the pH in the lower segment falls, due to the reabsorption of hydrogencarbonates, the uric acid precipitates out as crystals*

Water and solutes are filtered from the haemolymph into the end sac by the hydrostatic pressure of the blood. As this filtrate passes through the spaces in the glandular lining of the labyrinth and along the nephridial canal, useful materials are selectively reabsorbed into the haemolymph and further waste substances, including nitrogenous waste, are secreted into the filtrate.

Astacus has a lower solute potential than its environment and takes in water through any permeable surface especially the gills. Large volumes of urine, which is less concentrated than the haemolymph, are produced to counteract this osmotic influx. Most of the nitrogenous waste is lost as ammonia but some urea is also produced.

Carcinus lives in the intertidal zone of the sea-shore, surrounded for most of the time by sea water. It has antennal glands similar to those of *Astacus* which it uses to eliminate waste nitrogenous material, especially ammonia. In common with many other marine species, parts of its surface are permeable to salts and water and the body fluids are isosmotic with sea water. This is an economical measure for marine organisms as they do not need to expend energy maintaining their body fluids at a higher or lower solute potential than their environment. However, even though they are isosmotic, the ionic concentration of the body fluids may be maintained at a different level from that of the sea, and energy is required for ionic regulation.

Carcinus is found in a wide range of habitats. It can tolerate the more concentrated conditions which may be encountered in rock pools on sea shores and salt pans in salt marshes as water evaporates from them on hot days. In these conditions it acts as an osmoconformer and decreases the solute potential of its body fluids by retaining salts which the tissues tolerate. In these conditions the urine is more concentrated than the body fluids. *Carcinus* is able to tolerate the changing conditions found in estuaries and, in keeping with many species found in estuaries, it is euryhaline. As the salt concentration of the water decreases due to the diluting effects of river water or rainfall the body fluids of *Carcinus* become more concentrated than the surrounding medium (fig 19.12). Water tends to enter by osmosis and solutes leave by diffusion. Under these conditions *Carcinus* becomes an osmoregulator and maintains the body fluid composition at a steady state by actively secreting sodium from the urine back into the haemolymph through the cells of the antennal gland. Some water will be retained as the sodium is reabsorbed but the overall volume of the organism is prevented from increasing due to the tough cuticle. In these conditions the urine is isosmotic with the body fluids.

19.4.6 Effects of changes in the environment shown by non-vertebrates

Non-vertebrates which live in sea water, such as sea anemones, are isosmotic with their environment. If placed in diluted sea water they immediately take up water

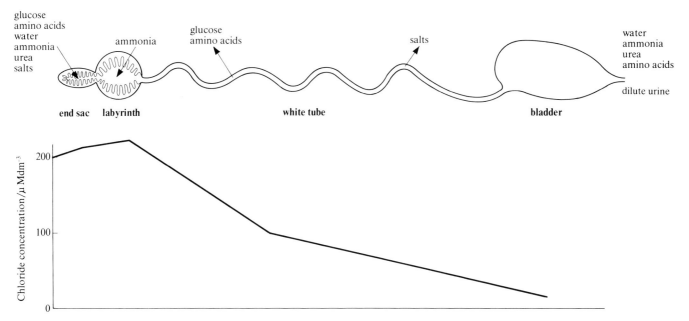

Fig 19.11 *Diagram summarising the structure and function of the antennal (green) gland of* Astacus. *The graph indicates changes in the solute potential of the filtrate. (After Peters from Barrington)*

and lose ions. This is also seen by exposing *Arenicola* to decreasing salinities. After an initial increase in mass the mass returns to normal. This is explained by the fact that water enters by osmosis faster than ions are lost. After a short while conditions become stable due to loss of ions, the body fluids become isosmotic with the environment and the mass returns to normal provided the salinity does not fall too low. *Nereis* is normally found in marine conditions in sand and mud but it can osmoregulate down to salinities of 10% sea water and inhabit estuaries. It is an osmoregulator and is able to remain more concentrated than the environment because of the reduced permeability of its body surface and its ability to take up chloride ions from its environment (fig 19.12).

There are some marine species that have a higher solute potential than sea water, such as the shrimps *Palaemonetes* and *Leander* (fig. 19.12). They have overcome problems of water loss and uptake of ions by drinking water and actively secreting ions back into the sea through their gills. These mechanisms of control are so efficient that shrimps are able to maintain their body fluid level at a steady state in external concentrations ranging from 2 to 110% sea water. It is thought that this ability reflects the freshwater ancestry of the species which have secondarily invaded sea water.

The brine shrimp (*Artemia*) has body fluids less concentrated than the high salinities of its environment and maintains its body fluids in a dilute state by continually removing sodium and chloride ions from the concentrated medium which it drinks. It does this by eliminating them from the haemolymph through the epithelium of the gills. It is also able to maintain its body fluids at a steady state despite fluctuations of 10–1 000% sea water in the external environment.

Some brackish water species, such as the mussel (*Mytilus*), are able to maintain the intracellular composition of their cells at a fairly steady state despite changes in the composition of the external environment and the extracellular fluid. This is thought to be due to regulation of the fluid composition by individual cells.

Many freshwater species, such as *Astacus*, are thought to have developed from marine species via brackish water species by progressive improvements in the efficiency of water and ion regulation.

Small freshwater non-vertebrate animals have a relatively large surface area to volume ratio. Since they have a lower water potential than their environment they tend to take in water and lose salts more rapidly than comparable larger non-vertebrates, such as *Astacus*, that have a smaller surface area to volume ratio. They have overcome this problem, to a certain extent, by having body fluids with a lower ionic concentration than larger forms.

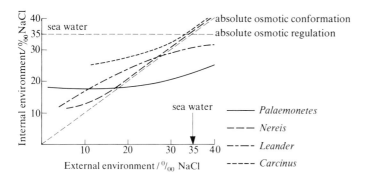

Fig 19.12 *Graph showing the relationship between internal and external environments for osmotic conformers, osmotic regulators and four marine species, the prawns,* Leander *and* Palaemonetes, *the ragworm,* Nereis *and the shore-crab,* Carcinus

19.4.7 Echinoderms

All echinoderms are marine. Nitrogenous waste is removed from the gills and tube-feet by diffusion as ammonia and urea. Echinoderms have a water vascular system containing sea water with which the cells are isosmotic. There is no problem of osmoregulation.

19.4.8 Vertebrates

All three nitrogenous waste products are excreted by vertebrates and, with few exceptions, the form of the waste product is related to the environmental availability of water. Osmoregulatory mechanisms in vertebrates are more efficient than non-vertebrates because of the reduced permeability of the body surface and the development of the kidney. Biologists are uncertain as to whether the earliest fish originated in the sea or in fresh water. Many biologists favour a marine origin and see the kidney as a later development necessary for survival in the higher solute potential conditions of fresh water. In this environment it provides a mechanism for the removal of excess water and the retention of salt. Subsequent development of the kidney is related to the environment of the organism, and shows a progressive increase in complexity throughout the vertebrate classes from the fish to mammals. This increase in complexity is associated with colonisation of the terrestrial environment. The increased efficiency of these mechanisms maintains the internal composition of the body fluids within narrower limits than in the non-vertebrates.

The basic unit of the kidney is the **nephron**. Nephrons are segmental structures formed from mesodermal nephrotomes (section 21.8) which have become intimately associated with blood vessels from the aorta and are linked to the coelom by a ciliated funnel. The nephrons of fish larvae show their most primitive arrangement where several of them open into the pericardial cavity and form a collective structure known as the **pronephros** (fig 19.13). All adult fish and amphibia lose the pronephros and have a more compact structure made up of many more nephrons and found in the abdominal and tail regions of the organisms. This is called a **mesonephric kidney**. Its nephrons have lost their connections with the coelom and are linked together by a collecting duct which leads to the urinogenital opening. Such a structure is ideal for the production of dilute urine produced predominantly by organisms living in a freshwater environment.

Reptiles, birds and mammals are adapted to life on land where problems of water removal experienced by fish and amphibians are replaced by problems of water retention. These organisms have an even more compact structure, the **metanephric kidney** which contains far more nephrons with longer tubules for water reabsorption. These tubules eventually release concentrated urine into the central cavities of the kidney. From here it passes to the **bladder** by a tube known as the **ureter**. (The detailed structure and function of the mammalian kidney is described in section 19.5.)

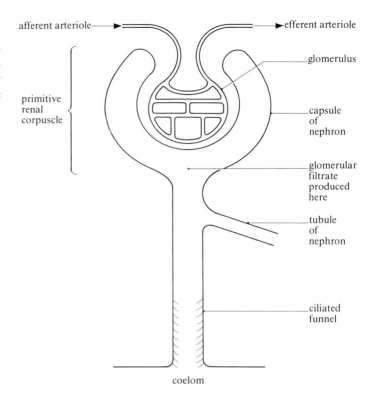

Fig 19.13 *Structure of a primitive nephron. Filtrate produced from the glomerulus passes to the coelom via the ciliated funnel or joins up with other nephrons via connecting tubules*

The vertebrate kidney relies on the principles of ultrafiltration, selective reabsorption and active secretion for the production of urine. **Urine** is a liquid containing nitrogenous waste, water and ions in excess of those required by the body. Ultrafiltration does not discriminate between those substances which are useful to the body and those which are not and energy is expended in reabsorbing 99% of the solutes back into the blood. However, despite the apparent inefficiency in terms of energy, this mechanism gives vertebrates greater flexibility to exploit new habitats since it permits 'foreign' or 'new' substances to be excreted as they are encountered. It does not require the development of new secretory mechanisms to remove these substances.

Fish

The excretory and osmoregulatory organs of the fish are gills and kidneys. Both structures are permeable to water, nitrogenous waste and ions and have a large surface area to facilitate exchange. The kidney, unlike the gill, is separated from the external environment by the body wall, the body tissues and extracellular body fluid, and can therefore exercise control over the steady-state composition of the body fluids. Despite the fact that fish live in an aquatic environment there are enough differences between the mechanisms of excretion and osmoregulation in freshwater and marine species for them to be described separately.

Freshwater fish. Freshwater bony fish have an internal osmotic concentration approximately

$300\,\text{mOsm dm}^{-3}$ and are more concentrated than their environment. Despite having a relatively impermeable outer covering of scales and mucus there is a considerable osmotic influx of water and loss of ions through the highly permeable gills, which also serve as the organs for the excretion of the waste nitrogenous substance ammonia. In order to maintain the body fluids at a steady state, freshwater fish have to continually lose a large volume of water. They do this by producing a large volume of glomerular filtrate from which solutes are removed by selective reabsorption into the capillaries surrounding the kidney tubules. The kidneys produce a large volume of very dilute urine (of higher solute potential than blood) which contains some ammonia and a number of solutes. Up to one-third of the body mass can be lost per day as urine. Ions which are lost from the body fluids are replaced from food and by active uptake from the external environment by special cells in the gills.

Marine fish. Fish are thought to have originated in the sea and, having successfully invaded the freshwater environment, secondarily re-invaded the sea and given rise to the cartilaginous fish and marine bony fish. Whilst in the freshwater environment many of the basic metabolic activities and organ functions evolved based on a solute potential of the body fluids at a level between one-third and one-half that of sea water. On their return to the sea the body fluids retained the ancestral solute potential and this produced problems of maintaining the body fluids at a steady level in an environment of lower solute potential (fig 19.14).

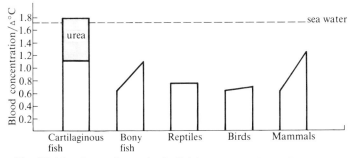

Fig 19.14 *Approximate body fluid concentrations of marine vertebrates. Cartilaginous fish are the only vertebrates with a body fluid more concentrated than the environment but as the graph shows the basic osmotic concentration is a little higher than that of bony fish. The retention of urea increases the solute potential to that of sea water, as shown by freezing point depressions ($\Delta\,°C$ = change in $°C$)*

Cartilaginous fish. The basic solute potential of body fluids in cartilaginous fish is approximately the same as that of marine bony fish, that is equivalent to a 1% salt solution. In order to prevent excessive water loss to the more concentrated sea water cartilaginous fish have decreased the solute potential of their body fluids by synthesising and retaining urea within their tissues and body fluids. The majority of the cells in the body, with the exception of brain cells, appear capable of synthesising urea and their metabolic activities appear not only to depend on its presence but also to be able to tolerate high levels of it. Investigations carried out on isolated shark hearts have shown that they will only beat if perfused with a balanced salt solution containing urea. The body fluids contain between 2 and 2.5% urea, which is about 100 times the concentration which can be tolerated by other vertebrates. High concentrations of urea normally disrupt the hydrogen bonding between amino acids and denature proteins so inhibiting enzyme activity, but not, for some reason, in the cartilaginous fish. Urea, together with inorganic ions and another nitrogenous waste substance trimethylamine oxide $((CH_3)_3N{=}O)$ which is less toxic than ammonia, increases solute potential of the body fluids above that of sea water (Δ sea water $-1.7\,°C$, Δ cartilaginous fish $-1.8\,°C$) (fig 19.14). Cartilaginous fish, having body fluids slightly more concentrated than the environment, take in water by osmosis through their gills. This is eliminated along with excess urea and trimethylamine oxide by the kidneys in a urine which is slightly less concentrated than the body fluids. The kidney has long tubules which are used for the selective reabsorption of urea but not for the elimination of salts which enter with the diet. Excess sodium and chloride ions are removed from the body fluids by active secretion into the rectum by the cells of the rectal gland, which is a small gland attached to the rectum by a duct. The gills are relatively impermeable to nitrogenous waste and any which is lost from the body is controlled by the kidney. In this way the solute potential of the body fluids is maintained at a high level.

Bony fish. Marine bony fish maintain their bodies at a solute potential which is less concentrated than sea water (fig 19.14). The body surfaces are relatively impermeable to water and ions due to scales and mucus, but the body fluids lose water and gain ions freely through the gills. In order to regulate the composition of the body fluids bony fish drink sea water, and secretory cells in the gut remove salts by active transport into the blood. **Chloride secretory cells** in the gills actively remove chloride ions from the blood into the sea and sodium ions follow to maintain electrochemical neutrality. The other major ions in sea water, magnesium and sulphate, are removed in the small volume of isosmotic urine which is produced by the kidney. The kidneys lack glomeruli and are therefore unable to carry out ultrafiltration. All the contents of the urine – such as the nitrogenous substance trimethylamine oxide which gives fish their characteristic smell – and salts, are secreted into the kidney tubules and water follows by osmosis.

Euryhaline fish. There are several euryhaline fish which not only tolerate slight changes in salinity but are able to adapt totally to freshwater and marine conditions for major periods of their lives. Depending upon the direction in which they move to spawn these fish are described as anadromic or catadromic. **Anadromic** (*ana*, up; *dramein*, to run) species such as the salmon (*Salmo salar*) hatch in fresh water and migrate to the sea

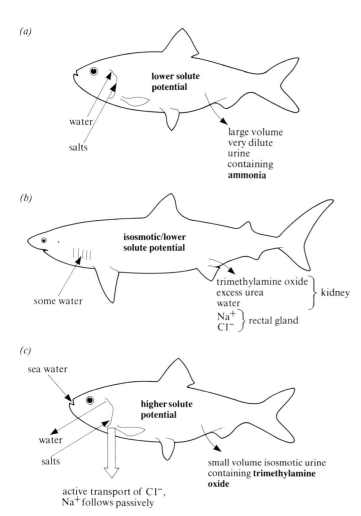

(a)

lower solute
potential

water

salts

large volume
very dilute
urine
containing
ammonia

(b)

isosmotic/lower
solute potential

some water

trimethylamine oxide
excess urea
water } kidney

Na⁺
Cl⁻ } rectal gland

(c)

sea water

higher solute
potential

water

salts

small volume isosmotic urine
containing **trimethylamine
oxide**

active transport of Cl⁻,
Na⁺ follows passively

Fig 19.15 *Excretion and osmoregulation in* (a) *freshwater bony fish,* (b) *cartilaginous fish,* (c) *marine bony fish*

where they mature before returning to fresh water to spawn. **Catadromic** (*cata*, down) species such as the eel (*Anguilla vulgaris*) move in the opposite direction. They hatch in sea water and migrate to fresh water where they mature before returning to the sea to breed. When the eel moves from fresh water to sea water it loses about 40% of its body mass in ten hours. To compensate for this and remain less concentrated it drinks sea water and eliminates ions by active secretion from the gills. When the eel moves from sea water to fresh water the mass initially increases as water enters by osmosis but it is able to achieve an osmotic steady state after only two days. Whilst in fresh water, salts are taken up by active transport through the gills.

These two species show that the active transport mechanisms in the gills are able to work in two directions. Whether this involves a change in the direction of pumping of the same cells or the operation of different sets of cells is not known. It is thought that hormones from the pituitary gland and the adrenal cortex may influence these mechanisms. In both types of fish a period of 'lying up' is necessary when they enter freshwater environments to allow their osmoregulatory mechanisms to adapt to the new surroundings.

Amphibians

Amphibians are believed to have developed from an ancestral stock of freshwater fish, and have inherited similar problems of osmoregulation in that their blood fluids are more concentrated than their freshwater environment. The skin of a frog is permeable to water, and most of the water from the environment is absorbed across the skin. The excess water which enters the body fluids is removed by ultrafiltration through the many large glomeruli of the kidney.

The amphibian kidney has been extensively used in investigating the physiology of the kidney because its large glomeruli are situated near the surface of the kidney. These are accessible to micropipettes which can be inserted into the glomerulus and tubules and the filtrate removed for analysis. In this way the effectiveness of ultrafiltration and selective reabsorption can be demonstrated. Amphibia produce a large volume of very dilute urine (less concentrated than the body fluids). This contains urea which is eliminated by secretion into the tubule as well as by ultrafiltration. The advantage of this mechanism is that it allows amphibians, in dry conditions, to reduce the amount of ultrafiltration by the glomerulus and thereby reduce water loss in the urine; at the same time the tubules continue to receive blood from the renal portal system from which they still actively secrete urea into the tubule. In this respect the mechanism is opposite to that seen in cartilaginous fish where urea is actively reabsorbed by the tubule.

Some salts are inevitably lost in the urine and by diffusion through the skin, but these are replaced from the diet and by their active uptake from the environment by the skin which is the main organ of osmoregulation. The larval stage of the amphibia, the tadpole, is completely aquatic and excretes ammonia through its gills, but at metamorphosis both the nitrogenous product and the mechanism of excretion changes, as described earlier in this section.

Frogs are able to store water in their bladders and the many subcutaneous lymph spaces. This replaces water lost by evaporation during periods when they are on land. Toads are able to tolerate dry conditions for longer periods of time because their skin is less permeable to water and because their kidneys are able to reabsorb water from the glomerular filtrate and produce a more concentrated urine. The permeability of amphibian skin is known to be controlled by an antidiuretic hormone produced by the posterior pituitary gland. The mechanism of control of permeability is thought to be similar to that of the mammalian kidney tubule.

Water balance in terrestrial organisms

The efficient functioning of animal cells relies on the maintenance of the steady state of the intracellular fluid of cells. Homeostatic exchanges in water content between cells, tissue fluid, lymph, plasma and the environment present problems to both aquatic and terrestrial forms of life. Aquatic organisms gain or lose water by osmosis through all permeable parts of the body surface depending on whether the environment is dilute or concentrated. Terrestrial organisms have the problem of losing water and many mechanisms are employed to maintain a steady-state water balance as summarised in table 19.15. This steady state is achieved by balancing loss and water gain, as shown in table 19.6.

Table 19.5. Summary of water conservation mechanisms shown by terrestrial organisms

Organism	Water conservation mechanism
insect	impermeable cuticle trachea and spiracles Malpighian tubules uric acid as nitrogenous waste cleidoic egg
reptile	scales and keratinised skin lungs metanephric kidney uric acid as nitrogenous waste cloacal reabsorption cleidoic egg behavioural responses to heat physiological tolerance to dehydration
bird	feathers lungs metanephric kidney uric acid as nitrogenous waste cleidoic egg cloacal reabsorption
mammal	keratinised skin and hair lungs metanephric kidney hypertonic urine containing urea viviparity behavioural response to heat restricted ecological range physiological tolerance to dehydration

Table 19.6. Summary of water balance mechanisms in terrestrial organisms

water loss from body	=	water gained by body
evaporation from body surface evaporation from gaseous exchange surface water in faeces water in urine water in secretions such as tears		drinking water in food uptake through body surface respiration (metabolic water)

Reptiles

Reptiles are primarily adapted to life in the terrestrial environment and show many morphological, biochemical and physiological adaptations to life on land. However, all three orders, the turtles, lizards and snakes, and crocodiles and alligators, have species which are secondarily adapted to life in the freshwater and marine environments. In all cases the excretory and osmoregulatory mechanisms of these organisms show adaptations to these environments.

Terrestrial reptiles reduce their water loss by having a relatively impermeable skin covered by keratinised scales. The gaseous exchange organs are lungs situated inside the body to reduce water loss. The tissues produce insoluble uric acid which can be excreted without the loss of much water. Excess sodium and potassium ions require water for their removal but, since conservation of water is critical, these combine with uric acid to form insoluble sodium and potassium urates which are excreted with uric acid. The glomeruli are small and produce only enough filtrate to wash out the uric acid from the kidney tubules into the cloaca where more water is reabsorbed. Many terrestrial reptiles have no glomeruli at all.

There is no special mechanism for the removal of salts in terrestrial reptiles and the tissues are able to tolerate increases of up to 50% the normal level of salts following the ingestion of food or when water loss is excessive. Marine reptiles, such as the Galapagos iguana and the edible turtle (*Chelone mydas*) obtain a great deal of salt from their food. Their kidneys are unable to remove the rapid influx of salt from the body fluids and rely on specialised **salt glands** in the head. These glands are able to secrete a concentrated solution of sodium chloride which is several times stronger than sea water. In the turtle the salt glands are found in the orbit of the eye and ducts lead from them to the eyes. They give the impression of 'crying' and produce tears with a very high salt concentration.

The cleidoic egg

An important characteristic of both reptiles and birds which has enabled them to become totally independent of water in their life cycle is the **cleidoic egg** (fig 20.52). This is an egg enclosed in a tough shell which protects the embryo from dehydration. During embryonic development an outgrowth of the hindgut produces a sac-like structure called the **allantois** which stores uric acid produced by the embryo. Since uric acid is insoluble and non-toxic it forms an ideal storage excretory material for the embryo. In the later stages of development the allantois becomes vascularised and pressed up against the shell where it functions as a gaseous exchange organ.

Birds

Birds are believed to have developed from a stock of terrestrial reptiles, such as snakes and lizards, and inherited the same problems. The skin of birds is relatively impermeable to water and the evaporation rate is kept low by the presence of feathers and the absence of sweat glands. However water loss from gaseous exchange surfaces is considerable due to the high ventilation rate and the maintenance of a relatively high body temperature. As a consequence of the increased metabolic rate some small birds may lose up to 35% of their body mass per day.

Nitrogenous waste is eliminated as uric acid in urine which is hypertonic to the body fluids. The urine passes into the cloaca where more water is removed from the urine and faeces before the almost solid residue is released from the body.

The kidney of birds has small glomeruli and all the blood supplying the tubule, where reabsorption of water and secretion of salts occurs, comes from the glomerulus, which relies on a relatively high blood pressure for efficient functioning. Consequently the production of a large volume of glomerular filtrate and the subsequent reabsorption of most of its water and salts have become linked. The surface area of the tubule is increased, to facilitate this reabsorption, by the development of a **loop of Henle**. The physiology of this structure enables the concentration of uric acid in the urine to reach 21% which is approximately three thousand times its concentration in the body fluids.

Some marine birds, such as the penguin, gannet, cormorant and albatross, which feed on fish and sea water, absorb large quantities of salts. These are removed from the body fluids by specialised salt-secreting cells in the **salt**, or **nasal**, **gland**. The nasal glands are similar to those of marine reptiles and are situated in the orbit. They secrete a sodium chloride solution that is four times stronger than that of the body fluids. The nasal glands are composed of many lobules made up of a large number of secretory tubules that open into a central cavity leading to the nasal cavity where the salt is released as large droplets or blown out in a fine spray.

19.5   The mammalian kidney

The kidney is the major excretory and osmoregulatory homeostatic organ of the mammalian body and has functions which include removal of metabolic waste products and 'foreign' molecules; regulation of the chemical composition of body fluids by removal of substances in excess of immediate requirements; regulation of the water content of body fluids, and thus the volume of the body fluids, and regulation of the pH of body fluids.

The kidney has a rich blood supply and regulates the blood composition at a steady state. This ensures that the composition of the tissue fluid, and consequently the cells bathed by it, is maintained at a level which coincides with the optimal conditions of the cells and enables them to function effectively and efficiently at all times.

19.5.1   Position and structure of kidneys

There are a pair of kidneys in humans situated at the back of the abdominal cavity, on either side of the vertebral column, in the region of the thoracic and lumbar vertebrae. Each kidney weighs about 0.5% of the total body mass, and the left kidney lies slightly anterior to the right.

The kidneys receive blood from the aorta via the **renal arteries**, and the **renal veins** return blood to the inferior vena cava. Urine formed in the kidneys passes by a pair of **ureters** to the **urinary bladder** where it is stored until it can be released conveniently via the **urethra**.

Fig 19.16 *TS through mammalian kidney showing the position of a cortical nephron and a juxtamedullary nephron*

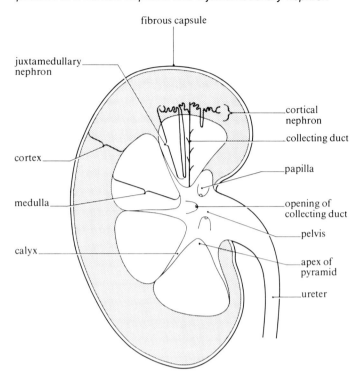

A transverse section of the kidney shows two distinct regions, an outer **cortex** and an inner **medulla** (fig 19.16). The cortex is covered by a fibrous capsule, and contains glomeruli which are just visible to the naked eye. The medulla is composed of tubules, collecting ducts and blood vessels grouped together to form **renal pyramids**. The apices of the pyramids are called **papillae**, and they project into the **pelvis** which is the expanded origin of the ureter (fig 19.16). A large number of blood vessels run through the kidney and supply a vast network of blood capillaries.

19.5.2   Nephron – gross structure and blood supply

The basic structural and functional unit of the kidney is the nephron and its associated blood supply. Each kidney, in a human, contains an estimated one million nephrons each having an approximate length of 3 cm. This offers an enormous surface area for the exchange of materials.

Each nephron is composed of six regions having strikingly different anatomical features and physiological functions:
(1) renal corpuscle (Malpighian body), composed of Bowman's capsule and glomerulus,
(2) proximal convoluted tubule,
(3) descending limb of the loop of Henle,
(4) ascending limb of the loop of Henle,
(5) distal convoluted tubule, and
(6) collecting duct.
The structural relationship between these regions is shown in fig 19.17.

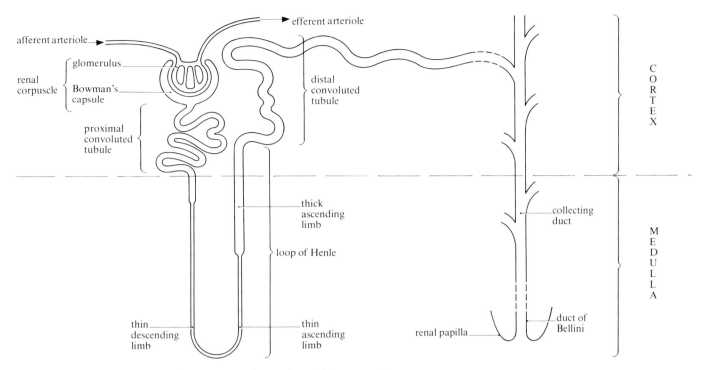

Fig 19.17 *Diagram showing the structure of a nephron. (Not to scale.)*

There are two types of nephrons, cortical nephrons and juxtamedullary nephrons, which differ in their positions in the kidney. **Cortical nephrons** are found in the cortex and have relatively short loops of Henle which just extend into the medulla. **Juxtamedullary nephrons** have their renal corpuscle close to (= *juxta*) the junction of the cortex and medulla. They have long descending and ascending tubules of the loop of Henle which extend deep into the medulla (fig 19.18). The significance of the two types of nephrons relates to differences in their use. Under normal conditions of water availability the cortical nephrons deal with the control of plasma volume, whereas when water is in short

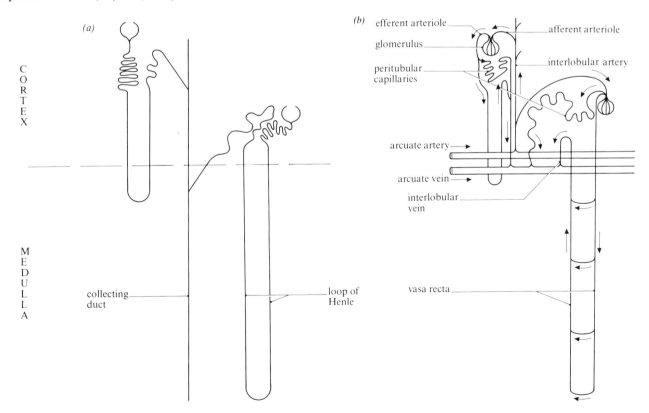

Fig 19.18 *Nephrons and their associated blood supply; (a) cortical nephron, (b) juxtamedullary nephron*

713

supply increased water retention occurs through the juxtamedullary nephrons.

Blood enters the kidney by the renal artery which progressively branches into interlobar arteries, arcuate arteries and interlobular arteries before passing to the glomerulus of the renal corpuscle as an afferent arteriole. A reduced volume of blood leaves the glomerulus by an efferent arteriole and flows through a network of peritubular capillaries in the cortex which surround the proximal and distal convoluted tubules of all nephrons and the loop of Henle of cortical nephrons. Arising from these capillaries are the capillaries of the vasa recta which run parallel to the loops of Henle and the collecting ducts in the medulla. The function of both of these vascular networks is to return blood, containing substances which are useful to the body, to the general circulation. Blood flow through the vasa recta is much less than through the peritubular capillaries and this enables a high solute potential to be maintained in the interstitial tissue of the medulla. This high solute potential is vital in producing a concentrated urine.

19.5.3 The role of the kidney

Apart from their function in the removal of metabolic waste, the kidneys are **homeostatic** organs and maintain the body fluid composition at a steady state despite wide fluctuations in water and salt uptake. A shortage of water, excess water uptake, excessive sweating, a shortage of salts or excess of salts would all have serious consequences for the body if the kidney was unable to adapt its function to these changes. Yet it is only the last two regions of the nephron, the distal convoluted tubule and the collecting ducts, where changes in function occur to regulate the body fluid composition. The rest of the nephron up to the distal convoluted tubule is *stereotyped* and functions in the same way in all physiological states. The waste product of kidney function is urine whose volume and composition varies, reflecting the physiological state of the body. Normally there is a copious supply of dilute urine, but at times when the body is short of water a concentrated urine is produced.

19.5.4 Basic principles of kidney function

A logical explanation of kidney function based on following the course of filtrate through the nephron is made difficult because events in one region of the nephron have important consequences for events in its other regions.

Urine formation and the regulation of the steady state of the body is a dynamic process involving the removal of substances from one part of the nephron to another, such as the collecting duct to ascending limb, and from nephron to capillaries surrounding the nephron.

The purpose of this section is to outline the general principles which underlie nephron function in terms of processes and mechanisms. This provides a background for the detailed study of later sections.

Processes

(1) **Ultrafiltration.** All small molecules, such as water, glucose and urea, are filtered out of the blood plasma in the glomerulus and produce a filtrate in Bowman's capsule which passes into the tubule of the nephron.

(2) **Selective reabsorption.** All substances useful to the body and required to maintain the water and salt composition of the body fluid at a steady state are removed from the filtrate and reabsorbed into the blood capillaries, for example glucose in the proximal convoluted tubule.

(3) **Secretion.** Further substances not required by the body may be secreted into the filtrate, by cells of the nephron, before it leaves the kidney as urine, for example K^+, H^+ and NH_4^+ in the distal convoluted tubule.

Mechanisms

(1) **Active transport.** Molecules and ions are secreted into and out of the filtrate as described in (2) and (3) above, for instance the uptake of glucose into the peritubular capillaries surrounding the proximal tubule and the removal of NaCl from the thick ascending limb.

(2) **Differential permeability.** Various regions of the nephron are selectively permeable to ions, water and urea, for example the proximal tubules are relatively impermeable compared with the convoluted tubule; the permeability of the collecting duct can be modified by hormones.

(3) **Concentration gradients.** A concentration gradient, varying from 300 mOsm kg^{-1} of water in the cortex to 1 200 mOsm kg^{-1} of water at the papillae, is maintained within the interstitial region of the medulla in humans as a result of (1) and (2) above.

(4) **Passive diffusion and osmosis.** Sodium and chloride ions and urea molecules will diffuse either into or out of the filtrate, according to the concentration gradient, wherever the nephron is permeable to them. Water molecules will pass out of the filtrate into a concentrated fluid in the interstitial region of the kidney wherever the nephron is permeable to water.

(5) **Hormonal control.** The regulation of water balance in the body and salt excretion is achieved by the effects of hormones acting on the distal convoluted tubule and collecting ducts, such as anti-diuretic hormone, aldosterone and other hormones.

19.5.5 Methods of study of kidney function

Investigations into the functioning of the kidney may be carried out directly on the exposed kidney, as in the case of studying the formation of urine, or indirectly, by analysing the relative composition of plasma and urine.

The American physiologist A. N. Richards showed that the composition of plasma and glomerular filtrate was similar, by inserting micropipettes into the renal corpuscles of amphibian kidneys and removing samples of filtrate for analysis. Amphibian kidneys were used for these studies because their renal corpuscles are relatively large and near to the surface of the kidney. This technique of **renal micropuncture** and withdrawal of fluid has been extended to other parts of the nephron and to mammals where it has yielded much information concerning the functions of these various regions.

Despite these advances there are still many kidney functions which are far from clear, for example the function of the loop of Henle. In these cases current knowledge is only hypothetical and based upon models of how these functions *may* be carried out.

Various techniques, based on the measurement of plasma clearance, have been used to investigate the rates of filtration and reabsorption by the kidney and the rate of blood flow to the kidney. **Plasma clearance** is a measure of the rate at which substances are removed from the plasma by the kidney.

The rate at which plasma is filtered by the glomeruli, the **glomerular filtration rate** (GFR) can be calculated directly from the plasma clearance value for a substance, such as the polysaccharide inulin $(C_6H_{10}O_5)_n$, which is filtered from the blood and not reabsorbed or secreted. In humans the glomerular filtration rate for both kidneys is about 125 cm³ per minute.

19.5.6 Nephron – structure and function

The **renal corpuscle** consists of a blind-ending tube which invaginates to form a double-walled epithelial capsule called **Bowman's capsule**. This encloses the **glomerulus**, consisting of a knot of about 50 parallel capillaries originating from a single afferent arteriole and rejoining to form an efferent arteriole (fig 19.19). The entire structure of the renal corpuscle is related to its function of filtering blood. The capillary walls are composed of a single layer of endothelial cells with openings between them of diameter 50–100 nm. These cells are pressed up against a **basement membrane** (basal lamina) which completely envelops each capillary and forms the only continuous structure separating the blood in the capillary from the lumen of Bowman's capsule (fig 19.20). The inner layer of Bowman's capsule is composed of cells called **podocytes** (*podos*, foot; *cytos*, cell) and these resemble starfish in having arms (**primary processes**) which give off structures resembling tube-feet called **secondary** or **foot processes**. The foot processes support the basement membrane and capillary beneath it and gaps of 25 nm between the foot processes, called **slit-pores**, facilitate the process of filtration. The outer cells of Bowman's capsule are unspecialised squamous epithelial cells (figs 19.21 and 19.22).

Ultrafiltration is the removal from the blood of all substances with a molecular mass (**RFM**) less than 68 000 and the formation of a fluid called **glomerular filtrate**.

Both kidneys receive a total of about 1 200 cm³ of

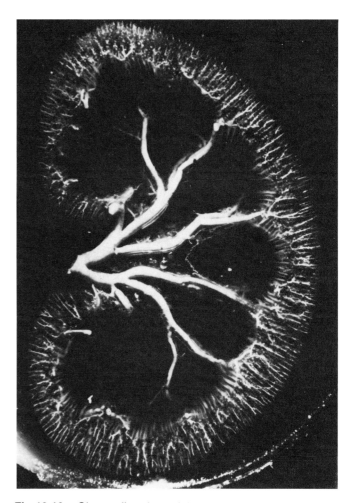

Fig 19.19 *Glomeruli and arterioles of dog kidney injected with silicone rubber. The tissues have been dissolved away*

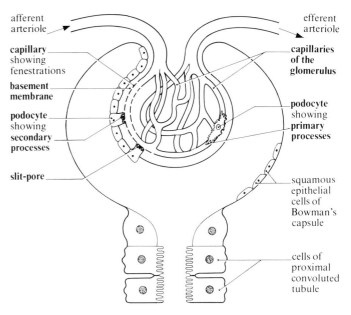

Fig 19.20 *Diagram of a renal corpuscle showing typical cells of the glomerulus and Bowman's capsule*

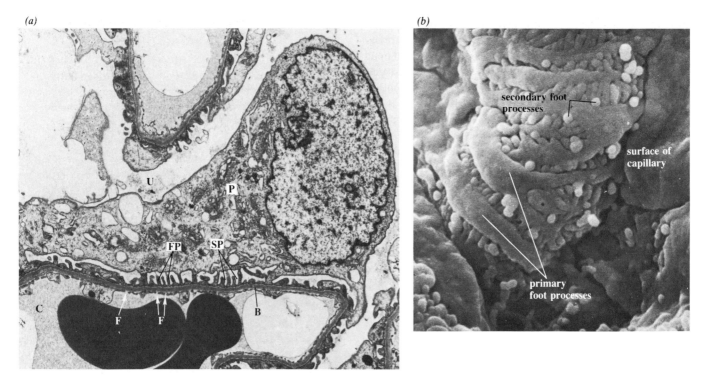

Fig 19.21 *(a) Electronmicrograph showing the structure of the glomerular capillary and wall of Bowman's capsule. Lumen of capillary (C) contains plasma which passes through fenestrations in the capillary wall as indicated by the arrows. (B) is the basement membrane which acts as the filter between the capillary (C) and the cavity of Bowman's capsule (U). Foot processes (FP) of a podocyte (P) rest on the basement membrane and slit-pores (SP) can be seen between the foot processes. (b) Scanning electron micrograph of glomerular capillary*

Fig 19.22 *Diagram showing the filtration path between the plasma in a glomerular capillary and the filtrate within the lumen of Bowman's capsule*

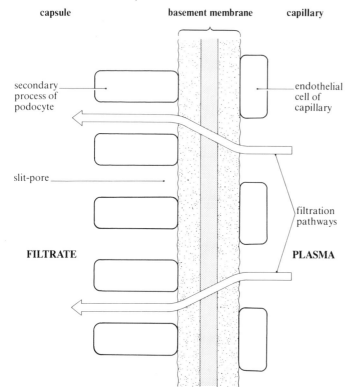

blood per minute which means that all the blood in the circulatory system passes through the kidney every 4–5 minutes. This volume of blood contains 700 cm^3 of plasma of which 125 cm^3 per minute is filtered out in the renal corpuscle. The substances forced out of the glomerular capillaries pass through the capillary fenestrations, basement membrane and slit-pores by the pressure developed within the capillaries. Most of the pressure is derived from the hydrostatic pressure of the circulating blood, but the effective pressure forcing fluid out of the glomerulus, the **filtration pressure**, is the result of a balance of other pressures shown in fig 19.23 and summarised by the expression:

$$\frac{\text{filtration}}{\text{pressure}} = \frac{\text{hydrostatic glomerular}}{\text{blood pressure}} - \left(\frac{\text{colloid solute}}{\text{potential}} + \frac{\text{hydrostatic glomerular}}{\text{filtrate pressure}}\right)$$

The blood pressure in the glomerular capillary can be varied by changes in the diameter of the afferent and efferent arterioles which are under nervous and hormonal control. Constriction of the efferent arteriole decreases the blood flow out of the glomerulus, raises the hydrostatic pressure within the glomerulus and, if the condition persists, it leads to substances with molecular masses (RFM) greater than about 68 000 entering the glomerular filtrate.

Glomerular filtrate has a chemical composition similar to

that of blood plasma. It contains glucose, amino acids, vitamins, some hormones, urea, uric acid, creatinine, ions and water. White and red blood corpuscles, platelets and plasma protein molecules, such as albumins and globulins, are prevented from passing out of the glomerulus by the basement membrane which acts as a filter. Blood passing from the glomerulus has an increased colloid solute potential due to the increased concentration of plasma proteins and a reduced hydrostatic pressure.

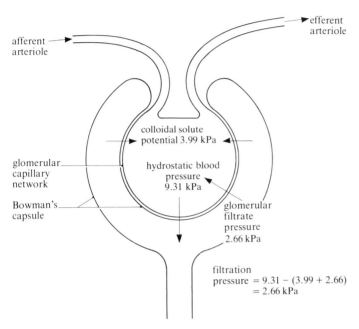

Fig 19.23 *The direction and magnitude of pressures influencing the filtration pressure in the human glomerulus*

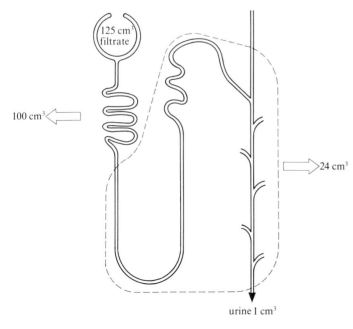

Fig 19.24 *Diagram showing the principal regions of reabsorption of renal filtrate*

The kidney tubules and selective reabsorption and secretion

Ultrafiltration produces a steady supply of glomerular filtrate, about 125 cm³ per minute in humans. If this was removed as urine it would produce 180 dm³ per day. Since only 1 500 cm³ of urine is produced each day, a great deal of reabsorption must occur. In fact, of the 125 cm³ of filtrate produced per minute 124 cm³ is reabsorbed. The main regions of reabsorption are shown in fig 19.24.

Ultrafiltration is an entirely passive and indiscriminate (in terms of substances which are valuable) process. Substances which are useful and vital are removed from the plasma along with excretory and other 'waste' substances. The function of the kidney tubules is to selectively reabsorb substances of further use to the body and those required to maintain the composition of the body fluids at a steady rate. Further waste substances may be added to the tubules by active secretion from the blood capillaries surrounding the tubules.

Proximal convoluted tubule. The proximal convoluted tubule is the longest (14 mm) and widest (60 μm) part of the nephron and conveys filtrate from Bowman's capsule to the loop of Henle. It is composed of a single layer of epithelial cells with extensive microvilli about 1 μm in length forming a brush border on the surface lining the tubule. The outer membrane of the epithelial cell rests on a basement membrane and is invaginated to form a labyrinth of **basal channels**. Adjacent membranes of tubule cells are separated by intercellular spaces and fluid circulates through basal channels and intercellular spaces as shown in fig 19.25. This fluid bathes and links the cells of the proximal convoluted tubule and the surrounding network of peritubular capillaries. The proximal convoluted tubule cells have numerous mitochondria concentrated near the basement membrane where they provide ATP for membrane-bound carrier molecules involved in active transport.

Selective reabsorption. The large surface area, the numerous mitochondria of the proximal convoluted tubule cells and the proximity of the peritubular capillaries are adaptations for the reabsorption of substances from the glomerular filtrate. Over 80% of the glomerular filtrate is reabsorbed here, including all the glucose, amino acids, vitamins, hormones and 85% of the sodium chloride and water. The mechanism of reabsorption occurs as follows. (1) Glucose, amino acids and ions that have diffused into the cells of the proximal convoluted tubule from the filtrate are actively transported out of the cells and into the intercellular spaces and basal channels by carrier mechanisms in the cell membranes. (2) Once in these spaces and channels they enter the extremely permeable peritubular capillaries by diffusion and are carried away from the nephron. (3) The constant removal of these substances from the proximal convoluted tubule cells creates a diffusion gradient between the filtrate in the

Fig 19.25 *Diagram showing the suggested mechanism of reabsorption of glomerular filtrate solutes, such as glucose, from the lumen of the proximal convoluted tubule into the surrounding peritubular capillaries. The carrier molecules of active transport mechanisms are thought to be situated in the basement membrane. The numbers apply to the description of glucose uptake given in the text*

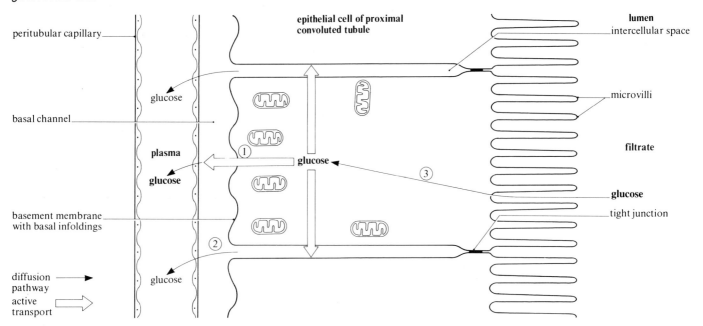

lumen and the cells, down which further substances pass. Once inside the cells they are actively transported into the spaces and channels and the cycle continues.

The active uptake of sodium and accompanying anions reduces the solute potential in the tubular filtrate and an equivalent amount of water passes into the peritubular capillaries by osmosis. Most of the filtered solutes and water are removed from the filtrate at a fairly constant rate. This produces a filtrate in the tubule which is isosmotic with blood plasma in the peritubular capillaries.

About 50% of the urea from the filtrate is reabsorbed, by diffusion, into the peritubular capillaries and passes back into the general circulation whilst the remainder is excreted in the urine.

Small molecular mass (RFM) proteins, that is those less than 68 000, passing into the tubule during ultrafiltration are removed by pinocytosis at the base of the microvilli. They are enclosed in pinocytotic vacuoles to which primary lysosomes (section 7.2.8) are attached. Hydrolytic enzymes in the lysosomes digest the proteins to amino acids which are either utilised by the tubule cells or passed on, by diffusion, to the peritubular capillaries.

Finally, active secretion of creatinine and 'foreign' substances occurs in this region. These substances are transported from the interstitial fluid bathing the tubules into the tubular filtrate and eventually removed in the urine.

19.5.7 Urine formation

Urine is formed by the exchange of solutes and water between the filtrate leaving the proximal convoluted tubule and all the structures distal to it (table 19.7).

Table 19.7 The composition of plasma and urine and changes in concentration occurring during urine formation in humans.

	Plasma %	Urine %	Increase
water	90	95	—
protein	8	0	—
glucose	0.1	0	—
urea	0.03	2	67×
uric acid	0.004	0.05	12×
creatinine	0.001	0.075	75×
Na^+	0.32	0.35	1×
NH_4^+	0.0001	0.04	400×
K^+	0.02	0.15	7×
Mg^{2+}	0.0025	0.01	4×
Cl^-	0.37	0.60	2×
PO_4^{3-}	0.009	0.27	30×
SO_4^{2-}	0.002	0.18	90×

The ability to produce a urine of lower solute potential is found only in the two groups of vertebrates, the birds and mammals, which possess a loop of Henle. The concentration of urine produced is directly related to the length of the loop of Henle and the thickness of the medulla relative to the cortex, which both increase progressively in animals living in drier habitats. For example, the beaver (*Castor*), a semi-aquatic mammal, has a thin medulla, a short loop of Henle and produces a large volume of dilute urine (600 mOsm kg^{-1} of water), whereas the desert-dwelling kangaroo rat (*Dipodomys*) and the jerboa (hopping mouse – *Dipus*) have thick medullas, long loops of Henle and produce small volumes of highly concentrated urine (6 000 and 9 000 mOsm kg^{-1} of water, respectively).

Descending and ascending limbs of the loop of Henle

Before describing the structure and detailed function of the various regions of the loop of Henle it is necessary to describe its overall function. The loop of Henle, in conjunction with the capillaries of the vasa recta and collecting duct, creates and maintains an increasing osmotic gradient in the medulla from the cortex to the papilla due to the build-up of increasing concentrations of sodium chloride and urea. This, in turn, provides the conditions for the progressive removal of water, by osmosis, from the tubule into the interstitial region of the medulla. The reabsorbed water is then removed from the medulla by the blood vessels of the vasa recta. Consequently a more concentrated urine is produced in the collecting duct.

At present the precise mechanism by which the loop of Henle concentrates sodium chloride towards the papilla of the medulla is not completely understood. The extent of the permeability of the descending tubule to sodium chloride is not yet understood, and whilst this affects the precise details of the mechanism it does not alter what has been described above, or what follows. The movement of ions, urea and water between the loop of Henle, vasa recta and collecting duct is described by the following points which refer to fig 19.26. (1) The first part of the descending limb is short, relatively wide (30 μm) and impermeable to ions, urea and water. It conveys filtrate from the proximal convoluted tubule to the longer, **thin** (12 μm) **descending**

Fig 19.26 *Summary diagram showing the movement of ions, urea and water in the medulla that produce an increasing osmotic gradient within the medulla. The numbers in boxes are the osmotic concentrations in mOsm kg^{-1} water. The numbers in circles refer to details in the text. The tonicity shown in various regions of the nephron is relative to blood plasma outside the kidney*

limb which is freely permeable to water. (2) Since the interstitial region of the medulla is more concentrated due to high concentrations of sodium chloride and urea, water is drawn out of the filtrate by osmosis and carried away by the vasa recta. (3) This reduces the volume of the filtrate by 5% and makes it more concentrated. At the apex of the medulla (the papilla) the descending limb of the loop of Henle makes a hairpin turn and becomes the ascending limb which is impermeable to water along its entire length. (4) The first part of the ascending limb, the **thin ascending limb**, is permeable to sodium chloride and urea. Sodium chloride diffuses out of the limb as it passes away from the more concentrated region of the medulla towards the cortex whereas urea diffuses into the limb. (5) The epithelium of the **thick ascending limb** is composed of flattened cuboidal cells with a rudimentary brush border and many mitochondria. These cells are the site of the active transport of sodium and chloride ions out of the filtrate. (6) The loss of sodium and chloride ions from the filtrate increases the concentration of the medulla and results in a more dilute filtrate passing to the distal convoluted tubule.

The loop of Henle as a countercurrent multiplier

The loop of Henle functions as a countercurrent multiplier for the following reasons:
(1) the close proximity of the descending and ascending limbs,
(2) the permeability of the descending limb to water,
(3) the impermeability of the descending limb to solutes,
(4) the permeability of the thin ascending limb to solutes, and
(5) the active transport mechanisms of the thick ascending limb.

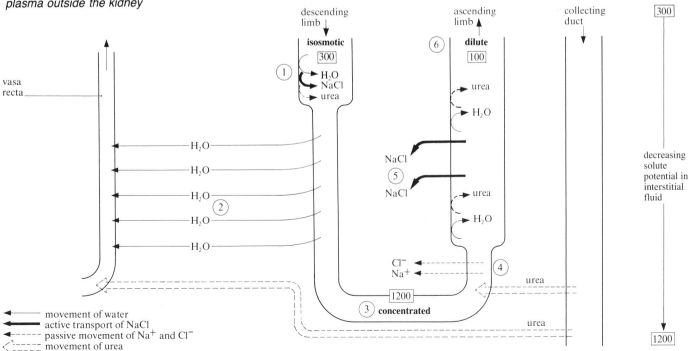

719

The values for osmotic concentrations of the filtrate in both limbs also suggest that the loop of Henle functions as a countercurrent multiplier. In such a system the concentration difference at any given level between the fluids in the ascending and descending limbs may be slight, but as this is maintained over a long distance, as in the loop of Henle, the difference becomes additive so that the final concentration of filtrate at the base of the loop is much greater than at either end. The longer the loop the greater the concentration difference.

The removal of sodium chloride from the ascending limb increases the concentration of the interstitial region of the medulla and water is drawn out of the descending limb. This water immediately passes into the vasa recta, thereby maintaining high concentrations of solutes in the interstitial region and in the filtrate, as shown in fig 19.27. Filtrate flows around the loop and countercurrent exchange continues. The constant cycling of solutes, both passively and actively, ensures a permanently high concentration of sodium chloride in the medulla. At the same time another system, a **countercurrent exchange** system (see below), operates in the vasa recta, and these two countercurrent mechanisms operate together to ensure the gradient of concentration in the medulla.

Fig 19.27 *Model illustrating the countercurrent multiplier formed by the tubules of the loop of Henle. Na$^+$ and Cl$^-$ ions are actively transported out of the thick ascending limb into the interstitial region. The solute concentration of the interstitial region rises. Water leaves the descending limb. The numbers indicate the osmotic concentration in mOsm kg^{-1} water. An arbitrary concentration gradient of 200 mOsm kg^{-1} water exists between descending and ascending limbs in the model*

The vasa recta as a countercurrent exchanger

The narrow descending capillary and wider ascending capillary of the vasa recta run parallel to each other and give off branched loops at different levels along their length. They are situated close to the limbs of the loop of Henle but substances are *not* transferred directly from limbs to blood vessels. Instead they pass through the interstitial region of the medulla where, due to the slow rate of blood flow through the vasa recta, sodium chloride and urea are trapped and an osmotic gradient is maintained. The cells of the vasa recta are freely permeable to ions, urea and water, and as the vessels run side by side they function as a countercurrent exchange system. As the descending capillary *enters* the medulla the progressively decreasing solute potential of the interstitial region draws water out of the plasma in the capillary by osmosis, and sodium chloride and urea enter by diffusion (fig 19.28). As blood flows from the medulla in the ascending capillary the reverse happens and the increasing solute potential of the interstitial region enables water to re-enter the plasma whilst sodium chloride and urea leave. The adaptive significance of this mechanism is that it allows the osmotic concentration of plasma *leaving* the kidney to remain at a steady state irrespective of the osmotic concentration of plasma *entering* the kidney. Finally, and most importantly, since all the movements of solutes and water are passive, the vasa recta countercurrent exchanger makes no metabolic demand on the kidney.

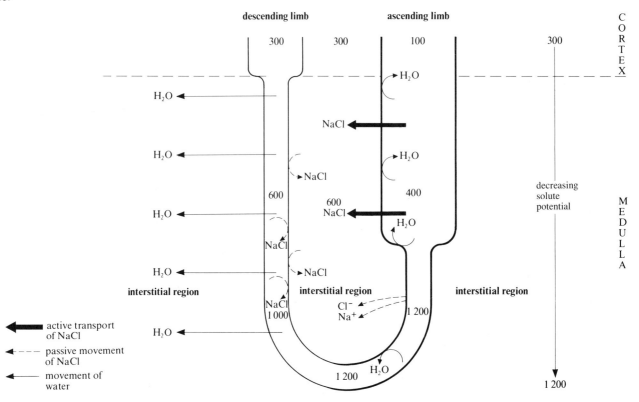

Fig 19.28 *The passive movement of water, ions and urea between adjacent vessels of the vasa recta and between these and the interstitial fluid of the medulla. The vessels of the vasa recta form a countercurrent exchange system. All values are given in mOsm kg^{-1} water*

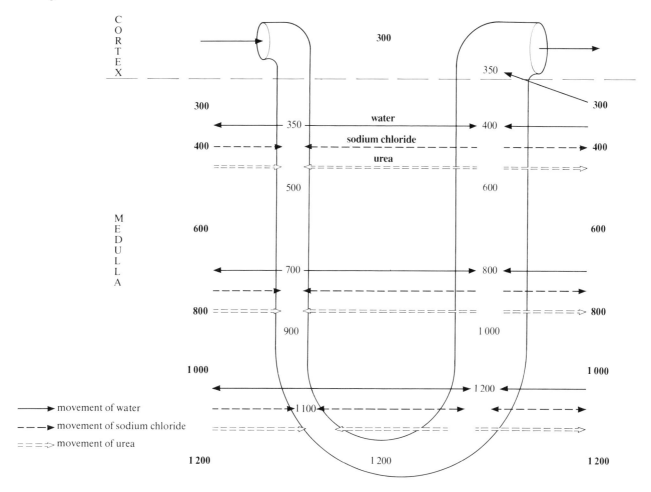

Distal convoluted tubule

The distal convoluted tubule loops backward towards the renal corpuscle and passes through the cortex. The cells of the distal tubule have brush borders and abundant mitochondria and this region is the site of the mechanisms for the fine control of salt, water and pH balance of the blood. The hormonal control of the permeability of the distal convoluted tubule to water is linked to that of the collecting duct; the two are described later. The control of salt and pH balance are described in section 19.7.

Collecting duct

The collecting tubule passes from the distal convoluted tubule in the cortex down through the medulla where it joins up with several other ducts to form larger ducts, the **ducts of Bellini**. The permeability of the walls of the duct to water and urea is controlled by **anti-diuretic hormone** (ADH), and together with the distal convoluted tubule these structures can produce a concentrated or dilute urine according to the body's demand for water.

19.6 Anti-diuretic hormone (ADH) and the formation of a concentrated or dilute urine

The body maintains the solute potential of the blood at an approximately steady state by balancing water uptake from the diet with water lost in evaporation, sweating, egestion and urine. The precise control of solute potential, however, is achieved primarily by the effect of ADH on the permeability of the distal convoluted tubule and collecting duct.

When small amounts of water are ingested, or excessive sweating occurs, or large amounts of salt are ingested, osmoreceptors in the hypothalamus detect a fall in blood solute potential. Nerve impulses are set up and pass to the posterior pituitary gland where ADH (vasopressin) is released. ADH increases the permeabilities of the distal convoluted tubule and collecting duct, water is withdrawn from the filtrate into the cortex and medulla and a reduced

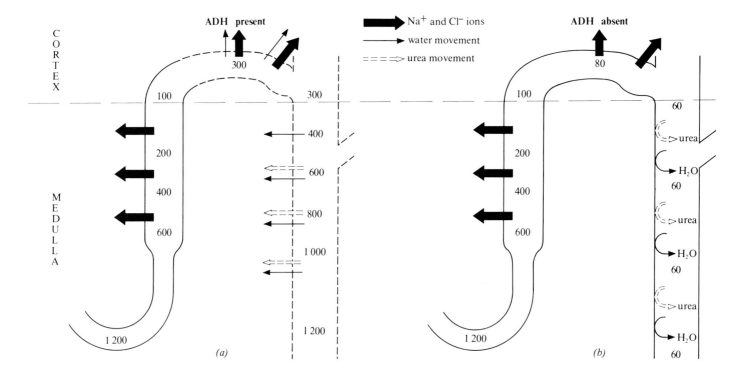

Fig 19.29 *Diagram illustrating the effect of ADH on the permeabilities of the distal convoluted tubule and collecting duct to water and urea*

volume of concentrated urine ($1\,000\,\text{mOsm}\,\text{kg}^{-1}$ of water) is released from the kidney.

ADH also increases the permeability of the collecting duct to urea, which diffuses out of the urine into the interstitial region of the medulla. Here it increases the osmotic concentration resulting in the removal of an increased volume of water from the thin descending limb (fig 19.29).

When there is a high intake of water and the solute potential of the blood begins to rise ADH release is inhibited, the walls of the distal convoluted tubule and collecting duct become impermeable to water, less water is reabsorbed as the filtrate passes through the medulla and a large volume of dilute urine is excreted (fig 19.29).

Table 19.8 shows a summary of the events involved in regulating water balance, and the control mechanisms involved in regulating water and salt balance are shown in fig 19.30.

Failure to release sufficient ADH leads to a condition known as **diabetes insipidus** in which large quantities of dilute urine are produced (diuresis). The fluid lost in the urine has to be replaced by excessive drinking.

Table 19.8. Summary of the changes produced in the epithelium of the distal convoluted tubule and collecting duct in response to ADH

Blood solute potential	ADH	Epithelium	Urine
falls	released	permeable	concentrated
rises	not released	impermeable	dilute

19.7 Control of blood sodium level

The maintenance of the plasma sodium level at a steady state is controlled by the hormone **aldosterone** which secondarily influences water reabsorption. A decrease in blood volume stemming from a loss of sodium stimulates a group of secretory cells, the **juxtaglomerular complex**, situated between the distal convoluted tubule and the afferent arteriole to release an enzyme, **renin**. Renin activates a plasma globulin, produced in the liver, to form the active hormone **angiotensin** and this releases aldosterone from the adrenal cortex. This stimulates the active uptake of sodium from the filtrate into the plasma in the peritubular capillaries. This uptake of sodium ions causes the reabsorption of an osmotically equivalent amount of water.

19.7.1 Homeostatic control of plasma, water and sodium levels

When the body has free access to water and a normal sodium diet, no ADH or aldosterone is released and the epithelium of the distal convoluted tubule and collecting duct remains impermeable to ions, urea and water and the urine is copious and dilute, a condition known as diuresis. The homeostatic control mechanisms are summarised in fig 19.30.

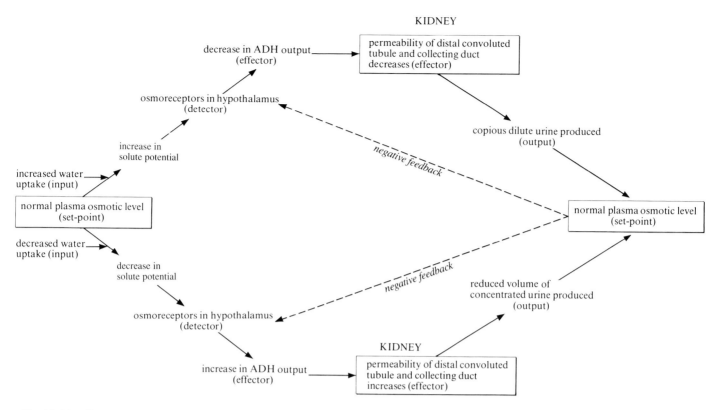

Fig 19.30 *Summary diagram of the control of plasma solute potential*

19.8   Control of blood pH

Hydrogencarbonate and phosphate buffers in the blood prevent excess hydrogen ions (H^+), produced by metabolic activities, from decreasing the pH of the blood. Carbon dioxide released into the blood during respiration is regulated by this system and prevented from causing changes in plasma pH prior to its excretion from the lungs. Excessive changes in blood chemistry which would change the plasma pH from its normal level of 7.4, however, are counteracted by the distal convoluted tubule. This excretes hydrogen ions and retains hydrogencarbonate ions if the pH falls, and excretes hydrogen carbonate ions and retains

hydrogen ions if the pH rises. This may produce changes in the pH of the urine from 4.5 to 8.5. A fall in pH also stimulates the kidney cells to produce the base ion ammonia (NH_4^+) which combines with acids brought to the kidney and is then excreted as ammonium salts.

Computer program. NEPHRON (CUP Micro Software) allows the user to investigate the functioning of the kidney at three structural levels. Changes in the composition of the glomerular filtrate during its passage from the glomerulus to the collecting ducts, for different initial conditions, can be followed, as well as investigation of special cases such as water diabetes and sugar diabetes.

Chapter Twenty

Reproduction

The ability to reproduce, that is to produce a new generation of individuals of the same species, is one of the fundamental characteristics of living organisms. It involves the transmission of genetic material from the parental generation to the next generation, thereby ensuring that the characteristics, not only of the species but also of the parental organisms, are perpetuated. The significance of reproduction in a given species is to replace those members of the species that die, thus ensuring continuity of the species, and also to allow increase in total numbers of the species where conditions are suitable.

A new individual normally has to go through a period of growth and development before it reaches the stage at which it can reproduce itself (chapter 21). Some members of a species will die before they reach reproductive age, due to predation, disease and accidental death, so that a species will only survive if each generation produces more offspring than the parental generation. Population sizes will fluctuate according to the balance between rate of reproduction and rate of death of individuals (section 12.6). There are a number of different reproductive strategies, all with certain advantages and disadvantages which are described in this chapter.

20.1 Asexual and sexual reproduction

There are two basic types of reproduction, asexual and sexual. **Asexual** reproduction is reproduction by a single organism without production of gametes. It usually results in the production of identical offspring, the only genetic variation arising as a result of random mutations among the individuals.

Genetic variation is advantageous to a species because it provides the 'raw material' for natural selection, and hence evolution. Offspring showing most adaptations to the environment will have a competitive advantage over the other members of the species and be more likely to survive and pass on their genes to the next generation. The species therefore has the capacity to change, that is to undergo speciation (section 25.7). Increased variation can be achieved by the mixing of genes from two different individuals, a process known as genetic recombination. This is the essential feature of **sexual** reproduction and occurs in a primitive form in some bacteria (section 2.2.4).

20.1.1 Asexual reproduction

Asexual reproduction is the production of offspring from a single organism without the fusion of gametes. Except in plants with alternation of generations (section 3.3.1), meiosis is not involved and the offspring are identical to the parent. Identical offspring from a single parent are referred to as a **clone**. Members of a clone only differ genetically as a result of random mutation. Most animal species do not naturally reproduce asexually, though recent successful attempts, discussed later, have been made to clone certain species artificially.

There are several types of asexual reproduction. Further details of the process in some of the individuals referred to below are given in the relevant sections of chapters 2, 3 and 4.

Fission

Fission occurs in unicellular organisms and is the division of the cell into two or more daughter cells identical to the parent cell. Replication of DNA and, in the case of eukaryotes, nuclear division precedes cell division. Normally two identical daughter cells are produced, a process called **binary fission**. This occurs in bacteria, many protoctistans, such as *Amoeba* and *Paramecium*, and in some euglenoid flagellates, for example *Euglena*. Under suitable conditions it results in rapid population growth, as described in section 2.2.4 for bacteria.

Multiple fission, in which repeated divisions of the parent nucleus are followed by division into many daughter cells, occurs in the Apicomplexa, a group of protoctistans including the malaria parasite *Plasmodium*. The stage undergoing multiple fission is called the schizont and the splitting process schizogony. In *Plasmodium* schizogony occurs imediately after infection when the parasite enters the liver. About 1 000 daughter cells are released, each capable of invading a red blood cell and producing up to a further 24 daughter cells by schizogony. Such prolific powers of reproduction compensate for the large losses associated with the difficulties of successful transfer between hosts, namely humans and the vector organism, the mosquito.

Spore formation (sporulation)

A spore is a small reproductive unit which is usually microscopic and unicellular, containing a small amount of cytoplasm and a nucleus. Spores are produced by bacteria, protoctistans, all groups of algae and green plants and all groups of fungi. They vary in type and function and are

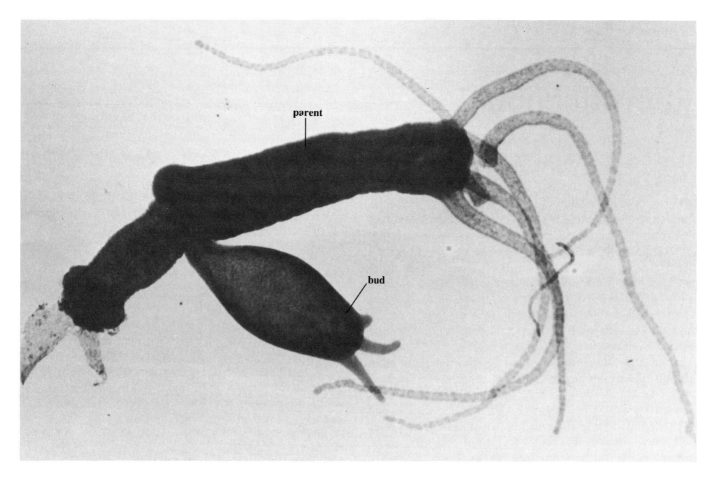

parent

bud

often produced in special structures. For example, spores of *Rhizopus* and *Dryopteris* are produced in sporangia; the microspores (pollen) and megaspores (embryo sacs) of seed-bearing plants are produced in sporangia called pollen sacs and ovules respectively.

Often spores are produced in large numbers and are very light, being dispersed easily by air currents as well as by animals, particularly insects. Being small they usually have minimal food stores and there is great wastage as many fail to find a suitable place for germination. In these cases they are primarily a means of rapid multiplication and spread of species, particularly of fungi.

Strictly speaking, the spores of bacteria are not reproductive structures but means of surviving adverse conditions, since each bacterium produces only one spore. Bacterial spores are among the most resistant known. For instance, they will often survive strong disinfectants and boiling in water.

Although this section is concerned with asexual reproduction, it should be pointed out that some spores are sexual spores, that is they take part in sexual reproduction. Examples are the zoospores of *Chlamydomonas* which sometimes function as gametes, and the zygospores of *Rhizopus* and *Spirogyra*. Zygospores are products of sexual reproduction and are relatively large spores with food stores and a protective outer coat. They can remain dormant during periods of adverse conditions.

Fig 20.1 *(above) Budding of* Hydra, *a cnidarian*

Fig 20.2 *(below) Asexual reproduction in* Bryophyllum. *Young plantlets are seen along the leaf margins*

Note that one organism may produce more than one type of spore, for example *Rhizopus* produces sexual and asexual spores, whilst most other plants produce micro- and megaspores in an asexual process.

Budding

Budding is a form of asexual reproduction in which a new individual is produced as an outgrowth (bud) of the parent, and is later released as a self-supporting, identical copy of the parent. It takes place in a number of groups of organisms, notably the cnidarians, for example *Hydra* (fig 20.1), and unicellular fungi, such as yeasts. In the latter case budding differs from fission, which also occurs, in that the two parts produced are not of equal size.

An unusual form of budding is shown by the succulent plant *Bryophyllum*, a xerophyte commonly used as a decorative houseplant. It forms miniature plants, complete with small roots, along the margins of its leaves (fig 20.2). These 'buds' eventually fall off and establish themselves as independent plants.

Fragmentation

Fragmentation is the breaking of an organism into two or more parts, each of which grows to form a new individual. Fragmentation occurs in filamentous algae, such as *Spirogyra*. Here breakage into two may occur anywhere along the length of the filament.

Fragmentation also occurs among certain lower animals which, unlike less differentiated animals, retain strong powers of regeneration from relatively undifferentiated cells. For example, the bodies of ribbon worms, a group of primitive, mainly marine worms, break up particularly easily into many pieces, each of which can regenerate a new individual. While in this case the process is a natural and controlled one, there are examples of animals that normally only regenerate as a result of accidental fragmentation, such as starfish. These animals have been the subjects of experiments on regeneration, a commonly used example being the free-living flatworm *Planaria*. These experiments have contributed to our understanding of the process of differentiation (section 22.8).

Vegetative propagation (vegetative reproduction)

Vegetative propagation or vegetative reproduction is a form of asexual reproduction in which a relatively large, usually differentiated part of a plant body becomes detached and develops into an independent plant. In essence it is similar to budding. Specialised structures often develop for the purpose, including bulbs, corms, rhizomes, stolons and tubers. Some of these also store food and are means of surviving adverse conditions, such as cold periods or drought. Plants possessing them can therefore survive from one year to the next and are either biennial, flowering and dying in their second year, or perennial, surviving from year to year. The structures are called **perennating organs**, and include bulbs, corms, rhizomes and tubers.

Perennating organs may be stems, roots, or whole shoots (buds), but in all cases the food stored is derived mainly from photosynthesis of the current year's foliage leaves. The food is translocated to the storage organ and then usually converted to an insoluble storage product such as starch. During the period of adverse conditions the aerial parts of the plant die and the perennating organ undergoes a period of dormancy underground. At the beginning of the next growing season the food reserves are mobilised by enzymes and buds become active, growing at the expense of the stored food. If more than one bud grows reproduction has taken place. This sequence of events is synchronised closely with the seasons, being controlled by such factors as day length (photoperiod) and temperature, environmental variables whose profound effects on growth and development are described in chapter 15.

Some of the organs of vegetative propagation and perennation are described below.

Bulb. A modified shoot, for example onion (*Allium*), daffodil (*Narcissus*) and tulip (*Tulipa*). An organ of perennation as well as vegetative propagation.

A bulb has a very short stem and fleshy storage leaves. It is surrounded by brown scaly leaves, the remains of previous year's leaves after their food stores have been used. The bulb contains one or more buds. If more than one grows, each forms a shoot which produces a new bulb at the end of the growing season, this being vegetative propagation. Roots are adventitious, that is they grow from the stem with no tap root.

A typical bulb is illustrated in fig 20.3.

Fig 20.3 *Diagrammatic section through a dormant bulb*

Corm. A short, swollen, vertical underground stem, as in *Crocus* and *Gladiolus*. An organ of perennation as well as vegetative propagation.

A corm consists of the swollen base of a stem surrounded by protective scale leaves; there are no fleshy leaves, unlike bulbs. Scale leaves are the remains of the previous season's foliage leaves. Roots are adventitious. At the end of the growing season contractile roots pull the new corm down into the soil. The corm contains one or more buds which may result in vegetative propagation (compare bulb).

A typical corm is illustrated in fig 20.4.

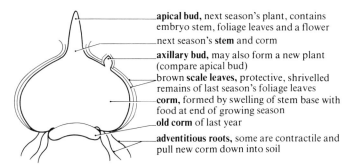

Fig 20.4 *Diagrammatic section through a dormant corm*

apical bud, next season's plant, contains embryo stem, foliage leaves and a flower

next season's **stem** and corm

axillary bud, may also form a new plant (compare apical bud)

brown **scale leaves**, protective, shrivelled remains of last season's foliage leaves

corm, formed by swelling of stem base with food at end of growing season

old corm of last year

adventitious roots, some are contractile and pull new corm down into soil

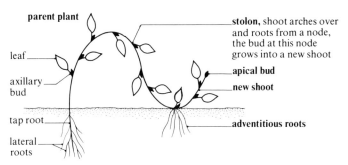

Fig 20.6 (above) *Generalised plan of a stolon*

parent plant

leaf

axillary bud

tap root

lateral roots

stolon, shoot arches over and roots from a node, the bud at this node grows into a new shoot

apical bud

new shoot

adventitious roots

Fig 20.7 (below) *Plan of a strawberry runner*

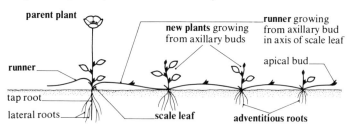

parent plant

runner

tap root

lateral roots

new plants growing from axillary buds

scale leaf

runner growing from axillary bud in axis of scale leaf

apical bud

adventitious roots

Rhizome. A horizontally growing underground stem, such as in *Iris*, Solomon's seal (*Polygonatum*), where it is short and swollen with stored food, and couch grass (*Agropyron repens*), mint (*Mentha*) and Michaelmas daisy (*Aster* spp.) where it is long and thin. It is usually an organ of perennation as well as vegetative propagation.

A rhizome bears leaves, buds, and adventitious roots. The leaves may be scale-like (small and thin, whitish or brownish in colour) as in couch grass, green foliage leaves only as in *Iris*, or a mixture of green and scale leaves as in Solomon's seal, where both types are borne on aerial shoots. An *Iris* rhizome is illustrated in fig 20.5.

Stolon. A creeping, horizontally growing stem that grows along the surface of the ground, for example blackberry (*Rubus*), gooseberry, blackcurrant and redcurrant (all *Ribes* spp.). It is not an organ of perennation. (See also runner below.) Roots are adventitious, growing from nodes.

A plan of a typical stolon is illustrated in fig 20.6.

Runner. A type of stolon that elongates rapidly, as in strawberry (*Fragaria*) and creeping buttercup (*Ranunculus repens*).

A runner bears scale leaves with axillary buds and the buds give rise to adventitious roots and new plants. The runners eventually decay once the new plants are estab-

lished. The runner may represent the main stem or grow from one of the lower axillary buds on the main stem, as illustrated in fig 20.7. In strawberry, scale leaves and axillary buds occur at every node, but roots and foliage leaves arise only at every other node. All axillary buds may give rise to new runners.

Tuber. A tuber is an underground storage organ, swollen with food and capable of perennation. Tubers survive only one year and shrivel as their contents are used during the growing season. New tubers are made at the end of the growing season, but do not arise from old tubers (in contrast to corms, which arise from old corms).

Stem tubers are stem structures produced at the tips of thin rhizomes, as in potato (*Solanum tuberosum*) and artichoke (*Helianthus tuberosum*). Their stem structure is revealed by the presence of axillary buds in the axils of scale leaves. Each bud may grow into a new plant during the next growing season.

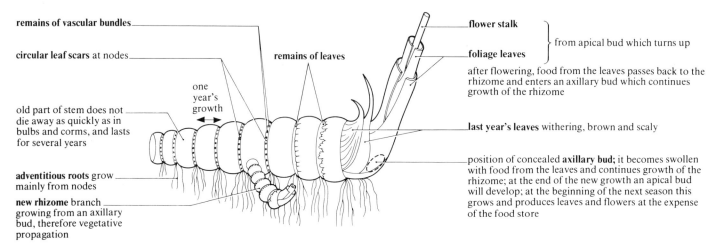

remains of vascular bundles

circular leaf scars at nodes

old part of stem does not die away as quickly as in bulbs and corms, and lasts for several years

adventitious roots grow mainly from nodes

new rhizome branch growing from an axillary bud, therefore vegetative propagation

one year's growth

remains of leaves

flower stalk

foliage leaves

from apical bud which turns up

after flowering, food from the leaves passes back to the rhizome and enters an axillary bud which continues growth of the rhizome

last year's leaves withering, brown and scaly

position of concealed **axillary bud**; it becomes swollen with food from the leaves and continues growth of the rhizome; at the end of the new growth an apical bud will develop; at the beginning of the next season this grows and produces leaves and flowers at the expense of the food store

Fig 20.5 *Diagrammatic structure of an Iris rhizome*

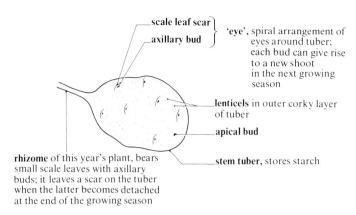

Fig 20.8 (above) Stem tuber of potato

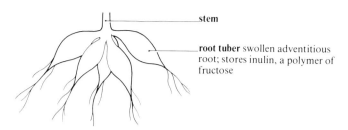

Fig 20.9 (above) Root tubers of Dahlia

Fig 20.10 (below) Tap roots of carrot and turnip

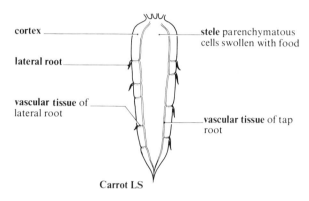

Carrot LS

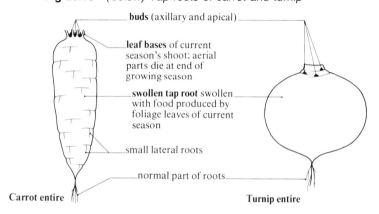

Root tubers are swollen adventitious roots, for example *Dahlia* and lesser celandine (*Ranunculus ficaria*). New plants develop from axillary buds at the base of the old stem.

A stem tuber of potato is illustrated in fig 20.8 and root tubers of *Dahlia* in fig 20.9.

Swollen tap roots. A tap root is a main root that has developed from the radicle, the first root of the seedling. Tap root systems are characteristic of dicotyledonous plants. Tap roots may become swollen with parenchymatous food-storing tissue, as in carrot (*Daucus*), parsnip (*Pastinaca*), swede (*Brassica napus*), turnip (*Brassica rapa*) and radish (*Raphanus sativus*). Together with buds at the base of the old stem, just above the tap root, they form organs of perennation and vegetative propagation. Two types of swollen tap root are shown in fig 20.10.

Swollen tap roots are characteristic of biennial plants, plants that grow vegetatively during the first year of growth and survive winter by means of an underground storage organ. They produce flowers and seeds during the second year of growth, at the end of which they die.

Apart from the specialised organs of vegetative propagation described above, some unmodified plant parts have the ability to regenerate new plants if detached from the parent plant, such as the fallen leaves of the succulent plant *Sedum*. The taking of cuttings by gardeners and horticulturalists can be regarded as a form of vegetative propagation.

Budding

Most roses are propagated by budding onto a suitable wood stock; a rapid method for satisfying the demand of the commercial markets for one of the world's most popular border plants. Vegetative buds are grafted onto, in July or August, the wood stock (either wild dog rose or rugosa). Garden roses do not breed true to type from seed. However all new roses (new introductions) are obtained by handmade crosses between selected parents.

Cuttings

Cuttings from blackcurrant bushes are taken in the autumn from well-ripened shoots formed in the previous summer. The cutting, about 20 cm long, is trimmed at the base just below a joint and inserted firmly in good soil outdoors. The cuttings root readily and can be transferred to their fruiting area the following autumn. Blackcurrants succeed well in most areas and are grown as a specialist crop for the home garden or commercially for their high content of vitamin C (fruit cordials).

Chrysanthemums, described as the queen of the autumn flowers and second only to the rose in popularity, are also propagated by cuttings, preferably taken from shoots which come through the soil directly from the roots.

Grafting

The original basis for the propagation of apple trees by grafting was that the plants could not easily be grown from soft cuttings and that the seedlings varied too much to be of any commercial value. By suitable choice of stock, to suit the variety of the apple being propagated and the commercial purposes for which it is required, the fruit grower can avoid problems such as unnecessary pruning later on.

Tissue culture and cloning of plants and animals

Tissue culture developed from earlier experiments which showed that the growth of cambial tissue excised from plants could be stimulated by the addition of nutrients and IAA. These new cells could be subcultured, but for continued cell division cytokinins were also required in the growth medium. The use of liquid culture allows continuous culturing of cells in the same vessel. Tissue culture is now widely used for the rapid propagation of desired varieties (such as date oil palms) or for varieties difficult to propagate by cuttings. Similar techniques have been developed for the tissue culture of animal cells.

Organisms produced from a single cell by subculturing (cloning) have an identical genetic constitution unless a mutation occurs among them. Cloning has the advantage that all the offspring behave similarly (for example uniform ripening of crops making harvesting easier) but should disease break out, no resistant strains or plants are present to lessen the impact. The use of cloned cells allows a quantitative study of the action of hormones, drugs and antibodies to be made on cells. Such a technique is a useful substitute for investigating the effects of drugs, cosmetics and pharmaceutical products on animal cells without exposing laboratory organisms such as rats, cats and dogs to these chemicals.

Cell hybridisation involves the fusion of the protoplasts or nuclei from two different cells and it is used for gene mapping and the study of the differentiation of cells during development.

Since the early 1960s techniques have been developed which have allowed successful cloning of certain plants and animals. These arose from attempts to demonstrate that the nuclei of mature, non-developing cells still contain all the information required to code for an entire organism and that cells become specialised as a result of the switching on and off of genes rather than by the loss of certain genes (section 22.7). The first success was achieved by Professor Steward of Cornell University, who showed that individual cells from a carrot root (the part we eat), when grown in a medium containing suitable nutrients and hormones, could be induced to start dividing again and to produce new carrot plants.

Success with higher animals followed shortly when Gurdon, working at Oxford University, achieved the first successful cloning of a vertebrate. The process does not occur naturally among vertebrates but, by taking a cell from the intestine of a frog and introducing its nucleus into an egg cell whose own nucleus had been destroyed by ultra-violet radiation, he was able to grow a tadpole, and

thence a frog, identical to the parent from which the nucleus was transplanted (fig 20.11).

Not only did experiments like these establish that differentiated (specialised) cells still contain all the information needed to make the whole organism, but they suggested that similar techniques might successfully be used in cloning more advanced vertebrates, including humans. The cloning of desirable animals such as prize bulls, racehorses and so on, might be as advantageous as the cloning of plants which it has been noted already takes place. However the application of the technique to humans would be open to serious moral question. Theoretically any number of genetically identical copies of the same man or woman might be made. Although superficially it might seem that, for example, brilliant scientists might be perpetuated in this way, it has to be remembered that the degree to which environment influences development is not fully known, and any cloned cell would have to go through all the phases of development once again including, in the case of a human embryo, fetus, baby and childhood.

20.1.2 Sexual reproduction

Sexual reproduction is the production of offspring by the fusion of the genetic material of haploid nuclei. Usually these nuclei are contained in specialised sex cells, or **gametes**, and at fertilisation they unite to form a diploid **zygote** which develops into the mature organism. Gametes are haploid, carrying a set of chromosomes derived by meiosis, and they provide the link between one generation and the next. (Sexual reproduction in flowering plants involves fusion of nuclei rather than cells but generally these nuclei are referred to as gametes.)

Meiosis is an essential feature of life cycles in which sexual reproduction occurs because it provides a mechanism for reducing the amount of genetic material by half. This ensures constancy in the amount of genetic material in each sexually reproducing generation, since fertilisation doubles the amount of genetic information. During meiosis random segregation of chromosomes (**independent assortment**) and exchange of genetic material between homologous chromosomes (**crossing-over**) results in new combinations of genes being brought together in the gamete and this reshuffling increases genetic diversity (section 22.3). The fusion of haploid gametic nuclei is called **fertilisation** or **syngamy** and it results in the production of a diploid zygote, that is a cell containing a set of chromosomes from each parent. This combination of two unique sets of chromosomes (**genetic recombination**) in the zygote forms the genetic basis of variation within species. The zygote grows and develops into the mature organism of the next generation. Sexual reproduction, therefore, involves the alternation, within the life cycle, of diploid and haploid phases, and the form adopted by the organism in each of these phases varies according to species, as shown in fig 20.13, p. 734.

Gametes are usually of two types, male and female, but

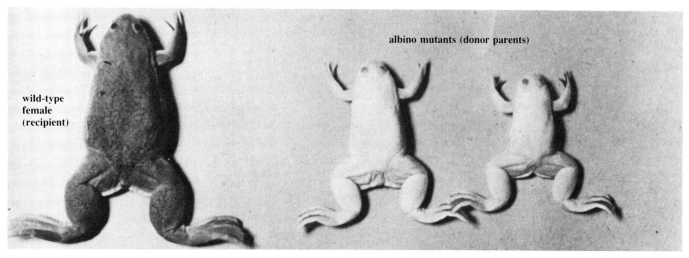

albino mutants (donor parents)

wild-type female (recipient)

Fig 20.11 *A clone of toads* (Xenopus laevis) *produced by nuclear transplantation. (above) A single tail-bud embryo was obtained from a cross between two albino mutants (donor parents). Its cell were dissociated and their nuclei transplanted into u.v.-treated (nucleus destroyed) unfertilised eggs of the wild-type female (recipient) shown.*

(below) The group of 30 toads (nuclear-transplant clone) are all female and albino; they were obtained from a total of 54 nuclear transfers

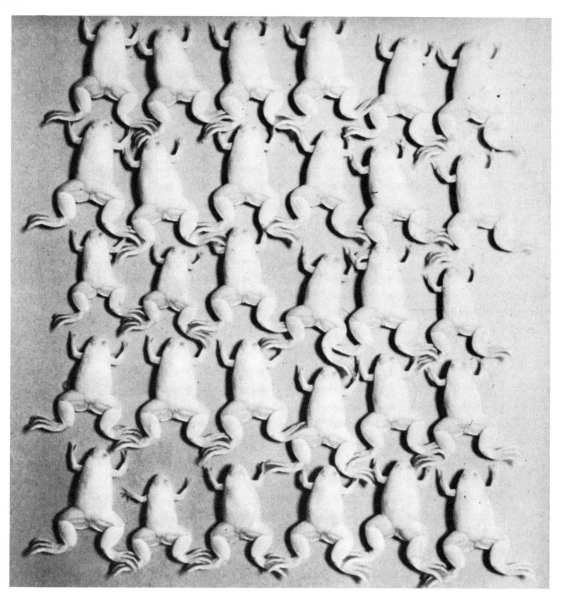

in some primitive organisms they are of one type only. (See isogamy, anisogamy and oogamy in section 20.2). If the gametes are of two types, they may be produced by separate male and female parents or by a single parent bearing both male and female reproductive organs. Species that have separate male and female individuals are described as **unisexual**, such as *Homo* (human) and most other animals. Some flowering plants are unisexual and in the case of **monoecious** plants there are separate male and female flowers on the *same* plant, for example *Corylus* (hazel) and *Cucurbita* (cucumber), whilst in *dioecious* plants one plant bears male flowers only and the other female flowers only, as in *Ilex* (holly) and *Taxus* (yew).

Hermaphroditism

Species capable of producing both male and female gametes within the same organism are described as **hermaphrodite**, or **bisexual**. Many protozoans, for example *Paramecium*, cnidarians such as *Obelia*, platyhelminths such as *Taenia* (tapeworm), oligochaetes such as *Lumbricus* (earthworm), crustacea such as *Balanus* (barnacle), molluscs such as *Helix* (garden snail), some fish, lizards and birds, and most flowering plants are hermaphrodite. This is thought to be the most primitive form of sexual reproduction and is seen in many primitive organisms. It represents an adaptation to sessile, slow-moving and parasitic modes of life. One of the advantages of hermaphroditism is the ability to carry out self-fertilisation, an essential for certain endoparasites, such as *Taenia*, which live a solitary existence. However, in the majority of species fertilisation of gametes from different organisms occurs, and many genetic, anatomical and physiological adaptations exist which prevent self-fertilisation and favour cross-fertilisation. For example, self-fertilisation is prevented in many protozoans by 'genetic incompatability', in many flowering plants by the structure of the androecium and gynaecium and in many animals by the production of eggs and sperm at different times by the same organism.

Parthenogenesis

Parthenogenesis is a modified form of sexual reproduction in which a female gamete develops into a new individual without being fertilised by a male gamete. The process occurs naturally in both animal and plant kingdoms and has the advantage, in some cases, of accelerating the normal reproductive rate.

There are two forms of parthenogenesis, haploid and diploid, depending upon the chromosome number of the female gamete. Many insect species, including ants, bees, and wasps, utilise **haploid parthenogenesis** for the production of specific types of organism within the social group. In these species meiosis occurs and haploid gametes are formed. Some eggs undergo fertilisation and develop normally into diploid females, whereas unfertilised (haploid) eggs develop into fertile haploid males. For example, the queen honeybee (*Apis mellifera*) lays fertilised eggs ($2n = 32$) which develop into females (queens or workers) and unfertilised eggs ($n = 16$) which develop into males (drones) which produce sperm by mitosis and not meiosis. The details of the development of the three types of honeybee are summarised in fig 20.12. In social insects this mechanism has the adaptive significance of controlling the numbers of each type of offspring.

Aphids show **diploid parthenogenesis** in which the egg-producing cells of the female undergo a modified form of meiosis involving total non-disjunction (section 22.3). All the chromosomes enter the egg cell and not the polar bodies. The egg cells develop within the mother and young females are released **viviparously**, that is the parents do not lay eggs but bear live young. This can occur for several generations, particularly during the summer, until a cell undergoes almost complete non-disjunction and produces a cell containing all the autosomes plus a single X chromosome. This cell develops parthenogenically into a male aphid. These autumn stage males and parthenogenically produced females, having undergone meiosis, produce haploid gametes for sexual reproduction. Fertilisation occurs and the diploid eggs laid by the females overwinter and hatch to produce parthenogenic females in the spring. These offspring are viviparous. The parthenogenic generations alternate with a normal sexually reproduced generation which introduces genetic recombination and variation into the population. The main advantage of parthenogenesis in aphids is the speed with which the population can increase its numbers, since all mature members of the population are egg-layers. This is particularly important at times when the environment is favourable and can support a large population, as during the summer months.

Among plants parthenogenesis occurs widely and takes various forms. One form is called **apomixis**, but it is not strictly a form of sexual reproduction, it only mimics its action. It occurs in some flowering plants in which a diploid cell of the ovule, either from the nucellus or megaspore, develops into a functional embryo in the absence of a male gamete. The rest of the ovule develops into the seed and the ovary into the fruit. In other forms a pollen grain is

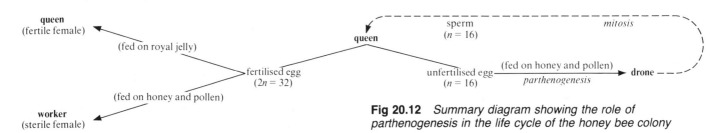

Fig 20.12 *Summary diagram showing the role of parthenogenesis in the life cycle of the honey bee colony*

necessary to trigger parthenogenesis, even though the pollen grain does not grow. In such cases the pollen grain induces the hormonal changes necessary for embryo development, and such cases are, in practice, difficult to distinguish from true sexual reproduction.

20.1.3 The origins of sexual reproduction

Any discussion based upon events occurring at an unknown stage in the history of life is purely speculative and any conclusions which emerge from the discussion must be tentative. The origins of sexual reproduction represent such a situation. It is thought that asexual methods of reproduction represent the primitive form of reproduction which existed as a means of 'copying' generations which were genetically identical. At a later stage, mechanisms are thought to have arisen enabling nucleic acid to be exchanged between organisms. This may have involved the fusion of whole organisms followed by meiosis and, indeed, this possibility would appear to precede the production and fusion of gametes. It is thought that the mechanisms involved in the exchange of genetic material as shown by bacteria and described in section 2.2.4 represent a primitive stage in the development of sex. The advantage of phenotypic variation resulting from meiosis and genetic recombination doubtless played a major role in the development of more complex forms of life and types of

Table 20.1. Comparison of asexual reproduction with sexual reproduction

Asexual reproduction	Sexual reproduction (omitting bacteria)
One parent only	Usually two parents
No gametes are produced	Gametes are produced. These are haploid and nuclei of two gametes fuse (fertilisation) to form a diploid zygote
Meiosis absent	Meiosis present at some stage in life cycle to prevent chromosome doubling in every generation*
Offspring identical to parent	Offspring are *not* identical to parents. They show genetic variation as a result of genetic recombination
Commonly occurs in plants, less differentiated animals and micro-organisms Absent in more differentiated animals	Occurs in the majority of plant and animal species
Often results in rapid production of large numbers of offspring	Less rapid increase in numbers

*A common source of confusion is the role played by mitosis and meiosis in reproduction. A proper discussion of this depends on a study of different life cycles and the points at which the two types of nuclear division occur in the life cycles. These are shown in fig 20.13 and described in section 20.1.4.

gametes, ranging from identical gametes (**isogametes**) to the heterogametic stage of motile male gametes, represented by sperms and antherozoids, and non-motile female gametes, represented by eggs (ova). The fact that every major group of organisms carries out sexual reproduction suggests that it has advantages over asexual reproduction, the latter though rare in animals more differentiated than platyhelminths, is retained in plants. Indeed the majority of plant species show alternation of asexual and sexual modes of reproduction in their life cycles, as described in section 20.2. One reason for this is that sessile organisms have problems of exchanging gametes and in many cases retain the option of reproducing asexually. Likewise the ecological problem of finding favourable habitats for offspring is aided by parents established in a habitat reproducing asexually. Problems of overcrowding, however, work counter to this and help limit the size of plant populations.

A summary of some of the essential and typical features of asexual and sexual reproduction is given in table 20.1.

20.1.4 Variety of life cycles

The various stages of development through which the members of a species pass from the zygote of one generation to the zygote of the next are called the **life cycle**. Life cycles vary in complexity and in some cases involve two or more generations that differ in their morphology (appearance) and reproduction, a phenomenon sometimes known as **alternation of generations**. This term is better confined to land plants and some algae which show alternation between a diploid, spore-producing generation called the **sporophyte** and a haploid, gamete-producing generation called the **gametophyte** (section 3.6.1). An alternation of asexual and sexual generations also occurs in some cnidarians, but here both generations are diploid and the haploid stage is represented only by the gametes. This form of alternation of generations is sometimes described as **metagenesis** (section 4.3.3.). During the life cycle of these cnidarians, different forms of the individuals of the species alternate with each other, a phenomenon known as **cyclic polymorphism**. In *Obelia*, for example, three forms occur in the life cycle, namely two types of polyp and a medusa (fig 4.3). Polymorphism occurs in some other organisms, for example, the primrose (*Primula*) has two types of flower, thrum-eyed and pin-eyed.

The life cycles of parasites are often complex and may involve several generations. Each generation is adapted to a particular situation, either for survival within a host or for transfer between hosts (for example, the life cycle of *Fasciola*, section 4.4.3). The additional generations produced by asexual reproduction (**polyembryony**) serve to increase the numbers of the species. Some representative life cycles are shown in fig 20.13.

Confusion sometimes occurs over the respective roles played by mitosis and meiosis in asexual and sexual

A e.g. *Chlamydomonas,*
Spirogyra, Rhizopus
The adult (sexual) organism
is haploid. The only diploid
stage is the zygote. The first
nuclear division of the
germinating zygote is by
meiosis, resulting in a return
to the haploid condition.

NB Gametes are *not*
produced by meiosis.

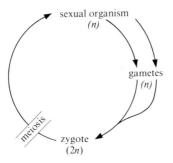

C e.g. *Obelia*
Three different
morphological forms occur
(polymorphism). All are
diploid. The diploid sexual
generation alternates with a
diploid asexual generation.
The only haploid cells are
the gametes.
Gametes *are* produced by
meiosis.

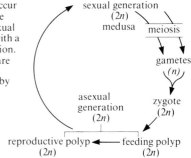

B e.g. *Fucus,*
vertebrates and most other
animals
The only haploid cells are
the gametes.
Gametes *are* produced by
meiosis.

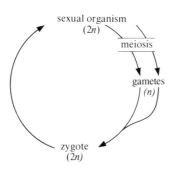

D e.g. *Laminaria* (a brown
alga), all land plants i.e.
mosses, ferns, conifers
and flowering plants.
Alternation of haploid and
diploid generations occurs.
NB Gametes are *not*
produced by meiosis.

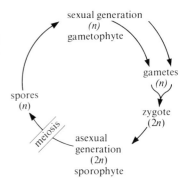

Fig 20.13 *Representative life cycles. A, B, C, D represent four different, commonly occurring, types of life cycle. Note that meiosis only occurs once in each life cycle. Asexual reproduction of the sexual organism is not shown in A, B and D, though may be possible depending on the species. (n = haploid; 2n = diploid.)*

reproduction and for this reason the significance of each within the life cycle is described again here in the context of life cycles. Meiosis occurs only in life cycles in which sexual reproduction occurs. When two haploid gametic nuclei fuse, the zygote produced has the diploid number of chromosomes and starts the next life cycle. Unless meiosis occurs somewhere in this life cycle, the gametic nuclei produced will be diploid and the zygote would then be **tetraploid** (have four sets of chromosomes). Meiosis is therefore necessary to prevent chromosome doubling in every generation in those life cycles in which sexual reproduction occurs. It does not necessarily occur immediately before gamete formation, as life cycles A and D in fig 20.13 show. An additional advantage of meiosis is that it contributes to variation by the processes of independent assortment of chromosomes and crossing-over of chromosomes (section 22.3). As a direct result, as in life cycles B and C, or indirectly, as in A and D, the gametes show variation. In the special case of alternation of generations (life cycle D) meiosis occurs in the production of spores and not gametes. Variation therefore occurs among the spores and the gametophytes that develop from the spores. This variation is passed on to the gametic nuclei which are produced in the gametophyte by mitosis. In all cases, however, meiosis can be said to form the basis of sexual reproduction. In life cycles A, B and C, that is life cycles where alternation of generations does *not* occur, asexual

reproduction results in the production of genetically identical offspring, and involves mitosis.

> **20.1** (*a*) Which one of the following statements is true, according to the information given so far in this chapter?
> (i) Asexual reproduction always results in the production of identical offspring
> (ii) Gametes are always haploid.
> (iii) Gametes are always produced by meiosis.
> (iv) Meiosis always produces haploid cells and mitosis always produces diploid cells.
> (v) Mitosis occurs only in diploid cells.
> (*b*) Give examples of exceptions to the other four statements.

20.2 Sexual reproduction in plants

All green plants that live on land, together with some well differentiated algae, show alternation of generations in which a haploid gametophyte generation alternates with a diploid sporophyte generation as shown in fig 20.13D. It is the gametophyte which undergoes sexual reproduction, producing gametes by mitosis.

The remaining green plants are all algae, and show a

range of types of sexual reproduction which are summarised in section 3.2.3. In more primitive types the gametes are all identical and the process is called **isogamy**; more complex (or advanced) types show **ansiogamy** in which dissimilar gametes are found, the extreme form of anisogamy being **oogamy**, where a motile male gamete swims to a sedentary female gamete.

On leaving water, both plants and animals have evolved strategies over millions of years to cope with dry land. Flowering plants and mammals owe much of their success to adaptations for sexual reproduction, and certain analogies can be drawn between the two groups. For example, the bringing together of male and female gametes does not rely on gametes being released into water, as it does for example with bryophytes or amphibians, and there is protection and nourishment of the developing embryo by the parent. A fundamental difference is the origin of gametes by mitosis from a gametophyte generation in flowering plants, whereas in mammals there is not alternation of generations and gametes are produced by meiosis from a diploid parent. As will be shown, however, the gametophyte generation of flowering plants is extremely reduced.

20.2.1 The life cycle of flowering plants (angiosperms)

The ways in which flowering plants have adapted to life on land have been described in chapter 3. The major adaptations made in reproduction are the production of seeds and fruits to nourish and protect the embryo plants and to aid in their dispersal, the absence of swimming male gametes, and the extreme reduction of the sexual gametophyte generation. Male gametes are carried inside pollen grains to the female parts of the plant, a process called **pollination** which is followed by the production of a pollen tube carrying male nuclei.

An outline of the life cycle of flowering plants is given in fig 3.38, where it is compared with representative life cycles of other plant groups. There is still an alternation of generations in the life cycle, as is shown more simply in fig 20.13D. Since the gametophyte generation is virtually non-existent and is not free-living, it would be difficult to realise that alternation of generations occurs were it not for the comparison that can be made with more primitive ancestors. The life cycle of flowering plants is described in more detail below and, strictly speaking, involves asexual reproduction of the dominant sporophyte generation (the flowering plant) and sexual reproduction of the gametophyte generation.

20.2.2 The structure and functions of the flower

The common use of the term, 'flowering plants to describe the angiosperms is a reference to the uniqueness of this group in producing flowers.

Flowers are reproductive structures whose evolutionary origins are unclear, but which are sometimes regarded as collections of highly specialised leaves, analogous to the cones of conifers in that they carry the spore-producing structures. They can be regarded as organs of both asexual and sexual reproduction, asexual because they produce spores (pollen grains and embryo sacs) and sexual because gametes are later produced within the spores. They are commonly referred to simply as organs of sexual reproduction. In areas where there are distinct seasons, flowering is usually synchronised with a particular season and time of year. Its environmental and hormonal control is described in section 15.5.

The parts of the flower are arranged spirally (in a few primitive flowers) or in whorls around the upper part (receptacle) of a flower stalk (pedicel). A generalised flower and the arrangement of flowers in groups (inflorescences) are shown in fig 20.14, and some of the terms used to describe the flower parts are explained below.

Parts of a flower

The **inflorescence** is a collection of flowers borne on the same stalk, the **peduncle** (see fig 20.14b). A collection of flowers may be more attractive to pollinating insects than a small solitary flower.

The **receptacle** is the end of the flower stalk (**pedicel**) from which the perianth, gynaecium and androecium arise. The receptacle and flower are described as hypogynous if the stamens and perianth are inserted below the gynaecium as in fig 20.14a, epigynous if stamens and perianth are inserted above the ovary, and perigynous if the receptacle is flattened or cup-shaped with the gynaecium at the centre and the stamens and perianth attached round the rim. (See also inferior and superior ovaries under gynaecium below.)

The **perianth** consists of two whorls of leaf-like parts called perianth segments. In monocotyledons the two whorls are usually similar, for instance daffodil (*Narcissus*), tulip (*Tulipa*) and bluebell (*Endymion non-scripta*). In dicotyledons the two whorls are usually different, consisting of an outer whorl of sepals called the calyx and an inner whorl of petals called the corolla.

The **calyx** is the collection of sepals. Sepals are usually green and leaf-like structures that enclose and protect the flower buds. Occasionally they are brightly coloured and petal-like, serving to attract insects for pollination.

Polysepalous – having free (unfused) sepals

Gamosepalous – having sepals that are at least partly fused into a tube.

The **corolla** is the collection of petals. In insect-pollinated flowers the petals are usually large and brightly coloured, serving to attract insects. In wind-pollinated flowers the petals are usually reduced in size and green, or may be entirely absent.

Polypetalous – having free (unfused) petals, for example pea (*Pisum*), rose (*Rosa*) and buttercup (*Ranunculus*)

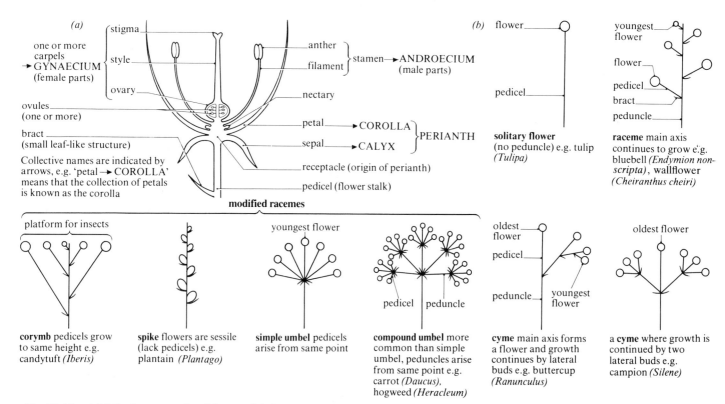

Fig 20.14 (a) LS of a generalised flower. (b) Arrangement of flowers in groups (inflorescences) or in isolation. Some common types of inflorescence are shown which can be described as racemose or cymose

Gamopetalous or Sympetalous – having petals that are at least partly fused into a tube, for example foxglove (*Digitalis*), primrose (*Primula*), dandelion (*Taraxacum*) and white deadnettle (*Lamium album*)

The **androecium** is the collection of stamens, forming the male reproductive organs of the flower. Each stamen consists of an **anther** and a **filament**. The anther contains the pollen sacs, in which pollen is made. The filament contains a vascular bundle that carries food and water to the anther.

The **gynaecium** or **pistil** is the collection of carpels, forming the female reproductive organs of the flower. A carpel consists of a stigma, style and ovary. The stigma receives the pollen grains during pollination and the style bears the stigma in a suitable position in the flower to receive the pollen. The ovary is the swollen, hollow base of the carpel and contains one or more ovules. Ovules are the structures in which the embryo sacs develop and which, after fertilisation, become seeds. Each is attached to the ovary wall by a short stalk called the funicle and the point of attachment is called the placenta.

The carpels of a flower may be separate and free, the apocarpous condition, as in buttercup, or fused to form a single structure, the syncarpous condition, as in white deadnettle. The ovary formed by fusion of carpels may have a single chamber or loculus (unilocular) or several loculi (multilocular) with one loculus formed by each constituent carpel. The styles of syncarpous flowers may be fused or separate.

Superior ovary – an ovary inserted above the other

flower parts on the receptacle, that is the ovary of a hypogynous or perigynous flower

Inferior ovary – an ovary inserted below the other flower parts on the receptacle, that is the ovary of an epigynous flower

The **nectaries** are glandular structures that secrete nectar, a sugary fluid that attracts animals for pollination, usually insects, but also birds and bats in the tropics.

The following terms are applied to whole plants and flowers.

Hermaphrodite (bisexual) plants – male and female sex organs borne on the same plant

Monoecious plants – separate male and female flowers borne on the same plant, such as oak (*Quercus*), hazel (*Corylus*), beech (*Fagus*) and sycamore (*Acer pseudoplatanus*)

Dioecious (unisexual) plants – male and female sex organs borne on separate plants, that is the plants are either male or female, for example yew (*Taxus*), willow (*Salix*), poplar (*Populus*) and holly (*Ilex*)

Hermaphrodite (bisexual) flowers – male and female sex organs in the same flower, such as in buttercup, white deadnettle, bluebell and pea

Unisexual flowers – separate male and female flowers, for example oak, hazel, yew, willow, poplar and holly

Symmetry of flowers

If the flower parts are arranged in radial symmetry around the receptacle, the flower is said to be regular or **actinomorphic**, for instance buttercup and bluebell. If the

stamen
numerous and spirally arranged on the receptacle;
collection of stamens forms the **androecium**

filament
white, short

anther
yellow

stigma
curved

style
very short

sepal
five form **calyx**; green, hairy,
curved round petal, free

ovary
apocarpous, superior, one
carpel, one locule, one ovule;
collection of carpels forms the
gynaecium; carpels are spirally
arranged on the receptacle

petal
five form **corolla;**
bright yellow,
glossy upper
surface, free
(polypetalous)

nectary
covered by a
small scale at
base of petal

} perianth

receptacle

pedicel

Phylum: Angiospermatophyta
Class: Dicotyledoneae
Family: Ranunculaceae

flower shows bilateral symmetry only, it is said to be irregular or **zygomorphic**, as in white deadnettle and pea.

Representative flowers. Some representative insect-pollinated flowers are illustrated in figs 20.15–20.18. Fig 3.39 illustrates the floral morphology of a typical grass, a wind-pollinated monocotyledon.

The structure of a flower is best illustrated by means of a half-flower, a view of the flower obtained by cutting the flower vertically into two equal halves (along the median plane, so as to split the pedicel in two longitudinally) and drawing one half, showing the cut surface as a continuous line.

Fig 20.15 *Half-flower of meadow buttercup (*Ranunculus acris*), a polypetalous dicotyledon. It is a herbaceous perennial common in damp meadows and pastures. It perennates by means of a rhizome. Flower: actinomorphic and hypogynous. Flowers appear April to September. Pollination: insects such as flies and small bees. Fruit: each carpel contains one seed and forms a fruit called an achene. No special dispersal mechanism*

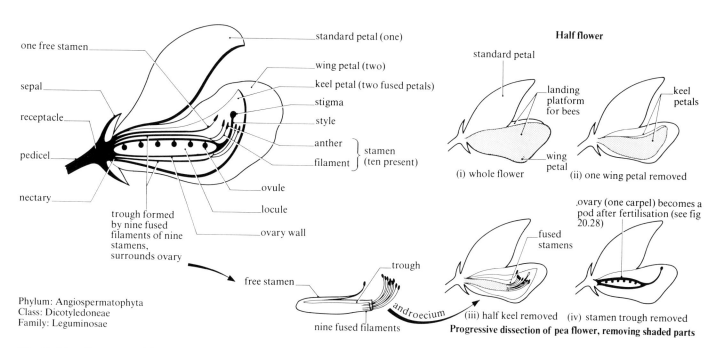

one free stamen

sepal

receptacle

pedicel

nectary

trough formed
by nine fused
filaments of nine
stamens,
surrounds ovary

free stamen

nine fused filaments

standard petal (one)

wing petal (two)

keel petal (two fused petals)

stigma

style

anther

filament

} stamen
(ten present)

ovule

locule

ovary wall

trough

androecium

Half flower

standard petal

landing
platform
for bees

wing
petal

(i) whole flower

keel
petals

(ii) one wing petal removed

.ovary (one carpel) becomes a
pod after fertilisation (see fig
20.28)

fused
stamens

(iii) half keel removed

(iv) stamen trough removed

Progressive dissection of pea flower, removing shaded parts

Phylum: Angiospermatophyta
Class: Dicotyledoneae
Family: Leguminosae

Fig 20.16 *Structure of flower of sweet pea (*Lathyrus odoratus*), a polypetalous dicotyledon. Flower: actinomorphic and polypetalous. Flowers appear in July. Calyx: five sepals. Corolla: five petals, one standard petal, two wing petals, two fused keel petals interlocking with wing petals. May be white or coloured. Pollination: bees are attracted by colour, scent and nectar. The standard petal is especially conspicuous. The two wing petals act as a landing platform. When a bee lands, its weight pulls them down together with the keel to which they are linked. The style and stigma emerge, striking the undersurface of the bee that may be carrying pollen from another flower. As the bee searches for nectar at the base of the ovary with its long proboscis, the anthers may rub pollen directly on to the undersurface of the style, from where it may be passed to the bee. Self-pollination may also occur. The garden pea (*Pisum sativum*) is similar, but more commonly self-pollinated. Fruit: a pod consisting of one carpel with many seeds. (See fig 20.28 for self-dispersal.)*

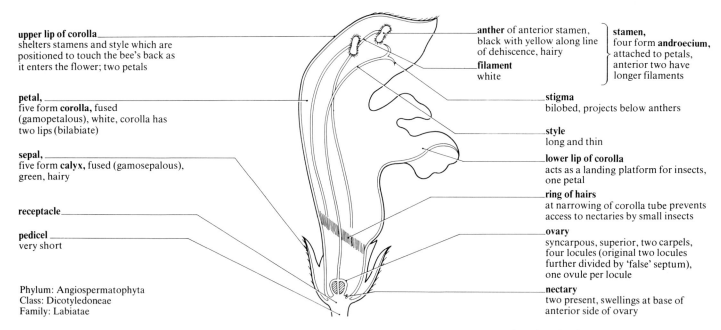

upper lip of corolla shelters stamens and style which are positioned to touch the bee's back as it enters the flower; two petals

petal, five form **corolla**, fused (gamopetalous), white, corolla has two lips (bilabiate)

sepal, five form **calyx**, fused (gamosepalous), green, hairy

receptacle

pedicel very short

Phylum: Angiospermatophyta
Class: Dicotyledoneae
Family: Labiatae

anther of anterior stamen, black with yellow along line of dehiscence, hairy

filament white

stamen, four form **androecium**, attached to petals, anterior two have longer filaments

stigma bilobed, projects below anthers

style long and thin

lower lip of corolla acts as a landing platform for insects, one petal

ring of hairs at narrowing of corolla tube prevents access to nectaries by small insects

ovary syncarpous, superior, two carpels, four locules (original two locules further divided by 'false' septum), one ovule per locule

nectary two present, swellings at base of anterior side of ovary

Fig 20.17 *Half-flower of white deadnettle* (Lamium album), *a sympetalous dicotyledon. The plant is a herbaceous perennial common in hedgerows and on waste ground. It perennates by means of a rhizome. Flower: zygomorphic (irregular) and hypogynous. Flowers appear in April to June and autumn. Pollination: mainly bumblebees. A bee lands on the lower lip and as it enters the flower its back, which may be carrying pollen, touches the stigma first, thus favouring cross-pollination, although self-pollination is possible. Fruit: four nutlets, each with a hard wall and containing one seed. The fruit is called a carcerulus*

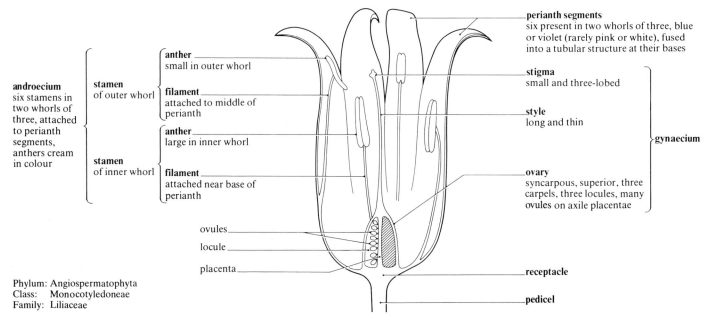

androecium six stamens in two whorls of three, attached to perianth segments, anthers cream in colour

stamen of outer whorl

stamen of inner whorl

anther small in outer whorl

filament attached to middle of perianth

anther large in inner whorl

filament attached near base of perianth

ovules

locule

placenta

perianth segments six present in two whorls of three, blue or violet (rarely pink or white), fused into a tubular structure at their bases

stigma small and three-lobed

style long and thin

ovary syncarpous, superior, three carpels, three locules, many ovules on axile placentae

gynaecium

receptacle

pedicel

Phylum: Angiospermatophyta
Class: Monocotyledoneae
Family: Liliaceae

Fig 20.18 *Half-flower of bluebell* (Endymion non-scripta), *a monocotyledon. The plant is an herbaceous perennial, common in woods and hedgerows, favouring shady positions and light, acid soils. It perennates by means of a bulb. Flower: actinomorphic and hypogynous. Parts are in threes, as is typical of monocotyledons. Flowers appear in April to May. Pollination: insects such as the honey bee. The flower is slightly scented and nectar is produced at the top of the ovary. Fruit: a capsule dehiscing into three valves*

Development of pollen grains

Each stamen consists of an **anther** in which four pollen sacs produce pollen, and a **filament** which contains a vascular bundle supplying food and water to the anther. Fig 20.19 illustrates the internal structure of an anther, with its four pollen sacs containing spore mother cells. Each spore

mother cell undergoes meiosis to form four pollen grains as shown in fig 20.20.

Immediately after meiosis the young pollen grains are seen in tetrads (groups of four). Each grain develops a thick wall, often with an elaborate sculptured pattern characteristic of the species or genus. The outer wall, or **exine**, is made of a substance related to cutin and suberin (sporopol-

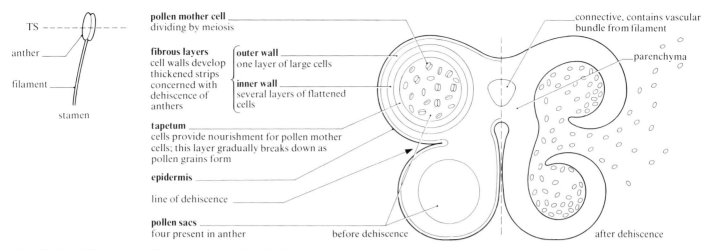

Fig 20.19 *TS mature anther before and after dehiscence*

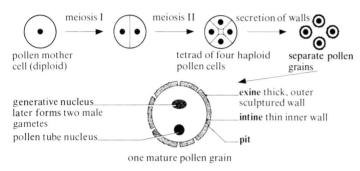

Fig 20.20 *Development of pollen grains*

lenin) but is more durable than either. It is one of the most resistant substances in nature and allows grain coats to survive unchanged over long periods of time, sometimes millions of years. This fact, together with the ease of identifying the parent genus or species which produced the grain, has given rise to the science of palynology or pollen analysis. By studying pollen grains from a particular time and place it is possible to determine what plants were growing and thus to gain information about, for example, the ecosystems (including animals) and climate of that time. A particularly abundant source of pollen grains is peat, which accumulates to great depths over long periods of time in peat bogs. Cores of peat can be extracted using special peat borers.

> **20.2** How might pollen grains be useful as indicators of (*a*) past climate, (*b*) past human activities?

The pollen grain at this stage is equivalent to a microspore, as discussed in chapter 3. Its nucleus divides into two by mitosis to form a generative nucleus and a pollen tube nucleus (fig 20.20). As soon as this happens, the contents of the pollen grain can be regarded as equivalent to a male gametophyte, because male gametes will be formed from the generative nucleus.

20.2.3 Development of the embryo sac and female gamete

Each carpel consists of a stigma, style and ovary. Within the ovary one or more ovules develop, each attached to the ovary wall at a point called the placenta by a short stalk or funicle through which food and water pass to the developing ovule. Often, as it develops, the ovule bends over so that its tip is facing downwards near the base of the funicle. If this occurs, the ovule is described as **anatropous**; if the funicle and ovule remain straight, then the ovule is described as **orthotropous**.

The main body of the ovule is the **nucellus**, enclosed and protected by two sheaths or **integuments**. A small pore is left at one end of the ovule, the **micropyle**. The other end of the ovule, where the funicle joins to the nucellus and integuments, is called the **chalaza**.

Within the nucellus, at the end nearest the micropyle, one spore mother cell develops, known as the embryo sac mother cell. This diploid cell undergoes meiosis and gives rise to a haploid megaspore or embryo sac as shown in fig 20.21. The embryo sac grows and as soon as its nucleus divides by mitosis its contents can be regarded as a female gametophyte. Continued mitotic divisions result in the production of eight nuclei, one of which is the nucleus of the female gamete.

Two polar nuclei migrate to the centre of the embryo sac and fuse to become a single diploid nucleus (in some cases they fuse later at fertilisation). The remaining six nuclei, three at each end, become separated by thin cell walls and only one of these, the female gamete, appears to serve any further function.

The final appearance of the mature carpel at fertilisation is shown in fig 20.22.

20.2.4 Pollination

After formation of pollen grains in the pollen sacs, the cells in the walls of the anther begin to dry and shrink, setting up tensions that eventually result in splitting

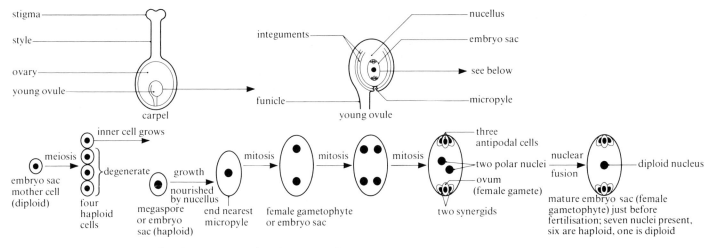

Fig 20.21 *Development of embryo sac and female gamete (in an anatropous ovule)*

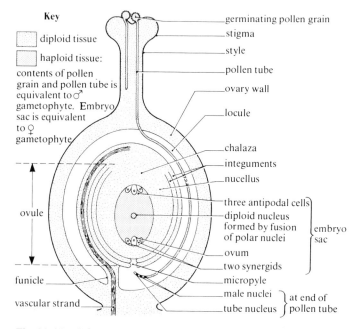

Key

- □ diploid tissue
- ▨ haploid tissue:

contents of pollen grain and pollen tube is equivalent to ♂ gametophyte. Embryo sac is equivalent to ♀ gametophyte

Labels on figure: germinating pollen grain, stigma, style, pollen tube, ovary wall, locule, chalaza, integuments, nucellus, three antipodal cells, diploid nucleus formed by fusion of polar nuclei, ovum, two synergids, micropyle, male nuclei } at end of tube nucleus } pollen tube, ovule, funicle, vascular strand

Fig 20.22 *LS carpel at fertilisation. The ovule illustrated is anatropous. Note that the ovule, which becomes the seed after fertilisation, contains both diploid parent tissue and haploid embryo sac tissue*

(dehiscing) of the anther down the sides along two lines of weakness (fig 20.19). The pollen grains are thus released.

The transfer of pollen grains from an anther to a stigma is called **pollination**. This must be achieved if the male gametes, which develop inside the pollen grains, are to reach the female gamete, and special, often elaborate, mechanisms have evolved that ensure successful pollination.

Transfer from an anther to a stigma of the same flower, or a flower on the same plant, is called **self-pollination**. Transfer of pollen from the anther of one plant to the stigma of another plant is called **cross-pollination**. Cross-pollination leads to cross-fertilisation and has the advantage of increasing the chances of variation. It is thus a form

of outbreeding. There are often special features to encourage it, some of which are described below.

Self-pollination leading to self-fertilisation has the advantage of greater reliability, particularly where members of the species are uncommon and are separated by large distances. This is because it is not dependent on an external agency, such as wind or insects, to deliver the pollen. However, self-fertilisation is the extreme form of inbreeding and can result in less vigorous offspring as described in section 25.4. Self-pollination is used in groundsel (*Senecio*) and chickweed (*Stellaria*), which produce no nectar or scent.

Both cross- and self-pollination have advantages and disadvantages and many plants balance the advantages by devices which favour cross-pollination but allow selfing to occur if crossing fails. For example, *some* of the buds produced by violet (*Viola*) and wood sorrel (*Oxalis*) never open, so that self-pollination inside these is inevitable.

Features favouring cross-pollination

Dioecious plants. Self-pollination in dioecious plants is impossible. Monoecious species, where separate male and female flowers occur on the same hermaphrodite plant, also favour cross-pollination but selfing may also occur.

> **20.3** Dioecious plants are rare, despite the advantages of cross-pollination. Suggest two possible reasons for this.
>
> **20.4** Dioecism (separate sexes) is common in animals. Why is the phenomenon more successful in animals than in flowering plants?

Dichogamy. Sometimes anthers mature and stigmas become receptive at different times, a condition known as dichogamy. If the anthers mature first, this is described as **protandry**, if the stigmas mature first it is

Fig 20.23 *A bee entering a flower of meadow sage. The stamens are hinged to a plate and, as the head of the bee pushes against this, the stamens are lowered. This brushes pollen onto the bee's abdomen. The stigma of the flower increases in length as the flower ages. If a bee now enters an older flower, it will come into contact with the stigma and the pollen will be transferred from its abdomen to the stigma. This series of activities causes cross-pollination to take place*

protogyny. Protandrous flowers are much more common, for example white deadnettle, dandelion, rosebay willowherb (*Epilobium angustifolium*); see also sage (*Salvia*) (fig 20.23).

Protogyny occurs in bluebell and figwort (*Scrophularia*). In most cases of dichogamy there is an overlapping period when both anthers and stigmas are ripe, thus allowing selfing if crossing has been unsuccessful. A similar mechanism for ensuring cross-fertilisation exists in some hermaphrodite animals, for instance *Hydra*, where the testes ripen before the ovary.

Self-incompatibility (self-sterility). Even if self-pollination does occur, the pollen grain often does not develop, or develops very slowly, so preventing or discouraging self-fertilisation. In all such cases there is a specific inhibition of pollen penetration of the stigma, or of pollen tube growth down the style, and this is genetically determined by self-incompatibility genes.*

When self-incompatibility occurs, the extent of compatible cross-pollination is variable and again is genetically determined. For most efficient use of the pollen, a high proportion of crosses should be compatible. An extreme example is clover, where all plants are self-incompatible, but cross-incompatibility occurs between less than one in 22 000 pairs. A less efficient system occurs where the compatible types are characterised by differences in floral morphology. An example is the primrose (*Primula*), discussed below.

> **20.5** Self-incompatibility is controlled by multiple alleles. Assuming (*a*) that there are three alleles, S_1, S_2 and S_3, and (*b*) that self-incompatibility occurs if the pollen grain and the style tissue have an allele in common, what proportion of the pollen grains from a plant with the genotype S_1S_2 would be capable of successfully germinating on a plant with the genotype S_2S_3?

Special floral structures. In most hermaphrodite flowers there are structural features that favour cross-pollination.

In the case of insect-pollinated flowers the stigma is usually borne above the anthers, thus removing the possibility of pollen falling on to the stigma of the same flower. A visiting insect, possibly carrying pollen from another plant, will touch the stigma first as it enters the flower. Later, while the insect is seeking nectar, pollen is either brushed against it or falls on to it before it leaves the flower. This occurs in white deadnettle (fig 20.17). A more primitive mechanism may ensure that the stigma brushes against the insect as it lands, as in pea (see fig 20.16 for details). Such mechanisms are generally reinforced by

* The genetics of self-incompatibility and its commercial implications are outside the scope of this book, but are dealt with in *Sexual Incompatibility in Plants*, Institute of Biology, Studies in Biology, No. 110; Lewis, Dan; Arnold, (1979).

dichogamy and the flowers are often complex and zygomorphic in shape.

Flowers attract insects by providing a source of food (nectar or pollen) and stimulating the senses of sight and smell of the insects. Those characteristics that enable flowers to do this are discussed below.

In the case of wind-pollinated flowers the stamens, the whole flower, or the inflorescence may hang downwards so that falling pollen will drop clear of the plant before being blown away, for example hazel catkins.

> **20.6** Fig 20.24 shows two types of primrose flower. They occur naturally in roughly equal numbers and differ in length of style (heterostyly) and position of anthers. (*a*) Given that bees collect nectar from the base of the corolla tube, explain how cross-pollination between pin-eyed and thrum-eyed flowers rather than between flowers of the same type, is favoured. (*b*) What is the advantage of such a system?

Although the heterostyly described in question 20.6 and fig 20.24 apparently favours outbreeding, a much more important difference between pin-eyed and thrum-eyed primroses is a self-incompatibility mechanism which is more effective in restricting cross-fertilisation to pin-eye/thrum-eye crosses. The genes that control incompatibility, style length and anther height lie close together on the same chromosome and behave as a single inheritable unit.

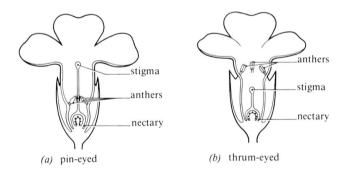

(a) pin-eyed   *(b)* thrum-eyed

Fig 20.24 *Heterostyly in primrose* (Primula) *flowers*

Wind pollination and insect pollination

Pollen grains are spores, but unlike the spores of the non-seed bearing plants they cannot germinate on land and must be transferred to the female parts of either cones, in the case of conifers, or flowers in the case of angiosperms. The original agent of spore dispersal was wind, but this is very inefficient in pollen transfer because the mechanism relies solely on chance interception of the pollen grains by the cones or the flowers. All conifers, and many flowering plants such as grasses and most temperate trees, such as oak and hazel, still rely on wind, but it is at the expense of producing enormous quantities of pollen, a drain on the plant's materials and energy. Insect pollination was rapidly exploited once flowers evolved because the insect is a much more precise agent of dispersal. It can carry a small amount of pollen from the anthers of one flower and deposit it precisely on the stigma of another flower. As a result, special relationships between flowers and insects have evolved, the reward the insects receive from the flowers being food in the form of nectar, and for some, pollen. The insects specialised for flower-feeding appeared at the same time as the flowering plants, and include bees, wasps, butterflies and moths. In a few particular cases the insect and the plant it pollinates are so interdependent that neither species can survive without the other, such as the yucca plant and its associated moth.

Insect pollination has the important additional advantage that it encourages cross-pollination and hence cross-fertilisation, so the modifications of flowers to encourage insect pollination described below could be added to the list of features favouring cross-pollination.

In order to attract insects, flowers generally are large, with brightly coloured petals or, if small, are grouped into inflorescences. Insects can see ultra-violet wavelengths that are invisible to humans so flowers that appear white to us may, in fact, appear coloured to insects. Often there are markings on the petals such as lines, spots or an increased intensity of colour that guide insects to the nectaries, as in violet and pansy (*Viola*), or orchids (*Orchis* and other genera) and foxgloves (*Digitalis*).

More specific than colours are the scents produced by flowers some of which, like lavender and rose, are used by humans in perfumes. Smells of rotting flesh that attract carrion-eating insects are also produced by some plants: the arum lily (*Arum maculatum*) attracts dung flies. Specificity for recognition is also provided by flower shape.

One of the most complex and bizarre mechanisms for ensuring cross-pollination is the sexual impersonation of female wasps by certain orchids. The flower parts mimic the shape, colourings and even the odour of the female wasp, and the impersonation is so convincing that the male wasps attempt to copulate with the flower (fig 20.25). While

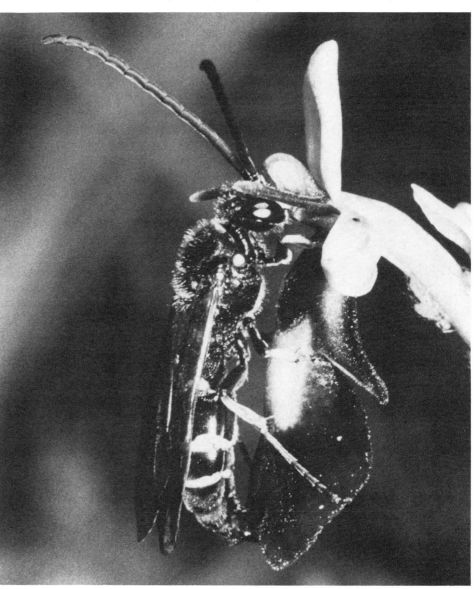

Fig 20.25 *A digger wasp* (Argogorytes mystaceus) *copulating with the fly orchid* (Ophrys insectifera)

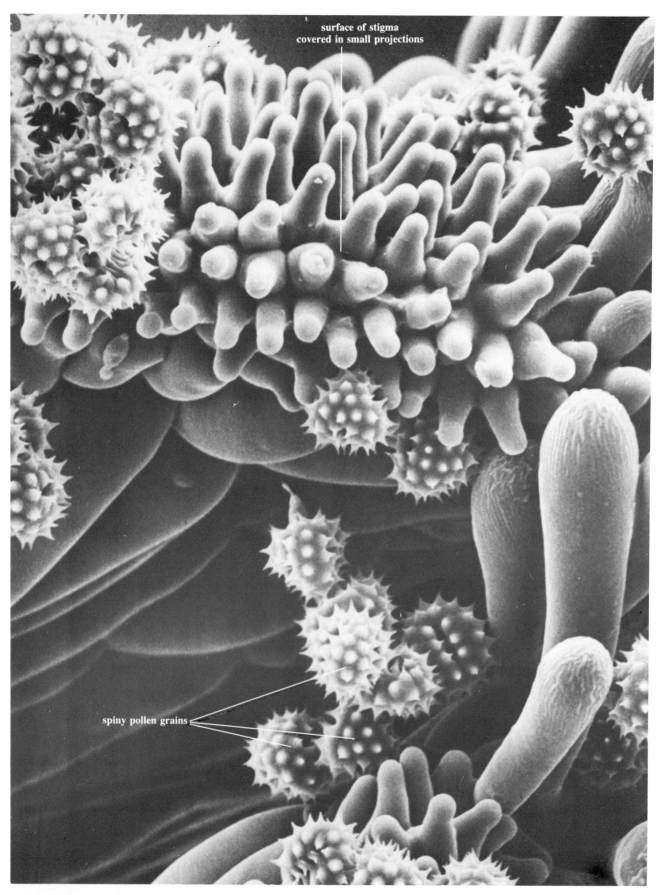

surface of stigma
covered in small projections

spiny pollen grains

Fig 20.26 *Scanning electron micrograph of pollen grains on the stigma of a flower. The spiked surface of the grains is typical of insect-pollinated flowers*

Table 20.2. Summary of typical differences between wind- and insect-pollinated flowers

Typical wind-pollinated flower	Typical insect-pollinated flower
Small petals not brightly coloured (usually green), or petals absent; flowers therefore inconspicuous	Large coloured petals; flowers therefore conspicuous. If flowers relatively inconspicuous they may be gathered together in inflorescences
Not scented	Scented
Nectaries absent	Nectaries present
Large branched and feathery stigma hanging outside flower to trap pollen	Small stigma, sticky to hold pollen and enclosed within flower
Pendulous stamens hanging outside flower to release pollen	Stamens enclosed within flower
Anthers versatile, i.e. attached only at midpoints to tip of filament so that they swing freely in air currents	Anthers fixed at their bases (basifixed) or fused along their backs to the filaments (dorsifixed) so that they are immovable
Large quantities of pollen owing to high wastage	Less pollen produced
Pollen grains relatively light and small; dry, often smooth, walls	Pollen grains relatively heavy and large. Spiny walls and stickiness help attachment to insect body (fig 20.26)
Flower structure relatively simple	Elaborate structural modifications for particular insects often occur
Flowers borne well above foliage on long stalks (e.g. grasses) or appear before leaves (e.g. many British trees)	Position and time of appearance variable in relation to foliage, though often borne above it for increased conspicuousness

doing so they deposit pollen and, on leaving the flower, collect fresh pollen to take to the next flower.

A summary of the typical differences between wind-pollinated and insect-pollinated flowers is given in table 20.2.

20.2.5   Fertilisation

Once a pollen grain has landed on the stigma, a sucrose solution secreted by epidermal cells of the stigma stimulates germination of the grain and possibly supplies food (fig 20.26). A pollen tube emerges from one of the pores in the wall of the pollen grain and grows rapidly down the style to the ovary. Its growth involves secretion of digestive enzymes and is controlled by the tube nucleus of the pollen grain, which is found at the growing tip of the tube. Growth is stimulated by auxins produced by the gynaecium, and the pollen tube is directed towards the ovary by certain chemicals, an example of chemotropism. It is probably also negatively aerotropic, that is it grows away from air. Growth depends on compatibility between the pollen and the style tissue as already described.

During growth of the pollen tube the generative nucleus of the pollen grain divides by mitosis to produce two male nuclei that represent the male gametes (fig 20.22). They are non-motile, unlike the sperms of lower plants, and depend on the pollen tube to reach the female gamete which is located in the embryo sac of the ovule. The pollen tube enters the ovule through the micropyle, the tube nucleus degenerates and the tip of the tube bursts, releasing the male gametes in the vicinity of the embryo sac which they enter. One nucleus fuses with the female gamete, forming a diploid zygote, and the other fuses with the two polar nuclei (or diploid nucleus if the latter have already fused) forming a triploid nucleus known as the primary endosperm nucleus. This double fertilisation is unique to flowering plants.

If, as is often the case, more than one ovule is present in the gynaecium, each must be fertilised by a separate pollen grain if it is to become a seed. Thus each seed may have been fertilised by a pollen grain from a different plant.

Experiment 20.1: To investigate the growth of pollen tubes

Stigmas secrete a solution containing sucrose ranging in concentration from about 2 to 45%. This helps to stick pollen grains to the stigma and to promote their germination. The addition of borate to the experimental solution helps to prevent osmotic bursting of pollen tube tips and stimulates growth.

Materials

microscope
cavity slide
flowers containing dehiscing anthers, such as dead-nettle or wallflower
10–20% (w/v) sucrose solution also containing sodium borate to a concentration of 0.01%
acetocarmine or neutral red

Method

Place a drop of sucrose solution in the central depression of a cavity slide and add pollen grains by touching the drop with the surface of a dehisced anther. Observe the slide at intervals over a period of 1–2 hours. The nuclei at the tip of growing tubes may be stained by irrigating with a drop of acetocarmine or neutral red.

20.2.6   Development of the seed to dormancy

Immediately after fertilisation, the ovule becomes known as the **seed** and the ovary the **fruit**.

The zygote grows by mitotic divisions to become a multicellular embryo which consists of a first shoot, the **plumule**, a first root, the **radicle**, and either one or two seed-leaves called **cotyledons** (one in monocotyledons and two in dicotyledons). These cotyledons are simpler in structure than the first true foliage leaves and may become swollen with food to act as storage tissue, as in the pea and

Table 20.3. Summary of the changes that occur after fertilisation in flowering plants

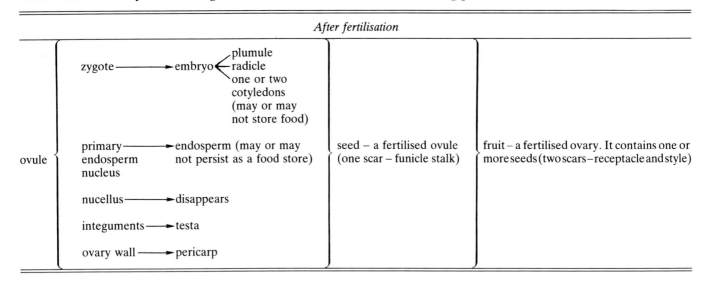

	After fertilisation		
ovule	zygote → embryo < plumule / radicle / one or two cotyledons (may or may not store food)	seed – a fertilised ovule (one scar – funicle stalk)	fruit – a fertilised ovary. It contains one or more seeds (two scars – receptacle and style)
	primary endosperm nucleus → endosperm (may or may not persist as a food store)		
	nucellus → disappears		
	integuments → testa		
	ovary wall → pericarp		

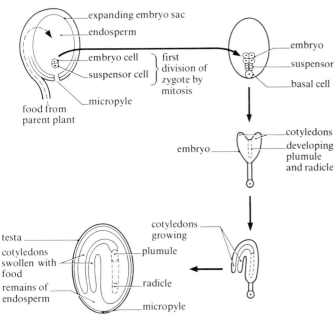

Fig 20.27 *Growth of an embryo in a non-endospermous dicotyledon seed, such as shepherd's purse (Capsella bursa-pastoris)*

broad bean (*Vicia faba*). The plumule consists of a stem, the first pair of true foliage leaves and a terminal bud. The triploid primary endosperm nucleus undergoes repeated divisions (mitotic) to form the **endosperm**, a mass of triploid nuclei which are separated from one another by thin cell walls. In some seeds this remains as the food store, as in maize (*Zea mays*).

If the cotyledons act as a food store they grow at the expense of the endosperm, which may disappear altogether. Some seeds store food in both endosperm and cotyledons.

Thus within the developing seed, both embryo and in some cases the endosperm, grow within the embryo sac. As their growth continues the surrounding nucellus becomes disorganised and breaks down, supplying nutrients for growth. Further nutrients are supplied by the vascular bundle in the stalk (funicle) of the ovule. There are close analogies here with the mammal, where food passes from the parent to the developing embryo via the placenta. As already noted, the term placenta is also used for the point of attachment of the funicle to the ovary wall.

The micropyle remains a small pore in the testa through which oxygen and water will enter when the seed germinates. The testa is a thin but tough protective layer derived from the integuments. The final stages in seed maturation involve a reduction in the water content of the seed from the normal levels for plant tissues of about 90% by mass to about 10–15% by mass. This markedly reduces the potential for metabolic activity and is an essential step in ensuring seed dormancy.

While the seeds develop, the ovary becomes a mature fruit, its wall being known as the **pericarp**. The changes that occur vary with species, but generally the fruit is adapted to protect the seeds and to aid in their dispersal as discussed in section 20.2.8.

The remaining flower parts wither and die and are abscissed in a controlled manner, just as leaves are in deciduous plants. In a few cases structures such as the receptacle, style or sepals are retained and contribute to dispersal. If the receptacle is involved, as in strawberry (*Fragaria*), the structure is called a **false fruit**.

The hormonal control of fruit development is discussed in section 15.3.5.

Some of the changes that occur after fertilisation are summarised in table 20.3.

Some stages in the development of the embryo are shown in fig 20.27.

20.2.7 Advantages and disadvantages of reproduction by seed

The seed is the characteristic product of sexual reproduction in the spermatophytes, being defined as a fertilised ovule. It contains an embryo plant with one or more cotyledons, sometimes an endosperm, and is surrounded by a protective testa.

Advantages

(1) The plant is independent of water for sexual reproduction and therefore better adapted for a land environment.
(2) The seed protects the embryo.
(3) The seed contains food for the embryo (either in cotyledons or in the endosperm).
(4) The seed is usually adapted for dispersal.
(5) The seed can remain dormant and survive adverse conditions.
(6) The seed is physiologically sensitive to favourable conditions and sometimes must undergo a period of after-ripening so that it will not germinate immediately (see chapter 15).
(7) The seed is a product of sexual reproduction and therefore has the attendant advantages of genetic variation.

Disadvantages

(1) Seeds are relatively large structures because of the extensive food reserves. This makes dispersal more difficult than by spores.
(2) Seeds are often eaten by animals for their food reserves.
(3) There is a reliance on external agents such as wind, insects and water for pollination. This makes pollination (and hence fertilisation) risky, particularly wind pollination.
(4) There is a large wastage of seeds because the chances of survival of a given seed are limited. The parent sporophyte must therefore invest large quantities of material and energy in seed production to ensure success.

(5) The food supply in a seed is limited, whereas in vegetative reproduction food is available from the parent plant until the daughter plant is fully established.
(6) Two individuals are required in dioecious species making the process more risky than reproduction in which only one parent is involved. However, dioecious plants are relatively rare.

The information provided above can be used to compare the advantages and disadvantages that seed-bearing plants have compared with non-seed-bearing plants, or to compare the relative merits of sexual reproduction and vegetative propagation within the seed-bearing plants.

20.2.8 Fruit and seed dispersal

After seed development either the entire fruit or the seed(s) contained within it are dispersed from the parent sporophyte. If the pericarp (wall) of the fruit becomes hard and dry it is called a dry fruit and if it becomes fleshy, a succulent fruit. Dry fruits may be dehiscent or indehiscent according to whether they do or do not release seeds by splitting. Alternatively dry fruits may split into a number of one-seeded portions and are then described as schizocarpic.

The further the seeds are dispersed, the less chance there is of competition from the parent plant. There is also more chance of finding a fresh area to colonise, thus increasing in time the overall population size. However, there is an attendant risk of the seed not finding a suitable place for germination if it is dispersed some distance from the parent.

There are three major external agents of dispersal, namely wind, animals and water. In addition self-dispersal mechanisms exist, often involving an explosive release of seeds from the fruit. Examples of all these types of dispersal are given below, fig 20.28, pages 745–8.

Fig 20.28 *Examples of different types of fruit and seed and their methods of dispersal*

ANIMAL DISPERSAL Animal dispersal is in general more reliable than wind dispersal because animals tend to frequent fertile places suitable for seed germination

(a) **Hooked fruits** e.g. goosegrass *(Galium)*, avens *Geum*, burdock *(Arctium)*, carrot *(Daucus)*, buttercup *(Ranunculus)*, bur-marigold *(Bidens)*, agrimony *(Agrimonia)*

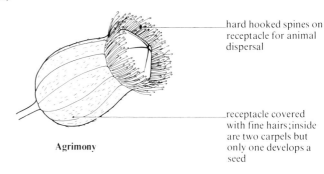

Goosegrass or cleavers
(Galium aparine)

two one-seeded portions of fruit

hooked pericarp

pedicel

Agrimony

hard hooked spines on receptacle for animal dispersal

receptacle covered with fine hairs; inside are two carpels but only one develops a seed

Agrimony has hard hooked spines on its receptacle.

Hooked or spiny fruits become attached to the skin, fur or wool of passing animals and may be carried some distance before dropping off or being scratched off. The hooks or spines develop from various parts of the fruit or surrounding structures. In *Geum* the style is hooked. In burdock a collection of small fruits is surrounded by hooked bracts (modified leaves) forming one structure. In addition, small stiff hairs break off and penetrate the skin, causing irritation and scratching with consequent removal of the fruits. Goosegrass, carrot and buttercup all have hooked pericarps. In bur-marigold the fruit has a pappus like the dandelion, but with strong barbs.

747

(a) Cont.

Scanning electron micrograph of the fruit of goosegrass, showing the numerous small hooks which develop from the pericarp. The hooks cling very effectively to the skin, fur or wool of passing animals

(b) **Succulent fruits** e.g. plum *(Prunus)*, blackberry *(Rubus)*, tomato *(Lycopersicum)*, apple *(Malus)*, strawberry *(Fragaria)*

Succulent fruits have fleshy parts that provide food for animals, including birds. They usually attract animals by becoming brightly coloured and scented as they ripen. The fruit is eaten and digested but the seeds are resistant to digestive enzymes and pass unharmed through the gut of the animal, to be deposited in the faeces, often on fertile soil. Nutrients from the decomposition of the faeces may increase the fertility around the seed. Representative examples of different types of fruit structure are illustrated below.

Section through blackberry – a collection of drupes formed from one flower

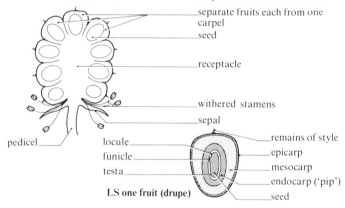

LS one fruit (drupe)

Plum

The plum is an example of a fruit called a **drupe** in which the pericarp has three layers, an **epicarp** (protective skin), a **mesocarp** (succulent) and an inner woody **endocarp,** ('stone') that protects the seed and resists digestion.

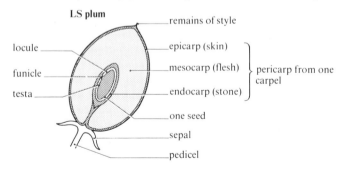

LS plum

Other examples of drupes are peach, cherry and almond (also *Prunus* spp.), elder *(Sambucus)* and coconut *(Cocos nucifera)* (fibrous mesocarp). Almonds sold in shops have normally had the epicarp and mesocarp removed.

Tomato

The tomato is an example of a fruit called a **berry**. It resembles a drupe, but the endocarp is fleshy not stony.

LS tomato
fusion of two, three or four carpels

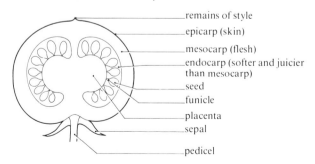

Other examples of berries are blackcurrant and gooseberry *(Ribes* spp.), marrow *(Cucurbita),* orange and lemon *(Citrus* spp.), banana *(Musa),* grape *(Vitis),* date *(Phoenix dactylifera)* (in date the single seed is woody).

(c) **False succulent fruits**

Sometimes the receptacle becomes swollen and fleshy and itself resembles a fruit. Such fruits are called false fruits. Examples are apple and strawberry.

Apple

The apple is an example of a false fruit called **a pome**. In pomes the flesh of the fruit is formed from the hollow receptacle which surrounds and encloses the carpels. The pericarp of the true fruit becomes the 'core' which contains the seeds ('pips'). Other examples are pear *(Pyrus)* and hawthorn *(Crataegus)*.

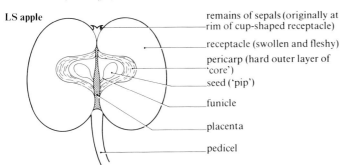

LS apple

- remains of sepals (originally at rim of cup-shaped receptacle)
- receptacle (swollen and fleshy)
- pericarp (hard outer layer of 'core')
- seed ('pip')
- funicle
- placenta
- pedicel

carpels 3-5 and fused, two seeds per carpel

Strawberry

The receptacle becomes swollen and bears on its surface small green fruits called **achenes** ('pips'), each of which contains a single seed.

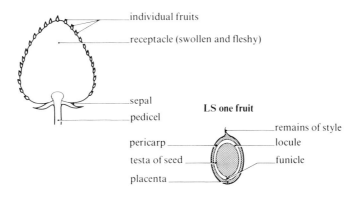

LS strawberry

- individual fruits
- receptacle (swollen and fleshy)
- sepal
- pedicel

LS one fruit

- remains of style
- pericarp
- locule
- testa of seed
- funicle
- placenta

(d) **Nuts** e.g. oak *(Quercus)*, beech *(Fagus)*, chestnut *(Castanea)* Nuts are relatively large, dry fruits that do not split open to allow seed dispersal (indehiscent). The whole fruit is dispersed, often as a result of being collected for food stores by animals, particularly by rodents such as squirrels.

Oak The nut is called an acorn.

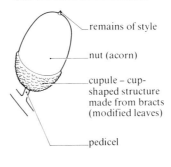

- remains of style
- nut (acorn)
- cupule – cup-shaped structure made from bracts (modified leaves)
- pedicel

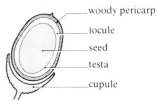

LS acorn
three fused carpels but only one seed develops

- woody pericarp
- locule
- seed
- testa
- cupule

(a) **Parachute mechanism** e.g. seeds of willowherb *(Epilobium)*, willow *(Salix)*, cotton *(Gossypium hirsutum)*, fruit of dandelion *(Taraxacum)*, 'old man's beard' *(Clematis)*

Dandelion

flower
- corolla
- stigma
- anthers
- pappus
- ovary

structures above pappus drop off after fertilisation

pappus
white hairs formed from sepals after fertilisation, large surface area aids wind dispersal

stalk
grows after fertilisation

fruit
(two fused carpels) from inferior ovary, small and light

- small hooks
- line of fusion of two carpels visible on **pericarp**
- scar of attachment to receptacle

LS fruit
- testa
- seed
- placenta
- locule
- pericarp
- funicle

749

(a) Cont.

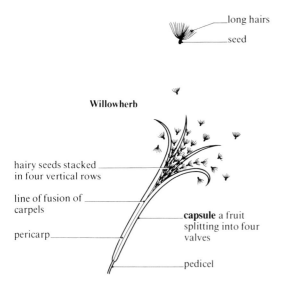

Willowherb

long hairs
seed

hairy seeds stacked
in four vertical rows

line of fusion of
carpels

pericarp

capsule a fruit
splitting into four
valves

pedicel

(b) **Wings** e.g. seeds of *Pinus* (a gymnosperm), fruit of elm *(Ulmus)*, ash *(Fraxinus)*, sycamore *(Acer)*, hornbeam *(Carpinus)*

Sycamore *(Acer pseudoplatanus)*

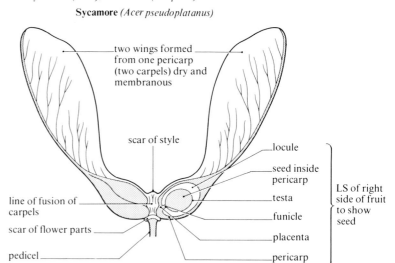

two wings formed
from one pericarp
(two carpels) dry and
membranous

scar of style

line of fusion of
carpels

scar of flower parts

pedicel

locule

seed inside
pericarp

testa

funicle

placenta

pericarp

LS of right
side of fruit
to show
seed

One fruit of sycamore Either before or after wind dispersal the fruit separates into two halves along the line of fusion of the carpels (the fruit is described as schizocarpic); as the fruit falls it rotates and is carried by the wind

(c) **Censer mechanism*** e.g. poppy *(Papaver)*, love-in-a-mist *(Nigella)*, foxglove *(Digitalis)*, campion *(Lychnis)* (all these examples have fruits called capsules)

Poppy

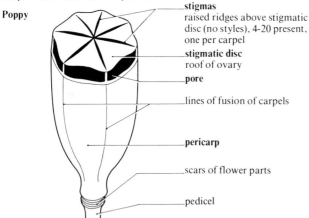

stigmas
raised ridges above stigmatic
disc (no styles), 4-20 present,
one per carpel

stigmatic disc
roof of ovary

pore

lines of fusion of carpels

pericarp

scars of flower parts

pedicel

The fruit, called a **capsule**, is borne at the end of a long pedicel which sways in the wind, causing the numerous small seeds to escape from the pores at the top of the capsule (* A censer is a vessel in which incense is burnt and is swayed from side to side as it is carried)

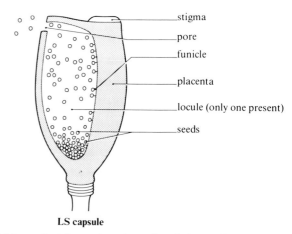

stigma

pore

funicle

placenta

locule (only one present)

seeds

LS capsule

(d) Some plants have extremely small seeds that are light enough to be distributed by wind without the aid of special appendages to increase surface area, e.g. orchids

SELF-DISPERSAL   The most common self-dispersal mechanisms involve dehiscent fruits.

Dehiscent fruits
These dry and break open, often by splitting lines of weakness, e.g. pods. Seeds may be forcibly ejected with varying degrees of violence or may simply drop out. The seeds released may also be modified for wind dispersal (e.g. willowherb). Capsules are also dehiscent (see poppy and willowherb under wind dispersal) and some release seeds violently, e.g. violet *(Viola)*.

Pods e.g. pea *(Pisum)*, broad bean *(Vicia)*, runner bean *(Phaseolus)*, gorse *(Ulex)* broom and laburnum *(Cytisus* spp.)
Pods are the characteristic fruits of the legume family (Leguminosae). Pods consist of one carpel containing many seeds. The pericarp splits along two sides.

Broom, laburnum or pea

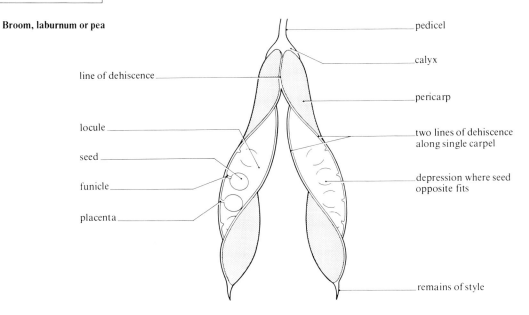

(see also fig 20.16 for earlier stages in development of pea pod)
The pericarp twists on drying due to oblique layers of fibrous tissue. As the twisting tension builds up, the pod may split suddenly along lines of dehiscence, forcibly ejecting some of the seeds. Others are released less forcibly as twisting continues.

WATER DISPERSAL

Few fruits and seeds are specialised for water dispersal, though water may act as a chance agent of dispersal. Those that are specialised are made buoyant by structures possessing air cavities. The coconut *(Cocos nucifera)* is a drupe (compare plum) whose mesocarp is fibrous and contains numerous air spaces. The water lily *(Nymphaea)* has a spongy outgrowth of its seed (the aril) derived from the funicle.

Water lily

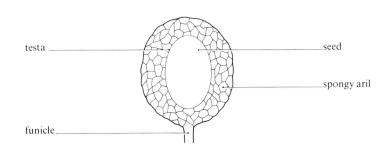

CHANCE DISPERSAL

The categories of wind, animal and self-dispersal are by no means rigid and the degree of specialisation of fruits and seeds for particular methods of dispersal is very variable. An element of chance is therefore bound to be involved in many cases, and more than one of the three dispersal methods could be used by a given fruit or seed. Humans are one of the chief agents of chance dispersal, with the possibility of seeds clinging to clothing etc. or being carried in cargoes or by machinery. Contamination of grain crops by weed seeds is a common phenomenon worldwide. Caches of nuts stored by rodents may be forgotten and germinate the following spring. Chance floods, hurricanes, etc. may carry seeds further than usual.

20.3 Human sexual reproduction

20.3.1 The human male reproductive system

The male reproductive system is composed of a pair of testes, genital ducts, accessory glands and the penis. The **testis** is an ovoid-shaped compound tubular gland surrounded by a capsule, the **tunica albuginea**, enclosing about 1 000 highly coiled **seminiferous tubules** embedded in connective tissue containing **Leydig cells** (interstitial cells). The tubules of the testis produce the male gametes, **spermatozoa** (commonly referred to as sperm), and Leydig cells produce the male sex hormone **testosterone**. The testes are situated outside the abdominal cavity in the **scrotal sac** and, as a result, temperatures at which sperm develop are 2–3 °C lower than the core temperature. The lower temperature in the scrotal sac is partly due to its position and partly due to the vascular plexus formed by the spermatic artery and vein acting as a countercurrent heat exchange system. The **dartos muscle** of the scrotal sac moves the testes towards or away from the body according to the outside temperature in order to maintain sperm production at an optimum level. Males passing through puberty with undescended testes (a condition called **cryptorchidism**) become permanently sterile and men persistently wearing tight underpants or taking very hot baths may have such a reduced sperm count that it leads to infertility. Whales and elephants are two of the few mammalian species with testes retained in the abdominal cavity.

The seminiferous tubules are approximately 50 cm long and 200 µm in diameter, situated in regions of the testis called **testicular lobules**. Both ends of the tubule are connected to the central region of the testis, the **rete testis**, by short **tubuli recti**. From here 10–20 **vasa efferentia** collect sperm and transfer them to the head of the **epididymis** where they are concentrated by reabsorption of fluid secreted from the seminiferous tubule. Sperm mature in this region of the epididymis before passing 5 m along the coiled tubule to the base of the epididymis where they are stored for a short period before entering the **vas deferens**. The vas deferens is a straight tube about 40 cm long forming, with the spermatic artery and vein, the 'spermatic cord' and conveying sperm to the urethra which traverses the penis. The relationship between these structures and the male accessory glands and penis is shown in figs 20.29 and 20.30.

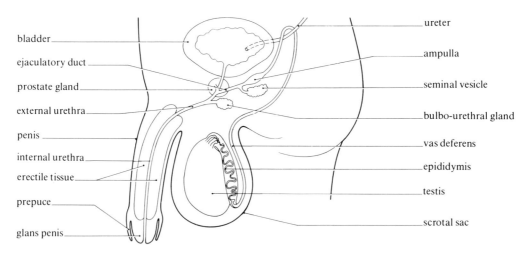

bladder

ejaculatory duct

prostate gland

external urethra

penis

internal urethra

erectile tissue

prepuce

glans penis

ureter

ampulla

seminal vesicle

bulbo-urethral gland

vas deferens

epididymis

testis

scrotal sac

Fig 20.29 (above) *Diagram of the human male reproductive system*

Fig 20.30 (below) *Simplified diagram showing the structure of the human testis and ducts conveying sperm from seminiferous tubules to the urethra*

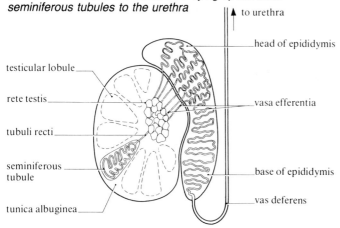

to urethra

head of epididymis

testicular lobule

rete testis

tubuli recti

seminiferous tubule

tunica albuginea

vasa efferentia

base of epididymis

vas deferens

Gamete formation (gametogenesis)

Cells of the germinal epithelium in both male and female gonads undergo a sequence of mitotic and meiotic divisions, called gametogenesis to produce mature male gametes (spermatogenesis) and female gametes (oogenesis). In both cases the process involves three stages, a multiplication stage, a growth stage, and a maturation stage. The multiplication stage involves repeated mitotic divisions producing many spermatogonia and oogonia. Each undergoes a period of growth in preparation for the first meiotic division and subsequent cytokinesis. This marks the beginning of the maturation stage during which the first and second meiotic divisions occur followed by differentiation of the haploid cells and the formation of mature gametes.

Development of spermatozoa (spermatogenesis)

Spermatozoa are produced by a sequence of cell divisions called **spermatogenesis** followed by a complex process of differentiation called **spermiogenesis** (fig 20.31). Spermatozoa production takes approximately 70 days and 10^7 spermatozoa are produced per gram of testis per day. The epithelium of the seminiferous tubule consists of an outer layer of **germinal epithelial cells** and about six layers of cells produced by repeated cell divisions of this layer (figs 20.32 and 20.33). These represent successive stages in the development of spermatozoa. Initial divisions of the germinal epithelial cells give rise to many **spermatogonia** which increase in size to form **primary spermatocytes**. These undergo the first meiotic division to form haploid **secondary spermatocytes** and the second meiotic division to form **spermatids**. Between these 'strands' of developing cells are large **Sertoli** or **nurse cells** stretching from the outer layer of the tubule to the lumen.

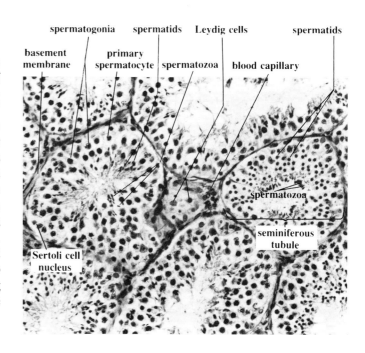

Fig 20.32 (right) *Photomicrographs of a section through the human testis showing seminiferous tubules and Leydig (interstitial) cells*

Fig 20.31 (below) *Summary diagram of the process of human spermatogenesis and spermiogenesis, not drawn to scale*

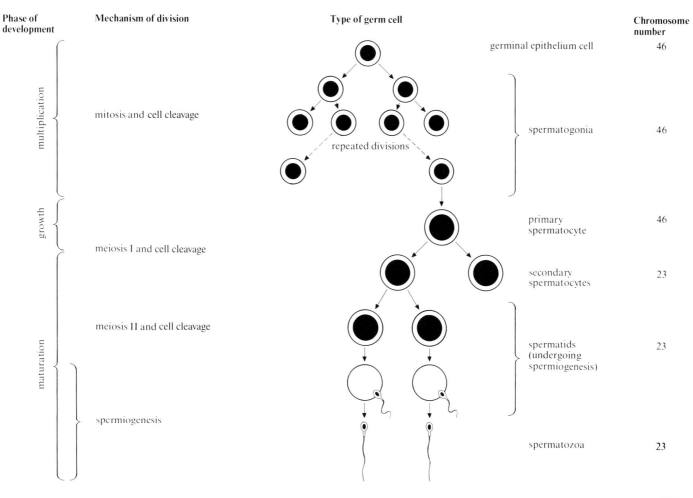

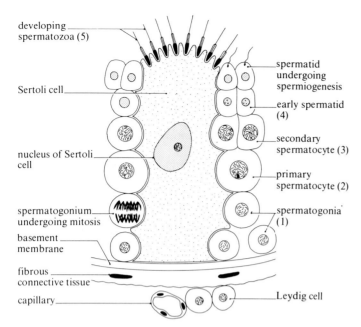

Fig 20.33 *Diagram showing the structure of part of the wall of a seminiferous tubule and interstitial cells. Cells in various stages of spermatogenesis and spermiogenesis are shown*

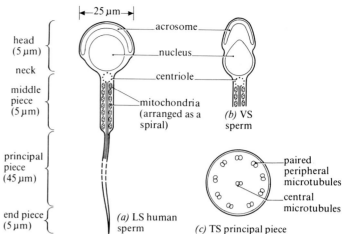

Fig 20.34 *Diagram showing the structure of a mature human spermatozoon*

20.7 Sertoli cells contain abundant smooth endoplasmic reticulum, Golgi apparatus and many mitochondria and lysosomes. In view of the structure of these cells what can you suggest about their function?

Spermatocytes become embedded in the many invaginations in the lateral margins of the Sertoli cells where they develop into spermatids before passing to the edge of the cell bordering the lumen where they mature as **spermatozoa**. The Sertoli cells are thought to provide mechanical support, protection and nourishment during maturation of the spermatozoa. All nutrients, oxygen and waste substances exchanged between the developing gametes and the blood vessels surrounding the tubules pass through the Sertoli cells. The fluid carrying spermatozoa through the tubules is secreted by the Sertoli cells.

Spermatozoa

Spermatozoa are minute, motile male gametes produced by the male gonads, the testes, and released in millions. They have various shapes according to species but share a common structure. Each spermatozoon is composed of five regions as shown in fig 20.34. The head consists of a nucleus, containing the haploid number of chromosomes, covered by a membrane-enclosed structure, the **acrosome**. This contains hydrolytic enzymes which will be involved in the penetration of the oocyte by the sperm immediately prior to fertilisation. Functionally, therefore, it may be thought of as an enlarged lysosome. The short neck region contains a pair of centrioles lying at right-angles to each other. The microtubules of one of the centrioles elongate

and run the entire length of the rest of the spermatozoon forming the **axial filament** of the flagellum. The middle piece is enlarged by the presence of many mitochondria arranged in a spiral surrounding the flagellum. The energy released by the mitochondria is used in the contractile mechanisms which bring about movement of the flagellum. The principal and end pieces of the spermatozoon are flagellate and in transverse section show the characteristic arrangement of nine pairs of peripheral microtubules surrounding a central pair of microtubules.

Human sperm have a rounded head in plan view and are flattened in a lateral view. Activation of the flagellum is described in section 20.3.2, but it is known that flagellar movement is insufficient to cover the distance from the vagina to the site of fertilisation. The principal locomotory function of sperm is to cluster around the oocyte and to orientate themselves prior to penetration of the oocyte membranes.

Endocrine function of the human testis

The growth, development and maintenance of the testis is controlled by the pituitary gonadotrophins, **follicle stimulating hormone (FSH)** and **luteinising hormone (LH)**. FSH stimulates the development of spermatozoa and LH stimulates the synthesis of the steroid hormone testosterone by the Leydig cells of the testis. LH exerts its influence on the Leydig cells by releasing membrane-bound cyclic AMP (adenosine monophosphate) into the cytoplasm which then passes to the nucleus where it stimulates the synthesis of enzymes involved in the synthesis of testosterone from cholesterol. (LH is sometimes referred to as **interstitial cell stimulating hormone (ICSH)** in males, because of its site of action.)

Testosterone is the principal androgenic hormone and it affects both primary and secondary sexual characteristics. Both testosterone and FSH are required for the successful production of sperm whereas testosterone alone controls the development of the secondary sexual characteristics during puberty and maintains these throughout adult life. These characteristics include the development of the male external genitalia and the accessory glands of the reproductive tract, increased muscle development, enlargement of the larynx producing deepening of the voice, the growth and distribution of hair and behavioural activities associated with mating and parental concern.

20.3.2 The human female reproductive system

Female involvement in reproduction is greater than that of the male and it involves reciprocal interrelationships between the pituitary gland, ovary, uterus and foetus. The female reproductive system is composed of paired ovaries and fallopian tubes, the uterus, vagina and external genitalia (fig 20.35).

The **ovaries** are attached to the wall of the body cavity by a fold in the peritoneum and have the dual function of producing female gametes and secreting female sex hormones. They are about the size and shape of an almond and consist of an outer **cortex** and inner **medulla** surrounded by a connective tissue sheath, the **tunica albuginea**. The outer layer of cells of the cortex is composed of germinal epithelial cells from which gamete cells are produced. The cortex is composed of developing follicles

and the medulla is composed of **stroma**, containing connective tissue, blood vessels and mature follicles (fig 20.38).

The **fallopian tube** is a muscular tube about 12 cm long and conveys female gametes from the ovary to the uterus. The opening of the fallopian tube is expanded and split into **fringes** or **fimbriae** which move nearer to the ovary at ovulation. The lumen of the fallopian tube is lined with ciliated epithelium and female gametes move towards the uterus aided by peristaltic movements of the muscle wall of the fallopian tube.

The **uterus** is a thick-walled organ about 7.5 cm long and 5 cm wide and composed of three main layers. The outer covering is called the **serous coat** and this encloses the middle layer, the **myometrium**, which forms the bulk of the wall. The myometrium is composed of bundles of smooth muscle cells which are sensitive to oxytocin during birth. The inner layer, the **endometrium**, is soft and smooth and composed of epithelial cells, simple tubular glands and spiral arterioles supplying the cells. The cavity of the uterus is capable of extending 500 times during pregnancy, that is from 10 cm^3 to 5 000 cm^3. The lower entrance to the uterus is the **cervix** which separates the uterus from the **vagina**. The vaginal orifice, the urethral orifice and the clitoris are protected by two folds of tissue called the **vulva** composed of the **labia majora** and **labia minora**. The **clitoris** is a small erectile structure which is homologous with the male penis. Within the walls of the vulva are the **vestibular glands** which release mucus when the female is sexually aroused and this helps to lubricate the penis during intercourse.

Development of human ova (oogenesis)

Unlike the production of spermatozoa in males which only begins at puberty, the production of ova in females begins before birth and is completed only after fertilisation. The stages in oogenesis are shown in fig 20.36. During fetal development primordial cells undergo repetitive mitotic division and produce many larger cells called **oogonia**. These undergo mitosis and form **primary oocytes** which remain at prophase of this stage until just before ovulation. Primary oocytes are enclosed by a single layer of cells, the **membrana granulosa**, and form structures known as **primordial follicles**. Approximately 2×10^6 of these follicles exist in the fetal female just before birth but only about 450 ever develop into secondary oocytes which are released from the ovary during the oestrous cycle. Prior to ovulation the primary oocyte undergoes the first meiotic division to form the haploid **secondary oocyte** and the **first polar body**. The second meiotic division proceeds as far as metaphase but does not continue until a sperm fuses with the oocyte. At fertilisation the secondary oocyte undergoes the second meiotic division producing a large cell, the **ovum**, and a **second polar body**. All polar bodies are small cells. They have no role in oogenesis and they eventually degenerate.

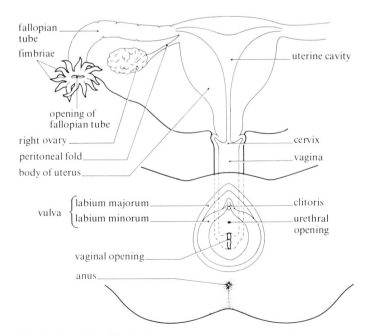

Fig 20.35 *Simplified diagram showing the human female reproductive system. The uterus and vagina are shown in section, and the external genitalia, urethral and anal openings are shown in surface view with the labia parted*

Phase of development	Mechanism of division	Type of germ cell	Stage in life cycle	Chromosome number

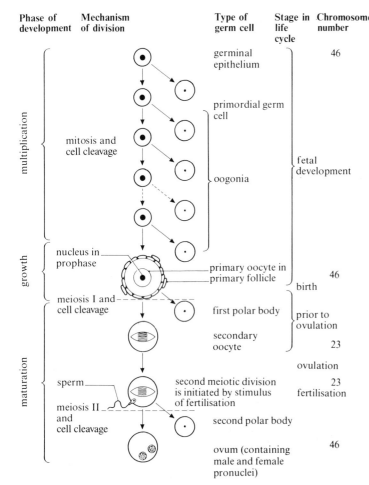

Fig 20.36 *Summary diagram of the process of human oogenesis*

Menstrual cycle

In males, gamete production and release is a continuous process beginning at puberty and lasting throughout life. In females, it is a cyclical activity with a periodicity of approximately 28 days and involves changes in the structure and function of the whole reproductive system. It is called the **menstrual cycle** and can be divided into four

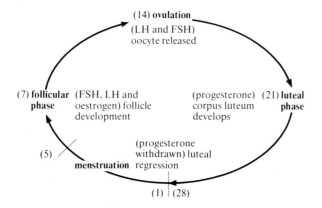

Fig 20.37 *Summary of the main phases of the human menstrual cycle. (Figures in brackets indicate days coinciding with phases of the cycle)*

phases as shown in fig 20.37. The events of the menstrual cycle involve the ovaries (the **ovarian cycle**) and the uterus (the **uterine cycle**) and these are regulated by hormones secreted by the ovary which in turn is regulated by pituitary gonadotrophins.

Ovarian cycle

In an adult female the ovarian cycle, which is summarised in fig 20.38, begins with the development of several primary follicles (containing primary oocytes) induced by the release of follicle stimulating hormone (FSH) from the anterior pituitary gland. Only one of these follicles continues to grow whilst the rest break down by a degenerative process known as **follicular atresia**. The cells of the membrana granulosa of the follicle proliferate to produce an outer fibrous layer several cells thick, known as the **theca externa**, and an inner vascular layer, the **theca interna**. The granulosa cells secrete a fluid which collects and forms a space, the **antrum**, within the follicle. Luteinising hormone (LH) released from the pituitary gland stimulates the cells of the thecae to produce steroids, the principal one being **17β-oestradiol**. Increasing levels of oestradiol during the follicular phase feed back negatively on the pituitary gland causing a decrease in FSH levels in the blood (days 4–11); LH levels remain unchanged. Oestrogen levels reach a maximum about three days before ovulation and at this time have a positive feedback action on the pituitary gland causing the release of both FSH and LH.

It is thought that FSH is necessary to stimulate the growth of follicles but that the continued follicular development is controlled mainly by LH. The granulosa cells line the periphery with the ovum displaced to one side of the follicle but still surrounded by a layer of granulosa cells. This mature follicle, known as the **Graafian follicle**, is about 1 cm in diameter and protrudes from the surface of the ovary giving it a warty appearance (fig 20.39). The exact mechanism of ovulation is unknown but LH, FSH and prostaglandins are thought to be involved.

At ovulation the secondary oocyte detaches from the wall of the follicle, is released into the peritoneal cavity and passes into the fallopian tube. Usually only one oocyte is released each month by one of the ovaries so that ovulation alternates between the pair of ovaries. The ovulated oocyte consists of a cell whose nucleus is in metaphase I of meiosis surrounded by a cell layer known as the **zona pellucida** and a layer of granulosa cells known as the **corona radiata** which protects the oocyte up to fertilisation.

Following ovulation, LH levels fall to follicular levels, and in the presence of another gonadotrophin, **prolactin**, the cells of the ruptured follicle change to form the **corpus luteum** (yellow body). This begins to secrete and release another female hormone, **progesterone**, and smaller amounts of oestrogen. These two hormones maintain the structure of the endometrium of the uterus and inhibit FSH and LH release by negative feedback on the hypothalamus.

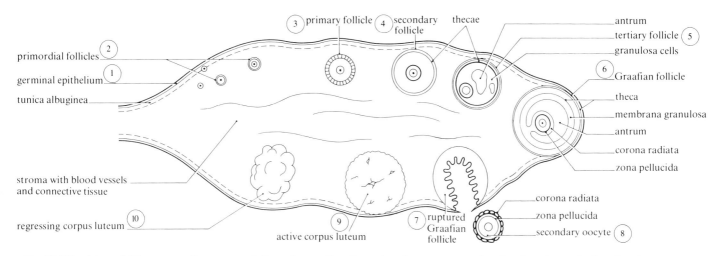

Fig 20.38 (above) *Diagrammatic representation of a section through a human ovary showing the stages in the development of a Graafian follicle, ovulation and the formation and regression of the corpus luteum. Not all these stages would be seen together. The numbers indicate the sequence of the stages*

Fig 20.39 (below) *Photomicrograph of mature human Graafian follicle*

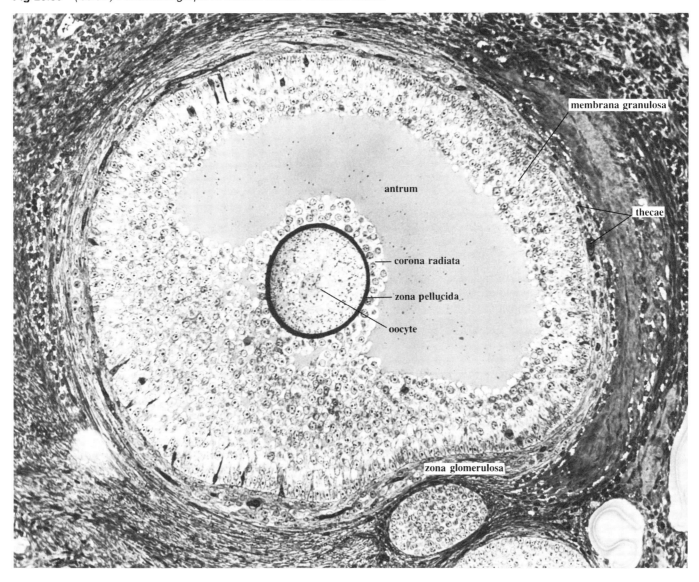

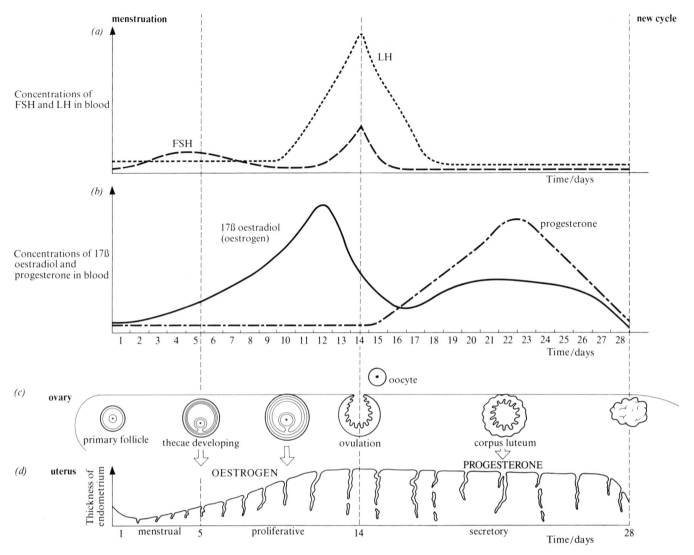

Fig 20.40 *Summary diagram showing the relationship between (a) pituitary gonadotrophins, (b) ovarian steroids, (c) follicle and corpus luteal development and (d) the thickness of the endometrium during the human oestrous cycle*

If fertilisation does not occur factors described later cause the regression of the corpus luteum, which persists as a 'scarred' area, the **corpus albicantus**, and the consequent decrease in progesterone and oestrogen levels. As these levels fall FSH release is no longer inhibited, and as the FSH level rises a new cycle of follicle development occurs. The relationship between the activity of the pituitary gland, ovary and uterus is shown in fig 20.40.

20.8 During a post-mortem carried out on a woman of 22 years of age it was noticed that her ovaries were unequal in size. Analyses of the ovaries revealed the following results:

Smaller ovary	Larger ovary
contained 17 000 follicles	contained 25 000 follicles
" 4 corpora lutea	" 5 corpora lutea
" 10 corpora albicanti	" 48 corpora albicanti

Most of the follicles were small but 219 were over 100 μm in diameter. Five follicles contained two oocytes each and 2% of the oocytes contained two nuclei each. Assuming that each follicle produces a corpus luteum,

(*a*) (i) at what age did the woman commence ovulation?

(ii) for approximately how many years would ovulation have continued?

(iii) how many potential sets of twins could this woman have produced and what type of twins would they be?

(*b*) What process accounts for the presence of two nuclei in some of the oocytes (section 22.3)?

Uterine cycle

The uterine cycle consists of three phases represented by structural and functional changes of the endometrium. These are as follows.

Menstrual phase. This is the shedding of the epithelial lining of the endometrium. Just prior to this phase the blood supply to this region is reduced by constriction of spiral arterioles in the wall of the uterus as a result of the fall in the progesterone level in the blood following the regression of the corpus luteum. This leads to the death of the epithelial cells. Following the period of constriction the spiral arterioles then dilate and the increased blood flow detaches the lining of the uterus and it is shed together with a variable amount of blood in the **menstrual flow**.

Proliferative phase. This coincides with the follicular phase of the oestrous cycle and involves the rapid proliferation of endometrial cells causing the thickening of the endometrium under the control of oestrogen from the developing follicle.

Secretory phase. During this phase progesterone from the corpus luteum stimulates the secretion of mucus from tubular glands and this maintains the lining of the uterus in a receptive state for the implantation of a fertilised ovum.

The effect of failure of fertilisation on the oestrous cycle

If fertilisation does not occur within 24 h of ovulation the secondary oocyte undergoes autolysis in the fallopian tube, as do any spermatozoa remaining in the female genital tract. The corpus luteum persists for 10–14 days following ovulation (usually up to day 26 of the cycle) but then it stops secreting progesterone and oestrogen, as a result of inadequate LH circulating in the blood, and undergoes autolysis. Recent evidence has suggested that in some species the wall of the uterus not containing a fertilised ovum produces a factor known as **luteolysin** which is a prostaglandin, **prostaglandin F2α**. This is thought to pass via the bloodstream to the ovary where it causes regression of the corpus luteum, by rupturing lysosomes within the granulosa cells of the corpus luteum, which then undergoes autolysis.

The effect of fertilisation

If fertilisation occurs the zygote develops into a **blastocyst** which embeds itself into the wall of the uterus within eight days of ovulation. The outer cells of the blastocyst, the **trophoblastic cells**, then begin to secrete a hormone, **human chorionic gonadotrophin** (HCG), which has a similar function to LH. This function includes prevention of autolysis of the corpus luteum and the secretion by it of increased amounts of progesterone and oestrogens which cause increased growth of the endometrium of the uterus. Loss of the lining of the endometrium is inhibited and the

absence of menstrual bleeding (the 'period') is the earliest sign of pregnancy. (Chorionic gonadotrophin has an interstitial cell stimulating effect on the male fetus and causes the secretion of testosterone by the fetal testes which induces growth of the male sex organs.) The placenta begins to assume greater importance in about week 10 of pregnancy when it begins to secrete most of the progesterone and oestrogen essential for a normal pregnancy. Premature failure of the corpus luteum before the secretory ability of the placenta is established fully is a common cause of miscarriage at about 10–12 weeks of pregnancy.

During pregnancy HCG may be detected in the urine and this forms the basis of pregnancy testing. The current test used is called the **agglutination-inhibition test** and involves the addition of chorionic gonadotrophin-coated latex particles to a mixture of urine and an antiserum that will agglutinate with chorionic gonadotrophin. If chorionic gonadotrophin is present in the urine it will react with the agglutinating antiserum and not with the latex particles. The absence of agglutination of the latex particles indicates pregnancy and can be used from 14 days after the missed period.

20.3.3 Copulation

Internal fertilisation is an essential part of reproductive cycles in terrestrial organisms and this is facilitated in many organisms, including humans, by the development of an **intromittent** organ, the penis, which is inserted into the vagina and releases gametes as high as possible within the female reproductive tract. Erection of the penis occurs as a result of a local increase in blood pressure in erectile tissue of the penis, due to parasympathetic nervous activity producing constriction of the veins and dilation of the arterioles following some form of sexual excitement. In this state the penis can be inserted into the vagina where the friction, produced by the rhythmic movements of sexual intercourse, increases the tactile stimulation of sensory cells at the tip of the penis. This activates sympathetic neurones which lead to closure of the internal sphincter of the bladder and contraction of the smooth muscle of the epididymis, vas deferens, and the male accessory glands, the seminal vesicle, prostate and bulbo-urethral glands. This action discharges sperm and seminal fluids into the proximal (internal) urethra where they mix to form **semen**. The increased pressure of these fluids in the proximal urethra leads to reflex activity in the motor neurones supplying the muscles at the base of the penis. Rhythmic wave-like contractions of these muscles force semen out through the distal (external) urethra during **ejaculation** which marks the climax of copulation. The other physiological and psychological sensations associated with this climax in both males and females are called **orgasm**. Lubrication is provided during intercourse partly by a clear mucus secreted by the male bulbo-urethral glands following erection but mainly by glands in the vagina and vulva. The secretions of the male accessory glands are alkaline and contain mucus, fructose, vitamin C, citric acid, prostaglandins and various clotting enzymes, and these increase the normally more acidic pH of the vagina to 6–6.5 which is the optimum pH for sperm motility following ejaculation. Approximately 3 cm³ of semen is discharged during ejaculation of which only 10% comprises sperm. Despite this low percentage, semen contains about 10^8 sperms cm^{-3}.

20.3.4 Fertilisation

Sperm are deposited high up the vagina close to the cervix. Investigations have shown that sperm pass from the vagina through the uterus and to the top of the fallopian tube within five minutes as a result of contractions of the uterus and fallopian tubes. These contractions are thought to be initiated by the release of oxytocin during sexual intercourse and the local action of prostaglandins, present in semen, on the uterus and fallopian tubes. Sperm are viable in the female genital tract for 24–72 h but are only highly fertile for 12–24 h. Sperm can only fertilise the

oocyte after spending several hours in the female genital tract, usually seven hours, during which time they undergo a process known as **capacitation**. This involves a change in the properties of the membrane covering the acrosome and enables fertilisation to proceed. Fertilisation usually occurs high up the fallopian tube.

When a sperm reaches the oocyte (fig 20.41), the outer membrane of the sperm covering the acrosomal region and the membranes of the acrosome rupture enabling **hyaluronidase** and **protease** enzymes stored in the acrosome to 'digest' away the cell layers, including the zona pellucida, surrounding the oocyte. These changes in the sperm head are known as the **acrosome reaction**. Subsequent changes in the sperm head evert the inner membrane of the acrosome allowing penetration of the zona pellucida and the cell surface membrane of the oocyte and, in humans, entry of the entire sperm. Once one sperm has entered the oocyte, cortical granules beneath the cell surface membrane, beginning at the point of sperm entry, rupture, releasing a substance which causes the zona pellucida to thicken and separate from the cell surface membrane. This is called the **cortical reaction** and spreads over the entire surface of the

(a)

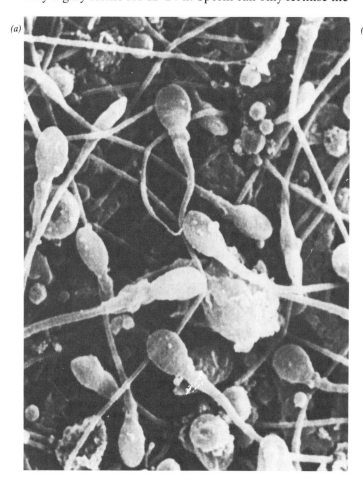

(b)

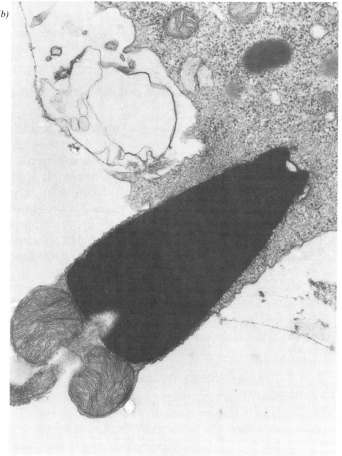

Fig 20.41 (a) Scanning electron micrograph of human sperms clustered around secondary oocyte
(b) The precise moment of fertilisation as a sperm penetrates the membrane of a sea-urchin's egg. The dark wedge is the head of the sperm, which contains the genetic code. The grey shape behind it is where energy is released that provides power for the tail. The sperm has digested the egg's surface coating of sugary protein and entered. Now the egg's internal fluid welds itself to the outside of the sperm, and draws it in to complete the mating. In some unknown way, the entry of one sperm prevents any others getting in, probably because of rapid changes in the egg's surface coating

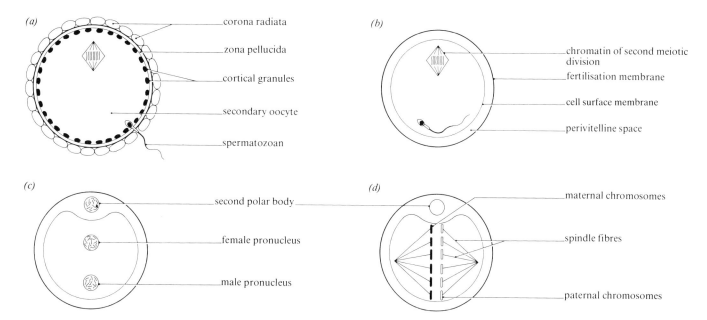

Fig 20.42 *Simplified diagrams illustrating fertilisation. (a) A spermatozoon having undergone capacitation is able to penetrate the zona pellucida of the secondary oocyte and cause the breakdown of cortical granules. (b) The cortical reaction has converted the zona pellucida into the fertilisation membrane which moves off the cell surface membrane creating the perivitelline space. (c) The second meiotic division produces the second polar body and is followed by the formation of the female pronucleus and male pronucleus. (d) The nuclear envelopes of the pronuclei break down and maternal and paternal chromosomes align themselves along the equator of the ovum attached to spindle fibres. This is metaphase of the first mitotic division of the zygote*

oocyte causing the zona pellucida to form an impenetrable barrier called the **fertilisation membrane** which prevents the entry of further sperm, that is preventing **polyspermy**.

The entry of a sperm acts as the stimulus for completion of the second meiotic division of the secondary oocyte which produces the ovum and the second polar body. The second polar body immediately degenerates, and the tail of the sperm is lost within the cytoplasm of the ovum. Sperm and ovum nuclei form **pronuclei** which are drawn together. The membranes of the pronuclei break down and the paternal and maternal chromosomes attach to spindle fibres which have formed. Both haploid sets of chromosomes by this stage have undergone replication and align themselves as 46 pairs of chromatids along the equator of the spindle as in metaphase of mitosis. This fusion of pronuclear chromosomes is termed **fertilisation**. At this point the diploid number of chromosomes is restored and the fertilised ovum is now called a **zygote**.

Anaphase and telophase of the zygote cell follow and complete the first mitotic division of the zygote. The zygote then undergoes cytokinesis and produces two diploid daughter cells. The process of fertilisation is summarised in fig 20.42.

20.3.5 Implantation

As the zygote passes down the fallopian tube it cleaves by successive nuclear and cell divisions to produce a collection of cells called the **morula**. Cleavage at this stage does not result in an increase in size of the morula because

the cells continue to be retained within the zona pellucida. The cleaved cells are called **blastomeres** and they form a wall of cells enclosing a central cavity in the morula, called the **blastocoel**, which fills with liquid from the oviduct. The outer layer of blastomeres is called the **trophoblast** and this differentiates at one point to form a thickened mass of cells, the **inner cell mass**. This stage is called the **blastocyst** and is reached about 4–5 days following ovulation. The structure of the blastocyst is shown in fig 20.43.

When the blastocyst arrives in the uterus it spends about two days in the lumen during which the zona pellucida gradually disappears enabling the cells of the trophoblast to make contact with the cells of the endometrium. The trophoblast cells multiply in the presence of nourishment from the endometrium and between the sixth and ninth days after ovulation the blastocyst becomes embedded

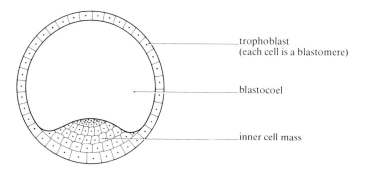

Fig 20.43 *Simplified diagram of a human blastocyst four days after ovulation*

761

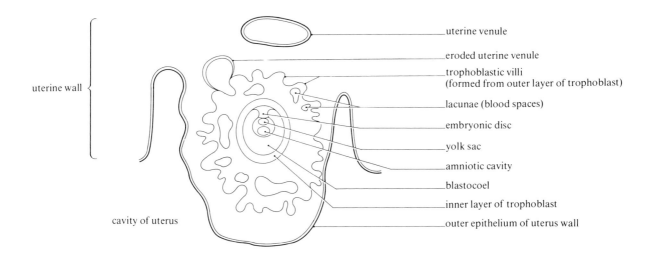

uterine wall	uterine venule
	eroded uterine venule
	trophoblastic villi (formed from outer layer of trophoblast)
	lacunae (blood spaces)
	embryonic disc
	yolk sac
	amniotic cavity
	blastocoel
	inner layer of trophoblast
cavity of uterus	outer epithelium of uterus wall

Fig 20.44 (above) *Simplified diagram showing a recently implanted human blastocyst in the endometrium of the uterus. Enzymes produced by the syncitium of the outer trophoblast break down the blood vessels of the endometrium producing lacunae containing blood which are used in the nourishment and excretion of the blastocyst*

within cells of the endometrium. This process is called **implantation**. The cells of the trophoblast differentiate into two layers and the cell membranes of cells of the outer layer of the trophoblast break down to form the **trophoblastic villi** which grow into the endometrium (fig 20.44). The areas of the endometrium between these villi form interconnecting cavities, called **lacunae**, which give this region of the endometrium a spongy appearance. Hydrolytic enzymes released by this multinucleate structure cause the arterial and venous blood vessels in the endometrium to break down and blood from them fills the lacunae. In the early stages of development of the blastocyst, exchange of nourishment, oxygen and excretory materials between the cells of the blastocyst and the maternal blood in the uterus wall occurs through the trophoblastic villi. Later in development this function is taken over by the placenta.

20.3.6 Early embryonic development

The outer cells of the blastocyst, the trophoblast, grow and develop into an outer membrane called the **chorion** which plays a major role in nourishing and removing waste from the developing embryo. Two cavities appear within the inner cell mass and the cells lining these give rise to two membranes, the **amnion** and the **yolk sac**. The amnion is a thin membrane covering the embryo and has a protective function. Secretion of **amniotic fluid** by the cells of the amnion fill the amniotic cavity between amnion and the embryo. As the embryo increases in size the amnion expands so that it is always pressed up against the uterus wall. The amniotic fluid supports the embryo and protects it from mechanical shock. The yolk sac has no significant function in humans but is important in reptiles and birds for the absorption of food from the yolk and its transfer to the midgut of the developing embryo.

The cells of the inner cell mass, beneath the early amnion, and the yolk sac form a structure called the **embryonic disc**, which gives rise to the embryo. The cells of the disc differentiate at an early stage (when the diameter is less than 2 mm) and form an outer layer of cells, the **ectoderm**, and an inner layer, the **endoderm**. At a later

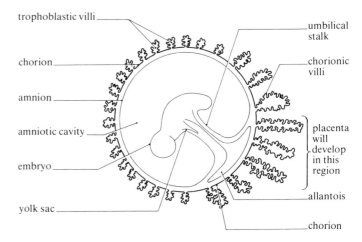

trophoblastic villi	umbilical stalk
chorion	chorionic villi
amnion	
amniotic cavity	placenta will develop in this region
embryo	
yolk sac	allantois
	chorion

Fig 20.45 *Simplified diagram showing the relationship between the human embryo and extra-embryonic membranes about five weeks after ovulation. The area of the allanto-chorion becomes the placenta*

stage the **mesoderm** is formed and these three germ layers give rise to all the tissues of the developing embryo as described in section 21.8.

During the early stages of embryonic development exchange of materials between embryo and mother across he trophoblastic villi is adequate, but soon a fourth membrane, the **allantois**, develops from the embryonic hindgut. The chorion, amnion, yolk sac and allantois are called **extra-embryonic membranes**, or **fetal membranes** (fig 20.45). The allantois grows outwards until it comes into contact with the chorion where it forms a richly vascularised structure, the **allanto-chorion**, which contributes towards the development of a more efficient and effective exchange structure, the **placenta**.

Placenta

The placenta is a temporary organ found only in eutherian mammals and is the only organ in animals composed of cells derived from two different organisms, the fetus and the mother. It is a point of close association between maternal and fetal circulations and facilitates the transfer of nutrients, oxygen and metabolic waste products between fetus and mother. The placenta is a discrete disc-shaped structure localised in one region of the uterus wall and as it develops it takes over from the trophoblastic villi as the principal site of exchange of materials after 12 weeks.

The fetal part of the placenta consists of connective tissue cells of the chorion which invade the trophoblastic villi in one region of the uterus wall and produce larger projections called **chorionic villi**. The inner regions of the chorionic villi become invaded with looped capillary networks derived from two blood vessels of the fetus, the umbilical artery and the umbilical vein. These blood vessels are derived from the allantois and run between fetus and uterus wall in the **umbilical cord** which is a tough structure about 40 cm long covered by cells derived from the amnion and chorion (fig 20.46).

The maternal part of the placenta is composed of outward projections of the outer layers of the endometrium, the **decidua**. Between these and the chorionic villi are lacunae supplied with arterial blood from the uterine arterioles and drained by venules of the uterine vein. The direction of blood flow through the lacunae is determined by the difference in pressure between arterial and venous vessels.

The cell membranes in the wall of the chorionic villi bathed by maternal blood bear microvilli, which increase their surface area, for the exchange of substances by diffusion and other methods of transport. Numerous mitochondria are found in these cells whose membranes contain carrier molecules used in the uptake of materials into the villi by active transport. The presence of numerous small vesicles within the cells of the villi suggests that materials are taken up from the maternal body by pinocytocis (section 7.2.2). A number of mechanisms of uptake are necessary since the distance between fetal and maternal blood is large, for example ten times that across the alveolar membranes of the lung. Water, glucose, amino acids, simple proteins, lipids, mineral salts, vitamins, hormones, antibodies and oxygen pass from mother to fetus, and water, urea and other nitrogenous waste materials, hormones and carbon dioxide pass from fetus to mother across the 'placental barrier'. Potentially harmful substances such as bacteria, viruses, toxins and drugs can pass to the fetus, but this is offset by certain antibodies, globulins, antibiotics and antitoxins passing in the same direction. This ensures that the baby is born with **passive immunity** (section 14.14.6) to certain diseases.

The placental barrier not only protects the fetus from many harmful situations which may occur to the mother but also shields the fetal circulation from the high blood

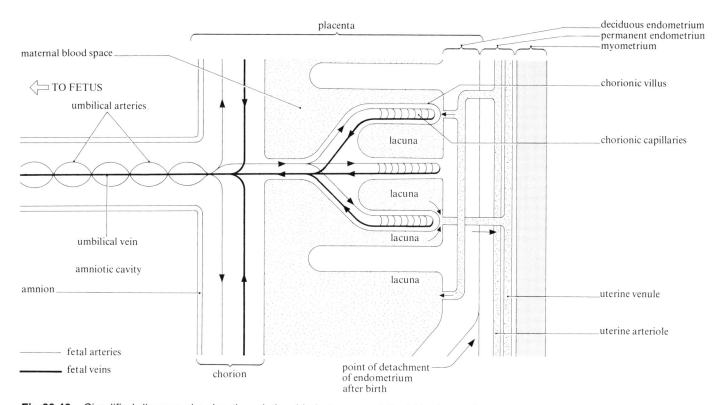

Fig 20.46 *Simplified diagram showing the relationship between umbilical blood vessels, capillaries of the chorionic villi and the blood spaces of the lacunae of the human placenta. This structure forms the link between the circulatory systems of the fetus and the mother*

pressure of the maternal circulation. It cannot function, however, as an immunological barrier, and since the fetus carries paternal genes it will produce antigens foreign to the mother who will produce antibodies against them. The mechanisms accounting for the remarkable ability of the fetus (or, in immunological terms, the **homograft**) to resist rejection for the 40 weeks of gestation is not known but is thought to involve the production of immune suppressive substances which circulate in the maternal plasma.

The continual passage of oxygen from mother to fetus is vital to the life and development of the fetus and this is ensured by the difference in affinity for oxygen between fetal and maternal haemoglobins as described in section 14.13.1.

The placenta is an endocrine organ whose major secretions are chorionic gonadotrophin, oestrogens, progesterone and **human placental lactogen**. The latter hormone stimulates mammary development in preparation for lactation. The site of secretion of all these hormones is the connective tissue of the chorion.

Sexual development in the embryo

The genetic sex of the embryo is determined at fertilisation by the sex chromosomes carried by the father's sperm, X in the case of a female and Y in the case of a male. Despite this, it would appear that the basic disposition of the human body is towards being female, largely as a result of the presence of an X chromosome in both sexes. In the early stages of embryonic development a pair of undifferentiated embryonic gonads, the **genital ridges**, and both rudimentary female and male reproductive systems develop in the embryo. As a result of this, all embryos are potentially bisexual up to the sixth week of development.

Recent investigations have revealed a possible mechanism whereby the sex chromosomes determine which of these systems is activated and lead to the phenotypic expression of the embryo's sex.

The X chromosome carries a gene, the **Tfm gene (testicular feminisation gene)** which specifies the production of an **androgen-receptor protein molecule** in the cells of the developing reproductive system. Since both male and female embryos carry at least one X chromosome, this molecule is present in both sexes.

The Y chromosome carries a gene called the **Y-linked testis-determining gene** specifying the production of a protein molecule, the **H-Y antigen** which stimulates the cells of the embryonic genital ridges to differentiate into seminiferous tubules and interstitial cells. Testosterone released into the embryonic circulatory system reacts with the androgen-receptor molecules in the target cells of the potential reproductive system. The androgen-receptor/testosterone complex formed passes to the nuclei where it activates genes associated with the development of the tissues. Testosterone will activate only those tissues which give rise to the male reproductive system and therefore an XY embryo will develop into a male fetus. The tissues of the potential female reproductive system are not activated

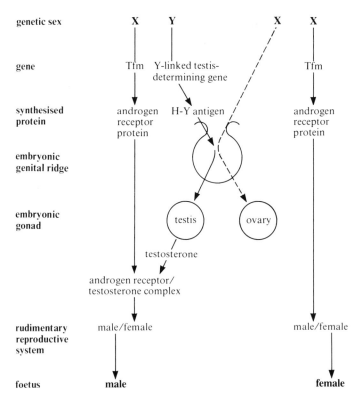

Fig 20.47 *Summary diagram showing the events involved in the differentiation of the embryonic genital ridge and rudimentary reproductive system into the specific gonad and reproductive system of the fetus*

and do not develop. In an XX embryo, the absence of testosterone allows the reproductive system to develop in its inherent direction towards that of female.

Thus it may be concluded that placental influences will direct the development of the embryo in the direction of a female unless diverted by a mechanism initiated by the Y chromosome. A summary of these events is shown in fig 20.47.

20.3.7 Birth

From the beginning of the third month of pregnancy the human embryo is referred to as the **fetus** and it normally completes a total of 40 weeks of development, the **gestation period**, before birth occurs. Most of the major organs are formed by the twelfth week of pregnancy and the remainder of the gestation period is taken up by growth.

Throughout pregnancy oestrogen and progesterone are secreted in progressively greater amounts, first by the corpus luteum and then principally by the placenta. In the last three months of pregnancy oestrogen secretion increases faster than progesterone secretion and, immediately prior to birth, the progesterone level declines and the oestrogen level increases. The functions of these hormones in pregnancy are summarised in table 20.4.

It was thought that hormonal activities within the mother controlled the timing of birth but recent evidence obtained from research on several mammals has suggested there is a

Table 20.4. Summary of major functions of human oestrogen and progesterone during pregnancy

Oestrogen	Progesterone
Growth of mammary glands	Growth of mammary glands
Inhibits FSH release	Inhibits FSH release
Inhibits prolactin release	Inhibits prolactin release
Prevents infection in uterus	Inhibits contraction of myometrium
Increases size of uterine muscle cells	
Increases ATP and creatine phosphate formation	
Increases sensitivity of myometrium to oxytocin	

high degree of fetal involvement in the timing of birth. This would seem to have profound adaptive survival value in ensuring birth of the fetus at a stage in development at which it can lead a relatively independent existence. The initial stages of birth are believed to result from stimuli, as yet undefined, influencing the fetal hypothalamus to release ACTH from the fetal pituitary. One area of current thought concerning the initial birth stimuli is that of 'fetal stress' brought about by an immunological rejection of the mature fetus by the tissues of the mother. As fetal ACTH is released it stimulates the fetal adrenal gland to release corticosteroids which cross the placental barrier and enter the maternal circulation causing a decrease in

progesterone production and an increase in secretion of prostaglandins. The reduction in progesterone level allows the maternal posterior pituitary gland to release the octapeptide hormone, oxytocin, and removes the inhibitory effect on contraction of the myometrium. Whilst oxytocin causes contraction of the smooth muscle of the myometrium, prostaglandins increase the power of the contractions. The release of oxytocin occurs in 'waves' during labour' and provides the force to expel the fetus from the uterus. The onset of contractions of the myometrium, so-called 'labour pains', are accompanied by the dilation of the cervix, the rupture of the amnion and chorion releasing amniotic fluid from the cervix, and the stimulation of stretch receptors in the walls of the uterus and cervix. The latter activate the autonomic nervous system and autonomic reflexes induce contraction of the uterus wall. Other impulses pass up the spinal cord to stimulate the hypothalamus to release oxytocin from the posterior pituitary gland. The pressure of the head of the fetus 'engaged' in the pelvis pressing against the cervix with its face towards the mother's anus, irritates the cervix and leads to stronger contractions of the myometrium.

Uterine contractions spread down over the uterus and are strongest from top to bottom, thus pushing the baby downwards. Throughout these contractions the cervix gradually dilates and the time between bouts of contractions decreases. This is the **first stage** of labour and it ends when the cervix has the same diameter as the head. The

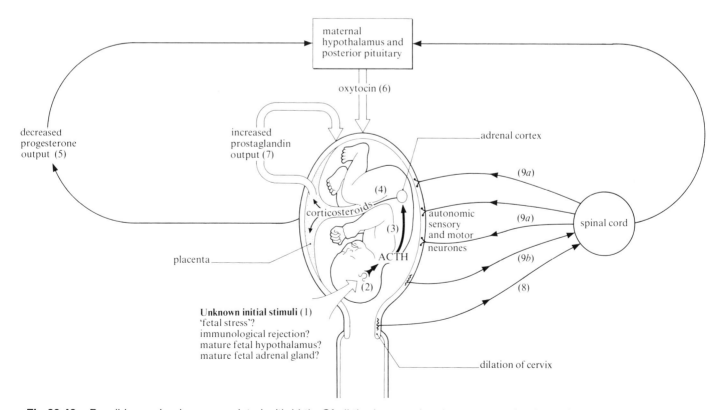

Fig 20.48 *Possible mechanisms associated with birth. Of all the hormonal and nervous mechanisms shown above, only the effect of oxytocin on the uterus wall has been clearly demonstrated. Numbers 1–7 show the possible sequence of events inducing contraction of the uterus wall and 8, 9a and 9b show the possible reflex pathways involved in the control of the contractions*

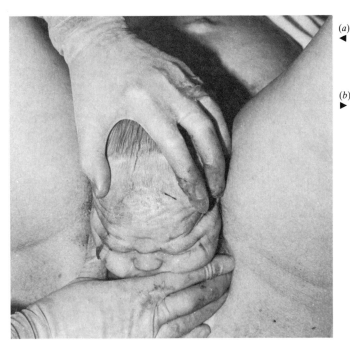

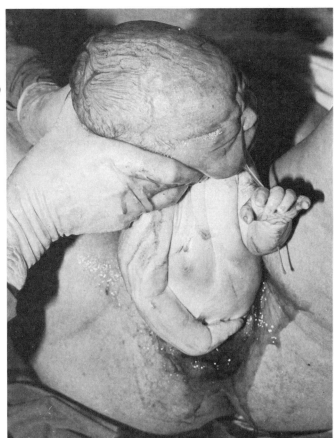

Fig 20.49 (a) (above) The baby's head has been guided through the vagina by the doctor attending the birth and it is now fully emerged. (b) (right) The body of the baby is now partially emerged. The legs are still inside and the umbilical cord remains attached. (c) (below) The baby has been cleaned and is resting on the mother. At this stage the umbilical cord is intact and the baby is still attached to the placenta

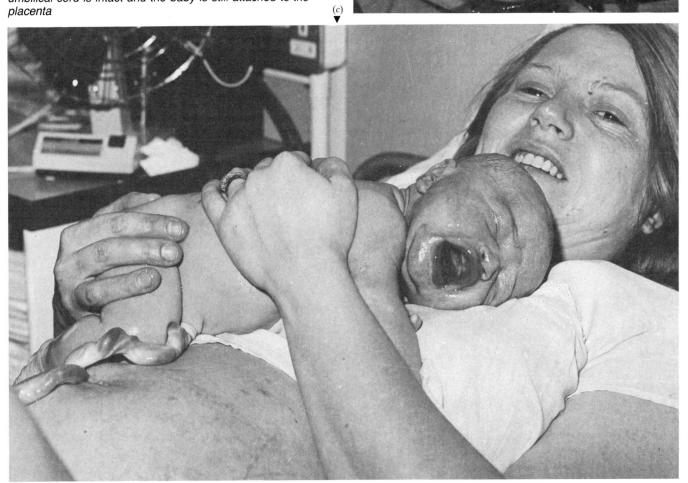

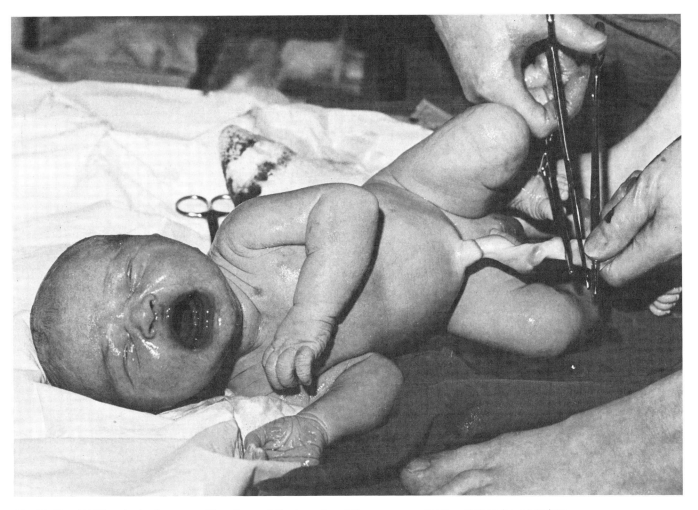

Fig 20.49 *(d) The doctor is now cutting the umbilical cord and the process of birth will then be complete*

second stage of labour involves the passage of the head and body through the vagina and the delivery of the baby. The umbilical cord is ligatured in two places close to the baby and a cut made between the ligatures allowing the baby to be now totally separated from any immediate physiological reliance on the mother. Within 10–45 minutes after birth the uterus contracts dramatically and separates the placenta from the wall of the uterus and the placenta then passes out through the vagina. This is the **third stage** of labour. Bleeding, throughout this period, is limited by contraction of smooth muscle fibres which completely surround all uterine blood vessels supplying the placenta. Average blood loss is kept to about 350 cm³.

20.3.8 Lactation

The **mammary glands**, or breasts, consist of two types of tissue, glandular tissue and supporting tissue or stroma. Glandular epithelial cells line small sacs called alveoli arranged in 15 lobules within the breast. The alveoli are surrounded by a layer of myoepithelial (contractile) tissue involved in the release of milk. Milk is produced by the glandular cells and passes, via a series of ducts and sinuses which store milk, to separate openings in the nipple.

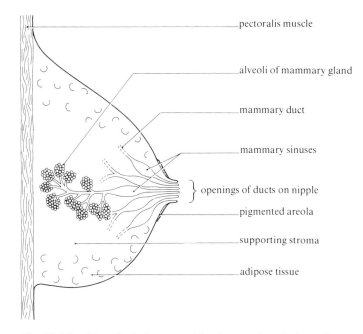

pectoralis muscle

alveoli of mammary gland

mammary duct

mammary sinuses

openings of ducts on nipple

pigmented areola

supporting stroma

adipose tissue

Fig 20.50 *Simplified diagram of the human female breast showing the glandular alveoli where milk is secreted and the ducts and sinuses conveying milk to the nipple.*

767

During puberty the breasts enlarge due to development of the stroma under the influence of oestrogen and progesterone. Internal changes in the nature of the stroma and secretory ducts, and in the amount of fat in the breasts, occur throughout the menstrual cycle, enlarging slightly during the luteal phase, but during pregnancy there is greater increase in size and activity of the breasts.

The increase in the size of the breasts during pregnancy is due to the development of the secretory areas under the influence of oestrogen, progesterone, corticosteroids, growth hormone, placental lactogen and prolactin. However, throughout pregnancy the presence of progesterone inhibits the formation of milk (**lactogenesis**). At birth, when the progesterone level falls, prolactin is no longer inhibited and it stimulates the alveoli to secrete milk.

Human milk contains fat, lactose (milk sugar) and the proteins lactalbumin and casein which are all easily digestible. The milk is synthesised from metabolites circulating in the blood, such as lactose from glucose under the influence of the enzyme **lactose synthetase**, protein from amino acids, and fats from fatty acids, glycerol and acetates. This food alone is adequate to produce weight gains in the baby of 25–30 g per day.

In between breast feeds prolactin stimulates milk production for the next feed. Oestrogen is necessary for the continued production of milk, but artificially induced high levels of oestrogen have been used to inhibit lactogenesis in mothers not wishing to breast feed. (It is common practice now to use a drug called **bromocriptine** instead of oestrogen.)

The ejection of milk from the nipple involves a simple reflex action, the **milk ejection reflex**. The sucking of the baby on the breast stimulates sensory receptors in the nipple to set up impulses passing via the spinal cord to the hypothalamus which releases oxytocin from the posterior pituitary gland. This causes contraction of the myoepithelial tissue surrounding the alveoli and forces milk through the ducts and sinuses and out of the nipples.

The initial secretion of the breasts, following birth, is not milk but **colostrum**. This has a yellow colour and contains cells from the alveoli and is rich in the protein, globulin, but low in fat. It is believed to be a means of passing antibodies, particularly IgA (section 14.14.4), from mother to baby.

20.3.9 Changes in fetal circulation at birth

Throughout development in the uterus the fetal lungs and digestive tract do not function, since gaseous exchange and nutrition are provided by the mother via the placenta. Most of the oxygenated blood returning to the fetus via the umbilical vein by-passes its liver in a vessel, the **ductus venosus**, which shunts blood into the inferior vena cava and passes it to the right atrium (fig 20.51). Some blood from the umbilical vein flows directly to the liver; blood entering the right atrium, therefore, contains a mixture of oxygenated and deoxygenated blood. From

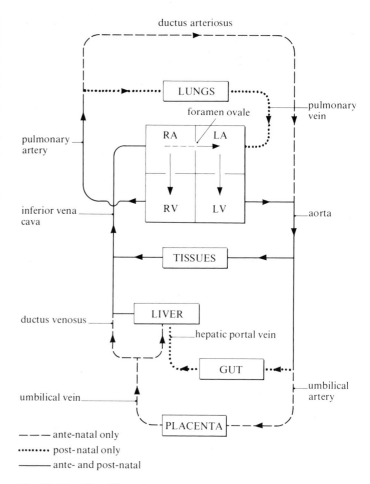

Fig 20.51 *Simplified diagram showing ante-natal (fetal) and post-natal circulatory systems. (The period when the blood vessels are functional are indicated on the diagram)*

here most of the blood passes through an opening in the atrial septum, the **foramen ovale**, into the left atrium. Some blood passes from the right atrium into the right ventricle and into the pulmonary artery but does not pass to the lungs. Instead it is shunted via the **ductus arteriosus** directly to the aorta thereby by-passing lungs, pulmonary vein and the atrium and ventricle of the left side of the heart. Blood from the left atrium passes into the left ventricle and into the aorta which supplies blood to the head, upper limbs, trunk and lower limbs and the umbilical artery. Pressure in the fetal circulatory system is greatest in the pulmonary artery and this determines the direction of blood flow through the fetus and placenta.

20.9 Describe a major change that would occur in the fetal circulation if blood pressure were highest in the aorta.

At birth the sudden inflation of the lungs reduces the resistance to blood flow through the pulmonary capillaries and blood flows through them in preference to the ductus arteriosus; this reduces the pressure in the pulmonary artery. Simultaneously the tying of the umbilical cord prevents blood from flowing through the placenta, and this increases the volume of blood flowing through the body of the baby and leads to a sudden increase in blood pressure in the aorta, left ventricle and left atrium. This pressure change causes the small valves guarding the foramen ovale, which open to the left atrium, to close, preventing the short-circuiting of blood from right to left atrium. Within a few months these valves fuse to the atrial septum and close the foramen ovale completely. If this does not occur the baby is left with a 'hole in the heart' and will require surgery to correct the defect.

The increased pressure in the aorta and decreased pressure in the pulmonary artery forces blood backwards along the ductus arteriosus into the pulmonary artery and hence to the lungs, thereby boosting its supply. After a few hours muscles in the wall of the ductus arteriosus constrict under the influence of the rising partial pressure of oxygen in the blood and close off this blood vessel. A similar mechanism of muscular contraction closes off the ductus venosus and increases blood flow through the liver. The mechanism of closing down the ductus venosus is not known but is essential in transforming the ante-natal (before birth) circulation into the post-natal (after birth) condition.

20.4 Phylogenetic review of sexual reproduction in vertebrates

Sexual reproduction occurs in every animal phylum and, whilst the basic processes of gamete formation, fertilisation and zygote formation are common to all groups, there is considerable variation in the anatomical, physiological and behavioural aspects of sexual reproduction. Many examples of the variations shown by the non-vertebrate phyla are described in chapter 4.

In vertebrates, too, tremendous variation exists in many of the aspects of sexual reproduction, and some of these, together with selected examples, are summarised in table 20.5. The phylogeny of the vertebrates shows a gradual adaptation to life on land. One of the major problems to overcome in making the transition from an aquatic existence to a terrestrial existence involved reproduction. The majority of fish shed their gametes directly into water, fertilisation is external, eggs contain a considerable amount of yolk, larval stages are common and any degree of parental care is rare. In the amphibia there are several examples of adaptations to terrestrial life but few of these involve mechanisms of reproduction. Amphibia have to

Table 20.5. Summary table showing variations in the mechanisms of sexual reproduction in selected vertebrates

Organism	Number of female gametes released per year	Diameter of egg/mm	Site of fertilisation	Site of embryonic development	Degree of parental care
Cod	$3–7 \times 10^6$	0.13	external	Sea as larvae, oviparous*	None, very little yolk in egg
Stickleback	60	2.0	external	Nest, built by male, oviparous	Male occupies territory, courts female; eggs laid and fertilised in nest; young protected in nest
Spotted dogfish (*Scyliorhinus canaliculus*)	144	15.0	internal	Egg case, 'Mermaids purse'; no larval stage, oviparous	Mating occurs near surface of water, large supply of yolk in egg
Frog (*Rana temporaria*)	2 000	2	external	Water, collectively as 'frog spawn', oviparous; larval (tadpole) stage undergoes metamorphosis	Simple courtship, mating occurs; Moderate amount of yolk in egg; no after-care
Sand lizard (*Lacerta agilis*)	6	8.0	internal	Amniote egg in holes in sand or soil, oviparous	Simple courtship, mating occurs; large amount of yolk; no after care
Robin (*Erithacus rubecula*)	5	20.0	internal	Amniote egg in nest built by female, oviparous	Male occupies territory, elaborate courtship, mating occurs, female incubates eggs for 14 days, fledgling fed by both parents, offspring independent after six weeks

*Offspring *laid* or spawned as eggs.

return to water to mate, and the early stages of their development take place there also. There are, however, many amphibian species that show elaborate behavioural patterns associated with parental care. For example, the male *Pipa* toad spreads the fertilised eggs over the back of the female where they stick, become 'embedded' in the skin and develop into tadpoles. After about three weeks they escape from the mother's back and lead an independent existence.

Reptiles were the earliest group of vertebrates to overcome the problems of fertilisation and development on land. Clearly shedding of gametes in a terrestrial situation is impossible, so the first requirement of totally land-dwelling organisms must have been the introduction of male gametes into the female body, that is internal fertilisation. Internal fertilisation occurs in reptiles and the increased chances of fertilisation reduces the numbers of gametes which it is necessary to produce. Once fertilised, the zygote develops within a specialised structure, the **amniote (cleidoic) egg**, which provides the embryo with a fluid-filled cavity in which it can develop on land. The outer shell provides immediate protection from mechanical damage and envelops the four membranes which surround the embryo. These four extra-embryonic membranes, the yolk sac, amnion, chorion and allantois are derived from ectoderm, endoderm and mesoderm and provide the embryo with protection and facilitate many of its metabolic activities including nutrition, respiration and excretion. The **yolk sac** develops as an outgrowth of the embryonic gut and encloses the yolk which is gradually absorbed by the blood vessels of the yolk sac. When the yolk has been used up the yolk sac is withdrawn into the gut. The **amnion** forms from an upgrowth of the cells beneath the embryo and completely encloses the embryo in the **amniotic cavity** which becomes filled with **amniotic fluid** secreted by the cells of the amnion. This provides the embryo with an immediate fluid environment (a replica of the ancestral aquatic environment of the amphibian) in which the

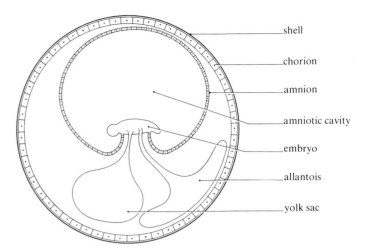

Fig 20.52 *Simplified diagram of the amniote egg*

embryo can develop. All reptiles, birds and mammals have an amnion and are called **amniotes**. As the embryo grows the amnion is pushed out until it fuses with the third embryonic membrane, the **chorion**, which lies immediately within the shell and prevents excessive water loss from the amnion. The **allantois** is an outgrowth of the embryonic hindgut and rapidly expands, in reptiles and birds, to underlie the chorion. Here it functions primarily as a 'bladder' for storing excretory products and as the gaseous exchange organ of the embryo, facilitating the transfer of respiratory gases between the environmental atmosphere and the amniotic fluid via the porous shell. The structure of the amniote egg is shown in fig 20.52.

Birds and primitive egg-laying mammals called monotremes, such as the duck-billed platypus, *Ornithorhyncus*, all produce an amniotic egg and, whilst the shell of the egg is lost in higher mammals, the four extra-embryonic membranes are retained; two of them, the chorion and allantois, give rise to the placenta in eutherian (placental) mammals (section 20.3.6).

Chapter Twenty-one

Growth and development

Growth is a fundamental characteristic of all living organisms. It is often thought of simply as an increase in size, but careful consideration shows this to be an inadequate definition. For example, the size of a plant cell may increase as it takes up water by osmosis, but this process may be reversible and cannot then be thought of as genuine growth. Also, during cleavage of the zygote and in the early embryo there is an increase in cell numbers without an increase in size (volume or mass). This is the result of cell division without subsequent increase in size of daughter cells. The process is a developmental one and so perhaps should be regarded as growth despite the fact that no increase in size occurs.

The process of development is so closely linked with growth that the phrase 'growth and development' is commonly used to describe the processes which are normally thought of as growth. Starting with an individual cell, growth of a multicellular organism can be divided into three phases:

(1) **cell division (hyperplasia)** – an increase in cell number as a result of mitotic division and cell division;
(2) **cell expansion (hypertrophy)** – an irreversible increase in cell size as a result of the uptake of water or the synthesis of living material;
(3) **cell differentiation** – the specialisation of cells; in its broad sense, growth also includes this phase of cell development.

However, each of these processes can occur at separate points in time. The example of cleavage has already been mentioned above. An increase in volume without change in cell numbers may also occur, as in the region of cell elongation behind the root and shoot tips of plants. In the case of single-celled organisms, such as bacteria, cell division results in *reproduction* (not growth) of the *individual* and *growth* of the *population*.

All stages of growth involve biochemical activity. Protein synthesis is particularly important since it is the means by which the DNA message is expressed in terms of enzymes synthesised by the cell. Enzymes control cell activities. Changes at the cell level bring about changes in overall form and structure, both of individual organs and of the organism as a whole, and this process is known as **morphogenesis**.

A definition of growth should satisfy the criterion of increase in size that occurs in all organisms from single-celled organisms to the most differentiated plants and animals, as well as reflecting the metabolic activity associated with growth. Growth can therefore be defined as **an irreversible increase in dry mass of living material**. This in turn reflects an increase in the amount of protein which has been synthesised, and the fact that the process of protein synthesis forms the basis of growth.

Growth may be positive or negative. **Positive growth** occurs when anabolism exceeds catabolism, whereas **negative growth** occurs when catabolism exceeds anabolism (chapter 11). For example, in the course of germination of a seed and the production of a seedling various physical parameters increase in magnitude, such as cell number, cell size, fresh mass, length, volume and complexity of form, whilst others such as dry mass may actually *decrease*. From the definition, germination in the latter case is therefore strictly a time of negative growth.

21.1 Measurement of growth

Growth occurs at many levels of biological organisation from the community level down to the molecular level. In all cases if the increase in measurable parameter is plotted against time an S-shaped growth curve is obtained. Fig 21.1 shows a variety of growth curves produced by plotting different parameters such as length, height, mass and surface area, volume and numbers against time. The shape of these curves is described as **sigmoid**, meaning S-shaped.

A sigmoid curve can be divided into four parts. The initial phase is the **lag phase** during which little growth occurs. This leads into the second phase, the **log phase** (grand period of growth) during which growth proceeds exponentially. During this phase the rate of growth is at its maximum and at any point the rate of growth is proportional to the amount of material or numbers of cells or organisms already present.

In all cases of growth the exponential increase declines and the rate of growth begins to decrease. The point at which this occurs is known as the **inflexion point**. The third phase is the **decelerating phase** (self-retarding phase) during which time growth becomes limited as a result of the effect of some internal or external factor, or the interaction of both. The final phase is the **plateau phase** or **stationary phase**. This usually marks the period where overall growth has ceased and the parameter under consideration remains constant. The precise nature of the curve during this phase may vary depending on the nature of the parameter, the

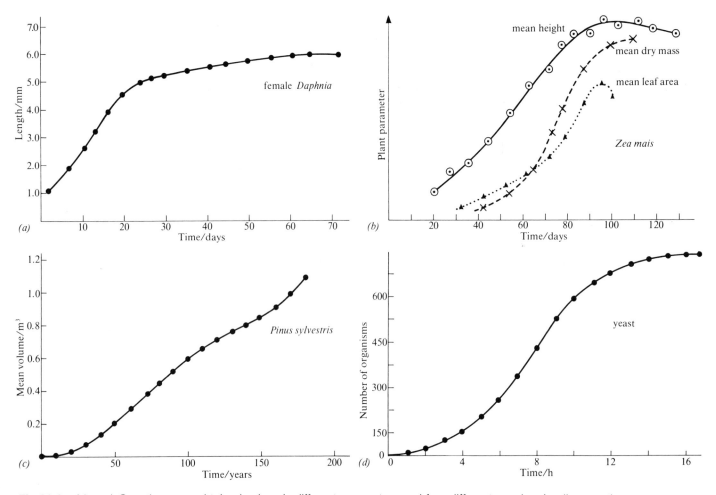

Fig 21.1 (above) *Growth curves obtained using six different parameters and four different species. In all cases the curves are sigmoid. ((b) After Kreusler. (c) Indicates growth of trees, after Tischendorf. (d) After Knopf.)*

Fig 21.2 (below) *A typical sigmoid growth curve showing the four characteristic growth phases and the inflexion point. (a) Lag phase; (b) log phase; (c) inflexion point; (d) decelerating phase; (e) plateau or stationary phase*

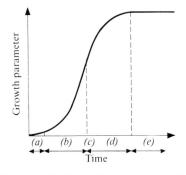

21.1.1 Methods of measuring growth

Growth can be measured at various levels of biological organisation, such as growth of a cell, organism or population. The numbers of organisms in a population at different times can be counted and plotted against time to produce a population growth curve as shown in fig 21.1*d* (also section 12.7.3). At the level of the organism there are a variety of parameters which may be measured; length, area, volume and mass are commonly used. In plants, growth curves for roots, stems, internodes and leaf area are often required, and length and area are the parameters chosen. In the case of growth in animals and entire plants length and mass are two commonly measured parameters. With regard to mass there are two values that can be used, namely fresh (wet) mass and dry mass. Of the two, fresh mass is the easier parameter to measure since it requires less preparation of the sample and has the advantage of not causing any injury to the organism, so that repeated measurements of the same organism may be taken over a period of time.

The major disadvantage of using fresh mass as a growth parameter is that it may give inconsistent readings due to fluctuations in water content. True growth is reflected by

species and internal factors. In some cases the curve may continue to increase slightly until the organism dies as is the case with monocotyledonous leaves, many non-vertebrates, fish and certain reptiles. This indicates **positive growth**. In the case of certain cnidarians the curve flattens out indicating no change in growth whilst other growth curves may tail off indicating a period of **negative growth**. The latter pattern is characteristic of many mammals, including humans, and is a sign of physical senescence associated with increasing age.

changes in the amounts of constituents other than water and the only valid way to measure these is to obtain the dry mass. This is done by killing the organism and placing it in an oven at 110 °C to drive off all the water. The specimen is cooled in a desiccator and weighed. This procedure is repeated until a constant mass is recorded. This is the dry mass. In all cases it is more accurate to obtain the dry mass of as large a number of specimens as is practicable and from this calculate the mean dry mass. This value will be more representative than that obtained from a single specimen.

21.1.2 Types of growth curve

Plotting data obtained from any one of the physical parameters described above, such as dry mass (m), against time (t) produces a growth curve which is known as the **actual** or **absolute growth curve** (fig 21.3). The usefulness of this curve is that it shows the overall growth pattern and the extent of growth. Data from this graph enable the growth curves in figs 21.3–5 to be constructed.

Plotting the change in parameter against time produces an **absolute growth rate curve** (fig 21.4). (The same curve

Fig 21.3 *Actual or absolute growth curve obtained by plotting live mass against age for sheep. (Data from L. R. Wallace (1948)* J. Agric. Sci., **38**, *93 and H. Pálsson & J. B. Vergés (1952)* J. Agric. Sci., **42**, *93)*

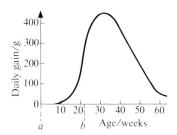

Fig 21.4 *Absolute growth rate curve plotted from data shown in fig 21.3*

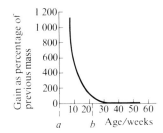

Fig 21.5 *Relative growth rate curve plotted from data shown in fig. 21.3*

could be obtained by calculating the slope of the absolute growth curve $\left(\dfrac{dm}{dt}\right)$ at various points and plotting these against time).

This curve shows how the rate of growth changes during the time of the study. In particular it shows the period when growth is most rapid and this corresponds to the steepest part of the absolute growth curve. The peak of the absolute growth curve marks the point of inflexion after which the rate of growth decreases as the adult size is attained.

Dividing each of the above values for the absolute rate of growth by the amount of growth at the beginning of each time period $\left(\dfrac{dm}{dt}\cdot\dfrac{1}{m}\right)$ and plotting these values against time produces a **relative rate of growth curve** (or **specific rate of growth curve**) (fig 21.5). This is a measure of the efficiency of growth.

A comparison of relative rate of growth curves for organisms grown or reared under different conditions shows clearly the most favourable conditions for rapid growth and for growth over an extended period. In the case of mammals the absolute growth curve is sigmoid but the exact shape of the curve appears to be related to the time taken to reach sexual maturity. In the rat the curve is steep and truly sigmoid since sexual maturity is reached quickly (within 12 months) whereas in humans the absolute growth curve shows four distinct phases of increased growth (fig 21.6).

21.1 What conclusions, regarding growth in humans, may be drawn from the three curves shown in fig 21.6?

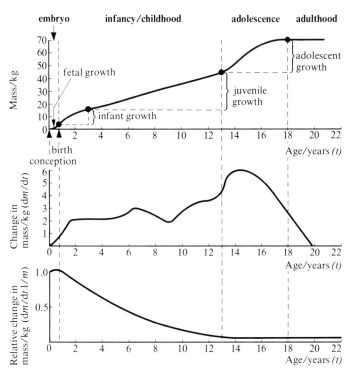

Fig 21.6 *Three types of growth curve for humans*

21.2   Patterns of growth

Various patterns of growth occur among organisms.

21.2.1   Isometric and allometric growth

Isometric (*isos*, same; *metron*, measure) growth occurs when an organ grows at the same mean rate as the rest of the body. In this situation change in size of the organism is not accompanied by a change in shape or external form of the organism. The proportions of the two structures remain the same. This type of growth pattern is seen in fish and certain insects, such as locusts (except for wings and genitalia) (fig 21.7). In such cases as these there is a simple relationship between linear dimension, area, volume and mass. The area increases as the square of linear dimension ($A \propto l^2$) whereas volume and mass increase as the cube of linear dimension ($V \propto l^3$ and $M \propto l^3$). Animals showing little change in overall shape with time therefore show a marked change in mass: an increase in length of only 10% is accompanied by a 33% increase in mass.

Allometric (*allos*, other; *metron*, measure) growth occurs when an organ grows at a different rate from the rest of the body. This produces a change in size of the organism which is accompanied by a change in shape of the organism. This pattern of growth is characteristic of mammals and illustrates the relationship between growth and development. Fig 21.8 shows how the relative proportions of various structures in humans change as a result of simultaneous changes in patterns of growth and development. In almost all animals the last organs to develop and differentiate are the reproductive organs. These show allometric growth and can be observed only in those organisms with external genital organs, hence they are not seen in many species of fish where growth appears to be purely isometric. Fig 21.9 shows the degree of variation in patterns of growth of different organs of a human. Again it can be seen that the last organs to develop are the reproductive organs.

The shapes of absolute growth curves for whole organisms as represented by length or mass show remarkable similarities and generally conform to the sigmoid shape described in section 21.1. However, several groups of organisms show variations on the general pattern which reflect adaptations to particular modes of life and environments as described in sections 21.2.2–21.2.3.

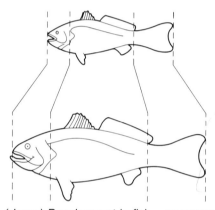

Fig. 21.7 *(above) Development in fish – an example of isometric growth. The external structures retain their shape and spatial relationships as a result of a proportional growth rate. (After Batt (1980) Influences on animal growth and development,* Studies in Biology, *No. 116, Arnold.)*

Fig 21.8 *(below) Development in humans – an example of allometric growth. To show the relative rates of growth from the age of two months to 25 years each stage has been given a constant height. (After Stratz, cited in J. Hammond (ed.) (1955) Progress in the physiology of farm animals,* **2**, 431, *Butterworths.)*

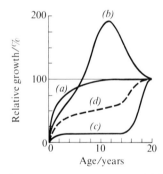

Fig 21.9 *(above) Relative growth rates of (a) brain, (b) thymus and (c) reproductive organs of humans. Each curve is drawn relative to the absolute growth curve of the whole body (d). (After Scammon)*

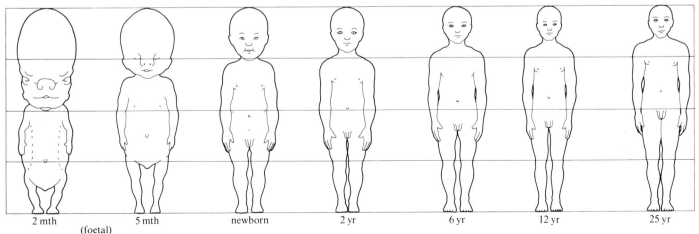

| 2 mth | 5 mth | newborn | 2 yr | 6 yr | 12 yr | 25 yr |

(foetal)

774

21.2.2 Limited and unlimited growth

Studies of the duration of growth in plants and animals show that there are two basic patterns, called limited (definite or determinate) growth and unlimited (indefinite or indeterminate) growth.

Growth in annual plants is limited and after a period of maximum growth, during which the plant matures and reproduces, there is a period of negative growth or senescence before the death of the plant. If the dry mass of the annual plant is plotted against time then an interesting variation on the sigmoid curve of fig 21.2 is seen, as shown in fig 21.10.

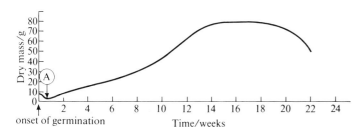

Fig 21.10 *Growth curve of a broad bean (*Vicia faba*) planted in March – an annual plant*

> **21.2** Examine fig 21.10 and answer the following questions, based on your knowledge of the life cycle of an annual plant.
> (a) Why is there negative growth initially during the germination of the seed?
> (b) Describe the appearance of the seedling when positive growth occurs at A.
> (c) What physiological process occurs here to account for positive growth?
> (d) Why is the decrease in dry mass after 20 weeks very sudden?

Several plant organs show limited growth but do not undergo a period of negative growth, for example fruits, organs of vegetative propagation, dicotyledonous leaves and stem internodes. Animals showing limited growth include insects, birds and mammals.

Woody perennial plants on the other hand show unlimited growth and have a characteristic growth curve which is a cumulative series of sigmoid curves (fig 21.11), each of which represents one year's growth. With unlimited growth, some slight net growth continues until death.

Other examples of unlimited growth are found among fungi, algae, and many animals, particularly non-vertebrates, fishes and reptiles. Monocotyledonous leaves show unlimited growth.

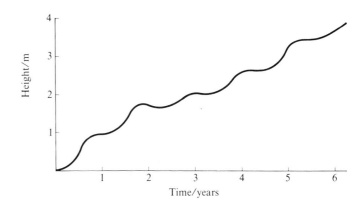

Fig 21.11 *Growth curve of a birch tree – a woody perennial*

21.2.3 Growth in arthropods

A striking and characteristic growth pattern is associated with crustacea and other arthropods, such as hemimetabolous insects and the larvae of holometabolous insects. Due to the inelastic nature of their exoskeletons they appear to grow only in spurts interrupted by a series of moults (**discontinuous growth**). A typical hemimetabolous growth pattern is shown in fig 21.12. It is growth curves such as these, based on length, which do not give a true reflection of growth. If a growth curve is plotted for the same insect, using dry mass as the growth parameter, a normal sigmoid curve is produced demonstrating that true growth, as represented by increase in living material, is continuous.

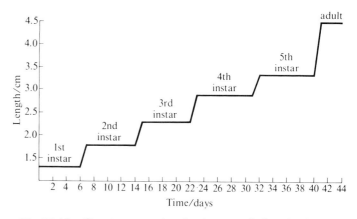

Fig 21.12 *Growth curve showing increase in length of the short-horned grasshopper. (After R. Soper & T. Smith (1979)* Modern Biology, *Macmillan.)*

21.3 Control of growth and development

The process of growth and development in an organism is controlled ultimately by the information contained in its DNA. Growth, however, is the result of the interaction between the DNA and the internal and external environments of the organism. Important external influences include availability of food, light, heat and water. The internal environment includes chemicals such as hormones and recently discovered cytoplasmic proteins ('transcription factors') that influence gene expression either directly or indirectly. External factors can influence internal factors, for example lack of iodine in the human diet leads to an inability to make the hormone thyroxine with a consequent reduction in growth rate.

Table 21.1. Summary of factors inflencing growth and development

External factors	Process affected
Light (intensity, quality and duration)	Photosynthesis – energy source (ch. 9) Photomorphogenesis (ch. 15) Phototropism (ch. 15) Greening (ch. 15) Photoperiodism (chs 15 and 16) Synthesis of vitamin D in humans
Short wavelength electromagnetic radiation (X-rays, γ-rays etc.)	Mutagenesis (ch. 23)
Nutrients	Autotrophic nutrition – carbon dioxide, water, inorganic salts required – deficiency diseases in absence (ch. 9) Heterotrophic nutrition – organic compounds, water and inorganic salts required (ch. 10); deficiency diseases in absence (chs 9 and 10)
Temperature	Affects growth via effect on enzymes (ch. 6 and fig 21.13): thermoperiodism (ch. 15)
Oxygen	Needed by aerobic organisms for respiration: particularly important for active uptake of ions by plant roots and fetal development (ch. 12)
Water	Essential for many processes (ch. 5)
Seasonal influences	Dormancy of buds, seeds and perennating organs (ch. 15) Leaf fall (ch. 15) Reproduction (chs 15, 16 and 20) Photoperiodism and thermoperiodism (chs 15 and 16)
Metabolic waste products	Not normally a problem, but may be inhibitory, e.g. in bacterial colonies

Internal factors	Process affected
Genes	Protein synthesis (ch. 23), hence enzyme synthesis and control of cell chemistry
Hormones and growth substances	Many processes (chs 15 and 16)

Recent experiments involving transplantation of tissues from species with different patterns of growth have revealed the occurrence of a form of control of growth resulting from tissue interaction. If each tissue were to grow at its normal rate discrepancies would occur and the organ would show malformations. Instead the growth rates of both tissues complement each other and growth of the organ is normal. The conclusion drawn from these studies is that one of the tissues determines the growth rate of the other.

Some of the factors affecting growth and development are summarised in table 21.1 (see also fig 21.13).

> **21.3** From the data shown in fig 21.13 explain fully why body mass is at its lowest level at times of maximum food intake.

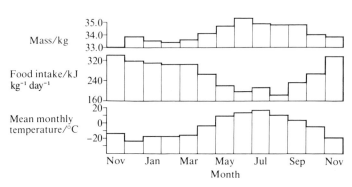

Fig 21.13 *Graphs showing the effects of food intake and temperature on body mass of a husky dog. (Data from J. L. Durrer & J. P. Hannon (1962) Am. J. Physiol.,* **202**, *375.)*

21.4 Development

In its broadest sense, growth includes not only an irreversible increase in dry mass as a result of cell division and increase in cell size, but also the subsequent process of development. During development cells become specialised for particular functions within the organism, a process known as **differentiation**. In other words, division of labour occurs among the cells. **Morphogenesis** also takes place, as mentioned earlier. The extent of cell differentiation is linked with the level of phylogenetic organisation as shown in table 21.2.

One of the intriguing problems of differentiation is the mechanism by which it occurs. Cell division is a major contributory factor in growth, and in all multicellular organisms this occurs by mitosis. The implication of this is that every cell derived from the original zygote or spore has an identical genetic composition (genotype) and therefore ought to have identical structure and function. That the latter is not the case in mature organisms is self-evident. What then are the mechanisms bringing about differences between cells, tissues, organs and organ systems? Cell structure and function are determined by the expressed activity of genes, and if cells differ in their structure and

Table 21.2. The approximate numbers of cells and cell types reflecting the degree of differentiation seen at different levels of phylogenetic organisation

Organism	Approximate number of cells	Approximate number of cell types
Protozoa	10^{-1}	10^{-1}
Porifera	$>10^3$	>10
Hydra	10^8	$10-20$
Annelids	10^{12}	10^2
Insects	10^{12}	10^2
Human	10^{15}	10^3

function this would appear to be due to a differential expression of genes. There are two possible reasons for this. Either cells specialise by losing certain genes, retaining only those needed for the specialised function, or specialisation involves 'switching' on and off different genes in different cells. It became obvious in the early 1960s that the latter was the case, at least in plants. Professor Steward of Cornell University showed that when differentiated cells of a carrot plant, such as phloem cells, were placed in a suitable culture medium they were capable of growing into new carrot plants and therefore still possessed all the relevant information. In 1967 Gurdon, working at Oxford University, showed the same to be true of animals when he transplanted nuclei from the intestinal epithelium of the African clawed toad, *Xenopus*, into eggs of the same species whose own nuclei had been destroyed by ultra-violet radiation. He found that normal development through the tadpole to the adult stage occurred in a small number of these transplants, suggesting that reactivation of genes is possible even in differentiated cells, provided the genes are placed in a suitable environment. Less differentiated cells from an early embryonic stage of development, such as the blastula, gave a higher success rate, and any number of genetically identical frogs can be produced using this technique. Identical offspring from a single parent are referred to as **clones**, and the technique described above is called **cloning** (section 20.1.1).

It is difficult to grow isolated mammalian cells in culture, and even more difficult to induce differentiation. This reflects the highly specialised nature of mammalian cells.

Differentiation may reach such a level of complexity that even growth is prevented. This situation is found in neurones. On the other hand, liver cells remain relatively unspecialised and are able to perform a great many functions (section 18.5). An adult mammalian liver, which has had two-thirds of its mass removed, will regenerate in three weeks to its original size and shape. This evidence not only demonstrates the extent of regenerative growth, but also indicates that the growth of organs and tissues is to a predetermined size and shape.

If nuclei lose none of their genetic potential as a result of differentiation that would suggest that the cytoplasm has a role in regulating differentiation. Spemann and Mangold investigated the influence of cytoplasmic factors on the

course of development. By transplanting tissue from a donor embryo into a host embryo they were able to demonstrate that the donor tissue was able to change the course of development of the host. This process is known as **induction** and the areas of the donor which bring about induction are known as **organisers**. A fuller account of the process, and of Spemann and Mangold's experiments, is given in section 22.8.2. The exact way in which the influence is exerted is not entirely clear but it is thought to involve the differential repression and activation of genes in different cells. This is discussed in detail in section 22.8.3.

Another factor affecting differentiation is hormones. Specific examples of growth hormones in plants and a range of animals are described later in this chapter and in chapters 15 and 16. Whilst the action of growth hormones in plants may be variable, there is evidence that certain aspects of growth hormone activity are common to all organisms. Hormones may act directly or indirectly on the genes and exert their influence by 'switching' genes 'on' or 'off' in a sequential manner which determines the pattern of development. Studies carried out on the giant chromosomes from the salivary glands of dipteran fly larvae show 'puffing' in various regions of the chomosomes (sections 22.8.5 and 23.5.1). The positions of these puffs correspond to certain stages in the development of the fly. These regions are genes and are the sites of active messenger RNA synthesis which results in the synthesis of substances vital to certain stages in the life cycle of the fly. Injections of insect growth hormones can induce 'puffing' in larvae which have had their growth-hormone-producing glands removed. Alternatively the injection of supra-optimal levels of growth hormone can alter the normal sequence of 'puffing' and hasten the development of the adult fly form. These studies suggest that hormones sometimes act by 'switching on' genes associated with development.

21.5 Morphogenesis

During the course of development differentiated cells come to occupy specific regions within the organism where they undergo further growth and cell division. This process is part of morphogenesis because it results in cells, tissues and organs, which give form and structure to the mature organism, coming to occupy their characteristic positions. The exact nature of the morphogenic movements is species-specific, but some characteristic examples of morphogenesis in plants and animals are described in the next two sections. The major morphogenic events in plants occur during the development of the stem, root, leaves and flower. In animals there are many spectacular examples of morphogenesis, but those described here are limited to showing the striking changes in form associated with metamorphosis and the increasing tissue complexity which accompanies vertebrate development.

21.6 Growth and development in the flowering plant

21.6.1 Seed dormancy

Certain environmental conditions, namely availability of water, optimum temperature and oxygen, must be present before the embryo of a seed will grow. However, in the presence of these factors, some apparently mature seeds will not germinate and must undergo certain internal changes which can generally be described as **after-ripening**. These changes ensure that premature germination does not occur. For example, seedlings produced immediately from seeds shed in summer or autumn would probably not survive winter. In other words, mechanisms exist which ensure that germination is synchronised with the onset of a season favourable for growth.

These mechanisms often involve the outer layers of seeds, which may contain growth inhibitors, being impervious to water or the passage of oxygen, or being physically strong enough to prevent growth of the embryo as in many legumes. Sometimes physical damage (**scarification**) to the seed coat can remove this restriction, a process which can be induced artificially by removing the testa or simply pricking it with a pin. Under natural circumstances, bacteria may have the same effect. More usually, however, the restriction is removed by some physiological change, involving the following factors.

Growth inhibitors. Many fruits or seeds contain chemical growth inhibitors which prevent germination. Abscisic acid often has this role, for instance in ash seeds. Thorough soaking of the seeds might remove the inhibitor or its effect may be overridden by an increase in a growth promoter such as gibberellin.

Light. The dormancy of some seeds is broken by light after water uptake, a phytochrome-controlled response. This is associated with a rise in gibberellin levels within the seed. Less commonly, germination is inhibited by light, such as in *Phacelia* and *Nigella*. (For a relevant experiment, refer to the foot of table 15.5, section 15.4.2.)

Temperature. As noted in section 15.5.1, seeds commonly require a cold period, or **stratification**, before germination will occur. This is common among members of the rose family (Rosaceae) and cereals. It is associated with a rise in gibberellin activity and sometimes a reduction in growth inhibitors.

Exactly how light and cold treatments affect seeds is not clear, but increased permeability of the seed coat, as well as changes in levels of growth substances, may be involved.

> **21.4** Seeds which require a stimulus of light for germination are usually relatively small. What could be the significance of this?

> **21.5** The light which passes through leaves is enriched in green and far-red light relative to the light which strikes the leaf surface.
> (a) Why is this?
> (b) What ecological significance might this have in relation to seeds like lettuce, where germination is a phytochrome-controlled response? (Read section 15.4.2 if necessary.)

21.6.2 Germination

Germination is the onset of growth of the embryo, usually after a period of dormancy. The structure of the seed at germination has been described in section 20.2.

Environmental conditions needed for germination

Water. The initial uptake of water by a seed is by a process called **imbibition**. It takes place through the micropyle and testa and is purely a physical process caused by the **adsorption** of water by colloidal substances within the seed. These include proteins, starch and cell wall materials such as hemicelluloses and pectic substances. The swelling of these substances can lead to strong imbibitional forces sufficient to rupture the testa or pericarp surrounding the seed. Water subsequently moves from cell to cell by osmosis. It is required to activate the biochemical reactions associated with germination, because these take place in aqueous solution. Water is also an important reagent at this stage in the hydrolysis (digestion) of food stores.

Minimum or optimum temperature. There is usually a characteristic temperature range outside which a given type of seed will not germinate. This will be related to the normal environment of the plant concerned and will be within the range 5–40 °C. Temperature influences the rate of enzyme-controlled reactions as described in section 6.4.3.

Oxygen. This is required for aerobic respiration, although such respiration can be supplemented with anaerobic respiration if necessary.

Physiology of germination

A typical seed stores carbohydrates, lipids and proteins, either in its endosperm or in the cotyledons of the embryo. Usually lipids in the form of oils form the major food reserves of the seed, though notable exceptions are the Leguminosae (legumes) and Gramineae (grasses, including cereals) where starch is the major food reserve. These two groups form the principal crops of humans and thus we get the bulk of our carbohydrates from them. Legumes are also especially rich in proteins, particularly soya bean; hence the use of the latter as a source of protein in new foods. In addition, seeds contain high levels of minerals, notably phosphorus, as well as normal cytoplasmic constituents such as nucleic acids and vitamins.

As a result of imbibition and osmosis the embryo becomes hydrated, and this activates enzymes such as the enzymes of respiration. Other enzymes have to be synthesised, possibly using amino acids provided by the digestion of stored proteins.

Broadly speaking, there are two centres of activity in the germinating seed, the **storage centre** (food reserve) and the **growth centre** (embryo). The main events in the storage centre, with the exception of enzyme synthesis, are catabolic, that is concerned with breakdown.

Digestion of the food reserves proceeds mainly by hydrolysis as below:

$$\text{proteins} \xrightarrow{\text{proteases}} \text{amino acids}$$

$$\text{polysaccharides} \xrightarrow{\text{carbohydrases}} \text{sugars}$$

$$\text{for example starch} \xrightarrow{\text{amylase}} \text{maltose} \xrightarrow{\text{maltase}} \text{glucose}$$

$$\text{lipids} \xrightarrow{\text{lipases}} \text{fatty acids} + \text{glycerol}$$

The soluble products of digestion are then translocated to the growth regions of the embryo. The sugars, fatty acids and glycerol may be used to provide substrates for respiration in both the storage and the growth centres. They may also be used for anabolic reactions in the growth centre, that is, reactions concerned with synthesis. Of particular importance in these reactions are glucose and amino acids. A major use of glucose is for the synthesis of cellulose and other cell wall materials. Amino acids are used mainly for protein synthesis, proteins being important as enzymes and structural components of protoplasm. In addition, mineral salts are required for the many reasons given in table 9.10.

Both storage and growth centres obtain the energy for their activities from respiration. This involves oxidation of a substrate, usually sugar, to carbon dioxide and water. A net loss in dry mass of the seed therefore occurs, since carbon dioxide is lost as a gas, and water does not contribute to dry mass. This loss will continue until the seedling produces green leaves and starts to make its own food (section 21.2.2).

A well-studied example of germination of a polysaccharide-rich seed is the barley grain, where it has been shown that the synthesis of α-amylase and other enzymes takes place in the outer layers of the endosperm in response to gibberellin secreted by the embryo. These outer layers contain stored protein which is the source of amino acids for protein synthesis. The process is described and experimentally investigated in section 15.2.6. Fig 15.21 shows an example of the role of hormones in early germination. The appearance of amylase in germinating barley grains can also be investigated by grinding them in water, filtering and centrifuging to obtain a clear extract and testing the activity of the extract on starch solution. By using samples of barley grains at different times from germination, increase in amylase activity per grain over a period of a week can be determined.

21.6 Explain the results shown in fig 21.14

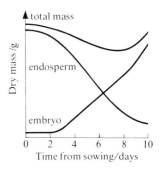

Fig 21.14 *Relative changes in dry mass of endosperm and embryo during germination of barley*

Those seeds which store lipids convert them to fatty acids and glycerol. Each molecule of lipid yields three molecules of fatty acid and one of glycerol (section 5.3.1). Fatty acids are either oxidised directly in respiration or converted to sucrose, which is then translocated to the embryo. The latter involves the glyoxylate cycle (section 11.5.5).

21.7 (This question tests some basic knowledge of chemistry and of the chemistry of lipids. The latter is covered in section 5.3.)

Suppose 51.2 g dry mass of seeds containing 50% fatty acid by mass, converted all the fatty acid to sugar in the following reaction:

$$\underset{\text{fatty acid}}{C_{16}H_{32}O_2} + 11O_2 \longrightarrow \underset{\text{sugar}}{C_{12}H_{22}O_{11}} + 4CO_2 + 5H_2O + \text{energy}$$

(*a*) Assuming that no other changes occurred which might affect dry mass, calculate the gain or loss in dry mass of the seeds.

(Relative atomic masses: C = 12, H = 1, O = 16.)

(*b*) What other important change might affect dry mass?

(*c*) Calculate the volume of carbon dioxide evolved from the seeds at STP (standard temperature and pressure).

(1 mole of gas at STP occupies 22.4 dm³.)

(*d*) How can fatty acid be obtained from a lipid, and what would be the other component of the lipid?

(*e*) How many carbon atoms would one molecule of the parent lipid have contained if $C_{16}H_{32}O_2$ was the only fatty acid produced?

(*f*) What is the identity of the sugar formed in the reaction shown?

(*g*) How does the oxygen reach the storage tissue?

Respiration in germinating seeds

Respiratory rates in both storage tissues and embryo are high owing to the intense metabolic activity in both regions. Substrates for respiration may differ in each region and may also change during germination. This is revealed by changes in the respiratory quotient (section 11.7.7).

21.8 When castor oil seeds were analysed for lipid and sugar content during germination in darkness, the results shown in fig 21.15 were obtained.

The RQ of the seedlings was measured at day 5 and the embryo was found to have an RQ of about 1.0, while the remaining cotyledons had an RQ of about 0.4–0.5.
(a) Suggest as full an explanation of these results as you can (refer to section 21.6.2 for relevant information).
(b) What would you expect the RQ of the whole seedling to be on day 11? Explain very briefly.

21.9 The RQ of peas is normally between 2.8 and 4 during the first seven days of germination, but is 1.5–2.4 if the testas are removed. In both cases ethanol accumulates in the seeds, but in much smaller amounts when the testas are removed. Account for these observations.

Growth of the embryo

Within the embryo growth occurs by cell division, enlargement and differentiation. Amounts of proteins, cellulose, nucleic acids and so on increase steadily in the growing regions while dry mass of the food store decreases. The first visible sign of growth is the emergence of the embryonic root, the **radicle**. This is positively geotropic and will grow down and anchor the seed. Subsequently, the embryonic shoot, the **plumule**, emerges and being negatively geotropic (and positively phototropic if above ground) will grow upwards.

There are two types of germination according to whether or not the cotyledons grow above ground or remain below it. In dicotyledons, if that part of the shoot axis, or internode, just below the cotyledons (**the hypocotyl**) elongates, then the cotyledons are carried above ground. This is **epigeal** germination. If the internode just above the cotyledons (the **epicotyl**) elongates, then the cotyledons remain below ground. This is **hypogeal** germination.

In epigeal germination, the hypocotyl remains hooked as it grows through the soil, as shown in fig 21.16 (b), thus meeting the resistance of the soil rather than the delicate plumule tip, which is further protected by being enclosed by the cotyledons. In hypogeal germination of dicotyledons the epicotyl is hooked, again protecting the plumule tip, as shown in fig 21.16c. In both cases the hooked structure immediately straightens on exposure to light, a phytochrome-controlled response.

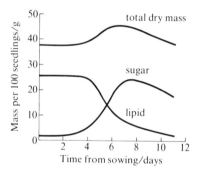

Fig 21.15 *Changes in lipid and sugar content of castor oil seeds during germination in the dark. (Based on data from R. Desveaux & M. Kogane-Charles (1952) Annls. Inst. natn. Rech. Agron., Paris, 3, 385–416; cited by H. S. Street & H. Opik (1976) The physiology of flowering plants 2nd ed., Arnold.)*

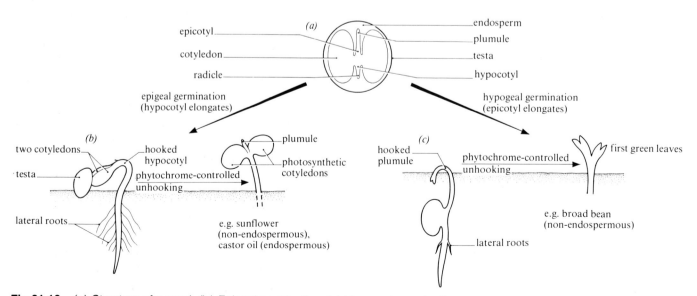

Fig 21.16 *(a) Structure of a seed, (b) Epigeal germination, (c) Hypogeal germination*

Table 21.3. Types of meristem and their functions

Type of meristem	Location	Role	Effect
Apical	Root and shoot apex	Responsible for primary growth, giving rise to primary plant body	Increase in length
Lateral (cambium)	Laterally situated in older parts of the plant parallel with the long axis of organs, e.g. cork cambium (phellogen), vascular cambium	Responsible for secondary growth. Vascular cambium gives rise to secondary vascular tissue; phellogen gives rise to the periderm, which replaces the epidermis and includes cork	Increase in girth
Intercalary	Between regions of permanent tissue, e.g. at nodes of many monocotyledons, such as bases of grass leaves	Allows growth in length to occur in regions other than tips. This is useful if the tips are susceptible to damage or destruction, e.g. eating by herbivores (grasses), wave action (kelps). Branching from the main axis is not then necessary	Increase in length

In the grasses, which are monocotyledons, the plumule is protected by a sheath called the **coleoptile**, which is positively phototropic and negatively geotropic as described in section 15.1.1. The first leaf grows out through the coleoptile and unrolls in response to light. On emerging into light a number of phytochrome-controlled responses rapidly occur, collectively known as **photomorphogenesis**. The overall effect is a change from etiolation (section 15.4.1) to normal growth. The major changes involved are summarised in table 15.5 and include expansion of the cotyledons or first true foliage leaves, as well as formation of chlorophyll ('greening'). At this point photosynthesis begins and net dry mass of the seedling starts to increase as it finally becomes independent of its food reserves and assumes an autotrophic existence. Once exposed to light, the shoot also shows phototropic responses although these are not phytochrome controlled.

21.6.3 Growth of the primary plant body

Meristems

In contrast to animals, growth in multicellular plants, with the exception of the young embryo, is confined to certain regions known as meristems. A meristem is a group of cells which retain the ability to divide by mitosis, producing daughter cells which grow and form the rest of the plant body. The daughter cells form the permanent tissue, that is, cells which have lost the ability to divide. There are three types of meristem, described in table 21.3. Two types of growth are mentioned in table 21.3, namely primary and secondary growth.

Primary growth is the first form of growth to occur. A whole plant can be built up by primary growth, and in most monocotyledonous plants and herbaceous dicotyledons it is the only type of growth. It is a result of the activity of the apical, and sometimes intercalary, meristems. The anatomy of mature primary roots and stems is dealt with in section 14.3.9.

Some plants continue with **secondary growth** from lateral meristems. This is most notable in shrubs and trees, which are sometimes described as **arborescent** to distinguish them from plants which lack extensive secondary growth,

namely **herbaceous** plants or **herbs**. A few herbaceous plants show restricted amounts of secondary thickening, as in the development of additional vascular bundles in *Helianthus* (sunflower).

Apical meristems and primary growth

A typical apical meristem cell is relatively small, cuboid, with a thin cellulose cell wall and dense cytoplasmic contents. It has a few small vacuoles rather than the large vacuoles characteristic of parenchyma cells, and the cytoplasm contains small, undifferentiated plastids called proplastids. Meristematic cells are packed tightly together with no obvious air spaces between the cells.

The cells are called **initials**. When they divide by mitosis one daughter cell remains in the meristem while the other increases in size and differentiates to become part of the permanent plant body.

21.6.4 Primary growth of the shoot

The structure of a typical apical shoot meristem is illustrated in figs 21.17 and 21.18. Fig 21.18 shows the approximate division of the shoot apex into regions of cell division, cell expansion and cell differentiation. There is more overlap in these zones than in the root. Passing back from the dome-shaped apical meristem, the cells get progressively older, so that different stages of growth can be observed simultaneously in the same apex. Thus it is relatively easy to study developmental sequences of plant tissue.

Three basic types of meristematic tissue are recognised, namely the **protoderm**, which gives rise to the epidermis; the **procambium**, giving rise to the vascular tissues, including pericycle, phloem, vascular cambium and xylem; and the **ground meristem**, producing the parenchyma **ground tissues**, which in the dicotyledons are the cortex and pith. These meristematic types are laid down by division of the initials in the apex. In the zone of expansion, the daughter cells produced by the initials increase in size, mainly by osmotic uptake of water into the cytoplasm and then into the vacuoles. Increase in the length of stems and roots is mainly brought about by elongation of cells during this stage. The process is illustrated in fig 21.19.

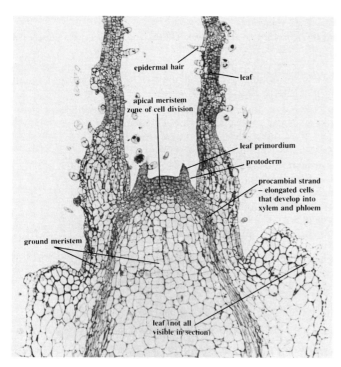

Fig 21.17 (above) The apical meristem

Fig 21.18 (below) LS shoot tip of a dicotyledon showing apical meristem and regions of primary growth. For simplicity, vascular tissue to leaves and buds has been omitted

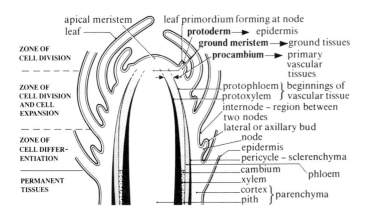

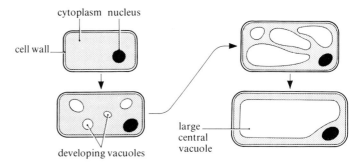

Fig 21.19 Expansion phase of growth of a meristematic cell

The small vacuoles increase in size, eventually fusing to form a single large vacuole. The pressure potential developed inside the cells stretches their thin walls and the orientation of cellulose microfibrils in the walls helps to determine the final shape assumed by the cells. The final volume of cytoplasm may not be significantly greater than in the original meristematic cell, but is now confined to the cell periphery by the vacuole. As expansion nears completion, many cells develop additional thickening of the cell walls, either of cellulose or lignin, depending on the type of cell being formed. This may restrict further expansion, but does not necessarily prevent it. Collenchyma cells in the cortex, for example, can continue elongating while extra cellulose is laid down in columns on the inside of the original walls. Thus they can give support to the plant while

still growing. In contrast, developing sclerenchyma cells deposit thick layers of lignin on their walls and soon die. Thus their differentiation does not start until expansion is virtually completed.

The procambium forms a series of longitudinally running strands whose cells are narrower and longer than those of the ground meristem. The first cells to differentiate in the procambium are those of the protoxylem to the inside, and protophloem to the outside. These are the parts of the primary xylem and phloem respectively which form before elongation is complete. The protoxylem typically has only annular or spiral thickenings of lignin on tracheids (section 8.2.1) which, being discontinuous, allow extension and stretching of the cellulose between the thickenings as the surrounding tissue elongates. Both protoxylem and protophloem elements soon die and generally get crushed and stretched to the point of collapse as growth continues around them. Their function is taken over by later-developing xylem and phloem in the zone of differentiation.

In the zone of differentiation each cell becomes fully specialised for its own particular function, according to its position in the organ with respect to other cells. The greatest changes occur in the procambial strands, which differentiate into vascular bundles. This involves lignification of the walls of sclerenchyma fibres and xylem elements, as well as development of the tubes characteristic of xylem vessels and phloem sieve tubes. The final forms of these tissues are described in section 8.2. Sclerenchyma and xylem now supplement the support previously given by collenchyma and turgid parenchyma. Between the xylem and phloem there are cells which retain the ability to divide. They form the vascular cambium, whose activities are described later, with secondary thickening.

Leaf primordia and lateral buds

Development of the shoot also includes growth of leaves and lateral buds. Leaves arise as small swellings or ridges called leaf primordia, shown particularly clearly in fig 21.17. The swellings contain groups of meristematic cells and appear at regular intervals, their sites of origin being called **nodes** and the regions between **internodes**. The pattern of leaf arrangement on the stem varies and is called **phyllotaxis**. Leaves may arise in whorls with two or more leaves at each node, or singly, either in two opposite ranks or in a spiral pattern. Generally, however, they are arranged to minimise overlapping, and hence shading, when fully grown so that they form a **mosaic**.

The primordia elongate rapidly, so they soon enclose and protect the apical meristem, both physically and by the heat they generate in respiration. Later they grow and increase in area to form the leaf blades. Cell division gradually ceases but may continue until they are about half their mature size.

Soon after the leaves start to grow, buds develop in the axils between them and the stem. These are small groups of meristematic cells which normally remain dormant, but retain the capacity to divide and grow at a later stage. They form branches or specialised structures such as flowers and underground structures such as rhizomes and tubers. They are thought to be under the control of the apical meristem (see apical dominance, section 15.3.3).

21.6.5 Primary growth of the root

The structure of the typical apical root system is illustrated in fig 21.20.

At the very tip of the apical meristem is a **quiescent centre**, a group of **initials** (meristematic cells) from which all other cells in the root can be traced, but whose rate of cell division is much slower than their daughter cells in the apical meristem around them. To the outside, the cells of the **root cap** are formed. These become large parenchyma cells which protect the apical meristem as the root grows through the soil. They are constantly being worn away and replaced. They also have the important additional function of acting as gravity sensors, since they contain large starch

grains which act as statoliths, sedimenting to the bottoms of cells in response to gravity. Their role is described in more detail in section 15.2.2.

Behind the quiescent centre, orderly rows of cells can be seen and the meristematic regions already described in the shoot, namely protoderm, ground meristem and procambium, can be distinguished (fig 21.20). In the root the term procambium is used to describe the whole central cylinder of the root, even though at maturity this contains the non-vascular tissues of the pericycle and the pith, if present.

The zone of cell division typically extends 1–2 mm back from the root tip, and overlaps slightly with the zone of cell elongation. Root tips are convenient material for observation of mitosis and a procedure for this is described in section 22.2. Behind this zone, growth is mainly by cell elongation, cells increasing in size in the manner described for the shoot and shown in fig 21.19. The zone of elongating cells extends to a point about 10 mm behind the root tip and their increase in length forces the root tip down through the soil.

Some cell differentiation begins in the zone of cell division, with the development of the first phloem sieve tube elements (fig 21.20). In longitudinal sections, neat files of developing sieve tube elements can be seen, getting progressively more mature further back from the root tip, until they become mature sieve tubes. Development of phloem is from the outside inwards.

Further back in the zone of elongation, the xylem vessels start to differentiate, also from the outside inwards (exarch xylem) in contrast to the stem (endarch xylem). The first-formed vessels are protoxylem vessels, as in the stem, and they show the same pattern of lignification and ability to stretch as cells around them grow. Their role is taken over by metaxylem, which develops later and matures in the zone of differentiation after elongation has ceased. The xylem often spreads to the centre of the root, in which case no pith develops.

Development is easier to examine in roots than in shoots. In the latter procambial strands to the leaves complicate the distribution of developing tissues. Development of xylem, in particular, is easily seen by squashing apical portions of fine roots such as those of cress seedlings and staining appropriately.

After all cells have stopped elongating, further differentiation is completed. This includes the development of root hairs from the epidermis.

Lateral roots

Branching from the main root may occur but not by means of buds, in contrast to the shoot. Instead, a small group of pericycle cells in the zone of differentiation resumes meristematic activity and forms a new root apical meristem. It then grows, forcing its way out through the endodermis, cortex and epidermis as shown in fig 21.20. Such development is termed endarch, compared with exarch development of lateral buds.

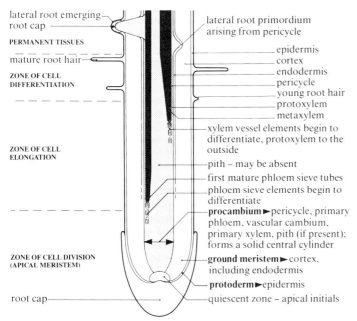

Fig 21.20 *LS apical meristem of a typical root. Xylem differentiation is shown to the right and phloem differentiation to the left. In reality xylem and phloem alternate round the root and would be on different radii. (See fig 14.16). Also, in reality, the zone of elongation would be longer*

Adventitious growth

Adventitious structures are those growing in uncharacteristic positions. Adventitious roots and buds may arise in a variety of situations as a result of certain cells resuming meristematic activity. **Adventitious roots** develop independently of the original primary root and form the main rooting system of monocotyledons, arising from nodes on the stem. Rhizomes and runners are stem structures from which adventitious roots arise directly. Adventitious roots are also important in propagation of plants by stem cuttings. Ivy clings by adventitious roots.

Adventitious buds may develop on roots, stems or leaves. For example African violets can be propagated from leaf cuttings, which develop adventitious roots and buds. Trees may develop new branches adventitiously from buds that arise in the trunk.

21.6.6 Lateral meristems and secondary growth

Secondary growth is that growth which occurs after primary growth as a result of the activity of lateral meristems. It results in an increase in girth. It is usually associated with deposition of large amounts of secondary xylem, called **wood**, which completely modifies the primary structure and is a characteristic feature of trees and shrubs.

There are two types of lateral meristem, the **vascular cambium** which gives rise to new vascular tissue, and the **cork cambium** or **phellogen**, which arises later to replace the ruptured epidermis of the expanding plant body.

Vascular cambium

There are two types of cell in the vascular cambium, the **fusiform initials** and the **ray initials**, illustrated in fig 21.21. Fusiform initials are narrow, elongated cells which divide by mitosis to form **secondary phloem** to the outside or **secondary xylem** to the inside. The amount of xylem produced normally exceeds the amount of phloem. Successive divisions are shown in fig 21.22. Secondary phloem contains sieve tubes, companion cells, sclerenchyma fibres and sclereids, and parenchyma.

Ray initials are almost spherical and divide by mitosis to form parenchyma cells which accumulate to form rays between the neighbouring xylem and phloem.

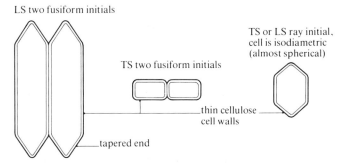

Fig 21.21 *Fusiform and ray initials*

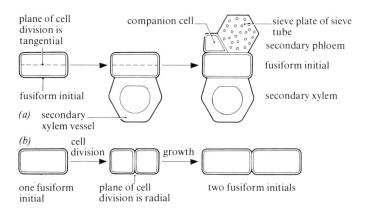

Fig 21.22 (a) *Two successive divisions of a fusiform initial to form xylem and phloem, seen in TS. In reality, differentiation of xylem and phloem to the stages shown would take some time, during which more cells would be produced. (b) Division of a fusiform initial to form a new fusiform initial, seen in TS*

Secondary growth in woody dicotyledon stems

The vascular cambium is originally located between the primary xylem and primary phloem of the vascular bundles, its derivation from the apical meristem being shown in fig 21.18. It becomes active very soon after primary cell differentiation is complete. Fig 21.23 summarises the early stages in secondary thickening of a typical woody dicotyledon stem.

Fig 21.23*a* shows the original primary stem structure, omitting the pericycle for simplicity. Fig 21.23*b* shows the development of a complete cylinder of cambium. Fig 21.23*c* shows a complete ring of secondary thickening. Here, fusiform initials have produced large quantities of secondary xylem, and lesser quantities of secondary phloem, while the ray initials have produced rays of parenchyma. As the stem increases in thickness, so the circumference of the cambium layers must increase. To achieve this, radial divisions of the cambial cells occur, as shown in fig 21.22. The original ray initials produce primary medullary rays which run all the way from pith to cortex, unlike the secondary medullary rays produced by later ray initials. The rays maintain a living link between the pith and cortex. They help to transmit water and mineral salts from the xylem, and food substances from the phloem, radially across the stem. Also, gaseous exchange can occur by diffusion through intercellular spaces. The rays may also be used for food storage, an important function during periods of dormancy, as in winter. In three dimensions they appear as radially–longitudinally running sheets because the ray initials occur in stacks one above the other, as shown in fig 21.24. Fig 21.24 illustrates the appearance of wood (secondary xylem) and the rays it contains in the three planes TS, TLS and RLS.

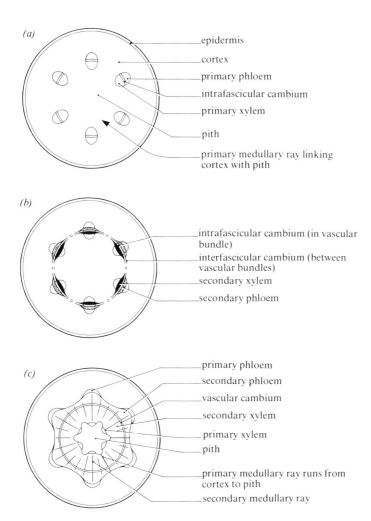

(a)
- epidermis
- cortex
- primary phloem
- intrafascicular cambium
- primary xylem
- pith
- primary medullary ray linking cortex with pith

(b)
- intrafascicular cambium (in vascular bundle)
- interfascicular cambium (between vascular bundles)
- secondary xylem
- secondary phloem

(c)
- primary phloem
- secondary phloem
- vascular cambium
- secondary xylem
- primary xylem
- pith
- primary medullary ray runs from cortex to pith
- secondary medullary ray

Fig 21.23 *Early stages in secondary thickening of a typical woody dicotyledon stem. (a) Primary structure of stem. (b) Cambium forms a complete cylinder as parenchyma cells in the medullary rays become meristematic, spreading outwards from the vascular bundles. Meanwhile secondary xylem and phloem are already being formed by the existing cambium. (c) A complete ring of secondary thickening has developed. Thickening is most advanced at the sites of the original vascular bundles where cambial activity first started*

Fig 21.25 shows part of the stem of a woody dicotyledon in its third year of growth, revealing the large amounts of secondary xylem produced. Fig. 21.26 shows photographs of a three-year-old and a five-year-old stem of *Tilia*, the lime tree.

Annual rings

Each year in temperate climates, growth resumes in the spring. The first vessels formed are wide and thin-walled, being suitable for the conduction of large quantities of water. Water is required to initiate growth, particularly the expansion of new cells, as in developing leaves. Later in the year, fewer vessels are produced and they are narrower with thicker walls. During winter the cambium remains dormant. The autumn wood produced at the end of one year, as growth ceases, will therefore be immediately next to the spring wood of the following year and will differ markedly in appearance. This contrast is seen as the **annual ring** and is clearly visible in fig 21.26. Where vessels are concentrated in the early wood it is said to be **ring porous**, as opposed to **diffuse porous** wood, where they are evenly distributed, and where it is more difficult to see annual rings. In tropical climates, seasonal droughts may induce similar fluctuations in cambial activity.

The width of an annual ring will vary partly according to climate, a favourable climate resulting in production of more wood and hence a greater distance between rings. This has been used in two areas of science, namely dendroclimatology and dendrochronology. **Dendroclimatology** is the study of climate using tree ring data. Applications vary from correlation of recent climatic records with tree growth, of possible interest in a specific locality, to investigations of more distant climatic events several hundreds or even thousands of years in the past. The oldest-known living trees, the bristlecone pines, are about 5 000 years old, and fossil wood of even greater age can be found.

Dendrochronology is the dating of wood by recognition of the pattern of annual rings. This pattern can act as a

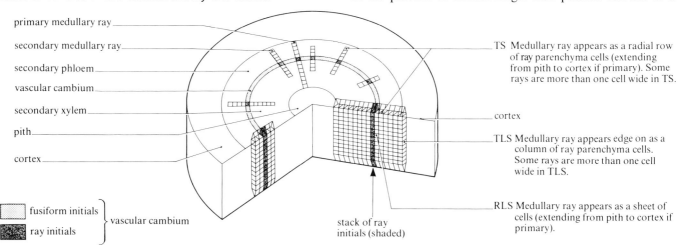

- primary medullary ray
- secondary medullary ray
- secondary phloem
- vascular cambium
- secondary xylem
- pith
- cortex

- fusiform initials
- ray initials
} vascular cambium

stack of ray initials (shaded)

TS Medullary ray appears as a radial row of ray parenchyma cells (extending from pith to cortex if primary). Some rays are more than one cell wide in TS.

cortex

TLS Medullary ray appears edge on as a column of ray parenchyma cells. Some rays are more than one cell wide in TLS.

RLS Medullary ray appears as a sheet of cells (extending from pith to cortex if primary).

Fig 21.24 *Diagrammatic representation of primary and secondary medullary rays in a typical woody dicotyledonous stem. A primary ray is shown to the right and a secondary ray to the left. (TLS, transverse longitudinal section; RLS, radial longitudinal section.)*

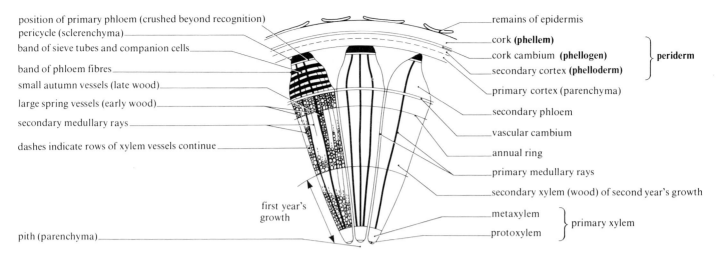

position of primary phloem (crushed beyond recognition)
pericycle (sclerenchyma)
band of sieve tubes and companion cells
band of phloem fibres
small autumn vessels (late wood)
large spring vessels (early wood)
secondary medullary rays
dashes indicate rows of xylem vessels continue
first year's growth
pith (parenchyma)

remains of epidermis
cork **(phellem)**
cork cambium **(phellogen)** ⎫ periderm
secondary cortex **(phelloderm)** ⎭
primary cortex (parenchyma)
secondary phloem
vascular cambium
annual ring
primary medullary rays
secondary xylem (wood) of second year's growth
metaxylem ⎫ primary xylem
protoxylem ⎭

Fig 21.25 (above) *TS of a typical woody dicotyledonous stem in the third year of growth (age two years), such as* Tilia. *Details of secondary phloem, secondary xylem and secondary medullary rays are shown only in the left-hand sector*

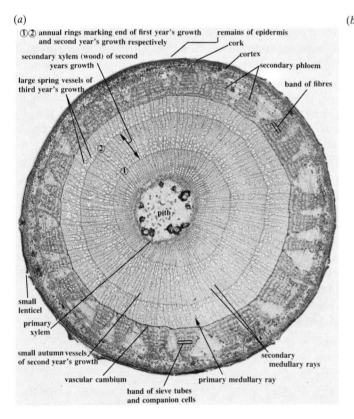

(a)
①② annual rings marking end of first year's growth and second year's growth respectively
secondary xylem (wood) of second years growth
large spring vessels of third year's growth
remains of epidermis
cork
cortex
secondary phloem
band of fibres
small lenticel
primary xylem
small autumn vessels of second year's growth
vascular cambium
band of sieve tubes and companion cells
primary medullary ray
secondary medullary rays
pith

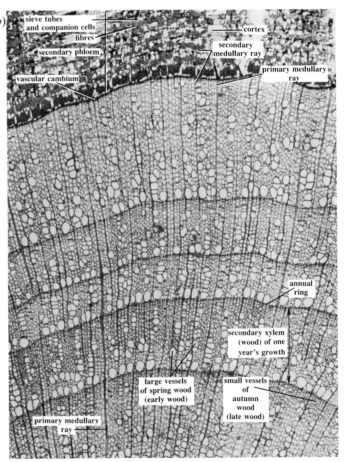

(b)
sieve tubes and companion cells
fibres
secondary phloem
vascular cambium
cortex
secondary medullary ray
primary medullary ray
annual ring
secondary xylem (wood) of one year's growth
large vessels of spring wood (early wood)
small vessels of autumn wood (late wood)
primary medullary ray

Fig 21.26 (a) TS of a two-year-old (third year) twig of Tilia vulgaris (× 2.2). (b) Part of a TS of a five-year-old (sixth year) twig of Tilia vulgaris (× 11.5)

'fingerprint', pinpointing the time during which the wood was growing. Dating of timbers at archaeological sites, in old buildings and ships and so on thus becomes feasible, provided enough data are available.

Heartwood and sapwood

As a tree ages, the wood at the centre may cease to serve a conducting function and become blocked with darkly staining deposits such as tannins. It is called **heartwood**,

whereas the outer, wetter conducting wood is called **sapwood**.

Cork and lenticels

As the secondary xylem grows outwards, so the tissues outside it become increasingly compressed, as well as being stretched sideways by the increasing circumference. This affects the epidermis, cortex, primary phloem and all but the most recent secondary phloem. The epidermis even-

786

tually ruptures and is replaced by cork as the result of the activity of a second lateral meristem, the **cork cambium** or **phellogen**. It generally arises immediately below the epidermis. **Cork** (or **phellem**) is produced to the outside of the cork cambium, while to the inside one or two layers of parenchyma are produced. These are indistinguishable from the primary cortex and form the **phelloderm** or secondary cortex. The phellogen, cork and phelloderm together comprise the periderm (fig 21.25).

As the cork cells mature, their walls become impregnated with a fatty substance called suberin which is impermeable to water and gases. The cells gradually die and lose their living contents, becoming filled either with air or with resin or tannins. The older, dead cork cells fit together around the stem, preventing desiccation, infection and mechanical injury. They become compressed as the stem increases in girth and may eventually be lost and replaced by younger cells from beneath. If the cork layer were complete, the respiratory gases oxygen and carbon dioxide could not be exchanged between the living cells of the stem and the environment, and the cells would die. At random intervals, however, slit-like openings, or **lenticels**, develop in the cork containing a mass of loosely packed, thin-walled dead cells, lacking suberin. They are produced by the cork cambium and have large intercellular air spaces allowing gaseous exchange.

Fig 21.27 shows a diagram of cork and lenticels.

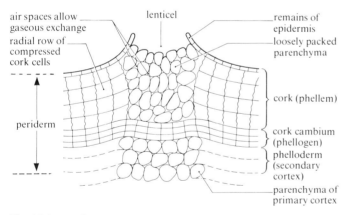

Fig 21.27 *VS lenticel (cell contents omitted)*

Bark

Eventually a woody stem becomes covered with a layer commonly known as bark. The term bark is an imprecise one which is used to refer either to all the tissues outside the vascular system, or more strictly to those tissues outside the cork cambium. Peeling bark from a tree generally strips tissues down to the vascular cambium, a thin layer of cells which is easily ruptured.

It is usual for the cork cambium to be renewed each year as the girth of the stem increases. Often a cork cambium arises in the secondary phloem, in which case the bark will, over a number of years, build up a layered appearance due to alternating layers of secondary phloem and bark.

Secondary growth in roots of dicotyledons

Most dicotyledons that show secondary growth of the stem also show secondary growth of the roots. In the case of plants with storage roots, such as carrots and turnip, it may be more conspicuous than in the stem, although parenchyma predominates in the xylem and phloem of the examples given. The process of secondary growth is summarised in fig 21.28 and is similar in principle to secondary growth in stems.

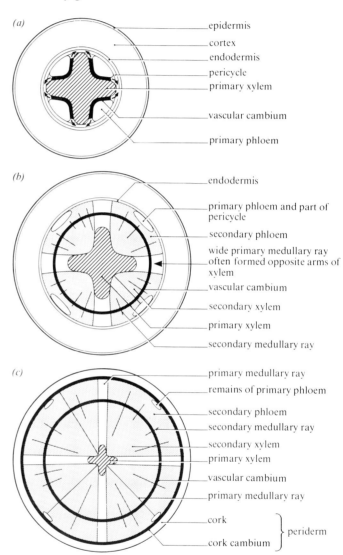

Fig 21.28 *Stages in the secondary growth of a dicotyledonous root. (a) The vascular cambium develops from cells of the procambium (fig 21.23) which have remained meristematic. The cambium continues to grow to form a complete ring (see arrows) as cells of the pericycle outside the xylem arms become meristematic. (b) The cambium produces rows of secondary xylem vessels internally and secondary phloem externally. Growth of secondary xylem starts earlier and is more rapid between the arms of the xylem, until the cambium becomes circular, rather than wavy, in outline. (c) As growth continues, the increasing girth stretches and tears the endodermis, cortex and epidermis, and these are sloughed off. A cork cambium develops from the pericycle. ((c) is drawn to a smaller scale than (a) and (b).)*

787

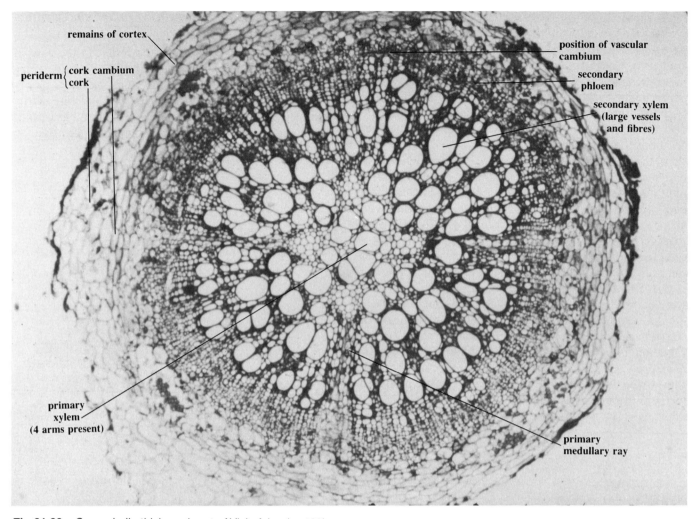

remains of cortex

periderm { **cork cambium** **cork** }

position of vascular cambium

secondary phloem

secondary xylem (large vessels and fibres)

primary xylem (4 arms present)

primary medullary ray

Fig 21.29 *Secondarily thickened root of* Vicia faba *(× 120)*

Development of secondary xylem, secondary phloem and medullary rays is basically similar to that in stems, and annual rings are usually formed as in stems. A cork cambium develops from the pericycle and serves the same function as in the stem. A phelloderm may be produced, but is indistinguishable from the pericycle. As with the stem, the original cork cambium may be replaced at intervals by cork cambium arising further inside the root. Fig 21.29 is a photograph of a transverse section through a root with secondary thickening.

21.7 Metamorphosis

The term metamorphosis (*meta*, between; *morphe*, form) applies to those rapid changes which occur during the transition from larval to adult form. This is the process of postembryonic maturation and is found in many non-vertebrate groups, especially amongst insects, echinoderms, hemichordates, urochordates, cephalochordates and some fish and amphibian species. Table 21.4 lists various animal groups and names of their larval stages.

Table 21.4. Some larval stages found in the animal kingdom

Animal group	*Larval stage*
cnidarians	planula
trematodes	miracidium/redia/cercaria
cestodes	hexacanth/cysticercus
polychaetes	trochophore
crustacea	nauplius/cypris/zoaea
insects	caterpillar (maggot, grub) or nymph
molluscs	trochophore/veliger
echinoderms	dipleurula/pluteus
urochordates	ascidian tadpole
lamprey	ammocoete
amphibia	tadpole

21.7.1 Adaptive significance of larval stages

Larvae generally act as a dispersal phase for the distribution of species. This is very important to sessile organisms as it provides a means of preventing overcrowding of the parental organisms by their offspring. Overcrowding would lead to increased competition for food and other resources and this could be harmful to the survival of the species. For example, many sessile marine organisms such as barnacles and mussels produce vast numbers of larvae which are planktonic and are dispersed by ocean currents. At a certain stage they settle on solid objects, a phenomenon known as 'spat-fall', and continue their development.

Larvae usually occupy a different habitat from the adult forms and have different feeding habits, forms of locomotion and behavioural patterns which enable the species to exploit the potential of two ecological niches during the life cycle. This increases the chances of survival of the species between the egg and adult stages. Many species, for example the dragonfly, only feed and grow during their larval stages which form the longest period of their life.

Another feature of larvae is their ability to act as a transition stage during which the species has time to adapt to the new conditions that will be encountered in the adult habitat. Physiological hardiness is another attribute which allows larvae to act as a dormant stage during adverse conditions. For example, some insects overwinter in the soil as larvae but most exist as another metamorphic stage, the pupa, and the physiological changes which accompany these stages are described in section 21.7.3.

A final advantage of larval stages is that they may provide an opportunity for the numbers of larvae to be increased. This is common in the life cycles of certain platyhelminths (section 4.4.3).

However, larvae should not be thought of as incompletely developed forms. In many cases they are highly developed, as shown by insect larval stages, where the only undeveloped structures are the reproductive organs. An interesting example of a fully developed larval stage which has attained sexual maturity, the axolotl, is described in section 21.7.4.

21.7.2 Characteristics of metamorphosis

The structural and functional changes which occur during metamorphosis prepare the organism for adult life in a new habitat or environment. In some cases these new adaptations may appear whilst the organism still retains the larval form and occupies the larval habitat. In other words metamorphosis is not entirely a response to a change in environment but a *preparation* for a change. For example, tadpoles, living in water where desiccation is not a problem, lose approximately 80% of their nitrogenous waste as ammonia. In the later stages of metamorphosis, whilst still living in water, tadpoles begin to excrete urea. By the time the young frogs are ready to leave the water they are excreting 80% of their nitrogenous waste as urea.

Whilst growth and differentiation may be influenced by hormones, metamorphosis is *entirely* controlled and regulated by endocrine secretions. In some cases metamorphosis is a response to increasing hormone levels and in other cases it is the result of different responses by different target organs to the same level of hormone. These responses may involve either cell death and reduction in size of an organ (involution) or cell division, differentiation and the growth of an organ.

21.7.3 Hormonal control of ecdysis and moulting in insects

The involvement of hormones in ecdysis and moulting was first described by Wigglesworth in Cambridge. In a series of experiments he was able to show that moulting is controlled by a **moulting hormone** (MH) which is released in response to a specific stimulus. The result of the moulting, in terms of stage in the life cycle, may be modified by another hormone, **juvenile hormone** (JH), which prevents the appearance of the adult form.

Wigglesworth chose to investigate insect growth hormone in *Rhodnius prolixus*, a blood-sucking hemipteran from South America. *Rhodnius* is an insect with five nymphal stages and no pupal stage, an example of incomplete metamorphosis. During each nymphal stage only one large blood meal is required and this acts as the stimulus for moulting. Wigglesworth was able to demonstrate that stretch receptors in the abdominal wall, activated by distension, set up nerve impulses which are transmitted to the brain. These impulses initiate a series of coordinated endocrine secretions which result in moulting. In the case of the moult from 4th to 5th instar this occurs within 14 days of feeding and 28 °C.

If the insect is decapitated within four days of a blood meal and the wound plugged with wax it will live for 18 months without showing any further growth or development. If decapitation occurs after this four-day period it will continue to grow but no moulting will occur. These observations suggest that it takes four days for impulses from the gut to be passed to the brain and hormones to be released which affect the growth and differentiation of the target tissues, including the epidermal cells.

In his experiments Wigglesworth transplanted the brain from an insect which was just about to moult, into the abdomen of a starved decapitated insect which then proceeded to moult. Transplanting brain tissue from a moulting insect into an insect without head or thorax did not result in moulting. Clearly then, a substance from the brain was influencing a region in the thorax which produced the moulting response. Previous studies on silkworm caterpillars had revealed the presence of a gland in the first thoracic segment, the **prothoracic gland**, which could induce moulting if implanted into the posterior region of a silkworm which was separated from the thorax by a ligature. This suggested that moulting in *Rhodnius* is also controlled by a hormone from the prothoracic gland.

Moulting hormone was isolated in 1953 and is a steroid with a similar structure to cholesterol (section 5.3.6). The hormone was named **ecdysone**, and because of the presence of more hydroxyl groups than cholesterol it is water-soluble. Since then it has been synthesised and produces all the responses normally associated with moulting when injected into insects.

Ecdysone is thought to activate genes controlling the production of enzymes involved in growth. This response is most marked in epidermal cells which undergo a series of changes associated with ecdysis and are described in fig 21.30.

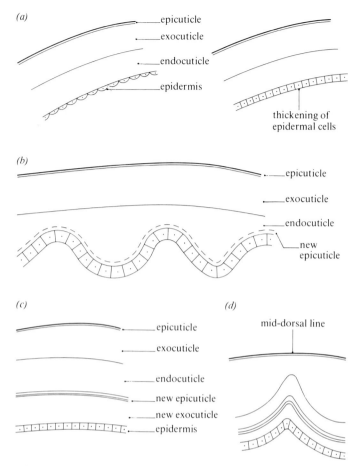

(a)
epicuticle
exocuticle
endocuticle
epidermis

thickening of
epidermal cells

(b)
epicuticle
exocuticle
endocuticle
new
epicuticle

(c)
epicuticle
exocuticle
endocuticle
new epicuticle
new exocuticle
epidermis

(d)
mid-dorsal line

Fig 21.30 *(a) TS* Rhodnius *cuticle. Without blood meal, epidermis thin and flattened. Following blood meal the epidermis starts to thicken out and separate from the endocuticle above. (b) New epicuticle then forms over the epidermis. Chitinase and proteinase enzymes are secreted by epidermis and break down the old cuticle. New cuticle is shielded from enzymes by the formation of a new epicuticle. Old digested endocuticle is absorbed by the epidermis and incorporated into new endocuticle. (c)* Rhodnius *takes in air, expands itself and breaks the old cuticle and moults. The new cuticle is soft and hardens by tanning. (d) Moulting occurs by splitting of the old cuticle along the mid-dorsal line which is specially thinned*

The addition of ecdysone to insect larvae with 'giant chromosomes' produces 'puffing' in specific regions of the chromosomes. These are sites of messenger RNA synthesis and this evidence suggests that ecdysone works directly at the level of genetic transcription.

In a further series of experiments Wigglesworth obtained data which suggested that the head region of *Rhodnius* larvae produces another hormone which promotes the retention of nymphal characteristics, thus preventing development into the adult form. Investigations revealed that a region just behind the brain, the **corpus allatum**, produced this response. Implantation of the corpus allatum from a third- or fourth-stage nymph into a fifth-stage produces a sixth-stage giant nymph and not an adult. Implantation of the corpus allatum of a fifth-stage nymph does not have this effect.

The corpus allatum produces a hormone called **juvenile hormone** or **neotonin**. Growth and metamorphosis in arthropods is now seen to be controlled by the interaction of ecdysone and juvenile hormone. The latter is believed to cause the retention of larval or nymphal characteristics by activating genes responsible for these characters and suppressing genes responsible for producing adult cuticle and structure.

The release of ecdysone and juvenile hormone is controlled by yet another hormone, which is produced by the brain. The mechanism of release may be described with reference to the locust (fig 21.31).

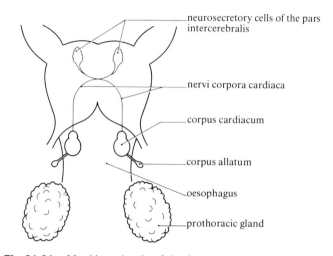

neurosecretory cells of the pars intercerebralis
nervi corpora cardiaca
corpus cardiacum
corpus allatum
oesophagus
prothoracic gland

Fig 21.31 *Moulting glands of the locust*

Neurosecretory cell bodies situated in the **pars intercerebralis** of the brain secrete a hormone, **prothoracicotrophic hormone (PTTH)**, which passes down the axons of the neurosecretory cells through the **nervi corpora cardiaca** possibly by axoplasmic streaming (section 16.6.2). The hormone is stored in a pair of glands, the **corpora cardiaca**, which are situated immediately behind the brain. The stimulus to moult, whatever it may be, sets up nerve impulses in the brain which pass down the nervi corpora cardiaca and cause the release of prothoracicotrophic hormone into the blood (fig 21.32). This passes to the prothoracic gland and ecdysone is released which stimulates, in turn, the epidermal cells to produce a new cuticle.

A similar pattern of events is involved in the control of ecdysis and moulting in *Rhodnius* but the corpora cardiaca and corpora allata are not bilateral structures, having fused together to form single structures situated in the mid-line of the body.

In insects showing **complete metamorphosis** the formation of the pupal stage occurs in the presence of a very low level of juvenile hormone whereas the absence of juvenile hormone results in a direct metamorphosis into the adult form. If the corpus allatum is removed from a second, third or fourth nymphal stage of an insect with **incomplete metamorphosis** it will moult into a miniature adult. Therefore, the increase in size and the attainment of sexual

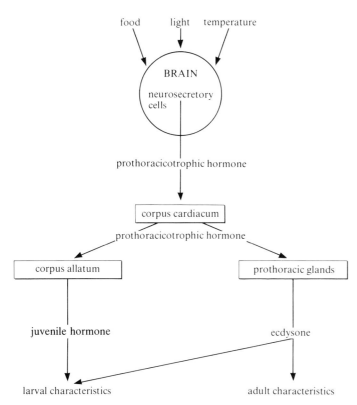

Fig 21.32 *The hormonal control of ecdysis and moulting in insects*

maturity in the insect may possibly result from falling levels of juvenile hormones. The control of growth and metamorphosis in the two types of life cycles of insects is summarised in fig 21.33.

Once the adult form has been attained in winged insects the prothoracic glands atrophy and disappear, preventing any further ecdyses or moults. This does not occur in wingless insects. In all adult insects the corpus allatum becomes active again and juvenile hormone is secreted. In females it is necessary for the deposition of yolk in the egg and in males it is required for the normal functioning of the accessory glands which produce the **spermatophore**, the capsule used to transfer sperm to the female.

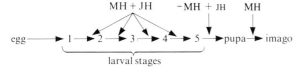

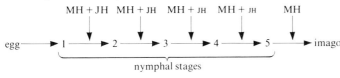

Fig 21.33 *The influence of growth hormones on complete and incomplete insect life cycles (MH moulting hormone, JH juvenile hormone. The height of the letters JH indicates relative concentration.)*

21.7.4 Metamorphosis in amphibia

Metamorphosis in amphibia involves the transition of an aquatic larva into a semi-terrestrial adult. The mechanisms of metamorphosis are controlled by endocrine secretions in an analogous way to those described in insects. Gudernatsch, a German biologist, discovered in 1911 that tadpoles feeding on extracts of mammalian thyroid glands would rapidly change into miniature frogs. This precocious metamorphosis, under the influence of thyroid extract, implicated the hormone thyroxine as the factor responsible for the many anatomical, physiological, biochemical and behavioural changes in the life cycle of the frog. Further investigations involved the removal of the thyroid gland in some animals and the pituitary gland in others. In both cases metamorphosis was prevented but was restored by feeding with thyroxine.

The initial stimulus for metamorphosis is thought to be a change in the environmental conditions such as increase in temperature or daylength. These external stimuli are transmitted to the brain and activate the hypothalamus which secretes **thyrotrophin releasing hormone** (TRH). This enters the blood vessels of the hypothalamico-hypophyseal portal system (section 16.6.2) and passes to the anterior pituitary gland. Here **thyroid stimulating hormone** or **thyrotrophin** (TSH) is released which enters the general circulation and stimulates the thyroid gland to release **thyroxine (tetraiodothyronine)** and **triiodothyronine**. These hormones act directly on all metamorphosing tissue and produce varying responses such as the atrophy of the larval tail and gills, accelerated growth of the limbs and tongue and differentiation of the skin to form gland cells and chromatophores (pigment-containing cells). The direct or local effects of thyroxine on metamorphosis at the tissue and biochemical levels were demonstrated by applying thyroxine in a fatty base to the left side of the tail and the left eye of several tadpoles. Pure fatty base was added to the right side to act as a control. After a few days, regression of the tails on the left side and a change from the larval visual pigment **porphyropsin** to the adult visual pigment **rhodopsin** had occurred in the left eyes. No change had occurred in the control tissues.

The early stages of metamorphosis are controlled by positive feedback, that is to say increasing amounts of thyroxine released by the growing thyroid gland stimulate the further production of thyroxine. As the level of circulating thyroxine increases, different target organs respond by showing cell death, cell division or cell differentiation, as described in the examples quoted above. Once the adult form has been attained thyroxine secretion is controlled by negative feedback (section 16.6.5). The sequence of external morphological changes shown by the tadpole during its metamorphosis is summarised in table 21.5.

The Mexican axolotl, *Amblystoma mexicanum* (fig 21.34), does not normally undergo metamorphosis due to a failure of the pituitary gland to produce thyroid stimulating

Fig 21.34 *The axolotl*

Table 21.5. Changes in external features in frog during metamorphosis. Times and sizes can only be approximate as the rate of metamorphosis depends upon food supply, temperature and internal factors

Time/ weeks	Size/ mm	Stages in development
0	—	Fertilisation
1	7	Hatches from jelly. External gills, tail, mouth with horny jaws. Mucus glands beneath mouth
2	9	External gills begin to atrophy, operculum grows over gills. Eyes prominent
4	12	External gills and mucus gland lost. Spiracle develops. Tail widens to aid swimming
7	28	Hindlimbs appear as buds
9	35	Hindlimbs fully formed but not used for swimming. Head begins to broaden
11–12	35	Left limb emerges through spiracle. Right limb enclosed by operculum. Hindlimbs used for swimming
13	25	Eyes become prominent and mouth widens.
14	20	Tail begins to be reabsorbed
16	15	All external larval features have disappeared. Frog emerges on to land

hormone (TSH). Instead, the axolotl attains sexual maturity whilst retaining larval characteristics such as external gills, tail fins and a light coloration. This is an example of **neoteny**, the attainment of sexual maturity whilst retaining larval characteristics. Neoteny is believed to have played a significant role in the physiological development of many animal groups, for example, the earliest vertebrates, which are thought to have descended from neotenous larval forms of sea-squirts.

The axolotl can be induced to metamorphose by the addition of the correct concentration of thyroxine to the water in which it is living. The visible effects of this are loss of gills and most of the tail fin and the assumption of the shape and features of a close relative, the land salamander.

21.8 Development in vertebrates

The preceding section on metamorphosis in amphibia described the morphological changes which occur during the development of the larval form into the adult form. Whilst these changes are spectacular and have tremendous adaptive significance in preparing the organism to meet the demands of the adult habitat, they appear trivial when compared to the events following fertilisation of the ovum. For example, of the 47 generations of cell division estimated to occur during the development of humans, 42 occur during the period of development which precedes birth. The study of embryonic development is known as *embryology* and the events which occur during this time are fundamentally the same in all animal species. They increase our understanding of the origins and functional relationships between tissues, organs and organ systems. This development is conveniently divided into three main phases, but it should be appreciated that the overall process of embryonic development is continuous and one stage passes imperceptibly into the next. These stages and their main features and implications are as follows.

Cleavage (or *segmentation*) This is the series of mitotic divisions of the zygote nucleus and cytoplasm that follows fertilisation. In the frog, the point of sperm entry into the egg prior to fertilisation imposes symmetry on the future embryo and marks the position of the future dorsal lip of the blastopore. Fertilisation stimulates cleavage which produces daughter cells or **blastomeres** forming a hollow ball of cells, the **blastula**, enclosing a cavity called the **blastocoel**.

By injecting cells with different coloured dyes (a technique known as **intra vitam staining**) the fate of the cells of the blastula can be followed throughout the next two processes of gastrulation and organogeny. Vogt has used this technique and produced **fate maps** which show the **prospective** or **presumptive** fate of cells of different regions, as shown in fig 21.35.

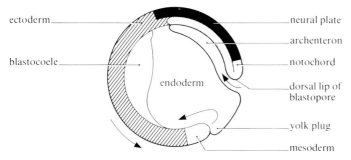

Fig 21.35 *VS of developing gastrula showing presumptive areas. Later growth and cell migration of the ectoderm and mesoderm is indicated by arrows. Mesoderm spreads inwards and occupies a position beneath the ectoderm*

Gastrulation. The onset of gastrulation is marked by the appearance of a circular opening, the **blastopore**. In the frog, cells of the blastula divide rapidly, differentiate, and by a series of **morphogenic** movements buckle inwards (*invaginate*) through the blastopore and obliterate the blastocoel forming a new cavity, the **archenteron**. The cells become rearranged as three distinct layers, called **primary germ layers**, within a double-layered structure called the **gastrula**. The germ layers, the ectoderm, mesoderm and endoderm, are now spatially organised so as to undergo organogeny.

Organogeny (organogenesis). Further cell division, growth and differentiation occurs involving many complex morphogenic activities including the formation of the notochord, the formation of the central nervous system and the development of the mesoderm. In vertebrates these give rise to the tissues, organs and organ systems of the embryo as shown in figs 21.36 and 21.37. Organogeny is terminated by the hatching or birth of the embryo.

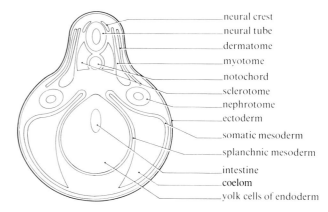

Fig 21.36 *Diagram of TS of newly hatched frog tadpole showing derivatives of the germ layers shown in fig 21.37. The tadpole is still dependent upon food provided by yolk since the ectoderm has not differentiated sufficiently to form the complete alimentary canal*

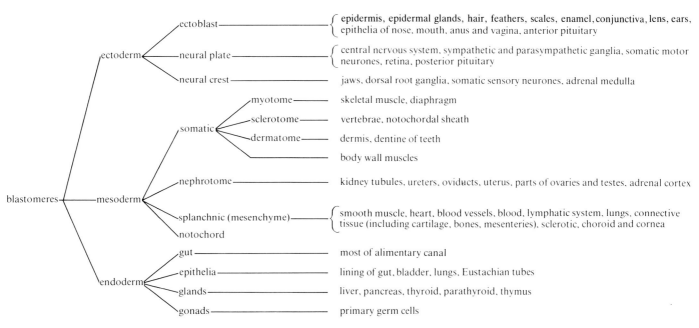

Fig 21.37 *The embryological fate of the three germ layers in vertebrates*

793

21.8.1 Mammalian growth hormones

There are four glands which secrete hormones influencing growth and development; they are the thyroid, liver, adrenal cortex and gonads. In all cases these glands secrete hormones under the control of other hormones released from the pituitary gland. The pituitary gland in turn is under the influence of specific releasing and inhibiting factors produced by the hypothalamus (section 16.6.2). Examples of these three levels of hormonal control are described with reference to the release of the growth hormone, **somatomedin** by the liver.

During the early part of this century numerous experiments involving ablation (removal) of the pituitary gland and replacement therapy confirmed the role of the pituitary in determining the rate and extent of growth in animals. A pituitary extract was isolated which increased body mass when injected into animals. This substance was called 'growth hormone'. Subsequent research has revealed that this is a trophic hormone, **somatotrophin**, which is released from the pituitary gland under the influence of two other hormones produced by the hypothalamus. These are **somatostatin**, a peptide made up of 40 amino acids and **growth hormone releasing factor (GH-RF)**. These two hormones are thought to have an antagonistic effect, with somatostatin being an inhibitor and GH-RF a stimulator of somatotrophin release. The former is thought to have a dominant influence over the latter.

Human somatotrophin is a protein of 190 amino acids. It acts via receptor sites in the hepatocytes of the liver, and stimulates synthesis and release of somatomedin into the hepatic vein. Somatomedin stimulates growth throughout the body by increasing the synthesis of nucleic acids in preparation for mitosis and increasing the amino acid uptake into cartilage and muscle. It also produces a rise in the intracellular levels of potassium, phosphorus, calcium and sodium, and changes in blood glucose and lipid levels aimed at providing extra metabolites for cell synthesis and growth. Synthesis of human somatotrophin by techniques of genetic engineering is described in section 2.5.4.

21.9 Repair and regeneration

Cell growth does not cease with the attainment of adult size. The loss of cells and tissues as a result of ageing, damage sustained by disease, accident or attack by other organisms can act as a stimulus for cell division and differentiation, resulting in the healing, repair and replacement of damaged or missing tissues.

Many tissues in mammals, such as skin, gut epithelial cells and blood cells, are continuously replaced throughout life at a steady rate determined by the normal rate at which they are lost. Other tissues, for example the liver, thyroid and pancreas, normally show a very low rate of cell division in the adult stage. If any part of these organs is lost in any way, the remaining tissues will undergo rapid cell division

and differentiation to restore the size of the organ. This process is known as **compensatory hypertrophy**. The cells of the central nervous system, on the other hand, are incapable of regeneration if damaged or lost.

Regeneration is the replacement, by growth, of parts of an organism lost for one of the reasons stated above. It is common in plants, particularly in the angiosperms where whole plants can be grown from cuttings which involve no more than a single leaf and its petiole, such as *Tradescantia*. The regenerative power of plants is used as a means of vegetative propagation (section 20.1.1).

The degree to which animals are able to regenerate new structures appears to be related to their structural complexity. Sponges, cnidarians and flatworms have remarkable powers of regeneration. Sponges and some cnidarians, such as *Hydra*, are capable of being macerated and regenerating complete organisms. *Planaria* can be cut in half longitudinally or transversely and then regenerate new halves. Another flatworm, *Dugesia*, can completely regenerate from a small piece cut from an adult. Most species of annelids are able to regenerate missing regions of the body, for example the earthworm can regenerate the first five segments if they are lost and a substantial portion of the posterior end. Crustacea, insects and echinoderms can regenerate new limbs and arms, just as amphibia and lizards are able to regenerate limbs and tails as the result of attack by others of the species or predators. Lizards with their long tails are able to shed them if attacked. The wriggling movements of the detached tail act as a diversion enabling the lizard to escape. This ability to voluntarily shed limbs is shared by lobsters and crabs and is called **autotomy**.

21.10 Dormancy

During their life cycle many plants and animals undergo periods when metabolic activity is reduced to a minimum and growth ceases. This is **dormancy**. It is a physiologically determined behavioural response and may involve the adult organism, a development stage such as the pupa, or a specialised reproductive body such as a spore. Dormancy is induced by environmental changes and has the biological significance of enabling the species to survive periods when the supply of energy is inadequate for normal growth and metabolism.

Most plant species of tropical and temperate zones, and all arctic plant species, exhibit dormancy in response to changing light, temperature and moisture conditions. The mechanisms of control of dormancy by plant growth regulator substances are described in section 15.5.

Animals show three forms of dormancy involving physiological adaptations which enable them to tolerate environmental extremes, and these are considered here. Some animals though, because of well-developed mechanisms of locomotion, are able to avoid unfavourable environmental conditions by moving to more favourable regions, such as by migration. These responses, although coordinated by physiological mechanisms, are strictly behavioural and are described in section 16.8.

21.10.1 Diapause

Diapause is a form of arrested development shown by insects, but this term is also used to describe the period of inactivity shown by protozoan cysts and the winter eggs of many freshwater aquatic organisms. Insect life cycles are adapted to produce offspring at times when food is plentiful for the larval and nymphal stages. Diapause is a means of coordinating these two events. Development can be arrested at any stage in the life cycle, egg, larva, pupa or adult, and for any species the exact stage or stages is determined genetically. Some insects always undergo a period of diapause known as **obligatory diapause**, for example the locust *Nomadacris*, whereas others enter diapause only if conditions become unfavourable, such as the locust *Schistocerca*, and this is termed **facultative diapause**.

The main factor inducing diapause in all species is daylength (photoperiod), but food availability, temperature and moisture may be influential. In order for diapause to be effective, the factor inducing diapause must act *in advance* of the adverse conditions. Therefore the mechanism of synchronisation often acts on a stage preceding that which undergoes diapause. For example, diapause in the egg stage of the silkworm, *Bombyx mori*, is the result of the photoperiod experienced by the female parent during development of the egg. Adult diapause, on the other hand, is induced by light conditions occurring during the early larval stages.

Light is thought to have a direct effect upon the brain which, in turn, influences the activity of the neurosecretory system. In aphids, light is thought to act directly on neurosecretory cells. In the case of the giant silkworm, *Hyalophora cecropia*, the short photoperiod of autumn inactivates neurosecretory cells in the brain which produce prothoracicotrophic hormone. This prevents the release of ecdysone from the thoracic glands and, in the absence of further development, the species overwinters in the pupal stage. Normal secretion and further development is only restored after an extended period of exposure to low temperatures. Paradoxically, it is the adverse conditions themselves, which diapause avoids, which act as the stimulus to break the period of dormancy (fig 21.38).

> **21.10** Using the experimental data presented in fig 21.38, account for the mechanisms which terminate diapause.

Most species of insect exposed to long periods of daylight undergo continuous growth and development and produce several generations per year, for example the black bean aphid, *Aphis fabae*. These species do not undergo diapause if artificially maintained in conditions of long daylength.

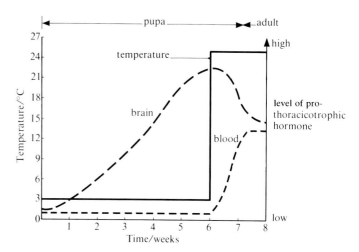

Fig 21.38 *Graph showing the relationship between the levels of prothoracicotrophic hormone in the brain and blood of silkworm at 3 °C and 25 °C*

They show a **long-day response** and only enter diapause if exposed to periods of short daylength. Other species, such as the silkworm, *Bombyx mori*, which has an embryonic diapause (egg stage), grow and develop normally during periods of short daylength and only enter diapause following exposure to periods of long daylength. This is a **short-day response**. Diapause eggs of the silkworm begin to grow and develop during the short daylengths of spring, and the adult emerges during early summer. As development occurs during periods of short daylength the eggs laid by these adults hatch and develop during the summer *without* entering diapause. However, the eggs laid by these summer silkworms enter diapause in preparation for winter. Since long photoperiods induce diapause in this type of insect this limits the number of generations per year. In the case of the silkworm there are two, as shown in fig 21.39.

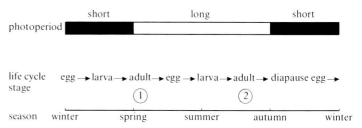

Fig 21.39 *Diagram showing the relationship between daylength, diapause and stages in the life cycle of* Bombyx mori. *This is an example of a short-day response*

Investigations have revealed the existence of a **diapause hormone** in *Bombyx* which determines whether or not the egg will undergo diapause. The long photoperiods of summer stimulate the brain to release a diapause hormone from a pair of neurosecretory cells situated in the suboesophageal ganglion. This has a direct effect on the ovary which releases darkly pigmented eggs which undergo diapause. Silkworms which develop during the short

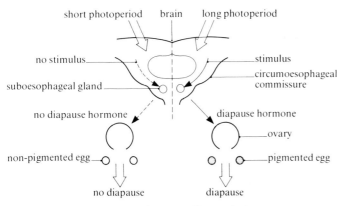

Fig 21.40 *Diagram showing the effects of photoperiod on the production of eggs in* Bombyx mori

photoperiods of later winter and spring do not release diapause hormone and lay non-pigmented eggs which do not undergo diapause (fig 21.40).

21.10.2 Aestivation

Aestivation (*aestas*, summer) is a particular form of dormancy found in certain fish and amphibia in response to hot dry periods. In such cases the organisms bury themselves in mud whilst it is still soft and undergo a period of metabolic inactivity which enables them to survive conditions of extreme dehydration. During this time they breathe atmospheric air. Normal metabolic activities are restored only when the river, pool or lake floods again following the period of drought. Two of the three genera of lungfish, *Lepidosiren* in South America and *Protopterus* in Africa, are able to aestivate for at least six months when the rivers they inhabit dry up.

21.10.3 Hibernation

Hibernation (*hiber*, winter) is a period of relatively low metabolic activity associated with periods of low temperature. This enables hibernating species of amphibia, reptiles, birds and mammals to survive at times when food is in short supply by reducing their energy demands to a low level. This is especially important in the case of homeotherms, which normally require a high metabolic rate to maintain their core temperature. True hibernation involves a fall in body temperature to that of the environment (the ambient temperature) and a reduction in heart rate, ventilation rate, metabolic rate, growth and development. In such conditions animals become almost poikilothermic. Examples of organisms showing true hibernation include insectivores such as shrews and hedgehogs: rodents including marmots, ground squirrels, dormice and hamsters: insectivorous bats and a few birds. Most other species which show some form of hibernation are in fact in a state of **torpor**, sleep or pseudohibernation. These include snakes, lizards, tortoises, salamanders, toads, newts and frogs. During this period the organism

may wake up, if the environmental temperature rises, in order to feed on supplies kept in the burrow or to urinate and defaecate.

The onset of hibernation is related to decreasing environmental temperature and photoperiod and the accumulation of adequate supplies of stored food. There is some experimental evidence that suggests a metabolite is present in the blood which could trigger hibernation, since blood taken from a hibernating ground squirrel induced hibernation in a non-hibernating squirrel within 48 h. Likewise hibernation has been induced in ground squirrels at times of the year when they are normally active by injecting blood from a hibernating squirrel. Some species such as the woodchuck, *Arctomys*, enter hibernation within a few hours whereas other species allow their core temperature to fall steadily over a period of several nights before achieving their hibernation temperature.

As the body temperature falls to about 1–2 °C above the environmental temperature the heart rate may fall from 400 to 8 beats per minute, as in the ground squirrel, and the basal metabolic rate may fall to less than 2% of the non-hibernating rate. Hibernating animals are unable to withstand a considerable drop in temperature, but they avoid freezing conditions by hibernating in nests or burrows where the microclimate is several degrees above freezing. Curling up the body aids in reducing the body surface area and conserving heat, as does burying the nose and mouth into the fur. If conditions become severe and body temperature falls to about 2 °C there is a danger of tissue damage by frost. The animal prevents this either by waking up and becoming active, thereby raising its temperature, or by increasing its metabolic rate without waking.

Many hibernating animals store energy as lipid droplets in a special type of adipose tissue known as **brown fat**. These cells contain many spherical mitochondria, and it is the presence of these that gives the cells their characteristic colour. Lipids in these cells are stored throughout the cytoplasm as droplets and not as a solid. Throughout hibernation stored lipids are used up steadily, but as animals come out of hibernation the metabolic activity of these cells rises sharply. This release of energy enables the animal to shiver vigorously and generate heat, which is dispersed by the blood system as the heart rate increases. The heart, brain and lungs receive this heat first as a result of vasoconstriction of blood vessels to other parts of the body. This is initiated by the sympathetic nervous system. Gradually the whole body warms up and normal metabolic and physiological activities are resumed.

Some small birds and mammals with large surface area to volume ratios have extremely high metabolic rates, and in order to survive they lower their body temperatures at night when they are unable to feed. This is known as **diurnal hibernation** and is seen in humming birds and small insectivorous bats.

Chapter Twenty-two

Continuity of life

The development of the cell theory by Schleiden and Schwann is described at the beginning of chapter 7. Rudolph Virchow extended this theory in 1855 by declaring that '*omnis cellula e cellula*' ('every cell is from a cell'). Recognition of the continuity of life stimulated further workers throughout the later part of the nineteenth century to investigate the structure of the cell and the mechanisms involved in cell division. Improved techniques of staining and better microscopes with increased resolution revealed the importance of the nuclei, and in particular the chromosomes within them, as being the structures providing continuity between one generation of cells and another. In 1879 Boveri and Flemming described the events occurring within the nucleus leading to the production of two identical cells, and in 1887 Weismann suggested that a specialised form of division occurred in the production of gametes. These two forms of division are called mitosis and meiosis respectively. The basic processes are almost identical but the outcome is entirely different.

Mitosis is the process by which a cell nucleus divides to produce two daughter nuclei containing identical sets of chromosomes to the parent cell. It is usually followed immediately by an equal division of the cytoplasm, the re-formation of a cell surface membrane and cell wall (plants), or cell membrane only (animals), and separation of the two daughter cells. This process is known as **cell division**. Mitosis with cell division results in an increase in cell numbers and is the method by which growth, replacement and repair of cells occurs in most animals and plants. In the unicellular organisms, mitosis provides the mechanism of asexual reproduction leading to an increase in their numbers.

Meiosis is the process by which a cell nucleus divides to produce four daughter nuclei each containing half the number of chromosomes of the original nucleus. An alternative name for meiosis is **reduction division** since it reduces the number of chromosomes in the cell from the diploid number ($2n$) to the haploid number (n). The significance of the process lies in the fact that it enables the chromosome number of a sexually reproducing species to be kept constant from generation to generation. Meiosis occurs only during gamete formation in animals and during spore formation in plants showing alternation of generations (section 20.2). It produces haploid nuclei that fuse together during fertilisation to restore the diploid number of chromosomes.

Chromosomes are the most significant structures in the cell during division since they are responsible for the transmission of hereditary information from generation to generation and have a regulatory role in cell metabolism (section 23.2). The chromosomes of eukaryotic cells are composed of DNA, proteins and small amounts of RNA (section 5.6). In non-dividing cells the chromosomes are extremely long and thin and are dispersed throughout the nucleus. Individual chromosomes cannot be seen, but the chromosomal material may stain with certain basic dyes (appendix A2.4.2.) and is known as **chromatin** (coloured threads). During cell division the chromosomes shorten and the stain intensifies so that individual chromosomes can be seen. In their extended form the chromosomes are involved in controlling the synthesis of all materials in the cell, but during cell division this function ceases.

In all forms of cell division the DNA of each chromosome undergoes replication so that two identical polynucleotide chains of DNA are produced (section 22.4.2). These become 'surrounded' by a protein 'coat' and at the onset of cell division appear as two identical strands lying side by side. Each strand is called a **chromatid** and they are attached to each other by a non-staining region called the **centromere**, associated with which is the **kinetochore**, the structure to which the microtubules of the spindle are attached.

22.1 The cell cycle

The sequence of events which occurs between the formation of a cell and its division into daughter cells is called the cell cycle. It has three main stages.

(1) **Interphase.** This is a period of intense synthesis and growth. The cell produces many materials required for its own growth and carrying out all the functions peculiar to it. DNA replication occurs during interphase.

(2) **Mitosis.** This is the process of nuclear division involving the separation of chromatids and their redistribution as chromosomes into daughter cells.

(3) **Cell division.** This is the process of division of the cytoplasm into two daughter cells.

The entire cycle is laid out in fig 22.1. The length of the cycle depends on the type of cell and external factors such as temperature, food and oxygen supplies. Bacteria may divide every 20 min, epithelial cells of the intestine wall every 8–10 h, onion root-tip cells may take 20 h whilst many cells of the nervous system never divide.

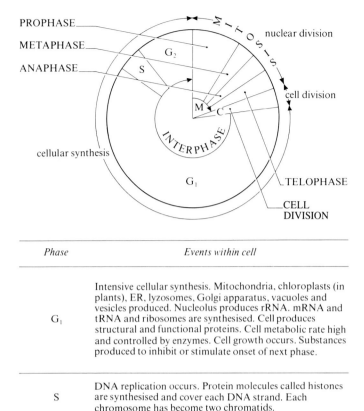

Phase	Events within cell
G₁	Intensive cellular synthesis. Mitochondria, chloroplasts (in plants), ER, lyzosomes, Golgi apparatus, vacuoles and vesicles produced. Nucleolus produces rRNA. mRNA and tRNA and ribosomes are synthesised. Cell produces structural and functional proteins. Cell metabolic rate high and controlled by enzymes. Cell growth occurs. Substances produced to inhibit or stimulate onset of next phase.
S	DNA replication occurs. Protein molecules called histones are synthesised and cover each DNA strand. Each chromosome has become two chromatids.
G₂	Intensive cellular synthesis. Mitochondria and chloroplasts divide. Energy stores increase. Mitotic spindle begins to form.
M	Nuclear division occurs in four phases.
C	Equal distribution of organelles and cytoplasm into each daughter cell.

Fig 22.1 *The cell cycle*

Experiment 22.1: To investigate the phases of mitosis

Chromosomes can normally be observed only during nuclear division. The apical meristem of roots (root tips) of garlic ($2n=16$), onion ($2n=16$) and broad bean ($2n=12$) provide suitable material for the experiment. The material is set up so that root development is initiated and the root tips are removed, fixed, stained and macerated so that the chromosomes may be observed under the microscope.

Materials

pins	pair of fine needles
test-tube containing water	several sheets of
scalpel	blotting paper
small corked tube	clove of garlic
forceps	distilled water
2 Petri dishes	acetic alcohol
water bath and test-tube	molar hydrochloric acid
microscope slide	Feulgen stain
cover-slip	

Method

(1) Place a pin through a clove of garlic and suspend in a test-tube full of water so that the base of the clove is covered with water. Leave for 3–4 days without any disturbance as this is likely to inhibit cell division temporarily.

(2) When several roots have grown 1–2 cm, remove the clove and cut off the terminal 1 cm of the root.

(3) Transfer the roots to a small corked tube containing acetic alcohol and leave overnight at room temperature to fix the material.

(4) Remove the root tips with forceps by grasping the cut end of the root, transfer to a Petri dish containing distilled water and wash for a few minutes to remove the fixative.

(5) Transfer the root tips to a test-tube containing molar hydrochloric acid which is maintained at 60 °C for 3 min (6–10 min for onion, peas and beans). This breaks down the middle lamellae holding the cells together and hydrolyses the DNA of the chromosomes to form deoxyribose aldehydes which will react with the stain.

(6) Pour the root tips and acid into a Petri dish. Remove the roots into another Petri dish containing distilled water and wash to remove the acid. Leave for 5 min.

(7) Transfer the roots to a small tube containing Feulgen stain and cork. Leave in a cool dark place (preferably a refrigerator) for a minimum of 2 h.

(8) Remove a root tip and place in a drop of acetic alcohol on a clean microscope slide.

(9) Cut off the terminal 1–2 mm of the root tip and discard the rest of the root.

(10) Tease out the root tip using a pair of fine needles and cover with a cover-slip. Place the slide on a flat surface, cover with several sheets of blotting paper and press down firmly over the cover-slip with the ball of the thumb. Do not allow the cover-slip to move sideways.

(11) Examine the slide under the low and high powers of the microscope and identify cells showing different phases of mitosis.

(12) Draw and label nuclei showing the various phases.

22.2 Mitosis

The events occurring within the nucleus during mitosis are usually observed in cells which have been fixed and stained (appendix A2.4.2). Whilst this shows the phases through which chromosomes pass during cell division, it fails to reveal the continuity of the process. The use of the phase-contrast microscope and time-lapse photography has enabled the events of nuclear division to be seen in the living cell as they happen. By speeding up the film, mitosis is seen as a continuous process which occurs in four active stages. The changes occurring during these stages in an animal cell are described in fig 22.2.

Interphase
Often mistakenly called **resting stage**. Variable duration depending upon function of the cell. Period during which cell normally carries out synthesis of organelles and increases in size. The nucleoli are prominent and actively synthesising ribosomal material. Just prior to cell division the DNA and histone of each chromosome replicates. Each chromosome now exists as a pair of **chromatids** joined together by a **centromere**. The chromosomal material will stain and is called **chromatin** but structures are difficult to see.

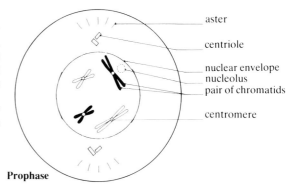

Prophase
Usually the longest phase of division. Chromatids shorten (to 4% of their original length) and thicken by **spiralisation** and condensation of the DNA protein coat. Staining shows up the chromatids clearly but the centromeres do not stain. The position of the centromere varies in different chromatid pairs. In animal cells and some plants the **centrioles** move to opposite poles of the cell. Short **microtubules** may be seen radiating from the centrioles. These are called **asters** (*astra*, a star). The **nucleoli** decrease in size as their nucleic acid passes to certain pairs of chromatids. At the end of prophase the nuclear envelope fragments into small vesicles which disperse and a spindle is formed.

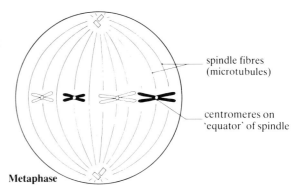

Metaphase
The pairs of chromatids become attached to the spindle by **spindle fibres** at their centromeres. The chromatids move upwards and downwards along the spindle until their centromeres line up across the '*equator*' of the spindle and at right-angles to the spindle axis.

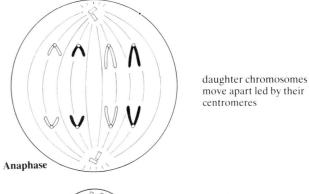

Anaphase
This stage is very rapid. The centromeres split into two and the spindle fibres pull the daughter centromeres to opposite poles. The separated chromatids, now called **chromosomes**, are pulled along behind the centromeres.

Telophase
The chromosomes reach the poles of the cell, uncoil, lengthen and lose the ability to be seen clearly. The spindle fibres disintegrate and the centrioles replicate. A nuclear envelope re-forms around the chromosomes at each pole and the nucleoli reappear. Telophase may lead straight into **cytokinesis** (cell division).

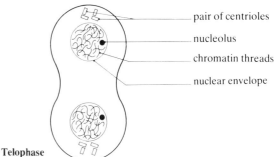

Fig 22.2 *Summary notes and diagrams of the stages of mitosis in an animal cell*

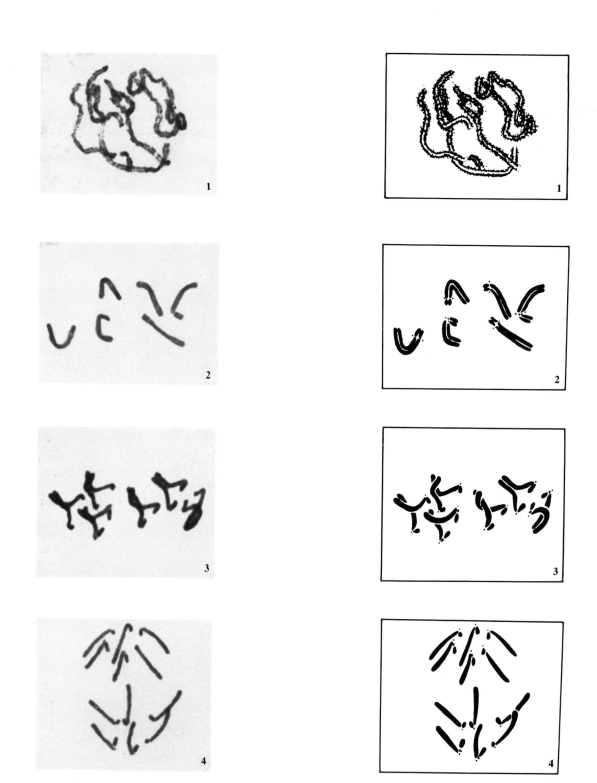

Mitosis

Four stages of mitotic cell division from root-tip cells of the plant Crocus balansae *(2n = 6). These are from squash preparations with only the stained chromosomes showing clearly. Details of nucleoli, spindles and cytoplasm are unstained and not visible*

At the start of division (1) the chromosomes are long, thin, but visibly double. They coil up and shorten. When fully contracted the nuclear envelope breaks down and the chromosomes become orientated on the spindle (2: polar view). After a while, spindle fibre activity on the centromeres (dotted in drawings) pulls the sister chromatids (3). Spindle fibres pull centromeres and chromatids to the poles (4) with the formation of two identical polar groups. Following cell division these form the nuclei of the two daughter cells

Fig 22.2 (continued) *Photomicrographs and drawings based on them showing the stages in mitosis in plant cells. (Courtesy of Dr S. A. Henderson, Department of Genetics, University of Cambridge)*

22.2.1 Centrioles and spindle formation

Centrioles are organelles situated in the cytoplasm close to the nuclear envelope in animal and certain plant cells. They occur in pairs and are double structures which lie at right-angles to each other.

Each centriole is approximately 500 nm long and 200 nm in diameter and is composed of nine groups of microtubules arranged in triplets. Adjacent triplets are believed to be attached to each other by fibrils (fig 22.3).

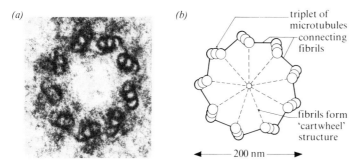

Fig 22.3 *(a) Electron micrograph of a TS of a centriole from embryonic chick pancreas. (b) Diagram of TS through a centriole as seen under the electron microscope*

Centrioles also occur at the bases of cilia and flagella, where they are known as **basal bodies** (section 17.6.2).

Spindle fibres are tubular and have a diameter of approximately 25 nm. They form during mitosis and meiosis, and are composed of microtubules made up of the protein **tubulin** and other protein molecules. At one time it was thought that the function of the centrioles was to act as organisers of the spindle fibres, but this is not now thought to be the case. The majority of plant cells lack centrioles but are capable of producing spindle fibres made up of microtubules identical to those found in animal cells. Some spindle fibres run from pole to pole, others are bound to the centromeres in bundles. It is thought that the relative movement of these spindle fibres accounts for the separation of daughter chromosomes during anaphase of mitosis. Electron microscopy provides evidence of the presence of cross-bridges between the two types of fibre. These **cross-bridges** suggest that the fibres may slide past each other during nuclear division using a ratchet-type mechanism similar to that associated with the movement of muscle fibrils (section 17.4.6).

The addition of **colchicine** (section 23.9.1) to actively dividing cells inhibits spindle formation and the chromatid pairs remain in their metaphase positions. This technique enables the number and structure of chromosomes to be examined under the microscope.

22.2.2 Cell division

Cytokinesis is the division of the cytoplasm. This stage normally follows telophase and leads into the G_1 phase of interphase. In preparation for division, the cell

organelles become evenly distributed towards the two poles of the telophase cells along with the chromosomes. In animal cells the cell membrane begins to invaginate during telophase towards the region previously occupied by the spindle equator. Microfilaments in the region are thought to be responsible for drawing in the cell membrane to form a continuous furrow around the equatorial circumference of the cell. The cell surface membranes in the furrow eventually join up and completely separate the two cells.

In plant cells the spindle fibres begin to disappear during telophase everywhere except in the region of the equatorial plane. Here they move outwards in diameter and increase in number to form a barrel-shaped region known as the **phragmoplast**. Microtubules, ribosomes, mitochondria, endoplasmic reticulum and Golgi apparatus are attracted to this region and the Golgi apparatus produces a number of small fluid-filled vesicles. These appear first in the centre of the cell and, guided by microtubules, coalesce to form a **cell plate** which grows across the equatorial plane (fig 7.23). The contents of the vesicles contribute to the new middle lamella and cell walls of the daughter cells, whilst their membranes form the new cell membranes. The spreading plate eventually fuses with the parent cell wall and effectively separates the two daughter cells. The new cell walls are called **primary cell walls** and may be thickened at a later stage by the deposition of further cellulose and other substances such as lignin and suberin to produce a **secondary cell wall** (fig 22.4). In certain areas the vesicles of the cell plate fail to fuse and cytoplasmic contact remains between the daughter cells. These cytoplasmic channels are lined by the cell surface membrane and form structures known as **plasmodesmata**.

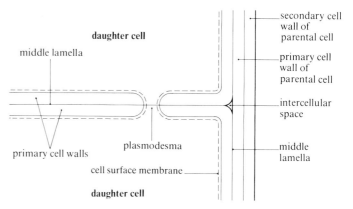

Fig 22.4 *The structure of the plant cell wall formed as a result of the cytokinesis of a parental cell*

22.2.3 Mitosis in animal and plant cells

The most important event occurring during mitosis concerns the equal distribution of duplicate chromosomes between the two daughter cells. This process is almost identical in animal and plant cells but there are a number of differences, and these are summarised in table 22.1.

Table 22.1. Differences between mitosis in plant and animal cells

Plant	Animal
No centriole present	Centrioles present
No aster forms	Asters form
Cell plate forms	No cell plate forms
No furrowing of cytoplasm at cytokinesis	Furrowing of cytoplasm at cytokinesis
Occurs mainly at meristems	Occurs in tissues throughout the body

The rate of mitosis varies in different organisms and tissues, being greatest in bacteria and embryonic stages of multicellular organisms and least in highly differentiated cells. Isolated cells taken from plants or animals and grown in nutrient culture solutions providing optimum conditions for cell division show the highest rate of mitosis. Such a population of cells derived from a single parent cell is known as a **clone** (section 20.1.1). The cells found in a clone need not be identical in structure or function. For example, single cells taken from an organism can give rise to a new organism or to a new tissue identical to that from which it was taken, such as a single lung cell giving rise to lung tissue having alveoli and ducts.

22.2.4 Significance of mitosis

The following points outline the main significances of mitosis.

Genetic stability. Mitosis produces two nuclei which have the same number of chromosomes as the parent cell. Moreover, since these chromosomes were derived from parental chromosomes by the exact replication of their DNA, they will carry the same hereditary information in their genes. Daughter cells are genetically identical to their parent cell and no variation in genetic information can therefore be introduced during mitosis. This results in genetic stability within populations of cells derived from parental cells, as in a clone.

Growth. The number of cells within an organism increases by mitosis (a process called **hyperplasia**) and this is a basic component of growth (chapter 21).

Asexual reproduction, regeneration and cell replacement. Many animal and plant species are propagated by asexual methods involving the mitotic division of cells. These methods of vegetative reproduction are described more fully in section 20.1.1. In addition to asexual reproduction, regeneration of missing parts, such as legs in crustacea, and cell replacement occurs, to varying degrees, in multicellular organisms.

22.3 Meiosis

Meiosis (*meio*, to reduce) is a form of nuclear division involving a reduction from the diploid number ($2n$) of chromosomes to the haploid number (n). In its simplest terms it involves a single duplication of chromosomes (DNA replication, as in mitosis) in the parent cell followed by two cycles of nuclear divisions and cell divisions (the **first meiotic division** and the **second meiotic division**). Thus a single diploid cell gives rise to four haploid cells as shown in outline in fig 22.5.

Meiosis occurs during the formation of sperm and ova (gametogenesis) in animals (sections 20.3.1 and 2) and during spore formation in most plants (those showing alternation of generation, section 20.2.2). Some plants do not show alternation of generations and meiosis occurs here at gamete formation. The stages of meiosis can be seen in spermatocyte nuclei from the testes of locust or grasshopper or nuclei in immature pollen sacs of *Crocus*.

Like mitosis, meiosis is a continuous process but is conveniently divided into prophase, metaphase, anaphase and telophase. These stages occur once in the first meiotic division and again in the second meiotic division. The behaviour of chromosomes during these stages is illustrated in fig 22.6, which shows a nucleus containing four chromosomes ($2n=4$), that is two homologous pairs of chromosomes.

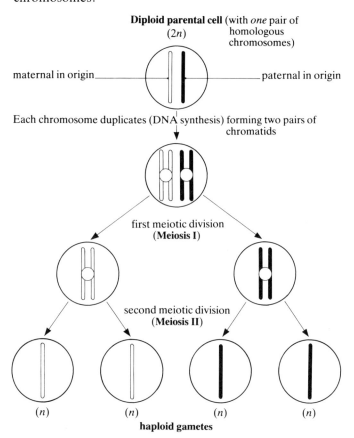

Fig 22.5 *The basic characteristics of meiosis showing one chromosome duplication followed by two nuclear and cell divisions*

Interphase

Variable length depending upon species. Replication of cell organelles and increase in size of cell. Most of the DNA and histone is replicated in premeiotic interphase but some is delayed and prolonged into early meiotic prophase I. Each chromosome now exists as a pair of chromatids joined together by a centromere. Chromosomal material will stain but no structure clear except prominent nucleoli (see fig 22.2 as for mitosis).

Prophase I

The longest phase. It is often described in five stages called **leptotene**, **zygotene**, **pachytene**, **diplotene**, and **diakinesis** but will be considered here as a progressive sequence of chromosomal changes.

(*a*) Chromosomes shorten and become visible as single structures. In some organisms they have a beaded appearance due to regions of densely stained material called **chromomeres** alternating with non-staining regions. Chromomeres are regions where the chromosomal material is tightly coiled.

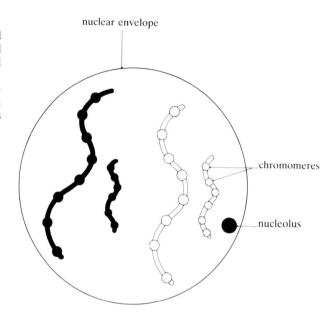

(a) *early prophase I*

(*b*) Chromosomes derived from maternal and paternal gamete nuclei come together and pair up. These are **homologous chromosomes**. Each pair is the same length, their centromeres are in the same positions and they usually have the same number of genes arranged in the same linear order. The chromomeres of the homologous chromosomes lie side by side. The pairing process is called **synapsis** and it may begin at several points along the chromosomes which then completely unite as if zipped up together. The paired homologous chromosomes are often described as **bivalents**. The bivalents shorten and thicken. This involves both molecular packaging and some visible coiling (or **spiralisation**). Each chromosome and its centromeres can now be seen clearly.

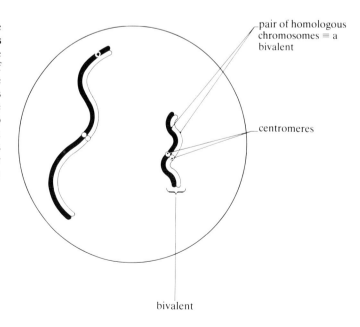

Fig 22.6 (a) – (k) *Summary notes and diagrams of the stages of meiosis in an animal cell.*

(b) *prophase I*

(c) The homologous chromosomes of the bivalents now fall apart and appear to repel each other partially. Each chromosome is now seen to be composed of two **chromatids**. The two chromosomes are seen to be joined at several points along their length. These points are called **chiasmata** (chiasma, a cross). It can be seen that each chiasma is the site of an exchange between chromatids. It is produced by breakage and reunion between two of the four strands present at each site. As a result, genes from one chromosome (e.g. paternal, **A**, **B**, **C**) become attached to genes from the other chromosome (maternal, **a**, **b**, **c**) leading to new gene combinations in the resulting chromatids. This is called **genetic crossing over.** The two chromosomes do not fall apart after crossing over (chiasma formation) because sister chromatids (of *both* chromosomes) remain firmly associated until anaphase.

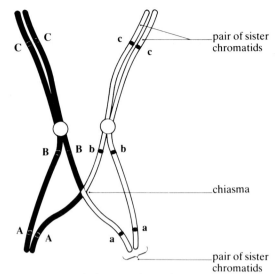

(c) *crossing over during prophase 1*

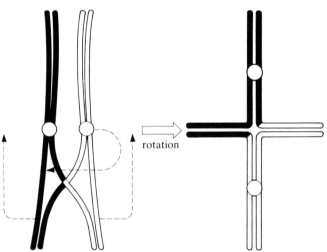

(d) (i) *Bivalent with a single chiasma*
Rotation of arms usually occurs during diplotene so that the X-shaped chiasma at the start of chiasma formation ends up looking like an open cross.

(d) The chromatids of homologous chromosomes continue to repel each other and bivalents assume particular shapes depending upon the number of chiasmata. Bivalents having a single chiasma appear as open crosses, two chiasmata produce a ring shape and three or more chiasmata produce loops lying at right-angles to each other. By the end of prophase I, all chromosomes are fully contracted and deeply stained. Other changes have occurred within the cell including: the centrioles (if present) migrate to the poles, the nucleoli and nuclear envelope disperse and then the spindle fibres form.

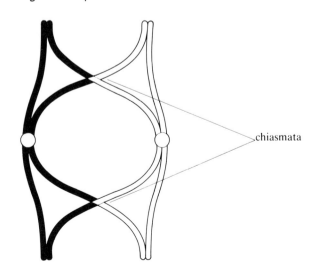

(d) (ii) *Bivalent with double chiasmata*
Rotation of the arms produces a ring shape.

Fig 22.6 (*continued*)

Metaphase I

The bivalents become arranged across the equatorial plate of the spindle. Their centromeres (though often visibly double) behave as though single and organise spindle fibres pointing towards only one of the poles. Gentle pulling from these fibres places each bivalent on the equator, with each centromere equidistant above and below it.

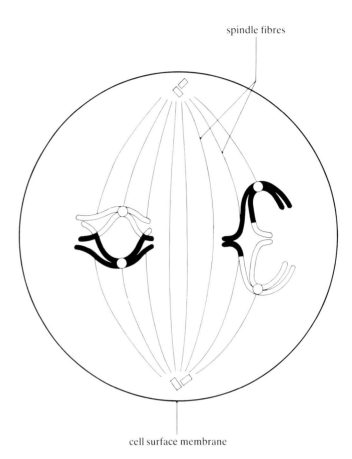

(e) *late metaphase I*

Anaphase I

The two centromeres of each bivalent do not divide, but sister chromatid adhesion ends. Spindle fibres pull whole centromeres, each attached to two chromatids, towards opposite poles of the spindle. This separates the chromosomes into two haploid sets of chromosomes in the daughter cells.

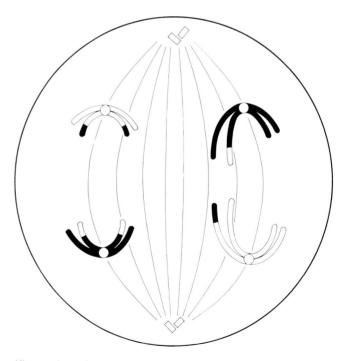

(f) *anaphase I*

Fig 22.6 (*continued*)

Telophase I

The arrival of homologous centromeres and their pairs of chromatids at opposite poles marks the end of the first meiotic division. Reduction of chromosome number has occurred but each pole possesses chromosomes composed of two chromatids.

As a result of crossing over, or chiasma formation, these chromatids are not genetically identical and must be separated in the second meiotic division. Spindles and spindle fibres usually disappear.

In animals and some plants the chromatids usually uncoil and a nuclear envelope re-forms at each pole and the nucleus enters interphase. Cleavage (animals) or cell wall formation (plants) then occurs as in mitosis. In many plants there is no telophase, cell wall formation or interphase and the cell passes straight from anaphase I into prophase of the second meiotic division.

Interphase II

This stage is present usually only in animal cells and varies in length. There is no S-phase and no further DNA replication occurs. The processes involved in the second meiotic division are mechanically similar to those of mitosis. They involve separation of the chromatids of both daughter cells produced during the first meiotic division. The second meiotic division differs from mitosis mainly in that (a) these sister chromatids are often widely separated at metaphase II (not at mitosis) and (b) the haploid number of chromosomes is present.

Prophase II

This stage is absent from cells omitting interphase II. The length of the stage is inversely proportional to the length of telophase I. The nucleoli and nuclear envelope disperse and the chromatids shorten and thicken. Centrioles, if present, move to opposite poles of the cells and spindle fibres appear. They are arranged with their axes at right-angles to the spindle axis of the first meiotic division.

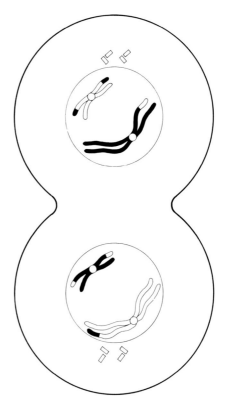

(g) *telophase I in an animal cell*

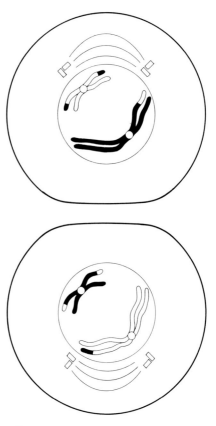

(h) *prophase II*

Fig 22.6 (*continued*)

Metaphase II

At this division the centromeres now behave as structurally double. They organise spindle fibres on each side to *both* poles and hence become aligned on the equator of the spindle.

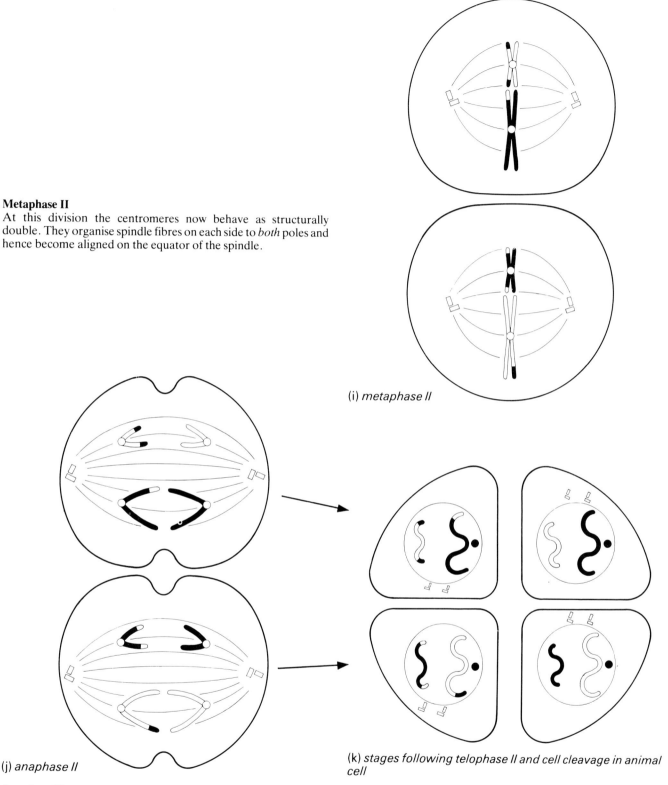

(i) *metaphase II*

(j) *anaphase II*

Anaphase II

The centromeres divide and the spindle fibres pull the two double centromeres to opposite poles. The separated chromatids, now called chromosomes, are pulled along behind the centromere.

Fig 22.6 (*continued*)

(k) *stages following telophase II and cell cleavage in animal cell*

Telophase II

This stage is very similar to that found at mitosis. The chromosomes uncoil, lengthen and become very indistinct. The spindle fibres disappear and the centrioles replicate. Nuclear envelopes re-form around each nucleus which now possess half the number of single chromosomes of the original parent cell (haploid). Subsequent cleavage (animals) or cell wall formation (plants) will produce four daughter cells from the original single parent cell.

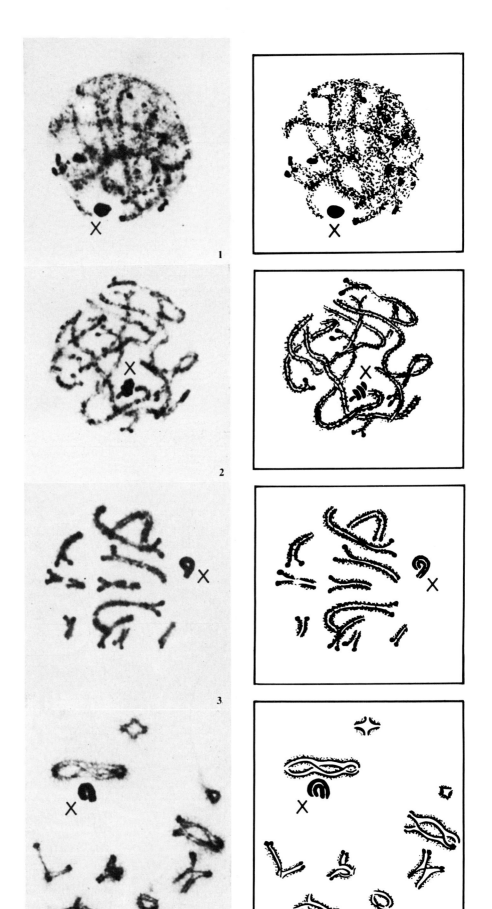

Fig 22.7 *(a) Eight stages of meiosis from spermatocytes of the desert locust* Schistocerca gregaria *(2n = 22 + X ♂). As at mitosis, these are from squash preparations with only the stained chromosomes showing clearly. Details of nucleoli, spindles and cytoplasm are unstained and not visible. At the start of the first meiotic division (1) the chromosomes are long, thin, fuzzy and not clearly visible, while the* **X** *is deeply staining. Pairing of homologous (maternal and paternal) chromosomes takes place with the formation of the haploid number (11) of* **bivalents** *and the* **X** *(2,3). Molecular exchange occurs between maternal and paternal chromosomes when intimately paired. They then fall apart along their length except at points where exchanges took place (4). These are called* **chiasmata**. *(part (b) overleaf)*

808

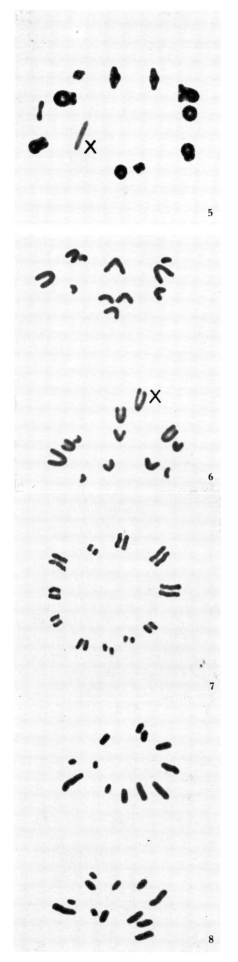

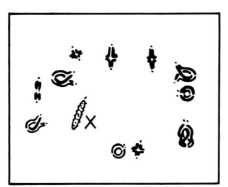

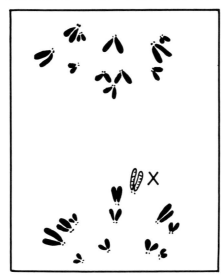

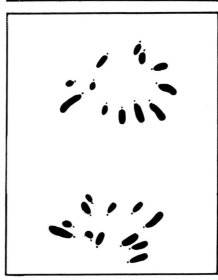

Fig 22.7 (b) Further contraction produces short, fat bivalents which, following breakdown of the nuclear membrane, become attached to the spindle by their centromeres (5: polar view). Spindle fibre activity pulls the haploid number of chromosomes apart (6: side view). The **X**, which is now weakly staining, goes undivided to one pole. At the second meiotic division the haploid number of chromosomes lie on the equatorial plate (7: polar view) and single chromatids are pulled to the poles by spindle fibre activity (8: side view) (Photomicrographs and drawings by courtesy of Dr S. A. Henderson, Department of Genetics, University of Cambridge)

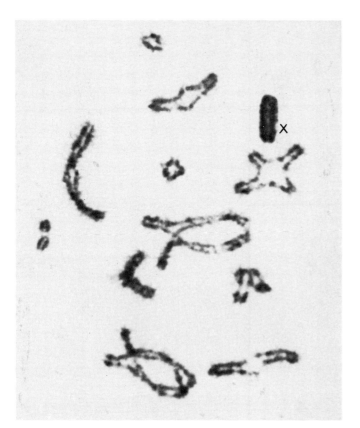
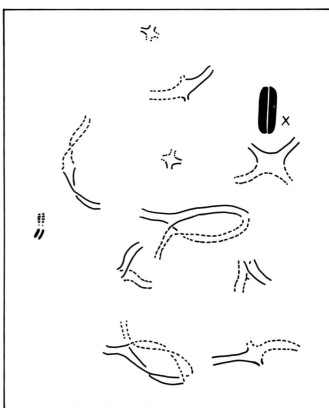

Fig 22.8 *Diplotene (prophase I) showing chiasmata. The chromosomes from a single cell at diplotene in the locust* Locusta migratoria, *showing bivalents with one or two chiasmata. Maternal and paternal chromosomes are represented by solid and dotted lines in the drawing. At each chiasma a genetic exchange has occurred. The shape of the bivalent will vary from rod-shaped, to cross-shaped or ring-shaped, depending on the number and position of chiasmata. The unpaired* **X** *chromosome is deeply staining at this stage (Dr S. A. Henderson)*

Fig 22.9 *Meiosis in living cells. Pairing and cell division at meiosis in living spermatocytes of the locust* Locusta migratoria. *These preparations are photographed with an optical technique known as Nomarski interference contrast, which uses polarised light and produces images of remarkably 3–D appearance in living, unstained cells. Two cells show chromosome pairing in early prophase I nuclei, with chromomere alignment (arrowed). The other two cells are at the end of the first meiotic division. It can be seen that, after the two polar groups have formed, cleavage of the cell takes place and two approximately equal daughter cells are produced. The fibrous structures stretching between the two polar groups, at cleavage pinched in two like a wheat sheaf, are the microtubules*

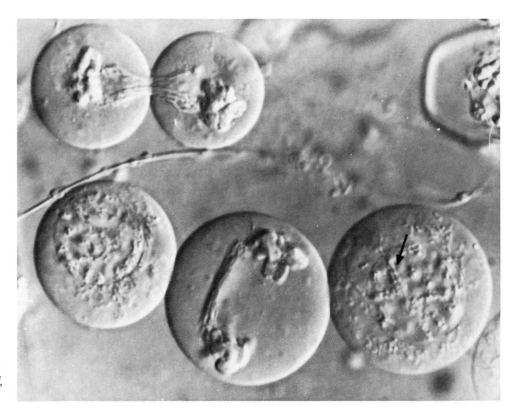

22.3.1   Significance of meiosis

The following points outline the main significances of meiosis.

Sexual reproduction Meiosis results in the formation of four daughter cells, each with half the number of chromosomes of the parent cell in all organisms carrying out sexual reproduction. During fertilisation the nuclei of the two gamete cells fuse and produce a zygote which has a fixed number of chromosomes for each species. In all organisms this number of chromosomes represents the diploid condition (2n). If meiosis did not occur fusion of gametes would result in a doubling of the chromosomes for each successive sexually reproduced generation. (An exception to this is shown in polyploidy which is described in section 23.9.) This situation is prevented in the life cycle of all sexually reproducing organisms by the occurrence, at some stage, of cell division involving a reduction in the diploid number of chromosomes (2n) to the haploid number (n).

22.1   The amount of DNA present per cell during several nuclear divisions is represented diagrammatically in fig 22.10.

(a) Which type of nuclear division is represented by fig 22.10?

(b) What phases are represented by the dashed lines W, X and Y?

(c) What type of cells are represented by the line Z?

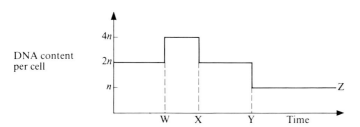

DNA content per cell

Fig 22.10   *Diagram for use in question 22.1*

Genetic variation Meiosis also provides opportunities for new combinations of genes to occur in the gamete cells. This leads to genetic variation in the genotype and phenotype of offspring produced by the fusion of gametes. The mechanisms of meiosis that contribute to this variation may be summarised as follows:

(1) The reduction of chromosomes from the diploid to the haploid number segregates (separates) alleles so that each gamete cell carries only one allele for a particular gene locus (section 23.2).

(2) The orientations on the equatorial spindle of bivalents during metaphase I and of chromosomes in metaphase II are random. The subsequent separation of these during anaphase I and II respectively produces new allelic recombinations in gamete cells. This is called **independent assortment** and results in the random

assortment of maternal and paternal chromosomes between daughter nuclei. This is the basis of Mendel's second law (section 23.1.3).

(3) As a result of chiasmata, crossing over of segments of chromatids occurs between homologous chromosomes during prophase I, leading to the formation of new combinations of alleles on chromosomes of the gamete cells. This breaks established linkage groups and produces new ones.

The significance of these three mechanisms in the process of inheritance and the production of variation is described in detail in section 23.8.4.

22.3.2   Similarities and differences between mitosis and meiosis

The main similarities between mitosis and meiosis involve the mechanisms by which the chromosomes and other cell organelles replicate and are manoeuvred within the cell prior to and during cell division. The mechanism of cell division, too, is similar in mitosis and meiosis.

The differences between the two processes are shown in table 22.2.

22.4   The structure of chromosomes

Histochemical and cytological analyses of chromosomes of eukaryotic cells have shown them to be composed of deoxyribonucleic acid (DNA) and protein, with small amounts of chromosomal RNA. (The 'chromosomes' of prokaryotic cells (bacteria) are composed of DNA only.) DNA has negative charges distributed along its length, and positively charged (basic) protein molecules called **histones** are bonded to it. This DNA protein complex is called chromatin.

Electron micrographs taken of lampbrush chromosomes (so-called because of their resemblance to brushes which were used to clean the glass of oil lamps) of amphibian oocytes during metaphase show that each chromatid appears to be composed of a tightly coiled axis with several lateral loops made up of a single DNA double helix (fig 22.11). These loops may represent DNA which has been exposed for the purpose of transcription (section 22.6.6).

The large amount of DNA in cells means that there is a packaging problem. A human cell, for example, contains about 2.2 m of DNA distributed among 46 chromosomes. Each chromosome therefore contains about 4.8 cm (48 000 μm) of DNA. Human chromosomes are on average about 6 μm long, a packing ratio of 8 000:1. In order to maintain a high degree of organisation when the DNA is folded, the histone proteins form a precise architectural 'skeleton' for the DNA.

Recent investigations suggest that the DNA helix combines with groups of eight histone molecules to form structures known as **nucleosomes** having the appearance of 'beads on a string'. These nucleosomes, and the DNA

Table 22.2. Differences between stages of mitosis and meiosis

	Mitosis	*Meiosis*
Prophase	Chromomeres not visible Homologous chromosomes remain separate No chiasmata formation No crossing over	Chromomeres visible Homologous chromosomes pair up Chiasmata occur Crossing over may occur
Metaphase	Pairs of chromatids line up on the equator of the spindle Centromeres line up in the same plane on the equator of the spindle	Pairs of chromatids line up on the equator only in second meiotic division Centromeres lie equidistant above and below the equator in the first meiotic division
Anaphase	Centromeres divide Chromatids separate Separating chromatids identical	Centromeres divide only during second meiotic division Chromatids separate only in the second meiotic division. In the first division whole chromosomes separate. Separating chromosomes may not be identical due to crossing over
Telophase	Same number of chromosomes present in daughter cells as parent cells Both homologous chromosomes present in daughter cells if diploid	Half the number of chromosomes present in daughter cells Only one of each pair of homologous chromosomes present in daughter cells
Occurrence	May occur in haploid, diploid or polyploid cells Occurs during the formation of somatic cells and some spores. Also occurs during the formation of gametes in plants with alternation of generations	Only occurs in diploid or polyploid cells In formation of gamete cells or spores

(a)

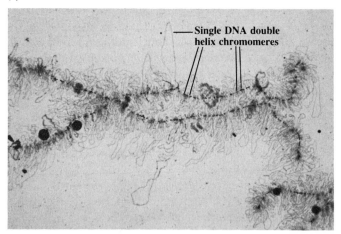

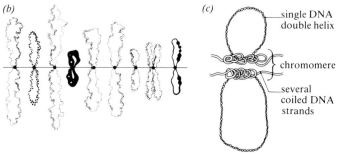

Fig 22.11 *(a) Lampbrush chromosomes of amphibian oocyte showing centromere and three chiasmata. (b) and (c) The effects of stretching lampbrush chromosomes to show the central filament of DNA and the loops of DNA where mRNA synthesis takes place. The dense regions are thought to be chromomeres. Each chromomere and its associated loop is thought to be associated with a specific gene locus. (From H. G. Callan (1963) Int. Rev. Cytology, 15, 1.)*

strands linking them, are packed closely together to produce a 30 nm diameter helix with about six nucleosomes per turn. The proposed structure of the chromosome' is shown in fig 22.12.

In the chromosomes of sperm of some species, such as salmon and herring, protamines replace histones as the proteins bound to the DNA.

22.4.1 Evidence for the role of DNA in inheritance

Following the proposal by Sutton and Boveri at the beginning of this century that chromosomes were the structures by which genetic information passed between generations (section 23.2), it took many years to clarify whether the genetic material was the DNA or the protein of the chromosomes. In a series of experiments, Alfred Mirsky demonstrated that all the somatic cells of a given species contain the same amount of DNA, and this is double the amount found in gamete cells. However, the same applies to the protein content of the chromosomes so this knowledge did little to clarify the nature of the genetic material.

It was suspected that protein might be the only molecule with sufficient variety of structure to act as genetic material.

Frederick Griffith, an English bacteriologist, made an observation in 1928 which was later to prove significant in resolving the problem. In the days before the development of antibiotics, pneumonia was often a fatal disease. Griffith was interested in developing a vaccine against the bacte-

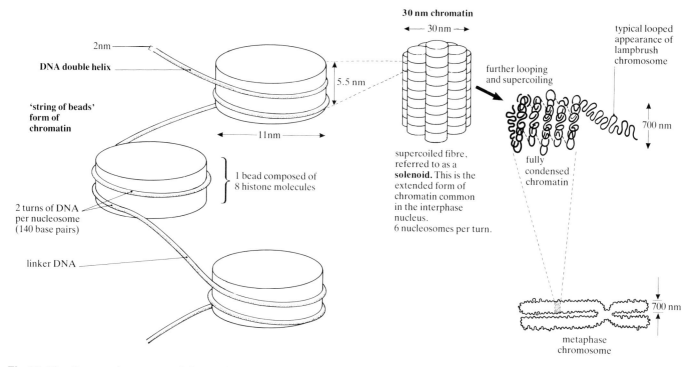

Fig 22.12 *Proposed structure of the nucleosome and its relationship to the chromosome and the DNA molecule*

rium *Pneumococcus* which causes one form of pneumonia. Two forms of *Pneumococcus* were known, one covered with a gelatinous capsule and virulent (disease-producing) and the other non-capsulated and non-virulent. The ability of these bacteria to cause pneumonia appeared to be related to the presence of the gelatinous capsule. Griffith hoped that by injecting patients with the non-capsulated, or heat-killed encapsulated forms, their bodies would produce antibodies which would afford protection against pneumonia. In a series of experiments Griffith injected mice with both forms of *Pneumococcus* and obtained the results shown in table 22.3. Post mortems carried out on the dead mice revealed the presence within their bodies of live encapsulated forms. On the basis of these results Griffith concluded that something must be passing from the heat-killed encapsulated forms to the live non-capsulated forms which caused them to develop capsules and become virulent. However, the nature of this **transforming principle**, as it was known, was not isolated and identified until 1944. For ten years Avery, McCarty and McCleod analysed

and purified the constituent molecules of heat-killed encapsulated pneumococcal cells and tested their ability to bring about transformation in live non-encapsulated cells. Removal of the polysaccharide capsule and the protein fraction from the cell extracts had no effect on transformation, but the addition of the enzyme deoxyribonuclease (DNAase), which breaks down (hydrolyses) DNA, prevented transformation. The ability of extremely purified extracts of DNA from encapsulated cells to bring about transformation finally demonstrated that Griffith's principle was in fact DNA. Despite this evidence many scientists still refused to accept that DNA, not protein, was the genetic material. In the early 1950s a wealth of irrefutable evidence, based upon the study of viruses, eventually demonstrated the ubiquitous nature of DNA as the carrier of hereditary information.

Viruses became one of the major experimental materials in genetic research in the 1940s and since then experiments involving their use have become as classic as those involving the garden pea, the fruit fly and, as will be **described** later, the bread mould *Neurospora*. Virus particles have an extremely simple structure consisting of a mainly protein coat enclosing a molecule of nucleic acid, either DNA or RNA (section 2.3.2). As such they provided ideal research material to investigate whether protein or nucleic acid is the genetic material. In 1952 Hershey and Chase began a series of experiments involving a particular type of virus which specifically attacks bacterial cells and is called a **bacteriophage**. Bacteriophage T_2 attacks the colon bacillus *Escherichia coli* (*E. coli*) and causes it to produce large numbers of T_2-phage particles in a very short time.

Table 22.3. Results of Griffith's experiments

Injected form of Pneumococcus	Effect
Live non-capsulated	mice live
Live capsulated	mice die
Heat-killed capsulated	mice live
Heat-killed capsulated + live non-capsulated	mice die

813

The essence of Hershey and Chase's experiment involved growing T₂-phage particles in *E. coli* which had been grown on a medium containing radioactive isotopes of either sulphur (^{35}S) or phosphorus (^{32}P). The phage particles formed in *E. coli* labelled with radioactive sulphur had incorporated this into their protein coats, whereas those formed in phosphorus-labelled *E. coli* contained radioactively labelled ^{32}P DNA. This selective distribution of isotopes is due specifically to the fact that proteins do not contain phosphorus and nucleic acids do not contain sulphur. The labelled T₂-phage particles were allowed to infect non-radioactively labelled *E. coli* and after a few minutes the cells were agitated in a blender or liquidiser which stripped off the phage particles from the bacterial walls. The bacteria were then incubated and examined for radioactivity. The results are shown in fig 22.13.

On the basis of these results Hershey and Chase concluded that it was the phage DNA which entered the bacterial cell and gave rise to large numbers of phage progeny. These experiments had demonstrated that DNA is the hereditary material. Confirmatory evidence that only the DNA contained within the phage is introduced into the bacterial cell has been provided by electron microscopy and increased knowledge of the life cycle of viruses. (The life cycle of virus and phage particles is described in sections 2.3.3 and 2.3.4.)

22.4.2 DNA replication

The double helical structure of DNA, as determined by Watson and Crick, is described in section 5.6.3. One of its most attractive features is that it immediately suggests a method by which replication could occur. Watson and Crick proposed that the two strands were capable of unwinding and separating, and acting as templates to which a complementary set of nucleotides would attach by base pairing. In this way each original DNA molecule would give rise to two copies with identical structures.

In 1956 Kornberg succeeded in demonstrating the in vitro synthesis of a DNA molecule using a single strand of DNA as a template. (This technique was used by later researchers to investigate the nature of the genetic code (section 22.5).) Kornberg extracted and purified an enzyme from *E. coli* which was capable of linking free DNA nucleotides, in the presence of ATP as an energy source, to form a complementary strand of DNA. This

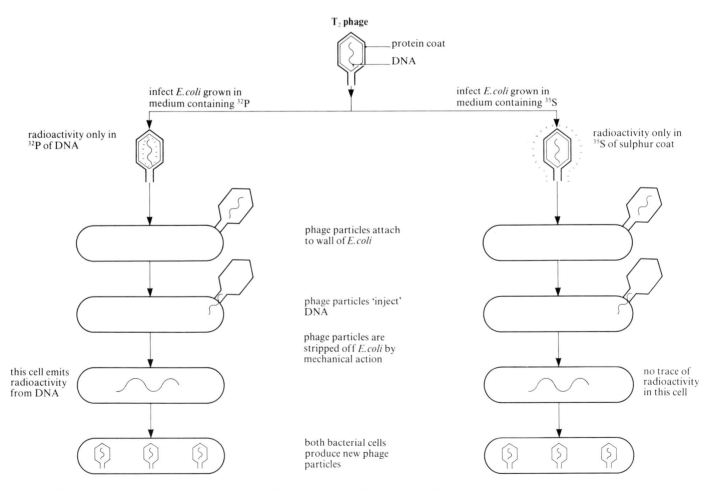

Fig 22.13 *Summary diagrams of Hershey and Chase's work on T₂ phage and* E. coli

enzyme he named **DNA polymerase**. In subsequent experiments Kornberg used nucleoside triphosphates (ATP, GTP, TTP, CTP) instead of nucleotides and ATP, and they too produced a complementary strand of DNA. Later evidence confirmed that this is the form in which nucleotides readily attach themselves to the DNA template and each other. As the nucleoside triphosphates link up, the two terminal phosphate groups are broken off. The remaining phosphate group of the nucleotide and the energy released are used to form the ester linkage between the $5 \rightarrow 3$ carbon atoms of the sugar molecules of adjacent nucelotides (fig 22.14).

Kornberg later demonstrated, in 1967, that DNA polymerase only adds nucleotides to the strand running in the $5 \rightarrow 3$ direction. Since the two DNA strands lie in

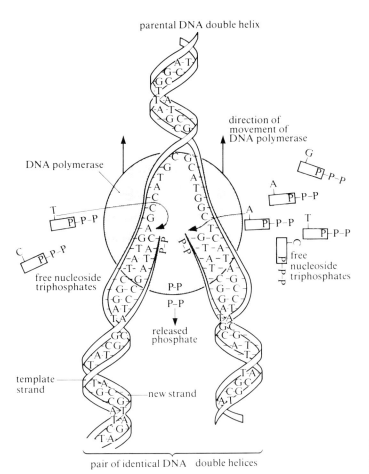

parental DNA double helix

direction of movement of DNA polymerase

DNA polymerase

free nucleoside triphosphates

released phosphate

free nucleoside triphosphates

template strand

new strand

pair of identical DNA double helices

Fig 22.14 *Replication of the DNA double helix. The parental DNA helix unwinds and the complementary strands separate due to the breaking of weak hydrogen bonds between complementary bases. The DNA polynucleotide chains do not break due to the strength of their phosphodiester linkages. Base pairing occurs between the bases of the template strands and free nucleoside triphosphates link up to form a polynucleotide chain. In this way two identical DNA molecules are produced. The enzyme DNA polymerase is involved in the separation of the parental strands and the formation of the new polynucleotide chain but other enzymes are also thought to influence replication*

opposite directions, that is are anti-parallel as shown in fig 22.12, DNA polymerase can only continuously produce one new DNA molecule at a time. Short sections of the other daughter DNA molecule are produced by the action of DNA polymerase moving in the opposite direction. These short sections of newly synthesised polynucleotide chains are joined together by the action of another enzyme called **DNA ligase** (fig 22.15). DNA molecules produced by in vitro synthesis in the presence of DNA ligase are biologically active and can be used in protein synthesis. Those DNA molecules produced in 1956 by Kornberg, whilst having the correct DNA structure, were biologically inactive due to the failure of sections of the synthesised $5 \rightarrow 3$ chain to connect up.

The method of DNA replication proposed by Watson and Crick and shown in fig 22.16 is known as **semiconservative replication** since each new double helix retains one strand of the original DNA double helix. The evidence for this mechanism was provided by a series of classic experiments carried out by Meselson and Stahl in 1958. *E. coli* has a single circular chromosome, and when cultures of these cells were grown for many generations in a medium containing the heavy isotope ^{15}N all the DNA became labelled with ^{15}N. These cells containing DNA labelled with ^{15}N were transferred to a culture medium containing the normal isotope of nitrogen (^{14}N) and allowed to grow. After periods of time corresponding to the generation time for *E. coli* (50 min at 36 °C) samples were removed and the DNA extracted and centrifuged at 40 000 times gravity for 20 h in a solution of caesium chloride (CsCl). During centrifugation the heavy caesium chloride molecules began to sediment to the bottom of the centrifuge tubes producing an increasing density gradient from the top of the tube to the bottom. The DNA settles out where its density equals that of the caesium chloride solution. When examined under ultra-violet light the DNA appeared in the centrifuge tube as a narrow band. The positions of the bands of DNA extracted from cells grown in ^{15}N and ^{14}N culture media and the interpretation of their structure are shown in fig 22.16. These experiments conclusively demonstrated that DNA replication is semi-conservative.

22.2 There were three hypotheses advanced to explain the process of DNA replication. One of these is known as semi-conservative and is described above and in fig 22.14. The other hypotheses are known as conservative replication and dispersive replication and are summarised in fig 22.17.

Draw diagrams to show the distribution of the different types of DNA in a density gradient which Meselson and Stahl would have found in the first two generations if these latter hypotheses had been correct.

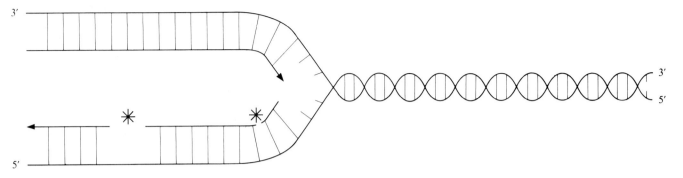

Fig 22.15 (above) The role of DNA ligase in DNA replication. The arrows show the direction in which DNA polymerase moves in producing new DNA double helices. DNA ligase is active in joining short sections of polynucleotide chains at the points labelled with an asterisk

Fig 22.16 (right) The results and interpretation of Meselson and Stahl's experiment into the process of DNA replication. The widths of the DNA bands in the centrifuge tubes reflect the proportions of the various types of DNA molecules as shown in the diagrams (right). In C the ratio of the width is 1:1 and in D the ratio is 3:1

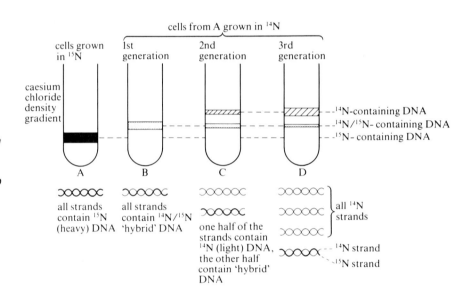

Fig 22.17 (below) Diagrams explaining two further theories of DNA replication

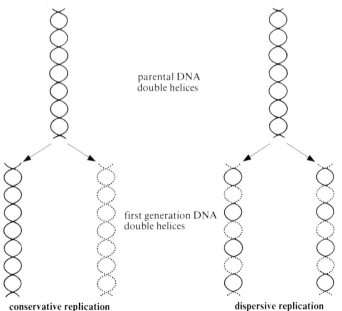

22.5 The nature of genes

The **particulate** nature of heredity has always been a feature of the study of inheritance. Mendel proposed in 1866 that the characteristics of organisms were determined by hereditary units called '**elementes**'. These were later termed **genes** and shown to be located on, and transmitted from generation to generation, by chromosomes (section 23.2).

Despite our current knowledge of chromosomes and the structure and function of DNA, it is still extremely difficult to give a precise definition of a gene. Investigations into the nature of the gene have so far produced three possible definitions of a gene and these are outlined below, since they have implications in the fields of genetics and evolution.

A unit of recombination. From his studies of chromosome mapping in *Drosophila* (section 23.3), Morgan postulated that a gene was **the shortest segment of a chromosome which could be separated from adjacent segments by crossing-over**. This definition regards the gene as a large unit, a specific region of the chromosome determining a distinct characteristic in the organism.

A unit of mutation. Investigations into the nature of mutations revealed that changes in characteristics occurred as a result of random and spontaneous alterations in the structure of a chromosome, a sequence of bases or even a single base (section 23.9). It seemed therefore that a gene might be as small as a single pair of complementary bases in the nucleotide sequence of DNA, that is **the shortest segment of a chromosome which could undergo mutation.**

A unit of function. Since genes were known to determine structural, physiological and biochemical characteristics of organisms it was suggested that a gene was **the shortest segment of a chromosome responsible for the production of a specific product.**

The third definition is the most acceptable but it lacks precision concerning the nature of the specific product. In some cases one 'gene' is known to affect several characteristics (section 23.1.1) whilst in other cases several 'genes' (polygenes) may determine one specific characteristic (section 23.7.6).

It was, however, as a result of research carried out by Beadle and Tatum that the third definition of the gene gained recognition. This became known as the **one gene, one enzyme hypothesis** and was largely substantiated by the development of a new field of biology called **molecular genetics.** (Subsequent research has narrowed this functional concept to that of the one cistron, one polypeptide hypothesis (section 22.5.1).)

22.5.1   Genes and enzymes

The relationship between genes and enzymes was first suggested, although not in those terms, by an English physician, Sir Archibald Garrod in 1908. Garrod postulated that certain 'inborn errors of metabolism' were the result of the failure of the body to produce certain important chemical substances which, in turn, were determined by hereditary mechanisms. It was almost 40 years later that the full extent of this hypothesis was demonstrated and found to be true as a result of the pioneer work in molecular genetics.

Initial investigations in molecular genetics involved establishing the various compounds and enzymes of metabolic pathways. Certain metabolic disorders produce defects in organisms which behave as though controlled by single genes. They may appear spontaneously, as in the case of mutations, or be inherited according to conventional genetic mechanisms. For example, the amino acids phenylalanine and tyrosine are normally used in the manufacture of cell proteins and other structural and physiological compounds, and the excess is broken down into carbon dioxide, water and nitrogenous wastes. In all cases their fate is determined by simple metabolic pathways

involving a series of enzymes. Defective enzymes or lack of enzymes at four points in these pathways produce the metabolic disorders **phenylketonuria**, **goitrous cretinism**, **albinism** and **alkaptonuria**. In all four cases these disorders are inherited in such a way as to suggest that they are each controlled by a single recessive gene.

Further important evidence supporting the one gene, one enzyme hypothesis was gained from work begun by Beadle and Tatum in 1941, investigating the mechanisms of inheritance of enzymes in the pink bread-mould *Neurospora crassa*. In common with Mendel and Morgan they were careful in their choice of experimental organism. *Neurospora* is an ascomycete fungus and has the following advantages for genetic research:
(1) it is easy to grow,
(2) it can be bred in large numbers,
(3) it has a very short life cycle (10 days),
(4) it has a haploid vegetative stage.

The latter point is very significant. Since only one set of chromosomes is present for most of the life cycle there is no masking of recessive genes. If a mutation arises and produces a recessive gene the effects of the mutation will be seen immediately. *Neurospora* normally produces asexual spores (**conidia**) which germinate and give rise to a **mycelium.** Segments of mycelia of opposite mating strains may fuse and produce a diploid zygote. This immediately undergoes a meiotic division followed by a single mitotic division to form an **ascus** or fruiting body containing eight haploid **ascospores**, four of these ascospores being derived from each parental strain. Each ascospore may germinate and produce a new mycelium. A mycelium can therefore arise from an asexually produced conidium or a sexually produced ascospore (fig 22.18).

Neurospora can grow on a culture medium containing only agar, sugars, salts and the vitamin biotin. This is known as **minimal medium**. Growth under these conditions demonstrates that *Neurospora* is able to synthesise all the carbohydrates, fats, amino acids and vitamins essential for its growth using enzymes produced by its cells.

Beadle and Tatum carried out the following procedure in their investigations:
(1) Conidia were exposed to X-rays in order to increase the mutation rate.
(2) These conidia were transferred to **complete medium** (containing all the necessary amino acids and vitamins for normal growth) and grown.
(3) The mycelia which formed were then crossed with mycelia from conidia not exposed to X-rays ('wild type').
(4) The asci produced contained four ascospores from each parental mycelial strain (mutant and wild type).
(5) The ascospores were dissected out and separately transferred to complete medium where they all grew.
(6) Samples of mycelia were placed on vitamin-enriched minimal medium. In some cases no growth occurred.
(7) The strains which did not grow were unable to

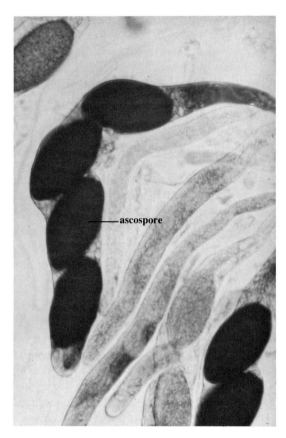

Fig 22.18 *Ascospores in an ascus*

synthesise certain amino acids. In order to determine which amino acids could not be synthesised, these strains were then transferred to a series of minimal media cultures each containing a single different amino acid.

(8) The specific medium in which growth occurred therefore contained the amino acid which the strain of *Neurospora* was unable to synthesise. In this way mutant strains of *Neurospora* were identified. Analysis of the results showed that in all cases where half of the ascospores from a given ascus produced a mutant strain, the other half were able to grow in minimal medium.

This suggested that the mutant gene behaved as a single recessive gene and was transmitted according to the rules of normal Mendelian inheritance. Beadle and Tatum interpreted these results as demonstrating that, in each case, the X-rays had induced a mutation in one gene controlling the production of one enzyme necessary in the synthesis of an amino acid. This formed the basis of their 'one gene, one enzyme' hypothesis (fig 22.19).

This early work established the experimental procedure of using minimal media which has been used and modified in microbial genetics to produce a vast amount of information concerning the role of genes.

It is now clearly established that genes exercise control within the cell by the synthesis of enzymes and other proteins. These enzymes in turn direct the synthesis of all other materials within the cell.

Over the years, however, the exact definition of the gene has been modified. Research carried out by Benzer in 1955 into the structure of genes in the bacteriophage T₄ gave rise to the concept of the cistron as a unit of function. A **cistron** is a region of DNA carrying information for the production of a polypeptide chain. This may function on its own as a biologically active molecule or may form part of a larger macromolecule. Current views on the nature of the gene have moved from the 'one gene, one enzyme' concept to the '**one cistron, one polypeptide**' concept.

22.5.2 The genetic code

When Watson and Crick proposed the double helical structure for DNA in 1953 they also suggested that the genetic information which passed from generation to generation, and which determined cell metabolism, might reside in the sequence of bases of the DNA molecule. Once it had been demonstrated that DNA only specified the production of protein molecules it became clear that the DNA nucleotide base sequence must determine the amino acid sequence of protein molecules. This relationship between bases and amino acids is known as the **genetic code**. The problems remaining were to demonstrate that a nucleotide code existed, to break the code and determine how the code is translated into the amino acid sequence of a protein molecule.

22.5.3 The code

There are four nucleotide bases in the DNA molecule, **adenine** (A), **guanine** (G), **thymine** (T) and **cytosine** (C) (section 5.6). They are arranged as a polynucleotide strand that can be indicated by the initial letters of the bases. This 'alphabet' of four letters is responsible for carrying the code that results in the synthesis of a potentially infinite number of different protein molecules. If one base determined the position of a single amino acid in the primary structure of a protein, the protein could only contain four amino acids. If a combination of pairs of bases coded for each amino acid then 16 amino acids could be specified into the protein molecule.

> **22.3** Using different pairs of the bases A, G, T and C list the 16 possible combinations of bases that can be produced.

Only a code composed of three bases could incorporate all 20 amino acids into the structure of protein molecules. Such a code would produce 64 combinations of bases.

> **22.4** If four bases used singly would code for four amino acids, pairs of bases code for 16 amino acids and triplets of bases code for 64 amino acids, deduce a mathematical expression to explain this.

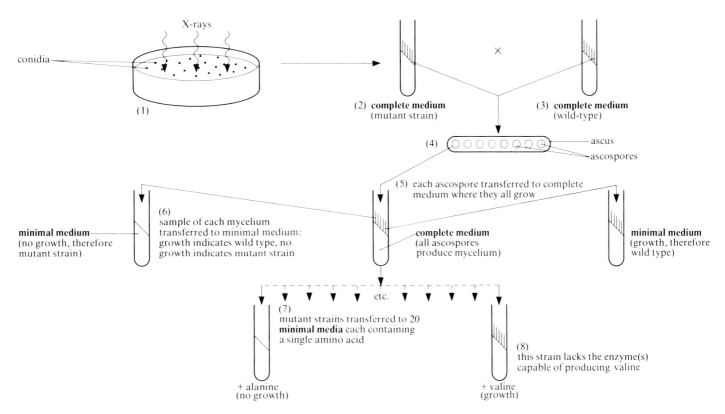

Fig 22.19 *Flow diagram illustrating the main steps in identifying mutant alleles controlling the synthesis of enzymes involved in amino acid production. Full details are given in the text. (The numbers on the diagram correspond with those in the text.)*

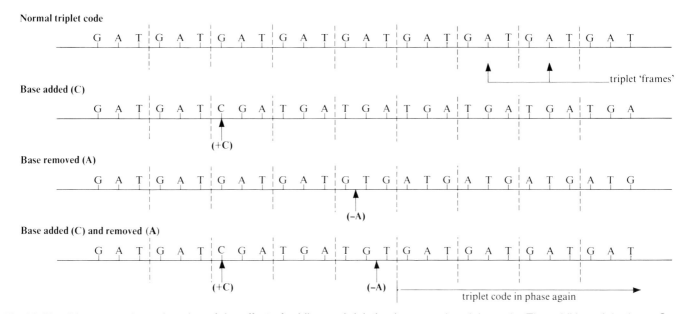

Fig 22.20 *Diagrammatic explanation of the effect of adding and deleting bases to the triplet code. The addition of the base C produces a frame shift which makes the original message GAT, GAT, . . . read as TGA, TGA, . . . The deletion of the base A produces a frame shift changing the original message from GAT, GAT, . . . to ATG, ATG, . . . The addition of the base C at the point indicated and the deletion of the base A at the point indicated restores the original message GAT, GAT. (After F. H. C. Crick (1962) The genetic code I, Scientific American Offprint No. 123, Wm. Saunders & Co.)*

Evidence for the existence of a **triplet code** was provided by Francis Crick in 1961 by producing mutations involving the addition or deletion of bases in T₄ phages. These additions and deletions which produced **frame-shifts** in the code, as shown in fig 22.20, were expressed in T₄ phages as mutations. These frame-shifts produced base triplet sequences which failed to result in the synthesis of protein molecules with the original amino acid sequence (primary

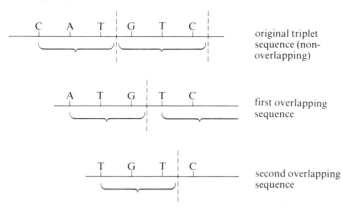

original triplet sequence (non-overlapping)

first overlapping sequence

second overlapping sequence

structure). Only by adding a base and deleting a base at specific points could the original base code sequence be restored. Restoring the original base sequence prevented the appearance of mutants in the experimental T₄ phages. These experiments also demonstrated that the code is **non-overlapping**, that is to say no base of a given triplet contributes to part of the code of the adjacent triplet (fig 22.21).

22.5 Using repeated sequences of the triplet GTA and the base C show that the sequence of triplets can only be restored by adding or deleting three bases. (Set out your answer as in fig 22.20.)

Computer program. The double software package BEADLE & TATUM, MUTATION (CUP Micro Software) permits the experimental determination of metabolic pathways by using mutants, and the consequences of deletion and substitution of DNA bases.

22.5.4 Breaking the code

In order to understand the experimental procedures used to determine which triplet base sequence codes for which amino acid (that is, break the genetic code) it is necessary to appreciate, in outline, the mechanism by which the triplet code is translated into the structure of a protein molecule.

Protein synthesis involves the interaction of two types of nucleic acid, deoxyribonucleic acid, DNA and ribonucleic acid, RNA. There are three kinds of RNA: messenger RNA (**mRNA**), ribosomal RNA (**rRNA**) and transfer RNA (**tRNA**). Apart from a number of organelles such as mitochondria and chloroplasts, DNA is confined to the nucleus where its base sequence is copied (**transcribed**) on to strands of messenger RNA (mRNA) which leave the nucleus. These become attached to ribosomes in the cytoplasm where the base sequence of mRNA is **translated**

into an amino acid sequence. Specific amino acids become attached to tRNA molecules which link up with complementary triplet bases on the mRNA. Adjacent amino acids brought together in this way react together to form a polypeptide chain. The process of protein synthesis, therefore, depends upon the presence of DNA, mRNA, ribosomes, tRNA, amino acids, ATP as an energy source and various enzymes and cofactors which catalyse each stage in the process.

Nirenberg used this information and various research techniques which had been developed during the late 1950s and designed a series of experiments to break the code. The essence of his experiments involved using a known base sequence of mRNA as a coded message and analysing the amino acid sequence of the polypeptide chain produced from it. Nirenberg was able to synthesise a mRNA molecule that consisted of the same triplet (UUU) repeated many times. This was called **polyuridylic acid** (poly-U) and acted as a code. A series of 20 test-tubes was prepared, each containing cell-free extracts of *E. coli* including ribosomes, tRNA, ATP, enzymes and a different radioactive labelled amino acid. Poly-U was added to each test-tube and left to allow in vitro synthesis of polypeptides to occur. Analysis of the contents of the test-tubes showed that a polypeptide had been formed only in the test-tube containing the amino acid phenylalanine. Thus the genetic code had been partly solved. Nirenberg had shown that the base triplet of the mRNA, or **codon**, UUU, determines the position of phenylalanine in a polypeptide chain. Nirenberg and his co-workers then began preparing synthetic polynucleotide molecules of all 64 possible codons and by 1964 had translated the codes for all 20 amino acids (table 22.4).

As can be seen from table 22.4 some amino acids have several specified codons. This type of code where the number of amino acids is less than the number of codons is termed **degenerate**. Analysis of the code also shows that for many amino acids only the first letters appear to be significant. Three of the codons shown in table 22.4 act as 'full stops' in determining the end of the code message. These presumably mark the end-point of a functional unit of the DNA, a cistron. In all of these experiments involved in breaking the genetic code, mRNA was used as the source of triplet bases. The 'genetic code', however, is transmitted from cell to cell and between generations by the triplet base sequence of DNA. Since mRNA is formed directly on the DNA polynucleotide strand by the method of complementary base pairing, the inheritable DNA genetic code is the complement of the mRNA code. This code can be obtained by translating the RNA bases into their complementary DNA bases according to the rules shown in table 22.5.

22.6 Write out the base sequence of mRNA formed from a DNA strand with the following sequence

A T G T T C G A G T A C C A T G T A A C G

Table 22.4. The base sequences of the triplet code and the amino acids for which they code

NB These are **codons**, i.e. base sequences of mRNA and not DNA. The DNA genetic code would have complementary bases and T would replace U.

	Second base				
First base	**U**	**C**	**A**	**G**	**Third base**
U	UUU ⎱ phe UUC ⎰ UUA ⎱ leu UUG ⎰	UCU ⎱ UCC ⎰ ser UCA ⎱ UCG ⎰	UAU ⎱ tyr UAC ⎰ UAA c.t.* UAG c.t.*	UGU ⎱ cys UGC ⎰ UGA c.t.* UGG trp	U C A G
C	CUU ⎱ CUC ⎰ leu CUA ⎱ CUG ⎰	CCU ⎱ CCC ⎰ pro CCA ⎱ CCG ⎰	CAU ⎱ his CAC ⎰ CAA ⎱ gln CAG ⎰	CGU ⎱ CGC ⎰ arg CGA ⎱ CGG ⎰	U C A G
A	AUU ⎱ AUC ⎰ ileu AUA ⎱ AUG met	ACU ⎱ ACC ⎰ thr ACA ⎱ ACG ⎰	AAU ⎱ asn AAC ⎰ AAA ⎱ lys AAG ⎰	AGU ⎱ ser AGC ⎰ AGA ⎱ arg AGG ⎰	U C A G
G	GUU ⎱ GUC ⎰ val GUA ⎱ GUG ⎰	GCU ⎱ GCC ⎰ ala GCA ⎱ GCG ⎰	GAU ⎱ asp GAC ⎰ GAA ⎱ glu GAG ⎰	GGU ⎱ GGC ⎰ gly GGA ⎱ GGG ⎰	U C A G

*c.t., chain termination codon, equivalent to a full stop in the message.

Table 22.5. The RNA bases which are complementary to those of DNA

DNA bases	Complementary RNA bases
A (adenine)	U (uracil)
G (guanine)	C (cytosine)
T (thymine)	A (adenine)
C (cytosine)	G (guanine)

One of the remarkable features of the genetic code is that it is thought to be universal. All living organisms contain the same 20 common amino acids and the same five nitrogenous bases, A, G, T, C and U. Nirenberg demonstrated that introducing mRNA from species A into a cell-free system from species B produced the same polypeptide as would normally be produced in species A. For example, mammalian haemoglobin molecules have been synthesised in cell-free extracts of *E. coli* supplied with mammalian haemoglobin mRNA.

Certain codons act as 'start signals' for the initiation of polypeptide chains, such as AUG (methionine), whereas others, such as UAA, are 'nonsense' codons and do not code for amino acids but act as 'stop signals' for the termination of polypeptide chains.

Advances in molecular biology have reached the point now where it is becoming possible to determine the base sequences for whole genes, and the genetic code for an entire organism, the phage ΦX174, has been determined. This represented a major landmark and whole genes can now be synthesised artificially, a practice which is of use in genetic engineering (section 2.5.4).

The main features of the genetic code are summarised below.

(1) A **triplet** of bases in the polynucleotide chain of DNA is the code for the incorporation of one amino acid into a polypeptide chain.

(2) It is **universal**: the same triplets code for the same amino acids in all organisms. (A few triplet codes in mitochondrial DNA differ from the 'universal code'.)

(3) It is **degenerate**: a given amino acid may be coded for by more than one codon.

(4) It is **non-overlapping**: for example, an mRNA sequence beginning AUGAGCGCA is not read AUG/UGA/

GAG . . . (an overlap of two bases) or AUG/GAG/GCG . . . (an overlap of one base). (However, recent studies have shown overlapping of certain genes in the bacteriophage ΦX174. This seems likely to be exceptional and may be an economy measure since it has very few genes.)

22.6 Protein synthesis

From the information given so far in this chapter it may be seen that the only molecules capable of being synthesised directly from the hereditary material of the cell are proteins. These may have a structural role, such as keratin and collagen, or a functional role, as in insulin, fibrinogen and most importantly enzymes, which are responsible for controlling cell metabolism. It is the particular range of enzymes in the cell which determines what type of cell it becomes. The 'instructions' for the manufacture of these enzymes and all other proteins are located in the DNA, which is generally confined to the nucleus; but, as was shown in the early 1950s, the actual synthesis occurs in the cytoplasm and involves ribosomes. This led to the realisation that a mechanism had to exist for carrying the genetic information from nucleus to cytoplasm. In 1961 two French biochemists, Jacob and Monod, postulated, on theoretical grounds, the existence of a specific form of RNA functioning as an intermediate molecule in the synthesis of protein. This compound was identified later as mRNA.

22.6.1 The role of RNA

RNA exists as a single-stranded molecule in all living cells. It differs from DNA in possessing the pentose sugar ribose instead of deoxyribose and the pyrimidine uracil instead of thymine. Analysis of the RNA content of cells has shown the existence of three types of RNA which are all involved in the synthesis of protein molecules. These are messenger RNA (mRNA), transfer RNA (tRNA) and ribosomal RNA (rRNA). All three types are synthesised directly on DNA, which is said to act as a template for RNA production, and the amount of RNA in each cell is directly related to the amount of protein synthesis.

22.6.2 Messenger RNA

Analyses of cells have shown that 3–5% of the total RNA of the cell is mRNA. This is a single-stranded molecule formed on a single strand of DNA by a process known as **transcription**. In the formation of mRNA only one strand of the DNA molecule is copied. As yet the mechanism determining which strand is to be copied has not been demonstrated. It may involve the activity of a promoter gene and operator gene (section 22.7.1). RNA nucleotides are attracted to the DNA strand according to

the rules of base pairing and link up to form an mRNA polynucleotide strand under the influence of the enzyme **RNA-polymerase**. The base sequence of mRNA is a complementary copy of the template DNA strand and varies in length according to the length of the polypeptide chain for which it codes. The smallest mRNA molecule is approximately 300 nucleotide units long. Most mRNA exists within the cell for a short time. In the case of bacteria this may be a matter of minutes whereas mammalian reticulocytes, which lose their nuclei as they become red blood cells, may continue to produce haemoglobin for several days.

22.6.3 Ribosomal RNA

Ribosomal RNA was the first RNA to be identified, and it makes up approximately 80% of the total RNA of the cell. It is synthesised by genes present on the DNA of several chromosomes found within a region of the nucleolus known as the **nucleolar organiser**. The base sequence of rRNA is similar in all organisms from bacteria to higher plants and animals. It is found in the cytoplasm where it is associated with protein molecules which together form the cell organelles known as ribosomes (see section 7.2.6).

Ribosomes are the site of protein synthesis. Here the mRNA 'code' is **translated** into a sequence of amino acids in a growing polypeptide chain. Ribosomes are often found in clusters linked together by a strand of mRNA. This complex is known as a polyribosome or **polysome** and enables several molecules of the same polypeptide to be produced simultaneously.

22.6.4 Transfer RNA

The existence of transfer RNA (tRNA) (or soluble RNA (sRNA) as it is sometimes referred to) was postulated by Crick and demonstrated by Hoagland in 1955. Each amino acid has its own tRNA molecule which transfers amino acids present in the cytoplasm to the ribosome. Consequently it acts as an intermediate molecule between the triplet code of mRNA and the amino acid sequence of the polypeptide chain. It constitutes about 15% of the total RNA of the cell and, having on average 80 nucleotides per molecule, it is the smallest of all the RNAs. There are more than 20 different tRNA molecules (60 have so far been identified) carrying specific amino acids. All tRNA molecules have the same basic structure as shown in fig 22.22.

The 5′-end of the tRNA always ends in the base guanine whilst the 3′-end always ends in the base sequence of CCA. The nucleotide sequence of the rest of the molecule is variable and may include some 'unusual bases' such as inosine (I) and pseudouracil (ψ). The triplet base sequence at the anticodon (fig 22.22) is directly related to the amino acid carried by that tRNA molecule. Each amino acid is attached to its specific tRNA by its own form of the enzyme

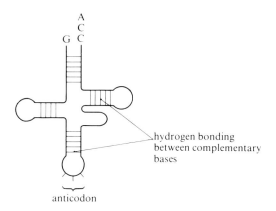

Fig 22.22 *A proposed model for the structure of transfer RNA (tRNA). The whole molecule is composed of 80 nucleotides but only 20 show complementary base pairing*

amino-acyl-tRNA synthetase. This produces an amino acid–tRNA complex with sufficient energy in the bond between the terminal A nucleotide (of CCA) and the amino acid to later form a peptide bond with the carboxyl group of the adjacent amino acid. In this way a polypeptide chain is synthesised. Experiments using ribosomes from rat liver cells in a cell-free extract of *E. coli* have shown that *E. coli* proteins can be manufactured despite the presence of 'foreign' ribosomes. This demonstrates the universal nature of coding mechanisms involving mRNA, tRNA and rRNA in the production of proteins.

22.6.5   The mechanism of protein synthesis

Information from various sources and involving a variety of experimental techniques carried out on a range of organisms from viruses to mammals has shown that protein synthesis is a two-stage process which may be summarised by fig 22.23.

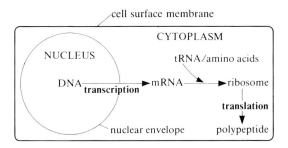

Fig 22.23 *Summary diagram of the main steps involved in protein synthesis*

22.6.6   Transcription

Transcription is the mechanism by which the base sequence of a cistron of a DNA strand is converted into the complementary base sequence of mRNA. The histone coat protecting the DNA double helix in the region of the cistron is thought to be stripped away, exposing the polynucleotide sequences of the DNA molecule. The

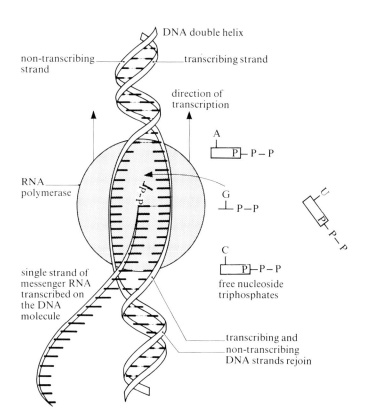

Fig 22.24 *Diagram showing the mechanism of transcription. In the presence of RNA polymerase the DNA double helix unwinds by breakage of the hydrogen bonds between complementary bases, and a polynucleotide strand of mRNA is formed from free RNA nucleoside triphosphates which link up opposite complementary DNA bases on the transcribing strand of template DNA. (After E. J. Ambrose & D. M. Easty (1977)* Cell biology, *2nd ed., Nelson.)*

double helix unwinds by breakage of the relatively weak hydrogen bonds between the bases of complementary strands exposing single strands of DNA. By some mechanism, as yet not understood, one of these strands is selected as a **template** for the formation of a complementary single strand of mRNA. This molecule is formed by the linking of free ribonucleotides under the influence of RNA polymerase and according to the rules of base pairing between DNA and RNA (table 22.5 and fig 22.24).

The exact nature of the copying of DNA bases into RNA bases has been demonstrated using synthetic DNA composed solely of thymine nucleotides (TTT). When introduced into a cell-free system containing RNA polymerase and all four nucleotides (A, U, C and G) the messenger RNA formed was composed entirely of adenine nucleotides.

When the mRNA molecules have been synthesised they leave the nucleus via the nuclear pores and carry the genetic code to the ribosomes. When sufficient numbers of mRNA molecules have been formed from the cistron the RNA polymerase molecule leaves the DNA, the two

823

strands 'zip' up re-forming the double helix and the protective protein coat is added again.

22.6.7 Translation

Translation is the mechanism by which the triplet base sequences of mRNA molecules are converted into a specific sequence of amino acids in a polypeptide chain. This occurs on ribosomes. Several ribosomes may become attached to a molecule of mRNA like beads on a string and the whole structure is known as a **polysome**. These structures, which can be seen under the electron microscope (fig 22.25) have a common strand with a diameter of 1.5 nm. This is the diameter of a single strand of mRNA. The advantage of such a complex is that it allows several polypeptides to be synthesised simultaneously (section 22.6.3). Each ribosome is composed of a small and a large subunit, resembling a 'cottage loaf' (fig 7.18). Messenger RNA is thought to form a reversible attachment to the surface of the small subunit in the presence of magnesium ions (Mg^{2+}). Having become attached to the ribosome it is thought that two mRNA codons are exposed to the larger ribosome subunit. The first codon binds the tRNA molecule having the complementary anticodon and which is carrying the first amino acid (usually methionine) of the polypeptide being synthesised. The second codon then attracts a tRNA–amino acid complex showing the complementary anticodon (figs

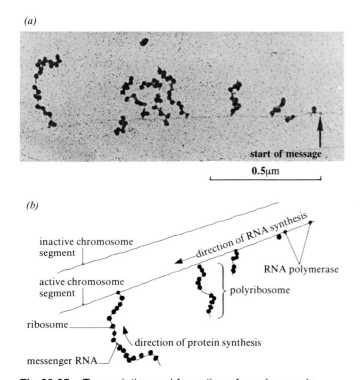

(a)

(b)

Fig 22.25 *Transcription and formation of a polysome in bacteria. (a) Electron micrograph of a chromosome segment showing stages in the development of mRNA and the attachment of ribosomes. (b) Diagrammatic representation of the structure shown in the electron micrograph in (a)*

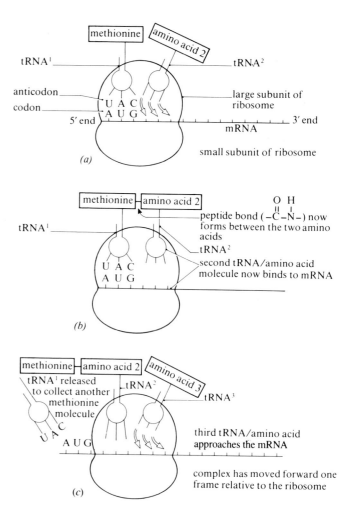

Fig 22.26 *(a) and (b) Consecutive stages in the attachment of tRNA/amino acid complexes by their anticodons to the codons on mRNA and the formation of a peptide bond between adjacent amino acids. (c) The relative movements of mRNA and ribosome exposing a new triplet (frame) for the attachment of the tRNA/amino acid complex. The initial tRNA molecule is now released from the ribosome and cycles back into the cytoplasm to be reactivated by enzymes to form a new tRNA/amino acid complex*

22.26*a* and *b*). The function of the ribosome is to hold in position the mRNA, tRNA and the associated enzymes controlling the process until a peptide bond forms between the adjacent amino acids.

Once the new amino acid has been added to the growing polypeptide chain the ribosome moves along the mRNA to enclose a new codon. The tRNA molecule which was previously attached to the polypeptide chain now leaves the ribosome and passes back to the cytoplasm to be reconverted into a new tRNA–amino acid complex (fig 22.26*c*).

This sequence of the ribosome steadily 'reading' and 'translating' the mRNA code continues until it comes to a codon signalling 'stop'. These terminating codons are UAA, UAG and UGA. At this point the polypeptide chain, now with its primary structure as determined by the DNA cistron, leaves the ribosome and translation is complete. The main steps involved in translation may be summarised under the following headings:

(1) binding of mRNA to ribosome,
(2) amino acid activation and attachment to tRNA,
(3) polypeptide chain initiation,
(4) chain elongation,
(5) chain termination,
(6) fate of mRNA,

and the process is summarised in fig 22.27.

As the polypeptide chains leave the ribosome they may immediately assume either secondary, tertiary or quaternary structures (section 5.5.3).

Evidence that it is the complementary base pairing between the mRNA codon and the tRNA anticodon which determines the incorporation of an amino acid into the polypeptide chain, and not the amino acid, was demonstrated by the following experiment. The tRNA–cysteine complex normally pairs up, via its anticodon ACA, with the mRNA codon UGU. Exposure of this tRNA–cysteine complex to a catalyst, Raney nickel, converted the cysteine to the amino acid alanine. When the new tRNA–alanine complex (carrying the tRNA–cysteine anticodon) was placed in a cell-free system containing poly-UGU–mRNA

the polypeptide chain formed contained only alanine. This experiment demonstrated the importance of the role of the mRNA-codon–tRNA-anticodon mechanism in translating the genetic code.

The whole sequence of protein synthesis occurs as a continuous process and is summarised in fig 22.28.

22.7 Genetic control

In this chapter the mechanisms whereby cells transfer genetic material from generation to generation have been described. The structure and methods of functioning of the genetic material are now known in considerable detail, but there are still many areas of genetics where there are many questions and few answers. Genetic research has come a long way in the last 30 years and produced many answers to fundamental questions. The major breakthroughs were undoubtedly the discovery of the structure of DNA and the breaking of the genetic code. Both of these provided inspiration and incentive to other scientists to delve deeper into understanding the apparent mysteries of molecular genetics. Most of these

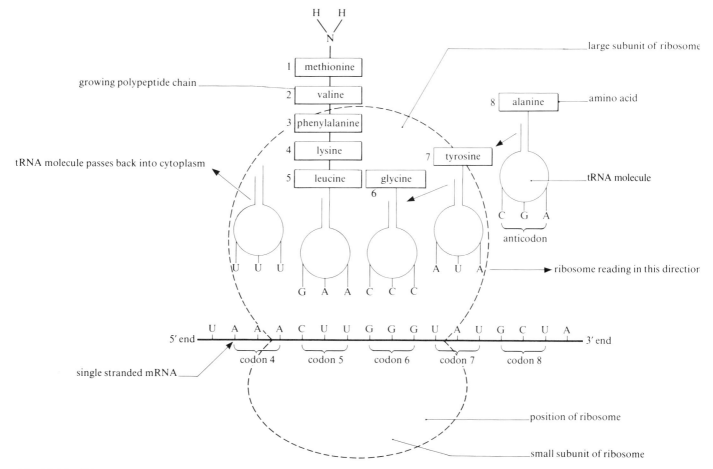

Fig 22.27 *Diagrammatic representation of translation. The anticodon of each specific tRNA/amino acid complex pairs with its complementary bases of the mRNA codon in the ribosome. In the example above a peptide bond would form between leucine and glycine and in this way an additional amino acid would be added to the growing polypeptide chain*

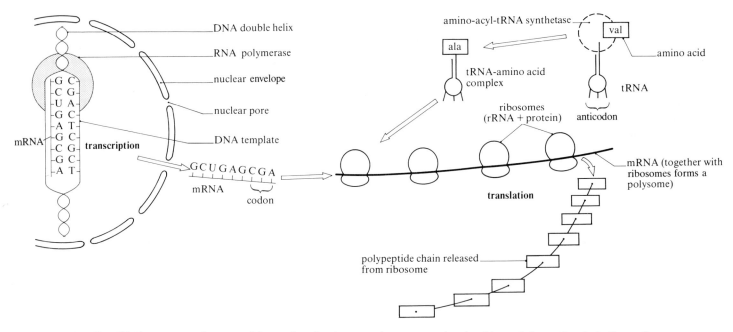

Fig 22.28 *Simplified summary diagram of the major structures and processes involved in protein synthesis in the cell*

unsolved problems which face molecular geneticists are concerned with the mechanisms by which gene activity is controlled in the processes of metabolism, development and differentiation.

Classical genetics has demonstrated that all somatic cells of an organism carry the same genetic complement, that is they contain the same number of chromosomes carrying the same alleles. Despite this, cells in a multicellular organism show wide variation in structure and function. Even within a single cell the rate at which certain protein molecules are synthesised varies according to circumstances and demand. Evidence for the mechanism by which genes are regulated within the cell was first obtained from studies into the control of enzyme synthesis in *E. coli*.

In 1961 Jacob and Monod carried out a series of experiments to investigate the nature of induction of enzyme synthesis in *E. coli*. Of the 800 enzymes thought to be synthesised by *E. coli* some are synthesised continuously and are called **constitutive enzymes**; others are synthesised only in the presence of an inducer compound, which may not be the substrate, and are called **inducible enzymes**. One of the latter enzymes is called β-**galactosidase**.

E. coli will grow rapidly on a culture medium containing glucose. When transferred to a medium containing lactose instead of glucose it will not grow immediately but after a short delay begins to show the same growth rate as seen on a glucose medium. Investigations revealed that growth on lactose medium required the presence of two substances not normally synthesised, called β-galactosidase, which hydrolyses lactose to glucose and galactose, and **lactose permease**, which enables the cell to take up lactose. This is an example of where a change in environmental conditions, lactose instead of glucose, has induced the synthesis of a particular enzyme. Other experiments involving *E. coli* showed that high concentrations of the amino acid **tryptophan** in the culture medium suppressed the production of the enzyme **tryptophan synthetase** used to synthesise tryptophan. β-galactosidase synthesis is an example of **enzyme induction**, whereas the suppression of tryptophan synthetase is an example of **enzyme repression**. On the basis of these observations and experiments, Jacob and Monod proposed a mechanism to account for induction and repression, the mechanism by which genes are 'switched on and off'.

22.7.1 The Jacob–Monod hypothesis of genetic control

The genetic blueprint determining the amino acid sequence of the proteins described above is located on **structural genes**, those for β-galactosidase and lactose permease being closely linked on the same chromosome. The activity of these genes is controlled by another gene called a **regulator gene** which is thought to prevent the structural genes from becoming active. This may be situated some distance from the structural genes. Evidence for the existence of a regulator gene comes from studies of mutant *E. coli* which lack this gene and as a consequence produce β-galactosidase continuously. The regulator gene carries the genetic code which results in the production of a **repressor molecule** that prevents the structural genes from being active. The repressor molecule does not directly affect the structural genes but is thought to influence a gene immediately adjacent to the structural genes known as the **operator gene**. The operator and structural genes are collectively known as the **operon** (fig 22.29).

The repressor molecule is thought to be a particular type of protein known as an **allosteric protein** which can either bind with the operator gene and suppress its activity ('switch it off') or not bind and permit the operator gene to become active ('switch it on'). When the operator gene is 'switched on' the structural genes carry out transcription and mRNA is formed which the ribosomes and tRNA translate into polypeptides. When the operator gene is 'switched off' no mRNA is formed and no polypeptides are formed (fig 22.29).

The mechanism controlling whether or not the allosteric protein binds to the operator gene is simple, yet sensitive to varying intracellular conditions. It is thought that the repressor molecule has at least two active sites to which either an inducer molecule or a co-repressor molecule may become attached, depending upon their relative concentrations at any given time, as described in section 22.7.4.

22.7.2 Enzyme induction

The binding of an inducer molecule to its active site on the repressor molecule alters the tertiary structure of the repressor (allosteric effect) (section 6.6) so that it cannot bind with the operator gene and repress it. The operator gene becomes active and 'switches on' the structural genes.

In the case of *E. coli* grown on glucose medium, the regulator gene produces a repressor substance which combines with the operator gene and switches it 'off'. The structural genes are not activated and no β-galactosidase and lactose permease are produced. When transferred to a lactose medium the lactose is thought to act as an inducer of protein synthesis by combining with the repressor molecule and preventing it combining with the operator gene. The structural genes become active, mRNA is produced and proteins are synthesised. Lactose is thus an inducer of its own breakdown (fig 22.30).

22.7.3 Enzyme repression

If a co-repressor molecule binds with its active site on the repressor molecule it reinforces the normal binding response of the repressor molecule with the operator gene. This inactivates the operator gene which, in effect, prevents the structural genes from being 'switched on'.

E. coli synthesises the amino acid tryptophan in the presence of the enzyme tryptophan synthetase. When the cell contains an excess of tryptophan some of it acts as a co-repressor of enzyme synthesis by combining with the repressor molecule. Co-repressor and repressor molecules combine with the operator gene and inhibit its activity. The structural genes are 'switched off', no mRNA is produced and no further tryptophan synthetase is synthesised. This is an example of feedback inhibition acting at the gene level (fig 22.31).

22.7.4 Control of metabolic pathways

This dual mechanism enables the cytoplasm and nucleus to interact in a delicate control of cell metabolism. In the case of a simple metabolic pathway as shown in fig 22.32 the initial substrate and final product can act as inducer and co-repressor respectively. This mechanism enables the cell to produce the amount of enzyme required at any given time to maintain the correct level of product. This method of metabolic control is highly economical. Negative feedback involving the inactivation of the initial enzyme (*a*) by combination with the end-product (*E*) would rapidly halt the pathway but would not prevent the continued synthesis of the other enzymes (*b*, *c* and *d*). In the system proposed by Jacob and Monod, the end-product (*E*), by combining with the repressor molecule to increase its repressive effect on the operator gene, would prevent the synthesis of all enzymes (*a*, *b*, *c* and *d*) and halt the pathway.

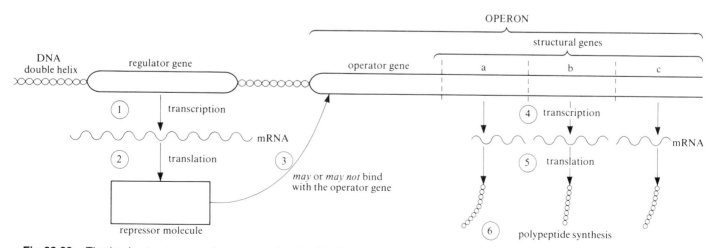

Fig 22.29 *The basic structures and processes involved in the control of protein synthesis according to the hypothesis produced by Jacob and Monod. The numbers indicate the sequence of events*

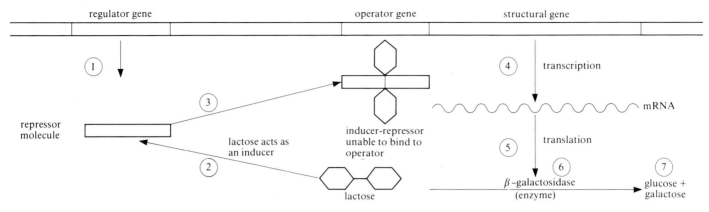

Fig 22.30 (above) *The method of induction of ß-galactosidase synthesis according to the Jacob–Monod hypothesis. The numbers indicate the sequence of events*

Fig 22.31 (below) *The mechanism of repression of tryptophan synthetase synthesis according to the Jacob–Monod hypothesis. The numbers indicate the sequence of events. Solid lines indicate actual processes. The dotted lines represent repressed stages*

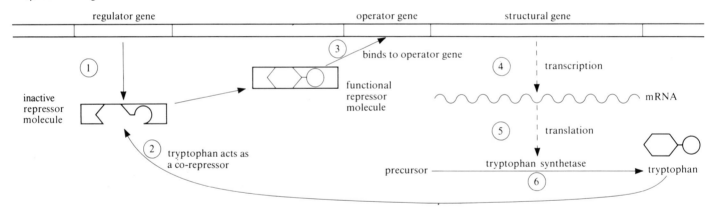

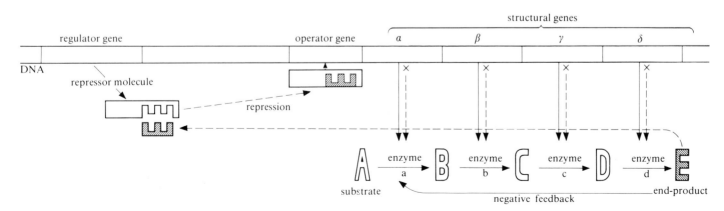

Fig 22.32 *Mechanisms of control of the metabolic pathways A→E. The solid lines represent the mechanism operating during negative feedback. The dotted lines represent the mechanisms operating during repression. X represents blocks in the enzyme synthesis*

22.7.5 Modification to the 'operon' hypothesis

Since 1961 when Jacob and Monod suggested a mechanism by which genes are 'switched on and off', further evidence has accumulated which has helped to clarify aspects of the mechanism. Genetic evidence has suggested the existence of a **promoter gene** situated adjacent to the operator gene which acts between it and the regulator gene. It is thought to have two functions. First the promoter gene is the site to which RNA polymerase binds before moving along the DNA to begin the transcription of mRNA on the structural genes. This movement will, of course, depend upon whether the operator gene is 'operational' or not. Secondly, the base sequence of the promoter gene determines which strand of the DNA double helix attracts the RNA polymerase. In this way the promoter gene determines which strand of the DNA double helix acts as the template for mRNA transcription.

22.8 The genetic control of development

The life cycle of the majority of multicellular animals and plants begins with a single cell, the zygote. This undergoes repeated mitotic and cytoplasmic divisions to give rise to a highly differentiated organism. This process is known as **growth and development** and includes the process of **differentiation**. Differentiation, that is the process whereby cells assume particular structures which enable them to carry out a restricted number of particular functions more efficiently, is one of the remarkable events of development. Why should the cells of an organism produced by repeated cell divisions and containing identical genetic material show the range of diversity which typifies higher multicellular organisms? The answer is far from clear but must involve the induction and repression of genes, perhaps by mechanisms similar to those described in the previous section. Evidence has suggested that there are three factors which act together in various ways to bring about differentiation. They are the nucleus, the cytoplasm and the environment.

22.8.1 The role of the nucleus

The importance of the nucleus as the storage site of the genetic material and its primary role in determining phenotypic characteristics has been appreciated for a long time. The German biologist Hammerling was one of the earliest workers to demonstrate the primary role of the nucleus. He chose as his research organism the unusually large acellular marine alga *Acetabularia*. There are two closely related species, *A. mediterranea* and *A. crenulata*, which differ only in the shape of their 'head' region (fig 22.33).

In a series of experiments, including some that involved separating the 'head' region from the 'basal' region (which

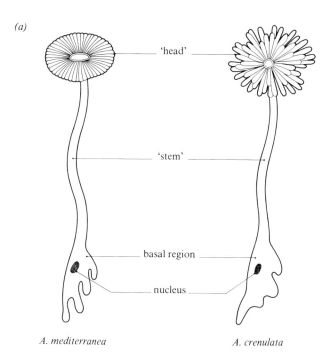

'head'

'stem'

basal region

nucleus

A. mediterranea   *A. crenulata*

Fig 22.33 *The marine alga* Acetabularia *used by Hammerling to demonstrate the role of the nucleus.* (a) *Two species of* Acetabularia. (b) *Transplant and excision experiments carried out by Hammerling*

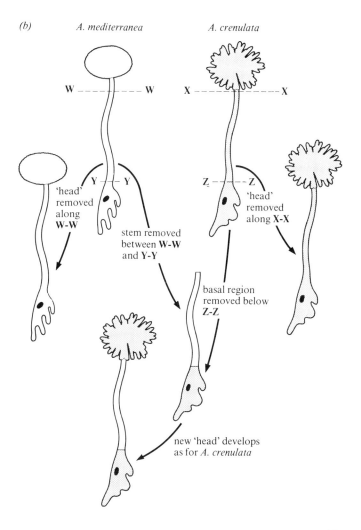

A. mediterranea   *A. crenulata*

W — — — W   X — — — X

Y — Y   Z — — — Z

'head' removed along **W-W**

stem removed between **W-W** and **Y-Y**

'head' removed along **X-X**

basal region removed below **Z-Z**

new 'head' develops as for *A. crenulata*

contained the nucleus), he was able to demonstrate the necessity of the nucleus for normal development. Further experiments involving the reciprocal grafting of the nucleus-containing 'basal' region of one species to the enucleate stalk region of the other species always produced hybrids that developed the 'head' which was characteristic of the nucleate portion of the graft.

However, in considering this model of nuclear control, due regard must be taken of the primitive nature of the organism used. Later experiments performed by two American scientists, Briggs and King, in 1952, made use of the technique of grafting but in this case they used cells from the frog *Rana pipiens*. The nuclei were removed from unfertilised egg cells and replaced with nuclei from late blastula cells which showed signs of differentiation. In most cases the recipient cells developed and grew into normal adult frogs.

22.7 What did the results of the above experiments demonstrate?

22.8.2 The role of the cytoplasm

Further evidence for the role of the cytoplasm is provided by embryological studies. From an early stage in the embryological development of many organisms from algae to mammals the egg cytoplasm is not homogeneous. The cytoplasm appears to be stratified, with less dense material at the upper pole and dense granular material at the lower pole. In those species, where the early cleavage planes are vertical, such as amphibia, all resulting cells, if separated, give rise to normal offspring. In other species where early cleavage planes are horizontal, such as molluscs, the cells, if separated, do not undergo normal development. In the former case all cells contain an equal distribution of the different layers of cytoplasm, whereas in the latter there is an unequal distribution of cytoplasm. Eggs where the cytoplasm is differentiated in this way in order to give rise to certain regions of the embryo are known as **mosaic eggs**. In all cases the nuclei of the cells contain the same genetic complement. Differential developments would therefore appear to result from some form of cytoplasmic influence on the genes.

In a series of now classic embryological experiments, Spemann and Mangold demonstrated in 1924 that differentiation is largely controlled by the cytoplasmic influence which one cell type has over another. In one of their experiments, they removed tissue from the dorsal lip of the blastopore of an amphibian gastrula (fig 22.34) and implanted it into a ventral region of another gastrula (the host). The cells of the dorsal lip normally develop into the notochord, mesodermal somites (myotomes) and neural tube. The host gastrula in this experiment developed a secondary notochord, extra myotomes and a neural tube in the region of the transplant which gave rise to a second tadpole as shown in fig 22.34.

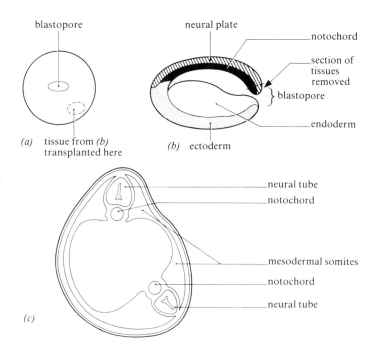

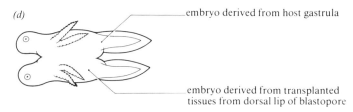

Fig 22.34 *Technique and results of Spemann and Mangold's experiments on embryonic induction. (a) Surface view of the developing gastrula showing the blastopore. (b) LS through gastrula of an amphibian showing the region of the dorsal lip of the blastopore which is excised and transplanted into gastrula (a). (c) TS through the developing embryo showing the development of two identical groups of embryological tissues. (d) 'Siamese' embryos produced by transplanting tissue from the dorsal lip of the blastopore*

On the basis of these observations Spemann and Mangold advanced a hypothesis of differentiation known as **embryonic induction**. According to this hypothesis certain cells act as **organisers** of other cells described as **competent** (or **determined**). Organisers are capable of inducing competent cells to develop into cell types having a structure and function different from those which would appear in the absence of organisers. These misplaced structures are described as **atopic** (*a*, without; *topos*, place).

In the embryological development of organisms a certain region known as the **primary organiser** determines the entire further course of development. In the case of amphibia this is the dorsal lip of the blastopore, whereas in birds it is a region known as the primitive streak. These primary organisers establish the **embryonic axis** and induce other tissues to act as secondary and tertiary organisers and so on until all the organs and organ systems of the embryo have differentiated and developed in their normal positions.

22.8.3 The nature of the organiser

Experiments have been carried out involving the removal of a tissue known to act as an organiser and placing it on a piece of agar for several hours. Implantation of the agar into regions known to be competent has induced them to differentiate as directed by the organiser tissue. This technique demonstrates that the organiser is a chemical substance which has diffused into the agar. Attempts to isolate the substance have so far produced no clear-cut result. Steroids, proteins and nucleic acids have all been suggested as likely organiser substances. Paul and Gilmour have observed that DNA molecules in different tissues are differentially 'coated' with histone and non-histone proteins. They suggest that histones 'cover' those regions of the DNA which are non-functional, that is their genes are irreversibly repressed, whilst non-histone proteins 'cover' those genes which are to be transcribed. This idea fits in well with the situation in mosaic eggs where a distribution of histones throughout the cytoplasm would lead to the production of cells with different regions of DNA 'blocked off'. In this way various genes would be effectively 'switched off' in different cells and this would provide a possible mechanism of differentiation.

22.8.4 The role of the environment

It is largely as a result of experiments such as those of Jacob and Monod that the extent of environmental influence can be seen on development. For example, lactose is an environmental factor that has a direct influence on the functioning of genes in *E. coli*. Light, temperature, water, nutrients and gas supplies can all influence the extent of development and growth in plants and animals as described in chapters 9, 10, 15, 16 and 21. The effect of the environment on differentiation is probably normally through an intermediate influence on the cytoplasm which in turn has a direct effect on the genes.

22.8.5 The role of genes in development

The relationship between specific regions of the DNA molecule and morphological development has been studied extensively in organisms possessing **giant chromosomes**. These are found, for example in the salivary glands of many dipteran larvae, including *Drosophila*. The reasons for the size of these **polytene chromosomes** are given in section 23.5.1. They are relatively easy to see under the light microscope and show distinct banding patterns when stained with Feulgen stain. During metamorphosis the *Drosophila* larvae pass through several stages, or instars, each separated by a period of intense cellular activity called ecdysis followed by moulting of the old cuticle. The final two ecdyses are the most dramatic and

produce the pupal stage and the imago (adult) stage. These are stages of intense metabolic activity and differentiation. Metamorphosis is controlled by hormones as described in section 21.4. During metamorphosis 'bands' along the chromosomes enlarge and form structures known as **chromosome puffs** or **rings of Balbiani** (after the scientist who first observed them in 1890). Specific stains which show up RNA, and autoradiographic studies involving labelled RNA nucleotides have shown these 'puffs' to be regions of RNA synthesis. The size of the 'puffs' has also been shown to be directly related to the rate of RNA synthesis. The puffing effect is thought to be produced by the unwinding of DNA molecules, the separation of complementary strands and the formation of mRNA during transcription.

There is a definite sequence of puffing during metamorphosis and this is induced by the moulting hormone ecdysone. During the various larval stages and the pupal stage different regions of the chomosomes show 'puffing', suggesting that the puffs correspond to the structural genes postulated in the Jacob–Monod hypothesis. Evidence that regions of puffing correspond to regions of genetic activity was produced by Beerman using two species of midge belonging to the genus *Chironomus*. Certain cells in the salivary gland of one species are granulated whereas those of the other species are non-granulated. Genetic mapping based upon crosses between these two species has shown that the alleles determining these characteristics are situated near the centromere of one of the chromosomes and the allele for granulated cells is dominant. Examination of the chromosomes of these species showed that puffing is only seen in the region where this gene is located in the species producing granulated cells. Furthermore, in the case of midges which are heterozygous for this characteristic, puffing at this locus is only seen in the chromosome carrying the dominant allele.

Further evidence for the link between chromosome puffs and mRNA synthesis is provided by the effect of injecting the drug actinomycin D into organisms having giant chromosomes. Actinomycin D inhibits transcription by preventing the synthesis of mRNA, and no puffing is seen in organisms treated in this way (fig 22.35).

Another factor influencing growth and development in plants and animals is hormones. In many cases this occurs at the level of transcription of mRNA. The exact way in which a given hormone affects transcription and protein synthesis is extremely variable, but some are thought to exert their influence on receptor sites on the cell membrane. Following binding of the hormone on to the receptor site, thought to be the enzyme **adenylate cyclase**, cyclic AMP is released into the cytoplasm and this acts as a second messenger which induces transcription. Further details of this mechanism are described in section 16.6.1.

This chapter has attempted to describe some of the processes associated with the continuity of life. Living systems appear to require both short-term genetic stability and long-term genetic flexibility. Genetic stability is seen to

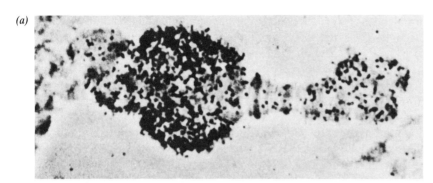

(a)

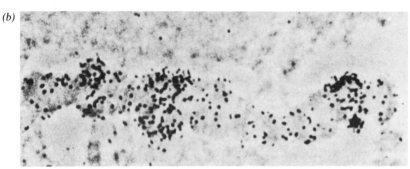

(b)

Fig 22.35 *The relationship between puffing and mRNA synthesis is clearly demonstrated by these autoradiograms of chromosome IV of the midge* Chironomus tentans. *The black dots indicate the position of radioactive uridine taken up during mRNA synthesis. (a) shows that RNA synthesis is closely related to the region of puffing. (b) Very little puffing and uridine uptake has occurred following the addition of small amounts of actinomycin D which inhibits mRNA synthesis. (From W. Beerman & U. Clever (1964) Chromosome puffs,* Scientific American *Offprint No. 180. Wm. Saunders & Co)*

be achieved by the mechanisms of mitosis, whereas the mechanisms of meiosis introduce an enormous amount of genetic variation, enabling organisms to adapt to changing environments.

Having established the cytological mechanisms of inheritance, research has shifted to considerations of the nature of the genetic material and the mechanisms involved in its control of cellular activities such as development, growth and differentiation. The next chapter describes the ways in which characteristics are inherited, the rules governing these processes and the way variations are introduced into populations.

Chapter Twenty-three

Variation and genetics

Genetics may rightly be claimed to be one of the most important branches of biology. For thousands of years, humans have used the techniques of genetics in the improvement of domestic animals and crops without having any real knowledge of the mechanisms which underlie these practices. Various pieces of archaeological evidence dating back 6 000 years suggest that humans understood that certain physical characteristics could be transmitted from one generation to another. By selecting particular organisms from wild stocks and interbreeding these, humans have been able to produce improved varieties of plants and animals to suit their needs.

It is only since the beginning of this century, though, that scientists have begun to appreciate fully the principles and mechanisms of heredity. Whilst advances in microscopy have revealed that the sperm and the ova transmitted the hereditary characteristics from generation to generation, the problem nevertheless remained of how minute particles of biological material could carry the vast number of characteristics that make up an individual organism.

The first really scientific advance in the study of inheritance was made by the Austrian monk Gregor Mendel who published a paper in 1866 which laid the foundations for the present-day science of genetics. He demonstrated that characteristics do not blend but pass from parents to offspring as discrete units. These units, which appear in the offspring in pairs, remain discrete and are passed on to subsequent generations by the male and female gametes which each contain a single unit. The Danish botanist Johannsen called these units **genes** in 1909, and the American geneticist Morgan, in 1912, demonstrated that they are carried on the chromosomes. Since the early 1900s the study of genetics has made great advances in explaining the nature of inheritance at both the level of the organism and at the level of the gene.

23.1 Mendel's work

Gregor Mendel was born in Moravia in 1822. In 1843 he joined an Augustinian monastery at Brünn in Austria (now Brno, in Czechoslovakia) where he took Holy Orders. From there he went to the University of Vienna where he spent two years studying natural history and mathematics before returning to the monastery in 1853. This choice of subjects undoubtedly had a significant influence on his subsequent work on inheritance in pea plants. Whilst in Vienna, Mendel had become interested in

the process of hybridisation in plants and, in particular, the different forms in which hybrid progeny appear and the statistical relationships between them. This formed the basis of Mendel's scientific investigations on inheritance which he began in the summer of 1856.

Mendel's success was due, in part, to his careful choice of experimental organism, the garden pea, *Pisum sativum*. He ascertained that it had the following advantages over other species:

(1) There were several varieties available which had quite distinct characteristics.
(2) The plants were easy to cultivate.
(3) The reproductive structures were completely enclosed by the petals so that the plant was normally self-pollinating. This led to the varieties producing the same characteristics generation after generation, a phenomenon known as **pure breeding**.
(4) Artificial cross-breeding between varieties was possible and resulting hybrids were completely fertile. From the 34 varieties of garden pea, Mendel selected 22 varieties which showed clear-cut differences in characteristics and used these in his breeding experiments. The seven basic characteristics, or **traits**, that Mendel was interested in were length of stem, shape of seed, colour of seed, shape and colour of pod, position and colour of flower.

Many scientists before Mendel had performed similar experiments on plants but none had produced results which had the accuracy and detail of Mendel's, nor were they able to explain their results in terms of a mechanism of inheritance. The reasons for Mendel's success may be taken as a model of how to carry out a scientific investigation. They may be summarised as follows:

(1) Preliminary investigations were carried out to obtain familiarity with the experimental organism.
(2) All experiments were carefully planned so that attention was focussed on only one variable at any time, thus simplifying the observations to be made.
(3) Meticulous care was taken in carrying out all techniques, thus preventing the introduction of contaminating variables (see below for details).
(4) Accurate records were kept of all the experiments and the results obtained.
(5) Sufficient data were obtained to have statistical significance.

As Mendel stated,

'The value and utility of any experiment are

determined by the fitness of the material to the purpose for which it is used.'

However, it is worth stating that there was an element of luck in Mendel's choice of experimental organism. The characters chosen by Mendel lacked many of the more complex genetic features which were later discovered, such as codominance (section 23.7.1), characteristics controlled by more than one pair of genes (section 23.7.6) and linkage (section 23.3).

23.1.1 Monohybrid inheritance and the principle of segregation

Mendel's earliest experiments involved selecting plants of two varieties which had clearly differentiated characteristics, such as flowers distributed along the main stem (axial) or flowers at the tip of the stem (terminal). These plants, showing a single pair of contrasted characteristics, were grown for a number of generations. Seeds collected from axial plants always produced plants with axial flowers, whilst those from terminal plants always produced terminal flowers. This demonstrated to Mendel that he was using pure-breeding plants. With this information he was in a position to carry out hybridisation experiments (experimental crosses) using these plants. His experimental technique involved removing the anthers from a number of plants of one variety before self-fertilisation could have occurred. These he called 'female' plants. Pollen was then transferred, by means of a brush, from the anthers of another plant of the same variety to the stigmas of the 'female' plant. The experimental flowers were then enclosed in a small bag to prevent pollen from other plants reaching their stigmas. **Reciprocal crosses** were carried out by transferring pollen grains from axial plants to terminal plants and pollen grains from terminal plants to axial plants. In all cases the seeds subsequently collected from both sets of plants gave rise to plants with axial flowers. This characteristic, 'axial flower', shown by these first generation hybrid plants (subsequently called the **first filial generation** or **F₁ generation** by Bateson and Saunders in 1902) was termed **dominant** by Mendel. None of the F₁ plants produced terminal flowers.

The F₁ plants then had their flowers enclosed in bags (to prevent cross-pollination occurring) and were left to self-pollinate. The seeds collected from these F₁ plants were counted and planted the following spring to produce the **second filial generation** or **F₂ generation**. (An F₂ generation is always the result of allowing the F₁ generation to inbreed or, as in this case, to self-pollinate.) When these plants flowered, some bore axial flowers and others terminal flowers. In other words, the characteristic 'terminal flower', which was absent in the F₁ generation, had reappeared in the F₂ generation. Mendel reasoned that the terminal characteristic must have been present in the F₁ generation but as it failed to be expressed in this generation he termed it **recessive**. Of the 858 F₂ plants that Mendel obtained, 651 had axial flowers and 207 had terminal flowers. Mendel carried out a series of similar experiments involving in each case the inheritance of a single pair of contrasting characteristics. Seven pairs of contrasting characteristics were studied and the results of the experimental crosses are shown in table 23.1. In all cases the analyses of the results revealed that the ratios of dominant to recessive characteristics in the F₂ generation were approximately 3:1.

The example quoted above is typical of all Mendel's experiments involving the inheritance of a single characteristic (**monohybrid inheritance**) and may be summarised as follows.

Observations

Parents   axial flowers × terminal flowers
F₁   all axial flowers
F₂   651 axial flowers   207 terminal flowers
F₂ ratio   3   :   1

On the basis of these, and similar results, Mendel drew the following conclusions.
(1) Since the original parental stocks were pure breeding, the axial variety must have possessed *two* axial factors and the terminal variety *two* terminal factors.
(2) The F₁ generation possessed *one* factor from **each** parent which were carried by the gametes.
(3) These factors do not blend in the F₁ generation but retain their individuality.

Table 23.1 The results of Mendel's experiments on the inheritance of seven pairs of contrasted characteristics. (The observed ratio of dominant to recessive characteristics approximates to the theoretical value of 3:1.)

| Characteristic | Parental appearance | | F₂ appearance | | Ratio |
	(dominant)	(recessive)	(dominant)	(recessive)	
length of stem	tall	dwarf	787	277	2.84:1
shape of seed	round	wrinkled	5 474	1 850	2.96:1
colour of seed	yellow	green	6 022	2 001	3.01:1
shape of pod	inflated	constricted	882	299	2.95:1
colour of pod	green	yellow	428	152	2.82:1
position of flower	axial	terminal	651	207	3.14:1
colour of flower	red	white	705	224	3.15:1
total			14 949	5 010	2.98:1

(4) The axial factor is dominant to the terminal factor which is recessive.

The separation of the pair of parental factors, so that one factor is present in each gamete, became known as **Mendel's first law**, or the **principle of segregation**. This states that

> the characteristics of an organism are determined by internal factors which occur in pairs. Only one of a pair of such factors can be represented in a single gamete.

We now know that these factors determining characteristics, such as flower position, are regions of the chromosome known as **genes**.

The foregoing experimental procedure carried out by Mendel in the investigation of the inheritance of a *single* pair of contrasted characteristics is an example of a **monohybrid cross**. This may be represented in terms of symbols and placed in a modern context of gamete formation and fertilisation. By convention, the initial letter of the dominant characteristic is used as the genotypic symbol and its capital form (e.g. **A**) represents the dominant allele and the lower case (e.g. **a**) represents the recessive allele. All of the terms and symbols described above are used in genetics and are summarised in table 23.2.

Fig 23.1 shows the correct way to describe a monohybrid cross or arrive at the solution to a genetics problem involving the inheritance of a single pair of contrasted characteristics.

The ratio of dominant phenotypes to recessive phenotypes of 3:1 is called the **monohybrid ratio**. Mendel's conclusions regarding the transfer of a single characteristic by each gamete and the genotypic appearance can be demonstrated by mathematical probability. The probability of a gamete cell from a heterozygous F_1 parent containing either the dominant allele **A** or the recessive allele **a** is 50% or $\frac{1}{2}$. If each gamete is represented by $\frac{1}{2}$, the

Let:

    A represent axial flower (dominant)
    a represent terminal flower (recessive)

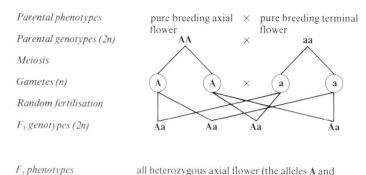

F₁ phenotypes   all heterozygous axial flower (the alleles **A** and **a** remain distinct in spite of the dominance of **A**)

The F_1 generation were self-pollinated

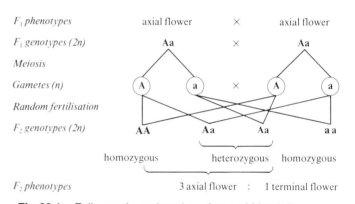

Fig 23.1 *Full genetic explanation of one of Mendel's monohybrid crosses. (2n represents the diploid condition, n represents the haploid condition; see section 22.3.)*

Table 23.2 Glossary of common genetic terms with examples based on fig 23.1.

Genetic term	Explanation	Example
gene	The basic unit of inheritance for a given characteristic	flower position
allele	One of a number of alternative forms of the same gene responsible for determining contrasting characteristics	**A** or **a**
locus	Position of an allele within a DNA molecule	
homozygous	The diploid condition in which the alleles at a given locus are identical	**AA** or **aa**
heterozygous	The diploid condition in which the alleles at a given locus are different	**Aa**
phenotype	The characteristics of an individual usually resulting from the interaction between the genotype and the environment in which development occurs	axial, terminal
genotype	The genetic constitution of an organism with respect to the alleles under consideration	**AA, Aa, aa**
dominant	The allele which influences the appearance of the phenotype even in the presence of an alternative allele	**A**
recessive	The allele which influences the appearance of the phenotype only in the presence of another identical allele	**a**
F_1 generation	The generation produced by crossing homozygous parental stocks	
F_2 generation	The generation produced by crossing two F_1 organisms	

number of possible combinations of F$_2$ genotypes is represented by $\frac{1}{2} \times \frac{1}{2} = \frac{1}{4}$. Hence there are four possible F$_2$ genotypes. The statistical probability of the **A** and **a** containing gametes combining by random fertilisation is shown in fig 23.2. As a result of dominance the phenotypic appearance will be 3 dominant phenotypes: 1 recessive phenotype. The results of Mendel's breeding experiments bear out this theoretical ratio as shown in table 23.1.

Let the probability of the alleles **A** and **a** appearing in the heterozygote (**Aa**) = 1,
therefore **A** = ½,
a = ½

Using these values the probability of each genotype and phenotype appearing in the F$_2$ generation can be demonstrated as shown below:

F$_1$ genotypes (2n)   **Aa**   ×   **Aa**

Meiosis

Gametes (n)   (A) (a)   ×   (A) (a)

(In terms of probability)   (½)(½)   ×   (½)(½)

Random fertilisation

F$_2$ genotypes (2n)   ¼ **AA**   ¼ **Aa** + ¼ **Aa**   ¼**aa**

F$_2$ phenotypes   ¾ dominant: ¼ recessive
i.e. 3 dominant: 1 recessive

Fig 23.2 *Explanation of the 3:1 Mendelian monohybrid ratio in terms of probability*

23.1 If a pure strain of mice with brown-coloured fur are allowed to breed with a pure strain of mice with grey-coloured fur they produce offspring having brown-coloured fur. If the F$_1$ mice are allowed to interbreed they produce an F$_2$ generation with fur colour in the proportion of three brown-coloured to one grey.
(a) Explain fully these results.
(b) What would be the result of mating a brown-coloured heterozygote from the F$_2$ generation with the original grey-coloured parent?

23.1.2   Test cross

The genotype of an F$_1$ organism, produced by the breeding of homozygous dominant and homozygous recessive parents, is heterozygous but shows the dominant phenotype. An organism displaying the recessive phenotype must have a genotype which is homozygous for the recessive allele. In the case of F$_2$ organisms showing the dominant phenotype the genotype may be either homozygous or heterozygous. It may be of interest to a breeder to know the genotype and the only way in which it can be determined is to carry out a breeding experiment. This involves the use of a technique known as **test cross**. By crossing an organism having an unknown genotype with a homozygous recessive organism it is possible to determine an unknown genotype within one breeding generation. For example in the fruit fly, *Drosophila*, long wing is dominant to vestigial wings. The genotype of a long wing *Drosophila* may be homozygous (**LL**) or heterozygous (**Ll**). In order to establish which is the correct genotype the fly is testcrossed with a double recessive (**ll**) vestigial wing fly. If the test cross offspring are all long wing the unknown genotype is homozygous dominant. A ratio of 1 long wing: 1 vestigial wing indicates that the unknown is heterozygous (fig 23.3).

23.2 Why is it not possible to use a homozygous dominant organism (such as **TT**) in a test cross experiment to determine the genotype of an organism showing the dominant phenotype? Illustrate your answer fully using appropriate genetic symbols.

23.1.3   Dihybrid inheritance and the principle of independent assortment

Having established that it was possible to predict the outcome of breeding crosses involving a single pair of contrasted characteristics, Mendel turned his attention to the inheritance of two pairs of contrasted characteristics. Since two pairs of alleles are found in

Let: **L** represent long wing (dominant)
l represent vestigial wing (recessive)

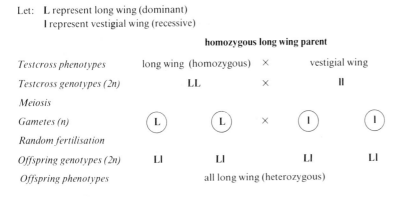
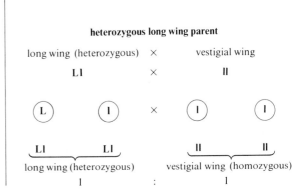

Fig. 23.3 *A full genetic explanation of how to determine the genotype of an organism showing a dominant characteristic. This technique is known as a test cross, and produces offspring phenotypes as shown*

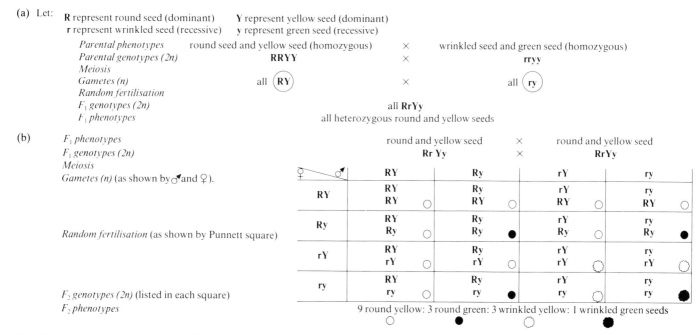

(a) Let: **R** represent round seed (dominant) **Y** represent yellow seed (dominant)
         r represent wrinkled seed (recessive) **y** represent green seed (recessive)

Parental phenotypes	round seed and yellow seed (homozygous)	×	wrinkled seed and green seed (homozygous)
Parental genotypes (2n)	**RRYY**	×	**rryy**
Meiosis			
Gametes (n)	all **RY**	×	all **ry**
Random fertilisation			
F₁ genotypes (2n)	all **RrYy**		
F₁ phenotypes	all heterozygous round and yellow seeds		

(b) *F₁ phenotypes*   round and yellow seed   ×   round and yellow seed
     F₁ genotypes (2n)   **Rr Yy**   ×   **RrYy**
     Meiosis
     Gametes (n) (as shown by ♂ and ♀).

Random fertilisation (as shown by Punnett square)

F₂ genotypes (2n) (listed in each square)
F₂ phenotypes   9 round yellow: 3 round green: 3 wrinkled yellow: 1 wrinkled green seeds

Fig 23.4 (a) Stages in the formation of F₁ phenotypes from homozygous parents. This is an example of a dihybrid cross since two characteristics are being considered. (b) Use of the Punnett square to show all possible combinations of gametes to form F₂ genotypes

the heterozygotes, this condition is known as **dihybrid inheritance.**

In one of his experiments Mendel used pea shape and pea cotyledon colour as the characteristics. Using the same techniques as described in section 23.1.1, he crossed pure-breeding (homozygous) plants having round and yellow peas with pure-breeding plants having wrinkled and green peas. The F₁ generation seeds were round and yellow. Mendel knew that these characteristics were dominant from earlier monohybrid breeding experiments but it was the nature and number of organisms of the F₂ generation produced from the self-pollination of the F₁ plants that now interested him. He collected a total of 556 F₂ seeds from the F₁ generation which showed the following characteristics:

> 315 round and yellow,
> 101 wrinkled and yellow,
> 108 round and green and
> 32 wrinkled and green.

The proportions of each phenotype approximated to a ratio of 9:3:3:1. This is known as the **dihybrid ratio**. Mendel made two deductions from these observations.

(1) Two new combinations of characteristics had appeared in the F₂ generation: wrinkled and yellow, and round and green.

(2) The ratios of each pair of allelomorphic characteristics (phenotypes determined by different alleles) appeared in the monohybrid ratio of 3:1, that is 423 round to 133 wrinkled, and 416 yellow to 140 green.

On the basis of these results Mendel was able to state that the two pairs of characteristics (seed shape and colour),

whilst combining in the F₁ generation, separate and behave independently from one another in subsequent generations. This forms the basis of **Mendel's second law** or the **principle of independent assortment** which states that,

> any one of a pair of characteristics may combine with either one of another pair.

The above experiment can be written out in terms of our present knowledge of genetics as shown in fig 23.4a. As a result of separation (segregation) of alleles (**R**, **r**, **Y** and **y**) and their independent assortment (rearrangement or **recombination**) four possible arrangements of alleles can be found in each of the male and female gametes. In order to demonstrate all the possible combinations of gametes that occur during random fertilisation a **Punnett square** is used. This is a grid named after the Cambridge geneticist R. C. Punnett and its value lies in minimising the errors which can occur when listing all possible combinations of gametes. It is advisable when filling in the Punnett square to enter all the 'male' gametes first in the vertical squares and then enter all the 'female' gametes in the horizontal squares. Likewise, when determining the F₂ phenotypes, it is advisable to mark off identical phenotypes in some easily identifiable way, as shown in fig 23.4b. From figs 23.4a and b, which are based on Mendel's first and second laws, it can be seen that each F₁ male and female genotype can give rise to gametes with the following combination of alleles;

R can only be present with **Y** or **y** (not **r**), that is **RY** or **Ry**,

r can only be present with **Y** or **y** (not **R**), that is **rY** or **ry**.
Thus there is a 1 in 4 chance of any gamete containing any of the four allele combinations shown above.

From a consideration of monohybrid inheritance, where $\frac{3}{4}$ of the F_2 phenotypes show the dominant allele and $\frac{1}{4}$ the recessive allele, the probability of the four alleles appearing in any F_2 phenotype is as follows:

round (dominant) $\frac{3}{4}$
yellow (dominant) $\frac{3}{4}$
wrinkled (recessive) $\frac{1}{4}$
green (recessive) $\frac{1}{4}$

Hence the probability of the following combinations of alleles appearing in the F_2 phenotypes is as follows:

round and yellow $= \frac{3}{4} \times \frac{3}{4} = \frac{9}{16}$
round and green $= \frac{3}{4} \times \frac{1}{4} = \frac{3}{16}$
wrinkled and yellow $= \frac{1}{4} \times \frac{3}{4} = \frac{3}{16}$
wrinkled and green $= \frac{1}{4} \times \frac{1}{4} = \frac{1}{16}$

The results of Mendel's breeding experiments with two pairs of contrasted characteristics approximated to the theoretical values shown above.

> **23.3** In the guinea pig, (*Cavia*), there are two alleles for hair colour, black and white, and two alleles for hair length, short and long. In a breeding experiment all the F_1 phenotypes produced from a cross between pure-breeding, short black-haired and pure-breeding, long white-haired parents had short black hair. Explain (*a*) which alleles are dominant, and (*b*) the expected proportions of F_2 phenotypes.
>
> **23.4** Flower colour in sweet pea plants is determined by two allelomorphic pairs of genes (**R,r**, and **S,s**). If at least one dominant gene from each allelomorphic pair is present the flowers are purple. All other genotypes are white.
> If two purple plants, each having the genotype **RrSs**, are crossed, what will be the phenotypic ratio of the offspring?

23.1.4 Summary of Mendel's hypotheses

The following summary includes terms taken from our present knowledge of the nature of genetics.
(1) Each characteristic of an organism is controlled by a pair of alleles.
(2) If an organism has two unlike alleles for a given characteristic, one may be expressed (the dominant allele) to the total exclusion of the other (the recessive allele).
(3) During meiosis each pair of alleles separates (segregates) and each gamete receives one of each pair of alleles (*the principle of segregation*).
(4) During gamete formation in each sex, either one of a pair of alleles may enter the same gamete cell (combine randomly) with either one of another pair (*the principle of independent assortment*).

(5) Each allele is transmitted from generation to generation as a discrete unchanging unit.
(6) Each organism inherits one allele (for each characteristic) from each parent.
NB The mechanism of dihybrid inheritance, the examples quoted in this section and the typical dihybrid ratio of 9:3:3:1 only apply to characteristics controlled by genes on *different* chromosomes. Genes situated on the *same* chromosome may not show this pattern of independent assortment as described in section 23.3.

23.2 The chromosomal basis of inheritance

Mendel published his research data and hypotheses in 1866 in a journal, *The Proceedings of the Brünn Natural History Society*, which was sent to most of the learned scientific societies throughout the world. In all cases they failed to appreciate the importance of his findings, possibly because scientists at the time were unable to relate them to any physical structures in the gametes by which the hereditary factors might be transmitted from parent to offspring.

By 1900, as a result of improvements in the optical properties of microscopes and advances in cytological techniques, the behaviour of chromosomes in gametes and zygotes had been observed. In 1875 Hertwig noted that during the fertilisation of sea urchin eggs two nuclei, one from the sperm and one from the egg, fused together. Boveri, in 1902, demonstrated the importance of the nucleus in controlling the development of characteristics in organisms, and in 1882 Flemming clarified the chromosomal events involved in mitosis.

In 1900 the significance of Mendel's work was realised almost simultaneously by three scientists, de Vries, Correns and Tschermak. In fact, it was Correns who summarised Mendel's conclusions in the familiar form of two principles and coined the term '**factor**', Mendel having used the term '*elemente*' to describe the hereditary unit. It was an American, William Sutton, however, who noticed the striking similarities between the behaviour of chromosomes during gamete formation and fertilisation, and the transmission of Mendel's hereditary factors. These have been summarised in table 23.3.

On the basis of the evidence suggested above, Sutton and Boveri proposed that chromosomes were the carriers of Mendel's factors, the so-called **chromosome theory of heredity**. According to this theory, each pair of factors is carried by a pair of homologous chromosomes, with each chromosome carrying one of the factors. Since the number of characteristics of any organism vastly outnumbers the chromosomes, as revealed by microscopy, each chromosome must carry many factors.

The term **factor** as the basic unit of heredity was replaced by Johannsen, in 1909, with the term **gene**. Whilst gene is used to describe the unit of heredity, it is the alternative

Table 23.3 A summary of the similarities between events occurring during meiosis and fertilisation and Mendel's hypotheses.

Meiosis and fertilisation	Mendel's hypotheses
Diploid cells contain *pairs* of chromosomes (homologous chromosomes)	Characteristics are controlled by *pairs* of factors
Homologous chromosomes *separate* during meiosis	Pairs of factors *separate* during gamete formation
One homologous chromosome passes into each gamete cell	Each gamete receives *one* factor
Only the *nucleus* of the male gamete fuses with the egg cell nucleus	Factors are transmitted from generation to generation as *discrete units*
Homologous pairs of chromosomes are restored at fertilisation, each gamete (♂ and ♀) contributing *one* homologous chromosome	Each organism inherits *one* factor from each parent

forms of the gene or **alleles** which influence phenotypic expression. Alleles are the alternative forms in which a gene may exist and they occupy corresponding positions or **loci** (singular **locus**) on **homologous chromosomes**, as shown in fig 23.5.

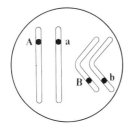

Fig 23.5 *A cell showing two pairs of homologous chromosomes. The positions of two different gene loci are indicated by circles. In this example two gene loci are shown situated on different pairs of homologous chromosomes and each gene is present as two alleles*

Mendel's principle of segregation of factors could now be explained in terms of the separation (segregation) of homologous chromosomes which occurs during anaphase I of meiosis and the random distribution of alleles into gamete cells. These events are summarised in fig 23.6.

23.2.1 Chromosomal explanation of independent assortment

Mendel's principle of independent assortment may also be explained in terms of the movement of chromosomes during meiosis. During gamete formation the distribution of each allele from a pair of homologous chromosomes is entirely independent of the distribution of alleles of other pairs. This situation is described in fig 23.7. It is the random alignment or assortment of homologous chromosomes on the equatorial spindle during metaphase I of meiosis, and their subsequent separation during metaphase I and anaphase I, that leads to the variety of allele recombinations in the gamete cells. It is possible to predict the number of allele combinations in either the male or female gamete using the general formula 2^n, where $n =$ haploid number of chromosomes. In the case of humans, where $n = 23$, the possible number of different combinations is $2^{23} = 8\,388\,608$.

> **23.5** The deposition of starch in pollen grains in maize is controlled by the presence of one allele of a certain gene. The other allele of that gene results in no starch being deposited. Explain why half the pollen grains produced by a given maize plant contain starch.
>
> **23.6** Calculate the number of different combinations of chromosomes in the pollen grains of the crocus (*Crocus balansae*) which has a diploid number of six ($2n = 6$).

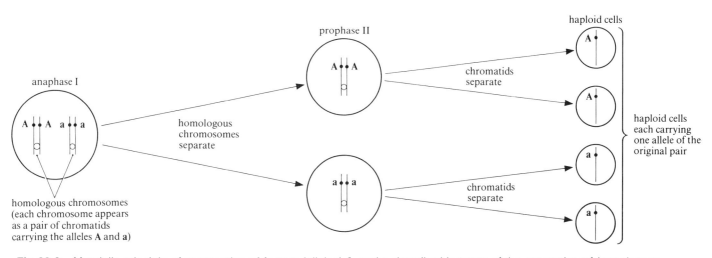

Fig 23.6 *Mendel's principle of segregation of factors (alleles)* **A** *and* **a** *described in terms of the separation of homologous chromosomes which occurs during meiosis*

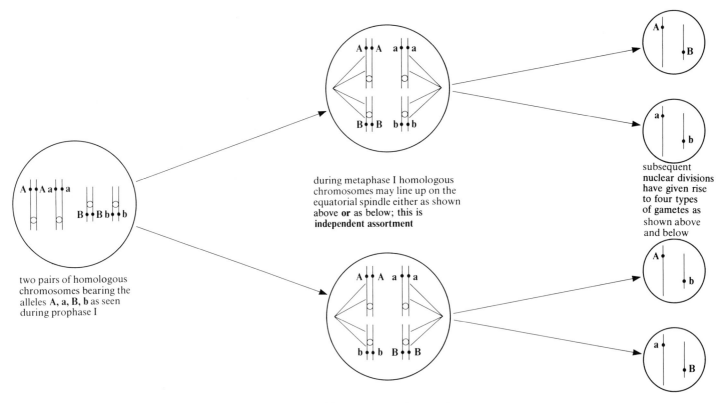

Fig 23.7 *Mendel's principle of independent assortment of factors (alleles)* **A, a, B, b,** *described in terms of the separation of homologous chromosomes which occurs during meiosis*

23.3 Linkage

All the situations and examples discussed so far in this chapter have dealt with the inheritance of genes situated on different chromosomes. Cytological studies have revealed that humans possess 46 chromosomes in all the somatic (body) cells. Since humans possess thousands of characteristics such as blood group, eye colour and the ability to secrete insulin, it follows that each chromosome must carry a large number of genes.

Genes situated on the same chromosome are said to be **linked**. All genes on a single chromosome form a **linkage group** and usually pass into the same gamete and are inherited together. As a result of this, genes belonging to the same linkage group usually do not show independent assortment. Since these genes do not conform to Mendel's principle of independent assortment they fail to produce the expected 9:3:3:1 ratio in a breeding situation involving the inheritance of two pairs of contrasted characteristics (dihybrid inheritance). In these situations a variety of ratios are produced which may be explained quite simply now that we possess a basic understanding of the mechanisms of inheritance as revealed by Mendel. (At this point it is worth re-emphasising Mendel's good fortune in choosing to study the inheritance of pairs of characteristics located on *different* chromosomes.) In *Drosophila* the genes for body colour and wing length have the following **allelomorphs** (phenotypic characteristics determined by

different alleles): grey and black body, and long and vestigial (short) wings. Grey body and long wing are dominant. If pure-breeding grey-bodied long-winged *Drosophila* are crossed with black-bodied vestigial-winged *Drosophila*, the expected F_2 phenotypic ratio would be 9:3:3:1. This would indicate a normal case of Mendelian dihybrid inheritance with random assortment resulting from the genes for body colour and wing length being situated on non-homologous chromosomes. However this result is not obtained. Instead the F_2 show an approximately 3:1 ratio of parental phenotypes. This may be explained by assuming that the genes for body colour and wing length are found on the same chromosome, that is they are linked, as shown in fig 23.8.

In practice, though, this 3:1 ratio is never achieved and four phenotypes are invariably produced. This is because **total** linkage is rare. Most breeding experiments involving linkage produce approximately equal numbers of the parental phenotypes and a significantly smaller number of phenotypes showing new combinations of characteristics, also in equal numbers. These latter phenotypes are described as **recombinants**. From this it is possible to produce the following definition of linkage.

Two or more genes are said to be linked when phenotypes with new gene combinations (recombinants) occur less frequently than the parental phenotypes.

The events leading to the discovery of linkage by the American Thomas H. Morgan may be summarised in one

Let:
  G represent grey body (dominant)
  g represent black body (recessive)
  L represent long wing (dominant)
  l represent vestigial wing (recessive)

Parental phenotypes   grey body, long wing   ×   black body, vestigial wing

Parental genotypes (2n)

   ×

Meiosis

Gametes (n)

      ×

Random fertilisation

F₁ genotypes (2n)

F₁ phenotypes   all heterozygous grey body, long-winged offspring

The F₁ generation was allowed to interbreed

F₁ phenotypes   grey body, long wing   ×   grey body, long wing

F₁ genotypes (2n)

×

Meiosis

Gametes (n)

   ×

Random fertilisation

F₂ genotypes (2n)

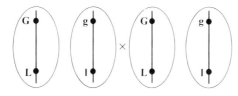

F₂ phenotypes   3 grey body, long wing: 1 black body, vestigial wing

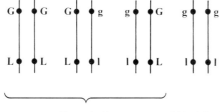

Fig 23.8 *Genetic explanation of the 3:1 ratio produced in F₂ phenotypes as a result of linkage*

of his experiments in which he predicted the results of a test cross between heterozygous grey-bodied, long-winged *Drosophila* (the F₁ generation of the experimental cross shown in fig 23.8) and homozygous recessive black-bodied vestigial-winged *Drosophila*. The two possible outcomes were predicted as follows:

(1) If the four alleles for grey and black body, and long and vestigal wings, were on different pairs of chromosomes (that is *not* linked) they should show independent assortment and produce the following phenotypic ratios:

1 grey body, long wing: 1 grey body, vestigial wing: 1 black body, long wing: 1 black body, vestigial wing.

(2) If the alleles for body colour and wing length were situated on the same pair of chromosomes (that is linked) the following phenotypic ratio would be produced:

1 grey body, long wing:1 black body, vestigial wing.

An explanation of these predictions is given in fig 23.9.

Morgan carried out this test cross several times and never obtained either of the predicted outcomes. Each time he obtained the following results:

41.5% grey body long wing
41.5% black body vestigial wing
8.5% grey body vestigial wing
8.5% black body long wing

On the basis of these results he postulated that:
(1) the genes were located on chromosomes,
(2) both the genes were situated on the same chromosome, that is linked,
(3) the alleles for each gene were on homologous chromosomes,
(4) alleles were exchanged between homologous chromosomes during meiosis.

The reappearance of recombinant alleles in 17% of the offspring was explained in terms of point (4). This is known as **crossing-over**.

23.7 A homozygous purple-flowered short-stemmed plant was crossed with a homozygous red-flowered long-stemmed plant and the F₁ phenotypes had purple flowers and short stems. When the F₁ generation was test crossed with a double homozygous recessive plant the following progeny were produced.

52 purple flower, short stem
47 purple flower, long stem
49 red flower, short stem
45 red flower, long stem

Explain fully these results.

(a) If the four alleles are situated on different pairs of chromosomes

Testcross phenotypes grey body, long wing × black body, vestigial wing
 (heterozygous) (homozygous)

Testcross genotypes (2n) **GgLl** × **ggll**

Meiosis

Gametes (n)
(as shown by
♂ and ♀)

Random fertilisation
(as shown in Punnett
square)

♀ \ ♂	GL	Gl	gL	gl
gl	GL gl	Gl gl	gL gl	gl gl

Offspring genotypes (2n)
(listed in each square)

Offspring phenotypes 1 grey body, long wing: 1 grey body, vestigial wing:
 1 black body, long wing: 1 black body, vestigial wing

(b) If the four alleles are situated on the same pair of chromosomes

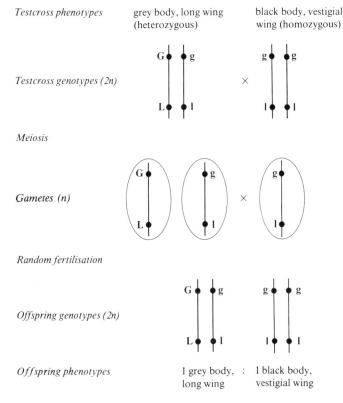

Testcross phenotypes grey body, long wing black body, vestigial
 (heterozygous) wing (homozygous)

Testcross genotypes (2n)

Meiosis

Gametes (n)

Random fertilisation

Offspring genotypes (2n)

Offspring phenotypes 1 grey body, : 1 black body,
 long wing vestigial wing

Fig 23.9 (a) and (b) Genetic explanation of Morgan's
predictions

23.3.1 Crossing-over and crossover values

In 1909 the Belgian cytologist Janssens
observed **chiasmata formation** during prophase I of meiosis

(section 22.3). The genetic significance of this process was
clarified by Morgan who proposed that crossing-over of
alleles occurred as a result of the breakage and recombination
of homologous chromosomes during chiasmata.
Subsequent research based on the microscopic examination
of cells and recombinant phenotypic ratios has
confirmed that crossover of genetic material occurs
between virtually all homologous chromosomes during
meiosis. The alleles of parental linkage groups separate
and new associations of alleles are formed in the
gamete cells, a process known as **genetic recombination**.
Offspring formed from these gametes showing 'new'
combinations of characteristics are known as **recombinants**.
Thus crossing-over is a major source of observable
genetic variation within populations.

The behaviour of a pair of homologous chromosomes in
Drosophila, carrying the alleles grey body and long wing
(both dominant) and black body and vestigial wing (both
recessive), during formation of chiasmata may be used to
illustrate the principle of crossing-over. A cross between a
male homozygous grey-bodied long-winged *Drosophila*
and a female homozygous black-bodied vestigial-winged
Drosophila produced heterozygous F₁ offspring with
grey bodies and long wings as shown in fig 23.10.

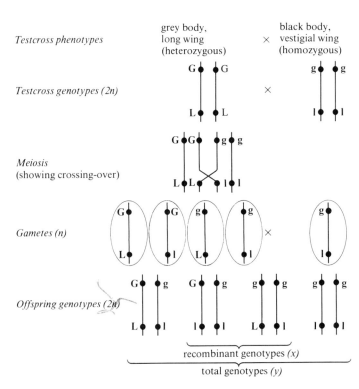

Testcross phenotypes grey body, black body,
 long wing × vestigial wing
 (heterozygous) (homozygous)

Testcross genotypes (2n)

Meiosis
(showing crossing-over)

Gametes (n)

Offspring genotypes (2n)

recombinant genotypes (x)
total genotypes (y)

Fig 23.10 *Genetic explanation of crossing-over and the
reappearance of recombinant genotypes. The recombination
frequency can be calculated by counting the number of
individuals showing recombination and the total number of
individuals and applying the following formula:*

$$recombination\ frequency\ (\%) = \frac{x}{y} \times 100$$

Test crossing the F_1 generation flies with homozygous double recessive flies produced the following results.

Parental phenotypes $\left\{\begin{array}{ll}\text{grey body, long wing} & 965 \\ \text{black body, vestigial wing} & 944\end{array}\right.$

Recombinant phenotypes $\left\{\begin{array}{ll}\text{black body, long wing} & 206 \\ \text{grey body , vestigial wing} & 185\end{array}\right.$

These results indicate that the genes for body colour and wing length are linked. (Remember that a dihybrid cross between an F_1 heterozygote and a double homozygous recessive would have produced a 1:1:1:1 phenotypic ratio if the genes had been situated on different chromosomes and therefore had undergone random assortment.) Using the figures obtained from the above cross it is possible to calculate the recombination frequency of the genes for body colour and wing length.

The **recombination frequency** is calculated using the formula

$$\frac{\text{number of individuals showing recombination}}{\text{number of offspring}} \times 100$$

From the example above the recombination frequency (%) is

$$\frac{(206 + 185)}{(965 + 944) + (206 + 185)} \times 100$$

$$= \frac{391 \times 100}{2300}$$

$$= 17\%.$$

This value indicates the number of crossovers which have occurred during gamete formation. A. H. Sturtevant, a student of Morgan, postulated that the recombinant frequency or **crossover frequency (crossover value (COV))** demonstrated that genes are arranged linearly along the chromosome. More importantly, he suggested that the crossover frequency reflects the relative positions of genes on a chromosome because the further apart linked genes are on the chromosomes, the greater the possibility of crossing-over occurring between them, that is the greater the crossover frequency (fig 23.11).

Fig 23.11 *Three gene loci represented by* **A**, **B** *and* **C** *are shown on the chromosome. Crossing-over and separation of genes is more likely to occur between* **A** *and* **C** *than between* **B** *and* **C** *or* **A** *and* **B** *since the frequency of crossing-over is related to the distance between the genes*

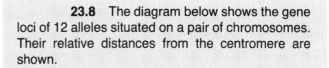

23.8 The diagram below shows the gene loci of 12 alleles situated on a pair of chromosomes. Their relative distances from the centromere are shown.

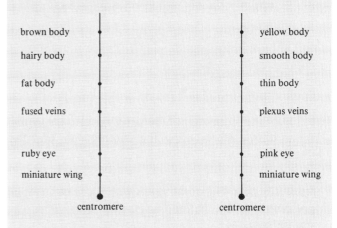

(a) What term is used to describe the chromosomes shown above?
(b) Crossing-over would probably occur most frequently between which two gene loci?
(c) Will crossing-over occur between the genes for eye colour and antenna shape? Explain your answer.

Computer program. The relationship between gene positions, recombination frequency and crossover frequency for two-point and three-point crosses, and single or double crossovers, can be investigated using the computer program CROSSOVER (CUP Micro Software).

23.4 Gene mapping

The major significance of calculating crossover frequencies is that it enables geneticists to produce maps showing the relative positions of genes on chromosomes. Chromosome maps are constructed by directly converting the crossover frequency or value between genes into hypothetical distances along the chromosome. A crossover frequency or value (COV) of 4% between genes **A** and **B** means that those genes are situated 4 units apart on the same chromosome. A COV of 9% for a pair of genes **A** and **C** would indicate that they were 9 units apart, but it would not indicate the linear sequence of the genes, as shown in fig 23.12.

Fig 23.12 *Possible gene loci of* **A**, **B** *and* **C** *on the basis of the data presented*

In practice it is usual to determine crossover values for at least three genes at once, as this **triangulation** process enables the sequence of the genes to be determined as well as the distances between them. Consider the following crossover values as determined by a series of breeding experiments involving four genes **P**, **Q**, **R** and **S**.

$$\mathbf{P} - \mathbf{Q} = 24\%$$
$$\mathbf{R} - \mathbf{P} = 14\%$$
$$\mathbf{R} - \mathbf{S} = 8\%$$
$$\mathbf{S} - \mathbf{P} = 6\%$$

To calculate the sequence and distances apart of the genes, a line is drawn representing the chromosome and the following procedure carried out.

(1) Insert the positions of the genes with the least COV in the middle of the chromosome, that is $\mathbf{S} - \mathbf{P} = 6\%$ (fig 23.13*a*).
(2) Examine the next largest COV, that is $\mathbf{R} - \mathbf{S} = 8\%$, and insert both possible positions of **R** on the chromosome, relative to S (fig 23.13*b*).
(3) Repeat the procedure for the next largest COV, that is $\mathbf{R} - \mathbf{P} = 14\%$. This indicates that the right-hand position of **R** is incorrect (fig 23.13*c*).
(4) Repeat the procedure for the COV for $\mathbf{P} - \mathbf{Q} = 24\%$ (fig 23.13*d*). The position of **Q** cannot be ascertained without additional information. If, for example, the COV for $\mathbf{Q} - \mathbf{R} = 10\%$ this would confirm the left-hand position for gene **Q**.

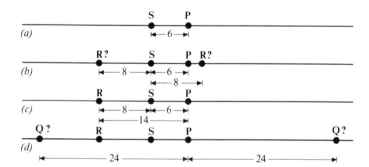

Fig 23.13 *Use of the triangulation process to establish the positions of genes P, Q, R and S on a chromosome*

A problem which arises in preparing chromosome maps is that of **double crossover**, particularly when considering genes which are widely separated, since the number of apparent crossovers will be less than the actual number. For example, if crossovers occur between alleles **A** and **B** and **B** and **C** in fig 23.14, **A** and **C** will still appear linked, but the chromosome will now carry the recessive allele **b**.

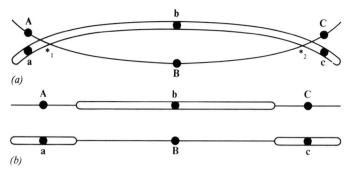

Fig 23.14 *(a) A pair of homologous chromatids, one carrying the dominant alleles* **A**, **B** *and* **C** *and the other carrying the recessive alleles* **a**, **b** *and* **c***. Crossing-over occurs at two points* *₁ *and* *₂*. (b) The result of separation of the chromatids in which the sequences of alleles are different, although the sequences of gene loci and the distances between them remain the same*

23.9 In maize the genes for coloured seed and full seed are dominant to the genes for colourless seed and shrunken seed. Pure-breeding strains of the double dominant variety were crossed with the double recessive variety and a test cross of the F_1 generation produced the following results.

coloured, full seed	380
colourless, shrunken seed	396
coloured, shrunken seed	14
colourless, full seed	10

Calculate the distance in units between the genes for coloured seed and seed shape on the chromosomes.

23.5 Linkage groups and chromosomes

Much of the evidence presented in this chapter so far has shown how our knowledge of the mechanics of inheritance has gradually increased. Most of the research into genetics in the early part of this century involved establishing the role of genes in inheritance. Morgan's research with the fruit fly (*Drosophila melanogaster*) established that the majority of phenotypic characteristics were transmitted together in four groups and these were called **linkage groups**. It was observed that the number of linkage groups corresponded to the number of pairs of chromosomes.

Studies on other organisms produced similar results. Breeding experiments using a variety of organisms revealed that some linkage groups were larger then others (that is they carried more genes). Examination of chromosomes in these organisms showed that they varied in length. Morgan demonstrated that there was a distinct relationship between these observations. This provided further confirmatory evidence that genes were located on chromosomes.

23.5.1   Giant chromosomes and genes

In 1913 Sturtevant began his work on mapping the positions of genes on the chromosomes of *Drosophila* but it was 21 years before there was a possibility of linking visible structures on chromosomes with genes. In 1934, it was observed that the chromosomes in the salivary gland cells of *Drosophila* were about 100 times larger than chromosomes from other body cells. For some reason these chromosomes duplicate without separating until there are several thousand lying side by side. When stained they can be seen with the light microscope and appear to be made up of alternating light and dark bands. Each chromosome has its own distinctive pattern of bands (fig 23.15). It was originally thought, or rather hoped, that these bands were genes, but this is not the case. Phenotypic abnormalities may be artificially induced in *Drosophila* and these correlate with changes in chromosomal banding patterns, as observed with the microscope. These phenotypic and chromosomal abnormalities in turn correlate with gene loci shown on chromosome maps which have been constructed on the basis of crossover values obtained from breeding experiments. Therefore it is possible to say that the bands on the chromosomes indicate the *positions* of genes but are not themselves genes.

23.6   Sex determination

The technique of relating phenotypic characteristics of organisms to the structure of their chromosomes, as described in earlier sections, is seen most clearly in the determination of sex. In *Drosophila* the observed phenotypic differences between the two sexes appear to be related to the differences in the size of their chromosomes, as shown in fig 23.16. Examination of the chromosome structure of a range of animals revealed that males and females showed certain chromosomal differences. Pairs of

Fig 23.16 *Structure of chromosomes in male and female* Drosophila melanogaster. *Four pairs of chromosomes are shown. The sex chromosomes are numbered I*

chromosomes (homologous chromosomes) are found in all cells, but one pair of chromosomes always shows differences between the sexes. These are the **sex chromosomes** or **heterosomes**. All other chromosomes are known as **autosomal chromosomes** or **autosomes**. As can be seen in fig 23.16, *Drosophila* has four pairs of chromosomes. Three pairs appear identical in both sexes (numbers II, III and IV), but the other pair, whilst appearing identical in the female, differ in the male. The chromosomes are known as X and Y chromosomes, and the genotype of the female is XX and that of the male is XY (fig 23.17). These characteristic sex genotypes are found in most animals, including humans; but in the case of birds (including poultry), moths and butterflies the sex genotypes are reversed: the females are XY and the males are XX. In some insects, such as the grasshopper the Y chromosome may be absent entirely and so the male has the genotype XO.

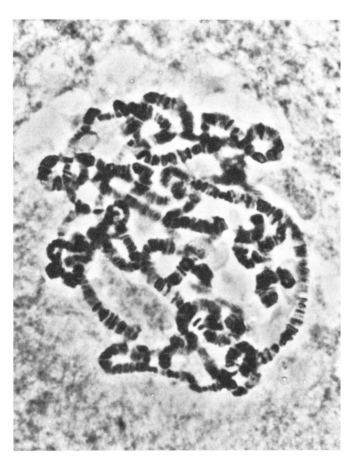

Fig 23.15 *Giant chromosomes from the salivary glands of* Drosophila melanogaster. *Four pairs of chromosomes are shown joined at their centromeres*

Fig 23.17 *Human sex chromosomes as they appear during metaphase of mitosis*

Fig 23.18 *Genetic explanation of the sex ratio in humans*

Parental phenotypes	female (♀)	×	male (♂)
Parental genotypes (2n)	XX	×	XY
Meiosis			
Gametes(n)	Ⓧ Ⓧ	×	Ⓧ Ⓨ
Random fertilisation			
Offspring genotypes (2n)	XX XY		XX XY
Offspring phenotypes	♀ ♂		♀ ♂

sex ratio 1 female : 1 male

In the production of gametes the sex chromosomes segregate in typical Mendelian fashion. For example, in mammals each ovum contains an X chromosome; in males one half of the sperms contains an X chromosome and the other half contains a Y chromosome as shown in fig 23.18. The sex of the offspring depends upon which type of sperm fertilises the ovum. The sex having the XX genotype is described as **homogametic** as it produces gamete cells containing only X chromosomes. Organisms with the XY genotype are described as **heterogametic** since half their gametes contain the X chromosome and half the Y chromosome. In humans, the genotypic sex of an individual is determined by examining non-dividing cells. One X chromosome always appears in the active state, which has the normal appearance. If another is present, it is seen in a resting state as a tightly coiled dark-staining body called the **Barr body**. The number of Barr bodies is always one less than the number of X chromosomes present, that is male (XY) = 0, female (XX) = 1. The function of the Y chromosome appears to vary according to species. In humans the presence of a Y chromosome controls the differentiation of the testis which subsequently influences the development of the genital organs and male characteristics (section 20.3.1). In some organisms, however, the Y chromosome does not carry genes concerned with sex. In fact it is described as genetically inert or genetically empty since it carries so few genes. In *Drosophila* it is thought that the genes determining male characteristics are carried on the autosomes and their phenotypic effects are masked by the presence of a pair of X chromosomes. Male characteristics, on the other hand, appear in the presence of a single X chromosome. This is an example of **sex-limited inheritance**, as opposed to sex-linked inheritance, and in humans is thought to cause suppression of the genes for growth of beard in females.

Morgan and his co-workers noticed that inheritance of eye colour in *Drosophila* was related to the sex of the parent flies. Red eye is dominant over white eye. A red-eyed male crossed with a white-eyed female produced equal numbers of F_1 red-eyed females and white-eyed males (fig 23.19a). A white-eyed male, however, crossed with a red-eyed female produced equal numbers of F_1 red-eyed males and females (fig 23.19b). Inbreeding these F_1 flies produced red-eyed females, red-eyed males and white-eyed males but *no* white-eyed females, (fig 23.19c). The fact that male flies showed the recessive characteristic more frequently than female flies suggested that the white eye recessive allele was present on the X chromosome and that the Y chromosome lacked the eye colour gene. To test this hypothesis Morgan crossed the original white-eyed male with an F_1 red-eyed female (fig 23.19d). The offspring included red-eyed and white-eyed males and females. From this Morgan rightly concluded that only the X chromosome carries the gene for eye colour. There is no gene locus for eye colour on the Y chromosome. This phenomenon is known as **sex linkage**.

23.10 In *Drosophila* the genes for wing length and for eye colour are sex-linked. Normal wing and red eye are dominant to miniature wing and white eye.

(a) In a cross between a miniature wing, red-eyed male and a homozygous normal wing, white-eyed female, explain fully the appearance of (i) the F_1 and (ii) the F_2 generations.

(b) Crossing a female from the F_1 generation above with a miniature wing, white-eyed male gave the following results:

normal wing, white-eyed males and females	35
normal wing, red-eyed males and females	17
miniature wing, white-eyed males and females	18
miniature wing, red-eyed males and females	36

Account for the appearance and numbers of the phenotypes shown above.

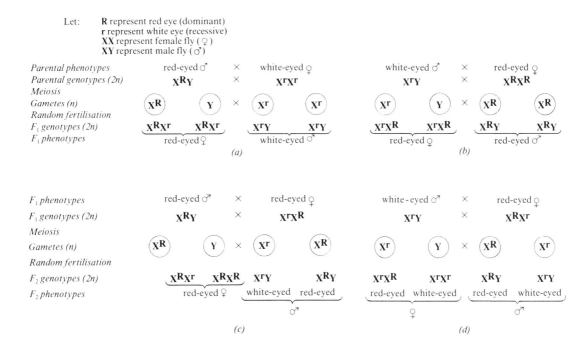

Let: **R** represent red eye (dominant)
      r represent white eye (recessive)
      XX represent female fly (♀)
      XY represent male fly (♂)

(a)

(b)

(c)

(d)

Fig 23.19 *(a) and (b) Morgan's reciprocal experimental crosses between red-eyed and white-eyed Drosophila. Note the low frequency of appearance of white eyes. (c) Morgan's confirmatory inbreeding experimental cross between an F₁ red-eyed male and an F₁ (heterozygous) red-eyed female. (d) The experimental cross between a white-eyed male and an F₁ (heterozygous) red-eyed female. Note the appearance of the white-eyed characteristic only in homozygous white-eyed female flies*

23.6.1 Sex linkage

Genes carried on the sex chromosomes are said to be sex-linked. In the case of the heterogametic sex there is a portion of the X chromosome for which there is no homologous region of the Y chromosome (fig 23.20).

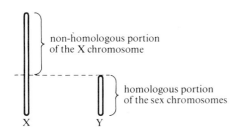

non-homologous portion
of the X chromosome

homologous portion
of the sex chromosomes

X   Y

Fig 23.20 *Homologous and non-homologous regions of the sex chromosomes*

Characteristics determined by genes carried on the non-homologous portion of the X chromosome therefore appear in males even if they are recessive. This special form of linkage explains the inheritance of **sex-linked traits** such as red–green colour blindness, premature balding and haemophilia. Haemophilia or 'bleeder's disease' is a sex-linked recessive condition which prevents the formation of factor VIII, an important factor in increasing the rate of blood clotting. The gene for substance VIII is carried on the non-homologous portion of the X chromosome and can appear in two allelomorphic forms: normal (dominant) and mutant (recessive). The following possible genotypes and phenotypes can occur.

genotype	phenotype
$X^H X^H$	normal female
$X^H X^h$	normal female (carrier)
$X^H Y$	normal male
$X^h Y$	haemophiliac male

In all sex-linked traits, females who are heterozygous are described as **carriers** of the trait. They are phenotypically normal but half their gametes carry the recessive gene. Despite the father having a normal gene there is a 50% probability (probability $\frac{1}{2}$) that sons of carrier females will show the trait. In the situation where a carrier haemophiliac female marries a normal male they may have children with phenotypes as shown in fig 23.21.

Let: **H** represent normal allele for blood clotting (dominant)
      h represent allele for haemophilia (recessive)
      XX represent female chromosomes
      XY represent male chromosomes

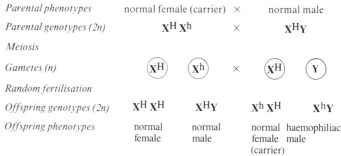

Fig 23.21 *Mechanism of inheritance of the sex-linked allele for haemophilia*

847

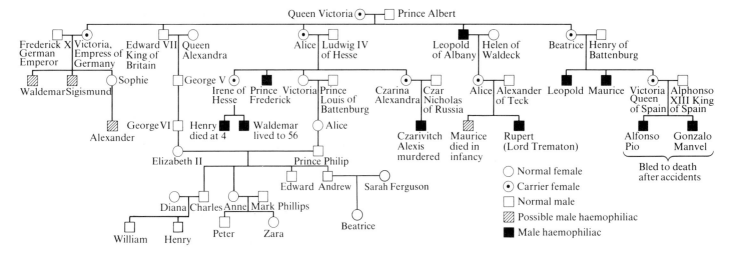

One of the best-documented examples of the inheritance of haemophilia is shown by the descendants of Queen Victoria. It is thought that the gene for haemophilia arose as a mutation in Queen Victoria or one of her parents. Fig 23.22 shows how the haemophilia gene was inherited by her descendants.

Fig 23.22 *Transmission of haemophilia in the descendants of Queen Victoria. In the diagram only those descendants involved in the transmission and appearance of haemophilia have been shown. The ancestry of the British Royal Family has been given to show why haemophilia is absent from seven generations of Queen Victoria's descendants*

23.11 Body colour in cats and magpie moths is controlled by a sex-linked gene on the X chromosome. The following data were obtained in two breeding experiments where the homogametic sex was homozygous for body colour in the parental generation.

	Magpie moth (normal colour dominant to pale colour)	Cat (black colour dominant to yellow colour)
Parental phenotypes	pale male × normal female	black male × yellow female
Offspring phenotypes	1 normal male : 1 pale female	1 yellow male : 1 black female

Which is the heterogametic sex in each of these organisms?

23.7 Gene interactions

The topics in this chapter so far have represented the simpler aspects of genetics: dominance, monohybrid and dihybrid inheritance, linkage, sex determination and sex linkage. There are many situations in genetics where genes interact in ways other than those already described and it is probable that the majority of phenotypic characteristics in organisms result from these. Several types of gene interaction will now be considered.

23.7.1 Codominance

There are several conditions where two or more alleles do not show complete dominance or recessiveness due to the failure of any allele to be dominant in the heterozygous condition. This state of **codominance** is an exception to the situation described by Mendel in his monohybrid breeding experiments. It is fortunate that he did not select organisms which show this condition as it may have unnecessarily complicated his early work.

Codominance is found in both plants and animals. In most cases the heterozygote has a phenotype which is intermediate between the homozygous dominant and recessive conditions. An example is the production of blue Andalusian fowls by crossing pure-breeding black and splashed white parental stocks. The presence of black plumage is the result of the possession of an allele for the production of the black pigment melanin. The splashed white stock lack this allele. The heterozygotes show a partial development of melanin which produces a blue sheen in the plumage.

As there are no accepted genotypic symbols for alleles showing codominance, the importance of specifying symbols in genetic explanations is apparent. For example, in the case of the Andalusian fowl, the following genotypic symbols may be used to illustrate the alleles: black – **B**; splashed white – **b**, **W**, **B**^{W} or **B**^{BW}. The results of a cross between black and splashed white homozygous fowl are shown in fig 23.23.

Let:
    B represent the black allele
    B^W represent the splashed white allele

Parental phenotypes	black (homozygous)	×	splashed white (homozygous)
Parental genotypes (2n)	**BB**	×	**B**^{W}**B**^{W}
Meiosis			
Gametes (n)	Ⓑ Ⓑ	×	Ⓑ^{W} Ⓑ^{W}
Random fertilisation			
F$_1$ genotypes (2n)	**BB**^{W} **BB**^{W}		**BB**^{W} **BB**^{W}
F$_1$ phenotypes	all 'blue' heterozygotes		

Fig 23.23 *The production of F$_1$ hybrids of Andalusian fowl*

If the F$_1$ generation are allowed to interbreed, the F$_2$ generation shows a modification of the normal Mendelian phenotypic monohybrid ratio of 3:1. In this case a phenotypic ratio of 1:2:1 is produced where half the F$_2$ generation have the F$_1$ genotype (fig 23.24). This ratio of 1:2:1 is characteristic of examples of codominance. Other examples are shown in table 23.4.

F$_1$ phenotypes	blue	×	blue
F$_1$ genotypes (2n)	**BB**^{W}	×	**BB**^{W}
Meiosis			
Gametes (n)	Ⓑ Ⓑ^{W}	×	Ⓑ Ⓑ^{W}
Random fertilisation			
F$_2$ genotypes (2n)	**BB** **BB**^{W} **BB**^{W} **B**^{W}**B**^{W}		
F$_2$ phenotypes	black blue splashed white		
	1 : 2 : 1		

Fig 23.24 *The production of F$_2$ hybrids of Andalusian fowl*

Table 23.4 Examples of codominance.

Characteristic	Alleles	Heterozygous phenotype
Antirrhinum flower (snapdragon)	red × white	pink
Mirabilis flower (four-o'clock flower)	red × white	pink
Short-horn cattle	red × white	roan
Angora and rex rabbits	long hair and short hair	intermediate silky fur

23.7.2 Multiple alleles

In all the cases studied so far, each characteristic has been controlled by a gene which may have appeared in one of two forms or alleles. There are several conditions where a single characteristic may appear in several different forms controlled by three or more alleles, of which any two may occupy the same gene loci on homologous chromosomes. This is known as the **multiple allele** (or **multiple allelomorph**) condition and it controls such characteristics as coat colour in mice, eye colour in mice and blood group in humans.

Inheritance of blood groups

Blood group is controlled by an autosomal gene. The gene locus is represented by the symbol **I** (which stands for isohaemagglutinogen) and there are three alleles represented by the symbols **A**, **B** and **o**. The alleles **A** and **B** are equally dominant and **o** is recessive to both. The genotypes shown in table 23.5 determine the phenotypic appearance of blood groups. The presence of a single dominant allele results in the blood producing a substance called agglutinin which acts as an antibody. For example, the genotype $I^A I^o$ would give rise to the agglutinogen **A** on the red blood cell membrane, and the plasma would contain the agglutinin **anti-B** (the blood group would be A). Blood-grouping is described in section 14.14.6.

Table 23.5 Human blood group genotypes.

Genotype	Blood group (phenotype)
$I^A I^A$	A
$I^A I^o$	A
$I^B I^B$	B
$I^B I^o$	B
$I^A I^B$	AB
$I^o I^o$	O

23.12 In cats, the genes controlling the coat colour are carried on the X chromosomes and are codominant. A black-coat female mated with a ginger-coat male produced a litter consisting of black male and tortoiseshell female kittens. What is the expected F$_2$ phenotypic ratio? Explain the results.

23.13 (a) Explain, using appropriate genetic symbols, the possible blood groups of children whose parents are both heterozygous, the father being blood group A and the mother B.

(b) If these parents have non-identical twins, what is the probability that both twins will have blood group A?

Fig 23.26 *Variation in comb shape in domestic fowl* (top left) *single comb,* (top right) *pea comb,* (bottom left) *rose comb,* (bottom right) *strawberry comb*

23.7.3   Lethal genes

There are several examples of conditions where a single gene may affect several characteristics, including mortality. In the case of humans and other mammals a certain recessive gene may lead to internal adhesions of the lungs resulting in death at birth. Another example involving a single gene affects the formation of cartilage and produces congenital deformities leading to fetal and neonatal death.

In chickens which are homozygous for an allele controlling feather structure called 'frizzled', several phenotypic effects result from the incomplete development of the feathers. These chickens lack adequate feather insulation and suffer from heat loss. To compensate for this they exhibit a range of structural and physiological adaptations, but these are largely unsuccessful and there is a high mortality rate.

The effects of a lethal gene are clearly illustrated by the inheritance of fur colour in mice. Wild mice have grey-coloured fur, a condition known as agouti. Some mice have yellow fur. Cross-breeding yellow mice produces offspring in the ratio 2 yellow fur : 1 agouti fur. These results can only be explained on the basis that yellow is dominant to agouti and that all the yellow coat mice are heterozygous. The atypical Mendelian ratio is explained by the fetal death of *homozygous* yellow coat mice (fig 23.25). Examination of the uteri of pregnant yellow mice from the

Let:
Y represent yellow fur (dominant)
y represent agouti fur (recessive)

Parental phenotypes	yellow fur	×	yellow fur
Parental genotypes (2n)	**Yy**	×	**Yy**
Meiosis			
Gametes (n)	(Y) (y)	×	(Y) (y)
Random fertilisation			
Offspring genotypes (2n)	YY Yy Yy		yy
Offspring phenotypes	1 yellow fur: 2 yellow fur : 1 agouti fur		
	die before birth		

Fig 23.25 *Genetic explanation of fur colour inheritance in mice showing the lethal genotype* **YY**

above cross revealed dead yellow fetuses. Similar examination of the uteri of crosses between yellow fur and agouti fur mice revealed no dead yellow fetuses. The explanation is that this cross would not produce homozygous yellow (**YY**) mice.

23.7.4   Gene-complex

The presence of a pair of alleles occupying a given gene locus and controlling the production of a single phenotypic characteristic is true in some cases only and exceptional in most organisms. Most characteristics are determined by the interaction of several genes which form a '**gene-complex**'. For example, a single characteristic may

be controlled by the interaction of two or more genes situated at different loci. In the case of the inheritance of the shape of the comb in domestic fowl there are genes at two loci situated on different chromosomes which interact and give rise to four distinct phenotypes, known as pea, rose, walnut and single combs (fig 23.26). The appearance of pea comb and rose comb are each determined by the presence of their respective dominant allele (**P** or **R**) and the absence of the other dominant allele. Walnut comb results from a modified form of codominance in which at least one dominant allele for pea comb and rose comb is present (that is **PR**). Single comb appears only in the homozygous double recessive condition (that is **pprr**). These phenotypes and genotypes are shown in table 23.6.

The F_2 genotypes and F_2 phenotypic ratios resulting from crossing a pure-breeding pea-comb hen with a pure-breeding rose-comb cock are shown in fig 23.27.

Table 23.6 Phenotypes and possible genotypes associated with comb shape in poultry.

Phenotype	*Possible genotypes*
pea	**PPrr, Pprr**
rose	**RRpp, Rrpp**
walnut	**PPRR, PpRR, PPRr, PpRr**
single	**pprr**

23.14 In poultry, the allele for white feather (**W**) is dominant over the allele for black feather (**w**). The alleles for pea comb, **P**, and rose comb, **R**, produce the phenotypes stated. If these alleles are present together they produce a phenotype called walnut comb and if their recessive alleles are present in the homozygous condition they produce a phenotype called single comb.

A cross between a black rose-comb cock and a white walnut-comb hen produced the following phenotypes:
3 white walnut-comb, 3 black walnut-comb, 3 white rose-comb, 3 black rose-comb, 1 white pea-comb, 1 black pea-comb, 1 white single-comb and 1 black single-comb.

What are the parental genotypes? Show clearly how they give rise to the phenotypes described above?

23.7.5   Epistasis

A gene is said to be **epistatic** (*epi*, over) when its presence suppresses the effect of a gene at another locus. Epistatic genes are sometimes called '**inhibiting genes**' because of their effect on the other genes which are described as **hypostatic** (*hypo*, under).

Fur colour in mice is controlled by a pair of genes occupying different loci. The epistatic gene determines the

851

Let:
    P represent presence of pea comb (dominant)
    p represent absence of pea comb (recessive)
    R represent presence of rose comb (dominant)
    r represent absence of rose comb (recessive)

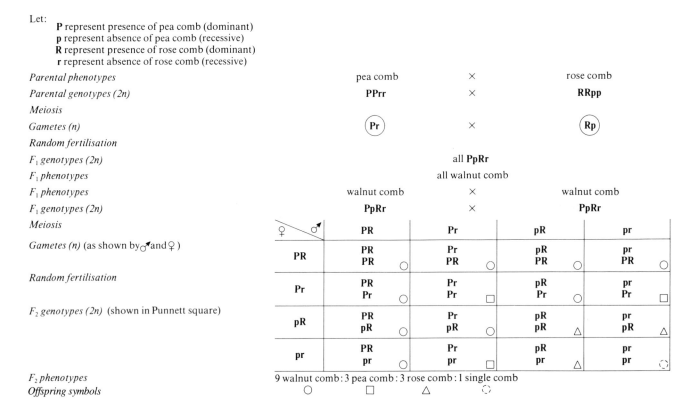

Parental phenotypes — pea comb × rose comb

Parental genotypes (2n) — **PPrr** × **RRpp**

Meiosis

Gametes (n) — (Pr) × (Rp)

Random fertilisation

F₁ genotypes (2n) — all **PpRr**

F₁ phenotypes — all walnut comb

F₁ phenotypes — walnut comb × walnut comb

F₁ genotypes (2n) — **PpRr** × **PpRr**

Meiosis

Gametes (n) (as shown by ♂ and ♀)

Random fertilisation

F₂ genotypes (2n) (shown in Punnett square)

F₂ phenotypes — 9 walnut comb : 3 pea comb : 3 rose comb : 1 single comb
Offspring symbols — ○ □ △ ◌

Fig 23.27 *Genetic explanation of comb inheritance in fowl*

Let:
    A represent agouti fur (dominant)
    a represent black fur (recessive)
    C represent coloured fur (dominant)
    c represent albino fur (recessive)

Parental phenotypes — agouti × albino

Parental genotypes (2n) — **AaCc** × **Aacc**

Meiosis

Gametes (n) (as shown by ♂ and ♀)

Random fertilisation

Offspring genotypes (2n) (as shown in Punnett square)

Offspring phenotypes — 3 agouti : 4 albino : 1 black
Offspring symbols — ○ □ △

Fig 23.28 *A genetic explanation of how unusual phenotypic ratios can be produced in the case of epistatic genes*

presence of colour and has two alleles, coloured (dominant) and albino (white) (recessive). The hypostatic gene determines the nature of the colour and its alleles are agouti (grey) (dominant) and black (recessive). The mice may have agouti or black fur depending upon their genotypes, but this will only appear if accompanied by the allele for coloured fur. The albino condition appears in mice that are homozygous recessive for colour even if the alleles for agouti and black fur are present. Three possible phenotypes can occur and they are agouti, black and albino. A variety of phenotypic ratios can be obtained depending on the genotypes of the mating pair (fig 23.28 and table 23.7).

Table 23.7 Some examples of the range of phenotypic ratios which can be produced as a result of epistatic gene interactions (see fig 23.28 for explanation of alleles).

Parental phenotypes	Genotypes	Phenotypic ratios
agouti × agouti	**AaCc × AaCc**	9 agouti : 3 black : 4 albino
agouti × black	**AaCc × aaCc**	3 agouti : 3 black : 2 albino
agouti × albino	**AaCc × Aacc**	3 agouti : 1 black : 4 albino
agouti × albino	**AaCc × aacc**	1 agouti : 1 black : 2 albino
agouti × albino	**AACc × aacc**	1 agouti : 1 albino
agouti × black	**AaCc × aaCC**	1 agouti : 1 black
albino × black	**AAcc × aaCC**	all agouti
albino × black	**AAcc × aaCc**	1 agouti : 1 albino

23.7.6 Polygenic inheritance

Many of the most obvious characteristics of organisms are produced by the combined effect of many different genes. These genes form a special gene complex known as a **polygenic system**. Whilst the effect of each gene alone is too small to make any significant impression on the phenotype, the almost infinite variety produced by the combined effect of these genes (**polygenes**) has been shown to form the genetic basis of **continuous variation**, which is described further in section 23.8.2.

23.8 Variation

The term variation describes the difference in characteristics shown by organisms belonging to the same natural population or species. It was the amazing diversity of structure within any species that caught the attention of Darwin and Wallace during their travels. The regularity and predictability with which these differences in characteristics were inherited formed the basis of Mendel's research. Whilst Darwin recognised that particular characteristics could be developed by selective breeding, as described in section 24.4.2, it was Mendel who explained the mechanism by which selected characteristics were passed on from generation to generation.

Mendel described how hereditary factors determine the genotype of an organism which in the course of development becomes expressed in the structural, physiological and biochemical characteristics of the phenotype. Whilst the phenotypic appearance of any characteristic is ultimately determined by the genes controlling that characteristic, the extent to which certain characteristics develop may be influenced by the environment.

A study of phenotypic differences in any large population shows that two forms of variation occur, discontinuous and continuous. Studies of variation in a character involve measuring the expression of that characteristic in a large number of organisms within the population, such as height in humans. The results are plotted as a histogram or a graph which reveals the **frequency distribution** of the variations of that characteristic within the population. Typical results obtained from such studies are shown in fig 23.29 and they highlight the difference between the two forms of variation.

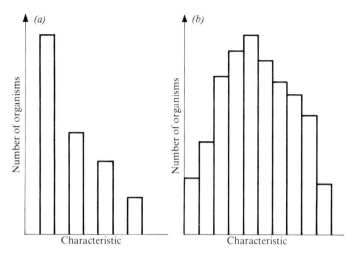

Fig 23.29 *Histograms representing frequency distribution in the case of (a) discontinuous variation and (b) continuous variation*

23.8.1 Discontinuous variation

There are certain characteristics within a population which exhibit a limited form of variation. Variation in this case produces individuals showing clear-cut differences with no intermediates between them, such as blood groups in humans, wing lengths in *Drosophila*, melanic and light forms in *Biston betularia*, style length in *Primula* and sex in animals and plants. Characteristics showing discontinuous variation are usually controlled by one or two major genes which may have two or more allelic forms and their phenotypic expression is relatively unaffected by environmental conditions.

Since the phenotypic variation is restricted to certain clear-cut characteristics, this form of variation is alternatively known as **qualitative inheritance**, as opposed to **quantitative inheritance** which is characteristic of continuous variation.

23.8.2 Continuous variation

Many characteristics in a population show a complete gradation from one extreme to the other without any break. This is illustrated most clearly by characteristics such as mass, linear dimension, shape and colour of organs and organisms. The frequency distribution for a characteristic exhibiting continuous variation is a **normal distribution curve** (section A2.7.3). Most of the organisms in the population fall in the middle of the range with approximately equal numbers showing the two extreme forms of the characteristic. Characteristics exhibiting continuous variation are produced by the combined effects of many genes (polygenes) and environmental factors. Individually each of these genes has little effect on the phenotype but their combined effect is significant.

23.8.3   Environmental influences

The ultimate factor determining a phenotypic characteristic is the genotype. At the moment of fertilisation the genotype of the organism is determined, but the subsequent degree of expression allowed to this genetic potential is influenced greatly by the action of environmental factors during the development of the organism. For example, Mendel's tall variety of garden pea normally attained a height of six feet. However, it would only do so if provided with adequate light, water and soil conditions. A reduction in the supply of any of these factors (**limiting factors**) would prevent the gene for height exerting its full effect. It was the Danish geneticist Johanssen who demonstrated the effect of the interaction of genotypic and environmental factors on phenotype. In a series of experiments on the mass of dwarf bean seeds he selected the heaviest and lightest seeds from each generation of self-pollinating dwarf bean plants and used these to produce the next generation. After repeating these experiments for several years he found only small differences in the mean mass of seeds from the same selected line, that is heavy or light, but large differences in mean mass of seeds from different selected lines, that is heavy and light. This suggested that both heredity and environment were influencing the phenotypic appearance of the characteristic. From these results it is possible to describe continuous phenotypic variation as being '**the cumulative effect of varying environmental factors acting on a variable genotype**'. The results also indicated that the extent to which a characteristic is inherited is determined primarily by the genotype. In the development of human characteristics such as personality, temperament and intelligence, there is evidence to suggest that both **nature** (hereditary factors) and **nurture** (environmental factors) interact to varying degrees in different individuals to influence the final appearance of the characteristic. It is these genetic and environmental differences which act to produce phenotypic differences between individuals. There is no firm evidence, as yet, to suggest that one factor is universally more influential than the other, but the environment can never increase the extent of the phenotype beyond that determined by the genotype.

23.8.4   Sources of variation

It will be appreciated that, as a result of the interaction between discontinuous and continuous variations and the environment, no two organisms will possess identical phenotypes. Replication of DNA is so nearly perfect that there is little possibility of variation occurring in the genotypes of asexually reproducing organisms. Any apparent variation between these organisms is therefore almost certainly the result of environmental influences. In the case of sexually reproducing organisms there is ample opportunity for genetic variation to arise. Two processes occurring during meiosis and the fusion of gametes during fertilisation provide the means of introducing unlimited genetic variation into the population. These may be summarised as follows:

(1) Reciprocal crossing-over of genes between chromatids of homologous chromosomes may occur during prophase I of meiosis. This produces new linkage groups and so provides a major source of genetic recombination of alleles (section 23.3 and 22.3).

(2) The orientation of the chromatids of homologous chromosomes (bivalents) on the equatorial spindle during metaphase I of meiosis determines the direction in which the pairs of chromatids move during anaphase I. This orientation of the chromatids is random. During metaphase II the orientation of pairs of chromatids once more is random and determines which chromosomes migrate to opposite poles of the cell during anaphase II. These random orientations and the subsequent independent assortment (segregation) of the chromosomes gives rise to a large calculable number of different chromosome combinations in the gametes (section 23.2.1)

A third source of variation in sexual reproduction results from the fact that the fusion of male and female gametes containing complementary sets of haploid chromosomes to produce a diploid zygotic nucleus is completely random (at least in theory). Thus, any male gamete is potentially capable of fusing with any female gamete.

These sources of genetic variation account for the routine '**gene reshuffling**' which is the basis of continuous variation. The environment acts on the range of phenotypes produced and those best suited to it thrive. This leads to changes in allele and genotypic frequencies as described in chapter 25. However, these sources of variation do not generate the major changes in genotype which are necessary in order to give rise to new species as described by evolutionary theory. These changes are produced by mutations.

23.9   Mutation

A mutation is a change in the amount or the structure of the DNA of an organism. This produces a change in the genotype which may be inherited by cells derived by mitosis or meiosis from the mutant cell. A mutation may result in the change in appearance of a characteristic in a population. Mutations occurring in gamete cells are inherited, whereas those occurring in somatic cells can only be inherited by daughter cells produced by mitosis. The latter are known as **somatic mutations**.

A mutation resulting from a change in the amount or arrangement of DNA is known as a **chromosomal mutation** or **chromosomal aberration**. Some forms of these affect the chromosomes to such an extent that they may be seen under the microscope. Increasingly the term mutation is being used to describe a change in the structure of the DNA at a single locus and this is known as a **gene mutation** or **point mutation**.

The concept of mutation as the cause of the sudden appearance of a new characteristic was first proposed by the Dutch botanist Hugo de Vries in 1901, following his work on inheritance in the evening primrose *Oenothera lamarckiana*. Nine years later T. H. Morgan began a series of investigations into mutations in *Drosophila* and, with the assistance of geneticists throughout the world, identified over 500 mutations.

23.9.1   Mutation frequency and causes of mutation

Mutations occur randomly and spontaneously; that is to say that any gene can undergo mutation at any time. The rates at which mutations occur vary between organisms.

As a result of the work of H. J. Müller in the 1920s it was observed that the frequency of mutation could be increased above the spontaneous level by the effects of X-rays. Since then it has been shown that the mutation rates can be significantly increased by the effects of high energy electromagnetic radiation such as ultra-violet light, X-rays and gamma rays. High-energy particles, such as α and β particles, neutrons and cosmic radiation, are also **mutagenic**, that is cause mutations. A variety of chemical substances, including mustard gas, caffeine, formaldehyde, colchicine, certain constituents of tobacco and an increasing number of drugs, food preservatives and pesticides, have been shown to be mutagenic.

23.9.2   Chromosome mutations

Chromosomal mutations may be the result of changes in the number or structure of chromosomes. Certain forms of chromosomal mutation may affect several genes and have a more profound effect on the phenotype than gene mutations. Changes in the number of chromosomes are usually the result of errors occurring during meiosis but they can also occur during mitosis. These changes may involve the loss or gain of single chromosomes, a condition called **aneuploidy**, or the increase in entire haploid sets of chromosomes, a condition called **euploidy** (**polyploidy**).

Aneuploidy

In this condition half the daughter cells produced have an **extra** chromosome $(n +1)$, $(2n + 1)$ and so on, whilst the other half have a chromosome missing $(n - 1)$, $(2n - 1)$ and so on. Aneuploidy can arise from the failure of a pair, or pairs, of homologous chromosomes to separate during anaphase I of meiosis. If this occurs, both sets of chromosomes pass to the same pole of the cell and separation of the homologous chromosomes during anaphase II may lead to the formation of gamete cells containing either one or more chromosomes too many or too few as shown in fig 23.30. This is known as **non-disjunction**.

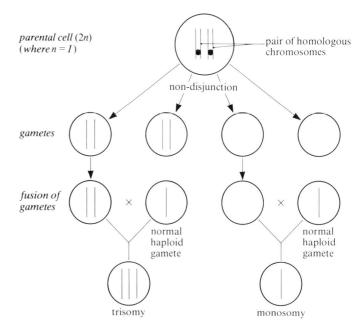

Fig 23.30 *Non-disjunction in gamete cell formation and the results of fusion of these abnormal gametes with normal haploid cells. The resulting cells may show a form of polysomy where the chromosome number may be (2n + 1) trisomy, (2n + 2) tetrasomy, (2n + 3) pentasomy etc., or monosomy (2n − 1) depending upon the number of homologous chromosomes which fail to separate normally*

Fusion of either of these gametes with a normal haploid gamete produces a zygote with an odd number of chromosomes.

Zygotes containing less than the diploid number of chromosomes usually fail to develop, but those with polysomic chromosomes may develop. In most cases where this occurs in animals it produces severe abnormalities. One of the commonest forms of chromosomal mutation in humans resulting from non-disjunction is a form of trisomy called Down's syndrome ($2n = 47$). The condition, which is named after the doctor who first described it in 1866, is due to the non-disjunction of the G21 chromosomes (fig 23.31). The symptoms of **Down's syndrome** include mental retardation, reduced resistance to disease, congenital heart abnormalities, a short stocky body and thick neck and the characteristic folds of skin over the inner corner of the eye which produce a superficial facial similarity to Mongolians. The syndrome used to be rather cruelly termed mongolism. Down's syndrome and other related chromosomal abnormalities occur more frequently in children born to older women. The exact reason for this is unknown but appears to be related to the age of the mother's egg cells.

Non-disjunction of the male and female sex chromosomes may also occur and produce aneuploidy affecting secondary sexual characteristics, fertility and, in some cases, intelligence (table 23.8).

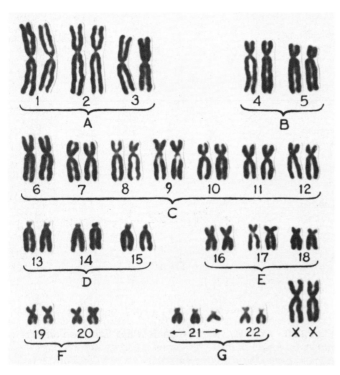

Fig 23.31 *The chromosomes of a female suffering from Down's syndrome. The non-disjunction of chromosomes G21 in one of the gametes has led to these chromosomes being trisomic in this female. A photograph, such as the one above, shows a complete set of chromosomes for an individual known as a karyotype*

Table 23.8 Phenotypic abnormalities resulting from non-disjunction of the sex chromosomes.

Condition/ Genotype	Symptoms	Frequency in Western populations
Klinefelter's syndrome (XXY)	♂, possessing some ♀ secondary sexual characteristics, sterile, testes very small, little facial hair, breasts may develop, usually low intelligence	0.02%
Turner's syndrome (XO)	♀, lacking normal secondary sexual characteristics and very short, nipples close together	0.03%
XXX	♀, normal appearance, fertile, but mentally retarded	0.12%
XYY	♂, tall, variable intelligence, may possess psychopathic traits or tendency for petty criminal acts	0.1%

Euploidy (polyploidy)

Gamete and somatic cells containing multiples of the haploid number of chromosomes are called **polyploids**, and the prefixes tri-, tetra-, and so on, indicate the extent of polyploidy, for example 3*n* is triploid, 4*n* is tetraploid, 5*n* is

pentaploid and so on. Polyploidy is much more common in plants than in animals. For example, approximately half the 300 000 known species of angiosperms are polyploid. The relatively low occurrence in animals is explained by the fact that the increased number of chromosomes in polyploids makes normal gamete formation during meiosis much more prone to error. Since most plants are capable of propagating themselves vegetatively they are able to reproduce despite being polyploid. Polyploidy is often associated with advantageous features such as increased size, hardiness and resistance to disease. This is called **hybrid vigour** (section 25.4.2). Most of our domestic plants are polyploids producing large fruits, storage organs, flowers or leaves.

There are two forms of polyploidy, autopolyploidy and allopolyploidy.

Autopolyploidy. This condition may arise naturally or artificially as a result of an increase in number of chromosomes within the same species. For example, if chromosomes undergo replication (during interphase) and the chromatids separate normally (during anaphase) but the cytoplasm fails to cleave (during cytokinesis), a **tetraploid** (4*n*) cell with a large nucleus is produced. This cell will undergo division and produce tetraploid cells. The amount of cytoplasm in these cells increases to preserve the nucleo-cytoplasmic volume ratio and leads to an increase in the size of the whole plant or some part of it. Autopolyploidy can be induced by the use of a drug called **colchicine** which is extracted from the corm of the autumn crocus (*Colchicum*). Concentrations of the order of 0.01% inhibit spindle formation by disrupting microtubules so that the chromatids fail to separate during anaphase. Colchicine and related drugs have been used in the breeding of certain varieties of economically important crops such as tobacco, tomatoes and sugarbeet. Autopolyploids can be as fertile as diploids if they have an even number of chromosome sets.

A modified form of polyploidy can occur in animals and give rise to cells and tissues which are polyploid. This process is called **endomitosis** and involves chromosome replication without cell division. The giant chromosomes in the salivary glands of *Drosophila* and tetraploid cells in the human liver are produced by endomitosis.

Allopolyploidy. This condition arises when the chromosome number in a sterile hybrid becomes doubled and produces fertile hybrids. F_1 hybrids produced from different species are usually sterile since their chromosomes cannot form homologous pairs during meiosis. This is called **hybrid sterility**. However, if multiples of the original haploid number of chromosomes, for example $2(n_1 + n_2)$, $3(n_1 + n_2)$ and so on (where n_1 and n_2 are the haploid numbers of the parent species) occur, a new species is produced which is fertile with polyploids like itself but infertile with both parental species.

Most allopolyploid species have a diploid chromosome number which is the sum of the diploid numbers of their parental species; for example rice grass (*Spartina anglica* (2n = 122) is a fertile allopolyploid hybrid produced from a cross between *Spartina maritima* (*stricta*) (2n = 60) and *Spartina alterniflora* (2n = 62). (The F₁ hybrid formed from the latter two species is sterile and is called *Spartina townsendii* (2n = 62)). Most allopolyploid plants have different characteristics from either parental species, and include many of our most economically important plants. For example, the species of wheat used to make bread, *Triticum aestivum* (2n = 42), has been selectively bred over a period of 5 000 years. By crossing a wild variety of wheat, einkorn wheat (2n = 14), with 'wild grass' (2n = 14) a different species of wheat, emmer wheat (2n = 28), was produced. Emmer wheat was crossed with another species of wild grass (2n = 14) to produce *Triticum aestivum* (2n = 42) which actually represents the hexaploid condition (6n) of the original einkorn wheat. Another example of interspecific hybridisation involving crossing the radish and cabbage is described in section 25.9.

Allopolyploidy does not occur in animals because there are fewer instances of cross-breeding between species. Polyploidy does not add new genes to a gene pool (section 25.1.1) but gives rise to a new combination of genes.

Structural changes in chromosomes

Crossing-over during prophase I of meiosis involves the reciprocal transfer of genetic material between homologous chromosomes. This changes the allele sequence of parental linkage groups and produces recombinants, but no gene loci are lost. Similar effects to these are produced by the structural changes in chromosomes known as inversions and translocations. In other forms of change, such as deletions and duplications, the number of gene loci on chromosomes is changed, and this can have profound effects on the phenotypes. Structural changes in chromosomes resulting from inversion, deletion and duplication, and in some cases from translocation, may be observed under the microscope when homologous chromosomes attempt to pair during prophase I of meiosis. Homologous genes undergo synapsis (pairing) (section 22.3) and a loop or twist is formed in one of the homologous chromosomes as a result of the structural change. Which chromosome forms the loop and the arrangement of its genes depends upon the type of structural change.

Inversion occurs when a region of a chromosome breaks off and rotates through 180° before rejoining the chromosome. No change in genotype occurs as a result of inversion but phenotypic changes may be seen (fig 23.32). This suggests that the order of gene loci on the chromosome is important; a phenomenon known as the **position effect**.

Translocation involves a region of a chromosome breaking off and rejoining either the other end of the same chromosome or another non-homologous chromosome (fig 23.32). The position effect may again be seen in the phenotype. Reciprocal translocation between non-homologous chromosomes can produce two new homologous pairs of chromosomes. In some cases of Down's

syndrome, where the diploid number is normal, the effects are produced by the translocation of an extra G21 chromosome onto a larger chromosome, usually D15.

The simplest form of chromosomal mutation is **deletion**, which involves the loss of a region of a chromosome, either from the ends or internally. This results in a chromosome becoming deficient in certain genes (fig 23.33). Deletion can affect one of a homologous pair of chromosomes, in which case the alleles present on the non-deficient chromosome will be expressed even if recessive. If deletion affects the same gene loci on both homologous chromosomes the effect is usually lethal.

In some cases a region of a chromosome becomes duplicated so that an additional set of genes exists for the region of **duplication**. The additional region of genes may be incorporated within the chromosome or at one end of

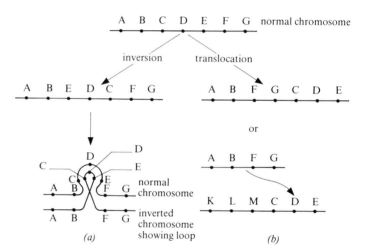

Fig 23.32 *Diagrammatic representation of inversion and translocation and their effects on the positions of genes A–G. (a) Looping in prophase due to inversion. (b) Part of the chromosome carrying genes C, D and E has broken off and become attached to the chromosome carrying genes K, L and M*

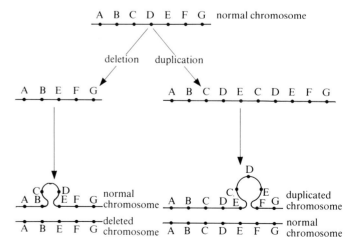

Fig 23.33 *Diagrammatic representations of deletion and duplication and their effects on the positions of genes A–G. In both cases looping can be seen*

the chromosome, or become attached to another chromosome (fig 23.33).

23.9.3 Gene mutations

Sudden and spontaneous changes in phenotype, for which there are no conventional genetic explanations or any microscopic evidence of chromosomal mutation, can only be explained in terms of changes in gene structure. A **gene mutation** or **point mutation** (since it applies to a particular gene locus) is the result of a change in the nucleotide sequence of the DNA molecule in a particular region of the chromosome. Such a change in the base sequence of the gene is transmitted to mRNA during transcription and may result in a change in the amino acid sequence of the polypeptide chain produced from it during translation at the ribosomes (section 22.6).

There are a variety of forms of gene mutation involving the addition, loss or rearrangement of bases in the gene. These mutations take the form of the **duplication**, **insertion**, **deletion**, **inversion** or **substitution** of bases. In all cases they change the nucleotide sequence and result in the formation of a modified polypeptide. For example, deletion causes a **frame shift** and the implications of this are described in section 22.5.

Gene mutations occurring during gamete formation are transmitted to all the cells of the offspring and may be significant for the future of the species. Somatic gene mutations which arise in the organism are inherited only by those cells derived from the mutant cells by mitosis. Whilst they may affect that organism, they are lost on the death of the organism. Somatic mutations are probably very common and go unnoticed, but in some cases they may produce cells with an increased rate of growth and division. These cells may give rise to a tumour which may be **benign** and not affect other tissues, or **malignant**, which lives parasitically on healthy cells, a condition known as **cancer**.

The effects of gene mutation are extremely variable. Most minor gene mutations pass unnoticed in the phenotype since they are recessive, but there are several cases where a change in a single base in the genetic code can have a profound effect on the phenotype. **Sickle cell anaemia** in humans is an example of **base substitution** mutation affecting a base in one of the genes involved in the production of haemoglobin. The respiratory pigment haemoglobin of adults is made up of four polypeptide chains (two α chains and two β chains) attached to the prosthetic group haem. The polypeptide chains influence the oxygen-carrying capacity of the haemoglobin molecule. A change in the base sequence of the triplet coding for one particular amino acid out of the 146 in the β chains gives rise to the production of sickle cell haemoglobin (HbS). The amino acid sequences for the normal and abnormal β chains differ in the substitution of **valine** for **glutamic acid** at one point in the abnormal polypeptide chains of **haemoglobin S**. Such a minor change causes haemoglobin S to crystallise at low oxygen concentrations. The histological effect of this is

to cause haemoglobin-S-containing red blood cells to distort and appear sickle-shaped. The physiological effect is to lower the amount of oxygen which can be carried by these cells, leading to acute anaemia. This not only causes physical weakness, but may lead to heart and kidney failure and an early death in individuals homozygous for the mutant allele. In the heterozygous condition individuals show the **sickle cell trait**. The red blood cells appear normal and only about 40% of the haemoglobin is abnormal. This produces only mild anaemia and in parts of the world where malaria is endemic, Africa and Asia in particular, it prevents carriers of the trait from contracting the disease. This is because the protozoan *Plasmodium*, which causes malaria, cannot live in red blood cells containing the abnormal haemoglobin (section 25.1.5).

23.9.4 Implications of mutation

The effects of chromosome and gene mutations are very variable. In many cases the mutations are lethal and prevent development of the organism, for example in humans about 20% of pregnancies end in natural abortion before 12 weeks and of these about 50% exhibit a chromosome abnormality. Some forms of chromosome mutation may bring certain gene sequences together, and that combined effect may produce a 'beneficial' characteristic. Another significance of bringing certain genes closer together is that they are less likely to be separated by crossing-over and this is an advantage with beneficial genes.

Gene mutation may lead to several alleles occupying a specific locus. This increases both the heterozygosity and size of the gene pool of the population and leads to an increase in variation within the population. Gene reshuffling as a result of crossing-over, independent assortment, random fertilisation and mutations, may increase the amount of continuous variation but the evolutionary implications of this are often short-lived since the changes produced may be rapidly diluted. Certain gene mutations, on the other hand, increase discontinuous variation and this has the more profound effect on changes in the population. Most gene mutations are recessive to the 'normal' allele which has come to form genetic equilibrium with the rest of the genotype and the environment as a result of successfully withstanding selection over many generations. Being recessive the mutant alleles may remain in the population for many generations until they come together in the homozygous condition and are expressed phenotypically. Occasionally a dominant mutant allele may arise in which case it will appear immediately in the phenotype (section 25.5, *Biston betularia*).

The information provided in this chapter accounts for the origins of variation within populations and the mechanisms by which characteristics are inherited, but it does not explain how the amazing diversity of living organisms described in chapters 2–4 may have arisen. Possible answers to this problem form the basis of the next two chapters.

Chapter Twenty-four

Evolution – history of life

The nature of life, its origin, the diversity of living organisms and the unifying structural and functional relationships which underlie this diversity form a focal point within the study of biology.

This chapter attempts to describe and discuss the many theories concerning the origin of life and the possible ways in which species have originated. Traditionally the study of the history of life has been fraught with allegations of indoctrination. Indoctrination may be defined as a conscious effort to inculcate an unshakeable commitment to a belief or doctrine. Such an approach is not only anti-scientific but also intellectually dishonest, and efforts to avoid this have been made in this text. A brief outline of the main theories on the origin of life is presented in this chapter so that students are aware that there is diversity of opinion as to the nature of this event. Much of the evidence on which these theories are based is metaphysical, that is to say it is impossible to repeat the exact events of the origin of life in any demonstrable way. This is true of both scientific and theological accounts. However, one theory, evolution, is increasingly being seen not as a single metaphysical theory but as a collection of individual scientific hypotheses each of which is capable of being tested, as described in section A2.1.

In this chapter, and in chapter 25, scientific facts have been selected to produce a coherent account of the processes underlying the origins and diversity of forms of life. Because of the necessity to be selective this account lacks absolute objectivity; indeed, this is inevitably true of any account, be it historical, scientific or metaphysical. However, by stressing the limitations and assumptions associated with the evidence presented here, this account may have a degree of objectivity and tentativeness which characterises good scientific writing. It must be stressed that the evidence presented in this chapter, and the conclusions drawn from it, represent current views. These are constantly under review and their validity is limited by the knowledge available to us at any given time.

24.1 Theories of the origin of life

Theories concerned with the origin of the Earth, and indeed the Universe, are diverse and uncertain. Steady-state cosmologists maintain that the Universe never had an origin. Other hypotheses suggest that it may have begun as a ball of neutrons, exploded in a 'big bang', emerged from one of several black holes, or may be the design of a Creator. Science, contrary to popular belief, cannot contradict the idea of a divine origin for the early universe, nor do theological views necessarily dismiss the view that during the origins of life, life acquired those characteristics explained by the natural laws of science.

The major theories accounting for the origin of life on Earth are:
(1) life was created by a supernatural being at a particular time (**special creation**);
(2) life arose from non-living matter on numerous occasions (**spontaneous generation**);
(3) life has no origin (**steady-state**);
(4) life arrived on this planet from elsewhere (**cosmozoan**);
(5) life arose according to chemical and physical laws (**biochemical evolution**).

24.1.1 Special creation

This theory is upheld by most of the world's major religions and civilisations and attributes the origin of life to a supernatural event at a particular time in the past. Archbishop Ussher of Armagh calculated in 1650 that God created the world in October 4004 BC, and finished with Man at 9.00 a.m. on the morning of the 23rd. He achieved this figure by adding up the ages of all the people in the biblical genealogies from Adam to Christ (the 'begats'). Whilst the arithmetic is sound, it places Adam as having lived at a time when archaeological evidence suggests that there was a well-established urban civilisation in the Middle East.

The traditional Judaeo-Christian account of creation, given in Genesis 1:1–26, has attracted, and continues to attract, controversy. Whilst all Christians would agree that the Bible is God's word to Man, there are differences of interpretation concerning the length of the 'day' mentioned in Genesis. Some believe that the world and all species were created in six days of 24 hours duration. They reject any other possible views and rely absolutely on inspiration, meditation and divine revelation. Other Christians do not regard the Bible as a scientific textbook and see the Genesis account as the theological revelation of the Creation of all living things through the power of God, described in terms understandable to men in all ages. For them the Creation account is concerned with answering the question 'Why?' rather than 'How?'. Whilst science broadly relies on observation and experiment to seek truth, theology draws its insights from divine revelation and faith.

'Faith is the substance of things hoped for, the

evidence of things not seen ... by faith ... we understand that the universe was created by God's word, so that what can be seen was made out of what cannot be seen.' (Hebrews 11:1, 3)

Faith accepts things for which there is no evidence in the scientific sense. This means that logically there can be no intellectual conflict between scientific and theological accounts of creation, since they are mutually exclusive realms of thought. Scientific truth to the scientist is tentative, but theological truth to the theist is absolute.

Since the process of special creation occurred only once and therefore cannot be observed, this is sufficient to put the concept of special creation outside the framework of scientific investigation. Science concerns itself only with observable phenomena and as such will never be able to prove or disprove special creation.

24.1.2 Spontaneous generation

This theory was prevalent in ancient Chinese, Babylonian and Egyptian thought as an alternative to special creation, with which it coexisted. Aristotle (384–322 BC), often hailed as the founder of biology, believed that life arose spontaneously. On the basis of his personal observations he developed this belief further in relating all organisms to a continuum, a *scala natura* (ladder of life).

'For nature passes from lifeless objects to animals in such unbroken sequence, interposing between them, beings which live and yet are not animals, that scarcely any difference seems to exist between neighbouring groups, owing to their close proximity.' (Aristotle)

In stating this he reinforced the previous speculations of Empedocles on organic evolution. Aristotle's hypothesis of spontaneous generation assumed that certain 'particles' of matter contained an 'active principle' which could produce a living organism when conditions were suitable. He was correct in assuming that the active principle was present in a fertilised egg, but incorrectly extrapolated this to the belief that sunlight, mud and decaying meat also had the active principle.

'Such are the facts, everything comes into being not only from the mating of animals but from the decay of earth ... And among plants the matter proceeds in the same way, some develop from seed, others, as it were, by spontaneous generation by natural forces; they arise from decaying earth or from certain parts of plants.' (Aristotle)

With the spread of Christianity, the spontaneous generation theory fell from favour, except among those who believed in magic and devil-worship, although it remained as a background idea for many more centuries.

Van Helmont (1577–1644), a much-acclaimed and successful scientist, described an experiment which gave rise to mice in three weeks. The raw materials for the experiment were a dirty shirt, a dark cupboard and a handful of wheat grains. The active principle in this process was thought to be human sweat.

24.1 What did Van Helmont omit from his experiment?

In 1688 Francesco Redi, an Italian biologist and physician living in Florence, took a more rigorous approach to the problem of the origin of life and questioned the theory of spontaneous generation. Redi observed that the little white worms seen on decaying flesh were fly larvae. By a series of experiments he produced evidence to support the idea that life can arise only from pre-existing life, the concept of **biogenesis**.

'Belief would be vain without the confirmation of experiment, hence in the middle of July, I put a snake, some fish, some eels of the Arno and a slice of milk-fed veal in four large, wide-mouthed flasks; having well closed and sealed them, I then filled the same number of flasks in the same way, leaving only these open.' (Redi)

Redi reported his results as follows.

'It was not long before the meat and the fish, in these second vessels (the unsealed ones), became wormy and the flies were seen entering and leaving at will; but in the closed flasks I did not see a worm, though many days had passed since the dead fish had been put in them.'

24.2 What do you consider was Redi's basic assumption?

These experiments, however, did not destroy the idea of spontaneous generation and, whilst the old theory took a setback, it continued to be the dominant theory within the secular community.

Whilst Redi's experiments appeared to refute the spontaneous generation of flies, the pioneer work in microscopy by Anton van Leeuwenhoek appeared to reinforce the theory with regard to micro-organisms. Whilst not entering the debate between biogenesis and spontaneous generation, his observations with the microscope provided fuel for both theories and finally stimulated other scientists to design experiments to settle the question of the origin of life by spontaneous generation.

In 1765 Lazzaro Spallanzani boiled animal and vegetable broths for several hours and sealed them immediately. He then removed them from the source of heat. After being set aside for several days, none of them, on examination, showed any signs of life. He concluded from this that the high temperature had destroyed all forms of living organisms in his vessel and without their presence no life could appear.

24.3 Suggest another reason why Spallanzani's experiment might have prevented the growth of organisms.

In 1860 Louis Pasteur turned his attention to the problem of the origins of life. By this stage he had demonstrated the existence of bacteria and found the solutions to the economic problems of the silk and wine industries. He had also shown that bacteria were ubiquitous and that non-living matter could easily become contaminated by living matter if all materials were not adequately sterilised.

24.4 What were Pasteur's basic assumptions about the origins of life?

In a series of experiments based upon those of Spallanzani, Pasteur demonstrated the theory of biogenesis and finally disproved the theory of spontaneous generation.

The validation of biogenesis however raised another problem. Since it was now clear that a living organism was required in order to produce another living organism, where did the first living organism come from? The steady-state hypothesis has an answer for this but all the other theories imply a transition from non-living to living at some stage in the history of life. Was this a primeval spontaneous generation?

Experiment 24.1: To investigate the origin of micro-organisms in terms of spontaneous generation and biogenesis

The objectives of this experiment are to repeat the experiments of Spallanzani and Pasteur and carry out further guided experiments which take into account the criticisms of their experimental techniques, and to evaluate objectively the hypotheses of spontaneous generation and biogenesis.

Materials

8 × 30 cm³ boiling tubes	straight glass tubing
boiling tube rack	0.5 × 6 cm
120 cm³ nutrient broth	air-lock (S-shaped) glass
5 cotton wool plugs	tubing 0.5 × 10 cm
aluminium foil	access to: autoclave,
water bath	incubator set at 32 °C

Method

(1) Autoclave eight boiling tubes.
(2) Place 15 cm³ of nutrient broth into each of these boiling tubes, labelled 1–8.
(3) Set up tubes 1–8 as outlined below.

Pair A
Tube 1 – Leave unplugged, do not heat.
Tube 2 – Plug with cotton wool and cover top with aluminium foil. Do not heat.

Pair B
Tube 3 – Leave unplugged. Heat in a boiling water bath for 10 min.
Tube 4 – Plug with cotton wool and cover top with aluminium foil. Heat in a boiling water-bath for 10 min.

Pair C
Tube 5 – Leave unplugged. Autoclave at 15 lb pressure for 20 min.

Tube 6 – Plug with cotton wool and cover top with aluminium foil. Autoclave at 15 lb pressure for 20 min.

Pair D
Tube 7 – Surround straight glass tubing with cotton wool and plug boiling tube. Autoclave at 15 lb pressure for 20 min.
Tube 8 – Surround S-shaped glass tubing with cotton wool and plug boiling tube. Autoclave at 15 lb pressure for 20 min.

(4) Place all boiling tubes in an incubator at 32 °C.
(5) Examine all boiling tubes every two days for ten days. Record observations in the form of a table.
(6) After ten days remove a drop of broth from each tube using sterile techniques and examine under the high power of the microscope. Record observations in the form of a table.
(7) Draw conclusions from these observations.

24.5 Clearly state the hypothesis which would account for the appearance of micro-organisms in the nutrient broth.

24.6 List the variables (factors) which may influence the appearance of micro-organisms in the broth.

24.7 Which variable differs between each of the tubes 1 and 2, 3 and 4, 5 and 6, and 7 and 8?

24.8 Which variable differs between the pairs of tubes A, B, C and D?

24.9 Which tubes repeat the experiments of Spallanzani and Pasteur?

24.10 Which tubes act as controls?

24.11 Do you consider that the experiments carried out above meet all the criteria of a scientific investigation, and what degree of validity would you attach to your conclusions?

24.1.3 Steady-state theory

This theory asserts that the Earth had no origin, has always been able to support life, has changed remarkably little, if at all, and that species had no origin.

Estimates of the age of the Earth have varied greatly from the 4004 BC calculation of Archbishop Ussher to the present-day values of $5\,000 \times 10^6$ years based on radioactive decay rates. Improved scientific dating techniques (Appendix 5) give increasing ages for the Earth, and extrapolation of this trend provides advocates of this theory with the hypothesis that the Earth had no origin. Whilst generally discrediting the value of geochronology in giving a precise age for the Earth, the steady-state theory uses this as a basis for supposing that the Earth has always existed. This theory proposes that species, too, never originated, they have always existed and that in the history of a species the only alternatives are for its numbers to vary, or for it to become extinct.

The theory does not accept the palaeontological evidence that presence or absence of a fossil indicates the origin or extinction of the species represented and quotes, as an example, the case of the coelacanth, *Latimeria*. Fossil evidence indicates that the coelacanths died out at the end of the Cretaceous period, 70 million years ago. The discovery of living specimens off the coast of Madagascar has altered this view. The steady-state theory claims that it is only by studying living species and comparing them with the fossil record that extinction can be assumed and then there is a high probability that this may be incorrect. The palaeontological evidence presented in support of the steady-state theory describes the fossil's appearance in ecological terms. For example, the sudden appearance of a fossil in a particular stratum would be associated with an increase in population size or movement of the organism into an area which favoured fossilisation. Most evidence for this theory is based on discredited aspects of evolutionary theory such as the gaps in the fossil record and is best studied, in detail, alongside it.

24.1.4 Cosmozoan theory

This theory does not offer a mechanism to account for the origin of life but favours the idea that it had an extraterrestrial origin. It does not therefore, constitute a theory of origin as such, but merely transposes the problem to elsewhere in the Universe.

The theory states that life could have arisen once or several times, at various times and in various parts of the Galaxy or Universe. Its alternative name is the theory of **panspermia**. Repeated sightings of UFOs, cave-drawings of rocket-like objects and 'spacemen' and reports of encounters with aliens provide the background evidence for this theory. Russian and American space probes have provided evidence that the likelihood of finding life within our Solar System is remote but cannot comment on the nature of life outside our Solar System. Research into meteoritic and cometary materials has revealed the presence of many pre-vital organic molecules, such as cyanogen and hydrocyanic acid, which may have acted as 'seeds' falling on a barren Earth. There are several claims that objects bearing resemblances to primitive forms of life on Earth have been found in meteorites but they have yet to gain any real credibility in scientific circles.

24.1.5 Biochemical evolution

It is generally agreed by astronomers, geologists and biologists that the Earth is some $4.5–5.0 \times 10^9$ years old.

Many biologists believe that the original state of the Earth bore little resemblance to its present-day form and had the following probable appearance: it was hot (about 4 000–8 000 °C) and as it cooled carbon and the less volatile metals condensed and formed the Earth's core; the surface was probably barren and rugged as volcanic activity, continuous earth movements and contraction on cooling, folded and fractured the surface.

The atmosphere is believed to have been totally different in those days. The lighter gases hydrogen, helium, nitrogen, oxygen and argon would have escaped because the gravitational field of the partially condensed planet would not contain them. However, simple compounds containing these elements (amongst others) would have been retained, such as water, ammonia, carbon dioxide and methane, and until the earth cooled below 100 °C all water would have existed as vapour. The atmosphere would appear to have been a 'reducing atmosphere', as indicated by the presence of metals in their reduced form (such as iron(II)) in the oldest rocks of the Earth. More recent rocks contain metals in their oxidised form (for example iron(III)). The lack of oxygen in the atmosphere would probably be a necessity, since laboratory experiments have shown, paradoxically, that it is far easier to generate organic molecules (the basis of living organisms) in a reducing atmosphere than in an oxygen-rich atmosphere.

In 1923 Alexander Oparin suggested that the atmosphere of the primeval Earth was not as we know it today but fitted the description given above. On theoretical grounds he argued that organic compounds, probably hydrocarbons, could have formed in the oceans from more simple compounds, the energy for these synthesis reactions probably being supplied from the strong solar radiation (mainly ultra-violet) which surrounded the Earth before the formation of the ozone layer, which now blocks much of it out. Oparin argued that if one considered the multitude of simple molecules present in the oceans, the surface area of the Earth, the energy available and the time scale, it was conceivable that oceans would gradually accumulate organic molecules to produce the 'primeval soup', in which life could have arisen. This was not a new idea, indeed Darwin himself expressed a similar thought in a letter he wrote in 1871:

'It is often said that all the conditions for the first production of a living organism are now present, which could ever have been present. But if, (and oh what a big if) we could conceive of some warm little pond, with all sorts of ammonia and phosphoric salts, light, heat, electricity, etc., present that a protein compound was chemically formed ready to undergo still more complex changes, at the present day, such matter would be constantly devoured or absorbed, which could not have been the case before living creatures were formed.'

In 1953 Stanley Miller, in a series of experiments, simulated the proposed conditions on the primitive Earth. In his experimental high-energy chamber (fig 24.1) he successfully synthesised many substances of considerable biological importance, including amino acids, adenine and simple sugars such as ribose. More recently Orgel at the Salk Institute has succeeded in synthesising nucleotides six units long (a simple nucleic acid molecule) in a similar experiment.

It has since been suggested that carbon dioxide was present in relatively high concentrations in the primeval

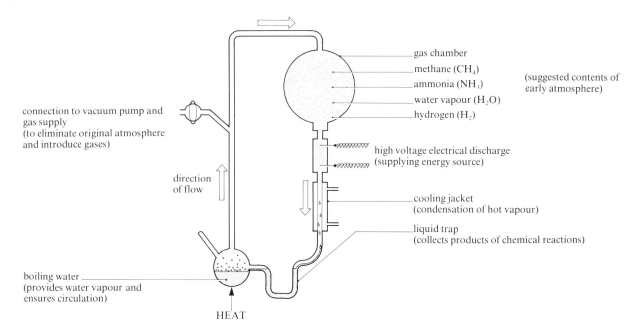

connection to vacuum pump and gas supply
(to eliminate original atmosphere and introduce gases)

direction of flow

gas chamber
methane (CH$_4$)
ammonia (NH$_3$)
water vapour (H$_2$O)
hydrogen (H$_2$)

(suggested contents of early atmosphere)

high voltage electrical discharge
(supplying energy source)

cooling jacket
(condensation of hot vapour)

liquid trap
(collects products of chemical reactions)

boiling water
(provides water vapour and ensures circulation)

HEAT

atmosphere. Recent experiments using Miller's apparatus but containing mixtures of carbon dioxide and water and only traces of other gases have produced similar results to those of Miller. Oparin's theory has been widely accepted, but major problems remain in explaining the transition from complex organic molecules to living organisms. This is where the theory of a process of biochemical evolution offers a broad scheme which is acceptable to the majority of contemporary biologists. However, there is no agreement as to the precise mechanism by which it may have occurred.

Oparin considered that protein molecules were crucial to the transformation from inanimate to animate. Because of the zwitterionic nature of protein molecules they are able to form colloidal hydrophilic complexes which attract, and become surrounded by, envelopes of water molecules. These bodies may separate from the body of the liquid in which they are suspended (aqueous phase) and form a type of emulsion. Coalescence of these structures produces a separation of colloids from their aqueous phase, a process known as **coacervation** (*coacervus*, clump or heap). These colloid-rich coacervates may have been able to exchange substances with their environment and selectively concentrate compounds within them, particularly crystalloids. The colloid composition of a coacervate would depend on the composition of the medium. The varying composition of the 'soup' in different areas would lead to variation in the chemical composition of coacervates, producing the raw material for 'biochemical natural selection'.

It is suggested that substances within the coacervates may have undergone further chemical reactions and, by absorbing metal ions into the coacervates, formed enzymes. The alignment of lipid molecules (complex hydrocarbons) along the boundary between the coacervates and the external medium would have produced a primitive cell membrane which conferred stability on the coacervates. Thus the incorporation of a pre-existing molecule capable of self-replication into the coacervate, and an internal

Fig 24.1 *Stanley Miller's apparatus in which he synthesised amino acids from gases under conditions thought to have been present in the primeval atmosphere. The gases and vapours were circulated under pressure and exposed to a high voltage for one week. At the end of the period the liquid products in the trap were analysed by paper chromatography. A total of 15 amino acids was isolated including glycine, alanine and aspartic acid*

rearrangement of the lipid-coated coacervate, may have produced a primitive type of cell. Increase in size of coacervates and their fragmentation possibly led to the formation of identical coacervates which could absorb more of the medium and the cycle could continue. This possible sequence of events would have produced a primitive self-replicating heterotrophic organism feeding on an organic-rich primeval soup.

Whilst this account of the origin of life is widely accepted by many scientists, the astronomer Sir Fred Hoyle has recently argued that the probability of random molecular interactions giving rise to life as described above is

'as ridiculous and improbable as the proposition that a tornado blowing through a junk yard may assemble a Boeing 747'.

24.2 The nature of the earliest organisms

Current evidence suggests that the first organisms were heterotrophs as these were the only organisms capable of utilising the external supplies of available energy locked up within the complex organic molecules present in the 'soup'. The chemical reactions involved in synthesising food substances appear to have been too complex to have arisen within the earliest forms of life.

As more complex organic molecules arose through 'biochemical evolution', it is assumed that some of these were able to harness solar radiation as an energy source and use it to synthesise new cellular materials. Incorporation of these molecules into pre-existing cells may have enabled the cells to synthesise new cellular materials without the need for them to absorb organic molecules, hence becoming autotrophic. Increasing numbers of heterotrophs would have reduced the available food resources in the primeval soup and this competition for resources would hasten the appearance of autotrophs.

The earliest photosynthetic organisms, whilst utilising solar radiation as their energy source, lacked the biochemical pathways to produce oxygen. At a later stage, it is believed that oxygen-evolving photosynthetic organisms developed, similar to existing blue-green bacteria (section 3.2), and this resulted in the gradual build-up of oxygen in the atmosphere. The increase in atmospheric oxygen and its ionisation to form the ozone layer would reduce the ultra-violet radiation striking the Earth. Whilst decreasing the rate of synthesis of new complex molecules, the decrease in radiation would confer some stability on otherwise successful forms of life. A study of the physiology of present-day organisms reveals a great diversity in biochemical pathways associated with energy capture and release, which may mirror many of Nature's early experiments with living organisms.

Despite the simplified account given above, the problem of the origin(s) of life remains. All that has been outlined is speculative and, despite tremendous advances in biochemistry, answers to the problem remain hypothetical. The above account is a simplified amalgam of present-day hypotheses. No 'ruling hypothesis' has yet achieved the status of an all-embracing theory (section A2.1). Details of the transition from complex non-living materials to simple living organisms remain a mystery.

24.3 Summary of the 'theories' of the origin of life

Many of these 'theories' and the way they explain the existing diversity of species cover similar ground but with varying emphases. Scientific theories may be ultra-imaginative on the one hand and ultra-sceptical on the other. Theological considerations too, may fit into this framework depending upon one's religious views. One of the major areas of controversy, even before the days of Darwin was the relationship between scientific and theological views on the history of life.

Diagrams (a)–(e) in fig 24.2 represent straightforward descriptions of theories, hypotheses or beliefs on the history of life, whereas (f) and (g) represent an attempt to combine certain aspects of three theories, (b), (c) and (d), into an alternative acceptable to many people. The practices of science and religion are not, therefore, necessarily mutually exclusive, as witnessed by the number of scientists who hold religious beliefs.

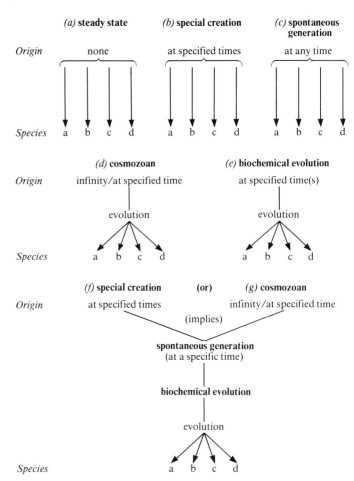

Fig 24.2 *Diagrammatic representation of various theories of the origin of life and the formation of species*

24.4 The theory of evolution

The term 'evolution' has a special place in the study of the history of life. It has become the unifying concept which underpins the whole study of biology. Evolution implies an overall gradual development which is both ordered and sequential. In terms of living organisms it may be defined as '**the development of differentiated organisms from pre-existing less differentiated organisms over the course of time**'.

The concept of evolution did not begin with Darwin and the publication of *On the Origin of Species*. Long before Darwin, attempts to explain the obvious diversity of living organisms which surround us had, paradoxically, led people to consider the basic structural and functional similarities which exist between organisms. Evolutionary hypotheses had been proposed to account for this and these ideas have themselves 'evolved' since the time of Darwin as knowledge has advanced.

The historical background to the development of the theory of evolution, as outlined in table 24.1, shows that the concept of continuity or gradual development of more complex species from pre-existing simpler forms had

Table 24.1 The history of evolutionary thought.

Ancient Chinese

Confucius	Life originated from a single source through a gradual unfolding and branching

Greek and Mediaeval period

Diogenes	All things are differentiations of the same thing and are the same thing
Empedocles	Air, earth, fire and water are the four roots of all things. Life arose by the action of the forces of attraction and repulsion on the four elements. Explained origin of Universe, plants, animals and humans (produced the germ of the idea of organic evolution)
Democritus	Living things arose by spontaneous generation from the slime of the Earth
Anaxogoras	Organisms sprang from atmospheric germs
Thales (640–546 BC)	All life came from water
Anaximander	Plants, then animals and finally humans arose from the mud of the emerging Earth
Aristotle (384–322 BC)	Proposed theory of continuous and gradual evolution from lifeless matter, based on his observations of animals. Recognised a 'scala natura' for animals
Dark Ages (400–1400 AD)	All theories based on those above or acceptance of special creation

Age of speculation (1400–1790)

John Ray (1627–1705)	Developed concept of species
Carl Linnaeus (1707–78)	Formalised 'binomial classification' system. Suggested genera were created separately and species were variants of them
Buffon (1707–88)	Suggested different types of animals had different origins at different times. Recognised influence of external environment. Believed in acquired inheritance
James Hutton (1726–97)	Theory of uniformitarianism. Gave age of Earth in millions of years

Age of formulation (1790–1900)

Erasmus Darwin (1731–1802)	Life arose from one single 'filament' made by God. Did not accept the preformation of humans. The filament evolved by acquired characteristics
Jean-Baptiste Lamarck (1744–1829)	Inheritance of acquired characteristics. Environment acts on organisms. Phenotype changes are passed on. Concept of use and disuse of organs
Georges Cuvier (1769–1832)	Established palaeontological evidence. Fossils the results of 'catastrophes' by which new species arose
William Smith (1769–1838)	Opposed Cuvier's theory of catastrophism on basis of continuity of similar species in related strata
Charles Lyell (1797–1875)	Demonstrated the progressive history of fossil evidence
Charles Darwin (1809–82)	Influenced by Lyell and Malthus. Established a theory of evolution by means of natural selection
Alfred Russel Wallace (1823–1913)	Similar theory to Darwin, but excepted humans from his theory
Hugo de Vries (1848–1935)	Recognised existence of mutations which were heritable as a basis for discontinuous variation and regarded species as arising by mutation
August Weismann (1834–1914)	Showed that the reproductive cells of animals are distinct and therefore unaffected by the influences acting on somatic tissues
Gregor Mendel (1822–84)	Work on genetics (published 1865) only came to light after 1900. Laws of inheritance

Developments in twentieth century (neo-Darwinism)

W. L. Johannsen	Phenotype characteristics are determined by genotype and environmental factors
T. Henry Morgan	Developed chromosome theory of heredity on basis of cytological evidence
H. J. Muller (1927)	Genotype can be altered by X-rays: induced mutation
R. A. Fisher (1930)	No difference between change investigated by geneticists and change shown in the fossil record
G. W. Beadle and and E. L. Tatum (1941)	Demonstrated the genetic basis of biochemical synthesis (following A. E. Garrod (1909) and J. B. S. Haldane (1935))
J. Lederberg and A. D. Hershey (1951)	Demonstrated value of using bacteria in studying changes in genotype
J. D. Watson and F. H. C. Crick (1953)	Proposed molecular structure of DNA and its mechanism of replication
F. Jacob and J. Monod (1961)	Proposed a mechanism for regulation of gene activity

occurred to several philosophers and natural historians before the formal declarations of evolutionary hypotheses were advanced in the early nineteenth century.

24.4.1 Lamarckian evolution

The French biologist Lamarck proposed, in 1809, a hypothesis to account for the mechanism of evolution based on two conditions: the use and disuse of parts, and the inheritance of acquired characteristics. Changes in the environment may lead to changed patterns of behaviour which can necessitate new or increased use (or disuse) of certain organs or structures. Extensive use would lead to increased size and/or efficiency whilst disuse would lead to degeneracy and atrophy. These traits acquired during the lifetime of the individual were believed to be heritable and thus transmitted to offspring.

According to Lamarckism, as the theory came to be known, the long neck and legs of the modern giraffe were the result of generations of short-necked and short-legged ancestors feeding on leaves at progressively higher levels of trees. The slightly longer necks and legs produced in each generation were passed on to the subsequent generation, until the size of the present-day giraffe was reached. The webbed feet of aquatic birds and the shape of flat fish could be explained similarly. In aquatic birds the constant spreading of the toe bones and the skin between them in order to swim to find food and escape predators gave rise to their webbed feet. Likewise adaptations resulting from fish lying on their sides in shallow water were proposed to explain the shape of flat fish. Whilst Lamarck's theory helped prepare the way for acceptance of the concept of evolution, his views on the mechanism of change were never widely accepted.

However, Lamarck's emphasis on the role of the environment in producing phenotypic changes in the individual was correct. For example, body-building exercises will increase the size of muscles, but these acquired traits, whilst affecting the phenotype, are non-genetic, and having no influence on the genotype cannot be inherited. To demonstrate this, Weismann cut off the tails of mice over many successive generations. According to Lamarckism, the enforced disuse of tails should have led to progeny with smaller tails. This was not the case. Weismann postulated that somatic (body) acquired characteristics (resulting in phenotypic changes) did not directly affect the germ (gamete) cells which were the means by which characteristics are passed on to the next generation. His theory of the 'Continuity of the Germ-Plasm' was a historical necessity before the inheritance of genetic characteristics by sexual reproduction could be accepted.

24.4.2 Darwin, Wallace and the origin of species by natural selection

Charles Darwin was born in 1809, the son of a wealthy doctor, and like many great people he had an undistinguished academic career. In 1831 he accepted an unpaid post as naturalist on the survey ship H.M.S. *Beagle*, which spent the next five years at sea charting the East Coast of South America. The *Beagle* returned to Falmouth in October 1836 via the coast of Chile, the Galapagos Islands, Tahiti, New Zealand, Tasmania and South Africa. For most of this time Darwin was concerned with studying geology, but during a five-week stay on the Galapagos Islands he was struck by the similarities shown by the flora and fauna of the islands and mainland. In particular he was intrigued by the characteristic distributions of species of tortoises and finches (section 24.7.2). He collected a great deal of biological data concerned with variation between organisms which convinced him that species were not immutable. On his return home his work on the selective breeding of pigeons and other domestic animals gave him a clue to the concept of artificial selection, but he was unable to appreciate how this could operate in the wild. An earlier *Essay on the Principles of Population* by the Reverend Thomas Malthus, published in 1778, had highlighted the consequences of the reproductive potential of humans. Darwin applied this to other organisms and saw that despite this the numbers within populations remained relatively constant. Having collated a vast amount of information he began to realise that under the intense competition of numbers in a population, any variations which favoured survival in a particular environment would increase that individual's ability to reproduce and leave fertile offspring. Less favourable variations would be at a disadvantage and organisms possessing them would therefore have their chances of successful reproduction decreased. These data provided Darwin with the framework to formulate, by 1839, a theory of evolution by natural selection, but he did not publish his findings at that time. Indeed Darwin's greatest contribution to science was not so much to show that evolution occurs but how it might occur.

In the meantime, another naturalist, Alfred Russel Wallace, who had travelled widely in South America, Malaya and the Eastern Indian archipelago, and also read Malthus, had come to the same conclusions as Darwin regarding natural selection.

In 1858, Wallace wrote a 20-page essay outlining his theory and sent it to Darwin. This stimulated and encouraged Darwin and in July 1858, Darwin and Wallace presented papers on their ideas at a meeting of the Linnean Society in London. Over a year later, in November 1859, Darwin published *On the Origin of Species by Means of Natural Selection*. All 1 250 printed copies were sold on the day of publication and it is said that this book has been second only to the Bible on its impact on human thinking.

24.5 Natural selection

Darwin and Wallace proposed that natural selection is the mechanism by which new species arise from pre-existing species. This hypothesis/theory is based on three observations and two deductions which may be summarised as follows.

Observation 1: Individuals within a population have a great reproductive potential.

Observation 2: The numbers of individuals in a population remain approximately constant.

Deduction 1: Many individuals fail to survive or reproduce. There is a 'struggle for existence' within a population.

Observation 3: Variation exists within all populations.

Deduction 2: In the 'struggle for existence' those individuals showing variations best adapted to their environment have a 'reproductive advantage' and produce more offspring than less well-adapted organisms.

Deduction 2 offers a hypothesis called natural selection which provides a mechanism accounting for evolution.

24.5.1 Evidence for natural selection

Observation 1: It was Malthus who highlighted the reproductive potential of humans and observed that human populations are able to increase exponentially (section 12.7.3). The capacity for reproduction is basic to all living organisms, and is a fundamental drive which ensures continuance of the species. This applies to other organisms as shown in table 24.2. If every female gamete was fertilised and developed to maturity, the Earth would be totally overcrowded in a matter of days.

Table 24.2 Reproductive potential of selected species.

Crassostrea virginica	American oyster	1.0×10^6 eggs per season
Lycoperdon sp.	giant puff ball	7.0×10^{11} spores
Papaver rhoeas	poppy capsule	6.0×10^3 seeds
Carcinus maenas	shore crab	4.0×10^6 eggs per season

Observation 2: All population sizes are limited or checked by various environmental factors, such as food availability, space and light. Populations tend to increase in size until the environment supports no further increase and an equilibrium is reached. The population fluctuates around this equilibrium, as discussed in section 12.7.3. Hence population sizes generally remain approximately constant over a period of time related to the length of the organism's life cycle.

Deduction 1: The continuous competition between individuals for environmental resources creates a 'struggle for existence'. Whether this competition occurs within a species (**intraspecific competition**) or between members of different species (**interspecific competition**) may be immaterial in affecting the size of the individual population (section 12.7.5), but it will still imply that certain organisms will fail to survive or reproduce.

Observation 3: Darwin's study of beetles whilst an undergraduate at Cambridge, his subsequent journey in the *Beagle* and his knowledge gained through the selective breeding of certain characteristics in pigeons convinced

him of the importance of intraspecific variation. Likewise the adaptive significance of the interspecific variation seen in Galapagos finches (genus *Geospiza*) gave Darwin a clue to his second deduction. Data collected by Wallace in the Malayan archipelago provided further evidence of variation between populations. Darwin and Wallace, however, were unable to account for the sources of the variation. This was not to be clarified until Mendel's work on the particulate nature of inheritance demonstrated how genetic variation is conserved.

Deduction 2: Since all individuals within a population exhibit variation and a 'struggle for existence' has been clearly established, it follows that some individuals possessing particular variations will be more suited to survive and reproduce. The key factor in determining survival is adaptation to the environment. Any variation, however slight, be it physical, physiological or behavioural, which gives one organism an advantage over another organism will act as a **selective advantage** in the 'struggle for existence'. (The term 'selective advantage' is less emotive than that coined by the social philosopher, Herbert Spencer, who described natural selection as 'survival of the fittest'. The term 'fit' has irrelevant human connotations, which have given an erroneous impression of natural selection.) Favourable variations will be inherited by the next generation. Unfavourable variations are 'selected out' or 'selected against', their presence conferring a **selective disadvantage** on that organism. In this way natural selection leads to increased vigour within the species and, in phylogenetic terms, ensures the survival of that species (assuming environmental conditions remain constant). The whole of Darwin's and Wallace's hypothesis of natural selection is summed up most succinctly in Darwin's own words:

'As many more individuals of each species are born than can possibly survive, and as, consequently, there is a frequently recurring struggle for existence, it follows that any being, if it vary however slightly in any manner profitable to itself, under the complex and sometimes varying conditions of life, will have a better chance of surviving and thus be naturally selected. From the strong principle of inheritance, any selected variety will tend to propagate its new and modified form.' (Darwin, 1859)

Many misconceptions have grown up around the theory of evolution as outlined by Darwin and they may be summarised as follows.

(1) Darwin made no attempt to describe how life originated on the Earth: his concern was with how new species might arise from pre-existing species.

(2) Natural selection is not simply a negative, destructive force, but can be a positive mechanism of innovation within a population (section 25.5). The 'struggle for existence' described by Darwin was popularised by the coining of unfortunate terms such as 'survival of the fittest' and 'elimination of the unfit' by the philosopher Herbert Spencer and the press of the day.

(3) The misconception that humans were 'descended from the apes' by some process of linear progression was over-sensationalised by the press and offended both the religious and secular communities. The former saw this as an insult to their belief that 'Man' was created in the 'image of God', whilst the latter were outraged by the apparent undermining of the 'superior position' of humans within the animal kingdom.

(4) The apparent contradiction between the Genesis six-day Creation account and that of a progressive origin for species was exacerbated by the meeting of the British Association for the Advancement of Science in June 1860. Bishop Samuel Wilberforce of Oxford vehemently attacked the conclusions of Darwin as outlined in *On the Origin of Species* but not being a biologist his address lacked accuracy. In concluding, he turned to Professor Thomas Henry Huxley, a proponent of Darwin's theory, and asked whether he claimed his descent from a monkey through his grandfather or grandmother. Huxley replied by expounding the more important ideas of Darwin and correcting the misconceptions of Bishop Wilberforce. In conclusion he implied that he would prefer to have a monkey for an ancestor than 'to be connected with a man who used great gifts to obscure the truth'. This unfortunate controversy has continued as the Genesis versus Evolution debate. Professor R. J. Berry has summarised the extremes of the debate as:

(*a*) those who are awed by scientists and believe that the Bible has been disproved;

(*b*) those who cling to the inspiration of Scripture and their own interpretations of it, and shut their eyes to the fact that God's work can be studied by scientific methods.

24.6 Modern views on evolution

The theory of evolution as proposed by Darwin and Wallace has been extended and elaborated in the light of contemporary evidence from genetics, molecular biology, palaeontology, ecology and ethology and is known as **neo-Darwinism** (*neo*, new, adding to the notion of). This may be defined as *the theory of organic evolution by the natural selection of genetically determined characteristics.*

The term 'evolution' may mean the result, or the process, of the above and different types of evidence support different aspects of this theory. In order to accept neo-Darwinian evolutionary theory, as defined above, for the historical development of life it is necessary to:

(1) establish the fact of change through time (**past evolution**);

(2) demonstrate a mechanism which produces evolutionary change (**natural selection of genes**);

(3) observe evolution happening today ('**evolution in action**').

Evidence for past evolution comes from many sources based on geology, such as fossils and stratigraphy. Evidence for a mechanism is found in the experimental and observational data of the natural selection of heritable characteristics, such as the selection of shell colour in *Cepaea* (section 25.5.1), and the mechanism of inheritance demonstrated by Mendelian genetics, as in Mendel's work on peas. Finally, evidence for the action of these processes occurring today is provided by studies of present populations, such as speciation in the herring gull (section 25.8.4), and the results of artificial selection and genetic engineering, as in the cultivation of wheat and the production of monoclonal antibodies.

There are no laws of evolution, only well-corroborated hypotheses which collectively add together to form a well-attested theory. The premature acceptance of current concepts as dogmatic truths at any level of scientific inquiry may stifle intellectual growth and the search for truth. The uncritical acceptance of evolutionary theory is a case in point. Some of the events presented as evidence for evolutionary theory can be reproduced under laboratory conditions, but that neither implies nor confirms that they did take place in the past; it merely indicates the possibility that these events occurred. Contemporary scientific debates on evolution are not concerned that evolution takes place but that it takes place according to natural selection of randomly generated mutations.

24.7 Evidence for the theory of evolution

Evidence associated with current views on the theory of evolution, is provided from many sources, the main ones being palaeontology, geographical distribution, classification, plant and animal breeding, comparative anatomy, adaptive radiation, comparative embryology and comparative biochemistry.

Much of the evidence presented in this chapter was unavailable to Darwin and Wallace at the time of publication of their papers on the origin of species by natural selection. Whilst great scientists are often characterised more by their powers of induction than those of deduction based on observation and experiment, Darwin and Wallace appear to have had a judicious blend of both. Darwin sums up both of these approaches in his statement:

'In October 1838, that is, 15 months after I had begun my systematic enquiry, I happened to read, for amusement, Malthus on Population, and being well prepared to appreciate the struggle for existence which everywhere goes on from long-continued observation of the habits of animals and plants, it at once struck me that under these circumstances favourable variations would tend to be preserved, and unfavourable ones to be destroyed. The result of this would be the formation of new species. Here, then, I had at last got a theory by which to work.'

The evidence presented here largely, but tentatively, supports the theory of evolution by natural selection as

Table 24.3 Types of fossils, their formation and examples

Fossil	Fossilisation process	Examples
Entire organism	Frozen into ice during glaciation	Woolly mammoths found in Siberian permafrost
,, ,,	Encased in the hardened resin (amber) of coniferous trees	Insect exoskeletons found in Oligocene rocks in Baltic coast
,, ,,	Encased in tar	'Mummies' found in asphalt lakes of California
,, ,,	Trapped in acidic bogs: lack of bacterial and fungal activity prevents total decomposition	'Mummies' found in bogs and peat in Scandinavia
Hard skeletal materials	Trapped by sedimentary sand and clay which form sedimentary rocks, e.g. limestone, sandstone and silt	Bones, shells and teeth (very common in British Isles)
Moulds and casts	Hard materials trapped as above. Sediments harden to rock. The skeleton dissolves leaving its impression as a mould of the organism. This can be infilled with fine materials which harden to form a cast. Great detail is thus preserved	Gastropods from Portland Stone, Jurassic. Casts of giant horsetails (*Calamites*) of Carboniferous forests. Internal casts of mollusc shells showing muscle attachment points
Petrifaction	Gradual replacement by water-carried mineral deposits, such as silica, pyrites, calcium carbonate or carbon. Slow infilling as organism decomposes producing fine detail	Silica replacements of the echinoderm *Micraster*
Impressions	Impressions of remains of organisms in fine-grained sediments on which they died	Feathers of *Archaeopteryx* in Upper Jurassic. Jellyfish in Cambrian found in British Columbia. Carboniferous leaf impressions
Imprints	Footprints, trails, tracks and tunnels of various organisms made in mud are rapidly baked and filled in with sand and covered by further sediments	Dinosaur footprints and tail scrapings indicate size and posture of organisms
Coprolites	Faecal pellets prevented from decomposing, later compressed in sedimentary rock. Often contain evidence of food eaten, e.g. teeth and scales	Cenozoic mammalian remains

outlined in section 24.5. It draws on data obtained from many sources, and in all cases is interpreted in terms that assume the validity of the concept of evolution. Much of the evidence is also supportive of other sources of evidence. Circular arguments and exceptions to the evidence abound and alternative interpretations can be found, but the broad concept of evolution is backed up by a wealth of scientific evidence which, at this level, is difficult to present in a form which is comprehensible yet not indoctrinatory.

24.7.1 Palaeontology

Palaeontology is the study of fossils. Fossils are any form of preserved remains thought to be derived from a living organism. They may include the following: entire organisms, hard skeletal structures, moulds and casts, petrifactions, impressions, imprints and coprolites (fossilised faecal pellets) (table 24.3).

Fossil evidence alone is inadequate to uphold an evolutionary theory, but it supports a theory of progressive increase in complexity of organisms and denies the fixity of species. Fossils were well known before evolution was generally accepted. They were interpreted either as the remains of former creations or as artefacts inserted into the rocks by God. Most of the remains found so far can be classified into the same taxonomic groups (phyla and classes) as living species, but whether they represent the ancestors of present-day forms can only be debated, not proved.

The oldest fossil-bearing rocks contain very few types of fossilised organisms and they all have a simple structure. Younger rocks contain a greater variety of fossils with increasingly complex structures. Throughout the fossil record many species which appear at an early stratigraphic level disappear at a later level. This is interpreted in evolutionary terms as indicating the times at which species originated and became extinct.

Geophysical evidence suggests that geographical regions and climatic conditions have varied throughout the Earth's history. Since organisms are adapted to particular environments, the constantly changing conditions may have favoured a mechanism for evolutionary change that accounts for the progressive changes in the structure of organisms as shown by the fossil record. Ecological considerations also fit in with the fossil evidence. For example, plants appeared on land before animals, and insects appeared before insect-pollinated flowers.

One of the major criticisms of using fossil evidence in support of an evolutionary theory is the lack of a continuous fossil record. Gaps in the fossil record ('missing links') are taken as strong evidence against a theory of descent by modification. However, there are several explanations for the incompleteness of the fossil record. These include the facts that:

Fig 24.3 *Photograph of trilobite fossil in Cambrian rocks*

(1) dead organisms decompose rapidly;
(2) dead organisms are eaten by scavengers;
(3) soft-bodied organisms do not fossilise easily;
(4) only a small fraction of living organisms will have died in conditions favourable for fossilisation;
(5) only a fraction of fossils have been unearthed.

Support for an evolutionary process increases as more and more possible 'missing links' are discovered, either as fossils, such as *Seymouria* (amphibia/reptile), *Archaeopteryx* (reptile/bird) and *Cynognathus* (reptile/mammal), or as living organisms representing groups with close structural similarities, such as *Peripatus* (fig 24.18) and *Latimeria*.

Alternatively, there exists the possibility that new species appeared so suddenly that intermediate forms in the lineage do not exist. Eldredge and Gould have proposed a process called '**punctuated equilibria**' which accounts for the sudden appearance of species. According to this proposal species remain unchanged for long periods of time before giving rise to new species in comparatively short periods of time. This process depends on the fact that evolutionary rates are variable and that certain new species arise rapidly with the palaeontological consequence of an incomplete fossil record. These apparent 'jumps' in the evolutionary sequence have given rise to the term '**saltatory evolution**' (*saltare*, to jump). Darwin himself considered this possibility and stated as much in the *Origin of Species*:

'I do not suppose that the process (speciation) . . . goes on continuously; it is far more probable that each form remains for long periods unaltered, and then again undergoes modification.'

The fossil history of the horse

The history of the horse provides one of the best examples of phylogeny based on an almost complete fossil record found in North American sedimentary deposits from the early Eocene to the present.

The earliest recognisable perissodactyls (odd-toed, hoofed mammals) appeared about 54×10^6 years ago and present-day perissodactyls include horses, tapirs and rhinoceroses. The oldest recognisable horse-like fossils belong to a genus called *Hyracotherium* which was widely distributed throughout North America and Europe during the early Eocene. By the beginning of the Oligocene it was extinct everywhere except North America. It was a small animal, lightly built and adapted for running. The limbs were short and slender and the feet elongated so that the digits were almost vertical. There were four digits in the forelimbs and three digits in the hindlimb. The incisors were small and the molars had low crowns with rounded cusps covered in enamel.

The probable course of development of horses from *Hyracotherium* to *Equus* involved at least twelve genera and several hundred species. The major trends seen in the development of the horse were concerned with locomotion and feeding. They represent adaptations to changing environmental conditions and may be summarised as follows:

(1) increase in size,
(2) lengthening of limbs and feet,
(3) reduction of lateral digits,
(4) increase in length and thickness of the third digit,
(5) straightening and stiffening of the back,
(6) better-developed sense organs,
(7) increase in size and complexity of the brain associated with point (6) above,
(8) increase in width of incisors,
(9) replacement of premolars by molars,
(10) increase in tooth length,
(11) increase in crown height of molars,
(12) increased lateral support of teeth by cement,
(13) increased surface area of cusps by exposure of enamel ridges.

A dominant genus from each geological epoch of the Cenozoic has been selected to show the progressive development of the horse in fig 24.4. However there is no evidence that the forms illustrated are direct relatives of each other.

The significance of the fossil sequence shown in fig 24.4 is that it supports a theory of progressive change based on homologous structures such as limbs and teeth. Each of the species shown in fig 24.4 represents a stage of development which was successful for several million years (as judged by the abundance of fossils) before becoming extinct. The extinction of a species did not, however, represent the disappearance of the family line. The fossil evidence reveals that another closely related species always superseded its extinction. As all the species in the sequence show structural and ecological similarities, this gives support to a theory of descent with modification. Other fossils found in the same rock strata suggest changing climatic conditions which, together with other evidence, indicates that each species was adapted to prevailing conditions.

The history of the horse does not show a gradual transition regularly spaced in time and locality, and neither is the fossil record totally complete. It would appear that several offshoots occurred from the line represented in fig 24.4, but they all became extinct. All modern horses appear to be descended from *Pliohippus*. The modern genus *Equus* arose in North America during the Pleistocene and migrated into Eurasia and Africa where it gave rise to zebras and asses as well as the modern horse. Paradoxically, having survived in North America for millions of years, the horse became extinct there several thousand years ago, at a time which coincided with the arrival of humans. Cave-paintings from other parts of the world suggest that the earliest use for the horse was as a source of food. The horse was absent from 'North America' until its reintroduction by the Spaniards almost 500 years ago.

24.7.2 Geographical distribution

All organisms are adapted to their environment to a greater or lesser extent. If the abiotic and biotic factors (section 12.2) within a habitat are capable of supporting a particular species in one geographical area, then one might assume that the same species would be found in a similar habitat in a similar geographical area, for example lions in the savannah of Africa and the pampas of South America. This is not the case. Plant and animal species are discontinuously distributed throughout the world. Ecological factors often account for this discontinuous distribution, but evidence from the successful colonisation of habitats by plant and animal species introduced there by humans suggest that factors other than those of ecological adaptation are involved. Rabbits are not endemic (naturally occurring) species in Australia, yet their rapid increase in numbers following their introduction by humans indicates the suitability of the Australian habitat. Similar examples of this principle are illustrated by the spread of domestic animals and plants by humans, such as sheep, corn, potatoes and wheat. A rational explanation for the discontinuous distribution of organisms is based on the concept of species originating in a given area and their subsequent dispersal outwards from that point. The extent of the dispersal will depend upon the success of the organisms, the efficiency of the dispersal mechanism and the existence of natural barriers such as oceans, mountain ranges and deserts. Wind-blown spores and seeds and flying animals would appear to have the best adaptations for dispersal over land and sea.

In contrast to, and despite the general principle of organisms being naturally confined to certain parts of the world, many related forms are found in widely separated regions, for example the three remaining species of lungfish (order Dipnoi) are found separately in tropical areas of South America (*Lepidosiren*), Africa (*Protopterus*) and Australia (*Neoceratodus*); camels and llamas (family Camelidae) are distributed in North Africa, Asia and

Epoch and age of oldest rocks	Genus	Body form (all heights are ground to shoulder)	Bones of right forelimb	Mode of life, climate and structural modification
Pleistocene 1×10^6 yr	*Equus*	up to 1.6m	hock — carpals — splintbones — cannon bone — 3rd digit — pastern — hoof	Adapted to life in dry grasslands. Very efficient at running. Metacarpals and metatarsals lengthened. Hoof formed from broadened phalanx 3 covering soft pad and all covered by claw. Teeth with large surface area. Enamel exposed where cement worn away. Premolars replaced by molars. Grind food.
Pliocene 7×10^6 yr	*Pliohippus*	1.0m	4 2 / 3	Increased reliance on speed. Digits 2 and 4 very much reduced. Thickening of metacarpals and metatarsals (hindlimb) for support. Phalanx 3 forms hoof. High-crowned teeth for eating grass.
Miocene 26×10^6 yr	*Merychippus*	up to 1.0m	4 2 / 3	Very dry conditions: prairies. Speed more important. Reduction of digits 2 and 4. Running on digit 3. Increase in length of remaining metacarpal and metatarsal. Taller with longer neck. Teeth longer with cement on crown.
Oligocene 38×10^6 yr	*Mesohippus*	up to 0.6m	4 2 / 3	Dry conditions: forests and prairies. Speed important to escape enemies. Only three digits very obvious. Third digit much enlarged.
Eocene 54×10^6 yr	*Hyracotherium*	about 0.4m	5 4 2 / 3 metacarpals (numbered as shown)	Size of fox. Lived on soft ground near streams. Four digits in forelimb and three digits in hindlimb increase surface area for support. Low-crowned molar teeth adapted to browsing on soft lush vegetation.

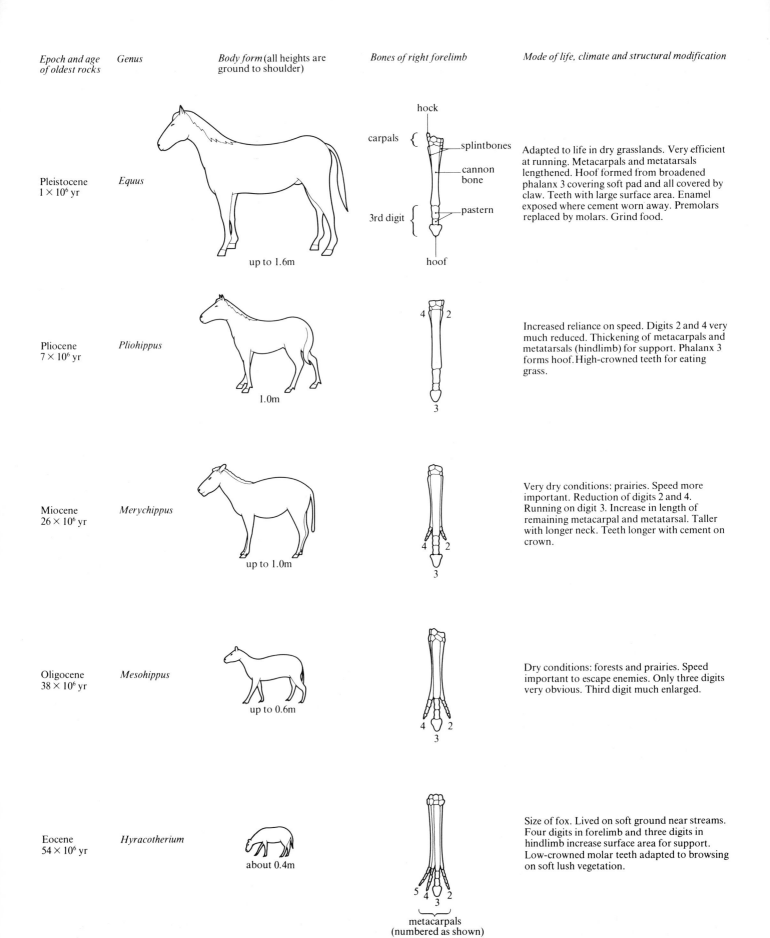

Fig 24.4 *Evolution of the modern horse*

872

South America; and racoons are widely found in North and South America and a small area of south-east Asia. Fossil evidence indicates that the distribution of these organisms was not always as seen today and that in the past they were more widely distributed.

Whilst none of this evidence has any immediate significance for evolutionary theory, it does point to the fact that the distribution of land masses was not always as it is today, as explained below.

It used to be believed that the world had always been as it now is and that the present continents and oceans had never changed positions. Early geologists, such as Hutton and Lyell (table 24.1), accounted for the existence of sedimentary rocks in terms of the periodic rise and fall of the sea. Later it was suggested that there were once two large continental masses, one in the Northern Hemisphere called Laurasia and one in the Southern Hemisphere called Gondwanaland, linked by extensive land bridges across which animals and plants could migrate and disperse. Subsequent geological research has modified this idea and favours the hypothesis of **continental drift**, based on the concept of **plate tectonics**. The hypothesis of continental drift was first proposed by Snider in 1858 but developed by Taylor in America and Wegener in Germany in the late 1800s. Wegener proposed that, during Carboniferous times, Laurasia and Gondwanaland formed one large land mass called Pangaea (Greek, all earth) which floated on the denser molten core of the Earth. It is now believed, though, that continents have drifted apart as a result of convection currents within the Earth spreading upwards and outwards, dragging plates on which the continents float. This hypothesis would account for the continuous movements of land masses and the present distribution of species such as those of the lungfishes (fig 24.5).

Fig 24.5 (a) Relative positions of South America, Africa and Australia during early stages of continental drift, indicating proximity of areas where lungfish may have originated. (b) Present distribution of species of lungfish

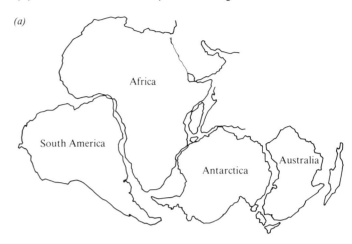

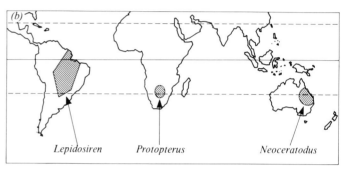

In the case of the camels and llamas it is believed that they arose from a common ancestor which fossil evidence suggests had its origin in North America. During the Pleistocene this ancestor spread southwards into South

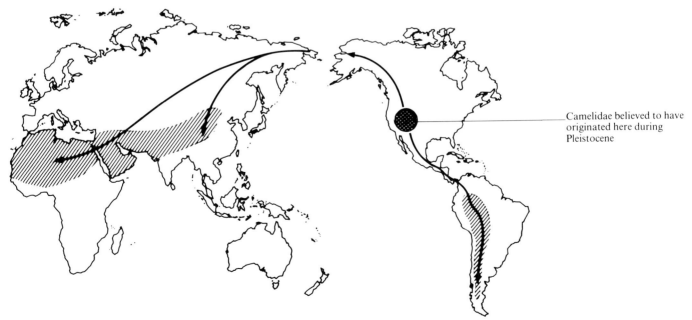

Fig 24.6 Map of the world showing distribution of present members of the family Camelidae, the camels in North Africa and Asia and the llamas in South America. During Pleistocene times the Camelidae were distributed throughout North and South America and much of Asia and North Africa. This distribution is based on fossil evidence. Solid black lines indicate possible migration routes. (Based on Matthews (1939) Climate of evolution, Vol. 1, 2nd ed., NY Acad. of Sci.)

America via the Isthmus of Panama, and northwards into Asia before changes in sea-level separated it from North America (fig 24.6). Throughout this time it is thought that progressive changes within the Camelidae occurred, producing the two genera *Camelus* and *Lama* at the extremes of their Pleistocene migration. Forms intermediate between the present camels and llamas exist in the fossil record throughout North America, Asia and North Africa. The fossil record indicates that other animals of the Camelidae in other parts of the world became extinct at the close of the last Ice Age.

Another example of discontinuous distribution as a result of geographical isolation is provided by the monotremes and marsupials of Australasia. Australasia is believed to have broken away from the other land masses during the late Jurassic, just after the appearance of primitive mammals. The mammals are divided into three orders: Monotremata, Marsupialia and Eutheria. In Australasia only the monotremes and marsupials developed. Here they coexisted and underwent adaptive radiation to produce the characteristic Australasian fauna represented by the monotremes *Tachyglossus* and *Zaglossus* (the spiny anteaters) and *Ornithorhynchus* (the duck-billed platypus), and 45 genera of marsupials. Elsewhere in the world the more advanced eutherian (placental) mammals also developed. As they spread out over the continents it is believed that they ousted the more primitive monotremes and marsupials from their ecological niches, except where geographical barriers disrupted their dispersal, as into Australasia.

These points may be summarised as:
(1) species originated in a particular area;
(2) species dispersed outwards from that area;
(3) dispersal could only occur for most species where land masses were close enough together to permit dispersal;
(4) the absence of more advanced organisms from a region usually indicates the prior separation of that region from the area of origin of those organisms.

Whilst none of the evidence presented above indicates the mechanism by which species are thought to have originated, it does suggest that various groups have originated at various times and in various regions. Fossil evidence reveals the ways in which these organisms have undergone gradual modification, but again gives no indication of the possible mechanism.

Evidence for a possible mechanism of the origin of species by natural selection is supplied by the distribution of plants and animals on oceanic islands. Both Wallace and Darwin were struck by the amazing diversity of species found on such islands, such as the Hawaiian and the Galapagos groups. Geological evidence indicates that these islands were formed by oceanic volcanic activity which thrust them up above sea level, so that they have never had any direct geographical links with any land mass. Plant species must have arrived on the islands by wind dispersal as spores and seeds, or water dispersal as floating seeds and masses of vegetation. Aquatic and semi-aquatic

organisms are believed to have been carried there by ocean currents, whilst terrestrial organisms may have been carried clinging to logs or floating masses of vegetation. Birds, bats and flying insects would have fewer problems of dispersal to these islands.

The Galapagos Islands are situated in the Pacific Ocean on the equator almost 1 000 km west of Ecuador and form an archipelago described further in section 25.8.3. When Darwin visited the islands in 1835, he noticed the similarity of the species found there to those on the nearest mainland, a fact he had also observed on the Cape Verde Islands off the coast of West Africa. However, the plant and animal species on oceanic islands were noticeably larger in most cases. This may be accounted for by the lack of competition from larger, and more dominant, advanced species which were absent from the islands, but which co-habited with smaller related species on the mainland. For example, the giant tortoise (*Geochelone elephantopus*), nearly 2 m long and weighing 260 kg, feeding on the plentiful vegetation found on the islands presumably attained this size due to the absence of competition from various mammalian species which existed on the mainland. Darwin noticed too that iguana lizards on the Galapagos Islands were abundant and again much larger than related mainland species. Lizards are terrestrial reptiles, but on the Galapagos Islands, where two species were found, one was aquatic. The aquatic form, *Amblyrhyncus cristatus*, fed on marine algae and showed adaptations for locomotion in water such as a laterally-flattened tail and well-developed webs of skin between the toes of all four limbs (fig 24.7). Competition for food, space and a mate within the terrestrial form is thought to have exerted a selection pressure on the lizards and favoured those showing variations with aquatic adaptations. This mechanism of environmental factors operating on a variable genotype is called **natural selection** and is described above. It could have been the process

Fig 24.7 *Giant aquatic lizard of the Galapagos Islands*

(a) Types of finch	Beak shape	Food source	Habitat	Number of species
large ground finch (ancestral)	typical main land type: short and straight	crushing seed	coastal	1
ground finches	various, but short and straight as above	seeds/insects	coast/lowlands	3
cactus ground finches	long slightly curved, split-tongue	nectar of prickly-pear cactus	lowland	2
insectivorous tree finches	parrot-like	seeds/insects	forest	3
vegetarian tree finch	curved, parrot-like	fruit/buds/soft fruit	forest	1
warbler finch	slender	insects in flight	forest	1
woodpecker finches	large, straight, (uses cactus spine or stick to poke insects out of holes in wood)	larvae insect	forest	2

which gradually gave rise to the aquatic species. It was, however, the diversity of adaptive structure shown by the 13 species of finches found within the archipelago which had the greatest influence on Darwin's thinking on the mechanism of the origin of species. Only one type of finch existed on the mainland of Ecuador and its beak was adapted to crushing seeds. On the Galapagos Islands, six major beak types were found, each adapted to a particular method of feeding. The various species, their feeding methods and numbers of species are summarised in fig 24.8.

Darwin postulated that a group of finches from the mainland colonised the islands. Here they flourished, and the inevitable competition produced by increase in numbers, and the availability of vacant ecological niches, favoured occupation of niches by those organisms showing the appropriate adaptive variations. Differences between species relate to small differences in body size, feather colour and beak shape. Several species of finch are found on all the bigger islands. The ground and warbler finches, thought to be the most primitive types, are found on most islands. The tree and vegetarian/tree finches are missing from the outlying islands, and the woodpecker finches are confined to the central group of islands. The actual species distribution is interesting and has been explained by Lack on the basis of adaptive radiation and geographical isolation. For example, on the central islands there are

Fig 24.8 (a) Adaptive radiation of Darwin's finches. (After Lack) (b) A male cactus finch (Geospiza scandens)

(b)

875

many species of several different types of finch, such as ground, tree warbler and woodpecker, rather than several species of the same type. Even where several species of only one type of finch are present, as on the outlying islands, each species differs in its ecological requirements. This fits in with the Gaussian exclusion principle (section 12.7) which states that two or more closely related species will not occupy the same area unless they differ in their ecological requirements.

24.7.3 Classification

The system of classification described in Appendix 3 was proposed by Linnaeus before the time of Darwin and Wallace, but has implications for the origin of species and evolutionary theory. Whilst it is possible to conceive that all species, both living and extinct, were created separately at a specific time or had no origin, the structural similarities between organisms, which forms the basis of a natural system of **phylogenetic classification**, suggest the existence of an evolutionary process. These similarities and differences between organisms may be explained as the result of progressive adaptation by organisms within each taxonomic group to particular environmental conditions over a period of time.

Numerical taxonomists, working mainly from comparative phenotypic characters have found it possible to construct a **phenetic classification** system (Appendix 3) which is consistent, to the extent of present knowledge, with the concept of evolution. These systems of classification are capable of standing in their own right as a basis for biological organisation, but they also strongly suggest that an evolutionary process has occurred.

24.7.4 Plant and animal breeding

One of the earliest features of human civilisation was the cultivation of plants and domestic animals from ancestral wild stocks. By selecting those members of the species which showed a favourable variation, such as increased size or improved flavour, and artificially breeding them by selective mating, selective propagation or selective pollination, the desired characteristics were perpetuated. Continued selective breeding by humans has produced the varieties of domestic animals and plants of agricultural importance seen today. It is known from archaeological remains that early humans were proficient in rearing cattle, pigs and fowl, and cultivating cereal crops and certain vegetables. Until the revelation of Mendel's work on genetics the theoretical basis of inheritance and breeding was not clear, but this has not limited human practical endeavour. In terms of genetics, humans are preserving those genes which are considered desirable and eliminating those which are undesirable for their purposes. This selection exploits naturally occurring gene variation, together with any fortuitous mutations which occur from time to time.

Whilst varieties of dogs, cats, birds, fish and flowers have been produced for sporting or decorative purposes, it is

(a)

(b)

Fig 24.9 *The result of selective breeding. The wild pig (a) is native to Europe, Asia and Africa but has been selectively bred to produce a variety of breeds, of which the English Large White pig (b) with its high quality of meat yield, is an example*

economically important varieties of animals and plants which have been studied most by plant and animal breeders (fig 24.9). Some specific examples of phenotypic characteristics which have been artificially selected are shown in table 24.4. A recently developed form of artificial selection is the selection for resistance to antibiotics, pesticides and herbicides shown respectively by pathogens, pests and weeds. A vicious circle is produced as new strains of organisms become immune to the ever-increasing number of chemical substances produced to contain and control them.

Table 24.4 Selected phenotypic characteristics and examples of them.

Phenotypic characteristic	Example
Hardiness	Sweetcorn grown in England
Size	Potato, cabbage
Increased yield	Milk, eggs, wool, fruit
Earlier maturity	Cereal crops (two per season)
Lengthened season	Strawberries
Taste/eating quality	Apples, seedless grapes
Harvesting ease	Peas
Length of storage	Beans/peas for freezing
Increased ecological efficiency	Protein from plants, e.g. soyabean
Resistance to disease	Rust and mildew (fungi)-resistant wheat

Since characteristics can be 'produced' by our ability to selectively breed, as in the case of breeds of dogs or pigeons, Darwin used this as evidence for a mechanism by which species might arise naturally. In the latter case the environment rather than humans were believed to act as the agent of selection. Artificially selected forms probably would not have arisen in the 'wild'; in most cases they are unable to compete successfully with closely related non-domesticated forms.

24.7.5 Comparative anatomy

Comparative study of the anatomy of groups of animals or plants (morphology) reveals that certain structural features are basically similar. For example, the basic structure of all flowers consists of sepals, petals, stamens, stigma, style and ovary; yet the size, colour, number of parts and specific structure are different for each individual species. Similarly, the limb-bone pattern of all tetrapods from amphibia to mammals has the same structural plan: it is called the **pentadactyl limb** (fig 17.11). This basic structure has been modified in several ways as illustrated in fig 24.10. In each case, the particular structure is adapted to a certain method of locomotion in a particular environment.

Organs having a similar basic structure, a similar topographic relationship as structures in other species, the same histological appearance and a similar embryonic development are said to be **homologous**, a term introduced in 1843 by Richard Owen.

Homologous structures showing adaptations to different environmental conditions and modes of life are examples of adaptive radiation. The ecological significance of these processes is considered in section 24.7.6. The specific functions that these structures carry out may vary in different organisms. These differences reflect the particu-

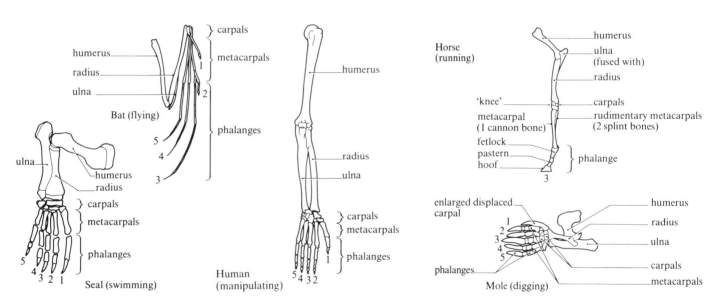

Fig 24.10 *Adaptations of the pentadactyl limb shown by mammals*

lar ways the organisms are adapted to their environments and modes of life. Other examples of homology are given below.

Branchial arches/Ear ossicles. Certain bones of the jaw in fish can be traced through other vertebrates, where they are involved in jaw suspension, to mammals where they appear as the ear ossicles, the malleus, incus and stapes (fig 24.11).

Halteres. The hind pair of wings typical of most insects have been modified in the Diptera into little rods, the halteres, which serve as gyroscopic organs helping to maintain balance in flight.

Pericarp. The ovary wall in flowering plants becomes modified, following fertilisation of the ovules, in a variety of ways to aid seed dispersal (figs 20.28 and 24.12).

Whilst homology does not prove that evolution has occurred, the existence of homology within a group of organisms is interpreted as evidence of their descent from a common ancestor and indicates close phylogenetic relationships.

Linnaeus used homology as the basis for his system of classification. The more exclusive the shared homologies, the closer two organisms are related and hence the lower the rank of the taxonomic group in which they are placed.

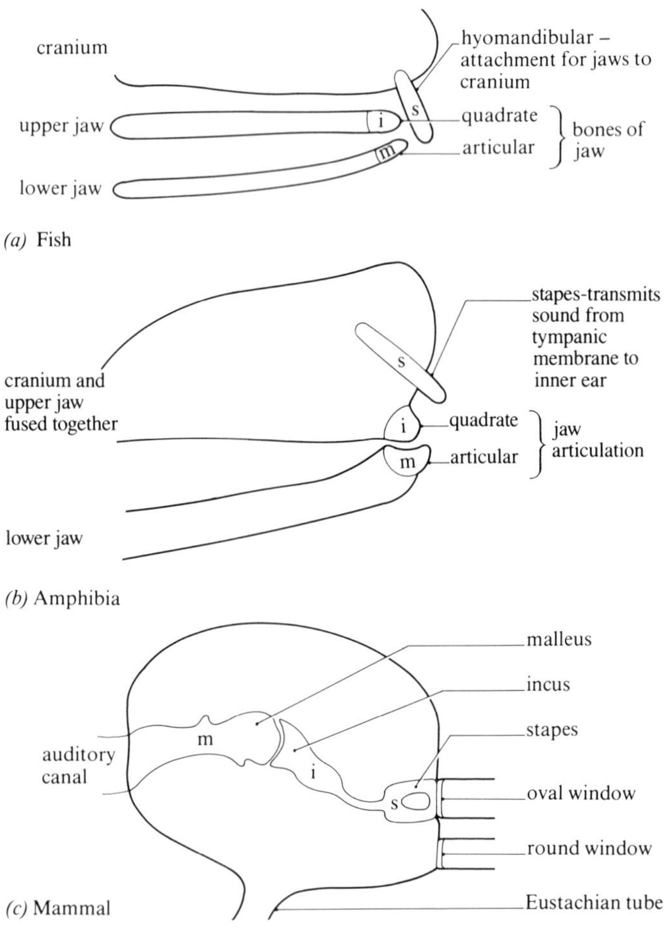

Fig 24.11 *Relative positions and functions of bones of the mammalian ear ossicles as seen in fish and amphibia*

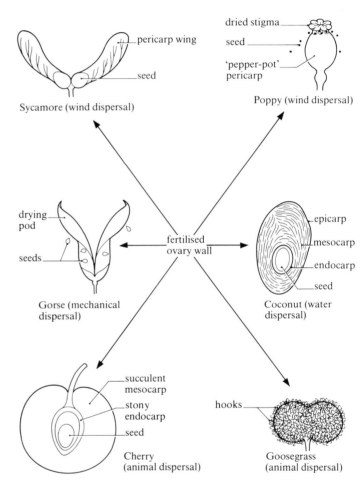

Fig 24.12 *Variation in pericarp structure for different methods of seed dispersal*

For example, butterflies and moths belong to the same order (Lepidoptera) whereas wasps and bees belong to another order (Hymenoptera).

Certain homologous structures in some species have no apparent function and are described as **vestigial organs**. The human appendix, although not concerned with digestion, is homologous with the functional appendix of herbivorous mammals. Likewise, certain apparently non-functional bones in snakes and whales are thought to be homologous with the hip bones and hindlimbs of quadruped vertebrates. The vertebrae of the human coccyx are thought to represent vestigial structures of the tail possessed by our ancestors and embryos. It would be very difficult to explain the occurrence of vestigial organs without reference to some process of evolution.

24.7.6 Adaptive radiation

When a group of organisms share a homologous structure which is differentiated to perform a variety of different functions, it illustrates a principle known as **adaptive radiation**. Adaptive radiation may be demonstrated within all taxonomic groups higher than the species. For example, all organisms belonging to a particular class share a number of diagnostic characteristics. Additionally, variations between different species within the class enable them to have modes of life adapted to particular habitats. For instance, the mouthparts of insects consist of the same basic structures: a labrum (upper lip), a pair of mandibles, a hypopharynx (floor of mouth), a pair of maxillae and a labium (fused second pair of mandibles, lower lip). Insects are able to exploit a variety of food materials, as shown in fig 24.13, because some of the above structures are enlarged and modified, others reduced and lost. This produces a variety of feeding structures.

The relatively high degree of adaptive radiation shown by insects reflects the adaptability and utility of the basic features of the group. It is this 'evolutionary plasticity' which has permitted them to occupy such a range of ecological niches. This is one of a group of related criteria used to describe the biological success of a taxonomic group, such as a phylum or class. Other criteria include the evolutionary age of the group and the number of species within the group.

The presence of a structure or physiological process in an ancestral organism, which has become greatly modified in more differentiated, apparently related organisms, may be interpreted as indicating a process of descent by modification which is the basis of evolutionary theory as defined in section 24.4.2. The significance of adaptive radiation is

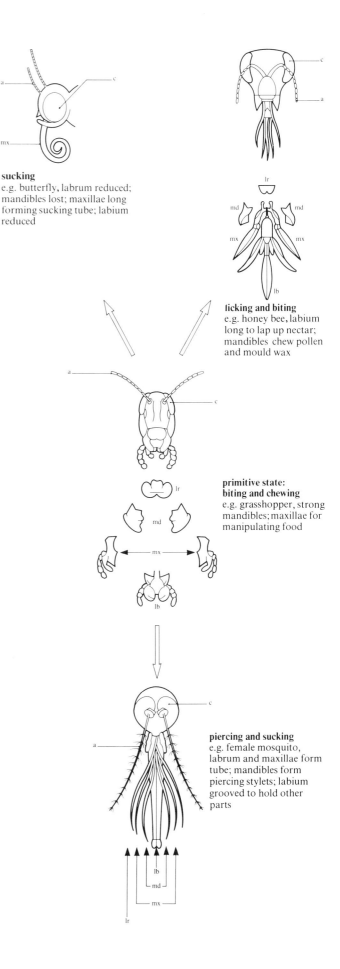

sucking
e.g. butterfly, labrum reduced; mandibles lost; maxillae long forming sucking tube; labium reduced

licking and biting
e.g. honey bee, labium long to lap up nectar; mandibles chew pollen and mould wax

primitive state: biting and chewing
e.g. grasshopper, strong mandibles; maxillae for manipulating food

piercing and sucking
e.g. female mosquito, labrum and maxillae form tube; mandibles form piercing stylets; labium grooved to hold other parts

Fig 24.13 *Adaptive radiation of insect mouthparts; a, antennae; c, compound eye; lb, labium; lr, labrum; md, mandibles; mx, maxillae*

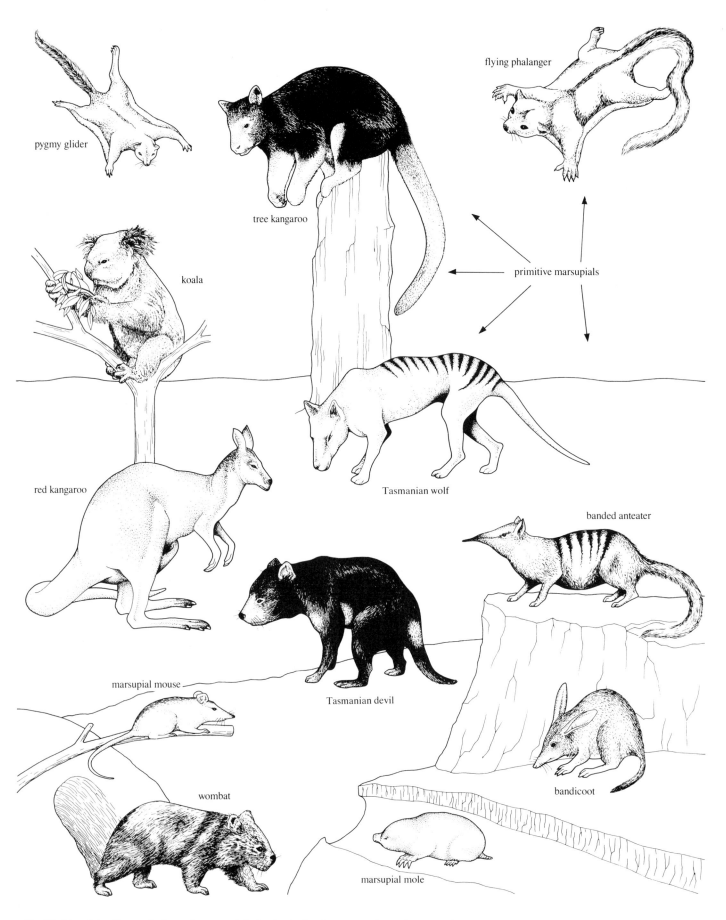

pygmy glider

flying phalanger

tree kangaroo

koala

primitive marsupials

red kangaroo

Tasmanian wolf

banded anteater

marsupial mouse

Tasmanian devil

bandicoot

wombat

marsupial mole

Fig 24.14   *Adaptive radiation of marsupials in Australia (from a variety of sources)*

that it suggests the existence of divergent evolution based on modification of homologous structures.

Similar structures, physiological processes or modes of life in organisms apparently bearing no close phylogenetic links but showing adaptations to perform the same functions are described as **analogous**. Examples include the eyes of vertebrates and cephalopod molluscs, the wings of insects and bats, the jointed legs of insects and vertebrates, the presence of thorns on plant stems and spines on animals, and the existence of vertebrate neuroendrocrines, such as acetylcholine, 5-hydroxytryptamine and histamine, in nettle stings. Analogous structures only bear superficial similarities. For example, the wings of insects are supported by toughened veins composed of cuticle, whereas both bats and birds have hollow bones for support. Likewise the embryological development of the cephalopod and vertebrate eyes is different. The former produces an erect retina with photoreceptors facing the incoming light, whereas the latter has an inverted retina with photoreceptors separated from incoming light by their connecting neurones (fig 16.33). Thus the vertebrate eye has a blind spot which is absent in cephalopods.

The existence of analogous structures suggests the occurrence of **convergent evolution**. Convergent evolution may be explained in terms of the environment, acting through the agency of natural selection, favouring those variations which confer increased survival and reproductive potential on those organisms possessing them.

The significance of divergent evolution, suggesting an evolutionary process, and convergent evolution, suggesting an evolutionary mechanism, is highlighted by the **parallel evolution** of marsupial and placental mammals. Both groups are thought to have undergone convergent evolution and come to occupy identical ecological niches in different parts of the world (fig 24.14 and table 24.5).

Table 24.5 Examples of parallel evolution shown by marsupial and placental mammals.

Marsupial mammals (Australasia)	Placental mammals (elsewhere)
Marsupial mole	Mole
Marsupial mouse	Mouse
Banded anteater	Anteater
Wombat	Prairie dog
Kangaroo	Antelope
Bandicoot	Rabbit
Flying phalanger	Flying squirrel
Koala	Sloth
Tasmanian wolf	Hyena

24.7.7 Comparative embryology

A study of the embryonic development of the vertebrate groups by Von Baer (1792–1867) revealed striking structural similarities occurring in all the groups, particularly during cleavage, gastrulation and the early stages of differentiation (section 21.5). Haeckel (1834–1919) suggested that this had an evolutionary significance. He formulated the principle that 'ontogeny recapitulates phylogeny', that is the developmental stages through which an organism passes repeats the evolutionary history of the group to which it belongs. Whilst this principle overgeneralises the situation, it is attractive and has a degree of demonstrable validity. Examination alone of the embryos and fetal stages of all the vertebrate groups reveals that it is impossible to identify the group to which they belong. Fig 24.15 shows that it is only in the later stages of development that they begin to assume some similarity to their adult form. At comparable stages the vertebrate embryos all possess the following.

(1) External branchial grooves (visceral clefts) in the pharyngeal region and a series of internal paired gill pouches. These join up in fishes to form the gill slits involved in gaseous exchange. In the other vertebrate groups the only perforation that develops in adults becomes the Eustachian tube and auditory canal involved in hearing.

(2) Segmental myotomes are evident in the tail-like structure which is retained in certain species only.

(3) There is a single circulation which includes a two-chambered heart showing no separation into right and left halves, a situation retained completely only in fishes.

As development proceeds in the vertebrate embryo, changes occur which produce the characteristics of fish, amphibian, reptile, bird or mammal depending upon the embryo's parentage. The interpretation placed on these

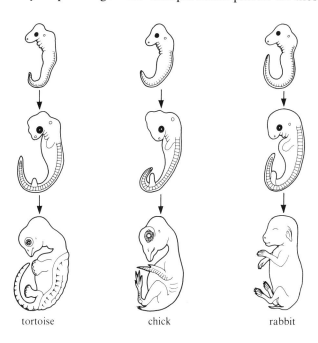

tortoise   chick   rabbit

Fig 24.15 *Stages in embryological development as shown by examples from three vertebrate classes*

881

observations is that these embryos, and hence the groups to which they belong, had a common ancestor. There seems little point in an organism having developmental structures which are apparently non-functional in the adult unless they are the remaining stages of ancestral structures. However the principle of recapitulation cannot be accepted entirely since no living organisms can show all the features of their proposed evolutionary ancestors. What appears to be probable is that organisms retain the inherited developmental mechanisms of their ancestors. Hence at various stages in development it is likely that an organism will show structural similarities to the embryos of its ancestors. Subsequent adaptations to different environmental conditions and modes of life will modify later stages of the developmental process. Observation reveals that the closer the organisms are classified on the basis of common adult homologous structures the longer their embryological development will remain similar. Organisms showing adaptations to certain modes of life and environments not typical of the major group to which they belong show fewer similarities to other members of the group during their embryonic development. This is clearly seen in the development of the parasitic platyhelminths (flatworms) *Fasciola* and *Taenia*, where a series of larval stages showing adaptations to secondary hosts exist which do not appear in the development of the free-living turbellarian platyhelminths, such as *Planaria*. Similarly, the terrestrial earthworm *Lumbricus* does not possess the ciliated trochophore larva which is typical of more ancestral annelids. This evidence highlights the imitations of Haeckel's principle of recapitulation.

Study of the embryological development of major groups of organisms reveals structural similarities evident in the embryonic and larval stages which are not apparent in the adult stages. These observations are interpreted as suggesting phylogenetic relationships between various groups of organisms and the implication underlying this is that an evolutionary process exists. On the basis of the cleavage patterns of the zygote and the fate of the blastopore, triploblastic animals may be divided into two groups, the protostomes and deuterostomes. **Protostomes**

show spiral cleavage and their blastopore becomes the mouth of the adult. This pattern of development is seen in the annelids, molluscs and arthropods. **Deuterostomes** show radial cleavage and their blastopore becomes the anus of the adult. The echinoderms and chordates show this pattern of development. These differences are shown in fig 24.16. It is evidence such as this which has helped clarify problems of the phylogenetic affinities of the echinoderms. The adult structure of echinoderms suggests that they are a non-vertebrate phylum, but their deuterostomic embryological development confirms their affinities with the chordate line of development. This example illustrates the principle that phylogenetic relationships should not be decided purely on evidence of adult homologous structures.

Evidence of the progressive development of various groups on the basis of embryological evidence can be seen within the plant kingdom, but examples are less well documented than for the animal kingdom. The early gametophyte of mosses and ferns, as represented by the protonema produced by germination of the spores, has a similar structure, physiology and pattern of growth to the filamentous green algae from which they are therefore thought to have developed. The principle of alternation of generations in plant life cycles, and the homologous variations upon it reflecting adaptations to various environmental conditions, may be interpreted as examples of homology and provide further evidence for evolutionary relationships between plant groups.

The cone-bearing plants represent a group which show features intermediate between those plants adapted to a terrestrial existence and those plants which still require water for the transfer of gametes. In the cycads the male gametophyte resembles the light dry microspore (pollen grain) of the angiosperms in that it is distributed by wind. As the male gametophyte develops, a pollen tube is formed as in angiosperms, but instead of this conveying a non-motile male gamete to the archegonium the terminal (antheridial) cell gives rise to two flagellated antherozoids (sperms) which swim to the ovule to bring about fertilisation (fig 24.17). The cycads therefore appear to represent an intermediate group between the non-vascular plants and the angiosperms and this suggests that a phylogenetic continuum exists within the plant kingdom. The existence of a group of organisms possessing features common to two other groups showing different levels of complexity, or adapted to different environments, may be interpreted as

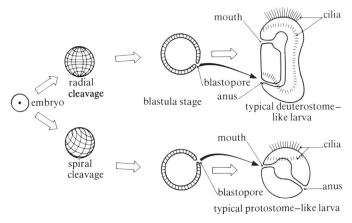

Fig 24.16 *Early developmental stages of deuterostomes and protostomes*

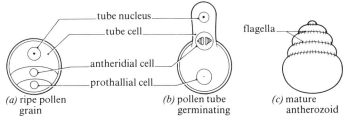

Fig 24.17 *Development of motile male gametes from pollen grain in* Cycas

Fig 24.18 *The primitive arthropod* Peripatus

suggesting phylogenetic continuity between the three organisms based on the descent of one group (such as the angiosperms) from another (the non-vascular plants) via the intermediate form (the cycads). Many of these intermediate forms are extinct and it is only by studying the fossil record that a progressive developmental sequence can be deduced. In many cases intermediate forms have not been found. These are equivalent to the 'missing links' but appear as gaps in the fossil record. It may be that these links do not exist, according to the hypothesis of punctuated equilibria (section 24.7.1). However, if one accepts the adage '*Natura non facit saltum*' ('Nature does not make leaps'), their absence may be explained by the possibility that they do not fossilise, have not yet been found, or even did not exist. In the case of the phylogenetic link between the annelids and the arthropods there is one group of organisms, the Onychophora, characterised by the genus *Peripatus*, which has features of both annelids and arthropods (fig 24.18). The annelid features include a body wall containing circular and longitudinal muscles, non-jointed parapodia-like limbs, segmental nephridia-like excretory tubules and a double ventral nerve cord. The arthropod features include a chitinous cuticle, spiracles and tracheae and an open blood system. Another 'living fossil' intermediate form is represented by the Dipnoi (lung fish) which suggests a link between fish and amphibians

Whilst much of this evidence suggests that some form of evolutionary process has occurred, it must be appreciated that there is no conclusive proof that it did occur.

24.7.8 Comparative biochemistry

As techniques of biochemical analysis have become more precise, this field of research has shed new light on evolutionary ideas. The occurrence of similar molecules in a complete range of organisms suggests the existence of biochemical homology in a similar way to the anatomical homology shown by organs and tissues. Again, this evidence for an evolutionary theory is supportive of other evidence rather than confirmatory in its own right. Most of the research which has been carried out on comparative biochemistry has involved analyses of the primary structure of widely distributed protein molecules, such as cytochrome *c* and haemoglobin, and more recently of nucleic acid molecules, particularly ribosomal RNA. Slight changes in the genetic code as a result of gene mutation produce subtle variations in the overall structure of a given protein or nucleic acid. This forms a basis for determining phylogenetic relationships if the following assumption is made: the fewer the differences in the molecular structure, the fewer the mutations which have occurred and the greater the affinity between organisms containing the molecule. Large differences in the molecular structure represent large differences in the DNA and predictably this situation exists in organisms showing fewer anatomical homologies.

Cytochromes are respiratory proteins situated in the mitochondria of cells and are responsible for the transfer of electrons along the respiratory pathway which produces water and liberates the energy required to synthesise ATP molecules (section 11.5.4). Cytochrome *c* is one such protein from the pathway. It is a conjugated protein composed of an iron-containing prosthetic group surrounded by a polypeptide chain containing between 104 and 112 amino acids, depending upon species. Modern techniques of computerised mass spectrometry have enabled the primary structure of the cytochrome *c* polypeptide chain to be worked out for a range of

Table 24.6 Cytochrome _c_ amino acid sequences for 21 species.

Species	70	1	2	3	4	5	6	7	8	9	80	1	2	3	4	5	6	7	8	9	90	1	2	3	4	5
Human	D	T	L	M	E	Y	L	E	N	P	K	K	Y	I	P	G	T	K	M	I	F	V	G	I	K	K
Rhesus monkey	D	T	L	M	E	Y	L	E	N	P	K	K	Y	I	P	G	T	K	M	I	F	V	G	I	K	K
Horse	E	T	L	M	E	Y	L	E	N	P	K	K	Y	I	P	G	T	K	M	I	F	A	G	I	K	K
Pig, bovine, sheep	E	T	L	M	E	Y	L	E	N	P	K	K	Y	I	P	G	T	K	M	I	F	A	G	I	K	K
Dog	E	T	L	M	E	Y	L	E	N	P	K	K	Y	I	P	G	T	K	M	I	F	A	G	I	K	K
Grey whale	E	T	L	M	E	Y	L	E	N	P	K	K	Y	I	P	G	T	K	M	I	F	A	G	I	K	K
Rabbit	D	T	L	M	E	Y	L	E	N	P	K	K	Y	I	P	G	T	K	M	I	F	A	G	I	K	K
Kangaroo	D	T	L	M	E	Y	L	E	N	P	K	K	Y	I	P	G	T	K	M	I	F	A	G	I	K	K
Chicken, turkey	D	T	L	M	E	Y	L	E	N	P	K	K	Y	I	P	G	T	K	M	I	F	A	G	I	K	K
Penguin	D	T	L	M	E	Y	L	E	N	P	K	K	Y	I	P	G	T	K	M	I	F	A	G	I	K	K
Pekin duck	D	T	L	M	E	Y	L	E	N	P	K	K	Y	I	P	G	T	K	M	I	F	A	G	I	K	K
Snapping turtle	E	T	L	M	E	Y	L	E	N	P	K	K	Y	I	P	G	T	K	M	I	F	A	G	I	K	K
Bullfrog	D	T	L	M	E	Y	L	E	N	P	K	K	Y	I	P	G	T	K	M	I	F	A	G	I	K	K
Tuna	D	T	L	M	E	Y	L	E	N	P	K	K	Y	I	P	G	T	K	M	I	F	A	G	I	K	K
Screwworm fly	D	T	L	F	E	Y	L	E	N	P	K	K	Y	I	P	G	T	K	M	I	F	A	G	I	K	K
Silkworm moth	D	T	L	F	E	Y	L	E	N	P	K	K	Y	I	P	G	T	K	M	I	F	A	G	L	K	K
Wheat	N	T	L	Y	D	Y	L	L	N	P	K	K	Y	I	P	G	T	K	M	V	F	A	G	L	K	K
Fungus (_Neurospora_)	N	T	L	F	E	Y	L	E	N	P	K	K	Y	I	P	G	T	K	M	V	F	P	G	L	K	K
Fungus (_baker's yeast_)	N	N	M	S	E	Y	L	T	N	P	K	K	Y	I	P	G	T	K	M	A	F	G	G	L	K	K
Fungus (_Candida_)	P	T	M	S	D	Y	L	E	N	P	K	K	Y	I	P	G	T	K	M	A	F	G	G	L	K	K
Bacterium (_Rhodospirillum_)	A	N	L	A	A	Y	V	K	N	P	K	A	F	V	L	E	S	K	M	T	F	K	-	L	T	K

Key to amino acids

A	alanine	F	phenylalanine	K	lysine
C	cysteine	G	glycine	L	leucine
D	aspartic acid	H	histidine	M	methionine
E	glutamic acid	I	isoleucine	N	asparagine

P	proline	T	threonine
Q	glutamine	V	valine
R	arginine	W	tryptophan
S	serine	Y	tyrosine

After Dayhoff, M. O. and Eck, R. V. (1967–8) _Atlas of protein sequence and structure_, National Biomedical Research Foundation, Silver Spring, Md.

organisms, including bacteria, fungi, wheat, screwworm fly, silkworm, tuna, penguin, kangaroo and primates. The similarity in cytochrome _c_ amino acid sequence between 21 organisms studied in this way is surprisingly high. In 20 out of the 21 organisms studied, ranging from the athlete's-foot fungus to humans, the amino acids in positions 78–88 were identical (table 24.6). The amino acid sequence for cytochrome _c_ of humans and chimpanzees is identical and differs from the rhesus monkey by only one amino acid. The computer studies, based on amino acid sequences of cytochrome _c_, have produced plant and animal phylogenetic trees which show close agreement with phylogenetic trees based on anatomical homologies.

Similar results have been obtained from the study of the globin proteins, haemoglobin and myoglobin, involved in oxygen transport and storage. The similarities and differences between the haemoglobin molecules of four primate species are shown in table 24.7. The relationships between the various globins, based on amino acid sequences, and their occurrence in organisms is shown in fig 24.19. Variations in the amino acid sequence of cytochrome _c_ and the globins are thought to have arisen by mutations of ancestral genes.

Immunological research has also produced evidence of phylogenetic links between organisms. Protein molecules,

Table 24.7 Similarities and differences between the polypeptide chains of haemoglobin in four primate species.

Species	_α-haemoglobin_ (141 amino acids)	_Polypeptide chains_ _β-haemoglobin_ (146 amino acids)	_γ-haemoglobin_
Human	+	+	+
Chimpanzee	+	+	1
Gorilla	1	1	1
Gibbon	3	3	2

Haemoglobin is composed of four polypeptide chains, made up of α, β, and γ polypeptides. + indicates no difference in amino acid sequence from that of human, figures indicate number of amino acid differences.

present in serum, act as antigens when injected into the bloodstream of animals that lack these proteins. This causes the animal to produce antibodies against them which results in an antigen/antibody interaction (section 14.14). This immune reaction depends upon the host animal recognising the presence of foreign protein structures in the serum. Human serum injected into rabbits sensitises them to human serum and causes them to produce antibodies against human serum proteins. After a period of time, if human serum is added to a sample of

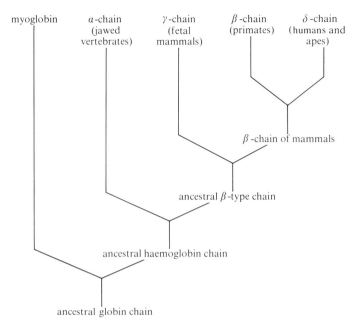

myoglobin   α-chain   γ-chain   β-chain   δ-chain
             (jawed   (fetal   (primates)   (humans and
             vertebrates)   mammals)   apes)

β-chain of mammals

ancestral β-type chain

ancestral haemoglobin chain

ancestral globin chain

Fig 24.19 *Supposed origins of myoglobin and vertebrate globin polypeptide chains. All five types are found in humans (After V. M. Ingram, (1963)* Haemoglobins in genetics and evolution, *Columbia University Press.)*

sensitised rabbit serum, antigen/antibody complexes form which settle out as a precipitate that can be measured. Adding serum from a variety of animals to samples of rabbit serum containing antibodies against human serum produces varying amounts of precipitate. Assuming that the amounts of precipitate are directly related to the amounts of 'foreign' protein present, this method can be used to establish affinities between animal groups as shown in table 24.8.

This technique of comparative serology has been used extensively to corroborate phylogenetic links. For example, zoologists were uncertain as to the classification of the king crab (*Limulus*). When various arthropod antigens were added to *Limulus* serum the greatest amount of precipitate was produced by arachnid antigens. This evidence reinforced morphological evidence, and *Limulus* is now firmly established in the class Arachnida. Similar

Table 24.8 Amounts of precipitate produced by adding serum from the following mammals to rabbit serum containing anti-human antibodies against human serum (amount of precipitate produced with human serum taken as 100%).

Human	100%
Chimpanzee	97%
Gorilla	92%
Gibbon	79%
Baboon	75%
Spider monkey	58%
Lemur	37%
Hedgehog	17%
Pig	8%

work has clarified many phylogenetic uncertainties amongst the mammals.

The separation of animal phyla into protostomes and deuterostomes on the basis of embryological development has been reinforced by analysis of the phosphate-containing storage molecules found in muscle and used in the synthesis of ATP. Protostomes, represented by annelids, molluscs and arthropods contain arginine phosphate, whilst deuterostomes represented by echinoderms and chordates, contain creatine phosphate.

A final example of biochemical homology is provided by the presence of similar or identical hormones in vertebrates where they carry out a range of different functions. For example, a hormone similar to mammalian prolactin occurs in all vertebrate groups where it is produced by the pituitary gland. Although it has been reported that there may be 90 distinct effects of prolactin, these can be arranged under two broad headings, reproduction and osmoregulation (table 24.9).

Table 24.9 Action of prolactin in vertebrates.

Group	Reproduction	Osmoregulation
Bony fish	Secretion of skin mucus	Increases urine production
Amphibia	Secretion of 'egg jelly'	Increases skin permeability to water
Reptiles	Suppresses egg production	Stimulates water loss in turtles
Birds	Production of 'crop milk'	Increases water uptake
Mammals	Mammary development and lactation	ADH-like activity

24.7.9 Conclusion

Neo-Darwinian evolutionary theory is based on evidence from a broad range of sources and supported by a mass of otherwise unrelated observations. This constitutes to the scientist the strongest type of evidence for the 'validity' of the theory. Evolution is widely accepted amongst scientists but there is still much work to be done in refining the theory and its application to all observed circumstances.

All scientific accounts, hypotheses and theories of the history of life are tentative and, as long as we remain objective in our search for truth, will remain so.

Since evolution forms a focal point within the study of biology it would be remiss to conclude this chapter without relating evolution to the perspective of the natural world. To do this it is fitting to quote from Darwin's final paragraph of the *Origin of Species*,

'There is a grandeur in this view of life, with its several powers, having been originally breathed by the Creator into a few forms or into one; and that, whilst this planet has gone cycling on according to the fixed law of gravity, from so simple a beginning endless forms most beautiful and most wonderful have been and are evolving.'

885

24.8　Human evolution

The course of human phylogeny can be followed only by means of the fossil record which is itself incomplete. However, the fragmentary fossil evidence recovered has enabled **palaeoanthropologists** to piece together an almost complete phylogeny for primates, though the validity of this phylogeny rests heavily on interpretation and conjecture.

The early stages of human evolution are studied by means of the comparative anatomy of fossils and the evidence of the comparative biochemistry of present-day humans and other mammalian species. Later stages of human evolution are studied using additional evidence from archaeological investigations. The existence of **artefacts** (objects made by humans) such as stone tools, pottery and fire hearths, provides us with insights into the ways in which modern humans have developed into the technological genius of the late-twentieth century.

Undoubtedly the greatest problem in studying human phylogeny is finding adequate fossil remains. Some excellent remains have been found, for example those in the sediments of the **Olduvai Gorge** in northern Tanzania by Louis, Mary and Richard Leakey, but invariably these consist of the skull and teeth only. These structures persist due to their extreme thickness and great hardness (fig 24.20).

Initially fossils are dated with respect to the age of the strata of rocks in which they are found and the ages of those above and below. This gives a **relative dating** for the fossils. **Absolute dating** is achieved by radioactive dating techniques as described in Appendix 5. Age estimates based upon both techniques are usually preferable to either in isolation.

Whatever conclusions we hold regarding humans and their probable ancestors must be tentative and open to revision in the light of new discoveries. Despite these cautions, there is a generally accepted view of human phyogeny which is presented below.

24.8.1　Human phylogeny

Humans belong to an order of mammals called **primates** which also includes tarsiers, lorises, lemurs, monkeys and apes (see table 24.10). The characteristics of this order show adaptations to life in a forest environment, and it was these requirements for an aboreal (tree-dwelling) existence which **preadapted** human ancestors for their evolutionary development. This enabled them to exploit the new ecological niches which appeared as the luscious forests of the Miocene period gave way to the drier grassland savannahs of the Pliocene period.

Within the order Primates are three groups of animals called **anthropoids**. These include the **New World monkeys** (marmosets and spider monkeys), the **Old World monkeys** (baboons and proboscis monkeys) and **hominoids** (apes and humans). Humans and their ancestors are more clearly

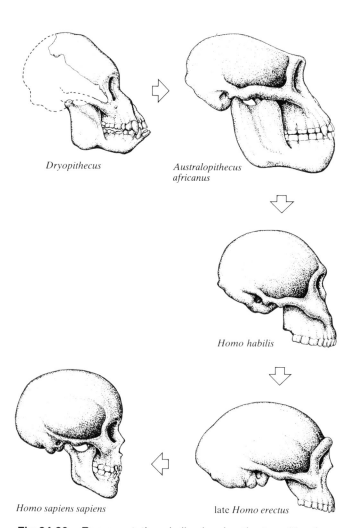

Fig 24.20　*Representative skulls showing the transition from* Dryopithecus *to* Homo sapiens

Table 24.10 Characteristics of the order Primates.

Grasping limbs	opposable thumb with grip for power and precision
Rotating forelimb	hand can rotate through 180°
Stereoscopic vision	eyes close together on face with parallel optical axes
Visual acuity	increased numbers of rods/cones with own nerve cells
Reduced olfaction	reduced snout allowing flatter face
Enlarged skull	expanded area for cerebrum, ventral foramen magnum
Large brain	increased sensory/motor areas, deeply fissured
Few offspring	longer gestation period, increased parental care
Social dependency	corporate activities, group cohesion

related to apes than any other anthropoid, and apes, in turn, are closer in phylogeny to Old World monkeys than to New World monkeys (see table 24.8).

It is generally accepted that the ape/human stock probably diverged from that of monkeys about 25–30

886

Table 24.11 Summary of the main features associated with human phylogeny.

Genus	Age of appearance/ million years ago	Skull	Brain capacity/cm^3	Teeth	Diet	Posture	Significance
Dryopithecus (earliest fossil ape)	25 (Miocene)	large muzzle	?	large canines, incisors, molars square	soft fruit, leaves	knuckle walker	earliest fossil ape, persisted until 10 million years ago
Ramapithecus	15 (Miocene)	deeper jaw	?	small canines, flattened molars, thicker enamel	seeds, nuts	partially upright	earliest hominid ground-dwelling in savannah
Australopithecus afarensis ('Lucy')	4.0 (Pliocene)	large jaws	450	small canines, small incisors	herbivorous	fully erect	still at home in trees but savannah dwellers
A. africanus	2.5	ventral foramen	450	small canines	carnivorous	fully erect	small game hunter, many variant forms
Homo habilis	2.0 (Pleistocene)	lighter jaw	700	small canines	carnivorous	fully erect	earliest stone tools, began hunting for meat, major increase in brain size foreshadowing social attributes
Homo erectus ('Peking Man')	1.5	thick, low forehead brow ridges	880	small canines	omnivorous	5–6 feet tall	beginning of cultural evolution, stone tools, cooperative hunting in bands, rudimentary language, used fire
Homo sapiens	0.25			small canines	omnivorous	5–6 feet tall	
(Swanscombe)	0.25	heavy jaw	1 200				cave-dweller
(Neanderthal)	0.08	face long and narrow, brow ridges, enlarged nasal cavity	1 500	heavier than modern teeth, wisdom teeth	omnivorous	5–6 feet tall	buried their dead, flint flake tools
(Cro-Magnon, modern man)	0.03	vaulted cranium, shorter skull, reduced jaws	1 400	teeth closer together, wisdom teeth	omnivorous	5–6 feet tall	polyphyletic origin giving rise to geographical races, arose by neoteny, cave-painting

million years ago, during the Oligocene period, and the subsequent separation of apes and human ancestors occurred between 5 and 10 million years ago in the middle of the Miocene period. From that time onwards, the family **Pongidae** (fossil forms and present-day gibbons, orang utans, gorillas and chimpanzees) and the family **Hominidae** (fossil forms and modern humans) have evolved along different lines. (Recent evidence, based on comparative biochemistry (section 24.7.8), has suggested that gorillas and chimpanzees may have diverged from human stock as recently as 5 million years ago. It is too early to uphold this claim as no supporting fossil evidence exists as yet.)

The gradual appearance of humans (*Homo sapiens sapiens*) from a common ape-ancestor took about 23 million years. During this time various fossil forms, represented in table 24.11 by four genera and six species, showed a transition in biological features such as skull appearance, tooth structure, brain size, upright posture and diet.

Of particular significance in the evolution of humans was the development of an upright posture (bipedalism) and the increase in brain size.

The transition from walking on four legs to walking on two legs (**bipedalism**) had implications far beyond those affecting the skeleton and muscles. It is now believed that the acquisition of an upright posture and the accompanying changes in the nervous system facilitated the subsequent enlargement of the cerebral hemispheres. The common ancestors of humans and apes are likely to have used all four limbs for movement, something akin to chimpanzees, but with the establishment of *Ramapithecus* more time was spent in an upright posture. By about 4 million years ago our hominid ancestors were bipedal and fully erect.

Freedom of the hands from locomotion enabled them to be used for carrying objects and manipulating the environment, all vital activities preadapting hominids for later dextrous activities associated with their cultural evolution. In addition, an upright posture gave the hominids increased height and range of vision which would have had advantages for them living, as they did, in the open savannah.

Along with the advantages of bipedalism was the **increasing brain size** as recorded by cranial capacities. Table 24.11 shows that the cranial capacities of hominids increased from about 450 cm^3 to about 1 400 cm^3. However, sheer volume alone does not give a complete picture of the brain potential which developed during human evolution. The complex infolding of the outer cortical tissue increased the surface area to give a much greater working area for the brain. This increase in effective area enabled control and coordination to be exercised over the newly developing behavioural activities such as tool-making, hunting and speech. Memory and intelligence – the ability to relate objects and events – rely on the provision of brain cells and nerve networks but these need to be programmed. It appears that this process of programming the human brain took a long time, during which time knowledge was acquired slowly and transmitted to subsequent generations by instruction.

The course of human evolution is remarkable in that the gradual transition in physical features (skeleton, movement, diet) were paralleled by an accelerating development in social behaviour. The process of becoming human is called **hominisation** and it is believed to have been influenced by: the development of *manipulative skills* and *speech*; changes in sexual behaviour allowing *pair bonding* and increased *parental supervision* of children; the establishment of *communal organisation* and *social responsibility*, arising from the principle of *food sharing*.

These essentially biological changes were accompanied by changes in information and behaviour transmitted from person to person by communication rather than inherited genetically. They signalled the development of *culture* which is defined as 'a store of information and set of behaviour patterns, transmitted, not by genetical inheritance, but by learning, by imitation, by instruction or by example.'* Culture embraces many different aspects of the life of people including customs, rituals, shared knowledge, language, beliefs, laws, religion, food and employment. Our knowledge of early human cultural evolution is limited to artefacts which archaeologists have recovered. Most of these are stone stools but their study gives useful insights into early human activities.

24.8.2   Stone tools

The increased brain size of *Homo habilis*, the dissociation of the hands from locomotion and the ability of the hands to achieve both power and precision grips led to the development of **stone tools**. *Homo habilis* (literally 'handy man') at first probably used pebble tools and sticks in much the same way as do present-day chimpanzees and gorillas. Gorillas strip leaves from twigs before inserting the twig into termite holes. When the termites climb onto the twig it is withdrawn and the termites eaten. The earliest human artefacts were made by *Homo habilis* (2 million years ago) and these were *chopping tools, hammer stones*, and *percussion flakes* made from lava or quartz and used for scraping. Later artefacts produced by *Homo erectus* (1.5 million years ago) required greater skill in manufacture and included *hand-held axes* having two cutting edges leading to a point. Sophisticated tools made from flint, bone and wood, however, did not appear until the Upper Palaeolithic, 35 000 years ago. The physical ability to make

* Stephen Tomkins (1984), *Origin of Mankind*, CUP.

888

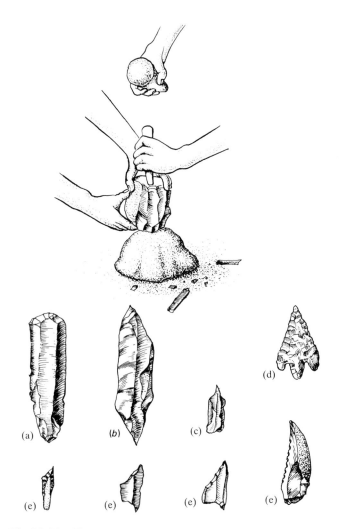

Fig 24.21   *The Upper Palaeolithic tool kit of Cro-Magnon Man. Using a hammer stone and antler tine punch, long-bladed flakes were struck from a flint core placed on a stone anvil. Flakes were then retouched to make such things as (a) end scraper, (b) burin chisel, (c) microburin drill, (d) arrowhead, (e) microliths (barbs). (After S. Tomkins (1984) The Origins of Mankind, Cambridge University Press)*

tools clearly requires sophisticated coordination of hand and eye. Such biological activities must be associated with the knowledge required to select materials, impart the skills to others and use these tools, the so-called cultural components of human development (fig 24.21).

The rate of progress in design, manufacture and use of hand tools from the pebbles of 2.5 million years ago to the hand-axes of 0.2 million years ago seems incredibly slow when compared to human technological achievements of the last 100 years. Since 1890 we have witnessed the origin of aircraft and sent people to the Moon, conquered most infectious diseases with antibiotics, transplanted organs and created artificial limbs and organs, developed computing to a sophisticated level, extended our senses with electron microscopes and radio telescopes, harnessed nuclear energy and exploited the potentials of biotechnology. This rapid increase in technology is not associated with increasing brain size but results from advances in research and development based on knowledge and skills transmitted from the previous generation. A child brought up by animals in total isolation from other humans (as in the case of the fabled Tarzan) would have no greater technological expertise than our hominid ancestors. It is through education alone, that is the transmission of culture, that humans are capable of the exponential technology advancement witnessed in the last 100 years.

24.8.3 Language

Oral communication is not unique to humans. Birds sing, porpoises 'beep', bats 'chirp' and monkeys and apes chatter, grunt and howl. Humans alone have developed spoken and written languages which are used to facilitate intraspecific communication and formulate abstract concepts of art, science, philosophy and religion. It is doubtful if we shall ever know when speech began but we suspect that its development was associated with cooperative hunting. Whatever the origins, the basic anatomical structures associated with speech had to be present in our ancestors. These include the lips, tongue and larynx and three areas of the brain, the speech motor cortical area (controlling the delivery of speech) and two further areas also in the left side of the cerebrum. One of these areas stores auditory, visual and verbal information and, the other is involved in formulating statements and response, that is putting words together. Studies of imprints of blood vessels and brain convolutions present in fossil skulls (**endocasts**) show that there was a substantial development of these areas in both *Australopithecus africanus* and *Homo habilis*.

24.8.4 Social behaviour in humans

Social behaviour in humans is developed to a greater extent than in any other species and extends beyond pair formation and family life to the establishment of communities at the levels of bands, tribes, chiefdoms and states.

The course of the evolution of human social behaviour was intimately linked with the development of culture and both were categorised by:
(1) establishment of the family (monogamy or polygyny);
(2) prolonged childhood (up to half of life) during which time children could acquire the prevailing culture;
(3) increased use of speech for communication;
(4) development of the concepts of a home base and food-sharing;
(5) competition for food replaced by cooperation in food-gathering enterprises;
(6) division of labour by age and sex, with older males hunting in bands to increase efficiency of hunting; women stay together to 'educate' children and gain protection from danger;
(7) stabilisation of a broader social structure where the

dominance hierarchy was replaced by kinship and prohibition of incest;
(8) extension of geographical range by tolerance of less optimal environments;
(9) use of simple tools and eventually the manufacture of complex tools;
(10) use of fire in cracking rocks, hardening wood, cooking food and defence against animals;
(11) development of folk wisdom, art, religion, philosophy, science and technology.

Thus we see the basic biological needs of food, sex and safety were satisfied more efficiently by the development of group activities based on a common economic–political–sexual structure enriched and supported by the rapid development of culture.

Indeed it can be said that current human evolution is based more on cultural development than on social behaviour.

24.8.5 Art and religion

Whilst humans share many aspects of behaviour with other primates and non-primates, there are some which are unique to the species and these include art, religion and free-will.

The earliest examples of representations of animals and humans come from the Upper Palaeolithic (30 000 years ago). Some are carved in wood and ivory and some are carved on cave walls. The significance of the early art is not known, but we do know that such activities required tools, skill, observation, thought, motivation and possibly leisure. Most of the best-known *cave paintings*, such as those at Lascaux in France, are no older than 20 000 years and used earth pigments, soot and burnt animal residues. What is interesting about these paintings is the variety of abstractions and techniques which are employed and the significance of work. Were they connected with rituals, religious beliefs, simply 'art for art's sake' or an early attempt at graffiti?

In some cases the art forms depicted animals and sex and these were often associated with death and birth respectively. Whether they had religious significance is not clear, but current opinion suggests they were not associated with religious figures as we know them today. *Religion* is believed to have developed at about the same time as cave painting as evidenced by the form of burials found in various parts of the world. In many cases the dead were buried along with offerings such as food, tools and decorative ornaments. A woman buried in Czechoslovakia had the paws of an arctic fox in one hand and its teeth in the other and her body was covered in red ochre. It is believed that this symbolism indicates established religious practices. Such a development requires the involvement of conscious intelligent thought, one of the most sophisticated aspects of cultural development. Religion as it is perceived today is fairly recent, the earliest shrines and temples and their accompanying artefacts being less than 10 000 years old.

Chapter Twenty-five

Mechanisms of speciation

The previous chapter described how Darwin came to appreciate that heritable variations occurred in natural populations as well as in artificial breeding situations. He perceived that these heritable variations were significant in evolutionary theory but had no means of accounting for the mechanism by which variations could appear and characteristics remain discrete. It was only with the reappearance of the work of Mendel on inheritance, and the appreciation of its importance in the understanding of evolutionary theory, that many of these problems could be resolved. Modern explanations of variation between organisms are a blend of evolutionary theory based on the work of Darwin and Wallace and genetic theory based on principles expounded by Mendel. Variation, inheritance and evolutionary theory may now be explained by evidence from a branch of biology known as **population genetics**.

25.1　Population genetics

A population is a group of organisms of the same species usually found in a clearly defined geographical area. Darwin was concerned how natural selection worked at the level of the individual organism in bringing about evolutionary change. Following the rediscovery of Mendel's demonstration of the particulate nature of inheritance, the importance of the genotype became significant in the study of variation, inheritance and evolutionary change. Bateson, the scientist who introduced the term 'genetics' in 1905, saw genetics as

> 'the elucidation of the phenomena of heredity and variation'.

It is the study of population genetics which forms the basis of modern views of evolutionary theory, a theory called **neo-Darwinism**, or the **synthetic theory of evolution**.

Genes acting independently, or in conjunction with environmental factors, determine the phenotypic characteristics of organisms and produce variation within populations. Phenotypes adapted to the environmental conditions or 'ecological framework' are '**selected for**', whereas nonadaptive phenotypes are '**selected against**' and eventually eliminated. Whilst natural selection operating on the phenotypic characteristics of individual organisms determines the fate of its genotype, it is the collective genetic response of the whole population that determines not only the survival of the species but also the formation of new species. Only those organisms which successfully reproduce before dying contribute to the future of the species. The fate of an individual organism is relatively insignificant in the history of a species.

25.1.1　Gene pool

A gene pool is the total variety of genes and alleles present in a sexually reproducing population, and in any given population the composition of the gene pool may be constantly changing from generation to generation. New combinations of genes produce unique genotypes which, when expressed in physical terms as phenotypes, undergo environmental selection pressures which continually select and determine which genes pass on to the next generation.

A population whose gene pool shows consistent change from generation to generation is undergoing evolutionary change. A static gene pool represents a situation where genetic variation between members of the species is inadequate to bring about evolutionary change.

25.1.2　Allele frequency

The appearance of any physical characteristic, for example coat colour in mice, is determined by one or more genes. Several forms of each gene may exist and these are called alleles (table 23.2). The number of organisms in a population carrying a particular allele determines the **allele frequency** (which is sometimes, incorrectly, referred to as the gene frequency). For example, in humans the frequency of the dominant allele for the production of pigment in the skin, hair and eyes is 99%. The recessive allele, which is responsible for the lack of pigment, a condition known as **albinism**, has a frequency of 1%. It is usual in population genetic studies to represent gene or allele frequencies as decimals rather than percentages or fractions. Hence this dominant allele frequency is 0.99 and the recessive albino allele frequency is 0.01. Since the total population represents 100% or 1.0 it can be seen that:

dominant allele frequency + recessive allele frequency = 1
　　　0.99　　　　+　　　　0.01　　　= 1

In terms of Mendelian genetics the dominant allele would be represented by a letter, say **N** (for normal pigmentation), and the recessive allele would be represented by **n** (the albino condition). In the example above, **N** = 0.99 and **n** = 0.01.

Population genetics has borrowed two symbols from the mathematics of probability, p and q, to express the frequency with which a pair of dominant and recessive alleles appear in the gene pool of the population. Therefore,

$$p + q = 1$$

where p = dominant allele frequency, and q = recessive allele frequency.

In the case of pigmentation in humans, $p = 0.99$ and $q = 0.01$,

$$\text{since} \quad p + q \quad = 1$$
$$0.99 + 0.01 = 1$$

The value of the above equation lies in the fact that if the frequency of either allele is known, the frequency of the other may be determined. For example, if the frequency of the recessive allele is 25% then q = 25% or 0.25.

$$\text{Since} \quad p + q \quad = 1$$
$$p + 0.25 = 1$$
$$p \quad = 1 - 0.25$$
$$p \quad = 0.75$$

That is, the frequency of the dominant allele is 0.75 or 75%.

25.1.3   Genotype frequencies

The frequencies of particular alleles in the gene pool are of importance in calculating genetic changes in the population and in determining the frequency of genotypes. Since the genotype of an organism is the major factor determining its phenotype, calculations of genotype frequency are used in predicting possible outcomes of particular matings or crosses. This has great significance in horticulture, agriculture and medicine.

The mathematical relationship between the frequencies of alleles and genotypes in populations was developed independently in 1908 by an English mathematician G. H. Hardy and a German physician W. Weinberg. The relationship known as the **Hardy–Weinberg equilibrium** is based upon a principle which states that

'the frequency of dominant and recessive alleles in a population will remain constant from generation to generation provided certain conditions exist.'

These conditions are:
(1) the population is large;
(2) mating is random;
(3) no mutations occur;
(4) all genotypes are equally fertile, so that no selection occurs;
(5) generations do not overlap;
(6) there is no emigration or immigration from or into the population, that is, there is no gene flow between populations.

Any changes in allele or genotype frequencies must therefore result from the introduction of one or more of the conditions above. These are the factors that are significant

in producing evolutionary change, and when changes occur the **Hardy–Weinberg equation** provides a means of studying the change and of measuring its rate.

25.1.4   The Hardy–Weinberg equation

Whilst the Hardy–Weinberg equation provides a simple mathematical model of how genetic equilibrium can be maintained in a gene pool, its major application in population genetics is in calculating allele and genotype frequencies.

Starting with two homozygous organisms, one dominant for allele **A** and one recessive for allele **a**, it can be seen that all offspring will be heterozygous (**Aa**).

Let	**A** = dominant allele			
	a = recessive allele			
Parental phenotypes	homozygous dominant	×	homozygous recessive	
Parental genotypes (2n)	**AA**	×	**aa**	
Meiosis				
Gametes (n)	(A) (A)	×	(a) (a)	
Random fertilisation				
F₁ genotypes (2n)	**Aa** **Aa**		**Aa** **Aa**	
F₁ phenotypes	all heterozygous			

If the presence of the dominant allele **A** is represented by the symbol p and the recessive allele **a** by the symbol q, the nature and frequency of the genotypes produced by crossing the F₁ genotypes above are seen to be:

F₁ phenotypes	heterozygous	×	heterozygous
F₁ genotypes (2n)	**Aa**	×	**Aa**
Meiosis			
Gametes (n)	(A) (a)	×	(A) (a)

Random fertilisation	**A** (p)	**a** (q)
A (p)	**AA** (p^2)	**Aa** (pq)
a (q)	**Aa** (pq)	**aa** (q^2)

F₂ genotypes (2n)	**AA** (p^2)	**2Aa** $(2pq)$	**aa** (q^2)
F₂ phenotypes	homozygous dominant,	heterozygous,	homozygous recessive

Since **A** is dominant, the ratio of dominant to recessive genotypes will be 3:1, the Mendelian monohybrid cross ratio. From the cross shown above it can be seen that the following genotypes can be described in terms of the symbols p and q:

$$p^2 = \text{homozygous dominant}$$
$$2pq = \text{heterozygous}$$
$$q^2 = \text{homozygous recessive}$$

The distribution of possible genotypes is statistical and based on probability. Of the three possible genotypes resulting from such a cross it can be seen that they are represented in the following frequencies:

$$\begin{array}{ccc} \textbf{AA} & \textbf{2Aa} & \textbf{aa} \\ \frac{1}{4} & \frac{1}{2} & \frac{1}{4} \end{array}$$

In terms of genotype frequency the sum of the three genotypes presented in the above population equal one, or, expressed in terms of the symbols p and q, it can be seen that the genotypic probabilities are:

$$p^2 + 2pq + q^2 = 1$$

(In mathematical terms $p + q = 1$ is the mathematical equation of probability and $p^2 + 2pq + q^2 = 1$ is the binomial expansion of that equation (that is $(p + q)^2$)).

To summarise, since

p = dominant allele frequency
q = recessive allele frequency
p^2 = homozygous dominant genotype
$2pq$ = heterozygous genotype
q^2 = homozygous recessive genotype

it is possible to calculate all allele and genotype frequencies using the expressions:

allele frequency $\qquad p + q = 1$, and
genotype frequency $p^2 + 2pq + q^2 = 1$.

However, in most populations it is only possible to estimate the frequency of the two alleles from the proportion of homozygous recessives, as this is the only genotype that can be identified directly from its phenotype.

For example, one person in 10 000 is albino, that is to say that the albino genotype frequency is 1 in 10 000. Since the albino condition is recessive, that person must possess the homozygous recessive genotype and in terms of probability it can be seen that

$$q^2 = \frac{1}{10\ 000}$$
$$= 0.0001$$

Knowing that $q^2 = 0.0001$ the frequencies of the albino allele (q), the dominant pigmented allele (p), the homozygous dominant genotype (p^2) and the heterozygous genotype ($2pq$) may be determined in the following manner.
Since

$$q^2 = 0.0001$$
$$q = \sqrt{0.0001}$$
$$= 0.01,$$

the frequency of the albino allele in the population is 0.01 or 1%.
Since

$$p + q = 1$$
$$p = 1 - q$$
$$= 1 - 0.01$$
$$= 0.99,$$

the frequency of the dominant allele in the population is 0.99 or 99%.
Since

$$p = 0.99$$
$$p^2 = (0.99)^2$$
$$= 0.9801,$$

the frequency of the homozygous dominant genotype in the population is 0.9801, or approximately 98%.
Since

$$p = 0.99 \text{ and } q = 0.01,$$
$$2pq = 2 \times (0.99) \times (0.01)$$
$$= 0.0198,$$

the frequency of the heterozygous genotype is 0.0198, or approximately 2% of the population carry the albino allele either as heterozygotes or albino homozygotes.

These calculations reveal a surprisingly high value for the frequency of the recessive allele in the population considering the low number of individuals showing the homozygous recessive genotype.

Heterozygous individuals showing normal phenotypic characteristics but possessing a recessive gene capable of producing some form of metabolic disorder when present in homozygous recessives are described as **carriers**. Calculations based on the Hardy–Weinberg equation show that the frequency of carriers in a population is always higher then would be expected from estimates of the occurrence of the disorder in the phenotype. This is shown in table 25.1.

Table 25.1 Some metabolic disorders and the frequencies of homozygous recessive and heterozygous genotypes.

Metabolic disorder	Approximate frequency of homozygous recessive genotype (q^2)	Frequency of 'carrier' heterozygous genotype ($2pq$)
albinism (lack of pigmentation in body)	1 in 10 000 (in Europe)	1 in 50
alkaptonuria (urine turns black upon exposure to air)	1 in 1 000 000	1 in 503
amaurotic family idiocy (leads to blindness and death)	1 in 40 000	1 in 100
diabetes mellitus (failure to secrete insulin)	1 in 200	1 in 7.7
phenylketonuria (may lead to mental retardation if not diagnosed)	1 in 10 000 (in Europe)	1 in 50

25.1.5 Implications of the Hardy–Weinberg equation

The Hardy–Weinberg equation shows that a large proportion of the recessive alleles in a population exist in carrier heterozygotes. In fact, the heterozygous genotypes maintain a substantial potential source of genetic variability. As a result of this, very few of the recessive alleles can be eliminated from the population in each generation. Only the alleles present in the homozygous recessive organism will be expressed in the phenotype and so be exposed to environmental selection and possible elimination. Many recessive alleles are eliminated because they confer disadvantages on the phenotype. This may result from the death of the organism prior to breeding or **genetic death**, that is the failure to reproduce. Not all recessive alleles, however, are disadvantageous to the population. For example, in human blood groups the commonest phenotypic characteristic in the population is blood group O, the homozygous recessive condition. This phenomenon is also clearly illustrated in the case of sickle-cell anaemia. This is a heritable disease of the blood common in certain populations in Africa, India, certain Mediterranean countries and amongst North American negroes. Homozygous recessive individuals usually die before reaching adulthood thereby eliminating two recessive alleles from the population. Heterozygotes, on the other hand, do not suffer the same fate. Studies have revealed that the sickle-cell allele frequency has remained relatively stable in many parts of the world. In some African tribes the genotype frequency is as high as 40%, and it was thought that this figure was maintained by the appearance of new mutants. Investigations have revealed that this is not the case, and in many parts of Africa where malaria is a major source of illness and death, individuals possessing a single sickle-cell allele have increased resistance to malaria. In malaria regions of Central America the selective advantage of the heterozygous genotype maintains the sickle-cell allele in the population at frequencies between 10 and 20%. The maintenance of a fairly constant frequency for a recessive allele which may be potentially harmful is known as **heterozygote advantage**. In the case of North American negroes who have not been exposed to the selection effect of malaria for 200–300 years the frequency of the sickle-cell allele has fallen to 5%. Some of this loss may be accounted for by increased gene flow resulting from black–white marriages, but an important factor is the removal of the selection pressure for the heterozygote due to the absence of malaria in North America. As a result of this the recessive allele has slowly been eliminated from the population. This is an example of evolutionary change in action. It clearly shows the influence of an environmental selection mechanism on changes in allele frequency, a mechanism which disrupts the genetic equilibrium predicted by the Hardy–Weinberg principle. It is mechanisms such as these that bring about the variations in populations which lead to evolutionary change.

Computer program. Changes in genotype percentages and gene frequencies over many generations, and the effects of mutation, selection, migration and genetic drift, can be investigated with the computer program HARDY–WEINBERG (CUP Micro Software).

25.2 Factors producing changes in populations

The Hardy–Weinberg equilibrium principle states that given certain conditions the allele frequencies remain constant from generation to generation. Under these conditions a population will be in genetic equilibrium and there will be no evolutionary change. However the Hardy–Weinberg equilibrium principle is purely theoretical because natural populations show the conditions necessary for equilibrium to exist (section 25.1.3).

The four major sources of genetic variation within a gene pool were described in detail in section 23.8.4, and they are crossing-over during meiosis, independent segregation during meiosis, random fertilisation and mutation. The first three sources of variation are often collectively referred to as **sexual recombination**, and they account for **gene reshuffling**. These processes however, whilst producing new genotypes and altering genotype frequencies, do not produce any changes in the existing alleles, hence the allele frequencies within the population remain constant. Many evolutionary changes, however, usually occur following the appearance of new alleles and the major source of this is mutation.

Other situations in which the conditions for the Hardy–Weinberg equilibrium principle do not exist are when there is non-random breeding, when the population is small and leads to genetic drift, when genotypes are not equally fertile so there is genetic load, and when gene flow occurs between populations. These situations are discussed below.

25.2.1 Non-random breeding

Mating in most natural populations is non-random. Sexual selection occurs whenever the presence of one or more inherited characteristics increases the likelihood of bringing about successful fertilisation of gametes. There are many structural and behavioural mechanisms in both plants and animals which prevent mating from being random. For example, flowers possessing increased size of petals and amounts of nectar are likely to attract more insects and increase the likelihood of pollination. Colour patterns in insects, fishes and birds, and behavioural patterns involving nest-building, territory possession and courtship, all increase the selective nature of breeding.

An experimental investigation with *Drosophila* illustrated the effect of non-random mating on genotype and allele frequencies. A culture of fruit flies containing equal numbers of red-eyed and white-eyed males and females was set up and within 25 generations all white-eyed fruit flies were eliminated from the population. Observation revealed that both red-eyed and white-eyed females preferred mating with red-eyed males. Thus sexual selection, as a mechanism of non-random mating, ensures that certain individuals within the population have an increased reproductive potential so their alleles are more likely to be passed on to the next generation. Organisms with less favourable characteristics have a decreased reproductive potential and the frequency of their alleles being passed on to subsequent generations is reduced.

25.2.2 Genetic drift

This refers to the fact that variation in gene frequencies within populations can occur by chance rather than by natural selection. Random genetic drift or the **Sewall Wright effect** (named after the American geneticist who realised its evolutionary significance) may be an important mechanism in evolutionary change in small or isolated populations. In a small population not all the alleles which are representative of that species may be present. Chance events such as premature accidental death prior to mating of an organism which is the sole possessor of a particular allele would result in the elimination of that allele from the population. For example, if an allele has a frequency of 1% (that is $q = 0.01$) in a population of 1 000 000 then 10 000 individuals will possess that allele. In a population of 100 only one individual will possess that allele so the probability of losing the allele from a small population by chance is much greater.

Just as it is possible for an allele to disappear from a population it is equally possible for it to drift to a higher frequency simply by chance. Random genetic drift, as its name implies, is unpredictable. In a small population it can lead to the extinction of the population or result in the population becoming even better adapted to the environment or more widely divergent from the parental population. In due course this may lead to the origin of a new species by natural selection. Genetic drift is thought to have been a significant factor in the origin of new species on islands and in other reproductively isolated populations.

A phenomenon associated with genetic drift is the **founder principle**. This refers to the fact that when a small population becomes split off from the parent population it may not be truly representative, in terms of alleles, of the parent population. Some alleles may be absent and others may be disproportionally represented. Continuous breeding within the **pioneer** population will produce a gene pool with allele frequencies different from that of the original parent population. Genetic drift tends to reduce the amount of genetic variation within the population, mainly as a result of the loss of those alleles which have a low

frequency. Continual mating within a small population decreases the proportion of heterozygotes and increases the number of homozygotes. Examples of the founder principle were shown by studies carried out on the small populations of religious sects in America who emigrated from Germany in the eighteenth century. Some of these sects have married almost exclusively amongst their own members. In these cases they show allele frequencies which are uncharacteristic of either the German or American populations. In the case of the Dunkers, a religious sect in Pennsylvania, each community studied was made up of about 100 families, a population so small as to be likely to lead to genetic drift. Blood group analyses produced the following results:

	Blood group A
indigenous Pennsylvanian population	42%
indigenous West German population	45%
Dunker population	60%

These values would appear to be the result of genetic drift occurring within small populations.

Whilst genetic drift may lead to a reduction in variation within a population it can increase variation within the species as a whole. Small isolated populations may develop characteristics atypical of the main population which may have a selective advantage if the environment changes. In this way genetic drift can contribute to the process of speciation.

25.2.3 Genetic load

The existence within the population of disadvantageous alleles in heterozygous genotypes is known as **genetic load**. As mentioned in section 25.1.5, some recessive alleles which are disadvantageous in the homozygous genotype may be carried in the heterozygous genotype and confer a selective advantage on the phenotype in certain environmental conditions, such as the sickle-cell trait in regions where malaria is endemic. Any increase in recessive alleles in a population as a result of deleterious mutations will increase the genetic load of the population.

25.2.4 Gene flow

Within the gene pool of a given cross-fertilising population there is a continual interchange of alleles between organisms. Providing there are no changes in allele frequency as a result of mutation, gene reshuffling will confer genetic stability or equilibrium on the gene pool. If a mutant allele should arise it will be distributed throughout the gene pool by random fertilisation.

Gene flow is often used loosely to describe the movement of alleles within a population as described above, but strictly speaking it refers to the movement of alleles from one population to another as a result of interbreeding between members of the two populations. The random introduction of new alleles into the **recipient** population and their removal from the **donor** population affects the allele frequency of both populations and leads to increased genetic variation. Despite introducing genetic variation into populations, gene flow has a conservative effect in terms of evolutionary change. By distributing mutant alleles throughout all populations, gene flow ensures that all populations of a given species share a common gene pool, that is it reduces differences between populations. The interruption of gene flow between populations therefore is a prerequisite for the formation of new species.

The frequency of gene flow between populations depends upon their geographical proximity, and the ease with which organisms or gametes can pass between the two populations. For example, two populations may be situated so close together that interbreeding is continuous and they may be considered in genetic terms as being one population since they share a common gene pool, for example two snail populations in adjacent gardens separated by a privet hedge.

It is relatively easy for flying animals and pollen grains to be actively or passively dispersed into new environments. Here they may interbreed or cross with the resident population, thereby introducing genetic variation into that population.

25.3 Selection

This is a mechanism that can be thought of as occurring at two interrelated levels, at the level of the organism and at the level of the alleles.

Selection is the process by which those organisms which appear physically, physiologically and behaviourally better adapted to the environment survive and reproduce; those organisms not so well adapted either fail to reproduce or die. The former organisms pass on their successful characteristics to the next generation, whereas the latter do not. Therefore selection can be seen to operate through the processes of **differential mortality** and **differential reproductive potential**. Selection has an adaptive significance in perpetuating those organisms most likely to ensure survival of the species and depends upon the existence of phenotypic variation within the population.

When a population increases in size, certain environmental factors become limiting, such as food availability in animals and light in the case of plants. This produces competition for resources between members of the population. Those organisms exhibiting characteristics which give them a competitive advantage will obtain the resource, survive and reproduce. Organisms without those characteristics are at a disadvantage and may die before reproducing. Both environmental limiting factors and population size operate together to produce a **selection pressure** which can vary in intensity.

Therefore, selection is the process determining which alleles are passed on to the next generation by virtue of the

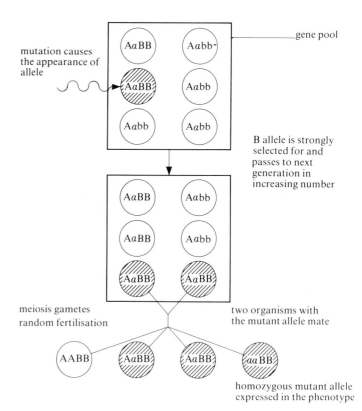

Fig 25.1 *Diagram showing the increased rate of spreading of a mutant allele (α) through a population if linked to a dominant allele (B) which is strongly selected for*

differential advantages they exhibit when expressed as phenotypes. Selection pressure can then be seen as a means of increasing or decreasing the spread of an allele within the gene pool and these changes in allele frequency can lead to evolutionary change. Major changes in genotype arise from the spread of mutant alleles through the gene pool.

The extent and timing of selection will depend upon the nature of the mutant allele and the degree of effect it has upon the phenotypic trait. If the allele is dominant, it will appear in the phenotype and be selected for or against. If the allele is recessive, as is the case with most mutants, it will not undergo selection until it appears in the homozygous state. The chances of this occurring immediately are slight and the allele may be 'lost' from the gene pool before appearing in the homozygous condition. An allele which is recessive in a given environment may persist until changes in the environment occur where it may have a dominant effect. These effects would probably appear first in the heterozygote and selection would favour its spread throughout the population, as in the case of sickle-cell anaemia.

A recessive mutant allele may spread rapidly through a population if it occupies a position (locus) on a chromosome very close (linked) to a functionally important dominant allele which is strongly selected for. In this 'linked' condition the chances of the mutant allele combining with another mutant allele to produce the homozygous condition are increased (fig 25.1).

The influence of a given mutant allele can vary. Those mutations affecting alleles controlling important functions are likely to be lethal and removed from the population immediately. Evolutionary change is generally brought about by the gradual appearance of many mutant alleles which exert small progressive changes in phenotypic characteristics.

There are three types of selection process occurring in natural and artificial populations and they are called stabilising, directional and disruptive. They may be best explained in terms of the normal distribution curve associated with the continuous phenotypic variation found in natural populations (fig 25.2).

25.3.1 Stabilising selection

This operates when phenotypic features coincide with optimal environmental conditions and competition is not severe. It occurs in all populations and tends to eliminate extremes from the population. For example, there is an optimum wing length for a hawk of a particular size with a certain mode of life in a given environment. Stabilising selection, operating through differential reproductive potentials will eliminate those hawks with wing spans larger or smaller than this optimum length.

Karn and Penrose carried out a study on the correlation between birth weight and post-natal mortality on 13 730 babies born in London between 1935 and 1946. Of these 614 were still-born or died within one month of birth. Fig 25.3 shows that there is an optimum birth weight of about 3.6 kg. Babies heavier or lighter than this are at a selective disadvantage and have a slightly increased rate of

mortality. From these results it is possible to calculate the intensity of selection pressure.

If 614 babies died at birth or within one month this represents a mortality of 4.5%. Even at the optimum birth weight 1.8% of babies died. Hence the selection pressure for weight at birth for babies of 3.6 kg is 4.5% − 1.8% = 2.7% or 0.027. At a birth weight of 1.8 kg there is a 34% mortality giving an intensity of selection pressure at this weight of approximately 30% or 0.3. It should be pointed out, however, that advances in paediatric medicine have considerably reduced post-natal mortality since 1946.

Stabilising selection pressures do not promote evolutionary change but tend to maintain phenotypic stability within the population from generation to generation.

25.3.2 Directional selection

This form of selection operates in response to gradual changes in environmental conditions. It operates on the range of phenotypes existing within the population and exerts selection pressure which moves the mean phenotype towards one phenotypic extreme. Once the mean phenotype coincides with the new optimum environmental conditions stabilising selection will take over.

This kind of selection brings about evolutionary change by producing a selection pressure which favours the increase in frequency of new alleles within the population. Directional selection forms the basis of artificial selection where the selective breeding of phenotypes showing desirable traits increases the frequency of those phenotypes within the population (section 25.4). In a series of experiments, D. S. Falconer selected the heaviest mice

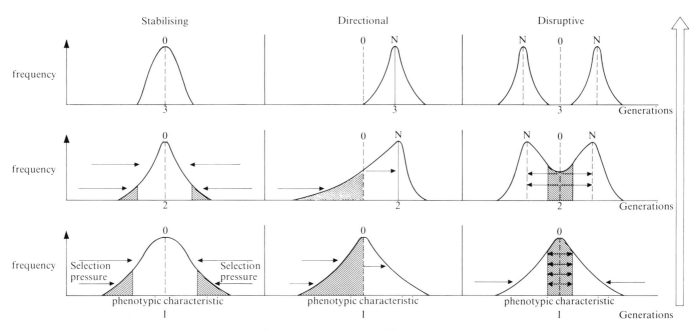

Fig 25.2 *Diagrams showing the three types of selection operating within populations. O indicates the original coincidence between optimum phenotype and optimum environmental conditions; N indicates the new position of coincidence of optimum phenotype and optimum environmental conditions. Organisms possessing characteristics in the shaded portions of the normal distribution are at a selective disadvantage and are eliminated by selection pressure. (The numbers 1–3 indicate the order of generations.)*

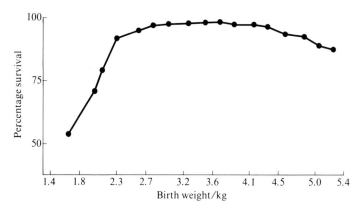

Fig 25.3 *The relationship between percentage survival and birth weight in human babies. (After M. N. Karn & L. S. Penrose (1951) Ann. Eugen., London, 16, 147–64.)*

from a population at six weeks and let them inbreed. He also selected the lightest mice and allowed them to inbreed. This selective breeding according to mass resulted in the production of two populations, one increasing in mass and the other decreasing (fig 25.4). After termination of selective breeding neither group returned to the original population mass of approximately 22 g. This suggested that the artificial selection of phenotypic characteristics led to some genotypic selection and some loss of alleles from each population. Many classic examples of natural directional selection can be seen in evidence today and they are discussed in section 25.5.

25.3.3 Disruptive selection

This is probably the rarest form of selection but can be very important in bringing about evolutionary change. Fluctuating conditions within an environment, say associated with season and climate, may favour the presence of more than one phenotype within a population. Selection pressures acting from within the population as a result of increased competition may push the phenotypes away from the population mean towards the extremes of the population. This can split a population into two sub-populations. If gene flow between the subpopulations is prevented, each population may give rise to a new species. In some cases this form of selection can give rise to the appearance of different phenotypes within a population, a phenomenon known as **polymorphism** (*poly*, many; *morphos*, form), and is discussed in section 25.5.1. Within a species organisms with different phenotypes, or **ecotypes**, may show adaptations to particular environmental conditions (section 25.6.2). When a species occupies an extremely large geographical range, organisms distributed along it may show local changes in phenotypic characteristics which are intermediate between those at the extremes of the range. This continuous gradation of characteristics along a geographical range is usually a phenotypic response to climate and/or edaphic (soil) variables and is known as a **cline** (section 25.6.3).

25.3.4 Intensity of selection pressure

The intensity of selection pressure within a population varies at different times and in different places and may be produced by changes in external or internal factors. External factors may include an increase in numbers of predators or pathogens or competition from other species (**interspecific competition**) for food and breeding space in the case of animals, and light, water and mineral salts in the case of plants. Changes in climatic conditions or the state of the habitat in which organisms live may exert new selection pressures. Internal factors such as a rapid increase in the size of the population can result in increased competition for environmental resources (**intraspecific competition**). As the population size increases, so do the numbers of parasites and predators. Pathogens, too, are more easily transmitted from organism to organism as the host population rises and diseases spread very rapidly. All of these factors may not only affect the intensity of the selection pressure but also the direction of the pressure. 'New' phenotypes (and genotypes) are selected for, and poorly adapted organisms are eliminated from, the population. The organisms to be eliminated first are those at the non-adaptive extremes of the phenotypic range.

One result of increased selection pressure is that it may cause organisms to become **specialised** to certain modes of life or narrower environmental conditions. This may be a disadvantage for the future of that species. Increased uniformity and dependency by a species increases the likelihood of that species becoming extinct should environmental conditions change. The fossil record contains many extinct organisms that were bizarre and overspecialised.

> **25.2** How might a knowledge of selection pressure and mode of life be useful in the eradication of a **named** parasite?

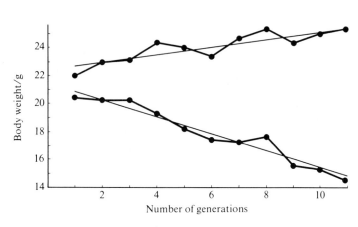

Fig 25.4 *Changes in weight in two mouse populations in successive generations undergoing selection for body weight. (After D. S. Falconer (1953) J. Genetics, 51 470–501.)*

From what has been said it can be seen that increased selection pressure is a conservative mechanism selecting for the phenotype best adapted to the prevailing environmental condition (the optimum phenotype).

A reduction in the intensity of selection pressure usually has the opposite effects to those described above. It may be produced by an absence of predators, pathogens, parasites and competing species or an increase in optimum environmental conditions. These conditions are usually found when an organism is introduced into a new environment. It is conditions such as these which are believed to have favoured the diversity of finch species found on the Galapagos Islands.

25.4   Artificial selection

Humans have practised artificial selection in the form of the domestication of animals and plants since the earliest times of civilisation. Darwin used evidence from artificial selection to account for the mechanism whereby changes in species could arise in natural populations, that is natural selection. The basis of artificial selection is the isolation of natural populations and the selective breeding of organisms showing characteristics or traits which have some usefulness to humans. In the case of cattle, the Hereford and Aberdeen Angus breeds have been selected for the quality and quantity of their meat, whereas Jersey and Guernsey cows are favoured for their milk yield. Hampshire and Suffolk sheep mature early and

produce a good quality meat but lack the hardiness and foraging ability of the Cheviot and Scotch Blackface. The latter examples show that no single breed has all the characteristics necessary for the best economic yield under all conditions and therefore a planned programme of selective breeding is often practised to increase the quality of the breed and the yield.

In artificial selection humans are exerting a directional selection pressure which leads to changes in allele and genotype frequencies within the population. This is an evolutionary mechanism which gives rise to new breeds, strains, varieties, races and subspecies. In all cases these groups have isolated gene pools, but they have retained the basic gene and chromosomal structure which is characteristic of the species to which they still belong.

25.4.1   Inbreeding

This involves selective reproduction between closely related organisms, for example between offspring produced by the same parents, in order to propagate particularly desirable characteristics. Inbreeding is a particularly common practice in the breeding of 'show' animals such as cats and dogs. It was used by livestock breeders to produce cattle, pigs, poultry and sheep with high yields of milk, meat, eggs and wool respectively, but for reasons stated below inbreeding is not now widely practised.

Prolonged inbreeding can lead to a reduction in fertility and this is a particular problem in the breeding of livestock.

(a)   (b)

Fig 25.5 An example of hybrid vigour. Photograph (a) shows two parental maize stalks which when interbred produce the hybrid shown in the centre of the photograph. The ear shown in the centre of the photograph (b) was produced by hybridisation of parental stocks with ears A and B as shown on the left and right of the photograph. (Photograph by D. F. Jones, Connecticut Agricultural Experiment Station.)

Intensive inbreeding reduces the variability of the genome (the sum of all the alleles of an individual) by increasing the number of homozygous genotypes at the expense of the number of heterozygous genotypes. In order to overcome these problems breeders resort to outbreeding after several generations of inbreeding. For example, a dairy farmer may use his own bull and successive generations of his own cows to produce cows with a high milk yield. Before the cattle begin to show signs of decreased resistance to disease and reduced fertility, the farmer will use another bull or artificially inseminate his breeding cows with semen acquired from a cattle-breeding centre. This introduces new alleles into the herd, thereby increasing the heterozygosity of the breeding population.

25.4.2 Outbreeding

This is particularly useful in plant breeding, but is being used increasingly in the commercial production of meat, eggs and wool. It involves crossing individuals from genetically distinct populations. Outbreeding usually takes place between members of different varieties or strains, and in certain plants between closely related species. The progeny are known as **hybrids**, and have phenotypes showing characteristics which are superior to either of the parental stocks. This phenomenon is known as **hybrid vigour** or **heterosis**. Hybrids produced from crossing homozygous parental stocks from different populations are called F_1 hybrids and show advantages such as increased fruit size and number, increased resistance to disease and earlier maturity. In maize (sweet corn), hybridisation has increased the grain yield of the F_1 hybrids by 250% over the parental stocks (fig 25.5). In the case of double-cross hybridisation, the hybrids produced by crossing two inbred strains are themselves crossed. The resulting hybrid produces ears having the quality and yield which more than covers the costs involved in a two-year breeding programme (fig 25.6).

Increased vigour results from the increased heterozygosity which arises from gene mixing. For example, whilst each homozygous parent may possess some, but not all, of the dominant alleles for vigorous growth, the heterozygote produced will carry all the dominant alleles, as shown in fig 25.7.

Increased vigour in certain varieties may not result simply from the increased prominence of dominant alleles,

Fig 25.6 *The phenotypes produced by double-cross hybridisation in maize. The maize crop on the right was produced by crossing the hybrids of the inbred strain (shown on the left)*

Fig 25.7 *A simple genetic explanation of increased vigour in F₁ hybrids*

Parental genotypes (2n)	FFgghhIIjj × FFGGHHiiJJ
Meiosis	
Gametes (n)	(F g h I J) × (F G H i J)
Random fertilisation	
F₁ genotypes (2n)	FfGgHhIiJj
F₁ phenotypes	This carries a dominant allele for each gene

but also from some form of interaction between particular combinations of alleles in the heterozygote.

If F₁ phenotypes are continually inbred the vigour will decrease as the proportion of homozygotes increases (fig 25.8).

Selective hybridisation can induce changes in chromosome number (chromosomal mutation), a phenomenon known as **polyploidy**, which can lead to the production of new species. An example of this is described in section 23.9.2.

25.4.3 Artificial selection in humans

Recent advances in human knowledge of the structure of the gene, the genetic code, the mechanisms of heredity and the prenatal diagnosis of genetic defects, have opened up the possibilities of selecting or eliminating certain characteristics in humans. The science of **eugenics** is concerned with the possibilities of 'improving' the 'quality' of the human race by the selective mating of certain individuals. This is a very emotive topic and raises all sorts of objections. Aldous Huxley in his book *Brave New World*, published in 1932, fictionalised the day when eugenics would be taken to its extreme possibilities and particular types of individuals would be produced according to the needs of society at that time. Whilst these ideas are repugnant to societies in which the freedom and rights of the individual are paramount, there are strong arguments for the exercise of limited forms of eugenic practice. In medicine, **genetic counselling** is becoming more acceptable as a means of informing couples with family histories of genetic abnormalities about the possible risks involved in

Fig 25.8 *Maize stalks of eight generations. The seven stalks on the right demonstrate loss of hybrid vigour as a result of inbreeding from the hybrid shown on the left. The last three generations show reduced loss of vigour as a result of their becoming homozygous. (Photograph by D. F. Jones, Connecticut Agricultural Experiment Station.)*

having children. By applying the Hardy–Weinberg equation it is possible to calculate the number of carriers of metabolic disorders such as phenylketonuria or abnormalities of the blood, such as thalassaemia, sickle-cell anaemia or haemophilia. Known carriers can be advised as to the likelihood of marrying another carrier and the possibilities of producing offspring affected by the disorder. Such forms of preventive medicine offer advice rather than dictate policy. Any scientific advances which reduce suffering must receive sympathetic appreciation. The dangers of eugenics lie in their possible abuse.

25.5 Natural selection

Natural selection, as postulated by Darwin and Wallace, represented a hypothesis based on historical evidence. For Darwin, the time span involved in the evolutionary change of a population was such that it could not be observed directly. Recent changes accompanying the industrial, technological and medical revolutions have produced such strong directional and disruptive pressures that we can now observe the results of dramatic changes in genotypic and phenotypic characteristics of populations within days. The introduction of antibiotics in the 1940s provided a strong selection pressure for strains of bacteria that have the genetic capability of being resistant to the effects of the antibiotics. Bacteria reproduce very rapidly, producing many generations and millions of individuals each day. Random mutation may produce a resistant organism in the population which will thrive in the absence of competition from other bacteria which have been eliminated by the antibiotic. As a result, new antibiotics have to be developed to eliminate the resistant bacteria, and so the cycle continues. Other examples of the effects of chemicals in producing selection pressure have been seen with DDT on body-lice and mosquitoes and the effect of the anticoagulant warfarin on rats. Following the development of resistant strains they spread very rapidly throughout the population.

Perhaps the classic example of evolutionary change is provided by the response of moth species to the directional selection pressure produced by the atmospheric pollution which accompanied the industrial revolution. Within the last 100 years darkened forms of about 80 species of moths have appeared in varying frequencies throughout the United Kingdom. This is a phenomenon known as **industrial melanism.** Up to 1848 all reported forms of the peppered moth (*Biston betularia*) appeared creamy-white with black dots and darkly shaded areas (fig 25.9). In 1848 a black form of the moth was recorded in Manchester, and by 1895, 98% of the peppered moth population in Manchester was black. This black 'melanic' form arose by a recurring random mutation, but its phenotypic appearance had a strong selective advantage in industrial areas for reasons put forward and tested by Dr H. B. D. Kettlewell.

The moths fly by night and during the day they rest on the

Fig 25.9 *Polymorphic forms of peppered moth,* Biston betularia. *(a) The normal form,* Biston betularia typica*; (b) the melanic form,* Biston betularia carbonaria. *(From E. B. Ford (1973)* Evolution studied by observation and experiment, *Oxford Biology Readers,* **55**, *Oxford University Press.)*

trunks of trees. The normal form of the moth is extremely well camouflaged as its colouration merges with that of the lichens growing on the trunks. With the spread of the industrial revolution sulphur dioxide pollution from the burning of coal killed off the lichens growing on trees in industrial areas, exposing the darker bark which was further darkened by soot deposits (fig 25.10).

Kettlewell, in the 1950s released known numbers of marked light and dark forms into two areas, one a polluted area near Birmingham where 90% of the population was the black form, and the other an unpolluted area in Dorset where the dark form was rarely found. On recapturing the moths using a light trap he obtained the following results:

	Birmingham	Dorset
Percentage marked dark form	34.1	6.3
Percentage marked light form	15.9	12.5

Kettlewell demonstrated using cine-film that robins and thrushes feed on the moths. This is a form of natural selection known as **selective predation**, and it acts as a selection pressure on the distribution of the melanic and non-melanic forms.

The results show that the melanic form of the moth, *Biston betularia carbonaria*, has a selective advantage in industrial areas over the lighter form, *Biston betularia typica*, whereas the lighter form has the selective advantage in non-polluted areas.

Subsequent research has demonstrated that the colouration of the dark form is due to the presence of a dominant melanic allele. Fig 25.11 shows a recent distribution of the two forms in the British Isles.

The presence of melanic forms in non-industrial areas of the east of England is explained by the distribution of melanic forms by prevailing westerly winds. Since the introduction of the Clean Air Act in 1956 the proportion of non-melanic forms has increased slightly as the selection pressure on these forms has been reduced in industrial areas.

25.5.1 Polymorphism

Polymorphism plays a significant role in the process of natural selection. It demonstrates many of the principles outlined earlier in the chapter regarding the relationship between genotype frequency within the population and variations in selection pressure. It is defined as the existence of two or more forms of the same species within the same population, and can apply to biochemical, morphological and behavioural characteristics. There are two forms of polymorphism, transient polymorphism and balanced, or stable, polymorphism.

A classic quantitative study of balanced polymorphism was carried out by Cain, Currey and Shepherd on the common land snail *Cepaea nemoralis*. The shells of this species may be yellow (and appear green with the living snail inside), brown, or various shades including pale fawn, pink, orange and red. The lip of the shell may be dark brown, pink or white and the whole shell may have up to five dark brown bands following the contours of the shell (fig 25.12). Both colouration and banding pattern are determined genetically. The colours are determined by multiple alleles with brown being dominant to pink and both being dominant to yellow. Banding is recessive.

Studies have revealed that the snails are predated upon by thrushes which carry the snails to a nearby stone which they use as an 'anvil' to crack open the shell; the snail inside is then eaten. By studying the proportions of types of shell found near an anvil with those in the immediate habitat, Cain, Currey and Shepherd demonstrated that selective forces were at work within the population. In areas where the background was fairly uniform, such as grass and woodland litter, the yellow and brown unbanded shells had a selective advantage as fewer of these shells were found near the anvil (fig 25.13). In areas where the ground cover was tangled and mottled, as in rough pasture or hedgerows, the darker banded shells had a selective advantage. The

(a)

(b)

Fig 25.10 *Melanic and non-melanic forms of* Biston betularia *on tree trunks in (a) an area near Birmingham, and (b) an area in Dorset. (Courtesy of Dr H. B. D. Kettlewell, Department of Zoology, University of Oxford.)*

Fig 25.11 *The distribution of melanic and non-melanic forms of* Biston betularia *in the British Isles in 1958. (After H. B. D. Kettlewell (1978)* Heredity, **12**, *51–72.)*

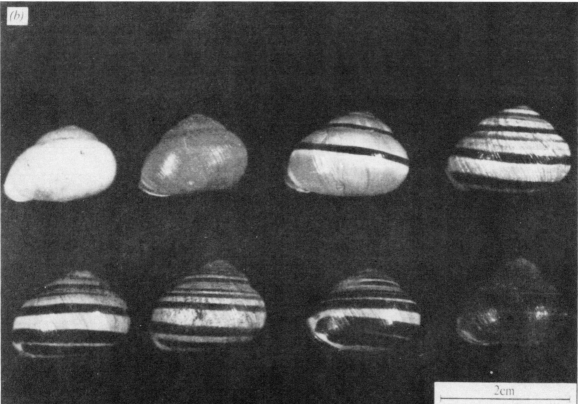

Fig 25.12 *Colour and banding pattern variation in the shells of* Cepaea nemoralis. *The extremes of colour and banding are shown as a progression from yellow unbanded (top left) to brown banded (bottom right). Photographs (a) and (b) show top and side views of the same shells. (After Tribe, Tallan & Erant (1978)* Basic Biology Course, *Book 12, Cambridge University Press.)*

904

Fig 25.13 *Unbanded shells of* Cepaea nemoralis *against a background of leaf litter. The shell on the extreme right is yellow, the shell at the top of the photograph is pink and the two shells on the left are brown. (After E. B. Ford (1973)* Evolution studied by observation and experiment, Oxford Biology Reader, **55**, *Oxford University Press.)*

forms suffering the greatest predation in any area were those which were visually conspicuous to the thrushes. A large population of polymorphic snails may include several areas with a range of backgrounds. Seasonal effects also produce changes in background colour and pattern. Although predation of conspicuous forms is continuous there is no overall selective advantage for any form, hence the numbers of each form within a population remain fairly constant from year to year.

The balance in numbers of each form may not be determined purely by colour and banding pattern. There is evidence to suggest that physiological effects may help to maintain the polymorphic equilibrium. In some areas where the soil is calcareous and dry and the background cover is light, the dominant forms are not always those with the least conspicuous colour and banding pattern. The genetic basis for the polymorphism shown by *Cepaea* is thought to rely on the existence of a special form of gene linkage. The genes for colour and banding pattern are linked and form a **super-gene** which acts as a single genetic unit and is inherited as such. These genes determine characteristics which have such a selective advantage that they are maintained within the population. It is the variety of allelic forms of these genes, maintained by the

heterozygotes which forms the basis of the polymorphism. The added linkage of genes controlling certain physiological effects is also thought to contribute to the maintenance of the balanced polymorphism. The existence of a number of distinct inherited varieties coexisting in the same population at frequencies too great to be explained by recurrent mutations, as in the case of *Cepaea*, is called **genetic polymorphism.**

Transient polymorphism

This arises when different forms, or **morphs**, exist in a population undergoing a strong selection pressure. The frequency of the phenotypic appearance of each form is determined by the intensity of the selection pressure, such as the melanic and non-melanic forms of the peppered moth. Transient polymorphism usually applies in situations where one form is gradually being replaced by another.

Balanced polymorphism

This occurs when different forms coexist in the same population in a stable environment. It is illustrated most clearly by the existence of the two sexes in animals and plants. The genotypic frequencies of the various forms exhibit equilibrium since each form has a selective advantage of equal intensity. In humans, the existence of the A, B, AB and O blood groups are examples of balanced polymorphism. Whilst the genotypic frequencies within different populations may vary, they remain constant from generation to generation within that population. This is because none of them have a selective advantage over the others. Statistics reveal that white men of blood group O have a greater life expectancy than those of other blood groups, but, interestingly, they also have an increased risk of developing a duodenal ulcer which may perforate and lead to death. Red–green colour blindness in humans is another example of polymorphism, as is the existence of workers, drones and queens in social insects and pin-eyed and thrum-eyed forms in primroses.

25.6 The concept of species

A species represents the lowest taxonomic group which is capable of being defined with any degree of precision. It may be defined in a variety of ways and some of these are summarised in table 25.2.

Organisms belonging to a given species rarely exist naturally as a single large population. It is usual for a species to exist as small interbreeding populations, called **demes**, each with its own gene pool. These populations may occupy adjacent or widely dispersed geographical areas. Spatial separation of populations means that the species may encounter a variety of environmental conditions and degrees of selection pressure. Mutation and selection within the isolated populations may produce the following degrees of phenotypic variation within the species.

25.6.1 Geographical races

Populations which are distributed over a wide geographical range or have occupied well-separated geographical habitats for a long period of time may show considerable phenotypic differences. These are usually based on adaptations to climatic factors. For example, the gypsy moth (*Hymantria dispar*) is distributed throughout the Japanese Islands and eastern Asia. Over this range a variety of climatic conditions are encountered, ranging from subarctic to subtropical. Ten geographical races have been recognised which differ from each other with regard to the timing of hatching of their eggs. The northern races hatch later than the southern races. The phenotypic variations shown by the ten races are thought to be the result of climatic factors producing changes in gene frequencies within their gene pools. The evidence that these variations are genetically controlled is shown by the fact that under identical environmental conditions the different races still hatch at different times.

25.6.2 Ecological races (ecotypes)

Populations adapted to ecologically dissimilar habitats may occupy adjacent geographical areas; for example the plant species *Gilia achilleaefolia* occurs as two

Table 25.2 Alternative ways of defining a species.

Biological aspect	Definition
Breeding	A group of organisms capable of interbreeding and producing fertile offspring
Ecological	A group of organisms sharing the same ecological niche; no two species can share the same ecological niche
Genetic	A group of organisms showing close similarity in genetic karyotype
Evolutionary	A group of organisms sharing a unique collection of structural and functional characteristics

races along the coast of California. One race, the 'sun' race, is found on exposed southerly facing grassy slopes, whilst the 'shade' race is found in shaded oak woodlands and redwood groves. These races differ in the size of their petals, a characteristic which is determined genetically.

25.6.3 Clines

A species exhibiting a gradual change in phenotypic characteristics throughout its geographical range is referred to as a **cline**. More than one cline may be exhibited by a species and they may run in opposite directions as shown by fig 25.14.

Species exhibiting marked phenotypic variation within a population according to their degree of geographical isolation are known as **polytypic species**. One classic form of a polytypic species is illustrated by gulls belonging to the genus *Larus* (section 25.8.4).

All cases of phenotypic variation described above represent varying degrees of genetic dissimilarity which may interfere with the breeding potential of members of the populations if brought together.

25.7 Speciation

This is the process by which one or more species arise from previously existing species. A single species may give rise to new species (**intraspecific speciation**), or, as is common in many flowering plants, two different species may give rise to a new species (**interspecific hybridisation**). If intraspecific speciation occurs whilst the populations are separated it is termed **allopatric speciation**. If the process occurs whilst the populations are occupying the same geographical area it is called **sympatric speciation**.

25.8 Intraspecific speciation

There are several factors involved in intraspecific speciation, but in all cases gene flow within populations must be interrupted. As a result of this each subpopulation becomes genetically isolated. Changes in allele and genotype frequencies within the populations, as a result of the effects of natural selection on the range of

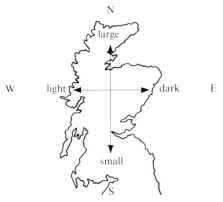

Fig 25.14 *Phenotypic variation in size and fur colour shown by the wood mouse* (Apodemus) *in Scotland*

phenotypes produced by mutation and sexual recombination, lead to the formation of races and subspecies. If the genetic isolation persists over a prolonged period of time and the subspecies then come together to occupy the same area they may or may not interbreed. If the breeding is successful they may still be considered to belong to the same species. If the breeding is unsuccessful, then speciation has occurred and the subspecies may now be considered to be separate species. This is the way in which it is believed evolutionary change can be brought about.

An initial factor in the process of speciation may be the reduction in the intensity of selection pressure within the population. This may lead to increased intraspecific variability. These new phenotypes may enable the population to increase its geographical range if the phenotypes show adaptations to environmental conditions found at the extremes of the range. Providing there is no reduction in gene flow throughout the population, the species, whilst exhibiting the localised phenotypic variation (ecotypes), will still share the same gene pool and continue to exist as a single species. This is the situation found in a cline.

Speciation will only occur as a result of the formation of barriers which lead to reproductive isolation between members of the population. Reproductive isolation is brought about by some form of what the geneticist Theodosius Dobzhansky called **isolating mechanism**.

25.8.1 Isolating mechanisms

An isolating mechanism is a means of producing and maintaining reproductive isolation within a population. This can be brought about by mechanisms acting before or after fertilisation. Dobzhansky suggested a classification of isolating mechanisms which has been modified and is shown in table 25.3.

25.8.2 Allopatric speciation

Allopatric (*allos*, other; *patria*, native land) speciation is characterised by the occurrence, at some stage, of spatial separation. Geographical barriers such as mountain ranges, seas or rivers, or habitat preferences, may produce a barrier to gene flow because of spatial

Table 25.3 Isolating mechanisms (after Dobzhansky).

Prezygotic mechanisms (barriers to the formation of hybrids)	
Seasonal isolation	Occurs where two species mate or flower at different times of the year; for example in California *Pinus radiata* flowers in February whereas *Pinus attenuata* flowers in April
Ecological isolation	Occurs where two species inhabit similar regions but have different habitat preferences; for example *Viola arvensis* grows on calcareous soils whereas *Viola tricolor* prefers acid soils
Behavioural isolation	Occurs where animals exhibit courtship patterns, mating only results if the courtship display by one sex results in acceptance by the other sex; for example certain fish, bird and insect species
Mechanical isolation	Occurs in animals where differences in genitalia prevent successful copulation and in plants where related species of flowers are pollinated by different animals
Postzygotic mechanisms (barriers affecting hybrids)	
Hybrid inviability	Hybrids are produced but fail to develop to maturity; for example hybrids formed between northern and southern races of the leopard frog (*Rana pipiens*) in North America
Hybrid sterility	Hybrids fail to produce functional gametes; for example the mule ($2n = 63$) results from the cross between the horse (*Equus equus*, $2n = 60$) and the ass (*Equus hemionus*, $2n = 66$)
Hybrid breakdown	F_1 hybrids are fertile but the F_2 generation and backcrosses between F_1 hybrids and parental stocks fail to develop or are infertile, for example hybrids formed between species of cotton (genus *Gossypium*)

separation. This inability of organisms or their gametes to meet leads to reproductive isolation. Adaptations to new conditions or random genetic drift in small populations lead to changes in allele and genotype frequencies. Prolonged separation of populations may result in them becoming genetically isolated even if brought together. In this way new species may arise. For example, the variety and distribution of the finch species belonging to the family Geospizidae on the islands of the Galapagos archipelago are thought to be the result of allopatric speciation. David Lack suggested that an original stock of finches reached the Galapagos Islands from the mainland of South America and, in the absence of competition from endemic species (representing relaxed selection pressure), adaptive radiation occurred to produce a variety of species adapted to particular ecological niches. The various species are believed to have evolved in geographical isolation to the point that when dispersal brought them together on certain islands they were able to coexist as separate species.

25.8.3 Sympatric speciation

Genetic differences may accumulate allopatrically in populations which have been geographically isolated for a much shorter period of time. If these populations are brought together, hybrids may form where these overlap. For example, both the carrion crow (*Corvus corone*) and the hooded crow (*Corvus corone cornix*) are found in the British Isles. The carrion crow is completely black and is common in England and southern Scotland. The hooded crow is black with a grey back and belly and is found in the north of Scotland. Hybrids formed from the mating of carrion and hooded crows occupy a narrow region extending across central Scotland (fig 25.15). These hybrids have reduced fertility and serve as an efficient reproductive barrier to gene flow between the populations of the carrion and hooded crows.

In time, selection against cross-breeding may occur, leading to speciation. Since such speciation occurs finally in the same geographical area, this is called **sympatric** (*sym*, together; *patria*, native land) **speciation**.

Sympatric speciation does not involve geographical separation of populations at the time at which genetic isolation occurs. It requires the development of some form of reproductive isolating mechanism which has arisen by selection within a geographically confined area. This may be structural, physiological, behavioural or genetic.

Sympatric speciation is more commonly thought of as providing an explanatory mechanism of how closely related species, which probably arose from a common ancestor by temporary isolation, can coexist as separate species within the same geographical area. For example, in the Galapagos archipelago the finch *Camarhyncus pauper* is found only on Charles Island, where it coexists with a related form *C. psittacula* which is widely distributed throughout the central islands (fig 25.16). The finch species appear to choose their mates on the basis of beak size. The range of beak sizes of *C. pauper* on Charles Island and *C. psittacula*

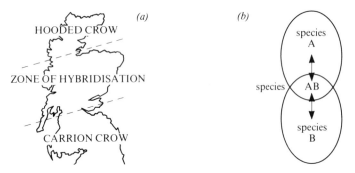

Fig 25.15 *Hybrid barrier as a means of preventing gene flow between two populations. The maintenance of the two crow species is shown to be due to the existence of a zone of hybridisation extending across Scotland as shown in (a). The existence of hybrid barriers between adjacent populations is common and functions as follows. Where the geographical ranges of A and B overlap, mating produces a hybrid with lowered fertility. A will interbreed freely with AB and AB with B but the existence of AB prevents free interbreeding of A and B populations*

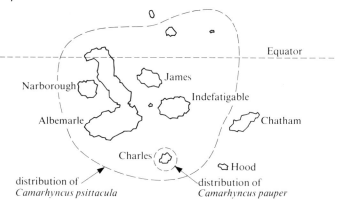

Fig 25.16 *The Galapagos Islands and the distribution of two species of finch illustrating coexistence following allopatric speciation*

on Albemarle Island are approximately equal, but on Charles Island *C. psittacula* has a longer beak. This difference is significant enough to ensure that the two species, which feed on different foods, appear unattractive to each other during the breeding season. In this way the species remain distinct and are able to coexist.

25.8.4 Ring species

This is a special form of sympatric speciation which occurs at the point where two populations at the extremes of a cline meet up and inhabit the same area, thus 'closing' the ring. For example, gulls of the genus *Larus* form a continuous population between latitudes 50–80 °N, encircling the North Pole. A ring of ten recognisable races or subspecies exist which principally differ in size and in the colour of their legs, back and wings. Gene flow occurs freely between all races except at the point where the 'ends of the ring' meet at the British Isles. Here, at the extremes of the geographical range, the gulls behave as distinct species, that is the herring gull (*Larus argentatus*) and the lesser black-backed gull (*L. fuscus*). These have a different appearance, different tone of call, different migratory patterns and rarely interbreed. Selection against cross-breeding is said to occur sympatrically.

Sympatric speciation without geographical isolation in sexually reproducing species is unlikely. However, in asexually reproducing organisms, including vegetatively propagated angiosperms, a single mutant so different from its parent population as to be genetically isolated could give rise to a new species sympatrically. An example is polyploidy in *Spartina* (section 23.9.2).

25.3 Ten subspecies of the *Larus argentatus–fuscus* population form a continuous ring extending from the British Isles through Scandinavia, Russia, Siberia, across the Bering Straits, through Alaska and Canada and back to the British Isles. If the subspecies inhabiting the Bering Straits and Alaska was eliminated what predicted effects might this have on the population?

25.9   Interspecific hybridisation

This is a form of sympatric speciation which occurs when a new species is produced by the crossing of individuals from two unrelated species. Fertile hybrids usually appear only in cases of interspecific hybridisation as a result of a form of chromosome mutation known as **allopolyploidy** (section 23.9.2). An example of this was demonstrated by Karpechenko in the case of hybrids formed between the cabbage and the radish. The genetic changes involved in this hybridisation are shown in fig 25.17.

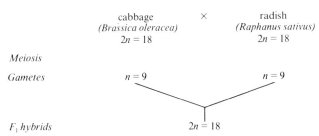

Meiosis

Gametes

F$_1$ hybrids

During meiosis in the F$_1$ hybrids chromosomes from each parent cannot pair together to form homologous chromosomes. The F$_1$ hybrids are therefore sterile. Occasionally non-disjunction of the F$_1$ hybrids produces gametes with the diploid set of chromosomes ($2n = 18$).

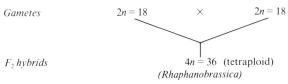

Gametes

F$_2$ hybrids

The F$_2$ hybrids are fertile. Homologous pairing can occur in meiosis as two sets of parental chromosomes are present. Diploid gametes ($2n = 18$), are produced which possess 9 chromosomes from the parental cabbage and 9 chromosomes from the parental radish.

Fig 25.17   *Stages involved in the hybridisation of the cabbage and the radish*

Answers and discussion

Chapter 14

14.1 (*a*) Solution B (*b*) Solution A (*c*) From B to A (*d*) (ii) $-1\,000\,kPa$. If you find this confusing remember $-1\,000$ is nearer zero than $-2\,000$. Zero is the maximum, or highest, ψ that can occur. (*e*) Solution B (*f*) Solution B (remember 'higher' means less negative in this case, that is nearer zero) (*g*) The lower the ψ_s of a solution the lower the ψ (in practice $\psi_s = \psi$ for a solution at atmospheric pressure).

14.2 The external solution. Remember that the cell wall is freely permeable to solutions.

14.3 Zero. The protoplast is not exerting pressure against the cell wall.

14.4 Prokaryotes and fungi. Although prokaryotes lack vacuoles, they have the same osmotic properties as plant cells and fungi.

14.5 At the start $\psi^{cell} = \psi_s + \psi_P$, $\psi^{solution} = \psi_s^{\,solution} = -1\,200\,kPa$; $\psi_P = 0$ because the cell is at incipient plasmolysis; $\psi_s^{cell} = -2\,000\,kPa$; $\psi^{cell} = -2\,000\,kPa + 0\,kPa = -2\,000\,kPa$. At the start, ψ of the solution is greater than ψ of the cell. Water therefore moves from the solution into the cell by osmosis. The only term that changes significantly as water enters the cell is ψ_P. As water enters, ψ_P, and hence ψ, increases until it prevents any further net entry of water. At this point ψ of the cell = ψ of the solution, and the cell is turgid.

Therefore, at equilibrium $\psi^{cell} = -1\,200\,kPa$. $\psi = \psi^s + \psi_P$ so $\psi_P = \psi^{cell} - \psi_s^{cell} = -1\,200\,kPa - -2\,000\,kPa = 800\,kPa$.

14.6 $\psi_s^{cell} = -1\,100\,kPa$; ψ pure water $= 0$; $\psi^{cell} = 0$ at equilibrium. $\psi_P = \psi - \psi_s = 0\,kPa - -1\,100\,kPa = 1\,100\,kPa$.

14.7 (*a*) ψ^{cell} at transfer $= \psi$ pure water $= 0$, ψ sucrose solution $= -800\,kPa$, so the difference in ψ between cell and external solution $= 800\,kPa$.
(*b*) Water would leave the cell (from higher to lower ψ).
(*c*) ψ_P would decrease.

14.8 (*a*) Cell B (*b*) From cell B to A
(*c*) The cells must have the same ψ at equilibrium and this will be the average of the two initial ψ_s, that is $-1\,000\,kPa$.
(*d*) Cell A at equilibrium: $\psi_P = \psi - \psi_s$
$= -1\,000\,kPa - -2\,000\,kPa$
$= 1\,000\,kPa$
Cell B at equilibrium: $\psi_P = \psi - \psi_s$
$= -1\,000\,kPa - -1\,400\,kPa$
$= 400\,kPa$

14.9 $-1\,060\,kPa$. For intermediate values between those shown in table 14.4, plot a graph of molarity of sucrose solution against solute potential.

14.10 Average ψ_s of beetroot cells is about $-1\,400\,kPa$.

14.11 ψ beetroot is about $-940\,kPa$.

14.12 A more accurate result can be obtained by taking the mean value of two or more replicates. Some indication of the variation that can be expected between strips is given in table 14.6.

14.13 To prevent evaporation of water, with subsequent increase in concentration of sucrose solutions, and possible drying up of beetroot strips.

14.14 $\psi_P = \psi - \psi_s$
$= -950\,kPa - -1\,400\,kPa$
$= 450\,kPa$.
Note that different beetroots may have different values of ψ_s and ψ.

14.15 (*a*) The cells of the intact scape are turgid and their walls are therefore tending to expand as pressure potential increases. The thick walls of the epidermal cells are less capable of stretching than the thin walls of the cortex cells and therefore exert a restraining influence on expansion of the cortical cells. The latter are under compression. Cutting the epidermis removes the restraint, each cortical cell expands slightly and there is an overall increase in volume of the cortex which causes the strip to curve outwards.
(*b*) Distilled water has a higher water potential than the scape cells. Water therefore enters the tissue from the distilled water by osmosis, inflating the cortical cells even further and causing outward curvature.
(*c*) The concentrated sucrose solution has a lower water potential than the scape cells. Water therefore leaves the tissue by osmosis, causing greater shrinkage of the cortical cells than the epidermal cells and a bending inwards of the tissue.
(*d*) The dilute sucrose solution must have the same water potential as the scape cells. There is therefore no net gain or loss of water by solution or tissue.
(*e*) Water potential. An outline of the experiment is as follows.

Prepare a dilution series of sucrose solutions from 1 M to distilled water (such as distilled water, 0.2 M, 0.4 M, 0.6 M, 0.8 M and 1.0 M). The typical curvature of freshly cut dandelion scapes should be recorded by drawing and then two pieces of scape placed in each solution in separate labelled petri dishes (two pieces are preferred so that an average can be obtained). Observe and accurately record curvatures (such as by drawing) after equilibrium has been reached (about 30 min). The solution which induces no change in curvature has the same ψ as the average dandelion scape cell immediately after the cut was made.

14.16 Outlines of two suitable experiments are as follows.
Effect of temperature. Cut cubes of fresh beetroot, wash to remove the red pigment from broken cells, and place in beakers of water at different temperatures over a range, say, from 20–100 °C. The appearance of red pigment in the water would indicate destruction of the partial permeability of the tonoplast (vacuole membrane) and cell surface membrane, attended by diffusion of the pigment from the cell sap to the water. The time taken for the appearance of a standard amount of pigment would give an indication of the rapidity of breakdown of membrane structure. The colour could be measured in a colorimeter or simply by eye.
Effect of ethanol. Method as above, using a range of ethanol concentrations instead of a range of temperatures.

14.17 (*a*) Leaves contain a very large number of stomata for gaseous exchange and there is little resistance to movement of water vapour through these pores.

(b) Leaves have a large surface area (for trapping sunlight and exchanging gases). The greater the surface area, the greater will be the loss of water by transpiration.

14.18 Light intensity increases as the Sun rises, reaching a maximum at midday when the Sun attains its highest point in the sky. Air temperature rises similarly, but it takes about two hours for the heating effect of the Sun to be reflected in a rise in air temperature (mainly because the soil has to heat up first and then radiate heat to the air). The initial rise in transpiration rate between 3 a.m. and 6 a.m., before air temperature rises is due to opening of the stomata in the light. From 6 a.m. onwards transpiration rate is closely correlated with temperature for reasons explained in the text. It is not closely correlated with light intensity, presumably because the stomata are now fully open and any further increase in light intensity has no effect.

During the afternoon, light intensity decreases as the Sun sinks, followed by a drop in temperature with the same lag of about two hours. Transpiration rate decreases both as a result of decreasing temperature and decreasing light intensity, but it is much more closely correlated with a decrease in the latter, probably because this induces stomatal closure. By about 7.30 p.m. it is dark and the stomata are probably closed. Any remaining transpiration is probably cuticular and still influenced by temperature.

14.19 See table 14.19(ans).

Table 14.19(ans)

Dicots	Monocots
Vascular bundles arranged in a ring	Vascular bundles scattered
Endodermis (starch sheath) present	Endodermis absent
Separate pith and cortex	Ground tissue not split into pith and cortex
Pericycle forms a cap to vascular bundle	Pericycle surrounds vascular bundle
Metaxylem has many vessels	Metaxylem has few vessels (commonly two or three)
Protoxylem present	Most protoxylem breaks down to leave a lysigenous canal
Cambium present and secondary thickening may occur later (some herbaceous plants, such as *Helianthus*, develop secondary vascular bundles; perennials develop wood, rays, annual rings, cork)	No cambium, therefore no secondary thickening (very few exceptions where monocotyledon stems develop a tree-like form)

14.20 (a) Hollow cylinder
(b) Solid rod/cylinder providing support
(c) Solid rod/cylinder providing support
(d) Solid cylinder

14.21 (1) Long tubes formed by joining of neighbouring cells, with breakdown of cross-walls between them.
(2) No living contents, so less resistance to flow.
(3) Tubes have high tensile strength so do not collapse.
(4) Fine tubes are necessary to prevent water columns from physically collapsing.

14.22 See table 14.22(ans).

14.23 ψ soil solution > root hair cell > cell C > cell B > cell A > xylem sap

14.24 (a) There is a rapid initial uptake of potassium (K^+) at both temperatures (during the first 10–20 min). After 20 min there is a continuous gradual uptake of K^+ at 25 °C but no further uptake at 0 °C. Uptake at 25 °C is inhibited by KCN.

Table 14.22(ans)

Dicots	Monocots
Piliferous layer quickly lost	Piliferous layer remains
Few protoxylem groups (few arms of metaxylem) 2–8, commonly four (tetrarch) or 5 (pentarch)	Many protoxylem groups (polyarch)
Pith not common. Xylem forms a solid cylinder at the centre of the root	Central pith. Xylem forms rods around the pith
Cambium often present, making secondary thickening possible	Cambium rarely present; therefore no secondary thickening

(b) There are two distinct phases of uptake. In the initial rapid phase, K^+ diffuses into the free spaces of the root. It enters through the cell walls at the piliferous layer, which are exposed to the solution, and diffuses through the apoplast, possibly entering the intercellular spaces where these contain solution. The results show that this phase is more or less independent of temperature and therefore not dependent on metabolism (enzyme-controlled reactions would proceed faster at 25 °C than 0 °C). This first phase is a passive process.

The second phase is temperature-dependent, and does not occur at 0 °C when the rate of metabolism is very low. This suggests that the process is dependent on metabolism, and its inhibition by KCN indicates that it is dependent on respiration. The second phase is therefore an active transport across cell membranes into cells.

14.25 Rise in respiratory rate is accompanied by a rise in KCl uptake. Once KCl is available, it is therefore apparently taken up by active transport, the energy being supplied by an increased respiratory rate.

14.26 KCN inhibits respiration and thence active transport of KCl into the carrot discs.

14.27 Much of the phosphate inside the root was in the free space and could therefore diffuse out to the water outside, reversing passive uptake.

14.28 No. The endodermis is a barrier to movement of water and solutes through the apoplast pathway (see section 14.5.2, apoplast pathway).

14.29 Autoradiography reveals the location of the ion in thin sections. Treat one plant with an inhibitor of active transport (such as low temperature or KCN) and have an untreated control plant; allow them both to take up the radioactive ion. In the treated plant ions will move only passively by way of the cell walls. Autoradiography should show that the radioactive ion tends to penetrate the root only as far as the endodermis, whereas the control should show much greater movement of ions to the tissue inside the endodermis.

14.30 (a) See table 14.30(ans).

Table 14.30(ans).

Plant part	Percentage distribution when upper leaf treated	Percentage distribution when lower leaf treated
apical region of shoot	4.8	3.6
^{14}C-treated leaf	48.4	53.9
other leaves	1.0	0.8
stem	3.5	5.5
pod	38.7	23.4
roots	3.6	12.8

Similarities in ^{14}C export from upper and lower leaves.
Similar proportions of assimilates are exported by both leaves (compare results for '^{14}C-treated leaf') and similar proportions pass to the other leaves. The major destination of the assimilates in both cases is the pod.

Differences in ^{14}C export from upper and lower leaves.
The pattern of export from a given leaf is affected by its position on the plant. The upper leaf exports a higher proportion of its assimilates to the pod and apical region than the lower leaf, which correspondingly exports a greater proportion to the roots.

(*b*) Once a pod is formed, it becomes a sink of considerable importance for carbon compounds, particularly from the leaves in its proximity. There are two other important sinks in the mature plant, namely the apical region of the shoot and the roots. The lower leaves export mainly to the roots and the upper leaves mainly to the apex.

14.31 0.72 s. The answer is obtained as follows:
100 cm = 1 000 mm = 1 000 000 μm = 10^6 μm
therefore sucrose moves at 10^6 μm h^{-1},
= 1 μm in $1/10^6$ h,
= 200 μm in $200/10^6$ h = $2/10^4$ h = $(2 \times 3\,600)/10^4$ s = 2×0.36 s
= 0.72 s.

14.32 2 500 sieve plates per metre:
$$1 \text{ m} = 10^6 \ \mu\text{m},$$
$$400 \ \mu\text{m} = 4 \times 10^2 \ \mu\text{m},$$
$$10^6/(4 \times 10^2) = 10^4/4 = 2\,500.$$

14.33 Oxygenated blood can be delivered to the tissues rapidly enough to satisfy the increased metabolic demands of the body. Various organs such as the kidney and the capillaries rely on a high blood hydrostatic pressure for effective and efficient functioning.

14.34 This means that oxygenated blood of the systemic circulation reaches the body capillaries at a much higher pressure. This is essential for the efficient function of organs and tissue fluid formation and permits active chemical processes and a high body temperature to be maintained. It is essential that a much lower pressure is developed in the pulmonary artery in order to prevent rupture of the delicate pulmonary capillaries.

14.35 Local vasodilation in the wounded area enables more blood carrying oxygen and nutrients to arrive there and speed up the process of repair and replacement. Increased body blood pressure prepares the body of the animal to respond to any further stress more readily and efficiently.

14.36 **Before the race.** Adrenaline is secreted in anticipation of the race. This stimulates vasoconstriction throughout the body in all but the most vital organs. Hence blood pressure is raised. Heart rate is also increased. Extra blood is passed to the general circulation from the spleen.

During the race. Increased metabolic activity takes place during the race, especially in the skeletal muscles. Increased carbon dioxide levels in these regions promote local vasodilation. The increased body temperature further enhances vasodilation. However the general increase in carbon dioxide level in blood is noted by the chemoreceptors of the aorta and carotid bodies which in turn stimulate the vasomotor centre to promote vasoconstriction. This increases blood pressure and therefore speeds up blood flow. Heart rate is also increased and a more complete emptying of the ventricles occurs. Towards the end of the race the muscles will be respiring anaerobically and producing lactic acid (section 11.3.8). Strong contractions of the muscles knead the veins and promote faster venous return to the heart.

Recovery. The oxygen debt is paid off and lactic acid removed from the blood system. Tissues subside in activity and the carbon dioxide level decreases. Consequently there is a return to normal of heartbeat and blood pressure.

14.37 In tissues which are respiring actively the partial pressure of carbon dioxide will be high. This leads to a reduced pH and to the displacement of the oxygen dissociation curve to the right. Analysis of fig 14.62 shows that as this occurs it facilitates the delivery of increased quantities of oxygen from the blood to the cells which can be used by respiratory processes for the production of energy. Looked at another way, haemoglobin takes up oxygen less readily initially but when saturated releases it quickly.

Increased metabolic activity increases the temperature in a part of the body. This produces a reduction in the affinity of oxygen for haemoglobin and an increased dissociation of oxygen. Thus the dissociation curve is again shifted to the right. This is physiologically advantageous as more oxygen is delivered to the active regions. The oxygen dissociation curve is not exactly the same for all animals. For example, compared with humans, the curve for small mammals is displaced to the right. Small mammals possess a much higher metabolic rate than humans and therefore it is appropriate that oxygen should be released much more readily.

14.38 The position of the curve of the fetus relative to that of its mother means that its blood has a greater affinity for oxygen than the maternal blood. This has to be so, as the fetus must obtain all of its oxygen from its mother's blood at the placenta. So, at any given partial pressure of oxygen the fetal blood will take up oxygen from the maternal blood and will always be more saturated with oxygen than the maternal blood.

14.39 This means that the blood has a high affinity for oxygen and that it is able to combine with it at the low oxygen tensions experienced at high altitude. This is another good example of physiological adaptation.

14.40 (1) Carboxyhaemoglobin reaches the lungs and takes up oxygen and forms oxyhaemoglobin,
(2) Oxyhaemoglobin is a weaker base than carboxyhaemoglobin and releases hydrogen ions.
(3) Hydrogen ions combine with hydrogencarbonate ions in the erythrocyte so forming carbonic acid.
(4) Carbonic acid dissociates into carbon dioxide and water.
(5) As a result of the loss of hydrogencarbonate ions from the erythrocyte, further hydrogencarbonate ions diffuse into the erythrocyte from the plasma.
(6) More carbonic acid is formed which dissociates into more carbon dioxide and water.
(7) Carbon dioxide diffuses out of the erythrocyte and is eventually excreted from the body via the lungs.

Chapter 15

15.1 Locomotion is primarily associated with the need to search for food (and is closely associated with the development of a nervous system). Green plants are autotrophic, that is make their own organic requirements, so do not need to search for food.

15.2 See table 15.2(ans) (next page).

15.3 Growth could be inhibited on the contact side, or stimulated on the opposite side, or a combination of these effects might occur. In fact, growth is slowed down (cells become less elongated) on the contact side and growth on the opposite side is stimulated 40–200 fold.

15.4 Various methods are possible. A simple experiment is illustrated in fig 15.4(ans).

15.5 (*a*) *Spirogyra* (or any other filamentous green alga).
(*b*) The bacteria are aerobic and positively aerotactic. Therefore they swim towards oxygen along a gradient from

low oxygen concentration to high oxygen concentration. The highest oxygen concentrations are around the edges of the cover-slip, where oxygen is diffusing into the water from the atmosphere, and adjacent to the algal filament where oxygen is being released as a waste product of photosynthesis.

Table 15.2(ans).

Example	Advantage
Shoots and coleoptiles positively phototropic	Leaves exposed to the light which is the source of energy for photosynthesis
Roots negatively phototropic	Exposed roots more likely to grow towards soil or equivalent suitable substrate
Shoots and coleoptiles negatively geotropic	Shoots of germinating seeds will grow upwards through soil towards light
Roots positively geotropic	Roots penetrate soil
Rhizomes, runners diageotropic	Helps plants colonise new areas of soil
Dicotyledonous leaves diageotropic	Flat surface of leaf will gain maximum exposure to sunlight (at right-angles to incident radiation)
Lateral roots plagiogeotropic	Large volume of soil exploited and the arrangement of roots provides support (similar to guy-ropes supporting a tent)
Branches plagiogeotropic	Larger volume of space occupied for exploitation of light
Hyphae positively chemotropic	Grow towards food
Pollen tubes positively chemotropic	Grow towards ovule, where fertilisation takes place
Roots and pollen tubes positively hydrotropic	Water essential for all living processes
Tendrils positively haptotropic	Essential for their function of support
Sundew tentacles positively haptotropic	Enables plant to imprison insects which walk over the tentacles (section 9.12.2)
Pollen tubes negatively aerotropic	Another mechanism ensuring that initial growth of the pollen tube is towards the tissue of the style (away from air)

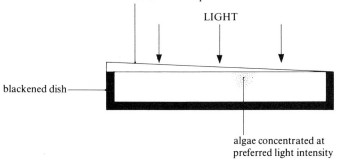

Fig 15.4(ans) *Experiment to demonstrate preferred light intensity of* Euglena *or* Chlamydomonas

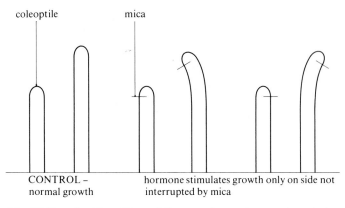

Fig 15.8(ans) *Repetition of Boysen-Jensen's experiments in uniform light. Three experiments are shown; treatment left, result right, in each case*

(c) Leave the slide in the dark for about 30 min and re-examine. All the bacteria should now be around the edges of the cover-slip because the alga cannot photosynthesise in the dark.

15.6 (a) The stimulus of light is detected by the coleoptile tip. Some kind of signal is transmitted from the tip (the receptor) to the region behind the tip (the effector).
(b) Experiment c was a check on the result from experiment b which could have been the result of injury to the coleoptile.

15.7 Further evidence of the existence of a signal, presumably a chemical transmitter substance (hormone), has been obtained. It cannot pass through an impermeable barrier. It moves mainly down the shaded side of the coleoptile. In experiment b mica prevented this movement. Light therefore either inhibits production of the hormone, causes its inactivation (stimulates its breakdown) or causes it to be redistributed laterally.

15.8 See fig 15.8(ans).

15.9 The coleoptile tip produces a chemical which diffuses into the agar. It can stimulate growth in the region behind the tip and restores normal growth (experiment a). There is little or no lateral transmission of the chemical (experiment b) under conditions of uniform illumination or darkness.

15.10 The coleoptile would have grown to the left.

15.11 A 100 ppm   B 10 ppm   C 1 ppm   D 0.1 ppm
E 0.01 ppm   F zero

15.12 A relatively high auxin concentration stimulates growth of coleoptiles (or shoots) but inhibits growth of roots. This supports the conclusions drawn from experiment 15.1.

15.13 See section 16.5.6.

15.14 (a) Abscisic acid can be transported away from root tips, undergo lateral transport in root tissues in response to gravity, and inhibit growth.
(b) IAA is probably not involved in the geotropic response of maize since it is apparently not transported away from the root tip.

15.15 (a) starch
(b) maltose
(c) maltase
(d) The main food reserve of cereal seeds is starch, stored in the endosperm.

15.16 Storage proteins are digested (hydrolysed) to provide amino acids, the basic units of proteins. These are reassembled to produce enzymes (which are always proteins), such as α-amylase, which are then used to digest the food stores of the endosperm.

15.17 The amylase activity could be associated with micro-organisms present on the fingers or with saliva which has been transferred from mouth to fingers. Note the importance, therefore, of not handling the seeds after their surface sterilisation in this kind of experiment.

15.18 Incubate seeds with radioactive (^{14}C-labelled) amino acids. This results in production of labelled amylase. Alternatively, incubation of seeds with inhibitors of protein synthesis (such as cycloheximide) prevents synthesis of amylase and no amylase activity is then recorded.

15.19 Dissection of the seeds into aleurone and non-aleurone portions should show that the initial appearance of labelled amylase is in the aleurone layer. Alternatively, separate incubation of endosperm with aleurone layers and endosperm without aleurone layer, with starch–gibberellin agar would result in amylase production only in the former (difficult to do in practice).

15.20 One of the best bioassays for gibberellin (quick, reliable and sensitive) involves incubating embryo halves of barley grains with the substance being assayed. After two days the amount of reducing sugar present is proportional to the amount of gibberellin present.

15.21 (a) The amino acid is retained by the young leaf and does not move very far from the point of application. In the old leaf some of it is exported via the veins and midrib.
(b) The young leaf would use the amino acid to make protein in growth. The old leaf is no longer growing and so is exporting nutrients to other parts of the plant such as roots and young leaves.
(c) Amino acids are retained by, or move towards, tissues treated with kinetin. (The reasons for this are unknown, but presumably connected with the maintenance or stimulation of normal cell activity by kinetin.)

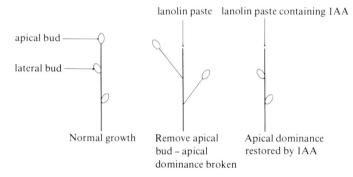

Fig 15.23(ans) *Experiment to show role of IAA in apical dominance*

15.22 One solution would be to take a plant where applied gibberellin is known to affect stem growth and remove its source of auxin by removing the shoot apex. Gibberellin should then prove ineffective. It is important to demonstrate that the response can be restored by addition of auxin (such as IAA in lanolin paste) as injury might be the reason for lack of response to gibberellins, or another chemical might be involved. Such experiments do demonstrate a total dependence on auxin.

15.23 (a) Auxin (IAA)
(b) See fig 15.23(ans).

15.24 Small leaves offer less resistance to passage through the soil (leaves of grasses remain inside the coleoptile). The hooked plumule of dicotyledonous plants protects the delicate apical meristem from soil particles. Elongated internodes ensure the maximum chance of reaching light.

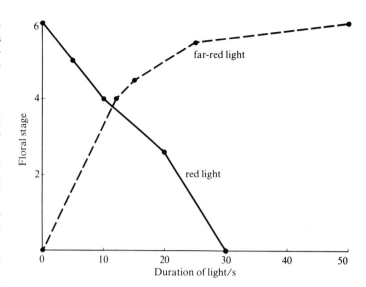

Fig 15.26(ans) *Effects of red light and red/far-red light interruptions of long night on flowering of cocklebur*

15.25 See chapter 9.

15.26 The graph is shown in fig 15.26(ans).
The opposite effects of red and far-red light are demonstrated. Red light exposure of 30 s, at the intensity used in the experiment, completely nullifies the inductive effect of a long night. The effectiveness of red light increases with time of exposure up to 30 s. The red light effect is reversed by far-red light, although a longer exposure (50 s) was needed to completely reverse the effect. These results suggest that phytochrome is the photoreceptor involved.

15.27 There are several possible methods. Fig 15.27(ans) illustrates one simple solution. Boxes represent light-proof covers, used as appropriate to give short days.

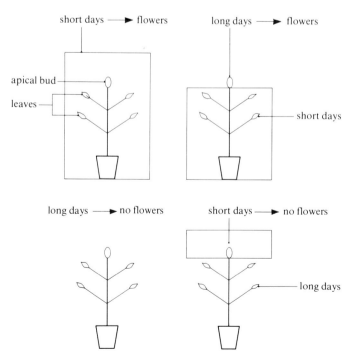

Fig 15.27(ans) *Experiment to determine whether leaves or floral apex are sensitive to the photoperiod that stimulates flowering*

15.28 Lateral bud inhibition or apical dominance is largely controlled by auxins. (See apical dominance, section 15.3.3.)

Chapter 16

16.1 (*a*) A steep concentration gradient of Na$^+$ ions exists between the outside and inside of the axon and Na$^+$ ions rapidly diffuse down this gradient.
(*b*) The relatively high negative potential within the axon encourages the inward movement of the positively charged Na$^+$ ions.

16.2 If the outflow of positive K$^+$ ions from the axon balanced the inflow of positive Na$^+$ ions into the axon there would be no change, or perhaps only a slight decrease, in the resting potential. Such a slight change would be insufficient to reach the threshold required to produce an action potential.

16.3 (*a*) Normal sea water
(*b*) One-half sea water
(*c*) One-third sea water
The amplitude of the action potential spike in (*a*) and the depolarised membrane potentials shown in (*b*) and (*c*) is determined by the number of Na$^+$ ions entering the axon from the extracellular fluid. The solutions in which (*a*), (*b*) and (*c*) were recorded contained progressively fewer Na$^+$ ions.

16.4 Sodium ions are pumped out of the axon and potassium ions are pumped in. The movements of the ions are linked (coupled) and mediated by the cation pump.

16.5 The longitudinal resistance of axoplasm decreases with increasing diameter of the axon. As the resistance decreases, the length of the membrane influenced by the local circuit increases and this lengthens the distance between adjacent depolarisations and leads to an increase in conduction velocity.

16.6 The frog is a cold-blooded (poikilothermic) organism, active within the temperature range 4–25 °C, whereas the cat, being warm-blooded (homeothermic), maintains a constant temperature of 35 °C. This increase in temperature increases the speed of conduction of the nerve impulses by a factor of three.

16.7 Graph (*a*) indicates that the frequency of impulses in the sensory neurone is directly related to the stimulus applied to the muscle spindle. It is known that the stimulus produces a depolarisation known as the generator potential and, as shown in graph (*b*), the magnitude of this potential is directly related to the frequency of sensory impulses. It may be concluded from these data that increasing stimuli produce increasing generator potentials whose amplitudes are directly related to the frequency of impulses in the sensory neurone.

16.8 The path taken by light as it passes through the eye is as follows: conjunctiva→cornea→aqueous humour→ lens→ vitreous humour→retina.

16.9 Light from an object falling onto several rods which are linked to the brain by separate neurones may not have sufficient energy to produce a propagated action potential in each neurone and therefore the light may not be detected. If, however, the same light falls on three rods which are linked to the same neurone supplying the brain, the separate generator potentials produced by the rods would summate and produce a propagated action potential which would be registered in the brain as light.

16.10 When looking directly at an object, light reflected from it passes along the optical axis of the eye and strikes the retina at the fovea which contains cones only. During daylight this will produce a detailed image in the brain due to the high light intensity activating the cones. At night the light intensity would be too low to activate the cones. By looking slightly to one side of the object the reflected light from it will not strike the fovea but a point on the retina to the side of it where there are rods. At night these will be activated by the low light intensity and an image will be produced in the brain.

16.11 The object will appear yellow. Each retina will distinguish one colour only. In one eye, green cones will be stimulated by light of 530 nm and, in the other, red cones will be stimulated by light of 620 nm. Mixing will occur in the brain due to equal stimulation by these colours and the object will appear to be the colour of the average of the combined wavelengths, that is $\dfrac{530 + 620}{2}$ nm = 575nm, which corresponds to yellow.

Chapter 17

17.1 The femur is basically a hollow bone. When a compression force is exerted on one side of the bone, the other side is subjected to tension. Along the central axis of the bone the forces diminish and are neutralised. The material in the centre of the bone consequently does not need to contribute to its strength. Reduction in weight of the bone due to the absence of bone along its central axis is advantageous to the animal as it lightens the weight of the femur without reducing its mechanical efficiency. The perimeter of the femur is composed of compact bone which resists the tension and compressional forces. Spongy bone at the head of the femur is a meshwork of interconnecting bony struts. They maintain the rigidity of the bone but with the minimum of weight.

Cartilage acts as a cushion between two articulating bones. Its matrix can be deformed by compression but will return to its original shape because it possesses good powers of extensibility. The cartilage also reduces friction between the smooth, moving articular surfaces.

The tendons consist of inextensible, white fibrous tissue and attach the muscles to the femur. The pull of the muscle is concentrated over a small area. Tendon organs operate to prevent muscle rupture if the muscle is suddenly subjected to a heavy load.

Ligaments are also composed of inextensible, white fibrous tissue and connect the femur to bones articulating with it at joints. They confine the movement of the components of each joint to a specific direction and therefore promote the efficiency of its operation. Ligaments also strengthen the joint.

17.2 (*a*) It allows free movement of the rib cage of the mammal.
(*b*) The flexible suspension enables the animal to withstand the shock sustained by the forelimbs when it lands at the end of a jump.
(*c*) The forelimbs possess a wide range of movement, which is useful for such activities as climbing, cleaning the face, manipulating food and digging.

17.3 A band remains the same length; H band becomes shorter; I band becomes shorter.

17.4 The myosin filaments (constituting the A band) remain the same length whilst actin filaments slide over them towards each other. This effectively shortens the H and I bands.

17.5 (*a*) The central non-contractile portion of the muscle spindle is stretched. Nerve impulses are fired from the annulo-spiral nerve endings and pass to the central nervous system. Impulses are propagated from the central nervous system via efferent neurones to the extrafusal fibres causing them to contract. This is the stretch reflex.
(*b*) The muscle spindle is no longer stretched and the number of impulses fired from the central non-contractile region of the spindle is diminished.

(c) Impulses are fired from the tendon organs which reach inhibitory neurones in the spinal cord. When these are activated this causes a reflex inhibition of contraction of the muscle that is being stretched. Therefore active resistance to stretching is decreased. This mechanism offers a form of protection to the muscles, preventing possible rupture when they are suddenly overloaded.

(d) The central region of the spindle is stretched and fires impulses to the spinal cord. Motor neurones are stimulated to carry impulses to the extrafusal fibres of the muscle causing contraction. When contraction in the intrafusal fibres is matched by an equal contraction of the extrafusal fibres, the central region of the spindle is stretched no further and a state of equilibrium is reached. This mechanism is very important as it sets the tone of muscles. It ensures that the muscle is not completely slack, and by increasing the stretching of the spindle so increases the muscle's response. If the muscle was slack when a heavy load was applied, the muscle could suffer considerable damage.

17.6 It allows greater movement of Ca^{2+} ions needed for muscle contraction.

17.7 Synchronous. This type of muscle has much more sarcoplasmic reticulum because it requires more nervous impulses to operate it, and each nerve impulse depends on the release of Ca^{2+} ions by the sarcoplasmic reticulum.

17.8 (a) Streamlined shape
(b) Smooth surface – scales overlap each other in an appropriate direction
– mucus/oily covering thus reducing friction
(c) Various types of fin to promote forward propulsion and stability during swimming
(d) Highly muscular body
(e) Lateral line (table 4.11)
(f) Swim bladder in bony fishes
(g) Highly coordinated neuromuscular activity

17.9 (a) Large, powerful flight muscles
(b) Streamlined body shape
(c) Sharp narrow wings, designed for low drag
(d) Large wings possess mostly primary feathers (for forward propulsion)
(e) Fast wing beat (10 per second)
(f) Forward thrust achieved by both the downbeat and upbeat of the wings.

17.10 This position increases the effective length of their limbs. Consequently each stride taken is longer and so propels the body forward over a greater distance. Assuming that the speed of movement of the limbs remains the same, the sprinter will therefore move forwards at a faster pace.

Chapter 18

18.1 Hyperventilation increases the tidal movements of air, carbon dioxide is expelled from the lungs and the carbon dioxide tension of the alveolar air decreases. The carbon dioxide level of the blood comes to a new equilibrium with the alveolar air as it passes through the pulmonary capillaries. This reduces the carbon dioxide tension of the blood and increases the blood pH. The abnormal alkalinity of the blood produces symptoms of dizziness and fainting and the inhibitory effect of lack of stimulation of the chemoreceptors supplying the respiratory centres decreases the ventilation rate.

18.2 The rates of transpiration and evaporation are inversely proportional to the level of atmospheric humidity. When humidity is high the rates of transpiration and evaporation

are low and the plant cannot lose latent heat and reduce its temperature.

18.3 19.6%

18.4 During this period the subject was allowed to equilibrate with his surroundings.

18.5 There is a direct relationship between these two variables which suggests that the rate of sweating is controlled by activity of the hypothalamus.

18.6 The direct relationship between skin temperature and evaporation during the first 20 min established that an equilibrium exists between the two. As the evaporation rate falls, due to the action of the hypothalamus in response to the ingestion of iced water, latent heat of evaporation is not being lost from the skin and this accounts for the observed rise in skin temperature.

18.7 'Fever' is due to the resetting of the hypothalamic 'thermostat' at a higher temperature. Until the core temperature rises to that temperature there is a discrepancy between 'normal' body temperature and the cold conditions. In these conditions the body responds by shivering and the body continues to feel cold until the core temperature reaches the temperature of the hypothalamic thermostat.

Chapter 20

20.1 (a) The true statement is (ii), 'Gametes are always haploid'. Even this is not always true since polyploid parent cells would give rise to gamete cells with more than the haploid number of chromosomes; for example the gametes of hexaploid wheat plants would be triploid.
(b) Exceptions to statements (i), (iii), (iv) and (v):
(i) Asexual reproduction in plants with alternation of generations involves meiosis, so the gametophytes produced show variation.
(iii) Gametes are produced by mitosis in life cycles A and D (fig 20.13).
(iv) Meiosis does always produce haploid cells (except in polyploid organisms). Mitosis can produce haploid cells, as in the growth of multicellular haploid organisms (such as *Spirogyra*, life cycle A, and growth of gametophyte, life cycle D, fig 20.13). It can also produce diploid cells as in the growth of multicellular diploid organisms.
(v) Mitosis can occur in haploid cells, as in the examples given in (iv) above.

20.2 (a) If the parent plants that produced the pollen grains can be identified, then certain deductions can be made about the climate that such plants would have grown in.
(b) Any human interference with the natural vegetation would be reflected in the pollen record. For example, pollen of weed species and agricultural plants, such as wheat, would indicate clearance of natural vegetation for agriculture. Similarly, absence of pollen from trees in some areas would indicate forest clearance.

20.3 If a plant species is dioecious, half of its individuals do not produce seeds. Also, there is a large wastage of pollen which is a disadvantage in terms of material and energy resources.

20.4 Separate sexes is more economic in animals than in plants because there is less risk in transferring male gametes as a result of locomotion and behaviour patterns.

20.5 $\frac{1}{2}$ (50%). Remembering that the pollen grain is haploid:

Parent plant genotype	Possible pollen genotypes
S_1S_2	$\left.\begin{matrix} S_1 \\ S_2 \end{matrix}\right\}$ in equal numbers

S_1 pollen grains would be compatible with S_2S_3 style tissue
S_2 pollen grains would be incompatible with S_1S_3 style tissue

Note that neither S_1 nor S_2 pollen grains would be compatible with the style of the parent plant (S_1S_2), so that self-fertilisation is impossible.

20.6 (a) The part of the bee's body receiving most pollen will be that which brushes against the anthers while the bee is taking nectar. Thus pollination will generally occur between anthers and stigmas at the same height within the flower, that is between pin-eyed and thrum-eyed flowers.

(b) It encourages outbreeding.

20.7 The functions of the cell organelles suggest that the cells manufacture materials for use within the cell. The raw materials for these processes come from the breakdown of materials entering the cell, using enzymes stored in the lysosomes. The synthesised products are packaged by the Golgi apparatus and stored for subsequent usage.

20.8 (a) Adding the numbers of corpora lutea and corpora albicanti together shows the number of ovulations which have occurred, that is 67 in all. Assuming one oocyte was released from each follicle per month this gives the *reproductive* age at 5 years 7 months. Hence the 22-year-old woman began ovulating at approximately the age of $16\frac{1}{2}$ years.

(b) Of the 42 000 follicles only 219 were primary oocytes, having a diameter over 100 μm. Again, assuming one oocyte would be released per month, the potential number of years for ovulation would be 18 years, 3 months.

(c) Five follicles contained two oocytes each, therefore potentially five pairs of twins might have been produced which would not be identical twins.

(d) Non-disjunction occurring during anaphase I of meiosis.

20.9 Blood would flow in the reverse direction along the ductus arteriosus.

Chapter 21

21.1 The following conclusions may be drawn from these curves:

(a) relative growth is greatest during embryological development,

(b) rate of growth is greatest during infancy and adolescence,

(c) maximum growth, in terms of a particular parameter, such as height, is greatest in the adult.

21.2 (a) There is loss of mass due to respiration of food reserves in the seed.

(b) Green leaves have grown and opened above the ground.

(c) Photosynthesis. Its rate must now be greater than respiration.

(d) This is due to dispersal of fruits and seeds.

21.3 Body mass averages about 33.5 kg from November to March at a time when the average daily intake is 320 kJ. Throughout this period the mean monthly temperature does not rise above −10 °C. In order to maintain a constant blood temperature of approximately 35 °C, despite a temperature difference of 45 °C, the husky, a homeotherm, must have an extremely high metabolic rate. This places a great demand on an adequate supply of food to provide the energy sources for respiratory activity. Since the data show that the average body mass throughout the winter period is below that of the summer, this provides extra evidence of the metabolic demands imposed on maintaining a constant body temperature.

21.4 Small seeds have relatively small food reserves; it is therefore important that the growing shoot reaches light quickly so that photosynthesis can start before the reserves are exhausted.

21.5 (a) Chlorophyll strongly absorbs red and blue light, but not green and far-red light (see chlorophyll absorption spectrum fig 9.9).

(b) Red light stimulates lettuce seed germination, but far-red light inhibits it (section 15.4.2). Seeds under a leaf canopy, where the light will be enriched in far-red, might therefore be inhibited from germinating until a break in the canopy ensures that they will not be too shaded for efficient photosynthesis and growth.

21.6 At the onset of germination, food reserves in the barley grain, principally starch, with some protein, are mobilised. Starch is converted to sugars, and proteins to amino acids, and these are translocated to the embryo for use in growth. Therefore, endosperm dry mass decreases while embryo dry mass increases.

At the same time there is an overall loss in dry mass during the first week. This is due to aerobic respiration, which consumes sugar, in both endosperm and embryo (though to a greater extent in the latter). At about day 7 the first leaf emerges and starts to photosynthesise. The resulting increase in dry mass more than compensates for respiration losses so that a net increase in dry mass is observed. At the same time the rate of growth of the embryo, now a seedling, increases.

21.7 (a) There is a gain in dry mass of 8.6 g, calculated as follows.

Mass of seeds = 51.2 g

Mass of fatty acid = 51.2/2 = 25.6 g

M_r fatty acid = 256

Therefore 1 mole = 256 g, so 25.6 g = 0.1 mole

From the equation,

0.1 mole fatty acid → 0.1 mole sugar + 0.5 mole water + 0.4 mole carbon dioxide

M_r sugar = 342

Therefore 25.6 g fatty acid → 34.2 g sugar + water + carbon dioxide

Water is not included in the dry mass and carbon dioxide is lost as a gas, therefore the gain in dry mass = (34.2 − 25.6) g = 8.6 g.

(b) Respiration would result in a decrease in dry mass. In reality there would still be an increase in dry mass.

(c) Volume of carbon dioxide evolved from the seeds = 8.96 dm^3 at STP, calculated as follows:

from the equation, 0.1 mole fatty acid → 0.4 mole carbon dioxide. 0.4 mole carbon dioxide occupies 0.4×22.4 dm^3 at STP = 8.96 dm^3.

(d) By hydrolysis, catalysed by a lipase. The other component of the lipid is glycerol.

(e) 51 carbon atoms (the lipid would be tripalmitin; the fatty acid is palmitic acid). Each lipid molecule comprises three fatty acid molecules, each with 16 carbon atoms, plus one glycerol molecule with three carbon atoms.

(f) Sucrose or maltose.

(g) Oxygen reaches the storage tissue by diffusion through the testa and micropyle.

21.8 (a) The dominant food store is lipid, which comprises about 70% of the dry mass of the seeds before germination. By day 4 the mass of lipid is starting to decrease and the mass of sugar to rise. Lipid is therefore being converted to sugar and translocated to the embryo. Note that no sugars can be formed by photosynthesis since germination occurs in darkness. At day 5 the RQ of the embryo = 1, indicating that the embryo is respiring the sugar derived from the lipids. At the same time, the cotyledons (RQ = 0.4−0.5) are gaining energy from the conversion of lipid to sugar, and possibly from oxidation of sugar and fatty acids.

$$C_{18}H_{34}O_3 + 13O_2 \rightarrow C_{12}H_{22}O_{11} + 6CO_2 + 6H_2O + \text{energy}$$
ricinoleic   sucrose
acid (fatty
acid derived
from a lipid)

RQ = 6/13 = 0.46

Conversion of lipid to sugar takes place with an increase in dry mass, so total dry mass of the seedlings increases up to 6 or 7 days. Beyond this point, the lipid reserves are running low, so rate of use of sugar starts to exceed the rate of production. Net mass of sugar, and total mass of seedlings, then starts to decrease. Sugar is used in respiration and in anaerobic reactions.

(b) At day 11, the RQ of the whole seedlings would probably be slightly less than 1.0. It is a combination of two reactions: the main one is the oxidation of sugar in respiration, RQ = 1, but there would probably still be a small contribution from the conversion of lipid to sugar, RQ 0.4−0.5.

21.9 Normally insufficient oxygen is able to penetrate the testa to allow exclusively aerobic respiration; the RQ is a combination of the RQ for aerobic respiration (probably about 1.0) and that for anaerobic respiration, which is infinity (∞). Removal of the testa allows more rapid penetration of oxygen by diffusion, with a consequent increase in aerobic respiration and decrease in RQ. Ethanol is a product of anaerobic respiration so less accumulates when the testas are removed.

21.10 During exposure of the pupa to a constant low temperature of 3 °C for 6 weeks thoracicotropin is produced and stored by neurosecretory cells in the brain. Transferring the pupa to a constant temperature of 25 °C causes the release of thoracicotropin into the blood which activates the thoracic glands to produce moulting hormone, diapause is broken and pupal–adult metamorphosis occurs.

Chapter 22

22.1 (a) Meiosis
  (b) W – interphase
     X – telophase I
     Y – telophase II
  (c) Gamete cells

22.2 See fig 22.2(ans).

22.3

Bases	A	G	T	C
A	AA	AG	AT	AC
G	GA	GG	GT	GC
T	TA	TG	TT	TC
C	CA	CG	CT	CC

22.4 4 bases used once = $4 \times 1 = 4^1 = 4$
  4 bases used twice = $4 \times 4 = 4^2 = 16$
  4 bases used three times = $4 \times 4 \times 4 = 4^3 = 64$
  therefore the mathematical expression is x^y where
  x = number of bases and y = number of bases used.

22.5 See fig 22.5(ans).

22.6 UAC AAG CUC AUG GUA CAU UGC

22.7 This suggests that the process of differentiation does not involve the loss of, or damage to, the genetic material (DNA) but the switching off of selected genes. The DNA was still able to function given the new environment of an undifferentiated cell. Further experiments involving transplanting donor nuclei from cells at a later stage of development did not produce viable embryos. This was taken as evidence that certain irreversible changes occur in the genetic material during development which influence differentiation by causing genes to be switched off irreversibly. However, later experiments carried out by Gurdon at Oxford in the 1960s involved transplanting nuclei from endothelial cells of tadpole intestine into enucleate egg cells from a mature frog. In many cases the eggs developed into normal frogs with the characteristics of the nucleus-donor tadpoles. This technique is known as cloning and suggested that whilst the nucleus

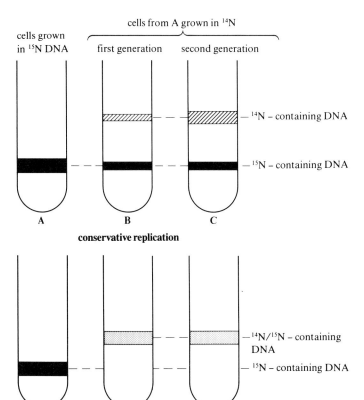

Fig 22.2(ans) *Diagrams explaining two further theories of DNA replication. The appearance of DNA in a caesium chloride density gradient according to the theories presented in Fig 22.14*

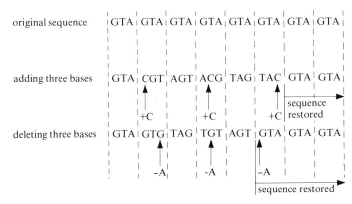

Fig 22.5(ans) *Answer to question expressed diagrammatically. The general principle behind restoring the normal triplet sequence by the addition or deletion of 3 bases is to add or delete three bases at any position along the length of the polynucleotide code*

plays the dominant role in the process of development, the cytoplasm (in this case the egg cytoplasm) plays a major role in determining the extent of the genetic expression of the nuclear material, that is differentiation. In this case it induced the nucleus to fulfil its complete genetic potential and produce a complete organism.

Chapter 23

23.1 See fig 23.1(ans) below.

(a) Let:

B represent brown fur (dominant)
b represent grey fur (recessive)

Parental phenotypes	brown fur	×	grey fur
Parental genotypes (2n)	**BB**	×	**bb**

Meiosis

Gametes (n) (B) (B) × (b) (b)

Random fertilisation

F₁ genotypes (2n)	**Bb**	**Bb**	**Bb**	**Bb**
F₁ phenotypes		all brown fur		

F₁ phenotypes	brown fur	×	brown fur
F₁ genotypes (2n)	**Bb**	×	**Bb**

Meiosis

Gametes (n) (B) (b) × (B) (b)

Random fertilisation

F₂ genotypes (2n)	**BB**	**Bb**	**Bb**	**bb**
F₂ phenotypes	3 brown fur	:		1 grey fur

(b)

Experimental phenotypes	brown fur	×	grey fur
Experimental genotypes (2n)	**Bb**	×	**bb**

Meiosis

Gametes (n) (B) (b) × (b) (b)

Random fertilisation

Offspring genotypes (2n)	**Bb**	**Bb**	**bb**	**bb**
Offspring phenotypes	1 brown fur	:		1 grey fur

In the case of monohybrid inheritance, the offspring from a heterozygous genotype crossed with a homozygous recessive genotype produce equal numbers of offspring showing each phenotype: in this case 50% brown fur and 50% grey fur.

23.2 If an organism having an unknown genotype is testcrossed with a homozygous dominant organism, all the offspring will show the dominant characteristic in the phenotype, as shown in fig 23.2(ans) below.

Let:

T represent a dominant allele

t represent a recessive allele

Testcross phenotypes	homozygous × homozygous	heterozygous × homozygous
Testcross genotypes (2n)	**TT** × **TT**	**Tt** × **TT**

Meiosis

Gametes (n)	(T)(T) × (T)(T)	(T)(t) × (T)(T)

Random fertilisation

Offspring genotypes (2n)	**TT TT TT TT**	**TT TT Tt Tt**
Offspring phenotypes	all tall (homozygous)	all tall (½ homozygous, ½ heterozygous)

23.3 *(a)* If short black hair appeared in the F₁ phenotypes, then short hair must be dominant to long hair and black hair must be dominant to white.
(b) See fig 23.3(ans) below.

Let:

B represent black hair
b represent white hair
S represent short hair
s represent long hair

F₁ phenotypes   short black hair × short black hair
F₁ genotypes (2n)   **SsBb** × **SsBb**

Meiosis

♀\♂	(SB)	(Sb)	(sB)	(sb)
(SB)	SB SB ■	Sb SB ■	sB SB ■	sb SB ■
(Sb)	SB Sb ■	Sb Sb □	sB Sb ■	sb Sb □
(sB)	SB sB ■	Sb sB ■	sB sB ■	sb sB ■
(sb)	SB sb ■	Sb sb □	sB sb ■	sb sb □

Gametes (n) (as shown by ♂ and ♀)

Random fertilisation (as shown by Punnett square)

F₂ genotypes (2n) (as shown in each square)

F₂ phenotypes	9 short black hair	:	3 short white hair	:	3 long black hair	:	1 long white hair

(Symbols)	■	□	▮	▯

23.4 See fig 23.4(ans) below.

Let:

R,r and **S,s** represent two allelomorphic pairs of genes controlling flower colour.

Parental phenotypes   purple × purple
Parental genotypes (2n)   **RrSs** × **RrSs**

Meiosis

♀\♂	(RS)	(Rs)	(rS)	(rs)
(RS)	RS RS ●	Rs RS ●	rS RS ●	rs RS ●
(Rs)	RS Rs ●	Rs Rs ○	rS Rs ●	rs Rs ○
(rS)	RS rS ●	Rs rS ●	rS rS ○	rs rS ○
(rs)	RS rs ●	Rs rs ○	rS rs ○	rs rs ○

Gametes (n) (as shown by ♂ and ♀)

Random fertilisation (as shown by Punnett square)

Offspring genotypes (2n) (as shown in each square)

Offspring phenotypic ratio	9 purple : 7 white

(Symbols)	●	○

23.5 The two alleles segregate during metaphase I and anaphase I.

23.6 The number of different combinations of chromosomes in the pollen gamete cells is calculated using the formula 2^n, where n is the haploid number of chromosomes.
In crocus, since $2n = 6$, $n = 3$.
Therefore, combinations $= 2 = 8$.

23.7 The F_1 phenotypes show that purple flower and short stem are dominant and red flower and long stem are recessive. The approximate ratio of 1:1:1:1 in a dihybrid cross suggests that the two genes controlling the characteristics of flower colour and stem length are not linked and the four alleles are situated on different pairs of chromosomes (fig 23.7(ans) below).

Let:

P represent purple flower
p represent red flower
S represent short stem
s represent long stem

Since the parental stocks were both homozygous for both characters the F_1 genotypes must be **PpSs**.

Testcross phenotypes	purple flower, short stem × red flower, long stem			
Testcross genotypes (2n)	PpSs		×	ppss

♀\♂	PS	Ps	pS	ps
ps	PS ps	Ps ps	pS ps	ps ps

Meiosis
Gametes (n)
(as shown by ♂ and ♀)

Random fertilisation
(as shown in Punnett square)

Offspring genotypes (2n)
(listed in each square)

Offspring phenotypes 1 purple flower, short stem: 1 purple flower, long stem: 1 red flower, short stem: 1 red flower, long stem

23.8 (*a*) Homologous chromosomes
(*b*) Body colour and wing length
(*c*) This cannot be concluded from the data since the position of the antenna shape gene is not shown.

23.9 Out of the 800 seeds produced, only 24 show the results of crossing-over between the genes for seed colour and seed shape. In the other 776, the alleles for seed colour and seed shape have remained linked as shown by their approximate 1:1 ratio.
Hence the crossover value is $(24/800) \times 100 = 3\%$. Therefore the distance between the genes for seed colour and seed shape is 3 units.

23.10 See fig 23.10(ans) below.

(a) Let:

N represent normal wing (dominant)
n represent miniature wing (recessive)
R represent red eye (dominant)
r represent white eye (recessive)
XX represent female fly (♀)
XY represent male fly (♂)

(i) *Parental phenotypes* miniature wing, red eye ♂ × normal wing, white eye ♀

Parental genotypes (2n) $X^{nR}Y$ × $X^{Nr}X^{Nr}$

Meiosis

Gametes (n) X^{nR} Y × X^{Nr} X^{Nr}

Random fertilisation

F_1 genotypes (2n) $X^{nR}X^{Nr}$ $X^{nR}X^{Nr}$ $X^{Nr}Y$ $X^{Nr}Y$

F_1 phenotypes normal wing, red eye ♀ normal wing, white eye ♂

(ii) Assuming no crossing-over between the genes for wing length and eye colour in the female, the following results are likely to appear:

F_1 phenotypes normal wing, white eye ♂ × normal wing, red eye ♀

F_1 genotypes (2n) $X^{Nr}Y$ × $X^{nR}X^{Nr}$

Meiosis

Gametes (n) X^{Nr} Y × X^{nR} X^{Nr}

Random fertilisation

F_2 genotypes (2n) $X^{Nr}X^{nR}$ $X^{Nr}X^{Nr}$ $X^{nR}Y$ $X^{Nr}Y$

F_2 phenotypes normal wing, red eye ♀ normal wing, white eye ♀ miniature wing, red eye ♂ normal wing, white eye ♂

(b) The lack of a 1:1:1:1 ratio of phenotypes resulting from this cross indicates crossing-over between the genes for wing length and eye colour in the female.

Testcross phenotypes normal wing, red eye ♀ × miniature wing, white eye ♂

Testcross genotypes (2n) $X^{nR}X^{Nr}$ × $X^{nr}Y$

Meiosis

Gametes (n)
(as shown by ♀ and ♂)

♂\♀	X^{nR}	X^{Nr}	X^{nr}	X^{NR}
X^{nr}	$X^{nR}X^{nr}$ ♀	$X^{Nr}X^{nr}$ ♀	$X^{nr}X^{nr}$ ♀	$X^{NR}X^{nr}$ ♀
Y	$X^{nR}Y$ ♂	$X^{Nr}Y$ ♂	$X^{nr}Y$ ♂	$X^{NR}Y$ ♂

Random fertilisation
(as shown in Punnett square)

Offspring genotypes (2n)
(as listed in squares)

Offspring phenotypes				
wing:	miniature	normal	miniature	normal
eye:	red	white	white	red
Experimental results	36	35	18	17

The alleles for wing length and eye colour are shown on the two F_1 female (X) chromosomes in the explanation above. Crossing-over between the alleles will give the recombinant genotypes shown above. Out of 106 flies, 35 show recombination of alleles (18 + 17), therefore the crossover value is 35/106 = approximately 30%.

23.11 See fig 23.11(ans) below.

Magpie moth

Let:

> N represent normal colour (dominant)
> n represent pale colour (recessive)

Parental phenotypes   pale colour male × normal colour female

Parental genotypes (2n)

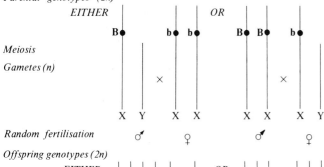

Meiosis

Gametes (n)

EITHER   OR

Random fertilisation

Offspring genotypes (2n)

EITHER   OR

Offspring phenotypes   normal colour ♀   normal colour ♂   normal colour ♂   pale colour ♀

From the results for the offspring phenotypes it is seen that the heterogametic sex in the magpie moth is the female.

Cat

Let:

> B represent black colour (dominant)
> b represent yellow colour (recessive)

Parental phenotypes   black colour male × yellow colour female

Parental genotypes (2n)

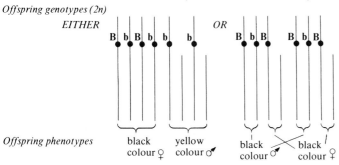

Meiosis

Gametes (n)

EITHER   OR

Random fertilisation

Offspring genotypes (2n)

EITHER   OR

Offspring phenotypes   black colour ♀   yellow colour ♂   black colour ♂   black colour ♀

From the results for the offspring phenotypes it is seen that the heterogametic sex in the cat is the male.

23.12 See fig 23.12(ans) below.

Let:

> B represent black coat colour
> G represent ginger coat colour
> XX represent female cat
> XY represent male cat

Parental phenotypes	ginger-coat male	×	black-coat female
Parental genotypes (2n)	X^GY	×	X^BX^B

Meiosis

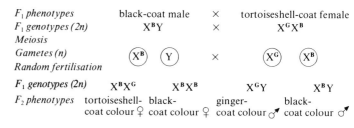

Gametes (n) (X^G) (Y) × (X^B) (X^B)

Random fertilisation

F_1 genotypes (2n) X^GX^B X^GX^B X^BY X^BY

F_1 phenotypes   tortoiseshell-coat colour ♀   black-coat colour ♂

(The parental female must be homozygous for black coat colour since this is the only condition to produce a black-coat colour phenotype).

F_1 phenotypes	black-coat male	×	tortoiseshell-coat female
F_1 genotypes (2n)	X^BY	×	X^GX^B

Meiosis

Gametes (n) (X^B) (Y) × (X^G) (X^B)

Random fertilisation

F_1 genotypes (2n) X^BX^G X^BX^B X^GY X^BY

F_2 phenotypes   tortoiseshell-coat colour ♀   black-coat colour ♀   ginger-coat colour ♂   black-coat colour ♂

23.13 (a) See fig 23.13(ans) below.
(b) There is a probability of ¼ (25%) that each child will have blood group A. So the probability that both will have blood group A is ¼ × ¼ = 1/16 (6.25%).

Let:

> I represent the gene for blood group
> A represent the allele A ⎱ (equally dominant)
> B represent the allele B ⎰
> o represent the allele O (recessive)

Parental phenotypes	blood group A	×	blood group B
Parental genotypes (2n)	I^AI^o	×	I^BI^o

Meiosis

Gametes (n) (I^A) (I^o) × (I^B) (I^o)

Random fertilisation

Offspring genotypes (2n) I^AI^B I^AI^o I^oI^B I^oI^o

Offspring phenotypes blood groups AB   A   B   O

23.14 See fig 23.14(ans) below.

Let:

> **P** represent pea comb
> **R** represent rose comb
> a single **P** allele and a single **R** allele occurring together produce walnut comb
> a double homozygous recessive genotype produces single comb
> **W** represent white feathers (dominant)
> **w** represent black feathers (recessive)

If eight different phenotypes are produced from the cross, each parent must possess as many heterozygous alleles as possible. Hence the genotypes are as shown below:

Parental phenotypes	black, rose-comb cock	×	white, walnut-comb hen
Parental genotypes (2n)	**wwRrpp**	×	**WwRrPp**

Meiosis

Gametes (n)
(as shown by ♀ and ♂)

♂ \ ♀	WRP	WRp	WrP	Wrp	wRP	wRp	wrP	wrp
wRp	WRP wRp ○	WRp wRp △	WrP wRp ○	Wrp wRp △	wRP wRp ●	wRp wRp ▲	wrP wRp ●	wrp wRp ▲
wrp	WRP wrp ○	WRp wrp △	WrP wrp □	Wrp wrp ◌	wRP wrp ●	wRp wrp ▲	wrP wrp ■	wrp wrp ✦

Random fertilisation
(as shown in Punnet square)

Offspring genotypes (2n)
(as shown in squares)

Offspring phenotypes:
(Symbols)

3 white, walnut-comb: 3 black, walnut-comb: 3 white, rose-comb: 3 black, rose-comb: 1 white, pea-comb:

○　　●　　△　　▲　　□

1 black, pea-comb: 1 white, single-comb: 1 black, single-comb

■　　◌　　✦

23.15 Since both dominant alleles, **W**, white, and **B**, black, are present in the heterozygous F₁ genotype, and the phenotype is white, it may be concluded that the alleles show an epistatic interaction where the white allele represents the epistatic gene and the black allele represents the hypostatic gene. The F_2 generation is shown in fig 23.15(ans) below.

Using the symbols given in the question,

F_1 *phenotypes*	white cock × white hen	
F_1 *genotypes (2n)*	**WwBb** × **WwBb**	

Meiosis
(as shown by ♂ and ♀)

Gametes (n)
(as listed in Punnett square)

♀ \ ♂	WB	Wb	wB	wb
WB	WB WB ○	Wb WB ○	wB WB ○	wb WB ○
Wb	WB Wb ○	Wb Wb ○	wB Wb ○	wb Wb ○
wB	WB wB ○	Wb wB ○	wB wB ●	wb wB ●
wb	WB wb ○	Wb wb ○	wB wb ●	wb wb ⊘

Random fertilisation

F_2 *genotypes (2n)*
(as listed in the squares)

F_2 *phenotypes*	12 white colour: 3 black colour: 1 brown colour	
(Symbols)	○　　●　　⊘	

Chapter 24

24.1 A control experiment in which each variable was systematically eliminated.

24.2 Redi's basic assumption was that the presence of 'worms' was due to the entry of the flies through the open flasks.

24.3 Sealing the broths would prevent the entry of organisms to the vessels. Lack of air within the vessels may have deprived organisms of oxygen for respiration.

24.4 Pasteur's basic assumptions were that each generation of organisms develops from the previous generation and not spontaneously.

24.5 Micro-organisms develop in the nutrient broth due to contamination of the broth by organisms in the atmosphere.

24.6 Sealed tubes, boiling, autoclaving, direct access to atmosphere, indirect access to the atmosphere.

24.7 Access to atmosphere.

24.8 Pair A are not heated, pair B are boiled for 10 min, pair C are autoclaved at 15 lb pressure for 20 min, pair D have differential access to the atmosphere.

24.9 Spallanzani – tubes 3 and 4
Pasteur – tubes 7 and 8

24.10 Tubes 1, 3, 5 and 7

24.11 The experimental design takes full account of scientific method. There is a hypothesis and the experimental design includes appropriate controls and systematically eliminated experimental variables. If identical experiments yield consistent results these data may be regarded as valid. The degree of validity attached to conclusions based on these, or any data, depends upon how accurately they interpret the data.

Chapter 25

25.1 The carrier genotype is the heterozygous genotype. The Hardy–Weinberg equation is used to calculate genotype frequencies. The equation may be represented as

$$p^2 + 2pq + q^2 = 1$$

where

p^2 = frequency of homozygous dominant genotype,
$2pq$ = frequency of heterozygous genotype,
q^2 = frequency of homozygous recessive genotype.

The incidence of cystic fibrosis in the population appears in individuals with the homozygous recessive genotype, hence q^2 is 1 in 2 000 or 1/2 000 = 0.0005.

Therefore $q = \sqrt{0.0005}$
$\qquad = 0.0224.$
Since $p + q = 1$
$\qquad p = 1 - q$
$\qquad\quad = 1 - 0.0224$
$\qquad\quad = 0.9776.$

The frequency of the heterozygous genotype ($2pq$) is therefore

$$2 \times (0.9776) \times (0.0224)$$
$$= 0.044$$
$$= 1 \text{ in } 23$$
$$\simeq 5\%$$

Approximately 5% of the population are carriers of the recessive gene for cystic fibrosis.

25.2 *Fasciola hepatica*, the liver fluke, is a parasite which infests sheep. It has an intermediate host, the snail *Limnaea truncatula*, which lives in fresh water and damp pastures. Draining ponds and wet areas would bring about a change in environmental conditions which would exert a selection pressure tending to eliminate *Limnaea*. As the numbers of the snail fall this would reduce the numbers of available hosts which would lead to a decrease in the numbers of the parasite, *Fasciola*.

25.3 Reduced selection pressure at the extremes of each new population would favour increased variability. New phenotypes may show adaptations to the areas previously occupied by the eliminated subspecies and spread inwards to occupy the vacated ecological niche. The initial geographical separation of the cline may have initiated allopatric speciation. If the ring was reformed, gene flow may be impossible due to genetic isolation and each subpopulation would diverge genetically even further to form distinct species, as is the present case in the British Isles where the species exist sympatrically. If the genetic isolation between the two subpopulations was not too great, hybrids may form when the subpopulations were reunited. This zone of hybridisation may act as a reproductive barrier as is the case with the carrion and hooded crows.

Appendix 1
Biological chemistry

A1.1   Elementary chemistry

An **atom** is the smallest part of an element that can take part in a chemical change. An **element** is a substance which cannot be split into simpler substances by chemical means, for example the elements carbon, oxygen and nitrogen. A **compound** is a substance which contains two or more elements chemically combined, as shown below.

Compounds	Elements
water	hydrogen and oxygen
glucose	carbon, hydrogen and oxygen
sodium chloride	sodium and chlorine

A **molecule** is the smallest part of an element or compound which can exist alone under normal conditions, such as H_2, O_2, CO_2 and H_2O.

A1.1.1   Structure of the atom

All elements are made up of atoms. The word 'atom' comes from the Greek word *atomos* meaning indivisible.

The particles which make up atoms are protons, neutrons and electrons, details of which are given in table A1.1. Protons and neutrons have equal mass, and together make up the mass of the nucleus. The electrons have very much lower mass than the protons or neutrons, and when the mass of an atom is being considered, usually only the mass of the nucleus is taken into account.

A neutron is composed of a proton and an electron bound together, so that its charge is neutral.

Atoms are electrically neutral because the number of protons in a nucleus equals the number of electrons orbiting around it.

The number of protons in the nucleus of an atom is called the **atomic number** of that element. It also equals the

Table A1.1 The locations, masses and charges of protons, neutrons and electrons.

Particle	Location	Mass	Charge
proton	the dense central core of the atom, forming the nucleus which has a diameter about $1/100\,000$ that of the atom	1 unit $(1.7 \times 10^{-24}\,g)$	positive $(+1)$
neutron		1 unit	neutral (0)
electron	in 'orbits' around the nucleus	$1/1870$ unit $(9.1 \times 10^{-28}\,g)$	negative (-1)

number of electrons in an atom. For an individual atom, the number of protons plus the number of neutrons equals the **mass number**.

The atoms of some elements exist in different forms called **isotopes** which have different mass numbers (section A1.3). The average mass of an atom is the **relative atomic mass** (A_r) and is usually an average value for a natural mixture of the isotopes. For example, chlorine is made up of a mixture of isotopes of mass numbers 35 and 37; the proportions of the isotopes are such that naturally occurring chlorine has a relative atomic mass of 35.5.

The known elements, of which there are over 100, can be listed in order of ascending atomic number as shown in table A1.2. As indicated in the table the electrons are arranged in successive shells around the nucleus. The first shell can hold up to two electrons (being nearest the nucleus it is the smallest), the second shell can hold up to eight electrons, the third shell can hold up to 18 electrons and the fourth shell can hold up to 32 electrons.

Table A1.2 The first 20 elements in order of ascending atomic number.

Atomic number	Mass number	Relative atomic mass*	Element	Symbol	Arrangement of electrons
1	1	1.0	hydrogen	H	1
2	4	4.0	helium	He	2
3	7	6.9	lithium	Li	2, 1
4	9	9.0	beryllium	Be	2, 2
5	11	10.8	boron	B	2, 3
6	12	12.0	carbon	C	2, 4
7	14	14.0	nitrogen	N	2, 5
8	16	16.0	oxygen	O	2, 6
9	19	19.0	fluorine	F	2, 7
10	20	20.2	neon	Ne	2, 8
11	23	23.0	sodium	Na	2, 8, 1
12	24	24.3	magnesium	Mg	2, 8, 2
13	27	27.0	aluminium	Al	2, 8, 3
14	28	28.1	silicon	Si	2, 8, 4
15	31	31.0	phosphorus	P	2, 8, 5
16	32	32.1	sulphur	S	2, 8, 6
17	35	35.5	chlorine	Cl	2, 8, 7
18	40	39.9	argon	Ar	2, 8, 8
19	39	39.1	potassium	K	2, 8, 8, 1
20	40	40.1	calcium	Ca	2, 8, 8, 2

* Relative atomic mass (A_r) was formerly atomic weight.
Figures for A_r are given to the nearest decimal place.
The symbols for some common elements are, in ascending order of atomic number, chromium (Cr), manganese (Mn), iron (Fe), cobalt (Co), nickel (Ni), copper (Cu), zinc (Zn), arsenic (As), bromine (Br), molybdenum (Mo), silver (Ag), cadmium (Cd), iodine (I), barium (Ba), platinum (Pt), mercury (Hg), lead (Pb), radium (Ra), uranium (U), plutonium (Pu).

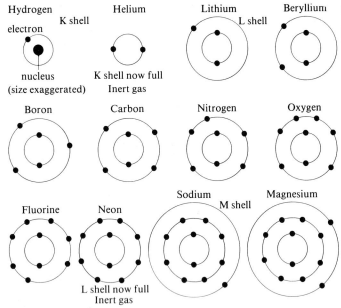

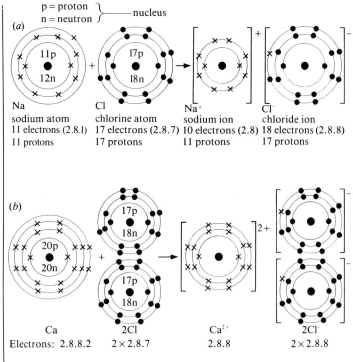

Fig A1.1 *The arrangement of electrons in shells for the first 12 elements. (The nucleus is omitted from all except hydrogen.)*

There are also further shells in the larger atoms, but these need not be considered here. The arrangements of electrons in shells for the first 12 elements are shown in fig A1.1.

Any element with an electronic configuration in which the outermost shell is full is particularly unreactive. Hence helium and neon (table A1.2) are so unreactive that they seldom form compounds with other atoms. Thus they are called noble gases.

The tendency of all other elements is to attain full electron shells through reaction with other elements. When two atoms react to form a compound there are basically two types of bond that can form between them, ionic and covalent bonds.

A1.1.2 Ionic bonding

This is a process in which electrons are transferred from one atom to another. Consider sodium reacting with chlorine (fig A1.2*a*). The sodium atom loses an electron and therefore has an overall positive charge of +1 (its nucleus contains 11 positively charged protons and is surrounded by 10 negatively charged electrons). Similarly the chlorine atom has gained an electron and now has an overall negative charge of −1. Both have full, and therefore stable, electron shells.

These charged particles are no longer true atoms and instead are called **ions**. Hence the sodium ion is represented as Na^+ and the chloride ion as Cl^-. Positively charged ions are called **cations**, and negatively charged ions **anions**. The resulting compound is sodium chloride (formula NaCl) but no molecules of NaCl exist. Instead there is an association of sodium and chloride ions in equal

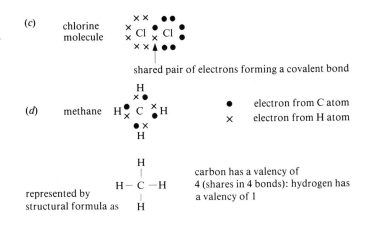

(c) chlorine molecule

shared pair of electrons forming a covalent bond

(d) methane

• electron from C atom
× electron from H atom

represented by structural formula as

carbon has a valency of 4 (shares in 4 bonds): hydrogen has a valency of 1

(e) In ethene (ethylene), C_2H_4, there are two pairs of shared electrons between carbon atoms:

ethene

• × electrons from C atom
○ electron from H atom

The two pairs of shared electrons are represented by a double bond, thus

Fig A1.2 *(a) Formation of sodium chloride. (b) Formation of calcium chloride. (c) Formation of the covalent chlorine molecule. (d) Formula of methane. (e) Formula of ethene. For clarity, electrons from different atoms have been given different symbols (×, • or ○). In reality, all electrons are indistinguishable. Only the outer shells of electrons are shown in (c), (d) and (e)*

numbers (ionic formula Na^+Cl^-). Compounds like this which are formed by the transfer of electrons are called **ionic compounds**. They are usually formed when metals react with non-metals. The metal produces a cation and the non-metal an anion. Salts are all ionic compounds.

Another typical example is calcium chloride (formula $CaCl_2$) (fig A1.2*b*). Here two electrons are lost from the calcium atom, and one gained by each chlorine atom. Therefore the calcium ion is represented as Ca^{++} or Ca^{2+}.

The number of electrons transferred (lost or gained) is the **valency**, sometimes called the **combining power**. Therefore sodium and chlorine have a valency of one and calcium has a valency of two. The number of plus or minus signs shown for an ion is therefore equal to its valency; for example, potassium and hydroxyl ions have a valency of one and so are written as K^+ and OH^-, magnesium and sulphate ions have a valency of two and so are written as Mg^{2+} and SO_4^{2-}, and aluminium has a valency of three and so is written as Al^{3+}

Ionic formulae

Ionic compounds do not exist as molecules but as collections of ions. The ionic formula shows the ratio in which elements are combined in an ionic compound; for example, the formula for the compound aluminium oxide is Al_2O_3, meaning that Al^{3+} and O^{2-} ions are in the ratio of 2 : 3. If an ion with more than one atom is present, such as in SO_4^{2-} (sulphate), the number of that ion present, if more than one, is indicated by using brackets, for example $Al_2(SO_4)_3$; but Na_2SO_4 needs no brackets as only one sulphate ion is involved.

A1.1.3   Covalent bonding

In this type of bonding electrons are not donated or received by the atoms concerned; instead, they are shared. Consider two chlorine atoms; each has seven electrons in its outer shell (electron configuration 2,8,7). In covalency, two chlorine atoms contribute one electron each to a shared pair of electrons, making a chlorine molecule, formula Cl_2. In this way both atoms obtain an approximation to the noble gas configuration and molecules are produced, not ions (fig A1.2*c*). The shared pair of electrons is conventionally written as a single bond thus $Cl-Cl$. Chlorine is said to have a covalency of one (it shares one of its electrons). Another example is methane, CH_4. Carbon has an atomic number of six with four electrons in its outer shell (2,4); hydrogen has an atomic number of one and has only one electron (fig A1.2*d*).

In ethene (ethylene), C_2H_4, there are two pairs of shared electrons between carbon atoms, and the two pairs are represented by a double bond (fig A1.2*e*). In some compounds there are three pairs of shared electrons, a triple bond, such as in ethyne (acetylene), C_2H_2.

Covalent compounds are far more common than ionic compounds in biological systems.

The valencies of some common elements and the charges on common ions are given in table A1.3.

Formulae of covalent compounds

For simple covalent compounds the formula represents the number of each type of atom present in one molecule; for example CO_2 (carbon dioxide) means that one atom of carbon is combined with two atoms of oxygen.

A1.1.4   Chemical equations

When chemical equations are written, not only must the correct formulae for the chemicals be used but also the equations must be balanced, that is there must be the same number of atoms of each element on the right-hand side of the equation as on the left. This can be done in the following way.
(1) Write a word equation, for example
   methane + oxygen → carbon dioxide + water
(2) Write the correct formulae.
   $$CH_4 + O_2 \quad \rightarrow \quad CO_2 \quad + H_2O$$
(3) Ask if the equation balances. The equation in (2) does not, for there are three oxygen atoms on the right side and only two on the left; also there are four hydrogen atoms on the left and two on the right.
(4) Balance the equation, if necessary, using large numbers in front of the relevant formulae and remembering that the formulae cannot be altered.
   $$CH_4 + 2O_2 \rightarrow CO_2 + 2H_2O$$
($2O_2$ means two molecules of oxygen (4 atoms of oxygen); $2H_2O$ means two molecules of water (4 atoms of hydrogen, 2 atoms of oxygen).)

Ionic equations

Equations for reactions between ionic compounds can be written simply as ionic equations. Consider the following reaction:
$$2NaOH + H_2SO_4 \rightarrow Na_2SO_4 + 2H_2O$$
sodium   sulphuric   sodium   water
hydroxide acid   sulphate
(All three compounds are aqueous.)
The equation can be rewritten to show the ions present:
$$2Na^+ + 2OH^- + 2H^+ + SO_4^{2-} \rightarrow 2Na^+ + SO_4^{2-} + 2H_2O$$
Removing ions common to both sides of the equation (not involved in the reaction) gives the ionic equation:
$$2OH^- + 2H^+ \rightarrow 2H_2O$$
This is the only reaction which has taken place.

A1.1.5   Acids, bases, salts, pH and buffers

A hydrogen atom consists of one electron and one proton. If the electron is lost it leaves a proton, and a proton may therefore be regarded as a hydrogen ion, usually written H^+. An **acid** is a substance which can act as a **proton donor** and this is a substance which can ionise to form H^+ as the cation. For the purpose of this book an acid will be defined as a substance which ionises in water to give H^+ ions as the cation. A **strong** acid, such as hydrochloric acid, is one which undergoes almost complete **dissociation** (separation of its constituent ions). It is therefore a more

Table A1.3 Valencies of some elements and charges of some ions.

(a) Valencies of some elements

1	2	3	4
F	O	N	C
Cl	S	P	Si

(b) Charges of some ions of single elements

−2	−1	+1	+2	+3
O^{2-}	F^-	H^+	Mg^{2+}	Al^{3+}
	Cl^-	Na^+	Ca^{2+}	
	Br^-	K^+	Zn^{2+}	
			Ba^{2+}	
	I^-	Cu^+		
		copper(I)	Cu^{2+} copper(II)	
			Fe^{2+} iron(II)	Fe^{3+} iron(III)
			Pb^{2+} lead(II)	

(c) Charges of some ions of more than one element

−3	−2	−1	+1
PO_4^{3-} phosphate (V)	SO_4^{2-} sulphate	NO_3^- nitrate	NH_4^+ ammonium
	CO_3^{2-} carbonate	NO_2^- nitrite	
		OH^- hydroxyl or hydroxide	
		HCO_3^- hydrogen-carbonate (formerly bicarbonate)	

efficient proton donor than a **weak** acid, such as ethanoic acid or carbonic acid, in which only a small proportion of the acid molecules dissociate to give hydrogen ions:

$HCl \rightleftharpoons H^+ + Cl^-$ $CH_3 COOH \rightleftharpoons CH_3 COO^- + H^+$
hydrochloric acid   ethanoic acid

Typical properties of acids are as follows.
(1) Many acids react with the more reactive metals such as magnesium or zinc to produce hydrogen.
(2) Acids are neutralised by bases to give salts and water only.
(3) Almost all acids react with carbonates to give carbon dioxide.
(4) Acids have a sour taste in dilute solution, for example ethanoic acid (vinegar).
(5) Solutions of acids give a characteristic colour with **indicators**; for example, they turn blue litmus red.

A **base** is a substance which reacts with an acid to form a salt and water only (otherwise defined as a **proton acceptor**). Most bases are insoluble in water. Those that are soluble in water form solutions called **alkalis**, such as sodium hydroxide, calcium hydroxide and ammonia solutions. Other typical properties are as follows.
(1) Bases usually have little action on metals.
(2) Bases react with aqueous solutions of the salts of most metals to precipitate an insoluble hydroxide.
(3) Reaction with ammonium salts gives ammonia.

(4) Solutions of alkalis give a characteristic colour with indicators; for example, they turn red litmus blue.

A **salt** is a compound in which the replaceable hydrogen of an acid has been partly or wholly replaced by a metal. An example is sodium chloride where the hydrogen atom of hydrochloric acid has been replaced by an atom of sodium. When a salt dissolves in water its constituent ions dissociate, that is they become free ions separated from one another by water molecules.

The pH scale

The acidity or alkalinity of a solution is related to the concentration of hydrogen ions in the solution. This is expressed as its pH (p represents a mathematical operation, H represents hydrogen). The pH is defined as the logarithm to the base 10 of the reciprocal of the hydrogen ion concentration. Pure water contains 1×10^{-7} moles of hydrogen ions per decimetre cubed (litre). The pH of water is therefore $\log (1/10^7) = 7$.

A pH of 7.0 represents a neutral solution (at room temperature). A pH of less than 7.0 represents an acidic solution, and a pH of more than 7.0 represents an alkaline solution.

The pH scale ranges from about −1 to about 15 (usually 0–14). The scale is logarithmic, so a change in pH of one unit represents a ten-fold change in hydrogen ion concentration.

928

Cells and tissues normally require a pH value close to 7 and fluctuations of more than one or two units from this cannot be tolerated. Mechanisms therefore exist to keep the pH of body fluids as constant as possible. This is partly achieved by buffers.

Buffers

A **buffer solution** is a solution containing a mixture of a weak acid and its soluble salt. It acts to resist changes in pH. Such changes can be brought about by dilution, or by addition of acid or alkali.

As acidity (hydrogen ion concentration) increases, the free anion from the salt combines more readily with free hydrogen ions, removing them from solution. As acidity decreases, the tendency to release hydrogen ions increases. Thus the buffer solution tends to maintain a constant, balanced hydrogen ion concentration. For example

$$HPO_4^{2-} + H^+ \underset{\text{high pH}}{\overset{\text{low pH}}{\rightleftharpoons}} H_2PO_4^-$$

hydrogen   dihydrogen
phosphate   phosphate

Some organic compounds, notably proteins, can function as buffers and they are particularly important in blood.

A1.2   Oxidation and reduction

All biological processes require energy to drive them and the biologist must be aware of the various reactions that make energy available for such processes. Chemical reactions which liberate energy are termed **exothermic** or **exergonic**, whilst those that use energy are **endothermic** or **endergonic**. Synthetic (anabolic) processes are endergonic (such as photosynthesis), whilst breakdown (catabolic) processes are exergonic (such as respiration). The sum of the catabolic and anabolic reactions of the cell occurring at any one moment represents its metabolism.

A cell obtains the majority of its energy by oxidising food molecules during the process of respiration. **Oxidation** is defined as the loss of electrons. The opposite process, in which electrons are gained, is called **reduction**. The two always occur together, electrons being transferred from the **electron donor**, which is thereby oxidised, to the **electron acceptor**, which is thereby reduced. Such reactions are called **redox** reactions, and they are widespread in the chemical processes of biological systems. Several mechanisms of oxidation and reduction exist, as described in the following sections.

A1.2.1   Oxidation

Oxidation may occur directly by the addition of molecular oxygen to a substance, which is then said to be oxidised.

$$A + O_2 \rightarrow AO_2$$

However, the most common form of biological oxidation is

when hydrogen is removed from a substance (**dehydrogenation**).

$$AH_2 + B \xrightarrow[\text{dehydrogenase}]{\text{dehydrogenation}} A + BH_2$$

A has been oxidised and B reduced.

A cell possesses a number of substances called **hydrogen carriers** which act like B in the equation above. Each dehydrogenation is catalysed by a specific dehydrogenase enzyme and the carriers are arranged in a linear order such that their level of potential energy (section A1.6.2) decreases from one end of the line (which is where the hydrogen atoms enter) to the other. This means that each time hydrogen atoms are transferred from one carrier to another of lower potential energy, a small quantity of energy is liberated. In some cases this can be incorporated into ATP.

In some reactions, each atom of hydrogen (which can be regarded as a hydrogen ion or proton, H^+, plus one negatively charged electron, e^-) is not transferred as a whole. Here the process only involves the transfer of electrons. For example

$$2FeCl_2 + Cl_2 \rightleftharpoons 2FeCl_3$$
iron(II)   iron(III)
chloride   chloride

Iron(II) ions are oxidised to iron(III) ions by the loss of one electron per ion, or

$$Fe^{2+} \rightleftharpoons Fe^{3+} + e^-$$
reduced   oxidised

The electrons are transferred to the chlorine molecule which is thereby reduced and forms two chloride ions. So the complete ionic equation is

$$2Fe^{2+} + Cl_2 \rightleftharpoons 2Fe^{3+} + 2Cl^-$$
reduced   oxidised   oxidised   reduced

Cytochromes, which contain iron, work in mitochondria and convey electrons (derived from hydrogen atoms which have split into hydrogen ions and electrons) along an electron transport chain. Here the electrons are passed from less electronegative atoms to more electronegative ones. The products of such reactions possess less potential energy than the reactants and the difference is liberated as energy which is utilised in one form or another. At the end of the chain is a cytochrome that also contains copper. This copper transfers its electrons directly to atmospheric oxygen and is thereby oxidised itself.

$$2Cu^+ - 2e^- \rightleftharpoons 2Cu^{2+}$$
$$2H^+ + 2e^- + \tfrac{1}{2}O_2 \rightleftharpoons H_2O$$
$$\overline{2H^+ + 2Cu^+ + \tfrac{1}{2}O_2 \rightleftharpoons 2Cu^{2+} + H_2O}$$

A1.2.2   Reduction

Reduction occurs when molecular oxygen is removed from a substance, or hydrogen atoms are gained by a substance, or when an electron is gained by a substance.

A1.3   Isotopes

Atoms of some elements exist in more than one form, the different forms being called **isotopes** (*iso*, same; *topos*, place: same position in the periodic table of elements). All the isotopes of a given element have the same number of protons and electrons (same atomic number) and therefore have identical chemical properties. However, they differ in the neutron content of their nuclei and therefore have different masses. To distinguish between isotopes, mass number is added to the symbol of the element; for example oxygen has three naturally occurring isotopes, ^{16}O, ^{17}O and ^{18}O. One isotope is usually much commoner than the others; for example the ratio of presence of $^{16}O:^{17}O:^{18}O$ is $99.759\%:0.037\%:0.204\%$.

Some combinations of protons and neutrons give nuclei which can exist without change for a long time. These nuclei are said to be stable. Other combinations give unstable nuclei, that is they tend to break up or decay, emitting particles and radiation. Such nuclei are said to be radioactive and can easily be detected using various instruments such as Geiger–Müller tubes and counters, scintillation counters, and so on. As the atomic number of the nucleus increases, so the relative number of neutrons needed for stability increases. For example, the 92 protons of uranium need 138 neutrons to be stable. Isotopes of uranium with larger numbers of neutrons are radioactive, their nuclei being unstable.

The rate of decay is often expressed as the **half-life**. This is the time during which, on average, half the atoms present will decay. For example, ^{14}C has a half-life of 5 570 years.

Radioactive isotopes can emit 'rays' of particles and radiation of three kinds.

(1) **α particles**. These are identical to helium nuclei, that is they consist of two protons plus two neutrons. They have two positive charges.

An example of α-particle emission is given below (see also fig A5.1). (The upper number on the left-hand side of each element's symbol is the mass number and the lower is the atomic number.)

$$^{238}_{92}U \rightarrow {}^{234}_{90}Th + {}^{4}_{2}H$$

The ^{238}U nucleus ejects an α particle, thus losing four units of mass and two of charge and becoming an isotope of thorium.

(2) **β particles**. These are fast-moving electrons derived from the nucleus when a neutron changes to a proton. β particles have a single negative charge (see also fig A5.1).

An example of β-particle emission is

$$^{234}_{90}Th \rightarrow {}^{234}_{91}Pa + \beta(e^-)$$

The thorium nucleus ejects an electron; one of its neutrons therefore becomes a proton. Its atomic mass is unchanged, but its atomic number (number of protons) is increased by one, and it becomes an isotope of protactinium.

(3) **γ rays**. These are very short wavelength electromagnetic waves associated with α and β decay. They have a high energy and are very difficult to stop, passing, for example, through thick sheets of lead.

α particles are easily stopped, for example by air or by a thin sheet of paper. β particles have a greater penetrating power but are stopped by a thick sheet of aluminium or a thin sheet of lead. The particles and the radiation can be harmful to living organisms if they are in close enough proximity to cells.

A1.4   Solutions and the colloidal state

Solutions have at least two parts or phases: the **continuous (dispersion)** phase or **solvent**, in which the **disperse** phase or **solute** is supported or dissolved.

In 1861 Graham distinguished between two types of solute which he called **crystalloids** and **colloids**. These he differentiated according to whether the solute molecules were capable of passing through a parchment (partially permeable) membrane. In fact, in biological systems there is no clear distinction between them since the biological solvent is always water and the properties of any water-based solution depend upon the size of the solute molecule and the effect of gravity. Three types of solution may be identified.

(1) **True solution**. In this, solute particles are small and comparable in size to the solvent molecules, forming a homogeneous system, and the particles do not separate out under the influence of gravity; for example salt solution and sucrose solution. Such solutions are regarded by chemists as forming one phase.

(2) **Colloidal solution**. The solute particles are large by comparison with those of the solvent, forming a heterogeneous system, but the particles still do not separate out under gravity; for example clay in water.

(3) **Suspension** or **emulsion**. The solute particles are so large that they cannot remain dispersed against gravitational force unless the suspension is stirred continuously. A suspension has solid particles whereas an emulsion has liquid particles in the disperse phase, for example a silt suspension.

The three systems above can be described as **dispersion systems** because the particles are dispersed through a medium. Dispersion systems can involve all three states of matter, namely solid, liquid and gas; for example gas in water (soda water), sodium chloride in water (salt solution) and solid in solid (copper in zinc as brass). All can be called solutions, but generally this term refers to those systems that have a liquid solvent.

Many biological systems exist as colloidal solutions

which are either hydrophobic or hydrophilic: a **hydrophobic sol** is water-hating, such as clay or charcoal in water, and a **hydrophilic sol** is water-loving, such as starch, table jelly, gelatin and agar-agar. Most of the colloidal solutions occurring in organisms, such as protein solutions, are hydrophobic sols. The viscosity of a hydrophilic sol, such as table jelly, can be increased by making it more concentrated or by lowering the temperature. As viscosity increases, the sol may set and is then called a **gel**. A gel is a more or less rigid colloidal system, although there is no sharp distinction between sol and gel. Ionic composition, pH and pressure are other factors which can affect sol–gel transformations and all may be important in living cells under certain circumstances.

Characteristics of the colloidal state are shown in table A1.4.

A1.5   Diffusion and osmosis

Molecules and ions in solution can move passively and spontaneously in a particular direction as a result of diffusion. Osmosis is a special type of diffusion. Such movements in living organisms do not require the expenditure of energy, unlike active transport. Another type of movement, namely mass flow, is considered in chapter 14.

A1.5.1   Diffusion

Diffusion involves the random and spontaneous movement of individual molecules and ions. For example, if a bottle of concentrated ammonia solution is left on a bench and the stopper removed, the smell of

Table A1.4 Characteristics of the colloidal state.

Phenomenon	Physical properties	Biological properties
Dialysis (the separation of particles by partially permeable membranes)	Colloids cannot pass through such membranes	Colloidal cytoplasm is retained within the cell surface membrane. Large molecules cannot pass through and therefore must be changed to smaller molecules such as starch to glucose
Brownian movement	Very small particles viewed under a microscope vibrate without changing position. This movement is due to the continuous bombardment of the molecules by the solvent molecules, for example Indian ink in water	All living cytoplasm is colloidal and minute particles in the cell can be seen to exhibit Brownian movement
Filtration	The movement of particles during this process depends on the size of the molecule. The actual size of the particles can be measured by varying the size of the filter pores	
Solute potential (osmotic potential)	Hydrophobic colloids develop extremely small solute potentials in solution. Hydrophilic colloids develop small but measurable solute potentials in solution	
Precipitation	Hydrophobic colloids can be precipitated (coagulation). A positively charged colloid will precipitate a negatively charged colloid. Electrolytes have the same effect	Dilute acids or rennet coagulate casein of milk, as in cheese-making. Precipitation of pectin from cell walls occurs during jam-making. Heat irreversibly coagulates egg albumen
Surface properties	Colloidal particles present an enormous surface area to the surrounding solvent. The surface energy is considerable here and this energy can cause molecules to aggregate at the surface interface. This is called **adsorption**. For example, charcoal is used to adsorb gases in respirators, or dyes from solution. This phenomenon can be used for stabilising colloidal sols, such as in the addition of egg to mayonnaise, or soap to oil-based insecticides	Adsorption of molecules occurs in the cell colloids particularly in cells near to, or concerned in the uptake of, ions, such as cortical cells of the root
Gel to sol and reverse changes	The sol state is fluid and the gel state is solid; for example, starch in hot water is a colloidal sol but when cooled it becomes a colloidal gel. Change of pH, temperature, pressure and the presence of metallic ions can also be equally effective	Clotting of blood is a sol to gel change with the gelation of the protein fibrinogen. Heat changes egg albumen from sol to gel
Imbibition	The absorption of fluid by colloids is called **imbibition**; for example gelatin taking in water	The testa of a dry seed or cellulose in cell walls take up water by imbibition. The release of gametes from sex organs, such as antheridia, is due to imbibitional swelling

ammonia soon penetrates the room. The process by which the ammonia molecules spread is diffusion, and although individual molecules may move in any direction, the net direction is outwards from the concentrated source to areas of lower concentration. Thus diffusion may be described as the *movement of molecules or ions from a region of their high concentration to a region of their low concentration down a concentration gradient*. In contrast to mass flow it is possible for the net diffusion of different types of molecule or ion to be in different directions at the same time, each type moving down its own concentration gradient. Thus in the lungs, oxygen diffuses into the blood at the same time as carbon dioxide diffuses out into the alveoli; mass flow of blood through the lungs, however, can be in one direction only. Also, smaller molecules and ions diffuse faster than larger ones, assuming equal concentration gradients. There is a modified form of diffusion called facilitated diffusion which is described in section 7.2.2.

A1.5.2   Osmosis

Osmosis is *the passage of solvent molecules from a region of their high concentration to a region of their low concentration through a partially permeable membrane*. The solvent in all biological systems is water.

Certain membranes, previously known as **semi-permeable membranes**, allow the passage of solvent molecules only and completely exclude solute molecules or ions. The membranes of living cells, however, allow the passage of certain solute molecules or ions in a selective manner, depending on the nature of the membrane. They are therefore best described as **partially permeable** rather than semi-permeable.

Imagine a situation in which an aqueous solution A, with a high concentration of solute, is separated by a differentially permeable membrane from an aqueous solution B with a low concentration of solute. In this situation, there will be a net movement of water (solvent) molecules through the membrane from solution B to solution A by osmosis. This will continue until equilibrium is reached, at which point there is no further net movement of water. Two solutions of the same osmotic concentration are described as **isosmotic**.

In the example given, water moves from B to A because solution B has a higher concentration of water molecules than solution A. In other words, water moves by diffusion. Osmosis is therefore best regarded as a special kind of diffusion in which equilibrium is attained by movement of solvent molecules only. The effects of different solutions on red blood cells are shown in fig A1.3.

Sea water is more concentrated than the fluids in the majority of living organisms (salinity is 34.5 parts per thousand) and fresh water is less concentrated (salinity less than 0.5 parts per thousand). Animals and plants living in estuaries have particular problems and the nature of these and their solutions are described in section 19.3.4.

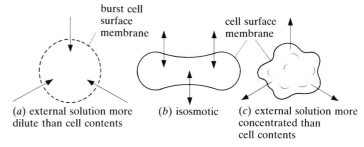

(a) external solution more dilute than cell contents

(b) isosmotic

(c) external solution more concentrated than cell contents

Fig A1.3 *The relative directions of movement of water molecules across the cell surface membrane of red blood cells placed in solutions of different concentrations. In (a) there is a net entry of water into the cell and the pressure set up bursts the membrane. This is called haemolysis. In (b) there is no change in the volume of the cell since equal quantities of water flow across the membrane in both directions. In (c) there is a net loss of water from the cell, the membrane 'collapses' and the appearance is described as 'crenated'*

If a solution is separated by a partially permeable membrane from pure water, the hydrostatic pressure required to resist the osmotic flow of water into the solution is called the **osmotic pressure** of that solution. The higher the concentration of a solution the higher is the osmotic pressure. The osmotic pressure of a solution can only be measured as a *real* pressure in a piece of apparatus called an **osmometer**. In normal situations the osmotic pressure of a solution is only a *potential* pressure and the term **osmotic potential** or **solute potential** is preferable to osmotic pressure. Osmotic or solute potential is, by convention, given a negative sign (section 14.1.4). For example, a molar solution of sucrose at 20 °C has an osmotic pressure of 3 510 kPa, but an osmotic or solute potential of −3 510 kPa. The more concentrated a solution, the higher is its osmotic pressure and the lower its osmotic or solute potential. Unfortunately, the terms 'osmotic pressure' and 'osmotic potential' are often used interchangeably and more concentrated solutions are mistakenly described as having higher osmotic potentials. For this reason the term **solute potential** is used throughout these books.

A1.6   Laws of thermodynamics

All chemical changes are governed by the laws of thermodynamics. The first law, called the **law of conservation of energy**, states that for any chemical process the total energy of the system and its surroundings always remains constant. This means that energy is neither created nor destroyed, and that if the chemical system gains energy then that quantity of energy must have been provided by the surroundings of the system, and vice versa. Therefore energy may be redistributed, converted into another form or both, but never lost.

The second law states that when left to themselves, systems and their surroundings usually approach a state of maximum disorder (**entropy**). This implies that highly ordered systems will readily deteriorate unless energy is used to maintain their order. All biological processes obey, and are governed by, these two laws of thermodynamics.

A1.6.1 Energy relations in living systems

Consider the decomposition of hydrogen peroxide into water and oxygen:

$$2H_2O_2 \rightleftharpoons 2H_2 + O_2$$

Generally, pure hydrogen peroxide will persist for a long time with no significant decomposition. For decomposition to occur, molecules must, on collision, have energy greater than a certain level, called the **activation energy**, E_a. Once this energy is reached, changes in the bonding pattern of the molecules occur and the reaction may generate enough energy to proceed spontaneously. The activation energy required varies with different reactants.

Addition of heat energy is the most common way in which activation energy is reached, and most reactants require quantities far greater than that provided by normal temperatures. For example, it is only when hydrogen peroxide is heated to 150 °C that it decomposes rapidly enough to cause an explosive reaction. Water and oxygen are produced and energy is liberated. The overall energy change which occurs in this reaction is called the free energy change (ΔG). As the reaction is very rapid, and the products water and oxygen generally do not re-unite to form hydrogen peroxide, the energy liberated is actually lost from the chemical system to the environment. Therefore ΔG is negative (fig A1.4).

Obviously high temperatures would be lethal to biological systems and so enzymes are used instead. Acting as catalysts, they reduce the activation energy required by the reactants and therefore increase the rates of chemical reactions without addition of energy, such as a rise in temperature, to the system. Catalase is the enzyme that promotes rapid decomposition of aqueous solutions of hydrogen peroxide in living systems.

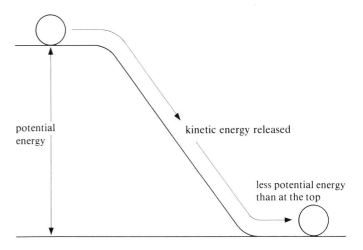

Fig A1.5 *Potential and kinetic energy*

A1.6.2 Potential energy

This is defined as the energy which a system possesses because of its position and condition. Consider a stationary ball at the top of a slope (fig A1.5). The ball possesses an amount of gravitational potential energy equal to the work done to place it there originally. When it rolls down the slope some of the potential energy of the ball is converted into kinetic energy. When the ball comes to rest at the bottom of the slope it possesses less potential energy than it had at the top. In order to restore the ball's potential energy to its original value, energy from the environment must be used to raise it once more to the top of the slope.

Potential energy for biological systems is built up by green plants during the production of sugar when photosynthesis occurs (fig A1.6). During this process, solar energy boosts certain electrons from their orbits with the result that they acquire potential energy. When oxidation of the sugar takes place during respiration, the potential energy of the electrons is used in various forms by living systems.

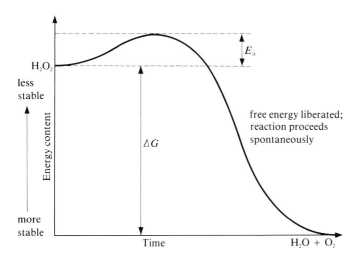

Fig A1.4 *Activation energy*

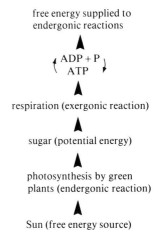

Fig A1.6 *Movement of energy through biological systems*

A1.7 The electromagnetic spectrum

The Sun emits energy in the form of electrical and magnetic vibrations, called **electromagnetic waves** or **electromagnetic radiation**. The complete range of electromagnetic radiation is called the **electromagnetic spectrum** (fig A1.7), and includes gamma- and X-rays, ultra-violet and visible light, infra-red radiation and radio waves. The differences between these forms of radiation are determined by their frequency, which is the rate (frequency) at which the waves are produced. Wavelength is inversely proportional to frequency. Thus a high frequency corresponds to a short wavelength. The shortest waves are the cosmic gamma-rays, whilst the longest are the long radio waves.

Even though the various types of waves differ in their wavelengths, they all possess the following common features:

(1) they travel across a vacuum at the same speed, 3×10^8 m s^{-1};
(2) they are transverse waves;
(3) they can be plane-polarised;
(4) they demonstrate the wave effects of interference and diffraction.

The visible spectrum occupies a very narrow part of the electromagnetic spectrum (wavelengths between 380–760 nm). This is the only part that can be perceived as light by the naked eye.

Fig A1.7 *The electromagnetic spectrum*

A1.8 Chromatography

Chromatography is a technique used for the separating of mixtures into their components. The technique depends upon the differential movement of each component through a stationary medium under the influence of a moving solvent. For example, the green pigment in plants, when dissolved in a suitable solvent and allowed to pass through a stationary medium such as powdered chalk, separates into a number of different coloured pigments. A similar experiment is described in experiment A1.3.

There are three basic types of chromatography, depending on the nature of the stationary medium: **paper chromatography**, **adsorption column chromatography** and **thin-layer chromatography**. Paper chromatography is used in experiments A1.1–1.3 and is also described further in section 9.4.3.

The various techniques of chromatography are now widely used in chemistry, biology, biochemistry and such specialist sciences as forensic medicine.

Electrophoresis

Electrophoresis is a modified form of chromatography used to separate charged molecules. An electric current is applied across a chromatographic medium such that one end has a positive charge and the other a negative charge. Individual molecules in the mixture move outwards through the medium towards the ends depending on their relative masses and charges. Electrophoresis is commonly used in the isolation and identification of amino acids, where the technique is improved further by adjusting the pH of the medium.

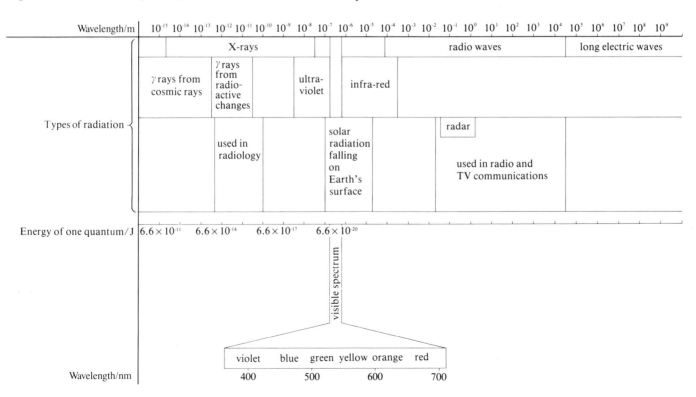

A1.8.1 The concept of R_f values

The movement of the solute relative to the solvent front on a chromatographic system is constant for that solute. This can be expressed in the term R_f as shown below.

$$R_f = \frac{\text{distance moved by solute}}{\text{distance moved by solvent front}}$$

If the solvent front goes off the end of the paper then it is possible to express the movement of a particular solute in comparison with the movement of another standard solute.

$$\text{Thus } R_x = \frac{\text{distance moved by solute}}{\text{distance moved by standard solute } x}$$

See fig A1.8c.

A1.8.2 Two-dimensional paper chromatography

Complex mixtures of solutes cannot always be separated efficiently by chromatography in one direction only. Thus a further separation must be carried out using a second solvent at right-angles to the first for a better separation of the spots (fig A1.8d).

A square sheet of paper is used. The test solution is applied to the base line near one end and the first separation is carried out. The paper is removed, dried and turned through 90° and a further chromatographic run is made with a different solvent. As a result the partially separated solutes of the first run are further separated in the second solvent which has different characteristics from the first. The paper is removed, dried, and the solutes located with a suitable reagent. The identification of a given compound can be made by comparison of its position with that of known standard compounds. This was the technique used by Calvin during his experiments to identify the initial products of the photosynthetic process (section 9.1.3).

Before running chromatograms of biological interest, it is helpful to practise the technique using coloured inks or indicators. The following experiments will show that the smaller, that is the more concentrated, the spot of origin, the better the separation. They also show that the longer the chromatogram runs, the better the separation of the samples.

Experiment A1.1: Separation of indicators

Materials

Whatman no. 1 or no. 3 filter paper	petri dish
methyl orange (screened)	pipette
bottle of 880 ammonia	

Method

Place a drop of screened methyl orange in the centre of the filter paper. Wave the paper in the air to dry it, hold it over an open bottle of 880 ammonia for a short while and then place the paper over a petri dish (fig A1.8a). Add one drop of water to the spot of the indicator.

Observations

The two indicators present in the methyl orange move outwards at different rates, the blue ring moving faster than the yellow ring. The blue ring is the indicator bromothymol blue and the yellow is methyl orange.

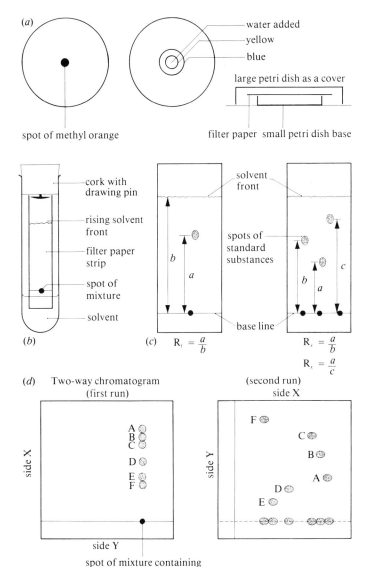

Fig A1.8 *Techniques of chromatography*

Experiment A1.2: Separation of coloured inks into their various components

Materials

boiling tube	drawing pin
cork	water-soluble felt-tip pens
filter paper	distilled water

935

Method

(1) Obtain a boiling tube and cork as shown in fig A1.8b. Pin a rectangle of filter paper to the underside of the cork by means of a drawing pin. Draw a pencil line across the free end of the filter paper about 1 cm up from the end.

(2) Mark crosses at equal intervals across the paper on the origin line, one cross for each ink being tested.

(3) Using water-soluble felt-tip pens of different colours, spot a sample ink on each cross and label the spot in pencil below the origin. The spot should be no larger than 2 mm. Allow the spots to dry.

(4) Suspend the paper in the boiling tube so that the origin is close to the surface of the solvent with the end of the paper just immersed. The solvent is distilled water.

(5) Allow the chromatogram to run until the solvent front is 1 cm from the top of the paper. Remove the chromatogram and allow to dry, having marked the end of the solvent front in pencil.

(6) If larger scale chromatography tanks are available these can be used for either ascending or descending runs.

Experiment A1.3: To separate plant pigments by paper chromatography

Materials

leaves of nettle or spinach	Buchner funnel
	separating funnel
blender or knife	light petroleum
90% propanone (acetone)	(BP 37.8–48.9 °C)
mortar and pestle	boiling tube
small piece of capillary	filter paper
tube	drawing pin

Method

Mince some leaves of nettle (*Urtica dioica*) or spinach in a blender (or simply cut them up into small pieces by chopping with a knife). Grind up the leaves with 90% propanone (acetone) in a mortar. Filter the extract through a Buchner funnel into a separating funnel. Add an equal volume of light petroleum. Shake the mixture thoroughly. Wash through with water several times and each time discard the water layer with its contents. The solvent for running the chromatogram is 100 parts of light petroleum: 12 parts of 90% propanone. Use a boiling tube and filter paper as described in the previous experiment. In the same manner rule a pencil line about 1 cm from the bottom of the filter paper. By means of a small piece of capillary tube, spot the mixture of pigments in the centre of the pencil line. Pour the solvent into the boiling tube to a depth of about 2 cm and then fix the cork and paper into the tube. The solvent should be allowed to run until it is just below the cork. This should take about 1–2 h. The tube should be placed in dim light.

Results

The following colour bands should be shown.

Colour of spot	R_f value	Pigments present
yellow	0.95	carotene
yellow-grey	0.83	phaeophytin
yellow-brown	0.71	xanthophyll (often differentiates into two spots)
blue-green	0.65	chlorophyll *a*
green	0.45	chlorophyll *b*

Appendix 2
Biological techniques

A2.1 Scientific method

Science may be defined in terms of either knowledge or method. Scientific **knowledge** is the total body of factual material which has been accumulated (by scientific **method**) relating to the events of the material world.

'Science is almost wholly the outgrowth of pleasurable intellectual curiosity.' A. N. Whitehead

In order to satisfy their curiosity, scientists must continually pose questions about the world. The secret of success in science is to ask the right questions.

'The formulation of a problem is often more essential than its solution, which may be mainly a matter of mathematical or experimental skill. To raise new questions, new possibilities, to regard old problems from a new angle, requires creative imagination and marks real advance in science.' Albert Einstein

Scientific investigations may begin in response to observations made by scientists or in response to some internal 'inductive' process on the part of scientists. Those aspects of knowledge which are described as scientific must, as the contemporary philosopher of science Karl Popper has stated, be capable of 'refutation'. This means that the facts of scientific knowledge must be testable and repeatable by other scientists. Thus it is essential that all scientific investigations are described fully and clearly as described in section A2.5. If investigations yield identical results under identical conditions, then the results may be accepted as valid. Knowledge which cannot be investigated as described above is not scientific and is described as 'metaphysical'.

Facts are based on **observations** obtained directly or indirectly by the senses or instruments, such as light or radio telescopes, light or electron microscopes and cathode ray oscilloscopes, which act as extensions of our senses. All the facts related to a particular problem are called **data**. Observations may be **qualitative** (that is describe colour, shape, taste, presence and so on) or **quantitative**. The latter is a more precise form of observation and involves the measurement of an amount or quantity which may have been demonstrated qualitatively.

Observations provide the raw material which leads to the formulation of a hypothesis (fig A2.1). A **hypothesis** is an assumption or question based on the observations, that may provide a valid explanation of the observations. Einstein stated that a hypothesis has two functions.

(1) It should account for all the observed facts relevant to that problem.
(2) It should lead to the prediction of new information. New observations (facts, data) which support the hypothesis will strengthen it. New observations which contradict the hypothesis must result in it being modified or even rejected.

In order to assess the validity of a hypothesis it is necessary to design a series of experiments aimed at producing new observations which will support or contradict the hypothesis. In most hypotheses there are a number of factors which may influence the observation; these are called **variables**. Hypotheses are objectively tested by a series of experiments in which each one of the hypothetical variables influencing the observations is systematically eliminated. The experimental series is said to be **controlled** and this ensures that only one variable of the problem is tested at a given time.

The most successful hypothesis becomes a **ruling hypothesis**, and if it withstands attempts at falsification and continues to be successful in predicting previously unexplained facts and relationships it may become a **theory**.

The trend throughout scientific study is to achieve higher levels of predictability (probability). When a theory has proved invariable under all circumstancs, or such variations as occur are systematic and predictable, then it may be accepted as a **law**.

As knowledge increases and techniques of investigation improve, hypotheses and even well-established theories may be challenged, modified and even rejected. Science is dynamic and controversial and the objective methods of science are always exposed to challenge.

A2.2 Recording by biological drawing

Purpose

(1) To provide a record of work for future reference.
(2) To supplement observation and to enable you to see more fully and accurately the studies that you are investigating.
(3) To aid memory of what you see by actively recording.

Principles

(1) Notebook or drawing paper of suitable thickness and quality must be used. It must be capable of standing some erasure of incorrect pencil lines.
(2) Pencils should be sharp and of HB quality. No coloured pencils should be used.

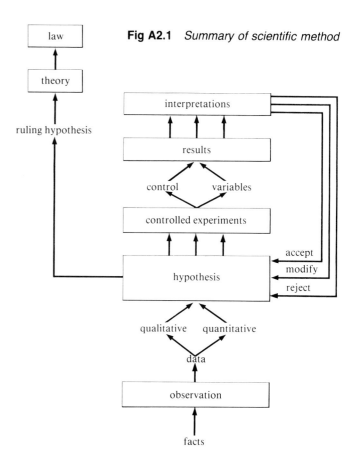

Fig A2.1 *Summary of scientific method*

(3) Drawings must be:
  (*a*) large enough – the greater the number of parts the larger the drawing;
  (*b*) simple – include the outline of the structure and other useful landmarks to show topography and relationship of parts;
  (*c*) accurate – if the subject has several similar parts, draw a small portion accurately;
  (*d*) drawn with lines sharp and clear – each line should be considered and then drawn without removing the pencil from the paper; shading and colour should be avoided;
  (*e*) labelled – these should be as complete as possible with label lines that do not cross; space labels around the figure.
(4) Make two drawings if necessary: (*a*) a simple drawing of the main features, and (*b*) details of small parts only. For example, a low power plan of a plant section, and a high power detail of the cells in a wedge or quadrant of the plan.
(5) Draw what you see and not what you think you see, and certainly not a textbook copy.
(6) Every drawing should have a title, magnification, viewpoint of the specimen (such as TS, RLS and so on) and explanatory notes (fig A2.2).
(7) Drawings of apparatus should be as a vertical section showing clearly where there can be a flow of gases from vessels, through tubes and valves.

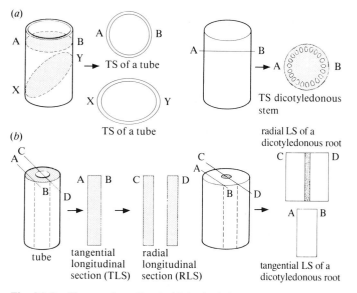

(a)

TS of a tube

TS of a tube

TS dicotyledonous stem

radial LS of a dicotyledonous root

(b)

tube

tangential longitudinal section (TLS)

radial longitudinal section (RLS)

tangential LS of a dicotyledonous root

Fig A2.2 *Types of section in biological drawings: (a) transverse sections, (b) longitudinal sections*

A2.3 Use of the hand lens and the microscope

A2.3.1 The hand lens

This is a convex lens mounted in a frame. The frame may be of small size (pocket lens), or much larger for aiding dissection (tripod lens). The hand lens should be held close to the eye and the object brought towards the lens until an enlarged image can be seen. If a drawing is to be made from the object under investigation, then the magnification of the drawing in relation to the size of the object must be calculated.

$$\text{Drawing magnification} = \frac{\text{linear dimension of the drawing}}{\text{linear dimension of the object}}$$

$$\text{For example} = \frac{6}{2} = 3$$

This can be written as ×3.

A2.3.2 The microscope

The microscope uses the magnifying powers of two convex lenses to produce a magnified image of a very small object. Examine a microscope and identify the parts shown in fig A2.3. The microscope is an expensive instrument and should be handled carefully, paying attention to the following.

(1) Keep the instrument in a box (or under a cover) when not in use in order to maintain it in a dust-free state.
(2) Remove it from the box using two hands and place it on the bench gently to avoid unnecessary jarring.
(3) The lenses must be kept clean by wiping with a lens tissue.
(4) The microscope must **always** be focussed **upwards**,

never downwards. It is very easy to pass through the plane of focus when looking through the microscope and focussing downwards, and as a result damage the slide.

(5) Keep both eyes open and use each eye in turn.

Adjustment of the microscope for low power work

(1) Place the microscope on the bench and sit behind it in a comfortable position. The object on the stage must be illuminated and this can be done with light from a built-in light source, from a window or a bench lamp. Light from the latter two sources shines on the understage mirror such that the curved surface reflects it up through the hole in the stage. The flat mirror is used to shine light through a sub-stage condenser, if there is one fitted.
(2) Using the coarse adjustment screw, rack up the tube and turn the nosepiece until the lowest power objective (×10 or 16 mm) clicks into line with the microscope tube.
(3) Place the slide to be examined on the microscope stage such that the material under the cover-slip is in the middle of the aperture of the stage.
(4) Viewing the stage and the slide from the side, rack down the coarse adjustment until the low power objective is about 5 mm from the slide.
(5) Looking through the microscope, rack up by means of the coarse adjustment until the object is in focus.

Adjustment of the microscope for high power work

(1) High power work needs artificial light for sufficient illumination. Use a bench lamp or microscope lamp with an opal bulb. If a filament bulb is used, it is

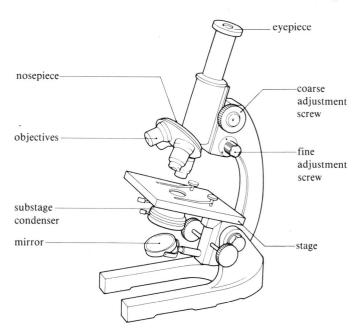

Fig A2.3 *A modern compound light microscope*

938

necessary to place a sheet of paper between the bulb and the microscope. Swing the mirror so that the flat surface is uppermost and the light is thrown up into the microscope.

(2) To focus the condenser, leave the slide on the stage. Rack up the sub-stage condenser until within 5 mm of the stage. Look down the microscope and rack up the coarse adjustment until the object comes into focus. Now adjust the focus of the condenser until the image of the lamp is just superimposed on the slide. Put the condenser just out of focus so that the lamp image disappears. The lighting should now be at its optimum. Incorporated with the condenser is the diaphragm. This adjusts the opening through which light passes and the aperture should be as wide as possible. The definition will then be at its best (see fig A2.3).

(3) Turn the nosepiece until the high power objective lens (×40 or 4 mm) clicks into place. If focus has already been achieved under low power, the nosepiece should automatically bring the high power lens into approximate focus. Adjust carefully using the fine adjustment and always focussing upwards.

(4) If the focus is still not correct after moving the higher power objective lens then use the following procedure. Look at the stage from the side, lower the tube until the objective lens is almost touching the slide. Watch the reflection of the objective lens in the slide and then aim to make the lens and its image almost meet.

(5) Look into the microscope and rack up slowly using the fine adjustment until the object is in focus.

Magnification

The magnification of the object is the multiple of eyepiece and objective lens magnifications (table A2.1).

Table A2.1 Magnification of the microscope.

Objective lens	Eyepiece lens	Magnification of the object
×10	×6	×60
×40	×6	×240
×10	×10	×100
×40	×10	×400

Oil immersion

For higher magnification than normal high power work (×400) an oil immersion lens can be used. The light gathering properties of the lens are greatly enhanced by placing a fluid between the objective lens and the cover-slip. The fluid must have the same refractive index as the lens itself so that the fluid used is generally cedarwood oil.

(1) Place the slide on the stage and focus as normal for high power work. Replace the objective lens with an oil immersion lens.

(2) Place a drop of cedarwood oil on top of the glass cover-slip over the top of the object to be examined.

(3) Focus the object again under low power, then swing in the oil immersion objective lens so that the tip is in contact with the oil.

(4) Look down the microscope and very carefully adjust the lens using the fine adjustment. Remember that at the plane of focus the lens is only 1 mm from the cover-slip of the slide.

(5) After use, clean the oil from the lens with soft tissue.

A2.4 Microscope techniques

A2.4.1 Preparation of material for the microscope

Biological specimens may be examined in a living or preserved form. In the latter case material can be sectioned for closer examination and treated with a wide variety of stains to reveal and identify different structures. Preparations of freshly killed material may be temporary or permanent.

A2.4.2 Permanent preparations

(1) **Fixation.** This is the preservation of material in a life-like condition. Tissues must be killed rapidly and this is best achieved with small pieces of living material. The agent used is called a **fixative**. By this method the original shape and structure are maintained and the tissue hardens so that thin sections can be cut.

(2) **Dehydration.** Dehydration, or removal of water, is done to prepare the material for infiltration with an embedding medium (see 4 below) or mounting medium (see 7 below) with which water is not miscible. Also, bacterial decay would eventually occur if water were present. For preservation of fine detail, dehydration should be gradual and accomplished by a series of increasingly concentrated ethanol/water or propanone (acetone)/water mixtures, finishing in 'absolute' (pure) ethanol or propanone.

(3) **Clearing.** Alcohol is not miscible with some of the common embedding and mounting media. Where this is the case, it is subsequently replaced with a medium (**clearing agent**) which is miscible, such as xylol. This also renders the material transparent.

(4) **Embedding.** Very thin sections are cut by a microtome, providing that the material is embedded in a supporting medium. For light microscopy, embedding involves impregnating the material with molten wax which is then allowed to set. A harder material (plastic or resin) must be used for electron microscopy because thinner sections are required, demanding more rigid support when cutting.

(5) **Sectioning.** Most pieces of material are too thick to allow sufficient light to pass through for microscopic investigation. It is usually necessary to cut very thin slices of the material (**sections**) and this may be done

with a razor or a microtome. Hand-sectioning is performed with a razor which must be of shaving sharpness. For ordinary work, sections should be 8–12 µm thick. The tissue must be held firmly between two pieces of elder pith. The razor is wetted with some of the liquid in which the tissue is stored and the cut is made through pith and tissue keeping the razor horizontal and drawing it towards the body with a long oblique sliding movement. Cut several sections fairly rapidly. Be content with the thinnest sections showing representative portions of the tissue.

Table A2.2 Common stains for plant and animal tissues.

Stain	Final colour	Suitable for:
Permanent stains		
aniline blue (cotton blue) in lactophenol	blue	fungal hyphae and spores
borax carmine	pink	nuclei; particularly for whole mounts (large pieces) of animal material, e.g. *Obelia* colony
eosin	pink	cytoplasm (see haematoxylin)
	red	cellulose
Feulgen's stain	red/ purple	DNA; particularly useful for showing chromosomes during cell division
haematoxylin	blue	nuclei; mainly used for sections of animal tissue with eosin as counterstain* for cytoplasm; also for smears
Leishman's stain	red-pink	blood cells
	blue	white blood cell nuclei
light green or fast green	green	cytoplasm and cellulose (see safranin)
methylene blue	blue	nuclei (0.125% methylene blue in 0.75% NaCl solution suitable as a vital stain)
safranin	red	nuclei; lignin and suberin of plants; mainly used for sections of plant tissue with light green as counterstain* for cytoplasm
Temporary stains		
aniline hydrochloride or aniline sulphate	yellow	lignin
iodine solution	blue-black	starch
phloroglucinol + conc. HCl	red	lignin
Schulze's solution (chlor-zinc-iodine)	yellow	lignin, cutin, suberin, protein
	blue	starch
	blue or violet	cellulose

* counterstain: two stains may be used (double staining) in which case the second is called the counterstain.

Embedded tissues can be sectioned with a **microtome**. For light microscopy, sections a few micrometres thick can be cut from wax-embedded tissues using a steel knife. The **ultramicrotome** is used for cutting extremely thin sections (20–100 nm) for electron microscopy, and a diamond or glass knife must be used.

The need for embedding can be avoided in light microscopy by using a **freezing microtome** which keeps the specimen frozen, and therefore rigid, during cutting.

(6) **Staining.** Most biological structures are transparent, so that some means of obtaining contrast between different structures must be employed. The most common method is staining. Some of the stains used in light microscopy are shown in table A2.2.

Certain stains when used in low concentrations are non-toxic to living tissue and can therefore be used on living material. These are called **vital stains**, for example methylene blue and neutral red.

To stain wax-embedded sections, the wax is dissolved away and the material partially rehydrated before staining.

(7) **Mounting.** For light microscopy, the final stained sections are 'mounted' on a glass slide in a resinous medium which will exclude air and protect them indefinitely, such as Canada balsam or euparol. The mounted specimen is covered with a glass cover-slip.

The sequence of events described above is typical for preparations of thin sections for permanent preparations. However, two common variations in the order of events are:
(a) if hand-cut sections of fresh material are used, sectioning precedes fixation;
(b) staining may follow fixation and be carried out at the appropriate stage of the dehydration sequence, for example a stain dissolved in 50% ethanol would be used after dehydration in 50% ethanol.

The above procedures are similar in principle for both light and electron microscopy, although details differ as outlined in table A2.3.

A2.4.3 Temporary preparations

Temporary preparations of material for light microscopy can be made rapidly, unlike permanent preparations. They are suitable for quick preliminary investigations. The stages involved are fixation, staining and mounting. Sectioning may precede fixation, or macerated material, such as macerated wood, may be used. Fresh material may be hand-sectioned with a razor directly into 70% alcohol as a fixative. For staining and mounting, a number of temporary stains may be used; some suitable for plant materials are shown in table A2.2. In each case the material should be placed on a clean glass slide (wipe clean with alcohol) and a few drops of stain added. In the case of phloroglucinol, one drop of concentrated hydrochloric acid is also added. The specimen is then covered with a thin

Table A2.3 Differences in preparation of material for light and electron microscopes.

Treatment	For light microscopes	For electron microscopes
Fixation	As for electron microscopy, or for example 99 parts ethanol: 1 part glacial ethanoic acid ('alcohol/acetic'), or 70% ethanol (but this causes shrinkage and damage to delicate structures)	Glutaraldehyde or mixture of glutaraldehyde and osmic acid (OsO_4) is often used. OsO_4 also stains lipids, and hence membranes, black. Smaller pieces of material fixed for more rapid and better preservation of fine structure
Dehydration	◄──────── Ethanol or propanone series ────────►	
Embedding	Wax	Resin (e.g. araldite, epon) or plastic
Sectioning	Metal knife	Only diamond or glass knives are sharp enough to cut the ultrathin sections required
	Microtome used	Ultramicrotome used
	Sections are few micrometres thick	Sections 20–100 nm thick
Staining	Coloured dyes (reflect visible light)	Heavy metals, e.g. compounds of osmium, uranium, lead (reflect electrons)

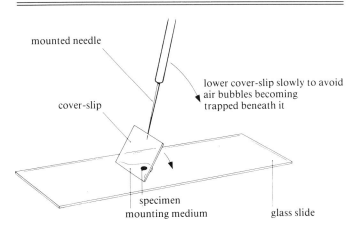

Fig A2.4 *Mounting a specimen and lowering a cover-slip on a glass slide*

mounted needle

lower cover-slip slowly to avoid air bubbles becoming trapped beneath it

cover-slip

specimen
mounting medium

glass slide

glass cover-slip to exclude air and dust, and to protect high power microscope objectives (fig A2.4). If the specimens begin to dry out, or if it is known that prolonged examination (longer than 10 min) is required, specimens should be mounted in glycerine after staining.

A2.5 The electron microscope

The resolving power of a light microscope is limited by the wavelength of light. The maximum possible resolution obtainable is equal to half the wavelength of light used; any objects smaller than this cannot be resolved.

The average wavelength of visible light is about 550 nm, and by the end of the nineteenth century it was possible to obtain a resolution of about 200 nm. Marginal improvements in resolution were gained by using specially designed microscopes with ultra-violet light of wavelength 250 nm, giving a resolution of about 100 nm. However, many cell structures are smaller than this. Progress was held up until the revolutionary development during the 1930s and 1940s of the electron microscope. Instead of using light as a radiation source, radiation of a much shorter wavelength and hence of much greater resolving power was used, namely electrons. The wavelength of electrons depends upon the voltage used to generate the electron beam, but in practice a resolution of about 0.5 nm can be obtained, about 500 times better than a light microscope and powerful enough to see large molecules. The limiting factor in progress was (and is) no longer resolution of the microscope but the methods used in preparing material for examination.

In essence the electron microscope operates on the same principle as the light microscope in that a beam of radiation is focussed by means of a condenser lens through the specimen and the image obtained is magnified by further lenses. Table A2.4 summarises some of the similarities and differences. Remember also that preparation of material for examination follows the same principles but again with important differences (table A2.3).

The operator sits at a console faced by the column down which the electrons are passed (fig A2.5). The microscope is upside down relative to the light microscope, with the

Table A2.4 Comparison of light and electron microscopes.

	Transmission electron microscope	Light microscope
Radiation source	electrons	light
Wavelength	e.g. 0.005 nm at 50 kV	400–700 nm
Max. useful magnification	×250 000 (on screen)	×1 500
Max. resolution in practice	0.5 nm	200–250 nm
in theory	0.2 nm	200 nm
Lenses	electromagnets	glass (quartz for ultra-violet radiation)
Specimen	non-living, dehydrated, relatively small or thin	living or non-living
	supported on a small copper grid in a vacuum	usually supported on a glass slide
Common stains	contain heavy metals to reflect electrons	coloured dyes
Image	black and white	usually coloured

From *A Dictionary of Life Sciences* ed. E. A. Martin (1976) Macmillan and Pan Books Ltd.

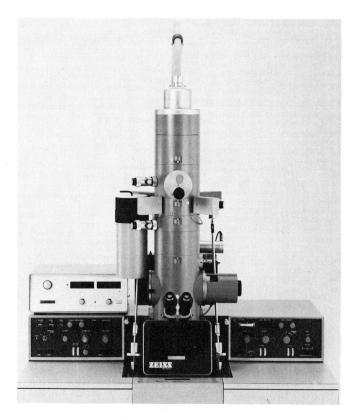

Fig A2.5 (left) *A modern transmission electron microscope*

Fig A2.6 (below) *Pathway of the electron beam in the transmission electron microscope*

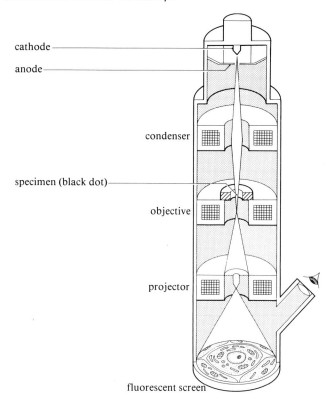

source of radiation (electrons) at the top of the column and the point at which the specimen is observed at the bottom (fig A2.6). A high voltage (such as 50 000 V) is passed through a tungsten filament at the top of the column, and the filament emits a stream of electrons. In order to focus the electrons (bend their path) electromagnets must be used rather than glass lenses. The inside of the column is under a high vacuum to minimise both electron scattering through collision with air particles and the subsequent heating that would occur. In the **transmission electron microscope** electrons are focussed through the specimen. Only very thin sections or particles can be observed because electrons are easily scattered or absorbed by the object. Portions of the specimen with high relative molecular mass cause most scattering, so heavy metals such as lead and uranium are used in the staining of specimens to increase contrast. The specimen is usually supported on a small copper grid (about 2 mm diameter) which may be covered with a thin plastic film for extra support. After passing through the specimen, electrons are collected and focussed by further electromagnetic lenses. Electrons cannot be observed with the human eye and so they are either focussed on to a fluorescent screen which produces a visible image, or allowed to pass directly on to a photographic film for a permanent photograph (**electron micrograph**).

Various techniques, described briefly below, are used to prepare material for observation but in all cases the material must be dead since it is observed in a vacuum, is quickly heated up and would be destroyed in the electron beam. Photographs must be taken for a permanent record if prolonged study of the specimen is required.

(1) **Heavy metal staining of ultrathin sections.** Sections are cut with an ultramicrotome and stained with heavy metal compounds, such as lead nitrate, uranyl acetate or osmic acid. Stained areas are opaque to electrons and therefore appear dark in micrographs.

(2) **Negative staining.** With negative staining the background is stained, whereas the specimen is not treated. The technique is particularly useful for examining surface details of small particles, such as ribosomes, viruses, and fragments of isolated organelles and membranes, since the stain penetrates between surface features.

(3) **Shadowing.** The specimen is sprayed with atoms of a heavy metal, such as gold or platinum, from a particular direction and angle. Exposed surfaces are coated with a layer of metal which is opaque to electrons. Sheltered areas, including a 'shadow' beyond the specimen, remain uncoated and relatively electron-transparent. These appear white (they allow the passage of electrons, equivalent to light). Since the human brain is used to seeing and interpreting black shadows, the photographs are usually published as negatives. Shadowing is used to show the surface structure of small objects such as viruses, molecules and cell walls. If a specimen is too thick to allow penetration of the electron beam, the organic material must be dissolved away after it has been shadowed, leaving only the metal **replica** of the surface. This is

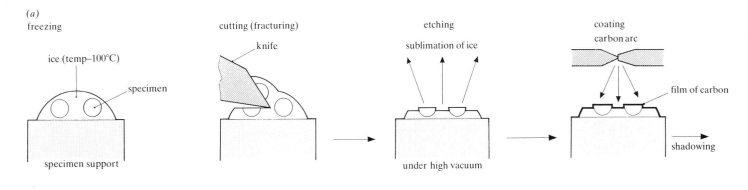

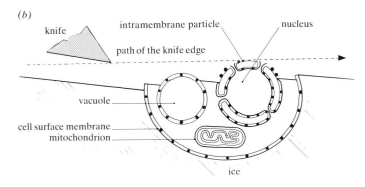

Fig A2.7 *(a) Diagrammatic representation of the stages in the preparation of cells by freeze-etching. (b) Exposure of cell membranes by the cutting process*

reinforced by coating with a film of carbon so that it can be picked up and placed on a standard grid.

(4) **Freeze-fracturing and freeze-etching.** A fragment of tissue is rapidly frozen at a very low temperature and then fractured with a sharp metal blade. The tissue fractures along planes of weakness which often run through membranes (fig A2.7). The specimen is kept cold and in a high vacuum, where ice sublimes away leaving an etched surface.

A replica of this surface is made by depositing a layer of carbon over it. This carbon replica is shadowed with a heavy metal and the tissue below the replica destroyed, usually with a strong acid at normal atmospheric pressure. The technique is useful for observing membrane structure (see figs 7.15 and 9.13). It has the advantage that the living tissue is killed rapidly and not exposed to chemical treatment that might affect its structure. It is likely, therefore, that the cells are preserved in a life-like form, thus confirming structures seen by conventional sectioning and staining techniques.

A recent modification of freeze etching has been introduced called **deep etching**. Here the specimen is frozen extremely rapidly, thus preventing formation of damagingly large ice crystals and improving resolution. Then extensive freeze-drying is carried out which results in deep etching of the ice. Structures inside the cell, notably the cytoskeleton, are then seen with exceptional clarity.

A2.5.1 Scanning electron microscope

With the scanning electron microscope (s.e.m.) a finely focussed beam of electrons scans to and fro across the specimen and electrons that are reflected from the surface (not transmitted) are collected and form the basis of a television-like image on a cathode ray tube. The advantage of the technique is that the surface features are shown with a great depth of field, giving a three-dimensional effect (see figs 9.8 and 14.13). Resolution is poorer than for the transmission electron microscope (5–20 nm) but specimens can be larger.

A2.5.2 High voltage electron microscope

More recently high voltage electron microscopes (500 000–1 000 000 V) have been introduced into biology. The high speed of acceleration of electrons allows penetration and observation of relatively thick sections (1–5 μm), with better understanding of three-dimensional structures at high resolution. Techniques that allow brief examination of living specimens are being introduced and should provide important information.

A2.5.3 Electron microprobe X-ray analysis

This is a powerful analytical tool which is still being developed in which the spectrum of X-rays reflected from particular elements when struck by a beam of electrons enables identification of the elements. It is used for studying the chemistry of materials, including biological specimens. The main areas of application are identification of foreign bodies, for example asbestos fibres in lung tissues, localisation of cell components (such as enzymes) or chemicals (for example drugs) and comparisons of pathological and normal tissues.

A2.6 Laboratory work and writing up an experiment

Before beginning any experimental investigation, the aim of the experiment should be made clear. This may involve the testing of a hypothesis, such as 'The germination of seeds requires the presence of water, oxygen and an optimum temperature', or a more open-ended investigation, such as 'What is the effect of light on the behaviour of woodlice?'. In both cases the experiment must be designed so that it can be performed, and the data produced should be reliable, relevant to the aim and hopefully used in producing a conclusion.

All experiments should follow a logical progression in the reporting or writing up of the experiment.
(1) **Title.** This should be a clear statement outlining the problem to be investigated. For example '*Experiment to investigate the effect of pH on enzyme activity*'. It should be a broad statement of intent which is made specific by the hypothesis or aim.
(2) **Hypothesis or aim.** This is a statement of the problem or the posing of a question. It may include an indication of the variables under examination and the possible outcome of the investigation. For example '*To investigate the effect of solutions of pH 2–10 on the rate of digestion of the protein albumin by the enzyme pepsin and to determine the optimum pH of the reaction*'.
(3) **Method or procedure.** This is an account of the activities carried out during the performance of the experiment. It should be concise, precise and presented logically in the order in which the apparatus was set up and the activities performed during the experiment. It should be written in the past tense and not in the first person. Using the information given, another scientist should be able to repeat the experiment.
(4) **Results and observations.** These may be qualitative or quantitative and should be presented as clearly as possible in some appropriate form or forms, such as verbal description, tables of data, graphs, histograms, bar charts, kite diagrams and so on. If several numerical values are obtained for repeated measurements of one variable, the mean ($\bar{x}$) of these values should be calculated and recorded.
(5) **Discussion.** This should be brief and take the form of the answer(s) to possible questions posed by the hypothesis, or confirmation of the aim. The discussion should not be a verbal repetition of the results, but an attempt to relate theoretical knowledge of the experimental variables to the results obtained.

A **conclusion** may be included if there is clear-cut verification of the stated aim. For example, for the aim given in (2) above a conclusion could state that there is 'a relationship between pH and enzyme activity and for this reaction the optimum pH is x'. The discussion of the results of this same experiment should include such theoretical aspects as the nature of the reaction and the possible chemical and physical aspects of the effects of pH on the three-dimensional structure of enzyme molecules.

A2.7 Presenting data

As a result of qualitative and quantitative investigations, observations are made and numerical data obtained. In order for the maximum amount of information to be gained from investigations, they must be planned carefully and the data must be presented comprehensively and analysed thoroughly.

A2.7.1 Tabulations

Tables form the simplest way of presenting data and consist of columns displaying the values for two or more related variables. This method gives neither an immediate nor clear indication of the relationships between the variables, but is often the first step in recording information and forms the basis for selecting some subsequent form of graphical representation.

A2.7.2 Graphical representation

A graph is a two-dimensional plot of two or more measured variables. In its simplest form a graph consists of two axes. The vertical y axis bears values called **ordinates** which show the magnitude of the **dependent** variable. This is the 'unknown quantity', that is the variable whose value is not chosen by the experimenter. The horizontal x axis bears values called **abscissae** which show the magnitude of the **independent** variable, which is the known quantity, that is the variable whose value is chosen by the experimenter.

The following stages are used in constructing a graph.
(1) The scale and intervals for each axis should match the magnitude of the variables being plotted and fill the graph paper as completely as possible.
(2) Each axis should begin at 0, but if all the values for one variable are clustered together, such as ten points lying between 6.12 and 6.68, a large scale will be required to cover these points. In this case, still begin with the axis at 0 but mark a break in the axis, marked as —//—, just beyond 0.
(3) Each axis must be fully labelled in terms of the variable, for example 'temperature/°C', and have equally spaced intervals covering the range of the interval, such as 0–60 at 12 five-unit intervals.
(4) The points plotted on the graph are called **coordinates**

and represent the corresponding values of the two variables, such as when $x = a$ and $y = b$.

(5) Actual points should be marked by an X or ⊙ and never by a dot only.

(6) The points marked on the graph are the record of the actual observations made and may be joined by a series of straight line segments drawn with a ruler, by a smooth curve or, in some cases, a regression line (a line of best fit) (section A2.8.3). These graphs are called **line graphs**. Straight line segments and smooth curves are preferable to a regression line.

(7) The graph should have a full title, such as 'Graph showing the relationship between . . . . .'.

(8) Only the points on the graph represent actual data, but estimates of other values can be obtained from reading off coordinates at any point on the line. This is called **interpolation**. Similarly coordinates outside the range of the graph may be determined by extending the line of the graph, a technique known as **extrapolation**. In both cases it must be stressed that these values are only estimates.

In graphs where the x axis is 'time', the steepness of the curve or **gradient** at any point can be calculated and

this gives a measure of the rate of change of the variable under investigation. For example, in the graph shown in fig A2.8 the rate of growth is calculated by drawing a tangent to the curve at the desired point and completing a triangle with the tangent at the hypotenuse, as shown in fig A2.9. The value of the y interval is then divided by the value of the x interval and this gives the rate of change in terms of the units used in labelling the graph.

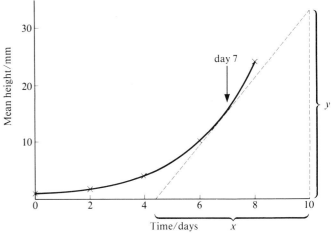

From the graph: $y = 33\,\text{mm}$
$\qquad\qquad\qquad x = 5.6\,\text{days}$

Therefore rate of growth $= \dfrac{y}{x} = \dfrac{33}{5.6}$

$\qquad\qquad\qquad\qquad = 5.9\,\text{mm day}^{-1}$

Fig A2.9 (below) *Method of calculating rate of change at a given point, for example day 7*

A2.7.3 Frequency distributions

Many relationships exist where each value of the dependent variable, corresponding to the independent variable, represents the number of times the latter value occurs, that is its frequency. Such relationships form a **frequency distribution** or **distribution**, for example lengths of earthworms in a population.

If the value of the independent variable can assume any value within a given range, its frequency distribution can be represented by a conventional graph as described above. These graphs are called **frequency curves** and may take one of the following forms depending upon how the data are presented. If the data are presented as numbers of individuals within defined intervals as shown in fig A2.10a, the distribution is known as a **continuous distribution** and the total area beneath the curve represents the total frequency.

(1) **Normal distribution curve.** Here the frequency distribution is symmetrical about a central value and examples include physical parameters such as height and mass of biological structure. This type of distribution is shown in fig A2.10.

(a)

Time/days	0	2	4	6	8	10	12	14	16	18	20	22	24	26
Mean height/mm	1	2	4	11	24	43	73	92	105	112	117	122	124	126

(b)

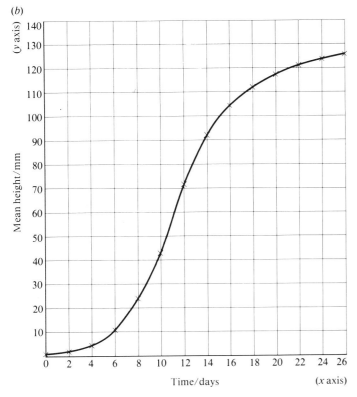

Fig A2.8 (above) *(a) Two sets of data relating to mean heights of oat seedlings and time. (b) Graph showing the relationship between mean heights of oat seedlings and time*

(a)

Mass class/kg	50-52	52-54	54-56	56-58	58-60	60-62	62-64	64-66	66-68	68-70	70-72
Frequency	4	7	11	16	24	29	26	16	8	4	2

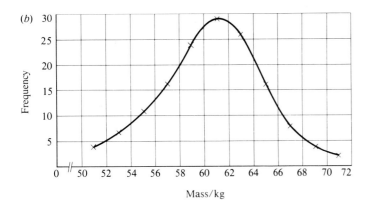

Fig A2.10 *(a) Number of 18-year-old males falling into 2 kg mass classes and represented as a table. (b) The graph representing the data from (a) forms a normal distribution curve*

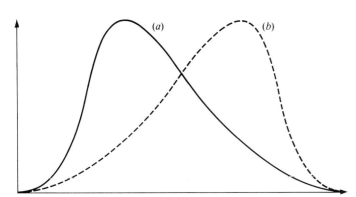

Fig A2.11 *(a) Positive skewed distribution. (b) Negative skewed distribution*

(2) **Positive skew.** Here the curve is asymmetrical, with the highest frequencies of the independent variable corresponding to its lower values and with a 'tail off' towards the higher values as shown in fig A2.11*a*. Examples include number of children per family, clutch size in birds and density of phytoplankton with depth.

(3) **Negative skew.** Here the highest frequencies of the independent variable correspond to the higher values and 'tail off' towards the lower values, as shown in fig 2.11*b*. This form of distribution is rarer than positive skew and represents a distribution showing some form of bias. Examples include optimum temperature for enzyme-controlled reactions and the output of thyroid-stimulating hormone in response to thyroxine.

(4) **Bimodal distribution.** Here there are two peaks (or modes), and it usually indicates the presence of two

(a)

Mass/kg	50	52	54	56	58	60	62	64	66	68	70	72
Cumulative frequency	0	4	11	22	38	62	91	117	133	141	145	147

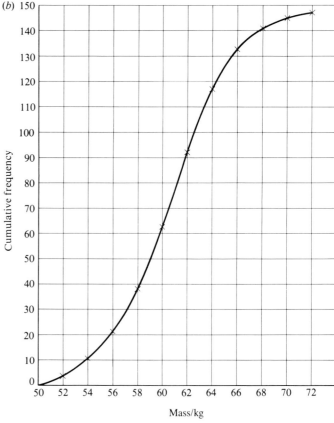

Fig A2.12 *Data (a) and graph (b) based upon fig A2.10a showing the cumulative frequency distribution of mass in 18-year-old males*

populations each exhibiting a partial normal distribution.

(5) **Cumulative frequency distribution.** The data presented in fig A2.10 may be presented as in fig A2.12, where the cumulative number of individuals below certain arbitrary class boundaries are shown. Where these data are presented graphically a cumulative frequency curve is produced.

If the values of the independent variable assume discrete values, that is whole numbers such as 3 and 5 (as in the numbers of petals of a dicotyledon), or represent physical traits such as blood groups, they exist as only discrete values and the distribution is described as **discontinuous**. In these cases it is inappropriate to plot a continuous graph and other forms of graphical representation are used as described below.

(1) **Column graph.** This shows the frequency with which distinct characteristics occur within a population, such as human blood groups (see fig A2.13*a*).

(2) **Histogram.** This represents continuous values of the independent variable which have been grouped into

946

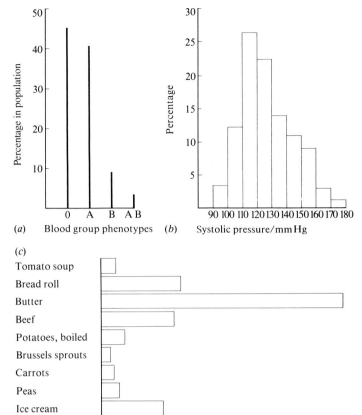

(a) Blood group phenotypes   (b) Systolic pressure/mm Hg

(c)

Tomato soup
Bread roll
Butter
Beef
Potatoes, boiled
Brussels sprouts
Carrots
Peas
Ice cream
Peaches, canned
Cheese, cheddar
Biscuits, plain
Coffee, black

1000   2000   3000
Energy content per 100g/kJ

Fig A2.13 (above) *Methods of presenting data. (a) Column graph showing frequency of blood group phenotypes in the population. (b) Histogram showing systolic blood pressure frequencies in women aged 30–9 years. (c) Bar chart showing energy content of foods in a three-course meal*

Fig A2.14 (below) *(a) and (b) method of constructing a kite diagram*

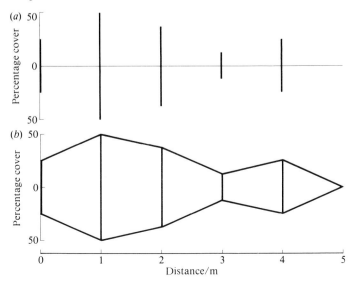

classes of equal widths. Where classes of equal width are chosen, for example 0–5, 5–10, 10–15, and so on, the limits of the interval are conventionally represented by the lower integer, that is 0–4.99, 5–9.99, 10–14.99 and so on. This is a useful way of representing data from a small sample and superficially resembles a column graph (fig A2.13b).

(3) **Bar graph.** This is a modified form of histogram usually representing the relationship between a continuous dependent variable, such as energy content, and a non-numerical independent variable, for example various foods (fig A2.13c). A modified form of bar graph is used in presenting ecological data and this is called a **presence–absence graph**. An example of this is shown in fig 13.21.

(4) **Kite diagram.** This is a special type of bar graph that provides an extremely clear visual display of the change in frequency of non-numerical variables which are continuously distributed within an area. A kite diagram is constructed by plotting the frequencies of each variable as a line symmetrically placed astride the x axis as shown in fig A2.14a. Once all of the frequencies have been plotted along the x axis, the adjacent limits of the lines are joined together by straight lines, as in a line graph, as shown in fig A2.14b. The enclosed area is usually shaded to present a clearer visual display. The use of kite diagrams is described in section 13.4.3.

Each one of the methods of presenting data described above is applicable to different biological situations, and all are represented in the chapters in these books. All methods have their relative merits, and the choice of which to use should be made on the basis of which will accurately and efficiently reveal relationships and patterns between variables.

A2.8 Elementary statistical methods in biology

When data are recorded as a series of values representing variables, such as heights or heart rate, it is useful to know both the average value and the spread of values. Estimates of the average value are called 'measures of central tendency' and these include the mean, the median and the mode. Estimates of the spread of values are called 'measures of dispersion' and they include variance and standard deviation.

A2.8.1 Measures of central tendency

Mean (arithmetic mean)

This is the 'average' of a group of values and is obtained by adding the values together and dividing the total by the number of individual values. For example, the mean ($\bar{x}$) for values $x_1, x_2, x_3, x_4, \ldots\ldots x_n$ is given by

$$\bar{x} = \frac{x_1 + x_2 + x_3 \ldots \ldots + x_n}{n},$$

$$\text{or } \bar{x} = \frac{\Sigma x}{n}$$

where Σ = sum or total of, x = individual values and n = number of individual values.

If the same value of x occurs more than once, the mean ($\bar{x}$) can be calculated using the expression $\bar{x} = \frac{\Sigma fx}{\Sigma f}$ where Σ_f = the sum of the frequencies of x, or simply, n.

Median

This represents the middle or central value of a set of values. For example, if five values of x are arranged in ascending order as x_1, x_2, x_3, x_4 and x_5, the median value would be x_3 since there are as many values above it as below it. If there are an even number of values of x, for example x_1 to x_6, the median is represented as the mean of the two middle values ($(x_3 + x_4)/2$).

Mode

This is the most frequently occurring value of a set of values. For example if the numbers of children in 10 families is 1,1,1,2,2,2,2,3,4, the mode or modal value is 2.

Each of the three values described above has its relative advantages, disadvantages and applicability. One example of the use of mean and mode is illustrated by reference to the number of children per family. The mean number of children per family is 2.4, but as children are discrete beings it is more usual to describe the number of children per family in whole numbers, thus using the modal value which is 2.

In a normal frequency distribution the values of the mean, the median and the mode coincide as shown in fig A2.15a, whereas in cases where the frequency distribution is skewed, these values do not coincide as shown in fig A2.15b.

A2.8.2 Measures of dispersion

Measures of dispersion are used in conjunction with measures of central tendency to give an indication

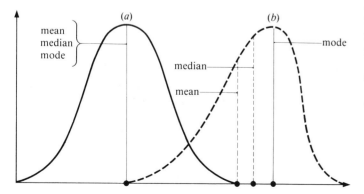

Fig A2.15 (above) *Distributions of mean, median and mode in (a) a normal distribution and (b) a skewed distribution*

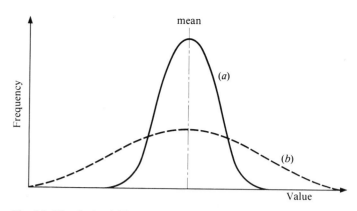

Fig A2.16 (below) *Two normal distribution curves showing the distribution of two sets of data (possibly populations) with identical total frequencies (that is the areas under the curves are equal). Curve (a) has a restricted range and is clustered around the mean. Curve (b) represents a wider range and is not clustered around the mean*

of the extent to which values are 'spread' or 'clustered' around the 'average'. This is illustrated with respect to a normal distribution by the curves shown in fig A2.16. In statistical analysis, one of the most useful measures of dispersion is the root mean square deviation or standard deviation, since it may be applied both to predicting the distribution of values about the average and to determining whether two sets of data are significantly different from one another and the degree of difference between them.

Standard deviation

The standard deviation (s) of a set of values is a measure of the variation from the arithmetical mean of these values and is calculated using the expression

$$s = \sqrt{\left(\frac{\Sigma fx^2}{\Sigma f} - \bar{x}^2\right)}$$

where Σ = sum of, f = frequency of occurrence of, x = specific values, and $\bar{x}$ = mean of the specific values.

For example, a sample of ten common limpet shells (*Patella vulgaris*) from a rocky shore have the following maximum basal diameters in millimetres: 36, 34, 41, 39, 37, 43, 36, 37, 41, 39. In order to calculate the mean maximum basal diameter and the standard deviation it is necessary to calculate f, fx^2 and $\bar{x}^2$ as shown in the following table:

x	f	fx	fx^2
34	1	34	1 156
36	2	72	2 592
37	2	74	2 738
39	2	78	3 042
41	2	82	3 362
43	1	43	1 849

$$\Sigma f = 10 \qquad \Sigma fx = 383 \qquad \Sigma fx^2 = 14\,739$$

Therefore $\bar{x} = 38.3$
$$\bar{x}^2 = 1\,466.9$$

Since
$$s = \sqrt{\left(\frac{\Sigma f x^2}{\Sigma f} - \bar{x}^2\right)}$$
$$= \sqrt{\left(\frac{14\,739}{10} - 1\,466.9\right)}$$
$$= \sqrt{(1\,473.9 - 1\,466.9)}$$
$$= \sqrt{7}$$

Therefore $s = 2.65$.

In this population of the common limpet the mean maximum basal diameter of the shell is 38.3 mm, with a standard deviation of 2.7 mm (correct to one decimal place). If these values are applied to a larger population of the common limpet then it may be assumed, on statistical grounds, that approximately 68% of the population will have a basal diameter of the shell of 38.3 mm plus and minus one standard deviation (2.7 mm), that is they will lie within a range 35.6–41.0 mm; approximately 95% of the population will have a basal diameter of the shell of 38.3 plus and minus two standard deviations (5.4 mm), that is they will lie within the range 32.9–43.7 mm, and practically 100% will lie within plus and minus three standard deviations.

The value of calculating the standard deviation is that it gives a measure of the spread of values from the mean. A small standard deviation indicates that there is little dispersion or variation from the mean and that the population is fairly homogeneous, as shown by the curve (a) in fig A2.16. As the value of the standard deviation increases, the degree of variation within the population increases as shown by curve (b) in fig A2.16.

Variance

The **variance** is the square of the standard deviation and the variance for a set of numbers is calculated using the expression:

$$\text{variance } (s^2) = \frac{\Sigma f x^2}{\Sigma f} - \bar{x}^2$$

where f is the number of values in the set.

Variance is useful in ecological investigations involving nutrition, reproduction and behaviour since it gives an indication of how organisms are dispersed within the population. Populations may be:
(a) randomly dispersed,
(b) aggregated into clusters, or
(c) regularly dispersed.

To determine the type of population dispersion within an area, the area is divided up into a number of equal-sized quadrats (section 13.2) and the number of individuals within the population, per quadrat, is counted. From these data the mean and variance are calculated using the expressions:

$$\text{mean } (\bar{x}) = \frac{\Sigma f x}{f}, \qquad \text{variance } (s^2) = \frac{\Sigma f x^2}{\Sigma f} - \bar{x}^2$$

where f is the number of quadrats containing $\bar{x}$ individuals. Using the following expression:

$$\text{population dispersion} = \frac{\text{variance}}{\text{mean}}$$

the three types of dispersion can be determined as shown in fig A2.17.

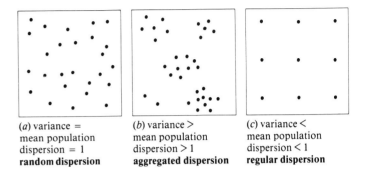

(a) variance = mean population dispersion = 1 **random dispersion**

(b) variance > mean population dispersion > 1 **aggregated dispersion**

(c) variance < mean population dispersion < 1 **regular dispersion**

Fig A2.17 *Types of dispersion*

A2.8.3 Relationships between variables

Data should always be presented in such a way as to reveal relationships between two or more sets of data. The simplest way of doing this is to plot a graph showing the relationship between variables, but this is only valuable if one of the variables (the independent variable) is under the control of the experimenter, as for example in the case of data shown in fig A2.8.

In other cases, where both variables are dependent, the value of one variable is plotted against the corresponding value of the other variable as, for example, in the case of heights and masses of 20 sixth-form students given in fig. A2.18a. These values are plotted and shown in fig A2.18b, which is called a **scatter diagram**. Visual inspection shows that there is some form of relationship between the two variables but this cannot be described more accurately until a relationship, represented by a straight line, can be drawn through the points.

This single line is called a **'line of best fit'** or a **regression line** and the proximity of the points to the line gives an indication of the degree of correlation between the two variables. The position of the line of best fit should pass through the point representing the mean values of mass and height ($\bar{x} = 65.7$ kg and $\bar{y} = 165.8$ cm) and the distribution of points above and below the line should be approximately equal. From this line the predicted values of height corresponding to mass can be calculated.

Correlation

The relationship between the two variables, x and y, described above may be represented by a term called **correlation**. Varying degrees of correlation may exist

(a)

Mass/kg	51	51	53	55	59	60	62	60	58	64	67	69	71	68	74	75	77	79	79	81
Height/cm	154	155	156	158	158	159	161	162	163	165	166	168	169	170	172	173	174	176	177	180

$\bar{x} = 65.7$ $\qquad$ $\bar{y} = 165.8$

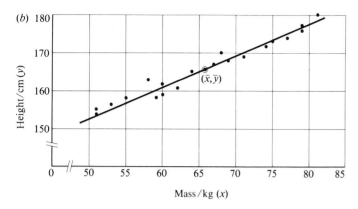

Fig A2.18 *Data showing mass and corresponding heights of 20 16-year-old male students, represented as a table (a) and a scatter diagram (b). The regression line is drawn*

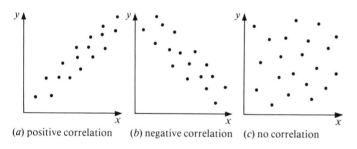

(a) positive correlation $\qquad$ (b) negative correlation $\qquad$ (c) no correlation

Fig A2.19 *Patterns of correlation: (a) positive correlation; (b) negative correlation; (c) no correlation*

between x and y as shown by the scatter diagrams in fig A2.19.

Presenting data in the form of a scatter diagram is not a reliable way of demonstrating the significance of the correlation since it is subjective. It is possible to represent correlation in terms of a statistical measure called the **correlation coefficient**. This can vary between -1 and $+1$; -1 represents a perfect negative correlation, such as oxygen tension in the atmosphere and rate of spiracle opening in insects; 0 represents no correlation, such as size of tomato fruits and number of seeds; $+1$ represents a perfect positive correlation, such as age and body length in the locust.

Appendix 3
Classification

The science of classification is called **taxonomy** and it involves the naming of organisms (**nomenclature**) and the systematic placing of organisms into groups or **taxa**

(**systematics**) on the basis of certain relationships between organisms. Biological nomenclature is based on the **binomial system** pioneered by the work of the Swedish naturalist Carl Linnaeus (1707–78). In this system each organism has two Latin names: a **generic** name beginning with a capital letter and a **specific** name beginning with a lower case letter. For example, humans are named *Homo sapiens*. The binomial system classifies organisms into groups at various hierarchical levels on the basis of easily observable, shared structural features, such as shape, number of, and position of, limbs and so on. It has since been extended, and the main hierarchical taxa now used in this system are as follows, in descending order of size:

kingdom
phylum (division in plants)
class
order
family
genus
species

Each taxon may contain a number of the taxon units below it, for example one phylum may contain six classes or a genus three species, but each taxon can only belong to the single taxon immediately above it, for example an order can only belong to the class above it (fig A3.1).

Within each hierarchical level there may be several taxa, but each is distinct in that whilst the members of each taxon

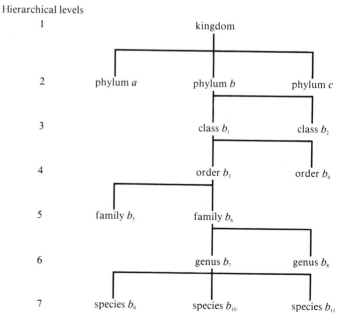

Fig A3.1 *Example of hierarchical taxonomic groups based on the Linnean system of classification*

950

share a common set of diagnostic features also possessed by *all* organisms at preceding taxonomic levels (higher levels), each taxon possesses diagnostic features *unique* to that taxon. For example, organisms belonging to family b_6 will possess all the diagnostic features of order b_3, class b_1 and phylum b (fig A3.1)

Taxa may be further subdivided into **subtaxa**, such as subclass or grouped together into **supertaxa**, such as superclass. Other taxa may also be formed by splitting taxa into **infrataxa** or **tribes**, or grouping taxa into **cohorts**.

The most natural group of organisms is the **species** and this is the lowest taxon in the Linnean system. Each species possesses its own distinct structural, behavioural and ecological characteristics. Definitions of the term 'species' are given in section 25.6. Members of sexually reproducing species, however, are unique in possessing a genotype shared neither by their ancestors nor descendants.

At each level of the hierarchy, rising from species to kingdom, the number of similarities between members of each taxon decreases. For example members of the same genus have more features in common than members of the same family or order.

There are two types of classification, artificial and natural. An **artificial classification** (also termed **arbitrary** or **utilitarian**) is based upon one or a few easily observable characteristics, and is devised and used for a limited number of special purposes where convenience and speed are important. For example, the characteristics could be colour, mode of locomotion, habit, habitat and so on. An example of an artificial classification of fish would be to group them as freshwater fish, brackish-water fish and marine fish on the basis of the environment, and this would be convenient for the purpose of investigating their mechanisms of osmoregulation.

A **natural classification** may be either **phylogenetic** or **phenetic** depending upon the criteria on which the classification is based. The most commonly used form of classification is **phylogenetic** and it reflects possible evolutionary relationships based on ancestry and descent. In such a system organisms belonging to the same taxa are believed to have a common ancestor, and may be represented in the form of a family tree, in this case called a **cladogram** (see fig 2.1).

A **phenetic** classification is based upon evidence presented by numerical taxonomists who consider masses of data relating to present-day morphological, cytological and biochemical similarities between organisms. This may reflect possible evolutionary relationships but is not constructed with this in view. A family tree based upon phenetic classification is called a **dendrogram**.

A3.1 Specimen identification and keys

A key is a convenient method of enabling a biologist to identify and name an organism. In its simplest form it involves listing the observable morphological characteristics of the organism and matching them with those features which are diagnostic of a particular taxon. Most of the characteristics used in identification are based on easily observable features such as shape, colour and numbers of appendages, segments and so on. Hence identification is *artificial* and *phenetic* since it relies purely on the appearance (phenotype) of the organism. Despite this, most **diagnostic keys** enable organisms to be identified into a taxon which is part of a **natural phylogenetic** hierarchical classification system.

There are various types of diagnostic keys, but the simplest is called a **dichotomous key**. This is made up of pairs of statements called **leads**, numbered 1, 2, 3 and so on, where each lead deals with a particular observable characteristic. The paired statements of each lead should be *contrasting* or *mutually exclusive* and, by considering these in order a large group of organisms may be broken down into progressively smaller groups until the unknown organism is identified at the lowest taxonomic group possible.

The characteristics used in keys should be readily observable morphological features, and may be **qualitative**, such as shape of abdomen and colour, or **quantitative**, such as number of hairs and length of stem. Either may be used, but the characteristic must be constant for that species and not subject to variation as a result of environmental influences. In this respect size and colour are often bad examples to use since both can be influenced by the environment, the season, the age or state of the organism at the time of identification. Characteristics chosen should, if possible, exist in two or more states. For example, the characteristic 'stem shape' may exist in one of the two states, 'round' or 'square'.

After each statement there is a number referring to the next lead to be considered. If the statement described in the lead matches the appearance of the specimen, the number following the statement indicates the next lead to consider.

Table A3.1 Extract of key to cultivated Leguminosae.

1 Woody trees and shrubs	2
Herbaceous and annual plants	15
2 Climbing	3
Non-climbing	4
3 Flowers bright red	Lobster claw
Flowers mauve, sometimes white, forming sprays	Wisteria
4 Flowers all or partly yellow	5
Flowers not yellow	8
5 Branches with thorns and spines	6
Branches without thorns and spines	7
6 Leaves absent, plant spiny all over	Gorse
Leaves present on young shoots, spines on older branches	Needle-whin
7 Young stem square, leaves small with three leaflets	Broom
Stems not square, leaves longer than one inch	9
8 etc.	

For example in the simple key to the cultivated Leguminosae shown in table A3.1, if the specimen has been keyed as far as lead 5 and it possesses branches without thorns or spines, the next lead to consider would be lead 7, and so on.

Appendix 4
Nomenclature and units

A4.1 Alphabetical list of common current names of chemicals

Old name	New name (nc = no change)
acetaldehyde	ethanal
acetamide	ethanamide or nc
acetic acid	ethanoic acid or nc
acetoacetic acid	3-oxobutanoic acid
acetone	propanone
acetylene	ethyne
adenine	nc
adenosine	nc
adipic acid	hexanedioic acid
alanine	2-aminopropanoic acid
alcohol (ethyl)	ethanol
alcohol (wood)	methanol
aldehyde	nc
aldol	3-hydroxybutanal
aliphatic	nc
alkyl	nc
ammonium hydroxide	ammonia solution
p-amino benzoic acid	{ 4-aminobenzoic acid / 4-aminobenzenecarboxylic acid
aspartic acid	aminobutanedoic acid
benzaldehyde	benzenecarbaldehyde or nc
benzene	nc
benzoic acid	benzenecarboxylic acid or nc
bicarbonate	hydrogencarbonate
butyric acid	butanoic acid
camphor	nc
cane sugar	sucrose
carbon tetrachloride	tetrachloromethane
carboxylic acids	nc
chloroform	trichloromethane
citric acid	2-hydroxypropane-1,2,3 -tricarboxylic acid
cobalt chloride	cobalt(II) chloride
dextrose	(+) glucose
ethyl acetate	ethyl ethanoate or nc
ethyl alcohol	ethanol
ethylene	ethene
ferric	iron(III)
ferrous	iron(II)
formaldehyde	methanal
fructose	nc
fumaric acid	*trans*-butanedoic acid
glucose	nc
glutamic acid	2-aminopentanedoic acid
glycerine/glycerol	propane-1,2,3-triol
glycine	{ aminoethanoic acid / aminoacetic acid

glycollic acid	{ hydroxyethanoic acid / hydroxyacetic acid
glyoxyllic acid	{ oxoethanoic acid / oxoacetic acid
indoleacetic acid (IAA)	indolylethanoic acid
isopropyl alcohol	propan-2-ol
lactic acid	2-hydroxypropanoic acid
lactose	nc
malic acid	2-hydroxybutanedioic acid
malonic acid	propanedioic acid
maltose	nc
nitric acid	nc
oleic acid	*cis*-octadec-9-enoic acid
oxalic acid	ethanedioic acid
palmitic acid	hexadecanoic acid
phenol	nc
phosphate	phosphate(V)
phosphoric acid	phosphoric(V) acid
phosphorous acid	phosphoric acid
potassium permanganate	potassium manganate(VII)
pyridine	nc
pyrogallol	benzene-1,2,3-triol
pyruvic acid	2-oxopropanoic acid
quinol	benzene-1,4-diol
stearic acid	octadecanoic acid
succinic acid	butanedoic acid
sucrose	nc
1-tartaric acid	(−) 2,3-dihydroxybutanedioic acid
thiourea	thiocarbamide or nc
toluene	methylbenzene
urea	carbamide or nc
n-valeric acid	pentanoic acid
xylene	dimethylbenzene

A4.2 Units, symbols, abbreviations and conventional terms

absolute	abs.
adenosine 5′-pyrophosphate	ADP *use* adenosine diphosphate
adenosine 5′-triphosphate	ATP *use* adenosine triphosphate
adrenocorticotrophic hormone	ACTH
angstrom	Å *preferably* use SI units 10 Å = 1 nm
anterior	ant.
antidiuretic hormone	ADH
approximately equal	≈
basal metabolic rate	b.m.r. or BMR
calciferol	vitamin D_2 preferred for biological activity (vitamin D is the generic term)
calorie	cal *use* SI unit joule 1 cal = 4.2 J
Centigrade	*use* Celsius (°C)
central nervous system	CNS
cerebrospinal fluid	c.s.f. or CSF
chi-squared	χ^2
coenzyme A	CoA
degree Celsius	°C
deoxyribonucleic acid	DNA
endoplasmic reticulum	ER

extracellular fluid — e.c.f. or ECF
figure (diagram) — fig
Geiger–Müller tube — GM
gram — g (gramme is continental spelling)
growth hormone — GH
haemoglobin — Hb
joule — J
kilo ($10^3 \times$) — k
Krebs cycle — or tricarboxylic acid cycle
luteinising hormone — LH
mass — m
maximum — max.
mean value of x (statistics) — $\bar{x}$
minimum — min.
minute — min
molar (concentration) — M (mol dm^{-3})
   molar means 'divided by amount of substance'
mole (unit of amount of substance) — mol replaces gram-molecule, gram-ion, gram-atom etc.
negative logarithm of hydrogen ion concentration — pH, plural – pH values
newton — N
normal saline — avoid *use* isosmotic saline
number of observations — n (or f)
parts per million — ppm
petroleum ether — avoid *use* light petroleum
pressure — p
red blood corpuscle — r.b.c. or RBC
respiratory quotient — r.q. or RQ
ribonucleic acid — RNA
solidus — / expressed in units of
solution — soln.
species — sp. (singular), spp. (plural)
standard deviation
  (of hypothetical population) — s
  (of observed sample) — S or s.d.
sum (statistics)
  (of hypothetical population) — Σ
  (of observed sample) — S or Σ
temperature (quantity) — T (absolute)
  — t (other scales)
thyroid-stimulating hormone — TSH
time — t
variety (biology) — var.
volume — vol.
white blood corpuscle — w.b.c. or WBC

A4.3 SI Units

A4.3.1 Names and symbols for SI units

Physical quantity	Name of SI unit	Symbol
length	metre	m
mass	kilogram	kg
time	second	s
electric current	ampere	A
thermodynamic temperature	kelvin	K
luminous intensity	candela	cd
amount of substance	mole	mol
solid angle	steradian	sr

A4.3.2 Derived units from SI units

Quantity	SI unit	Symbol	Expressed in terms of SI units
work, energy, quantity of heat	joule	J	$\mathrm{kg\,m^2\,s^{-2}}$; $1\,\mathrm{J} = 1\,\mathrm{N\,m}$
force	newton	N	$\mathrm{kg\,m\,s^{-2}}$; $= \mathrm{J\,m^{-1}}$
power	watt	W	$\mathrm{kg\,m^2\,s^{-3}}$; $= \mathrm{J\,s^{-1}}$
quantity of electricity	coulomb	C	A s
electric potential	volt	V	$\mathrm{kg\,m^2\,s^{-3}\,A^{-1}}$; $\mathrm{W\,A^{-1}}$
luminous flux	lumen	lm	cd sr
illumination	lux	lx	$\mathrm{cd\,sr\,m^{-2}}$ or $\mathrm{lm\,m^{-2}}$
area	square metre	m^2	
volume	cubic metre	m^3	
density	kilogram per cubic metre	kg m^{-3}	

A4.3.3 Special units still in use (should be progressively abandoned)

Quantity	Unit name and symbol		Conversion factor to SI
length	angstrom	Å	$10^{-10}\,\mathrm{m} = 0.1\,\mathrm{nm}$
length	micron	μm	$10^{-6}\,\mathrm{m} = 10^{-3}\,\mathrm{mm} = 1\,\mu\mathrm{m}$
volume	litre	l	$10^{-3}\,\mathrm{m^3} = 1\,\mathrm{dm^3}$
mass	tonne	t	$10^3\,\mathrm{kg} = \mathrm{Mg}$
pressure	millimetres of mercury	mmHg	$10^2\,\mathrm{mmHg} = 13.3\,\mathrm{kPa}$

A4.3.4 Prefixes for SI units

These are used to indicate decimal fractions of the basic or derived SI units.

Multiplication factor	Prefix	Symbol
$0.000\,000\,000\,001 = 10^{-12}$	pico	p
$0.000\,000\,001 = 10^{-9}$	nano	n
$0.000\,001 = 10^{-6}$	micro	μ
$0.001 = 10^{-3}$	milli	m
$1\,000 = 10^3$	kilo	k
$1\,000\,000 = 10^6$	mega	M
$1\,000\,000\,000 = 10^9$	giga	G
$1\,000\,000\,000\,000 = 10^{12}$	tera	T

Thus 1 nanometre (nm) $= 1 - 10^{-9}$ m,
also 1 centimetre (cm) $= 1 \times 10^{-2}$ m.
Note that the kilogram is somewhat out of place in the above table since it is a basic SI unit. In the school laboratory the most convenient units are grams (g) and cubic centimetres (cm³). Where possible the basic SI units should be used.

A4.3.5 Rules for writing SI units

(1) The symbol is not an abbreviation and thus a full stop is not written after the symbol except at the end of a sentence.
(2) There is no plural form of a unit; thus 20 kg or 30 m, not 20 kgs or 30 ms.
(3) Capital initial letters are never used for units except when named after famous scientists, such as N (Newton), W (Watt) and J (Joule).
(4) Symbols combined in a quotient can be written as, for example, metre per second or $m\,s^{-1}$. The use of the solidus (stroke, /) is restricted to indicating the unit of a variable, such as temperature /°C.

(5) The raised decimal point is not correct. The internationally accepted decimal sign is placed level with the feet of the numerals, for example 3.142. The comma is no longer used to separate groups of three digits but a space is left instead so that figures appear as 493 645 189 not as 493,645,189.

Appendix 5
The geological time scale

The history of the Earth is divided for convenience into a series of four geological **eras** and eleven

Table A5.1 Geological time scale and history of life (age = years $\times 10^6$)

Era	Period	Epoch	Age	Animal groups	Plant groups
CENOZOIC (*cenos*, recent)	Quaternary	Recent (Holocene)	0.01	Dominance of humans	
		Glacial (Pleistocene)	2	Origin of humans	
	Tertiary	Pliocene	7	Adaptive radiation of mammals	Adaptive radiation of flowering plants, especially herbaceous types
		Miocene	26	Dogs and bears appeared	
		Oligocene	38	Apes and pigs appeared	
		Eocene	54		
		Palaeocene	65	Horses, cattle and elephants	
MESOZOIC (*mesos*, middle)	Cretaceous		135	Extinction of ammonites and dinosaurs; origin of modern fish and placental mammals	Dominance of flowering plants
	Jurassic		195	Dinosaurs dominant; origin of birds and mammals; insects abundant	Origin of flowering plants
	Triassic		225	Dinosaurs appear; adaptive radiation of reptiles	Abundance of cycads and conifers
PALAEOZOIC (*palaeos*, ancient)	Permian		280	Adaptive radiation of reptiles; beetles appear; extinction of trilobites	Origin of conifers
	Carboniferous		350	Origin of reptiles and insects; adaptive radiation of amphibia	Abundance of tree-like ferns, e.g. *Lepidodendron*, forming 'coal forests'
	Devonian		400	Origin of amphibia and ammonites; spiders appear; adaptive radiation of fish (cartilaginous and bony)	Earliest mosses and ferns
	Silurian		440	Origin of jawed fish; earliest coral reefs	Earliest spore-bearing, vascular plants
	Ordovician		500	Origin of vertebrates, jawless fish; trilobites, molluscs and crustacea abundant	
	Cambrian		570	Origin of all non-vertebrate phyla and echinoderms	
ARCHEOZOIC	Pre-Cambrian		1 000	*Selected organisms* primitive metazoans	
			2 000	primitive eukaryotes	
			3 000	blue-green bacteria (prokaryotes), bacteria	
			3 500?	origins of life ?	
			5 000?	origin of Earth?	

periods. The two most recent periods are further divided into seven systems or **epochs**.

The rocks of the Earth's crust are stratified, that is they lie layer upon layer. Unless disrupted by earth movements, the rocks get progressively younger towards the top of a series of layers (strata). William Smith in the eighteenth century noticed an association between fossil groups and particular strata. The sequence of fossils revealed a gradual increase in complexity of organisms from the lower strata to the highest, indicating that over geological periods of time some organisms have advanced in complexity.

Radioactive dating has established an approximate age for the oldest rocks belonging to each period. The geological time scale and the distinctive biological events associated with each period, as revealed by fossil evidence, are shown in table A5.1.

A5.1 The age of the Earth

Current estimates are that the planet Earth is about 4.6–4.9×10^9 years old. These estimates are based mainly on the dating of rocks (**geochronology**) by radioactive dating techniques.

In section A1.3 it was explained that atoms of some elements exist in a number of forms called isotopes, some of which are radioactive. Radioactive elements 'decay' at a constant rate which is independent of temperature, gravity, magnetism or any other force. The rate is measured in terms of the 'half-life'.

Three principal methods of radioactive dating are currently used, as shown in fig A5.1. Methods (1) and (2) are used for determining the ages of rocks in the Earth's crust, whereas the third method, radiocarbon dating, is used for dating fossils and has direct relevance in discussions of the history of life.

Radiocarbon dating

The normal non-radioactive isotope of carbon is ^{12}C. The radioactive isotope, ^{14}C, occurs in minute quantities ($< 0.1\%$) in air, surface waters and living organisms. It is continually being produced in the atmosphere by the action of cosmic rays on nitrogen and oxygen nuclei, and there is good evidence to suggest that the rate of ^{14}C production has been constant for several thousand years. An equilibrium has been set up whereby production of ^{14}C balances ^{14}C loss by radioactive decay. ^{14}C is found occurring freely as $^{14}CO_2$ and the ratio of $^{14}C:^{12}C$ compounds remains theoretically constant. Living organisms absorb ^{14}C either as carbon

dioxide or as organic molecules throughout life. At death no more carbon is taken in and the ^{14}C continues to decay according to the rate shown by the half-life. By calculating the amount of ^{14}C in the dead organism and comparing it with the amount of ^{14}C in a living organism, the age of the dead organism can be estimated. For example, if the amount of ^{14}C in a fossil mammalian bone was found to be one-quarter that in the same bone from a recently killed mammal and the half-life is 5.6×10^3 years, the estimated age of the fossil bone would theoretically be 11.2×10^3 years. Using this technique, organic remains can be dated back, fairly accurately, for up to 10.0×10^4 years.

There are many sources of error involved in radiometric dating, so ages determined by these methods are only approximate. However, these methods have proved to be of great value in extending our knowledge of the Earth.

(1) Uranium/thorium methods
Uranium and thorium are generally found occurring together in the same rocks

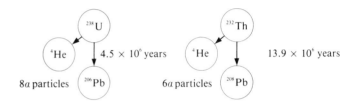

(2) Potassium/argon methods

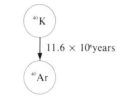

(3) Radiocarbon dating methods

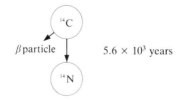

Fig A5.1 *Radiometric dating techniques*

Index

Numbers in italic denote figures.

α-helix, 151
abiotic environment, organisms interactions, 401–2
abomasum, 321
abscisic acid, 551, 558–9, 674
    antagonism to auxin, 561
    role in plant growth/development, 556
abscission, 561–2
    fruit drop associated, 562
    layer, 561
    zone, 561
absorption spectrum, 257, 563
absorption, 289
acclimatisation, 357
accommodation (eye), 596
acetic acid (ethanoic acid), *126*
acetylcholine, 177, 572, 574, 575, 645
acetylcholinesterase, 177, 572–3, 645
acid rain, *429–30, 431*
acinus, 687
acoelomate condition, 98
Acquired Immune Deficiency Syndrome (AIDS), 31, 536–8
acrosome reaction, 760
ACTH (adrenocorticotrophic hormone; corticotrophin), 604, 607, 611
    fetal, 765
actin, 210, 639–40, 642
Actinopterygii, *122*
action potential, 569, 570, 571
action spectrum, 257, 563
activation energy, 168, 933
active transport, 196–8, 701
adaptive radiation, 879–81
adenine, 463, *557*, 698, 818
adenosine diphosphate (ADP), 157
adenosine monophosphate (AMP), 157, *171*
adenosine triphosphatase (ATPase), 338
adenosine triphosphate (ATP), 157, *171*, 178, 324–5, 467, 639, 641, 642–3, 650
    sodium–potassium pump driven by, 196–7
    synthesis, 337–8
adenovirus, *14*
adenyl cyclase, 606, 831
adipose tissue, 238, 678
adrenal glands, 610–12
    cortex, 604, 611
    medulla, 604, 611–12
adrenaline (epinephrine), 526, 604, 606, 611–12
    molecular structure, *611*
    physiological effects, 611
adrenergic receptors, 612
adrenocorticotrophic hormone (ACTH; corticotrophin), 604, 607, 611
adrenocorticotrophin releasing factor (CRF), 607
aerobic bacteria, 292
aerobic respiration, 327–8, 330
    photosynthesis compared, 468
aerotaxis, 544
aerotropism, 543
aestivation, 796

agar, 47
Agaricus (*Psalliota*), 18, 19, 24, 25
ageing (senescence), 406
agglutination–inhibition test, 759
agglutinogens, 539
aggression (agonistic behaviour), 618–19, 621–2
Agnatha, *122*
agranulocytes (mononuclear leucocytes), 513–14
agriculture, 419–20
    land loss, 432
AIDS (acquired immune deficiency syndrome), 13, 536–8
alanine, 144
albedo, 365
albinism, 817, 891
albumin, serum, 513
albumins, 148
Alcaligenes, 35
alcohol groups, primary/secondary, 129
alcohol(s), 140
alcoholic fermentation, 330
aldehyde group, 129
aldohexoses, 463
aldoses, 130–2, *132*
aldosterone, 604, 722
aldrin, 376
algae, 40–9
    harmful effects, 48–9
alginic acid, 47
alimentary canal, cat, 320
alimentary canal, human, 304–7
    endocrine control of secretions, 319
alimentary canal, sheep, 320–1
alkalaemia, 356
alkali, 928
alkaptonuria, 817
allantochorion, 762
allantoic acid, 698
allantoin, 698
allantois, 711, 762, 770
alleles, 835, 839
    frequency, 891–2
    multiple, 849
allelochemical interactions, 416
allelomorphs, 840
allelopathy, 416
Allen's rule, 684, *685*
allograft, 540
allopolyploidy, 856–7, 909
allosteric activators, 178
allosteric effectors, 178
allosteric enzymes, 178–9
allosteric inhibitors, 178
alternation of generations, 59, 92, 733
altruism, 624
alveolar air, percentage composition of gases, 353
alveolar tubes, 349
alveolar ventilation, 354
alveoli, 349
amacrine cell, 597
ameloblasts, 309

amino acids, 127, 129, 143–6, 914, 915
amino sugar, 131
amino-acyl-tRNA synthetase, 823
aminopeptidase, 314
Ammophila (marram grass), 486, *487*
amnion, 762
amniotic cavity, 770
amniotic fluid, 762
Amoeba proteus, 52, 53–4, 292–3
Amoore's theory of olfaction, 594
AMP (adenosine monophosphate), 157, 171
Amphibia (amphibians), 121, *122*, 462
amphibia, 710
    metamorphosis, 791–2
ampulla, 602
amylase, 147, 181, 314
amyloglucosidase, 181
amylopectin, 137
amyloplasts, 214
amylose, 137
anabolic reactions, 323
anaemia, sickle cell, 858
anaerobes, 330
anaerobic respiration, 326, 330–1
analogous structures, 881
anaphase, *799, 805, 807*
androecium, 736
androgen-receptor protein molecule, 764
anemometer, 444
aneuploidy, 855
angiosperms (flowering plants), 75, 78–80, *83*, 357
    adaptation to life on land, 81
angiotensin, 611, 722
animals, 85
    breeding, 876–7
    coordination/control in, 567–626
    ectothermic, 675, 676–7
    endothermic, 675, 677–82
    general characteristics, 86–8
    homeothermic (homoiothermic), 675
    light-involved processes, 396
    plants compared, 39
    poikilothermic, 675
    resources, sustainable use, 434
    sources of heat, 675
    temperature influence on growth/distribution, 675
anion, 926
anisogamy, 42, 735
Annelida, 100–6, 507–8, 703–5
    body wall compared with arthropod wall, *109*
annual rings, 785–6
annuals, 78
Anopheles sp. (mosquito), 299–300
anoxia (hypoxia), 356
antagonism, 559–62
antennal glands, 706, 707
antheridium, 42
antherozoids (spermatozoids), 42–3
Anthozoa, 90
anthrocyan, 213
anthrocyanin, 213

anthropocentrism, 613
anthropoids, 886
anthropomorphism, 613
antibiotics, 26–7
antibody, 533, *535*, 538
antidiuretic hormone (ADH; vasopressin), 604, 607, 721–2
antigen (immunogen), 533–4
antigibberellins, 555, 565
apical dominance, 560–1
Apicomplexa, 51, 53
apocrine glands, 234, 679
apoenzyme, 169
apomixis, 732
apoplast, 482, 494–5
appendix, 317
    human, 879
apple scab, 34
aqueous humour, 595
arabinan, 139
Arachnida, 110
arachnoid membrane, 580, *581*
archaebacteria, *4*, *5*
archegonium, 42
archenteron, 98
area sampling, 449–50
areolar tissue, 236–7
argentaffine cells, 313
arginase, optimum pH, 174
arginine, 144
Aristotle, 860, 865
aromatic bases, 127
arteriole, 507, 516, *517*
artery, 507, 514–16
Arthropoda, 106–13, 705–6
    blood vascular system, 508
    body wall compared with annelid body wall, *109*
    limb, *628*
arthropodin, 107
arthropodisation, 107
ascidian tadpole, 119, *120*
Ascomycota, 23–4
ascorbic acid (vitamin C), 305
asexual reproduction, 725–30
asparagine, 144
aspartic acid, 144
aspergillosis (farmer's lung), 34
Aspergillus, 19, 23, 26, 34
assimilation, 289
association areas, 584–5
astrocytes, 247
atherosclerosis, 673, 691
athlete's foot, 19, 34
atlas, 633
atmosphere, 396
    pollution, 429
atom, 925
ATP (adenosine triphosphate), 157, *171*, 178, 324–5, 467
ATPase (adenosine triphosphatase), 338
atrio-ventricular node, 523
atrium, 508
atropine, 575
Auerbach's plexus, 307
autecological investigation, 456–9
autecology, 359
autocatalysis, 313
autograft, 540
autolysis, 208
autophagy, 208
autopolyploidy, 856
autosomes (autosomal chromosomes), 843
autotomy, 794
autotrophic bacteria, 13
autotrophic nutrition, 39, 249–87

autotrophs, 249, 251, 323
auxins, 545–8
    commercial applications, 551, 552
    fruit set associated, 562
    geotropism associated, 549–60
    role in plant growth/development, 556
Aves, 121, *122*
axis, 633
axolotl, 791–2
axoneme, 649
axons, 244, 567, 568, 570
Azotobacter, 6, *8*

β-configuration, 150
β-oxidation of fatty acids, 339
B cell, 534–5
baby foods, 181
Bacillus, 6, *8*, 27
bacteria, 4–12, 280–90
bacterial diseases, human, 32
bacterial experiments, 35–8
bacteriochlorophyll, 289
bacteriology, 4
bacteriophages, 15, *16*, 17, 813–14
Baermann funnel, 446, *448*
baking, 26
balance, 601–2
balding, premature, 847
bar graph, 947
barbs, 660
barbules, 660
bark, 787
barnacles, *111*
baroreceptors, 526
Barr body, 846
basal bodies (kinetosomes), 209, 801
basal ganglia, 586
basal metabolic rate (BMR), 354, 680
base, 928
basement membrane, 231, 715
Basidiomycota, 24
basking heliotherms, 677
basophils, 513, *514*
batch fermentation, 331
batch reactor, 182
beating tray, 446
bees *see* honeybees
behaviour (ethology), 613–26
    altruistic, 624
    ethological approach, 613
    innate, 613–24
    kin selected, 624
    learned, 624–6
    mechanistic approach, 613
    territorial, 618–19
    vitalistic approach, 613
behavioural thermoregulation, 677
belt transect, 449
Benedict's test, 136, 162, 463
benzene, *126*
benzoic acids, 552
Bergman's rule, 684
Bernard, Claude, 667
betaglucanase, 181
biennials, 80
bile duct, *686*, 687
bile ductules, 687
bile salts, 314, 315
bile, 315, 691–2
bilirubin, 513, 691
biliverdin, 513, 691
binary fission, 725
binocular vision, 599
bioassay, 547
biochemical identifications, 160–4
biochemical oxygen demand (BOD), 385–7

    industrial wastes, 387
    water quality, 387
biochips, 183
biogas, 27
biogeochemical cycles (mineral cycles), 24, 364, 377–80
    fluid reservoirs, 379
    sedimentary reservoirs, 379
biological control, 620
    of pests, 423–4
biological detergents, 181
biological molecules, 126–9
biological oxidation, 325
biological rhythms, 616, 617–18
biomass, 27, 369, 374, 401
    standing (standing crop), 369
bioreactors (fermenters), 26, 331, *332*
biosensors, 182–3
biosphere (ecosphere), 359
    major cycles, *378*
biotechnology, 26–8
biotic analysis, 444–52
biotic climax, 400
biotic potential, 407
biotin (vitamin H), 305
bipedal gait, 630, 666, 887
birds, 121, *122*
    brain, 582
    circulatory system, 511
    water balance, 711
birth (human), 764–7
birth rate (natality), 405
biting mouthparts, 297
biuret test, 161
Bivalvia (Pelycopoda), 107
bladder, 708, 712
blastocoel, 761, 793
blastocyst, 759
blastula, 793
bleaching, 598
blind spot, 596
blood
    cells, 512–14
    control of metabolites in, 672
    control of respiratory gases in, 670–1
    frog, 511
    functions, 526–33
        carbon dioxide carriage, 529–30
        clotting, 530–1
        defensive, 530–3
        oxygen carriage *see under* oxygen
        phagocytosis, 531
        wound healing, 532–3
    mammalian, 511–14
    pH control, 723
    plasma, 511–12, 513
    storage in liver, 691
blood groups, 539–40, 849
    inheritance, 849
    universal donors, 540
    universal recipients, 540
blood pressure, *523*, 525–6, 672–3
    control, 673
blood vessels, 507
blue-green bacteria (Cyanobacteria), *5*, 280, 281, 292
body cavities, 98–100
Bohr effect (shift), 528
bolus, 311
bomb calorimeter, 300
bombykol, 620
bone, 239–42, 629–30, 916
    deposition, factors controlling, 630
    development, 630
    growth, dentine growth, *242*
    Haversian system, 240, *241*

trabeculae, 629
Volkman's canals, 240
bone marrow tissue, 243
boring mouthparts, 297
boron, 284, 286
botulinum toxin, 575
botulism, 33
Bowman's capsule, 712
Boysen-Jensen's experiments, 546–7
brachiation, 630–1
bradycardia, 672
brain, 582–7
    association areas, 584–5
    birds, 582
    cerebellum, 586
    cerebrum, 584–6
    fish, 582
    forebrain, 582, 583
    hindbrain, 582, 583
    human, 584–7
    mammals, 582
    prefrontal lobes, 585
    sensory areas, 584
    silent areas, 585
    size, 887–8
    speech area, 889
    speech motor centre, 585
    ventricles, 580
branchial arches, 878
bread mould (*Rhizopus stolonifer*), 20, 21–3
breasts (mammary glands), 776–8
breathing centre, 352
breeding
    artificial selection, 893
    inbreeding, 893–4
    non-random, 888–9
    outbreeding, 894–5
    plant and animal, 874–5
    pure, 833
brittle star, *118*
Broads, Norfolk, phosphate levels, 383–4
bronchi, 349
bronchioles, 349
brown earths (brown forest soils), 394
brown fat, 680, 796
brown rot, 34
Brunner's glands, 313
Bryophyta, 59–64
buccal cavity, 311
bud, adventitious, 784
bud-break, 566
budding 726, 727
    propagation by, 729
buffer, 929
bulb, 727
bulbs of Krause, 593
bundle of His, 524

C_3 plants, 279
C_4 plants, 276–80
cabbage white butterfly (*Pieris brassicae*), *117*, 298–9
calcicoles, 395
calciferol (vitamin D), 305
calcifuges, 394
calcitonin, 604, 608, 610
calcium, 285
callose, 137
calorie (gram calorie), 365
calorigenesis, 609
calorimeter, *303*
Calvin cycle, 264, 492
cambium, 784
    cork, 786, 787
    vascular, 784, 785, 786, 787, 788
camel, 686

capacitation, 760
capillarity, 492
capillary, 507, 515, *517*
capsid, 14
capsomeres, 14
capture–recapture technique, 451–2
carbamino-haemoglobin compound, 529
carbohydrates (saccharides), 130–8, 325
    classification, *130*
    synthesis, 266
carbon, 125–6
    atoms, asymmetry of, *133*
    bonds, *126*, 126
    energy source, 249
    fixation, 47
carbon cycle, 249, *251*, 380–2
carbon dioxide, 249, 380–2
    carriage by blood, 529–30
    effect on heart muscle, 526
    pump, 466
    role in photosynthesis, 251, 260, 264–72, 274, 275–80
carbon monoxide, 529
carbonic acid, 529
carbonic anhydrase, 512, 529
carboxyhaemoglobin, 529
carboxyl group, 129
carbonyl group, 129
carboxylase, 265
carboxypeptidase, 314, 315
cardiac cycle, 521–3
cardiac muscle, 243, *244*
cardiac output, 524
cardiovascular centre, 671
carnivores, 289, 366
carnivorous (insectivorous) plants, 286
carotenes, 256, 257
carotenoids, 257
carotid body, *526*, 670
carotid sinus, *526*
carpel, 740
carpometacarpus, 661
carrageenin (carragheen), 47
carrion feeders, 366
carrying capacity, 408
cartilage, 238–9, 629, 916
cascade effect, 605
Casparian strip, 219, 494, *495*
caste system, 623
castor bean, 140
catabolic reactions, 323
catalase, 181, 208, *464*
    optimum pH, 174
catalysts, 167–8
catecholamines, 611
cation, 926
cation exchange capacity, 389
cation (sodium) pump, 568
cave paintings, 889
cavitation, 493
cell(s), 185–214
    respiration, 325
cell cycle, 797, *798*
cell differentiation, 771
cell division (hyperplasia), 771, 801, 802
cell expansion (hypertrophy), 771
cell structure
    animal, *186*, *188–9*
    general, 192–211
    historical events, 185
    plant, *187*, *190–1*, 211–14
cell surface membrane, 189, 192–8
    structure, 193–4
    transport across, 195–8
cell wall, 211–13
cellulase, 18, 181

cellulose, 18, *136*, 137, 462
    digestion in ruminants, 321
centrioles, 209, 801
centromere, 797
centrum, 628
cephalisation, 587
Cephalochordata, 121
Cephalopoda, 117
Ceratocystis ulmi (parasite causing Dutch elm disease), 19
cerebellum, 586
cerebral cortex, 584
cerebral ganglia, 587
cerebrospinal fluid, 580
cerebrum, 584–6
Cestoda, 93
chaetae, 651
chaffinch song, 615
Chandler Biotic Score, 385
cheese manufacture, 26
chemical 'building blocks', 127
chemicals
    of life, 127–62
    toxic, 28
chemoautotrophs, 13, 249, 251
chemoheterotroph, *250*, 251
chemoheterotrophism, 12, 13, 464
chemoreceptors, 353, 588, 593–5, 670
chemosynthesis, 281
chemotaxis, 544
chemotherapy, 176
chemotropism, 543
chewing mouthparts, 297
chiasmata *804*, *808*, 810, 842
Chilopoda, 110
chitin, 138, 628
Chlamydomonas, 43, 44–5
chloramphenicol, 26
chlorenchyma, 219
chloride secretory cell, 709
chloride shift, 530
chlorine, 285
chlorocruorin, 343
chlorofluorocarbons, 429
chlorophyll, 255–6, 465, 918
    electron donor, 259
Chlorophyta (green algae), 41, 44; *see also Chlamydomonas*
chloroplasts, 191, 214, 253, *254*, 255, *262*, 465, 466
chlorosis, 270, 284
choice chamber, 614
cholecystokinin (pancreozymin), 319, 604, 692
cholera, 32
cholesterol, *143*, 193, 611, 691–2
cholic acid, *143*
choline, 127
Chondrichthyes, 121, *122*
chondroblasts, 239
chondrocytes, 239
chondroitin sulphate, 139
Chondrostei, *122*
Chordata, 119–22
    Vertebrata, *see* Vertebrata
chorion, 762, 763
chorionic gonadotrophin, 604
choroid plexuses, 580, 586, 587
choroid, 595
chromatid, 797
chromatin, 200, 797, 811
chromatogram, *318*
chromatography, 934–6
    electrophoresis, 934
    two-dimensional paper, 935
chromatophores, 237

chromium, 284
chromoplasts, 214
chromoprotein, 148
chromosomes, 200, 797, 811–15, 838–9
  autosomal (autosomes), 845
  deletion, 857
  DNA *see* DNA
  duplication, 857–8
  giant, 845
  homologous *803–4*, 839
  independent assortment explanation, 839
  inversion, 857
  mutation, 854–5
  non-disjunction, 855
  puffs (rings of Balbiani), 831, *832*
  sex (heterosomes), 845
  structural changes, 857–8
  translocation, 857
  see also genes, 844
chylomicrons, 315
chyme, 313
chymotrypsin(ogen), 314, 315
  optimum pH, 174
Chytridiomycota, 19
cilia, 54–6, 649–51
ciliary body, 595
ciliary feeding, 293–4, 294–5
ciliary muscle, 595
ciliated epithelium, 231, *232*
Ciliophora, 51, 53, 54–8
circadian rhythm, 618
circulatory system, 506
  Amphibia, 510–11
  Annelida, 507–8
  Arthropoda, 508
  birds, 511
  closed vascular system, 507
  mammals, 511, 514–26
  open vascular system, 507
  Reptilia, 511
  vertebrate, 508–11
circumoesophageal connectives, 587
circumpharyngeal connectives, 587
cistron, 818
classification of living organisms, *4*
classification of organisms, 876
  phenetic, 876
  phylogenetic, 876
classification, 950–1
clavicle, 634
clay–humus complex, 389
cleavage, 793
cleidoic egg, 711
climacteric (fruit), 562
climax community, 398, 399–401
climax woodland, 401
cline, 898, 906
clitoris (human), 755
clone, 725, 777, 802
cloning, 730, *731*
Clostridium, *8*, 33, 330
clover root nodules, 282, 287
club mosses (Lycopodophyta), 65, 67–71, *83*
Cnidaria (Coelenterata), *87*, 88–92
coacervation, 863
cobalt, 284, 286
cocci, *8*
coccyx (human), 879
cochlea, 601
cockroach, blood vascular system, 508
codominance, 848–9
codons, 820, 821
coelom, 98–9
coelomic fluid, 99
coenzyme Q, 330
coenzymes, 170–2

co-evolution, 416
cohesion–tension theory, 482, 492
colchicine, 209, 801
cold sores, 31
collagen, 532
  triple-helix structure, *152*
collenchyma, 216, 220, *221*
colloidal state, 930–1
colonial theory, 86
colostrum, 768
colour blindness, 598–9, 847
colour vision, 598
columnar epithelium, 231, *232*
combining power (valency), 927
commensalism, 290, 291
common cold, 31
community ecology, 398–404
companion cells, 220, *229*, 230
comparative anatomy, 877–9
comparative biochemistry, 883–5
comparative embryology, 881–3
compartmentation, 192
compensation point, 274–5
competition, interspecific/intraspecific, 619, 867, 898
competitive exclusion, 415
competitive exclusion principle (Gaussian exclusion principle), 416
composite materials, 211
compound eye, 599
conditioning (conditioned reflex), 625
cones, 597
conifers (Coniferophyta), 75, 76–8
  adaptation to life on land, 81
conjugation, 45
conjunctiva, 595
connective tissue, animal, 234–43
  adipose, 238
  areolar, 236–7
  bone, *see* bone
  cartilage, *see* cartilage
  white fibrous, 237–8, *240*
  yellow elastic, 238
conservation agencies, 437–8
conservation, 427–8, 433–4
  genetic variety, 428
  rare/endangered species, 433
  United Kingdom, 435–7
consumers, 365–6
contagion, 31
continental drift, 873
continuous culture, 331
contractile vacuole, 702, *703*, *704*
control
  biological, 423
  herbicides, 420
  integrated, 425
  pesticides, 420
control systems, 667–9
  feedback, 668
  thryoxine production, 669
conus arteriosus, 509
coordination, nervous/endocrine compared, 612
copper, 284, 286
coppice system, 435–6
copulation (human), 759–60
coracoid, 634
Cori cycle, 689
cork, 787
corm, 727, *728*
cornea, 595
corolla, 735
coronary thrombosis, 531
corpora cardiaca, 788
corpora quadrigemina, 586

corpus albicantus, 758
corpus allatum, 790
corpus callosum, 584
corpus luteum, 604, 756
  premature failure, 759
correlation, 561
corticospinal (pyramidal) tract, 585
corticosterone, *143*
corticotrophin (adrenocorticotrophic hormone: ACTH), 604, 607, 611
cortisol, 604
cotyledons, 745
countercurrent heat exchanger, 685
courtship, 620–1
covalent bonding, 927
cranium, 631
creatine phosphate, 324
creatine, 698
creatinine, 698
cretinism, goitrous, 817
Crick, F.H.C., 865
crop rotation, 420
crossing-over, 842–3
Crossopterygii (lobe-finned fish), 119, *122*
crown gall, 30
Crustacea, 110
cryptorchidism, 752
crystalline cone, 599
cubical epithelium, 231
cultural control of pests, 423
cupula, 602
curare, 575
cuticle (plant), 482, 487–8
cuttings, 729
cuttlefish (squid; *Sepia officinalis*), *106*, 395–6
cyanobacteria, *5*
cybernetics, 667
cyclic AMP (3,5-adenosine monophosphate), 606
cyclic polymorphism, 733
cysteine, 144
cytochrome(s), 328, 330, 883
cytochrome *c*, 883–4
cytochrome oxidase, 328
cytogenetics, 185
cytokinins, 557–8, 560
  role in plant growth/development, 556
cytology, 185
cytoplasm, 200, 830–1
cytoplasmic streaming, 200
cytosine, 463, 818
cytoskeleton, 208–11
cytosol, 200

daily food requirements, 365
dairy industry, 181
Daphnia pulex (common water flea), 294, *295*
dark adaptation, 598
dark reaction, 264, *267*
dark respiration, 275
Darwin, Charles, 545, 862, 864, 866–8, 874–5
data presentation, 944–7
day-neutral plants, 564
DCMU (dichlorophenyl dimethyl urea), 270
DDT (dichlorophenyltrichloroethane), 376–7, 469
  effects on crop/soil fauna, *422*
  lethal dose, mammals, 421–2
dead space air, 353
deamination, 689
death rate (mortality), 405, 406
decarboxylation, oxidative, 328
decidua, 763
deciduous plants, 80
decomposers, 13, 18, 367

decremental conduction, 587
defaecation, 317
deforestation, 432, 469
demes, 906
demography, 405
denaturation, of enzymes, 173
dendrites, 245, 571
dendrochronography, 785–6
dendroclimatology, 785
dendrons, 244
denitrification, 283
density-dependent (density-conditioned) growth, 408, 412
density-independent growth, 408
dental disease, *310*, 311
dentine, 242, 309
dentition, human, 307–11
deoxy sugar, 131
deoxyribose nucleic acid, *see* DNA
depolarisation, 569, 571
desert animals, 140–1
desertification, 432
detritivores, 367
detritus, 367, 375
Deuteromycota (Fungi imperfecti), 19
deuterostomes, 882
development, 776–7
    control, 776
      factors influencing, 776
      vertebrates, 792–3
dextro-rotatory substances, 133
diabetes insipidus, 722
diabetes mellitus, 612
diapause hormone, 795
diapause, 795
diapedesis, 513, 531
diaphragm, 349
diaphysis, 629
diastole, 521
diatom, 48
diatomite (kieselguhr), 47
dicarboxylic acids, 277
dicotyledons, 78, 79, *80*
dieldrin, 376
diencephalon, 583, 586
dietary requirements, of humans, 297–304
differentiation, 776
    hormones effect, 777
diffusion, 195, 474, 931–2
    facilitated, 195
digestion, 289
digestive secretions, 314
    control, 318–19
dihybrid inheritance, 836–8
dihydroxyacetone, 130, *132*, 462
diisopropylfluorophosphate (DFP), 177
dinucleotide, *156*, 157
dioecious plants, 732, 740
dipeptidase, 314
dipeptide, 145, 146
1,3 diphosphoglycerate, 324
diphtheria, 32
diplococci, *8*
diploid, 60–2, 68, 79
Dipnoi (lung fish), 883
Dipodomys (kangaroo rat), 701
disaccharides, *130*, *136*, 135–7
discrimination, 575, 590
disease
    bacterial, 30–3
    deficiency, 284–6, 304, 305
    fungal, 33, 34
    transmission, 30–3
    viral, 30–3
displacement activity, 622
disulphide bond, 146

diurnal rhythm, 618
diversity index, 445
DNA (deoxyribose nucleic acid), 154, 156–60, 161, 185, 189–91, 198, 200, 669, 811–15, *816*, 919
    bacterial, 6, 7, 10–12
    inheritance role, 812–14
    nucleotide bases, 818
    polymerase, 815
    prokaryote, 3
    recombinant, 10
    recombinant technology, *see* genetic engineering
    replication, 814–15
    structure of, 157–60
    transcription, 823–4
    transduction, 12
    viral, 13–14, 16
dogfish
    circulatory system, 508–10
    locomotion, 656–7
    respiratory system, 345–6
dominance hierarchy, 622
dopamine, 575
dormancy, 566, 794–5
dormin, 674
dorsal light reaction, 614
dorsal root ganglion, 582
Down's syndrome, 855, *856*, 857
downstream processing, 332
drag, 661
droplet infection, 30–1
drought, adaptation to, 701
drought endurers, 700
drought evaders, 700
ducts of Bellini, 721
duodenum, 313
    hormone secretion, 604
dura mater, 580, *581*
Dutch elm disease, 34
dynein, 649
dysentery, bacterial, 32

ear, mammalian, 600–2
    cochlea, 600
    inner, 600
    middle, 600
    outer, 600
    semicircular canals, 602
    vestibular apparatus, 601
earliest organisms, 863
Earth, age, 955
earthworm
    blood vascular system, 507–8
    locomotion, 651–2
    urine formation, *704*
eccrine gland, 679
ecdysis, 628, 789–91
ecdysone (moulting hormone), 789–90
Echinodermata, 118, 119, 708
Echinoidea, 118
ecological niche, 362
ecological pyramids, 369–73
    biomass, 369–71
    criticisms, 372–3
    energy, 372
    numbers, 369, *370*
ecological races (ecotypes), 898, 906
ecological research projects/investigations, 452–3
ecological succession, 398–404
    primary, 398
    secondary, 398, 403
    underlying features, 401
ecology, 359–62
    production, 373–6

quantitative, 439–59
ecosphere, *see* biosphere
ecosystem, 359, 360, 363
    abiotic component, 359, 387–97
    biotic component, 359
    climatic factors, 395–7
    rational cropping of, 376
ectoderm, 762
ectoparasites, 292
ectoplasm, 648
ectosymbiont, 291
ectotherms, 675, 767–7
edaphic factors, 387–90
effector cells, 567
effector, 668
egesta, 373
egestion, 289, 695
elastase, 314
elastic fibres, 238, 239
elastin, 237
electrochemical gradients, 196
electrochemical proton gradient, 338
electroencephalogram, 582–3
electromagnetic spectrum, 934
electron acceptor, 257
electron carriers, 329–30
electron donor, 259
electron microprobe X-ray analysis, 943–4
electron microscope, 941–4
    high voltage, 943
    scanning, 943
electron, 925
electro-osmosis, 506
electroreceptor, 588
element, 925
elements found in living organisms, 125
Embden–Meyerhof pathway, 325
embryo (human), 762
    sexual development, 764
embryonic induction, 830
emigration, 406
endocrine glands, 234
endocrine system, 603–12
endocytosis, 198
endoderm, 762
endodermis, 216, 219–20
endolymph, 600, 601
endometrium, 755, 761
endomitosis, 856
endomysium, 574
endoparasites, 292
endopeptidases, 314
endoplasm, 648
endoplasmic reticulum (ER), 189, 200–2
endorphin(s), 576
endoskeleton, 627–8
endosperm, 746, 747
endosymbiont, 39, 254–5, 291
endotherms, 675, 677–86
end-plate potential, 574
end-product inhibition (negative feedback inhibition), 179
energy, 323–57
    chemical, 323
    endergonic reaction, 323
    environment–heterotrophic cell transfer, *323*
    expenditure by humans measurement, 300
    flow through food chain, *373*, *375*
    food value measurement, 300
    new sources, 434–5
    pyramid, 372
    recommended daily intake, 301
    source, 249
    Sun as source, 364–5, 434–5

energy—*cont.*
    transfer efficiency, 373
    utilisation, 323–57
energy relations in living systems, 933
energy units, 364, 365
engram, 624
enkephalins, 576
enterogastrone, 319
enterokinase, 314, 315
    optimum pH, 174
entropy, 364, 932
environment
    external, 667
    genes role in, 831
    internal, 667, 669–70, *670*
    role, 831
environmental changes, effect on
    non-vertebrates, 706–7
    vertebrates, 708–12
environmental factors measurement, 439,
    441–3
environmental resistance, 407
enzyme(s), 167–82
    activators, 170
    active site, 168
    allosteric, *see* allosteric enzymes
    classification, 180
    cofactors, 169–70
    constitutive, 826
    designer, 182
    immobilisation, 182
    inducible, 826
    induction, 827
    industrial uses, 181
    inhibition, 176
    mechanisms of action, 168–9
    membrane-bound, 313, 314
    metabolism control, 179
    multi-enzyme complex, 179
    rate of reactions/factors affecting, 172–4
    repression, 827
    substrate, 168
    technology, 28, 180–3
eosinophils, 513, *514*
ependymal cells, 247
epidermis, 216, 217–19, 678–9
epididymis (human), 752
epiglottis, 349
epilepsy, 583
epinasty, 544
epinephrine *see* adrenaline
epiphysis (bone), 629
epiphysis (pineal gland), 608
episomes, 12
epistasis, 851–2
epithelial tissues, animal, 230–4
ER (endoplasmic reticulum), 189, 200–2
erector pili muscle, 679
ergot, 33, 34
erythroblasts, 243
erythrocytes (red blood cell), 512–13, *514,
532*
    formation, 691
erythropoiesis, 691
Escherichia coli, 6, 8
    bacteriophage-infested, *17*
    conjugation, 10–11
    vitamin synthesis, 25
eserine, 575
essential elements, 284
esters, 138
ethanoic acid (acetic acid), *126*
ethanol, 27–8, 435
ethene, 551, 557, 559
    role in plant growth/development, 556
ethephon, 555, 557

ethology *see* behaviour
etiolation, 562
etioplast, 562
eubacteria, *5*
euchromatin, 200
eugenics, 901
Euglena, 49–50, 249
euglenoid motion, *650, 651*
euglenoids, 49
eukaryotes, 3–4, 39, 255
euploidy (polyploidy), 856–7, 901
eutrophication, 48, 382–7
evergreen plants, 80
evolution, 859–89
    convergent, 881
    human, 886
    Lamarckian, 866
    modern views, 868
    natural selection, 866–7
    saltatory, 870
evolutionary ecology, 362
excitable cells, 567
excreta, 373
excretion, 2, 695–8
    animals, 696–7
    nitrogenous products, 697–8
    plants, 696
    products, 696
exergonic reaction, 323
exocrine glands, 234, *235*
exocytosis, 198, 208, 572
exopeptidases, 314
exoskeleton, 627, 628
exotoxins, 539
expiration, 352
expiratory centre, 352
expiratory reserve volume, 353
expired air, percentage composition of gases,
    353
exteroceptor, 588
extracellular fluid, 698
extra-embryonic membranes, 762
extrapyramidal tract, 585
eye
    arthropod, 599–600
    human, 595–9
        accommodation, 596
        depth of focus, 596
        visual acuity, 592
    mammalian, 595

F_1 generation, 835
F_2 generation, 835
factor VIII, 847
FAD (flavin adenine dinucleotide), 157, 170,
    171, 330
faecal contamination, 33
faeces, 317
fallopian tube (human), 755
false fruit, 746
family-scale digester, Chinese, 27
farmer's lung (aspergillosis), 34
Fasciola hepatica, 95–8
fat(s), 325
    as respiratory substrate, 339
fat cell, 237
fatty acids, 127, 138–40, 339
feathers, *659*, 660–1
fecundity, 405
Fehling's test, 136, 162
femur, 916; *see also* bone
fermentation, industrial, 331–2
fermenters (bioreactors), 26, 331, *332*
ferns (Filicinophyta), 65, 65–7, *83*
ferritin, 513, 691
fertilisation (human), 759, 760–1

fertilisation membrane, 761
fetal circulation changes at birth, 768–9
fetal stress, 765
fetus, 764
fever, 917
fibrin, 531, *532*
fibrinogen, 513, 531
fibroblasts, 237, 532
ficin, 181
filter feeding, 294–5
fimbriae (pili), 6
fireblight, 30
fish, 708–10
    bony, 709
    cartilaginous, 709
    euryhaline, 709–10
    freshwater, 708–9
    locomotion 655–8
    marine, 709
fisheries, 417–19
fission (unicellular organisms), 725
flagella, 6, 7, 45, 49, 649–51
flagellin, 6
flame cells, 92
flavoproteins, 148, 330
flight (bats), 664–5
flight (birds), 661–4
    flapping, 662–3
    gliding, 664
    hovering, 664
    soaring, 664
florigen, 565
flower, 735–7, *738*
    actinomorphic, 736
    hermaphrodite (bisexual), 736
    parts, 735–6
    unisexual, 736
    zygomorphic, 737
flowering plants, *see* angiosperms
fluid feeders, 290
    mouthparts, 298–300
flukes, 95
fluorescence, 257
    sensitised, 259
fluorine, 284, 286
fluxes, 379
FMN (flavin mononucleotide), 170
folic acid (vitamin M(Bc)), 176, 305
follicle stimulating hormone (FSH), 604, 607,
    754, 756, *758*
food
    composition per, 100g edible portion,
        302–3
    deterioration, 30
    energy value measurement, 300
    fate of absorbed food materials, 319
    recommended daily intake, 301
    regulation of intake in humans, 319–20
    vacuole, 52–5
food chain, 365–7
    concentration effects, 376–7
    energy loss, 374
food poisoning, bacterial, 32, 33
food webs, 367, *368*
foodborne diseases, 33
foramen ovale, 768
forebrain, 582, 583
forest maintenance, 428
fossils, 859–70
    absolute dating, 886
    horse, 870–1, *872*
    'living', 883
    relative dating, 886
founder principle, 895
fovea, 592, 596
fragmentation, 727

freezing point, 699
frequency distributions, 945–7
Frisch, Karl von, 623
frog, 710, 916
    blood circulatory system, 510–11
    locomotion, 658
    metamorphosis, 792
frond, 66–7
fructose, *132*
fruit fly (*Drosophila melanogaster*), 412
fruit
    climacteric, 562
    ripening, 562
    set, 562
fucoxanthin, 47
Fucus, 46–7
fumagillin, 26
Funaria, 61–3
fungi, 17–24
    diseases due to, 33
    practical work, 38
Fungi imperfecti (phylum Deuteromycota), 19
fungicides, 420
furanose ring, 134
fusiform initials, 784

galactose, *132*
β-galactosidase, 826, *828*
Galapagos Islands, 874–6
gall bladder, 315
gametangia, 42
gametes, *42*, 730–1
    human, 752
gametogenesis, 752
gametophyte (*see also* sporophyte), 60–76,
    79, 733
gamma aminobutyric acid (GABA), 575
gas gangrene, 33
gas gland, 657
gaseous exchange, 340–51
    in Amphibia, 347–8
    in Annelida, 342
    in Arthropoda, 344
    in Aves (birds), 348–9
    in Chondrichthyes (cartilaginous fish),
        345–6
    in Cnidaria, 342
    in Mammalia, 349–51
    in Osteichthyes (bony fish), 346–7
    in Platyhelminthes, 342
    in Reptilia, 348–9
gasohol, 27, 435
gastric juice, 312, 314
gastrin, 319, 604
Gastropoda, 107
gastrula, 793
gastrulation, 793
Gaussian exclusion principle (competitive
    exclusion principle), 416
gene(s), 816–18, 835
    codominance, 848–9
    crossover frequency (value), 843
    development role, 831–2
    double crossover, 844
    enzymes related, 817–18
    epistatic (inhibiting), 851–2
    interactions, 848–53
    lethal, 851
    linkage, 840–1
    linkage groups, 844
    mapping, 843–4
    mutations, 854–5, 858
    operator, 826
    recombination frequency, 843
    regulator, 826
    see also chromosomes

gene bank, 433
gene cloning, *see* genetic engineering
gene complex, 851
gene flow, 895–6
gene pool, 891
gene reshuffling, 894
generation time, 8
generator (receptor) potential, 588
genetic code, 818–22
    breaking, 820–1
genetic control, 825–32
    Jacob–Monod hypothesis *see* Jacob–
        Monod hypothesis
    of development, 829
genetic counselling, 901–2
genetic death, 894
genetic drift (Sewall–Wright effect), 895
genetic engineering, 28–30
genetic load, 895
genetic polymorphism, 905
genetic recombination, 10, 730, 842
genetic resources for human use, 433–4
genetic terms, 835
genome, 7
genotype, 835, *836*
    frequencies, 892
geochronology, 955
geographical distribution of organisms, 871–6
geographical races, 906
geological time scale, 954–5
geotaxis, 544
geotropism, 543, 549–50, 551
germ layers, 793
German measles (rubella), 31
germination, 778–81
    epigeal, 780
    hypogeal, 780
gestation period (human), 764
gibberellic acid, 552, *553*, 555, 557, 565
gibberellins, 551–3, 560
    commercial applications, 555
    mode of action, 555
    role in plant growth/development, 556
gill, 343, 345, 346
gland, endocrine/exocrine, 603
glands, 234, *235*
glandular cells, 93
glandular epithelium, 234
Glisson's capsule, 686
globin, 691
globin proteins, 884, *885*
globulins, 148
    serum, 513
glomerular filtration rate, 715
glomerulus, 715
glottis, 349
glucagon, 604, 612
glucanases, 181
glucoamylases, 181
glucocorticoids, 604
gluconeogenesis, 689
glucosans, 137
glucose, *132*, *135*
    isomers, *134*
glucose-6-phosphate, 324
glucose isomerase, 181
glutamic acid, 144
    oxidative deamination, *340*
glutamine, 144
glyceraldehyde, 130, *132*, 462
    optical isomers, *134*
glyceraldehyde-3-phosphate, 327, 339
glycerate-3-phosphate, 265–8
glycerol, 127, 140, 339, *340*
glycine, 144
glycogen, 137

glycogenesis, 689
glycogenolysis, 689
glycolipids, 138, 141, 142, 193
glycolysis, 325–6, *327*
glycoproteins, 138, 148
glycosidic bond, 135
glycosylation, 206
glyoxylate cycle, 339
glyoxysomes, 208, 339
glypure, 620
glysophosine, 555
goitre, 610
Golgi apparatus, 189, 203–6
gonorrhoea, 31, 32
Graafian follicle, 604, 756, *757*
grafting, 729–30
Gram negative bacteria, 5, 6
Gram positive bacteria, 4, 5, 6
gramicidin, 27
Gram's stain, 4
granulocytes (polymorphonuclear
    leucocytes), 513, *514*
grasslands, 436
gravity-sensing mechanism, 550
green glands, 706, *707*
green revolution, 425–7
greenhouse effect, 381–2
grey matter, 582
griseofulvin, 26
growth, 771–6
    adventitious, 784
    allometric, 774
    arthropods, 775
    control, 776
    discontinuous, 775
    factors influencing, 776
    isometric, 774
    limited/unlimited, 775
    measurement, 771–3
    negative, 771, 772
    positive, 771, 772
    secondary, 784–5
    types of curve, 773
growth hormone (GH), 30, 604, 607
growth hormone release-inhibiting hormone
    (GHRIH; somatostatin), 607, 794
growth hormone releasing factor (GHRF),
    607, 794
growth regulators (plants), 551
    crop value increasing, 557
    growth retardants, 557
    quality improving, 555–7
    yield increasing, 555
growth substances (plants), 544–59
guanine, 463, 698, 818
guard cells, 217, 218, 489
gums, 139
gustation *see* taste
guttation, 493
gynaecium, 736
gypsy moth, biological control, 620

habitat, 361, 362
Haeckel, Ernst H., 881
haem, 170, 328, *527*, 691
haemerythrin, 343
haemocoel, 100, 507
haemocyanin, 343
haemocytoblasts, 243
haemoglobin, 147, *154*, 343, 512, 527
    breakdown, 691
    carbon monoxide combination, 529
    polypeptide chains, 884
haemophilia, 531, 847, 848
haemopoiesis, 512
haemopoietic tissue, 242–3, 512

hair follicles, 679
halophytes, 699–700
halosere, 398
halteres, 878
hand lens, 938
hand sorting, 446
haploid
    gametophyte, 60, 68
    spores, 61, 67
haptonastic movements, 544
haptotropism (thigmotropism), 543
hard pan (iron pan), 393–4
Hardy–Weinberg equation, 892–4, 924
harvest index, 374
harvestable dry matter, 374
harvesting, 420
Hatch–Slack pathway, 277
heart, mammalian, 519–21
    atrio-ventricular node, 523
    bundle of His, 524
    excitation/contraction mechanism, 523–4
    exercise effect on rate, 525
    Purkyne tissue, 524
    rate regulation, 524–5, 672
    refractory period, 524
    sino-atrial node, 523
    sounds, 521
    tetanus, 524
    see also cardiac cycle; cardiac output
heartwood, 786
heat, 673
    balance, 682–4
    body, production by liver, 693
    conduction, 676
    convection, 676
    evaporation, 676
    loss, 680–2
    radiation, 676
    sources for animals, 675, 680
heat load, 685–6
heaths, lowland, 362
hedgerows, 436
helicotrema, 609
hemicelluloses, 139, 211
Hemichordata, 121
heparin, 139, 237, 531
Hepaticae, 59, 60, 61, 83, 462
hepatocytes, 686–7
herbicides, 420
herbivores, 289, 366
hermaphroditism, 732
heroin, 575
Herpes simplex, 31
heterochromatin, 200
heterosis (hybrid vigour), 856, 900
heterosomes (sex chromosomes), 845
heterospory, 64–5, 74
heterostyly, 742
heterothallic fungi, 21
heterothermism, 674
heterotrophic nutrition, 39, 287–320
heterotrophs, 249, 251, 289
heterozygote advantage, 894
heterozygous, definition of, 835
hexosans, 137
hexose(s), 131, 462, 462–3
hexose monophosphate shunt (pentose
    phosphate shunt), 339
hibernation, 796
    diurnal, 796
Hill reaction, 262, 465
hindbrain, 582, 583
Hirudinea, 101, 102
histamine, 237, 531
histidine, 144
histiocyte (macrophage), 237

histology, 215–44
histones, 148, 200, 811
historical ecology, 362
HIV virus (human immunodeficiency virus)
    536–7, 542
holdfast, 46, 47
holocrine glands, 234
holoenzyme, 169
holophytic (photoautotrophic) organisms, 249
Holostei, 122
Holothuroidea, 118
holozoic nutrition, 289–90
homeostasis, 360, 667
homeotherm, 675
homeothermy, 683
Hominidae, 887
hominisation, 888
Homo (human), 121
homograft, 764
homology, 877–9
homospory, 65
homothallic fungi, 21
homozygous, 835
honeybees, 623, 624
    dances, 623
hormones, 544, 603–6
    growth (mammalian), 794
    see also specific hormones
horse, evolution of, 870–1, 872
horsetails (Sphenophyta), 65, 71–3, 83
horticulture, 419–20
host–parasite relationship, 415
housefly (Musca domestica)
    feeding methods, 289, 299
    life cycle, 116
human chorionic gonadotrophin (HCG), 759
human placental lactogen, 604
humidity, measurement of, 443
Humulin, 28
humus, 24, 389
hyaluronic acid, 139
hybrid, 900
hybrid barrier, 908
hybrid sterility, 856
hybrid vigour (heterosis), 856, 900
Hydra, 295
hydranth, 91
hydrocarbons, 429
hydrochloric acid, 313, 314
hydrogen bond, 127, 146
hydrogen carriers, 329–40
hydrogen pump, 466
hydrolase, 180
hydrological cycle, 379, 396
hydrophobic molecules, 127
hydrophytes, 699
hydroponics, 427
hydrosere, 398
hydrotheca, 88, 89
hydrotropism, 543
hydroxyl group, 129
5-hydroxytryptamine (serotonin), 531, 575
Hydrozoa, 90
hyperglycaemia, 672
hyperparathyroidism, 608
hyperplasia (cell division), 771, 801, 802
hypertension, 673
hyperthyroidism, 610
hypertrophy (cell expansion), 771
    compensatory, 794
hyperventilation, 917
hypoglycaemia, 672
hyponasty, 544
hypothalamo-hypophysial portal system, 607
hypothalamus, 319, 320, 586, 606–7
    heat gain centre, 680, 683

heat loss centre, 680, 683
    hormone production, 604, 607
hypothyroidism, 610
hypoxia (anoxia), 356
H–Y antigen, 764

igneous rocks, 391
ileum, 313
immigration, 406
immunisation (vaccination), 539
immunity, 533–9
    acquired active, 539
    acquired passive, 538
    cell-mediated response, 534, 535
    humoral immune response, 534, 535
    natural active, 538
    natural passive, 538, 763
    secondary response, 535
immunofluorescence microscopy, 209
immunogen (antigen), 533–4
immunoglobulins, 533, 538
immunological memory, 538
immunosuppression, 541
implantation (human), 761–2
imprinting, 625
inbreeding, 899–900
individual-characteristic behaviour, 615
indoleacetic acid (IAA), 547, 548
induced fit hypothesis, 169, 170
induction, 777
industrial melanism, 902
infant mortality, 406
infection control, 673
influenza, 15, 31
infundibulum, 607
ingestion, 289
inheritance
    blood group, 849
    chromosomal basis, 838
    dihybrid, 836
    monohybrid, 834
    polygenic, 853
    sex-limited, 847
inhibitory reflexes, 647–8
initials, 781
innate releasing mechanisms, 617
insect(s), 108–113
    eusocial, 624
    hormonal control of moulting, 789–91
    long-day/short-day response, 795
    metamorphosis, complete/incomplete,
        790–1
    walking, 653
insectivorous (carnivorous) plants, 286
insight learning, 625
inspiration, 351–2
inspiratory centre, 352
inspiratory volume, 353
inspired air, percentage composition of
    gases, 353
inflorescence, 735
inflammation, 531–2
instincts, 615
insulin, 28–9, 147, 150, 604, 606, 612
integrated control of pests, 425
intelligence, 585
intensity discrimination, 601
intercellular fluid, 518, 519
intercostal muscles, 349, 351
interferon, 30, 541
intermediate filaments, 211
interoceptor, 588
interphase 799, 803, 806
interspecific competition, 414, 415
interstitial cell stimulating hormone (ICSH;
    luteinising hormone), 604, 607, 754, 758

intervertebral discs, 631
intestinal juice (succus entericus), 313, 314
intestine
    active transport in, 198
      large, 316–17
      small, *see* small intestine
intracellular fluid, 698
intracellular transport, 209
intraspecific interactions, 414
intraspecific competition, 619
intrinsic gastric factor, 313
inulin, 137
involuntary muscle, 243, *244*
iodine, 284, 286
ion, 926
ionic binding, 926–7
ionic bond, 146
ionic compounds, 927
ionic equations, 927
ionic formulae, 927
iris, 595
iron, 284, 285, 285–6
irritability (sensitivity), 567
islets of Langerhans, 204, 604, 612
isogamete, 733
isogamy, 22, 42, 735
isograft, 540
isolating mechanisms, 907
isoleucine, 144
isomerase, 180
isomerism, 132–5
    optical, 132, 133, 134
    stereo, 132
    structural, 132
isotope, 930

Jacob–Monod hypothesis, 826–9
jaundice, 691
joints, 636–7
joule, 364, 365
J-shaped growth curves, 407, 408, 409
juvenile hormone (neotonin), 789, 790
juxtaglomerular complex, 722

Kaibab Plateau deer, 415
kangaroo rat (*Dipodomys*), 701
keratin, 150, 233, 679
keto group, 129
ketohexoses, 463
ketone, 129
ketoses, 130–2, *132*
key factor analysis, 412
kick sampling, 446
kidney, 708
    active transport in, 198
    birds, 712
    mammals, 712
      blood supply, 712
      function, 714–18
      glomerular filtrate, 716–17
      nephron, 712–13, 715–18
      structure, 712
    mesonephric, 708
    metanephric, 708
    renin secretion, 604
kinesis, 544, 614
kinetic energy, *933*
kinetic response, 614–15
kinetin, 557, 558, 560
kinetochore, 797
kinin, 557
kite diagram, 947
kite net, 446
Klinefelter's syndrome, 856
klinostat, 549
klinotaxic responses, 614

Kranz anatomy, 277
Krebs cycle, 327–8
K-species (strategies), 410, 411
Kupffer cells, 688
kymograph, 640

labia majora/minora (human), 755
labium, 108, 297
labour, 764–7
labrum, 108, 297
lactase, 181, 314
lactate fermentation, 330
lactate, 643
lactation (human), 767–8
lactifers, 213
lactogenesis, 768
lactose, 135, 831
lacuna(e), 239
laevo-rotatory substances, 133
lakes, 382–5
Lamarck, Jean-Baptiste, 865, 866
lamellae, 345
land restoration, 428
language, 889
large intestine, 316–17
larva, 113, 116, 117, 118, 121
larval stages, 788–9
larynx, 349
latent heat of evaporation, 482
lateral buds, 782–3
latex, 213
laws of conservation of energy, 249, 364,
    932
leaching, 390
    bacterial, 28
leaf
    chlorotic, 270
    movement of water through *see* water
    primordia, 782–3
    scar, 82
    structure, 251–3
leaf area index, 374
leaf mosaic, 30
learning, 578, 626
    associative, 625
    insight, 625
    latent (exploratory), 625
    trial-and-error (operant conditioning),
      625
lens (eye), 595
lenticel, 482, 787
leprosy, 31
lethal dose, 50 (LD_{50}), 421
leucine, 144
leucocytes (white blood cells), 513–14
leucoplasts, 214
Leydig cells, 752, 754
lichens, 19–21
life cycles, 733–4
ligaments, 916
ligase, 180
light, 395
    compensation point, 274
    intensity, 912
    measurement, 444
    perception by plant, 565
    quality, 564–5
    quantity, 564–5
    reactions, in photosynthesis, 260–2, 267
    responses to, 563–5
    transmission by plant, 565
light trap, 446
lignification, 212
lignin, 120
limbs, mammalian, 635–6
Lincoln index, 451

line transect, *448*, 449
Linnaeus, Carl, 865, 878, 950
lipase, 181, 314, 315
lipid(s), 138–42, 918–19
    bilayer, 193
    energy store, 140
    functions, 142
    synthesis, 266
    tests, 163
lipidoplasts, 214
lipoproteins, 141, 142, 148
litter, 389
liver, mammalian, 686–93
    blood supply, 687
    functions, 688–93
      bile production, 691–2
      blood storage, 691
      carbohydrate metabolism, 688–9
      cholesterol production, 691
      detoxification, 692
      erythrocyte formation, 691
      excretion, 697
      fat metabolism, 691
      haemoglobin breakdown, 691
      heat production, 693
      hormone production/breakdown, 692
      mineral storage, 691
      plasma protein production, 690–1
      protein metabolism, 689–90
      vitamin storage, 691
    lymph from, 688
    position, 686
    structure, 686–8
liverworts, 60, 61, *83*, 462
lizards, body temperature regulation, 677
lobe-finned fish (Crossopterygii), 119, *122*
lobster appendages, *109*
lock and key hypothesis, 168–9
locomotion, 627, 913
    amoeboid, 648
    crayfish (*Astacus fluviatilis*), 653
    dog, 665–6
    dogfish, 656–7
    earthworm (*Lumbricus terrestris*), 651–2
    euglenoid, *650*, 651
    fish, 655–8
    frog, 658
    herring, 657–8
    insects, 653–4
    Paramecium 651
    ragworm (*Nereis*), 652–3
locus, 835
long-day plants, 564
loops of Henlé, 712–14, 719–20
Lorenz, Konrad, 615, 617
Lumbricus terrestris (common earthworm),
    102, 104–6, 298, 651–2
    agricultural importance, 106
lung, 349–51
    excretion by, 697
    volumes/capacities, 353
lung fish (Dipnoi), 883
luteinising hormone (LH; interstitial cell
    stimulating hormone), 604, 607, 754, *758*
luteinising hormone releasing hormone
    (LHRH), 607
luteolysin (prostaglandin F2α), 759
luteotrophin (LTH; prolactin), 604, 607, 756,
    885
lyase, 180
Lycopodophyta (club mosses), 65, 67–71, *83*
lymph, 518, *519*
lymph nodes, 518, *519*, *520*
lymphatic system, 518, *519*, *520*
lymphoblasts, 243
lymphocytes, 514, 518

lymphoid tissue, 243
lymphokines, 534
lysergic acid diethylamide (LSD), 575
lysine, 144
lysogenic bacteria, 17
lysosomes, 189, 206–8
lysozyme, 6, 147, *150*, 311, 531

macroglia, 247
macromolecules, 129
macronutrients, 284
macrophage (histiocyte), 237, 531
macrophagous feeders, 290, 295–300
maculae, 601
magnesium, 285
magnetotaxis, 544
maize, 426
malaria eradication, 377
malate shunt, 277
male fern (*Dryopteris filix-mas*), 65, *66*, *70*
malnutrition, 300
Malpighian layer, 678
Malpighian tubules, 112, 705
maltase, 314
maltose, 135, 314
mammal trap, 446, *447*
Mammalia (mammals), 121, *122*
    diving, 357
    nutrition, 300–4
mammalian growth hormones, 794
mammary glands (breasts), 767–8
mandible, 108, 297
manganese, 284, 285
mannan, 139
mannose, *132*
marker gene, 28
marram grass (*Ammophila*), 486, *487*
marsupials, adaptive radiation, 870
mass flow, 473
    systems, 473
mast cells, 237
materials, deterioration, 30
mating, 620–1
maximum sustainable yield, 376
measles, 31
mechanoreceptor, 588, 592–3
medulla oblongata, 587
medusa, 88, *89*, 90, 91–2
megakaryocytes, 243, 514
megasporangium, 65, 68, 72, 76
megaspore, 64, 65, 71, 72, 74, 76
meiosis (reduction division), 44, 45, 71, 72,
    730, 797, 802–11
    genetic variation, 811
    mitosis compared, 811, *812*
    sexual reproduction, 811
Meissner's corpuscle, 593
Meissner's plexus, 307
melatonin, 608
membrane(s)
    alcohol effect, 480
    heat effect, 480
membrane potential, 567
memory, 624–6
    long-term, 625
    short-term, 625
memory cells, lymphatic, 535
Mendel, Gregor, 833–8, *839*
    first law (principle of segregation), 835,
        839
    second law (principle of independent
        assortment), 837, *840*
meninges, 580, *581*
menstrual cycle, 756
mercury vapour lamp, *447*
meristem, 781

apical, 228, 781, *782*
    lateral, 784
merocrine glands, 234
mescaline, 575
mesencephalon, 583, 586
mesenchyme cells, 237
mesenteries, 99, 307
mesoderm, 92, 762, *793*
mesogloea, 88
mesophyll, *187*, 216, 219, 252
mesophytes, 486, 700
mesosomes, 7, 8
messenger RNA (mRNA), 160, 202, 203,
    820, 822
metabolic pathways, 167, 179
    control, 827, *828*
metabolic rate measurement, 354
metabolism, 323
metacercaria, 98
metachronal rhythm, 650
metagenesis, 92, 733
metal(s), extraction from minerals/solutions,
    28
metameric segmentation, 102, 104
metamorphosis, 104, 113–17, 788–92
    amphibia, 791–2
    frog, 792
    insects, complete/incomplete, 790–1
metaphase, *799*, *805*, *807*
metaphloem, 230
metaxylem, 228
metencephalon, 583, 586
metenkephalin, 576
methane, 24, 124
methanogens, 27
methionine, 144
microbodies (peroxisomes), 208
microclimates, 397
microglia, 247
micronutrients, 284
micro-organisms
    benefits, 24
    harmful, 30–3
    mutualism involved, 292
    mutualistic, 25–6
    soil fertility effects, 24
    uses, 24
    see also bacteria; viruses
microphagous feeders, 289, 290, 292–300
microscope, 938–41
    electron *see* electron microscope
microfilaments, 210
microtubules, 208–10
microvilli, 211
midbrain, 582, 583
middle lamella, 191
mildews, 18, 33, 34
milk, 304
    bacterial content, 33–5
milk (human), 768
milk ejection reflex, 768
Miller, Stanley, 862, *863*
Millon's test, 165
mineral(s)
    cycles, *see* biogeochemical cycles
    deficiency diseases, 284
    element deficiencies, 284–6
    plant/animal nutrition, 284
    salts, 301
mineralocorticoids, 604
minimal medium, 817
miracidium, 95
mistletoe, 292
mitochondria, 189, 211, 255, 334–7
    assembly, 336
    evolution, 336–7

mitosis, 44, 45, 71, 72, 205, 797, 798–802
    animal cells, 801–2
    meiosis compared, 811, *812*
    plant cells, 801–2
molar teeth, 308–9, 320, 321
Mollusca, 106, 107
molybdenum, 284, 286
monoamine oxidase inhibitors, 575
monoblasts, 243
monoclimax hypothesis, 399
monocotyledons, 78, 79, *80*
monocytes, 514
monoecious plants, 732
monohybrid cross, 835
monohybrid inheritance, 834, *836*
monomers, 129
mononuclear leucocytes (agranulocytes)
    513–14
monosaccharides, 127, 129, 130–5, *136*
    derivatives, 131
    functions, 131
morph, 905
morphine, 575
morphogenesis, 771, 776, 777
mortality (death rate), 405, 406
morula, 761
mosquito (*Anopheles* sp.), 299–300
mosses, 60, 61–4, *83*
    adaptation to land, 63–4, 462
motivation, 615
motor end-plate, 644–5
motor neurone, 244, 245
motor unit, 644
motorium, 651
moulds, 33, 34
moulting hormone (ecdysone), 789–90
mouthparts, of insects, 108, 293, 297
mucilages, 139
mucin, 206, 311
Mucor, 18, 19, 20, 21, 290
mucus, 206
mull, 394
multiple alleles, 859
multiple-enzyme complex, 179
mumps, virus, 15, 31
Münch's hypothesis, 504–5
murein, 6, 139
Musca domestica (housefly), *116*, 298, *299*
muscarine, 575
muscle, 637–46
    cardiac, 637
    skeletal *see* skeletal muscle
    smooth, 646
muscle spindle, 593, 646–7, 916–17
muscle tissue, 243–4, *244*
    active transport in, 198
muscle tone, 647
muscularis externa, 306–7
mushrooms, *see Agaricus*, 25
mutation, 855–8
    gene, 854, 858
mutualism, 13, 290, 291
    fungal, 19
    micro-organisms involving, 292
mycelium, 17, 20
mycobacteria, 5
mycology, 4, 17
mycoplasma (pleuro-pneumonia-like
    organisms), 5
mycoprotein, 27
mycorrhizas, 286–7
myelencephalon, 583, 586–7
myelin, 570–1
myelin sheath, 245
myelocytes, 243
myeloid tissue, 243

myofibril, 638
myoglobin, 147, *152*, 529, 642, 884, *885*
myogram, 640
myosin, 639, 642
myotomes, 655
myxoedema, 610

NAD (nicotinamide adenine dinucleotide), 157, 170, *171*, 329–30
NAD dehydrogenase, 330
NADP (nicotinamide adenine dinucleotide phosphate), 157, *171*, 329–30
nasty, 544
natality (birth rate), 405
natural selection, 902–3
negative feedback inhibition (end-product inhibition), 179
nematoblast, 88, 90
Nematoda, 100
neo-Darwinism, 865, 868, 891
neoteny, 119, 792
neotonin (juvenile hormone), 789, 790
nephridium, 703
nephron, 712–14
Nereis diversicolor, 102, *102*–4, 652–3
    trochophore larva, 104
nerve cells, 567
    active transport in, 198
nerve cord, 576, 587
nerve impulse, 567–71
    action potential, 569–71
    depolarisation, 569
    frequency code, 571
    ionic movements, 568
    positive feedback, 569
    repolarisation of membrane, 569
    resting potential, 567–8
    speed of conduction, 570
    temperature effect on rate, 571
nerves, 245–7
    cranial, 576, 577
    spinal, 576
    vagus, 576
nervous system, 567
    autonomic, 579–80
    central, 580–7
    parasympathetic, 579–80, 581
    peripheral, 576–9
    phylogenetic development, 587
    sympathetic, 579–80, 581
    vertebrate, 576–87
net assimilation rate (unit leaf rate), 374
neurilemma, 245
neuroendocrine reflex, 608
neuroendocrine response, 608
neuroglia, 247
neurohaemal organ, 607
neuromuscular junction, 574–6
    chemical influences on, 575–6
neurones, 244, 245, 567
    adrenergic, 572
    afferent (sensory), 576
    cholinergic, 572
    efferent (motor), 576
    excitatory motor, 579, 585
    inhibitory motor, 579, 585
neurophysins, 607
neurosecretory cells, 607
Neurospora crassa 817–18
neurotransmitter substances, 572
neutron, 925
neutrophils, 513, *514*
niacin (nicotinic acid; vitamin B₃), 305
nicotine, 575
nicotinic acid (niacin), 305
nitrate(s), 385

nitrate fertilisers, 281–2
nitrification, 282–3
nitrogen, 285
    cycle, 24, 281–2
    fixation, 281–2
nodes of Ranvier, 245, 571
non-random breeding, 894–5
non-sulphur bacteria, 280, 289
non-swimming male gametes, 75
noradrenaline (norepinephrine), 572, 575, 611–12
notochord, 119
nuclear envelope, 4, 198–200
nuclease, 314, 315
nucleic acids, 154–60, 698
nucleocapsid, 15
nucleolar organiser, 200
nucleolus, 200
nucleoprotein, 148
nucleoside, 157, 315
nucleosomes, 811
nucleotidase, 314
nucleotides, 154, 156, 155–7
nucleus, 4, 186–9, 198–200, 829–30
nurse cell, 753
nutrients
    cycles (biogeochemical cycles), 24, 364, 377–80
    recommended daily intake, 301
nutrition, 1, 13, 249–304
nyctinasty (sleep movement), 544

Obelia, 88–92
obligate symbiont, 291
oceanic thermocline, 381, *383*
octane, *126*
oedema, 532
oesophagus, 311–12, 317
oestradiol, *143*, 604, 756
oestrogen, 604, 756, *758*
    human, function during pregnancy, 765
oestrone, *143*
Oligochaeta, 101, *102*, 104–6
oligodendrocytes, 247
ommatidia, 591, 599
omnivores, 289, 367
oocyte, 755
oogamy, 42, 735
oogenesis, 755, *756*
oogonium, 42
oomycetes, 49–51
oosphere, 42
operant conditioning (trial-and-error learning), 625
operator gene, 826
operon, 826, *827*, 829
Operophthera brumata (winter moth), 411, 412–14
Ophiuroidea, 118
opsonins, 531
optic chiasma, 599
optic nerve, 596
optical isomerism, 132–5
organ, 85
organ of Corti, 601
organ system, 85
organisers, 777, 830–1
organisms
    interactions between, within community, 404
    interactions with abiotic environment, 401–4
    methods of collection, 445–9
organophosphates, 422
organophosphorous weedkillers/insecticides, 575

organs of Ruffini, 593
origin of life theories, 859–63
    biochemical evolution, 862–3
    cosmozoan theory, 862
    special creation, 859–60
    spontaneous generation, 860
    steady-state theory, 861–2
ornithine cycle, 690, 697
orthokinesis, 615
osmoconformer, 699
osmoregulation, 197, 695, 698, 701
    mechanical, 699
    mechanisms, 699
    plants, 699–700
osmoregulator, 699
osmosis, 195, 474–7, 932
    movement of water between cells, 477
    movement of water between solutions and cells, 477
    plant cells, 475, *476*
ossicles of ear, 878
ossification, 630
Osteichthyes, 121, *122*
osteoblasts, 240, 241, 630
osteoclasts, 208, 241, 630
osteocytes, 241
ostia, 111
otoconium, 601, *602*
outbreeding, 900–1
ova (human) development (oogenesis), 755, *756*
ovarian cycle, 756–8
ovary, 94, 96
    human, 755, *757*
organ, 85
overcrowding, 412–14
overnutrition, 300
overfishing, 418–19
ovule, 74
ovule development, 740
oxidation, 929
oxidation ponds, 48
oxidative deamination, 340
oxidative decarboxylation, 328
oxidative phosphorylation, 260, 326, 328–9
oxidoreductase, 180
oxygen
    algae source, 48
    carriage by blood, 527–8
    cycle, 284
    haemoglobin binding to, 528
oxygen dissociation curve, 527, *528*
oxyhaemoglobin, 512, 527, 530
oxyntic (parietal) cells, 313
oxytocin, 604, 607, *765*
ozone layer, 381
    depletion, 429

Pacinian corpuscle, 588, *589*, 593
palaentology *see* fossils
palisade cells, 219, 252–3
pancreas, 315, *316*, 612
    acinar cells, *204*
    hormone secretion, 612
pancreatic juice, 314, 315
pancreatic lipase, optimum pH, 174
pancreozymin (cholecystokinin), 319, 604, 692
pantothenic acid (vitamin B₅), 305
paper industry, 181
parallel flow system, in gills, 345, 346
Paramecium, 54–8, 293–4, 651
parasites, 13, 292–3, 366
    facultative, 13, 292
    obligate, 13, 292
    specialisations, 293

parasitic fungi, 18–19
parasitism, 291–2
parathormone, 604, 608
parathyroid glands, 608
parenchyma, 215–20, 228, 230
Parkinson's disease, 586
parthenocarpy, 562
parthenogenesis, 732
Pasteur, Louis, 860–1
pathogens, 13, 30
pecking order (social hierarchies), 622–3
pectin(s) (pectic substances), 139, 211
pectinases, 181
pectoral girdle, 634
pedology, 387
pellagra, 305
Pellia, 60, 61
pelvic girdle, 635
Pelycopoda (Bivalvia), 107
penicillin, 26
penicillinase, 12
Penicillium, 18, 19, 23, 23–4, 26
penis (human), 752, 759
pentadactyl limb, 877
pentosans, 137
pentose(s), 131, 462, 462–3
pentose-phosphate shunt (hexose-
    monophosphate shunt), 339
peppered moth (*Biston betularia*), 902
pepsin(ogen), 313, 314
    optimum pH, 174
peptide bond, 145
perennating organs, 727–9
perennials, 80
pericarp, 878
perichondrium, 239
pericycle, 216, 220
perilymph, 600
periodontal disease, 311
periosteum, 240, 630
peristalsis, 315–16, 646
peritoneum, 99
peroxisomes (microbodies), 208
personality, 585
pesticides, 376–7, 420–5
    ecosystem effects, *424*
    lethal dose, 421
    residues, 422
pH, 928–9
Phaeophyta (brown algae), 41, 45–7
phage, *see* bacteriophage
phagocytes, 198
phagocytosis, 531, *533*
pharynx, 349
phellem, 787
phelloderm, 787
phellogen, 787
phenotype, 835
    recombinants, 840
phenoxyacetic acids, 551, 552
phenylalanine, 144, 817
phenylketonuria, 817
pheromones, 425, 594–5, 620
pH
    and amino acids, 145, 154
    in enzyme reactions, 174–6
    of soil, 393, 441
phloem, 216, 228–30, 497
    mineral salts in, 497
    organic solutes translocation, 497–9, 500–1
    sieve plates, 502, 506
    sieve tubes, *500*, 501–2
        loading/unloading, 505
    transcellular strands, 506
    transfer cells, 505
    translocation in, 504–6

phloem protein (P-protein), 502, 506
phosphate compounds, 324
phosphate levels in lakes, Norfolk Broads, 384
    removal at sewage works, 384
phosphocreatine, 642
phosphofructokinase, 178
phospholipids, 141, *142*, 193
phosphophenylpyruvate, 324
phosphoprotein, 148
phosphorescence, 257
phosphoric acid, 155
phosphorus, 285
    cycle, *283*, 284
photoautographs, *250*, 251
photoautotrophic (holophytic) organisms, 249
photoheterotrophs, 251, 289
photomorphogenesis, 562, 564
photonasty, 544
photoperiod, 617
photoperiodism, 563–4, 566
photophosphorylation, 260
    cyclic, 261–2
    non-cyclic, 261
photoreception, 597–8
photoreceptor, 562–3, 588
photorespiration, 275–6, 279–80
photosynthesis, 250–75
    aerobic respiration compared, 468
    dark reactions, 264, 267
    factors affecting, 268–70
    light reactions, 260–2, 267
    pea plant, 499–500
    prokaryotes/eukaryotes compared, 280
photosynthetic pigments, 255–9
photosystems, 259
phototaxis, 544
phototrophs, 249
phototropism, 543, 545–8
phyllotaxis, 782
phylogeny, human, 886–8
phytochrome, 563
    mode of action, 565
    plant responses controlled by, 564
Phytophthora infestans, 49–51
phytoplankton, 382, 383
pia mater, 580, *581*
Pieris (white butterflies), *117*, 298–9, 422
pigments, 257–9
pili (fimbriae), 6
pin moulds, 21
pineal gland (epiphysis), 608
pitch discrimination, 601
pitfall trap, 446, *447*
pituitary dwarfism, 30
pituitary gland, 607–8
    anterior (adenohypophysis), 604, 607
    posterior (neurohypophysis), 604, 607
placenta (human), 763–4
    hormone secretion, 604, 764
plagioclimax, 400
plague, 31
Planaria lugubris, 92–5, *93*, *94*
plankton, 48
plankton net, 446
plant tissues, 215–30
plants, 59–83
    adaptation to climatic extremes, 486–7, 674, 700
    adaptation to dry conditions, 397
    animals compared, 39
    bolting, 565
    breeding, 876–7
    comparison of main groups, *83*
    day-length sensitivity, 564
    fertilisation independent of water, 75

flowering, movement of water through 481–2
flowering, *see* angiosperms
fossil, 64
gametophyte/sporophyte generations, *74*
gravity-sensing mechanism, 550
growth of primary body, 781–2
light-involved processes, 396
movements, 543–4
    nasties, 544
    pulvinus, 544
    taxes, 543, 544
    tropisms, 543
photosynthetic slump, 674
resources, sustainable use, 436
shoot growth, 560
support in, 666
tissues, *see* plant tissues
transition from aquatic to terrestrial environment, 59
wilting, 674
plasma, 511–12, 513, 718
plasma cells, 237, 535
plasma clearance, 715
plasmids, 12, 28
plasmolysis, 476–7
    incipient, 476, 478
plastids, 214
platelets, 514
Platyhelminthes, 92–8, 702–3, *704*
pleura, 351
pleural cavity, 351
pleuro-pneumonia-like organisms (mycoplasmas), 5
ploughing, 419
pneumococci (*Diplococcus pneumoniae*), 8
podocytes, 715
podzols, 392–4
poikilothermic animals, 463
poikilotherms, 675
point quadrat (pin frame), 450
polar bodies, 755
polarimeter, 133
poliomyelitis (polio), 31
pollarding, 435
pollen analysis, British, 399
pollen grains, 738–9, *740*
    fertilisation, 745
pollen tube growth, 562, 745
pollination, 75, 739–45
    cross-, 740, 740–2
    insect, 743–5
    self-, 740
    self-incompatibility (self-sterility), 742
    wind, 742–3, 745
pollution, 379, 381–2, 429–32, 433
    atmospheric, 429
    water, 431–2
Polychaeta, 101, *102*, 102–4
polychlorinated biphenyls (PCBs), 422
polyclimax, 399
polyembryony, 733
polymorphism, 92, 623, 898, 903
    balanced, 905–6
    transient, 905
polymorphonuclear leucocytes (granulocytes), 513, *514*
polynucleotides, 154, 157
polyp, hydroid, 88, *89*, 90
polypeptide, 145, 146, *149*
polyploidy (euploidy), 856–7, 901
polysaccharides, 130, 136–8
    related compounds, 138
polysome, 824
polytypic species, 906
polyuridylic acid, 820

Pongidae, 887
pons, 586
pooter, 446, *449*
population, 404
    dynamics, 405
    ecology, 404–19
    factors affecting size, 411–19
    growth curves, 407–10
    size estimation, 450–2
    strategies, 410–11
    survivorship curves, 406–7
population genetics, 891
Porifera (sponges), 85
porphyrin ring, 170
porphyropsin, 791
post-synaptic membrane, 572
potassium, 285
potato blight, 34, 49, 50–1
potential energy, 933
potometer, 484
P-protein (phloem protein), 502, 506
precapillary sphincter, 516
predator(s), 366
predator–prey relationships, 414–15
prefrontal lobes, 585
prefrontal lobotomy, 586
pregnancy test, 759
pre-reproductive mortality, 406
presence–absence graph, 947
pressure potential, 475, 477
presynaptic membrane, 572
prickly pear (*Opuntia*), 424
primary structure, protein, 147
primates, 886
principle of independent assortment, 837,
    840
Proalcool programme, 27
procambium, 781, 782, 783
producers, 365
production ecology, 373–6
productivity
    primary, 373
    secondary, 374–6
proenzyme (zymogen), 206
progesterone, *143*, 604, 756, *758*
    human, function during pregnancy, 765
proinsulin, 30
prokaryotes, 3–4, 5, 255
prolactin (luteotrophin; LTH), 604, 607, 756,
    885
prolactin inhibiting factor, 607
prolactin releasing factor (PRF), 607
proline, 144
promoter gene, 829
pronephros, 708
prophage (provirus), 17
prophase, *799, 803*, 806
proplastids, 214, 253
proprioceptor, 588, 670
profile transect, 449
prostaglandin F2α (luteolysin), 759
protandry, 740, 741
proteases, 181
protein(s), 146–54, 155, 325
    animal, 375
    dietary, 300–1
    respiratory substrate, 339, 340
    synthesis, 266–8
protein engineering, 182
protein synthesis, 820, 822, 823, *826, 827*
protein-synthesising machinery, 154–5
proteoplasts, 214
prothallus, 64
prothoracic gland, 789
prothoracicotrophic hormone (PTTH), 790
prothrombin, 513

Protoctista (protoctists), 39, 40
protogny, 742
proton, 925
proton-motive force, 339
protoplasm, 192
protostome, 882
protozoa, 52, 53, 702
protozoans, 702
Pruteen, 27, 331, 332
pseudocoelom, 99
pseudopodia, *53*, 54, 648
pseudopodia, 648
pseudopodial feeding, 292–3
pseudostratified epithelium, 232, *233*
Psilopsida, 64
pulmonary ventilation, 354
pulvinus, 544
punctuated equilibria, 870
Punnett square, 837
pupil, 595, 596
Purkyne tissue, 524
pyramidal (corticospinal) tract, 585
pyranose ring, 134
pyrenoid, 43, 45
pyridoxine (vitamin B_6), 305
pyrogen, 684
pyruvate, 267, 278, 326, 327, 643
pyruvic acid, 330, 331

quadrat, 449–50
quaternary structure, protein, 152–4

races
    ecological (ecotypes), 898, 906
    geographical, 906
rachis, 660
radiocarbon dating, 955
radioimmunoassay, 603
radula, 297
ray initials, 784
rays, 784, 785, 786, 787, 788
reaction centre, 259
receptor (generator) potential, 588
recessive character, 835
reclamation from industrial/urban dereliction,
    435
recombinant DNA, 10
recycling, 428, 434
red blood cells *see* erythrocytes
    membrane, *193*
    sodium–potassium pump, *197*
red grouse, territorial size, 619
redia, 96
redox reactions, 328
reduction, 929
reduction division *see* meiosis
refractory period, 524, 570
    absolute, 570
    relative, 570, 640
regeneration, tissue, 794
regulator gene, 826
Reissner's membrane, 601
relative growth rate, 374
releaser, 616
renal threshold, 612
rendzinas, 394–5
renin, 181, 314, 604, 611, 722
reproduction, 725–70
    asexual, 725–30
        sexual reproduction compared, 733
    in algae, 41–5
    in animals, 53, 56, 58, 89–90, 95, 104,
        107
    in bacteria, 8
    in fungi, 23–6
    in plants, 60–74, 76–7, 79

    sexual, 730–4
        plants, 734–5; *see also* flower; pollen;
            pollination
        vertebrates, 769–70
reproductive system, human female, 755–9
reproductive system, human male, 725–5
reptiles, 711
Reptilia, 121, *122*
reserpine, 575
residual air, 353
resilin, 107
resistance factors (R plasmids/R factors), 12
resource partitioning, 404
respiration, 1, 324
    activity measurement, 353–4
    aerobic, 327–8, 330, 331
    anaerobic, 326, 330–1
    cell, 325
    in germinating seed, 780
    major metabolic pathways, *341*
respiratory centres, 670
respiratory chain, 326, 328–9
respiratory distress syndrome, 350
respiratory gases, control, in blood, 670–1
respiratory pigments, 342, 343
respiratory quotient (RQ), 354–5, 780
respiratory rate, 354
respiratory structures, special, 342
respiratory surface types, *343*
reflex(es), 576
    conditioned, 578
    inhibitory, 647–8
    monosynaptic, 577
    polysynaptic spinal/brain, 577–8
    simple (vertebrates), 615
    spinal, 577, *578*, 615
    stretch, 647
    visceral, 579
reflex arc, *577, 578*
resting potential, 567
restriction endonucleases, 28
reticular activating system, 585
reticular formation, 585
reticular fibres, 237
reticulo-endothelial system, 237, 688
reticulospinal tract, 585
retina, 595, 596–7
retinene (retinol), 597
rhabdites, 93
rhabdome, 599
rhabdoviruses, 15
rheotaxis, 544
rhesus factor, 540
Rhiphidistia, *122*
rhizome, 728
Rhizopoda, 51, 53, 53–4
Rhizopus stolonifer (bread mould), 19, *20,*
    21–3
rhodopsin (visual purple), 597–8, 791
rib, 349
riboflavin (vitamin B_2), 170
ribonuclease, 147, *169*
ribonucleic acid *see* RNA
ribose, *132, 135*
ribosomes, 189, 202–3
ribulose, *132*
ribulose bisphosphate, 265
ribulose bisphosphate carboxylase, 265
rickettsias, *5*
ring species, 908
ring structures, 134–5
rings of Balbiani (chromosome puffs), 831,
    832
ringworm, 19, 34
RNA (ribonucleic acid), 160, 811, 822
    bases, 821

RNA—cont.
  messenger (mRNA), 160, 202, 203, 820, 822
  ribosomal (rRNA), 202, 822
  transfer (tRNA), 160, 202, 820, 822–3
  translation, 824–5
robin, aggressiveness, 618
rods, 597
root cap, 783
root nodules, 282, 287
roots
  adventitious, 784
  lateral, 783
  mineral salts uptake, transport, translocation, 495–7
  primary growth, 783
  secondary growth, 787–8
  water uptake, 493
rough endoplasmic reticulum (RER), 186, 187, 189, 200–2
roughage, 304
royal jelly, 623
r-species (strategies), 410, 411
rubella (German measles), 31
rumen, 321
runner, 728
rusts, 19, 33, 34

saccharides, *see* carbohydrates
salinity, 396
saliva, 314
salivary amylase, 170, *172*, 311, 314
  optimum pH, 174
salivary glands, 311
Salmonella food poisoning, 30, 33
salt, 928
salt gland, 711, 712
sampling methods, 449–52
saprotrophs (saprophytes), 12–13, 18, 290
sapwood, 493, 786
sarcolemma, 574, 638
sarcomere, 639
sarcoplasmic reticulum, 638
scent post, 619
schizocoelom, *99*
schizogony, 725
Schwann cells, 245, 247
scientific method, 936–7
sclera, 595
sclereids, *223*, 225, 230
sclerenchyma, *216*, 220–5
scleroproteins, 148
scotopsin, 597
scour, 284
scraping mouthparts, 297
scurvy, 305
Scyliorhinus (dogfish), 297–8
Scyphozoa, 90
seal, 357, 422
seaweed fertiliser, 48
sebaceous gland, 679
sebum, 679
secondary structure, protein, 150–1
secretin, 319, 604
secretion, 695, 701
seed-bearing plants, 73–82
seeds, 74–5, 745–7, *748*
  advantages/disadvantages, 746–7
  dispersal, 747, 748–51
  dormancy, 778
  embryo growth, 780–1
  germination, 778–80
  scarification, 778
  stratification, 778
seismonasty, 544
seizing/swallowing mouthparts, 297–8

Selaginella, 67–70, *71*, *72*
selection, 896–9
  artificial, 899, 901–2
  directional, 897–8
  disruptive, 898
  intensity of selection pressure, 898
  natural, 902–3
  stabilising, 897
selective reabsorption, 701
semen, 759, 760
semicircular canals, 602
seminiferous tubules, 752
senescence (ageing), 406
sensitised fluorescence, 259
sensitivity (irritability), 567, 590
sensory neurone, 244, 245
sensory receptors, 567, 588
  feedback control, 591
  lateral inhibition, 591
  phasic, 590
  properties, 590–2
  spontaneous activity, 591
  tonic, 590
seral communities, 398
sere, 398
serine, 144
serotonin (5-hydroxytryptamine), 531, 575
Sertoli cells, 753, 754
serum, 531
setose feeding, 294
sewage disposal, 24, 48, 434
Sewall–Wright effect (genetic drift), 895
sex determination, 845–6
sex hormones
  female, 755, 756, 758, 764, 765, 768
  male, 754, 755
sex linkage, 847
sexual recombination, 894
sexual reproduction, *see* reproduction
sexual reproduction, human, 752–69
Sharpey–Schafer fibres, 240
short-day plants, 564
shuttle systems, 332–3
SI units, 953–4
sickle cell anaemia, 858, 894
sieve plate, 501
sieve tubes, 228–30, 501, 502, 504, 506
sign stimuli, 616
  motivational, 616
  releasing (releasers), 616
  terminating, 616
silicon, 286
silk fibroin, 150
single cell protein (SCP), 27
sino-atrial node, 523
sinus venosus, *509*
sinuses, 508, 510
sinusoids, 687
skeletal muscle (striped, striated, voluntary muscle), 637–46
  absolute refractory period, 640
  all-or-nothing action, 640
  antagonists, 637, 638
  composition, 638–40
  contraction, 640–2
    isometric, 640
    isotonic, 640
    mechanical summation, 641
    sliding filament theory, 641–2
    cramp, 643
  energy supply, 642–3
  excitation–contraction coupling, 642
  exercise effect, 643–4
  fast (twitch) muscle fibres, *645*, 646
  innervation, 644–5
  motor unit, 644

oxygen debt, 643
relative refractory period, 640
slow (tonic) muscle fibres, 645, 646
synergists, 637
tetanus, 641
tone, 647
T system, 638
skeleton, 627–37
  endo-, 627, 628–9
  exo-, 627, 628
  functions, 627
  hydrostatic, 627–8
  rabbit, 631–7
    appendicular skeleton, 634–6
    axial skeleton, 631–6
  vertebrate, 629
skin, 679–80
  excretion by, 696
  functions, 680
  human, 678–9
  vertebrate, 679
skin cancer, 429
skull, 631
slash-and-burn system, 420
slime layer, 4
small intestine, 313–15, *316*, 317
  flora, 25
smallpox, 31
smell, 594
  insects, 594–5
smooth endoplasmic reticulum (SER), 186, 187, 189, 200–2
smooth muscle, 646
smuts, 19, 33, 34
snail, feeding methods, 297
social behaviour, 622
  human, 889
social hierarchies (pecking order), 622–3
social organisation, 623–4
sodium, 285
  blood level, 722
sodium (cation) pump, 568
sodium–potassium pump, 196–7
soft rot, 19, 21, 33, 34
soil, 387–95
  erosion, 432–3
  formation, 390–2
  hard pan (iron pan), 393–4
  measurement, 439
  structure, 387–90
  types, 392–5
solenocyte, 703
solifluction, 391
solute potential, 475
solution, 930–1
somatomedin, 609, 692, 794
somatostatin (growth hormone release-inhibiting hormone; GHRIH), 607, 794
somatotrophin (growth hormone), 30, 692, 794
sound, 600–1
  pitch/intensity discrimination, 601
soya bean, 140
speciation, 906
  allopatric, 907
  interspecific, 909
  intraspecific, 906–7
  sympatric, 908
species, 906
  polytypic, 906
  ring, 908
species-characteristic behaviour, 615
species cover, 451
species density, 450
species frequency, 451
specimen identification, 951–2

Speman and Mangold's hypothesis, 830
spermatheca, 106
spermatogenesis, 753–4
spermatophore, 791
spermatozoa (human), 44, 752, 754
   development (spermatogenesis), 753–4
spermatozoids (antherozoids), 42–3
Sphenophyta (horsetails), 65, 71–3, *83*
sphincter, 306
sphygmomanometer, 672–3
spinal cord, 582
spindle formation, 801
spiracles, 112, 344
spirochaetes, *8*
spirometer, 353–4, *355*
sponges (Porifera), 85
sporangia, 65–72
spore formation (sporulation), 725–7
spores
   bacterial, 8
   plant, 64, 65
sporocyst, 95–6
sporophyte (*see also* gametophyte), 60–76,
   79, 733
squamous epithelium, *230*, 231, 232
squid (cuttlefish; *Sepia officinalis*), *106*, 295–6
starch, 137
   industry, 181
   test, 163
starch–statolith hypothesis, 550
Starling's law, 525
statistics, 947–50
   correlation, 949–50
   correlation coefficient, 950
   mean (arithmetic mean), 947–8
   measure of dispersion, 948
   median, 948
   mode, 948
   relationships between variables, 949–50
   standard deviation, 948
   variance, 949
statocyte, 550
statolith, 550
Stelleroidea, 118
stem
   primary growth, 781–4
   secondary growth, 784–8
stereoisomerism, 132
stereoscopic vision, 599
sternum, 349
steroid hormones, 604, 605, 606
steroids, 141, 142, *143*
sterols, 193
sticky trap, 446
stolon, 728
stomach, 312–13, 317
   secretion phases, *320*
stoma(ta), 217, *218*, 482, 484, 488
   densities, 488
   opening–closing mechanism, 489–92
stone tools, 888–9
storage, *379*
storage of crops, 420
stratification (seeds), 566
stratification in woodland ecology, 402
stratified epithelium, 232–3
streptococci, *8*, 33, 34, 35
   lactic acid, 26
streptomycin, 26–7
stretch reflex, 647
stridulation, 620
structural isomerism, 132
strychnine, 575
subarachnoid space, 580
suberin, 219, 494
subliminal stimulus, 640

succinic dehydrogenase, *176*, 330
succus entericus (intestinal juice), 313, 314
sucrase, 314
   optimum pH, 174
sucrose, 135
   test, 163
sugar(s), 127, *130*
sugar acid, 131
sugar alcohol, 131
sugar phosphate, 265
sulphonamides, 176
sulphur, 285
   bacteria, 5, *280*, 281, 283
   cycle, 283–4
sulphur dioxide, 429, 430
super-gene, 905
surfactant, 350
survivorship curves, 406–7
suspensory ligament, 595
Svedberg unit(s), 202
swallowing, 311, *312*
sweat glands, 679
sweep net, 446
swim bladder, open/closed, 657
sympathetic ganglion, 579
sympathetic nervous system, 579, 646
symplast, 482, 493
synapse, 244, 571–6
   axodendritic, 571
   axosomatic, 571
   chemical, 572
   chemical influences on, 575–6
   electrical, 575, 574
   excitation–secretion coupling, 572
   excitatory, 573
   excitatory postsynaptic potential, 573
   functions, 574–5
   inhibitory, 573
   inhibitory postsynaptic potential, 573
   summation, 573
   transmission mechanisms, 572–3
syncitial theory, 86
synecological investigation, 453–6
synecology, 359
synergism, 559–62
synovial fluid, 636–7
syphilis, 32
systole, 521

T cell, 534, 541
   HIV particles producing, *542*
T system, 574, 638
tachycardia, 672
tannins, 213
tap root, swollen, 729
taste bud, 593, *594*
taste (gustation), 593
   insects, 593–4
taste hair, 594
taxis, 543, 544, 614
teeth
   cat, 320
   human, 309–10
   sheep, 320–1
telencephalon, 583, 584–6
teleology, 613
Teleostei, *122*
telophase *799*, *806*, 807
temperature, 395–6, 673–6
   adaptations to extreme climates, 684–5
   body, 675–6
   core, 675
   homeostatic control, *684*
   influence on growth/distribution of
      animals, 675
   measurement, 443

   plant adaptations to high/low
      temperatures, 674
tendons, 238, 916
tentacles, 88–91
tentacular feeding, 295–6
terpenes, 141, 142
territorial behaviour, 618–19
territoriality (territorial behaviour), 412
tertiary structure, protein, 152
test cross, 836
testis (human), 752
   endocrine function, 754–5
   testosterone secretion, 604
   undescended, 752
testosterone, *143*, 604, 752, 755
   embryonic, 764
   male aggressiveness associated, 619
tetanus toxin, 575
tetanus, 32, 33
tetracyclines, 26
tetroses, 131
thalamus, 586
Thallophyta, 17
thallus, 17
thermal gradient, 676
thermistor, 443–4
thermodynamics, laws, 932–3
thermonasty, 544
thermoreceptor, 588, 593
thiamin (vitamin B_1), 305
thigmotropism (haptotropism), 543
thorax, 351
threonine, 144
thrombin, 531
thromboplastin, 530
thrombosis, 531, 673
thrombus, 531
through conduction tract, 587
thymine, 818
thymosin, 534
thymus gland, 534
thyroglobulin, 208, 608
thyroid gland, 608–9
   C cells, 619
   hormone secretion, 604, 609–10
   overactivity (hyperthyroidism), 610
   underactivity (hypothyroidism), 610
thyroid stimulating hormone (TSH), 208,
   604, 607, 609, 791
thyrotrophin releasing hormone (TRH), 607,
   609, 791
thyroxine (T_4), 604, 606, 608, 609, 791
tidal volume, 353
tissue culture, 730
tobacco callus cultures, 560
tobacco mosaic virus (TMV), *15*, 30, 147
tocopherol (vitamin E), 305
tomato bushy stunt virus, 30
tomato spotted wilt virus, 30
tonoplast, 475
topography, 397–8
torpor, 796
touch, 592–3
toxoids, 32, 539
trace elements, 284
trachea, 349
tracheids, 225–6
tracheoles, insect, 344–5
trachoma, 31
transamination, 268, 330, 340, *341*
transcription, 823–4
transducer, 183, 588
transducing particles, 12
transduction mechanism, 588
transect, 419
transfer cells, 505

transfer RNA (tRNA), 160, 202, 820, 822–3
transferase, 180
transforming principle, 813
transitional epithelium, 233, *234*
translocation, 473
    mineral salts through plants, 495–7
    organic solutes in phloem, 497–506
    water through plants, 481–95
transpiration, 482
    cohesion–tension theory, 482, 492
    environmental factors effects, 486
    functions, 488–9
    measurement of rate, 484
    plant/internal factors effects, 486–8
transplantation, 540
    graft rejection prevention, 541
transport, 473
    animals, 506–33
    plants, 473–506
Trematoda, 93, 95–8
Trent Biotic Index, 385, 386
triad, 638
triglycerides, 140
triiodothyronine (T_3), 604, 608, 609, 791
trimethylamine oxide, 698
triose(s), 131
triose phosphate, 266–8
triplet code, 818–20
trochophore, 104
trophallaxes, 623
trophic levels, 365–7
trophoblast, 762
tropisms, 543
tropocollagen, 151
tropomyosin, 639–40
troponin, 639, 640
trypsin(ogen), 181, 314, 315
tryptophan, 144, 826
tryptophan synthetase synthesis repression
  828
tryptophan systhetase, 826
TSH (thyroid stimulating hormone), 208
tuber, 728–9
tuberculosis, 31, 32
tuberculum, 633
tubulin, 801
Tullgren funnel, 446, 448
tumours, benign/malignant, 858
Turbellaria, 92–5
Turner's syndrome, 856
turnip yellow mosaic virus, 30
turnover rate, 379–80
twitch fibres, 646
typhoid fever, 32
typhus, 32
tyrosine, 144, 817

ultrafiltration, 700
umbilical cord, 763
underfishing, 418
undernutrition, 300
unit leaf rate (net assimilation rate), 374
units, 952–3
    SI, 953–4
uracil, 821
urea, 690, 697
ureter, 708, 712
urethra, 712
uric acid, 697–8
urine, 708
    composition, 718

formation, 718–19
Urochordata, 121
uterine cycle (human), 759
uterus (human), 755

vaccination (immunisation), 19, 539
vaccines, 30, 539
vacuole, 213
vacuum activity, 622
vagina (human), 755
valency (combining power), 927
valine, 144
vanadium, 284
variation, 853–4
    continuous, 853
    discontinuous, 853
    sources, 854
vas deferens, 94–6, 105, 106, 752
vas efferens, 752
vascular cambium, 784
vascular plants, 64
vascular wilt, 34
vasoconstriction, 525
vasodilation, 525
vasomotor centre, 526
vasopressin (antidiuretic hormone, ADH),
  604, 607, 721–2
vectors, 31
vegetative propagation (reproduction),
  727–30
vein, 507, 514, *515*, 516–17
    muscle contraction effect, *517*
    semilunar valve, 516–17
    structure, 514, *515*
venereal diseases, 31
ventilation
    acclimatisation effect, 357
    altitude effect, 356–7
    human, 351–3
ventral nerve cord, 587
ventricle, 508
venule, 507
vernalin, 565–6
vernalisation, 565–6
vertebrae, 630
    caudal, 634
    cervical, 632
    lumbar, 634
    sacral (sacrum), 634
    thoracic, 633
Vertebrata, 121–2
vesicle, 198
vessels, in plant vascular system, 226–8
vestibular glands (human), 755
vestigial organs, 879
vibrio, *8*
villi, 313–16
virology, 4
viruses, 13–17, 30–31
visible spectrum, 595, 598
vision
    binocular, 599
    stereoscopic, 599
visual acuity, 592
visual cortex, 599
visual pathways, 599
visual purple (rhodopsin), 597–8, 791
vital capacity, 353
vitamin C, 532
vitamins, 25, 164, 176, 305
vitrellar cell, 599

vitreous humour, 596
Volkman's canals, 240
voluntary muscle, 243, 244

Wallace, Alfred R. (1823–1913), 865, 866–7
wart disease of potato, 19, 33
waste recycling, 428, 434
water, 127–8, 301–4, 396
    ascent in xylem, 492–3
    biochemical oxygen demand (BOD),
      385–7
    cohesion–tension theory of movement
      482, 492
    guttation, 493
    molecules, 492
    movement through flowering plant,
  481–2
    movement through leaf, 482–4
    organic discharge effect on oxygen
      content, *386*
    root uptake, 493
    vapourisation, 482
water balance, terrestrial organisms, 710–12
water current measurement, 443
water potential, 474–5, 480
waterborne diseases, 33
waxes, 141, 142
weed control, 420
whirling hygrometer, 443, *444*
white fibrous tissue, 238
whooping cough, 32
wilting, 674
wind pollination, 742
wind speed/direction measurement, 444
wine manufacture, 26
winter moth (*Operophthera brumata*), 411,
  412–14
wood, 225, 784
woodland, 400–2, 435
woody dicotyledon stem, 785
wound contamination, 33
wound healing, 532–3

X chromosome, 764
xanthophylls, 256, 257
xenobiotics, 28
xenograft, 540
xerophytes, 486, 674, 700
XXX syndrome, 856
xylem, 216, 225–8
    mineral salts in, 497
    water ascent in, 492–3
XYY syndrome, 856

Y chromosome, 764
yaws, 31
yeast (*Saccharomyces*), 19
yellow elastic tissue, 238
yellow fever, 31
yolk sac, 762, 770

zeatin, 557
zinc, 284, 285
zonation, 46, *398*, 399
Zoomastigina, 52–3, 53
zoospores, 45
zygapophyses, 631
Zygomycota, 21–3
zygote, 60–1, 63, 67, 70, 71, 74, 79, 730
zygotic nucleus, 56
zymogen (proenzyme), 206